THIS SUBMARINE
WAS BUILT IN OUR SHIPYARD

ADDRESS:

BRODOGRADILIŠTE I TVORNICA DIESEL · MOTORA · SPLIT

SPLIT-JUGOSLAVIJA

JANE'S FIGHTING SHIPS

25200

Edited by Raymond V. B. Blackman
MBE, CEng, MIMarE, MRINA

(623.825)

Order of Contents

World Sales Distribution

Jane's Yearbooks,

Paulton House, Shepherdess Walk, London, N1, England

All the World
except

North, Central and South America:
McGraw-Hill Book Company,
330 West 42nd Street, New York, NY

and

Canada:
McGraw-Hill Company of Canada Ltd, 330 Progress Avenue, Scarborough, Ontario

---

Editorial communication to:

The Editor, Jane's Fighting Ships
Jane's Yearbooks, Paulton House, Shepherdess Walk,
London N1, England
Telephone 01-251-0787

Advertisement communication to:

Jane's Advertising Department
Haymarket Publishing Group,
Gillow House, 5 Winsley Street,
London W1, England
Telephone 01-636-3600

---

*Classified List of Advertisers

The various products available from the advertisers in this edition are listed alphabetically in about 350 different headings. In order to increase the usefulness of the Classified List a section is incorporated, on tinted paper, listing the product headings in French and German, alphabetically in those languages. The identification letter and number corresponding to the English-language listing is shown against each item.

Alphabetical list of advertisers
1971/72 edition

Digital systems for fighting ships

FERRANTI Digital Systems are now in service or on order for almost every type of ship or craft from aircraft carriers to submarines.

Large centralised multi-computer systems for AIO and weapon control, like the ADAWS (Action Data Automation Weapon Systems) for HMS BRISTOL and the Type 42 destroyers. Specialised Action Information Systems like CAAIS (Computer Assisted Action

Information System) for a variety of ships from frigates to helicopter carriers. Weapon-control systems like WSA4 (Weapon System Automation, Mk. 4) for control of guns and Seacat in the new AMAZON class frigates (Type 21). Submarine systems for fleet submarines and also for conventional submarines like the OBERON class. Digital Data Links to provide reliable high-speed exchange of data between ships.

Ferranti Digital Systems, based on the FM1600 range of integrated circuit computers and associated equipment, have been chosen by the Royal Navy for all types of operational requirement. And by several overseas navies, too. On current plans, well over 200 FM1600 series computers will be at sea in the late 1970's.

Ferranti systems provide training as well. The first stage of the Royal Navy's new Combined Tactical Trainer is already in operation. It comprises an operations room model of an ADA fitted guided missile

destroyer and a 20-cubicle Action Speed Tactical Trainer. Stage 2, including model operations rooms for the new ADAWS and CAAIS systems, is now in production. Other systems are on order for maintenance training, and other specialised roles.

FERRANTI

NAVAL DIGITAL SYSTEMS

Ferranti Limited,
Digital Systems Department,
Bracknell, Berkshire,
England, RG12 1RA.

Alphabetical list of advertisers

1971/72 edition—*continued*

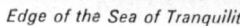

The only sea not patrolled by Paxman power

And given some briny, Paxman engines would no doubt make their appearance there as well! In the meantime the need for lightweight, compact, reliable diesel power for defence and patrol vessels on our own troubled waters remains unchanged; a need met in all respects by Paxman Ventura and Napier Deltic diesels, covering 450-2400 bhp and 1650-4140 bhp respectively.

If fast boat designers and naval architects had to design diesel engines as well as hulls they would come up with something very like the Ventura and Deltic. Both types meet their most exacting requirements in terms of approval by authorities; in meeting naval shock standards, and having low profile dimension, and ultra-low weights—we're talking about 6 lb per bhp for the Ventura vee-form engine and less than 4 lb per bhp for the Deltic opposed-piston engine. Then you can add to this the unseen benefits—lower capital cost over other propulsion systems, cheaper high speed cruise operation, interchangeability of wearing parts over different engine sizes, longer periods between overhaul, and, most important, speedy and simplified routine maintenance procedures.

It's no surprise that Paxman diesels already power over 100 fast patrol boats, corvettes, MTBs and police and customs vessels on all the seven seas.

If you're considering new construction, consider Ruston Paxman diesel propulsion. Call for our engineers for planning meetings or write for our comprehensive brochures on Paxman Ventura and Napier Deltic high speed diesels.

Edge of the Sea of Tranquility

Ruston Paxman Diesels Limited

A MANAGEMENT COMPANY OF ENGLISH ELECTRIC DIESELS LIMITED

Naval Department Paxman Works Colchester Essex England
Telephone: 0206 5151, Telex: 98151

N3 © D.915

mtu power to the power of experience

If we — the MTU Group — speak about motive power, we mean high-speed, high-performance diesel engines, gas turbines and highly sophisticated and advanced aero-engines.

We think about the impulses which have been given to the propulsion technique by M.A.N., Maybach and Daimler-Benz with their epochal developments. And, we think about the exacting technology of the aero-engine fields.

Today, we — the MTU Group — are working on the technology of tomorrow. On motive power requirements which are imposed on us by the demands of the future. The bases of our activities is the experience gained through decades and throughout the world.

Not without good reason, wherever the need for sophisticated motive power systems and reliable maximum performance arises, the demand is: Drive by MTU

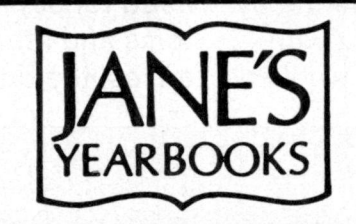

DIESEL ENGINE SPECIALISTS

Hedgehogs hog-tie a pig-boat...

1944: WW II's greatest ASW accomplishment by a single ship occurs during 12 days in May. The "hedgehog"— firing destroyer-escort USS England K.O.'s five Japanese subs, logs a major assist on a sixth. Introduced in late 1941, the "hedgehog" is a multi-spigot mortar salvoing *24 projectiles each with 31 pounds of high explosive. The missiles strike a ring pattern 250 yards ahead of the ship, explode only on contact. Armed with it, ASW ships now attack while sonar information is hot, with no need to consider sub's depth.*

We have a commitment.

Our twenty-six years in antisubmarine warfare have provided the background, the technology, and the climate for our current involvement in 20 distinct sectors of ASW research and development, con- cepts and operations. We have a commitment...to shape out of to- day's technology, even more ad- vanced Naval Combat Systems for tomorrow.
Write: Singer - Librascope, De- partment 10-415; 808 Western Avenue, Glendale, Calif. 91201.

SINGER
LIBRASCOPE

LISTE CLASSIFIEE DES ANNONCEURS

Le numéro de référence accompagnant chaque rubrique ci-dessous indique la rubrique anglaise équivalente en pages 17-31

E3, E5	Accessoires électriques	G9	Engrenages à denture en V
F11	Accessoires pour navires	G6	Engrenages, conico-hélicoïdaux
S25	Acier allié et spécial	G13	Equipement d'entretien d'engins guidés
S27	Acier au manganèse résistant à l'usure	G4	Engrenages divers
H4	Aéroglisseurs	G8	Engrenages droits
G18	Affûts de canons	E18	Engrenages épicycloïdaux
N3	Aides radio à la navigation	G5	Engrenages, hypoïdes
R16	Ailettes anti-roulis	G7	Engrenages, réducteurs-inverseurs
A7	Alternateurs	T16	Enregistreurs de profondeur et de roulis des torpilles
R1	Antennes de radar	S11	Ensembles à bagues collectrices
C25	Appareillage de commande	F8 ⎫	Equipement de commande et de contrôle de déviation
M17	Appareillage de commande moteur	T17 ⎭	des torpilles
E7	Appareillages de commutation électrique	D6	Equipement d'injection de moteurs Diesel
S28	Appareils de pilotage	M6	Equipement de manutention des matériaux
T23	Appareils de pilotage	T6	Equipement de télécommunications
G19	Appareils de pointage et d'indication d'altitude	U2	Equipement de télévision sous-marine
M4	Architectes marins	S35	Equipement de topographie
O6	Armements	E9	Equipement électronique
E8	Auxiliaires electrohydrauliques	L8	Equipement haut-parleur
S6	Banc d'essais des compas magnétiques de navires	H9	Equipement hydrographique
H8	Bateaux à aile portante	H7	Equipement hydraulique
G1	Bateaux à turbine à gaz	M8	Equipement microphonique
F7	Bateaux-pompes et de sauvetage	S16	Equipement radar ultrasonique
C3	Cabestans et treuils	S17	Equipement radar ultrasonique, appareils sur coque et
E2	Câbles électriques		systèmes hydrauliques
C2	Caissons	R6	Equipement radio
G16	Canonnières	R5	Equipement radio d'avions
N1	Canons de bord	S20	Equipement stabilisateur
G17	Canons et affûts	S21	Equipement stabilisateur pour le contrôle du tir
P4	Carénages de périscope	T12	Equipement d'essai des systemès de contrôle du tir
G3	Carters d'engrenages	T20	Equipement d'instruction
T21	Chalutiers	E4	Equipement électrique
F13	Chariots élévateurs à fourche	F10	Equipement mécanique de navires
B2	Chaudières	E19	Escourteurs
W3	Chaudières à tube d'eau	I11	Etude d'intérieurs et d'aménagements de navires
C15	Commande centralisée et automatique	M16	Fabricants de maquettes
E13	Commandes de démarrage et d'arrêt moteurs	H2	Fenêtres réchauffées
E12	Commandes de vitesse moteurs	F4	Ferry-boats
G20	Compas gyroscopiques	C4	Ferry-boats pour voitures
I5	Composants d'instruments (Mécaniques)	U1	Feux de plongée sous marine
P18	Composants de pompes	T13	Fibres textiles
C18	Compresseurs	M22	Fiches à broches multiples
A2	Compresseurs d'air	P9	Fiches et douilles
O2	Compresseurs exempts d'huile	S14	Fiches et douilles à broches multiples
C22	Condenseurs	S13	Fiches et douilles électriques étanches à l'eau
A17	Conduite et pilotage automatiques	O5	Filtres optiques Fondeurs de cuivre pour navires
S8	Construction de systèmes pour navires		Foreuses de pétrole
T15	Constructeurs de vedettes lancetorpilles	S8	Fonderie de cuivre pour navires
S3	Constructions et réparations de navires	F15	Frégates
S30	Contrôle du tir dans les sous-marins	G10	Génératrices électriques
C7	Contrôleurs de l'espace réservés au frêt	R17	Gouvernails
C28	Croiseurs	C27	Grues de navires
C26	Corvettes	P13	Hélices pour navires
C17	Démarreurs à air comprimé pour turbines à gaz et	I2	Indicateurs de feux de navigation
	moteurs Diesel	S12	Indicateurs de fumée
M18	Démarreurs moteurs	H3	Indicateurs de gouvernail
S5	Dessin de navires et de sous-marins	I1	Indicateurs électriques
D2	Destroyers	I4	Injecteurs
A3	Dispositif de freinage à la descente (Avion)	F16	Injecteurs de mazout
S15	Douilles	A5	Instruments d'avions
L1	Douilles de lampes	I10	Instruments d'équipement d'essai
D9	Dragues	I9	Instruments de précision
M10	Dragueurs de mines	I6	Instruments électroniques
C16	Dragueurs de mines côtiers et d'intérieur	I7	Instruments nautiques ⎤
N5	Dragueurs de mines nonmagnétiques	S2	Instruments scientifiques
H1	Echangeurs de chaleur	M12	Installations d'engins
D8	Ecluses de docks	E6	Installations et réparations électriques
E1	Economiseurs	R15	Inverseurs
P16	Editeurs	B1	Jumelles
L5	Elévateurs hydrauliques	L6	Lampes et éclairage
S29	Elimination des tensions	A11	Lance-roquettes anti-sous-marins
A14	Embarcations d'assaut	T18	Lance-torpilles latéraux
F6	Embarcations et autres produits en fibre de verre	B3	Livres de marine
R7	Emetteurs et récepteurs radio	B3a	Livres de marine épuisés
G15	Engins guidés	A18	Machines auxiliaires

B1	Machines de pont	C24	Pupitres de commande (électriques)
S4	Machines de navires	R2	Radar de contrôle de tir
P15	Machines de propulsion	R3	Radar de surveillance des ports
H6	Machines hydrauliques	M5	Radar marin
D7	Matériel de plongée	N2	Radar naval
I3	Matériaux infra-rouges	R4	Radar pour la navigation et pour l'avertissement menant à l'interception
S22	Matériel classique de production de vapeur		
F14	Matériel de distillation d'eau fraîche	T11	Ravitailleurs
C5	Matériel de manutention de charges	O3	Réchauffeurs de combustibles
H5	Matériel hydraulique	F3	Réchauffeurs d'eau d'alimentation
S23	Matériel nucléaire de production de vapeur	P14	Recherche relative aux hélices de navires
M15	Modéliste	P11	Récipients sous pression
E16	Moteurs à turbines à gaz	R13	Réducteurs, inverseurs, à commande à huile hydraulique
E17	Moteurs à turbines à vapeur		
E14	Moteurs d'avions	G11	Régulateurs
E15	Moteurs Diesel	E10	Régulateurs de moteur et enregistreur de données
D3	Moteurs Diesel auxiliaires	G12	Régulateurs de vitesse moteur
D4	Moteurs Diesel principaux de propulsion	T22	Remorqueurs
M20	Moteurs électriques	W1	Réparations de navires de guerre
R14	Moteurs réversibles actionnés à la vapeur ou à l'air comprimé	T4	Réservoirs de stockage de pétrole et d'eau
		A12	Roquettes anti-sous-marins
M9	Mouilleurs de mines	C19	Service de calcul
A8	Munitions	F2	Service d'étude de navires de guerre rapides
D10	Navires à cargaisons sèches	S10	Simulateurs
C23	Navires à containers	T1	Simulateurs d'entraînement tactique
G14	Navires à engins guidés	W6	Soudure à l'arc, à l'arc en atmosphere d'argon ou au gaz
M14	Navires à missiles		
P2	Navires à passagers	S32	Sous-marins
C6	Navires-cargos	S33	Sous-marins (conventionnels)
T2	Navires-citernes	M21	Stabilisateurs à poids mobiles
T3	Navires-citernes (petits)	S7	Stabilisateurs de navires
A15	Navires d'assaut	R8	Statoréacteurs
M3	Navires d'entretien et de réparations	S34	Surchauffeurs
W2	Navires de guerre	W4	Systèmes d'armements
R12	Navires de recherche	W5	Systèmes d'armements (composants de radar ultrasonique)
S1	Navires de sauvetage et de barrage		
M7	Navires marchands	O4	Systèmes de bruleurs de mazout
I12	Onduleurs et chargeurs de batterie	A16	Systèmes de commande automatiques
C20	Ordinateurs	M11	Systèmes de commande de missiles
S36	Panneaux de commande	T14	Systèmes de commande de torpilles
S37	Panneaux de commande et appareillage de commutation	N4	Systèmes d'huile combustible et brûleurs
		A1	Systèmes d'instruction pour le combat
A10	Patrouilleurs anti-sous-marins	M13	Systèmes de lancement d'engins
F1	Patrouilleurs rapides	L4	Systèmes Laser
P3	Patrouilleurs, vedettes, ravitailleurs et péniches	T7	Systèmes télégraphiques
		I8	Tableaux à instruments
L2	Péniches de débarquement	R10	Télécommandes
P5	Périscopes	R9	Télémètres
S31	Périscopes de sous-marins	L3	Télémètres à Laser
F12	Phares d'éclairage	T8	Télémoteurs
C14	Pièces coulées en acier	T10	Téléphone à hautparleur
C8	Pièces coulées en aluminium-bronze	T9	Téléphone sans pile
C11	Pièces coulées en coquille	L7	
C9	Pièces coulées en fer à grand rendement	T19	} Torpilles et tubes lance-torpilles
C12	Pièces coulées en fer à graphite sphéroïdal	B4	Transporteurs en vrac
C13	Pièces coulées en fer "Ni-resist" à graphite sphéroïdal	X1	Travaux aux rayons X
		W7	Treuils
C10	Pieces coulées en métaux non ferreux	A9	Treuils à munitions
S26	Pièces de forge, plaques et sections, pièces estampées	C21	Tubes de condenseurs
		C1	Tubes pour câbles (avec ou sans)
D5	Pièces de forge, plaques et sections, pièces estampées an acier	T24	Turbines
		T25	Turbines à gaz d'echappement
E11	Pièces de rechange pour moteurs Diesel	G2	Turbines à gaz
E11 P1		T26	Turbines à gaz marines
P11 R11	} Pièces pour moteurs Diesel	S24	Turbines à vapeur
S18		T27	Turbines à vapeur marines
M1	Pièces usinées en métaux ferreux	P7	Tuyaux d'eau de mer
M2	Pièces usinées en métaux non ferreux	P6	Tuyaux en cuivre et en laiton
P8	Pistons, segments et axes de pied de bielle	V3	Vannes automatiques à plaque ou à disque
A13	Plaque de blindage	V1	Vannes et robinets
P17	Pompes	V2	Vannes et robinets hydrauliques
F9	Pompes à incendie		
P10	Pontons automoteurs	M19	Vedettes lance-torpilles
A4	Porte-avions	S19	Vedettes rapides
F5	Produits optiques réalisés à partir de fibres	A6	Véhicules à coussin d'air
D11	Propriétaires de cales sèches	Y1	Yachts (à moteur)
P12	Propulsifs		
T5	Publications techniques		

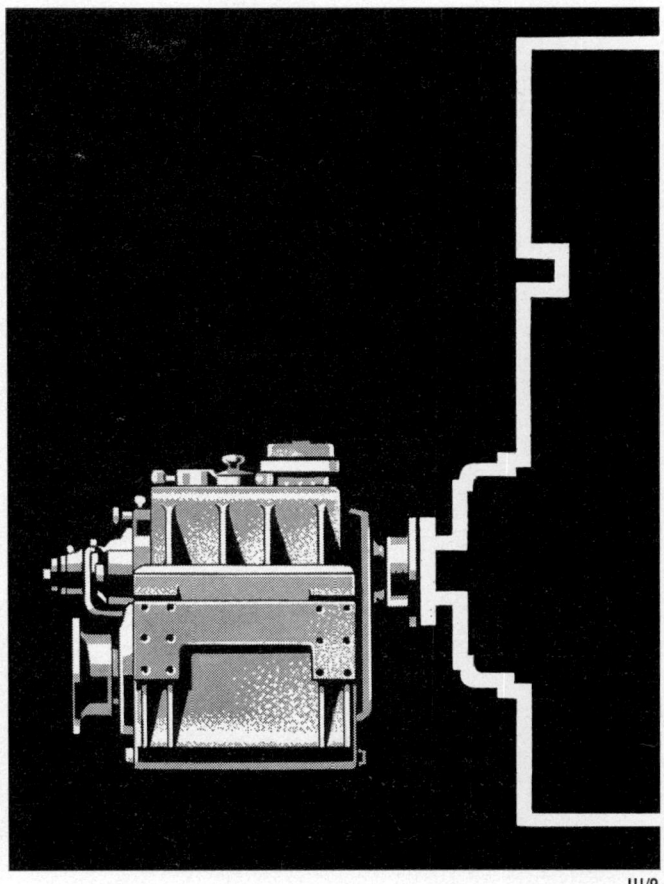
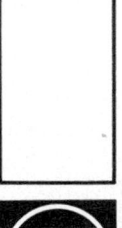

A 1. ACTION INFORMATION SYSTEMS
Plessey Radar Ltd.

A 2. ACTION INFORMATION TRAINERS
Ferranti Ltd.
Plessey Radar Ltd.
Rhine-Schelde

A 3. AIR COMPRESSORS
Hawker Siddeley Group
Split Shipyard

A 4. AIRCRAFT ARRESTING GEAR
MacTaggart, Scott & Co. Ltd.

A 5. AIRCRAFT CARRIERS
Netherlands United Shipbuilding
  Bureaux Ltd.

A 6. AIRCRAFT INSTRUMENTS
British Aircraft Corporation
Ferranti Limited
Hawker Siddeley Group
Thomson C. S. F.

A 7. AIR-CUSHION VEHICLES
British Hovercraft Corporation Ltd.
S.E.D.A.M.
Vosper Thornycroft Group, The

A 8. ALTERNATORS
Hawker Siddeley Group
Laurence, Scott & Electromotors Ltd.
Sofrexan

A 9. AMMUNITION
AB Bofors
D.T.C.N.
Sofrexan

A 10. AMMUNITION HOISTS
Blohm + Voss AG
MacTaggart, Scott & Co. Ltd.

A 11. ANTI-SUBMARINE LAUNCHES
Boatservice Ltd. A/S
Brooke Marine Ltd.
Cantiere Rodriquez
Netherlands United Shipbuilding
  Bureaux Ltd.
Sofrexan
Vosper Thornycroft Group, The
Yarrow (Shipbuilders) Ltd.

A 12. ANTI-SUBMARINE ROCKET LAUNCHERS
AB Bofors

A 13. ANTI-SUBMARINE ROCKETS
AB Bofors
D.T.C.N.
British Aircraft Corporation
Sofrexan

A 14. ARMOUR PLATES
AB Bofors

A 15. ASSAULT CRAFT
Blohm + Voss AG
British Hovercraft Corporation
Brooke Marine Ltd.
Cantiere Rodriquez
Hawker Siddeley Group
Vosper Thornycroft Group, The
Yarrow (Shipbuilders) Ltd.

A 16. ASSAULT SHIPS
Blohm + Voss AG
Boatservice Ltd, A/S
Brooke Marine Ltd.
Cantiere Rodriquez
D.T.C.N.
Sofrexan
Vosper Thornycroft Group, The
Yarrow (Shipbuilders) Ltd.

A 17. AUTOMATIC CONTROL SYSTEMS
British Aircraft Corporation
Ferranti Ltd.
Laurence, Scott & Electromotors Ltd.
Litton Systems (Canada) Ltd.
Hawker Siddeley Group
Hollandse Signaalapparaten N.V.
Sofrexan
Thomson C. S. F.
Vosper Thornycroft Group, The

A 18. AUTOMATIC STEERING
Hawker Siddeley Group
Rhine-Schelde
Sofrexan
Thomson C. S. F.

A 19. AUXILIARY MACHINERY
Blohm + Voss AG
Hawker Siddeley Group
Korody-Colyer Corporation
Laurence Scott & Electromotors Ltd.
M.T.U.—Motoren und Turbinen Union
Sofrexan

B 1. BINOCULARS
Barr & Stroud Ltd.
Rhine-Schelde

B 2. BOILERS
Blohm + Voss AG
D.T.C.N.
Netherlands United Shipbuilding
  Bureaux Ltd.
Yarrow (Shipbuilders) Ltd.

B 3. BOOKS (NAVAL)
Alnavco
Antheil Booksellers

B 3a. BOOKS (NAVAL) OUT OF PRINT
Antheil Booksellers

B 4. BULK CARRIERS
Blohm + Voss AG
Fr Lürssen Werft
Rhine-Schelde
Split Shipyard
Todd Shipyards Corporation

C 1. CABLE LOOMS (WITH OR WITHOUT)
Laurence Scott & Electromotors Ltd

C 2. CAISSONS

C 3. CAPSTANS AND WINDLASSES
MacTaggart, Scott & Co. Ltd.

C 4. CAR FERRIES
Blohm + Voss AG
British Hovercraft Corporation
Brooke Marine Ltd.
Fr. Lürssen Werft
Rhine-Schelde
Vosper Thornycroft Group, The
Yarrow (Shipbuilders) Ltd.

C 5. CARGO HANDLING EQUIPMENT
Blohm + Voss AG
British Hovercraft Corporation Ltd.
Laurence, Scott & Electromotors Ltd.
MacTaggart, Scott & Co. Ltd.

C 6. CARGO SHIPS
Blohm + Voss AG
Boatservice Ltd. A/S
Brooke Marine Ltd.
Fr Lürssen Werft
Rhine-Schelde
Todd Shipyards Corporation
Yarrow (Shipbuilders) Ltd.

C 7. CARGO SPACE MONITORS
Brooke Marine Ltd.

C 8. CASTINGS, ALUMINIUM-BRONZE
Barr & Stroud Ltd.

C 9. CASTINGS, HIGH DUTY IRON
Barr & Stroud Ltd.

C 10. CASTINGS, NON-FERROUS
Barr & Stroud Ltd.
Hawker Siddeley Group

C 11. CASTINGS, SHELL, MOULDED
Ferranti Ltd.

C 12. CASTINGS S.G. IRON
Ferranti Ltd.

C 13. CASTINGS S.G. NI-RESIST IRON
Ferranti Ltd.

C 14. CASTINGS, STEEL
AB Bofors
Rhine-Schelde

C 15. CENTRALISED AND AUTOMATIC CONTROL
Ferranti Ltd.
Hawker Siddeley Group
Hollandse Signaalapparaten N.V.
Laurence Scott & Electromotors Ltd.
M.T.U.—Motoren und Turbinen Union
Sofrexan
Todd Shipyards Corporation
Thomson C.S.F.
Vosper Thornycroft Group, The

C 16. COASTAL AND INSHORE MINESWEEPERS
Boatservice Ltd. A/S
Brooke Marine Ltd.
D.T.C.N.
Netherlands United Shipbuilding
  Bureaux Ltd.
Rhine-Schelde
Vosper Thornycroft Group, The
Yarrow (Shipbuilders) Ltd.

C 17. COMPRESSED AIR STARTERS FOR GAS TURBINES AND DIESEL ENGINES

C 18. COMPRESSORS
Hawker Siddeley Group
Rhine-Schelde
Split Shipyard

C 19. COMPUTER SERVICES
Contraves AG
Ferranti Ltd.
Hollandse Signaalapparaten N.V.
Litton Systems (Canada) Ltd.
Marconi Co. Ltd., The
Thomson C. S. F.
Yarrow & Co. Ltd.

C 20. COMPUTERS
Ferranti Limited
Hawker Siddeley Group
Hollandse Signaalapparaten N.V.
Litton Systems (Canada) Ltd.
Marconi Communications
Thomson C. S. F.
Yarrow & Co. Ltd.

Marconi
complete naval
communications

The Marconi comprehensive range of s.s.b/i.s.b naval communications equipment meets all present and foreseeable requirements for voice and automatic telegraphy.

The complete range conforms to Royal Naval standards of resistance to shock, vibration and climatic conditions, and has been NATO codified by the British Defence Department. It is in wide use by the Royal Navy and in the modernization of ten other navies.

Marconi Communication Systems Limited also has a complete range of communications equipment available for shore stations; shipborne, mobile and static space communication earth terminals; digital transmission, and airborne communications.

In addition the Company is able to assist naval departments and shipbuilders with the planning, fitting, testing and tuning of complete ship communications installation.

Marconi Communication Systems Limited

Radio Communications Division, Chelmsford, Essex, CMI IPL

A GEC-Marconi Electronics Company

LTD/H88

C 21. CONDENSER TUBES

C 22. CONDENSERS
Blohm + Voss AG
D.T.C.N.
Yarrow & Co. Ltd.

C 23. CONTAINER SHIPS
Blohm + Voss AG
Brooke Marine Ltd.
Fr. Lürssen Werft
Split Shipyard
Todd Shipyards Corporation
Yarrow (Shipbuilders) Ltd.

C 24. CONTROL DESKS (ELECTRIC)
Laurence, Scott & Electromotors Ltd.
Plessey Company Limited, The
Vosper Thornycroft Group, The

C 25. CONTROL GEAR
Hawker Siddeley Group
Korody Colyer
Laurence Scott & Electromotors Ltd.
Thomson C. S. F.
Vosper Thornycroft Group, The

C 26. CORVETTES
Blohm + Voss AG
Brooke Marine Ltd.
D.T.C.N.
Fr. Lürssen Werft
Netherlands United Shipbuilding
    Bureaux Ltd.
Sofrexan
Vosper Thornycroft Group, The
Yarrow (Shipbuilders) Ltd.

C 27. CRANES, SHIPS'
Hawker Siddeley Group

C 28. CRUISERS
Cantiere Rodriquez
D.T.C.N.
Netherlands United Shipbuilding
    Bureaux Ltd.
Sofrexan

C 29. COUPLINGS
Flexibox Ltd.

D 1. DECK MACHINERY
Hawker Siddeley Group
Laurence, Scott & Electromotors Ltd.
MacTaggart, Scott & Co. Ltd.
Vosper Thornycroft Group, The

D 2. DESTROYERS
Blohm + Voss AG
D.T.C.N.
Netherlands United Shipbuilding
    Bureaux Ltd.
Sofrexan
Vosper Thornycroft Group, The
Yarrow (Shipbuilders) Ltd.

D 3. DIESEL ENGINES, AUXILIARY
Blohm + Voss AG
Chantiers de L'Atlantique
Coventry Climax Engines Ltd.
C.R.M. Fabbrica Motori Marini
Hawker Siddeley Group
Korody-Colyer Corporation
M.T.U.—Motoren und Turbinen Union
Netherlands United Shipbuilding
    Bureaux Ltd.
Ruston Paxman Diesels
    (Naval Division)

D 4. DIESEL ENGINES, MAIN PROPULSION
Blohm + Voss AG
Chantiers de L'Atlantique
C.R.M., Fabbrica Motori Marini
Hawker Siddeley Group
Korody-Colyer Corporation
M.T.U.—Motoren und Turbinen Union
Netherlands United Shipbuilding
    Bureaux Ltd.
Ruston Paxman Diesels
    (Naval Division)
Sofrexan
Split Shipyard

D 5. DIESEL ENGINE SPARE PARTS
Blohm + Voss AG
Chantiers de L'Atlantique
C.R.M., Fabbrica Motori Marini
Hawker Siddeley Group
Korody-Colyer Corporation
Fr. Lürssen Werft
M.T.U.—Motoren und Turbinen Union
Netherlands United Shipbuilding
    Bureaux Ltd.
Split Shipyard

D 6. DIESEL FUEL INJECTION EQUIPMENT
Korody-Colyer Corporation

D 7. DIVING EQUIPMENT
Sofrexan
Thomson C. S. F.

D 8. DOCK GATES
D. T. C. N.
Vosper Thornycroft Group, The

D 9. DREDGERS
Brooke Marine Ltd.

D 10. DRY CARGO VESSELS
Blohm + Voss AG
Boatservice Ltd. A/S
Brooke Marine Ltd.
Fr Lürssen Werft
Todd Shipyards Corporation
Split Shipyard
Yarrow (Shipbuilders) Ltd.

D 11. DRY DOCK PROPRIETORS
Blohm + Voss AG
Netherlands United Shipbuilding
    Bureaux Ltd.

E 1. ECONOMISERS
Netherlands United Shipbuilding
    Bureaux Ltd.
Yarrow & Co. Ltd.

E 2. ELECTRIC CABLES
Hawker Siddeley Group

E 3. ELECTRICAL AUXILIARIES
Hawker Siddeley Group
Laurence, Scott & Electromotors Ltd.
Vosper Thornycroft, Group The

E 4. ELECTRICAL EQUIPMENT
Hawker Siddeley Group
Laurence, Scott & Electromotors Ltd.
Plessey Company Limited, The
Sofrexan
Vosper Thornycroft Group, The
Whipp & Bourne Ltd.

E 5. ELECTRICAL FITTINGS
Hawker Siddeley Group
Vosper Thornycroft Group, The

E 6. ELECTRICAL INSTALLATIONS AND REPAIRS
Hawker Siddeley Group
Vosper Thornycroft Group, The
Yarrow (Shipbuilders) Ltd.

E 7. ELECTRICAL SWITCHGEAR
Hawker Siddeley Group
Laurence, Scott & Electromotors Ltd.
Vosper Thornycroft Group, The
Whipp & Bourne Ltd.

E 8. ELECTRO-HYDRAULIC AUXILIARIES
MacTaggart, Scott & Co. Ltd.
Vosper Thornycroft Group, The

E 9. ELECTRONIC EQUIPMENT
Barr & Stroud Ltd.
British Aircraft Corporation
British Hovercraft Corporation Ltd.
Decca Radar Ltd.
Edo Corporation
Ferranti Limited
Hawker Siddeley Group
Hollandse Signaalapparaten N.V.
Laurence, Scott & Electromotors Ltd.
Marconi Communications System Ltd.
Plessey Company Limited, The
Thomson C. S. F.
Van der Heem Electronics
Vosper Thornycroft Group, The

E 10. ELECTRONIC EQUIPMENT REFITS
Plessey Radar Ltd.

E 11. ENGINE MONITORS AND DATA LOGGERS
Decca Radar Ltd.
M.T.U.—Motoren und Turbinen Union
Thomson C. S. F.
Vosper Thornycroft Group, The

E 12. ENGINE PARTS, DIESEL
Chantiers de L'Atlantique
C.R.M. Fabbrica Motori Marini
Hawker Siddeley Group
Korody-Colyer Corporation
M.T.U.—Motoren und Turbinen Union
Netherlands United Shipbuilding
    Bureaux Ltd.

E 13. ENGINE SPEED CONTROLS
Hawker Siddeley Group
Vosper Thornycroft Group, The

E 14. ENGINE START AND SHUT-DOWN CONTROLS
Hawker Siddeley Group
Vosper Thornycroft Group, The

E 15. ENGINES, AIRCRAFT
M.T.U.—Motoren und Turbinen Union
Ruston Paxman Diesels
    (Naval Division)
Sofrexan

Where quality is critical...EDO

EDO Corporation originates, engineers and builds top quality systems
for a variety of military applications throughout the free world.
EDO systems are widely used in antisubmarine warfare..oceanography..airborne
mine countermeasures..strike warfare..airborne navigation and instrumentation
..hydrodynamics and airframes..command and control.
Today, as for the past 46 years, EDO QUALITY means the best there is.

**EDO
CORPORATION**
College Point, N. Y. 11356, U.S.A.

[20]

E 16. ENGINES, DIESEL
Blohm + Voss AG
Chantiers de L'Atlantique
Coventry Climax Engines Ltd.
C.R.M., Fabbrica Motori Marini
Fiat
Hawker Siddeley Group
Korody-Colyer Corporation
M.T.U.—Motoren und Turbinen Union
Netherlands United Shipbuilding
   Bureaux Ltd.
Rhine-Schelde
Sofrexan

E 17. ENGINES, GAS TURBINE
Rhine-Schelde
Sofrexan

E 18. ENGINES, STEAM TURBINE
Blohm + Voss AG
D.T.C.N.
Netherlands United Shipbuilding
   Bureaux Ltd.
Sofrexan
Yarrow & Co. Ltd.

E 19. EPICYCLIC GEARS
Barr & Stroud Ltd.
D.T.C.N.
Sofrexan
Zahnradfabrik Friedrichshafen AG

E 20. ESCORT VESSELS
Blohm + Voss AG
Brooke Marine Ltd.
D.T.C.N.
Fr Lürssen Werft
Netherlands United Shipbuilding
   Bureaux Ltd.
Sofrexan
Vosper Thornycroft Group, The
Yarrow (Shipbuilders) Ltd.

F 1. FAST PATROL BOATS
Boatservice Ltd. A/S
British Hovercraft Corporation
Brooke Marine Ltd.
Cantiere Rodriquez
Hollandse Signaalapparaten N.V.
Korody Marine Corporation
Fr. Lürssen Werft
Netherlands United Shipbuilding
   Bureaux Ltd.
Sofrexan
Vosper Thornycroft Group, The
Yarrow & Co. Ltd.

F 2. FAST WARSHIP DESIGN SERVICE
Brooke Marine Ltd.
D.T.C.N.
Sofrexan
Vosper Thornycroft Group, The
Yarrow (Shipbuilders) Ltd.

F 3. FEED WATER HEATERS
Blohm + Voss AG
Yarrow & Co. Ltd.

F 4. FERRIES
British Hovercraft Corporation
Brooke Marine Ltd.
Rhine-Schelde
Vosper Thornycroft Group, The
Yarrow (Shipbuilders) Ltd.

F 5. FIBRE OPTICS
Barr & Stroud Ltd.
Ferranti Ltd.

F 6. FIBREGLASS VESSELS AND OTHER PRODUCTS
Blohm + Voss AG
Boatservice Ltd. A/S
D.T.C.N.
Netherlands United Shipbuilding
   Bureaux Ltd.
Sofrexan
Vosper Thornycroft Group, The
Yarrow (Shipbuilders) Ltd.

F 7. FIRE AND SALVAGE VESSELS
Brooke Marine Ltd.
Cantiere Rodriquez
Sofrexan
Yarrow (Shipbuilders) Ltd.

F 8. FIRE CONTROL AND GUNNERY EQUIPMENT
Barr & Stroud Ltd.
AB Bofors
Contraves AG
Ferranti Limited
Hollandse Signaalapparaten N.V.
Laurence, Scott & Electromotors Ltd.
Marconi Co. Ltd., The
Plessey Company Limited, The
Sofrexan
Thomson C. S. F.

F 9. FIRE PUMPS
Coventry Climax Engines Ltd.

F 10. FITTINGS, SHIP

F 11. FLEXIBLE CONDUIT COVERINGS

F 12. FLOODLIGHTS

F 13. FORK LIFT TRUCKS
Coventry Climax Engines Ltd.
Hawker Siddeley Group

F 14. FRESH WATER DISTILLING PLANT
Netherlands United Shipbuilding
   Bureaux Ltd.
Sofrexan

F 15. FRIGATES
Blohm + Voss AG
Brooke Marine Ltd.
D.T.C.N.
Fr Lürssen Werft
Netherlands United Shipbuliding
   Bureaux Ltd.
Rhine-Schelde
Vosper Thornycroft Group, The
Yarrow (Shipbuilders) Ltd.

F 16. FUEL OIL INJECTORS
Korody-Colyer Corporation

G 1. GAS TURBINE BOATS
Blohm + Voss AG
British Hovercraft Corp.
Brooke Marine Ltd.
Netherlands United Shipbuilding
   Bureaux Ltd.
Sofrexan
Vosper Thornycroft Group, The
Yarrow (Shipbuilders) Ltd.

G 2. GAS TURBINES
Hawker Siddeley Group
Rhine-Schelde
Sofrexan
Yarrow & Co. Ltd.

G 3. GEAR CASINGS
Korody-Colyer Corp.
Sofrexan
Yarrow & Co. Ltd.

G 4. GEARS AND GEARING
Barr & Stroud Ltd.
Korody Colyer Corporation
Laurence, Scott & Electromotors Ltd.
Netherlands United Shipbuilding
   Bureaux Ltd.
Sofrexan
Vosper Thornycroft Group, The
Yarrow & Co. Ltd
Zahnradfabrik Friedrichshafen AG

G 5. GEARS—HYPOID
Barr & Stroud Ltd.
Korody Colyer Corp.

G 6. GEARS—SPIRAL BEVEL
Korody-Colyer Corp.
Laurence, Scott & Electromotors Ltd.
Vosper Thornycroft Group, The

G 7. GEARS, REVERSE-REDUCTION
Korody-Colyer Corporation
M.T.U.—Motoren und Turbinen Union
Netherlands United Shipbuilding
   Bureaux Ltd.
Vosper Thornycroft Group, The
Zahnradfabrik Friedrichshafen AG

G 8. GEARS—SPUR
Barr & Stroud Ltd.
Korody Colyer Corp.
Laurence, Scott & Electromotors Ltd.

G 9. GEARS, VEE DRIVE
Korody-Colyer Corp.
Vosper Thornycroft Group, The

G 10. GENERATORS, ELECTRIC
Hawker Siddeley Group
Laurence, Scott & Electromotors Ltd.
Sofrexan

G 11. GOVERNORS
Korody-Colyer Corporation

G 12. GOVERNORS, ENGINE SPEED
Hawker Siddeley Group
Korody-Colyer Corporation

G 13. GUIDED MISSILE SERVICING EQUIPMENT
Aerospatiale (S.N.I.A.S.)
British Aircraft Corporation
D.T.C.N.
Fr Lürssen Werft
Hawker Siddeley Group
Sofrexan
Thomson C. S. F.

G 14. GUIDED MISSILE SHIPS
Blohm + Voss AG
British Hovercraft Corporation
Brooke Marine Ltd.
D.T.C.N.
Netherlands United Shipbuilding
   Bureaux Ltd.
Sofrexan
Vosper Thornycroft Group, The
Yarrow (Shipbuilders) Ltd.

Protection for a better world

Patrol Boats by Vosper Thornycroft

45ft

60ft

These 45ft and 60ft craft have hulls of g.r.p. which is exceptionally strong and not liable to rot, corrosion or damage from marine borers. Maintenance, therefore, is minimal. With diesel machinery and speeds up to 25 knots, these craft are widely used in many countries for inshore patrol, customs & police launches and similar duties.

100ft

Derived from the "Brave" class, these gas turbine powered craft have maximum speeds of 55 knots and can be heavily armed. Diesels are also fitted for long range cruising. More than twenty have been built for five navies.

VOSPER THORNYCROFT

103ft

Of steel construction and diesel machinery, these 103ft and 110ft craft have proved most successful for routine patrol duties in open waters. With maximum speeds of 25-30 knots, they can be armed with simple and sophisticated weapons according to need. More than 40 have been built for six navies.

110ft

Below – The fast patrol boat of the future, combining all the best features of the boats above and carrying a powerful modern armament of guided missiles and guns. Long endurance and fine seakeeping are important features of this very sophisticated 40 knot fast patrol boat.

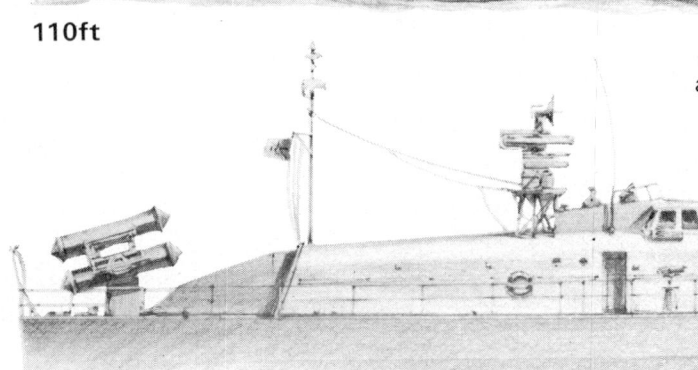

142ft

For further information on Vosper Thornycroft Frigates, Corvettes and Fast Patrol Boats, see:
ABU DHABI, BRAZIL, BRUNEI, CEYLON, DENMARK, GHANA, GREECE, IRAN, KENYA, KUWAIT, LIBYA, MALAYSIA, NIGERIA, PERU, SINGAPORE, TRINIDAD & TOBAGO, UNITED KINGDOM.

◁B A subsidiary of the David Brown Corporation Ltd.

PAULSGROVE, PORTSMOUTH, ENGLAND.
Tel: Cosham 79481 Telex 86115.

Triton radar antenna
surveillance radar of Vega system

VEGA

surveillance, target designation and fire control system for surface vessels

VEGA CASTOR - VEGA POLLUX - Fire control against sea, air or shore targets (all caliber guns).

VEGA POLLUX PC - Fire control against air or sea targets (gun caliber lower than or equal to 40 mm).

VEGA POLLUX PCE - Fire control against air or sea targets (gun caliber lower than or equal to 40 mm).
Guidance of EXOCET surface-to-surface missile.

VEGA CASTOR ET - VEGA POLLUX ET - Fire control against air, sea or shore targets (all caliber guns).
Guidance of EXOCET surface-to-surface missile.
Guidance of wire guided torpedoes.

VEGA POLLUX PCET - Fire control against air or sea targets (gun caliber lower than or equal to 40 mm).
Guidance of EXOCET surface-to-surface missile.
Guidance of wire guided torpedoes.

VEGA TRITON E - Guidance of EXOCET surface-to-surface missile.

VEGA TRITON T - Guidance of wire guided torpedoes.

THOMSON-CSF

DIVISION RADARS DE SURFACE
1, RUE DES MATHURINS - 92 BAGNEUX - FRANCE
TEL. 655.11.22

G 15. GUIDED MISSILES
AB Bofors
Aerospatiale (S.N.I.A.S.)
British Aircraft Corporation
Contraves AG
D.T.C.N.
Hawker Siddeley Group
Sofrexan
Thomson C. S. F.

G 16. GUN BOATS
Boatservice Ltd. A/S
Brooke Marine Ltd.
Cantiere Rodriquez
D.T.C.N.
Fr Lürssen Werft
Netherlands United Shipbuilding
    Bureaux Ltd.
Sofrexan
Vosper Thornycroft Group, The
Yarrow (Shipbuilders) Ltd.

G 17. GUNS AND MOUNTINGS
AB Bofors
Contraves AG
D.T.C.N.
F.M.C. Northern Ordnance Division
Sofrexan

G 18. GUN MOUNTS
AB Bofors
F.M.C. Northern Ordnance Division
Sofrexan

**G 19. GUN-SIGHTING APPARATUS
AND HEIGHT FINDERS**
Barr & Stroud Ltd.
British Aircraft Corporation
Thomson C. S. F.

G 20. GYROSCOPIC COMPASSES
British Aircraft Corporation
Ferranti Ltd.
Hawker Siddeley Group
Sofrexan
Thomson C. S. F.

H 1. HEAT EXCHANGERS
Blohm + Voss AG
Korody-Colyer Corporation
Vosper Thornycroft Group, The

H 2. HEATED WINDOWS
Barr & Stroud Ltd.

H 3. HELM INDICATORS
Hawker Siddeley Group
Laurence, Scott & Electromotors Ltd.

H 4. HOVERCRAFT
British Hovercraft Corporation Ltd.
Vosper Thornycroft Group, The

H 5. HYDRAULIC EQUIPMENT
D.T.C.N.
MacTaggart, Scott & Co. Ltd.
Mingori
Vosper Thornycroft Group, The

H 6. HYDRAULIC MACHINERY
MacTaggart, Scott & Co. Ltd.
Vosper Thornycroft Group, The

H 7. HYDRAULIC PLANT
MacTaggart, Scott & Co. Ltd.

H 8. HYDROFOILS
Blohm + Voss AG
Cantiere Rodriquez
Hawker Siddeley Group

**H 9. HYDROGRAPHIC SURVEY
EQUIPMENT**
British Aircraft Corporation
Laurence, Scott & Electromotors Ltd.
Plessey Company Limited, The
Thomson C. S. F.

I 1. INDICATORS, ELECTRIC
Korody-Colyer Corporation.
Laurence Scott, & Electromotors Ltd.

I 2. IFF Mk 10 SYSTEMS
Plessey Radar Ltd.

I 3. INFRA-RED MATERIALS
Barr & Stroud Ltd.
Thomson C. S. F.

I 4. INJECTORS
Korody-Colyer Corporation

**I 5. INSTRUMENT COMPONENTS
(MECHANICAL)**
Laurence, Scott & Electromotors Ltd.
Thomson C. S. F.

I 6. INSTRUMENTS, ELECTRONIC
AB Bofors
British Aircraft Corporation
British Hovercraft Corporation
Columbia Electronics International
    Inc.
Barr & Stroud Ltd.
Decca Radar Ltd.
Ferranti Limited
Korody Marine Corporation
Laurence Scott & Electromotors Ltd.,
Plessey Company Limited, The
Thomson C. S. F.
Vosper Thornycroft Group, The

I 7. INSTRUMENTS, NAUTICAL
Columbia Electronics International,
    Inc.
Hawker Siddeley Group
Plessey Company Limited, The

I 8. INSTRUMENT PANELS
Korody-Colyer Corporation
Laurence, Scott & Electromotors Ltd.
Thomson C. S. F.
Vosper Thornycroft Group, The

I 9. INSTRUMENTS, PRECISION
Barr & Stroud Ltd.
British Aircraft Corporation
Ferranti Limited
Hawker Siddeley Group
Korody Colyer Corporation
Laurence, Scott & Electromotors Ltd.

**I 10. INSTRUMENTS, TEST
EQUIPMENT**
British Aircraft Corporation
Columbia Electronics International,
    Inc.
Ferranti Ltd.
Hollandse Signaalapparaten N.V.
Korody Colyer Corporation
Laurence, Scott & Electromotors Ltd.
Thomson C.S.F.

**I 11. INTERIOR DESIGN AND
FURNISHING FOR SHIPS**
Blohm + Voss AG
Brooke Marine Ltd.
Vosper Thornycroft Group, The

**I 12. INVERTERS AND BATTERY
CHARGERS**
Ferranti Ltd.
Vosper Thornycroft Group, The

L 1. LAMPHOLDERS
Hawker Siddeley Group

L 2. LANDING CRAFT
British Hovercraft Corporation
Brooke Marine Ltd.
D.T.C.N.
Korody Marine Corporation
Netherlands United Shipbuilding
    Bureaux Ltd.
Sofrexan
Vosper Thornycroft Group, The
Yarrow (Shipbuilders) Ltd.

L 3. LASER RANGEFINDERS
AB Bofors
Barr & Stroud Ltd.
Ferranti Ltd.
Sofrexan
Thompson C. S. F.

L 4. LASER SYSTEMS
Barr & Stroud Ltd.
Ferranti Ltd.
Sofrexan
Thomson C. S. F.

L 5. LIFTS—HYDRAULIC
MacTaggart Scott & Co. Ltd.

L 6. LIGHTS AND LIGHTING
Hawker Siddeley Group
Korody Marine Corporation

**L 7. LIQUID PETROLEUM GAS
CARRIERS**
Fr. Lürssen Werft
Rhine-Schelde

L 8. LOUDSPEAKER EQUIPMENT
Thomson C. S. F.

M 1. MACHINED PARTS, FERROUS
Blohm + Voss AG
Vickers Limited
Vosper Thornycroft Group, The
Yarrow & Co. Ltd.

**M 2. MACHINED PARTS,
NON-FERROUS**
Barr & Stroud Ltd.
Blohm + Voss AG
Vickers Limited
Vosper Thornycroft Group, The
Yarrow & Co. Ltd.

**M 3. MAINTENANCE AND REPAIR
SHIPS**
Brooke Marine Ltd.
D.T.C.N.
Fr. Lürssen Werft
Rhine-Schelde
Vosper Thornycroft Group, The
Yarrow (Shipbuilders) Ltd.

M 4. MARINE ARCHITECTS
Ingenieurkontor Lübeck

M 5. MARINE RADAR
Decca Radar Limited
Marconi Radar Systems Ltd.
Sofrexan
Thomson C. S. F.

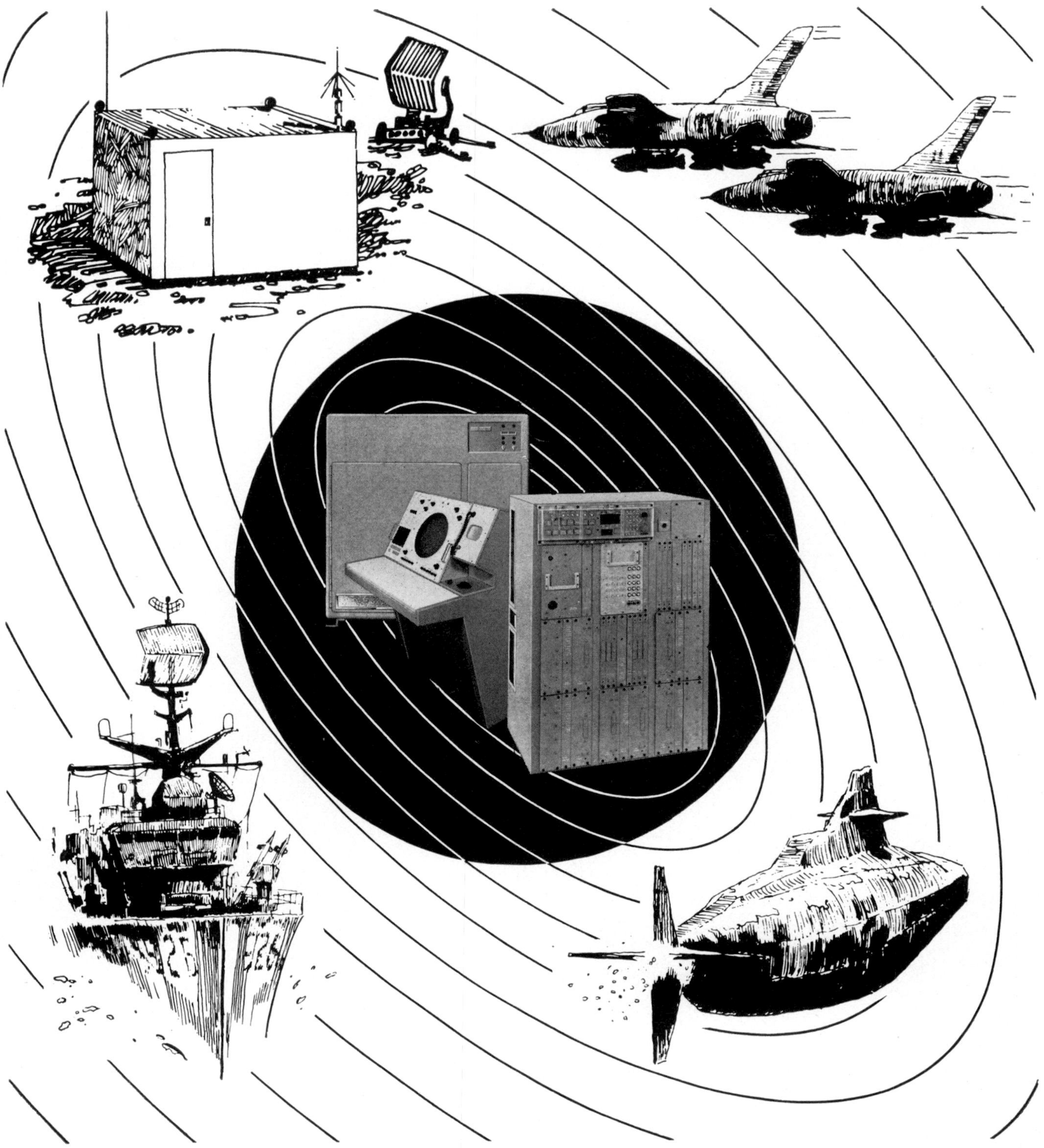

HAVE YOU GOT A TACTICAL DECISION-MAKING PROBLEM?

Litton has tactical data systems able to make decisions in any area whether it be land, sea or air. Our systems are microminiaturized, flexible and completely mobile. If your problem is in the field, the computer and displays are placed in an operational environment, transportable by helicopter or by transport aircraft to the operation site. The whole system is designed for rapid field deployment and optimum utilization of personnel and equipment. ☐ If your problem is at sea, Litton Systems capability for shipborne applications covers the spectrum from large command and control systems to special-purpose systems for ASW and missile control. And if your problem is in the air, Litton systems are fully operational in airborne roles—relieving the operator for decision-making functions. ☐ Have you got a tactical decision-making problem? If the problem is complex, Litton can simplify it.

LITTON SIMPLIFIES
THE COMPLEX

LITTON SYSTEMS (CANADA) LIMITED, TORONTO, ONTARIO ■ DIVISION OF LITTON INDUSTRIES

M 6. MATERIALS HANDLING EQUIPMENT

British Hovercraft Corporation
Coventry Climax Engines Ltd.
Decca Radar Ltd.
MacTaggart, Scott & Co. Ltd.

M 7. MERCHANT SHIPS

Blohm + Voss AG
Boatservice Ltd. A/S
Brooke Marine Ltd.
Fr. Lürssen Werft
Split Shipyard
Todd Shipyards Corporation
Yarrow (Shipbuilders) Ltd.

M 8. MICROPHONE EQUIPMENT

Columbia Electronics International
 Inc.
Hawker Siddeley Group
R.F. Communications
Sofrexan
Thomson C. S. F.

M 9. MINE LAYERS

Blohm + Voss AG
Boatservice Ltd. A/S
British Hovercraft Corporation
Brooke Marine Ltd.
D.T.C.N.
Netherlands United Shipbuilding
 Bureaux Ltd.
Sofrexan
Vosper Thornycroft Group, The
Yarrow (Shipbuilders) Ltd.

M 10. MINESWEEPERS

Blohm + Voss AG
Boatservice Ltd. A/S
Brooke Marine Ltd.
D.T.C.N.
Netherlands United Shipbuilding
 Bureaux Ltd.
Sofrexan
Vosper Thornycroft Group, The
Yarrow (Shipbuilders) Ltd.

M 11. MISSILE CONTROL SYSTEMS

Aerospatiale (S.N.I.A.S.)
British Aircraft Corporation
Contraves AG
Decca Radar Ltd.
Ferranti Ltd.
Hollandse Signaalapparaten N.V.
Litton Systems (Canada) Ltd.
Marconi Co. Ltd., The
Sofrexan
Thomson C. S. F.

M 12. MISSILE INSTALLATIONS

Aerospatiale (S.N.I.A.S.)
British Aircraft Corporation
Hawker Siddeley Group
Sofrexan
Thomson C. S. F.
Vosper Thornycroft Group, The

M 13. MISSLE LAUNCHING SYSTEMS

Aerospatiale (S.N.I.A.S.)
British Aircraft Corporation
F.M.C. Northern Ordnance Division
Hawker Siddeley Group
Sofrexan
Thompson C. S. F.

M 14. MISSILE SHIPS

Blohm + Voss AG
Brooke Marine Ltd.
D.T.C.N.
Fr. Lürssen Werft
Netherlands United Shipbuilding
 Bureaux Ltd.
Sofrexan
Vosper Thornycroft Group, The
Yarrow (Shipbuilders) Ltd.

M 15. MODELMAKERS

Alnavco
Split Shipyard
Vosper Thornycroft Group, The
Yarrow (Shipbuilders) Ltd.

M 16. MODEL TEST TOWING TANK SERVICE

D.T.C.N.
Vosper Thronycroft Group, The

M 17. MOTOR CONTROL GEAR

Hawker Siddeley Group
Korody-Colyer Corporation
Laurence, Scott & Electromotors Ltd.
Thomson C. S. F.
Vosper Thornycroft Group, The

M 18. MOTOR STARTERS

Hawker Siddeley Group
Korody-Colyer Corporation
Laurence, Scott & Electromotors Ltd.
Thomson C. S. F.
Vosper Thornycroft Group, The

M 19. MOTOR TORPEDO BOATS

Boatservice Ltd. A/S
British Hovercraft Corporation
Brooke Marine Ltd.
Cantiere Rodriquez
Fr. Lürssen Werft
Sofrexan
Vosper Thornycroft Group, The
Yarrow (Shipbuilders) Ltd.

M 20. MOTORS, ELECTRIC

Ferranti Limited
Hawker Siddeley Group
Laurence, Scott & Electromotors Ltd.
Sofrexan
Thomson C. S. F.

M 21. MOVING WEIGHT STABILISERS

Vosper Thornycroft Group, The

M 22. MULTI-PLAN PLUGS

N 1. NAVAL GUNS

AB Bofors
Contraves AG
D.T.C.N.
F.M.C. Northern Ordnance Division
Sofrexan

N 2. NAVAL RADAR

Contraves AG
Decca Radar Limited
Hollandse Signaalapparaten N.V.
Marconi Radar Systems Ltd.
Plessey Radar Ltd.
R. F. Communications
Sofrexan
Thomson C. S. F.

N 3. NAVIGATION AIDS

Barr & Stroud Ltd.
British Aircraft Corporation
Decca Navigator Co. Ltd., The
Decca Radar Limited
Ferranti Limited
Hawker Siddeley Group
Laurence, Scott & Electromotors Ltd.
Marconi Radar Systems Ltd.
Plessey Company Limited, The
Sofrexan
R. F. Communications
Thomson C. S. F.

N 4. NIGHT VISION SYSTEMS

Barr & Stroud Ltd.
Sofrexan
Thomson C. S. F.

N 5. NON-MAGNETIC MINESWEEPERS

Boatservice Ltd. A/S
Netherlands United Shipbuilding
 Bureaux Ltd.
Sofrexan
Vosper Thornycroft Group, The
Yarrow (Shipbuilders) Ltd.

O 1. OCEANOGRAPHIC SURVEY SHIPS

Yarrow (Shipbuilders) Ltd.

O 2. OIL DRILLING RIGS

Hawker Siddeley Group

O 3. 'OILFREE' COMPRESSORS

Hawker Siddeley Group

O 4. OIL FUEL HEATERS

Blohm + Voss AG
Vosper Thornycroft Group, The

O 5. OIL FUEL SYSTEMS AND BURNERS

Todd Shipyards Corporation
Vosper Thornycroft Group, The

O 6. OPTICAL FILTERS

Barr & Stroud Ltd.

O 7. ORDNANCE

AB Bofors
D.T.C.N.
F.M.C. Northern Ordnance Division
Sofrexan

P 1. PARTS FOR DIESEL ENGINES

Blohm + Voss AG
Chantiers de L'Atlantique
C.R.M., Fabbrica Motori Marini
Hawker Siddeley Group
Korody-Colyer Corporation
M.T.U.—Motoren und Turbinen Union
Netherlands United Shipbuilding
 Bureaux Ltd.

P 2. PASSENGER SHIPS

Blohm + Voss AG
Boatservice Ltd. A/S
Brooke Marine Ltd.
Cantiere Rodriquez
Split Shipyard
Vosper Thornycroft Group, The
Yarrow (Shipbuilders) Ltd.

P 3. PATROL BOATS, LAUNCHES, TENDERS AND PINNACES

Boatservice Ltd. A/S
British Hovercraft Corporation
Brooke Marine Ltd.
Cantiere Rodriquez
Korody Marine Corporation
Fr. Lürssen Werft
Netherlands United Shipbuilding
 Bureaux Ltd.
Vosper Thornycroft Group, The
Yarrow (Shipbuilders) Ltd.

P 4. PERISCOPE FAIRINGS

Edo Corporation
MacTaggart, Scott & Co. Ltd.
Sofrexan

P 5. PERISCOPES

Barr & Stroud Ltd.
D.T.C.N.
Plessey Radio Systems Division

P 6. PIPES, COPPER AND BRASS

Mingori
Plessey Radio Systems Division
Vickers Limited

P 7. PIPES, SEA WATER

Mingori
Plessey Radio Systems Division

P 8. PIPE BENDING MACHINES

Mingori

P 9. PISTONS, PISTON RINGS, AND GUDGEON PINS

Korody-Colyer Corporation

P 10. PLUGS AND SOCKETS

Ferranti Limited
Thomson C. S. F.

P 11. PONTOONS, SELF PROPELLED

Brooke Marine Ltd.
Yarrow (Shipbuilders) Ltd.

P 12. PRESSURE VESSELS

D.T.C.N.
Netherlands United Shipbuilding
   Bureaux Ltd.
Vickers Limited
Vosper Thornycroft Group, The
Yarrow & Co. Ltd.

P 13. PROPELLENTS

AB Bofors

P 14. PROPELLERS, SHIPS'

AB Bofors
Split Shipyard

P 15. PROPELLERS, SHIPS' RESEARCH

Sofrexan
Vosper Thornycroft Group, The

P 16. PROPULSION MACHINERY

Blohm + Voss AG
D.T.C.N.
Flexibox Ltd.
Hawker Siddeley Group
Korody-Colyer Corporation
Laurence, Scott & Electromotors Ltd.
M.T.U.—Motoren und Turbinen Union
Netherlands United Shipbuilding
   Bureaux Ltd.
Sofrexan
Yarrow & Co. Ltd.

P 17. PUBLISHERS

Alnavco
Antheil Booksellers
B.P.C. Publishing Ltd.
McGraw-Hill Book Company
Sampson Low, Marston & Co. Ltd.

P 18. PUMPS

F.M.C. Northern Ordnance Division
Hawker Siddeley Group
Korody Colyer Corporation
MacTaggart, Scott & Co. Ltd.

P 19. PUMPS, COMPONENT PARTS

Flexibox Ltd.
F.M.C. Northern Ordnance Division
Korody-Colyer Corporation

P 20. PLOTTING TABLES

Laurence Scott & Electromotors Ltd.

R 1. RADAR AERIALS

Barr & Stroud Ltd.
British Aircraft Corporation
Decca Radar Limited
Hollandse Signaalaparaten N.V.
Marconi Radar Systems Ltd.
Plessey Radar Ltd.
R. F. Communications
Sofrexan
Thomson C. S. F.

R 2. RADAR FOR FIRE CONTROL

Contraves AG
Decca Radar Ltd.
Ferranti Ltd.
Hollandse Signaalapparaten N.V.
Marconi Radar Systems Ltd.
Sofrexan
Thomson C. S. F.

R 3. RADAR FOR HARBOUR SUPERERVISION

Decca Radar Limited
Ferranti Ltd.
Hollandse Siggnaalapparaten N.V.
Marconi Co. Ltd., The
Plessey Radar Ltd.
Thomson C. S. F.

R 4. RADAR FOR NAVIGATION WARNING INTERCEPTION

Decca Radar Limited
Ferranti Ltd.
Hollandse Signaalapparaten N.V.
Marconi Radar Systems Ltd.
Plessey Radar Ltd.
Thomson C. S. F.

R 5. RADIO, AIR

Marconi Communication Systems Ltd.
Plessey Company Limited, The
R. F. Communications
Thomson C. S. F.

R 6. RADIO EQUIPMENT

Hawker Siddeley Group
Marconi Communication Systems Ltd.
Plessey Company Limited, The
R. F. Communications
Sofrexan
Thomson C. S. F.

R 7. RADIO TRANSMITTERS AND RECEIVERS

Marconi Communication Systems Ltd,
Plessey Company Limited, The
R. F. Communications
Sofrexan
Thomson C. S. F.

R 8. RAMJETS

Aerospatiale (S.N.I.A.S.)
British Aircraft Corporation
Sofrexan

R 9. RANGEFINDERS

Barr & Stroud Ltd.
Sofrexan
Thomson C. S. F.

R 10. REMOTE CONTROLS

Laurence, Scott & Electromotors Ltd.
Plessey Company Limited, The
Sofrexan
Thomson C. S. F.
Vosper Thornycroft Group, The

R 11. REPLACEMENT PARTS FOR DIESEL ENGINES

Blohm + Voss AG
Chantiers de L'Atlantique
C.R.M., Fabbrica Motori Marini
Hawker Siddeley Group
Korody-Colyer Corporation
M.T.U.—Motoren und Turbinen Union
Netherlands United Shipbuilding
   Bureaux Ltd.

R 12. RESEARCH SHIPS

Brooke Marine Ltd.
Fr. Lürssen Werft
Sofrexan
Thomson C. S. F.
Vosper Thornycroft Group, The
Yarrow (Shipbuilders) Ltd.

R 13. REVERSE REDUCTION GEARS, OIL OPERATED

C.R.M., Fabbrica Motori Marini
Korody-Colyer Corporation
M.T.U.—Motoren und Turbinen Union
Vosper Thornycroft Group, The
Zahnradfabrik Friedrichshafen AG

R 14. REVERSING ENGINES, STEAM AND AIR OPERATED

MacTaggart, Scott & Co. Ltd.

R 15. REVERSING GEARS

C.R.M., Fabbrica Motori Marini
Korody-Colyer Corporation
M.T.U.—Motoren und Turbinen Union
Vosper Thornycroft Group, The
Zahnradfabrik Friedrichshafen AG

R 16. ROLL DAMPING FINS

Blohm + Voss AG
Vosper Thornycroft Group, The

R 17. RUDDERS

Yarrow (Shipbuilders) Ltd.

S 1. SALVAGE AND BOOM VESSELS

Brooke Marine Ltd.
Vosper Thornycroft Group, The
Yarrow (Shipbuilders) Ltd.

S 2. SCIENTIFIC INSTRUMENTS

Barr & Stroud Ltd.
Decca Radar Ltd.
Ferranti Limited
Thomson C. S. F.

S 3. SEALS (MECHANICAL)

Flexibox Ltd.

S 4. SHIP BUILDERS AND SHIP REPAIRERS

Blohm + Voss AG
Boatservice Ltd. A/S
Brooke Marine Ltd.
Cantiere Rodriquez
D.T.C.N.
Fr. Lürssen Werft
Netherlands United Shipbuilding
   Bureaux Ltd.
Split Shipyard
Todd Shipyards Corporation
Vosper Thornycroft Group, The
Yarrow (Shipbuilders) Ltd.

S 5. SHIP & SUBMARINE DESIGN

Ingenieurkontor Lübeck

CLASSIFIED LIST OF ADVERTISERS—*continued*

S 6. SHIP MACHINERY
Blohm + Voss AG
D.T.C.N.
M.T.U.—Motoren und Turbinen Union
Netherlands United Shipbuilding
   Bureaux Ltd.
Sofrexan
Yarrow & Co. Ltd.

S 7. SHIPS MAGNETIC COMPASS TEST TABLES
Barr & Stroud Ltd.

S 8. SHIP STABILISERS
Blohm + Voss AG
Vosper Thornycroft Group, The

S 9. SHIP SYSTEMS ENGINEERING
D.T.C.N.
Ferranti Ltd.
Hawker Siddeley Group
Netherlands United Shipbuilding
   Bureaux Ltd.
Vosper Thornycroft Group, The
Yarrow & Co. Ltd.

S 10. SHIPS' BRASSFOUNDRY

S 11. SIMULATORS
British Aircraft Corporation
Ferranti Limited
Hawker Siddeley Group
Laurence, Scott & Electromotors Ltd.
Sofrexan
Van der Heem Electronics
Vosper Thornycroft Group, The

S 12. SLIP RING, ASSEMBLIES

S 13. SMOKE INDICATORS
Barr & Stroud Ltd.

S 14. SOCKETS AND PLUGS, ELECTRIC WATERTIGHT
Thomson C. S. F.

S 15. SOCKETS AND PLUGS, MULTI PIN PATTERNS
Thomson C. S. F.

S 16. SOCKET TERMINATIONS
Thomson C. S. F.

S 17. SONAR EQUIPMENT
British Aircraft Corporation
Columbia Electronics International,
   Inc.
Edo Corporation
Decca Radar Ltd.
Laurence Scott & Electromotors Ltd.
Plessey Company Limited, The
Rhine-Schelde
Sofrexan
Thomson C. S. F.
Van der Heem Electronics

S 18. SONAR EQUIPMENT, HULL FITTINGS AND HYDRAULICS
Decca Radar Ltd.
D.T.C.N.
Laurence Scott & Electromotors Ltd.
Thomson C. S. F.
Vosper Thornycroft Group, The

S 19. SPARE PARTS FOR DIESEL ENGINES
Blohm + Voss AG
Chantiers de L'Atlantique
C.R.M., Fabbrica Motori Marini
Hawker Siddeley Group
Korody-Colyer Corporation
M.T.U.—Motoren und Turbinen Union
Netherlands United Shipbuilding
   Bureaux Ltd.

S 20. SPEED BOATS
Brooke Marine Ltd.
Boatservice Ltd. A/S
Cantiere Rodriquez
Fr. Lürssen Werft
Vosper Thornycroft Group, The
Yarrow (Shipbuilders) Ltd.

S 21. STABILISING EQUIPMENT
Blohm + Voss AG
Ferranti Ltd.
Hollandse Signaalapparaten N.V.
Vosper Thornycroft Group, The

S 22. STABILISING EQUIPMENT FOR FIRE CONTROL
British Aircraft Corporation
Contraves AG
Ferranti Ltd.
Hollandse Signaalapparaten N.V.

S 23. STEAM-RAISING PLANT, CONVENTIONAL
Blohm + Voss AG
D.T.C.N.
Netherlands United Shipbuilding
   Bureaux Ltd.
Rhine-Schelde
Yarrow & Co. Ltd.

S 24. STEAM-RAISING PLANT, NUCLEAR
D.T.C.N.
Netherlands United Shipbuilding
   Bureaux Ltd.

S 25. STEAM TURBINES
Blohm + Voss AG
D.T.C.N.
Netherlands United Shipbuilding
   Bureaux Ltd.
Sofrexan
Yarrow & Co. Ltd.

S 26. STEEL, ALLOY AND SPECIAL
AB Bofors

S 27. STEEL FORGINGS, PLATES AND SECTIONS, STAMPINGS
AB Bofors

S 28. STEEL, MANGANESE, WEAR RESISTING
AB Bofors

S 29. STEERING GEAR
Hastie & Co. Ltd., John
MacTaggart, Scott & Co. Ltd.
Vosper Thornycroft Group, The

S 30. STRESS RELIEVING
F.M.C. Northern Ordnance Division
Vosper Thornycroft Group, The
Yarrow & Co. Ltd.

S 31. SUBMARINE FIRE CONTROL
Ferranti Ltd.
Hollandse Signaalapparaten N.V.
Laurence Scott & Electromotors Ltd.
Plessey Company Ltd., The
Rhine-Schelde
Sofrexan
Thomson C. S. F.

S 32. SUBMARINE PERISCOPES
Barr & Stroud Ltd.
Rhine-Schelde
Sofrexan
Thomson C. S. F.

S 33. SUBMARINES
D.T.C.N.
Netherlands United Shipbuilding
   Bureaux Ltd.
Sofrexan
Split Shipyard

S 34. SUBMARINES (CONVENTIONAL)
D.T.C.N.
Netherlands United Shipbuilding
   Bureaux Ltd.
Sofrexan
Thomson C. S. F.

S 35. SUPERHEATERS
Blohm + Voss Ltd.
Yarrow & Co. Ltd.

S 36. SURVEY EQUIPMENT
British Aircraft Corporation
Thomson C. S. F.

S 37. SWITCHBOARDS
Blohm + Voss AG
Hawker Siddeley Group
Laurence, Scott & Electromotors Ltd.
Vosper Thornycroft Group, The
Whipp & Bourne Ltd.

S 38. SWITCHBOARDS AND SWITCHGEAR
Hawker Siddeley Group
Laurence, Scott & Electromotors Ltd.
Vosper Thornycroft Group, The
Whipp & Bourne Ltd.

T 1. TACTICAL TRAINING SIMULATORS
Ferranti Ltd.
Laurence Scott & Electromotors Ltd.
Plessey Radar Ltd.
Sofrexan
Thomson C. S. F.

T 2. TANKERS
Blohm + Voss AG
Fr. Lürssen Werft
Rhine-Schelde
Split Shipyard
Yarrow (Shipbuilders) Ltd.

T 3. TANKERS (SMALL)
Brooke Marine Ltd.
Fr Lürssen Werft
Rhine-Schelde
Split Shipyard
Yarrow (Shipbuilders) Ltd.

T 4. TANKS, OIL AND WATER STORAGE
Rhine-Schelde
Split Shipyard
Vosper Thornycroft Group, The

One merit alone...
to satisfy your demands

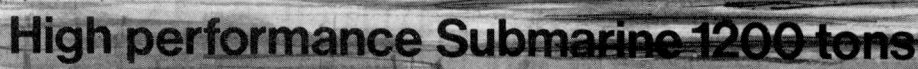

High performance Submarine 1200 tons

T 5. TECHNICAL PUBLICATIONS

B.P.C. Publishing Ltd.
Ferranti Ltd.
McGraw-Hill Book Company
Plessey Radar Ltd.
Sampson Low, Marston & Co. Ltd.

T 6. TELECOMMUNICATION EQUIPMENT

Columbia Electronics International Inc.
Ferranti Limited
Hawker Siddeley Group
Korody Marine Corporation
Marconi Co. Ltd., The
R. F. Communications
Sofrexan
Thomson C. S. F.

T 7. TELEGRAPH SYSTEMS

Columbia Electronics International, Inc.
Hawker Siddeley Group

T 8. TELEMOTORS

MacTaggart, Scott & Co. Ltd.

T 9. TELEPHONES, BATTERY-LESS

Hawker Siddeley Group

T 10. TELEPHONES, LOUD-SPEAKING

Hawker Siddeley Group
Korody Marine Corporation

T 11. TENDERS

Blohm + Voss AG
Brooke Marine Ltd.
Fr. Lürssen Werft
Vosper Thornycroft Group, The
Yarrow (Shipbuilders) Ltd.

T 12. TEST EQUIPMENT FOR FIRE CONTROL SYSTEMS

Barr & Stroud Ltd.
British Aircraft Corporation
Columbia Electronics International, Inc.
Contraves AG
Ferranti Limited
Hollandse Signaalapparaten N.V.
Laurence, Scott & Electromotors Ltd.
Thompson C. S. F.

T 13. TEXTILE FIBRES

Dupont Co.

T 14. TORPEDO CONTROL SYSTEMS

Barr & Stroud Ltd.
Ferranti Ltd.
Hollandse Signaalapparaten N.V.
Laurence, Scott & Electromotors Ltd.
Sofrexan
Thomson C. S. F.

T 15. TORPEDO CRAFT BUILDERS

Boatservice Ltd. A/S
Brooke Marine Ltd.
Cantiere Rodriquez
Fr. Lürssen Werft
Netherlands United Shipbuilding Bureaux Ltd.
Vosper Thornycroft Group, The
Yarrow (Shipbuilders) Ltd.

T 16. TORPEDO DEPTH AND ROLL RECORDERS

Barr & Stroud Ltd.

T 17. TORPEDO ORDER AND DEFLECTION CONTROL

Barr & Stroud Ltd.
Laurence, Scott & Electromotors Ltd.
Thompson C. S. F.

T 18. TORPEDO SIDE-LAUNCHERS

D.T.C.N.
F.M.C., Northern Ordnance Division
Sofrexan
Vosper Thornycroft Group, The

T 19. TORPEDOES AND TORPEDO TUBES

D.T.C.N.
Netherlands United Shipbuilding Bureaux Ltd.
Plessey Company Limited, The
Vosper Thornycroft Group, The

T 20. TRAINING EQUIPMENT

Ferranti Ltd.
Hollandse Signaalapparaten N.V.
Korody Marine Corporation
Laurence, Scott & Electromotors Ltd.
Plessey Company Limited, The

T 21. TRAWLERS

Brooke Marine Ltd.
Vosper Thornycroft Group, The
Yarrow (Shipbuilders) Ltd.

T 22. TUGS

Brooke Marine Ltd.
D.T.C.N.
Todd Shipyards Corporation
Vosper Thornycroft Group, The
Yarrow (Shipbuilders) Ltd.

T 23. TURBINE GEARS

D.T.C.N.
Netherlands United Shipbuilding Bureaux Ltd.
Sofrexan

T 24. TURBINES

Blohm + Voss AG
D.T.C.N.
Netherlands United Shipbuilding Bureaux Ltd.
Sofrexan
Yarrow & Co. Ltd.

T 25. TURBINES, EXHAUST

D.T.C.N.
Netherlands United Shipbuilding Bureaux Ltd.

T 26. TURBINES, GAS MARINE

Sofrexan
Yarrow & Co. Ltd.

T 27. TURBINES, STEAM MARINE

Blohm + Voss AG
D.T.C.N.
Netherlands United Shipbuilding Bureaux Ltd.
Sofrexan
Yarrow & Co. Ltd.

U 1. UNDERWATER LIGHTS

U 2. UNDERWATER TELEVISION EQUIPMENT

Barr & Stroud Ltd.
Marconi Communications System Ltd.
Thomson C. S. F.

V 1. VALVES AND COCKS

Cockburns Ltd.
Vickers Limited

V 2. VALVES AND COCKS, HYDRAULIC

MacTaggart, Scott & Co. Ltd.

V 3. VALVES, AUTOMATIC PLATE OR DISC

W 1. WARSHIP REPAIRERS

Blohm + Voss AG
Brooke Marine Ltd.
D.T.C.N.
Fr. Lürssen Werft
Netherlands United Shipbuilding Bureaux Ltd.
Todd Shipyards Corporation
Vosper Thornycroft Group, The
Yarrow (Shipbuilders) Ltd.

W 2. WARSHIPS

Blohm + Voss AG
Brooke Marine Ltd.
D.T.C.N.
Fr. Lürssen Werft
Netherlands United Shipbuilding Bureaux Ltd.
Sofrexan
Vosper Thornycroft Group, The
Yarrow (Shipbuilders) Ltd.

W 3. WATER TUBE BOILERS

Blohm + Voss AG
D.T.C.N.
Netherlands United Shipbuilding Bureaux Ltd.
Yarrow (Shipbuilders) Ltd.

W 4. WEAPON SYSTEMS

AB Bofors
Aerospatiale (S.N.I.A.S.)
British Aircraft Corporation
Contraves AG
Decca Radar Ltd.
D.T.C.N.
Ferranti Limited
F.M.C., Northern Ordnance Division
Hawker Siddeley Group
Hollandse Signaalapparaten N.V.
Laurence, Scott & Electromotors Ltd.
Marconi Communications Ltd.
Plessey Radar Ltd.
Sofrexan
Thomson C. S. F.

W 5. WEAPON SYSTEMS (SONAR COMPONENTS)

British Aircraft Corporation
Edo Corporation
Laurence, Scott & Electromotors Ltd.
Plessey Company Limited, The
Sofrexan
Thomson C. S. F.

W 6. WELDING, ARC, ARGON ARC OR GAS

Vosper Thornycroft Group, The
Yarrow & Co. Ltd.

W 7. WINCHES

Hawker Siddeley Group
Laurence, Scott & Electromotors Ltd.
MacTaggart, Scott & Co. Ltd.
Vosper Thornycroft Group, The

X 1. X-RAY WORK

Split Shipyard
Vosper Thornycroft Group, The
Yarrow & Co. Ltd.

Y 1. YACHTS (POWERED)

Boatservice Ltd. A/S
Brooke Marine Ltd.
Cantiere Rodriquez
Fr. Lürssen Werft
Vosper Thornycroft Group, The
Yarrow (Shipbuilders) Ltd.

INSERENTEN-BRANCHENVERZEICHNIS

Die Verweisungszahl bei jedem nachstehend aufgeführten Gegenstand gibt die entsprechende englische Überschrift auf den Seiten 17-31

A1	Aktionsübermittlungs-Schulungsgeräte	F14	Frischwasserdestillieranlagen
E13	Anfahr- und Abstellsteuerungen für Schiffsmaschinen	R6	Funkanlagen
C3	Ankerwinden und Auflaufhaspeln	R7	Funksender und -empfänger
P15	Antriebsmaschinen	F13	Gabelstapler
P12	Antriebsmittel	G2	Gasturbinen
I1	Anzeigegeräte, Elektrische	G1	Gasturbinenschiffe
L5	Aufzüge, hydraulische	E19	Geleitschiffe
T20	Ausbildungsgeräte	G10	Generatoren, Elektro-
S10	Ausbildungsgeräte (Simulatoren)	G17	Geschütze und Lafettierung
F10	Ausrüstung, Schiffs-	G18	Geschützlafetten
C4	Autofähren	G19	Geschützrichtaufsätze und Höhensucher
A16	Automatische Regelsysteme	G7	Getriebe, Rückwärts-, Reduktions-
A17	Automatische Steuerung	G3	Getriebegehäuse
D9	Bagger	G4	Getrieberäder und Getriebe
M1	Bearbeitete Eisenteile	F6	Glasfaserboote und andere Erzeugnisse
M2	Bearbeitete Nichteisenteile	B4	Großtransporter
C23	Behälterschiffe	C12	Gußeisenteile, Kugelgraphit
H2	Beheizte Fenster	C13	Grußeisenteile, Kugelgraphit-, Ni-Resist
T11	Beiboote	C8	Gußteile, Aluminium-Bronze-
E5	Beleuchtungskörper (Armaturen)	C9	Gußteile, Hochfeste Eisen-
S1	Bergungs- und Hafensperren-Verlegungsschiffe	C11	Gußteile, maskengeformte
F11	Biegsame Leitungsummantelungen	C10	Gußteile, Nichteisen-
O4	Brennölanlagen und Brenner	C14	Gußteile, Stahl-
F16	Brennöleinspritzanlagen	M7	Handelsschiffe
B3	Bücher (nautische)	A18	Hilfsmaschinen
B3a	Bücher (nautische) vergriffen	H4	Hovercraft (Luftkissenfahrzeuge)
C20	Computer	H7	Hydraulische Anlagen
C19	Computer, Wartung und Verkauf	H5	Hydraulische Geräte
S23	Dampferzeugungsanlage, Atom-	H6	Hydraulische Maschinen
S22	Dampferzeugungsanlage, herkömmlich	G5	Hypoidgetriebe
B2	Dampfkessel	I3	Infrarot-Werkstoffe
S24	Dampfturbinen	I6	Instrumente, Elektronische
D1	Deckmaschinenanlagen	I10	Instrumente für Versuchseinrichtungen
D6	Dieselkraftstoffeinspritzanlagen	I7	Instrumente, Nautische
D4	Dieselmotoren, Hauptantriebs-	I9	Instrumente, Präzisions-
D3	Dieselmotoren, Hilfs-	I8	Instrumententafeln
D5	Dieselmotoren-Ersatzteile	I5	Instrumententeile (Mechanische)
D8	Docktore	Y1	Jachten (Motor-)
P11	Druckgefäße	C1	Kabelgeflechte (mit oder ohne)
C17	Druckluftanlasser für Gasturbinen und Dieselmotoren	W4	Kampfanlagen
S16	Echolotausrüstungen	W5	Kampfanlagen (Unterwasserortungsteile)
I4	Einspritzausrüstung	G16	Kanonenboote
E1	Ekonomiser	G9	Keilriemenantriebe
E4	Elektroausrüstung	P8	Kolben, Kolbenringe und Kolbenbolzen
E3	Elektrohilfmaschinen	O2	Kompressoren für ölfreie Luft
E8	Elektrohydraulische Zusatzgeräte	C26	Korvetten
E6	Elektroinstallation und Reparatur	C27	Kräne, Schiffs-
E2	Elektrokabel	G20	Kreiselkompasse
E9	Elektronische Ausrüstung	C28	Kreuzer
E7	Elektroschaltanlagen	W2	Kriegsschiffe
R9	Entfernungsmesser	W1	Kriegsschiff-Reparaturbetriebe
F2	Entwerfen von schnellen Kriegsschiffen	C16	Küsten- und Flachwasser-Minensuchboote
R11	Ersatzteile für Dieselmotoren	C5	Ladungsumschlageinrichtungen
F4	Fähren	L6	Lampen und Beleuchtung
F5	Faseroptik	L1	Lampenhalter (Fassungen)
G15	Ferngelenkte Flugkörper	A15	Landungsboote und -schiffe
G13	Ferngelenkte Flugkörper, Wartungsausrüstung	A14	Landungsfahrzeuge
G14	Ferngelenkte Flugkörper-Schiffe	L2	Landungsfahrzeuge
B1	Ferngläser	L3	Laser-Entfernungsmesser
T6	Fernmeldeanlagen	L4	Lasersysteme
R10	Fernsteuerungen	L8	Lautsprecheranlagen
F8	Feuerleitungs- und Schießausrüstung	M13	Lenkwaffenabschußsysteme
F7	Feuerlösch- und Bergungsfahrzeuge	M12	Lenkwaffenanlagen
F9	Feuerlöschpumpen	A6	Luftkissenfahrzeuge
T21	Fischdampfer	A2	Luftverdichter
R5	Flugfunk	M4	Marinarchitekten
M14	Flugkörper-Schiffe	N1	Marinegeschütze
A5	Flugzeuginstrumente	N2	Marineradar
A3	Flugzeuglandebremsvorrichtungen	G11	Maschinenregler
A4	Flugzeugträger	M6	Materialverladeanlagen
L7	Flüssiggasbehälter (Petroleum-)	M22	Mehrpolstecker
R12	Forschungsschiffe	M8	Mikrophonanlagen
C7	Frachtraumüberwachungsgeräte	M9	Minenleger
C6	Frachtschiffe	M10	Minensuchboote
F15	Fregatten	M15	Modellhersteller

M16	Modellschleppversuchsdienst
M18	Motoranlasser
S19	Motorboote
E12	Motordrehzahlregler
G12	Motordrehzahlregler
E17	Motoren, Dampfturbinen-
E15	Motoren, Diesel-
M20	Motoren, Elektro-
E16	Motoren, Gasturbinen-
M17	Motorkontrollanlagen
E10	Motorkontrollgeräte und Datenschreiber
E11	Motorteile, Diesel-
M19	Motortorpedoboote
A8	Munition
A9	Munitionsaufzüge
N4	Nachtsichtsysteme
N3	Navigationsanlagen
H9	Nautische Vermessungsgeräte
O1	Ölbohranlagen
O5	Optische Filter
A13	Panzerplatten
P2	Passagierschiffe
P3	Patrouillenschiffe, -Barkassen, -Beiboote und -Pinassen
F1	Patrouillenschnellboote
P5	Periskope
P4	Periskopverkleidungen
E18	Planetengetriebe
P10	Pontons, selbstfahrende
I2	Positionslampen
S6	Prüftische für Schiffsmagnetkompaß
P17	Pumpen
P18	Pumpen, Einzelteile
R2	Radar für Feuerleitung
R3	Radar für Hafenaufsicht
R4	Radar für Navigation, Warnung, Abfang
R1	Radarantennen
M11	Raketensteueranlagen
S12	Rauchmarkierungsvorrichtungen
P6	Rohre, Kupfer- und Messing-
P7	Rohre, Seewasser-
X1	Röntgenarbeiten
R13	Rückwärts-Reduktionsgetriebe, ölbetrieben
H3	Rudermelder
C24	Schaltpulte (elektrische)
S36	Schalttafeln, Schaltschränke
S37	Schalttafeln (Schaltschränke) und Schaltanlagen
F12	Scheinwerfer
S8	Schiffsanlagentechnik
S3	Schiffsbauer und Instandsetzungsbetriebe
I11	Schiffsinneneinrichtung und -ausbau
S4	Schiffsmaschinen
S9	Schiffsmessinggiesserei
S5	Schiffs und U-boot Entwerf
P14	Schiffspropeller-Forschungsdienst
M5	Schiffsradar
S11	Schleifringe
T22	Schlepper
S7	Schlingerdämpfungsanlagen
P13	Schrauben, Schiffs-
W6	Schweissen, elektrisch, Argon-Lichtbogen-oder Gas-
C2	Senkkästen
S29	Spannungsentlastung
F3	Speisewasservorwärmer
G6	Spiralzahnkegelrad
M21	Stabilisieranlagen mit verschiebbaren Massen
S20	Stabilisierungsanlagen
S21	Stabilisierungsanlagen für Feuerleitung
R16	Stabilisierungsflossen
S27	Stahl, Mangan-, widerstandsfähig gegen Abnutzung
S25	Stahl- und Speziallegierungen
S26	Stahlschmiedestücke, -platten und -teile, Preßstücke
R8	Staustrahlturbinen
S13	Steckdosen und Stecker, elektrische, wasserdicht
S14	Steckdosen und Stecker, mehrpolige Typen
S15	Stecker
P9	Stecker und Steckdosen
C25	Steuer- (Regelungs-) Anlagen
S28	Steuergeräte
R17	Steuerruder
G8	Stirnräder
N5	Suchboote für Nichtmagnetminen
T4	Tanks, Öl- und Wasservorrats-
T2	Tankschiffe
T3	Tankschiffe (klein)
D7	Tauchausrüstung
T5	Technische Veröffentlichungen
P1	Teile für Dieselmotoren
T7	Telegraphenanlagen
T8	Telemotoren
T9	Telephone, batterielose
T10	Telephone, Lautsprecher-
T12	Testgeräte für Feuerleitungsanlagen
T13	Textilfäsern
T15	Torpedobootbauer
T19	Torpedos und Torpedorohre
T18	Torpedo-Seitenabschußvorrichtungen
T14	Torpedosteuersysteme
T17	Torpedosteuerungs und -abweichungskontrolle
T16	Torpedo-Tiefen- und Schlingeraufzeichner
H8	Tragflächenboote
O3	Treibölvorwärmer
E14	Triebwerke, Flugzeug-
D11	Trockendockinhaber
D10	Trockenfrachter
T24	Turbinen
T25	Turbinen, Auspuff-
T27	Turbinen, Schiffs-Dampf-
T26	Turbinen, Schiffs-Gas-
T23	Turbinenvorgelege
S34	Überhitzer
A10	U-Bootabwehrboote
A12	U-Bootabwehrraketen
A11	U-Bootabwehr-Raketenabschußvorrichtungen
S30	U-Boot-Feuerleitung
S31	U-Boot-Periskope
R15	Umkehrgetriebe
R14	Umkehrmotoren, dampf- und luftbetrieben
S32	Unterseeboote
S33	Unterseeboote (herkömmlich)
U2	Unterwasserfernsehgeräte
S17	Unterwasser-Schallmessanlagen, Rumpfeinbauten und hydraulische Einrichtungen für
U1	Unterwasserscheinwerfer
V3	Ventile, automatische Platten- und Teller-
V1	Ventile und Absperrvorrichtungen
V2	Ventile und Absperrvorrichtungen, hydraulische
C18	Verdichter
C22	Verflüssiger
C21	Verflüssigerrohre
P16	Verleger
S35	Vermessungsgeräte
O6	Waffen
H1	Wärmeaustauscher
M3	Wartungs- und Reparaturschiffe
W3	Wasserröhrenkessel
I12	Wechselrichter und Batterieladegeräte
A7	Wechselstromerzeuger
W7	Winden
S2	Wissenschaftliche Instrumente
C15	Zentralisierte und automatische Steuerung
D2	Zerstörer

for new ships and conversions, all types of naval surface vessels, modern fast patrol craft and submarines,

apply to :

SOFREXAN

which associates the facilities of
the French Naval Shipyards
and of world-known Weapon Systems Manufacturers.

Shareholders of SOFREXAN

French Navy
Dubigeon-Normandie
Constructions Mécaniques de Normandie
Chantiers Navals Franco-Belges
Chantiers Navals de l'Estérel

Alcatel
Cie des Ateliers et Forges de la Loire
Société Nationale Industrielle Aérospatiale
Thomson-CSF
Cie de Signaux et Entreprises Electriques

SOFREXAN

47, rue de Monceau - PARIS (8ᵉ)
Tél. : 522 12-52   Télex 28.756 F

SERCAD PUBLICITÉ

Action!
Action!

Submarine Command Team Trainer puts you where the action is

Submarine attack team personnel and sonar teams can be trained in the full use of their equipment, under simulated "live" action conditions, by the Ferranti Submarine Command Team Trainer. This equipment can also be used for tactical training of the submarine command in the co-ordination and direction of attacks or defensive manoeuvres.

Equipments are made to specific requirements and one recently supplied by Ferranti can simulate an exercise involving two manned submarines and up to five other unmanned vessels of types which can be selected at the start of an exercise and can be either surface ships or submarines.

The submarines can attack in consort or can oppose each other, or two separate exercises can be conducted simultaneously with the five unmanned vessels shared between the two submarine exercises.

During the course of the exercise, the instructor can control the manoeuvring of the unmanned vessels and can also initiate an attack against the submarines, using torpedoes, mortars and other weapons as appropriate.

A particular feature of this trainer is the simulation of the view through the attack periscopes of the submarines. Great realism is obtained by using television techniques and small models of the target ships which appear correctly positioned in the field of view of the periscope, as to bearing, waterline elevation, angle-on-the-bow, range and speed under the control of the computer.

For further information, contact
**Ferranti Limited,
Electronic & Display Equipment Division,
Simonsway, Wythenshawe,
Manchester, M22 5LA**
Telephone: 061-437 5291. Telex: 669045.

FERRANTI

ED. ED 1 [rb]

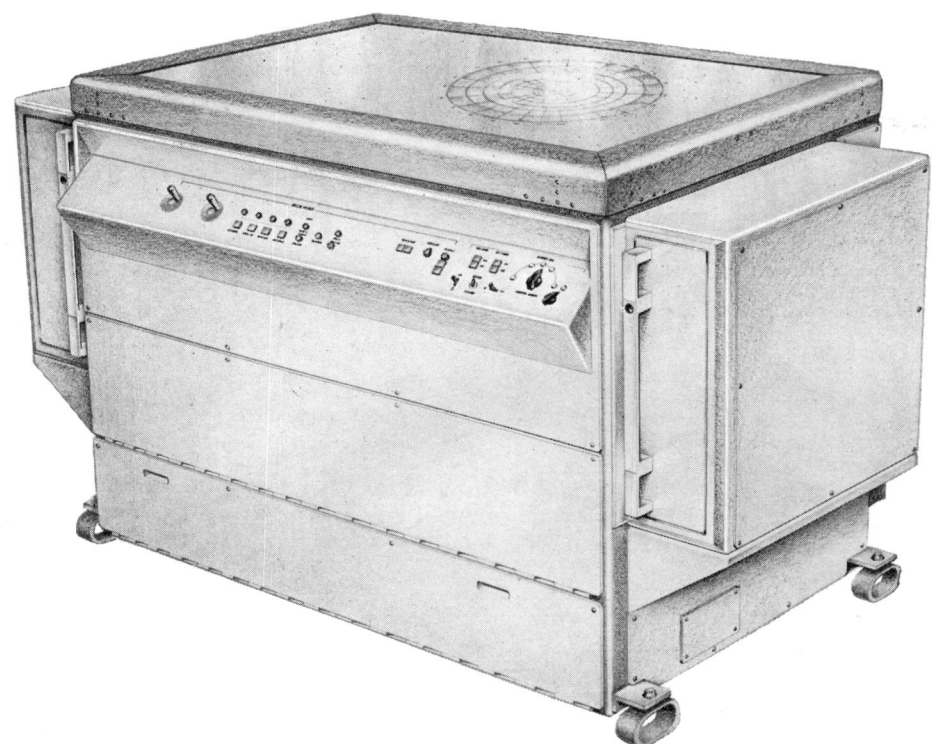

A 'radar true plot' or radar plotting table, an L.S.E. product developed jointly with Signaal (Netherlands)

PRECISION ELECTRONIC AND ELECTRO-MECHANICAL EQUIPMENT

True motion indication and transmission units; radar true plots; navigational plotting tables; weapon control apparatus; sonar equipment; attack teachers and simulators; steering trainers; hydrographic winches and control gear.

A specially-designed twin-dynamometer test rig for high-power contra-rotating torpedo motors

Instruments & Special Products Division

LAURENCE, SCOTT & ELECTROMOTORS LIMITED
NORWICH, NOR 85A   Telephone 28333

Training personnel? We know the problem -it's one of ours!

Only we solve it <u>our</u> way: by developing and manufacturing the most suitable electronic radar and sonar simulating equipment.

One example: our Shipborne Sonar Simulator type SSS-03, which simulates into realistic detail two echo sources, their true positions and movements.

Possibilities: moving surface or submarine targets, moving torpedoes, bubble echo and false echo.

And there are even more - all described in detail in our SSE/SSS literature we'll be glad to mail to you. Just ask for it.

SSS-03

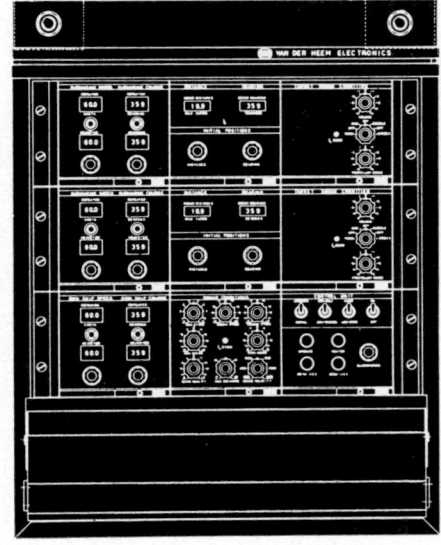

Shore based training system

 PHILIPS underwater systems

VAN DER HEEM ELECTRONICS N.V.
P.O. BOX 1060, THE HAGUE,
THE NETHERLANDS

A MEMBER OF THE
PHILIPS GROUP OF COMPANIES

PHILIPS

DIESEL SERVICE

our specialty

Our long experience in serving the free world's Navies, operating U.S.-made Diesel Equipment, is at your complete disposal, including:

Supply of Spares

Technical Assistance

Instruction and Parts Book Library

Special Tools and Test Equipment

Preserving, Packaging and Packing to U.S. Navy Specifications

Yearly Maintenance Contracts

Complete Replacement and Exchange Engines, Transmissions and other Major Components

Cut-Away Instruction Models

SERVING THE NAVIES OF | *THE FREE WORLD*

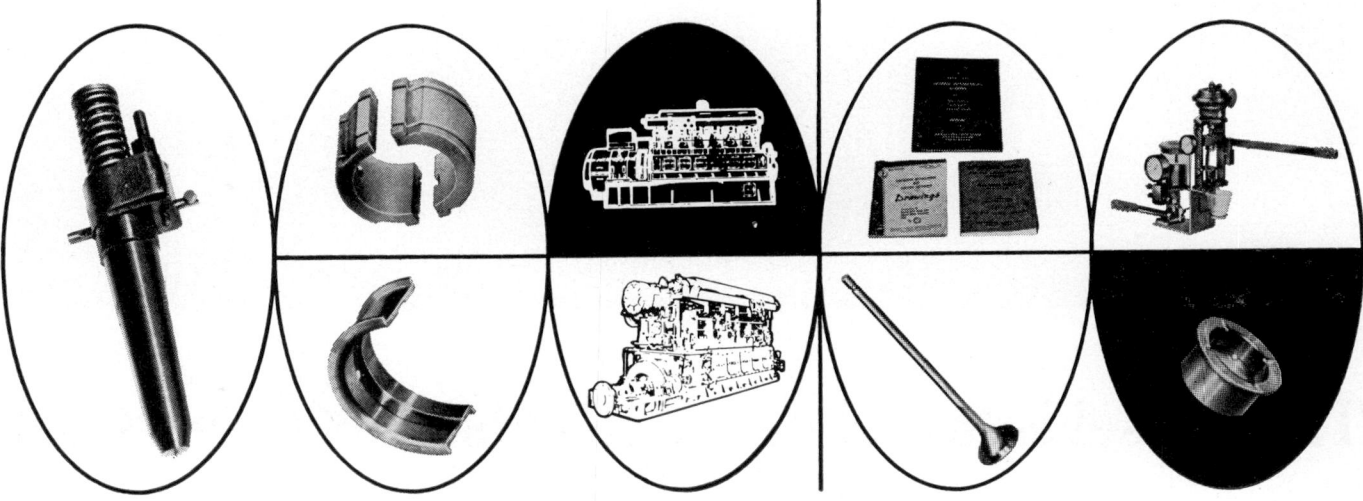

WESTERN EUROPEAN BRANCH WAREHOUSE AT HAVAM, HERUNGERWEG, VENLO, HOLLAND

ADDRESS ALL CORRESPONDENCE TO:

KORODY-COLYER CORPORATION
112 NORTH AVALON BOULEVARD, WILMINGTON, CALIFORNIA
TELEPHONE (213) 830-0330.   CABLE: KORODIESEL

This vessel is brand new... it's also 1,000 years old

The double-hull principle used by early Polynesians is now being applied to the new T-AGOR-16 catamaran you see above. Built for the Navy by Todd, she is the largest, most technologically advanced of America's oceanographic research vessels.

The shipbuilding business is one of the oldest in the world...but the importance of ships is still so great that they participate in the most modern ventures of man. Todd is proud to play a part in the conquering of inner space...a world even more unknown to us at present than the moon.

Executive offices: One Broadway, New York, N. Y. 10004. (212) 344-6900. Cable "Robin" New York.

TODD
SHIPYARDS CORPORATION
SHIPYARDS: Brooklyn · New Orleans · Galveston
Houston · Los Angeles · San Francisco · Seattle

SEAWOLF

the anti-missile
naval defence system

A warship that can only defend itself against aircraft is severely handicapped. Unless it can also counter the anti-ship *missile,* it cannot remain an effective fighting unit.

A Seawolf-armed ship will be able to counter small, fast missiles as well as aircraft and still mount full offensive armament.

The compact Seawolf missile, now under development for the Royal Navy, incorporates techniques used in British Aircraft Corporation's successful and inexpensive Rapier missile. It will use a light-weight, multi-barrel Vickers launcher. In association with high performance Marconi GWS 25 radars, Seawolf will be fitted extensively in new and existing ships of the Royal Navy from the mid-1970s onwards.

The Seawolf missile and launcher can also be associated with other surveillance and tracking systems in small ships.

 **BRITISH AIRCRAFT CORPORATION**
the most powerful aerospace company in Europe
Guided Weapons Division Stevenage Herts England

GWN 6

[38]

Navies the world over have installed
Whipp & Bourne switchgear
for over sixty years

WHIPP and BOURNE LIMITED CASTLETON · ROCHDALE · LANCASHIRE · TELEPHONE : ROCHDALE 32051 (10 lines) TELEX : 63442

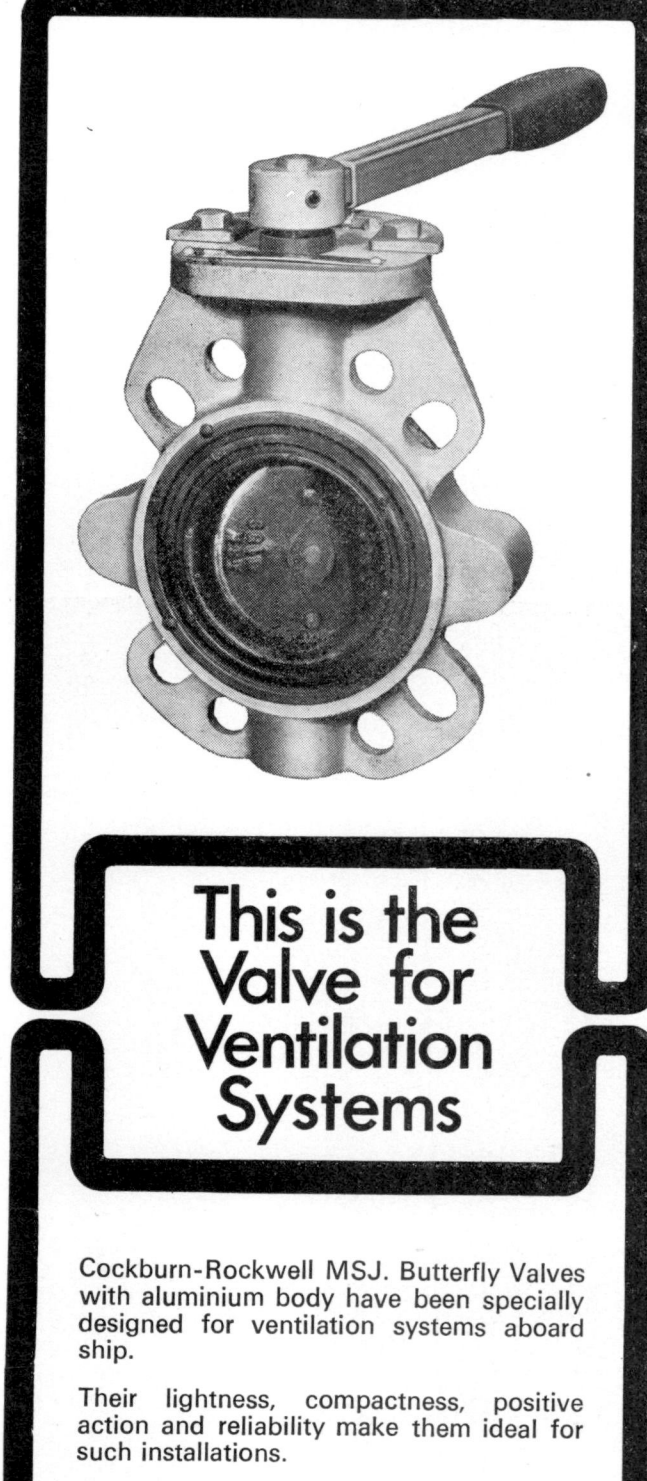

EXOCET

4 EXOCET MISSILES

1 OPERATOR

The EXOCET surface-to-surface weapon system is replacing the conventional 380 mm gun in all modern navies, on all types of warships, from high-speed launches or hydrofoils to big ships.

In the development of guidance equipment and missile installation, AEROSPATIALE cooperates fully with each user to meet his specific requirements in the best cost effectiveness conditions.

EXOCET provides new-class warships with unprecedented fire power and brings less recent-type ships modern tactical capability.

a new dimension in defence flexibility...

BHC 'real' hovercraft

Already, BHC "real" hovercraft are in service with the defence forces of the U.S., Iran, Italy, Brunei and the U.K. Further orders are in hand from Iran and Saudi Arabia.

Military versions of the SRN6 and BH7 are in series production at BHC and their fully amphibious capability lends a new defence flexibility for fast attack, logistic support, reconnaissance, casualty evacuation, offshore interception, tactical assault, patrol and many other roles often denied to other vehicles.

BHC "real" hovercraft — a new dimension in defence flexibility.

Decca
world leaders in marine electronics

Decca Transar Radar
Decca ISIS 300 Integrated
Ship Instrumentation System
Decca Navigator System
Arkas Automatic Pilot

Decca Radar Limited
The Decca Navigator Company Limited
Decca House, Albert Embankment
London SE1

DR 415

The New Bofors 57mm Dual-Purpose Gun, L/70

has a high combat effect against targets of all types: surface vessels, aircraft, air-to-surface missiles and surface-to-surface missiles.

The ammunition for this all-automatic gun has been optimized to give the highest possible effect:
for aerial targets-prefragmented shells with proximity fuzes, for naval targets-armour-piercing ammunition.

AB BOFORS
S 690 20 Bofors, Sweden

Powerful

Versatile

Economical

The YARROW FRIGATE

Its high armament/displacement weight ratio makes the Yarrow Frigate a very powerful and compact warship. The machinery installation of diesel engine and gas turbine permits both high speed performance and long range cruising.

Automated control results in a low manning requirement, and this with the machinery arrangement, gives moderate operational costs.

YARROW
(SHIPBUILDERS) LTD
SCOTSTOUN · GLASGOW

Dramatic Deadly

that's the new Vosper Thornycroft fast patrol Hovercraft!

With a full speed of 46 knots and exceptional stability and manoeuvrability in rough weather, this patrol vessel provides a fast and stable weapons platform, or it can float on its raft ready for instant action. The weapons load is 22 tons on a 100 ton displacement, and includes four Exocet guided missiles with a range of about 20 kilometres. The forward gun is a twin barrelled 35mm Oerlikon. Both controlled by Contraves fire control equipment.

The VT1 series Hovercraft has been exhaustively tested and evaluated for seakeeping and reliability for several hundred hours, many of them in the rough winter waters between the Channel Islands and the French coast. Installed power is about 5000 hp, or around one third of power needed for a conventional patrol boat of comparable performance.

Its shallow draft and high speed make it difficult to hit with torpedoes. The low silhouette offers a poor visual target. The performance is virtually unaffected by skirt damage from splinters or small arms. If emergency repairs are needed, then the hovercraft can be beached on any sloping surface, or berthed alongside a jetty like a normal boat.

The ideal heavily armed, short range vessel

For the full drama behind this fast patrol hovercraft, contact:

VOSPER THORNYCROFT
PAULSGROVE, PORTSMOUTH, ENGLAND
Telephone Cosham 79481. Telex 86115

1966
1961

▷B A SUBSIDIARY OF THE DAVID BROWN CORPORATION LIMITED

[49]

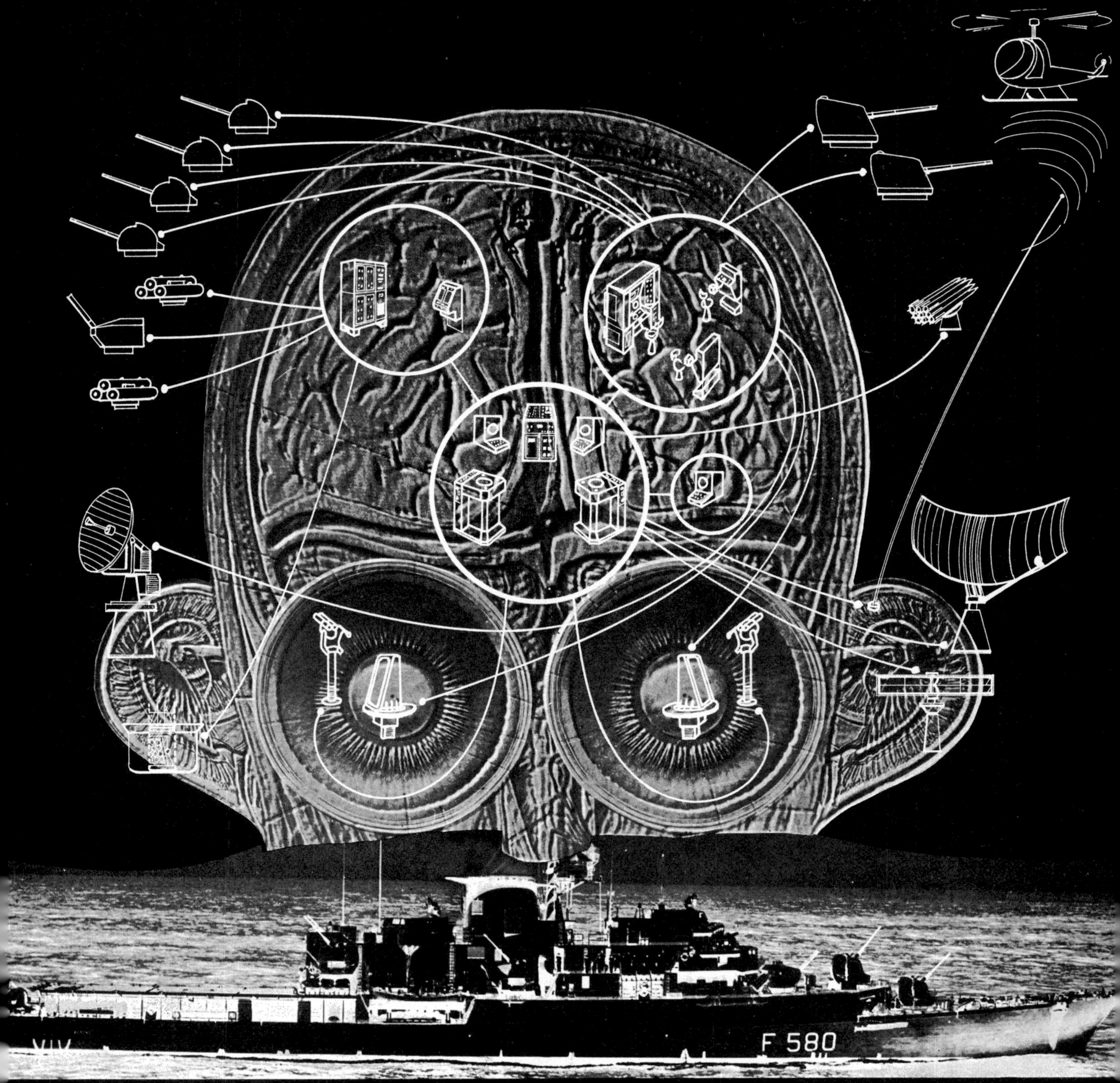

Compact Frigate - 675 tons

speed 25 knots

223 x 28¹/₃ x 9

ELECTRONIQUE MARCEL DASSAULT
55, QUAI CARNOT - 92 - SAINT-CLOUD - 603 89-00

Practice at Sea

H.M.S. Hampshire

H.M.S. Juno

H.M.S. Rothesay

Hastie Steering Gear is installed in all classes of ships of the Royal Navy and many overseas navies

JOHN HASTIE & CO. LTD.
P.O. BOX 18
GREENOCK, SCOTLAND
Telephone: Greenock 22286 (7 lines)
Telex: 77194

OERLIKON/OTO *35 mm. Naval Twin Mounting.*

76/62 OTO COMPACT *Anti-Ship and Anti-Aircraft Mounting.*

OTOMAT *Anti-Ship Missile System.*

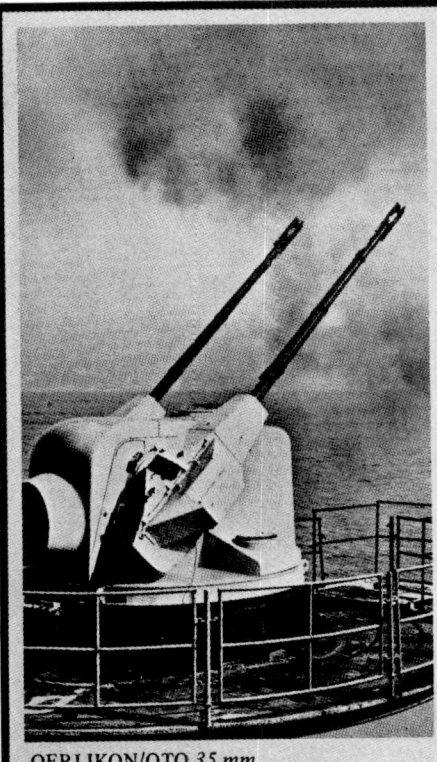

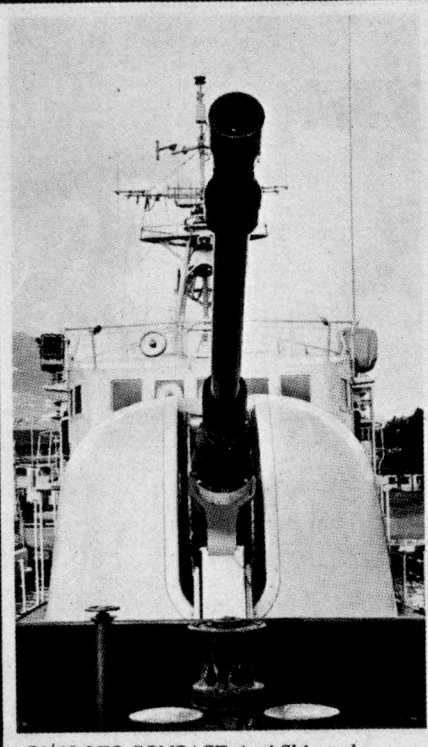

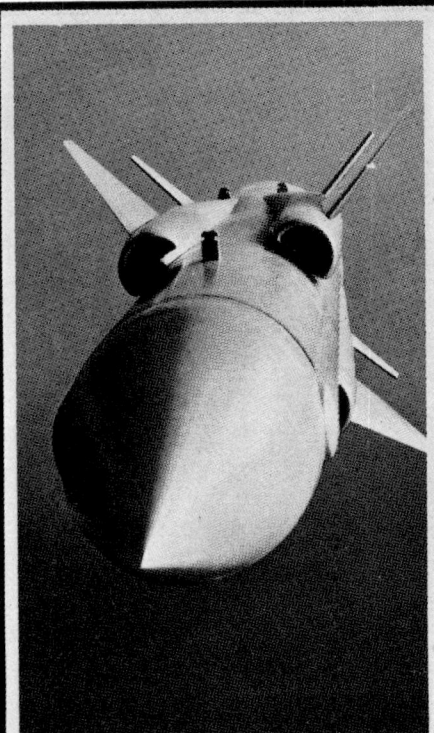

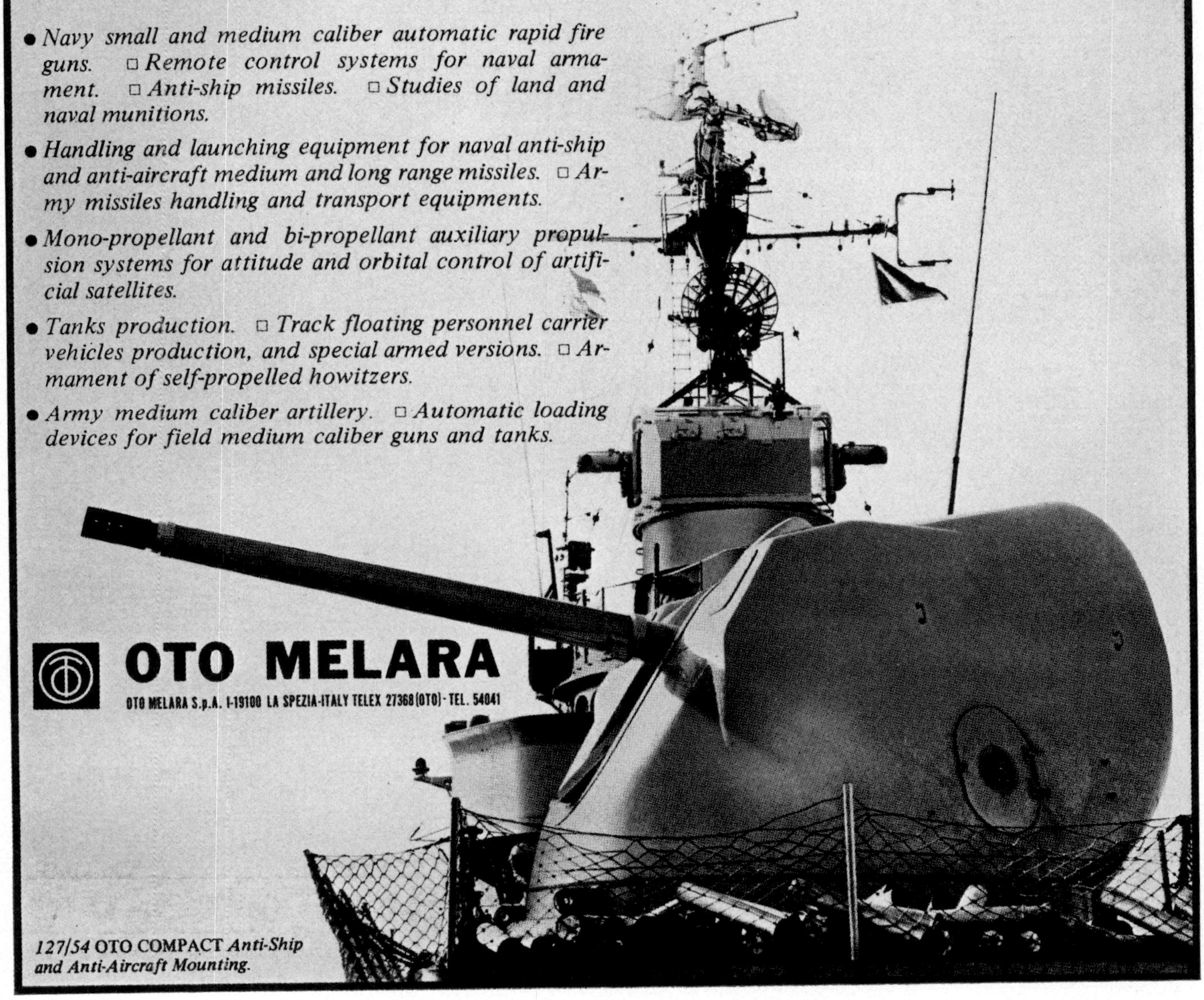

127/54 OTO COMPACT *Anti-Ship and Anti-Aircraft Mounting.*

e Limited

ESTABLISHED 1874

CONSULTING NAVAL ARCHITECTS

A DOWSETT COMPANY

37.5 m Seal Class
Long Range
Patrol Craft.

63m. A/S
Corvette (with
varied armament),
has anti-frigate
capability.

12 m. Fast Patrol
Craft. Now building
five further craft
for overseas
governments

THE QUEEN'S AWARD
TO INDUSTRY 1968

Changing Naval Tactics

Operating from the helicopter platform of a cruiser the Hawker Siddeley Harrier, high performance V/STOL fighter, affords instant protection against stand-off attack; a rapid

HAWKER SIDDELEY AVIATION

lift-off and a form dably armed defensive weapon is on its way. Recovery is just as simple. The Harrier is a fixed wing transonic fighter aircraft, with the versatility of a helicopter.

The HS Harrier

The Harrier is already in service with the Royal Air Force and the United States Marine Corps and is in quantity production for both.

Kingston upon Thames, England
Hawker Siddeley Group supplies mechanical, electrical and aerospace equipment with world-wide sales and service.

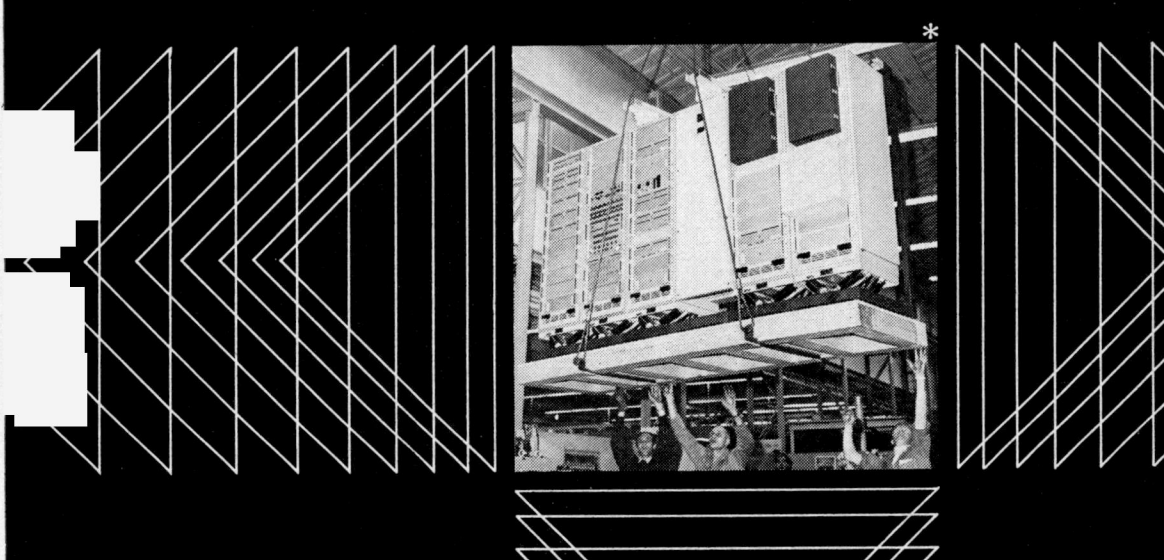
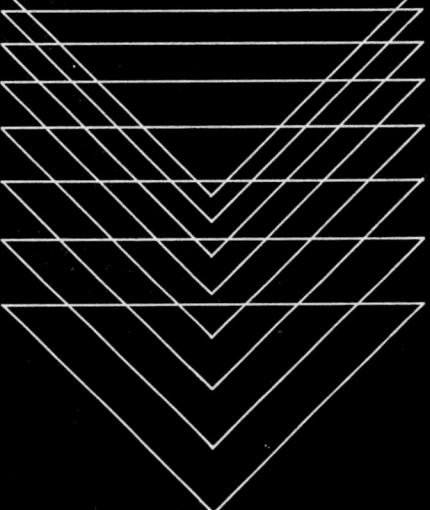

FR. LÜRSSEN WERFT
BREMEN

Telex: 24 44 84   GERMANY   *Telephone: 667017*

Lightest automatic 5" gun mount tested and accepted for ship installation

The Mark 45, a 5-inch/ 54 caliber automatic gun mount, has been test fired more than three years, including 18 months aboard ship, and has been accepted by the U.S. Navy for service use. Weighing less than 50,000 lbs., it is designed for installation on frigates, destroyers and destroyer escorts, as well as larger ships. It fits the same mounting foundation as the 5-inch/38 caliber single mount Mark 30.

Train, elevation and firing sequence of the Mark 45 can be automatically controlled by one man from a remote control panel below deck. Sustained firing beyond twenty rounds can be maintained by an additional crew of five. It stows, loads and fires all existing types of 5-inch/54 caliber semi-fixed ammunition without adjustment.

Total environmental protection is provided by an aluminum shield with thermal insulation.

For complete details about the Mark 45, write:

Marconi
radar systems
for warships

Crown copyright

- ■ **Surveillance Radars**
- ■ **Tracking and Missile Guidance Radars**
- ■ **Weapon System Management**
- ■ **Radar Data Processing and Display Equipment**
- ■ **Control Systems**

Marconi Radar Systems Limited
A GEC-Marconi Electronics Company
New Parks, Leicester, England LE3 1UF

LTD/GMO3

20121 milano via manzoni 12 tel. 708 326 / 708 327 telegr. cremme

DIESEL ENGINES LIGHT AND POWERFUL

ITALIAN COASTGUARD'S PATROL VESSEL "APPUNTATO MEATTINI" POWERED BY TWO 18 CYLINDER 1350 HP CRM 18 D/S TYPE DIESEL ENGINES DEVELOPING A SPEED OF OVER 30 KNOTS.

PRODUCTION RANGE:

DIESEL ENGINES FROM 100 TO 1350 HP
GASOLINE ENGINES FROM 1000 TO 2000 HP
INVERSION, REDUCTION GEARS - V. DRIVES

Selenia has developed a new and very advanced line of shipborne surveillance radars which will completely fulfil the operational requirements of modern electronic warfare. Main features of the new equipments are: advanced ECCM capabilities - high subclutter visibility - extreme reliability. The range of Selenia activities in the field of tracking radars covers monopulse, pulse - doppler and conical scan systems. Modern digital technology has been widely applied to these radars in order to give a substantial performance enhancement.

selenia search and fire control radars

SELENIA - INDUSTRIE ELETTRONICHE
ASSOCIATE SpA
RADAR DIVISION
ROME, ITALY

High and medium speed DIESEL ENGINES for

— marine and submarine propulsion
— and electric generating sets

from **900** HP   to **17 100** HP.

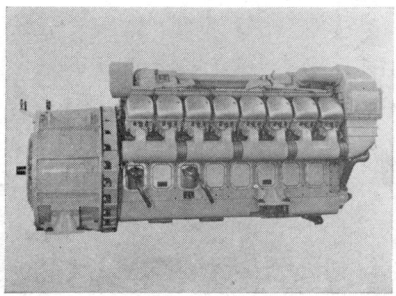

PA type	— 1500 rpm
— PA4-185 :	900 to 3 000 HP
— PA4-200 :	1 400 to 3 550 HP

PA6 type	— 1050 rpm
	4 200 to 6 300 HP

PC type	— 420/500 rpm
— PC2 :	3 000 to 9 000 HP
— PC2-5 :	7 200 to 10 800 HP
— PC3 :	11 400 to 17 100 HP

2 300 S.E.M.T.-PIELSTICK engines in service or in order in the world for a total output of over **8** millions HP.

CHANTIERS DE L'ATLANTIQUE

DÉPARTEMENT-MOTEURS

2, QUAI DE SEINE - 93 - SAINT - DENIS

Tel: 752.19.44
243.18.93

Telex: 62 333 F
MOTLAN

[65]

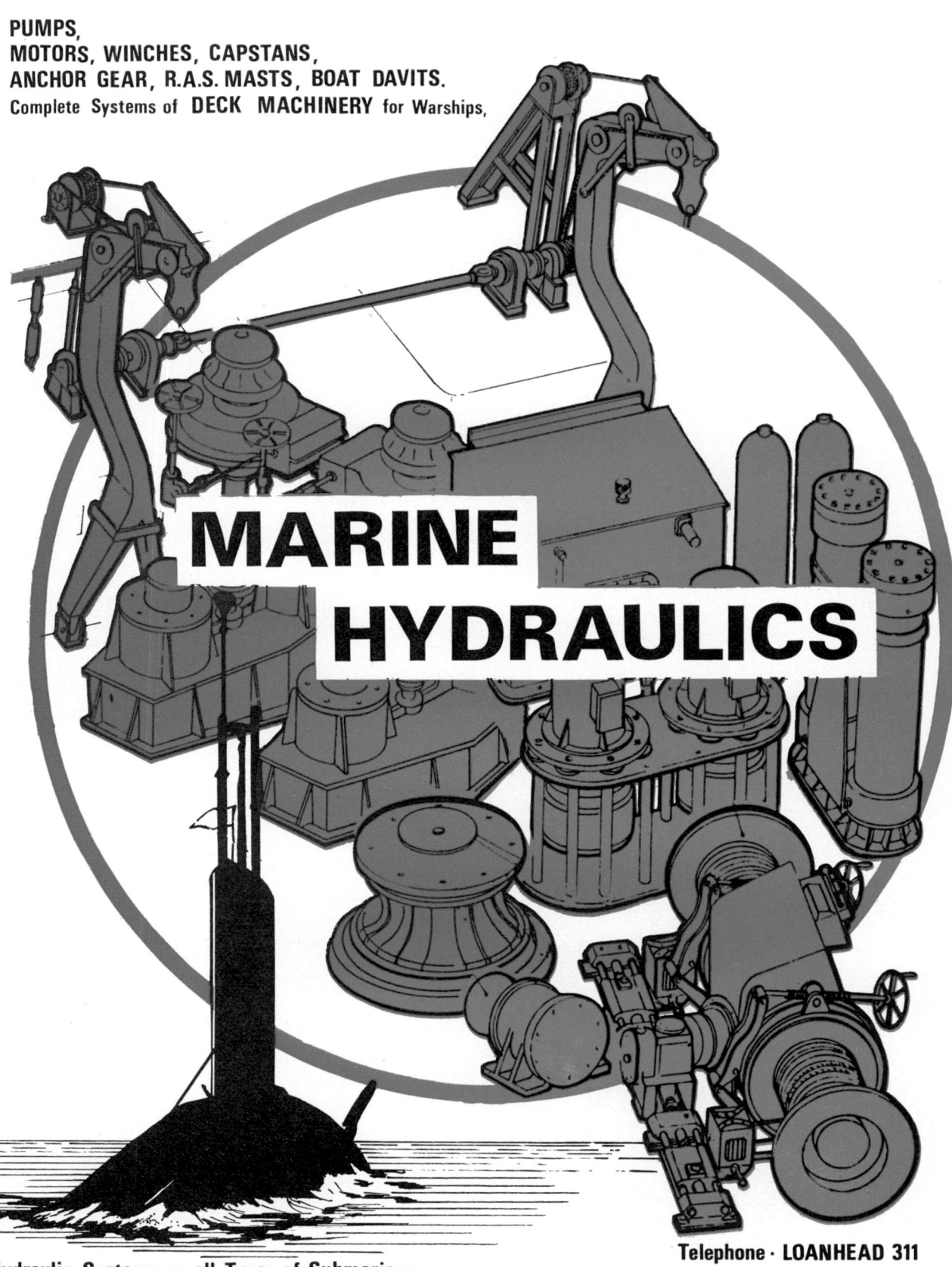

FOR EVERY LIBRARY—
AUTHORITATIVE REFERENCES,
ACCLAIMED WORLD-WIDE

JANE'S ALL THE WORLD'S AIRCRAFT
John W. R. Taylor, Editor

"The outstanding, one-volume definitive work on aircraft. If you could have only one volume in your aviation library, this should be the one".—*The Flyer*. Covers aircraft, drones, gliders and sailplanes, space vehicles, rocket weapons, aero-engines. Over 1,600 illustrations.

JANE'S FIGHTING SHIPS
Raymond V. B. Blackman, Editor

"The authoritative . . . standard work of reference on the world's navies."—*The New York Times*. More than 15,000 ships of 105 nations throughout the world, including the USSR, are covered in detail. Full specifications are given of all vessels in naval service from major warships to tugs. Also described and illustrated are all types of shipborne aircraft and helicopters, land-based naval reconnaissance aircraft and shipborne naval Missiles The book concludes with a table showing the naval strength of each country. Approximately 2,800 photographs, plans and silhouettes.

JANE'S FREIGHT CONTAINERS
Patrick Finlay, Editor

"A reference as broad as the-container movement itself and will prove invaluable to shippers, carriers and government agencies".—*Via Port of New York*. Reports on all aspects of containerization on a global scale: ports, container ship-owners, air freight, manufacturers. Valuable new additions on ship charterers, fork lift trucks, new inventions and forecasts. Over 1,400 photographs, diagrams and maps.

JANE'S MAJOR COMPANIES OF EUROPE
Lionel F. Gray, Editor

Invaluable to the business man with international interest. Over 1,000 companies in 13 countries are listed by industry activity. Listing includes management, capital structure, subsidiaries, major shareholders, balance sheets and results. This year the entries are being substantially expanded to give more information on each company than has ever been given before.

JANE'S SURFACE SKIMMERS
Roy McLeavy, Editor

The definitive standard work on hydrofoils, hovercraft and other air cushion vehicles—records with specifications and standardized descriptions all products in three main fields. Includes ACV licensing authorities, worldwide directory of world's hover clubs and associations, and an illustrated technical glossary. Approximately 600 photographs and plans.

JANE'S WEAPON SYSTEMS
Ronald Pretty and D. H. R. Archer, Editors

Detailed specifications and descriptions on three major weapons categories: systems, platforms (land, sea and air vehicles used for transport and launching) and auxiliary equipment. A section on the world's balance of power is included. A must for the armed services and those in the weapons industry. Approximately 900 photographs and diagrams.

JANE'S WORLD RAILWAYS
Henry Sampson, Editor

"The most complete compilation on railways available anywhere." —*Railway Age*. This internationally-accepted, standard reference details 1400 railways by operational and physical characteristics, operational and financial results, physical improvements, container and piggy back growth. Also includes 400 manufacturers and suppliers of railway equipment in 29 countries and rapid transit systems (including underground) in 58 cities in 27 countries. Approximately 1,300 photographs, maps and loading gauge diagrams.

JANE'S WORLD MINING
Who Owns Whom
Peter Angeloni, Editor

This reference for the financial/investment community lists all major mining and mineral exploration companies. Details include overseas affiliates, major stockholders, and holdings. Included are elaborate pull-out diagrams of corporate "family trees," showing interlocking relationships in three big mining groups. The diagrams will be of special interest to stockbrokers helping them devise similar charts for other companies.

For further information write- Trade Division

McGraw-Hill Book Company
330 West 42nd Street, New York, N.Y. 10036

Whose editions of Jane's are marketed in the United States, its Dependencies and the Philippine Islands; the Dominion of Canada and in Central and South America.

New Soviet "Krivak" class

JANE'S

FIGHTING SHIPS

FOUNDED IN 1897 BY FRED T. JANE

EDITED BY
RAYMOND V. B. BLACKMAN, M.B.E., C.Eng., M.I.Mar.E., M.R.I.N.A

1971-72

S.B.N. 354 00096 9

JANE'S YEARBOOKS

LONDON
SAMPSON LOW MARSTON & Co., LTD

Couplings for the next decade of fighting ships

Metastream main propulsion couplings are being fitted to Type 42 machinery for the next generation of fighting ships. They accommodate misalignment due to thermal expansion, hull flexure and distortion from underwater shock. The non-lubricated dry couplings maintain their high degree of dynamic balance, minimising vibration in high speed and arduous conditions.

The world's first all gas-turbine major warship, H.M.S. Exmouth, uses Metastream couplings in her main propulsion machinery of two Proteus and one Olympus gas turbines.

METASTREAM FLEXIBLE COUPLINGS ARE ALSO USED IN:

ROYAL NAVY	G.P. Frigates. One gas and one steam turbine. H.M.S. Zulu, Nubian, Gurkha, Eskimo, Tartar, Ashanti, Mohawk. G.M.D. Destroyers. Four gas and four steam turbines. H.M.S. London, Hampshire, Kent, Devonshire, Fife, Glamorgan. Type 82 Destroyer. Two steam and two Olympus turbines. H.M.S. Bristol.

IRANIAN NAVY	**LIBYAN NAVY**	**MALAYSIAN NAVY**
Mark 5 Frigates Olympus turbine	Mark 7 Frigates Olympus turbine	Yarrow Frigate Olympus turbine

METASTREAM flexible couplings for main propulsion machinery up to 30,000 s.h.p.

FLEXIBOX LIMITED Head Office: Nash Road, Trafford Park, Manchester M17 ISS. Telephone: 061-872 1477 Telex: 667281

Associated Companies in: Australia, Canada, France, Germany, Holland, Italy, Spain, Sweden, South Africa, U.S.A.

JANE'S FIGHTING SHIPS 1971-72

Compilation of the various sections of this edition has been undertaken by:

R. V. B. Blackman   THE MAIN SHIP REFERENCE SECTION

except

Norman Polmar   UNITED STATES OF AMERICA

and

Michael J. H. Taylor   NAVAL AIRCRAFT AND MISSILES

CONTENTS

...*getting navy system*

under way...

Plessey equips modern fighting ships with
electronic eyes, and ears . . . and claws.

By developing and manufacturing new radars,
sonars, communications, weapons . . . ; and
integrating them into total Weapons Electronics
systems, including Action Information
Organization command and control facilities.

Which means this. Whatever your requirement
– whether it is to design, engineer and commission
a new Weapons Electronics system, to carry out
a complete refit, or to fit a single sonar, a radar
display or a radio transceiver – Plessey Electronics
gets you under way.

PLESSEY Electronics

The Plessey Company Limited
Surrey House, Temple Place,
Victoria Embankment, London WC2R 3BZ,
England. Telephone: 01-836 7722

PE 449

Electric truck with full free lift mast working 'tween decks.

Diesel truck operating on dockside.

Truck being lowered into hold ready for operation.

Climax handling costs less

On waterfronts throughout the world — and even in ships' holds — where mechanical handling is an essential part of cargo operations, Climax fork trucks are lifting, loading, stacking. And saving money for their operators. Climax fork trucks are available from 2,000 lb to 18,000 lb capacity; there are electric and mechanical versions. There's a model for every job. And on most electric trucks you can specify SCR '72 — the world's most up-to-date fork truck electronic control system. Cuts your costs even more.

Climax can solve *your* handling problems and show you how mechanical handling can cost you less.

BRITISH
LEYLAND
Climax

Coventry Climax Engines Limited Coventry CV1 4DX England

FOREWORD

Since last year's edition of this annual was published two factors have projected from the maritime defence concept which could influence the composition and deployment of many navies in the immediate future.

One is a somewhat belated but now acute awareness evinced by hitherto quite autonomous navies of the need for international co-operation and mutual security.

The other is the recognition, not only by major powers but also by smaller countries, of the tactical power and strategic influence of the fast and diminutive warship armed with the optimum payload of guided missiles.

Ironically it is the new world sea power of the Soviet Union which has engendered the yen for co-operation, and it is the Soviet Navy which has pointed the way to the ascendency of the missile boat over much larger orthodox warships.

As regards international naval co-operation, the North Atlantic Treaty Organisation is, of course, now well established, and there is a Standing Naval Force Atlantic, a permanent, multi-national squadron, albeit not nearly as powerful as it could and should be; but there is no comparable multi-national naval force in the Indian Ocean.

Recently, however, there has been a change in the climate of opinion. From last year, when it seemed that few countries officially showed the slightest interest in the void created by a combination of the prospective withdrawal of British warships from the Far East and the preoccupation of United States naval forces in Vietnam and the Mediterranean: to this year when, not only several navies, but almost every thinking-ahead authority, is suggesting or formulating ways of filling the Indian Ocean gap from Cape Town to Singapore.

If the arms for South Africa controversy has done nothing else it has shed light on the problems of sustaining the European ocean trade routes round the Cape to India, Pakistan, Malaysia, Hong Kong and Australasia, and has brought home to all countries on the Indian Ocean seaboard the extent to which they are laid open to foreign maritime infiltration and influence.

The prime necessity would appear to be a multi-national Standing Naval Force East comprising warships seconded from each of the countries with military or commercial interests in that oceanic hemisphere from South Africa to Indonesia. Ideally this Standing Naval Force would include ships from U.S.A., Britain, Australia, New Zealand, India, Pakistan, Malaysia, Singapore, Portugal and South Africa.

As regards the new era of guided missile boats in spate it is quite remarkable how many of the smaller countries as well as the major powers have seen the light and have taken up the small fast boat with the long-reach big-punch.

An alarming feature of the past decade has been the progressively increasing cost of fighting ships of the categories to be found in most navies: destroyers, frigates and escorts. When confronted with this escalation problem several of the smaller countries decided that the answer was smaller and cheaper vessels.

This policy was given impetus after the sinking of the Israeli destroyer *Eilath* by an Egyptian missile boat, and several western navies became aware of the possibilities of equipping small and fast vessels with modern guided missile systems for the surface-to-ship role.

Of particular interest are the missile boat flotillas created by Norway, which represent a considerable increase in the effectiveness of her navy. Adopting the indigenously designed "Penguin" system, four missile launchers are being installed in six new fast torpedo boats and six missile launchers have been or will be installed in 20 existing fast gunboats in addition to their present armament.

Germany has also taken up guided missile boats in a very decided way. Abandoning what seemed to be a firm project to build four guided missile frigates of 3,500 tons, the German Navy is instead to build ten guided missile boats of 350 tons and 20 guided missile boats of 250 tons.

Among the other countries which have or are building missile boats are Denmark, Israel, Italy, Greece and Malaysia; and Algeria, China, Cuba, Egypt, Finland, East Germany, Indonesia, Poland, Romania, Syria and Yugoslavia, indeed most of the satellite countries who take their marine armaments from the Soviet Union.

Much the same as the submarine was in the past reckoned to be the weapon of the weaker power, so the diminutive missile boats with surface-to-surface systems will give smaller navies an offensive power out of all proportion to their modest overall size.

In fact, viz-a-viz a country with a much greater fleet of larger warships without missiles the smaller country with missile boats could hold the balance of deterrent power and exert a containing influence. And withall the missile boats are cheaper and quicker to build, easier to maintain and much more economical in manpower.

Yet there is seeming reluctance on the part of some of the larger maritime powers to build missile boats. The British Navy, for instance, has no missile boats and has not shown any inclination to operate such craft, although at the time of writing the Royal Navy is temporarily using the guided missile boat *Tenacity* built by Vosper Thornycroft. The two fast patrol boats of the "Brave" class have been laid up and Britain's representatives of the Coastal Forces are three new fast but unarmed training boats. However, these are eminently suitable for arming with missiles and doubtless would be if emergency required.

A great volume of new facts and figures and a large number of pictures have been added in this edition, the 74th year of issue of *Jane's Fighting Ships*. For the fourth successive year the Soviet section has been considerably enlarged and is now three times the size that it was in the late sixties, reflecting the growing size and power of the Soviet Navy. And the volume is again issued earlier in the year, the earliest publication date in the 23 years of the present editorship. More than 1,100 new illustrations have been added in this issue, including over 200 scale drawings. Altogether there are some 3,200 illustrations in the book comprising nearly 2,700 photographs and nearly 500 drawings. Particulars are given of over 15,000 ships and craft in 110 navies or sea-defence forces.

USA

Norman Polmar, editor and compiler of the American section, has given an outline of the American naval scene:

'The size and relative capabilities of the United States Navy continue to decline at what many authorities consider to be an alarming rate. This situation, hitherto discussed in closed sessions of naval officials and in this annual, is now being addressed openly. The Chief of Naval Operations has told Congress that the Navy has "a lower than prudent level of current forces" and has "been falling well behind a responsible replacement rate".

The force levels of the Fiscal Year 1972 budget reduce several categories of warships to their lowest strengths for over a decade. The situation is evident in the planned force of 13 attack aircraft carriers (one with a mixed attack/anti-submarine air wing) compared to 16 attack carriers three years ago; three anti-submarine carriers instead of

six in 1969; 160 cruisers, frigates (leaders) and destroyers decreased from 240; and 93 attack submarines, a drop of ten boats since 1969. The number of nuclear-powered attack (fleet) submarines has increased from 41 to 57 during the past three years, but this is limited compensation for the reduction in destroyer-type ships and ASW carriers with their air groups.

Despite the wind-down of the Vietnam War, the responsibilities of the US Navy remain. The Navy will long be engaged in supporting US and South Vietnamese forces on the Indochina peninsula; the "Nixon Doctrine" for foreign policy in the 1970s calls for meeting overseas military commitments and responsibilities, but with a "low profile" of US forces overseas, an obvious mandate for the astute employment of sea power. Simultaneously, US strategy calls for maintaining a capability for countering the other super-power at sea. But the Soviet Navy has already exceeded the United States in active surface ship and submarine numbers, including near parity in nuclear submarine strength (and a larger nuclear submarine construction programme). In some respects the characteristics and capabilities of the Soviet ships obviously are superior to those of their US Navy counterparts. Expanding Soviet naval operations during the past few years, notably the 200-ship-plus "Okean" exercise of April 1970, demonstrate that the Soviets have developed the ability to operate these ships on the high seas; regular deployments of warships to the Caribbean, Mediterranean, and Indian Ocean areas demonstrate that the Soviets are in fact using these ships as politico-economic-military forces.

The only category of warship in which the US Navy now *and for the near future* maintains a decisive advantage is the aircraft carrier. No other ship or even combination of surface ships can match the versatility, striking power and range, or endurance of the modern attack carrier and her 80 to 90 aircraft. Yet even this margin over the Soviet Navy is narrowing as the number of attack carriers in commission is being reduced, the construction of a fourth nuclear-powered carrier (the CVAN 70) is in doubt, and the adequacy of the F-14 ship-borne fighter (successor to the F-4 Phantom) is being questioned.

In their stead, some naval authorities are advocating smaller and lower-cost air capable ships, hydrofoil missile boats, and surface effect ships for a variety of missions. However, it seems questionable to consider even a squadron of air capable ships, each with perhaps six Harrier V/STOL attack aircraft and six SH-3 helicopters, as comparable to a single attack carrier.

But if the United States is seriously to address the question of countering the Soviet Union at sea, or indeed the Soviet allies equipped with advanced aircraft, missile boats, and submarines, the question of maintaining *and even increasing* attack carrier strength must be considered and difficult decisions have to be made. The aircraft carrier has been viable for so long, proved itself so often in hot and cold wars, and is so versatile that its place in modern warfare should be understood and properly evaluated.

The cost of modern air power—both land-based and sea-based is rising at an awesome rate. The costs of aircraft, ordnance, support equipment, manpower, and bases all are increasing. The CVAN 70 probably will cost more than $800 million dollars if constructed under the Fiscal Year 1972 or 1973 programme; the cost will most likely be a *billion* dollars if delayed until 1975. However, this cost is comparable if not actually less than the cost of supporting an equivalent number of aircraft at land bases overseas in view of vulnerability, political considerations, support and logistics. Korea and Vietnam have amply demonstrated this comparison.

Solutions to the problem of maintaining a strong Navy with limited funds are difficult to devise. However, there are some alternatives that warrant consideration: To maintain carrier strength the Navy could consider a halt to the construction of destroyers and frigates—which are being criticised for poor design as well as increasing costs—to permit carrier construction and operation. This would result in fewer screening ships, but this partially could be compensated by increased use of ship-based early warning and anti-submarine aircraft and helicopters, operating nuclear submarines as ASW escorts for carriers, and expansion of passive defensive activities (e.g. operating the carriers under conditions of electronic silence). Imaginative concepts of operation can compensate for shortages of escorts as long as carriers are available to provide the increased reconnaissance and strike capabilities over opposing naval forces.

All of the above is predicated on the thesis that a naval confrontation with the Soviet Union is possible (or could be avoided by strong US naval forces); similarly, sea-based tactical air would be the key in supporting US and allied operations ashore, and in operations against other naval and air forces. The North Korean capture of the US intelligence ship *Pueblo* and downing of a naval reconnaissance plane have called attention to the "other" military threats to US activities.

In the strategic/nuclear balance of forces the USSR has gained superiority over the United States in numbers of ICBMs and the megatonnage that can be delivered; and the current Soviet ballistic missile submarine construction rate of at least six submarines per year could give the USSR parity if not superiority in "Polaris" type submarines by 1975. (In addition to which the USSR has a number of nuclear powered and diesel-driven submarines with shorter-range missiles). Soviet progress in the strategic weapons area is of utmost concern to US defense leaders because improved guidance and multiple warhead technology (MIRV) could permit the predicted Soviet strategic forces of the mid-1970s to destroy virtually all US land-based ICBMs in a surprise first-strike attack; simultaneously, Soviet missile submarines could destroy most US manned bombers before they could become airborne. Accordingly, the US Navy's 41 Polaris/Poseidon submarines are acknowledged as the *most survivable* US strategic deterrent forces for the foreseeable future.

Arguments for partially or entirely replacing the land-based missiles and bombers with additional missiles at sea are being countered by arguments for maintaining the "triad" of deterrence—the combination of land-based bombers, land-based missiles, and sea-based missiles that have been the premise of US strategic forces for more than a decade. Although modern technology argues against this "triad", political and separate service concepts survive. Increasing the sea-borne portion of deterrence, either in submarines or surface ships, would increase weapon survivability, remove strategic targets from the heartland of the United States, and eliminate or reduce the need for the Safeguard Anti-Ballistic Missile (ABM) system that will have the primary purpose of protecting land-based Minuteman ICBMs.

The US Navy is receiving the largest portion of the proposed Fiscal Year 1972 defense budget allocation to the services, 34·56 per cent compared to 33·77 per cent for the Air Force and 31·66 per cent for the Army (about $500 million more than the Air Force and $2 billion more than the Army). This is the first budget since the "unification" of the armed services in 1947 that the Navy has received the largest share. However, the FY 1972 military budget represents the smallest portion of the Federal budget (32·1 per cent) and the smallest portion of the Gross National Product (6·8 per cent) since before the Korean War of 1950-1953. A comparison of FY 1972 defense spending in terms of constant dollars represents a decrease of $23·9 billion from FY 1968, the Vietnam War peak.

a new factory built on a wealth of experience

In 1971, Fiat Grandi Motori will gradually transfer all its diesel engine activities—design, production, marketing, sales and after-sales service— to Grandi Motori Trieste : the fifty-fifty joint stock company formed by Fiat and I.R.I.

The new factory will be among the largest and most modern in the world, the increased diesel engine production of Fiat Motori—Turin and I.R.I. (Ansaldo—Genova and C.R.D.A.—Trieste) centred on the new Trieste factory amounting up to a million b.h.p. annually.

Grandi Motori Trieste
Fiat—Ansaldo—C.R.D.A.
Via San Nicolo 6—34121 Trieste—Italy
Teleph. 61301—755055
Telegr. Grandimotoritrieste
Telex G.M.T. 46274

The situation for the US Navy is serious: winding down the war in Indochina will make sea duty and its family separation less attractive; there is increasing hostility toward the military in the United States; reductions in ship strength make deployments longer and more arduous; commitments are continuing and, in some areas, increasing; inflation and real cost increases are making ship and aircraft procurement difficult; and new ships with relatively inferior capabilities are compounding the problems. There are no simple answers. The US Secretary of Defense declares: "I pledge that I shall continue to urge actions which will assure the supremacy of the US naval power". The President of the United States avers: "What the Soviet Union needs in terms of military preparedness is different from what we need. They are a land power, primarily, with a great potential enemy on the East. We are primarily, of course, a sea power, and our needs, therefore, are different." '

USSR

By any standards the Soviet Fleet now represents the super-navy of a super-power. This tends to serve as the red rag to the bull to some countries whose spheres of influence, commensurate with their declining navies, are shrinking, while in step with her expanding navy Soviet spheres of influence are widening.

But it might well be the case that the Soviet Union is just as concerned about what she considers to be a threat to her overseas trade and ultimate security, namely the knitting together of NATO navies and the deployment of the fleets of western countries the breadth of the Atlantic and the breadth of the Pacific away from their own domains, as the USA is worried about the expansion and broad-scattering of the Soviet Navy.

After all, seen through Soviet eyes, the naval squadrons of the USSR are only just off their own Baltic doorstep in the North Sea, only just off their own Black Sea doorstep in the Eastern Mediterranean, and only just off their own Vladivostok doorstep in the China Seas. It is only in their recent forays into the Indian Ocean that Soviet warships are off limits and even then the excuse could justifiably be made that they are on passage from one part of the Soviet Union to another.

Whereas, also from the Soviet point of view, the USA maintains a powerful fleet in the Mediterranean 4,000 miles from New York and a huge fleet in South East Asia 5,000 miles from San Francisco.

So the USSR probably fears the overseas extension of the USA and the constant liaison of the British, French, Italian and German navies, through NATO, as much as the USA fears the ever widening ripples of Soviet sea power all round the world. And the USSR can always say that they are merely "showing the flag", much the same as the US Navy have done since the Second World War and the British Navy did when it had a comparable navy.

"The Soviet Navy on the seas and oceans reliably guarantees the USSR's security and its state interests", says the Soviet Minister of Defence. The men of the Soviet Navy were tirelessly improving their military and political knowledge, successfully mastering modern combat equipment and weapons, and enhancing vigilance and combat preparedness. They were ready at all times to defend the sea frontiers of the socialist motherland. The shipbuilding industry was reaching new achievements in equipping the Navy with combat ships and formidable armaments.

"Our strong ocean-going Navy is the basis of the might of our country" says the Commander-in-Chief of the Soviet Navy. "Soviet fighting ships are systematically present on the seas, including the areas where the shock navies of NATO are present. The presence of our ships in these areas binds the hands of the imperialists and deprives them of the possibility of unhindered interference in the internal affairs of peoples. This situation is undoubtedly not to the liking of the imperialist 'hawks' who are trying to distort the purpose of the voyages of Soviet ships and to diminish their importance for the cause of peace. Of decisive importance in present day conditions is not only the number of ships, but mainly the quality of their nuclear missile, weapons and technical capabilities and the high morale and fighting capabilities of their personnel.

"In this respect our Navy is up to the level of present day demands. Its equipment and the vigilance of the crews protect our country from all kinds of surprises. The pride of our Navy is our nuclear submarines, which are fitted out with a variety of missiles which can be launched from under water. Our submarines, together with the Navy's missile-carrying and anti-submarine high speed, long range aircraft, are the basis of the striking might of the Navy. Up-to-date surface ships, equipped with the most modern weapons, are assigned a major role in carrying out the Navy's tasks. The Soviet Navy is an impressive deterrent in the way of imperialist reaction and adventures. At the same time the Soviet Navy is a symbol of our fraternal assistance to the friendly and freedom-loving peoples," declared the Commander-in-Chief.

Friend or foe will read what they will from this peroration, but it sounds very much like "show the flag and police the world", which is what Britain did until the Second World War and what the United States has been trying to do ever since.

Every year for the last decade or so a new class of rocket cruisers, missile destroyers, submarines, escorts, minesweepers, missile boats and/or torpedo boats has appeared in the Soviet Navy and most western observers have been impressed by their sophistication and novelty.

The past year has been no exception. Not only has a new class of missile cruisers appeared, the "Kresta II" class, bristling with their missile and radar control complex, but a new type of general purpose destroyer leader, the "Krivak" class, see photographs in the Late Addenda, and two new classes of nuclear-powered submarines have been operationally deployed, and a new class of guided missile corvettes is being built.

So prolific has the Soviet naval shipbuilding effort been that the USSR is now able to maintain a standing naval force in the Mediterranean five times stronger than five years ago to counter the American Sixth Fleet. Recently a US admiral remarked to the Editor of this annual with some bitterness that he could count more guns in the Soviet Fleet in the Mediterranean than he could in his own fleet there.

Again, five years ago the USSR had no warships in the Indian Ocean, but today there are a score of surface ships alone, and there is no telling how many Soviet submarines are in the area. The Soviet Navy is believed to be completing nuclear powered submarines at the rate of one every long month. (There was a gap of three years between the completion of Britain's third nuclear powered fleet submarine *Warspite* and the completion of the fourth, *Churchill*).

The United States is very worried about the growth of the Soviet Navy's mounting strength in the Mediterranean, along North Africa and in the Indian Ocean. But while the USA is shackled to an enervating war elsewhere she expects the countries of NATO in general and the countries bordering the Mediterranean in particular to increase their naval contribution to the common effort.

It is estimated that the strength of the Soviet Fleet now comprises 83 nuclear powered submarines, 318 conventionally powered submarines, 2 cruiser helicopter carriers, 26 cruisers including missile ships, 100 destroyers including missile armed vessels, 130 escorts of the small frigate and corvette type, 270 coastal escorts and patrol vessels, 320 minesweepers, 125 missile boats, 325 torpedo boats, 125 amphibious ships and 75 smaller landing craft excluding minor LCMs. Support ships, auxiliaries and service craft run into thousands.

This navy list constitutes a very formidable force indeed, both as a strategic deterrent and for conventional sea warfare. It indicates the transition of the USSR from a land power to a sea power, and suggests that the Soviet Union is just as concerned about the ganging up of smaller Western navies, which have little power individually but immense power collectively, as the United States Navy is about the growing spread of the Soviet Navy all over the world.

United Kingdom

The bald statement in the 1971 Defence Estimates that "Work continues on the design of a through-deck cruiser" was hardly calculated to inspire credibility in the fashioning of the Royal Navy of the 1970s, to encourage those in the Fleet Air Arm to perfect their skill in those incredibly efficient dual-element machines *Ark Royal* and *Eagle*, or to aid recruiting.

With a change of Government it seems likely that *Ark Royal* will continue in service until the end of the decade and that *Eagle* will not now disappear from the naval scene until her economical life is expended. In which case, providing the so-called "through-deck cruiser" is completed and in operational service by 1980, the viability of the Fleet Air Arm would be assured in continuity.

From the first picture impression, (see this edition, page 343) the new through-deck cruiser appears to be quite an aircraft carrier in its own right, capable of operating vertical and short take off fixed wing aircraft as well as helicopters. "What's in a name? That which we call a rose By any other name . . . ."

In this particular case there is quite a lot in a name. Had it been generally known at the time of the great Fleet Air Arm controversy, when the late Government was cutting down Britain's aircraft carriers right and left under the expedient euphemism of "phasing out", that the new through-deck cruisers, of which three are envisaged eventually, were going to be so viable for operating aircraft it would have been realised that it was in the nation's interests to maintain at parity, or even above par, the recruitment of pilots and aircrew into the Royal Navy, thus ensuring a continuity of training and expertise right through from the passing of the great angled-deck carriers to the advent of the smaller through-deck, aircraft-carrying cruisers.

Smaller or not, however, the new style cruiser-carrier does not appear to be any the less complex or cheaper, judging by the time it is taking to get it off the drawing board and the figures mentioned as being the likely eventual cost. £50,000,000 was the estimate for the projected fixed-wing aircraft carrier CVA 01 which was cancelled a few years ago on the grounds of economy, but the first through-deck cruiser will probably give no change from that. The constant fear of the Royal Navy is that it will price itself out of existence.

Perhaps it could be forgiven if the question were posed as to why the "thing", as it has been both bitterly and affectionately called, has to be so costly. A few years ago, the Americans wanted a class of ships quickly "in the vertical envelopment concept" to support the Marine Corps. The US naval architects simply took a wall-sided mercantile hull of the C 2 type, virtually an oblong steel box sharpened at one end and faired-off at the other, and fitted in all the offices and shops required to operate and maintain helicopters around this platform which of its own nature provided the large hangar in its belly for the stowage and servicing of helicopters and the long flat top for a flight deck. The resulting first "amphibious assault ship", essentially a helicopter carrier, but a potential take-off-and-landing strip for vertical fixed-wing aircraft, was the *Iwo Jima*, built for only $40,000,000/£16,000,000, less than the cost of a modern British destroyer. Six more ships of the class have been built since in an average time of only two years. So it can indeed be said that the USA got its amphibious/helicopter carrier squadron cheaply and quickly. Yet it serves the purpose. That splendid acrobatic flying machine, the Harrier, capable of hovering, lifting and dropping vertically, and crabbing sideways, could be operated from simple ships of this type as well as helicopters. And the flight deck is ample for a short take-off to save fuel and boost the payload.

It is greatly to be trusted that the three through-deck cruisers will materialise and not only for strategic and tactical reasons. There is a lot in prestige. Prestige is power, and power is a deterrent, the last stop deterrent before the nuclear one. But there is little prestige in an entirely small ship navy, desirable though smaller and cheaper ships are in many ways. There must be the leaven of the capital ship whatever form it may take. When Britain ceases to have big ships she will have lost face for ever and she will have no voice at the conference table.

Of the few big ships remaining in the Royal Navy; the former fixed wing aircraft carrier *Hermes* (Britain's youngest carrier, completed only eleven years ago) is being converted into a commando ship/helicopter carrier; and the conventional cruiser *Tiger's* conversion to a *commandement* helicopter ship is nearing completion, but the conversion of her sister ship *Lion* has been cancelled.

The fixed-wing aircraft carrier *Centaur*, only fifteen years old, and originally a sister ship of *Hermes*, is regrettably being scrapped: the question could logically be posed why she is not also being converted into a commando ship/helicopter carrier (for *Albion* and *Bulwark* have now been running almost continually for a decade or so and must eventually be retired) or at least into some form of amphibious ship combined with a vertical take-off interim role, until the new through-deck cruisers materialise.

The last two of the class of eight "County" class guided missile armed destroyers, *Antrim* and *Norfolk* have been completed, and *Bristol*, the only guided missile armed destroyer of her type, is nearing completion. The first of a new class of guided missile armed destroyers, *Sheffield*, has been launched.

Work continues on the design of a new class of general purpose frigates, the "Type 22". The last two of the 26 very successful general purpose frigates of the "Leander" class, *Apollo* and *Ariadne*, are being completed. The first of the new "Type 21" frigates, *Amazon* has been launched.

In the underwater field, the fifth and sixth nuclear-powered fleet submarines, *Conqueror* and *Courageous* are being accepted from the builders; the seventh, eighth and ninth, *Swiftsure*, *Sovereign* and *Superb*, are under construction; and the tenth is being ordered. But a matter of concern is that the number of submarines being produced is not nearly keeping pace with the number being scrapped. The "T" class diesel-powered submarines have gone, even though 13 were reconstructed and converted in recent years, and only a handful of the 16 "A" class conventional submarines remain in service.

So the backbone of the Royal Navy's submarine patrol service, apart from deterrent and strategic considerations, are the 21 diesel powered boats of the "Oberon" and "Porpoise" classes. The need is clearly pointed for the urgent building of more medium sized diesel-electric boats of about 1,000 tons for normal operational patrol, fleet exercises and routine training.

Raymond V. B. Blackman

ACKNOWLEDGEMENTS

There has been a good response this year from our *Fighting Ships* correspondents, in the East as well as the West, and with the goodwill and co-operation of all except one or two of the 110 naval and maritime authorities concerned there has been a steady flow of data and photographs to this annual, providing the latest pictorial and descriptive portraits of newly built warships, reconstructed vessels and converted units, maintaining the tradition of *Fighting Ships*, established in 1897, of presenting a comprehensive panorama of "All The World's Fighting Ships" (the original title) together with their support ships, auxiliary vessels and service craft.

It would perhaps be of assistance to both official and honorary correspondents to be more fully acquainted with the *Fighting Ships* preparation schedule. Copy is sent to the printers in alphabetical order of countries, starting with e.g. Argentina and Australia early in January and finishing with Vietnam and Yugoslavia in late April. This is designed to allow machining of the whole book by late May, binding in June and distribution and publication in July. It follows therefore that updating of data and new photographs are ideally received by late December for the ABC countries and by early April for the XYZ countries. Late information is, of course, where possible, embodied in the galley and page proof stages, but unavoidably this can only be done in a limited way to avoid upsetting format, final layout and pagination. And inevitably some sections are on the machines when late information or pictures arrive, in which case they are inserted in the Addenda. But in order to obviate discrepancies in co-related data between the early printed sections and the national chapters going to press later it is desirable that all information and pictures should come in by the date requested by the Editor.

As usual *Fighting Ships* is much indebted to the Naval Boards, Navy Departments and Ministries of Marine and Defence who furnished information and photographs. This was facilitated by the kindness of the Ambassadors and Naval Attachés in London, including Vice-Admiral Carlos Coda, Argentine Navy; Lt.-General Avi. Baron Michel Donnet, CVO, DFC, Belgian Embassy; Rear-Admiral Fernando Ernesto Carneiro Ribeiro, Brazilian Navy; Rear-Admiral Adolfo F. Walbaum, Chilean Navy; Rear-Admiral Paul C. L. Delahousse, French Navy; Rear-Admiral Alberto Benvenuto, Peruvian Navy; Rear-Admiral M. R. Terry-Lloyd, South African Embassy; Rear-Admiral Fillmore B. Gilkeson, United States Navy; Rear-Admiral Pablo Cohen Guerrero, Venezuelan Navy; Commodore S. L. Ahren, Royal Swedish Navy; Captain K. A. I. Ruusuvuori, Finnish Navy; Captain K. T. Raeder, Federal German Navy; Captain A. Glykis, Royal Hellenic Navy; Captain Corrado Vittori, Italian Navy; Captain K. Ohashi, Japanese Embassy; Captain F. de Blocq van Kuffeler, Royal Netherlands Navy; Captain O. E. Aslaksrud, Royal Norwegian Navy; Captain J. B. Pinheiro de Azevedo, Portuguese Navy; Captain R. D. Kingon, South African Navy; Captain Chinda Chai-Udom, Royal Thai Navy; Captain Hasan Sarioglu, Turkish Navy; Colonel H.R.H. Prince Georg of Denmark, CVO, Royal Danish Embassy; Colonel Witold Lokuciewski, Polish Embassy; Colonel Svetozar Oro, Yugoslav Embassy; Commander Don Salvador Moreno, Spanish Navy.

Grateful acknowledgement is made of the kind co-operation of Captain (Rear-Admiral designate) Andrew John Miller, Director of Public Relations (Naval), Ministry of Defence, London; Chief of Naval Information, Washington; Commandant, US Coast Guard; Commander R. S. Harney, USN, Public Affairs Officer for the Commander-in-Chief United States Naval Forces Europe;

Commodore K. D. Gray, DFC, Australian Naval Representative, London; Captain P. H. Cayley, CD, RCN, Senior Canadian Naval Liaison Officer, Canadian Defence Staff, London; Commodore N. P. Datta, IN, Indian Naval Adviser, London; Commodore J. L. N. Mungavin, PN, Pakistan Naval Adviser, London; Commodore E. C. Thorne, Senior New Zealand Naval Liaison Officer, London;

M. Henri le Masson, Editor of "Flottes de Combat", Herr Gerhard Albrecht, Editor of "Weyers Flottentaschenbuch"; Dr. Giorgio Giorgerini, Editor of "Almanaco Navale"; Vice-Admiral Alberto Zamboni, Editor of "Rivista Marittima"; Captain Allan Kull, Editor of "Marinkalender";

Dr Luigi Accorsi; Rear-Admiral M. J. Adam, CVO, CBE; Professor Alfredo Aguilera; Dr Giorgio Arra; Lieutenant Erminio Bagnasco; Mrs R. V. B. Blackman; Herr Siegfried Breyer; Mr William H. Davis; Dr Aldo Fraccaroli; Constructor Lt-Commander Shizuo Fukui; Commander Alvin H. Grobmeier; Lt-Commander A. Hague, VRD, RNR; Captain T. D. Manning, CBE, VRD, RNVR; Ing Augusto Nani; Mr George A. S. Ransome; Mr C. W. E. Richardson; Mr John S. Rowe; Captain Aluino Martins da Silva; Captain R. Steen Steenson, RDN; Herr Stefen Terzibaschitsch; Mr Godfrey H. Walker; and many others whom it would be invidious to mention or who prefer to remain anonymous.

For the fourth year Mr Norman Polmar has compiled the US chapter in direct liaison with the Navy Department of the Pentagon, evidence of which can be seen in that extensively revised section. He is grateful to the many individuals in the US Navy and Coast Guard and American industry who have provided assistance in preparing this year's edition, especially Mr Samuel L. Morison of the Naval History Division; Lieutenant Commander Richard McEwen, Chief Yeoman Ronald G. Woll, Mr Robert Carlisle, Miss Anna Urband, and Miss Judith Van Benthuysen of the Office of Navy Information; Captain Stephen De La Mater, Director Naval Air Warfare Analysis, Captain Wayne L. Zimmerman, Head Mine Warfare Branch, and Commander Detlow M. Marthinson Jnr, Assistant for Riverine Craft in the Office of the Chief of Naval Operations; Commander Don Walsh of the Office of the Secretary of the Navy; Mr Richard C. Bassett of the Naval Ship Systems Command; Lieutenant Commander Ronald Black of the Naval Ordnance Systems Command; Chief Journalist C. T. Brown of the Strategic Systems Project Office; Mr Kenneth Robinson and Mr Stuart Nelson of the Office of the Oceanographer of the Navy; Mr Larry Manning of the Military Sealift Command; Commander Berry Meaux, Chief Warrant Officer Joseph Greco, and Miss Elizabeth Segedi of the Coast Guard Office of Public Information; Mr Raymond Wilcover of the National Ocean Survey; and Captain S. Robert Foley, Commanding Officer of the USS *Coronado*.

No illustration may be reproduced without permission; but the Press may reproduce information and official photographs at sight provided *Jane's Fighting Ships* is fully acknowledged. Photographs credited to professional photographers are copyright and should not be reproduced without their permission. Their addresses are: Wright & Logan, Albert Road Junction, Portsmouth, England; Skyfotos, Lympne Airport, Kent, England; and A. & J. Pavia, 40 Ordnance Street, Valletta, Malta.

Photographs or information for the next edition, the preparation of which starts immediately, should be sent as soon as possible to the Editor, JANE'S FIGHTING SHIPS, care of Jane's Yearbooks, Sampson Low, Marston & Co., Paulton House, 8 Shepherdess Walk, London, N.1., England.

Raymond V. B. Blackman.

RADAR INSTALLATION NOTES

Radar development started during the mid nineteen-thirties, and the need for secrecy then and during the 1939 to '45 war resulted in the use of code names and symbols to identify various equipments. As a result alpha-numeric symbols are still widely used to define types of radar. Similarly, the radio frequency bands are designated by letters.

British naval radars are defined by a number, for example Type 293. US naval radars are designated by an alpha-numeric symbol, for example SPS 10. Alpha-numeric identification systems are also used by Italian, Dutch and French navies. The radars fitted in ships of the USSR are identified by code names such as HAYMARKET since the USSR has never released data on their radar or its nomenclature.

The vast majority of radars found in ships of navies of other than those mentioned above are supplied by either British, Dutch, French, Italian, United States or USSR sources.

There are five main frequency bands in general use for naval radar systems. These are designated by letters; and the table below shows typical frequencies in the bands and corresponding wavelengths.

Wave Band	Frequency	Wavelength
P	220 MHz	1·4 metres
L	1,300 MHz	23 cms
S	3,000 MHz	10 cms
C	5,500 MHz	5·5 cms
X	9,000 MHz	3·3 cms

In general long range early warning radars operate in P or L bands; shorter range and tactical radars operate in S band, and navigation and weapon fire control radars operate in C or X band.

Additional data on naval radars may be found in the associated JANES Year book "JANE'S WEAPON SYSTEMS".

The following list, which is not fully comprehensive, gives the designation and purpose of many of the radars to be found in most of the ships of the worlds' navies. The list is arranged in countries of origin.

France

DRBV 20 and 22	Long range early warning air
DRBV 11 and 23	Medium range air and surface warning
DRBI 10 and 23	Three dimensional target indication
DRBN series	Navigational radars
DRBC series	Fire control radars

Italy

Italy follows US conventions; but certain radars can be identified from the initials RAN for search radars and RTN for fire control radars.

Netherlands

LWO 1, 2, 3 etc.	Long range early warning air
DA 02	Medium range air and surface warning
V 1	Height finder
M 20 and 40 series	Fire control systems using X band radars

United Kingdom

Type 960, 965	Long range air early warning
Type 984	Three dimensional
Type 277 and 278	Height finder and surface warning
Type 293, 993	Air and surface warning
Type 974, 978	Navigational radars also used for tactical display

United States

SPS 6 and 12 SPS 40 and 43	Long range early warning air
SPS 5 and 10	Close range air and surface search
SPS 30	Height finder
SPS 32 and 39	Three dimensional
SPG 49, 51, 55, 56	Fire control radars for missile systems

USSR

Aldgate Aldwych Holborn Kingsway Strand	Long and medium range air warning
Cornhill Knightsbridge	Surface search radars
Knightsbridge	Three dimensional
Bankside Barbican Cheapside Millbank Piccadilly	Fire control radars

ABU DHABI

SEA WING, ABU DHABI DEFENCE FORCE

Administration

Sea Wing Commander:
  Commander G. A. St. G. Poole

The Sea Wing of the Abu Dhabi Defence Force was formed in March 1968. The Wing's function is to patrol territorial waters and oil installations in Abu Dhabi marine areas. The Wing is locally recruited with the exception of some ex-Royal Naval Officers, and Officers on secondment from the Pakistan Navy.

PATROL CRAFT

3 "KAWKAB" TYPE

BANIYAS (July 1969)   **KAWKAB** (Jan 1969)   **THOABAN** (Jan 1969)

Displacement, tons	32
Dimensions, feet	57 × 16·5 × 4·5
Guns	2—20 mm
Main engines	2 Caterpillar diesels. 750 bhp = 19 knots
Radius, miles	300
Complement	2 officers, 9 men

A photograph of *Kawkab* appears in the 1969-70 edition.

CONSTRUCTION. Built by Keith Nelson & Co Ltd, Bembridge, Isle of Wight. Launch dates above. Of glass fibre hull construction.

THOABAN   *1970, Abu Dhabi Defence Force, Official*

6 "DHAFEER" TYPE

DHAFEER (Feb 1968)   **HAZZA** (May 1968)
DURGHAM (Sep 1968)   **MURAYJIB** (Feb 1970)
GHADUNFAR (May 1968)   **TIMSAH** (Sep 1968)

Displacement, tons	10
Dimensions, feet	41 × 12 × 3·5
Guns	1 × ·5 in mg
Main engines	2 Cummins diesels; 370 bhp = 19 knots
Radius, miles	150
Complement	6 (1 officer, 5 men)

CONSTRUCTION. All built by Keith Nelson & Co Ltd, Bembridge, Isle of Wight. Of glass fibre hull construction. Launch dates above. A sixth craft of this class is under construction.

DURGHAM   *1970, Abu Dhabi Defence Force, Official*

ALGERIA

Personnel

1971: Total 3 025 (275 officers and cadets, and 2 750 petty officers and men)

Mercantile Marine

Lloyd's Register of Shipping: 9 vessels of 28 929 tons gross

COASTAL ESCORTS

6 Ex-SOVIET "SOI" CLASS

Displacement, tons	215 light; 250 normal
Dimensions, feet	138 pp; 147 oa × 20 × 10
Guns	4—25 mm (2 twin mounts)
Main engines	3 diesels; 3 500 bhp = 28 knots
Complement	30

Delivered by USSR on 7 and 8 Oct 1967, first two, and the other four since 1968.

MISSILE BOATS

2 Ex-SOVIET "OSA" CLASS

Displacement, tons	160 standard; 200 full load
Dimensions, feet	131 5 oa × 23 × 6·5
Missiles	4 "Styx" surface to surface
Guns	4—25 mm
Main engines	3 diesels; 4 800 bhp = 35 knots

One boat was delivered by USSR on 7 Oct 1967. Two or three others have been reported since.

8 Ex-SOVIET "KOMAR" CLASS

Displacement, tons	75 standard; 100 full load
Dimensions, feet	82 × 20 × 6
Missiles	2 "Styx" surface to surface
Guns	2—25 mm
Main engines	3 diesels; 4 800 bhp = 40 knots

Acquired in 1967 from USSR. The number of serviceable boats is reported to be six or seven.

TORPEDO BOATS

6 Ex-SOVIET "P6" CLASS

Displacement, tons	66 standard; 75 full load
Dimensions, feet	85·3 × 20·0 × 6·0
Tubes	2—21 inch
Guns	2—25 mm
Main engines	Diesels; 5 000 bhp = 45 knots

Acquired from the USSR. Two more boats are reported to be in reserve.

COASTAL MINESWEEPER

SIDI FRADJ (ex-*Darfour*)

Displacement, tons	215 standard; 270 full load
Dimensions, feet	136 oa × 24·5 × 6
Guns	1—3 in; 2—20 mm AA
Main engines	Diesels; 1 000 bhp = 13 knots

Two ex-US BYMS type coastal minesweepers were presented to Algeria by Egypt to form the nucleus of the new Algerian Navy. Both *Darfour* (ex-BYMS 2041) and *Tor* (ex-BYMS 2175) arrived in Algiers on 4 Nov 1962, being officially handed over on 6 Nov and renamed *Sidi Fradj* and *Djebel Aures*, respectively, but the latter was wrecked off Algiers in Apr 1963. Now considered obsolescent.

It is reported that there are also: 2 minesweepers of the "T 43" type, 2 former Egyptian torpedo boats, six patrol vessels, 1 old surveying trawler of the "Sekstan" type, 1 torpedo recovery vessel, several coastguard boats and some small auxiliaries.
But is is not clear whether these craft, all former Soviet vessels, are actually incorporated in the Algerian Navy or are lent for a limited period by the USSR or Egypt.

SIDI FRADJ   *Ex-U.A.R.*

ALBANIA

Strength of the Fleet

Mercantile Marine

4 Submarines	12 Torpedo Boats	16 Coastal Patrol Craft	2 Oilers	Lloyd's Register of Shipping:
2 Fleet Minesweepers	6 Inshore Minesweepers	1 Degaussing Ship	20 Small Auxiliaries	17 vessels of 56 472 tons gross
4 Patrol Vessels				

SUBMARINES

4 Ex-USSR "W" CLASS

Displacement, tons	1 030 surface; 1 180 submerged
Dimensions, feet	240 × 22 × 15
Tubes	6—21 in (4 bow, 2 stern)
Main engines	Diesels; 4 000 bhp = 17 knots surface
	Electric motors; 2 500 hp = 15 knots submerged

Three of the four "W" class submarines are operational. Two were transferred from the USSR in 1960, and two others were reportedly seized from the USSR in mid-1961 upon the withdrawal of Soviet ships from their Albanian base.

FLEET MINESWEEPERS

2 Ex-USSR "T 43" CLASS

Displacement, tons	500 standard; 600 full load
Dimensions, feet	200 × 27·5 × 9
Guns	4—37 mm AA; 8—13 mm AA MG
Main engines	Diesels; 2 shafts; speed = 18 knots

"T 43" class fleet minesweepers acquired from the USSR in 1960.

"T 43" Class   Ex-USSR

PATROL VESSELS

4 Ex-USSR "KRONSTADT" CLASS

Displacement, tons	300 standard; 350 full load
Dimensions, feet	167·3 × 19·3 × 9
Guns	1—3·9 in; 2—37 mm AA; 3—20 mm AA
A/S weapons	Depth charge projectors
Main engines	Diesels; 2 shafts = 23 knots

"Kronstadt" class submarine chasers. Fitted for minelaying. Four were transferred from the USSR in 1958, but two of these were exchanged for newer vessels in 1960.

"KRONSTADT" Class   Ex-USSR

TORPEDO BOATS

12 Ex-USSR "P-4" CLASS

Displacement, tons	50
Dimensions, feet	85·3 × 20 × 6
Guns	4—25 mm AA MG
Tubes	2—18 in
Main engines	Diesels; 2 000 bhp = 42 knots

Soviet built fast patrol boats acquired in 1955. It is reported that there are 12 motor torpedo boats in the Albanian Navy, all of the Soviet P-4 class but some may have been supplied by the Chinese.

"P-4" Class   Ex-USSR

INSHORE MINESWEEPERS

6 Ex-USSR "T 301" CLASS

Displacement, tons	130 standard; 180 full load
Dimensions, feet	100 × 16 × 4·5
Guns	2—37 mm AA; 2—25 mm AA
Main engines	Diesels; 2 shafts; 480 bhp = 10 knots

"T 301" class inshore minesweepers acquired from the USSR in 1957-60. Another photograph of "T 301" class appears in the 1962-63 edition.

"T 301" Class   Ex-USSR

"T 301" Class   Ex-USSR

COASTAL PATROL CRAFT

16 CG TYPE

Displacement, tons	40 to 45 standard; 45 to 50 full load
Dimensions, feet	82·0 × 16·7 × 5·6
Guns	2—25 mm or 2—13 mm
Main engines	Diesels = 30 to 42 knots

Not all of the same type. Some are of the Soviet PO-2 class. There are also reported to be a number of coastguard cutters. The two gunboats of the armoured type were deleted from the list in 1971.

DEGAUSSING SHIP

1 Ex-USSR "SEKSTAN" CLASS

Dimensions, feet	134 × 40 × 14 max

Transferred from the USSR. Built in Finland in 1956. The two landing craft of the utility transport type were deleted from the list in 1971.

OILERS

2 Ex-USSR "KHOBI" CLASS

Measurements, tons	1 600 deadweight
Dimensions, feet	220 × 33 × 15 max
Main engines	2 diesels; 1 600 bhp = 12 knots

Transferred from the USSR. Launched in 1956. In addition to the above there are reported to be a number of small auxiliaries.

TENDERS

There are reported to be a dozen harbour and port tenders including a water carrier and a torpedo recovery vessel.

The "Atrek" class submarine tender transferred from USSR in 1961 as a depot ship was converted into a merchant ship.

TUGS

Several small tugs are employed in local duties or harbour service.

ARGENTINA

Administration

Commander in Chief of the Navy:
Almirante Pedro A. J. Gnavi

Chief of Naval Staff:
Vicealmirante Juan Carlos Gonzalez Llanos

Chief of Naval Operations:
Vicealmirante Raúl Francos

Diplomatic Representation

Chief of Naval Commission in Europe and Naval Attaché in London and The Netherlands:
Vicealmirante Carlos Go. N. Coda

Naval Attaché in Washington:
Contraalmirante Carlos Alvarez

Naval Attaché in Paris:
Capitan de Navio Julio A. Guidi

Strength of the Fleet

  1 Aircraft Carrier
  2 Submarines (Conventionally Powered)
  3 Cruisers
  6 Destroyers
  3 Frigates
  2 Corvettes
  4 Coastal Minesweepers
  2 Minehunters (ex-Coastal Minesweepers)
  9 Patrol Vessels
  3 Coastal Patrol Craft
  3 Survey Ships
  5 Landing Ships
 29 Landing Craft and Minor Landing Craft
  1 Mine Support Vessel
  1 Salvage Vessel
  1 Training Ship
  4 Transports
  3 Oilers
  1 Icebreaker (Antarctic Research Ship)
 13 Tugs

Ships

The names of all Argentine warships and naval auxiliary vessels are prefaced by "A.R.A." (Armada Republica Argentina).

New Construction Programme

2 Type 42 Guided Missile Destroyers
2 Hunter-Killer (A/S) Submarines
2 Fast Patrol Vessels
1 Tank Landing Ship (BDT)

Personnel

1971: 33 300 (2 300 officers, 31 000 ratings) including 11 000 conscripts)

Mercantile Marine

Lloyd's Register of Shipping:
327 vessels of 1 265 510 tons gross

Scale: 150 feet = 1 inch (1 : 1 800)

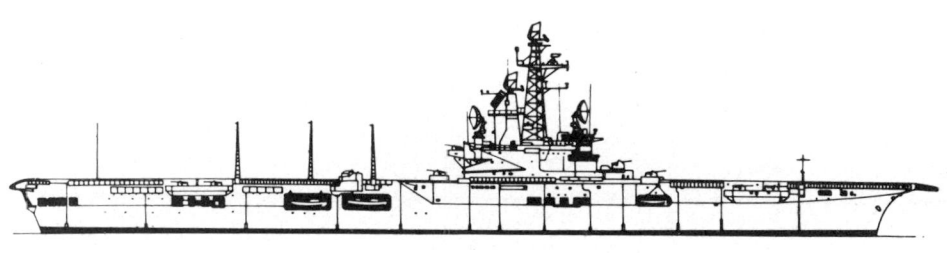

25 DE MAYO

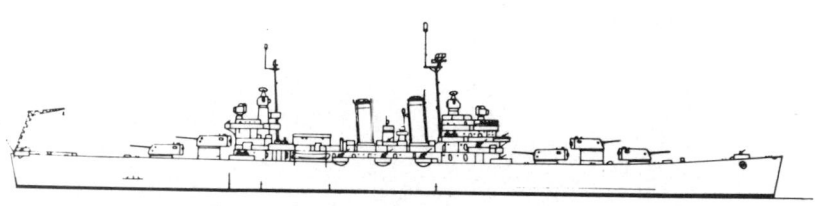

GENERAL BELGRANO, 9 DE JULIO

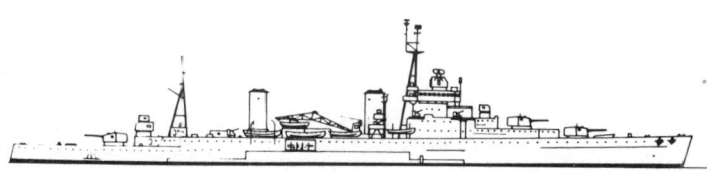

LA ARGENTINA

TYPE 42

BUENOS AIRES Class

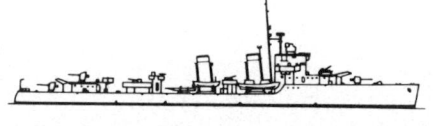

ENTRE RIOS, SAN JUAN, SANTA CRUZ

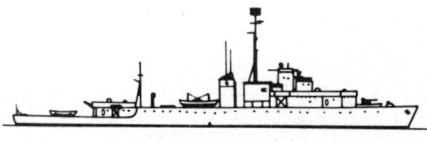

JUAN B. AZOPARDO

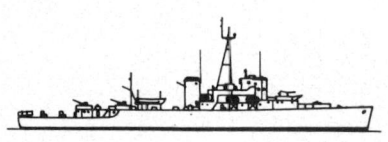

AZOPARDO, PIEDRABUENA

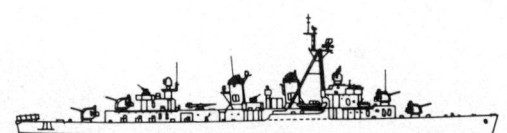

BROWN, ESPORA, ROSALES

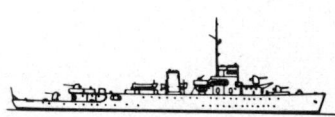

KING, MURATURE

AIRCRAFT CARRIERS (*Portaviones*)

Name		*Builders*	*Laid down*	*Launched*	*Completed*
25 DE MAYO (ex-*HrMs Karel Doorman*, ex-*HMS Venerable*)		Cammell Laird & Co Ltd Birkenhead	3 Dec 1942	30 Dec 1943	17 Jan 1945

1 Ex-BRITISH "COLOSSUS" CLASS

Displacement, tons	15 892 standard; 19 896 full load
Length, feet (*metres*)	630 (*192·0*) pp 693·2 (*211·3*) oa
Beam, feet (*metres*)	80 (*24·4*)
Draught, feet (*metres*)	25 (*7·6*)
Width, feet (*metres*)	121·3 (*37·0*) overall
Hangar:	
Length, feet (*metres*)	455 (*138·7*)
Width, feet (*metres*)	52 (*15·8*)
Height, feet (*metres*)	17·5 (*5·3*)
Aircraft	Capacity 21; normal complement: 14 (8 fixed-wing and 6 helicopters)
Guns, AA	10—40 mm
Boilers	4 three-drum; working pressure 400 psi (*28·1 kg/cm²*); Superheat 700°F (*371°C*)
Main engines	Parsons geared turbines; 40 000 shp; 2 shafts
Speed, knots	24·25 designed
Radius, miles	12 000 at 14 knots
Oil fuel, tons	3 200
Complement	1 500

Purchased from Great Britain on 1 Apr 1948 and commissioned in the Royal Netherlands Navy on 28 May 1948. Badly damaged by boiler room fire on 29 Apr 1968. Sold to Argentina on 15 Oct 1968 and refitted at Rotterdam by N. V. Dok en Werf Mij Wilton Fijenoord. Commissioned in the Argentine Navy on 12 Mar 1969. Completed refit on 22 Aug 1969 and sailed for Argentina on 1 Sep 1969.

RECONSTRUCTION. Underwent extensive refit modernisation in 1955-1958 including angled flight deck and steam catapult, mirror sight landing system, and new anti-aircraft battery of ten 40 mm guns, at the Wilton-Fijenoord Shipyard, at a cost of 25 million guilders. Conversion completed in July 1958.

RADAR
Search: Two Philips LWO series early warning radars with associated height finders for air interception.
Tactical: S Band tactical and navigation radar.

ENGINEERING. The turbine sets and boilers are arranged *en echelon*, the two propelling-machinery spaces having two boilers and one set of turbines in each space, on the unit system. She was reboilered in 1965-1966 with boilers removed from HMS *Leviathan*. During refit for Argentina in 1968-1969 she received new turbines, also from HMS *Leviathan*.

APPEARANCE. With modified island superstructure and bridge, lattice tripod radar mast, and tall raked funnel, she differs considerably from her former appearance and from her original sister ships in the British, French and Brazilian Navies.

DISPOSALS
It was officially stated in Jan 1971 that the aircraft carrier *Independencia* (ex-HMS *Warrior*), No V 1, a near-sister-ship of *25 de Mayo*, was no longer operational and had been withdrawn from service (see full particulars, history, photographs, and plan and elevation drawing in the 1970-71 and earlier editions).

DRAWING. Starboard elevation and plan. Redrawn in 1971. Scale: 125 feet = 1 inch (1 : 1 500).

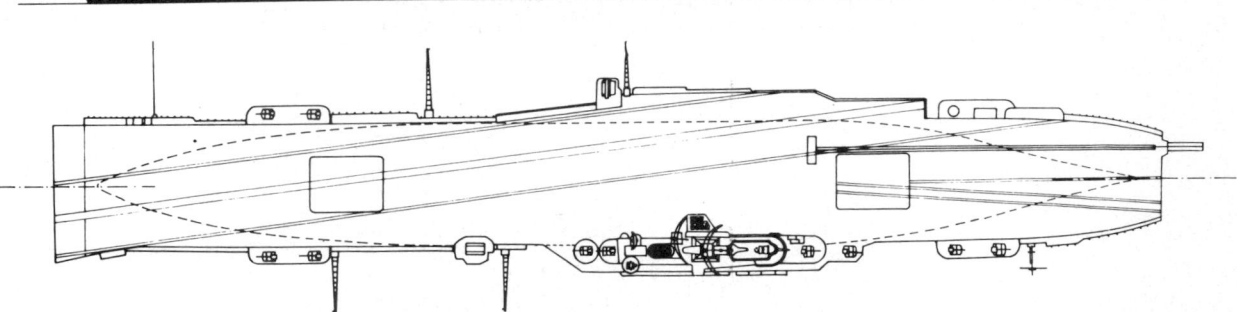

25 DE MAYO

1970, Wright & Logan

25 DE MAYO (Harrier VTOL aircraft demonstration on flight deck)

1970, Argentine Navy, Official

SUBMARINES

2 NEW CONSTRUCTION

Displacement, tons	450
Length, feet (metres)	144·4 (44·0)
Beam, feet (metres)	15·1 (4·6)
Torpedo tubes	8—21 in (in bow)
Speed, knots	10 on surface

It is reported that two submarines are being built in
Argentina using material and pre-fabricated sections of
Federal German construction.

2 Ex-US "BALAO" CLASS

SANTA FE (ex-USS Lamprey, SS 372) S 11
SANTIAGO DEL ESTERO
(ex-USS Macabi, SS 375) S 12

Displacement, tons	1 526 standard; 1 816 surface; 2 425 submerged
Length, feet (metres)	311·5 (94·9)
Beam feet (metres)	27 (8·2)
Draught, feet (metres)	17 (5·2)
Torpedo tubes	10—21 in (533 mm); 6 bow. 4 stern. 24 Mk 14 torpedoes
Main engines	6 500 hp GM 2-stroke diesels (surface); 4 610 hp electric motors (submerged)
Speed, knots	20 on surface; 10 submerged
Radius, miles	12 000 at 10 knots
Oil fuel (tons)	300
Complement	82

Both built by Manitowoc SB Co, launched on 8 June
and 19 Sep 1944 and completed on 17 Nov 1944 and
29 Mar 1945 respectively. Transferred at Mare Island
Naval Shipyard after refit on 27 July and 11 Aug 1960.

SANTIAGO DEL ESTERO

1969, Argentine Navy, Official

SANTA FE

1969, Argentine Navy, Official

CRUISERS

Name	No.	Builders	Laid down	Launched	Completed
GENERAL BELGRANO (ex-17 de Octubre, ex-Phoenix, CL 46)	C 4	New York S.B. Corp Camden	15 Apr 1935	12 Mar 1938	18 Mar 1939
NUEVE DE JULIO (ex-Boise, CL 47)	C 5	Newport News S.B. & D.D. Co	1 Apr 1935	3 Dec 1936	1 Feb 1939

2 Ex-US "BROOKLYN" CLASS

Displacement, tons	Gen. Belgrano: 10 800 standard; 12 650 normal; 13 645 full load Nueve de Julio: 10 500 standard 12 300 normal; 13 645 full load
Length, feet (metres)	608·3 (185·4) oa
Beam, feet (metres)	69 (21·0)
Draught, feet (metres)	24 (7·3) max
Aircraft	2 helicopters
Missiles, AA	2 quadruple "Sea Cat" launchers (General Belgrano only).
Guns, surface	15—6 in (153 mm) 47 cal; 8—5 in (127 mm) 25 cal.
Guns, AA	28—40 mm; 16—20 mm;
Guns, saluting	4—47 mm
Armour	Belt 4 in—1½ in (100—38 mm) Decks 3 in+2 in (76+51 mm) Turrets 5 in—3 in (127—76 mm) Conning Tower 8 in (203 mm)
Boilers	8 Babcock & Wilcox Express type
Main Engines	Westinghouse geared turbines 100 000 shp; 4 shafts
Speed, knots	32·5
Radius, miles	7 600 at 15 knots
Oil fuel (tons)	2 200
Complement	1 200

Former "light" cruisers of the United States Navy
"Brooklyn" class. Superstructure was reduced, bulges
added, beam increased, and mainmast derricks and
catapults removed. Purchased from the United States
in 1951 at a cost of $7 800 000 representing 10 per cent
of their original cost ($37 000 000) plus the expense of
reconditioning them. Both were transferred to the
Argentine Navy on 12 Apr 1951. General Belgrano was
commissioned under the name 17 de Octubre at Philadelphia on 17 Oct 1951. 9 de Julio was commissioned
into the Argentine Navy at Philadelphia on 11 Mar 1952.

PHOTOGRAPHS. A starboard bow aerial view of
9 de Julio appears in the 1954-55 to 1958-59 editions, a
large port quarter surface view of 9 de Julio in the
1957-58 edition, a port broadside view of General
Belgrano in the 1957-58 to 1963-64 editions, and a starboard broadside surface view of 9 de Julio in the 1964-65
and 1965-66 editions and a port broadside in the 1965-66
to 1968-69 editions.

HISTORICAL. 9 de Julio refers to 9 July 1816, when the
Argentine provinces signed the Declaration of Independence. 17 de Octubre was renamed General Belgrano in
1956 following the overthrow of President Peron the
year before.

HANGAR. The hangar in the hull right aft accommodates two helicopters together with engine spares and
duplicate parts, though 4 aircraft was the original complement. The incorporation of this hangar resulted in a

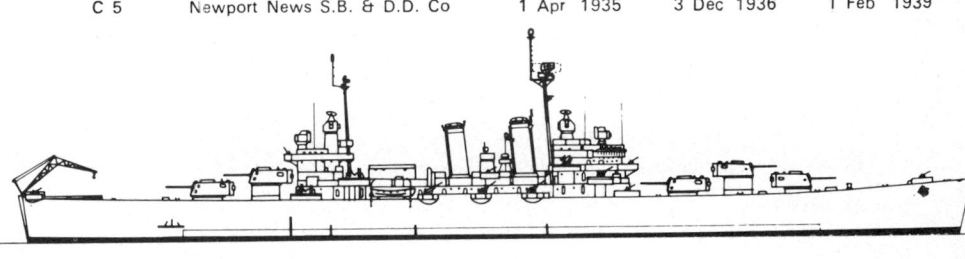

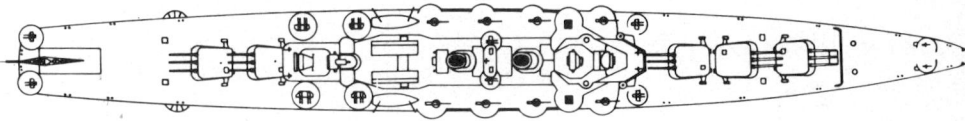

DRAWING: Starboard elevation and plan. Re-drawn
in 1971. Scale 125 feet = 1 inch. (1 : 1 500). "Sea-
cats" abreast fore control in General Belgrano only.

RADAR
Search: L Band early warning radar, Type SPS 12.
Tactical: Probably SPS 10.

9 DE JULIO.

1969, Argentine Navy, Official

very wide and nearly flat counter and high freeboard aft
and also gave the after guns higher command. Above
the hangar a revolving crane is placed at the stern

extremity overhanging the hangar hatch. The two
aircraft catapults, originally mounted above the hangar as
far outboard as possible, and the aircraft were removed.

Name	No.
LA ARGENTINA	C 3

Displacement, tons	6 000 standard ; 7 610 normal
	8 630 full load
Length, feet (*metres*)	510 (*155·5*) pp ; 541·2 (*164·9*) oa
Beam, feet (*metres*)	56·5 (*17·2*)
Draught, feet (*metres*)	16·5 (*5·0*) max
Guns, surface	9—6 in (*153 mm*)
Guns, AA	14—40 mm
Torpedo tubes	6—21 in (*533 mm*), tripled
Armour	Side and C.T. 3 in (*76 mm*) ;
	deck and gunhouses 2 in (*51 mm*)
Boilers	4 Yarrow ; 300 psi (*21 kg/cm²*)
Main engines	Parsons geared turbines
	54 000 shp ; 4 shafts.
Speed, knots	30
Radius, miles	7 500 at 12 knots
Oil fuel (tons)	1 500
Complement	800

Designed as Training Cruiser. Cost 6 000 000 gold pesos (about £1 750 000). Best recent speed 25 knots.

Cruisers—*continued*

Builders	Laid down	Launched	Completed
Vickers-Armstrongs Ltd, Barrow-in Furness	Jan 1936	16 Mar 1937	31 Jan 1939

GUNNERY. Original 4 inch guns were removed in 1950 and 40 mm guns added.

DRAWING. Starboard elevation and plan. Re-drawn in 1971. Scale 125 feet = 1 inch (1 : 1 500).

LA ARGENTINA

1969. Argentine Navy, Official

DESTROYERS

2 NEW CONSTRUCTION TYPE 42

Displacement, tons	3 500
Length, feet (*metres*)	410·0 (*125·0*)
Beam, feet (*metres*)	47·0 (*14·3*)
Missile launchers	2 "Sea Dart" (1 twin)
Aircraft	1 anti-submarine helicopter
Guns	1—4·5 in automatic
Main engines	Rolls Royce Olympus gas turbines for full power ; Rolls Royce Tyne gas turbines for cruising ; 2 shafts
Speed, knots	30 designed

Guided missile armed destroyers of the British "Sheffield" class. The Argentine Navy signed the contract with Vickers Ltd, Barrow-in-Furness, announced on 18 May 1970, for the construction of two "Type 42" destroyers or frigates, one to be built in Great Britain and the other in Argentina with British oversight of construction.

Name	No.	Builders	Laid down	Launched	Completed
BROWN (ex-USS *Heerman*, DD 532)	D 20	Bethlehem Steel Co, San Francisco	8 May 1942	5 Dec 1942	6 July 1943
ESPORA (ex-USS *Dortch*, DD 670)	D 21	Federal S.B. & D.D. Co, Port Newark	1942	20 June 1943	16 July 1943
ROSALES (ex-USS *Stembel*, DD 644)	D 22	Bath Iron Works Corporation, Bath, Maine	21 Dec 1942	8 May 1943	7 Aug 1943

3 Ex-US "FLETCHER" CLASS

Displacement, tons	2 100 standard ; 3 050 full load
Length, feet (*metres*)	376·5 (*114·8*) oa
Beam, feet (*metres*)	39·5 (*12·0*)
Draught, feet (*metres*)	12·2 (*3·7*) mean ; 18 (*5·5*) max
Guns, surface	4—5 in (*127 mm*) 38 cal.
Guns, AA	6—3 in (*76 mm*) 50 cal.
Torpedo tubes	5—21 in (*533 mm*) quintupled
A/S depth charges	2 fixed Hedgehogs ; 1 DC rack
A/S torpedo racks	2 side-launching
Boilers	4 Babcock & Wilcox
Main engines	2 sets GE geared turbines
	60 000 shp ; 2 shafts
Speed, knots	35
Radius, miles	6 000 at 15 knots
Oil fuel (tons)	650
Complement	300

All were transferred to the Argentine Navy on 1 Aug 1961. *Espora* is of the later "Fletcher" class.

PHOTOGRAPHS. A photograph of *Espora* appears in the 1969-70 and 1970-71 editions and of *Brown* in the 1965-66 to 1968-69 editions.

RADAR
Search: L Band SPS 6.
Tactical: C Band SPS 10.
Fire Control: X Band, antenna on Director.

ROSALES

1971

Destroyers—continued

Name	No.	Builders	Laid down	Launched	Completed
ENTRE RIOS	D 7	Vickers-Armstrongs Ltd, Barrow-in-Furness	1936	21 Sep 1937	Mar 1938
SAN JUAN	D 9	John Brown & Co Ltd, Clydebank	1936	24 June 1937	Mar 1938
SANTA CRUZ	D 12	Cammell Laird & Co Ltd, Birkenhead	1936	3 Nov 1937	Oct 1938

ENTRE RIOS   1971

3 "BUENOS AIRES" CLASS

Displacement, tons	1 375 standard; 1 820 to 1 850 normal; 1 980 to 2 010 full load
Length, feet (metres)	312 (95·1) pp; 320 (97·5 wl; 323 (98·5) oa
Beam, feet (metres)	34·8 (10·6)
Draught, feet (metres)	10·7 (3·3) mean
Guns, surface	3 or 4—4·7 in (120 mm)
Guns, AA	6—40 mm; 5 MG
A/S weapons	1 Hedgehog; 4+DCT
Torpedo tubes	4—21 in (533 mm) quadrupled
Boilers	3 three-drum type
Main engines	Parsons geared turbines 34 000 shp; 2 shafts
Speed, knots	35
Radius, miles	4 100 at 14 knots
Oil fuel, tons	450
Complement	200

Classification changed from Exploradores to Torpederos in 1952 and to Destructores in 1957. One quadruple torpedo mount removed in 1956. Corrientes of this class was lost by collision with the cruiser Almirante Brown on 3 Oct 1941. Buenos Aires, Misiones and San Luis were withdrawn from service in 1971.

PHOTOGRAPHS. A photograph of Santa Cruz appears in the 1967-68 and 1968-69 editions and of San Juan in the 1953-54 to 1958-59 editions.

FRIGATES

Name	No.	Builders	Laid down	Launched	Completed
AZOPARDO	P 35	Astillero Nav. Rio Santiago	Nov 1950	11 Dec 1953	7 July 1957
PIEDRABUENA	P 36	Astillero Nav. Rio Santiago	Nov 1950	17 Dec 1954	16 Dec 1958

AZOPARDO   1966, Argentine Navy, Official

2 "AZOPARDO" CLASS

Displacement, tons	1 160 standard; 1 400 full load
Length, feet (metres)	278·5 (84·9)
Beam, feet (metres)	31·5 (9·6)
Draught, feet (metres)	10·2 (3·1)
Guns, surface	1—4·1 in (105 mm)
Guns, AA	6—40 mm
A/S weapons	1 Hedgehog; 4 DC mortars
Boilers	2 water tube 3-drum type
Main engines	2 Parsons geared turbines; 5 000 shp; 2 shafts
Speed, knots	20 max
Radius, miles	5 400 at 12 knots
Oil fuel, tons	340
Complement	160

Both built at Astillero Nav. Rio Santiago. Improved "King" type. Azopardo is named after the Argentine naval hero.

Ex-US PF TYPE

JUAN B AZOPARDO (ex-Hercules, ex-USS Ashville, ex-HMCS Nadur, ex-HMS Adur) GC 11

Displacement, tons	1 445 standard; 1 920 normal; 2 415 full load
Length, feet (metres)	285·5 (87·2) wl; 304 (92·7) oa
Beam, feet (metres)	37·5 (10·1)
Draught, feet (metres)	13·7 (4·2)
Guns, AA	2—40 mm
Boilers	2 three-drum type
Main engines	Triple expansion 5 500 ihp; 2 shafts
Speed, knots	19 (max now 14)
Radius, miles	7 800 at 12 knots
Oil fuel, tons	700
Complement	175

Former US patrol escort of the "Tacoma" class, built by Canadian Vickers, Montreal; laid down on 10 Mar 1942, launched on 22 Aug 1942 and completed on 1 Dec 1942. Operated by National Maritime Prefectura and bears prefix P.N.M. to name.

Of sister ships Santisima Trinidad, P 34 (ex-HMS Caicas, ex-Hannam) was reclassified as a survey ship in 1963. and Heronia (ex-USS Reading, PF 66) was withdrawn from active service and scrapped in 1966. Sarandi (ex-USS Uniontown, ex-Chattanooga, PF 65) was withdrawn from service in 1968.

JUAN B. AZOPARDO   1969, Argentine Navy, Official

CORVETTES

Name	No.	Builders	Laid down	Launched	Completed
KING	P 21	Astillero Nav. Rio Santiago	Dec 1938	Dec 1943	28 July 1946
MURATURE	P 20	Astillero Nav. Rio Santiago	June 1938	July 1945	18 Nov 1946

2 "KING" CLASS

Displacement, tons	913 standard; 1 000 normal; 1 032 full load
Length, feet (metres)	252·7 (77·0)
Beam, feet (metres)	29 (8·8)
Draught, feet (metres)	7·5 (2·3)
Guns, surface	3—4·1 in (105 mm)
Guns, AA	4—40 mm Bofors; 2—MG
A/S	4—DCT
Main engines	2—Werkspoor 4-stroke diesels; 2 500 bhp; 2 shafts
Speed, knots	18
Radius, miles	6 000 at 12 knots
Oil fuel (tons)	90
Complement	130

Both built at Astillero Nav. Rio Santiago. Named after Captain John King, an Irish follower of Admiral Brown, who distinguished himself in the war with Brazil, 1826-28; and Captain Murature, who performed conspicuous service against the Paraguayans at the Battle of Cuevas on Aug. 6 1865.

KING   1970, Argentine Navy, Official

PHOTOGRAPHS. A photograph of Murature appears in the 1964-65 to 1966-67 editions.

The corvette Republica was withdrawn from service on 5 Aug 1967 and scrapped in 1968.

FAST PATROL VESSELS

2 NEW CONSTRUCTION

It was officially stated by the Argentine Navy in Jan 1971 that two fast patrol vessels are under construction.

COASTAL MINESWEEPERS

6 Ex-BRITISH "TON" CLASS

CHACO (ex-HMS *Rennington*)	M 5
CHUBUT (ex-HMS *Santon*)	M 3
FORMOSA (ex-HMS *Ilmington*)	M 6
NEUQUEN (ex-HMS *Hickleton*)	M 1
RIO NEGRO (ex-HMS *Tarlton*)	M 2
TIERRA DEL FUEGO (ex-HMS *Bevington*)	M 4

Displacement, tons	360 standard; 425 full load
Dimensions, feet	140 pp; 153 oa × 28·8 × 8·2
Guns	1—40 mm AA
Main engines	2 diesels; 2 shafts; 3 000 bhp = 15 knots
Oil fuel (tons)	45
Radius, miles	2 300 at 13 knots
Complement	Minesweepers 27; Minehunters 36

Former British coastal minesweepers of the "Ton" class. Of composite wooden and non-magnetic metal construction. Purchased in 1967. In 1968 *Chaco* and *Formosa* were converted into minehunters in HM Dockyard, Portsmouth, and the other four were refitted and modernised as minesweepers by the Vosper Thornycroft Group with Vosper activated fin stabiliser equipment.

DISPOSALS
Of the eight former minesweepers of the "Bouchard" class, *Drummond*, *Parker* and *Spiro* were stricken into reserve and laid up in 1963, and *Granville*, *Py*, *Robinson* and *Seaver* were deleted from the list on the 20 Nov 1967. *Py* and *Seaver* were transferred to the Paraguayan Navy in 1969, and *Bouchard* and *Parker* in 1964.

CHACO (hunter)   1970, Wright & Logan

FORMOSA (hunter)   1969, Wright & Logan

TIERRA DEL FUEGO (sweeper)   1969, Wright & Logan

DISPOSALS OF MTBS
The motor torpedo boats *P 82* and *P 84* have been removed from service, at was officially stated in Mar 1970. Of the other seven boats of the "Higgins" type P 86 and P 88 were officially stricken from the list in 1966, and P 81, P 83, P 85, P 87 and P 89 in 1963.

PATROL VESSELS (*Avisos*)

2 Ex-US TUG TYPE

THOMPSON (ex-US *Sombrero Key*) A 4   **GOYENA** (ex-US *Dry Tortugas*) A 3

Displacement, tons	1 863 full load
Dimensions, feet	191·3 × 37 × 18
Guns	2—40 mm (1 twin) Bofors; 2—20 mm, 70 cal (single)
Main engines	2 Enterprise diesels; 2 250 bhp = 12 knots
Oil fuel (tons)	532
Complement	60

Built by Pendleton Shipyard Co., New Orleans. Launched in 1943 and leased to the Argentine Navy in 1965.

2 Ex-US ATF TYPE

COMMANDANTE GENERAL IRIGOYEN (ex-USS *Cahuilla*, ATF 152)   A 1
COMMANDANTE GENERAL ZAPIOLA (ex-USS *Arapaho*, ATF 68)   A 2

Displacement, tons	1 235 standard; 1 675 full load
Dimensions, feet	195 wl; 205 oa × 38·2 × 15·3
Guns	1—3 in; 4—40 mm AA; 2—20 mm AA originally
Main Engines	4 sets diesels with electric drive; 3 000 bhp = 16 knots
Complement	85

Former US fleet ocean tugs of the "Apache" class. Fitted with powerful pumps and other salvage equipment. Both built by Charleston S.B. & D.D. Co., Charleston, S.C. Launched on 2 Nov. 1944 and 22 June 1942, respectively, and completed on 10 Mar. 1945 and 20 Jan. 1943. Transferred to Argentina at San Diego, California, in 1961 Classified as tugs until 1966 when they were re-rated as patrol vessels (avisos).

COMMANDANTE GENERAL IRIGOYEN   1969, Argentine Navy, Official

4 Ex-US ATA TYPE

CHIRIGUANO (ex-US *ATA* 227) A7   **SANAVIRON** (ex-US *ATA* 228) A 8
DIAGUITA (ex-US *ATA* 124) A5   **YAMANA** (ex-US *ATA* 126) A 6

Displacement, tons	689 standard; 800 full load
Dimensions, feet	133·7 wl; 143 oa × 34 × 12
Guns	2—20 mm AA
Main Engines	Diesel-electric; 1 850 bhp = 12·5 knots
Oil fuel (tons)	154
Radius, miles	16 500
Complement	49

Former US auxiliary ocean tugs. Built by Levingstone Shipbuilding Co., Orange Texas, USA, in 1945. *Diaguita* and *Yamana* are fitted as rescue ships. All four of above ships bear names of South American Indian tribes. Classified as ocean salvage tugs until 1966 when they were re-rated as patrol vessels (avisos).

YAMANA   1969, Argentine Navy, Official

Patrol Vessels—*continued*

SPIRO GC 12

Displacement, tons	560 normal ; 650 full load
Dimensions, feet	197 oa (59·7) × 24 (7·32) × 11½ (3·5)
Guns	4 × 40 mm
Main engines	2 MAN Diesels ; 2 000 bhp = 13 knots
Complement	77

Former minesweeper of the "Bouchard" class, now operated by the Prefectura Nacional Maritima. Built by the Rio Santiago Navy Yard. Launched on 7 June 1937. Sister ships *Bouchard, Parker, Py* and *Seaver* were transferred to the Paraguayan Navy. They were the first warships built in Argentine yards.

SPIRO   *1969, Argentine Navy, Official*

COASTAL PATROL CRAFT

3 "LYNCH" TYPE

EREZCANO GC 23   **LYNCH** G3 21   **TOLL** GC 22

Displacement, tons	100 normal ; 117 full load
Dimensions, feet	90 × 19 × 6
Guns	1 × 20 mm
Main engines	2 Maybach Diesels ; 2 700 bhp = 22 knots
Complement	16

Patrol craft operated by the Prefectura Nacional Maritima. Pennant numbers GC 23, GC 21, and GC 22, respectively, were assigned when they were under construction at Rio Santiago shipyards in 1964. There is also GC 31, see photograph below.

LYNCH   *1969, Argentine Navy, Official*

GC 31   *1971*

MINELAYER SUPPORT VESSEL

CORRIENTES (ex-BDM 2)

Displacement, tons	743 light ; 1 095 full load
Dimensions, feet	196·5 wl ; 203·5 oa × 33·8 × 8
Main engines	2 diesels ; 2 shafts ; 2 800 bhp = 13 knots
Oil fuel, tons	170
Radius, miles	4 100 at 12 knots
Complement	66

Former Medium Landing Ship (ex-USN *LSM 86*). Converted at Naval Shipyard, Buenos Aires during 1968.

SURVEY SHIPS (*Buques Oceanograficos*)

1 Ex-CANADIAN FLOWER CLASS

CAPITAN CANEPA (ex-HMCS *Barrie*) Q 8

Displacement, tons	995 standard ; 1 265 full load
Dimensions, feet	208 × 33·5 × 16·5
Main Engines	Triple expansion ; 2 750 ihp = 15 knots
Boilers	2
Oil fuel (tons)	271
Complement	54

Former Canadian corvette (frigate) of the "Flower" class. Launched in Canada on 12 Nov. 1940. Completed on 12 May 1941. A photograph of *Capitan Canepa* appears in the 1958-59 to 1964-65 editions.

CAPITAN CANEPA   *1969, Argentine Navy, Official*

1 TRANSPORT TYPE

USHUAIA No. Q 10

Displacement, tons	1 275 standard ; 1 500 full load
Dimensions, feet	211 × 31·5 × 11·5
Guns	Removed
Main Engines	2 sets diesels ; 2 shafts ; 1 200 bhp = 12·7 knots
Oil fuel (tons)	60
Radius, miles	3 500
Complement	65

Built at Rio Santiago. Launched in 1939. Named after the capital of the territory of Tierra del Fuego. Formerly rated as a transport until 1959, when she was reclassified as a survey ship. She is also a buoy ship for the laying and servicing of buoys and lights.

USHUAIA   *1969, Argentine Navy, Official*

DISPOSAL

The survey ship *Comodoro Augusto Lassere*, Q 9, (ex-frigate *Santisima Trinidad*, P 34, ex-HMS *Caicos*, ex-USS *Hannam*) was deactivated in 1968 and officially withdrawn from further service in 1970, see photograph in the 1965-66 to 1968-69 editions.

1 SAIL TYPE

EL AUSTRAL (ex-US *Atlantis*) Q 7

Displacement, tons	571
Dimensions, feet	110 pp 141 oa × 27 × 20
Main engines	Diesel ; 400 bhp
Oil fuel (tons)	22
Complement	19

Built by Burmeister & Wain, Copenhagen. Launched and completed in 1931. Incorporated into the Argentine Navy on 30 April, 1966. Acquired from USA. Officially rated as *Buque Oceanografico*.

LANDING SHIPS

1 NEW CONSTRUCTION

CABO SAN ANTONIO

Displacement, tons	4 300 light; 8 000 full load
Dimensions, feet	445 oa × 62 × 16·5
Guns	6—3 in (3 twin)
Main engines	Diesels; 2 shafts; 13 700 hbp = 11 knots
Complement	124

Built at the Naval Shipyard in Rio Santiago. Reported to be designed to carry a helicopter and two landing craft.

5 Ex-US LST TYPE

CABO SAN BARTOLOME	BDT 1	**CABO SAN ISIDRO**	BDT 6
CABO SAN GONZALO	BDT 4	**CABO SAN PIO**	BDT 10

Displacement, tons	2 366 beaching; 4 080 full load
Dimensions, feet	316 wl; 328 oa × 50 × 14
Guns	4—40 mm (2 twin) *Cabo San Bartolome* only
Main Engines	2 diesels; 2 shafts; 1 800 bhp = 11 knots
Oil fuel (tons)	700
Radius, miles	9 500 at 9 knots
Complement	80

Ex-US LST's 875, 998, 872, 919. Built by Puget Sound Bridge and Dredging Co., Seattle, USA. Launched in 1944. Have two rudders. BDT 5, BDT 8, BDT 9, and BDT 12, were withdrawn from service in 1958-60, and BDT 2, BDT 7, BDT 11 and BDT 13 in 1964. *Cabo San Francisco de Paula*, BDT 3 has been used as a store ship since 1966. *Cabo San Vicente* BDT 14 (Q 52) was withdrawn from service in 1971.

MEDIUM LANDING SHIPS

Of the former United States landing ships, medium, BDM 2 (ex-USN *LSM* 86) was converted into a minelayer support vessel in 1968, see previous page; and BDM 1 (Q 69), ex-USN *LSM* 267, was withdrawn from service, it was officially stated in Jan 1971.

LANDING CRAFT

BDI 1 Q 54 (ex-USS *LCIL* 583)		**BDI 4** Q 57 (ex-USS *LCIL* 606)	

Displacement, tons	230 light; 387 full load
Dimensions, feet	153 wl; 159 oa × 23·2 × 5
Guns	2—20 mm AA (only in BDI 4)
Main engines	8 sets diesels; 3 200 bhp = 14 knots. Two reversible propellers
Oil fuel, tons	110
Radius, miles	6 000 at 12 knots
Complement	30

Former US Navy large infantry landing craft. BDI 3, BDI 6, BDI 8, BDI 9, BDI 11 and BDI 13 were withdrawn from service in 1958. BDI 1 and BDI 4 were given new Q numbers as shown above instead of Q 64 and 67. BDI 10 (Q 63) was converted into an oiler in 1960 and renamed *Punta Lara*. BDI 5, BDI 7, BDI 12 and BDI 14 were officially deleted from the list in 1961, BDI 2 in 1963, and BDI 15 (Q 68) in 1971.

BDI   *1970. Argentine Navy, Official*

BDI 4   *1960, Giorgio Arra*

SALVAGE VESSEL (*Buque de Salvamento*)

GUARDIAMARINA ZICARI (ex-*Tehuelche*, ex-HMS *Kingfisher*, ex-*King Salvor*)

Displacement, tons	1 600
Dimensions, feet	200·2 pp; 216 oa × 37·8 × 13
Main engines	Triple expansion. 2 shafts; 1 500 ihp = 12 knots
Oil fuel (tons)	310
Complement	82

Former British submarine rescue ship. Built as an Admiralty ocean salvage vessel by Wm. Simons & Co. Ltd. Renfrew, Scotland, and laid down on 17 May 1941, launched on 18 May 1942 and completed on 17 July 1942. Converted into a Submarine Rescue Bell and Target Ship in 1953-54. Paid off as Bell Rescue Ship in 1958 and subsequently employed as a Submarine Support Ship and Tender. Purchased from Great Britain in Dec 1960, and sailed from Chatham to Argentina in Apr 1961, and renamed *Tehuelche*. Again renamed *Guardiamarina Zicari* in Apr 1963. Pennant No. Q 81.

GUARDIAMARINA ZICARI   *Argentine Navy, Official*

TRAINING SHIP (*Buques Esquela*)

LIBERTAD Q 2

Displacement, tons	3 025 standard; 3 765 full load
Dimensions, feet	262 wl; 301 oa × 47 × 21·8
Guns	1—3 in; 4—40 mm AA; 4—47 mm saluting
Main engines	2 Sulzer diesels; 2 400 bhp = 13·5 knots
Radius	15 000 miles
Complement	370 (crew) plus 150 cadets

Built in the State-owned shipyards at Rio Santiago. Launched on 30 June 1956. The former training ship *Madryn* was removed from the list on 29 June 1967.

LIBERTAD   *1971*

MINOR LANDING CRAFT

LCM 1	**LCM 2**	**LCM 3**	**LCM 4**

It was officially stated in Jan 1971 that four LCMs have been incorporated in the Fleet.

EDVP	**EDVP**	**EDVP**	**EDVP**	**EDVP**	**EDVP**	**EDVP**	**EDVP**

Units incorporated into the Argentine Navy at the end of 1970 included eight vehicle and personnel landing craft.

EDVP 1, 3, 4, 5, 6, 7, 8, 9, 10, 11, 12, 13, 20, 21, 22, 24, 27, 28, 29

Displacement, tons	12
Dimensions, feet	39·5 × 10·5 × 5·5
Main engines	Diesel, 9 knots

Ex USN LCVPs. EDVP Numbers 16, 23, 25 and 26 were withdrawn from service in 1966.

TRANSPORTS (*Transportes*)

BAHIA AGUIRRE   **BAHIA BUEN SUCESO**   **BAHIA THETIS**

Displacement, tons	3 100 standard; 5 000 full load
Dimensions, feet	334·7 × 47 × 13·8
Guns	2—4·1 in; 2—40 mm Bofors AA; 2—20 mm AA; 4—47 mm saluting
Main engines	2 sets Nordberg diesels; 2 shafts; 3 750 bhp = 16 knots
Oil fuel (tons)	500 (*Bahia Thetis*); 442 (*Bahia Buen Suceso*), 355 (*Bahia Aguirre*)
Radius, miles	15 000
Complement	100

Built in Canada by Halifax shipyards. *Bahia Buen Suceso* was completed at Halifax, Nova Scotia, in June 1950. Nos Q 2, Q 6 and Q 8, respectively. The first two are troop transports, *Bahia Thetis* was used as a training ship and carried guns (see above).

BAHIA AGUIRRE   *1970, Argentine Navy, Official*

BAHIA THETIS   *Added 1967, Werner Schiefer*

BAHIA BUEN SUCESO   *1969, Argentine Navy, Official*

SAN JULIAN (ex-*FS* 281) B 7

Displacement, tons	930
Dimensions, feet	176 × 32·5 × 11
Main engines	2 sets diesels; 2 shafts; 1 000 bhp = 10 knots
Oil fuel (tons)	75
Complement	40

Ex-US Army small cargo carrier. Built by Wheeler Shipbuilding Corpn. Launched in 1944. It was officially stated in May 1960 that this vessel, formerly rated as a transport was to be converted into a salvage vessel, but in Dec 1961 it was officially stated that she would continue to be a transport ship.

LA PATAIA B 10

Displacement, tons	3 825 standard; 6 000 full load
Dimensions, feet	335·2 × 50·2 × 23
Main engines	2 sets diesels; 2 shafts; 3 400 bhp = 16 knots
Oil fuel (tons)	500
Radius, miles	15 000
Complement	100

Built in Italy by C. R. del Adriatico (CRDA). Laid down on 25 Apr 1948, launched on 25 June 1949, completed in June 1950 and delivered on 2 Oct 1951. Troop transport. Being withdrawn from service in 1971. Sister ships *Le Maier* and *Les Eclaireurs* were scrapped in 1964.

LA PATAIA   *1970, Argentine Navy, Official*

DOCK LANDING SHIP

CANDIDO DE LASALA Q 43 (ex-USS *Gunston Hall*, LSD 5)

Displacement, tons	5 480 standard; 9 375 full load
Dimensions, feet	457·8 oa × 72·2 × 18·0
Guns	12—40 mm AA
Main engines	2 Skinner Unaflow; 2 shafts; 7 400 shp = 15·4 knots
Boilers	2 two drum single pass
Complement	Accommodation for 326 (17 officers and 309 men)

Built by Moore Dry Dock Co, Oakland, Calif. Laid down on 28 Dec 1942, launched on 1 May 1943 and completed on 10 Nov 1943. Transferred from the US Navy on 1 May 1970.

OILERS (*Buques Tanques*)

PUNTA MEDANOS B 18

Displacement, tons	14 352 standard; 16 331 full load
Measurement, tons	8 250 deadweight
Dimensions, feet	470 pp; 502 oa × 62 × 28·5
Main engines	Double reduction geared turbines. 2 shafts; 9 500 shp = 18 knots (over 19 knots attained on trials)
Boilers	2 Babcock & Wilcox two-drum integral furnace water-tube
Oil fuel (tons)	1 500
Radius, miles	13 700
Complement	99

Built by Swan, Hunter & Wigham Richardson Ltd, Wallsend on-Tyne. Launched on 20 Feb 1950. Completed on 10 Oct 1950. A unit of the Argentine Navy available as a training vessel for personnel. She embodied experience gained in previous fleet oilers, and was then the finest equipped and fastest of her type afloat. Fitted for fuelling warships at sea. Boilers built under licence by the Wallsend Slipway & Engineering Company. Steam conditions of 400 lb. per sq. in pressure and 750 deg F

PUNTA MEDANOS   *1969, Argentine Navy, Official*

Oilers—*continued*

PUNTA Class   *Official*

PUNTA DELGADA (ex-*Sugarland*, ex-*Nanticoke*, AOG 66) B 16

Displacement, tons	5 930 standard; 6 090 full load
Dimensions, feet	325 × 48·2 × 20
Main engines	Westinghouse diesel; 1 shaft; 1 400 bhp = 11·5 knots
Oil fuel, (tons)	150
Radius, miles	9 000
Complement	72

Named after geographical location. USMS type T1-M-BT1. Built by St. John's River SB Corp, Jacksonville, Fla. Launched on 7 Apr 1945.
Of two sister ships of this class *Punta Ninfas* (ex-*Black Bayou*, ex-*Michigamme*, AOG 65) was scrapped in 1964, and *Punta Loyola* (ex-*Capitain*, ex-*Klickitat*, AOG 64) was withdrawn from active service in 1966.

PUNTA DEL GADA   *1971*

DISPOSALS
Punta Ciguena (ex-*Sulphur Bluff*) was officially deleted from the list in 1961, and sister ship *Punta Rasa* (ex-*Salt Creek*) B 20 in 1971. *Punta Lara* (ex-BDI 10, ex-USS *LCIL* 688) was withdrawn from service in 1971.

PUNTA ALTA B 12

Displacement, tons	1 600 standard; 1 900 full load
Measurement, tons	800 deadweight
Dimensions, feet	210 × 33·8 × 12·5
Main engines	Diesel; 1 shaft; 1 850 bhp = 8 knots
Oil fuel (tons)	146
Radius, miles	4 700

Built at Puerto Belgrano. Launched in 1937. Named after a headland.

ICEBREAKER (*Rompehielo*)

GENERAL SAN MARTIN Q 4

Displacement, tons	4 854 standard; 5 301 full load
Measurement, tons	1 600 deadweight
Dimensions, feet	279 × 61 × 21
Guns	1—4 in; 2—40 mm AA Bofors
Aircraft	1 reconnaissance aircraft and 1 helicopter
Main engines	4 diesel-electric; 2 shafts; 7 100 hp = 16 knots
Range, miles	35 000 at 10 knots
Oil fuel (tons)	1 100
Complement	160

Built by Seebeck Yard of Weser AG. Launched on 24 June 1954. Completed in Oct 1954. Used by the Antarctic Institute. Fitted for research. Specially insulated against cold.

GENERAL SAN MARTIN   *1970, Argentine Navy, Official*

TUGS (*Remolcadores*)

GUAYCURU R 33   QUILMES R 32

Displacement, tons	368 full load
Dimensions, feet	107·2 × 24·4 × 12·5
Main engines	Skinner Unaflow engines; 645 ihp = 9 knots
Boilers	Cylindrical (Scotch)
Oil fuel (tons)	52
Radius, miles	2 200 at 7 knots
Complement	14

"Quilmes" class tugs built at Rio Santiago, Argentina, in the State Naval Shipyards. Laid down on 23 Aug and 15 Mar 1956, respectively launched on 27 Dec 1959 and 8 July 1957 and completed on 29 July and 30 Mar 1960.

PEHUENCHE   R 29   TONOCOTE   R 30

Displacement, tons	330
Dimensions, feet	105 × 24·7 × 12·5
Main engines	Triple expansion; 600 ihp = 11 knots
Boiler	2
Oil fuel (tons)	36
Radius, miles	1 200
Complement	13

Both built in Rio Santiago Naval Yard. Commissioned for service in 1954.

MATACO   R 3   TOBA   R 4

Displacement, tons	600
Measurement, tons	339 gross
Dimensions, feet	130·5 pp; 137 wl; 139 oa × 28·5 × 11·5
Main engines	Triple expansion; 2 shafts; 1 200 ihp = 12 knots
Boilers	2
Oil fuel (tons)	95 tons
Radius, miles	3 900
Complement	34

Both built by Hawthorn Leslie, Ltd, Hebburn-on-Tyne. Launched on 24 Jan 1928 and 23 Dec 1927, respectively. Both completed in Mar 1928.

HUARPE   R 12

Displacement, tons	370
Dimensions, feet	107 × 27·2 × 12
Main engines	Triple expansion; 800 ihp
Boilers	1 cylindrical (Howaldt Werke)
Oil fuel (tons)	58
Complement	13

Built by Howaldt Werke in 1927. Entered service in the Argentine Navy in 1942. Sister ship *Puelche*, R 13, was withdrawn from service, it was officially stated in Jan 1971.

QUERANDI   R 2

Displacement, tons	615
Measurements, tons	345 gross
Dimensions, feet	134·5 × 30 × 11
Main engines	Triple expansion; 1 300 ihp = 12 knots
Boilers	2
Oil fuel (tons)	115
Radius, miles	2 400
Complement	34

Built by John I. Thornycroft & Co. Ltd., Woolston, Southampton. Launched in July 1914. Being withdrawn from service in 1971.

CALCHAQUI   R 6   MOCOVI   R 5
CAPAYAN   R 16   MORCOYAN   R 19
CHULUPI   R 10   QUIQUIYAN   R 18

Displacement, tons	70
Dimensions, feet	67 × 14 × 13
Main engines	Diesel; 310 bhp = 10 knots
Oil fuel, tons	8·7
Complement	5

Built in USA and officially allocated the above pennant numbers in 1969.

DISPOSALS
The former tug *Ona* was deleted from the list on 11 July 1967.
The salvage tug *Ranquel* was withdrawn from Service and deleted from the list in May 1960.
The salvage tug *Charrua* (ex-US Army LT 224) was officially stricken from the list in 1963. Her sister ship *Guarani* was lost without trace in the Straits of Magellan on 15 Oct 1958.

AUSTRALIA

Naval Board

President: Minister for the Navy:
Dr. Malcolm George Mackay

First Naval Member and Chief of Naval Staff:
Vice Admiral Richard Innes Peek, CB, OBE, DSC

Second Naval Member and Chief of Naval Personnel:
Rear-Admiral Hugh David Stevenson, CBE

Third Naval Member and Chief of Naval Technical Services:
Rear-Admiral Bryan J. Castles

Fourth Naval Member and Chief of Supply:
Rear-Admiral William D. Graham, CBE

Secretary, Department of the Navy:
Mr. Samuel Landau, CBE, MA

Senior Appointments

Flag Officer Commanding Australian Fleet:
Rear-Admiral William John Dovers, CBE, DSC

Deputy Chief of the Naval Staff:
Rear-Admiral Anthony Monkton Synnot

Diplomatic Representation

Australian Naval Representative in London:
Commodore Kenneth Douglas Gray, DFC, RAN

Naval Attaché in Washington:
Commodore Bruce H. Loxton, RAN

Strength of the Fleet

2 Aircraft Carriers (1 as Transport Ship)
4 Submarines (Diesel Powered)
7 Destroyers (3 armed with guided missiles)
7 Destroyer Escorts
6 Coastal Minesweepers and Minehunters
20 Patrol Craft
5 Oceanographic Research Ships
10 Fleet Support Ships

New Projected Construction Programme

1 Small Helicopter Carrier
2 Diesel Electric Submarines
3 Guided Missile Armed Destroyers
10 Light Fleet Destroyers (Escorts)
1 Fleet Replenishment Ship, 20 000 tons
1 Small Hydrographic Vessel

Ensign

On 1 Mar 1967 the British White Ensign was replaced by the Australian White Ensign. This retains the Union Jack in the top left canton but replaces the red cross of St. George with the five stars of the Southern Cross and the Federal Star, all blue, on a white field.

Pennant Numbers

There was a re-allocation of pennant numbers within the R.A.N. on 1 Jan 1969. Surface ships bear the numbers without category prefix letters, similar to the system of bare hull numbers in the US Navy. Only auxiliaries now have the prefix letter painted on. Submarines do not display their numbers.

Navy Estimates

	$A		$A
1954-55:	96 330 000	1962-63:	97 780 000
1955-56:	97 668 000	1963-64:	109 018 000
1956-57:	78 130 000	1964-65:	138 424 000
1957-58:	87 582 000	1965-66:	190 934 000
1958-59:	84 802 000	1966-67:	234 634 000 *
1959-60:	85 224 000	1967-68:	232 687 000 *
1960-61:	89 432 000	1968-69:	223 721 500 *
1961-62:	96 038 000	1969-70:	239 252 100 *
		1970-71:	243 010 000 *

*Includes United States Credits

Personnel

1 January 1960: 10 594 officers and sailors
1 January 1961: 10 547 officers and sailors
1 January 1962: 10 832 officers and sailors
1 January 1963: 11 228 officers and sailors
1 January 1964: 11 908 officers and sailors
1 January 1965: 12 822 officers and sailors
1 January 1966: 13 960 officers and sailors
1 January 1967: 15 247 officers and sailors
1 January 1968: 16 125 officers and sailors
1 January 1969: 16 638 officers and sailors
1 January 1970: 17 030 officers and sailors
1 January 1971: 17 090 officers and sailors

Mercantile Marine

Lloyd's Register of Shipping:
344 vessels of 1 074 112 tons gross

DESIGN STUDIES AND PROJECTED SHIPS

Several new ships are projected or are under study to re-enforce the Australian Fleet. Design studies have been put in hand for a new light destroyer to supplement the present strength as American and Canadian designs are adjudged unnecessarily large for Australian requirements, while British designs do not fully meet the high speed and cruising range commitments that the Fleet requires. Present thinking envisages a hull of approx 360 feet with twin screw marine gas turbine propulsion and a crew of under 200 to produce a relatively small and economical fleet escort. On this basis a design could be developed for a ship with a limited, but all round anti-aircraft, anti-submarine and anti-ship capability or a common hull to be equipped for a major role in one of the three capabilities with the other two taking a minor role. Currently an operational research study is being made concurrently with the design study to evaluate probable requirements.

A $42 000 000 provision has been made to supply the R.A.N. with a Fleet Replenishment Ship (designation AOE) not dissimilar from the Canadian Defence Services Provider. To be built in Australia, she would be approximately 20 000 tons, length 540 feet and beam 72 feet. Twin controllable pitch screws would be powered by four medium speed diesels. In addition to all types of marine fuels, provision will be made to stow and supply naval stores, machinery spares and all forms of victualling

supplies. Ammunition stowage will also be provided with the normal naval magazine control and flooding arrangements.

"At Sea" transfers will be made both by the normal jackstay transfer for stores and slung hose arrangements for fuels and in addition two helicopters will be housed onboard to provided vertical replenishment facilities.

Budgetry provision for the ship includes cost of construction, spares and shore support facilities.

HMAS *Diamantina* will reach the end of her useful life in 1974 and it is intended to replace her by new construction similar to HMAS *Moresby*. Design by the RAN is in hand and the ship will be built in Australia at a cost of approximately $11 958 000. Spares, shore support and initial maintenance will increase the cost to $17 732 000. Design calls for a ship of 2 300 tons. 315 feet overall, 44 feet beam, carrying a helicopter and hangar for use in the hydrographic role. Provision is made for dual hydrographic/oceanographic research and accommodation will include research facilities for up to 13 scientists in addition to the ships company. She will be diesel engined.

Recent hydrographic requirement led to the conversion of a motor stores lighter, HMAS *Paluma*, for this service and replacement is now urgently required. It is therefore intended to build a replacement of similar design to the Philippine *Atyimba* recently completed in Australia. Diesel engined, she will displace 700 tons with length 150 feet and beam 33 feet, and will be named HMAS *Flinders*. Complement 36 officers and sailors.

The re-institution of the Submarine Service in the R.A.N. gives rise to problems of training as much of the detailed Command Team instruction must necessarily be conducted ashore. At present R.A.N. personnel receive this instruction in the Command Team Trainers of the Royal Navy but the continuation of this for a long period is undesirable due to the loss of time involved in sending key personnel long distances overseas. It is intended therefore to set up an Australian Submarine Service training facility, probably in the Sydney area in the near future to provide the necessary facilities.

In addition to the improved training that will be available for submarine crews, it is intended to place an overseas order for a much improved passive sonar system to be fitted in all four of the "O" class submarines now in service.

Sonar can be used in two forms, one the obvious one of transmission of a sound signal to be reflected and received from the target under investigation; and the other by using the set as a pure hydrophone to receive emissions from other sources. This latter has, of course the advantage of not revealing the presence of the listening vessel. The effectiveness of this role can be judged by the fact that large inherently noisy naval vessels steaming at high speed can be located and identified at ranges in excess of 100 miles. The fitting of these sets to the "O" class submarines, in themselves one of the quietest types of submarine ever developed, will vastly increase their value and also the safety factor of the ships themselves.

HULL NUMBERS

Carriers

Melbourne	21
Sydney	p214

Submarines

Oxley	57
Otway	59
Ovens	70
Onslow	60

Destroyers

Brisbane	41
Hobart	39
Perth	38
Vampire	11
Vendetta	08
Duchess	154
Anzac	59

Destroyer Escorts

Derwent	49
Parramatta	46
Stuart	48
Swan	50
Torrens	53
Yarra	45
Queenborough	57

Support Ships

Supply	o195
Stalwart	d215

Survey Ships

Moresby	gs73
Barcoo	gs245
Paluma	gsc337
Diamantina	gor266
Kimbla	gor314
Gascoyne	gor276

Minehunters

Curlew	1121
Snipe	1102

Coastal Minesweepers

Gull	1185
Hawk	1139
Ibis	1183
Teal	1152

Patrol Boats

Acute	81
Adroit	82
Advance	83
Aitape	84
Archer	86
Ardent	87
Arrow	88
Assail	89
Attack	90
Aware	91
Bandolier	95
Barbette	97
Barricade	98
Bayonet	101
Bombard	99
Buccaneer	100
Ladava	92
Lae	93
Madang	94
Samarai	85

Auxiliaries

Banks	g244
Bass	g247

Scale 150 feet = 1 inch (1 : 1800)

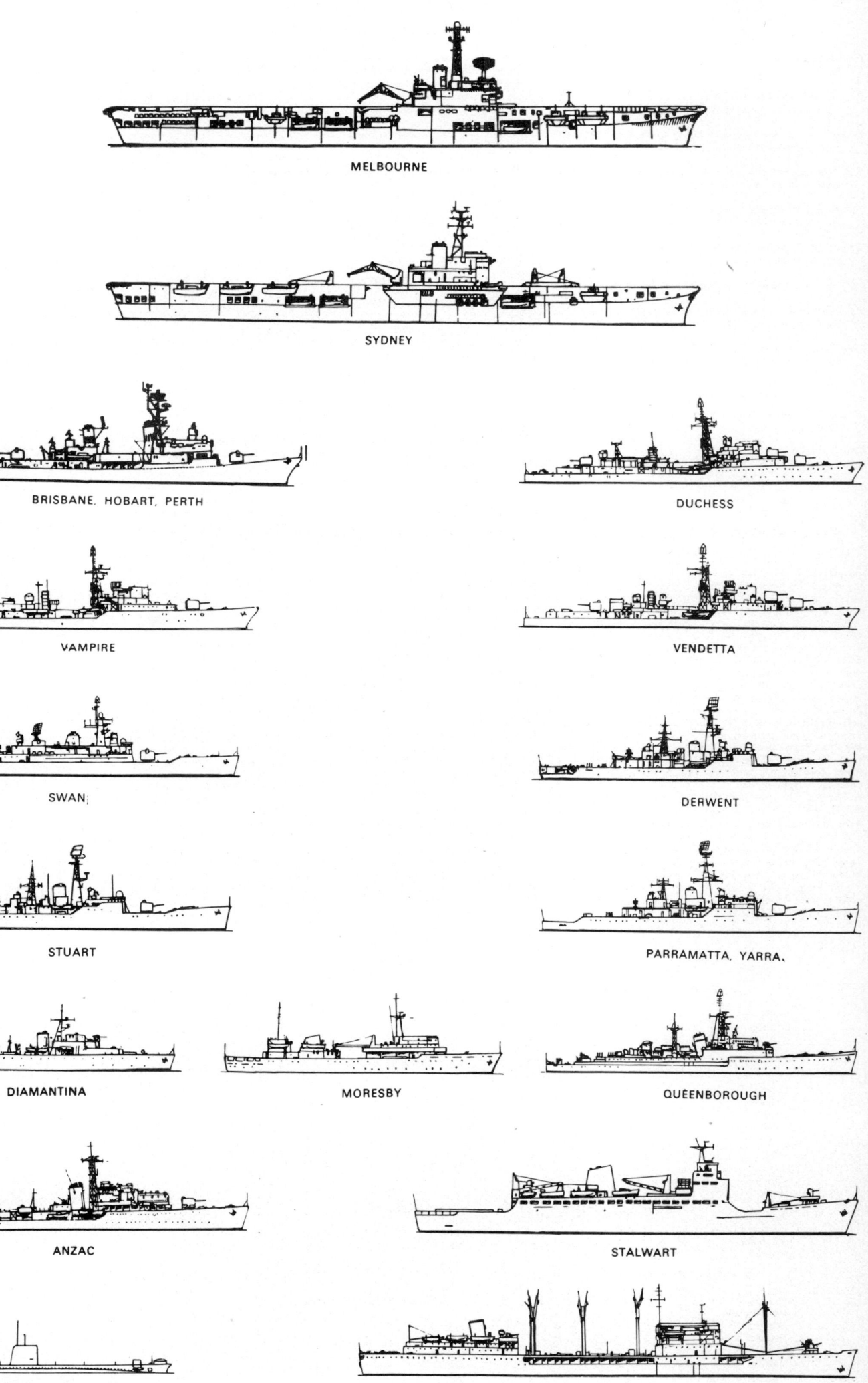

MELBOURNE

SYDNEY

BRISBANE. HOBART. PERTH

DUCHESS

VAMPIRE

VENDETTA

SWAN

DERWENT

STUART

PARRAMATTA, YARRA,

DIAMANTINA

MORESBY

QUEENBOROUGH

ANZAC

STALWART

ONSLOW, OTWAY, OVENS, OXLEY

SUPPLY

AIRCRAFT CARRIER

Name	No.	Builders	Laid down	Launched	Completed
MELBOURNE (ex-*Majestic*)	21	Vickers-Armstrongs, Barrow-in-Furness	15 Apr 1943	28 Feb 1945	8 Nov 1955

1 MODIFIED "MAJESTIC" CLASS

Displacement, tons	16 000 standard; 19 966 full load
Length, feet (*metres*)	650·0 (*198·1*)wl; 701·5 (*213·8*)oa
Beam, feet (*metres*)	80·2 (*24·5*) hull
Draught, feet (*metres*)	25·5 (*7·8*)
Width, feet (*metres*)	80·0 (*24·4*) flight deck 126·0 (*38·4*) oa including 6 deg angled deck and mirrors
Hangar, feet (*metres*)	444×52×17·5 (*135·3×15·8×5·3*)
Aircraft	4 Sky Hawk jet fighters; 6 Tracker aircraft; 10 Westland Wessex A/S helicopters (see *Aircraft* notes)
Guns, AA	12—40 mm (4 twin, 4 single) Bofors
Boilers	4 Admiralty 3-drum type
Main engines	Parsons single reduction geared turbines; 2 shafts; 42 000 shp
Speed, knots	24; sea speed 23 max
Complement	1 350 (150 officers and 1 200 sailors) with air group embarked; 1 070 (75 officers and 995 sailors) as Flagship

At the end of the Second World War, when she was still incomplete, work on this ship was virtually brought to a standstill pending a decision as to future naval requirements. When full-scale work was resumed during 1949-55, and after her design had several times been re-cast, she underwent reconstruction and modernisation in Great Britain, including the fitting of the angled deck, steam catapult and mirror deck landing sights, and was transferred to the RAN on completion. She was commissioned and renamed at Barrow-in-Furness on 28 Oct 1955, sailed from Portsmouth on 5 Mar 1956, and arrived at Fremantle, Australia, on 23 April 1956. She became flagship of the Royal Australian Navy at Sydney on 14 May 1956. She cost £A8 309 000.

MODERNISATION. *Melbourne* completed her extended refit during 1969 at a cost of over $A8 750 000 (25 per cent over estimate) to enable her to operate with S2E Tracker and A4E Skyhawk aircraft, and to improve habitability.

ENGINEERING. Boilers work at a pressure of 430 lb per sq in and a temperature of 700 degrees Fahrenheit of superheat.

MELBOURNE   1970, Royal Australian Navy, Official

AIRCRAFT. The aircraft complement formerly comprised 8 Sea Venom jet fighters, 17 Gannet turbo-prop anti-submarine aircraft, and 2 Sycamore helicopters, later 4 Sea Venom, 6 Gannet and 10 Wessex A/S helicopters. Fourteen S2E Tracker anti-submarine aircraft and ten A4E Skyhawk fighter/bombers were purchased in 1966 in the USA (in service 1967) at a cost of £A46 000 000.

RADAR
Search: Philips LWO series early warning and associated height finders for aircraft direction.
Tactical: Type 293 Target Indication and surface warning.
E.W.: Electronic intelligence and warfare equipment also fitted.

PHOTOGRAPHS. A port bow oblique aerial view of *Melbourne* appears in the 1957-58 to 1964-65 editions. a large port quarter aerial oblique view in the 1962-63 and 1963-64 editions, a port quarter surface view in the 1961-62 edition, a dead overhead aerial view showing angled deck in the 1956-57 to 1961-62 editions, a large port bow surface view in the 1955-56 to 1960-61 editions, a port near broadside view in the 1964-65 to 1968-69 editions, port broadside aerial in the 1965-66 to 1969-70 editions.

DRAWING. Starboard elevation and plan as converted with the angled deck. Scale: 128 feet = 1 inch.

MELBOURNE   1970, Royal Australian Navy, Official

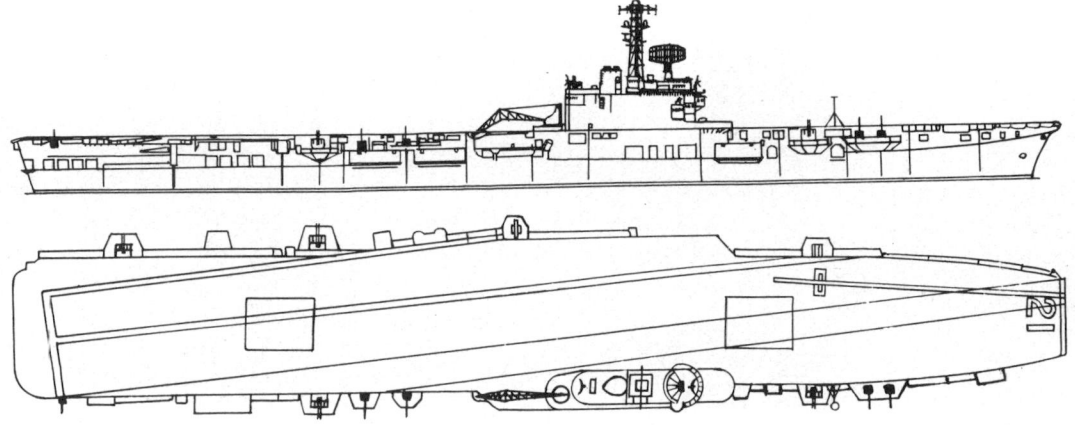

FAST TRANSPORT (ex-Aircraft Carrier)

Name	No.	Deck Letter	Builders	Laid down	Launched	Completed
SYDNEY (ex-*Terrible*)	P 214 (ex-A 214, ex-R 17)	S (ex-K)	H.M. Dockyard, Devonport	19 Apr 1943	30 Sep 1944	5 Feb 1949

1 "MAJESTIC" CLASS

Displacement, tons	12 569 standard; 17 233 full load (revised official figure)
Length, feet (*metres*)	630·0 (*192·0*)pp; 696·8 (*212·4*)oa
Beam, feet (*metres*)	80·0 (*24·4*)
Draught, feet (*metres*)	18·25 (*5·6*) mean; 25·0 (*7·6*) max
Flight deck,	
Length, feet (*metres*)	690·7 (*210·5*)
Width, feet (*metres*)	112·5 (*34·3*)
Guns, AA	4—40 mm, single mountings
Boilers	4 Admiralty 3-drum; 400 psi; 700°F
Main engines	Parsons single reduction geared turbines; 2 shafts; 42 000 shp
Speed, knots	24·5
Complement	608 (40 officers, 568 sailors) as transport. 550 (36 officers and 514 sailors) as training ship.

This ship was handed over to the Royal Australian Navy on 16 Dec 1948, accepted for service on 5 Feb 1949, sailed from Devonport on 12 April and arrived in Australia in May 1949.

ORIGINAL SCHEME. As an operational aircraft carrier she displaced 15 740 tons standard, carried Seafury fighters and Firefly anti-submarine and reconnaissance squadrons, with a stowage capacity of 37 machines, mounted 30 Bofors 40 mm AA guns, and her complement was 1 100 officers and sailors (peace), 1 300 (war).

RADAR
Search: Type 293 combined air and surface warning.

SYDNEY   *1970, Royal Australian Navy, Official*

PHOTOGRAPHS. A starboard bow oblique aerial view of *Sydney* as an aircraft carrier appears in the 1954-55 to 1961-62 editions, a port quarter surface view in the 1957-58 edition, a starboard broadside view in the 1957-58 to 1962-63 editions, and a starboard quarter oblique aerial view in the 1958-59 to 1963-64 editions. A starboard bow surface view of *Sydney* as a troop transport appears in the 1963-64 to 1965-66 editions. A port bow aerial view, as a troop transport, appears in the 1964-65 to 1967-68 editions, and a starboard dead broadside surface view in the 1966-67 to 1969-70 editions.

TRAINING AND CONVERSION. It was officially announced on 4 Apr 1957 that she would have a flying training role, but the ship was converted to a fast military transport in 1962, and was recommissioned after conversion on 7 Mar 1962. She also serves as a training ship, and can operate Wessex anti-submarine helicopters.

DRAWINGS. A plan and port elevation drawing of *Sydney*, as an operational aircraft carrier, drawn to a scale of 128 feet = 1 inch, appears in the 1949-50 to 1963-64 editions, and a silhouette drawing in the 1949-50 to 1965-66 editions.

SYDNEY   *1971, Royal Australian Navy, Official*

SYDNEY   *1970, Royal Australian Navy, Official*

SUBMARINES

4 "OXLEY" CLASS

(BRITISH "OBERON" TYPE)

Displacement, tons	1 610 standard; 2 196 surface; 2 417 submerged (revised official figures)
Length, feet (*metres*)	241 (*73·5*) pp; 295·5 (*90·1*) oa
Beam, feet (*metres*)	26·5 (*8·1*)
Draught, feet (*metres*)	18 (*5·5*)
Torpedo tubes	8—21 in (*533 mm*) for homing torpedoes
Main engines	2 Admiralty Standard Range diesels, 3 600 bhp; 2 shafts; 2 electric motors, 6 000 shp; Electric drive
Speed, knots	16 surface; 18 submerged (official figures)
Oil fuel, tons	300
Radius, miles	12 000 at 10 knots
Complement	62 (7 officers, 55 sailors)

Name	Builders	Laid down	Launched	Completion
ONSLOW	Scotts' Shipbuilding & Eng Co Ltd, Greenock	4 Dec 1967	3 Dec 1968	23 Dec 1969
OTWAY	Scotts' Shipbuilding & Eng Co Ltd, Greenock	29 June 1965	29 Nov 1966	26 Apr 1968
OVENS	Scotts' Shipbuilding & Eng Co Ltd, Greenock	17 June 1966	4 Dec 1967	15 Apr 1969
OXLEY	Scotts' Shipbuilding & Eng Co Ltd, Greenock	2 July 1964	24 Sep 1965	27 Mar 1967

It was officially announced by the Minister for the Navy in Canberra, Australia, on 22 Jan 1963 that four submarines of the "Oberon" class were to be built in British shipyards under Admiralty supervision at an overall cost of £A5 000 000 each, with deliveries spread over 3 years. *Oxley* commissioned on 18 Apr 1967, *Otway* on 23 Apr 1968, *Ovens* on 18 Apr 1969 and *Onslow* on 22 Dec 1969. These constitute the 1st Submarine Squadron, R.A.N.

NEW CONSTRUCTION. It was officially announced in the 1970-71 Defence Programme that two further units would be ordered for the RAN.

OXLEY   *1971, Royal Australian Navy, Official*

PHOTOGRAPHS. A port broadside surface view of *Oxley* appears in the 1967-68 to 1969-70 editions, a starboard bow surface view of *Otway* in the 1969-70 and 1970-71 editions, and a port near broadside surface view of *Ovens* in the 1970-71 edition.

R.N. SQUADRON. The last unit of the Fourth Submarine Squadron of the Royal Navy, *Trump*, was withdrawn in Jan 1969.

But in 1970 RN submarines were again based on Sydney, "on detachment" from the Far East Fleet, and one British submarine will be maintained on station from 1971, it was officially stated in the 1971-72 Navy Estimates.

OVENS   *1971, Royal Australian Navy, Official*

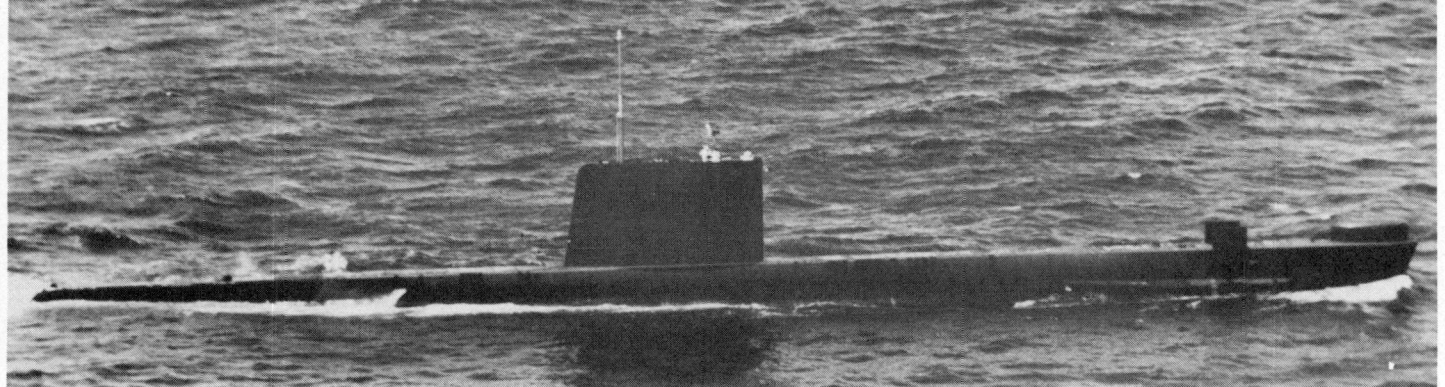

OTWAY   *1971, John Mortimer*

GUIDED MISSILE ARMED DESTROYERS

3 "PERTH" CLASS (DDG)

Displacement, tons	3 370 standard; 4 618 full load
Length, feet (metres)	431 (131·4) wl; 437 (132·2) oa
Beam, feet (metres)	47·1 (14·3) revised official figures
Draught, feet (metres)	20·1 (6·1)
Missiles, AA	For "Tartar", single launcher
Missiles, A/S	For long range "Ikara" system with two single launchers
Guns, dual purpose	2—5 in (127 mm) 54 cal, single-mount, rapid fire
Torpedo tubes	6 (2 triple banks) for A/S torpedoes
Boilers	4 Foster Wheeler "D" type; 1 200 psi; 950°F
Main engines	2 GE double reduction turbines; 2 shafts; 70 000 shp
Speed, knots	35
Complement	333 (21 officers, 312 sailors)

Name	No.	Builders	Laid down	Launched	Completed
BRISBANE	41	Defoe Shipbuilding Co, Bay City, Mich.	15 Feb 1965	5 May 1966	24 Jan 1968
HOBART	39	Defoe Shipbuilding Co, Bay City, Mich.	26 Oct 1962	9 Jan 1964	18 Dec 1965
PERTH	38	Defoe Shipbuilding Co, Bay City, Mich.	21 Sep 1962	26 Sep 1963	22 May 1965

HOBART   1970, Royal Australian Navy, Official

On 6 Jan 1962, in Washington, US defence representatives and Australian military officials (on behalf of the Royal Australian Navy) and executives of the Defoe Shipbuilding Company, of Bay City, Michigan, signed a £A12 863 350 ($A25 726 700 in Australian decimal currency introduced in 1966) contract for the construction of two guided-missile destroyers (shipbuilding cost only). On 22 Jan 1963 it was officially announced by the Navy Minister in Canberra, Australia, that a third guided-missile destroyer was to be built in USA for Australia. The first of their kind for the Australian Navy, they constitute the 1st Destroyer Squadron, RAN. In addition to the "Tartar" missiles, with a range of 15 to 20 miles, they are equipped with long range anti-submarine weapons. These versatile ships are intended to work with hunter killer groups in attacking submarines and to protect vital ocean convoys.

RADAR. Search: SPS 40 and 3 D SPS 52 for aircraft. Tactical: SPS 10 surface search and tactical radar. Fire Control: C Band for Tartar system, X band for guns.

DESIGN. Generally similar to the US "Charles F. Adams" class, but they differ by the addition of a broad deckhouse between the funnels enclosing the "Ikara" anti-submarine torpedo-carrying missile system, and the mounting of a single-arm launcher, instead of a twin, for the "Tartar" surface-to-air guided missiles. As compared with previous destroyers, the ships have greater length overall, more beam and heavier displacement. They have a new hull design with aluminium superstructures. The most recent habitability improvements have been incorporated into their constructoin, including air conditioning of all living spaces.

PERTH   1971, Royal Australian Navy, Official

COMMISSIONING. The first ship, *Perth*, commissioned at Boston Navy Shipyard, Mass on 17 July, 1965; arriving to join the R.A.N. at Brisbane on 4 Mar 1966. *Hobart* commissioned on 18 Dec 1965 and *Brisbane* on 16 Dec 1967, at Boston Navy Shipyard.

COST. Original estimate £A6 400 000 to £A7 000 000 each (with missiles and electronics £A20 000 000 each). Decimal currency: $A12 800 000 to $A14 000 000 each (with missiles and electronics $A40 000 000 each). The total cost of *Perth* was reported to be $A50 000 000.

BRISBANE   1970, Royal Australian Navy, Official

DESTROYERS

3 "DARING" CLASS (DD)

Displacement, tons	2 800 standard; 3 600 full load
Length, feet (metres)	366 (111·3) pp; 388·5 (118·4) oa
Beam, feet (metres)	43 (13·1)
Draught, feet (metres)	12·8 (3·9)
Guns, surface	6—4·5 in (115 mm) in 3 twin turrets, two forward and one aft (Vampire see Gunnery and Modernisation notes)
Guns, AA	6—40 mm (2—40 mm in Duchess)
A/S weapons	1 3-barrelled DC mortar (see Design notes)
Boilers	2 Foster Wheeler; 650 psi; 850°F
Main engines	English Electric geared turbines; 2 shafts; 54 000 shp
Speed, knots	30·5
Radius, miles	3 700 at 20 knots
Oil fuel, tons	584
Complement	320 (14 officers, 306 sailors)

Name	No.	Builders	Begun	Launched	Completed
VAMPIRE	11	Cockatoo Island Dockyard, Sydney	1 July 1952	27 Oct 1956	23 June 1959
VENDETTA	08	HMA Naval Dockyard, Williamstown	4 July 1949	3 May 1954	26 Nov 1958
DUCHESS	154	John I. Thornycroft & Co, Southampton	2 July 1948	9 Apr 1951	23 Oct 1952

VENDETTA   1970, Royal Australian Navy, Official

The above particulars refer to Vampire and Vendetta. For slightly different data applying to Duchess, which has "Squid" instead of "Limbo" depth charge mortars, see under "Daring" class in the United Kingdom section. The three ships constitute the 2nd Destroyer Squadron, R.A.N.

All-purpose ships, equipped for surface engagements, anti-aircraft defence, and anti-submarine warfare, Vampire and Vendetta are the largest destroyers ever built in Australia. They were ordered in 1946. The ships are powerfully equipped for both offensive and defensive purposes. Their sister ship, Voyager, the prototype of the class, collided with the aircraft carrier Melbourne and sank off the southern coast of New South Wales on the night of 10 Feb 1964. She was replaced by the British destroyer Duchess, lent to Australia by the United Kingdom for four years on 8 May 1964, later extended to 1971 et seq.

MODERNISATION. Vampire and Vendetta, already comprehensively overhauled, underwent further extended refits in 1970-71 and 1971-72, respectively.

RADAR
Search: Type 293 S Band air and surface warning radar.
Fire Control: X Band for both forward and after systems.

DESIGN. Vampire and Vendetta were of similar design, including all welded construction, to that of the "Daring" class, built in Great Britain, but were modified to suit Australian conditions and have "Limbo" instead of "Squid" anti-submarine mortars.

GUNNERY. "B" and "X" 4·5-inch twin turrets were removed from Vampire during her 1968 refit, pending major refit in 1970-71.

TUBES. The five 21-inch torpedo tubes in a quintuple mounting in Duchess were removed in 1970.

CONSTRUCTION. The superstructure is of light alloy, instead of steel, to reduce weight.

CLASS. Four large destroyers of this type were originally projected, to have been named after the Royal Australian Navy's famous "Scrap Iron Flotilla" of destroyers which won renown in the Mediterranean on the Tobruk ferry run and in other areas during the Second World War, but Waterhen was cancelled in 1954, and Voyager was lost in collision with Melbourne on 10 Feb 1964.

VAMPIRE (with only one 4·5 inch turret)   1970, Royal Australian Navy, Official

DUCHESS   1970, Royal Australian Navy, Official

Destroyers—*continued*

1 "BATTLE" CLASS (DD)

Displacement, tons	2 400 standard; 3 400 full load
Length, feet (*metres*)	355 (*108·2*) pp; 379 (*115·5*) oa
Beam, feet (*metres*)	41·0 (*12·5*)
Draught, feet (*metres*)	17·5 (*5·3*) max
Guns, surface	2—4·5 in (1 twin turret)
Guns, AA	5—40 mm
A/S weapons	1 "Squid" 3-barrelled DC mortar
Boilers	2 Admiralty 3-drum 400 psi; 650°F
Main engines	Parsons geared turbines; 2 shafts; 50 000 shp
Speed, knots	31
Oil fuel, tons	680
Radius, miles	3 000 at 20 knots
Complement	332 (20 officers, 312 sailors)

Anzac became fleet training ship in Mar 1961. She was modernised to warning role in May 1963 with deckhouse aft and director removed.

Name	No.	Builders	Laid down	Launched	Completed
ANZAC	59	Williamstown Naval Dockyard	23 Sep 1946	20 Aug 1948	14 Mar 1951

Ordered in 1946. Originally similar to the "Battle" class destroyers in the Royal Navy, but several alterations were incorporated, including sleeping accommodation for officers and men fore and aft, improved mess layout and other amenities, modern radar fire control, close range Staag armament (new type of twin 40 mm Bofors gun mounting) and contemporary anti-submarine weapons.

GUNNERY. *Anzac* had the first "Daring" type 4·5 inch guns and mountings of completely Australian manufacture (weight of twin mount is approx 50 tons). They are fully automatic, with a rate of fire of 25 rounds per minute, and an accurate range of over ten miles, firing a shell weighing 53 lb. (The 4·5 inch guns for *Tobruk* were imported from Great Britain).

Original main armament was two twin 4·5 inch turrets. In 1966 "B" turret in *Anzac* was suppressed and replaced by a chartroom for training purposes. In *Tobruk*, guns from "B" turret, torpedo tubes and 40 mm guns were removed.

RADAR. Search: Type 293 S Band combined air and surface warning radar.

DISPOSALS
Sister ship *Tobruk* was placed on the disposal list in 1970. Of the three destroyers of the "Tribal" class, *Bataan* was listed for disposal in 1957 (and scrapped), *Warramunga* in 1962, and *Arunta* in 1968, (*Arunta* sank on 13 Feb, 1969, off E. Australia whilst in tow to breakers in Taiwan).

ANZAC ("B" turret replaced by chartroom)   1971, John Mortimor

DESTROYER ESCORT (*Converted Destroyer*)

1 "QUEENBOROUGH" CLASS

Displacement, tons	2 020 standard; 2 750 full load
Length, feet (*metres*)	358·2 (*109·2*)
Beam, feet (*metres*)	35·7 (*10·9*)
Draught, feet (*metres*)	17·0 (*5·2*) max
Guns, AA	2—40 mm
A/S weapons	2 "Limbo" 3-barrelled DC mortars
Boilers	2 Admiralty 3-drum; 300 psi; 650°F
Main engines	Parsons geared turbines; 2 shafts; 40 000 shp
Speed, knots	31·25
Complement	146 (10 officers, 136 sailors)

Formerly in the Royal Navy, lent to the Royal Australian Navy on 20 May 1946. Permanent transfer and intended conversion similar to Type 15 frigates of the R.N. announced in June 1950. Converted at Williamstown Dockyard, completing on 7 Dec 1954. The 4-inch twin turret was removed in 1965.

RADAR. Search: Type 293 S Band and Type 277 S Band height finder. Fire Control X Band.

DISPOSALS
Of this class, *Quality*, loaned on 25 Jan 1946, and not converted, was sold on 10 Apr 1958 to Mitsubishi Co, for scrap; *Quadrant*, lent on 15 Oct 1945 and converted by 16 July 1953 into Type 15, was sold to Kinoshita Co for scrap in Jan 1963. *Quiberon*, lent on 6 July 1942, and *Quickmatch*, lent on 14 Sep 1942, both transferred outright in June 1950 and converted by 18 Dec 1957 and 23 Sep 1955 respectively, were placed on the disposal list in 1970.

Name	No.	Builders	Laid down	Launched	Completed
QUEENBOROUGH	57 (ex- 02)	Swan, Hunter & W. R. Ltd, Wallsend	6 Nov 40	16 Jan 42	10 Dec 42

QUEENBOROUGH   1971, Royal Australian Navy, Official

DESTROYER ESCORTS (Type 12 Anti-Submarine Frigates)

Name	No.	Builders	Laid down	Launched	Completed
DERWENT	49	Williamstown Naval Dockyard, Melbourne	17 June 1959	17 Apr 1961	23 Apr 1964
PARRAMATTA	46	Cockatoo Island Dockyard, Sydney	31 Jan 1957	31 Jan 1959	4 July 1961
STUART	48	Cockatoo Island Dockyard, Sydney	8 Mar 1959	8 Apr 1961	27 June 1963
YARRA	45	Williamstown Naval Dockyard, Melbourne	30 Apr 1956	30 Sep 1958	25 July 1961
SWAN	50	Williamstown Naval Dockyard, Melbourne	16 Feb 1965	16 Dec 1967	17 Apr 1970
TORRENS	53	Cockatoo Island Dockyard, Sydney	28 Aug 1965	28 Sep 1968	17 Jan 1971

6 "RIVER" CLASS

Displacement, tons	2 100 standard; 2 700 full load
Lenght, feet (*metres*)	360 (*109·7*) pp; 370 (*112·8*) oa
Beam, feet (*metres*)	41 (*12·5*)
Draught, feet (*metres*)	17·3 (*5·3*) max
Missiles, AA	1 quadruple launcher for "Seacat"
A/S weapons	1 launcher for "Ikara" long range system
	1 "Limbo" 3-barrelled DC mortar
Guns, dual purpose	2—4·5 in (*115 mm*)
Boilers	2 Babcock & Wilcox; 550 psi; 850°F
Main engines	2 double reduction geared turbines; 2 shafts; 30 000 shp
Speed, knots	30
Complement	247 (13 officers, 234 sailors)in *Swan* and *Torrens*; 250 (13 officers, 237 sailors) in other four ships

The design is generally similar to that of British "Type 12" anti-submarine frigates, but modified by the Royal Australian Navy to incorporate improvements in equipment and habitability. The enclosed tower foremast differs from that in "Rothesay" class frigates in the Royal Navy. All six ships are being standardised to uniform armament and layout.
Stuart was the first ship fitted with the "Ikara" anti-submarine guided missile, trial ship for the system. *Derwent* was the first RAN ship to be fitted with "Seacat". The variable depth sonar has been removed from *Derwent* and *Stuart*.

RADAR. Search: All ships fitted with Philips LWO series of L Band early warning radars. Type 293 combined air and surface warning, except *Swan* which has Philips/HSA X Band radar.
Fire Control: MRS 3 or HSA systems, X Band radar.

CLASS. Although *Swan* and *Torrens* differ from *Derwent*, *Parramatta*, *Stuart* and *Yarra* and closely resemble the British *Leander* type, it is officially stated that the above figures apply to all ships and all six ships are of the same class.

PHOTOGRAPHS. Other photographs of *Parramatta* appear in the 1961-62 to 1963-64, 1966-67 and 1968-69 editions, and 1969-70 and 1970-71 editions, of *Yarra* in the 1962-63 and 1969-70 editions, and of *Derwent* in the 1964-65, 1965-66, 1968-69 and 1969-70 editions.

STUART   *1970, Royal Australian Navy, Official*

TORRENS   *1971, John Mortimor*

DERWENT   *1970, Royal Australian Navy, Official*

SWAN   *1970, Royal Australian Navy, Official*

DESTROYER TENDER

STALWART 215

Displacement, tons	10 000 standard ; 15 500 full load
Length, feet (*metres*)	515·5 (*157·1*) oa
Beam, feet (*metres*)	67·5 (*20·6*)
Draught, feet (*metres*)	29·5 (*9·0*)
Guns, AA	4—40 mm (2 twin)
Main engines	2 Scott-Sulzer 6-cyl turbo-diesels
	2 shafts ; 14 400 bhp
Speed, knots	20
Complement	395 (23 officers and 273 sailors)

Largest naval vessel built in Australia. Built at Cockatoo Island Dockyard by Vickers (Australia) Pty Ltd, Sydney. Ordered on 11 Sep 1963. Laid down in June 1964 and launched on 7 Oct 1966. Completed 8 Feb 1968. Designed to maintain destroyers and frigates and advanced weapons systems, including guided missiles. She has a helicopter flight deck and is defensively armed. High standard of habitability. Commissioned on 9 Feb 1968. Formerly rated as Escort Maintenance Ship. Redesignated Destroyer Tender in 1968. Cost officially estimated at just under $A15 000 000.

STALWART   1970, Royal Australian Navy, Official

OCEANOGRAPHIC RESEARCH SHIPS

1 NEW CONSTRUCTION

COOK

Displacement, tons	1 750 standard; 2 500 full load
Length, feet (*metres*)	315·0 (*90·6*)
Beam, feet (*metres*)	44·0 (*13·4*)
Draught, feet (*metres*)	15·1 (*4·6*)
Aircraft	1 helicopter
Main engines	Diesels ; 2 shafts ; 4 000 bhp
Speed, knots	20 approx
Oil fuel, tons	400
Radius, miles	10 000 at 10 knots
Complement	140 including 13 scientists

Intended to replace HMAS *Diamantina*, the design is basically similar to that of HMAS *Moresby*. Her cost is estimated to be nearly $12 000 000 (nearly $18 000 000 with spares), shore support and initial maintenance. The helicopter and hangar will provide facilities for use in the hydrographic role, but the ship will have a dual oceanographic and hydrographic research capacity with accommodation and laboratory research facilities for up to 15 scientists in addition to the ship's company.

COOK   Official Illustration

Name	No.	Builders	Laid down	Launched	Completed
DIAMANTINA	266 (ex-F 377)	Walkers Ltd, Maryborough, Queensland	12 Apr 43	6 Apr 44	27 Apr 45

Displacement, tons	1 340 standard ; 2 127 full load
Length, feet (*metres*)	283 (*86·3*) pp; 301·3 (*91·8*) oa
Beam, feet (*metres*)	36·7 (*11·2*)
Draught, feet (*metres*)	12·5 (*3·8*)
Guns	1—40 mm
Boilers	2 Admiralty 3-drum
Main engines	Triple expansion
	5 500 ihp ; 2 shafts
Speed, knots	19·5
Complement	125 (6 officers, 119 sailors)

Frigate converted in 1959-60 for survey and completed conversion for oceanographic research in June 1969. The conversion included the provision of special laboratories. Sister ship *Lachlan* was sold to the Royal New Zealand Navy.

GUNNERY. The two 4-inch guns and two "Squid" A/S mortars in "B" position were removed. The forward 4-inch gun was in "A" position with the 40 mm gun superimposed.

DISPOSALS
Of the six other ships of this class, *Burdekin* and *Hawkesbury* were sold in Sep 1961 ; *Barwon*, sold Jan 1962, left Sydney for Japan on 17 Aug 1962 ; *Macquarie* was sold on 5 July 1962, *Barcoo* awaits disposal and *Gascoyne* was placed on the disposal list in 1970.
Of the four frigates of the "Bay" class, *Condamine* was scrapped in Japan in Dec 1961, *Murchison* and *Shoalhaven* were declared for disposal in 1962 and *Culgoa* was placed on the disposal list in 1970.

"SWAN" CLASS FRIGATES
Swan, latterly cadet training ship, was paid off in Nov 1962 and sold on 5 June 1964. *Warrego*, latterly survey ship, was paid off into reserve in Aug 1963 and broken up at Sydney in 1966.

OCEAN MINESWEEPERS. The last four ocean minesweepers of the "Bathurst" class were *Castlemaine*, placed on the disposal list in 1970. *Colac*, now a tank cleaning vessel, *Mildura* and *Wagga*. These were survivors of a group of 32, four of which were given to New Zealand. For names and disposals of the remaining ships see 1961-62 edition.

DIAMANTINA   1968. Royal Australian Navy. Official

MORESBY (see page 24)   Royal Australian Navy, Official

COASTAL MINESWEEPER AND MINEHUNTERS

CURLEW (ex-HMS *Chediston*, ex-*Montrose*) 1121 **IBIS** (ex-HMS *Singleton* 1183
GULL (ex-HMS *Swanston*) 1185 **SNIPE** (ex-HMS *Alcaston*) 1102
HAWK (ex-HMS *Somerleyton*, ex-*Camston*) 1139 **TEAL** (ex-HMS *Jackton*) 1152

Displacement, tons	375 standard; 445 full load (revised official figures)
Dimensions, feet	140 pp; 152 oa × 28·8 × 8·2
Guns	2—40 mm AA, *Curlew* and *Snipe* 1—40 mm
Main engines	Napier Deltic diesels; 2 shafts; 3 000 bhp = 16 knots
Complement	4 officers; 29 sailors; Minehunters 37 (3 officers, 34 sailors)

"Ton" class coastal minesweepers Purchased from the United Kingdom in 1961, and modified in British Dockyards to suit Australian conditions. Turned over to the Royal Australian Navy, commissioned and re-named on 21 Aug, 19 July, 18 July, 7 Sept, 11 Sept, and 30 Aug 1962 respectively. Mirrlees diesels were replaced by Napier Deltic, and ships air conditioned and fitted with stabilisers. Sailed from Portsmouth to Australia on 1 Oct 1962. Constitute the 1st Mine Countermeasures Squadron. *Curlew* and *Snipe* have been converted into minehunters. A photograph of *Ibis* appears in the 1968-69 and 1969-70 editions.

HAWK   *1970, Royal Australian Navy, Official*

PATROL BOATS

New Guinea
AITAPE 84 **LADAVA** 92 **LAE** 93 **MADANG** 94 **SAMARAI** 85
Australia
ACUTE 81 **ARCHER** 86 **ASSAIL** 89 **BANDOLIER** 95 **BAYONET** 101
ADROIT 82 **ARDENT** 87 **ATTACK** 90 **BARBETTE** 97 **BOMBARD** 99
ADVANCE 83 **ARROW** 88 **AWARE** 91 **BARRICADE** 98 **BUCCANEER** 100

Displacement, tons	146 full load
Dimensions, feet	107·5 oa × 20 × 7·3 (max)
Guns	1—40 mm; 2 medium MG (no guns in *Aware, Bandolier* and *Madang*)
Main engines	Paxman 16 YJCM Diesels; 2 shafts = 21-24 knots
Complement	19 (3 officers, 16 sailors). New Guinea boats: 2 officers 14 sailors

Five patrol boats for the formation of the New Guinea coastal security force and fifteen for general duties have been built. Steel construction. Builders: Evans Deakin & Co, Pty. Ltd, Brisbane, and Walkers Ltd, Maryborough. Ordered in Nov 1965. First vessel was originally scheduled for delivery in Aug 1966, but was not launched until Mar 1967. All now completed. Cost $A800 000 each. *Aware, Bandolier* and *Madang* are unarmed. A photograph of *Attack* appears in the 1968-69 to 1970-71 editions.

AWARE   *1970, Royal Australian Navy, Official*

BUCCANEER   *1971, Royal Australian Navy, Official*

SEAWARD DEFENCE BOATS

SDB 1321 Y 295   **SDB 1324** Y 296   **SDB 1325** Y 297

Displacement, tons	59 standard, 64 full load
Dimensions, feet	80·2 oa × 16·1 × 5·5
Guns	1—40 mm AA
Main engines	2 Buda diesels; 2 shafts; 390 bhp max = 11 knots
Complement	12

Originally known as Harbour Defence Motor Launches (HDML) and afterwards as Seaward Defence Motor Launches (SDML). 1321 was modified with a two berth C.O.'s cabin added, and covered bridge in place of an open bridge. *SDML 1322* was stricken off in 1953. Remaining four were redesignated Seaward Defence Boats (*SDB*) in 1957. SDB 1327 was stricken from the list in 1960. Used for training.

SDB 1321   *Royal Australian Navy Official*

OCEANOGRAPHIC RESEARCH SHIPS

(ex-*Boom Defence Vessel*)

KIMBLA A 314

Displacement, tons	762 standard; 1 021 full load
Dimensions, feet	150 pp; 179 oa × 32 × 12 mean
Main engines	Triple expansion; Oil fuel; 1 shaft; 350 ihp = 9·5 knots
Complement	40 (4 officers and 36 sailors)

Built as a boom defence vessel by Walkers Ltd., Maryborough Laid down on 4 Nov 1953. Launched 23 Mar 1955. Completed on 26 Mar 1956 Converted to a Trials Vessel in 1959. Is now employed on Science Oceanography Guns removed (1—40 mm AA; 2—20 mm AA).

KIMBLA   *1970, Royal Australian Navy, Official*

BOOM DEFENCE VESSELS

Of the "Kangaroo" class, *Karangi* was deleted from the list in 1965, *Kangaroo* was put up for sale in July 1966, and *Koala* was declared for disposal in 1968. *Kookaburra*, of the "Net" type, was stricken in 1965.

ARCHER (see Col. 1)   *1971, John Mortimer*

SURVEY SHIPS

MORESBY

Displacement, tons	1 714 standard; 2 351 full load
Dimensions, feet	284·5 pp; 314·0 oa × 42·0 × 15·0
Guns	2—40 mm Bofors AA (single)
Aircraft	1 Westland Scout helicopter
Main engines	Diesel-electric; 3 diesels; 3 990 bhp; 2 electric motors; 2 shafts; 5 000 shp = 19 knots
Complement	140 (13 officers, 127 sailors)

The Royal Australian Navy's first specifically designed survey ship. Built at the State Dockyard, Newcastle, New South Wales, at a cost of £A2 000 000 ($A4 000 000.) Laid down in June 1961. Launched on 7 Sep 1963. Commissioned on 6 Mar 1964. Fitted with modern hydrographic equipment. A larger broadside view appears on page 22.

MORESBY   *1970, Royal Australian Navy, Official*

PALUMA

Displacement, tons	336 (official figure)
Dimensions, feet	120 × 24 × 6·8 mean
Main engines	Ruston & Hornsby diesels; 2 shafts = 9·5 knots
Complement	3 officers and 25 sailors

Built at the Newcastle State Dockyard during the Second World War as a motor stores lighter. Commissioned on 18 March 1957. Conversion into a survey vessel was completed on 10 May 1959.

PALUMA   *1970, Royal Australian Navy, Official*

DIVING TENDERS

OTTER (ex-*Wintringham*) Y 299   **SEAL** (ex-*Popham*) Y 298
TORTOISE (ex-*Neasham*)

Displacement, tons	120 standard; 159 full load
Dimensions, feet	100 pp × 22 × 5·8
Main engines	2 Paxman diesels; 1 100 bhp = 14 knots

Transferred from Royal Navy, these ex-inshore Minesweepers were converted to Diving Tenders and attached to the Diving School at Sydney.

SEAL   *1971, Royal Australian Navy, Official*

FAST COMBAT SUPPORT SHIPS (AO*MI*)
1 PROJECTED

PROTECTOR

Displacement, tons	20 000 approx (official figure)
Length, feet (*metres*)	540 (*164·6*)
Beam, feet (*metres*)	72 (*21·95*)
Aircraft	2 helicopters
Main engines	4 medium speed diesels driving 2 controllable pitch propellers through reduction gearing.

To be built in Australia. Designed to replenish ships of all sizes. Will carry all kinds of fuel oils, ammunition, consumable stores and machinery spares. Estimated cost: $42 000 000.

PROJECTED AOM   *1970, Royal Australian Navy, Official*

FLEET OILER

SUPPLY (ex-*Tide Austral*)

Displacement, tons	15 000 standard; 25 941 full load
Measurement, tons	17 600 deadweight; 11 200 gross
Dimensions, feet	550 pp; 583 oa × 71 × 32 max
Guns	6—40 mm AA (2 twin, 2 single)
Main engines	Double reduction geared turbines; 15 000 shp = 17·25 knots
Complement	13 officers, 187 sailors

Built for Australia by Harland & Wolf, Ltd., Belfast. Launched 1 Sep 1954, completed March 1955. British "Tide" Class. Lent to Great Britain until 1 Sep 1962, when *Tide Austral* was re-named HMAS *Supply* and commissioned in the Royal Australian Navy at Portsmouth 15 Aug 1962. Sailed for Australia 1 Oct 1962.

SUPPLY   *1970, Australian Navy, Official*

SUPPLY SHIP

JEPARIT

Measurement, tons	3 790 net; 6 341 gross
Dimensions, feet	435·5 × 56·5 × 24
Main engines	4 500 bhp
Speed	13 knots

Ex-cargo vessel of Australian National Line, built by Evans Deakin and Co Pty, Brisbane and completed in 1964, used for supplying Vietnam forces. Owing to difficulties in handling the ship, she was purchased and commissioned in the Royal Australian Navy at Sydney on 11 Nov 1969

GENERAL PURPOSE VESSELS

BANKS		BASS
Displacement, tons	207 standard; 255 and 260 full load respectively	
Dimensions, feet	90 pp; 101 oa × 22 × 8	
Main engines	Diesel; speed = 10 knots	
Complement	14 (2 officers, 12 sailors)	

"Explorer" class. Of all steel construction. *Banks* was fitted for fishery surveillance and *Bass* for surveying, but both were used for other duties. Reserve training.

TUG

BRONZEWING

Displacement, tons	250
Dimensions, feet	98·8 oa × 21·2 × 8·2
Main engines	Diesel; 1 shaft; 480 bhp = 10 knots

Launched by Mort's Dock, Sydney 25 June 1946.

DISPOSAL
Sprightly, ex-US tug, was declared for disposal in 1969.

BELGIUM

Administration	New Construction Plan For 1975	Personnel

Administration

Chief of Naval Staff
  Commodore L. J. J. Lurquin

Diplomatic Representation

Naval, Military and Air Attaché in London:
  Lt. General Avi Baron M. Donnet

Naval, Military and Air Attaché in Washington:
  Lt. General Avi. van Rolleghem

Naval, Military and Air Attaché in Paris:
  General Major Laurent

New Construction Plan For 1975

4 ASW Frigates, 1,300 tons, 28 knots
1 Training Corvette projected, service by 1975

Strength of the Fleet

7 Ocean Minesweepers (Non-Magnetic)
2 Command and Logistic Support Ships
9 Coastal Minesweepers (Non-Magnetic)
12 Inshore Minesweepers
6 River Patrol Boats
2 Research Ships
13 Auxiliaries and Service Craft

Personnel

1971: 316 officers and 3,969 other ranks
1970: 330 officers and 4,500 other ranks
1969: 330 officers and 4,400 other ranks
1968: 335 officers and 4,800 other ranks

Mercantile Marine

Lloyd's Register of Shipping:
230 vessels of 1 062 152 tons gross

OCEAN MINESWEEPERS

Name	Pennant No.	Builders	Laid down	Launched	Completed	Transferred
A.F. DUFOUR (ex-*Lagen*, M 950 ex-*MSO* 498)	M 903	Bellingham Shipyard Inc, Wash	1954	13 Aug 1954	27 Sep 1955	15 Apr 1966
ARTEVELDE (ex-*MSO* 503, ex-*AM* 503)	M 907	Tacoma Boatbuilding Co, Tacoma, Wash	1953	19 June 1954	15 Dec 1955	15 Dec 1955
BREYDEL (ex-*MSO* 504, ex-*AM* 504)	M 906	Tacoma Boatbuilding Co, Tacoma, Wash	1954	25 Mar 1955	15 Feb 1956	15 Feb 1956
DE BROUWER (ex-*Namsen*, M 951, ex-*MSO* 499)	M 904	Bellingham Shipyard Inc, Wash	1954	15 Oct 1954	1 Nov 1955	15 Apr 1966
F. BOVESSE (ex-*MSO* 516, ex-*AM* 516)	M 909	Tampa Shipbuilding Co Inc, Tampa, Fla.	1954	2 Aug 1956	25 Jan 1957	25 Jan 1957
G. TRUFFAUT (ex-*MSO* 515, ex-*AM* 515)	M 908	Tampa Shipbuilding Co Inc, Tampa, Fla.	1955	11 Nov 1955	12 Oct 1956	12 Oct 1956
VAN HAVERBEKE (ex-*MSO* 522)	M 902	Petersen Builders Inc, Sturgeon Bay, Wisc.	1959	29 Oct 1959	7 Nov 1960	9 Dec 1960

7 U.S. MSO (Ex-AM) TYPE 498

Displacement, tons	720 light; 730 full load
Length, feet (*metres*)	165 (*50·3*) wl; 172·5 (*52·6*) oa
Beam, feet (*metres*)	35 (*10·7*)
Draught, feet (*metres*)	11 (*3·4*)
Guns, AA	1—40 mm
Main engines	2 GM diesels
	1 600 bhp; 2 shafts
Speed, knots	14 max
Radius, miles	2 400 at 12 knots
Oil fuel (tons)	50
Complement	72

Wooden hulls and non-magnetic equipment. Capable of sweeping mines of any type. Diesels of non-magnetic stainless steel alloy. Controllable pitch propellers.

DELIVERY. *Artevelde* and *Breydel* were transferred at Seattle, Wash. *Van Haverbeke* berthed at Ostend on 2 May 1961, *F. Bovesse* in Sep 1957, *G. Truffaut* in Aug 1957, *Breydel* in Sep 1956, and *Artevelde* in June 1956.

TRANSFERS. *A.F. Dufour* (ex-*Lagen*) and *De Brouwer* (ex-*Namsen*). handed over by USA to Norway on 27 Sep and 1 Nov 1955, respectively, were transferred to Belgium in 1966.

PHOTOGRAPHS. A photograph of *Breydel* appears in the 1966-67 edition, of *G. Truffaut* in the 1968-69 edition, and of *Artevelde* in the 1968-69 and 1969-70 editions.

DISPOSALS OF COASTAL ESCORTS
Of the four former ocean minesweepers reclassified as coastal escorts in 1959, *A. F. Dufour* (ex-HMCS *Winnipeg*) and *De Brouwer* (ex-HMCS *Spanker*) were stricken in 1966 and *De Moor* (ex-HMS *Rosario*) and *G. Lecointe* (ex-HMCS *Wallaceburg*) were officially deleted from the list in March 1969.

DISPOSAL OF COMMAND SHIP
The command and logistical support ship for mine-sweepers, *Kamina* (ex-*Royal Harold*, ex-*Herman von Wissmann*), A 957 (ex-AP 907), former German sub-marine parent ship, was officially removed from the effective list in Sep 1967.

VAN HAVERBEKE   *1971, Giorgio Arra*

F. BOVESSE   *1970, John G. Callis*

ZINNIA A 961

Displacement, tons	1 705 light; 2 435 full load
Length, feet (*metres*)	299·2 (*91·2*) pp; 309 (*94·2*) wl;
	326·4 (*99·5*) oa
Beam, feet (*metres*)	45·9 (*14·0*)
Draught, feet (*metres*)	11·8 (*3·6*)
Guns	3—40 mm AA (single)
Aircraft	1 helicopter
Main engines	2 Cockerill V 12 TR 240 CO diesels;
	5 000 bhp; 1 shaft
Speed, knots	20 max; 18 sea
Oil fuel (tons)	500
Radius, miles	4 400 at 14 knots
Complement	125

Laid down at Hoboken by J. Cockerill on 8 Nov 1966. Launched on 6 May 1967. Completed on 12 Sep 1967 Controllable pitch propeller. Design includes a platform and a retractable hangar for one light liaison-helicopter. Rated as Command and Logistic Support Ship.

ZINNIA   *1970, Lt. Cdr. (R) J. F. van Puyvelde*

Support Ships—*continued*

COASTAL MINESWEEPERS

GODETIA A 960

Displacement, tons	1 700 light ; 2 300 full load
Dimensions, feet	289 wl ; 301 oa × 46 × 11·5
Guns	4—40 mm (2 twin) AA
Aircraft	Provision for light helicopter
Main engines	4 ACEC—MAN diesels ; 2 shafts ; 5.400 bhp = 19 knots max
Oil fuel (tons)	500
Radius (miles)	4 500 at 15 knots
Complement	100 plus 35 spare billets

Built at Temse by J. Boel and Sons. Laid down on 15 Feb 1965, launched on 7 Dec 1965 and completed on 2 June 1966. Controllable pitch propellers. Provided with a platform which can take a light liaison-helicopter, and has Royal Apartments.

PHOTOGRAPHS. A starboard broadside view of *Godetia* appears in the 1966-67 edition, a port overhead view in the 1966-67 and 1967-68 editions, a starboard bow surface view in the 1967-68 edition, and a port bow aerial view in the 1968-69 and 1969-70 editions.

DISPOSAL
The support ship *Adrien de Gerlache* (ex-HMS *Liberty*), A 954, former British ocean minesweeper of the "Algerine" class, subsequently reclassified as a coastal escort and again re-rated as a command and logistic support ship for minesweepers, was officially deleted from the list on 20 June 1969 and sold in 1970.

9 U.S. MSC (ex-AMS) TYPE 60

M 929 HEIST	M 930 ROCHEFORT
M 931 KNOKKE	M 927 SPA
M 933 KOKSIJDE	M 928 STAVELOT
M 932 NIEUWPOORT	M 934 VERVIERS (ex-*MSC* 259)
	M 935 VEURNE (ex-*MSC* 260)

Displacement, tons	330 light ; 390 full load
Dimensions, feet	139 pp ; 144 oa × 27·9 × 7·5 (8 max)
Guns	1—40 mm AA
Main engines	2 GM Diesels ; 2 shafts ; 880 bhp = 13·5 knots max
Oil fuel (tons)	28
Range, miles	2 700 at economical speed (10·5 knots)
Complement	39

Coastal minesweepers with wooden hulls and constructed throughout of materials with the lowest possible magnetic attraction to attain the greatest possible safety factor when sweeping for magnetic mines. M 910-925, 934 and 935 were built in USA, under MDAP, and M 926-933 of same type were built in Belgium under MAP with machinery and equipment from USA. M 934 (ex-MSC 259) turned over 19 June 1956, M 935 (ex-MSC 260) was transferred on 7 Sep 1956. M 926 to 933 were all laid down in 1953-54 and launched and completed in 1954-55.

RECLASSIFICATION. *Mechelen*, M 926, former coastal minesweeper of this class was re-rated as a research ship and re-numbered A 962 in 1968 (see next page).

TRANSFERS. M 914, *Roeselaere* (ex-*MSC* 103), M 915, *Arlon* (ex-*MSC* 104) and M 916, *Bastogne* (ex-*MSC*·151) were transferred to the Royal Norwegian Navy in summer 1966 by the Belgian Naval Force. M 910, *Diest* (ex-*MSC* 77), M 911, *Eekloo* (ex-*MSC* 101), M 912, *Lier* (ex-*MSC* 63), M 913, *Maaseik* (ex-*MSC* 78), M 917, *Charleroi* (ex-*MSC* 152), M 918, *St. Niklaas* (ex-*MSC* 64), M 920, *Diksmuide* (ex-*MSC* 65) and M 925, *De Panne* (ex-*MSC* 131) were handed over to the USA and transferred to Nationalist China (Taiwan) on 30 Oct 1969. Five were handed over to the USA and transferred to Greece, M 919, *St. Truiden* (ex-*MSC* 169) and M 921, *Herve* (ex-*MSC* 153) on 29 July 1969, and M 922, *Malmedy* (ex-*MSC* 154), M 923, *Blankenberge* (ex-*MSC* 170) and M 924, *Laroche* (ex-*MSC* 171) on 26 Sep 1969.

PHOTOGRAPHS. A photograph of *Rochefort* appears in the 1961-62 to 1967-68 editions, of *Charleroi* in the 1967-68 edition, of *Heist, Spa* and *Stavelot* in the 1968-69 and 1969-70 editions, and of *Verviers* in the 1969-70 and 1970-71 editions.

GODETIA   *1970, Belgian Navy, Official*

ROCHEFORT   *1970, Belgian Navy, Official*

VEURNE (see next column)   *1971, Belgian Navy, Official*

KOKSIJDE   *1970, Belgian Navy, Official*

KNOKKE   *1970, Belgian Navy, Official*

NIEUWPOORT   *1970, Belgian Navy, Official*

INSHORE MINESWEEPERS

(Dragueurs de Mines de Petits Fonds)

12 "HERSTAL" CLASS MSI

M 485 ANDENNE (ex-*MSI* 97) May 1958	**M 483 OUGREE** (ex *MSI* 95) 16 Nov
M 484 DINANT (ex-*MSI* 96) 5 Apr 1958	1957
M 478 HERSTAL (ex-*MSI* 90) 6 Aug 1956	**M 480 SERAING** (ex-*MSI* 92) 16
M 479 HUY (ex-*MSI* 91) 17 Nov 1956	Mar 1957
M 473 LOKEREN 18 May 1957	**M 475 TONGEREN** 16 Nov 1957
M 476 MERKSEM 5 Apr. 1958	**M 474 TURNHOUT** 7 Sep 1957
M 477 OUDENAERDE May 1958	**M 482 VISE** (ex-*MSI* 94) 7 Sep 1957

Displacement, tons	160 light (190 full load)
Dimensions, feet	106·7 pp; 113·2 oa × 22·3 × 6 (7 max)
Guns	1—13 mm AA
Main engines	2 diesels; 2 shafts; 1 260 bhp = 15 knots max
Oil fuel (tons)	18
Range, miles	2 300 at 10 knots
Complement	17

MSI type. Modified AMI "100-foot" class. All built in Belgium. The first four MSI were launched in 1956. *Herstal* and *Temse* were both launched at the Mercantile Marine Yard, Kruibche, on 6 Aug 1956, followed by another pair in 1956, and four more pairs in 1957 (see launch dates above). *Herstal* was completed in June 1957. The first group of eight (M 478 to 485) was a United States "off shore order", the remaining eight (M 470 to 477) being financed under the Belgian Navy Estimates.

PHOTOGRAPHS. A photograph of *Kortrijk* appears in the 1959-60 to 1964-65 editions, of *Tongeren* in the 1964-65 to 1967-68 editions, of *Seraing* in the 1963-64 to 1968-69 editions, of *Andenne* in the 1966-67 to 1968-69 editions, of *Temse* in the 1969-70 edition, and of *Ougree* in the 1968-69 to 1970-71 editions.

TRANSFERS
Of this class M 470, *Temse*, M 471, *Hasselt*, M 472. *Kortrijk*, and M 481, *Tournai* (ex-MSI 93) were officially deleted from the list in 1970 and are being handed over to the USA.

TURNHOUT   *1970, John G. Callis*

VISE   *1971, Belgian Navy, Official*

HERSTAL   *1971, John G. Callis*

RIVER PATROL BOATS *(Vedettes Fluviales)*

LEIE   LIBERATION   MEUSE   SAMBRE   SCHELDE SEMOIS

Displacement, tons	25 light; 27·5 full load
Dimensions, feet	75·5 pp; 82 oa × 12·5 × 3 feet (*Liberation* 85·5 × 13·1 × 3·2)
Guns	2—13 mm MG
Main engines	2 diesels; 2 shafts; 440 bhp = 19 knots
Complement	7

Built at the Theodor Shipyards of Regensburg, Germany, in 1953, except *Liberation* in 1954. *Dender, Ourthe* and *Rupel* were officially deleted from the list in 1965. *Yser* was deleted from the list on 27 Aug 1969 and sold on 9 Sep 1969. A photograph of *Sambre* appears in the 1966-67 to 1969-70 editions.

LEIE   *1970, John G Callis*

RESEARCH SHIPS *(Bâtiments d'Études)*

MECHELEN A 962 (ex M 926)

Displacement, tons	330 light; 390 full load
Dimensions, feet	139 pp; 144 oa × 27·9 × 7·5 (8 max)
Main engines	2 GM diesels; 2 shafts; 880 bhp 13 5 knots max
Oil fuel (tons)	28
Radius (miles)	2 700 at economical speed (10 5 knots)
Complement	39

Former coastal minesweeper built in 1954. Re-rated as a research ship in 1968. A photograph of *Mechelen* as the coastal minesweeper M 926 appears in the 1968-69 edition.

MECHELEN   *1970. Belgian Navy. Official*

ZENOBE GRAMME A 958

Displacement, tons	149
Dimensions, feet	92/76 × 22·5 × 7 feet
Main engines	1 MWM diesel; 1 shaft; 200 bhp = 10 knots
Complement	14

Auxiliary sail schooner. Built by J. Boel in Temse, Belgium, in 1961. Designed for scientific research. A photograph appears in the 1966-67 and 1967-68 editions.

DISPOSAL
The research ship *Eupen* (ex-*Eureka*, ex-*BYMS 11*, ex-*Young Joe*), former coastal minesweeper, was officially deleted from the list in 1964 as she had become obsolete.

TUGS *(Remorqueurs)*

SUB-LIEUTENANT VALCKE A 950

Displacement, tons	110
Dimensions, feet	78·8 pp 95 oa × 21 × 5·5
Main engines	1 diesel; 1 shaft; 600 bhp = 12 knots
Complement	14

Built in Haarlem, Netherlands in 1951. A photograph of *Sub-Lieutenant Valcke* appears in the 1966-67 to 1968-69 editions.

There are also two port tugs. *Bij* and *Krekel*, displacement 71 tons, length 57·8 feet. 2 Voith-Schneider propellers, 400 hp; three harbour tugs, *Hommel* and *Wesp*, displacement 22 tons, length 43 feet, with 300 bhp diesels and Voith-Schneider propellers; built in Germany in 1953; and *Mier*, displacement 17·5 tons, length 41 feet, with 90 bhp diesels of Voith-Schneider propellers, built in Belgium in 1962.

AUXILIARY CRAFT

HARBOUR CRAFT. There are three barges, namely *FN 4, FN 5* and *FN 6*, displacement 300 tons, length, 105 feet, built in the Netherlands; the ammunition ship *Ekster*, displacement 140 tons, length 118 feet, built in Belgium in 1953; two diving cutters, ZM 3 and ZM 4, displacement 8 tons, length 33 feet; built in Belgium in 1953; and the harbour transport cutter *Spin*, displacement 32 tons, length 47·8 feet, with 250 bhp diesels = 8 knots and Voith-Schneider propeller, built in the Netherlands in 1958.

BRAZIL

Administration

Minister of the Navy:
Admiral Adalberto de Barros Nunes

Chief of Naval Staff:
Admiral Antonio Borges da Silveira Lobo

Diplomatic Representation

Naval Attaché in London:
Captain Hugo Regis Veiga

Naval Attaché in Washington:
Rear Admiral Eddy Sampaio Espellet

Naval Attaché in Paris:
Captain Murillo Rubens Habema de Maia

Strength of the Fleet

1 Aircraft Carrier
2 Submarines (Diesel Powered)
2 Cruisers (Conventional)
11 Fleet Destroyers
5 Frigates (Destroyer Escorts)
2 Coastal Minesweepers
10 Corvettes (Fleet Tug Type)
6 Survey Ships (2 Frigate Type)
3 Seaward Defence Craft
2 River Monitors
6 Coastal Gunboats
12 Support Ships and Service Craft

1971 to 1979 Construction Programme

4 Submarines (Diesel Powered)
6 Guided Missile Leaders (Mk 10 Frigates)
10 Destroyer Escorts
26 Coastal Minesweepers
25 Fast Patrol Vessels
5 River Patrol Boats
1 Dock Amphibious Ship
1 Submarine Rescue Ship
1 Hydrographic Survey Ship
1 Fleet Tug

Naval Bases

There are naval bases at Rio de Janeito, Belem, Natal, Ricife and Salvador, and a River base at Ladario.

Naval Aviation

A Fleet Air Arm was formed on 26 January 1965, exclusively of helicopters. Fixed wing aircraft afloat are operated by the Brazilian Air Force.

Personnel

1971: 40 600 (3 800 officers and 36 800 men) including marines

Mercantile Marine

Lloyd's Register of Shipping:
422 vessels of 1 381 458 tons gross

Scale: 150 feet = 1 inch (1 : 1 800)

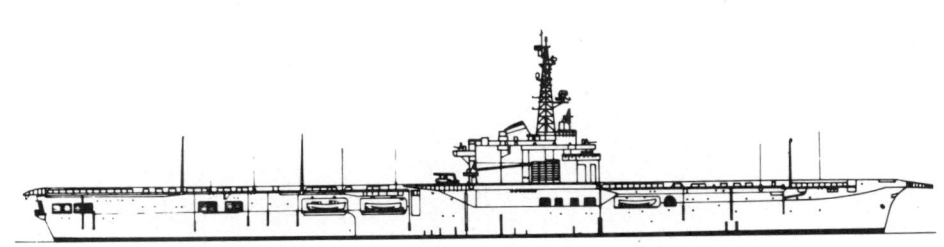

MINAS GERAIS

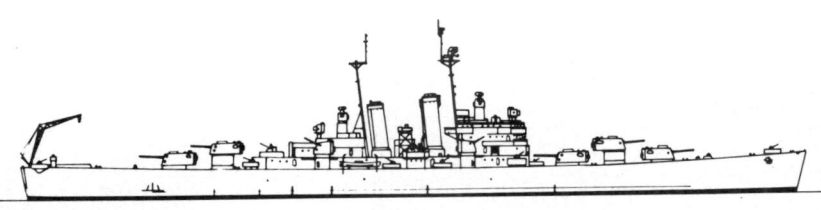

TAMANDARE

PERNAMBUCO

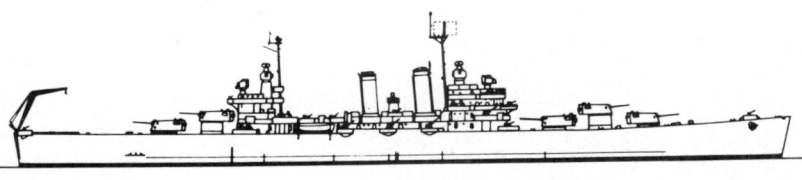

BARROSO

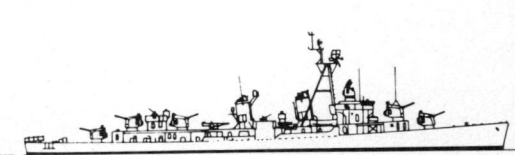

PARA *Class*

NITHEROI *Class*

MARIZ E BARROS

AMAZONAS *Class*

IMPERIAL MARINLEIRO *Class*

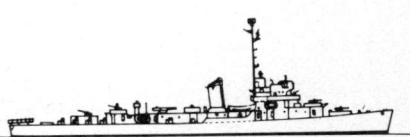

BERTIOGA *Class*

AIRCRAFT CARRIER (NAel)

	Pennant No.	Builders	Laid down	Launched	Completed	Reconstructed
MINAS GERAIS (ex-HMS *Vengeance*)	A 11	Swan, Hunter & Wigham Richardson, Ltd, Wallsend-on-Tyne	16 Nov 1942	23 Feb 1944	15 Jan 1945	Verolme Dock, Rotterdam, 1957-60

1 Ex-BRITISH TYPE ("COLOSSUS" CLASS)

Displacement, tons	15 890 standard; 17 500 normal; 19 890 full load (see *Displacement* note)
Length, feet (*metres*)	630 (*192·0*) pp; 695 (*211·8*) oa
Beam, feet (*metres*)	80 (*24·4*)
Draught, feet (*metres*)	21·5 (*6·6*) mean
Flight deck,	
Length, feet (*metres*)	690 (*210·3*)
Width, feet (*metres*)	121 (*37·0*) oa as reconstructed
Height, feet (*metres*)	39 (*11·9*) above water line
Catapults	1 steam
Aircraft	21 capacity
Guns, AA	10—40 mm (2 quadruple, 1 twin)
Guns, saluting	2—47 mm
Boilers	4 Admiralty 3-drum type; Working pressure 400 psi (*28 kg/cm²*); max superheat 700°F (*371°C*)
Main engines	Parsons geared turbines; 2 shafts; 40 000 shp
Speed, knots	25; sea 24·25; 25·3 on trials after reconstruction
Radius, miles	12 000 at 14 knots; 6 200 at 23 knots
Oil fuel, tons	3 200
Complement	1 000 (1 300 with air group)

MINAS GERAIS   *1971, Brazilian Navy, Official*

Served in the British Navy from 1945 onwards. Insulated for tropical service and partially air-conditioned. Fitted out in late 1948 to early 1949 for experimental cruise to the Arctic. Lent to the Royal Australian Navy early in 1953, but returned to the Royal Navy in Aug 1955. Purchased by the Brazilian Government on 14 Dec 1956. (date announced by British Admiralty). Reconstructed at Verolme Dock, Rotterdam (Verolme United Shipyard's Rozenburg yard) from summer 1957 to Dec 1960. The conversion and overhaul included the installation of the angled deck, steam catapult, mirror sight deck landing system, armament fire control and radar equipment. The ship was purchased for $9 000 000 and the reconstruction cost $27 000 000. Commissioned in the Brazilian Navy at Rotterdam on 6 Dec 1960. Left Rotterdam for Rio de Janeiro on her maiden voyage as *Minas Gerais* on 13 Jan 1961. Used primarily for anti-submarine aircraft and helicopters.

RADAR. Search: SPS 8 and SPS 12 systems
Tactical: SPS 10.

ELECTRICAL. During reconstruction an alternating current system was installed with a total of 2 500 kW supplied by four turbo-generators and one diesel generator.

DAMAGE CONTROL. No great measure of vertical sub-division on the sandwich system as it was reckoned that it is better for ships to settle evenly in the event of damage and flooding than to foster capsizing.

ENGINEERING. Engines and boilers arranged *en echelon*, the two propelling machinery spaces having one set of turbines and two boilers installed side by side in each space, on the unit system. Maximum speed at 120 rpm. Steam capacity was increased when the boilers were retubed during reconstruction in 1957-60.

OPERATIONAL. Single track catapult for launching, and arrester wires for recovering, 20 000 lb aircraft at 60 knots. Catapult accelerator gear port side forward. Flight deck originally designed for 14 000 lb aircraft reinforced to take heavier machines.

HANGAR. Dimensions: length, 445 feet; width, 52 feet; clear depth, 17·5 feet. Aircraft lifts: 45 feet by 34 feet. During reconstruction in 1957-60 new lifts replaced the original units.

DISPLACEMENT. Before reconstruction: 13 190 tons standard; 18 010 tons full load.

DRAWING. Starboard elevation and plan. Re-drawn in 1971. Scale: 125 feet = 1 inch (1 : 1 500).

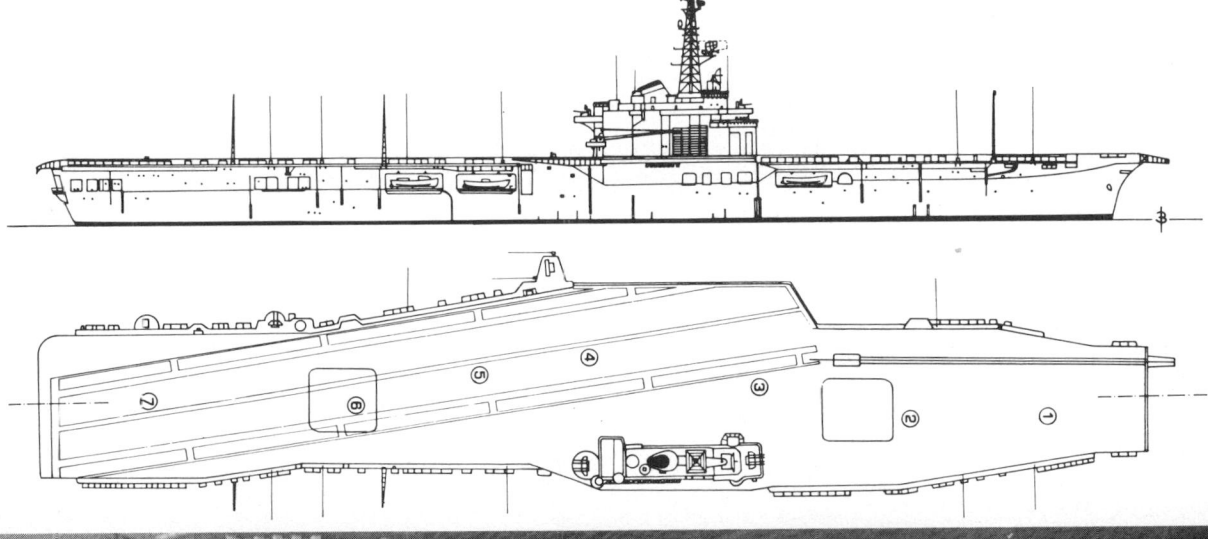

MINAS GERAIS   *1969, Brazilian Navy, Official*

Aircraft Carrier —*continued*

MINAS GERAIS see previous page   *1970, Brazilian Navy, Official*

SUBMARINES (*Submarinos*)

2 NEW CONSTRUCTION
BRITISH "OBERON" CLASS

HUMAITA   **TONELEROS**

Displacement, tons	1 610 standard estimated ;
	2 060 full buoyancy surface ;
	2 200 normal surface ;
	2 420 submerged, official figure
Length, feet (*metres*)	295·5 (*90·1*) overall
Beam, feet (*metres*)	26·5 (*8·1*)
Draught, feet (*metres*)	18·0 (*5·5*)
Tubes	8—21 in (*533 mm*), 6 bow and
	2 stern for homing torpedoes
Main engines	2 Admiralty Standard Range 1
	diesels ; 3 680 bhp ;
	2 electric motors ; 6 000 shp ;
	2 shafts ; electric drive
Speed, knots	15 on surface max ;
	17·5 submerged designed
Complement	70 (6 officers and 64 men)

It was officially stated that two submarines of the British "Oberon" class were ordered from Vickers, Barrow in 1969. They are expected to be in service in 1972 and 1973.

HISTORICAL. The name *Humaita* commemorates a naval action in the river war against Paraguay on 21 Feb 1868. It was previously borne by a submarine of much the same dimensions launched in 1927.

RIO GRANDE DO SUL   *1971, Brazilian Navy, Official*

2 Ex-US "BALAO" CLASS

BAHIA (ex-USS *Plaice*, SS 390) S 12
RIO GRANDE DO SUL (ex-USS *Sand Lance*, SS 381, ex-*Orca*, ex-*Orjanco*) S 11

Displacement, tons	1 526 standard ; 1 816 surface ;
	2 400 submerged
Length, feet (*metres*)	311·5 (*94·9*)
Beam, feet (*metres*)	27 (*8·2*)
Draught, feet (*metres*)	17 (*5·2*)
Torpedo tubes	10—21in (*533 mm*); 6 bow, 4 stern
Main engines	6 500 bhp FM 2-stroke diesels ;
	5 500 hp electric motors
Speed, knots	20 on surface ; 10 submerged
Radius, miles	12 000 at 10 knots
Oil fuel, tons	300
Complement	85

Both built by Portsmouth Navy Shipyard. Launched on 15 Nov and 25 June 1943 and completed on 12 Feb 1944 and 9 Oct 1943, respectively. Lent to Brazil for five years after overhaul at Pearl Harbour Navy Shipyard in Sep 1963 and subsequently extended at regular intervals.

Of the two submarines of the "Gato" class, *Humaita*, S 14 (ex-US *Muskallung*, SS 262) was returned to the USN in late 1967 and expended in the Pacific as a target in 1968 and *Riachuelo* S 15 (ex-USS *Paddle*) was broken up in Brazil in 1968.

BAHIA   *1968, Brazilian Navy, Official*

CRUISERS (CL)

TAMANDARE (ex-USS *St. Louis*, CL 49)	Pennant No. C 12	Builders Newport News S.B. & DD.. Co.	Laid down 10 Dec 1936	Launched 15 Apr 1938	Completed 10 Dec 1939

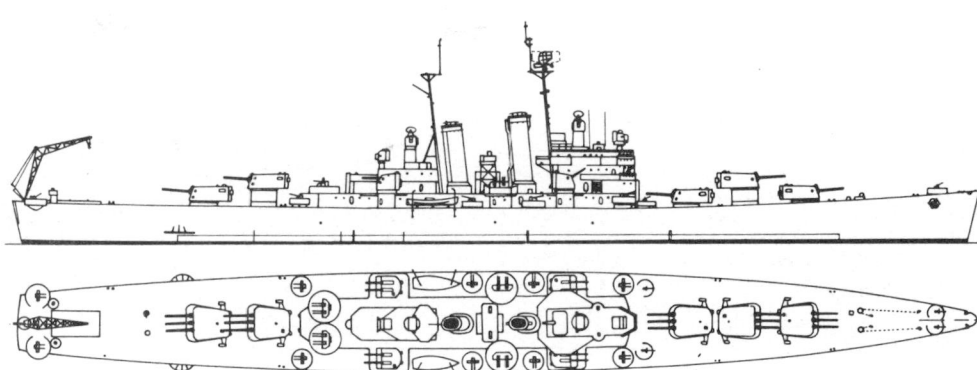

Displacement, tons	10 000 standard ; 13 500 full load
Length, feet (*metres*)	608·5 (*185·5*) oa
Beam, feet (*metres*)	69 (*21·0*)
Draught, feet (*metres*)	24 (*7·3*) max
Aircraft	1 Helicopter (see *Hangar* notes)
Guns, surface	15—6 in (*153 mm*) 47 cal (5 triple)
Guns, dual purpose	8—5 in (*127 mm*) 38 cal (4 twin)
Guns, AA	28—40 mm, 8—20 mm
Armour, inches (*mm*)	Belt 5 in—1½ in (*127 mm—38 mm*) ; Decks 3 in+2 in (*76 mm+ 51 mm*) ; Turrets 5 in—3 in (*127 mm—76 mm*) ; C.T. 8 in (*203 mm*)
Boilers	8 Babcock & Wilcox Express
Main engines	Westinghouse geared turbines 100 000 shp; 4 shafts
Speed, knots	32·5
Radius, miles	14 500 at 15 knots
Oil fuel, tons	2 100
Complement	975

"St Louis" class. Transferred from USA on 29 Jan 1951. Differs from *Barroso* in having 5-inch guns paired in roomy gunhouses on high bases, different boat stowage, small tripod mast immediately abaft 2nd funnel, and after gunnery control redistributed. SPS 12 search and SPS 10 tactical radar.

HANGAR. The hangar in the hull right aft could originally accommodate 6 aircraft if necessary together with engine spares and duplicate parts, though 4 aircraft was the normal capacity. The incorporation of this hangar resulted in a very wide and nearly flat counter and high freeboard aft and also gave the after guns higher command. Above the hangar two catapults were mounted as far outboard as possible, and a revolving crane was placed at the stern extremity overhanging the aircraft hatch.

PHOTOGRAPHS. A port bow oblique aerial view appears in the 1969-70 and 1970-71 editions.

DRAWING. Starboard elevation and plan: Re-drawn in 1971. Scale: 125 feet = 1 inch. (1 : 1 500).

TAMANDARE

1971, Brazilian Navy, Official

BARROSO (ex-USS *Philadelphia*, CL 41)	Pennant No. C 11	Builders Philadelphia Navy Yard	Laid down 28 May 1935	Launched 17 Nov 1936	Completed 28 July 1938

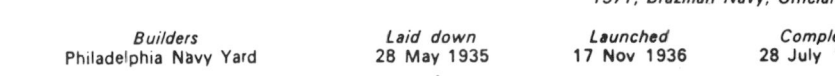

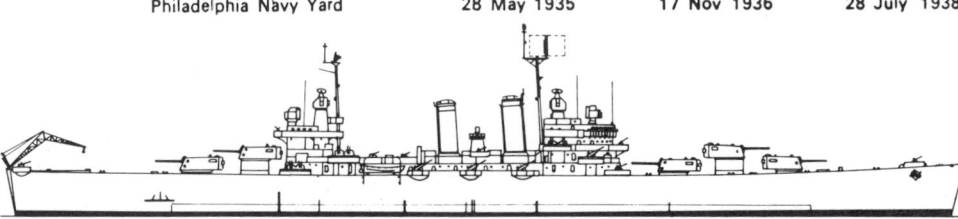

Displacement, tons	9 700 standard ; 13 000 full load
Length, feet (*metres*)	600 (*182·9*) wl ; 608·5 (*185·5*) oa
Beam, feet (*metres*)	69 (*21·0*) with bulges
Draught, feet (*metres*)	19·8 (*6·0*) mean ; 24 (*7·3*) max
Aircraft	1 Helicopter
Guns, surface	15—6 in (*153 mm*) 47 cal (5 triple) 8—5 in (*127 mm*) 38 cal single
Guns, AA	28—40 mm, 20—20 mm
Armour, inches (*mm*)	Belt 4 in—1½ in (*102—38*) ; decks 3 in and 2 in (*76 and 51*) ; Turrets 5 in—3 in (*127—76*) ; C.T. 8 in (*203*)
Boilers	8 Babcock & Wilcox Express
Main engines	Westinghouse geared turbines 100 000 shp; 4 shafts
Speed, knots	32·5
Radius, miles	14 500 at 15 knots
Oil fuel (tons)	2 100
Complement	888

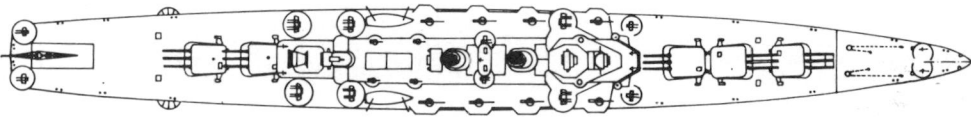

"Brooklyn" class. Purchased from the United States in 1951. Originally two catapults were mounted on the quarter deck for launching the aircraft (see *Hangar Notes* under *Tamandare*). Commissioned in the Brazilian Navy on 21 Aug 1951.

RADAR. Search: SPS 12. Tactical: SPS 10.

CLASS SISTERS. Originally a sister ship of *General Belgrano* (ex-*17 de Octubre*, ex-USS *Phoenix*) and *Nueve de Julio* (ex-USS *Boise*) in the Argentine Navy, and *O'Higgins* (ex-USS *Brooklyn*) and *Prat* (ex-USS *Nashville*) in the Chilean Navy.

DRAWING. Starboard elevation and plan. Re-drawn in 1971. Scale: 125 feet = 1 inch. (1 : 1500).

PHOTOGRAPHS. A starboard dead broadside view of *Barroso* appears in the 1962-63 to 1968-69 editions.

BARROSO

1971, Brazilian Navy, Official

GUIDED MISSILE LEADERS (Contratorpedeiros Oceanicos) DLGs

NITHEROI   1971, Vosper Thornycroft Group and Brazilian Navy, Official

6 "NITHEROI" CLASS
VOSPER THORNYCROFT MARK 10
CAMPISTA   DEFENSORA   ISABEL
CONSTITUICAD IMPERATRIZ   NITHEROI

Displacement, tons	3 300 standard; 3 900 full load
Length, feet (metres)	400 (124·9) wl; 424 (129·2) oa
Beam, feet (metres)	44·0 (13·4)
Draught, feet (metres)	18·0 (5·5)
Aircraft	1 helicopter armed with homing torpedo
Missile launchers	"Exocet" surface-to-surface in General Purpose version; "Seacat" surface-to-air; "Ikara" in Anti-Submarine version
Guns	2—4·5 inch Mark 8 in General Purpose version; 1—4·5 inch Mark 8 in Anti-Submarine version
Main engines	CODOG system; 2 Rolls Royce gas turbines = 30 knots; 4 MAN diesels = 22 knots
Endurance, miles	5 300 nautical at 17 knots; 1 300 nautical at 29 knots
Complement	200 officers and ratings

All the above technical particulars were kindly furnished by the Brazilian naval authorities. A very interesting design of singularly handsome, symmetrical, raked and low-lying clean-out appearance. The moulded depth is 28 feet (8·5 metres). Exceptionally economical in personnel complement, amounting to a fifty per cent reduction of manpower in relation to previous warships of this size and complexity.

CONTRACT. A contract, announced on 29 Sep 1970, valued at about £100 000 000, was signed between the Brazilian Government and Vosper Thornycroft Ltd, Portsmouth, England for the design and building of these six Vosper Thornycroft Mark 10 frigates comparable with the British type 42 guided missile destroyers being built for the Royal Navy.

CONSTRUCTION. Four of the ships will be built at Vosper Thornycroft's Woolston, Southampton shipyard and two by the Naval Dockyard in Brazil with materials, equipment and lead-yard services supplied by Vosper Thornycroft. Of the four ships to be built in Great Britain two will be general purpose fleet escorts equivalent to destroyer leaders and the other two will be highly specialised anti-submarine DLG type vessels.

The two ships to be built in Brazil will both be anti-submarine destroyers. Building practice will be generally similar to that for the Royal Navy but modified to suit Brazilian naval requirements.

DELIVERY. It is expected that design work will be completed for construction of the first British-built ship to be started at Woolston early in 1972. The estimated building time for each ship will be about four years, ships being laid down at yearly intervals so that the last of these six vessels will be completed in 1979.

CLASS. It is envisaged that the originally formulated new construction scheme for six units of this "Nitheroi" class might be extended eventually to ten ships. In that case Vosper Thornycroft might build the first six of the Mark 10 Type and the remaining four might be assembled in the Naval Dockyard in Brazil, as the Brazilian Government is anxious to establish the construction of such ships in Brazil.

NOMENCLATURE. The name Nitheroi was previously borne by the Brazilian Submarine chaser João Pessoa Nitheroi built at Rio in 1943.

DESTROYERS (Contratorpedeiros) (CT)

4 "AMAZONAS" CLASS

Name	Laid down	Launched	Completed
ACRE	28 Dec 40	30 May 45	10 Dec 51
AMAZONAS	20 July 40	29 Nov 43	10 Nov 49
ARAGUAIA	20 July 40	24 Nov 43	3 Sep 49
ARAGUARI	28 Dec 40	14 July 46	23 June 51

Displacement, tons	1 450 standard; 2 180 full load
Length, feet (metres)	323·0 (98·5) oa
Beam, feet (metres)	35·0 (10·7)
Draught, feet (metres)	10·5 (3·2)
Guns, surface	3—5 in (127 mm) 38 cal
Guns, AA	4—40 mm (2 twin); 2—20 mm
A/S weapons	4 DCT
Torpedo tubes	6—21 in (533 mm), two triple
Boilers	3 three-drum type
Main engines	Parsons geared turbines; 2 shafts; 34 000 shp
Speed, knots	35·5 designed; 34 sea
Radius, miles	6 000 at 15 knots
Oil fuel, tons	450
Complement	190

All built by Ilha das Cobras, Rio de Janeiro, to British design. Named after rivers. Refitted with tripod mast. Nos. respectively, D 10, D 12, D 14, D 15. A photograph of Amazonas appears in the 1963-64 to 1968-69 editions. Of this class, Ajuricaba, D 11 and Apa, D 13, were removed from the list in 1964.

RADAR. Search: SPS 6. Tactical: SPS 10.

1 "MARCILIO" DIAS CLASS

MARIZ E BARROS D 26

Displacement, tons	1 500 standard; 2 200 full load
Length, feet (metres)	360 (109·7) oa
Beam, feet (metres)	35 (10·7)
Draught, feet (metres)	12 (3·7)
Guns, dual purpose	2—5 in (127 mm) 38 cal
Guns, AA	4—40 mm
Missile launchers	1 quadruple "Seacat"
A/S weapons	2 hedgehogs; 4 DCT
Torpedo tubes	4—21 in (533 mm) quadruple
Boilers	4 Babcock & Wilcox Express
Main engines	GE geared turbines; 2 shafts; 42 800 shp
Speed, knots	36·5 designed, now 32 max
Radius, miles	6 000 at 15 knots
Oil fuel, tons	500
Complement	190

Built at Ilha das Cobras, Rio de Janeiro, with design, guns and material from USA. Laid down in 1937, launched on 28 Dec 1940, commissioned on 29 Nov 1943, and completed in 1944.

ACRE   1969, Brazilian Navy, Official

MARIZ E BARROS   1971, Brazilian Navy, Official

GUIDED WEAPONS. British Seacat missile launcher was installed in place of former X position 5 in gun.

Sister ships Greenhalgh, D 24 and Marcilio Dias, D 25, were deleted from the list in 1966.

Destroyers—continued

Name	Pennant No.	Builders	Laid Down	Launched	Completed
PARA (ex-USS *Guest*, DD 472)	D 27	Boston Navy Yard	27 Sep 1941	20 Feb 1942	15 Dec 1942
PARAIBA (ex-USS *Bennett*, DD 473)	D 28	Boston Navy Yard	10 Dec 1941	16 Apr 1942	9 Feb 1943
PARANA (ex-USS *Cushing*, DD 797)	D 29	Bethlehem Steel Co (Staten Island)	3 May 1943	30 Sep 1943	17 Jan 1944
PERNAMBUCO (ex-USS *Hailey*, DD 556)	D 30	Seattle-Tacoma S.B. (Corpn, Seattle)	1 Apr 1942	9 Mar 1943	30 Sep 1943
PIAUI (ex-USS *Lewis Hancock*, DD 675)	D 31	Federal S.B. & D.D Co.	24 Sep 1942	1 Aug 1943	24 Sep 1943
SANTA CATERINA (ex-USS *Irwin* DD 794)	D 32	Bethlehem Steel Co (San Pedro)	14 Feb 1943	31 Oct 1943	14 Feb 1944

7 Ex-US "FLETCHER" TYPE
"PARA" CLASS

Displacement, tons	2 100 standard; 3 050 full load
Length, feet (*metres*)	376·5 (*114·8*) oa
Beam, feet (*metres*)	39·3 (*12·0*)
Draught, feet (*metres*)	18 (*5·5*) max
Guns, dual purpose	5—5 in (*127 mm*) 38 cal; except *Pernambuco*: 4—5 in
Guns AA	10—40 mm (2 quadruple and 1 twin) except *Pernambuco* 6—3 in (*76 mm*) 50 cal (3 twin) and *Para*: 6—40 mm (3 twin)
Torpedo tubes	5—21 in (*533 mm*)
A/S weapons	2 Hedgehogs; 1 DC rack; 2 side launching torpedo racks
Boilers	4 Babcock & Wilcox
Main engines	2 GE geared turbines; 2 shafts; 60 000 shp
Speed, knots	35
Radius, miles	6 000 at 15 knots
Oil fuel, tons	650
Compliment	260

PERNAMBUCO (four 5-inch guns)   *1969, Brazilian Navy, Official*

Parana, Piaui and *Santa Caterina* are of the later "Fletcher" class and *Para, Paraiba, Pernambuco* are of the "Fletcher" class. *Para, Paraiba, Parana* and *Pernambuco* were acquired from USA on loan for five years, subsequently extended. *Para* was transferred to Brazil on 5 June 1959. *Paraiba* on 15 Dec 1959 at Bremerton, Washington, *Parana* and *Pernambuco* on 20 July 1961, at Norfolk Naval Shipyard, Portsmouth, Virginia, *Piaui* was transferred on 1 Aug 1967 and *Santa Caterina* on 10 May 1968.
Sister ships *Yarnall* (DD-541) and *Irwin* (DD-794) were selected as replacements for *Sigsbee* (DD 502) and *Melvin* (DD 680), originally scheduled for transfer; but in the event *Yarnall* was transferred to Taiwan China.

RADAR. Search: SPS 6. Tactical: SPS 10. Fire Control: X Band.

PHOTOGRAPHS. A starboard broadside view of *Para* (five 5-inch) guns appears in the 1969-70 edition.

PARANA   (five 5-inch guns)   *1970, courtesy Engineer Captain Aluino Martins de Silva, P.N.*

FRIGATES (Destroyer Escorts) (Officially rated as *Avisos Oceanicos*)

Name		Laid down	Launched	Completed
BAEPENDI (ex-USS *Cannon*, DE 99)	U 27 (ex-D 17)	14 Nov 1942	25 May 1943	26 Sep 1943
BAURU (ex-USS *Reybold*, DE 177)	U 28 (ex-D 18)	17 May 1943	22 Aug 1943	11 Oct 1943
BENEVENTE (ex-USS *Christopher*, DE 100)	U 30 (ex-D 20)	7 Dec 1942	June 1943	23 Oct 1943
BOCAINA (ex-USS *Marts*, DE 174)	U 32 (ex-D 22)	26 Apr 1943	8 Aug 1943	3 Sep 1943
BRACUI (ex-USS *McAnn*, DE 179)	U 31 (ex-D 23)	3 May 1943	5 Sep 1943	24 Sep 1943

5 Ex-US DE TYPE
"BERTIOGA" CLASS

Displacement, tons	1 240 standard; 1 900 full load
Length, feet (*metres*)	306 (*93 3*) oa
Beam, feet (*metres*)	37 (*11·3*)
Draught, feet (*metres*)	12 (*3·7*)
Guns, dual purpose	3—3 in (*76 mm*)
Guns, AA	2—40 mm, 4—20 mm
Torpedo tubes	3—21 in (*533 mm*)
A/S weapons	2 DC racks
Main engines	4 GE diesels; 2 electric motors; diesel-electric drive; 2 shafts; 6 000 bhp
Speed, knots	19
Radius, miles	11 500 at 11 knots
Oil fuel, tons	300
Complement	200

BAEPENDI   *1970, Brazilian Navy, Official*

Former US "Bostwick" class destroyer escorts, transferred in 1944. Built by Dravo, Wilmington, Del. (*Baependi*) and Federal, Port Newark (other four). Formerly designated CTE (Destroyer Escorts) but reclassified as *Avisos Oceanicos* in 1965.

PHOTOGRAPHS. A photograph of *Bocaina* appears in the 1962-63 edition.

CLASS.
Of this class, *Babitonga*, D 16 (ex-USS *Alger*, DE 101) and *Bertioga*, D 21 (ex-USS *Pennenill*, DE 175) were officially removed from the list in 1964, and *Beberibe* D 19 (ex-USS *Herzog*, DE 178) in 1968.

BRACUI   *1969, Brazilian Navy, Official*

COASTAL MINESWEEPERS (NV)

4 NEW CONSTRUCTION "SCHÜTZE" CLASS

ANHATOMIRIN   **ARACATUBA**   **ARATU**   **ATALAIA**

Displacement, tons	230 standard; 280 full load
Dimensions, feet	154·9 × 23·6 × 6·9
Guns	1—40 mm AA
Main engines	4 Maybach diesels; 2 shafts; 4 500 bhp = 24 knots

Builders: Conasa S.A. de Cabadelo, Paraiba and Abeking & Rasmussen, Lemwerder. Ordered in Apr 1969. Six more are projected.

2 Ex-US MSCo TYPE "JAVARI" CLASS

JURUENA (ex-USS *Grackle*) M 14   **JURUA** (ex-USS *Jackdaw*) M 13

Displacement, tons	270 standard; 350 full load
Dimensions, feet	136 × 24·5 × 8 max
Guns	4—20 mm in two twin mountings
A/S weapons	2 DCT
Main engines	2 GM diesels; 2 shafts; 1 000 bhp = 15 knots
Oil fuel (tons)	16
Radius, miles	2 300 at economical speed
Complement	50

Coastal minesweepers of wooden construction. Both launched in 1942-43. Originally known in USA as Auxiliary Motor Minesweepers (AMS). Reclassified as Minesweepers, Coastal (old), MSC (o), in Feb 1955, *Javari*, ex-*Cardinal*, MSCo 4, and *Jutai*, ex-*Egret*, MSCo 13, were transferred to Brazil by USA at Charleston Naval Shipyard on 15 Aug 1960 as the nucleus of a Brazilian mine force, and renamed after Brazilian rivers. *Jackdaw* MSCo 21, was transferred in Jan 1963, and *Grackle* MSCo 13, in Apr 1963. Used for patrol and escort duties, *Javari*, M 11, and *Jutai*, M 12, were declared for disposal in 1969.

JURUA   *1970, Brazilian Navy, Official*

SURVEY SHIPS (*Navios Hidrograficos*) (NH)

2 FRIGATE TYPE

Name	Pennant No.	Laid down	Launched	Completed
CANOPUS	H 22	13 Dec 1956	20 Nov 1957	15 Mar 1958
SIRIUS	H 21	13 Dec 1956	30 July 1957	1 Jan 1958

Displacement, tons	1 463 standard; 1 800 full load
Measurement, tons	1 600 gross
Dimensions, feet	236·2 pp; 246 wl; 255·7 oa × 39·3 × 12·2
Guns	1—3 in AA; 4—20 mm MG
Main engines	2 Sulzer diesels; 2 shafts; 2 700 bhp = 15·75 knots
Radius, miles	12 000 at cruising speed of 11 knots
Complement	102

Built by Ishikawajima Heavy Industries Co. Ltd., Tokyo, Japan. Helicopter platform aft. Special surveying apparatus, echo sounders, Raydist equipment, sounding machines installed and helicopter, landing craft (LCVP), jeep, and survey launches carried. All living and working spaces are air-conditioned. Controllable pitch propellers.

CANOPUS   *1969, Brazilian Navy, Official*

SIRIUS   *1970, Brazilian Navy, Official*

Survey Ships—*continued*

3 COASTAL TYPE

Name	Pennant No.	Laid down	Launched	Completed
ARGUS	H 31	12 Dec 1955	6 Dec 1957	29 Jan 1959
ORION	H 32	12 Dec 1955	5 Feb 1958	11 June 1959
TAURUS	H 33	12 Dec 1955	7 Jan 1958	23 Apr 1959

Displacement, tons	250 standard; 300 full load
Dimensions, feet	138 pp; 147·7 oa × 20 × 6·6
Guns	2—20 mm AA
Main engines	2 diesels coupled to two shafts; 1 200 bhp = 15 knots
Oil fuel, tons	35
Radius	1 200 miles at 15 knots

All built by Arsenal da Marinha, Rio de Janeiro and commissioned on dates shown as completed in table above. A photograph of *Orion* appears in the 1961-62 to 1965-66 editions.

ARGUS   *1966, Brazilian Navy, Official*

ALMIRANTE SALDANHA U 10 (ex-NE 1)

Displacement, tons	3 325 standard; 3 825 full load
Dimensions, feet	262 pp; 307·2 oa × 52 × 18·2 mean
Main engines	Diesel; 1 400 bhp = 11 knots
Radius, miles	12 000
Complement	356

Former training ship with a total sail area of 25 990 sq ft and armed with four 4-in guns, one 3-in AA gun and four 3-pounders. Built by Vickers Armstrongs, Ltd, Barrow, Launched on 19 Dec 1933. Cost £314 500. Instructional minelaying gear was included in equipment. The single 21-in torpedo tube was suppressed. Re-classified as an Oceanographic Ship (NOc) Aug 1959, and completely remodelled by 1964. A photograph as sailing ship appears in the 1952-53 to 1959-60 editions.

ALMIRANTE SALDANHA   *1971, Brazilian Navy, Official*

CORVETTES (*Corvetas*) (CV)

10 "IMPERIAL MARINHEIRO" CLASS

ANGOSTURA	V 20	**FORTE DE COMBRA**	V 18	**IPIRANGA**	V 17
BAHIANA	V 21	**IGUATEMI**	V 16	**MEARIM**	V 22
CABOCLO	V 19	**IMPERIAL MARINHEIRO**	V 15	**PURUS**	V 23
				SOLIMOES	V 24

Displacement, tons	911 standard
Dimensions, feet	184 × 30·5 × 11·7
Guns	1—3 in, 50 cal; 4—20 mm AA
Main engines	2 Sulzer diesels; 2 160 bhp = 16 knots
Oil fuel (tons)	135
Complement	60

All built in the Netherlands, launched in 1954-55, and incorporated into the Brazilian Navy in 1955. Actually fleet tugs. A photograph of *Imperial Marinheiro* appears in the 1956-57 and 1957-58 editions and *Ipiranga* in the 1958-59 to 1968-69 editions.

ANGOSTURA   *1969, Brazilian Navy, Official*

RIVER MONITORS (*Monitores*) (M)
1 THORNYCROFT TYPE

PARNAIBA U 17 (ex-P 2)

Displacement, tons	620 standard; 720 full load
Dimensions, feet	180·5 oa × 33·3 × 5·1 max
Guns	1—3 in, 50 cal; 2—47 mm; 2—40 mm AA; 6—20 mm AA
Armour	3 in side and partial deck protection
Main engines	2 Thornycroft triple expansion; 2 shafts; 1 300 ihp = 12 knots
Boilers	2 three drum type, working pressure 250 psi
Oil fuel, tons	70
Complement	90

Built at Rio de Janeiro. Laid down on 11 June 1936. Launched on 2 Sep 1937 and completed in Nov 1937. In Matto Grosso Flotilla. Rearmed with the above guns in 1960. For former armament see 1959-60 edition.

PARNAIBA   *1971, Brazilian Navy, Official*

1 WHITE TYPE

PARAGUACU (ex-*Victoria*, ex-*Espiriot Santo*) U 16 (ex-P 3)

Displacement, tons	430 standard; 500 full load
Dimensions, feet	146·5 × 34·8 × 4·9
Guns	1—3 in, 50 cal; 2—47 mm; 2—40 mm AA; 6—20 mm AA
Main engines	2 White triple expansion; 1 100 ihp = 13 knots
Boilers	2 three drum type
Oil fuel, tons	40
Complement	70

Built at Rio de Janeiro. Launched on 22 Dec 1938. In Matto Grosso Flotilla. Rearmed with the above guns in 1960. For former armament see 1959-60 edition.

PARAGUACU   *1966, Brazilian Navy, Official*

COASTAL GUN BOATS
6 "PIRATINI" CLASS

PAMPEIRO	PENEBO	PARATINI
PARATI	PIRAJA	POTI

Dimensions, feet	95 × 19 × 6 (official figures)
Main engines	4 diesels; 1 100 bhp

It is officially stated that six coastal gunboats of the "Piratini" class are being built in the Arsenal de Marinha do Rio de Janeiro; the first vessel entered service in Nov 1970 and the other five are expected to be ready for service during 1971.

PGM 109   PGM 110   PGM 118   PGM 119   PGM 120   PGM 121

Originally scheduled to be built in the United States for transfer to Brazil under MAP

PIRAQUE (see top of Col. 2)   *1968, Brazilian Navy, Official*

SEAWARD DEFENCE CRAFT (NPa)
3 "P" CLASS

PIRAJU J 28 (ex-P 1)   **PIRANHA** J 30 (ex-P 3)   **PIRAQUE** J 32 (ex- P4)

Displacement, tons	130 standard
Dimensions, feet	128 × 19·5 × 6
Guns	1—3 in, 23 cal.; 2—20 mm AA
A/S weapons	30 DC
Main engines	Diesels; 3 shafts; 1 890 bhp = 20 knots
Complement	30

All launched in 1947-48. Built at Rio de Janeiro. The hulls are of wooden construction. A photograph of *Piranha* appears in the 1950-51 to 1960-61 editions.

Of this class *Pirambu* P 2, and *Pirapia*, P 5, were officially removed from the list in 1964, and *Pirauna*, P 6, in 1960.

DISPOSALS

The six small gunboats of the "Rio" class were deleted from the list in 1968.

PIRANHA   *1970, Brazilian Navy, Official*

REPAIR SHIPS

BELMONTE G 24 (ex-USS *Helios*, ARB 12, ex-*LST 1127*)

Displacement, tons	1 625 light; 2 030 standard; 4 100 full load
Dimensions, feet	316 wl; 328 oa × 50 × 11
Guns	8—40 mm AA
Main engines	GM diesels; 2 shafts; 1 800 bhp = 11·6 knots
Oil fuel, tons	1 000
Radius, miles	6 000 at 9 knots

Former United States battle damage repair ship. Built by Maryland DD Co, Baltimore Md. Laid down on 23 Nov 1944. Launched on 14 Feb 1945. Completed on 26 Feb 1945. Loaned to Brazil by USA in Jan 1962 under MAP.

BELMONTE   *1969, Brazilian Navy, Official*

SURVEY LAUNCHES

CAMOCIS	ITACURUSSA	PARAIBANO
CARABELAS	JACEGUAI	RIO BRANCO

Displacement, tons	32 standard; 50 full load
Dimensions, feet	52·5 + 15·1 + 4·3
Main engines	1 diesel; 165 bhp = 11 knots

Small wooden hulled survey launches for coastal and external duties. Built by Borman, Rio in 1968-71.

AUXILIARY VESSEL

CEARA (ex-*ARD 14*)

Displacement, tons	5 200
Length, feet	402
Beam, feet	81

Formerly the United States auxiliary repair dry dock *ARD* 14. Transferred from the US Navy to the Brazilian Navy and allocated the name *Ceara*.

OILERS (*Navios-Tanques*) (NT)

MARAJO G 27

Measurement, tons	10 500 deadweight
Dimensions, feet	440·7 × 63·3 × 24
Main engines	Diesel; one shaft = 13·6 knots
Capacity, cu metres	14 200
Complement	80

Laid down on 13 Dec 1966 and launched on 31 Jan 1968. Built by Ishikawajima Do Brasil-Estaleisos SA. Completed on 22 Oct 1968.

DISPOSALS
It is officially stated that the two former United States gasoline tankers of the USMC type T1-M-A2 built in 1944-45, *Raza* (ex-*Klaskanine*, AOG 63) G 19 (ex-*R 2*) and *Rijo* (ex-*Gualula*, AOG 28) G 20 (ex-*R 1*), were deleted from the list in 1970.

MARAJO   *1969, Brazilian Navy, Official*

POTENGI G 17

Displacement, tons	600
Dimensions, feet	175·5 pp; 178·8 oa × 24·5 × 6
Main engines	Diesels; 2 shafts; 550 bhp = 10 knots
Oil, tons	450
Complement	19

Built at the Papendrecht yard in the Netherlands. Launched on 16 Mar 1938. Employed in the Matto Grosso Flotilla on river service.

DISPOSALS
The four small tankers *Anita Garibaldi*, *Gastão Moutinho*, *Mataripe* and *Taubate* and the two water carriers *Itaupra* and *Paulo Afonso* were deleted from the list in 1963.

TRANSPORTS (*Navios-Auxiliares*) (NTr)

SOARES DUTRA   *1970, Brazilian Navy, Official*

4 "PEREIRA" CLASS

Name	Pennant No.	Laid down	Launched	Completed
ARY PARREIRAS	G 21	13 Dec 1955	24 Aug 1956	29 Dec 1956
BARROSO PEREIRA	G 16	13 Dec 1953	10 Aug 1954	1 Dec 1954
CUSTÓDIO DE MELLO	U 26	13 Dec 1953	10 June 1954	30 Dec 1954
SOARES DUTRA	G 22	13 Dec 1955	13 Dec 1956	23 Mar 1957

Displacement, tons	4 800 standard; 7 300 full load
Measurement, tons	4 200 deadweight; 4 879 gross (Panama)
Dimensions, feet	362 pp; 391·8 oa × 52·5 × 20·5 max
Guns	2—20 mm AA
Main engines	Ishikawajima double reduction geared turbines; 2 shafts; 4 800 shp = 17·67 knots (sea speed 15 knots)
Boilers	2 Ishikawajima two drum water tube type, oil fuel
Complement	127 (Troop capacity 1 972)

All built in Japan by Ishikawajima Heavy Industries Co. Ltd, Tokio. Transports and cargo vessels. Flush deckers with forecastle and long poop. Elevator type helicopter landing platform laid on aft. Normal troop carrying capacity for 497 personnel, with commensurate medical, hospital and dental facilities. All working and living quarters are mechanically ventilated with partial air conditioning. Refrigerated cargo space of 15 500 cubic feet. Can carry 4 000 tons of cargo. *Barroso Pereira* and *Custódio de Mello* were incorporated into the Brazilian Navy on 22 Mar 1955 and 8 Feb 1955, respectively. Formerly armed with eight 40 mm AA guns. *Custodio de Mello* has been classified as a training ship since July 1961.

The training ship *Albatros* was deleted from the list in 1968.

Transports—continued

CUSTODIO DE MELLO   *1969, Brazilian Navy, Official*

ARY PARREIRAS   *1968, Brazilian Navy, Official*

TUGS (*Rebocadores*) (R)

TRIDENTE (ex-*ATA 235*)   **TRITÃO** (ex-*ATA 234*)   **TRIUNFO** (ex-*ATA 236*)

Displacement, tons	534 standard; 835 full load
Dimensions, feet	133·7 wl; 143 oa × 33 × 13·2
Guns	2—20 mm AA
Main engines	GM diesel-electric; 1 500 hp = 13 knots

All built by Gulfport Boiler & Welding Works, Inc, Port Arthur, Texas, and launched in 1954. Ex-US *ATRs*. Nos. *Tridente* R 22, *Tritão* R 21, *Triunfo* R 23 (ex-R 1, R 2, R 3). A photograph of *Tridente* appears in the 1950-51 to 1957-58 editions.

TRITAO   *1968, Brazilian Navy, Official*

BRUNEI
FAST PATROL BOAT

PAHLAWAN

Displacement, tons	95 standard; 114 full load
Dimensions, feet	90 pp; 96 wl; 99 oa × 25·2 × 7
Guns	1—40 mm; 2—20 mm
Main engines	3 Bristol Siddeley Proteus gas turbines; 3 shafts; 12 750 bhp = 57 knots max; 2 diesels for cruising and manoeuvring
Radius, miles	450 at full speed; 2 300 at 10 knots
Complement	20

Ordered from Vosper Ltd, Portsmouth, England, on 10 Dec 1965. Launched on 5 Dec 1966. Completed on 19 Oct 1967. Constructed of resin bonded timber with aluminium alloy superstructure.

PAHLAWAN   *1968, Vosper Limited*

BULGARIA

Administration

Commander-in-Chief, Navy:
Vice-Admiral Dobrev

Diplomatic Representation

Naval Attaché in London:
Lt. Colonel Dimiter Simov

Strength of the Fleet

2 Submarines, Conventionally Powered,
2 Medium Escorts
8 Coastal Escorts
2 Fleet Minesweepers
4 Inshore Minesweepers
8 Torpedo Boats
10 Landing Craft
26 Training and Service Craft

Personnel

1971: 6 000 officers and ratings

Mercantile Marine

Lloyd's Register of Shipping:
139 vessels of 686 104 tons gross

SUBMARINES

2 "W" TYPE

Displacement, tons	1 030 surface; 1 180 submerged
Length, feet (metres)	245 (74.7) oa
Beam, feet (metres)	23.6 (7.2)
Draught, feet (metres)	14.8 (4.5)
Guns, AA	4—25 mm
Torpedo tubes	6—21 in (533 mm), 4 bow, 2 stern
Main engines	4 000 hp diesels (surface)
	2 500 hp electric motors (submerged)
Speed, knots	17 on surface, 15 submerged
Radius, miles	13 000
Complement	60

Transferred from the Soviet Navy in 1958. The coastal submarine of the Soviet "MV" type was deleted from the list in 1967.

"W" Type   *Added 1966*

MEDIUM ESCORTS

"Riga" Type   *Added 1967*

2 "RIGA" TYPE

DRUZKI	SMELI

Displacement, tons	950 standard; 1 200 full load
Length, feet (metres)	295.3 (90) oa
Beam, feet (metres)	31.5 (9.6)
Draught, feet (metres)	10.2 (3.1)
Guns AA	3—3.9 in (100 mm); 4—37 mm
Tubes	3—21 in (533 mm)
A/S weapons	4 DCT
Mines	50
Main engines	Geared turbines
	24 000 shp; 2 shafts
Speed, knots	27

Transferred from the Soviet Navy in 1957 and 1958. Fitted with S Band search radar.

COASTAL ESCORTS

6 "SOI" TYPE

Displacement, tons	215 light; 250 normal
Dimensions	138 pp, 147 oa × 20 × 10 max
Guns	4—25 mm (2 twin)
A/S weapons	4 five-barrelled ahead throwing rocket launchers
Main engines	3 diesel; 3 500 bhp = 28 knots
Complement	30

Steel hulled patrol vessels or submarine chasers reportedly transferred from the USSR in 1963.

2 "KRONSTADT" TYPE

Displacement, tons	300 standard; 350 full load
Dimensions, feet	167 × 19.3 × 9
Guns	1—3.4 in; 2—37 mm AA; 3—20 mm AA
A/S weapons	Depth charge throwers
Main engines	Diesels; 2 shafts; 27 knots
Oil fuel (tons)	20
Complement	40

"Kronstadt" class submarine chasers transferred from the USSR in 1957.

MINESWEEPERS

2 "T 43" TYPE

Displacement, tons	500 standard; 600 full load
Dimensions, feet	200 × 27.2 × 9.5
Guns	4—37 mm AA; 8—13 mm MG
Main engines	Diesels; 2 shafts; 3,200 bhp = 18 knots
Complement	60

Three "T" class minesweepers are reported to have been transferred from the USSR in 1953, of which one was cannibalised.

INSHORE MINESWEEPERS

4 "T 301" TYPE

Displacement, tons	130 standard; 180 full load
Dimensions, feet	100 × 16 × 4.5
Guns	2—37 mm AA; 2—25 mm AA
Main engines	Diesels; 2 shafts; 480 bhp = 10 knots
Complement	30

"T" 301 class inshore minesweepers reported to have been transferred from the USSR in 1955.

TORPEDO BOATS

8 "P 4" TYPE

Displacement, tons	50
Dimensions, feet	85.3 × 20 × 6
Guns	4—25 mm AA
Torpedoes	2
Main engines	Diesels; 2 000 bhp = 42 knots

Motor torpedo boats of the "P 4" class reported to have been transferred from the USSR in 1956. The fast patrol boats of the Soviet "PA 2" type, of which there were originally reported to have been 12, were deleted from the list in 1967.

MINESWEEPING BOATS

24 "PO-2" TYPE

Ex-Soviet craft. 12 are reported to have been acquired in 1950 and 12 in 1956 for harbour, coastal, inshore and estuarial employment and general purpose duties.

LANDING CRAFT

10 LCU TYPE

Displacement, tons	164 oa
Guns	1—37 mm AA

Ten utility landing craft are reported to have been built in Bulgaria in 1954. Based on a German Second World War design.

TRAINING VESSEL

VESELITZ (ex-*Asen*)

Displacement, tons	240
Guns	2—65 mm; 1 MG
Main engines	120 hp = 7 knots

Auxiliary sail training vessel. Launched in 1912. Refitted in 1933-34. *Kamicia* deleted in 1968.

TUG

A former Soviet tug of the fleet type with an overall length of 135 feet.

BURMA

Administration

Vice-Chief of Staff, Defence Services (Navy):
Commodore Thaung Tin

Diplomatic Representation

Naval, Military and Air Attaché in London:
Captain Chit Ko Ko

Naval, Military and Air Attaché in Washington:
Colonel Tin Htut

Strength of the Fleet

1 Frigate
1 Escort Minesweeper
2 Patrol vessels (Escort, Fleet Minesweeper)
5 Torpedo Boats
4 Support Gunboats (Landing Craft)
13 Patrol Gunboats
21 River Gunboats
14 Auxiliary Ships and Service Craft

Personnel

1971: 6 200 (300 officers and 5 900 ratings) including reserves

Mercantile Marine

Lloyd's Register of Shipping:
35 vessels of 51 221 tons gross

Name	Builders	Laid down	Launched	Completed
MAYU (ex-HMS *Fal*)	Smiths Dock Co Ltd, South Bank-on-Tees, Middlesborough, England	20 May 1942	9 Nov 1942	2 July 1943

1 Ex-BRITISH "RIVER" CLASS

Displacement, tons	1 460 standard; 2 170 full load
Length, feet (*metres*)	283 (*86·3*) pp; 301·3 (*91·8*) oa
Beam, feet (*metres*)	36·7 (*11·2*)
Draught, feet (*metres*)	12 (*3·7*)
Guns, dual purpose	1—4 in (*102 mm*)
Guns, AA	4—40 mm
Boilers	2—three drum type
Main engines	Triple expansion 5 500 ihp; 2 shafts
Speed, knots	19
Radius, miles	4 200 at 12 knots
Oil fuel (tons)	440
Complement	140

"River" class frigate. Acquired from Great Britain and renamed in March 1948.

MAYU — *Burmese Navy, Official*

ESCORT MINESWEEPER

Name	Builders	Laid down	Launched	Completed
YAN MYO AUNG (ex-HMS *Mariner*, ex-*Kincardine*)	Port Arthur Shipyards, Canada	26 Aug 1943	9 May 1944	23 May 1945

1 Ex-BRITISH "ALGERINE" CLASS

Displacement, tons	1 040 standard; 1 335 full load
Length, feet (*metres*)	225 (*68·6*) pp; 235 (*71·6*) oa
Beam, feet (*metres*)	35·5 (*10·8*)
Draught, feet (*metres*)	11·5 (*3·5*)
Guns, surface	1—4 in (*102 mm*)
Guns, AA	4—40 mm
Boilers	2 three-drum type
Main engines	Triple expansion 2 000 shp; 2 shafts
Speed, knots	16·5
Radius, miles	4 000
Complement	140

Former ocean minesweeper in the British Navy, of the corvette type and used as escort vessel. *Mariner*, M 380 was transferred from Great Britain in 1957. Handed over to Burma in London and renamed *Yan Myo Aung*, on 18 Apr 1958. Fitted for minelaying and can carry 16 mines, eight on each side.

YAN MYO AUNG — *1964, Burmese Navy, Official*

TORPEDO BOATS

5 BRITISH-BUILT CONVERTIBLE TYPE

T 201 (ex-*PTS 101*)	**T 203** (ex-*PTS 103*)	**T 205** (ex-*PTS 105*)
T 202 (ex-*PTS 102*)	**T 204** (ex-*PTS 104*)	

Displacement, tons	50 standard; 64 full load
Dimensions, feet	67 pp; 71·5 oa × 19·5 × 6 max
Guns	As MGB: 1—4·5 in; 1—40 mm AA; As MTB: 2—20 mm AA
Tubes	As MTB: 4—21 in
Main engines	2 Napier Deltic diesels; 5 000 shp = 42 knots
Complement	13

Interchangeable motor torpedo boats/motor gunboats built by Saunders Roe (Anglesey) Ltd, England. Convertible craft of aluminium construction, with riveted skin and aluminium alloy framework. As well as main engines, auxiliary power is also provided by diesels. The Saunders-Roe slow-speed electric drive was fitted to facilitate manoeuvring in the confined inland waters where the craft may be required to operate. Armament and layout of the vessels were similar to the British fast patrol boats of the "Dark" Class. The cost including engines, equipment and spares, of the five boats was over £1 800 000. T 201 was launched 24 Mar 1956. All were completed in 1956-57. A photograph of T 201 of this class appears in the 1956-57 to 1961-62 editions.

T 202 — *1966, Burmese Navy, Official*

SUPPORT GUNBOATS

4 Ex-BRITISH LCG (M) TYPE

	INDAW	INLAY	INMA	INYA
Displacement, tons	381			
Dimensions, feet	154·5 oa × 22·5 × 7·8			
Guns	2—25 pdr; 2—2 pdr			
Main engines	Paxman Ricardo diesels; 2 shafts; 1 000 bhp = 13 knots			
Complement	39			

Former British *LCG* (M), Landing craft, gun medium. Employed as gunboats. A photograph of *Inlay* of this class appears in the 1950-51 to 1961-62 editions.

INMA — *Burmese Navy, Official*

PATROL VESSELS

YAN TAING AUNG, PCE 41 (ex-USS *Farmington*, PCE 894)

Displacement, tons	640 standard; 903 full load
Dimensions, feet	180 wl; 184 oa × 33 × 9·5
Guns	1—3 in, 50 cal dp; 2—40 mm AA (1 twin); 8—20 mm AA (4 twin)
A/S weapons	1 hedgehog; 2 DCT; 2 DC tracks
Main engines	GM diesels; 2 shafts; 1 800 bhp = 15 knots

Former US patrol ship (escort). Built by Willamette Iron & Steel Corp, Portland, Oregon. Laid down on 7 Dec 1942, launched on 15 May 1943 and completed 10 Aug 1943. Transferred on 18 June 1965.

Patrol Vessels—continued

YAN GYI AUNG, PCE 42 (ex-USS *Craddock*, MSF 356)

Displacement, tons	650 standard; 945 full load
Dimensions, feet	180 wl; 184·5 oa × 33 × 9·8 max
Guns	1—3 in 50 cal single forward; 4—40 mm AA (2 twin); 4—20 mm AA (2 twin)
Main engines	Diesels; 2 shafts; 1 710 shp = 14·8 knots

Former US steel hulled fleet minesweeper of the "Admirable" class. Built by Willamette Iron & Steel Corp, Portland, Oregon. Laid down on 10 Nov 1943 and launched on 22 July 1944. Transferred at San Diego on 31 Mar 1967.

RIVER GUN BOATS

2 BURMESE-BUILT LARGE TYPE

NAGAKYAY　　　　　　　　　　　　　　**NAWARAT**

Displacement, tons	400 standard; 450 full load
Dimensions, feet	163 × 26·8 × 5·8
Guns	2—25 pdr QF; 2—40 mm AA
Main engines	2 Paxman-Ricardo turbo-charged diesels; 2 shafts; 1 160 bhp = 12 knots
Complement	43

Built at the Government Dockyard, Dawbon, Rangoon, Burma, *Nagakyay* was completed on 3 Dec 1960 and *Nawarat* on 26 Apr 1960.

NAGAKYAY　　　　　　　　　1962, Burmese Navy, Official

10 YUGOSLAVIAN BUILT "Y" TYPE

Y 301　Y 302　Y 303　Y 304　Y 305　Y 306　Y 307　Y 308　Y 309　Y 310

Displacement, tons	120
Dimensions, feet	100 pp; 104·8 oa × 24 × 3
Guns	2—40 mm AA; 1—2 pdr
Main engines	2 Mercedes-Benz diesels; 2 shafts; 1 000 bhp = 13 knots
Compliment	29

All ten of these boats were completed in 1958 at the Shipyard "Uljanik", Pula, in Yugoslavia. For detailed building dates see 1966-67 and earlier editions. A photograph of Y 301 appears in the 1962-63 and 1963-64 editions.

Y 310　　　　　　　　　　1964, Burmese Navy, Official

9 CONVERTED TRANSPORT TYPE

HINTHA	SAGU	SETKAYA	SHWEPAZUN
SABAN	SEINDA	SETYAHAT	SHWETHIDA
			SINMIN

Displacement, tons	98
Dimensions, feet	94·5 × 22 × 4·5
Guns	1—40 mm; 3—20 mm
Main engines	Crossley ERL—6 diesel; 160 bhp = 12 knots
Complement	32

A photograph of *Sagu* appears in the 1964-65 to 1970-71 editions, and of *Saban* in the 1962-63 and 1963-64 editions.

SHWEPAZUN　　　　　　　　1971, Burmese Navy, Official

PATROL GUNBOATS

6 US-BUILT PGM TYPE

PGM 401　　**PGM 402**　　**PGM 403**　　**PGM 404**　　**PGM 405**　　**PGM 406**

Displacement, tons	100
Dimensions, feet	95 × 19 × 5
Guns	1—40 mm AA; 2—0·5 US Browning MG
Main engines	4 GM diesels; 2 shafts; 1 000 bhp = 16 knots
Complement	17

Built by the Marinette Marine Corporation, USA. Ex-US PGM 43-46, 51 and 52 respectively. Machinery comprises 2-stroke, 6-cylinder, tandem geared twin diesel propulsion unit—1 LH and 1 RH; 500 bhp per unit.

PGM 401　　　　　　　　　1962, Burmese Navy, Official

MOTOR GUNBOATS

7 Ex-UNITED STATES CGC TYPE

MGB 101　MGB 102　MGB 104　MGB 105　MGB 106　MGB 108　MGB 110

Displacement, tons	49 standard; 66 full load
Dimensions, feet	78 pp; 83 oa × 16 × 5·5
Guns	1—40 mm AA; 1—20 mm AA
Main engines	4 GM diesels; 2 shafts; 800 bhp = 11 knots
Complement	16

Ex-USCG 83-ft type cutters with new hulls built in Burma. Completed in 1960. For detailed building dates see 1966-67 and earlier editions. Machinery comprises 2-stroke, 6 cylinder, tandem geared, twin diesel propulsion units—1 LH and 1 RH drive; 400 bhp per unit.

MGB 102　　　　　　　　1962, Burmese Navy, Official

TRANSPORTS

PYIDAWAYE

Measurement, tons	2 217·31 gross
Dimensions, feet	270 × 47 × 15
Main engines	Fleming & Ferguson triple expansion 2 000 ihp
Boilers	2 Scotch (return type)
Radius, miles	2 000
Complement	88

Former passenger ship. In service since 1962. Wears the Burmese naval ensign.

PYIDAWAYE　　　　　　　　1964, Burmese Navy, Official

LCU 1626 (ex-USS *LCU 1626*)

Displacement, tons	200 light; 342 full load
Dimensions, feet	135·2 oa × 29 × 5·5
Main engines	Diesels; 2 shafts; 1 000 bhp = 11 knots

Ex-US utility landing craft. Transferred under MAP in 1967. Used as transport.

LCM 701	**LCM 702**	**LCM 703**	**LCM 704**	**LCM 705**	**LCM 707**
				LCM 706	**LCM 708**

Displacement, tons	28
Dimensions, feet	56 × 14 × 4
Main engines	2 Gray Marine diesels; 225 bhp

US-built LCM type landing craft. Used as local transports for stores and personnel.

TUGS

YTL 423　　　**YTL 557**　　　**YTL 560**　　　**TYL 592**

Four small tugs were transferred from the USN during 1968 under MAP.

CAMBODIA
MARINE ROYAL KHMERE

The Marine Royal Khmere was established on 1st March 1954.

Chief of Staff of Marine Royal Khmere (MRK): Capitaine de Corvette Vong Sarendy

Personnel

1971: Navy: 1 350 officers and men.   Marine Corps: 150 officers and men.

Mercantile Marine

1971: Lloyd's Register of Shipping: 3 vessels of 4 230 tons gross

PATROL VESSELS
2 Ex-US PC TYPE

E 311 (ex-*Flamberge, P 631,* ex-*PC 1086*)   **E 312** (ex-*L'Inconstant, P 636,* ex-*PC 1171*)

Displacement, tons	325 standard; 400 full load
Dimensions, feet	170 wl; 173·7 oa × 23 × 6·5
Guns	1—3 in dp; 1—40 mm AA, 4—20 mm AA
Main engines	2 GM diesels, 2 shafts; 3 600 bhp = 18 knots
Oil fuel (tons)	62
Radius, miles	6 000 at 10 knots
Complement	63

Former US submarine chasers of the PC type. Transferred from the US Navy to the French Navy in 1951 and served in Indo-China and again transferred to the Marine Royal Khmere in 1955-56. Built of steel.

E 312   *Official*

SUPPORT GUNBOATS
1 Ex-US LSIL TYPE

P 111 (ex-*LSIL 9039,* ex-*LSIL 875*)

Displacement, tons	230 standard; 387 full load
Dimensions, feet	169 × 23·7 × 5·7
Guns	1—3 in; 1—40 mm AA; 2—20 mm AA
Main engines	2 GM diesels; 2 shafts; 1 000 bhp = 15 knots
Oil fuel (tons)	100
Radius, miles	8 000 at 12 knots
Complement	58

Former US infantry landing ship of the LSIL type. Transferred from the US Navy to the French Navy, on 2 Mar 1951 and stationed in Indo-China; and again transferred to the Marine Royal Khmere in 1957.

1 ex-US LCI TYPE

P 112 (ex-*Medicin Capitaine Le Gall*)

Displacement, tons	230 standard; 350 full load
Dimensions, feet	160 × 23 × 6
Guns	1—3 in; 5—20 mm AA
Main engines	8 GM diesels; 2 shafts; 1 800 bhp = 15 knots
Oil fuel	120 tons
Radius, miles	8 000 at 12 knots
Complement	40

TORPEDO BOATS
2 Ex-YUGOSLAV 108 TYPE

VR I   **VR II**

Displacement, tons	55 standard; 60 full load
Dimensions, feet	69 pp; 78 oa × 21·3 × 7·8
Guns	1—40 mm AA; 4—12·7 mm MG
Tubes	2
Main engines	3 Packard petrol motors; 5 000 bhp = 36 knots
Complement	14

Torpedo boats presented by Yugoslavia in 1965 and numbered by the Cambodian Navy.

PATROL BOATS
2 Ex-US AVR TYPE

VR 3   **VR 4**

Displacement, tons	30
Dimensions, feet	63 × 13 × 4·6
Guns	4—12·7 mm MG
Main engines	GM Diesel 500 bhp = 15 knots
Complement	12

Patrol Boats—*continued*
3 Ex-CHINESE CPB TYPE

VC 4   **VC 5**   **VC 6**

Displacement, tons	7·7 standard; 9·7 full load
Dimensions, feet	42 × 9 × 3·9
Guns	2—12·7 mm MG
Main engines	Diesel, 300 bhp = 20 knots
Complement	10

Coastal patrol boats transferred from the People's Republic of China in Jan 1968. A photograph of these in company appears in the 1969-70 edition.

1 Ex-HDML TYPE

VP 212 (ex-*VP 748,* ex-*HDML 1223*)

Displacement, tons	46 standard; 54 full load
Dimensions, feet	72 oa × 16 × 5·5
Guns	2—20 mm AA; 4—7·5 mm MG
Main engines	2 diesels; 2 shafts; 300 bhp = 10 knots
Oil fuel (tons)	6
Radius, miles	2 200 at 10 knots
Complement	8

Former British harbour defence motor launch of the HDML type. Transferred from the British Navy to the French Navy in 1950 and again transferred from the French Navy to the Marine Royal Khmere in 1956. VP 749 and VP 642 were discarded in 1968.

LANDING CRAFT
1 EDIC TYPE

T 916 (ex-*EDIC 606*)

Displacement, tons	292 standard; 650 full load
Dimensions, feet	193·5 × 39·2 × 4·5
Guns	1—81 mm mortar; 2—12·7 mm MG
Main engines	2 MGO diesels; 2 shafts; 1 000 bhp = 10 knots
Complement	16 (1 officer, 15 men)

Completed and transferred from the French Government in Aug 1969.

3 Ex-US LCU TYPE

T 913 (ex-USS *LCU 1577*) **T 914** (ex-USS *LCU 783*) **T 915** (ex-USS *LCU 1421*)

Displacement, tons	180 standard; 360 full load
Dimensions, feet	115 wl; 119 oa × 34 × 6
Guns	2—20 mm AA
Main engines	3 diesels; 3 shafts; 675 bhp = 8 knots
Oil fuel (tons)	12
Radius, miles	750 at 7 knots
Complement	12

Former US utility landing craft of the LCU type. LCU 783 and LCU 1421 were transferred on 31 May 1962. Former LCT(6)s 9085 (ex-622) and 9091 (ex-720) were deleted from the list in 1969, with ex-LCU 9073 (ex-USS *LCU* 1420.)

T 913   *1969, Marine Royal Khmere, Official*

CAMEROON

Complete independence was proclaimed on 1 Jan 1960

Mercantile Marine

Lloyd's Register of Shipping: 9 vessels of 1 688 tons gross

PATROL BOATS

VIGILANTE   (ex-*VC 6,* P 756)   (ex- VC 8, P 758)

Displacement, tons	75 standard; 82 full load
Dimensions, feet	104·2 × 15·5 × 5·5
Guns	2—20 mm AA
Main engines	Mercedes-Benz diesels; 2 shafts; 2 700 bhp = 28 knots
Radius, miles	1 500 at 15 knots
Complement	15

Former French seaward defence motor launches of the VC type. Built by Constructions Mécaniques de Normandie, Cherbourg. Completed in 1958. *Vigilante* was officially handed over from France to the Republic of Cameroon on 7 Mar 1964.

PATRIE DU CAMEROUN (ex-*VP 768,* ex-*HDML 1228*)

Displacement, tons	40 standard; 52 full load
Dimensions, feet	71 × 15·2 × 6
Guns	2—20 mm AA; 4 MG
Main engines	2 diesels; 2 shafts; 300 bhp = 12 knots
Radius, miles	2 200 at 10 knots
Complement	11

Former British HDML type. Launched in 1943. Transferred from the British Navy to the French Navy in 1950 for service in Indo-China; again transferred from the French Navy to the Cameroon Government in 1963 to replace ex-VP 747, ex-HDML 1423.

BRIGADIER M'BONGA TOUNDA

Displacement, tons	20 full load
Dimensions, feet	60 × 13·5 × 4
Guns	1—12·7 mm MG
Main engines	Caterpillar Diesel; 2 shafts; 540 bhp = 21 knots
Complement	8

Built by Ch Navals de L'Esterel in 1967.

CANADA

Administration

Minister of National Defence:
The Hon. Donald S. Macdonald, MP

On 1 Aug 1964 the Naval Board was dissolved, and Naval Headquarters was integrated with Canadian Forces Headquarters. On 1 Feb 1968, the Canadian Forces Reorganization Act unified the three branches of the Canadian Forces and the title Royal Canadian Navy was dropped. Maritime Command, one of five commands comprising the Canadian Armed Forces, is made up of the bulk of what was the Royal Canadian Navy plus Maritime Patrol aircraft squadrons and bases.

Senior Naval Appointments

Commander Maritime Command:
Vice Admiral H. A. Porter, CD

Commander Maritime Forces Pacific:
Rear Admiral R. H. Lier, C.D.

Commander Canadian Flotilla Atlantic:
Commodore W. P. Hayes, CD

Diplomatic Representation

Senior Naval Liaison Officer, London:
Captain (N) P. H. Cayley, CD

Canadain Forces Attaché and Senior Naval Liaison Officer, Washington:
Commodore R. J. Pickford, CD

History

The Royal Canadian Navy officially came into being on 4 May 1910, when Royal Assent was given to the Naval Service Act.

Ships of the Royal Canadian Navy served in three wars. During the First World War the Canadian naval strength was 9 600 officers and men and 100 ships. During the Second World War the RCN expanded to 95 000 officers, men and wrens; and 392 ships, Canada's major naval effort being devoted to the Battle of the Atlantic. Canadian destroyers served in the Far East throughout the Korean War.

Flag

On 15 Feb 1965 a new Canadian flag replaced the Red, White and Blue ensigns :—
Official description: A red flag of the proportions two by length and one by width, containing in its centre a white square the width of the flag, with a single red maple leaf centred therein.

With the proclamation of the new national flag on 15 Feb 1965 Canadian ships no longer wear the Red, White or Blue Ensigns, the national flag being worn on the ensign staff aft. In Feb 1968 a naval jack was approved to be flown by Canadian Warships.
Official description: A white flag of the proportions two by length and one by width, containing in the top left corner, the Canadian flag and centred on the flag the naval crown, fouled anchor and eagle combined in dark blue.

Ships

The senior ship of a squadron wears a command broad pennant. This is a swallow-tailed pennant, white, with blue borders top and bottom, and bearing the squadron number in blue. "Barber pole" stripes are painted on the lower structure of the foremast of ships of the Fifth Canadian Escort Squadron, in the tradition of the "Barber Pole Brigade", mid-ocean escort group of the Second World War.

Strength of the Fleet

  4 Submarines (Diesel Powered)
 20 Destroyer Escorts and Helicopter Escorts
  3 Operational Support (Helicopter) Ships
  2 Escort Maintenance Ships
  1 Large Diving Tender (ex-Ocean Escort)
  6 Coastal Minesweepers
  6 Oceanographic Research Vessels
  1 Hydrofoil Anti-Submarine Craft
  4 Gate Vessels (Boom Defence Netlayers)
 42 Auxiliaries and Service Craft
  2 Sailing Ketches (Cadet Training)

Personnel

1970: 14 770 (1 691 officers and 13 079 men) in Maritime Command)

1971: 16 906 (2 379 officers and 14 527 men and women)

Navy Estimetas

1962-63: $287 466 000	1965-66: $292 565 000
1963-64: $306 184 000	1966-67: $295 000 000
1964-65: $272 892 000	1967-68: $300 000 000

1968-69: $283 201 000 (Maritime Command)
1969-70: $359 701 000 (Maritime Command)
1970-71: $360 000 000 (Maritime Command)
1971-72: Estimates by command are no longer calculated, it was officially stated in Feb 1971.

Mercantile Marine

Lloyd's Register of Shipping:
1 266 vessels of 2 399 949 tons gross

Scale: 150 feet = 1 inch (1 : 1 800)

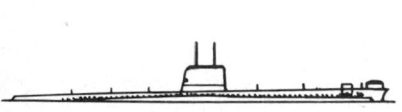
OJIBWA, OKANAGAN, ONONDAGA

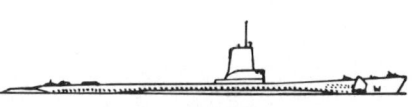
RAINBOW

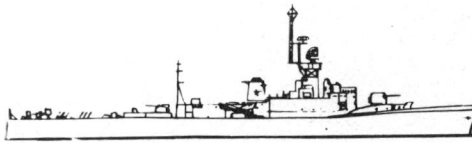
CHAUDIERE, COLUMBIA, ST. CROIX

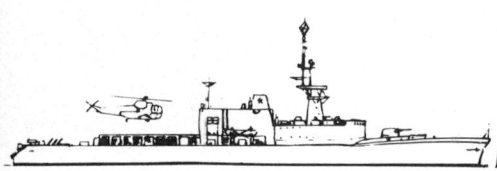
ANNAPOLIS, NIPIGON

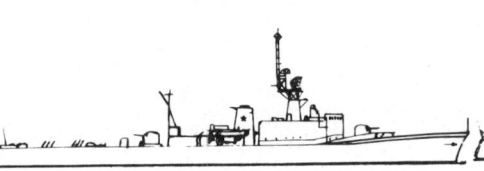
QU'APPELLE

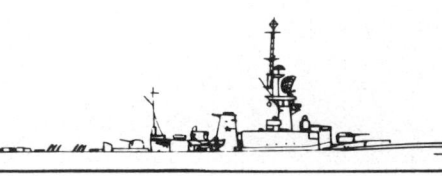
MACKENZIE, YUKON

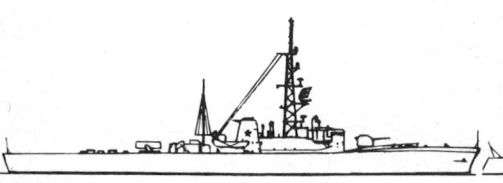
RESTIGOUCHE (Asroc)

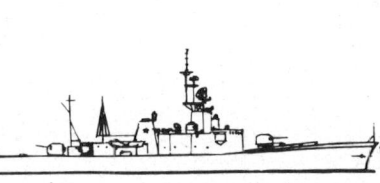
GATINEAU

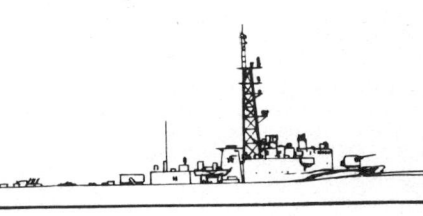
TERRA NOVA (Asroc and Limbo)

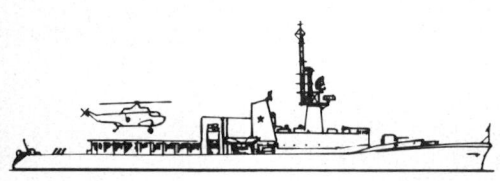
ASSINIBOINE, ST. LAURENT, SAGUENAY, SKEENA

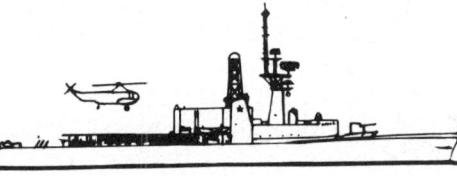
FRASER

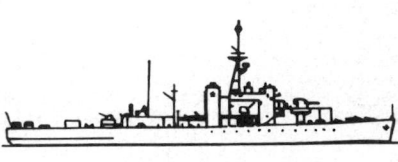
GRANBY

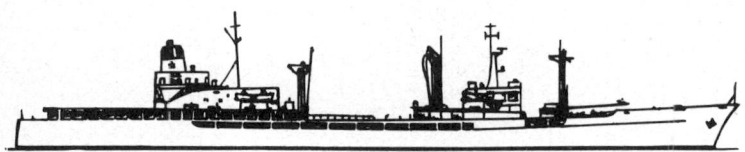
PROVIDER

CAPE BRETON (CAPE SCOTT similar but mainpost before after superstructure)

SUBMARINES (SS)

3 BRITISH-BUILT "OBERON" TYPE

Displacement, tons	2 060 full buoyancy surface;
	2 200 normal surface;
	2 420 submerged
Length, feet (metres)	241 (73·5) pp; 294·2 (90·0) oa
Beam, feet (metres)	26·5 (8·1)
Draught, feet (metres)	18 (5·5)
Torpedo tubes	8—21 in (533 mm), 6 bow and
	2 stern
Main engines	2 400 hp Admiralty Standard
	Range diesels; 3 600 hp electric
	motors (submerged)
Speed, knots	12 on surface; 16 submerged
Complement	65 (7 officers, 58 ratings)

Name	No.	Builders	Laid down	Launched	Commissioned
OJIBWA (ex-*Onyx*)	72	HM Dockyard, Chatham	27 Sep 1962	29 Feb 1964	23 Sep 1965
OKANAGAN	74	HM Dockyard, Chatham	25 Mar 1965	17 Sep 1966	22 June 1968
ONONDAGA	73	HM Dockyard, Chatham	18 June 1964	25 Sep 1965	22 June 1967

The procurement of three submarines for the Royal Canadian Navy was announced by the Minister of National Defence on 11 Apr 1962, all of the "Oberon" class built in Great Britain. The first of these patrol submarines was obtained by the Canadian Government from the Royal Navy construction programme. She was laid down as *Onyx* but launched as *Ojibwa*. The other two were specifically Canadian procurements. There were some design changes to meet specific new requirements including installation of RCN communications equipment and enlargement of de-icing and air-conditioning systems to meet the wide extremes of climate encountered in Canadian operating areas.

NOMENCLATURE. The name *Ojibwa* is that of a tribe of North American Indians now widely dispersed in Canada and the USA and one of the largest remnants of aboriginal population. *Okanagan* and *Onondaga* are also well known Canadian Indian tribes.

OPERATIONAL. This class of oceangoing submarines have improved detection equipment and are capable of higher submerged speeds. They are capable of maintaining continuous underwater patrols in any part of the Pacific or Atlantic oceans. All are equipped to fire homing torpedoes.

ELECTRONICS. The equipments include sonar with forecastle mounted array and X band surveillance radar installations.

OKANAGAN   *1969, Canadian Maritime Command, Official*

ONONDAGA   *1970 Canadian Maritime Command Official*

DISPOSALS

The aircraft carrier *Bonaventure* paid off on 1 Apr 1970 and was transferred to the Crown Assets Disposal Commission (CADC) for ultimate disposal. She was sold for scrap to M. W. Kennedy, Ltd of Vancouver, B.C.

The training submarine *Grilse* (ex-USS *Burrfish*) was returned to the USN in Dec 1968 after having been on loan to Canada since May 1961.

1 Ex-US "TENCH" TYPE

RAINBOW SS 75 (ex-*USS Argonaut* SS 475)

Displacement, tons	1 526 standard; 1 800 surface;
	2 500 submerged
Length, feet (metres)	311·2 (95·0)
Beam, feet (metres)	27·2 (8·2)
Draught, feet (metres)	17 (5·2)
Torpedo tubes	10—21 in (533 mm) 6 fwd 4 aft
Main engines	6 500 hp diesels (surface)
	4 610 hp electric motors
	(submerged)
Speed, knots	20 on surface; 10 submerged
Radius, miles	14 000 at 10 knots
Oil fuel (tons)	300
Complement	82 (8 officers, 74 men)

OJIBWA   *1971, Canadian Forces, Official*

Former US submarine of the "Tench" class. Built by Navy Yard, Portsmouth, New Hampshire. Laid down on 28 June 1944, launched on 1 Oct 1944 and completed on 15 Jan 1945. Purchased in Dec 1968 as a replacement for *Grilse*. Commissioned on 2 Dec 1968. Based at Esquimalt for anti-submarine training with aircraft and ships of Pacific Maritime Command.

RAINBOW   *1970, Canadian Maritime Command, Official*

DESTROYER HELICOPTER ESCORTS (DDH)

4 "IROQUOIS" CLASS

Displacement, tons	4 050 full load
Length, feet (metres)	398 (121·3); 426 (129·8) oa
Beam, feet (metres)	50 (15·2)
Draught, feet (metres)	14 (4·3)
Aircraft	2 "Sea King" CHSS-2 A/S helicopters
Guns, dual purpose	1—5 in (127 mm) LA, single
A/S	1 A/S Mortar Mk X
Torpedo tubes	2 triple for A/S homing torpedoes
Main engines	Gas turbines; 2 Pratt & Whitney FT4; 44 000 shp + 2 Pratt & Whitney FT 12 6 200 shp for cruising; 2 shafts
Speed, knots	27 designed
Radius, miles	4 500 at economical speed

Name	No.	Builders	Laid down	Launched	To Complete
ALGONQUIN	283	Davie SB Co, Lauzon	1 Sep 1969	mid Apr 1971	30 June 1973
ATHABASKAN	282	Davie SB Co, Lauzon	1 June 1969	mid Apr 1971	30 Sep 1972
HURON	281	Marine Industries Ltd, Sorel	15 Jan 1969	27 Nov 1970	30 June 1973
IROQUOIS	280	Marine Industries Ltd, Sorel	15 Jan 1969	28 Nov 1970	30 Aug 1972

It will be observed that these ships have the same hull design, dimensions and basic characteristics as the large general purpose frigates cancelled at the end of 1963 (see particulars and illustration in the 1963-64 edition). Designed as anti-submarine ships, they will be fitted as leaders, with variable depth and conventional sonar, landing deck equipped with double hauldown and beartrap, Flume type anti-rolling tanks to stabilise the ships at low speed, pre-wetting system to counter radio-active fallout, enclosed citadel, and bridge control of machinery which will comprise gas turbines, instead of the steam originally projected.

DESIGN. Plans have been changed over the last few years, see illustrations in the 1966-67, 1967-68 and 1968-69 to 1970-71 editions.

MISSILES. Sea Sparrow anti-aircraft missile will be fitted.

IROQUOIS   *1971, Canadian Forces, Official*

Name	No.	Builders	Work Commenced	Launched	Completed
ANNAPOLIS	265	Halifax Shipyards Ltd, Halifax	July 1960	27 Apr 1963	19 Dec 1964
NIPIGON	266	Marine Industries Ltd, Sorel Q	Apr 1960	10 Dec 1961	30 May 1964

NIPIGON   *1971, Canadian Forces, Official*

2 "ANNAPOLIS" CLASS

Displacement, tons	2 400 standard; 3 000 full load
Length, feet (metres)	371·0 (113·1) oa
Beam, feet (metres)	42·0 (12·8)
Draught, feet (metres)	14·4 (4·4)
Aircraft	1 CHSS-2 "Sea King" helicopter
Guns, AA	2—3 in (76 mm) 50 cal (1 twin)
A/S weapons	1 Mk 10 three-barrelled mortar (Limbo) in after well
Boilers	2 water tube
Main engines	Geared turbines; 2 shafts; 30 000 shp
Speed, knots	28 (official figure) 30 trials
Complement	246 (12 officers, 234 ratings)

These two ships represented the logical development of the original "St Laurent "class, through the "Restigouche" and "Mackenzie" designs. Due to the erection of a helicopter hangar and flight deck, and variable depth sonar only one "Limbo" mounting could be installed. Also the 50 cal 3 inch mounting had to be moved forward to replace the 70 cal mounting in the original design.

RADAR. Search: SPS 12. Tactical: SPS 10. Fire Control: X Band.

CONSTRUCTION. As these, like preceding DDEs are largely prefabricated no firm laying down date is officially given. Work on hull units commenced under cover long before components were laid on the slip. "Work Commencement" schedule dates are therefore used in the Laid down column.

PHOTOGRAPHS. Other views of Annapolis and Nipigon appear in the 1965-66 to 1969-70 editions.

ANNAPOLIS   *1970, Canadian Maritime Command, Official*

DESTROYER ESCORTS (DDE) Anti-Submarine Frigate Type

Name	No.	Builders	Laid down	Launched	Completed
MACKENZIE	261	Canadian Vickers Ltd, Montreal	15 Dec 1958	25 May 1961	6 Oct 1962
QU'APPELLE	264	Davie Shipbuilding & Repairing	14 Jan 1960	2 May 1962	14 Sep 1963
*SASKATCHEWAN	262	Victoria Machinery (and Yarrow)	16 July 1959	1 Feb 1961	16 Feb 1963
YUKON	263	Burrard DD & Shipbuilding	25 Oct 1959	27 July 1961	25 May 1963

4 "MACKENZIE" CLASS

Displacement, tons	2 380 standard; 2 890 full load
Length, feet (metres)	366·0 (111·5) oa
Beam, feet (metres)	42·0 (12·8)
Draught, feet (metres)	13·5 (4·1)
Guns, AA	4—3 in (76 mm) 2 twin
A/S weapons	2 Mk 10 "Limbo" in well aft
Boilers	2 water tube
Main engines	Geared turbines; 2 shafts; 30 000 shp
Speed, knots	28
Complement	245 (12 officers, 233 ratings)

RADAR. Search: SPS 12. Tactical: SPS 10. Fire Control: X Band.

PHOTOGRAPHS. Starboard broadside aerial view of *Saskatchewan* in 1963-64 editions, Port quarter oblique aerial view of *Mackenzie* in the 1963-64 and 1964-65 editions, and starboard broadside surface view in 1966-67 to 1969-70 editions, port broadside view of *Yukon* in the 1964-65 and 1965-66 editions.

Saskatchewan was launched by Victoria Machinery Depot Co Ltd, but completed by Yarrow's Ltd.

MACKENZIE   1970, Canadian Maritime Command, Official

Name	No.	Builder	Laid down	Launched	Completed
GATINEAU	236	Davie Shipbuilding & Repairing	30 Apr 1953	3 June 1957	17 Feb 1959
KOOTENAY	258	Burrard DD & Shipbuilding	21 Aug 1952	15 June 1954	7 Mar 1959
RESTIGOUCHE	257	Canadian Vickers, Montreal	15 July 1953	22 Nov 1954	7 June 1958
TERRA NOVA	259	Victoria Machinery Depot Co	14 Nov 1952	21 June 1955	6 June 1959

4 "RESTIGOUCHE" CONVERSIONS

Displacement, tons	2 390 standard; 2 900 full load
Length, feet (metres)	371·0 (113·1)
Beam, feet (metres)	42·0 (12·8)
Draught, feet (metres)	14·1 (4·3)
Guns, AA	2—3 in (76 mm) 70 cal forward
A/S weapons	ASROC aft and 1 Mk 10 ("Limbo") three-barrelled depth charge mortar in after well
Boilers	2 water tube
Main engines	Geared turbines; 2 shafts; 30 000 shp
Speed, knots	28 plus
Complement	250 (13 officers, 237 ratings)

CONVERSION. These four ships were refitted with anti-submarine rocket launcher aft and lattice foremast, *Terra Nova* commencing in Sep 1967. Work included removing the after 3 inch 50 cal twin gun mounting and one "Limbo" A/S Mk 10 triple mortar, provision of ASROC and variable depth sonar, Dates of refits, *Terra Nova* was completed on 18 Oct 1968; *Gatineau* commenced on 15 Sep 1969, *Kootenay* in May 1970 and *Restigouche* in Aug 1970. *Kootenay* was severely damaged by an engine room explosion in Oct 1969.

RADAR. Search: SPS 12. Tactical: SPS 10. Fire Control: X Band.

PHOTOGRAPHS. A starboard broadside view of *Restigouche* before conversion appears in the 1958-59 edition, a starboard bow oblique aerial view of *Terra Nova* in the 1960-61 to 1962-63 editions, a port broadside aerial view of *Kootenay* in the 1959-60 to 1962-63 editions, and a port broadside surface view of *Gatineau* in the 1963-64 and 1964-65 editions.

TERRA NOVA   1970, Canadian Maritime Command, Official

Name	No.	Builder	Laid down	Launched	Completed
CHAUDIERE	235	Halifax Shipyards Ltd	30 July 1953	13 Nov 1957	14 Nov 1959
COLUMBIA	260	Burrard DD & Shipbuilding	11 June 1953	1 Nov 1956	7 Nov 1959
ST. CROIX	256	Marine Industries Ltd, Sorel, Q	15 Oct 1954	17 Nov 1957	4 Oct 1958

3 "RESTIGOUCHE" CLASS

Displacement, tons	2 370 standard; 2 880 full load
Length, feet (metres)	366·0 (111·5) oa
Beam, feet (metres)	42·0 (12·8)
Draught, feet (metres)	13·5 (4·1)
Guns, AA	4—3 in (76 mm) 2 twin
A/S weapons	2 Mk 10 triple barrelled mortar (Limbo) in well aft
Boilers	2 water tube
Main engines	Geared turbines; 2 shafts; 30 000 shp
Speed, knots	28
Complement	248 (12 officers, 236 ratings)

RADAR. Search: SPS 12. Tactical: SPS ·10. Fire Control: X Band.

PHOTOGRAPHS. A port quarter surface view of *Columbia* appears in 1960-61 to 1962-63 editions.

CHAUDIERE   1970, Canadian Maritime Command, Official

Destroyer Escorts (DDH ex-DDE) Anti-Submarine Frigate Type—*continued*

7 "ST. LAURENT" CLASS

Name	No.	Builders	Laid down	Launched	Completed
ST. LAURENT	DDE 205	Canadian Vickers, Ltd, Montreal	22 Nov 1950	20 Nov 1951	29 Oct 1955
SAGUENAY	DDE 206	Halifax Shipyards, Ltd, Halifax	4 Apr 1951	30 July 1953	15 Dec 1956
SKEENA	DDE 207	Burrard Dry Dock & Shipbuilding	1 June 1951	19 Aug 1952	30 Mar 1957
OTTAWA	DDE 229	Canadian Vickers, Ltd, Montreal	8 June 1951	29 Apr 1953	10 Nov 1956
MARGAREE	DDE 230	Halifax Shipyards Ltd, Halifax	12 Sep 1951	29 Mar 1956	5 Oct 1957
*FRASER	DDE 233	Yarrows, Ltd, Esquimalt, B.C.	11 Dec 1951	19 Feb 1953	28 June 1957
ASSINIBOINE	DDE 234	Marine Industries Ltd, Sorel, Q	19 May 1952	12 Feb 1954	16 Aug 1956

Displacement, tons	2 260 standard ; 2 800 full load
Length, feet (*metres*)	366·0 (*111·5*) oa
Beam, feet (*metres*)	42·0 (*12·8*)
Draught, feet (*metres*)	13·2 (*4·0*)
Guns, AA	2—3 in (*76 mm*) 50 cal (1 twin)
A/S weapons	1 "Limbo" 3-barrelled depth charge mortar in after well
Boilers	2 water tube
Main engines	English Electric geared turbines; 2 shafts; 30 000 shp
Speed, knots	28·5 (official figure)
Complement	250 (13 officers, 237 ratings)

The first major warships to be designed in Canada. Escort vessels built primarily for detection and destruction of fast submarines. In design, much assistance was received from the Royal Navy (propelling machinery of British design) and the US Navy. In function they supersede the frigates of the Second World War and like the latter they were designed so that in the event of emergency they could be produced rapidly and in quantity. With speed, manoeuvrability and weapons for anti-submarine sea warfare, the design provided for flush deck, low bridge, considerable use of aluminium instead of steel for superstructure, fittings and furniture, and compartmented hull. All ships have long range sonar to probe for submarines and improved armament and electronic equipment as submarine chasers.

* *Fraser* was launched by Burrard Dry Dock & Shipbuilding but completed by Yarrows Ltd.

RADAR. Search: SPS 12. Tactical: SPS 10.

RECONSTRUCTION. All have helicopter platforms and VDS. *St. Laurent* was equipped with VDS in 1961 and platform added later. Twin funnels were stepped to permit forward extension of the helicopter hangar. Gunhouses are of fibreglass. In providing helicopter platforms and hangars it was possible to retain only one three barrelled "Limbo" mortar and only one twin 3-inch gun mounting. Dates of recommissioning after conversion: *Assiniboine* 28 June 1963, *St. Laurent* 4 Oct 1963, *Ottawa* 21 Oct 1964, *Saguenay* 14 May 1965, *Skeena* 15 Aug 1965, *Margaree* 15 Oct 1965, *Fraser* 31 Aug 1966.

GUNNERY. Original armament was 4—3 inch, 50 cal AA (2 twin), 2—40 mm AA (single), and 2 "Limbo" mortars.

PHOTOGRAPHS. A photograph of *Ottawa* appears in the 1965-66 edition, of *Saguenay* in the 1966-67 and 1967-68 editions, of *St. Laurent* in the 1964-65 to 1967-68 editions, and of *Assiniboibe* in the 1964-65 to 1970-71 editions.

MARGAREE   1971, Canadian Forces, Official

FRASER   1970 Canadian Maritime Command, Official

OVERHEAD PLAN VIEW   1971, Canadian Forces, Official

SKEENA   1971, Wright & Logan

OPERATIONAL SUPPORT SHIPS (AOR)

Name	No.	Builders	Laid down	Launched	Completed
PRESERVER	AOR 510	Saint John Dry Dock Co Ltd, N.B.	17 Oct 1967	29 May 1969	30 July 1970
PROTECTEUR	AOR 509	Saint John Dry Dock Co Ltd, N.B.	17 Oct 1967	18 July 1968	30 Aug 1969

Displacement, tons	9 000 light ; 24 000 full load
Measurement, tons	22 100 gross ; 13 250 deadweight
Length, feet (metres)	546 (168·4) oa
Beam, feet (metres)	76 (23·2)
Draught, feet (metres)	30 (9·1)
Guns, AA	1—3 in (76 mm)
A/S launcher	1 Sea Sparrow fitted
Aircraft	3 CHSS-2 helicopters
Boilers	2 forced draught water tube
Main engines	Geared turbine
	21 000 shp; 1 shaft
Radius, miles	4 100 at 20, 7 500 at 11·5 knots
Complement	227 (15 officers, 212 ratings)

PRESERVER   *1971, Canadian Forces, Official*

Provided for under the Five Year Programme. Contract price $47 500 000 for both ships. In design they are an improvement on that of the prototype *Provider*. They increase the ability of Canadian anti-submarine forces to remain continuously on station in emergency. Alternatively they could carry spare anti-submarine helicopters, military vehicles and bulk equipment for sealift purposes. 12 000 tons fuel, 1 250 tons ammunition.

PROVIDER AOR 508

Displacement, tons	7 300 light ; 22 700 full load
Measurement, tons	20 000 gross ; 14 700 deadweight
Length, feet (metres)	523 (159·4) pp ; 555 (169·2) oa
Beam, feet (metres)	76 (23·2)
Draught, feet (metres)	32 (9·8) max
Aircraft	3 HSS 2 helicopters
Boilers	2 water tube
Main engines	Double reduction geared turbine
	21 000 shp; 1 shaft
Speed, knots	20
Radius, miles	5 000 at 20 knots
Oil fuel, (tons)	1 200
Complement	142 (11 officers, 131 ratings)

PROTECTEUR   *1971, courtesy Mr. Michael D. J. Lennon*

Authorised (announced) on 15 Apr 1958. Built by Davie Shipbuilding Ltd, Lauzon, Quebec. Preliminary construction work began in Sep 1960. Laid down on 1 May 1961. Launched on 5 July 1962. Commissioned for service on 28 Sep 1963. Cost $15 700 000.

DESIGN. The clean, streamlined hull was designed for speed while replenishing the fleet on operations. The forward bridge structure contains the commanding officer's accommodation as well as a modern 8-berth hospital. In the superstructure also are the wheelhouse, chartroom and three positions for control of this ship—the command control and the two bridge wings. The helicopter flight deck is aft with the hangar on this deck and immediately below the funnel. At least three Sikorsky helicopters can be accommodated in the hangar. The flight deck can receive the largest and heaviest helicopters. Immediately below the flight deck are two accommodation decks for the ship's company including the main galley and combined mess-recreation spaces for chief and petty officers and men. An unusual feature is the Self-Propelled Vehicle (SPV) fitted at number 6 station for the transfer of solid stores. A total of 20 electro-hydraulic winches are fitted on deck for ship-to-ship movements of cargo and supplies, as well as shore-to-ship requirements when alongside.

PROVIDER   *1968, courtesy Mr. Godfrey H. Walker*

NOMENCLATURE. Formerly rated as Fleet Replenishment Ship, but reclassified as Operational Support Ship in 1965. *Provider* was the name of the RCN parent ship for Fairmile motor launches in World War II.

ESCORT MAINTENANCE SHIPS (ARE)

2 "CAPE" CLASS

Displacement, tons	8 580 standard ; 11 270 full load
Dimensions, feet	441·5 × 57 × 20 mean at standard displacement
Main engines	Triple expansion ; 1 shaft ; 2 500 ihp = 11 knots
Boilers	2 Foster Wheeler
Complement	*Cape Breton* 220 ; *Cape Scott* 270 officers and men

Name	No.	Builders	Laid down	Launched	Completed
CAPE BRETON	100	Burrard Dry Dock Co, Vancouver, BC	5 July 1944	7 Oct 1944	25 Apr 1945
CAPE SCOTT	101	Burrard Dry Dock Co, Vancouver, BC	8 June 1944	27 Sep 1944	20 Mar 1945

Cape Breton formerly served in the Royal Navy as the escort maintenance ship *Flamborough Head*; but she returned from the United Kingdom in 1951 and was acquired by the Royal Canadian Navy and renamed *Cape Breton* on 31 Jan 1953, serving as a training establishment for technical apprentices at Halifax until 1958 when she sailed for Esquimalt for conversion to her present function. On 16 Nov 1959 she was commissioned on the West Coast as the second mobile repair ship; but was paid off to reserve on 10 Feb 1964.

Cape Scott served in the Royal Navy as *Beachy Head* until 1947, when she was lent to the Royal Netherlands Navy and renamed *Vulkaan*; but she was returned to the Royal Navy in 1950, and acquired by the Royal Canadian Navy in 1952, being renamed *Cape Scott* in 1953. On 28 Jan 1959 she was commissioned at Halifax as the Royal Canadian Navy's first mobile repair ship.

Both ships are equipped with a helicopter landing platform, a decompression chamber for the ship's divers, engineering, electrical and electronic repair shops, diesel, engine repair shop, battery shop, sheet metal shop, welding shop, pipe and coppersmith's shop, plate shop and blacksmith's shop. Each ship contains an eight-berth hospital, large sick bay, operating theatre, X-ray room, small medical laboratory, dental clinic and dental laboratory.

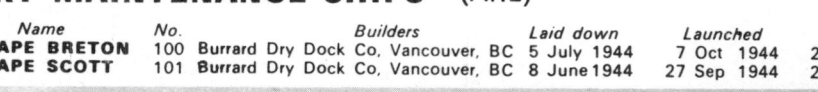

CAPE SCOTT   *1971, Canadian Forces, Official*

CAPE BRETON   *Official*

DIVING DEPOT SHIP

GRANBY　　　　　　　　*1968, Canadian Maritime Command, Official*

GRANBY FSE 180 (ex-*Victoriaville*, DE 320)

Displacement, tons	1 570 standard; 2 360 full load (as frigate)
Dimensions, feet	310·5 oa × 36·5 × 16·0
Guns, surface	2—4 in (1 twin)
Guns, AA	6—40 mm (4 single, 1 twin) as frigate
A/S weapons	2 "Squid" triple barrelled depth charge mortars
Boilers	2 Admiralty 3-drum type
Main engines	Triple expansion; 2 shafts; 5 500 ihp = 19 knots max
Radius, miles	9 600 at 12 knots
Oil fuel, tons	720 bunkerage capacity
Complement	140 (as frigate)

Depot ship for Fleet Diving Unit, Atlantic. Sole survivor of the 21 of this class, all built in Canada, which originally of similar design to the British "River" class frigates, including three transferred to Norway, were modernised and reconstructed to flush deckers (completed anti-submarine conversion in 1953-58). All redesignated FFE (instead of PF) in 1953. Again redesignated, DE, in 1964 and FSE in 1968.

Lauzon was declared surplus in 1963, *Buckingham, Fort Erie* and *Lanark* in 1965, *Cap de la Madeleine, inch Arran, La Hulloise* and *Outremont* in 1966, *Antigonish, Jonquiere, New Glasgow, New Waterford, Ste. Theresa, Stettler, Sussexvale* and *Swansea* in 1967, and *Beacon Hill* in 1968.

TRANSFERS. *Penetang* (ex-*Rouyn*), *Prestonian* (ex-*Beauharnois*), and *Toronto* (ex-*Gifford*) were lent to Norway in 1956, being renamed *Draug, Troll* and *Garm,* respectively, and transferred outright on 27 June 1958.

RESEARCH VESSELS (AGOR)

BLUETHROAT (AGOR 114)

Displacement, tons	785 standard; 870 full load
Dimensions, feet	150·7 pp; 157 oa × 33 × 10
Main engines	Diesel; 2 shafts; 1 200 bhp = 13 knots

Authorised under 1951 Programme. Built by Geo. T. Davie & Sons Ltd, Lauzon PQ. Laid down on 31 Oct 1952. Launched on 15 Sep 1955. Completed on 28 Nov 1955. Built as Mine and Loop Layer, but under NATO standardised nomenclature listed as Harbour Mineplanter. In 1957 she was rated Controlled Minelayer, NPC 114. Redesignated as Cable Layer (ALC) in 1959, and as Research Vessel (AGOR) in 1964.

BLUETHROAT　　　　　　　　　　　*Official*

SACKVILLE (AGOR 113)

Displacement, tons	1 085 standard; 1 350 full load
Dimensions, feet	190 pp; 205 oa × 33 × 14·5
Main engines	Triple expansion; 2 750 ihp = 16 knots
Boilers	2 SE

Built by St. John Dry Dock Co, NB. Launched an 15 May 1941. Completed on 30 Dec 1941. "Ex-Flower" class frigate (corvette) converted to loop layer. Employed by Naval Research Laboratories for oceanographic work. Formerly designated AN 113, but rated ALC in 1959, as cable layer under NATO nomenclature. Redesignated Research Vessel (AGOR) in 1964. Photograph in the 1964-65 to 1969-70 editions.

FORT FRANCES (AGOR 170)

Displacement, tons	1 040 standard; 1 335 full load
Dimensions, feet	225 oa × 35 × 11 max
Main engines	Triple expansion; 2 shafts; 2 000 ihp = 16·5 knots
Boilers	2, of 3-drum type

Built by Port Arthur Shipbuilding Co, Ontario. Launched on 30 Oct 1943. Former "Algerine" class Ocean Minesweeper (AM). Redesignated Coastal Escort (FSE) in 1953. Refitted as survey ship and redesignated AGH in 1959. Again redesignated AGOR in 1964. A photograph appears in the 1964-65 to 1966-67 editions. Sister ship *Oshawa*, AGOR 174 was disposed of when *Endeavour* commissioned. *Kapuskasing*, FSE 171, was lent to Dept of Mines and Technical Surveys. *New Liskeard* was discarded on 1 Dec 1969.

OCEANOGRAPHIC RESEARCH VESSELS

QUEST (AGOR 172)

Displacement, tons	2 130 (official figure)
Dimensions, feet	235 oa; 253 wl × 42 × 15·5
Aircraft	Light helicopter
Main engines	Diesel electric; 2 shafts; 2 950 shp = 16 knots max; Bow thruster propeller
Radius, miles	10 060 at 12 knots
Complement	55

Built by Burrard Dry Dock Co, Vancouver for the Naval Research Establishment of the Defence Research Board for acoustic hydrographic and general oceanographic work, in particular as related to anti-submarine warfare. Capable of operating in heavy ice in the company of an icebreaker. A large 5-ton crane is fitted forward so that the jib-head can be lowered to surface level and thus reduce the swing on scientific instruments. Design is slightly enlarged version of *Endeavour* (see below) with similar main engines, speed and range. Construction began in 1967. Launched on 9 July 1968. Completed on 21 Aug 1969. Based at Halifax.

QUEST　　　　　　　　*1970, Canadian Maritime Command, Official*

ENDEAVOUR (AGOR 171)

Displacement, tons	1 560 (official figure)
Dimensions, feet	215 wl; 236 oa × 38·5 × 13
Aircraft	1 light helicopter
Main engines	Diesel electric; 2 shafts; 2 960 shp = 16 knots
Radius, miles	10 000 at 12 knots
Complement	10 officers, 13 scientists, 25 ratings (plus helicopter pilot and engineer)

A naval research ship specifically designed to meet the scientific requirements for undertaking programmes in anti-submarine research. Flight deck 48 by 31 feet. Stiffened for operating in ice-covered areas. Designed by the Director General Ships and the Pacific Naval Laboratory. Built by Yarrows Ltd, Esquimalt, BC. Contract let in Nov 1963. Accepted for service on 9 Mar 1965. She is able to turn in 2·5 times her own length. Her crowsnest is fitted with engine and steering controls for navigation in ice. A bulbous bow reduces pitch and she has anti-roll tanks. Two 9-ton Austin-Weston telescopic cranes are fitted. There are two oceanographical winches each holding 5 000 fathoms of 5·16 in wire, two bathythermograph winches and a deep-sea anchoring and coring winch. She has acoustic insulation in her machinery spaces.

ENDEAVOUR　　　　　　　　*1970, Canadian Maritime Command, Official*

LAYMORE (AGOR 516)

Measurement, tons	560 gross, 262 net
Dimensions, feet	176·5 × 32 × 8
Main engines	GM diesels; 1 000 bhp = 10·8 knots

Former coastal supply vessel, rated as fleet auxiliary and designated AKS. Converted to research vessel 2 Aug 1965 to Mar 1966 and reclassified AGOR. Her original sister ship *Eastore* was sold on 30 July 1964.

LAYMORE　　　　　　　　*1971, Canadian Forces, Official*

COASTAL MINESWEEPERS (MCB)
6 "BAY" CLASS

Name	No.	Builders	Laid down	Launched	Completed
CHALEUR	164	Marine Industries	20 Feb 56	17 Nov 56	12 Sep 57
CHIGNECTO	160	Geo. T. Davie	25 Oct 55	26 Feb 57	1 Aug 57
COWICHAN	162	Yarrows	10 July 56	26 Feb 57	19 Dec 57
FUNDY	159	Davie Shipbuilding	7 Mar 55	14 June 56	27 Nov 56
MIRAMICHI	163	Victoria Machinery	2 Feb 56	22 Feb 57	28 Oct 57
THUNDER	161	Port Arthur	1 Sep 55	27 Oct 56	3 Oct 57

Displacement, tons	390 standard ; 412 full load
Dimensions, feet	140·0 pp ; 152·0 oa × 28·0 × 7·0 aft
Guns	1—40 mm AA
Main engines	2 GM V-12 diesels ; 2 shafts ; 2 400 bhp = 16 knots
Oil fuel, tons	52
Range, miles	4 500 at 11 knots
Complement	38 (3 officers, 35 ratings)

Extensively built of aluminium, including frames and decks. There were originally 14 vessels of this class. Named after Canadian straits and bays. Designation changed from AMC to MCB in 1954. *Chaleur, Chignecto, Cowichan* and *Miramichi* are employed as training ships, *Thunder* and *Fundy* commissioned for midshipman training in summer 1970. A photograph of *Gaspe* appears in the 1954-55 to 1957-58 editions. and of *Miramichi* in the 1958-59 to 1968-69 editions.

TRANSFERS. *Chaleur* (144), *Chignecto* (156), *Cowichan* (147), *Fundy* (145), *Miramichi* (150), and *Thunder* (153), of this class were transferred to the French Navy in 1954 ; but six more of the same class with the same names were built for the Royal Canadian Navy to replace those transferred. *Comax* (146), *Gaspe* (143), *Trinity* (157), and *Ungava* (148) of this class were transferred to the Turkish Navy in 1958.

Fortune, James Bay, Quinte and *Resolute* were declared surplus in 1965. *Fortune* (renamed *Offshore*) and *James Bay* were sold commercially for oil exploration.

CHALEUR   *1969, Canadian Maritime Command, Official* .

GATE VESSELS (YMG)
4 "PORTE" CLASS

Name	No.	Builders	Laid down	Launched	Completed
PORTE DE LA REINE	184	Victory Machinery	4 Mar 51	28 Dec 51	19 Sep 52
PORTE QUEBEC	185	Burrard Dry Dock	15 Feb 51	28 Aug 51	7 Oct 52
PORTE ST. JEAN	180	Geo. T. Davie	16 May 50	21 Nov 50	4 June52
PORTE ST. LOUIS	183	Geo. T. Davie	21 Mar 51	22 July 52	28 Aug 52

Displacement, tons	429 full load
Dimensions, feet	125·5 × 26·3 × 13
Guns	1—40 mm AA
Main engines	Diesel ; A/C Electric ; 1 shaft ; 600 bhp = 11 knots
Complement	3 officers ; 20 ratings

Of trawler design. Multi-purpose vessels used for operating gates in A/S booms, fleet auxiliaries, anti-submarine netlayers for entrances to defended harbours. Can be fitted for minesweeping. Designation changed from YNG to YMG in 1954. All four used during summer for training Reserves. *Port Dauphine* was taken over by the Coast Gurad. Photographs of *Porte St. Jean* appear in the 1952-53 to 1960-61 and 1962-63 to 1965-66 editions, of *Porte Quebec* in the 1961-62 edition, of *Porte St. Louis* in the 1966-67 to 1970-71 editions.

PORTE DE LA REINE   *1971, Canadian Forces, Official*

ANTI-SUBMARINE HYDROFOIL (FHE)
BRAS D'OR (FHE 400)

Displacement, tons	180
Dimensions, feet	150·8 oa × 21·5 × 15 (hull depth) ; 23 (hull-borne draught) ; 7·5 (60 knots draught) ; foil base 90
Main engines	Pratt & Whitney FT4A—2 gas turbine when foil-borne ; 22 000 shp = 50 to 60 knots
	Davey-Paxman diesel when hull-borne, 2 000 shp = 12 to 15 knots
	P & W. ST-6A gas turbine for hull-borne boost and foil-borne auxiliary power ; 390 shp

De Havilland Aircraft of Canada Ltd, Toronto, designed this prototype all-weather. ocean-going hydrofoil craft. Completion was delayed by fire on 7 Nov 1966. Designated FHE for Fast Hydrofoil Escort. The supercavitating bow foil has a 22·5 ft span and the delayed cavitation main-foil has a 65 ft span. Marine Industries Ltd, Picton, Que, were the sub-contractor for the assembly and outfitting of the vessel, of welded all-aluminium construction. Named *Bras d'Or* in recognition of early work on hydrofoils by Alexander Graham Bell and F. W. Baldwin on Bras d'Or Lake, Cape Breton Island. Photograph showing foils in the 1968-69 edition.

BRAS d'OR   *1969, Canadian Maritime Command, Official*

DISPOSALS

All four ships of the "Bird" class patrol craft, *Blue Heron, Cormorant, Loon* and *Mallard* were declared surplus in 1970 for disposal. Photographs of *Loon* appeared in the 1956 57 to 1963 64 editions and of *Cormorant* in the 1964-65 to 1969-70 editions.

DIVING TENDERS

YMT 11   **YMT 12**

Displacement, tons	110
Dimensions, feet	88 × 20 × 4·8 mean
Main engines	GM diesels ; 228 bhp = 10·75 knots

YMT 11 was completed in Jan 1962 and YMT 12 on 7 Aug 1963, both by Ferguson Industries Ltd, Picton, Nova Scotia. They can dive four men at a time to a depth of 250 feet and are fitted with a recompression chamber. A photograph of YMT 11 appears in the 1962-63 edition. There are small diving tenders YMT 6, YMT 8, YMT 9 and YMT 10, 70 tons, 75 × 18·5 × 8·5 feet, 2 diesels 165 bhp, YMT 1 (46 ft) was transferred to the Naval Research Establishment as a yard craft. YMT 3 and YMT 5 were declared surplus and sold in 1963. YMT 2 and YMT 7 are 46-ft. wooden hulled single screw vessels. Two new diving tenders, YSD 1 and YSD 2, entered service in 1965. Also torpedo recovery vessels *Nimpkish*, YMR 120, and *Songhee*, YMR 1. The yacht *Oriole*, QW 3, used for officer cadet training, has been in commission since 1953.

OILERS (AO)
2 "DUN" CLASS

DUNDALK (AOC 50)   **DUNDURN (AOC 502)**

Displacement, tons	950
Dimensions, feet	178·8 × 32·2 × 13
Main engines	Diesel ; 700 bhp = 10 knots

Small vessels designated tankers, and classed as fleet auxiliaries. A photograph of *Dundalk* appears in the 1949-50 to 1959-60 editions.

DUNDURN   *1969, courtesy Mr. G. R. Hooper (Master)*

TUGS

3 "SAINT" CLASS

Name	No.	Laid down	Launched	Completed
SAINT ANTHONY	ATA 531	15 July 1954	2 Nov 1955	22 Feb 1957
SAINT CHARLES	ATA 533	28 Apr 1954	10 July 1956	7 June 1957
SAINT JOHN	ATA 535	1 Dec 1953	14 May 1956	23 Nov 1956

Displacement, tons	840 full load
Dimensions, feet	151·5 × 33 × 17
Guns	2—40 mm Bofors AA
Main engines	Diesel; 1 shaft; 1 920 bhp = 14 knots

Ocean tugs. Authorised under the 1951 Programme. All built by the St. John Dry Dock Co.

SAINT JOHN   1970, Canadian Maritime Command, Official

3 "TON" CLASS

CLIFTON (ATA 529)   **HEATHERTON** (ATA 527)   **RIVERTON** (ATA 528)

Displacement, tons	462
Dimensions, feet	104 pp; 111·2 oa × 28 × 11
Main engines	Dominion Sulzer diesel; 1 000 bhp = 11 knots
Complement	17

Large harbour tugs. *Clifton* was launched on 31 July 1944. A photograph of *Heatherton* appears in the 1952-53 to 1959-60 editions.

5 "GLEN" CLASS

GLENBROOK   GLENDYNE   GLENEVIS   GLENLIVIT II   GLENSIDE

Dimensions, feet	80 × 20·7 × 7·2 (aft full load)
Main engines	Diesel; 300 bhp = 9 knots

Big harbour tugs. *Glenlivit II* is loaned to Halifax Department of Public Works. Hull numbers are YTB 501 503, 502, 504 and 500, respectively. Sister tugs *Glendevon*, Y 505 and *Glendon*, Y 506 were taken out of service on 31 Mar 1964 and sold to commercial interests.

3 "WOOD" CLASS

EASTWOOD   **GREENWOOD**   **OAKWOOD**

Dimensions, feet	60 oa × 16 × 5 (aft full load)
Main engines	250 hp = 10 knots

Medium harbour tugs. Used as A/S Target Towing Vessels. Launched 1944. Hull numbers are YMT 550, 551 and 554 respectively. *Wildwood* was stricken from the Navy List in 1959. *Lakewood* was declared surplus in 1966. Other medium harbour tugs are:

FT1, FT2. Employed as fire tugs, Hull numbers YMT 556 and 557 respectively. Sister fire tug FT3, YMT 558, was taken out of service on 31 Mar 1964 and transferred to Dept of Public Works, St. John's Newfoundland.

13 "VILLE" CLASS

ADAMSVILLE	**LISTERVILLE**	**MARYSVILLE**	**PARKSVILLE**
BEAMSVILLE	**LOGANVILLE**	**MERRICKVILLE**	**PLAINSVILLE**
LAWRENCEVILLE	**MANNVILLE**	**OTTERVILLE**	**QUEENSVILLE**
			YOUVILLE

Dimensions, feet	40 × 10·5 × 4·8
Main engines	Diesel; 1 shaft; 150 bhp

Small harbour tugs. Majority employed on towing duties at Esquimalt and Halifax; Hull numbers are YTS 582, 583, 584, 578, 589, 577, 585, 581, 590, 579, 587, 586 and 588 respectively. Sister tugs *Colville*, Y 576, and *Eckville*, Y 580, were taken out of service on 31 Mar 1964 for disposal. The small harbour tugs *Shoveller* and *Valliant* Nos YTS 591 and 575, were disposed of in 1966.

The diving depot ship *Granby*, YMT 180, originally a "Bangor" (Diesel) class fleet minesweeper (AM), redesignated coastal escort (FSE) in 1953 and clearance diving depot ship (YMT) in 1959 after having been employed as a submarine rescue vessel, was declared surplus in 1967 and replaced by the ocean escort *Victoriaville*, converted to a diving depot ship and renamed *Granby* (see previous page).

The supply vessel *Seatari* (ex-*Malahat*), AKS 514, was officially deleted from the list in 1969.

R.C.M.P. MARINE DIVISION

1 "FORT" CLASS

FORT STEELE MP 34

Displacement, tons	85
Dimensions, feet	110 wl; 118 oa × 21 ×` 7
Main engines	Two Paxman Ventura 12 YJCM diesels; 2 shafts; Kamewa controllable pitch propellers; 2 800 bhp = over 18 knots.
Complement	16

Completed by Canadian Shipbuilding & Engineering Ltd in Nov 1958. Patrol craft on the east coast. Built of steel with aluminium superstructure. Twin rudders.

The large "Commissioner" class patrol vessel of the corvette type, *Wood*, MP 17, was transferred from the Royal Canadian Mounted Police Division to the Ministry of Transport in 1971, see Coast Guard, page 54.

1 "BIRD" CLASS

VICTORIA MP 31

Displacement, tons	66 full load
Dimensions, feet	92 × 17 × 5·3
Main engines	2 diesels; 1 200 bhp = 14 knots
Complement	20

Victoria was built for the RCMP by Yarrows Limited, Victoria. Completed in Dec 1955. She was a steel copy of the wooden "Bird" class inshore patrol vessels built for the Navy.

VICTORIA   1971, Official

2 75 ft "DETACHMENT" CLASS

STAND OFF   **NICHOLSON**

Displacement, tons	55
Dimensions, feet	75 oa × 17 × 6·5
Main engines	2 diesel; 1 400 bhp = 16 knots
Complement	5

Both of wood construction. Both built by Smith & Rhuland, Lunenburg NS and completed in 1967 and 1968 respectively. Intended for service on the Atlantic coast.

13 65 ft "DETACHMENT" CLASS

ACADIAN	**ALERT**	**CAPTOR**	**INTERCEPTOR**	**TAHSIS**
ADVERSUS	**BURIN**	**DETECTOR**	**MASSET**	**TOFINO**
		GANGES	**NANAIMO**	**WESTVIEW**

Displacement, tons	48
Dimensions, feet	65 × 15 × 4
Main engines	1 Cummins diesel; 1 shaft; 410 bhp = 12 knots

Coastal patrol police boats built for service on the east and west coasts.

2 "TURBOJET" TYPE

LITTLE BOW II   **SIDNEY**

Displacement, tons	27
Dimensions, feet	55 × 14 × 4
Main engines	2 General Motors turbojet engines; 600 bhp = 16 knots

These turbojet craft were built as an experiment and no additions are contemplated.

6 "DETACHMENT" CLASS (GREAT LAKES)

CARNDUFF II	**CUTKNIFE II**	**SHAUNAVON II**
CHILCOOT II	**MOOSOMIN II**	**TAGISH II**

Dimensions, feet	50 × 15 × 3
Main engines	2 diesel engines; 600 bhp = over 17 knots

A class of small, fast patrol craft built for service on the Great Lakes.
There are also *Advance, Athabasca, Beaver, Fort Erie, Fort Francis II, Kenora III, Sorel* and *Valleyfield*, 26 to 36 feet in length with petrol motors, speeds up to 27 knots. Six are on the Great Lakes and four on the West Coast. In addition to these there are also the following, *Battleford, Slide Out, Dauphine, Lac La Ronge, Moose Jaw, Bruce* and *Reliance*.

CANADIAN COAST GUARD

Administration

Minister of Transport:
Hon Don Jamieson PC, MP

Deputy Minister of Transport:
Mr. O. G. Stoner, BA

Administrator, Marine Transportation Administration:
Dr. P. Camu

Director Marine Operations (Canadian Coast Guard):
Rear Admiral Anthony H. G. Storrs, DSC & Bar, CD, RCN (Ret'd)

Establishment

In January 1962 all ships owned and operated by the Federal Department of Transport with the exception of pilotage and canal craft, were amalgamated into the Canadian Coast Guard, a civilian service.

Ships

The Canadian Coast Guard is comprised 150 vessels of all types (including 61 barges), of which about 60 are of watch-keeping size. They operate in Canadian waters from the Great Lakes to the northernmost reaches of the Arctic Archipelago.

There are heavy icebreakers, icebreaking ships for tending buoys and lighthouses, marine survey craft, weather-oceanographic ships, and many specialized vessels for tasks such as search and rescue, cable lifting and repair, marine research and shallow-draft operations in areas such as the Mackenzie River system and some parts of the Arctic.

The Ship Building and Heavy Equipment Branch of the Department of Defence Productions arranges for the design, construction and repair of Coast Guard ships and also provides this service for a number of other Canadian Government departments.

Principal bases for the ships are the department's 11 District offices, located at—St. John's, Newfoundland; Dartmouth, N.S.; Saint John, N.B.; Charlottetown, P.E.I.; Quebec and Sorel, Que.; Prescott and Parry Sound, Ont.; Victoria and Prince Rupert, B.C.; and at Hay River, on Great Slave Lake.

Missions

The Canadian Coast Guard carries out the following missions:
1. Icebreaking and Escort. Icebreaking is carried out in the Gulf of St. Lawrence and River St. Lawrence and the Great Lakes in winter to assist shipping and for flood control, and in Arctic waters in summer.
2. Icebreaker-Aids to Navigation Tenders. Installation, supply and maintenance of fixed and floating aids-to-navigation in Canadian waters.

3. Organize and provide icebreaker support and some cargo vessels for the annual Northern sealift which supplies bases and settlements in the Canadian Arctic and Hudson Bay.
4. Provide and operate special patrol cutters and lifeboats for marine search and rescue.
5. Provide and operate survey and sounding vessels for the St. Lawrence River Ship Channel.
6. Provide and operate weatherships for Ocean Station "Papa" in the Pacific.
7. Provide and operate vessel for the repairing of undersea cables.
8. Provide and operate vessel for environmental research.
9. Provide and operate vessel for Marine Traffic Control on the St. Lawrence river.
10. Operate a small fleet of aircraft primarily for aids to navigation ice reconnaissance, and pollution control work.

Fleet Strength

Heavy Icebreakers	5
Medium Icebreakers	1
Medium Icebreaking aids to Navigation Vessels	8
Light icebreaking aids to navigation vessels	5 (+1 reserve)
Ice strengthened aids to navigation vessels	4
Aids-to-navigation tenders	12 (+2 reserve)
Agency tenders and workboats	10
Northern supply vessels	4
Sealift stevedore depot vessel	1
Search and Rescue—Offshore patrol cutters	6
Great Lakes patrol cutters	3
Shore-based hovercraft	1
Shore-based lifeboats	6
Shore-based launches	6
St. Lawrence light icebreaking survey and sounding vessel	1
St. Lawrence ship channel survey and sounding vessels	6
Weather ships for ocean station Papa in the Pacific	2
Cable repair ship	1
Environmental research vessel	1
St. Lawrence River marine traffic control vessel	1
Training vessels (inactive)	2
Total	**86 (+3 reserves)**

Aircraft

Fixed wing	1
Helicopters	25
Total	**26**

WEATHER SHIPS

VANCOUVER

1970, Canadian Coast Guard, Official

Name	Laid down	Launched	Completed
QUADRA	Feb 1965	4 July 1966	Mar 1967
VANCOUVER	Mar 1964	29 June 1965	4 July 1966

Displacement, tons	5 600 full load
Dimensions, feet	361·2 pp; 404·2 oa × 50 × 17·5
Aircraft	1 helicopter
Main engines	Turbo-electric; 2 shafts; 7 500 shp = 18 knots.
Boilers	2 automatic Babcock & Wilcox D type
Range, miles	8 400 at 14 knots
Complement	96

New type, turbo-electric twin screw weather and oceanographic vessels for Pacific Ocean service. Both built by Burrard Drydock Limited, North Vancouver, B.C. They replace the Coast Guard weather ships, former frigates, which have been in service for many years, on loan from the Royal Canadian Navy, for Ocean Station "Papa" 900 miles west of the British Colombia coast. They have bow water jet reaction system to assist steering at slow speeds. Flume stabilization systems are fitted. They are turbo-electric powered, with oil-fired boilers to provide the quiet operation needed for vessels housing much scientific equipment. Their complement includes 15 technical officers such as meteorologists, oceanographers and electronics technicians.

QUADRA

1969, Canadian Coast Guard, Official

DISPOSALS
The three former "River" class frigates, *St. Catherines, Stonetown* and *St Stephen,* acquired by the Department of Transport from the Royal Canadian Navy and converted into weather ships in 1950, were taken out of service in 1968 and sold in 1969.

CABLE REPAIR SHIPS

JOHN CABOT

Displacement, tons	6 375 full load
Dimensions, feet	313·3 × 60 × 21·5
Aircraft	1 helicopter
Main engines	Diesel-electric; 2 shafts; 9 000 shp = 15 knots
Range, miles	10 000 at 12 knots
Complement	85 officers and men

Combination cable repair ship and icebreaker. Built by Canadian Vickers Limited, Montreal. Laid down in May 1963, launched on 15 Apr 1964 and completed in July 1965. Designed to repair and lay cable over the bow only. For use in East Coast and Arctic waters. Bow water jet reaction manoeuvring system, heeling tanks and Flume stabilisation system. Three circular storage holds handle a total of 400 miles of submarine cable. Personnel include technicians and helicopter pilots, the ship being designed for use with that type of aircraft.

JOHN CABOT   1970, Canadian Coast Guard, Official

NORTHERN SUPPLY VESSELS

4 FORMER TANK LANDING CRAFT (LCT 8s)

EIDER   PUFFIN   RAVEN   SKUA

Measurement, tons	1 083 to 1 104 gross
Dimensions, feet	225 pp; 231·2 oa × 38 × 3
Main engines	Diesel; 1 000 shp = 9 knots

Converted LCT (8)s, acquired from Great Britain in 1957-61. Built by Harland & Wolff, Belfast (Puffin and Raven) and Sir Wm. Arrol & Co Ltd, Glasgow (Eider). All completed in 1946.
Sister ship Nanook, officially rated as a Northern Service Depot Ship, was disposed of in 1969. Auk and Gannet were declared for disposal in 1970. Skua is reclassified as an Aid to Navigation vessel.

GANNET   1970, Canadian Coast Guard, Official

SKUA   Canadian Coast Guard, Official

MARMOT   MINK

Displacement, tons	586 full load
Dimensions, feet	187·2 × 33·8 × 4
Main engines	Diesel; 920 shp = 8 knots

Converted LCT (4)s acquired from Great Britain in 1958. Completed in 1944. Formerly officially rated as Steel Landing Craft for Northern Service, now re-rated as Aids to Navigation Tenders, in reserve.

MINK   1963, Canadian Coast Guard, Official

MARMOT unloading on beach   1967, Canadian Coast Guard, Official

ICEBREAKERS

NORMAN MCLEOD ROGERS

Displacement, tons	6 320 full load
Dimensions, feet	295 oa × 62·5 × 20
Aircraft	1 helicopter
Landing craft	2
Main engines	4 diesels and 2 gas turbines powering 2 electric motors; 2 shafts; 12 000 shp = 15 knots service
Complement	55

A new type of icebreaker for use in the Gulf of St Lawrence and East Coast waters. Built at the yard of Canadian Vickers Limited, Montreal. This is the world's first application of gas turbine electric propulsion for booster power in an icebreaker. Completed in Oct 1969. Officially rated as a Heavy Icebreaker.

NORMAN MCLEOD ROGERS   1970, Canadian Coast Guard, Official

Icebreakers—continued

LOUIS S. ST. LAURENT

Displacement, tons	13 000 full load
Dimensions, feet	366·5 oa 80 × 31
Aircraft	2 helicopters
Main engines	Turbo-electric; 3 shafts; 24 000 shp = 17·75 knots *trials*
Range, miles	16 000 miles at 13 knots cruising speed
Complement	Total accommodations for 216

This new icebreaker for service in the Arctic and the Gulf of St. Lawrence was built at Canadian Vickers Limited, Montreal. She is larger than any of the former Coast Guard icebreakers. This triple screw ship with a steam turbo-electric propulsion system is the world's most powerful non-nuclear powered icebreaker. She has a helicopter hangar below the flight deck, with an elevator to raise the two helicopters to the deck when required. She was launched on 3 Dec 1966 and completed in Oct 1969. She is officially rated as a heavy icebreaker.

LOUIS S. ST. LAURENT   *1971, Canadian Coast Guard, Official*

JOHN A. MACDONALD

Displacement, tons	9 160 full load
Measurement, tons	6 186 gross
Dimensions, feet	315 × 70 × 28
Main engines	Diesel-electric; 15 000 shp = 15·5 knots designed

Completed by Davie Shipbuilding Limited, Lauzon, Port Quegec, in Sep 1960. Officially rated as a heavy icebreaker.

JOHN A. MACDONALD   *1971, Canadian Coast Guard, Official*

WOLFE (see top of Col. 2)   *1963, Canadian Coast Guard, Official)*

MONTCALM   WOLFE

Displacement, tons	3 005 full load
Measurement, tons	2 022 gross
Dimensions, feet	220 × 48 × 16
Main engines	Steam reciprocating; 4 000 ihp = 13 knots designed

Wolfe was built by Canadian Vickers Limited, Montreal, and completed in Nov 1959, *Montcalm* was built by Davie Shipbuilding Ltd, Lauzon, P.Q., and completed in June 1957. Officially rated as Medium Icebreaking Aids to Navigation Vessels.

MONTCALM   *1967, Canadian Coast Guard, Official*

CAMSELL

Displacement, tons	3 072 full load
Measurement, tons	2 020 gross
Dimensions, feet	223·5 × 48 × 16
Main engines	Diesel-electric; 4 250 shp = 13 knots designed

Completed by Burrard Dry Dock Company Limited, Vancouver, BC in Oct 1959. Officially rated as Medium Icebreaking Aids to Navigation Vessel.

CAMSELL   *1967, Canadian Coast Guard, Official*

DISPOSAL
The old icebreaker *Saurel* was removed from the Canadian Coast Guard list and disposed of in 1967.

SIR HUMPHREY GILBERT

Displacement, tons	3 000 full load
Measurement, tons	1 930 gross
Dimensions, feet	220 × 48 × 16·3
Main engines	Diesel-electric; 4 250 shp = 13 knots designed

Completed by Davie Shipbuilding Limited, Lauzon, Port Quebec, in June 195? Officially rated as Medium Icebreaking Aids to Navigation Vessel.

SIR HUMPHREY GILBERT   *1970, Canadian Coast Guard, Official*

Icebreakers—*continued*

LABRADOR

Displacement, tons	6 490 full load
Measurement, tons	3 823 gross
Dimensions, feet	269 pp; 290 oa × 63·5 × 29
Aircraft	Provision for 2 helicopters
Main engines	Diesel-electric 10 000 shp = 16 knots designed

Built by Marine Industries Limited, Sorel, Quebec. Ordered in Feb 1949, laid down on 18 Nov 1949, launched on 14 Dec 1951 and completed for the Royal Canadian Navy on 8 July 1954, but transferred to the Department of Transport in Feb 1958. Officially rated as a Heavy Icebreaker. A photograph of *Labrador* as an Arctic Patrol Vessel in the Royal Canadian Nevy appears in the 1966-67 and earlier editions.
When commissioned in the Royal Canadian Navy *Labrador* was rated as Arctic Patrol Vessel, Helicopter Carrier and Icebreaker. Her original designation was AGB, changed to AW 50 in 1954. She was the first naval vessel to traverse the North West Passage and circumnavigate Norht America, when she was Canada's largest and most modern icebreaker. High-tensile steel sides 1·6 inches thick, and heeling tanks. Aircraft hangar and flight deck aft for operating helicopters. Carries two landing craft hangar and flight deck for operating helicopters. Carries two landing craft strengthened to resist ice. Latest navigational devices, and equipped with instruments for hydrography, oceanography, meteorology, cosmic ray research, ice reconnaissance and other scientific purposes. Fitted with Denny Brown stabilisers. Propelling machinery can be controlled from bridge. She was transferred, on loan, to the Department of Transport and subsequently acquired from the Royal Canadian Navy outright. Mounting for two 40 mm guns forward, but guns were removed.

LABRADOR   *1970, Canadian Coast Guard, Official*

d'IBERVILLE

Displacement, tons	9 930 full load
Measurement, tons	5 678 gross
Dimensions, feet	310 × 66·5 × 30·2
Main engines	Steam reciprocating; 10 800 ihp = 15 knots designed

Completed by Davie Shipbuilding Limited, Lauzon, Port Quebec, in May 1953. Officially rated as a Heavy Icebreaker.

d'IBERVILLE   *1967, Canadian Coast Guard, Official*

ERNEST LAPOINTE

Displacement, tons	1 675 full load
Measurement, tons	1 179 gross
Dimensions, feet	184 × 36 × 15·5
Main engines	Steam reciprocating; 2 000 ihp = 13 knots designed

Completed by Davie Shipbuilding Limited, Lauzon, Port Quebec, in Feb 1941. Officially rated as St. Lawrence Ship Channel Icebreaking Survey and Sounding Vessel.

ERNEST LAPOINTE   *1971, Canadian Coast Guard, Official*

N. B. McLEAN

Displacement, tons	5 034 full load
Measurement, tons	3 254 gross
Dimensions, feet	277 × 60·5 × 19·6
Main engines	Steam reciprocating; 6 500 ihp = 13 knots max

Completed by Halifax Shipyards, Limited, Halifax, NS, in 1930. Officially rated as Medium Icebreaker.

GRIFFON

Displacement, tons	3 096
Dimensions, feet	234 × 49 × 15·5
Main engines	Diesel; 4 000 bhp; 13·5 knots designed

Completed in Dec 1970. Officially rated as a Medium Icebreaking Aids to Navigation Vessel.

J. E. BERNIER   *1971, Canadian Coast Guard, Official*

J. E. BERNIER

Displacement, tons	3 096
Dimensions, feet	231 × 49 × 16
Aircraft	1 helicopter
Main engines	Diesel Electric; 4 250 bhp = 13·5 knots (trial speed)

Built by Davie Shipbuilding Co, Ltd, Lauzon, Quebec; completed in Aug 1967. Officially rated as Medium Icebreaking Aids to Navigation Vessel.

SIMCOE

Displacement, tons	1 300 full load
Dimensions, feet	179·5 × 38 × 12
Main engines	Diesel-electric; 2 000 shp = 12 knots

Completed by Canadian Vickers in 1962. Photograph in the 1963-64 edition. Officially rated as Ice Strengthened Aids to Navigation Vessel.

SIMON FRASER   TUPPER

Displacement, tons	1 876 full load
Measurement, tons	1 357 gross
Dimensions, feet	204·5 × 42 × 14
Main engines	Diesel-electric; 2 900 shp = 13·5 knots designed

Simon Fraser was completed by Burrard Dry Dock Company Limited, N. Vancouver in Feb 1960 and *Tupper* by Marine Industries Limited, Sorel, Quebec in Dec 1959. Both officially rated as Light Icebreaking Aids to Naviagtion Vessels.

THOMAS CARLETON   *1970, Canadian Coast Guard, Official*

THOMAS CARLETON

Displacement, tons	1 532 full load
Dimensions, feet	180 × 42 × 13
Main engines	Diesel; 2 000 bhp = 12 knots designed

Built by Saint John Dry Dock Limited, Saint John, NB. Completed in 1960. Officially rated as a Light Icebreaking Aids to Navigation Vessel.

Icebreakers—continued

ALEXANDER HENRY

Displacement, tons	2 497 full load
Measurement, tons	1 647 gross
Dimensions, feet	210 × 43·5 × 16
Main engines	Diesel; 3 550 bhp = 13 knots designed

Built by Port Arthur Shipbuilding Limited, Port Arthur. Completed in July 1959. Officially rated as a Medium Icebreaking Aids to Navigation Vessel.

SIR WILLIAM ALEXANDER   *1970, Canadian Coast Guard, Official*

SIR WILLIAM ALEXANDER

Displacement, tons	3 555 full load
Measurement, tons	2 153 gross
Dimensions, feet	227·5 × 45 × 17·5
Main engines	Diesel electric; 4 250 shp = 15 knots designed

Built by Halifax Shipyards, Limited, Halifax. Completed in June 1959. Equipped with Flume Stabilisation System. Officially rated as a Medium Icebreaking Aids to Navigation Vessel.

WALTER E. FOSTER   *1970, Canadian Coast Guard, Official*

WALTER E. FOSTER

Displacement, tons	2 715 full load
Measurement, tons	1 672 gross
Dimensions, feet	229·2 × 42·5 × 16
Main engines	Steam reciprocating; 2 000 ihp = 12·5 knots designed

Built by Canadian Vickers, Limited, Montreal. Completed in Dec 1954. Officially rated as a Light Icebreaking Aids to Navigation Vessel.

EDWARD CORNWALLIS   *1971, Canadian Coast Guard, Official*

EDWARD CORNWALLIS

Displacement, tons	3 700 full load
Measurement, tons	1 965 gross
Dimensions, feet	259 × 43·5 × 18
Main engines	Steam reciprocating; 2 800 ihp = 13·5 knots designed

Built by Canadian Vickers Limited, Montreal. Completed in Dec 1949. Photograph in the 1963-64 to 1965-66 editions. In reserve. Officially rated as a Light Icebreaking Aide to Navigation Vessel.

DISPOSAL
The Arctic Service Vessel *C. D. Howe* was officially deleted from the Coast Guard List in 1969. Photograph in the 1969-70 edition.

DEPOT SHIP

NARWHAL

Measurement, tons	2 064 gross
Dimensions, feet	251·5 × 42·0 × 12·0
Main engines	Diesel; 2 000 bhp
Complement	32

Built by Canadian Vickers, Montreal. Completed in July 1963. Officially rated as Sealift Stevedore Depot Vessel. Cruising range: 9 200 miles.

NARWHAL   *1970, Canadian Coast Guard, Official*

SEARCH AND RESCUE CUTTERS

ALERT

Displacement, tons	2 025
Dimensions, feet	234·3 × 39·9 × 15·1
Aircraft	1 helicopter
Main engines	Diesel Electric; 7 716 hp = 18·75 knots
Radius, miles	6 000

Ordered from Davie Ship building Ltd, Lauzon Feb 1967. For offshore duties.

ALERT   *1971, Canadian Coast Guard, Official*

RACER   RALLY   RAPID   READY   RELAY   RIDER

Measurement, tons	153 gross
Dimensions, feet	95·2 × 20 × 6·5
Main engines	Diesel; 2 400 bhp = 20 knots *designed*

Built by Yarrows Ltd, Esquimalt, BC; Davie Shipbuilding Ltd, Lauzon, PQ; Ferguson Industries, Picton, NS; Burrard Dry Dock, Vancouver; and Kingston Shipyard, respectively. All completed in 1963. A photograph of *Relay* (now Marine Traffic Control Cutter) appears in the 1964-65 to 1968-69 editions. *Rider*, completed for the Dept of Fisheries, was taken over by the Coast Guard in Mar 1969.

RACER   *1969, Canadian Coast Guard, Official*

SPINDRIFT   SPRAY   SPUME

Measurement, tons	57 gross
Dimensions, feet	70 × 16·8 × 4·7
Main engines	2 diesels; 1 500 bhp = 19 knots *designed*

Built by Cliff Richardson Boats Ltd, Meaford, Ont; J. J. Taylor & Sons, Ltd, Toronto; and Grew Ltd, Penetanguishene, Ont, respectively. Completed in 1963-64 for service on Great Lakes Patrol.

SPINDRIFT   *1966, Canadian Coast Guard, Official*

SUPPLY VESSELS

BARTLETT   *1971, Canadian Coast Guard, Official*

BARTLETT   PROVO WALLIS

Displacement, tons	1 620
Dimensions, feet	189·3 × 42·5 × 12·5
Engines	Diesel; 1 760 bhp = 12 knots

In service since 1970. Classed as Ice Strengthened Aids to Navigation Vessels.

MONTMORENCY

Displacement, tons	1 006 full load
Measurement, tons	750 gross
Dimensions, feet	163 × 34 × 11
Main engines	Diesel; 1 200 bhp

Built by Davie Shipbuilding Limited, Lauzon, Port Quebec. Completed in Aug 1957. Officially rated as an Ice Strengthened Aids to Navigation Vessel. A photograph of *Montmorency* appears in the 1963-64 to 1968-69 editions.

MONTMAGNY   *1970, Canadian Coast Guard, Official*

MONTMAGNY

Displacement, tons	565 full load
Dimensions, feet	148·0 × 29·0 × 8·0
Main engines	Diesels; 1 000 bhp

Built by Russel Bros. Owen Sound, Ont. Completed in May 1963.

VERENDRYE

Displacement, tons	400 full load
Dimensions, feet	125·0 × 26·0 × 7·0
Main engines	Diesels; 760 bhp

297 tons gross. Built by Geo. T. Davie & Sons, Ltd, Lauzon. Completed in Oct 1959.

SIR JAMES DOUGLAS   *1970, Canadian Coast Guard, Official*

ALEXANDER MACKENZIE   SIR JAMES DOUGLAS

Displacement, tons	720 full load
Dimensions, feet	150·0 × 30·0 × 10·3
Main engines	Diesels; 1 000 bhp

564 tons gross. Built by Burrard Dry Dock Vancouver and completed 1950 and Nov 1956 respectively. These two, and *Montmagny* and *Verendrye* are officially rated as Aids to Navigation Tenders.

PATROL VESSEL

WOOD Ex-MP 17

Displacement, tons	600 standard
Dimensions, feet	178 oa × 29 × 9·2
Main engines	2 Fairbanks-Morse diesels; 2 shafts; 2 660 bhp = 16 knots
Complement	60 as RCMP vessel

Corvette type. Built by Geo. T. Davie and Sons Ltd, Lauzon, Levis, Quebec. Completed in July 1958. Used for patrol on the east coast of Canada, this ship is built of steel, strengthened against ice, with aluminium superstructure. Transferred from the Royal Canadian Mounted Police Marine Division to the Ministry of Transport in 1971.

WOOD   *1966, Director of Marine Services, Official*

SURVEY AND SOUNDING VESSELS

VILLE MARIE

Displacement, tons	493 full load
Dimensions, feet	134·0 × 28·0 × 9·5
Main engines	Diesel electric; 1 000 hp

BEAUFORT

Displacement, tons	776 full load
Dimensions, feet	167·5 × 24·0 × 9·0
Main engines	Diesels; 1 280 bhp

NICOLET

Displacement, tons	935 full load
Dimensions, feet	166·5 × 35·0 × 9·6
Main engines	Diesels; 1 350 bhp

DETECTOR

Displacement, tons	584 full load
Dimensions, feet	140·0 × 35·0 × 10·0
Main engines	Steam reciprocating

Completed in 1915. *Beaufort* and *Ville Marie* were completed in 1960. There are also two smaller vessels *Glenada* and *Jean Bourdon* for the St. Lawrence Ship Channel.

ENVIRONMENTAL RESEARCH VESSEL

PORTE DAUPHINE   *1970, Canadian Coast Guard, Official*

PORTE DAUPHINE

Displacement, tons	447
Dimensions, feet	119·3 × 25 × 11·3
Main engines	Diesel; 1 shaft; 600 bhp = 12·5 knots

Former gate vessel of the "Porte" class in the Royal Canadian Navy, taken over in 1958.

DUMIT   ECKALOO   MISKANAW   TEMBAH

Four vessels to assist navigation in Mackenzie River operations. Small tug/buoy tender type.

MALLARD   MOORHEN

Shore based craft: For search and rescue and patrol duties: Six lifeboats (CG 101-106), six launches (*Mallard, Moorhen*, CG 110-113) and one Hovercraft (CG 021).

DISPOSALS
Supply vessels: *Estevan* was for disposal in 1970, *Brant* deleted from list in 1967 and *Chesterfield* in 1968, *Grenville* sank in St. Lawrence River in Dec 1968 due to ice action.

CEYLON

Administration

The Royal Ceylon Navy was formed on 9 Dec 1950 when the Navy Act was proclaimed.

Captain of the Navy:
Commodore D. V. Hunter

Diplomatic Representation

Services Attaché in London:
Withdrawn from 1 November 1970

Naval Base

The Naval Base is established at Trincomalee, which was a British base from 1795 until 1957.

Strength of the Fleet

1 Frigate	27 Patrol Boats
1 Hydrofoil Craft	1 Tug

Personnel

1971: 1 980 (160 officers and 1 820 sailors)

Mercantile Marine

Lloyd's Register of Shipping:
26 vessels of 10 039 tons gross

FRIGATE

Name	No.	Builders	Launched
GAJABAHU (ex-*Misnak*, ex-HMCS *Hallowell*)	F 232	Canadian Vickers Ltd, Montreal	8 Aug 1944

1 Ex-CANADIAN "RIVER" CLASS

Displacement, tons	1 445 standard; 2 360 full load
Length, feet (*metres*)	283 (*86·3*) pp; 295·5 (*90·1*) wl; 310·5 (*91·9*) oa
Beam, feet (*metres*)	36·5 (*11·1*)
Draught, feet (*metres*)	13·8 (*4·2*)
Guns, surface	1—4 ln (*102 mm*)
Guns, AA	3—40 mm
Boilers	2 three-drum type
Main engines	Triple expansion; 5 500 ihp; 2 shafts
Speed, knots	20
Radius, miles	6 000 at 12 knots
Oil fuel, tons	585
Complement	160

Acquired by Israel in 1950 and sold by Israel to Ceylon in 1959. Guns above replaced 3—4·7 inch, 8—20 mm in 1965. Sister ship *Mahasena* (ex-*Mivtakh*, ex-Canadian *Violetta*, ex-HMCS *Orkney*) was sold early in June 1964 to a Hong Kong shipbreaker.

GAJABAHU   *1971, Royal Ceylon Navy Official*

PATROL BOATS

21 THORNYCROFT TYPE

Displacement, tons	15
Dimensions, feet	45·5 × 12 × 3
Main engines	2 boats: Thornycroft K6SMI engines; 500 bhp = 25 knots
	7 boats: General Motors 6-71 Series; 560 bhp = 25 knots

Fast twin screw motor launches built by Thornycroft (Malaysia) Limited in Singapore. The hulls are of hard chine type with double skin teak planking. Equipped with radar, radio, searchlight etc. Two ordered in 1965 and completed in 1966. Seven ordered in 1966 and completed in 1967. 12 more assembled in Ceylon and completed by Sep 1968. A photograph of PC 97 appears in the 1967-68 to 1969-70 editions

SERUWA   *1971, Royal Ceylon Navy, Official*

1 SHORT HYDROFOIL TYPE

Dimensions, feet	22·2 × 9·9 hull; 10·2 oa. Depth over side moulded: 3; Draught at anchor: 3·7; Draught at speed: 1·7, official figures.
Main engines	2 Volvo Penta Aquamatic 100 hp engines. Total 200 hp = 40 knots

A short type of hydrofoil craft added to the Royal Ceylon Navy List in 1964.

PC 102   *1970, Royal Ceylon Navy, Official*

HANSAYA   LIHINIYA

Displacement, tons	36
Dimensions, feet	63·5 pp; 66 oa × 14 × 4
Main engines	3 General Motors diesels; 450 bhp = 16 knots

"Hansaya" class long patrol boats built at Venice by the Korody Marine Corporation. A photograph of *Lihiniya* appears in the 1967-68 to 1970-71 editions.

HYDROFOIL CRAFT   *1964, Royal Ceylon Navy, Official*

TUG

ALIYA (ex-*Adept*, ex-*Empire Barbara*)

Displacement, tons	503 full load
Dimensions, feet	105 × 26·5 × 12·8
Main engines	Triple expansion; 850 ihp = 10 knots

Built by Cochrane & Sons Ltd, Selby, Yorks, England. Transferred from Great Britain. Decommissioned in 1964 to be sold, but this intention was rescinded. She was recommissioned in 1966 and underwent major refit in 1967.

ESCORT MINESWEEPERS. *Parakrama* (ex-HMS *Pickle*) was sold in June 1964 to a Hong Kong scrapyard and *Vijaya* (ex-HMS *Flyingfish*, ex-*Tillsonburg*) was returned to Britain.

SEAWARD DEFENCE BOAT. *Kotiya* (ex-HMS *Doxford*) sank in Trincomalee Harbour during the cyclone of 22 Dec 1964, and was disposed of after salvaging.

BOOM DEFENCE VESSEL. *Baron* was purchased from Great Britain by the Colombo Port Commission.

HANSAYA   *1971, Royal Ceylon Navy, Official*

DIYAKAWA   KORAWAKKA   SERUWA   TARAWA

Displacement, tons	13
Dimensions, feet	46 pp; 48 oa × 12 × 3
Main engines	2 Foden FD.6 diesels; 240 bhp = 15 knots

Diyakawa and *Korawakka* were rated as harbour launches in June 1970. *Seruwa* and *Tarawa* were rated as hydrographic vessels.

CHILE

Administration	Diplomatic Representation	Strength of the Fleet

Administration

Minister of National Defence:
Sr Alejandro Rios V.

Commander-in-Chief of the Navy:
Admiral Raul Montero

Chief of the Naval Staff:
Rear-Admiral Pablo Weber

Diplomatic Representation

Chief of the Chilean Naval Mission in Great Britain and Naval Attaché in London, Paris, The Hague and Stockholm:
Rear Admiral Adolfo F. Walbaum

Chief of the Chilean Naval Mission in USA and Naval Attaché in Washington:
Rear-Admiral Victor Bunster

Strength of the Fleet

2 Submarines (Diesel Powered)
2 Cruisers
4 Destroyers
4 Escort Destroyers
1 Helicopter Support Ship
4 Torpedo Boats
5 Patrol Vessels
5 Landing Craft
13 Support Ships and Service Craft

New Construction

Two submarines of the British "Oberon" class.
Two frigates of the British "Leander" class.

Personnel

1971: 15 000 (1 000 officers and 14 000 men)

Mercantile Marine

Lloyd's Register of Shipping:
134 vessels of 307 560 tons gross

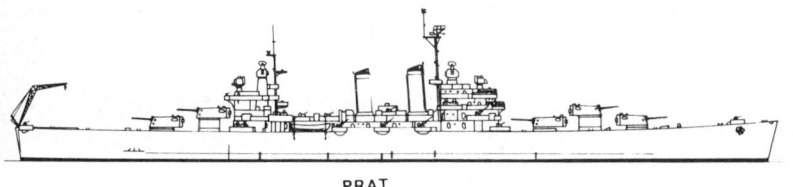

PRAT

RIVEROS

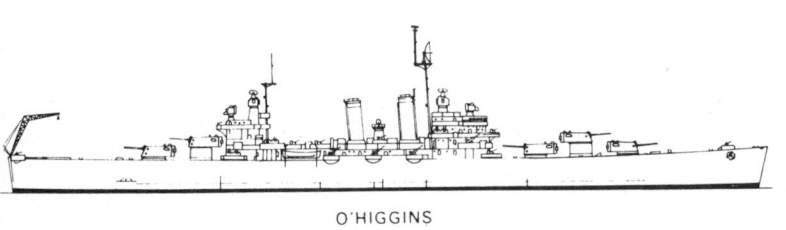

O'HIGGINS

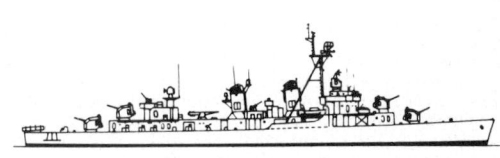

BLANCO ENCALADA, COCHRANE

SUBMARINES

2 NEW CONSTRUCTION

BRITISH "OBERON" CLASS

CONDELL SS 23   **O'BRIEN** SS 22

Displacement, tons	1 610 standard; 2 030 surface; 2 410 submerged
Length, feet (*metres*)	241 (*73·5*) pp (295·2 (*90*) oa
Beam, feet (*metres*)	26·5 (*8·1*)
Draught, feet (*metres*)	18 (*5·5*)
Torpedo tubes	8—21 in (*533 mm*)
Main engines	2 diesels 3 680 bhp 2 electric motors 6 000 shp 2 shafts, electric drive
Speed, knots	12 surface, 17 submerged

Ordered from Scott's Shipbuilding & Engineering Co, Ltd, Greenock, late 1969 as part of a new fleet replacement and modernisation programme.

2 Ex-US "BALAO" CLASS

SIMPSON SS 21 (ex-USS *Spot*, SS 413)
THOMSON SS 20 (ex-USS *Springer*, SS 414)

Displacement, tons	1 526 standard; 1 816 surface; 2 425 submerged
Length, feet (*metres*)	311·6 (*95·0*)
Beam, feet (*metres*)	27 (*8·2*)
Draught, feet (*metres*)	17 (*5·2*)
Torpedo tubes	10—21 in (*533 mm*), 6 bow and 4 stern
Main engines	6.500 hp GM 2-stroke diesels; 4 610 hp electric motors
Speed, knots	20 on surface, 10 submerged
Radius, miles	12 000 at 10 knots
Oil fuel (tons)	300
Complement	80

Both built at Mare Island Navy Yard. *Thomson* launched on 3 Aug 1944, completed on 18 Oct 1944, was transferred at San Francisco, on 23 Jan 1961, and overhauled in USA in 1966 during which a high sail was installed. *Simpson*, launched on 20 May 1944 and completed on 3 Aug 1944, was transferred end of 1961.

THOMSON   *1971, Chilean Navy, Official*

SIMPSON   *1969, Chilean Navy, Official*

O'HIGGINS (see next page)   *1969, Chilean Navy, Official*

CRUISERS (Cruceros)

Name	No.	Builders	Laid down	Launched	Completed
O'HIGGINS (ex-USS *Brooklyn*, CL 40)	CL 02	New York Navy Yard	12 Mar 1935	30 Nov 1936	18 July 1938
PRAT (ex-USS *Nashville*, CL 43)	CL 03	New York S.B. Corp.	24 Jan 1935	2 Oct 1937	25 Nov 1938

2 "PRAT" CLASS
Ex-US "BROOKLYN" CLASS

Displacement, tons	
O'Higgins	9 700 standard ; 13 000 full load
Prat	10 000 standard ; 13 500 full load
Length, feet (*metres*)	608·3 (*185·4*) oa
Beam, feet (*metres*)	69 (*21·0*)
Draught, feet (*metres*)	24 (*7·3*) max
Aircraft	1 Bell helicopter (see *Hangar*)
Guns, surface	15—6 in (*153 mm*) 47 cal (5 triple) ; 8—5 in (*127 mm*) 25 cal (single)
Guns, AA	28—40 mm ; 24—20 mm
Armour, inches (*mm*)	Belt 4 in—1½ in (*102—38*) ; Decks 3 in+2 in (*76+51*) ; Turrets 5 in—3 in (*127—76*) ; C.T. 8 in (*203*)
Boilers	8 Babcock & Wilcox Express type
Main engines	Westinghouse geared turbines 100 000 shp ; 4 shafts
Speed, knots	32·5
Range, miles	14 500 at 15 knots
Oil fuel (tons)	2 100
Complement	888 to 975 (peace)

PRATT   *1971 Chilean Navy, Official*

Former "light" cruisers of the US "Brooklyn" Class. Purchased from the United States in 1951 at a price representing 10 per cent of their original cost (*$37 000 000*) plus the expense of reconditioning them.

HANGAR. The hangar in the hull right aft could accommodate 6 aircraft if necessary together with engine spares and duplicate parts, though 4 aircraft was the normal capacity. The existence of this hangar resulted in a very wide and nearly flat counter and high freeboard aft and also gave the after guns higher command. Above the hangar two catapults were mounted as far outboard as possible, and a revolving crane was placed at the stern extremity overhanging the aircraft hatch.

RADAR
Search: SPS 12. Tactical: SPS 10.

DRAWING. Starboard elevation and plan. Drawn in 1971. Scale: 125 feet = 1 inch (1 : 1 500).

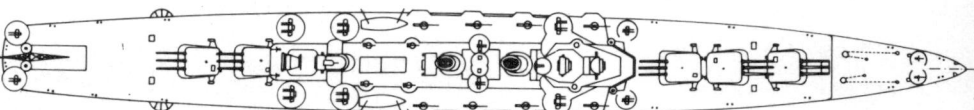

2 "ALMIRANTE" CLASS

Displacement, tons	2 730 standard ; 3 300 full load
Length, feet (*metres*)	402 (*122·5*) oa
Beam, feet (*metres*)	43 (*13·1*)
Draught, feet (*metres*)	13·3 (*4·0*)
Missiles, AA	Quadruple launcher for "Seacat"
Guns, AA	4—4 in (*102 mm*) ; 6—40 mm
A/S	2 Squid 3-barrelled DC mortars
Torpedo tubes	5—21 in (*533 mm*) quintupled
Boilers	2 Babcock & Wilcox
Main engines	Parsons Pametrada geared turbine 54 000 shp ; 2 shafts
Speed, knots	34·5
Range, miles	6 000 at 16 knots
Complement	266

DESTROYERS (Destructores)

Name	No.	Builders	Laid down	Launched	Completed
RIVEROS	DD 18	Vickers-Armstrongs Ltd, Barrow	12 Apr 1957	12 Dec 1958	31 Dec 1960
WILLIAMS	DD 19	Vickers-Armstrongs Ltd, Barrow	20 June 1956	5 May 1958	26 Mar 1960

Ordered in May 1955. Layout and general arrangements are conventional. Bunks fitted for entire crew.

OPERATIONAL. The Operations Room and other similar spaces are air-conditioned. There are twin rudders for exceptional manoeuvrability. The ventilation and heating systems have been designed to suit the Chilean coastline, extending from the tropics to Cape Horn. The latest type of warship radar is fitted, specially developed for these ships to work in conjunction with new fire control systems developed by Vickers-Armstrongs.

GUNNERY. The 4-inch guns are disposed in four single mountings, two superimposed forward and two aft. They are automatic with a range of 12 500 yards (11 400 metres) and an elevation of 75 degrees.

RADAR. Search: Metric wavelength. Tactical: S and X Band. Fire Control: X Band.

WILLIAMS   *1969, Chilean Navy, Official*

MISSILES. British "Seacat" radar controlled short range surface-to-air weapon installations were fitted at the Chilean Navy Yard at Talcahuano in 1964.

ELECTRICAL. The electrical system is on alternating current. Galleys are all electric. There is widespread use of fluorescent lighting. Degaussing cables are fitted.

RIVEROS   *1971, Chilean Navy, Official*

Name
BLANCO ENCALADA (ex-USS *Wadleigh* DD 689)
COCHRANE (ex-USS *Rooks*, DD 804)

2 Ex-US "FLETCHER" CLASS

Displacement, tons	2 100 standard; 2 750 full load
Length, feet (*metres*)	376·5 (*110·5*) oa
Beam, feet (*metres*)	39·5 (*12·0*)
Draught, feet (*metres*)	18 (*5·5*) max
Guns, dual purpose	4—5 in (*127 mm*) 38 cal.
Guns, AA	6—3 in (*76 mm*) 50 cal.
Torpedo tubes	5—21 in (quintupled)
A/S	2 Hedgehogs; 2 side launching torpedo racks; 1 DC rack; 6 "K" DCT
Boilers	4 Babcock & Wilcox
Main engines	2 GE geared turbines 60 000 shp; 2 shafts
Range, miles	6 000 at 15 knots
Oil fuel (tons)	650
Speed, knots	35
Complement	250 (14 officers, 236 men). Accommodation for 324 (24 officers, 300 men)

Former United States destroyers of the "Fletcher" class. Transferred to Chile under the Military Aid Program in 1963.

RADAR
Search.: SPS 6.
Tactical: SPS 10.
Fire Control: X Band.

TRANSFERS. Three more destroyers were scheduled for transfer from the United States Navy to the Chilean Navy under a new transfer law signed by the President of the United States in 1966 whereby the United States was lending or donating warships to friendly nations. The ships were to have been refitted and modernised and adapted to Chilean requirements before transfer to the new flag, but the four escort destroyers of the *Serrano* class were transferred instead.

DISPOSALS
Of the six destroyers of the "Serrano" class, all built by John Thornycroft & Co Ltd, Southampton, in 1927-29, *Hyatt, Orella, Riquelme* and *Serrano* were stricken from the Navy List in Jan 1963, and *Aldea* and *Videla* in 1958.

Destroyers—continued

No.	Builder	Launched	Completed
DD 14	Bath Iron Works Corpn, Bath	7 Aug 1943	19 Oct 1943
DD 15	Todd Pacific Shipyards	6 June 1944	2 Sep 1944

BLANCO ENCALADA   *1970, Chilean Navy, Official*

COCHRANE   *1969, Chilean Navy, Official*

---

2 NEW CONSTRUCTION BRITISH "LEANDER" CLASS

LATORRE PF 06   **LYNCH** PF 07

Displacement, tons	2 500 standard; 3 000 full load
Dimensions, feet	372 oa × 43 × 18 max
Aircraft	1 light helicopter
Missile launchers, AA	1 quadruple "Seacat"
Guns, dual purpose	2—4·5 in (1 twin)
A/S weapons	1 "Limbo" 3-barrel DC mortar
Main engines	2 geared turbines; 30 000 shp
Speed, knots	30

Two frigates of the British "Leander" design have been ordered from Yarrow & Co Ltd, Scotstoun as part of the modernisation programme of the Chilean Navy.

4 DE TRANSPORT TYPE

SERRANO DE 26 (ex-USS *Odum* APD 71, ex-DE 670)
ORELLA DE 27 (ex-USS *Jack C. Robinson* APD 72, ex-DE 671)
RIQUELME DE 28 (ex-USS *Joseph E. Campbell* APD 49, ex-DE 70)
URIBE DD 29 (ex-USS *Daniel Griffin* APD 38, ex-DE 54)

Displacement, tons	1 400 standard; 2 130 full load
Dimensions, feet	300 wl; 306 oa × 37 × 12·6
Guns	1—5 in 38 cal dp; 6—40 mm AA
Main engines	GE turbo-electric; 2 shafts; 12 000 shp = 23·6 knots 2 turbines 6 000 hp each 2 generators 4 500 kW each
Boilers	2 Foster Wheeler "D" type

These former destroyer escort transports were purchased from the USA, transferred at Orange, Texas 25 Nov 1966 (first three) and Norfolk Va 1 Dec 1966 (*Uribe*) They have been modernised for use as escort destroyers.

Of the three ex-Canadian frigates of the "River" class, *Baquedano* (ex-*Esmerelda*, ex-HMCS *Glace Bay*) and *Iquique* (ex-HMCS *Joliette*) both purchased 3 Jan 1946, were sold for scrap 29 Nov 1968. *Covadonga* (ex-HMCS *Seacliffe*, ex-*Megantic*) purchased 3 Mar 1946 was declared surplus in 1968 to be disarmed and sold in due course. Of the three ex-Canadian corvettes of the "Flower" class, *Papudo* (ex-HMCS *Thorlock*), was sold for scrap 17 July 1967, and *Casma* (ex-*Stellarton*) and *Chipana* (ex-*Strathroy*) were sold for scrap 2 July 1969.

FRIGATES

SERRANO   *1969, Chilean Navy, Official*

ORELLA   *1970, Chilean Navy, Official*

PATROL VESSELS

PAPUDO

Displacement, tons	450
Dimensions, feet	170 × 33 × 6
Complement	69 (40 officers, 65 men)

Under construction in Asmar, Talcahuano, Chile. Launched on 7 Jan 1970. Rated as a PC.

	Pennant No.	Launched
LAUTARO (ex-USS *ATA 122*)	PP 62	27 Nov 1942
LIENTUR (ex-USS *ATA 177*)	PP 60	5 June 1944

Displacement, tons	534 standard; 835 full load
Dimensions, feet	134·5 wl; 143 oa × 33 × 13·2 max
Guns	1—3 in AA; 2—20 mm AA
Main engines	GM diesel-electric; 1 500 shp = 12·5 knots
Oil fuel, tons	187
Complement	33

Former United States Navy auxiliary ocean tugs of the ATA type ("Maricopa" class), originally ocean rescue tugs (ATRs), transferred to the Chilean Navy and reclassified as patrol vessels. Launch dates above. Built by Levingstone Shipbuilding Co, Orange, Texas, USA.
LOSS. Sister ship *Leucoton* (ex-USS *ATA 200*) PP 61 ran aground on a sand bank on 15 Aug 1965 and was lost as a result of a heavy coastal storm during salvage operations

LAUTARO   *1969, Chilean Navy, Official*

HELICOPTER SUPPORT SHIP
(*BARCAZA PORTA-HELICOPTERO*)

AGUILA ARV 135 (ex-USS *Aventinus*, ARVE 3, ex-LST 1092)

Displacement, tons	1 625 light; 4 100 full load
Dimensions, feet	316 wl; 328 oa × 50 × 11·2
Guns	8—40 mm AA
Main engines	GM diesels; 2 shafts; 1 800 bhp = 11·6 knots

Former United States aircraft repair ship (engine). Built by American Bridge Co, Ambridge, Pa. Laid down on 8 Jan 1945, launched on 24 Mar 1945, and completed on 19 May 1945. Transferred to the Chilean Navy by USA in 1963 under the Military Aid Program. Also used as destroyer tender and submarine repair ship.
There is also *Mutilla*, ARD.132, former US auxiliary repair dry dock *ARD 32*, leased to Chile on 15 May 1960: 5 200 tons displacement, 492 × 84 × 5·7 to 33·2 feet.

AGUILA   *1971, Chilean Navy, Official*

SURVEY SHIP

YELCHO (ex-USS *Tekesta*, ATF 93) Pennant No. AGS 64

Displacement, tons	1 235 standard; 1 675 full load
Dimensions, feet	195 wl; 205 oa × 38·5 × 15·3 max
Guns	1—3 in; 4—40 mm AA; 2—20 mm AA
Main engines	4 diesels with electric drive; 3 000 bhp = 16·5 knots
Complement	85

Former United States fleet ocean tug of the ATF type ("Apache" class) fitted with powerful pumps and other salvage equipment. *Yelcho* was built by Commercial Iron Works, Portland, Oregon, laid down on 7 Sep 1942, launched on 20 Mar 1943, completed on 16 Aug 1943, and loaned to Chile by the USA on 15 May 1960, having since been employed as Antarctic research ship and surveying vessel. A photograph appears in the 1963-64 to 1970-71 editions.

LOSS Sister ship *Janequeo* (ex-USS *Potawatomi*, ATF 109) AGS 65 sank with all hands on 15 Aug 1965 during the salvage operations on *Leucoton*, see above.

TORPEDO BOATS

FRESIA 81	**GUACOLDA** 80	**QUIDORA** 82	**TEGUALDA** 83

Displacement, tons	134
Dimensions, feet	118·1 × 18·4 × 7·2
Guns	2—40 mm AA
Tubes	4—21 in
Main engines	Diesels; 2 shafts; 4 800 bhp = 32 knots
Radius, miles	1 500 at 15 knots
Complement	20

Built in Spain at Cadiz to German Lürssen design. *Fresia* and *Guacolda* were delivered on 9 Dec 1965 and 30 July 1965, respectively, *Quidora* and *Tegualda* in 1966. A photograph of *Guacolda* appears in the 1968-69 edition, and of *Quidora* in the 1969-70 and 1970-71 editions.

FRESIA   *1971, Chilean Navy, Official*

LANDING CRAFT

ASPIRANTE MOREL LSM 92 (ex-USS *Aloto*, LSM 444)

Displacement, tons	743 standard; 1 095 full load
Dimensions, feet	196·5 wl; 203·5 oa × 34·5 × 7·3
Main engines	Diesel; 2 shafts; 2 800 bhp = 12 knots
Oil fuel (tons)	60
Radius, miles	2 500
Complement	60

Former United States medium landing ship launched in 1945. *Aspirante Morel* (ex-*Aloto*) was leased to Chile on 2 Sep 1960 at Pearl Harbour to replace the older LSM of the name.
Sister ships, *Aspirante Morel* (ex-USS *LSM 417*) was withdrawn from service in 1958 *Guardiamarine Contreras* (ex-USS *LSM 113*) in 1959, and *Aspirante Izaza* (ex-USS *LSM 259*) in 1965. *Aspirante Goicolea* (ex-USS *LSM 400*) withdrawn in 1967

ASPIRANTE MOREL   *1971, Chilean Navy, Official*

ELICURA LSM 90	**OROMPELLO** LSM 94

Displacement, tons	290 light; 750 full load
Dimensions, feet	138 wl; 145 oa × 34 × 12·8
Main engines	Diesels; 2 shafts; 900 bhp = 10·5 knots
Oil fuel (tons)	77
Radius, miles	2 900
Complement	20

Orompello was built for the Chilean Government by Dade Drydock Corporation, Miami, Florida, and transferred on 15 Sep 1964. *Elicura* was built at Talcahuano, launched on 21 April 1967, and handed over on 10 December 1968.

OROMPELLO   *1971, Chilean Navy, Official*

GRUMETE DIAZ LCU 96	**GRUMETE TELLEZ** LCU 93

Displacement, tons	143 to 160 light; 309 to 329 full load
Dimensions, feet	105 wl; 119 oa × 32·7 × 5 max
Main engines	Diesel; 3 shafts; 675 bhp = 10 knots
Oil fuel (tons)	11
Radius, miles	700 at 7 knots
Complement	12

Former United States tank landing craft of the LCT (6) type. *Grumete Diaz* and *Grumete Tellez* are ex-LCU 1396 and ex-LCU 1458. Launched in 1944. Transferred in 1960. *Grumete Bolados* LCU 95 was withdrawn from service it was officially stated in 1971.
Of the six landing craft of the "Cabo Bustos" class, *Cabo Bustos* was converted into a harbour ammunition barge and *Eduardo Llanos* and *Soldado Canaves* were officially withdrawn from service in 1965; and sister ships *Grumete Bolados*, *Grumete Diaz* and *Grumete Tellez* were withdrawn from service in 1959.

SMALL PATROL VESSELS

FUENTEALBA WPC 75   **ODGER** WPC 76

Displacement, tons	215 max
Dimensions, feet	80 × 21 × 9
Guns	1—20 mm AA
Main engines	One Cummins diesel 340 hp = 9 knots
Radius; miles	2 600

Both these vessels were built in Chile by Astilleros Y Maeslronzas De La Armada (ASMAR); *Fuentealba* was completed 22 July 1966 and *Odger* 21 April 1967. A photograph of *Fuentealba* appears in the 1968-69 to 1970-71 editions.

TRANSPORTS

AQUILES AP-47 (ex-Danish *Tjaldur*)

Displacement, tons	2 660 registered; 1 462 net; 1 395 dw
Dimensions, feet	288 × 44 × 17
Main engines	1 Slow Burmeister and Wain Diesel; 3 600 bhp = 16 knots
Range, miles	5 500
Complement	60 crew plus 447 troops

Ex-Danish MV built in 1953 by Aalborg Verft, Denmark, bought by Chile in 1967.

AQUILES   *1968, Chilean Navy, Official*

PILOTO PARDO AP 45

Displacement, tons	1 250 light; 2 000 standard; 3 000 full load
Dimensions, feet	269 × 39 × 15
Aircraft	1 helicopter
Main engines	2 diesel-electric; 2 000 hp = 14 knots
Complement	44 (plus 24 passengers)

Built by Haarlemsche Scheepsbouw Mij, Haarlem, Netherlands. Antarctic patrol ship, transport and research vessel with reinforced hull to navigate in ice. For special service in Southern Ocean. Officially listed as transport. Delivered in 1959.

The former transport *Presidente Pinto*, AKA 41 (ex-USS *Zenobia*, AKA 52), latterly employed as a training ship, was relegated for use as an auxiliary harbour ship in 1968. The transport *Angamos*, AP 48, was officially deleted from the list in 1968 to await disposal.

PILOTO PARDO   *1969, Chilean Navy, Official*

OILERS

ARAUCANO AO 53

Displacement, tons	17 300
Measurement, tons	18 030 deadweight
Dimensions, feet	497·6 × 74·9 × 28·8
Guns	4—40 mm
Main engines	B and W diesels; 10 800 bhp = 14·5 knots (17 on trials)
Range, miles	12 000

Naval tanker built by Burmeister & Wain, Copenhagen, Denmark. Launched on 21 June 1967. Sailed on 19 Jan 1967 from Copenhagen to Chile.

ARAUCANO   *1968, Chilean Navy, Official*

Oilers—*continued*

ALMIRANTE JORGE MONTT AO 52

Displacement, tons	9 000 standard; 17 500 full load
Measurement, tons	11 800 gross; 17 750 deadweight
Dimensions, feet	548 × 67·5 × 30
Main engines	Rateau Bretagne geared turbine; 1 shaft; 6 300 shp = 14 knots
Boilers	2 Babcock & Wilcox
Radius, miles	16 500 at 14 knots

Naval squadron supply tanker. Built by Ateliers et Chantiers de la Seine Maritime, Le Trait, France. Laid down in 1954. Launched on 14 Jan 1956. Completed in Mar 1956.

ALMIRANTE JORGE MONTT   *1969, Chilean Navy, Official*

TRAINING SHIP

ESMERALDA (ex-*Don Juan de Austria*) BE 43

Displacement, tons	3 040 standard; 3 673 full load
Dimensions, feet	308·8 oa; 260 pp × 43 × 23 max
Guns	2—57 mm
Sail area	Total 26 910 sq feet
Main engines	1 Fiat auxiliary diesel. 1 shaft; 1 400 bhp = 11 knots
Range, miles	8 000
Complement	271 plus 80 cadets

Four-masted schooner completed in 1952. Built in Spain by the Echevarrieta Yard, Cadiz, and originally intended for the Spanish Navy. Transferred to Chile on 12 May 1953. Near sister ship of *Juan Sebastian de Elcano* in the Spanish Navy. Similar to the Brazilian training ship *Almirante Saldanha* before her major reconstruction. Replaced transport *Presidente Pinto* as training ship.

ESMERALDA   *1971, A. & J. Pavia*

TUGS

COLOCOLO ATA 73

Displacement, tons	790
Dimensions, feet	126·5 × 27 × 12 mean
Main engines	Triple expansion; 1 050 shp = 11 knots
Fuel, tons	130 coal

Built by Bow, McLachlan & Co, Paisley. Formerly classed as coastguard vessel. Of four sister ships *Janequeo* was withdrawn from service in 1958, *Sobenes* in 1965, *Galvarino* in 1968, and *Cabrales* in 1971.

ANCUD (YT 104)   **CORTEZ** (YT 128)   **REYES** (YT 120)
CAUPOLICAN (YT 127)   **MONREAL** (YT 105)

Fortuna (YT 123) and *Galvez* (YT 102) were withdrawn from service in 1965, *Moctezuma* (YT 108) in 1968 and *Ugarte* (YT 107) in 1971. *Yagan* (YT 126) was lost in 1964 while assisting a merchant ship during a storm.

Of the two harbour tugs of the "Huemul" class, *Contramaestre Brito* (ex-*Pelantaro*) was lost, and *Huemul* was disposed of in 1968.

CHINA (People's Republic)

Administration

Commander-in-Chief of the Navy:
Vice-Admiral Hsiao

Pennant Numbers

Block numbering system:—
Submarines: 100 series; Major Surface Ships: 200 series;
Amphibious Ships: 300 series.

Strength of the Fleet

35	Submarines (Diesel Powered)
4	Destroyers (Minelaying)
9	Destroyer Escorts (Small Frigates)
11	Escorts (Sloops and Corvettes)
10	Fast Missile Boats
31	Submarine Chasers (Patrol Vessels)
160	Fast Gunboats
240	Fast Torpedo Boats
22	Coast and River Defence Vessels
27	Medium and Coastal Minesweepers
54	Amphibious Types (Landing Ships and Craft)
33	Auxiliaries and Support Ships
375	Miscellaneous and Service Craft

Personnel

1971: 150 000 officers and men, including 16 000 naval air force and 28 000 marines.

Mercantile Marine

Lloyd's Register of Shipping:
274 vessels of 867 994 tons gross

SUBMARINES

NEW CONSTRUCTION

It is reported that there may be up to three nuclear powered submarines in various stages of construction designed for a displacement of 3 000 tons and an armament of missiles and torpedoes. First vessel begun in 1969.

1 "G" CLASS
BALLISTIC MISSILE TYPE

Displacement, tons	2 350 surface; 2 800 submerged
Length, feet (*metres*)	320·0 (*97·5*)
Beam, feet (*metres*)	28·2 (*8·6*)
Draught, feet (*metres*)	22·0 (*6·7*)
Missile launchers	3 vertical tubes
Torpedo tubes	6—21 in (*533 mm*) bow
Main engines	3 diesels, total 6 000 hp Electric motors
Speed, knots	17·6 surface, 17 submerged
Radius, miles	22 700 surface cruising
Complement	86 (12 officers, 74 men)

Ballistic missile submarine similar to the Soviet "G" class. Built at Dairen in 1964. Missiles have 380 miles range. The missile tubes are fitted in the conning tower.

21 SOVIET "W" CLASS

Displacement, tons	1 300 surface; 1 600 submerged
Length, feet (*metres*)	272·3 (*83·0*) oa
Beam, feet (*metres*)	24·3 (*7·3*)
Draught, feet (*metres*)	15·7 (*4·8*)
Torpedo tubes	6—21 in (*533 mm*); 4 bow 2 aft (20 torpedoes or 40 mines)
Main engines	Diesel-electric; 2 shafts; 4 000. bhp diesels; 2 500 hp electric motors
Speed, knots	17 surface; 15 submerged
Radius, miles	13 000
Complement	60

Medium size streamlined, long range submarines similar to the "W" class built in the USSR. Equipped with snort. Fitted for minelaying. Assembled from Soviet components in Chinese yards between 1956 and 1964.

"G" class   1966, col. Breyer

6 "R" CLASS

Displacement, tons	1 100 surface; 1 600 submerged
Length, feet (*metres*)	246·0 (*75·0*)
Beam, feet (*metres*)	27·9 (*8·5*)
Draught, feet (*metres*)	14·1 (*4·3*)
Torpedo tubes	6—21 in (bow) 18 torpedoes
Main engines	Diesels; electric motors
Speed, knots	18·5 surface; 15 submerged

The Chinese are now thought to be building their own Soviet design "R" class submarines. At least six of this type are probably now in service.

4 Ex-SOVIET "S-1" CLASS

Displacement, tons	840 surface; 1 050 submerged
Length, feet (*metres*)	256 (*78·0*)
Beam, feet (*metres*)	21 (*6·4*)
Draught, feet (*metres*)	13 (*4·0*)
Torpedo tubes	6—21 in (*533 mm*)
Main engines	4 200 hp diesels; 2 200 hp electric motors
Speed, knots	19 surface; 8·5 submerged
Radius, miles	9 800 at 9 knots
Oil fuel, tons	105
Complement	50

All launched in 1937-40. Particulars of individual boats vary slightly. Transferred from the USSR in 1954-55.

3 Ex-SOVIET "M-V" CLASS

Displacement, tons	350 surface; 420 submerged
Length, feet (*metres*)	167·3 (*51·0*)
Beam, feet (*metres*)	16·0 (*4·9*)
Draught, feet (*metres*)	12·1 (*3·7*)
Guns, AA	1—45 mm 1 MG;
Torpedo tubes	2—21 in (*533 mm*)
Main engines	1 000 hp diesels; 800 hp electric motors
Speed, knots	13 surface; 10 submerged
Radius, miles	4 000 at 8·5 knots
Oil fuel, tons	21
Complement	24

Designed for coastal operations, Latterly used for training and instruction but nearing the end of their usefulness owing to age. Four were transferred from the USSR in 1954-55, but M 200 was deleted from the list in 1963.

The four ex-Soviet "Shshuka" class medium type submarines (see particulars in the 1962-63 and earlier editions) were deleted from the list in 1963.
The two smaller submarines built for coastal operations, one of the ex-Soviet "M IV" class, and one of the ex-Soviet "M 1" class, latterly used only for training and instructions, were deleted from the list in 1963.

DESTROYERS

4 Ex-SOVIET "GORDY" CLASS

ANSHAN	CHI LIN
CHANG CHUN	FU CHUN

Displacement, tons	1 657 standard; 2 150 full load
Length, feet (*metres*)	357·7 (*109·0*) pp; 377 (*114·9*) oa
Beam, feet (*metres*)	33·5 (*10·2*)
Draught, feet (*metres*)	13 (*4·0*)
Guns, surface	4—5·1 in (*130 mm*)
Guns, AA	8—37 mm
A/S	8 DCT
Torpedo tubes	6—21 in (*533 mm*) tripled
Boilers	3-drum type
Main engines	Tosi geared turbines 50 000 shp; 2 shafts
Speed, knots	36
Oil fuel (tons)	500
Complement	250

CHANG CHUN   Hajime Fukaya

Of Odero-Terni-Orlando design. All launched in 1936-41. Fitted for minelaying.

The old light cruiser *Pei Ching* (ex-*Huang Ho*, ex-*Victory*, ex-*Chungking*, ex-HMS *Aurora*), became a hulk.

DESTROYER ESCORTS

5 "KIANGNAN" CLASS

No. 209

Displacement, tons	1 350 standard; 1 800 full load
Length, feet (*metres*)	298 (*90·8*)
Beam, feet (*metres*)	33·5 (*10·2*)
Draught, feet (*metres*)	12 (*3·7*)
Guns, dual purpose	6—3·9 in (*100 mm*) (3 twin)
Speed, knots	30

Built at Canton since 1968. Of different design to original destroyer escort class with two twin guns forward and one aft.

4 "RIGA" CLASS

CH'ENG TU	KUEI YANG
KUEI LIN	K'UN MING

Displacement, tons	1 200 standard; 1 600 full load
Length, feet (*metres*)	295 (*89·9*) oa
Beam, feet (*metres*)	31·5 (*9·6*)
Draught, feet (*metres*)	10 (*3·0*)
Guns, dual purpose	3—3·9 in (*100 mm*) single mounts
Guns, AA	4—37 mm
A/S	4 DC projectors
Torpedo tubes	3—21 in (*533 mm*); 3 torpedoes
Mines	50 capacity, fitted with rails
Boilers	2
Main engines	Geared turbines 24 000 shp; 2 shafts
Speed, knots	28
Oil fuel (tons)	300

First of the class, launched on 28 Apr 1956 at Hutang Shipyard, Shanghai, had light tripod mast, but was later converted with heavier mast and larger bridge as in the other three. Second vessel was launched on 26 Sep. 1956. Third vessel was built at Shanghai and the fourth in 1957. Somewhat similar to the Soviet "Riga" class destroyer escorts. Two were redesigned with modified superstructure.

ESCORTS (Corvettes)

CHANG PAI — *Hajime Fukaya*

1 Ex-JAPANESE "UKURU" CLASS

HUI AN (ex-*Shisaka*)

Displacement, tons	940 standard; 1 020 full load
Length, feet (*metres*)	255 (*77·7*) wl; 258·5 (*78·8*) oa
Beam, feet (*metres*)	30 (*9·1*)
Draught, feet (*metres*)	10 (*4·0*)
Guns, surface	2 4·7 in (*120 mm*); 6 MG
Main engines	2 diesels; 4 200 bhp; 2 shafts
Speed, knots	19·5
Complement	150

Ex-Japanese "Ukuru" class escort destroyer. Launched in 1943. Completed in 1945. Rearmed in 1955.

1 Ex-JAPANESE "ETOROFU" CLASS

CHANG PAI (ex-Japanese *Oki*, ex-Chinese *Ku An*)

Displacement, tons	870 standard; 1 020 full load
Length, feet (*metres*)	237·9 (*72·5*) pp; 250 (*76·0*) wl 255 (*77·7*) oa
Beam, feet (*metres*)	30 (*9·1*)

Draught, feet (*metres*)	10 (*4·0*)
Guns, surface	2—3·9 in (*100 mm*)
Guns, AA	2—45 mm
Main engines	2 diesels; 4 200 bhp; 2 shafts
Speed, knots	19·7
Complement	150

Ex-Japanese Type A or "Etorofu" class. Built by Uraga Dock Co Ltd. Laid down on 27 Feb 1942. Launched on 20 Oct 1942. Completed on 31 Mar 1943. Rearmed in 1955. One raked funnel, two pole masts with tripod bases. Sister ship of *Lin An* in Taiwan (National Republic of China) Navy.

1 Ex-JAPANESE SLOOP TYPE

NAN CHANG (ex-Chinese *Chang Chi*, ex-Japanese *Uji*)

Displacement, tons	950 standard; 1 206 full load
Length, feet (*metres*)	249·5 (*76·1*) pp; 257·5 (*78·5*) wl 264 (*80·5*) oa
Beam, feet (*metres*)	31 (*9·4*)
Draught, feet (*metres*)	8·7 (*2·6*)
Guns, surface	2—3·9 in (*100 mm*)
Guns, AA	2—3 in (*76 mm*); 4—37 mm
Boilers	2
Main engines	2 turbines; 4 600 shp; 2 shafts
Speed, knots	20·15
Radius, miles	3 460 at 14 knots
Complement	170

NAN CHANG — *K. Long*

Former Japanese sloop or gunboat. Built at Sakurajima Works, Osaka. Launched on 25 Sep 1940. Completed in 1941. Rearmed in 1955. The 37 mm guns replaced 20 mm guns. The bridge was refitted.

1 Ex-JAPANESE "C" CORVETTE

SHEN YANG (ex-*Yuang An*, ex-*Mukden*, ex-*No. 81*)

Displacement, tons	745 standard; 810 full load
Length, feet (*metres*)	206·7 (*63·0*) pp; 216·5 (*66·0*) wl; 221·5 (*67·5*) oa
Beam, feet (*metres*)	27·5 (*8·4*)
Draught, feet (*metres*)	9·5 (*2·9*)
Guns, surface	2—3·9 in (*100 mm*)
Guns, AA	4—37 mm
Main engines	2 diesels; 1 900 bhp; 2 shafts
Speed, knots	16·5
Radius, miles	6 500 at 14 knots
Complement	136

CHI NAN — *Hajime Fukaya*

Ex-Japanese C or No. 1 type. Built in 1944-45. Rearmed in 1955. Sister ship *Chi An* became a hulk.

4 Ex-JAPANESE "D" CORVETTES

CHANG SHA (ex-Chinese *Chieh 12*, ex-*No. 118*)
CHI NAN (ex-*Wei Hei*, ex-*Chieh 6*, ex-*No. 194*)
HSI AN (ex-Chinese *Chieh 14*, ex-Japanese *No. 198*)
WU CHANG (ex-Chinese *Chien 5* ex-Japanese *No. 14*)

Name	Chang Sha	Hsi An
Builders	Kawasaki Sensha Works	Mitsubishi, Zosen Co, Nagasaki
Laid down	8 June 1944	17 Jan 1945
Launched	18 Oct 1944	26 Feb 1945
Completed	27 Dec 1944	31 Mar 1945

Displacement, tons	740 standard; 900 full load
Length, feet (*metres*)	213·2 (*54·2*) pp; 223 (*56·7*) wl; 228 (*57·9*) oa
Beam, feet (*metres*)	28·2 (*8·6*)
Draught, feet (*metres*)	10 (*3·0*)
Guns, surface	2—3·9 in (*100 mm*), or 2—4·7 in (*120 mm*)
Guns, AA	3—3 in (*76 mm*), or 3 or 6—37 mm; 4—25 mm, or 3—20 mm
Main engines	Steam turbine; 2 500 shp
Speed, knots	17·5
Radius, miles	4 500 at 14 knots
Complement	160

CHANG SHA — *Hajime Fukaya*

Ex-Japanese Type D or Kaibokan Class No. 2 Type. Thin trunked funnel amidships. Pole masts with tripod bases.

1 Ex-CANADIAN CORVETTE TYPE

KUANG CHOU (ex-Chinese *Yuan Pei*, ex-HMCS *Bowmanville*, ex-*Nunney Castle*)

Displacement, tons	1 100 standard; 1 580 full load
Length, feet (*metres*)	252 (*76·8*) oa
Beam, feet (*metres*)	36·7 (*11·2*)
Draught, feet (*metres*)	15·2 (*4·6*)
Guns, surface	2—5·1 in (*130 mm*)
Guns, AA	1—45 mm
Boilers	2 three-drum type
Main engines	Triple expansion; 2 800 ihp
Speed, knots	16·5
Radius, miles	8 400 at 10 knots
Oil fuel (tons)	480
Complement	100

Built by Wm Pickersgill & Sons, Ltd, Sunderland. Laid down on 12 Aug 1943. Launched on 26 Jan 1944. Completed in 8 Oct 1944.

2 Ex-BRITISH CORVETTE TYPE

KAI FENG (ex-SS *Cloverlock*, ex-HMS *Clover*)
LIN I (ex-SS *Ziang Teh*, ex-HMS *Heliotrope*, ex-USS *Surprise*)

Displacement, tons	1 020 standard; 1 280 full load
Length, feet (*metres*)	190 (*57·9*) pp; 205 (*62·5*) oa
Beam, feet (*metres*)	33 (*10·1*)
Draught, feet (*metres*)	14·5 (*4·4*)
Guns, surface	2—3·9 in (*100 mm*)
Guns, AA	Kai Feng: 1—45 mm; 4—37 mm Lin 1: 2—37 mm
Boilers	2 S.E.
Main engines	Triple expansion; 2 750 ihp
Speed, knots	16
Radius, miles	7 000 at 10 knots
Fuel (tons)	350 coal
Complement	78

Both built in 1940-41. Converted from merchant vessels by Chinese Republicans and re-armed. Existence of sister ship, former corvette, converted, ex-*Coppercliffe* (ex-*Wan Lee*, ex-*Ta Lun*) is doubtful.

FAST MISSILE BOATS
7 SOVIET "OSA" CLASS

Displacement, tons	160 standard; 200 full load
Dimensions, feet	131·5 oa × 23 × 6·5
Missiles, surface	4 "Styx" type launchers in two pairs abreast aft
Guns	4—25 mm (2 twin, 1 forward and 1 aft)
Main engines	3 diesels; 5 000 bhp = 35 knots

It was reported in Jan 1965 that one "Osa" class guided missile patrol boat had been incorporated in the Navy. Four more were acquired in 1966-67, and two in 1968.

"Osa" Class   1969

3 SOVIET "KOMAR" CLASS

Displacement, tons	75 standard; 100 full load
Dimensions, feet	82 oa × 20 × 6
Missiles, surface	2 "Styx" type launchers with 15 miles range
Guns	2—25 mm AA (1 twin forward)
Main engines	Diesels; 2 shafts; 4 800 bhp = 40 knots

One "Komar" class guided missile boat is reported to have joined the fleet in 1965. Two more were delivered in 1967.

"Komar" Class   S. Breyer

PATROL VESSELS

Ex-USSR   1969

24 "KRONSTADT" CLASS SUBMARINE CHASERS

579	611	612	615	618	622

Displacement, tons	300
Dimensions, feet	167·5 × 19·3 × 9
Guns	1—3·9 in; 2—37 mm AA; 3—20 mm AA
Main engines	Diesels; 2 shafts; speed 27 knots

Six built in 1950-53 were received from USSR in 1956-57. Remainder were built at Shanghai and Canton, with 12 completed by 1956. The last was assembled in 1957. Flush decked, squat funnel, slightly raked, block bridge structure.

The six old former Soviet patrol vessels of the "Artillerist" class, and the three former British patrol trawlers of the "Isles" class were deleted from the list in 1967, and the two former Soviet submarine chasers of the "S.O.1." class in 1969.

FAST GUN BOATS
103 "SHANGHAI II" CLASS

Displacement, tons	120 full load
Dimensions, feet	130 × 18 × 5·6
Guns	4—37 mm, 2 twin, 1 forward, 1 aft
	4—25 mm, 2 twin aft of bridge
	1 chaser mortar forward
Torpedo tubes	2 (not fitted in later boats)
Main engines	4 diesels; 5 000 bhp = 30 knots
Complement	25

Two centreline trainable torpedo tubes were mounted abaft the superstructure. Over a hundred boats of this class have been built, with construction continuing at Shanghai. Intended as interchangeable gunboats or fast patrol boats. Designed for series construction in China. Three units were transferred to North Korea and four to North Vietnam.

NEW SHANGHAI Class   1970

12 "SHANGHAI" TYPE

Displacement, tons	100 full load
Dimensions, feet	120 × 18 × 5·5
Guns	4—37 mm in twin mountings fore and aft
Main engines	4 diesels; 4 800 bhp = 28 knots
Complement	21

The prototype of these convertable motor gun/torpedo boats appeared in 1959.

SHANGHAI Type   1969

45 "SWATOW" TYPE

Displacement, tons	67 full load
Dimensions, feet	83·5 × 20 × 6
Guns	4—37 mm. in twin mountings; 2—12·7 mm
A/S weapons	8 depth charges
Main engines	4 diesels; 4 800 bhp = 40 knots
Complement	17

"P 6" type motor torpedo boat hulls with torpedo tubes removed. In 1958 "P-6" hulls were converted to "Swatow" class motor gunboats at Dairen, Canton, and Shanghai.

MGB   1969

FAST TORPEDO BOATS

40 HYDROFOIL TYPE

Dimensions, feet	100 × 25 × 12 (moulded depth)
Torpedo tubes	4 fixed (two on each side)
Guns	4 light (two twin)
Complement	20 /

At least 25 motor torpedo boats of the hydrofoil type were reported to be in the South China Fleet in 1968. Of all-metal construction with a bridge well forward and a low superstructure extending aft. The four guns are in horizontally paired mountings, one on the main deck and one on the superstructure. Forward pair of foils can apparently be withdrawn into recesses in the hull. Painted olive green.

50 "HUCHWAN" CLASS

Displacement, tons	45
Dimensions, feet	73 × 16 × 3·1
Torpedo tubes	2—21 inch
Guns	2—12·7 mm

Hydrofoil torpedo boat, designed and built by China, at least 26 having been constructed since 1966. One unit reported transferred to North Vietnam.

70 "P4" TYPE

Displacement, tons	25
Dimensions, feet	63 × 11 × 3
Guns	2 or 4—25 mm AA
Main engines	Diesels, 2 000 bhp = 45 knots

This class have aluminium hulls. The German-built *Kual 102* was deleted from the list in 1963.

PTBs   *1969*

80 "P6" TYPE

153	**154**	**155**	**159**

Displacement, tons	66
Dimensions, feet	82 × 20 × 6
Guns	4—25 mm AA
Torpedo tubes	2—21 in
Main engines	Diesels, 5 000 bhp = 40 knots
Complement	25

This class have wooden hulls. Some were constructed in Chinese Republican yards. All have been built since 1966. Above pennant numbers observed *en flotille*.

MTB   *1969*

PATROL CRAFT

5 "HAINAN" CLASS

Dimensions, feet	135 × 20 × 10
Guns	4—37 mm (2 pairs superimposed, 1 forward, 1 aft)
	4—25 mm (2 pairs superimposed, amidships)

Chinese built improved Soviet "S.O.I." type but smaller for seaward defence. Low freeboard. The 25 mm guns are abaft the bridge.

2 Ex-JAPANESE TYPE

Ex-KWANG KUO	Ex-HSIEN FENG
(ex-Japanese No. 223)	(ex-Chinese *Koo Ming*, ex-Japanese

Displacement, tons	135
Dimensions, feet	96 × 19 × 9

SC Type. Built in 1942-43. (The ex-British harbour defence motor launches were lost).

MEDIUM MINESWEEPERS

20 SOVIET "T 43" CLASS

Displacement, tons	410 standard; 530 full load
Dimensions, feet	200 × 27·2 × 9
Guns	4—37 mm AA
Main engines	Diesels = 18 knots

Two were acquired from USSR in 1954-55. Eighteen more were built in Chinese shipyards, two in 1956, and the remainder since. The construction of "T 43" class fleet minesweepers was terminated at Wuchang, but continued at Canton.

1 Ex-BRITISH "BATHURST" CLASS

Ex-SS **CHEUNG HING** (ex-HMAS *Bendigo*)

Displacement, tons	815 standard; 1 025 full load
Dimensions, feet	162 pp; 186 oa × 31 × 8·5
Guns	2—5·1 in; 2—37 mm AA
Main engines	Triple expansion; 2 shafts; 1 800 ihp = 15 knots
Boilers	2 Admiralty 3-drum small tube type
Oil fuel (tons)	170
Radius, miles	4 300 at 10 knots

Built as a fleet minesweeper but employed as an escort vessel. Launched in Mar 1941 at Sydney, Australia. Disposed of as surplus after the Second World War. Converted from a merchant vessel.

COASTAL MINESWEEPERS

4 Ex-US YMS TYPE

Ex-**YMS 346**	Ex-**YMS 367**	Ex-**YMS 393**	Ex-**YMS 2017**

Displacement, tons	270 standard; 350 full load
Dimensions, feet	136 × 24·5 × 6
Guns	1—3 in; 2—20 mm; 2 DCT
Main engines	2 GM Diesels; 1 000 bhp = 13 knots

Built of wood in USA in 1942-43, and transferred to the Chinese Navy in 1948. Some are fitted as gunboats. Ex-YMS 339 was deleted from the list in 1963.

2 Ex-JAPANESE AMS TYPE

Ex-**No. 4**   **No. 201** (ex No. 14)

Displacement, tons	222
Dimensions, feet	97·1 oa × 19·3 × 7·3 max
Guns	1—3·1 in; 4—25 mm (No. 201, 1—40 mm; 1—25 mm;
	2—13 mm; 3—7·7 mm)
Main engines	1 Diesel; 300 bhp = 9·5 knots
Radius, miles	1 700 at 9·5 knots

Ex-Japanese auxiliary minesweepers. Trawler type No. 201, completed in 1943, was delivered to China at Tsingtau on 3 Oct 1947, and taken over by the Chinese Republic.

COAST DEFENCE VESSELS

Ex-**YUNG SUI**

Displacement, tons	650
Dimensions, feet	225 × 30 × 7 max
Guns	1—3 in AA; 1—40 mm AA; 4 MG
Main engines	Triple expansion; 2 shafts; 4 000 shp = 12 knots
Boilers	2 Yarrow; Coal fired

Built by Kiangnan Dock Co, Shanghai. Launched in 1929. Salvaged and repaired after sinking in 1949. *Yung Sui* is ex-Chinese Nationalist name. A photograph appears in the 1969-70 and earlier editions.

Ex-**AN TUNG** (ex-Japanese *Ataka*, ex-*Nakosa*)

Displacement, tons	727
Dimensions, feet	222 × 32 × 7·5
Guns	2—3 in; 5—25 mm; 6 MG
Main engines	Triple expansion; 1 700 ihp = 11 knots
Boilers	2 Kampon

Former Japanese. Built at Yokohama Dock. Launched in April, 1922. Coal burning. Ex-*Yen An*, ex-*Yung Chi*, ex-*Asuka*, ex-*Yung Chi* was discarded.

AN TUNG   *Official*

Coast Defence Vessels—*continued*

3 Ex-US TYPE

Ex-**PGM 12**	Ex-**PGM 14**	**KAN TANG** (ex-*PGM 15*)

Displacement, tons	280 standard; 348 trial; 450 full load
Dimensions, feet	170 wl; 173·3 oa × 23 × 11 max
Guns	1—3 in 50 cal dp; 2—40 mm AA (twin)
Main engines	GM diesel; 2 shafts; 2 800 bhp = 20 knots

Former US submarine chasers or patrol vessels (gunboats).

CH'ANG CHIANG (ex-*Ming Chuan*)

Displacement, tons	464
Dimensions, feet	176·8 × 26 × 6·5 max
Guns	4—40 mm (2 twin, 1 forward, 1 aft);
	4—25 mm (2 twin, 1 port, 1 starboard)
Main engines	Triple expansion; 2 shafts; 2 200 ihp = 12 knots
Boilers	2 Yarrow
Coal, tons	280

Built by Kiangnan Dock Co., Shanghai. Launched in 1929. Rearmed in 1967.

CHIANG YUAN

Displacement, tons	550
Dimensions, feet	170 pp; 180 oa × 28 × 7
Guns	1—20 mm AA
Main engines	Triple expansion; 2 shafts; 4 000 ihp = 12 knots
Boilers	Watertube
Coal, tons	113

Built by Kawasaki Co, Kobe. Launched in 1905. Former armament removed.

CHIANG YUAN   *Official*

TING HSIN	**TUNG TEH**

Displacement, tons	500 standard
Guns	1—3 in; 4—47 mm
Main engines	Speed: 11 knots
Fuel	Coal

Both captured by the People's Republic of China Navy in 1949.

RIVER DEFENCE VESSELS

2 Ex-JAPANESE TYPE

Ex-**YUNG AN** (ex-*Futami*)	Ex-**YUNG PING** (ex-*Atami*)

Displacement, tons	170
Dimensions, feet	148·5 × 22 × 4·7
Guns	1—47 mm AA; 5—25 mm AA; 3 MG
Main engines	2 sets triple expansion; 2 shafts; 1 200 ihp = 12 knots
Boilers	2 Kampon
Oil fuel (tons)	53

Built by Tama, Fujinagata. Both launched in 1929. Former Japanese river gunboats.

YUNG PING   *Official*

Ex-CHANG TEH (ex-*Seta*)

Displacement, tons	305
Dimensions, feet	180 × 27 × 3
Guns	2—3 in; 6 MG
Main engines	Triple expansion; 2 shafts; 2 100 ihp = 14 knots
Boilers	2 Kampon
Oil fuel (tons)	85

Japanese prize, built at Harima yard. Launched in 1923. Reported to have been discarded. Ex-Japanese *Katado* of the same class may still exist.

River Defence Vessels—*continued*

2 Ex-JAPANESE TYPE

FU CHIANG (ex-*Chiang Feng*, ex-Chinese *Kiang Shih*, ex-Japanese *Fushima*)
Ex-**CHIANG HSI** (ex-Chinese *Nan Chang*, ex-Japanese *Sumida*)

Displacement, tons	373·6 tons, official Japanese figure, 320 standard
Dimensions, feet	159·1 pp; 164 wl; 165 oa × 32·2 × 4·1
Guns	1—3·1 in HA short cal; 8—25 mm
Main engines	2 geared turbines; 2 shafts; 2 200 shp = 16·7 knots
Boilers	2 Kampon
Radius, miles	1 496 at 14 knots

Both ships were built by Fujinagata Co, Osaka. Launched on 26 Mar 1939 and 30 October 1939, respectively. Completed on 15 July 1939 and 31 May 1940, respectively. Were the latest river gunboats in the Japanese Navy. *Fushima* bombed and bottomed at Anking on 29 Nov 1944, was salvaged and towed to Shanghai for repairs and was moored there at the end of the war. *Sumida* was at Shanghai at the end of the war; her armament has been removed for land batteries.

FU CHIANG   *Official*

Ex-YING HAO (ex-HMS *Sandpiper*)

Displacement, tons	185
Dimensions, feet	160 × 30·7 × 2 mean
Guns	1—3·7 in howitzer; 9 smaller
Main engines	2 sets triple expansion; 2 shafts; 600 ihp = 11 knots
Boilers	1, of Admiralty 3-drum type

Built by John I. Thornycroft & Co Ltd, Southampton. Launched on 9 June 1933. Presented to Nationalist China by Great Britain in Feb 1942, and subsequently taken over by the Republicans. Now has mainmast.

Ex-NAN CHIANG (ex-*Ying Teh*, ex-*Lung Huan*, ex-HMS *Falcon*)

Displacement, tons	372
Dimnesions, feet	150 × 28·7 × 5 mean
Guns	1—3·7 in howitzer; 2—6 pdr; 10 MG
Main engines	Parsons geared turbines; 2 250 shp = 15 knots
Boilers	2, of Admiralty 3-drum type
Fuel oil, tons	84

Built by Yarrow & Co, Ltd, Scotstoun, Glasgow. Launched in 1931. Presented to Nationalist China by the British Government in Feb 1942, and subsequently taken over by the Republicans.

Ex-YING SHAN (ex-HMS *Gannet*)

Displacement, tons	310
Dimensions, feet	177 wl; 184·7 oa × 29 × 3·2
Guns	2—3 in AA; 8 MG
Main engines	Geared turbines; designed 2 250 shp = 16 knots
Boilers	Yarrow
Fuel oil (tons)	60

Designed by Yarrow. Built by Yarrow & Co, Ltd, Scotstoun, Glasgow. Launched in 1927. Presented to Nationalist China by Great Britain in Feb 1942, and subsequently taken over by the Republicans.

2 Ex-US TYPE

Ex-**MEI YUAN** (ex-USS *Tutuila*) Ex-**TAI YUAN** (ex-*Tatara*, ex-USS *Wake*, ex-*Guam*)

Displacement, tons	370 standard
Dimensions, feet	150 wl × 159·5 oa × 27 × 5·2 mean—fresh water); (6 max)
Guns	2—3 in 23 çal; 10 MG
Main engines	Triple expansion; 1 950 ihp = 12 knots
Oil fuel (tons)	75

Built by Kiangnan Dock Co, Shanghai. Launched on 14 June and 28 May 1927 respectively. *Mei Yuan* was presented to China by the US Government in March 1942. Sister ship was recovered from Japanese hands and presented to China in 1946.

TAI YUAN   *Official*

River Defence Vessels—*continued*

Ex-KIANG KUN (ex-Japanese *Narumi*, ex-Italian *Ermanno Carlotto*)

Displacement, tons	180 standard
Dimensions, feet	160 × 24·5 × 2·8
Guns	2—3 in; 6 MG
Main engines	Designed 1 100 ihp = 14 knots max
Boilers	2 Yarrow
Oil (tons)	56

Built by Shanghai Dock & Engineering Co. Launched in 1921. Completed in 1921. Shallow draught river gunboat. Twin screws in tunnels.

Ex-FAKU (ex-French *Balny*)

Displacement, tons	201
Dimensions, feet	167·2; 179 oa × 23 × 5
Guns	1—3 in AA; 2—1 pdr; 4 MG
Main engines	Triple expansion; 920 ihp = 14 knots
Boilers	2 Fouche water tube
Fuel (tons)	45 coal
Range, miles	900 at 14 knots

Built by Chantiers de Bretagne, Nantes. Launched in 1920. Completed in 1921.

Ex-HO HSEUH (ex-Chinese *Yang Ch'i*, ex-Japanese *Toba*)

Displacement, tons	215
Dimensions, feet	180 × 27 × 2·5 mean; (4 max)
Guns	3—3 in; 3—25 mm AA; 3 MG
Main engines	Triple expansion; 2 shafts; 900 ihp = 9 knots
Boilers	2 Kampon
Coal (tons)	80

Former Japanese shallow draught river gunboat. Built by Sasebo, Japan. Launched in 1911.

Official

BOOM DEFENCE VESSELS

1 Ex-BRITISH "BAR" TYPE

Ex-Japanese No. 101 (ex-HMS *Barlight*)

Displacement, tons	750 standard; 1 000 full load
Dimensions, feet	150 pp; 173·8 oa × 32·2 × 9·5
Guns	1—3 in dp; 6 MG
Main engines	Triple expansion; 850 ihp = 11·75 knots
Boilers	2 single-ended

Boom defence vessel of British "Bar" Class. Built by Lobnitz & Co Ltd, Renfrew. Launched on 10 Sep 1938. Captured by Japanese in 1941. Acquired by China in 1945.

5 Ex-US "TREE" CLASS

Displacement, tons	560 standard; 805 full load
Dimensions, feet	146 wl; 163 oa × 30·5 × 11·8
Guns	1—3 in AA
Main engines	Diesel-electric; 800 bhp = 13 knots

Former United States netlayers of the "Tree" class taken over by the People's Republic.

SURVEY CRAFT

Ex-CHUNG NING (ex-Japanese *Takebu Maru*)

Displacement, tons	200 standard
Dimensions, feet	115 × 16 × 6
Main engines	Speed; 10 knots

Former Japanese. Employed for hydrographic and general purpose duties.

Ex-FUTING

Displacement, tons	160 standard
Dimensions, feet	90 × 20 × 8
Main engines	Speed: 11 knots

REPAIR SHIP

TAKU SHAN (ex-*Hsing An*, ex-USS *Achilles*, ARL 41, ex-*LST* 455)

Displacement, tons	1 625 light; 4 100 full load
Dimensions, feet	316 wl; 328 oa × 50 × 11
Guns	1—3 in; 8—40 mm AA
Main engines	Diesel-electric; 2 shafts; 1 800 bhp = 11 knots

Launched on 17 Oct 1942. Burned and grounded in 1949, salvaged and refitted

LANDING SHIPS

16 Ex-US LST TYPE

CHANG PAI SHAN	Ex-CHUNG 122 (ex-*Ch'ing Ling*)
CHING KANG SHAN	Ex-CHUNG 125
CHUNG (ex-USS *LST* 355)	I MENG SHAN (ex-*Chung* 106 ex-USS
Ex-CHUNG 101 (ex-USS *LST* 804)	*LST* 589)
Ex-CHUNG 102 (ex-USS *LST*)	No. 16
Ex-CHUNG 107 (ex-USS *LST* 1027)	No. 258
Ex-CHUNG 110	TA PIEH SHAN
Ex-CHUNG 111 (ex-USS *LST* 805)	TAI HSING SHAN
Ex-CHUNG 116 (ex-USS *LST* 406)	SZU CH'ING SHAN

Displacement, tons	1 653 standard; 4 080 full load
Dimensions, feet	316 wl; 328 oa × 50 × 14
Main engines	Diesel; 2 shafts; 1 700 bhp = 11 knots

There were reported to be 20 ex-US LSTs in naval service, but several are out of commission. Eleven other ex-US LSTs were in the merchant service.

13 Ex-US LSM TYPE

Ex-CHUAN SHIH SHUI	Ex-HUA 209 (ex-USS *LSM* 153)
Ex-HUA 201 (ex-USS *LSM* 112)	Ex-HUA 211
Ex-HUA 202 (ex-USS *LSM* 248)	Ex-HUA 212
Ex-HUA 204 (ex-USS *LSM* 430)	Ex-HUAI HO (ex-Chinese *Wan Fu*)
Ex-HUA 205 (ex-USS *LSM* 336)	Ex-HUANG HO (ex-Chinese *Mei Sheng*,
Ex-HUA 207 (ex-USS *LSM* 282)	ex-USS *LSM* 433)
Ex-HUA 208 (ex-USS *LSM* 42)	Ex-YUN HO (ex-Chinese *Wang Chung*)

Displacement, tons	743 beaching; 1 095 full load
Dimensions, feet	196·5 wl; 203·5 oa × 34·5 × 8·8
Main engines	Diesel; 2 shafts; 2 800 = 12 knots

Built in USA in 1944-45. Some were converted for minelaying. Armament varies.

LANDING CRAFT

15 Ex-US LSIL TYPE

Ex-CHU TIEN (ex-Chinese *Lien Kuang*	MIN 312
ex-USS *LCI* 517)	MIN 313
Ex-KU CHOU	MIN 319
Ex-USS LCI 488	MIN 321
Ex-LIEN PI (ex-USS *LCI* 514)	MIN 325
MIN 301	MIN 331
MIN 303	Ex-YUNG KAN (ex-Chinese *Lien Yung*,
MIN 306	ex-USS *LCI* 632)
MIN 311	

Displacement, tons	230 light; 387 full load
Dimensions, feet	159 × 23·7 × 5·7
Main engines	Diesel; 2 shafts; 1 320 bhp = 14 knots

Built in USA in 1943-45. Reported to be fitted with rocket launchers. Some are fitted as minesweepers. Armament varies.

10 Ex-US LCU (ex-LCT) TYPE

Ex-HO CHIEN (ex-USS *LCT* 515)	Ex-HO YUNG (ex-USS *LCT* 1171)

Displacement, tons	160 light; 320 full load
Dimensions, feet	105 wl; 119 oa × 33 × 5
Main engines	Diesel; 3 shafts; 475 bhp = 10 knots
Oil fuel (tons)	80

Former United States Navy Tank Landing Craft later reclassified as Utility Landing Craft. There are reported to be ten utility landing craft comprising two of the ex-British LCT (3) class and eight of the ex-US LCT (5) and LCT (6) class.

SUPPLY SHIPS

8 Ex-US ARMY FS TYPE

Ex-US Army FS 146 (ex-*Clover*)	Ex-US Army FS——
Ex-US Army FS 155 (ex-*Violet*)	Ex-US Army FS——
Ex-TA CHEN (ex-US)	

Displacement, tons	1 000 standard
Dimensions, feet	175 oa × 32 × 10
Main engines	GM diesels; 1 000 bhp = 12 knots

Built in USA in 1944-54. Two are reported to be employed as motor torpedo boat tenders. The transport *Chiao Jen* was stricken from the list in 1967.

OILERS

There are reported to be two ex-US "Mattawee" Class petrol tankers and three ex-US 174 ft yard oilers of the "YO" type.

TUGS

There are reported to be at least two tugs of the USSR type, two of the US Navy ATA type, two of the US Army type, and five of the US Army harbour tug type.

SERVICE CRAFT

There are also reported to be 125 armed motor junks, 100 armed motor launches and 150 service craft and miscellaneous boats.

CHINA (Taiwan)

Administration

Commander-in-Chief Chinese Nationalist Navy:
    Vice-Admiral Feng Chi-Chung

Fleet Commander:
    Vice-Admiral Li Tan-Chien

Diplomatic Representation

Naval Attaché in Washington:
    Rear Admiral Chien Tsou

Ships

Chinese (Nationalist) ship's names are prefaced by "RCN" (Republic of China Navy).

Strength of the Fleet

11	Destroyers	1	Repair Ship
17	Frigates	50	Coastal Craft
1	Escort Transport	6	Transports
4	Escort Vessels	4	Oilers
2	Fleet Minesweepers	21	LSTs
1	Minelayer	15	LSMs
21	Submarine Chasers	5	LSIs
1	Gunboat	3	LSLs
15	Coastal Minesweepers	21	LCUs
2	Inshore Minesweepers	2	Survey Ships
1	Dock Landing Ship	1	Floating Dock
2	Amphibious Flagships	12	Support Ships

Personnel

1971: Total: 62 000 officers and men including 27 000 of the Marine Corps.

The Chinese Nationalist Navy undergoes training with the United States Military Assistance Advisory Group on Taiwan.
United States Marine Corps advisers train Chinese Nationalist marines on Taiwan in amphibious operations.

Mercantile Marine

Lloyd's Register of Shipping:

274 vessels of 1 166 230 tons gross

DESTROYERS

	Builders	Launched	Completed
(ex-USS Bristol, DD 857)	Bethlehem (San Pedro)	29 Oct 1944	17 Mar 1945
(ex-USS Brush, DD 745)	Bethlehem (Staten Is)	28 Dec 1943	17 Apr 1944
(ex-USS Haynsworth, DD 700)	Federal SB & DD Co	15 Apr 1944	22 June 1944
(ex-USS Samuel N. Moore, DD 747)	Bethlehem (Staten Is)	23 Feb 1944	24 June 1944

4 Ex-US "ALLEN M. SUMNER" CLASS

Displacement, tons	2 200 standard; 3 320 full load
Length, feet (metres)	376·5 (114·8) oa
Beam, feet (metres)	40·9 (12·4)
Draught, feet (metres)	19 (5·8)
Guns	6—5 inch (127 mm) 38 calibre dual purpose (twin); 4—3 inch (76 mm) 50 calibre AA (twin)
A/S weapons	2 fixed hedgehogs; depth charges
Main engines	2 geared turbines 60 000 shp; 2 shafts
Boilers	4
Speed, knots	34
Complement	274

Three ships were purchased from the USN on 9 Dec 1969, and transferred on 11 Dec 1969 (ex-Brush and ex-Samuel N. Moore) and 23 Dec 1969 (ex-Bristol). A fourth ship, USS Haynsworth DD 700, was purchased on 12 May 1970.

ex-BRUSH   Added 1970, Official

Name	No.
AN YANG (ex-USS Kimberley DD 521)	18
KUN YANG (ex-USS Yarnall, DD 541)	19

Builders	Laid down	Launched	Completed
Bethlehem (Staten Is)	27 July 1942	4 Feb 1943	22 May 1943
Bethlehem (San Francisco)	5 Dec 1942	25 July 1943	30 Dec 1943

2 ex-USS "FLETCHER" CLASS

Displacement, tons	2 100 standard; 3 050 full load
Length, feet (metres)	376·5 (114·7) oa
Beam, feet (metres)	35·9 (11·9)
Draught, feet (metres)	18 (5·5)
Guns	5—5 inch (127 mm) 38 calibre dual purpose 60—4 mm AA (twin)
A/S weapons	2 fixed hedgehogs, depth charges
Torpedo tubes	5—21 inch (533 mm) quintruple in Kun Yang only
Main engines	2 geared turbines; 60 000 shp; 2 shafts
Boilers	4
Speed, knots	35
Complement	249

An Yang was recommissioned at Boston, Mass in 1967 and transferred on 1 June 1967. Kun Yang purchased on 10 June 1968. Before transfer An Yang had the

AN YANG   1971, courtesy Toshio Tamura

quintuple torpedo mounting aft of the funnels removed but retained the original pole mast. Kun Yang retains

the torpedo tubes and has a tripod foremast, see photograph in the 1970-71 edition.

Name	No.	Builders	Laid down	Launched	Completed
HSUEN YANG (ex-USS Rodman, DD 456, ex-DMS 21)	16	Federal SB & DD Co	2 Dec 1940	26 Sep 1941	27 Jan 1942
NAN YANG (ex-USS Plunkett, DD 431)	17	Federal SB & DD Co	1 Mar 1939	9 Mar 1940	16 July 1940

2 Ex-US "GLEAVES" CLASS

Displacement, tons	1 700 standard; 2 575 full load
Length, feet (metres)	341 (104·0) wl; 348·3 (106·2) oa
Beam, feet (metres)	36 (11·0)
Draught, feet (metres)	18 (5·5)
Guns, surface	4—5 in, 38 cal
Guns, AA	8—40 mm (Hsuen Yang 4—40 mm); 2—20 mm
A/S weapons	2 Hedgehogs
Boilers	4 Babcock & Wilcox
Main engines	GE geared turbines 50 000 shp; 2 shafts
Speed, knots	34
Radius, miles	5 000 at 15 knots
Oil fuel (tons)	600
Complement	250

Transferred on loan from the US Navy, Rodman on 28 July 1955 and Plunkett on 16 Feb 1959. Now have tripod foremasts. In 1963 a fourth 5 inch gun was mounted in Hsuen Yang.

HSUEN YANG (tripod foremast)   1970, Toshio Tamura

PHOTOGRAPHS. An official photograph of the destroyer Nan Yang, with pole foremast, a starboard dead broadside view, appears in the 1962-63 to 1969-70 editions.

Name
HAN YANG (ex-USS *Hilary P. Jones*, DD 427)
LO YANG (ex-USS *Benson*, DD 421)

2 Ex-US "MAYO" TYPE

Displacement, tons	1 620 standard; 2 450 full load
Length, feet (*metres*)	340 (*103·6*) wl; 348·2 (*106·2*) oa
Beam, feet (*metres*)	35·3 (*10·8*)
Draught feet (*metres*)	18·0 (*5·5*)
Guns, surface	4—5 in (*127 mm*) 38 cal
Guns, AA	4—40 mm; 6—20 mm
A/S weapons	DC mortar; DC throwers
Main engines	2 GE geared turbines; 2 shafts; 50 000 shp
Boilers	4 high pressure
Speed, knots	34
Radius, miles	5 000 at 15 knots
Oil fuel, tons	600
Complement	230

Transferred from USN at Charleston, South Carolina, on 26 Feb 1954. A photograph of *La Yang* appears in the 1954-55 to 1957-58 editions.

1 Ex-JAPANESE "KAGERO" TYPE

TAN YANG (ex-*Yukikaze*) 12

Displacement, tons	2 050 standard; 2 490 full load
Length, feet (*metres*)	388·0 (*118·3*) oa
Beam, feet (*metres*)	35·5 (*10·8*)
Draught, feet (*metres*)	12·3 (*3·8*)
Guns, dual purpose	3—5 in (*127 mm*) 38 cal; 2—3 in (*76 mm*)
Guns, AA	6—40 mm
A/S weapons	DC racks
Main engines	2 geared turbines; 2 shafts; 52 000 shp
Boilers	3 Kampon
Speed, knots	27·5 on trials
Radius, miles	5 000 at 18 knots
Complement	250

1 Ex-US "RUDDEROW" TYPE

TAI YUAN (ex-USS *Riley*, DE 579) 27

Displacement, tons	1 450 standard; 2 230 full load
Length, feet (*metres*)	306·0 (*93·3*) oa
Beam, feet (*metres*)	37·0 (*11·3*)
Draught, feet (*metres*)	14·0 (*4·3*)
Guns, dual purpose	2—5 in 38 calibre
Guns, AA	6—40 mm (3 twin); 5—20 mm
Main engines	Turbo electric drive; GE geared turbines; 2 shafts; 12 000 shp
Boilers	2 Foster Wheeler
Speed, knots	24
Oil fuel, tons	378
Radius, miles	5 000 at 15 knots
Complement	180

Built by Bethlehem-Hingham. Launched on 29 Dec 1943 and completed on 13 Mar 1944. Transferred at Seattle, Wash on 10 July 1968.

4 Ex-US "BOSTWICK" TYPE

Displacement, tons	1 240 standard; 1 900 full load
Length, feet (*metres*)	306·0 (*92·3*) oa
Beam, feet (*metres*)	36·8 (*11·2*)
Draught, feet (*metres*)	12·0 (*3·7*)
Guns	4—3 in (*76 mm*) (*Tai Ho* 2—5 in)
Guns, AA	3 or 4—40 mm; 6 to 10—20 mm
A/S weapons	8 DCT
Torpedo tubes	3—21 in (*533 mm*) triple (*Tai Ho* 2 triple A/S; *Tai Ho* none)
Main engines	Diesel-electric; 2 shafts; 6 000 bhp
Speed, knots	19
Radius, miles	11 500 at 11 knots
Oil fuel, tons	300
Complement	150

Transferred on 31 Dec 1948. *Tai Ho*: bridge refitted, 3 inch replaced by 5 inch guns, new radar, in 1964.

1 Ex-US "EVARTS" TYPE

TAI KANG (ex-USS *Wyffels*, DE 6) 21

Displacement, tons	1 150 standard; 1 430 full load
Length, feet (*metres*)	289·5 (*88·2*) oa
Beam, feet (*metres*)	35·0 (*10·7*)
Draught, feet (*metres*)	10·7 (*3·3*)
Guns, dual purpose	3—3 in (*76 mm*) 50 cal
Guns, AA	4—40 mm; 11—20 mm
A/S weapons	9 DCT
Main engines	Diesel-electric; 2 shafts; 6 000 bhp
Speed, knots	19
Radius, miles	5 500 at 14 knots
Complement	120,

Built by Boston Navy Yard. Completed on 21 Apr 1943. Transferred in 1946. Sister ship *Tai Ping* (ex-USS *Decker* DE 47), was torpedoed and sunk by Chinese Republican torpedo boats off Tachen Island on 14 Nov 1954.

Destroyers—*continued*

No.	Builders	Laid down	Launched	Completed
15	Philadelphia Navy Yard	16 Nov 1938	14 Dec 1939	7 Sep 1940
14	Bethlehem (Quincy)	16 May 1938	15 Nov 1939	25 July 1940

HAN YANG　　　　　　　　　　　　　　　　*Official*

TAN YANG　　　　　　　　　　　*1970, Toshio Tamura*

Built by Sasebo, Japan, launched in 1939 and completed in 1940. Large refit in 1951-52, trials in Feb 1953. Rearmed with US guns in 1959. Now used as a training ship.

FRIGATES

TAI YUAN　　　　　　　　　　　*1971, Iain G. B. Lovie*

Name	No.	Launched	Completed
TAI CHAO (ex-USS *Carter*, DE 112)	26	29 Feb 1944	2 May 1944
TAI HO (ex-USS *Thomas*, DE 102)	23	31 July 1943	21 Nov 1943
TAI HU (ex-USS *Breeman*, DE 104)	25	31 July 1943	12 Dec 1943
TAI TSANG (ex-*Bostwick*, DE 103)	24	30 Aug 1943	21 Dec 1943

TAI HO (5 inch guns, bridge refitted)　　　　　*1970, Toshio Tamura*

Frigates—continued

12 Ex-US APD TYPE

CHUNG SHAN PF 44 (ex-*Blessman*, APD 48, ex-*DE* 69)
FU SHAN PF 35 (ex-*Truxton*, AP 98, ex-*DE* 282)
HENG SHAN PF 39 (ex-*Raymond W. Herndon*, APD 121, ex-*DE* 688)
HUA SHAN PF 33 (ex-*Donald W. Wolf*, APD 129, ex-*DE* 713)
KANG SHAN PF 43 (ex-*George W. Ingram*, APD 43, ex-*DE* 62)
LU SHAN PF 36 (ex-*Bull*, APD 78, ex-*DE* 693)
SHOU SHAN PF 37 (ex-*Kline*, APD 120, ex-*DE* 687)
TAI SHAN PF 38 (ex-*Register*, APD 92, ex-*DE* 233)
TIEN SHAN 315 (ex-*Kleinsmith*, APD 134, ex-*DE* 718)
WEN SHAN PF 34 (ex-*Gantner*, APD 42, ex-*DE* 60)
YU SHAN PF 44 (ex-*Kinzer*, APD 120, ex-*DE* 687)
PF 45 (ex-*Schmidt*, APD 761)

Displacement, tons	1 400 standard; 2 130 full load
Length, feet (*metres*)	300 (*91·4*) wl; 306 (*93·3*) oa
Beam, feet (*metres*)	37 (*11·3*)
Draught, feet (*mètres*)	12·7 (*3·9*)
Guns, dual purpose	1—5 in (*127 mm*) 38 cal. 2—5 in in *Heng Shan* and *Kang Shan*
Guns, AA	6—40 mm
Boilers	2 Express
Main engines	GE geared turbines, electric drive 12 000 shp; 2 shafts
Speed, knots	23
Radius, miles	5 500 at 15 knots
Oil fuel (tons)	350
Complement	204

HUA SHAN

1971, Iain G. B. Lovie

Former destroyer escorts converted by the USA and officially rated as High Speed Transports. *Kleinsmith* was transferred from the United States Navy to Nationalist China at Tsoyin, Taiwan, on 16 May 1960. Her new name *Tien Shan* means Heavenly Mountain. *Gantner* and *Walter B. Cobb* were transferred to Taiwan on 15 Mar 1966 at San Francisco, California, but *Walter B. Cobb* was lost at sea while under tow to Taiwan, and was replaced by *Bull*. *Donald W. Wolf*, *Kinzer*, *Kline*, and *Truxtun*, were transferred in 1965, *Raymond W. Herndon* and *Register* on 11 July 1966. *Blessman* and *George W. Ingram* on 19 May 1967. Only *Tien Shan* is rated as APD, the others as frigates. *Rendour* APD 102, (ex-DE 592) was not in the event transferred to Taiwan China, but to Mexico. A photograph of *Tien Shan* appears in the 1962-63 to 1970-71 editions, and of *Tai Kang* in the 1970-71 and earlier editions, For disposals of the older frigates, see 1970-71 and earlier editions.

ESCORT VESSELS

1 Ex-US PCE TYPE

WEI YUAN (ex-*Yung Hsiang*, ex-*PCE* 869, 6 Feb 1943) 42

Displacement, tons	640 standard; 903 full load
Dimensions, feet	180 wl; 184·5 × 33 × 9·5 max
Guns	2—3 in dp; 3—40 mm AA; 6—20 mm AA
Main engines	Diesel; 2 shafts; 1 800 bhp = 17 knots
Complement	110

Built by Albina Engine and Machinery Works, Portland, Ore. One 3 inch 50 cal gun was added in 1955. Rated as gunboat. *Yung Tai*, PCE 62 (ex-41, ex-USS *PCE* 867) was damaged in action on 14 Nov 1965 and later discarded.

YUNG TAI

1963, Official

3 Ex-US MSF TYPE

CHU YUNG (ex-USS *Waxwing*, MSF 389) PCE 67
PING CHING (ex-USS *Steady*, MSF 118) PCE 70
WU SHENG (ex-USS *Redstart*, MSF 378) PCE 66

Displacement, tons	890 standard; 1 250 full load
Dimensions, feet	215 wl; 221·2 oa × 32·5 × 10·8 max
Guns	2—3 in 50 cal (single); 4—40 mm AA (2 twin); 4—20 mm AA (2 twin)
A/S weapons	1 ASW projector, 1 triple ASW torpedo tube mounting 2 DC projectors; 2 DCT
Main engines	2 shafts; 3 530 bhp = 18 knots
Complement	95

Former US Fleet Minesweepers of the "Auk" Class. Steel hulled. Built by American SB Co. Cleveland, Ohio (*Waxwing*) and Savannah Mach & Foundry Co (*Redstart*) Launched and completed in 1964-65. Minesweeping gear removed so that the ships can be employed as Escort Patrol Vessels. *Redstart* and *Waxwing* were transferred on 22 July 1965 and 14 Oct 1965, respectively, at Seattle, Washington. *Steady* was purchased on 15 Aug 1967 and transferred in 1968.

FLEET MINESWEEPERS

3 Ex-US MSF (ex-AM) TYPE

47 YUNG CHIA	(ex-USS *Implicit*,	AM 246, 6 Sep 1943)	2 rated as
48 YUNG HSIU	(ex-USS *Pinnacle*,	AM 274, 11 Sep 1943)	Minesweepers
50 YUNG FENG	(ex-USS *Prime*,	AM 279, 22 Jan 1944)	(Minelayer)

Displacement, tons	650 standard; 945 full load
Dimensions, feet	180 wl; 184·5 oa × 33 × 9·8 max
Guns	1—3 in dp; 3—40 mm AA; 6—20 mm AA
Main engines	Diesel; 2 shafts; 1 710 bhp = 14·8 knots
Complement	104

All MSF (ex-AM) type fleet minesweepers acquired from the US Navy. Launch dates above. *Yung Feng* is fitted for minelaying with tracks on her stern and is rated as a coastal minelayer. *Yung Hsing* served as a maritime customs vessel. *Yung Ting* was converted to a survey ship, see later page.

DISPOSALS
Sister ships *Yung Chun* No. 52 (ex-USS *Gavia*, AM 363), *Yung Ho*, No. 53 (ex-USS *Delegate*, AM 217) and *Yung Kang*, No. 54 (ex-USS *Elusive*, AM 225), all rated as gunboats, and *Yung Hsing*, No. A 4 (ex-USS *Embattle*, AM 226) in the Coastguard, were scrapped in 1964. *Yung Ning*, No. 46 (ex-USS *Magnet*, AM 260), rated as a minesweeper, was discarded in 1963. *Yung Sheng*, No. 43 (ex-USS *Lance*, AM 257), *Yung Shou* (ex-USS *Pivot*, AM 276) and *Yung Shun* (ex-USS *Logic*, AM 258) rated as minesweepers, were discarded in 1968.

LOSSES
Yung Chang (ex-USS *Refresh*, AM 287) 51, of this class, rated as a gunboat, was sunk off Southern China on 14 Nov 1965 by a Chinese Communist escort.
Chein Men (ex-USS *Toucan*, MSF 387) PCE 45, transferred from the US Navy to the Taiwan Navy on 22 Dec 1964, was sunk by Communist Chinese warships south of Quemoy on 6 Aug 1965.

YUNG CHANG

196? Official

PATROL VESSELS
(Submarine Chasers)
12 EX-US PC TYPE

109 CHIH KIANG	(ex-US PC 1078), 8 Aug 1942	
116 CHING KIANG	(ex-US PC 1168), 3 July 1943	
115 CHUNG KIANG	(ex-US PC 1262), 27 Mar 1943	
105 FUKIANG	(ex-Hwangpu, ex-US PC 492) 29 Dec 1941	
108 HSIANG KIANG	(ex-US PC 786) 6 Feb 1943	
120 HSI KIANG	(ex-USS Susanville, ex-PC 1149)	
113 KUNG KIANG	(ex-USS PC 1233), 11 Jan 1943	
111 LI KIANG	(ex-US PC 1208), 15 Sep 1943	
122 PEI KIANG	(ex-USS Hanford, ex-PC 1142)	
114 PO LIANG	(ex-US PC 1254), 31 Oct 1942	
125 TO KIANG	(ex-USS Milledgeville, ex-PC 1263)	
119 TUNG KIANG	(ex-USS Placerville, ex-PC 1087)	

Displacement, tons	280 standard; 450 full load
Dimensions, feet	173·7 oa × 23 × 10·8 max
Guns	1—3 in, 50 cal; 1—40 mm AA; 5—20 mm AA
Main engines	Diesel; 2 880 bhp = 20 knots
Oil fuel, tons	60
Radius, miles	5 000 at 10 knots
Complement	65

Launch dates above. *Hanford, Placerville, Escondido* and *Vandalia* were transferred from US Navy on 15 July 1957 and *Milledgeville* in July 1959. *Chien Fang* and *Wu Sung* were discarded in 1951-52, and *Chialing* (ex-US PC 1247) in 1964. *Yuan Kiang* was officially deleted from the list in 1966. *Chang Kiang* (ex-US PC 1232) PC 118, was sunk by Chinese Republican warships south of Quemoy on 6 Aug 1965. *Liu Kiang* and *Han Kiang* were discarded locally in 1969.

CHUNG KIANG   *United States Navy, Official*

9 Ex-US SC TYPE

SC 502 (ex-*Chu Chien*, ex-*SC 708*)	SC 503 (ex-103 *Chu Chien*, ex-*SC 698*)
Ex-SC 518 Ex-SC 648	Ex-SC 722 Ex-SC 735
Ex-SC 637 Ex-SC 703	Ex-SC 723

Displacement, tons	95 standard; 148 full load
Dimensions, feet	107·5 wl; 110·9 oa × 17 × 6·5
Guns	1—40 mm AA
Main engines	Diesel; 2 shafts; 800 bhp = 15·5 knots
Complement	28

PATROL VESSEL
(Gunboat Ex-Submarine Chaser)
1 Ex-US PGM (ex-PC) TYPE

117 CHU KIANG (ex-USS PGM 31, ex-PC 1567)

Displacement, tons	295 standard; 470 full load
Dimensions, feet	170 wl; 173·7 oa × 23 × 11
Guns	1—3 in; 1—40 mm AA; 4—20 mm AA
Main engines	2 GM diesels; 2 800 bhp = 19 knots
Oil fuel, tons	60
Radius, miles	5 000 at 9 knots
Complement	80

Built by Leatham D. Smith SB Co, Sturgeon Bay, Wis. Laid down on 18 July 1944, launched on 23 Sep 1944 and completed on 17 Jan 1945. Transferred from the US Navy in 1954. *Ling Chiang* 103 (ex-*Tung Ting*, ex-USS PGM 13) was torpedoed and sunk by Chinese Republican torpedo boats on 10 Jan 1955. *Ying Chiang* 101 (ex-*Pao Ying*, ex-USS PGM 20) was torpedoed by Republican torpedo boats on 20 Jan 1955, and was subsequently scrapped as beyond economical repair.

Sister ship *Ou Chang*, 102 (ex-*Hung Tse*, ex-USS PGM 26), *Chu Chiang*, 106 (ex-*Ya Ling*, ex-49, ex-*Hai Hung*, SC 401), ex-Japanese type, and the very old gunboat *Chu Kuan*, 75, Japanese built, were scrapped in 1964.
The old gunboat *Yung Hsiang*, also Japanese built, and the old auxiliary minelayer *Chieh 29* (ex-*Kuroshimu*), Japanese built, were previously deleted from the active list.

CHU KIANG   *1962, Official*

COASTAL MINESWEEPERS
7 Ex-US MSC TYPE

YUNG AN,	MSC 56 (ex-USS MSC 140)
YUNG CHI,	MSC 160 (ex-USS MSC 300)
YUNG CHUAN,	MSC 58 (ex-USS MSC 278)
YUNG HSIN,	MSC 59 (ex-USS MSC 302)
YUNG LO,	MSC 161 (ex-USS MSC 306)
YUNG NIEN,	MSC 57 (ex-USS MSC 277)
YUNG PING,	MSC 55 (ex-USS MSC 123)

Displacement, tons	335 light; 378 full load
Dimensions, feet	138 pp; 145 oa × 27 × 8·5
Guns	2—20 mm AA
Main engines	2 GM diesels; 2 shafts; 880 bhp = 14 knots
Complement	40 (5 officers, 35 men)

"Bluebird" class non-magnetic and wooden hull construction. Built in USA. MSC 123 and MSC 140 were transferred to Taiwan on 4 June 1955. MSC 227, launched on 30 June 1958, and MSC 278, launched on 1 Aug 1958, both built by the Tacoma Boatbuilding Co, were transferred at Seattle on 10 June and 10 July respectively, in 1959. MSC 302 transferred on 5 Mar 1965, MSC 300 on 15 Apr 1965, MSC 306 on 18 May 1966.

YUNG NIEN   *1963, Official*

JAPANESE TYPE
The coastal minesweepers *Chiang*, No. 541, and *Chiang Yung*, No. 542, former Japanese auxiliary minesweepers No. 22 and No. 19, respectively, were discarded in 1968

8 ex-US MSC (ex-AMS) TYPE

(ex-*Charleroi*, ex-*AMS* 152)	(ex-*Diksmude*, ex-*AMS* 65)
(ex-*De Panne*, ex-*AMS* 131)	(ex-*Lier*, ex-*AMS* 63)
(ex-*Diest*, ex-*AMS* 77)	(ex-*Maasieck*, ex-*AMS* 78)
(ex-*Eekloo*, ex-*AMS* 101)	(ex-*St. Nicholas*, ex-*AMS* 64)

Displacement, tons	330 light; 390 full load
Dimensions, feet	139 pp; 144 oa × 27·9 × 7·5 (8 max)
Guns	1—40 mm AA
Main engines	2 GM diesels; 2 shafts; 880 bhp = 13·5 knots max
Oil fuel tons	28
Range, miles	2 700 at 10·5 knots
Complement	39

Formerly units of the Belgian Navy, built in the US and in Belgian yards under MAP. Returned to the USN as surplus to Belgian requirements and re-allocated to China in 1969.

Ex-CHARLEROI   *1971 John G. Callis*

INSHORE MINESWEEPERS
2 ex-US MSI TYPE

Displacement, tons	160 light; 190 full load
Dimensions, feet	106·7 pp; 113·2 oa ×22·3 × 6 (7 max)
Guns	1—20 mm AA
Main engines	2 diesels; 2 shafts; 1 260 bhp = 15 knots max
Oil fuel (tons)	18
Range, miles	2 300 at 10 knots
Complement	17

Former inshore minesweepers of the Belgian Navy built as a US "offshore procurement". Returned to US custody and retransferred in 1969.

DOCK LANDING SHIP

1 Ex-US "ASHLAND" CLASS

TUNG HAI LSD 191 (ex-USS *White Marsh*, LSD 8)

Displacement, tons	4 790 standard; 8 700 full load
Dimensions, feet	454 wl; 457·8 oa × 72 × 18
Guns	12—40 mm AA
Main engines	Skinner Unaflow; 2 shafts; 7 400 ihp = 15·6 knots
Boilers	2, of 2-drum type
Complement	326 (total accommodation)

Built by Moore Dry Dock Co. Launched on 19 July 1943. Designed to serve as parent ship for landing craft and coastal craft. Transferred from the US Navy to the Chinese (Taiwan) Navy on 17 Nov 1960 at Long Beach, California, under the Military Aid Programme.

TUNG HAI   1965, Official

AMPHIBIOUS FORCE FLAGSHIPS

2 Ex-US LST TYPE

AGC 1 **KAO HSIUNG** (ex-LST *Chung Hsi*, ex-USS *LST 735 USS Dukes County*)
AGC 2 ex-LST *Chung Shi*, ex-USS *LST 1010*

Converted from LST type, *Kao Hsiung* in 1964, AGC 2 in 1968

KAO HSIUNG (ex-*Chung Hai*) as LST   Official

TANK LANDING SHIPS

21 Ex-US LST TYPE

216 **CHUNG KUANG** (ex-USS *LST* 503)
227 **CHUNG MING** (ex-USS *Sweetwater County*, LST 1152)
231 **CHUNG YEA** (ex-USS *Sublette County*, LST 1144)
218 **CHUNG CHIH** (ex-USS *Berkeley County*, LST 279)
221 **CHUNG CH'UAN** (ex-*Wan Yiu*, ex-*Lu Yi*, ex-*LST* 640)
224 **CHUNG CHENG** (ex-USS *Lafayette County*, LST 859)
206 **CHUNG CHI** (ex-*LST* 1017)
205 **CHUNG CHIEN** (ex-*LST* 716)
225 **CHUNG CHIANG** (ex-USS *San Bernadino County*, LST 1110)
230 **CHUNG BANG** (ex-USS *LST* 578)
223 **CHUNG FU** (ex-USS *Iron County*, LST 840)
201 **CHUNG HAI** (ex-*LST* 755)
204 **CHUNG HSING** (ex-*LST* 557)
208 **CHUNG SHUN** (ex-*Wan Kuo*, ex-*LST* 732)
209 **CHUNG LIEN** (ex-*LST* 1050)
222 **CHUNG SHENG** (ex-*LST* 1033)
228 **CHUNG SUO** (ex-USS *Bradley County*, LST 400)
203 **CHUNG TING** (ex-*LST* 537)
229 **CHUNG WAN** (ex-*LST* 535)
215 **CHUNG YU** (ex-*Wan Li*, ex-*LST* 520
210 **CHUNG YUNG** (ex-*LST* 574)

Displacement, tons	1 653 standard; 4 080 full load
Dimensions, feet	316 wl; 328 oa × 50 × 14 max
Guns	6—40 mm AA; 12—20 mm AA
Main engines	Diesel; 2 shafts; 1 700 bhp = 11 knots
Complement	119

LST 218, 400 and 735 transferred to Nationalist China at San Diego, in July 1955 and 1960 (*Dukes County*), LST 216 at San Diego 29 April 1955, LST 226 and LST 227 at Seattle on 21 Oct 1958, LST 520, 535 and 578 in Sep 1958, LST 213, 224 and 225 in 1958, LST 231 at Charleston, SC, on 21 Sep 1961. Ex-US LST 732 and ex-US LST 1152 are on loan to US with Chinese crews. An LST was torpedoed and sunk by Chinese Republican torpedo boats off Quemoy on 25 Aug 1958. LST 208 *Chung Shun* (ex-*LST* 993) is believed to have been lost, since a newly acquired LST has been numbered 208. Five of above (200, 202, 308, 313, 315) were acquired from the merchant service in 1955. LST 313 *Chung Kung* (ex-*Chung* ex-*LST* 945) was scrapped in 1956, LST 207 *Chung Cheng* in 1958. *Chung Hsi* ex-LST 219, ex-USS *LST* 735 and *Chung Shih*, ex-LST 236, ex-USS *LST* 1010, both converted to Amphibious Force Flagships

REPAIR SHIP (ARL ex-LST)

1 Ex-US LST TYPE

336 **SHUNG SHAN** (ex-*Vulcain*, ex-USS *Agenor*, ARL 3, ex-*LST 490*)

Displacement, tons	1 625 light; 4 080 full load
Dimensions, feet	328 oa × 50 × 14·5
Guns	8—40 mm AA; 8—20 mm AA
Main engines	2 diesels; 1 700 bhp = 10·8 knots
Oil fuel, tons	1 060
Radius, miles	6 000 at 9 knots

Former US ocean tank carrier with bow doors. Built by Kaiser Co, Inc, Vancouver, Wash. Laid down on 24 Jan 1943. Launched on 3 Apr 1943. Completed on 20 Aug 1943. Transferred from the US Navy to France in 1951 for service in Indo-China. Returned to the USA by France, and then transferred to (Taiwan) China by the USA on 15 Sep 1957.

MEDIUM LANDING SHIPS

15 Ex-US LSM TYPE

241 **MEI CHIN** (ex-*LSM* 155)   249 **MEI CHIEN** (ex-*LSM* 76)
245 **MEI HENG** (ex-*LSM* 456)   250 **MEI HWA** (ex-*LSM* 256)
248 **MEI HO** (ex-*LSM* 13)   251 **MEI CHEN** (ex-*LSM* 422)
244 **MEI PENG** (ex-*LSM* 431)   252 **MEI KUN** (ex-*LSM* 478)
246 **MEI HUNG** (ex-*LSM* 442)   253 **MEI PING** (ex-USS *LSM* 471)
247 **MEI SUNG** (ex-*LSM* 457)   254 **MEI WEN** (ex-*LSM* 472)
243 **MEI I** (ex-*LSM* 285)   255 **MEI HAN** (ex-*LSM* 474)
                                     256 **MEI LO** (ex-USS *LSM* 362)

Displacement, tons	743 standard; 1 095 full load
Dimensions, feet	196·5 wl; 203·5 oa × 34·5 × 7·3
Guns	2—40 mm AA; 4—20 mm AA
Main engines	Diesel; 2 shafts; 2 800 bhp = 12 knots
Complement	59 (*Mei Lo* 6 officers and 46 men)

Mei Lo 242 (ex-*LSM* 157) was destroyed by Chinese Communist artillery and beached on Quemoy Island on 8 Sep 1958. *Mei Wen*, 254, and *Mei Han*, 255, were transferred from the United States Navy at Seattle, Wn, on 6 Feb 1959. LSM 242, LSM 471 and LSM 478 were also loaned to Nationalist China by the USA in 1959. *Mei Lo* 256 (ex-*LSM* 362) was transferred at Bremeston, Wash in May 1962.

MEI KUN   1962. Official

LANDING CRAFT

5 LSIL TYPE

264 **LIEN CHENG** (ex-*LSIL* 630)   261 **LIEN CHU** (ex-*LSIL* 233)
265 **LIEN HUA** (ex-*LSIL* 631)   262 **LIEN LI** (ex-*LSIL* 417)
                                      263 **LIEN SHENG** (ex-*LSIL* 418)

Displacement, tons	227 standard; 387 full load
Dimensions, feet	159 × 23·7 × 5·7
Guns	2—20 mm AA
Main engines	Diesel; 2 shafts; 1 320 bhp = 14 knots
Complement	28

Former United States Landing Craft Infantry (Gunboat), and Landing Craft Infantry (Mortar). Armament varies. China (Taiwan) received ex-US LSIL 818, 1017, 1092 from the United States under MDAP (they were formerly on loan to France from the USA for service in Indo-China) to be used only for cannibalization.

LIEN HUA   1963, Official

Landing Craft—*continued*

3 LSSL TYPE

| 472 LIEN CHIH (ex-USS *LSSL* 81) | 473 LIEN JEN (ex-USS *LSSL* 95) |
| | 427 LIEN YUNG (ex-USS *LSSL* 56) |

Displacement. tons	227 standard; 387 full load
Dimensions. feet	153 wl; 158 oa × 28·7 × 5·7
Guns	6—40 mm AA (twin); 10 rocket launchers
Main engines	GM diesels; 2 shafts; 1,320 bhp = 14·4 knots
Complement	78

Ex-US LSSL's formerly LCS(L) 3. Landing Craft Support (Large) transferred at Yokosuka. Japan. on 19 Feb 1954. Taiwan received ex-US LSSL 2 and 28 from USA under MDAP (they were formerly on loan to France from USA for service in Indo-China) to be used for cannibalization.

LIEN Type   *Added 1971*

21 LCU (ex-LCT) TYPE

485 HO CHANG (ex-*LCT* 512)	505 HO FENG (ex-*LCU* 1397)
506 HO CHAO (ex-*LCU* 1429)	502 HO HOEI (ex-*LCU* 1218)
486 HO CHENG (ex-*LCT* 1145)	491 HO MENG (ex-*LCU* 1599)
501 HO CHI (ex-*LCU* 1212)	492 HO MOU (ex-*LCU* 1600)
496 HO CHIEN (ex-*LCU* 1278)	490 HO SENG (ex-*LCU* 1598)
489 HO CHUAN (ex-*LCU* 489)	488 HO SHAN (ex-*LCU* 1596)
481 HO CHUN (ex-*LCT* 892)	493 HO SHOU (ex-*LCU* 1601)
484 HO CHUNG (ex-*LCT* 849)	507 HO TENG (ex-*LCU* 1452)
482 HO CH'UNG (ex-*LCT* 1213)	503 HO YAO (ex-*LCU* 1244)
504 HO DENG (ex-*LCU* 1367)	495 HO YUNG (ex-*LCU* 1271)
	494 HO (ex-*LCU* 1225)

Displacement. tons	143 standard; 285 full load
Dimensions. feet	114·2 × 32·7 × 3·5
Guns	2—20 mm AA
Main engines	Diesel; 3 shafts; 675 bhp = 10 knots
Complement	11

In 1964 ex-LCU 1212, 1218, 1367, 1397, and 1452 transferred from USA under MAP.

SURVEY SHIPS

362 YANG MING (ex-45 *Yung Ting*, ex-USS *Lucid*, AM 259)

Displacement. tons	650 standard; 945 full load
Dimensions. feet	180 wl; 184·5 oa × 33 × 9·8 max
Main engines	Diesels; 2 shafts; 1 710 bhp = 14·8 knots

Former US fleet minesweeper converted into a survey ship. Launched 5 June 1943.

266 LIEN CHING

Former US landing craft of the LSIL type converted into a survey ship. See particulars at bottom of Col 2 on the previous page.

PATROL CRAFT

521 HAI LI	546 CHIANG LIEN	591 P'AO 111	635 P'AO 5
522 HAI NING	547 CHIANG P'ING	592 P'AO 112	636 P'AO 6
523 HAI YAO	548 CHIANG FENG	593 P'AO 113	637 P'AO 7
524 HAI WEI	549 CHIANG KUNG	594 P'AO 114	638 P'AO 8
525 HAI AN	550 CHIANG LUN	595 P'AO 115	639 P'AO 9
526 HAI CHING	551 CHIANG CH'ENG	596 P'AO 116	640 P'AO 10
542 CHIANG YUNG	581 P'AO 101	631 P'AO 1	641 P'AO 11
543 CHIANG HSIU	584 P'AO 104	632 P'AO 2	642 P'AO 12
544 CHIANG TING	587 P'AO 107	633 P'AO 3	643 P'AO 13
545 CHIANG MING	588 P'AO 408	634 P'AO 4	646 P'AO 16

6 Ex-HDML TYPE

681 FANG I	684 FANG SEU	686 FANG LIU
682 FANG SAN	685 FANG CHI	687 FSNG PA

Displacement. tons	46 standard; 54 full load
Dimensions. feet	72 × 15·9 × 4·8
Guns	1—40 mm; 1—20 mm; 4 MG
Main engines	2 Diesels; 230 bhp = 11 knots

Former harbour defence motor launches. Built in Great Britain in 1942-43.

2 MTB TYPE

FU CHOU (PT 511)   **HSUEH CHIH** (PT5 12)

Built by Mitsubishi Zosen Co, Japan in 1957. Armed with 18-inch torpedo tubes and 1—20 mm AA gun aft.

2 HIGGINS TYPE

PT 32   **PT 33**

Former US PT boats, now used as submarine chasers.

OILERS

307 CHANG PEI (ex-USS *Pecatonica*, AOG 57)

Displacement. tons	1 850 light; 4 335 full load
Measurement. tons	2 575 deadweight
Dimensions. feet	292 wl; 310·8 oa × 48·5 × 15·7 max
Guns	4—3 in dp 50 cal
Main engines	Diesel-electric; 2 shafts; 3 300 bhp = 14 knots

Former US petrol carrier of the "Patapsco" class. Built by Cargill, Inc, Savage, Minn. Laid down on 6 Dec 1944. Launched on 17 Mar 1945. Transferred to Taiwan China under MAP .on 24 Apr 1961 at Tsoying, Taiwan. Crew 124.

306 KUAI CHI (ex-*Soviet Tuapse*)
Petrol Tanker. Captured in 1954. Commissioned in Nationalist Navy in Feb 1956.

304 SZU MING (ex-USS *YO* 198)

Displacement. tons	1 400 full load
Dimensions. feet	174 oa × 32 × 15
Guns	1—25 mm; 2—20 mm; 2 MG
Main engines	Diesel; 560 bhp = 11 knots

Built in USA in 1954 by Manitowoc SB Co, Wis. Capacity 6 570 barrels. Ex-USS YO 175 was transferred under MAP in March 1967.

302 HSIN KAO (ex-*Tai Hwa*, ex-USS *Towaliga*, AOG 42)

Displacement. tons	700 standard; 2 700 full load
Measurement. tons	1 453 deadweight
Dimensions. feet	212·5 wl; 220·5 oa × 37 × 12·8
Guns	1—3 in; 2—40 mm AA; 3—20 mm AA
Main engines	Diesel; 1 shaft; 800 bhp = 10 knots

Ex-US. TI-M-A2 type, "Mettawee" class. Launched by East Coast Shipyards on 29 Oct 1944. Sister ship *Yu Chuan*, No. 303 (ex-*Wautanga*, AOG 22, ex-*Conrol*, ex-USS *Sakatonchee*, YOG 52) and the oiler *Ho Lan*, No 305 (ex-Polish oiler *Praca*) were scrapped in 1964.

DISPOSALS.
The oiler *Omei* was scrapped at Kaoshiung Naval Base Aug to Sept 1967.

TRANSPORTS

311 WULING (ex-*Shirasaki*)

Displacement. tons	950
Dimensions. feet	203 × 31·2 × 10·2
Guns	1—3 in; 1—40 mm AA; 8—25 mm AA; 4 MG
Main engines	2 diesels; 600 bhp = 15 knots

Former Japanese. Refrigerated cargo ship. Destroyer hull.

313 TIEN CHU	315 CHIU HUA	HUEI FENG
316 TIEN TAI	317 CHUNG SHAN	

Displacements and other particulars vary in individual ships. *Tien Chu* is ex-Polish cargo ship *Prezedent Gottwald* captured by China while trading with the Communists.

TUGS

TA TUNG (ex-USS *Chickasaw*, ATF 83) ATF 548

Displacement. tons	1 235 standard; 1 675 full load
Dimensions. feet	195 wl; 205 oa × 38·5 × 15·4 max
Guns	1—3 in; 2—20 mm
Main engines	GM diesel electric; 1 shaft; 3 000 bhp = 16·5 knots

US fleet ocean tug of the "Apache" class transferred on loan in Jan 1966. Used as a gunboat.

342 TA WU (ex-*Wu Kung*, ex-*Pei Chi* No. 1, ex-*LT*) **343 TA MING** (ex-*LT* 000)

Displacement. tons	570 light; 967 full load
Dimensions. feet	149 oa × 33 × 15
Guns	1—40 mm; 2—20 mm
Main engines	Reciprocating. Oil fuel. 1 200 hp = 12 knots

Built in USA in 1943. *Ta Ch'ing* reported decommissioned on 1 June 1951.

345 TA YU (ex-*LT* 310)   **347 TA SHUEH** (ex-USS *Tonkowa*, ATA 176)
                              TA (ex-USS *Geronimo*, ATA 207)

Displacement. tons	534 standard; 835 full load
Dimensions. feet	133·7 wl; 143 oa × 33·9 × 13·2
Guns	2—25 mm; 2 MG; (*Ta Sueh* 1—3 in)
Main engines	Diesel-electric; 1 500 hp = 12·5 knots

Ta Yu is a former US Army tug. *Ta Shueh* is a former US Navy tug of the "Marikopa" class built by Levingstone SB Co, Orange, Texas, completed on 19 Aug 1944, and transferred on 5 Apr 1962. *Geronimo* was transferred on loan on 8 Feb 1969 from the United States Coast Guard.
(There are small harbour tugs YTL 427, YTL 428, YTL 454, YTL 584 and YTL 585 transferred by USA in 1963-64).
Floating Drydock, ex-USS PAD 9 was transferred under MAP in Oct 1967.

COLOMBIA

Administration

Fleet Commander:
Vice Admiral Jaime Parra Ramirez

Chief of Naval Operations
Rear Admiral Eduardo Wills Olaya

Chief of Naval Staff:
Rear Admiral Magin Ortiga Sanclemente

Diplomatic Representation

Naval Attaché in Washington:
Captain Gabriel R. Reyes Cardenas

Strength of the Fleet

3 Destroyers
4 Destroyer Escort Transports
9 Coast Guard Patrol Vessels
5 River Gunboats
2 Surveying Vessels
10 Patrol Motor Launches
5 Transports
5 Oilers.
8 Support Ships and Service Craft
11 Tugs

Designation

Ships names are prefaced by the letters "ARC" (Armada Republica de Colombia)

Personnel

1971: 700 officers and 6 500 men

Mercantile Marine

Lloyd's Register of Shipping:
49 vessels of 234 526 tons gross

DESTROYERS (Destructores)

Name	No.	Builders	Laid down	Launched	Completed
SIETE DE AGOSTO	06	Götaverken, Göteborg	Nov 1955	19 June 1956	31 Oct 1958
VEINTE DE JULIO	05	Kockums Mek Verkstads A/B, Malmo	Oct 1955	26 June 1956	15 June 1958

2 MODIFIED "HALLAND" TYPE

Displacement, tons	2 650 standard; 3 100 full load
Length, feet (*metres*)	380·5 (*116·0*) pp; 397·2 (*121·1*) wl
Beam, feet (*metres*)	40·7 (*12·4*)
Draught, feet (*metres*)	12·5 (*3·8*)
Guns, surface	6—4·7 in (*120*) mm, 3 twin turrets
Guns, AA	4—40 mm, single mounts
Torpedo tubes	4—21 in (*533 mm*)
A/S weapons	1 quadruple DC rocket launcher
Boilers	2 Penhöet, Motala Verkstad; 568 psi; 840°F
Main engines	De Laval double reduction geared turbines; 55 000 shp; 2 shafts
Range, miles	445 at 35 knots
Oil fuel (tons)	524
Speed, knots	30 nominal, 16 economical
Complement	260 (20 officers, 240 men)

Modified Swedish "Halland" type ordered in 1954. The hull and machinery are similar but they have different armament (six 4·7 inch instead of four, no 57 mm guns, four 40 mm guns instead of six, and four torpedo tubes instead of eight) and different accommodation arrangements. They have an anti-submarine rocket projector, more radar and communication equipment, and air conditioned living spaces, having been designed for the tropics.

RADAR
Search. HSA LWO 3—SGR 114.
Tactical. HSA DA 02—SGR 105.
Fire Control. X Band, probably HSA M 20 series.

NOMENCLATURE. The change of name from *13 de Junio* to *7 de Agosto* was decreed by the Colombian Navy in July 1957.

ENGINEERING. Although the designed speed was 35 knots it is officially stated that the maximum sustained speed does not exceed 25 knots.

7 DE AGOSTO   *1971, Colombian Navy, Official*

20 DE JULIO   *1970, Colombian Navy, Official*

Name	No.	Builders	Laid down	Launched	Completed
ANTIOQUIA (ex-USS *Hale*, DD 642)	DD 01	Bath Iron Works Corporation, Bath, Maine	23 Nov 1942	4 Apr 1943	15 June 1943

Displacement, tons	2 100 standard; 2 952 full load
Length, feet (*metres*)	369 (*112·5*) pp; 376 (*114·8*) oa
Beam, feet (*metres*)	39·5 (*12·0*)
Draught, feet (*metres*)	12·3 (*3·8*) mean; 18·0 (*5·5*) max
Guns, surface	4—5 in (*127 mm*) 38 cal.
Guns, AA	6—3 in (*76 mm*) 50 cal.
Torpedo tubes	5—21 in (*533 mm*) quintrupled
A/S weapons	2 fixed Hedgehogs; 1 DC rack 2 side-launching torpedo racks
Boilers	4 Babcock & Wilcox; 615 psi; 850°F
Main engines	2 sets GE geared turbines 60 000 shp; 2 shafts
Speed, knots	35 designed, 37 max. 14 econ
Radius, miles	6 000 at 14 knots
Oil fuel (tons)	650
Complement	300 (peace); 350 (war)

Former US destroyer of the "Fletcher" class. Transferred from the US Navy at Boston, Massachusetts, on 23 Jan 1961, and renamed *Antioquia*.

RADAR
Search. SPS 6.
Tactical. SPS 10.
Fire Control. X Band.

Of the three frigates of the US "Tacoma" class, similar to the original British "River" type, *Capitan Tono*, FG 12 (ex-USS *Bisbee*, PF 46) was discarded in Dec 1962, *Almirante Padilla*, FG 11 (ex-USS *Groton*, PF 29) in Jan 1965, and *Almirante Brion*, FG 14 (ex-USS *Burlington*, PF 51) in 1968.

ANTIOQUIA   *1970, Colombian Navy, Official*

DESTROYER TRANSPORTS

ALMIRANTE PADILLA   *1971, Colombian Navy, Official*

ALMIRANTE BRION   *1971, Colombian Navy, Official*

ALMIRANTE BRION (ex-*USS Burke APD* 65, ex-*DE* 215)   DT 07
ALMIRANTE PADILLA (ex-*USS Tollberg APD* 103, ex-*DE* 593)   DT 12
ALMIRANTE TONO (ex-*USS Bassett APD* 73, ex-*DE* 672)
CORDOBA (ex-*USS Ruchamkin LPR* 89, ex-*APD* 89, ex-*DE* 228)   DT 15

Displacement, tons	1 400 standard ; 2 130 full load
Dimensions, feet	300 wl ; 306 oa × 37 × 12·7 max
Guns	1—5 in, 38 cal dp ; 6—40 mm AA
Main engines	GE turbo-electric ; 2 shafts ; 12 000 shp = 23·6 knots
Boilers	2 "D" Express
Oil fuel (tons)	350
Radius, miles	5 500 at 15 knots
Complement	204 accommodation plus 162 troop capacity

Former US high speed transports (converted destroyer escorts). *Almirante Padilla* was built by Bethlehem SB Co, Hingham, Mass, laid down on 30 Dec 1943, launched on 12 Feb 1944, completed on 31 Jan 1945 and transferred on 14 Aug 1965. *Almirante Tono* was built by Consolidated Steel Co, Orange, Tex, laid down on 28 Nov 1943, launched on 15 Jan 1944, completed on 23 Feb 1945 and transferred at Boston, Mass, on 6 Sep 1968. *Almirante Brion* was built by Philadelphia Navy Yard, laid down on 1 Jan 1943, launched on 3 Apr 1943, completed on 20 Aug 1943 and transferred on 8 Dec 1968. *Cordoba* was built by Philadelphia Navy Yard, laid down on 14 Feb 1944, launched on 15 June 1944 and transferred on 24 Nov 1969.

CORDOBA   *1971, Columbian Navy, Official*

ALMIRANTE PADILLA   *1969. Official*

COAST GUARD VESSELS

CARLOS ALBAN

CARLOS ALBAN   *1971, Colombian Navy, Official*

CARLOS E. RESTREPO	**ESTEBAN JARAMILLO**	**PEDRO GUAL**
Displacement, tons	123·5	
Dimensions, feet	107·8 pp × 18 × 6	
Guns	1—20 mm AA	
Main engines	2 Maybach diesels ; 2 450 bhp = 26 knots	

Built by Werft Gebr. Schurenstedt KG Bardenfleth in 1964. Pennant Nos. AN 206, AN 205 and AN 204, respectively.

PEDRO GUAL   *1965. Colombian Navy, Official*

OLAYA HERRERA

Displacement, tons	40
Dimensions, feet	68·8 pp × 12·8 × 3·5
Guns	1—·50 Browning AA
Main engines	2 Merbens diesels ; 570 bhp

Built by Astilleros Magdalena, Barranquilla, in 1960. Pennant No. AN 203.

GENERAL RAFAEL REYES	**GENERAL VASQUES COBO**
Displacement, tons	146
Dimensions, feet	118 pp ; 124·7 oa × 23 × 5
Guns	1—40 mm
Main engines	2 Maybach diesels ; 2 400 bhp = 18 knots

Built by Lürssen Werft, Vegesack. Launched on 10 Nov and 27 Sep 1955, respectively. Delivered in May 1956. Pennant Nos. AN 01 and AN 02 respectively. Photograph of *General Vasques Cobo* in the 1957-58 to 1964-65 editions.

ESPARTANA

Displacement, tons	50
Dimensions, feet	90 wl ; 96 oa × 13·5 × 4
Guns	1—20 mm AA
Main engines	2 diesels ; 300 bhp = 13·5 knots

Launched on 22 June 1950 at Cartagena Naval Dockyard. Pennant No. GC 100. Photographs of *Espartana* appear in the 1953-54 to 1968-69 editions.

CAPITAN BINNEY

Displacement, tons	23
Dimensions, feet	67 × 10·7 × 3·5
Main engines	Diesels ; 115 bhp = 13 knots

Built at Cartagena in 1947. Buoy and lighthouse inspection boat. Named after first head of Colombian Naval Academy, Lt-Commander Ralph Douglas Binney, RN. Pennant No. GC 101.

CAPITAN BINNEY   *1971, Colombian Navy, Official*

RIVER GUNBOATS

3 "ARAUCA" CLASS

ARAUCA CF 37   **LETICIA** CF 36   **RIOHACHA** CF 35

Displacement, tons	184
Dimensions, feet	163·5 oa × 23·5 × 2·8
Guns	2—3 in, dp, 50 cal; 4—20 mm
Main engines	2 Caterpillar engines; 916 bhp = 13 knots
Range, miles	1 000
Complement	43

Built by Union Industrial de Barranquilla (Unial) Colombia. Launched in 1955. Completed in 1956. A photograph of *Arauca* appears in the 1957-58 to 1960-61 editions. *Leticia* has been equipped as a hospital ship.

LETICIA   *1971, Colombian Navy, Official*

RIOHACHA   *1966, Colombian Navy, Official*

BARRANQUILA CF 31   **CARTAGENA** CF 33

Displacement, tons	142
Dimensions, feet	130 pp; 137·8 oa × 23·5 × 2·8 max
Guns	2—3 in; 1—20 mm AA; 4 MG
Main engines	2 Gardner semi-diesels; 2 shafts; working in tunnels; 600 hp = 15·5 knots
Oil fuel (tons)	24
Complement	39

Both built by Yarrow & Co. Ltd. Scotstoun, Glasgow, and launched on 10 May 1930, and 26 Mar 1930, respectively. *Barranquilla* was modernised in Cartagena with new armament, engines, auxiliaries and superstructure. Sister ship *Santa Marta*, CF 32, was withdrawn from service in Dec 1962.

CARTAGENA   *1971, Colombian Navy, Official*

BARRANQUILA   *1961, Colombian Navy, Official*

There are also *Rodriguez Zamora* (ex-USN *ARD* 28), 6 700 tons full load, 488·7 oa × 81 feet, crew 109, transferred from the United States Navy, officially rated as auxiliary floating dry dock; *Capitan Eloy Mantilla* (ex-USN *YR* 66), 516 tons standard, 150 oa × 34 feet, crew 24 transferred from the US Navy, rated as floating workshop; floating dock *Manuel Laro* and repair boat *Victor Cubillos*.

SURVEY VESSELS

SAN ANDRES (ex-USS *Rockville*, PCER 851)

Displacement, tons	640 standard; 900 full load
Dimensions, feet	180 wl; 184·5 oa × 33 × 9·5
Main engines	Diesel; 2 shafts; 1 800 bhp = 15 knots
Complement	60

Former US patrol rescue escort vessel built by Pullman Standard Car Mfg Co, Chicago, laid down on 18 Oct 1943, launched on 22 Feb 1944, completed on 15 May 1944. acquired on 5 June 1969 for conversion to a surveying vessel.

TENDERS

GORGONA FB 161

Displacement, tons	560
Dimensions, feet	135 × 29·5 × 9·3
Main engines	2 Nohab diesels; 910 bhp = 13 knots

Built by Astillero Lidingoverken. Launched in May 1954. Pennant No. FB 161. Formerly classified as a tender. Recently employed in the hydrographic service. The tender *Jamary* was deleted from the official list in 1970.

GORGONA   *1971, Colombian Navy, Official*

RAFAEL MARTINEZ

Displacement, tons	38
Dimensions, feet	56 pp; 57·5 oa × 15 × 8
Main engines	2 six-cylinder diesels; 120 bhp

SMALL TRANSPORTS

CIUDAD DE QUIBDO TM 43

Displacement, tons	633
Dimensions, feet	165 × 23·5 × 9
Main engines	1 Mai diesel; 1 shaft; 390 bhp = 11 knots
Oil fuel (tons)	32
Complement	12

Built by Gebr. Sander Delfzijl, in the Netherlands.

CIUDAD DE QUIBDO   *1971, Colombian Navy, Official*

BELL SALTER (ex-*Souris*, ex-*Leccarmaro II*). TM 41.

Displacement, tons	60
Dimensions, feet	82 × 14 × 5·5
Main engines	2 GM diesels; 1 500 rpm; speed 8 knots

HERNANDO GUTIERREZ   *1971, Colombian Navy, Official*

HERNANDO GUTIERREZ TF 52   **MARIO SERPA** TF 51
                                         SOCORRO (ex-*Alberto Gomez*)

Displacement, tons	70
Dimensions, feet	82 × 18 × 2·8
Main engines	2 GM diesels; 260 bhp = 9 knots
Oil fuel (tons)	4
Complement	10 (berths for 56 troops)

River transports. Launched at Cartagena in 1954, 1953 and 1955 respectively. Named after Army Officers. *Socorro* was converted in July 1967 into a floating surgery. *Hernando Gutierrez* and *Mario Serpa* were also converted into dispensary ships in 1970.

OILERS

BARRANCABERMEJA BT 66   **TUMACO** BT 57

Displacement, tons	9 214 light ; 22 316 full load
Dimension feet	602·3 × 76 × 32·1
Main engines	Rush-Sultzer diesel ; 1 shaft ; 10 500 bhp = 15·5 knots
Complement	65 (10 officers, 55 men)

Barrancabermeja was built by Sociedad Española de Construccion Naval, Cadiz. Laid down on 1 Feb 1965, launched on 1 Aug 1965, completed on 1 June 1966.

BARRANCABERMEJA   *1970, Colombian Navy, Official*

COVENAS (ex-*M/T Randfonn*) BT 65

Measurement, tons	22 096 gross ; 5 096 net ; 14 000 deadweight
Dimensions, feet	515·3 oa × 64 × 30·5 max
Main engines	Diesel ; 1 shaft ; 6 000 bhp = 14·5 knots
Complement	49 (7 officers, 42 men)

Built by Gotaverken in 1950. Acquired in 1966. Capacity 136 250 barrels. The oiler *Antonio de Arevalo* was withdrawn from service in 1967.

COVENAS   *1971, Colombian Navy, Official*

MAMONAL (ex-US *Tonti*, AOG 76) BT 62
SANCHO JIMENO (ex-*Transmere*, ex-USS *Kiamichi* AOG 73) BT 63

Displacement, tons	5 984 full load
Measurement, tons	3 150 gross ; 3 925 deadweight ; 2 063 net
Dimensions, feet	309 wl, 325 oa × 48·2 × 21·7
Main engines	Diesel ; 1 shaft ; 1 400 bhp = 10 knots
Complement	33

Built by Todd Shipyard, Houston, and St. John's River S.B. Corp., Jacksonville respectively. *Sancho Jimeno* was purchased in 1952. *Mamonal* was transferred in Jan 1965. A photograph pf *Mamonal* appears in the 1965-66 to 1969-70 editions.

SANCHO JIMENO   *1970, Colombian Navy, Official*

TRAINING SHIP

GLORIA

Displacement, tons	1 300
Dimensions, feet	212 × 34·8 × 21·7
Main engines	Auxiliary diesel ; 500 bhp = 10·5 knots

Sail training ship. Built at Bilbao in 1968. Barque rigged. Hull is entirely welded. Sail area: 1 675 sq yards (*1,400 sq. metres*).

GLORIA   *1971, Colombian Navy, Official*

PATROL LAUNCHES

ALBERTO RESTREPO (1 Oct 1952)   **HUMBERTO CORTES** (26 Nov 1952)
CARLOS GALINDO (1954)   **JUAN LUCIO** (2 May 1953)

Displacement, tons	35
Dimensions, feet	76·8 pp ; 81·8 oa × 12 × 2·8
Guns	1—20 mm AA ; 4 MG
Main engines	2 GM diesels ; 260 bhp = 13 knots
Complement	13

Built at Cartagena. Launch dates above. Nos. LR 125, 128, 126 and 122 respectively. A photograph of *Alberto Restrepo* appears in the 1957-58 to 1964-65 editions, and of *Humberto Cortes* in the 1965-66 to 1970-71 editions.

ALFONSO VARGAS (3 July 1952)   **FRITZ HAGALE** (19 July 1952)

Displacement, tons	33
Dimensions, feet	72 pp ; 76 oa × 12 × 2·8
Guns	1—20 mm AA ; 4 GM
Main engines	2 GM ; diesels 280 bhp = 13 knots
Complement	10

Built at Cartagena naval base. Designed for operations on rivers. Named after naval officers. Launch dates above. Pennant Nos LR 123 and 124 respectively. A photograph of *Fritz Hagale* appears in the 1956-57 to 1963-64 editions.

DILIGENTE   **PALACE**   **TRIUNFANTE**   **VENGADORA**

Launched at the Naval Base, Cartagena, in 1942-54. The boats vary in detail. Pennant Nos. LR 138, 130, 133, and 139 respectively.

TUGS

PEDRO DE HEREDIA (ex-USS *Choctaw*, ATF 70) RM 72

Displacement, tons	1 235 standard ; 1 764 full load
Dimensions, feet	195 wl ; 205 oa × 38·5 × 15·5 max
Main engines	4 diesels, electrical drive ; 3 000 bhp = 16·5 knots

Former United States ocean tug of the "Apache" class. Launched on 18 Oct 1942.

PEDRO DE HEREDIA   *1971, Colombian Navy, Official*

TENIENTE SORZANO

Displacement, tons	54
Dimensions, feet	60 pp ; 65·7 oa × 17·5 × 9
Main engines	6-cylinder diesel ; 240 bhp

ANDAGOYA RM 71

Displacement, tons	100
Main engines	Caterpillar diesel ; 80 bhp = 8 knots

Launched in 1928. Re-engined in 1955. Photograph in 1957-58 edition.

ABADIA MENDEZ

Displacement, tons	39
Dimensions, feet	52·5 × 11 × 4
Main engines	Caterpillar diesel ; 80 bhp = 8 knots

Built in Germany in 1924. Harbour tug. There are also the harbour tug, *La Colombiana* and the river tug *Joves Fiallo*, RR 90.

CANDIDO LEGUIZAMO   **CAPITAN RIGOBERTO GIRALDO**
CAPITAN ALVARO RUIZ   **CAPITAN VLADIMIR VALEK**
CAPITAN CASTRO   **TENIENTE LUIS BERNAL**

Displacement, tons	50
Dimensions, feet	63 × 14 × 2·5
Main engines	2 GM diesels ; 260 bhp = 9 knots

TENIENTE MIGUEL SILVA

Dimensions, feet	73·3 × 17·5 × 3
Main engines	2 diesels ; 260 bhp = 9 knots

River tug. Built by Union Industrial (Unial) of Barranquila. Pennant No. 89.

CONGO (ex-Belgian)

CONGO (ex-*President Mobuto*, ex-*General Olsen*)
River boat, 260 ft oa, renamed 3 Sep 1967. A force for Lake Tanganyika was formed in 1967 consisting of two 50 ft patrol boats, four 21 ft speed boats and a converted trawler. Four small patrol craft were reported transferred by Communist China.

CONGO (ex-French)

The Republic of Congo (formerly Middle Congo, of French Equatorial Africa), which became independent on 15 Aug 1960, formed a naval service, but the patrol vessel *Reine N'Galifowou* (ex-French P 754) which was transferred 16 Nov, 1962, was returned to France on 18 Feb, 1965 and then re-transferred to Senegal as *Siné Saloum*.

COSTA RICA

The Coast Guard includes two 90 ft wooden patrol boats and an armed tug.

CUBA

Strength of the Fleet

4 Frigates (including 1 ex-*Crucero*)
2 Escort Patrol Vessels
18 Patrol Vessels (Submarine Chasers)
18 Missile Boats
24 Torpedo Boats
13 Coast Guard Cutters
21 Auxiliaries and Service Craft

Naval Establishments

Naval Acadamy:
　At Mariel, for Officers and cadets

Naval School:
　At Morro Castle, for petty officers and men

Personnel

1971: 6 000 (380 officers, 220 subordinate officers, and
5 400 men)

Mercantile Marine

Lloyd's Register of Shipping:
236 vessels of 332 906 tons gross

FRIGATES (*Fragatas*)

Name	Pennant No.	Builders	Laid down	Launched	Completed
ANTONIO MACEO (ex-USS *Peoria*, PF 67)	F 302	Leathem D. Smith, S.B. Co, Sturgeon Bay, Wisconsin	4 June 1943	2 Oct 1943	15 Oct 1944
JOSÉ MARTI (ex-USS *Eugene*, PF 40)	F 301	Consolidated Steel, Los Angeles, California	12 June 1943	6 July 1943	15 Jan 1944
MAXIMO GOMÉZ (ex-USS *Grand Island*, PF 14)	F 303	Kaiser Cargo Inc, Richmond, California	27 Nov 1943	19 Feb 1944	27 May 1944

3 Ex-US PF TYPE

Displacement, tons	1 430 standard; 2 415 full load
Length, feet (*metres*)	285·5 (*87·0*) wl; 304·0 (*92·7*) oa
Beam, feet (*metres*)	37·5 (*11·4*)
Draught, feet (*metres*)	13·7 (*4·2*)
Guns, dual purpose	3—3 in (*76 mm*)
Guns, AA	*Antonio Maceo:* 4—40 mm; 4—12·7 mm *José Matri:* 4—40 mm; 6—20 mm *Maximo Gomez:* 4—40 mm; 9—20 mm
A/S weapons	Hedgehog; DCT; racks
Boilers	2 three-drum type
Main engines	Triple expansion; 2 shafts; 5 500 ihp
Speed, knots	18
Radius, miles	9 500 at 12 knots
Complement	135 (*José Marti*)

MAXIMO GOMEZ　　　　　　　　　　*Added 1966, Cuban Navy, Official*

All three were acquired from the US Navy in 1947. Refitted in 1956 at Key West. *José Marti* was fitted as flagship.

A photograph of *José Marti* appears in the 1955-56 to 1959-60 editions, and of *Antonio Maceo* in the 1960-61 to 1965-66 editions.

CUBA

Displacement, tons	2 055
Length, feet (*metres*)	260 (*79·3*) pp
Beam, feet (*metres*)	39 (*11·9*)
Draught, feet (*metres*)	14 (*4·3*)
Guns, surface	2—4 in (*102 mm*); 2—3 in (*76 mm*)
Guns, AA	4—57 mm; 5—20 mm
Boilers	2 Foster Wheeler 3-drum type
Main engines	Triple expansion; 6 000 ihp
Speed, knots	14

Originally rated as a *crucero* (cruiser). Built by Cramp, Philadelphia. Launched on 10 Aug 1911. Reconstructed in 1936-37. Converted from coal to oil burning. Completed further-reconstruction in 1956.

CUBA　　　　　　　　　　*Added 1964, Cuban Navy, Official*

PATROL ESCORTS (*Buques de Patrulla y Escolta*)

2 Ex-US PCE TYPE ESCORT PATROL VESSELS

Name	**CARIBE** (ex-USS *PCE* 872)	**SIBONEY** (ex-USS *PCE* 893)
Pennant No.	PE 201	PE 302
Builders	Albina Eng. & Mach. Works. Portland. Oreg	Williamette Iron & Steel Corp., Portland. Oreg.
Laid down	30 Jan 1943	27 Oct 1942
Launched	24 Mar 1943	8 May 1943
Completed	29 Nov 1943	25 July 1944

Displacement, tons	640 standard; 903 full load
Dimensions, feet	180 wl; 184·5 oa × 33 × 9·5
Guns	1—3 in dp; 3—40 mm AA; 4—20 mm AA
A/S weapons	Hedgehog. DCT and racks
Main engines	12 cylinder diesels; 2 shafts; 1 800 bhp = 14 knots
Complement	99

Built in USA. Former United States escort patrol vessels. Box deck-house amidship was removed from *Caribe* in 1953. Both completed a refit in 1956 at Key West Naval Base. when new anti-submarine armament and equipment were installed.
The old sloop *Patria*, at Mariel as a permanent installation of the Naval Academy for training midshipmen, has been removed from the effective list.

CARIBE　　　　　　　　　　*Cuban Navy Official*

MISSILE BOATS

18 Ex-USSR "KOMAR" TYPE

Displacement, tons	75 standard; 100 full load
Dimensions, feet	88 oa × 21 × 6
Guided weapons	2 launchers for missiles of 10 to 15 miles range
Main engines	Speed = 40 knots

Former Soviet boats. Twelve transferred in 1962. Last two arrived Dec 1966.

PATROL VESSELS (Submarine Chasers)

12 Ex-USSR "SOI" TYPE

Displacement, tons	215
Dimensions, feet	147·7 × 18 × 6·5
Guns	4—25 mm (2 twin)
A/S weapons	4 five-barrelled rocket launchers
Main engines	3 diesels; 3 500 bhp = 26 knots

Six were transferred from the USSR by Sep 1964, and six more in 1967.

6 Ex-USSR "KRONSTADT" TYPE

Displacement, tons	300 standard; 350 full load
Dimensions, feet	167·3 × 19·3 × 9
Guns	1—3·9 in; 2—37 mm AA; 3—20 mm AA; DC
Mines	6 on two racks at the stern
Main engines	2 diesels; 2 shafts; speed = 22 knots

Former Soviet submarine chasers reported transferred from the USSR in 1962.

TORPEDO BOATS

12 Ex-USSR "P 6" TYPE

Displacement, tons	75 standard; 100 full load
Dimensions, feet	88 ×21 × 6
Guns	4—25 mm AA (two twin)
Tubes	2—21 in (two single)
Main engines	Speed = 45 knots

12 Ex-USSR "P 4" TYPE

Displacement, tons	50
Dimensions, feet	85·3 × 20 × 6
Guns	4—25 mm AA (2 twin)
Main engines	Diesels; 2 000 bhp = 42 knots

Former Soviet motor torpedo boats, transferred from the USSR in 1962-64.

COAST GUARD CUTTERS (*Guardacostas*)

HABANA *GC* 107 (ex-*SC* 1291) **ORIENTE** *GC* 104 (ex-*SC* 1000)
LAS VILLAS *GC* 106 (ex-*SC* 1290) **PINAR DEL RIO** *GC* 108 (ex-*SC* 1301)

Displacement, tons	95
Dimensions, feet	107·5 wl ; 111 oa × 17 × 6·5
Guns	2—20 mm AA
Main engines	GM diesels ; 2 shafts, 1 000 bhp = 15 knots

Built in the United States by Dingle Boat Works (*Oriente*), W. A. Robinson, Inc, Ipswich, Mass. (*Havana* and *Las Villas*), and Perkins & Vaughan, Inc, Wickford, RI (*Pinar del Rio*). *Camaguey GC* 105, was removed from the effective list in 1960.

HABANA *Cuban Navy, Official*

LEONCIO PRADO GC 101

Displacement, tons	80
Dimensions, feet	110 × 17·7 × 6·2
Guns	1—20 mm AA
Main engines	2 sets 8-cycle, 2 stroke diesels ; 1 000 bhp = 15 knots
Oil	2 232 gallons for a cruising radius of 16 000 miles

Built at Havana. Launched in 1946. Of wooden hulled construction.

LEONCIO PRADO *Added 1966, Cuban Navy, Official*

GC 11 (ex-USCGC 83351) **GC 13** (ex-USCGC 83385) **GC 14** (ex-USCGC 83395)

Displacement, tons	45
Dimensions, feet	83 × 16 × 4·5
Guns	1—20 mm AA
Main engines	2 Sterling Viking petrol motors ; 1 200 hp = 18 knots
Complement	12

Former *CS* of same numbers. Built in USA. Ex-Coast Guard Cutters. Launched in 1942-43. Of wooden hulled construction. Received from US Navy in March 1943. Rated as *Guardacostas*, 83 ft. GC 12 and GC 22 were disposed of.

GC 13 *Cuban Navy, Official*

GC 32 (ex-USCGC 56191) **GC 33** (ex-USCGC 56190) **GC 34** (ex-USCGC 56192)

Displacement, tons	45
Dimensions, feet	83 × 16 × 4·5
Guns	1—20 mm AA
Main engines	2 Superior diesels ; 460 bhp = 12 knots
Complement	12

Built in USA. Ex-Coast Guard Cutters. Launched in 1942-43. Of wooden hulled construction. A photograph of GC 32 appears in the 1955-56 to 1959-60 editions. GC 31 was disposed of.

DONOTIVO (ex-*Capitan Fernandez Quevedo*) GC 102

Displacement, tons	130
Dimensions, feet	101 × 18 × 7
Main engines	2 sets diesels ; 360 bhp = 12 knots

Built at Havana. Launched in 1932. Photograph in 1947-48 to 1959-60 editions.

MATANZAS *GC* 103

Displacement, tons	80
Dimensions, feet	100 × 18 × 6
Guns	1—1 pdr
Main engines	2 Fairbanks Morse diesels ; 180 bhp = 12 knots

Wooden hulled. Built at Havana. Launched in 1912. A photograph appears in the 1947-48 to 1959-60 editions. Both of the above are rated *Guardacostas Auxiliares*.

MOTOR LAUNCHES

R 41 (ex-*PT* 715) **R 42** (ex-*PT* 716)

Displacement, tons	35
Dimensions, feet	71 × 19·2 × 5
Guns	2 MG
Main engines	2 Packard gas engines ; 3 shafts ; 3 600 bhp = 35 knots

Former US motor torpedo boats of the PT type. Built in the USA by Annapolis Yacht Yard Inc, Annapolis, Md. Launched on 9 July 1945 (R 41) and 17 July 1945 (R 42). Sunk during a hurricane on 5 Oct 1948, but were salvaged and put into service as sea-air rescue craft. Rated as *Buques-Auxiliares*, ex-*Torpederos*. Sister R 43 sank on 6 May 1961 after hitting a submerged object off Western Cuba.

SV 7	**SV 8**	**SV 9**	**SV 10**	**SV 12**	**SV 14**
Dimensions, feet		Length 40			
Guns		1—50 cal MG			
Main engines		2 GM diesels ; speed 25 knots			

Later boats of the SV type assigned to naval stations for coastal vigilance, to deal with contraband, and for auxiliary services, rescue and navigation. Equipped with radar.

SV 1	**SV 2**	**SV 3**	**SV 4**	**SV 5**	**SV 6**
Displacement, tons		6·15			
Dimensions, feet		32 × 10 × 2·8			
Main engines		2 Chrysler Crown, 230 bhp	18 knots		

Auxiliary patrol boats for port vigilance, launched in 1953. A photograph of *SV* 6 appears in the 1957-58 edition.

LIGHTHOUSE TENDERS
(*Buque de Servicia de Faros*)

ENRIQUE COLLAZO (ex-*Joaquin Godoy*)

Displacement, tons	815
Dimensions, feet	211 × 34 × 9
Main engines	Triple expansion ; 2 shafts ; 672 ihp = 8 knots

Built at Paisley, Scotland. Launched in 1906. Acquired in 1950 from Cuban mercantile marine. A photograph appears in the 1953-54 to 1957-58 editions.

BERTHA

Displacement, tons	98
Dimensions, feet	104 × 19 × 11
Main engines	2 Gray Marine diesels ; 450 bhp = 10 knots

Launched in 1944. Pennant No. SF 10. A photograph appears in the 1957-48 edtiion.

AUXILIARY VESSELS (*Buques-Auxiliares*)

GRANMA A 11
Yacht which landed in Cuba on 2 Dec 1956 with Dr Fidel Castro and the men who began the liberation war. Historical vessel incorporated into the Navy as an auxiliary. The former Presidential Yacht *10 de Marzo* (ex-*Wakitty*) was removed from the list.

A1 **A2** **A3**

Displacement, tons	60
Dimensions, feet	74 × 15 × 5
Guns	1 MG
Main engines	2 diesel engines

Formerly yachts. A photograph of A3 appears in the 1954-55 to 1957-58 editions.

RESCUE AND SALVAGE VESSELS

10 DE OCTUBRE (ex-*ATR* 4)

Displacement, tons	852 standard ; 1 315 full load
Dimensions, feet	155 wl ; 165·5 oa × 33·3 × 16
Main engines	Triple expansion ; 1 600 ihp = 12 knots
Boilers	2 Babcock & Wilcox D-type ; oil burning

Former US ocean rescue tug. Built in the USA. Launched in 1943. Largely of wooden construction. Guns removed. Pennant No. RS 210. Rated as *Buque de Rescate y Salvamento*. Sister ship *20 de Mayo* was removed from the effective list.

CYPRUS

Mercantile Marine

Lloyd's Register of Shipping: 207 vessels of 1 138 229 tons gross

PATROL BOATS
6 "P 4" CLASS

Displacement, tons	25
Dimensions, feet	63 × 11 × 3
Guns	2—4 25 mm
Main engines	Diesels ; 2 000 bhp = 45 knots

Four of these were transferred by USSR in Oct 1964 and two in Feb 1965. Also reported that two extra engines have been supplied since that time.

2 Ex-GERMAN "R" TYPE

Displacement, tons	125
Dimensions, feet	124 × 19 × 4·5
Guns	1—40 mm ; 1—20 mm
Main engines	2 MAN diesels ; 1 800 bhp = 20 knots

Originally three of this class were taken up from mercantile use and re-armed. One was destroyed by Turkish air attack on 8 Aug 1964 at Xeros. It was reported that there were 10 small craft of about 50 tons, armed with one or two 20 mm guns.

DENMARK

Administration

Commander in Chief:
Vice-Admiral S. Thostrup, RDN

Diplomatic Representation

Defence Attaché, London:
Colonel H.R.H. Prince Georg of Denmark, CVO

Assistant Defence Attaché, London:
Commander Jorgen Haack-Moeller

Naval Attaché, Washington:
Captain Hjort Jensen

Strength of the Fleet

4 Submarines (Diesel Powered)
6 Frigates (4 for Fishery Protection)
4 Minelayers
4 Corvettes
3 Coastal Minelayers
8 Coastal Minesweepers
9 Seaward Defence Craft
16 Torpedo Boats
4 Inshore Minesweepers
27 Patrol Craft
10 Support Ships and Service Craft

Navy Estimates

1961-62: 177 100 000 Kr.	1966-67: 371 900 000 Kr.
1962-63: 210 100 000 Kr.	1967-68: 376 450 000 Kr.
1963-64: 231 000 000 Kr.	1968-69: 390 900 000 Kr.
1964-65: 279 100 000 Kr.	1969-70: 400 000 000 Kr.
1965-66: 291 500 000 Kr.	1970-71: 418 800 000 Kr.

Personnel

January 1971: 7 000 officers and men

Mercantile Marine

Lloyd's Register of Shipping:
1 210 vessels of 3 314 320 tons gross

SUBMARINES

2 "NARHVALEN" CLASS

Displacement, tons	370 surface; 450 submerged
Length, feet (*metres*)	144·4 (*44·0*)
Beam, feet (*metres*)	15 (*4·6*)
Draught, feet (*metres*)	12·5 (*3·8*)
Torpedo tubes	8—21 in (*533 mm*) bow, internal
Main engines	Diesels; 1 200 bhp surface; Elec. motors, 1 200 hp submerged
Speed, knots	10 surface; 17 submerged
Complement	21

These coastal submarines are similar to the German "U-4" class and are being built under licence at the Royal Dockyard, Copenhagen. They are conventionally powered, and fitted with schnorkel installation. "Teardrop" hull. Originally numbered S 330 and S 331.

Name	No.	Laid down	Launched	Completed
NARHVALEN	S 320	16 Feb 1965	10 Sep 1968	27 Feb 1970
NORDKAPEREN	S 321	20 Jan 1966	1970	Dec 1970

NARHVALEN   *1970, Royal Danish Navy, Official*

4 "DELFINEN" CLASS

Displacement, tons	550 standard; 595 surface 643 submerged
Length, feet (*metres*)	117·2 (*54·0*)
Beam, feet (*metres*)	15·4 (*4·7*)
Draught, feet (*metres*)	13·1 (*4·0*)
Torpedo tubes	4—21 in (*533 mm*)
Main engines	2 Burmeister & Wain diesels 1 200 bhp surface; Electric motors, 1 200 hp submerged
Speed, knots	15 surface and submerged
Range, miles	4 000 at 8 knots
Complement	33

Built in the Royal Dockyard, Copenhagen. Engined with diesels of a new type. Equipped with Schnorkel.

PHOTOGRAPHS. A photograph of *Springeren* appears in the 1967-68 edition, and of *Delfinen* and *Spaekhuggeren* in the 1968-69 and 1969-70 editions.

Name	No.	Laid down	Launched	Completed
DELFINEN	S 326	1 July 1954	4 May 1956	16 Sep 1958
SPÆKHUGGEREN	S 327	1 Dec 1954	20 Feb 1957	27 June 1959
SPRINGEREN	S 329	3 Jan 1961	26 Apr 1963	22 Oct 1964
TUMLEREN	S 328	22 May 1956	22 May 1958	15 Jan 1960

TUMLEREN   *1970, Royal Danish Navy, Official*

FAST FRIGATES

Name	No.	Builders	Laid down	Launched	Completed
HERLUF TROLLE	F 353	Helsingörs J. & M.	18 Dec 1964	8 Sep 1965	16 Apr 1967
PEDER SKRAM	F 352	Helsingörs J. & M,	25 Sep 1964	20 May 1965	30 June 1966

2 "PEDER SKRAM" CLASS

FF (ex-DE) TYPE

Displacement, tons	2 030 standard; 2 720 full load (officially revised figures)
Length, feet (*metres*)	354·3 (*108*) pp; 396·5 (*112·6*) oa
Beam, feet (*metres*)	39·5 (*12*)
Draught, feet (*metres*)	11·8 (*3·6*)
Guns, surface	4—5 in (*127 mm*) 38 cal US
Guns, AA	4—40 mm
A/S weapons	DC
Main engines	CODAG; 2 shafts:— 2 GM 16-567 D diesels; 4 800 hp; 2 Pratt & Whitney PWA GG 4A-3 gas turbines; 44 000 hp total output
Speed, knots	28 designed; over 30 max; 18 economical sea
Complement	112

Fast frigates of Danish design built at Helsingör. They were to have been armed, additionally to guns, with three 21 inch torpedo tubes and the "Terne" anti-submarine weapon. There is space on the quarter deck for possible future surface-to-air guided missile launcher installation.

PENNANT NOS. The pennant numbers allocated originally were D 320 (see illustration in the 1963-64 to 1965-66 editions) and D 321, when they were designated DE (Destroyer Escorts). US/NATO procurement numbers PC 1644 and PC 1645, respectively.

RADAR.
Search. Two S Band air and surface search.
Tactical. X Band.
Fire Control. Three X Band and HSA or Contraves.

HERLUF TROLLE   *1968, Royal Danish Navy, Official*

PEDER SKRAM   *1970, Royal Danish Navy, Official*

FRIGATES

Name	No.	Builders	Laid down	Launched	Completed
FYLLA	F 351	Aalborg Værft	27 June 1962	18 Dec 1962	10 July 1963
HVIDBJØRNEN	F 348	Aarhus Flydedok	4 June 1961	23 Nov 1961	15 Dec 1962
INGOLF	F 350	Svendborg Værft	5 Dec 1961	27 July 1961	27 July 1963
VÆDDEREN	F 349	Aalborg Værft	30 Oct 1961	6 Apr 1962	19 Mar 1963

4 "HVIDBJORNEN" CLASS
FF TYPE

Displacement, tons	1 345 standard; 1 650 full load
Length, feet (metres)	219·8 (67·0) pp; 238·2 (72·6) oa
Beam, feet (metres)	38·0 (11·6)
Draught, feet (metres)	16 (4·9)
Aircraft	1 Alouette III helicopter
Guns, dual purpose	1—3 in (76 mm)
Main engines	4 GM 16—567C diesels; 6 400 bhp; 1 shaft
Speed, knots	18
Range, miles	6 000 at 13 knots
Complement	75

Ordered in 1960-61. Of frigate type for fishery protection and surveying duties in the North Sea, Faroe Islands, and Greenland waters. They are equipped with a helicopter platform aft. The prototype ship of the class was built by Aarhus Flydedok og Maskinkompagni.

PHOTOGRAPHS. A photograph of Fylla appears in the 1969-70 and 1970-71 editions and of Ingolf in the 1968-69 and 1969-70 editions.

RADAR
Search. S Band combined air and surface.
Navigation. X Band.

DISPOSALS OF "FLOWER" CLASS
The former British frigate of the "Flower" class, Thetis (ex-HMS Geranium) was discarded in 1963.

DISPOSALS OF "HUITFELDT" CLASS
Of the two patrol vessels, formerly coastal destroyers, of the "Huitfeldt" class, Huitfeldt (ex-Nymfen) was discarded in 1965, and Willemoes (ex-Najaden) was officially deleted from the Navy List in 1966. Both were scrapped at Antwerp in 1966.

HVIDBJØRNEN · 1970, Royal Danish Navy, Official

VÆDDEREN · 1971, Royal Danish Navy, Official

CORVETTES

Name	No.	Builders	Launched	Transferred
BELLONA	F 344	Naval Meccanicia, Castellammare	9 Jan 1955	31 Jan 1957
DIANA	F 345	Cantiere del Tirreno, Riva, Trigoso	19 Dec 1954	30 July 1955
FLORA	F 346	Cantiere del Tirreno, Riva, Trigoso	25 June 1955	28 Aug 1956
TRITON	F 347	Cantiere Navali di Taranto	12 Sep 1954	10 Aug 1955

4 "TRITON" CLASS

Displacement, tons	760 standard; 873 full load
Length, feet (metres)	242·8 (74·0) pp; 250·3 (76·3) oa
Beam, feet (metres)	31·5 (9·6)
Draught, feet (metres)	9 (2·7)
Guns, surface	2—3 in (76 mm)
Guns, AA	1—40 mm
A/S	2 Hedgehogs; 4 DCT
Main engines	2 Ansaldo Fiat 409T diesels 4 400 bhp; 2 shafts
Speed, knots	18 designed, 20 max 16 sea
Range, miles	2 400 at 18 knots
Complement	110

All four vessels were built in Italy for the Danish Navy under the United States "offshore" account in the Mutual Defence Assistance Program.

RADAR
Search. Plessey AWS 1.
Navigation. S Band.

CLASSIFICATION. Officially classified as corvettes in 1954, but have "F" pennant numbers like frigates.

PHOTOGRAPHS. A photograph or Triton appears in the 1956-57 to 1962-63 editions and of Diana in the 1968-69 and 1969-70 editions.

BELLONA · 1970, Royal Danish Navy, Official

MINELAYERS

Name	No.	Builders	Laid down	Launched	Completed
FALSTER	N 80	Nakskov Skibsvaerft	12 Apr 1962	19 Sep 1962	7 Nov 1963
FYEN	N 81	Frederikshavn Værft	12 Apr 1962	3 Oct 1962	18 Sep 1963
MØEN	N 82	Frederikshavn Værft	4 Oct 1962	6 Mar 1963	29 Apr 1964
SJÆLLAND	N 83	Nakskov Skibsvaerft	17 Jan 1963	14 June 1963	7 July 1964

4 "FALSTER" CLASS

Displacement, tons	1 900 full load
Length, feet (metres)	238 (72·5) pp; 252·6 (77·0) oa
Beam, feet (metres)	41 (12·5)
Draught, feet (metres)	10 (3·0)
Guns, dual purpose	4—3 in (76 mm), 2 twin mountings
Mines	400
Main engines	2 GM—567D 3 diesels; 4 800 shp 2 shafts
Speed, knots	17
Complement	120

Minelayers of a novel Scandinavian-NATO design. Ordered in 1960-61. All are named after Danish Islands. The steel hull is flush decked with a raking stem, a full stern, and a prominent knuckle forward. The superstructure has a block outline surmounted by a squat streamlined funnel, two light lattice masts, high angle director control towers fore and aft and whip aerials. The hull is sub-divided by watertight bulkheads and flats to isolate damage, and has been specially strengthened for ice navigation.

RADAR
Search. C Band low coverage.
Navigation. S and X Band.

PHOTOGRAPHS. A photograph of Fyen appears in the 1967-68 edition and of Falster in the 1968-69 and 1969-70 editions.

MØEN · 1970, Wright & Logan

COASTAL MINELAYERS

LANGELAND   *1971, Royal Danish Navy, Official*

LANGELAND N 42

Displacement, tons	310 standard; 232 full load
Dimensions, feet	133·5 oa; 128·2 pp × 23·7 × 7·2
Guns	2—40 mm. 2—20 mm Madsen
Main engines	Diesel; 2 shafts; 385 bhp = 11·6 knots
Complement	37

Built at the Royal Dockyard, Copenhagen. Laid down in 1950. Launched on 17 May 1950. Completed in 1951.

LOUGEN   *1971, Royal Danish Navy, Official*

2 "LOUGEN" CLASS

LAALAND N 40   **LOUGEN** N 41

Displacement, tons	240 standard; 260 full load
Dimensions, feet	105·5 × 21·2 × 6·5
Guns	2—20 mm AA
Main engines	B. & W. diesel; 2 shafts; 350 bhp = 10 knots
Complement	31

Built at the Royal Dockyard, Copenhagen. Both laid down in 1940, launched in 1941 and completed in 1946. A photograph of *Lougen* appears in the 1965-66 and 1966-67 editions.

LAALAND   *1968, Royal Danish Navy, Official*

DISPOSAL
The old coastal minelayer *Lindormen*, N 39, was officially stricken from the list in 1970.

COASTAL MINESWEEPERS
8 "SUND" CLASS

AARØSUND	(ex-*AMS* 127) M 571	**GULDBORGSUND** (ex-*MSC* 257) M 575	
ALSSUND	(ex-*AMS* 128) M 572	**OMØSUND**	(ex-*MSC* 221) M 576
EGERNSUND	(ex-*AMS* 129) M 573	**ULVSUND**	(ex-*MSC* 263) M 577
GRØNSUND	(ex-*MSC* 256) M 574	**VILSUND**	(ex-*MSC* 264) M 578

Displacement, tons	350 standard; 376 full load
Dimensions, feet	138 pp; 144 oa × 27 × 8·5
Guns	2—20 mm
Main engines	Diesels; 2 shafts; 1 200 bhp = 13 knots
Complement	35

MSC (ex-AMS) 60 class NATO coastal minesweepers all built in USA. Completed in 1954-56. *Aarøsund* was transferred on 24 Jan 1955, *Alssund* on 5 Apr 1955, *Egernsund* on 3 Aug 1955, *Grønsund* on 21 Sep 1956, *Guldborgsund* on 11 Nov 1956. *Omøsund* on 20 June 1956, *Ulvsund* on 20 Sep 1956 and *Vilsund* on 15 Nov 1956. A photograph of *Omøsund* appears in the 1966-67 and 1967-68 editions and of *Aarosund* in the 1968-69 and 1969-70 editions.

ALSSUND   *1970, Royal Danish Navy, Official*

SEAWARD DEFENCE CRAFT
9 "DAPHNE" CLASS

Name	Pennant No.	Laid down	Launched	Completed
DAPHNE	P 530	1 Apr 1960	10 Nov 1960	19 Dec 1961
DRYADEN	P 531	1 July 1960	1 Mar 1961	4 Apr 1962
HAVFRUEN	P 533	15 Mar 1961	4 Oct 1961	20 Dec 1962
HAVMANDEN	P 532	15 Nov 1960	16 May 1961	30 Aug 1962
NAJADEN	P 534	20 Sep 1961	20 June 1962	26 Apr 1963
NEPTUN	P 536	1 Sep 1962	29 May 1963	18 Dec 1963
NYMFEN	P 535	1 Apr 1962	1 Nov 1962	4 Oct 1963
RAN	P 537	1 Dec 1962	10 July 1963	15 May 1964
ROTA	P 538	19 July 1963	25 Nov 1963	20 Jan 1965

Displacement, tons	170
Dimensions, feet	121·3 × 20 × 6·5
Guns	1—40 mm AA
A/S weapons	2—51 mm rocket launchers. depth charges
Main engines	Diesels; 2 shafts; 2 600 bhp = 20 knots (plus 1 cruising engine; 100 bhp)
Complement	23

All built at the Royal Dockyard, Copenhagen. A photograph of *Havmanden* appears in the 1963-64 to 1965-66 editions, of *Najaden* in the 1966-67 and 1967-68 editions, and of *Daphne* in the 1968-69 and 1969-70 editions.

NEPTUN   *1970, Royal Danish Navy, Official*

ROYAL YACHT

DANNEBROG A 540

Displacement, tons	1 130
Dimensions, feet	246 oa × 34 × 11·2
Guns	2—37 mm
Main engines	2 sets Burmeister & Wain 8 cylinder; 2 cycle diesels. 1 800 bhp = 14 knots
Complement	57

Built at the Royal Dockyard, Copenhagen. Launched on 10 Oct 1931.

DANNEBROG   *1971, Royal Danish Navy, Official*

TORPEDO BOATS (Torpedobaade)

6 "SØLØVEN" CLASS

Name	Pennant No.	Laid down	Launched	Completed*
SØLØVEN	P 510	27 Aug 1962	19 Apr 1963	June 1964*
SØRIDDEREN	P 511	4 Oct 1962	22 Aug 1963	June 1964*
SØBJORNEN	P 512	9 July 1963	19 Aug 1964	Sep 1965
SØHESTEN	P 513	5 Sep 1963	31 Mar 1965	June 1966
SØHUNDEN	P 514	18 Aug 1964	12 Jan 1966	Dec 1966
SØULVEN	P 515	30 Mar 1965	27 Apr 1966	Mar 1967

Displacement, tons	95 standard; 114 full load
Dimensions, feet	90 pp; 96 wl; 99 oa × 25·5 × 7
Guns	2—40 mm Bofors AA
Tubes	4—21 in (side)
Main engines	3 Bristol Siddeley Proteus gas turbines; 3 shafts; 12 750 bhp = 54 knots
	GM diesels on wing shafts for cruising = 10 knots
Complement	29

The design is a combination of the "Brave" class hull form and "Ferocity" type construction. *Søløven* ("Sea Lion") and *Søridderen* ("Sea Knight") were built by Vosper Limited, Portsmouth, England (*delivered to the Royal Danish Navy on 12 and 10 Feb 1965, respectively); and the remaining four under licence by the Royal Dockyard, Copenhagen. A photograph of *Søløven* appears in the 1964-65 and 1965-66 editions, of *Søridderen* in the 1966-67 and 1967-68 editions, and of *Søhunden* in the 1968-69 and 1969-70 editions.

SØULVEN   1970, Royal Danish Navy, Official

4 "FALKEN" CLASS

Name	Pennant No.	Laid down	Launched	Completed
FALKEN	P 506	1 Nov 1960	19 Dec 1961	4 Oct 1962
GLENTEN	P 507	3 Jan 1961	15 Mar 1962	15 Dec 1962
GRIBBEN	P 508	15 May 1961	18 July 1962	26 Apr 1963
HØGEN	P 509	1 Sep 1961	4 Oct 1962	6 June 1963

Displacement, tons	119
Dimensions, feet	118 × 17·8 × 6
Guns	1—40 mm AA; 1—20 mm AA
Tubes	4—21 in (side)
Main engines	3 diesels; 3 shafts; 9 000 bhp = 40 knots
Complement	23

Ordered under US offshore procurement in the Military Aid Programme. All built at the Royal Dockyard, Copenhagen. Named after birds. A photograph of *Falken* appears in the 1963-64 to 1965-66 editions, and of *Glenten* in the 1968-69 and 1969-70 editions.

GRIBBEN   1970, Royal Danish Navy, Official

6 "FLYVEFISKEN" CLASS

FLYVEFISKEN	P 500	HAVKATTEN	P 502	MAKRELEN	P 504
HAJEN	P 501	LAXEN	P 503	SVÆRDFISKEN	P 505

Displacement, tons	110
Dimensions, feet	120 × 18 × 6
Guns	1—40 mm AA; 1—20 mm AA
Tubes	2—21 in
Main engines	3 diesels; 3 shafts; 7 500 bhp = 40 knots
Complement	22

Three built in Royal Dockyard, Copenhagen, three in Frederikssund Vaerft. All units are named after fishes. Ordered in 1952, laid down in 1953 and launched in 1954-55. A photograph of *Flyvefisken* appears in the 1956-57 to 1963-64 editions, of *Hajen* in the 1964-65 and 1965-66 editions, of *Laxen* in the 1966-67 to 1967-68 editions and of *Havkatten* in the 1968-69 and 1969-70 editions.

SVÆRDFISKEN   1970, Royal Danish Navy, Official

INSHORE MINESWEEPERS (Minestrygere)

4 "VIG" CLASS

Name	Pennant No.	Laid down	Launched	Completed
ASVIG	M 579	22 Apr 1959	11 May 1960	6 Sep 1961
MOSVIG	M 580	22 Apr 1959	14 Sep 1960	25 Oct 1961
SANDVIG	M 581	11 May 1960	1 Mar 1961	1 Feb 1962
SÆLVIG	M 582	14 Sep 1960	14 July 1961	30 Apr 1962

Displacement, tons	180
Dimensions, feet	113·5 × 22·5 × 6·2
Guns	2—20 mm AA
Main engines	2 diesels; 2 shafts; 11 000 bhp = 13 knots
Complement	18

All built at the Royal Dockyard, Copenhagen. A photograph of *Asvig* appears in the 1969-70 edition.

MOSVIG   1970, Royal Danish Navy, Official

PATROL CRAFT (Orlogskuttere)

6 "BARSØ" CLASS

BARSØ	Y 300	DREJØ	Y 301	ROMSØ	Y 302	THURØ	Y 304
				SAMSØ	Y 303	VEJRØ	Y 305

Displacement, tons	155
Dimensions, feet	83·7 × 19·7 × 9·8
Speed	11 knots

Rated as patrol cutters. All launched and completed in 1969.

BARSØ   1970, Royal Danish Navy, Official

2 "MAAGEN" CLASS

MAAGEN (Y 384)	MALLEMUKKEN (Y 385)

Displacement, tons	190
Dimensions, feet	88·5 × 21·7 × 9·5
Guns	1—40 mm AA
Main engines	385 hp; 1 shaft; speed 11 knots

Of steel construction. Built at Helsingor, laid down 15 Jan 1960, launched 1960.

TEJSTEN (Y 383)

Displacement, tons	130
Dimensions, feet	82 × 20·7 × 9·4
Guns	1—37 mm
Main engines	Alfa Diesel; 180 bhp = 9 knots

Of wooden construction. Built by Holbaek Skibsbyggeri. Launched 1951. Sister boat *Skarven*, Y 382, was disabled by grounding in the Faroes on 7 May 1966 and officially deleted from the list. All three above for service in Greenland waters.

2 "ALHOLM" CLASS

ALHOLM Y 369 (ex-*MSK 1*)	ERTHOLM Y 371 (ex-*MSK 3*)

Displacement, tons	70
Dimensions, feet	69 × 17 × 9
Guns	1—20 mm AA
Main engines	Diesel; 120 bhp = 10 knots

Built by Frederikssund Vaerft. All launched in 1945. A photograph of *Alholm* appears in the 1968-69 edition. Sister boat *Birkholm* Y 370 (ex-MSK 2) was officially deleted from the list in 1969.

LINDHOLM Y 374 (ex-*MSK 6*)

Displacement, tons	68
Dimensions, feet	65·7 × 16·8 × 7·5
Main engines	Diesel; 120 bhp = 9 knots

Built by Sydhavns Vaerft. Launched in 1945. Of sister boats *Græsholm* Y 373 (ex-MSK 5) was officially deleted from the list in 1968 and *Fyrholm* T 372 (ex-MSK 4) in 1969. A photograph of *Lindholm* appears in the 1969-70 edition.

COAST GUARD CUTTERS
7 "FÆNØ" CLASS

ASKØ MHV 81 (ex-Y 386, ex-M 560, ex-MS 2)
BAAGØ MHV 84 (ex-Y 387, ex-M 561, ex-MS 3)
ENØ MHV 82 (ex-Y 388, ex-M 562, ex-MS 5)
FÆNØ MHV 69 (ex-M 563, ex-MS 6)
HJORTØ MHV 85 (ex-Y 389, ex-M 564, ex-MS 7)
LYØ MHV 86 (ex-Y 390, ex-M 565, ex-MS 8)
MANØ MHV 83 (ex-Y 391, ex-M 566, ex-MS 9)

Displacement, tons	74
Dimensions, feet	78·8 × 21 × 5
Guns	1—20 mm
Main engines	Diesel; 1 shaft; 350 bhp = 11 knots

Of wooden construction. All launched in 1941. Former inshore minesweepers. Used by the Maritime Home Guard.

FÆNO   *1969, Royal Danish Navy, Official*

MHV 70   **MHV 71**   **MHV 72**

Displacement, tons	76
Guns	1—20 mm AA
Main engines	200 bhp = 10 knots

Built in 1958. Patrol boats and training craft for the Naval Home Guard. Of the fishing cutter type. Formerly designated DMH, but allocated MHV numbers in 1969. A photograph of DMH 71 appears in the 1968-69 edition. In addition there are some 20 small vessels of the trawler and other types.

5 "Y" TYPE

Y 338   **Y 339**   **Y 343**   **Y 354**   **Y 359**

Miscellaneous patrol cutters (ex-fishing vessels) all built in 1944-45. Y 342 and Y 347 were officially stricken from the list in 1971.

ICEBREAKERS (*Isbrydere*)

DANBJØRN   **ISBJØRN**

Displacement, tons	3 685
Dimensions, feet	252 × 56 × 20
Main engines	Diesels; Electric drive; 11 880 bhp = 14 knots
Complement	34

Built in 1965. The old two-funnelled icebreaker *Isbjørn* was discarded in 1969. A photograph of the new *Isbjørn* appears in the 1969-70 edition.

DANBJØRN   *1970, Danish Royal Navy, Official*

ELBJØRN

Displacement, tons	893 standard; 1 400 full load
Dimensions, feet	156·5 × 40·3 × 14·5
Main engines	Diesels; electric drive; 3 600 bhp = 12 knots

Built in 1953. A photograph appears in the 1956-57 to 1960-61 editions.

STOREBJØRN

Displacement, tons	2 540
Dimensions, feet	197 × 49·2 × 19

Built in 1931. Icebreakers are controlled by the Ministry of Trade and Shipping.

LILLEBJØRN

Displacement, tons	1 000
Dimensions, feet	144·3 × 36·5 × 18

Built in 1926. The small icebreaker *Mjolner* was stricken from the list in 1960.

DEPOT SHIPS (*Depotskibe*)

HJÆLPEREN (ex-US *LSM 500*) A 563

Displacement, tons	1 030 standard; 1 170 full load
Dimensions, feet	203·5 oa × 34·5 × 8·3
Guns	2—40 mm
Main engines	Diesels; 2 shafts; 2 800 bhp = 12 knots
Complement	60

Former United States medium landing ship. Built by Brown Shipbuilding Co, Houston, Texas. Laid down on 17 Mar 1945. Launched on 7 Apr 1945. Completed on 17 May 1945. Transferred to the Royal Danish Navy on 15 May 1953. Depot and Repair ship for motor torpedo boats.
DISPOSAL
The depot ship *Aegir*, ex-German *Tanga*, was officially deleted from the list in Jan 1967.

HJÆLPEREN   *1971, Royal Danish Navy, Official*

HENRIK GERNER (ex-M/S *Hammershus*) A 542

Displacement, tons	2 200 standard
Dimensions, feet	252·7 × 40 × 18·3
Guns	6—40 mm AA
Main engines	Burmeister & Wain diesel; speed = 15 knots
Complement	230

Former Danish passenger ship. Built in 1936. Transferred to the Royal Danish Navy on 8 Jan 1964, refitted at the Royal Dockyard, Copenhagen, and commissioned as a depot ship for submarines.

HENRIK GERNER   *1971, Royal Danish Navy, Official*

OILERS (*Tankfartøjer*)

RIMFAXE (ex-US *YO 226*) A 568   **SKINFAXE** (ex-US *YO 229*) A 596

Displacement, tons	422 light; 1 390 full load
Dimensions, feet	174 oa × 32 × 13·2
Main engines	1 GM diesel; 560 bhp = 10 knots
Complement	23

Yard oilers transferred to the Royal Danish Navy from the USA on 2 Aug 1962. A photograph of *Skinfaxe* appears in the 1968-69 to 1970-71 editions.

RIMFAXE   *1971, Royal Danish Navy, Official*

DISPOSAL
The tenders *Hollaenderdybet* (ex-*Den Lille Havfrue*) A 554, and *Kongedybet* (ex-*Kirsten Pill*), A 555, were officially stricken from the list in 1970.

DOMINICAN REPUBLIC

Administration	Strength of the Fleet		Personnel
Under Secretary For The Navy: Commodore Miguel A. Cintron Romero	1 Destroyer 3 Frigates 5 Corvettes	2 Minesweepers 3 Patrol vessels 24 Auxiliary and Service Craft	1971: Total 4 000 (370 officers and 3 630 men)
Chief of Naval Staff: Commodore Ramon E. Jiménez Hijo			
Vice-Chief of Naval Staff: Captain Luis A. Pimentel	**New Construction** Five corvettes are projected to replace the "Flower" Type.		**Mercantile Marine** Lloyd's Register of Shipping: 16 vessels of 8 493 tons gross

DESTROYERS (*Destructores*)

Name	Pennant No.	Builders	Laid down	Launched	Completed
DUARTE (ex-*Trujillo*, ex-HMS *Hotspur*)	501 (ex-D 101	Scotts' S.B. & Eng. Co. Ltd., Greenock	27 Feb 1935	23 Mar 1936	29 Dec 1936

1 Ex-BRITISH "H" TYPE

Displacement, tons	1 340 standard; 2 020 full load
Length, feet (*metres*)	312 (*95·1*) pp; 320 (*97·5*) wl 323 (*98·5*) oa
Beam, feet (*metres*)	33 (*10·0*)
Draught, feet (*metres*)	15 (*4·6*) max (props)
Guns, surface	3—4·7 in (*120 mm*)
Guns, AA	4—20 mm
A/S weapons	4 DCT
Torpedo tubes	4—21 in (*533 mm*)
Boilers	3 Admiralty 3-drum
Main engines	Parsons geared turbines; 2 shafts; 34 000 shp
Speed, knots	36; sea 25
Radius, miles	5 700 at 15 knots
Oil fuel, tons	455
Complement	145

Former British destroyer of the "H" flotilla which served in the Royal Navy until Nov 1948 when she was purchased and renamed *Trujillo*. Renamed *Duarte* in 1962. Her Pennant No. was changed from D 101 to 501 in 1968. To be removed from the effective list 1971.

DUARTE

Added 1970, Wright & Logan

FRIGATES (*Fragatas*)

Name	Pennant No.	Builders	Laid down	Launched	Completed
CAP. GENERAL PEDRO SANTANA (ex-*Presidente Peynado*, ex-USS *Pueblo*, PF 13)	453 (ex-F 104)	Kaiser S.Y. Richmond, Cal.	14 Nov 1943	20 Jan 1944	27 May 1944
GREGORIO LUPERON (ex-*Presidente Troncoso*, ex-USS *Knoxville*, PF 64)	452 (ex-F 103)	Leatham D. Smith S.B. Co, Wis.	15 Apr 1934	10 July 1943	29 Apr 1944

2 Ex-US "RIVER" TYPE

Displacement, tons	1 430 standard; 2 415 full load
Length, feet (*metres*)	298 (*90·8*) wl; 304 (*92·7*) oa
Beam, feet (*metres*)	37·5 (*11·4*)
Draught, feet (*metres*)	12 (*3·7*)
Guns, surface	3—3 in (*76 mm*)
Guns, AA	4—40 mm (2 twin); 6—20 mm; 4—0·5 in (*12·7 mm*) MG
Boilers	2 three-drum type
Main engines	Triple expansion; 2 shafts; 5 500 ihp
Speed, knots	16
Oil fuel, tons	760
Complement	140

Formerly United States patrol frigates, PF, of the "Tacoma" class similar to the contemporary British frigates of the "River" class. Transferred from the US Navy to the Dominican Republic Navy in 1949. Renamed *Capitan General Pedro Santana* and *Gregorio Luperon* in 1962.

GREGORIO LUPERON

Official

PENNANT NUMBERS. Pennant numbers were changed from F 104 and F 103 to 453 and 452 respectively, in 1968.

LOSS. The Canadian built frigate *Juan Pablo Duarte*, formerly the USS *Natchez*, rx-HMS *Annam*, of practically the same design as the British frigates of the "River" type and otherwise similar in most respects to the training frigate *Mella*, see next page, was lost.

DISPOSAL. The destroyer *Sanchez* (ex-*Generalisimo*), D 102, formerly the British destroyer *Fame*, was removed from the effective list in 1968, see photograph in the 1961-62 to 1968-69 editions. She was originally a near sister ship of *Duarte*, see above.

CAP GENERAL PEDRO SANTANA

1969, Dominican Navy, Official

Frigates—continued

1 Ex-CANADIAN "RIVER" TYPE

MELLA (ex-*Presidente Trujillo*, ex-HMS *Carlplace*)

Displacement, tons	1 400 standard; 2 125 full load
Length, feet (*metres*)	301·5 (*91·9*)
Beam, feet (*metres*)	36·7 (*11·2*)
Draught, feet (*metres*)	12 (*3·7*) mean
Boilers	2 three-drum
Main engines	Triple expansion; 2 shafts; 5 500 ihp
Speed, knots	20
Oil fuel, tons	645
Complement	195 (15 officers, 130 men, 50 midshipmen)

Built by Davis SB & Repairing Co, Lauzon, Canada. Launched on 6 July 1944. Completed on 13 Dec 1944. Transferred to the Dominican Navy in 1946. Original Dominican frigate. Modified for use as Presidential Yacht with extra accommodation and deck-houses built up aft. Pennant number as a frigate was F 101, but as the Presidential Yacht she no longer wore it. Now carries pennant number 451 as training ship. Renamed *Mella* in 1962. Used for training midshipmen.

MELLA   *1958, Official*

CORVETTES (*Corbetas*)

Name	Pennant No.	Builders	Launched	Completed
CRISTOBAL COLON (ex-HMCS *Lachute*)	401 (ex-C 101)	Morton Ltd, Quebec City, P.Q.	9 June 1944	26 Oct 1944
GERARDO JANSEN (ex-HMCS *Peterborough*)	404 (ex-C 104)	Kingston Shipbuilding Co, Kingston, Ontario	15 Jan 1944	1 June 1944
JUAN ALEJANDRO ACOSTA (ex-HMCS *Louisbourg*)	402 (ex-C 102)	Morton Ltd, Quebec City, P.Q.	13 July 1943	13 Dec 1943
JUAN BAUTISTA CAMBIASO (ex-HMCS *Belleville*)	403 (ex-C 103)	Kingston Shipbuilding Co, Kingston, Ontario	17 June 1944	19 Oct 1944
JUAN BAUTISTA MAGGIOLO (ex-HMCS *Riviere du loup*)	405 (ex-C 105)	Morton Ltd, Quebec City, P.Q.	2 July 1943	21 Nov 1943

5 Ex-CANADIAN "FLOWER" TYPE

Displacement, tons	1 060 standard; 1 350 full load
Length, feet (*metres*)	193 (*58·8*) pp; 208 (*63·4*) oa
Beam, feet (*metres*)	33 (*10·0*)
Draught, feet (*metres*)	14·5 (*4·4*) mean
Guns, surface	C. Colon: 1—3 in (*76 mm*) Others: 1—4 in (*102 mm*)
Guns, AA	C. Colon: 2—40 mm (twin) 6—20 mm; 4—0·5 in MG (2 twin) Others: 1—40 mm; 6—20 mm; 2—0·5 in MG
Boilers	2 three-drum type
Main engines	Triple expansion; 2 750 ihp
Speed, knots	16
Oil fuel, tons	282
Complement	53

All built in Canadian shipyards under the Emergency Construction programme during the Second World War. Transferred to the Dominican Navy in 1947. The sixth ship, *Asbestos*, was wrecked *en route* from Canada. Pennant numbers were changed in 1968, 300 being added to all numbers and letter C suppressed. A photograph of *Juan Maggiolo* appears in the 1951-52 to 1957-58 editions, of *Cristobal Colon* in the 1951-52 to 1960-61 editions, and of *Gerardo Jansen* in the 1961-62 to 1965-66 editions.

JUAN BAUTISTA CAMBIASO   *1966, Official*

PATROL VESSELS (*Patrulleros*)

3 Ex-USCG WPC TYPE

	Pennant No.	Launched
INDEPENDENCIA (ex-USCGC *Icarus*)	204 (ex-P 105)	1931
LIBERTAD (ex-*Rafael Atoa*, ex-USCGC *Thetis*)	205 (ex-P 106)	1931
RESTAURACION (ex-USCGC *Galathea*)	203 (ex-P 104)	1932

Displacement, tons	334-337
Dimensions, feet	165 × 25·2 × 9·5
Guns	1—3 in; 1—40 mm; 1—20 mm
Main engines	2 Diesels; 1 280 bhp = 15 knots
Complement	35 (*Independencia*, 4 officers, 25 men)

Ex-US Coastguard Cutters. *Independencia* was completed by Bath Iron Works in 1932, and *Restauracion* by John H. Machis & Co, Camden, NJ, in 1933. Pennant numbers were changed from P 105, P 106, P 104 to 200 series in 1968.

DISPOSALS
Of the three patrol vessels of the ex-US PC type, *27 de Febrero* (ex-*PC 613*), *Constitucion* (ex-*Cibas*, ex-*Engage*, ex-*PC 1597*) were discarded in 1968; and *Patria* (ex-*Capitan Wenceslas Arvels*, ex-*PC 1202*) in 1962.

INDEPENDENCIA   *1964, Dominican Navy, Official*

RESTAURACION   *1969, Dominican Navy, Official*

LIBERTAD   *1970, Dominican Navy, Official*

FLEET MINESWEEPERS

2 Ex-US MSF TYPE

SEPARACION (ex-USS *Skirmish*, MSF 302) BM 454) **TORTUGERO** (ex-USS *Signet*, MSF 303) BM 455)

Displacement, tons	650 standard ; 945 full load
Dimensions, feet	180 wl ; 184·5 oa × 33 × 10
Guns	1—3 in dp ; 4—40 mm AA
Main engines	Diesel ; 2 shafts ; 1 710 bhp = 15 knots

Former US fleet minesweepers of the "Admirable" class. Purchased on 13 Jan 1965.

MEDIUM LANDING SHIP

(Barcazas de Desembarco)

1 Ex-US LSM TYPE RATED AS AUXILIARY

(Buque Auxiliar)

SIRIO (ex-USS *LSM 483*) 301 (ex-BA 104)

Displacement, tons	734 standard ; 1 100 full load
Dimensions, feet	196 wl ; 203·5 oa × 34 × 10 mean
Main engines	2 General Motors diesels ; 2 shafts ; 1 800 bhp = 14 knots
Oil fuel, tons	164
Complement	30

Ex-United States *LSM* (Medium Landing Ship). Built by Brown Shipbuilding Co Houston, Texas. Laid down on 17 Feb 1945, launched on 10 Mar 1945 and completed on 13 April 1945. Transferred to the Dominican Navy in 1960. Pennant number changed from BA 104 to 301 in 1968.

SIRIO   1964, Dominican Navy, Official

UTILITY LANDING CRAFT

(Barcazas de Desembarco)

2 LCT TYPE RATED AS AUXILIARY

(Lanchas Auxiliares)

ENRIQUILLO (ex-*17 de Julio*) 303 (ex-LA 3)   **SAMANA** 302 (ex-LA 2)

Displacement, tons	150 standard ; 310 full load
Dimensions, feet	105 wl ; 119·5 oa × 36 × 3 mean
Guns	1 AA, 50 cal
Main engines	3 General Motors diesels ; 441 bhp = 8 knots
Oil fuel, tons	80
Complement	17

Both built by Astilleros Navales Dominicanos in 1957-58. The new *Samana*, LA 2, replaced the *Samana* LA 2 lost in bad weather. *Enriquilla* (ex-*17 de Julio*) was launched on 24 Oct 1957. Renamed in 1962. Pennant numbers changed from LA 3 and LA 2 to 303 and 302, respectively, in 1968.

ENRIQUILLO   1964, Dominican Navy, Official

COAST GUARD VESSELS (Guardacostas)

1 US PGM TYPE

BETELGEUSE (ex-US *PGM* 77) GC 102

Displacement, tons	107
Dimensions, feet	94·5 × 20·7 × 5
Guns	1—40 mm ; 4—20 mm (2 twin) ; 2—0·5 in MG
Main engines	4 diesels ; 2 shafts ; 2 200 bhp = 21 knots
Radius, miles	1 500 at 10 knots

Built in the USA and transferred to the Dominican Republic under the Military Aid Programme. Completed in 1966 by Peterson Builders. Transferred on 14 Jan 1966.

RIGEL 101

Displacement, tons	50
Dimensions, feet	80 × 18 × 5
Guns	1 MG
Main engines	Speed = 18·5 knots maximum

DISPOSALS
The former GC 102, *Las Carreras*, ex-*Sanchez*, ex-*Patria*, ex-*SC 1153*, and her sister boat GC 101, *30 de Marzo*, ex-*Mella*, ex-*Rosa*, ex-*SC 1351*, were discarded in 1966-67. *Las Calderas* (ex-*Luberon*, GC 9) and *Bahia Ocoa* (ex-*22 de Junio*, GC 10) were discarded in 1968. Sister boat *Bahia Manzanillo* GC 11 (ex-*16 de Agosto*, ex-USCG cutter 56199) was discarded in 1962. The coastguard vessel *Trinidad*, GC 8, was also discarded in 1962, and *Boya*, GC 2, in 1960. The training ship *Duarte* (ex-*Nueva Tioditie*), GA 1 was discarded in 1962.

RIGEL   1969. Dominican Navy, Official

3 "BELLATRIX" CLASS

BELLATRIX GC 106   **CAPELLA** GC 108   **PROCION** GC 103

Displacement, tons	60
Dimensions, feet	85 × 19 × 5
Guns	3—·5 mg
Main engines	2 GM Diesels ; 1 000 bhp = 19·5 knots

Officially added to the Dominican Republic Coast Guard list in 1969.

BELLATRIX   1970, Dominican Navy, Official

PROCION   1969, Dominican Navy, Official

LIGHTHOUSE AND BUOY TENDER

(Buque de Faros y Boyas-Boyero)

CAPOTILLO (ex-*Camillia*) 1 (ex-FB 101)

Displacement, tons	337
Dimensions, feet	117 × 24 × 7·8
Main engines	2 Diesels; 880 bhp = 10 knots
Complement	40

Built in the United States in 1911. Acquired from the United States Coast Guard in 1949.

CAPOTILLO   *Dominican Navy, Official*

MOTOR LAUNCHES (Lanchas Auxiliare)

1 HYDROGRAPHIC SURVEY TYPE

MAIMON LA 5

Dimensions, feet	53 × 9 × 4
Main engines	2 motors; 500 hp = 14 knots
Complement	4

Acquired for the Hydrographic Service of the Navy in 1960.

MAIMON   *1971, Official*

2 "ATLANTIDA" TYPE
PUERTO HERMOSO LA 7   **ATLANTIDA** LA 8

The motor launch *Altogracia*, LA-1 (ex-*Laura*), was discarded in 1960 and *Najaya*, LA 4, in 1962.

RESCUE LAUNCH (Lancha de Rescate)

CAPITAN ALSINA 105 (ex-LR 101)

Displacement, tons	100 standard
Dimensions, feet	92 wl; 104·8 oa × 19·2 × 5·8
Guns	2—20 mm AA; 2 MG
Main engines	Diesel; 2 shafts; 1 000 hp = 17 knots
Complement	20

Of wooden construction. Launched in 1944. Named as above in 1957. LR 102 was lost in 1956. Sister boat *Capitan Maduro*, LR 103, was discarded in 1968.

CAPITAN ALSINA   *Official*

DISPOSALS
The auxiliary ships (*Buques Auxiliares*) *18 de Decembre*, BA-101 (ex-US *WPC* 587), converted patrol vessel, and *Leonor*, BA-102 (ex-*Romanita*), were discarded in 1960. The Presidential yacht *Patria* (ex-*Angelita*) was sold in 1968.

OILERS

2 Ex-US YO TYPE COASTAL TANKERS

CAPITAN W ARVELO BT 4   **CAPITAN BEOTEGUI** BT 5
(ex-USS *YO 215*)   (ex-US *YO 213*)

Displacement, tons	370 light; 1,095 full load
Dimensions, feet	156·5 × 30 × 13·3
Guns	1—20 mm
Main engines	1 Fairbanks-Morse diesel; 525 bhp = 8 knots max
Capacity	6 570 barrels
Complement	27

Former United States self propelled fuel oil barges. Both built by Ira S. Bushey & Sons, Inc, Brooklyn, New York. Loaned by the USA in Mar 1964.

CAPITAN W. ARVELO   *1969, Dominican Navy, Official*

DISPOSALS
The oiler *San Carlos*, BT 102, was officially deleted from the list in Feb 1965 and *Ulises Heureaux* (ex-*24 de Octubre*, ex-*YO 2*) BT 101, in 1968.

TUGS (Remolcadores)

2 "HERCULES" TYPE

HERCULES 12 (ex-R 2)   **GUACANAGARIX 13** (ex-R 5)

Dimensions, feet	70 × 18·5 × 9·0
Main engines	1 Caterpillar motor; 500 hp; 1 225 rpm
Complement	8 to 11

Small tugs of coastal type built by Astilleros Navalis Dominicos in 1960.

HERCULES   *1971, Official*

1 US TYPE

ISABELA 20 (ex-R 1)

Displacement, tons	40
Dimensions, feet	65 × 14 × 9
Main engines	2 diesel motors; 300 bhp = 8 knots
Complement	8

Built in the United States. Named *Isabela* in 1957. A photograph appears in the 1951-52 to 1957-58 editions. The tug *Hercules* (ex-*Heracles*), Pennant No. R 2, transferred from the Dominican mercantile marine in 1952, was lost in 1956.

6 "BERGANTIN" TYPE

BERGANTIN R 14	**CONSUELO** R 18	**RIO HAINA** R 17
CALDERAS R 19	**MERCEDES** R 16 (ex-R 10)	**SANTANA** R 15 (ex-R 7)

Small tugs for harbour and coastal use. Not all of uniform type and dimensions.

DISPOSALS
The tugs *Bergantin*, R-6, *Catalina*, R-3, *Leonidas*, R-8 and *Luperon*, R-4 were discarded in 1960-62.

ECUADOR

Administration

Minister of Defence:
Senor Jorge Acosta Velasco

Commander-in-Chief of the Navy:
Rear Admiral Jorge Cruz

Diplomatic Representation

Naval Attaché in London:
Captain Guillermo Jarrin N.

Naval Attaché in Washington:
Captain Reinaldo Vallejo

Strength of the Fleet

1 Patrol Frigate ("River" Type)
2 Escort Destroyers ("Hunt" Type)
1 Modified Destroyer Escort
2 Escort Patrol Vessels (PCE Type)
2 Motor Gunboats (PGM Type)
6 Patrol Boats (Motor Launches)
2 Medium Landing Ships (LSM Type)
1 Supply Ship (Cargo)
1 Survey Ship (ex-Netlayer)
1 Water Carrier (YW Type)
3 Tugs (1 Ocean, 2 Harbour)

Ships

The names of Ecuadorian naval vessels are prefaced by "BAE"

Establishments

The Naval Academy is in Salinas

Naval Bases

In Galápagos, Guayaquil, Salinas, and San Lorenzo

Personnel

1971: Total 4 000 (360 officers and 3 640 men)

Mercantile Marine

Lloyd's Register of Shipping:
18 vessels of 45 451 tons gross

FRIGATE

Name	Pennant No.	Builders	Laid down	Launched	Completed
GUAYAS (ex-USS *Covington*, PF 56)	E 21 (ex-E 01)	Globe S.B. Co, Superior, Wis.	1 Mar 1943	15 July 1943	7 Aug 1944

1 Ex-US PF TYPE

Displacement, tons	1 430 standard; 2 415 full load
Length, feet (*metres*)	304·0 (*92·7*) oa
Beam, feet (*metres*)	37·5 (*11·4*)
Draught, feet (*metres*)	13·7 (*4·2*)
Guns, surface	2—3 in (*76 mm*) single
Guns, AA	2—40 mm; 4—20 mm
A/S weapons	3 DCT
Boilers	2 small tube
Main engines	Triple expansion; 2 shafts; 5 500 ihp
Speed, knots	19 max; 16 sea
Radius, miles	9 500 at 12 knots
Oil fuel, tons	290 normal; 645 max
Complement	150

Former US patrol frigate of the PF type. Purchased from the USA in 1947. Similar in design to British "River" class frigates of the time.

GUAYAS   *1967, Ecuadorian Navy, Official*

ESCORT DESTROYERS

Name	Pennant No.	Builders	Laid down	Launched	Completed
PRESIDENTE ALFARO (ex-HMS *Quantock*)	D 01	Scotts' S.B. & Eng Co Ltd, Greenock	26 July 1939	22 Apr 1940	6 Feb 1941
PRESIDENTE VELASCO IBARRA (ex-HMS *Meynell*)	D 02	Swan Hunter & Wigham Richardson, Wallsend	10 Aug 1939	7 June 1940	30 Dec 1940

2 Ex-BRITISH "HUNT" CLASS
(TYPE 1) ESCORT DESTROYERS

Displacement, tons	1 000 standard; 1 490 full load
Length, feet (*metres*)	272·3 (*83·0*) pp; 280 (*85·4*) oa
Beam, feet (*metres*)	29 (*8·8*)
Draught, feet (*metres*)	14 (*4·3*)
Guns, surface	4—4 in (*102 mm*)
Guns, AA	2—20 mm
A/S weapons	DC throwers; DC racks
Boilers	2 Admiralty 3-drum
Main engines	Parsons geared turbines (by Wallsend Slipway in *Presidente Velasco Ibarra*) 19 000 shp; 2 shafts
Speed, knots	23 sea
Radius, miles	2 000 at 12 knots 800 at 25 knots
Oil fuel (tons)	280
Complement	146

PRESIDENTE VELASCO IBARRA   *1965, Ecuadorian Navy, Official*

Former British frigates (ex-escort destroyers) of the "Hunt" class, Type 1, purchased by Ecuador from Great Britain on 18 Oct 1954, and refitted by J. Samuel White & Co, Ltd, Cowes, Isle of Wight. *Quantock* was taken over by the Ecuadorian Navy in Portsmouth Dockyard on 16 Aug 1955, when she was renamed *Presidente Alfaro*. Sister ship *Meynell* was transferred to the Ecuadorian Navy and renamed *Presidente Velasco Ibarra* in Aug 1955.

PRESIDENTE ALFARO   *1970, Ecuadorian Navy, Official*

Escort Destroyers—*continued*

1 Ex-US APD- TYPE

HIGH SPEED TRANSPORT

25 DE JULIO E 12 (ex-*Enright*, APD 66, ex-DE 216)

Displacement, tons	1 400 standard; 2 130 full load
Dimensions, feet	306·0 oa × 37·0 × 12·6
Guns	1—5 in 38 cal; 4—40 mm
Boilers	2 "D" Express
Main engines	GE geared turbines with electric drive; 2 shafts; 12 000 shp = 23 knots
Complement	204

Former US high speed transport (modified destroyer escort). Built by the Navy Yard, Philadelphia, Pa. Laid down on 22 Feb 1943, launched on 29 May 1943 and completed on 21 Sep 1943. Transferred to Ecuador on 14 July 1967 under MAP. Could carry 162 troops.

25 DE JULIO

1968, *Ecuadorian Navy, Official*

ESCORT PATROL VESSELS

2 Ex-US PCE TYPE

Name	ESMERALDAS	MANABI
	(ex-USS *Eunice*, PCE 846)	(ex-USS *Pascagoula*, PCE 874)
Pennant No.	E 22 (ex-E 03)	E 23 (ex-E 02)
Builders	Pullman Standard Car	Albina Eng & Mach
	Manufacturing Co. Chicago, Ill	Works, Portland, Oreg
Laid down	10 Aug 1943	1 Mar 1943
Launched	20 Dec 1943	11 May 1943
Completed	4 Mar 1944	31 Dec 1943
Transferred	29 Nov 1960	5 Dec 1960

Displacement, tons	640 standard; 903 full load
Dimensions, feet	180 wl; 184·5 oa × 33 × 9·5
Guns	1—3 in dual purpose; 6—40 mm AA
A/S weapons	4 DCT
Main engines	GM diesels; 2 shafts; 1 800 bhp = 15·4 knots
Complement	100 officers and men

Former United States patrol vessels (180 ft Escorts) transferred from the US Navy to the Ecuadorian Navy on 29 Nov and 5 Dec 1960, respectively. A photograph of *Manabi* appears in the 1963-64 and 1964-65 editions.

ESMERALDAS

1965, *Ecuadorian Navy, Official*

GUN BOATS

2 Ex-US PGM TYPE

GUAYAQUIL (ex-US *PGM 76*) LC 73   **QUITO** (ex-US *PGM 75*) LC 71

Displacement, tons	101
Dimensions, feet	95 oa × 19 × 5
Guns	1—40 mm AA; 2—20 mm
Main engines	4 diesels; 2 shafts; 2 200 bhp = 21 knots
Radius, miles	1 500 at cruising speed
Complement	15

US built. Transferred to the Ecuadorian Navy under MAP on 30 Nov 1965.

GUAYAQUIL

1967, *Ecuadorian Navy, Official*

PATROL BOATS

6 ML TYPE

LSP 1   LSP 2   LSP 3   LSP 4   LSP 5   LSP 6

Displacement, tons	45 standard; 64 full load
Dimensions, feet	76·8 × 13·7 × 4·2 mean (6·3 max)
Guns	Light MG AA
Main engines	Bohn & Kähler diesel; 2 shafts; 1 200 bhp = 22 knots
Range, miles	550 at 16 knots
Complement	9

Built by Hermann Havighorst, Bremen-Blumenthal. Ordered in 1954. First two were delivered in Aug 1954 and the remainder in 1955. Pennant Nos. LP 81 to LP 86. A photograph of LSP 1 appears in the 1955-56 edition.

LP 6

1963, *Ecuadorian Navy Official*

POWER VESSELS

5 Ex-US APD TYPE

Although not on the Navy List of Ecuador the hulls of the former US Navy high speed transports (modified destroyer escorts) *Reeves* APD 52, *Frament*, APD 77, *Crosley* APD 87, *Hunter Marshall*, APD 112, and *Walter S. Gorka*, APD 114, were transferred from the United States in July and Aug 1961 for use as floating power plants.

MEDIUM LANDING SHIPS

2 Ex-US LSM TYPE

JAMBELI (ex-USS *LSM 539*) T 31   **TARQUI** (ex-USS *LSM 555*) T 32

Displacement, tons	743 beaching; 1 095 full load
Dimensions, feet	196·5 wl; 203·5 oa × 34·5 × 8·3
Guns	2—40 mm AA
Main engines	Diesels; 2 shafts; 2 800 bhp = 12·5 knots

Former US Landing Ships, Medium. *Jambeli* was laid down by Brown S.B. Co, Houston, on 10 May 1945. *Tarqui* was laid down by the Navy Yard, Charleston, SC on 3 Mar 1945 and launched on 22 Mar 1945. Purchased from USA in 1958 and transferred to the Ecuadorian Navy at Green Cove Springs, Florida in Nov 1958. Crew 60. A photograph of *Tarqui* appears in the 1963-64 to 1966-67 editions.

JAMBELI

1967 *Ecuadorian Navy, Official*

SUPPLY SHIP

CALICUCHIMA (ex-US *FS* 525) T 42

Displacement, tons	650 light; 950 full load
Dimensions, feet	176 × 32 × 14 max
Main engines	Diesels; 2 shafts; 500 bhp = 11 knots

Former United States small cargo ship of the Army FS type. Leased to Ecuador on 8 Apr 1963. Provides service to the Galapagos Islands.

CALICUCHIMA   1970, Ecuadorian Navy, Official

WATER CARRIER

ATAHUALPA (ex-US *YW* 131) T 41 (ex-A 01)

Displacement, tons	415 light; 1 235 full load
Dimensions, feet	174·0 × 32·0 × 15·0
Main engines	GM diesels; 750 bhp = 11·5 knots

Built by Leatham D. Smith SB Co, Sturgeon Bay in 1945. Transferred from USA in Mar 1963. Acquired by the Ecuadorian Navy on 2 May 1963.

DOCK VESSELS

AMAZONAS (ex-US *ARD* 17)

Measurement, tons	3 500 lifting capacity
Dimensions, feet	491·7 oa × 81·0 oa × 32·9 max

Former United States auxiliary floating dock. Built in 1943-44. Transferred on loan on 7 Jan 1961. Suitable for docking destroyers and landing ships. Dry Dock companion craft YFND 20 was leased on 2 Nov. 1961.

SURVEY SHIP

ORION (ex-USS *Mulberry*, AN 27) 101

Displacement, tons	560 standard; 805 full load
Dimensions, feet	146 wl; 163 oa × 30·5 × 11·8 max
Guns	1—3 in AA
Main engines	Diesel-electric; 800 bhp = 13 knots
Complement	48

Former United States netlayer. Built by Commercial Iron Works, Portland, Oregon. Launched on 26 Mar 1941. Loaned by US under MAP. Transferred to Ecuador in Nov 1965.

ORION   1970, Ecuadorian Navy, Official

TUGS

CAYAMBE (ex-*Los Rios*, ex-USS *Cusabo*, ATF 155) R 51 (ex-R 01)

Displacement, tons	1 235 standard; 1 675 full load
Dimensions, feet	195 oa × 205 oa × 38·5 × 15·5 max
Guns	1—3 in; 4—40 mm AA; 2—20 mm AA
Main engines	4 diesels with electric drive; 3 000 bhp = 16·5 knots
Complement	85

Former US "Apache" class fleet ocean tug. Launched on 26 Feb 1945. Fitted with powerful pumps and other salvage equipment. Transferred to Ecuador by lease on 2 Nov 1960 and renamed *Los Rios*. Again renamed *Cayambe* in 1966.

CAYAMBE   1970, Ecuadorian Navy, Official

COTOPAXI (ex-*R. T. Ellis*) R 52

Displacement, tons	150
Dimensions, feet	82 × 21 × 8
Main engines	Diesel; 1 shaft; 650 bhp = 9 knots

Former US tug. Built by Equitable Building Co, Incorp. Purchased from the United States in 1947.

COTOPAXI   1970, Ecuadorian Navy, Official

SANGAY (ex-*Loja*) R 53

Displacement, tons	295 light; 390 full load
Dimensions, feet	107 × 26 × 14
Main engines	Fairbanks Morse diesel; speed = 12 knots

Built in 1952. Acquired by the Ecuadorian Navy in 1964. Renamed in 1966.

SANGAY   1970, Ecuadorian Navy, Official

EGYPT

SUBMARINES

6 Ex-USSR "R" TYPE

Displacement, tons	1 100 surface; 1 600 submerged
Length, feet (metres)	246·0 (75·0)
Beam, feet (metres)	24·0 (7·3)
Draught, feet (metres)	14·5 (4·4)
Torpedo tubes	6—21 in (533 mm) bow
Main engines	Diesels, 4 000 bhp
	Electric motors, 2 500 hp
Speed, knots	18·5 surface; 15 submerged
Complement	65

Two "R" class units replaced two "W" class boats which returned to the USSR in May 1966. Another "R" class boat was transferred to Egypt in Feb 1966, and five "R" class submarines had been delivered by the end of 1966. Six "R" boats were transferred by 1969.

6 Ex-USSR "W" TYPE

Displacement, tons	1 030 surface; 1 180 submerged
Length, feet (metres)	240 (73·2) oa
Beam, feet (metres)	22 (6·7)
Draught, feet (metres)	15 (4·6)
Guns, AA	4—25 mm
Torpedo tubes	6—21 in (533 mm); 4 forward
	2 aft
Main engines	4 000 bhp diesels; 2 500 hp electric motors
Speed, knots	17 on surface; 15 submerged
Radius, miles	13 000
Complement	60

The first "W" class units were transferred from the Soviet Navy to the Egyptian Navy in June 1957. Three more arrived at Alexandria on 24 Jan 1958. Another was transferred to Egypt at Alexandria in Jan 1962.

4 Ex-USSR "SKORYI" TYPE

AL NASSER	DUMYAT
AL ZAFR	SUEZ

Displacement, tons	2 600 standard; 3 500 full load
Length, feet (metres)	393·7 (120·0) pp; 420 (128·0) oa
Beam, feet (metres)	41 (12·5)
Draught, feet (metres)	13·1 (4·0)
Guns, surface	4—5·1 in (130 mm)
Guns, AA	2—3 in (76 mm); 7—37 mm
A/S weapons	4 DCT
Torpedo tubes	10—21 in (533 mm) quintupled
Mines	80 can be carried
Boilers	3
Main engines	Geared turbines; 2 shafts; 70 000 shp
Speed, knots	38
Radius, miles	4 000 at 15 knots
Complement	250

Former "Skoryi" class destroyers of the Soviet Navy. Launched in 1951. Al Nasser and Al Zafr were delivered to the Egyptian Navy on 11 June 1956 at Alexandria. The implication of each name in Arabic is "victory".

1 Ex-BRITISH "Z" TYPE

EL FATEH (ex-HMS Zenith)

Displacement, tons	1 730 standard; 2 575 full load
Length, feet (metres)	350 (106·8) wl; 362·8 (110·6) oa
Beam, feet (metres)	35·7 (10·9)
Draught, feet (metres)	17·1 (5·2) max
Guns, dual purpose	4—4·5 in (115 mm)
Guns, AA	6—40 mm
A/S weapons	4 DCT
Boilers	2 Admiralty 3-drum
Main engines	Parsons geared turbines; 2 shafts; 40 000 shp
Speed, knots	36·75 designed; 31·25 sea
Radius, miles	2 800 at 20 knots
Oil fuel, tons	580
Complement	250

Former "Z" class destroyer in the British Navy. Built by Wm. Denny & Bros Ltd, Dumbarton. Laid down on 19 May 1942, launched on 5 June 1944 and completed on 22 Dec 1944. Purchased from Great Britain in 1955. Before being taken over by Egypt. El Fateh was refitted by John I. Thornycroft & Co Ltd, Woolston, Southampton in July 1956.

RADAR
Search: Type 960 Metric wavelength. Tactical: Type 293 S Band. Fire Control: X Band.

Strength of the Fleet

13	Submarines	19	Missile Boats
5	Destroyers	12	Patrol Vessels
4	Escorts	36	Torpedo Boats
2	Corvettes	16	Amphibious Ships
6	Minesweepers	5	Auxiliaries

Personnel

1971: 14 000 officers and men, including the Coast Guard

Mercantile Marine
Lloyd's Register of Shipping:
124 vessels of 238 282 tons gross

R Type   1968, Skyfotos

1 Ex-USSR "MV" TYPE

Displacement, tons	350 surface; 420 submerged
Length, feet (metres)	167·3 (51·0)
Beam, feet (metres)	16 (4·9)
Draught, feet (metres)	12 (3·7)
Guns, AA	1—45 mm; 1 MG
Torpedo tubes	2—21 in (533 mm)

Main engines	1 000 bhp diesels; 800 hp electric motors
Speed, knots	13 on surface; 10 submerged
Radius, miles	4 000 at 8 knots
Complement	24

Launched in 1950. Transferred from the USSR to Egypt in June 1957. There is no evidence of new construction in Egypt.

DESTROYERS

SKORYI Type   Added 1966

It was reported in Dec 1959 that six destroyers were being transferred from the USSR to Egypt. Two were delivered at Alexandria in Jan 1962.

RADAR. Search: Probably S Band. Tactical: Probably C Band. Fire Control: X Band.

It was reported that the USSR would supply the Egyptian Navy with destroyers armed with 150 miles range sea-surface missiles, presumably of the "Krupny" or "Kildin" class.

EL FATEH

MODERNISATION. Refitted and modernised by J. Samuel White & Co Ltd, at Cowes, Isle of Wight from May 1963 until July 1964.

LOSS
Sister ship El Qaher (ex-HMS Zenith) was sunk by Israeli aircraft on 16 May 1970.

ESCORTS

1 Ex-BRITISH "BLACK SWAN" TYPE

Displacement, tons	1 490 standard; 1 925 full load
Length, feet (metres)	283 (86·3) pp; 299·5 (91·3) oa
Beam, feet (metres)	38·5 (11·7)
Draught, feet (metres)	14·0 (4·3) max
Guns, surface	6—4 in (102 mm)
Guns, AA	4—40 mm; 2—20 mm
A/S weapons	4 DCT
Boilers	2 three-drum type
Main engines	Geared turbines; 2 shafts; 4 300 shp
Speed, knots	19·75 designed; 18 sea
Radius, miles	4 500 at 12 knots
Oil fuel, tons	370
Complement	180

Former "Black Swan" class sloop (later re-rated as frigate) in the British Navy. Transferred from Great Britain in Nov 1949. As flotilla leader she had a broad band painted on her funnel and a thinner flotilla band.

1 Ex-BRITISH "RIVER" TYPE

Displacement, tons	1 490 standard; 2 216 full load
Length, feet (metres)	283 (86·3) pp; 301·5 (91·9) oa
Beam, feet (metres)	36·7 (11·2)
Draught, feet (metres)	14·1 (4·3)
Guns, surface	1—4 in (102 mm)
Guns, AA	2—40 mm; 6—20 mm
A/S weapons	4 DCT
Boilers	2 Admiralty 3-drum type
Main engines	Triple expansion; 2 shafts; 5 500 ihp
Speed, knots	18
Radius, miles	9 500 at 12 knots
Oil fuel, tons	640
Complement	180

Former "River" class frigate of the British Navy. Purchased from Great Britain in Nov 1948. Refitted by Willoughby (Plymouth) Ltd. Sailed for Egypt in Apr 1950. Formerly mounted two 4-inch guns.

CLASS. Of her two sister ships Abikir (ex-HMS Usk) was sunk as a blockship in the Suez Canal in Nov 1956. (raised and dumped in Apr 1957); and Domiat (ex-HMS Nith) was sunk by the British cruiser Newfoundland off Suez on 1 Nov 1956.

1 Ex-BRITISH "HUNT" TYPE

Displacement, tons	1 000 standard; 1 490 full load
Length, feet (metres)	273 (83·2) wl; 280 (85·3) oa
Bean, feet (metres)	29 (8·8)
Draught, feet (metres)	15·1 (4·3) max
Guns, surface	4—4 in (103 mm)
Guns, AA	2—40 mm; 2—20 mm
A/S weapons	2 DCT
Boilers	2 three-drum type
Main engines	Parsons geared turbines; 2 shafts; 19 000 shp
Speed, knots	25 max
Radius, miles	2 000 at 12 knots
Oil fuel, tons	280
Complement	146

Former British "Hunt" Class, Type 1 escort destroyer (later re-rated as frigate). Served in the British Navy from 1940. Transferred from the British Navy to the Egyptian Navy in July 1950; Sailed for Egypt in April 1951, after a nine months' refit by J. Samuel White & Co Ltd, Cowes. She was first renamed Ibrahim el Awal but was renamed Mohamed Ali el Kebir about 1951.

1 Ex-BRITISH "FLOWER" TYPE

Displacement, tons	1 060 standard; 1 340 full load
Length, feet (metres)	190 (57·9) pp; 205 (62·5) oa
Beam, feet (metres)	33 (10·0)
Draught, feet (metres)	14·5 (4·4) max
Guns, surface	1—4 in (102 mm)
Guns, AA	2—20 mm
Boilers	2 SE
Main engines	Triple expansion; 2 750 shp
Speed, knots	16
Radius, miles	7 000 at 10 knots
Oil fuel (tons)	230
Complement	85

Former "Flower" class corvette (later re-rated as frigate) of the British Navy. Taken over by Yugoslavia in 1943 (loaned). Returned to the British Navy early in 1949 and transferred to Egypt on 28 Oct 1949.

CLASS. Sister ship Misr (ex-SS Malrouk) was rammed and sunk by collision south of Suez 16th-17th May 1953.

None of the above four old WW2-built vessels are any longer of considerable military value.

Name	No.	Builders	Laid down	Launched	Completed
TARIK (ex-El Malek Farouq, ex-HMS Whimbrel)	42	Yarrow & Co Ltd, Glasgow	31 Oct 1941	25 Aug 1942	13 Jan 1943

TARIK   Added 1966

Name	No.	Builders	Laid down	Launched	Completed
RASHID (ex-HMS Spey)	43	Smith's Dock Co Ltd, Middlesbrough	18 July 1941	10 Dec 1941	19 May 1942

RASHEED   1968

	No.	Builders	Laid down	Launched	Completed
PORT SAID (ex-Mohamed Ali, ex-Ibrahim el Awal, ex-HMS Cottesmore)	11	Yarrow & Co, Ltd, Scotstoun, Glasgow	12 Dec 1939	5 Sep 1940	29 Dec 1940

PORT SAID (ex-Mohamed Ali)   Added 1966

CLASS. Sister ship Ibrahim el Awal served in the British Navy as HMS Mendip until 1948, when she was transferred to the Chinese Navy and renamed Lin Fu; she was returned to the British Navy at Hong Kong a year later and reverted to her original name, but was transferred to the Egyptian Navy in Nov 1949, when she was first renamed Mohamed Ali el Kebir but was afterwards again renamed Ibrahim el Awal, exchanging names with her sister ship about 1951-52. Ibrahim el Awal surrendered to Israeli forces off Haifa on 31 Oct 1956; she was rehabilitated and incorporated into the Israeli Navy and renamed Haifa (see later page).

Name	Builders	Laid down	Launched	Completed
EL SUDAN (ex-Mallow, ex-Partizanka ex-Nada, ex-HMS Mallow)	Harland & Wolff, Ltd, Belfast	14 Nov 1939	22 May 1940	2 July 1940

EL SUDAN   A. & J. Pavia

CORVETTES (ex-FLEET MINESWEEPERS)

2 Ex-BRITISH "BANGOR" TYPE

Name	Builders	Laid down	Launched	Completed
MATROUH (ex-HMS *Stornoway*)	Henry Robb, Ltd, Leith	17 July 1940	10 June 1941	17 Nov 1941
NASR (ex-HMS *Bude*)	Lobnitz & Co. Ltd, Renfrew	2 Apr 1940	4 Sep 1940	12 Dec 1941

Displacement, tons	672 standard; 900 full load
Dimensions, feet	180 oa × 28·5 × 9·5
Guns	1—4 fn; 1—3 ln; 2—40 mm AA; (4—20 mm in *Matrouh*)
A/S weapons	2 DCT
Main engines	Triple expansion; 2 shafts; 2 400 ihp = 16 knots (designed) sea speed 14 knots
Boilers	2 Admiralty 3-drum type
Oil fuel (tons)	170
Radius, miles	4 300 at 10 knots
Complement	60

Former "Bangor" class fleet minesweepers acquired from Great Britain. Now rated as corvettes. Sister ship *Sollum* sank in heavy weather off Alexandria on 7 Mar 1953.

MATROUH   *Egyptian Navy, Official*

FLEET MINESWEEPERS

6 Ex-USSR "T 43" TYPE

ASSIUT	CHARKIEH	GARBIA
BAHAIRA	DAQHALIA	SINAI

Displacement, tons	410 standard; 530 full load
Dimensions, feet	200 × 27·2 × 9
Guns	4—37 mm AA
Main engines	Diesel = 18 knots

Four were transferred from the Soviet Navy and delivered to Egypt in 1956. and two others later. *Miniya* was sunk by Israeli air attack in the Gulf of Suez on 6 Feb 1970. Sister ships *Hittine* and *Yarmouk* were allocated to Syria.

INSHORE MINESWEEPERS

2 Ex-USSR "T 301" TYPE

EL FAYUH	EL HANUFIEH

Displacement, tons	130 standard; 180 full load
Dimensions, feet	100 × 16 × 4·5
Guns,	2—37 mm AA; 2—25 mm AA
Main engines	Diesels; 2 shafts; 480 bhp = 10 knots
Complement	30

Reported to have been transferred by the USSR to Egypt in 1962; possibly a third ship transferred also.

BYMS TYPE
Of the wooden coastal minesweepers, *Gaza* (ex-*BYMS* 2013) was lost on 26 July 1950, as a result of fuel-tank explosion off Mersa Matrouh, sister ships *Darfour* (ex-*BYMS* 2041) and *Tor* (ex-*BYMS* 2175) were transferred to the Algerian Navy on 6 Nov 1962, and the remaining six, *Arish* (ex-*BYMS* 2028), *Kaisaria* (ex-*BYMS* 2075), *Kordofan* (ex-*BYMS* 2212), *Malek Fuad* (ex-*BYMS* 2035), *Naharia* (ex-*BYMS* 2069) and *Rafah* (ex-*BYMS* 2149) are no more than mouldering hulks.

PATROL VESSELS

12 Ex-USSR "SOI" TYPE

Displacement, tons	215 light; 220 full load
Dimensions, feet	138 pp; 147 oa × 20 × 10 max
Guns	4—25 mm (2 twin mountings)
A/S weapons	4 five-barrelled ahead throwing rocket launchers
Main engines	3 diesels; 3 500 bhp = 28 knots

Former Soviet submarine chasers. Eight reported to have been transferred by the USSR to Egypt in 1962 to 1967 and four others later.

ROCKET ASSAULT SHIPS

2 Ex-USSR "POLNOCNY" TYPE

Displacement, tons	900 to 1 000
Dimensions, feet	246 × 39·3 × 9·8
Armament	Rocket projector
Main engines	Diesels, 4 000 bhp = 15 knots

A new type of Soviet amphibious vessel basically similar to the United States medium rocket landing ships of the LSMR type. This TRV type, which can carry eight to ten tanks, was delivered by the USSR to the Egyptian Navy in 1965-66.

MISSILE BOATS

12 Ex-USSR "OSA" TYPE

Displacement, tons	160 standard; 200 full load
Dimensions, feet	121·3 pp; 131·5 oa × 23 × 6·5
Guided weapons	4 large hood type missile launchers in two pairs abreast with range of 15 to 18 miles
Guns	4—25 mm (2 twin, 1 forward, 1 aft)
Main engines	3 diesels; 4 800 bhp = 35 knots

Reported to have been delivered to Egypt by the Soviet Navy in 1966.

7 Ex-USSR "KOMAR" TYPE

Displacement, tons	75 standard; 100 full load
Dimensions, feet	88 oa × 21 × 6
Guided Missiles	2 launchers with missiles of 10 to 15 miles range
Main engines	Speed = 40 knots

Former Soviet missile boats transferred from the USSR in 1962 to 1967. One of this type was sunk by Israeli jets on 16 May 1870. Two patrol boats named *Nisr* 1 and 2 110 tons, are reported to have been launched at Port Said on 16 May 1963 *et seq* by the Castro Naval Shipyard.

KOMAR Type   *1966, Col. Bjorn Borg*

TORPEDO BOATS

6 Ex-USSR "SHERSHEN" TYPE

Displacement, tons	150
Dimensions, feet	131·5 × 23 × 6·5
Guns	4—25 mm AA (2 twin)
Torpedo tubes	4—21 in (single)
Main engines	Gas turbines; speed = 40 knots

One delivered from USSR in Feb 1967, two more (326,329) in Oct 1967, and three since.

24 Ex-USSR "P" 6 TYPE

Displacement, tons	50
Dimensions, feet	85·5 × 20 × 6
Guns	4—25 mm AA MG
Tubes	2—21 in
Main engines	Speed = 42 knots

The first twelve boats arrived at Alexandria on 19 Apr 1956. Two boats were destroyed by British naval aircraft on 4 Nov 1956, two were sunk by the Israeli destroyer *Elath* off Sinai on 12 July 1967, two by Israeli MTBs off Sinai coast on 11 July 1967 and two by Israeli air attacks in 1969.
The above particulars refer to the early arrivals. Six former Soviet motor torpedo boats of the "P6" class are reported to have been transferred by the USSR in 1960.

6 Ex-YUGOSLAVIAN TYPE

Displacement, tons	56 full load
Dimensions, feet	78 × 20·7 × 5·2
Guns	1—40 mm AA
Tubes	4
Main engines	3 Packard motors; 3 shafts; 4 500 bhp = 35 knots

Purchased from Yugoslavia in 1956. Similar to the boats of the US Higgins type.

The two motor torpedo boats of the British Fairmile "D" type, *El Naser* and *El Zafer*, are reported to have been disposed of, and the three motor launches of the British Fairmile "B" type, *Hamza* (ex-ML 134), *Sab el Bahr* and *Saker el Bahar* are hulks. The transport *El Quseir* (ex-*El Amira Fawzia*) and the yachts *Ntisar* (ex-*Fakhr le Bihar*) and *El Horria* (ex-Royal yacht *Mahroussa*), latterly used as training ship, were deleted from the list in 1967, although the latter was still in service in 1970.

LANDING CRAFT

8 Ex-USSR "VIDRA" TYPE

Displacement, tons	300 standard; 500 full load
Dimensions, feet	164 × 26·2 × 7·2
Main engines	2 diesels; 2 shafts; 400 bhp = 15 knots

Can carry and land up to 250 tons of military equipment and stores.

6 Ex-USSR "SMB 1" TYPE

Displacement, tons	200 standard; 420 full load
Dimensions, feet	157·5 × 19·7 × 5·6
Main engines	Diesels. Speed = 11 knots

Several utility landing craft of the MP-SMB 1, delivered to the Egyptian Navy in 1965. Predecessors of the "Vidra" type. Can carry 150 tons of military equipment.

(The tank landing ship *Aka* (ex-LST 178) was sunk as a block-ship near Lake Timsah in the Suez Camal on 1 Nov 1956). The LCM type were deleted in 1971.

FLEET TUGS

Ex-USSR "OKHTENSKY" TYPE

A number of Soviet fleet tugs were reported transferred to the Egyptian Navy in 1966

ETHIOPIA

Administration

The Imperial Ethiopian Navy, founded in 1955, is one of the three Services under the Ministry of National Defence. The Commander-in-Chief is His Imperial Majesty. The Deputy Commander-in-Chief has his Naval Headquarters in Addis Ababa.

Deputy Commander-in-Chief of the Imperial Ethiopian Navy:
    Commodore H.I.H. Prince Alexander Desta
Chief of Staff:
    Colonel Taye Telahun
Naval Adviser:
    Capitaine de Fregate M. Vasseur FN
Commanding Officer, Haile Selassie I Naval Base, Massawa:
    Captain J. E. Farnol, DSC, RN(Retd)

Naval Establishments

"Haile Selassie I" Massawa: Naval Base and College, established in 1956.
Embaticalla: Marine Commando Training School.
Assab: Naval Base, expanding to include a ship repair facility.

Personnel

1971: 210 National officers and cadets, 15 Warrant officers, 987 National enlisted men.

Mercantile Marine

Lloyd's Register of Shipping: 25 vessels of 49 266 tons gross

COASTAL MINESWEEPERS

1 Ex-NETHERLANDS "WILDERVANK" CLASS

ELST

Displacement, tons	373 standard; 417 full load
Dimensions, feet	149·8 oa × 28·0 × 7·5
Guns	2—40 mm AA
Main engines	2 diesels; 2 shafts; 2 500 bhp = 14 knots
Oil fuel, tons	25 tons
Radius, miles	2 500 at 10 knots
Complement	38

Western Union type non-magnetic coastal minesweeper of the "Wildervank" class built in the Netherlands in 1954-56. Purchased by Ethiopia and transferred from the Royal Netherlands Navy in 1971.

WILDERVANK Class   1971, Official

TRAINING SHIP

ETHIOPIA (ex-USS *Orca*, AVP A9) A 01

Displacement, tons	1 766 standard; 2 800 full load
Dimensions, feet	300 wl; 310·8 oa × 41 × 13·5 max
Guns	1—5 in 38 cal; 5—40 mm AA (but guns vary)
Main engines	2 sets diesels; 2 shafts; 6 080 bhp = 18·2 knots
Complement	215

Former United States seaplane tender. Built by Lake Washington Shipyard, Houghton Wash. Laid down 13 July 1942, launched on 4 Oct 1942 and completed on 23 Jan 1944. Transferred from the US Navy in Jan 1962.

ETHIOPIA   1967, Imperial Ethiopian Navy, Official

Ethiopia—continued

PATROL BOATS
5 PGM TYPE

PC 11 (ex-USN *WVP* 95304)		**PC 13** (ex-USN *PGM* '53)	
PC 12 (ex-USN *WVP* 95310)		**PC 14** (ex-USN *PGM* 54)	
		PC 15 (ex-USN *PGM* 58)	

Displacement, tons	101
Dimensions, feet	95 oa × 19 × 5
Guns	1—40 mm AA; 1—·50 cal MG
Main engines	4 diesels; 2 shafts; 2 200 bhp = 21 knots
Radius, miles	1 500 at cruising speed
Complement	15

Ex-*PGM* 53 and ex-*PGM* 54 were built by Petersen Builders for transfer on 25 Aug 1961 and ex-*PGM 58* built by Marinette was transferred on 19 July 1962, under MAP. All are steel-hulled and twin-screwed. A photograph of PC 14 appears in 1962-63 to 1966-67 editions, and of PC 11 in the 1967-68 to 1969-70 editions.

PC 12   1970, Imperial Ethiopian Navy, Official

HARBOUR DEFENCE CRAFT
4 "CAROLINE" CLASS

CAROLINE	GB 22	**JOHN**	GB 21
JACQUELINE	GB 24	**PATRICK**	GB 23

Length, feet	40
Guns	2—·50 calibre machine guns
Speed, knots	20 approx
Complement	7

Patrol craft or very light gunboats. Built by Steward Seacraft Inc, Berwick, La. *Caroline* and *John* were delivered in 1966, *Jacqueline* and *Patrick* in 1967. Their complement is 3 officers and 4 ratings or 2 officers and 5 ratings.

JOHN   1970, Imperial Ethiopian Navy, Official

LANDING CRAFT

There are 2 of the US LCM type, with 2 more to be delivered by the USN in mid-1971.

DISPOSALS
The former Yugoslavian motor torpedo boats *Barracuda* and *Shark*, received in Jan 1960, were removed from the Ethiopian Navy List in 1969.

EL SALVADOR

Mercantile Marine

Lloyd's Register of Shipping: 11 vessels of 1 650 tons gross

PATROL BOATS

GC 1 (ex-*Fle-Ja-Lis*)		**GC 2** (ex-*Nohaba*)	

Displacement, tons	46
Dimensions, feet	72 oa × 16 × 5·5
Guns	1—20 mm
Main engines	2 diesels; 2 shafts; speed = 12 knots
Complement	16

Former British HDML type. Purchased from commercial sources in 1959.

FINLAND

Administration
Commander-in-Chief, Finnish Navy:
Rear-Admiral J. Pirhonen

Diplomatic Representation
Naval Attaché in London:
Captain Kai Ruusuvuori, FN

Naval Attaché in Washington:
Colonel Martti Frick

Naval Attaché in Moscow:
Colonel Henrick Antilla

Naval Attaché in Paris:
Lieutenant-Colonel Niilo Palmén

Strength of the Fleet

3 Frigates (1 for Training)
2 Corvettes (Fast Gunboats)
2 Coastal Minelayers
1 Missile Craft
4 Coast Guard Patrol Vessels
15 Fast Patrol Boats
14 Patrol Boats
5 Patrol Boats, ex-Inshore Minesweepers
1 Cable Ship
14 Support Ships and Service Craft
9 Icebreakers

Treaty Limitations
The Finnish Navy is limited by the treaty of Paris 1947 to 10,000 tons of ships and 4 500 personnel. Submarines and motor torpedo boats are prohibited.

Personnel
1971: 2 000 officers and ratings

Mercantile Marine
Lloyd's Register of Shipping:
388 vessels of 1 397 232 tons gross

FRIGATES (*SAATTAJAT*)

2 "UUSIMAA" CLASS

HÄMEENMAA   **UUSIMAA**

Displacement, tons	950 standard; 1,350 full load
Length, feet (*metres*)	278·8 (*85·0*) pp 295·2 (*90·0*) oa
Beam, feet (*metres*)	32·2 (*9·8*)
Draught, feet (*metres*)	11 (*3·4*)
Guns, dual purpose	3—3·9 in (*100 mm*) single
Guns, AA	2—40 mm
A/S weapons	1 Hedgehog; 4 DC projectors
Torpedo tubes	3—21 in (*533 mm*)
Mines	50 (capacity)
Boilers	2
Main engines	Geared turbines
	25 000 shp; 2 shafts
Speed, knots	28
Complement	150

Former Soviet frigates of the "Riga" class. Purchased from the USSR and transferred to the Finnish Navy on 28 Apr 1964 and 12 May 1964, respectively.

RADAR
Search: S Band.
Fire Control: X Band.

PHOTOGRAPHS. A starboard near broadside view of *Hämeenmaa* appears in the 1967-68 edition and a starboard quarter oblique view showing the minelaying stern in the 1968-69 edition.

HÄMEENMAA   *1971, Finnish Navy, Official*

UUSIMAA   *1969, Finnish Navy, Official*

Name	Builders	Laid down	Launched	Completed
MATTI KURKI (ex-HMS *Porlock* Bay, ex-*Loch Sea-forth*, ex-*Loch Muick*)	Charles Hill & Sons, Ltd, Bristol	22 Nov 1944	14 June 1945	8 Mar 1946

Displacement, tons	1 580 standard; 2 420 full load
Length, feet (*metres*)	286 ((*87·2* pp; 307·5 (*93·7*) oa
Beam, feet (*metres*)	38·5 (*11·7*)
Draught, feet (*metres*)	15·2 (*4·6*)
Guns, surface	4—4 in (*102 mm*)
Guns, AA	6—40 mm
Boilers	2 Admiralty 3-drum
Main engines	Triple expansion
	5 500 ihp; 2 shafts
Speed, knots	18
Radius, miles	9 500 at 12 knots
Oil fuel (tons)	724
Complement	160

Former British frigate of the "Bay" class. Transferred in Mar 1962. Employed as a training ship (*Koululaiva*).

RADAR. Search and Tactical. Type 293.

MATTI KURKI   *1969, Finnish Navy, Official*

CORVETTES (*Tykkiveneet*)

KARJALA   **TURUNMAA**

Displacement, tons	650
Dimensions, feet	243·1 × 25·6 × 7·9
Guns	1—4·7 in automatic dp forward; 2—40 mm AA (single); 2—30 mm AA (1 twin) aft
A/S weapons	Depth charge projectors
Main engines	CODOG (combined diesel or gas turbine). Rolls Royce Olympus gas turbine; 22 000 hp = 35 knots
Complement	70

Fast gunboats for trade protection ordered on 23 Feb 1956 from Wärtsilä-yhtymä Oy Shipyard, Helsinki. Flush decked. Rocket flare guide rails on sides of 4·7 in turret. Fitted with Vosper Thornycroft fin stabiliser equipment. *Karjala* was launched on 16 Aug 1967 and completed on 21 Oct 1968. *Turunmaa* was launched on 11 July 1967 and completed on 29 Aug 1968. A photograph of *Karjala* appears in the 1969-70 and 1970-71 editions.

RADAR. Search and Tactical. X Band.

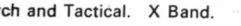

TURUNMAA   *1971, Finnish Navy, Official*

MISSILE CRAFT

ISKU

Displacement, tons	115
Dimensions, feet	86·5 × 28·6 × 6·6
Missile launchers	4 "Styx" surface-to-surface in two pairs abreast
Guns, anti-aircraft	2—30 mm (1 twin)
Main engines	4 diesels; 4 800 bhp = 25 knots

Guided missile craft of novel design completed for the Finnish Navy in 1970. Built at the "Reposaaren kenepoja". The construction combines a missile boat armament on a landing craft hull. The missile launchers are of similar type to those mounted in the Soviet "Osa" class.

ISKU   1970, B. Borg

COASTAL MINELAYERS (MIINALAIVAT)

KEIHÄSSALMI

Displacement, tons	360
Dimensions, feet	168 × 23 × 6
Guns	2—40 mm AA; 2—20 mm AA
Mines	Up to 100 capacity
Main engines	2 Wärtsilä diesels; 2 shafts; 2 000 bhp = 15 knots
Complement	60

Of improved "Ruotsinsalmi" type, built at Valmet Oy Shipyard, Helsinki under contract dated June 1955. Launched on 16 Mar 1957. Diesel type officially revised in 1971. X Band Search and Tactical radar.

KEIHASSALMI   1971, Finnish Navy, Official

RUOTSINSALMI

Displacement, tons	310
Dimensions, feet	150 × 23 × 5
Guns	2—40 mm AA; 2—20 mm AA
Mines	Up to 100 capacity
Main engines	2 MAN diesels; 2 shafts; 1 200 bhp = 15 knots
Complement	60

Built by Crichton-Vulcan Shipyard, Turku. Laid down in 1937. Launched in May 1940. Completed in Feb 1941. Diesel type officially revised in 1971.

RUOTSINSALMI   1969, Finnish Navy, Official

PATROL VESSELS (Vartiolaivat)

VALPAS

Displacement, tons	540
Dimensions, feet	159·1 × 27·9 × 12·5.
Main engines	Diesel; 1 800 bhp = 15 knots

Officially stated to be slightly larger than the Coast Guard vessel Silmä, see below. Scheduled to be completed in May 1971.

SILMÄ

Displacement, tons	500
Dimensions, feet	160·8 × 27·2 × 11·8
Main engines	1 800 bhp = 15 knots

Coast Guard vessel built by Laivateollisuus Oy, Turku, in 1962-63. Prototype for an improved patrol vessel, see Valpas above.

SILMÄ   1964, Finnish Navy, Official

UISKO

Displacement, tons	400
Dimensions, feet	141 × 24 × 12·8
Main engines	1 800 bhp = 15 knots

Coast Guard vessel built by Valmet Oy, Helsinki. Launched in 1958. Completed in 1959.

UISKO   Finnish Navy, Official

TURSAS

Displacement, tons	400
Dimensions, feet	131·2 × 23·5 × 14
Guns	1—3 in; 1—40 mm AA; 2—20 mm AA
Main engines	Diesel; 620 bhp = 12 knots

Built by Crichton-Vulkan. Launched in 1933. Belongs to the Coast Guard, under the Ministry of the Interior. The Coast Guard vessel Merikotka was officially deleted from the list in 1960. The old Coast Guard vessel Aura, has been removed from the effective list, it was officially stated in 1971.

TURSAS   1968, Finnish Navy, Official

FAST PATROL BOATS (NOPEAT VARTIOVENEET)

13 "NOULI" CLASS

NUOLI 1	NUOLI 3	NUOLI 5	NUOLI 8	NUOLI 11
NUOLI 2	NUOLI 4	NUOLI 6	NUOLI 9	NUOLI 12
		NUOLI 7	NUOLI 10	NUOLI 13

Displacement, tons	40
Dimensions, feet	72·2 × 21·7 × 5
Guns	1—40 mm; 1—20 mm AA
Main engines	3 diesels; 2 700 bhp = 40 knots
Complement	15

Designed and built by Laivateollisuus Oy, Turku. First four were launched in 1961, five more in 1962, and two more in 1963. A photograph of *Nuoli 1* appears in the 1962-63 to 1968-69 editions, and another photograph of *Nuoli 6* in the 1965-66 to 1968-69 editions.

NUOLI 10   *1969, Finnish Navy, Official*

NUOLI 6   *Finnish Navy, Official*

2 "VASAMA" CLASS

VASAMA 1   **VASAMA 2**

Displacement, tons	70
Dimensions, feet	67 pp; 71·5 oa × 19·5 × 6
Guns	2—40 mm AA
Main engines	2 Napier Deltic diesels; 5 000 bhp = 42 knots
Complement	20

British "Dark" type built by Saunders Roe (Anglesey) Ltd, Beaumaris, England, in 1955-57. A photograph of *Vasama 1* appears in the 1967-68 to 1969-70 editions.

VASAMA 2   *1970, Finnish Navy, Official*

DISPOSALS
The former Italian fast patrol boats *Hurja 1, Hurja 2, Hurja 3, Hurja 4* and *Hurja 5* were scrapped in 1963. Of the fast patrol boats of the "Taisto" class, *Taisto 2, Taisto 4* and *Taisto 5* were scrapped in 1963 and *Taisto 3, Taisto 6, Taisto 7* and *Taisto 8* were removed from the effective list in 1966.

CABLE SHIP (Kaapelialus)

PUTSAARI

Displacement, tons	430
Dimensions, feet	147·6 × 38·5 × 9·8 (officially revised figures)
Main engines	Diesel; 450 bhp = 10 knots

Built by Rauma-Repola Oy Shipyard, Rauma. Launched in Dec 1965.

PUTSAARI   *1971, Finnish Navy, Official*

PATROL BOATS (VARTIOVENEET)

VIIMA

Displacement, tons	135
Dimensions, feet	118·1 × 21·7 × 7·5
Guns	1—20 mm AA
Main engines	3 diesels; 4 050 bhp = 24 knots

Coast guard patrol boat built by Laivateollisuus Oy Ab, Turku, Finland in 1964. Formerly rated as *Vartiomoottoriveneet*.

VIIMA   *1971, Finnish Navy, Official*

8 "KOSKELO" CLASS

KAAKKURI	KOSKELO	TELKKA	KURKI
KIILSA	KUOVI	KUIKKA	TAVI

Displacement, tons	75 standard; 97 full load
Dimensions, feet	95·1 × 16·4 × 4·9
Guns	2—20 mm AA
Main engines	2 Mercedes-Benz diesels; 2 shafts; 1 000 bhp = 16 knots
Complement	8

Built of steel and strengthened against ice, *Koskelo* and *Kuikka* were completed in 1956. Remaining six were completed in 1958-60. All the above patrol boats belong to the Coast Guard which is under the Ministry of the Interior. A photograph of *Koskelo* appears in the 1957-58 to 1963-64 editions and of *Tavi* in the 1964-65 to 1967-68 editions.

KUIKKA   *1968, Finnish Navy, Official*

VMV COAST GUARD TYPES
The Coast Guard *Vartiomoottoriveneet* VMV 11, VMV 13, VMV 19 and VMV 20 are removed from the effective list, it was officially stated in 1970. VMV 18 was stricken from the list in 1958. For other disposals see 1966-67 edition.

Patrol Boats—*continued*
5 "R" CLASS

RAISIO (No. 4)	RÖYTTA (No. 5)	RUISSALO (No. 3)

Displacement, tons	110 standard; 130 full load
Dimensions, feet	108·3 × 18 × 5·9 (officially revised figures)
Guns	1—40 mm Bofors; 1—20 mm Masden
Main engines	2 Mercedes-Benz diesels; 2 500 bhp = 17 knots

Built by Laivateollisuus, Turku, in 1959. Brake horse power rating officially revised in 1971. A photograph of *Ruissalo* appears in the 1967-68 edition, and of *Raisio* in the 1965-66 to 1968-69 editions.

RÖYTTA   *1969, Finnish Navy, Official*

RIHTNIEMI (No. 1)	RYMÄTTYLÄ (No. 2)

Displacement, tons	90 standard; 110 full load
Dimensions, feet	101·7 × 18·7 × 5·9
Guns	1—40 mm Bofors; 1—20 mm Masden
Main engines	2 Mercedes-Benz diesels; 1 400 bhp = 15 knots

Built by Rauma-Repela Oy Shipyard. Ordered in July 1955, launched in 1956 and delivered on 20 May 1957. Controllable pitch propellers. Formerly rated as *Raivaajat* (Inshore Minesweepers) but, it was officially stated in Dec 1969, reclassified as *Vartioveneet* (Small Patrol Boats). Brake horse power rating officially revised in 1971. A photograph of *Rymättglä* appears in the 1960-61 to 1963-64 editions.

RIHTNIEMI   *1968, Finnish Navy, Official*

DISPOSALS (COASTAL MINESWEEPERS)
Of the four ex-US BYMS type, *Tammenpää* and *Vahterpää* were sold for scrap in 1958, *Purunpää* was discarded in 1959, and *Katanpää* scrapped in 1960.

DISPOSALS (MOTOR MINESWEEPING BOATS)
Kallanpää was scrapped in 1963, and her sister *Ajonpää* in 1959. Of the "Kuha" class, *Kuha* 2, *Kuha* 5, *Kuha* 7, *Kuha* 8, *Kuha* 12, *Kuha* 13, *Kuha* 14, *Kuha* 15, *Kuha* 16 *Kuha* 17 and *Kuha* 18 were scrapped in 1963, *Kuha* 10 and *Kuha* 11 in 1961, and *Kuha* 1, *Kuha* 4 and *Kuha* 9 in 1969-60. Of the "Ahven" class, *Ahven* 2, *Ahven* 3, *Ahven* 4 and *Ahven* 6 were scrapped in 1963, *Ahven* 1 and *Ahven* 5 in 1961.

STAFF SHIP

KORSHOLM

Displacement, tons	650
Dimensions, feet	160·8 × 27·9 × 10·8
Speed, knots	10·5

Adapted merchant ship of the small passenger and cargo type. Built in 1931.

KORSHOLM   *1970, Finnish Navy, Official*

TRANSPORT CRAFT *(KULJETUSALUKSET)*
6 "KALA" CLASS

KALA 1	KALA 2	KALA 3	KALA 4	KALA 5	KALA 6

Displacement, tons	60
Dimensions, feet	81·8 × 26·2 × 6
Main engines	2 diesels; 360 bhp = 9 knots

Launched in 1956. Completed in 1959. Of LCU (utility landing craft) type. Officially classed as transport craft. A photograph of *Kala 2* appears in the 1959-60 to 1962-63 editions

KALA 6   *1963, Finnish Navy, Official*

SEILI (ex-F 177)

Displacement, tons	180
Dimensions feet	143 × 20 × 4 (officially revised figures)
Guns	1—1·4 in (*105 mm*)
Main engines	Speed = 10 knots

Former German MFP type landing craft converted and armoured. Launched in 1942. *Lonna* was scrapped in 1963.

SEILI   *1970, Finnish Navy, Official*

3 "PANSIO" CLASS (TUG TYPE)

PANSIO (1947)	PORKKALA (1940)	PUKKIO (1939)

Displacement, tons	162
Dimensions, feet	92 × 21·5 × 9
Guns	1—40 mm; 1—20 mm AA
Main engines	Diesel; 300 bhp = 9 knots

Built by Valmet Oy, Turku. Launch dates above. Vessels of the tug type used as transports, minesweeping tenders, minelayers and patrol vessels. Can carry 20 mines. A photograph of *Porkkala* appears in the 1962-63 edition.

TRAINING SHIP
The training ship *Suomen Joutsen* (ex-*Oldenburg*, ex-*Laennec*) was converted into a stationary seaman's school ship, and sold to the Finnish Mercantile School in 1960.

TUGS *(HINAAJAT)*
3 "PIRTTISAARI" CLASS

PIRTTISAARI (ex-DR 7)	PYHTÄÄ (ex-DR 2)	PURHA (ex-DR 10)

Displacement, tons	106
Dimensions, feet	69 × 20 × 8·5
Guns	1—20 mm
Main engines	1 diesel; 400 bhp = 9 knots

Former US Army Tugs. Launched in 1943-44. General purpose vessels used as minesweepers, minelayers, patrol vessels, tenders, tugs or personnel transports. *DR 2* and *DR 7*, were adapted as the Coast Artillery transports *Pyhtää* and *Pirttisaari* in 1958 and 1959, respectively. A photograph of *Pyhtää* (DR 2) appears in the 1953-54 to 1962-63 editions.

PIRTTISAARI   *1970, Finnish Navy, Official*

ICEBREAKERS (JÄÄNMURTAJAT)

1 NEW CONSTRUCTION

Displacement, tons	7 800
Dimensions, feet	337·9 × 77·1 × 24·6
Main engines	Diesel-electric; 20 000 bhp

It was officially stated in Jan 1971 that an icebreaker of new construction is planned considerably larger than "Tarmo" class icebreakers. She is scheduled to be completed towards the end of 1974.

3 "TARMO" CLASS

TARMO   **VARMA**   **APU**

Displacement, tons	4 890
Dimensions feet	281 × 71 × 21
Main engines	Wärtsilä-Sulzer diesels; electric drive; 4 shafts (2 screws forward 2 screws aft); 12 000 bhp = 17 knots

Built by Wärtsilä-yhtymä Oy Shipyard, Helsinki. *Tarmo* was completed in 1963, *Varma* in 1968 (launched 29 Mar) and *Apu* on 25 Nov 1970.

TARMO   *1968, Finnish Navy, Official*

3 (4) "KARHU" CLASS

KARHU   **MURTAJA**   **SAMPO**

Displacement, tons	3 540
Dimensions, feet	243·2 × 57 × 20
Main engines	Diesel-electric; 4 shafts; 7 500 bhp = 16 knots

Built by Wärtsilä-yhtymä Oy Shipyard, Helsinki. *Karhu* was launched on 22 Oct 1957, and completed at the end of 1958. *Murtaja* was launched on 23 Sep 1958. *Sampo* was completed in 1960. There is also the combined Finnish/West German owned, Finnish manned, icebreaker *HANSA*, of the "Sampo" class, completed on 25 Nov 1966, which operates off Germany in winter and off Finland otherwise.

KARHU   *1968*

SAMPO   *1970, Finnish Navy, Official*

MURTAJA   *1968*

VOIMA

Displacement, tons	4 415
Dimensions, feet	254·8 wl; 274 oa × 63·7; 61·3 wl × 20·3
Main engines	Diesels with electric drive; 4 shafts; 14 000 bhp = 16·5 knots
Oil fuel (tons)	740

Built by Wärtsilä-yhtymä Oy Shipyard, Helsinki. Launched and completed in 1953. Built for deep-sea work. Two propellers forward and aft. Transferred to the Board of Navigation in 1956.

VOIMA   *1968, Finnish Navy, Official*

SISU

Displacement, tons	2 075
Dimensions, feet	194·8 wl; 210·2 oa × 46·5 × 16·8
Guns	2—3·9 in AA
Main engines	3 sets Atlas Polar Diesels with electric drive; 2 shafts and a bow propeller; 4 000 hp = 16 knots
Complement	100

Built by Wärtsilä-yhtymä Oy Shipyard, Helsinki. Launched on 24 Sep 1938.

SISU   *1968, Finnish Navy, Official*

OTSO

Displacement, tons	900
Dimensions, feet	134·5 pp; 144·3 oa × 37·5 × 16·5
Main engines	Triple expansion, with bow propeller; 1 860 iph = 13 knots
Oil fuel, tons	60

Launched in 1936. Belongs to the town of Helsinki. Photograph in the 1953-54 and earlier editions.

It was officially stated in March 1969 that the icebreaker *Apu* (ex-*Tarmo*, ex-*Sampo II*) was steaming her last winter period and would be scrapped or at least removed from the effective list. (Her name was changed when *Sampo* and *Tarmo* were allocated successively as names for new icebreakers). A photograph of this ship (as *Tarmo*) appears in the 1958-59 to 1963-64 editions. In December 1969 it was officially stated that the ship was acting as a museum ship in Helsinki with her former name *Tarmo* (old), the name *Apu* having been allocated to an icebreaker under construction. All the above icebreakers belong to the Board of Navigation, except the *Otso*, which belongs to the town of Helsinki.

DISPOSALS
The old and less powerful icebreakers *Apu* and *Murtaja* were scrapped in Spring 1959 and 1958, respectively. The old icebreaker *Sampo* was scrapped in 1961.

FRANCE

Administration

Chief of the Naval Staff:
Amiral A. M. G. L. S. Storelli

Assistant Chief of Naval Staff:
Vice-Amiral M. S. B. De Joybert

*C in C Atlantic Theatre (CECLANT) and Prefet Maritime
of the Second Region (PREMAR DEUX):*
Vice-Amiral d'Escadre Rousselot

Prefet Maritime of the First Region (PREMAR UN):
Vice-Amiral Bouillant

*C in C Mediterranean Theatre (CECMED) and Prefet
Maritime of the Third Region (PREMAR TRIOS):*
Vice-Amiral d'Escadre de Scitivaux de Greishe

Diplomatic Representation

Naval Attaché in London:
Contre-Amiral Paul Delahousse

Naval Attaché in Washington:
Contre-Amiral N. M. Houot

Naval Attaché in Moscow:
Captain Leroux

Naval Attaché in Ottawa:
Colonel Cazillet

Strength of the Fleet

2 Aircraft Carriers
1 Helicopter Carrier
1 Helicopter Cruiser (Training/Commando)
1 Nuclear Powered Ballistic Missile Submarine
20 Submarines (Diesel Powered)
1 Anti Aircraft Missile Cruiser
1 Command Ship (Converted Cruiser)
3 Guided Missile Armed Frigates
4 Guided Missile Armed Destroyers
13 Destroyers (A/S, AD, and Command)
27 Frigates
2 Ex-Frigates (Experimental)
1 Experimental Guided Missile Ship
2 Assault Landing Ships
1 Minehunter (New Construction)
14 Ocean Minesweepers
61 Coastal Minesweepers
15 Patrol Vessels
15 Inshore Minesweepers
4 Experimental Ships
9 Survey Ships
4 Maintenance Ships
6 Patrol Boats
12 Transports and Logistic Support Ships
5 Landing Ships
18 Landing Craft
100 Support Ships and Service Craft

1971-75 New Construction Plan

2 Nuclear Powered Ballistic Missile Submarines
4 Diesel-Electric Powered Conventional Submarines
3 Guided Missile Frigates ("Corvettes") "C 70" Type
3 Guided Missile Firgates ("Corvettes") "C 67" Type
1 Guided Missile Frigate ("Corvette") "Aconit" Type
14 Corvettes (officially rated as *Avisos*)
5 Minehunters

Personnel

1969: 70,200 (5,400 officers, 64,800 ratings)
1970: 69,300 (4,880 officers, 64,420 ratings)
1971: 68,586 (4,732 officers, 63,854 ratings)

Mercantile Marine

Lloyd's Register of Shipping:
1 420 vessels of 6 457 900 tons gross

FRENCH CARRIER-BORNE AIRCRAFT

Name	Maker	Type	Dimensions		Power Plant	Armament	Performance
JAGUAR M	Breguet/BAC	Single-seat Attack Bomber	Wing Span Length	27 ft 10¼ in 50 ft 11 in	Two Rolls-Royce/ Turboméca Adour turbofan	Two 30 mm cannon, 3 000 lb of bombs or missiles	Max speed 729 knots. Range 2 430 nautical miles
ETENDARD IV-M	Dassault	Single-seat Interceptor and Fighter-Bomber	Wing Span Length	31 ft 6 in 47 ft 3 in	One SNECMA Atar 8 turbojet	Two 30 mm cannon, 3 000 lb of bombs or missiles	Max speed 673 mph at 36 000 ft. Range 370-1 000 miles
ETENDARD IV-P	Dassault	Single-seat Reconnaissance/ Flight Refuelling Tanker Aircraft	Wing Span	31 ft 6 in	One SNECMA Atar 8 turbojet	Cameras in nose and underfuselage pack	Max speed 673 mph at 36 000 ft. Range 370-1 000 miles
Br 1050 ALIZÉ	Breguet	Three-Seat Anti-Submarine Aircraft	Wing Span Folded Length	51 ft 2 in 22 ft 11 in 45 ft 6 in	One Rolls-Royce Dart R. Da. 7 turboprop	Two AS torpedoes. Up to five depth charges. Six rockets or two missiles	Max speed 322 mph. Normal endurance 4 hr 30 min.
CRUSADER F8E-FN	Ling Temco Vought	Single-Seat All Weather Interceptor	Wing Span Length	35 ft 2 in 54 ft 6 in	One Pratt & Whitney J 57. P 20 A turbojet with post combustion	Two 20 mm cannon, Four air-to-air missiles (Sidewinder of Matra 530)	Max speed Mach 1·8 at 36 000 ft. Endurance 2 hr 10 min.
SA 321G SUPER FRELON	Sud-Aviation	Anti-Submarine and Transport Helicopter	Rotor dia Length (blades and tail folded)	62 ft 56 ft.	Three Turboméca Turmo III C3 shaft Turbines	Anti-Submarine attack weapons	Max speed 165 mph. Range 584 miles
HSS 1	Sikorsky	Anti-Submarine Warfare, helicopter	Rotor dia Length	56 ft 65 ft 10 in	One Wright R 1820-84	Anti-Submarine weapons	Max speed 130 knots Endurance 4 hr.

FRENCH NAVAL GUIDED MISSILES

Type	Name	Maker	Length ft	Propulsion	Speed Mach.	Range miles	Guidance System	Notes
SURFACE-TO-SEA	Malafon	Latécoère	19·66	Two solid boosters only. Unpowered in cruise	0·6	7	Command	Aeroplane configuration. Built around 21 in. acoustic homing torpedo. In service.
SURFACE -TO-AIR	Masurca Mk 2	Ruelle Arsenal	28·2	Two-stage solid propellent	2·5	25	Semi-active radar	To be standard naval anti-aircraft armament
UNDERWATER-TO- SURFACE	MSBS	S.E.R.E.B.	34·12	Two-Stage propellent		1 250 to 1 600	Inertial	Sixteen to be carried by each Nuclaer powered ballistic missile submarine. Under development. Nuclear warhead.
ANTI-SURFACE	MM 38 Exocet	Nord Aviation	16·4	Solid propellent	0·9	20	Auto	For C 67 Type frigates (corvettes). In production.

PENNANT NUMBERS

R Aircraft and Helicopter Carriers

95 Arromanches
97 Jeanne d'Arc
98 Clemenceau
99 Foch

S Submarines

610 Le Foudroyant
611 Le Redoutable
612 Le Terrible
613 L'Indomptable
631 Narval
632 Marsouin
633 Dauphin
634 Requin
635 Aréthuse
636 Argonaute
637 Espadon
638 Morse
639 Amazone
640 Ariane
641 Daphné
642 Diane
643 Doris
645 Flore
646 Galatée
648 Junon
649 Venus
650 Psyche
651 Sirene
655 Gymnote

C Cruisers and Command Ships

610 de Grasse
611 Colbert

D Missile Leaders and Destroyers

602 Suffren
603 Duquesne
621 Surcouf
622 Kersaint
623 Cassard
624 Bouvet
625 Dupetit Thouars
626 Chevalier Paul
627 Maillé Brézé
628 Vauquelin
629 D'Estrées
630 Du Chayla
631 Casabianca
632 Guépratte
634 La Bourdonnais
635 Forbin
636 Tartu
637 Jauréguiberry
638 La Galissonniere

F Frigates, Escorts and Corvettes

703 Aconit
725 Victor Schoelcher
726 Commandant Bory
727 Amiral Charner
728 Doudart de Legrée
729 Balny
733 Commandant Rivière
740 Commandante Bourdais
748 Protet
749 Ensigne de Vaisseau Henry
761 Le Corse
762 Le Brestois
763 Le Boulonnais
764 Le Bordelais
765 Le Normand
766 Le Picard
767 Le Gascon

F Frigates, Escorts—*continued*

768 Le Lorrain
769 Le Bourguignon
770 Le Champenois
771 Le Savoyard
772 Le Breton
773 Le Basque
774 L'Agenais
775 Le Béarnais
776 L'Alsacien
777 Le Provencal
778 Le Vendéen

M Coastal and Inshore Minesweepers

609 Narvik
610 Ouistreham
612 Alencon
613 Berneval
615 Cantho
616 Dompaire
617 Garigliano
618 Mytho
619 Vinh-long
620 Berlaimont
621 Origny
622 Autun
623 Baccarat
624 Colmar
632 Pervenche
633 Pivoine
635 Réséda
638 Acacia
639 Acanthe
640 Marjolaine
667 Ajonc
668 Azalée
669 Begonia
670 Bleuet
671 Camélia
672 Chrysanthème
673 Coquelicot
674 Cyclamen
675 Eglantine
676 Gardénia
677 Giroflée
678 Glaieul
679 Glycine
681 Laurier
680 Jacinthe
682 Lilas
683 Liseron
684 Lobelia
685 Magnolia
687 Mimosa
688 Muguet
701 Sirius
702 Rigel
703 Antarès
704 Algol
705 Aldebaran
706 Régulus
707 Véga
710 Pégase
712 Cybele
713 Calliope
714 Clio
715 Circe
716 Ceres
726 La Dunkerquoise
727 La Malouine
728 La Bayonnaise
729 La Paimpolaise
730 La Dieppoise
731 La Lorientaise
734 Croix du Sud
735 Etoile Polaire
736 Altair

M Minesweepers—*continued*

737 Capricorne
740 Cassiopée
741 Eridan
743 Sagittaire
746 Arcturus
747 Bételgeuse
748 Persée
749 Phénix
750 Bellatrix
751 Dénébola
754 Canopus
755 Capella
756 Céphée
757 Verseau
758 Aries
759 Lyre
765 Mercure
771 Tulipe
772 Armoise
773 Violette
774 Oeillet
775 Paquerette
776 Jasmin
781 Aubepine
782 Capucine
783 Hortensia
784 Geranium
785 Hibiscus
786 Dahlia
787 Jonquille
788 Myosotis
789 Petunia

P Patrol Vessels, Coastal Escorts

630 L'Intrépide
635 L'Ardent
637 L'Etourdi
638 L'Effronté
639 Le Frondeur
640 Le Fringant
641 Le Fougueux
642 L'Opiniatre
643 L'Agile
644 L'Adroit
645 L'Alerte
646 L'Attentif
647 L'Enjoué
648 Le Hardi
730 La Combattante
780 Oiseau des Isles

L Landing Ships

9003 Argens
9004 Bidassoa
9007 Trieux
9008 Dives
9009 Blavet
9021 Ouragan
9022 Orage
9097 Issole

A Auxiliaries and Support Ships

603 Henry Poincaré
607 Arago
608 Moselle
610 Ile d'Oléron
611 Maine
612 Médoc

A Auxiliaries—*continued*

614 Falleron
615 Loire
617 Garonne
618 Rance
619 Aber Wrac'h
620 Acheron
621 Rhin
622 Rhone
626 La Charente
627 La Seine
628 La Saone
629 Lac Chambon
630 Lac Tonle Sap
631 Lac Tchad
633 Duperré
634 Verdon
635 Rummel
637 Maurienne
638 Sahel
643 Aunis
644 Berry
645 Anjou
646 Triton
647 Ingénieur Elie Monnier
648 Archimede
649 Etoile
650 Belle Poule
652 Mutin
653 La Grande Hermine
660 Hippopotame
661 Infatigable
665 Goliath
666 Eléphant
667 Hercule
668 Rhinocéros
669 Tenace
670 Implacable
673 Lutteur
674 Acharné
675 Isére
678 La Coquille
682 Alidade
683 Octant
*684 Coolie
685 Robuste
686 Actif
687 Laborieux
688 Valeureux
692 Travailleur
698 Petrel
699 Pelican
706 Courageux
718 Pachyderme
719 Bélier
724 Belouga
727 Araignée
728 Scorpion
729 Tarentule
733 Saintonge
749 La Prudente
750 Liamone
755 Commandant Robert Giraud
756 L'Esperance
757 D'Entrecasteaux
758 La Recherche
759 Marcel Le Bihan
760 Cigale
761 Criquet
762 Fourmi
763 Grillon
764 Scarabée
765 Locuste
777 Luciole
780 Astrolabe
781 Boussole
789 Archeonaute
791 Corail

Scale: 150 feet = 1 inch (1 : 1 800)

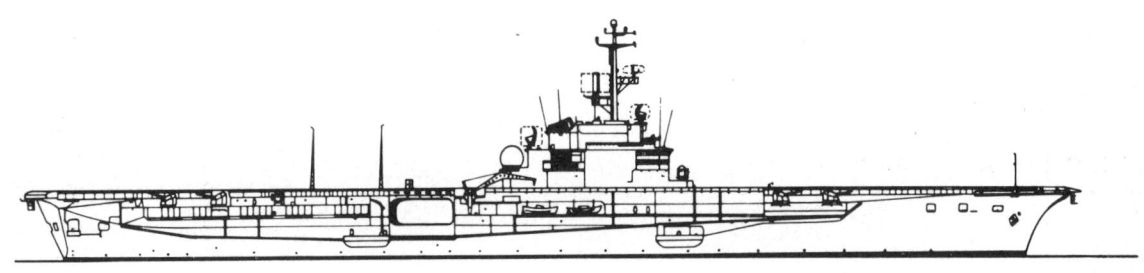

CLEMENCEAU, FOCH

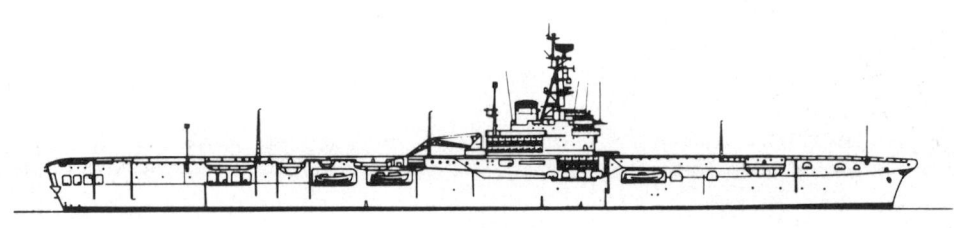

ARROMANCHES

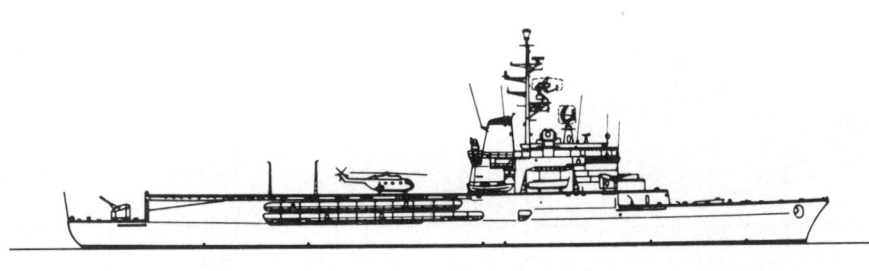

JEANNE D'ARC

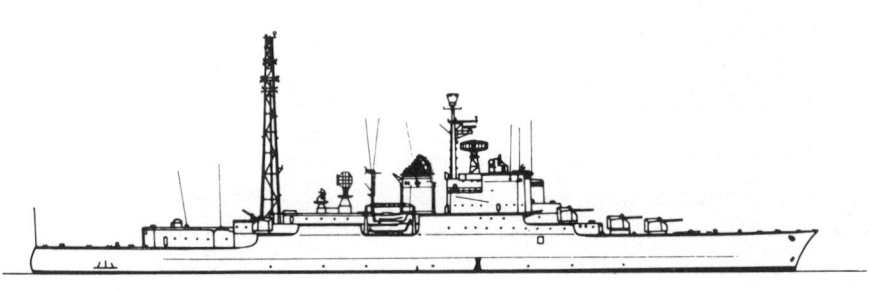

DE GRASSE

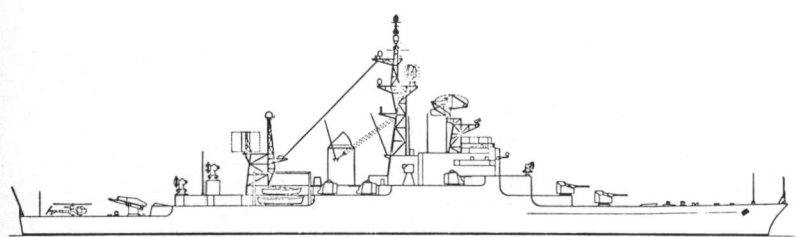

COLBERT (scheme after refit 1970-73)

ILE D'OLERON

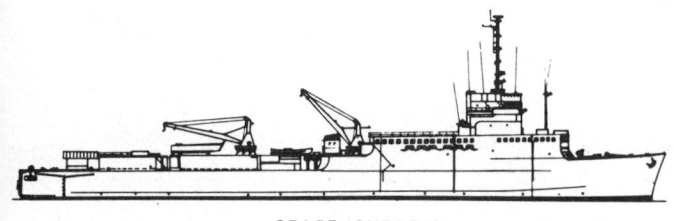

ORAGE, OURAGAN

DUQUESNE, SUFFREN

Destroyers, Escorts

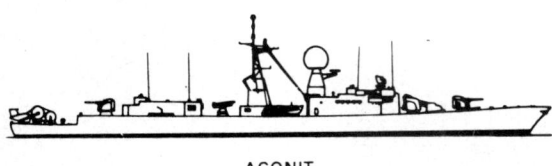

ACONIT

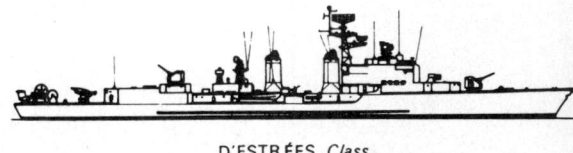

D'ESTRÉES *Class*

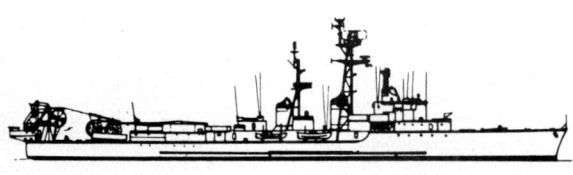

DUPERRÉ. Experimental Ship

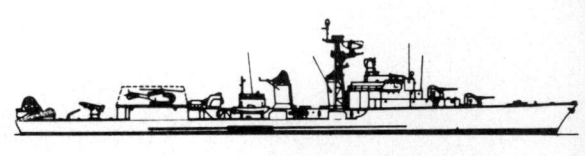

LA GALISSONIÈRE

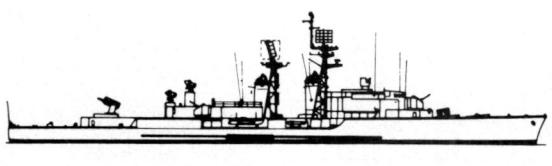

DU CHAYLA *Class*

L'ALSACIEN, LE PROVENCAL, LE VENDEEN

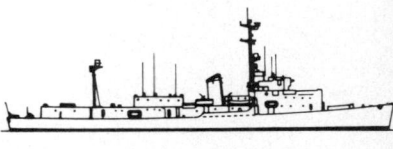

ARAGO

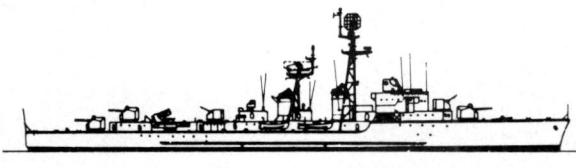

FORBIN *Class*

L'AGENAIS, LE BÉARNAIS, LE BRETON

COMMANDANT ROBERT GIRAUD

SURCOUF *Class*. Command Type

LE NORMAND *Class* E 52 Type

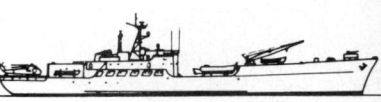

RHIN

COMMANDANT RIVIÈRE *Class*

LE CORSE *Class*, E 50 Type

RHONE

AIRCRAFT CARRIERS (Porte-Avions)

2 "CLEMENCEAU" CLASS

Name	No.	Builders	Laid down	Launched	Completed
CLEMENCEAU (PA 54)	R 98	Brest	Nov 1955	21 Dec 1957	22 Nov 1961
FOCH (PA 55)	R 99	Penhoet-Loire & Brest	Feb 1957	23 July 1960	15 July 1963

Displacement, tons	22 000 standard ; 32 800 full load
Length, feet (metres)	780·8 (238·0) pp (864·8 (263·6)oa
Beam, feet (metres)	104·1 (31·7) hull with bulges
Width, feet (metres)	168 (51·2) oa
Draught, feet (metres)	25·3 (7·7) ; 28 (8·56) screws
Catapults	2 Mitchell-Brown steam, Mk BS 5
Aircraft	Capacity 30, including jet aircraft. Each carries 3 Flights—1 of Etendard IV, 1 of Crusader, 1 of Breguet Alizé. See Aircraft notes
Armour	Flight deck, island superstructure and bridges, hull (over machinery spaces and magazines)
Guns, AA	8—3·9 in (100 mm) automatic in single turrets
Boilers	6 ; steam pressure 640 psi (45 kg/cm²), superheat 842°F (450°C)
Main engines	2 sets Parsons geared turbines 126 000 shp; 2 shafts
Speed, knots	31 max (33·4 trials) ; 24 sustained sea
Radius, miles	6,400 at 18 knots 3 500 at full power
Oil fuel (tons)	3 600
Complement	2 150

The first aircraft carriers designed as such and built from the keel to be completed in France. Authorised in 1953 and 1955 respectively. Clemenceau was ordered from Brest Dockyard on 28 May 1954 and begun in Nov 1955. Foch began construction at Chantiers de l'Atlantique a St. Nazaire, Penhoet-Loire, in a special dry dock (the contract provided for the construction of the hull and propelling machinery) and was completed by Brest Dockyard.

RADAR

Search: DRBV 20 Metric wavelength, DRB1 10 3D S Band.
Tactical: DRBV 23 L Band.
Fire Control: X Band
Miscellaneous: NRBA 50 Carrier Controlled approach radar. Various Electronic Warfare equipments.

CLEMENCEAU   1971, Dr. Giorgio Arra

FLIGHT DECK. They have the angled deck incorporated, two lifts, measuring 52·5 × 36 feet, one of them on the starboard deck edge, two steam catapults for aircraft up to 11 tons, and two mirror sight deck landing aids. The flight deck measures 543 × 96·8 feet and is angled at 8 degrees.

HANGAR. Dimensions of the hangar are: 497·7 × 87 × 28 feet.

GUNNERY. These aircraft carriers were originally to have been of the light fleet type with an armament of 24—2·25 inch guns in twin mountings, but the armament was revised to 12—3·9 inch (100 mm) in 1956 and to 8—3·9 inch (100 mm) in 1958. The 100 mm guns are of a new design. Rate of fire 60 rounds per minute.

BULGES. Foch was completed with bulges. These having proved successful during trials, Clemenceau was modified similarly during her first refit, increasing her beam by 6 feet.

DRAWING. Starboard elevation and plan. Redrawn in 1970. Scale: 125 feet = 1 inch (1 : 1 500).

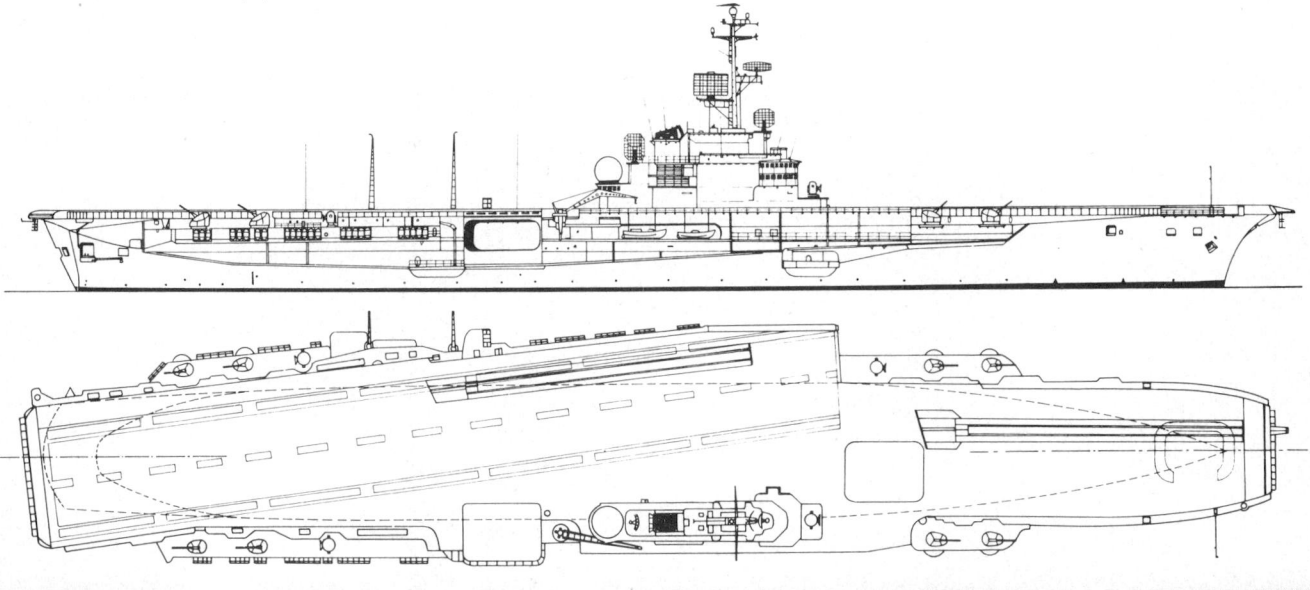

FOCH   1971, French Navy, Official

HELICOPTER CARRIER   (*Porte-Hélicoptères*)

Name	*Pennant No.*	*Builders*	*Laid down*	*Launched*	*Completed*
ARROMANCHES (ex-HMS *Colossus*)	R 95	Vickers-Armstrongs Ltd, Newcastle-on-Tyne	1 June 1942	30 Sep 1943	16 Dec 1944

1 Ex-BRITISH "COLOSSUS" CLASS

Displacement, tons	14 000 standard ; 18 500 full load
Length, feet (*metres*)	694·5 (*211·7*) oa
Beam, feet (*metres*)	80·2 (*24·5*)
Width, feet (*metres*)	118 (*36·0*) oa
Draught, feet (*metres*)	23 (*7·0*)
Aircraft	24 Helicopters
Boilers	4 three-drum type ; 400 psi (*28 kg/cm²*) ; 680°F (*360°C*)
Main engines	Parsons geared turbines 40 000 shp ; 2 shafts
Speed, knots	23·5
Radius, miles	12 000 at 14 knots
Oil fuel (tons)	3 200
Complement	1 019 (42 officers and 777 men, plus 200 for air service)

This ship was lent to the French Navy for five years from August 1946 with the option of purchase in 1951. This was taken up, and she was permanently transferred from Great Britain in that year. Extensively refitted 1950-51 ; and again refitted in 1957-58.

RECONSTRUCTION. Modernised and partially rebuilt in 1957-58 with the angled deck at 4 degrees, and mirror sight deck landing aid sponsons, the overall width being increased from 112·5 feet to just over 118 feet (*36 metres*). In consequence of these modifications the ship was able to receive Breguet Alizé ASM aircraft of the 1050 type. Extensively refitted in 1968 and rearmed in Sep 1969, being redesignated a helicopter carrier for several years more service in a quadruple role ; to operate intervention and anti-submarine helicopters, as a fast operational transport and a sea training carrier.

ENGINEERING. Engines and boilers are arranged *en echelon*, one set of turbines and two boilers being installed side by side in each of the two main propelling machinery spaces, on the unit system, so that the starboard propeller shaft is longer than the port.

RADAR
Search: DRBV 22 Air and surface surveillance.

GUNNERY. She formerly mounted 43—40 mm AA guns (as refitted) but these were removed when she became a training and helicopter carrier.

DRAWING. Starboard elevation and plan. Redrawn in 1970. Scale: 125 feet = 1 inch (1 : 1 500).

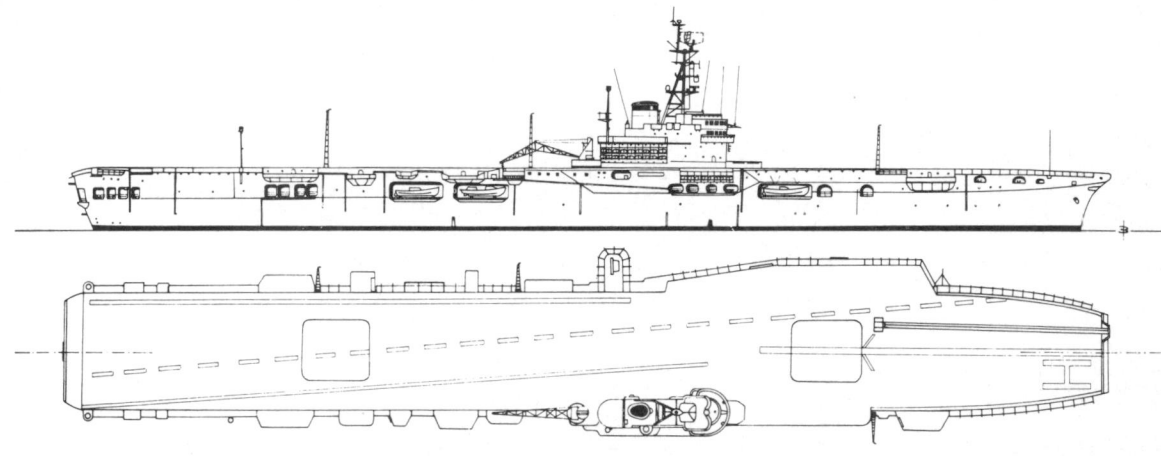

ARROMANCHES   *1971, French Navy, Official*

ARROMANCHES   *1971, Official*

ARROMANCHES   *1971, Dr. Giorgio Arra*

HELICOPTER CARRIER CRUISER (*Croiseur Porte-Hélicoptères*)

Name	*No.*	*Builders*	*Ordered*	*Laid down*	*Launched*	*Completed*
JEANNE D'ARC (ex-*La Résolue*)	R 97	Brest Dockyard	8 Mar 1957	7 July 1960	30 Sep 1961	1 July 1963 (trials) 30 June 1964 (service)

1 TRAINING/COMMANDO TYPE

Displacement, tons	10 000 standard ; 12 360 full load
Length, feet (*metres*)	597·1 (*182·0*) oa
Beam, feet (*metres*)	78·7 (*24·0*) hull
Draught, feet (*metres*)	21·6 (*6·6*) max
Flight deck	230 × 85 ft (*70 × 26 m*)
Aircraft	Heavy A/S helicopters (4 in peacetime as training ship 8 in wartime)
Guns, AA	4—3·9 in (*100 mm*) single
Boilers	4 ; working pressure 640 psi (*45 kg/cm²*) ; 842°F (*450°C*)
Main engines	Rateau-Bretagne geared turbines 40 000 shp ; 2 shafts
Speed, knots	26·5 designed
Radius, miles	6 000 at 15 knots
Oil fuel (tons)	1 360
Complement	906 (44 officers, 670 ratings and 192 cadets)

Authorised under the 1957 estimates. Used for training officer cadets in peacetime in place of the old training cruiser *Jeanne d'Arc* (which was decommissioned on 28 July 1964 and sold for scrap in Dec 1965 at Brest). In wartime, after rapid modification, she would be used as a commando ship, helicopter carrier or troop transport with commando equipment and a battalion of 700 men. The lift has a capacity of 12 tons. The ship is almost entirely air-conditioned.

GUNNERY. She was originally designed to mount six 100 mm (3·9 inch) guns (now four).

ELECTRONICS. The ship is almost as well equipped with electronic apparatus as the aircraft carrier *Clemenceau*. She also has long range sonar gear.

RADAR
Search: DRBI 10 3D and DRBV 23.
Tactical: S Band with cheese type antenna.
Fire Control. X Band.

NOMENCLATURE. The name *La Résolue* was only a temporary one until the decommissioning of the training cruiser *Jeanne d'Arc* which was relieved by *La Résolue* in 1964 when the latter ship took the name *Jeanne d'Arc*, on 16 July.

MODIFICATIONS. Between first steaming trials and completion for operational service the ship was modified with a taller funnel to clear the superstructure and obviate the smoke and exhaust gases swirling on to the bridges. After completion, in 1964, the whaleboat emplacement was plated in.

PHOTOGRAPHS of *Jeanne d'Arc* (as *La Résolue*), before modification with taller funnel, appear in the 1963-64 edition: near broadside surface view, starboard quarter surface view, and port quarter oblique aerial view showing hangar open. The latter view also appears in the 1964-65 edition. A port bow view and a starboard quarter view, both before the whaleboat emplacement was plated in, appear in the 1964-65 and 1965-66 editions. A starboard quarter oblique aerial view appears in the 1965-66 to 1968-69 editions.

JEANNE D'ARC *1969 French Navy Official*

JEANNE D'ARC *1970, French Navy, Official*

JEANNE D'ARC *French Navy, Official*

SUBMARINES

Name	No.	Builders	Laid down	Launched	Completion	Operational
LE REDOUTABLE	SNLE 1 (S 611)	Cherbourg Naval Dockyard	30 Mar 1964	29 Mar 1967	Trials 1969	1971
LE TERRIBLE	SNLE 2 (S 612)	Cherbourg Naval Dockyard	24 June 1967	12 Dec 1969	Trials 1971	Scheduled 1972
LE FOUDROYANT	SNLE 3 (S 610)	Cherbourg Naval Dockyard	1969	1971	Scheduled 1973	Scheduled 1974
L'INDOMPTABLE	SNLE 4 (S 613)	Cherbourg Naval Dockyard	Scheduled 1971	Scheduled 1973	Scheduled 1975	Scheduled 1976

NUCLEAR POWERED BALLISTIC MISSILE TYPE

Displacement, tons	7 500 surface; 9 000 submerged
Length, feet (*metres*)	420 (*128·0*)
Beam, feet (*metres*)	34·8 (*10·6*)
Draught, feet (*metres*)	32·8 (*10·0*)
Missile launchers	16 tubes amidships for "Polaris" type ICBM's; range 1 900 miles
Torpedo tubes	4 (18 torpedoes)
Nuclear reactors	1 pressurised water-cooled
Main engines	2 turbo-alternators; 1 electric motor; 15 000 hp; 1 shaft
Auxiliary propulsion	1 diesel
Speed, knots	20 on surface; 25 submerged (conservative estimate)
Complement	Two alternating crews each of 142 (12 officers, 130 men)

Le Redoutable was the first French nuclear powered, ballistic missile armed submarine and the prototype of the "*Force de dissuasion*" of four, or five, such vessels which the Navy plans to have in the late 1970s. The vessels have a submerged cruise duration of about three months. The ballistic missiles are comparable with the United States "Polaris" weapons, but are of French manufacture each with a weight of 15 tons. The diesel has oil bunkerage for a range of 5 000 miles. The decision to build a fourth unit of this class was officially announced on 7 Dec 1967. It is reported that a fifth deterrent submarine of this type is envisaged for which the tentatively suggested name is *Le Formidable*.

LE REDOUTABLE   *1970, French Navy, Official*

LE REDOUTABLE   *1970, French Navy, Official*

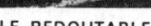

LE REDOUTABLE   *1970, French Navy, Official*

LE REDOUTABLE   *1970, French Navy, Official*

Submarines—continued

GYMNOTE

1 EXPERIMENTAL MISSILE TYPE

Displacement, tons	3 000 surface; 3 250 submerged
Lenght, feet (metres)	275·6 (84·0)
Beam, feet (metres)	34·7 (10·6)
Draught, feet (metres)	25 (7·6)
Missile launchers	4 tubes for "Polaris" type ICBM
Main engines	4 sets 620 kW diesel electric. 2 electric motors; 2 shafts; 2 600 hp
Speed, knots	11 surface; 10 submerged
Complement	78 (8 officers, 70 men)

An experimental submarine for testing ballistic missiles for the first French nuclear powered deterrent submarines, and for use as an underwater laboratory to prove equipment and arms for nuclear powered submarines.

HULL. *Gymnote* was the hull laid down in 1958 as the nuclear powered submarine Q 244 which was cancelled in 1959. The hull was still available when a trials vessel for the French "Polaris" type missiles was required and was completed as *Gymnote*.

RESCINDMENT. The projected nuclear powered fleet submarine of a new hunter-killer type, allocated the name *Rubis*, was officially taken out of the list in 1968.

PHOTOGRAPHS. A starboard view of *Gymnote* appears in the 1966-67 to 1968-69 editions, and an oblique aerial view showing jurymast in the 1969-70 edition.

4 NEW CONSTRUCTION

Displacement, tons,	1 200 surface
Length, feet (metres)	213·3 (65·0)
Beam, feet (metres)	22·3 (6·8)
Draught, feet (metres)	16·4 (5·0)
Tubes	4—21·7 in (550 mm) 14 torpedoes
Main engines	Diesel-electric; 1 shaft
Speed, knots	21 submerged
Radius, nautical miles	9 000 at 10 knots with Schnorkel
Complement	50

New type conventional submarines the building of which was officially announced in 1970.

9 "DAPHNE" CLASS

Name	No.	Launched	Completed
DAPHNÉ	S 641	20 June 1959	1 June 1964
DIANE	S 642	4 Oct 1960	20 June 1964
DORIS	S 643	14 May 1960	26 Aug 1964
FLORE	S 645	21 Dec 1960	21 May 1964
GALATÉE	S 646	22 Sep 1961	25 July 1964
JUNON	S 648	11 May 1964	25 Feb 1966
VENUS	S 649	24 Sep 1964	1 Jan 1966
PSYCHÉ	S 650	28 June 1969	7 June 1970
SIRENE	S 651	28 June 1969	3 Sep 1970

Displacement, tons	869 surface; 1 043 submerged
Length, feet (metres)	189·6 (57·8)
Beam, feet (metres)	22·3 (6·8)
Draught, feet (metres)	15·1 (4·6)
Torpedo tubes	12—21·7 in (550 mm) 8 bow 4 stern
Main engines	SEMT-Pielstick diesel-electric 1 300 bhp surface; 1 600 hp motors submerged; 2 shafts
Speed, knots	13·5 surface; 16 submerged
Complement	45 (6 officers, 39 men)

BUILDERS. *Daphné* and *Diane* were built by Dubigeon, Nantes, *Doris, Flore, Galatée, Junon* and *Venus* by Cherbourg and *Psyché* and *Sirene* by Brest.

COMPLETION. The completion dates above are the dates of "admission to active service" listed officially.

PHOTOGRAPHS. A photograph of *Flore* appears in the 1961-62 edition, of *Daphné* in the 1967-68 and 1968-69 editions, of *Galatée* in the 1965-66 to 1969-70 editions, of *Venus* in the 1968-69 to 1970-71 editions, and of *Diane* in the 1970-71 edition.

LOSSES. Of the "Daphne" class *Minerve*, S 647 was lost in the Western Mediterranean on 27 Jan 1968 and *Eurydice*, S 644, was lost in that area on 4 Mar 1970.

Name	No.	Builders	Laid down	Launched	Completed
GYMNOTE	S 655	Cherbourg Naval Dockyard	17 Mar 1963	17 Mar 1964	17 Oct 1966

GYMNOTE (missile being shipped)

DORIS

JUNON

PSYCHE

4 "ARÉTHUSE" CLASS

Displacement, tons	400 standard; 543 surface; 669 submerged
Length, feet (metres)	162·7 (49·6)
Beam, feet (metres)	19 (5·8)
Draught, feet (metres)	13·1 (4·0)
Torpedo tubes	4—21·7 in (550 mm) bow
Main engines	12-cyl. SEMT-Pielstick diesel-electric; 1 060 bhp surface; 1 300 hp motors submerged; 1 shaft
Speed, knots	16 surface; 18 submerged
Complement	40 (6 officers, 34 men)

All built at Cherbourg. Submarine-killer type for hunting enemy submarines. Streamlined hull, silent motors, and up-to-date electronic and detection equipment.

PHOTOGRAPHS. A photograph of *Amazone* appears in the 1964-65 and 1965-66 editions, and of *Arethuse* in the 1967-68 to 1969-70 editions.

DISPOSALS OF "S" CLASS
Of the former British submarines of the "S" class, *Siréne* was returned to Great Britain at Gosport on 24 Oct 1958. and reverted to the original name *Spiteful*, and *Sultane* was returned to Great Britain at Rosyth on 5 Nov 1959, and reverted to her original name *Statesman*. *Saphir* (ex-*Satyr*) was also returned to Great Britain on 11 Aug 1961 to await disposal at Rosyth. *Sibylle* (ex-*Sportsman*) was lost accidentally with all hands on 23 Sep 1952. near Toulon.

DISPOSALS OF GERMAN TYPES
Blaison (ex-U 123), former German Type IX B, was discarded in 1957. *Bouan* (ex-U 510), former German Type IXC, was scrapped in 1958.
Of the two former German Type VII C boats, *Laubie* (ex-U 766) was withdrawn on 17 Oct 1961 (seriously damaged by collision and scrapped) and *Mille* (ex-U 471) in Aug 1963.
Roland Morillot (ex-U 2518) S 613, former German oceangoing Type XXI, was officially deleted from the list in 1968.

6 "NARVAL" CLASS

Displacement, tons	1 200 standard; 1 640 surface 1 910 submerged
Length, feet (metres)	257·2 (78·4)
Beam, feet (metres)	25·6 (7·8)
Draught, feet (metres)	18·5 (5·65)
Torpedo tubes	6—21·7 in (550 mm) bow; 20 torpedoes
Main engines	Three 750 kW 12-cyl SEMT-Pielstick diesels; two 2 400 hp electric motors; 2 shafts
Speed, knots	16 surface; 18 submerged
Radius, miles	15 000 at 8 knots with schnorkel
Complement	67 (7 officers, 60 men)

Designed as oceangoing submarines. Improved versions of the German XXI type. *Dauphin, Marsouin, Narval* and *Requin* were built in seven prefabricated parts each of 10 metres in length.

NOMENCLATURE. *Dauphin* means Dolphin, *Espadon* means *Swordfish*, *Marsouin* means Porpoise, *Morse* means Walrus, *Narval* means Narwhal, and *Requin* means Shark.

PHOTOGRAPHS. A photograph of *Narval* as first completed without bulbous bow appears in the 1957-58 edition, of *Requin* in the 1959-60 and 1960-61 editions, of *Narval* with bulbous bow and of *Dauphine* in the 1957-58 to 1965-66 editions, of *Marsouin* surfacing in the 1966-67 to 1969-70 editions, of *Morse* in the 1966-67 to 1970-71 editions and of *Espadon* in the 1967-68 to 1970-71 editions (all before reconstruction).

RECONSTRUCTION. During a five-year reconstruction programme, officially announced in 1965 and completed by the end of 1970, these submarines, *Requin* in Spring 1967 and *Espadon* and *Morse* in succession at Lorient followed by the other three, were given a new diesel electric power plant as well as new weapon and detection equipment. It is reported that this reconstruction has been very successful. See altered appearance of *Requin* and *Narval*.

ENGINEERING. New main propelling machinery installed on reconstruction during 1965 to 1970 includes diesel-electric drive on the surface with SEMT-Pielstick diesels. The original main engines comprised Schneider 4 000 bhp 7 cyl. 2 str. diesels for surface propulsion and 5 000 hp electric motors submerged.

"LA CRÉOLE" CLASS. *L'Africaine* was withdrawn from service on 1 July 1961 (reported worn out), *Le Créole* was officially deleted from the list in Mar 1963, *L'Androméde* and *L'Astrée* in 1965, and *L'Artémis* in 1966.

Submarines—*continued*

Name	No.	Programme	Builders	Laid down	Launched	Completed
AMAZONE	S 639	1954	Cherbourg	Dec 1955	3 Apr 1958	1 July 1959
ARÉTHUSE	S 635	1953	Cherbourg	Mar 1955	9 Nov 1957	23 Oct 1958
ARGONAUTE	S 636	1653	Cherbourg	Mar 1955	29 June 1957	11 Feb 1959
ARIANE	S 640	1954	Cherbourg	Dec 1955	12 Sep 1958	16 Mar 1960

ARGONAUTE   *1970, French Navy, Official*

ARIANE   *1970, French Navy, Official*

Name	No.	Programme	Builders	Laid down	Launched	Completed
DAUPHIN	S 633	1950	Cherbourg	Jan 1952	17 Sep 1955	1 Aug 1958
ESPADON	S 637	1954	Normand	Mar 1957	15 Sep 1958	2 Apr 1960
MARSOUIN	S 632	1949	Cherbourg	Nov 1951	21 May 1955	1 Oct 1957
MORSE	S 638	1954	Seine Maritime	Dec 1956	10 Dec 1958	2 May 1960
NARVAL	S 631	1949	Cherbourg	Oct 1951	11 Dec 1954	1 Dec 1957
REQUIN	S 634	1950	Cherbourg	Feb 1952	3 Dec 1955	1 Aug 1958

REQUIN (as reconstructed)   *1969. French Navy. Official*

NARVAL   *1971, French Navy, Official*

MARSOUIN   *1971, Wright & Logan*

ANTI-AIRCRAFT CRUISER (*Croiseur Anti-Aérien*)

Name	Pennant No.	Builders	Laid down	Launched	Completed	Commissioned	Reconstruction
COLBERT	C 611	Brest Dockyard	Dec 1953	24 Mar 1956 (floated out of dry dock)	1958 (trials end of 1957)	5 May 1959	Apr 1970-Jan 1973

Displacement, tons	8 500 standard ; 11 300 full load
Length, feet (*metres*)	593·2 (*180·8*) oa
Beam, feet (*metres*)	64·6 (*19·7*)
Draught, feet (*metres*)	25·2 (*7·7*) screws
Aircraft	1 Helicopter
Missile launchers	1 twin "Masurca" surface-to-air aft (after reconstruction)
Guns	2—3·9 in (*100 mm*) single automatic ; 12—57 mm in 6 twin mountings, 3 on each side (after reconstruction)
Armour	Has some protection. See notes
Boilers	4 Indret multiturbular ; 640 psi (*45 kg/cm²*) ; 842°F (*450°C*)
Main engines	2 sets CEM-Parsons geared turbines ; 2 shafts ; 86 000 shp
Speed, knots	32·4 max (33·7 trials) ; 15 economical sea
Radius, miles	4 000 at 25 knots
Oil fuel, tons	1 492
Complement	800 (70 officers, 730 men) as Flagship after reconstruction

COLBERT (1970-73 rearmament model) 1971, French Navy, Official

Provision was made in the original design for her to be fitted with guided missiles. New scheme of protection, and platform for helicopter. She was equipped as command ship and for radar control of air strikes.

REARMAMENT. *Colbert* has been undergoing a major refit since Apr 1970. Her armament will include an anti-aircraft "Masurca" guided missile system, but she will not now have the pre-1970 envisaged scheme of six MM 38 surface-to-surface launchers and the associated "Exocet" guided missile system and six 3·9 inch (*100 mm*) guns. Four of the latter are being suppressed in favour of twelve 57 mm guns. She will have SENIT tactical information system, new radar including decimetric improved DRB 23 as in *Foch*, and air-conditioned accommodation. The ship will be operational in 1973.

GUNNERY. Prior to Apr 1970 the armament comprised sixteen 5 inch (*127 mm*) dual purpose guns in eight twin mountings, and twenty 57 mm Bofors anti-aircraft guns in ten twin mountings.

PHOTOGRAPHS of *Colbert* before modification and the suppression of the whaleboat emplacement appear in the 1965-66 and earlier editions.

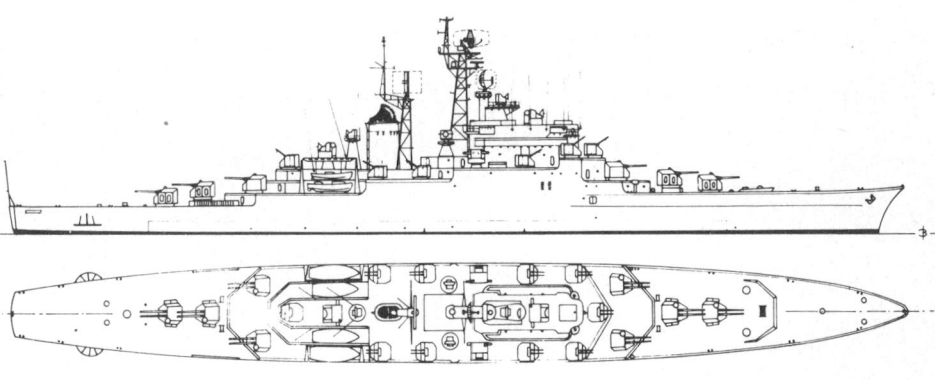

COLBERT (before rearmament) Starboard elevation and plan. Scale 125 feet = 1 inch (1 : 1 500).

COMMAND CRUISER (*Bâtiment de Commandement*)

Name	Pennant No.	Builders	Laid down	Launched	Completed	Commissioned
DE GRASSE	C 610	Lorient Dockyard and Brest Dockyard (see notes)	Nov 1938	11 Sep 1946	Aug 1955 (trials)	3 Sep 1956 (operational)

Displacement, tons	9 000 standard ; 12 350 full load
Length, feet (*metres*)	617·8 (*188·3*) oa
Beam, feet (*metres*)	69·9 (*21·3*)
Draught, feet (*metres*)	21·4 (*6·53*) aft
Guns, dual purpose	12—5 in (*127 mm*) ; 6 twin mountings
Boilers	4 A & C de B Indret multitubular ; 500 psi (*35 kg/cm²*) ; 725°F (*385°C*)
Main engines	2 sets Rateau-Chantiers de Bretagne geared turbines 105 000 shp ; 2 shafts
Speed, knots	33 max (33·8 trials) ; 18 cruising
Radius, miles	5 200 at 18 knots ; 2 500 at full power
Oil fuel (tons)	1 900 normal
Complement	560 plus accommodation for 120 engineers and technicians after modifications

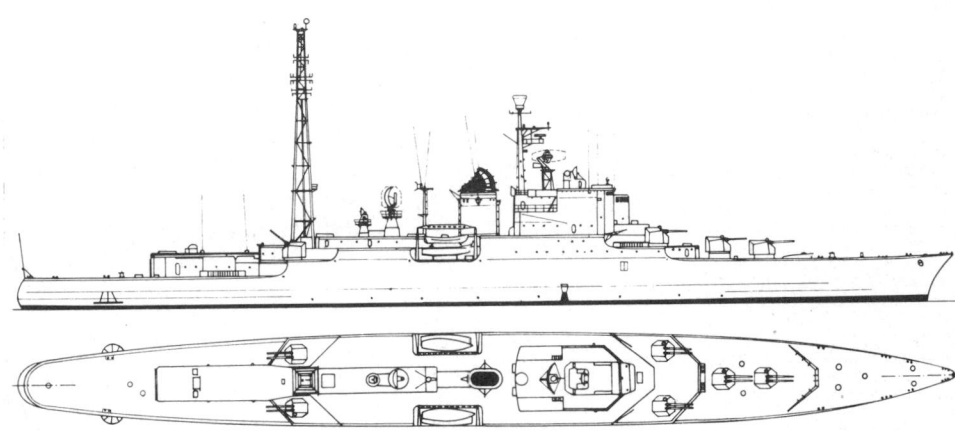

Ordered under the 1937 Estimates. Her construction was suspended during the German occupation of Lorient, but was resumed in 1946 until her launch when building was stopped. Construction was again resumed on 9 Jan 1951. Completed in Brest Dockyard as an anti-aircraft cruiser to a modified design. She is equipped as a fleet command ship and for radar control of air strikes.

MODIFICATIONS. Refitted at Brest as Flagship of the Pacific Experimental Nuclear Centre in 1966. Signal department enlarged, and several turrets suppressed.

RADAR.
Search : DRBI 10 3D and DRVB 23.
Fire Control : X Band.

GUNNERY. All the 57 mm Bofors AA guns (six twin mountings) and two twin 5 inch guns were suppressed during the conversion as flagship of the Pacific Experimental centre.

PHOTOGRAPHS of *De Grasse* before conversion from anti-aircraft cruiser to command ship appear in the 1965-66 and earlier editions.

DRAWING. Starboard elevation and plan. Redrawn in 1970. Scale: 125 feet = 1 inch (1 : 1 500).

DE GRASSE 1967, French Navy, Official

GUIDED MISSILE FRIGATES (*Fregates Lance-Engins*)

2 "SUFFREN" CLASS (FLE 60 TYPE)

Name	No.	Builders	Laid down	Launched	Trials	Operational
DUQUESNE	D 603	Brest Dockyard	Nov 1964	12 Feb 1966	Oct 1968	Jan 1969
SUFFREN	D 602	Lorient Dockyard	Dec 1962	15 May 1965	Dec 1965	July 1968

Displacement, tons	5 100 standard; 6 000 full load
Length, feet (*metres*)	517·0 (*157·6*) oa
Beam, feet (*metres*)	50·8 (*15·5*)
Draught, feet (*metres*)	20·0 (*6·1*)
Missiles, AA	"Masurca", twin launcher
A/S weapons	"Malafon" rocket/homing torpedo single launcher 13 missiles carried
Guns, AA	2—3·9 in (*100 mm*) automatic, single 2—30 mm (automatic, single)
Torpedo launchers	4 (2 each side) for A/S homing torpedoes
Boilers	4 automatic; working pressure 640 psi (*45 kg/cm²*); superheat 842°F (*450°C*)
Main engines	Double reduction geared turbines 70 000 shp; 2 shafts
Speed, knots	34
Radius, miles	5 000 at 18 knots
Complement	446 (39 officers, 407 men)

DUQUESNE   *1971, Wright & Logan*

Ordered under the 1960 Programme. The structure provides best possible resistance to atomic blast. Fitted with detection devices, two sonars including VDS, and SENIT tactical information system. Studied habitability. Equipped with stabilisers.

RADAR
Search: DRBI 23 3D. Tactical: S Band. Fire Control: DRBR 51 C and X Band for Masurca, X Band for guns.

SUFFREN   *1970, French Navy, Official*

NEW CONSTRUCTION (C 70 TYPE)

Displacement, tons   3 500

A new type of lighter corvette is projected. Two or three are included in the 1971-75 construction programme. To be gas turbine powered.

NEW CONSTRUCTION

3 "TOURVILLE" CLASS (C 67 TYPE)

DUGUAY-TROUIN   **TOURVILLE**

Displacement, tons	4 580 standard; 5 300 full load
Length, feet (*metres*)	498·7 (*152·0*) oa
Beam, feet (*metres*)	50·2 (*15·3*)
Missiles, surface	6 "MM 38" ("Exocet")
A/S weapons	"Malafon" rocket/homing torpedo
Guns, AA	3—3·9 in (*100 mm*)
Torpedoes	Auto guided
Aircraft	2 WG 13 ON ASW helicopters
Main engines	Geared turbines; 2 shafts; 58 000 shp
Speed, knots	30
Radius, miles	5 000 at 18 knots
Boilers	4 automatic
Complement	274 (20 officers, 254 men)

TOURVILLE model   *1971, French Navy, Official*

Derived from the "Aconit" design. *Tourville* was laid down at Lorient on 16 Mar 1970 for launching in May 1972 and completion in 1974. *Duguay-Trouin* was laid down in Jan 1971 for launching in 1973 and completion in 1975. Third ship to be begun in 1971. Officially rated as corvettes, but will be comparable with the "Suffren" class frigates.

ACONIT

Displacement, tons	3 000 standard; 3 560 full load
Length, feet (*metres*)	416·7 (*127·0*) oa
Beam, feet (*metres*)	44·0 (*13·4*)
Missiles, A/S	"Malafon" rocket/homing torpedo
Guns, AA	2—3·9 in (*100 mm*)
A/S weapons	1 quadruple 12 in (*305mm*) mortar
Torpedoes	Auto-guided
Main engines	Geared turbines; 1 shaft; 27 200 shp
Boilers	2 automatic
Speed, knots	27 max
Radius, miles	5 000 at 18 knots
Complement	240 (20 officers, 220 men)

ACONIT model   *1971, French Navy, Official*

Officially rated as a "Corvette" but from her size and armament must logically be described as a frigate. Laid down at Lorient in Jan 1966 and launched on 7 Mar 1970 for trials in 1971 and operations in 1972. SENIT equipment fitted. See photograph of ship nearing completion in ADDENDA.

DESTROYERS (Rated as Escorteurs d'Escadre)

Name	Pennant No.	Builders	Laid down	Launched	Completed
LA GALISSONNIÈRE	D 638	Lorient Naval Dockyard	Nov 1958	12 Mar 1960	July 1962

1 ANTI-SUBMARINE (T 56) TYPE

Displacement, tons	2 750 standard ; 3 910 full load ;
Length, feet (metres)	435·7 (132·8) oa
Beam, feet (metres)	41·7 (12·7)
Draught, feet (metres)	15·4 (4·7) aft ; 18·0 (5·5) screws
Aircraft	1 A/S helicopter
A/S	"Malafon" rocket/homing torpedoes, 1 launcher
Guns, AA	2—3·9 in (100 mm) automatic, single
Torpedo tubes	6—21·7 in (550 mm) ASM, 2 triple
Boilers	4 A & C de B Indret ; 500 psi (35 kg/cm²) ; 716°F (380°C)
Main engines	2 sets geared turbines ; 2 shafts 63 000 shp (72 000 on trials, light)
Speed, knots	34·5 (38·2 on trials, light), 15 sea
Radius, miles	4 900 at 18 knots
Oil fuel (tons)	725
Complement	333 (20 officers, 313 men)

Designed as a squadron escort and flotilla leader. She has extensive sonar and anti-submarine apparatus, including variable depth sonar and homing torpedoes. Particularly well developed anti-aircraft and radar equipment. T 56 type. Same characteristics as regards hull and machinery as T 47 and T 53 R types, but different armament. She has a hangar and a platform for landing a helicopter. When first commissioned she was used as an experimental ship for new sonars and anti-submarine weapons.

ARMAMENT. She is fitted with French makes of guided missiles and was the first French combatant ship to be so armed. This is the reason for the two 3·9 in (100 mm) guns instead of the 3 or 4 previously planned. As redesigned she was France's first operational guided missile ship.

RADAR
Search: DRBV 22. Tactical: S Band.
Fire Control: X Band.

PHOTOGRAPHS of La Galissonniere as first completed appear in the 1962-63 edition, and a starboard bow view in the 1963-64 to 1965-66 editions.

LA GALISSONNIÈRE   1969, French Navy, Official

Name	Pennant No.	Builders	Laid down	Launched	Completed (commissioned)
DUPERRÈ	A 633	Lorient Naval Dockyard	Nov 1954	2 July 1955	8 Oct 1957
FORBIN	D 635	Brest Naval Dockyard	Aug 1954	15 Oct 1955	1 Feb 1958
JAURÈGUIBERRY	D 637	Forges et Chantiers de la Gironde	Sep 1954	5 Nov 1955	July 1958
LA BOURDONNAIS	D 634	Brest Naval Dockyard	Aug 1954	15 Oct 1955	Mar 1958
TARTU	D 636	Ateliers et Chantiers de Bretagne	Nov 1954	2 Dec 1955	5 Feb 1958

4 AIRCRAFT DIRECTION (T53) TYPE
1 EXPERIMENTAL ("DUPERRÈ")

Displacement, tons	2 750 standard ; 3 750 full load
Length, feet (metres)	422 (128·6) oa
Beam, feet (metres)	41·7 (12·7)
Draught, feet (metres)	15·0 (4·6) aft ; 17·7 (5·4) screws
Guns, dual purpose	6—5 in (127 mm), twin mounts
Guns, AA	6—2·25 in (57 mm) Bofors 2 or 4—20 mm
A/S	Sextuple Bofors lance roquettes howitzer
Torpedo tubes	6—21·7 in (550 mm) ASM, 2 triple (also able to launch ordinary torpedoes)
Boilers	4 Indret or A & C de B in two boiler rooms separated by turbine compartment. Working pressure 500 psi (35·2 kg/cm²) ; superheat 725°F (385°C)
Main engines	2 ACL geared turbines 63 000 shp ; 2 shafts
Speed, knots	34 max (35 trials)
Radius, miles	5 000 at 18 knots
Oil fuel (tons)	700
Complement	281 (19 officers, 262 men)

TARTU   1971, Wright & Logan

Radar Picket Destroyers. Modified "Surcouf" Class or "T 53 R" Type fitted as aircraft direction and command ships. Radar equipment more comprehensive and prominent than in the original "Surcouf" or "T 47" Anti-Aircraft Type. Classed as Escorteurs Rapides in 1953, but re-rated as Escorteurs in 1955. Latest electronic appliances. Named after famous sailors Duperré was reclassified as trials ship in 1967, all armament removed.

RADAR
Search: DRBI 10 and DRBV 22.
Fire Control: X Band.

CONSTRUCTION. Hull entirely welded. Light alloys used extensively for upperworks.

GUNNERY. The 5 inch guns are able to use standard American ammunition.

PHOTOGRAPHS. A photograph of Forbin appears in the 1958-59 to 1962-63 editions, and of La Bourdonnais in the 1970-71 edition.

DUPERRE   1970, French Navy, Official

Destroyers—*continued*

12 "SURCOUF" CLASS

Bouvet	Rearmed
Du Chayla	with
Dupetit Thouars	guided
Kersaint	missiles
Cassard	Converted to
Chevalier Paul	command
Surcouf	ships
Casabianca	Original
D'Estrées	anti-aircraft
Guépratte	T 47 type
Maillé Brézé	converted to
Vauquelin	anti-submarine

Name	No.	Builders	Laid down	Launched	Completed
BOUVET	D 624	Lorient Naval Dockyard	June 1952	3 Oct 1953	13 May 1956
CASABIANCA	D 631	A. C. Bretagne	Oct 1953	13 Nov 1954	4 May 1957
CASSARD	D 623	A. C. Bretagne	Nov 1951	12 May 1953	14 Apr 1956
CHEVALIER PAUL	D 626	F. C. Gironde	Feb 1952	28 July 1953	22 Dec 1956
D'ESTRÉES	D 629	Brest Naval Dockyard	May 1953	27 Nov 1954	19 Mar 1957
DU CHAYLA	D 630	Brest Naval Dockyard	July 1953	27 Nov 1954	4 June 1957
DUPETIT THOUARS	D 625	Brest Naval Dockyard	Mar 1952	4 Feb 1954	15 Sep 1956
GUÉPRATTE	D 632	F. C. Gironde	Aug 1953	9 Nov 1954	6 June 1957
KERSAINT	D 622	Lorient Naval Dockyard	Nov 1951	3 Oct 1953	20 Mar 1956
MAILLÉ BRÉZÉ	D 627	Lorient Naval Dockyard	Oct 1953	26 Sep 1954	4 May 1957
SURCOUF	D 621	Lorient Naval Dockyard	July 1951	3 Oct 1953	1 Nov 1955
VAUQUELIN	D 628	Lorient Naval Dockyard	Mar 1953	26 Sep 1954	3 Nov 1956

Displacement, tons	2 750 standard; 3 850 full load
Length, feet (*metres*)	421·3 (*128·4*) oa
Beam, feet (*metres*)	42·6 (*13·0*)
Draught, feet (*metres*)	15·8 (*4·8*) aft; 18·3 (*5·6*) screws
Missiles, AA	Single "Tartar" Mark 13 (40 missiles) in *Bouvet*, *Du Chayla*, *Dupetit Thouars* and *Kersaint* only
Guns, dual purpose	6—5 in (*127 mm*), twin mounts (see *Conversion* notes)
Guns, AA	6—57 mm; 6—20 mm
Torpedo tubes	12—21·7 in (*550 mm*) in 4 triple mounts (6 ordinary, 6 ASM)
Boilers	4 Indret; 500 psi (*35·2 kg/cm²*); superheat 725°F (*385°C*)
Main engines	2 Parsons geared turbines 63 000 shp; 2 shafts
Speed, knots	35 max
Radius, miles	5 000 at 18 knots
Oil fuel (tons)	800
Complement	293 (336 with command staff)

Designed as Escorteurs Rapides Anti-aériens but re-rated Escorteurs Prèmiere Classe in 1951, Escorteurs Rapides in 1953 and Escorteurs d'Escadre in 1955. Named after famous French sailors. Hull entirely welded, assembled from 84 prefabricated sections. Light alloys used extensively for upper-works. Two boiler rooms alternate with two engine rooms.

CONVERSION. In 1968 *D'Estrées* was converted into an anti-submarine vessel, *Maillé Brézé* 1969, *Vauquelin*, *Casabianca* and *Guépratte* in 1969-70. New armament 2—3·9 in (*100 mm*) AA, 1 Malafon missile launcher, 6 A/S tubes (2 triple), 1 Bofors rocket launcher, variable depth sonar and bow sonar. The four SAM conversions lost all their 5 inch guns. *Cassard*, *Chevalier Paul* and *Surcouf*, refitted as flotilla leaders, retained their 6—5 inch guns but only 4—57 mm AA and 6 tubes for ASM torpedoes.

RADAR
Search: DRBV 20A and SPS 52 in "Tartar" ships. Others have DRBV 11 or 22 and S Band radars.
Fire Control: C Band for guided weapons, X Band for guns.

PHOTOGRAPHS. A photograph of *Vauquelin* appears in the 1957-58 to 1962-63 editions, of *Guépratte* in the 1959-60 to 1961-62 editions, of *Cassard* in the 1962-63 to 1965-66 editions, of *Dupetit Thouars* (firing guided missiles) in the 1966-67 and 1967-68 editions, of *Bouvet* in the 1967-68 to 1969-70 editions, of *Maillé Brézé* before conversion in the 1968-69 to 1970-71 editions, and of *D'Estrées* in the 1969-70 and 1970-71 editions.

MAILLE BRÉZÉ (as converted to anti-submarine)   1971, French Navy, Official

DU CHAYLA   1970, French Navy, Official

SURCOUF   1971, French Navy, Official

DUPETIT THOUARS   1970, French Navy, Official

DUAL PURPOSE FRIGATES (Rated as *Avisos Escorteurs*)

ENSEIGNE DE VAISSEAU HENRY

1971, courtesy Mr. John Mortimer

9 "COMMANDANT" RIVIERE CLASS

	Launched	Completed
AMIRAL CHARNER	12 Mar 60	15 Dec 62
BALNY	17 Mar 62	31 Mar 69
COMMANDANT BORY	11 Oct 58	5 Mar 64
COMMANDANT BOURDAIS	15 Apr 61	1 Mar 63
COMMANDANT RIVIÈRE	11 Oct 58	4 Dec 62
DOUDART DE LAGRÈE	15 Apr 61	1 Mar 63
ENSEIGNE DE VAISSEAU HENRY	14 Dec 63	1 Jan 65
PROTET	7 Dec 62	1 May 64
VICTOR SCHOELCHER	11 Oct 58	15 Oct 62

Displacément, tons	1 750 standard.; 1 950 full load
Length, feet (*metres*)	321·5 (*98·0*) pp; 338 (*103*) oa
Beam, feet (*metres*)	37·8 (*11·5*)
Draught, feet (*metres*)	12·5 (*3·8*) mean; 14·1 (*4·3*) max
Aircraft	1 light helicopter can land aft
Guns, AA	3—3·9 in (*100 mm*) automatic, singles (*Balny* 2 only); 2—30 mm
A/S	1—12in (*305mm*) quadruple mortar
Torpedo tubes	6—21 in (*533mm*) ASM
Main engines	4 SEMT-Pielstick diesels; 16 000 bhp; 2 shafts; except *Commandant Bory*: Sigma free piston generators and gas turbines *Balny*: CODAG; 1 shaft
Speed, knots	25·4 max (26·4 trials)
Radius, miles	4 500 at 15 knots
Complement	214 (15 officers, 199 men)

All built by Lorient Dockyard. Formerly classed as *Escorteurs d'Union Francaise*. Officially rerated as *Avisos Escorteurs* on 1 Apr 1959. *Commandant Bourdais* commissioned as fishery protection ship for Newfoundland and Greenland in Mar 1963. *Victor Schoelcher* acts as training ship.

RADAR
Search: DRBV 22. Tactical: S Band.
Fire Control: X Band.

PHOTOGRAPHS. A photograph of *Commandant Rivière* appears in the 1960-61 to 1964-65 editions, of *Doudart de la Grée* in the 1964-65 and 1965-66 editions, of *Enseigne de Vaisseau Henry* in the 1965-66 to 1967-68 editions, of *Commandant Bory* in the 1966-67 to 1968-69 editions, of *Protet* in the 1968-69 and 1969-70 editions.

COMMANDANT BORY

1971, French Navy, Official

COMMANDANT BOURDAIS

1970, French Navy, Official

BALNY (with CODAG propulsion system and only two 3·9 inch guns)

1971, Wright & Logan

FAST FRIGATES (Rated as *Escorteurs Rapides*)

14 "LE NORMAND" CLASS
(E 52 TYPE)

Name	No.	Builders	Laid down	Launched	Completed
LE NORMAND	F 765	F. Ch. de la Medit	July 1953	13 Feb 1954	3 Nov 1956
LE LORRAIN	F 768	F. Ch. de la Medit	Feb 1954	19 June 1954	1 Jan 1957
LE PICARD	F 766	A. C. Loire	Nov 1953	31 May 1954	20 Sep 1956
LE GASCON	F 767	A. C. Loire	Feb 1954	23 Oct 1954	29 Mar 1957
LE CHAMPENOIS	F 770	A. C. Loire	May 1954	12 Mar 1955	1 June 1957
LE SAVOYARD	F 771	F. Ch. de la Medit	Nov 1953	7 May 1955	14 June 1956
LE BOURGUIGNON	F 769	Penhoët	Jan 1954	28 Jan 1956	11 July 1957
LE BRETON	F 772	Lorient Navy Yard	June 1954	2 Apr 1955	20 Aug 1957
LE BASQUE	F 773	Lorient Navy Yard	Dec 1954	25 Feb 1956	18 Oct 1957
L'AGENAIS	F 774	Lorient Navy Yard	Aug 1955	23 June 1956	14 May 1958
LE BÉARNAIS	F 775	Lorient Navy Yard	Dec 1955	23 June 1956	18 Oct 1958
L'ALSACIEN	F 776	Lorient Navy Yard	July 1956	26 Jan 1957	27 Aug 1960
LE PROVENCAL	F 777	Lorient Navy Yard	Feb 1957	5 Oct 1957	6 Nov 1959
LE VENDÈEN	F 778	F. Ch. de la Medit	Mar 1957	27 July 1957	1 Oct 1960

Displacement, tons	1 295 standard; 1 795 full load
Length, feet (*metres*)	311·7 (*95·0*) pp; 325·8 (*99·3*) oa
Beam, feet (*metres*)	33·8 (*10·3*)
Draught, feet (*metres*)	11·2 (*3·4*) aft; 13·5 (*4·1*) screws
Guns, AA	6—2·25 in (*57 mm*), in twin mountings (4 only in F 776, 777, 778); 2—20 mm
A/S	Heavy sextuple Bofors ASM (*lance-roquettes*) mortar of Hedgehog type forward (except F 776, 777, 778 with 1—12 in (*305 mm*) quadruple mortar) 2 DC mortars; 1 DC rack
Torpedo tubes	12 ASM (4 triple mountings aft) for homing torpedoes
Boilers	2 Indret; pressure 500 psi (*35·2 kg/cm²*); superheat 725°F (*385°C*)
Main engines	Parsons or Rateau geared turbines 20 000 shp
Speed, knots	28 (on trials they exceeded 29 kts)
Radius, miles	4 500 at 12 knots
Oil fuel (tons)	310
Complement	175 peace; 200 war

The E 52a type have similar characteristics to the E 50 type as regards hull and machinery but are easily distinguished in that they have the ASM tubes aft and the heavy hedgehog or ASM howitzer forward while the E 50 type have the ASM torpedo tubes forward. *L'Agenais, L'Alsacien, Le Béarnais, Le Provençal* and *Le Vendèen* have a different arrangement of bridges. *L'Alsacien, Le Provençal,* and *Le Vendèen* have the Strombos-Velensi type modified funnel cap, and differ in armament, with a 12-inch quadruple mortar in place of the sextuple Bofors' howitzer and only 4—57 mm AA guns.

RADAR
Search: DRBV 22. Fire Control: X Band.

PHOTOGRAPHS of *Le Gascon* appear in the 1957-58 to 1959-60 editions, of *L'Agenais* in the 1958-59 and 1960-61 to 1963-64 editions, of *Le Bourguignon* in the 1962-63 and 1963-64 editions, of *Le Savoyard* in the 1964-65 and 1965-66 editions, of *Le Vendèen* in the 1964-65 to 1966-67 editions, of *Le Breton* in the 1966-67 edition, of *Le Champenois* in the 1967-68 to 1969-70 editions.

Of the "*L'Aventure*" class, *La Croië de Lorraine* (ex-HMS *Strule*, ex-*Glenarm*), *L'Ailette* (ex-*L'Escarmouche*, ex-HMS *Frome*) and *La Confiance* (ex- *Toniknois*, ex-HMS *Malaya*) were condemned in Sep 1961. *L'Aventure* was withdrawn from service on 15 Dec 1961. *La Surprise* was sold to Morocco in June 1964. *La Decouverte* (ex-HMS *Windrush*) replaced *Lucifer* (ex-German M 227) as experimental ship at Cherbourg.

LE LORRAIN and LE BOURGUIGNON   *1968. Skyfotos*

LE BEARNAIS   *1970, French Navy, Official*

LE NORMAND   *1971, French Navy, Official*

LE PROVENCAL (showing Strombos-Velensi modified funnel cap)   *1971, Dr. Giorgio Arra*

FAST FRIGATES (Rated as *Escorteurs Rapides*)

4 "LE CORSE" CLASS (E 50 TYPE)

Name	No.	Builders	Laid down	Launched	Completed
LE BORDELAIS	F 764	F. Ch. de la Medit	May 1952	11 July 1953	7 Apr 1955
LE BOULONNAIS	F 763	A. C. Loire	Mar 1952	12 May 1953	5 Aug 1955
LE BRESTOIS	F 762	Lorient Navy Yard	Nov 1951	16 Aug 1952	19 Jan 1956
LE CORSE	F 761	Lorient Navy Yard	Oct 1951	5 Aug 1952	15 Apr 1955

Displacement, tons	1 290 standard; 1 528 for trials; 1 680 full load
Length, feet (*metres*)	311·7 (*95·0*) pp 325·5 (*99·2*) oa
Beam, feet (*metres*)	33·8 (*10·3*)
Draught, feet (*metres*)	13·5 (*4·1*) screws
Guns, AA	6—2·25 in (*57 mm*), 3 twin 2—20 mm
A/S weapons	2 mortars; 1 DC rack; 1 sextuple "lance roquettes"
Torpedo tubes	12 ASM tubes (four triple mounts forward) for homing torpedoes
Boilers	2 Indret; pressure 500 psi (*35·2 kg/cm²*); superheat 725°F (*385°C*)
Main engines	Rateau A & C de B geared turbines 20 000 shp
Speed, knots	28·5 max, 28·9 trials (*Bordelais* 29·5 on trials); economical sea speed 14
Radius, miles	4 000 at 15 knots
Oil fuel, tons	292
Complement	174

LE BRESTOIS (showing 100 mm gun)   *1971, Dr. Giorgio Arra*

Seagoing convoy escort vessels with a large radius of action. Designed as Escorteurs Rapides Anti-Sous-marins. Re-rated as Escorteurs de Deuxième Classe in 1951, as Escorteurs in 1953, and as Escorteurs Rapides in 1955. *Le Bordelais* has Strombos-Velensi type modified funnel cap. *Le Brestois* has similar mainmast to that in *Le Provencal*. *Le Boulonnais* and *Le Corse* normal reserve status on 1 Dec 1964, *Le Bordelais* since Aug 1966.

RADAR. Search: DRBV 22.

GUNNERY. *Le Brestois* had a single 3·9 in (*100 mm*) automatic AA gun mounted in place of the after twin 57 mm mounting for experimental purpose, and after her refit completed in 1963 she retained this mounting.

PHOTOGRAPHS of *Le Boulonnais* appears in the 1956-57, 1957-58, 1963-64, 1964-65 and 1965-66 editions, and of *Le Corse* in tne 1966-67 to 1969-70 editions.

LE BORDELAIS   *Added 1971, Stefan Terzibaschitsch*

EXPERIMENTAL EX-FRIGATES (Rated as *Avisos*) Ex-*Escorteurs*

Ex-US DESTROYER ESCORT TYPE 1 "ARABE" CLASS

Name	No.	Builders	Launched	Completed
ARAGO (ex-*Somali*, ex-USS DE 111)	A 607	Dravo Corp, Willmington	12 Feb 1944	9 Apr 1944

Displacement, tons	1 300 standard; 1 650 full load
Length, feet (*metres*)	300 (*91·4*) pp; 306 (*93·3*) wl
Beam, feet (*metres*)	36·8 (*11·2*)
Draught, feet (*metres*)	10·7 (*3·3*)
Guns	All removed
Main engines	4 GE diesels, 2 electric motors; diesel-electric drive 6 000 bhp; 2 shafts
Speed, knots	19 (economical speed 12 kts)
Radius, miles	11 500 at 11 knots
Complement	150 peace;

Sole survivor of 14 "Bostwick" class destroyer escorts acquired from the United States in 1944-1952, was converted into an experimental vessel in 1956 and her armament landed, her pennant number subsequently being changed from F 703 to A 607. Her name was changed from *Somali* to *Arago* on 1 Apr 1968. Fitted with S band combined air and surface search radar.

COMMANDANT ROBERT GIRAUD
(ex-*Immelmann*) A 755 (ex-F 755)

Displacement, tons	1 000 standard; 1 380 full load
Length, feet (*metres*)	239 (*72.9*) pp; 256 (*78·0*) oa
Beam, feet (*metres*)	36 (*11·0*)
Draught, feet (*metres*)	12 (*3·7*)
Main engines	4 MAN diesels 8 800 bhp; 2 shafts
Speed, knots	20·5
Radius, miles	7 800 at 12 knots
Oil fuel (tons)	236

ARAGO (ex-*Somali*)   *1968, French Navy, Official*

Former dépanneur d'hydravions, ex-German aircraft tender. Built by Norderwerft, Hamburg. Launched in 1941. Completed in Dec 1941. Transferred by Great Britain in Aug 1946, with *Paul Goffeny*. Re-rated as Escorteur de Deuxième Classe early in 1953, as Aviso Escorteur on 11 Aug 1953, as Aviso in 1955, as *Gabarre* in 1963, and *Aviso Hydrograph* in 1969. Formerly used as patrol and escort vessel, support gunboat and carrier for commandos. The diesels are coupled two by two by hydraulic transmission on two shafts. Sister ship *Paul Goffeny* was officially deleted from the list in 1969. Of the *Avisos Hydrographes*, ex-frigates, *Amiral Mouchez* F 752, was condemned in Sep 1965, *Beautemps-Beaupré* A 752 (ex-F 751) and *La Pérouse* A 753 (ex-F 750) were officially deleted from the list in 1969.

COMMANDANT ROBERT GIRAUD   *1969, Official*

EXPERIMENTAL GUIDED MISSILE SHIP (ex-Transport)

ILE d'OLERON (ex-*München*, ex-*Mur*)

Displacement, tons	3 280 standard ; 7 500 full load
Length, feet (*metres*)	350 (*106·7*) pp ; 377·5 (*115·2*) oa
Beam, feet (*metres*)	50 (*15·2*)
Draught, feet (*metres*)	21·3 (*6·5*)
Main engines	MAN 6-cylinder diesels 3 500 bhp, 1 shaft
Speed, knots	14·5
Oil fuel (tons)	340
Radius, miles	7 200 at 12 knots
Complement	195 (15 officers, 180 men)

Launched in Germany in 1939. Taken as a war prize. Formerly rated as a transport. Converted into an experimental guided missiles ship in 1957-58 by Chantiers de Provence et l'Arsenal de Toulon. Commissioned as a test bed early in 1959. Equipped with stabilisers.

EXPERIMENTAL. When converted she was designed for experiments with two launchers for ship to air missiles, the medium range "Masurca" and the long range "Masalca", and one launcher for ship to shore missiles, the "Malaface". Latterly fitted with one launcher for target planes. Now fitted for the trials of MM 38.

ILE d'OLÉRON   1970, French Navy, Official

RADAR. The photograph shows the ship fitted with an L band early warning radar and an S band stacked beam air and surface 3 D radar. The missile system tracking radar operates in C band.

COMMAND SHIP. The command ship *Gustav Zede* (ex-*Saar*) A 641, former German submarine depot ship and latterly flagship of the 3rd Fast Escort Flotilla (Anti-Submarine Group) was officially deleted from the list in 1971.

ASSAULT LANDING SHIPS (Transports de chalands de debarquement)

ORAGE TCD 2   **OURAGAN** TCD 1

Displacement, tons	5 800 light ; 8 500 full load ; 15 000 when fully immersed
Length, feet (*metres*)	489 (*149·0*)
Beam, feet (*metres*)	70·5 (*21·5*)
Draught, feet (*metres*)	15 (*4·6*) ; 28·5 (*8·7*) max
Guns, surface	2—4·7 in (*120 mm*) mortars
Guns, AA	6—30 mm
Main engines	2 diesels ; 8 000 bhp ; 2 shafts
Speed, knots	17
Radius, miles	8 000 at 15 knots
Complement	341 (14 officers, 327 men)

Built at Brest Dockyard. *Ouragan* was laid down in June 1962, launched on 9 Nov 1963, completed for trials in 1964, and commissioned in Jan 1965. Bridge is on the starboard side. Fitted with a platform for three heavy helicopters. Able to carry EDICs loaded with eleven light tanks each, or 18 loaded LCMs, also 1 500 tons of material and equipment handled by two 35 tons cranes. Allocated to the Pacific Nuclear Experimental Centre. *Orage* was launched on 22 Apr 1967 and completed in Mar 1968.

OURAGAN   1970, courtesy Admiral M. Adam

ORAGE   1969, French Navy, Official

CORVETTES (rated as avisos)

2 NEW CONSTRUCTION

Displacement, tons	950 standard ; 1 200 full load
Length, feet (*metres*)	249·3 (*76·0*) oa
Beam, feet (*metres*)	33·8 (*10·3*) revised official figure
Draught, feet (*metres*)	9·8 (*3·0*)
Guns, AA	1—3·9 in (*100 mm*) ; 2—20 mm
A/S weapons	1 sextuple mortar (375 mm) ; 4 fixed torpedo throwers
Main engines	2 Pielstick diesels ; 2 shafts ; 11 000 bhp
Speed, knots	24 (revised official figure)
Radius, miles	4 500 at 15 knots
Complement	66 (4 officers, 62 men)

Small escorts of a new type. The first pair were ordered in 1971.

OURAGAN   1971, French Navy, Official

MINEHUNTERS (Chasseurs de Mines)

5 NEW CONSTRUCTION "CIRCE" CLASS

CALLIOPE	CERES	CIRCE	CLIO	CYBELE

Displacement, tons	460 standard; 495 normal; 510 full load
Dimensions, feet	152·6 × 29·2 × 8·0
Guns	1—20 mm
Main engines	Diesels; single axial screw; designed for 15 knots
Radius, miles	3 000 at 12 knots
Complement	50 (5 officers, 45 men)

A new design. Ordered in 1968. Built by Constructions Mecaniques de Normandie, Cherbourg. Active rudder on each side for working at slow speeds. *Circe* was launched on 15 Dec 1970.

CIRCE   *1971, French Navy, Official*

OCEAN MINESWEEPERS

14 US MSO (ex-AM) TYPE "BERNEVAL" CLASS

ALENCON (ex-*AM* 453	DOMPAIRE (ex-*AM* 454)
AUTUN (ex-*AM* 502)	GARIGLIANO (ex-*AM* 452)
BACCARAT (ex-*AM* 505)	MYTHO (ex-*AM* 475)
BERLAIMONT (ex-*AM* 500)	NARVIK (ex-*AM* 512)
BERNEVAL (ex-*AM* 450)	ORIGNY (ex-*AM* 501)
CANTHO (ex-*AM* 476)	OUISTREHAM (ex-*AM* 513)
COLMAR (ex-*AM* 514)	VINH LONG (ex-*AM* 477)

Displacement, tons	700 standard; 795 full load
Dimensions, feet	165 wl; 171 oa × 35 × 10·3
Guns	1—40 mm AA
Main engines	2 GM diesels; 2 shafts; 1 600 bhp = 13·5 knots
Radius, miles	3 000 at 10 knots
Complement	54

The USA transferred to France eight new AMs in 1953, and four in 1954. Three more transferred in 1956. *Bir Hacheim* transferred in Feb 1954, *Garigliano* in Apr 1954 and *Vinh Long* in 1955. *Origny* was launched on 25 Feb 1955. *Autun* on 6 May 1955, *Baccarat* on 6 Aug 1955 and *Berlaimont* on 7 Jan 1955. *Origny* is classified and fitted as an oceanographic research vessel but is Navy owned and manned. *Bir Hacheim* M 614 (ex-*AM* 451) was returned to the US Navy at Brest on 4 Sep 1970 and transferred to the Uruguayan Navy, being renamed *Maldonado*.

APPEARANCE. *Autun, Baccarat, Berlaimont, Colmar, Narvik, Origny* and *Ouistreham* have a taller tunnel.

PHOTOGRAPHS. A photograph of *Garigliano* appears in the 1955-56 edition, of *Alençon* in the 1956-57 to 1958-59 editions, of *Narvik* in the 1959-60 edition, of *Vinh Long* in the 1960-61 to 1963-64 editions, of *Colmar* in the 1962-63 to 1966-67 editions, of *Berneval* in the 1964-65 to 1968-69 editions, of *Berlaimont* in the 1967-68 to 1969-70 editions.

MYTHO (short funnel type)   *1969, French Navy, Official*

AUTUN (tall funnel type)   *1971, A. & J. Pavia*

COASTAL MINESWEEPERS (Dragueurs Côtiers)

27 BRITISH TYPE "SIRIUS" CLASS

ALDÉBARAN (27 June 53)	CAPELLA (6 Sep 55)	LYRE (3 May 56)
ALGOL (15 Apr 53)	CASSIOPÉE (16 Nov 53)	PEGASE (21 June 55)
ALTAIR (27 Mar 56)	CASTOR (19 Nov 53)	PERSÉE (23 May 55)
ANTARÈS (21 Jan 54)	CÉPHÉE (3 Jan 56)	PHÉNIX (23 May 55)
ARCTURUS (12 Mar 54)	CROIX DU SUD	RÉGULUS (18 Nov 52)
ARIES (13 Mar 56)	(13 June 56)	RIGEL (13 May 53)
BELLATRIX (21 July 55)	DÉNÉBOLA (12 July 56)	SAGITTAIRE (12 Jan 55)
BÉTELGEUSE (12 July 54)	ERIDAN (18 May 54)	SIRIUS (6 Oct 52)
CANOPUS (31 Dec 53)	ETOILE POLAIRE	VEGA (14 Jan 53)
	(5 Mar 57)	VERSEAU (26 Apr 56)

Displacement, tons	365 standard; 424 full load
Dimensions, feet	140 pp; 152 oa × 28 × 8·2
Guns	1—40 mm Bofors AA; 1—20 mm Oerlikon AA (several have 2—20 mm AA)
Main engines	SIGMA free piston generators and Alsthom or Rateau-Bretagne gas turbines or SEMT-Pielstick 16-cyl fast diesels; 2 shafts; 2 000 bhp = 15 knots (11·5 knots when sweeping)
Oil fuel (tons)	48
Radius, miles	3 000 at 15 knots
Complement	38

Of wooden and aluminium alloy construction. Launch dates above. Of same general characteristics as the British "Ton" class, but of different hull construction. Propelled by Alsthom or Rateau gas turbines with SIGMA free piston generators, except *Altair, Arcturus, Aries, Bételgeuse, Canopus, Capella, Céphée, Croix du Sud, Etoile Polaire, Lyre, Phénix* and *Verseau,* which have SEMT-Pielstick light diesels. Similar to ships built in Great Britain and Netherlands of which the plans were basically similar. The original design was developed In close collaboration with John I. Thornycroft & Co. Ltd, Southampton, and the Royal Navy. 16 vessels were built under the "off-shore" programme. *Altair, Arcturus* and *Croix de Sud* have been station-ships in the West Indies since 1960. D 25, D 26 and D 27 were allocated to Yugoslavia. *Fomalhaut, Orion, Pollux* and *Procyon* were returned to the USN in 1970, *Achernar Capricorne* and *Centaure* in 1971.

PHOTOGRAPHS. A photograph of *Régulus* appears in the 1957-58 to 1959-60 editions, of *Vega* in the 1954-55 to 1963-64 editions, of *Altair* in the 1964-65 to 1966-67 editions, of *Aldébaran* in the 1967-68 to 1970-71 editions.

ANTARES   *1971, courtesy Admiral M. Adam*

27 US MSC (Ex-AMS) TYPE. "ACACIA" CLASS

ACACIA (ex-*AMS* 69)	GLYCINE (ex-*AMS* 118)
ACANTHE (ex-*AMS* 70)	JACINTHE (ex-*AMS* 115) LAYER
AJONC (ex-*AMS* 71)	LAURIER (ex-*AMS* 86)
AZALÉE (ex-*AMS* 67)	LILAS (ex-*AMS* 93)
BEGONIA (ex-*AMS* 83)	LISERON (ex-*AMS* 98)
BLEUÊT (ex-*AMS* 116)	LOBELIA (ex-*AMS* 96)
CAMÉLIA (ex-*AMS* 68)	MAGNOLIA (ex-*AMS* 87)
CHRYSANTHEME (ex-*AMS* 113)	MARJOLAINE (ex-*Aconit*, ex-*AMS* 66)
COQUELICOT (ex-*AMS* 84)	MIMOSA (ex-*AMS* 99)
CYCLAMEN (ex-*AMS* 119)	MUGUET (ex-*AMS* 97)
EGLANTINE (ex-*AMS* 117)	PERVENCHE (ex-*AMS* 141)
GARDÉNIA (ex-*AMS* 114)	PIVOINE (ex-*AMS* 125)
GIROFLÉE (ex-*AMS* 85)	RESEDA (ex-*AMS* 126)
GLAIEUL (ex-*AMS* 120)	

Displacement, tons	370 standard; 405 full load
Dimensions, feet	136·2 pp; 141 oa × 26 × 8·3
Guns	2—20 mm AA
Main engines	2 GM diesels; 2 shafts; 1 200 bhp = 13 knots (8 sweeping)
Oil fuel, tons	40
Radius, miles	2 500 at 10 knots
Complement	38 (3 officers, 35 men)

The USA agreed in Sep 1952 to allocate to France in 1953, 36 new AMS (later re-designated MSC) under the Mutual Defence Assistance Programme, but only 30 were finally transferred to France in 1953-55. Three were returned to the USA after delivery to Saigon for Indo-China, and two of these were allocated to Japan (AMS 95 and 144). Three (AMS 139, 140, 143) were not delivered, having been allocated to Spain. Constructed throughout of wood or other materials with the lowest possible magnetic attraction to attain the greatest possible safety factor when sweeping for magnetic mines. All built in USA in 1951-54. All named after flowers. *Aconit* was renamed *Marjolaine* in 1967 (name *Aconit* assigned to new frigate). *Jacinthe* was converted into a minelayer on 1968. *Marguerite* (ex-*AMS* 94) was returned to the USN at Toulon in Nov 1969 and transferred to the Uraguayan Navy, renamed *Rio Negro*. *Pavot* and *Renocule* were returned to the USN on 24 Mar and transferred to the Turkish Navy.

PHOTOGRAPHS. A photograph of *Coquelicot* appears in the 1954-55 to 1959-60 editions, of *Pavot* in the 1965-66 to 1967-68 editions, of *Laurier* in the 1968-69 to 1970-71 editions. See photograph of *Pervenche* at the top of column 1, next page.

Coastal Minesweepers—continued

PERVENCHE (see previous page)   1971, Dr. Giorgio Arra

1 SPECIAL TYPE

MERCURE

Displacement, tons	333 light ; 362 normal ; 380 full load
Dimensions, feet	137·8 pp ; 145·5 oa × 27 × 8·5
Guns	2—20 mm AA
Main engines	2 Mercedes-Benz diesels ; 2 shafts ; Kamewa variable pitch propellers ; 4 000 bhp = 15 knots
Oil fuel (tons)	48
Radius, miles	3 000 at ·15 knots
Complement	48

Ordered in France from Mécaniques de Normandie (who have built six sister ships for the Federal German Navy) under the "off-shore" programme. Laid down in Jan 1955. Launched on 21 Dec 1957. Completed in Dec 1958. Somewhat different from the "Sirius" class and with the same method of construction as the United States-built "Acacia" class. Stated to be a very successful model.

MERCURE   1968, French Navy, Official

6 Ex-CANADIAN "BAY" TYPE "LA DUNKERQUOISE" CLASS

LA BAYONNAISE (ex-*Chignecto*)		**LA LORIENTAISE** (ex-*Miramachi*)	
LA DIEPPOISE (ex-*Chaleur*)		**LA MALOUINE** (ex-*Cowichan*)	
LA DUNKERQUOISE (ex-*Fundy*)		**LA PAIMPOLAISE** (ex-*Thunder*)	

Displacement, tons	390 standard ; 412 full load
Dimensions, feet	140 pp ; 152 oa · 28 · 8·7
Guns	1—40 mm AA
Main engines	General Motors diesels ; 2 shafts ; 2 400 bhp = 16 knots max
Oil fuel (tons)	52
Radius, miles	4 500 at 11 knots
Complement	43 (4 officers, 39 men)

La Bayonnaise (launched 12 May 1952) *La Malouine* (launched 12 Nov 1951) and *La Paimpolaise* (launched 17 July 1953) were tranferred to the French flag at Halifax on 1 Apr 1954, *La Dunkerquoise* (launched Apr 1953) on 30 Apr 1954, and *La Dieppoise* (launched 21 June 1952) and *La Lorientoise* (launched in 1953) on 10 Oct 1954. All similar to the "Bay" class in the Royal Canadian Navy. *La Bayonnaise* and *La Dunkerquoise* left Brest in Apr 1961 for the Pacific to relieve *Lotus* and *Tiare* in New Caledonia and Tahiti, respectively. *La Dieppoise* is at Djibouti, *La Malouine* is at Diego Suarez, and *La Lorientaise* and *La Paimpolaise* are in New Caledonia and Tahiti, respectively.

As these ships are used on "colonial" service they have been air conditioned. A photograph of *La Dunkerquoise* appears in the 1968-69 to 1970-71 editions.

LA DIEPPOISE   1971, French Navy, Official

PATROL VESSELS (*Escorteurs Cotiers*)

14 "LE FOUGUEUX" CLASS

L'ADROIT (6 Sep 1958)	L'ETOURDI (5 Feb 1958)
L'AGILE (26 June 1954)	LE FOUGUEUX (31 May 1954)
L'ALERTE (5 Oct 1957)	LE FRINGANT (6 Feb 1958)
L'ATTENTIF (10 July 1958)	LE FRONDEUR (26 Feb 1959)
L'ARDENT (17 July 1958)	LE HARDI (17 Sep 1958)
L'EFFRONTÉ (27 Jan 1959)	L'INTRÉPIDE (12 Dec 1958)
L'ENJOUE (5 Oct 1957)	L'OPINIATRE (4 May 1954)

Displacement, tons	325 standard ; 400 full load
Dimensions, feet	170 pp × 23 × 6·5
Guns	2—40 mm Bofors AA ; 2—20 mm AA
A/S weapons	1 hedgehog ; 4 DC mortars (and 2 DC racks) ; Sonar in *L'Agile*, *Le Fougueux*, *L'Opiniatre* ; others have a new 120 mm ASM mortar forward ; 2 DCT ; 1 DC rack
Tubes	*L'Intrépide* has a tube mounted on the stern
Main engines	4 SEMT-Pielstick light and fast diesel engines coupled 2 by 2 3 240 bhp = 18·7 knots (22 knots on trial)
Radius, miles	3 000 at 12 knots ; 2 000 at 15 knots
Complement	62 (4 officers, 58 men)

L'Agile, *Le Fougueux* and *L'Opiniatre* were built in France under a USA offshore order. Five more were built under the 1955 and six under the 1956 estimates. These have a different armament, slightly different appearance, and modified bridge. *L'Agile* is employed on fishery protection duties in the North Sea, English Channel, Bristol Channel, off Shetland and Orkney Islands and Norway.

PHOTOGRAPHS. A photograph of *L'Opiniatre* appears in the 1958-59 and 1959-60 editions, of *L'Adroit* in the 1960-61 to 1966-67 editions, of *Le Fougueux* in the 1967-68 to 1969-70 editions.

L'ENJOUE   1970, French Navy, Official

LA COMBATTANTE

Displacement, tons	182 standard ; 201 full load
Dimensions, feet	147·8 × 24·2 × 6·5
Guns	1—30 mm AA
Guided weapons	1 quadruple rocket launcher for SS 11 1 sextuple rocket launcher
Main engines	2 SEMT-Pielstick diesels ; 2 shafts ; variable pitch propellers 3 200 bhp = 23 knots
Radius, miles	2 000 at 12 knots
Complement	25

Patrouilleur garde-côte or light patrol vessel. Authorised under the 1960 Programme. Built by Construction Mécaniques de Normandie. Laid down in Apr 1962, launched on 20 June 1963, and completed on 1 Mar 1964. Of wooden and plastic laminated non-magnetic construction. Fitted for the trials of the MM 38 missile system (1971).

LA COMBATTANTE   1970, French Navy, Official

PATROL LAUNCHES (*Chasseurs de Sousmarins*)

1 Ex-US SC TYPE

M 691 (ex-*CH 101*, ex-*SC 524*)

Displacement, tons	110 standard ; 138 full load
Dimensions, feet	107·5 wl ; 110·6 oa × 18·8 × 6·5
Main engines	2 GM diesels ; 2 shafts ; 1 000 bhp = 15 knots

Of wooden construction. Launched in 1943. Acquired from the USN in 1944. Formerly rated as Submarine Chasers, but re-rated as patrol vessels in 1951. *P 690*, *691*, *695*, *696*, *697*, *711*, *713*, *714*, *715* were converted into inshore minesweepers in 1954, but were discarded as such in 1958-59. *P 706* was officially deleted from the list in 1969. For full list of disposals see 1967-68 and earlier editions

TRANSFERS
P 699 was transferred to the Ivory Coast Republic and re-named *Patience* and *P 700* was transferred to the Senegalian Republic and re-named *Senegal*.

1 FAIRMILE ML TYPE

OISEAU DES ILES P 78C

Displacement, tons	130
Dimensions, feet	111·5 × 18·4 × 4·3
Speed, knots	11·5

This former Fairmile motor launch was seized by the Customs Authority and allocated to the Navy for training frogmen.

MAINTENANCE SHIPS

5 LOGISTIC SUPPORT TYPE

GARONNE Repair Workshop (*Bâtiment de soutien logistique, version Atelier*)
LOIRE Minesweeper Support (*Bâtiment de soutien logistique, version Dragueurs*)
RANCE Damage Control (*Bâtiment de soutien logistique, version Sécurité*)
RHIN Electronic Service (*Bâtiment de soutien logistique, version Électronique*)
RHONE Submarine Depot (*Bâtiment de soutien logistique, version Sousmarins*)

Displacement, tons	2 075 standard ; 2 375 full load ; see notes
Dimensions, feet	3C0 × 43 × 12 (*Garonne* 333 × 45·2 × 12·7)
Guns	3—40 mm AA
Aircraft	2 Alouette helicopters
Landing craft	2 (LCP)
Main engines	2 SEMT-Pielstick diesels ; 1 shaft ; 3 300 bhp = 16 knots
Radius, miles	6 000 at 12 knots
Complement	71 (5 officers, 66 men) plus circa 100 technicians, except *Garonne* 221 (10 officers, 211 men)

All these maintenance and logistic support ships have the same basic characteristics, hull and machinery, differing only in their respective specialisation, except *Garonne* which has one more deck, larger workshops and a heavier displacement of 2 320 tons standard, as a repair ship for the Pacific Nuclear Experimental Station (CEP), and *Rance*, radiological security ship (radioactive decontamination) with extended bridge and different silhouette and hangar for three helicopters. All were built by Lorient

Name	No.	Programme	Laid down	Launched	Completed
Garonne	A 617	1963	Nov 1963	8 Aug 1964	1 Sep 1965
Loire	A 615	1962	July 1965	1 Oct 1966	10 Oct 1967
Rance	A 618	1963	Aug 1964	15 May 1965	5 Feb 1966
Rhin	A 621	1959	May 1961	17 Mar 1962	1 Mar 1964
Rhone	A 622	1960	Feb 1962	8 Dec 1962	1 Dec 1964

LOIRE   *1970, French Navy, Official*

RHIN   *1969, French Navy, Official*

RANCE   *1969, French Navy, Official*

RHONE   *1971, French Navy, Official*

GARONNE   *French Navy, Official*

4 CONVERTED LINERS

MAINE (ex-*El Mansour*) A 611

Displacement, tons	5 420 standard ; 6 000 full load
Measurement, tons	5 818 gross ; 1 320 deadweight
Dimensions, feet	399·2 × 53·8 × 18
Main engines	2 Parsons turbines ; 2 shafts ; 7 500 shp = 15 knots
Boilers	2 (2 landed)
Complement	115 (9 officers, 106 men)

A photograph of *Maine* appears in the 1965-66 edition. Near sister ship *Morvan* (ex-*Sidi Mabrouk*) A 613, 4 750 tons full load, built by J. S. White (launched on 22 Apr 1948) was officially deleted from the list in 1971. See photograph and full particulars in the 1969-70 and 1970-71 editions.

MEDOC (ex-*Sidi Ferruch*) A 612

Displacement, tons	4 430 standard ; 5 300 full load
Measurement, tons	3 988 gross
Dimensions, feet	372·2 × 49·2 × 23
Main engines	2 Rateau turbines ; 2 shafts ; 4 750 shp = 15 knots
Boilers	2
Complement	123 (8 officers, 115 men)

The above two passenger vessels designed and built for Algeria by F. C. Medit. Launched on 22 Oct 1932 *Maine*, Bretagne/Loire (launched on 14 May 1949) *Medoc*, were purchased in Sep 1963 and fitted out as barrack and accommodation ships for the maintenance of the Nuclear Establishment of Polynesia, the experimental base in the Pacific where they are manned by naval personnel.

MEDOC   *1969, French Navy, Official*

MAURIENNE (ex-M/S *Brazza*) A 637   **MOSELLE** (ex-*Foucauld*) A 608

Displacement, tons	8 700 standard ; 9 100 full load
Measurement, tons	9 065 gross ; 5 946 deadweight
Dimensions, feet	480 oa × 62 × 22·3
Main engines	2 Doxford diesels ; 2 shafts ; 8 800 bhp = 17·5 knots

Former motor passenger ships of the *Chargeurs Réunis* (West Africa Coast Service). Built by Swan, Hunter & Wigham Richardson Ltd, Wallsend-on-Tyne. Launched on 14 Oct and 17 July 1947. Completed in 1948. *Maurienne* was purchased in Nov 1964, converted at Brest in 1965 and admitted to active service on 8 Mar 1966 (left Brest the following day for the Pacific Nuclear Experimental Centre), helicopter landing platform aft. *Moselle* was converted in 1967 (no platform).

MAURIENNE   *9 Mar 1966, courtesy Admiral M. Adam*

RHIN helo lift (see Col. 1)   *1969, French Navy, Official*

SURVEY SHIPS (Annexes Hydrographiques)

1 NEW CONSTRUCTION

D'ENTRECASTEAUX A 757

Displacement, tons	2 200
Dimensions, feet	295·2 × 42·7 × 12·8
Main engines	2 diesel-electric; 1 000 Kw; 2 controllable pitch propellers; Speed—15 knots
Auxiliary engines	2 Schottel orientable and retractable
Complement	125 (8 officers, 79 men + 38 scientists)

This ship was specially designed for oceanographic surveys. She will be completed in 1971.

D'ENTRECASTEAUX　　　　　　1971, Courtesy Admiral M. Adam

2 TROPICAL TYPE

ASTROLABE A 780 (ex-P 680)　　　　**BOUSSOLE** A 781 (ex-P 681)

Displacement, tons	250 standard; 440 full load
Dimensions, feet	137·8 × 27 × 8·2
Guns	1—40 mm AA; 2 MG
Main engines	2 Baudouin DV.8 diesels. 1 shaft; controllable pitch propeller; 800 bhp = 13 knots max
Radius, miles	4 000
Complement	34 (3 officers, 31 men)

Authorised under the 1961 Programme. Specially designed for the Hydrographic Service for surveys in tropical waters. Built by Chantiers de la Seine Maritime, Le Trait. Laid down in 1962. launched on 27 May and 11 Apr 1963 respectively, and commissioned in 1964.

ASTROLABE　　　　　　1970, French Navy, Official

AIRCRAFT TENDER TYPE. *Paul Goffeny* was officially deleted from the list in 1969, but her sister ship *Commandant Robert Giraud* was reinstated in her place as a survey ship. see earlier page.

1 RESEARCH TYPE

LA RECHERCHE (ex-*Guyane*) A 758 (ex-P 660)

Displacement, tons	780 standard; 1 047 full load
Measurement, tons	965 gross
Dimensions, feet	203·5 pp; 221·5 oa × 34·2 × 13
Main engines	1 Werkspoor diesel; 1 535 bhp = 13·5 knots
Complement	72 (5 officers and 67 men)

Former passenger motor vessel built by Chantiers Zeigler at Dunkirk. Launched on 17 Sep 1951. Purchased in 1960 and converted by Cherbourg Dockyard into a surveying ship. Commissioned into the French Navy in Mar 1961 and her name changed from *Guyane* to *La Recherche*. To improve stability she was fitted with bulges.

LA RECHERCHE　　　　　　1970, French Navy, Official

Survey Ships—continued

2 CONVERTED TRAWLER TYPE

ESPERANCE (ex-*Jacques Coeur*) A 756　　**ESTAFETTE** (ex-*Jacques Cartier*)

Displacement, tons	800 standard; 1 400 full load
Dimensions, feet	196·1 × 32·2 × 14·8
Main engines	MAN diesels; 1 850 bhp = 15 knots
Complement	41 (5 officers, 36 men)

Former trawlers built in 1962 and purchased in 1968-69 and adapted as survey ships.

1 EXPERIMENTAL TYPE

LA COQUILLE (ex-*Atlantic Dolphin*) A 678

Displacement, tons	394 standard; 555 full load
Dimensions, feet	121·3 × 26·2 × 14·1
Main engines	Paxman diesel-electric; 1 shaft; speed 12 knots
Complement	23 (2 officers, 21 men)

Former British trawler. Built by J. S. Doig, Grimsby, in 1963. Purchased in May 1965 and converted by Cherbourg Dockyard as a survey and scientific research ship for the Pacific Nuclear Experimental Centre.

OCTANT　　　　　　1970. Official

2 TENDER TYPE

ALIDADE (ex-*Evelyne Marie*) P 682　　**OCTANT** (ex-*Michel Marie*) P 683

Displacement, tons	110 standard; 120 full load
Dimensions, feet	Length 78
Main engines	2 diesels; 1 shaft; controllable pitch; 250 bhp = 9 knots
Complement	11 men

Two small fishing trawlers purchased by the Navy and converted into survey craft of a new type by the Constructions Mécaniques de Normandie at Cherbourg as tenders to *La Recherche*. Wooden hull and steel upperworks. *Alidade* floated up after conversion on 15 Nov 1962 and *Octant* on 20 Dec 1962. Commissioned in 1963.

LARGER SURVEY SHIPS. Ex-frigates *Beautemps-Beaupré*, A 752 (ex-751), and *La Pérouse*, A 753 (ex-F 750) used as survey ships, were deleted from the list in 1969. The old frigate type survey ship *Amiral Mouchez*, F 752, was discarded in 1965.

ALIDADE　　　　　　1969, Official

AMMUNITION SHIP

1 NEW CONSTRUCTION

ACHERON A 620

Displacement, tons	6 485 standard; 10 250 full load
Dimensions, feet	482·2 × 70·5 × 21·3
Main engines	2 SEMT-Pielstick diesels; 1 shaft; 11 500 bhp = 18 knots

Provided for under the 1961 Programme. Under construction at Brest Dockyard. To be launched in 1970 and completed in 1972.

TORPEDO RECOVERY CRAFT

PELICAN (ex-*Kerfany*)　　　　　　**PETREL** (ex-*Cap Lopez*)

Measurement, tons	395 (*Pelican*); 263 (*Petrel*)

Purchased and converted from tuna clippers into torpedo recovery craft.

INSHORE MINESWEEPERS

(*Dragueurs de Rade et d'Estuaire*)

15 Ex-BRITISH "HAM" CLASS

ARMOISE (ex-*Wexham*)	M 772	JASMIN (ex-*Stedham*)	M 776
AUBEPINE (ex-*Rendlesham*)	M 781	JONQUILLE (ex-*Sulham*)	M 787
CAPUCINE (ex-*Petersham*)	M 782	MYOSOTIS (ex-*Ripplingham*)	M 788
DAHLIA (ex-*Whippingham*)	M 786	OEILLET (ex-*Isham*)	M 774
GERANIUM (ex-*Tibenham*)	M 784	PAQUERETTE (ex-*Kingham*)	M 775
HIBISCUS (ex-*Sparham*)	M 785	PETUNIA (ex-*Pineham*)	M 789
HORTENSIA (ex-*Mileham*)	M 783	TULIPE (ex-*Frettenham*)	M 771
		VIOLETTE (ex-*Mersham*)	M 773

Displacement, tons	120 standard; 140 full load
Dimensions, feet	100 pp; 106·5 oa × 21·2 × 5·5
Guns	1—40 mm Bofors AA or 1—20 mm Oerlikon AA forward
Main engines	2 Paxman diesels; 550 bhp = 14 knots (9 knots when sweeping)
Oil fuel (tons)	15
Complement	12 (2 officers, 10 men)

Former British inshore minesweepers of the "Ham" class transferred to France under the US "off-shore" procurement programme. The first, M 771, was delivered in Dec 1954, and the last, M 789, was handed over at Hythe on 10 Nov 1955.

ARMOISE   *1969, courtesy Dr. Giorgio Arra*

VIOLETTE   *M. Henri Le Masson*

PETUNIA   *1970, French Navy, Official*

SEAWARD PATROL CRAFT

4 VC Type (*Vedettes de Surveillance Côtière*

VC 1 P 751		**VC 2** P 752		**VC 3** P 753	**VC 10** P 760

Displacement, tons	75 standard; 82 full load
Dimensions, feet	104·2 × 15·5 × 5·5
Guns	2—20 mm AA
Main engines	2 Mercedes-Benz diesels; 2 shafts; 2 700 bhp = 28 knots
Radius, miles	1 500 at 15 knots
Complement	15

Seaward defence motor launches of new type. All completed in 1958 and 1959. Built by the Construction Mécaniques de Normandie, Cherbourg (VC 3 and 10), and Lürrsens in Germany (VC 1 and 2). A photograph of VC 3 appears in the 1967-68 and 1968-69 editions.

VC 11 (P 761) was transferred to the Tunisian Navy on 22 Sep 1959; VC 12 (P 762) to the Royal Moroccan Navy on 15 Nov 1960 and renamed *Es Sabiq*; VC 4 (P 754) to the Republic of the Congo on 16 Nov 1962; VC 5 (P 755) to Senegal on 19 Jan 1963; VC 9 (P 759) to Cote d'Ivoire (Ivory Coast) in 1963; VC 8 (P 758) to Madagascar in 1963 and renamed *Mailaka*; VC 6 (P 756) to Cameroon on 7 Mar 1964, VC 7 (P 757) to Mauritania in 1966.

VC 10   *1971, Dr. Giorgio Arra*

VC 2   *1968*

PATROL BOATS (*Ex-Flotilla du Rhin*)

P 9785   P 9786

Displacement, tons	45
Dimensions, feet	79·3 × 14·8 × 4·2
Guns	8—0·5 MG (four twin mountings)
Main engines	2 Daimler-Benz diesels; 2 shafts; 1 000 bhp = 18 knots

Built by Burmeister-Brême (P 9785) and Bodenwerft-Kressbronn. Completed in 1954. Sister boats P 9783, P 9784, P 9787 and P 9788 were officially deleted from the list in 1969.

The auxiliary patrol launch *Rambervillers* was deleted from the list in 1963. She was a war prize with the *Ormont* which was retired from service in Feb 1958. The former Rhine Flotilla support ships *Hoche*, L 981, *Kleber*, L 982, and *Marceau*, L 980, were officially deleted from the list in 1965. The former Rhine Flotilla patrol boats P 9781 and P 9782 (35 tons, duralumin hull), P 9796 (ex-41), P 9787 (ex-42) and P 9798 (ex-43), all 23 tons, P 9740, P 9741, P 9742 and P 9743 (12 tons, peralumin hull), P 9794 (10 tons, hydrofoil), and P 9790 and P9791 (2 tons, fixed foils) were also officially deleted from the list in 1965, and P 9792 and P 9793 (6 tons, fixed foils) in 1966. The patrol boats *Enclume* A 790, old German LCM, and *Amiral Exelmans* (ex-*Germania*), A 73, ex-river passenger boat used for training pilots, were officially deleted from the list in 1969.

TRAINING SHIPS (*Voiliers-École*)

LA BELLE-POULE A 650	**L'ÉTOILE** A 649

Displacement, tons	227
Dimensions, feet	128 oa × 23·7 × 11·8
Main engines	Sulzer diesel; 120 bhp = 6 knots

Auxiliary sail vessels. Built by Chantiers de Normandie (Fécamp) in 1932. Accommodation for 3 officers, 30 cadets, 5 petty officers, 12 men. Attached to Navy School.

LA GRANDE HERMINE (ex-*Menestral*) A 753

Ex-fishing boat built in 1936. Purchased in 1963 in replacement for *Dolphin* (ex-*Simone Marcelle*) as the School of Manoeuvre Training ship.

MUTIN A 652

A small coastal tender attached to l'École de pilotage (the School of Pilotage).

TRANSPORTS

ANJOU   *1970, French Navy, Official*

ANJOU (ex-*Leoville*) A 645   **BERRY** (ex-M/S *Médoc*) A 644

Displacement, tons	2 700
Measurement, tons	1 203 gross; 1 552 deadweight
Dimensions, feet	284·5 oa × 38 × 15
Main engines	2 MWM diesels coupled on one shaft; 2 400 bhp = 15 knots

Built by Roland Werft Bremen. Launched on 10 Sep and 10 May 1958, respectively. Purchased in Jan 1966 and Oct 1964 from Cie. Worms for the Pacific experimental station, renamed in 1966 and 1964 and refitted in 1966 and 1965. Classed as refrigerated transports. For CEP (Centre Experimental Pacific).

BERRY   *1969. French Navy. Official*

AUNIS (ex-*Regina Pacis*) A 643

Displacement, tons	2 700 full load
Measurement, tons	1 250 gross
Dimensions, feet	284·5 × 31 × 15
Main engines	2 4-str 8-cyl oil geared to 1 shaft; 2 000 bhp = 16·6 knots

Built by Roland Werft, Bremen. Launched on 3 July 1956. Purchased in Nov 1966 from Seatto, Ambrosino & Pugliese for Pacific Experimental Station.

LUTIN (ex-*George Clemenceau*)

Displacement, tons	68
Main engines	400 hp = 10 knots

Purchased in 1965. Ex-vedette. Detection school, Toulon.

SSBN TENDER. A 1 200-ton service lighter of 1 000 hp for nuclear fuel elements of SSBNs was launched on 26 Oct 1967 for delivery in May 1968.

VERDON (ex-*Josta*) A 634

Displacement, tons	6 500
Measurement, tons	3 100 gross; 4 275 deadweight
Dimensions, feet	344·8 × 48·8 × 20
Main engines	1 B & W 5-cyl diesel; 1 shaft

Former Norwegian motor ship. Built in 1952. Purchased in June 1964 by the Army white and light products carrier service but manned and commissioned by the Navy for CEP.

ARIEL Y 604   **KORRIGAN** Y 661

Displacement, tons	225 full load
Dimensions, feet	132·8 × 24·5 × 10·8
Main engines	MGO diesels; 2 shafts; 1 640 bhp = 16 knots

Ariel was laid down in Dec 1963, launched on 27 Apr 1964 and delivered in Dec 1964 by Villeneuve (La Garonne). *Korrigan* was launched on 6 Mar 1964.

SYLPHE Y 710

Displacement, tons	171 standard; 189 full load
Dimensions, feet	126·5 × 22·7 × 8·2
Main engines	MGO diesel; 1 shaft; 600 bhp = 12 knots

Small transports for personnel, built by Chantiers Franco-Belge in 1959-60 (*Sylphe*) and 1963-64 (*Ariel* and *Korrigan*).

SAINTONGE (ex-*Santa Maria*) A 733

Measurement, tons	294 gross; 500 deadweight
Dimensions, feet	177 × 28 × 10·5
Main engines	1 diesel; 1 shaft; 520 bhp = 9 knots

Built by Chantiers Duchesne et Bossière, Le Havre, for a Norwegian owner under the name of *Sven Germa*. Launched on 12 July 1956. Purchased in Apr 1965 from the firm of H. Beal & Co, Fort de France for the Pacific Nuclear Experimental Centre. The CEP support transports Guyenne (ex-*Douce France*, ex-*Sunfarer*) A 735 and Tarn (ex-*Orgeval*, ex-*Colomb Bechar*, ex-*Maria Laetitia*) A 771 were officially deleted from the list (*Tarn* sunk as target ship off Tahiti on 18 June 1970).

Transports—*continued*

FALLERON (ex-German *Welle*) A 614

Displacement, tons	210 standard; 429 full load
Dimensions, feet	128·0 × 22·0 × 7·8
Main engines	1 Sulzer diesel; 280 bhp = 8 knots

Cap Ferrat was stricken in 1960. *Ter* (ex-German *Heinrich*) was condemned in 1964. *Moléne* (ex-German B 262, ex-V 620, ex-*Köln*) was officially deleted from the list in Aug 1963, and *Gapeau* (ex-German B 264, ex-V 625, ex-*Johan Shultz*) in 1969.

MÉLUSINE Y 736   **MERLIN** Y 735

Displacement, tons	170
Dimensions, feet	103·3 × 23·2 × 7·9
Main engines	MGO diesels; 2 shafts; 960 bhp = 11 knots

Small transports for 400 personnel built in 1966 by Chantiers Navals Franco-Belges at Chalon sur Saône. Both laid down in Dec 1966 and accepted on 1 June 1968. *Méluisne* was launched on 23 Dec 1967 and *Merlin* on 8 Nov 1967. Their home port is Toulon.

TRÉBÉRON (ex-*B* 254) Y 712

Displacement, tons	120 standard; 140 full load
Dimensions, feet	82·0 × 19·7 × 9·5
Main engines	Diesel; 1 shaft; 120 bhp = 8·5 knots

Former German danlayer used as small personnel transport for local port service.

EXPERIMENTAL SHIPS
(*Bâtiments-Réceptacle d'Engines d'Experimentation*)

HENRI POINCARE (ex-*Maina Marasso*) A 603

Displacement, tons	20 000 full load
Measurement, tons	12 835 gross
Dimensions, feet	565 × 74 × 31
Main engines	1 double reduction turbine; 1 shaft; speed = 15 knots
Boilers	2 high pressure water tube

Built by Cantieri Riuniti de Adriatico, Monfalcone. Launched in Oct 1960. Former Italian tanker. Purchased in Sep 1964. Arrived in Brest dockyard on 1 Oct 1964 to undergo conversion into a radar picket ship and guidance vessel for the experimental guided missile station in the Landes (SW France). The conversion was completed in March 1968. Named after the mathematician and scientist.

HENRI POINCARE   *1969, French Navy, Official*

TRITON A 646

Displacement, tons	1 300 standard; 1 500 full load
Dimensions, feet	223·1 × 39·4 × 11·8
Main engines	Diesels 2 Voith Schneider = 13 knots
Radius, miles	4 000 at 13 knots
Complement	50 (4 officers, 29 men + 17 scientists)

Under sea recovery and trials ship to replace *Élie Monnier*. To be equipped with a helicopter. Launched at Lorient on 7 Mar 1970 and completed by 1971.

TRITON   *1971, French Navy, Official*

PORT DEPOT SHIPS

Former warships, now obsolete, are classed as port depot ships:—
There are the heavy cruiser *Ocean* (ex-*Suffren*) and the light cruiser *Montcalm* at Toulon, used as barracks. Also the flotilla leaders (ex-light cruisers) *Chateaurenault* and *Guichen*, and a number of other ships including *Voltigeur* and *Gustav Zede* (ex-*Saar*) former command ship and submarine depot ship.

LANDING SHIPS

BIDASSOA   1970, Skyfotos

TRIEUX   1970, French Navy, Official

ARGENS BDC 2	BIDASSOA BDC 5	DIVES BDC 4
	BLAVET BDC 3	TRIEUX BDC 1

Displacement, tons	1 400 standard; 1 765 normal; 4 000 full load
Dimensions, feet	328 oa × 50 × 14
Guns	2—40 mm AA; 2—40 mm AA (Bidassoa, Blavet, Dives, 1—4·7 in mortar); 3—40 mm AA
Main engines	SEMT-Pielstick diesels; 2 shafts; 2 000 bhp = 11 knots
Radius, miles	18 500 at 10 knots
Complement	85 (6 officers and 79 men). Plus 170 troops (normal)

Built by Chantiers Seine Maritime (Bidassoa, Dives) and Chantiers de Bretagne, Nantes (others). Launched on 7 Apr 1959, 30 Dec 1960, 15 Jan 1960, 29 June 1960 and 6 Dec 1958, respectively. All commissioned in 1960-61. Can carry: 4 LCVP's, 1 800 tons of freight, 335 (up to 870 if required) troops (329 in bunks, 552 in hammocks). Blavet and Trieux are fitted with a helicopter platform. A photograph of Dives appears in the 1967-68 to 1970-71 editions.

ARGENS   1971, Dr. Giorgio Arra

The former US tank landing ships Chéliff (ex-US LST 874) and Odet (ex-US LST 815) were officially deleted from the list in 1970 and 1969, respectively.

LANDING SHIP DOCK. The dock landing ship Foudre (ex-Greek Okeanos, ex-British Oceanway, ex-US LSD 12), A 646, was officially deleted from the list in 1969.

LANDING CRAFT

11 EDIC (ENGINS DE DEBARQUEMENT INFANTERIE CHARS)

L 9091 (7 Jan 1968)	L 9094 (24 July 1958)	L 9071 (30 Jan 1968)
L 9092 (21 Feb 1958)	L 9095 (11 Apr 1958)	L 9072 (1968)
L 9093 (17 Apr 1958)	L 9096 (11 Oct 1958)	L 9073 (1968)
	L 9070 (30 Oct 1967)	L 9074 (1970)

Displacement, tons	292 standard; 642 full load
Dimensions, feet	193·5 × 39·2 × 4·5
Guns	2—20 mm AA
Main engines	MGO diesels; 2 shafts; 1 000 bhp = 8 knots
Complement	16 (1 officer, and 15 men)

9091, 9094, 9070 were built by C. N. Franco Belges, 9095, 9096 by Toulon Dockyard, 9071 by La Perrière. Launch dates above.

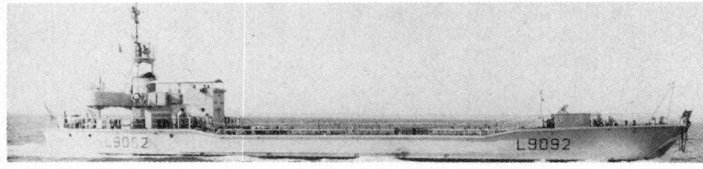

L 9092   1970, French Navy, Official

4 EDA (Engins de Debarquement Ateliers)

Same hull and engine characteristics as the EDIC type, but equipped as repair ships. Built in 1964 and 1965. No names allocated.

Landing Craft—continued

ISSOLE L 9097

Displacement, tons	600 full load
Dimensions, feet	160·8 × 23 × 7·2
Main engines	2 diesels; 1 000 bhp = 12 knots

Built at Toulon in 1957-58. Coaster with bow doors and ramp.

ISSOLE   1969, courtesy Godfrey H. Walker, Esq.

LCT 9099

Former British tank landing craft. Fitted as a workshop in 1964. LCT 9062, LCT 9063 (ex-Alkyon), LCT 9064 (ex-Salvor), LCT 9098 deleted from list in 1969.

LCT 9061 (ex-HMS Buttress, LCT(8) 4099)

Former British tank landing craft purchased in July 1965, see LCT(8)s, UK section.

L 9081 and L 9082 are bâtiments-annexe atelier (B A A), L 9083 is bâtiment-annexe-électronique (B A E), L 9084 is bâtiment-annexe-magasin électrique (B A M E).

DIVING TENDERS
(Bâtiment de Récherches Sous Marines)

INGENIERU ÉLIE MONNIER A 647 (ex-German trawler Albatross)

Displacement, tons	320 standard; 350 full load
Dimensions, feet	111·5 × 24 × 10·2
Main engines	Diesels; 1 shaft; 600 bhp = 12·5 knots
Radius, miles	1 500 at 12 knots
Complement	19 (1 officer, 18 men)

Built by D. W. Kremer Schiffwert Elmshom in 1944. Fitted for ocean research.

INGENIUR ELIE MONNIER   1971, Dr. Giorgio Arra

BELOUGA A 724 (ex-Cote d'Argent)

Tuna clipper built 1958, purchased in 1966 for conversion into a diving tender.

WATER CARRIERS

LIAMONE (ex-Arrosoir) A750

Displacement, tons	450 light; 1 369 full load
Dimensions, feet	184 × 28·9 × 13·8
Main engines	Sulzer diesels; 1 000 bhp = 11·5 knots

Rated as regional supply ship. Crew 27. Renamed Liamone in Mar 1954. Photograph in 1957-58 edition. Of two sister ships Giboulée was officially deleted from the list in 1969 and Hanap in 1971.

RUMMEL A 635   SAHEL A 638

Displacement, tons	630 light; 1 450 full load
Measurement, tons	650 deadweight
Dimensions, feet	176·2 × 29·5 × 14·5
Guns	2—20 mm AA
Main engines	2 diesels; 700 bhp = 12 knots

Sahel was completed in Aug 1951, Rummel in 1952 by Chantiers Naval de Caen. Photograph of Sahel in 1957-58 and earlier editions.

OASIS A 751

Displacement, tons	335 standard; 683 full load
Displacement, feet	164·8 × 27 × 9
Guns	2—20 mm AA
Main engines	Triple expansion; 1 shaft; 800 ihp = 10 knots

Built by A. C. Bretagne. In reserve. Sister Torrent was scrapped in 1964.

CATARACTE

Small water carrier of 330 tons. Cascade, Durance and Fraiche were scrapped in 1957, Aube in 1958, Ardèche in 1960, Casamance and Zöghouan in 1963, Aiguade in 1964, Benzene in 1967, Bruine in 1969, Averse, Deluge, Fontaine, Formene, Mirage and Ondee in 1970.

BOOM DEFENCE VESSELS

LA FIDÈLE A 751   **LA PERSÉVÉRANTE** A 750   **LA PRUDENTE** A 749

Displacement, tons	446 standard; 626 full load
Dimensions, feet	142·8 × 32·8 × 9·2
Main engines	2 Badouin diesels; 1 shaft; 620 bhp = 10 knots
Radius, miles	4 000 at 10 knots
Complement	30 (1 officer, 29 men)

Net layers and tenders built by Atel. Ch. La Manche, Dieppe, (*La Fidéle* and *La Prudente*) and Atel. Ch. La Rochelle (*La Persévérante*). Launched on 13 May 1968 (*La Fidéle*), 14 May 1968 (*La Persévérante*) and 26 Aug 1968 (*La Prudente*). Diesel-electric drive, 440 kW.

LA PRUDENTE   1970, French Navy, Official

5 "GRILLON" CLASS

CIGALE (ex-*AN* 98) A 760   **FOURMI** (ex-*AN* 97) A 762
CRIQUET (ex-*AN* 96) A 761   **GRILLON** (ex-*AN* 95) A 763
                               SCARABÉE (ex-*AN* 94) A 764

Displacement, tons	770 standard; 850 full load
Dimensions, feet	151·9 oa × 33·5 × 10·5
Guns	1—40 mm Bofors AA; 4—20 mm AA
Main engines	2, 4-stroke diesels, electric drive, 1 shaft; 1 600 bhp = 12 knots
Complement	45

US type off-shore orders. Sister ship *G 6* was allocated to Spain. *Criquet* was launched on 3 June 1954, *Cigale* on 23 Sep 1954, *Fourmi* on 6 July 1954, *Grillon* on 18 Feb 1954 and *Scarabée* on 21 Nov 1953. Rated as *Garbarres* (*Mouilleur de Filets*). A photograph of *Criquet* appears in the 1957-58 to 1964-65 editions, and of *Scarabée* in the 1968-69 to 1970-71 editions.

CIGALE   1971, French Navy, Official

5 Ex-US-AN TYPE NETLAYERS

ARAIGNÉE (ex-*Hackberry*, ex-*Maple*, AN 727)	A 727
LOCUSTE (ex-*Locust*, AN 765)	A 765
LUCIOLE (ex-*Sandalwood*, AN 32)	A 777
SCORPION (ex-*Yew*, AN 37)	A 728
TARENTULE (ex-*Pepperwood*, ex-*Walnut*, AN 729)	A 729

Launched on 6 Mar 1941, 1 Feb 1941, 6 Mar 1941, 25 Sep 1941 and 25 Aug 1941, respectively. *Locuste* was purchased in 1966 and *Luciole* in 1967. The three others were transferred in 1944.

ARAIGNÉE   1970, French Navy, Official

Boom Defence Vessels—*continued*

MARCEL LE BIHAN (ex-German *Greif*) A 759

Displacement, tons	800 standard; 1 000 full load
Dimensions, feet	236·2 × 34·8 × 10·5 max
Guns	4—20 mm AA
Main engines	2 GM diesels; 2 shafts, 4 400 bhp = 16 knots
Radius, miles	2 000 at 13 knots

Former German aircraft tender. Built by Lubecker Fleudewerke. Launched in 1936. Completed in 1937. Transferred by USA in Feb 1948. Re-rated Escorteur de Deuxième Classe early 1953, Aviso Escorteur 11 Aug 1953, Aviso 1955 and Gabarre 1 Nov 1959, 4·1 in gun and 2—40 mm removed. Tender for bathysphere *Archimede*.

Commandant Robert Giraud (ex-German *Immelmann*) A 755 (see earlier page,) former German aircraft tender, escort vessel, and boom defence vessel, successively, was reinstated as a survey ship in 1969 in place of her sister ship *Paul Goffeny*.

MARCEL LE BIHAN   1971, Dr. Giorgio Arra

PATIENTE A 737   **PERSISTANTE** A 731

Patiente 305 tons, 500 hp = 7 knots. *Persistante* 350 tons, 500 hp = 8 knots. *Girafe* and *Persévérante* were scrapped in 1957. *Fidéle* in 1958, *Puissant* in 1960, *Agissante* in 1961, *Victorieuse* in 1964.

1 Ex-BRITISH "NET" CLASS

LA DECOUVERTE (ex-*Amalthee*, ex-*Plantagenet*, ex-*Barwood*)

Displacement, tons	605 standard; 790 full load
Dimensions, feet	159·7 × 30·7 × 13
Main engines	Triple expansion; 850 ihp = 10 knots
Boilers	Cylindrical

Formerly the British boom defence vessel HMS *Plantagenet* (ex-*Barwood*) built by Lobnitz & Co Ltd, Renfrew and launched on 23 Feb 1939. She became the commercial oil research ship *Amalthee* under the French flag in 1960. She was purchased for the French Navy in 1969 and converted as a survey ship.

LA DECOUVERTE   1970, courtesy Admiral M. Adam

OILERS (*Transports Petroliers*)

LA CHARENTE (ex-*Beaufort*) A 626

Displacement, tons	7 084 light; 26 000 full load
Measurement, tons	12 373 gross; 18 800 deadweight
Dimensions, feet	587·2 × 72 × 30·3
Main engines	1 General Electric geared turbine
Boilers	2

Former Norwegian tanker built by Kaldnes Mek. Verksted Tönsberg, in 1957. Purchased by the French Navy in May 1965 and adapted for the Pacific Experimental Station.

LA CHARENTE   1969, courtesy Admiral M. Adam

Oilers—*continued*

ISERE (ex-*La Mayenne*, ex-*Caltex Strasbourg*) A 675

Displacement, tons	10 172 light
Measurement, tons	18 000 deadweight
Dimensions, feet	559 × 71·2 × 30·3
Main engines	1 single geared Parsons turbine; 8 260 shp = 16 knots
Boilers	2

Built by Seine Maritime. Launched on 22 June 1959. Former French tanker. Purchased late in 1964 for the Pacific Nuclear Experimental Centre.

LAC CHAMBON (ex-*Anticline*) A 629   **LAC TONLÉ-SAP** (ex-*Pumper*) A 630
LAC TCHAD (ex-*Syncline*) A 631

Displacement, tons	800 light 2 670 full load
Dimensions, feet	235 × 37 × 15·8
Guns	3—20 mm AA
Main engines	2 Fairbanks-Morse diesels; 1 150 bhp = 11 knots

Ex-US oil barges. Acquired in Dec 1944 and Mar 1945. *Lac Noir* was scrapped in 1951 and *Lac Pavin* in 1953. A photograph of *Lac Tchad* appears in the 1968-69 to 1970-71 editions.

LAC TONLE SAP   *1971, French Navy, Official*

LA SAÖNE A 628   **LA SEINE** A 627

Displacement, tons	7 350 light; 23 800 full load
Measurement, tons	16 870 deadweight
Dimensions, feet	525 × 72·5 × 33
Main engines	Parsons geared turbines; 2 shafts; 15 800 shp = 17 knots
Boilers	3 Penhoët

Ordered as fleet tankers. Completed as merchant tankers after the second World War. Returned to the French Navy from charter company in Sep 1953. *La Seine* was fitted as a fleet replenishment ship in 1961, *La Saöne* in 1962. Now rated as *Petroliers Ravitailleurs d'Escadre*. They carry 11 500 tons of fuel, 300 tons of food and have 75 000 tanks of wine.

LA SEINE   *1970, French Navy, Official*

LA SAÖNE   *1971, courtesy Godfrey H. Walker, Esq.*

ABER-WRAC'H (ex-*CA 1*) A 619

Displacement, tons	1 380 standard; 3 400 full load
Dimensions, feet	284 oa × 40 × 15·8
Guns	1—40 mm AA
Main engines	1 diesel; controllable pitch propeller; 2 000 bhp = 12 knots

Built at Cherbourg. Authorised in 1956. Ordered in 1959. Laid down in 1961. The after part with engine room was launched on 24 Apr 1963. The fore part was built on the vacated slip, launched and welded to the after part. Complete hull floated up on 21 Nov 1963 Commissioned in 1964.

ABER WRACH   *1970, French Navy, Official*

FLEET TUGS

ACTIF	A 686	**HERCULE**	A 667	**ROBUSTE**	A 685
COURAGEUX	A 706	**LABORIEUX**	A 687	**TRAVAILLEUR**	A 692
		LUTTEUR	A 673	**VALEUREUX**	A 688

Displacement, tons	230
Dimensions, feet	92 × 26 × 13
Main engines	1 MGO diesel; 1 050 bhp = 11 knots
Radius, miles	2 400 nautical
Complement	15

Courageux, Hercule, Robuste and *Valeureux* were completed in 1960 and the other four in 1962-63 at Le Havre, F. Ch. de la Mediterranee for service at Cherbourg (*Lutteur*), Toulon (*Actif, Robuste* and *Travailleur*) and Brest (*Hercule, Laborieux* and *Valeureux*).

HIPPOPOTAME (ex-*Utrecht*) A 660

Displacement, tons	640
Measurement, tons	524 gross
Main engines	Diesel-electric; 1 850 shp

Former Netherlands high sea tug. Built in 1943. Purchased by the French Navy in Jan 1964 to be used at the Experimental Base in the Pacific. Admitted to active service on 5 Mar 1964.

BÉLIER A 719   **PACHYDERME** A 718

Displacement, tons	900 standard; 1 185 and 1 115 full load, respectively
Main engines	2 000 ihp = 12 knots
Oil fuel (tons)	180
Radius, miles	3 000

A photograph of *Pachyderme* appears in the 1957-58 edition.

BUFFLE A 700

Displacement, tons	900 standard; 1 180 full load
Dimensions, feet	167·5 × 33 × 10
Main engines	2 sets triple expansion; 2 000 ihp = 12 knots
Complement	32

Launched on 4 May 1939. *Erable* was officially deleted from the list in 1969.

ACHARNÉ A 674

Displacement, tons	500 standard; 682 full load
Dimensions, feet	114·8 × 27·8 × 10
Main engines	Triple expansion; 1 000 ihp = 11 knots

Both laid down in 1937-38. *Acharné* by Brest, *Utile* by F. & C. de la Gironde, Bordeaux, *Actif, Applique* and *Capét* were scrapped in 1957-58. *Contentin* was withdrawn from service in 1960. *Champion* was condemned in 1961, *Obstiné* in 1965, *Enténté* and *Tetu* in 1966, *Utile* in 1969.

INFATIGABLE (ex-*Polangen*) A 661

Displacement, tons	715
Main engines	1 300 ihp = 11 knots

Coolie was officially deleted from the list in 1969 and sister tug *Malabar* in 1969.

IMPLACABLE (ex-*Fohn II*) A 670

Displacement, tons	800
Main engines	1 300 ihp = 11 knots

DISPOSALS
Intraitable (ex-*Nordergrunde*) was condemned in Mar 1961, and *Mammouth* in July 1963. *Imbattable* (ex-*Nesserland*) was officially deleted in 1965.

ÉLÉPHANT (ex-*Bar*) A 666

Displacement, tons	810 standard; 1 180 full load
Main engines	2 000 ihp = 12 knots

The tug *Samson* (ex-German *Suder Hever*) was officially condemned Mar 1961.

RHINOCÉROS A 668

Displacement, tons	640
Main engines	Diesels; 1 850 bhp = 12 knots

A photograph of *Rhinocéros* appears in the 1953-54 to 1957-58 editions.

TENACE (ex-*ATA 226*) A 669

Displacement, tons	450
Main engines	Diesels; 1 600 bhp = 10 knots

DISPOSALS. *Locmine* was condemned in 1964, and *Efficace* was officially deleted from the list in 1966.

HARBOUR TUGS. *Acajou, Balsa Bouleau Charme Chene Cormier Equeurdreville, Erable, Frene, Hetre Hevea, Latanier, Melcze, Merisier Okoume, Olivier Peuplier Pin, Platane Saule Sycomore*

Chataignier Manguier, Marronnier, Noyer Paletuvier, Papayer:
Built at Cherbourg in 1967 for service at Brest (*Chataignier, Manguier, Papayer*) Toulon (*Marronnier, Noyer*) and Cherbourg (*Paletuvier*) 700 hp.

Ana, Bengali, Eider, Grand Duc, Macreuse Marabort, Martin Pecheur:
All eight 60·2 × 18·8 × 9 feet, diesel 250 hp = 9 knots. Five based at Lorient, three at St. Malo. *Alouette, Sarcelle, Vanneau* and three more ordered in Oct 1967.

GERMANY (Federal Republic)

Bundesmarine Administration

Chief of Naval Staff, Federal German Navy:
Vice-Admiral Gert Jeschonnek

Commander-in-Chief of the Fleet:
Vice-Admiral Armin Zimmermann

Diplomatic Representation

Naval Attaché in London:
Captain Karl Theodor Raeder

Naval Attaché in Washington:
Captain Paul Brasack

Naval Attaché in Paris:
Captain W. Toepser

Strength of the Fleet

12 Submarines (Diesel Powered)
12 Destroyers (Two Missile)
 8 Frigates (Six Fast)
13 Escort and Support Ships
 1 Training Ship (Cruiser Type)
 6 Corvettes (Chaser Type)
24 Coastal Minesweepers
30 Fast Minesweepers
21 Inshore Minesweepers
40 Torpedo Boats
 2 Minelayers (ex-Landing Ships)
24 Landing Craft
39 Supply Ships and Auxiliaries
28 Service Craft

New Construction

Guided missile craft under construction include:
10 Fast patrol boats of circa 350 tons displacement
20 Fast patrol boats of circa 250 tons displacement

Personnel

1961: 23 100 (2 100 officers, 21 000 men)
1965: 33 000 (3 000 officers, 30 000 men)
1968: 36 600 (3 300 officers, 33 270 men)
1969: 37 500 (3 750 officers, 33 750 men)
1970: 39 000 (3 900 officers, 35 100 men)
1971: 35 000 (3 200 officers, 31 800 men)

Mercantile Marine

Lloyd's Register of Shipping:
2 868 vessels of 7 881 000 tons gross

Scale: 150 feet = 1 inch (1 : 1800)

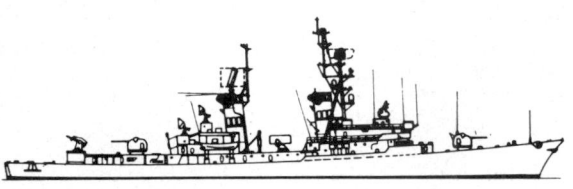

LÜTJENS *Class*

DEUTSCHLAND

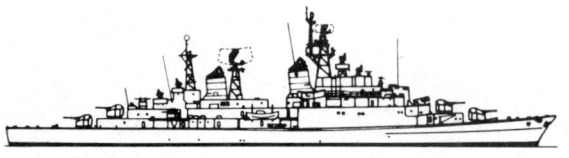

HAMBURG *Class*

SCHARNHORST

GNEISENAU

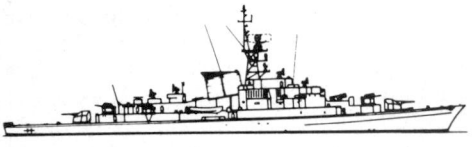

KÖLN *Class*

Z1 *Class*

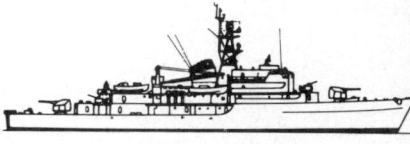

RHEIN *Class*

SUBMARINES

12 NEW CONSTRUCTION TYPE 206

| U 13 | U 15 | U 17 | U 19 | U 21 | U 23 |
| U 14 | U 16 | U 18 | U 20 | U 22 | U 24 |

Displacement, tons   400 surface

U 13-24 are of similar design to U 9-12. Ordered on 7 June 1969 from Howaldtswerke/Deutsche Werft and Reinstahl/Nordseewerke for completion in 1972-73.

11 COASTAL TYPE 205

U 1 (21 Oct 1961) S 180	U 7 (29 May 1963) S 186
U 2 (25 Jan 1962) S 181	U 8 (11 Oct 1963) S 187
U 4 (22 Aug 1962) S 183	U 9 (20 Oct 1966) S 188
U 5 (22 Nov 1962) S 184	U 10 (20 July 1967) S 189
U 6 (22 Apr 1963) S 185	U 11 (9 Feb 1968) S 190
	U 12 (10 Sep 1968) S 191

Displacement, tons	370 surface; 450 submerged
Length, feet (*metres*)	142·7 (*43·5*) oa
Beam, feet (*metres*)	15·1 (*4·6*)
Torpedo tubes	8 in bow
Main engines	2 MB diesels; total 1 200 bhp
	2 electric motors, total 1 700 bhp
Speed, knots	10 on surface; 17 submerged
Complement	21

All built by Howaldtswerke, Kiel in floating docks. Original launch dates above. "Teardrop" Hull. Fitted with schnorkel. First submarines designed and built by Germany since the end of the Second World War.

DESIGN IMPROVEMENT. U 4-12 were built to a heavier and improved design, U 1 and U 2 were modified accordingly and refloated on 17 Feb 1967 and 15 July 1966, respectively. U 1 was completely reconstructed from late 1963 to 4 Mar 1965. (See original appearance in the 1962-63 and 1963-64 editions.) U 4-8 are sheathed with zinc. U 9-12 have hulls of different steel alloys of non-magnetic propensity. U 7 and U 11 were put into service on 22 May 1968 and 21 June 1968, respectively. U 12 was completed on 14 Jan 1969.

PHOTOGRAPHS. A photograph of U 2 appears in the 1962-63 and 1963-64 editions, of U 6 in the 1964-65 to 1967-68 editions, of U 8 and U 9 in the 1968-69 and 1969-70 editions, of U 10 in the 1970-71 edition.

U 11   *1970, Official*

U 12   *1971, Official*

U 3 of this class lent to Norway on 10 July 1962 and temporarily named *Kobben* (S 310), was returned to Germany in 1964 and decommissioned on 15 Sep 1967 for disposal.

The schedule of six oceangoing hunter-killer U-boats, U 25 to U 30, of 1 000 tons, authorised on 9 Oct 1963 for delivery from German shipyards by 1967 was not implemented and officially deleted from the list in 1970.

Submarines—continued

1 CONVERTED TYPE XXI

WILHELM BAUER (ex-U 2540) Y 880

Displacement, tons	1 620 surface; 1 820 submerged
Length, feet (metres)	252·7 (77·0) pp
Beam, feet (metres)	21·7 (6·6)
Draught, feet (metres)	20·3 (6·2)
Torpedo tubes	4—21 in (533 mm) in bow
Main engines	Diesel-electric drive
	2 diesels total 4 200 bhp
	2 electric motors total 5 000 hp
Speed, knots	15·5 surface; 17·5 submerged

Launched in 1944 by Blohm & Voss. Hamburg. Sunk on 3 May 1945. Raised in 1957. Rebuilt in 1958-59 at Howaldtswerke, Kiel. Commissioned on 1 Sep 1960. Used for experiments on electronic equipment in the *Erpobungsstelle fur Marinewaffen* (Experimental Station for Naval Weapons). Conning tower was modified.

WILHELM BAUER   1971, Official

The Type XXIII coastal submarine *Hecht* (Pike), S 171, ex-*UW* 21, ex-*U* 2367, was removed from the effective list on 30 Sep 1968. Her sister ship *Hai* (Shark), S 170, ex-*UW* 20, ex-*U* 2365 was lost off the Dogger Bank on 14 Sep 1966 and although raised was not rehabilitated. She was scrapped at Emden in 1969.

DESTROYERS

Name	No.	Builders	Laid down	Launched	Completion
LÜTJENS	D 185 (USN-DDG 28)	Bath Iron Works Corp	1 Mar 1966	11 Aug 1967	12 Mar 1969
MÖLDERS	D 186 (USN-DDG 29)	Bath Iron Works Corp	12 Apr 1966	13 Apr 1968	12 Sep 1969
ROMMEL	D 187 (USN-DDG 30)	Bath Iron Works Corp	22 Aug 1967	1 Feb 1969	24 Apr 1970

MODIFIED ADAMS CLASS DDG

Displacement, tons	3 370 standard; 4 500 full load
Length, feet (metres)	431 (131·4) wl; 440 (134·1) oa
Beam, feet (metres)	47 (14·3)
Draught, feet (metres)	20 (6·1)
Missile launchers	1 "Tartar" single
Guns, dual purpose	2—5 in (127 mm) single
A/S launchers	"Asroc"; 2 triple torpedo; 1 DCT
Boilers	4 Combustion Engineering; 1 200 psi (84·4 kg/cm²)
Main engines	Geared steam turbines 70 000 shp; 2 shafts
Speed, knots	36
Complement	340 (21 officers, 319 men)

Destroyers of the "Charles F. Adams" type. 1965 contract. Cost $43 754 000.

RADAR
Search. SPS 40 and SPS 52 3D.
Fire Control. SPG 51 for Tartar; GFCS 68 for guns.

LÜTJENS   1970, Official

4 "HAMBURG" CLASS

Name	No.	Builders	Laid down	Launched	Completed
BAYERN	D 183	H. C. Stülcken Sohn, Hamburg	1962	14 Aug 1962	6 July 1965
HAMBURG	D 181	H. C. Stülcken Sohn, Hamburg	1959	26 Mar 1960	23 Mar 1964
HESSEN	D 184	H. C. Stülcken Sohn, Hamburg	1962	4 May 1963	8 Oct 1968
SCHLESWIG-HOLSTEIN	D 182	H. C. Stülcken Sohn, Hamburg	1959	20 Aug 1960	12 Oct 1964

Displacement, tons	3 340 standard; 4 330 full load
Length, feet (metres)	420 (128) wl; 439·7 (134·0) oa
Beam, feet (metres)	44 (13·4)
Draught, feet (metres)	17 (5·2)
Guns, dual purpose	4—3·9 in (100 mm) single
Guns, AA	8—40 mm, 4 twin
A/S weapons	2 Bofors 4-barrel DC Mortars
Torpedo tubes	5—21 in (533 mm), 3 bow and 2 stern; 2—12 in for AS torpedoes
Boilers	4 Wahodag; 910 psi (64 kg/cm²), 860°F (460°C)
Main engines	2 Wahodag dr geared turbines; 68 000 shp; 2 shafts
Speed, knots	35·8 max; 18 economical sea
Complement	280 (17 officers, 263 men)

All named after countries of the German Federal Republic.

RADAR
Search. HSA LWO 3.
Tactical. HSA DA 02.
Fire Control. BSA M 40 Series systems.

PHOTOGRAPHS. Photographs of *Hessen* and *Schleswig-Holstein* appear in the 1969-70 and 1970-71 editions.

HAMBURG with replacement radar screen   1971, Stefan Terzibaschitsch

BAYERN   1971, Wright & Logan

Destroyers—*continued*

Name	No.	Builders	Laid down	Launched	Completed	German commissioned
Z 1 (ex-USS *Anthony*, DD 515)	D 170	Bath Iron Works Corporation, Maine	17 Aug 1942	20 Dec 1942	26 Feb 1943	17 Jan 1958
Z 2 (ex-USS *Ringgold*, DD 500)	D 171	Federal SB & DD Co, Port Newark	25 June 1942	11 Nov 1942	24 Dec 1942	14 July 1959
Z 3 (ex-USS *Wadsworth*, DD 516)	D 172	Bath Iron Works Corporation, Maine	18 Aug 1942	10 Jan 1943	16 Mar 1943	6 Oct 1959
Z 4 (ex-USS *Claxton*, DD 571)	D 178	Consolidated Steel Corporation, Orange	25 June 1941	1 Apr 1942	8 Dec 1942	15 Dec 1959
Z 5 (ex-USS *Dyson*, DD 572)	D 179	Consolidated Steel Corporation, Orange	25 June 1941	15 Apr 1942	30 Dec 1942	23 Feb 1960

5 Ex-US "FLETCHER" CLASS

Displacement, tons	2 100 standard; 2 750 full load
Length, feet (*metres*)	368·4 (*112·3*) wl; 376·5 (*114·8*) oa
Beam, feet (*metres*)	39·5 (*12*)
Draught, feet (*metres*)	18 (*5·5*) max
Guns, dual purpose	4—5 in (*127 mm*) 38 cal.
Guns, AA	6—3 in (*76 mm*) 50 cal., 3 twin mountings
A/S	2 hedgehogs; 1 DC rack
Torpedo tubes	5—21 in (*533 mm*), quintuple bank; 2 ASW tubes
Boilers	4 Babcock & Wilcox; 569 psi (*40 kg/cm²*); 851°F (*455°C*)
Main engines	2 sets GE geared turbines 60 000 shp; 2 shafts
Speed, knots	34 max; 17 economical sea speed
Radius, miles	6 000 at 15 knots
Oil fuel (tons)	650
Complement	280

Z 1   *1971, Official*

Former US "Fletcher" class destroyers. Their loan from the United States for five years was extended. *Anthony*, now Z 1 (NATO *Pennant No.* D 170) arrived at Bremerhaven on 14 Apr 1958. *Ringgold* was transferred by the USA at Charleston, S.C., on 14 July 1959.

RADAR
Search. SPS 6.
Tactical. SPS 10.
Fire Control. GFCS 56 and 68.

PHOTOGRAPHS. A photograph of Z 4 appears in the 1967-68 edition, of Z 3 in the 1968-69 and 1969-70 editions, of Z 2 in the 1968-69 to 1970-71 editions.

DISPOSALS
Z6, No. D 180 (ex-USS *Charles Ausburn*, DD 570) was decommissioned on 15 Dec 1967 and scrapped in 1969.

Z 5   *1970, Official*

FAST FRIGATES

6 "KOLN" CLASS

Displacement, tons	2 100 standard; 2 550 full load
Length, feet (*metres*)	360·9 (*110*)
Beam, feet (*metres*)	36·1 (*11·0*)
Draught, feet (*metres*)	11·2 (*3·4*)
Guns, dual purpose	2—3·9 in (*100 mm*)
Guns, AA	6—40 mm; 2 twin and 2 single
A/S	2 Bofors 4-barrel DC mortars (rocket launchers)
Torpedo tubes	2 for ASW torpedoes
Main engines	Combined diesel and gas turbine plant: 4 MAN 16-cyl. diesels, total 12 000 bhp; 2 Brown-Boveri gas turbines, 26 000 bhp 38 000 shp; 2 shafts
Speed, knots	30 max; 23 economical sea speed;
Radius, miles	920 at full power
Oil fuel, tons	333
Complement	210

Name	No.	Builders	Launched	Completed
AUGSBURG	F 222	H. C. Stülcken Sohn, Hamburg	15 Aug 1959	7 Apr 1962
BRAUNSCHWEIG	F 225	H. C. Stülcken Sohn, Hamburg	3 Feb 1962	16 June 1964
EMDEN	F 221	H. C. Stülcken Sohn, Hamburg	21 Mar 1959	24 Oct 1961
KARLSRUHE	F 223	H. C. Stülcken Sohn, Hamburg	24 Oct 1959	15 Dec 1962
KÖLN	F 220	H. C. Stülcken Sohn, Hamburg	6 Dec 1958	15 Apr 1961
LUBECK	F 224	H. C. Stülcken Sohn, Hamburg	23 July 1960	6 July 1963

Streamlined and flushdecked fast anti-submarine frigates or escort destroyers with low freeboard aft. Ordered in Mar 1957. All ships of this class are named after towns of West Germany.

RADAR
Search. HSA DA 02.
Fire Control. X Band.

KARLSRUHE   *1970, Official*

ENGINEERING. Each of the two shafts is driven by two diesels coupled and geared to one BBC gas turbine. Controllable pitch propellers. A speed of 32 knots is reported to have been attained on full power trials.

CATEGORY. These ships were originally designated *Geleitboote*, but are now rated as *Fregatten*.

PHOTOGRAPHS. A photograph of *Köln* appears in the 1961-62 to 1966-67 editions, of *Emden* in the 1966-67 and 1967-68 editions, of *Lubeck* in the 1968-69 and 1969-70 editions. A photograph of *Braunschweig* appears on the next page.

CANCELLATION. The project to build four guided missile frigates of 3 500 tons, see full particulars and drawings in the 1970-71 edition, has been abandoned, it is officially stated.

AUGSBURG   *1970, Official*

Frigates—*continued*

BRAUNSCHWEIG (see previous page)

1971, Skyfotos

Name	No.	Builders	Laid down	Launched	Completed
GNEISENAU (ex-HMS *Oakley*, ex-*Tickham*)	F 212	Yarrow & Co Ltd, Scotstoun, Glasgow	19 Aug 1940	15 Jan 1942	7 May 1942

Displacement, tons	1 050 standard; 1 610 full load
Length, feet (*metres*)	264·2 (*80·5*) pp; 280 (*85·3*) oa
Beam, feet (*metres*)	31·5 (*9·6*)
Draught, feet (*metres*)	14 (*4·3*)
Guns, dual purpose	1—3·9 in (*100 mm*)
Guns, AA	4—40 mm
Boilers	2 Admiralty 3-drum; 299 psi (*21 km/cm²*); 660°F (*350°C*)
Main engines	2 Parsons double reduction geared turbines; 19 000 shp; 2 shafts
Speed, knots	25·5 max.12 economical sea speed
Radius, miles	3 600 at 14 knots
Oil fuel (tons)	345
Complement·	130

Former British frigate (ex-escort destroyer) of "Blankney" class ("Hunt" class, Type II). Purchased Nov 1957. Officially taken· over after refit at Langton Branch Dock, Harland & Wolff, Liverpool, 2 Oct 1958. Commissioned and renamed at Bremerhaven, 18 Oct 1958. Fitted with stabiliser and cowl funnel. Modified 1961. Anti-submarine weapons removed. Refitted by Howaldts-werke, Hamburg, 1962-64. In reserve.

RADAR.
Search. HSA DA 02.
Fire Control. HSA M 40 Series systems.

GNEISENAU

1967, Official

The two former British frigates (ex-escort destroyers) of "Hunt" class, Type III, *Brommy* (ex-HMS *Eggesford*), F 218, and *Raule* (ex-HMS *Albrighton*), F 217, were decommissioned in 1968 and scrapped in 1969.

Name	No.	Builders	Laid down	Launched	Completed
SCHARNHORST (ex-HMS *Mermaid*)	F 213	Wm Denny & Bros Ltd, Dumbarton	8 Sep 1942	11 Nov 1943	12 May 1944

Displacement, tons	1 490 standard; 1 975 full load
Length, feet (*metres*)	283 (*86·3*) pp; 300 (*91·44*) oa
Beam, feet (*metres*)	38·5 (*11·7*)
Draught, feet (*metres*)	11·5 (*3·5*) mean
Guns, dual purpose	2—3·9 in (*100 mm*)
Guns, AA	4—40 mm
A/S	1 DCT; 1 DC rack; 40 DC
Boilers	2 Admiralty 3-drum; 250 psi (*17·5 km/cm²*); 400°F (*205°C*)
Main engines	2 Parsons double reduction geared turbines; 4 300 shp; 2 shafts
Speed, knots	18
Radius, miles	4 500 at 12 knots
Oil fuel (tons)	370
Complement	180

Former British frigate (ex-sloop) of the Modified "Black Swan" class.· Handed over at Vickers-Armstrongs, Tyne, on 5 May 1959. Latterly employed for gunnery training. Now in reserve.
RADAR
Search. HSA DA 02.
Fire Control.· HSA M 40 Series systems.

CONVERSION. *Scharnhorst* was converted by Stülcken Sohn, Hamburg, from June 1961 to July 1962, with French type 100 mm guns (her former armament was 6—4 inch AA, 2—40 mm AA).

SCHARNHORST

1968, Official

Of this class *Graf Spee* (ex-HMS *Flamingo*), F 215 and *Hipper* (ex-HMS *Actaeon*), F 214 were officially stricken from the active list on 31 July 1964 to be scrapped.

Scheer (ex-HMS *Hart*), F 216, converted into a radar picket training ship, was decommissioned in 1968 and scheduled to be scrapped.

ESCORT AND SUPPORT SHIPS

13 "RHEIN" CLASS

DONAU	69	**LECH**	56	**RHEIN**	58
ELBE	61	**MAIN**	63	**RUHR**	64
ISAR	64	**MOSEL**	67	**SAAR**	65
LAHN	55	**NECKAR**	66	**WERRA**	68
				WESER	62

Displacement, tons	2 370 standard ; 2 540 full load except *Lahn* and *Lech* 2 460 standard ; 2 680 full load
Length, feet (*metres*)	304·5 (*92·8*) wl ; 323·5 (*98·6*) oa
Beam, feet (*metres*)	38·8 (*11·8*)
Draught, feet (*metres*)	11·2 (*3·4*)
Guns, AA	2—3·9 in (*100 mm*) ; none in *Lahn*, *Lech* ; 4—40 mm
Main engines	6 Maybach or Daimler diesels ; Diesel-electric drive in *Isar*, *Lahn*, *Lech*, *Mosel*, *Saar* 11 400 bhp ; 2 shafts
Speed, knots	21·7 max, 15 economical sea speed
Radius, miles	1 625 at 15 knots
Oil fuel, tons	334
Complement	110 (accommodation for 200)

SAAR 1971, *Official*

Elbe, *Mosel*, *Rhein*, and *Ruhr* were built by Schlieker-werft, Hamburg, *Isar* by Blohm & Voss, Hamburg, *Weser* by Elsflether Werft, *Neckar* by Lürssen, Bremen-Vegesack, *Saar* by Norderwerft, Hamburg, *Donau* by Schlichting, Travemünde, *Lahn* and *Lech* by Flender, Lübeck, *Main*, *Werra* by Lindenau, Kiel-Friedrichsort. All completed in 1961-64. Rated as *Belgleitschiffe* (tenders) for mine-sweepers (*Isar*, *Mosel*, *Saar*), submarines (*Lahn*, *Lech*), training (*Donau*, *Ruhr*, *Weser*), and motor torpedo boats (others) but these handsome and symmetrical ships of very interesting design, with their 3·9 in (100 mm) guns and comparatively high speed could obviously be used in lieu of frigates, although their flag superior is A.

DONAU 1970, *Official*

RADAR
Search. HSA DA 02 or X Band.
Fire Control. HSA M 40 Series systems.

STATUS. Five of these comparatively new ships, namely *Donau*, *Isar*, *Lahn*, *Lech* and *Weser*, were placed in reserve by July 1968 it was officially stated. This was part of the economy programme announced by the Federal German Navy in Sep 1967.

PHOTOGRAPHS. A photograph of *Rhein* appears in the 1962-63 edition, of *Weser* in the 1963-64 edition, of *Elbe* in the 1964-65 to 1967-68 editions, of *Lahn* and *Ruhr* in the 1967-68 edition, of *Lech* in the 1968-69 to 1970-71 editions.

NECKAR 1970, *Official*

TRAINING SHIP

1 LIGHT CRUISER TYPE	Name **DEUTSCHLAND**	No. A 59	Builders Nobiskrug, Rendsburg	Laid down 1959	Launched 5 Nov 1960	Completed 25 May 1963

Displacement, tons	4 880 normal ; 5 500 full load	Main engines	6 680 bhp diesels (2 Daimler-Benz and 2 Maybach) ; 2 shafts 8 000 shp double reduction MAN geared turbines ; 1 shaft	First West German naval ship to exceed the post-war limit of 3 000 tons. Designed with armament and machinery of different types for training purposes. The
Length, feet (*metres*)	452·8 (*138·0*) pp ; 475·8 (*145·0*) oa			
Beam, feet (*metres*) .	52·5 (*16·0*)			
Draught, feet (*metres*)	15·7 (*4·8*)			name originally planned for this ship was *Berlin*. Ordered
A/S weapons	2 Bofors 4-barrel rocket launchers	Speed, knots	22 max (3 shafts) ; 17 (2 shafts) 14 economical (1 shaft)	in 1956. Carried out her first machinery sea trials on
Guns, dual purpose	4—3·9 in (*100 mm*) single			15 Jan 1963.
Guns, AA	6—40 mm ; 2 twin and 2 single	Radius, miles	1 700 at 17 knots	RADAR.
Torpedo tubes	4 for A/S ; 2 for surface	Oil fuel, tons	230 furnace ; 410 diesel	Search. HSA LWO 3. Tactical. HSA DA 02.
Boilers	2 Wahodag ; 768 psi (*54km/cm²*) ; 870°F (*465°C*)	Complement	554 (33 officers, 271 men, 250 cadets.)	Fire Control. HSA M 40 Series systems.

DEUTSCHLAND 1970, *Skyfotos*

MISSILE BOATS

10 NEW CONSTRUCTION TYPE 143

Displacement, tons	*circa* 350
Length, feet	200
Guided weapons	4 launchers for "Tartar" surface-to-surface missiles
Guns	2—76 mm AA (Italian Oto Melara)
Torpedoes	2—21 in wire guided
Speed, knots	*circa* 38
Complement	40

Builders: Fr. Lürssen, Bremen-Vegesack. Designed as fast patrol boats. Ordered in 1971. To be completed from 1975 onwards to replace ten torpedo boats of the "Jaguar" class.

MODEL   *1970, Official*

20 NEW CONSTRUCTION TYPE 148

Displacement, tons	*circa* 250 full load
Dimensions, feet	154·2 × 23 × 5·9
Guided weapons	4 "Exocet" surface-to-surface
Guns	1—76 mm AA (Italian Oto Melara) ; 1—40 mm AA (Bofors)
Main endings	4 MTU diesels = 38 knots
Complement	40

Designed as fast patrol boats. Ordered in Dec. 1970. To be completed from 1973 onwards to replace 20 torpedo boats of the "Jaguar" class. Builders: Constructions Mecaniques de Normandy, Cherbourg.

CORVETTES

HANS BÜRKNER Y 879

Displacement, tons	982 standard ; 1 100 full load
Dimensions, feet	265·2 oa × 30·8 × 10
Guns	2—40 mm AA (twin mounting)
A/S weapons	1 DC mortar (four-barrelled) ; 2 DC racks
Main Engines	4 MAN diesels ; 2 shafts ; 13 600 shp = 25 knots
Complement	50

Torpedofangboot. Built by Atlaswerke, Bremen. Launched on 16 July 1961 Completed on 18 May 1963. Named after designer of German pre First World War battleships.

HANS BÜRKNER   *1970, Official*

5 "THETIS" CLASS

HERMES P 6112	THESEUS P 6115	TRITON P 6114
NAJADE P 6113	THETIS P 6111	

Displacement, tons	564 standard ; 680 full load
Dimensions, feet	229·7 × 27 × 7·5
Guns	2—40 mm AA (twin mounting)
A/S weapons	Bofors DC mortar (*Hermes* 2 tubes)
Main engines	2 MAN diesels ; 2 shafts ; 6 800 bhp = 24 knots
Complement	48

Submarine chasers. Built by Roland Werft, Bremen-Hemelingen. Some have computer house before bridge. *Thetis* commissioned on 1 July 1961, *Hermes* on 16 Dec 1961, *Najade* on 12 May 1962, *Triton* on 10 Nov 1962, *Theseus* on 15 Aug 1963. Photographs of *Hermes, Thetis* and *Triton* appear in the 1968-69 and 1969-70 editions.

NAJADE (forebridge type)   *1970, Skyfotos*

TORPEDO BOATS

10 NEW CONVERSION TYPE 142

DACHS	P 6094	HERMELIN	P 6095	OZELOT	P 6101
FRETTCHEN	P 6100	HYÄNE	P 6099	PUMA	P 6097
GEPARD	P 6098	NERZ	P 6096	WIESEL	P 6093
				ZOBEL	P 6092

Displacement, tons	225 full load
Dimensions, feet	137·8 × 23 × 7·5
Guns	2—40 mm AA Bofors L 70 (single)
Tubes	2—21 in wire guided
Main engines	4 Mercedes-Benz 20 cyl diesels ; 4 shafts ; 12 000 bhp = 40 knots
Complement	38

Originally units of the "Jaguar" class, but now officially known as the modernised "Zobel" class.

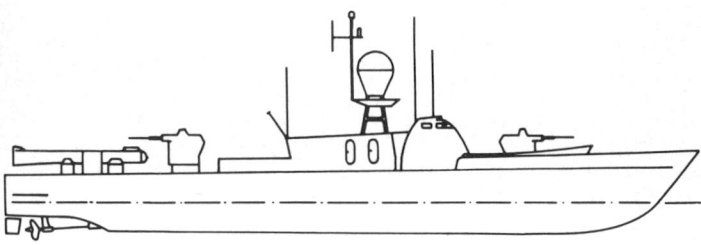

30 "JAGUAR" CLASS

ALBATROS *	P 6069	HÄHER	P 6087	PANTHER	P 6064
ALK	P 6084	ILTIS	P 6058	PELIKAN	P 6086
BUSSARD *	P 6074	JAGUAR	P 6059	PINGUIN	P 6090
DOMMEL	P 6091	KONDOR *	P 6070	REIHER	P 6089
ELSTER	P 6088	KORMORAN *	P 6077	SEEADLER *	P 6068
FALKE *	P 6072	KRANICH	P 6083	SPERBER *	P 6076
FUCHS	P 6066	LEOPARD	P 6060	STORCH	P 6085
GEIER *	P 6073	LÖWE	P 6065	TIGER	P 6063
GREIF *	P 6071	LUCHS	P 6061	WEIHE	P 6082
HABICHT *	P 6075	MARDER	P 6067	WOLF	P 6062

Displacement, tons	160 standard ; 190 full load
Dimensions, feet	138 × 22 × 5
Guns	2—40 mm AA Bofors L 70 (single)
Tubes	4—21 in (2 torpedo tubes can be removed for 4 mines)
Main engines	Mercedes-Benz 20 cyl or Maybach 16 cyl diesels ; 4 shafts ; 12 000 bhp = 42 knots
Complement	38

32 boats were built by Fr. Lürssen, Bremen-Vegessack in 1957-62 and eight by Kröger-werft Rendsburg in 1958-64. Of composite construction, with steel frames, mahogany diagonal carvel hulls, alloy bulkheads and superstructure. Units marked * are Type 141 with Maybach diesels. Remaining 20 are Type 140 with Mercedes-Benz diesels. Ten were converted into Type 142, see above.

PHOTOGRAPHS. A photograph of *Jaguar* appears in the 1958-59 to 1961-62 editions, of *Häher* in the 1962-63 to 1966-67 editions, of *Gepard* in the 1964-65 to 1966-67 editions, of *Wolf* in the 1964-65 to 1967-68 editions, of *Zobel* in the 1967-68 edition, of *Dachs* and *Geier* in the 1968-69 and 1969-70 editions, of *Habicht* in the 1968-69 to 1970-71 editions, of *Hermelin* and *Puma* in the 1970-71 edition.

DOMMEL   *1971, Giorgio Arra*

THESEUS (blockbridge type) see column 1   *1970, Official*

COASTAL MINESWEEPERS
18 "LINDAU" CLASS

CUXHAVEN	M 1078	KONSTANZ	M 1081	TÜBINGEN	M 1074
DÜREN	M 1079	LINDAU	M 1072	ULM	M 1083
FLENSBURG	M 1084	MARBURG	M 1080	VÖLKLINGEN	M 1087
FULDA	M 1068	MINDEN	M 1085	WEILHEIM	M 1077
GÖTTINGEN	M 1070	PADERBORN	M 1076	WETZLAR	M 1075
KOBLENZ	M 1071	SCHLESWIG	M 1073	WOLFSBURG	M 1082

Displacement, tons	370 standard ; 425 full load
Dimensions, feet	137·8 pp ; 147·7 oa × 27·2 × 8·5
Guns	1—40 mm AA
Main Engines	Maybach diesels ; 2 shafts ; 4 000 bhp = 17 knots
Complement	46

Lindau, first German-built vessel for the Federal German Navy since the Second World War, launched on 16 Feb 1957. Built by Yacht- & Bootswerft, Burmester, Bremen-Burg. Seventeen similar Kustenminensuchboote were built in German yards in 1958-60. The hull is of wooden construction, laminated with plastic glue. The engines are of non-magnetic materials. The first six, *Göttingen, Koblenz, Lindau, Schleswig, Tübingen* and *Wetzlar,* were modified with lower bridges in 1958-59. *Schleswig* was lengthened by 6·8 feet in 1960, and all others in 1960-64. *Flensburg* and *Fulda* were converted into minehunters in 1968-69.

PHOTOGRAPHS. Photographs of *Weilheim* appear in the 1959-60 to 1961-62 editions, and of *Schleswig* in the 1962-63 to 1967-68 editions.

FLENSBURG   *1970, Official*

LINDAU   *1968*

FULDA   *1970, Official*

6 "VEGESACK" CLASS

DETMOLD	M 1252	PASSAU	M 1255	VEGESACK	M 1250
HAMELN	M 1251	SIEGEN	M 1254	WORMS	M 1253

Displacement, tons	362 standard ; 378 full load
Dimensions, feet	137·8 pp ; 144·3 oa × 26·2 × 9
Guns	2—20 mm AA
Main Engines	2 Mercedes-Benz diesels ; 2 shafts ; 1,500 bhp = 15 knots Kamewa controllable pitch propellers

Built in Cherbourg. All launched and completed in 1959-60. A photograph of *Vegesack* appears in the 1960-61 to 1963-64 editions. of *Hameln* in the 1964-65 to 1966-67 editions, of *Detmold* in the 1967-68 edition.

PASSAU   *1969, Official*

FAST MINESWEEPERS
30 "SCHUTZE" CLASS

ALGOL	M 1068	MARS	M 1058	SCHUTZE	M 1062
ATAIR	M 1067	MIRA	M 1050	SIRIUS	M 1055
CAPELLA	M 1098	NEPTUN	M 1093	SKORPION	M 1060
CASTOR	M 1051	ORION	M 1053	SPICA	M 1059
DENEB	M 1064	PEGASUS	M 1066	STEINBOCK	M 1091
FISCHE	M 1096	PERSEUS	M 1090	STIER	Y 849
GEMMA	M 1097	POLLUX	M 1054	URANUS	M 1099
HERKULES	M 1095	PLUTO	M 1092	WAAGE	M 1063
JUPITER	M 1065	REGULUS	M 1057	WEGA	M 1089
KREBS	M 1055	RIGEL	M 1056	WIDDER	M 1094

Displacement, tons	200 standard ; 226 full load
Dimensions, feet	144·5 pp ; 154·5 oa × 22·3 × 7·2
Guns	1—40 mm AA (some still have the designed 2—40 mm) *Pegasus* have 2—40 mm
Main engines	Maybach diesels ; 2 shafts ; Escher-Wyss propellers 3 600 bhp = 24·5 knots
Complement	39

Algol, Capella, Castor, Fische, Gemma, Krebs, Mars, Mira, Orion, Pollux, Regulus, Rigel, Schütze, Sirius, Skorpion, Spica, Steinback, Stier, Waage and *Wega* were built by Abeking & Rasmussen, Lemwerder; *Deneb, Jupiter, Pluto, Uranus* and *Widder* by Schurenstedt, Bardenfl; *Atair, Herkules, Neptun, Pegasus* and *Perseus* by Schlichting, Travemünde. The design is a development of the "R" boats of the Second World War. All this class are named after stars. *Stier,* former hull number M 1061, carries no weapons, but has a decompression chamber, being security vessel for submarines. All completed in 1959-64. Formerly classified as inshore minesweepers, but re-rated as fast minesweepers in 1966.

PHOTOGRAPHS. A photograph of *Schultze* appears in the 1959-60 edition, of *Gemma* in the 1960-61 to 1962-63 editions, of *Pegasus* in the 1963-64 to 1966-67 editions, of *Jupiter* in the 1966-67 and 1967-68 editions, of *Pluto* in the 1967-68 edition, of *Gemma* in the 1968-69 and 1969-70 editions, of *Capella* and *Wega* in the 1968-69 to 1970-71 editions.

MARS   *1971, Official*

STEINBOCK   *1971, Official*

PERSEUS   *1970, Official*

Of the remaining fast minesweepers of the "R" types *Alderbaran* M 1088 (ex-R 131, ex-R 91), mine-diving vessel; *Merkur* W 68 (ex-M 1066, ex-R 134), security vessel for submarines; and OT 1, W 52 (ex-*Jupiter,* ex-R 146), for sonar training duties, when not required for ancillary purposes will be scrapped. UW 4 (ex-R 149, ex-R 102) and UW 5, W 47 (ex-R 150) both training vessels for the submarine weapons school were scrapped in 1969.

COASTAL PATROL BOATS. Of the remaining coastal patrol boats FM 1 (ex-W 7, ex-*Pierre Mené*) and FM 2 (ex- W 8, ex-*Malgré Tout*), both for telecommunications training ; TM 1 (ex-UW 3, ex-W 12, ex-No. 186) and TM 2 (ex-UW 2, ex-W 11, ex-*Miss Andrée*) both for diving training ; UW 1 (ex-W 10, ex- *Adrien Magnier*) for underwater training, all of the motor minesweeper (MMS 1) type; KW 15, KW 16, KW 17, KW 18, KW 19 (gunnery training) and KW 20, of the frontier patrol boat type; and KW 1, KW 2, KW 3, KW 6, KW 7 and KW 8, of the harbour defence boat type, were in 1968 either scrapped or used as experimental vessels, training hulks and barges for various agencies. KW 4, KW 5, KW 9 and KW 10 were given to Tanzania (shipped on 8 Dec 1963) and handed over to commercial interests).

INSHORE MINESWEEPERS

10 "FRAUENLOB" CLASS

ACHERON	Y 1661	FRAUENLOB	Y 1652	MEDUSA	Y 1655
ATLANTIS	Y 1660	GEFION	Y 1654	MINERVA	Y 1657
DIANA	Y 1658	LORELEY	Y 1659	NAUTILUS	Y 1653
				UNDINE	Y 1656

Displacement, tons	204 standard ; 230 tons full load
Dimensions, feet	124·7 × 27·2 × 7·2
Guns	1—40 mm AA
Main engines	Diesels = 14 knots
Complement	24

Built by Kröger Werft, Rendsburg. Launched in 1965-67. Completed in 1965-68. Originally designed as *Küstenwachboote* or ·coastguard boats with "W" pennant numbers : W 31 to W 38 (*Frauenlob, Nautilus, Gefion, Medusa, Undine, Minerva, Diana Loreley*, respectively) and rated as patrol boats of the seaward defence craft type ; but officially re-rated as inshore minesweepers in 1968 with the "M" hull numbers M 2671 to M 2680 (*Frauenlob, Nautilus, Gefion, Medusa, Undine Minerva, Diana, Lorely, Atlantis, Acheron*, respectively). Re-allocated "Y" numbers in 1970.

FRAUENLOB   *1970, Stefan Terzibaschitsch*

NAUTILUS   *1971, Official*

HOLNIS Y 836 (ex- M 2651)

Displacement, tons	180
Dimensions, feet	116·8 × 24·3 × 6·9
Guns	1—20 mm AA
Main engines	2 Mercedes-Benz diesels ; 2 shafts ; 2 000 bhp = 14·5 knots
Complement	21

Now serving for test and evaluation purposes, *Holnis* was launched on 22 May 1965 and completed in 1966 by Abeking & Rasmussen, Lemwerde, as the prototype of a new design of *Binnenminensuchboote* projected as a class of 20 such vessels but she is the only unit of this type, the other 19 boats having been cancelled. Hull number changed from M 2651 to Y 836 in 1970.

HOLNIS   *1969, Official*

2 "NIOBE" CLASS

HANSA Y 806, ex-W 22 (18 Nov 1957)

NIOBE Y 1643, ex-W 21 (18 Aug 1957)

Displacement, tons	150 standard ; 180 full load
Dimensions, feet	115·2 × 21·3 × 5·6
Guns	1—40 mm AA
Main engines	*Hansa:* 1 Mercedes-Benz diesel ; 1 shaft ; 950 bhp = 14 knots
	Niobe: 2 Mercedes-Benz diesels ; 2 shafts ; 1 900 bhp = 16 knots
Complement	*Hansa* 19 ; *Niobe* 22

Built by Kröger Werft, Rendsburg. . Launch dates above. Completed in 1958. The post-war prototype vessels of the category, formerly designated *Küstenwachboote* or coastal patrol vessels but re-rated as *Binnenminensuchboote* or inshore minesweepers in 1966. Named after former cruisers. *Hansa* serves as support ship for minedivers. *Niobe* (photograph in the 1967-68 edition) serves for test and evaluation purposes.

HANSA   *1970, Stefan Terzibaschitsch*

8 ARIADNE CLASS

AMAZONE	(27 Feb 1963) Y 1650		HERTHA	(18 Feb 1961) Y 1647
ARIADNE	(23 Apr 1960) Y 1644		NIXE	(3 Dec 1962) Y 1649
FREYA	(25 June 1966) Y 1645		NYMPHE	(20 Nov 1962) Y 834
GAZELLE	(14 Aug 1963) Y 1651		VINETA	(17 Sep 1960) Y 1646

Displacement, tons	184 standard ; 210 full load
Dimensions, feet	124·3 × 27·2 × 6·6
Guns	1—40 mm AA
Main engines	2 Mercedes-Benz diesels ; 2 shafts ; 2 000 bhp = 14 knots
Complement	23

Launch dates above. Former Pennant Nos. W 29, 23, 24, 30, 26, 28, 27, 25 respectively. All completed by Krögerwerft, Rendsburg, in 1960-63. All named after former cruisers, 1897-1900. Formerly classified as patrol boats (*Küstenwachboote*) but re-rated as inshore minesweepers in 1966, and given new M hull numbers in Jan 1968 (2669, 2663, 2664, 2670, 2666, 2668, 2667, 2665, respectively), and Y hull numbers in 1970. In reserve.

Photographs of *Amazone* and *Ariadne* appear in the 1968-69 and 1969-70 editions.

FREYA   *1970, Official*

GAZELLE   *1970, Official*

MINELAYER

BOCHUM (ex-USS *Rice County*, *LST* 1089) *N* 120 (ex-A 1404)
BOTTROP (ex-USS *Saline County*, *LST* 1101) *N* 121 (ex-A 1504)

Displacement, tons	1 653 standard; 4 080 full load
Dimensions, feet	316 wl; 328 oa × 50 × 14
Guns	6—40 mm (2 twin, 2 single)
Main Engines	2 GM diesels; 2 shafts; 1 700 bhp = 11 knots
Oil fuel (tons)	600
Radius, miles	15 000 at 9 knots

Former United States tank landing ships of the 511-1152 series transferred in 1961, and converted into minelayers. Commissioned on 6 Feb 1964. The third ship of this type, *Bamberg*, N 122 (ex-A 1403, ex-USS *Greer County*, LST 799) was scrapped in 1968.

BOTTROP   *1970, Official*

BOCHUM   *1969, Official*

MEDIUM LANDING SHIPS

2 Ex-US LSM TYPE

EIDECHSE (ex-USS *LSM* 491) L 751   **KROKODIL** (ex-USS *LSM* 537) L 750

Displacement, tons	743 light; 1 095 full load
Dimensions, feet	196·5 wl; 203·5 oa × 34·5 × 8·3
Guns	2—40 mm AA (1 twin)
Main engines	GM diesel; 2 shafts; 2 800 bhp = 12·5 knots

Rated as Lundungsboote. Survivors of six medium landing ships (two LSM(R) and four LSM) purchased from USA for about $6 000 000 and transferred to Germany on 5 Sep 1958 at Charleston SC. Refitted in 1959.

DISPOSALS.
Two medium landing ships of this class, *Salamander* (ex-USS *LSM* 553) L 752 and *Viper* (ex-USS *LSM* 558) L 753 were officially deleted from the list in Feb and Mar 1969. The two medium landing ships (rocket) of the US LSMR type, *Natter* L 755 (ex-*Thames River*, LSM(R) 534 and *Otter* L 754 (ex-*Smyrna River*, LSM(R) 532), were decommissioned on 15 Dec 1967 and scrapped.

KROKODIL (helicopter deck aft)   *Wright & Logan*

EIDECHSE   *Official*

LANDING CRAFT

22 LCU TYPE

BARBE	L 790	**FELCHEN**	L 793	**LACHS**	L 762	**SALM**	L 799
BRASSE	L 789	**FLUNDER**	L 760	**MAKRELE**	L 796	**SCHLEIE**	L 765
BUTT	L 788	**FORELLE**	L 794	**MURANE**	L 797	**STOR**	L 766
DELPHIN	L 791	**INGER**	L 795	**PLOTZE**	L 763	**TUMMLER**	L 767
DORSCH	L 792	**KARPFEN**	L 761	**RENKE**	L 798	**WELS**	L 768
				ROCHEN	L 764	**ZANDER**	L 769

Displacement, tons	200 light; 403 tull load
Dimensions, feet	136·5 × 28·9 × 5·2
Guns	1—20 mm AA
Main engines	GM diesels; 2 shafts; 1 380 bhp = 12 knots
Complement	17

Similar to the United States LCU (Landing Craft, Utility) type. Provided with bow and stern ramp. Built by Howaldt, Hamburg, all launched in 1965-66. A photograph of *Delphin* appears in the 1967-68 to 1969-70 editions.

The utility landing craft LCU 1 (ex-USS LCU 779, ex-LCT(6) 779), transferred from the USA under MAP was scrapped in 1968.

SCHLEIE   *1970, Stefan Terzibaschitsch*

REPAIR SHIPS

ODIN (ex-USS *Diomedes*, ARB 11, ex-*LST* 1119) A 512
WOTAN (ex-USS *Ulysses*, ARB 9, ex-*LST* 967) A 513

Displacement, tons	1 625 light; 3 600 full load (revised official figures)
Dimensions, feet	316 wl; 328 oa × 50 × 11
Guns	4—40 mm AA
Main Engines	2 GM diesels; 2 shafts; 1 800 bhp = 11·6 knots
Oil fuel (tons)	600
Radius, miles	15 000 at 9 knots

Transferred under MAP in June 1961. *Odin* commissioned in Jan 1966 and *Wotan* on 2 Dec 1965.

The two landing ships of the former United States LST type, ex-USS *Millard County*, LST 987, and ex-USS *Montgomery County*, LST 1041, purchased in 1960 for conversion into repair ships similar to the US ARB type, above, were scrapped in 1968.

WIELAND Y 804   **MEMMERT** Y 805

The two small repair ships, *Wieland* Y 804, 130 tons, rated as a *Schwimmwerkstattschiff* or floating workshop, and *Memmert* Y 805 (ex-USN 106, ex-*India*, ex-BP 34), 165 tons, rated as a *Torpedoklarmachschiff* or torpedo repair ship, salvage vessel with a derrick, were officially stated in 1971 to be still in service and on the Navy List.

ODIN   *1971, Official*

WOTAN   *1970, Official*

TENDER

EIDER (ex-*Catherine*, ex-*Docnet*) A 50   **TRAVE** (ex-*Caroline*, ex-*Flint*) A 51

Displacement, tons	480 standard ; 750 full load
Dimensions, feet	164 pp ; 177·2 oa × 27·5 × 14
Guns	1—40 mm AA ; 1—20 mm AA
Main Engines	*Eider*: Triple expansion ; 1 shaft ; 750 ihp = 12 knots
	Trave: Mercedes-Benz diesels ; 1 shaft ; 900 bhp = 12 knots
Fuel (tons)	*Trave*: 153 ; *Eider*: 130

Former British "Isles" type minesweeping trawlers. Built in Canada by Davie & Sons, Lauzon, in 1942. *Trave* was converted from steam (triple expansion) to diesel-electric propulsion in 1952-54. *Eider* is employed as a mine clearance training vessel, she has been civilian manned since 1 Jan 1968.

TRAVE   *1970, Stefan Terzibaschitsch*

EIDER   *1969, Official*

OSTE (ex-USN 101, *Puddefjord*) A 52

Measurement, tons	567 gross
Dimensions, feet	160 × 29·7 × 17
Guns	2—20 mm AA
Main Engines	2 Sulzer diesels ; 1 shaft ; 1 400 bhp = 14 knots

Built in 1943 at Akers Mekaniske Vaerkstad, Oslo. Taken over from the US Navy. Converted into a radar research and testing vessel in 1968.

OSTE (as radar testing ship)   *1970, Stefan Terzibaschitsch*

EMS (ex-USN 104, ex-*Harle*) A 53

Measurement, tons	660 gross
Dimensions, feet	185·7 oa × 29 × 15·5
Guns	4—20 mm
Main engines	Sulzer diesels ; 1 000 bhp = 12 knots

Built in 1941 by Kremer & Sohn, Elmshorn. Officially stated in 1971 to be still in service with the Navy.

The depot ship WS 1 (ex-*City of Havana*, ex-*José Marti*, ex-*Northway*, ex-*LSD* 11), former US Landing Ship, Dock, then a West Indian fruit carrier, latterly employed by the West German Navy as an accommodation ship, was sold to Greek mercantile interests in 1966.

SUPPLY SHIPS   (*Tross-Schiffe*)

2 MINE CARRIER TYPE

SACHSENWALD A 1437   **STEIGERWALD** A 1438

Displacement, tons	3 850 full load
Dimensions, feet	363·5 × 45·6 × 11·2
Guns	4—40 mm AA (two twin mountings)
Main engines	2 diesels ; 2 shafts ; 5 600 hp = 17 knots (revised official figure)
Radius, miles	3 500 nautical
Complement	65

Built by Blohm & Voss, Hamburg as mine transports. Laid down on 1 Aug 1966 and 9 May 1966. Launched on 10 Dec 1966 and 10 Mar 1967. Both commissioned on 20 Aug 1969. Rated as *Minentransporter*. Have mine ports in the stern and can be used as minelayers.

CANCELLATIONS. The project for *Torpedotransporter*, designed as a supply ship and transport for torpedoes, etc. was abandoned in 1968. The project for three *Grosse Versorger*, or heavy maintenance, support and provision ships, was abandoned in 1970.

SACHSENWALD   *1970, Official*

STEIGERWALD   *1971, Stefan Terzibaschitsch*

2 "WESTERWALD" CLASS

ODENWALD A 1436   **WESTERWALD** A 1435

Displacement, tons	3 460
Dimensions, feet	347·8 × 46 × 12·2
Guns	4—40 mm AA
Main engines	Diesels ; 5 600 bhp = 17 knots
Complement	60

Ammunition transports built by Lübecker Masch in 1966-67. *Odenwald* was launched on 5 May 1966 and commissioned on 23 Mar 1967 and *Westerwald* was launched on 25 Feb 1966 and commissioned on 1 Feb 1967. Rated as *Munitionstransporter*.

ODENWALD   *1971, Official*

WESTERWALD   *1968, Official*

Supply Ships—*continued*

8 "LÜNEBURG" CLASS

COBURG	A 1412	**LÜNEBURG**	A 1411	**OFFENBURG**	A 1417
FREIBURG	A 1413	**MEERSBURG**	A 1418	**SAARBURG**	A 1415
GLÜCKSBURG	A 1414	**NIENBURG**	A 1416		

Displacement, tons	3 254
Dimensions, feet	341·2 × 43·3 × 13·8
Guns	4—40 mm AA
Main engines	2 Maybach diesels; 2 shafts; 5 600 bhp = 17 knots
Complement	103

Lüneburg, Coburg, Glücksburg, Meersburg and *Nienburg* were built by Flensburger Schiffbau and Vulkan, Bremen, others by Blohm & Voss, Hamburg. Commissioned on 9 July, 27 May, 9 July, 9 July, 25 June, 1 Aug, 27 May and 30 July, respectively, 1968.

NIENBURG   *1971, Official*

SAARBURG   *1970, Official*

LUNEBURG   *1968, Stefan Terzibaschitsch*

2 "ANGELN" CLASS

ANGELN (ex-*Borée*) A 1408		**DITHMARSCHEN** (ex-*Hébé*) A 1409	

Measurement, tons	2 101 gross
Dimensions, feet	296·9 × 43·6 × 20·3
Main engines	Pielstick diesels; 1 shaft; 3 000 bhp = 14 knots (revised official figure)
Complement	57

Both built by Ateliers et Chantiers de Bretagne, Nantes. Purchased from shipowners S. N. Caënnaise, Caen. Launched on 9 Oct 1954 and 7 May 1955 and commissioned on 27 Nov 1959 and 19 Dec 1959, respectively. Rated as Materialtransporter. A photograph of *Angeln* appears in the 1968-69 to 1970-71 editions.

DITHMARSCHEN   *1968, Stefan Terzibaschitsch*

Supply Ships—*continued*

SCHWARZWALD (ex-*Amalthee*) A 1400

Measurement, tons	1 667 gross (revised official figure)
Dimensions, feet	263·1 × 39 × 15·1
Guns	4—40 mm AA Bofors
Main engines	Sulzer diesel; 3 000 bhp = 15 knots (official figure)

Built by Ch. Dubigeon, Nantes. Launched on 31 Jan 1956. Purchased from the Soc Navale Caënnaise in Feb 1960. Commissioned as an ammunition transport.

SCHWARZWALD   *1971, Official*

DISPOSALS

Three supply ships were stricken from the Navy List: *Pfälzerland* (ex-*Lucetta*) Y 831 on 15 Apr 1969; *Siegerland* (ex-*Leuchtenburg 3*) Y 832 on 31 March 1969; and *Sauerland* (ex-*Rolandseck*) Y 830 on 14 May 1969.

SAIL TRAINING SHIPS

GORCH FOCK

Displacement, tons	1 760 standard; 1 870 full load
Dimensions, feet	229·7 wl; 257 oa × 39·2 × 15·8
Main Engines	Auxiliary MAN diesel; 800 bhp = 11 knots
Sail area, sq ft	21 141 (speed of up to 15 knots under sail)
Radius, miles	1 990
Complement	206 (10 officers, 56 ratings, 140 cadets)

Sail training ship of the improved "Horst Wessel" type. Barque rig. Launched by Blohm & Voss, Hamburg, on 23 Aug 1958 and commissioned on 17 Dec 1958. A photograph appears in the 1968-69 to 1970-71 editions.

NORDWIND

Displacement, tons	100
Dimensions, feet	78·8 × 22 × 9
Main Engines	Diesel; 150 bhp = 8 knots. (Sail area 2 037·5 sq ft)

Ketch, ex-Kreigsfischkutter (KFK). Photograph in the 1954-55 edition. There are over 70 other sailing vessels of various types serving for sail training and recreational purposes. *Achat, Alarich, Amsel, Argonaut, Borasco, Brigant, Dankwart, Diamont Dietrich, Drossel, Dompfaff, Fafnir, Fink, Flibustier, Freibeuter, Gernot, Geiserich, Geuse, Giselher, Gödicke, Gunnar, Gunter, Hadubrand, Hagen, Hartnaut Hildebrand, Horand, Hunding, Jaspis, Kaper, Klipper, Korsar, Kuchkuch, Lerche, Likendeeler, Magellan, Michel, Mime, Meise, Mistral, Monsun, Nachtigall, Ortwin, Ostwind, Pampero, Pirol, Ruediger, Samum, Saphir, Schirocco, Seeteufel, Siegfried, Siegmund, Siegura. Smaragd, Star, Stieglitz, Störtebecker, Taifun, Teja, Topas, Tornadon, Totila, Vitalienbrüder, Volker, Walter, Wate, Westwind, Wiking, Wittigo, Zeisig.*

EXPERIMENTAL VESSELS

WALTHER VON LEDEBUR

Displacement, tons	725
Dimensions, feet	219·8 × 34·8 × 8·9
Main engines	Maybach diesels; 2 shafts; 5 000 bhp = 19 knots

Wooden hulled vessel. Built by Burmester, Bremen-Berg. Launched on 30 June 1966. The largest of several civilian manned experimental vessels including *Friedrich Voge* (ex-*Kurefjord*) Y 888, former tug, 179 tons gross; *Karl Kolls* (ex-*Salmo*, ex-*Gerda 1*, ex-*Margarethe*, ex-*Nora*) Y 887, former small freighter, 189 tons gross; *Otto Meycke* Y 882, former trawler; *Whilelm Pullwer* Y 838; and *Wilhelm Laudahn* Y 839 (ex-*UW 9*, ex-*Seeschwalbe* P 6057, ex-*S 3*) serving different agencies.

WALTHER VON LEDEBUR   *1971, Official*

Experimental Vessels—continued

4 Ex-COASTAL MINESWEEPERS

ADOLF BESTELMEYER (ex-*BYMS* 2213) **HERMAN VON HELMOLTZ**
H. C. OERSTED (ex-*Vinstra*, ex-*NYMS* 247) **RUDOLF DIESEL** (ex-*BYMS* 2279)

Displacement, tons	270 standard; 350 full load
Dimensions, feet	136 × 24·5 × 8
Main Engines	2 diesels; 2 shafts; 1 000 bhp = 15 knots;

Of US YMS type. Built in 1943. *Adolf Bestelmeyer*, Y 881, and *Rudolph Diesel* Y 889, are used for gunnery purposes. *H. C. Oersted*, Y 877, was acquired from the Royal Norwegian Navy. *Herman von Helmholtz*. Y 878, commissioned on 18 Dec 1962, is used as a degaussing ship. A photograph of *H. C. Oersted* appears in the 1967-68 edition, and of *Adolf Bestelmeyer* in the 1968-69 to 1970-71 editions.

RUDOLF DIESEL   *1971, Offiical*

SURVEYING VESSELS include *Planet* (1967), military research ship temporarily commissioned as a survey ship, Y 843, in the Bundesmarine; and *Meteor* (1964), *Süderoog, Gauss, Hooge, Ruden, Atair, Rungholt, Alkor* and *Wega*, administered by the Federal Ministry of Transport.

TRIALS VESSELS include *Viktoria* (ex-*Herzog Friederich*) Y 808; TF 101 (Y 883), TF 102 (Y 884), TF 103 (Y 885), TF 104 (Y886) and TF 105 (Y 835); TF 25 (Y 806) and TF 26 (Y 807) ; and EF 1 (ex-*Süderoog*) Y 890, but these were all officially deleted from the strength in 1968 as none of them are on the Navy List, all being manned by civilians as experimental vessels for various agencies, as are the four YMS type vessels above which are retained in this edition, however, since as former minesweepers they are still naval defence potential.

FISHERY PROTECTION VESSELS include *Poseidon, Anton Dohrn, Meerkatze, Frithjof Walther Herwig* and *Uthorn*, administered by the Federal Ministry for Agriculture and Fisheries.

TANK CLEANING VESSELS include *Forde* and *Jade* of 1 100 tons completed in late 1967.

RESCUE LAUNCHES
4 "KW" TYPE

FL 5 Y 857 (ex-W 11)   **FL 7** Y 859 (ex-W 13)
FL 6 Y 858 (ex-W 12)   **FL 8** Y 860 (ex-W 14)

Displacement, tons	45 standard; 60 full load
Dimensions, feet	83 pp; 93·5 oa × 15·5 × 4
Main Engines	2 Mercedes-Benz diesels; 2 000 bhp = 25 knots
Complement	14

Built 1951-52. All are similar to US Coast Guard 93-ft type. Formerly rated as harbour defence vessels, but re-rated as Flugsicherungsboote (employed as air/sea rescue launches) in 1959. Guns removed. Formerly H 11 (ex-P 1), H 12 (ex-P 2), H 13 (ex-P3) and H 14 (ex-P 4) respectively.

FL 1 (ex-*FL 51*, ex-*MSM 2*) was disposed of in 1962. *FL 4* (ex-*Falke*, ex-*FL 4*), a smaller type of aircraft rescue boat, was also disposed of in 1962. *FL 2* (ex-*FL 52*, ex-*MSM 3*) and *FL 3* (ex-*FL 50*, ex-*MSM 1*), ex-German Air Force sea rescue launches, were disposed of on 2 Aug and 1 Aug 1963 respectively.

FL 6   *1968, Official*

FL 9 Y 861 (ex-D 2763)   **FL 10** Y 862 (ex-D 2765)   **FL 11** Y 963 (ex-D 2766)

Displacement, tons	70
Dimensions, feet	95·2 × 16·5 × 4·2
Main Engines	Maybach diesels; 2 shafts; 3 200 bhp = 30 knots
Radius, miles	600 at 20 knots

Built by Kröger, Rendsburg. Former Flugsicherungsboote of the RAF station List/Sylt Commissioned on 1 Sep 1961.

OILERS

AMMERSEE	A 1425	**WALCHENSEE**	A 1424
TEGERNSEE	A 1426	**WESTENSEE**	A 1427

Displacement, tons	2 000 (revised official figure)
Dimensions, feet	233 × 36·7 × 13·5
Main engines	Diesels; 2 shafts; 1 400 bhp = 12·6 knots

Built by Lindenau, Friedrichsort. Launched on 22 Sep 1966, 22 Oct 1966, 10 July 1965 and 25 Feb 1966 and commissioned on 2 Mar 1967, 23 Mar 1967, 29 June 1966 and 6 Oct 1967 respectively.
A photograph of *Tegernsee* appears in the 1968-69 to 1970-71 editions.

WESTENSEE   *1971, Official*

EIFEL (ex-*Friedrich Jung*) A 1429

Displacement, tons	2 279 light; 4 700 full load
Measurement, tons	3 444 gross; 4 720 deadweight
Dimensions, feet	334 × 47·2 × 23·3
Main Engines	3 360 hp = 14 knots

Built by Norder-Werft. Hamburg. Launched on 29 Mar 1958. Purchased in 1963 for service as an oiler in the Bundesmarine. Commissioned on 27 May 1963.

EIFEL   *1970 Official*

HARZ (ex-*Claere Jung*) A 1428

Displacement, tons	1 308 light; 3 696 full load
Measurement, tons	2 594 gross; 3 755 deadweight
Dimensions, feet	303·2 × 43·5 × 21·7
Main Engines	2 520 hp = 13 knots

Built in 1953 by Norder-Werft, Hamburg. Purchased in 1963 for service as an oiler in the Bundesmarine. Commissioned on 27 May 1963.

HARZ   *1970, Official*

FRANKENLAND (ex-*Münsterland*, ex-*Powell*) Y 827

Displacement, tons	16 310
Measurement, tons	11 700 gross
Dimensions, feet	521·8 × 70·2 × 37·5
Main Engines	Diesels; 5 800 bhp = 13·5 knots

Built by Lithgows, Glasgow. Launched in 1950. Commissioned on 29 Apr 1959.

FRANKENLAND   *1968, courtesy Mr Godfrey H. Walker*

Oilers—continued

BODENSEE (ex-*Unkas*) A 1406   **WITTENSEE** (ex-*Sioux*) A 1407

Displacement, tons	1 200
Measurement, tons	1 230 deadweight : 980 gross
Dimensions, feet	208·3 × 32·5 × 15
Main Engines	Diesels ; 1 050—1 250 bhp = 12 knots

Built by P. Lindenau, Kiel-Friedrichsort. Launched on 19 Nov 1955 and an 23 Sep 1958, respectively. Commissioned on 26 Mar 1959. These ships are nearly identical.

BODENSEE   1968

BORKUM (ex-USN 105, ex- *Borkum*) Y 824

Displacement, tons	450
Measurement, tons	265 gross
Dimensions, feet	124·7 × 26·5 × 12
Main Engines	Diesels ; Speed = 6 knots

Built by Flender Lübeck. Launched in 1939. Former German motor tanker.

EUTIN (ex-*Ramsöy*) Y 825

Displacement, tons	410
Main engines,	Speed = 6 knots

Built by Menzer, Geesthact. Launched in 1943. Commissioned on 1 July 1956.

EMSLAND (ex-*Antonio Zotti*) Y 828   **MÜNSTERLAND** (ex-*Angela Germona*) Y 829

Measurement, tons	6 200 gross (*Emsland*) ; 6 191 (*Münsterland*)
Dimensions, feet	461 × 54·2 × 25·8
Main Engines	Diesel ; CRDA ; 4 800 bhp (*Emsland*) ; Fiat 5 500 bhp (*Münsterland*) = 13 knots

Built by CRDA Monfalcone, and Ansaldo, Genoa, respectively. Both launched in 1943. Completed in 1947 and 1946, respectively. Purchased in 1960 from Italian owners. Converted in 1960-61 by Schliekerwerft, Hamburg, and Howaldtswerke, Hamburg, respectively. Commissioned 7 Nov 1961 and 16 Oct 1961. Civilian crew.

EMSLAND   1970, Official

MUNSTERLAND   1968, Skyfotos

FW 1   **FW 2**   **FW 3**   **FW 4**   **FW 5**   **FW 6**

Displacement, tons	590 (revised official figure)
Dimensions, feet	144·4 × 25·6 × 8·2
Main engines	MWM diesel, 230 bhp = 9 knots

Built by Germania in 1963-64. Actually employed as Frischwasserboote. The oiler *Jeverland* (ex-*Ammerland*, ex-*Kongsdal*) Y 826 was sold in Dec 1968 and broken up at Santander, Spain early in 1969.

FW 2   1970, Official

TUGS

BALTRUM   **LANGEOOG**   **SPIEKEROOG**
JUIST   **NORDERNEY**   **WANGEROOGE**

Displacement, tons	854 standard ; 1 024 full load
Dimensions, feet	170·6 × 39·4 × 12·8
Guns	1—40 mm AA
Main engines	Diesel-electric ; 2 shafts ; 2 400 hp = 13·6 knots
Complement	35

Built by Schichau, Bremerhaven. *Wangerooge*, prototype, salvage tug, was launched on 4 July 1966. *Wangerooge* commissioned on 9 Apr 1968, *Langeoog* and *Spiekeroog* on 14 Aug 1968, *Baltrum* on 8 Oct 1968.

FEHMARN A 1458   **HELGOLAND** A 1457

Displacement, tons	1 310 standard ; 1 619 full load
Dimensions, feet	223·1 × 41·7 × 14·4
Guns	1—40 mm AA
Main engines	Diesel-electric ; 4 MWM diesels ; 2 shafts ; 3 800 hp = 16·6 knots

Bergungsschlepper or salvage tugs. Built by Unterweser, Bremerhaven. Launched on 25 Nov 1965 and 8 Apr 1965 and commissioned on 1 Feb 1967 and 8 Mar 1966.

FEHMARN   1968, Official

AMRUM Y 822   **FÖHR** Y 821   **NEUWERK** Y 823   **SYLT** Y 820

Displacement, tons	262 standard
Dimensions, feet	100·7 oa × 25·2
Main engines	1 Deutz diesel 1 100 bhp = 12 knots

Built by Fr. Schichau, Bremerhaven. Launched in 1961. All completed in 1962-63.

DISPOSALS

Passat (ex-USN 103, ex-*Passat*) Y 800 was scrapped in 1968. *Pellworm* (ex-USN 102, ex-*Pellworm*) Y 801 was stricken from the active list in 1968. *Plön* (ex-*Bombay*, ex-*Bodden*) Y 802 was stricken from the list in 1970.

HARBOUR TYPE

There are also nine small harbour tugs all completed in 1958-60 :—*Blauort* Y 803, *Knechtsand* Y 814, *Langeness* Y 819, *Lütje Hörn* Y 812, *Mellum* Y 813, *Nordstrand* Y 817, *Scharhörn* Y 815, *Trischen* Y 818 and *Vogelsand* Y 816.

ICEBREAKERS

HANSE

Displacement, tons	3 700
Dimensions, feet	243·2 × 57 × 20
Main engines	Diesel-electric ; 4 shafts ; 7 500 bhp = 16 knots

Built by Wärtsilä Oy, Helsinki, Finland. Laid down on 12 Jan 1965. Launched on 17 Oct 1966. Completed on 25 Nov 1966. Commissioned on 13 Dec 1966. Although owned by West Germany she sails under the Finnish flag, manned by a Finnish crew. Only when the winter is so severe that icebreakers are needed in the southern Baltic will she be transferred under the German flag and command. She is of improved "Karhu" class. She does not belong to the Bundesmarine.

EISBAR A 1402   **EISVOGEL** A 1401

Displacement, tons	560 standard
Dimensions, feet	125·3 oa × 31·2 × 7·9 (15·1 max)
Guns	Can carry 1—40 mm AA Bofors
Main Engines	2 Maybach diesels ; 2 shafts ; 2 400 bhp = 13 knots

Built by J. G. Hitzler, Lauenburg. Launched on 9 June and 28 Apr 1960, and commissioned on 1 Nov and 11 Mar 1961, respectively. Icebreakers and tugs.

EISVOGEL   1970, Official

GERMANY (Democratic Republic)

Administration

Commander-in-Chief, Volksmarine:
Vice Admiral Willi Ehm

Chief of Naval Staff:
Rear Admiral Johannes Streubel

Strength of the Fleet

2 Escorts
16 Fleet Minesweepers
12 Fast Missile Boats
62 Fast Torpedo Boats
26 Patrol Vessels
15 Coastal Minesweepers
18 Inshore Minesweepers
20 Coast Guard Boats
18 Landing Craft
7 Oilers
10 Tugs
20 Auxiliary Vessels

Personnel

1971: 1 450 officers and 14 550 men

Mercantile Marine

Lloyd's Register of Shipping:
432 vessels of 988 640 tons gross

ESCORTS
2 Ex-SOVIET "RIGA" TYPE

ERNST THÄLMANN 121   **KARL MARX** 122

Displacement, tons	1 050 standard; 1 350 full load
Dimensions, feet	278·9 oa × 31·2 × 9
Guns	3—3·9 in single; 4—37 mm AA paired vertically
Tubes	3—21 in
A/S weapons	4 depth charge projectors
Main Engines	Geared turbines; 2 shafts; 24 000 shp = 28 knots
Oil fuel (tons)	300
Complement	190

Designed to carry 50 miles. Fitted with Haymarket search radar. Sister ships *Friedrich Engels* 124 and *Karl Liebnecht* 123 have been scrapped it was stated in 1971. A fifth ship of this type was burnt out at the end of 1959 and became a total wreck.

1965, Werner Kähling

ERNST THÄLMANN

FLEET MINESWEEPERS
"PASEWALK" CLASS

PASEWALK

Pasewalk is reported to be the prototype of a class of dual purpose minelayers and minesweepers (*Minenlege-und-Räumschiffe*), MLR.

10 "KRAKE" CLASS

BERLIN	GERA	LEIPZIG
ERFURT	HALLE	MAGDEBURG
FRANKFURT/ODER	KARL-MARX-STADT	POTSDAM
		ROSTOCK

Displacement, tons	650 standard
Dimensions, feet	229·7 × 26·5 × 12·2
Guns	1—3·4 in; 10—25 mm AA paired vertically
A/S weapons	4 DCT
Main engines	Diesels; 2 shafts; 34 000 bhp = 18 knots
Complement	90

Built in 1956-58 at Peenewerft, Wolgast. Four completed in 1958, were originally for Poland. Appearance is different compared with the first type, the squat wide funnel being close to the bridge with lattice mast and radar. Fitted for minelaying. On 1 Mar 1961 they were given the names of the capitals of districts etc, of East Germany. Pennant numbers 221 to 225 and 241 to 245.

"Krake" Class No. 222   1970, Niels Gartig

Fleet Minesweepers—*continued*
2 "HABICHT" II CLASS

211   **212**

Displacement, tons	550 standard
Dimensions, feet	213 oa × 26·5 × 11·8
Guns	1—3·4 in; 8—25 mm AA paired vertically
A/S weapons	4 DCT
Main engines	2 diesels; 2 shafts; 2 800 bhp = 17 knots
Complement	80

The design was a modification of that of the "Habicht 1" class, but lengthened by 20 feet amidships. Built at Wolgast Peene Yard. Both completed in 1955-56. All welded. Fitted for minelaying. Four vessels of this class were deleted from the list in 1970.

"Habicht II" Class   1969

6 "HABICHT I" CLASS

213   **214**   **215**   **216**   **R11**   **R 21**

Displacement, tons	500 standard
Dimensions, feet	193·5 oa × 26·2 × 11·8
Guns	1—3·4 in; 8—25 mm AA; 2—20 mm AA
A/S weapons	4 DCT
Main engines	Diesels; 2 shafts; 2 400 bhp = 17 knots
Complement	70

Modified German M 40 type minesweepers but with diesel propulsion. Prefabricated in five sections and assembled at Volkswerft, Stralsund. Laid down in 1952-53, launched in 1952-54 and completed in 1952-54. All welded. Fitted to carry 18 mines. MLR G-33 sank early in 1958 but was salvaged and repaired in 1959 and serves as a rescue ship. Four ships are employed as patrol escort ships as well as minesweepers, the other two having been converted to rescue ships in 1961 and numbered R 11 and R 21. "Habicht" means Hawk.

"Habicht I" Class

R 21   1968, Werner Kähling

FAST MISSILE BOATS
12 SOVIET "OSA" CLASS

ALBERT GAST	KARL MESEBERG	PAUL WIECZOREK
ALBIN KÖBIS	MAX REICHPIETSCH	RICHARD SORGE
AUGUST LÜTTGENS	PAUL EISENSCHNEIDER	RUDOLF EGELHUFER
FRITZ GAST	PAUL SCHULZ	WALTER KRÄMER

Displacement, tons	160 standard; 200 full load
Dimensions, feet	121·3 pp; 131·5 oa × 28 × 6·5 max
Missile launchers	4 large hooded mountings in 2 pairs abreast aft for "Styx" surface-to-surface guided missiles
Guns	4—25 mm (2 twin, 1 forward, 1 aft)
Main engines	3 diesels; speed = 35 knots

A development of the hybrid fast patrol boat—motor torpedo boat—motor gunboat type. Reported to have been launched in 1964 onwards.   Fitted with Aldgate and Minories search radar.

OSA Type   1965, Reinecke

FAST TORPEDO BOATS
4 SOVIET "SHERSHEN" CLASS

ARTHER BECKER   EDGAR ANDRÉ

Displacement, tons	150 standard
Dimensions, feet	132 × 32 × 6·5
Guns	4—25 mm (2 twin)
Tubes	4—21 in (single)
Main engines	Diesels; 7 500 bhp = 38 knots

Acquired from the USSR. Four were reported to have been delivered in 1968-69, probably the first instalment of a flotilla.   They do not differ in any way from the Soviet boats of the class.   Pennant numbers run in an 840 series.

SHERSHEN Class   1970, Niels Gartig

P 6 Class No. 864   1970, Niels Gartig

P 6 Class   1970

Torpedo Boats—continued
40 "ILTIS" CLASS

Displacement, tons	28 to 30
Dimensions, feet	49·2 × 10·0 × 2·6
Tubes	2—21 in (torpedoes fired over stern). Some have three tubes
Main engines	Diesels; 3 000 bhp = 30 knots

Leichte Torpedoschnellboote or light torpedo fast boats of the PT type. No anti-aircraft guns. Numbered in a 900 series.

No. 912   1971, S. Breyer

18 Ex-SOVIET "P6" CLASS

Displacement, tons	75
Dimensions, feet	85·3 × 20 × 6 max
Guns	4—25 mm (2 twin mountings)
Tubes	2—21 in
Main Engines	4 diesels; 4 800 bhp = 43 knots max

Interchangeable torpedo/gunboats acquired in 1957-60 from the USSR. Wooden hull. Pennant numbers run in an 800 series. A photograph of No. 914 appears in the 1968-69 to 1970-71 editions. The motor torpedo boats of the "PA 3" Class were deleted from the list in 1968.

No. 308   1971, S. Breyer

No 808   1968

P 6 Class

No. 306   1965, Werner Kähling

COASTAL MINESWEEPERS

15 "KONDOR" CLASS

Displacement, tons	245
Dimensions, feet	150·9 × 23·0 × 6·6
Guns	2—25 mm or 2—30 mm
Main engines	Diesels; speed = 24 knots

A new class of medium fast minesweepers and patrol vessels built at Peenewerft. Five units were operational in 1970. The pennant numbers run in a 300 series. They will replace the small minesweepers of the "Schwalbe" class.

W 316   1971

PATROL VESSELS

12 USSR "SOI" TYPE

ADLER	HABICHT	KRANICH	SCHWALBE
BUSSARD	HAI	MÖWE	SPERBER
FALKE	KORMORAN	REIHER	WEIHE

Displacement, tons	215 standard; 250 full load
Dimensions, feet	138 pp; 147·7 oa × 20 × 10 max
Guns	4—25 mm AA (2 twin mounts)
A/S weapons	4 ahead throwing launchers; 2 DCT
Main Engines	3 diesels; 3 500 bhp = 28 knots
Complement	30

Submarine chasers. Fitted with mine rails. Pennant numbers run in a G 20, G 40 and G 60 series. These vessels now belong to the Coast Guard.

G 22   1970, Niels Gartig

No. 411   1964, courtesy Herr Werner Kähling

14 "HAI" CLASS

Displacement, tons	300 standard; 370 full load
Dimensions, feet	174 pp; 187 oa × 19 × 10
Guns	4—25 or 37 mm (2 twin)
A/S weapons	2—4 barrelled rocket launchers
Main engines	2 gas turbines; diesels; 8 000 bhp = 25 knots
Complement	45

Submarine chasers built at Peenewerft, Wolgast. The prototype vessel completed construction in 1963. All were in service by the end of 1969, and the programme is now completed. Pennant numbers are in the 400 series.

Patrol Vessels—continued

HAI No. 433 (see column 1)   1970, Niels Gartig

INSHORE MINESWEEPERS

18 "SCHWALBE II" CLASS

Displacement, tons	100 standard
Dimensions, feet	105 oa × 18 × 3·5 max
Main Engines	2 diesels; 380 bhp = 12·5 knots

Small minesweepers of medium speed built in 1955-57 at VEB Yachtwerft, Berlin. The pennant numbers run in 300 series. Being phased out and replaced by "Kondor" class coastal minesweepers, see column 1. Six boats were deleted from the list in 1971. A number of units of this class are used as torpedo retrievers and buoy tenders and seven in the Coast Guard.

The minesweeping boats of the original "Schwalbe" class were deleted from the effective list in 1968.

No. 34   1968

"SCHWALBE" Class

SURVEY VESSELS

JOHANN L. KRÜGER (1951)   **HELMUT JUST** (1952)

Displacement, tons	475
Measurement, tons	260 gross
Dimensions, feet	128 × 24 × 11
Main engines	Diesel; 400 bhp = 10·5 knots

Built at VEB Rosslauer Shipyard, Rosslau. River Elbe. Launch dates above. Also *Alfred Merz* and *Karl F. Gauss* (1952-55), 200 tons, 9·5 knots (seiner type); *Jordan* and *Magnetologe* (1954), 135 tons 10 knots, (German KFK type); *Arkona, Darsser Ort* and *Stubbenkammer* (1956), 55 tons, 10 knots (cutter type); and *Flaggtief* (ex-*Stralsund*) and *Hydrograph* (1953) 30 tons, 8 knots.
Hydrograph is also reported as an electronic intelligence collection trawler based at Warnemuende and employed in the Baltic.
The surveying vessel *Meteor* was deleted from the list in 1968 as she is not on the Navy List, being civilian manned and administered. See particulars in the 1967-68 edition.

LANDING CRAFT

6 "ROBBE" CLASS

| EBERSWALDE | GRIMMEN | LÜBBEN |
| EISENHÜTTENSTADT | HOYERSWERDA | SCHWEDT |

Displacement, tons   600 standard; 800 full load
Dimensions, feet   196·8 × 32·8 × 6·6
Guns   2—45 mm AA (1 twin); 4—25 mm AA (2 twin)
Main Engines   Diesels = 12 knots

Amphibious vessels of a type midway between the landing ship and landing craft categories. Launched in 1962-64.

"ROBBE" Class   1971, S. Breyer

12 "LABO" CLASS

| GERHARD PRENZLER | HEINZ WILKOWSKI | ROLF PETERS |

Displacement, tons   150 standard; 200 full load
Dimensions, feet   131·2 × 27·9 × 5·9
Guns   4—25 mm AA (2 twin)
Main engines   Diesels = 10 knots

Landing craft of a lighter type. Built by Peenewerft, Wolgast. Launched in 1961-63

"LABO" Class   1970, S. Breyer

"LABO" Class   1969, S. Breyer

TUGS

There are at least ten tugs of various types all with the prefix "A" before the pennant numbers.

TUG   1970, Niels Gartig

COAST GUARD BOATS

18 "DELPHIN/TUMMLER" CLASS

Displacement, tons   50 to 60
Dimensions, feet   95·1 × 13·8 × 3·9
Guns   2—25 mm AA or 4—15 mm AA
A/S weapons   4 DC
Main engines   Jumo diesels; 1 000 bhp = 25 knots

Küsten-und Reede Schutzboote (Coastal and harbour defence boats) of all metal construction. These boats now belong to the *Grenzbrigade Kuste* or Coast Guard. All the craft used by this force are called gunboats and have the prefix G before the pennant numbers. Twelve operational and remainder for training. A photograph of this KRS type appears in the 1963-64 to 1968-69 editions.
The coastal defence boats of the "Sperber" class were deleted from the list in 1968. The remaining two boats of the "Forelle" class have not been observed for some considerable time and are presumed scrapped in 1971.

PIONIER   1969

| PARTISAN | PIONIER |

Displacement, tons   79
Main engines   Speed = 13 knots

Built in 1957. Coastal boats rated as *schulschiffe* or training vessels. The 20 boats of the "KS 1" class in the Coast Guard were deleted from the list in 1971.

OILERS

| HIDDENSEE | POEL | RIEMS | RUDEN |

Displacement, tons   1 000 full load
Dimensions, feet   195 oa × 29·5 × 12·5 max
Main Engines   2 diesels; 2 800 bhp = 14 knots

Built at Peenewerft, Wolgast, in 1960-61. Crew 26. Speed in service 9 knots.

RIEMS   1971, S. Breyer

| RÜGEN | USEDOM | VILM |

Displacement, tons   585
Main engines·   Speed = 9 knots

Built by Mathias-Thesen-W, Wismor in 1955 to 1957.

USEDOM   1970, Niels Gartig

TRAINING SHIPS

WILHELM PIECK

Displacement, tons   200
Main Engines   Diesel; 1 shaft; 106 bhp = 8 knots

Brigantine employed as a school ship. Built in 1951. A photograph appears in the 1955-56 edition. Also yachts, *Ernst Thälmann*, 150 tons, *Jonny Scheer*, 120 tons, *Max Riechpietsch* and *Knechtsand*.
The old training ship *Albin Köbis* (ex-escort vessel *Ernst Thälmann*, ex-*Dorsch*, ex-Danish fishery protection ship *Hvidbjornen*, was deleted from the list in 1968.

The fishery protection vessels *Robert Koch, Professor Henking* (ex-*Neues Deutschland*) and *Dr Friedrich Wolf* were deleted from the Navy List in 1968.
The tenders H 41 and H 43, the netlayer H 42, and the experimental vessels *Karl Liebknecht, Rosa Luxemburg* and *Saturn* were also deleted in 1968.

GHANA

Administration	Personnel	Mercantile Marine
Commander of the Navy: Commodore P. F. Quaye	1971: 1 100 (100 officers, 1 000 ratings)	Lloyd's Register of Shipping: 73 vessels of 166 465 gross tons

CORVETTES

KROMANTSE   *1971, Official*

2 "KROMANTSE" CLASS

KROMANTSE F 17   **KETA** F 18

Displacement tons	380 light ; 440 standard ; 500 full load
Dimensions feet	162 wl ; 177 oa × 28·5 × 13 (props)
Guns	1—4 in. 1—40 mm AA (see notes)
A/S weapons	1 Squid triple-barrelled depth charge mortar
Main engines	2 Bristol Siddeley Maybach diesels ; 2 shafts ; 390 rpm ; 7 100 bhp = 20 knots (5 700 hp = 18 knots sea)
Oil fuel. tons	60
Radius. miles	2 000 at 16 knots
Complement	54 (6 + 3 officers. 45 ratings)

Anti-submarine vessels of a novel type designed by Vosper Ltd, Portsmouth. a joint venture with Vickers-Armstrongs, Ltd. one ship being built by each company. Comprehensively fitted with sonar, air and surface warning radar. Vosper roll damping fins. and air conditioning throughout excepting machinery spaces. Generators 360 kW The electrical power supply is 440 volts, 60 cycles ac. The originally proposed twin 40 mm mounting was suppressed to save top weight. A very interesting patrol vessel design. an example of what can be achieved on a comparatively small platform to produce an inexpensive and quickly built anti-submarine vessel. *Kromantse* was launched by Vosper Ltd at the Camber Shipyard. Portsmouth, on 5 Sep 1963. and commissioned on 27 July 1964. *Keta* was launched at Newcastle on 18 Jan 1965. and commissioned on 18 May 1965.

RADAR
Search. Plessey AWS 1.

RESCINDMENT. The order to Yarrow & Co Ltd, Scotstoun, Glasgow for the construction of a frigate (see full particulars and photograph of the model in the 1966-67 edition) was rescinded in 1966, but the ship was launched without ceremony or name on Clydeside on 29 Dec 1966 and completed in 1968 for sale. She is still the subject of discussions going on between the builders and the Ghana Government, it is officially stated.

COASTAL MINESWEEPERS

1 "TON" CLASS

EJURA (ex-*Aldington*) M 16

Displacement, tons	360 standard ; 425 full load
Dimensions, feet	140 pp ; 153 oa × 28·8 × 8·2
Guns	1—40 mm AA forward ; 2—20 mm AA aft
Main Engines	Deltic diesels ; 2 shafts ; 3 000 bhp = 15 knots max
Oil fuel (tons)	45
Complement	27

Former Royal Navy non-magnetic type vessel. Lent to Ghana by Britain in 1964

EJURA   *1971, Ghana Navy, Official*

INSHORE MINESWEEPERS

AFADZATO (ex-*Ottringham*) M 12   **YOGAGA** (ex-*Malham*) M 11

Displacement, tons	120 standard ; 159 full load
Dimensions, feet	100 pp ; 107·5 oa × 22 × 5·8
Guns.	1—10 mm AA
Main Engines	2 Paxman diesels ; 1 000 bhp = 14 knots
Oil fuel, tons	15
Complement	22

Malham, commissioned on 2 Oct 1959, and *Ottringham*. commissioned on 30 Oct 1959. sailed for Ghana on 31 Oct 1959, and were officially transferred from the Royal Navy to the Ghana Navy at Takoradi at the end of Nov 1959 and renamed after hills in Ghana. Now fitted with funnel.

KETA   *1966, Wright & Logan*

YOGAGA   *1966, Ghana Navy, Official*

KROMANTSE   *1969, Ghana Navy, Official*

AFADZATO   *Ghana Navy, Official*

SEAWARD DEFENCE BOATS

ELMINA and KOMENDA (rear)   *Official*

2 "FORD" CLASS

ELMINA P 13   **KOMENDA** P 14

Displacement, tons	120 standard; 160 full load
Dimensions, feet	100 wl; 117·5 oa × 20·5 × 5
Guns	1—40 mm, 60 cal Bofors AA
A/S weapons	Depth charge throwers
Main engines	2 Davey Paxman diesels; 2 shafts; 1 000 bhp = 16·5 knots
Complement	19

Built for Ghana by Yarrow & Co Ltd, Scotstoun, Glasgow. Both laid down on 18 Oct 1961. *Komenda* was launched on 17 May 1962 and commissioned on 1 Nov 1962. *Elmina* was commissioned on 29 Nov 1962. Fitted with roll damping fins. It was officially stated in 1967 that the Foden diesel and centre shaft have been removed.

ELMINA   *1966, Ghana Navy, Official*

KOMENDA   *1969, Ghana Navy, Official*

PATROL BOATS

3 USSR BUILT

P 20   **P 21**   **P 23**

Displacement, tons	86 standard; 91 full load
Dimensions, feet	98 pp × 15 × 4·8
Guns, AA	2—14·5 mm (twin mounting)
Main engines	2 Model M50-3 diesels; 2 shafts; 1 600 rpm; 1 200 bhp = 18 knots
Oil fuel, tons	9·25
Radius, miles	460 at 17 knots
Complement	16 (2 officers, 14 ratings)

Built in the USSR. Completed in Aug 1963. Acquired in 1967. Sister boat *P 22* has been scrapped, it was officially stated in 1970.

P 23   *1969, Ghana Navy, Official*

TRAINING SHIP

ACHIMOTA (ex-*Kantamento*, ex-*Radiant*) A 15

Displacement, tons	600
Dimensions, feet	174 oa × 28 × 14
Main engines	Diesels; 2 shafts; speed = 13 knots max
Oil fuel, tons	60
Complement	35 (with additional accommodation for 30)

Built in 1927 by Camper & Nicholsons, Ltd, England for the Commodore of the Royal Yacht Squadron. Converted into an anti-submarine vessel during the Second World War. After hostilities sold to the Abingdon Steamship Co Ltd, for Mediterranean cruises. Later re-engined and modernised. The Ghana Government then purchased her for use as a State Yacht. In Feb 1963 she was transferred to the Ghana Navy and converted into Training Depot Ship.

ACHIMOTA   *1968, Ghana Navy, Official*

ACHIMOTA   *1971, Official*

MAINTENANCE REPAIR CRAFT

ASUANTSI (ex-*MRC* 1122)

Displacement, tons	657
Dimensions, feet	225 pp; 231·3 oa × 39 × 3·3 forward, 5 aft
Main engines	4 Paxman, 1 840 bhp = 9 knots cruising

Acquired from Britain in 1965 and arrived in Ghana waters in July 1965. Used as a base workshop at Tema Naval Base. Is kept operational, and does a fair amount of seatime in general training and exercise tasks.

ASUANTSI   *1966, Ghana Navy, Official*

GREECE

Administration

Commander-in-Chief, Royal Hellenic Navy:
Vice-Admiral K. Margaritis, RHN

Deputy Commander-in-Chief:
Rear-Admiral G. Petmezas, RHN

Commander of the Fleet:
Rear-Admiral G. Moralis, RHN

Personnel

1971: 18 000 (1 640 officers and 16 360 ratings)
(conscript, 18 months or enlistment)

Strength of the Fleet

2 Submarines (Diesel Powered)
9 Destroyers
4 Frigates (Destroyer Escorts)
5 Corvettes (Ocean Minesweepers)
2 Minelayers (ex-Medium Landing Ships)
5 Patrol Vessels (2 ex-Support Landing Ships)
21 Coastal Minesweepers
13 Fast Patrol Boats (Torpedo Boats)
13 Landing Ships (6 medium)
43 Support Ships and Service Craft

New Construction

4 Submarines (Diesel Powered)
3 Frigates (3 more later)
4 Missile Boats (Fast Gunboats)

Diplomatic Representation

Naval Attaché in London:
Captain A. Glykis, RHN

Naval Attaché in Washington:
Captain S. Kapsalis, RHN

Naval Attaché in Cairo:
Captain Mitsakos, RHN

Naval Attaché in Bonn:
Captain A. Damiralis, RHN

Mercantile Marine

Lloyd's Register of Shipping:
1 850 vessels of 10 951 993 tons gross

Scale: 150 feet = 1 inch (1 : 1 800)

NAVARINON, THYELLA

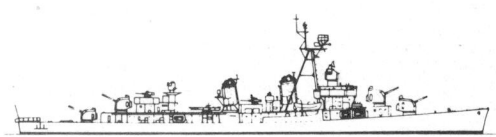

ASPIS, LONCHI, SFENDONI, VELOS

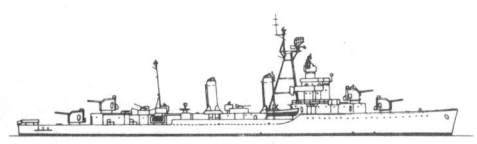

DOXA, NIKI

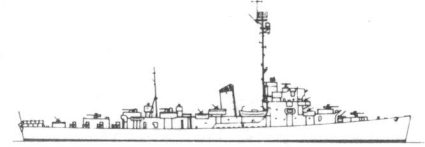

AETOS, IERAX, LEON, PANTHIR

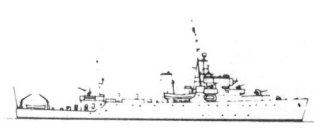

PIRPOLITIS

SUBMARINES

NEW CONSTRUCTION

GLAVKOS   PROTEUS
NIREUS   TRITON

Greece ordered four 1 000-ton submarines from Howaldts-werke/Deustche Werft AG in Kiel. Germany asked the WU for permission to build these boats but this had not been granted by early 1970. However, when late in 1969 construction had advanced to sections being placed on the slip Germany announced that these boats would be built anyway under the permission received to build U 25 to U 30, German boats of which construction had not yet commenced.

1 Ex-US "BALAO" CLASS

TRIAINA (ex-USS Scabbardfish, SS 397) S 86

Displacement, tons	1 526 standard; 1 816 surface; 2 425 submerged
Length, feet (metres)	311·5 (94·9) oa
Beam, feet (metres)	27 (8·2)
Draught, feet (metres)	17 (5·2)
Torpedo tubes	10—21 in (533 mm), 6 bow, 4 stern
Main engines	6 500 bhp diesels (surface) 4 610 hp electric motors (submerged)
Speed, knots	20 on surface, 10 submerged
Radius, miles	12 000 at 10 knots
Oil fuel (tons)	300
Complement	80

Built at Portsmouth Navy Yard, USA. Launched on 27 Jan 1944 and completed on 29 Apr 1944. Transferred on 26 Feb 1965 at San Francisco (lent by US in 1964).

1 Ex-US "GATO" CLASS

POSEIDON (ex-Lapon) S 78 (ex-Y 16)

Displacement, tons	1 525 standard; 1 816 surface; 2 425 submerged
Length, feet (metres)	311·7 (95·0)
Beam, feet (metres)	27 (8·2)
Draught, feet (metres)	17 (5·2)
Guns, dual purpose	1—5 in (127 mm) 25 cal.
Torpedo tubes	10—21 In (533 mm), 6 bow, 4 stern
Main engines	6 500 bhp GM 2-stroke diesels (surface); 2 750 hp electric motors (submerged)
Speed, knots	21 on surface; 10 submerged
Complement	85

Built by Electric Boat Division of General Dynamics Corp, Groton, Conn. Laid down on 21 Feb 1942, launched on 27 Oct 1942 and completed on 23 Jan 1943. Lent by USA in 1957 (transferred on 8 Aug). Sister Amfitriti (ex-USS Jack, SS 259) was returned to US and expended as a target in Sep 1967.

GLAVKOS   1971, Royal Hellenic Navy, Official

TRIAINA   1970, Royal Hellenic Navy, Official

POSEIDON   1969, Royal Hellenic Navy, Official

DESTROYERS

Name	No.	Builder	Laid down	Launched	Completed
ASPIS (ex-USS *Conner*, DD 582)	D 06	Boston Navy Yard	16 Apr 1942	18 July 1942	8 June 1943
LONCHI (ex-USS *Hall*, DD 583)	D 56	Boston Navy Yard	16 Apr 1942	18 July 1942	6 July 1943
NAVARINON (ex-USS *Brown*, DD 546)	D 63	Bethlehem (S. Pedro)	27 June 1942	22 Feb 1943	10 July 1943
SFENDONI (ex-USS *Aulick*, DD 569)	D 85	Consolidated Steel Corp, Texas	14 May 1941	2 Mar 1942	27 Oct 1942
THYELLA (ex-USS *Bradford*, DD 545)	D 28	Bethlehem (S. Pedro)	28 Apr 1942	12 Dec 1942	12 June 1943
VELOS (ex-USS *Charette*, DD 581)	D 16	Boston Navy Yard	20 Feb 1941	3 June 1942	18 May 1943
***THEMISTOCLES** (ex-USS *Forrest Royal*, DD 872)		Bethlehem (Staten Island)	**Gearing Class** 17 Jan 1946		29 June 1946

6 Ex-US "FLETCHER" CLASS

Displacement, tons	2 100 standard; 3 050 full load
Length, feet (*metres*)	376·5 (*114·7*) oa
Beam, feet (*metres*)	39·5 (*12·0*)
Draught, feet (*metres*)	18 (*5·5*) max
Guns, dual purpose	4—5 in (*127 mm*) 38 cal. in *Aspis, Lonchi, Sfendoni* and *Velos*, 5 in *Navarinon* and *Thyella*
Guns, AA	6—3 in (*76 mm*), 3 twin, in *Aspis, Lonchi, Sfendoni* and *Velos*. 10—40 mm (2 quadruple, 1 twin) in *Navarinon* and *Thyella*
A/S weapons	Hedgehogs; DC's
Torpedo tubes	5—21 in (*533 mm*), quintuple bank, in *Aspis, Lonchi, Sfendoni* and *Velos*, none in *Navarinon* and *Thyella*
Torpedo racks	Side-launching for A/S torpedoes
Boilers	4 Babcock & Wilcox; 615 psi (*43·3 km/cm²*) 800°F (*427°C*)
Main engines	2 sets GE geared turbines; 2 shafts; 60 000 shp
Speed, knots	35 designed, 30 to 32 max
Radius, miles	6 000 at 15 knots; 1 260 to 1 285 at 30 to 32 knots
Oil fuel, tons	506
Complement	250

Transferred from USA, *Aspis*, *Lonchi* and *Velos* at Long Beach, Cal, on 15 Sep 1959, 9 Feb 1960 and 15 June 1959, respectively, *Sfendoni* at Philadelphia on 21 Aug 1959, *Navarinon* and *Thyella* at Seattle, Wash, on 27 Sep 1962. *Aspis* means Shield. *Another ex-US destroyer to be taken over has been named *Themistocles* (see details under "Gearing" class in US section).

RADAR. Search: SPS 6, SPS 10. Fire Control: GFCS 56 and 68 systems.

PHOTOGRAPHS. A photograph of *Thyella* appears in the 1963-64 to 1967-68 editions, of *Aspis* in the 1967-68 edition, of *Velos* in the 1968-69 and 1969-70 editions, of *Lonchi* in the 1968-69 to 1970-71 editions.

NAVARINON   1970, Royal Hellenic Navy, Official

SFENDONI   1971, Major Aldo Fraccaroli

Name	No.	NATO No.	Builders	Laid down	Launched	Completed
DOXA (ex-USS *Ludlow*, DD 438)	20	D 220	Bath Iron Works Corpn	18 Dec 1939	11 Nov 1940	5 Mar 1941
NIKI (ex-USS *Eberle*, DD 430)	65	D 225	Bath Iron Works Corpn	12 Apr 1939	14 Sep 1940	4 Dec 1940

2 Ex-US "GLEAVES" CLASS

Displacement, tons	1 700 standard; 2 580 full load
Length, feet (*metres*)	348·2 (*106·1*) oa
Beam, feet (*metres*)	36·1 (*11·0*)
Draught, feet (*metres*)	18 (*5·5*) max
Guns, surface	4—5 in (*127 mm*), 38 cal
Guns, AA	12—40 mm (2 quadruple, 2 twin), (see *Gunnery* notes)
A/S weapons	Hedgehogs; DC's
Torpedo tubes	Removed
Torpedo racks	Side-launching for A/S torpedoes
Boilers	4 Babcock & Wilcox; 580 psi (*40·8 kg/cm²*); 850°F (*455°C*)
Main engines	2 sets GE geared turbines; 2 shafts; 50 000 shp
Speed, knots	36·5 designed, actually 30 max
Radius, miles	5 000 at 15 knots; 1 500 at 30 knots
Oil fuel, tons	440
Complement	188

Taken over from the United States Navy on 18 Apr 1952. A tripod foremast was stepped during modernisation. For former appearance with pole foremast, see photograph of *Niki* in the 1956-57 to 1964-65 editions. Names mean "Glory" and "Victory" respectively. Scheduled to be discarded in the near future as they are of pre-Second World War design and over 30 years old.

GUNNERY. The six 20 mm AA guns first installed were removed in 1962.

TUBES. The five 21-inch torpedo tubes originally mounted in a quintuple bank were removed.

RADAR. Search: SPS 6, SPS 10. Fire Control: GFCS 68 system.

PHOTOGRAPHS. A port quarter oblique view of *Doxa* appears in the 1965-66 to 1968-69 editions, and a starboard surface dead broadside view in the 1964-65 to 1970-71 editions.

CRUISER. *Elli*, formerly the Italian light cruiser *Eugenio di Savoia*, was officially deleted from the list in 1964.

NIKI   1969, Royal Hellenic Navy, Official

DOXA   1971, Royal Hellenic Navy, Official

FRIGATES (Destroyer Escorts)

Name	No.	NATO No.	Builders	Laid down	Launched	Completed
AETOS (ex-USS *Slater*, DE 766)	01	D 212	Tampa SB Co	9 Mar 1943	13 Feb 1944	1 May 1944
IERAX (ex-USS *Elbert*, DE 768)	31	D 213	Tampa SB Co	1 Apr 1943	23 May 1944	12 July 1944
LEON (ex-USS *Eldridge*, DE 173)	54	D 217	Federal SB & DD Co	22 Feb 1943	25 June 1943	27 Aug 1943
PANTHIR (ex-USS *Garfield Thomas*, DE 193)	67	D 227	Federal SB & DD Co	23 Sep 1943	12 Dec 1943	24 Jan 1944

4 Ex-US "BOSTWICK" DE TYPE

Displacement, tons	1 240 standard ; 1 900 full load
Length, feet (*metres*)	306 (*93·3*) oa
Beam, feet (*metres*)	36·7 (*11·2*)
Draught, feet (*metres*)	14 (*4·3*)
Guns, dual purpose	3—3 in (*76 mm*) 50 cal.
Guns, AA	6—40 *mm*, 3 twin
	14—20 *mm*, 7 twin
A/S weapons	Hedgehog ; 8 DCT ; 1 DC rack
Torpedo racks	Side launching for A/S torpedoes
Main engines	4 sets GM diesel-electric
	6 000 bhp ; 2 shafts
Speed, knots	19·25 max
Radius, miles	11 500 at 11 knots ; 6 920 at 17·5 knots
Oil fuel (tons)	316
Complement	220 (war)

Former US destroyer escorts of the "Bostwick" class. *Aetos* and *Ierax* were transferred on 15 Mar 1951 and *Leon* and *Panthir* on 15 Jan 1951. Their 3—21 inch torpedo tubes in a triple mount were removed. Meanings of names are Eagle, Falcon, Lion and Panther, respectively.

PHOTOGRAPHS. A photograph of *Leon* appears in the 1962-63 to 1965-66 editions, and of *Aetos* in the 1966-67 to 1969-70 editions.

3 + 3 PROJECTED

Greece is negotiating with British shipyards for the construction of three frigates, with three more to follow later on.

DISPOSALS OF "HUNT" CLASSES
Of the ex-British "Hunt" Type III frigates (escort destroyers) *Adrias* (ex-*Border*) was scrapped after a mine blew away her forecastle on 22 Oct 1943, *Kanaris* (ex-*Hatherleigh*) and *Pindos* (ex-*Bolebroke*) were returned to Britain on 12 Dec 1959 and sold for scrap in Greece, *Miaoulis* (ex-*Modbury*) was similarly disposed of in 1960 ; *Adrios* (ex-*Tanatside*) and *Astings* (ex-*Catterick*) were discarded in 1963 and sold by the British Admiralty. The ex-British "Hunt" Type II frigates (escort destroyers). *Aegaion* (ex-*Lauderdale*) ; *Kriti* (ex-*Hursley*) and *Themistocles* (ex-*Bramham*) were returned to Britain on 12 Dec 1959 and sold for scrap in Greece.

5 Ex-BRITISH "ALGERINE" TYPE

Displacement, tons	1 030 standard ; 1 325 full load
Length, feet (*metres*)	225 (*68·6*) oa
Beam, feet (*metres*)	35·5 (*10·8*)
Draught, feet (*metres*)	11·5 (*3·5*) max
Guns, dual purpose	2—3 in (*76 mm*) US Mark 21 (1 in *Pirpolitis*, none in *Mahitis*)
Guns, AA	4—20 mm (US), 2MG
A/S weapons	2 to 4 DCT
Main engines	2 triple expansion ; 2 shafts ; 2 700 ihp = 16 knots max
Boilers	2 Yarrow, 250 psi (*17·6 kg cm²*)
Oil fuel, tons	235
Radius, miles	5 000 at 10 knots ; 2 270 at 14·5 knots
Complement	85

Former British ocean minesweepers of the "Algerine" class. Acquired from the Executive Committee of Surplus Allied Material. Latterly employed as Corvettes. The armament of *Mahitis* was removed when she became a training ship. *Armatolos* and *Navmachos* were used as auxiliaries and others as personnel transports. Photographs of *Pyrpolitis* appear in the 1957-58 to 1970-71 editions.

IERAX
1970, Skyfotos

PANTHIR
1970, A. & J. Pavia

CORVETTES (Ocean Minesweepers)

Name	No.	Builders	Launched
ARMATOLOS (ex-HMS *Aries*)	M 12	Toronto Shipyard	19 Sep 1942
MAHITIS (ex-HMS *Postillion*)	M 58	Redfern Construction Co	14 Nov 1942
NAVMACHOS (ex-HMS *Lightfoot*)	M 64	Redfern Construction Co	31 Aug 1942
POLEMISTIS (ex-HMS *Gozo*)	M 74	Redfern Construction Co	18 Mar 1943
PYRPOLITIS (ex-HMS *Arcturus*)	M 76	Redfern Construction Co	27 Jan 1943

POLEMISTIS
1971, Royal Hellenic Navy, Official

MINELAYERS (Ex-Landing Ships)

AKTION (ex-*LSM* 301) N 04   AMVRAKIA (ex-*LSM* 303) N 05

Displacement, tons	720 standard ; 1 100 full load
Dimensions, feet	196·5 wl ; 203·5 oa × 34·5 × 8·3 max
Guns	8—40 mm dp (4 twin) ; 6—20 mm AA (single)
Mines	Capacity 100 to 130
Main Engines	2 diesels ; 2 shafts ; 3 600 bhp = 12·5 knots
Radius, miles	3 000 at 12 knots
Complement	65

Former US Medium Landing Ships. Both built at Charleston Naval Shipyard. *Aktion* was launched on 1 Jan 1945 and *Amvrakia* on 14 Nov 1944. Converted in the USA into all purpose seagoing minelayers for the Royal Hellenic Navy. Underwent extensive rebuilding from the deck up. Twin rudders. The Greek flag was hoisted on 1 Dec 1953. A photograph of *Aktion* appears in the 1965-66 to 1967-68 editions.

AMVRAKIA
1970, Royal Hellenic Navy, Official

MISSILE BOATS

4 + 2 NEW CONSTRUCTION

CALYPSO	EUNICE	KOMOTOTHOI	MAUSITHOI

Displacement, tons	220 standard; 250 full load
Dimensions, feet	154·2 x· 23·3 × 8·2
Missiles	MM 38 Exocet surface-to-surface
Guns	1—40 mm
Main engines	4 diesels; 2 shafts; 14 000 bhp = 40 knots
Radius, miles	800 at 30 knots

Ordered in 1969 from Constructions Mecaniques de Normandy, Cherbourg. Similar to the Israeli "Saar" class. First units to be completed in 1971.

PATROL VESSELS

ANTIPLOIARKHOS PEZOPOULOS (ex-*PGM* 21, ex-*PC* 1552)   P 70
PLOTARKHIS ARSLANOGLOU (ex-*PGM* 25, ex-*PC* 1556)   P 14
PLOTARKHIS CHANTZIKONSTANDIS (ex-*PGM* 29, ex-*PC* 1565) P 96

Displacement, tons	335 standard; 439 full load
Dimensions, feet	170 wl; 174·7 oa × 23 × 10·8 (max)
Guns	1—3 in; 6—20 mm AA
A/S weapons	Hedgehog; side launching torpedo racks; depth charges
Main engines	2 GM diesels; 2 shafts; 3 600 bhp = 19 knots

All launched in 1943-44. Acquired from USA in Aug 1947. The two 40 mm AA guns were removed and a hedgehog was installed in 1963. Of these sister ships *Plotarkhis Blessas* (ex-PGM 28, ex-PC 1559) P 61, was sole in 1963 and *Antiploiarkhos Laskos* (ex-PGM 16, ex-PC 1448) P 53 and *Ploiarkhos Meletopoulos* (ex-PC 1553) P 57 were out of service in 1971.

ANTIPLOIARKHOS PEZOPOULOS   *1970, Royal Hellenic Navy, Official*

PLOTARKHIS MARIDAKIS (ex-USS *LSSL* 65)   14 Nov 1944   P 94
PLOTARKHIS VLACHAVAS (ex-USS *LSSL* 35)   17 Sep 1944   P 95

Displacement, tons	257 standard; 395 full load
Dimensions, feet	157 × 23·2 × 5·7
Guns	1—3 in; 4—40 mm AA (2 twins); 4—20 mm AA
Main Engines	Diesel, 2 shafts; 1 600 bhp = 14·4 knots

Built by Albina Engine & Machinery Works Inc, Portland, Oreg, and Commercial Iron Works, Portland, respectively. *Plotarkhis Vlachavas* was transferred from USA on 12 Aug 1957 and *Plotarkhis Maridakis* in June 1958.

PLOTARKHIS VLACHAVAS   *1969, Royal Hellenic Navy, Official*

TORPEDO BOATS

ANDROMEDA	P 21	KASTOR	P 23	PIGASSOS	P 25
INIONOS	P 22	KYKONOS	P 24	TOXOTIS	P 26

Displacement, tons	69 standard; 76 full load
Dimensions, feet	75 pp; 80·4 oa × 24·6 × 6·9
Torpedo tubes	4—21 In
Guns	2—40 mm AA
Main engines	2 Napier Deltic T 18-37 K diesels; 3 100 bhp = 43 knots
Complement	22

Andromeda and *Inionos* were taken over in Feb 1967 from Mandal, Norway. *Kastor* and *Kykonos*, and the third pair, *Pigassos* and *Toxotis*, were delivered in succession in 1967. A photograph of *Inionos* appears in the 1967-68 to 1970-71 editions.

ANDROMEDA   *1971, Royal Hellenic Navy, Official*

Torpedo Boats—*continued*

ASTRAPI P 20 (ex-*Strahl* P 6194)

Displacement, tons	95 standard; 110 full load
Dimensions, feet	96 (full); 99 oa × 25 × 7 (props)
Torpedo chutes	4—21 in side launching
Guns	2—40 mm AA
Main engines	3 Bristol Siddeley Marine Proteus gas turbines; 3 shafts; 12 750 bhp = 55·5 knots

Built by Vosper, Portsmouth. Launched on 10 Jan 1962. Commissioned in Federal German Navy on 21 Nov 1962. Transferred to Royal Hellenic Navy in Apr 1967. Refitted by Vosper in 1968. Of similar design to British "Brave" class.

ASTRAPI   *1969, Royal Hellenic Navy. Official*

AIOLOS P 19 (ex-*Pfeil* P 6193)

Displacement, tons	75 standard; 80 full load
Dimensions, feet	92 wl; 95 oa × 23·9 × 6·5
Torpedo chutes	4—21 in side launching
Guns	2—40 mm AA
Main engines	2 Bristol Siddeley Marine Proteus gas turbines; 2 shafts; 8 500 bhp = 50 knots

Built by Vosper, Portsmouth. Launched on 26 Oct 1961. Commissioned in German Navy on 27 June 1962. Transferred to Royal Hellenic Navy in Apr 1967. Refitted by Vosper in 1968. Based on design of Vosper prototype *Ferocity*.

AIOLOS   *1969, Royal Hellenic Navy, Official*

DELPHIN (ex-*Sturmmöwe*)	**PHOENIX** (ex-*Eismöwe*)
DRAKEN (ex-*Silbermöwe*)	**POLIKOS** (ex-*Raubmöwe*)
	POLYDVEKIS (ex-*Wildschwan*)

Displacement, tons	190 standard; 155 full load
Dimensions, feet	116·1 × 16·7 × 5·9
Armament	2—21 in torpedo tubes; 4—20 mm AA guns
Main engines	4 diesels; 9 000 bhp

Old S-Boote taken over from Germany in 1969. Built by Lurssen, Vegesack, 1951-56.

COASTAL MINESWEEPERS

AIDON (ex-*MSC* 310)	M 248	DAPHNI (ex-*MSC* 307)	M 247
AIGLI (ex-*MSC* 299)	M 246	DORIS (ex-*MSC* 298)	M 245
ARGO (ex-*MSC* 317)	M 213	KICHLI (ex-*MSC* 308)	M 241
AVRA (ex-*MSC* 318)	M 214	KICHU (ex-*MSC* 314)	M 249
(ex-*MSC* 319)		KISSA (ex-*MSC* 309)	M 242

Displacement, tons	320 standard; 370 full load
Dimensions, feet	138 pp; 144 oa × 28 × 8·5
Guns	2—20 mm AA (twin)
Main engines	2 GM diesels; 2 shafts; 880 bhp = 13 knots
Complement	39

Built in USA for Greece. *Aidon, Aigli, Daphni, Doris, Kichli* and *Kissa*, were completed and transferred in 1964-65, *Argo* and *Avra* in 1968, *Kichu* and MSC 319 in 1969-70. Built of wood and non-magnetic materials. A photograph of *Kichli* appears in the 1966-67 edition and of *Daphni* in the 1967-68 to 1970-71 editions.

DORIS   *1971, Royal Hellenic Navy, Official*

Coastal Minesweepers—*continued*

M 254   *1971, Michael D. J. Lennon*

ANTIOPI (ex-Belgian *Herve*, M 921, ex-USS *MSC* 153)
ATALANTI (ex-Belgian *St. Truiden*, M 919, ex-USS *MSC* 169)
NIOVI (ex-Belgian *Laroche*, M 924, ex-USS *MSC* 171)
PHEDRA (ex-Belgian *Malmedy*, M 922, ex-USS *MSC* 154)
THALIA (ex-Belgian *Blankenberge*, M 923, ex-USS *MSC* 170)

Displacement, tons	330 light; 402 full load
Dimensions, feet	145 oa × 27·9 × 8 feet
Guns	2—20 mm Oerlikon (1 twin)
Main engines	2 GM diesels; 2 shafts; 900 bhp = 14 knots
Oil fuel, tons	28 capacity
Radius, miles	2 700 at ecomical speed (10·5 knots)
Complement	38 officers and men

Former Belgian vessels taken over on 29 July 1969 (*Herve* and *St. Truiden*) and 26 Sep 1969 (*Laroche*, *Malmedy* and *Blankenberge*). Of standard USN *MSC* (ex-*AMS*) Type 60. Nos 206, 210, 254.

AFROESSA   *1971, Royal Hellenic Navy, Official*

AFROESSA (ex-*BYMS* 2185)	M 209	**KERKYRA** (ex-*BYMS* 2172)	M 208
KALYMNOS (ex-*BYMS* 2033)	M 201	**PARALOS** (ex-*BYMS* 2066)	M 204
KARTERIA (ex-*BYMS* 2065)	M 203	**ZAKYNTHOS** (ex-*BYMS* 2209)	M 212

Displacement, tons	270 standard; 350 full load
Dimensions, feet	136 × 24·5 × 8
Guns	1—3 in; 2—20 mm AA; 4 MG; 2 DCT
Main Engines	Diesel; 1 000 bhp = 12 knots
Complement	33

Of wooden construction. All the names are conventional and are not mentioned in signals or correspondence. Known by numbers, *Karteria* was launched on 21 Dec 1942. *Ithaki* (ex-*BYMS* 2240). *Kefallinia* (ex-*BYMS* 2171), *Lefkas* (ex-*BYMS* 2086), *Patmos* (ex-*BYMS* 2229), *Salaminia* (ex-*BYMS* 2067), and *Simi* (ex-*BYMS* 2190) were deleted from the list in 1966 and *Leros* (ex-*BYMS* 2186) and *Paxi* (ex-*BYMS* 2056) in 1969. A photograph of *Paralos* appears in the 1955-56 to 1962-63 editions. and of *Leros* in the 1963-64 to 1965-66 editions.

TANK LANDING SHIPS

IKARIA   *1970, Royal Hellenic Navy, Official*

Tank Landing Ships—*continued*

IKARIA (ex-USS *Potter County*, LST 1086)	L 154	
LESBOS (ex-USS *Boone County*, LST 389)	L 172	
RODOS (ex-USS *Bowman County*, LST 391)	L 157	
SYROS (ex-USS LST 325)	L 144	

Displacement, tons	1 653 standard; 4 080 full load
Dimensions, feet	316 wl; 328 oa × 50 × 14 max
Guns	8—40 mm AA; 6—20 mm AA; (*Rodos:* 10—40 mm)
Main Engines	GM diesels; 2 shafts; 1 700 bhp = 11·6 knots
Complement	119 (accommodation for 266)

Former United States tank landing ships. *Ikaria, Lesbos* and *Rodos* were transferred to the Royal Hellenic Navy on 9 Aug 1960. *Syros* was transferred on 29 May 1964 at Portsmouth, Virginia, under MAP. Cargo capacity 2 100 tons.

Of the original LST (3) type landing ships on loan from Great Britain, *Alfios* (ex-*LST* 3020), *Axios* (ex-*LST* 3007) and *Strymon* (ex-LST 3502) were returned to the Royal Navy, refitted at Malta and taken over by the Ministry of Transport. *Acheloos* (which replaced *Acheloos*, ex-LST 2503 in 1964) and *Aliakmon* L 104 (ex-LST 3002) were officially deleted from the list in 1969, and *Pinios* L 171 (ex-*LST* 3506) in 1971.

SYROS   *1969, Royal Hellenic Navy, Official*

CHIOS L 195 (ex-*LST* 35) **LIMNOS** L 158 (ex-*LST* 36) **SAMOS** L 179 (ex-*LST* 33)

Displacement, tons	1 625 standard; 4 080 full load
Dimensions, feet	316 wl; 328 oa × 50 × 14 max
Guns ,	1—3 in; 6—20 mm AA
Main Engines	Diesel; 2 shafts; 1 700 bhp = 11 knots
Oil fuel (tons)	595
Complement	119

All launched in 1943. Acquired from the US Navy in 1943, on Lend-lease terms. *Lesvos* (ex-LST 322) was returned to the British Government in 1953. A photograph of *Chios* appears in the 1952-53 to 1960-61 editions.

SAMOS   *1969, Royal Hellenic Navy, Official*

MEDIUM LANDING SHIPS

IPOPLIARKHOS CRYSTALIDIS (ex-USS *LSM* 541)	L 165
IPOPLIARKHOS DANIOLOS (ex-USS *LSM* 227)	L 163
IPOPLIARKHOS GRIGOROPOULOS (ex-USS *LSM* 45)	L 161
IPOPLIARKHOS MERLIN (ex-USS *LSM* 577)	L 166
IPOPLIARKHOS ROUSSEN (ex-USS *LSM* 399)	L 164
IPOPLIARKHOS TOURNAS (ex-USS *LSM* 102)	L 162

Displacement, tons	743 beaching; 1 095 full load
Dimensions, feet	196·5 wl; 203·5 oa × 34·2 × 8·3
Guns	2—40 mm AA; 8—20 mm AA
Main engines	Diesel direct drive; 2 shafts; 3 600 bhp = 13 knots

Former US Medium Landing Ships. *LSM* 541 and *LSM* 557 were handed over to Greece at Salamis on 30 Oct 1958 and *LSM* 45, *LSM* 102, *LSM* 227 and *LSM* 399 at Portsmouth, Virginia on 3 Nov 1958. All were renamed after naval heroes killed during World War 2. A photograph of *Ipopliarkhos Crystalidis* appears in the 1961-62 to 1966-67 editions and of *Ipopliarkhos Grigoropoulos* in the 1967-68 to 1970-71 editions.

IPOPLIARKHOS TOURNAS   *1971, Royal Hellenic Navy, Official*

REPAIR SHIP

SAKIPIS (ex-*KNM Ellida*, ex-USS *ARB* 13, ex-USS *LST* 50) A 329

Displacement, tons	3 800 standard; 5 000 full load
Dimensions, feet	316 wl; 328 oa × 50 × 11 max
Guns	12—40 mm AA; 12—20 mm AA
Main Engines	GM diesels; 2 shafts; 1 800 bhp = 10 knots
Complement	200

Former US tank landing ship. Built by Dravo Corporation, Pittsburgh. Laid down on 29 Aug 1943, launched on 16 Oct 1943, completed on 27 Nov 1943. Converted to a battle damage repair ship in 1952 by Puget Sound Bridge & Dry Dock Co. Taken over by the Royal Norwegian Navy at Seattle on 14 Nov 1952 to serve as a battle damage repair ship for surface vessels. Returned to the US Navy on 1 July 1960. Transferred to Greece on 16 Sep 1960 at Bergen, Norway.

SAKIPIS   *1969, Royal Hellenic Navy, Official*

MINESWEEPER DEPOT SHIP

HERMES (ex-*Product*, ex-*Port Jackson*) A 324

Displacement, tons	550 standard; 650 full load
Dimensions, feet	133 × 27·8 × 11
Main Engines	Diesel; 4-stroke; 560 bhp = 11 knots

Former British trawler. Launched on 1941. On loan from Great Britain.

HERMES   *1969, Royal Hellenic Navy, Official*

BOOM DEFENCE VESSELS

THETIS (ex-USS *AN* 103) A 307

Displacement, tons	680 standard; 805 full load
Dimensions, feet	146 wl; 169·5 oa × 33·5 × 11·8 max
Guns	1—40 mm AA; 4—20 mm AA
Main engines	MAN diesels; 1 shaft; 1 400 bhp = 12 knots
Complement	48

Netlayer of the US type. Built by Kröger, Rendsburg, as a US offshore order. Launched in 1959. Taken over by the Royal Hellenic Navy on 9 Apr 1960.

THETIS   *1971, Royal Hellenic Navy, Official*

OCEAN SALVAGE VESSELS

SOTIR (ex-*Salventure*) A 384

Displacement, tons	1,440 standard; 1 700 full load
Measurement, tons	1 112 gross
Dimensions, feet	216 oa × 37·8 × 13 max
Main Engines	Triple expansion; 2 shafts; 1 500 ihp = 12 knots
Oil fuel (tons)	310
Complement	60

Former British Royal Fleet Auxiliary ocean salvage vessel of the "Salv" class. On loan from Great Britain. Equipped with a decompression chamber.

SOTIR   *1969, Royal Hellenic Navy, Official*

DOCK LANDING SHIP

NAFKRATOUSSA (ex-USS *Fort Mandan*, LSD 21)

Displacement, tons	4 790 light; 9 375 full load
Dimensions, feet	457·8 oa × 72·2 × 18 max
Guns	8—40 mm AA
Main engines	Geared turbines; 2 shafts; 7 000 shp = 15·4 knots
Boilers	2

Built at Boston Navy Yard. Laid down on 2 Jan 1945. Launched on 22 May 1945. Completed on 31 Oct 1945. This dock landing ship to be taken over from USA in 1971 has been named *Nafkratoussa*, replacing the previous *Nafkratoussa* (ex-*Hyperion*, ex-*LSD* 9) out of service in 1971 as Headquarters ship of Captain, Landing Forces.

NAFKRATOUSSA (ex-*LSD* 9)   *1970, A. & J. Pavia*

LANDING CRAFT

LCU 763 (*Kithnos*)	**LCU 827** (*Sciathos*)	**LCU 1229** (*Kea*)
LCU 655 (*Sifnos*)	**LCU 852** (*Scopelos*)	**LCU 1379** (*Karpathos*)
	LCU 971 (*Kimolos*)	**LCU 1382** (*Kassos*)

Displacement, tons	143 standard; 309 full load
Dimensions, feet	105 wl; 119 oa × 32·7 × 5 max
Guns	2—20 mm AA
Main Engines	Diesel; 3 shafts; 440 bhp = 8 knots
Complement	13

Former US Utility Landing Craft of the *LCU* (ex-*LST* (6)) type. *Sciathos* and *Scopelos* were acquired in 1959. *Kea*, *Kithnos* (original No. 149) and *Sifnos* were transferred from USA in 1961. and *Karpathos* (original No. 146) *Kassos* and *Kimolos* in 1962. These LCUs are referred to by their hull numbers and not by name. There are also 13 LCMs and 34 *LCVPs*, all transferred from USA.

KITHNOS, LCU 763 (L 149)   *1971, Royal Hellenic Navy, Official*

Greece—*continued*
OILERS

ARETHOUSA (ex-USS *Natchaug*, AOG 54) A 377

Displacement, tons	1 850 light; 4 335 full load
Measurement, tons	2 575 deadweight; cargo capacity 2 040
Dimensions, feet	232 wl; 310·8 oa × 48·5 × 15·7 max
Guns	4—3 in dp; 50 cal
Main engines	GM diesels; 2 shafts; 3 300 bhp = 14 knots
Complement	43 (6 officers, 37 men)

Former US petrol carrier. Built by Cargill Inc, Savage, Minn. Laid down on 15 Aug 1944. Launched on 6 Dec 1944. Transferred from the USA to Greece under the Mutual Defense Assistance Program at Pearl Harbour, Hawaii, in July 1959.

ARETHOUSA   1968, A. & J. Pavia

ZEUS (ex-YOG 98) A 372

Dimensions, feet   165 × 35 × 10

Former US yard petrol carrier. Launched in 1944. Capacity 900 tons.

SIRIOS (ex-*Poseidon*, ex-*Empire Faun*) A 345

Formerly on loan from Great Britain, but purchased outright in 1962. This ship was renamed *Sirios* when the name *Poseidon* was given to the submarine *Lapon* acquired from the USA in 1958 (see earlier page). Capacity 850 tons.

VIVIIS A 471

Originally a water carrier but now employed as an oiler. Capacity 687 tons.

PROMETHEUS A 374

Small yard oil tanker. Launched in 1959. Capacity 520 tons.

KRONOS (ex-*Islay*, ex-*Dresden*) A 373

Displacement, tons   311

Capacity 110 tons. *Khalki* and *Xanthi* were officially stricken from the list in 1958.

ORION (ex-US tanker Y 126) A 376

Formerly small United States yard tanker. Capacity 700 tons.

ORION   1969, Royal Hellenic Navy, Official

GABON

Mercantile Marine

Lloyd's Register of shipping: 4 vessels of 1 182 tons gross

PATROL BOAT

PRESIDENT LEON M'BA GCO 1

Displacement, tons	85 standard
Dimensions, feet	92 × 20·5 × 5
Guns	1 × 75 mm; 1 12·7 mm MG
Main engines	Diesel = 12·5 knots

Built in Gabon, launched on 16 Jan 1968, as a replacement for the former British SDB *Bouet-Willaumez*, ex- *VP 775*, ex- *VP 25*, ex-*HDML* 1021, which was returned to France in 1968 after service with Gabon since 1961.

FLEET TUGS

ACCHILEUS (ex-*Confident*)   **ATROMITOS** A 410   **PERSEUS** (ex-*ST772*)
AEGEVS   **CIGAS**   **ROMALEOS**
AIAS   **MINOTAVROS**   **TITAN**
ANTAIOS (ex-*Busy*)   (ex-*Theseus*, ex-*ST* 539) **SAMSON** (ex-*F* 16)
ATLAS (ex-*F* 5)

Heraklis was officially deleted from the list in 1966, *Aegeus* in 1968, and *Kentravros* in 1969.

LIGHTHOUSE TENDERS

ST LYKOUDIS (ex-*Chania*, ex-HMS *Nasturtium*) A 481

Displacement, tons	1 020 standard; 1,280 full load
Dimensions, feet	190 pp; 205 oa × 33 × 14·5
Main Engines	Triple expansion; 2 750 ihp = 14 knots
Boilers	2 SE
Oil fuel (tons)	230

Former corvette of the British "Flower" type. Launched in 1940. Sold to Greece as a merchant ship in 1948.

ST. LYKOUDIS   1969, Royal Hellenic Navy, Official

SKYROS A 485   **SERRAI** (ex-*Anna Raeder*) A 487

Displacement, tons   350   Displacement, tons   725

WATER CARRIERS

ILIKI   KALIROE   KASTORIA   STYMPHALIA   TRIHONIS   VOLVI

Capacity 120 tons, except *Trihonis* 300. *Volvi* 350. *Kastoria* 520 tons.

COASTAL SURVEY VESSELS

VEGAS (ex-*BYMS* 2078)

Former coastal minesweeper of the wooden hulled BYMS type, see sister ships on previous page. Of eight sister ships used as coastal patrol vessels, *Aura* (ex-*BYMS* 2054) was deleted from the list in 1962, *Andromeda* (ex-*BYMS* 2261), *Kleio* (ex-*BYMS* 2152) and *Thalia* (ex-*BYMS* 2252) in 1967, *Lambadias* (ex-*BYMS* 2182), *Pigassos* (ex-*BYMS* 2221) and *Prokyon*) ex-*BYMS* 2076) in 1968, and *Ariadne* (ex-*BYMS* 2058) in 1971.

ANEMOS

Officially added to the Royal Hellenic Navy List in 1969. The coastal survey vessel *Alykoni* was discarded in 1961.

GUYANA

Mercantile Marine

Lloyd's Register of Shipping: 6 vessels of 12 212 tons gross

PATROL LAUNCHES

Dimensions, feet	44·5 × 11·5 × 6·3;
Guns	7·62 mm general purpose machine guns
Main engines	D 336A diesels

It was officially reported that four launches for this force were launched on 15 Feb 1968. They have steel hulls with aluminium superstructures.

GUATEMALA

On 5 Jan 1959 Guatemala announced the establishment of a navy, with the primary duty of routing poaching fishing boats and smugglers. In addition to the patrol vessel below there are four small patrol craft (ex-US 40 ft Coast Guard cutters). A 63 ft aircraft rescue boat (AVR) was transferred from USA to Guatemala on 8 Oct 1964.

Personnel

80 officers, non-commissioned officers and men

Mercantile Marine

1971: Lloyd's Register of Shipping: 2 vessels of 3 629 tons gross

PATROL BOATS

JOSÉ FRANCISCO BARRUNDIA (ex-*Snapphanen*)

Displacement, tons	310 standard; 370 full load
Dimensions, feet	170·8 × 19·8 × 9·2
Guns	2—3 in; 2—25 mm AA
Main Engines	De Laval geared turbines; 2 shafts; 3 600 shp = 23 knots
Boilers	2 Vancon-Normand
Oil fuel (tons)	50
Complement	40

Built by Karlskrona Dockyard. Launched on 2 Nov 1933. Former minesweeper in the Royal Swedish Navy until 1959 when she was transferred to the new Guatemalan Navy as the first warship. Now has lower mast (lattice), bridge and funnel (squat, thicker and streamlined) and shields on her 12-pounder guns. One of the 25 mm guns was moved aft. She is painted a very light grey, nearly white. In 1964 she was reported to be inoperative.

JOSE FRANCISCO BARRUNDIA   1959, Official

GUINEA

Mercantile Marine

Lloyd's Register of Shipping: 41 vessels of 14 214 tons gross

Coast Guard

Several "P 6" class MTBs were reported to have been received since Aug 1967. Observed in Conakry Harbour late Oct 1970; Three "P 6" class MTBs, two patrol boats of the same type as P 20, P 21 and P 23 in the Ghana Navy with the numbers P 215 and P 425, and two small landing craft.

HAITI

COAST GUARD VESSELS

DESSALINES (ex-USS *Tonawanda*, AN 89) GC 10

Displacement, tons	650 standard; 785 full load
Dimensions, feet	168·5 × 33 × 10·8
Main Engines	Busch-Sulzer diesel-electric; 1 500 shp = 12 knots

Former United States Navy netlayer of the "Cohoes" class. Built by Leatham D. Smith S.B. Co. Launched on 14 Nov 1944. Loaned to Haiti in 1960 for five years.

AMIRAL KILLICK   Official

AMIRAL KILLICK (ex-USCG *Black Rock*, WAGL 367) GC 7

Displacement, tons	160
Dimensions, feet	Length 114

Former buoy tender purchased from the US Coast Guard in 1955, commissioned in Jan 1956.

LA CRETE A PIERROT (ex-USCG 95315) GC 8   VERTIERES GC 9

Displacement, tons	100
Dimensions, feet	95 × 19 × 5
Guns	1—40 mm AA
Main Engines	4 diesels; 2 shafts; 2 200 bhp = 21 knots
Radius, miles	1 500
Complement	15

Former US Coast Guard steel cutters. Built at US Coast Guard Yard, Curtiss Bay, Maryland. *La Crete a Pierrot* was acquired on 26 Feb 1956. *Vertieres* was transferred to Haiti at Norfolk, Virginia, in Oct 1956 and commissioned in Dec 1956.

16 AOUT 1946 (ex-*SC* 453) GC 2

Displacement, tons	110 standard; 138 full load
Dimensions, feet	110·5 × 18·8 × 6·5
Guns	2—40 mm; 2—20 mm
Main Engines	Diesels; 2 shafts; 1 000 bhp = 15 knots

Submarine chaser of the SC type acquired during 1947 from the US Navy. Launched in 1943. Laid up in reserve. *Amiral Killick*, GC 4, was discarded in 1954, *Toussaint L'Ouverture* (ex-*SC* 1064) was sold in 1959.

SAVANNAH GC 1

Displacement, tons	47
Dimensions, feet	83 × 16 × 4·2
Main Engines	Diesels; 2 shafts; 200 bhp = 9 knots
Complement	12

Ex-USCG cutter 56200, built in the USA in 1944 and acquired in 1944.

ARTIBONITE (ex-US *LCT*) GC 5

Displacement, tons	134 standard; 285 full load
Dimensions, feet	120·3 oa × 32 × 4·2
Main Engines	3 diesels; 675 bhp = 8 knots
Complement	12

Former US tank landing craft. Salvaged by Haitian Coast Guard after grounding and converted. Laid up in reserve having been damaged by grounding in Mar 1956. *Vertieres* GC 6 (ex-USS *APC* 92) was lost at sea.

SANS SOUCI (ex-*Captain James Taylor*)

Displacement, tons	161
Main Engines	Diesels; 2 shafts; 300 bhp = 10 knots

Employed, when required, as the Presidential Yacht.

HONDURAS

Coast Guard

There are three small coastguard cutters.

Mercantile Marine

Lloyd's Register of Shipping: 52 vessels of 60 216 tons gross

HUNGARY

Mercantile Marine

Lloyd's Register of Shipping: 20 vessels of 31 325 tons gross

River Guard

Until late in 1968 naval vessels listed included the river patrol vessel *Baya* (ex-*Barsch*), the parent ship *Csobanc*, the training ship *Badacsony*, ten patrol launches, ten river minesweepers, and two minesweeping launches (see full particulars of all these vessels in the 1968-69 and earlier editions); but in 1969 it was officially stated by the Hungarian Embassy in London that there were no longer any fighting ships in Hungary since the small fleet had been dispersed, and in 1970 it was stated that there were no plans to enter new naval vessels into service. But it is reported that there still remains a residue of a flotilla of river monitors and watch pickets forming the River Guard under the Ministry of the Interior which constitutes a para-military marine service, and Army vessels are very active along the Danube.

Former Sweeper   River Guard

ICELAND

Duties

The Coast Guard Service (Landhelgisgaezlan) deals with fishery protection, salvage, rescue, hydrographic research, surveying, and lighthouse duties.

Personnel

1971: 120 officers and men (official)

Strength of the Coast Guard

5 Patrol Vessels; Prefix: v/s; colour: dark grey.
1 Patrol Aircraft and helicopter

Mercantile Marine

Lloyd's Register of Shipping:
279 vessels of 119 305 tons gross

COAST GUARD PATROL VESSELS

ÆGIR

Displacement, tons	1 150
Dimensions, feet	204 × 33 × 13
Guns	1—57 mm
Main engines	2 diesels; 2 shafts; 8 000 bhp = 19 knots
Complement	22

The first new construction patrol vessel for the Icelandic Coast Guard Service for about eight years. Projected in Feb 1965. Built by Aalborg Vaerft, Denmark. Laid down in May 1967. Completed in 1968.

ÆGIR   *1969, Icelandic Coast Guard Service. Official*

ODINN

Measurements, tons	1 000
Dimensions, feet	187 pp × 33 × 13
Guns	1—57 mm
Main Engines	2 diesels; 2 shafts; 5 000 bhp = 18 knots
Complement	22.

Designed as a coast guard vessel. Built at Aalborg Vaerft A/S, Denmark. Laid down in Jan 1959. Launched in Sep 1959. Completed in Jan 1960.

ODINN   *1967, Icelandic Coast Guard Service, Official*

ALBERT

Measurement, tons	200 gross
Dimensions, feet	Length: 111·2
Guns	1—47 mm
Main engines	1 Nohab diesel; 650 bhp = 12·5 knots
Complement	15

Launched in 1956. Completed and commissioned for service in Apr 1957.

ALBERT   *1967, Icelandic Coast Guard Service, Official*

THOR

Displacement, tons	920
Dimensions, feet	183·3 pp; 206 oa × 31·2 × 13
Guns	1—57 mm
Main engines	2 diesels; 3 200 bhp = 17 knots
Complement	22

Built at Aalborg, Denmark. Launched in 1951. Completed and commissioned in late 1951. Rated as coastal inspection and salvage vessel.

THOR   *1969, Icelandic Coast Guard Service, Official*

ARVAKUR

Displacement, tons	716
Dimensions, feet	106 × 33 × 13
Guns	1 small to be mounted
Main engines	1 diesel; 1 000 bhp = 12 knots
Complement	12

Built as a lighthouse tender in the Netherlands in 1962. Acquired by Iceland for duty in the Coast Guard Service in 1969.

ARVAKUR   *1969, Icelandic Coast Guard Service, Official*

DISPOSALS
Gautur (ex-*Odinn*) was officially deleted from the Coast Guard List on 1 Jan 1963, *Tyr* in 1964, and *Sæbjorg* in Aug 1965. The old *Aegir* (built in 1929) was broken up in 1968, and the small *Maria Julia* was sold in 1969.

LOSS. The fishery protection patrol vessel and lighthouse tender *Hermodur* foundered off the south-west coast of Iceland on 17 Feb 1959.

INDIA

Administration

Chief of the Naval Staff:
Admiral S. M. Nanda, PVSM

Flag Officer C in C, West Coast:
Vice-Admiral N. Krishnan, PVSM

Flag Officer Commanding Western Fleet:
Rear-Admiral V. A. Kamath

Flag Officer C in C, East Coast:
Vice-Admiral K. B. Nair, PVSM

Diplomatic Representation

Naval Adviser in London:
Commodore N. P. Datta

Naval Attaché in Paris and Bonn:
Commodore B. K. Dang

Naval Attaché in Washington:
Brigadier F. Mehta
Naval Attaché in Moscow:
Commodore S Prakash

Strength of the Fleet

 1 Aircraft Carrier
 4 Submarines (Diesel Powered)
 2 Cruisers
 3 Destroyers
 3 Escort Destroyers
19 Frigates
 4 Survey Ships (3 ex-Frigates)
 1 Ocean Minesweeper
 4 Coastal Minesweepers
 4 Inshore Minesweepers
 6 Torpedo Boats
15 Patrol Craft (Seaward Defence)
16 Support Ships and Service Craft

Colour of Warships

In 1969 the active vessels of the Indian Fleet assumed a darker shade of grey than previously used.

Personnel

1971: 20 000 (1 800 officers, 18 200 ratings)

Naval Bases and Establishments

Bombay (C in C Western Fleet, barracks and main Dockyard);
Vishakapatnam (C in C Eastern Command, submarine base, dockyard and barracks);
Cochin (Naval Air Station, barracks and professional schools);
Lonavala and Jamnagar (professional schools);
Calcutta, Goa, and Port Blair small bases only.

Mercantile Marine

Lloyd's Register of Shipping:
399 vessels of 2 401 656 tons gross

Scale: 150 feet = 1 inch   (1 : 1 800)

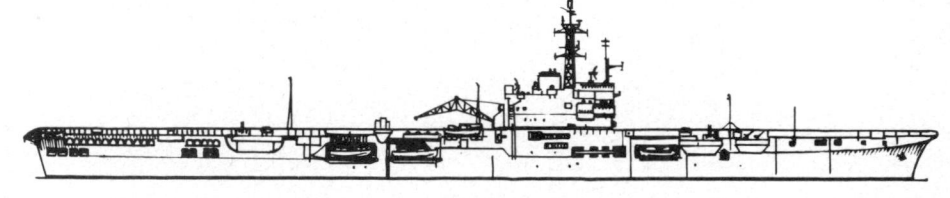

VIKRANT

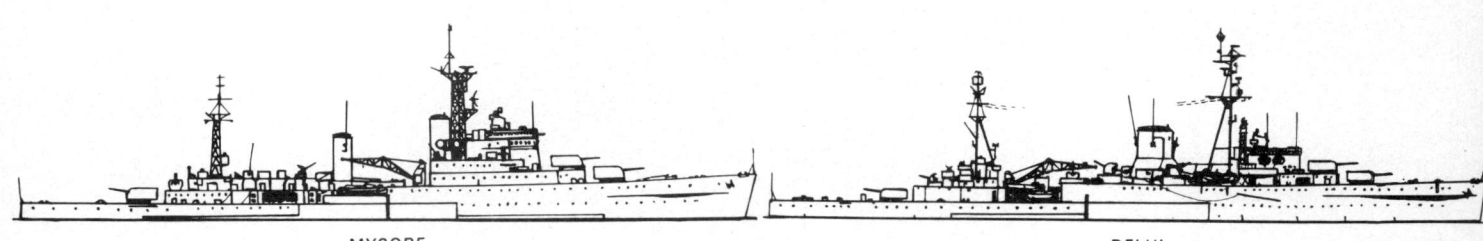

MYSORE   DELHI

RANA

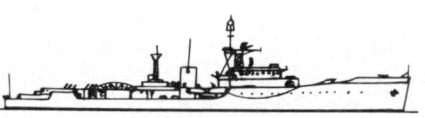

KHUKRI, KIRPAN, KUTHAR

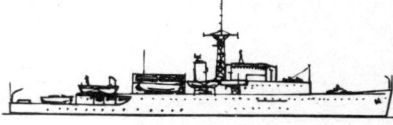

JUMNA

RAJPUT   RANJIT

KADMATT

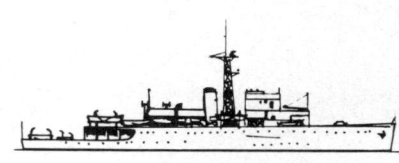

SUTLEJ

TALWAR, TRISHUL

GANGA, GODAVARI, GOMATI

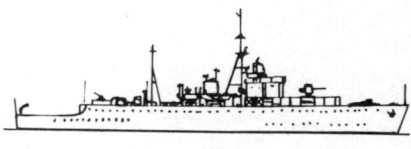

TIR

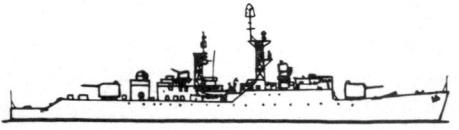

BEAS, BETWA, BRAHMAPUTRA

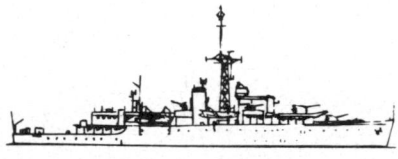

KAVERI, KISTNA

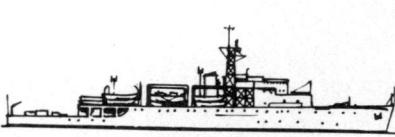

INVESTIGATOR

DARCHAK

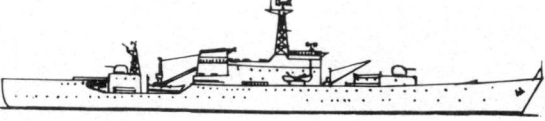

AMBA

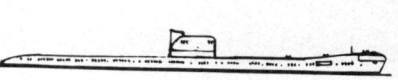

KALVARI

AIRCRAFT CARRIER

Name	No.	Builders	Engineers	Laid down	Launched	Completed
VIKRANT (ex-HMS *Hercules*)	R 11	Vickers-Armstrong Ltd, Tyne	Parsons Marine Steam Turbine Co	14 Oct 1943	22 Sep 1945	4 Mar 1961

1 Ex-BRITISH "MAJESTIC" CLASS

Displacement, tons	16 000 standard ; 19 500 full load
Length, feet (*metres*)	630 (*192·0*) pp ; 700 (*213·4*) oa
Beam, feet (*metres*)	80 (*24·4*) hull
Width, feet (*metres*)	128 (*39·0*)
Draught, feet (*metres*)	24 (*7·3*)
Aircraft	21 capacity
Guns, AA	15—40 mm ; 4 twin, 7 single
Boilers	4 Admiralty 3-drum ; 400 psi ; 700°F
Main engines	Parsons single reduction geared turbines ; 40 000 shp ; 2 shafts
Speed, knots	24·5 designed
Complement	1 343, designed accommodation

Acquired from Great Britain in Jan 1957 after having been suspended in May 1946 when structurally almost complete and 75% fitted out. Taken in hand by Harland & Wolff Ltd, Belfast, in Apr 1957 for completion in 1961 Commissioned on 4 Mar 1961 and renamed *Vikrant*.

HABITABILITY. Partially air-conditioned and insulated for tropical service, the ship's sides being sprayed with asbestos cement instead of being lagged. Separate messes and dining halls.

ENGINEERING. Engines and boilers are arranged *en echelon*, one set of turbines and two boilers being installed side by side in each of the two propelling machinery spaces, on the unit system, so that the starboard propeller shaft is longer than the port.

FLIGHT DECK. The aircraft including strike and anti-submarine aircraft, operate from an angled deck with steam catapult, landing sights and two electrically operated lifts.

VIKRANT   *1971, Indian Navy, Official*

RADAR
Search: Type 960, Type 277.
Tactical: Type 293.
Miscellaneous: Type 963 Carrier Controlled Approach.

CLASS. Originally a sister ship of *Leviathan* (structurally almost finished and 80 per cent fitted out but never wholly completed and broken up in 1968) ; *Magnificent* (which served in the Royal Canadian Navy 1946-57) of the Royal Navy, scrapped in 1965 ; *Sydney* (ex-*Terrible*) and *Melbourne* (ex-*Majestic*) in the Royal Australian Navy ; and *Bonaventure* (ex-*Powerful*) in the Royal Canadian Navy. decommissioned in 1970.

DRAWING. Starboard elevation and plan. Drawn in 1971. Scale: 125 feet = 1 inch (1 : 1 500).

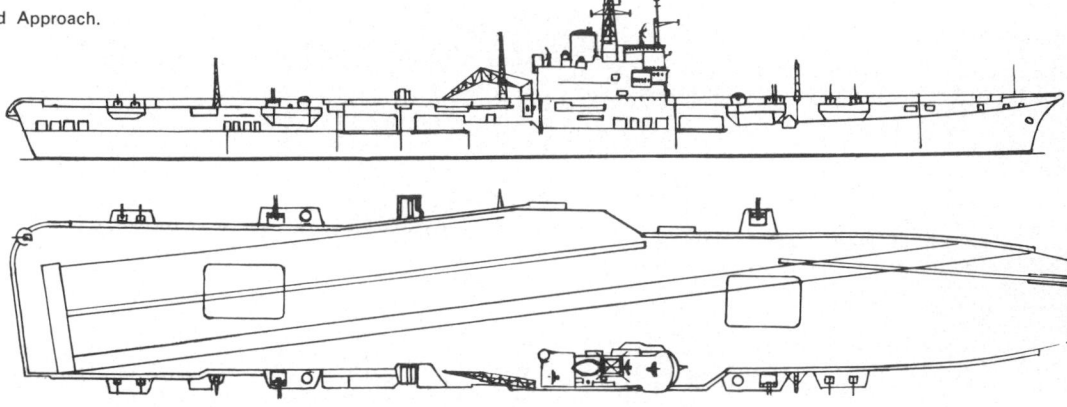

VIKRANT   *1971, John G. Callis*

SUBMARINES

4 EX SOVIET "F" CLASS

KALVARI   **KARANJ**   **KURSURA**
KANDERI

Displacement, tons	2 000 surface ; 2 300 submerged
Dimensions, feet	300 × 27 × 19
Tubes	8—21 in (20 torpedoes carried)
Main engines	Diesel 3 shaft 10 000 bhp = 20 knots surface
	Electric motors 4 000 hp = 15 knots submerged

Kalvari arrived in India on 16 July 1968 and *Kanderi* in 1969. *Kanderi* commissioned at Riga in Jan 1969. A photograph of *Kanderi* appears in the 1969-70 and 1970-71 editions.

KANDERI   *1971, Dr. Louis Th. Berge*

CRUISERS

Name	No.	Builders	Engineers	Laid down	Launched	Completed
MYSORE (ex- HMS *Nigeria*)	C 60	Vickers-Armstrongs, Ltd, Tyne	Parsons	8 Feb 1938	18 July 1939	23 Sep 1940

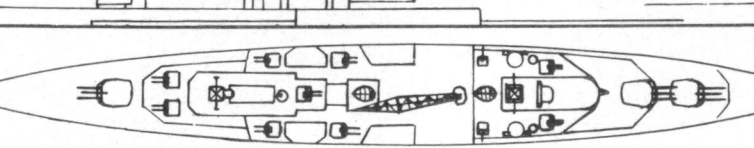

Displacement, tons	8 700 standard ; 11 040 full load
Length, feet (*metres*)	538 (*164·0*) ,pp ; 549 (*167·3*) wl
	555·5 (*169·3*) oa
Beam, feet (*metres*)	62 (*18·9*)
Draught, feet (*metres*)	21 (*6·4*) max
Guns, surface	9—6 in (*152 mm*)
Guns, AA	8—4 in (*102 mm*)
	12—40 mm ; 5 twin and 2 single
Armour	Side 4½ in—3 in (*114—76 mm*) ;
	Deck 2 in (*51 mm*) ;
	Conning tower 4 in (*102 mm*) ,
	Turrets 2 in (*51 mm*)
Boilers	4 Admiralty 3-drum
Main engines	Parsons geared turbines
	72 500 shp ; 4 shafts
Speed, knots	31·5
Complement	800

Formerly a "Colony" class cruiser in the Royal Navy. Purchased from Great Britain on 8 Apr 1954 for £300 000. Extensively refitted and reconstructed by Cammell Laird & Co Ltd, Birkenhead, before commissioning. Formerly handed over to the Indian Navy at Birkenhead and renamed *Mysore* on 29 Aug 1957.

RADAR
Search: Type 960, Type 277.
Tactical: Type 293.
Fire Control: X Band.

RECONSTRUCTION. Ship formerly had tripod masts. During reconstruction the triple 6 inch turret in "X" position and the 6—21 inch torpedo tubes (tripled) were removed, the bridge was modified, two lattice masts were stepped, all electrical equipment was replaced and the engine room and other parts of the ship were refitted.

DRAWING. Starboard elevation and plan. Drawn in 1971. Scale: 125 feet = 1 inch (1 : 1 500).

PHOTOGRAPHS. A port bow surface view of *Mysore* appears in the 1957-58 to 1960-61 editions, a port oblique aerial view in the 1961-62 to 1965-66 editions, and a port broadside surface view in the 1966-67 to 1960-71 editions.

MYSORE

1971, Roland Rodwell

Name	No.	Builders	Laid down	Launched	Completed
DELHI (ex HMS *Achilles*)	C 74	Cammell Laird & Co Ltd, Birkenhead	11 June 1931	1 Sep 1932	5 Oct 1933

Displacement, tons	7 114 standard , 9 740 full load
Length, feet (*metres*)	522 (*159·1*) pp ; 544·5 (*166·0*) oa
Beam, feet (*metres*)	55·2 (*16·8*)
Draught, feet (*metres*)	20·0 (*6·1*) max
Guns, surface	6—6 in (*152 mm*)
Guns, AA	8—4 in (*102 mm*) , 14—40 mm
Guns, saluting	4—3 pdr
Armour	4 in-2 in side, 1 in gunhouses, 1 in
	bridge, 2 in deck
Main engines	Parsons geared turbines ; 4 shafts
	72 000 shp ; 32 knots
Boilers	4 Admiralty 3-drum type
Oil fuel, tons	1 800
Complement	800

Formerly a "Leander" class light cruiser in the Royal Navy. Purchased from Great Britain and delivered on 5 July 1948. Refitted in 1955.

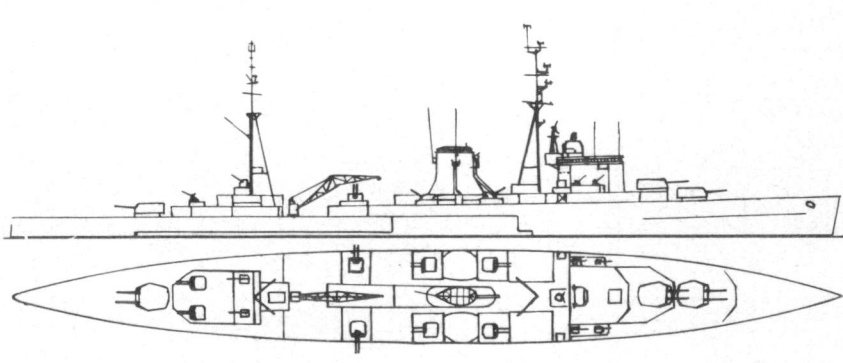

RADAR
Search: Type 960, Type 277.
Tactical: Type 293.
Fire Control: Early design.

TORPEDO TUBES. In 1958 the original eight 21 inch torpedo tubes, in two quadruple banks, were removed, their emplacement was suppressed, and the forecastle deck plating was consequently extended aft to the twin 40 mm AA gun mounting abreast the boat stowage.

HISTORICAL. As HMS *Achilles*, then lent to the Royal New Zealand Navy, this ship, with HMS *Ajax* and HMS *Exeter*, defeated the German battleship *Admiral Graf Spee* in the Battle of the River Plate on 13 Dec 1939.

DRAWING. Starboard elevation and plan. Drawn in 1971. Scale: 125 feet = 1 inch (1 : 1 500).

DELHI

Added 1971

DESTROYERS

Name	No.	Builders	Begun	Launched	Completed	Transferred
RANA (ex-HMS *Raider*)	D 115	Cammell Laird & Co Ltd, Birkenhead	16 Apr 1941	1 Apr 1942	16 Nov 1942	9 Sep 1949
RAJPUT (ex-HMS *Rotherham*)	D 209	John Brown & Co Ltd, Clydebank	10 Apr 1941	21 Mar 1942	27 Aug 1942	29 July 1949
RANJIT (ex-HMS *Redoubt*)	D 141	John Brown & Co Ltd, Clydebank	19 June 1941	2 May 1942	1 Oct 1942	4 July 1949

Displacement, tons	1 725 standard ; 2 424 full load
Dimensions, feet	339·5 wl ; 362 oa × 35·7 × 16 max
Guns, surface	4—4·7 in (*120 mm*)
Guns, AA	4—40 mm
A/S weapons	4 DCT
Torpedo tubes	8—21 in (2 quadruple) in *Rana*
Main engines	Parsons geared turbines ; 2 shafts 40 000 shp = 32 knots
Boilers	2 Admiralty 3-drum type
Oil fuel (tons)	490
Radius, miles	2 500 at 20 knots
Complement	240

First British destroyers with officers' accommodation forward instead of aft. Refitted and modernised before transfer. Arrived in Indian waters in Jan 1950. Constitute 11th Destroyer Squadron of which *Rajput* is Leader.

RADAR
Search: Type 293.
Fire Control: Early design.

PHOTOGRAPHS. A photograph of *Rana* appears in the 1957-58 edition and of *Ranjit* in the 1966-67 edition.

RAJPUT

ESCORT DESTROYERS

Name	No.	Builders	Laid down	Launched	Completed
GANGA (ex-HMS *Chiddingfold*)	D 94	Scott's Shipbuilding & Engineering Co Ltd, Greenock	1 Mar 1940	10 Mar 1941	16 Oct 1941
GODAVARI (ex-HMS *Bedale*, ex-*Slazak*, ex-*Bedale*)	D 92	R. & W. Hawthorn, Leslie & Co Ltd, Hebburn	29 May 1940	5 Sep 1941	18 June 1944
GOMATI (ex-HMS *Lamerton*)	D 93	Swan, Hunter & Wigham Richardson Ltd, Wallsend	10 Apr 1939	14 Dec 1940	16 Aug 1944

3 "HUNT" CLASS. TYPE II

Displacement, tons	1 050 standard ; 1 610 full load
Length, feet (*metres*)	264·2 (*80·5*) pp 280 (*85·3*) oa
Beam, feet (*metres*)	31·5 (*9·6*)
Draught, feet (*metres*)	14 (*4·3*)
Guns, dual purpose	6—4 in (*102 mm*)
Guns, AA	4—20 mm
Boilers	2 Admiralty 3-drum
Main engines	Parsons geared turbines 19 000 shp ; 2 shafts
Speed, knots	25
Radius, miles	3 700 at 14 knots
Oil fuel (tons)	280
Complement	150

GANGA   *Added 1971, A. & J. Pavia*

Former "Hunt" class, Type II frigates F 131, F 126 and F 88, respectively, (ex-Escort Destroyers). Transferred from Great Britain in Apr/May 1953. Lent to the Indian Navy for three years, subject to extension by agreement.

Officially rated as destroyers with D pennant Nos. Constitute the 22nd Destroyer Squadron of which *Godavari* is Leader.

A photograph of *Godavari* appears in the 1953-54 to 1955-56 editions, and of *Gomati* in the 1966-67 to 1970-71 editions.

GENERAL PURPOSE FRIGATES

6 NEW CONSTRUCTION
"LEANDER" CLASS

HIMGIRI   **NILGIRI**

Displacement, tons	2 450 standard ; 2 800 full load
Length, feet (*metres*)	360 (*109·7*) wl ; 372 (*113·4*) oa
Beam, feet (*metres*)	43 (*13·1*)
Draught, feet (*metres*)	18 (*5·5*)

Aircraft	1 Wasp helicopter
Missiles, AA	2 "Seacat" quadruple launchers
Guns, dual purpose	2—4·5 in (*115 mm*) 1 twin
A/S weapons	1 "Limbo" 3 barrelled DC mortar
Boilers	2
Main engines	2 geared turbines ; 30 000 shp
Speed, knots	30 max
Oil fuel, tons	460

First major warships built in Indian yards. Of similar design to later (broad beam) "Leander" class general purpose frigates in the Royal Navy. All ordered from Mazagon Docks Ltd, Bombay. *Nilgiri* was laid down in Oct 1966, launched on 23 Oct 1968 for commissioning in July 1971. *Himgiri* was launched on 6 May 1970. The third ship was laid down on 14 Sep 1970. Three further ships of the class are projected, it was stated in 1970.

ANTI-AIRCRAFT FRIGATES

Name	No.	Builders	Launched	Completed
BEAS	F 137	Vickers-Armstrongs Ltd, Newcastle-on-Tyne	9 Oct 1958	24 May 1960
BETWA	F 139	Vickers-Armstrongs Ltd, Newcastle-on-tyne	15 Sep 1959	8 Dec 1960
BRAHMAPUTRA (ex-*Panther*)	F 31	John Brown & Co Ltd, Clydebank	15 Mar 1957	28 Mar 1958

3 "LEOPARD" CLASS

Displacement, tons	2 251 standard ; 2 515 full load
Dimensions, feet	320 pp ; 330 wl ; 339·8 oa × 40 × 12·7 max
Guns, surface	4—4·5 in (*114 mm*), 2 twin turrets
Guns, AA	4—40 mm
A/S weapons	1 Squid 3-barrelled DC mortar
Main engines	Admiralty standard range diesels 2 shafts ; 12 380 bhp = 25 knots
Oil fuel (tons)	230
Complement	210

Brahmaputra (Leader), originally ordered as *Panther* for the Royal Navy on 28 June 1951, was the first major warship to be built in Great Britain for the Indian Navy since India became independent. All three ships are generally similar to the British frigates of the "Leopard" class, but modified to suit Indian conditions.

RADAR
Search : Type 960.
Tactical : Type 293.
Fire Control: X Band forward and aft.

BRAHMAPUTRA   *1971, Indian Navy, Official*

PHOTOGRAPHS.
A photograph of *Beas* appears in the 1966-67 to 1970-71 editions, and a starboard bow view of *Betwa* in the 1961-62 to 1965-66 editions.

ANTI-SUBMARINE FRIGATES

2 "WHITBY" CLASS. 1st RATE

Displacement, tons	2 144 standard; 2 545 full load (*Talwar*), 2 557 (*Trishul*)
Length, feet (*metres*)	360 (*109·7*) pp 369·8 (*112·7*) oa
Beam, feet (*metres*)	41 (*12·5*)
Draught, feet (*metres*)	17·8 (*5·4*)
Guns, surface	2—4·5 in (*115 mm*)
Guns, AA	4—40 mm (1 twin before "Limbos", 2 singles abaft funnel)
A/S weapons	2 "Limbo" 3-barrelled DC mortars
Boilers	2 Babcock & Wilcox
Main engines	2 sets geared turbines; 30 000 shp; 2 shafts
Speed, knots	30 max
Oil fuel, tons	400
Complement	231 (11 officers, 220 men)

Built in Great Britain and generally similar to the British frigates of the "Whitby" class, but slightly modified to suit Indian conditions. Talwar is a common weapon in India.

RADAR. Tactical: Type 293. Fire Control: X Band.

Name	No.	Builders	Launched	Completed
TALWAR	F 140	Cammell Laird & Co Ltd, Birkenhead	18 July 1958	1960
TRISHUL (*Leader*)	F 143	Harland & Wolff Ltd, Belfast	18 June 1959	1960

TALWAR   *Added 1971, A. & J. Pavia*

TORPEDO TUBES. Provision was made in the original design for twelve 21 inch (eight single A/S and two twin) but they were not fitted.

PHOTOGRAPHS. A photograph of *Trishul* appears in the 1960-61 edition, and other views of *Talwar* in the 1961-62 to 1970-71 editions.

3 "BLACKWOOD" CLASS 2nd RATE

Displacement, tons	1 180 standard; 1 456 full load
Length, feet (*metres*)	300 (*91·4*) pp; 310 (*94·5*) oa
Beam, feet (*metres*)	33 (*10·0*)
Draught, feet (*metres*)	15·5 (*4·7*)
Guns, AA	3—40 mm (single)
A/S weapons	2 "Limbo" 3-barrelled DC mortars
Boilers	Babcock & Wilcox
Main engines	1 set geared turbines; 15 000 shp; 1 shaft
Speed, knots	27·8 max; 24·5 sustained sea
Oil fuel, tons	300
Complement	150

Built in Great Britain, and generally similar to the British frigates of the "Blackwood" class, but slightly modified to suit Indian requirements. Kirpan means Sword.

RADAR. Fitted with S band air and surface surveillance radar.

Name	No.	Builders	Launched	Completed
KHUKRI	F 149	J. Samuel White & Co Ltd, Cowes, Isle of Wight	20 Nov 1956	16 July 1958
KIRPAN	F 144	Alex Stephen & Sons Ltd, Govan, Glasgow	19 Aug 1958	July 1959
KUTHAR	F 146	J. Samuel White & Co Ltd, Cowes, Isle of Wight	14 Oct 1958	1959

KUTHAR   *Added 1971, A. & J. Pavia*

TORPEDO TUBES. Provision was made for four 21-inch (2 twin) but they were not fitted.

PHOTOGRAPHS. A photograph of *Kuthar* appears in the 1966-67 to 1970-71 editions.

FRIGATES

2 "KISTNA" CLASS

Displacement, tons	1 470 standard; 1 925 full load
Length, feet (*metres*)	283 (*86·3*) pp; 295·5 (*90·1*) wl 299·5 (*91·3*) oa
Beam, feet (*metres*)	38·5 (*11·7*)
Draught, feet (*metres*)	11·2 (*3·4*)
Guns, surface	4—4 in (*102 mm*)
Guns, AA	4—40 mm
A/S weapons	2 DCT
Boilers	2 three-drum type
Main engines	Parsons geared turbines 4 300 shp; 2 shafts
Speed, knots	19
Radius, miles	4 500 at 12 knots
Oil fuel (tons)	370
Complement	210

Former sloops of the British "Black Swan" class built for India and modified to suit Indian conditions. *Cauvery* was renamed *Kaveri* in 1968. A photograph of *Kaveri* appears in the 1955-56 to 1959-60 editions.

RADAR. Fitted with S band air and surface surveillance radar and ranging radar for the gunfire control system.

Name	No.	Builders	Laid down	Launched	Completed
KAVERI	F 110	Yarrow & Co. Ltd, Scotstoun, Glasgow	28 Oct 1942	15 June 1943	21 Oct 1943
KISTNA	F 46	Yarrow & Co. Ltd, Scotstoun, Glasgow	14 July 1942	22 Apr 1943	23 Aug 1943

KISTNA   *1962, Edward Rodwell*

1 "RIVER" CLASS

TIR F 256 (ex-HMS *Bann*)

Displacement, tons	1 463 standard; 1 934 full load
Length, feet (*metres*)	283 (*86·3*) pp; 303 (*92·4*) oa
Beam, feet (*metres*)	36·7 (*11·2*)
Draught, feet (*metres*)	14·5 (*4·4*)
Guns, surface	1—4 in (*102 mm*)
Guns, AA	1—40 mm; 2—20 mm
Boilers	2 Admiralty 3-drum
Main engines	Triple expansion 5 500 ihp; 2 shafts
Speed, knots	18
Radius, miles	3 100 at 12 knots
Oil fuel (tons)	385
Complement	120

Former "River" class frigate in the Royal Navy. Built by Charles Hill & Sons Ltd, Bristol. Laid down on 18 June 1942, launched on 29 Dec 1942, completed on 7 May 1942 and transferred on 3 Dec 1945. Converted to a Midshipman's Training Frigate by Bombay Dockyard in 1948. Originally the sister ship of *Investigator*, see under Survey Ships.

TIR   *1971, Indian Navy, Official*

5 "PETYA" CLASS

KADMATT	**KAMORTA**	**KAVARATTI**
	KATCHAL	**KILTAN**

Displacement, tons	1 050 standard; 1 200 full load
Length, feet (metres)	250 (76·2) wl; 262·5 (80) oa
Beam, feet (metres)	32 (9·8)
Draught, feet (metres)	9·8 (3·0)
Guns, dual purpose	4—3 in (76 mm) 2 twin
Torpedo tubes	5—21 in (533 mm)
Main engines	2 gas turbines, 10 000 hp; 2 diesels, 4 000 hp; 2 shafts
Speed, knots	30

Transferred to Indian Navy during 1969. Reported that a sixth unit is to be transferred. Pennant numbers of two units are reported to be P 179 and P 181.

1 INDIAN BUILT

DARSHAK

Displacement, tons	2 790
Length, feet (metres)	319 (97·2) oa
Beam, feet (metres)	49 (14·9)
Draught, feet (metres)	28·8 (8·8)
Main engines	2 diesel-electric units, 3 000 bhp
Speed, knots	16
Complement	150

First ship built by Hindustan Shipyard, Vizagapatam for the Navy. Launched on 2 Nov 1959 and commissioned on 28 Dec 1964. Operated by the hydrographic branch for marine survey of Indian coastline and harbours. Provision was made to operate a helicopter. The ship is all welded.

1 "RIVER" CLASS (Ex-Frigate)

INVESTIGATOR F 243 (ex-Khukri, ex-HMS Trent)

Displacement, tons	1 460 standard; 1 930 full load
Length, feet (metres)	283 (86·3) pp; 303 (92·4) oa
Beam, feet (metres)	36·7 (11·2)
Draught, feet (metres)	14 (4·3)
Boilers	2 Admiralty 3-drum
Main engines	Triple expansion 5 500 shp; 2 shafts
Speed, knots	18 max
Radius, miles	5 000 at 10 knots
Oil fuel, (tons)	400
Complement	120

Former "River" class frigate in the Royal Navy. Built by Charles Hill & Sons Ltd, Bristol. Laid down on 31 Jan 1942, launched on 10 Oct 1942, completed on 15 Feb 1943, and transferred in April 1946. Converted to a survey ship and renamed Investigator in 1951. Originally the sister ship of the training frigate Tir, see previous page.

2 "SUTLEJ" CLASS
(Ex-Frigates, Ex-Sloops)

JUMNA F 11	**SUTLEJ** F 95

Displacement, tons	1 300 standard; 1 750 full load
Length, feet (metres)	276 (84·1) wl; 292·5 (89·2) oa
Beam, feet (metres)	37·5 (11·4)
Draught, feet (metres)	11·5 (3·5)
Boilers	2 Admiralty 3-drum
Main engines	Parsons geared turbines 3 600 shp; 2 shafts
Speed, knots	18
Radius, miles	5 600 at 12 knots
Oil fuel (tons)	370
Complement	150

Former frigates employed as survey ships since 1957 and 1955 respectively. Both ships are generally similar to the former British frigates of the "Egret" class. Jumna and Sutlej together with Kaveri and Kistna (see previous page) formerly constituted the 12th Frigate Squadron.

CONSTRUCTION. Both built by Wm. Denny & Bros Ltd, Dumbarton. Jumna was laid down on 20 Feb 1940, launched on 16 Nov 1940 and completed on 13 May 1941. Sutlej was laid down on 4 Jan 1940, launched on 10 Oct 1940 and completed on 23 Apr 1941.

DISPOSAL
Afonso de Albuquerque, the former Portuguese frigate disabled and taken in the Goa conquest in Dec 1961, was sold for scrap late in 1966.

Frigates—continued

"PETYA" CLASS   Ex-Soviet

SURVEY SHIPS

DARSHAK   1967 Official

INVESTIGATOR   1965. Indian Navy. Official

JUMNA   1971, Indian Navy, Official

SUTLEJ   Official

OCEAN MINESWEEPERS

1 "BANGOR" CLASS

KONKAN (ex-HMS *Tilbury*) M 228

Displacement, tons	656 standard; 825 full load
Dimensions, feet	171·5 pp; 180 oa × 28·5 × 9·5
Guns	1—2 pdr, 4 MG
Main Engines	Triple expansion; 2 shafts; 2 000 ihp = 16·5 knots
Boilers	2 Admiralty 3-drum
Complement	87

Built by Lobnitz & Co Ltd, Renfrew. Laid down on 15 Aug 1941. Launched on 18 Feb 1942. Completed on 12 June 1942. Scheduled for decommissioning for the last several years, but still in the Navy List in Spring 1971.
Three ocean minesweepers of the "Bathurst" class, *Bengal*, *Bombay* and *Madras*, all reciprocating engine type, built in Sydney, Australia, and three of the "Bangor" class, *Rohilkhand*, steam turbine type, *Konkan* and *Rajputana*, all built in Scotland, constituted the 31st Minesweeping Squadron.
Rajputana and *Rohilkhand* were disposed of in 1960 and *Bombay* and *Madras* in 1962. *Bengal* was discarded in 1967.

KONKAN   *Official*

COASTAL MINESWEEPERS

4 "TON" CLASS

CANNANORE (ex-*Whitton*)	M 1191	**KAKINADA** (ex-*Durweston*)		M 1201
CUDDALORE (ex-*Wennington*)	M 1190	**KARWAR** (ex-*Overton*) Leader		M 1197

Displacement, tons	360 standard; 425 full load
Dimensions, feet	140 pp; 153 oa × 28·8 × 8·2
Guns	1—40 mm AA, 2—20 mm AA
Main Engines	Napier Deltic diesels; 2 shafts; 1 250 bhp = 15 knots
Oil fuel (tons)	45
Complement	40

"Ton" class coastal minesweepers of wooden construction built for the Royal Navy, but transferred from Great Britain to the Indian Navy in 1956. *Cannanore* was built by Fleetlands Shipyard, Ltd Gosport and launched 30 Jan 1956; *Karwar* was built by Camper & Nicholson, Ltd, Gosport, and launched 30 Jan 1956. *Cuddalore*, built by J. S. Doig Ltd, Grimsby, and *Kakinada*, built by Dorset Yacht Co Ltd, Hamworthy were taken over in Aug 1956, and sailed for India in Nov/Dec 1956. Named after minor ports in India. Constitute the 18th Mine Counter Measures Squadron, together with the inshore minesweepers. Four more were reportedly to be acquired.
A photograph of *Cannanore* appears in the 1957-58 to 1963-64 editions and of *Kakinada* in the 1967-68 to 1970-71 editions.

KARWAR   *Added 1971, Wright & Logan*

CUDDALORE   *Added 1971, A. & J. Pavia*

INSHORE MINESWEEPERS

4 + 2 "HAM" CLASS

BASSEIN (ex-*Littleham*)	M 2707	**BIMLIPTAN** (ex-*Hildersham*)	M 2705
BHATKAL M 89		**BULSAR**	

Displacement, tons	120 standard; 170 full load
Dimensions, feet	98 pp; 107 oa × 22 × 6·7
Guns	1—20 mm AA
Main Engines	2 Paxman diesels; 550 bhp = 14 knots (9 knots sweeping)
Oil fuel (tons)	15
Complement	16

"Ham" class inshore minesweepers of wooden construction built for the Royal Navy but transferred from Great Britain to the Indian Navy in 1955. *Bassein* was built by Brooke Marine Ltd, Oulton Broad, Lowestoft, and launched on 4 May 1954; *Bimlipitan* was built by Vosper Ltd, Portsmouth, and launched on 5 Feb 1954. Two further units were built at Magazon Dockyard Bombay. *Bhaktal* was launched in Apr 1967, and *Bulsar* on 17 May 1969. Two more ships are projected.
Barq (ex-*MMS* 132), *MMS* 130 and *MMS* 154, former British motor minesweepers of the "105 ft" type of wooden construction, transferred from Great Britain, are employed as yard craft. *MMS* 1632 and *MMS* 1654 are yard craft in Bombay.

BIMLIPITAN   *Added 1966, A. & J. Pavia*

BASSEIN   *Added 1971, A. & J. Pavia*

PATROL CRAFT

PANBAN	**PANAJI**	**PANVEL**	**PULICAT**	**PURI**

Displacement, tons	120 standard
Dimensions, feet	97 × 20 × 6

Six were ordered from USSR five of which were reportedly delivered in 1967.

4 HDML TYPE

SPC 3110 (ex-*HDML* 1110)	**SPC 3117** (ex-*HDML* 1117)
SPC 3112 (ex-*HDML* 1112)	**SPC 3118** (ex-*HDML* 1118)

Displacement, tons	48 standard; 54 full load
Dimensions, feet	72 oa × 16 × 4·7
Guns	2—20 mm AA
Main Engines	Diesel; 2 shafts; 320 bhp = 12 knots
Complement	14

Former British Harbour Defence Motor Launches. These boats, formerly known as Seaward Defence Motor Launches, constitute the 321st Sea/Land Patrol Craft Squadron.

The seaward patrol craft *SPC 6420* (ex-*ML* 6420, ex-*ML* 420) of the Fairmile "B" motor launch type, was stricken from the Navy list in 1963.

SPC 3112   *Indian Navy, Official*

SEAWARD DEFENCE BOATS

3 "AJAY" CLASS

ABHAY	AJAY	AJIT	AKSHAY	AMAR

Displacement, tons	120 standard; 151 full load (*Ajay* 146)
Dimensions, feet	110 pp; 117·2 oa × 20 × 5
Guns	1—40 mm AA
Main Engines	2 diesels; speed = 18 knots

Generally similar to the "Ford" class in the Royal Navy. *Ajay* was built by Garden Reach Workshop, Calcutta and commissioned on 21 Sep 1960. *Abhay* and *Akshay* were both built by Hoogly Docking and Engineering Company Ltd. Calcutta and commissioned on 13 Nov 1961 and 8 Jan 1962, respectively.

AJAY   *1964, Indian Navy, Official*

2 "SHARADA" CLASS

SHARADA SPB 3133	SUKANYA SPB 3132

Displacement, tons	86
Dimensions, feet	103·2, length
Guns	Small arms
Main Engines	Diesels

Built in Yugoslavia. Commissioned on 5 Dec 1959 and 12 Dec 1959, respectively.

SHARADA   *1964, Indian Navy, Official*

4 "SAVITRI" CLASS

SAVITRI SPB 3128	SHARAYU SPB 3129	SUBHADRA SPB 3130
		SUVARNA SPB 3131

Displacement, tons	63
Dimensions, feet	85·3 pp; 90·2 oa × 20 × 5
Guns	Small Arms
Main Engines	2 diesels; 2 shafts; 1 900 bhp = 21 knots

Built in Italy. Commissioned on 6 Feb 1958, 28 Oct 1957, 20 Aug 1957 and 28 Aug 1957, respectively. Constitute the 322nd SDB Squadron. *Sharayu* is Leader.

SAVITRI   *1964, Indian Navy, Official*

REPAIR SHIPS

DHARINI A 306 (ex-*Hermine*)

Displacement, tons	4 625
Dimensions, feet	328 × 46 × 19
Main Engines	Triple expansion
Oil fuel (tons)	621

Cargo ship converted to a tender. Officially rated as a repair and store ship. Commissioned in May 1960.

DHARINI   *1964 Indian Navy, Official*

TORPEDO BOATS

6 "OSA" TYPE

MTB 1	MTB 2	MTB 3	MTB 4	MTB 5	MTB 6

Displacement, tons	150
Dimensions, feet	131·5 × 23 × 5·6
Main engines	3 diesels; 3 shafts; 4 800 bhp = 35 knots

Reported to be of similar type to the Soviet missile boats of the "Osa" class.

LANDING SHIPS

MAGAR (ex-HMS *Avenger*, LST (3) 3011)

Displacement, tons	2 256 light; 4 980 full load
Dimensions, feet	347·5 oa × 55·2 × 11·2
Guns	2—40 mm AA; 6—20 mm AA; (2 twin, 2 single)
Main Engines	Triple expansion; 2 shafts; 5 500 ihp = 13 knots
Complement	180

Former British tank landing ship of the LST (3) type transferred in 1949.

MAGAR   *Added 1964, A. & J. Pavia*

SOVIET "POLOCNY" CLASS

GHARIAL 1 (1966)	GULDAR 2 (1966)	LSMR 3	LSMR 4

Displacement, tons	900 to 1 000
Dimensions, feet	246 × 39·3 × 9·8
Armament	Rocket projector
Main Engines	Diesels; 4 000 bhp = 15 knots

The two later landing craft received from the USSR are of the "Polocny II" class.

POLNOCNY class   *1967, col. Breyer*

LCT 4294 (Ex-LCT 1294) Yard Craft

Displacement, tons	200
Dimensions, feet	187·2 × 38·8 × 3·5
Main engines	Speed 9·5 knots

SUBMARINE TENDER

AMBA A 14

Displacement, tons	6 000 light; 9 000 full load
Dimensions, feet	370 pp; 420 oa × 65 × 20
Aircraft	Provision for helicopter
Guns, dual purpose	4—2·3 in (*57 mm*) 2 twin
Main engines	Diesels; 2 shafts; 7 000 bhp = 17 knots

Modified "Ugra" type acquired from the Soviet Union in 1968.

OILERS

SHAKTI A 136

Displacement, tons	3 500
Dimensions, feet	323 × 44 × 20
Main Engines	Diesel; speed: 13 knots max; 9 knots economical

Rated as Fleet Replenishment Group Tanker. Acquired from Italy in Nov 1953.

CHILKA	**SAMBHAR**
Displacement, tons	1 530 (oil capacity 1 000)
Dimensions, feet	202 × 30·7 × 13
Main Engines	Triple expansion; 809 ihp = 9 knots

Chilka built by Blythwood Shipbuilding Co, Scotstoun. *Sambhar* by A. & J. Inglis, Ltd, Glasgow, launched 1942. Both acquired in 1948. Engined by David Rowan & Co. Two steam dynamos, two steam pumps, ballast pump. Rated as yard craft.

DEEPAK A 1750

On charter to Indian Navy from Mogul Lines. Fleet replenishment tanker. Fitted with a helicopter landing platform aft, but no hangar.

TUG

HATHI

Displacement, tons	668
Dimensions, feet	147·5 × 23·7 × 15
Main Engines	Triple expansion; speed = 13 knots

Built by the Taikoo Dock & Engineering Company, Hong Kong. Launched in 1932.

INDONESIA

Administration	Strength of the Fleet	Diplomatic Representation

Administration

*Commander-in-Chief of the Navy and
Chief of the Naval Staff:*
  Vice-Admiral R. Sudomo

Deputy Chief of the Naval Staff (Operations):
  Rear-Admiral L. M. Abdul Kadir

Inspector General of the Navy:
  Commodore Subroto Judono

Chief for Naval Material:
  Commodore Sudiomo

Chief for Naval Personnel:
  Rear Admiral Suprapto

Commander of Navy Marine Corps:
  Major General Mukijat

Commander-in-Chief Indonesian Fleet:
  Reat-Admiral Samsjul Bachri

Strength of the Fleet

12 Diesel Powered Submarines
 1 Cruiser
 8 Destroyers
12 Frigates
18 Patrol Vessels
12 Missile Boats
21 Torpedo Boats
 6 Fleet Minesweepers
14 Coastal Minesweepers
19 Patrol Boats
18 Coastal Gunboats
25 Seaward Defence Boats
 8 Landing Ships
10 Landing Craft
 1 Training Ship
11 Support Ships
10 Oilers
55 Auxiliary and Service Craft.

Diplomatic Representation

Naval Attaché and Naval Attaché for air in London:
  Colonel D. U. Martojo

Naval Attaché and Naval Attaché for Air in Washingon:
  Colonel Sukardjo D. Saroso

Personnel

Navy: 25 000; (including Fleet Air Arm); and 14 000
  Marine Commando Corps

Mercantile Marine

Lloyd's Register of Shipping:
489 vessels of 642 530 tons gross

SUBMARINES

12 Ex-USSR "W" CLASS

ALUGORO 406	PASOPATI 410
BRAMASTRA 412	TJAKRA 401
HENDRADJALA 405	TJANDRASA 408
NAGABANDA 403	TJUNDMANI 411
NAGARANGSANG 404	TRISULA 402
NANGGALA 407	WIDJAJADANU 409

Displacement, tons	1 030 surface; 1 180 submerged
Length, feet (*metres*)	240 (*73·1*) oa
Beam, feet (*metres*)	22 (*6·7*)
Draught, feet (*metres*)	15 (*4·6*) max
Guns, AA	2—2·4 in (*57 mm*); 2—25 mm
Torpedo tubes	6—21 in (*533 mm*) 4 forward, 2 aft; 14 torpedoes carried
Mines	40, or 20 additional torpedoes
Main engines	4 000 bhp diesels; 2 500 hp electric motors, diesel-electric drive; 2 shafts
Speed, knots	17 on surface; 15 submerged
Radius, miles	13 000 to 16 500
Complement	60

TJAKRA   *Indonesian Navy, Official*

Former Soviet submarines of the medium sized, long range "W" class. *Nanggala* and *Tjakra* were purchased from Poland and transferred to the Indonesian Navy in Aug 1959. *Nanggala* was overhauled at Surabaja in 1960. The four Soviet submarines of the "W" class, which arrived in Indonesia on 28 June 1962, brought the total number of this class transferred to Indonesia by the USSR to 14 units, but it was reported that only six would be maintained operational, while six would be kept in reserve and two used for spare parts. *Nanggala*, *Tjundmani* and *Tjakra* were placed in reserve in 1969.

CRUISER

1 Ex-USSR "SVERDLOV" CLASS

IRIAN (ex-*Ordzhonikidze*) 201

Displacement, tons	15 450 standard; 19 200 full load
Length, feet (*metres*)	650 (*198·0*) pp; 689 (*210·0*) oa
Beam, feet (*metres*)	70 (*21·3*)
Draught, feet (*metres*)	16 (*4·9*) mean; 24·5 (*7·5*) max
Guns, surface	12—6 in (*152 mm*), 4 triple 12—3·9 in (*100 mm*), 6 twin
Guns, AA	32—37 mm, 16 twin mounts
Torpedo tubes	10—21 in (*533 mm*), 2 quintuple
Mines	140 to 250 capacity

Armour	Belt 4 in to 1½ in (*100 to 38 mm*) CT 6 in (*150 mm*); turrets 5 in (*125 mm*); deck 3 in to 1 in (*75 to 25 mm*)
Boilers	6
Main engines	Geared steam turbines; 2 shafts; 130 000 shp
Speed, knots	34·5
Radius, miles	5 000 at 20 knots
Oil fuel, tons	4 000 capacity bunkerage
Complement	1 050 officers and men

Ordzhonikidze was built at the Baltiski Yard, Leningrad in 1950-53. She was renamed *Irian* and transferred from the USSR to Indonesia where she arrived in Oct 1962. A second Soviet cruiser was to have been acquired by the end of 1963, according to the Indonesian (then) Deputy Chief of Naval Staff. She was being modified to suit Indonesian requirements and conditions in the equatorial climate, and her armament was to be different from that of her sister ship. But in fact only one "Sverdlov" class cruiser had been transferred from the USSR to Indonesia by 1971.

IRIAN   *Added 1963, Wright & Logan*

DESTROYERS

8 Ex-USSR "SKORI" CLASS

BRAWIDJAJA 306	**SILIWANGI**
DIPONEGORO 307	**SINGAMANGARADJA** 302
SANDJAJA	**SUTAN BADARUDIN** 303
SAWUNGGALING 308	**SULTAN ISKANDARMUDA** 304

Displacement, tons	2 600 standard; 3 500 full load
Length, feet (metres)	393·8 (120·0) pp; 420 (128·0) oa
Beam, feet (metres)	41 (12·5)
Draught, feet (metres)	13·1 (4·0)
Guns, surface	4—5·1 in (130 mm); 2 twin
Guns, AA	2—3 in (76 mm); 7—37 mm; certain ships have 8—37 mm (4 twin)
A/S weapons	4 DCT
Torpedo tubes	10—21 in (533 mm)
Mines	Could carry up to 80
Boilers	3
Main engines	Geared turbines; 2 shafts; 70 000 shp
Speed, knots	38
Radius, miles	4 000 at 15 knots
Complement	250

Former Soviet destroyers of the "Skori" type. Built in 1951-56. Four (201, 202, 203, 204) were purchased from Poland and transferred to the Indonesian Navy in 1959. *Singamangaradja* means. Gannet. *Sawunggaling* was originally named *Sarwadjala*. *Iskandandarmuda* was transferred in 1962 and *Brawidjaja* and *Diponegoro* in 1964. *Sandjaja*, *Siliwangi* and *Singamangaradja* were withdrawn from active service in 1969.

PHOTOGRAPHS. A starboard broadside surface view of *Siliwangi* appears in the 1963-64 to 1967-68 editions and a port quarter surface view of *Diponegoro* in the 1968-69 to 1970-71 editions.

SINGAMANGARADJA   *Commodore A. Dipo*

SANDJAJA

Indonesian Navy, Official

FRIGATES

8 Ex-USSR "RIGA" CLASS

HANG TUAH 358	**MONGINSIDI**
JOS SUDARSO 351	**NGURAH RAI** 353
KAKIALI 539	**NUKU** 360
LAMBUNG MANGKURAT 357	**SLAMET RIJADI** 352

Displacement, tons	1 200 standard; 1 600 full load
Length, feet (metres)	273·8 (85·0) pp; 295 (90·0) oa
Beam, feet (metres)	34·5 (10·5)
Draught, feet (metres)	9·5 (2·9)
Guns, dual purpose	3—3·9 in (100 mm) single mounts
Guns, AA	4—37 mm
A/S weapons	4 DC projectors
Torpedo tubes	3—21 in (533 mm)
Mines	Fitted with mine rails
Boilers	2
Main engines	Geared steam turbines; 2 shafts; 25 000 shp
Speed, knots	28

Two "Riga" class frigates pennant Nos. 405 and 406, were transferred from the USSR to Indonesia with the cruiser *Irian* in Sep. 1962. Two more were transferred in 1963 and three more in 1964. *Mongonsidi* was placed in reserve in 1969.

RIGA Class   *Sergei Romanov*

2 "SURAPATI" CLASS

Name	No.	Builders	Laid down	Launched	Completed
IMAN BONDJOL	250	Ansaldo, Leghorn	8 Jan 1956	5 May 1956	19 May 1958
SURAPATI	251	Ansaldo, Leghorn	8 Jan 1956	5 May 1956	28 May 1958

Displacement, tons	1 150 standard; 1 500 full load
Length, feet (metres)	295·2 (90·0) pp 325 (99·0) oa
Beam, feet (metres)	36 (11·0)
Draught, feet (metres)	8·5 (2·6)
Guns, AA	4—4 in (102 mm) 46 cal., 2 twin mounts; 6—30 mm, 3 twin;
A/S weapons	2 Hedgehogs; 4 DCT
Torpedo tubes	3—21 in (533 mm)
Boilers	2 Foster Wheeler
Main engines	2 sets Parsons geared turbines; 2 shafts; 24 000 shp
Speed, knots	32
Radius, miles	2 800 at 22 knots cruising speed
Oil fuel, tons	350
Complement	200

Fast frigate or light destroyer type. A photograph of *Surapati* appears in the 1959-60 to 1966-67 editions.

IMAN BONDJOL   *courtesy Dr Ing Luigi Accorsi*

Frigates—continued

2 "PATTIMURA" CLASS

	Launched	Completed
PATTIMURA	1 July 1956	28 Jan 1958
SULTAN HASANUDIN	24 Mar 1957	8 Mar 1958

Displacement, tons	950 standard; 2 200 full load
Length, feet (metres)	246 (75·0) pp; 270·2 (82·4) oa
Beam, feet (metres)	34 (10·4)
Draught, feet (metres)	9 (2·7)
Guns, AA	2—3 in (76 mm) 40 cal. 2—30 mm 70 cal twin
A/S weapons	2 Hedgehogs; 4 DCT
Main engines	3 Ansaldo-Fiat diesels; 3 shafts; 6 900 bhp
Speed, knots	22
Radius, miles	2 400 at 18 knots cruising speed
Oil fuel, tons	100
Complement	110

Small sloop or fast corvette type. Both laid down on 8 Jan 1956 by Ansaldo, Leghorn. Nos. 252 and 253. A photograph of *Sultan Hasanudin* appears in the 1963-64 to 1965-66 editions.

PATTIMURA — *Dr Ing Luigi Accorsi*

PATROL VESSELS

14 Ex-USSR "KRONSTADT" TYPE

BARAKUDA 817	**LAPAI**	**PANDRONG** 814
KAKAP 816	**LUMBA LUMBA**	**SURA** 815
KATULA 811	**MADIDIHANG**	**TOHOK** 829
LANDJURU	**MOMARE**	**TONGKOL**
	PALU 818	**TJUTJUT**

Displacement, tons	300
Dimensions, feet	167·3 × 19·3 × 9
Guns	1—3·9 in; 2—37 mm AA; 3—20 mm AA
A/S weapons	Depth bomb projectors
Mines	Fitted for laying
Main engines	Diesels; 2 shafts; bhp = 27 knots
Oil fuel, tons	20
Complement	40

Former Soviet submarine chasers of the "Kronstadt" type. Built in 1951-54. Transferred to the Indonesian Navy on 30 Dec 1958. *Landjru, Lapai, Lumba Lumba, Madidihang Momare* and *Tongkol* were withdrawn from active service in 1970.

"Kronstadt" Class — *1961, Indonesian Navy, Official*

4 Ex-US PC TYPE

HUI (ex-USS *Malvern*, PC 580)	**TJAKALANG** (ex-USS *Pierre*, PC 1141)
TENGGIRI (ex-USS PC 1183)	**TORANI** (ex-USS *Manville*, PC 581)

Displacement, tons	280 standard; 450 full load
Dimensions, feet	170 wl; 173·7 oa × 23 × 10·8 max
Guns	1—3 in; 1—40 mm AA; 2—20 mm AA; 4 DCT
Main engines	2 GM diesels; 2 shafts; 2 880 bhp = 20 knots
Oil fuel, tons	60
Radius, miles	5 000 at 10 knots
Complement	54 (4 officers, 50 men)

Former US submarines chaser of the steel-hulled PC type. Built in 1942-43. *Pierre* transferred from the US Navy at Pearl Harbour, Hawaii in Oct 1958 and *Malvern* and *Manville* in Mar 1960. Pennant Nos. 318, 309, 313 and 317 respectively. Sister ship *Alu-Alu* (ex-USS PC 787) was removed from the effective list in 1961.

TENGGIRI — *1966, Indonesian Navy, Official*

Of the four corvettes, former Australian ocean minesweepers, *Hang Tuah* (ex-*Morotai*, ex-*Ipswich*) was reported sunk by rebel aircraft off Balikpapan, East Borneo on 28 Apr 1958; *Banteng* and *Radjawali* arrived at Hong Kong for scrapping in Apr 1968; and *Pati Unus*, latterly a ratings training ship, was disposed of in 1969.

TORPEDO BOATS

7 GERMAN-BUILT "JAGUAR" TYPE

ADJAK	**BIRUANG**	**MADJAN KUMBANG**	**SERIGALA**
ANOA	**HARIMAU**		**SINGA**

Displacement, tons	150
Dimensions, feet	131 pp; 138 oa × 25 × 5
Guns	2—40 mm AA (single)
Torpedo tubes	4—21 in
Main engines	4 Daimler-Benz diesels; 4 shafts; 12 000 bhp = 40 knots
Complement	39

Built by Lürssen, Bremen-Vegesack in 1959-60. The first four boats had wooden hulls, but the second four were built of steel. Pennant Nos. 601, 602, 603, 604, 605, 607 and 608. A photograph of *Singa* appears in the 1961-62 to 1967-68 editions. *Matian Tutul* 606 of this class was sunk on 15 Jan 1962 by Dutch warships off Borneo.

HARIMAU — *Indonesia*

14 Ex-USSR "P6" TYPE

ANGIN BADAI	**ANGIN GRENGGONG**	**ANGIN RIBUT**
ANGIN BOHOROK	**ANGIN KUMBANG**	**ANGIN TAUFAN**
ANGIN BRUBU	**ANGIN PASAT**	**ANGIN TONGGI**
ANGIN GENDING	**ANGIN PRAHARA**	**ANGIN WAMANDAIS**
	ANGIN PUJUH	**ANGIN WAMBRAU**

Displacement, tons	75 standard; 100 full load
Dimensions, feet	88 × 21 × 5·2
Guns	4—25 mm AA (2 twin)
Tubes	2—21 in (single)
Main engines	Diesels; speed 42 knots max

Former Soviet interchangeable torpedo boats of the "P 6" class. A total of 14 were reported delivered since 1961, including eight in 1961, and six in 1962.

ANGIN KUMBANG — *1968, Indonesian Navy, Official*

FLEET MINESWEEPERS

PULAU RANI	**PULAU RATENO**	**PULAU ROON**
PULAU RADJA	**PULAU RONDO**	**PULAU RORBAS**

Displacement, tons	500 standard; 600 full load
Dimensions, feet	200 × 27·2 × 9
Guns	4—37 mm AA; 8—13 mm AA
Main Engines	Diesels; 2 shafts; speed = 17 knots

Former Soviet fleet minesweepers of the "T 43" type transferred to Indonesia by the USSR, four in 1962 and two in 1964. *Pulau Rondo* is in reserve.

COASTAL MINESWEEPERS

10 "R" CLASS (RAUM-BOATS)

PULAU RAAS	PULAU REMPANG	PULAU ROMA
PULAU RANGSANG	PULAU RENGAT	PULAU ROTI
PULAU RAU	PULAU RINDJA	PULAU RUPAT
		PULAU RUSA

Displacement, tons	139·4 standard
Dimensions, feet	129 × 18·7 × 5
Guns	1—40 mm AA; 2—20 mm AA
Main engines	2 MAN diesels; 12 cyl; 2 800 bhp = 24·6 knots
Complement	26

Built by Abeking & Rasmussen Yach-und Bootswerft, Lemwerder 10 in 1945-57. These boats have a framework of light metal covered with wood. *Palau Raas, Palau Rempang* and *Palau Roti* in reserve in 1969.

PULAU ROTI   *Indonesian Navy, Official*

DJAMPEA	DJOMBANG	ENGGANO (ex-*Hino Maru*)	FLORES

Displacement, tons	175
Dimensions, feet	106·7 pp; 113·7 (*Flores*) 114·1 oa × 18·8 × 6·2
Main Engines	1 Enterprise diesel; 360 bhp = 12·5 knots

First three were commissioned in 1941. *Flores* was completed by the Japanese during the occupation of Java. First were two built at Droogdok Maatschappij, and the other two at Droogdok Mij, Tandjong Priok. Used as auxiliary minesweepers by the Royal Netherlands Navy. *Enggano* was re-named by Japanese. These ships were recovered after the war. *Enggano* in reserve in 1969.

PATROL BOATS

6 Ex-YUGOSLAVIAN "KRALJEVICA" TYPE

BUBARA	KRAPU	LEMADANG
DORANG	LAJANG	TODAK

Displacement, tons	190 standard; 245 full load
Dimensions, feet	134·5 × 20·8 × 7
Guns	1—3 in; 1—40 mm AA; 6—20 mm AA
A/S weapons	DC
Main Engines	2 MAN diesels; 2 shafts; 3 300 bhp = 20 knots
Oil fuel (tons)	15
Radius, miles	1 500 at 12 knots
Complement	54

Former Yugoslavian submarine chasers of the "Kraljevica" class. Purchased and transferred on 27th Dec 1958. Nos 310, 311 (*Dorang*), 312 (*Lajang*) and 314 to 316. A photograph of *Lajang* appears in the 1961-62 to 1967-68 editions. *Bubara* was withdrawn from active service in 1970.

DORANG   *1968, Indonesian Navy, Official*

3 "MAWAR" CLASS

KALAHITAM	KELABANG	KOMPAS

Displacement, tons	147
Guns	40 mm AA
Main engines	2 diesels; speed 21 knots

Indonesia was reported to be building five submarine chasers of the "Mawar" class in her own yards. Similar to the prototype *Kelabang*. At least two, *Kompas* and *Kalahitam*, have been completed.

KALAHITAM   *1968, Indonesian Navy, Official*

MISSILE BOATS

12 Ex-USSR "KOMAR" CLASS

GRIWIDJAJA	KATJABOLA	SAROTAMA
HARDADALI	KOLAPLINTAH	SARPAMINA
KALAMISANI	PULANGGENI	SARPAWISESA
KALANADA	NAGAPASA	TRITUSTA

Displacement, tons	75 standard; 100 full load
Dimensions, feet	88 × 21 × 5·2
Guns	2—25 mm AA (1 twin)
Guided weapons	2 launchers in twin housing with missiles of 10 to 15 nautical miles range
Main engines	Diesels; speed = 40 knots

Former Soviet guided missile patrol boats of the "Komar" class. Six were transferred to Indonesia in 1961-63, four more in Sep 1964 and two in 1965.

COASTAL GUNBOATS

18 Ex-USSR "BK" CLASS

Displacement, tons	120
Dimensions, feet	124·7 × 19 × 4·6
Guns,	1—85 mm; 4—25 mm AA
Main engines	Diesels; speed 20 knots

Reported to have been transferred from the USSR to Indonesia in 1962. Fitted with large gun mounting. Ten Soviet-built gunboats were reported to have been transferred to Indonesia at Djakarta 11 Oct 1961.

PGM TYPE. Three USN PGM type, 55-57 were intended for transfer to Indonesia as *Silungkang, Waitatire* and *Kalukuang* respectively, but were handed over to Philippines instead as *Yacha, Yanga* and *Yundi* in 1965.

SEAWARD DEFENCE BOATS

25 Ex-HDML PATROL BOAT TYPES

PP 01	PP 06	PP 011	PP 016	PP 021
PP 02	PP 07	PP 012	PP 017	PP 022
PP 03	PP 08	PP 013	PP 018	PP 023
PP 04	PP 09	PP 014	PP 019	PP 024
PP 05	PP 10	PP 015	PP 020	PP 025

Displacement, tons	46 standard; 54 full load
Dimensions, feet	72 × 16 × 5·5
Guns	1—37 mm; 2—20 mm Oerlikon MG
Main Engines	2 diesels; 2 shafts; 300 bhp = 11 knots
Complement	10

All ex-Netherlands patrol boats. Built in 1943-46. Formerly British HDML type *RP 109, RP 111, RP 112, RP 114,* and *RP 118* ex-*HDML 1451, HDML 1472, HDML 1473, HDML 1454* and *HDML 1449*).

Displacement, tons	44 standard; 56 full load
Dimensions, feet	62 oa × 18·3 × 4
Guns	1—20 mm AA; 1 MG
Main Engines	1 diesel; 165 bhp = 10 knots
Complement	10

Built in 1945-46. Former American Higgins type motor launches, later Netherlands *RP 120, RP 121, RP 122, RP 125, RP 127, RP 128, RP 130, RP 134,* and *RP 136,* transferred to Indonesia in 1950.

Displacement, tons	54
Guns	1—40 mm AA; 2—20 mm AA
A/S weapons	3 DCT
Main Engines	Speed = 11 knots
Complement	10

Former Netherlands motor launch *RP 138,* transferred by the Royal Netherlands Navy in 1950. A photograph of this type appears in the 1951-52 to 1960-61 editions.

TRAINING SHIP

DEWARUTJI

Displacement, tons	810 standard; 1 500 full load
Dimensions, feet	191·2 oa; 136·2 pp × 31·2 × 13·9
Main Engines	MAN diesel engines; 600 bhp = 10·5 knots
Complement	110 (32 + 78 midshipmen)

Built in Germany by H. C. Stülcken & Sohn, Hamburg. Launched on 24 Jan 1953. Completed on 9 July 1953. Barquentine of iron construction. Sail area, 1 305 sq yds (*1 091 sq metres*). Speed with sails 12·8 knots. The training ship *Nanusa* a former freighter, has been returned to mercantile service.

DEWARUTJI   *Indonesia*

SUBMARINE SUPPORT SHIPS

MULTATULI

Displacement, tons	3 220
Dimensions, feet	338 pp; 365·3 oa × 52·5 × 23
Guns	1—85 mm; 4—40 mm (single mountings)
Main engines	B & W diesel; 5 500 bhp = 18·5 knot max
Oil fuel (tons)	1 400
Radius, miles	6 000 at 16 knots cruising speed
Complement	134

Built in Japan by Ishikawajima-Harima Heavy Industries Co Ltd, as a submarine tender. Launched on 15 May 1961. Delivered to Indonesia in Aug 1961. Pennant No. 476. Flush decker. Capacity for replenishment at sea (fuel oil, fresh water, provisions, ammunition, naval stores and personnel). Medical and hospital facilities. Equipment for supplying compressed air, electric power and distilled water to submarines. Air conditioning and mechanical ventilation arrangements for all living and working quarters. A photograph of *Multatuli* appears in the 1962-63 to 1967-68 editions.

1 Ex-USSR "DON" CLASS

RATULANGI

Displacement, tons	4 750 standard; 6 000 full load
Dimensions, feet	450 × 49 × 17
Guns	4—3·9 in; 12—37 mm AA
Main Engines	Diesels; speed = 21 knots approx
Complement	300

A submarine support ship, escort vessel and maintenance tender of the "Don" class, transferred from the USSR to Indonesia in 1962, arriving in Indonesia in July with Soviet pennant No. 441.

RATULANGI　　　　　　　　　*1968, Indonesian Navy, Official*

1 Ex-USSR "ATREK" CLASS

THAMRIN

Displacement, tons	3 500 standard
Measurement, tons	3 258 gross
Dimensions, feet	336 × 49 × 20
Main engines	Steam expansion and exhaust turbine; 2 450 ihp = 13 knots
Boilers	2
Radius, miles	3 500

Former Soviet advanced submarine parent ship of the smaller tender type. Built in 1955-57 and converted to naval use from a mercantile freighter. Arrived in Indonesia on 28 June 1962 as a transfer from the USSR "Atrek" class.

SURVEY SHIPS

BURUDJULASAD	HIDRAL	JALANIDHI

Displacement, tons	2 150 full load
Dimensions, feet	269·5 × 37·4 × 11·5
Machinery	4 MAN diesels; 2 shafts; 6 850 bhp = 19·1 knots
Complement	78

Burudjulasad was launched in 1966; her equipment includes laboratories for oceanic and meteorological research, a cartographic room, and a helicopter. The names *Hidral* and *Jalanidhi* were officially listed, but it is not clear whether they are of the same type or employed on surveying.

BURUDJULASAD　　　　　　　*1968, Indonesian Navy, Official*

BURDIAMHAL

Displacement, tons	1 200 full load
Dimensions, feet	211·7 oa; 192 pp × 33·2 × 10
Main engines	2 Werkspoor diesels; 1 160 bhp = 10 knots
Complement	90

Built by Schweepserf De Waal, Zalthomme. Launched on 6 Sep 1952. Completed on 6 July 1953. A photograph appears in the 1954-55 to 1960-61 editions.

SAMUDERA

Measurement, tons	200 gross
Dimensions, feet	125·2 × 21·5 × 9·8
Main engines	Werkspoor diesel engines; 450 bhp

Built by Ferus Smit, Foxol. Launched on 28 May 1952. Completed on 28 Aug 1952. Same type as "Bango" class motor patrol vessels. Equipped as a laboratory ship, used for deep sea exploration in Indonesian waters. A photograph appears in the 1953-54 to 1960-61 editions. Another survey ship, *Dewa Kembar*, was laid up in reserve.

LANDING SHIPS

TANDUNG NUSANIVE	TELUK KAU	TELUK MENADO
TELUK BAJUR	TELUK LANGSA	TELUK RATAI
		TELUK TOMINI

7 Ex-US LST "511-1152" TYPE

Displacememt, tons	1 653 standard; 4 080 full load
Dimensions, feet	316 wl; 328 oa × 50 × 14
Guns	7—40 mm AA; 2—20 mm AA
Main Engines	GM diesels; 2 shafts; 1 700 bhp = 11·6 knots
Oil fuel (tons)	600
Radius, miles	7 200 at 10 knots
Cargo capacity	2 100 tons
Complement	119 (accommodation for 266)

1 JAPANESE TYPE

TELUK AMBOINA LST 869

Displacement, tons	2 200 standard; 4 800 full load
Dimensions, feet	327 × 50 × 15
Guns	2—85 mm; 4—40 mm
Main Engines	MAN diesels; 2 shafts; 3 000 bhp = 13·1 knots
Oil fuel (tons)	1 200
Radius, miles	4 000 at 13·1 knots
Complement	88 (accommodation for 300)

Built in Japan. Launched on 17 Mar 1961 and transferred in June 1961.

LANDING CRAFT

3 Ex-US LCT TYPE

AMAHAI (ex-*Tropenvogel*, LCI 467) 864	MARICH (ex-*Zeemeeuw*) 866
	PIRU (ex-*Zeearend*, LCI 420) 868

Displacement, tons	250 standard; 381 full load
Dimensions, feet	158 × 23 × 7
Guns	1—37 mm; 2 Vickers MG
Main engines	GM diesels; 1 800 bhp = 15 knots
Complement	60

Former US infantry landing craft. Turned over from Netherlands East Indies Government on formation of Indonesian Navy in 1950. Sister ships *Baruna* (ex-*Jjsvogel*, LCI 948) and *Namlea* (ex-*Stormvogel*) LCI 588, were rerated as pilot ship and light ship in 1961.

4 Ex-YUGOSLAVIAN LCT TYPE

TELUK KATURAI	TELUK WEDA
TELUK WADJO	TELUK WORI

Displacement, tons	110 standard; 250 full load
Dimensions, feet	166 × 21·5 × 5·5
Guns	1—40 mm; 2—20 mm
Main engines	2 diesels; 2 shafts; 375 bhp = 7 knots
Oil fuel (tons)	6
Complement	†5

Transferred from Yugoslavia on 1 Nov 1958. Nos 862, 860, 861 and 863. *Teluk Wadjo* and *Teluk Weda* in reserve in 1969.

2 Ex-"LCVT" TYPE

DORE	AMURANG

Displacement, tons	182 standard; 275 full load
Dimensions, feet	125·7 × 32·8 × 5·9
Main engines	Diesels; 210 hp = 8 knots
Complement	17

1 Ex-USSR LCT TYPE

TELUK PARIGI

Displacement, tons	600 standard; 800 full load
Dimensions, feet	246·0 × 39·3 × 9·8
Main engines	Diesels; 2 shafts; 2 200 hp = 10 knots

CABLE SHIP

BIDUK

Displacement, tons	1 250 standard
Dimensions, feet	213·2 oa × 39·5 × 11·5
Main Engines	1 Triple expansion engine; 1 600 ihp = 12 knots
Complement	66

Cable Layer, Lighthouse Tender, and multi-purpose naval auxiliary. Built by J. & K. Smit, Kinderijk. Launched on 30 Oct 1951. Completed on 30 July 1952. A photograph of this ship appears in the 1953-54 to 1960-61 editions.

TRANSPORTS

2 "BANGGAI" TYPE

BANGGAI (ex-*Biscaya*)	NUSA TELU (ex-*Casa Blanca*)

Measurement, tons	750
Dimensions, feet	168 × 27·9 × 7·8

Dual purpose troop and cargo ships. Renamed in 1961. Pennant Nos 925, 924.

MOROTAI TYPE. The transports *Halmahera*, No 921, and *Merotai*, No. 922, reverted to the Merchant Navy as *Djati Roto* and *Djati Bono* in 1968. Acquired from merchant service on 23 Nov 1957. A photograph of *Moratai* appears in the 1961-62 to 1968-69 editions.

AUXILIARY PATROL CRAFT

5 DKN TYPE

DKN 901	DKN 902	DKN 903	DKN 904	DKN 905

Displacement, tons	140
Dimensions, feet	128 × 19 × 5·2
Guns	4—20 mm AA
Main Engines	Maybach diesels; 2 shafts; 3 000 bhp = 24·5 knots

Patrol craft and police boats. Projected as a class of ten units. 901, 902 and 904 were built by Lürssen, Vergesack, 903 and 905 by Abeking & Rasmussen Lemwerder.

1 + 1 KELABANG TYPE

KELABANG

Displacement, tons	147
Main engines	2 diesels; speed 21 knots

Launched on 22 Aug 1960 at Surabja. A sister ship was scheduled to be built.

6 "PAT" CLASS

PAT 01	PAT 02	PAT 03	PAT 04	PAT 05	PAT 06

Dimensions, feet	91·9 pp; 100 oa × 17 × 6
Main Engines	2 Caterpillar diesels; 340 bhp

6 "BALAM" CLASS

BALAM	BARAU	BEKAKA	BELATIK	BENDALU	BOGA

Measurement, tons	200 gross
Dimensions, feet	125·2 oa × 21·3 × 6·5
Main Engines	Werkspoor diesel engine; 400-430 bhp = 11 knots

All launched in 1953. *Balam* and others were commissioned for service in 1953.

7 "BANGO" CLASS

BANGO	BABUT	BEO	BETTET	BIDO	BLEKOK	BLIBIS

Measurement, tons	194 gross
Dimensions, feet	120·5 pp; 125·2 oa × 21·3 × 6·6
Main Engines	Werkspoor diesel engine; 430 bhp = 11 knots

All launched in 1952. A photograph of *Bettet* appears in the 1953-54 to 1960-61 editions.

7 "DURIAN" CLASS

DAIK	DAGONG	DAMARA	DATA	DUATA	DUKU	DURIAN

Displacement, tons	90
Dimensions, feet	78·2 × 16 × 6·8
Main Engines	Caterpillar diesel; 190 bhp

All launched in 1952.

12 "ALKAI" CLASS

ALKAI	ALULU	AMPIS	ANKANG	ANTANG	ARYAT
ALLAP	AMPOK	ANDIS	ANKLOENG	AROKWES	ATTAT

Displacement, tons	143; 247 full load
Dimensions, feet	124·3 × 18·5 × 5·5
Guns	1—37 mm AA; 4 MG
Main engines	Enterprise diesel; 400-450 = 12 knots
Complement	20

Built in the Netherlands. *Ampok* and *Alkai* were shipped to Indonesia on 17 Mar 1950. *Ampis* in reserve in 1969.

3 Ex-US SC TYPE

BHAYAMKARA 1	BHAYAMKARA II	BHAYAMKARA III

Displacement, tons	116 (trials); 148 full load
Dimensions, feet	107·5 wl; 110·8 oa × 17 × 6·5
Main Engines	Diesel; 800 bhp = 15·5 knots

Former US submarine chasers of the 110 SC type. Operated by Indonesian Marine Police. A photograph appears in the 1954-55 to 1960-61 editions.

2 MERABU TYPE

MERABU (ex-*Merbaboe*)   **RINDJANI**

Displacement, tons	80
Dimensions, feet	74·5 × 14·5 × 5
Main Engines	Diesel; 135 bhp = 10 knots
Complement	20

Merabu is laid up in reserve it was officially stated in 1969 (removed from the effective list).

SALVAGE VESSELS

TRITON (ex-*Mutsunoura Maru*)

Displacement, tons	384
Measurement, tons	383 gross
Dimensions, feet	182·5 × 30 × 15
Main Engines	Triple expansion reciprocating; 700 ihp = 7 knots
Complement	43

Former Japanese vessel renamed. Launched in 1941. Pennant No. 926. Laid up in reserve in 1969.

OILERS

2 Ex-USSR TYPE

BUNJU   **SAMBU**

Displacement, tons	2 170 standard; 6 170 full load
Dimensions, feet	350·5 × 49·2 × 20·2
Guns	2—20 mm
Main Engines	Polar diesel; 1 shaft; 2 650 bhp = 10 knots
Oil fuel (tons)	390
Cargo capacity	4 739 tons
Complement	71

Former Soviet tankers transferred to the Indonesian Navy on 29 June 1959. Pennant Nos. 904 and 903. Both laid up in 1969.

TJEPU (ex-*Scandus*, ex-*Nordhem*)

Displacement, tons	1 372
Measurement, tons	1 042 gross
Dimensions, feet	226·5 × 34 × 14·2
Main Engines	Polar diesel; 1 shaft; 850 bhp = 11 knots

Built in Sweden in 1949. Acquired in 1951. Pennant No. 901. Laid up in 1969.

PLADU

Displacement, tons	1 412 standard; 4 062 full load
Dimensions, feet	294·7 × 42·2 × 15·5
Guns	2—20 mm
Main Engines	Compound engines; 1 700 ihp = 10 knots
Oil fuel (tons)	449
Cargo capacity, tons	3 132
Complement	70

Purchased from Singapore in 1958. Pennant No. 902. Withdrawn from active service in 1970.

6 Ex-USSR TYPE

BALIKAPAN	PANGKALAN BRANDAN	WONOKROMO

Dispalcement, tons	3 500 standard; 7 115 full load
Dimensions, feet	400·3 × 52·5 × 21·0
Main engines	Diesels; 2 shafts; 4 500 bhp = 17 knots max

TARAKAN   **BULA**

Displacement, tons	1 340 full load
Dimensions, feet	352·0 × 37·7 × 14·8
Main engines	Diesels; 1 shaft; 1 500 bhp = 13 knots

PAKAN BARU

Displacement, tons	1 500 full load
Dimensions, feet	63 × 11·5 × 4·5
Main engines	Diesels; 2 shafts; 800 bhp = 11 knots

TUGS

RAKATA (ex-USS *Menominee*, ATF 73)

Displacement, tons	1,235 standard; 1,675 full load
Dimensions, feet	195 wl; 205 oa × 38·5 × 15·5 max
Guns	1—3 in; 4—40 mm AA; 2—20 mm AA
Main engines	4 diesels with electric drive; 3 000 bhp = 16 5 knots
Complement	85

Former American fleet ocean tug of the "Apache" class. Launched on 14 Feb 1942. Transferred from the United States Navy to the Indonesian Navy at San Diego in Mar 1961. Pennant No. 928.

LAMPO BATANG

Displacement, tons	250
Dimensions, feet	92·3 oa; 86·7 pp × 23·2 × 11·3
Main engines	2 diesels; 1 200 bhp = 11 knots
Oil fuel (tons)	18
Radius, miles	1 000 at 11 knots
Complement	43

Ocean tug. Built in Japan. Launched in April 1961. Delivered in Nov 1961. Pennant No. 934.

GANDENG

Measurement, tons	610 gross
Main Engines	Speed = 7·5 knots

Launched in 1940. Reported to have been given a new Indonesian name.

BROMO   **TAMBORA**

Displacement, tons	150
Dimensions, feet	71·7 wl; 79 oa × 21·7 × 9·7
Main Engines	MAN diesel; 2 shafts; 600 bhp = 10·5 knots
Oil fuel (tons)	9
Radius, miles	690 at 10·5 knots
Complement	15

Harbour tugs. Built in Japan. Launched in June 1961. Delivered in Aug 1961. Pennant Nos 936 and 935.

IRAN

Administration	Strength of the Fleet	Personnel
Administration		**Personnel**

Administration
Commander-in-Chief Imperial Iranian Navy:
Admiral Farajollah Rassai

Diplomatic Representation
Naval Attaché in London:
Commander Djamshid Pourzand

Naval Attaché in Washington:
Commander S. Anoushirarani

Strength of the Fleet

1	Destroyer	16	Patrol Boats
4	Fast Frigates	12	Hovercraft
1	Training Frigate	2	Landing Craft
4	Corvettes	1	Repair Ship
1	Escort Minesweeper	2	Yachts
4	Coastal Minesweepers	1	Oiler
2	Inshore Minesweepers	2	Auxiliaries

Personnel

1971: 7 000 officers and men

Mercantile Marine

Lloyd's Register of Shipping:
56 vessels of 129 025 tons

Scale: 150 feet = 1 inch (1 : 1 800)

ARTEMIZ

SAAM *Class*

BAYANDOR *Class*

DESTROYERS

Name	Builders	Laid down	Launched	Completed
ARTEMIZ (ex-HMS *Sluys*, D 60) D 5	Cammell Laird & Co Ltd, Birkenhead	24 Nov 1943	28 Feb 1945	30 Sep 1946

1 Ex-BRITISH "BATTLE" CLASS

Displacement, tons	2 325 standard ; 3 360 full load
Length, feet (*metres*)	355 (*108·2*) pp ; 379 (*115·5*) oa
Beam, feet (*metres*)	40·5 (*12·3*)
Draught, feet (*metres*)	17·5 (*5·2*)
Guns, surface	4—4·5 in (*115 mm*) 2 twin forward
Guns, AA	8—40 mm Bofors
Missile launchers, AA	1 quadruple "Seacat" aft
A/S weapons	1 "Squid" 3-barrelled DC mortar
Main engines	Parsons geared turbines ; 2 shafts ; 50 000 shp
Speed, knots	35·5 max ; 31 sustained sea
Complement	270

Transferred to Iran at Southampton on 26 Jan 1967, and handed over to the Imperial Iranian Navy after a 3-year modernisation refit by the Vosper Thornycroft Group.
New Acquisitions. 2 destroyers, USS *Gainard*, DD 706 and *Zellars*, DD 777, to be transferred to Iran in 1972 after refit and renamed *Babr* (Panther) and *Palang* (Tiger).
RADAR. Search: Plessey AWS 1. Fire Control: X Band.

ARTEMIZ

1971, Official

FRIGATES

4 "SAAM" CLASS

Displacement, tons	1 110 standard ; 1 290 full load
Length, feet (*metres*)	310 (*94·4*) oa
Beam, feet (*metres*)	34 (*10·4*)
Draught, feet (*metres*)	10·5 (*3·2*)
Guns, surface	1—4·5 in (*115 mm*) 1 Mk 8
Guns, AA	2—35 mm Oerlikon (twin)
Missile launchers, SS	1 Quintuple "Seakiller"
Missile launchers, AA	1 triple "Seacat"
A/S weapons	2 "Limbo" 3-barrelled DC mortars
Main engines	2 Rolls-Royce "Olympus" gas turbines ; 2 Paxman diesels ; 2 shafts ; 46 000 + 3 800 shp
Speed, knots	40 designed
Complement	125 (accommodation for 146)

Name	Builders	Laid down	Launched	Completed
FARAMARZ	Vosper Thornycroft, Woolston	25 July 1968	30 July 1969	28 Feb 1972
ROSTAM	Vickers, Newcastle & Barrow	10 Dec 1967	4 Mar 1969	31 Mar 1972
SAAM	Vosper Thornycroft, Woolston	22 May 1967	25 July 1968	1 Feb 1971
ZAAL	Vickers, Barrow	3 Mar 1968	4 Mar 1969	1 Mar 1971

It was announced on 25 Aug 1966 that Vosper Ltd, Portsmouth, had received an order for four "destroyers" for the Iranian Navy. Of small frigate type, one main gun forward, anti-aircraft and anti-submarine weapons, high speed from gas turbines, with diesels for long range cruising. Air conditioned throughout, and fitted with Vosper stabilisers. *Rostam* was towed to Barrow for completion.

RADAR. Search: Plessey AWS 1. Fire Control: Contraves Sea Hunter.

SAAM

1971, Wright & Logan

Name	Builders	Laid down	Launched	Completed
BABR (ex-HMS *Derby Haven*, ex-*Loch Assynt*)	Swan, Hunter & Wigham Richardson, Ltd Wallsend on-Tyne	11 Feb 1944	14 Dec 1944	2 Aug 194

1 Ex-BRITISH "LOCH" TYPE

Displacement, tons	1 650 standard ; 2 160 full load
Length, feet (*metres*)	286 (*87·2*) pp ; 309 (*94·2*) oa
Beam, feet (*metres*)	38·5 (*11·7*)
Draught, feet (*metres*)	14·5 (*4·4*) max
Guns, surface	2—4 in (*102 mm*)
Guns, AA	4—40 mm
Boilers	2 Admiralty 3-drum
Main engines	Triple expansion 5 500 ihp ; 2 shafts
Speed, knots	19·5
Radius, miles	9 500 at 12 knots
Oil fuel (tons)	725
Complement	140

Modified "Loch" class frigate acquired from Great Britain in 1949 "Babr" means "Panther".

BABR

Added 1966, courtesy Dr Giorgio Arra

CORVETTES

4 US PF TYPE

BAYANDOR F 25   **NAGHDI** F 26
KAHNAMUIE F 28   **MILANIAN** F 27

Displacement, tons	900 standard; 1 135 full load
Length, feet (metres)	275 (83·8) oa
Beam, feet (metres)	33 (10·0)
Draught, feet (metres)	10 (3·0)
Guns, surface	2—3 in (76 mm)
Guns, AA	2—40 mm
A/S weapons	Hedgehog
Main engines	F-M diesels; 6 000 bhp
Speed, knots	20 max
Complement	140

Built by Levingstone Shipbuilding Co, Bayandor, PF 103, laid down 20 Aug 1962, launch July 1963, transfer 18 May 1964. Naghdi, PF 104, laid down 12 Sep 1962, launch Oct 1963, transfer 22 July 1964. Milanian, PF 105, and Kahnamuie, PF 106, laid down on 1 May 1967, 12 June 1967, launched 4 Jan 1968, 4 Apr 1968 respectively, Milanian and Kahnamuie completed 13 Feb 1969. A photograph of Byandor appears in the 1964-65 to 1968-69 editions.

NAGHDI   1969, Imperial Iranian Navy, Official

ESCORT MINESWEEPER

	Name	Builders	Laid down	Launched	Completed
1 Ex-BRITISH "ALGERINE" TYPE	PALANG (ex-HMS Fly)	Lobnitz & Co Ltd, Renfrew	6 Oct 1941	1 June 1942	10 Oct 1942

ESCORT MINESWEEPER

Displacement, tons	1 040 standard; 1 235 full load
Length, feet (metres)	225 (68·6) oa
Beam, feet (metres)	35·5 (10·8)
Draught, feet (metres)	13 (4·0)
Guns, surface	2—4 in (102 mm) single
Guns, AA	4—40 mm Bofors
A/S weapons	2 depth charge throwers
Main engines	Triple expansion 2 000 ihp; 2 shafts
Speed, knots	16·5
Radius, miles	5 000 at 10 knots
Oil fuel (tons)	270
Complement	85

Former "Algerine class ocean minesweeper and escort vessel acquired from Great Britain in 1949. "Palang" means "Tiger". Now out of service.

PALANG   1966, Official

COASTAL MINESWEEPERS

4 MSC TYPE

KARKAS (ex-USS MSC 292) 34   **SHAHROKH** (ex-USS MSC 276) 31
SHAHBAZ (ex-USS MSC 275) 32   **SIMORGH** (ex-USS MSC 291) 33

Displacement, tons	320 light; 378 full load
Dimensions, feet	138 pp; 145·8 oa × 28 × 8·3
Guns	1—20 mm
Main Engines	2 GM diesels; 2 shafts; 890 bhp = 12·8 knots
Oil fuel (tons)	27
Radius, miles	2 400 at 11 knots
Complement	40 (4 officers, 2 midshipmen, 34 men)

Built by Bellingham Shipyards Co (Shahbaz and Shakrokh), Petersen Builders Inc. (Karkas) and Tacoma Boatbuilding Co, (Simorgh). Of wooden construction. Launch-ed in 1958-61 and transported from US to Iran under MAP in 1959-62. "Shahbaz" means Eagle and "Shahrokh" means Bird of Prey.

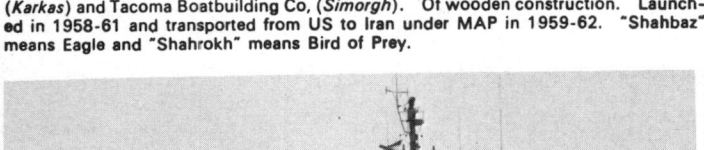

SHAHROKH   1971, John G. Callis

INSHORE MINESWEEPERS

2 US MSI TYPE

HARISCHI (ex-Kahnamuie) 301 (ex-MSI 14)   **RIAZI** 302 (ex-MSI 13)

Displacement, tons	180 standard; 235 full load
Dimensions, feet	111 × 23 × 6
Guns	MG
Main engines	Diesels; 650 bhp = 13 knots
Oil fuel, tons	20
Radius, miles	1 000 at 9 knots
Complement	23 (5 officers, 18 men)

Built in USA by Tacoma Boatbuilding Co and delivered to Iran under MAP. Laid down on 22 June 1962 and 1 Feb 1963, and transferred at Seattle, Washington, on 3 Sep 1964 and 15 Oct 1964, respectively. In Aug 1967 Kahnamui was renamed Harischi as the name Kahnamuie was required for one of the new US PFs, see above. A photograph of Harischi appears in the 1969-70 and 1970-71 editions.

RIAZI   1971, Official

PATROL BOATS

3 IMPROVED PGM TYPE

BAHRAM   **NAHID**   **PARVIN** (ex-*PGM* 103)

Displacement, tons	105 standard; 146 full load
Dimensions, feet	100 × 22 × 10
Guns	1—40 mm; 2—20 mm, 2—50 cal MG
Main engines	8 MG diesels; 2 000 bhp = 15 knots

Motor gunboats of an enlarged design, compared with the "Keyvan" class below. Built in USA by Tacoma Boatbuilding Co of Tacoma and Petersen Builders Inc of Sturgeon Bay, Wisconsin, and transferred to Iran under MAP in 1970 (PGM 103 and PGM 112)

PARVIN   *1971, Official*

4 PGM TYPE

KEYVAN (MDA1) **MAHAN** 64 **MEHRAN** **TIRAN**

Displacement, tons	85 standard; 107 full load
Dimensions, feet	90 pp; 95 oa × 20·2 × 6·8 max
Guns,	1—40 mm AA
A/S weapons	8-barrelled 7·2 in projector, 8—300 lb depth charges
Main Engines	4 Cummins diesels; 2 shafts; 2 200 bhp = 20 knots
Radius, miles	1 500 cruising range
Complement	15

Keyvan, built in USA in 1955, was delivered to Iran on 14 Jan 1956. In the Persian Gulf. *Tiran* was built by the US Coast Guard at Curtis Bay, Maryland, and transferred to Iran in 1957. *Mahan* and *Mehran* were delivered to Iran in 1959.

It was officially stated in 1971 that all the nine coast guard cutters of the "Azar" class *Azar, Chahab, Darakhsh, Navak, Peykan, Tondbad, Tondar, Toufan* and *Tousan*, see particulars in the 1970-71 and earlier editions, were out of service.

MAHAN   *1969. Imperial Iranian Navy. Official*

REPAIR SHIP

1 Ex-US ARL (Ex-LST) TYPE

SOHRAB (ex-USS *Gordlus*, ARL 36, ex-*LST* 1145)

Displacement, tons	1 625 light; 4 100 full load
Dimensions, feet	316 wl; 328 oa × 50 × 11·2
Guns	8—40 mm AA
Main Engines	GM diesels; 2 shafts; 1 800 bhp = 11·6 knots

Former US repair ship for landing craft. Built by Chicago Bridge & Iron Co, Seneca Ill. Laid down on 5 Feb 1945. Launched on 7 May 1945. Completed on 18 May 1945. Transferred by the USA under the Military Aid Programme in Sep 1961.

SOHRAB   *1971, Official*

HOVERCRAFT

2 + 2 WELLINGTON (BH.7) CLASS

101   **102**   103   104

Displacement, tons	50 max weight, 33 empty
Dimensions, feet	76 × 45 × 42 (height inflated)
Guns	2 Browning MG
Main engines	1 Proteus 15 M/541 gas turbine = 60 knots max
Oil fuel tons	10 max

Two more of this Wellington class Mk 4 type are under construction.

101   *1971, Official*

8 WINCHESTER (SR.N6) CLASS

01 **02** **03** **04** **05** **06** **07** **08**

Displacement, tons	10 normal gross weight (basic weight 14 200 lbs; disposable load ·8 200 lbs)
Dimensions, feet	48·4 × 25·3 × 15·9 (height)
Main engines	1 Gnome Model 1050 gas turbine = 58 knots max. 1 Peters diesel as auxiliary power unit.

The Imperial Iranian Navy has the world's largest fully operational hovercraft squadron, which is used for coastal defence and logistic duties.

03   *1971, Official*

LANDING CRAFT

GHASM (ex-USS *LSIL*)

Displacement, tons	210 light; 393 full load
Dimensions, feet	153 wl; 159 oa × 23·7 × 5·7 max
Guns	4—20 mm AA
Main Engines	GM diesels; 2 shafts; 1 800 bhp = 14·4 knots
Oil fuel (tons)	80
Radius, miles	5 000 at 12 knots
Complement	40

Former US Landing Ship, Infantry, Large, built in 1944. *Ghasm* was added to the fleet in 1964. It was officially stated in 1971 that sister ships *Hengam*, 41 (ex-French *LSIL* 9037, ex-USS LSIL 768) and *Larak*, 42 (ex-USS *LSIL* 710) were out of service.

GHESHNE (ex-USS *LCU* 1431)

Displacement, tons	160 light; 320 full load
Dimensions, feet	119 × 32 × 5·7
Guns	2—20 mm AA
Main engines	Diesels; 675 bhp = 10 knots
Complement	14

LCU 1431 was transferred to Iran by US in 1964 under the Military Aid Programme.

GHESHNE   *1971, Official*

IMPERIAL YACHTS

KISH

Displacement, tons	178
Dimensions, feet	122 × 25 × 7
Main engines	2 sets by Motor and Turbinen Union Friedrichshafen GMBH MAN-Maybach-Mercedes-Benz; 2 920 hp

A smaller and more modern Imperial Yacht built by Yacht und Bootswerft, Burmester, Germany. Commissioned in 1970. In the Persian Gulf.

KISH   1971, Official

SHASAVAR

Displacement, tons	530
Dimensions, feet	176 × 25·3 × 10·5
Main Engines	2 sets diesels; 1 300 bhp

Built by N. V. Boele's Scheepwerven, Boines, Netherlands. Engined by Gebr Stork of Hengelo. Launched in 1936. In the Caspian Sea.

SHAHSAVAR   1971, Imperial Iranian Navy, Official

COASTAL LAUNCHES

3 CASPIAN TYPE

BABOLSAR	GORGAN	SEFIDROUDE

Displacement, tons	28 to 32
Dimensions, feet	68·5 × 12·5 × 5·2
Guns	1—47 mm (Skoda); 1 MG
Main Engines	2 Krupp diesels; 2 shafts; 300 bhp = 14 knots

Built in 1935 by Cant Nav Riuniti Palermo, Italy. Employed in the Caspian Sea.

6 HARBOUR TYPE

MAHNAVI-HAMRAZ	MAHNAVI-VAHEDI	MORVARID
MAHNAVI-TAHERI	MARDJAN	SADAF

Displacement, tons	10
Dimensions, feet	40 × 11 × 3·7
Guns	MG
Main Engines	2 GM diesels.

Small launches for port duties. Not all in active service in 1969 and 1970.

SEWARD DEFENCE CRAFT

It was officially stated in 1971 that the two former British motor launches of the harbour (seaward) defence type, Asalon (ex-HMS SML 323, ex-HDML1081), latterly employed on surveying duties, and Tahmadou, FDB 65 (ex-FDB 58, ex-HMS SDML 1389), recently used as despatch boats, were out of service.

OILERS

HORMUZ 43

Displacement, tons	1 250 standard; 1 700 full load
Dimensions, feet	171·2 wl; 178·3 oa × 32·2 × 14
Main engines	1 Ansaldo Q 370, 4 cycle diesel
Oil fuel, tons	25

Hormuz was built by Cantiere Castellamare di Stabia. Own oil fuel: 25 tons. Cargo oil capacity: 5 000 to 6 000 barrels.

HORMUZ   1970, Imperial Iranian Navy, Official

WATER CARRIER

LENGEH 46 (ex-USS YW 88)

Displacement, tons	1 250 standard
Dimensions, feet	178 × 32 × 14
Main engines	Diesels; speed = 10 knots

Transferred to Iran by US in 1964. Similar to oiler Hormuz above. The former British tender Sirry (ex-MFV 1513), rated as a 90 ft fire extinguishing boat, was out of service, it was officially stated in 1971.

LENGEH   1969, Official

TUGS

BAHMANSHIR 45

Harbour tug (ex-US Army ST 1002), 150 tons, transferred in 1962. The tug Yadakbar (ex-Neyrou) was officially deleted from the list in 1971.

IRAQ

Diplomatic Representation

Military Attaché in London: Colonel Saadoon Hilmy

PATROL VESSELS

3 Ex-USSR "SOI" TYPE

Displacement, tons	215 light; 220 normal
Dimensions, feet	138 pp; 147 oa × 20 × 10 max
Guns	4—25 mm AA
A/S weapons	4 five-barrelled ahead-throwing rocket launchers.
Main Engines	3 diesels; 3 500 bhp = 25 knots

Former Soviet submarine chasers delivered by the USSR to Iraq in 1962.

TORPEDO BOATS

12 Ex-USSR "P 6" TYPE

Displacement, tons	50
Dimensions, feet	82 × 20 × 6
Guns	4—13 mm AA MG
Tubes	2—21 in
Main Engines	Speed = 40 knots

Presented by the USSR. Two were received in 1959, four in Nov 1960, and six in Jan 1961. Some remain non-operational.

LIGHTHOUSE TENDER

FAISAL 1 (ex-*Sans Peur,* ex-*Restless*)

Displacement, tons	1 025
Dimensions, feet	186 × 29·5 × 14·5
Main Engines	Triple expansion; 2 shafts; 850 ihp = 13 knots
Boilers	1 oil-fired

Former Royal Yacht. Designed by G. L. Watson Ltd. Built by John Brown & Co Ltd, Clydebank. Launched in 1923. A photograph appears in the 1937 to 1959-60 editions.

PRESIDENTIAL YACHT

AL THAWRA (ex-*Melike Aliye*)

Displacement, tons	746
Main Engines	Diesels; 2 shafts; 1 800 shp = 14 knots

Royal Yacht before assassination of King Faisal II in 1958, after which she was renamed *Al Thawra* (*The Revolution*) instead of *Malike Aliye* (*Queen Aliyah*)

AL THAWRA   Added 1966, Aldo Fraccaroli

Mercantile Marine

Lloyd's Register of Shipping: 35 vessels of 36 576 tons gross

PATROL BOATS

	No. 1	No. 2	No. 3	No. 4
Displacement, tons	67			
Dimensions, feet	100 × 17 × 3 mean			
Guns	1—3·7 in howitzer; 2—3 in mortars; 4 MG			
Main Engines	2 Thornycroft diesels; 2 shafts; 280 bhp = 12 knots			

Protected by bullet-proof plating. All built by John I. Thornycroft & Co Ltd, Woolston, Southampton. All launched, completed and delivered in 1937.

No. 1   *John I. Thornycroft & Co. Ltd*

6 Ex-USSR SMALL TYPE

Six small patrol boats are also reported to have been delivered by the USSR.

8 PORTS ADMINISTRATION TYPE

Length, feet	36
Main engines	1 diesel; 125 bhp

Patrol boats built by John I. Thornycroft & Co for the Iraqi Ports Administration.

4 PILOT DESPATCH TYPE

Length, feet	21
Main engines	1 diesel; 40 bhp

Pilot despatch launches built by John I. Thornycroft & Co for the Iraqui Ports Administration.

TUG

ALARM (ex-*St Ewe*)

Displacement, tons	570 standard; 820 full load
Dimensions, feet	135 × 30 × 14·5
Main Engines	Triple expansion; 1 shaft; 1 200 ihp = 12 knots
Boilers	2 oil-fired

Former British "Rescue" type tug of the "Saint" class. Built by Murdock & Murray. Launched in 1919.

IRELAND (REPUBLIC OF)

Administration

The Irish Naval Service is administered by the Director on Haulbowline Island in Cork Harbour, under the Department of Defence in Dublin.

Personnel

Estimate 1971: Total *circa* 500 officers and men

Mercantile Marine

Lloyd's Register of Shipping: 86 vessels of 174 977 tons gross

NEW CONSTRUCTION. It was officially stated in Feb 1969 that the Irish Government had authorised the purchase of two new vessels for the Naval Service. One would be a fast naval ship which would also have a fishery protection potential. The other would be primarily a fishery protection vessel suited for conditions off the Irish coasts. The planning, design and construction of the vessels were expected to take about two years.

CORVETTES

	No.	Laid down	Launched	Completed
MAEV (ex-HMS *Oxlip*)	01	9 Dec 1940	28 Aug 1941	28 Dec 1941

Displacement, tons	1 020 standard; 1 280 full load
Dimensions, feet	190 pp; 205 oa × 33 × 14·5
Guns	1—4 in
Main engines	Triple expansion; 2 750 ihp = 16 knots (designed); maximum sea speed now 10 to 12 knots
Boilers	2 SE
Oil fuel (tons)	230 (average bunkerage)
Complement	48 (accommodation for 78)

Formerly a British "Flower" class corvette. Purchased from Great Britain in 1946 (with sister ships *Cliona* and *Macha*). *Maev* was built by A. & J. Inglis Ltd, Pointhouse, Glasgow. The lattice mast was stepped in 1953. She was refitted for fishery protection duties in 1968-69. Her secondary guns were suppressed and she is no longer equipped with "Hedhegog" anti-submarine mortar, depth charges or 2-pounder Oerlikon guns. She was still in service in March 1971, it was officially stated, but it was proposed that she would be withdrawn from service in the near future and offered for sale.

DISPOSALS
Sister ships *Cliona* (ex-HMS *Bellwort*) and *Macha* (ex-HMS *Borage*), both built by George Brown & Co (Marine) Ltd, Greenock, were sold for breaking up in 1970-71.

MAEV (after refit)   *1970, Irish Naval Service, Official*

TENDERS

JOHN ADAMS

Measurement, tons	94 gross
Dimensions, feet	85 × 18·5 × 7
Main engines	Diesel; 125 bhp = 8 knots

Built by Richard Dunston, Ltd, Thorne, Doncaster, Yorks. Launched in 1934.

GENERAL McHARDY

Measurement, tons	100 gross
Dimensions, feet	76·5 × 18 × 9·5
Main engines	Compound reciprocating; 200 ihp = 9 knots

Built by Philip & Son, Ltd, Dartmouth, Devon, launched in 1928. Ferry tender. It was officially stated in Jan 1971 that she has been offered for sale.

DISPOSAL. The tender *Nyndham* was sold in 1968 and subsequently broken up.

FISHERY PROTECTION VESSEL

1 NEW CONSTRUCTION

Displacement, tons	1 020 approx designed (official figure)
Dimensions, feet	180·0 pp; 200·0 oa × 33·0 × 14·0
Main engines	Designed for a speed of 18 knots

It was officially stated on Jan 1971 that "One fishery protection vessel is under construction for delivery in 1972". Designed as an all weather ship. Being built by Verolme, Cork. The first vessel ever built for the Naval Service in the Republic of Ireland.

BANBA (ex-*Alverton*)   *1971, Wright & Logan*

COASTAL MINESWEEPERS

3 Ex-BRITISH "TON" CLASS

BANBA (ex-HMS *Alverton*)		**FÓLA** (ex-HMS *Blaxton*)
		GRAINNE (ex-HMS *Oulston*)

Displacement, tons	360 standard; 425 full load
Dimensions, feet	140·0 pp; 153·0 oa × 28·8 × 8·2
Guns	1—40 mm AA; 2—20 mm AA (but armament is under review)
Main engines	2 diesels; 2 shafts; 3 000 bhp = 15 knots max
Oil fuel, tons	45
Radius, miles	2 300 at 13 knots
Complement	30 average

Former British "Ton" class coastal minesweepers. Built in 1954-59. Double mahogany hulls and otherwise constructed of aluminium alloy and other materials with the lowest possible magnetic attraction to attain the greatest possible safety factor when sweeping. Purchased from Great Britain in 1971. See fuller particulars of the numerous "Ton" class in the United Kingdom section on later page. To be used for fishery protection duties in replacements for the old corvettes. Scheduled to arrive in Irish Republican waters in Spring 1971.

Grainne after transfer   *April 1971, Wright & Logan*

FÓLA (ex-*Blaxton*)   *1971, A. & J. Pavia*

ISRAEL

Administration
Commander-in-Chief of the Israeli Navy:
Rear Admiral A. Botzer
Diplomatic Representation
Naval, Military and Air Attaché in London and Paris:
Major General S. Eyal

Naval, Military and Air Attaché in Washington:
Major General E. Zaira

Strength of the Fleet

3 Submarines (Diesel Powered)
2 Destroyers (including 1 Escort Type)
9 Fast Torpedo Boats
12 Fast Missile Boats
9 Patrol Vessels (including 1 Submarine Chaser)
10 Landing Craft
12 Patrol Boats (Small PBR Type)
1 Transport

Personnel

2 200 (200 officers and 2 000 men)

Mercantile Marine

Lloyd's Register of Shipping:
108 vessels of 713 867 tons gross

SUBMARINES

Name	No.	Builders	Laid down	Launched	Completed
LEVIATHAN (ex-HMS *Turpin*)	75	HM Dockyard, Chatham	24 May 1943	5 Aug 1944	18 Dec 1944
DOLPHIN (ex-HMS *Truncheon*)	77	HM Dockyard, Devonport	5 Nov 1942	22 Feb 1944	25 May 1945

2 Ex-BRITISH "T" CLASS

Displacement, tons	*Dolphin:* 1 310 standard; 1 535 surface; 1 740 submerged *Leviathan:* 1 280 standard; 1 505 surface; 1 700 submerged
Length, feet (*metres*)	*Dolphin:* 293·5 (*89·5*) oa *Leviathan:* 285·5 (*87·0*) oa
Beam, feet (*metres*)	26·5 (*8·1*)
Draught, feet (*metres*)	14·8 (*4·5*)
Torpedo tubes	6—21 m (*533 mm*) 4 bow, 2 stern
Main engines	Diesels; 2 500 bhp (surface); Electric Motors: 2 900 hp (submerged)
Speed, knots	15·25 on surface; 15 to 18 submerged
Complement	*Dolphin:* 65 *Leviathan:* 69

Both of these modernised submarines originally had the 265 pp and 273·5 overall length of the standard "T" class. But during the rebuilding of these boats of the "Conversion Type" the pressure hull was severed at the engine room section, the two halves moved apart and a new section built in. The extra space accommodated a second pair of electric motors, clutches between which and the original motors made electric drive possible, and a fourth battery section was added to give a submerged speed of 15 to 18 knots (the original submerged speed was 9 knots). All guns and external torpedo tubes were removed. Improved periscopes, sonar and radar were installed with a periscope snort mast. In the initial drastic reconstruction the bridge was reduced to a small cramped cab before the fin conning tower, but later the bridge was built into the huge fin or "sail" which houses two periscopes, two radar masts, two snort masts and an aerial. As *Turpin* the *Leviathan* was lengthened by 12 feet, and as *Truncheon* the *Dolphin* was lengthened by 20 feet. They have welded pressure hulls.

TRANSFERS. *Leviathan* (meaning whale) was handed over to Israel in Portsmouth Dockyard on 19 May 1967. *Dolphin* was transferred from the Royal Navy at Gosport on 9 Jan 1968.

LOSS. Original sister ship *Dakar* (ex-HMS *Totem*), handed over to Israel on 10 Nov 1967, was lost in the Eastern Mediterranean on 25 Jan 1968.

DOLPHIN   *1971, Israeli Navy, Official*

LEVIATHAN (reconstructed)   *1967, Skyfotos*

Name	No.	Builders	Laid down	Launched	Completed
TANIN (ex-HMS *Springer*)	71	Cammell Laird Birkenhead	8 May 1944	14 May 1945	2 Aug 1945

1 Ex-BRITISH "S" CLASS

Displacement, tons	715 standard; 814 surface; 1 000 submerged
Length, feet (*metres*)	202·5 (*61·7*) pp; 217 (*66·2*) oa
Beam, feet (*metres*)	23·8 (*7·2*)
Draught, feet (*metres*)	10·5 (*3·2*)
Guns, surface	1—4 in (*102 mm*)
Torpedo tubes	6—21 in (*533 mm*)
Main engines	1 900 hp diesels (surface); 1 300 hp electric motors (submerged)
Speed, knots	14·7 on surface; 9 submerged
Complement	57

Purchased by Israel in Oct 1958, handed over to the Israeli Navy in Portsmouth on 9 Oct 1958 and renamed *Tanin* (Crocodile). Refitted in Great Britain and delivered in Dec 1959. Fitted with "Snort" mast. Sister ship *Rahav* (ex-HMS *Sanguine*), delivered to Israel after refit in May 1960, was discarded as worn out in 1968 and was cannibalised to keep *Tanin* in commission, but the latter herself will be reduced to training.

TANIN   *1970, Israeli Navy, Official*

DESTROYERS

Name	No.	Builders	Laid down	Launched	Completed
YAFFO (ex-HMS *Zodiac*)	42	Thornycroft, Southampton	7 Nov 1942	11 Mar 1944	25 Oct 1944

1 Ex-BRITISH "Z" CLASS

Displacement, tons	1 710 standard; 2 555 full load
Length, feet (*metres*)	362·2 (*110·4*) oa
Beam, feet (*metres*)	35·5 (*10·8*)
Draught, feet (*metres*)	17 (*5·2*)
Guns, dual purpose	4—4·5 in (*115 mm*)
Guns, AA	6—40 mm
A/S weapons	4 DCT
Torpedo tubes	8—21 in (*533 mm*)
Main engines	Parsons geared turbines; 2 shafts; 40 000 shp
Boilers	2 Admiralty 3-drum
Speed, knots	31
Complement	250

Transferred to Israel on 15 July 1955 in Cardiff Docks. Refitted before going to Israel in 1956 by Crichtons in Trafalgar Dock, Liverpool. Now used as a training ship. Sister ship *Elath* sank off Sinai coast on 21 Oct 1967 after missile boat attack.

YAFFO   *1968, A. & J. Pavia*

Destroyers—*continued*

Name	No.	Builders	Laid down	Launched	Completed
HAIFA (ex-*Ibrahim el Awal*, ex-*Lin Fu*, ex-*Mendip*)	38	Swan, Hunter & Wigham Richardson, Ltd Wallsend	10 Aug 1939	9 Apr 1940	12 Oct 1940

1 Ex-EGYPTIAN "HUNT" TYPE 1

Displacement, tons	1 000 standard; 1 490 full load
Length, feet (*metres*)	273·3 (*83·3*) pp; 280·0 (*85·3*) oa
Beam, feet (*metres*)	29·0 (*8·8*)
Draught, feet (*metres*)	14 (*4·3*) max
Guns, surface	4—4 in (*102 mm*)
Guns, AA	2—40 mm; 3—20 mm
A/S weapons	2 DCT
Main engines	Parsons geared turbines; 2 shafts; 19 000 shp
Boilers	2 three-drum type
Speed, knots	25
Oil fuel, tons	280
Endurance, miles	3 000 at 14 knots
Complement	190

HAIFA   *1971, Israeli Navy, Official*

Former escort destroyer, later reclassified as anti-aircraft frigate, of the British "Hunt" class, Type 1. Engined by the Wallsend Slipway & Engineering Co Ltd, Wallsend-on-Tyne. Captured from Egypt off Haifa on 31 Oct 1956 and renamed *Haifa*. Classified by Israel as a destroyer.

HISTORY: This ship, first named *Mendip*, served with the British Navy from Oct 1940 until May 1948 when she was transferred to the Chinese Navy and renamed *Lin Fu*. She was returned to the British Navy at Hong Kong a year later and reverted to the name *Mendip* but was transferred to the Egyptian Navy in Nov 1949 and renamed *Mohamed Ali el Kebir* but was again renamed *Ibrahim el Awal* in 1951. She was captured from Egypt off Haifa by Israeli forces on 31 Oct 1956 and renamed *Haifa*. Commissioned in the Israeli Navy in Jan 1957.

MISSILE BOATS

12 "SAAR" CLASS

ACCO	HEEREV	MISHAK	SAAR
EILATH	HETZ	MIVTACH	SOUFA
GAASH	MISGAN	MIZNAK	YAVIT

Displacement, tons	220 standard; 250 full load
Dimensions, feet	147·6 oa × 23·0 × 5·9 (8·2 max)
Missile launchers	8 "Gabriel" surface-to-surface
Guns, AA	1—40 mm
Tubes	2 side launchers for 21 in torpedoes (surface or A/S)
Main engines	4 diesels; 13 500 bhp = 40 knots
Oil fuel, tons	30
Range, miles	800 at 30 knots cruising
Complement	35 to 40

Built by Ch de Normandie, Cherbourg, completed between 1967 and 1970. Final five ships were delivered from France to Israel in Jan 1970.

YAVIT   *1971, Israeli Navy, Official*

PATROL VESSELS

1 "PC" TYPE

NOGAH (ex-USS *PC* 1188) P 22

Displacement, tons	295 standard; 450 full load
Dimensions, feet	170·0 pp; 173·7 oa × 23·0 × 10·0
Guns	1—4 in; 1—40 mm AA; 3—20 mm AA
A/S weapons	4 DCT
Main engines	2 diesels; 2 shafts; 1 764 bhp = 18 knots
Complement	70

Former United States patrol vessel (submarine chaser) of the steel-hulled PC type. Built by Gibbs Gas Engine Co, Jacksonville, Fla. Laid down on 12 July 1943, launched on 31 Jan 1944 and completed on 5 Sep 1944.

NOGAH   *Israeli Navy, Official*

TORPEDO BOATS

3 "OPHIR" CLASS

OPHIR T 150	SHVA T 151	TARSHISH T 152

Displacement, tons	40
Dimensions, feet	70 × 17 ×₌5
Guns,	1—40 mm AA; 2—20 mm AA
Torpedoes	2—17·7 in
Main Engines	High octane petrol engines; 4 000 bhp = 40 knots.

Motor Torpedo Boats/Gunboats built for the Israeli Navy by Cantieri Baglieto, Varrazze, Italy, in 1956-57.

SHVA   *1964, Israeli Navy, Official*

6 "AYAH" CLASS

AYAH T 200	DAYA T 202	TAHMASS T 204
BAZ T 201	PERESS T 203	YASOOR T 205

Displacement, tons	62 standard
Dimensions, feet	85·3 oa × 20·7 × 5
Guns	1—40 mm; 4—20 mm AA
Torpedoes	2—17·7 in
Main Engines	2 Napier Deltic diesels; 2 shafts; 4 600 bhp = 42 knots
Complement	15

Built by Chantiers de Meulan, France. Launched in 1950-56. A photograph of T 208 appears in the 1953-54 to 1957-58 editions, of T 207 in the 1953-54 to 1960-61 editions.

PERESS   *Israeli Navy, Official*

TAHMASS   *1965, Israeli Navy, Official*

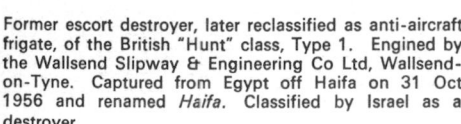

PATROL BOATS

4 "KEDMA" CLASS

KEDMA 46   **NEGBA** 52   **YAMA** 48   **ZAFONA** 60

Displacement, tons	32
Dimensions, feet	67·0 × 15·0 × 4·8
Guns	2—20 mm
Main engines	2 diesels; 2 shafts; 1 540 bhp = 25 knots
Complement	10

Built in Japan during 1968. Handy boats of the small seaward defence type.

KEDMA   *1970, Israeli Navy, Official*

2 "YAR" CLASS

YARDEN 42   **YARKON** 44

Displacement, tons	96 standard; 109 full load
Dimensions, feet	100 × 20 × 6
Guns,	2—20 mm AA
Main Engines	Diesels; 2 shafts; speed 22 knots
Complement	16

Both built by Yacht & Bootswerft, Burmester Bremen-Burg, Germany. *Yarkon* was launched on 25 July 1955 and *Yarden* in 1957.

YARKON   *Israeli Navy, Official*

YARDEN   *Israeli Navy, Official*

12 "PBR" TYPE

Displacement, tons	7·5
Length, feet	30·2 oa
Guns	1—0·5 MG
Main engines	Diesels; speed = 24 knots
Complement	5

New vessels in service with the Israeli Navy and added to the official list in 1971.

2 "HDML" TYPE

DROR 21   **TIRTSA** 25

Displacement, tons	46 standard; 54 full load
Dimensions, feet	72 oa × 16 × 5·5
Guns	2—20 mm AA
A/S	8 DC
Main Engines	2 diesels; 2 shafts; 320 bhp = 12 knots
Complement	12

Former British harbour defence motor launches. Built in Great Britain in 1943.

LANDING CRAFT

3 "ASH" CLASS

ASHDOD 61   **ASHKELON** 63   **ACHZIV** 65

Displacement, tons	400 standard; 730 full load
Dimensions, feet	180·5 pp; 205·5 oa × 32·8 × 5·8
Guns	2—20 mm AA
Main engines	3 MWM diesels; 3 shafts; 1 900 bhp = 10·5 knots
Oil fuel, tons	37
Complement	20

These three landing craft were completed during 1966-67 by Israel Shipyards, Haifa.

ASHDOD   *Israeli Navy, Official*

3 "LC" TYPE

ETZION GUEBER 51   **SHIKOMONA** 53   **LC** 55

Displacement, tons	182 standard; 230 full load
Dimensions, feet	120·0 × 23·2 × 4·7
Guns, AA	2—20 mm
Main engines	2 diesels; 2 shaft;s 1 280 bhp = 10 knots
Complement	12

In lieu of the landing craft of the LCI and LCT types, which were taken out of commission for disposal (with the exception of one LCT, which was given to the Israeli National Museum in Haifa) three new landing craft were built in the Israeli Dockyard.

SHIKOMONA   *Israeli Navy, Official*

3 "LCM" TYPE

LCM

Displacement, tons	22 tons standard; 60 full load
Dimensions, feet	50 × 14 × 3·2
Main Engines	2 diesels; 450 bhp = 11 knots

Former United States vessels of the LCM (Landing Craft Mechanised) type. There are a number of other landing craft.

BEIT SHAFEI

Dimensions, feet	225·0 × 38·9 × 5·0
Capacity	16 tanks
Speed	12·5 knots

TRANSPORTS

3 "BAT" TYPE

BAT GOLIM   **BAT SHEVA**   **BAT YAM**

Displacement, tons	900 (official figure for *Bat Sheva*), others 1 200
Dimensions, feet	311·7 × 36·7 × 26·9
Guns	4—20 mm AA
Main engines	Diesels; speed = 10 knots
Complement	26

BAT SHEVA   *1971, Israeli Navy, Official*

ITALY

Administration

Chief of Naval Staff:
Ammiraglio di Squadra Giuseppe Roselli Lorenzini

Commander, Allied Naval Forces, Southern Europe
(Commander Navy, South Malta):
Ammiraglio di Squadra Gino Birindelli

Commander-in-Chief of Fleet:
Ammiraglio di Squadra Eugenio Henke

Director General Navy Personnel:
Ammiraglio di Squadra Mario Gambetta

Deputy Chief of Naval Staff:
Ammiraglio di Divisione Gino De Giorgi

Diplomatic Representation

Naval Attaché in London:
Captain Corrado Vittori, ItN

Naval Attaché in Washington:
Captain Claudio Boido, ItN

Naval Attaché in Moscow:
Captain Carlo Moriani, ItN

Naval Attache in Paris:

Captain Giuseppe Colombo, ItN

Strength of the Fleet

10	Diesel Powered Submarines
4	Guided Missile Armed Cruisers
2	Guided Missile Armed Destroyers
1	Destroyer Leader (ex-Light Cruiser)
4	Destroyers
1	Experimental Destroyer
13	Frigates
20	Corvettes
4	Ocean Minesweepers
1	Patrol Vessel
37	Coastal Minesweepers
7	Fast Gunboats
7	Torpedo Boats
20	Inshore Minesweepers
5	Transports
1	Landing Ship
4	Training Ships
6	Support Gunboats (ex-Landing Ships)
138	Support Ships and Service Craft

New Construction Programme

2 Diesel Powered Submarines
2 Guided Missile Armed Destroyers
5 Missile Boats
1 Nuclear Powered Fast Fleet Replenishment Ship of new design
1 Hydrofoil Missile Gunboat

Navy Estimetas

1966: 201,333,181,000 Lire
1967: 213,557,581,000 Lire
1968: 82,700,000,000 Lire *
1969: 91 500,000,000 Lire *
1970: 86 500,000,000 Lire *
1971: 88,000,000,000 Lire *

*Under the Defence budget reorganisation the Navy retained direct control only of sufficient funds to modernise and operate the Fleet. The cost of all other requirements became the direct responsibility of the Defence Ministry.

Personnel

1966: 39,000 officers and ratings
1967: 40,000 officers and ratings
1968: 40,000 officers and ratings
1969: 40,000 officers and ratings
1970: 41,000 officers and ratings
1971: 42,500 officers and ratings

Mercantile Marine

Lloyd's Register of Shipping:
1 639 vessels of 7 447 610 tons gross

Scale: 150 feet = 1 inch (1 : 1800)

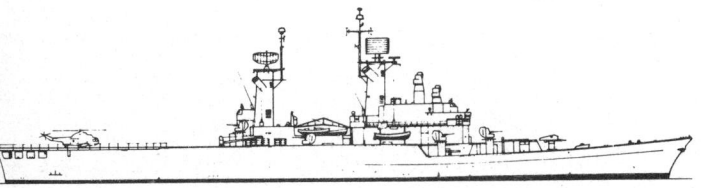
VITTORIO VENETO

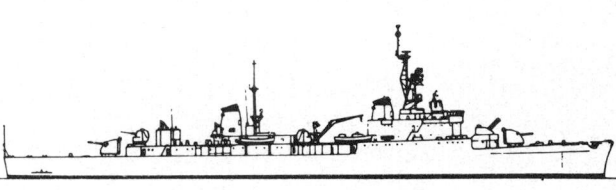
ARDITO *Class*

ANDREA DORIA, CAIO DUILIO

SAN MARCO

GIUSEPPE GARIBALDI

SAN GIORGIO

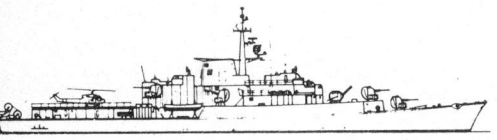
ALPINO, CARABINIERE

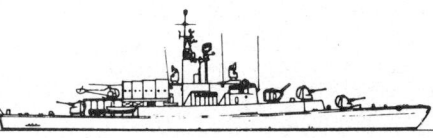
BERGAMINI *Class*

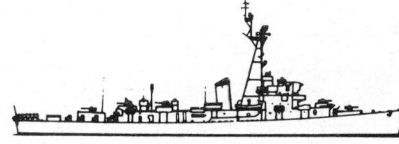
ALTAIR *Class*

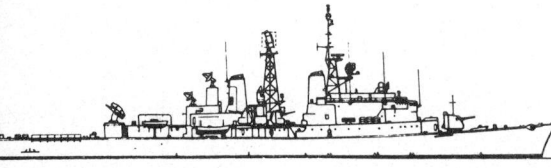
IMPAVIDO, INTREPIDO

CENTAURO *Class* as converted

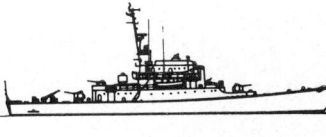
ALBATROS *Class*

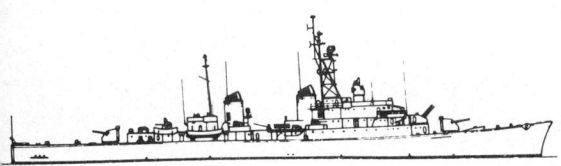
IMPETUOSO, INDOMITO

DE CRISTOFARO *Class*

CENTAURO *Class* original

SUBMARINES

Name	No.	Builders	Laid down	Launched	Completed
BAGNOLINI	S 505	CRDA Monfalcone	15 Apr 1965	26 Aug 1967	16 June 1968
DANDOLO	S 513	CRDA Monfalcone	10 Mar 1967	16 Dec 1967	25 Sep 1968
MOCENIGO	S 514	CRDA Monfalcone	12 June 1967	20 Apr 1968	11 Jan 1969
TOTI	S 506	CRDA Monfalcone	15 Apr 1965	12 Mar 1967	22 Jan 1968

4 "TOTI" CLASS

Displacement, tons	460 standard; 524 surface; 582 submerged
Length, feet (*metres*)	153·2 (*46·7*)
Beam, feet (*metres*)	15·4 (*4·7*)
Draught, feet (*metres*)	13·1 (*4·0*)
Torpedo tubes	4—21 in
Main engines	2 Fiat MB 820 N/I diesels, 1 electric motor, Diesel-electric drive; 2 200 hp; 1 shaft
Speed, knots	9 on surface; 14 submerged
Radius, miles	3 000 at 5 knots
Complement	24

Italy's first native-built submarines since the Second World War. The design was recast several times, being finalised as coastal submarines of the hunter-killer type. The above figures were officially revised in 1969.

SONAR, RADAR. Fitted with large sonar on forecastle and probably with some form of air detection radar.

PHOTOGRAPHS. A photograph of *Toti* appears in the 1968-69 and 1969-70 editions. and of *Bagnolini* in the 1969-70 and 1970-71 editions.

NEW CONSTRUCTION. The two projected oceangoing hunter-killer submarines, officially deleted from the New Construction Programme in 1968, were restored to the building scheme in 1970. Names under consideration: *Cesare Battisti, Guglielmo Marconi, Nazario Sauro.*

DANDOLO   *1971, Italian Navy, Official*

MOCENIGO   *1970, Italian Navy, Official*

Name	No.	Builders	Launched	Completed	Transferred
ALFREDO CAPPELLINI (ex-USS *Capitaine*, SS 336)	S 513	Electric Boat Div, General Dynamics Corpn	1 Oct 1944	26 Jan 1945	5 Mar 1966
EVANGELISTA TORRICELLI (ex-USS *Lizardfish*, SS 373)	S 512	Manitowoc SB Co, Manitowoc, Wisconsin	16 July 1944	30 Dec. 1944	9 Jan 1960
FRANCESCO MOROSINI (ex-USS *Besugo*, SS 321)	S 514	Electric Boat Div, General Dynamics Corpn	27 Feb 1944	19 June 1944	31 Mar 1966

3 Ex-US "BALAO" CLASS

Displacement, tons	1 600 standard; 1 816 surface: 2 425 submerged
Length, feet (*metres*)	311·5 (*95·0*)
Beam, feet (*metres*)	27 (*8·2*))
Draught, feet (*metres*)	17 (*5·2*)
Torpedo tubes	10—21 in (*533 mm*) 6 bow and 4 stern
Main engines	4 GM 16/278 diesels, 6 000 hp; 4 electric motors; 2 750 hp
Speed, knots	18 on surface; 10 submerged
Radius, miles	14 000 at 10 knots
Oil fuel (tons)	300
Complement	85

Former US oceangoing submarines. *Lizardfish* was originally to have been renamed *Luigi Torelli*. The 3-inch gun is no longer mounted. A photograph of *Alfredo Cappellini* appears in the 1968-69 and 1969-70 editions.

EVANGELISTA TORRICELLI   *1970, Italian Navy, Official*

Name	No.	Builders	Laid down	Launched	Completed	Transferred
LEONARDO DA VINCI (ex-USS *Dace*, SS 247)	S 510	Electric Boat Div, General Dynamics Corpn	22 July 1942	25 Apr 1943	23 July 1943	15 Dec 1954
ENRICO TAZZOLI (ex-USS *Barb*, SS 220)	S 511	Electric Boat Div, General Dynamics Corpn	7 June 1941	2 Apr 1942	8 July 1942	31 Jan 1955

2 Ex-US "GATO" CLASS

Displacement, tons	1 525 standard; 1 816 surface: 2 425 submerged
Length, feet (*metres*)	307·4 (*93·7*)
Beam, feet (*metres*)	27·3 (*8·3*)
Draught, feet (*metres*)	17 (*5·2*)
Torpedo tubes	10—21 in (*533 mm*) 6 bow and 4 stern
Main engines	4 GM diesels, 6 000 hp; 2 electric motors, 2 750 hp
Speed, knots	18 on surface; 10 submerged
Radius, miles	12 000 at 10 knots
Oil fuel (tons)	300 tons
Complement	85

ENRICO TAZZOLI   *1970, Italian Navy, Cfficial*

Former United States oceangoing submarines. Transferred to Italy by the USA after conversion to guppy snorkel in 1953-54. Modified structure and fairwater. Loan by US was extended for 5 years in 1959. A photograph of *Leonardo da Vinci* appears in the 1968-69 and 1969-70 editions.

Name	No.	Builders	Laid down	Launched	Completed	Rebui
PIETRO CALVI (ex-*Bario*, ex-*Uit 7*, ex-*Bario*)	S 503	CRDA Trieste (1944); CN Taranto (1961)	15 Mar 1943	23 Jan 1944	Dec 1957	1961

1 "FLUTTO" CLASS

Displacement, tons	800 standard; 905 surface 1 107 submerged
Length, feet (*metres*)	216·5 (*66·0*)
Beam, feet (*metres*)	23 (*7·0*)
Draught, feet (*metres*)	13·2 (*4·0*)
Torpedo tubes	4—21 in (*533 mm*)
Main engines	2 MAN diesels, 2 700 hp; 3 electric motors; 1 shaft
Speed, knots	14 on surface; 14 submerged
Radius, miles	10 000 at 8 knots
Complement	60

Sunk by Allied air-raid on 16 Mar 1945 after having been renamed *Uit* 7. She was reconstructed with a tear drop bow and modernised during 1957-59, being re-launched on 21 June 1959. In Mar 1961 her original name *Bario* was changed to *Pietro Calvi*.

PIETRO CALVI   *1970, Italian Navy, Official*

DISPOSALS. The submarine *Vortice* of the "Flutto" class was officially deleted from the list in 1967. The submarine *Giada* of the "Acciaio" class was removed from the effective list in 1965.

GUIDED MISSILE CRUISERS (CG)

Name	No.	Builders	Laid down	Launched	Completed
VITTORIO VENETO	C 550	Navalmeccanica Castellammare di Stabia	10 June 1965	5 Feb 1967	30 Apr 1969

1 HELICOPTER CARRIER TYPE

Displacement, tons	7,500 standard; 8,850 full load (official figures)
Length, feet (metres)	557·7 (170·0) oa
Beam, feet (metres)	63·6 (19·4)
Draught, feet (metres)	17·2 (5·2)
Aircraft	9 A/B 240B ASW helicopters
Missiles, AA	1 "Terrier"/"Asroc" twin launcher forward
Guns, AA	8—3 in (76 mm) 62 cal.
Torpedo tubes	2 triple for A/S torpedoes
Boilers	4 Foster-Wheeler; 711 psi (50 kg/cm²); 842°F (450°C)
Main engines	2 Tosi double reduction geared turbines; 73 000 shp; 2 shafts
Speed, knots	32 designed
Radius, miles	6 000 at 20 knots
Oil fuel, tons	1 200
Complement	530 (60 officers, 470 men)

Multi-purpose guided missile armed cruiser and helicopter carrier. Developed from the "Doria" class, but with much larger helicopter squadron and improved facilities for anti-submarine operations. Projected under the 1959-60 New Construction Programme, but her design was recast several times, see official artist's impression in the 1963-64 to 1966-67 editions. She was commissioned for service on 12 July 1969.

VITTORIO VENETO

1970 Italian Navy, Official

VITTORIO VENETO

1970 Italian Navy, Official

RADAR. Fitted with long range 3 D radar for air surveillance and designation, with antenna mounted on the foremast. The mainmast carries an antenna for an S band surface and air tactical radar. The "Terrier" missiles are controlled from directors mounted in tandem above the bridge and have C band radar. The guns are controlled by two systems, one forward and one aft, which employ X band tracker radars.

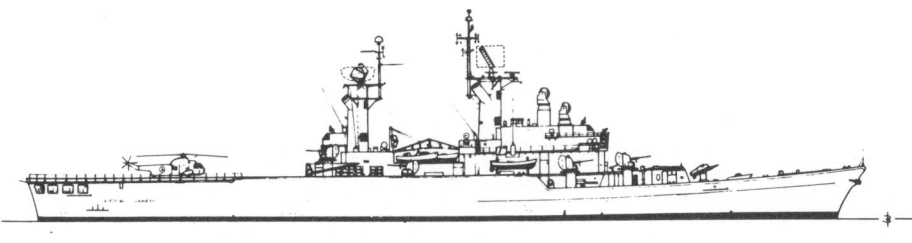

DRAWING. Redrawn in 1970. Scale 125 feet = 1 inch (1 : 1 500)

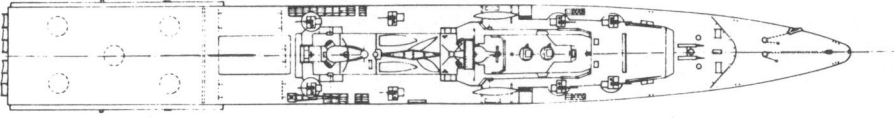

RESCINDMENT. The projected improved guided missile cruiser/helicopter carrier/assault ship *Trieste* (ex-*Italia*) was officially deleted from the New Construction Programme in 1968.

GUIDED MISSILE ESCORT CRUISERS (CG)

Name	No.	Builders	Laid down	Launched	Completed
ANDREA DORIA	553	Cantieri del Tirreno, Riva Trigoso	11 May 1958	27 Feb 1963	23 Feb 1964
CAIO DUILIO	554	Navalmeccanica Castellammare di Stabia	16 May 1958	22 Dec 1962	30 Nov 1964

2 "ANDREA DORIA" CLASS

(officially rated as *Incrociatori di Scorta*)

Displacement, tons	5 000 standard ; 6 500 full load (official figures)
Length, feet (*metres*)	489·8 (*149·3*) oa
Beam, feet (*metres*)	56·4 (*17·2*)
Draught, feet (*metres*)	16·4 (*5·0*)
Aircraft	4 A/B 204B ASW helicopters
Missiles, AA	1 "Terrier" twin launcher forward
Guns, AA	8—3 in (*76 mm*) 62 cal.
Torpedo tubes	2 triple for 12 in (*305 mm*) A/S torpedoes
Boilers	4 Foster-Wheeler ; 711 psi (*50 kg/cm²*) ; 842°F (*450°C*)
Main engines	2 double reduction geared turbines 60 000 shp ; 2 shafts
Speed, knots	31 designed, 30 sustained
Radius, miles	6 000 at 20 knots
Oil fuel, tons	1 100
Complement	478 (53 officers, 425 men)

Escort cruisers of novel design and generous beam with a good helicopter capacity in relation to their size. *Enrico Dandolo* was the name originally allocated to *Andrea Doria*.

GUNNERY. The anti-aircraft battery includes eight 3-inch fully automatic guns of a new pattern, disposed in single turrets, four on each side amidships abreast the funnels and the bridge.

HELICOPTER PLATFORM. Helicopters operate from a large platform aft measuring 98·5 feet by 52·5 feet (*30 by 16 metres*).

ROLL DAMPING. Both ships have Gyrofin-Salmoiraghi stabilisers.

RADAR
Search: SPS 12 and SPS 39 3 D.
Fire Control: SPG 55 for "Terrier", ELSAG NA 9 systems with X Band radar for guns.

VTOL HARRIER. The Harrier, the world's first operational VTOL close support fighter aircraft, designed and built by Hawker Siddeley, demonstrated its capabilities of operating from shipborne platforms when it completed a two-day demonstration watched by Italian service chiefs, with a vertical landing on the comparatively small helicopter flight deck of the *Andrea Doria* over which it had arrived at almost the speed of sound and from which it took off again vertically to fly back to England via Pisa, see photograph in the 1969-70 edition.

ANDREA DORIA *1970, Italian Navy, Official*

CAIO DUILIO *1971 Stefan Terzibaschitsch*

CAIO DUILIO *Added 1971, Dr Aldo Fraccaroli*

ANDREA DORIA *Added 1971, Dr. Aldo Fraccaroli*

GUIDED MISSILE LIGHT CRUISERS (CG)

Name	No.	Builders	Laid down	Launched	Completed	Reconstruction
GIUSEPPE GARIBALDI	C 551	C.R. dell'Adriatico, Trieste	Dec 1933	21 Apr 1936	Dec 1937	Dec 1957-Nov 1962

Displacement, tons	9 800 standard; 11 335 full load
Length, feet (metres)	593 (180·7) wl; 613·5 (187·0) oa
Beam, feet (metres)	61·7 (18·8) oa
Draught, feet (metres)	22 (6·7)
Missiles, surface	4 tubes for ICBM's aft in "Y" position. See Missile Systems notes below
Missiles, AA	1 "Terrier" twin launcher
Guns, dual purpose	4—5·3 in (135 mm), 53 cal., 2 twin, see Gunnery notes
Guns, AA	8—3 in (76 mm) 62 cal., singles
Armour	Belt 4·5 in (115 mm); deck 2·25 in (57·5 mm); turrets 4 in (100 mm); CT 5 in (125 mm)
Boilers	6 CRDA Yarrow three-drum type; 356 psi (25 kg/cm²); 608°F (320°C)
Main engines	2 Parsons single reduction geared turbines; 100 000 shp; 2 shafts
Speed, knots	30
Radius, miles	4 000 at 20 knots
Oil fuel (tons)	1 700
Complement	694 (43 officers, 651 men)

Originally a sister ship of the light cruiser *Luigi di Savoia Duca degli Abruzzi* (removed from the effective list in Apr 1961).

G. M. RECONSTRUCTION. From Dec 1957 *Giuseppe Garibaldi* was converted into a guided missile cruiser. The appearance of the ship was completely altered, with a single large trunked funnel and lattice masts. She was commissioned for operational service in Nov 1962, and became Flagship of the Commander-in-Chief.

MISSILE SYSTEMS. The ballistic missile tubes are installed aft in "Y" position, the "Terrier" system being superimposed in "X" position, a deck higher. *Giuseppe Garibaldi* practice launched "Terrier" and ballistic missiles off La Spezia in late 1961 and 1962. Her initial launches were made in the Caribbean Sea on 8 Nov 1962 first with "Terrier" and then with ballistic missiles.

GUNNERY. The armament includes four 5·3 inch dual purpose guns of a new automatic model disposed in two twin turrets forward, and an anti-aircraft battery of eight 3-inch automatic guns, also of a new pattern, built by O.T.O. La Spezia, disposed in single turrets, four on each side amidships abreast the funnel and bridge.

ENGINEERING. On her original trials this ship developed 104 030 shp and a speed of 33·6 knots. During reconstruction her machinery was completely refitted.

FUNNEL. Early in 1963 the top of the funnel cowl was modified, increasing the height.

OPERATIONAL. This ship, with the missile destroyers *Impavido* and *Intrepido*, form the 4th Naval Division.

A/S CONVERSION. The further conversion of *Giuseppe Garibaldi* into an Anti-Submarine Warfare Command Ship was rescinded due to lack of funds.

RADAR
Search: Selenia ARGOS 5 000 and SPS 39 3 D.
Fire Control: SPG 55 for "Terrier". NSG with X Band radar for guns.

PHOTOGRAPHS. A photograph taken from "X" position over "Y" position, showing vertical tubes aft for four ballistic missiles, appears in the 1963-64 to 1970-71 editions.

DRAWING. Starboard elevation and plan. Drawn in 1969. Scale: 125 feet = 1 inch (1 : 1500).

GIUSEPPE GARIBALDI (missiles aft silhouetted) — 1969, Italian Navy, Official

GIUSEPPE GARIBALDI — 1971, Dr. Giorgio Arra

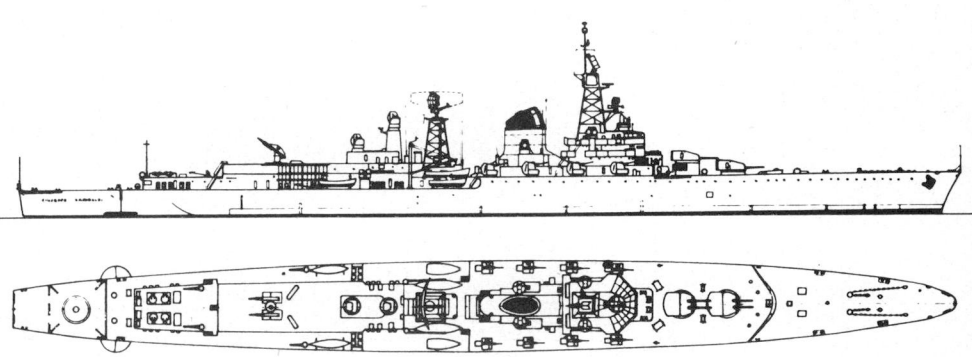

GIUSEPPE GARIBALDI — 1968, Dr. Giorgio Arra

GUIDED MISSILE ARMED DESTROYERS (DDG)

2 "AUDACE" CLASS BUILDING

ARDITO	**AUDACE**	Missiles, AA	1 "Tartar" launcher aft	

Displacement, tons	3 500 standard; 4 400 full load	
Length, feet (metres)	446·4 (136·6)	
Beam, feet (metres)	46·7 (14·2)	
Draught, feet (metres)	15 (4·6)	
Aircraft	2 light A/S helicopters	

Missiles, AA	1 "Tartar" launcher aft
Guns, dual purpose	2—5 in (127 mm) 54 cal single
Guns, AA	4—3 in (76 mm) 62 cal
Torpedo tubes	6 A/S (two tripled)
Boilers	4 Foster Wheeler type
Main engines	2 geared turbines; 73 000 shp
Speed, knots	33

It was announced in Apr 1966 that two new guided missile destroyers would be built. They are basically similar to, but an improvement in design on that of the "Impavido" class, and measurably larger, with an extended flight deck so that they can operate two A/B 204 B ASW helicopters. Officially rated as *Caccia Lanciamissile* and designated DDG. *Ardito* was laid down on 10 July 1968.

Name	No.	Builders	Ordered	Laid down	Launched	Completed
IMPAVIDO	D 570	Cantieri del Tirreno, Riva Trigoso	Jan 1957	10 June 1957	25 May 1962	16 Nov 1963
INTREPIDO	D 571	Ansaldo, Leghorn	1959	16 May 1959	21 Oct 1962	30 Oct 1964

2 "IMPAVIDO" CLASS

Displacement, tons	3 201 standard; 3 941 full load
Length, feet (metres)	429·5 (130·9)
Beam, feet (metres)	44·7 (13·6)
Draught, feet (metres)	14·8 (4·5)
Aircraft	1 A/S light helicopter
Missiles, AA	1 "Tartar" launcher, aft
Guns, AA	2—5 in (127 mm) 38 cal. forward 4—3 in (76 mm) 62 cal.
Torpedo tubes	2 triple for A/S torpedoes
Boilers	4 Foster Wheeler; 711 psi (50 kg/cm²); 842°F (450°C)
Main engines	2 double eduction geared turbines 70 000 shp; 2 shafts
Speed, knots	34 designed, see Engineering
Radius, miles	3 300 at 20 knots
Oil fuel, tons	650
Complement	344 (15 officers, 319 men)

Rated as *Caccia Lanciamissili*. Built under the 1956-57 and 1958-59 programmes, respectively. Both ships have stabilisers.

IMPAVIDO

1970, Italian Navy, Official

ANTI-SUBMARINE WARFARE. The helicopters are of the weapons carrier type (Italian).

ENGINEERING. On first full power trials *Impavido*, at light displacement, reached 34·5 knots (33 knots at normal load). Sustained sea speed: 30 knots.

RADAR
Search: SPS 12 and SPS 39 3 D.
Fire Control: SPG 51 for "Tartar", X Band for guns.

INTREPIDO

1968. Dr. Giorgio Arra

IMPAVIDO

1968. Dr. Giorgio Arra

DESTROYER LEADER (ex-LIGHT CRUISER) DL

Name	No.	Builders	Laid down	Launched	Completed
SAN GIORGIO (ex-*Pompeo Magno*)	D 562	Cantieri N. Riuniti Ancona	23 Sep 1939	28 Aug 1941	24 June 1943

Displacement, tons	4 450 full load
Length, feet (*metres*)	455·2 (*138·8*) wl ; 466·5 (*142·3*) oa
Beam, feet (*metres*)	47·2 (*14·4*)
Draught, feet (*metres*)	21 (*6·4*)
Guns, surface	4—5 in (*127 mm*) 38 ; 3—3 in (*76 mm*) 62
A/S weapons	1 three-barrelled mortar ; 2 triple torpedo tubes
Main engines	2 Tosi Metrovick gas turbines, 15 000 hp ; and 4 Fiat diesels ; 16 600 bhp ; 2 shafts
Speed, knots	20 (diesels only), 28 (diesel and gas)
Radius, miles	4 800 at 20 knots
Oil fuel, tons	500 (diesel oil)
Complement	314 plus 130 cadets

SAN GIORGIO

1970, Italian Navy, Official

Built as *Esploratore Oceanice* (Ocean Scout), but re-rated light cruiser of the Roman Captains (*Capitani Romani*) class. Converted into fleet destroyer in 1951 by Cantieri del Tirreno, Genova, being completed 1 July 1955. Re-rated *Esploratore* (scout) in 1957, and *Cacciatorpediniere Conduttore* (destroyer leader) in 1958. Underwent complete re-construction at the Naval Dockyard, La Spezia, in 1963-65. The modernisation included her adaptation as a Training Ship for 130 cadets of the Accademia Navale. Changes were made in the armament and new machinery was fitted, gas turbines and diesels replacing steam turbines and boilers.

RADAR
Search: SPS 6.
Fire Control: X Band.

DISPOSAL
Original sister ship *San Marco*, D 563 (ex-*Giulio Germanico*) was officially deleted from the list in Jan 1971.

SAN GIORGIO

1971, courtesy R. P. de Kerbrech, Esq.

DESTROYERS

Name	No.	Builders	Ordered	Laid down	Launched	Completed
IMPETUOSO	D 558	Cantieri del Tirreno, Riva Trigoso	Nov 1950	7 May 1952	16 Sep 1956	25 Jan 1958
INDOMITO	D 559	Ansaldo, Leghorn (formerly OTO)	Nov 1950	24 Apr 1952	7 Aug 1955	23 Feb 1958

2 "IMPETUOSO" CLASS

Displacement, tons	2 755 standard ; 3 800 full load
Length, feet (*metres*)	405 (*123·4*) pp ; 418·7 (*127·6*) oa
Beam, feet (*metres*)	43·5 (*13·3*)
Draught, feet (*metres*)	17·5 (*5·3*)
Guns, AA	4—5 in (*127 mm*) 38 cal. 16—40 mm, 56 cal.
A/S weapons	1 three-barrelled mortar ; 4 DCT ; 1 DC rack
Tubes	6 (2 triple) for A/S torpedoes
Main engines	2 double reduction geared turbines ; 2 shafts ; 65 000 shp
Boilers	4 Foster-Wheeler ; 711 psi (50 kg/cm²) wroking pressure ; 842°F (*450°C*) superheat temperature
Speed, knots	34, see *Engineering* notes
Radius, miles	3 400 at 20 knots
Oil fuel, tons	650
Complement	393 (25 officers, 368 men)

INDOMITO

Added 1971, Dr. Aldo Fraccaroli

Italy's first destroyers built since Second World War. Officially rated as *Cacciatorpediniere* or torpedo boat destroyers. Armament if and when converted: 1 single "Tartar" launcher, 2—5 in, 4—3 in guns.

ENGINEERING. On their initial sea trials these ships attained a speed of 35 knots at full load.

RADAR
Search: SPS 6.
Fire Control: GFCS 63.

IMPETUOSO

1970, Italian Navy, Official

FANTE (ex-USS *Walker*, DD 517)
GENIERE (ex-USS *Pritchett*, DD 561)

3 Ex-US "FLETCHER" CLASS

Displacement, tons	2 080 standard; 2 940 full load
Length, feet (*metres*)	376·5 (*114·3*) oa
Beam, feet (*metres*)	39·5 (*12·0*)
Draught, feet (*metres*)	18 (*5·5*)
Guns, surface	2—5 inch, 38 cal, (4 in *Geniere*)
Guns, AA	4—3 inch, 50 cal (6 in *Geniere*) in twin mountings
A/S weapons	1 DC rack, 2 side-launching torpedo racks, 2 fixed Hedgehogs
Main engines	GE geared turbines; 2 shafts; 60 000 shp
Boilers	4 Babcock & Wilcox
Speed, knots	35 designed (32 sea)
Oil fuel, tons	650
Radius, miles	6 000 at 15 knots
Complement	250

TRANSFER
Walker was transferred from the United States Navy and commissioned as *Fante* on 2 July 1969. *Prichett* was transferred at San Diego on 17 Jan 1960 and renamed *Geniere*. She left San Francisco Navy Yard for Italy in the late summer 1970. All the above particulars were officially furnished.

TORPEDO TUBES. The five 21-inch torpedo tubes (originally ten, in two quintuple banks) were removed.

RADAR
Search: SPS 6 and SPS 10.
Fire Control. GFCS 68.

DEACTIVATION. A third destroyer of this class, *Lanciere*, D 560 (ex-USS *Taylor*, DD 468) was transferred from the United States Navy on 2 July 1969 (with *Fante*, ex-*Walker*, see above) and commissioned into the Italian Navy, see official photograph and full particulars in the 1970-71 edition; but in Jan 1971 she was officially deleted from the list as she has been removed from the status of an active ship. It has been stated that this 30-year-old veteran will probably be cannibalised to provide spare parts to keep her two almost equally old sister ships in effective condition.

DISPOSAL
The former United States "Mayo" class destroyer *Artigliere*, D 553 (ex-USS *Woodworth*, DD 460), latterly used as a depot ship for motor torpedo boat flotillas, was officially deleted from the list in Jan 1971 as she is 30 years old and no longer retains her active ship status.

Destroyers—*continued*

No.	Builders	Laid down	Launched	Completed
D 561	Bath Iron Works Corpn	31 Aug 1942	31 Jan 1943	2 Apr 1943
D 555	Seattle-Tacoma SB Corpn	20 July 1942	31 July 1943	15 Jan 1944

GENIERE   *1971, Italian Navy, Official*

FANTE   *1970, Italian Navy, Official*

EXPERIMENTAL DESTROYER

Name	No.	Builders	Laid down	Launched	Completed
AVIERE (ex-USS *Nicholson*, DD 442)	D 554	Boston Navy Yard	1 Nov 1939	31 May 1940	3 June 1941

Displacement, tons	1 700 standard; 2 580 full load
Length, feet (*metres*)	341 (*103·9*) wl; 348·3 (*106·1*) oa
Beam, feet (*metres*)	36·0 (*11·0*)
Draught, feet (*metres*)	18 (*5·5*) max
Guns, surface	4—5 in (see *Gunnery*)
Guns, AA	12—40 mm; 6—20 mm
A/S weapons	4 DC throwers; 2 DC racks
Main engines	GE geared turbines; 2 shafts; 50 000 shp
Boilers	4 Babcock & Wilcox
Speed, knots	30 (26 sustained)
Oil fuel, tons	600
Radius, miles	6 000 at 12 knots
Complement	240

Former US "Gleaves" class destroyer. Transferred from USA and commissioned on 25 May 1951. Officially turned over to Italy on 11 June 1951. The 5—21 in torpedo tubes were removed.

GUNNERY. In 1970 she was fitted with OTO Melara 127/54 (5-inch) gun mounting in "B" position and new OTO Melara 76/62 (3-inch) gun mounting in "X" position, these new mountings having been adopted by the Italian navy.

AVIERE (before experimental rearmament)   *1969, Italian Navy, Official*

RADAR
Search: SPS 6.
Fire Control: GFCS 68.

STATUS. Classification officially changed from Fleet Destroyer to Experimental Ship in 1971.

FRIGATES *(Fregate)*

Name	No.	Builders	Laid down	Launched	Completed
ALPINO (ex-*Circe*)	F 580	Cantiere Navali del Tirreno, Riva Trigoso	27 Feb 1963	10 June 1967	14 Jan 1968
CARABINIERE (ex-*Climene*)	F 581	Cantiere Navali del Tirreno, Riva Trigoso	9 Jan 1965	30 Sep 1967	28 Apr 1968

2 "ALPINO" CLASS

Displacement, tons	2 700 full load
Length, feet (*metres*)	349·0 (*106·4*) pp; 352·0 (*107·3*) wl; 371·7 (*113·3*) oa
Beam, feet (*metres*)	43 (*13·1*)
Draught, feet (*metres*)	12·7 (*3·9*)
Aircraft	2 A/B 204B ASW helicopters
Guns, dual purpose	6—3 in (*76 mm*) 62 cal single
A/S weapons	1 single-barrelled DC mortar
Tubes	6 (2 triple) 12 in (*305 mm*) for A/S torpedoes
Main engines	4 Tosi diesels = 16 800 hp; 2 Tosi Metrovick gas turbines = 15 000 hp; 31 800 hp; 2 shafts
Speed, knots	22 (diesel only), 28 (diesel and gas)
Radius, miles	4 200 at 18 knots
Oil fuel (tons)	275
Complement	254 (21 officers, 233 men)

CARABINIERE   *1968, Dr. Ing. Luigi Accorsi*

Circe and *Climene* were provided for under the 1959-60 programme. The original "Circe" class project was modified in 1962, in respect of both machinery and armament. The originally allocated names *Circe* and *Climene* were changed to *Alpino* and *Carabiniere*, respectively in June 1965. The new design is an improved version of that of the "Centauro" class combined with that of the "Bergamini" class. They have similar basic characteristics but a heavier displacement and increased engine power. Two other ships of the same type, to have been named *Perseo* and *Polluce* were provided for under the 1960-61 programme, but they were suspended owing to fiscal considerations, and new names reported are *Bersagliere* and *Granatiere*.

RADAR
Search: SPS 6.
Fire Control: ELSAG NA 9 systems with X Band radar.

ALPINO   *1970, Italian Navy, Official*

4 "BERGAMINI" CLASS

Name	No.	Builders	Laid down	Launched	Completed
CARLO BERGAMINI	F 593	San Marco, CRDA Trieste	19 May 1957	16 June 1960	23 June 1962
CARLO MARGOTTINI	F 595	Navalmeccanica, Castellammare	26 May 1957	12 June 1960	5 May 1962
LUIGI RIZZO	F 596	Navalmeccanica, Castellammare	26 May 1957	6 Mar 1957	15 Dec 1961
VIRGINIO FASAN	F 594	Navalmeccanica, Castellammare	6 Mar 1960	9 Oct 1960	10 Oct 1962

Displacement, tons	1 650 full load
Length, feet (*metres*)	308·4 (*94*) oa
Beam, feet (*metres*)	37·4 (*11·4*)
Draught, feet (*metres*)	10·2 (*3·1*)
Aircraft	1 A/B-47-J3 helicopter
Guns, AA	3—3 in (*76 mm*) ·62 cal single
A/S weapons	1 single-barrelled depth charge mortar
Tubes	6 (2 triple) 12 in (*305 mm*) for A/S torpedoes
Main engines	4 diesels (Fiat in *Fasan* and *Margottini*, Tosi in others); 2 shafts; 15 000 bhp
Speed, knots	26 max; 24·5 sustainad
Radius, miles	4 000 at 10 knots
Complement	160

Light frigates of novel type with diesel instead of steam propulsion. Originally rated as *Corvette Veloci*.

RADAR
Search: SPS 6.
Fire Control. X Band.

CONVERSION. The anti-submarine capability was augmented in *Carlo Margottini* in 1968, *Virginio Fasan* in 1969 and *Carlo Bergamini* in 1970 by the allocation of an AB-204 A/S helicopter for the operation of which the enlargement of the flight deck was necessary together with the removal of the single gun and mountings astern (see photograph of *Carlo Margottini*). The same conversion is planned for *Luigi Rizzo*.

CONSTRUCTION. *Carlo Bergamini* was originally to have been built by Cantieri Navali di Taranto; but the order was cancelled and she was begun at CRDA di Trieste Yard in May 1959 (built until she was launched in San Marco yard, Trieste, but completed in Monfalcone Yard, both of CRDA).

ANTI-SUBMARINE WEAPONS. The single-barrelled automatic depth charge mortars have a range of 1 000 yards. Rate of fire is 15 DC per minute. The 12-inch torpedoes have a life of six minutes at 30 knots.

PHOTOGRAPHS. A photograph of *Carlo Bergamini* appears in the 1966-67 and 1967-68 editions, and of *Luigi Rizzo* in the 1966-67 to 1969-70 editions.

VIRGINIO FASAN (before conversion)   *1968, Italian Navy, Official*

CARLO MARGOTTINI   *1970, Italian Navy, Official*

ENGINEERING. The diesels are coupled to the shafts by reduction gearing and Vulcan joints.

ROLL DAMPING. Two Denny-Brown stabilisers reduce inclination in heavy seas from 20 to 5 degrees.

4 "CENTAURO" CLASS

Displacement, tons	1 807 standard; 2 196 full load (revised official figures)
Length, feet (metres)	308·4 (94) pp; 338·4 (103·1) oa
Beam, feet (metres)	39·5 (12)
Draught, feet (metres)	12·6 (3·8)
Guns, AA	3—3 in (76 mm) 62 cal single
A/S weapons	1 three-barrelled depth charge mortar
Tubes	6 (2 triple) 12 in (305 mm) for A/S torpedoes
Main engines	2 double reduction geared turbines 2 shafts; 22 000 shp
Speed, knots	26
Boilers	2 Foster Wheeler; 626 psi (44 kg/cm²) working pressure; 842°F (450°C) superheat temperature
Oil fuel, tons	400
Radius, miles	2 500 at 20 knots
Complement	255 (16 officers, 239 men)

The above refers to Castore and Canopo, see Conversion.

Cigno (US hull No. DE 1020) and Castore (DE 1031) were built to Italian plans and specifications under the US off-shore programme. All four ships have automatic anti-submarine and medium anti-aircraft armament, and are fitted with US sonar gear.

RADAR
Search: SPS 6.
Fire Control: X Band.

PENNANT NUMBERS. In 1960 these four ships, which originally had D pennant numbers, were given F numbers. The formerly allocated F number of Canopo was 552.

CONVERSION. Castore underwent medium anti-aircraft conversion in 1966-67, Canopo in 1968-69, and the other two ships are being similarly converted. See former particulars in the 1966-67 and earlier editions. The changes include the mounting of three 3-inch 62 cal single guns, replacing the two 2 barrelled 76 mm 62 cal and the four 40 mm 70 cal AA guns.

GUNNERY. The 3 inch guns originally mounted were in twin gunhouses of a new type with the two barrels in the vertical plane, one superfiring over the other. They were Italian designed and built by OTO, La Spezia.

Frigates—continued

Name	No.	Builders	Laid down	Launched	Completed
CANOPO	F 551 (ex-D 570)	Cantieri Navali di Taranto	15 May 1952	20 Feb 1955	1 Apr 1958
CENTAURO	F 554 (ex-D 571)	Ansaldo, Leghorn	31 May 1952	4 Apr 1954	5 May 1957
CIGNO	F 555 (ex-D 572)	Cantieri Navali di Taranto	10 Feb 1954	20 Mar 1955	7 Mar 1957
CASTORE	F 553 (ex-D 573)	Cantieri Navali di Taranto	14 Mar 1955	8 July 1956	14 July 1957

CIGNO — 1970, Italian Navy, Official

CASTORE — 1967, Italian Navy, Official

Their rate of fire was 60 rounds per minute with 3 200 feet per second muzzle velocity.

PHOTOGRAPHS. A photograph of Centauro appears in the 1967-68 to 1969-70 editions.

CANOPO with new armament — 1971, Major Aldo Fraccaroli

Name	No.	Builders	Laid down	Launched	Completed
ALDEBARAN (ex-USS Thornhill, DE 195)	F 590	Federal SB & DD Co, P. Newark	7 Oct 1943	30 Dec 1943	1 Feb 1944
ALTAIR (ex-USS Gandy, DE 764)	F 591	Tampa SB Co	1 Mar 1943	12 Dec 1943	7 Feb 1944
ANDROMEDA (ex-USS Wesson, DE 184)	F 592	Federal SB & DD Co, P. Newark	29 July 1943	17 Oct 1943	11 Nov 1943

Displacement, tons	1 900 full load
Length, feet (metres)	306 (93·3) oa
Beam, feet (metres)	36·7 (11·2)
Draught, feet (metres)	14 (4·3)
Guns, surface	3—3 in (76 mm) 50 cal.
Guns, AA	6—40 mm; 18—20 mm
A/S weapons	1 Hedgehog; 8 DCT; 2 DC racks
Main engines	GM diesel-electric; 2 shafts; 6 000 hp
Speed, knots	21 designed; 16·5 actual sea
Radius, miles	11 500 at 11 knots
Oil fuel, tons	300
Complement	160

Ex-US destroyer escorts of the "Bostwick" class. Transferred on 10 Jan 1951. In 1956 a pentapod foremast was stepped in place of the former polemast. A photograph of Aldebaran is in the 1967-68 edition.

RADAR
Search: SPS 6
Fire Control: X Band.

ALTAIR — 1968, Aldo Fraccaroli

CORVETTES

Name	No.	Builders	Laid down	Launched	Completed
LICIO VISINTINI	F 546	CRDA Monfalcone	30 Sep 1963	30 May 1965	25 Aug 1966
PIETRO DE CRISTOFARO	F 540	Cantiere Navali de Tirreho, Riva Tregoso	30 Apr 1963	29 May 1965	19 Dec 1965
SALVATORE TODARO	F 550	Cantiere Ansaldo, Leghorn	21 Oct 1962	24 Oct 1964	25 Apr 1966
UMBERTO GROSSO	F 541	Cantiere Ansaldo, Leghorn	21 Oct 1962	12 Dec. 1964	25 Apr. 1966

4 "DE CRISTOFARO" CLASS

Displacement, tons	850 standard ; 940 full load
Length, feet (metres)	246 (75·0) pp ; 263·2 (80·2) oa
Beam, feet (metres)	33·7 (10·3)
Draught, feet (metres)	9 (2·7)
Guns, dual purpose	2—3 in (76 mm), 62 cal, single
A/S weapons	1 single-barrelled DC mortar
Tubes	2 triple for A/S torpedoes
Main engines	2 diesels = 8 400 bhp ;·2 shafts
Speed, knots	23·5 max ; 21·5 sustained sea
Radius, miles	4 000 at 18 knots
Oil fuel, tons	100
Complement	131 (8 officers, 123 men)

The design is an improved version of that of the "Albatros" class.

PHOTOGRAPHS. A photograph of *Pietro de Cristofaro* appears in the 1966-67 and 1967-68 editions and of *Umberto Grosso* in the 1968-69 and 1969-70 editions.

SALVATORE TODARO   1970, Italian Navy. Official

RADAR. Air and surface surveillance radar with antenna mounted at top of foremast. Gunfire control system has director mounted aft, above compass platform, with X band tracker radar.

RESCINDMENT. The projected improved type of "corvette" *circa* 1 200 tons, gas turbines, 20 000 hp, 30-31 knots, was officially deleted from the New Construction Programme in 1968.

Name	No.
AIRONE (ex-*PCE* 1921)	F 545
ALBATROS (ex-*PCE* 1919)	F 543
ALCIONE (ex-*PCE* 1920)	F 544
AQUILA (ex-*Lynx*, ex-*PCE* 1626)	F 542

Builders	Launched	Completed
Navalmeccanica, Castellammare di Stabia	21 Nov 1954	29 Dec 1955
Navalmeccanica, Castellammare di Stabia	18 July 1954	1 June 1955
Navalmeccanica, Castellammare di Stabia	19 Sep 1954	23 Oct 1955
Breda Marghera Yard, Mestre, Venice	31 July 1954	2 Oct 1956

4 "ALBATROS" CLASS

Displacement, tons	800 standard ; 950 full load
Length. feet (metres)	250·3 (76·3) oa
Beam feet (metres)	31·5 (9·6)
Draught, feet (metres)	9·2 (2·8)
Guns, AA	4—40 mm 70 cal. Bofors (see Gunnery)
A/S weapons	2 Hedgehogs Mk II ; 2 DCT ; 1 DC rack
Tubes	2 triple A/S to be fitted
Main engines	2 Fiat diesels ; 2 shafts ; 5 200 bhp
Speed, knots	19
Radius, miles	2 400 at 18 knots
Oil fuel, tons	100
Complement	109

Eight ships of this class were built in Italy under US offshore MDAP orders. 3 for Italy, 4 for Denmark and 1 for the Netherlands, *Aquila*, laid down on 25 July 1953, which was ceded to the Italian Navy on 18 Oct 1961 at Den Helder.

ALCIONE   1970, Italian Navy, Official

GUNNERY. The two 3-inch guns originally mounted, one forward and one aft, were temporarily replaced by two 40 mm guns in 1963. The ultimate armament will include two 3-inch guns of the OTO Melara model.

TUBES. All four ships will receive two triple ASW.
PHOTOGRAPHS. A photograph of *Airone* appears in the 1959-60 to 1961-62 editions, and of *Aquila* in the 1962-63 to 1969-70 editions.

12 "APE" CLASS

BAIONETTA	F 578	GABBIANO	F 571
BOMBARDA	F 549	IBIS	F 561
CHIMERA	F 569	SCIMITARRA	F 564
CORMORANO	F 575	SFINGE	F 579
CRISALIDE	F 547	SIBILLA	F 565
FARFALLA	F 548	URANIA	F 570

Displacement, tons	670 standard ; 771 full load
Length, feet (metres)	192·8 (58·8) wl ; 212·6 (64·8) oa
Beam, feet (metres)	28·5 (8·7)
Draught, feet (metres)	8·9 (2·7)
Guns, AA	4—40 mm 56 cal in 4 ships ; 3—40 mm 56 cal in 6 ships ; 2—40 mm 56 cal in 2 ships ; see Gunnery
A/S weapons	1 Hedgehog Mk 10 (see notes) ;
Torpedo tubes	2—17·7 in (450 mm), see notes
Main engines	2 Fiat diesels ; 2 shafts ; 3 500 bhp
Speed, knots	15
Radius, miles	2 800 at 15 knots
Oil fuel, tons	64
Complement	100,

FARFALLA   1971, Italian Navy, Official

All launched in 1942-48. Originally fitted for minesweeping. Armament is subject to change. All modified with navigating bridge. The vessels attached to Command Training School had torpedo tubes.

GUNNERY. *Chimera. Cormorano, Sibilla* and *Sfinge* 4—40 mm 56 cal AA. *Bombarda* and *Gabbiano* 2—40 mm 56 cal AA and 2—20 mm 70 cal AA. Remainder 3—40 mm 56 cal AA. *Cormorano* and *Sibilla* have no hedgehog.

RADAR
Search: SPS 6 in *Sfinge*.

PHOTOGRAPHS. A photograph of *Scimitarra* appears in the 1957-58 edition, of *Cormorano* in the 1963-64, 1964-65 and 1965-66 editions, of *Cristalide* in the 1966-67 to 1969-70 editions, of *Bombarda* in the 1970-71 edition.

DISPOSALS
Ape, F 567, *Fenice*, F 577, *Folga*, F 576, and *Pomona*, F 573, were officially deleted from the list in 1965, *Driade*, F 568, on 1 Aug 1966, *Danaide*, F 563, in 1968, *Minerva*, F 562, in 1969, *Flora*, F 572, *Gru*, F 566, and *Pellicano*, F 574, in 1970.

SFINGE   1968, Aldo Fraccaroli

MISSILE BOATS

5 NEW CONSTRUCTION

Displacement, tons	300
Missile launchers	Surface-to-surface system
Guns	1—3 inch (76 mm)
Main engines	All gas turbine propulsion

Vessels of the large MGB type projected under the 1969 new construction programme.

1 PROJECTED HYDROFOIL MISSILE-GUN TYPE

To be built at La Spesia. 60 tons, 72 × 24 feet, 2 short range missiles, 1-76 mm AA Gun, Rolls Royce Proteus gas turbines, 4500 hp=50 knots. See photo of model in Addenda.

OCEAN MINESWEEPERS

4 "SALMONE" CLASS (Ex-US MSO TYPE)

SALMONE (ex-*MSO* 507) M 5430 **SQUALO** (ex-*MSO* 518) M 5433
SGOMBRO (ex-*MSO* 517) M 5432 **STORIONE** (ex-*MSO* 506) M 5431

Displacement, tons	665 standard; 750 full load
Dimensions, feet	165 wl; 173 oa × 35 × 10
Guns	1—40 mm; 56 cal AA
Main engines	2 diesels; 2 shafts; 1 600 bhp = 14 knots
Oil fuel, tons	46
Radius, miles	3 000 at 10 knots

Former US "Agile" class. Wooden hulls and non-magnetic diesels of stainless steel alloy. Controllable pitch propellers. *Storione*, launched on 13 Nov 1954, was built by Martinolich SB Company, San Diego, and transferred on 23 Feb, 1956. *Salmone*, launched on 19 Feb 1955 was built by Martinolich SB Co, and transferred at San Diego, on 17 June 1956. *Sgombro* and *Squalo* were delivered in June 1957. A photograph of *Squalo* appears in the 1963-64 to 1967-68 editions.

STORIONE *1969, Italian Navy, Official*

SGOMBRO *Aldo Fraccaroli*

SALMONE *1968, Italian Navy, Official*

PATROL VESSELS

VEDETTA (ex-*Belay Deress*, ex-USS *PC* 1616) F 597

Displacement, tons	325 standard; 450 full load
Dimensions, feet	170 pp; 174 oa × 23 × 10
Guns	2—40 mm; 56 cal Bofors AA; 2—20 mm AA
Main engines	4 diesels; 2 shafts; 3 240 bhp = 19 knots
A/S weapons	1 Hedgehog ; 4 DCT; 2 DC racks
Radius, miles	3 000 at 12 knots
Complement	60

Built at Brest, France, as a United States off-shore order under the Mutual Defense Assistance Program. Laid down on 17 Dec 1953. Launched on 30 Sep 1954. Completed on 23 Aug 1955. Originally intended for Germany, but a change in US plans resulted in the ship never being delivered, and she was finally given to Ethiopia under the Military Aid Programme. Transferred to Ethiopia at Bremerhaven, Germany, by the US Navy in Jan 1957. Officially taken over from the US flag at Massawa, Ethiopia, in mid-1957. Later, the ship was found to be too sophisticated for Ethiopia, and she was returned to the US Navy. She was then sold to Italy, being transferred on 3 Feb 1959, and officially classified as a *nave pattuglia* (patrol vessel). Air-conditioning equipment is installed. Refitted in La Spezia Navy Yard in 1959. Employed as a Fishery Protection Vessel.

VEDETTA *1969, Italian Navy, Official*

TORPEDO BOATS *(Motosiluranti)*

MS 441 (ex-841) **MS 443** (ex-843) **MS 453** (ex-853)

Displacement, tons	64 full load
Dimensions, feet	78 × 20 × 6
Guns	1—40 mm, 56 cal; 2 or 3—20 mm, 70 cal
Torpedoes	2—17·7 in (no tubes)
Main engines	3 petrol motors; 3 shafts; 4 500 bhp = 34 knots
Radius, miles	1 000 at 20 knots

Former US PT boats of Higgins type. Refitted in Italy in 1949-53. New radar installed. MS 441 converted into a fast transport for commandos and frogmen. MS 442 (ex-842), MS 451 (ex-851) and MS 452 (ex-852) transferred to Customs in 1966, and MS 444 (ex-844) was removed from the effective list in 1966.

MS 453 *1969, Italian Navy, Official*

MS 472 (ex-612) **MS 473** (ex-813) **MS 474** (ex-614) **MS 481** (ex-615)

Displacement, tons	72 full load
Dimensions, feet	92 × 15 × 5
Guns	1 or 2—40 mm, 56 cal
Tubes	2—17·7 in
Main Engines	Petrol motors; 3 shafts; 3 450 bhp = 27 knots
Radius, miles	600 at 16 knots

Built in 1942-43 at CRDA Monfalcone yard; converted as MV (motovedette) with no tubes under the Peace Treaty. Reconverted in 1951-53. MS 472 and MS 473 were refitted as convertible boats in 1960 and MS 474 and MS 481 in 1961. A photograph of MS 473 appears in the 1966-67 to 1969-70 editions.

MS 482 (ex-616), MS 483 (ex-617) and MS 484 (ex-618) were removed from the effective list in 1963, and MS 471 (ex-611) and MS 475 (ex-619) in 1965.

The British MTBs *Dark Avenger*, *Dark Biter*, *Dark Hunter* and *Dark Invader* were taken over in 1967 for the Guardia di Finanza.

MS 481 *1971, Dr. Giorgio Arra*

COASTAL MINESWEEPERS
18 "ABETE" CLASS

ABETE	M 5501	**FAGGIO**	M 5507	**OLMO**	M 5512
ACACIA	M 5502	**FRASSINO**	M 5508	**ONTANO**	M 5513
BETULLA	M 5503	**GELSO**	M 5509	**PINO**	M 5514
CASTAGNO	M 5504	**LARICE**	M 5510	**PIOPPO**	M 5515
CEDRO	M 5505	**MANDORLO**	M 5519	**PLATANO**	M 5516
CILIEGIO	M 5506	**NOCE**	M 5511	**QUERCIA**	M 5517

Displacement, tons	378 standard; 405 full load
Dimensions, feet	138 pp; 144 oa × 26·5 × 8·5
Guns	2—20 mm, 70 cal AA
Main Engines	2 diesels; 2 shafts; 1 200 bhp = 13·5 knots
Oil fuel (tons)	25
Radius, miles	2 500 at 10 knots

Wooden hulled *Dragomine Costieri* constructed throughout of materials with the lowest possible magnetic attraction to attain the greatest safety factor when sweeping for magnetic mines. All transferred by the US in 1953-54. Original hull numbers AMS 72-76, 79-82, 88-90, 133-137. *Mandorlo* (ex-*Salice*, ex-USS *MSC 280*), transferred at Seattle on 16 Dec 1960, is of slightly different type and is used as MHC (minehunter). A photograph of *Ciliegio* appears in the 1956-57 to 1961-62 editions, and of *Frassino* in the 1965-66 edition.

MANDORLO   *1970, Italian Navy, Official*

PIOPPO   *1969, Italian Navy, Official*

19 "AGAVE" CLASS

AGAVE	M 5531	**GLICINE**	M 5537	**BAMBÙ**	*M 5521
ALLORO	M 5532	**LOTO**	M 5538	**EBANO**	*M 5522
EDERA	M 5533	**MIRTO**	M 5539	**MANGO**	*M 5523
GAGGIA	M 5534	**TIMO**	M 5540	**MOGANO**	*M 5524
GELSOMINO	M 5535	**TRIFOGLIO**	M 5541	**PALMA**	*M 5525
GIAGGIOLO	M 5536	**VISCHIO**	M 5542	**ROVERE**	*M 5526
				SANDALO	*M 5527

Displacement, tons	375 standard; 405 full load
Dimensions, feet	144 oa × 26·5 × 8·5
Guns	2—20 mm; 70 cal AA
Main Engines	2 diesels; 2 shafts; 1 200 bhp = 13·5 knots
Oil fuel (tons)	25
Radius, miles	2 500 at 10 knots

Non-magnetic minesweepers of composite wooden and alloy construction similar to those transferred from the US but built in Italian yards. *Last 7 were built by CRDA, Monfalcone, and launched in 1956.
A photogrpah of *Alloro* appears in the 1959-60 to 1961-62 editions, of *Sandalo* in the 1962-63 to 1965-66 editions, of *Gaggia* and *Palma* in the 1966-67 to 1968-69 editions.

AGAVE   *1969, Italian Navy, Official*

FAST GUN BOATS *(Motocannoniere)*
4 "FRECCIA" CLASS CONVERTIBLE TYPE

DARDO (ex-*MC* 592, ex-493)	P 495	**SAETTA** (ex-*MC* 591)	P 494
FRECCIA (ex-*MC* 590)	P 493	**STRALE** (ex-*MC* 593, ex-494)	P 496

Displacement, tons	188 standard; 215 full load
Dimensions, feet	150 × 23·8 × 5·5
Guns	*As Gunboat:* 3—40 mm, 70 cal or 2—40 mm, 70 cal
	As Fast Minelayer: 1—40 mm AA with 8 mines
	As Torpedo Boat: 1—40 mm, 70 cal
Tubes	*As Torpedo Boat:* 2—21 in
Main engines	2 diesels; 7 600 bhp; 1 Bristol Siddeley Proteus gas turbine. 4 250 shp; Total hp 11 850 = 40 knots

Freccia was laid down by Cantiere del Tirreno, Riva Trigosa on 30 Apr 1963, launched on 9 Jan 1965 and commissioned on 6 July 1965. *Saetta* was laid down by CRDA, Monfalcone on 11 June 1963, launched on 11 Apr 1965. and completed in 1966. *Dardo* was laid down by Taranto Navy Yard on 10 May 1964. Special convertible version designed to carry mines or depth charges. Can be converted in 24 hours to gunboat, torpedo boat, fast minelayer, or missile boat. Fitted with S band navigation and tactical radar employing a slotted waveguide antenna. The gunfire control system has a driector with X band tracker radar. *Saetta* has been experimentally armed with 5 short range missiles (range 10 000 metres). See photograph.

SAETTA experimentally armed with 5 short range missiles   *1970, Official*

FRECCIA   *1969, Dr. Aldo Fraccaroli*

2 "LAMPO" CLASS CONVERTIBLE TYPE

BALENO (ex-*MC* 492) P 492		**LAMPO** (ex-*MC* 491) P 491	

Displacement, tons	170 standard; 206 full load
Dimensions, feet	131·5 × 21 × 5
Guns	*As Gunboat:* 3—40 mm, 70 cal or 2—40 mm, 70 cal
	As Torpedo Boat: 1—40 mm, 70 cal
Tubes	*As Torpedo Boat:* 2—21 in
Main engines	2 Fiat diesels, 1 Metrovick gas turbine; 3 shafts; total 11 700 hp = 39 knots.

Convertible gunboats, improved versions of the *Folgore* prototype. Both built by Arsenale MM Taranto. *Lampo* was laid down on 4 Jan 1958, launched on 22 Nov 1960 and commissioned in July 1963. A photograph of her as torpedo boat appears in the 1968-69 edition. *Baleno* was laid-down on the same slip on 22 Nov 1960, launched on 10 May 1964 and commissioned on 16 July 1965. She has been converted to an improved design.

LAMPO   *1970, Italian Navy, Official*

BALENO   *1969, Italian Navy, Official*

Fast Gunboats—*continued*

FOLGORE (ex-*MC 490*) P 490

Displacement, tons	160 standard; 190 full load
Dimensions, feet	129·5 × 19·7 × 5
Guns	2—40 mm AA
Tubes	2—21 in
Main Engines	4 diesels; 4 shafts; 10 000 bhp = 38 knots
	(accelerating from 20 knots to full speed very rapidly)

Authorised in Nov 1950, launched on 21 Jan 1954 from CRDA Monfalcone Yard, and commissioned on 21 July 1955. Two rudders. A port quarter oblique aerial view of *Folgore* appears in the 1963-64 to 1966-67 editions, and a port broadside view in the 1967-68 and 1968-69 editions.

The old motor gunboat MC 485 (ex-*MS 621*, ex-*Toros*), former German S-boat, was officially deleted from the list in 1965, and the submarine chaser/corvette/gunboat *Fulmine* (ex-*Sentinella*, ex-*VAS 470*) P 499 (ex-*F 598*) in 1970.

FOLGORE   *1969, Dr. Aldo Fraccaroli*

INSHORE MINESWEEPERS

(Dragamine Litoranei)

20 "ARAGOSTA" CLASS

ARAGOSTA	M 5450	**GAMBERO**	M 5457	**POLIPO**	M 5463
ARSELLA	M 5451	**GRANCHIO**	M 5458	**PORPORA**	M 5464
ASTICE	M 5452	**MITILO**	M 5459	**RICCIO**	M 5465
ATTINIA	M 5453	**OSTRICA**	M 5460	**SCAMPO**	M 5466
CALAMARO	M 5454	**PAGURO**	M 5461	**SEPPIA**	M 5467
CONCHIGLIA	M 5455	**PINNA**	M 5462	**TELLINA**	M 5468
DROMIA	M 5456			**TOTANO**	M 5469

Displacement, tons	119 standard; 130 full load
Dimensions, feet	106 × 21 × 6
Main Engines	2 diesels; 1 000 bhp = 14 knots
Oil fuel (tons)	15
Radius, miles	2 000 at 9 knots
Complement	14

Similar to the British "Ham" class. All constructed in Italian yards to the order of NATO in 1955-57. All names of small sea creatures. Designed armament of one 20 mm gun not mounted. *Polipo* was originally named *Polpo*. A photograph of *Ricco* appears in the 1958-59 to 1961-62 editions, of *Aragosta* in the 1962-63 and 1963-64 editions.

POLIPO   *1971, Italian Navy, Official*

TELLINA   *1969, Dr. Aldo Fraccaroli*

DISPOSALS OF BYMS TYPE

Of the 17 coastal minesweepers of the BYMS type, *Begonia* and *Dalia* were transferred to the Custom House Guard Sea Service in Apr 1966, and the other nine vessels of the "Azalea" class (one funnel), *Azalea, Fiordaliso, Gardinia, Gladiolo, Magnolia, Orchidea, Primula, Tulipano, Verbena*, were removed from the effective list at the end of 1966 with the six units of the "Anemone" class (two funnels), *Anemone, Biancospino, Geranio, Mughetto, Narciso* and *Oleandro*, see full particulars in the 1966-67 and earlier editions.

SURVEY SHIPS (Navi Idrografiche)

STAFFETTA (ex-*Elbano*, ex-USS *Prudent*, PG 96, ex-HMS *Privet*) A 5307

Displacement, tons	1 020 standard; 1 280 full load
Dimensions, feet	205 oa × 33 × 14·5
Guns	2—20 mm AA
Main Engines	Triple expansion; 2 750 ihp = 15 knots
Boiler	2 cylindrical
Oil fuel (tons)	250
Radius, miles	5 500 at 8 knots

Former British "Flower" class corvette (later re-rated frigate). Built by Morton Engine & DD Co, Montreal, Canada, engined by Port Arthur SB Co. Laid down on 14 Aug 1942. Launched on 4 Dec 1942. Completed on 16 Aug 1943. Converted for hydrographic duties and commissioned in 1953.

The oceanographic vessel *Bannock* (ex-USS *Bannock*, ATF 81), former US fleet ocean tug was converted and is manned by the National Research Council and is not on the Navy List; she wears the mercantile flag. (See data in the 1964-65 edition.)

STAFFETTA   *1971, A. & J. Pavia*

NETLAYERS (Posareti)

2 "ALICUDI" CLASS

ALICUDI A 5304 (ex-USS AN 99)   **FILICUDI** A 5305 (ex-USS AN 100)

Displacement, tons	680 standard; 834 full load
Dimensions, feet	151·8 pp; 165·3 oa × 33·5 × 10·5
Guns	1—40 mm, 70 cal AA; 4—20 mm, 70 cal AA
Main Engines	Diesel-electric; 1 200 hp = 12 knots

Built to the order of NATO. Laid down on 22 Apr 1954 and 19 July 1954, respectively by Ansaldo, Leghorn, launched on 11 July 1954 and 26 Sep 1954.

ALICUDI   *Italian Navy, Official*

LANDING SHIP

QUARTO

Displacement, tons	764 standard; 980 full load
Dimensions, feet	226·4 × 31·3 × 6
Guns	4—40 mm AA (2 twin)
Main engines	3 diesels; 2 300 bhp = 13 knots
Radius, miles	1 300 at 13 knots

Quarto was laid down on 19 Mar 1966 at Taranto Naval Shipyard and launched on 18 Mar 1967. The design is intermediate between that of LSM and LCT. Two more ships of this class, *Lombardo* and *Piemonte*, were officially deleted from the New Construction Programme in 1968, and it was officially stated in Jan 1971 that the construction of the other two, *Caprera* and *Marsala* had also been cancelled.

QUARTO   *1971, Dr. Aldo Fraccaroli*

TRANSPORTS *(Navi Trasporto)*

ANDREA BAFILE (ex-USS *St. George*, AV 16)   A 5314

Displacement, tons	8 510 standard ; 14 000 full load
Dimensions, feet	492 oa × 69·5 × 26 max
Main engines	Allis-Chalmers geared turbines ; 1 shaft ; 8 500 shp = 18·7 knots
Boilers	2 Foster-Wheeler

Former USN seaplane carrier, launched on 14 Feb 1944. Purchased and commissioned in the Italian Navy on 17 May 1969 and modified. Troop transport and Command Ship. Serves as a depot ship for "Special Forces" (frogmen etc).

ANDREA BAFILE   *1970, Italian Navy, Official*

STROMBOLI A 5330   **VESUVIO** A 5329

Displacement, tons	2 848 light ; 4 713 standard ; 6 160 full load
Dimensions, feet	334·1 oa × 46 × 21·7
Guns	*Stromboli:* 1—3·9 in ; 4—40 mm, 56 cal
	Vesuvio: 2—40 mm AA ; forward only
Main engines	1 double reduction geared turbine ; 3 000 shp = 15 knots
Boilers	3 water tube
Radius, miles	3 340 at 11 knots

Both built by Odero-Terni-Orlando yard, La Spezia. *Stromboli* was completed in 1948 and *Vesuvio* in 1954. *Stromboli* was latterly Flagship of the Logistic Support Group. The 3·9 inch gun aft was removed from *Vesuvio*, converted into a tender for helicopters served by a hangar abaft the funnel and a flight deck laid on right aft. Taken out of commission and removed from the list of active ships in 1971.

VESUVIO   *1970, Italian Navy, Official*

STROMBOLI   *1970, Italian Navy, Official*

Transports—*continued*

1 AKA TYPE

ETNA (ex-USS *Whitley*, AKA 91) A 5328

Displacement, tons	7 430 light ; 14 200 full load
Measurement, tons	5 145 gross ; 7 700 deadweight
Dimensions, feet	435 wl ; 459·2 oa × 63 × 26·3 max
Main Engines	GE geared turbines ; 1 shaft ; 6 000 shp = 16·5 knots
Boilers	2 Combustion Engineering

Former US attack cargo ship of the "Andromeda" class. Built by Moore DD Co, Oakland, California, launched on 22 June 1944. Completed on 21 Sep 1944. C2—S—B 1 type. Transferred to Italy in Feb 1962. Rated as *Nave trasporto mezzi da sbarco.*

ETNA   *1970, Italian Navy, Official*

1 AVB TYPE

ANTEO (ex-USS *Alameda County*, AVB 1, ex-*LST* 32) A 5306

Displacement, tons	1 625 light ; 2 366 beaching ; 4 080 full load
Dimensions, feet	316 wl ; 328 oa × 50 × 14 max
Guns	7—40 mm AA ; 2—20 mm AA
Main Engines	GM diesels ; 2 shafts ; 1 700 bhp = 11·6 knots max

Former US tank landing ship. Built by Dravo Corp, Neville Island, Pa. Laid down on 17 Feb 1943. Launched on 23 May 1943. Completed on 12 July 1943. Re-classified from LST 32 to AVB 1 (Advance Aviation Base ship) on 28 Sep 1957. Transferred to the Italian Navy in Nov 1962 as a transport.

ANTEO   *1970, Italian Navy, Official*

SUPPORT SHIPS *(Nave appogio)*

PIETRO CAVEZZALE (ex-USS *Oyster Bay*, AVP 28, ex-*AGP* 6) A 5301

Displacement, tons	1 766 standard ; 2 800 full load
Dimensions, feet	300 wl ; 311·8 oa × 41 × 13·5 max
Guns	2—40 mm, 56 cal AA
Main Engines	2 sets diesels ; 2 shafts ; 6 080 bhp = 16 knots
Oil fuel (tons)	400
Radius, miles	10 000 at 11 knots
Complement	200

Former United States seaplane tender (previously motor torpedo boat tender) of the "Barnegat" class, built at Lake Washington Shipyard and launched on 7 Sep 1942. Transferred to the Italian Navy on 23 Oct 1957 and renamed.

PIETRO CAVEZZALE   *1968, Italian Navy, Official*

TRAINING SHIPS (Navi Scuola)

AMERIGO VESPUCCI A 5312

Displacement, tons	3 543 standard; 4 146 full load
Dimensions, feet	229·5 pp; 270 oa hull; 330 oa bowsprit × 51 × 22
Guns	4—3 in, 50 cal; 1—20 mm
Main Engines	Two Fiat diesels with electric drive to 2 Marelli motors. 1 shaft; 2 000 hp = 10 knots
Sail area	22 604 square feet
Endurance	5 450 miles at 6·5 knots
Complement, tons	400 + 150 midshipmen

Built at Castellammare. Launched on 22 March 1930 and completed in 1931. Hull, masts and yards are of steel. Loud speakers and echo-sounding gear are included in her equipment. Extensively refitted at La Spezia Naval Dockyard in 1964.

AMERIGO VESPUCCI   1968, Italian Navy, Official

PALINURO (ex-Commandant Louis Richard) A 5311.

Displacement, tons	1 042 standard; 1 450 full load
Measurement, tons	858 gross
Dimensions, feet	204 pp; 226·3 oa × 32 × 18·7
Main engines	1 diesel; 1 shaft; 450 bhp = 7·5 knots
Endurance, miles	5 390 at 7·5 knots
Sail area, square feet	1 152

Barquentine, Ex-French, launched in 1920. Purchased in 1950. Rebuilt and commissioned in Italian Navy on 16 July 1955.

PALINURO   1968, Italian Navy, Official

CORSARO II

Measurement, tons	41
Dimensions, feet	68·6 × 15·4 × 9·5
Auxiliary engines	1 Mercedes-Benz diesel, 96 bhp
Sail area	2117 square feet

Special yacht for sail training and oceanic navigation. RORC class. Built by Costaguta Yard, Voltri, in 1959-60.

STELLA POLARE

Measurement, tons	47
Dimensions, feet	6 9 × 15·4 × 9·8
Sail area, square feet	2 200
Complement	14

Yawl. Built by Santgerm. Chiavari in 1964-65 as a sail training vessel for the Italian Navy.

The training ship Gazzella (ex-B 3, ex-M 801), former German fleet minesweeper, subsequently used as an auxiliary ship, then a patrol ship, later a coastal escort (corvette) and then navi idrografiche, was removed from the effective list in 1966 with sister ship Daino (ex-B 2, ex-M 802), former minesweeper, etc. and survey ship.

MOTOR TRANSPORTS (Mototrasporti)

Ex-GERMAN MFP TYPE

MTC 1001	MTC 1004	MTC 1006	MTC 1008	MTC 1010
MTC 1003	MTC 1005	MTC 1007	MTC 1009	MTC 1102

Displacement, tons	240 standard
Dimensions, feet	164 × 21·3 × 5·7
Guns	2 or 3—20 or 37 mm
Main Engines	2 or 3 diesels; 500 bhp = 10 knots

Moto-Trasporti Costieri, MTC 1001 to 1010 are Italian MZ (Motozattere). MTC 1102 and 1103 are ex-German built in Italy. MTC 1002 was removed from the effective list in 1964, MTC 1101 and MTC 1104 in 1970, and MTC 1103 in 1971. A photogrpah of MTC 1003 appears in the 1965-66 to 1970-71 editions.

MTC 1010   1971, Dr. Giorgio Arra

23 Ex-US LCM TYPE

MTM 9901	MTM 9905	MTM 9911	MTM 9916	MTM 9921
MTM 9902	MTM 9906	MTM 9912	MTM 9917	MTM 9922
MTM 9903	MTM 9908	MTM 9913	MTM 9918	MTM 9923
MTM 9904	MTM 9909	MTM 9914	MTM 9919	MTM 9924
	MTM 9915	MTM 9920		MTM 9925

Displacement, tons	20 standard
Dimensions, feet	49·5 × 14·8 × 4·2
Guns	2—20 mm AA
Main Engines	Diesels; speed 10 knots

Rated as Moto-Trasporti Medi. Former US landing craft of the LCM type. MTM 9907 was removed from the effective list in 1967, and MTM 9910 in 1971.

39 Ex-US LCVP TYPE

MTP 9701	MTP 9709	MTP 9717	MTP 9726	MTP 9734
MTP 9702	MYP 9710	MTP 9718	MTP 9727	MTP 9735
MTP 9703	MTP 9711	MTP 9719	MTP 9728	MTP 9736
MTP 9704	MTP 9712	MTP 9720	MTP 9729	MTP 9737
MTP 9705	MTP 9713	MTP 9721	MTE 9730	MTP 9738
MTP 9706	MTP 9714	MTP 9722	MTP 9731	MTP 9739
MTP 9707	MTP 9715	MTP 9723	MTP 9732	MTP 9740
MTP 9708		MTP 9724	MTP 9733	MTP 9741

Displacement, tons	8 to 10 standard
Dimensions, feet	36·5 × 10·8 × 3
Guns	2 MG
Main engines	Diesels; Speed: 10 knots

Rated as Moto-Trasporti Piccoli. MTP 9701 to 9724 are former US landing craft of the LCVP type. MTP 9726 of 10 tons displacement and similar characteristics is of Italian construction. MTP 9725 was officially removed from the effective list in 1963, and MTP 9716 in 1971.

LIGHTHOUSE TENDERS

BUFFOLUTO A 5327

Displacement, tons	930 standard
Dimensions, feet	172·5 pp; 184·2 oa × 29·5 × 11
Main Engines	2 triple expansion; 1 400 ihp = 10 knots
Boilers	2 Thornycroft

Built by S. Giorgio, La Spezia. Launched in 1922. Sister ship Panigaglia blew up in July 1947.

RAMPINO A 5309

Displacement, tons	350 standard; 645 full load
Dimensions, feet	158·8 × 24·2 × 13
Main Engines	Triple expansion = 7 knots

Buoy tender. Of netlayer type. Built at Osaka. Classed as Nave Ausiliarie.

3 Ex-BRITISH LCT(3) TYPE

MTF 1301	MTF 1302	MTF 1303

Displacement, tons	296 light; 700 full load
Dimensions, feet	192 × 31 × 7
Guns	1—40 mm, 56 cal AA; 2—20 mm, 70 cal AA
Main Engines	Diesel; 1 shaft; speed = 8 knots

Converted landing craft of the British LCT (3) type. Lighthouse motor transports (Moto-Trasporti Fari). NATO Pennant Nos.: A 5361, A 5362 and A 5363.

MFT 1301   1968, Italian Navy, Official

SUPPORT GUN BOATS *(Cannoniere d'appoggio)*
6 "ALANO" CLASS
(Ex-US LANDING SHIPS, SUPPORT/LARGE)

ALANO (ex-*LSSL* 34) **MASTINO** (ex-*LSSL* 62) **SEGUGIO** (ex-*LSSL* 64)
BRACCO (ex-*LSSL* 38) **MOLOSSO** (ex-*LSSL* 63) **SPINONE** (ex-*LSSL* 118)

Displacement, tons	246 standard; 430 full load
Dimensions, feet	153 wl; 158·5 oa × 23·7 × 5·7
Guns	5—40 mm; 56 cal; 4—20 mm, 70 cal; 4—12·7 mm
Main engines	8 Gray Marine diesels; 2 shafts; 1 800 bhp = 12 knots
Oil fuel, tons	87
Radius, miles	8 000 at 10 knots

Transferred from the USN on 25 July 1951, under the Mutual Defense Assistance Program. NATO pennant numbers L 9851 to L 9856, respectively. A photograph of *Alano* appears in the 1955-56 to 1957-58 editions, of *Segugio* in the 1967-68 to 1968-69 editions, of *Mastino* in the 1963-64 to 1967-68 editions, and of *Spinone* in the 1968-69 and 1969-70 editions.

MOLOSSO　　　　　　　　　1970, Italian Navy, Official

SALVAGE SHIP *(Nave Salvataggio)*

PROTEO (ex-*Perseo*, ex-*Proteo*) A 5310

Displacement, tons	1 865 standard; 2 147 full load
Dimensions, feet	220·5 pp; 248 oa × 38 × 21 max
Main Engines	2 diesels; 4 800 bhp = 16 knots (see Notes)
Radius, miles	7 500 at 13 knots

Laid down at Cantieri Navali Riuniti, Ancona, in 1943. Suspended in 1944. Seized by Germans and transferred to Trieste. Construction recommenced at Cantieri Navali Riuniti, Ancona, in 1949. Diesels at 250 rpm drive a single propeller through hydraulic couplings and reduction gearing. Formerly mounted one 3·9 inch AA gun and two 20 mm, 70 cal AA guns.

PROTEO　　　　　　　　　1969, Italian Navy, Official

REPAIR CRAFT *(Motoofficine Costiere)*

MOC 1201　**MOC 1203**　**MOC 1205**　**MOC 1208**
MOC 1202　**MOC 1204**　**MOC 1207**

Displacement, tons	350 standard; 640 full load
Dimensions, feet	192 × 31 × 7
Guns	2—40 mm; 2—20 mm (2 ships have 2—40 mm and 1 ship has 3—20 mm)
Main Engines	Diesel = 8 knots

Former British LCT (3) type landing craft converted to repair craft. MOC 1207 and 1208 are ammunition transports. NATO Nos.: A 5331 to 5338, respectively. A photograph of MOC 1201 appears in the 1955-56 to 1966-67 editions, of MOC 1208 in the 1967-68 and 1968-69 editions, and of MOC 1202 in the 1969-70 and 1970-71 editions.

MOC 1205　　　　　　　　　1971, Dr. Giorgio Arra

FAST REPLENISHMENT SHIP (AOR)
1 NEW CONSTRUCTION NUCLEAR POWERED TYPE
ENRICO FERMI

Displacement, tons	18 000
Dimensions, feet	574·2 × 72·2 × 26·3
Aircraft	8 helicopters
Main engines	Nuclear reactor; steam turbines = 21 knots
Range, cruising	300 000 miles
Complement	350 officers and ratings

Italy's first nuclear powered ship. Scheduled to come into service in 1970-71. A Fiat-Ansaldo project, with Fiat building the reactor and some of the main components, under the aegis of the Italian Navy which will be responsible for her operation. A hangar for all types of helicopters will be built aft, and a large workshop constructed on the forecastle for the maintenance of submarines. Will carry 4 850 tons of black oil, 1 550 tons of diesel oil, 340 tons of petrol and 150 tons of aviation spirit.

OILERS *(Navi Cisterna per Nafta)*
1 Ex-US "T2" TYPE

STEROPE (ex-*Enrico Insom*) A 5368

Displacement, tons	5 350 light; 21 800 full load
Dimensions, feet	523·5 oa × 68 × 30·8
Main Engines	Turbo-electric; 6 000 shp = 15 knots
Boilers	2 Babcock & Wilcox

Former United States built oiler of the T 2 type acquired by the Italian Navy in 1959 and refitted at La Spezia Navy Yard in April 1959.

STEROPE　　　　　　　　　1970, Aldo Fraccaroli

1 QUARNARO TYPE

DALMAZIA A 5367

Displacement, tons	1 466 light; 3 216 standard; 5 000 full load
Dimensions, feet	260 × 32·5 × 15·2
Guns	1—4·7 in; 2—20 mm AA
Main Engines	Triple expansion; 2 shafts; 1 450 ihp = 10 knots
Boilers	2 Thornycroft oil-fired
Cargo, tons	1 800

Built by Quarnaro Yard, Fiume, launched in 1922. Formerly classified as a water carrier. Reclassified as a fleet oiler in 1958. A photograph of *Dalmazia* appears in the 1967-68 and earlier editions.

DALMAZIA　　　　　　　　　1970, Italian Navy, Official

WATER CARRIERS *(Navi Cisterna per Acqua)*

BASENTO A 5256　　**BRADANO** A 5357　　**BRENTA** A 5358

Displacement, tons	1 914
Dimensions, feet	216·9 × 33 × 12·8 ·0
Main engines	2 Fiat A 236 diesels; 2 shafts; 1 730 hp = 12·5 knots
Water capacity, tons	1 200
Radius	1650 miles at 12·5 knots

Built by Inma di La Spezia. (The tanker ex-US YO 247 was officially deleted from the list in Jan 1971).

Water Carriers—*continued*

PO A 5365   **VOLTURNO** A 5366

Displacement, tons	1 556 light; 3 541 standard; 6 000 full load
Dimensions, feet	270·7 × 38·8 × 16·8
Guns	1—4 in, 35 cal; 2—40 mm; 2—20 mm (*Po*)
	1—4·7 in, 45 cal; 2—40 mm; 2—20 mm AA (*Volturno*)
Main Engines	Triple expansion; 1 700 ihp = 11·5 knots
Boilers	2 oil-fired watertube
Oil fuel (tons)	226
Cargo capacity, tons	2 200

Po was launched by Cant Nav Riuniti, Ancona, on 21 Dec 1936. *Volturno* was built by Cantieri del Tirreno, Riva, Trigoso, in 1936-37, and rebuilding was completed in 1951. *Volturno* has radar mast. A photograph of *Volturno* appears in the 1967-68 and earlier editions.

PO   *1970, Italian Navy, Official*

ADIGE (ex-*YW* 92)   **ISONZO** (ex-*YW* 77)   **TICINO** (ex-*YW* 79)
FLEGETONTE (ex-*YW* 95)   **TANARO** (ex-*YW* 99)

Displacement, tons	436 standard; 1 470 full load
Guns	3—20 mm, 70 cal AA
Main engines	2 deisels; 315 hp = 8 knots
Water capacity, tons	850

Ex-US Army YW type. NATO Pennant Nos.: A 5369, A 5371, A 5372, A 5376 and A 5377, respectively.

SESIA A 5375

Displacement, tons	1 050
Dimensions, feet	213·2 × 33 × 11·2
Guns	3—20 mm, 70 cal AA
Main Engines	Fiat diesels; 2 shafts; 600 bhp = 8 knots

Built by Adriatico. Launched in 1933. Fitted for minelaying.

METAURO A 5373

Displacement, tons	592
Dimensions, feet	133·2 × 26·5 × 10·5
Guns	1—20 mm, 70 cal AA
Main Engines	Tosi diesels; 400 bhp = 8 knots

Built by C. N. Quarnaro-Fiume. Launched in 1933

METAURO   *1968, Aldo Fraccaroli*

ARNO A 5370

Displacement, tons	634
Dimensions, feet	138·8 × 26 × 10
Guns,	1—20 mm, 70 cal AA
Main Engines	1 Fiat diesel; 350 bhp = 8 knots

Built by Odero-Terni-Orlando, La Spezia. Launched in 1929.

MINCIO A 5374

Displacement, tons	645
Dimensions, feet	138·5 × 26·2 × 10
Guns	1—20 mm, 70 cal AA
Main Engines	Tosi diesels; 350 bhp = 8 knots

Built in Venice. Launched in 1929.

Water Carriers—*continued*

TIMAVO

Displacement, tons	265
Main Engines	1 Tosi diesel; 200 bhp = 8 knots

Built by COMI, Venezia, 1926. Sister ship *Vipacco* was removed from the effective list in 1961.

FRIGIDO (ex-*Fukuiu Maru*)

Displacement, tons	398
Dimensions, feet	116·5 × 21·5 × 10
Guns	2 MG
Main Engines	Triple expansion; 221 ihp = 7 knots
Boilers	1 cylindrical

Built by Osaka. Launched in 1912. Purchased in 1916.

OFANTO

Displacement, tons	250
Dimensions, feet	105·5 × 19·7 × 7·5
Main Engines	1 Triple expansion; 165 ihp = 6 knots
Boilers	1

Built by SEB, Riva Trigoso, 1913-14.

LENO   **SIMETO**   **SPRUGOLA**   **STURA**

Small water carriers of 270, 167, 212 and 126 displacement, respectively. *Tronto* was officially deleted from the list in 1970.

TUGS   *(Rimorchiatori)*

PORTO D'ISCHIA   **RIVA TRIGOSO**

Displacement, tons	296 full load
Dimensions, feet	83·7 × 23·3 × 10·8
Main engines	Diesel; 1 shaft; 850 bhp = 12·1 knots

Both launched in Sep 1969. Controllable pitch propeller.

CIRCEO   **TAVOLARA**

Both completed in 1955. Minor tugs for local and general purposes.

AUSONIA   **PANARIA**

Displacement, tons   240

Both launched in 1948. Coastal tugs for general utility duties.

CICLOPE A 5319   **TITANO** A 5320

Displacement, tons	1 200
Dimensions, feet	157·5 × 32·5 × 13
Main Engines	Triple expansion; 1 shaft; 1 000 ihp = 8 knots

Both were launched in 1948. Sister ship *Nereo* was discarded in 1957.

MISENO   **MONTE CRISTO**

Displacement, tons   285

Former United States Navy harbour tugs. The tug *Atlante* A 5317 was officially deleted from the list in 1970.

GAGLIARDO A 5322   **ROBUSTO** A 5323

Displacement, tons	389 standard; 506 full load
Main Engines	1 000 ihp = 8 knots

Both launched in 1939.

PORTO EMPEDOCLE

Displacement, tons	330 standard
Main Engines	500 ihp = 11 knots

Launched in 1934. Employed as a harbour tug. Armament of 1—3 in gun removed.

PORTO FOSSONE   **PORTO RECANATI**   **PORTO VECCHIO**
PORTO PISANO   **PORTO TORRES**   **SALVORE**
                                           TINO

Displacement, tons	226 to 270
Dimensions, feet	88·8 × 22 × 10
Main Engines	600 ihp = 9 knots

All launched in 1936-37, except *Tino*, 1931. Principally employed as harbour tugs. Armament of 1—3 inch gun removed. *Porto Rosso* was deleted from the list in 1965.

ATLETA (ex-*LT* 152)   **FORTE** (ex-*LT* 159)
COLOSSO (ex-*LT* 214)   **TENACE** (ex-*LT* 154)

Displacement, tons	525 standard; 835 full load
Dimensions, feet	142·8 × 32·8 × 11
Main Engines	2 diesel-electric; 690 hp = 11 knots

Ex-US Army. Pennant Nos.: A 5318, A 5320, A 5321, A 5324, respectively.

LIPARI   **VENTIMIGLIA**

Displacement, tons	254 (*Lipari*); 230 (*Ventimiglia*)
Dimensions, feet	108·2 × 23 × 7·2 (*Lipari*)
Main Engines	(*Lipari*) 500 hp = 9 knots; (*Ventimiglia*) 550 = 10 knots

Lipari was built in 1917. There are also 55 harbour tugs, ferry tugs, lagoon tugs, numbered tugs and minor tugs.

IVORY COAST

Mercantile Marine

Lloyd's Register of Shipping: 27 vessels of 26 064 tons gross

PATROL BOATS

1 FRANCO-BELGE TYPE

LE VIGILANT

Displacement, tons	235 normal
Dimensions, feet	149·3 pp; 155·8 oa × 23·6 × 8·2
Dimensions, (metres)	47·5 oa × 7 × 2·5
Guns	2—40 mm AA
Missiles	8 SS12
Main engines	2 diesels; 1 shaft; 2 400 bhp
Speed, knots	18·5
Range, miles	2 000 at 15 knots
Complement	25 (3 officers and 22 men)

Built by Franco-Belge. Laid down in Feb 1967. Launched on 23 May 1967. Scheduled for completion in 1968. Sister ship to *Malaika* of Madagascan Navy.

1 Ex-FRENCH VC TYPE

PERSEVERANCE (ex-*VC 9*, *P 759*)

Displacement, tons	75 standard; 82 full load
Dimensions, feet	104·5 × 17 × 6
Dimensions, (metres)	21·6 × 4·65 × 1·8
Guns	2—20 mm AA
Main Engines	2 Mercedes-Benz diesels; 2 shafts; 2 700 bhp = 28 knots
Oil fuel (tons)	10
Radius, miles	1 100 at 16·5 knots; 800 at 21 knots
Complement	15

Former French seaward defence motor launch. Built by Constructions Mecaniques de Normandie. Cherbourg. Completed in 1958. Transferred from France to Ivory Coast 26 April 1963.

PERSEVERANCE   *1964, Ivory Coast Armed Forces, Official*

1 Ex-US SC TYPE

PATIENCE (ex-*P 699*, ex-*CH 71*, ex-US *SC 1337*)

Displacement, tons	110 standard; 138 full load
Dimensions, feet	107·5 wl; 110·8 oa × 17 × 6·5
Dimensions (metres)	33·7 × 5·7 × 2
Guns	1—40 mm AA; 3—20 mm AA
Main Engines	2 GM diesels; 2 shafts; 1 000 bhp = 15 knots
Oil fuel (tons)	15
Radius, miles	2 000 at 10 knots; 1 150 at 15 knots
Complement	25

Former United States wooden submarine chaser. Transferred from the USA to France on 29 Dec 1943, and from France to Ivory Coast in 1961.

PATIENCE   *1964, Ivory Coast Armed Forces, Official*

LANDING CRAFT

There are two landing craft of the LCVP type, 7 tons, 2 machine guns, 200 hp, 9 knots.

JAMAICA

Defence Force Coast Guard

Jamaica, which became independent within the Commonwealth, on 6 Aug 1962, formed the Coast Guard as the Maritime Arm of the Defence Force.
The Jamaican Government signed an agreement with the USA for the transfer of a small number of coastguard vessels for the new navy.
Great Britain lent several RN petty officers for technical assistance. The British Mission included a technical team to survey sites for the establishment of local naval bases.

Administration

Officer Commanding Jamaican Defence Force Coast Guard:
Lieutenant-Commander G. B. L. Copland

Personnel

1971: 9 officers, 43 men

Mercantile Marine

Lloyd's Register of Shipping: 6 vessels of 12 899 tons gross

PATROL BOATS

DISCOVERY BAY P 4   **HOLLAND BAY** P 5   **MANATEE BAY** P 6

Displacement, tons	60
Dimensions, feet	85 × 18·8 × 5·9
Guns	3—·50 cal Browning
Main Engines	2 GM 16 V71 N diesels; 2 shafts; 700 bhp = 21 knots
Oil fuel, tons	13
Radius, miles	500 at 12 knots
Complement	10

Built by Sewart Seacraft Inc, Berwick, La, USA. All aluminium construction. *Discovery Bay*, the prototype was launched in Aug 1966 and named and commissioned on 3 Nov 1966. *Holland Bay*, commissioned 4 Apr 1967, and *Manatee Bay*, commissioned 9 Aug 1967, were supplied under the US Military Assistance Programme.

DISCOVERY BAY   *1968, Jamaica Coast Guard*

DISCOVERY BAY   *1967, courtesy ALCOA*

AVR TYPE

The former ex-US AVR type patrol boats, *Mandingo* P 1 and *Coromantee* P 2 have been disposed of.

JORDAN

Coastal Guard

It was officially stated in 1969 that Jordan had no naval force known as such, but the Jordan Coastal Guard, sometimes called the Jordan Sea Force, took orders direct from the Director of Operations at General Headquarters.
The force of two Bertram fibre glass patrol boats, two Polson aluminium motor boats and four wooden motor boats is based at Aqaba. There is no flotilla in the Dead Sea.

JAPAN

Administration

Chief of the Maritime Staff, Defence Agency:
Admiral Kazutomi Uchida

Commander-in-Chief, Self-Defence Fleet:
Vice Admiral Seizaburo Hoshino

Chief Administration Division Maritime Staff Office:
Rear Admiral Kiyonori Kunishima

Diplomatic Representation

Defence (Naval) Attaché in London:
Captain Keizo Ohashi

Defence (Naval) Attaché in Washington:
Captain Yasuhiro Tamagawa

Defence Attaché in Moscow:
Colonel Keitaro Watanabe

Defence Attaché in Paris:
Colonel Akira Kashiwagi

Five Year Defence Build-up Plan

Under the third 5-year defence programme (from 1968 to 1972). Japan planned to build 56 new warships aggregating 48 000 tons, including 2 destroyers (equipped with anti-submarine helicopters) of 4 700 tons, 1 destroyer (with surface-to-air missiles) of 3 900 tons, 3 destroyers of 2 000 tons, 8 destroyer escorts of 1 450 tons and 5 submarines of 1 800 tons.

New Construction Programmes

1971: 2 Destroyers with ASW helicopters (4 700 tons)
1 Destroyer (2 100 tons)
5 Destroyer Escorts (1 470 tons)
3 Submarines (1 800 tons)
1 Minelayer (2 000 tons)
4 Minesweepers (380 tons)
2 Torpedo Boats (100 tons)
1 Tank Landing Ship (1 450 tons)
1 Minesweeping Tender (2 000 tons)

1970: 1 Destroyer with ASW helicopters (4 700 tons)
3 Destroyer Escorts (1 470 tons)
2 Submarines (1 800 tons)
4 Minesweepers (380 tons)
1 Torpedo Boat (100 tons)

Strength of the Fleet

10 Submarines (Diesel Powered)
27 Destroyers (including 1 Guided Missile Type)
13 Frigates (11 Destroyer Escorts)
20 Fast Patrol Vessels
2 Minelayers (Cablelayer, Minesweeper)
2 Training Ships (1 Turbine, 1 Diesel)
35 Coastal Minesweepers
10 Torpedo Boats
4 Tank Landing Ships (1 Medium)
93 Support Ships and Service Craft

Personnel

1971: 43 065 (7 151 officers, 31 174 men, 4 740 civil)
1970: 42 590 (6 990 officers, 30 843 men, 4 757 civil)
1970: 42 590 (6 974 officers, 30 839 men, 4 757 civil)
1969: 42 572 (6 974 officers, 30 839 men, 4 759 civil)
1967: 41 626 (6 589 officers, 30 002 men, 5 035 civil)
1966: 40 160 (6 300 officers, 28 880 men, 4 980 civil)
1965: 39 943 (6 210 officers, 28 832 men, 4 901 civil)

Names

The practice of painting the ship's names on the broadsides of the hulls was discontinued in 1970.

Coast Guard

10 Large patrol vessels	169 Coastal craft
77 Patrol vessels	26 Surveying vessels
42 Patrol craft	26 Tenders

Mercantile Marine

Lloyd's Register of Shipping:
8 402 vessels of 27 003 704 tons gross

Scale: 150 feet = 1 inch (1 : 1 800)

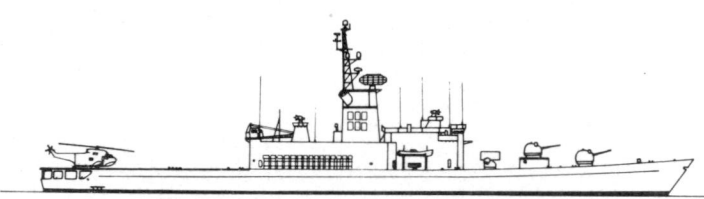

HARUNO (DDU Helocarrier)

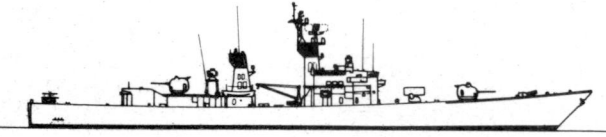

TAKATSUKI *Class*

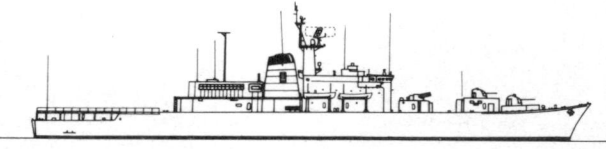

KATORI

AMATSUKAZE

KITAKAMI, OI

ISUZU, MOGAMI

AKIZUKI, TERUZUKI

MINEGUMO *Class*

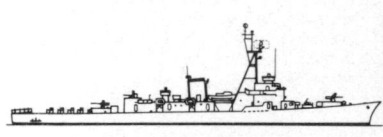

IKAZUCHI, INAZUMA

HARUSAME, MURASAME, YUDACHI

YAMAGUMO *Class*

AKEBONO

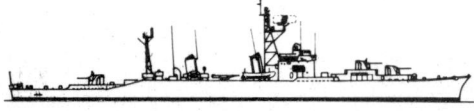

AYANAMI *Class*

ARIAKE

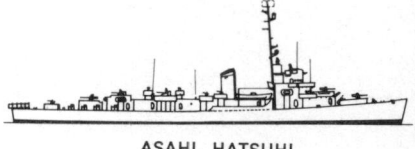

ASAHI, HATSUHI

HARUKAZE, YUKIKAZE

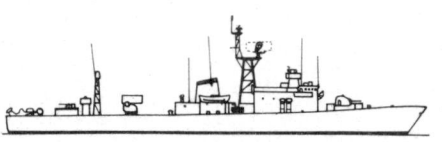

CHIKUGO *Class*

WAKABA

SUBMARINES

3 + 2 NEW CONSTRUCTION

UZUSHIO

Displacement, tons	1 850 standard
Length, feet (*metres*)	236·2 (*72·0*)
Beam, feet (*metres*)	32·5 (*9·9*)
Draught, feet (*metres*)	24·6 (*7·5*)
Torpedo tubes	6—21 in (*533 mm*); bow
Main engines	2 diesels; 3 400 bhp; 1 shaft; 1 electric motor; 7 200 hp
Speed, knots	12 on surface, 20 submerged
Complement	80

Uzushio was built by Kawasaki. Laid down on 25 Sep 1968, launched on 11 Mar 1970. Name means "Whirl Current".

5 "OSHIO" CLASS

Displacement, tons	1 650 standard; *Oshio* 1 600
Length, feet (*metres*)	288·7 (*86·0*)
Beam, feet (*metres*)	26·9 (*8·2*)
Draught, feet (*metres*)	16·2 (*4·9*), *Oshio* 15·4 (*4·7*)
Torpedo tubes	8—21 in (*533 mm*); 6 bow 2 stern
Main engines	2 diesels; 2 300 bhp; 2 shafts; 2 electric motors; 6 300 hp
Speed, knots	14 on surface; 18 submerged
Complement	80

Oshio was built under the 1961 programme, *Asashio* 1963. Cost $5 600 000. A bigger design to obtain improved seaworthiness, a larger torpedo capacity and more comprehensive sonar and electronic devices. Capable of deep diving, the first submarines of this propensity of all submarines built before or after the Second World War in Japanese yards. *Asashio* means "Morning Tide" and *Oshio* means "Flood Tide" or "Big Tide".

PHOTOGRAPHS. A photograph of *Oshio* appears in the 1965-66 to 1967-68 editions, and of *Harushio* in the 1969-70 and 1970-71 editions.

4 "HAYASHIO" CLASS

Displacement, tons	750 standard (SS 521, 522); 780 standard (SS 523, 524)
Length, feet (*metres*)	193·6 (*59·0*) oa (SS 521, 522); 200·1 (*61·0*) oa (SS 523, 524)
Beam, feet (*metres*)	21·3 (*6·5*)
Draught, feet (*metres*)	13·5 (*4·1*)
Torpedo tubes	3—21 in (*533 mm*); bow
Main engines	2 diesels, total 1 350 hp; 2 shafts 2 electric motors, total 1 700 hp
Speed, knots	11 on surface; 14 submerged
Complement	40

Medium submarines of improved type, with more efficient sonar devices, giving them slightly increased displacement. Very handy and successful boats, with a large safety factor, complete air conditioning and good habitability.

CONSTRUCTION. *Hayashio* and *Wakishio* were built under the 1959 fiscal year new construction programme and *Natsushio* and *Fuyushio* under the 1961 programme.

NOMENCLATURE. *Fuyushio* means "Winter Tide", *Hayashio* "Swift Tide", *Natsusnio* "Summer Tide", and *Wakashio* "Young Tide".

PHOTOGRAPHS. A photograph of *Wakashio* appears in the 1964-65 to 1966-67 editions and of *Hayashio* in the 1968-69 to 1970-71 editions.

NUCLEAR POWER STUDY. The Director of the Japanese Defence Agency stated on 5 May 1955 that Japan was studying the possibility of building a nuclear powered submarine. In the meantime, conventional submarines would be ordered.

1 "OYASHIO" CLASS

OYASHIO SS 511

Displacement, tons	1 130 surface; 1 420 submerged
Length, feet (*metres*)	258·5 (*78·8*)
Beam, feet (*metres*)	23 (*7·0*)
Draught, feet (*metres*)	15·2 (*4·6*)
Torpedo tubes	4—21 in (*533 mm*); 10 torpedoes
Main engines	2 diesels, total 2 700 hp 2 electric motors, total 5 960 hp
Speed, knots	13 on surface; 19 submerged
Radius, miles	5 000 at 10 knots
Complement	65

Ordered under the 1956 Programme. Built by Kawasaki Jyuko Co Kobe. Laid down on 25 Dec 1957, launched on 25 May 1959 and completed on 30 June 1960. The first submarine built in a Japanese shipyard after the Second World War, *Oyashio* is the name of a tide stream in the Pacific off Honshu. First estimated to cost £2 718 000. but this figure was exceeded.

"GATO" CLASS. The former US "Gato" class submarine, *Kuroshio* SS 501 (ex-USS *Mingo*, SS 261) was officially taken out of commision on 31 Mar 1966.

ARASHIO   *1971, Japanese Maritime Self-Defence Force, Official*

Name	No.	Builders	Laid down	Launched	Completed
ARASHIO	SS 565	Mitsubishi Jyuko, Kobe	5 July 1967	24 Oct 1968	25 July 1969
ASASHIO	SS 562	Kawasaki Jyuko Co, Kobe	10 Oct 1964	27 Nov 1965	13 Oct 1966
HARUSHIO	SS 563	Mitsubishi Jyuko Co, Kobe	12 Oct 1965	25 Feb 1967	21 Dec 1967
MICHISHIO	SS 564	Kawasaki Jyuko, Kobe	26 July 1966	5 Dec 1967	29 Aug 1968
ŌSHIO	SS 561	Mitsubishi Jyuko Co, Kobe	29 June 1963	30 Apr 1964	31 Mar 1965

ASASHIO   *1969, Japanese Maritime Self-Defence Force Official*

Name	No.	Builders	Laid down	Launched	Completed
FUYUSHIO	SS 524	Kawasaki Jyuko Co, Kobe	6 Dec 1961	14 Dec 1962	17 Sep 1963
HAYASHIO	SS 521	Shin Mitsubishi Jyuko Co, Kobe	6 June 1960	31 July 1961	30 June 1962
NATSUSHIO	SS 523	Shin Mitsubishi Jyuko Co, Kobe	5 Dec 1961	18 Sep 1962	29 June 1963
WAKASHIO	SS 522	Kawasaki Jyuko Co, Kobe	7 June 1960	28 Aug 1961	17 Aug 1962

NATSUSHIO   *1971, Japanese Maritime Self-Defence Force, Official*

FUYUSHIO   *1970, Japanese Maritime Self-Defence Force, Official*

OYASHIO   *1971, Japanese Maritime Self-Defence Force Official*

DESTROYERS

KIKUZUKI   1971, S. Woodrifle

1 PROJECTED MISSILE TYPE

Displacement, tons	3 900 (official figure)
Missile launchers	Surface-to-air; surface-to-surface
Aircraft	1 helicopter
Speed, knots	30

Projected under the Five Year Defence Build-up Plan.

1+1 NEW CONSTRUCTION DDH TYPE

HARUNA

Displacement, tons	4 700 (official figure)
Length, feet (metres)	502·0 (153·0)
Beam, feet (metres)	57·4 (17·5)
Draught, feet (metres)	16·7 (5·1)
Aircraft	3 anti-submarine helicopters
A/S weapons	Asroc multiple launcher
Guns	2—5 in (127 mm) single, rapid fire
Torpedo tubes	6—21 in (533 mm) 2 triple
Main engines	70 000 shp
Speed, knots	32
Complement	364

Ordered under the third five-year defence programme
(from 1968 to 1972. Laid down in 1970 and 1971.
Type 2401.

4 IMPROVED "MOON" CLASS

Displacement, tons	3 050 (official figure)
Length, feet (metres)	446·2 (136·0) oa
Beam, feet (metres)	44·0 (13·4)
Draught, feet (metres)	14·5 (4·4)
Aircraft	1 helicopter
A/S weapons	Octuple Asroc; 1 four barrelled rocket launcher
Guns, dual purpose	2—5 in (127 mm) 54 cal. single
Torpedo launchers	2 triple for A/S homing torpedoes
Boilers	2 Mitsubishi CE
Main engines	2 Mitsubishi WH geared turbines 60 000 shp; 2 shafts
Speed, knots	32
Complement	270

Anti-submarine type. Takatsuki (High Moon) was
provided under the 1963 programme. Equipped with
drone anti-submarine helicopter and hangar.

PHOTOGRAPHS. A photcgraph of Takatsuki appears
in the 1968-69 edition.

RADAR
Search: Metric wavelength.
Tactical: Probably C Band.
Fire Control: GFCS 56 with X Band.

Name	No.	Builders	Laid down	Launched	Completed
KIKUZUKI	DD 165	Mitsubishi Jyuko Co, Nagasaki	15 Mar 1966	25 Mar 1967	27 Mar 1968
MOCHIZUKI	DD 166	Ishikawajima Jyuko Co, Tokyo	25 Nov 1966	15 Mar 1968	25 Mar 1969
NAGATSUKI	DD 167	Mitsubishi Jyuko Co, Nagasaki	2 Mar 1968	19 Mar 1969	12 Feb 1970
TAKATSUKI	DD 164	Ishikawajima Jyuko Com Tokyo	8 Oct 1964	7 Jan 1966	15 Mar 1967

NAGATSUKI   1971, Japanese Maritime Self-Defence Force, Official

Name	No.	Builders	Laid down	Launched	Completed
ASAGUMO	DD 115	Maizuru Jyuko Co, Maizuru	24 June 1965	25 Nov 1966	29 Aug 1967
MAKIGUMO	DD 114	Uraga Dock Co, Yokosukia	10 June 1964	26 July 1965	29 Nov 1966
MINEGUMO	DD 116	Mitsui Zozen Co, Tamano	14 Mar 1967	18 Dec 1967	31 Aug 1968
MURAKUMO	DD 118	Maizuru Jyuko Co	19 Oct 1968	15 Nov 1969	31 Aug 1970
NATSUGUMO	DD 117	Uraga Dock Co, Yokosukia	26 June 1967	25 July 1968	25 Apr 1969
YAMAGUMO	DD 113	Mitsui Zozen Co, Tamano	23 Mar 1964	27 Feb 1965	30 Oct 1966
AOKUMO	DD 119	Mtsu Zozen Co, Tamano	1970	1971	1972

6 + 1 + 3 "CLOUD" CLASS

Displacement, tons	2 050 (official figure); Murakumo 2 150
Length, feet (metres)	374 (114·0)
Beam, feet (metres)	38·7 (11·8)
Draught, feet (metres)	12·8 (3·9)
A/S	Octuple Asroc; 1 four-barrelled rocket launcher in Asagumo, Makigumo and Yamagumo; DASH installation in lieu of Asroc in Minegumo, Natsugumo and Murakumo
Guns, AA	4—3 in (76 mm) 50 cal, 2 twin
Torpedo launchers	2 triple for A/S homing torpedoes
Main engines	6 Mitsui (Yamagumo and Murakumo), Mitsubishi (Asagumo, Makigumo) B & W diesels; 26 500 bhp; 2 shafts
Speed, knots	27
Complement	210

MURAKUMO   1971, Japanese Maritime Self-Defence Force, Official

Yamagumo was ordered under the 1962 fiscal year new
construction programme. Makigumo under the 1963
programme, and Asagumo under the 1964 programme.
Makigumo means "Rolling Cloud", and Yamagumo means
"Mountain Cloud". Seventh ship ordered under the
1967 construction programme.

RADAR.
Search: Metric wavelength.
Tactical: Probably C Band.
Fire Control: GFCS 56 with X Band.

PHOTOGRAPHS. A photograph of Makigumo appears
in the 1968-69 edition, and of Minegumo in the 1969-
70 and 1970-71 editions.

YAMAGUMO   1969, Japanese Maritime Self-Defence Force, Official

Destroyers—continued

1 GUIDED MISSILE ARMED TYPE

AMATSUKAZE   DD 163

Displacement, tons	3 050 standard ; 4 000 full load
Length, feet (metres)	429·8 (131·0)
Beam, feet (metres)	44 (13·4)
Draught, feet (metres)	13·8 (4·2)
Missiles, A/A	1 single "Tartar" launcher (US)
Guns, AA	4—3 in (76 mm) 50 cal, 2·twin
A/S	ASROC
Torpedo dropping gear	1 each side for A/S short torpedoes
Boilers	2 Ishikawajima Foster Wheeler
Main engines	2 Ishikawajima GE geared turbines 60 000 shp; 2 shafts
Speed, knots	33
Oil fuel (tons)	900
Complement	290

Ordered under the 1960 programme. Built by Mitsubishi, Nagasaki. Laid down on 29 Nov 1962, launched on 5 Oct 1963 and completed on 15 Feb 1965. The largest naval vessel completed in Japan after the Second World War, and the first armed with guided missiles. Distinguished by clean lines, flush deck and minimum superstructure. Equipped with surface-to-air guided missiles supplied from USA. Designed to carry and operate a helicopter. *Amatsukaze* means "Heaven Wind".

RADAR
Search: SPS 37 and SPS 39 3 D.
Fire Control: SPS 51 for "Tartar", X Band for guns.

2 "MOON" CLASS
(US "OFF-SHORE" PROGRAMME)

Displacement, tons	2 350 standard ; 2 890 full load
Length, feet (metres)	387·2 (118·0) oa
Beam, feet (metres)	39·4 (12·0)
Draught, feet (metres)	13·1 (4·0)
Guns, dual purpose	3—5 in (127 mm) 54 cal. single
Guns, AA	4—3 in (76 mm) 50 cal., 2 twin
Torpedo tubes	4—21 In (533 mm) quadrupled
A/S	1—US model Mk 108 rocket launcher ; 2 hedgehogs ; 2 Y-mortars ; 2 DCT
Boilers	2 Mitsubishi CE type
Main engines	2 geared turbines :— *Akizuki*: Mitsubishi Escher-Weiss *Teruzuki*: Westinghouse 45 000 shp, 2 shafts
Speed, knots	32
Complement	330

Destroyers of unusual design with long forecastle hull. Received from USA as part of the 1957 Military Aid Programme, but built in Japanese shipyards under an off-shore procurement agreement. US Navy hull numbers DD 960 and DD 961. They were designed as flotilla leaders to serve as senior officers' ships, and are equipped with two homing torpedo launchers, two radar systems and two sonar installations. *Akizuki* means "Autumn Moon"; *Teruzuki* means "Shining Moon"

RADAR
Search: SPS 6. Tactical: SPS 10. Fire Control: X Band

ANTI-AIRCRAFT TYPE

3 "RAIN" CLASS

Displacement, tons	1 800 standard ; 2 500 full load
Length, feet (metres)	354·3 (108·0) oa
Beam, feet (metres)	36 (11·0) oa
Draught, feet (metres)	12·2 (3·7)
Guns, dual purpose	3—5 in (127 mm) 54 cal
Guns, AA	4—3 in (76 mm) 50 cal, 2 twin
A/S	8 short torpedoes ; 1 Hedgehog 1 DC rack ; 1 Y-gun
Boilers	2 (see *Engineering* notes)
Main engines	2 sets geared turbines 30 000 shp; 2 shafts
Speed, knots	30
Complement	250

Murasame and *Yudachi* were built under the 1956 Programme, *Harusame* 1957 Programme, *Harusame* means "Spring Rain" *Murasame* means "Shower".

ENGINEERING. *Murasame* has Mitsubishi Jyuko turbines and Mitsubishi CE boilers; and the other two have Ishikawajima Harima Jyuko turbines and Ishikawajima FW-D boilers.

RADAR
Search: SPS 6. Tactical: SPS 10. Fire Control: X Band.

PHOTOGRAPHS. A photograph of *Murasame* appears in the 1963-64 to 1965-66 editions and of *Yudachi* in the 1966-67 to 1969-70 editions.

AMATSUKAZE   *1970, Japanese Maritime Self-Defence Force, Official*

TERUZUKI   *1971, courtesy Mr. Michael D. J. Lennon*

Name	No.	Builders	Laid down	Launched	Completed
AKIZUKI	DD 161	Mitsubishi Zosen Co, Nagasaki	31 July 1958	26 June 1959	13 Feb 1960
TERUZUKI	DD 162	Shin Mitsubishi Jyuko Co, Kobe	15 Aug 1958	24 June 1959	29 Feb 1960

AKIZUKI   *1969, Japanese Maritime Self-Defence Force, Official*

MURASAME   *1971, JMSDF, Official*

Name	No.	Builders	Laid down	Launched	Completed
HARUSAME	DD 109	Uraga Dock Co, Yokosuka	17 June 1958	18 June 1959	15 Dec 1959
MURASAME	DD 107	Mitsubishi Zosen Co, Nagasaki	17 Dec 1957	31 July 1958	28 Feb 1959
YUDACHI	DD 108	Ishakawajima Jyuko Co, Tokyo	16 Dec 1957	29 July 1958	25 Mar 1959

HARUSAME   *1970, courtesy Toshio Tamura*

Destroyers—continued

Name	No.	Builders	Laid down	Launched	Completed
AYANAMI	DD 103	Mitsubishi Zosen Co, Nagasaki	20 Nov 1956	1 June 1957	12 Feb 1958
ISONAMI	DD 104	Shin Mitsubishi Jyuko Co, Kobe	14 Dec 1956	30 Sep 1957	14 Mar 1958
MAKINAMI	DD 112	Iino Jyuko Co, Maizuru	20 Mar 1959	25 Apr 1960	30 Oct 1960
ONAMI	DD 111	Ishikawajima Jyuko Co, Tokyo	20 Mar 1959	13 Feb 1960	29 Aug 1960
SHIKINAMI	DD 106	Mitsui Zosen Co, Tamano	24 Dec 1956	25 Sep 1957	15 Mar 1958
TAKANAMI	DD 110	Mitsui Zosen Co, Tamano	8 Nov 1958	8 Aug 1959	30 Jan 1960
URANAMI	DD 105	Kawasaki Jyuko Co, Tokyo	1 Feb 1957	29 Aug 1957	27 Feb 1958

ANTI-SUBMARINE ("A" TYPE DDK)

7 "WAVE" CLASS

Displacement, tons	1 700 standard; 2 500 full load
Length, feet (metres)	357·6 (109·0) oa
Beam, feet (metres)	35·1 (10·7)
Draught, feet (metres)	12 (3·7) max
Guns, AA	6—3 in (76 mm) 50 cal. 3 twin
A/S	2 US Model Mk 15 Hedgehogs; 2 Y-mortars
Torpedo tubes	4—21 in (533 mm) quadrupled
Torpedo launchers	4 fixed, for A/S homing torpedoes
Boilers	2 (see Engineering)
Main engines	2 Mitsubishi Escher-Weiss geared turbines
	35 000 shp; 2 shafts
Speed, knots	32
Complement	230

Built under the 1955 Programme (Ayanami, Isonami, Shikinami, Uranami); 1957 Programme (Takanami) and 1958 Programme (Ōnami, Makinami).

ANTI-SUBMARINE. The Hedgehog type depth charge throwers are mounted on turntables before the bridge. Four torpedo loading racks are mounted in pairs abreast the after funnel. Droppers for anti-submarine homing torpedoes are mounted on the quarter deck.

GUNNERY. To facilitate ammunition supply the armament was designed to take standard US shell.

RADAR Search: SPS 12. Tactical: SPS 10. Fire Control: X Band.

ENGINEERING. Types of boilers installed are as follows: Mitsubishi CE in Ayanami, Isonami and Uranami; Hitachi Babcock & Wilcox in Ōnami, Shikinami and Takanami; Kawasaki Jyuko BD in Makinami.

CLASS. Reported to be very successful ships. The largest batch of destroyers of a single design put in hand since the Second World War.

NOMENCLATURE. Ayanami means "Weave Wave", Isonami means "Shore Wave", Shikinami means "Spread Wave", Takanami means "High Wave", Uranami means "Small Bay Wave", Ōnami means "Billow Wave" and Makinami means "Roller Wave".

PHOTOGRAPHS of Uranami appear in the 1958-59 to 1960-61 editions, of Isonami and Murasame (Addenda) in the 1959-60 editions, of Ōnami (Addenda) in the 1960-61 edition and the 1966-67 to 1968-69 editions and of Takanami in the 1961-62 and 1962-63 editions and the 1966-67 to 1968-69 editions. A starboard broadside surface view, of Makinami appears in the 1963-64 to 1965-66 editions, and a port broadside view in the 1966-67 to 1968-69 editions.

AYANAMI   1969, Japanese Maritime Self-Defence Force, Official

SHIKINAMI   1969, Japanese Maritime Self-Defence Force, Official

URANAMI   1969, Japanese Maritime Self-Defence Force, Official

2 "WIND" CLASS

Displacement. tons	1 700 standard; 2 340 full load
Length. feet (metres)	347·8 (106 0) wl; 358·5 (109·3) oa
Beam feet (metres)	34·5 (10·5)
Draught. feet (metres)	12·0 (3·7)
Guns dual purpose	3—5 in (127 mm) 38 cal.
Guns. AA	8—40 mm (2 quadruple)
A/S	Tubes for short homing torpedoes; 2 Hedgehogs; 1 DC rack; 4 K-guns
Boilers	Harukaze: 2 Hitachi-Babcock Yukikaze: 2 Combustion Engineering
Main engines	2 sets geared turbines; Harukaze: 2 Mitsubishi Escher Weiss Yukikaze: 2 Westinghouse
	30 000 shp; 2 shafts
Speed knots	30
Radius miles	6 000 at 18 knots
Oil fuel (tons)	557
Complement	240

Authorised under the 1953 programme. First destroyer hulled vessels built in Japan after the Second World War. Electric welding was extensively used in hull construction; development of weldable high tension steel in main hull and light alloy in superstructure were also novel. Harukaze means "Spring Wind" and Yukikaze means "Snow Wind".

Name	No.	Builders	Laid down	Launched	Completed
HARUKAZE	DD 101	Mitsubishi Zosen Co, Nagasaki	15 Dec 1954	20 Sep 1955	26 Apr 1956
YŪKIKAZE	DD 102	Mitsubishi Jyuko Co, Kobe	17 Nov 1954	20 Aug 1955	31 July 1956

YŪKIKAZE   1970, Japanese Maritime Self-Defence Force, Official

RADAR Search: L Band. Tactical: SPS 10. Fire Control: X Band.

PHOTOGRAPHS. A photograph of Harukaze appears in the 1963-64 to 1965-66 editions.

ANTI-SUBMARINE. Armament was modified in Mar 1969 when homing torpedo tubes were mounted and depth charge equipment correspondingly reduced. Nearly all the armament was supplied from the USA under the MSA clause.

Destroyers—continued

Name	No.	Builders	Launched	Completed
ARIAKE (ex-USS *Heywood L. Edwards*, DD 663)	DD 183	Boston Navy Yard	6 Oct 1943	26 Jan 1944
YUGURE (ex-USS *Richard P. Leary*, DD 664)	DD 184	Boston Navy Yard	6 Oct 1943	23 Feb 1944

US LATER "FLETCHER" TYPE

2 "TWILIGHT" CLASS

Displacement, tons	2 050 standard ; 3 040 full load
Length, feet (*metres*)	376·5 (*114·8*)
Beam, feet (*metres*)	39·3 (*12·0*)
Draught, feet (*metres*)	18 (*5·5*) max
Guns, dual purpose	*Ariake:* 3—5 in (*127 mm*) 38 cal.
	Yugure: 4—5 in (*127 mm*) 38 cal.
Guns AA	10—40 mm
A/S weapons	*Ariake:* Mk 108 rocket launcher dropping gear for short homing torpedoes on each side ; *Yugure:* 2 Hedgehogs
Boilers	4 Foster Wheeler
Main engines	GE geared turbines 60 000 shp ; 2 shafts
Speed, knots	35
Complement	300

Transferred on loan from the US Navy on 10 Mar 1959 and towed to Japan for refit, during which No. 3 5 inch gun was removed. *Ariake* means "Dawn Twilight" *Yugure* means "Evening Dusk".

RADAR
Search: SPS 12.
Tactical: SPS 10.
Fire Control: Probably GFCS 68.

ARIAKE   *1970, Japanese Maritime Self-Defence Force, Official*

CONVERSION. Both ships completed conversion in Mar 1962 with improved bridges, larger combat information centre, newer radar aerials and tripod masts. No. 2 5 inch gun in *Ariake* was replaced by Weapon A.
A photograph of *Yugure* appears in the 1964-65 and 1965-66 editions.

The destroyers *Asakaze* (ex-USS *Ellyson*) and *Hatakaze* (ex-USS *Macomb*) taken over on 19 Oct 1954 were returned to the United States Navy in 1969.

FRIGATES

DESTROYER ESCORT TYPE

1 + 2 + 5 NEW CONSTRUCTION

AYASE 216   **MIKUMA** DE 217
CHIKUGO DE 215

Displacement, tons	1 470 standard ; 1 750 full load
Length, feet (*metres*)	305·5 (*93·0*) oa
Beam, feet (*metres*)	35·5 (*10·8*)
Draught, feet (*metres*)	11·5 (*3·5*)
Guns, dual purpose	2—3 in (*76 mm*) 50 cal, (1 twin)
Guns, AA	2—40 mm (1 twin)
A/S weapons	Octuple ASROC
Torpedo launchers	2 triple 12·7 in (*324 mm*)
Main engines	4 Mitsui B & W diesels ; 2 shafts ; 16 000 shp
Speed, knots	25
Complement	180

Chikugo was built by Mitsui Zozen Co, Tamano, under the 1967 New Construction Programme. Laid down on 9 Dec 1968 and launched on 13 Jan 1970. DE 216 was ordered under the 1968 Programme and DE 217 under the 1969 Programme. Five more are projected under the Five Year Defence Build-up Plan.

CHIKUGO   *1971, Official*

DESTROYER ESCORT TYPE (DE)

4 "RIVER" CLASS

Name	No.	Builders	Laid down	Launched	Completed
ISUZU	DE 211	Mitsui Zosen Co, Tamano	16 Apr 1960	17 Jan 1961	29 July 1961
KITAKAMI	DE 213	Ishikawajima-Harima Co, Tokyo	7 June 1962	21 June 1963	27 Feb 1964
MOGAMI	DE 212	Mitsubishi Zosen Co, Nagasaki	4 Aug 1960	7 Mar 1961	28 Oct 1961
ŌI	DE 214	Maizuru (former lino) Co, Maizuru	10 June 1962	15 June 1963	22 Jan 1964

Displacement, tons	1 490 standard ; 1 700 full load
Length, feet (*metres*)	308·5 (*94·0*) oa
Beam, feet (*metres*)	34·2 (*10·4*)
Draught, feet (*metres*)	11·5 (*3·5*)
Guns, dual purpose	4—3 in (*76 mm*) 50 cal. 2 twin
A/S weapons	1 4-barrelled rocket launcher ; 1 DCT ; 1 DC rack *Isuzu* Mk 108 rocket launcher (Weapon A)
Torpedo tubes	4—21 in (*533 mm*) quadrupled
Torpedo launchers	2 triple for A/S homing torpedoes
Main engines	4 diesels, Mitsui in *Oi, Isuzu,* Mitsubishi in *Kitakami, Mogami;* 16 000 hp ; 2 shafts
Speed, knots	25
Complement	180

Isuzu and *Mogami* were built under the 1959 new construction programme and *Kitakami* and *Ōi* under the 1961 new construction programme.

RADAR
Search: SPS 6.
Tactical: SPS 10.

CLASS VARIATION. The second pair of this type, *Kitakami* and *Ōi*, have a number of improvements in armament and equipment and are of slightly different dimensions.

NOMENCLATURE. New frigates of the destroyer escort (DE) type were named after rivers, like the old light cruisers. This naming system applied on 1 Oct 1960.

PHOTOGRAPHS. A photograph of *Mogami* appears in the 1961-62 edition, of *Isuzu* in the 1962-63 to 1966-67 editions and of *Kitakami* in the 1967-68 to 1969-70 editions.

ISUZU   *1970, courtesy, Toshio Tamura*

ŌI   *1970, Japanese Maritime Self Defence Force, Official*

Frigates—continued

Name	No.	Builders	Laid down	Launched	Completed
IKAZUCHI	DE 202	Kawasaki Jyuko Co, Kobe	18 Dec 1954	6 Sep 1955	29 May 1956
INAZUMA	DE 203	Mitsui Zosen Co Tamano	25 Dec 1954	4 Aug 1955	5 Mar 1956

DIESEL "B" TYPE ESCORT
2 "THUNDER" CLASS

Displacement, tons	1 070 standard ; 1 300 full load
Length, feet (metres)	287 (87·5) wl ; 288·7 (88·0) oa
Beam, feet (metres)	28·5 (8·7)
Draught, feet (metres)	10·2 (3·1)
Guns, dual purpose	2—3 in (76 mm) 50 cal.
Guns, AA	2—40 mm
A/S	1 Hedgehog ; 8 K-guns ; 2 DC racks
Main engines	12 000 hp diesels ; Mitsubishi in Ikazuchi ; Mitsui B & W in Inazuma ; 2 shafts
Speed, knots	25
Complement	160

Diesel powered "B" type DE Escort Vessels. Authorised by Congress under 1953 fiscal year programme. Unlike the turbine boat, Akebono (see below) which has two funnels, these diesel boats have only one funnel.

NOMENCLATURE. Ikazuchi means "Thunder" and Inazuma means "Thunderbolt".

GUNNERY. The original 2—3 inch guns and 4—40 mm guns were removed in Mar 1959 and replaced by 2—3 inch quick firing guns and 2—40 mm guns.

RADAR
Search: SPS 6.
Tactical: SPS 10.
Fire Control: X Band.

PHOTOGRAPHS. A dead broadside view of Inazuma appears in the 1961-62 to 1966-67 editions.

IKAZUCHI   1967, Japanese Maritime Self-Defence Force. Official

INAZUMA   1967, Japanese Maritime Self-Defence Force, Official

Name	No.	Builders	Laid down	Launched	Completed
AKEBONO	DE 201	Ishikawajima Jyuko Co, Tokyo	10 Dec 1954	15 Oct 1955	20 Mar 1956

STEAM TURBINE "B" TYPE

Displacement, tons	1 060 standard ; 1 350 full load
Length, feet (metres)	295 (90·0) oa
Beam, feet (metres)	28·5 (8·7)
Draught, feet (metres)	11 (3·4) max
Guns, AA	2—3 in (76 mm) 50 cal.
Boilers	2 Ishikawajima-Foster Wheeler
Main engines	Ishikawajima geared turbines 18 000 shp ; 2 shafts
Speed knots,	28
Complement	190

The only steam powered DE. Rated as "B" type Escort Vessel. Built under the 1953 Programme. Ordered on 20 Nov 1954. Akebono means "Dawn".

GUNNERY. The original 2—3 inch guns and 4—40 mm guns were removed in March 1959 when 2—3 inch quick firing guns were mounted.

RADAR
Search: SPS 6.
Tactical: SPS 10.
Fire Control: X Band.

AKEBONO   1967, Japanese Maritime Self-Defence Force, Official

Name	No.	Builders	Laid down	Launched	Completed
WAKABA (ex-Nashi)	DE 261	Kawasaki, Kobe	1 Sep 1944	17 Jan 1945	15 Mar 194

EXPERIMENTAL SHIP
FORMER ESCORT DESTROYER

Displacement, tons	1 250 standard ; 1 560 full load
Length, feet (metres)	322·2 (98·2) pp 329·8 (100·5) oa
Beam, feet (metres)	31·2 (9·5)
Draught, feet (metres)	10·7 (3·3)
Guns, AA	2—3 in (76 mm) 50 cal. aft
A/S	1 Hedgehog ; 4 K-guns ; 2 DCT
Boilers	2 Kanpon
Main engines	2 geared turbines ; 14 000 shp ; 2 shafts
Speed, knots	26 designed ; 24 present
Radius, miles	4 680 at 16 knots
Oil fuel (tons)	395
Complement	175

This former escort destroyer, Nashi was built under the War Programme of 1943 as one of the Modified "Matsu" type. She was sunk on 28 July 1945 off Hatajiri Point, Inland Sea, by carrier borne aircraft. She was officially scrapped on 15 Sep 1945, but was subsequently raised and repaired and purchased by the Maritime Self-Defence Force. She completed her first reconstruction at Kure Zosen on 12 May 1956, being renamed and commissioned on 31 May. "Wakaba means "Young Leaf". She was to be used as a training ship, but was converted into a radar, picket. Her second reconstruction commenced at Uraga Dock Co on 10 Sep 1957 and was completed on 28 Mar 1958. Her lattice foremast and tripod mainmast were stepped in 1958 ; large radar aerial fitted aft in 1961 ;

WAKABA   1967. Japanese Maritime Self-Defence Force, Official

various antennas fitted in experimental roles. Re-classified as an Experimental Ship in 1968.

A port broadside view of Wakaba appears in the 1961- to 1966-67 editions.

Frigates—*continued*

Name	No.	Builders	Laid down	Launched	Completed
ASAHI (ex-USS *Amick*, DE 168)	DE 262	Federal Port Newark	30 Nov 1942	27 May 1943	26 July 1943
HATSUHI (ex-USS *Atherton*, DE 169)	DE 263	Federal Port Newark	14 Jan 1943	27 May 1943	29 Aug 1943

DESTROYER ESCORTS
2 "SUN" CLASS

Displacement, tons	1 250 standard; 1 510 normal; 1 900 full load
Length, feet (*metres*)	306 (*93·3*) oa
Beam, feet (*metres*)	36·1 (*11·0*)
Draught, feet (*metres*)	12 (*3·7*) max
Guns, dual purpose	3—3 in (*76 mm*) 50 cal.
Guns, AA	6—40 mm; 8—20 mm
A/S	8 K-guns; 1 DCT
Main engines	GM diesels, electric drive 6 000 hp; 2 shafts
Speed, knots	20
Complement	220

Former US "Bostwick" class destroyer escorts. Taken over from the US Navy on 14 June 1955. *Asahi* means "Morning Sun"; *Hatsuhi* means "First Sun of the Year".

PHOTOGRAPHS. A photograph of *Asahi* appears in the 1961-62 to 1966-67 editions.

HATSUHI   *1967, Japanese Maritime Self-Defence Force, Official*

PATROL FRIGATES
2 "TREE" CLASS

KAYA (ex-USS *San Pedro*, PF 37)   P F 288
KEYAKI (ex-USS *Evansville*, PF 70)   P F 295

Displacement, tons	1 450 standard; 2 415 full load
Length, feet (*metres*)	285·5 (*87·0*) wl; 304 (*92·7*) oa
Beam, feet (*metres*)	37·5 (*11·4*)
Draught, feet (*metres*)	13·7 (*4·2*) max
Guns, dual purpose	3—3 in (*76 mm*) 50 cal.
Guns, AA	2—40 mm; 9—20 mm
A/S	1 Hedgehog; 8 K-guns; 2 DC racks.
Boilers	2 three-drum type; 240 psi (*16·9 kg/cm²*)
Main engines	Triple expansion 5 500 shp; 2 shafts
Speed, knots	18
Radius, miles	9 500 at 12 knots
Oil fuel (tons)	645
Complement	170

Launched in 1943. Transferred on loan from the United States in 1953. Technically returned to the US on 28 Aug 1962, but were transferred outright to the

KAYA   *1970, Japanese Maritime Self-Defence Force, Official*

Japanese Government the same day and became Japanese ships. Named after trees. *Keyaki* has a deckhouse added abaft the mainmast.

Ten sister ships were reclassified as moored training ships, *Buna* on 1 Feb 1965, *Kashi, Moni, Tochi* and *Ume* on 1 Apr 1965, and *Kaede, Maki, Matsu, Nara* and *Sakura* on 31 Mar 1966. *Kusu* was converted to a Drone Target Carrier in 1964, *Nire* and *Shii* were returned to the USN on 31 Mar 1970 and *Kiri* and *Sugi* were laid up on the same date.

MINELAYER

1 NEW CONSTRUCTION
SOOYA

Displacement, tons	2 150 standard	Torpedo tubes	6 anti-submarine type
Length, feet (*metres*)	318·2 (*97·0*)		Ordered under the 1971 New Construction Programme.
Guns	2—3 in (*76 mm*); 2—20 mm	Type 951.	

TRAINING SHIPS

AZUMA 4201

Displacement, tons	1 950 standard; 2 500 full load
Length, feet (*metres*)	325 (*99·0*)
Draught, feet (*metres*)	12·5 (*3·8*)
Guns	1—3 in (*76 mm*) 50 cal
A/S weapons	2 DC racks
Main engines	2 diesels; 2 shafts; 4 000 bhp
Speed, knots	18

Built by Maizuru Jyuko Co, Maizuru as a training support ship. Laid down on 13 July 1968, launched on 14 Apr 1969 and completed 21 Oct 1969.

KATORI 3501

Displacement, tons	3 372 standard; 4 000 full load
Length, feet (*metres*)	418·5 (*127·0*)
Beam, feet (*metres*)	49·3 (*14·6*)
Draught, feet (*metres*)	14·6 (*4·3*)
Aircraft	1 helicopter
Guns, dual purpose	4—3 in (*76 mm*) 50 cal
A/S weapons	1 four barrelled rocket launcher
Torpedo launchers	6 (2 triple mounts) for homing torpedoes
Main engines	Geared turbines; 2 shafts; 20 000 shp
Speed, knots	25
Complement	460 including trainees

An unusual design, closely approximating to an A/S frigate/convoy escort command ship with great potential in all roles. Ordered under the 1966 New Construction Programme. Built by Ishikawajima Harima, Tokyo. Launched on 19 Nov 1968 and completed on 10 Sep 1969. Provided with a landing deck aft for a helicopter.

RADAR Search: SPS 12. Tactical: SPS 10.

AZUMA   *1971, JMSDF Official*

KATORI   *1970, courtesy, Toshio Tamura*

FAST PATROL VESSELS

10 "MIZUTORI" CLASS SUBMARINE CHASERS (PC)

Name	No.	Builders	Laid down	Launched	Completed
HATSUKARI	315	Sasebo Shipyard	25 Jan 1960	24 June 1960	15 Nov 1960
HIYODORI	320	Sasebo Shipyard	29 Feb 1965	25 Sep 1965	28 Feb 1966
KASASAGI	314	Fujinagata, Osaka	18 Dec 1959	31 May 1960	31 Oct 1960
KUMATAKA	318	Fujinagata, Osaka	20 Mar 1963	21 Oct 1963	25 Mar 1964
MIZUTORI	311	Kawasaki, Kobe	13 Mar 1959	22 Sep 1959	27 Feb 1960
ŌTORI	313	Kure Shipyard	16 Dec 1959	27 May 1960	13 Oct 1960
SHIRATORI	319	Sasebo Shipyard	29 Feb 1964	8 Oct 1964	27 Feb 1965
UMIDORI	316	Sasebo Shipyard	15 Feb 1962	15 Oct 1962	30 Mar 1963
WAKATAKA	317	Kure Shipyard	5 Mar 1962	13 Nov 1962	30 Mar 1963
YAMADORI	312	Fujinagata, Osaka	14 Mar 1959	22 Oct 1959	15 Mar 1960

Displacement, tons	420 to 450 standard
Dimensions, feet	197 × 23·3 × 7·5
Guns	2—40 mm (1 twin)
A/S weapons	1 hedgehog; 1 DC rack; 2 homing torpedo launchers
Main Engines	2 MAN diesels; 2 shafts; 3 800 bhp = 20 knots
Oil fuel (tons)	24·5
Complement	70

Mizutori and *Yamadori* built under 1958 programme, *Ōtori*, *Kasasagi* and *Hatsukari* 1959, *Umidori* (Sea Bird) and *Wahataka* (Young Hawk) 1961, *Kumataka* 1962, *Shiratori* (White Bird) 1963, *Hiyodori* 1964. A photograph of *Hiyodori* appears in the 1967-68 to 1969-70 editions.

OTORI   *1970, courtesy Toshio Tamura*

2 "UMITAKA" CLASS SUBMARINE CHASERS (PC)

Name	No.	Builders	Laid down	Launched	Completed
ŌTAKA	310	Kure Shipyard	18 Mar 1959	3 Sep 1959	14 Jan 1960
UMITAKA	309	Kawasaki, Kobe	13 Mar 1959	25 July 1959	30 Nov 1959

Displacement, tons	440 to 480 standard
Dimensions, feet	197 × 23·3 × 8
Guns	2—40 mm (1 twin)
A/S weapons	1 hedgehog, 1 DC rack; 2 triple A/S torpedo launchers
Main Engines	2 B & W diesels; 2 shafts; 4 000 bhp = 20 knots
Oil fuel (tons)	24
Radius, miles	2 000 at 12 knots
Complement	70

Built under the 1957 programme. Design emphasises good sea-keeping qualities. *Ōtaka* means Great Hawk. *Umitaka* Sea Hawk.

ŌTAKA   *1967, Hajime Fukaya*

1 GAS TURBINE TYPE SUBMARINE CHASER (PC)

HAYABUSA 308

Displacement, tons	380 standard
Dimensions, feet	190·2 × 25·7 × 7
Guns	2—40 mm AA (1 twin)
A/S weapons	1 Hedgehog; 2 DC throwers; 2 DC racks
Main engines	1 Gas turbine 5,000 hp; 2 diesels 4,000 bhp; 3 shafts Total 9 000 hp = 26 knots
Complement	75

Built under the 1954 fiscal year programme by Mitsubishi Shipbuilding & Engineering Co Ltd, Nagasaki. Laid down on 23 May 1956. Launched on 20 Nov 1956. Completed on 10 June 1957. The gas turbine was installed in Mar 1962.

HAYABUSA   *1967, Japanese Maritime Self-Defence Force, Official*

Fast Patrol Vessels—*continued*

7 DIESEL TYPE SUBMARINE CHASERS (PC)

Name	No.	Builders	Laid down	Launched	Completed
KAMOME	305	Uraga	27 Jan 1956	3 Sep 1956	14 Jan 1957
KARI	301	Fujimagata, Osaka	18 Jan 1956	26 Sep 1956	8 Feb 1957
KIJI	302	Iino, Maizuru	14 Dec 1955	11 Sep 1956	29 Jan 1957
MISAGO	307	Uraga	27 Jan 1956	1 Nov 1956	11 Feb 1957
TAKA	303	Fujimagata, Osaka	18 Jan 1956	17 Nov 1956	11 Mar 1957
TSUBAME	306	Kure Shipyard	15 Mar 1956	10 Oct 1956	31 Jan 1957
WASHI	304	Iino, Maizuru	14 Dec 1955	12 Nov 1956	20 Mar 1957

Displacement, tons	330 standard; (*Kari, Kiji, Taka, Washi*, 310)
Dimensions, feet	173·3 oa × 21·8 × 6·8
Guns	2—40 mm (1 twin)
A/S weapons	1 hedgehog; 2-Y guns; 2 DC racks
Main Engines	2 diesels (*Kari, Kiji, Taka* and *Washi*, Kawasaki-MAN; others Mitsui-Burmeister & Wain). 2 shafts; 4 000 bhp = 20 knots
Oil fuel (tons)	21·5
Complement	70

Authorised under the 1954 programme. At the time they were an entirely new type of fast patrol vessels or submarine chasers, reminiscent of the United States PC type but modified and improved in many ways. *Kamome* means "Seagull". A photograph of *Kamome* appears in the 1957-58 to 1965-66 editions.

MISAGO   *1970, Japanese Maritime Self Defence Force, Official*

COASTAL MINELAYERS

MINELAYER AND CABLE LAYER (ARC)

TSUGARU 481

Displacement, tons	950 standard
Dimensions, feet	216·3 × 34·1 × 11
Guns	1—3 in, 50 cal dp; 2—20 mm AA;
A/S weapons	4 K-guns (DC mortars)
Mines	4 mine launchers, capacity of 40 mines
Main Engines	Diesel; 2 shafts; 3 200 bhp = 16 knots
Complement	100

Dual purpose cable layer and coastal minelayer. Built under the 1953 programme by Yokohama Shipyard & Engine Works, Mitsubishi Nippon-Heavy Industries Ltd. Laid down on 18 Dec 1954. Launched on 19 July 1955. Completed on 15 Dec 1955.

TSUGARU   *1966, Japanese Maritime Self-Defence Force, Official*

MINELAYER AND MINESWEEPER (AMC)

ERIMO 491

Displacement, tons	630 standard
Dimensions, feet	210 × 26 × 8
Guns	2—40 mm AA; 2—20 mm AA
A/S weapons	1 hedgehog; 2 K-guns; 2 DC racks
Main Engines	Diesel; 2 shafts; 2 500 bhp = 18 knots
Complement	80

Multi-purpose minelayer, ocean minesweeper (non-magnetic) and submarine chaser. Authorised under 1953 fiscal programme. Built by Uraga Dock Co. Laid down on 10 Dec 1954. Launched on 12 July 1955. Completed on 28 Dec 1955.

ERIMO   *1970, Japanese Maritime Self-Defence Force, Official*

COASTAL MINESWEEPERS

28 + 6 "KASADA" CLASS

Name	No.	Laid down	Launched	Completed
AMAMI	MSC 625	1 Mar 1966	31 Oct 1966	3 Mar 1967
CHIBURI	MSC 620	27 Mar 1963	29 Nov 1963	25 Mar 1964
HABUSHI	MSC 608	24 Mar 1959	19 June 1959	22 Sep 1959
HARIO	MSC 618	19 Mar 1962	10 Dec 1962	27 Mar 1963
HIRADO	MSC 614	14 Mar 1960	3 Oct 1960	17 Dec 1960
HOTAKA	MSC 616	22 Mar 1961	23 Oct 1961	24 Feb 1962
IBUKI	MSC 628	27 Feb 1967	2 Dec 1967	27 Feb 1968
IOU	MSC 631	21 Sep 1968	12 Aug 1969	22 Jan 1970
KANAWA	MSC 606	25 Aug 1958	22 Apr 1959	24 July 1959
KARATO	MSC 617	15 Mar 1962	11 Dec 1962	23 Mar 1963
KASADO	MSC 604	9 July 1956	19 Mar 1958	26 June 1958
KATSURA	MSC 629	10 Feb 1967	18 Sep 1967	18 Feb 1968
KOOZO	MSC 609	30 Mar 1959	12 Nov 1959	26 Feb 1960
KOSHIKI	MSC 615	20 Mar 1961	9 Nov 1961	29 Jan 1962
KUDAKO	MSC 622	17 Mar 1964	8 Dec 1964	24 Mar 1965
MIKURA	MSC 612	30 Mar 1959	14 Mar 1960	27 May 1960
MINASE	MSC 627	1 Feb 1966	10 Jan 1967	25 Mar 1967
MUTSURE	MSC 619	28 Mar 1963	16 Dec 1963	24 Mar 1964
OOTSU	MSC 621	25 Mar 1964	5 Nov 1964	24 Feb 1965
REBUN	MSC 624	27 Mar 1965	7 Dec 1965	25 Mar 1966
RISHIRI	MSC 623	9 Mar 1964	22 Nov 1965	5 Mar 1966
SAKITO	MSC 607	16 Aug 1958	22 Apr 1959	25 Aug 1959
SHIKINE	MSC 613	12 Jan 1960	22 July 1960	15 Nov 1960
SHISAKA	MSC 605	20 July 1956	20 Mar 1958	16 Aug 1958
TAKAMI	MSC 630	25 Sep 1968	15 July 1969	15 Dec 1969
TATARA	MSC 610	25 Aug 1958	14 Jan 1960	26 Mar 1960
TSUKUMI	MSC 611	24 Mar 1959	12 Jan 1960	27 Apr 1960
URUME	MSC 626	1 Feb 1966	12 Nov 1966	30 Jan 1967

Displacement, tons	340 standard ; 380 later ships
Dimensions, feet	150·9 × 27·6 × 7·5 ; 170·6 × 28·9 × 7·9 later ships
Guns	1—20 mm AA
Main engines	2 diesels ; 2 shafts ; 1 200 bhp, 1 440 later ships = 14 knots

Hull is of wooden construction. Otherwise built of non-magnetic materials. *Habushi, Kanawa* and *Kasado* were built by Hitachi, Kanawaga Works, *Shishaka* and *Sakito* by Nippon Steel Tube Co, Tsurumi. *Kasado* and *Shisaka* were ordered under the 1955 programme, *Habushi, Kanawa* and *Sakito* 1957, four 1958, two 1959, two 1960, two 1961, two 1962, two 1963, two 1964, three 1965, two 1967, two 1968, two 1969, four 1970. A photograph of *Shisaka* appears in the 1961-62 to 1966-67 editions and of *Rishiri* in the 1967-63 edition.

The six latest ships are of slightly different type:—

UTONE	632	AWAJI	634	TEURI	636
MIJAKE	633	TOOSHI	635	MUROTSU	637

KATSURA   *1968, Japanese Maritime Self-Defence Force, Official*

1 "YASHIRO" CLASS

YASHIRO MSC 603

Displacement, tons	230 standard ; 255 full load
Dimensions, feet	118 pp × 22·7 × 6·2
Guns	1—20 mm AA
Main Engines	Diesel ; 2 shafts ; 1 200 bhp = 13 knots

Built under the 1953 Programme by the Nippon Kokan Co, Tsurumi. Laid down on 22 June 1955, launched on 26 Mar 1956 and completed on 10 July 1956.

YASHIRO   *1970, Japanese Maritime Self-Defence Force, Official*

DISPOSALS
Of the nine coastal minesweepers of the "Ujishima" class, *Moroshima, Ogishima, Ninoshima, Yugoshima, Yurishima* were officially deleted from the list in 1957 ; *Etajima* and *Ujishima* in 1966 ; *Yakishima* was returned to USN on 31 Mar 1970. All ex-US AMS of the "Albatross" class.

2 "ATADA" CLASS

Name	No.	Laid down	Launched	Completed
ATADA	MSC 601	20 June 1955	12 Mar 1956	30 Apr 1956
ITSUKI	MSC 602	22 June 1955	12 Mar 1956	20 June 1956

Displacement, tons	240 standard ; 260 full load
Dimensions, feet	118 pp ; 123·3 oa × 21 × 6·8
Guns	1—20 mm AA
Main Engines	Diesel ; 2 shafts ; 1 200 bhp = 13 knots

Of wood and light metal construction. Authorised under the 1953 fiscal year programme. Built by the Hitachi Zosen Co. Named after small islands. A photograph of *Itsuki* appears in the 1960-61 to 1966-67 editions.

ATADA   *1970, Japanese Maritime Self-Defence Force, Official*

4 "YASHIMA" CLASS

HASHIMA (ex-USS AMS 95)	TSUSHIMA (ex-USS MSC, ex-AMS 255)
TOSHIMA (ex-USS MSC 258)	YASHIMA (ex-USS AMS 144)

Displacement, tons	335 standard ; 375 full load
Dimensions, feet	138 pp ; 144 oa × 26·5 × 8·3
Guns	1—20 mm AA
Main engines	2 GM diesels ; 880 bhp = 13 knots

Former US auxiliary minesweepers of non-magnetic construction. Transferred on 3 June 1955 (*Hashima*, MSC 625), 1 Feb 1957 (*Toshima*, MSC 654), 18 July 1956 (*Tsushima*, MSC 652), and 16 Dec 1954 (*Yashima*, MSC 651). *Hashima* and *Yashima* were reclassified as miscellaneous ships on 31 March 1970. A photograph of *Yashima* appears in the 1961-62 to 1965-66 editions.

TOSHIMA   *1966, Japanese Maritime Self-Defence Force, Official*

MINESWEEPING BOATS (*Sookaitei*)

No. 1	No. 2	No. 3	No. 4	No. 5	No. 6

Displacement, tons	40
Dimensions, feet	57·2 wl ; 62·3 oa × 16 × 4
Main Engines	Diesels ; 2 shafts ; 320 bhp = 10 knots
Complement	10

Nos. 1, 2 and 3 were launched in Jan and Feb 1957 and completed in Mar and Apr 1957. No. 4 was launched in Apr 1957 and completed in June 1957. Nos. 5 and 6 were laid down in Aug 1958 and completed in Feb-Mar 1959. Nos. 1 and 2 were built by Hitachi, Kanagawa; and the others by Nihon Kohan, Tsurumi. Named *Sokaitel* Nos. 1 to 6 and numbered MSB 701 to 706.

MB 5   *1963, Official*

TORPEDO BOATS *(Gyoraitei)*

New Construction: 2 torpedo boats of 100 tons are in the 1971 Programme.

PT 10

Displacement, tons	90 standard; 120 full load
Dimensions, feet	105 × 27·8 × 3·7
Guns	2—40 mm AA (1 forward, 1 aft)
Tubes	4—21 in (single, amidships)
Main Engines	3 Napier Deltic diesels; 9 400 bhp = 40 knots
Complement	26

1960 programme. Built by Mitsubishi, Shimonoseki. Laid down on 30 Jan 1961. Launched on 28 July 1961. Completed on 25 May 1962. Light metal hull.

PT 10   *1970, Japanese Maritime Self-Defence Force, Official*

PT9

Displacement, tons	55
Dimensions, feet	71·3 × 19·8 × 6
Tubes	2—21 in
Main Engines	2 Napier Deltic diesels; 5 000 bhp = 40 knots
Complement	14

Basically similar to the British "Dark" class MTBs. Built by Saunders-Roe (Anglesey) Ltd, Beaumaris. Delivered to Yokosuka Naval Base on 29 July 1957. Accepted into service on 2 Sep 1957. Has mounting for 1—40 mm AA (gun not fitted).

PT 9   *Saunders-Roe (Anglesey) Ltd*

PT 7   PT 8

Displacement, tons	100
Dimensions, feet	112 × 24·7 × 4
Guns	2—40 mm AA
Tubes	4—21 in
Main Engines	3 Mitsubishi diesels; 3 shafts; 6 000 bhp = 33 knots
Complement	30

Authorised in the 1954 fiscal year. Built by Mitsubishi Zosen Co, Shimonoseki Works. Both laid down on 23 Aug 1956, launched on 2 Feb and 20 July 1957, respectively, and completed on 19 Dec 1957 and 10 Jan 1958. Light metal hulls.
A photograph of PT 8 appears in the 1966-67 to 1970-71 editions.

PT 7   *1971, Japanese Maritime Self-Defence Force, Official*

PT 1   PT 2   PT 3   PT 4   PT 5   PT 6

Displacement, tons	75 (Nos 3 and 4: 70)
Dimensions, feet	82 × 20 × 6
Guns	1—40 mm AA
Tubes	2—21 in torpedo launchers
Main Engines	2 diesel engines; 4 000 bhp = 31 knots
Complement	18

Authorised under the 1953 fiscal year programme. Nos. 1 and 2 have wooden hulls, Nos. 5 and 6 have steel hulls, and Nos. 3 and 4 have light metal hulls. Builders: Azuma Zosen Co (Nos 5 and 6), Hitachi Zosen Co (Nos. 1 and 2), and Mitsubishi Zosen Co (Nos. 3 and 4). Numbers 801 to 809 were assigned on 1 Sep 1957.

PT 1   *1969 Japanese Maritime Self Defence Force, Official*

SUBMARINE RESCUE VESSEL   (ASR)

FUSHIMI ASR 402

Displacement, tons	1 430 standard
Dimensions, feet	249·5 × 41 × 12
Main engines	Diesel; 3 000 bhp = 16 knots

Building by Sumnitomo SB & Machinery Co, laid down on 5 Nov 1968. Will have a rescue chamber and two decompression tanks.

FUSHIMI (official sketch)   *1970, Official*

CHIHAYA ASR 401

Displacement, tons	1 340 standard
Dimensions, feet	239·5 × 39·3 × 12·7
Main Engines	Diesels; 2 700 bhp = 15 knots
Complement	90

Authorised under the 1959 fiscal year programme. The first vessel of her kind to be built in Japan. Laid down on 15 Mar 1960. Launched by Mitsubishi Nippon Heavy Industries Co, Yokohama on 4 Oct 1960. Completed on 15 Mar 1961. Has rescue chamber, decompression chamber, and four-point mooring equipment.

CHIHAYA   *1968, Japanese Maritime Self-Defence Force, Official*

DRONE TARGET CARRIER

KUSU PF 281 (ex-USS *Ogden*, PF 39)

Displacement, tons	1 450 standard; 2 415 full load
Dimensions, feet	285·5 wl, 304 oa × 37·5 × 13·7 max
Guns, AA	2—40 mm; 6—20 mm
Main engines	Triple expansion; 2 shafts; 5 500 ihp = 18 knots
Boilers	2 three-drum type; 240 psi

Former "Tree" class frigate, ex-US "Tacom" type patrol frigate, converted to Drone Target Carrier in 1964. The drone target carrier *Hamagiku* (ex-415, ex-USS *LSSL* 87) former US landing ship support, was deleted from the list in 1967.

ICEBREAKER   (AGB)

FUJI 5001

Displacement, tons	5 250 standard; 7 760 normal; 8 566 full load
Dimensions, feet	328 × 72·2 × 29
Aircraft	3 helicopters
Main engines	4 diesel-electric; 2 shafts; 12 000 shp = 16 knots
Radius, miles	5 000 at 15 knots
Complement	200 plus 35 scientists and observers

Antarctic Support Ship. Built by Tsurumi Shipyard, Yokohama, Nippon Kokan Kabushiki Kaisha. Laid down on 28 Aug 1964, launched on 18 Mar 1965, delivered on 15 July 1965. Hangar and flight deck aft. Named after the mountain.

FUJI   *1968, Japanese Maritime Self-Defence Force, Official*

SALVAGE VESSEL

SHOBO 41

Displacement, tons	45
Dimensions, feet	75 × 18 × 3·3
Main engines	4 diesels; Speed = 19 knots

A new fire defence boat. Built by Azumo Zosen, Yokosuka. Completed 28 Feb 1964.

PATROL BOATS

SHOOKAI 1, 2, 3, 4, 5, 6, 7   SHOOKAI 11, 12, 13, 14, 15, 16, 17

Displacement, tons	18
Dimensions, feet	45·5 × 13·7 × 3·2
Main Engines	2 diesels; 450 bhp = 16 knots

These vessels were transferred to Japan under the MAP programme in 1958.

TANK LANDING SHIPS

New Construction: 1 landing ship of 1 450 tons is in the 1971 Programme.

OOSUMI 4001   **SHIMOKITA** 4002   **SHIRETOKO** 4003

Displacement, tons	1 650 standard; 4 080 full load
Dimensions, feet	316 wl; 348 oa × 50 × 14
Guns	7—40 mm AA; 2—20 mm AA
Main engines	GM diesels; 2 shafts; 1 700 bhp = 11 knots
Complement	70

Former US *Dagget County, LST 689, Hillsdale County, LST 835,* and *Nansemond County, LST 1064,* built by Jeffersonville B. & M. Co, Ind; American Bridge Co, Ambridge; Pa, and Bethlehem Steel Co, Hingham, Mass. respectively, in 1954-55. Commissioned in the Japanese MSDF on 1 Apr 1961. Named after homeland peninsulars. A photograph of *Oosumi* appears in the 1962-63 to 1966-67 editions.

SHIRETOKO   *1967, Japanese Maritime Self-Defence Force, Official*

MEDIUM LANDING SHIP

LSM 3001 (ex-French *LSM 9013,* ex-USS *LSM 125*)

Displacement, tons	743 beaching; 1 095 full load
Dimensions, feet	196·5 wl; 203·5 oa × 34·5 × 5·2 beaching; (8·5 max)
Guns	2—40 mm AA; 6—20 mm AA
Main engines	Diesels; 2 shafts; 2 800 bhp = 12 knots
Complement	50

Transferred from USA to France in 1954 for use in Indo-China. Returned by France in 1957 to USA, and then transferred to Japan in 1958.

LSM 3001   *1971, Japanese Maritime Self-Defence Force, Official*

HIGH SPEED BOATS   *(Kosoku)*

KOSOKU 4   **KOSOKU 5**

Displacement, tons	26
Dimensions, feet	75·5 × 18 × 2·5
Main Engines	2 Packard engines; 3 000 bhp = 40 knots

Of aluminium construction. Laid down on 10 Oct 1958 and 11 Dec 1958 at Mitsubishi, Shimonoseki Works under the 1957 and 1958 Programme, launched on 11 **Dec** 1958 and 2 Mar 1959, and completed on 11 May 1959 and 12 June **1959**. respectivley. Pennant Nos. ASH 04 and 05.

KOSOKU 1   **KOSOKU 2**   **KOSOKU 3**

Displacement, tons	30
Dimensions, feet	65·7 × 17 × 2·7
Main Engines	2 Packard petrol engines; 3 000 bhp = 42 knots

ASH category. Of wooden construction. Former names of Kosoku 1 and 2 were YS 03, YS 04 as service craft. All are Maritime Delf-Sefence Force auxiliaries.

KOSOKU 22, 23, 24, 25, 26, 27, 28, 30

Displacement, tons	30
Dimensions, feet	63·2 × 15·2 × 6
Main Engines	2 petrol engines; 1 200 bhp = 33·5 knots

ASH 22-26 transferred under MAP in 1958-59, 27-30 in 1961-62.

MINESWEEPER TENDERS   (MST)

HAYASE

Displacement, tons	2 000 standard
Guns	2—3 in (76 mm); 2—20 mm
Torpedo tubes	6 anti-submarine warfare type

This minesweeper tender of Type 462 is in the 1971 new construction programme. She will be generally similar to the new Type 951 minelayer.

HAYATOMO (ex-USS *Hamilton County, LST* 802) MST 461

Displacement, tons	1 650 standard; 4 080 full load
Dimensions, feet	316 wl; 328 oa × 50 × 14
Guns	7—40 mm AA; 2—20 mm AA (original armament)
Main engines	GM diesels; 2 shafts; 1 700 bhp = 11 knots

Former US tank landing ship. Built by Jeffersonville B. & M. Co, Jeffersonville. Ind. Laid down on 2 Sep 1944, launched on 19 Oct 1944 and completed on 13 Nov 1944. Purchased from the US Navy on 30 June 1960. Rated as MSC Tender.

HAYATOMO   *1963, Tatuo Kamino*

2 "MIHO" CLASS

MIHO (ex-USS *FS* 524)   **NASAMI** (ex-USS *FS* 408)

Displacement, tons	706
Dimensions, feet	177 × 30 × 10
Main Engines	Diesels; 2 shafts; 1 000 bhp = 11 knots

Transferred from the United States in 1955. *Nasami* is rated as a minesweeper tender (MST). *Miho,* formerly rated as ASS, was refitted as an inshore minesweeper depot ship in August 1959. A photograph of *Nasami* appears in the 1957-58 edition.

LANDING CRAFT

LCU 2001   LCU 2002   LCU 2003   LCU 2004   LCU 2005   LCU 2006

Displacement, tons   187

Former US Navy LCU 1602, 1603, 1604, 1605, 1606 and 1607 transferred under MAP

42 Ex-U.S. LCM TYPE

LCM 1001—1042

Displacement, tons   22

55 landing craft comprising 6 LCUs of 187 tons, 29 LCMs of 22 tons and 20 LCVPs of 8 tons were transferred from the United States on 2 June 1955. 13 LCMs, Nos 1030—1042, were transferred from the United States under MAP in 1961.

OILERS   (AO)

HAMANA

Displacement, tons	2 900 light; 7 550 full load
Dimensions, feet	420 × 51·5 × 20·5
Guns	2—40 mm AA
Main Engines	Diesel; 5 000 bhp = 16 knots

Built by Uraga Dock Co under the 1960 programme. Laid down on 17 Apr 1961 launched on 24 Oct 1961, and completed on 10 Mar 1962. Named after the lake.

HAMANA   *Japanese Maritime Self-Defence Force, Official*

TOBA

Displacement, tons	390
Dimensions, feet	126·7 × 28 × 12
Main Engines	1 diesel; 1 200 bhp = 11 knots

AST category. Of wooden construction. Former name was LT 392.

SUMA

Displacement, tons	115
Dimensions, feet	70·5 × 19 × 5
Main Engines	1 diesel; 600 bhp = 12 knots

ATR category. Steel construction. Former name YLT 749. The small harbour tugs YTL 162, 167, 203, 244, 748, 749 and 750 were transferred by the USA.

MARITIME SAFETY AGENCY

Established in May 1948.   *Director General:* Takeshi Tsutsume   Personnel 1971: 11 000

LARGE PATROL VESSELS
2 "IZU" CLASS

IZU PL 31   **MIURA** PL 32

Displacement, tons	2 080 normal
Dimensions, feet	295·3 wl × 38 × 12·8
Main engines	Diesel ; 2 shafts; 10 400 bhp = 21·6 knots
Radius, miles	14 700 at 12·7 knots; 5 000 at 21 knots
Complement	72

Izu was laid down in Aug 1966, launched in Jan 1967 and completed in July 1967. *Miura*, built by Maizuru Jukogyo Ltd, was laid down in May 1968, launched in Oct 1968 and completed in Mar 1969. Employed in long range rescue and patrol and weather observation duties. Equipped with weather observation radar, various types of marine instruments. Ice proof hull for winter work. A photograph of *Izu* appears in the 1968-69 and 1969-70 editions.

MIURA   *1970, Japanese Maritime Safety Agency, Official*

ERIMO PL 13   **SATSUMA** PL 14

Displacement, tons	1 009 normal (official figures)
Dimensions, feet	239·5 wl × 30·2 × 9·9
Guns	1—3 in, 50 cal; 1—20 mm AA
Main Engines	Diesels; 2 shafts; 4 800 bhp = 19·78 knots

Both built by Hitachi Zosen Co Ltd. *Erimo* was laid down on 29 Mar 1965, launched on 14 Aug 1965 and completed on 30 Nov 1965. Her structure is strengthened against ice. Employed as a patrol vessel off northern Japan. *Satsuma*, completed on 30 July 1966, is assigned to guard and rescue south of Japan; she is not particularly strengthened against ice.

SATSUMA   *1970, Japanese Maritime Safety Agency, Official*

KOJIMA PL 21

Displacement, tons	1 100
Dimensions, feet	228·3 × 33·8 × 10·5
Guns	1—3 In; 1—40 mm AA; 1—20 mm AA
Main Engines	Diesels; 2 600 hp = 17 knots
Complement	17 officers, 42 men, 47 cadets

Maritime Safety Agency training ship. Completed on 21 May 1964 at Kure Zosen.

KOJIMA   *1965, Japanese Maritime Safety Agency, Official*

Large Patrol Vessels—*continued*
2 "NOJIMA" CLASS

NOJIMA PL 11   **OJIKA** PL 12

Displacement, tons	950 standard; 980 normal; 1 100 full load
Dimensions, feet	208·8 pp; 226·5 oa × 30·2 × 10·5
Main Engines	2 sets diesels; 3 000 bhp = 17·5 knots
Complement	51

Nojima was built by Uraga Dock Co Ltd. Laid down on 27 Oct 1961, launched on 12 Feb 1962, and completed on 30 Apr 1962. *Ojika* was completed on 10 June 1963 Both employed as patrol vessels and weather ships.

NOJIMA   *1968, Japanese Maritime Safety Agency, Official*

2 "MUROTO" CLASS

DAIO PL 02   **MUROTO** PL 01

Displacement, tons	750 standard; 840 normal
Dimensions, feet	182 pp; 200 oa × 30·5 × 10·2
Guns	1—3 in, 50 cal; 2—20 mm AA
Main engines	2—4 cycle single acting diesels; 1 500 bhp = 15·37 knots

Muroto, built by Uraga Dock Company Ltd, Tokyo, was laid down on 16 Aug 1949, launched on 5 Dec 1949, and delivered on 20 Mar 1950. Vertical tubular donkey boiler, three generators, wireless, radar, direction finder, echo-sounder, streamlined bridge wings.

MUROTO   *1970, Japanese Maritime Safety Agency, Official*

SOYA PL 107

Displacement, tons	4 364 normal; 4 818 full load
Dimensions, feet	259·2 wl × 51·9 (*including bulge*) × 18 9
Aircraft	4 helicopters (see *Notes*)
Main Engines	2 sets diesels; 4 800 bhp = 12·5 knots on trials
Radius, miles	16 400 at 11 knots
Complement	96

Originally a Lighthouse Supply Ship and Navigational Aid Vessel (LL) but converted by Nippon Kokan Kabashiki Kaisha, Asano into a South Pole Research Ship. Her first conversion, begun on 12 Mar 1956 was completed on 10 Oct 1956. The second conversion, begun on 1 July 1957, was completed on 30 Sep 1957. The third conversion was completed on 5 Oct 1958. She carried two Sikorsky S—58 helicopters and two Bell 47G-2 helicopters on a flight platform laid on the quarter deck for exploration and surveying in the Antarctic. She was designed for breaking ice more than 4 feet thick. Upon completion of her Antarctic research mission in 1963 she was assigned to guard and rescue service as a patrol vessel.

SOYA   *1970, Japanese Maritime Safety Agency, Official*

MEDIUM PATROL VESSELS
3 "KUNASHIRI" CLASS

KUNASHIRI PM 65   **MINABE** PM 66   PM 67

Displacement, tons	498 normal
Dimensions, feet	190·4 oa × 24 ·2 × 7·9
Guns	1—20 mm AA
Main engines	2 sets diesels; 2 600 bhp = 17·6 knots
Radius, miles	3 000 at 16·9 knots
Complement	40

Kunashiri was built by Maizuru Jukogyo Ltd. Laid down in Oct 1968, launched in Dec 1968 and completed in Mar 1969. *Minabe*, laid down in Oct 1969, and completed in Mar 1970. Sister ship under construction at *Maizura* was scheduled to be completed in Mar 1971.

KUNASHIRI   *1970, Japanese Maritime Safety Agency, Official*

5 "CHIFURI" CLASS

CHIFURI PM 18   **KOZU** PM 20   **SHIKINE** PM 21
DAITO PM 22   **KUROKAMI** PM 19

Displacement, tons	465 standard; 483 normal
Dimensions, feet	169 pp; 177 wl × 25·2 × 8·5 (normal)
Guns	1—3 in 50 cal; 1—20 mm AA
Main engines	2 sets diesels; 1 300 bhp = 15·8 knots
Radius, miles	4 400 at 12 knots

A photograph of *Chifuri* appears in the 1962-63 to 1965-66 editions.

DAITO   *1970, Japanese Maritime Safety Agency, Official*

14 "REBUN" CLASS

AMAKUSA	PM 09	**HIRADO**	PM 17	**NOTO**	PM 13
GENKAI	PM 07	**IKI**	PM 05	**OKI**	PM 06
HACHIJO	PM 08	**KOSHIKI**	PM 16	**OKUSHIRI**	PM 10
HEKURA	PM 14	**KUSAKAKI**	PM 11	**REBUN**	PM 04
		MIKURA	PM 15	**RISHIRI**	PM 12

Displacement, tons	450 standard; 488 trials; 495 normal
Dimensions, feet	155·2 pp; 164 wl; 170 oa × 26·5 × 8·5
Guns	1—3 in 50 cal; 1—20 mm AA
Main engines	2 sets diesels; 1 300 bhp = 15 knots
Radius, miles	3 000 at 12 knots

A development of the original "Awaji" class medium patrol vessel design. All completed in 1951. A photograph of *Mikura* appears in the 1961-62 to 1964-65 editions, and of *Genkai* in the 1963-64 to 1965-66 editions.

HACHIJO   *1969, Japanese Maritime Safety Agency, Official*

Medium Patrol Vessels—*continued*
3 "AWAJI" CLASS

AWAJI PM 01   **MIYAKE** PM 02   **SADO** PM 03

Displacement, tons	510 standard; 550 normal
Dimensions, feet	172 oa × 26·7 × 9·2
Guns	1—3 in 50 cal; 1—20 mm AA
Main engines	2 sets diesels; 1 300 bhp = 15 knots
Radius, miles	3 000 at 12 knots

Of a design resembling United States Coast Guard Cutters. All completed in 1950. A photograph of *Awaji* appears in the 1962 63-and 1963-64 editions and of *Sado* in the 1966-67 to 1970-71 editions.

MIYAKE   *1971, Maritime Safety Agency*

5 "MATSUURA" CLASS

AMAMI PM 62   **MATSUURA** PM 60   **SENDAI** PM 61
KARATSU PM 64   **NATORI** PM 63

Displacement, tons	420 standard; 425 normal
Dimensions, feet	163·3 pp; 181·5 oa × 23 × 7·5
Guns	1—20 mm AA
Main engines	2 sets diesels; 1 400 bhp = 16·5 knots (*Matsuura, Sendai*); 1 800 bhp = 16·8 knots (*Amami, Natori*); 2 600 bhp (*Karatsu*)
Radius, miles	3 500 at 13 knots
Complement	37

Matsuura and *Sendai* were built by Osaka Shipbuilding Co Ltd. *Matsuura* was laid down on 16 Oct 1960, launched on 24 Dec 1960 and completed on 18 Mar 1961. *Sendai* was laid down on 23 Aug 1961, launched on 18 Jan 1962 and completed on 21 Apr 1962. *Amami*, completed on 29 Mar 1965. *Natori*, completed in 1966, and *Karatsu*, delivered to MSA on 31 Mar 1967, were built by Hitachi Zosen Co Ltd.

MATSUURA   *1970, Japanese Maritime Safety Agency, Official*

TESHIO PM 53

Displacement, tons	421·5 normal
Dimensions, feet	149·4 pp; 159 wl × 23 × 8·2
Guns	1—40 mm AA
Main engines	2 sets diesels; 1 400 bhp = 15·71 knots
Radius, miles	3 690 at 12 knots
Complement	37

Built by Uraga Dock Co Ltd. Laid down on 15 Sep 1954, launched on 12 Jan 1955, completed on 19 Mar 1955. Photograph in the 1962-63 to 1965-66 editions.

6 "YAHAGI" CLASS

CHITOSE PM 56   **SORACHI** PM 57   **YAHAGI** PM 54
HORONAI PM 59   **SUMIDA** PM 55   **YUBARI** PM 58

Displacement, tons	333·15 standard; 375·7 normal
Dimensions, feet	147·3 pp; 157·2 wl × 24 × 7·4 (normal)
Guns	1—40 mm AA
Main engines	2 sets diesels; 1 400 bhp = 15·5 knots
Radius, miles	4 000 at 12 knots
Complement	37

All built by Niigata Engineering Co Ltd. *Yahagi* was laid down on 9 Dec 1955, launched on 19 May 1956 and completed on 31 July 1956. *Sumida* was completed on 30 June 1957. *Chitose* was laid down on 20 Sep 1957, launched on 24 Feb 1958 and completed on 30 Apr 1958. *Sorachi* was completed in Mar 1959, *Yubari* on 15 Mar 1960, *Horonai* on 4 Feb 1961. A photograph of *Yahagi* appears in the 1959-60 and 1960-61 editions, and of *Chitose* in the 1961-62 to 1966-67 editions.

HORONAI   *1967, Japanese Maritime Safety Agency, Official*

Medium Patrol Vessels—*continued*
2 "TOKACHI" CLASS

TATSUTA PM 52   **TOKACHI** PM 51

Displacement, tons	336 standard; 381 normal (*Tokachi*)
	324 standard; 369 normal (*Tatsuta*)
Dimensions, feet	157·5 pp; 164 wl; 170 oa × 21·9 × 11·2
Guns	1—40 mm AA
Main engines	2 sets of 4 cycle single acting diesels
	1 500 bhp ≈ 16 knots (max); 12 knots (service) (*Tokachi*)
	1 400 bhp = 15 knots (max); 12 knots (service) (*Tatsuta*)
Radius, miles	3 824 at 12 knots (*Takachi*); 3 930 at 12 knots (*Tatsuta*)
Complement	37

Tokachi was built by Harima Dockyard, Kure. Laid down on 14 Nov 1953, launched on 8 May 1954 and completed on 31 July 1954. *Tatsuta* was completed on 10 Sep 1954. A photograph of *Tokachi* appears in the 1962-63 to 1966-67 editions.

TATSUTA   *1967, Japanese Maritime Safety Agency, Official*

SMALL PATROL VESSELS
3 "NAGARA" CLASS

KITAKAMI PS 20   **NAGARA** PS 18   **TONE** PS 19

Displacement, tons	260
Dimensions, feet	131·2 × 23 × 7·2
Guns	1—40 mm AA
Main engines	2 diesels; 2 shafts; 800 bhp = 13·5 knots
Radius, miles	2 000 at 12 knots
Complement	35

Improved versions of the "Kuma" class. All launched and completed in 1952.

NAGARA   *1970 Japanese Maritime Safety Agency, Official*

17 "KUMA" CLASS

ABUKUMA	PS 08	**KIKUCHI**	PS 10	**NOSHIRO**	PS 13
CHIKUGO	PS 16	**KISO**	PS 14	**OYODO**	PS 07
FUJI	PS 02	**KUMA**	PS 01	**SAGAMI**	PS 06
ISHIKARI	PS 05	**KUMANO**	PS 17	**SHINANO**	PS 15
ISUZU	PS 04	**KUZURYU**	PS 09	**TENRYU**	PS 03
		MOGAMI	PS 11	**YOSHINO**	PS 12

Displacement, tons	258 standard; 275 normal
Dimensions, feet	122 pp; 126·3 wl; 132·2 oa × 23 × 7·5
Guns	1—40 mm AA
Main engines	2 sets diesels; 800 bhp = 13·6 knots
Radius, miles	2 000 at 12 knots
Complement	35

Kuma was built by Nippon Kokan Kabushiki Kaisha, Tsurumi Dockyard, laid down on 29 Sep 1950, launched on 12 Jan 1951 and completed on 24 Mar 1951.

MOGAMI   *1970, Japanese Maritime Safety Agency, Official*

Small Patrol Vessels—*continued*
13 "HIDAKA" CLASS

ASHITAKA	PS 43	**IBUKI**	PS 45	**ROKKO**	PS 35
AKIYOSHI	PS 37	**KAMUI**	PS 41	**TAKANAWA**	PS 36
HIDAKA	PS 32	**KUNIMI**	PS 38	**TAKATSUKI**	PS 39
HIYAMA	PS 33	**KURAMA**	PS 44	**TOUMI**	PS 46
				TSURUGI	PS 34

Displacement, tons	166·2 to 164·4 standard; 169·4 normal
Dimensions, feet	100 pp, 111 oa · 20·8 × 5·5
Main engines	1 set diesels; 1 shaft; 690 to 700 bhp = 13·5 knots
Radius, miles	1 100 at 12 knots

Hidaka was built by Azuma Shipbuilding Co. Laid down on 4 Oct 1961, launched on 2 Mar 1962 and completed on 23 Apr 1962. Both *Hiyama* and *Tsurugi* were completed in Mar 1963 by Hitachi Shipbuilding Co. *Kunimi* was built under the 1964 fiscal year programme by Hayashikane Shipbuilding & Engineering Co, Shimoneseki, laid down on 15 Nov 1964, launched on 19 Dec 1964 and completed on 15 Feb 1965. Three more local patrol ships were completed in 1965, two in 1966, two in 1967 and two in 1968. A photograph of *Hidaka* appears in the 1963-64 to 1965-66 editions.

TSURUGI   *1970, Japanese Maritime Safety Agency, Official*

5 SPECIAL RESCUE TYPE

AKAGI PS 40   **TSUKUBA** PS 31

Displacement, tons	65 (*Akagi* 42 normal)
Dimensions, feet	80·5 × 21·5 × 3·7; *Akagi* 78·8 oa × 17·8 × 3·2
Main engines	2 Niigata diesels; 1 800 bhp = 18·4 knots trials;
	Akagi: 2 Mercedes Benz diesels; 2 200 bhp = 28 knots
Radius, miles	230 at 15·6 knots; *Akagi*: 350 at 21 knots

Akagi and *Tsukuba* (photograph in the 1963-64 to 1965-66 editions) were built by Hitachi Zosen, Kanagawa, and completed in 1965 and on 30 Mar 1962 respectively.

ASAMA PS 47   **BIZAN** PS 42   **SHIRAMINE** PS 48

Displacement, tons	40 normal
Dimensions, feet	80·5 × 18·3 × 2·8
Guns	1 MG aft
Main engines	2 Mitsubishi diesels; 1 140 bhp = 21·6 knots
Radius, miles	400 at 18 knots

Bizan and *Asama* were built by Shimonoseki Shipyard & Engine Works, Mitsubishi Heavy Industries Ltd. Completed in Mar 1966 and in Feb 1969 respectively. *Shiramine* was built by the same shipyard and completed in Dec 1969. Of light metal construction.

The small patrol vessel *Kabashima*, PS 100, was scrapped in 1970. Of this group *Fujitaka*, PS 151, and *Hayabusa*, PS 153, were deleted from the list in 1965, and *Komadori*, PS 152, in 1966.

The six small patrol vessels of the "Kawachidori" type, *Asachidori, Hamachidori, Haruchidori, Miochidori, Sawachidori* and *Tomochidori* were officially deleted from the list in 1969. Previous disposals were *Namichidori* and *Sayochidori* in 1965, *Okichidori* and *Shimachidori* in 1966, *Kawachidori, Musachidori* and *Iwachidori* in 1967 and *Wakachidori* and *Isochidori* in 1968.

BIZAN   *1967, Japanese Maritime Safety Agency, Official*

FIRE FIGHTING CRAFT

2 "HIRYU" CLASS

HIRYU FL 01   **NANRYU** FL 03   **SHYORYU** FL 02

Displacement, tons	251 normal
Dimensions, feet	90·2 oa × 34·1 × 7·2
Main engines	2 sets diesels; 2 200 bhp = 13·5 knots
Radius, miles	395 at 13·4 knots
Complement	14

Hiryu, a catamaran type fire boat, was built by Nippon Kokan Kabushiki Kaisha, Asano Dockyard. Laid down in Oct 1968, launched in Feb 1969 and completed in Mar 1969. Designed and built for fire fighting services to large tankers. Seven water nozzles (6 000 1/min × 2, 3 000 1/min × 4 and 1 800 1/min ×1) are installed and fire extinguishing foamy liquid of 14·5 cubic meters is carried and to be discharged from these nozzles. A sister ship, *Shoryu* was completed in Mar 1970, and a third vessel *Nanryu*, in Mar 1971, both at the same Asano dockyard.

HIRYU   *1970, Japanese Maritime Safety Agency, Official*

PATROL CRAFT

7 "SHINONOME" CLASS   3 "HANAYUKI" CLASS

ASAGUMO	PC 34	**ISOYUKI**	PC 39	**NATSUGUMO**	PC 35
HANAYUKI	PC 37	**MAKIGUMO**	PC 32	**SHINONOME**	PC 30
HATAGUMO	PC 31	**MINEYUKI**	PC 38	**TATSUGUMO**	PC 36
				YAEGUMO	PC 33

Displacement, tons	43 to 46 normal (*Hanayuki* 37 to 40)
Dimensions, feet	69 × 17·2 × 3·2 (*Hatagumo, Makigumo, Shinonome, Yaegumo, Asagumo, Natsugumo, Tatsugumo*)
	68·9 oa × 16·7 × 3·1 (*Hanayuki, Mineyuki, Isoyuki*)
Main engines	2 diesels; 1 400 bhp = 20 knots
	2 diesels; 1 000 bhp = 18·8 knots (*Shinonome*)
	2 diesels; 1 500 bhp = 21 knots (*Hanayuki* class)
Complement	9 to 10

Isoyuki on 29 Feb 1960, *Hanayuki* and *Mineyuki* in Mar 1959, *Asagumo* on 15 Mar 1955, *Natsugumo* on 31 Mar 1955, *Tatsugumo* on 31 May 1955 and the others before Oct 1954. Of light alloy framework and wooden hulls.

HANAYUKI   *1970, Japanese Maritime Safety Agency, Official*

16 "MATSUYUKI" CLASS

ASAGIRI	PC 47	**SHIMAYUKI**	PC 41	**PC 48**		**PC 52**	
HAMAYUKI	PC 43	**TAMAYUKI**	PC 42	**PC 49**		**PC 53**	
KOMAYUKI	PC 45	**UMIGIRI**	PC 46	**PC 50**		**PC 54**	
MATSUYUKI	PC 40	**YAMAYUKI**	PC 44	**PC 51**		**PC 55**	

Displacement, tons	40 normal
Dimensions, feet	65·6 wl × 16·7 × 3·2
Guns	One 13 mm AA
Main engines	Two Mercedes Benz diesels; 2 200 bhp = 25·8 knots
Radius, miles	244 at 24·8 knots
Complement	10

Since 1964 two or three craft of this type have been built per year by Hitachi Kanagawa Factory, *Yamayuki* and *Komoyuki* in 1966-67. Built of light alloy frame-work and wooden hulls to give considerably reduced weight and increased speed. Four further craft of this type were completed in Mar 1970, and four in Mar 1971.

The ex-US PT boat *Hiryu*, was officially deleted from the list in 1969, as were PC 12, 16, 17, 18, 21 and 23, and all 24 craft of the "Hatsunami" type. Names, photographs and details appear in the 1969-70 edition. General purpose launch *Matsuki* was also discarded in 1970.

SURVEYING VESSELS

TENYO HM 05

Displacement, tons	181
Dimensions, feet	95 × 19·2 × 9·2
Main engines	Diesels; 230 bhp = 10 knots
Radius, miles	3 160 at 10 knots

HEIYO HM 04

Displacement, tons	69
Dimensions, feet	73·5 × 14·5 × 8
Main engines	Diesel; 150 bhp = 9 knots
Radius, miles	670 at 9 knots

Completed by Shimuzu Dockyard of Nippon Kokan Kabushiki Kaisha in Mar 1955. There are 21 other smaller vessels of HS type ranging from 5 to 8 tons displacement.

MEIYO HL 03

Displacement, tons	486 normal
Measurement, tons	360 gross
Dimensions, feet	133 wl; 146 oa × 26·5 × 9·5
Main engines	1 set diesel; 700 bhp = 12 knots
Radius, miles	4 500 at 10 knots
Complement	40

Built by Nagoya Shipbuilding & Engineering Co, Nagoya. Laid down on 14 Sep 1962, launched 22 Dec 1962 and completed 15 Mar 1963. Controllable pitch propeller. The old *Meiyo* (HL 01) was discarded on 1 Mar 1963 and replaced by the new *Meiyo*, HL 03.

MEIYO   *1971, Maritime Safety Agency*

TAKUYO HL 02

Displacement, tons	880 standard; 930 normal
Dimensions, feet	185 pp; 192·8 wl × 31·2 × 10·7 normal
Main engines	2 sets diesels; 1 300 bhp = 14 knots max
Radius, miles	8 000 at 12 knots

Built for the Maritime Safety Agency, by Niigata Engineering Co Ltd. Laid down on 19 May 1956, launched on 19 Dec 1956, and completed in March 1957.

TAKUYO   *1971, Japanese Maritime Safety Agency, Official*

KAIYO HM 06

Displacement, tons	378 normal
Dimensions, feet	132·5 wl; 146 oa × 26·5 × 7·8
Main engines	1 set diesels; 450 bhp = 12 knots
Radius, miles	6 100 at 11 knots

Built by Nagoya Shipbuilding & Engineering Co, Nagoya. Completed on 14 Mar 1964. Rated as Medium Surveying Vessel. Controllable pitch propeller.

TENDERS

WAKAKUSA   *1971, Maritime Safety Agency*

WAKAKUSA LL 01

Displacement, tons	1 815
Dimensions, feet	204 × 32·2 × 19·1
Main engines	1 850 hp

Built by Hitachi Innoshima Dockyard-in Mar 1946. Purchased from Osaka Shosen Kaisha, in Jan 1956. Rated as Navigation Aid Vessel (Lighthouse Supply Ship).

GINGA LL 12   HOKUTO LL 11   KAIO LL 13

Displacement, tons	500
Dimensions	128·7 × 31·2 × 13·9
Main engines	2 diesels; 420 bhp = 11·26 knots
Radius, miles	2 800 ·miles at 10 knots

The above three are not sister ships. The above particulars refer to *Ginga* which was built by Osaka Shipbuilding Co Ltd. Laid down on 11 Nov 1953, launched on 6 May 1954 and completed on 30 June 1954. Equipped with 15 ton derrick for laying buoys. Rated as Navigation Aid Vessels (Buoy Tenders). A photograph of *Ginga* appears in the 1955-56 to 1964-65´editions.

There are also 7 LMs (LM 101 to LM 109) and 15 navigation and buoy tenders for miscellaneous service.

GINGA   *1971, Maritime Safety Agency*

MYOJO LM 11

Displacement, tons	318 normal
Dimensions, feet	78·8 pp; 87·1 oa × 39·4 × 8·8
Main engines	2 sets diesels; 600 bhp = 11·1 knots
Radius, miles	3 697 at 10 knots

Built by Nippon Kokan Kabushiki Kaisha, Asano Dockyard. Laid down in Nov 1966, launched in Feb 1967 and delivered in Mar 1967. The first catamaran type buoy tender, propelled by controllable pitch propeller, this ship is employed in maintenance and position adjustment service to floating aids to navigation.

There are also 8 LM's for the same maintenance service, 87 LS's and 18 HS's. Eight LS class tenders were scrapped and eight replacements built, and one was purchased.

MYOJO   *1970, Japanese Maritime Safety Agency, Official*

UNDERWATER RESEARCH VESSEL

SHINKAI HU 06

Displacement, tons	91
Dimensions, feet	54·2 oa × 21·6 × 13
Main engines	1 set electric motor; 11 kW
Radius, hours	4·6 at 2·3 knots in water
Complement	4

Laid down in Sept 1967, launched in Mar 1968 and completed in March 1969 by Kawasaki Heavy Industries Ltd. An underwater vehicle designed for making researches of biological and underground resources of the continental shelves. With a main propeller and two auxiliary ones installed on each side of the hull, this ship can dive into the depth of 2 000 feet and stay on the sea bed for sampling, observing and photographing.

SHINKAI   *1970, Japanese Maritime Safety Agency, Official*

COASTAL PATROL CRAFT

96 MOTOR LAUNCH TYPE

SOYOKAZE	CL 03	HATAKAZE	CL 17	KOTOKAZE	CL 31
SAWAKAZE	CL 04	MATSUKAZE	CL 18	KITAKAZE	CL 32
OKIKAZE	CL 05	IWAKAZE	CL 19	ISOKAZE	CL 33
YAMAKAZE	CL 06	NATSUKAZE	CL 20	KISOKAZE	CL 34
MINEKAZE	CL 07	YUKEKAZE	CL 21	MICHIKAZE	CL 35
UMIKAZE	CL 08	SHIMAKAZE	CL 22	TSURUKAZE	CL 36
NOKAZE	CL 09	YUKAZE	CL 23	AMATSUKAZE	CL 37
NUMAKAZE	CL 10	YODOKAZE	CL 24	KUKIKAZE	CL 38
KAWAKAZE	CL 11	ASAKAZE	CL 25	SAGIKAZE	CL 39
TANIKAZE	CL 12	YAKAZE	CL 26	SHIOKAZE	CL 40
HATSUKAZE	CL 13	KIYAKAZE	CL 27	NIIKAZE	CL 41
ARAKAZE	CL 14	IYOKAZE	CL 28	TOMOKAZE	CL 42
HARUKAZE	CL 15	FUSAKAZE	CL 29	WAKAKAZE	CL 43
SACHIKAZE	CL 16	TACHIKAZE	CL 30	and CL 44-64	
				105-171	

CL 03 to **CL 64** (62 boats) and **CL 105** to **CL 171** (34 boats)

For coastal patrol and rescue duties. *Arakaze* CL 14, of light alloy construction, was laid down in Nov 1953, launched in Feb 1954 and completed in Mar 1954. The others are of steel or wooden construction. Eight sister boats were built in 1970 and six more completed in Mar 1971.

KUKIKAZE   *1971, Maritime Safety Agency*

HARBOUR PATROL CRAFT

CS 01 to **CS 58** (52 boats) and **CS 100** to **CS 126** (14 boats)
For harbour patrol and seaward defence duties. Of various types and displacements. CS 22, 50, 53, 54 and 56 were scrapped. A photograph of this type, *Isagiku* CS 63, appears in the 1960-61 to 1964-65 editions.

SERVICE CRAFT

CR 03 to **CR 10** (10 boats) and **CR 51** for rescue service. CR 02, 09, 14, 15, 16, 17, 18 were scrapped.

SALVAGE CRAFT

FS 01 to **FS 07** (7 boats) for fire-fighting service, rescue and salvage duties.

UTILITY LAUNCHES

There are 14 local and miscellaneous boats of various sizes and employment.

KENYA
Establishment

The Kenya Navy, which is based in Mombasa, was inaugurated on 12 Dec 1964, the first anniversary of Kenya's independence.

Administration

Commander, Kenya Navy: Commander William Alan Edward Hall, RN

Mercantile Marine

Lloyd's Register of Shipping: 23 vessels of 19 013 gross

SEAWARD DEFENCE BOATS

1 BRITISH "FORD" CLASS

NYATI (ex-HMS *Aberford*) P 3102

Displacement, tons	120 standard ; 160 full load
Dimensions, feet	110·0 pp ; 117·5 oa × 20·0 × 5·0
Guns	1—40 mm Bofors AA
Main engines	Davey Paxman diesels ; 1 100 bhp = 15 knots max
Oil fuel, tons	23
Complement	19

Transferred on loan from Great Britain in 1964, but acquired outright by Kenya in 1967. *Nyati* means Buffalo. It was officially stated in Apr 1971 that *Nyati* is in reserve.

NYATI 1970, Kenya Navy, Official

PATROL CRAFT

3 BRITISH VOSPER TYPE

CHUI P 3112   **NDOVU** P 3117   **SIMBA** P 3110

Displacement, tons	96 standard ; 109 full load
Dimensions, feet	95 wl ; 103 oa × 19·8 × 5·8
Guns	2—40 mm Bofors AA
Main engines	Paxman Ventura diesels ; 2 800 bhp = 24 knots
Radius, miles	1 000 at economical speed
Complement	23 (3 officers and 20 ratings)

The first ships specially built for the Kenya Navy. Designed and built by Vosper Ltd. Portsmouth. Ordered on 28 Oct 1964. *Simba* was launched on 9 Sep 1965 and completed on 23 May 1966. *Chui* was handed over on 7 July 1966 and *Ndovu* was handed over on 27 July 1966. All three left Portsmouth on 22 Aug 1966 and arrived at their base in Mombasa on 4 Oct 1966. Air conditioned. Fitted with modern radar communications equipment and roll damping fins. *Chui* means Leopard, *Ndovu* means Elephant, *Simba* means Lion.

NDOVU 1970, Kenya Navy, Official

CHUI 1967, A. & J. Pavia

KUWAIT
Mercantile Marine

Lloyd's Register of Shipping: 133 vessels of 591 660 tons gross

PATROL BOATS

8 "78 ft" TYPE. NEW CONSTRUCTION

AL-SALEMI	AMAN	MASHHOOR	MURSHED
AL-MUBARAKI	MARZOOK	MAYMOON	WATHAH

Displacement, tons	40
Dimensions, feet	78 oa × 15·5 × 4·5 mean
Main engines	2 Rolls Royce 8-cylinder 90° V form marine diesels. 1 340 shp at 1 800 rpm, 1 116 shp at 1 700 rpm = 20 knots
Guns	1 MG
Range	700 nautical miles at 15 knots cruising speed
Complement	12 (5 officers, 7 men)

Two were built by Thornycroft before the merger and six by Vosper afterwards (first two of which were ordered from the Group on 12 Sep 1966). Designed and built by John I. Thornycroft & Co Ltd, Woolston, Southampton, *Al-Salemi* and *Al-Mubaraki* were ordered in Aug 1965 and shipped to Kuwait on 8 Sep 1966. Specially designed for operational duties in the Arabian Gulf. Hulls are of welded steel construction, with superstructures of aluminium alloy. Twin hydraulically operated rudders, giving good manoeuvrability. Decca type D.202 radar. Two Lister Blackstone air-cooled diesel generators, 220 volts.

AL-MUBARAKI 1969, Vosper-Thornycroft

AL-SALEMI 1967, courtesy Vosper Thornycroft Group

PATROL LAUNCHES

Built by the Singapore yard of Thornycroft (Malaysia) Limited, now the Tanjong Rhu, Singapore, yard of Vosper Thornycroft Uniteers Private Ltd, subsidiaries of the David Brown Corporation Ltd, and part of the Vosper Thornycroft Group. Known as 50-foot patrol craft. Completed in 1962.

LANDING CRAFT

Two 88-ft landing craft have been built for the Ministry of the Interior, Kuwait, by Vosper Thornycroft Uniteers Private Ltd, Singapore.

SIMBA (see Col 1) 1969, Kenya Navy, Official

KOREA (North)

| **Administration**
Commander of the Navy: Rear Admiral Yu Chang Kwon | **Personnel**
1971: 9 000 (800 officers and 8 200 men) | **Mercantile Marine**
Lloyd's Register of Shipping: 11 vessels of 45 556 tons gross |

SUBMARINES
2 Ex-SOVIET "W" CLASS

Displacement, tons	1 030 surface; 1 180 submerged
Dimensions, feet	240 × 12 × 15
Tubes	6—21 in (4 bow, 2 stern); 18 torpedoes carried normally (or up to 40 mines)
Main engines	Diesel-electric; 2 shafts; Diesels: 4 000 bhp = 17 knots surface; Electric motors: 2 500 hp = 15 knots submerged
Radius, miles	13 000 to 16 500
Complement	60 to 70

FLEET MINESWEEPERS
2 Ex-SOVIET "T 43" TYPE

| Displacement, tons | 500 standard; 600 full load |
| Dimensions, feet | 200 oa × 27·5 × 9 |

Fleet Minesweepers received by the North Korean Navy from the USSR. Built 1954.

8 Ex-SOVIET "FUGAS" TYPE

Displacement, tons	440 standard; 550 full load
Dimensions, feet	203·5 oa × 23·7 × 8
Guns	1—3·9 in; 1—37 mm AA
Main engines	Diesels; 2 shafts; 2 800 bhp = 18 knots

Former Soviet minesweepers built in 1935-42. Fitted for minelaying. It is reported that most, if not all, of this type have been withdrawn from active service as newer vessels have been built or acquired.

"FUGAS" CLASS   *Ziro Kimata*

PATROL VESSELS
1 Ex-SOVIET "ARTILLERIST" TYPE

Displacement, tons	240 standard; 280 full load
Dimensions, feet	160·8 × 19 × 6·7
Guns	1—3·9 in; 2—37 mm AA
A/S weapons	2 depth charge throwers
Main engines	Diesels; 2 shafts; 3 300 bhp = 22 knots

Former Soviet patrol vessel or coastal escort, rated as a submarine chaser. Built in 1943. Sister ship was deleted from the list in 1971.

4 "SHANGHAI" TYPE

Displacement, tons	100 full load
Dimensions, feet	120 × 18 × 5·5
Guns	4—37 mm (2 twin); 2—25 mm (1 twin)

Fast patrol boats or motor gunboats reported acquired from China in 1967.

4 NEW CONSTRUCTION

| Displacement, tons | circa 160 |
| Dimensions, feet | Length 125 |

Two fast submarine chasers of medium size built for the North Korean Navy.

Patrol Vessels—*continued*
10 SOVIET "SO-1" TYPE

Displacement, tons	215 light; 250 normal
Dimensions, feet	147 oa × 20 × 10
Guns	4—25 mm (2 twin)
A/S weapons	4 five barrelled launchers
Main engines	3 diesels; 3 500 bhp = 26 knots

Soviet designed craft similar to the "SO-1" class steel hulled submarine chasers.

"SO-1" Type   *1971, Official*

10 PATROL TYPE

| Displacement, tons | circa 130 |
| Dimensions, feet | Length 100 |

Small craft for seaward defence and local duties; rated as submarine chasers.

4 Ex-SOVIET "MO 1" TYPE

Displacement, tons	50
Dimensions, feet	85·5 × 13 × 4·5
Guns	2—13 mm AA MG
Main engines	2 petrol engines; 2 shafts; 1 300 bhp

Former Soviet motor launches transferred in 1954. Rated as submarine chasers.

TORPEDO BOATS
3 PTF TYPE

Fast patrol craft of the motor torpedo boat type commissioned for service in 1967-68.

40 Ex-SOVIET "P 4" TYPE

Displacement, tons	50
Dimensions, feet	85·5 × 20 × 6
Guns	4—25 mm AA
Main engines	Diesels; 2 000 bhp = 42 knots

Former Soviet motor torpedo boats. Built in 1951-57. Aluminium hulls.

"P-4" Type   *1971, Official*

FAST GUNBOATS
7 MGB TYPE

Reported to have been incorporated into the North Korean Navy since 1 Jan 1967.

4 PTG TYPE

Larger vessels of the patrol gunboat type reported to have been acquired in 1967-68.

MINESWEEPING LAUNCHES
24 INSHORE TYPE

| Displacement, tons | 20 normal |
| Dimensions, feet | Length, 50 pp |

Very small minesweeping craft for inshore, coastal, estuarial and general utility duties.

KOREA
Strength of the Fleet

Administration

Chief of Naval Operations:
Admiral Chang, Chi-Su

Vice Chief, Naval Operations:
Vice Admiral Kim, Kwang-Ok

Commander-in-Chief of Fleet:
Rear Admiral Kim, Sang-Kil

Personnel

1971: 16 600 (2 300 officers and 14 300 men)

3 Destroyers
7 Frigates (3 Destroyer Escort Type)
6 Fast Transports (ex-Destroyer Escorts)
11 Escort Vessels (3 ex-Fleet Minesweepers)
6 Patrol Vessels (Submarine Chasers)
11 Coastal Minesweepers
8 Tank Landing Ships
12 Medium Landing Ships
1 Survey Ship
13 Fleet Support Ships and Service Craft.

Diplomatic Representation

Naval Attaché in London:
Colonel Dong Ho, Kim

Naval Attaché in Washington:
Commodore Chan Kuk Pak

Mercantile Marine

Lloyd's Register of Shipping:
329 vessels of 849 457 tons gross

DESTROYERS

Name	No.	Builders	Launched	Completed
CHUNG MU (ex-USS *Erben*, DD 631)	DD 91	Bath Iron Works Corpn, Bath, Maine	21 Mar 1943	28 May 1943
PUSAN (ex-USS *Hickox*, DD 673)	DD 93	Federal SB-DD Co, Port Newark	4 July 1943	10 Sep 1943
SEOUL (ex-USS *Halsey Powell*, DD 686)	DD·92	Bethelhem Co, Staten Island	30 June 1943	25 Oct 1943

3 Ex-US "FLETCHER" TYPE

Displacement, tons	2 100 standard; 3 050 full load
Length, feet (*metres*)	360·9 (*110·0*)wl; 376·5 (*114·8*)oa
Beam, feet (*metres*)	39·5 (*12·0*)
Draught, feet (*metres*)	18·1 (*5·5*) max
Guns, dual purpose	5—5 in (*127 mm*) 38 cal
Guns, AA	6—40 mm Bofors
A/S weapons	2 fixed Hedgehogs; 1 DC rack
Torpedo tubes	5—21 in (*533 mm*) quintupled
Torpedo racks	2 side launching for A/S torpedoes
Boilers	4 Babcock & Wilcox; 634 psi (*44·6 kg/cm²*); 850°F (*454°C*)
Main engines	2 GE geared turbines; 2 shafts; 60 000 shp
Speed, knots	35 max; 12 economical sea
Radius, miles	6 000 at 15 knots
Oil fuel, tons	650
Complement	300 (18 officers, 282 men)

Former United States destroyers, *Chung Mu* (laid down on 28 Oct 1942) of the "Fletcher" class, and *Pusan* and *Seoul* of the Later "Fletcher" class, transferred to Korea in May 1963, 27 April 1968 and 15 Nov 1968 respectively.

RADAR. Search: SPS 12. Tactical: SPS 10. Fire Control: GFCS 68 with X Band.

PHOTOGRAPHS. A starboard broadside surface view of *Chung Mu* appears in the 1964-65 to 1966-67 editions.

CHUNG MU *1967, Korean Navy, Official*

FRIGATES

Name	No.	Builders	Launched	Completed
KANG WON (ex-USS *Sutton*, DE 771)	DE 72	Tampa S.B. Co	6 Aug 1944	22 Dec 1944
KYONG KI (ex-USS *Muir*, DE 770)	DE 71	Tampa S.B. Co	4 June 1944	20 Aug 1944

2 Ex-US "BOSTWICK" TYPE
DESTROYER ESCORTS

Displacement, tons	1 240 standard; 1 900 full load
Length, feet (*metres*)	306·0 (*93·2*) oa
Beam, feet (*metres*)	36·8 (*11·2*)
Draught, feet (*metres*)	14·1 (*4·3*) max
Guns, dual purpose	3—3 in (*76 mm*) 50 cal.
Guns, AA	3—40 mm; 8—20 mm
A/S weapons	8 depth charge throwers
Torpedo tubes	Removed (see notes)
Main engines	GM diesels, electric drive; 2 shafts; 6 000 hp
Speed, knots	20
Radius, miles	11 500 at 11 knots
Oil fuel, tons	300
Complement	208

Former United States destroyer escorts of the "Bostwick" class. Transferred from the United States Navy at Boston in 1956 under MDAP. Renamed after Korean States.

RADAR. Equipped with metric wavelength search radar.

TORPEDO TUBES. These ships formerly carried three 21 inch torpedo tubes in a triple mounting.

PHOTOGRAPHS. A starboard bow surface view of *Kang Won* appears in the 1967-68 to 1970-71 editions.

KIONG KI *1971, Official*

Frigates—continued

1 Ex-US "RUDDEROW" TYPE
DESTROYER ESCORT

Displacement, tons	1 450 standard; 2 230 full load
Length, feet (metres)	306·0 (93·2) oa
Beam, feet (metres)	36·8 (11·2)
Draught, feet (metres)	14·1 (4·3) max
Guns, surface	2—5 in (127 mm) 38 cal.
Guns, AA	2—40 mm; 6—20 mm
A/S weapons	8 DCT
Boilers	2 Combustion Engineering
Main engines	GE geared turbines, electric drive; 2 shafts; 12 000 shp
Speed, knots	24
Radius, miles	5 000 at 15 knots
Oil fuel, tons	378
Complement	186 (6 officers, 180 men)

Former United States destroyer escort of the "Rudderow" class transferred to Korea at Seattle, Washington, on 16 June 1963 and renamed.

RADAR. Equipped with SPS 10 tactical radar set.

Name	No.	Builders	Launched	Completed
CHUNG NAM (ex-USS Holt. DE 706)	DE 73	Defoe Shipbuilding Co, Bay City	15 Dec 1943	9 June 1944

CHUNG NAM

1971, Official

Name	No.
DUMAN (ex-USS Muskogee, PF 49)	PF 61
IMCHIN (ex-USS Sausalito, PF 4)	PF 66
NAKTONG (ex-USS Hoquiam, PF 5)	PF 65
TAE DONG (ex-USS Tacoma, PF 3)	PF 63

Builders	Laid down	Launched	Completed
Consolidated Steel Corpn	18 Sep 1943	18 Oct 1943	16 Mar 1944
Kaiser Cargo Inc	7 Apr 1943	20 July 1943	4 Mar 1944
Permanente Metals Corpn	10 Apr 1943	31 July 1943	8 May 1944
Permanente Metals Corpn	10 Mar 1943	7 July 1943	6 Nov 1944

4 Ex-US "TACOMA" TYPE

Displacement, tons	1 430 standard; 2 435 full load
Length, feet (metres)	285·5 (87·0) wl; 304 (92·7) oa
Beam, feet (metres)	37·5 (11·4)
Draught, feet (metres)	13·7 (4·2)
Guns, dual purpose	3—3 in (76 mm) 50 cal.
Guns, AA	2—40 mm; 9—20 mm
A/S weapons	6 depth charge throwers
Boilers	2; 250 psi (17·6 kg/cm²); 425°F (218°C)
Main engines	Triple expansion; 2 shafts; 5 500 ihp
Speed, knots	18
Radius. miles	9 500 at 12 knots
Oil fuel, tons	645
Complement	181 (10 officers, 171 men)

Former United States patrol frigates, PF, of the "Tacoma" class. Transferred to the USSR under the Lend-Lease scheme during the Second World War. Returned to USA after hostilities and laid up at Yokosuka naval base. Reactivated on the outbreak of the Korean War. Apnok and Duman were loaned to the Korean Navy and commissioned on 5 Nov 1950. Naktong and Taedong were transferred on 8 Oct 1951 at Yokosuka. Apnok, ex-USS Rockford (PF 48), in collision on 21 May 1952, was decommissioned, returned to the USN and expended as a target in 1953. She was replaced by Imchin.

RADAR. Equipped with metric wavelength search radar.

NAK TONG

1967, Korean Navy, Official

PHOTOGRAPHS. A photograph of Tae Dong appears in the 1963-64 to 1966-67 editions.

USS Pasco PF6 was towed to Koera in Jan 1969. probably for cannibalisation for existing frigates. Reported USS Gloucester may also be similarly handed over.

ESCORT TRANSPORTS
6 Ex-US APD (ex-DE) TYPE

ASAN (ex-USS Harry L. Corl, APD 108, ex-DE 598) APD 82
CHR JU (ex-USS William M. Hobby, APD 95, ex-DE 236) PG 87
CHUN NAM (ex-USS Hayter, APD 80, ex-DE 212) PG 86
KYONG BUK (ex-USS Kephart APD 61, ex-DE 207) PG 85
KYONG NAM (ex-USS Cavallero, APD 128, ex-DE 712) APD 81
UNG PO (ex-USS Julius A. Raven, APD 110, ex-DE 600) APD 83

Displacement, tons	1 400 standard; 2 130 full load
Dimensions, feet	300 wl; 306 oa × 37 × 12·6
Guns	1—5 in, 38 cal dp; 6—40 mm AA
Main engines	GE turbines with electric drive; 2 shafts; 12 000 bhp = 23 knots
Boilers	2 "D" Express
Oil fuel (tons)	350
Radius, miles	5 500 at 15 knots
Complement	210 plus 162 troops

Former United States high speed transports, APD, modified destroyer escorts. Kyong Nam was built by the Defoe Shipbuilding Co, Bay City, Mich. Laid down on 28 Mar 1944. Launched on 15 June 1954. Completed on 13 Mar 1945. Transferred in 1959. Asan, laid down on 19 Jan 1944 and launched on 1 Mar 1944, and Ung Po, laid down on 26 Jan 1944 and launched on 3 Mar 1944, both by Bethlehem S.B. Co. Hingham, Mass, were transferred in 1966. Ex-USS Kephart, launched 6 Sep 1943, and ex-USS William M. Hobby, launched 11 Feb 1944, both transferred May 1967 under MAP. Chun Nam transferred Aug 1967.

ESCORTS
3 Ex-US "AUK" CLASS MSF TYPE

KOJE	(ex-USS Dextrous, MSF 341)	PCE 1003
SHIN SONG	(ex-USS Ptarmigan, MSF 376)	PCE 1001
SUNCHON	(ex-USS Speed, MSF 116)	PCE 1002

Displacement, tons	890 standard; 1 250 full load
Dimensions, feet	215 wl; 221 oa × 32·2 × 10·8 max
Guns	2—3 in, 50 cal dp (single); 4—40 mm AA (2 twin); 4—20 mm AA (2 pairs)
Tubes	3—21 In (pyramided)
A/S weapons	4 DCT (single) 2 DC tracks; 1 hedgehog
Main engines	2 GM diesel electric; 2 shafts; 3 532 bhp = 18 knots
Complement	117 total accommodation

Former United States steel-hulled fleet minesweepers. Shin Song was built by the Savannah Machinery & Foundry Co. Laid down on 9 Mar 1944, launched on 15 July 1944 and completed on 15 Jan 1945. Transferred from the US to the Republic of Korea Navy on 25 July 1963 at Seattle, Washington. Employed as a patrol escort ships (PCE).

KYONG NAM

1967, Korean Navy, Official

SHIN SONG

1964, Korean Navy, Official

Escorts—continued

8 Ex-US "180ft" STEEL PCE TYPE

HAN SAN (ex-USS *PCEC* 873)	PCEC 53
KOJIN (ex USS *Report* MSF 289)	PCEC 50
MYONG RYANG (ex-USS *PCEC* 896)	PCEC 52
OK PO (ex-USS *PCEC* 898)	PCEC 55
PYOK PA (ex-USS *Dania*, PCE 870)	PCE 57
RO RYANG (ex-USS *PCEC* 882)	PCEC 51
RYUL PO (ex-USS *Somerset* PCE 892)	PCE 58
SA CHON (ex-USS *Batesburg*, PCE 903)	PCE 59

Displacement, tons	640 standard; 967 full load
Dimensions, feet	180 wl; 184·5 oa × 33·1 × 10 max
Guns	1—3 in 50 cal, dp; 3—40 mm AA; 8—20 mm AA
Main engines	Diesels; 2 shafts; 2 000 bhp = 14·3 knots
Oil fuel (tons)	260
Radius, miles	4 300 at 10 knots
Complement	104

Former United States patrol ships, escorts, PCE (four were later redesignated control escorts, PCEC, on assignment to amphibious forces). Built in 1942-45 by Albina Engine and Machine Works, Portland, Oregon (*Han San*, *Pyok Pa*, *Ro Ryang*), and Willamette Iron & Steel Corp, Portland, Oregon (*Myong Ryang*, *Ok Po*, *Ryul Po*, *Sa Chan*). Transferred from the United States Navy in Feb 1955 (*Myong Ryang*, *Ro Ryang*), on loan, in 1956 (*Han Sen*, *Ok Po*) and 1961 (*Pyok Pa*, *Ryul Po*, *Sa Chon*, *Tang Po*). Sister ship *Tang Po*, PCE 56 (ex-USS *Maria*, PCE 842) was sunk by North Korean coastal batteries north of the demarcation line on 19 Jan 1967. A photograph of *Han San* appears in the 1959-60 and 1960-61 editions, and of *Ok Po* in the 1961-62 to 1966-67 editions

RO RYANG   *1967 Korean Navy, Official*

PATROL VESSELS

2 NEW CONSTRUCTION

On trials recently were two 100-ft patrol boats built in Korea for the Korean Navy equipped with Vosper stabilisers.

4 Ex-US "173 ft." STEEL PC TYPE

KUM CHONG SAN (ex-USS *Grosse Point*, PC 1546)	PC 708
MYO HYANG SAN (ex-*PC* 600)	PC 706
O TAE SAN (ex-USS *Winnemucca*, PC 1145)	PC 707
SOL AK (ex-USS *Chadron*, PC 546)	PC 709

Displacement, tons	280 standard; 450 full load
Dimensions, feet	170 wl; 173·7 oa × 23 × 10·8 max
Guns	1—3 in, 50 cal, dp; 1—40 mm AA; 4—20 mm
A/S weapons	2 ASW rocket launchers, mousetrap
Main engines	Diesels; 2 shafts; 2 880 bhp = 20 knots
Complement	71

Former United States submarine chasers, PC, of steel construction, built in 1941-42. *Kum Chong San* and *O Tae San* were transferred on loan at Seattle on 21 Nov 1960 and Nov 1 1960 respectively. *Pak Tu San*, PC 701 (ex *Ensign-Whitehead*, ex-PC 823), *Kum Kang San*, PC 702 (ex-*PC* 810) and *Sam Kak San*, PC 703 (ex-PC 802) were decommissioned on 21 Aug 1960 and scrapped. *Chirisan* PC 704, was mined and sank off Wonson, Korea, on 26 Dec 1951. *Han Ra San*, PC 705 (ex-USS PC 485) was sunk in a typhoon at Guam in Nov 1962 and although raised was scrapped in 1964. *Sol Ak* (ex-USS *Chadron*) was transferred at Guam on 22 Jan 1964.
A photograph of *Myo Hyang San* appears in the 1957-58 edition, and of *Sol Ak* in the 1964-65 to 1966-67 editions.

KUM CHONG SAN   *Korean Navy, Official*

Patrol Vessels—continued

2 Ex-US "136 ft" WOODEN PCS TYPE

HWA SEONG PCS 205 (ex-*PCS* 1448)   **KUM SEONG** PCS 202 (ex-*PCS* 1445)

Displacement, tons	251 standard; 338 full load
Dimensions, feet	130 wl; 136 oa × 24·5 × 8·5
Guns	1—40 mm; 2—20 mm
Main engines	2 GM diesels; 2 shafts; 800 bhp = 14 knots

Former United States submarine chasers, PSC type, of wooden construction, built in 1943-44. Acquired by Korea in 1952. *Suseong* PSC 201 (ex-USS *PCS* 1426) was returned to USA in Apr 1963. *Mok Seong* lent to the Hydrographic Office in Jan 1964, was returned to USN and discarded in Sept 1967.

9 Ex-CGC "95 ft" TYPE

CAPE DARBY	CAPE KIVANDA	CAPE ROSIER
CAPE FALCON	CAPE PORPOISE	CAPE SABLE
CAPE FLORIDA	CAPE PROVIDENCE	CAPE TRINITY

Displacement, tons	106
Dimensions, feet	95 × 19 × 6
Guns	1—20 mm
Main engines	4 diesels; 2 shafts; 2 200 bhp = 21 knots
Complement	14

Former Coast Guard cutters transferred to the USN, thence to Korea in 1968 and 1969. Bear designation PB in Korean service.

COASTAL MINESWEEPERS

7 Ex-US MSC TYPE

HA DONG MSC 527 (ex-*MSC* 296)	**KUM SAN** MSC 522 (ex-*MSC* 284)
KO HUNG MSC 523 (ex-*MSC* 285)	**NAM YANG** MSC 526 (ex-*MSC* 295)
KUM KOK MSC 525 (ex-*MSC* 286)	**SAM CHOK** MSC 528 (ex-*MSC* 316)

Displacement, tons	320 standard; 370 full load
Dimensions, feet	138 pp; 144 oa × 28 × 9 max
Guns	2—20 mm AA
Main engines	2 diesels; 2 shafts; 1 200 bhp = 14 knots
Complement	43

"Bluebird" class specially built by USA for transfer under the Military Aid Program. *Ko Hung* and *Kum San* were transferred to Korea in 1959, followed by *Kum Kok*, transferred at Long Beach, California, on 10 Nov 1959. *Ha Dong* and *Nam Yang* were transferred at Boston, Mass on 16 Nov 1963 and 7 Oct 1963 respectively. Both were built by Petersen Builders, Inc, Sturgeon Bay, Wisc. MSC 302 is building in USA for transfer to Korea under MAP. A photograph of *Kum Kok* appears in the 1961-62 to 1966-67 editions.
MSB 2 was transferred from the US Navy to the Korean Navy on 1 Dec 1961.

KUM SAN   *1967, Korean Navy, Official*

5 Ex-US YMS TYPE

KIM CHON MSC(O) 513	
KIM PO MSC(O) 520 (ex-USS *Kite*, ex-*MSC*(O) 22, ex-*AMS* 22, ex-*YMS* 369)	
KOCHANG MSC(O) 521 (ex-USS *Mockingbird*, ex-*MSC*(O) 22, ex-*YMS* 419)	
KUM HWA MSC(O) 519 (ex-USS *Curlew*, ex-*MSC*(O) 8, ex-*YMS* 218)	
KWANG CHE MSC(O) 503	

Displacement, tons	270 standard; 350 full load
Dimensions, feet	136 oa × 24·5 × 8 max
Guns	1—40 mm, 50 cal; 2—20·mm AA
Main engines	Diesels; 1 000 bhp = 15 knots
Complement	50

Former United States auxiliary motor minesweepers of wooden construction, built in 1941-42. All ex-YMS type. *Kum Hwa*, *Kim Po* and *Kochang* were transferred from the US Navy on 6 Sep 1956. *Kyong Chu*, MSC (O) 502 was decommissioned on 10 May 1962. *Kang Kyong* MSC(O) 510 was scrapped in 1964.

KOCHANG   *Korean Navy, Official*

TANK LANDING SHIPS

8 Ex-US LST TYPE

BI BONG LST 809 (ex-USS *LST* 218)
BUK HAN LST 815 (ex-USS *Lynn County LST* 900)
DUK BONG LST 808 (ex-*LST* 227)
HWA SAN LST 816 (ex-USS *Pender County LST* 1080)
KAE BONG LST 810 (ex-USS *Berkshire County LST* 288)
SU YONG LST 813 (ex-USS *Kane County LST* 853)
UN BONG LST 807 (ex-USS *LST* 1010)
WEE BONG LST 812 (ex-USS *Johnson County LST* 849)

Displacement, tons	1 653 standard; 2 366 beaching; 4 080 full load
Dimensions, feet	316·0 wl; 328·0 oa × 50·0 × 14·0
Guns	7—40 mm AA; 2—20 mm AA
Main engines	Diesels; 2 shafts; 1 700 bhp = 11 knots
Complement	110

Former United States tank landing ships. Cargo capacity 2 100 tons. *Duk Bong* and *Un Bong* were transferred on 22 Mar 1955 at S. Diego, *Kae Bong* on 5 May 1956 at Seattle, *Buk Han*, *Su Yong* and *Wee Bong* on 2 Dec 1958, 22 Dec 1958 and 13 Jan 1959, respectively, at Seattle, and *Hwa San* was transferred on 30 Oct 1958 at Long Beach. Photographs of *Su Yong* appear in the 1962-63 to 1970-71 editions.

KAE BONG   *1971, Official*

ROCKET LANDING SHIP

SI HUNG LSMR 311 (ex-USS *St Joseph River, LSMR* 527)

Displacement, tons	1 102 standard; 1 280 full load
Dimensions, feet	203·5 oa × 34·5 × 8·3 max
Guns	1—5 in; 2—40 mm AA; 2—20 mm AA
Launchers	8—5 in rocket projectors
Main engines	Diesels; 2 shafts; 2 800 bhp = 13 knots
Complement	142

Former US medium landing ship (rocket). Transferred to the Korean Navy at San Diego, Cal. on 15 Sep 1960. *Si Hung* means "The Beginning of Prosperity."

SI HUNG   *1967, Korean Navy, Official*

MEDIUM LANDING SHIPS

11 Ex-US LSM TYPE

BIYOUP LSM 607 (ex-USS *LSM* 96)   **PUNG DO** LSM(F)608 (ex-USS *LSM* 54)
KA DUK LSM 605 (ex-USS *LSM* 462)   **SIN-MI** LSM 612 (ex-USS *LSM* 316)
KI RIN LSM 610 (ex-USS *LSM* 19)   **TAE CHO** LSM 601 (ex-USS *LSM* 546)
KU MOON LSM 606 (ex-USS *LSM* 30)   **ULRYUNG** LSM 613 (ex-USS *LSM* 17)
NEUNG RA LSM 611 (ex-USS *LSM* 84)   **WOLMI** LSM 609 (ex-USS *LSM* 57)
                                              YEU DO LSM 602 (ex-USS *LSM* 268)

Displacement, tons	743 beaching; 1 095 full load
Dimensions, feet	196·5 wl; 203·5 oa × 34·5 × 8·5 max
Guns	1—40 mm AA; 4—20 mm AA
Main engines	Diesels, direct drive; 2 shafts; 2 880 bhp = 12·5 knots
Complement	62

LSM 19, 30, 54, 84 and 96 were transferred to the Korean Navy at Seattle in 1956. LSM 19, 84 transferred on 3 July 1956, LSM 17 on 18 Oct 1956, LSM 316 on 18 Nov 1956. *Pun Do*, (LSM(F) 608) was converted into a Mine Force Flagship. *Dok Do*, LSM 603 (ex-USS *LSM* 419) was decommissioned on 26 Feb 1963. A photograph of *Ku Moon* appears in the 1963-64 to 1966-67 editions.

YEO DO   *1967, Korean Navy, Official*

SURVEY SHIP

Hydrographic Survey Ship No. 3 (ex-USC and GSS *Hodgson*) transferred to Korea at Seattle, Washington, March 1968. This ex-YMS type, of 267 tons, 137 feet, built in 1943, is assigned to the Korean Hydrographic Office and not rated as a Navy ship.

LANDING CRAFT REPAIR SHIP

DUK SOO (ex-USS *Minotaur, ARL* 15, ex-*LST* 645)

Displacement, tons	2 366 standard; 4 100 full load
Dimensions, feet	316 wl; 328 oa × 50 × 11·2
Guns	2—40 mm AA
Main engines	GM diesels; 2 shafts; 1 800 bhp = 11·5 knots
Complement	277

Former United States landing craft repair ship. Built by Chicago Bridge & Iron Co Seneca, Del. Laid down on 20 June 1944. Launched on 20 Sep 1944. Completed on 30 Sep 1944

DUK SOO   *1963, Korean Navy. Official*

SUPPLY SHIPS

KIMHAE AKL 902   **MA SAN** AKL 909 (ex-USS *AKL* 35)
KUN-MI AKL 908   **MOCK PO** AKL 907 (ex-USCGC *Trillium, WAK* 170)
(ex-USS *Sharps, AKL* 10)   **WAEKWAN** AKL 903

Displacement, tons	520
Dimensions, feet	179 oa ×·32 × 10 max
Guns	1—40 mm AA; 2—30 mm AA
Main engines	Diesel; 2 shafts; 1 000 shp = 13 knots
Complement	43 *Kimhae*; 49 others

AKL 35 was transferred from the USA on 6 Sep 1956, *Kun San* on 3 Apr 1956, *Ma San* on 9 Sep 1956, and *Mack Po* in 1956. Ex-USS Army FS craft.

OILERS

CHUN-JI (ex-*Birk*) AO 2   **PUJON** (ex-*Hassel*) AO 3

Displacement, tons	1 400 standard; 4 160 full load
Measurement, tons	2 257 and 2 256 gross, respectively
Dimensions, feet	275 pp × 44·5 × 18·2
Guns	1—40 mm AA; 2—20 mm AA
Complement	73

Former Norwegian tankers. Both built by A/S Berken Mek Verks ·Bergen, Norway. in 1951. Taken over by Korean Navy at Rotterdam, Sep and July 1953, respectively.

KU RYONG YO 1, ex-YO 106 (ex-USS *YO* 118)

Displacement, tons	428 standard; 1 126 full load
Dimensions, feet	174 oa × 33 × 13 max
Main engines	Union diesel; 1 shaft; 500 shp = 7 knots
Complement	36

Former US self-propelled fuel oil barge. Transferred to Korea on 3 Dec 1946.

HWA CHON YO 5 (ex-*Paek Yeon*, AO 5, ex-USS *Derrick*, YO 59)

Displacement, tons	893 standard; 2 700 full load
Dimensions, feet	236 oa × 38 × 15 max
Guns	3—20 mm AA
Main engines	Fairbanks-Morse diesel; 1 shaft; 1 150 bhp = 10·5 knots
Complement	46

Former US self-propelled fuel oil barge. Loaned to Korea on 14 Oct 1955.

TUGS

DO BONG ATA 3 (ex-USS *Pinola, ATA* 206)
YONG MUN ATA 2 (ex-USS *Keosanqua, ATA* 198)

Displacement, tons	538 standard; 838 full load
Dimensions, feet	134·5 wl; 143 oa × 34 × 13·2 max
Guns	1—3 in; 4—20 mm AA
Main engines	GM diesel-electric; 1 shaft; 1 500 hp = 13·5 knots

Former United States auxiliary ocean tugs of the "Maricopa" class, ATA type. Built by Gulfport Boiler and Welding Works, Inc, Port Arthur, Texas (*Do Bong*) and Levingston Shipbuilding Co, Orange, in 1944-45. Transferred on 2 Jan 1962.

YONG MUN   *1967, Korean Navy, Official*

LAOS

Administration

Commander, Royal Lao Navy and Chief of Naval Staff:
Colonel Prince Sinthanavong Kindavong

RIVER PATROL CRAFT

7 LCM (6) Type	28 tons	4 in commission, 3 in reserve
6 Cabin Type	21 tons	2 in commission, 4 in reserve
2 Chris Craft Type	15 tons	2 in commission
12 11 metre Type	10 tons	5 in commission, 7 in reserve
8 8 metre Type	6 tons	8 in reserve
7 Cargo Transport	50 tons	1 in commission, 6 in reserve

It was officially stated in 1971 that the above river squadrons are extant.

LEBANON

Diplomatic Representation

Naval, Military and Air Attaché in London: Colonel Toufic Jalbout

Mercantile Marine

Lloyd's Register of Shipping: 79 vessels of 181 790 tons gross

PATROL BOATS

TARABLOUS

Displacement, tons	105 standard
Dimensions, feet	124·7 × 18 × 5·8
Guns	2—40 mm
Main engines	2 Mercedes-Benz diesels; 2 shafts; 2 700 bhp = 27 knots
Radius, miles	1 500
Complement	19 (3 officers, 16 men)

Tarablous was built by Ch. Navals de l'Estérel. Laid down in June 1958. Launched in June 1959. Completed in 1959.

TARABLOUS   *1968 Lebanese Navy, Official*

3 "BYBLOS" CLASS

BYBLOS 11   **SIDON** 12   **BEYROUTH** (ex-*T/R*) 13

Displacement, tons	28 standard
Dimensions, feet	66 × 13·5 × 4
Guns	1—20 mm AA; 2 MG
Main engines	General Motors diesels; 2 shafts; 530 bhp = 18·5 knots

French built ML type craft. Built by Ch. Navals de l'Estérel. Launched in 1954-55

BYBLOS   *1968, Lebanese Navy, Official*

DJOUNIEH

Displacement, tons	82 standard; 130 full load
Dimensions, feet	112 × 18 × 7·5
Guns	1—20 mm; 2—12·7 mm MG
Main engines	2 GM diesels; 2 shafts = 16 knots
Complement	16

Ex-Fairmile "B" motor launch of the Royal Navy built in 1940-41.

DJOUNIEH   *1970, Lebanese Navy, Official*

LANDING CRAFT

SOUR (ex-LCU 1474)

Displacement, tons	180 standard; 360 full load
Dimensions, feet	115 × 34 × 6
Guns	2—20 mm AA
Main engines	3 diesels; 3 shafts; 675 bhp = 10 knots

Former United States utility landing craft built in 1957, transferred in Nov 1958.

SOUR   *1968, Lebanese Navy, Official*

LIBERIA

Personnel

The small naval service or coast guard has about 200 officers and men.

Mercantile Marine

Lloyd's Register of Shipping: 1 869 vessels of 33 296 644 tons gross

MOTOR GUNBOATS

PGM 69   **PGM 102**

Displacement, tons	100
Dimensions, feet	95 oa × 19 × 5
Guns	1—40 mm AA
Main engines	4 diesels; 2 shafts; 2 200 bhp = 21 knots
Complement	15

PGM 102 (US number) is being built in the United States for transfer under the Military Aid Programme. PGM 69, sister boat, was the prototype for Liberia from USA.

PRESIDENTIAL YACHT

LIBERIAN (ex-*Virginia*)

Measurement, tons	742 (*Thames* measurement); 692·27 gross; 341·6 net
Dimensions, feet	173 wl; 209 oa × 29·7 × 13·1

Motor yacht of 742 tons (yacht measurement) built in 1930 by William Beardmore & Co Ltd, Dalmuir. Purchased by Liberia for use as the Presidential yacht in 1957. (Her previous owners were the Trustees of the Estate of the late Viscount Camrose). Extensively refitted by Cammell Laird & Co Ltd, Birkenhead, at the end of 1962.

LIBERIAN   *1964, Official*

PATROL BOATS

ML 4001   **ML 4002**

Displacement, tons	11·5
Dimensions, feet	40·5 oa × 11·5 × 3·5
Guns	2 MG
Main engines	2 GM diesels; 2 shafts; 380 bhp = 23 knots max

Coastguard cutters built at the United States Coast Guard Yard, Curtis Bay, Maryland. presented by the USA and transferred during 1957.

ML 4002   *courtesy Dr Giorgio Arra*

LANDING CRAFT

Landing craft reported to be used for transport and general utility purposes.

LIBYA

Establishment

The Libyan Navy was established in Nov 1962 when a British Naval Mission was formed and first recruits were trained at HMS *St Angelo*, Malta. Cadets were also trained at the Britannia Royal Naval College, Dartmouth, and technical ratings at HMS *Sultan*, Gosport, and HMS *Collingwood*, Fareham, England.

Personnel

1971: Total of 1 000 officers and ratings, including Coast Guard

Administration

Senior Officer, Libyan Navy: Lieutenant-Commander Mansur Bader

Head of the British Naval Mission: Captain Richard Clinton Mayne, RN

Mercantile Marine

1971: Lloyd's Register of Shipping: 11 vessels of 4 189 tons gross

FRIGATE

DAT-ASSAWARI   *1968, Vosper Thornycroft*

1 NEW CONSTRUCTION

DAT-ASSAWARI

Displacement, tons	1 325 standard; 1 625 full load
Length, feet (*metres*)	310·0 (*94·5*) pp; 330·0 (*100·6*) oa
Beam, feet (*metres*)	36·0 (*11·0*)
Draught, feet (*metres*)	11·2 (*3·4*)
Guns	1—4·5 in; 2—40 mm (twin)
Aircraft	1 helicopter
Missile launchers	6 (2 triple) "Seacat" close range ship-to-air
Main engines	CODOG arrangement; 2 shafts; 2 Rolls Royce gas turbines; 23 200 shp = 37·5 knots max 2 Paxman diesels; 3 500 bhp = 17 knots
Range, miles	5 700 at 17 knots economical cruising speed

The order was placed with Vosper Thornycroft on 6 Feb 1968 for this Mark 7 Fast Frigate. She will be generally similar in design to the two Iranian destroyers built by this firm, but larger and with different armament. She was launched without ceremony in Sep 1969. Scheduled to be completed in Dec 1972.

LOGISTIC SUPPORT SHIP

ZELTIN   *1969, Official*

1 DOCK TYPE

ZELTIN

Displacement, tons	2 200 standard; 2 470 full load
Ship:	
Length, feet (*metres*)	300·0 (*91·4*) wl; 324·0 (*98·8*) oa
Beam, feet (*metres*)	48·0 (*14·6*)
Draught, feet (*metres*)	10·2 (*3·1*); 19·0 (*5·8*) aft when flooded
Dock:	
Length, feet (*metres*)	135·0 (*41·1*)
Width, feet (*metres*)	40·0 (*12·2*)
Guns	2—40 mm AA
Main engines	2 Paxman 16 cyl diesels; 3 500 bhp; 2 shafts
Speed, knots	15
Range, miles	3 000 at 14 knots
Complement	As Senior Officer Ship: 101 (15 officers and 86 ratings)

The Vosper-Thornycroft Group received the order for this novel dock ship on 31 Jan 1967 (announced) for delivery in late 1968. She was designed and built by John I. Thornycroft & Co Ltd, at the Group's Woolston Shipyard. Launched on 29 Feb 1968. Commissioned (with *Sirte* and *Susa*) on 23 Jan 1969.

The ship provides full logistic support, including mobile docking maintenance and repair facilities for the Libyan fleet and acts as parent ship for the corvette *Tobruk* and the three fast patrol boats *Sebha*, *Sirte* and *Susa*. Craft up to 120 ft can be docked.

Fitted with accommodation for a flag officer or a senior officer and staff. Operational and administrative base of the squadron. Workshops with a total area of approx 4 500 sq ft are situated amidships with ready access to the dock, and there is a 3-ton travelling gantry fitted with outriggers to cover ships berthed alongside up to 200 feet long.

ZELTIN   *1969, Vosper Thornycroft*

CORVETTE

TOBRUK

Displacement, tons	440 standard; 500 full load
Dimensions, feet	162 wl; 177 oa × 28·5 × 10 mean (13 props)
Guns	1—4 in; 4—40 mm AA (single)
Main engines	2 Paxman Ventura 16 YJCM diesels; 2 shafts; 3 800 bhp = 18 knots
Radius, miles	2 900 at 14 knots
Complement	63 (5 officers and 58 ratings)

Designed and built by Vosper Limited, Portsmouth, in association with Vickers Limited. Launched on 29 July 1965, completed on 30 Mar 1966, commissioned for service at Portsmouth on 20 Apr 1966, sailed for Libya on 30 May 1966 and arrived in Tripoli on 15 June 1966. A gun corvette fitted with surface warning radar, Vosper roll damping fins and air-conditioning. Duties for which she was designed include protection of shipping from air and sea attack, training officers and men of the Libyan Navy, and State visiting. A suite of State apartments is included in the accommodation.

TOBRUK   *1971, A. & J. Pavia*

FAST PATROL BOATS

SUSA discharging one of her eight Nord-Aviation missiles   1969, Vosper

SEBHA   1969, Wright & Logan

SIRTE   1971, A. & J. Pavia

3 "SUSA" CLASS

SEBHA (ex-Sokna)	SIRTE	SUSA
Displacement, tons	95 standard; 114 full load	
Dimensions, feet	90·0 pp; 96·0 wl; 100·0 oa × 25·5 × 7·0	
Missiles	8—SS 12	
Guns	2—40 mm AA (single)	
Main engines	3 Bristol Siddeley "Proteus" gas turbines; 3 shafts; 12 750 bhp = 54 knots	
Complement	20	

The order for these three fast patrol boats from Vosper Limited, Portsmouth, England, was announced on 12 Oct 1966. They are generally similar to the motor torpedo boats designed and built by Vosper for the Royal Danish Navy. Built at the Vosper-Thornycroft Group's Portchester shipyard. Fitted with air conditioning and modern radar and radio equipment. *Susa* was launched on 31 Aug 1967, *Sirte* on 10 Jan 1968 and *Sokna* (renamed *Sebha*) on 29 Feb 1968. First operational vessels in the world to be armed with Nord-Aviation SS 12(M) guided weapons with sighting turret installation and other equipment developed jointly by Vosper and Nord. These weapons, of which eight can be fired by each boat without reloading, have a destructive power equivalent to a six-inch shell.

COAST GUARD VESSELS

SECURITY PATROL VESSELS. *Ar-Rakib* and *Farwa* were completed on 4 May 1967 by John I Thornycroft, Woolston, 100 tons, 100 × 21 × 5·5 feet, 3 Rolls Royce DV8TLM diesels, 1 740 bhp = 18 knots, 1—20 mm gun, 1 800 miles range at 14 knots, fuel 20 tons. Designed specifically for operation in North African waters. Welded steel construction. Four similar craft were ordered from the Vosper Thornycroft Group (announced on 3 Jan 1968), *Benina*, *Misurata*, both completed on 29 Aug 1968, *Akrama* and *Homs*, both completed early in 1969.

FARWA   1969, Thornycroft

INSHORE MINESWEEPERS

2 BRITISH "HAM" TYPE

BRAK (ex-HMS *Harpham*)   ZUARA (ex-HMS *Greetham*)

Displacement, tons	120 standard; 159 full load
Dimensions, feet	100 pp; 106 oa × 21·2 × 5·5
Guns	1—20 mm AA
Main engines	2 Paxman diesels; 1 100 bhp = 14 knots
Complement	15 to 22

Lent to Great Britain in 1963 to form the nucleus of a navy for Libya, and given outright to the Royal Libyan Navy in 1966. Given Libyan names in Sep 1966.

BRAK   A. & J. Pavia

ZUARA   1967, A. & J. Pavia

PATROL BOATS

4 "GARIAN" TYPE

GARIAN   KHAWLAN   MERAWA   SABRATHA

Displacenemt, tons	100
Dimensions, feet	102·0 × 20·0 × 5·0
Guns	1—40 mm; 1—20 mm
Main engines	2 Paxman 12 YJCM diesels; 3 600 bhp = 24 knots
Complement	20

Built by Brooke Marine, Lowestoft. Launched on 21 Apr, 29 May, 25 Oct and 30 Sep 1969, respectively, and completed on 30 Aug 1969 (*Garian* and *Khawlan*) and early in 1970 (other two).

KHAWLAN   1970, courtesy Brooke Marine

MAINTENANCE REPAIR CRAFT

ZLEITEN (ex-*MRC* 1013, ex-LCT)

Displacement, tons	657 standard; 900 approx full load
Dimensions, feet	225·0 pp; 231·3 oa × 39·0 × 3·3 forward, 5·0 aft
Main engines	4 Paxman diesels; 2 shafts; 1 840 bhp = 9 knots cruising

Built in 1944-45. Purchased from Great Britain on 5 Sep 1966. Depot ship for minesweepers.

CUSTOMS LAUNCHES

There are also three fast patrol launches for customs and fishery protection, see full particulars in the 1963-64 and 1964-65 editions.

MALAWI

It is reported that Great Britain is to supply Malawi with at least three gunboats to patrol the disputed waters of Lake Malawi (which has an extent of 11,460 sq miles and a length of 360 miles with an outlet to the River Zambesi)

MALAYSIA

Administration

Chief of the Naval Staff:
 Commodore Dato K. Thanabalasingam, DPMT, JMN, SMJ, RMN

Diplomatic Representation

Military Adviser in London:
 Brigadier General Unku Ahmed bin Abdul Rahman, DK, KMN

Strength of the Fleet

1 Frigate (New Construction, Gas Turbine)
1 Frigate (Training Ship)
6 Coastal Minesweepers
4 Fast Patrol Boats (Missile Craft)
24 Patrol Craft
1 Survey Vessel
1 Diving Tender

Personnel

1971: 4 400 (400 officers and 4 000 ratings)

Ships

The names of Malaysian warships are prefixed by KD.. (Kapal Diraja) meaning Royal Ship

Mercantile Marine

Lloyd's Register of Shipping:
89 vessels of 48 148 tons gross

FRIGATES

1 YARROW TYPE

RAHMAT (ex-*Hang Jebat*) F 24

Displacement, tons	1 250 standard; 1 600 full load
Length, feet (*metres*)	300·0 (*91·44*)pp; 308 (*93·9*) oa
Beam, feet (*metres*)	34·1 (*10·4*)
Draught, feet (*metres*)	14·8 (*4·5*)
Aircraft	1 helicopter
Missile launchers	1 quadruple "Seacat" surface-to-air
Guns, dual purpose	1—4·5 in (*114 mm*)
Guns, AA	2—40 mm
A/S weapons	1 "Limbo" three-barrelled mortar
Main engines	1 Bristol Siddeley Olympus gas turbine; 19 500 shp; Crossley Pielstick diesel; 3 850 bhp; 2 shafts
Speed, knots	26 boosted by gas turbine; 16 on diesel alone
Complement	140

General purpose frigate of new design developed by Yarrow. Fully automatic with saving in complement. Ordered from Yarrow & Co Ltd, Scotstoun, on 11 Feb 1966. Launched on 18 Dec 1967. The revised delivery date is mid 1971. *Hang Jebat* was the name of a Malay warrior of the 15th century.

RADAR. Search: HSA LWO 3. Tactical: HSA X band M 24. Fire Control: HSA M Series.

1 Ex-BRITISH "LOCH" CLASS

HANG TUAH (ex-HMS *Loch Insh*) F 433

Displacement, tons	1 575 standard; 2 400 full load
Length, feet (*metres*)	297·2 (*90·6*) wl; 307·0 (*93·6*) oa
Beam, feet (*metres*)	38·5 (*11·7*)
Draught, feet (*metres*)	14·8 (*4·5*)
Guns, AA	6—40 mm
Boilers	2 Admiralty 3-drum
Main engines	2 triple expansion; 5 500 ihp; 2 shafts
Speed, knots	19·5 designed
Complement	140

Built by Henry Robb Ltd, Leith. Laid down on 17 Nov 1943, launched on 10 May 1944 and completed on 20 Oct 1944. On transfer refitted with helicopter deck, air-conditioning, modern radar and extra accommodation in Portsmouth Dockyard. Re-commissioned on 12 Oct 1964. Sailed on 12 Nov 1964. Converted into a training ship in Apr 1971, the two 4-inch guns and the two "Squid" mortars having been removed. *Hang Tuah* was the name of a Malay Admiral of the 15th century.

RADAR: Search: Type 227.

HANG JEBAT 1970, courtesy Yarrow & Co Ltd, Scotstoun, Glasgow

HANG TUAH 1971, Michael D. J. Lennon

COASTAL MINESWEEPERS

6 Ex-BRITISH "TON" CLASS

BRINCHANG (ex-*Thankerton*) M 1172		**LEDANG** (ex-*Hexton*) M 1143	
JERAI (ex-*Dilston*) M 1168		**MAHAMIRU** (ex-*Darlaston*) M 1127	
KINABALU (ex-*Essington*) M 1134		**TAHAN** (ex-*Lullington*) M 1163	

Displacement, tons	360 standard; 425 full load
Dimensions, feet	140 pp; 152 oa × 28·8 × 8·2
Guns	1—40 mm AA forward; 2—20 mm AA aft
Main engines	Diesels; 2 shafts; 2 500 bhp = 15 knots max
Oil fuel, tons	45
Complement	39

Mahamiru transferred from the Royal Navy on 24 May 1960. *Ledang*, refitted at Chatham Dockyard before transfer, commissioned for Malaysia in Oct 1963. *Jerai* and *Kinabalu*, refitted in Great Britain, arrived in Malaysia summer 1964. *Brinchang* and *Tahan*, refitted in Singapore, transferred to Malaysian Navy in May and Apr 1966, respectively. A photograph of *Ledang* appears in the 1964-65 to 1966-67 editions, of *Mahamiru* in the 1967-68 edition.

KINABALU 1971, Michael D. J. Lennon

JERAI 1969, Michael D. J. Lennon

TAHAN 1971, Royal Malaysian Navy, Official

FAST MISSILE BOATS

4 "PERKASA" CLASS

GEMPITA P 152   **HANDALAN** P 151   **PENDEKAR** P 153   **PERKASA** P 150

Displacement, tons	95 standard ; 114 full load
Dimensions, feet	90 pp ; 96 wl ; 99 oa × 25·5 × 7
Guns	1—40 mm AA ; 1—20 mm AA
Missiles	8—SS 12(M) in 2 quadruple launchers
Main engines	3 Rolls Royce Proteus gas turbines ; 3 shafts ; 12 750 bhp = 54 knots
	GM diesels on wing shafts for cruising = 10 knots

The design is a combination of the "Brave" class hull form and "Ferocity" type construction. Ordered from Vosper Limited, Portsmouth, England, on 22 Oct 1964. Generally similar to the motor torpedo boats built by Vosper for the Royal Danish Navy. They can also operate in the gunboat rôle or a minelaying rôle. *Perkasa* (Valiant) was launched on 26 Oct 1965, *Handalan* (Reliant) on 18 Jan 1966, *Gempita* (Thunderer) on 6 Apr 1966, and *Pendekar* (Champion) on 24 June 1966. The hull is entirely of glued laminated wooden construction, with upperworks of aluminium alloy. Equipment includes Rover gas turbine generating sets, full air conditioning, Decca radar, and comprehensive navigation and communications system. The craft were shipped to Malaysia in mid-1967. They were re-armed with eight SS.12 missiles in place of four 21-inch t pedoes in 1971.

PENDEKAR   *1970, Royal Malaysian Navy, Official*

INSHORE MINESWEEPERS, "HAM" CLASS
Of the four inshore minesweepers transferred from Great Britain in 1958 and 1959, *Temasek* (ex-HMS *Brantingham*) M 2612 paid off in 1966, *Langka Suka* (ex-HMS *Bedham*) M 2606, *Sri Johor* (ex-HMS *Altham*) M 2602 and *Sri Perlis* (ex-HMS *Asheldham*) M 2604 in 1967. Their two sister ships transferred from the Royal Navy in Singapore in 1966, *Jerong* (ex-HMS *Boreham*) M 2627 and *Todak* (ex-HMS *Felmersham*) M 2610, were paid off in 1970 and sold.

SEAWARD DEFENCE BOATS
Of the original seven former British harbour defence motor launches (HDML) later known as seaward defence motor launches (SDML), *Sri Kedah* (SDML 3501) was scrapped in 1959, *Sri Selangor* (SDML 1509) in 1961, *Sri Pahang* (SDML 3505) and *Sri Kelantan* (SDML 3508) in 1965. *Sri Negri Sembilan* (SDML 3506) and *Sri Perak* (SDML 3507) for sale in 1966. *Sri Trengganu* (SDML 3502) was sold in Nov 1970.

PATROL CRAFT

6 "KEDAH" CLASS

SRI KEDAH	P 3138	**SRI PAHANG**	P 3141	**SRI SELANGOR**	P 3139
SRI KELANTAN	P 3142	**SRI PERAK**	P 3140	**SRI TRENGGANU**	P 3143

4 "SABAH" CLASS

SRI MELAKA	P 3147	**SRI SABAH**	P 3144
SRI NEGRI SEMBILAN	P 3146	**SRI SARAWAK**	P 3145

14 "KRIS" CLASS

BADEK	P 37	**KRIS**	P 34	**SERAMPANG**	P 41
BELADAU	P 44	**LEMBING**	P 40	**SRI JOHOR**	P 49
KELEWANG	P 45	**PANAH**	P 42	**SRI PERLIS**	P 47
KERAMBIT	P 43	**RENCHONG**	P 38	**SUNDANG**	P 36
		RENTAKA	P 46	**TOMBAK**	P 39

Displacement, tons	96 standard ; 109 full load
Dimensions, feet	95 wl ; 103 oa × 19·8 × 5·5
Guns	2—40 mm ; 70 cal AA
Main engines	2 Bristol Siddeley/Maybach MD 655/18 diesels ; 3 500 bhp = 27 knots max
Radius, miles	1 400 (*Sabah* class 1 660) at 14 knots
Complement	22 (3 officers, 19 ratings)

All 24 craft were built by Vosper Limited, Portsmouth. The first six boats, constituting the "Kedah" class were ordered in 1961 for delivery in 1963. The four boats of the "Sabah" class were ordered in 1963 for delivery in 1964. The remaining 14 boats of the "Kris" class were ordered in 1965 for delivery between 1966 and 1968. All are of prefabricated steel construction and are fitted with Decca radar, air conditioning and Vosper roll damping equipment. The difference between the three classes are minor, the later ones having improved radar, communications, evaporators and engines of Maybach, as opposed to Bristol Siddeley construction. *Sri Johor*, the last of the 14 boats of the "Kris" class, was launched on 22 June 1967. Originally the pennant numbers allocated were in a "3100" series, but the later boats were numbered in a two figure run as shown above. A photograph of *Sri Pahang* appears in the 1964-65 and 1965-66 editions, and of *Sri Perak* in the 1964-65 to 1966-67 editions.

SRI SARAWAK ("Sabah" Class)   *1971, A. & J. Pavia*

SRI KEDAH ("Kedah" Class)   *1970, Royal Malaysian Navy, Official*

KELEWANG ("Kris" Class)   *1969, John G. Callis*

DIVING TENDERS

DUYONG

Displacement, tons	120 standard ; 140 full load
Dimensions, feet	99·5 wl ; 110·0 oa × 21·0 × 5·8
Guns	1—20 mm
Main engines	2 Cummins diesels ; 1 900 rpm ; 500 bhp = 10 knots
Complement	23

Built by Kall Teck (Pte) Ltd, Singapore. Launched on 18 Aug 1970. Commissioned on 5 Jan 1971.

DUYONG   *1971, Royal Malaysian Navy, Official*

SURVEY VESSEL

PERANTAU (ex-HMS *Myrmidon*, ex-HMS *Edderton*) A 151

Displacement, tons	360 standard ; 420 full load
Dimensions, feet	153 oa × 28·8 × 8·5
Main engines	Diesels ; 2 shafts ; 3 000 bhp = 15 knots
Endurance, miles	2 300 at 13 knots
Complement	26

A former coastal minesweeper of the "Ton" type, converted by the Royal Navy into a survey ship, renamed *Myrmidon* in Apr 1964, and commissioned for service on 20 July 1964. Paid off in 1968 and purchased by Malaysia in 1969. Service in Malaysian waters since 1970. *Perantau* means "a rover".

PERANTAU   *1971, Royal Malaysian Navy, Official*

DISPOSALS
The landing craft *Sri Perlis* (ex-HMS *Pelandok*, ex-LCG(L) 450), and the trawler controlled minelayer *Sri Johor* (ex-HMS *Penyu*, ex-HMS *Dabchick*, ex-*Thorney*), were sold in 1959. The auxiliary *Panji* was returned to Singapore in 1965. The patrol craft *Sri Tanjong Merang* was returned to the Marine Dept, Malaya, in Oct 1966. The maintenance repair craft MRC 1401 (ex-*Sri Melaka*, ex-HMMS *Malaya*, ex-MCR 1401, ex-LST (E) 341) was scrapped in 1967. The former landing craft *Sri Langkawi* (ex-HMS *Counterguard*, ex-LCT (8) 4043) was sold in Feb 1968. The despatch and survey vessel *Mutiara* was sold in Sep 1969.

MEXICO

Administration	Diplomatic Representation	Strength of the Fleet

Administration

Secretary of the Navy:
Admiral C. G. Demn, Luis M. Bravo Carrera

Under-Secretary of the Navy:
Rear-Admiral Ing. M. N. Ricardo Chazaro Lara

Commander-in-Chief of the Navy:
Vice-Admiral C. G. Demn. Humberto Uribe Escandon

Chief of the Naval Staff:
Rear-Admiral C. G. Demn. Miguel A. Gomez Ortega

Director of Services:
Rear-Admiral C. G. Demn. Mario Artigas Fernandez

Diplomatic Representation

Naval Attaché in London:
Vice-Admiral Diego Mujica Narango

Naval Attaché in Washington:
Vice-Admiral Miguel Manzarraga

Strength of the Fleet

2 Destroyers
10 Frigates, Escort Transports and Gunboats
17 Escorts and Fleet Minesweepers
10 Patrol Boats and Launches
4 Support Ships and Auxiliaries

Personnel

1971: Total 11 566 (2 337 officers and 9 229 men including marines)

Mercantile Marine

Lloyd's Register of Shipping:
132 vessels of 381 096 tons gross

2 Ex-US "FLETCHER" CLASS

RATED AS *BUQUES ESCOLTAS*

Displacement, tons	2 100 standard; 3 050 full load
Length, feet (*metres*)	376·5 (*114·7*) oa
Beam, feet (*metres*)	39·5 (*11·9*)
Draught, feet (*metres*)	18·0 (*5·5*)
Guns (original)	5—5 in (*127 mm*); 14—40 mm; 10—20 mm (armament under review)
Torpedo tubes	5—21 in (*533 mm*) quintupled
A/S weapons	8 DCT
Main engines	2 geared turbines; 2 shafts; 60 000 shp
Boilers	4
Speed, knots	34
Oil fuel, tons	650
Endurance, miles	6 000 at 15 knots
Complement	250

Former US standard destroyers of the original "Fletcher" class taken out of the 1 May 1968 stricken (disposal) list and transferred to the Mexican Navy in 1971.

DESTROYERS

Name		Builders	Laid down	Launched	Completed
CUAUHTEMOC (ex-*John Rodgers*) DD 574		Consolidated Steel	25 July 41	7 May 42	9 Feb 43
CUITLAHUAC (ex-*Harrison* DD 573)		Consolidated Steel	25 July 41	7 May 42	25 Jan 43

FLETCHER CLASS   1971, Official

FRIGATES

Name	No.	Builders	Laid down	Launched	Completed
CALIFORNIA (ex-USS *Belet*, APD 109, ex-*DE* 599)	B 3 (ex-H 3)	Bethlehem SB Co, Hingham	26 June 1944	3 Mar 1944	15 June 1945
CHIHUAHUA (ex-USS *Earle B. Hall*, APD 107, ex-*DE* 597)		Bethlehem SB Co, Hingham	9 Jan 1944	1 Mar 1944	15 Mar 1945
COAHUILA (ex-USS *Barber*, APD 57, ex-*DE* 161)		Norfolk Navy Yard, Norfolk, Va	27 Apr 1943	20 May 1943	10 Oct 1943
PAPALOAPAN (ex-USS *Earhart*, APD 113, ex-*DE* 603)	B 4 (ex-H4)	Bethlehem SB Co, Hingham	20 Mar 1945	12 May 1945	26 July 1945
TEHUANTEPEC (ex-USS *Joseph M. Auman*, APD 117, ex-*DE* 74)	B 5 (ex-H 5)	Consolidated Steel Corp Orange	8 Nov 1943	5 Feb 1944	25 Apr 1945
USUMACINTA (ex-USS *Don O. Woods*, APD 118, ex-*DE* 721)	B 6 (ex-H 6)	Consolidated Steel Corp, Orange	1 Dec 1943	19 Feb 1944	28 May 1945

6 Ex-US "RUDDEROW" CLASS

RATED AS *FRAGATAS TRANSPORTES*

Displacement, tons	1 400 standard; 2 130 full load
Length, feet (*metres*)	300 (*91·5*) wl; 306 (*93·3*) oa
Beam, feet (*metres*)	37 (*11·3*)
Draught, feet (*metres*)	12·7 (*3·9*)
Guns, dual purpose	1—5 in (*127 mm*) 38 cal.
Guns, AA	6—40 mm, 3 twin; 6—20 mm
Boilers	2 Foster Wheeler "D" with superheater; 475 psi (*33·4 kg/cm²*) 750°F (*399°C*)
Main engines	GE turbo-electric 12 000 shp; 2 shafts
Speed, knots	23·6; 13 economical sea
Radius, miles	5 500 at 15 knots
Oil fuel (tons)	350
Complement	204 plus 162 troops

Former US converted destroyer escorts rated as high speed transports (APD) in the US Navy. Purchased by Mexico in 1971 (*Chihuahua, Coahuila*) and on 12 Dec 1963 (other four). The latter replaced the four ex-US "Tacoma" type frigates bearing the same names, which were stricken in June and Aug 1964. Photographs of *Papaloapan* appear in the 1965-66 to 1968-69 editions.

CALIFORNIA and *Papaloapan* (from *Guanajuato*)   1969, Mexican Navy, Official

Name	No.	Builders	Launched	Completed
DURANGO	B—1 (ex-128)	Union Naval de Levante, Valencia	28 June 1935	1936

1 "DURANGO" TYPE

RATED AS *TRANSPORTE DE GUERRA*

Displacement, tons	1 600 standard; 2 000 full load
Length, feet (*metres*)	282 (*86·0*) pp; 303 (*92·4*) oa
Beam, feet (*metres*)	40 (*12·2*)
Draught, feet (*metres*)	10 (*3·1*)
Guns, surface	2—4 in (*102 mm*); 2—2·24 in (*57 mm*)
Guns, AA	2—25 mm, twin; 4—20 mm
Main engines	2 Enterprise DMR-38 diesels, 5 000 bhp; electric drive; 2 shafts
Speed, knots	18 max, 12 sea (cruising)
Radius, miles	3 000 at 12 knots
Oil fuel (tons)	140
Complement	149 (24 officers and 125 men)

Originally designed primarily as an armed transport with accommodation for 20 officers and 450 men. The two Yarrow boilers and Parsons geared turbines of 6 500 shp installed when first built were replaced with two 2 500 bhp diesels in 1967 when the ship was re-rigged with remodelled funnel (see new appearance in photograph). Carries a lighter armament than the "Guanajuato" class (see below) which besides troop carrying and transport capacity are equivalent to frigates in many ways. *Durango* replaced *Zaragoza* as training ship in Mar 1964.

DURANGO   1969, Mexican Navy, Official

3 "GUANAJUATO" CLASS

RATED AS *CANONEROS (GUNBOATS)*

Name	No.	Builders	Launched
GUANAJUATO	C-7	Sociedad Espanol de Construction Naval, Ferrol	29 May 1934
POTOSI	C-9	Sociedad Espanol de Construction Naval, Motagorda, Cadiz	24 Aug 1934
QUERETARO	C-8	Sociedad Espanol de Construction Naval, Ferrol	29 June 1934

Displacement, tons	1 300 standard; 1 950 full load
Length, feet (*metres*)	264 (*80·5*) oa
Beam, feet (*metres*)	37·8 (*11·5*)
Draught, feet (*metres*)	10 (*3·0*)
Guns, surface	3—4 in (*102 mm*) singles
Guns, AA	6—20 mm, singles
Main engines	2 Enterprise DMR-38 diesels
	5 000 bhp; 2 shafts
Speed, knots	14
Oil fuel (tons)	140
Complement	140 (20 officers and 120 men)

Officially classified as gunboats (canoneros), but can be used as transports with berths for 120 troops. The Parsons geared turbines (2 shafts, 5 000 shp = 19 knots) and Yarrow boilers installed when originally built in 1934 were replaced with two diesels each of 2 500 bhp: *Querétaro* in 1958, *Potosi* in 1961, and *Guanajuato* in 1964. Former pennant numbers: *Querétaro* H 9 (ex-43); *Potosi* H 8 (ex-44). A photograph of *Querétaro* appears in the 1964-65 and 1965-66 editions and of *Potosi* in the 1966-67 to 1968-69 editions.

GUANAJUATO　　　　　　　1970, *Wright & Logan*

ESCORT MINESWEEPERS

16 Ex-MSF TYPE Rated as *DRAGAMINAS* and *ESCOLTAS*)

Name	No.	Ex-US Name & No.		Name	No.	Ex-US Name & No.	
DM-01	D-1	Jubilant	255	DM-13	E-3	Knave	256
DM-02	D-2	Hilarity	241	DM-14	E-4	Rebel	284
DM-03	D-3	Execute	232	DM-15	E-5	Crag	214
DM-05	D-5	Scuffle	298	DM-16	E-6	Dour	223
DM-06	D-6	Eager	224	DM-17	E-7	Diploma	221
DM-10	D-0	Instill	252	DM-18	E-8	Invade	254
DM-11	E-1	Device	220	DM-19	E-9	Intrigue	253
DM-12	E-2	Ransom	283	DM-20	E-0	Harlequin	365

Displacement, tons	650 standard; 945 full load
Displacement, feet	180 wl; 184·5 oa × 33 × 10
Guns	1—3 in, 50 cal dp; 4—40 mm AA
Main engines	2 diesels; 2 shafts; 1 710 bhp = 15 knots
Complement	104

Former US steel-hulled "180-ft" fleet minesweepers of the "Admirable" class, MSF, ex-AM type. All completed in 1943-44. Of the twenty vessels transferred at Orange, Texas, on 2 Oct 1962 ten were designated *dragaminas* for minesweeping duties, with D pennant numbers, and ten *escoltas* for escort and general purpose duties with E pennant numbers. A photograph of DM 02 appears in the 1964-65 to 1969-70 editions, of DM 19 in the 1964-65 to 1970-71 editions, and of DM 16 in the 1966-67 to 1970-71. DM 04 (D-4) ex-*Facility* 233, DM 07 (D-7) ex-*Recruit* 285, DM 08 (D-8) ex-*Success* 310, and DM 09 (D-9) ex-*Scout* 296 were officially stricken from the list in 1971.

DM 11　　　　　　　1966, *Mexican Navy, Official*

DM 17　　　　　　　1970, *Mexican Navy, Official*

PATROL VESSELS

1 Ex-US PCE TYPE

TOMAS MARIN (ex-*PCE 875*) C 3

Displacement, tons	600 standard; 903 full load
Dimensions, feet	180 wl; 184·5 oa × 33·1 × 9·5
Guns	1—3 in, 50 cal; 6—40 mm AA (3 twin); 4—20 mm AA (single)
A/S weapons	2 DCT
Main engines	GM diesels; 2 shafts; 1 800 bhp = 15 knots
Complement	80

Sole survivor of five former US patrol vessels of the PCE type, all completed in 1943-44 and purchased from the US Navy in 1947. Rated as *Corbeta*. Sister ships *Blass Godinez* (ex-*PCE* 871) C 2, *David Porter* (ex-*PCE* 847) C 4, *Pedro Saina de Baranda* (ex-*PCE* 844) C 1, and *Virgilio Uribe* (ex-*PCE* 868) C 5 were scrapped in 1965.

TOMAS MARIN　　　　　　　1966, *Mexican Navy, Official*

Of the PC type vessels of the "G 30" class GC 31 (ex-USS *PC* 820) GC 32 (ex-USS *PC* 608), GC 34 (ex-USS *PC* 794) and GC 36 (ex-USS *PC* 1224) were stricken in Mar 1964, GC 30 (ex-USS *PC* 820), GC 33 (ex-USS *PC* 813), GC 35 (ex-USS *PC* 824) and GC 37 (ex-USS *PC* 819) in 1966, and GC 38 (ex-USS *PC* 1210) in 1971.
Of the nine patrol vessels of the "G 20" class, G 29 was scrapped in 1952, G 20, G 21, G 23 G 26 and G 27 in 1954, G 22 and G 25 in 1956, and G 28 in 1966.

PATROL BOATS

2 "AZUETA" CLASS

AZUETA G 9　　　　　　　**VILLAPANDO** G 6

Dispalcement, tons	80 standard; 85 full load
Dimensions, feet	85·3 × 16·4 × 7·0
Guns	2—13·2 mm AA (1 twin)
Main engines	Superior diesels; 600 bhp = 12 knots

Of all steel construction. Built at Astilleros de Tampico in 1959 and 1960 respectively. A photograph of *Azueta* appears in the 1970-71 and earlier editions.

VILLAPANDO　　　　　　　1966, *Mexican Navy, Official*

5 RIVER TYPE

AM 4	AM 5	AM 6	AM 7	AM 8

Displacement, tons	35
Main engines	Diesel; speed = 10 knots

River patrol craft of steel construction. Built in Tampico and Veracruz. Entered service from 1960 to 1962.

Patrol Boats—continued

POLIMAR 1 G 1	POLIMAR 2 G 2	POLIMAR 3 G 3

Displacement, tons	37 standard; 57 full load
Dimensions, feet	60·1 × 15·1 × 4·0
Main engines	2 diesels; 456 bhp = 16 knots

Small patrol craft of steel construction. *Polimar 1* was built at Astilleros de Tampico in 1961 and entered service on 1 Oct 1962. *Polimar 2* and *Polimar 3* were built at Icacas Shipyard, Guerrero and entered service in 1966.

POLIMAR 1   *1969 Mexican Navy, Official*

TRANSPORT

ZACATECAS B 2

Displacement, tons	780 standard
Dimensions, feet	158 × 27·2 × 9
Guns	1—40 mm AA; 2—20 mm AA (single)
Main engines	1 MAN diesel; 560 hp = 10 knots
Complement	50 (13 officers and 37 men)

Built at Ulua Shipyard, Veracruz. Launched in 1959. Cargo ship type. The hull is of welded steel construction. Photograph in the 1966-67 to 1970-71 editions.

OILERS
2 Ex-US YO TYPE

AGUASCALIENTES (ex-YOG 6) 1 5	**TLAXCALA** (ex-YO 107) 1 6

Displacement, tons	440 light; 1 480 to 1 800 full load
Dimensions, feet	174·5 oa × 33·0 × 11·8 max
Main engines	Union diesel direct; 500 bhp = 8 knots
Capacity	6 570 barrels
Complement	26 (5 officers and 21 ratings)

Former US self-propelled fuel oil barges. Built by Geo. H. Mathis Co Ltd, Camden, N.J. and Geo. Lawley & Son, Neponset, Mass, respectively, in 1943. Purchased in 1964. Entered service in Nov 1964.

TLAXCALA   *1966, Mexican Navy, Official*

SURVEY SHIP

SOTAVENTO 1 A

Displacement, tons	300 standard; 400 full load
Dimensions, feet	165·5 × 28 × 10
Main engines	Diesels; 1 800 bhp = 17 knots

Built by Higgins, New Orleans. Launched in 1947. Handsome, streamlined, with truncated funnel, air conditioned and equipped with radar. Formerly the Presidential Yacht, but officially reclassified as *Buque Hidrografico* in 1966.

SOTAVENTO   *1967, Mexican Navy, Official*

TUGS

R-1 (ex-*Farallon*)	**R-3** (ex-*Vicent Point*)	**R-5** (ex-*Burnt Island*)
R-2 (ex-*Montauk Point*)	**R-4** (ex-*Moose Teak*)	

Remolcadores acquired by the Mexican Navy and added to the list in 1971.

MADAGASCAR

The *République Malgache* became an independent state on 26 June 1960.

Mercantile Marine
Lloyd's Register of Shipping: 26 vessels of 29 451 tons gross

PATROL VESSELS

MALAIKA

Displacement, tons	235 light
Dimensions, feet	149·3 pp; 155·8 oa × 23·6 × 8·2
Guns	2—40 mm AA
Main engines	2 MGO diesels; 1 shaft; 2,400 bhp = 18·5 knots
Radius, miles	2 000 at 18 knots

Ordered by the French Navy to be built by Chantiers Navals Franco-Belges for delivery to Madagascar. Laid down in Nov 1966, launched on 22 Mar 1967 and completed in Dec 1967.

FANANTENANA (ex-*Richelieu*)

Displacement, tons	1 040 standard; 1 200 full load
Dimensions, feet	183·7 pp; 206·4 oa × 30 × 14·8
Guns	2—40 mm AA
Main engines	2 Deutz diesels; 1 shaft; 1 060 + 500 bhp = 12 knots

Trawler purchased and converted in 1966-67 to Coast Guard and training ship. 691 tons gross. Built in 1959 by A. G. Weser, Bremen, Germany.

JASMINE (ex-*D* 385, ex-*D* 211, ex-*YMS* 31)

Displacement, tons	280 standard; 325 full load
Dimensions, feet	134·5 × 24·5 × 12
Main engines	2 diesels; 2 shafts; 1 000 bhp = 12 knots
Oil fuel, tons	22
Radius, miles	2 500·at 10 knots

Former coastal minesweeper of the YMS type launched on 10 Apr 1942 and acquired by France in 1954. Acquired by Madagascar on 19 Aug 1965 as a light tender. Same type originally at *Tanamasoandro* (ex-*Marjolaine*, ex-*D* 337, ex-*YMS* 69) discarded on delivery of *Malaika* (ex-*P* 758, *VC* 8) returned to the French Navy in 1967.

MAURITANIA

Mercantile Marine
Lloyd's Register of Shipping: 1 vessel of 711 tons gross

PATROL BOATS

DAR EL BARKA	**TICHITT**

Displacement, tons	75 standard; 82 full load
Dimensions, feet	104·3 × 15·4 × 5·5
Guns	2—20 mm AA
Main engines	2 Mercedes-Benz diesels; 2 shafts; 2 700 bhp = 28 knots
Radius, miles	1 500 at 15 knots

Built by Ch Navales de L Esterel, in service June and April 1969 respectively.

IM RAQ'NI	**SLOUGHI**

Displacement, tons	20
Dimensions, feet	59 × 13·5 × 3·8
Guns	1—12·7 mm
Main engines	2 GM diesels; 512 bhp = 21 knots
Radius, miles	860 at 12 knots

MUSCAT and OMAN
PATROL VESSELS

EL SAID

A patrol vessel with a length of 202 feet and a gun on her forecastle, built by Brooke Marine, Lowestoft, as flagship of the new navy. Originally launched in Apr 1969 as a yacht for the Sultan of Muscat and Oman, she was converted for a dual purpose role as flagship and as ship of state for delivery at the end of 1970. Powered by two 12 cylinder Paxman Ventura diesels.

EL SAID   *Brooke Marine, 1971*

FAST PATROL BOATS
3 BROOKE MARINE TYPE

Under construction. Each powered by two 16 cylinder Paxman Ventura Diesels.

NATO

North Atlantic Treaty Organisation (NATO) Naval Forces are:—
BELGIUM· CANADA, DENMARK, FRANCE, GERMAN FEDERAL REPUBLIC GREECE, ICELAND, ITALY, NETHERLANDS, NORWAY, PORTUGAL TURKEY, UNITED KINGDOM, UNITED STATES.

MOROCCO

Diplomatic Representation

Naval, Military and Air Attaché in London:
Commandant Mustapha Jabrane

Personnel

1971: 500 officers and ratings

Mercantile Marine

Lloyd's Register of Shipping:
31 vessels of 54 725 tons gross

FRIGATES

Name	Builders	Laid down	Launched	Completed
AL MAOUNA (ex-*La Surprise*, ex-HMS *Torridge*) 31 (ex-033)	Blyth Dry Docks & Ship building Co	17 Oct 1942	16 Aug 1943	6 Apr 1944

Displacement, tons	1 450 standard; 2 150 full load
Length, feet (*metres*)	283·0 (*86·3*) pp; 301·3 (*91·8*) oa
Beam, feet (*metres*)	36·5 (*11·1*)
Draught, feet (*metres*)	12·5 (*3·8*)
Aircraft	1 helicopter
Guns, surface	2—4·1 in (*105 mm*)
Guns, AA	3—40 mm; 2—20 mm
A/S weapons	1 "Hedgehog"; 4 DCT; 2 DC racks
Main engines	Triple expansion; 2 shafts; 5 500 ihp
Boilers	2 Admiralty 3-drum
Speed, knots	18
Oil fuel, tons	645
Radius, miles	7 700 at 12 knots
Complement	123 (10 officers, 113 men)

Former British "River" class frigate purchased by France in 1944. Sold to Morocco in June 1964 and converted as flagship and Royal yacht by Chantiers Dubigeon at Brest. A helicopter landing deck and extra accommodation were provided aft. SPS 6 search radar. Accepted on 5 March 1965.

AL MAOUNA   *1968, Royal Moroccan Navy, Official*

PATROL VESSELS

(*Escorteur Cotier*)

AL BACHIR 22 (ex-12)

Displacement, tons	125 light; 154 full load
Dimensions, feet	124·7 pp; 133·2 oa × 20·8 × 4·7
Guns	2—40 mm AA and MG
Main engines	2 SEMT-Pielstick diesels; 2 shafts; 3 600 bhp = 25 knots
Oil fuel, tons	21
Radius, miles	2 000 at 15 knots
Complement	23

Ordered in 1964 from Constructions Mécaniques de Normandie, Cherbourg, launched 25 Feb 1967, delivered 30 Mar 1967.

AL BACHIR   *1967, Royal Moroccan Navy, Official*

LIEUTENANT RIFFI 32

Displacement, tons	325 standard; 374 full load
Dimensions, feet	170 wl; 173·8 oa × 23 × 6·3
Guns	1—3 in dp; 2—40 mm AA
A/S weapons	2 ASM mortars; 1 DC rack
Main engines	SEMT-Pielstick diesels; 2 shafts; 3 600 bhp = 19 knots
Radius, miles	3 000 at 12 knots; 2 000 at 15 knots
Complement	59 (4 officers, 55 men)

Of modified "Fougueux" design. Built by Constructions Mécaniques de Normandie, Cherbourg. Laid down in May 1963. Launched on 1 Mar 1964. Completed in May 1964. Controllable pitch propellers.

VC Type   *Official*

LIEUTENANT RIFFI   *1969, Royal Moroccan Navy, Official*

The corvette (*aviso*) *El Lahiq* (ex-*Chamois*, ex-*Annamite*) was returned to France in 1967 and hulked as a breakwater at the Ile de Levant. She was transferred from the French Navy on 7 Nov 1961. The patrol vessel *Agadir* (ex-French *Gaumier*, ex-USS *PC* 545) was returned to France on 19 Aug 1964 and became Q 390. Sold for scrap at Brest on 15 Nov 1965.

SEAWARD PATROL CRAFT

(*Vedette de Port*)

ES SABIQ (ex-*P* 762, VC 12) 11

Displacement, tons	75 standard; 82 full load
Dimensions, feet	104·5 × 15·5 × 5·5
Guns	2—20 r..m AA
Main engines	Mercedes-Benz diesels; 2 shafts; 2 700 bhp = 28 knots
Radius, miles	1 500 at 15 knots
Complement	17

Former French seaward defence motor launch of the VC type. Built by Chantiers Navals d'Estérel. Launched on 13 Aug 1957. Completed in 1958. Transferred from the French Navy to the Moroccan Navy on 15 Nov 1960 and renamed *Es Sabiq*.

LANDING CRAFT

LIEUTENANT MALGHAGH 21

Displacement, tons	292 standard; 642 full load
Dimensions, feet	193·6 × 39·2 × 4·3
Guns	2—20 mm AA
Main engines	MGO diesels; 2 shafts; 1 000 bhp = 8 knots
Complement	16 (1 officer, 15 men)

Ordered early in 1963 from Chantiers Navals Franco-Belges and completed in 1964. Similar to the French landing craft of the EDIC type built at the same yard.

LIEUTENANT MALGHAGH   *1971, Royal Moroccan Navy, Official*

There are also the yacht *Essaoira*, 60 tons, from Italy in 1967, used as a training vessel for watchkeepers; and twelve customs boats, four of 40 tons, 82 feet, diesels 940 bhp = 23 knots, and eight 42·7 feet, all built in 1963. The *Murene*, Coast Guard Cutter, has also been reported.

NETHERLANDS

Organisation

The top policy making body of the Royal Netherlands Navy is the Admiralty Board. The senior naval officer is the Chief of Naval Staff, who also holds the appointment of Commander-in-Chief. Under him all ships, aircraft and establishments in the Netherlands are commanded by the Admiral Netherlands Home Command. Ships of the sea-going fleet form the Netherlands Task Group, which normally consists of one or two cruisers, from 5 to 8 destroyers and frigates, 2 or 3 submarines and a number of shorebased aircraft. Other submarines, aircraft, minesweepers, etc come under their respective type-commanders.

The Netherlands Naval Air Service—comprising just under 100 aircraft—carries out both maritime patrol (Neptunes—Atlantics) and shipboard (helicopters) operations. Also available are search and rescue, communications and training aircraft.

The Netherlands Marine Corps consists of about 2 800 men.

The defence of the Netherlands Antilles (West Indies) is entirely a naval responsibility under the Flag Officer Netherlands Antilles. A destroyer, some small craft, a naval air squadron and R. Neth. Marine units are normally available, and could be quickly re-inforced if needed.

Administration

Minister of Defence: W. den Toom

Chairman Joint Chiefs of Staff:
Admiral H. M. van den Wall Bake

Chairman Joint Services Material Board:
Vice-Admiral J. C. H. van den Bergh

Secretary of State for Defence (Navy): A. van Es

Chief of the Naval Staff and Commander-in-Chief:
Vice-Admiral J. B. M. J. Maas

Flag Officer Naval Personnel:
Vice-Admiral Jonkheer W. C. M. de Jonge van Ellemeet

Flag Officer Naval Material:
Rear-Admiral Mr. Ir. P. P. van de Vijver

Command

Admiral Netherlands Home Command:
Vice-Admiral A. van der Moer

Commander Netherlands Task Group:
Rear-Admiral E. Roest

Commandant Royal Netherlands Marine Corps:
Major-General C. C. Schoenzetter

Flag Officer Netherlands Antilles:
Commodore A. S. de Vries

Diplomatic Representation

Naval Attaché in London:
Captain F. de Blocq van Kuffeler

Naval Attaché in Washington and NLR SACLANT:
Raer-Admiral O. Cramwinckel

Naval Attaché in Paris:
Captain M. G. Zuidijk

Naval Attache in Bonn:
Captain H. A. Hes

Ships

Warships are painted greyish blue except submarines, which are dark grey overall. Ships of the Royal Netherlands Navy are referred to by the prefix "Hr. Ms".

Strength of the Fleet

- 5 Submarines (Diesel Powered)
- 2 Cruisers (1 Guided Missile Armed)
- 12 Destroyers (Anti-Submarine) Escorts
- 6 Frigates (General Purpose Type)
- 6 Corvettes (Patrol Escort Type)
- 3 MCM Command Support Ships (ex-Ocean Minesweepers)
- 3 Escorts (ex-Ocean Minesweepers)
- 5 Patrol Vessels (Submarine Chasers)
- 32 Coastal Minesweepers (Non-Magnetic)
- 4 Coastal Minehunters (Non-Magnetic)
- 5 Diving Vessels (Converted Coastal Minesweepers)
- 16 Inshore Minesweepers (Non-Magnetic)
- 37 Support Ships and Service Craft

New Construction Programme

- 1 nuclear powered fleet submarine, building postponed
- 2 diesel powered submarines, ocean-going type
- 2 guided missile frigates, DDG type
- 4 anti-submarine warfare frigates
- 1 fast combat support ship
- 1 oceanographic ship
- 2 small survey ships

Conversion Programme

- 1 coastal minesweeper to minehunter (1970-1971)
- 1 coastal minesweeper to minehunter (1971-1972)

Naval Aircraft

Brequet Atlantic
Lockheed Neptune
Grumman Tracker

Augusta Bell 204B
Westland Wasp

Missiles

Surface to air: US "Terrier"; British "Sea-Cat"
Air to Surface: French A.S.12

Personnel

1 January 1971: 20 200 officers and ratings (including the Navy Air Service, Royal Netherlands Marine Corps and about 360 officers and women of the W.R.NL.N.S.)

Navy Estimates

1961: f 445 000 000	1966: f 702 000 000
1962: f 564 000 000	1967: f 727 000 000
1963: f 542 000 000	1968: f 775 000 000
1964: f 627 000 000	1969: f 824 000 000
1965: f 660 000 000	1970: f 936 000 000
	1971: f 998 000 000

Mercantile Marine

Lloyd's Register of Shipping
1 598 vessels of 5 206 663 tons gross

Scale: 150 feet = 1 inch (1 : 1 800)

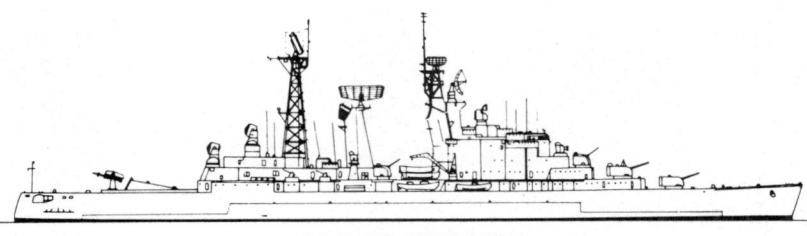

DE ZEVEN PROVINCIEN

FRIESLAND *Class*

DE RUYTER

HOLLAND *Class*

VAN SPEIJK *Class*

WOLFF *Class*

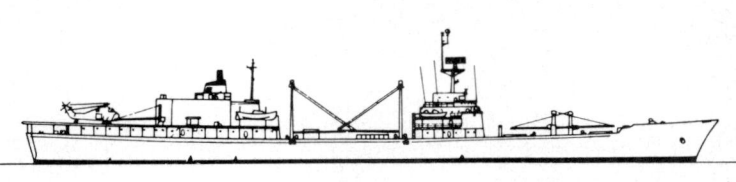

POOLSTER

SNELLIUS *Class*

LIST OF PENNANT NUMBERS

Submarines:

S 802 Walrus
S 804 Potvis
S 805 Tonijn
S 808 Dolfijn
S 809 Zeehond

Cruisers:

C 801 De Ruyter
C 802 De Zeven Provincien

Destroyers:

D 808 Holland
D 809 Zeeland
D 810 Noord Brabant
D 811 Gelderland
D 812 Friesland
D 813 Groningen
D 814 Limburg
D 815 Overijssel
D 816 Drenthe
D 817 Utrecht
D 818 Rotterdam
D 819 Amsterdam

Frigates:

F 802 Van Speijk
F 803 Van Galen
F 804 Tjerk Hiddes
F 805 Van Nes
F 814 Isaac Sweers
F 815 Evertsen

Corvettes;

F 817 Wolf
F 818 Fret
F 819 Hermelijn
F 820 Vos
F 821 Panter
F 822 Jaguar

Escorts;

A 854 Onversaagd
A 855 Onbevreesd
A 858 Onvervaard

MCM Command Support Ships

A 856 Onverschrokken
A 857 Onvermoeid
A 859 Onverdroten

Mine Hunters

M 801 Dokkum
M 818 Drunen
M 828 Staphorst
M 842 Veere

Coastal Minesweepers;

M 802 Hoogezand
M 803 Wildervank
M 806 Roermond
M 807 Waalwijk
M 808 Axel
M 809 Naaldwijk
M 810 Abcoude
M 811 Aalsmeer
M 812 Drachten
M 813 Ommen
M 814 Meppel
M 815 Giethoorn
M 817 Venlo
M 819 Goes
M 820 Woerden
M 822 Leersum
M 823 Naarden
M 826 Grijpskerk
M 827 Hoogeveen
M 830 Sittard
M 841 Gemert
M 844 Rhenen
M 845 Beemster
M 846 Bolsward
M 847 Bedum
M 848 Beilen
M 849 Borculo
M 850 Borne
M 851 Brummen
M 852 Breukelen
M 853 Blaricum
M 854 Brielle
M 855 Breskens
M 856 Bruinisse
M 857 Boxtel
M 858 Brouwershaveh

Inshore Minesweepers;

M 868 Alblas
M 869 Bussemaker
M 870 Lacomblé
M 871 Van Hamel
M 872 Van Straelen
M 873 Van Moppes
M 874 Chompff
M 875 Van Well·Groeneveld
M 876 Schuiling
M 877 Van Versendaal
M 878 Van Der Wel
M 879 Van 't Hoff
M 880 Mahu
M 881 Staverman
M 882 Houtepen
M 883 Zomer

Patrol Vessels:

P 802 Balder
P 803 Bulgia
P 804 Freijer
P 805 Hadda
P 806 Hefring

Auxiliary Ships:

A 829 Mercuur
A 830 Pelikaan
A 832 Woendi
A 835 Poolster
A 847 Argus
A 848 Triton
A 849 Nautilus
A 850 Hydra
A 870 Wamandai
A 871 Wambrau
A 872 Westgat
A 873 Wielingen
A 902 Luymes
A 903 Zeefakkel
A 907 Snellius
A 912 Dreg 4

Nos. 879 to 892 are allocated to
stationary accommodation ships.

LIMBURG

1971, Royal Netherlands Navy, Official

SUBMARINES (Onderzeeboten)

Name	Builders	Ordered	Laid down	Launched	Trials	Commission
TIJGERHAAI	Rotterdamse Droogdok Mij, Rotterdam	24 Dec 1965	14 July 1966	1971	1971	Late 1972
ZWAARDVIS	Rotterdamse Droogdok Mij, Rotterdam	24 Dec 1965	14 July 1966	2 July 1970	1971	Early 1972

2 NEW CONSTRUCTION

Displacement, tons	1 800 surface; 2 300 submerged
Length, feet (metres)	216·5 (66·0)
Beam, feet (metres)	27·5 (8·4)
Draught, feet (metres)	23·3 (7·1)
Torpedo tubes	6—21 in (533 mm)
Main engines	Diesel-electric; 1 shaft
Speed, knots	15 on surface; 25 submerged
Complement	68

In the 1964 Navy Estimates a first instalment was approved for the construction of two conventionally powered submarines. Scheduled to be launched in autumn 1970 and early spring 1971 and to be commissioned one year after launch. Construction of Tijgerhaai is about six months behind that of Zwaardvis, it is officially stated.

ZEEHOND   1971, Royal Netherlands Navy, Official

Name	No.	Builders	Laid down	Launched	Completed
POTVIS	S 804	Wilton-Fijenoord, Schiedam	17 Sep 1962	12 Jan 1965	2 Nov 1965
TONIJN	S 805	Wilton-Fijenoord, Schiedam	27 Nov 1962	14 June 1965	24 Feb 1966
DOLFIJN	S 808	Rotterdamse Droogdok Mij, Rotterdam	30 Dec 1954	20 May 1959	16 Dec 1960
ZEEHOND	S 809	Rotterdamse Droogdok Mij, Rotterdam	30 Dec 1954	20 Feb 1960	16 Mar 1961

2 "POTVIS" CLASS
2 "DOLFIJN" CLASS

Displacement, tons	1 140 standard; 1 494 surface; 1 826 submerged
Length, feet (metres)	260·9 (79·5)
Beam, feet (metres)	25·8 (7·8)
Draught, feet (metres)	15·8 (4·8)
Torpedo tubes	8—21 in (533 mm)
Main engines	2 MAN diesels, total 3 100 bhp Electric motors, 4 200 hp; 2 shafts
Speed, knots	14·5 on surface; 17 submerged
Complement	64

These submarines are of a triple-hulled design. Maximum depth 980 feet (300 metres). Potvis and Tonijn, originally voted for in 1949 with the other pair, but suspended for some years, had several modifications compared with Dolfijn and Zeehond and were officially considered to be a separate class; but modernisation of the first pair has been completed, and all four boats are now almost identical.

POTVIS   1970, Royal Netherlands Navy, Official

CONSTRUCTION. The hull consists of three cylinders arranged in a triangular shape. The upper cylinder accommodates the crew, navigational equipment and armament. The lower two cylinders house the propulsion machinery comprising diesel engines, batteries and electric motors. See Frontispiece of the 1959-1960 edition for scale models—cutaway longitudinal section showing double decker roominess, and cross section showing triple hull permitting greater diving depth.

DOLFIJN   1969, Royal Netherlands Navy, Official

PROJECTED NUCLEAR POWERED TYPE. In the "defence note" issued in June 1964 the construction of nuclear powered submarines was announced. In the defence note 1968 it was still considered that the nuclear vessel is the submarine of the future, but when one can be obtained is uncertain in view of presently available defence funds and required overall investments, and nuclear submarines are not considered within the present short term plans (official).

TONIJN   1969, Royal Netherlands Navy, Official

Name	No.	Builders	Laid down	Launched	Completed	Converted	Transferred
WALRUS (ex-Icefish)	S 802	Manitowoc SB Co, Wisconsin	1943	20 Feb 1944	10 June 1944	1952	21 Feb 1953

1 "WALRUS" CLASS

Displacement, tons	1 420 standard; 1 525 surface; 2 425 submerged
Length, feet (metres)	309 (94·2) oa
Beam, feet (metres)	27 (8·2)
Draught, feet (metres)	17 (5·2)
Torpedo tubes	10—21 in (533 mm), 6 bow and 4 stern
Main engines	4 GM 2-stroke diesels, total 6 500 bhp; Electric motors, 2 700 hp
Speed, knots	20 on surface; 10 submerged
Radius, miles	12 000 at 10 knots
Oil fuel (tons)	300
Complement	79

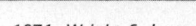

WALRUS   1971, Wright & Logan

Former "Balao" class submarine on loan from USA (for period of five years, subsequently extended) after having been streamlined with enclosed conning tower "fin". 24 torpedoes can be carried.

DISPOSAL
Sister submarine Zeeleeuw (ex-USS Hawkbill) S 803 was returned to the USN and sold for scrap in the Netherlands on 24 Nov 1970.

DISPOSALS OF "T" CLASS. Of the two submarines of the former British "T" class, Zwaardvis (ex-HMS Talent) was scrapped in July 1963 and Tijgerhaai (ex-HMS Tarn) was deleted from the list in 1966.

CRUISERS (*Kruisers*)

Name	No.	Builders	Laid down	Launched	Completed
DE RUYTER (ex-*Zeven Provincien*)	C 801	Wilton-Fijenoord, Schiedam	5 Sep 1939	24 Dec 1944	18 Nov 1953
DE ZEVEN PROVINCIEN (ex-*De Ruyter*, ex-*Eendracht*, ex-*Kijkduin*)	C 802	Rotterdam Drydock Co	19 May 1939	22 Aug 1950	17 Dec 1953

Displacement, tons	9 529 standard; 11 850 full load (*C 802*: 9 850 std; 12 250 load)
Length, feet (*metres*)	590·5 (*180·0*) pp; *C801*: 614·5 (*190·3*) oa; *C802*: 609 (*188·7*) oa
Beam, feet (*metres*)	56·7 (*17·3*)
Draught, feet (*metres*)	22 (*6·7*) max
Missiles, AA	*De Zeven Provincien* (*C802*) only: 1 twin "Terrier" launcher aft
Guns, surface	*C801*: 8—6 in (*152 mm*) in twin turrets; *C802*: 4—6 in (*152 mm*) in twin turrets
Guns. AA	*C801*: 8—57 mm in twin turrets; 8—40 mm; *C802*: 6—57 mm in twin turrets; 4—40 mm
Boilers	4 Werkspoor-Yarrow
Main engines	2 De Schelde-Parsons geared turbines; 85 000 shp; 2 shafts
Speed. knots	32
Complement	*De Ruyter*: 926 *De Zeven Provincien*: 940

Machinery by K. M. de Schelde. Construction resumed in 1946. Both hulls were nameless in 1945 and since the name *De Ruyter* was wanted back in the Navy as soon as possible that name was given to the hull already launched and therefore the most advanced. Tripod mast. originally abaft after funnel, is now before after funnel.

DE RUYTER — 1970, *Peter Carter*

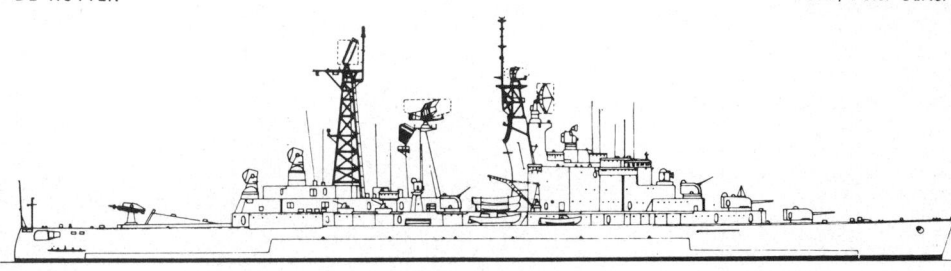

RADAR
Search: LWO 1, SPS 39 3 D, VI SGR 104 Height Finder. Tactical: DA 02.
Fire Control: HSA M 20 series for guns, SPG 55 for "Terrier".

GUIDED MISSILE CONVERSION. *De Zeven Provincien* was converted in 1962-64 by Rotterdamsche Droogdok Mij, Rotterdam with "Terrier" installation by NV Dok en Werf Mij Wilton-Fijenoord Schiedam. *De Ruyter* will not be converted. She will be replaced in 1975 by two guided missile armed frigates (DDG) the construction of which will commence in 1971.

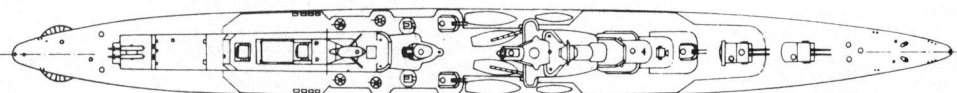

GUNNERY. Main armament has 60 degrees elevation. All guns are fully automatic and radar controlled. The 6 inch guns have a rate of fire of 15 rounds per minute.

TRANSFER OF AIRCRAFT CARRIER. H.N.L.M.S. *Karel Doorman* was sold to Argentina in Oct 1968 and renamed *Veinticinco de Mayo*.

DRAWING. Represents *De Zeven Provincien*. Starboard elevation and plan. *De Ruyter* has curved bow which accounts for the variation in overall length.

Scale 125 feet = 1 inch. (1 : 1 500) A port elevation and plan drawing of *De Ruyter* appears in the 1953-54 to 1965-66 editions.

DE RUYTER — 1969, *Stefan Terzibaschitsch*

DE ZEVEN PROVINCIEN converted with guide missile launcher aft — 1970, *Royal Netherlands Navy, Official*

GUIDED MISSILE FRIGATES

2 NEW CONSTRUCTION DDG TYPE

Displacement, tons	4 300 standard; 5 400 full load
Dimensions, feet	452·8 oa; 429·5 pp × 48·5 × 15·1
Guns	2—4·7 in (twin turret)
Missile launchers	1 "Tartar" aft; Point defence missile system
Aircraft	1 light weight helicopter armed with homing torpedoes
Main engines	2 main gas turbines, 40 000 hp; 2 cruising gas turbines, 8 000 hp
Speed, knots	circa 30 max
Complement	306

First design allowance was voted for in 1967 estimates. Ordered (announced on 27 July 1970) from Koninklijke Maatschappij De Schelde, Flushing, member of the Rhine Schelde Shipbuilding Group, for laying down in 1971 and completion in 1975 to replace the cruiser *De Ruyter*. Hanger and helicopter spot landing platform aft.

MISSILE FRIGATE DDG TYPE   *1971, Royal Netherlands Navy, Official*

FRIGATES (*Fregatten*)

Name	No.	Builders	Laid down	Launched	Completed
TJERK HIDDES	F 804	Nederlandse Dok en Scheepsbouw Mij, Amsterdam	1 June 1964	17 Dec 1965	16 Aug 1967
VAN GALEN	F 803	Koninklijke Maatschappij De Schelde, Flushing	25 July 1963	19 June 1965	1 Mar 1967
VAN NES	F 805	Koninklijke Maatschappij De Schelde, Flushing	25 July 1963	26 Mar 1966	9 Aug 1967
VAN SPEIJK	F 802	Nederlandse Dok en Scheepsbouw Mij, Amsterdam	1 Oct 1963	5 Mar 1965	14 Feb 1967
EVERTSEN	F 815	Koninklijke Maatschappij De Schelde, Flushing	6 July 1965	18 June 1966	21 Dec 1967
ISAAC SWEERS	F 814	Nederlandse Dok en Scheepsbouw Mij, Amsterdam	5 May 1965	10 Mar 1967	15 May 1968

6 "VAN SPEIJK" CLASS

Displacement, tons	2 200 standard; 2 850 full load
Dimensions, feet	360 wl, 372 oa × 41 × 18
Guns	2—4·5 in (twin turret)
Missile launchers	2 quadruple "Seacat" anti-aircraft
A/S weapons	1 "Limbo" three-barrelled depth charge mortar
Aircraft	1 lightweight helicopter armed with homing torpedoes
Boilers	2 Babcock & Wilcox
Main engines	2 double reduction geared turbines; 2 shafts; 30 000 shp
Speed, knots	28·5 sea, 30 max
Complement	254

Basically similar to British "Leander" class. Four ships were ordered in Oct 1962 and two later. Built to replace the six frigates of the "Van Amstel" class (DEs) returned to USA and subsequently scrapped.

DESIGN. Although in general these ships are based on the design of the British Improved Type 12 ("Leander" class), there are a number of modifications in accordance with the requirements of the Royal Netherlands Navy. As far as possible equipment of Netherlands manufacture was installed. This resulted in a number of changes in the ship's superstructure compared with the British "Leander" class. To avoid delay these ships were in some cases fitted with equipment already available, instead of going through long development stages.

RADAR. Search: LWO 3. Tactical: DA 02. Fire Control: HSA M Series.

PHOTOGRAPHS. A photograph of *Tjerk Hiddes* appears in the 1968-69 edition, and of *Van Nes* in the 1969-70 and 1970-71 editions.

VAN SPEIJK   *1971, Dr. Giorgio Arra*

EVERTSEN   *1970, Royal Netherlands Navy, Official*

VAN GALEN   *1971, Royal Netherlands Navy, Official*

ANTI-SUBMARINE ESCORTS DDE (*Onderzeebootjagers*)

Name	No.	Builders	Laid down	Launched	Completed
FRIESLAND	D 812	Nederlandse Dok en Scheepsbouw Mij, Amsterdam	17 Dec 1951	21 Feb 1953	22 Mar 1956
GRONINGEN	D 813	Nederlandse Dok en Scheepsbouw. Mij, Amsterdam	21 Feb 1952	9 Jan 1954	12 Sep 1956
LIMBURG	D 814	Koninklijke Maatschappij De Schelde, Flushing	28 Nov 1953	5 Sep 1955	31 Oct 1956
OVERIJSSEL	D 815	Dok-en-Werfmaatschappij Wilton-Fijenoord	15 Oct 1953	8 Aug 1955	4 Oct 1957
DRENTHE	D 816	Nederlandse Dok en Scheepsbouw Mij, Amsterdam	9 Jan 1954	26 Mar 1955	1 Aug 1957
UTRECHT	D 817	Koninklijke Maatschappij De Schelde, Flushing	15 Feb 1954	2 June 1956	1 Oct 1957
ROTTERDAM	D 818	Rotterdamse Droogdok Mij, Rotterdam	7 Jan 1954	26 Jan 1956	28 Feb 1957
AMSTERDAM	D 819	Nederlandse Dok en Scheepsbouw Mij, Amsterdam	26 Mar 1955	25 Aug 1956	10 Aug 1958

8 "FRIESLAND" CLASS

Displacement, tons	2 497 standard; 3 070 full load
Length, feet (*metres*)	370 (*112·8*) pp; 380·5 (*116·0*) oa
Beam, feet (*metres*)	38·5 (*11·7*)
Draught, feet (*metres*)	17 (*5·2*)
Guns, surface	4—4·7 in (*120 mm*) twin turrets
Guns, AA	4—40 mm (2 removed during recent refits)
A/S weapons	2 four-barrelled depth charge mortars
Boilers	4 Babcock
Main engines	2 Werkspoor geared turbines, 60 000 shp; 2 shafts
Speed, knots	36
Complement	284

These ships have side armour as well as deck protection. "Limbo" type anti-submarine rocket throwers. Twin rudders. Propellers 370 rpm. Named after provinces of the Netherlands, and the two principal cities. To be replaced by a new class of frigates after 1975.

RADAR. Search: LWO 3. Tactical: DA 02. Fire Control: HSA M Series.

GUNNERY. The 4·7 inch guns are fully automatic with a rate of fire of 50 rounds per minute. All guns are radar controlled. Originally six 40 mm guns were mounted.

AMSTERDAM   *1969, Royal Netherlands Navy, Official*

TORPEDO TUBES. *Utrecht* was equipped with eight 21 inch A/S torpedo tubes (single, four on each side) in 1960 and *Overijssel* in 1961, and the others were to have been, but the project was dropped and tubes already fitted were removed.

PHOTOGRAPHS. A photograph of *Friesland* appears in the 1967-68 to 1969-70 editions, of *Rotterdam* in the 1964-65 to 1966-67 editions and of *Utrecht* in the 1967-68 and 1968-69 editions.

DISPOSALS OF DE TYPE
The six frigates or destroyer escorts of the "Van Amstel" class, *De Bitter* (ex-USS *Rinehart, DE 196*) F 807, *De Zeeuw* (ex-USS *Eisner, DE 192*) F 810, *Dubois* (ex-USS *O'Neill, DE 188*) F 809, *Van Amstel* (ex-USS *Burrows, DE 195*) F 806, *Van Ewijck* (ex-USS *Gustafson, DE 182*) F 808, and *Van Zijll* (ex-USS *Stern, DE 187*) F 811, were returned to the US Navy and sold for scrap in Dec 1967.

LIMBURG   *1970, courtesy Admiral M. Adam*

FRIESLAND   *1971, Royal Netherlands Navy, Official*

DRENTHE   *1971, Dr. Giorgio Arra*

ANTI-SUBMARINE ESCORTS (DDE) —*continued*

Name	No.	Builders	Laid down	Launched	Completed
HOLLAND	D 808	Rotterdamse Droogdok Mij, Rotterdam	21 Apr 1950	11 Apr 1953	31 Dec 1954
ZEELAND	D 809	Koninklijke Maatschappji De Schelde, Flushing	12 Jan 1951	27 June 1953	1 Mar 1955
NOORD BRABANT	D 810	Koninklijke Maatschappji De Schelde, Flushing	1 Mar 1951	28 Nov 1953	1 June 1955
GELDERLAND	D 811	Dok-en-Werfmaatschappij Wilton-Fijenoord	10 Mar 1951	19 Sep 1953	17 Aug 1955

4 "HOLLAND" CLASS

Displacement, tons	2 215 standard; 2 765 full load
Length, feet (metres)	360·5 (109·9) pp; 371 (113·1) oa
Beam, feet (metres)	37·5 (11·4)
Draught, feet (metres)	16·8 (5·1)
Guns, surface	4—4·7 in (120 mm) twin turrets
Guns, AA	1—40 mm
A/S weapons	2 four-barrelled depth charge mortars
Boilers	4 Babcock
Main engines	Werkspoor Parsons geared turbines; 45 000 shp; 2 shafts
Speed, knots	32
Complement	247

Two ships of this class are equipped with engines of the pre-war "Callenburgh" class and two with similar engines built during the war in the Netherlands, intended for German destroyers that were never built. (The four "Callenburgh" class destroyers were being built in 1940. *Isaac Sweers* was towed to England and completed there. *Tjerk Hiddes* was completed by the Germans as ZH 1. The other two, *Callenburgh* and *Van Almonde*, were too severely damaged for further use and were scrapped, the engines being installed in the "Holland" class).

RADAR. Search: LWO 3. Tactical: DA 02. Fire Control: HSA M Series.

GUNNERY. The 4·7 inch guns are fully automatic with a rate of fire of 50 rounds per minute. All guns are radar controlled.

PHOTOGRAPHS. A photograph of *Gelderland* appears in the 1968-69 and 1969-70 editions.

4 NEW CONSTRUCTION ASW TYPE

Displacement, tons	circa 2 000
Speed, knots	30 approx

The 1970 Estimates included a vote for the construction of four new anti-submarine frigates to replace the four "Holland" class DDEs in 1976-77. Construction is now scheduled to start in 1972.

NOORD BRABANT   1969, Royal Netherlands Navy. Official

ZEELAND   1971, Dr. Giorgio Arra

HOLLAND   1970, courtesy Godfrey H. Walker, Esq

CORVETTES

Name	No.	Builders	Laid down	Launched	Completed
FRET (ex-*PCE 1604*)	F 818	General Shipbuilding and Engineering Works, Boston	18 Dec 1952	30 July 1953	4 May 1954
HERMELIJN (ex-*PCE 1605*)	F 819	General Shipbuilding and Engineering Works, Boston	2 Mar 1953	6 Mar 1954	5 Aug 1954
JAGUAR (ex-*PCE 1609*)	F 822	Avondale Marine Ways, Inc, New Orleans, Louisiana	10 Dec 1952	20 Mar 1954	11 June 1954
PANTER (ex-*PCE 1608*)	F 821	Avondale Marine Ways, Inc, New Orleans, Louisiana	1 Dec 1952	30 Jan 1954	11 June 1954
VOS (ex-*PCE 1606*)	F 820	General Shipbuilding and Engineering Works, Boston	3 Aug 1952	1 May 1954	2 Dec 1954
WOLF (ex-*PCE 1607*)	F 817	Avondale Marine Ways, Inc, New Orleans, Louisiana	15 Nov 1952	2 Jan 1954	26 Mar 1954

6 "WOLF" CLASS

Displacement, tons	808 standard; 975 full load
Length, feet (metres)	180 (54·9) pp; 184·5 (56·2) oa
Beam, feet (metres)	33 (10·0)
Draught, feet (metres)	9·5 (2·9) mean; 14·5 (4·4) max
Guns, dual purpose	1—3 in (76 mm)
Guns, AA	6—40 mm (Jaguar, Panter: 4—40 mm); 8—20 mm
A/S	1 Hedgehog; 2 DCT (Jaguar, Panter: 4); 2 DC racks
Main engines	2 GM diesels; 1 600 bhp; 2 shafts
Speed, knots	15
Complement	96

PCE type escorts built in USA. *Lynx* (ex-*PCE 1626*) of a different type, similar to the Italian "Albatros" and Danish "Triton" classes, was returned to USN on 18 Oct 1961 and handed over to the Italian Navy and renamed *Aquila*.

PHOTOGRAPHS. A photograph of *Fret* appears in the 1957-58 to 1960-61 editions, of *Jaguar* in the 1961-62 to 1967-68 editions, of *Panter* in the 1962-63 to 1967-68 editions, of *Wolf* in the 1968-69 and 1969-70 editions.

VOS   1970, Royal Netherlands Navy. Official

MCM SUPPORT SHIPS AND ESCORTS

Name	No.	Laid down	Completed
ONVERSAAGD (ex-AM 480)	A 854 (ex-M 884)	1952	27 May 1954
ONBEVREESD (ex-AM 481)	A 855 (ex-M 885)	1952	21 Sep 1954
ONVERSCHROKKEN (ex-AM 483)	A 856 (ex-M 886)	1952	22 July 1954
ONVERMOEID (ex-AM 484)	A 857 (ex-M 887)	1952	23 Sep 1954
ONVERVAARD (ex-AM 482)	A 858 (ex-M 888)	1952	31 Mar 1955
ONVERDROTEN (ex-AM 485)	A 859 (ex-M 889)	1952	22 Nov 1954

Displacement, tons	735 standard; 790 full load
Dimensions, feet	165·0 pp; 172·0 oa × 36·0 × 10·6
Guns	1—40 mm AA
A/S weapons	2 DC
Main engines	Diesels; 1 600 bhp = 15·5 knots
Oil fuel, tons	46
Radius, miles	2 400 at 12 knots
Complement	70

Built in USA for the Netherlands, *Onversaagd, Onbevreesd* and *Onvervaard* by Astoria Marine Construction Co and the remaining three by Peterson, Builders, Wisconsin. Of wooden and non-magnetic construction.

RECLASSIFICATION. Originally designed as Ocean Minesweepers (*Oceaan-mijnen vegers*) but used as Escorts and re-numbered with "A" pennants in 1966. Reclassified in 1968 as Escorts (*Escortevaartuigen*) for *Onversaagd, Onbevreesd* and *Onvervaard*, and MCM Group Command and Support Ships (*Hoofdkwartier-ondersteuningsachepen voor MB Groepen*) for *Onverschrokken, Onvermoeid* and *Onverdroten*.

ONVERVAARD (Escort type)   1969, Royal, Netherlands Navy, Official

ONVERDROTEN (Command Type)   Added 1971, Godfrey H. Walker

PATROL VESSELS (*Patrouillevaartuigen*)

Name	No.	Laid down	Launched	Completed
BALDER	P 802	12 Sep 1953	24 Feb 1954	6 Aug 1954
BULGIA	P 803	10 Oct 1953	24 Apr 1954	9 Aug 1954
FREYR	P 804	24 Feb 1954	21 July 1954	1 Dec 1954
HADDA	P 805	24 Apr 1954	2 Oct 1954	3 Feb 1955
HEFRING	P 806	21 July 1954	1 Dec 1954	23 Mar 1955

Displacement, tons	149 standard; 225 full load
Dimensions, feet	114·9 pp; 119·1 oa × 20·2 × 5·9
Guns	1—40 mm; 3—20 mm
A/S weapons	2 DGT, Mousetrap
Main engines	Diesels; 2 shafts; 1 050 shp = 15·5 knots
Radius, miles	1 000
Complement	27

Built in the Netherlands by Rijkswerf Willemsoord on US account. US submarine chaser type, SC Nos 1627-1631.

PHOTOGRAPHS. A photograph of *Hadda* appears in the 1960-61 edition, of *Balder* in the 1961-62 to 1965-66 editions, of *Freyr* in the 1966-67 to 1970-71 editions.

HEFRING   1971, Royal Netherlands Navy, Official

MINE COUNTERMEASURES VESSELS

18 "DOKKUM" CLASS

ABCOUDE	M 810	HOOGEZAND	M 802	ROERMOND*	M 806
DOKKUM	M 801 H	HOOGEVEEN	M 827	SITTARD	M 830
DRACHTEN	M 812	NAALDWIJK	M 809	STAPHORST	M 828 H
DRUNEN	M 818 H	NAARDEN	M 823	VEERE	M 842 H
GEMERT	M 841	OMMEN	M 813	VENLO	M 817
GIETHOORN	M 815	RHENEN*	M 844	WOERDEN*	M 820

9 "WILDERVANK" CLASS

AALSMEER	M 811	GOES	M 819	MEPPEL	M 814
AXEL	M 808	GRIJPSKERK	M 826	WAALWIJK*	M 807
ELST	M 829	LEERSUM*	M 822	WILDERVANK	M 803

Displacement, tons	373 standard; 417 full load
Dimensions, feet	149·8 oa × 28 × 6·5
Guns	2—40 mm
Main engines	2 diesels; Fyenoord MAN or Werkspoor; 2 500 bhp = 16 knots
Complement	38

Of 32 Western Union type non-magnetic coastal minesweepers built in the Netherlands (*Kustmynenvegers*), 18 were on US account as the "Dokkum" class, with MAN engines, and 14 on Netherlands account as the "Wildervank" class, with Werkspoor diesels. All launched in 1954-56 and completed in 1955-56. Named after small towns in the Netherlands. *Dokkum* and *Drunen* converted to minehunters *Mijnenjagers* (MHC) in 1968-70, *Veere* in 1970-71 and *Staphorst* in 1971-72. Five more conversions pending. *Leersum, Rhenen, Waalwijk* and *Woerden* were converted to MCM diving vessels (*Duikvaartuigen*) in 1962-65, and *Roermond* in 1968. A photograph of *Venlo* appears in the 1961-62 to 1965-66 editions, of *Aalsmeer* in the 1962-63 to 1966-67 editions, of *Meppel* in the 1966-67 to 1968-69 editions, of *Maaldwijk* in the 1967-68 and 1968-69 editions. *Gieten, Lisse, Lochem, Sneek* and *Steenwijk* of the "Wildervank" class were officially deleted from the list in 1970, and *Elst* was sold to Ethiopia in 1971.

HOOGEZAND (Sweeper)   1969, Wright & Logan

DOKKUM (Hunter)   1971, Royal Netherlands Navy, Official

14 "BEEMSTER" CLASS

BEEMSTER (ex-*AMS* 105)	M 845	BREUKELEN (ex-*AMS* 100)	M 852
BOLSWARD (ex-*AMS* 109)	M 846	BLARICUM (ex-*AMS* 112)	M 853
BEDUM (ex-*Beerta* ex-*AMS* 106)	M 847	BRIELLE (ex-*AMS* 167)	M 854
BEILEN (ex-*AMS* 110)	M 848	BRESKENS (ex-*AMS* 148)	M 855
BORCULO (ex-*AMS* 107)	M 849	BRUINISSE (ex-*AMS* 168)	M 856
BORNE (ex-*AMS* 108)	M 850	BOXTEL (ex-*AMS* 149)	M 857
BRUMMEN (ex-*AMS* 111)	M 851	BROUWERSHAVEN ex-*AMS* 150)	M 858

Displacement, tons	330 standard; 384 full load
Dimensions, feet	138 pp; 144·7 oa × 27·9 × 7·5
Guns	2—20 mm AA
Main engines	2 diesels; 880 bhp = 13·6 knots
Complement	37

All completed and transferred from USA in 1953-54. Of non-magnetic construction. Named after small towns in the Netherlands. A photograph of *Beemster* appears in the 1955-56 to 1960-61 editions, of *Brummen* in the 1966-67 and 1967-68 editions, of *Borcolo* in the 1968-69 to 1970-71 editions.

BROUWERSHAVEN   1971, courtesy Mr. Michael D. J. Lennon

INSHORE MINESWEEPERS

(Ondiepwater mijnenvegers)

16 "VAN STRAELEN" CLASS

ALBLAS	M 868	MAHU	M 880	VAN MOPPES	M 873
BUSSEMAKER	M 869	SCHUILING	M 876	VAN STRAELEN	M 872
CHÖMPFF	M 874	STAVERMAN	M 881	VAN VERSENDAAL	M 877
HOUTEPEN	M 882	VAN DER WEL	M 878	VAN WELL GROENEVALD	
LACOMBLÉ	M 870	VAN HAMEL	M 871		M 875
		VAN 'T HOFF	M 879	ZOMER	M 883

Displacement, tons	151 light; 169 full load
Dimensions, feet	90 pp; 99·3 oa × 18·2 × 5·2
Guns	1—20 mm AA
Main engines	Werkspoor diesels; 2 shafts; 1 100 bhp = 13 knots
Complement	12

Built, 6 by Werf de Noord at Albasserdam; 5 by N.V. de Arnhemse Scheepsbouw Maatschappij at Arnhem; and 5 by Amsterdamsche Scheepswerft G. de Vries Lentsch Jr at Amsterdam. Eight were built under the offshore procurement programme, with MDAP funds, and the remaining eight were paid for by Netherlands. All ordered in mid-1957. Built of non-magnetic materials. *Alblas*, the first, was laid down at Werf de Noord N.V. at Albasserdam on 26 Feb 1958, launched on 29 June 1959, started trials on 15 Jan 1960 and completed on 12 Mar 1960. All the others were laid down in 1958-61, launched in 1958-61 and commissioned in 1960-62.
A photograph of *Alblas* appears in the 1960-61 edition, of *Bussemaker* in the 1961-62 to 1965-66 editions, of *Van Straelen* in the 1966-67 to 1968-69 editions.

VAN HAMEL   *1969, Royal Netherlands Navy, Official*

ACCOMMODATION SHIPS (Logementschepen)

A 891 *Soemba*, former radar training ship, A 881 *Neptunus*, A 882 *Schorpioen*, A 884 *Buffel*, A887 *Haarlemmermeer*, A 888 *Hertog Hendrik* (reserve) and *Van Kinsbergen*, former frigate, ex-gunboat. A 877 (ex-*Flores*), former gunboat, and A 878 *Tromp*, former light cruiser, were scrapped in 1968; A 880 *Willem van der Zaan*, former minesweeper support ship, former frigate, former minelayer, and A 879 *Jacob can Heemskerck*, former light cruiser in 1970, and the old depot ship *Cornelius Drebble*, A 886, in 1971.

Cornelius Drebble is the name of the new "Boatel":—775 tons, length 206·7 feet, beam 38·7 feet, draught 3·6 feet, complement 200, cost 3m guilders. Ordered in 1969 from Scheepswerf Voorwaarts at Hoogezand, launched on 19 Nov 1970 and completed in 1971. Serves as accommodation vessel for crews of ships refitting at private yards in the Rotterdam area.

SUPPLY SHIPS (Voorraadschepen)

1 Ex-US LST TYPE

WOENDI (ex-*Steven van der Hagen*, ex-*LST V*, ex-*LST* 1034) A 832

Displacement, tons	1,625 light; 3,770 standard; 4 145 full load
Dimensions, feet	316 wl; 328 oa × 50 × 14 max
Guns	4—40 mm AA; 6—20 mm AA
Main engines	Diesel; 2 shafts; 1 800 bhp = 11 knots
Complement	105

Built at Boston, Mass, in 1944. Seagoing store ship at Den Helder. *Zuiderkrius* (ex-*Granston Victory*) A 853 was paid off in 1968 and sold for scrap in Spain.

1 Ex-BRITISH LST TYPE

PELIKAAN (ex-HMS *Thruster*, ex-*LST*) A 830

Displacement, tons	2 840 light; 4 250 standard; 6 538 full load
Dimensions, feet	390 × 49 × 13
Guns	2—40 mm AA; 10—20 mm AA
Main engines	Turbine; 7 000 shp = 17 knots
Oil fuel, tons	2 100 max
Complement	127

Built by Harland & Wolff Ltd, Belfast. Laid down on 31 July 1941. Launched on 24 Sep 1942. Completed on 14 Mar 1943. Purchased from Great Britain in 1947. Commissioned in the Royal Netherlands Navy in July 1948. Store ship at Den Helder.

PELIKAAN   *1969, Royal Netherlands Navy, Official*

SURVEY SHIPS (Opnemingsvaartuigen)

1 NEW CONSTRUCTION OCEANOGRAPHIC TYPE

The 1971 Estimates announce the construction of a new oceanographic ship to replace both survey ships, *Luymes* and *Snellius*.

2 NEW CONSTRUCTION PILOT CUTTER TYPE

Displacement, tons	1 050 tons (official figure)
Dimensions, feet	193·6 × 36·4 × 12·2
Main engines	Diesel electric; 2 100 hp (3 × 700) = 13 knots max
Complement	45

The projected two survey ships, the construction of which was announced in the 1971 Defence Estimates, were ordered in Feb 1971 from the yard of Boele Scheepswerven en Machinenfabriek, Bolnes. One of these will replace the old survey vessel *Zeefakkel*, see below. Their design is based on that of the very successful pilot cutters of the "Capella" class. To have a helicopter deck. Both ships primarily have been designed for survey work, but can also be used for limited oceanographic and meteorological work. They will operate mainly in the North Sea and other shallow waters of the continental shelf. Their cost is estimated to be 10·5 million guilders per ship. They will be completed in Jan and May 1973.

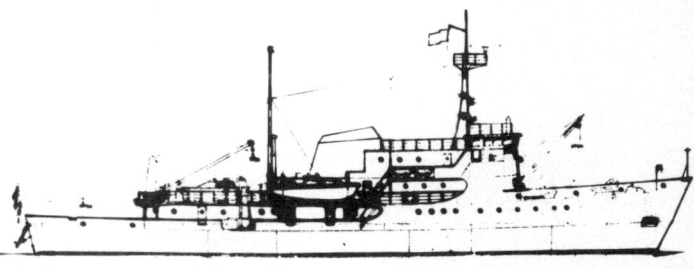

SURVEY SHIPS building   *1971, Official*

Name	No.	Builders	Laid down	Launched	Completed
LUYMES	A 902	Gusto, Schiedam	4 Apr 1949	21 Apr 1951	4 May 1952
SNELLIUS	A 907	P. Smit, Jr, Rotterdam	3 Jan 1949	14 Apr 1951	4 Feb 1952

Displacement, tons	1 100 standard; 1 540 full load
Dimensions, feet	234·2 × 35·5 × 12·8
Guns	1—40 mm AA; 2—20 mm AA
Main engines	2 Stork 6 cyl, 4 str diesels; 2 shafts; 2 000 bhp = 15 knots
Complement	80

Sloop type. Fitted for service in the tropics with special upper deck access and habitability. A photograph of *Snellius* appears in the 1970-71 edition.

LLUYMES   *1970, Royal Netherlands Navy, Official*

ZEEFAKKEL A 903

Displacement, tons	355 standard; 384 full load
Dimensions, feet	149·0 oa × 24·7 × 6·9 max
Guns	1—3 AA; 1—40 mm AA
Main engines	2 Smit 8 cyl, 4 str MAN diesels; 2 shafts; 640 bhp = 12 knots
Complement	29

Built by J. & K. Smit, Kinderdijk where she was laid down in Sep 1949, launched on 21 July 1950 and completed on 22 Mar 1951. Commissioned on 23 Mar 1951, for local service. Photographs appear in the 1957-58 to 1967-68 editions.

DREG IV A 920

Displacement, tons	46 standard; 48 full load
Dimensions, feet	65·7 × 15·1 × 4·9
Main engines	120 hp = 9·5 knots
Complement	10

Sister boats *Dreg I*, *Dreg II* and *Dreg III* of this class were scrapped in 1969-70.

DIVING VESSELS (Duikvaartuigen)

5 coastal minesweepers, *Rhenen*, *Roermond* and *Woerden* of the "Dokkum" class and *Leersum* and *Waalwijk* of the "Wildervank" class were converted to diving vessels. There are also four small harbour diving craft (*duiksloepen*), *Argus*, A 843, *Hydra*, A 850, *Nautilus*, A 849 and *Triton*, A 848.

WEATHER SHIPS

WEATHER SHIPS. The weather observation ships *Cirrus* (ex-USS *Abilene*, PF 58) and *Cumulus* (ex-USS *Forsyth*, PF 102), former patrol frigates, were replaced by a new weather observation ship, *Cumulus*, specially built for this work...In May 1962 her keel was laid at the yard of the NV Gebr van der Werf at Deest (near Nijmegen). Launched on 22 Dec 1962. Taken over on 18 Apr 1963. Measurement: 1 974 tons gross. Dimensions: Length 233·7 oa; 203·5 pp. Beam 41 feet. Draught 15 feet. Main engines: 6-cyl Werkspoor diesel; 1 400 bhp = 12 knots. Crew 62. She is operated by the Ministry of Transport and manned by mercantile personnel.

FAST COMBAT SUPPORT SHIP

1 NEW CONSTRUCTION

The 1971 Estimates include a vote for the construction of a second Fast Combat Support Ship. Will be similar but slightly larger and faster than *Poolster*.

POOLSTER A 835

Displacement, tons	16 800 full load
Measurement, tons	10 000 deadweight
Dimensions, feet	515 pp; 552·2 oa × 66·7 × 27
Guns	2—40 mm AA
Aircraft	Capacity: 5 helicopters (official complement 3 SH-34 J)
Main engines	22 500 shp turbines = 21 knots (18 service)

Fast fleet replenishment ship (*Bevoorradingsschip*). Built by Rotterdam Dry Dock Co. Laid down on 18 Sep 1962. Launched on 16 Oct 1963. Trials mid-1964. Commissioned on 10 Sep 1964. Helicopter deck aft. Funnel heightened by 4·5 m.

POOLSTER   *1969, Skyfotos*

LANDING CRAFT (*Landingsvaartuigen*)

L 9521   L 9526

Displacement, tons	20
Dimensions, feet	50 × 11·8 × 5·8
Main engines	2 Kromhout diesels; 75 bhp = 8 knots
Complement	3

Now officially rated as LCA Type. The landing craft L 9609 (ex-*Kais*) was sold in 1970.

L 9510	L 9512	L 9514	L 9517	L 9520
L 9511	L 9513	L 9515	L 9518	L 9522

Displacement, tons	13·6
Dimensions, feet	46·2 × 11·5 × 6
Main engines	Rolls Royce diesel; Schottel propeller; 200 bhp = 12 knots
Complement	3

New landing craft made of plastic (polyester), all commissioned in 1962-63, except L 9520 in 1964.

L 9510   *1969, Royal Netherlands Navy, Official*

TRAINING SHIPS (*Opleidingsvaartuigen*)

HENDRIK KARSSEN (ex-Y 807, ex-RC 11, ex-De Mok 1) Y 8102

Displacement, tons	172 standard; 185 full load
Dimensions, feet	137·8 oa; 114 pp × 20·7 × 5·5
Guns	2—20 mm AA
Main engines	2 Kromhout diesels; 180 bhp = 11 knots
Complement	18

Built by Rijkswerf Willemsoord. Launched in 1939. Equipped with water monitors for fire fighting. Renamed *Hendrik Karssen* in 1954. Training and ferry vessel for local use at Den Helder. A photograph appears in the 1966-67 and 1967-68 editions.

HOBEIN (ex-Doornbos, ex-German Dornbusch) Y 8101

Displacement, tons	132
Dimensions, feet	92 oa; 83·3 pp × 19·7 × 5·5
Guns	1—40 mm AA; 1—20 mm AA
Main engines	Diesel; 250 bhp = 8·5 knots
Complement	10

Navigational training ship for midshipmen and other naval personnel, and ferry vessel for local use at Den Helder. Renamed *Hobein* in July 1952.

URANIA (ex-Tromp) Y 8050

Displacement, tons	38
Dimensions, feet	72 × 16·3 × 10
Main engines	Diesel; 65 hp
Complement	15

Schooner used for training in seamanship. Commissioned on 23 Apr 1938.

TENDERS (*Hulpschepen*)

VAN BOCHOVE A 923

Displacement, tons	150
Dimensions, feet	97·2 × 18·2 × 6
Main engines	Kromhout diesel; Schottel propeller; 140 bhp = 8 knots
Complement	8

Torpedo recovery vessel. Built by Zaanlandse Scheepsbouw Mij, Zaandam. Ordered Oct 1961, launched on 20 July 1962 and completed in Aug 1962.

DIVING TENDER (NETLAYER)
The diving tender *Cerebus*, A 895, former netlayer, was returned to the US Navy on 17 Sep 1970. The ship was then immediately handed over to the Turkish Navy and named *AG 6*.

VAN BOCHOVE   *1968, Royal Netherlands Navy, Official*

MERCUUR A 829

Displacement, tons	274 standard; 290 full load
Dimensions, feet	137·5 pp; 140 oa × 23 × 9
Main engines	Diesels engine; 375 bhp = 12 knots (see *Notes*)
Complement	35

Built by Rijkswerf Willemsoord. Launched on 26 Feb 1936. Torpedo trials vessel. Rebuilt in 1960, triple expansion replaced by diesel, and guns removed.

TUGS (*Sleepboten*)

WESTGAT A 872   WIELINGEN A 873

Displacement, tons	185
Dimensions, feet	90·6 × 22·7 × 7·7
Guns	2—20 mm AA
Main engines	Bolnes diesel; 720 bhp = 12 knots

Built by Rijkswerf, Willemsoord. Launched on 22 Aug 1967 and 6 Jan 1968 and completed on 10 Jan 1968 and 4 Apr 1968, respectively. Equipped with salvage pumps and fire fighting equipment. Stationed at Den Helder. The tug *Hercules* (ex-*Walcheren XII*, ex-*Atlas*) A 828, was sold to private interests in 1968.

WAMANDAI   *1970, Royal Netherlands Navy, Official*

WAMANDAI A 870 (ex-Y. 8035)

Displacement, tons	159 standard; 185 full load
Dimensions, feet	89·2 × 21·3 × 7·5
Guns	2—20 mm AA
Main engines	Diesel; 500 bhp = 11 knots

Built by Rijkswerf, Willemsoord, Den Helder. Launched on 28 May 1960. Equipped with salvage pumps and fire fighting equipment. In the Netherlands Antilles since 1964.

WAMBRAU A 871

Displacement, tons	154 standard; 184 full load
Dimensions, feet	86·5 oa × 20·7 × 7·5
Guns	2—20 mm AA
Main engines	Werkspoor diesel and Kort nozzle; 500 bhp = 10·8 knots

Built by Rijkswerf Willemsoord. Launched on 27 Aug 1956. Completed on 8 Jan 1957. Equipped with salvage pumps and fire fighting equipment. Stationed at Den Helder.

BERKEL Y 8037   DINTEL Y 8038   DOMMEL Y 8039   IJSSEL Y 8040

Displacement, tons	139 standard; 163 full load
Dimensions, feet	82 oa × 20·5 × 7·3
Main engines	Werkspoor diesel and Kort nozzle; 500 bhp

Harbour tugs built by H. H. Bodewes, Millingen. Specially designed for use at Den Helder. Completed in 1956-57.

NEW ZEALAND

Defence Headquarters Naval Staff

Chief of the Naval Staff:
Rear Admiral L. G. Carr, CB, DSC

Deputy Chief of the Naval Staff:
Commodore R. T. Hale, OBE

The three New Zealand Service Boards were formally abolished in 1971 as part of the Defence Headquarters reorganization. The former three Service Headquarters and Defence Office have been reorganised into functional branches and offices.
On 1 June 1970 the command and control of the three New Zealand Services was vested in the Chief of Defence Staff who exercises this authority through the three Service Chiefs of Staff.

Diplomatic Representation

Head of New Zealand Defence Liaison Staff, London and Senior Naval Liaison Officer:
Commodore E. C. Thorne

Deputy Head of New Zealand Defence Staff, Washington and Naval Attaché:
Commander D. B. Domett, RNZN

Personnel

January 1969: 2 959 officers and ratings
January 1970: 3 074 officers and ratings
January 1971: 2 870 officers and ratings

Strength of the Fleet

4 Frigates
1 Survey Ship (former Frigate)
2 Escort Minesweepers (Ocean)
12 Seaward Patrol Craft
1 Antarctic Support Ship
1 Research Vessel
2 Tenders

Mercantile Marine

Lloyd's Register of Shipping:
122 vessels of 185 836 tons gross

Silhouettes

Scale: 150 feet = 1 inch (1 : 1 800)

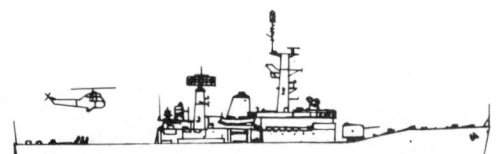

WAIKATO

OTAGO, TARANAKI

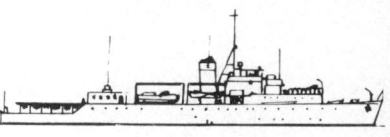

LACHLAN

FRIGATES

Name	No.	Builders	Laid down	Launched	Completed
CANTERBURY	F 421	Yarrow Ltd, Clyde	12 Apr 1969	6 May 1970	Late 1971
WAIKATO	F 55	Harland & Wolff Ltd, Belfast	10 Jan 1964	18 Feb 1965	19 Sep 1966

2 "LEANDER" CLASS
GENERAL PURPOSE
IMPROVED TYPE 12

Displacement, tons	2 305 standard; 2 640 normal; 2 800 full load
Length, feet (*metres*)	360 (*109·7*) pp; 372 (*113·4*) oa
Beam, feet (*metres*)	41 (*12·5*)
Draught, feet (*metres*)	13·8 (*4·2*)
Aircraft	1 Wasp helicopter armed with homing torpedoes
Missiles, AA	1 "Seacat" quadruple launcher
Guns, surface	2—4·5 in (*155 mm*) in twin turret; 2—20 mm
A/S	1 Limbo 3-barrelled DC mortar
Boilers	2 Babcock & Wilcox
Main engines	2 sets d.r. geared turbines 30 000 shp; 2 shafts
Speed, knots	30
Complement	248 (14 officers, 234 ratings)

Waikato, ordered in 14 June 1963 (announced by the High Commission for New Zealand in London). Commissioned on 16 Sep 1966, trials in the United Kingdom until spring 1967, arrived in New Zealand waters in May 1967. *Canterbury* was ordered in Aug 1968, for delivery late 1971.

RADAR. Long range metric wavelength air warning radar with antenna of "Mattress" type at top of mainmast. S band surface and close range air warning radar antenna mounted on top of foremast. X band navigation radar. Gunfire control system director, mounted above compass platform has X band tracker radar. Second fire control director, aft of the mainmast, employs X band tracker radar. IFF secondary rader.

PHOTOGRAPHS. A starboard broadside surface view of *Waikato* appears in the 1966-67 edition, a port quarter oblique aerial view in the 1967-68 and 1968-69 editions, and a broadside aerial view in the 1969-70 edition.

Blackpool, commissioned in the Royal New Zealand Navy on 16 June 1966, was returned to the Royal Navy in Apr 1971. To be replaced by *Canterbury*.

WAIKATO

1970, Royal New Zealand Navy, Official

WAIKATO

1971, Royal New Zealand Navy, Official

Frigates—continued

Name	No.	Builders	Launched	Completed
OTAGO (ex-*Hastings*)	F 111	John I. Thornycroft & Co, Ltd Woolston, Southampton	11 Dec 1958	22 June 1960
TARANAKI	F 148	J. Samuel White & Co Ltd, Cowes, Isle of Wight	19 Aug 1959	28 Mar 1961

2 "ROTHESAY" CLASS TYPE 12

Displacement, tons	2 144 standard; 2 557 full load
Length, feet (*metres*)	360 (*109·7*) pp; 370 (*112·8*) oa
Beam, feet (*metres*)	41 (*12·5*)
Draught, feet (*metres*)	12 (*3·7*)
Missiles, AA	1 "Seacat" quadruple launcher
Guns, surface	2—4·5 in (*115 mm*) in twin turret; 2—40 mm (*Taranaki* only)
A/S	2 Limbo 3-barrelled DC mortars
Torpedo tubes	Originally 12—21 in (*533 mm*), 8 single A/S, 2 twin (now suppressed)
Boilers	2 Babcock & Wilcox
Main engines	2 sets d.r. geared turbines 30 430 shp; 2 shafts
Speed, knots	over 30
Complement	240 (13 officers, 227 ratings)

Anti-submarine frigates. *Taranaki* was ordered direct (announced by J. Samuel White & Co on 22 Feb 1957). For *Otago* New Zealand took over the contract (officially stated on 26 Feb 1957) for *Hastings* originally ordered from John I. Thornycroft & Co in Feb 1956 for the Royal Navy). Both vessels are generally similar to those in the Royal Navy, but were modified to suit New Zealand conditions. *Otago* has had enclosed foremast since 1967 refit; *Taranaki* was similarly fitted during 1969.

OTAGO   1970, Royal New Zealand Navy, Official

DISPOSALS
Of the six anti-submarine frigates of the "Loch" class, purchased from Great Britain in 1948, and renamed after New Zealand lakes, *Taupo* and *Tutira* were sold for scrap on 15 Dec 1961, *Hawea* and *Pukaki* were sold for scrap at Hong Kong in Sep 1965, and *Rotoiti*, taken out of commission on 29 July 1965, and *Kaniere*, latterly used as an alongside training ship at Auckland, were scrapped in Hong Kong in Sept 1966.

TARANAKI   1971, Royal New Zealand Navy, Official

ESCORT MINESWEEPERS

2 "BATHURST" CLASS

Displacement, tons	790 standard; 1 025 full load
Length, feet (*metres*)	162 (*49·4*) pp; 186 (*56·7*) oa
Beam, feet (*metres*)	31 (*9·4*)
Draught, feet (*metres*)	9·5 (*2·9*)
Guns AA	2—40 mm
Boilers	2 Admiralty 3-drum small tube
Main engines	Triple expansion, 1 800 ihp; 2 shafts
Speed, knots	15
Complement	71

Name	No.	Builders	Laid down	Launched	Completed
INVERELL	M 233	Mort's Dock, Sydney	7 Dec 1941	2 May 1942	2 May 1943
KIAMA	M 353	Evans Deakins, Brisbane	2 Nov 1942	3 July 1943	26 Jan 1944

Originally four vessels of this class were given to New Zealand by Australia in 1952 (see disposal note below).

Kiama was recommissioned on 15 Mar 1966 for training and fishery protection duties, her 4-inch gun being replaced by a 40 mm AA gun, and a deckhouse being built aft.

Inverell was recommissioned on 15 Aug 1965 as a training ship for new entry ratings, replacing the frigate *Rotoiti*. Her sweeping gear was removed and her deckhouse extended further aft. 4-inch gun replaced by 40 mm.

PHOTOGRAPHS. A photograph of *Kiama* appears in the 1953-54, 1954-55 and 1955-56 editions.

DISPOSALS
Echuca was scrapped at Auckland in April 1968, and *Stawell* in Aug 1968.

COASTAL MINESWEEPERS. The Royal Navy coastal minesweepers HICKLETON and SANTON, which were manned by the Royal New Zealand Navy, commissioning at Singapore on 10 Apr 1965 for patrol duties in Malaysian waters, reverted to the Royal Navy in late 1966 and returned to the United Kingdom.

INVERELL   1969, Royal New Zealand Navy, Official

DISPOSALS OF LIGHT CRUISERS.
Of the two light cruisers of the improved "Dido" class lent to New Zealand by Great Britain, *Black Prince* reverted to Royal Navy control in Dec 1961 and was scrapped in Japan in May 1962, and *Royalist* was taken out of commission on 4 July 1966 and reverted to the control of the Royal Navy, prior to sale for scrapping in Japan, towed from Auckland Jan 1968.

SURVEY SHIPS *(Ex-Frigate)*

LACHLAN F 364

Displacement, tons	1 420 standard; 2 220 full load
Length, feet (*metres*)	301·2 (*91·8*)
Beam, feet (*metres*)	36·7 (*11·2*)
Draught, feet (*metres*)	12 (*3·7*)
Boilers	2 Admiralty 3-drum
Main engines	Triple expansion
	5 500 ihp; 2 shafts
Speed, knots	20
Complement	143

Former Australian "River" class frigate. Built by Mort's Dock, Sydney, NSW, launched on 25 Mar 1944, transferred on loan from RAN in 1948 and purchased outright in 1962. Her forecastle deck was subsequently extended aft from the shelter deck to the quarter deck. Guns were removed on conversion for survey duties. A helicopter platform 50 feet by 30 feet, 7 feet above the quarter deck, was laid in 1966.

LACHLAN

1971, John Mortimer

SEAWARD PATROL BOAT

12 HDML TYPE

HAKU P 3565 (ex-*Wakefield* ex-Q 1197)
KAHAWAI P3553 (ex-*Tamaki*)
KOURA P 3564 (ex-*Toroa* ex-Q 1350)
KUPARU P 3563 (ex-*Pegasus* ex-Q 1349)
MAKO P3551 (ex-Q 1183)
MANGA P3567 (ex-Q 1185)
MARORO P3554 (ex-*Irirangi* ex-Q 1192)
PAEA P3552 (ex-Q 1184)
PARORE P3562 (ex-Q 1190 ex *Olphert*)
TAKAPU P3556 (ex-Q 1188)
TAMURE P3555 (ex-*Ngapona* ex-Q 1193)
TARAPUNGA (P 3566 ex-Q 1387)

Displacement, tons	46 standard; 54 full load
Dimensions, feet	72 × 16 × 5·5
Guns	1—20 mm AA; several MG (not fitted at present)
Main engines	Diesel; 2 shafts; 320 bhp = 12 knots
Complement	9

Originally known as Harbour Defence Motor Launches. All built in various yards in the United States and Canada and shipped to New Zealand.

Takapu and *Tarapunga* are commissioned as surveying MLs and operate with *Lachlan*. All others have been converted with lattice masts surmounted by a radar aerial, *Mako*, *Paea*, *Maroro*, *Kahawai* and *Haku* are employed on Fishery Protection duties, others are attached to RNZNVR Divisions.

A photograph of *Mako* appears in the 1958-59 to 1962-63 editions, of *Paea* in the 1963-64 to 1965-66 editions and of *Manga* in the 1965-66 to 1969-70 edition.

KAHAWI and MAKO   1970, Royal New Zealand Navy, Official

TAMURE   1969, Royal New Zealand Navy, Official

TENDERS

ARATAKI   **MANAWANUI**

Dimensions, feet	Length: 75
Main engines	Diesel

Steel tugs. *Arataki* is used as a dockyard tug and *Manawanui* as a diving tender.

DISPOSALS
Of the two patrol vessels of the "Bird" class (anti-submarine and minesweeping trawlers of the corvette type) *Kiwi* was sold in 1962 and broken up at Auckland in 1965, and *Tui* was taken out of service in Dec 1967 and sold for scrap in the 1969.
The lighthouse tender *Hauraki* (ex-*Endeavour*) was deleted from the list in 1964.

The two Fairmile "B" Type motor launches *Maori* and *Philomel*, converted to local naval transports and passenger harbour craft, were deleted from the list in 1964.
Of the two naval stores vessels, *Lander 1* was deleted from the list in 1964, and *Coastguard* was sold as a fishing boat on 7 July 1961.
HMNZS *Endeavour* (ex-MV *John Biscoe*, ex-HMS *Pretext*, ex-USS *AN* 76), former netlayer, boom defence vessel, survey ship, and Antarctic support ship in turn, was declared surplus and sold in 1961.

RESEARCH VESSEL

TUI AGOR 5, ex-A 2 (ex-USNS *Charles H. Davis*, T-AGOR 5)

Displacement, tons	1 200 standard; 1 380 full load
Dimensions, feet	208·9 × 37·4 × 15·3
Main engines	Diesel-electric; 1 shaft; 10 000 hp = 12 knots
Complement	8 officers, 16 ratings, 15 scientists

Oceanographic research ship built by Christy Corp, Sturgeon Bay, Wis. Laid down on 15 June 1961, launched on 30 June 1962 and completed on 25 Jan 1963. On loan from US. Commissioned in the Royal New Zealand Navy on 11 Sep 1970. Bow propeller 175 hp.

TUI   1971, Royal New Zealand Navy, Official

ANTARCTIC SUPPORT SHIP

ENDEAVOUR A 184 (ex-USS *Namakagon*, AOG 53)

Displacement, tons	1 850 light; 4 335 full load
Dimensions, feet	292 wl; 310·8 oa × 48·7 × 15·7
Main engines	GM diesels; 2 shafts; 3 300 bhp = 14 knots
Complement	72 officers and ratings

Former US "Patapsco" class petrol carrier. Built by Cargill, Inc, Savage, Minn. Laid down on 1 Aug 1944. Launched on 4 Nov 1944. Refitted and strengthened for service in ice and transferred on loan to the Royal New Zealand Navy in Oct 1962

ENDEAVOUR   1971, John Mortimer

NICARAGUA
Mercantile Marine

Lloyd's Register of Shipping: 7 vessels of 15 933 tons gross

COAST GUARD BOATS *(Guardacostas)*

RIO CRUTA

Dimensions, feet	Length: 85
Guns	1—20 mm automatic cannon in bow
Main engines	Diesels; speed = 9 knots maximum
Complement	11

A wooden *guardacosta* of the Marine Section of the Guardia Nacional of Nicaragua. Another *guardacosta* without name or number is a diesel launch of approx 26 ft with a 20 mm gun, a designed speed of 25 knots and a crew of 5 or 6. Also reported were six wooden patrol boats, four 90 ft and two about 80 ft, and a former partol boat, 75 ft, wooden, built in 1925, used for training.

NIGERIA

Administration

Chief of the Naval Staff:
Rear-Admiral Joseph Etim Akinwole Wey, OFR

Naval Officer-in-Charge (Lagos):
Commodore Nelson Bossman Soroh

Chief of Staff:
Commander Mugibi Ayinde Adelanwa

Diplomatic Representation

Naval Attaché (Assistant Defence Adviser) in London:
Lieutenant Commander Emmanuel Oladipo Makinde

Strength of the Fleet

1 Frigate, 6 Seaward Defence Boats, 3 Fast Patrol Boats,
1 Landing craft, 2 Survey Craft.

Personnel

1968: 100 Officers and 1 200 ratings (official figures)
1970: 120 Officers and 1 600 ratings (official figures)
1971: 180 Officers and 2 000 ratings (official figures)

Mercantile Marine

Lloyd's Register of Shipping:
49 vessels of 98 634 tons gross

FRIGATE

Name	No.	Builders	Laid down	Launched	Completed
NIGERIA	F 87	Wilton, Fijenoord NV	9 Apr 1964	12 Apr 1965	16 Sep 1965

1 A/S AND AA TYPE

Displacement, tons	1 724 standard; 2 000 full load
Length, feet (*metres*)	341·2 (*104·0*) pp; 360·2 (*109·8*) oa
Beam, feet (*metres*)	37 (*11·3*)
Draught, feet (*metres*)	11 (*3·3*)
Guns, dual purpose	2—4 in (*102 mm*) twin mounting
Guns, AA	5—40 mm single mountings
A/S	1—triple-barrel DCM
Main engines	4 MAN diesels
	16 000 bhp; 2 shafts
Speed, knots	26
Complement	216

Anti-aircraft and anti-submarine frigate built in the Netherlands. Cost £3 500 000. Commissioned in Sep 1965. Helicopter platform laid on aft.

NIGERIA   *1970, Nigerian Navy, Official*

CORVETTES

2 Mk 3 VOSPER THORNYCROFT TYPE

DORINA   **OTOBO**

Displacement, tons	500 standard; 600 full load
Length, feet	202 oa
Guns	2—4 in (1 twin)
Main engines	2 MAN diesels = 23 knots max
Radius, miles	3 500 at 14 knots
Complement	66 (7 officers and 59 ratings)

Ordered on 28 Mar 1968. Laid down in 1970 for delivery in 1972. *Dorina* was launched on 16 Sep 1970 and *Otobo* in May 1971 (scheduled). Known as the "Hippopotamus" class as each name means "hippopotamus" in one of the principal Nigerian languages.

DORINA   *1971, Vosper Thornycroft*

SEAWARD DEFENCE BOATS

6 "FORD" CLASS

BENIN (ex-HMS *Hinksford*)   **KADUNA** (ex-HMS *Axford*) P 03
BONNY (ex-HMS *Difford*) P 3111   **SAPELE** (ex-HMS *Dubford*) P 3119
ENUGU P 3137   **IBADAN II** (ex-HMS *Bryansford*)

Displacement, tons	120 standard; 160 full load
Dimensions, feet	110 pp; 117·2 oa × 20 × 5
Guns	1—40 mm Bofors AA; 2—20 mm Oerlikon
A/S weapons	DC rails and DC
Main engines	Davey Paxman diesels; Foden engine on centre shaft; 1 100 bhp = 18 knots max; 15 knots sea speed
Complement	26

Enugu was the first warship built for the Nigerian Navy. Ordered from Camper and Nicholson's Gosport, in 1960. Completed on 14 Dec 1961. Sailed from Portsmouth for Nigeria on 10 Apr 1962. Fitted with Vosper roll damping fins. *Benin, Ibadan* and *Kaduna* were purchased from Great Britain on 1 July 1966 and transferred at Devonport on 9 Sep 1966. *Ibadan* was seized by the Eastern Region prior to its declaration of independence as the Republic of Biafra on 30 May 1967 and renamed *Vigilance* but was sunk at Port Harcourt on 10 Sep 1967 by Nigerian Navy, salved but later scrapped at Lagos. *Dubford* and *Gifford* were purchased from Great Britain during 1967-68 and *Bryansford* in 1968-69. A photograph of *Enugu* appears in the 1962-63 to 1969-70 editions.

KADUNA   *1970, Nigerian Navy, Official*

The seaward defence motor launch *Kaduna* (ex-HMS *SDML* 3515) was deleted from the Navy List in 1965. Presidential Yacht *Valiant* was transferred to Inland Waterways Department in 1966. Of the two minesweeping launches, *Sapele* (ex-*MSML* 2217) was disposed of in Feb 1967 and *Calabar* (ex-*MSML* 2223) was deleted from the list in 1969. The customs vessel *Challenger*, P 10, was deleted in 1970. The patrol vessel *Ogoja*, former Netherlands *Queen Wilhelmina*, ex-USS *PC* 468) was wrecked off Brass in October 1969.

FAST PATROL BOATS

3 Ex-SOVIET "P 6" CLASS

EKPEN   **EKUN**   **ELOLE**

Displacement, tons	69·6 standard; 79·5 full load
Dimensions, feet	83·7 × 20 × 9
Guns	4 × 25 mm (2 twin)
A/S Weapons	2 DCT; 2 DC racks
Engines	4 12 cyl diesels; 4 800 bhp = 38·5 knots
Complement	24

Soviet built fast patrol boats of the small submarine chaser type purchased from the USSR in 1967.

EKPEN   *1969, Nigerian Navy, Official*

LANDING CRAFT

LOKOJA (ex-*LCT* (4) 1213)

Displacement, tons	350 standard; 586 full load
Dimensions, feet	187·5 × 38·8 × 4·5
Guns	2—20 mm AA
Main engines	2 Paxman diesels; 920 bhp = 10 knots

Purchased from Great Britain in 1959. Allocated the name *Lokoja* in 1961. Underwent a major refit in 1966-67, including complete replating of the bottom.

LOKOJA   *1971, Nigerian Navy, Official*

SURVEY VESSELS

PATHFINDER P 06

Measurement, tons	544 gross
Dimensions, feet	154·2 × 27 × 11
Guns	1—40 mm AA
Main engines	2 triple expansion; 200 ihp = 8 knots

Built by J. Samuel White & Co Ltd, Cowes, Isle of Wight. Launched on 23 Oct 1953 and completed in 1954.

PENELOPE P 11

Measurement, tons	79 gross
Dimensions, feet	79·5 × 7·8 × 4·5
Main engines	2 Gardner diesels; speed 10 knots

Built by Aldous Successors, Brightlingsea in 1958. Used for local survey duties.

NORWAY

Administration

Commander-in-Chief (Inspector-General):
Rear Admiral Hans Sigurd Skjong, RNoN

Commander Coastal Fleet:
Commodore Øivind Schau, RNoN

Diplomatic Representation

Naval Attaché in London:
Captain Ole Andreas Aslaksrud, RNoN

Naval Attaché in Washington:
Captain Rolf Henningsen, DSC, RNoN

Naval Attaché in Moscow:
Captain Bjorn Erling Ytterhorn, RNoN

Strength of the Fleet

15 Coastal Submarines (Diesel Powered)
5 Frigates (Destroyer Escort Type)
4 Coastal Minelayers (ex-Ocean Minesweepers)
2 Patrol Vessels (Submarine Charers)
10 Coastal Minesweepers (Non-Magnetic)
26 Missile Torpedo Boats (Fast Patrol Boats)
20 Missile Gunboats (Fast Patrol Boats)
14 Fleet Support Ships and Service Craft

Ships

Norwegian warships are referred to officially with the prefix KNM, equivalent to HMS. Since Mar 1959 the suffix "RNoN" has been used instead of "RNorN".

Missile System

A Norwegian developed surface-to-ship guided missile system is the "Penguin" with a weight of 4 tons approx installed with 6 missiles. Missiles: Length 3 m (9·84 ft), Diameter 28 cm (11·0 in), Weight 330 kg (727·5 lbs), Warhead 120 kg (264·5 lbs), Range 20 km plus (over 13 miles) at high subsonic speed.

Personnel

1971: 9 000 officers and ratings
1970: 8 500 officers and ratings
1969: 7 200 officers and ratings
1968: 6 000 officers and ratings
1967: 6 000 officers and ratings
1966: 6 200 officers and ratings
1965: 6 000 officers and ratings
1964: 6 300 officers and ratings
1963: 6 300 officers and ratings
1962: 5 200 officers and ratings

Navy Estimates

1971: *ca* 600 000 000 kr. (official)

Mercantile Marine

Lloyds Register of Shipping:
2 808 ships of 19 346 911 tons gross

Scale: 150 feet = 1 inch (1˝ : 1 800)

OSLO *Class*

HAAKON VII

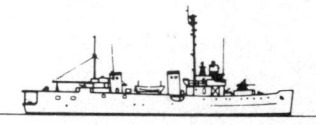

BRAGE, GOR, TYR, ULLER

SUBMARINES *(Undervannsbater)*

15 "KOBBEN" CLASS

Name	No.	Launched	Completed
KAURA	S 315	16 Oct 1964	5 Feb 1965
KINN	S 316	30 Nov 1963	8 Apr 1964
KOBBEN	S 318	25 Apr 1964	17 Aug 1964
KUNNA	S 319	16 July 1964	1 Oct 1964
KYA	S 317	20 Feb 1964	15 June 1964
SKLINNA	S 305	21 Jan 1966	27 May 1966
SKOLPEN	S 306	24 Mar 1966	17 Aug 1966
STADT	S 307	10 June 1966	15 Nov 1966
STORD	S 308	2 Sep 1966	9 Feb 1967
SVENNER	S 309	27 Jan 1967	1 July 1967
ULA	S 300	19 Dec 1964	7 May 1965
UTHAUG	S 304	8 Oct 1965	16 Feb 1966
UTSIRA	S 301	11 Mar 1965	1 July 1965
UTSTEIN	S 302	19 May 1965	9 Sep 1965
UTVAER	S 303	30 June 1965	1 Dec 1965

Displacement, tons	350 standard ; 472 submerged
Length, feet (*metres*)	149 (*45·4*)
Beam, feet (*metres*)	15 (*4·6*)
Draught, feet (*metres*)	14 (*4·3*)
Tubes	8—21 in (*533 mm*) bow
Main engines	2 MB 820 Maybach-Mercedes-Benz diesels ; 1 200 bhp ; electric drive ; 1 200 hp ; 1 shaft
Speed, knots	17
Complement	18 (5 officers, 13 men)

It was announced in July 1959 that the USA and Norway would share equally the cost of these submarines ordered under a modernisation programme, for delivery in 1964-67. All were built by Rheinstahl-Nordseewerke in Emden, West Germany. Of the same type as the German U 4 class but with stronger hulls to dive deeper.

NOMENCLATURE. These boats were given names perpetuating those of submarines which recently served in the Royal Norwegian Navy but have been discarded (see *Disposals* below), and some new names. The "U" group were named after features of the Norwegian seaboard, *Ula* being the name of the birthplace of Ulabrand the navigator.

PHOTOGRAPHS. A photograph of *Kya* appears in the 1964-65 to 1968-69 editions, of *Utstein* in the 1966-67 to 1968-69 editions, and of *Skolpen* in the 1968-69 and 1969-70 editions.

TRANSFER. The German submarine U 3, lent to the Royal Norwegian Navy in 1962 for training and temporarily named *Kobben*, S 310, was returned to the Federal German Navy in 1964. A new submarine for the Royal Norwegian Navy named *Kobben*, S 318 was completed in 1964 (see above).

DISPOSALS
Of the former British "U" class, *Utsira* (ex-HMS *Variance*) was stricken from the Navy List in Dec 1962, *Utstein* (ex-HMS *Venturer*) in Jan 1964, *Ula* (ex-HMS *Varne*) in July 1964, *Utvaer* (ex-HMS *Viking*) in Dec 1964, and *Uthang* (ex-HMS *Votary*) in Oct 1965.

DISPOSALS OF EX-GERMAN VII C TYPE
Of the ex-German VII C type, *Kinn* (ex-U 1202) was removed from the Royal Norwegian Navy List on 1 June 1961, *Kaura* (ex-U 995) in Jan 1963, and *Kya* (ex-U 926) in Mar 1964.

KINN   *1970, Royal Norwegian Navy, Official*

ULA   *1969, Royal Norwegian Navy, Official*

STADT   *1969, courtesy Godfrey H. Walker, Esq.*

5 "OSLO" CLASS

DESTROYER ESCORT TYPE

Displacement, tons	1 450 standard; 1 745 full load
Length, feet (metres)	308 (93·9) pp; 317 (96·6) oa
Beam, feet (metres)	36·7 (11·2)
Draught, feet (metres)	17·4 (5·3)
Guns, dual purpose	4—3 in (76 mm) 2 twin mounts
Missile Launches	"Penguin" to be installed in 1972
A/S weapons	"Terne" system
Torpedo launchers	2
Boilers	2 Babcock & Wilcox
Main engines	1 set De Laval Ljungstron double reduction geared turbines; 1 shaft; 20 000 shp
Speed, knots	25
Complement	151 (11 officers, 140 ratings)

Built under the five-year naval construction programme approved by the Norwegian "Storting" (Parliament) late in 1960. Although all the ships of this class were constructed in the Norwegian Naval Dockyard, half the cost was borne by Norway and the other half by the United States. The design of these ships is similar to that of the "Dealey" class destroyer escorts in the United States Navy, but slightly modified to suit Norwegian requirements. They have traditional Norwegian destroyer names or torpedo boat names.

RADAR. Search: DRBV 22. Tactical and Fire Control: HSA M 24 system.

ENGINEERING. The main turbines and auxiliary machinery were all built by De Laval Ljungstrom, Sweden at the company's works in Stockholm-Nacka.

PHOTOGRAPHS. A photograph of Oslo appears in the 1966-67 to 1969-70 editions and of Trondheim in the 1967-68 to 1970-71 editions.

DISPOSALS OF "Cr" CLASS
Of the former British destroyers of the "Cr" class, Trondheim (ex-HMS Croziers) was removed from the Navy List on 1 May 1961, D 303 (ex-Oslo, ex-HMS Crown) was removed from the list and scrapped in 1966, and Bergen (ex-HMS Cromwell, ex-Cretan) and Stavanger (ex-HMS Crystal) were stricken from the Navy List on 1 Jan 1967.

DISPOSAL OF "S" CLASS
The former British destroyer Stord (ex-HMS Success) of the "S" class, purchased from Great Britain in 1946 was stricken from the Navy List in 1959.

DISPOSAL OF "HUNT" CLASS
Of the three former British escort destroyers or frigates of the "Hunt" Class, Type II, Haugesund (ex-HMS Beaufort) and Tromso (ex-HMS Zetland) were removed from the list in 1965 and sold, and Arendal (ex-HMS Badsworth) was removed from the list on 1 May 1961. The former British escort destroyer Narvik (ex-HMS Glaisdale) of the "Hunt" class, Type III, was removed from the list on 1 May 1961.

DISPOSALS OF "RIVER" CLASS
Of the three former Canadian frigates of the "River" Class, Draug (ex-HMCS Penetang) was removed from the list and sold in 1966, and Garm (ex-HMCS Toronto) and Troll (ex-HMCS Prestonian) were converted, respectively, into Torpedo Boat Depot Ship and Submarine Depot Ship in 1964 and 1965 and renamed Valkyrien and Horten; see later page.

FRIGATES

Name	No.	Builders	Laid down	Launched	Completed
BERGEN	F 301	Marinens Hovedverft, Horten	1964	23 Aug 1965	15 June 1967
NARVIK	F 304	Marinens Hovedverft, Horten	1964	8 Jan 1965	30 Nov 1966
OSLO	F 300	Marinens Hovedverft, Horten	1963	17 Jan 1964	29 Jan 1966
STAVANGER	F 303	Marinens Hovedverft, Horten	1965	4 Feb 1966	1 Dec 1967
TRONDHEIM	F 302	Marinens Hovedverft, Horten	1963	4 Sep 1964	2 June 1966

STAVANGER   1970, Royal Norwegian Navy, Official

BERGEN   1971, Royal Norwegian Navy, Official

NARVIK   Lieut. K. M. Napier, RN

TRAINING SHIP

HAAKON VII (ex-US Gardiners Bay, AVP 39) A 537

Displacement, tons	1 766 standard; 2 800 full load
Length, feet (metres)	300 (91·4) wl; 310·8 (94·7) oa
Beam, feet (metres)	41·2 (12·7)
Draught, feet (metres)	13·5 (4·1) max
Guns, surface	1—5 in (127 mm)
Guns, AA	8—40 mm; 4—20 mm
Main engines	2 F-M diesels 6 080 bhp; 2 shafts
Speed, knots	18·2
Complement	215, plus 86 officer cadets and petty officer apprentices

Former US seaplane tender (small) of the AVP type, built by Lake Washington Shipyard, Houghton, Wash. Laid down on 14 Mar 1944, launched on 2 Dec 1944 and completed on 11 Feb 1945. Transferred from the US Navy to the Royal Norwegian Navy on 17 May 1958 and converted and rearmed as a training ship for midshipmen and naval cadets. Accommodation for 367.

HAAKON VII   1970, Royal Norwegian Navy, Official

COASTAL MINELAYER

4 "GOR" CLASS

BRAGE (ex-USS *Triumph*, MMC 3, ex-*MSF* 323, ex-*AM* 323) transferred 1960
GOR (ex-USS *Strive*, MMC 1 ex-*MSF* 117, ex-*AM* 117). transferred 1959
TYR (ex-USS *Sustain*, MMC 2, ex-*MSF* 119, ex-*AM* 119) transferred 1959
ULLER (ex-USS *Seer*, MMC 5, ex-*MSF* 112, ex-*AM* 112) transferred 1960

Displacement, tons	890 standard; 1 250 full load
Dimensions, feet	215 wl; 221·2 oa × 32·2 × 16 max
Guns	*Brage, Gor, Tyr:* 1—3 in, 50 cal; 4—20 mm AA (2 twin); *Uller:* 1—3 in, 50 cal; 1—40 mm AA
A/S weapons	*Brage, Gor, Tyr:* 2 Hedgehogs; 3 DCT *Uller:* "Terne" ASW system; 1 DCT
Main engines	GM diesels with electric drive; 2 shafts 2 070 bhp = 16 knots
Complement	83

Former US Coastal Minelayers (MMC) originally built as Ocean Minesweepers (AM) of the steel-hulled large type ("Auk" class) but reclassified as Fleet Minesweepers (MSF) in Feb 1955. *Gor, Tyr* and *Uller* were built by American Shipbuilding Co, Cleveland, Ohio, and *Brage* by Associated Shipbuilders. *Gor* and *Tyr* were converted into coastal minelayers at Charleston Naval Shipyard in 1959, and *Brage* at the same yard in 1960, but *Uller* was converted at a Norwegian shipyard. A photograph of *Brage* appears in the 1968-69 and 1969-70 editions.

Name	No.	Laid down	Launched	Completed
Brage	N 49	27 Oct 1942	25 Feb 1943	3 Feb 1944
Gor	N 48	17 Nov 1941	16 May 1942	27 Oct 1942
Tyr	N 47	17 Nov 1941	23 June 1942	9 Nov 1942
Uller	N 50	28 Nov 1941	23 May 1942	21 Oct 1942

ULLER   1970, Royal Norwegian Navy, Official

TYR   1969, Royal Norwegian Navy, Official

GOR   1970, Royal Norwegian Navy, Official

CONTROLLED MINELAYERS

BORGEN N 51

Displacement, tons	282 standard
Dimensions, feet	94·5 pp; 102·5 oa × 26·2 × 11
Main engines	2 GM diesels; 2 Voith-Schneider propellers; 330 bhp = 9 knots

PATROL VESSELS

2 "SLEIPNER" CLASS   CORVETTE TYPE

ÆGER P 951   **SLEIPNER** P 950

Displacement, tons	600 standard; 780 full load
Dimensions, feet	227·8 oa × 26·2
Guns	1—3 in; 1—40 mm
A/S weapons	"Terne" ASW system
Main engines	4 Maybach diesels; 2 shafts; 9 000 bhp = over 20 knots
Complement	62

Submarine chasers of the corvette type. Under the five-year programme only two instead of the originally planned five new patrol vessels were built. *Sleipner* was launched on 9 Nov 1963 at the Nylands Verksted shipyard, Oslo, and completed on 29 Apr 1965. *Aeger*, originally to have been named *Balder*, was launched on 24 Sep 1965. and completed on 31 Mar 1967.

ÆGER   1970, Royal Norwegian Navy, Official

SLEIPNER   1969, Royal New Zealand Navy. Official

COASTAL MINESWEEPERS

10 "SAUDA" CLASS

ALTA (ex-*Arlon* M 915, ex-*MSC* 104)		M 314	31 Jan 1953
GLOMMA (ex-*Bastogne* M 916, ex-*MSC* 151)		M 317	13 June 1953
KVINA		M 332	21 July 1954
OGNA		M 315	18 June 1954
SAUDA (ex-USS *AMS* 102)		M 311	July 1953
SIRA (ex-USS *MSC* 132)		M 312	26 Oct 1954
TANA (ex-*Roeselaere* M 914, ex-*MSC* 103)		M 313	6 Dec 1952
TISTA		M 331	1 June 1954
UTLA		M 334	2 Mar 1955
VOSSO		M 316	16 June 1954

Displacement, tons	333 standard; 384 full load
Dimensions, feet	144 × 28 × 8·5 max
Guns	2—20 mm AA
Main engines	GM diesels; 880 bhp = 13·5 knots
Oil fuel, tons	25
Complement	38

Sauda, built by Hodgeson Bros, Gowdy & Stevens, East Boothbay, Maine, was completed on 25 Aug 1953 and *Sira* on 28 Nov 1955. Hull of wooden construction. Five coastal minesweepers of the non-magnetic type were built in Norway with US engines. Launch dates above. Completed on 5 Mar 1955 (*Ogna*), 16 Mar 1955 (*Vosso*), 27 Apr 1955 (*Tista*), 12 July 1955 (*Kvina*) and 15 Nov 1955 (*Utla*). *Kvina, Ogna* and *Utla* were built by Båtservice Ltd, Mandal, *Tista* by Forende Batbyggeriex, Risör, and *Vosso* by Skaaluren Skibsbyggeri, Rosendal. A photograph of *Utla* appears in the 1966-67 to 1969-70 editions.

Alta, Glomma and *Tana* were taken over from the Royal Belgian Navy in May, Sep and Mar 1966, respectively, having been exchanged for two Norwegian ocean minesweepers of the US MSO type, *Lagen* (ex-*MSO* 498) and *Namsen* (ex-*MSO* 499).

VOSSO   1970, Royal Norwegian Navy, Official

MISSILE TORPEDO BOATS

6 "SNÖGG" CLASS

KJAPP	P 985	RAPP	P 981	SNAR	P 982
KVIKK	P 984	RASK	P 983	SNOGG (ex-Lyr)	P 980

Displacement, tons	100 standard; 125 full load
Dimensions, feet	120·0 × 20·5 × 5·0
Missile launchers	4 "Penguin" SSM; range 20 km plus
Guns	1—40 mm
Tubes	4—21 in
Main engines	2 Maybach diesels; 2 shafts; 7 200 bhp = 32 knots
Complement	18

These steel hulled torpedo boats of a new design ordered from Batservice Werft, A/S, Mandal, Norway, started coming into service in 1970. Hulls are similar to those of the "Storm" class gunboats, see next column. To be armed with missiles in addition to gun and tubes. The six torpedo boats of the "Rapp" class, of the same names, were deleted from the list in 1970.

SNÖGG   *1970, Royal Norwegian Navy, Official*

RAPP   *1971, Royal Norwegian Navy, Official*

TORPEDO BOATS

20 "TJELD" CLASS

DELFIN	P 386	HAI	P 381	LAKS	P 384	SKARV	P 344
ERLE	P 390	HAUK	P 349	LOM	P 347	SKREI	P 380
FALK	P 350	HVAL	P 383	LYR	P 387	STEGG	P 348
GEIR	P 389	JO	P 346	RAVN	P 357	TEIST	P 345
GRIBB	P 388	KNURR	P 385	SEL	P 382	TJELD	P 343

Displacement, tons	70 standard; 82 full load
Dimensions, feet	75·5 pp; 80·3 oa × 24·5 × 6·8 max
Guns	1—40 mm AA; 1—20 mm AA
Tubes	4—21 in
Main engines	2 Napier Deltic Turboblown diesels; 2 shafts; 6 200 bhp = 45 knots
Radius, miles	450 at 40 knots; 600 at 25 knots
Complement	18

Built by Boatservice Ltd, Oslo. The first boat, *Tjeld* commissioned in June 1960, and the last of the first group of twelve in 1962. The first of the second group of eight, *Sel*, was launched on 7 Mar 1963 and the last, *Delfin*, on 7 Jan 1966 (commissioned on 20 May 1966). A photograph of *Tjeld* appears in the 1961-62 and 1962-63 editions, of *Gribb* in the 1963-64 to 1965-66 editions, of *Teist* in the 1966-67 to 1968-69 editions, of *Jo* in the 1967-68 to 1969-70 editions.

HVAL   *1970, Royal Norwegian Navy, Official*

SKARV   *1969, Wright & Logan*

MISSILE GUN BOATS

20 "STORM" CLASS

ARG	P 968	DJERV	P 966	ODD	P 975	STEIL	P 969
BLINK	P 961	GLIMT	P 962	PIL	P 976	STORM	P 960
BRANN	P 970	GNIST	P 979	ROKK	P 978	TRAUST	P 973
BRASK	P 977	HVASS	P 972	SKJOLD	P 963	TROSS	P 971
BROTT	P 974	KJEKK	P 965	SKUDD	P 967	TRYGG	P 964

Displacement, tons	100 standard; 125 full load
Dimensions, feet	120·0 × 20·5 × 5·0
Missile launchers	6 "Penguin" SSM; range 20 km plus
Guns	1—3 in; 1—40 mm
A/S weapons	DC throwers
Main engines	2 Maybach diesels; 2 shafts; 7 200 bhp = 32 knots

The first of 20 (instead of the 23 originally planned) gunboats of a new design built under the five-year programme was *Storm*, launched on 8 Feb 1963, and completed on 31 May 1963, but this prototype was eventually scrapped and replaced by a new series construction boat as the last of the class. The first of the production boats was *Blink*, launched on 28 June 1965 and completed on 18 Dec 1965. Formerly known as Motor Gunboats, but officially reclassified as Gunboats in 1965. The first was armed with "Penguin" surface-to-surface guided missile launchers in 1970, in addition to originally designed armament.

TRAUST with 6 Penguins fitted   *1971, A/S Kongsberg Vapenfabrikk*

PENGUIN SSM missile being launched   *1971, A/S Kongsberg Vapenfabrikk*

DEPOT SHIPS

2 Ex-CANADIAN FRIGATE TYPE

HORTEN (ex-*Troll*, ex-*Prestonian*) Pennant No. 1530 (ex-F 314)
VALKYRIEN (ex-*Garm*, ex-*Toronto*) Pennant No. A 535 (ex-F 315)

Displacement, tons	1,570 standard; 2 240 full load
Dimensions, feet	301·3 × 36·5 × 16
Guns	*Horten:* 3—40 mm; *Valkyrien:* 2—4 in, 2—40 mm
Main engines	Triple expansion; 2 shafts; 5 500 ihp = 19 knots
Complement	*Horten:* 86; *Valkyrien:* 104

Former Canadian modernised "River" class frigates. Both built by Davie Shipbuilding Co., Lauzon, Port Quebec, Canada. Launched on 22 June 1944 and 18 Sep 1943, and completed on 13 Sep 1944 and 6 May 1944, respectively. Loaned to Norway on 10 Mar 1956 and renamed, transferred outright early in 1959, and converted for use as depot ships and again renamed in 1965 and 1964, respectively. *Horten* for submarine support, and *Valkyrien* as parent ship for torpedo boats and gunboats.

HORTEN   *1969, Royal Norwegian Navy, Official*

FISHERY PROTECTION SHIPS

NORNEN

Measurement, tons	930 gross
Dimensions, feet	201·8 × 32·8 × 15·8
Guns	1—3 in (76 mm)
Main engines	4 diesels; 3 500 bhp = 17 knots
Complement	32

Built by Mjellem & Karlsen, Bergen, Norway. Launched and completed in 1963.

NORNEN　　　　　　　　　　　1970, Royal Norwegian Navy, Official

FARM　　　　　　　　　　　　　　　　　　　　　　HEIMDAL

Measurement, .tons	600 gross
Dimensions, feet	177 × 26·2 × 16·5
Guns	1–3 in (76 mm)
Main engines	2 diesels; 2 700 bhp = 16 knots
Complement	29

Farm was built by Ankerlökken Veft, Fioro and *Heimdal* by Bolsones Verft, Molde, in 1962. A photograph of *Heimdal* appears in the 1966-67 to 1969-70 editions.

FARM　　　　　　　　　　　1970, Royal Norwegian Navy, Official

ANDENES　　　　　　　NORDKAPP　　　　　　　SENJA

Measurement, tons	500 gross
Dimensions, feet	186 × 31 × 16
Guns	1–3 in (76 mm)
Main engines	MAN diesel; 2 300 bhp = 16 knots
Complement	29

All three built in the Netherlands in 1957 as whalers. Acquired by Norway in 1965 and converted into Fishery Protection Ship. A photograph of *Andenes* appears in the 1966-67 to 1969-70 editions.

NORDKAPP　　　　　　　　　　1970, Royal Norwegian Navy, Official

WEATHER SHIPS

POLARFRONT I (ex-Saxifrage)　　　POLARFRONT II (ex-Bryony)

Displacement, tons	1 060 standard; 1 300 full load
Dimensions, feet	205 oa × 33 × 14·5 max
Main engines	Triple expansion; 2 750 ihp = 16·5 knots
Boilers	2 SE
Oil fuel (tons)	350
Radius, miles	7 000 at 10 knots
Complement	46

Former British "Flower" class corvettes (later re-rated as frigates). Built by Charles Hill & Sons Ltd, Bristol (*Saxifrage*) and Harland & Wolff Ltd, Belfast (*Bryony*). Laid down on 1 Feb 1941 and 16 Nov 1940, launched on 24 Oct 1941 and 15 Mar 1941, and completed on 6 Feb 1942 and 16 June 1942, respectively. Transferred to Norway and employed as weather ships, but not on the Navy List. A photograph of *Polarfront II* appears in the 1956-57 to 1969-70 editions.

OCEANOGRAPHIC RESEARCH SHIPS

H. U. SVERDRUP

Displacement, tons	400
Measurement, tons	295 gross
Dimensions, feet	127·7 oa; 111·5 pp / 25 × 13
Main engines	Wichmann diesel; 600 bhp = 11·5 knots
Oil fuel (tons)	65
Radius, miles	5 000 at 10 knots cruising speed
Complement	10 crew; 9 scientists

Built by Örens Mekaniske Verksted, Trondheim. Laid down in Sep 1959, launched in Feb 1960, completed on 15 June 1960. Financed by the US Mutual Weapon Development Programme and operated by the Norwegian Defence Research Establishment. Steel hull, welded construction, controllable pitch propeller. She does not belong to the Royal Norwegian Navy, but is a Defence project. A photograph appears in the 1964-65 to 1970-71 editions.

ROYAL YACHT

NORGE (ex-Philante) A 533

Measurement, tons	1 686 (Thames yacht measurement)
Dimensions, feet	250·2 pp; 263 oa × 28 × 15·2
Main engines	8-cyl diesels; 2 shafts; 3 000 bhp = 17 knots

Built by Camper & Nicholson's Ltd, Gosport, England, to the order of the late Mr T. O. M. Sopwith as escort and store vessel for the yachts *Endeavour I* and *Endeavour II*. Launched on 17 Feb 1937. Served in the British Navy as an anti-submarine escort during the Second World War, after which she was purchased by the Norwegian people for King Haakon at a cost of nearly £250 000 and reconditioned as a Royal Yacht at Southampton. Can accommodate about 50 people in addition to crew.

NORGE　　　　　　　　　　　1971, Royal Norwegian Navy, Official

There are also the landing craft *Kvalsund* and *Raftsund*, 590 tons, 164 × 33·8 × 5·9 feet, 11 knots, 2-20 mm guns, built in 1968-69.
A new naval icebreaker planned under the new construction programme is not being proceeded with for the time being.

PANAMA

Mercantile Marine
Lloyd's Register of Shipping: 886 ships of 5 645 877 tons gross

PATROL BOATS
2 VOSPER TYPE

PANQUIACO GC 10　　　　　　　　　　　　　LIGIA ELENA

Displacement, tons	96 standard; 123 full load
Dimensions, feet	95·0 wl; 103·0 oa × 18·9 × 5·8
Guns	2—20 mm
Main engines	2 Paxman Ventura 12 cyl diesels; 2 800 bhp = 24 knots
Complement	23

Constructed with hull of welded mild steel and upperworks of welded or buck-bolted aluminium alloy. Vosper fin stabiliser equipment. *Panquiaco* was launched on 22 July 1970 at Portchester, Portsmouth, England. Ordered from Vosper Thornycroft for delivery in 1971. Order is valued at £660 000 and was the first placed by Panama with the United Kingdom for many years.

PANQUIACO　　　　　　　　　　　1971, Vosper Thornycroft

2 US SMALL CG UTILITY TYPE

Displacement, tons	35
Dimensions, feet	69 × 14 × 5
Guns	1 MG
Main engines	400 hp = 13 knots
Complement	10

Transferred to Panama by the USA at the US Naval Station, Rodman, Canal Zone, in June 1962. Under the 1955 Treaty the USA occupied the Rio Hato base.

PAKISTAN

Administration

Commander-in-Chief, Pakistan Navy, and
Chief of the Naval Staff:
  Vice-Admiral Muzaffar Hasan, HQA, SK

Chief of Staff:
  Rear Admiral Rashid Ahmad, SK, TQA

Flag Officer Commanding P. N. Flotilla:
  Rear Admiral Mohammad Sharif, SK

Strength of the Fleet

4 Submarines (Conventional)	8 Coastal Minesweepers
1 Light Cruiser	6 Patrol Boats
5 Destroyers	1 Survey Ship
2 Frigates	7 Auxiliaries

Diplomatic Representation

Naval Adviser, High Commission, London:
  Commodore Leslie Norman Mungavin, SK

Naval Attaché in Washington:
  Captain Zafar Shamsie PN

Personnel

1963: 7 700 (700 officers; 7 000 ratings)
1964: 8 250 (750 officers; 7 500 ratings)
1965: 8 350 (790 officers; 7 560 ratings)
1966: 8 680 (820 officers; 7 860 ratings)
1967: 9 000 (820 officers; 8 180 ratings)
1968: 9 050 (800 officers; 8 250 ratings)
1969: 9 200 (850 officers; 8 350 ratings)
1970: 9 870 (870 officers; 9 000 ratings)
1971: 9 900 (900 officers; 9 000 ratings)

Mercantile Marine

Lloyd's Register of Shipping:
179 vessels of 566 022 tons gross

Scale: 150 feet = 1 inch (1 : 1 800)

BABUR

SHAH JAHAN

BADR, KHAIBAR

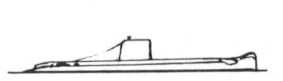

HANGOR, MANGRO, SHUSHUK

TIPPU SULTAN, TUGHRIL

ALAMGIR, JAHANGIR

GHAZI

ZULFIQUAR

SUBMARINES

Name	Pennant No.	Builders	Laid Down	Launched	Completed
HANGOR	S 131	Arsenal de Brest	1 Dec 1967	28 June 1969	1970
MANGRO	S 133	C. N. Ciotal (Le Trait)	8 July 1968	7 Feb 1970	1970
SHUSHUK	S 132	C. N. Ciotal (Le Trait)	1 Dec 1967	30 July 1969	12 Jan 1970

3 FRENCH "DAPHNE" CLASS

Displacement, tons	700 standard; 869 surface; 1 043 submerged
Length, feet (metres)	189·6 (57·8)
Beam, feet (metres)	22·3 (6·8)
Draught, feet (metres)	15·1 (4·6)
Torpedo tubes	12—21 in (550 mm) 8 bow, 4 stern (external)
Main engines	Diesel electric (SEMT-Pielstick); 1 300 bhp surface; electric motors 1 600 hp submerged; 2 shafts
Speed, knots	13 surface; 15·5 submerged
Complement	45

1 Ex-US "TENCH" CLASS

GHAZI S 130 (ex-USS *Diablo* AGSS 479, ex-*SS* 479)

Displacement, tons	1 570 standard; 1 864 surface; 2 410 submerged
Length, feet (metres)	311·7 (95·0) oa
Beam, feet (metres)	27·3 (8·3)
Draught, feet (metres)	16·3 (5·0)
Torpedo tubes	10—21 in (533 mm); 6 bow, 4 stern
Main engines	4 diesels, total 6 500 bhp; 4 electric motors, total 4 610 shp; 2 shafts
Speed, knots	20 surface; 10 submerged
Radius, miles	14 000 at 10 knots
Oil fuel, tons	300
Complement	85

Built by Portsmouth Navy Shipyard, New Hampshire. Launched on 30 Nov 1944 and completed on 31 Mar 1945.

Transferred on loan from the USA after extensive overhaul and refit at the Philadelphia Navy Shipyard, converting her into a Fleet Snorkel Type. Commissioned into the Pakistan Navy at the USN Submarine Base, New London, Connecticut on 1 June 1964. The name *Ghazi* means Defender of the Faith.

MANGRO   1971, courtesy Admiral M. J. Adam

GHAZI   1966, Pakistan Navy, Official

LIGHT CRUISER (Cadet Training Ship)

Name	No.	Builders and Engineers	Laid down	Launched	Completed
BABUR (ex-HMS *Diadem*)	84	R. & W. Hawthorn Leslie & Co Ltd, Hebburn-on-Tyne	15 Nov 1939	26 Aug 1942	6 Jan 1944

Displacement, tons	5 900 standard; 7 560 full load
Length, feet (*metres*)	485 (*147·9*) pp; 512 (*156·1*) oa
Beam, feet (*metres*)	52·0 (*15·8*)
Draught, feet (*metres*)	18·5 (*5·6*)
Guns, surface	8—5·25 in (*133 mm*) 4 twin
Guns, AA	14—40 mm
Torpedo tubes	6—21 in (*533 mm*) 2 triple
Armour	3 in (*76 mm*) sides; 2 in (*51 mm*) decks and turrets
Boilers	4 Admiralty 3-drum
Main engines	Parsons s.r. geared turbines; 4 shafts; 62 000 shp
Speed, knots	32
Oil fuel, tons	1 100
Complement	588

Former British Improved "Dido" class anti-aircraft light cruiser. Purchased on 29 Feb 1956. Refitted at HM Dockyard, Portsmouth and there transferred to Pakistan and renamed *Babur* on 5 July, 1957. Adapted as cadet training ship in 1961.

NOMENCLATURE. Renamed after Babur, the founder of the Mogul Empire. (*Diadem* means emblem of sovereignty).

Prefix C was dropped from the pennant number in 1963.

RADAR. Search: Type 960. Tactical: Type 293. Fire Control: Early British design.

DRAWING. Starboard elevation and plan. Redrawn in 1971. Scale: 125 feet = 1 inch (1 : 1 500).

BABUR   1966. Pakistan Navy, Official

DESTROYERS

Name	No.	Builders	Laid down	Launched	Completed
BADR (ex-HMS *Gabbard*)	161 (ex-D 47)	Swan, Hunter & Wigham Richardson Ltd, Wallsend-on-Tyne	2 Feb 1944	16 Mar 1945	10 Dec 1946
KHAIBAR (ex-HMS *Cadiz*)	163 (ex-D 79)	Fairfield Shipbuilding & Engineering Co Ltd, Govan, Glasgow	10 May 1943	16 Sep 1944	12 Apr 1946

2 "BATTLE" CLASS

Displacement, tons	2 325 standard; 3 361 full load
Length, feet (*metres*)	355 (*108·2*) pp; 379 (*115·5*) oa
Beam, feet (*metres*)	40·2 (*12·3*)
Draught, feet (*metres*)	17·0 (*5·2*)
Guns, surface	4—4·5 (*115 mm*)
Guns, AA	10—40 mm
A/S weapons	"Squid" triple DC mortar
Torpedo tubes	8—21 in (*533 mm*) quadrupled
Boilers	2 Admiralty 3-drum
Main engines	Parsons geared turbines; 2 shafts; 50 000 shp
Speed, knots	35·75 designed; 31 sea
Radius, miles	3 000 at 20 knots
Oil fuel, tons	680
Complement	270

Purchased from Britain on 29 Feb 1956. Modernised with US funds under MDAP. *Badr* was refitted at Palmers Hebburn, Yarrow, transferred to Pakistan on 24 Jan 1957 and sailed from Portsmouth for Karachi on 17 Feb 1957. *Khaibar* was refitted at Alex Stephen & Son Ltd, Govan, Glasgow, and handed over on 1 Feb 1957.

BADR   1966. Pakistan Navy, Official

RADAR. Search: Type 277. Tactical: Type 293. Fire Control: X Band.

PENNANT NOS. Were changed from D 47 and D 79 to 161 and 163, respectively, in 1963.

NOMENCLATURE. *Khaibar* was named in commemoration of a famous battle in the history of Islam which Prophet Mohammed won in Arabia over 1,350 years ago.

1 "CH" CLASS

SHAH JAHAN (ex-HMS *Charity*) 164 (ex-D 29)

Displacement, tons	1 710 standard; 2 545 full load
Length, feet (*metres*)	350 (*106·7*) wl; 362·7 (*110·5*) oa
Beam, feet (*metres*)	35·7 (*10·9*)
Draught, feet (*metres*)	17·0 (*5·2*)
Guns, surface	3—4·5 in (*115 mm*)
Guns, AA	6—40 mm
A/S weapons	2 "Squid" triple DC mortars
Torpedo tubes	4—21 in (*533 mm*) quadrupled
Boilers	2 Admiralty 3-drum
Main engines	Parsons geared turbines; 2 shafts; 40 000 shp
Speed, knots	36·75 designed; 31·25 sea
Complement	200

SHAH JAHAN   1963. Pakistan Navy, Official

Built by John I. Thornycroft, Co Ltd, of Woolston, laid down 9 July 1943, launched on 30 Nov 1944 and completed on 19 Nov 1945. Purchased by USA and handed over to Pakistan on 16 Dec 1958, under MDAP,

at yard of J. Samuel White & Co Ltd, Cowes who refitted her. Renamed *Shah Jahan* ("Emperor of the World") after the Fifth Emperor of the Mughal Dynasty who was ruler at the height of prosperity of the Mughal Empire.

RADAR. Tactical: Type 293. Fire Control: X Band.

PENNANT No. changed from D 29 to 164 in 1963. Sister ship *Taimur* (ex-HMS *Chivalrous*) was returned to the Royal Navy and scrapped in 1960-61.

Destroyers—continued

Name	No.	Builders	Laid down	Launched	Completed
ALAMGIR (ex-HMS *Creole*)	160 (ex-D 82)	J. Samuel White & Co Ltd, Cowes	3 Aug 1944	22 Nov 1945	14 Oct 1946
JAHANGIR (ex-HMS *Crispin*, ex-*Craccher*)	162 (ex-D 168)	J. Samuel White & Co Ltd, Cowes	1 Feb 1944	23 June 1945	10 July 1946

2 "CR" CLASS

Displacement, tons	1 730 standard; 2 560 full load
Length, feet (*metres*)	350 (*106·7*) wl 362·8 (*110·5*) oa
Beam, feet (*metres*)	35·7 (*10·9*)
Draught, feet (*metres*)	17·0 (*5·2*)
Guns, surface	3—4·5 in (*115 mm*)
Guns, AA	6—40 mm
A/S weapons	2 "Squid" triple DC mortars
Torpedo tubes	4—21 in (*533 mm*) quadrupled
Boilers	2 Admiralty 3-drum
Main engines	Parsons geared turbines; 2 shafts; 40 000 shp
Speed, knots	36·75 designed; 31·25 sea
Radius, miles	2 800 at 20 knots
Oil fuel, tons	580
Complement	200

ALAMGIR   *1965, Pakistan Navy, Official*

Purchased by Pakistan (announced by the Royal Navy) on 29 Feb 1956. Refitted and modernised in Great Britain by John I. Thornycroft & Co Ltd, Woolston, Southampton, in 1957-58 with US funds under MDAP. Turned over to the Pakistan Navy at Southampton in 1958 (*Crispin* on 18 Mar and *Creole* 20 June) and renamed.

RADAR. Tactical: Type 293. Fire Control: X Band.

GUNNERY. There was formerly a W/T cabin in place of "B" gun and a gun in "X" position, but during the refit before joining the Pakistan Navy the 4·5 inch gun was restored to "B" position, the 4·5 inch gun in "X" position was suppressed and two "Squids" were substituted.

PENNANT NOs. Changed from D 82 and D 168 to 160 and 162, respectively, in 1963.

JAHANGIR   *1963, Pakistan Navy, Official*

FAST ANTI-SUBMARINE FRIGATES (*Ex-Destroyers*)

Name	No.	Builders	Laid down	Launched	Completed
TIPPU SULTAN (ex-HMS *Onslow*, ex-*Pakenham*)	260 (ex-F 249)	John Brown & Co Ltd, Clydebank	1 July 1940	31 Mar 1941	8 Oct 1941
TUGHRIL (ex-HMS *Onslaught*, ex-*Pathfinder*)	261 (ex-F 204	Fairfield SB & Eng Co Ltd, Glasgow	14 Jan 1941	9 Oct 1941	19 June 1942

2 LIMITED CONVERSION TYPE 16

Displacement, tons	1 800 standard; 2 300 full load
Length, feet (*metres*)	328·7 (*100·2*) pp; 345 (*105·2*) oa
Beam, feet (*metres*)	35·0 (*10·7*)
Draught, feet (*metres*)	15.7 (*4·8*)
Guns, dual purpose	2—4 in (*102 mm*)
Guns, AA	5—40 mm
A/S weapons	2 "Squid" triple DC mortars
Torpedo tubes	4—21 in (*533 mm*)
Boilers	2 Admiralty 3-drum
Main engines	Parsons geared turbines; 2 shafts; 40 000 shp
Speed, knots	34
Complement	170

Originally three "O" class destroyers were acquired from Great Britain, *Tippu Sultan* being handed over on 30 Sep 1949; *Tariq* on 3 Nov 1949; and *Tughril* on 6 Mar 1951. An agreement was signed in London between Great Britain and USA for refit and conversion in the United Kingdom of *Tippu Sultan* and *Tughril* (announced 29 Apr 1957) with US funds. All three ships were scheduled for conversion into fast anti-submarine frigates. *Tippu Sultan* and *Tughril* were converted at Liverpool by Grayson Rolls & Clover Docks Ltd, Birkenhead, and C.

TIPPU SULTAN   *1963, Pakistan Navy, Official*

& H. Crighton Ltd, respectively. *Tariq* was not converted. She was handed back to Great Britain at Portsmouth on 10 July 1959 and broken up at Sunderland, arriving there in Oct 1959. Pennant Nos changed from D 49 and D 204 to F 249 and F 204 respectively, in 1959, and to 260 and 261 in 1963. Type 293 tactical radar.

SURVEY SHIP (*Ex-Frigate*)

Name	No.	Builders	Laid down	Launched	Completed
ZULFIQUAR (ex-*Dhanush*, ex-*Deveron*)	262 (ex-F 265)	Smith's Dock Co Ltd, South Bank-on-Tees	16 Apr 1942	12 Oct 1942	2 Mar 1943

1 "RIVER" CLASS

Displacement, tons	1 370 standard; 2 100 full load
Length, feet (*metres*)	283 (*86·3*) pp; 301·5 (*91·9*) oa
Beam, feet (*metres*)	36·7 (*11·2*)
Draught, feet (*metres*)	12·5 (*3·8*)
Guns, surface	1—4 in (*102 mm*)
Guns, AA	2—40 mm
Boilers	2 Admiralty 3-drum
Main engines	Triple expansion; 5 500 ihp
Speed, knots	20
Radius, miles	3 000 at 12 knots
Oil fuel, tons	400
Complement	150

Former British frigate of the "River" class converted into a survey ship, with additional charthouse aft. She has strengthened davits and carries survey motor boats. The after 4-inch gun was removed.

PENNANT NUMBER was changed from F 265 to 262 in 1963.

DISPOSAL
Sister ship *Shamsher* (ex-*Nadder*) of the "River" class (training ship) was disposed of in 1960.

ZULFIQUAR   *1965, Pakistan Navy, Official*

COASTAL MINESWEEPERS

8 MSC TYPE

MAHMOOD	(ex-*MSC* 267) M 160	**MUHAFIZ**	(ex-*AMS* 138) M 163
MOMIN	(ex-*MSC* 293) M 161	**MUJAHID**	(ex-*MSC* 261) M 164
MOSHAL	(ex-*MSC* 294) M 167	**MUKHTAR**	(ex-*MSC* 274) M 165
MURABAK	(ex-*MSC* 262) M 162	**MUNSIF**	(ex-*MSC* 273) M 166

Displacement, tons	335 light; 375 full load
Dimensions, feet	138 pp; 144 oa × 27 × 8·5
Guns	2—20 mm
Main engines	GM diesels; 2 shafts; 880 bhp = 14 knots
Complement	39

Transferred to Pakistan by the US under MAP. *Mukhtar* and *Munsif* on 25 June 1959, *Muhafiz* on 25 Feb 1955, *Mujahid* in Nov 1956, *Mahmood*, M 160, in May 1957, *Mubarak* in 1957, *Momin* in Aug 1962 and *Moshal* M 167, on 13 July 1963. A photograph of *Momin* appears in the 1964-65 edition.

MAHMOOD   1963, Pakistan Navy, Official

PATROL CRAFT

4 "TOWN" CLASS

ÇOMILLA P 142	**JESSORE** P 141	**RAJSHAHI** P 140	**SYLHET** P 143

Displacement, tons	115 standard; 143 full load
Dimensions, feet	100 wl; 107 oa ×' 20 × 5
Guns	2—40 mm; 70 cal Bofors AA
Main engines	2 Maybach/Mercedes MD 655/18 diesels; 3 400 bhp (tropical) = 24 knots
Complement	19

Fast patrol craft named after towns in East Pakistan, built by Brooke Marine Limited, Lowestoft, England, to the order of the Pakistan Government. The contract was placed on 5 Oct 1963, *Jessore* and *Comilla* were commissioned on 20 May,1965 and *Rajshahi* and *Sylhet* on 2 Aug 1965. The hulls are of special design, being longitudinally and traversely strengthened. All-welded steel construction with superstructures of all welded sea resistant aluminium alloy. A photograph of *Comilla* appears in the 1965-66 to 1970-71 editions.

JESSORE   Added 1971, A. & J. Pavia

SEAWARD DEFENCE MOTOR LAUNCHES

2 SDML TYPE

SDML 3517 (ex-*SDML* 1261)	**SDML 3520** (ex-*SDML* 1266)

Displacement, tons	46 standard; 54 full load
Dimensions, feet	72 oa × 15·8 × 15·3
Guns	1—3 pdr; 1—20 mm AA
Main engines	Diesels; 2 shafts; 320 bhp = 12 knots
Complement	14

Former British Harbour Defence Motor Launches of wooden construction, built under the emergency programme during the Second World War, and re-designated Seaward Defence Motor Launches after the war. SDML 3518 and SDML 3519 were scrapped in 1965. A photograph of SDML 3517 appears in the 1963-64 and 1964-65 editions.

SDML 3520   1965, Pakistan Navy, Official

OILERS

DACCA (ex-USNS *Mission Santa Clara*, AO 132) A 41

Displacement, tons	5 730 light; 22 380 full load
Dimensions, feet	503 wl; 523·5 oa × 68 × 30·9 max
Main engines	Turbo-electric; 6 000 shp = 15 knots
Boilers	2 Babcock & Wilcox
Oil capacity	20 000 tons (official figure); 134 000 barrel capacity
Complement	160 (15 officers and 145 men)

Former US fleet tanker of the "T2-SE-A1" Type ("Mission" Class). Transferred on loan to Pakistan under MDAP. Handed over from the US on 17 Jan 1963.

DACCA   1964. Pakistan Navy Official

ATTOCK (ex-USS YO 249) A 298

Displacement, tons	600 standard; 1,255 full load
Dimensions, feet	177·2 oa × 32 × 15 max
Main engines	Direct coupled diesel; speed 8·5 knots
Complement	26

A harbour oiler of 6 500 barrels capacity built in Trieste, Italy, in 1960 for the Pakistan Navy, under the Mutual Defence Assistance Programme of USA. A photograph appears in the 1964-63 to 1970-71 editions.

WATER CARRIERS

ZUM ZUM YW 15

Built in Italy under US off-shore procurement of the MDA Programme.

ZUM ZUM   1971, W. H. Davis

TUGS

MADADGAR (ex-USS *Yuma*, ATF 94) A 42

Displacement, tons	1 235 standard; 1 675 full load
Dimensions, feet	195 wl; 205 oa × 38·5 × 15·3 max
Main engines	4 GM diesels; electric drive; 1 shaft; 3 000 bhp = 16·5 knots
Complement	85

Ocean-going salvage tug. Built by Commercial Iron Works, Portland, Oregon. Laid down on 13 Feb 1943. Launched on 17 July 1943. Completed on 31 Aug 1943. Transferred from the US Navy to the Pakistan Navy on 25 Mar 1959 under MDAP. Fitted with powerful pumps and other salvage equipment. A photograph appears in the 1965-66 to 1970-71 editions.

RUSTOM

Dimensions, feet	105 × 30 × 11
Main engines	Crossley diesel; 1 000 bhp = 9·5 knots (max)
Radius, miles	1 500 endurance
Complement	21

General purpose tug for the Pakistan Navy originally ordered from Werf-Zeeland at Hansweert, Netherlands, in Aug 1952, but after the liquidation of this yard the order was transferred to Worst & Dutmer at Meppel. Launched on 29 Nov 1955. A photograph appears in the 1964-65 edition.

BHOLU   **GAMA**

These are small harbour tugs built under an "off-shore" order by Costaguta-Voltz.

PARAGUAY

Strength of the Fleet		Personnel	Mercantile Marine
2 River Defence Vessels	3 River Patrol Boats	1971: 1 900 officers and men including coastguard and marines.	Lloyd's Register of Shipping: Total 1971: 26 vessels of 21 884 tons gross
3 Patrol vessels	1 Tug		
2 Patrol launches			

RIVER DEFENCE VESSELS

RATED AS GUNBOATS (CANOUEROS)

2 "HUMAITA" CLASS

HUMAITA (ex-*Capitan Cabral*) C 2   **PARAGUAY** (ex-*Comodor Meya*) C 1

Displacement, tons	636 standard; 865 full load
Dimensions, feet	231 × 35 × 5·3
Guns	4—4·7 in; 3—3 in AA; 2—40 mm AA
Mines	6
Armour	·5 in side amidships; ·3 in deck; ·8 in CT
Main engines	Parsons geared turbines; 2 shafts; 3 800 shp = 17 knots
Boilers	2
Oil fuel, tons	150
Radius, miles	1 700 at 16 knots
Complement	86

Rated as gunboats but also fitted for minelaying. The armour is of high tensile steel. Both built by Odero, Genoa, laid down in Apr 1929, launched in 1930, and completed in May 1931.

PARAGUAY   *Official*

PATROL VESSELS

FORMER MEDIUM MINESWEEPERS

3 "GRANVILLE" CLASS

HERNANDEZ (ex-*Seaver*)   **MESA** (ex-*Parker*)   **NANAHUA** (ex-*Bouchard*)

Displacement, tons	450 standard; 620 normal; 650 full load
Dimensions, feet	164 pp; 137 oa × 24 × 8·5 max
Guns	4—40 mm Bofors AA; 2 MG
Main engines	2 sets MAN 2-cycle diesels; 2 000 bhp = 16 knots
Oil fuel, tons	50
Radius, miles	3 000 at 12 knots
Complement	70

Former Argentinian minesweepers of the "Bouchard" class. Built at Sanchez Shipyard, San Fernando, Rio Santiago Naval Yard, and Hansen & Puccini, San Fernando, respectively. Laid down in 1936, 1935 and 1937. Launched on 2 May 1937, 20 Mar 1936 and 18 Aug 1938. Can carry mines. Transferred from the Argentinian Navy to the Paraguayan Navy in Apr 1964 et seq.

NANAHUA (*Bouchard*)   *Official*

MESA (*Parker*)   *Official*

PATROL LAUNCHES (Launchas Patrulleras)

2 CG TYPE

P1 (ex-*USCGC 20417*)   **P 2** (ex-*USCGC 20418*)

Displacement, tons	16
Dimensions, feet	45·5 oa × 13·5 × 3·5
Guns	2—20 mm AA
Main engines	2 petrol motors; 2 shafts; 190 hp = 20 knots
Complement	10

Of wooden construction. Built in the United States in 1944. Acquired from the United States Coast Guard in 1944.

RIVER PATROL BOATS (Avisos de Guerra)

CORONEL MARTINEZ A 2

Displacement, tons	80
Dimensions, feet	71·5 × 18 × 8·2
Guns	1—3 in; 2—37 mm
Main engines	150 ihp = 6·5 knots

Medium type of river patrol boat, military transport, and general utility craft.

CAPITAN CABRAL (ex-*Adolfo Riquelme*) A 1

Displacement, tons	180 standard; 206 full load
Dimensions, feet	98·5 pp; 107·2 oa × 23·5 × 9·8
Guns	1—3 in Vickers; 2—37 mm Vickers; 4 MG
Main engines	Triple expansion; 1 shaft; 300 ihp = 9 knots
Complement	47

Former tug. Built by Werf-Conrad, Haarlem. Launched in 1907. Of wooden construction.

CAPITAN CABRAL   *Official*

TENIENTE HERREROS A 3

Displacement, tons	41
Dimensions, feet	63·2 × 11 × 6·8
Guns	4 MG
Main engines	300 ihp = 5·5 knots

Small type of river patrol boat and service craft. Built in the Netherlands in 1908.

TUGS

YLT 559 A 4

Dimensions, feet	66·2 × 17 × 5
Main engines	Diesel; 300 bhp

Small harbour tug YTL 559 transferred to Paraguay by the USA under the Military Aid Program in May 1963. Built by Everett Pacific SB & DD Co, Wash.

PERU

Administration

Minister of Marine and Chief of Naval Operations:
Vice Admiral Manuel Fernandez Castro

Chief of Naval Staff:
Vice Admiral Carlos Salmon Cavero

Commander-in-Chief of the Fleet:
Rear Admiral Jorge Bellina Eggerstedt

Strength of the Fleet

4 Submarine (Diesel Powered)
2 Cruisers (British "Ceylon" Class)
4 Destroyers (2 "Daring", 2 "Fletcher")
3 Destroyer Escorts ("Bostwick" Class)
2 Patrol Vessels (Corvettes) MSF Type
6 Fast Patrol Craft (Vosper Type)
2 Coastal Minesweepers (YMS Type)
2 Coastal Gunboats
4 Landing Ships (2 LST, 2 LSM)
7 River Gunboats
3 Patrol Launchers
3 Transports
6 Oilers
7 Support Ships and Service Craft

Diplomatic Representation

Naval Attaché in London and Paris:
Rear Admiral Alberto Benvenuto Cisneros

Naval Attaché in Washington:
Rear Admiral Armando Echeandia Ramos

Personnel

1971: 7 870 (720 officers, 7 150 men)

Mercantile Marine

Lloyd's Register of Shipping:
494 vessels of 377 812 tons gross

Scale: 150 feet = 1 inch (1 : 1 800).

ALMIRANTE GRAU

AGUIRRE, CASTILLA, RODRIGUEZ

CORONEL BOLOGNESI

DIEZ CANSECO, GALVEZ

FERRÉ, PALACIOS

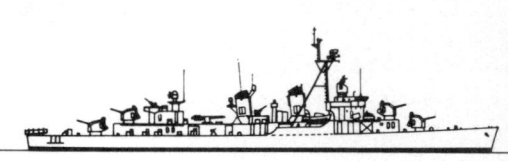

GUISE, VILLAR

SUBMARINES

4 "ABTAO" CLASS (US BUILT)

Displacement, tons	825 standard; 1 400 submerged
Length, feet (*metres*)	243 (*74·1*) oa
Beam, feet (*metres*)	22 (*6·7*)
Draught, feet (*metres*)	14 (*4·3*)
Guns, surface	1—5 in (*127 mm*) 25 cal (*Abtao* and 2 *de Mayo*)
Torpedo tubes	6—21 in (*533 mm*); 4 bow, 2 stern
Main engines	2 GM 278A diesels; 2 400 bhp; Electric motors; 2 shafts
Speed, knots	16 on surface; 10 submerged
Radius, miles	5 000 at 10 knots
Oil fuel (tons)	45
Complement	40

Name	No.	Laid down	Launched	Completed
ABTAO (ex-*Tiburon*)	42	12 May 1952	27 Oct 1953	20 Feb 1954
ANGAMOS (ex-*Atun*)	43	27 Oct 1955	5 Feb 1957	1 July 1957
DOS DE MAYO (ex-*Lobo*)	41	12 May 1952	6 Feb 1954	14 June 1954
IQUIQUE (ex-*Merlin*)	44	27 Oct 1955	5 Feb 1957	1 Oct 1957

All built by Electric Boat Division. General Dynamics Corporation, Groton, Connecticut. They are of modified US "Mackerel" class.

NOMENCLATURE. The names of all Peruvian submarines were changed in Apr 1957 by a supreme decree of the President of the Republic of Peru. The names now used are in honour of famous Peruvian naval battles. Previous names: *Lobo* means wolf, *Tiburon* shark.

PENNANT NUMBERS were changed from 5, 7, 6 and 8 to SS2, SS 3, SS 1 and SS 4 respectively in 1959, and were again changed to 42, 43, 41 and 44 respectively in 1960.

PHOTOGRAPHS. A photograph of all four submarines of this class together appears in the 1959-60 edition, of *Abtao* in the 1966-67 and 1967-68 editions and of *Angamos* in the 1968-69 to 1969-70 editions.

"R" CLASS
The four old submarines of the "R" class, *Arica* (ex-*R 4*), *Casma* (ex-*R 2*), *Islay* (ex-*R 1*) and *Pacocha* (ex-*R 3*) were scrapped in 1960.

DOS DE MAYO

1970, Peruvian Navy, Official

IQUIQUE

1970 Peruvian Navy, Official

CRUISERS

Name	No.	Builders	Laid down	Launched	Completed
ALMIRANTE GRAU (ex-HMS *Newfoundland*)	81	Swan, Hunter & Wigham Richardson, Ltd, Wallsend on-tyne	9 Nov 1939	19 Dec 1941	31 Dec 1942
CORONEL BOLOGNESI (ex-HMS *Ceylon*)	82	Alexander Stephen & Sons, Ltd, Govan, Glasgow	27 Apr 1939	30 July 1942	13 July 1943

2 "ALMIRANTE GRAU" CLASS

Displacement, tons	*Almirante Grau:* 8 800 standard; 11 090 full load *Col. Bolognesi:* 8 781 standard; 11 110 full load
Length, feet (*metres*)	538 (*164·0*) wl; 549 (*167·4*) wl; 555·5 (*169·3*) oa
Beam, feet (*metres*)	63·6 (*19·4*)
Draught, feet (*metres*)	16·5 (*5·0*) mean; 20·5 (*6·2*) max
Guns, surface	9—6 in (*152 mm*) three triple
Guns, dual purpose	8—4 in (4 twin)
Guns, AA	12—40 mm *Almirante Grau* 18—40 mm *Col. Bolognesi*
Armour	4 in (*102 mm*) sides and CT; 2 in (*51 mm*) turrets and deck
Boilers	4 Admiralty 3-drum; 400 psi (*28 km/cm²*); 720°F (*382°C*)
Main engines	Parsons s.r. geared turbines 72 500 shp; 4 shafts
Speed, knots	31·5
Radius, miles	6 000 at 13 knots; 2 800 at full power
Oil fuel (tons)	1 620
Complement	*Almirante Grau:* 743 *Col. Bolognesi:* 766

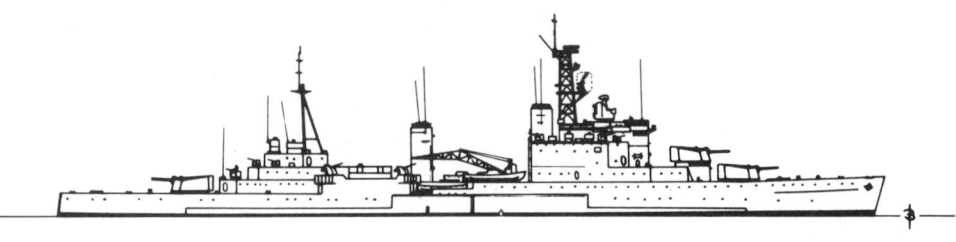

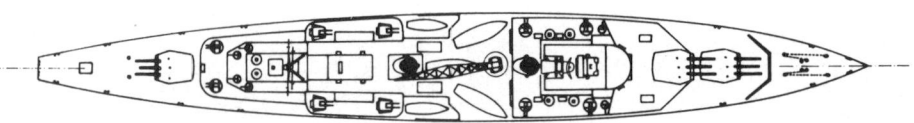

Former British cruisers of the "Ceylon" class, a modification of the original 8 000-ton "Colony" class design, one 6-inch turret having been suppressed, and the number of light AA. guns augmented *Almirante Grau* was engined by Wallsend Slipway & Engineering Co Ltd.

RECONSTRUCTION. *Almirante Grau* was reconstructed in 1951-53 at HM Dockyard. Devonport, with two lattice masts, new bridge and improved AA armament, her torpedo tubes being removed. *Coronel Bolognesi* was refitted with lattice foremast and covered modified bridge in 1955-56, and her torpedo tubes were removed.

RADAR
Search: Type 960, Type 277.
Tactical: Type 293.
Fire Control: S Band for surface fire, X Band for AA fire.

GUNNERY. The 4 inch guns of *Coronel Bolognesi* are radar-controlled.

APPEARANCE. *Almirante Grau* has HA director mounted on either side of bridge. *Coronel Bolognesi* was refitted with a lattice foremast and a tripod mainmast, whereas *Almirante Grau* was reconstructed with two lattice masts.

TRANSFER. *Almirante Grau* (incorporated in the Peruvian Navy on 19 Dec 1959) was formally transferred from the British Navy at Portsmouth on 30 Dec 1959 and *Coronel Bolognesi* was transferred from the British Navy at Portsmouth on 9 Feb 1960.

TORPEDO TUBES. Each ship originally mounted 6—21 inch torpedo tubes.

DRAWING. Starboard elevation and plan of *Coronel Bolognesi*. Re-drawn in 1971. Scale 125 feet = 1 inch. (1 : 1 500). *Almirante Grau* has lattice mainmast, see separate drawings on previous page.

ALMIRANTE GRAU

1971, Peruvian Navy, Official

CORONEL BOLOGNESI

1970, Peruvian Navy, Official

DESTROYERS

2 "FERRÉ" CLASS

Ex-BRITISH "DARING" CLASS

Name	Builders	Laid down	Launched	Completed
FERRÉ (ex-HMS *Decoy*)	Yarrow, Co Ltd, Scotstoun	22 Sep 1946	29 Mar 1949	28 Apr 1953
PALACIOS (ex-HMS *Diana*)	Yarrow, Co Ltd, Scotstoun	3 Apr 1947	8 May 1952	29 Mar 1954

FERRÉ (as HMS *Decoy*)   1970, *Skyfotos*

Displacement, tons	2 800 standard; 3 600 full load
Length, feet (*metres*)	366 (*111·7*) pp; 375 (*114·3*) wl; 390 (*118·9*) oa
Beam, feet (*metres*)	43 (*13·1*)
Draught, feet (*metres*)	18 (*5·5*) max
Guns, surface	6—4·5 in (*115 mm*); 2 twin fwd; 1 twin aft, Mk VI
Guns, AA	2—40 mm
A/S weapons	1 Squid 3 barrelled DC mortar
Torpedo tubes	5—21 in (*533 mm*)
Boilers	2 Foster Wheeler; Pressure 650 psi (*45·7 kg/cm²*); Superheat 850°F (*454°C*)
Main engines	English Electric dr geared turbines 2 shafts
Speed, knots	34·75 designed; 31·5 deep
Radius, miles	1 700 at full power; 4 400 at 20 knots
Oil fuel (tons)	580
Complement	297

Purchased by Peru in 1969 and refitting by Cammel Laird (Ship repairers) Ltd, Birkenhead, for further service. *Palacios* being towed from Plymouth for refit 9 Dec 1969. Formerly units of the "Daring" class of the Royal Navy, the largest orthodox destroyers ever built in Great Britain. Originally named *Dragon* and *Druid*. To be delivered to Peru mid 1971 (*Palacios*) and late 1971 (*Ferré*).

PALACIOS (as HMS *Diana*)   1970, *John R. Mortimer*

RADAR
Tactical: Type 293.
Fire Control: X band for both forward and after fire control systems.

Name	No.	Builders	Launched	Completed
GUISE (ex-USS *Isherwood*, DD 520)	72	Bethlehem Steel Co, Staten Island	24 Nov 1942	10 Apr 1943
VILLAR (ex-USS *Benham*, DD 796)	71	Bethlehem Steel Co, Staten Island	29 Aug 1943	20 Dec 1943

2 "VILLAR" CLASS

Ex-US "FLETCHER" CLASS

Displacement, tons,	2 120 standard; 2 715 normal; 3 050 full load
Length, feet (*metres*)	360·2 (*109·8*) pp; 370 (*112·8*) wl; 376·2 (*114·7*) oa
Beam, feet (*metres*)	39·7 (*12·1*)
Draught, feet (*metres*)	12·2 (*3·7*) mean; 18 (*5·5*) max
Guns, dual purpose	4—5 in (*127 mm*) 38 cal.
Guns, AA	6—3 in (*76 mm*) 50 cal., 3 twin
A/S weapons	2 fixed Hedgehogs; 1 DC rack
Torpedo tubes	5—21 in (*533 mm*) quintupled
Torpedo racks	2 side-launching for A/S torpedoes
Boilers	4 Babcock & Wilcox; 600 psi (*42 km/cm²*); 850°F (*455°C*)
Main engines	2 GE impulse reaction geared turbines; 60 000 shp; 2 shafts
Speed, knots	34 max; 15 economical sea
Radius, miles	6 000 at 15 knots; 900 at full power
Oil fuel (tons)	650
Complement	Allowance; 245 (15 officers and 230 men) Max accommodation: 275 (15 officers and 260 men) revised official figures

Former United States destroyers of the later "Fletcher" class (*Villar*) and "Fletcher" class (*Guise*).

GUISE   1970, *Peruvian Navy, Official*

RADAR
Search: SPS 6.
Tactical: SPS 10.
Fire Control: GFCS 68 system forward, GFCS 56 system aft.

TRANSFER. Transferred from the United States Navy to the Peruvian Navy at Boston. Massachusetts, on 15 Dec 1960, and at San Diego, California, on 8 Oct 1961 respectively.

VILLAR   1971, *Peruvian Navy, Official*

DESTROYER ESCORTS

3 "CASTILLA" CLASS

Ex-US "BOSTWICK" CLASS

Name	No.	Launched	Completed
AGUIRRE (ex-USS, *Waterman, DE* 740)	62	4 July 1943	31 Dec 1943
CASTILLA (ex-USS *Bangust, DE* 739)	61	6 June 1943	30 Oct 1943
RODRIGUEZ (ex-USS *Weaver, DE* 741)	63	20 June 1943	30 Nov 1943

Displacement, tons	1 240 standard; 1 900 full load
Length, feet (*metres*)	300 (*91·4*) pp; 302·2 (*92·1*) wl; 306 (*93·3*) oa
Beam, feet (*metres*)	36·9 (*11·2*)
Draught, feet (*metres*)	12 (*3·6*) mean; 14·1 (*4·3*) max
Guns, dual purpose	3—3 in (*76 mm*) 50 cal.
Guns, AA	6—40 mm, 3 twin; 10—20 mm
A/S weapons	1 Mk 10 ahead-throwing mortar; 8 K mortars; 2 DC racks aft
Main engines	4 GM diesel-electric sets 60 000 hp; 2 shafts
Speed, knots	21 designed; 19 max continuous
Radius, miles	10 500 at 12 knots; 3 000 at full power
Oil fuel (tons)	322
Complement	Allowance: 172 (12 officers and 160 men); Max accommodation: 212 (12 officers and 200 men) revised official figures

CASTILLA   *1970, Peruvian Navy, Official*

Former United States destroyer escorts, DE, of the "Bostwick" class. All built by the Western Pipe & Steel Co, San Pedro, California, in 1943. Transferred to Peru on 26 Oct 1951, under the Mutual Defence Assistance Programme. Reconditioned and modernised at Green Cove Springs and Jacksonville, Flor. Actually arrived in Peru on 24 May 1952.

PENNANT NUMBERS. Given "DE" instead of "D" pennant numbers in 1959. Pennant numbers were changed from 2, 1 and 3 to 62, 61 and 63 respectively, in 1960.

TORPEDO TUBES. The original three 21 inch torpedo tubes in a triple mounting were removed.

AGUIRRE   *1967, Peruvian Navy, Official*

PHOTOGRAPHS. A starboard quarter oblique aerial view of *Castilla* appears in the 1953-54 to 1959-60 editions, a port broadside surface view of *Rodriguez* in the 1960-61 to 1963-64 editions, a port bow surface view of *Aguirre* in the 1960-61 to 1965-66 editions, a starboard bow oblique aerial view of *Rodriguez* in the 1966-67 edition, a port broadside surface view of *Castilla* in the 1964-65 to 1969-70 editions, and a port dead broadside surface view of *Rodriguez* in the 1967-68 to 1970-71 editions.

RIVER CLASS
The two elderly frigates of the "Palacios" Class, *Ferré* (ex-HMCS *Poundmaker*) and *Palacios* (ex-HMCS *St. Pierre*), former frigates of the Canadian "River" class, were officially stricken from the Peruvian Navy List in 1966. The frigate *Galvez* (ex-USS *Woonsocket PF* 32), former patrol frigate of the United States "Tacoma" class, similar to the British "River" class, was scrapped in 1961.

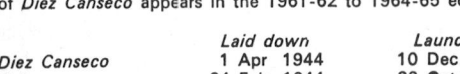

RODRIGUEZ   *1971, Peruvian Navy, Official*

PATROL VESSELS (*Corvettes*)

2 "GALVEZ" CLASS. Ex-US MSF TYPE

Name	No.
DIEZ CANSECO (ex-USS *Shoveler, MSF* 382)	69
GALVEZ (ex-USS *Ruddy, MSF* 380)	68

Displacement, tons	890 standard; 1 250 full load
Dimensions, feet	215 wl; 221·2 oa × 32·2 × 11 max
Guns	1—3 in, 50 cal dp; 2—40 mm AA
A/S weapons	1 hedgehog
Main engines	Diesel electric; 2 shafts; 3 532 bhp = 18 knots
Complement	100

Former US "Auk" class fleet minesweepers, MSF (ex-ocean minesweepers, AM), of the large steel hulled type. Both built by the Gulf Shipbuilding Corp. Activated at San Diego, California, and transferred to the Peruvian Navy under the Mutual Defence Assistance Programme on 1 Nov 1960. Sonar equipment was fitted so that they could be used as patrol vessels. The 3 inch gun director was removed. A photograph of *Diez Canseco* appears in the 1961-62 to 1964-65 editions.

	Laid down	Launched	Completed
Diez Canseco	1 Apr 1944	10 Dec 1944	28 June 1945
Galvez	24 Feb 1944	29 Oct 1944	28 Apr 1945

GALVEZ   *1970, Peruvian Navy, Official*

FAST PATROL CRAFT
6 VOSPER TYPE

DE LOS HEROS	23	**LARREA**	25	**SANTILLANA**	22
HERRERA	24	**SANCHEZ CARRION**	26	**VELARDE**	21

Displacement, tons	100
Dimensions, feet	103·7 wl; 109·7 oa × 21 × 5·7
Guns	2—20 mm AA
Main engines	2 Napier Deltic 18 cyl, turbocharged diesels; 6 200 bhp = 30 knots
Complement	25 (4 officers and 21 ratings)

Designed and built by Vosper Ltd, Portsmouth, England, for the Peruvian Navy. Of all-welded steel construction with aluminium upperworks. Designed for coastal patrol, air sea-rescue, and fishery protection. Equipped with Vosper roll damping fins, Decca Type 707 true motion radar, comprehensive radio, up-to-date navigation aids, sonar, depth charges in racks aft, and air-conditioning. The first boat, *Velarde*, was launched on 10 July 1964, the last, *Sanchez Carrion*, on 18 Feb 1965. Can be armed as gunboat, torpedo boat (four side-launched torpedoes) or minelayer. A twin rocket projector can be fitted forward instead of gun. A photograph of *Velarde* appears in the 1966-67 to 1970-71 editions.

SANCHEZ CARRION   *1971, Peruvian Navy, Official*

COASTAL MINESWEEPER
2 "BONDY" CLASS

BONDY (ex-*YMS* 25) 137		**SAN MARTIN** (ex-*YMS* 35) 138	

Displacement, tons	300 standard; 325 full load
Dimensions, feet	136 × 24·5 × 6
Guns	1—3 in; 2—20 mm AA
Main engines	2 GM diesels; 1 000 bhp = 13 knots; 11 knots econ)
Complement	30

Former US wooden motor minesweepers, YMS. *Bondy* was built by Greenport Basin & Construction Co, Long Island, NY, and launched on 28 Jan 1943, *San Martin* by C. Hilterbandt Drydock Co, Kingston, NY, and acquired from USA in 1947. Formerly known as *Alferez de Fragata Bondy* and *Guardiamarina San Martin*. Pennant Nos. changed from 27 and 29 to 137 and 06 respectively, in 1964 and the latter to 138 in 1965. A photograph of *San Martin* appears in the 1958-59 to 1965-66 editions.

BONDY   *1966, Peruvian Navy, Official*

PATROL LAUNCHES
3 "RIO" CLASS

RIO PIURA 04	**RIO TUMBES** 02	**RIO ZARUMILLA** 01

Displacement, tons	37 full load
Dimensions, feet	65·7 × 17 × 3·2
Guns	2—40 mm
Main engines	2 GM diesels; 2 shafts; 1 200 bhp = 18 knots

Built by Viareggio, Italy. Ordered in 1959, laid down on 15 July 1959, and entered service on 5 Sep 1960. *Rio el Salto*, 03, was deleted from the list in 1966.

RIO PIURA   *1967, Peruvian Navy, Official*

GUNBOATS

RIO SAMA   *1971, Peruvian Navy, Official*

RIO SAMA PC 11 (ex-USS *PGM* 78)   (ex-*PGM 111*)

Displacement, tons	145·5
Dimensions, feet	101 × 21 × 7
Guns	2—40 mm, 2—0·5 MG
Main engines	Diesel = 18 knots
Complement	15

Transferred in Sep 1966 from the United States under the Military Aid programme.

RIVER GUNBOATS
2 "MARANON" CLASS

MARAÑÓN	13	John I. Thornycroft & Co	23 Apr 1951	July 1951
UCAYALI	14	Ltd. Southampton, England	7 Mar 1951	June 1951

Displacement, tons	365 full load
Dimensions, feet	154·8 wl × 32 × 4 max
Guns	2—3 in, 50 cal dp; 7—20 mm AA (2 twin, 3 single)
Main engines	British Polar M 441 diesels; 800 bhp = 12 knots
Range, miles	6 000 without refuelling
Complement	40

Ordered early in 1950. Employed on police duties in Upper Amazon. Specially designed for carrying naval officers and men under tropical conditions. Very shallow draught. Superstructure of aluminium alloy. Mechanical ventilation. Based at Iquitos A photograph of *Maranon* appears in the 1962-63 to 1970-71 editions.

UCAYALI   *1971, Peruvian Navy, Official*

2 "LORETO" CLASS

AMAZONAS 11	**LORETO** 12

Displacement, tons	250 standard
Dimensions, feet	145 × 22 × 4
Guns	2—3 in; 1—47 mm; 2—20 mm AA
Main engines	Diesel; 750 bhp = 15 knots
Complement	35

Designed and built by the Electric Boat Co, Groton, Conn. Launched in 1934. A photograph of *Loreto* appears in the 1958-59 edition and of *Amazonas* in the 1959-60 to 1970-71 editions.

NAPO 301

Displacement, tons	98
Dimensions, feet	100 pp; 101·5 oa × 18 × 3
Main engines	Triple expansion; 250 ihp = 12 knots
Boilers	Yarrow
Complement	22

Built by Yarrow Co Ltd, Scotstoun, Glasgow. Launched in 1920. Built of steel. Converted from wood to oil fuel burning. In the Upper Amazon Flotilla. Pennant No. 16 was changed to 301 in 1967. Converted to a Dispensary Vessel in 1968.

AMERICA 15

Displacement, tons	240
Dimensions, feet	133 × 19·5 × 4·5
Guns	2—3 pdr; 4—12·7 mm AA
Main engines	Triple expansion; 350 ihp = 14 knots
Complement	26

Built by Tranmere Bay Development Co Ltd, Birkenhead. Built of steel. Launched and completed in 1904. Converted from coal to oil fuel burning. In the Upper Amazon Flotilla. The river gunboat *Iquitos* was discarded in 1967 after 92 years service.

LANDING SHIPS

CHIMBOTE (ex-M/S *Rawhiti*, ex-USS *LST 283*) 34

Displacement, tons	1 625 standard ; 4 050 full load
Dimensions, feet	316 wl ; 328 oa × 50 × 14·1
Guns	1—3 in
Main engines	GM diesels ; 2 shafts ; 1 700 bhp = 10 knots
Oil fuel, tons	600 oil tanks ; 1 100 ballast tanks
Radius, miles	24 000 at 9 knots
Complement	Accommodation for 16 officers and 130 men

Former US tank landing ship of the 1-510 Series. Built by American Bridge Co, Ambridge, Pennsylvania. Laid down on 2 Aug 1943, launched on 10 Oct 1943 and completed on 18 Nov 1943. Sold to Peru by a British firm in 1951.

CHIMBOTE   *1970, Peruvian Navy, Official*

PAITA (ex-USS *Burnett County*, LST 512) 35 (ex-*AT 4*)

Displacement, tons	1 653 standard ; 4 080 full load
Dimensions, feet	316 wl ; 328 oa × 50 × 14·5 max
Guns	6—40 mm AA ; 6—20 mm AA
Main engines	GM diesels ; 2 shafts ; 1 700 bhp = 10 knots
Complement	13 officers, 106 men

Former US tank landing ship of the 511-1152 Series. Built by Chicago Bridge & Iron Co, Seneca, Illinois. Laid down on 29 July 1943. Launched on 10 Dec 1943 and completed on 8 Jan 1944. Purchased by Peru in 1957.

PAITA   *1966, Peruvian Navy, Official*

2 "LOMAS" CLASS

ATICO (ex-USS *LSM 554*)   **LOMAS** (ex-USS *LSM 396*)

Displacement, tons	513 standard ; 913 full load
Dimensions, feet	196·5 wl ; 203·5 oa × 34·5 × 7
Guns	2—40 mm AA ; 4—20 mm AA
Main engines	Diesels ; 800 rpm ; 2 shafts ; 3 600 bhp = 12 knots
Oil fuel, tons	165 oil tanks
Complement	Accommodation for 116 (10 officers and 106 men)

Former US medium landing ships of the LSM type. Both built by Charleston Navy Yard, Charleston, SC, USA. Purchased in 1959. A photograph of *Atico* appears in ths 1960-61 to 1966-67 editions.

Name	No.	Laid down	Launched	Completed
Atico	37	3 Mar 1945	22 Mar 1945	14 Sep 1945
Lomas	36	13 Dec 1944	2 Jan 1945	23 Mar 1945

LOMAS   *1967, Peruvian Navy, Official*

TRANSPORTS

INDEPENDENCIA (ex-USS *Bellatrix*, *AKA 3*, ex-*Raven*, *SKA 20*) 31 (ex-21)

Displacement, tons	6 194 light
Measurement, tons	Maritime Commission deadweight, 8 656
Guns	1—5 in 38 cal ; 3—3 in 50 cal. 10—20 mm
Dimensions, feet	435 wl ; 459 oa × 63 × 26·5
Main Engines	1 Nordberg diesel ; 1 shaft ; 6 000 bhp = 16·5 knots

Former US attack cargo ship. Built by Tampa Shipbuilding Co, Tampa, Florida, in 1941. Transferred to Peru at Bremerton, Washington on 20 July 1963 under the Military Aid Program. Training ship for the Peruvian Naval Academy. Pennant number was changed from 21 to 31 in 1969.

INDEPENDENCIA   *1970, Peruvian Navy, Official*

ILO

Displacement, tons	18 400 full load
Measurement, tons	13 000 deadweight
Dimensions, feet	507·7 × 67·3 × 27·2
Main engines	Diesels ; Speed = 15·6 knots

The name *Ilo* was assigned to a new vessel launched on 15 July 1970 by the Servicio Industrial de la Marina in Callao. The new transport *Ilo* is now being completed and will be ready for sea in Dec 1971.
The old *Ilo* (ex-*Norlindo*) No. 133 (ex-33) was removed from the effective list in 1968.

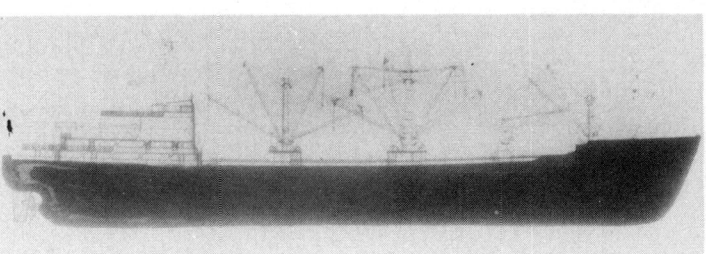

ILO   *1971, Peruvian Navy, Official*

CALLAO (ex-*Monserrate*) 132

Displacement, tons	7 790 full load
Measurement, tons	5 578 gross
Dimensions, feet	459 × 56 × 22
Main engines	2 diesel motors ; speed = 14 knots
Complement	100 (13 officers, 87 ratings)

Former Hamburg America liner. Built by Bremen Vulkan Yard, Bremen-Vegesack. Launched in 1938. Salved and seized on 1 Apr 1941 by the Peruvian Government after scuttling by the Germans. Employed as a troop transport and cargo carrier. Pennant No. changed from 32 to 132 in 1964.

CALLAO   *1965, Peruvian Navy, Official*

DISPOSALS

The German type transport *Rimac* (ex-*Eten*, ex-*Rhakotis*) was scrapped in July 1960. The fleet supply ships and oilers *Cabo Blanco* (ex-*Mariscall Castilla*, ex-*Preserver*) and *Organus* (ex-*Olaya*) of the Canadian type, were scrapped in 1961.

FLOATING DOCKS
The former US auxiliary floating dry dock *ARD 8* was transferred to Peru in Feb 1961: displacement 5 200 tons ; length 492 feet ; beam 84 feet ; draught 5·7 to 33·2 feet. Pennant No. changed from WY 20 to ADF 112 in 1964.
The former US floating dock *AFDL 33* launched in Oct 1964 was transferred to Peru in July 1959 displacement 1 900 tons ; length 288 feet ; beam 64 feet, draught 8·2 to 31·5 feet. Pennant No. changed from WY 19 to ADF 111 in 1964.

OILERS

2 "PARINAS" CLASS

Name	No.	Launched	Completed
PARINAS	155	2 May 1967	13 June 1968
PIMENTAL	156	30 Dec 1967	27 June 1969

Displacement, tons	3 434 light; 13 600 full load
Measurement, tons	10 000 deadweight
Dimensions, feet	410·9 × 63·1 × 26
Main engines	Burmeister and Wain Type 750 diesel; 5 400 bhp = 14·5 knots

Built by the Servicio Industrial de la Marina in the Naval Arsenal at Callao.   In service 1969.

PARINAS   *1970, Peruvian Navy, Official*

2 "SECHURA" CLASS

LOBITOS 159   **ZORRITOS** 158

Displacement, tons	8 700 full load
Measurement, tons	4 300 gross; 6 000 deadweight
Dimensions, feet	360·0 wl; 385·0 oa × 52·0 × 21·2 max
Main engines	Burmeister & Wain diesels; 2 400 bhp = 12 knots (13·25 knots on trials)
Boilers	2 Scotch with Thornycroft oil burners for cargo tank cleaning

Designed for transferring fuel to warships at sea.   *Zorritos*, built by Servicio Industrial de la Marina in the Arsenal Naval del Callao, Peru, was laid down on 8 Oct 1955 and launched on 8 Oct 1958.   Pennant No. was changed from 58 to 158 in 1964.   *Lobitos* built by Servicio Industrial de la Marina in the Arsenal Naval del Callao, Peru, was launched in May 1965.   Sister ship *Sechura*, No. 154 (ex-54) was laid up in 1968 (officially removed from the effective list).

LOBITOS   *1967, Peruvian Navy, Official*

TALARA 153

Displacement, tons	7 000
Measurement, tons	4 800 deadweight; (about 35 000 barrels)
Dimensions, feet	336·2 × 50·9 × 22·5
Main engines	Burmeister & Wain diesel; Type 562. *VT*-F115. 2 400 bhp = 12 knots

Built to requirements of Lloyd's Register.   Laid down in 1953 by Burmeister & Wain's Maskin-Og Skibsbygger, Copenhagen.   Completed in 1955.   No. changed from 53 to 153 in 1964.   A photograph appears in the 1955-56 to 1966-67 editions.   Laid up in reserve in 1969 (removed from the effective list).

MOLLENDO (ex-*Amalienborg*) ATP 151

Displacement, tons	6 084 standard; 25 670 full load
Dimensions, feet	534·8 × 72·2 × 30
Main engines	674-VTFS-160 diesels; 7 500 bhp = 14·5 knots

This Japanese built tanker, completed Sep 1962, was acquired by Peru in Apr 1967.

MOLLENDO   *1970, Peruvian Navy, Official*

WATER CARRIER

MANTILLA (ex-US *YW* 122) 141

Displacement, tons	1 235 full load
Dimensions, feet	174 × 32
Guns	1 MG forward
Capacity, gallons	200,000

Former US water barge.   Built by Henry C. Grebe & Co Inc, Chicago, Ill.   Lent to Peru in July 1963.

MANTILLA   *1970, Peruvian Navy, Official*

TUGS

RIOS (ex-USS *Pinto*. ATF 90) 123

Displacement, tons	1 235 standard; 1 675 full load
Measurement, tons	195 wl; 205 oa × 38·5 × 15·5 max
Main engines	4 GM diesel electric; 3 000 bhp = 16·5 knots

Former United States fleet ocean tug of the "Apache" class.   Launched on 5 Jan 1943.   Transferred to Peru in 1960 and delivered in Jan 1961.   Fitted with powerful pumps and other salvage equipment.

RIOS   *1967, Peruvian Navy, Official*

UNANUE (ex-USS *Wateree*. ATA 174) 136

Displacement, tons	534 standard; 852 full load; official revised figure
Dimensions, feet	133·7 wl; 143 oa × 33·9 × 13·2
Main engines	GM diesel-electric; 1 500 bhp = 13 knots

Former United States auxiliary ocean tug of the "Maricopa" class.   Built by Levingston SB Co. Orange, Texas.   Laid down on 5 Oct 1943, launched on 18 Nov 1943 and completed on 20 July, 1944.   Purchased from the USA in Nov 1961 under MAP

UNANUE   *1970, Peruvian Navy, Official*

PHILIPPINES

Administration	Strength of the Fleet		Ships

Administration

Flag Officer in Command, Philippine Navy:
Commodore Ismael C. Lomibao, PN

Diplomatic Representation

Naval, Military and Air Attaché in London:
Colonel Pedro L. Los Baños

Personnel

1971: 1 640 officers and 16 360 men including Coast
Guard and marine reserves

Strength of the Fleet

7 Escort Vessels   2 Coastal Minesweepers
7 Patrol Vessels   28 Patrol Boats
3 Command Ships   37 Support Ships, etc

Coast Guard

Established Oct 1967 as a specialised branch within the
Navy.

Commandant: Commodore Dioscero E. Papa

Ships

Names are those of geographical locations, mostly
provinces, and are prefixed by RPS (Republic of
Philippines Ship).

Mercantile Marine

Lloyd's Register of Shipping: 313 vessels of 946 400 tons

ESCORT VESSELS

2 PCE TYPE

CEBU	(ex-*PCE* 881) PS 28	**LEYTE**	(ex-*PCE* 885) PS 30
ILOILO	(ex-*PCE* 879) PS 32	**NEGROS OCCIDENTAL**	(ex-*PCE* 884) PS 29
		PANGASINAN	(ex-*PCE* 891) PS 31

Displacement, tons	640 standard; 903 full load
Dimensions, feet	180 wl; 184·5 oa × 33 × 9·5
Guns	1—3 in; 3—40 mm (E31, 6—40 mm); 4—20 mm
Main engines	2 GM diesels; 2 shafts; 1 800 bhp = 15 knots

Former US escorts. Built in Portland, Oregon, USA, by Albina Eng & Mach Works
(28, 29, 30) and Willamette Iron & Steel Corp (31, 32). All launched in 1943-44.
A photograph of *Leyte* appears in the 1956-57 to 1964-65 editions, of *Negros Occidental*
in the 1965-66 to 1968-69 editions and of *Iloilo* in the 1969-70 and 1970-71 editions.

CEBU   *1971, Official*

2 MSF TYPE

QUEZON (ex-USS *Vigilance*, MSF 324, ex-*AM* 324) PS 70
RIZAL (ex-USS *Murrelet*, MSF 372, ex-*AM* 372)   PS 69

Displacement, tons	890 standard; 1 250 full load
Dimensions, feet	215 wl; 221 oa × 32·2 × 10·8 max
Guns	2—3 in, 50 cal (single); 4—40 mm AA (2 twin)
A/S	1 mortar; 2 DCT
Main engines	Diesel-electric; 2 shafts; 3 532 bhp = 18 knots

Former US fleet minesweepers of the "Auk" class. *Quezon* was built by Associated
Shipbuilders and *Rizal* by Savannah Machine & Foundry Co. Launched on 5 Apr
1943 and 24 Dec 1944, respectively. *Rizal* was transferred on 18 June 1965 and
Quezon on 19 Aug 1967 at Seattle, Washington. Minesweeping gear removed.
A photograph of *Quezon* appears in the 1969-70 and 1970-71 editions.

RIZAL   *1971, Official*

PATROL VESSELS

5 PC TYPE

BATANGAS	(ex-*PC* 1134) PS 24	**NUEVA ECIJA**	(ex-*PC* 1241) PS 25
BOHOL	(ex-*PC* 1131) PS 22	**NUEVA VISCAYA**	(ex-USS *Altus*
CAPIZ	(ex-*PC* 1564) PS 27		*PC 568*) PS 80

Displacement, tons	330 standard; 450 full load
Dimensions, feet	173·7 oa × 23 × 10·8
Guns	1—3 in dp; 1—40 mm AA; 5—20 mm AA
Main engines	2 GM diesels; 2 shafts; 3 600 bhp = 18 knots

Former US submarine chasers of steel construction. Built in 1942-43. Transferred
in 1947-58. *Negros Oriental*, C 26 (ex-*PC* 1563), sunk in a typhoon at Guam in Nov
1962, was raised, but stricken on 24 Jan 1963. *Nueva Viscaya*, transferred in 1968
after service with the US Air Force, had been stricken from the USN list on 15 Mar 1963.

BOHOL   *1968, Philippine Navy, Official*

2 PCS TYPE

LAGUNA (ex-*PCS* 1403) PG 12   **TARLAC** (ex-*PCS* 1399, ex-*YMS* 450) PG 11

Displacement, tons	230 standard; 300 full load
Dimensions, feet	136 oa × 24·5 × 8·5
Guns	1—3 in; 4—20 mm
Main engines	2 GM diesels; 2 shafts; 800 bhp = 14 knots

Former US submarine chasers of wooden construction. Built in 1943-44. Transferred in Jan 1948. A photorgaph of *Laguna* appears in the 1956-57 to 1961-62
editions.

LAGUNA   *1969, Philippine Navy, Official*

COMMAND SHIPS

THE PRESIDENT (ex-*Roxas*, ex-*Lapulapu*) TP 777

Measurement, tons	2 200 gross
Guns	2—40 mm; 2—20 mm AA
Main engines	B. & W. diesels; 2 shafts; 5 000 bhp = 16·5 knots

Formerly the Presidential Yacht. Acquired from Japan as reparation. Built at Isha-
kawajima, Japan. Launched in 1958 and completed in 1959. Originally named
Lapu-Lapu after the chief who killed Magellan. On 9 Oct 1962 the ship was recommissioned and renamed *Roxas* after the late Manuel Roxas, first President of the
Philippine Republic. Renamed *The President* in 1967.

The command ship *Rajah Soliman* D 66 (ex-USS *Bowers*, APD 40, ex-DE 637), sunk
in a typhoon at Bataan National Shipyard in June 1964, was raised, but stricken on
3 Dec 1964.

THE PRESIDENT   *1968, Philippine Navy, Official*

DATU KALANTIAW (ex-USS *Booth* DE 170) FS 76

Displacement, tons	1 240 standard ; 1 900 full load
Dimensions, feet	306 × 36·6 × 14
Guns	2—3 in AA ; 6—40 mm (3 twin) 2—20 mm
ASW weapons	2 triple launchers
Main engines	Diesel Electric 6 000 shp = 21 knots
Complement	11 Officers, 154 men

Former US "Bestwick" class destroyer escort transferred to Philippine Navy 15 Dec 1967 at Philadelphia. Numbered as Destroyer Escort but also rated as Command Ship.

MOUNT SAMAT (ex-*Pagasa*, ex-*Santa Maria*, ex-*Pagasa*, ex-*Apo* 21, ex-USS *Quest*, AM 281) TP 21

Displacement, tons	650 standard ; 945 full load
Dimensions, feet	180 wl ; 184 ·5 oa × 33 × 9·8
Guns	1—3 in ; 4—20 mm AA
Main engines	Diesel ; 2 shafts ; 1 710 bhp = 14 knots

Former US fleet minesweeper. Built by Gulf SB Corpn. Launched on 16 Mar 1944. Converted into Presidential Yacht. Renamed *Mount Samat* in 1967.

MOUNT SAMAT   *1971, Official*

COASTAL MINESWEEPERS

ZAMBALES	(ex-USS *MSC* 218) PM 55
ZAMBOANGA DEL NORTE	(ex-USS *MSC* 210) PM 56

Displacement, tons	335 standard ; 375 full load
Dimensions, feet	138 pp ; 144 oa × 27 × 8·3
Main engines	GM diesels ; 2 shafts ; 880 bhp = 14 knots

Non-magnetic coastal minesweepers of the US "Bluebird" class. *Zambales* was built by Bellingham Shipyard Co, Washington, laid down in Aug 1954 and launched on 25 Feb 1955. Transferred on 7 Mar and 23 Apr 1956, respectively.

ZAMBALES   *1969, Philippine Navy, Official*

PATROL BOATS

		MISAMIS OCCIDENTAL (ex-*PGM* 38) G 53	
AGUSAN	(ex-*PGM* 39) G 61	**PALAWAN** (ex-*PGM* 42) G 64	
ANTIQUE	(ex-*PGM* 36) G 51	**ROMBLON** (ex-*PGM* 41) G 63	
CAMARINES SUR	(ex-*PGM* 33) G 48	**SULU** (ex-*PGM* 34) G 49	
CATAN DUANES	(ex-*PGM* 40) G 62	**YACHI** (ex-*PGM*) 55 G 57	
LA UNION	(ex-*PGM* 35) G 50	**YANGA** (ex-*PGM* 56) G 59	
MASBATE	(ex-*PGM* 37) G 52	**YUNDI** (ex-*PGM* 57) G 60	

Displacement, tons	95 standard ; 143 full load
Dimensions, feet	110 × 17 × 6·5
Guns	1—60 mm mortar ; 2—40 mm AA ; 4—50 cal MG
Main engines	Diesels ; 2 shafts ; 1 540 bhp = 18 knots

G 48-53 were built by Georgia Shipbuilding Co, St Mary's Georgia. Motor gunboats with the basic design of the former 110 ft SC type of the US Navy. The first four were delivered to the Philippine Navy in 1955 and G 52 and G 53 in 1956. G 61-64 were built by Tacoma Boatbuilding Co, Tacoma, Washington, for transfer under MAP. All steel, G 61, completed in Aug 1959, and G 62 were transported to the Philippines aboard ship in Feb 1960, followed by G 63 and G 64 in Apr 1960. A photograph of *Camarines Sur* appears in the 1956-57 to 1961-62 editions.

Patrol Boats—*continued*

ROMBLON   *1968, Philippine Navy, Official*

ALERT	(ex-*SC* 1267) P 16	**MALAMPAY SOUND**	(ex-*SC* 1274) P 20
CAVITE	(ex-*SC* 981) P 19	**MOUNTAIN PROVINCE**	(ex *SC* 736) P 15
		SURIGAO	(ex-*SC* 747) P 17

Displacement, tons	85 standard ; 130 full load
Dimensions, feet	111 oa × 17 × 6
Guns	1—40 mm AA ; 3—20 mm AA
Main engines	Diesels ; 2 shafts ; 1 000 bhp = 14·18 knots

Former US small submarine chasers of wooden construction. Built in 1942-43. Transferred in 1946-48.

6 US PCF TYPE

306 (ex-USS *PCF 33*)	**309** (ex-USS *PCF 84*)
307 (ex-USS *PCF 34*)	**310** (ex-USS *PCF 85*)
308 (ex-USS *PCF 83*)	**311** (ex-USS *PCF 86*)

Displacement, tons	22 full load
Dimensions, feet	50 × 13 × 3·5
Guns	2·50 cal mg
Main engines	2 geared diesels ; 960 shp = 25 knots

All transferred from the United States Navy on 15 Dec 1967.

PATROL BOAT 310   *1969, Philippine Navy Official*

HYDROFOIL PATROL BOATS

CAMIGUIN H 72		**SIQUIJOR** H 73

Displacement, tons	28
Measurement, tons	60 gross
Dimensions, feet	68·5 × 15·8 (24·3 foils) × 7
Guns	1—20 mm AA
A/S weapons	1 torpedo launcher
Main engines	Mercedes Benz diesel (MB 20, 12 cyl) ; 2 shafts ; 1 250 bhp = 38 knots

Built by Cantiere Navale Leopoldo Rodriquez, Messina, Sicily. Laid down on 26 May and 28 Oct 1964. Completed in Apr 1965. For military and police patrol.

CAMIGUIN   *1969, Philippine Navy, Official*

Hydrofoil Boats—*continued*

BALER H 75   **BONTOC** H 74

Displacement, tons	32 full load
Measurement, tons	60 gross
Dimensions, feet	68·9 × 15·7 × 24·6 over foils
Guns	MG fore and aft
Main engines	Ikegai-Mercedes Benz diesel; 3 200 bhp = 37·8 knots (32 cruising). Also auxiliary engine
Complement	15 (3 officers, 12 ratings)

Built by Hitachi Zosen, Kanagawa, Japan. Completed in Dec 1966. For smuggling prevention.

REPAIR SHIPS

AKLAN (ex-USS *Romulus*, ARL 22, ex-*LST 926*)

Displacement, tons	1 625 light; 4 100 full load
Dimensions, feet	316 wl; 328 oa × 50 × 11
Guns	8—40 mm AA
Main engines	GM diesels; 2 shafts; 1 800 bhp = 11·6 knots

Former US landing craft repair ship transferred under MAP in Nov 1961.

AKLAN   *1968, Philippine Navy, Official*

LANDING SHIPS

ALBAY (ex-*LST 865*) LT 39	**CADDO PARISH**	LST 515
BULACAN (ex-*LST 843*) LT 38	**HICKMAN COUNTY**	LST 825
MISAMIS ORIENTAL (ex-*LST 875*) LT 40	**MADERA COUNTY**	LST 905

Displacement, tons	1 625 light; 4 080 full load
Dimensions, feet	316 wl; 328 oa × 50 × 14 max
Guns	7—40 mm AA; 2—20 mm AA
Main engines	Diesel; 2 shafts; 1 800 bhp = 12 knots

Former US landing ships of the LST type. LST 515, LST 825 and LST 905 were transferred from USN on 26 Nov 1969.

MISAMIS ORIENTAL   *1968, Philippine Navy, Official*

BATANES (ex-USS *LSM 236*) LP 65   **ISABELA** (ex-USS *LSM 463*) LP 41
ORIENTAL MINDORO (ex-US *LSM 320*) LP 68

Displacement, tons	743 beaching; 912 full load
Dimensions, feet	196·5 wl; 204 oa × 34·5 × 8·3
Guns	2—40 mm AA
Main engines	Direct drive diesel; 2 shafts; 2 800 bhp = 12·5 knots

Former medium landing ships. *Batanes* was transferred on 15 Sep 1960. *Isabella* was refloated on 1 Jan 1964 after being aground since Sep 1963.

BATANES   *1962, courtesy Mr W. H. Davis*

OILERS

LAKE NAUJAN (ex-US *YO 173*) Y 43

Displacement, tons	521 standard; 1 400 full load
Dimensions, feet	174 oa × 32 × 13·2
Guns	2—20 mm
Main engines	Diesel; 560 bhp = 8 knots

Ex-US YO type. A photograph appears in the 1953-54 to 1960-61 editions.

SUPPLY SHIP

LIMASAWA (ex-USCGC *Nettle WAK 169*) 79

Displacement, tons	728
Dimensions, feet	176·5 × 32 × 10
Main engines	Diesel; 2 shafts; 1 000 bhp = 11 knots

Same basic design (USN FS type) as *Bojeadour* and *Lauis Ledge*. Transferred from USCG at Manilla 1968.

LIGHTHOUSE TENDERS

BOJEADUR (ex-US *FS 203*) L 46   **LAUIS LEDGE** (ex-US *FS 185*) L 45

Displacement, tons	470 standard; 811 full load
Dimensions, feet	180 oa × 32 × 10
Main engines	Diesel; 2 shafts; 1 000 bhp = 11 knots

Ex-US FS type.

LAUIS LEDGE   *1969, Philippine Navy, Official*

PEARL BANK (ex-US *OL 4*) L 47

Displacement, tons	162 standard; 301 full load
Dimensions, feet	120 oa × 24 × 8
Guns	2—20 mm AA
Main engines	Diesel; 2 shafts; 240 bhp = 6 knots

Ex-OL type. A photograph appears in the 1953-54 to 1957-58 editions.

WATER CARRIER

LAKE LANAO (ex-US *YW 125*) Y 42

Displacement, tons	1 235 full load
Dimensions, feet	174 oa × 32 × 15
Guns	2—20 mm AA
Main engines	Diesel; 640 bhp = 9 knots

LAKE LANAO   *1969, Philippine Navy, Official*

TUGS

IFUGAO (ex-US *ATR 96*) R 44

Displacement, tons	534 standard; 852 full load
Dimensions, feet	134·5 wl; 413 oa × 33 × 13·5
Guns	1—3 in; 2—20 mm
Main engines	Diesel-electric; 1 500 bhp = 13 knots

Rescue tug returned to US from United Kingdom, and then transferred to the Philippines. Photograph in the 1956-57 to 1957-58 editions.

IGOROT (ex-*YTL 572*) 222   **MARANAO** (ex-*YTL 574*) 221
                                         MANGYAN (ex-*ST 1312*) 223

Small harbour tugs. US YTL 429 and 449 were transferred under MAP in 1963.

COAST GUARD CUTTERS

COASTGUARD UTILITY BOATS. 15 ex-US CG Cutters, Nos 100-114. No names assigned.

AUXILIARY

A small auxiliary floating dry dock, AFDL 44, was transferred by US in 1968 under MAP.

POLAND

Administration

Commander-in-Chief of the Polish Navy:
Vice-Admiral Ludwik Janczyszyn

Chief of the Naval Staff:
Rear-Admiral Henryk Pietraszkiewicz

Diplomatic Representation

Naval, Military and Air Attaché in London:
Colonel Witold Lokuciewski

Naval, Military and Air Attaché in Washington:
Colonel Henryk Nowaczyk

Naval, Military and Air Attaché in Moscow:
Brigadier General Waclaw Jagas

Naval, Military and Air Attaché in Paris:
Colonel Marian Bugaj

Strength of the Fleet

5 Submarines (Diesel Powered)
3 Destroyers
24 Fleet Minesweepers (Medium)
12 Fast Missile Boats
8 Patrol Vessel (Submarine Chasers)
20 Fast Torpedo Boats
38 Patrol Boats
16 Landing Ships
27 Minesweeping Boats
8 Training Ships
6 Surveying Vessels
7 Oilers
12 Support Ships and Auxiliaries

Ships

Polish warships are referred to officially with the prefix ORP, equivalent to HMS, for Okrety Polska Rzeczpospolita

Naval Aviation

There is a Fleet Air Arm of about 50 fixed-wing aircraft and helicopters. A fighter division of two wings supports the Navy.

Personnel

1971: 20 000 (1 800 officers and 18 200 men)

Mercantile Marine

Lloyd's Register of Shipping:
516 vessels of 1 580 298 tons gross

SUBMARINES (Okrety Podwodne)

4 Ex-USSR "W" TYPE

BIELIK 295	**ORZEL** 292
KONDOR 294	**SOKOL** 293

Displacement, tons	1 030 surface; 1 180 submerged
Length, feet (metres)	240 (73·2)
Beam, feet (metres)	22 (6·7)
Draught, feet (metres)	15 (4·6)
Torpedo tubes	6—21 in (533 mm), 4 bow, 2 stern
	18 torpedoes carried
Mines	40 mines or 18 torpedoes
Main engines	Diesel electric, 4 000 hp; 2 shafts
	Electric motors, 2 500 hp
Speed, knots	17 on surface; 15 submerged
Radius, miles	1 300
Complement	60

A class of medium size long range submarines built in the USSR and transferred to the Polish Navy. One Polish submarine has borne the number 317.

NOMENCLATURE. Kondor means Condor, Orzel means Eagle and Sokol means Falcon.

PHOTOGRAPHS. A port oblique aerial view of Sokol appears in the 1966-67 to 1970-71 editions.

FORMER "WILK" CLASS
The three submarines of the "Wilk" class, Rys, Wilk and Zbik, were broken up in 1957.

"KASZUB" CLASS
It was officially stated in Feb 1970 that the six coastal submarines of the Ex-USSR "M" Type, Kaszub 301, Krakowiak 303, Kujawiak 305, Mazowsze (ex-Kurp) 306, Mazur 302, and Slazak (ex-Podhalanin) 304, were removed from the effective list.
Formerly the Soviet "MV" class M 100 to M 105 built in 1944 to 1950, they were transferred to the Polish Navy in 1956 and 1957. Kurp ran aground and was so badly damaged as to be at first sight reckoned a total loss, but she was refitted and renamed Mazowsze.
See photograph of Kaszub in the 1955-56 to 1967-68 editions and of Kujawiak in the 1968-69 and 1969-70 editions.

1 NETHERLANDS BUILT

SEP 219

Displacement, tons	1 092 surface; 1 450 submerged
Length, feet (metres)	273·5 (83·4) pp; 275·5 (84·0) oa
Beam, feet (metres)	22 (6·7)
Draught, feet (metres)	13 (4·0).
Guns, surface	1—4 in (105 mm)
Guns, AA	2—40 mm
Torpedo tubes	8—21 in (533 mm)
Main engines	2 Sulzer diesels, total 4 740 hp
	Electric motors, 1 000 hp
Speed, knots	19 on surface; 9 submerged
Complement	56

Built by Rotterdam Dry Dock Co. Laid down in 1936, launched on 17 Oct 1938 and completed in 1939. Sep means Vulture. Fitted for minelaying. Now over age and used for initial sea training purposes. Sister ship Orzel (Eagle) was lost in June 1940.

SOKOL   1971, Polish Navy, Official

KONDOR   1970, Skyfotos

BIELIK   1969, Official

ORZEL   1968, Official

SEP   1969, Official

DESTROYERS *(Niszczyciele)*

2 Ex-SOVIET "SKORY" CLASS

GROM (ex-*Smetlivy*)   **WICHER** (ex-*Skory*)

Displacement, tons	2 600 standard; 3 500 full load
Length, feet (*metres*)	393·8 (*120·0*) pp; 420 (*128·0*) oa
Beam, feet (*metres*)	41 (*12·5*)
Draught, feet (*metres*)	15 (*4·5*)
Guns, surface	4—5·1 in (*130 mm*), 2 twin mounts
Guns, AA	2—3 in (*76 mm*); 7—37 mm
A/S weapons	4 DCT
Torpedo tubes	10—21 in (*533 mm*) 2 quintuple
Mines	80 capacity
Boilers	4 high pressure
Main engines	Geared turbines; 2 shafts; 70 000 shp
Speed, knots	36
Radius, miles	4 000 at 15 knots
Oil fuel, tons	700
Complement	280

WICHER   1968. Official

Former Soviet destroyers of the first "Skory" type. *Wicher* was in fact the prototype of the class. Two were delivered by the USSR to Poland on 15 Dec 1957 (*Grom*) and 28 June 1958 (*Wicher*).

PENNANT NUMBERS. Former identification numerals were 53 and 54, respectively.

NOMENCLATURE. "Grom" means Thunderbolt, and "Wicher" means Hurricane.

RADAR
Search: Minories and an obsolescent S Band radar.
Tactical: Aldgate.
Fire Control: Obsolescent type.

GROM   1968. Official

1 BRITISH BUILT

BLYSKAWICA 271

Displacement, tons	2 144 standard; 3 383 full load
Length, feet (*metres*)	357 (*108·8*) pp; 374 (*114·0*) oa
Beam, feet (*metres*)	37 (*11·3*)
Draught, feet (*metres*)	10·2 (*3·1*)
Guns, dual purpose	8—4 in (*102 mm*)
Guns, AA	10—37 mm
A/S weapons	4 DCT; 22 DC and racks
Torpedo tubes	3—21 in (*533 mm*) tripled
Boilers	4 three-drum type
Main engines	Parsons geared turbines; 2 shafts; 54 000 shp
Speed, knots	39
Complement	180

Built by J. Samuel White & Co Ltd, Cowes, Isle of Wight. Laid down on 1 Oct 1935, launched on 1 Oct 1936 and completed on 1 Oct 1937. Name means Lightning. Originally fitted for minelaying, and could carry 7 mines; but no longer has minelaying capabilities. Bows were strengthened for ice navigation.

ARMAMENT. The original armament was 7—4·7 mm AA, 4 MG, 6—21 inch tubes (tripled), 2 DCT.

RECONSTRUCTION. The ship was completely dismantled in 1958 down to the hull, and superstructure was entirely rebuilt and armament modified in 1959-60.

ENGINEERING. Boilers work at 385 lbs per sq in pressure with 200 degrees of superheat. Ship exceeded her designed speed on trials.

NEW CONSTRUCTION. The project to build a new escort or frigate of the light destroyer type has apparently been rescinded.

PRESERVATION. The old destroyer **Burza**, 1 515 tons standard, 2 430 tons full load, was officially withdrawn from active service with the Polish Navy in 1962 and put in a state of preservation to be used as a museum ship.

BLYSKAWICA   1965. Polish Navy. Official

BURZA   1969. Official

FLEET MINESWEEPERS (TRALOWCE)

12 "KROGULEC" CLASS

ALBATROS	618	KORMORAN	616		619	622
CZAPLA	617	KROGULEC	614	TUKAN	620	623
JASTRAB	615	ORLIK	613		621	624

Displacement, tons	500
Dimensions, feet	190·3 × 24·6 × 8·2
Guns	6—25 mm AA
Main engines	Diesels; speed = 16 knots

Flushdecked minesweepers of a new type built at the Stocznia Yard from 1963 onwards.
Jastrab and *Orlik* commissioned in 1964.
A photograph of *Jastrab* appears in the 1966-67 and 1967-68 editions.

ALBATROS   *1968, Official*

12 SOVIET "T 43" TYPE

BIZON	605	DZIK	604	MORS	610	TUR	602
BOBR	606	FOKA	609	ROSOMAK	607	ZBIK	612
DELFIN	608	LOS	603	RYS	611	ZUBR	601

Displacement, tons	500 standard; 600 full load
Dimensions, feet	200 × 27·2 × 9
Guns	4—37 mm AA; 8—13 mm MG AA
Main engines	Diesels; 2 shafts; speed = 18 knots
Complement	60

Soviet "T43" type but built in Poland at Stocznia Gdynska. Gdynia in 1957-62.
A photograph of *Tur* appears in the 1958-59 edition, and of *Los* in the 1959-60 to
1964-65 editions.

DELFIN   *1969, Polish Navy, Official*

"BIRD" CLASS

It was officially stated in Feb 1970 that the three coastal minesweepers of the "Bird"
class, *Czaiku* 325, *Mewa* 326, and *Rybitwa* 327, were removed from the effective list.
Built in Poland in 1935 and recovered from German hands in 1945 they were latterly
no longer used for minesweeping, being known as coastal craft, and classed as general
utility auxiliaries, with all armament removed.
See photograph of *Mewa* in the 1958-59 to 1964-65 editions and of *Rybitwa* in the
1965-66 to 1969-70 editions.
Sister boat *Kompas* (ex-*Zuraw*) is used as a surveying vessel, see later page.

ZUBR   *1970*

MISSILE BOATS

12 SOVIET "OSA" TYPE

Displacement, tons	160 standard; 200 full load
Dimensions, feet	121·3 pp; 131·5 oa × 20 × 6·5
Guided weapons	4 large hood type missile launchers in two pairs abreast
Guns	4—25 mm (2 twin, 1 forward, 1 aft)
Main engines	3 diesels; 4 800 bhp = 35 knots
Complement	25

Fast vessels of the motor torpedo boat type but with a large hull and four missile
launchers in two pairs abreast the superstructure. Reported to have a surface-to-
surface missile range of about 15 miles.

RADAR. Search: Minories. Tactical: Aldgate. Fire Control: Bankside.

"Osa" class No. 080   *1970, Official*

"Osa" class No. 164   *1969, Official*

PATROL VESSELS

8 Ex-SOVIET "KRONSTADT" CLASS

CZUINY	368	NIEUGIETY	361	ZAWZIETY	363	ZWINNY	365
GROZNY	362	WYTRWALY	367	ZRECZNY	366	ZWROTNY	364

Displacement, tons	300 standard; 350 full load
Dimensions, feet	167·3 × 19·3 × 9
Guns	1—3·9 in; 2—37 mm AA; 4—13 mm MG AA
Main engines	2 diesels; speed = 27 knots
Complement	40

Former Soviet submarine chasers. Four built in 1953 were acquired by Poland in 1957.
Grozny, Wytrwaly, Zrecany. and *Zwinny* (Strong, Energetic, Clever and Speedy), were
delivered on 15 Dec 1957. A photograph of *Zwrotny* appears in the 1958-59 to 1964-65
editions.

ZAWZIETY   *1968, Official*

NIEUGIETY   *Official*

TORPEDO BOATS (*Scigacze torpedowe*)

No. 410 — *1971, Polish Navy Official*

No. 403 — *1971, Official*

20 Ex-SOVIET "P 6" TYPE

401	404	407	410	413	417
402	405	408	411	414	418
403	406	409	412	415	419
				416	420

Displacement, tons	68 full load
Dimensions, feet	83 × 20 × 6 max
Guns	4—25 mm AA; 8 DC
Tubes	2—12 in
Main engines	4 diesels; 4 800 bhp = 43 knots

Acquired from the USSR in 1957-58. A photograph of No. 409 appears in the 1965-66 to 1970-71 editions, of No. 405 in the 1966-67 to 1970-71 editions, and of No. 410 in the 1969-70 and 1970-71 editions.

No. 408 — *1970, Official*

Nos. 418 and 419 — *1969, Col Borg*

Torpedo Boats—continued

No. 416 — *1971, Polish Navy, Official*

No. 414 — *1968, Official*

PATROL BOATS

4 "OKSYWIE" CLASS

OP 301	OP 302	OP 303	OP 304

Displacement, tons	170 standard
Dimensions, feet	134·5 × 19 × 6·9
Guns	2 twin 37 mm
A/S weapons	Depth charge racks
Main engines	Diesels; Speed = 20 knots

In series construction. Are an improved version of the earlier patrol boats of this type.

OP 301 — *1969, Official*

5 "OBLUZE" CLASS

321	322	323	324	325

Displacement, tons	170
Dimensions, feet	134 × 19 × 7
Guns	2—37 mm AA

In series production since 1965 at Oksywie Shipyard. Some hulls differ.

9 "GDANSK" CLASS

311	313	315	317	319
312	314	316	318	

Displacement, tons	120
Dimensions, feet	124·7 × 19·2 × 5
Guns	2—37 mm AA
A/S	Depth charges
Main engines	Diesels; speed 20 knots

Nine submarine chasers of the "Gdansk" class were built in 1960.

20 "KP" TYPE

KP 118	KP 120	KP 122	KP 124	KP 126
KP 119	KP 121	KP 123	KP 125	

Displacement, tons	60
Guns	2 MG AA (in twin mounting)
Main Engines	3 motors; speed 15 knots

Small patrol boats reported to be under the jurisdiction of the Frontier Guard.

LANDING SHIPS

20 "POLNOCNY" CLASS

Displacement, tons	900 to 1 000
Dimensions, feet	246 × 39·3 × 9·8
Armament	Rocket projectors
Main engines	Diesels; 4 000 bhp = 15 knots

Polish built, in Gdansk, but same as the Soviet "Polnocny" type. Pennant numbers run in an 800 series.

LANDING CRAFT. It was officially stated by the Polish naval authorities in Feb 1971 that all of the landing craft of the US LCT (5) type have been removed from the effective list.

LSMR 894   *1969, Official*

MINESWEEPING BOATS

7 "TR 40" CLASS

Polish built minesweeping boats numbered in 800 series.

20 "K 8" CLASS

Minesweeping boats built in Poland. Pennant numbers run in 800 and 900 series.

TRAINING SHIPS (*Okrety szkolne*)

1 PROJECTED

Displacement, tons	8 900
Dimensions, feet	410 × 54·2 × 23
Main engines	Sulzer diesel; 4 000 bhp = 14 knots

It has been reported that a new training ship authorised would probably have a dual purpose role, but there is no official confirmation of this.

GRYF (ex-*Zetempowiec*, ex-*Opplem*, ex-*Omsk*, ex-*Empire Contees*, ex-*Irene Oldendorf*)

Measurement, tons	1 959 gross
Dimensions, feet	282·2 × 44·2 × 18·8
Guns	2—3·9 in; 4—37 mm AA
Main engines	Steam; 1 200 hp = 10 knots

Former German "Hansa" class ship. Built by Burmeister & Wain. Launched in 1944. Taken over in 1947. Transferred to the Navy in 1949. The name was changed from *Zetempowiec* to *Gryf* in 1957. Reported to be used as a hospital ship.

GRYF   *1969, Official*

HENRYK RUTKOWSKI

Measurement, tons	70 gross
Dimensions, feet	89·6 × 21·0 × 8·9
Main engines	Diesels; 135 bhp = 9 knots

Ketch of the German KFK type built in 1944 allocated to the Sea Fishery School.

Training Ships—*continued*

ISKRA (ex-*Pigmy*, ex-*Iskra*, ex-*St Blanc*, ex-*Vlissingen*)

Displacement, tons	560
Dimensions, feet	128 × 25 × 10
Main engines	Diesels; 250 bhp = 7·5 knots
Complement	30, plus 40 cadets

A three masted schooner with auxiliary engines. Built by Muller, Foxhol, Holland. Launched in 1917.

ISKRA   *1969, Official*

DAR POMORZA (ex-*Prinz Eitel Friedrich*

Displacement, tons	1 561
Measurement, tons	1 566 gross
Dimensions, feet	240 × 41 × 21
Main engines	Diesel

An auxiliary motored fully rigged sailing ship of the Polish mercantile Marine. Built by Blohm & Voss, Hamburg. Launched in 1909. Provides personnel and training for the Navy, but is not on the Polish Navy List.

DAR POMORZA   *Skyfotos*

HORYZONT

A training ship of about 1 000 tons for navigation instruction. Assigned to the Polish Navy, but not on the Polish Navy List.

PODHALANIN

A training boat of 93 tons gross with a speed of 12 knots built in 1957. Not on the Polish Navy list.

PAWEL FINDEP

A paddle steamer taken over for inland duty as an instructional vessel. Not on the Polish Navy list.

SURVEYING VESSELS (Okret hydrograficzne)

BALTYK

Displacement, tons	1 000
Measurement, tons	658 gross; 450 deadweight
Dimensions, feet	194·3 oa; 175·3 pp × 29·5 × 14
Main engines	Steam; 1 000 hp = 11 knots

Trawler of B-10 type. Built in 1944 in Glansk. Converted and structure altered. The hydrographic vessels *Zodiac* and *Koziorozec* (see details in the 1961-62 edition) are no longer on the Navy List. They belong to the Shipping Board of Gdansk.

BALTYK   *1968, Official*

1 "BIRD" CLASS

(Ex-COASTAL MINESWEEPER)

KOMPAS (ex-*Zuraw*)

Displacement, tons	140 standard; 183 full load
Dimensions, feet	139·5 × 21·3 × 5·5
Main engines	Diesel; 1 040 bhp = 15 knots
Complement	30

Built in Poland at Gdynia. Launched on 22 Aug 1938. Recovered from German hands in 1945. All armament removed. Formerly a coastal minesweeper of the "Bird" class, now used as a surveying vessel. Sister boats *Czaika*, *Mewa* and *Rybitwa* were removed from the effective list in 1970.

1 BYMS TYPE

(Ex-COASTAL MINESWEEPER)

ZODIAK

Displacement, tons	215 standard; 315 full load
Dimensions, feet	136 × 24·5 × 7·3
Main engines	2 diesels; 2 shafts; 1 000 bhp = 15 knots
Complement	15

Former British BYMS type coastal minesweeper but not now a naval vessel, being employed as a hydrographic vessel belonging to the shipping Board of Gdansk. Built in 1943-44.

ZODIAK   *Official*

HYDROGRAF   **KONTROLER**

Measurement, tons	82 gross
Dimensions, feet	78·7 × 21 × 7·9
Main engines	Speed = 9 knots

Built in 1956 and 1957. For hydrographic duties in coastal waters or estuaries, but not in the Polish Navy list.

KOZIOROZEC

Displacement, tons	219
Dimensions, feet	120 × 23 × 8
Main engines	Diesel; 450 bhp = 12 knots
Complement	15

Built in 1950 by the Finnboda Varv, Stockholm. Purchased by the Gdansk Maritime Office and used as a hydrographic vessel. No longer on the Navy List. Belongs to the Shipping Board of Gdansk.

OILERS (Ropowiec)

ZOLW (ex-*Stutthof*) Z 4

Displacement: 450 tons. Name changed from *Stutthof* to *Zolw* (Turtle) in 1961.

KRAB Z 1   **SLIMAK** Z 3

Measurement 300 tons deadweight. *Krab* means Crab and *Slimak* means snail. Small tankers built in 1958 at Gdansk.

MEDUZA Z 2

Dimensions, feet	98 × 15 × 8
Complement	8

Fuel oil and replenishment vessel for ships in ports and local waters.

Z 5   **Z 6**   **Z 7**

Lighters of 300 tons gross with diesels, converted into tankers for coastal service.

CABLE SHIP

KABLOWIEC

Measurement, tons	800 gross
Dimensions, feet	130 × 15 × 5

Cable ship and general naval auxiliary, converted from a freighter-bunker ship.

DEGAUSSING VESSELS

URAN   **URANIA**

Displacement, tons	254
Main engines	Speed = 8 knots

Degaussing vessel of the British MMS minesweeper 11 type, classed as auxiliaries.

ICEBREAKER

PERKUM

Displacement, tons	800
Main engines	Diesel-electric; 2 shafts; 3 500 bhp = 12 knots

Icebreaker built in 1962 by P. K. Harris & Sons, Appledore, Devon, England. Not a naval vessel but can be employed with and for the Navy.

TENDERS

JOWISZ   **JUPITER**   **MARS**   **ORION**

Displacement, tons	130
Dimensions, feet	100 × 16 × 4·2
Main engines	Diesel; 3 shafts; 400 bhp = 10 knots
Complement	32

All built in USSR in 1944-45. Soviet "T 301" type. Formerly named *Kormoran*, *Kania*, *Krogulec* and *Orlik*. Training tenders.

YACHTS

ZAWISZA CZARNY

Measurement, tons	150 gross
Dimensions, feet	107 × 23
Main engines	Diesel; 300 bhp = 9 knots

Three masted schooner with a sail area of 514 sq. yards. Built in 1952. Training yacht.

JANEK KRASNICKI   **ZEW MORZA**

Measurement, tons	70 gross
Dimensions, feet	82 × 21
Main engines	Diesel; speed 5 knots

Two masted schooners with a sail area of 418 sq. yards. Built at Neptun, Rostock. Formerly named *Edit* and *Jutta*. Training yachts.

MARIUS ZARUSKI (ex-*Kryssaren*)

Measurement, tons	71 gross
Dimensions, feet	83 × 19
Main engines	Petrol engine; 150 bhp = 5 knots

Ketch with a sail area of 368 sq. yards. Purchased from Sweden. Training boat.

PORTUGAL

Administration

Minister of Marine:
Vice-Admiral Manuel Pereira Crespo

Chief of Naval Staff:
Admiral Fernando Ornelas e Vasconcelos

Diplomatic Representation

Naval Attaché in London:
Captain J. B. Pinheiro Azevedo, PoN

Naval Attaché in Washington:
Captain Vasco Antonio Martins Rodrigues, PoN

Naval Attaché in Paris:
Commander Mario Dias Martins, PoN

Strength of the Fleet

4 Submarines (Diesel Powered)
10 Frigates
4 Corvettes (New Construction Small Frigates)
1 Corvette (ex-Fleet Minesweeper)
14 Patrol Vessels
5 Ocean Minesweepers (including 1 Trawler)
12 Coastal Minesweepers
6 Survey Ships (including 2 Launches)
1 Training Ship
4 Fishery Protection Vessels
47 Patrol Launches
79 Landing Craft
5 Support Ships and Auxiliaries

Personnel

1970: 17 700 (1 650 officers and 16 050 men) including
marines

1971: 18 300 (1 700 officers and 16 600 men) including
marines

Navy Estimates

1962: Escudos   605 496 335
1963: Escudos 1 056 903 256
1964: Escudos 1 250 324 896
1965: Escudos 1 278 093 329
1966: Escudos 1 746 984 109
1967: Escudos 2 012 275 632
1968: Escudos 2 266 012 273
1969: Escudos 2 423 004 584
1970: Escudos 2 948 698 359
1971: Escudos 3 232 133 630

Mercantile Marine

Lloyd's Register of Shipping:
376 vessels of 870 008 tons gross

Scale: 150 feet = 1 inch (1 : 1 800)

COMANDANTE JOAO BELO *Class*

ALVARES CABRAL *Class*

PERO ESCOBAR

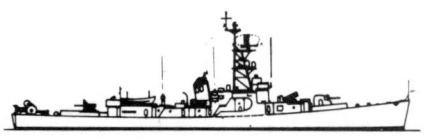

ALMIRANTE PEREIRA DA SILVA *Class*

JOÃO COUTINHO *Class*

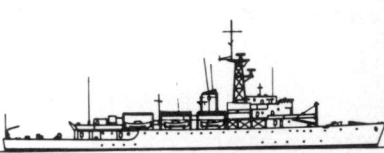

AFONSO DE ALBUQUERQUE

SUBMARINES

Name	No.	Builders	Laid down	Launched	Completed
ALBACORA	S 163	Dubigeon-Normandie	6 Sep 1965	13 Oct 1966	1 Oct 1967
BARRACUDA	S 164	Dubigeon-Normandie	19 Oct 1965	24 Apr 1967	4 May 1968
CACHALOTE	S 165	Dubigeon-Normandie	27 Oct 1966	16 Feb 1968	25 Jan 1969
DELFIM	S 166	Dubigeon-Normandie	12 May 1967	23 Sep 1968	1 Oct 1969

4 "ALBACORA" CLASS

(FRENCH "DAPHNE" TYPE)

Displacement, tons	869 surface; 1 043 submerged
Length, feet (*metres*)	190·2 (*58·0*)
Beam, feet (*metres*)	22·7 (*6·9*)
Draught, feet (*metres*)	15·5 (*4·7*)
Torpedo tubes	12—21·7 in (*550 mm*), 8 bow, 4 stern
Main engines	SEMT-Pielstick diesels, 1 300 hp Electric motors, 1 600 hp. 2 shafts
Speed, knots	16 on surface and submerged
Radius, miles	3 000 at 7 knots
Oil fuel (tons)	90
Complement	50 (5 officers; 45 men)

The prefabricated construction of these medium size
submarines was begun during 1 Oct 1964 to 6 Sep 1965
at the Dubigeon-Normandie Shipyard, Nantes, France.
They are basically similar to the French "Daphne" type,
but slightly modified to suit Portuguese requirements.

BARRACUDA   *1970, Captain Aluino Martins da Silva*

ALBACORA   *1969, Portuguese Navy, Official*

"NARVAL" CLASS
Of the three submarines of the "Narval" class, formerly
British "S" class, *Neptuno* (ex-HMS *Spearhead*) was
discarded on 1 Sep 1967, *Nautilo* (ex-HMS *Saga*) on
25 Jan 1969, and *Narval* (ex-HMS *Spur*) on 1 Oct 1969.

CACHALOTE   *1970, Portuguese Navy, Official*

FRIGATES (Fragatas)

Name	No.	Builders	Laid down	Launched	Completed
COMANDANTE HERMENEGILDO CAPELO	F 481	At et Ch de Nantes	13 May 1966	29 Nov 1966	26 Apr 1968
COMANDANTE JOÃO BELO	F 480	At et Ch de Nantes	6 Sep 1965	22 Mar 1966	1 July 1967
COMANDANTE ROBERTO IVENS	F 482	At et Ch de Nantes	13 Dec 1966	8 Aug 1967	23 Nov 1968
COMANDANTE SACADURA CABRAL	F 483	At et Ch de Nantes	18 Aug 1967	1 Apr 1968	1 July 1969

4 "COMANDANTE JOÃO BELO" CLASS

(FRENCH "COMMANDANT RIVIERE" TYPE)

Displacement, tons	1 650 standard; 2 180 full load
Length, feet (metres)	321·5 (98) pp; 338 (103·0) oa
Beam, feet (metres)	37·7 (11·5)
Draught, feet (metres)	12·5 (3·8) mean
Guns, AA	3—3·9 in (100 mm) singles; 2—40 mm
A/S	1—12 in (305 mm) quadruple
Torpedo tubes	6—21·7 in (550 mm) ASM, 2 triple
Main engines	SEMT-Pielstick diesels 16 200 bhp; 2 shafts
Speed, knots	25 (26·5 max)
Radius, miles	4 500 at 15 knots
Complement	200 (14 officers, 186 men)

COMANDANTE JOÃO BELO — 1971, Official·

CONSTRUCTION. The prefabricated construction of these medium fast frigates was begun on 1 Oct 1964 at the Ateliers et Chantiers de Nantes, France.

COMANDANTE ROBERTO IVENS — 1970, Portuguese Navy, Official

DESIGN. They are similar to the French "Commandant Riviere" type except for the 30 mm AA guns which were replaced by 40 mm AA guns.

DISPOSALS OF DESTROYERS

Of the five destroyers of the "Vouga" class, the only unconverted ship Douro, was discarded in Dec 1959. Of the converted ships Dao was discarded on 29 Nov 1960, Tejo on 9 Feb 1965, Lima on 16 Oct 1965, and Vouga on 3 June 1967.

DISPOSALS OF DESTROYER ESCORTS

Of the two fast frigates of the "Diogo Cao" class (former US destroyer escorts of the "John C. Butler" type) Corte Real (ex-USS McCoy Reynolds, DE 440) was discarded on 21 Oct 1968 and Diogo (Cão (ex-USS Formoe, DE 509) on 19 Nov 1968.

COMANDANTE JOÃO BELO — 1969, Portuguese Navy, Official

Name	No.	Builders	Laid down	Launched	Completed
ALMIRANTE GAGO COUTINHO	F 473 (ex-US DE 1042)	Estaleiros Navais Lisnave, Lisbon	2 Dec 1963	30 Aug 1965	1 Aug 1967
ALMIRANTE MAGALHÃES CORREA	F 474 (ex-US DE 1046)	Estaleiros Navais de Viana do Castelo	1 Sep 1963	26 Apr 1965	1 Dec 1967
ALMIRANTE PEREIRA DA SILVA	F 472 (ex-US DE 1039)	Estaleiros Navais Lisnave, Lisbon	14 June 1962	2 Dec 1963	20 Dec 1966

3 "ALMIRANTE PEREIRA DA SILVA" CLASS

(US "DEALY" DESTROYER ESCORT TYPE)

Displacement, tons	1 450 standard; 1 950 full load
Length, feet (metres)	314·6 (95·9)
Beam, feet (metres)	37 (11·3)
Draught, feet (metres)	14 (4·3)
Guns, dual purpose	4—3 in (76 mm) 50 cal.
A/S	2 Bofors 4-barrelled mortars; 2 DC throwers
Torpedo tubes	6 (2 triple) for A/S torpedoes
Boilers	2 Foster Wheeler, 300 psi, 850°F
Main engines	De Laval dr geared turbines 20 000 shp; 1 shaft
Speed, knots	26 designed
Radius, miles	4 500 at 15 knots
Oil fuel (tons)	400
Complement	166 (12 officers, 154 men)

ALMIRANTE PEREIRA DA SILVA — 1968, Portuguese Navy, Official

DESIGN. Medium-fast frigates similar to the United States destroyer escorts of the "Dealey" class, but modified to suit Portuguese requirements.

CONSTRUCTION. The prefabrication of Almirante Pereira da Silva and Almirante Gago Coutinho was begun in 1961 at Lisnave (formerly Navalis Shipyard, Lisbon) and of Almirante Magalhães Correa in 1962.

ALMIRANTE GAGO COUTINHO — 1970, Portuguese Navy, Official

Frigates—*continued*

Name	No.	Builders	Laid down	Launched	Completed
PERO ESCOBAR	F 335	Navalmeccanica, Castellammare di Stabia, Italy	7 Jan 1955	25 Sep 1955	1 July 1957

Displacement, tons	1 250 standard; 1 600 full load
Length, feet (*metres*)	295·2 (*90·0*) pp; 306·7 (*93·5*) wl; 321·5 (*98·0*) oa
Beam, feet (*metres*)	35·5 (*10·8*)
Draught, feet (*metres*)	10 (*3·0*)
Guns, dual purpose	4—3 in (*76 mm*) 50 cal.
A/S	2 "Squid" triple DC mortars
Torpedo tubes	6 (2 triple) for A/S torpedoes
Boilers	2 Ansoldo-Foster Wheeler "D" 32 kg/cm², 400°C
Main engines	2 Ansaldo-Genova sr geared turbines; 24 000 shp; 2 shafts
Speed, knots	32·6 max
Radius, miles	2 800 at 13·5 knots
Oil fuel (tons)	236
Complement	165 (10 officers, 155 men)

A "light destroyer" or fast anti-submarine escort built to the order of NATO for the Portuguese Navy.

GUNNERY. The armament before modernisation comprised two single 3 inch guns, two 40 mm AA (twin mount), four 20 mm AA (two twin mounts) and three 21 inch torpedo tubes.

MODERNISATION. Modernised in 1970-71, the alterations including the fitting of new guns, sonar and anti-submarine torpedo tubes similar to those in the "Almirante Pereira da Silva" class frigates.

PERO ESCOBAR   1969, Portuguese Navy, *Official*

Name					
ALVARES CABRAL (ex-HMS *Burghead Bay*)					
VASCO DA GAMA (ex-HMS *Mounts Bay*)					

No.	Builders	Laid down	Launched	Completed
F 336	Charles Hill & Sons Ltd, Bristol	21 Sep 1944	3 Mar 1945	20 Sep 1945
F 478	Wm. Pickersgill Ltd, Sunderland W	23 Oct 1944	8 June 1945	11 Apr 1949

2 "ALVARES CABRAL" CLASS
(Ex-BRITISH "BAY" CLASS)

Displacement, tons	1 600 standard; 2 580 full load
Length, feet (*metres*)	286 (*87·2*) pp; 307·5 (*93·7*) oa
Beam, feet (*metres*)	38·5 (*11·7*)
Draught, feet (*metres*)	15·5 (*4·7*)
Guns, surface	4—4 in (*102 mm*)
Guns, AA	6—40 mm
A/S	1 Hedgehog; 4 DCT; 2 DC racks
Boilers	2 Admiralty 3-drum, 225 psi
Main engines	Triple expansion 5 500 ihp; 2 shafts
Speed, knots	19·5
Radius, miles	7 500 at 10 knots
Oil fuel (tons)	680
Complement	171 (11 officers, 160 men)

Former British frigates of the "Bay" class, designed primarily for anti-aircraft escort duties.

W=Completed by J. Samuel White & Co Ltd, Cowes, Isle of Wight.

ALVARES CABRAL   1970, *courtesy Commander B. Ferreira Monteiro, P.N.*

TRANSFER. *Alvares Cabral* and *Pacheco Pereira* were purchased from Great Britain in Apr 1959 and officially transferred to the Portuguese Navy at Plymouth on 11 May 1959. *D. Francisco de Almeida* and *Vasco da Gama* were purchased from Great Britain in May 1961 and modernised before delivery by John I. Thornycroft & Co Ltd, Woolston, Southampton, where they were commissioned in the Portuguese Navy on 3 Aug 1961.

VASCO DA GAMA   1968, Portuguese Navy, *Official*

DISPOSALS
Of this class, *D. Francisco de Almeida* (ex-HMS *Morcombe Bay*) F 479 and *Pacheco Pereira* (ex-HMS *Bigbury Bay*) F 337 were discarded on 7 Sep 1970 and 6 July 1970, respectively.
Of the "Diogo Gomez" class, former British "River" class, F 332 *Nuno Tristão* (ex-HMS *Avon*) was discarded on 12 Jan 1970 and her sister ship *D. Fernando* (ex-*Diogo Gomez*, ex-HMS *Awe*) F 331 on 20 Apr 1969.
The depot ship *S. Cristovão* (former frigate *Bartolomeu Dias*) was discarded on 11 Oct 1969.

PHOTOGRAPHS. A photograph of *D. Francisco Almeida* appears in the 1963-64 to 1965-66 editions, and of *Pacheco Pereira* in the 1969-70 and 1970-71 editions.

ALMIRANTE PEREIRA DA SILVA (see previous page)   *Lietu. K. M. Napier, RN*

CORVETTES

Name		Builders	Launched	Completed
ANTÓNIO ENES	F 471	Empresa Nacional Bazan de Constructiones Navales Militares,	1 Sep 1969	14 Nov 1970
AUGUSTO DE CASTILHO	F 484	Empresa Nacional Bazan de Constructiones Navales Militares,		
GENERAL PEREIRA D'ECA	F 477	Blohm and Voss A.G., Hamburg, Germany	16 Aug 1969	10 Oct 1970
HONORIO BARRETO	F 485	Empresa Nacional Bazan de Constructiones Navales Militares,		
JACINTO CANDIDO	F 476	Blohm and Voss A.G., Hamburg, Germany	16 June 1969	16 June 1970
JOÃO COUTINHO	F 475	Blohm and Voss A.G., Hamburg, Germany	2 May 1969	7 Mar 1970

6 NEW CONSTRUCTION "JOÃO COUTINHO" CLASS

Displacement, tons	1 252 standard; 1 400 full load
Length, feet (metres)	227·5 (84·6)
Beam, feet (metres)	33·8 (10·3)
Draught, feet (metres)	10·0 (3·07)
Guns, AA	2—3 in (76 mm); 2—40 mm
A/S weapons	1 Hedgehog; 2 DC throwers; 2 DC tracks
Main engines	2 OEW 12 cyl. Pielstick diesels; 10 560 bhp
Speed, knots	22·3
Radius, miles	6 250 at 14 knots
Complement	97 (9 officers 88 men) plus 34 marine detachment

Escorts of the small frigate type. Officially rated as corvettes. Three were built in Spain. The three built in Germany were ordered in Apr, 1968 for delivery in Jan, Apr and Aug 1970.

JOÃO COUTINHO   1971, Portuguese Navy, Official

JOÃO COUTINHO   1971, Portuguese Navy, Official

1 Ex-BRITISH "BANGOR" CLASS

CACHEU F 470 (ex-Comandante Almeida Carvalho, A 527, ex-Fort York, ex-Mingon)

Displacement, tons	672 standard; 900 full load
Length, feet (metres)	171·5 (52·3) pp; 180 (54·9) oa
Beam, feet (metres)	28·5 (8·7)
Draught, feet (metres)	9·5 (2·9) max
Guns, dual purpose	1—3 in (76 mm)
Guns, AA	2—20 mm
Boilers	2 three-drum small tube type
Main engines	Triple expansion 2 400 ihp; 2 shafts
Speed, knots	16.
Oil fuel (tons)	160
Complement	83 (8 officers, 75 men)

Former British fleet minesweeper of the "Bangor" class, Originally a sister of Almirante Lacerda, see next page. Launched in Canada on 24 Aug 1941. Purchased from Great Britain in 1950. Served as survey ship until 1965 when she was converted into a corvette and her name and number changed from Comandante Almeida Carvalho.

CACHEU   1969, Portuguese Navy, Official

SURVEY SHIPS (Navios Hidrograficos) Ex-Frigate

AFONSO DE ALBUQUERQUE (ex-HMS Dalrymple, ex-Luce Bay, ex-Loch Glass) A 526

Displacement, tons	1 600 standard; 2 230 full load
Length, feet (metres)	286 (87·2) pp; 307 (93·6) oa.
Beam, feet (metres)	38·5 (11·7)
Draught, feet (metres)	14·2 (4·3)
Boilers	2 Admiralty 3-drum
Main engines	4-cylinder triple expansion 5 500 ihp; 2 shafts
Speed, knots	19·5
Radius, miles	5 000 at 10 knots
Oil fuel (tons)	580
Complement	140 (10 officers, 130 men)

Modified frigate of the "Bay" class. Built by Wm. Pickersgill & Sons Ltd, Sunderland, but completed at HM Dockyard, Devonport. Laid down on 29 Apr 1944. launched on 12 Apr 1945, and completed on 10 Feb 1949. Equipped with radar and sonar. Purchased by Portugal from Great Britain in Apr 1966. The main machinery was manufactured by George Clark Ltd. Sunderland. Power at 220 volts DC, is from two 120 kw turbogenerators and two 150 kw diesel generators.

AFONSO DE ALBUQUERQUE   1970, Portuguese Navy, Official

Survey Ships—*continued*

1 "PEDRO NUNES" CLASS (Ex-SLOOP)

PEDRO NUNES A 528

Displacement, tons	1 090 standard; 1 197 full load
Dimensions, feet	223 pp × 32·8 × 9·5
Guns	1—4·7 in, 50 cal; 4—20 mm AA (see *Gunnery*)
Main engines	2 sets MAN 8 cyl diesels; 2 400 bhp = 16·5 knots
Oil fuel, tons	110 normal; 126 max
Radius, miles	6 000 at 13 knots
Complement	51 (7 officers, 44 men)

Built as a second class sloop (aviso de segundo classe) at Lisbon Naval Yard. Laid down on 5 Nov 1931, launched on 17 Mar 1934 and completed on 11 Apr 1935. Converted into a survey ship (navio hidrografico) in 1956.

GUNNERY. The forward 4·7 inch gun was removed from *Pedro Nunes* in 1956. when she was converted into a survey ship.

DISPOSAL
Sister ship *Joao de Lisboa* (ex-*Infante D. Henrique*), A 5200, was discarded on 17 Aug 1966.

PEDRO NUNES   *1968, Portuguese Navy, Official*

1 Ex-BRITISH "FLOWER" CLASS FRIGATE

CARVALHO ARAUJO (ex-*Terje Ten*, ex-*Commandant Drogou*, ex-*Chrysanthemum*)
A 524

Displacement, tons	1 020 standard; 1 340 full load
Dimensions, feet	190 pp; 205 oa × 33 × 16·5
Guns	1—3 inch; 4—20 mm AA
Main engines	Triple expansion; 2 750 ihp = 16 knots
Boilers	2 cylindrical
Oil fuel, tons	288
Complement	49 (7 officers and 42 men)

Former British corvette (later re-rated as a frigate) of the "Flower" class. Built by Harland & Wolff Ltd, Belfast. Laid down on 17 Dec 1940, launched on 11 Apr 1941, and completed on 26 Jan 1942. Served in the French Navy during the Second World War. Sold out of the service after hostilities. Purchased by Portugal from the Hector Whaling Company, at Capetown, in Mar 1959, and later equipped as a survey ship for the Portuguese Navy to replace the former *Corvalho Araújo* (ex-British "Flower" class minesweeping sloop *Jonquil*) which was discarded in 1959.

DISPOSAL
The survey ship *Salvador Correia*, former minesweeper and patrol vessel *Baldaque da Silva*, ex-minesweeping trawler *Ruskholm* of the British "Isles" class, was discarded on 27 Mar 1967.

CARVALHO ARAUJO   *Added 1968, Admiral M. Adam*

1 Ex-BRITISH "BANGOR" CLASS FLEET MINESWEEPER

ALMIRANTE LACERDA (ex-*Caroquet*) A 525

Displacement, tons	672 standard; 900 full load
Dimensions, feet	171·5 pp; 180 oa × 28·5 × 9·5 max
Guns	1—3 in; 2—20 mm AA
Main engines	Triple expansion; 2 shafts; 2 400 ihp = 16 knots
Boilers	2, of 3-drum small-tube type
Oil fuel, tons	160
Complement	49 (7 officers, 42 men)

Former British fleet minesweeper of the "Bangor" class, steam type. Built in Canada, launched on 2 June 1941, and purchased from Great Britain in 1946.

Survey Ships—*continued*

ALMIRANTE LACERDA   *1969, Portuguese Navy, Official*

SURVEY LAUNCHES

CRUZEIRO DO SUL (ex-*Giroflée*)

Displacement, tons	100 standard
Dimensions, feet	93·2 × 17·8 × 8
Main engines	2 Gleenifer diesels; 320 bhp = 12 knots max
Radius, miles	2 000 at 10 knots (economical speed)
Complement	8 (1 officer, 7 men)

MIRA (ex-*Formalhaut*, ex-*Arrabida*)

Displacement, tons	23 standard
Dimensions, feet	62·9 × 1.5·2 × 4
Main engines	3 Perkins diesels; 300 bhp = 15 knots max
Radius, miles	650 at 8 knots (economical speed)
Complement	6 men

OCEAN MINESWEEPERS
(*Draga-minas oceânicos*)

4 "S. JORGE" CLASS

CORVO	(ex-USS *MSO* 487) M 418	**PICO**	(ex-USS *MSO* 479) M 416
GRACIOSA	(ex-USS *MSO* 486) M 417	**S. JORGE**	(ex-USS *MSO* 478) M 415

Name	Builders	Laid down	Launched	Completed
Corvo	Burger Boat Co	18 Aug 1953	28 July 1954	23 Nov 1955
Graciosa	Burger Boat Co	16 May 1953	19 Nov 1953	15 Aug 1955
Pico	Bellingham SY	1 Oct 1953	18 June 1954	1 June 1955
S. Jorge	Bellingham SY	26 Aug 1953	30 Apr 1954	24 Apr 1955

Displacement, tons	665 standard; 750 full load
Dimensions, feet	165 pp; 172 oa × 35 × 10 mean
Guns	1—40 mm AA
Main engines	2 GM diesels; 2 shafts; 1 600 bhp = 13·5 knots max
Oil fuel, tons	46
Radius, miles	3 800 at 10 knots (economical speed)
Complement	69 (5 officers, 64 men)

"MSO 421" class built in the USA under the Mutual Defense Assistance Programme by Burger Boat Co. Manitowoc, Wisconsin and Bellingham Shipyard Co. Constructed of wooden and non-magnetic materials. The diesels of non-magnetic stainless steel alloy, are model 8-278A, two stroke cycle, non-reversible 8-cylinder V engines. Controllable pitch propellers. A photograph of *Corvo* appears in the 1961-62 to 1969-70 editions, and of *Pico* in the 1967-68 to 1969-70 editions.

GRACIOSA   *1970, Portuguese Navy, Official*

S. JORGE   *1970, Portuguese Navy, Official*

PATROL VESSELS (Navios-Patrulhas)

5 PORTUGUESE BUILT "MAIO" CLASS

Name	No.	Builders	Launched	Completed
BOAVISTA	P 592	Est Nav do Mondego	10 July 1956	17 May 1957
BRAVA	P 590	EN de Viana do Castelo	2 May 1956	27 Dec 1956
FOGO	P 591	EN de Viana do Castelo	2 May 1956	11 Apr 1957
SANTA LUZIA	P 594	Arsenal do Alfeite	17 Jan 1957	24 Oct 1958
SANTO ANTÃO	P 593	Arsenal do Alfeite	8 June 1956	30 Dec 1957

Displacement, tons	366 standard ; 400 full load
Dimensions, feet	170 pp ; 173·8 oa × 23 × 10 mean
Guns	2—40 mm AA ; 2—20 mm AA
A/S weapons	1 Hedgehog, 4 DCT ; 2 depth charge tracks
Main engines	4 SEMT-Pielstick diesels (4-stroke, 14 cylinder V) ; 2 shafts ; 3 500 bhp = 19 knots
Oil fuel, tons	45
Radius, miles	3 900 at 19 knots
Complement	62 (5 officers, 57 men)

Built in Portugal under the US off-shore procurement programme. Of all-welded construction. A photograph of *Brava* appears in the 1958-69 to 1962-63 editions and of *Santa Luzia* in the 1968-69 and 1969-70 editions.

SANTO ANTÃO   *1970, Portuguese Navy, Official*

3 FRENCH BUILT "MAIO" CLASS

Name	No.	Builders	Launched
MAIO (ex-*Funchal*, ex-*P* 4)	P 587	Dubigeon, Nantes	27 Sep 1954
PORTO SANTO (ex-*P* 5)	P 588	Normand (Le Havre)	9 Feb 1955
S NICOLAU (ex-*P* 8)	P 589	Normand (Le Havre)	7 June 1955

Displacement, tons	366 standard ; 400 full load
Dimensions, feet	170 pp ; 173·7 oa × 23 × 10
Guns	2—40 mm AA ; 2—20 mm AA
A/S weapons	1 Hedgehog ; 4 DCT ; 2 depth charge tracks
Main engines	4 SEMT-Pielstick diesels ; 2 shafts ; 3 240 bhp = 17·5 knots
Radius, miles	4 000 at 10 knots
Complement	62 (5 officers, 57 men)

Of PC design, but built in France as a US offshore procurement order under the Mutual Defense Assistance Programme. Fitted with two mine rails. A photograph of *S. Nicolau* appears in the 1961-62 to 1969-70 editions.

PORTO SANTO   *1970, Portuguese Navy, Official*

S. NICOLAU   *Dr. Giorgio Arra*

Of the "Principe" class, *Santiago* was decommissioned on 1 July 1967, and *Sal* on 31 Aug 1968. *Madeira* and *Principe* (ex-*Flores*) were discarded on 6 Sep 1969. *S. Tomé* was discarded on 7 Apr 1970 and *S. Vicente* on 19 June 1970.

Patrol Vessels—continued

8 "CACINE" CLASS

CACINE	P 1140	CUANZA	P 1144	ROVUMA	P 1143
CUNENE	P 1141	GEBA	P 1145	ZAIRE	P 1146
		MANDOVI	P 1142	ZAMBEZE	P 1147

Displacement, tons	310 full load
Dimensions, feet	144 oa × 25·2 × 7·1
Guns	2—40 mm AA
	1—32 barrelled rocket-launcher 37 mm
Main engines	2 Maybach diesels ; 2 000 bhp = 20 knots
Complement	33 (3 officers, 30 men)

Cacine, Cunine, Mandovi and *Rovuma* were built in Arsenal do Alfeite, the other four in Estaleiros Navais do Mondego.

CACINE   *1970, Portuguese Navy, Official*

COASTAL MINESWEEPERS
(Draga-Minas Costeiros)

4 "S. ROQUE" CLASS (BRITISH "TON" TYPE)

Name	No.	Launched	Completed
LAGOA	M 403	15 Sep 1955	10 Aug 1956
RIBEIRA GRANDE	M 402	14 Oct 1955	8 Feb 1957
ROSARIO	M 404	29 Nov 1955	8 Feb 1956
S .ROQUE	M 401	5 Sep 1955	4 June 1956

Displacement, tons	360 standard ; 425 full load
Dimensions, feet	140 pp ; 152 oa × 28·8 × 7
Guns	1—40 mm AA ; 2—20 mm AA (twin mount)
Main engines	2 Mirrlees diesels ; 2 shafts ; 2 500 bhp = 15 knots
Complement	47 (4 officers, 43 men)

Similar to the British "Ton" class coastal minesweepers, but built in Portugal. All laid down at CUF Shipyard, Lisbon, on 7 Sep 1954, under the OSP-MAP. *Lagoa* and *S Roque* were financed by USA and the other two by Portugal. A photograph of *Lagoa* appears in the 1958-59 to 1960-61 editions, of *Ribeira Grande* in the 1961-62 to 1965-66 editions and of *S. Roque* in the 1966-67 to 1968-69 editions.

ROSARIO   *1969, Portuguese Navy, Official*

8 "PONTA DELGADA" CLASS

Name		No.
ANGRA DO HEROISMO	(ex-*AMS* 62)	M 407
HORTA	(ex-*AMS* 61)	M 406
LAJES	(ex-*AMS* 146)	M 411
PONTA DELGADA	(ex-*Adjutant*, AMS 60)	M 405
SANTA CRUZ	(ex-*AMS* 92)	M 409
S. PEDRO	(ex-*AMS* 147)	M 412
VELAS	(ex-*AMS* 145)	M 410
VILA DO PORTO	(ex-*AMS* 91)	M 408

Displacement, tons	375 standard ; 405 full load
Dimensions, feet	138 pp ; 144 oa × 27 × 8
Guns	2—20 mm AA (twin mount)
Main engines	GM diesels ; 900 bhp = 14 knots
Complement	40 (4 officers, 36 men)

Of wooden and non-magnetic construction. *Ponta Delgada* was transferred from USA on 7 Apr 1953. Four more were delivered in 1953-54 and remaining three in 1955. A photograph of *S. Pedro* appears in the 1961-62 to 1965-66 editions, of *Santa Cruz* in the 1966-67 to 1968-69 editions, of *Lajes* in the 1969-70 and 1970-71 editions.

HORTA   *1971, Portuguese Navy, Official*

FISHERY PROTECTION VESSELS

4 "AZEVIA" CLASS (Lanchas de Fiscalização da Pesca)

AZEVIA P595   **BICUDA** P596   **CORVINA** P 597   **DOURADA** P598

Displacement, tons	230; 270 full load
Dimensions, feet	134·5 pp; 139·8 oa × 21·3 × 7
Guns	2—20 mm AA
Main engines	2 7-cyl 2-stroke Sulzer diesels except first pair; 2 10-cyl 4-stroke MAN diesels; 2 shafts; 2 400 bhp = 17 knots
Oil fuel, tons	25
Radius, miles	3 700 at 11 knots; 850 at 17 knots
Complement	30 (2 officers, 28 men)

All launched in 1941-42. A Photograph of *Bicuda* appears in the 1953-54 to 1959-60 editions. Sister *Espadilha* was discarded on 20 Apr 1969.

AZEVIA   *1968, Portuguese Navy, Official*

PATROL LAUNCHES

10 "ARGOS" CLASS

ARGOS	P 372	**DRAGÃO**	P 374	**LIRA**	P 361
CASSIOPEIA	P 373	**ESCORPIÃO**	P 375	**ORION**	P 362
CENTAURO	P 1130	**HIDRA**	P 376	**PEGASO**	P 379
				SAGITARIO	P 1131

Displacement, tons	180 standard; 210 full load
Dimensions, feet	131·2 pp; 136·8 oa × 20·5 × 7
Guns	2—40 mm AA
Main engines	2 Maybach diesels; 1 200 bhp = 17 knots
Oil fuel, tons	16
Complement	24 (2 officers, 22 men)

Six built by Arsenal do Alfeite, Lisbon, and four by Estaleiros Navais de Viana do Castelo. All completed June 1963 to Sep 1965. Named after constellations. A photograph of *Dragão* appears in the 1964-65 to 1966-67 editions.

ARGOS   *1967, Portuguese Navy, Official*

2 "D. ALEIXO" CLASS

D. ALEIXO P 1148   **D. JEREMIAS** P 1149

Displacement, tons	60 full load
Dimensions, feet	82·1 oa × 17 × 5·2
Guns	1—20 mm AA
Main engines	2 Cummins diesels; 1 270 bhp = 16 knots
Complement	10 (1 officer)

D. Aleixo was commissioned on 7 Dec 1967, *D. Jeremias* on 22 Dec 1967.

DOM ALEIXO   *1969, Portuguese Navy, Official*

3 "ALVOR" CLASS

ALBUFEIRA P 1157   **ALJEZUR** P 1158   **ALVOR** P 1156

Displacement, tons	35·7 full load
Dimensions, feet	68 oa × 18 × 5·1
Guns	1—20 mm AA
Main engines	2 Cummins diesels; 235 bhp = 12·3 knots
Complement	7 (1 officer)

They were all built at Arsenal do Alfeite and commissioned in 1967-68.

ALVOR   *1968. Portuguese Navy, Official*

13 "BELLATRIX" CLASS

ALDEBARAN		**CANOPUS**	P 364	**POLLUX**	P 368
ALTAIR	P 377	**DENEB**	P 365	**PROCION**	P 1153
ARCTURUS		**ESPIGA**	P 366	**RIGEL**	P 378
BELLATRIX	P 363	**FOMALHAUT**	P 367	**SIRIUS**	P 1154
				VEGA	P 1155

Displacement, tons	23 light; 29 full load
Dimensions, feet	62·8 wl; 68 oa × 15·2 × 4
Guns	1—20 mm Oerlikon AA
Main engines	2 Cummins diesels; 470 bhp = 15 knots
Complement	7

The first eight were completed in 1961-62 in Germany by Beyerische Schiffbaugesell-schaft and the last five (*Arcturus, Aldebaran* and *Procion*, commissioned on 17 May 1968, *Sirius* and *Vega*) were built in Arsenal do Alfeite, Lisbon. A photograph of *Bellatrix* appears in the 1962-63 to 1967-68 editions, and of *Espiga* in the 1969-70 edition.

PROCION   *1970, Portuguese Navy, Official*

6 "JUPITER" CLASS

JUPITER	P 1132	**MERCURIO**	P 1135	**URANO**	P 1137
MARTE	P 1134	**SATURNO**	P 1136	**VENUS**	P 1133

Displacement, tons	32 full load
Dimensions, feet	69 oa × 16·5 × 4·3
Guns	1—20 mm Oerlikon AA
Main engines	2 Cummins diesels; 1 270 bhp = 20 knots
Complement	8

Built during 1964-65. All commissioned between 10 Mar and 12 Aug 1965. A photograph of *Jupiter* appears in the 1967-68 to 1969-70 editions.

URANO   *1970. Portuguese Navy, Official*

ALGOL P 1138

Displacement, tons	24
Dimensions, feet	50·3 × 13·3 × 2·5
Guns	2 MG
Main engines	2 Cummins diesels; 244 bhp

Built by Argibay, Lisbon in 1964. Crew varies, normally seven.

ALGOL   *1969, Portuguese Navy, Official*

Patrol Launches—*continued*

CASTOR P 580

Displacement, tons	22
Dimensions, feet	53·5 wl ; 58 oa × 13·1 × 3·3
Guns	1—20 mm Oerlikon AA
Main engines	2 Cummins diesels ; 500 bhp = 15 knots
Complement	7

Built at the Estaleiros Navais do Mondego and commissioned on 3 Feb 1964.

ANTARES P 360   REGULUS P 369

Displacement, tons	18
Dimensions, feet	56 oa ; 51·5 wl × 15·2 × 4 aft
Guns	1—20 mm Oerlikon quick firing AA
Main engines	2 Cummins diesels ; 2 shafts ; 460 bhp = 18·2 knots
Complement	7

Antares was built in 1959 by James Taylor (Shipbuilders) Ltd, Shoreham, Sussex, England. The hull is of Deborine resinglass fibre moulding. *Regulus* was built in Portugal by Navalis Shipyard, the hull being imported from England. Completed on 27 Jan 1962. Of this class, *Sirius* and *Vega* were lost in action in Dec 1961 during the Indian invasion of Goa.

ANTARES   *1970, Portuguese Navy, Official*

RIO MINHO P 370

Displacement, tons	14
Dimensions, feet	49·2 × 10·5 × 2·3
Guns	2 light MG
Main engines	2 Alfa Romeo ; 130 bhp = 9 knots
Complement	7

Built at Arsenal do Alfeite in 1955-57 for the River Minho on the Spanish border.

DISPOSALS
The gunboat *Dio* was discarded on 20 Apr 1969. The patrol launch *Tete*, P 371, former river gunboat, was discarded in 1971.

MINESWEEPER (*Caça-Mina*)

SANTA MARIA (ex-*P 4*, ex-*Whalsay*) M 392

Displacement, tons	560 standard ; 770 full load
Dimensions, feet	164 × 27·5 × 15
Guns	1—3 in ; 2—20 mm AA ; DC carried
Main engines	Triple expansion ; 850 ihp = 12 knots
Complement	52 (3 officers and 49 men)

"Isles" class trawler. Built by Cook, Welton & Gemmel, laid down 19 Dec 1941, launched 4 Apr 1942, completed 4 Sep 1942. Purchased from Great Britain in 1947, and named after island in the Azores. Originally classified as patrol vessel but later rated as minesweeper. Of five sister ships, *Miguel* (ex-*Brurey*) was discarded in 1956, *Terceira* (ex-*Haling*) in 1957, *Salvador Correia* (ex-*Saltarelo*) in 1961, and *Faial* (ex-*Mangrove*) M 391 was decommissioned in 27 Mar 1967. *Baldaque da Silva* (ex-*Ruskholm*) changed her name to *Salvador Correia* and was reclassified as a survey ship.

SANTA MARIA   *1966, Portuguese Navy, Official*

LANDING CRAFT (*Lanchas de desembarque*)

2 "BOMBARDA" CLASS LDG

ALABARDA LDG 202   BOMBARDA LDG 201 (ex-105)

The LDG *Alabarda* is under construction at the Estaleiros Navais do Mondego, *Bombarda* was commissioned in 1969.

BOMBARDA   *1970, Portuguese Navy, Official*

4 "ALFANGE" CLSSS LDG

ALFANGE LDG 101	CIMITARRA LDG 103
ARIETE LDG 102	MONTANTE LDG 104

Displacement, tons	500
Dimensions, feet	Length : 187
Main engines	2 diesels ; 1 000 bhp
Complement	20

Landing craft similar to the LCT (4) type built at the Estaleiros Navais do Mondego and commissioned during 1965.

ALFANGE   *1968, Portuguese Navy, Official*

16 LDM 400 CLASS

LDM 401	LDM 404	LDM 407	LDM 410	LDM 413
LDM 402	LDM 405	LDM 408	LDM 411	LDM 414
LDM 403	LDM 406	LDM 409	LDM 412	LDM 415
				LDM 416

13 LDM 300 CLASS

LDM 301	LDM 303	LDM 305	LDM 307	LDM 309	LDM 311
LDM 302	LDM 304	LDM 306	LDM 308	LDM 310	LDM 312
					LDM 313

5 LDM 200 CLASS

LDM 201	LDM 202	LDM 203	LDM 204	LDM 205

16 LDM 100 CLASS

LDM 101	LDM 104	LDM 107	LDM 110	LDM 113
LDM 102	LDM 105	LDM 108	LDM 111	LDM 114
LDM 103	LDM 106	LDM 109	LDM 112	LDM 115
				LDM 116

Displacement, tons	50 full load
Dimensions, feet	Length : 50 feet
Main engines	2 diesels ; 450 bhp

29 LCM type landing craft were commissioned in 1964 to 1966 setting up four classes in LDM 100, 200, 300, and 400 series as above. All built at the Estaleiros Navais do Mondego.

4 LDP 300 (Ex-LD) CLASS

LDP 301	LDP 302	LDP 303	LDP 304

16 LDP 200 CLASS

LDP 201	LDP 203	LDP 206	LDP 209	LDP 212	LDP 215
	LDP 204	LDP 207	LDP 210	LDP 213	LDP 216
	LDP 205	LDP 208	LDP 211	LDP 214	LDP 217

Thirteen LDP 200 class were commissioned in 1965-67, four in Jan-Feb 1969. Of this class LDP 202 was discarded on 9 Mar 1970.

3 LDP 100 (Ex-LD) CLASS

LDP 105	LDP 107	LDP 108

Displacement, tons	12 light ; 18 full load
Dimensions, feet	Length : 46 oa
Main engines	2 diesels ; 180 bhp

The nine LD class landing craft (of the LCA type) were redesignated LDP 103, 105, 107, 108 and 109 and LDP 301, 302, 303 and 304. Built at the Estaleiros Navais do Mondego and commissioned on 16 June 1961 (LDP 103), 22 Feb 1963 (LDP 105), 1964 (LDP 107, 108, 109, 301, 302, 303, 304). LPD 103 and LPD 109 were discarded on 15 Nov 1969.

TRAINING SHIP (Navio-Escola)

SAGRES (ex-*Guanabara*, ex-*Albert Leo Schlageter*) A 520

Displacement, tons	1 415 standard ; 1 869 full load
Dimensions, feet	229·7 pp ; 249 oa × 39·3 × 17
Main engines	2 MAN auxiliary diesels ; 1 shaft ; 750 bhp = 10 knots
Oil fuel, tons	52
Radius, miles	3 500 at 10 knots
Complement	163 (10 officers, 153 men)

Former German sail training ship. Built by Blohm & Voss, Hamburg. Launched in June 1937 and completed on 1 Feb 1938. Sister of US Coast Guard training ship *Eagle* (ex-German *Horst Wessel*). Taken by USA as a reparation after the Second World War in 1945 and sold to Brazil in 1948. Purchased from Brazil and commissioned in the Portuguese Navy on 2 Feb 1962 at Rio de Janeiro and renamed *Sagres*. Sail area 20 793 sq ft. Height of mast 142 ft.

SAGRES   1971, Portuguese Navy, Official

DEPOT SHIP (Navio Deposito)
Former Training Ship

SANTO ANDRÉ (ex-*Sagres*, ex-*Flores*, ex-*Max*, ex-*Rickmer Rickmers*) A 5207

Displacement, tons	3 067 standard ; 3 176 full load
Dimensions, feet	263·5 × 40·3 × 19
Guns	4—47 mm saluting
Main engines	2 Krupp diesels ; 2 shafts ; 700 bhp = 8 knots

Former German sailing vessel. Built at Bremerhaven. Launched in 1896. Captured during the First World War. Re-rigged as a barque and adapted as a naval training ship during 1924-27. Auxiliary motors were fitted in 1931. Reclassified as a depot ship and renamed *Santo André* by decree of 31 Jan 1962. Replaced on 8 Feb 1962 by the training ship *Guanabara*, purchased from Brazil which took the name and number of the former *Sagres*.

FLEET OILER (Navio Petroleiro)
S. GABRIEL A 5206

Displacement, tons	9 000 standard ; 14 200 full load
Measurement, tons	9 500 gross ; 9 000 deadweight
Dimensions, feet	452·8 pp ; 479 oa × 59·8 × 26·2
Main engines	1 Pametrada geared turbine ; 1 shaft ; 9 500 shp = 17 knots
Boilers	2
Radius, miles	6 000 at 15 knots
Complement	84 (10 officers, 74 men)

Built at Estaleiros de Viana do Castelo. Commissioned on 27 Mar 1963. The oiler *Cimarron* was officially deleted from the list in Mar 1971.

S. GABRIEL   1969, Portuguese Navy, Official

LOGISTIC SHIP (Navio de apoio Logistico)
1 Ex-US ARC/LSM TYPE

S. RAFAEL (ex-*Medusa*, ex-USS *Portunus*, ARC 1, ex-*LSM 275*, ex-*LCT* (7) 1773) A 5214

Displacement, tons	743 standard ; 1 220 full load
Dimensions, feet	196·5 pp ; 221·1 oa × 34·5 × 10·5
Guns	2—40 mm ; 2—20 mm
Main engines	GM direct drive diesel ; 2 shafts ; 2 800 bhp = 12 knots
Radius, miles	5 240 at 10 knots
Complement	56 (6 officers, 50 men)

Former US medium landing ship, LSM type. Built by Federal Shipbuilding and Drydock Co, Newark, New Jersey. Laid down on 1 Aug 1944, launched on 11 Sep 1944, and completed on 6 Oct 1944. Converted to a cable repairing or laying ship by the US Navy in 1952. Transferred to the Portuguese Navy under MAP in 1959. Delivered to Portugal on 16 Nov and commissioned on 18 Nov as a diving tender (*navio-apoio de mergulhadores*). Converted to a logistic ship in 1969 and guns mounted as above.

S. RAFAEL (ex-*Medusa*)   Portuguese Navy. Official

1 FLEET OILER TYPE

SAM BRAS A 523

Displacement, tons	5 766 standard ; 6,374 full load (officially revised figures)
Dimensions, feet	333·1 pp ; 356·8 oa × 47·3 · 16·5 (officially revised figures)
Guns	1—3 in (76 mm) ; 2—40 mm ; 2—20 mm
Main engines	B. & W. 2-stroke diesel ; 1 shaft ; 2 820 bhp = 12 knots
Oil fuel, tons	568
Radius, miles	11 000 at 12 knots
Complement	111 (11 officers, 90 men)

Built at Arsenal do Alfeite. Laid down on 22 Feb 1941. Launched on 17 Mar 1942. Former fleet oiler converted to logistic ship and armed as above in Arsenal do Alfeite.

S. BRAS   1971, Portuguese Navy, Official

TUG/BUOY TENDER
1 NEW CONSTRUCTION

Displacement, tons	900
Main engines	2 400 hp
Speed, knots	15

A dual purpose fleet tug and buoy tender is reported to have been ordered late in 1968 from the Alfeite Naval Yard

DISPOSAL
The old lighthouse tender *Almirante Schultz*, A 521, was discarded on 10 Nov 1969 See full particulars and photograph in the 1969-70 edition.

ROMANIA

Diplomatic Representation	*Commander-in-Chief of the Navy:* Vice-Admiral Grigore Martes	**Personnel** 1971: 5 000 officers and ratings

Strength of the Fleet

Naval, Military and Air Attaché in London: Lieutenant-Colonel D. Badea	4 Medium Minesweepers	22 Inshore Minesweepers
	5 Missile Boats	8 Minesweeping Boats
Naval, Military and Air Attaché in Washington: Colonel Nicolae Gheorghe Plesa	3 Patrol Vessels	2 Training Ships
	8 Torpedo Boats	25 Auxiliary Vessels

Mercantile Marine

Lloyd's Register of Shipping:
64 vessels of 338 242 tons gross

MISSILE BOATS

5 Ex-USSR "OSA" CLASS

Displacement, tons	160 standard; 200 full load
Dimensions, feet	131·5 oa × 23 × 6·5
Missile launchers	4 large hood type in two pairs abreast
Guns, AA	4—25 mm (2 twin, 1 forward, 1 aft)
Main engines	3 diesels; 4 800 bhp = 35 knots

Built since 1959. Reported to have a surface-to-surface range of 15 to 18 miles.

MINESWEEPERS

4 Ex-GERMAN "M 40" TYPE

DESCATUSARIA   DESROBIERA   DEMOCRATIA   DREPTATEA

Displacement, tons	543 standard; 775 full load
Dimensions, feet	188 pp; 203·5 oa × 28 × 7·5 (max)
Guns	6—37 mm AA (twin)
A/S weapons	2 DCT
Main engines	Triple expansion; 2 shafts; 2 400 ihp = 17 knots
Boilers	2 three-drum water tube
Fuel, tons	152 coal
Radius, miles	4 000 at 10 knots
Complement	80

Former German "M 40" type coal-burning minesweepers. Built in 1943. Taken over by USSR at the end of the Second World War. Transferred to Rumania in 1956-1957. Pennant numbers DB-13, DB-14, DB-15 and DB-16.

DB-15 and DB-16   *1968*

DB-14 and DB-15   *1964, P. H. Silverstone*

PATROL VESSELS

3 Ex-USSR "KRONSTADT" CLASS

V-1   V-2   V-3

Displacement, tons	300 standard; 350 full load
Dimensions, feet	167·3 × 19·3 × 9
Guns	1—3·4 in dual purpose forward; 2—37 mm AA single aft; 6—12·7 mm in twin mounts
A/S weapons	2 ahead throwing launchers; 2 side projectors; 2 depth charge tracks
Main engines	Diesels; 2 shafts; speed = 27 knots

Former Soviet submarine chasers transferred to Rumania from the USSR. There are also some patrol boats in the Black Sea and some launches on the Danube.

The two old patrol vessels rated as gunboats, *Locotenent-Comandor Stiki Eugen* (ex-French *Friponne*) and *Sublocotenent Ghiculescu* (ex-French *Mignonne*), were deleted, being over age and obsolete.

The two very old patrol boats, former Austrian torpedo boats (torpiloare), *Sborul* (ex-*T 81*) and *Smeul* (ex-*T 83*), considered of no further military value, were discarded for scrap.

Certain of the old river monitors *Ardeal*, *Basarabia*, *Bratianu* and *Bucovina* were reported to still exist, but *Lahoorai* and the old river gunboats *Closca*, *Cusan* and *Horia* were discarded.

TORPEDO BOATS

8 Ex-USSR "P 4" CLASS

Displacement, tons	50
Dimensions, feet	85·3 × 20 × 6
Guns	4—25 mm AA
Tubes	2—21 in
Main engines	Speed = 42 knots

Former Soviet motor torpedo boats transferred to Rumania from the USSR.

INSHORE MINESWEEPERS

22 Ex-USSR "T 301" CLASS

Displacement, tons	130
Dimensions, feet	100 × 16 × 4·5
Guns	2—45 mm AA; 4—12·7 mm MG
Main engines	Diesel; 480 bhp = 10 knots
Complement	30

Former Soviet coastal Minesweepers transferred to Rumania by the USSR in 1956-60.

TRAINING SHIP *(Navă Scoală)*

MIRCEA

Displacement, tons	1 604
Dimensions, feet	239·5 oa; 267·3 (with bowsprit) × 39·3 × 16·5
Sail area	18 830 sq ft
Main engines	Auxiliary MAN; 6-cylinder Diesel; 500 bhp = 9·5 knots
Complement	83 + 140 midshipmen for training

Built by Blohm & Voss, Hamburg. Laid down on 30 Apr 1938. Launched on 22 Sep 1938. Completed on 29 Mar 1939. Refitted at Hamburg in 1966.

MIRCEA   *1970, courtesy Mr. Michael D. J. Lennon*

RASARITUL (ex-*Taifun*)

Measurement, tons	34 (*Thames* measurement)
Dimensions, feet	54 × 12·5 × 3
Main engines	2 petrol motors; 2 shafts.

Built by J. Samuel White & Co Ltd, Cowes, Isle of Wight, England. Launched in 1938. Of wooden construction. Yacht used as sail training ship. The training ship *Liberatea* (ex-*Luceafarul*, ex-*Nahlin*), former Royal Yacht, and the training ship *Constanta* (former submarine depot ship) were removed from the list in 1968.

MINESWEEPING BOATS

8 "TR-40 CLASS"

VD-241   VD-242   VD-243   VD-244   VD-245   VD-246   VD-247   VD-248

Eight "TR-40" Class minesweeping boats are employed on shallow water and river duties. Two survey craft, ten landing craft, ten transports and three oilers are also reported.

The eight former Soviet submarines; the Rumanian built submarines *Requinul* (S 1) and *Marsuinul* (S 2); and the four former Soviet coastal submarines of the "M V" Type, were deleted from the list in 1967. All were over age and obsolescent and were discarded.

The very old destroyers D 9 (ex-D21, ex-*Letuchi*, ex-*Regina Maria*) and D 10 (ex-D 22, ex-*Likhol*, ex-*Regele Ferdinand*), over age and obsolescent, were deleted from the list in 1967.

Of the over-age and obsolete destroyers *Marasti* (ex-Italian *Sparvieto*) and *Marasesti* (ex-Italian *Nibbio*), one was scrapped at Constanta and the other reduced to a hulk. The old minelayer *Amiral Murgescu*, latterly used as a training ship, was deleted from the list in 1967, being worn out and not worth refitting.

SAUDI ARABIA

Mercantile Marine

Lloyd's Register of Shipping: 37 vessels of 48 543 tons gross

TORPEDO BOATS

Displacement, tons	170 standard
Dimensions, feet	131 wl; 139·5 oa × 23·0 × 7·3
Guns	2—40 mm
Torpedo tubes	4—21 in
Main engines	4 diesels; 12 000 bhp = 41 knots
Complement	33 (3 officers; 30 men)

Two reported. Of the "Jaguar" type. Built in Germany and delivered in 1969.

PATROL BOATS

RIYADH

Displacement. tons	100 standard
Dimensions, feet	95·0 × 19·0 × 6·0
Guns	1—40 mm AA
Main engines	4 diesels; 2 shafts; 2 200 bhp = 21 knots

Steel-hulled patrol boat of US CG design transferred to Saudi Arabia in 1960. There are also eight small patrol boats and two air-sea rescue boats.

SENEGAL

Mercantile Marine

Lloyd's Register of Shipping: 19 vessels of 9 058 tons gross

PATROL VESSELS

1 NEW CONSTRUCTION

SAINT LOUIS

Displacement, tons	235 standard
Dimensions, feet	149·3 pp; 155·8 oa × 23·6 × 8·2
Guns	2—40 mm AA
Main engines	2 MGO diesels; 1 shaft; 2 400 bhp = 18·5 knots
Complement	25 (3 officers, 22 men)

Ordered from Ch Navales Franco-Belges. Laid down on 20 Apr 1970, launched on 5 Aug 1970 and commissioned on 1 Mar 1971. Sister to *Malaika* of Madagascar and *Vigilant* of Ivory Coast.

PATROL BOATS

2 Ex-FRENCH "VC" TYPE

CASAMANCE (ex-*VC 5*, P 755)
SINE-SALOUM (ex-*Reine N'Galifourou*, ex-*VC 4*, P 754)

Displacement, tons	75 standard; 82 full load
Dimensions, feet	104·5 × 15·5 × 5·5
Guns	2—20 mm AA
Main engines	2 Mercedes-Benz diesels; 2 shafts; 2 700 bhp = 28 knots max

Former French patrol craft (Vedettes de Surveillance Côtière). Built by the Constructions Mécaniques de Normandie, Cherbourg. Completed in 1958. *Casamance* was transferred from France to Senegal in 1963. *Sine-Saloum* was given to Senegal on 24 Aug 1965 after having been returned to France by the Congo in Feb 1965.

SINE-SALOUM   *1967, Senegalese Navy, Official*

1 Ex-US "SC" TYPE

SÉNÉGAL (ex-*P 700*, ex-*CH 62*, ex-US *SC 1344*)

Displacement, tons	110 standard; 138 full load
Dimensions, feet	107·5 wl; 110·9 × 17 × 6·5
Guns	1—40 mm AA; 3—20 mm AA
Main engines	2 GM diesels; 2 shafts; 1 000 bhp = 13 knots max
Complement	25

Former US submarine chaser transferred to France on 19 Nov 1943, and from France to Senegal on 12 July 1961. First ship of Senegalese naval force.

SENEGAL   *1967, Senegalese Navy, Official*

SIERRA LEONE

Establishment

Sierra Leone became a sovereign and independent member state of the Commonwealth of Nations on 27 Apr 1961.

Mercantile Marine

1971: Lloyd's Register of Shipping: 4 vessels of 855 tons gross

PATROL VESSELS

It has been officially stated that Sierra Leone is acquiring at least one fighting vessel.

SOMALI REPUBLIC

Establishment

Somalia became an independent territory as the Somali Republic on 1 July 1960.

Mercantile Marine

Lloyd's Register of Shipping: 79 vessels of 369 118 tons gross

TORPEDO BOATS

12 Ex-USSR "P6" CLASS

Displacement, tons	66 standard; 76 full load
Dimensions, feet	88·3 × 20·0 × 6·0
Torpedo tubes	2—21 in
Guns	4—25 in AA
Main engines	4 diesels; 4 800 bhp = 45 knots

12 or more of the ex-USSR "P 6" type were to be transferred by the USSR or UAR.

PATROL BOATS

2 Ex-USSR "POLUCHAT" I CLASS

Displacement, tons	100 standard, 120 full load
Dimensions, feet	98·4 × 20·0 × 5·9
Guns	2—25 mm AA
Main engines	Diesels = 15 knots

Two of these boats are reported to have been transferred from the USSR in 1968.

SOUTHERN YEMEN

Mercantile Marine

Lloyd's Register of Shipping: 5 vessels of 1 417 tons gross

INSHORE MINESWEEPERS

3 "HAM" CLASS

Displacement, tons	120 standard; 160 full load
Dimensions, feet	106·5 oa × 21·2 × 5·5
Guns	1—20 mm AA
Main engines	2 Paxman diesels; 1 100 bhp = 14 knots
Oil fuel, tons	15
Complement	15 officers and men

The British inshore minesweepers *Bodenham*, *Blunham* and *Elsenham* were transferred to the South Arabian Navy established by the Federal Government.

HAM CLASS   *A. & J. Pavia*

PATROL BOATS

15 COASTAL TYPE

Fifteen small diesel engined patrol boats were ordered in the United Kingdom in 1969.

SINGAPORE

Establishment

The island became an independent sovereign state as the Republic of Singapore on 9 Aug 1965.

Mercantile Marine

Lloyd's Register of Shipping: 153 vessels of 424 417 tons gross

FAST PATROL CRAFT

6 VOSPER THORNYCROFT DESIGN

3 "TYPE B"

SOVEREIGNTY (25 Nov 1969) P 71 **DARING** (28 Nov 1970) P 74
            DAUNTLESS   P 73

Displacement, tons	100 standard; 130 full load
Dimensions, feet	103·6 wl; 109·6 × 21·0 × 5·6
Guns	1—76 mm Bofors; 1—20 mm Oerlikon
Main engines	2 Maybach MD 872 diesels; 2 × 3 600 bhp = 32 knots max; continuous sea speed over 25 knots
Range, miles	Over 1 000 nautical at 15 knots
Complement	19 (3 officers, 16 ratings)

Sovereignty was built by Vosper Thornycroft Ltd, Portsmouth, England and completed in 1971. *Daring* and *Dauntless* are being built by Vosper Thornycroft Private Ltd (formerly Uniteers Yard) in Singapore. Steel hulls of round bilge form with spray strake and spray deflecting knuckle extending for more than half the length. Aluminium alloy superstructure.

SOVEREIGNTY   *1971, Vosper Thornycroft*

3 "TYPE A"

INDEPENDENCE (15 July 1969) P 69 **FREEDOM** (18 Nov 1969) P 70
            JUSTICE (May 1970) P 72

Displacement, tons	100 standard
Dimensions, feet	110·0 × 21·0 × 6·5 max
Guns	1—40 mm AA (forward); 1—20 mm AA aft
Main engines	2 Maybach diesels; 2 × 3 500 bhp = 32 knots (max)
Range	"In excess of 1 000 miles" (official)
Complement	19 to 22

On 21 May 1968 the Vosper Thornycroft Group announced the receipt of an order for six of their 110-foot fast patrol boats for the Republic of Singapore. Two boats have been built at the Group's Portsmouth Yard and four at Vosper Thornycroft Uniteers Yard (now Vosper Thornycroft Private Ltd) in Singapore. The total value of the order is $30 000 000 Singapore (£4 000 000). This is the first time that such advanced patrol craft have been built in the Group's Singapore Yard. It marks a significant step towards meeitng further requirements for these very specialised craft in South East Asia. In design these vessels are of a hybrid type between that of the fast patrol craft built for the Malaysian Navy and those built for the Peruvian Navy. Two sub types, the first of each (*Independence* and *Sovereignty*) built in UK, the remainedr in Singapore. Second type have more advanced armament. *Independence* was completed in 1970.

INDEPENDENCE   *1971, Vosper Thornycroft*

SEAWARD DEFENCE BOAT

1 "FORD" TYPE

PANGLIMA P 48

Displacement, tons	119 standard; 134 full load
Dimensions, feet	117·0 × 20·0 × 6·0
Guns	1—40 mm; 60 cal AA forward
Main engines	Paxman YHAXM supercharged B 12 diesels = 14 knots
Oil fuel, tons	15
Complement	15 officers and men

Built by United Engineers, Singapore. Laid down in 1954. Launched on 14 Jan 1956. Accepted by the Singapore Government in May 1956. Similar to the British seaward defence boats of the "Ford" class. Transferred to the Royal Malaysian Navy on the formation of Malaysia. Transferred to the Singapore Government (independent Republic of Singapore) in 1967.

PANGLIMA   *1964, Official*

PATROL BOATS

PX 10	**PX 11**	**PX 12**	**PX 13**

Displacement, tons	40 standard
Length, feet	87·0
Guns	2—20 mm

Built by Vosper Thornycroft Group, Portsmouth, England for marine police duties. There is also the former Netherlands boat *Endeavor*, built in 1955.

LANDING SHIP

1 US LST TYPE

HOLMES COUNTY LST 836

Displacement, tons	1 653 light; 4 080 full load
Dimensions, feet	316·0 wl; 328·0 oa × 50·0 × 14·0
Guns	8—40 mm (4 twin)
Main engines	GM diesels; 2 shafts; 1 700 bhp = 11·6 knots
Complement	120

Tank landing craft to be transferred from the US Navy on 1 July 1971.

LANDING CRAFT

2 LCT (8) TYPE

CAIRNHILL (ex-*Ardennes*)   **TANGLIN** (ex-*Arromanches*)

Displacement, tons	657 light; 1 017 full load
Dimensions, feet	225·0 pp; 231·2 oa × 39·0 × 5·0
Main engines	4 Paxman diesels; 1 840 bhp = 12·6 knots max (9 knots economical cruising speed)
Complement	37

Originally in the Royal Navy but transferred to the British Army. Acquired by Singapore in 1970. There are also six small landing craft.

TANGLIN   *1971, A. & J. Pavia*

SOUTH AFRICA

Administration

Commander, Maritime Defence and Chief of the Navy:
Vice-Admiral H. H. Bierman, SSA, OBE

Chief of Naval Staff:
Rear-Admiral J. Johnson, SM, DSC

Diplomatic Representation

Armed Forces Attaché in London:
Rear Admiral M. R. Terry Lloyd, SM

Naval Attache in London:
Captain R. D. Kingon, SAN

Naval, Military and Air Attaché in Washington:
Brigadier H. J. P. Burger, SM

Strength of the Fleet

2 Destroyers (Helicopter Carrying)
6 Anti-Submarine Frigates
1 Escort Minesweeper (Training)
10 Coastal Minesweepers (Non-Magnetic)
5 Seaward Defence Craft
9 Support Ships and Auxiliaries
8 Air Sea Rescue Launchers

Naval Base

HM Dockyard at Simonstown was transferred to the Republic of South Africa on 2 Apr 1957.

New Construction Programme

3 Diesel-electric Submarines (French "Daphne" Class)
1 Survey Ship
1 Air/Sea Rescue Launch

Personnel

1971: Total 4 760 (420 officers, 3 140 ratings and 1 200 national service ratings)

Air Sea Rescue Base

The SAAF Maritime Group base at Langebaan was transferred to the South African Navy on 1 Nov 1969, becoming SAN Sea Rescue Base (SAS *Flamingo*). The ASR launches were recently given Naval Coastal Forces numbers to replace SAF "R" numbers. Their black hulls and buff upperworks are being repainted grey to conform to the naval scheme.

Mercantile Marine

Lloyd's Register of Shipping:
249 vessels of 510 504 tons gross

SUBMARINES

Name	*Builders*	*Laid down*	*Launched*	*Completed*
MARIA VAN RIEBEECK	Dubigeon—Normandie (Nantes-Chantenay	14 Mar 1968	18 Mar 1969	22 June 1970
JOHANNA VAN DER MERWE	Dubigeon—Normandie (Nantes-Chantenay)	24 Apr 1969	21 July 1970	21 July 1971
EMILY HOBHOUSE	Dubigeon—Normandie (Nantes-Chantenay)	18 Nov 1968	24 Oct 1969	25 Jan 1971

3 "FRENCH" "DAPHNE" CLASS

Displacement, tons	850 surface; 1 040 submerged
Length, feet (*metres*)	190·3 (*58*)
Beam, feet (*metres*)	22·3 (*6·8*)
Draught, feet (*metres*)	15·4 (*4·7*)
Torpedo tubes	12—21·7 in (*550 mm*) (8 bow, 4 stern)
Main engines	SEMT-Pielstick diesel electric; 1 300 bhp surface; 1 600 hp submerged; 2 shafts
Speed, knots	16 surface and submerged
Complement	47 (6 officers, 41 men)

First submarines ordered for the South African Navy. They are of the French "Daphne" design, similar to those built in France for Pakistan and Portugal. The names commemorate the wives of two early Boer Leaders, and an English Quakeress noted for her relief work in South Africa during the Anglo-Boer conflict of 1899 to 1902.

MARIA VAN RIEBEECK   *1971, South African Navy, Official*

DESTROYERS

Name	*No.*	*Builders*	*Laid down*	*Launched*	*Completed*
JAN VAN RIEBEECK (ex-HMS *Wessex*, ex-*Zenith*)	D 278	Fairfield SB & Eng Co Ltd. Govan, Glasgow	20 Oct 1942	2 Sep 1943	11 May 1944
SIMON VAN DER STEL (ex-HMS *Whelp*)	D 237	R. & W. Hawthorn Leslie & Co Ltd	1 May 1942	3 June 1943	25 Apr 1944

2 FORMER BRITISH "W" CLASS

Displacement, tons	2 205 standard; 2 850 full load
Length, feet (*metres*)	339·5 (*103·6*)pp; 362·8 (*110·6*)oa
Beam, feet (*metres*)	35·7 (*10·9*)
Draught, feet (*metres*)	17·1 (*5·2*) max (props)
Aircraft	2 Westland "Wasp" helicopters
Guns, surface	4—4 in (*102 mm*) 2 twin
Guns, AA	2—40 mm (single)
Guns, saluting	4—3 pdr.
Torpedo tubes	4—21 in (quadrople)
Torpedo tubes, A/S	6 (2 triple)
A/S weapons	2 DCT; 2 DC racks
Boilers	2 Admiralty 3-drum type; 300 psi; 670°F
Main engines	2 Parsons sr geared turbines; 2 shafts; 40 000 shp
Speed, knots	36·75 designed; 31·25 sea
Radius, miles	3 260 at 14 knots
Oil fuel, tons	579 (95%)
Complement	192 (11 officers, 181 men)

Purchased from Great Britain, *Jan van Riebeeck* was transferred to South Africa on 29 Mar 1950, and *Simon van der Stel* early in 1952.

MODERNISATION. *Simon Van der Stel* was modernised in 1962-64 and *Jab van Riebeeck* in 1964-66.

JAN VAN RIEBEECK   *South African Navy, Official*

RADAR. Search and Tactical. Type 293. Fire Control: X Band (NSG NA 9 system).

GUNNERY. The main armament formerly comprised four 4·7 inch guns.

SIMON VAN DER STEL   *1970, South African Navy, Official*

ANTI-SUBMARINE FRIGATES

3 "PRESIDENT" CLASS

Name	No.	Builders	Laid down	Launched	Completed
PRESIDENT KRUGER	F 150	Yarrow & Co. Scotstoun	6 Apr 1959	20 Oct 1960	1 Oct 1962
PRESIDENT PRETORIUS	F 145	Yarrow & Co. Scotstoun	21 Nov 1960	28 Sep 1962	4 Mar 1964
PRESIDENT STEYN	F 147	Alex Stephen & Sons. Govan	20 May 1960	23 Nov 1961	25 Apr 1963

Displacement, tons	2 250 standard; 2 800 full load
Length, feet (metres)	360 (109·7) wl; 370 (112·8) oa
Beam, feet (metres)	41·0 (12·5)
Draught, feet (metres)	17·1 (5·2) max (props)
Guns, surface	2—4·5 in (115 mm) 1 twin
Guns, AA	2—40 mm Bofors
Guns, saluting	4—3 pdr.
Aircraft	1 "Wasp" helicopter
A/S weapons	1 "Limbo" 3-barrel DC mortar
Boilers	2 Babcock & Wilcox; 550 psi; 850°F
Main engines	2 sets double reduction geared turbines; 2 shafts; 30 000 shp
Speed, knots	over 30 max, 28 sustained sea
Radius, miles	4 500 at 15 knots
Oil fuel, tons	430
Complement	203 (13 officers, 190 men)

Originally "Whitby" Type 12 frigates built in the United Kingdom as a part of the expansion programme. *President Kruger* arrived in South Africa on 27 Mar 1963.

CONVERSION. These ships have been converted to carry a "Wasp" A/S helicopter, complete with hangar installation and landing deck. In order to accommodate this, one "Limbo" A/S mortar was removed and the two single 40 mm remounted on the hangar roof. *President Kruger* completed refit and recommissioned on 5 Aug 1969, *President Steyn* completed refit in 1971, when *President Pretorius* was taken in hand. The refits were carried out at S.A. Naval Dockyard, Simonstown.

GUNNERY. The two 40 mm guns were on the main deck, a deck lower than in the "Whitby" class original design. As converted they are on top of the hangar.

ENGINEERING. Geared turbines of advanced design and high power start on a cruising turbine and switch over to the main turbines at a predetermined speed.

ELECTRICAL. System is alternating current, 440 bolts, three phase, 60 cycles per second.

RADAR. Search: DRBV 23 (*President Kruger*). Tactical: Type 293. Fire Control: X Band.

NAMES. Kruger was the last President of the Transvaal Republic. Steyn was last President of the old Orange Free State. Pretorious was first President of the Transvaal Republic: he built and named the capital Pretoria after his father, one of the "Great Trek" leaders.

PRESIDENT STEYN

1970, South African Navy, Official

PRESIDENT PRETORIOUS

1971, Official

PRESIDENT KRUGER

1971, South African Navy, Official

1 FORMER BRITISH TYPE 15

VRYSTAAT (ex-HMS *Wrangler*) F 157

Displacement, tons	2 240 standard; 2 880 full load
Length, feet (metres)	339·5 (103·5) pp; 362·8 (110·6) oa
Beam, feet (metres)	35·7 (10·9)
Draught, feet (metres)	17·1 (5·2) max props
Guns, surface	2—4 in (102 mm) 1 twin
Guns, AA	2—40 mm Bofors
Guns, saluting	4—3 pdr
A/S weapons	2 "Squid" triple DC mortars
Boilers	2 Admiralty 3-drum; 300 psi; 675°F
Main engines	Parsons single reduction geared turbines; 2 shafts; 40 000 shp
Speed, knots	36·75 designed; 31·25 sea
Radius, miles	3 200 at 14 knots
Oil fuel, tons	505
Complement	195 (13 officers, 182 men)

Built by Vickers-Armstrongs, Barrow. Laid down on 23 Sep 1942, launched on 30 Dec 1943, completed on 14 June 1944. Fully converted into a Type 15 fast anti-submarine frigate from a fleet destroyer of the "W" class in 1951-52 by Harland & Wolf Ltd, Belfast. Refitted by the Mount Stuart Dry Dock Ltd, Cardiff, and taken over from the Royal Navy on 29 Nov 1956 as a unit of the South African Navy and renamed *Vrystaat*. Sailed for South Africa at the end of Jan 1957.

VRYSTAAT

1970, South African Navy, Official

RADAR. Search: Type 277. Tactical: Type 293.
CLASS. Originally a sister ship of *Jan van Riebeeck* and *Simon van der Stel* (see previous page).

Frigates—continued

Name	No.	Builders	Laid down	Launched	Completed
GOOD HOPE (ex-HMS *Loch Boisdale*)	F 432	Blyth Dry Docks & SB Co Ltd	8 Nov 1943	5 July 1944	1 Dec 1944
TRANSVAAL (ex-HMS *Loch Ard*)	F 602	Harland & Wolff, Ltd. Belfast	20 Jan 1944	2 Aug 1944	21 May 1945

2 FORMER BRITISH "LOCH" CLASS

Displacement, tons	1 610 standard; 2 450 full load
Length, feet (*metres*)	286 (*87·2*) pp; 307 (*93·6*) oa
Beam, feet (*metres*)	38·5 (*11·7*)
Draught, feet (*metres*)	15·1 (*4·6*) max
Guns, surface	2—4 in (*102 mm*) 1 twin
Guns, AA	*Transvaal:* 6—40 mm Bofors
	Good Hope: 2—40 mm Bofors
Guns, Saluting	*Good Hope:* 4—3 pdr
A/S weapons	2 "Squid" triple DC mortars
Boilers	2 Admiralty 3-drum; 225 psi
Main engines	2 sets triple expansion; 2 shafts; 5 500 ihp
Speed, knots	19 max
Radius, miles	9 500 at 12 knots
Oil fuel, tons	720
Complement	165 (10 officers, 155 men)

These two "Loch" class anti-submarine frigates, and a sister ship, *Natal*, were presented to South Africa by Great Britain in 1944-45.

CONSTRUCTION. *Transvaal* was completed by Lobnitz & Co Ltd, Renfrew.

MODIFICATION. When *Transvaal* was modernised she had her forecastle deck extended aft to provide extra accommodation (see photograph).

CONVERSION. *Good Hope* was converted into a despatch vessel in 1955 as Administrative Flagship of the South African Navy. She has deckhouse superstructure for extra cabins, and reception platform above built on aft, and mainmast. Refitted in 1961. Sister ship *Natal* was converted into a survey ship in 1957.

RADAR. Equipment includes Type 277 search radar installation.

GOOD HOPE　　　　　　　　　　　1970, South African Navy, Official

TRANSVAAL　　　　　　　　　　　1971, South African Navy, Official

ESCORT MINESWEEPER

1 FORMER BRITISH "ALGERINE" CLASS

PIETERMARITZBURG (ex-HMS *Pelorus*) M 291

Displacement, tons	1 040 standard; 1 330 full load
Length, feet (*metres*)	212·5 (*64·8*) pp; 225 (*68·6*) oa
Beam feet (*metres*)	35·5 (*10·8*)
Draught, feet (*metres*)	11·5 (*3·5*)
Guns, surface	2—4 in (*102 mm*) 1 twin
Guns, AA	2—40 mm Bofors
A/S weapons	4 DCT
Boilers	2 three-drum type; 250 psi
Main engines	2 sets triple expansion; 2 shafts; 2 400 ihp
Speed, knots	16 max, 14 sustained
Radius, miles	5 500 at 10 knots
Oil fuel, tons	270
Complement	115 (8 officers, 107 men)

Built as ocean minesweeper by Lobnitz & Co Ltd. Renfrew. Laid down on 8 Oct 1942, launched on 18 June 1943, completed on 7 Oct 1943. Also used as escort vessel. Purchased from Great Britain in 1947 Re-commissioned as midshipmen's training ship on 30 Aug 1962. The twin 4 inch mount, replacing a single 4 inch, was fitted in 1958.
Sister ship *Bloemfontein* (ex-HMS *Rosamund*) was sunk as a target by *Johannesburg* and *President Kruger* on 5 June 1967 off Simonstown.

PIETERMARITZBURG　　　　　　　1969. South African Navy. Official

SURVEY SHIPS

1 YARROW NEW CONSTRUCTION

Displacement, tons	1 930 standard; 2 750 full load
Length, feet (*metres*)	235 (*71·6*); 260·1 (*79·3*)
Beam, feet (*metres*)	49·1 (*15·0*)
Draught, feet (*metres*)	15·1 (*4·6*)
Aircraft	1 helicopter
Main engines	4 Paxman/Ventura diesels geared to 1 shaft and controllable pitch propeller; 4 880 bhp

NATAL (ex-HMS *Loch Cree*) A 301

Displacement, tons	1 435 standard; 2,260 full load
Length, feet (*metres*)	286 (*87·2*) pp; 307·0 (*93·6*) oa
Beam, feet (*metres*)	38·5 (*11·7*)
Draught, feet (*metres*)	14·7 (*4·5*)
Boilers	2 Admiralty 3-drum
Main engines	Triple expansion; 2 shafts; 5 500 ihp
Speed, knots	19 max
Radius, miles	9 500 at 12 knots
Oil fuel, tons	720
Complement	124

"Lock" class frigate built by Swan, Hunter & Wigham Richardson Ltd, Tyne. Laid down on 18 Oct 1943, launched on 19 June 1944, completed on 8 Mar 1945. Presented by Great Britain in 1945. Converted into a survey ship in 1957 when guns and A/S weapons were removed. Type 277 search radar. Originally a sister ship of *Good Hope* and *Transvaal*.

Speed, knots	Designed for 16 on trials
Radius, miles	12 000 at 11 knots
Oil fuel, tons	560 bunkerage capacity
Complement	Total 123 (12 officers, 104 ratings plus 7 scientists)

An order was placed with Yarrow (Shipbuilders) Ltd, for a "Hecla" class survey ship on 7 Nov 1969. Equipped for hydrographic survey with limited facilities for the collection of oceanographical data and for this purpose fitted with special communications equipment, naval surveying gear, survey launches and facilities for helicopter operations. Hull strengthened for navigation in ice and fitted with a transverse bow thrust unit and passive roll stabilisation system. Capable of undertaking long ocean passages in any part of the world including winter passages in the North Atlantic. Scheduled for launch mid Mar 1971 and delivery Nov 1971.

NATAL　　　　　　　　　　　　South African Navy, Official

COASTAL MINESWEEPERS

10 BRITISH "TON" CLASS

DURBAN	M 1499	**MOSSELBAAI** (ex-*Oakington*)	M 1213
EAST LONDON (ex-*Chilton*)	M 1215	**PORT ELIZABETH** (*Dumbleton*)	M 1212
JOHANNESBURG (*Castleton*)	M 1207	**PRETORIA** (ex-*Dunkerton*)	M 1144
KAAPSTAD (ex-*Hazleton*)	M 1142	**WALVISBAAI** (ex-*Packington*)	M 1214
KIMBERLEY (ex-*Stratton*)	M 1210	**WINDHOEK**	M 1498

Displacement, tons	360 standard; 425 full load
Dimensions, feet	140·0 pp; 152·0 oa × 28·8 × 8·2
Guns	1—40 mm Bofors AA; 2—20 mm AA
Main engines	Mirrlees diesels in *Kaapstad* and *Pretoria*, 2 500 bhp; Deltic diesels in remainder; 3 000 bhp = 15 knots

Kaapstad and *Pretoria*, open bridge and lattice mast, were purchased in 1955. *Windhoek*, frigate bridge and tripod mast, was launched by Thornycroft, Southampton, on 27 June 1957. *Durban*, covered bridge and tripod mast, was launched at Camper & Nicholson, Gosport, on 12 June 1957. *East London* and *Port Elizabeth*, transferred from the Royal Navy at Hythe on 27 Oct 1958, sailed for South Africa in Nov 1958. *Johannesburg*, *Kimberley* and *Mosselbaai* were delivered in 1959. *Walvisbaai* was launched by Harland & Wolff, Belfast on 10 Dec 1958 and delivered in 1959. A photograph of *Pretoria* appears in the 1956-57 to 1962-63 editions, of *Windhoek* in the 1958-59 to 1963-64 editions, of *Kimberley* in the 1962-63 to 1966-67 editions, of *Walvisbaai* in the 1967-68 to 1969-70 editions and of *Port Elizabeth* in the 1970-71 edition.

DURBAN — Added, 1971

SEAWARD DEFENCE BOATS

5 BRITISH "FORD" CLASS

GELDERLAND (ex-*Brayford*)	P 3105	**NAUTILUS** (ex-*Glassford*)	P 3120
HAERLEM	P 3126	**OOSTERLAND**	P 3127
		RIJGER	P 3125

Displacement, tons	120 standard; 160 full load
Dimensions, feet	110·0 wl; 117·2 oa × 20·0 × 4·5
Guns	1—40 mm AA
A/S weapons	2 DCT in *Haerlem*, *Oosterland* and *Rijger*
Main engines	2 Davey Paxman diesels; Foden engine on centre shaft; 1 100 bhp = 18 knots max; sea speed 15 knots

Gelderland, built by A. & J. Inglis Ltd, Glasgow, was purchased from Britain, and handed over to South Africa at Portsmouth on 30 Aug 1954. Designed to detect, locate and destroy submarines, including midget submarines, in the approaches to defended ports. Modern electronic equipment and comprehensive electrical installation. Second ship, *Nautilus*, was purchased in 1955, *Rijger* was launched on 6 Feb 1958, *Haerlem* on 18 June 1958, *Oosterland* on 27 Jan 1959. All three of these later ships, built by Vosper Ltd, Portsmouth, are fitted with Vosper roll damping fins. *Haerlem* had a charthouse added aft (see photograph in the 1966-67 to 1970-71 editions) as an inshore survey boat. A photograph of *Gelderland* appears in the 1955-56 edition, of *Nautilus* in the 1956-57 to 1959-60 editions.

RIJGER — 1971

TRAINING VESSELS

HDML 1204

Displacement, tons	45 standard; 54 full load (revised official figures)
Dimensions, feet	72·0 × 15·5 × 5·3
Main engines	2 Gardner 8-cylinder diesels; 300 bhp = 11 knots

Sole survivor of the former British Admiralty type HDMLs (Harbour Defence Motor Launches) later designated Seaward Defence Motor Launches. Built in South Africa 1941-42. Guns removed. Attached to Military Academy, Saldanha, as Midshipmen's training vessel. SDML 1202 was converted to a gunnery target. SDML 1330 and 1331 were scrapped in 1953, SDML 1199 and 1201 in 1955, SDML 1198 in 1956, SDML 1332 in 1958 and SDMLs 1197, 1200, 1202 and 1203 in 1968.

NAVIGATOR

Navigational Training Vessel. 75 tons displacement; 63 × 20 feet; 2 Foden diesels, 200 bhp = 9·5 knots. Based at Naval College, Gordon's Bay. Round bilge fishing boat wooden hull. Built by Fred Nicholls (Pty) Ltd, Durban in 1964.

BOOM DEFENCE VESSELS

SOMERSET (ex-HMS *Barcross*) P 285

Displacement, tons	750 standard; 960 full load
Dimensions, feet	150 pp; 182 oa × 32·2 × 11·5
Main engines	Triple expansion; 850 ihp = 11 knots
Boilers	2 SE
Oil fuel, tons	186

Built by Blyth Dry Dock & SB Co Ltd. Laid down on 15 Apr 1941, launched on 21 Oct 1941, completed on 14 Apr 1942. Engined by Swan, Hunter & Wigham Richardson Ltd, Tyne. Renamed in 1951 after Dick King's horse. Sister ship *Fleur* (ex-HMS *Barbrake*) P 273 was sunk as a target in False Bay on 8th Oct 1965.

SOMERSET — 1971, Official

FLEET REPLENISHMENT SHIP

TAFELBERG (ex-*Annam*)

Measurement, tons	12 500 gross; 18 430 deadweight
Main engines	B & W diesels; 8 420 bhp = 15·5 knots
Complement	100 as naval vessel (40 as tanker)

Built by Nakskovs Skibsvaert as Danish East Asiatic Co tanker. Launched on 20 June 1958. Purchased by the Navy in 1965. Accommodation rehabilitated by Barens Shipbuilding & Engineering Co, Durban with extra accommodation, air conditioning, re-wiring for additional equipment, new upper RAS (replenishment at sea) deck to contain gantries, re-fuelling pipes. Provision for helicopters. Remainder of conversion by Jowies, Brown & Hamer, Durban. Name means Table Mountain.

TAFELBERG — 1970, South African Navy, Official

TORPEDO RECOVERY VESSEL

Displacement, tons	220 standard; 257 full load
Dimensions, feet	115·0 wl; 121·5 oa × 27·5 × 11·1
Main engines	2 Paxman Ventura diesels; 1 400 bhp

Built by Dorman Long (Africa) Ltd at Durban and completed on 29 Nov 1969. Combined Torpedo Recovery Vessel and Diving Tender.

FLEUR — 1970, South African Navy, Official

NAVAL TUGS

DE NEYS   **DE NOORDE**

Displacement, tons	180 and 170, respectively
Dimensions, feet	94·0 × 26·5 × 15·75 and 104·5 × 25·0 × 15·0
Main engines	2 Lister Blackstone diesels; 2 shafts; 608 bhp

Both built by Globe Engineering Works Ltd, Cape town. Completed on 23 July 1969 and Dec 1961.

AIR SEA RESCUE LAUNCHES (ex-*SAAF*)

P 1551 (ex-*R* 31)   **P 1552** (ex-*R* 30)   **P 1553** (ex-*R* 9)   **P 1554**

P 1554: New construction, 26 tons, 64 × 16 × 5 feet, 2 diesels, 1 120 bhp = 28 kts.
P 1551 & 1552: 87 tons, 96 × 19 × 5 feet, 2 diesels, 4 480 bhp = 30 kts (1962, 1961).
P 1553: 24 tons, 63 × 15 × 4 feet, 2 petrol engines, 1 000 bhp = 30 kts (built 1945).
There are also 2 ex-seaplane tenders, 41 ft, and 2 ex-marine tenders, 24 ft.

SPAIN

Administration

Minister of Marine:
Admiral Excmo Sr Don Adolfo Baturone Colombo

Chief of Naval Staff:
Admiral Excmo Sr Don Enrique Barbudo Duarte

Deputy Chief of Naval Staff:
Rear-Admiral Excmo Sr Don Gabriel Pita da Veiga Sanz

Commander-in-Chief of the Fleet:
Vice-Admiral Excmo Sr Don Juan

Diplomatic Representation

Naval Attaché in London:
Commander Sr Don Salvador Moreno Reyna

Naval Attaché in Washington:
Captain Sr Don Jorge Garcia-Parreño Kaden

Strength of the Fleet

1 Helicopter Carrier
5 Submarines (Diesel Powered)
1 Heavy Cruiser
18 Destroyers (16 Anti-Submarine)
4 Frigates
6 Frigate Minelayers
5 Corvettes
13 Medium Fleet Minesweepers
12 Coastal Minesweepers
14 Patrol and Coastguard Vessels
3 Fast Torpedo Boats
3 Anti-Submarine Launches
11 Landing Ships and Landing Craft
47 Support Ships and Service Craft

Personnel

1971: Total 52 300 (4 500 officers, 37 000 ratings, 4 800 civil branch, 6 000 marines)

Building Programme

Official Statement:—
New construction carried out in Spain includes 5 frigates of US design and 4 submarines of French design.
The construction of these ships is the most important step the Spanish shipbuilding industry has recently taken to carry out a naval programme in accordance with advanced designs and modern techniques. The programme includes training equipment and new maintenance facilities ashore.

Navy Estimates.

	pesetas		pesetas
1960:	2 655 833 903.00	1966:	4 500 000 000.00
1961:	2 658 479 733.00	1967:	5 679 600 000.00
1962:	3 314 590 252.00	1968:	6 852 000 000.00
1963:	3 559 743 625.00	1969:	6 852 000 000.00
1964:	3 904 880 558.00	1970:	8 743 592 000.00
1965:	4 000 000 000.00	1971:	9 402 981 000.00

Mercantile Marine

Lloyd's Register of Shipping:
2 234 vessels of 3 440 952 tons gross

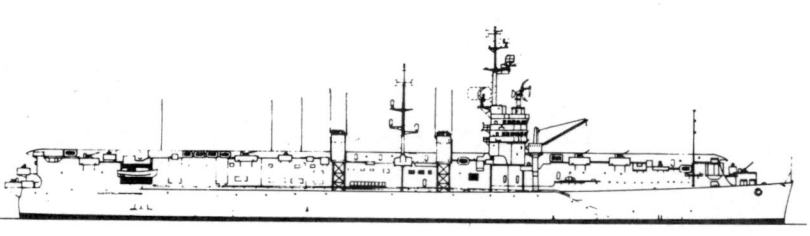

DÉDALO

MARQUÉS DE LA ENSENADA, ROGER DE LAURIA

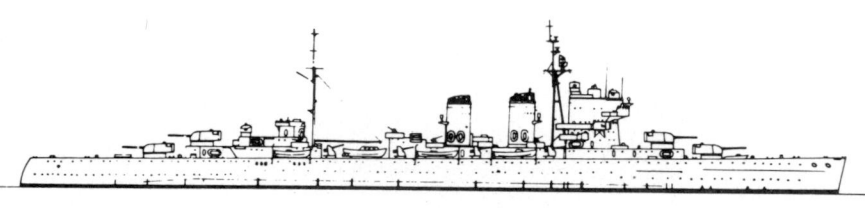

CANARIAS

OQUENDO

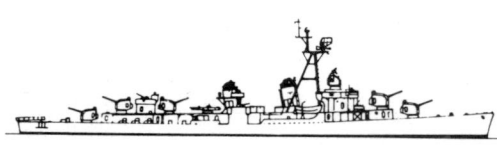

ALMIRANTE FERRANDIZ

AUDAZ *Class*

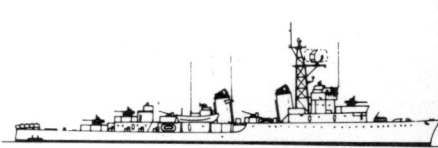

ALAVA, LINIERS

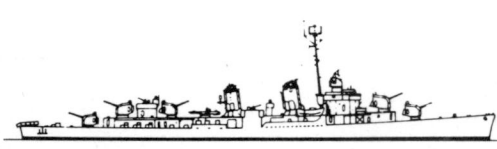

LEPANTO

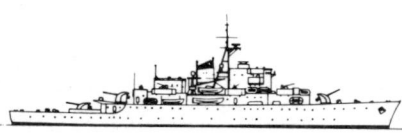

PIZARRO *Class*

JUPITER, VULCANO

ALCALA GALIANO, JORGE JUAN

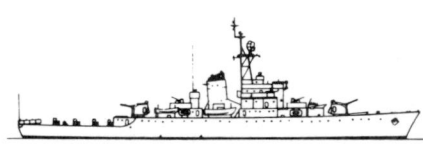

LEGAZPI, VICENTE YANEZ PINZON

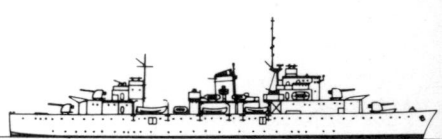

MARTE, NEPTUNO

ALMIRANTE VALDES

EOLO, TRITON

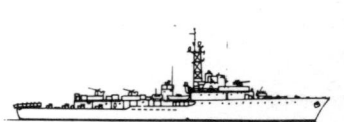

ATREVIDA *Class*

HELICOPTER CARRIER

Name	No.	Builders	Laid down	Launched	Completed
DÉDALO (ex-USS *Cabot*, ex-*Wilmington*, AVT 3, ex-CVL 28)	PH 01	New York Shipbuilding Corporation	16 Aug 1942	4 Apr 1943	24 July 1943

Ex-AIRCRAFT CARRIER (CVL)

Displacement, tons	11 000 standard ; 15 800 full load
Length, feet (*metres*)	600 (*182·8*) wl ; 623 (*189·9*) oa
Beam, feet (*metres*)	71·5 (*21·8*) hull
Width, feet (*metres*)	109 (*33·2*) extreme
Draught, feet (*metres*)	26 (*7·9*)
Aircraft	20 anti-submarine helicopters
Guns	16—40 mm AA
Boilers	4 Babcock & Wilcox
Main engines	GE geared turbines ; 100 000 shp ; 4 shafts
Speed, knots	32
Radius, miles	7 200 at 15 knots
Oil fuel, tons	1 800
Complement	800 (50 officers, 750 men)

Completed as an aircraft carrier from the hull of a "Cleveland" class cruiser. Originally carried over 40 aircraft. Converted to specialise in anti-submarine warfare, as a "Hunter-Killer Carrier", with strengthened flight and hangar decks, large port side catapult, revised magazine arrangements, new electronic gear, corrected stability to counter added top weight, and 26 aircraft. As a fixed-wing aircraft carrier the complement was 1 109 (159 officers and 950 men). Since conversion has only two of her original four funnels. Originally designed to include 4—5 inch guns in armament. Latterly mounted 26—40 mm AA. Reactivated and modernised at Philadelphia Naval Shipyard, where she was transferred to Spain on 30 Aug 1967, on loan for five years. SPS 6 and SPS 40 search radar ; SPS 10 tactical ; SPS 6 heightfinder.

DEDALO

1971, Official

DÉDALO

1969, Spanish Navy, Official

DÉDALO

1971, Official

SUBMARINES

"DAPHNE" TYPE — 1971, Official

ALMIRANTE GARCIA DE LOS REYES — 1969, Spanish Navy, Official

D 2 — 1966, Spanish Navy, Official

D 3 — 1971, Professor Alfredo Aguilera

SA 51 — 1970, Spanish Navy, Official

NEW CONSTRUCTION
4 FRENCH "DAPHNE" TYPE

Displacement, tons	870 surface; 1 040 submerged
Length, feet (metres)	189·6 (57·8)
Beam, feet (metres)	22·3 (6·8)
Draught, feet (metres)	15·1 (4·6)
Tubes	12—21·7 in (550 mm) (8 bow, 4 stern)
Main engines	SEMT- Pielstick diesel-electric; 1 300 bhp surface; 1 600 hp submerged; 2 shafts
Speed, knots	13 on surface; 15·5 submerged
Complement	50 (5 officers, 45 men)

It is officially stated that four submarines basically similar to the French "Daphne" class are being built with extensive French assistance in the Cartagena Yard. Originally five submarines of this class were envisaged, two to be built in the early 1970s and three later.

1 Ex-US "BALAO" TYPE
ALMIRANTE GARCIA DE LOS REYES E 1
(ex-USS *Kraken*, SS 370) S 31

Displacement, tons	1 880 surface; 2 060 submerged
Length, feet (metres)	311·5 (95·0)
Beam. feet (metres)	27·2 (8·2)
Draught, feet (metres)	17·2 (5·2)
Torpedo tubes	10—21 in (533 mm) 6 bow, 4 stern; 24 torpedoes
Main engines	4 diesels, total 6 400 bhp; Electric motors, 4 600 hp
Speed, knots	20 on surface; 10 submerged
Oil fuel, tons	300
Radius, miles	12 000 at 10 knots
Complement	80

Former US Navy submarine of the "Balao" class. Built by Manitowoc SB Co. Launched on 30 Apr 1944 and completed on 8 Sep 1944. Transferred on 24 Oct 1959 after modernisation and overhaul at Pearl Harbour.

PROJECTED ACQUISITIONS
The US "Balao" class submarines *Menhaden* SS 377 and *Ronquil* SS 396 (in July 1971) are to be formally transferred to Spain and after refit will join the fleet in 1972.

2 "D" CLASS

	No.	Laid down	Launched	Completed
D 2	S 21	Sep 1934	12 Dec 1944	2 Apr 1951
D 3	S 22	Sep 1945	20 Feb 1952	20 Feb 1954

Displacement, tons	1 200 surface; 1 480 submerged
Length, feet (metres)	276·5 (84·3)
Beam, feet (metres)	21·8 (6·65)
Draught, feet (metres)	13·5 (4·1)
Torpedo tubes	6—21 in (533 mm), 4 fwd, 2 aft
Main engines	2 Sulzer diesels, 5 000 bhp; Electric motors, 1 300 hp
Speed, knots	20·5 on surface; 9·5 submerged
Radius, miles	9 000 on surface
Complement	75

Ordered under the 1926 Programme. Both built at the Sociedad Española de Construcción Naval. Cartagena. Completed modernisation on 10 Dec and 14 Mar 1963 respectively. Diving limit, 50 fathoms. Allocated S pennant numbers in 1961.

CLASS. Sister ship D 1 (S 11), not modernised, was deleted from the list in 1966.

RECENT DISPOSAL
The old submarine G 7 (ex-U 573) S 01, the former German U-boat of the VII type, built by Blohm & Voss, Hamburg, interned in Spain in 1942 and purchased from Germany the following year, was removed from the effective list in 1971, it is officially stated.

2 "TIBURON" CLASS

SA 51   **SA 52**

Displacement, tons	78 surface; 81 submerged
Length, feet (metres)	70·5 (21·5)
Beam, feet (metres)	9 (2·7)
Draught, feet (metres)	9 (2·7)
Torpedo tubes	2—21 in (533 mm)
Main engines	Pegaso diesels, 400 hp; Electric motors, 400 hp
Speed, knots	10 on surface; 14·5 submerged
Complement	5

Midget submarines launched in 1958. Originally rated as *Submarinos Experimentales*, but in 1963 designated Assault Submarines with "SA" numbers.

ENGINEERING. The diesels were constructed by the ENASA (former Hispano-Suiza) Barcelona, 200 hp each, at 2 000 rpm, with reduction gear on the single screw disposed in a nozzle in continuation of the conic after hull.

RECENT DISPOSALS
The two midget submarines of 20 tons, SA 41 (F 1) and SA 42 (F 2), known as the "Foca" class, see full particulars in the 1970-71 and earlier editions, were officially removed from the effective list in 1971.

CRUISERS (*Crucero*)

Name	No.	Builders	Laid down	Launched	Completed
CANARIAS	C 21	Sociedad Espanola de Construction Naval, El Ferrol	15 Aug 1928	28 May 1931	1 Oct 1936

Displacement, tons	10 670 standard ; 13 500 full load
Length, feet (*metres*)	636·5 (*194·0*)
Beam, feet (*metres*)	64 (*19·5*)
Draught, feet (*metres*)	21·3 (*6·5*)
Guns, surface	8—8 in (*203 mm*) 50 cal.
	8—4·7 in (*120 mm*) 45 cal.
Guns, AA	4—1·5 in (*38 mm*) 70 cal. ;
	4—37 mm ; 2—20 mm
Armour	sides 1·5—2 in (*38—50 mm*) ;
	turrets 1 in (*25 mm*) ;
	magazines 4 in (*100 mm*)
Boilers	8 Yarrow
Main engines	Parsons geared turbines
	92 000 shp ; 2 shafts
Speed, knots	31 max, 11 economical sea
Radius, miles	7 800 at 11 knots
Oil fuel, tons	2 794
Complement	1 000 (40 officers, 960 men)

This ship was designed by the late Sir Philip Watts on the basic pattern of the contemporary British heavy cruisers of the later "County" classes. From initial completion until 1952 she had trunked funnels, but she emerged from refit in 1953 with two separate funnels, this being a reversion to the original design which had never been carried out. L Band search radar.

TORPEDO TUBES. The twelve 21 inch torpedo tubes in four triple mountings were removed in 1960.

GUNNERY. Elevation of the 8 inch guns is 70 degrees.

NOMENCLATURE. *Canarias* is named after the Canary Islands. Rated as *Crucero* Type 2.

CLASS. Only sister ship *Baleares* was torpedoed and sunk on 6 Mar 1938 during the Spanish Civil War.

RESCINDMENT. Was to have been completely overhauled as Flagship of the Spanish Navy, under the Naval Modernisation Programme (US MAP). But a combined US/Spanish survey of the ship found that complete modernisation was not feasible in view of her nearly 40 years afloat. Modernisation plans were therefore cancelled.

DRAWING. Starboard elevation and plan. Redrawn in 1970. Scale 125 feet = 1 inch (1 : 1 500).

DISPOSALS
The "Galicia" Class cruisers, *Almirante Cervera*, *Galicia* and *Miguel de Cervantes* were stricken from the Navy List in 1966, the anti-aircraft cruiser *Mendez Nuñez* in 1963, and the light cruiser *Navarra* in 1956.

CANARIAS

1971, Spanish Navy, Official

CANARIAS

1970, Spanish Navy, Official

CANARIAS

1966, Spanish Navy, Official

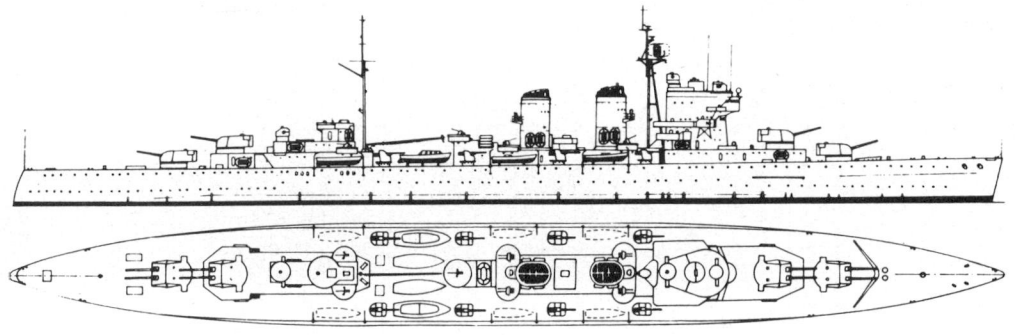

ANTI-SUBMARINE DESTROYERS (*Destructores Caza Submarinas*)

2 MODIFIED "OQUENDO" TYPE

Name	No.
MARQUÉS DE LA ENSENADA	D 43
ROGER DE LAURIA	D 42

Laid down	Launched		Completed
4 Sep 1951	15 July 1959	(D 43)	30 Aug 1970
4 Sep 1951	12 Nov 1958	(D 42)	22 Dec 1969

Displacement, tons	3 000 standard; 3 587 full load
Lenght, feet (*metres*)	391·5 (*119·3*)
Beam, feet (*metres*)	42·7 (*13·0*)
Draught, feet (*metres*)	18·4 (*5·6*)
Aircraft	1 anti-submarine helicopter
Guns	6—5 in (*127 mm*) 38 cal (3 twin)
A/S weapons	2 triple launchers for 324 mm torpedoes
Torpedo tubes	2—21 in (*533 mm*) single
Boilers	3 three-drum type
Main engines	2 Rateau-Bretagne geared turbines; 2 shafts; 6 000 shp
Speed, knots	31
Oil fuel, tons	673
Radius, miles	4 500 at 15 knots
Complement	300

Ordered at Ferrol in 1948. Originally of the same design as *Oquendo*, see next page. Towed to Cartagena for reconstruction to a new design. *Roger de Lauria* was re-launched after being lengthened and widened on 22 Aug 1967 and *Marqués de la Ensenada* on 2 Mar 1968. *Roger de Lauria* started trials on 30 May 1969 to join the fleet early in 1970. *Marqués de la Ensenada* started trials in Dec 1969, and both ships are in service in 1971.

RADAR
Search: SPS 40.
Tactical: Probably C Band.
Fire Control: GFCS 68 system, X Band.

8 "AUDAZ" CLASS

Displacement, tons	1 227 standard; 1 550 full load
Length, feet (*metres*)	295·2 (*90·0*) pp; 308·2 (*94·0*) oa
Beam, feet (*metres*)	30·5 (*9·3*)
Draught, feet (*metres*)	17·1 (*5·2*) max
Guns, AA	2—3 in (*76 mm*) 50 cal; 2—40 mm 70 cal,
A/S weapons	2 Hedgehogs; 8 mortars; 2 DC racks
Torpedo racks	2 side launching for A/S torpedoes (6 torpedoes)
Boilers	2 La Seine 3-drum type
Main engines	Rateau-Bretagne geared turbines; 2 shafts; 28 000 shp
Speed, knots	31·6 (see *Engineering*)
Radius, miles	3 200 at 14 knots
Oil fuel, tons	290
Complement	191

Based on the French "Le Fier" design. All built at Ferrol. Allocated D Pennant numbers in 1961, but still referred to officially and unofficially as fast frigates, see *Classification* note below.

MODERNISATION. Delivery dates after modernisation: *Audaz* 28 June 1961, *Furor* 9 Sep 1960, *Meteoro* 21 Feb 1963, *Osado* 21 Aug 1961, *Rayo* 21 Feb 1963. All fitted with US electronic and ASW equipment.

RADAR. Search: L Band. Fire Control: X Band.

GUNNERY. Before rearmament and modernisation these ships mounted 3—4·1 inch guns, 4—37 mm AA guns and 8—20 mm AA guns.

ENGINEERING. The boilers are in two compartments separated by the engine rooms. Steam is superheated to 375 degrees Fahrenheit. Working pressure is 500 lb. per sq in. Engines have developed 30 800 shp on trials and 32,500 shp max = 33 knots.

CLASSIFICATION. These ships were originally projected as conventional destroyers but their classification was changed to fast frigates in 1955, to anti-submarine frigates, in 1956, and to anti-submarine destroyers in 1961.

NOMENCLATURE. Meanings of names: *Audaz*, audacious; *Furor*, Fury; *Intrépido*, fearless; *Meteoro*, meteor; *Osado*, daring; *Rayo*, thunderbolt; *Relámpago*, lightning flash; *Temerario*, venturesome.

PHOTOGRAPHS. A photograph of *Osada* appears in the 1956-57 and 1957-58 editions, of *Rayo* in the 1956-57 to 1961-62 editions, of *Furor* and *Temerario* in the 1966-67 to 1969-70 editions and of *Meteoro* in the 1970-71 editions.

LOSS. Sister ship *Ariete* (battering ram) grounded on 25 Feb 1966 and was declared a total loss.

MARQUÉS DE LA ENSENADA — 1971, Spanish Navy, Official

ROGER DE LAURIA — 1970, Spanish Navy, Official

Name	No.	Laid down	Launched	Completed
AUDAZ	D 31	26 Sep 1945	24 Jan 1951	30 June 1953
FUROR	D 34	3 Aug 1945	24 Feb 1955	9 Sep 1960
INTRÉPIDO	D 38	14 July 1945	15 Feb 1961	25 Mar 1965
METEORO (ex-*Atrevido*)	D 33	3 Aug 1945	4 Sep 1951	30 Nov 1955
OSADO	D 32	3 Aug 1945	4 Sep 1951	25 Jan 1955
RAYO	D 35	3 Aug 1945	4 Sep 1951	25 Jan 1956
RELÁMPAGO	D 39	14 July 1945	26 Sep 1961	7 July 1965
TEMERARIO	D 37	14 July 1945	29 Mar 1960	16 Mar 1964

INTREPIDO — 1969, Spanish Navy, Official

AUDAZ — Official

Anti-Submarine Destroyers—continued

1 "OQUENDO" TYPE

Name	No.	Laid down	Launched	Completed
OQUENDO	D 41	15 June 1951	5 Sep 1956	22 Dec 1964

Displacement, tons	2 582 standard; 3 005 full load
Length, feet (metres)	382 (116·4)
Beam, feet (metres)	36·5 (11·1)
Draught, feet (metres)	12·5 (3·8)
Guns, surface	4—4·7 (120 mm) (2 twin)
Guns, AA	6—40 mm, 70 cal.
A/S weapons	2 Hedgehogs
Torpedo tubes	2 TT racks
Boilers	3 three-drum type
Main engines	2 Rateau-Bretagne geared turbines; 2 shafts; 60 000 shp
Speed, knots	32·4 max
Oil fuel, tons	659
Radius, miles	5 000 at 15 knots
Complement	Oquendo 249

Ordered at Ferrol in 1947. Oquendo was initially completed on 13 Sep 1960, and completed modernisation on 22 Dec 1964.

CONSTRUCTION. Designed as a conventional destroyer but modified during construction. Seven 21-inch torpedo tubes and two depth charge throwers were suppressed in favour of later anti-submarine weapons. Roger de Lauria and Marqués de la Ensenada, see previous page, were originally of the "Oquendo" design. Sister ships Bias de Laao, Blasco de Garay, Bonifaz, Gelmirez, Langara and Recalde were cancelled in 1953.

OQUENDO   1971, Spanish Navy, Official

RADAR. Search: Believed S Band. Tactical: X Band. Fire Control: X Band.

CLASSIFICATION. Re-classified as anti-submarine frigate in 1955, again re-rated as fast frigate in 1956, and as anti-submarine destroyer in 1961.

Name	No.	Builders	Laid down	Launched	Completed
ALCALA GALIANO (ex-USS Jarvis, DD 799)	D 24	Todd Pacific Shipyards	—	14 Feb 1944	3 June 1944
ALMIRANTE FERRANDIZ (ex-USS David W. Taylor DD 551)	D 22	Gulf SB Corpn, Chickasaw, Ala	12 June 1941	4 July 1942	18 Sep 1943
ALMIRANTE VALDÉS (ex-USS Converse, DD 509)	D 23	Bath Iron Works Corp, Maine	23 Feb 1942	30 Aug 1942	8 June 1943
JORGE JUAN (ex-USS McGowan, DD 678)	D 25	Federal SB & DD Co	—	14 Nov 1943	20 Dec 1943
LEPANTO (ex-USS Capps, DD 550)	D 21	Gulf SB Corpn, Chickasaw, Ala	12 June 1941	31 May 1942	23 June 1943

5 "LEPANTO" CLASS

Displacement, tons	2 080 standard; 2 750 normal; 3 050 standard
Length, feet (metres)	376·5 (114·8) oa
Beam, feet (metres)	39·5 (12·0)
Draught, feet (metres)	18 (5·5)
Guns, surface	D21, D22: 5—5 in (127 mm) 38 cal.; Others: 4—5 in (127 mm) single mounts
Guns, AA	D21, D22: 6—40 mm Bofors; D21: 12—20 mm Oerlikon (6 in D22); Others: 6—3 in (76 mm) 50 cal., 3 twin
A/S weapons	2 "Hedgehogs"; 6 DCT; 2 DC racks
Torpedo tubes	5—21 in (533 mm) quintupled
Torpedo racks	2 side launching for A/S torpedoes
Boilers	4 Babcock & Wilcox
Main engines	Allis Chalmers geared turbines; 2 shafts; 60 000 shp
Speed, knots	35, 16 economical sea
Radius, miles	5 800 at 16 knots
Oil fuel, tons	650
Complement	290 (17 officers, 273 men)

Former US fleet destroyers. Capps, renamed Lepanto, and David W. Taylor, renamed Almirante Ferrandiz, were the first units of the "Fletcher" class to be transferred to a foreign government: loaned to Spain for a period of five years, they were reconditioned at San Francisco, Cal, and there turned over to the Spanish Navy on 15 May 1957, sailing for Spain on 1 July 1957. Converse, renamed Almirante Valdes, was transferred to the Spanish Navy at Philadelphia on 1 July 1959. McGowan, renamed Jorge Juan, was transferred at Barcelona on 1 Dec 1960 and Jarvis at Philadelphia on 3 Nov 1960, both being of the Later "Fletcher" class and transferred on a five year renewable loan basis, under MAP. All five ships were allocated D pennant numbers in 1961.

RADAR. Search: SPS 6. Tactical: X Band. Fire Control: Obsolescent Metric type.

APPEARANCE. Alcala Galiano, Almirante Ferrandiz, and Jorge Juan have tripod mast, Almirante Valdés and Lepanto have pole mast. See also differing number of 5 inch guns in data table above.

PHOTOGRAPHS. A port bow oblique aerial view of Almirante Ferrandiz appears in the 1958-59 and 1959-60 editions, a port dead broadside surface view of Lepanto in the 1958-59 to 1961-62 editions, a starboard bow view of Almirante Valdes (as re-armed) in the 1960-61 edition, a starboard bow surface view of Alcalá Galiano in the 1961-62 to 1965-66 editions, a port broadside surface view of Almirante Ferrandiz in the 1962-63 to 1965-66 editions, a port quarter oblique surface view of Jorge Juan and a port near broadside-quarter view of Lepanto in the 1966-67 to 1968-69 editions, and a port rear broadside surface view of Almirante Valdes in the 1966-67 to 1969-70 editions.

JORGE JUAN (four 5 inch, tripod mast)   1969, Spanish Navy, Official

ALMIRANTE FERRANDIZ (five 5 inch, tripod mast)   1969, Spanish Navy, Official

LEPANTO (five 5 inch, pole mast)   1970, Spanish Navy, Official

2 "ALAVA" CLASS

Displacement, tons	1 842 standard; 2 287 full load
Length, feet (*metres*)	336·3 (*102·5*)
Beam, feet (*metres*)	31·5 (*9·6*)
Draught, feet (*metres*)	19·7 (*6·0*)
Guns, AA	3—3 in (*76 mm*) 50 cal, Mk 22; 3—40 mm, 70 cal
A/S weapons	2 "Hedgehogs"; 8 DC mortars; 6 DC racks
Torpedo racks	2 side launching, 6 A/S torpedoes
Boilers	3 Yarrow 3-drum type
Main engines	Parsons geared turbines; 2 shafts; 31 500 shp
Speed, knots	29 max, 12 economical sea
Radius, miles	3 500 at 16 knots
Oil fuel, tons	370
Complement	224 (17 officers, 207 men)

Ordered in 1936, but construction was held up by the Civil War. After being resumed, was again suspended in 1940, but restarted at Empresa Nacional Bazan in 1944.

RADAR. Search: L Band. Fire Control: X Band.

TORPEDO TUBES. These ships have had no tubes since modernisation in 1962. They formerly carried 6—21 inch (tripled), but now have torpedo racks.

GUNNERY. Before modernisation these ships mounted 4—4·7 inch, 6—37 mm AA and 3—20 mm AA guns.

PHOTOGRAPHS. A photograph of *Liniers* appears in the 1966-67 to 1969-70 editions.

DISPOSALS
All the pre-Second World War destroyers have now been disposed of. Of the "Churruca" Group 2, *Ciscar*, sunk in the Civil War in Oct 1937, but salved and refitted in 1938-39, grounded in fog and broke her back off El Ferrol on 17 Oct 1957 and was discarded in 1958. *Jorge Juan* was removed from the Navy List in 1959,

DESTROYERS (*Destructores*)

Name	No.	Builders	Laid down	Launched	Completed	Modernised
ALAVA	D 52 (ex-23)	Cartagena	21 Dec 1944	19 May 1947	21 Dec 1950	17 Jan 1962
LINIERS	D 51 (ex-21)	Cartagena	1 Jan 1945	1 May 1946	27 Jan 1951	18 Sep 1962

ALAVA   1970, Spanish Navy, Official

Escaño, Gravina and *Ulloa*'in 1964, *Almirante Antequera* in 1969 and *Almirante Miranda* in 1971.
Of "Churruca" Group 1, *Lepanto, Alcala Galiano* and *Almirante Valdes* were removed from the list in 1957,

Churruca in 1964, *Sanchez Barcaiztegui* in 1965, and *Jose Luiz Diez* in 1966.
Of the "*Alsedo*" class *Alsedo* and *Velasco* were removed from the list in 1957, and *Lazaga* in 1961.

FRIGATES (*Fragatas*)

LEGAZPI   1971, Spanish Navy, Official

5 NEW CONSTRUCTION

ANDALUCA	DEG 8	**BALEARES**	DEG 7
ASTURIAS	DEG 10	**CATALUNA**	DEG 9
		EXTREMADURA	DEG 11

Displacement, tons	2 640 standard; 3 420 full load
Length, feet (*metres*)	414·5 (*126·3*) oa
Beam, feet (*metres*)	44·2 (*13·5*)
Draught, feet (*metres*)	24·0 (*7·3*)
Aircraft	2 helicopters
Missile launchers	1 single for "Standard" missiles
Guns, dual purpose	1—5 in (*127 mm*) 54 cal
A/S weapons	ASROC; 2 twin torpedo launchers (Mk 32); 2 single torpedo launchers (Mk 25)
Boilers	2—1 200 psi (*84·4 kg/cm²*)
Main engines	1 geared turbine; 1 shaft; 35 000 shp
Speed, knots	27

In June 1966 Spain and the USA signed an agreement for the construction of five frigates in Spain with technical and material assistance by USA. Being built at El Ferrol del Caudillo. Generally similar to the US guided missile escort ships of the "Brooke" class. Equipped with weapons and electronic equipment furnished by USA, including anti-submarine warfare torpedoes and rockets. Fitted with three-dimensional search radar, one bow mounted sonar and one variable depth sonar. *Baleares* was laid down on 31 Oct 1958 and launched in Aug 1970, and *Andaluca* was laid down on 2 July 1969 and launched in 1971 when Cataluna was also expected to be launched.

4 "PIZARRO" CLASS

Displacement, tons	1 924 standard; 2 228 full load
Length, feet (*metres*)	279 (*85·0*) pp 312·5 (*95·30*) oa
Beam, feet (*metres*)	39·5 (*12·0*)
Draught, feet (*metres*)	17·7 (*5·4*)
Guns, surface	F41, F42: 2—5 in (*127 mm*) 38 cal. Others: 6—4·7 in (*120 mm*) 3 twin
Guns, AA	F41, F42: 4—40 mm, 70 cal. Others: 8—37 mm; 6—20 mm
A/S weapons	F41, F42: 2 "Hedgehogs"; 8 mortars; 2 racks Others: 4 DCT
Torpedo racks	F41, F42: 2 side launching for A/S
Boilers	2 Yarrow
Main engines	2 sets Parsons geared turbines; 2 shafts; 6 000 shp
Speed, knots	18·5
Radius, miles	4 000 at 14 knots
Oil fuel, tons	390
Complement	291 (14 officers, 277 men)

All built at Ferrol. Designed to carry 30 mines. Rated *Canoneras* until 1958 when re-rated *Fragatas*. Allocated F pennant numbers in 1961. *Legazpi* and *Vicente Yañez Pinzon* completed modernisation on 14 Jan and 25 Mar 1960 respectively. Of four sister ships *Martin Aloñso Pinzon* and *Pizarro* were discarded in 1968, and *Magallanes* and *Vasco Nuñez de Balboa* were officially removed from the effective list in 1971.

VICENTE YAÑEZ PINZON   1971, Spanish Navy, Official

Name	No.	Launched	Completed
HERNAN CORTES	F 32	3 Aug 1944	18 Sep 1947
LEGAZPI	F 42	8 Aug 1944	8 Aug 1951
SARMIENTO DE GAMBOA	F 36	8 Aug 1944	2 May 1950
VICENTE YAÑEZ PINZON	F 41	3 Aug 1944	5 Aug 1949

SARMIENTO DE GAMBOA   1971, Spanish Navy, Official

FRIGATE MINELAYERS (*Minadores*)

2 "EOLO" CLASS

Name	No.	Launched	Completed
EOLO	F 21	30 Sep 1939	1 Jan 1942
TRITON	F 22	26 Feb 1940	18 Oct 1943

Displacement, tons	1 723 standard; 1 942 full load
Length, feet (*metres*)	291·7 (*88·9*) oa
Beam, feet (*metres*)	38·5 (*11·7*)
Draught, feet (*metres*)	17·7 (*5·4*) max
Guns, dual purpose	4—4·1 in (*105 mm*)
Guns, AA	4—37 mm
A/S	2 DCT
Mines	Stowage for 170 *Eolo*, 180
Boilers	2 Yarrow
Main engines	Parsons geared turbines 5 000 shp; 2 shafts
Speed, knots	19·5 max, 12 economical sea
Oil fuel (tons)	300
Complement	224 (9 officers, 215 men)

TRITON   *1970, Spanish Navy, Official*

Both built by the Sociadad Española de Construccion Naval, Ferrol. Dual purpose frigates and minelayers. Allocated F pennant numbers in 1961. A photograph of *Eolo* appears in the 1967-68 to 1969-70 editions.

4 "JUPITER" CLASS

Name	No.	Launched	Completed
JUPITER	F 11	14 Sep 1935	1937
MARTE	F 01	19 June 1936	1937
NEPTUNO	F 02	17 Dec 1937	1939
VULCANO	F 12	12 Oct 1935	1937

Displacement, tons	2 103 standard; 2 245 full load
Length, feet (*metres*)	302·8 (*92·3*) pp; 328 (*100·0*) oa
Beam, feet (*metres*)	41·5 (*12·6*)
Draught, feet (*metres*)	11·5 (*3·5*)
Guns, surface	F 01 and F 02 only: 4—4·7 in (*120 mm*)
Guns, AA	F 01: 4—2·5 i n (*63 mm*); 4—20 mm; F 02: 4—37 mm; 3—20 mm F 11 and F 12 as modernised:— 4—3 in (*76 mm*) Mk 26, single; 4—40 mm, 70 cal
A/S weapons	F 11 and F 12 as modernised:— 2 "Hedgehogs"; 8 mortars; 2 DC racks
Mines	Stowage for 264 but normally less
Boilers	2 Yarrow
Main engines	2 sets Parsons geared turbines; 2 shafts; 5 000 shp
Speed, knots	17·4 max, 10 economical sea
Oil fuel, tons	280
Complement	243 (16 officers, 227 men)

All built by the Sociedad Española de Construccion Naval, Ferrol. Multi-purpose frigates or gunboats and cruising type minelayers. *Neptuno* is midshipmen's training ship. The modernisation of *Jupiter* with lattice mast and four 3-inch guns was completed on 28 Oct 1960, and of *Vulcano* on 28 Feb 1961. All allocated F pennant numbers in 1961.

PHOTOGRAPHS. A port bow view of *Jupiter* appears in the 1961-62 editions, a port broadside view of *Vulcano* in the 1962-63 to 1965-66 editions, a starboard quarter view of *Jupiter* in the 1964-65 and 1965-66 editions, a starboard quarter view of *Neptuno* in the 1966-67 and 1967-68 editions, a starboard quarter view of *Vulcano* in the 1966-67 to 1968-69 editions, a port bow view of *Neptuno* in the 1968-69 to 1970-71 editions.

DISPOSALS
The frigate *Canovas del Castillo* was stricken from the list in 1959, and the larger frigate *Calvo Sotelo* (ex-*Zacatecas*) in 1957.

VULCANO   *1971, Spanish Navy, Official*

JUPITER   *1969, Spanish Navy, Official*

5 "ATREVIDA" CLASS

Displacement, tons	997 standard; 1 135 full load
Length, feet (*metres*)	247·8 (*75·5*) oa
Beam, feet (*metres*)	33·5 (*10·2*)
Draught, feet (*metres*)	9·8 (*3·0*)
Guns, dual purpose	1—3 in (*76 mm*) 50 cal Mk 26
Guns, AA	3—40 mm, 70 cal
A/S weapons	2 Hedgehogs; 8 mortars; 2 DC racks
Mines	20 can be carried
Main engines	Sulzer diesels; 2 shafts; 3 200 bhp
Speed, knots	18·5 max
Radius, miles	8 000 at 10 knots
Oil fuel, tons	100
Complement	113

Atrevida commissioned on 19 Aug 1954. All have been modernised since 1959, *Princesa* being delivered on 3 Oct 1959, *Nautilus* on 15 Dec 1959, *Diana* on 13 May 1960, *Atrevida* on 14 June 1960 and *Villa de Bilbao* on 2 July 1960. Allocated F pennant numbers in 1961.

PHOTOGRAPHS. A photograph of *Diana* rearmed with lattice mast appears in the 1960-61 edition, of *Villa de Bilbao* as modernised in the 1961-62 to 1965-66 editions, of *Princesa* in the 1967-68 and 1968-69 editions, of *Nautilus* in the 1969-70 and 1970-71 editions.

RECENT DISPOSAL
The sixth ship of this class *Descubierta*, F 51 was officially removed from the effective list in 1971.

CORVETTES (*Corbetas*)

Name	No.	Laid down	Launched	Completed
ATREVIDA	F 61	26 June 1950	2 Dec 1952	19 Aug 1954
DIANA	F 63	27 July 1953	29 Apr 1955	13 May 1960
NAUTILUS	F 64	27 July 1953	23 Aug 1956	15 Dec 1959
PRINCESA	F 62	18 Mar 1953	31 Mar 1956	3 Oct 1959
VILLA DE BILBAO	F 65	18 Mar 1953	19 Feb 1958	2 July 1960

ATREVIDA   *1971, Michael D. J. Lennon*

FLEET MINESWEEPERS (*Dragaminas*)

7 "ALMANZORA" CLASS

Name	No.	Builders	Launched	Completed	Modernised
ALMANZORA	M 14	Cartagena	27 July 1953	Nov 1954	20 May 1960
EO	M 17	Cadiz	22 Sep 1953	Mar 1955	22 Mar 1961
EUME	M 13	Cartagena	27 July 1953	Dec 1953	20 July 1960
GUADALHORCE	M 16	Cartagena	18 Feb 1953	Dec 1953	18 Feb 1960
GUARDIARO	M 11	Cartagena	26 June 1950	Apr 1953	14 Dec 1959
NAVIA	M 15	Cadiz	28 July 1953	Mar 1955	22 Nov 1960
TINTO	M 12	Cartagena	26 June 1950	May 1953	28 July 1959

Displacement, tons	671 standard; 770 full load
Dimensions, feet	243·8 × 33·5 × 12·3 max
Guns	2—20 mm AA
Main engines	Triple expansion and exhaust turbines; 2 shafts; 2 400 hp = 16 knots
Boilers	2 Yarrow
Oil fuel, tons	90
Radius, miles	1 000 at 6 knots
Complement	79

Formerly DM 11, 13, 10, 14, 8, 12, 9, respectively. Allocated new M pennant numbers in 1961. Until modernisation the armament also included one 3·5 in gun and one 37 mm AA gun. A photograph of *Eume* appears in the 1962-63 and 1963-64 editions, of *Almanzora* in the 1964-65 to 1966-67 editions, of *Navia* in the 1967-68 and 1968-69 editions, and of *Eo* in the 1969-70 edition.

GUARDIARO   *1970, Spanish Navy, Official*

6 "BIDASOA" CLASS

Name	No.	Builders	Launched	Completed
BIDASOA	M 01	Cartagena	15 Sep 1943	5 Apr 1946
LEREZ	M 03	Cartagena	21 Dec 1944	12 Feb 1947
NERVION	M 02	Cartagena	15 Apr 1944	4 June 1946
SEGURA	M 05	Cartagena	6 Oct 1948	20 Dec 1948
TAMBRE	M 04	El Ferrol	18 Oct 1944	21 July 1946
TER	M 06	Cartagena	18 Feb 1948	22 July 1948

Displacement, tons	555 standard; 470 full load
Dimensions, feet	200·5 × 27·9 × 12·1 max
Guns	1—4·1 in; 1—37 mm AA; 2—20 mm AA
Main engines	Triple expansion and exhaust turbines; 2 shafts; 2 400 hp = 16·5 knots
Boilers	2 Yarrow
Fuel, tons	195 coal
Radius, miles	1 060 at 10 knots
Complement	82

German M-Boote 40 type. Named after rivers. Formerly DM 1, 5, 3, 2, 6, 4, 7, respectively. Allocated new M pennant numbers in 1961. *Guadalete*, of this class, which was employed as a coastguard vessel, sank in a gale 20 miles east of Gibraltar on 25 Mar 1954. A photograph of *Bidasoa* appears in the 1964-65 to 1967-68 editions, and of *Tambre* in the 1968-69 and 1969-70 editions.

LEREZ   *1970, Spanish Navy, Official*

PATROL BOATS

CABO FRADERA

Displacement, tons	25 standard; 28 full load
Dimensions, feet	58·5 × 14 × 5·2
Main engines	2 diesels; 760 bhp = 12 knots
Complement	9

Built at La Carraca, in 1963. (River patrol boat *Cabo Fradera* was disposed of)

COASTAL MINESWEEPERS
12 Ex-US AMS TYPE

DUERO (ex-*Spoonbill*, MSC 202)	M 28		NALÓN (ex-*AMS* 139)	M 21
EBRO (ex-*MSC* 269)	M 26		ODIEL (ex-*MSC* 288)	M 32
GENIL (ex-*MSC* 279)	M 31		SIL (ex-*Redwing*, MSC 200)	M 29
JUCAR (ex-*AMS* 220)	M 23		TAJO (ex-*MSC* 287)	M 30
LLOBREGAT (ex-*AMS* 143)	M 22		TURIA (ex-*AMS* 130)	M 27
MIÑO (ex-*AMS* 266)	M 22		ULLA (ex-*AMS* 265)	M 24

Displacement, tons	355 standard; 384 full load
Dimensions, feet	138 pp; 144 oa × 27·2 × 8
Guns	1—20 mm AA
Main engines	2 diesels; 2 shafts; 900 bhp = 14 knots
Oil fuel, tons	30
Radius, miles	2 700 at 10 knots
Complement	39

Non-magnetic minesweepers transferred from the USA, *Nalón* on 16 Feb 1954, *Llobregat* on 5 Nov 1954, *Turia* on 1 June 1955, *Jucar* on 22 June 1956, *Ulla* on 24 July 1956, *Miño* on 25 Oct 1956, *Redwing* and *Spoonbill* on 16 June 1959, *Ebro* on 19 Dec 1958, *Genil* on 11 Sep 1959, *Tajo* on 9 July 1959 and *Odiel* on 9 Oct 1959. A photograph of *Odiel* appears in the 1961-62 edition, of *Tajo* in the 1968-69 edition and of *Llobregat* in the 1969-70 edition.

EBRO   *1970, Spanish Navy, Official*

ULLA, Class B, with mainmast   *1971, Spanish Navy, Official*

PATROL VESSELS (*Patrulleros*)

CANDIDO PEREZ (ex-*SC* 679)

Displacement, tons	106 standard; 138 full load
Dimensions, feet	107·5 wl; 111 oa × 19 × 7
Guns	1—40 mm AA; 3—20 mm
A/S weapons	2 DCT
Main engines	GM diesels; 2 shafts; 1 000 bhp = 15·6 knots
Radius, miles	2 300

Former United States submarine chaser of the "110 ft" wooden type. Built by Walter E. Abrams Shipyard, Inc. Laid down on 4 mar 1942. Launched on 29 Aug 1942. Completed on 19 Dec 1942. Transferred to Spain in 1957.

RECENT DISPOSAL
The old patrol vessel, former US submarine chaser, *Javier Quiroga* (ex-*Blue Arrow* ex-USS *PC* 1211), was officially removed from the effective list in 1971.

CANDIDO PEREZ   *Spanish Navy, Official*

LANDING SHIPS (*Borcazas de Desembarco*)

LSM 1 (ex-USS *LSM* 329) **LSM 2** (ex-USS *LSM* 331) **LSM 3** (ex-USS *LSM* 343)

Displacement, tons	930 standard ; 1 094 full load
Dimensions, feet	196·5 wl × 203·5 oa × 34·5 × 8·3
Guns	1—40 mm AA ; 2—40 mm AA
Main engines	2 diesels ; 2 shafts ; 3 600 bhp = 12·5 knots
Complement	59

Medium landing ships transferred at Bremerton, Washington, on 25 Mar 1960. A photograph of LSM 2 appears in the 1965-66 to 1967-68 editions.

LSM 3   *1969, Official*

LANDING CRAFT

BDK 1   **BDK 2**   **BDK 3**   **BDK 4**   **BDK 5**

Displacement, tons	481 standard ; 868 full load
Dimensions, feet	187 × 38·8 × 5·5
Main engines	2 diesels ; 1 000 bhp = 7 knots

Built by Bazan, Ferrol. Of British LCT (4) Type, (There are also 13 LCMs (Lanchas de Desembarco), LCM 1 to LCM 13, and 5 LCPs, LCP 1 to LCP 5).

BDK 5   *1969, Spanish Navy, Official*

BDK 1   *1971, Spanish Navy, Official*

LANDING CRAFT

BDK 6   **BDK 7**   **BDK 8**

Displacement, tons	315 standard ; 665 full load
Dimensions, feet	193·5 × 39 × 5
Guns	1—20 mm AA ; 2—12·7 mm MG
Main engines	2 diesels ; 1 040 bhp = 9·5 knots
Radius, miles	1 500
Complement	17

Landing craft of the French EDIC type built at La Carraca. Completed in Dec 1966.

K 6   *1970, Spanish Navy, Official*

SURVEY SHIPS (*Buques Hidrografos*)

POLLUX   *1971, Spanish Navy, Official*

CASTOR H 4   **POLLUX** H 5

Displacement, tons	327 standard ; 383 full load
Dimensions, feet	111 pp ; 125·9 oa × 24·9 × 8·9
Main engines	1 Sulzer 4TD-36 diesel ; 720 hp = 11·7 knots
Radius, miles	3 620
Complement	36

Built by E. N. Bazan La Carraca. Completed on 10 Nov 1966 and 6 Dec 1966.

CASTOR   *1970, Spanish Navy, Official*

TOFINO

Displacement, tons	998 standard ; 1 255 full load
Dimensions, feet	224·5 × 35 × 11
Guns	1—37 mm
Main engines	Triple expansion ; 2 shafts ; 810 ihp = 12·5 knots
Boilers	2 Yarrow
Complement	181

Built by Ferrol. Launched on 21 Aug 1933. Sister ship *Malaspina* (ex-*Bausa*) was officially deleted form the effective list in 1971.

TOFINO   *1970, Professor Alfredo Aguileru*

JUAN DE LA COSA (ex-*Artabro*)

Displacement, tons	770 standard ; 1 100 full load
Dimensions, feet	188 × 35·5 × 8·8
Main engines	B. & W diesels ; electric drive ; 500 bhp = 9 knots

Launched by UNL, Valence in 1935. The small survey craft *H 2* and *H 3* (see photograph in the 1969-70 edition) were withdrawn from the active list in 1969-70.

JUAN DE LA COSA   *1969, Spanish Navy, Official*

TORPEDO BOATS (Lanchas Torpederas)

LT 30	LT 31	LT 32

Displacement, tons	100 standard; 116 full load
Dimensions, feet	114 × 16·8 × 5
Guns	1—20 mm AA
Tubes	2—21 in
Main engines	3 diesel; 3 shafts; 7 500 bhp = 41 knots
Oil fuel, tons	20
Radius, miles	650 at 30 knots
Complement	26

Built at La Carraca, Cadiz, to the design of Lurssens of Bremen. LT 31 was commissioned on 21 July 1956. L 32 was launched in 1956, (photograph in 1960-61 to 1966-67 editions). LT 27, LT 28 and LT 29 were discarded in 1963.

LT 31   1970, Spanish Navy, Official

ANTI-SUBMARINE LAUNCHES
(Launches Antisubmarinas)

LAS 10	LAS 11	LAS 12

Displacement, tons	63 normal, full load
Dimensions, feet	78·0 pp; 83·3 oa × 16·1 × 6·6
Guns	1—20 mm AA; 1—8 mm MG
Missile launchers	2 MR 20 for light rockets of "Hedgehog" type
A/S weapons	8 small depth charges
Speed, knots	15

Seaward defence vessels for surveillance of shipping lanes. Of wooden hull construction. First units built by F.N. Bazan, Cadiz in 1963-64. There are also five smaller launcher LBI 1 to LBI 5, of 25 tons, 16 knots, 46·0 × 15·4 feet.

LAS 10   1971, Official

DOCK SHIP

SAN MARCOS LSD 25

To be formally transferred from USA to Spain in July 1971 and after rehabilitation to join the fleet in 1972.

PATROL VESSELS (Guardacostas)

CENTINELA		SERVIOLA
Displacement, tons	255 standard; 282 full load	
Dimensions, feet	117·5 × 22·5 × 9·8	
Guns	2—37 mm	
Main engines	1 diesel; 430 bhp = 12 knots	

Completed at Ferrol, in 1953. Rated as Fishery Protection Vessels (Guardapescas).

1969, Spanish Navy, Official   SERVIOLA

Patrol Vessels—continued

PROCYON   1971, Spanish Navy, Official

PEGASO		PROCYON
Displacement, tons	436 standard; 498 full load	
Dimensions, feet	137·8 × 27 × 9·5	
Guns	2—20 mm AA	
Main engines	1 shaft; 532 bhp = 12 knots	

Both commissioned at Cartegena in Jan 1951. Rated as Coastguard Vessels (Guardacostas). Photograph of Procyon in the 1966-67 to 1969-70 editions.

PEGASO   1970 Spanish Navy, Official

AZOR

Displacement, tons	442 standard; 486 full load
Dimensions, feet	153 × 25·2 × 12·5
Main engines	2 diesels; 1 200 bhp = 12 knots

Fishery Protection Launch (Lancha Guardapescas). Used as the Caudillo's yacht.

AZOR   1969, Spanish Navy, Official

CIES		SALVORA
Displacement, tons	180 standard; 275 full load	
Dimensions, feet	107 × 20·5 × 9	
Guns	1 MG	
Main engines	1 Sulzer diesel; 400 bhp = 12 knots	

Purchased in Dec 1952. Rated as Fishery Protection Vessels (Guardapescas).

SALVORA   1969, Spanish Navy, Official

The patrol vessels, former "Mersey" type trawlers, Arcila (ex-William Doak), rated as a guardacosta, and Xauen (ex-Henry Cramwell), as an oceanographica, were officially deleted from the effective list in 1970.

TRANSPORTS

ALMIRANTE LOBO (ex-*Torrelaguna*)

Displacement, tons	5 662 standard ; 8 038 full load
Dimensions, feet	362·5 × 48·2 × 25·7
Guns	2—37 mm, 60 cal
Main engines	1 triple expansion ; 2 000 ihp = 12 knots

Ex-cargo vessel. Built at Astilleros Echevarrieta, Cadiz. Commissioned 4 Oct **1954.**

ALMIRANTE LOBO   *Official*

ARAGON (ex-USS *Noble*), AAP 218, TA 11

Displacement, tons	6 720 light ; 12 450 full load
Dimensions, feet	436·5 wl ; 455 oa × 63·5 × 24 max
Main engines	Geared turbines ; 8 500 shp = 17 knots
Boilers	2 Babcock & Wilcox

Former US Attack Transport, transferred at San Francisco on 19 Dec 1964.

ARAGON   *1971, Michael D. J. Lennon*

CASTILLA (ex-USS *Achernar*, AKA 53) TA 21

Displacement, tons	7,430 light ; 11 416 full load
Dimensions, feet	435 wl ; 457·8 oa × 63 × 24
Guns	1—5 in, 38 cal ; 8—40 mm, 60 cal
Main engines	2 GE geared turbines ; 12 000 shp = 16 knots
Boilers	2 Foster-Wheeler

Former US Attack Cargo Ship, transferred at New York on 2 Feb 1965.

CASTILLA   *1970, Spanish Navy, Official*

OILERS

TEIDE

Displacement, tons	2 747 light ; 8 030 full load
Dimensions, feet	385·5 × 48·5 × 20·3
Guns	1—4·1 in
Main engines	2 diesels ; 3 360 bhp = 12 knots

Ordered from Factoria de Bazan, Cartegena, in December 1952. Laid down on 11 Nov 1954. Launched on 20 June 1955. In service October 1956.

TEIDE   *1968. Spanish Navy, Official*

PP 1   **PP 2**

Displacement, tons	470
Dimensions, feet	138 pp ; 147·5 oa × 25 × 9·5
Main engines	Deutz diesel ; 220 bhp = 10 knots
Complement	12

Both built at Santander and launched in 1939. Small service tankers. The oiler *Pluton* (ex-*Campilo*) BP 01, was officially removed from the effective list in 1971.

TRAINING SHIP   (*Buque-Escuela*)

JUAN SEBASTIAN DE ELCANO

Displacement, tons	3 420 standard ; 3 754 full load
Dimensions, feet	269·2 pp ; 308·5 oa × 43 × 23 full load
Guns	2—37 mm
Main engines	1 Sulzer diesel ; 1 shaft ; 1 500 bhp = 9·5 knots
Oil fuel, tons	230
Endurance, miles	10,000 at 9·5 knots
Complement	224 + 80 cadets

Four-masted schooner. Named after the first circumnavigator of the world (1519-26) who succeeded to the command of the expedition led by Magallanes after the latter's death. Built by Echevarrieta Yard, Cadiz. Launched on 5 Mar 1927. Completed in 1928. A photograph appears in the 1952-53 to 1957-58 editions.

JUAN SEBASTIAN DE ELCANO   *1969, Spanish Navy, Official*

COASTAL LAUNCHES

V 2	Displacement :	22	tons	Guns : 1—7	mm	Speed : 6·7	knots
V 3	Displacement :	10	tons	Guns : 1—7	mm	Speed : 7·5	knots
V 4	Displacement :	65	tons	Guns : 1—7	mm	Speed : 9	knots
V 5	Displacement :	4·5	tons	Guns : 1—7	mm	Speed : 5	knots
V 7	Displacement :	20	tons	Guns : 1—7	mm	Speed : 8·5	knots
V 8	Displacement :	26·5	tons	Guns : 1—7	mm	Speed : 7·8	knots
V 9	Displacement :	15·6	tons	Guns : 1—7	mm	Speed : 9	knots
V 10	Displacement :	11·69	tons	Guns : 1—7	mm	Speed : 9·5	knots
V 11	Displacement :	11·69	tons	Guns : 1—7	mm	Speed : 9·5	knots
V 12	Displacement :	28	tons	Guns : 1—7	mm	Speed : 7·8	knots
V 13	Displacement :	45·1	tons	Guns : 1—7	mm	Speed : 7·8	knots
V 17	Displacement :	110·9	tons	Guns : 1—13	mm	Speed : 10·5	knots
V 18	Displacement :	116	tons	Guns : 1—13	mm	Speed : 6	knots
V 21	Displacement :	16	tons	Guns : 1—13	mm	Speed : 17·6	knots

LANZON (V 18)   *1969, Spanish Navy, Official*

There are also V 1 and V 6. Coastal launches employed on surveillance and fishery protection duties, lanchos guardapescas, except V 17, rated as patrullero. V 4 is named *Alcatraz*, V 12 *Esturian* and V 18 *Lanzon*. V 19 was officially stricken from the list in 1963, and V 20 in 1965.

V 21   *1969, Spanish Navy, Official*

BOOM DEFENCE VESSEL (Cala-Redes)

CR 1 (ex-G 6)

Displacement, tons	630 standard; 831 full load
Dimensions, feet	165·5 × 34 × 10·5
Guns	1—40 mm AA; 1—20 mm AA
Main engines	2 diesels with electric drive; 1 500 bhp = 12 knots

Built by Penhoët, France, as a US off-shore order. Launched on 28 Sep 1954. Transferred from the US in 1955 under MDAP.

CR 1   *Spanish Navy, Official*

AUXILIARY PATROL VESSELS

RR 10   RR 19   RR 20   RR 28   R 29

Displacement, tons	364 standard; 498 full load
Dimensions, feet	124 × 29 × 10
Guns	1—47 mm; 1—20 mm AA
Main engines	Triple expansion; 1 shaft; 800 ihp = 11·5 knots
Coal, tons	200
Radius, miles	620 at 10 knots

Former tugs. All launched in 1941-42. A photograph appears in the 1957-58 edition.

RR 19   *1969, Spanish Navy, Official*

TUGS (Remolcadores)

RR 50   RR 51   RR 52   RR 53   RR 54   RR 55

Displacement, tons	227
Dimensions, feet	91·2 × 23 × 11
Main engines	1 shaft; 1 400 shp

All built at Cartagena for naval service in 1963-66.

BS 1 (ex-RA 6)   **RA 4**   **RA 5**

Displacement, tons	951 standard; 1 069 full load
Dimensions, feet	183·5 × 32·8 × 15·8
Main engines	2 Sulzer diesels; 3 200 bhp = 15 knots

All built at La Carraca, in 1963. RA 6 was renumbered BS 1 when she became a frogman base.

BS 1 (ex-RA 6)   *1969, courtesy Professor Alfredo Aguilera*

Tugs—continued

RA 1   RA 2

Displacement, tons	757 standard; 1 039 full load
Dimensions, feet	184 × 33·5 × 12
Guns	2 MG
Main engines	2 Sulzer diesels; 3 200 bhp = 15 knots

Ordered in 1949. Built at Factoria de Bazan, Cartagena. Launched on 2 Sep 1954 and 5 Oct 1954, commissioned on 9 July 1955 and 12 Sep 1955, respectively.

RAI   *1970, Spanish Navy, Official*

RA 2   *1969, Spanish Navy, Official*

RA 3 (ex-Metinda III)

Displacement, tons	762 standard; 1 080 full load
Dimensions, feet	137 × 33·1 × 15·5
Main engines	Triple expansion; 12 knots max; 10 knots service

RA 3   *1969, Official*

RR 15   RR 16

Displacement, tons	434
Dimensions, feet	124 × 27·5 × 10
Main engines	800 ihp = 11·5 knots

Of this class RR 17 was officially deleted from the Navy List in 1968.

RR 11

Displacement, tons	279
Dimensions, feet	111·5 × 20 × 10
Main engines	600 ihp = 11 knots

SWEDEN

Administration

Commander-in-Chief of the Navy (including Coast Artillery):
Vice-Admiral Bengt Lundvall

President of the Navy Technical and Administrative Board:
Rear-Admiral Gunnar Grandin

Commander-in-Chief of Active Fleet:
Rear-Admiral Christer Kierkegaard

Chief of Naval Staff:
Major-General Gunnar Eklund

Chief of Staff Active Fleet:
Commodore Alf Berggren

Diplomatic Representation

Naval Attaché in London:
Captain N. U. Rydström

Naval Attaché in Washington:
Commodore N. L. Lindgren

Strength of the Fleet

22 Submarines (Diesel Powered)
8 Destroyers
6 Fast Anti-submarine Frigates
1 Minelayer and Submarine Depot Ship
1 Minelayer and Sea Training Ship
1 Submarine Support Ship
42 Torpedo Boats
18 Coastal Minesweepers (Non-Magnetic)
17 Inshore Minesweepers
9 Mining Tenders
1 Staff Communications Ship
2 Training Ships
23 Patrol Boats
7 Surveying Vessels
1 Salvage Vessel
2 Mine Transports
57 Landing Craft
5 Icebreakers
14 Support Ships and Service Craft

Personnel

1971: Active list of Navy and Coast Artillery:
16 000 officers and men, including conscripts

New Construction Programme

5 Conventional Submarines (New design A14 Type)
2 Anti-submarine Frigates (Rescinded 1971)
1 Minelayer and Submarine Depot Ship
12 Torpedo Boats (Modified T 131 type) Building
8 Fast Gunboats (New Design)
3 Coastal Minesweepers (Modified M 68 type)
1 Icebreaker (Diesel Electric)

Navy Estimates

kr.	kr.
1960-61: 389 500 000	1965-66: 532 770 000
1962-61: 409 000 000	1966-67: 652 300 000
1962-63: 423 000 000	1967-68: 672 000 000
1963-64: 469 000 000	1968-69: 670 000 000
1964-65: 490 250 000	1969-70: 722 000 000
	1970-71: 713 000 000

Mercantile Marine

Lloyd's Register of Shipping:
995 vessels of 4 920 704 tons gross

Scale: 150 feet = 1 inch (1 : 1 800)

OSTERGOTLAND *Class*

KARLSKRONA

HALLAND *Class*

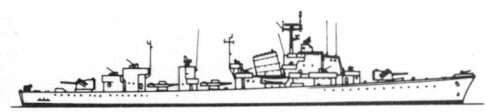

ÖLAND

VISBY *Class*

MODE

UPPLAND

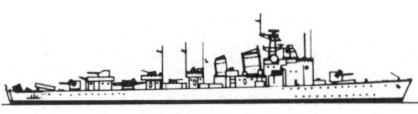

KALMAR

ÄLVSNABBEN

SJOBJORNEN   *1969, Royal Swedish Navy, Official*

NORDKAPAREN   *1969, Official*

SUBMARINES

NEW CONSTRUCTION
5 IMPROVED "A 14" CLASS

Displacement, tons	1 125 submerged
Length, feet (*metres*)	167·3 (*51·0*)
Beam, feet (*metres*)	20·0 (*6·1*)
Draught, feet (*metres*)	16·7 (*5·1*)
Torpedo tubes	21 in (*533 mm*)
Main engines	Diesels, electric motors

Five more submarines of a streamlined, long-range type, are included in the new construction programme. They will be conventional but with engines enabling them to stay submerged for a long time.

SJÖBJÖRNEN   *1971, Royal Swedish Navy, Official*

5 "SJOORMEN" CLASS

Name	Builders	Launched	Completed
SJÖORMEN	Kockums	25 Jan 67	31 July 67
SJÖLEJONET	Kockums	29 June 67	16 Dec 68
SJÖHUNDEN	Kockums	21 Mar 68	25 June 69
SJÖHÄSTEN	Karlskrona	6 Aug 68	15 Sep 69
SJÖBJÖRNEN	Karlskrona	9 Jan 68	28 Feb 69

Displacement, tons	700 standard; 800 surface; 1 110 submerged
Length, feet (*metres*)	167·3 (*51*)
Beam, feet (*metres*)	20 (*6·1*)
Draught, feet (*metres*)	19·7 (*6·0*)
Torpedo tubes	21 in (*533 mm*)
Main engines	Diesels; electric motors; 1 large 5-bladed propeller
Complement	23

Karlskrona is now a civilian yard. *Sjöbjörnen* means Seabea; *Sjöormen* Seaserpent, *Sjöhästen* Seahorse *Sjöhunden* Seadog, and *Sjölejonet* Sealion. Conning tower letters: Sor, Sbj, She, Shu, Sle.

SJÖORMEN   *1968, Royal Swedish Navy, Official*

SPRINGAREN   *1968, Royal Swedish Navy, Official*

6 "DRAKEN" CLASS

Name	Builders	Launched	Completed
DELFINEN	Karlskrona	7 Mar 61	7 June 62
DRAKEN	Kockums	1 Apr 60	4 Apr 62
GRIPEN	Karlskrona	31 May 60	28 Apr 62
NORDKAPAREN	Kockums	8 Mar 61	4 Apr 62
SPRINGAREN	Kockums	31 Aug 61	7 Nov 62
VARGEN	Kockums	20 May 60	15 Nov 61

Displacement, tons	770 standard; 835 surface
Length, feet (*metres*)	229·7 (*70*)
Beam, feet (*metres*)	16·7 (*5·1*)
Draught, feet (*metres*)	16·7 (*5·1*)
Torpedo tubes	4—21 in (*533 mm*) bow
Main engines	Diesels; electric motors
Speed, knots	16·75 surface; 25 submerged
Complement	36

These six submarines have fast-diving capabilities.

NOMENCLATURE. *Draken* means Dragon, *Gripen* Griffon, *Vargen* Wolf.

APPEARANCE. Distinctive letters painted on the conning tower are: De. *Delfinen*; Dra. *Draken*; Gri. *Gripen*; Nor. *Nordkaparen*; Spr. *Springaren*. Vgn. *Vargen*.

PHOTOGRAPHS. A photograph of *Draken* appears in the 1962-63 to 1964-65 editions, of *Gripen* in the 1967-68 and 1968-69 editions, and of *Vargen* in the 1969-70 edition.

NORDKAPAREN   *1971, Royal Swedish Navy, Official*

DELFINEN   *1969, Royal Swedish Navy, Official*

Submarines—continued

6 "HAJEN" CLASS

Name	Builders	Launched	Completed
BÄVERN	Kockums	11 Dec 1954	29 May 1957
HAJEN	Karlskrona	21 Apr 1955	28 Feb 1957
ILLERN	Kockums	3 Oct 1955	31 Aug 1957
SÄLEN	Kockums	14 Nov 1957	8 Apr 1959
UTTERN	Kockums	3 Feb 1958	31 Aug 1960
VALEN	Kockums	14 Nov 1958	4 Mar 1959

Displacement, tons	720 standard; 785 surface
Length, feet (metres)	216·5 (64·5)
Beam, feet (metres)	16·7 (5·1)
Draught, feet (metres)	14·8 (4·5)
Guns, AA	1—20 mm
Torpedo tubes	4—21 in (533 mm) bow (8 torpedoes)
Main engines	SEMT-Pielstick diesels; 1 700 bhp; Electric motors; electric drive on surface
Speed, knots	16 on surface, 20 submerged
Complement	44

All built by Kockums Mékaniska Verkstads Aktiebolag, Malmo, except *Valen* built by the Royal Swedish Naval Dockyard, Karlskrona.

OPERATIONAL. Equipped with Schnorkel, and have fast-diving capabilities.

NOMENCLATURE. *Bävern* means Beaver, *Hajen* Shark, *Illern* Polecat, *Sälen* Seal, *Uttern* Otter and *Valen* Whale.

APPEARANCE. Distinctive letters painted on the conning tower are: Bav, *Bävern*; H j, *Hajen*; Iln *Illern*; Sa, *Sälen*; Utn, *Uttern*; Val, *Valen*.

PHOTOGRAPHS. A photograph of *Hajen* appears in the 1957-58 to 1959-60 editions, of *Bävern* in the 1960-61 to 1965-66 editions, of *Illern* in the 1964-65 to 1966-67 editions, of *Uttern* in the 1966-67 to 1968-69 editions, of *Valen* in the 1967-68 and 1968-69 editions.

DISPOSALS
Of the nine old submarines of the "Sjölejonet" class, *Dykaren* (Diver), *Sjöborren* (Sea-urchin), *Sjöhunden* (Seadog), *Sjölejonet* (Sealion) and *Svärdfisken* (Swordfish) were stricken in 1960 and scrapped; and *Sjöbjörnen* (Seabear), *Sjöhästen* (Seahorse), *Sjöormen* (Seaserpent) and *Tumlaren* (Porpoise) were discarded on 1 Jan 1964.

The three old submarines of the "Najad" class, *Nacken* (Neck), *Najad* (Naiad) and *Neptun* (Neptune) were sold in 1969 to US commercial interests for oil and gas exploration off Alaska.

5 "ABBORREN" CLASS

ABBORREN (ex-U5)	LAXEN (ex-U8)
GÄDDAN (ex-U7)	MAKRILLEN (ex-U9)
	SIKEN (ex-U6)

Displacement, tons	420 standard; 430 surface; 460 submerged
Length, feet (metres)	164 (50·0)
Beam, feet (metres)	17·5 (5·3)
Draught, feet (metres)	17·5 (5·3)
Torpedo tubes	4—21 in (533 mm) 3 bow and 1 stern
Main engines	2 MAN diesels, total 1 500 hp Electric motor, 750 hp
Speed, knots	14 on surface; 9 submerged
Complement	23

All were built by Kockums Mek. Verkstads, Malmö (U 4, 5 June 1943, U 5, 8 July 1963, U 6 ,18 Aug 1943, U 7, 23 Nov 1943). and by Karlskrona Naval Dockyard (U 8, 25 Apr 1944, U 9, 23 May 1944) (original launch dates). Reconstructed in 1960-64. Launching dates after reconstruction: *Abborren* 1962, *Makrillen* 1963, *Forellen* 1963, *Laxen* 1964, *Gäddan* 1963, *Siken* 1964, All have been streamlined. Officially rated as *Kustubåtar* (coastal submarines) Distinctive letters Abb, For, Gad, Lax, Mak. Sik.

PHOTOGRAPHS. A photograph of *Laxen* appears in the 1965-66 to 1967-68 editions, of *Abborren* in the 1967-68 and 1968-69 editions, of *Siken* in the 1968-69 and 1969-70 editions, of *Forellen* in the 1970-71 edition.

DISPOSALS
Of four sister submarines of this class, *U 1* was scrapped in 1961, *U 2* was for sale in 1962, and *U 3* in 1964. *Forellen* (ex- *U 4*) was deleted officially from the list in 1971.

MIDGET
The midget submarine *Spiggen* (Stickleback), former British X-craft, was officially deleted from the list in 1970.

CRUISERS
The cruiser *Göta Lejon* was officially deleted from the list in 1970; she will be scrapped or sold in the near future. Her sister ship *Tre Kronor* was discarded on 1 Jan 1964.

HAJEN 1970, Royal Swedish Navy, Official

VALEN Royal Swedish Navy, Official

SALEN 1969, Royal Swedish Navy, Official

MAKRILLEN 1969, Royal Swedish Navy, Official

ABBORREN Royal Swedish Navy, Official

DESTROYERS (*Jagare*)

4 "ÖSTERGÖTLAND" CLASS

Name	No.	Builders	Laid down	Launched	Completed
GÄSTRIKLAND	J 22	Götaverken, Göteborg	1 Oct 1955	6 June 1956	14 Jan 1959
HÄLSINGLAND	J 23	Kockums Mek Verkstads A/B	1 Oct 1955	14 Jan 1957	17 June 1959
ÖSTERGÖTLAND	J 20	Götaverken, Göteborg	1 Sep 1955	8 May 1956	3 Mar 1958
SÖDERMANLAND	J 21	Eriksberg Mekaniska Verkstad	1 June 1955	28 May 1956	27 June 1959

Displacement, tons	2 150 standard ; 2 600 full load
Length, feet (*metres*)	367·5 (*112·0*) pp ; 380 (*115·8*) oa
Beam, feet (*metres*)	36·8 (*11·2*)
Draught, feet (*metres*)	12 (*3·7*)
Missile launchers	"Seacat" surface-to-air
Guns, surface	4—4·7 in (*120 mm*)
Guns, AA	Östergötland: 7—40 mm
	Hälsingland: 5—40 mm
	Others: 4—40 mm
A/S	Triple barrelled DC mortar
Torpedo tubes	6—21 in (*533 mm*)
Mines	60 can be carried
Boilers	2 Babcock & Wilcox
Main engines	De Laval turbines
	40 000 shp ; 2 shafts
Speed, knots	35
Radius, miles	2 200 at 20 knots
Oil fuel (tons)	330
Complement	244

These ships have improved anti-aircraft defence and anti-submarine weapons of the Bofors type. J (for *Jagare*) painted on bows with number in 1966.

PHOTOGRAPHS. A photograph of *Hälsingland* appears in the 1965-66 and 1966-67 editions, and of *Gastrikland* in the 1967-68 to 1969-70 editions.

ÖSTERGOTLAND   1970, Stefan Terzibaschitsch

MODERNISATION. *Södermanland* was modernised in 1962, and *Gästrikland* and *Östergötland* in 1963.

RADAR. Search and Tactical: S Band. Fire Control: X Band.

SODERMANLAND   1968. Royal Swedish Navy, Official

2 "HALLAND" CLASS

Name	No.	Builders	Laid down	Launched	Completed
HALLAND	J 18	Götaverken, Göteborg	1951	16 July 1952	8 June 1955
SMALAND	J 19	Eriksberg Mekaniska Verkstad, Göteborg	1951	23 Oct 1952	12 Jan 1956

Displacement, tons	2 800 standard ; 3 400 full load
Length, feet (*metres*)	380·5 (*116·0*) wl ; 397·2 (*121·0*) oa
Beam, feet (*metres*)	41·3 (*12·6*)
Draught, feet (*metres*)	14·8 (*4·5*)
Missiles, surface	1 rocket launcher
Guns, dual purpose	4—4·7 in (*120 mm*)
Guns, AA	2—57 mm ; 6—40 mm
A/S weapons	2 four-barrelled DC mortars
Torpedo tubes	8—21 in (*533 mm*)
Mines	Can be fitted for minelaying
Boilers	2
Main engines	De Laval double reduction geared
	turbines ; 58 000 shp ; 2 shafts
Speed, knots	35
Radius, miles	3 000 at 20 knots
Oil fuel, tons	500
Complement	290

Both ordered in 1948. The first Swedish destroyers of post-war design and construction. Fully automatic gun turrets forward and aft, ahead throwing anti-submarine weapons of the Bofors type forward, and ship-to-ship guided missiles launcher abaft the after funnel.

RADAR. Search: LWO 3. Tactical: S Band.. Fire Control: X Band.

SMALAND   1968. Royal Swedish Navy. Official

HALLAND   1968, Royal Swedish Navy, Official

Destroyers—continued

Name	No.	Builders	Laid down	Launched	Completed	Modernised
ÖLAND	J 16	Kockums Mek Verkstads A/B, Malmö	1943	15 Dec 1945	5 Dec 1947	1960
UPPLAND	J 17	Karlskrona Dockyard	1943	5 Nov 1946	31 Jan 1949	1963

2 "ÖLAND" CLASS

Displacement, tons	2 000 standard; 2 400 full load
Length, feet (metres)	351 (107·0) pp; 364·2 (111·0) oa
Beam, feet (metres)	36·8 (11·2)
Draught, feet (metres)	11·2 (3·4)
Guns, dual purpose	4—4·7 in (120 mm)
Guns, AA	6—40 mm
A/S weapons	1 triple-barrelled depth charge mortar
Torpedo tubes	6—21 in (533 mm) tripled
Mines	60
Boilers	2 Penhoët
Main engines	De Laval geared turbines 44 000 shp; 2 shafts
Speed, knots	35
Radius, miles	2 500 at 20 knots
Oil fuel (tons)	300
Complement	210

The superstructure and machinery spaces are lightly armoured. Fitted for minelaying. J (for *Jagare*) painted on bows with number in 1966.

GUNNERY. The 4·7 inch guns are semi-automatic with an elevation of 80 degrees. The 40 mm AA gun near the jackstaff was removed in 1962, and the eight 20 mm AA guns were suppressed in 1964.

RADAR. Search and Tactical: S Band. Fire Control: X Band.

UPPLAND   *1969, Royal Swedish Navy, Official*

RECONSTRUCTION. *Öland* was modernised in 1960 with new bridge, and *Uppland* with new bridge and helicopter platform in 1963.

DISPOSALS OF OLDER DESTROYERS *Klas Horn* was discarded in 1958. *Ehrensköld* and *Nordensköld* were discarded on 1 Apr 1963.

ÖLAND   *1970, Royal Swedish Navy, Official*

FAST ANTI-SUBMARINE FRIGATES (ex-Destroyers) Rated as *Fregatter*

KARLSKRONA F 79

Displacement, tons	1 250 standard; 1 400 full load
Length, feet (metres)	304 (92·7) wl; 310·5 (94·6) oa
Beam, feet (metres)	29·5 (9·0)
Draught, feet (metres)	12·5 (3·8)
Guns, dual purpose	3—4·7 in (120 mm);
Guns, AA	4—40 mm
A/S weapons	2 triple-barrelled DC mortars
Boilers	3 Penhoët
Main engines	De Laval geared turbines 32 000 shp; 2 shafts
Speed, knots	39
Radius, miles	1 200 at 20 knots
Oil fuel (tons)	150
Complement	130

Former torpedo boat destroyer. Built by Karlskrona Dockyard. Launched on 16 June 1939 and completed on 1 Sep 1940. Originally carried 20 to 60 mines. Refitted for anti-submarine warfare, and officially reclassified as frigate on 1 Jan 1961. Converted in 1963. F (for *Fregatter*) painted on bows with number in 196E.

RADAR. Equipped with Type 293 search radar installation.

DISPOSALS. Of this class *Göteborg* was discarded in 1958, *Stockholm* on 1 Jan 1964, *Malmö* and *Norrkoping* in 1967, and *Gavle* in 1969.

KARLSKRONA   *1970, Stefan Terzibaschitsch*

1 "MJOLNER" CLASS

MODE F 73

Displacement, tons	760 standard; 960 full load
Length, feet (metres)	243·8 (74·3) wl; 256 (78·0) oa
Beam, feet (metres)	26·2 (8·0)
Draught, feet (metres)	7·5 (2·3)
Guns, dual purpose	2—4·1 in (105 mm)
Guns, AA	2—40 mm
Boilers	2 three-drum type
Main engines	2 sets De Laval geared turbines 16 000 shp; 2 shafts
Speed, knots	30
Oil fuel (tons)	190
Complement	100

Built by Götaverken. Laid down in Sep 1941, launched on 11 Apr 1942 and completed in 1942. Formerly rated as seagoing torpedo boats or coastal destroyers (*kustjagare*). Originally fitted for minelaying.

MODE   *1971, Royal Swedish Navy, Official*

CONVERSION
Converted into fast anti-submarine frigate in 1955 and the 3—21 inch torpedo tubes removed.

DISPOSALS
Of three sister ships *Magne* and *Mjolner* were officially deleted from the list in 1967, and *Munin* in 1970.

Fast Anti-Submarine Frigates—*continued*

4 "VISBY" CLASS

Name	No.	Builders	Launched	Completed
HÄLSINGBORG	13	Götaverken	23 Mar 43	30 Nov 43
KALMAR	14	Eriksberg	20 July 43	3 Feb 44
SUNDSVALL	F 12	Eriksberg	20 Oct 42	17 Sep 43
VISBY	F 11	Götaverken	16 Oct 42	10 Aug 43

Displacement, tons	1 150 standard; 1 320 full load
Length, feet (*metres*)	310 (*94·5*) wl; 320 (*97·5*) oa
Beam, feet (*metres*)	30 (*9·1*)
Draught, feet (*metres*)	12·5 (*3·8*)
Aircraft	Nos. 11, 12: I helicopter
Guns, dual purpose	Nos. 13, 14: 3—4·7 in (*120 mm*)
Guns, AA	Nos. 11, 12: 2—57 mm;
	Nos. 13, 14: 3—40 mm
A/S	1 four-barrelled DC mortar
Torpedo tubes	Nos. 13 and 14: 5—21 in (*533 mm*) quintupled
Boilers	3 three-drum type
Main engines	De Laval geared turbines 36 000 shp; 2 shafts
Speed, knots	39
Radius, miles	1 600 at 20 knots
Oil fuel (tons)	150
Complement	140

SUNDSVALL   *1970, Royal Swedish Navy, Official*

Kalmar was laid down on 16 Nov 1942, and *Visby* on 29 Apr 1942. All were originally fitted for minelaying.

RADAR. Search: S Band. Fire Control: HSA M 24.

RECLASSIFICATION. Re-rated from destroyers to frigates on 1 Jan 1965.
PENNANT NUMBERS. F (for *Fregatter*) painted on bows with number in 1966.

PHOTOGRAPH. A photograph of *Kalmar* appears in the 1962-63 to 1966-67 editions, of *Hälsingborg*, in the 1963-64 to 1966-67 edition and of *Visby* in the 1969-70 edition.

MINELAYER AND SUBMARINE DEPOT SHIP

1 + 1 NEW CONSTRUCTION

ÄLVSBORG M 02   **M 03**

Displacement, tons	2 700
Length, feet (*metres*)	302·5 (*92·2*)
Beam, feet (*metres*)	49·2 (*15·0*)
Draught, feet (*metres*)	13·1 (*4·0*)
Guns, AA	3—57 mm Bofors
Main engines	Diesels; 4 200 bhp
Speed, knots	15
Cost	Estimated about 34 000 000 kr total
Complement	90 (accommodation for 210 more)

This new combined minelayer and submarine depot ship was ordered in 1968 from the Naval Dockyard in Karlskrona and launched on 11 Nov 1969. Scheduled to be completed in 1971.

The novel ship will replace both the minelayer *Alvsnabben*, and the submarine depot ship *Patricia*.

The adjacent artist's impression shows the unique multiple minelaying rail sloping transom.

ÄLVSBORG   *1969, Royal Swedish Navy, Official*

MINELAYER (*Minfartyg*) Cadets' Seagoing Training Ship

ÄLVSNABBEN M 01

Displacement, tons	4 250 standard;
Length, feet (*metres*)	317·5 (*96·8*) wl; 334·7 (*102·0*) oa
Beam, feet (*metres*)	44·5 (*13·5*)
Draught, feet (*metres*)	16 (*4·9*)
Guns, surface	2—6 in (*152 mm*)
Guns, AA	2—57 mm Bofors; 2—40 mm (+ mounts for 2 twin 40 mm)
Guns, saluting	4—35 mm
Main engines	Diesels; 1 shaft; 3 000 bhp
Speed, knots	14
Complement	255 (63 cadets)

Built on a mercantile hull by Eriksberg Mekaniska Verkstad Göteborg. Laid down in Oct 1942, launched on 19 Jan 1943, completed in Apr 1943. Employed as a training ship during 1953-58, and relieved the anti-aircraft cruiser *Gotland* as Cadet's Seagoing Training Ship in 1959. Re-armed in 1961. Formerly carried 4—6 inch, 8—40 mm AA, 6—20 mm AA.

RADAR. Equipped with S Band search radar installation.

ÄLVSNABBEN   *1969 Royal Swedish Navy, Official*

SUBMARINE DEPOT SHIP (*Ubåts depåfartyg*)

PATRICIA (ex- *Patris II*) A 206

Displacement, tons	4 950 standard;
Length, feet (*metres*)	335 (*102·0*)
Beam, feet (*metres*)	47·5 (*14·5*)
Draught, feet (*metres*)	20 (*6·0*)
Guns, AA	8—40 mm; 2—20 mm
Boilers	2
Main engines	Triple expansion; 1 shaft; 2 450 ihp
Speed, knots	14 (now less)
Complement	Accommodation for 500

Former Swedish-Lloyd merchant liner. Built by Swan, Hunter & Wigham Richardson Ltd, Wallsend-on-Tyne. Launched and completed in 1926. Acquired in 1940. She was reconstructed to increase the accommodation for about 500 men and to maintain and administer nine submarines. Will be scrapped in the near future.

PATRICIA   *1970, Royal Swedish Navy, Official*

TORPEDO BOATS (Torpedbatar)

12 NEW CONSTRUCTION "SPICA II" CLASS

T 131	T 133	T 135	T 137	T 139	T 141
T 132	T 134	T 136	T 138	T 140	T 142

6 "SPICA" CLASS

CAPELLA 123	SIRIUS 122	VEGA 125
CASTOR 124	SPICA 121	VIRGO 126

Displacement, tons	"Spica" class: 200 standard; "Spica II" class: 230 standard
Dimensions, feet	139·5 hull; 141 oa ("Spica II" class 144·4) × 23·3
Guns	1—57 mm Bofors AA
Torpedo tubes	6—21 in (single, fixed)
Missile launchers	For light-rockets
Main engines	3 Bristol Siddeley Proteus 1 274 gas turbines; 3 shafts; 12 720 shp = 40 knots
Complement	28 (7 officers, 21 ratings)

The lead vessel of a group of six, *Spica*, was completed in 1966 by Götaverken, Götenborg, who shared the contract for the series with Karlskronavarvet. Designed to operate in areas contaminated by nuclear fall-out. *Sirius* and *Capella* built by Götaverken; *Castor*, *Vega* and *Virgo* by Karlskronavarvet. The 57 mm gun is in a power operated turret controlled by a radar equipped director, with 57 mm rocket flare projector placed before, and a 10·3 mm launcher on each side, of the totally enclosed bridge. The turret is mounted in the centre of a long foredeck to give wide and clear arcs of fire. HSA M 24 fire control radar. Twelve more projected. A photograph of *Sirius* appears in the 1968-69 and 1969-70 editions, of *Spica* in the 1968-69 to 1970-71 editions, of *Castor* in the 1969-70 and 1970-71 editions.

CAPELLA *1970, Royal Swedish Navy, Official*

VEGA *1971, Royal Swedish Navy, Official*

VIRGO *1971, Royal Swedish Navy, Official*

11 "PLEJAD" CLASS MTB—MGB CONVERTIBLES

ALDEBARAN	T 107	ARCTURUS	T 110	POLARIS	T 103
ALTAIR	T 108	ARGO	T 111	POLLUX	T 104
ANTARES	T 109	ASTREA	T 112	REGULUS	T 105
		PLEJAD	T 102	RIGEL	T 106

Displacement, tons	155 standard; 170 ful load
Dimensions, feet	157·5 × 18·3
Guns	2—40 mm Bofors AA
Tubes	6—21 in (2 forward, 4 aft)
Main engines	3 Mercedes-Benz diesels; 3 shafts; 9 000 bhp = 37·5 knots
Range, miles	600 at 30 knots
Complement	33

All built at Lurssen, Vegesack, launched between 1954 and 1959 and completed by 1960. A photograph of *Plejad* emerging from camouflaged nuclear bomb-proof shelter appears in the 1962-63 to 1964-65 editions, of *Antares* in the 1960-61 to 1964-65 editions, of *Polaris* in the 1965-66 to 1967-68 editions, of *Rigel* in the 1968-69 and 1969-70 editions, of *Regulus* in the 1969 and 1970-71 editions.

Perseus, T 101, built at Karlskrona, completed in 1951, the first of a convertible type of torpedo and gunboat of experimental design, re-engined with Götaverken machinery to give greater power, differing in appearance from the other boats, but funnel later removed, was discarded in 1967.

Torpedo Boats—continued

ARGO *1971, Royal Swedish Navy, Official*

POLLUX *1970, Royal Swedish Navy, Official*

15 "T 42" TYPE

T 42	T 45	T 48	T 51	T 54
T 43	T 46	T 49	T 52	T 55
T 44	T 47	T 50	T 53	T 56

Displacement, tons	40 standard
Dimensions, feet	75·5 × 19·4 × 4·6
Guns	1—40 mm Bofors AA
Tubes	2—21 in
Main engines	Diesels; speed = 45 knots

Built by Kockums Mekaniska Verkstads Aktiebolag, Malmö. All launched between 1956 and 1959 and completed by 1960. A photograph of T 56 appears in the 1964-65 to 1966-67 editions, of T 42 in the 1967-68 and 1968-69 editions, and of T 49 in the 1969-70 edition.

T 45 *1970, Royal Swedish Navy, Official*

10 "T 32" TYPE

T 32	T 34	T 36	T 38	T 40
T 33	T 35	T 37	T 39	T 41

Displacement, tons	40 standard
Dimensions, feet	75·5 × 18·4 × 4·5
Guns	1—40 mm Bofors AA; 2 MG
Tubes	2—21 in
Main engines	Diesels; Speed 40 knots

Launched in 1950-52. Built by Kockums Mekaniska Verkstads Aktiebolag, Malmö. Of all welded steel construction. T 41, of slightly different design, provided under the 1952 Programme, was launched and completed in 1962. A photograph of T 38 appears in the 1953-54 to 1962-63 editions, of T 40 in the 1963-64 to 1966-67 editions, of T 41 in the 1966-67 to 1968-69 editions.

Of the small type of motor torpedo boats, T 21, T 22, T 23, T 24, T 25, T 26 and T 27 were scrapped in 1969, and T 28, T 29, T 30 and T 31 were scrapped in 1960. The older motor torpedo boats, T 15, T 16, T 17 and T 18 were discarded in 1957.

T 32 *1967, Royal Swedish Navy, Official*

COASTAL MINESWEEPERS

12 "ARKÖ" CLASS

ARKÖ	M 57	HASSLÖ	M 64	NÄMDÖ	M 67	STYRSÖ	M 61
ASPÖ	M 63	IGGÖ	M 60	SKAFTÖ	M 62	VÄLLÖ	M 66
BLIDÖ	M 68	KARLSÖ	M 59	SPÄRÖ	M 58	VINÖ	M 65

Displacement, tons	300 standard
Dimensions, feet	131 pp; 144·5 oa × 23 × 8
Guns	1—40 mm AA
Main engines	Mercedes-Benz diesels; 2 shafts; 2 000 bhp = 14·5 knots

Of wooden construction. There is a small difference in the deck-line between M 57-59 and M60-68. *Arkö* launched on 21 Jan 1957. *Arkö, Karlsö* and *Spårö* completed in 1957, *Iggö* in 1960. *Skaftö* in 1961, *Aspö, Haåslö, Vinö* and *Styrsö* in 1962, *Vällö* in 1963, *Bildö* and *Nämdö* in 1964. Six more in the new construction programme. A photograph of *Arkö* appears in the 1959-60 to 1965-66 editions, of *Aspö* in the 1966-67 to 1968-69 editions, of *Styrsö* in the 1968-69 and 1969-70 editions.

SPÄRÖ   1970, courtesy Godfrey H. Walker, Esq.

VALLÖ   1969, Royal Swedish Navy, Official

6 "HANÖ" CLASS

HANÖ	M 51	STURKÖ	M 54	TJURKÖ	M 53
ORNÖ	M 55	TÄRNÖ	M 52	UTÖ	M 56

Displacement, tons	270 standard
Dimensions, feet	131·2 × 23 × 8
Guns	2—40 mm AA
Main engines	Diesels; 2 shafts; 2 400 bhp = 14·5 knots

All of this class were built at Karlskrona and launched in 1953. A photograph of *Hanö* appears in the 1967-68 to 1969-70 editions and of *Ornö* in the 1968-69 to 1970-71 editions.

TÄRNÖ   1970, Royal Swedish Navy, Official

UTÖ   1971, Royal Swedish Navy, Official

MINING TENDERS *(Minutlaggare)*

MUL 12 (1952)	MUL 14 (1953)	MUL 16 (1956)	MUL 18 (1956)
MUL 13 (1952)	MUL 15 (1953)	MUL 17 (1956)	MUL 19 (1956)

Displacement, tons	245 standard
Dimensions, feet	102·3 × 24·3 × 10·2
Guns	1—40 mm AA
Main engines	1 Nohab diesel-electric; 360 bhp = 10·5 knots

Launch dates above. Coastal Artillery personnel. A photograph of *MUL 15* appears in the 1963-64 to 1966-67 editions, of *MUL 12* in the 1967-68 and 1968-69 editions, of *MUL 10* in the 1969-70 and 1970-71 editions.

MUL 11

Displacement, tons	200 standard
Dimensions, feet	98·8 × 23·7 × 11·8
Guns	2—20 mm AA
Main engines	2 Atlas diesels; 300 bhp = 10 knots

Launched in 1946. *MUL 10* was officially deleted from the list in 1970.

MUL 11 degaussing   1971, Royal Swedish Navy, Official

DISPOSALS OF MINESWEEPERS

Of the "Bredskar" class, *Ven* was scrapped in 1960, *Grönscär* was removed from the effective list on 1 Apr 1963, *Halmön Koster, Sandön* and *Vingo* were discarded on 1 Jan 1964, *Bredskär Bremön, Kullen, Arskär* and *Ramskär* by the end of 1967, and *Ulvön* in 1968. Of the "Arholma" class, *Arholma* was scrapped in 1959 and *Landsort* was officially discarded on 1 Jan 1964. Of the "Jägaren" class, *Snapphanen* was transferred to the Guatemalan Navy in 1959, and *Jägaren, Kaparen* and *Vaktaren* were scrapped in 1958.

STAFF SHIP *(Stabsfartyg)*

MARIEHOLM A 201

Displacement, tons	1 445 standard
Dimensions, feet	210 × 32·5 × 11·5
Aircraft	1 helicopter
Guns	2 MG (1—40 mm removed, see notes below)
Main engines	Steam reciprocating; 950 ihp = 12 knots

Former passenger ship. Completed in 1934. Converted during the Second World War to serve as a Base Communication Centre for the Commander-in-Chief of the Active Fleet. Recently used as a Staff Ship for the Commander-in-Chief in winter time, flying his flag. The ship had her mainmast removed and a helicopter platform installed aft in 1959 for employment as flagship of the Active Fleet (the "Coast Fleet"). The 40 mm Bofors on the forecastle has been landed for the time being.

MARIEHOLM   1970, Royal Swedish Navy, Official

TRAINING SHIPS *(Skonerter)*

FALKEN (12 June 1947)   GLADAN (14 Nov 1946)

Displacement, tons	220 standard
Dimensions, feet	93 wl; 129·5 oa × 23·5 × 13·5
Main engines	Auxiliary diesel; 120 bhp

Sail training ships. Schooners. Launch dates above. Sail area 5 511 square feet.

INSHORE MINESWEEPERS

9 "ORUST" AND "HISINGEN" CLASSES

BLACKAN	M 44	GILLÖGA	M 47	RÖDLÖGA	M 48
DÄMMAN	M 45	HISINGEN	M 43	SVARTLÖGA	M 49
GALTEN	M 46	ORUST	M 41	TJÖRN	M 42

Displacement, tons	Orust, Tjörn: 110 standard; Hisingen: 115; others 140
Dimensions, feet	Orust, Tjörn: 62·3 × 19·7 × 4·5; others 76·2 × 21 × 4·7
Guns	Orust, Tjron: 1—20 mm AA; others 1—40 mm AA
Main engines	2 diesels; 600 bhp = 9 knots

Orust and *Tjörn* were launched in 1948. Similar to fishing cutter type. *Blackan, Dämman, Galten* and *Hisingen* were launched in 1957. Three authorised in Apr 1962 were built in 1964. A photograph of *Galten* appears in the 1964-63 to 1966-67 editions, and of *Hisingen* in the 1967-68 to 1969-70 editions.

SVARTLOGA   1970, Royal Swedish Navy, Official

8 "M" TYPE

M 15	M 21	M 23	M 25
M 16	M 22	M 24	M 26

Displacement, tons	70 standard
Dimensions, feet	85·3 × 16·5 × 4·5
Guns	1—20 mm
Main engines	Diesel; 600 bhp = 13 knots

All launched in 1941. M 17, M 18 and M 20 of this large motor launch type were re-rated as tenders and renamed *Lommen, Spoven* and *Skuld* respectively, see later page. M 19 was officially deleted from the list in 1969.

M 22   1969, Royal Swedish Navy, Official

SALVAGE VESSEL (*Bärgningsfartyg*)

BELOS A 211

Displacement, tons	950 standard
Dimensions, feet	204 × 27 × 12
Aircraft	1 helicopter
Main engines	Diesel; 2 shafts; 1 200 bhp = 13 knots

A new salvage vessel built to succeed and take the name of the old *Belos*. Launched on 15 Nov 1961. Completed on 29 May 1963. Equipped with a decompression chamber. The old salvage vessel *Belos* (launched in 1885), then the world's oldest naval vessel in service (she helped to raise the 334-year old warship *Vasa* in 1961) was discarded on 1 Aug 1963.

BELOS   1969, Royal Swedish Navy, Official

PATROL BOATS (*Vedettbåtar*)

V 57

Displacement, tons	115 standard
Dimensions, feet	98 pp; 105 oa × 17·3 × 7·5
Guns	2—20 mm AA
Main engines	Diesel; 500 bhp = 13·5 knots
Complement	12

Built at Stockholm. Launched in 1953. Fitted for minelaying. In Coast Artillery. A photograph of *V 57* appears in the 1962-63 to 1969-70 editions.

DISPOSALS

V 51, V 52, V 53, V 54, V 55 and *V 56*, 125 tons coal burning triple expansion steam engined type manned by Coast Artillery, were officially discarded in 1967.

7 "70" SERIES

71	72	73	74	75	76	77

Displacement, tons	28 standard
Dimensions, feet	69 × 15 × 5
Guns	1—20 mm
Main engines	Diesel; speed = 18 knots

Launched in 1966-67 and completed in 1968. Rated as *Bevakningsbåtar*.

10 "60" SERIES

61	62	63	64	65	66	67	68	69	70

Displacement, tons	30 standard
Dimensions, feet	62·3 × 15 × 4
Guns	1—20 mm
Main engines	Diesel; speed = 19 knots

Guard boats of the coast artillery (*Bevakningsbåtar*) launched in 1960-61. A photograph of No. 62 appears in the 1967-68 to 1969-70 editions.

5 "SVK" TYPE

SVK 1	SVK 2	SVK 3	SVK 4	SVK 5

Displacement, tons	19 standard
Dimensions, feet	55·8 × 12·1 × 3·9
Guns	1—20 mm AA
Main engines	Diesels; 100 to 135 bhp = 10 to 11 knots

Patrol launches of the Sjovarnskarens type. All launched in 1944. Sjovarnskaren = RNVR. *Tumlaren*, a small fishing cutter, also belongs to the SVK.

M 7 and *M 8*, former inshore minesweepers of the medium motor launch type taken over as patrol boats, were sold in 1968.

WATER CARRIERS

FRYKEN A 217

Displacement, tons	307 standard
Dimensions, feet	105·0 × 18·7 × 8·9
Main engines	Diesels; 370 bhp = 10 knots

A naval construction water carrier. Launched in 1959 and completed in 1960. Former pennant number was 263.

1970, Royal Swedish Navy, Official

UNDEN A 216

Displacement, tons	500 standard
Dimensions, feet	121·4 × 23·3 × 9·8
Main engines	Steam reciprocating; 225 ihp = 9 knots

Launched in 1946. The pennant number of *Unden* was formerly 268.

GÄLNAN

Displacement, tons	98 standard
Dimensions, feet	95·1 × 19·0 × 9·2
Main engines	Speed = 8 knots

Launched in 1942. Small water tanker for harbour and local services.

SURVEY SHIPS (Sjömätningsfartyg)

JOHAN MÅNSSON

Displacement, tons	977 standard; 1 030 full load (official figure)
Dimensions, feet	183·7 × 36·1 × 11·5
Main engines	Diesels; 3 300 bhp = 15 knots

Launched on 14 Jan 1966. A new survey ship is planned in the near future.

JOHAN MANSSON   1971, Royal Swedish Navy, Official

RAN

Displacement, tons	285 standard
Dimensions, feet	98·4 × 23·0 × 8·5
Main engines	Diesels; 260 bhp = 9 knots

Ran was launched in 1945 and completed and commissioned for service in 1946.

GUSTAV AF KLINT

Displacement, tons	750 standard
Dimensions, feet	170·6 × 28·5 × 15·4
Main engines	Diesels; 640 bhp = 10 knots

Launched in 1941. Reconstructed in 1963. She formerly displaced 650 tons with a length of 154 feet.

GUSTAV AV KLINT   1970, Royal Swedish Navy, Official

ANDEN (ex-M 9)   MÄSEN (ex-M 3)

Displacement, tons	53 standard
Dimensions, feet	78·8 × 16·5 × 4·5
Main engines	Diesel; 400 bhp = 13 knots

Former inshore minesweepers of the motor launch type, launched in 1940 and subsequently converted into survey craft. M 7 and M 8 were taken over as patrol boats. Sister boats Grisslan (ex-M 6), Svärtan (ex-M 5), Tärnan (ex-M 4) and Viggen (ex-M 10) were officially deleted from the list in 1971.

JOHAN NORDENANKAR

Displacement, tons	260 standard
Dimensions, feet	98·5 × 22·3 × 8·2
Main engines	Diesels; 200 bhp = 8 knots

PETTER GEDDA

Displacement, tons	135 standard
Dimensions, feet	82·0 × 18·0 × 6·8

Both the above were launched in 1924. Ejdern was officially deleted from the list in 1970.

NILS STRÖMCRONA

Displacement, tons	140 standard
Dimensions, feet	88·6 × 17·0 × 8·2
Guns	None in peacetime
Main engines	Diesels; 300 bhp = 9 knots

Launched in 1894. The older survey ships will eventually be replaced.

SUPPLY SHIP

FREJA A 221

Displacement, tons	415 standard; 450 full load
Dimensions, feet	160·8 × 27·9 × 12·1
Main engines	Diesels; 600 bhp = 11 knots

Built by Kroger, Rendsburg. Launched in 1953. Employed as a provision ship.

ICEBREAKERS (Isbrytarfartyg)

1 NEW CONSTRUCTION

A new icebreaker is being built by the Wärtsilä concern in Finland.

NJORD

Displacement, tons	5 150 standard; 5 686 full load
Dimensions, feet	260·8 pp; 283·8 oa × 69·6 × 20·3
Main engines	Wärtsilä diesel-electric; 4 shafts, 2 forward, 2 aft; 12 000 hp = 18 knots

Built by Wärtsilä, Finland. Launched on 20 Oct 1968 and completed in Dec 1969 Near sister ship of Tor.

NJORD   1971, Royal Swedish Navy, Official

TOR

Displacement, tons	4 980 standard; 5 290 full load
Dimensions, feet	254·3 pp; 277·2 oa × 69·5 × 20·3
Main engines	Wärtsilä-Sulzer diesel-electric; 4 shafts; 2 forward; 2 aft 12 000 hp = 18 knots

Launched from Wärtsilä's Crichton-Vulcan yard, Turku, on 25 May 1963. Towed to Sandvikens Skeppsdocka, Helsingfors, for completion. Delivered on 31 Jan 1964. Larger but generally similar to Oden, and a near-sister to Tarmo built for Finland

TOR   1968, Royal Swedish Navy, Official

ODEN

Displacement, tons	4 950 standard; 5 220 full load
Dimensions, feet	256 pp; 273·5 oa × 63·7 × 22·7
Main engines	Diesel-electric; 4 shafts (2 forward); 10 500 bhp =
Oil fuel, tons	740 16 knots
Complement	75

Similar to the Finnish Voima and 3 Soviet icebreakers. 4 screws, 2 forward, 2 af Built at Sandviken, Helsingfors. Launched on 16 Oct 1956. Completed in 195

ODEN   1969, Royal Swedish Navy, Official

THULE

Displacement, tons	2 200 standard; 2 380 full load
Dimensions, feet	187·0 wl; 204·2 oa × 52·8 × 19·4
Main engines	Diesel-electric; 3 shafts (1 for'd); 4 800 bhp = 17 knots
Complement	43

Launched at the Naval Dockyard, Karlskrona, in Oct 1951. Completed in 1953. photograph appears in the 1969-70 and earlier editions. The icebreaker Atle w officially discarded in 1967.

Icebreakers—continued

YMER   *1969. Royal Swedish Navy, Official*

YMER

Displacement, tons	4 330 standard; 4 645 full load
Dimensions, feet	240 wl; 258 oa × 63·1 × 22·3
Main engines	6 Atlas diesel-electric; 9 000 hp = 16 knots
Complement	44

Launched by Kockums MV A/B, Malmö in 1932. First large icebreaker with diesel-electric propulsion. Designed to carry a seaplane for ice spotting and survey.

LANDING CRAFT

BORE   **GRIM**   **HEIMDAL**

Displacement, tons	380 standard
Dimensions, feet	118·1 × 27·9 × 8.5
Main engines	Diesels; 500 bhp = 12 knots

General utility landing craft of improved design. Launched in 1961 (*Grim*) and 1966. A photograph of *Grim* appears in the 1966-67 to 1968-69 editions.

BORE   *1969, Royal Swedish Navy, Official*

SKAGUL A 333   **SLEIPNER** A 335

Displacement, tons	335 standard
Dimensions, feet	114·8 × 27·9 × 9·5
Main engines	Diesels; 640 bhp = 12 knots

Sleipner was launched in 1959 and completed in 1960. *Skagul* was launched and completed in 1960. A photograph of *Skagul* appears in the 1962-63 to 1966-67 editions

Nos. 201-204   **205-238**   **239-243**

Displacement, tons	31
Dimensions, feet	69 × 13·8 × 4·2
Main engines	Speed = 18 knots

A series of 43 landing craft rated as Landstigningfarkoster. Launched in 1957 *et seq.*

200 Series   *1967, Royal Swedish Navy, Official*

L 51   **L 52**   **L 53**   **L 54**   **L 55**

Displacement, tons	32 standard
Dimensions, feet	50·8 × 16 × 3·2
Main engines	Diesel; 140 bhp = 8 knots

Landing craft of general utility type. Launched in 1948, L 53 and L 54 laid up 1960.

ANE   **BALDER**   **LOKE**   **RING**

Displacement, tons	135 standard
Dimensions, feet	91·9 × 26·2 × 6·0
Main engines	Speed = 8·5 knots; (*Loke* 9·2 knots)

MINE TRANSPORT

FÄLLAREN A 236   **MINÖREN** A 237

Displacement, tons	165 standard
Dimensions, feet	105 × 20·3 × 7·2
Main engines	Speed = 9 knots

Launched in 1941 and 1940 respectively. Rated as *Mintransportfartyg*.

OILERS   (*Tankfartyg*)

OLJAREN (ex-*Martha*) A 227

Displacement, tons	1 100 standard
Dimensions, feet	180·5 × 27·6 × 12·1
Guns	2—25 mm AA
Main engines	Diesels; 400 bhp = 10 knots

Launched in 1939. Cargo capacity 695 tons. Her pennant number was formerly 267. The oiler *Tankaren* (ex-*Lister*) 269 was officially deleted from the list in 1969 and the oiler *Eldaren* (ex-*Muron*) A 226 (ex-266) was deleted in 1970.

OLJAREN   *1971, Royal Swedish Navy, Official*

TENDERS

PELIKANEN A 247

Displacement, tons	100 standard
Dimensions, feet	108·2 × 19 × 6
Main engines	Speed = 15 knots

Torpedo recovery and rocket trials vessel. Launched in 1964.

ACHILLES A 251   **AJAX** A 252

Displacement, tons	450
Dimensions, feet	108·2 × 28·5 × 12
Main Engines	Diesel, 1650 bhp = 12 knots

Achilles was launched in 1962 and *Ajax* in 1963. Both are icebreaking tugs. Former pennant numbers were 276 and 277, respectively.

AJAX   *1970, Royal Swedish Navy, Official*

SIGRUN A 256

Displacement, tons	250 standard
Dimensions, feet	105·0 × 22·3 × 11·8
Main engines	Diesels; 320 bhp = 11 knots

Launched in 1961. Rated as *Tvättbytesfartyg*.

HECTOR A 321   **HERMES** A 253   **HEROS** A 323

Displacement, tons	185 standard
Dimensions, feet	75·5 × 22·6 × 11·1
Main engines	Diesels; 630 bhp = 11·5 knots

Launched in 1953-57. The pennant number of *Hermes* was changed from 318.

HÄGERN (ex-*Torpedbargaren*) A246

Displacement, tons	50 standard
Dimensions, feet	88·6 × 16·4 × 4·9
Main engines	Diesels; 270 bhp = 10 knots

Hägern was launched in 1951. Her pennant number was changed from 274 to 246.

LOMMEN (ex-*M* 17) A 231   **SKULD** (ex-*M* 20) A 371
                                           SPOVEN (ex-*M* 18) A 232

Displacement, tons	70 standard
Dimensions, feet	85·3 × 16·5 × 4·5
Main engines	Diesel; 600 bhp = 13 knots

Former inshore minesweepers of the large motor launch type. All launched in 1941.

EXPERIMENTAL CRAFT

URD (ex-*Capella*) A 271

Displacement, tons	63 standard; 90 full load
Dimensions, feet	73·8 × 18·3 × 9·2
Main engines	Diesels; 200 bhp = 8 knots

Experimental vessel added to the official list in 1970. Launched in 1929.

SUDAN

Establishment

The Navy was established in 1962 to guard the Red Sea coast.

Diplomatic Representation

Naval, Military and Air Attaché in London:
Brigadier Salah El-din Mohamed Said

Mercantile Marine

Lloyd's Register of Shipping: 12 vessels of 22 153 tons gross

PATROL BOATS

2 YUGOSLAV PBR 512 TYPE

PBR I   **PBR II**

Displacement, tons	190 standard; 245 full load
Dimensions, feet	134·5 × 20·7 × 7·0
Guns	2—40 mm AA; 2—20 mm AA
Main engines	Diesel; 2 shafts; 3 300 bhp = 20 knots

Submarine chasers of the "500" class. Transferred from the Yugoslavian Navy during 1969.

4 YOGOSLAV MOSOR PB TYPE

GIHAD PB 1   **HORRIYA** PB 2   **ISTIGLAL** PB 3   **SHAAB** PB 4

Displacement, tons	100
Dimensions, feet	115 × 16·5 × 5·2
Guns	1—40 mm AA; 1—20 mm AA; 2—7·6 mm MG
Main engines	Mercedes-Benz diesels; 2 shafts; 1 800 bhp = 20 knots
Radius, miles	1 400
Complement	20 officers and men

Built by Mosor Shipyard, Trogir, Yugoslavia, in 1961-62. Of steel construction. First craft acquired by the newly established Sudanese Navy. A photograph of *Horriya, Istiglal* and *Shaab* in company appears in the 1962-63 to 1965-66 editions, and of *Istiglal* and *Shaab* together in the 1967-68 and 1968-69 editions.

GIHAD   *Sudanese Navy, Official*

HORRIYA   *Sudanese Navy, Official*

LANDING CRAFT

Two ex-Yugoslavian landing craft of the DTK 221 type were taken over during 1969.

OILER

Ex-PN 17

Displacement, tons	420 standard; 650 full load
Dimensions, feet	141·5 × 22·8 × 13·6
Main engines	300 bhp = 7 knots

Former Yugoslavian oiler rehabilitated and transferred to the Sudanese Navy in 1969.

WATER CARRIER

A small water carrier, ex-PV 6, was transferred from Yugoslavia to the Sudanese Navy in 1969.

SURVEY SHIP

A small vessel, converted for service as a hydrographic ship, was acquired from Yugoslavia in 1969.

SYRIA

New Construction

The construction is planned of patrol vessels of 150 tons with a speed of 27 knots; motor torpedo boats; and seaward defence boats of 60 tons with a speed of 23 knots.

Acquisition Programme

One destroyer, two small submarines of the "M" type and six motor torpedo boats were expected from the USSR. Several small craft were received from France.

Mercantile Marine

Lloyd's Register of Shipping: 4 vessels of 1 020 tons gross

MINESWEEPERS

2 Ex-USSR "T 43" TYPE

HITTINE   **YARMOUK**

Displacement, tons	500 standard; 600 full load
Dimensions, feet	200 × 27·2 × 9
Guns	4—37 mm AA; 8—13 mm AA
Main engines	Diesel motors; 2 shafts; speed = 18 knots

Reported in 1962 to have transferred from the Soviet Navy to the Syrian Navy.

PATROL VESSELS

3 Ex-FRENCH "CH" TYPE

Name	Builders	Laid down	Launched	Completed
AKABA BEN NASEH	A. C. de France	1938	Jan 1940	Apr 1940
AL HARISSI	A.C. Seine Maut	1938	1939	1940
TAREK BEN SAID	A.C. Seine Maut	1938	1939	1940

Displacement, tons	107 standard; 131 full load
Dimensions, feet	116·5 pp; 121·8 oa × 17·5 × 6·5
Guns	1—3 in; 2—20 mm AA
A/S weapons	Depth charges
Main engines	MAN diesels; 2 shafts; 1 130 bhp = 16 knots
Oil fuel, tons	5
Radius, miles	1 200 at 8 knots; 680 at 13 knots
Complement	28

These former French submarine chasers were transferred in 1962 to form the nucleus of the Syrian Navy. Respectively ex-*Ch* 10, ex-*Ch* 19, and ex-*Ch* 130.

"Ch" Type   *M Henri Le Masson*

MISSILE BOATS

8 Ex-USSR "KOMAR" CLASS

Displacement, tons	75 standard; 100 full load
Dimensions, feet	82·0 × 20·0 × 6·0
Missile launchers	2 for "Styx" with 15 miles range
Guns	2—25 mm AA
Main engines	3 diesels; 4 800 bhp = 40 knots

Former Soviet missile patrol boats. See further particulars and photographs in the USSR section.

TORPEDO BOATS

15 Ex-USSR TYPE

Displacement, tons	45 standard; 50 full load
Tubes	2—21 in
Guns	2—25 mm AA
Main engines	Diesels; 2 400 bhp = 40 knots

Five torpedo boats were transferred from the USSR at Latakia on 7 Feb 1957, and at least ten subsequently.

TANZANIA

Mercantile Marine

Lloyd's Register of Shipping: 10 vessels of 17 722 tons gross

COASTAL PATROL BOATS

There are reported to be four small patrol boats, two of 50 tons and two of 27 tons. It was officially stated in 1967 that the four *Küstenwachboote* loaned to the Tanzania Government by the Federal Republic of Germany, KW 4, KW 5, KW 9 and KW 10, shipped from West Germany on 8 Dec 1963, and renamed *Rafiki, Papa, Uhura* and *Salama*, respectively, see full particulars in the 1966-67 edition, had been handed over to the Southern Engineering Company of Mombasa, Kenya.

THAILAND

Administration

Commander-in-Chief of the Navy:
Admiral Charoon Chalermtiarana

Chief of the Naval Staff:
Admiral Thavil Rayananon

Diplomatic Representation

Naval Attaché in London:
Captain Chinda Chai-Udom

Naval Attaché in Washington:
Captain Tada Ditbanjong

Strength of the Fleet

1 Destroyer Escort	15 Patrol Boats
4 Patrol Frigates	5 Coast Guard Vessels
1 Escort Minesweeper	7 Landing Ships
2 Coastal Minelayers	9 Landing Craft
17 Patrol Vessels	1 Survey Ship
4 Coastal Minesweepers	1 MCS Support Ship
11 Coastal Gunboats	15 Auxiliaries

New Construction

1 General Purpose Frigate (New Yarrow Design)
2 Corvette Frigates (US Small PF Type

Personnel

1971: Navy, 15 000 (2 000 officers) and 13 000 ratings)
Marine Corps: 6 400 (400 officers and 6 000 men)

Mercantile Marine

Lloyd's Register of Shipping:
60 vessels of 82 271 tons gross

DESTROYER ESCORTS

Name	No.	Builders	Launched	Completed
PIN KLAO (ex USS Hemminger) DE 746	3 (ex-1)	Western Pipe & Steel Co	12 Sep 1943	30 May 1944

Displacement, tons	1 240 standard; 1 900 full load
Length, feet (*metres*)	306·0 (*93·3*) oa
Beam, feet (*metres*)	37·0 (*11·3*)
Draught, feet (*metres*)	14·1 (*4·3*)
Guns, dual purpose	3—3 in (*76 mm*) 50 cal
Guns, AA	6—40 mm
A/S weapons	8 DCT
Torpedo tubes	6 (2 triple) for A/S torpedoes
Main engines	GM diesels with electric drive; 2 shafts; 6 000 bhp
Speed, knots	20
Radius, miles	11 500 at 11 knots
Oil fuel, tons	300
Complement	220

Ex-US "Bostwick" class. Transferred from US Navy to Royal Thai Navy at New York Navy Shipyard in July 1959 under MDAP. The 3—21 in torpedo tubes were removed and the 4—20 mm AA guns were replaced by 4—40 mm AA. The six A/S torpedo tubes were fitted in 1966.

PIN KLAO   1966, Royal Thai Navy, Official

FRIGATES

1 YARROW TYPE

Displacement, tons	1 780 official figure
Length, feet (*metres*)	320·0 (*97·6*)
Beam, feet (*metres*)	36·0 (*11·0*)
Draught, feet (*metres*)	18·0 (*5·5*)
Missile launchers	1 quadruple "Seacat" s-to-a
Guns, dual purpose	2—4·5 in (*114 mm*) single
Guns, AA	2—40 mm single
A/S weapons	1 triple barrelled "Limbo" mortar; 2 depth charge throwers
Main engines	1 Rolls-Royce "Olympus" gas Turbine; 24 000 shp; 1 Crossley-Pielstick diesel; 6 000 bhp
Speed, knots	26 approx
Complement	140

An order was placed with Yarrow & Co Ltd, Scotstoun, Glasgow on 21 Aug 1969 for a general purpose frigate. A long range vessel of a new design, developed by Yarrow resulting in a comparative low cost ship with an armament displacement ratio superior to that of any comparable warship. The ship is fully automatic with a consequent saving in complement. Scheduled for launching mid 1971, and delivery early 1973.

New Frigate (model)   courtesy Yarrow (Shipbuilders) Ltd

2 US NEW CONSTRUCTION CORVETTE TYPE

TAPI PF 107		PF 108

Displacement, tons	900 standard; 1 135 full load
Length, feet (*metres*)	275 (*83·8*) oa
Beam, feet (*metres*)	33 (*10·0*)
Draught, feet (*metres*)	10 (*3·0*)
Guns, surface	2—3 in (*76 mm*)
Guns, AA	2—40 mm
Main engines	FM Diesels; 6 000 bhp
Speed, knots	20

Both ordered from the American Shipbuilding Co, Toledo Ohio at the end of 1969. Of similar design to the Iranian corvettes of the "Bayandor" class.

PF Type   RTN

Frigates—continued

Name	No.	Builders	Laid down	Launched	Completed
PRASAE (ex-USS *Gallup*, PF 47)	2	Consolidated Steel Corpn, Los Angeles	18 Aug 1943	17 Sep 1943	29 Feb 1944
TAHCHIN (ex-USS *Glendale*, PF 36)	1	Consolidated Steel Corpn, Los Angeles	6 Apr 1943	28 May 1943	1 Oct 1943

2 "PRASAE" CLASS

Displacement, tons	1 430 standard; 2 100 full load
Length, feet (*metres*)	304·0 (*92·7*) oa
Beam, feet (*metres*)	37·5 (*11·4*)
Draught, feet (*metres*)	13·7 (*4·2*)
Guns, dual purpose	3—3 in (*76 mm*) 50 cal.
Guns, AA	2—40 mm; 9—20 mm
A/S weapons	8 DCT
Main engines	Triple expansion; 2 shafts; 5 500 ihp
Speed, knots	19
Boilers	2 small water tube 3-drum type
Oil fuel, tons	685
Radius, miles	9 500 at 12 knots
Complement	180

Former US patrol frigates of the "Tacoma" class. Delivered to the Royal Thai Navy on 29 Oct 1951. They were of similar design to the British frigates of the "River" class. A photograph of *Tachin* appears in the 1969-70 and 1970-71 editions.

PRASAE   *1971, Official*

1 Ex-BRITISH "FLOWER" CLASS

BANGPAKONG (ex-*Gondwana*, ex-HMS *Burnet*) PF 4

Displacement, tons	1 060 standard; 1 350 full load
Length, feet (*metres*)	193·0 (*58·8*) pp; 203·2 (*61·9*) oa
Beam, feet (*metres*)	33·0 (*10·0*)
Draught, feet (*metres*)	14·5 (*4·4*)
Guns, dual purpose	1—3 in (*76 mm*) 50 cal.
Guns, AA	1—40 mm; 6—20 mm
A/S weapons	4 DCT
Main engines	Triple expansion; 2 880 ihp
Speed, knots	16
Boilers	2 three-drum type
Oil fuel, tons	282
Radius, miles	4 800 at 12 knots
Complement	100

Built by Ferguson Bros, Port Glasgow as a "Flower" class corvette. Laid down on 2 Nov 1942, launched on 31 May 1943, completed on 23 Sept 1943. Served in Indian Navy before transfer to Royal Thai Navy on 15 May 1947. The 3 inch replaced a 4 inch gun, and the 40 mm replaced a 20 mm gun in 1966. Sister ship *Prasae* (ex-*Sind*, ex-*Betony*) was lost in the Korean War on 13 Jan 1951.

BANGPAKONG   *Royal Thai Navy, Official*

1 SLOOP TYPE

MAEKLONG No. 3

Displacement, tons	1 400 standard; 2 000 full load
Length, feet (*metres*)	269·0 (*82·0*)
Beam, feet (*metres*)	34·0 (*10·4*)
Draught, feet (*metres*)	10·5 (*3·2*)
Guns, surface	4—4·7 in (*120 mm*)
Guns, AA	3—40 mm; 3—20 mm
Main engines	Triple expansion; 2 shafts; 2 500 ihp
Speed, knots	14
Boilers	2 water tube
Oil fuel, tons	487
Radius, miles	8 000 at 12 knots
Complement	155 as training ship

Built by Uraga Dock Co, Japan. Laid down in 1936, launched on 27 Nov 1936, completed in June 1937. Designed as dual-purpose sloop and torpedo boat. Employed as training ship. The 4—18 inch torpedo tubes were removed. Sister ship *Tachin*, heavily damaged on 1 June 1945, was scrapped.

MAEKLONG   *1967, Royal Thai Navy, Official*

1 Ex-BRITISH "ALGERINE" CLASS

PHOSAMTON (ex-HMS *Minstrel*) MSF 1

Displacement, tons	1 040 standard; 1 335 full load
Length, feet (*metres*)	225·0 (*68·6*) oa
Beam, feet (*metres*)	35·5 (*10·8*)
Draught, feet (*metres*)	10·5 (*3·2*)
Guns, surface	1—4 in (*102 mm*)
Guns, AA	6—20 mm
A/S weapons	4 DCT
Main engines	Triple expansion; 2 shafts; 2 000 ihp
Speed, knots	16
Boilers	2 three-drum type
Oil fuel, tons	270
Radius, miles	5 000 at 10 knots
Complement	103

Former British "Algerine" class ocean minesweeper capable of fleet sweeping and escort duties. Built by Redfern Construction Co. Laid down in 1943, launched on 5 Oct 1944, completed in 1945. Transferred in Apr 1947. The 20 mm guns were increased from 3 to 6, and the DCTs from 2 to 4 in 1966.

PHOSAMTON   *1965, Royal Thai Navy, Official*

COASTAL MINELAYERS

BANGRACHAN   *Official*

2 "BANGRACHAN" CLASS

BANGRACHAN (No. 1)   **NHONG SARHAI** (No. 2)

Displacement, tons	368 standard; 408 full load
Dimensions, feet	160·8 × 25·9 × 7·2
Guns	2—3 in AA; 2—20 mm AA
Mines	142 capacity
Main engines	Burmeister & Wain diesels; 2 shafts; 540 bhp = 12 knots
Oil fuel, tons	18
Radius, miles	2 700
Complement	55

Launched by Cantiere dell'Adriatico, Monfalcone in 1936, *Nhong Sarhai* on 22 July. A photograph of *Nhong Sarhai* appears in the 1961-62 to 1965-66 editions.

ARMOURED GUNBOATS. Of the two armoured gunboats or coast defence monitors (1,000 tons with 6-inch guns) built by Vickers Armstrong in 1928-30, *Ratanakosindra* was withdrawn from service in 1968 and *Sukothai* was removed from the effective list in 1971.

PATROL VESSELS

7 "TRAD" CLASS

CHANDHABURI	16 Dec 1936	No. 22	**PUKET**	28 Sep 1935	No. 12
CHUMPORN	18 Jan 1937	No. 31	**RAYONG**	11 Jan 1937	No. 23
PATTANI	16 Oct 1936	No. 13	**SURASDRA**	28 Nov 1936	No. 21
			TRAD	26 Oct 1935	No. 11

Displacement, tons	318 standard; 470 full load
Dimensions, feet	219 pp; 223 oa × 21 × 7
Guns	2—3 in AA; 1—40 mm AA; 2—20 mm AA; *Chumporn, Puket* and *Trad* 2—40 mm
Tubes	4—18 in (2 twin); *Chumporn, Puket* and *Trad* 2—18 in (twin)
Main engines	Parsons geared turbines; 2 shafts; 9 000 hp = 31 knots
Boilers	2 Yarrow
Oil fuel, tons	102
Radius, miles	1 700 at 15 knots
Complement	70

Designed as torpedo boats, *Puket* and *Trad* were laid down on 8 Feb 1935 by Canteiri Riuniti dell'Adriatico, Monfalcone, for delivery by end of 1935. Launch dates above. Armament was supplied by Vickers-Armstrongs Ltd. First boat reached 32-34 knots on trials with 10 000 hp. All delivered by summer 1937. The 2 single 18 inch torpedo tubes and the 4—8 mm guns were removed.

TRAD   *Official*

CHANDHABURI   *1970, Royal Thai Navy, Official*

Patrol Vessels—*continued*

3 "SATTAHIB" CLASS

KANTANG No. 7   **KLONGYAI** No. 5   **SATTAHIB** No. 8

Displacement, tons	110 standard; 135 full load
Dimensions, feet	131·5 × 15·5 × 4
Guns	1—3 in; 1—20 mm
Tubes	2—18 in
Main engines	Geared turbines; 2 shafts; 1 000 shp = 19 knots
Boilers	2 water-tube
Oil fuel, tons	18
Complement	31

Sattahib was built by the Royal Thai Naval Dockyard, Bangkok, laid down on 21 Nov 1956, launched on 28 Oct 1957 and completed in 1958. The other two were built by Ishikawajima Co, Japan, both launched on 26 Mar 1937 and completed on 21 June 1937. A photograph of *Klongyai* appears in the 1956-57 to 1964-65 editions and of *Sattahib* in the 1965-66 to 1970-71 editions. *Takbai* No. 6 was removed from the effective list in 1971.

KANTANG   *1971, Official*

7 "LIULOM" CLASS

LIULOM (ex-*PC* 1253) **PHALI** (ex-*PC* 1185) **SUKRIP** (ex-*PC* 1218)
LONGLOM (ex-*PC* 570) **SARASIN** (ex-*PC* 495) **THAYANCHON** (ex-*PC* 575)
                                                      TONGPLIU (ex-*PC* 616)

Displacement, tons	280 standard; 400 full load
Dimensions, feet	174 oa × 23·2 × 6
Guns	1—3 in AA; 1—40 mm AA; 5—20 mm AA
A/S weapons	2 ASW torpedo tubes (except *Sarasin*)
Main engines	Diesel; 2 shafts; 3 600 bhp = 19 knots
Oil fuel, tons	60
Radius, miles	6,000 at 10 knots
Complement	62 to 71, *Sukeip* 69 (10 officers, 59 men)

Former US submarine chasers. Launched in 1941-43. Nos. PC 7, 8, 4, 1, 5, 2 and 6, respectively. A photograph of *Sukrip* appears in the 1956-67 to 1964-65 editions. and of *Longlom* in the 1965-66 to 1968-69 editions.

THAYANCHON   *1969, Royal Thai Navy, Official*

SURVEY SHIP

CHANTHARA

Displacement, tons	870 standard; 996 full load
Dimensions, feet	229·2 oa × 34·5 × 10
Guns	1—20 mm AA
Main engines	2 diesels; 2 shafts; 1 000 bhp = 13·25 knots
Radius	10 000 miles (cruising)
Complement	69

Built by C. Melchers & Co, Bremen, Germany. Laid down on 27 Sep 1960. Launched on 17 Dec 1960. Can also be used as training ship and yacht.

CHANTHARA   *1962, Royal Thai Navy, Official*

COASTAL MINESWEEPER

BANGKEO (ex-USS *MSC* 303) 6   **LADYA** (ex-USS *MSC* 297) 5
DONCHEDI (ex-USS *MSC* 313) 8   **TADINDENG** (ex-USS *MSC* 301) 7

Displacement, tons	330 standard ; 362 full load
Dimensions, feet	145·3 oa × 27 × 8·5
Guns	2—20 mm AA
Main engines	4 GM diesels ; 2 shafts ; 1 000 bhp = 13 knots
Complement	43 (7 officers and 36 men)

Built by Peterson Builders Inc, Sturgeon Bay, Wisc, (*Ladya* and *Donchedi*), Tacoma Boat building Co Tacoma, Wash. (*Tadindeng*) and Dorchester Shipbuilding Corp, Camden (*Bangkeo*). *Ladya* was transferred on 14 Dec 1963, *Bangkeo* on 9 July 1965, *Tadindeng* on 26 Aug 1965, and *Donchedi* on 17 Sep 1965 (last three launched in 1964, 1 July, 11 Apr, 22 Dec). A photograph of *Ladya* appears in the 1964-65 to 1966-67 editions, of *Tadindeng* in the 1967-68 and 1968-69 editions and of *Donchedi* in the 1969-70 and 1970-71 editions. Of the ex-US YMS type, *Bangkeo* (ex-YMS 384), *Ladya* (ex-YMS 138) and *Tadindeng* (ex-YMS 21) were removed from the effective list in 1964 and 1965.

BANGKEO   *1971, Official*

COASTAL GUNBOATS

T 91

Displacement, tons	87·5 standard
Dimensions, feet	104·3 × 17·5 × 5·5
Guns	1—40 mm AA ; 1—20 mm AA
Main engines	Diesels ; 1 600 bhp = 25 knots
Complement	21

Fast patrol boat type. Built by the Royal Thai Naval Dockyard, Bangkok.

T 91   *1970, Royal Thai Navy, Official*

T 11 (ex-US *PGM* 71)   **T 14** (ex-US *PGM* 116)   **T 17** (ex-US *PGM*)
T 12 (ex-US *PGM* 79)   **T 15** (ex-US *PGM* 117)   **T 18** (ex-US *PGM*)
T 13 (ex-US *PGM* 107)   **T 16** (ex-US *PGM* 115)   **T 19** (ex-US *PGM* 123)
                                                T i10 (ex-US *PGM* 124)

Displacement, tons	130 standard ; 147 full load
Dimensions, feet	99·0 wl ; 101·0 oa × 21·0 × 6·0
Guns	1—40 mm AA ; 4—20 mm AA ; 2—·50 cal
Main engines	Diesels ; 2 shafts ; 1 800 bhp = 18·5 knots
Complement	30

T 11 was built by Peterson Builders Inc, launched on 5 May 1965 and transferred to the Royal Thai Navy on 1 Feb 1966. T 13 was transferred 28 Aug 1967, T 14, T 15 on 18 Aug 1969 and 2 Oct 1969, T 16, T 17 and T 19 on 12 Feb 1970, T 19 and T 110 on 25 Dec 1970.

T 12   *1969, Royal Thai Navy, Official*

COAST GUARD VESSELS

CGC 13   **CGC 14**   **CGC 15**   **CGC 16**

Displacement, tons	95
Dimensions, feet	95 × 20·2 × 5
Guns	1—20 mm AA
A/S weapons	2 D.C. racks ; 2 mousetraps
Main engines	4 diesels ; 2 shafts ; 2 200 bhp = 21 knots
Boilers	1 500 miles cruising range
Complement	15

U.S. coastguard cutters transferred in 1954. Similar to those built for U.S.C.G. by U.S. Coast Guard Yard, Curtis Bay, in 1953. Cost £475,000 each.

CGC 14   *Royal Thai Navy Official*

CGC 11

Displacement, tons	44·5
Dimensions, feet	83·1 × 16 × 4·5
Guns	1—20 mm AA
A/S weapons	2 DC racks ; 2 mousetraps
Main engines	2 Viking petrol engines ; 1 300 bhp = 20·5 knots

Former US Coast Guard cutter of the YP class. Of wooden hulled construction. Sister CGC 12 disposed of in 1968. A photograph of CGC 11 appears in the 1967-68 to 1969-70 editions.

PATROL BOATS

SC 7 (ex-*SC* 31, ex-US *SC* 1632)   **SC 8** (ex-*SC* 32, ex-US *SC* 1633)

Displacement, tons	110 light ; 125 full load
Dimensions feet,	111 × 17 × 6
Guns	1—40 mm ; 3—20 mm
A/S weapons	Depth Charges, Mousetrap
Main engines	High-speed diesel = 18 knots

Former US wooden submarine chasers. Built by South Coast Co, Newport Reach, California, in 1954-55. SC 33 (ex-*SC* 1634) was scrapped 8 Mar 1962. A photograph of SC 8 appears in the 1959-60 to 1969-70 editions.

FAST PATROL CRAFT

T 21   **T 22**   **T 23**   **T 24**   **T 25**   **T 26**   **T 27**

Displacement, tons	20 standard ; 22 full load
Dimensions, feet	50 × 13
Guns	2—0·50 cal (1 twin)
Main engines	Diesels ; 2 shafts ; 480 bhp = 25 knots
Complement	5

T 23, T 24, T 25, T 26 and T 27 were transferred from US to Thailand on 21 Sep 1970.

RIVER PATROL CRAFT

T 31   **T 32**   **T 33**   **T 34**   **T 35**   **T 36**

Displacement, tons	10·4 standard ; 13·05 full load
Dimensions, feet	35 × 10
Guns	2—0·50 cal (1 twin) ; 2—0·30 cal
Main engines	Diesels ; 2 shafts ; 225 bhp = 14 knots
Complement	7

LANDING SHIPS
4 Ex-US LST TYPE

ANGTHONG (ex-USS *LST* 294) LST 1
CHANG (ex-USS *Lincoln County LST* 898) LST 2
LANTA (ex-USS *Stone County LST* 1141) LST 4
PANGAN (ex-USS *Stark County LST* 1134) LST 3

Displacement, tons	1 625 standard ; 4 080 full load
Dimensions, feet	316 wl ; 328 oa × 50 × 14
Guns :	6—40 mm ; 4—20 mm
Main engines	GM diesels ; 2 shafts ; 1 700 bhp = 11 knots
Complement	80

Angthong is employed as a transport. *Chang*, transferred to Thailand in 1962, was built by Dravo Corp, laid down on 15 Oct 1944, launched on 25 Nov 1944 and completed on 29 Dec 1944. *Pangan* was transferred on 16 May 1966 and *Lanta* on 12 Mar 1970. A photograph of *Angthong* appears in the 1956-57 to 1964-65 editions.

CHANG   *1965, Royal Thai Navy, Official*

LANDING CRAFT

3 Ex-US LSM TYPE

KRAM (ex-USS *LSM* 469) LSM 3   **KUT** (ex-USS *LSM* 333) LSM 5
PAI (ex-USS *LSM* 338) LSM 2

Displacement, tons	743 standard ; 1 095 full load
Dimensions, feet	196·5 wl ; 203·5 oa × 34·5 × 8·3
Guns	2—40 mm AA
Main engines	Diesel direct drive ; 2 shafts ; 2 800 bhp = 12·5 knots
Complement	55

Former United States landing ship of the LCM, later LSM (Medium Landing Ship), type. *Kram* was transferred to Thailand under MAP at Seattle, Wash, on 25 May 1962; she was built by Brown Shipbuilding Col, Houston, Tex, laid down on 27 Jan 1945, launched on 17 Feb 1945, and completed on 17 Mar 1945. A photograph of *Kut* appears in the 1956-57 to 1964-65 editions, and of *Kram* in the 1965-66 to 1969-70 editions.

NAKA LSSL 3 (ex-USS *LSSL* 102)

Displacement, tons	233 standard ; 287 full load
Dimensions, feet	152 wl ; 158 oa × 23 × 4·25
Guns	1—3 inch ; 4—40 mm AA ; 4—20 mm AA ; 4—81 mm mortar
Main engines	Diesels ; 2 shafts ; 1 320 bhp = 15 knots

Transferred in 1966. Acquired when Japan returned her to USA. Support gunboat.

2 Ex-US LCI TYPE

PRAB (ex-*LCI* 670) LC1 1   **SATAKUT** (ex-*LCI* 739) LCI 2

Displacement, tons	230 standard ; 387 full load
Dimensions, feet	157 × 23 × 6
Guns	2—20 mm AA
Main engines	Diesel ; 2 shafts ; 1 320 bhp = 14 knots
Complement	54

Former United States landing craft of the LCI (Infantry Landing Craft) type. A photograph of *Prab* appears in the 1957-58 and earlier editions.

SATAKUT   *Royal Thai Navy, Official*

6 LCU Ex-US LCT (6) TYPE

ARDANG (LCU 10)   **MATAPHON** (LCU 8)   **RAWI** (LCU 9)
KOLUM (LCU 12)   **PHETRA** (LCU 11)   **TALIBONG** (LCU 13)

Displacement, tons	134 standard ; 279 full load
Dimensions, feet	112 × 32 × 4
Guns	2—20 mm AA
Main engines	Diesel ; 3 shafts ; 675 bhp = 10 knots
Complement :	37

Former United States landing craft of the LCT(6) type. Employed as transport ferries A photograph of *Mataphon* appears in the 1950-51 to 1961-62 editions.

TRANSPORTS

SICHANG AKL 1

Displacement, tons	815 standard
Dimensions, feet	160 × 28 × 16
Main Engines	Diesel ; 2 shafts ; 550 bhp = 16 knots
Complement	30

Built by Harima Co, Japan. *Sichang* was launched on 10 Nov 1937. Completed in Jan 1938. A photograph of this ship appears in the 1953-54 to 1959-60 editions. Sister ship *Pangan* was deleted from the list in 1962.

KLED KEO A 7

Displacement, tons	382 standard ; 450 full load
Dimensions, feet	154·9 × 25·4 × 14
Guns	3—20 mm
Main engines	1 diesel ; 600 hp = 12 knots max
Complement	54

TRAINING SHIP (*Ex-Fleet Minesweeper*)

CHOW PRAYA (ex-HMS *Havant*)

Displacement, tons	680 standard ; 840 full load
Dimensions, feet	220·0 × 28·2 × 7·5
Guns	2—57 mm AA ; 1—40 mm AA
Main engines	Triple expansion ; 2 shafts ; 2 200 ihp = 16 knots
Boilers	Yarrow, converted to burn oil
Oil fuel, tons	160
Radius, miles	1 750 at 15 knots
Complement	65

Former British fleet minesweeper of the "Racecourse" class. Built by Eltringhams, South Shields. Launched on 24 Mar 1919. Purchased in Aug 1922 and reconstructed by John I. Thornycroft & Co. Ltd., Southampton. Guns are interchangeable for training. A photograph appears in the 1957-58 to 1969-70 editions.

OILERS

PROET

Displacement, tons	360 (official figure)
Dimensions, feet	122·7 × 19·7 × 8·7
Main engines	Diesels ; 500 bhp = 9 knots

Built by the Royal Thai Naval Dockyard, Bangkok. Commissioned on 16 Jan 1970.

SAMED

Displacement, tons	305 standard ; 485 full load
Dimensions, feet	108 × 20 × 10 feet
Main Engines	Diesel ; 500 bhp = 11 knots

Built by Royal Thai Naval Dockyard, Bangkok. Launched on 8 July 1966.

CHULA AO 2

Displacement, tons	2 395 standard
Dimensions, feet	328 × 43·2 × 25 feet
Main Engines	Steam turbine

This tanker and *Matra* (see below) were acquired for naval oiling and supply duties.

CHULA   *1969, Royal Thai Navy, Official*

MATRA AO 3

Displacement, tons	4 744
Dimensions, feet	328 × 45·2 × 20
Main Engines	Steam turbine

Employed as a freighting and fleet replenishment tanker and naval supply ship.

SAMUI YO 4

Displacement, tons	422 standard
Dimensions, feet	174·5 × 32 × 15
Main Engines	Diesel ; 2 shafts ; 600 bhp = 8 knots
Complement	49

Small tanker of the ex-YOG type. Employed as a fleet auxiliary attendant oiler. A photograph appears in the 1956-57 to 1969-70 editions.

PRONG

Displacement, tons	150 standard
Dimensions, feet	95 × 18 × 7·5
Main Engines	Diesel ; 150 bhp = 10 knots
Complement	14

Launched in 1938. Employed as a small naval auxiliary servicing tanker.

MINESWEEPER SUPPORT SHIPS

RANG KWIEN MCS 11 (ex-*Umihari Maru*)

Displacement, tons	586 standard
Dimensions, feet	162·3 × 31·2 × 13·0 max
Main engines	Triple expansion steam ; Speed = 10 knots

Built in 1944 by Mitsubishi Co as a tug. Acquired by Royal Thai Navy on 6 Sep 1967.

RANG KWIEN   *1969, Royal Thai Navy, Official*

WATER CARRIERS

CHUANG

Displacement, tons	305 standard ; 485 full load
Dimensions, feet	98 × 18 × 7·2 (official figures)
Main Engines	GM diesel ; 500 bhp = 11 knots
Complement :	29

Built by the Royal Thai Naval Dockyard, Bangkok. Launched on 14 Jan 1965.

CHAN YW 6

Displacement, tons	355 standard
Dimensions, feet	139·5 × 24 × 10
Main Engines	Diesel ; Speed = 6 knots

A photograph of this ship appears in the 1956-57 to 1959-60 editions.

TUGS

SAMAESAN (ex-*Empire Vincent*) YTB 7

Displacement, tons	503 full load
Dimensions, feet	105·0 × 26·5 × 13·0
Main engines	Triple expansion ; 850 ihp = 10·5 knots
Complement	27

Built by Cochrane & Sons Ltd, Selby, Yorks, England. Photograph in 1957-58 and earlier editions.

KLUENG BADAN   **MARN VICHAI**   **RAD**

Displacement, tons	63 standard (*Rad* 52 standard)
Dimensions, feet	64·7 × 16·5 × 6·0 (*Rad* 60·7 × 17·5 × 5·0)
Main engines	Diesels ; speed = 8 knots (*Rad* 6 knots)

TRINIDAD AND TOBAGO

COAST GUARD

Administration

Commanding Officer, T. & T. Coast Guard: Captain D. F. A. Bloom MOM, GM

Personnel

1971: 156 (18 officers, 138 men), 194 (22 officers, 172 men) by 1972

Mercantile Marine

Lloyd's Register of Shipping: 22 vessels of 20 734 tons gross

PATROL CRAFT

2 LATER VOSPER TYPE

BUCCO REEF   **CHAGUARAMAS**

Displacement, tons	100 standard; 125 full load
Dimensions, feet	95 wl; 103·0 × 19·8 × 5·8
Guns	1—40 mm Bofors
Main engines	2 Paxman Ventura diesels; 2 900 bhp = 24 knots
Oil fuel, tons	20
Radius, miles	2 000 at 13 knots
Complement	19 (3 officers, 16 ratings)

It is officially stated that an order has been placed with the Vosper Thornycroft Group, Portsmouth, for two new patrol craft of the "Trinity" class for delivery in Jan 1972.

2 VOSPER TYPE

COURLAND BAY CG 2   **TRINITY** CG 1

Displacement, tons	96 standard; 123 full load
Dimensions, feet	95 wl; 102·6 oa × 19·7 × 5·5
Guns:	1—40 mm Bofors
Main Engines	2 12-cyl Vee-form Paxman Ventura YJCM turbocharged diesels; 2 910 bhp 24·5 knots (max.)
Oil fuel (tons)	18
Radius, miles	1 800 at 13·5 knots
Complement	17 (3 officers; 14 ratings)

Designed and built by Vosper Limited, Portsmouth. Of steel construction with aluminium alloy superstructure. Up-to-date radar and navigation equipment is fitted, and the boats are air-conditioned throughout except the engine room. Vosper roll-damping equipment is fitted for improved sea-keeping and greater efficiency and comfort of the crews. Laid down Oct 1963. *Trinity* was launched on 14 Apr 1964. Both were commissioned at Portsmouth on 20 Feb 1965. *Trinity* is named after Trinity Hills, so named by Columbus on making his landfall in 1498, and *Courland Bay* after a bay in Tobago where a settlement was founded by the Duke of Courland in the 17th century.

COURLAND BAY   1970, Trinidad & Tobago Coast Guard, Official

TRINITY   1969, Trinidad & Tobago Coast Guard, Official

Patrol Craft—continued

1 60 ft TYPE

SEA HAWK

Dimensions, feet	60 × 17·3 × 3·5
Guns	1 machine gun
Main engines	2 Rolls Royce diesels; 250 hp = 14·5 knots
Radius, miles	400
Complement	6 (1 officer, 5 men)

Built by J. Taylor (Shipbuilders) Ltd, Shoreham-by-Sea. Extensively refitted in 1969; but taken out of service in 1971 and placed in reserve.

SEA HAWK   1970, Trinidad & Tobago Coast Guard, Official

1 45ft TYPE

SEA SCOUT

Length, feet	45·0
Main engines	1 GM 671 diesel; speed = 12 knots

Built by J. Taylor (Shipbuilders) Ltd, Shoreham-oy-Sea. Refitted in 1970 with a single GM 671 diesel in place of the former two Perkins diesels.

SEA SCOUT   1969, Trinidad & Tobago Coast Guard, Official

2 + 2 INSHORE TYPE

CG 5   CG 6

It is officially stated that two fibreglass fast runabouts, capable of speeds of 27 knots have recently been purchased for inshore patrol work in the Gulf of Paria, and it is anticipated that two similar type vessels will be built in 1971.

CG 6   1971, Trinidad & Tobago Coast Guard. Official

TOGO

PATROL BOATS

It was reported that Togo, which proclaimed independence on 27 April 1960, had acquired 3 steel 100 ft motor patrol boats and 1 steel 95 ft river gunboat and intended to acquire in the near future 1 steel 130·ft patrol vessel.

TUNISIA

Administration
Chief of Naval Staff: Capitaine de Fregate Jedidi Bechir

Mercantile Marine
Lloyd's Register of shipping: 17 vessels of 22 089 tons gross

CORVETTE *(Aviso)*

DESTOUR (ex-*Chevreuil* F 735) E 71

Displacement, tons	647 standard; 920 full load
Dimensions, feet	257 × 28·5 × 10·5
Guns	1—4·1 inch (*105 mm*); 1—40 mm AA; 4—20 mm AA
A/S weapons	4 DCT; 2 DC racks
Main engines	2 Sulzer diesels; 2 shafts; 4 000 bhp = 20 knots
Oil fuel, tons	105 capacity
Radius, miles	10 000 at 9 knots; 5 200 at 15 knots
Complement	100 (8 officers, 92 men)

Built at Lorient Dockyard. Laid down in Apr 1937, launched on 17 June 1939 and completed in Oct 1939. Transferred from the French Navy on 13 Oct 1959 and renamed.

DESTOUR   *1971, Tunisian Navy, Official*

PATROL CRAFT

AL JALA	P 203	JOUMHOURIA	P 202
ISTIKLAL (ex-*VC* 11, *P* 761)	P 201	REMADA	P 204

Displacement, tons	75 standard; 82 full load
Dimensions, feet	104·5 × 15·5 × 5·5
Guns	2—20 mm AA
Main engines	2 Mercedes-Benz diesels; 2 shafts; 2 400 bhp = 28 knots
Radius, miles	1 400 at 15 knots
Complement	17

Istiklal, seaward defence motor launch of the VC type, built by Lurssens in Germany, and completed in 1958, was transferred from the French Navy on 22 Sep 1959. A photograph of *Al Jala* appears in the 1970-71 edition.

ISTIKLAL   *1971, Tunisian Navy, Official*

PATROL VESSELS

SAKIET SIDI YOUSSEF (ex-*UW 12*)

Displacement, tons	325 standard; 400 full load
Dimensions, feet	170 pp × 23 × 6·5
Guns	1—40 mm; 2—20 mm
A/S weapons	1 hedgehog; 2 DCT; 2 DC racks
Main engines	4 Pielstick-SEMT diesels; 2 340 bhp = 19 knots
Complement	4 officers, 59 men

Patrol vessel of the "Fougueux"" type. Built in France by Dubigeon, Nantes, under US off-shore order. Purchased by Federal Germany in 1957 and served as A/S trials vessel. Transferred to Tunisia in Dec 1969.

SAKIET SIDI YOUSSEF   *1971, Tunisian Navy, Official*

PATROL LAUNCHES

V 102	V 103	V 104	V 105	V 107
			V 106	V 108

Displacement, tons	38
Dimensions, feet	83 × 15·6 × 4·1
Guns	1—20 mm
Main engines	2 twin GM diesels; 2 400 hp = 23 knots
Complement	11

Officially rated as *Vedettes Cotiers.* In general duties in harbour and off the coast. V 107 and V 108 were added to the flotilla in 1971.

V 104   *1970, Tunisian Navy, Official*

2 NEW CONSTRUCTION "P 48" TYPE

BIZERTE   **HORRIA** (*Liberte*)

Displacement, tons	250
Dimensions, feet	157·5 × 23·3 × 7
Guns	2—40 mm AA
Missiles	8 SS12 M
Main engines	2 diesels; 4 800 bhp = 20 knots

Built by Ch Franco-Belges (Villeneuve, la Garenne). *Bizeret* was launched on 20 Nov 1969. *Horria* means Liberte.

BIZERTE   *1971, Tunisian Navy, Official*

TUG

RAS ADAR (ex-*Zeeland*, ex-*Pan American*, ex-*Ocean Pride*. ex-HMS *Oriana*, BAT 1)

Displacement, tons	540 standard
Dimensions, feet	144·4 × 33 × 13·5

Built by the Gulfport Boilerworks & Eng Co in 1942 and lend leased to the Royal Navy in that year as BAT 1 HMS *Oriana*, returned and sold in 1946 as Ocean *Pride*, then *Pan America* in 1947, then *Zeeland* in 1956.

RAS ADAR   *1970, Tunisian Navy, Official*

TURKEY
Strength of the Fleet

10 Submarines	6 Patrol Vessels
10 Destroyers	13 Coastal Minesweepers
1 Minelayer	3 Inshore Minesweepers
18 Escorts	42 Motor Launches
11 Torpedo Boats	6 Boom Vessels
5 Coastal Minelayers	10 Support Ships

Personnel
1971: 37 230 (2 760 officers and 34 470 ratings)

Administration

Commander-in-Chief, Turkish Naval Forces:
Oramiral (Senior Admiral) Celal Eyiceoglu

Chief of Staff, Turkish Naval Forces:
Koramiral (Vice Admiral) Hilmi Firat

Commander of the Turkish Fleet:
Oramiral (Admiral) Kemal Kayacan

Diplomatic Representation

Naval Attaché in London:
Captain Hasan Sarioglu

Naval Attaché in Washington:
Captain Fikri Topsever

Mercantile Marine

Lloyd's Register of Shipping:
324 vessels of 696 824 tons gross

Scale: 150 feet = 1 inch (1 : 1 800)

PIYALE PASA

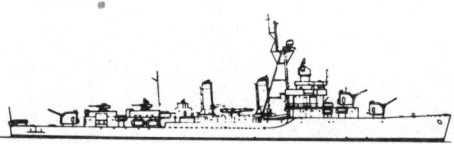
GELIBOLU, GIRESUN

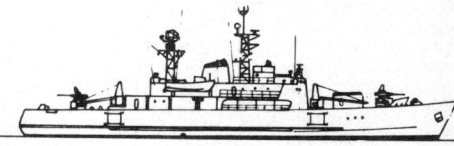
NUSRET

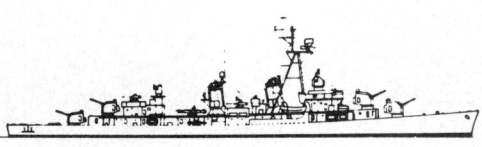
ISTANBUL, IZMIR

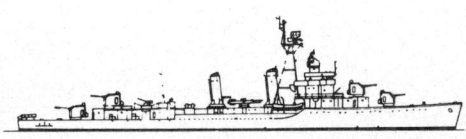
GAZIANTEP, GEMLIK

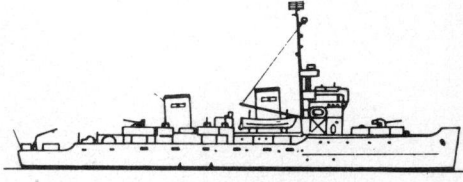
CANDARLI Class

SUBMARINES

PIRI REIS
1971, Official

4 PROJECTED

Under the scheme of German military assistance to South East European nations an agreement was reached in Jan 1970 whereby Germany will provide four submarines of 450 tons (officially revised figure) for Turkey, some being built in Germany and the remainder in Turkey with German assistance.

RECENT ACQUISITIONS. The following are being or will be transferred from USA to Turkey after refit:— Pomfret SS 391, Razorback SS 394, Seafox SS 402 (all three "Balao" class) and Thornback SS 418 ("Tench" class).

10 "GUR" CLASS

Displacement, tons	1 526 standard; 1 829 surface; 2 424 submerged
Length, feet (metres)	311·8 (95·0)
Beam, feet (metres)	27·2 (8·3)
Draught, feet (metres)	13·8 (4·2)
Guns, surface	1—5 in (127 mm) 25 cal., removed from most boats
Torpedo tubes	10—21 in (533 mm), 6 bow and 4 stern; 24 torpedoes carried
Main engines	GM 2-stroke diesels, total 6 500 hp Electric motors, total 2 750 hp
Speed, knots	20 on surface; 10 submerged
Radius, miles	12 000 at 10 knots
Oil fuel (tons)	300
Complement	85

Name	Nato No.	Builders	Launched	Completed
BIRINCI INÖNÜ (ex-USS Brill, SS 330)	S 330	Electric Boat Co	25 June 1944	26 Oct 1944
CANAKKALE (ex-USS Bumper, SS 333)	S 333	Electric Boat Co	6 Aug 1944	9 Dec 1944
CERBE (ex-USS Hammerhead, SS 364)	S 341	Manitowoc SB Co	27 Oct 1943	1 Mar 1944
GÜR (ex-USS Chub, ex-Bonat, SS 329)	S 334	Electric Boat Co	7 May 1944	28 Apr 1945
HIZIR REIS (ex-USS Mero, SS 378)	S 344	Manitowoc SB Co	17 Jan 1945	17 Aug 1945
IKINCI INÖNÜ (ex-USS Blueback, SS 326)	S 331	Electric Boat Co	21 May 1944	23 Sep 1944
PIRI REIS (ex-USS Mapiro, SS 376)	S 343	Manitowoc SB Co	9 Nov 1944	30 Apr 1945
PREVEZE (ex-USS Guitarro, SS 363)	S 340	Manitowoc SB Co	26 Sep 1943	16 Jan 1944
SAKARYA (ex-USS Boarfish, SS 327)	S 332	Electric Boat Co	18 June 1944	21 Oct 1944
TURGUT REIS (ex-USS Bergall, SS 320)	S 342	Electric Boat Co	16 Feb 1944	12 June 1944

Former US submarines of the "Balao" type acquired by Turkey in 1948-60. All built by the Electric Boat Company, Groton, Connecticut, except Cerbe, Hizir, Reis, Piri Reis and Preveze, by Manitowoc Shipbuilding Co. Of all-welded construction. High standard of accommodation including separate messing and sleeping compartments. Canakkale, officially transferred in 1950, was semi-streamlined before delivery. Dumlupinar (ex-Blower) was lost in the Dardanelles on 4 Apr 1953. Preveze semi-streamlined and Cerbe, fully streamlined, were transferred on 7 Aug 1954 and Oct 1954 respectively. Cerbe and Preveze are "guppy snorkel" conversions. Their loan was extended for five years in 1959, Sakarya was overhauled by the Electric Boat Division of the General Dynamics Corporation (formerly known as the Electric Boat Company), Groton, in 1957. Turgut Reis was transferred in Oct 1958 and Hizar Reis and Piri Reis on 20 Apr 1960 and 18 Mar 1960 at San Francisco Naval Shipyard.

PENNANT NUMBERS. It was officially stated in 1970 that the national numbers of submarines in the Turkish Navy have been suppressed.

PHOTOGRAPHS. A photograph of Turgut Reis appears in the 1959-60 to 1965-66 editions, of Hizir Reis in the 1964-65 to 1967-68 editions, of Sakarya and Ikinci Inonu in the 1966-67 to 1968-69 editions, of Cerbe in the 1968-69 and 1969-70 editions and of Prevese in the 1969-70 and 1970-71 editions.

EARLIER CLASSES. Burak Reis, Murat Reis and Oruc Reis, of the "Burak Reis" class, and Saldiray and Yildiray of the "Saldiray" class, were discarded in 1957.

BATTLE CRUISER. The old Turkish battle cruiser Yavuz (ex-German Goeben), decommissioned in 1960, was for sale at Golcuk naval base in 1970.

GÜR
1970, Turkish Navy, Official

BIRINCI INONU
1969, Official

CANAKKALE
1970, Turkish Navy, Official

DESTROYERS

Name	No.	Builders	Laid down	Launched	Completed
PIYALE PASA (ex-HMS *Meteor*)	D 351	Alex Stephen & Sons Ltd, Govan, Glasgow	14 Sep 1940	3 Nov 1941	12 Aug 1942

Displacement, tons	2 115 standard; 2 840 full load
Length, feet (*metres*)	354·0 (*107·9*)pp; 362·5 (*110·5*)oa
Beam, feet (*metres*)	36·8 (*11·2*)
Draught, feet (*metres*)	16·2 (*5·0*)
Guns, surface	5—4·7 in (*120 mm*)
Guns, AA	6—40 mm (1 twin, 4 single)
Guns, saluting	2—3 pdr
A/S weapons	1 "Squid" triple-barrel DC mortar
Torpedo tubes	4—21 in (*533 mm*)
Main engines	Parsons geared turbines; 2 shafts; 48 000 shp
Speed, knots	36
Boilers	2 Admiralty 3-drum
Oil fuel, tons	500
Radius, miles	1 700 at 20 knots
Complement	240

Formerly of the "Milne" class, one of the most successful and handsome types which ever served in the Royal Navy, and first British destroyers with three power worked turrets. Transferred to Turkey on 16 Aug 1957. Handed over to the Turkish Navy at Portsmouth on 29 June 1959 after refit, the after tubes and secondary armament having been removed and replaced by deckhouse, "Squid" and 40 mm guns. Type 293 search radar. Sister ships *Alp Arslan* (ex-HMS *Milne*), *Kilic Ali Pasa* (ex-HMS *Matchless*, and *Maresal Fevzi Cakmak* (ex-HMS *Marne*) were decommissioned in 1970 but it was officially stated in Mar 1971 that *Piyale Pasa* was still listed.

PIYALE PASA · · · · · · · · · 1970, Turkish Navy, Official

Name	No.	Builders	Laid down	Launched	Completed
GAZIANTEP (ex-USS *Lansdowne*, DD 486)	D 348 (ex-344)	Federal SB & DD Co, Port Newark	July 1941	20 Feb 1942	29 Apr 1942
GELIBOLU (ex-USS *Buchanan*, DD 484)	D 346	Federal SB & DD Co, Port Newark	11 Feb 1941	22 Nov 1941	21 Mar 1942
GEMLIK (ex-USS *Lardner*, DD 487)	D 347	Federal SB & DD Co, Port Newark	July 1941	20 Mar 1942	13 May 1942
GIRESUN (ex-USS *McCalla*, DD 488)	D 345	Federal SB & DD Co, Port Newark	July 1941	20 Mar 1942	27 May 1942

Displacement, tons	1 810 standard; 2 580 full load
Length, feet (*metres*)	341·0 (*103·9*)wl; 348·5 (*106·2*)oa
Beam, feet (*metres*)	36·0 (*11·0*)
Draught, feet (*metres*)	18·0 (*5·5*)
Guns, surface	D345, D346: 3—5 in (*127 mm*) 38 cal.; D344, D347: 4—5 in (*127 mm*) 38 cal.
Guns, AA	D345, D346: 4—3 in (*76 mm*); D344, D347: 4—40 mm
A/S weapons	2 Hedgehogs; homing torpedoes;
Torpedo tubes	5—21 in (*533 mm*)
Main engines	GE geared turbines; 2 shafts; 50 000 shp
Speed, knots	37 designed; 34 max
Boilers	4 Babcock & Wilcox
Oil fuel, tons	600
Radius, miles	5 000 at 15 knots
Complement	250

GAZIANTEP · · · · · · · · · 1970, Stefan Terzibaschitsch

Former US "Gleaves" class destroyers, acquired by Turkey early in 1949. *Gelibolu* and *Giresun* were formally taken over on 29 Apr 1949, and *Gaziantep* and *Gemlik* in 1950. Modernised in UAS in 1957-58 and fitted with tripod instead of pole foremast and raised bridge.

GUNNERY. The 5 in gun in "X" position, 40 mm AA and 20 mm AA guns in *Gelibolu* and *Giresun* were replaced by four 3-in AA guns in two twin mountings.

RADAR. Search: SPS 6. Tactical: SPS 10. Fire Control: GFCS 68.

PHOTOGRAPHS. A photograph of *Giresun* appears in the 1966-67 and 1967-68 editions, and of *Gemlik* in the 1968-69 and 1969-70 editions.

RECENT ACQUISITION. "Gearing" class:—**ADATEPE** D 353 (ex-USS *Forrest Royal*) DD 872 to join the Turkish fleet after refit in USA.

GELIBOLU · · · · · · · · · 1970, Turkish Navy, Official

Name	No.	Builders	Launched	Completed
IÇEL (ex-USS *Preston*, DD 795)	D 344	Bethlehem Company, San Pedro	12 Dec 1943	20 Mar 1944
ISKENDERUN (ex-USS *Boyd*, DD 544)	D 343	Bethlehem Company, San Pedro	29 Oct 1942	8 May 1943
ISTANBUL (ex-USS *Clarence K. Bronson*, DD 668)	D 340	Federal SB & DD Co, Port Newark	18 Apr 1943	11 June 1943
IZMIR (ex-USS *Van Valkenburgh*, DD 656)	D 341	Gulf Shipbuilding Corporation	19 Dec 1943	2 Aug 1944
IZMIT (ex-USS *Cogswell*, DD 651)	D 342	Bath Iron Works Corporation	5 June 1943	17 Aug 1943

Displacement, tons	2 050 standard; 3 000 full load
Length, feet (*metres*)	376·5 (*114·8*) oa
Beam, feet (*metres*)	39·5 (*12·1*)
Draught, feet (*metres*)	18·0 (*5·5*)
Guns, surface	4—5 in (*127 mm*) 38 cal
Guns, AA	6—3 in (*76 mm*)
A/S weapons	2 Hedgehogs
Torpedo tubes	5—21 in (*533 mm*) quintupled
Main engines	GE geared turbines; 2 shafts; 60 000 shp
Speed, knots	34
Boilers	4 Babcock & Wilcox
Oil fuel, tons	650
Radius, miles	6 000 at 15 knots
Complement	250

Istanbul and *Ismir* transferred from US on 14 Jan and 28 Feb 1967, *Iskenderun* and *Ismit* on 1 Oct 1969, *Icel* on 15 Nov 1969. A photograph of *Istanbul* appears in the 1967-68 and 1968-69 editions.

RADAR. Search: SPS 6. Tactical: SPS 10. Fire Control: GFCS 68.

IZMIR · · · · · · · · · 1969, Official

2 NEW CONSTRUCTION

Displacement, tons 1 450 standard; 1 950 full load
Length, feet (metres) 311·7 (95·0)
Beam, feet (metres) 38·7 (11·8)
Draught, feet (metres) 18·1 (5·5)

NUSRET N 110 (ex-N 108)

Displacement, tons 1 880 standard
Length, feet (metres) 246 (75·0) pp; 252·7 (77·0) oa
Beam, feet (metres) 41 (12·6)
Draught, feet (metres) 11 (3·4)
Guns, dual purpose 4—3 in (76 mm), 2 twin mountings
Mines 400 capacity
Main engines GM diesels, 4 800 hp; 2 shafts
Speed, knots 18
Complement 130

A new type of minelayer of special Scandinavian-NATO design. Built at Frederikshaven Dockyard, Denmark. Laid down in 1962, launched in 1964, and completed in 1965. Commissioned on 16 Sep 1964 at Copenhagen.

RADAR. Search: S band. Fire Control: X Band.

FRIGATES

Guns	4—3 in (76 mm) 2 twin
Tubes	6—12·6 in (320 mm) 2 triple
Aircraft	1 helicopter
Main engines	4 Fiat diesels; 2 shafts; 24 000 bhp
Speed, knots	25

First warships built in Turkey. The prototype was laid down in the Gölcük naval yard on 9 Mar 1967. Said to have been inspired by the destroyer escorts of the US "Claud Jones" class, but there is not a great deal of resemblance. Italian propelling machinery.

MINELAYER

NUSRET
1969, Official

ESCORTS

6 "CANDARLI" CLASS

CANDARLI (ex-Frolic, 22 July 1943)	A 593 (ex-AGS 2)	**CESME** (ex-Elfreda, 25 Jan 1943)	A 595
CARDAK (ex-Tourmaline, 4 Oct, 1942)	A 596	**EDINCIK** (ex-Grecian, 22 Sep 1943)	A 597 (ex-598)
CARSAMBA (ex-Tattoo, 27 Jan 1943)	A 594 (ex-AGS 1)	**EREGLI** (ex-Pique, 26 Oct 1942)	A 592

Displacement, tons 1 010 standard; 1 250 full load
Length, feet (metres) 215·0 (61·4) wl; 221·0 (67·4) oa
Beam, feet (metres) 32·0 (9·8)
Draught, feet (metres) 10·8 (3·3)
Guns 1—3 in (76 mm); 6—40 mm
Main engines Diesel electric; 2 shafts; 3 500 bhp
Speed, knots 18

Former US fleet minesweepers of the "Auk" type. Transferred to Great Britain while under construction. Transferred to Turkey in Apr 1947. Built by Associated Shipbuilders, Cleveland (Carsamba, Cesme and Edincik); General Engineering & DD Co, Alameda (Candarli) and Gulf Shipbuilding Corporation, Houston (Cardak and Eregli). Launch dates above. Named after Turkish ports. Erdemli (ex-Catherine) was withdrawn from active service in 1963, and Edremit (ex-Chance) in 1965. Cesme and Cardak are Headquarters Ships. Eregli is Logistic Support Ship, Edincik is Training Ship, Carsamba and Candarli are Survey Ships.

CANDARLI
1970, Turkish Navy, Official

3 "ALANYA" CLASS

Name	No.	Builders	Launched
ALANYA (ex-Broome)	A 589 (ex-M 501)	Evans Deakin, Brisbane	6 Oct 1941
AMASRA (ex-Pirie)	A 590 (ex-M 502)	Broken Hill, Whyalla	Dec 1941
AYVALIK (ex- Antalya, ex-Geraldton)	A 588 (ex-M 500)	Poole & Steele, Sydney	16 Aug 1941

Displacement, tons 790 standard; 1 025 full load
Length, feet (metres) 162·0 (49·4) pp; 186·0 (56·7) oa
Beam, feet (metres) 31·0 (9·4)
Draught, feet (metres) 8·5 (2·6)
Guns, surface 1—4 in (102 mm)
Guns, AA 1—40 mm; 4—20 mm
A/S weapons 2 DCT
Main engines Triple expansion; 2 shafts; 1 800 ihp
Speed, knots 15
Boilers 2 water tube
Oil fuel, tons 170
Radius, miles 4 500 at 10 knots
Complement 85

All Australian built, 1940-42. Served in the Royal Navy. Acquired from Great Britain in Aug 1946. Named after Turkish ports. All are now Logistic Support Ships. Hamit Naci (ex-Ayancik, ex-Launceston) was withdrawn from service in 1965, and Ayvalik (ex-Gawler) in 1963. A photograph of Alanya appears in the 1951-52 to 1963-64 editions and of Amasra in the 1964-65 to 1968-69 editions.

SAVARONA

Displacement, tons 5 100
Length, feet (metres) 349·5 (106·5)wl; 408·5 (124·5)oa
Beam, feet (metres) 53 (16·2)
Draught, feet (metres) 20·5 (6·2) mean
Guns, surface 4—3 in (76 mm)
Guns, AA 2—40 mm; 2—20 mm
Main engines 6 geared turbines; 2 shafts; 10 750 shp
Speed, knots 21 designed; about 18 now
Boilers 4 watertube; 400 psi
Oil fuel, tons 2 100
Radius, miles 9 000 at 15 knots
Complement 132 + 81 midshipmen

Built by Blohm & Voss, Hamburg. Launched on 28 Feb 1931. Formerly probably the most sumptuously fitted yacht afloat. Equipment includes Sperry gyro-stabilisers. Converted into a training ship in 1952, the saloons and dining rooms being adapted as classrooms, workshops and libraries for 120 midshipmen.

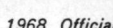

AYVALIK
1968, Official

TRAINING SHIP

SAVARONA
1968, A. & J. Pavia

COASTAL ESCORTS (ex-Fleet Minesweepers)

6 "BAFRA" CLASS

		Name	No.	Launched
Displacement, tons	672 standard; 900 full load	**BAFRA** (ex-HMCS *Nipigon*, FSE 188)	P 121	30 Sep 1940
Length, feet (*metres*)	171·5 (*52·3*) pp ; 180·0 (*54·8*) oa	**BANDIRMA** (ex-HMCS *Kenora*, FSE 191)	P 129	20 Dec 1941
Beam, feet (*metres*)	28·5 (*8·7*)	**BARTIN** (ex-HMCS *Kentville*, FSE 182)	P 130	18 Apr 1941
Draught, feet (*metres*)	12·5 (*3·8*) max	**BEYLERBEYI** (ex-HMCS *Mahone*, FSE 192)	P 123	15 Nov 1940
Guns, AA	1—40 mm; 6—20 mm	**BORNOVA** (ex-HMCS *Westmount*, FSE 187)	P 126	14 Mar 1942
A/S weapons	1 Hedgehog; 4 DCT	**BUYUKDERE** (ex-HMCS *Sarnia*, FSE 190)	P 128	21 Jan 1942
Main engines	Triple expansion; 2 shafts; 2 400 ihp			
Speed, knots	16·5			
Boilers	2 Admiralty 3 drum			
Complement	70			

Former Canadian "Bangor" class fleet minesweepers, rerated coastal escorts in 1953. Transferred to Turkey in 1957. *Bafra, Bandirma, Bartin* were turned over 29 Nov 1957 at Point Edward Naval Base, Sydney, NS, and *Beylerbeyi, Barnova, Buyukdere* early 1958. All sailed from Canada to Turkey on 19 May 1958. *Biga* (ex-MMCS *Medicine Hat*, FSE 197) was withdrawn from service in 1963, *Beykoz* (ex-HMCS *Blairmore*, FSE 195), *Bodrem* (ex-HMCS *Fort William*, FSE 195), *Bozcaada* (ex-HMCS *Swift Current*, FSE 185) in 1970.

RADAR. C Band search installation.

PHOTOGRAPHS. A photograph of *Beykoz* appears in the 1963-64 to 1965-66 editions, of *Bandirma* in the 1966-67 to 1968-69 editions and of *Bartin* in the 1969-70 edition.

BAFRA

1970, Turkish Navy, Official

COASTAL MINESWEEPERS

12 MSC TYPE

SAMSUN M 510 (ex-USA *MSC* 268)   **SEYHAN** M 509 (ex-USS *AMS* 142)
SAPANCA M 517 (ex-USS *MSC* 312)   **SEYMEN** M 507 (ex-USS *AMS*)
SARIYER M 518 (ex-USS *MSC* 315)   **SIGACIK** M 516 (ex-USS *MSC* 311)
SAROS M 515 (ex-USS *MSC* 305)   **SILIFKE** M 514 (ex-USS *MSC* 304)
SEDDULBAHIR M 513 (ex-*MSC* 272)   **SINOP** M 511 (ex-USS *MSC* 270)
SELCUK M 508 (ex-USS *AMS* 124)   **SURMENE** M 512 (ex-USS *MSC* 271)

Displacement, tons	320 standard; 370 full load
Dimensions, feet	138·0 pp ; 144·0 oa × 28·0 × 9·0
Guns	2—20 mm AA
Main engines	2 diesels; 2 shafts; 1 200 bhp = 14 knots
Oil fuel, tons	25
Radius, miles	2 500 at 10 knots
Complement	38 (4 officers, 34 men)

Built of non-magnetic materials. Transferred on 30 Sep 1958, 26 July 1965, 8 Sep 1967, 8 Nov 1965, 9 July 1959, 24 Mar 1970, 24 Mar 1970, 19 Nov 1970, 29 May 1965, 25 Oct 1965, 30 Jan 1959, 27 Mar 1959, respectively. A photograph of *Sinop* appears in the 1961-62 to 1965-66 editions, and of *Seddulbahir* in the 1966-67 to 1968-69 editions. Pennant numbers changed from 257, 266, 267, 264, 260, 265, 263, 258 and 259, respectively, in 1970. *Pavot* (ex-AMS 124) and *Renoncull* (ex-AMS 14) were transferred from France (via USA) on 24 Mar 1970 and *Seymen* from UK (via USA) on 19 Nov 1970.

SAMSUN

1969, Official

4 MCB TYPE

TIREBOLU M 532 (ex-HMCS *Comax*)   **TERME** M 531 (ex-HMCS *Trinity*)
TEKIRDAG M 533 (ex-HMCS *Ungava*)   **TRABZON** M 533 (ex-HMCS *Gaspe*)

Displacement, tons	390 standard; 412 full load
Dimensions, feet	140·0 pp ; 152·0 oa × 20·8 × 7·0
Guns	1—40 mm
Main engines	Diesels; 2 shafts; 2 400 bhp = 16 knots
Oil fuel, tons	52
Radius, miles	4 500 at 11 knots
Complement	40

Ex-Canadian MCBs. Sailed from Sydney, Nova Scotia, to Turkey on 19 May 1958. A photograph of *Terme* appears in the 1959-60 to 1966-67 editions, and of *Trabzon* in the 1967-68 to 1969-70 editions. Pennant numbers changed from 524, 525, 523 and 522, respectively in 1970.

TIREBOLU

1970, Turkish Navy, Official

COASTAL MINELAYERS

5 LSM TYPE

MARMARIS (ex-*LSM* 481) N 103 (ex-100)
MERIC (ex-*LSM* 490) N 102
MERSIN (ex-*LSM* 492) N 104 (ex-103)
MORDOGAN (ex-*LSM* 484) N 101
MUREFTE (ex-*LSM* 493) N 105 (ex-104)

Displacement, tons	743 standard; 1 100 full load
Dimensions, feet	196·5 wl; 203·2 oa × 34·5 × 8·5
Guns	2—40 mm AA; 2—20 mm AA
Main Engines	Diesels; 2 shafts; 2 880 bhp = 12 knots
Oil fuel (tons)	60
Radius, miles	2 500 at 10 knots
Complement	70

Ex-U.S. Landing Ships Medium. All launched in 1945, converted into coastal minelayers by the U.S. Navy in 1952 and taken over by the Turkish Navy (LSM 481, 484 and 490) and the Norwegian Navy (LSM 492 and 493) in Oct 1952 under MAP. LSM 492 (*Vale*) and LSM 493 (*Vidar*) were retransferred to the Turkish Navy on 1 Nov 1960 at Bergen, Norway. Pennant numbers changed in 1970. A photograph of *Marmaris* appears in the 1955-56 to 1968-69 edition.

MERSIN

1969, Official

1 YMP TYPE

MEHMEDCIK (ex-U.S.S. *YMP* 3)

Displacement, tons	540 full load
Dimensions, feet	130 × 35 × 6
Main Engines	Diesels; 2 shafts; 600 bhp = 10 knots
Complement	22

Former US motor mine planter. Built by Higgins Inc, New Orleans. Completed in 1958. Steel hulled. Transferred under MAP in 1958. For harbour defence. Former pennant number was N 105.

"K" CLASS

Of the "K" class, former US *YMS* type, *Kas* (ex-*YMS* 79) and *Kilimli* (ex-*YMS* 289) were withdrawn from service in 1963, *Kozlu* (ex-*YMS* 375) and *Kusadasi* (ex-*YMS* 468) in 1965, and *Karamursel* (ex-*Kulluck*, ex-*YMS* 348), *Kemer* (ex-*YMS* 228), *Kerempe* (ex-*YMS* 239) and *Kirte* (ex-*YMS* 307) in 1966.

MEHMEDCIK

1969, Official

PATROL VESSELS

6 "AKHISAR" CLASS

AKHISAR	P 114 (ex-*PC* 1641)	**SIVRIHISAR**	P 115 (ex-*PC* 1642)
DEMIRHISAR	P 112 (ex-*PC* 1639)	**SULTANHISAR**	P 111 (ex-*PC* 1638)
KOCHISAR	P 116 (ex-*PC* 1643)	**YARHISAR**	P 113 (ex-*PC* 1640)

Displacement, tons	280 standard ; 412 full load
Dimensions, feet	170 wl ; 173·7 oa × 23 × 10·2
Guns	1—3 inch dp ; 1—40 mm AA
A/S weapons	4 DCT
Main Engines	2 FM Diesels ; 2 shafts ; 2 800 bhp · 19 knots
Complement	65 (5 officers and 60 men)

Similar to US 173 ft class submarine chasers. Built by Gunderson Bros, Engineering Co, Portland, Oregon, except *Kochisar* built in Gölcük Dockyard, Turkey. Transferred on 3 Dec 1964, 22 Apr 1965, 22 Apr 1965, 2 May 1964, 24 Sep 1964 and 22 Apr 1965 respectively. PC 1645 is building in USA. A photograph of *Sultanhisar* appears in the 1966-67 to 1968-69 editions. PGM 72, 104, 105, 106, 108, 114, 115 were built in USA for transfer to Turkey.

KOCHISAR   *1969. Official*

TORPEDO BOATS

9 "KARTAL" CLASS

ALBATROS	P 325	**KARTAL**	P 324	**PELIKAN**	P 326
ATMACA	P 322	**KASIRGA**	P 329	**SAHIN**	P 323
DENIZKUSU	P 321	**MELTEM**	P 330	**SIMSEK**	P 332

Displacement, tons	160 standard ; 180 full laod
Dimensions, feet	140·5 × 23·5 × 7·2
Guns	2—40 mm AA
Tubes	4—21 inch
Main engines	4 Maybach diesels ; 4 shafts ; 12 000 bhp = 42 knots

Of the German "Jaguar" type. Built by Lürssen, Vegesack, in 1966-67 (P 321, 322, 323, 324, 329, 330, ex-P 336, 335, 334, 333, 338, 337, respectively), others in 1968.

KASIRGA   *1970, Turkish Navy, Official*

KARTAL   *1967, Turkish Navy, Official*

2 "NASTY" TYPE

DOGAN (ex-*Hugin*) P 327   **MARTI** (ex-*Munin*) P 328

Displacement, tons	70 standard ; 75 full load
Dimensions, feet	75·5 pp ; 80·3 oa · 24·5 × 6·8
Guns	1—40 mm AA
Tubes	2—21 inch
Main Engines	2 Napier Deltic turbo blown diesels ; 6 200 bhp — 43 knots

Transferred under a German-Turkish war reparations plan from West Germany and renamed. "Nasty" type, built by Boat Services Ltd, A/S in 1959-60.

DOGAN   *Turkish Navy, Official*

MOTOR LAUNCHES

AB 25 (P 1225)	**AB 27** (P 1227)	**AB 29** (P 1229)	**AB 32** (P 1232)
AB 26 (P 1226)	**AB 28** (P 1228)	**AB 30** (P 1230)	**AB 33** (P 1233)
		AB 31 (P 1231)	**AB 34** (P 1234)

Displacement, tons	170 (official figure)
Dimensions, feet	132 × 21 × 5·5
Guns	2—40 mm
Speed	22 knots

Officially stated to be newly designed patrol boats of the motor launch type. Built at Gölcük Naval Yard. First was launched on 9 Mar 1967.

AB 28   *1970, Turkish Navy, Official*

AB 21 (P 1221)	**AB 22** (P 1222)	**AB 23** (P 1223)	**AB 24** (P 1224)

Displacement, tons	142 (official figure)
Dimensions, feet	101 × 21 × 7·7

Motor launches of the patrol gunboat type supplied from the United States.

AB 23   *1970, Turkish Navy, Official*

J 12	**J 13**	**J 14**	**J 15**	**J 16**	**J 17**	**J 18**	**J 19**	**J 20**

Displacement, tons	70
Dimensions, feet	95 × 15·5 × 4·2
Main engines	4 MB diesels ; 2 shafts ; 2 700 bhp = 29 knots

Cutters of U.S.C.G. type built in 1960-61 by Schweers, Bardenfleth. A photograph of J 12 appears in the 1962-63 to 1965-66 editions.

J 19   *1970, Turkish. Navy, Official*

AB 1 (ex-*ML* 386)	P 1201 (ex-P 321)	**AB 4** (ex-*ML* 837) P 1204 (ex-P 324)
AB 2 (ex-*ML* 584)	P 1202 (ex-P 322)	**AB 6** (ex-*ML* 842) P 1206 (ex-P 326)
AB 3 (ex-*ML* 836)	P 1203 (ex-P 323)	**AB 7** (ex-*ML* 862) P 1207 (ex-P 327)

Displacement, tons	85 standard ; 115 full load
Dimensions, feet	112 × 17·8 × 4
Guns	1—3 pdr ; 2—20 mm AA ; 4 MG
Main engines	2 Hall-Scott engines ; 1 120 bhp = 21 knots
Oil fuel, tons	12
Complement	18

Fairmile B type. Launched in 1940-42. Transferred in 1947. Pennant numbers changed in 1970. A photograph of AB 2 appears in the 1947-48 to 1960-61 editions, and of AB 7 in the 1961-62 to 1965-66 editions. AB 5 and AB 8 were scrapped, it was officially stated in 1969.

AB 6   *1970, Turkish Navy, Official*

Motor Launches—*continued*

LS 9 P 1209 (ex-P 339) **LS 10** P 1210 (ex-P 308)
LS 11 P 1211 (ex-P 309) **LS 12** P 1212 (ex-P 310)

Displacement, tons	63 standard
Dimensions, feet	83·0 × 14·0 × 5·0
Guns	1—20 mm AA
A/S weapons	2 "Hedgehogs"
Main engines	2 Cummins diesels; 1 100 bhp = 20 knots

Ex-US type, transferred on 25 June 1953. Pennant numbers changed in 1970. A photograph of LS 12 (P 310) appears in the 1961-62 to 1967-68 editions.

LS 10   *1968, Aldo Fraccaroli*

MTB 1 P 311 **MTB 3** P 313 **MTB 6** P 316 **MTB 8** P 318
MTB 2 P 312 **MTB 4** P 314 **MTB 7** P 317 **MTB 9** P 319
                                                  MTB 10 P 320

Displacement, tons	70 standard
Dimensions, feet	71·5 × 13·8 × 8·5
Main engines	Diesel; 2 000 bhp = 10 knots

All launched in 1942. General purpose craft. P pennant numbers (NATO) above. Photograph of MTB 9 in the 1957-58 edition. MTB 5 (315) was scrapped.

SUBMARINE DEPOT SHIP

DONATAN (ex-USS *Anthedon*, AS 24)

Displacement, tons	8 100 standard
Dimensions, feet	492 × 69·5 × 26·5
Main engines	Geared turbines; 1 shaft; 8 500 shp = 14·4 knots
Boilers	2

Former US submarine tender of the "Aegir" class transferred to Turkey on 7 Feb 1969.

TENDERS

ERKIN A 591 (ex-*Trabzon*, ex-*Imperial*)

Displacement, tons	10 990 (official figure)
Dimensions, feet	441 × 58·5 × 23

Built in 1938. Purchased in 1968 and placed on the Navy List in 1970.

ERKIN   *1970, Turkish Navy, Official*

ISIN (ex-*Imia Layteri*) Y 1230 (ex- A 570)

Displacement, tons	200 standard; 390 full load
Dimensions, feet	110·0 × 24·0 × 7·0
Guns	1—20 mm AA
Main engines	Crossley diesels; 330 bhp = 10 knots
Oil fuel, tons	32

Built by James Pollock, Sons & Co, Faversham, England. Launched in 1941. Coaster type. Formerly employed in charging the batteries of submarines. Now a main diving ship. A photograph of *Isin* appears in the 1957-58 and earlier editions. The tenders *Akin* and *Dalgie* have been discarded, it is officially stated.

GATE VESSELS

Y 1216

Displacement, tons	360 (official figure)
Dimensions, feet	102·7 × 34 × 4·7

The gate vessels YNG 45, 46 and 47 were built by US for transfer to Turkey under MAP, and numbered Y 1201, 1202 and 1203.

PRESIDENTIAL YACHT

HALAS (ex-*Umur*)

Completed and commissioned for service in 1956. Renamed *Halas* in 1961.

INSHORE MINESWEEPERS

FATSA M 502 (ex-*MSI* 17) **FINIKE** M 503 (ex-*MSI* 18)
FETHIYE M 501 (ex-*MSI* 16) **FOCA** M 500 (ex-*MSI* 15)

Displacement, tons	180 standard; 235 full load (official figure)
Dimensions, feet	111·9 × 23·5 × 7·9
Guns	1—50 cal
Main engines	4 diesels; 2 shafts; 960 bhp = 13 knots
Complement	20

Built in USA and transferred under MAP at Boston, Mass, Aug-Sep 1967. *Finike* was delivered by Peterson Builders Inc. on 8 Nov 1967.

FOCA   *1970, Turkish Navy, Official*

REPAIR SHIPS

BASARAN (ex-*Patroclus*, ARL 19, ex-*LST* 955) A 582
ONARAN (ex-*Alecto*, AGP 14, ex-*LST* 558) A 581

Displacement, tons	1 625 standard; 3 960 to full load
Dimensions, feet	316 wl; 328 oa × 50 × 11
Guns	2—40 mm AA; 8—20 mm AA
Main Engines	Diesel; 2 shafts; 1 700 bhp = 11 knots
Oil fuel (tons)	1 000
Radius, miles	6 000 at 9 knots

Former US repair ship and MTB tender, respectively, of the LST type. *Basaran* was launched on 22 Oct 1944 by Bethlehem Hingham Shipyard, *Onaran* on 14 Apr 1944 by Missouri Valley Bridge & Iron Co. Acquired from the USA in 1952 and 1947, respectively.

ONARAN   *1967, Turkish Navy, Official*

BASARAN   *1970, Turkish Navy, Official*

SUBMARINE RESCUE SHIP

KURTARAN (ex-*Bluebird*, ASR 19, ex-*Yurak*) A 584

Displacement, tons	1 294 standard; 1 675 full load
Dimensions, feet	205·0 oa × 38·5 × 12·0
Guns	1—3 inch; 2—40 mm AA
Main engines	Diesel-electric; 3 000 bhp × 16 knots

Built by Charleston S.B. & D.D. Co. Launched in 1946. Former salvage tug, adapted as a submarine rescue vessel in 1947. Transferred from the US Navy on 15 Aug 1950.

KURTARAN   *1971, A. & J. Pavia*

BOOM DEFENCE VESSELS

AG 6 (ex-*Cerberus*, A 895)

Displacement, tons	780 standard; 902 full load
Dimensions, feet	165·0 × 33·0 × 10·0
Guns	1—3 in; 4—20 mm AA
Main engines	Diesel-electric; 1 shaft; 1 500 bhp = 12·8 knots

Netlayer built by Bethlehem Steel Co, Staten Island. Launched in May 1952 and completed on 10 Nov 1952. Transferred from USA to Netherlands in Dec 1952. Used first as a boom defence vessel and latterly as salvage and diving tender since 1961 but retained her netlaying capacity. Handed back to USN (formality) on 17 Sep 1970 but immediately turned over to the Turkish Navy.

EX-CERBERUS   *Official*

AG 5 P 305 (ex-P 306)

Displacement, tons	680 standard; 960 full load
Dimensions, feet	148·7 pp; 173·8 oa × 35·0 × 13·5
Guns	1—40 mm AA; 3—20 mm AA
Main engines	4 MAN diesels; 2 shafts; 1 450 bhp = 12 knots

Netlayer AN 104 built in US off-shore programme by Kröger, Rendsburg for Turkey. Launched on 20 Oct 1960. Delivered on 25 Feb 1961. A photograph appears in the 1964-65 to 1968-69 editions.

AG 4 (ex-*Larch*, ex-*AN* 21) P 304

Displacement, tons	560 standard; 805 full load
Dimensions, feet	146·0 wl; 163·0 oa × 30·5 × 10·5
Guns	1—3 inch AA
Main engines	Diesel-electric; 800 bhp = 12 knots

Former US netlayer of the "Aloe" class. Built by American S.B. Co, Cleveland. Laid down in 1940. Launched on 2 July 1941. Completed in 1941. Acquired in 1947.

AG 4.   *1969. Official*

3 "BAR" CLASS

AG 1 (ex-*Barbarian*, 21 Oct 1937) P 301   **AG 2** (ex-*Barbette*, 15 Dec 1937) P 302
AG 3 (ex-*Barfair*, 21 May 1938) P 303

Displacement, tons	750 standard; 1 000 full load
Dimensions, feet	150·0 pp; 173·8 oa × 32·2 × 9·5
Guns	1—3 inch AA
Main engines	Triple expansion; 850 ihp = 11·5 knots
Boilers	2 SE

Former British boom defence vessels. First two were built by Blyth S.B. Co and the third by J. Lewis & Sons. Launch dates above. A photograph of AG 1 appears in the 1957-58 edition, and of AG 2 in the 1966-67 editions.

AG 3   *1970, Turkish Navy, Official*

KALDIRAY P 306 (ex-P 305)

Measurement, tons	732 gross
Main engines	Steam reciprocating; 500 ihp = 10 knots
Complement	97

Built in 1938. Former French vessel. Purchased in 1964. A photograph of *Kaldiray* appears in the 1967-68 to 1970-71 editions.

OILERS

ULABAT   **VAN**

Displacement, tons	900
Main engines	Designed for a speed of 14·5 knots

Two small tankers for the Turkish Navy built in the Gölcük Dockyard, Izmit, in 1968-70.

ALBAY HAKKI BURAK A 572

Displacement, tons	3 800 full load
Dimensions, feet	251·3 pp; 274·7 oa × 40·2 × 18
Main Engines	2 GM diesels; electric drive; 4 400 bhp = 16 knots
Complement	88

Two new tankers for the Turkish Navy were ordered from Gölcük Dockyard, Izmit. *Alban Burak* was built in 1964.

ALBAY HAKKI BURAK   *1967, Turkish Navy, Official*

YUZBASI TOLUNAY A 571 (ex-A 586)

Displacement, tons	2 500 standard; 3 500 full load
Dimensions, feet	260 × 41 × 19·5
Main Engines	Atlas Polar-diesels; 2 shafts; 1 920 bhp = 14 knots

Built at Taskizak by Haskoy Naval D.Y., Istanbul. Launched on 22 Aug 1950.

YUZBASI TOLUNAY   *1967, Turkish Navy, Official*

AKAR (ex-*Istambul*, ex-*Adour*) A 570 (ex- A580)

Displacement, tons	4 289 light; 13 200 full load
Dimensions, feet	433 × 52·7 × 27 feet
Main Engines	Parsons geared turbines; 5 200 shp = 15 knots

A photograph of *Akar* appears in the 1959-60 to 1966-67 editions.

AKAR   *1970, Turkish Navy, Official*

AKPINAR (ex-*Chiwaukum*) A 574

Displacement, tons	700 light; 2 700 full load
Measurement, feet	1 453 deadweight
Dimensions, feet	212·5 wl; 220·5 oa × 37 × 12·8
Main Engines	Diesel; 800 bhp = 10 knots

Formerly the United States oiler *AOG 26*. Built by East Coast S.Y. Inc., Bayonne. Laid down on 2 Apr 1944. Launched on 5 May 1944. Completed on 22 July 1944. Transferred to Turkey in 1949. A photograph appears in the 1957-58 edition.

GOLCUK Y 1207 (ex-A 573)

Displacement, tons	1 255
Measurement, feet	750 deadweight
Dimensions, feet	185 × 31·1 × 10
Main Engines	B. & W. diesel; 700 bhp = 12·5 knots

Built by Gölcük Dockyard, Ismit. Launched on 4 Nov 1953. A photograph appears in the 1957-58 and earlier editions.

TUGS

ÖNCU   **ÖNDER**

Displacement, tons	500
Speed	12 knots

The US harbour tugs ex-YTL 155, 751 were transferred under MAP. A number of LCU type landing craft are building in Germany for transfer to Turkey.

UNITED KINGDOM

Chief of the Defence Staff:
Admiral of the Fleet Sir Peter Hill-Norton, GCB

Admiralty Board

Secretary of State for Defence (Chairman):
The Right Honourable Lord Carrington, KCMG, MC
Minister of State, Ministry of Defence (Vice-Chairman):
Lord Balniel, MP
Minister of State for Defence Procurement:
Mr Ian Gilmour, MP
Parliamentary Under-Secretary of State for Defence for the Royal Navy:
Mr Peter Kirk, MP
Chief of the Naval Staff and First Sea Lord:
Admiral Sir Michael Pollock, GCB, MVO, DSC
Chief of Naval Personnel and Second Sea Lord:
Vice-Admiral Sir Andrew Mackenzie Lewis, KCB (Vice-Admiral Leslie Derek Empson, CB, from Dec 1971)
Controller of the Navy:
Vice-Admiral Anthony Templer Frederick Griffith Griffin, CB
Chief of Fleet Support:
Rear-Admiral George Francis Allan Trewby, CEng, FIMechE, MIMarE, FRINA
Vice-Chief of the Naval Staff:
Vice-Admiral Terence Thornton Lewin, MVO, DSC
Chief Scientist (Royal Navy): Mr. Basil Wilfred Lythall, CB, MA
Deputy Under Secretary of State (Navy): Mr. Sydney Redman, CB
Second Permanent Under-Secretary for Administration: Sir Arthur Drew, KCB, JP
Second Permanent Under-Secretary for Equipment: Sir Martin Flett, KCB

Commanders-in-Chief

Commander-in-Chief, Naval Home Command:
Admiral Sir Horace Rochfort Law, KCB, OBE, DSC
Fleet Commander-in-Chief:
Admiral Sir William Donough O'Brien, KCB, DSC
(Admiral Sir Edward Beckwith Ashmore, KCB, DSC, from September 1971)

Flag Officers

Commander, Far East Fleet:
Rear Admiral John Anthony Rose Troup, DSC & Bar
Flag Officer, Naval Air Command:
Vice-Admiral Michael Frampton Fell, CB, DSO, DSC & Bar
Flag Officer, Scotland and Northern Ireland:
Rear-Admiral David Arthur Dunbar-Nasmith, CB, DSC
Flag Officer, Submarines:
Vice-Admiral John Charles Young Roxburgh, CB, CBE, DSO, DSC
Flag Officer, Carriers and Amphibious Ships:
Rear Admiral John Devereux Treacher
Flag Officer, Flotillas, Western Fleet:
Rear-Admiral Arthur MacKenize Power, MBE
Flag Officer, Medway, and Admiral Superintendent, H.M. Dockyard, Chatham:
Rear-Admiral Frederick Charles William Lawson, DSC & Bar, C.Eng, MIMechE
Rear-Admiral Colin Charles Harrison Dunlop, CBE, from Oct 1971
Flag Officer, Plymouth and Admiral Superintendent H.M. Dockyard, Devonport:
Vice-Admiral John Rae McKaig, CBE
Flag Officer, Second-in-Command, Far East Fleet:
Rear-Admiral David Williams
Flag Officer, Sea Training and in Command Portland Naval Base:
Rear-Admiral Edward Gerrard Napier Mansfield
Flag Officer, Malta:
Rear-Admiral John Atrill Templeton-Cotill
Flag Officer, Gibraltar, and Admiral Superintendent, H.M. Dockyard, Gibraltar:
Rear-Admiral Arthur Rodney Barry Sturdee
Flag Officer, Spithead and Admiral Superintendent, H.M. Dockyard, Portsmouth:
Rear-Admiral Peter George La Niece, CBE
Admiral Superintendent, H.M. Dockyard, Rosyth:
Rear-Admiral William Terence Colborne Ridley, CB, OBE, CEng, FIMechE, MIMarE

General Officers, Royal Marines

Commandant-General, Royal Marines:
General Sir Peter William Cradock, Hellings, KCB, DSC, MC
(Lieutenant-General Basil Ian Spencer Gourlay, OBE, MC, from Nov 1971)
Chief of Staff to Commandant-General, Royal Marines:
Major-General Patrick Richard Kay, MBE
Major General Commanding Headquarters Training Group, Royal Marines:
Major-General Basil Ian Spencer Gourlay, OBE, MC
Major-General Commanding Commando Forces Royal Marines:
Major-General Peter John Frederick Whiteley, OBE

Senior Appointments

Director-General Ships, Chief Naval Engineer Officer, Senior Naval Representative, Bath:
Vice-Admiral Robert George Raper, CB, CEng, FIMechE, MIMarE
Director-General Aircraft (Naval)
Rear-Admiral John Edward Dyer-Smith, CEng, FIMechE
Director-General Weapons (Naval):
Rear-Admiral Philip Alexander Watson, MVO
Assistant Controller (Polaris):
Rear-Admiral Charles William Haines Shepherd, CBE
Director of Warship Design:
Mr. W. Norman Hancock, CEng, MRINA, RCNC
Director of Engineering (Ships):
Rear Admiral Lionel Dorian Dymoke, CEng, FIMechE, MIMarE

Diplomatic Representation

British Naval Attaché in Washington:
Rear-Admiral William David Stewart Scott
American Naval Attaché in London:
Rear-Admiral Fillmore B. Gilkeson, US Navy
British Naval Attaché in Moscow:
Captain Henry Masterman Ellis, RN
British Naval Attaché in Paris:
Captain Cecil Robert Peter Charles Branson, RN

1971-72 New Construction Programme

1 Nuclear Powered Fleet Submarine. "Improved" Design. Ordered in 1971.
2 Frigates. "Type 21". Intention to order announced in 1971.
2 Small Fleet Tankers.

1971-72 Conversion Programme

1 Commando Carrier. *Hermes.* Conversion from fixed-wing aircraft carrier.
1 Frigate. "Type 12". *Leander.* Conversion to carry "Ikara".

1970-1971 New Construction Programme

1 Nuclear Powered Fleet Submarine. "Improved" Design. *Superb.* Ordered May 1970.
Design assistance contracts placed with the shipbuilding industry during 1970 for one Command Helicopter Cruiser.
3 Guided Missile Armed Destroyers. "Type 42". Ordered 1970.
3 Frigates. "Type 21". *Active, Ambuscade, Antelope.* Ordered 1970 (two on 30 April, one on 19 May).
1 Glass Reinforced Plastic Minehunter. *Wilton.* Contract placed 11 Feb 1970.

1970-1971 Conversion Programme

2 Anti-Submarine Frigates. *Brighton, Rhyl.* Conversion to operate helicopter.

1969-70 New Construction Programme

1 Frigate. Interim "Type 21". *Amazon.* Order announced 26 Mar 1969. Laid down 6 Nov 1969. Launched 26 Apr 1971.
Lead Items for Frigate. Standard "Type 22". Announced 26 Mar 1969.
1 Research and Development Vessel. *RDV 01. Crystal.* Ordered Dec 1969.

1969-70 Conversion Programme

1 Cruiser. *Lion.* Conversion to operate helicopters. Rescinded in 1970.
1 Anti-Submarine Frigate. *Berwick.* Conversion to operate helicopter.
1 Conventionally Powered Patrol Submarine. For training.

1968-69 New Construction Programme

1 Nuclear Powered Fleet Submarine. "Improved" Design. *Sovereign.* Ordered May 1969.
1 Guided Missile Armed Destroyer. "Type 42". *Sheffield.* Ordered 14 Nov 1968. Laid down 15 Jan 1970.
Design Study for Patrol Frigate. Announced 27 Feb 1968.
Lead Items for Minesweepers. New Design.
1 Experimental Trials Vessel. *ETV 01. Whitehead.* Order announced 3 Dec 1968.
3 Anti-Fast Patrol Boat Training Craft. *Cutlass, Sabre, Scimitar.*
2 Ocean Tugs. "Roysterer" Class. *Robust, Rollicker.*

1968-69 Conversion Programme

1 Conventionally Powered Patrol Submarine. *Oberon.* For Training.
1 Destroyer. For Trials. *Matapan.*
2 Anti-Submarine Frigates. *Falmouth, Lowestoft.* Conversion to operate helicopter.
1 Store Carrier. As Torpedo Recovery Vessel.

1967-68 New Construction Programme

1 Nuclear Powered Fleet Submarine. "Improved" Design. *Swiftsure.* Announced 16 Feb 1967. Ordered Nov 1967. Laid down June 1969.
2 General Purpose Frigates. "Leander Class". *Ariadne* and *Apollo.* Ordered (announced) 29 July 1968.
3 Small Fleet Tankers. New Design. "Rover" Class. Ordered Jan 1968.

1967-68 Conversion Programme

1 Aircraft Carrier. *Ark Royal.* 3-year, £3m special refit and modernisation.
1 Cruiser. *Tiger.* Conversion to operate Helicopters.
1 Anti-Submarine Frigate. *Londonderry.* Conversion to operate helicopter.
6 Minehunters. "Ton" Class. Conversion from Coastal Minesweepers.
1 Ice Patrol Ship. *Endurance (ex-Anita Dan).* Conversion from commercial ice operating ship.

1966-67 New Construction Programme

1 Aircraft Carrier. CVA 01. Cancelled.
2 Nuclear Powered Fleet Submarines. "Valiant" Class. Ordered 9 Aug 1966 (*Conqueror*) and 1 Mar 1967 (*Courageous, ex-Superb*).
2 General Purpose Frigates. "Leander" Class. *Achilles, Diomede.* Ordered 8 Mar 1967.

1966-67 Conversion Programme

1 Gas Turbine Powered Anti-Submarine Frigate. *Exmouth.* Conversion from steam.
2 Anti-Submarine Frigates. *Plymouth, Yarmouth.* Conversion to operate helicopter.
3 Minehunters. "Ton" Class. Conversion from Coastal Minesweepers.

1965-66 New Construction Programme

1 Guided Missile Armed Destroyer. "Type 82". *Bristol.* Ordered 4 Oct 1966.
1 Nuclear Powered Submarine. *Churchill.* Ordered 15 Oct 1955.
3 General Purpose Frigates. "Leander" Class. *Bacchante, Charybdis, Scylla.*
2 Medium Berthing Tugs.
2 Landing Craft Mechanised. Mk 9.

1965-66 Conversion Programme

1 Cruiser. *Blake.* Conversion to operate helicopters.
1 Anti-Submarine Frigate. *Rothesay.* Conversion to operate helicopter.
2 Minehunters. "Ton" Class. Conversion from Coastal Minesweepers.

Navy Estimates

1962-63: £422 273 000	1965-66: £589 040 000	1968-69: £668 715 000
1963-64: £439 951 600	1966-67: £597 129 000	1969-70: £642 043 000
1964-65: £487 690 000	1967-68: £648 043 500	1970-71: £659 378 500

Strength of the Fleet

2 Fixed Wing Aircraft Carriers	1 Heavy Repair Ship (ex-Aircraft Carrier)	5 Fast Training and Patrol Boats
3 Commando Ships and Helicopter Carriers	1 Submarine Parent Ship	2 Seaward Defence Boats
4 Nuclear Powered Ballistic Missile Submarines	1 Destroyer Depot Ship	10 Fleet Support and Supply Ships
5 Nuclear Powered Fleet Submarines	2 Maintenance Ships	27 Fleet Oilers
26 Diesel Powered Patrol Submarines	8 Survey Ships (including 4 Coastal Vessels)	23 Mooring, Salvage and Boom Vessels
2 Assault Ships (Amphibious Cruiser Type)	5 Inshore Survey Craft	1 Royal Yacht and Hospital Ship
3 Cruisers (including 2 Helicopter Cruisers)	49 Coastal Minesweepers (including 12 Hunters)	1 Diving Trials Ship
9 Guided Missile Armed Destroyers	24 Inshore Minesweepers (20 Auxiliary Services)	2 Cable Vessels
3 Destroyers (including 1 Experimental)	3 Controlled Minelayers	41 Fleet Tenders
65 Frigates	2 Landing Ships (LST Type)	10 Armament Carriers
6 Logistic Landing Ships	24 Landing Craft (LCT Type)	14 Water Carriers
1 Helicopter Support Ship	33 Minor Landing Craft	91 Fleet and Berthing Tugs
1 Ice Patrol Ship	6 Experimental Vessels (2 New Construction)	92 Auxiliaries and Service Craft.
1 Mine Countermeasures Support Ship		

Personnel

1960-61: 102 000	1964-65: 103 000	1968-69: 98 000
1961-62: 100 000	1965-66: 104 000	1969-70: 95 500
1962-63: 100 000	1966-67: 103 000	1970-71: 89 000
1963-64: 100 000	1967-68: 100 500	1971-72: 87 000

Mercantile Marine

Lloyd's Register of Shipping: 3 822 vessels of 25 824 820 tons gross

British Carrier Borne Aircraft

Name	Maker	Type	Dimensions	Power Plant	Armament	Performance
PHANTOM II (F-4K)	McDonnell (USA)	Two-seat All-Weather Interceptor and Attack Fighter	Wing Span 38 ft 5 in Folded 27 ft 6·5 in Length 58 ft 3 in	Two Rolls-Royce Spey 25 R Turbojets with afterburners	Sidewinder and Sparrow AAM's bombs, rockets	Maximum Speed Over Mach 2
SEA VIXEN F(AW)Mk 2	Hawker Siddeley	Two Seat All-Weather Fighter	Wing Span 50 ft Folded 22 ft 3 in Length 55 ft 7 in	Two Rolls-Royce Avon 208 Turbojets	Firestreak, Red Top or Bullpup missiles, bombs, rockets	Maximum Speed at (10,000 ft) 560 knots
BUCCANEER S.Mk 2	Hawker Siddeley	Two-seat All-Weather Strike and Reconnaissance Aircraft	Wing Span 44 ft Folded 19 ft 11 in Length 63 ft 5 in	Two RB168-IA Spey Turbofans	Nuclear Weapons, bombs, rockets, Bullpup missiles, Martel ASM's	Maximum Speed at 200 ft, Mach 0·85 approx
GANNET AEW Mk 3	Westland	Three-seat Early Warning Aircraft	Wing Span 54 ft 6 in Folded 19 ft 11 in Length 44 ft	One R-R Bristol Double Mamba 102 Turboprop	None	Maximum Speed approx 220 knots
SEA KING HAS.Mk I	Westland	Multi-Seat All-Weather Anti-Submarine and Transport Helicopter	Rotor dia 62 ft Length 72 ft 8 in Width Folded 16 ft 4 in Height (to rotor hub) 15 ft 6 in	Two R-R Bristol Gnome 1400 engines	Up to 840 lb of weapons including homing torpedoes	Maximum Speed 144 knots; Cruising Speed for max range 118 knots; Range with max fuel, 10% reserve 54 nautical miles
WESSEX HAS. Mk 3	Westland	Multi-Seat Anti-Submarine and General-Purpose Helicopter	Rotor dia 56 ft Length 65 ft 9 in	One Napier Gazelle NGa 22 Mk 165 Turbine engine	Anti-Submarine weapons	Maximum Speed 116 knots
WESSEX HAS. Mk I	Westland	Multi-Seat Anti-Submarine and General-Purpose	Rotor dia 56 ft Length 65 ft 9 in	One Napier Gazelle 161 Shaft-Turbine engine	Anti-Submarine Weapons, SS II Missiles	Maximum Speed 116 knots
WESSEX HU. Mk 5	Westland	Commando Assault and Transport Helicopter	Rotor dia 56 ft Length 65 ft 9 in	Two coupled R-R Bristol Gnome Shaft-Turbine engines	SS II missiles, guns, rockets	Maximum Speed 116 knots, Range 415 nautical miles
WASP HAS. Mk I	Westland	Two-Crew Anti-Submarine Helicopter	Rotor dia 32 ft 3 in Overall length 40 ft 4 in	One R-R Bristol Nimbus Shaft-turbine engine	Anti-Submarine homing torpedoes or missiles	Maximum Speed 104 knots, Range 234 nautical miles

British Naval Guided Missiles

Type	Name	Maker	Length	Propulsion	Speed Mach	Range N. Miles	Guidance System	Notes
SURFACE-TO-AIR	Seacat	Short Bros & Harland	4 ft 10·3 in	Solid Propellant			Radio command	Short-range Anti-aircraft missile
	Sea Dart	Hawker Siddeley	14 ft 3·5 in	R-R Bristol Odin ramjet, Solid Propellant booster		19½		Medium-range, area-defence, ship-to-ship missiles
	Seaslug	Hawker Siddeley	20 ft	ICI Solid propellant and solid boosters			Beamrider	Carried by "County" class destroyers. Capable of engaging low flying and surface targets
	Seawolf (PX 430)	British Aircraft Corporation						Close-range Anti-aircraft missile with aurface-to-surface capability
AIR-TO-AIR	Firestreak	Hawker Siddeley	10 ft 5·5 in	Solid propellant	2·0+	4·3	Infra-red	Carried by Sea Vixen fighters
	Sparrow	Raytheon (USA)	12 ft	Rocketdyne Mk 38 Solid propellant	3·5+	7+	Semi-active	Carried by Phantom aircraft
	Red Top	Hawker Siddeley	11 ft 5·7 in	Solid propellant	3·0	6	Infra-red	Carried by Sea Vixen Mk 2 fighters
	Sidewinder	Raytheon (USA)	9 ft 6·5 in	Rocketdyne Solid propellant	2·5	2	Infra-red	Carried by Phantom fighters, Buccaneers
AIR-TO-SURFACE	Bullpup	Maxson and European Consortium	10 ft 6 in	Thiokol LR58-4 Liquid propellant	1·8	6	Radio command	Carried by Phantom, Buccaneer, Sea Vixen
	Martel	Anglo-French	12 ft/13 ft 1½ in	Solid propellant			TV	Carried by Buccaneer and Nimrod
	SS II	Aérospatiale (France)	3 ft 11 in	Solid propellant	360 mph	1·75	Wire guidance	Carried by Wessex helicopters
ANTI-SUBMARINE	Ikara	Australian Department of Supply	11 ft	Solid propellant			Radio/radar Terminal homing	Mounted in frigate *Leander* and destroyer *Bristol*
SURFACE-TO-SURFACE	Polaris A3	Lockheed	31 ft	Solid propellant	10	2 500	Inertial	In nuclear powered submarines *Renown*, *Repulse*, *Resolution* and *Revenge*

LIST OF PENNANT NUMBERS

Aircraft Carriers

| R | 05 | Eagle |
| R | 09 | Ark Royal |

Commando Carriers

R	07	Albion
R	08	Bulwark
R	12	Hermes

Submarines

S	01	Porpoise
S	02	Rorqual
S	03	Narwhal
S	04	Grampus
S	05	Finwhale
S	06	Cachalot
S	07	Sealion
S	08	Walrus
S	09	Oberon
S	10	Odin
S	11	Orpheus
S	12	Olympus
S	13	Osiris
S	14	Onslaught
S	15	Otter
S	16	Oracle
S	17	Ocelot
S	18	Otus
S	19	Opossum
S	20	Opportune
S	21	Onyx
S	22	Resolution
S	23	Repulse
S	26	Renown
S	27	Revenge
S	49	Artemis
S	63	Andrew
S	67	Alliance
S	69	Auriga
S	72	Aeneas
S	101	Dreadnought
S	102	Valiant
S	103	Warspite
S	104	Churchill
S	105	Conqueror
S	106	Courageous
S	107	Swiftsure
S	108	Sovereign
S	109	Superb

Assault Ships

| L | 10 | Fearless |
| L | 11 | Intrepid |

Cruisers

C	20	Tiger
C	34	Lion
C	99	Blake

Destroyers

D	01	Caprice
D	02	Devonshire
D	06	Hampshire
D	12	Kent
D	16	London
D	18	Antrim
D	19	Glamorgan
D	20	Fife
D	21	Norfolk
D	23	Bristol
D	35	Diamond
D	43	Matapan
D	73	Cavalier
D	154	Duchess

Frigates

F	10	Aurora
F	12	Achilles
F	14	Leopard
F	15	Euryalus
F	16	Diomede
F	18	Galatea
F	27	Lynx
F	28	Cleopatra
F	32	Salisbury
F	34	Puma
F	36	Whitby
F	37	Jaguar
F	38	Arethusa
F	39	Naiad
F	40	Sirius
F	42	Phoebe
F	43	Torquay
F	45	Minerva
F	47	Danae
F	48	Dundas
F	52	Juno
F	53	Undaunted
F	54	Hardy
F	56	Argonaut
F	57	Andromeda
F	58	Hermione
F	59	Chichester
F	60	Jupiter
F	61	Llandaff
F	63	Scarborough
F	65	Tenby
F	69	Bacchante
F	71	Scylla
F	72	Ariadne
F	73	Eastbourne
F	75	Charybdis
F	77	Blackpool
F	78	Blackwood
F	80	Duncan
F	83	Ulster
F	84	Exmouth
F	85	Keppel
F	88	Malcolm
F	94	Pallister
F	97	Russell
F	99	Lincoln
F	101	Yarmouth
F	103	Lowestoft
F	104	Dido
F	106	Brighton
F	107	Rothesay
F	108	Londonderry
F	109	Leander
F	113	Falmouth
F	114	Ajax
F	115	Berwick
F	117	Ashanti
F	119	Eskimo
F	122	Gurkha
F	124	Zulu
F	125	Mohawk
F	126	Plymouth
F	127	Penelope
F	129	Rhyl
F	131	Nubian
F	133	Tartar
F	138	Rapid
F	197	Grenville

Minelayers

| N | 13 | Miner III |
| N | 21 | Abdiel |

Helicopter Support Ship

| K | 08 | Engadine |

Support Ships & Auxiliaries

A	00	Britannia
A	70	Echo
A	71	Enterprise
A	72	Egeria
A	75	Tidespring
A	76	Tidepool
A	77	Pearleaf
A	78	Plumleaf
A	79	Bayleaf
A	80	Orangeleaf
A	81	Brambleleaf
A	84	Reliant
A	85	Faithful
A	86	Forceful
A	87	Favourite
A	88	Agile
A	89	Advice
A	90	Accord
A	91	Griper
A	92	Grinder
A	93	Dexterous
A	94	Director
A	95	Typhoon
A	96	Tidereach
A	97	Tideflow
A	98	Tidesurge
A	108	Triumph
A	111	Cyclone
A	122	Olwen
A	123	Olna
A	124	Olmeda
A	130	Gold Ranger
A	133	Hecla
A	134	Rame Head
A	135	Nordenfelt
A	137	Hecate
A	144	Hydra
A	160	Fort Dunvegan
A	163	Black Ranger
A	169	Brown Ranger
A	171	Endurance
A	176	Bullfinch
A	179	Whimbrel
A	185	Maidstone
A	186	Fort Rosalie
A	187	Forth
A	191	Berry Head
A	194	Tyne
A	200	Vidal
A	204	Robert Dundas
A	207	Wave Prince
A	218	Samsonia
A	222	Spapool
A	223	Nimble
A	224	Spabrook
A	230	Fort Langley
A	231	Reclaim
A	232	Kingarth
A	240	Bustler
A	241	Robert Middleton
A	257	Spaburn
A	259	St. Margarets
A	260	Spalake
A	261	Eddyfirth
A	262	Hartland Point
A	264	Reward
A	265	Wave Chief
A	268	Green Rover
A	269	Grey Rover
A	270	Blue Rover
A	280	Resurgent
A	281	Kinbrace
A	288	Sea Giant
A	289	Confiance
A	290	Confident
A	293	Careful
A	316	Fort Sandusky
A	329	Retainer
A	332	Caldy
A	333	Coll
A	334	Bern
A	336	Lundy
A	338	Skomer
A	339	Lyness
A	340	Graemsay
A	342	Foulness
A	344	Stromness
A	345	Tarbatness
A	346	Switha
A	377	Maxim
A	378	Kinterbury
A	387	Girdle Ness
A	390	Samson
A	404	Bacchus
A	406	Hebe
A	480	Resource
A	482	Kinloss
A	486	Regent
A	494	Salvalour
A	497	Salveda
A	499	Salvestor
A	500	Salvictor
A	503	Sea Salvor
A	505	Succour
A	506	Swin
A	507	Uplifter
A	508	Capable

Boom Defence Vessels

P	190	Laymoor
P	191	Layburn
P	192	Mandarin
P	193	Pintail
P	194	Garganey
P	195	Goldeneye
P	201	Barbain
P	202	Barfoot
P	232	Barmond
P	284	Moorsman
P	294	Barfoil

Coastal Minesweepers

M	1103	Kilmorey (Alfriston)
M	1107	Beachampton
M	1109	Killiecrankie (Bickington)
M	1110	Bildeston
M	1113	Brereton
M	1114	Brinton
M	1115	Bronington
M	1124	St. David (Crichton)
M	1125	Cuxton
M	1126	Montrose (Dalswinton)
M	1130	Highburton
M	1133	Bossington
M	1136	Curzon (Fittleton)
M	1140	Gavinton
M	1141	Glasserton
M	1146	Venturer (Hodgeston)
M	1147	Hubberston
M	1150	Invermoriston
M	1151	Iveston
M	1153	Kedelston
M	1154	Kellington
M	1155	Monkton
M	1157	Kirkliston
M	1158	Laleston
M	1164	Maddiston
M	1165	Maxton
M	1166	Nurton
M	1167	Clyde (Repton)
M	1173	Mersey (Pollington)
M	1174	Puncheston
M	1175	Northumbria (Quainton)
M	1180	Shavington
M	1181	Sheraton
M	1182	Shoulton
M	1187	Upton
M	1188	Walkerton
M	1189	Wasperton
M	1192	Wilkieston
M	1193	Wolverton
M	1194	Thames (Woolaston)
M	1195	Wotton
M	1196	Yarnton
M	1198	Ashton
M	1199	Belton
M	1200	Soberton
M	1204	Stubbington
M	1205	Wiston
M	1208	Lewiston
M	1209	Chawton
M	1216	Solent (Crofton)

Inshore Minesweepers

M	304	Waterwitch (Powderham 2720)
M	2002	Aveley
M	2010	Isis (Cradley)
M	2603	Arlingham TRV (ex-PAS)
M	2611	Bottisham R
M	2614	Bucklesham TRV
M	2616	Chelsham R
M	2621	Dittisham TRV
M	2622	Downham TRV
M	2624	Elsenham TRV
M	2626	Everingham PAS
M	2628	Flintham TRV
M	2630	Fritham TRV
M	2635	Haversham TRV
M	2636	Lasham TRV
M	2716	Pagham RNXS
M	2717	Fordham DGV
M	2726	Shipham RNXS
M	2733	Thakeham RNXS
M	2735	Tongham PAS
M	2737	Warmingham DGV
M	2780	Woodlark (Yaxham)
M	2781	Portisham RNXS
M	2783	Odiham RNXS
M	2784	Puttenham RNXS
M	2785	Birdham RNXS
M	2790	Thatcham DGV
M	2793	Thornham

DGV = *Degaussing Vessels*
PAS = *Port Auxiliary Service*
RNXS= *Royal Naval Auxiliary Service*
TRV = *Torpedo Recovery Vessels*
R = *Reserve (ex-RAF)*

Aircraft Carriers

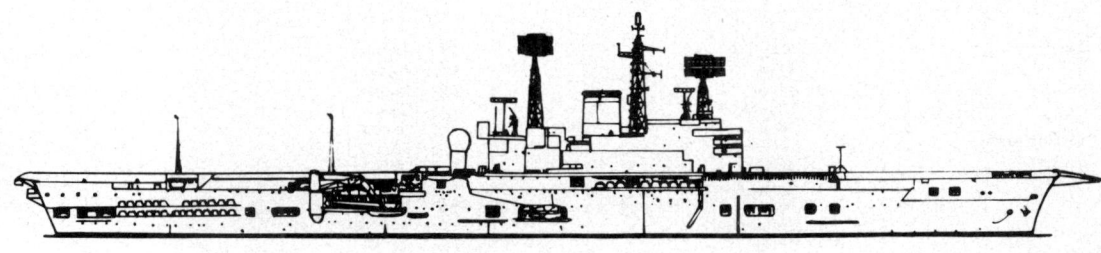

ARK ROYAL

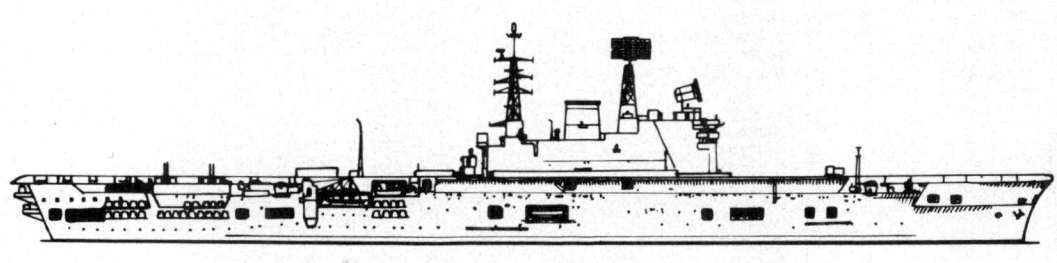

EAGLE

Commando Carriers

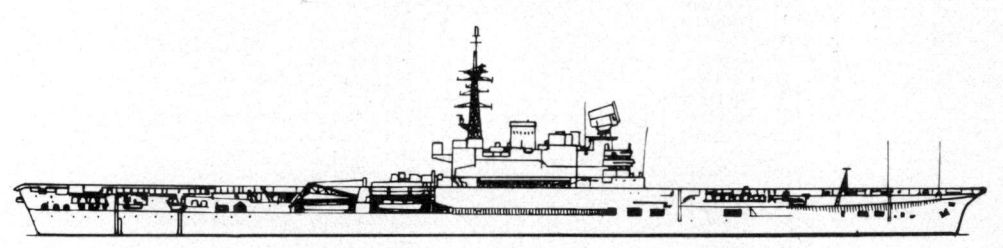

HERMES (as fixed wing aircraft carrier before conversion 1972)

ALBION

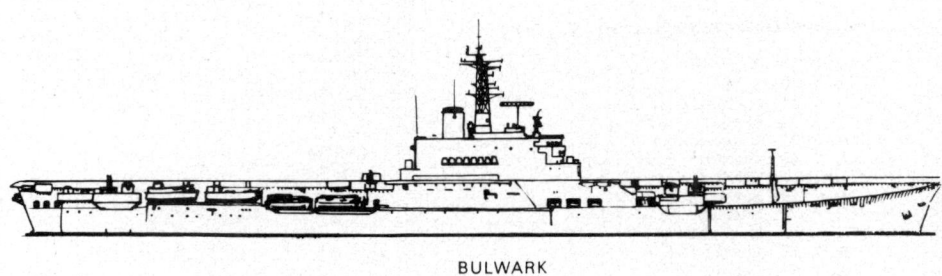

BULWARK

Escort Maintenance Ship

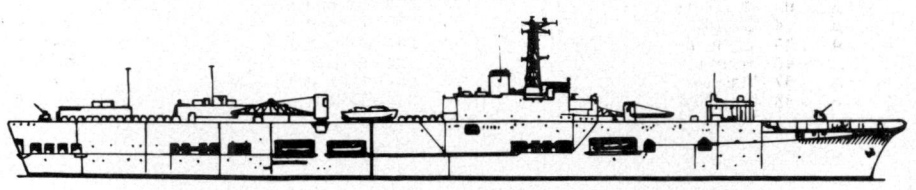

TRIUMPH (former Aircraft Carrier) Heavy Repair Ship

Scale: 150 feet = 1 inch

Cruisers, Guided Missile Destroyers, Nuclear Submarines, Support Ships

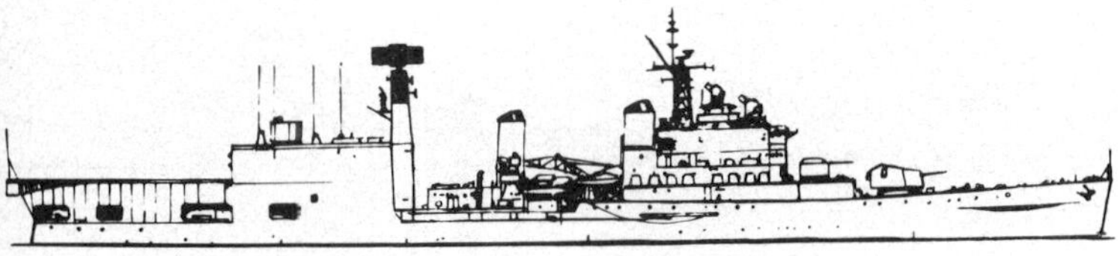

BLAKE, TIGER (Helicopter Cruisers)

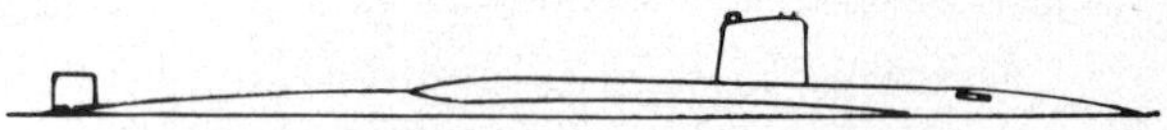

RENOWN, REPULSE, RESOLUTION, REVENGE

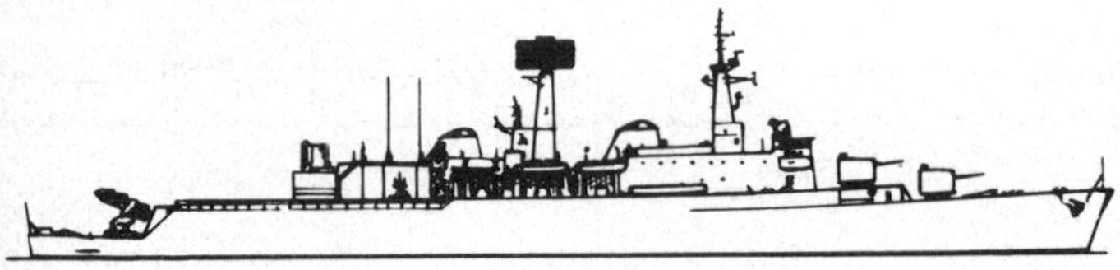

ANTRIM, NORFOLK

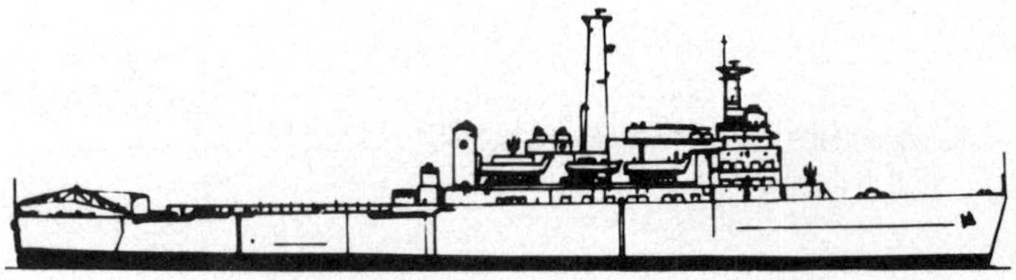

FEARLESS. INTREPID (Assault Ships)

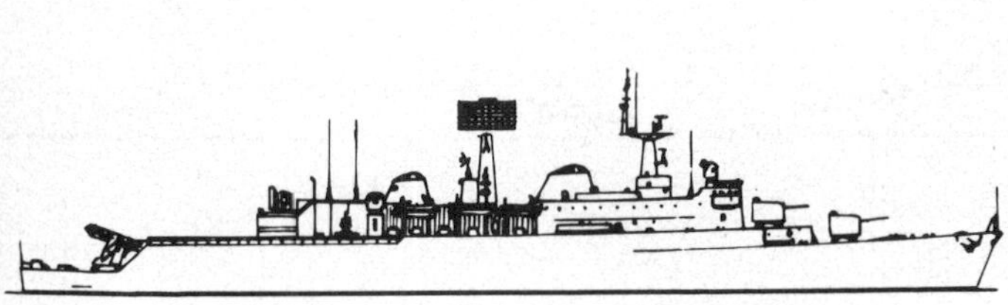

FIFE, GLAMORGAN

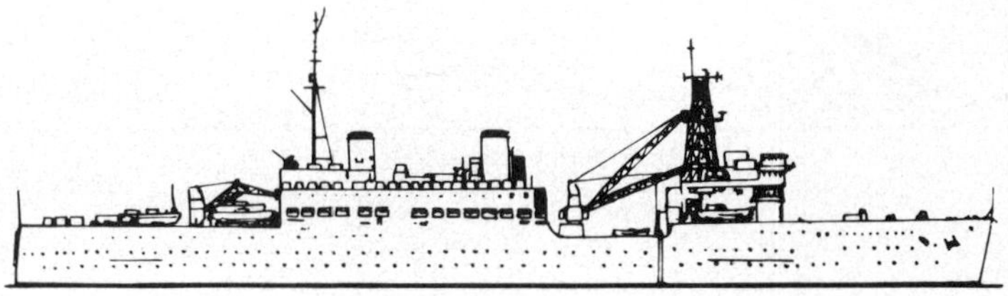

FORTH (Submarine Support Ship)

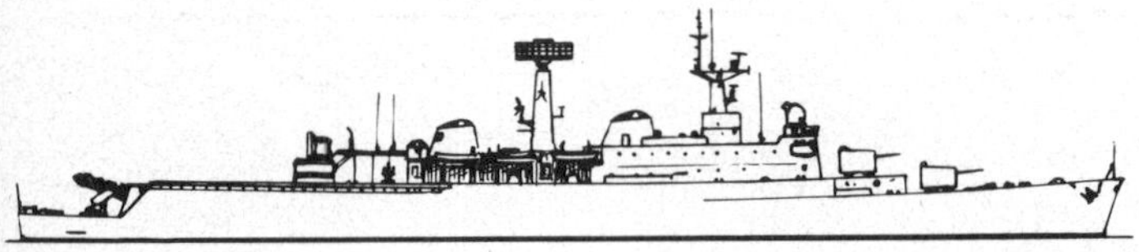

KENT, LONDON

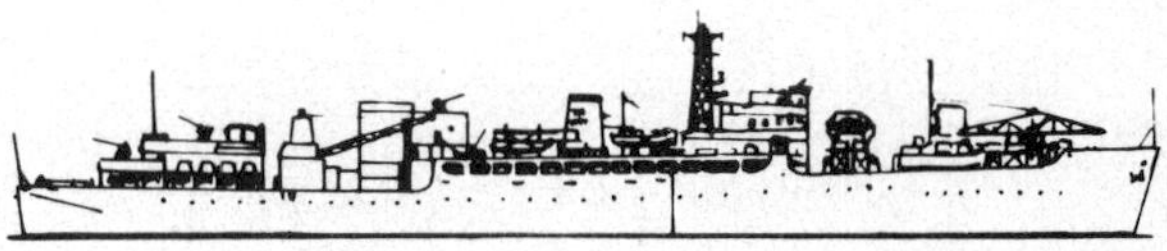

HARTLAND POINT

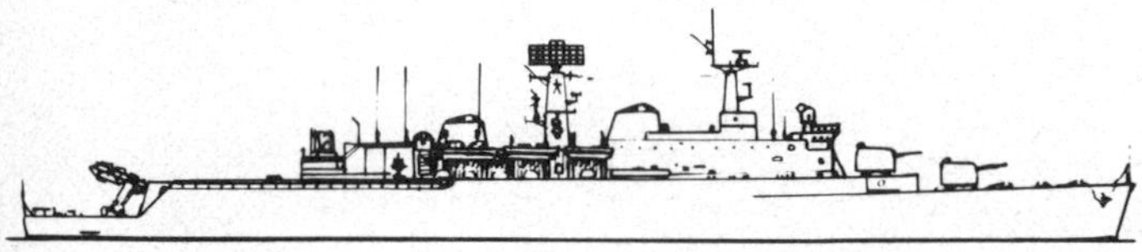

DEVONSHIRE, HAMPSHIRE

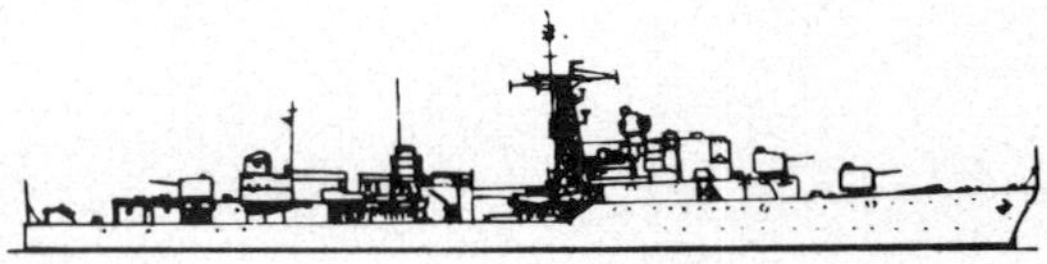

DIAMOND

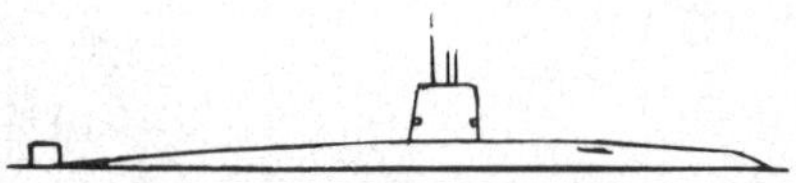

CHURCHILL, CONQUEROR, VALIANT, WARSPITE

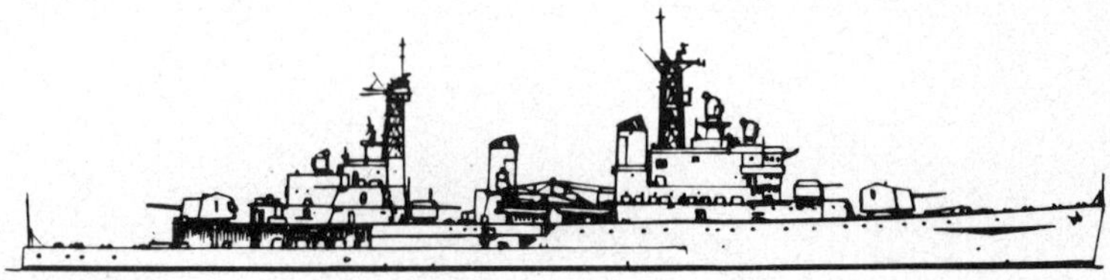

LION (Conventional Cruiser)

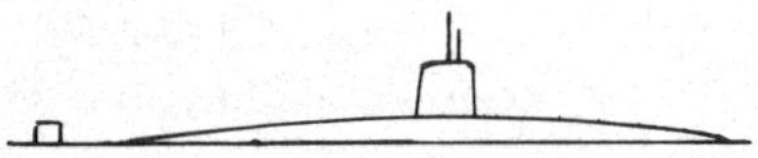

DREADNOUGHT

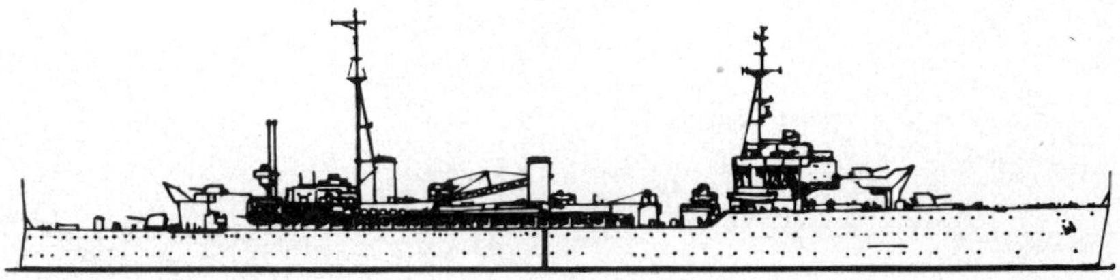

TYNE (Destroyer Depot Ship)

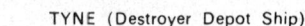

Scale: 150 feet = 1 inch

Diesel Submarines, Destroyers, Frigates, Survey Ships, Ice Patrol Ship

OBERON and PORPOISE *Classes*

Converted ROTHESAY *Class*

ULSTER

"A" *Class*

ROTHESAY *Class*

UNDAUNTED, helo deck aft

CAPRICE

WHITBY *Class* for training

RAPID

CAVALIER

JAGUAR, LEOPARD, LYNX, PUMA

GRENVILLE

LEANDER *Class* with "Seacat"

LINCOLN (CHICHESTER with aft structure as LLANDAFF)

ABDIEL (Minelayer)

LEANDER *Class* with AA guns

LLANDAFF (SALISBURY with aft structure as LINCOLN)

HECATE, HECLA, HYDRA (Survey)

"TRIBAL" *Class*

BLACKWOOD *Class*

VIDAL (Survey Ship)

"TRIBAL" *Class* with "Seacat"

EXMOUTH (Gas Turbines)

ENDURANCE (Ice Patrol Ship)

AIRCRAFT CARRIERS

Name	Deck Letter	No.	Builders	Laid down	Launched	Completed	Refitted
ARK ROYAL (ex-*Irresistible*)	R	R 09	Cammell Laird, Birkenhead	3 May 1943	3 May 1950	25 Feb 1955	Mar 1967-Feb 1970

Displacement, tons	43 060 standard; 50 786 full load
Length, feet (*metres*)	720·0 (*219·5*)pp; 845·0 (*275·6*)oa
Beam, feet (*metres*)	112·8 (*34·4*) hull
Draught, feet (*metres*)	36·0 (*11·0*)
Width, feet (*metres*)	166·0 (*50·6*)
Catapults	2 improved steam
Aircraft	30 fixed wing + 6 helicopters
Missile launchers	Fitted for four quadruple "Seacat"
Armour	4·5in belt; 4·in flight deck; 25in hangar deck; 1·5in hangar side
Boilers	8 Admiralty 3 drum pressure 400 psi (*28·1 kg/cm²*); superheat 600°F (*316°C*)
Main engines	Parsons single reduction geared turbines; 4 shafts; 152 000 shp
Speed, knots	31·5 designed max
Oil fuel, tons	5 500 capacity
Complement	260 officers (as Flagship) 2 380 ratings (with Air Staff)

ARK ROYAL (after three years special refit)

1970, Official

First British aircraft carrier with steam catapults. Had first side lift in a British aircraft carrier, situated amidships on the port side and serving the upper hangar but in 1959 this was removed, the deck park provided by the angled deck having obviated its necessity, leaving her with two centre line lifts. In 1961, the deck landing projector sight, "Hilo" long range guidance system, and more powerful steam catapults were installed. Ship originally cost £21 428 000.

MODERNISATION. A three-years "special refit" and modernisation costing £32 500 000, from Mar 1967 to Feb 1970, enables her to operate both Phantom and Buccaneer Mk 2 aircraft. A fully angled deck 8·5 degrees off the centre line was fitted, involving two large extensions to the flight deck, and the size of the island was increased. A new waist catapult with an increased launching speed allows her to operate aircraft at almost "nil" wind conditions. A new direct acting gear was installed to enable bigger aircraft to be landed on at greater speeds.

RADAR. Search: Type 965 (2 sets). Aircraft Direction: Type 982 and Type 983 height finder. Tactical: Type 993. Miscellaneous: Carrier Controlled Approach Radar.

GUNNERY. Originally mounted 16—4·5 inch guns in eight twin turrets, two on each beam forward and two on each beam aft, but the four on port side forward, were removed in 1956, the four on starboard side forward in 1959, four in two forward turrets on after sponsons in 1964 and the four aft in 1969.

DRAWING. Starboard elevation and plan. Drawn in 1970 after refit. Scale: 125 feet = 1 inch (1 : 1 500).

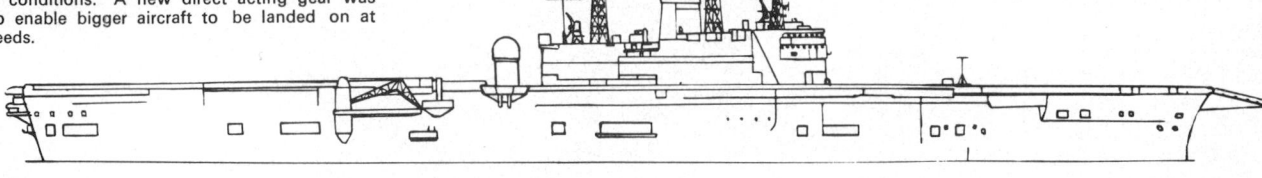

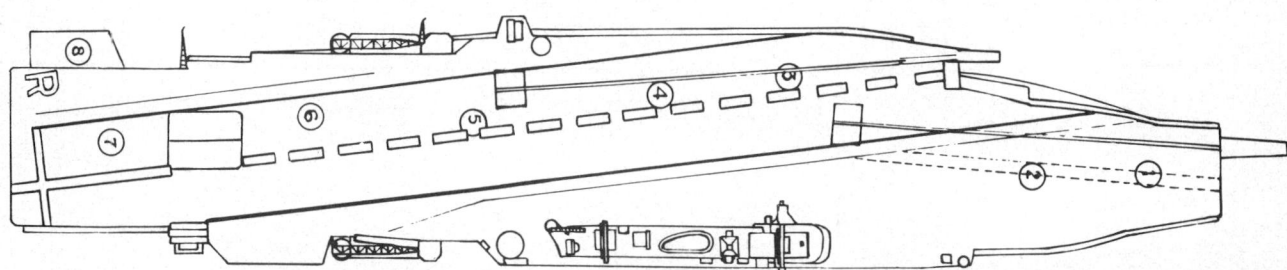

ARK ROYAL (after special refit)

1970 Official

ARK ROYAL

1971, Official

Aircraft Carriers—*continued*

Name	Deck Letter	No.	Builders	Laid down	Launched	Completed	Reconstructed
EAGLE (ex-*Audacious*)	E	R 05	Harland & Wolff, Belfast	24 Oct 1942	19 Mar 1946	1 Oct 1951	HM Dockyard Devonport, 1959-64

Displacement, tons	43 000 standard; 50 536 full load
Length, feet (*metres*)	720·0 (*219·5*)pp; 811·8 (*247·4*)oa
Beam, feet (*metres*)	112·8 (*34·4*) hull
Draught, feet (*metres*)	36·0 (*11·0*)
Width, feet (*metres*)	171·0 (*52·1*) overall
Catapults	2 steam (see *Reconstruction* note)
Aircraft	30 fixed wing + 6 helicopters
Missile launchers	6 quadruple "Seacat" (3 starboard), 2 port, 1 aft
Guns, dual purpose	8—4·5 in (*115 mm*), 2 twin starboard, 2 twin port)
Armour	4·5 in belt; 4 in flight deck; 2·5 in hangar deck; 1·5 in hangar side
Boilers	8 Admiralty 3-drum
Main engines	Parsons s.r. geared turbines; 4 shafts; 152 000 shp
Speed, knots	31·5
Complement	1 745 including ship's air staff; 2 750 max with air squadrons

Ordered on 19 May 1942. Accepted on 1 Mar 1952. Of 90 per cent welded construction. Damage control arrangements exceptionally complete. Originally cost £15 795 000. Modernisation cost £31 000 000.

RECONSTRUCTION. Fully angled flight deck at 8·5 degrees. New flight deck armour. Two steam (instead of hydraulic) catapults for launching the latest naval aircraft. Superstructure half as long again as former island. Lattice mast shorter and thicker than previously stepped. The most up-to-date living accommodation was also incorporated. Reconstructed from the end of 1959 to May 1964.

RADAR. Search: Type 965. Aircraft Direction: Type 984 3 D. Miscellaneous: Carrier controlled approach.

REFIT. During refit at HM Dockyard, Devonport, from Sep 1966 to Apr 1967, more powerful catapults and arrester gear were installed for Phantom aircraft.

ANTI-CONTAMINATION. Equipped with improved and built-in pre-wetting system to counteract contamination in the event of fallout or chemical hazard.

ELECTRICAL. During reconstruction the generating capacity was increased to 8 250 kW.

CLASS. Sister ship of *Ark Royal*, see previous page. Two more aircraft carriers of this type, *Africa* and original *Eagle*, and three much larger aircraft carriers, to have been named *Gibraltar*, *Malta* and *New Zealand*, were cancelled at the end of the Second World War.

DRAWING. Port elevation and plan. Scale: 125 feet = 1 inch (1 : 1 500).

EAGLE   *1971, Official*

EAGLE with *Phantom* landing   *1969, Official*

EAGLE   *1971, Official*

COMMANDO CARRIERS

Name	Deck Letter	No.	Builders	Laid down	Launched	Completed
HERMES (ex-*Elephant*)	H	R 12	Vickers-Armstrongs, Barrow-in-Furness	21 June 1944	16 Feb 1953	18 Nov 1959

Displacement, tons	23 900 standard; 28 700 full load
Length, feet (*metres*)	650·0 (*198·1*) pp; 744·3 (*226·9*) oa
Beam, feet (*metres*)	90·0 (*27·4*) hull
Draught, feet (*metres*)	29·0 (*8·8*)
Width, feet (*metres*)	160·0 (*48·8*) overall
Aircraft	20 helicopters
Armour	Reinforced flight deck
Missile launchers	2 quadruple "Seacat" surface-to-air systems
Boilers	4 Admiralty 3-drum type
Main engines	Parsons geared turbines; 2 shafts; 76 000 shp
Speed, knots	28 designed max
Oil fuel, tons	3 880 furnace; 320 diesel; 1 000 avgas
Complement	1 830 (190 officers, 1 640 men) 2 100 with air squadrons

HERMES as fixed-wing aircraft carrier

1971, Official

Originally name ship of a class including *Albion*, *Bulwark* and *Centaur*, but design was modified to a more advanced type, incorporating new equipment and improved arrangements, including five post-war developments—angled deck, steam catapult, landing sight, 3-D radar, and deck-edge lift. Air-conditioned. Embarked air squadrons and joined the Fleet summer 1960. Long refit 1964 to 1966, costing £10 000 000, when the "Alaskan Highway" was stepped out on the starboard side of the island, adding 15·5 feet to overall breadth, all ten 40 mm AA guns in five twin mountings suppressed two "Seacat" systems installed, and living accommodation improved. Refitted in 1969.

CONVERSION. It was officially announced on 17 Feb 1971 that a start was to be made on the conversion of HMS *Hermes* from a fixed-wing aircraft carrier to the Commando ship rôle. She was taken in hand at HM Dockyard, Devonport on 1 Mar 1971. Completion as LPH is expected in approx 2 years. Main features of conversion are:—Removal of steam catapults, arrester gear and fixed-wing aircraft facilities: Rearrangement to provide Commando accommodation and storage for their guns, ammunition, vehicles and communications; Changes to radar etc to meet the new role; Installation of additional air-conditioning, larger diesel generators, new auxiliary boilers and evaporators: Extension of automatic control of machinery: Modernisation of galley, bakery, laundry and stories facilities.

RADAR. Search: Type 293. Aircraft Direction: Type 984. Miscellaneous: Carrier controlled approach radar.

ENGINEERING. Remote control for engines, coupled with automatic feed for boilers, whereby with the entire complement of officers and men under cover and protected in "the citadel", a self-contained section proof against radio-active fall-out, the ship could be steamed through an atomic cloud.

FLIGHT DECK. Angled 6·5 deg off centre line of ship, the biggest angle that could be contrived in an aircraft carrier of the size. Strengthened to take Harrier aircraft.

ELECTRICAL. The plant is 440 volt, 3 phase, 60 cycle AC with a generating capacity of 5 440 kW.

DRAWING. Port elevation and plan as fixed-wing aircraft carrier Scale: 125 feet = 1 inch (1 : 1 500).

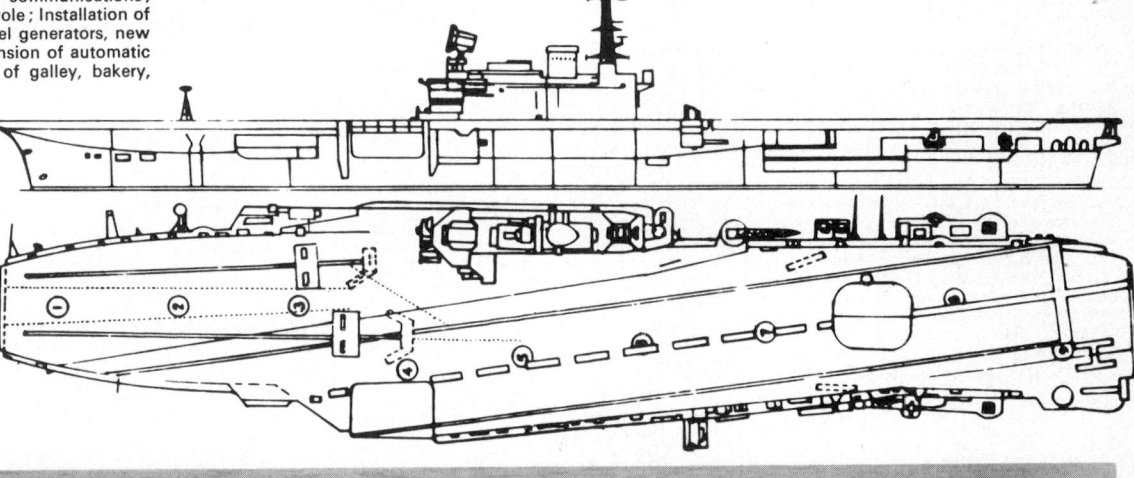

HERMES after conversion to commando carrier, artist's impression

1971, Official

Commando Carriers—*continued*

Name	Deck Letter	No.	Builders	Laid down	Launched	Completed	Converted
ALBION	A	R 07	Swan, Hunter & Wigham Richardsom	23 Mar 1944	6 May 1947	26 May 1954	1961-62
BULWARK	B	R 08	Harland & Wolff Ltd, Belfast	10 May 1945	22 June 1948	4 Nov 1954	1959-60

2 MODIFIED "CENTAUR" CLASS

Displacement, tons	23 300 standard ; 27 705 full load
Length, feet (*metres*)	650 (*198·1*) pp ; 737·8 (*224·9*) oa
Beam, feet (*metres*)	90 (*27·4*) hull
Draught, feet (*metres*)	28 (*8·5*)
Width, feet (*metres*)	123·5 (*37·7*) overall
Aircraft	20 helicopters .
Landing craft	4 LCVP
Missiles	2 sextuple rocket launchers
Guns, AA	8 40 mm ; 4 twin (2 single in Bulwark)
Boilers	4 Admiralty 3 drum
Main engines	Parsons geared turbines 76 000 shp ; 2 shafts
Speed, knots	28
Oil fuel, tons	3 880 furnace ; 320 diesel
Complement	1 035 plus 733 Royal Marine Commando and troops (900 in Bulwark) ; Accommodation for 1 923 to 1 937 officers and men

Former fixed-wing aircraft carriers. Converted into commando ships in Portsmouth Dockyard, Feb 1961 to 1 Aug 1962 (*Albion*) and Jan 1959 to 19 Jan 1960. (*Bulwark*). A full strength commando is available, which the ships can quickly transport and land with equipment. Their helicopters can disembark the commando's vehicles. The ships have sufficient stores and fuel to support the commandos in operations ashore, and can re-embark the unit speedily. They reinforce the traditionally close association of the Corps of Royal Marines with the Royal Navy, and give these versatile troops greater mobility and usefulness, enabling them to be fully self-supporting. The ships are fully convertible to the anti-submarine role. They can, at short notice, and entirely within their own resources, adapt their helicopters for anti-submarine work.

RADAR. Search: Type 965 in *Albion*, Type 293 in both ships. Aircraft Direction: Type 982 in *Bulwark*, Type 983 in both ships.

GUNNERY. Eight 40 mm AA guns were removed during the initial conversion of *Bulwark* to provide space for four vehicle personnel landing craft carried at built-in gantries, leaving her with 18—40 mm AA. guns. As converted *Albion* has one twin 40 mm mounting in each quadrant ; and *Bulwark* has since also been reduced to this armament.
ENGINEERING. The three-bladed propeller in *Bulwark* was replaced by a four-bladed propeller. At 28 knots the propellers work at 230 revolutions per minute. *Albion* was engined by Walsend Slipway & Engineering Co Ltd, Tyne, and *Bulwark* by her builders.

CONVERSION. Basically *Bulwark* was not changed during her initial conversion, although the fixed wing capability, arrester wires and catapults were removed. Alterations and modifications were. made to render the ship suitable as an all-helicopter troop carrier with

ALBION carrying 20 Wessex V helicopters

1970, Official

ALBION

1969, John G. Callis

16 Westland Whirlwind aircraft, replaced at a later date by the Wessex, and four landing craft (vehicle or personnel). The ship was fitted with the most extensive air conditioning system in the Royal Navy. In 1963 *Bulwark* was further refitted to the same standard as *Albion*, with slight variation in air conditioning. In her initial conversion *Albion* embodied a number of improvements and was able to carry Wessex helicopters and a larger military force. Her extensive modifications. included alteration to the angled flight deck and the removal of catapult and arrester gear.

DRAWING. Port elevation and plan of *Bulwark*. Scale: 125 feet = 1 inch (1 : 1 500).

CLASS. It was officially announced in Feb 1971 that *Centaur*, fixed wing aircraft carrier, originally of this class, is for disposal. Of the other five of this class originally ordered, *Arrogant*, original *Hermes*, *Monmouth* and *Polyphemus* were cancelled in 1945 ; and *Hermes* (ex-*Elephant*) was completed to a modified design (see previous page).

"MAJESTIC" CLASS. *Magnificent* (lent to Canada 1946 to 1957) was scrapped in 1965. *Powerful* (renamed *Bonaventure*) was completed for Canada ; *Majestic* (renamed *Melbourne*) was completed for Australia ; *Terrible* (renamed *Sydney*) was sold to Australia. *Hercules* was sold to India in 1957 for completion and renamed *Vikrant* in Mar 1961. *Leviathan* left Portsmouth on 23 May 1968 to be broken up at Faslane.

"COLOSSUS "CLASS. *Venerable* (renamed *Karel Doorman*) was sold to Netherlands in 1948 and to Argentina in 1968 (renamed *25 de Mayo*) ; *Colossus* (renamed *Arromanches*) was sold to France in 1951 ; *Perseus* and *Pioneer* (as maintenance aircraft carriers) were scrapped in 1958 and 1954 ; *Vengeance* was sold to Brazil in 1956 and commissioned as *Minas Gerais* in Dec 1960 ; *Warrior* was sold to Argentine in July 1958 and commissioned as *Independencia* in Jan 1959 ; *Glory* was scrapped in 1961 ; *Ocean* and *Theseus* in 1962. *Triumph* converted into a heavy repair ship, see later page.
VICTORIOUS. The aircraft carrier *Victorious* left Portsmouth on 11 July 1969 to be broken up at Faslane.

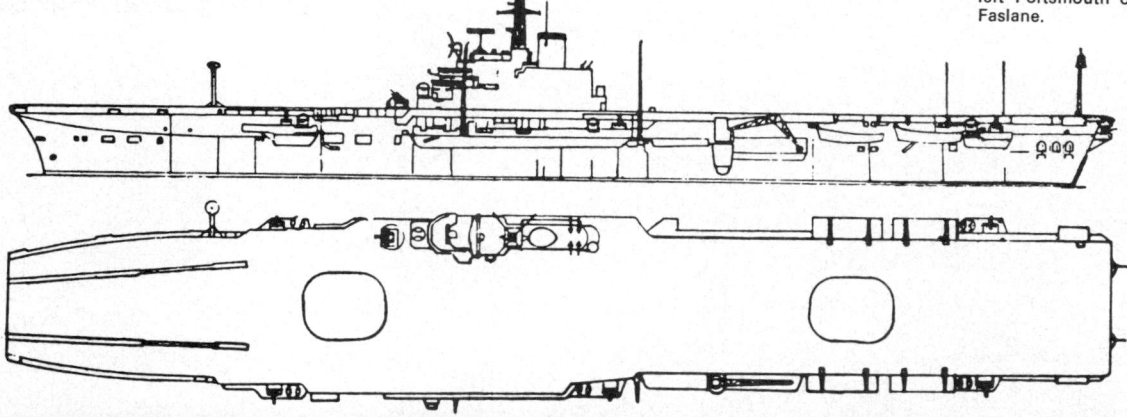

BULWARK

1971, Official

Name	No.	Builders	Laid down	Launched	Accepted
RENOWN	S 26	Cammell Laird & Co Ltd, Birkenhead	25 June 1964	25 Feb 1967	Feb 1969
REPULSE	S 23	Vickers-Armstrongs Ltd, Barrow-in-Furness	12 Mar 1965	4 Nov 1967	Oct 1968
RESOLUTION	S 22	Vickers-Armstrongs Ltd, Barrow-in-Furness	26 Feb 1964	15 Sep 1966	Oct 1967
REVENGE	S 27	Cammell Laird & Co Ltd, Birkenhead	19 May 1965	15 Mar 1968	Dec 1969

RESOLUTION   *1970, Official*

Nuclear Powered Ballistic Missile Submarines (SSBN)

4 "RESOLUTION" CLASS

Displacement, tons	7 500 surface; 8 400 submerged
Length, feet (*metres*)	360 (*109·7*) pp; 425 (*129·5*) oa
Beam, feet (*metres*)	33 (*10·1*)
Draught, feet (*metres*)	30 (*9·1*)
Missiles, surface	16 tubes amidships for "Polaris" A—3's IRBM's, range 2 500 nautical miles
Torpedo tubes	6—21 in (*533 mm*) forward
Nuclear reactors	1 pressurised water cooled
Main engines	Geared steam turbines; 1 shaft
Speed, knots	20 on surface; 25 submerged
Complement	141 (13 officers, 128 ratings); 2 crews (see *Personnel*)

In Feb 1963 it was officially stated that it was intended to order four or five 7 000 ton nuclear powered submarines, each to carry 16 "Polaris" missiles, and it was planned that the first would be on patrol in 1968. Their hulls and machinery would be of British design. As well as building two submarines Vickers-Armstrongs would give lead yard service (ie act as the "parent" firm) to the builders of the other two. Four "Polaris" submarines were in fact ordered on 8 May 1963 (date of official announcement). The intention to build a fifth Polaris submarine was confirmed by the then Ministry of Defence on 26 Feb 1964, but this intention was rescinded by a new Ministry of Defence on 15 Feb 1965. Britain's first "Polaris" armed submarine, *Resolution*, put to sea on 22 June 1967 and completed 6 weeks trial in the Firth of Clyde and Atlantic on 17 Aug 1967.

DESIGN. These submarines, the largest ever built for the Royal Navy differ in several respects from United States "Polaris" submarines, notably in having six torpedo tubes instead of four and modified habitability.

SONAR AND RADAR. Fitted with a large sonar array mounted in the "forehead" position and an X band short range surveillance radar.

PERSONNEL. Each submarine, which has accommodation for 19 officers and 135 ratings is manned on a two-crew basis, in order to get maximum operational time at sea on the pattern of the system in the United States "Polaris" submarines in which two complete crews relieve each other approximately every three months.

COST. £40 240 000, *Resolution*; £39 950 000, *Renown*; £37 500 000, *Repulse*; £38 600 000 *Revenge*; completed ships excluding missiles, £52 000 000 to £55 000 000 including weapon system.

REVENGE   *1970, Official*

REPULSE   *1971, Official*

RENOWN   *1971, Official*

Submarines—*continued*

Name	No.	Builder	Ordered	Laid down	Launched	Completed (Commissioned)
CHURCHILL	S 104	Vickers Ltd Shipbuilding Group, Barrow	21 Oct 1965	30 June 1967	20 Dec 1968	15 July 1970
CONQUEROR	S 105	Cammell Laird & Co Ltd, Birkenhead	9 Aug 1966	5 Dec 1967	28 Aug 1969	1971
COURAGEOUS	S 106	Vickers Ltd Shipbuilding Group, Barrow	1 Mar 1967	15 May 1970	7 Mar 1970	1972
VALIANT	S 102	Vickers Ltd Shipbuilding Group, Barrow	31 Aug 1960	22 Jan 1962	3 Dec 1963	18 July 1966
WARSPITE	S 103	Vicekrs Ltd Shipbuilding Group, Barrow	12 Dec 1962	10 Dec 1963	25 Sep 1965	18 Apr 1967
SWIFTSURE	S 107	Vickers Ltd Shipbuilding Group, Barrow	3 Nov 1967	6 June 1969		
SOVEREIGN	S 108	Vickers Ltd Shipbuilding Group, Barrow	16 May 1969	Jan 1970		
SUPERB	S 109	Vickers Ltd Shipbuilding Group, Barrow	20 May 1970	Jan 1971		
	S 110	Vickers Ltd Shipbuilding Group, Barrow	1971			

Nuclear Powered Fleet Submarines
5 "VALIANT" CLASS
3 + 1 "SWIFTSURE" CLASS

Displacement, tons	3 500 standard ; 4 500 submerged
Length, feet (*metres*)	285 (*86·9*)
Beam, feet (*metres*)	33·2 (*10·1*)
Draught, feet (*metres*)	27 (*8·2*)
Torpedo tubes	6—21 in (*533 mm*) homing
Nuclear reactors	1 pressurised water-cooled
Main engines	EE Geared steam turbines ; 1 shaft
Speed, knots	30 approx
Complement	103 (13 officers, 90 men)
	97 (12 and 85) in *Swiftsure*

It was announced on 31 Aug 1960 that the contract for a second nuclear powered submarine (*Valiant*) had been awarded to Vickers-Armstrongs (Shipbuilders Ltd), the principal sub-contractors being Vickers-Armstrongs (Engineers) Ltd, for the machinery and its installation, and Rolls Royce and Associates for the nuclear steam raising plant. Her hull is broadly of the same design as that of *Dreadnaught*, but she is slightly larger. She was originally scheduled to be completed in Sep 1965, but work was held up by the "Polaris" programme. The Intention to order the third nuclear powered submarine (*Warspite*) from Vickers-Armstrongs Ltd was announced by the Ministry of Defence on 10 Aug 1962, the intention to order the fourth (*Churchill*) on 13 Mar 1965, a fifth (*Conqueror*) on 4 Mar 1966, and a sixth (*Courageous*, ex-*Superb*) on 9 Nov 1966. The order for a seventh nuclear powered fleet submarine, of "Improved" type (*Swiftsure*) was in the 1967 Estimates, for the eighth (*Sovereign*) in 1968, ninth (*Superb*) in 1970 and tenth in 1971.

SONAR AND RADAR. Fitted with a large sonar array mounted in the "forehead" position around the bow. Also fitted with X band short range surveillance radar.

VALIANT

1971, Official

ENDURANCE. On 25 Apr 1967 *Valiant* completed the 12,000-mile homeward voyage from Singapore, the record submerged passage by a British submarine, after 28 days non-stop.

ENGINEERING. *Valiant's* reactor core was made in Great Britain, with machinery of British design and manufacture similar to the shore prototype installed in the Admiralty Reactor Test Establishment at Dounreay. The main steam turbines and condensers were designed and manufactured by the English Electric Company, Rugby, and the electrical propulsion machinery and control gear by Laurence, Scott & Electromotors Ltd.

ANTI-SUBMARINE WARFARE. *Valiant* and her sister ships are equipped to hunt and kill enemy submarines and surface warships, with sonar gear to detect at much greater ranges than that fitted in British Conventional submarines.

NOMENCLATURE. All the names given to British nuclear powered submarines (except *Churchill*, named after the late Sir Winston Churchill, First Lord of the Admiralty during the early part of both World Wars, famous wartime leader, and greatest Prime Minister) are former battleship names of the first and second world wars. The name originally chosen for the second nuclear submarine (*Valiant*) was *Inflexible*.

CHURCHILL (launch)   *Dec 1968, Official*

WARSPITE with *Wessex*

1969, Official

CHURCHILL

1971, Official

Submarines—*continued*

CONQUEROR
Aug 1969, Official

COURAGEOUS
March 1970, Official

COURAGEOUS (see previous page)
1970, Official

Name	No.	Builders	Engineers	Laid down	Launched	Commissioned
DREADNOUGHT	S 101	Vickers-Armstrongs, Barrow	Rolls-Royce and Westinghouse	12 June 1959	21 Oct 1960	17 April, 1963

1 PROTOTYPE NUCLEAR POWERED

Displacement, tons	3 000 standard; 3 500 surface; 4 000 submerged
Length, feet (*metres*)	265·8 (*81·0*)
Beam, feet (*metres*)	32·2 (*9·8*)
Draught, feet (*metres*)	26 (*7·9*)
Torpedo tubes	6—21 in (*533 mm*) bow, all internal
Nuclear reactor	1 S5W pressurised water-cooled
Main engines	Geared steam turbines; 1 shaft
Speed, knots	30 approx
Complement	88 (11 officers, 77 men)

DREADNOUGHT
1970, Official

The Royal Navy's first nuclear powered submarine, specially designed to hunt and destroy enemy underwater craft. A prominent feature of her design is her whale-shaped hull, the near-perfect streamlining giving maximum underwater efficiency, while the fin-like conning tower is also aimed at reducing "drag" to a minimum. She is capable of continuous high underwater speed and has long endurance. Her hull is British built, but her nuclear plant was manufactured in the United States. It was announced by the Navy on 10 Aug 1959 that the General Dynamics Corporation, USA had been awarded a contract for help in her construction. *Cost:* £18,455,000.

OFFICIAL STATEMENT. As originally planned *Dreadnought* was to have been fitted with a British designed and built nuclear reactor, but in 1958 an agreement was concluded with the United States Government for the purchase of a complete set of propulsion machinery of the type fitted in USS *Skipjack.* This agreement enabled the submarine to be launched far earlier. The supply of this machinery was made under a contract between the Westinghouse Electric Corporation and Rolls-Royce. The latter were also supplied with design and manufacturing details of the reactor and with safety information and set up a factory in this country to manufacture similar cores. *Dreadnought* has a hull of British design both as regards structural strength and hydrodynamic features, although the latter are based on the pioneering work of the US Navy in *Skipjack* and *Albacore*. From about amidships aft, the hull lines closely resemble *Skipjack* to accommodate the propulsion machinery. The forward end is wholly British in concept. In the Control Room and Attack Centre the instruments are fitted into consoles.

Almost every electrical and mechanical part of the propulsion machinery is installed in duplicate to minimise the inconvenience of breakdowns. In addition, every control feature of the power plant and of the boat is duplicated. These innovations ensure an extremely high standard of reliability which, combined with the need to refuel at only very long intervals, give her the ability to undertake patrols of particularly long endurance at continued high underwater speeds.
Accommodation for her crew is of a standard impossible to attain in any previous submarine. The improved water distilling plant for the first time provides unlimited fresh water for shower baths and for washing machines in the fully equipped laundry. Separate mess spaces are provided for senior and junior ratings, arranged on either side of a large galley, equipped for serving meals on the cafeteria system. Particular attention was paid to the decoration and furnishing of living quarters and to recreational facilities which include cinema equipment, an extensive library and tape recordings, features which help to offset the monotony associated with prolonged underwater voyages.
She is fitted with an inertial navigation system and with means of measuring her depth below ice.

SONAR AND RADAR. Fitted with a large sonar array mounted in the "forehead" position around the bow. Also fitted with X band short range surveillance radar.

ROLE. Her primary role is as a submarine hunter killer for which purpose she is equipped with the latest developments in underwater weapons and detection.

MANOEUVRABILITY. This submarine manoeuvres and travels underwater with movements similar to those of an aircraft banking in flight, as she has similar controls.

ENGINEERING. A complete nuclear reactor for installation in *Dreadnought* was purchased in the USA. The General Dynamics Corporation Provided design, material and technical assistance in the installation of the propulsion system. The propulsion plant itself was placed under contract to Westinghouse Electric Corporation by Rolls-Royce acting as agents for the Royal Navy.

REFUELLING and REFIT. Announced on 30 Jan 1969 at Rosyth Dockyard that the first refuelling of a nuclear powered submarine had been completed in *Dreadnought*. Officially stated refit was completed in 1970.

Patrol Submarines

13 "OBERON" CLASS

Displacement, tons	1 610 standard; 2 030 surface; 2 410 submerged
Length, feet (metres)	241 (73·5) pp; 295·2 (90·0) oa
Beam, feet (metres)	26·5 (8·1)
Draught, feet (metres)	18 (5·5)
Torpedo tubes	8—21 in (533 mm) for homing torpedoes
Main engines	2 ASR 1, 16 VMS diesels; 3 680 bhp; 2 electric motors; 6 000 shp; 2 shafts; electric drive
Speed, knots	12 surface, 17 submerged
Complement	68 (6 officers, 62 men)

This class have improved detection equipment and are capable of high underwater speeds. They are able to maintain continuous submerged patrols in any part of the world and are equipped to fire homing torpedoes.

CONSTRUCTION. For the first time in British submarines plastic was used in the superstructure construction. Before and abaft the bridge the superstructure is mainly of glass fibre laminate in most units of this class. The superstructure of Orpheus is of light alloy aluminium.

*The submarine of this class laid down on 27 Sep 1962 at HM Dockyard, Chatham, as Onyx for the Royal Navy was launched on 29 Feb 1964 as Ojibwa for the Royal Canadian Navy. She was replaced by another "Oberon" class submarine named Onyx for the Royal Navy built by Cammell Laird, Birkenhead.

SONAR AND RADAR. Fitted with sonar with forecastle mounted array; and X band surveillance radar.

GUNNERY. "O" class submarines serving in the Far East carry a small surface gun.

MODIFICATION. Oberon has been modified with deeper casing to house equipment for the initial training of personnel for nuclear powered submarines.

PHOTOGRAPHS. A photograph of Otter appears in the 1963-64 to 1966-67 editions, of Opportune in the 1965-66 and 1966-67 editions, of Onslaught in the 1967-68 editions, and of Ocelot, Osiris and Otus in the 1967-68 and 1968-69 editions, of Onyx in the 1968-69 and 1969-70 editions, of Opossum in the 1969-70 edition, of Olympus in the 1969-70 and 1970-71 editions.

TRANSFERS OF "T" CLASS. Talent (renamed Zwaardvis) and Tarn (renamed Tijgerhaai) were transferred to the Royal Netherlands Navy. Two lent to the Royal Netherlands Navy in June 1948 were returned to the Royal Navy in 1953, Tapir (Netherlands name Zeehond) on July 16 and Taurus (Netherlands name Dolfijn) on Dec 8. Totem and Turpin (converted boats) were transferred to the Israeli Navy in 1965 and renamed Dakar (Shark) and Leviathan (Whale), respectively. (Dakar was lost in the eastern Mediterranean on 25 Jan 1968). Truncheon (converted boat) was transferred to the Israeli Navy on 9 Jan 1968 and renamed Dolphin.

DISPOSALS OF "T" CLASS
Truculent sank after collision in the Thames Estuary on 12 Jan 1950, was salvaged on 14 Mar, but was scrapped on 5 Apr 1950. Tantalus, Tantivy and Templar were discarded in 1950. Tradewind was scrapped in 1955. Taurus and Thorough were approved to be scrapped in 1958 when they awaited tow to the shipbreakers or disposal otherwise as targets in 1960. Telemachus and Trespasser were scrapped in 1961, Thule (damaged in collision in 1960) in 1962, Tactician, Trenchant and Tudor in 1963. Tally Ho (latterly harbour training), Tapir and Tireless ("Streamlines") were for disposal in 1964 (and removed from the list in 1968). Teredo ("Streamline") was sold for scrap in 1965. Thermopylae (converted boat) and Talent and Token ("Streamlines") were approved for disposal in 1968, Tabard and Trump in 1969, and Taciturn and Tiptoe in 1970 (all converted boats).

SECOND WORLD WAR LOSSES OF "T" CLASS. Talisman, Tempest, Thorn, Thunderbolt (ex-Thetis), Tigais, Tarpon, Traveller, Trooper, Tetrach, Thistle, Triad, Triton, Triumph, Turbulent, P 311. Cancelled: Talent (1) (P 343), Theban, Thor, Threat, Tiara.

Submarines—continued

Name	No.	Builders	Laid down	Launched	Completed
OBERON	S 09	H.M. Dockyard, Chatham	28 Nov 1957	18 July 1959	24 Feb 1961
OCELOT	S 17	H.M. Dockyard, Chatham	17 Nov 1960	5 May 1962	31 Jan 1964
ODIN	S 10	Cammell Laird & Co Ltd, Birkenhead	27 Apr 1959	4 Nov 1960	3 May 1962
OLYMPUS	S 12	Vickers-Armstrongs Ltd, Barrow	4 Mar 1960	14 June 1961	7 July 1962
ONSLAUGHT	S 14	H.M. Dockyard, Chatham	8 Apr 1959	24 Sep 1960	14 Aug 1962
ONYX *	S 21	Cammell Laird & Co Ltd, Birkenhead	16 Nov 1964	18 Aug 1966	20 Nov 1967
OPOSSUM	S 19	Cammell Laird & Co Ltd, Birkenhead	21 Dec 1961	23 May 1963	5 June 1964
OPPORTUNE	S 20	Scotts' S.B. & Eng Co Ltd, Greenock	26 Oct 1962	14 Feb 1964	29 Dec 1964
ORACLE	S 16	Cammell Laird & Co Ltd, Birkenhead	26 Apr 1960	26 Sep 1961	14 Feb 1963
ORPHEUS	S 11	Vickers-Armstrongs Ltd, Barrow	16 Apr 1959	17 Nov 1959	25 Nov 1960
OSIRIS	S 13	Vickers-Armstrongs Ltd, Barrow	26 Jan 1962	29 Nov 1962	11 Jan 1964
OTTER	S 15	Scotts' S.B. & Eng Co Ltd, Greenock	14 Jan 1960	15 May 1961	20 Aug 1962
OTUS	S 18	Scotts' S.B. & Eng Co Ltd, Greenock	31 May 1961	17 Oct 1962	5 Oct 1963

OBERON (after refit)   1970, Wright & Logan

ORPHEUS   1970, Wright & Logan

ODIN   1970, Official

ORACLE   1971, courtesy Godfrey H. Walker, Esq

Submarines—continued

Patrol Submarines

8 "PORPOISE" CLASS

Name	No.	Builders	Laid down	Launched	Completed
CACHALOT	S 06	Scotts S.B. & Eng Co Ltd, Greenock	1 Aug 1955	11 Dec 1957	1 Sep 1959
FINWHALE	S 05	Cammell Laird & Co Ltd, Birkenhead	18 Sep 1956	21 July 1959	19 Aug 1960
GRAMPUS	S 04	Cammell Laird & Co Ltd, Birkenhead	16 Apr 1955	30 May 1957	19 Dec 1958
NARWHAL	S 03	Vickers-Armstrongs Ltd, Barrow	15 Mar 1956	25 Oct 1957	4 May 1959
PORPOISE	S 01	Vickers-Armstrongs Ltd, Barrow	15 June 1954	25 Apr 1956	17 Apr 1958
RORQUAL	S 02	Vickers-Armstrongs Ltd, Barrow	15 Jan 1955	5 Dec 1956	24 Oct 1958
SEALION	S 07	Cammell Laird & Co Ltd, Birkenhead	5 June 1958	31 Dec 1959	25 July 1961
WALRUS	S 08	Scotts' S.B. & Eng Co Ltd, Greenock	12 Feb 1958	22 Sep 1959	10 Feb 1961

Displacement, tons	1 605 standard; 2 030 surface; 2 405 submerged
Length, feet (metres)	241 (73·5) pp; 295·2 (90·0) oa
Beam, feet (metres)	26·5 (8·1)
Draught, feet (metres)	18 (5·5)
Torpedo tubes	8—21 in (533 mm), 6 bow, 2 stern 30 torpedoes carried
Main engines	2 ASR-1. 16 VMS diesel-electric sets, total 3 680 bhp; 2 shafts; 2 main batteries; electric drive; 6 000 shp
Speed, knots	12 on surface; 17 submerged
Complement	71 (6 officers, 65 men)

Porpoise was the first operational submarine designed since the Second World War to be accepted into service. Able to undertake continuous submerged patrol in any part of the world. The design of hull and superstructure gives capabilities of high underwater speed and great diving depth. Stress was also laid on long endurance, both on the surface and submerged, whether on batteries or snorting. Propelled on the surface, or when snorting by diesel-electric drive from Admiralty Standard Range diesels, and from large batteries driving the motors when submerged. The snort equipment was designed to give maximum snort-charging facilities and to operate in rough sea conditions. Both air and surface warning radar can be operated at periscope depth as well as when surfaced. The general habitability is of the highest standard, with strip lighting and air conditioning plant which provides drying and either heating or cooling of the air for arctic or tropical service. Oxygen replenishment and carbon dioxide and hydrogen eliminators make it possible to remain totally submerged without even using snort for several days. Apparatus to distil fresh water from sea water for drinking, and stowage for large quantities of stores and provisions enable the boats to remain on patrol for months without outside support.

SONAR AND RADAR. Fitted with sonar array on forecastle. Fitted with X band surveillance radar.

ENGINEERING. The propelling machinery was made by the builders except in *Cachalot* and *Walrus*, by HM Dockyard, Chatham.

ELECTRICAL. The electric propulsion system in all eight boats was manufactured by The English Electric Co Ltd, Rugby, and was of more advanced design than hitherto.

PHOTOGRAPHS. Photographs of *Finwhale*, *Narwhal* and *Porpoise* appear in the 1967-68 and 1968-69 editions, and a photograph of *Cachalot* appears in the 1969-70 edition.

DISPOSALS OF "S" CLASS
For transfers of "S" class and disposals of "S" class see 1969-70 edition, page 319.

DISPOSALS OF "EX" CLASS
Of the two experimental fast submarines with propelling machinery employing high test peroxide, the first submarines of post-war design to be built for the Royal Navy. *Explorer*, S 30 (machinery 14 000 shp) was discarded in 1963 and scrapped at Barrow in Feb 1965, and *Excalibur*, S 40, was listed for disposal by scrapping in 1965.

DISPOSALS OF MIDGET CLASS
The three "Midget" Type (X-craft), namely *Minnow* (X-54), *Shrimp* (X-52) and *Sprat* (X-53), were placed on the disposal list in 1961. Sister boat *Stickleback* (X-51) was sold to Sweden on 15 July 1958 and renamed *Spiggen* (Swedish equivalent of "Stickleback").

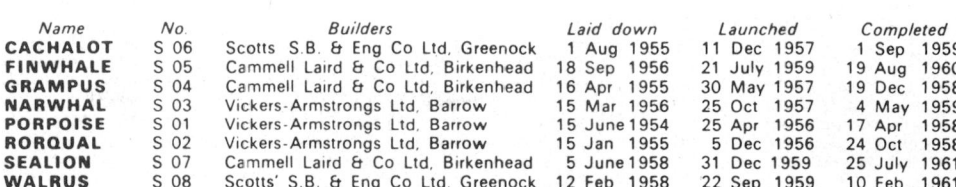

WALRUS   *1971, Wright & Logan*

RORQUAL   *1969, Official*

PORPOISE   *1971, Wright & Logan*

NARWHAL   *1971, Official*

Patrol Submarines
5 "A" CLASS

Displacement, tons,	1 120 standard ; 1 385 surface
	1 620 submerged
Length, feet (metres)	221 (67·4) pp ; 283 (86·3) oa
Beam, feet (metres)	22·2 (6·8)
Draught, feet (metres)	17 (5·2)
Guns	Removed (see Gunnery notes)
Torpedo tubes	6—21 (533 mm) internal, 4 bow,
	2 stern ; 16 torpedoes carried
	External tubes removed (see notes)
Main engines	8-cyl. diesel, 4 300 bhp
	Electric motors, 1 250 hp
Speed, knots	19 on surface, 8 submerged
Oil fuel (tons)	159
Complement	60 to 68 (5 officers, 63 men)

These submarines were originally designed for service in the Pacific, and had a different hull from the "T" class. Construction was entirely welded. All have "Snort" breathing equipment. *Alliance* and *Ambush*, so fitted, remained submerged for record periods in 1947-48. On 15 June 1953, *Andrew* completed a 2 500 sea miles underwater voyage from Bermuda to the English Channel in 15 days, a record for "snorting" in the Royal Navy.

SONAR AND RADAR. Fitted with sonar array on forecastle. Fitted with X Band surveillance radar. Type 955.

GUNNERY. Some boats of this class had the 4-inch guns removed before reconstruction. Others mounted the 4-inch gun temporarily after reconstruction. Some are fitted with a mounting for a gun. *Aeneas* had a 4-inch gun mounted in Feb 1960 and again carried a gun before the conning tower in 1966. *Artemis* mounted a 4-inch gun in 1960, after reconstruction. *Andrew* and *Auriga* carried a gun while in the Far East.

CONVERSION. The "A" class were rebuilt and streamlined with an enclosed fin conning tower 26·5 feet high. *Artful* was the first to undergo reconstruction in 1955 followed by the remainder of this class.

TORPEDO TUBES. Originally mounted 10—21 inch (4 external) as designed, and carried 20 torpedoes. External tubes (two bow and two stern) were removed.

PHOTOGRAPHS. A photograph of *Artemis* (after reconstruction) with gun appears in the 1960-61 and 1961-62 editions, of *Auriga* without gun in the 1960-61 to 1961-63 editions.

CLASS. *Affray* was lost in the English Channel on 17 April 1951. The following 30 units were cancelled, though some had actually been launched. *Abelard, Acasta, Ace, Achates, Adept, Admirable, Adversary, Agate, Aggressor, Agile, Aladdin, Alcestis, Andromache, Answer, Antaeus, Antagonist, Anzac, Aphrodite, Approach Arcadian, Argent, Argosy, Asgard, Asperity, Assurance, Astarte, Atlantis, Austere, Awake Aztec.*

PENNANT NOS. The pennant numbers of most of the "A" Class submarines (and all "O" class submarines) were changed on 1 May 1961.

DISPOSALS
Aurochs, the only one of the class not converted, was listed for disposal in Sep 1965, towed from Portsmouth on 9 May 1966, and broken up at Troon in Feb 1967. *Alderney* and *Anchorite* were officially listed in Feb 1968 for disposal by scrapping, *Amphion* and *Artful* in Feb 1969, *Alaric, Alcide, Ambush* and *Astute* in Feb 1970 and *Acheron* in Feb 1971.

Submarines—continued

Name	No	Builders	Laid down	Launched	Completed
AENEAS	S 72	Cammell Laird & Co Ltd. Birkenhead	10 Oct 1944	25 Oct 1945	31 July 1946
ALLIANCE	S 67	Vickers-Armstrongs Ltd. Barrow	13 Mar 1945	28 July 1945	14 May 1947
ANDREW	S 63	Vickers-Armstrongs Ltd. Barrow	13 Aug 1945	6 Apr 1946	16 Mar 1948
ARTEMIS	S 49	Scotts S.B. & Eng Co Ltd. Greenock	28 Feb 1944	26 Aug 1946	15 Aug 1947
AURIGA	S 69	Vickers-Armstrongs Ltd. Barrow	7 June 1944	29 Mar 1945	12 Jan 1946

AENEAS — 1971, Official

AURIGA with gun — 1969, Official

ARTEMIS — 1969, A. & J. Pavia

ANDREW with gun — 1969, Official

ALLIANCE — 1969, Wright & Llogan

ASSAULT SHIPS

Name	No.	Builders	Ordered	Laid down	Launched	Completion
FEARLESS	L 10 (ex-L 3004)	Harland & Wolff Ltd, Belfast	1 Dec 1961	25 July 1962	19 Dec 1963	25 Nov 1965
INTREPID	L 11 (ex-L 3005)	John Brown & Co. (Clydebank) Ltd	1 May 1962	19 Dec 1962	25 June 1964	11 Mar 1967

2 AMPHIBIOUS CRUISER TYPE

Displacement, tons	11 060 standard ; 12 120 full load 16 950 ballasted
Length, feet (metres)	500 (152·4) wl ; 520 (158·5) oa
Beam, feet (metres)	80 (24·4)
Draught, feet (metres)	20·5 (6·2)
Draught, ballasted	32 (9·8) aft ; 23 (7·0) fwd ; 27·5 (8·4) mean
Landing craft	4 LCM(9) in dock ; 4 LCVP at davits
Vehicles	Specimen load: 15 tanks, 7 three-ton and 20 quarter-ton trucks (20 three tonners on flight deck)
Aircraft	Flight deck facilities for 5 Wessex helicopters (6 operable)
Missiles, AA	4 "Seacat" systems
Guns, AA	2—40 mm Bofors
Boilers	2 Babcock & Wilcox
Main engines	2 EE turbines 22 000 shp ; 2 shafts
Speed, knots	21
Complement	556 (36 officers, 520 men) 111 Royal Marines and Army

INTREPID   1970, Official

These assault ships, with commando carriers, replace the former ships of the Amphibious Warfare Squadron. They carry landing craft which are floated through the open stern by flooding compartments of the ship and lowering her in the water ; are able to deploy tanks, vehicles and men ; have seakeeping qualities much superior to those of tank landing ships, and greater speed and range. Capable of operating independently. Also able to serve as Command Ships at sea for transit operations and as Headquarters Ships in the assault area. Another valuable feature is a helicopter platform which is also the deckhead of the converted well or dock from which the landing craft are floated out. The vessels have a hull combining features of both an escort aircraft carrier and a troop transport with the basic lines of a cruiser and a dock landing ship. Officially estimated building cost: Fearless £11 250 000 ; Intrepid £10 300 000. In the Defence Estimates these assault ships are listed after aircraft carriers and commando ships and before cruisers and destroyers.

INTREPID   1970, Official

RADAR. Fitted with Type 993 search radar.

ENGINEERING. The two funnels are staggered across the beam of the ship, indicating that the engines and boilers are arranged en echelon, two machinery spaces having one turbine and one boiler installed in each space, the starboard shaft being longer than the port. The main machinery is arranged in two self contained units, each driving one shaft. The turbines were manufactured by the English Electric Co, Rugby, the gearing by David Brown & Co Huddersfield. Boilers work at a pressure of 550 lbs per sq in and a temperature of 850 deg F. Two 5-bladed propellers, 12·5 feet diameter, 200 rpm in Fearless.

ELECTRICAL. Power at 440V 60 c/s 3-phase a.c. is supplied by four 1 000 kW AE1 turbo-alternators.

OPERATIONAL. Each ship is fitted out as a Naval Assault Group/Brigade Headquarters with an Assault Operations Room from which naval and military personnel, working in close co-operation, can mount and control the progress of an assault operation. Equipped with latest radio aids so that the Admiralty Board can send teleprinter messages wherever ships are operating. H.F. transmitters enable ships to communicate with Commonwealth or Allied receiving stations. Also able to maintain contact with other ships, aircraft, military authorities and associated landing craft which may be operating with them. Each ship operates with a Royal Marine Commando or infantry battalion.

TROOPS. Each ship can carry 380 to 400 troops at ship's company standards, and an overload of 700 marines and military personnel can be accommodated for short periods.

SATELLITE SYSTEM. The Royal Navy fitted its first operational satellite communication system in Intrepid in 1969, the contract having been awarded to Plessey Radar.

FEARLESS   1971, Skyfotos

1 PROJECTED

Displacement, tons	19 000 to 20 000 estimated
Length, feet (metres)	650·0 (198·1) approx
Beam, feet (metres)	84·0 (25·6) approx
Draught, feet (metres)	24·0 (7·3) approx
Aircraft	Helicopter squadron
Missile launchers	1 quadruple surface-to-surface; 2 twin "Sea Dart" surface-to-air
Main engines	"Olympus" gas turbines and "Tyne" gas turbines
Speed, knots	30 plus
Complement	750

It was officially stated in Feb 1971 that work continues on the design of a cruiser capable of providing a landing deck and hangar for helicopters, together with facilities for the command and control of naval and maritime air forces. The ship will be configured for a through deck, i.e. flight deck area and approach will be unobstructed by superstructure, providing a limited run for V/STOL aircraft. Two column masts and two funnels. Open forecastle head. See illustration on next page. Eventually three ships are envisaged.

3 "TIGER" CLASS

Displacement, tons	9 500 standard; 12 080 full load
Length, feet (metres)	538·0 (164·0)pp; 550·0 (167·6)wl 566·5 (172·8) oa as converted
Beam, feet (metres)	64·0 (19·5)
Draught, feet (metres)	23·0 (7·0)
Aircraft	4 helicopters in Blake, Tiger
Missile launchers	2 quadruple "Seacat" in Blake, Tiger
Guns	As converted: 2—6 in (152 mm) 1 twin; 2—3 in (76 mm) 1 twin Lion: 4—6 in (2 twin); 6—3 in (3 twin)
Armour	Belt 3·5 in—3·2 in (89—83 mm); deck 2 in (51 mm); turrets 3 in—1 in (76—25 mm)
Boilers	4 Admiralty 3-drum type
Main engines	4 Parsons geared turbines; 4 shafts; 80 000 shp
Speed, knots	31·5 max
Radius, miles	2 000 at 30 knots; 4 000 at 20 knots; 6 500 at 13 knots
Oil fuel, tons	1 850
Complement	Blake: 85 officers, 800 ratings

Originally designed to provide close cover and anti-aircarft support for convoys, aircraft carrier groups and assault landings, and for military and policing duties in any part of the world. Work on ships stopped in July 1946, for eight years. Decision to complete them announced 15 Oct 1954. Dismantled for resumption to new design in 1955. Tiger cost £13 113 000, Lion £14 375 000, Blake £14 940 000 (helicopter conversion £5 500 000).
CONVERSION. Blake was converted to command helicopter cruiser at HM Dockyard, Portsmouth from early 1965 until she recommissioned on 23 Apr 1969. The reconstruction involved the suppression of the after twin 6 inch turret and the two midship twin 3 inch turrets and the provision of a raised flight deck at the stern and hangar for operating Sea King anti-submarine helicopters. Tiger is being similarly converted but it is no longer planned to convert Lion.

RADAR. Search: Type 965 and Type 992. Height Finder: Type 277. Fire control: X Band.

GUNNERY. As originally designed guns included nine 6 inch, ten 4 inch. The 6 inch fully automatic guns of advanced design are equally effective in surface and anti-aircraft roles. Rate of fire is 20 rpm, more than twice that of any previous cruiser. The 3 inch guns are capable of 90 rpm. The guns have comprehensive direction system which enables all turrets to be controlled by radar. Each Mk 26 6 inch turret weighs 163 tons and each Mk 6 3 inch turret 38·5 tons.

OPERATIONAL. Ships are copned from totally enclosed bridge, the first fitted in British cruisers. 200-line automatic telephone exchange.

ENGINEERING. Main machinery is largely automatic and can be remotely controlled. Steam conditions 400 psi pressure and 640°F. Propellers 11 ft dia, 285 rpm.

CRUISERS

Name	No.	Builders and Engineers	Laid down	Launched	Completed
BLAKE (ex-Tiger, ex-Blake)	C 99	Fairfield SB & Eng Govan	17 Aug 42	20 Dec 45	8 Mar 61
LION (ex-Defence)	C 34	Scotts' SB & Eng, Greenock*	24 June 42	2 Sep 44	20 July 60
TIGER (ex-Bellerophon)	C 20	John Brown, Clydebank	1 Oct 41	25 Oct 45	18 Mar 59

*To launching stage. Completed by Swan, Hunter & Wigham Richardson Ltd, Wallsend-on-Tyne: Main machinery completed by the Wallsend Slipway & Engineering Co Ltd, Wallsend-on-Tyne.

BLAKE   1971, Official

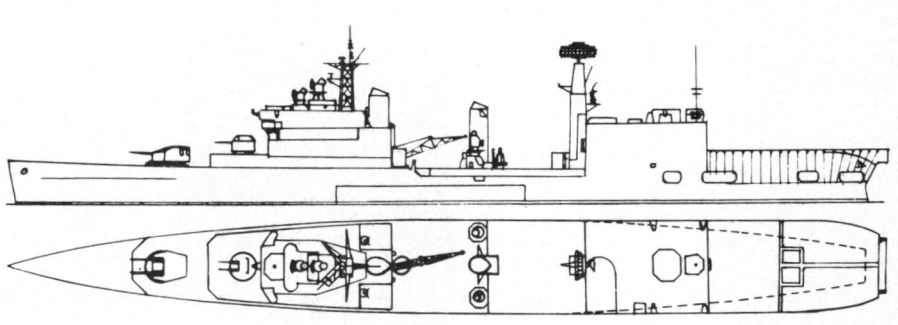

DRAWING. Port elevation and plan of Blake after conversion. Scale: 125 feet = 1 inch (1 : 1 500).

ELECTRICAL. 4 turbo-generators provide 4 000 kW ac, the first time this type power used in British cruisers.

NOMENCLATURE. The name of Defence was changed to Lion (announced 8 Oct 1957).

TORPEDOES. Originally designed to mount eight 21-inch torpedo tubes in two quadruple banks.

HABITABILITY. Complete air-conditioning is installed. Generous electrical equipment is provided for all domestic and recreational purposes. Accommodation is of a much higher standard than in previous cruisers.

CLASS. Hawke of this class, laid down in HM Dockyard, Portsmouth in Aug 1944, was cancelled in 1946, as was Bellerophon (ex-Tiger) a cruiser of enlarged design ordered from Vickers-Armstrongs.

"BELFAST" CLASS. Belfast was paid off in Mar 1971. Edinburgh was lost in action on 2 May 1942.

"SOUTHAMPTON" CLASS. Glasgow and Liverpool were scrapped in 1958, Newcastle in 1959, Birmingham in 1960 and Sheffield in 1967. Gloucester, Manchester and Southampton were lost in the Second World War.

"COLONY" CLASS. Jamaica was scrapped in 1960, Kenya in 1962, Bermuda and Mauritius in 1965, Gambia in 1968. Nigeria was sold to the Indian Navy in 1954 and renamed Mysore. Fiji and Trinidad were lost in the Second World War.

"CEYLON" CLASS. Newfoundland and Ceylon were transferred to the Peruvian Navy at Portsmouth on 30 Dec 1959 and 9 Feb 1960, respectively, and renamed Almirante Grau and Colonel Bolognesi.

LATER CRUISERS. Superb was scrapped in 1960, and Swiftsure in Oct 1962.

BLAKE showing conversion aft   1969 Official

Cruisers—continued

SCHEME FOR THROUGH DECK CRUISER (HELICOPTER CARRIER)
(see previous page)

1971, Official

LION (see previous page)

Added 1969, John G. Callis

TIGER before reconstruction (see previous page)

Skyfotos

GUIDED MISSILE ARMED DESTROYERS *(Gas Turbine)*

1 + 3 "TYPE 42"

NEW CONSTRUCTION

SHEFFIELD

Displacement, tons	3 500 approx full load
Length, feet *(metres)*	392·0 *(119·5)*wl; 410·0 *(125·0)* oa
Beam, feet *(metres)*	47·0 *(14·3)*
Aircraft	1 twin engined "Lynx" anti-submarine helicopter
Missile launchers	1 twin "Sea Dart" medium range surface-to-air (surface-to-surface capability)
Guns	1—4·5 in automatic, Mark 8, high rate of fire; 2—20 mm Oerlikon; 2 saluting
A/S weapons	Helicopter launched torpedoes
Main engines	COGOG arrangement of Rolls Royce Olympus gas turbines for full power; and 2 Rolls Royce Tyne gas turbines for cruising; 2 shafts; 50 000 shp; reversible pitch propellers for manoeuvering
Speed, knots	30 approx estimated max
Endurance	Over 4 000 miles at 18 knots
Complement	280 (20 officers and 260 ratings) (accommodation for 312)

The first "Type 42" all-gas turbine propelled destroyer with the Sea Dart guided missile as her main armament was ordered from Vickers Limited Shipbuilding Group, Barrow-in-Furness (announced 14 Nov 1968) and laid down 15 Jan 1970 for service in 1973. Smaller version of the original "Type 82" design. The helicopter will carry an air-to-surface weapon for use against lightly defended surface ship targets such as fast patrol boats. The gas turbine installation is a development of that in the frigate *Exmouth*. Benefits include rapid ability to reach maximum speed, reduction in space and weight, and 25 per cent reduction in technical manpower.

SHEFFIELD   *1971, Official*

High standard of accommodation, with living and working spaces fully air-conditioned. To cost £17 000 000 per ship.

RADAR and SONAR. Will be fitted with most up-to-date sonar and extensive radar and EW equipment.

SHEFFIELD, Artist's impression   *1969. Vickers Limited*

SHEFFIELD   *1970, Official*

GUIDED MISSILE ARMED DESTROYERS

1 "TYPE 82" NEW CONSTRUCTION

BRISTOL

Displacement, tons	5 650 standard (approx)
	6 750 full load
Length, feet (metres)	490·0 (149·4) wl; 507·0 (154·5) oa
Beam, feet (metres)	55·0 (16·8)
Draught, feet (metres)	22·5 (6·9)
Aircraft	Landing platform for 1 "Wasp" helicopter
Missile launchers	1 twin "Seadart" GWS 30 launcher aft
A/S weapons	1 "Ikara" single launcher forward; 1 "Limbo" three-barrelled depth charge mortar (Mark 10) aft
Guns	1—4·5 in (115 mm) forward
Guns, saluting	4
Boilers	2
Main engines	COSAG arrangement (combined steam and gas turbines) 2 sets Standard Range geared steam turbines, 30 000 shp; 2 Bristol-Siddeley marine "Olympus" gas turbines, 44 600 shp; 2 shafts; Total 74 600 shp
Speed, knots	30 approx estimated max
Endurance, miles	Over 4 500 at 18 knots
Complement	433 (33 officers, 400 ratings)

The design was originally intended to be an enlarged version of that of the "Leander" class general purpose frigate as a vehicle for the new "Seadart" guided weapons system, but the design turned out larger than that of the "County" class guided missile armed destroyers and has been referred to as escort cruiser. Three funnels, one amidships and two aft abreast the mainmast.

Designed around a powerful new weapons system. Hull capable of sea-keeping and high speeds in all weathers. Fully stabilised to present a steady weapon platform. Sleek, modern appearance. The gas turbines provide emergency power and high speed boost. The machinery is remotely controlled from a ship control centre. Automatic steering, obviating the need for a quartermaster. Many labour-saving items of equipment fitted to make the most efficient and economical use of manpower resulting in a smaller ships' company for tonnage than any previous warship. Living conditions highest obtainable in a warship, with full air-conditioning, modern electric galleys, multi-choice cafeteria messing, television and individual bunk sleeping in comfortable mess-decks. Capable of steaming and fighting without

BRISTOL model   *1971, Official*

discomfort to her crew when shut-down against nuclear fallout. Fitted with Action Data Automation Weapon System to compute information from the new 3D radar and other sensors, and control their various weapons to engage the targets selected, the latest Sonar system to provide the long-range information required for the Seadart and Ikara weapons.

The Seadart ship missile system, developed to meet the air threat of the 1970's and 1980's, also has a reasonable anti-ship capability. Its main advantages over the "Seaslug" system fitted in the "County" Class are: Considerably improved surface-to-air performance, particularly at very high and very low levels. Quicker reaction time. Considerably improved target handling capacity. It is lighter and takes up less space.

Ikara is a long-range anti-submarine weapon system, developed in Australia, designed to deliver homing torpedoes to a position where they can attack submarine targets. It is propelled by a rocket motor providing the missile with its long-range capability.

Officially stated on 23 Feb 1966 that Type 82 ships were to be ordered later that year, but only one was ordered (announced 4 Oct 1966) from Swan Hunter Group (Wallsend) Associated Shipbuilders, laid down on 15 Nov 1967 and launched on 30 June 1969.

RADAR and SONAR. Will be fitted with extensive radar and EW equipment and the latest sonar systems to provide long range information for "Seadart" and "Ikara".

BRISTOL, artist's impression   *1971, Official*

BRISTOL model   *1971, Official*

Guided Missile Armed Destroyers—continued

8 "COUNTY" CLASS

Displacement, tons	5 440 standard; 6 200 full load
Length, feet (metres)	505·0 (153·9)wl; 520·5 (158·7)oa
Beam, feet (metres)	54·0 (16·5)
Draught, feet (metres)	20·0 (6·1) max
Aircraft	1 "Wessex" helicopter
Missile launchers	1 twin "Seaslug" aft; 2 quadruple "Seacat" abaft after funnel; 2 sextuple 3 in, Mark 4
Guns	4—4·5 in (115 mm), 2 twin turrets forward; 2—20 mm, single
Boilers	2 Babcock & Wilcox
Main engines	Combined steam and gas turbines. 2 sets geared steam turbines, 30 000 shp; 4 gas turbines, 30 000 shp. 2 shafts; Total 60 000 shp; (see Engineering notes)
Speed, knots	32·5 max
Complement	471 (33 officers and 438 men)

Name	No.	Builders	Laid down	Launched	Completed
ANTRIM	D 18	Fairfield SB & Eng Co Ltd, Govan	20 Jan 66	19 Oct 67	14 July 70
DEVONSHIRE	D 02	Cammell Laird & Co Ltd, Birkenhead	9 Mar 59	10 June 60	15 Nov 62
FIFE	D 20	Fairfield SB & Eng Co Ltd, Govan	1 June 62	9 July 64	21 June 66
GLAMORGAN	D 19	Vickers-Armstrongs Ltd, Newcastle-on-Tyne	13 Sep 62	9 July 64	11 Oct 66
HAMPSHIRE	D 06	John Brown & Co (Clydebank) Ltd, Glasgow	26 Mar 59	16 Mar 61	15 Mar 63
KENT	D 12	Harland & Wolff Ltd, Belfast	1 Mar 60	27 Sep 61	15 Aug 63
LONDON	D 16	Swan, Hunter & Wigham Richardson, Wallsend	26 Feb 60	7 Dec 61	4 Nov 63
NORFOLK	D 21	Swan, Hunter & Wigham Richardson, Wallsend	15 Mar 66	16 Nov 67	7 Mar 70

The first pair, *Devonshire* and *Hampshire*, designed to embody developments in the destroyer field, were projected under the 1955-56 Estimates, and it was later found possible to arm this super-destroyer type with guided weapons instead of anti-aircraft guns, and to carry modern anti-submarine, radar and communication equipment. *Kent* and *London*, provided under the 1956-57 Estimates, have mainmast stepped further aft. *Fife* and *Glamorgan*, 1961-62 Estimates, and *Antrim* and *Norfolk*, 1964-65 Estimates, have the more powerful "Seaslug" II system, later to be fitted in the first four. All fitted with stabilisers. Their endurance gives them a considerable capacity for operating independently like cruisers. Photographs of *Devonshire* firing "Seaslug" appear in the 1962-63 to 1964-65 editions.

ANTI-SUBMARINE. In addition to anti-submarine homing torpedoes dropped by an anti-submarine helicopter the ships are fitted with modern underwater detection equipment for anti-submarine work.

GLAMORGAN   *1969, Official*

OPERATIONAL. Ships of this class have three main roles:—Escort duties with a task group, including the ability to provide anti-aircraft defence for the group and to augment its anti-submarine capability: Operations as part of a task unit of light forces with the ability to bombard in support of land forces and to attack light forces with gunfire: Police duties in any part of the world. The ships are designed to operate in "fall-out" areas. As many deck installations are under cover, the ships have clean lines, facilitating "washing down" in the event of nuclear attack.

GUNNERY. The 4—4·5 inch guns are radar controlled, fully automatic dual-purpose quick-firing for attack and defence against ships and aircraft. The 20 mm guns were added for picket duties in S.E. Asia; but have been retained for general close range duties.

ENGINEERING. These are the first ships of their size to have COSAG (combined steam and gas) turbine machinery. This is of exceptionally compact and light design, enabling the amount of fighting equipment to be increased. Boilers work at a pressure of 700 psi and a temperature of 950 deg F. The steam and gas turbines are geared to the same shaft. Each shaft set consists of a high pressure and low pressure steam turbine of 15 000 shp combined output plus two G.6 gas turbines each of 7 500 shp. The gas turbines provide a high concentration of compact power and are used to supplement the steam power for high speed work. They are also able to develop their full power from cold within a few minutes, providing unprecedented mobility, and enabling ships lying in harbour without steam to get under way instantly in emergency.

HELICOPTER. The helicopter is the first to be fitted as a complete "hunter killer". It carries dipping sonar and homing torpedoes.

HAMPSHIRE   *Added 1970, Wright & Logan*

ELECTRICAL. Two 1 000 kW turbo-alternators and three gas turbine alternators, total 3 750 kW, at 440 V.a.c.

RADAR. Search: Type 965 and Type 992. Height finder: Type 277. Fire Control: X Band.

HABITABILITY. All vessels have the latest accommodation standards and are fully air-conditioned.

LONDON   *1970, Wright & Logan*

NORFOLK (foremast modified since completion)   *1971, John G. Callis*

Guided Missile Armed Destroyers—*continued*

KENT   *1969. Official*

ANTRIM   *1971, Official*

FIFE   *1969, Official*

DEVONSHIRE   *Added 1970, courtesy Godfrey H. Walker, Esq.*

Destroyers—*continued*

1969, Official

4 "CA" CLASS

CAPRICE

Displacement, tons	2 106 standard ; 2 749 full load
Length, feet (*metres*)	339·5 (*103·5*) pp ; 350 (*106·7*) wl
	362·8 (*110·6*) oa
Beam, feet (*metres*)	35·7 (*10·9*)
Draught, feet (*metres*)	17·1 (*5·2*) max (props)
Missile launchers	1 quadruple "Seacat"
Guns	3—4·5 (*115 mm*) ; 4—40 mm
A/S weapons	2 "Squid" triple-barrelled DC mortars in "X" position
Torpedo tubes	4—21 in (*533 mm*) quadrupled ;
Boilers	2 Admiralty 3 drum ;
	Pressure 300 psi (*211 kg/cm²*)
	Temperature 640°F (*338°C*)
Main engines	Parsons geared turbines ; 2 shafts ; 40 000 shp
Speed, knots	36·75 designed ; 31·25 sea
Radius, miles	1 300 at full power ;
	2 800 at 20 knots
Oil fuel, tons	580
Complement	186 (10 officers, 176 ratings)

Name	No.	Builders	Laid down	Launched	Completed
CAPRICE	D 01	Yarrow & Co Ltd, Scotstoun	28 Sep 1942	16 Sep 1943	5 Apr 1944
CAVALIER	D 73	J. Samuel White & Co Ltd, Cowes	28 Feb 1943	7 Apr 1944	22 Nov 1944

The "C" group of destroyers were built as 4 flotillas, ie: "Càesar", "Chequers", "Cossack" and "Crescent" classes. *Caprice* is employed on trials and training duties (relieved *Manxman* as Marine Engineer Officers' Training ship at Devonport).

RECONSTRUCTION. Extensively refitted and modernised, with superstructure extended aft and modified bridge. *Cavalier* has a different bridge from *Caprice* which has "Leopard" type.

GUNNERY. Former armament was 4—4·5 inch and 6—40 mm guns (also 8—21 inch torpedo tubes). The 4·5 inch gun in "X" position was removed.

RADAR. Search: Type 293. Fire Control: X Band.

NOMENCLATURE. *Caprice* was originally allocated the name *Swallow*.

TRANSFERS. Of the "Cr" class, *Crescent* and *Crusader* were transferred to the Royal Canadian Navy in 1945. *Cromwell, Crown, Croziers* and *Crystal* were sold to Norway in 1946, and *Creole* and *Crispin* were sold to Pakistan in 1956. Of the "Ch" class, *Chivalrous* was transferred to Pakistan in 1953 and *Charity* in 1958.

DISPOSALS. *Ceasar, Carron, Cassandra* and *Cavendish* were scrapped in 1967. *Carysfort* was disposed of in Nov 1970. *Cambrian* was awaiting disposal in 1971.

EARLIER CLASSES. For disposals of the destroyers of the "Ch", "Co" and "Cr" classes, early "Battle" class, and older destroyers, see 1966-67 edition.

CAVALIER ("Seacat" on after superstructure)

1969, courtesy C. E. Taylor, Esq.

DISPOSALS OF "DARING" CLASS
Daring and *Delight* were officially approved for disposal during 1968-69 and *Dainty* and *Defender* during 1969-70. *Decoy* (renamed *Ferré*) and *Diana* (renamed *Palacios*) were sold to Peru in 1969 and refitted by Cammell Laird (Ship repairers) Ltd, Birkenhead, for delivery to Peru in mid 1971. and late 1971 *Diamond* is adapted for harbour training. *Duchess* is on loan to the Royal Australian Navy.

LATER "BATTLE" CLASS
Of the four radar pickets, *Aisne* was approved for disposal in 1969 and *Agincourt, Barrosa* and *Corunna* in 1971. Of the four standard destroyers, *Alamein, Dunkirk* and *Jutland* were scrapped in 1955 and *Matapan* is being converted into a Trials Ship, see later page.

"WEAPON CLASS"
Of the four Radar Picket Destroyers, *Battleaxe* was scrapped in 1964. *Broadswood* was expended as a target in 1968. *Crossbow* has been used as harbour training ship since 1967 (see particulars in 1965-66 edition). *Scorpion* is still being used for Naval Construction Research Establishment trials at Rosyth.

DIAMOND (training)

1971, Official

FAST FRIGATES (*Gas Turbine*)

(3 + 1 "TYPE 21") AMAZON CLASS
NEW CONSTRUCTION

**ACTIVE   AMAZON   AMBUSCADE
ANTELOPE**

Displacement, tons	2 500 full load
Length, feet (*metres*)	360·0 (*109·7*)wl; 384·0 (*117·0*)oa
Beam, feet (*metres*)	41·8 (*12·7*) max
Draught, feet (*metres*)	12·3 (*3·7*) deep
Aircraft	1 twin engined "Lynx" anti-submarine helicopter
Missile launchers	1 quadruple "Seacat" surface-to-air (later ships will have "Seawolf"
Guns	1—4·5 in, Mark 8; 2—20 mm Oerlikon
A/S weapons	Helicopter launched torpedoes
Torpedo tubes	6 (2 triple)
Main engines	COGOG arrangement of 2 Rolls Royce "Olympus" gas turbines for speed; 2 Rolls Royce "Tyne" gas turbines for cruising; 2 shafts; 50 000 shp; controllable pitch propellers for astern
Speed, knots	In excess of 30 estimated max
Endurance	Approx 4 500 nautical miles at 17 knots
Complement	170 (11 officers and 159 ratings)

AMAZON   1969, Vosper Thornycroft Group

The Navy awarded Vosper Thornycroft, Portsmouth and Southampton, a contract on 27 Feb 1968 for the design of a patrol frigate to be prepared in full collaboration with Yarrow Ltd, Scotstoun. The resulting first "Type 21" all-gas-turbine powered frigate, *Amazon*, was ordered from the Woolston Yard of Vosper Ltd on 26 Mar 1969 for completion in summer 1972. She was laid down on 6 Nov 1969 and launched on 26 Apr 1971. This is the first custom built gas turbine frigate (designed and constructed as such from the keel up, as opposed to conversion) and the first warship designed by commercial firms for many years. *Active* and *Antelope* (laid down on 23 Mar 1971) were ordered from Vosper on 30 Apr 1970 and 04 from Yarrow on 18 May 1970.

"TYPE 22" PROJECTED

Displacement, tons	3 000 approx (unofficial estimate)
Aircraft	1 "Lynx" helicopter
Missile launchers	"Sea Wolf" surface-to-air system; surface-to-surface system
Main engines	COGOG arrangement of Rolls Royce "Olympus" gas turbines and 2 Rolls Royce "Tyne" gas turbines driving 2 shafts
Speed, knots	30 approx estimated max

Designed as successors to the "Leander" class general purpose frigates the construction of which ceases with the completion of the scheduled programme of 26 ships.

AMAZON model   1969, Vosper Thornycroft Group

AMAZON artist's impression   1971, Vosper Thornycroft Group

AMAZON model   1371, Official

GENERAL PURPOSE FRIGATES (Anti-Submarine Versatile Type)

"LEANDER" CLASS

24 + 2 NEW CONSTRUCTION

Displacement, tons	2 450 standard; 2 860 full load (broad beam ships 2 500, 2 962)
Length, feet (metres)	360 (109·7) wl; 372 (113·4) oa
Beam, feet (metres)	41/43 (12·5/13·1) see Design
Draught, feet (metres)	18 (5·5) max (props)
Aircraft	1 Wasp helicopter armed with homing torpedoes
Missile launchers	1 or 2 quadruple "Seacat" and 2 sextuple 3" Mk 4 in later ships
Guns, dual purpose	2—4·5 in (115 mm), 1 twin
Guns, AA	2—40 mm, single; 2—20 mm, single in "Seacat" ships
A/S weapons	1 "Limbo" 3-barrelled DC mortar
Main engines	2 d.r. geared turbines; 2 shafts; 30 000 shp
Boilers	2
Speed, knots	30
Oil fuel, tons	460
Complement	263 (17 officers and 246 ratings)

Name	No.	Builders	Laid down	Launched	Completed
AJAX	F 114	Cammell Laird & Co Ltd, Birkenhead	12 Oct 59	16 Aug 62	10 Dec 63
DIDO	F 104	Yarrow & Co Ltd, Scotstoun, Glasgow	2 Dec 59	22 Dec 61	18 Sep 63
LEANDER	F 109	Harland & Wolff Ltd, Belfast	10 Apr 59	28 June 61	27 Mar 63
PENELOPE	F 127	Vickers-Armstrongs Ltd, Tyne	14 Mar 61	17 Aug 62	31 Oct 63
AURORA	F 10	John Brown & Co (Clydebank) Ltd	1 June 61	28 Nov 62	9 Apr 64
EURYALUS	F 15	Scotts' Shipbuilding & Eng, Greenock	2 Nov 61	6 June 63	16 Sep 64
GALATEA	F 18	Swan, Hunter & Wigham Richardson, Tyne	29 Dec 61	23 May 63	25 Apr 64
ARETHUSA	F 38	J. Samuel White & Co Ltd, Cowes	7 Sep 62	5 Nov 63	24 Nov 65
NAIAD	F 39	Yarrow & Co Ltd, Scotstoun, Glasgow	30 Oct 62	4 Nov 63	15 Mar 65
CLEOPATRA	F 28	HM Dockyard, Devonport	19 June 63	25 Mar 64	4 Jan 66
SIRIUS	F 40	HM Dockyard, Portsmouth	9 Aug 63	22 Sep 64	15 June 66
MINERVA	F 45	Vickers-Armstrongs Ltd, Tyne	25 July 63	19 Dec 64	14 May 66
PHOEBE	F 42	Alex Stephen & Sons Ltd, Glasgow	3 June 63	8 July 64	15 Apr 66
DANAE	F 47	HM Dockyard, Devonport	16 Dec 64	31 Oct 65	7 Sep 67
JUNO	F 52	John I. Thornycroft Ltd, Woolston	16 July 64	24 Nov 65	18 July 67
ARGONAUT	F 56	Hawthorn Leslie, Ltd, Hebburn-on-Tyne	27 Nov 64	8 Feb 66	17 Aug 67
ANDROMEDA	F 57	HM Dockyard, Portsmouth	25 May 66	24 May 67	2 Dec 68
JUPITER	F 60	Yarrow & Co Ltd, Scotstoun, Glasgow	3 Oct 66	4 Sep 67	9 Aug 69
HERMIONE	F 58	Alex Stephen & Sons Ltd, Glasgow	6 Dec 65	26 Apr 67	11 July 69
BACCHANTE	F 69	Vickers Ltd, High Walker, Newcastle	27 Oct 66	29 Feb 68	17 Oct 69
SCYLLA	F 71	HM Dockyard, Devonport	17 May 67	8 Aug 68	12 Feb 70
CHARYBDIS	F 75	Harland & Wolff Lto, Belfast	27 Jan 67	28 Feb 68	2 June 69
ACHILLES	F 12	Yarrow & Co Ltd, Scotstoun	1 Dec 67	21 Nov 68	9 July 70
DIOMEDE	F 16	Yarrow & Co Ltd, Scotstoun	30 Jan 68	15 Apr 69	2 Apr 71
APOLLO	F 70	Yarrow & Co Ltd, Scotstoun	1 May 69	15 Oct 70	28 Jan 72
ARIADNE	F 72	Yarrow & Co Ltd, Scotstoun	1 Nov 69	to be 71	28 June 72

This class embodies the qualities of the successful "Whitby" class anti-submarine frigates in a more versatile improved "Type 12". The main new features are long-range air warning radar, "Seacat" anti-aircraft missiles, improved anti-submarine detection equipment, and a lightweight helicopter armed with homing torpedoes. Air conditioning and better living conditions were also provided in this mainly anti-submarine but flexible and all-purpose type. Seven ships were initially provided for, three more were ordered in the 1961-62 Navy Estimates three in 1962-63, three 1963-64, three 1964-65 (Hermione was completed by Yarrow), three 1965-66, two 1966-67. The last two, Apollo and Ariadne were ordered from Yarrow (announced) on 29 July 1968.

GUIDED WEAPONS. Naiad was the first of the class to be completed with a "Seacat" missile launcher, followed by Arethusa, Cleopatra, Phoebe, Minerva, Sirius, Juno, Argonaut, and Danae. The 40 mm guns mounted in the earlier ships will be replaced by "Seacat".

DESIGN. These ships have hull and machinery similar to that in the "Whitby" class, but plans were revised for a composite anti-submaine, anti-aircraft and air direction role. Equipped with VDS (Variable Depth Sonar). Later ships have a two feet broader beam of 43 feet to improve stability. Andromeda was the first, followed by Jupiter, Hermione, Bacchante, Charybis, Scylla, Achilles, Diomede, Apollo and Ariadne.

ELECTRICAL. Alternating current, 440 volts, 60 cycles, 1 900 kW installation in early vessels and 2 500 kW in later vessels.

NOMENCLATURE. Ajax, Dido and Leander were originally to have been the last three frigates of the "Rothesay" class, Fowey, Hastings and Weymouth, respectively. Penelope was to have been the fifth frigate of the "Salisbury" class, Coventry.

PHOTOGRAPHS. A photograph of Leander appears in the 1963-64 and 1964-65 editions, of Ajax and Penelope in the 1964-65 edtions, of Euryalus in the 1967-68 1966-67 editions, of Arethusa and Minerva in the 1967-68 and 1968-69 editions, of Juno in the 1968-69 and 1969-70 editions, of Naiad and Sirius in the 1969-70 edition, and of Andromeda, Cleopatra, Dido and Galatea in the 1969-70 and 1970-71 editions.

RADAR. Search: Type 965 and Type 993. Fire Control: X Band.

CONVERSION. Leander is being fitted with the "Ikara" anti-submarine weapon during major refit at Devonport. Conversion of some other units of the class is under way.

ACHILLES   1971, Official

HERMIONE   1970, Wright & Logan

ARGONAUT   1969, courtesy Godfrey H. Walker, Esq.

General Purpose Frigates—*continued*   Improved Type 12

JUPITER   *1971, Official*

BACCHANTE   *1970, Official*

CHARYBDIS   *1970, Official*

SCYLLA   *1971, Official*

9 "ROTHESAY" CLASS

ANTI-SUBMARINE FRIGATES

Name	No.	Builders	Laid down	Launched	Completed
BERWICK	F 115	Harland & Wolff Ltd, Belfast	16 June 1958	15 Dec 1959	1 June 1961
BRIGHTON	F 106	Yarrow & Co Ltd, Scotstoun	23 July 1957	30 Oct 1959	28 Sep 1961
FALMOUTH	F 113	Swan Hunter, Wigham Richardson	23 Nov 1957	15 Dec 1959	25 July 1961
LONDONDERRY	F 108	J. Samuel White & Co Ltd, Cowes	15 Nov 1956	20 May 1958	22 July 1960
LOWESTOFT	F 103	Alex Stephen & Sons Ltd, Govan	9 June 1958	23 June 1960	18 Oct 1961
PLYMOUTH	F 126	HM Dockyard, Devonport	1 July 1958	20 July 1959	11 May 1961
RHYL	F 129	HM Dockyard, Portsmouth	29 Jan 1958	23 Apr 1959	31 Oct 1960
ROTHESAY	F 107	Yarrow & Co Ltd, Scotstoun	6 Nov 1956	9 Dec 1957	23 Apr 1960
YARMOUTH	F 101	John Brown & Co Ltd, Clydebank	29 Nov 1957	23 Mar 1959	26 Mar 1960

Displacement, tons	2 380 standard; 2 800 full load (as converted)
Length, feet (*metres*)	360·0 (*109·7*)wl; 370·0 (*112·8*)oa
Beam, feet (*metres*)	41·0 (*12·5*)
Draught, feet (*metres*)	17·3 (*5·3*) max (props)
Aircraft	1 "Wasp" helicopter armed with homing torpedoes (in converted ships)
Missile launchers	1 quadruple for "Seacat"; 2 sextuple 3 in Mark 4 rocket (in rearmed ships)
Guns, dual purpose	2—4·5 in (*115 mm*); 1 twin single in twin
Guns, AA	2—20 mm single in converted ships
A/S weapons	1 Limbo 3-barrelled DC mortar (in converted ships)
Boilers	2 Babcock & Wilcox
Main engines	2 double reduction geared turbines; 2 shafts; 30 000 shp
Speed, knots	30 max
Oil fuel, tons	400 approx
Complement	235 (15 officers and 220 ratings)

Provided under the 1954-55 programme. Basically similar to the "Whitby" class but with modifications in layout as a result of experience gained.

MISSILES. The "Rothesay" class have been or are being fitted with "Seacat" surface-to-air guided missiles as secondary armament in place of Bofors close range anti-aircraft guns.

CONVERSION. *Rothesay* was reconstructed and modernised at HM Dockyard, Rosyth, in May 1966 to May 1968 during which she was equipped to operate a Wessex Wasp lightweight anti-submarine helicopter armed with homing torpedoes, and fitted with "dipping" sonar. A flight deck and hangar were built on aft, necessitating the removal of one of her anti-submarine mortars. A "Seacat" replaced the 40 mm gun. *Yarmouth, Plymouth, Londonderry, Lowestoft, Falmouth* and *Berwick* have also undergone conversion with a hangar aft, and the remaining ships of this class, *Rhyl* and *Brighton* are being similarly converted as they come into dockyard for extended overhaul, on the pattern of the very successful general purpose frigates of the "Leander" class.

RADAR. Search: Some ships are fitted with Type 993 and others with Type 293. Fire Control: X Band.

PHOTOGRAPHS. A photograph of *Rhyl* appears in the 1963-64 and 1964-65 editions and of *Berwick* and *Brighton* in the 1967-68 to 1969-70 editions.

NOMENCLATURE. The "Rothesay" (and "Whitby") classes were named after seaside resorts and coastal towns. The ships laid down as *Fowey, Hastings* and *Weymouth* were re-designed as general purpose frigates of the "Leander" class and re-named *Ajax, Dido* and *Leander*, respectively, see earlier page.

ENGINEERING. Two Admiralty Standard Range turbines each rated at 15 000 shp. Propeller revolutions 220 rpm. Steam conditions 550 psi (*38·7 kg/cm²*) pressure and 850° F (*450°C*) temperature at boilers.

ELECTRICAL. Two turbo generators and two diesel generators in all ships. Total 1 140 kW. Alternating current, 440 volts, three phase, 60 cycles per second.

YARMOUTH (after conversion)   *1969. Official*

PLYMOUTH (after conversion)   *1970, Wright & Logan*

LOWESTOFT (after conversion)   *1971, Wright & Logan*

LONDONDERRY (after conversion)   *April 1970, Wright & Logan*

Anti-Submarine Frigates—*continued*   Converted Type 12

ROTHESAY after conversion   *1969, Official*

FALMOUTH after conversion   *1971, John G. Callis*

ROTHESAY *Wessex* Mk 3 refuelling,   *1969, Official*
Wasp about to land

ROTHESAY *Wasp* landed   *1969, Official*
Wessex above

Anti-Submarine Frigates—continued

6 "WHITBY" CLASS. TYPE 12

Displacement, tons	2 150 standard; 2 560 full load
Length, feet (metres)	360·0 (109·7)wl; 369·8 (112·7)oa
Beam, feet (metres)	41·0 (12·5)
Draught, feet (metres)	17 (5·2) max (props)
Guns, dual purpose	2—4·5 in (115 mm) 1 twin
Guns, AA	1—40 mm Bofors in Dartmouth four ships; 2—40 mm Bofors (1 twin) in others
A/S weapons	2 Limbo 3-barrelled DC mortars
Boilers	2 Babcock & Wilcox Pressure 550 psi (38·7 kg/cm²) Temperature 850°F (454°C)
Main engines	2 sets d.r. geared turbines; 2 shafts; 30 430 shp
Speed, knots	31 (29 sea)
Oil fuel, tons	370
Complement	225 (12 officers and 213 ratings)

Name	No.	Builders	Laid down	Launched	Completed
BLACKPOOL*	F 77	Harland & Wolff Ltd. Belfast	20 Dec 1954	14 Feb 1957	13 Aug 1958
EASTBOURNE†	F 73	Vickers-Armstrongs Ltd Tyne	13 Jan 1954	29 Dec 1955	9 Jan 1958
SCARBOROUGH	F 63	Vickers-Armstrongs Ltd. Tyne	11 Sep 1953	4 Apr 1955	10 May 1957
TENBY	F 65	Cammell Laird & Co Ltd, Birkenhead	23 June 1953	4 Oct 1955	18 Dec 1957
TORQUAY	F 43	Harland & Wolff Ltd, Belfast	11 Mar 1953	1 July 1954	10 May 1956
WHITBY	F 36	Cammell Laird & Co Ltd, Birkenhead	30 Sep 1952	2 July 1954	19 July 1956

*(Blackpool was lent to the Royal New Zealand Navy until Apr 1971)

Ordered in 1951. Primarily designed for locating and destroying submarines, these frigates were fitted with underwater detection equipment and anti-submarine weapons of post-war development. Good sea-keeping qualities enable them to maintain their high speed in rough seas. Their twin-rudders improve manoeuvrability. They are all welded and were specially designed with the lightest possible structure.

ENGINEERING. Propelling machinery includes geared turbines of Y 100 design and high power. Double reduction gearing allows low propeller revolutions of 220 rpm at high power and the propeller efficiency is correspondingly high. This, with improvements in hull design, enables these frigates to achieve over 30 knots on only 75 per cent of the power required by older destroyers of comparable displacement. Arrangement of the engine room machinery is outstandingly good.

RADAR. Search: Type 293 and Type 277 for surface search. Fire Control: X Band.

ANTI-SUBMARINE WARFARE. Have modern equipment for hunting and destroying submarines and facilities for directing anti-submarine aircraft.

TORPEDO TUBES. Provision was made in the design for mounting 12 A/S torpedo tubes (8 single, 2 twin), but earlier ships never carried them, and they were removed from later ships. Scarborough was the first to be fitted with tubes (four fixed on each side, and two swivel mountings).

ELECTRICAL. System is alternating current, 440 volts; three phase, 60 cycles per second. Two turbo alternators and two diesel alternators. Total 1 140 kilowatts.

OPERATIONAL. When completed they were considered to be the most useful class of ships of their size ever put into service. With high fo'c'sle and clean lines they ride well in a sea-way and are exceptionally dry. The enclosed bridge is spacious, with splendid vision, heated windows in the fore of the bridge being an asset in Arctic waters. The operations room was the finest ever put into a ship of the size.

APPEARANCE. Later ships were completed with thicker, raked back funnel with dome cap (there are two stacks inside the funnel) and early ships of the class, which had vertical funnel, were similarly altered.

TRAINING. Eastbourne, Scarborough, Tenby and Torquay, Dartmouth Training Squadron, are now slightly different in appearance. They have only a single 40 mm, not twin.

PHOTOGRAPHS. A photograph of Blackpool appears in the 1966-67 edition and of Torquay in the 1969-70 and 1970-71 editions.

SCARBOROUGH   1971, Official

WHITBY   1971, John Mortimer

EASTBOURNE   1970, Wright & Logan

TENBY   1970, courtesy Godfrey H. Walker, Esq

Anti-Submarine Frigates—continued

8 "BLACKWOOD" CLASS. TYPE 14

Name	No.	Builders	Laid down	Launched	Completed
DUNCAN	F 80	John I. Thornycroft & Co, Woolston	17 Dec 1953	30 May 1957	21 Oct 1958
DUNDAS	F 48	J. Samuel White & Co Ltd, Cowes	17 Oct 1952	25 Sep 1953	16 Mar 1956
EXMOUTH	F 84	J. Samuel White & Co Ltd, Cowes	24 Mar 1954	16 Nov 1955	20 Dec 1957
HARDY	F 54	Yarrow & Co Ltd, Scotstoun	4 Feb 1953	25 Nov 1953	15 Dec 1955
KEPPEL	F 85	Yarrow & Co Ltd, Scotstoun	27 Mar 1953	31 Aug 1954	6 July 1956
MALCOLM	F 88	Yarrow & Co Ltd, Scotstoun	1 Feb 1954	18 Oct 1955	12 Dec 1957
PALLISER	F 94	Alex Stephen & Sons Ltd, Govan	15 Mar 1955	10 May 1956	13 Dec 1957
RUSSELL	F 97	Swam, Hunter & Wighan Richardson	11 Nov 1953	10 Dec 1954	7 Feb 1957

Displacement, tons	1 180 standard; 1 456 full load
Length, feet (*metres*)	300 (*91·4*) wl; 310 (*94·5*) oa
Beam, feet (*metres*)	33·0 (*10·1*)
Draught, feet (*metres*)	15·5 (*4·7*) max (props)
Guns, AA	2—40 mm Bofors (see *Gunnery*)
A/S weapons	2 "Limbo" 3-barrelled DC mortars
Boilers	2 Babcock & Wilcox
	Pressure 550 psi (*38·7 kg/cm²*)
	Temperature 850°F (*454°C*)
Main engines	1 set geared turbines; 1 shaft;
	15 000 shp; (see *Machinery Conversion*)
Speed, knots	27·8 max; 24·5 sea
Radius, miles	4 000 at 12 knots
Oil fuel, tons	275
Complement	140 (8 officers and 132 ratings)

Anti-submarine utility type. Very lightly gunned. Of comparatively simple construction. Built in pre-fabricated sections. In 1958-59 their hulls were strengthened to withstand severe and prolonged sea and weather conditions on fishery protection in Icelandic waters.

ANTI-SUBMARINE WEAPONS. The Limbos each fire with great accuracy a pattern of large depth charges set to explode at a predetermined depth. They are trained over a wider arc than previous types of anti-submarine mortars, and have a much greater and more accurate range.

RADAR. Equipped with Type 978 search radar.

GUNNERY. The original gun armament was three 40 mm Bofors AA guns, but one was removed.

TORPEDOES. 4—21 inch tubes (2 twin) mounted in *Blackwood*, *Exmouth*, *Malcolm* and *Palliser* were removed.

ENGINEERING. All engined by their builders, except *Pellew* and *Russell*, by Wallsend Slipway & Eng Co Ltd, and *Grafton* and *Malcolm* by Parsons Marine Steam Turbine Co Ltd, Wallsend-on-Tyne. The turbines were of advanced design. The propelling machinery of *Hardy* and *Keppel* includes turbines of English Electric Co design. Four-bladed, 12 ft diameter propeller, 220 rpm.

FISHERY PROTECTION. *Duncan* (on completion as Leader in 1958), *Malcolm* (in 1959) *Palliser* (Apr 1958) and *Russell* (Jan 1958) originally formed the 1st Division of the Fishery Protection Squadron (now incorporated in the Western Fleet).

PHOTOGRAPHS. A photograph of *Palliser* appears in the 1959-60 edition, of *Dundas* in the 1967-68 edition, of *Hardy* in the 1968-69 and 1969-70 editions, and of *Keppel* in the 1970-71 editions.

NOMENCLATURE. Named after famous Captains of British naval history.

CLASS. Sister ships *Grafton* and *Pellew* were officially approved for disposal in 1968-69 and *Murray* in 1969-70.

TRAINING. *Blackwood* was also for disposal in 1969 but it was officially stated in 1969 that she had arrived at Portsmouth to join *Crossbow* as harbour training ship for the shore establishments *Sultan* and *Collingwood*.

RUSSELL   *1971, Wright & Logan*

DUNCAN   *1970, courtesy Michael D. J. Lennon*

MALCOLM   *1969, Wright & Logan*

MACHINERY CONVERSION. Conversion of *Exmouth* (announced on 10 Feb 1966) to all-gas turbine propulsion at HM Dockyard, Chatham, was completed on 20 July 1968. She provided the Royal Navy with the first major warship propelled entirely by gas turbines, heralding a new era in naval marine engineering. *Exmouth* has one BSE Olympus for full power, with two Proteus engines for cruising. The Olympus engine develops 22 500 hp and the two Proteus engines 3 250 each = 6 500 hp but only one system or the other will propel; they cannot be used together or for boost. Both these engines are marine versions of well-known and proven aircraft gas turbines and their use in warships benefits from the extensive research and development already completed for aircraft use, and from which they have evolved. The Olympus will be used in new classes of frigates and destroyers to come into service in the early 1970's. In the meantime *Exmouth* took the Olympus to sea as a main propulsion plant some years earlier and enables the operational characteristics and benefits of all-gas turbine propulsion to be fully evaluated in the rigours of naval service. These benefits include significant reductions in weight and space of machinery and fuel, and in operating and maintenance staffs. Gas turbine machinery installations in *Exmouth* and in future ships will be operated and controlled entirely from the bridge. Other new features in *Exmouth* are the use of a gas turbine developed by Centrax Ltd of Newton Abbot, Devon, for driving the main electric generator, and this incorporates a waste heat boiler to produce steam for auxiliary and domestic purposes. A controllable pitch propeller by Stone Manganese Marine Ltd, of Deptford, is fitted for astern operation. The new installation for *Exmouth* was designed by the Yarrow-Admiralty Research Department in conjunction with Bristol Siddeley Engines Ltd, under the overall direction of the Navy Department.

EXMOUTH (gas turbine propulsion)   *1971, Official*

GENERAL PURPOSE FRIGATES (Gas Turbine)

7 "TRIBAL" CLASS. TYPE 81

Displacement, tons	2 300 standard; 2 700 full load
Length, feet (*metres*)	350·0 (*106·7*)wl; 360·0 (*109·7*)oa
Beam, feet (*metres*)	42·3 (*12·9*)
Draught, feet (*metres*)	17·5 (*5·3*) max (props)
Aircraft	1 "Wasp" helicopter
Missile launchers	2 quadruple "Seacat" in *Gurkha* and *Zulu* (which also has 2 sextuple 3" Mk 4 rockets and 2—20 mm AA guns
Guns, dual purpose	2—4·5 in (*115 mm*) single
Guns, AA	2—40 mm single
A/S weapons	1 "Limbo" 3-barrelled DC mortar
Boilers	1 Babcock & Wilcox (plus 1 auxiliary boiler)
Main engines	Combined steam and gas turbine; Metrovick steam turbine; 12 500 shp. Metrovick gas turbine; 7 500 shp; 1 shaft; 20 000 shp
Speed, knots	28
Oil fuel, tons	400
Complement	253 (13 officers and 240 ratings)

Name	No.	Builders	Laid down	Launched	Completed
ASHANTI	F 117	Yarrow & Co Ltd, Scotstoun	15 Jan 1958	9 Mar 1959	23 Nov 1961
ESKIMO	F 119	J. Samuel White & Co Ltd, Cowes	22 Oct 1958	20 Mar 1960	21 Feb 1963
GURKHA	F 122	J. I. Thornycroft & Co Ltd ,Woolston	3 Nov 1958	11 July 1960	13 Feb 1963
MOHAWK	F 125	Vickers-Armstrongs Ltd, Barrow	23 Dec 1960	5 Apr 1962	29 Nov 1963
NUBIAN	F 131	HM Dockyard, Portsmouth	7 Sep 1959	6 Sep 1960	9 Oct 1962
TARTAR	F 133	HM. Dockyard, Devonport	22 Oct 1959	19 Sep 1960	26 Feb 1962
ZULU	F 124	Alex Stephen & Sons Ltd, Govan	13 Dec 1960	3 July 1962	17 Apr 1964

Designed to perform all frigate functions rather than for outstanding performance in any one specialised rôle, but capable of providing the main escort functions of anti-submarine protection, anti-aircraft defence, and aircraft direction. *Ashanti, Eskimo* and *Gurkha* were ordered under the 1955-56 Estimates, *Nubian* and *Tartar* 1956-57, and *Mohawk* and *Zulu* 1957-58. These versatile ships, designed as self-contained units for service in such areas as the Persian Gulf, air conditioned in all manned compartments. *Ashanti* cost £5 220 000.

RADAR. Search: Type 965 and Type 29. Fire Control: X Band.

SONAR. *Ashanti* and *Gurkha* were fitted with variable depth sonar equipment in the counter well in 1970, see photographs.

ENGINEERING. These ships have COSAG (combined steam and gas) turbine propelling machinery. The engines are right aft. The principle employed is that of highly efficient steam turbines and gas turbines geared to the same propeller shaft. The gas turbines provide a high concentration of power in a very compact form and are used to boost the steam turbines for sustained bursts of high speed. They are also able to develop full power from cold within a few minutes, thus providing unprecedented mobility. The steam turbine provides power for normal cruising and manoeuvering. The gas turbine driving on the same propeller shaft provides additional power for high speed, and also enables the ship lying in harbour without steam up to get under way instantly in emergency. The machinery is remotely controlled at all powers. The main boiler works at a pressure of 550 psi and a temperature of 850 deg F. Five-bladed propeller, 11·75 ft diameter, 280 rpm. The machinery installations were designed by the Yarrow-Admiralty Research Department. Metropolitan-Vickers designed and manufactured the steam turbines, gas turbines, gearing and control gear. This lightweight and compact machinery enabled more fighting equipment to be carried than with orthodox machinery. The forward funnel serves the boiler, the after one the gas turbine.

OPERATIONAL. Totally enclosed bridge and air-conditioned operations room. Fitted with stabilisers. Twin rudders.

PHOTOGRAPHS. A photograph of *Nubian* appears in the 1968-69 edition, of *Tartar* in the 1967-68 and 1968-69 editions and of *Mohawk* in the 1969-70 and 1970-71 editions.

ELECTRICAL. Generator capacity of 1 500 kW. Fluorescent lighting in all living accommodation.

CONSTRUCTION. All-welded prefabrication. Robust hull with special emphasis on prevention of corrosion. Denny Brown stabilisers fitted to reduce rolling in heavy seas. Good seakeeping qualities facilitate speed in rough weather..

ANTI-SUBMARINE. The first frigates designed to carry a helicopter for anti-submarine reconnaissance.

HABITABILITY. High standard of living accommodation. All manned compartments air-conditioned.

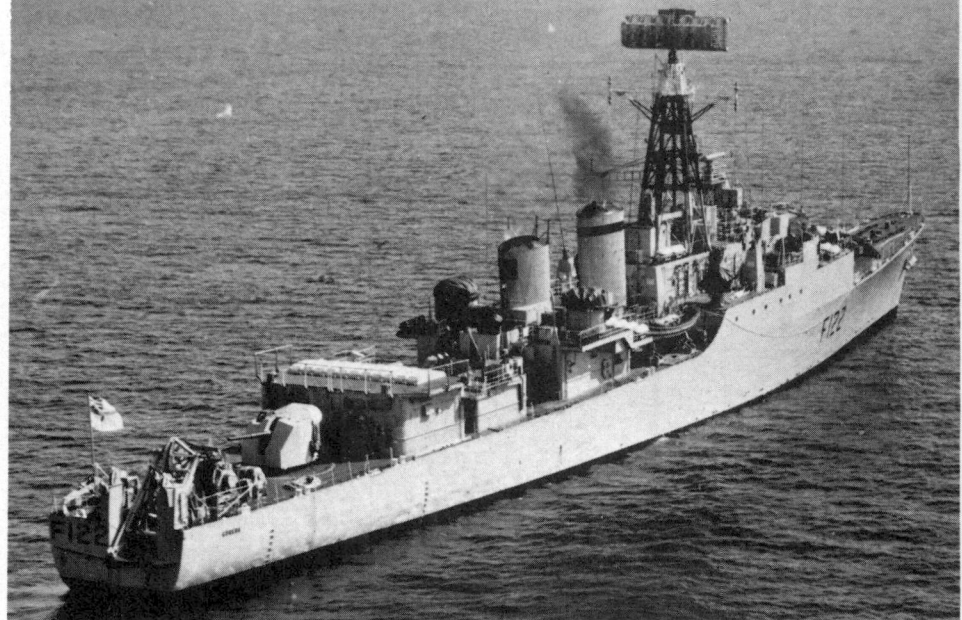

GURKHA (VDS aft)   1971, Official

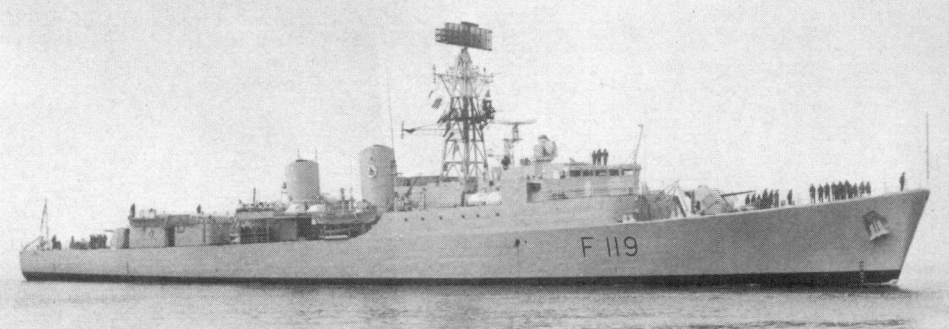

ESKIMO   1969, Wright & Logan

ZULU   1971, John G. Callis

ASHANTI (VDS in counter well)   1971, Official

ANTI-AIRCRAFT FRIGATES

4 "LEOPARD" CLASS. TYPE 41

Displacement, tons	2 300 standard, 2 520 full load
Length, feet (metres)	320 (97·5) pp; 330 (100·6) wl; 339·8 (103·6) oa
Beam, feet (metres)	40 (12·2)
Draught, feet (metres)	16 (4·9) max (props)
Guns, dual purpose	4—4·5 in (115 mm), 2 twin turrets
Guns, AA	1—40 mm
A/S weapons	1 Squid 3-barrelled DC mortar
Main engines	8 ASR 1 diesels in three engine rooms; 14 400 bhp; 2 shafts; 4 engines geared to each shaft.
Speed, knots	24
Radius, miles	2 300 at full power; 7 500 at 16 knots
Oil fuel (tons)	220
Complement	235 (15 officers, 220 ratings)

Name	No.	Builders	Laid down	Launched	Completed
JAGUAR	F 37	Wm Denny & Bros Ltd, Dumbarton	2 Nov 1953	30 July 1957	12 Dec 1959
LEOPARD	F 14	H.M. Dockyard, Portsmouth	25 Mar 1953	23 May 1955	30 Sep 1958
LYNX	F 27	John Brown & Co Ltd, Clydebank	13 Aug 1953	12 Jan 1955	14 Mar 1957
PUMA	F 34	Scotts' SB & Eng Co Ltd, Greenock	16 Nov 1953	30 June 1954	24 Apr 1957

Designed primarily for the protection of convoys against aircraft, but can also serve as a medium type of destroyers in offensive operations.

CONSTRUCTION. All welded. *Jaguar*, *Lynx* and *Puma* were ordered on 28 June 1951. Fitted with stabilisers. The construction of another ship ordered under the 1956-57 Navy Estimates to have been named *Panther*, was cancelled in the 1957 defence economies.

RADAR. Search: Type 965 and Type 993. Fire Control: X Band.

ENGINEERING. The propelling machinery comprises Admiralty Standard Range 1 diesels coupled to the propeller shafting through hydraulic gear boxes. These diesels are of light weight, about 17 lb/shp. *Puma's* engines, of Admiralty design, were manufactured by HM Dockyard, Chatham, and Polar Engines, Ltd, Glasgow, and installed by Scotts' Shipbuilding and Engineering Co Ltd. Engines of similar design used for driving the ship's electric generators were manufactured by Peter Brotherhood & Co Ltd, Peterborough. The engines of *Lynx*, manufactured by Crossley Brothers, Manchester, and British Polar Engines, Glasgow were installed by John Brown & Co Ltd, and the ship's electric generators made by Vickers-Armstrongs. The engines of *Leopard* were manufactured by Vickers-Armstrongs, Ltd, Barrow, and the engines of *Jaguar* by Crossley Motors Ltd, Manchester. *Jaguar* is the only ship of class to be fitted with controllable pitch propellers, 12 ft diameter 200 rpm. The fuel tanks have a compensating system, so that sea water replaces oil fuel as it is used.

RECONSTRUCTION. *Lynx* was extensively refitted in 1963 with new main "mack". *Puma* was similarly refitted in 1964, and *Leopard* in Oct 1964-Feb 1966, followed by *Jaguar*.

GUIDED MISSILES. "Seacat" missile launcher and director will replace the 40 mm gun mounting.

NOMENCLATURE. All ships of this class are named after big cats. The fifth and intended sixth ships of the class were successively to have been named *Panther* (see *Construction* notes above and *Class* notes below).

CLASS. A ship of this class, originally to have been named *Panther*, built by John Brown & Co Ltd, Clydebank, intended for the Royal Navy, was transferred to the Indian Navy and renamed *Brahmaputra*, see Indian section. Another *Panther* was projected to take her place, but this ship was not built as a unit of this class or under that name (see *Nomenclature* notes on following page).

PUMA   1969, Official

JAGUAR   1971, Wright & Logan

LEOPARD   1970, Wright & Logan

LYNX   1971, Wright & Logan

AIRCRAFT DIRECTION FRIGATES

4 "SALISBURY" CLASS. TYPE 61

Name	No.	Builders	Laid down	Launched	Completed
CHICHESTER	F 59	Fairfield SB & Eng Co Ltd, Govan	25 Jan 1953	21 Apr 1955	16 May 1958
LINCOLN	F 99	Fairfield SB & Eng Co Ltd, Govan	20 May 1955	6 Apr 1959	7 July 1960
LLANDAFF	F 61	Hawthorn Leslie Ltd, Hebburn-on-Tyne	27 Aug 1955	30 Nov 1955	11 Apr 1958
SALISBURY	F 32	HM Dockyard, Devonport	23 Jan 1952	25 June 1953	27 Feb 1957

Displacement, tons	2 170 standard ; 2 408 full load
Length, feet (*metres*)	320·0 (*97·5*) pp ; 330·0 (*100·6*) oa 339·8 (*103·6*) oa
Beam, feet (*metres*)	40·0 (*12·2*)
Draught, feet (*metres*)	15·5 (*4·7*) max (props)
Missile launchers	1 quadruple "Seacat" in *Lincoln* and *Salisbury* which also have 2 sextuple 3 in rocket launchers
Guns, dual puprose	2—4·5 in (*115 mm*)
Guns, AA	2—40 mm (see *Guided Missile* notes) ; 2—20 mm in *Lincoln* and *Salisbury*
A/S weapons	1 Squid triple-barrelled DC mortar
Main engines	8 ASR 1 diesels in three engine rooms ; 2 shafts ; 14 400 bhp
Speed, knots	24
Radius, miles	2 300 at full power ; 7 500 at 16 knots
Oil fuel, tons	230
Complement	237 (14 officers and 223 ratings)

Designed primarily for the direction of carrier-borne and shore based aircraft, but can also serve as a lighter type of destroyer in offensive operations.

CONSTRUCTION. Ordered on 28 June 1951 except *Salisbury*, the prototype ship. Construction was all welded and largely prefabricated. The construction of the fifth ship, *Exeter*, ordered under the 1956-57 Navy Estimates, was cancelled in the 1957 defence economies. Fitted with stabilisers (except *Lincoln*).

ENGINEERING. *Salisbury* is powered by Admiralty Standard Range 1 heavy oil engines coupled to the propeller shafts through hydraulic couplings and oil operated reverse and reduction gear boxes. These engines, designed to develop 1940 bhp at 920 rpm, were manufactured by Vickers-Armstrongs, Barrow, who also made engines of similar design for driving the ship's four 360 kW electric generators. Other ships have four 500 kW generators. *Llandaff* has similar main engines manufactured by British Polar, of Glasgow. Engines of similar design for driving the ship's electric generators were manufactured by Vickers-Armstrongs, Barrow. *Llandaff* is the only Type 61 frigate to have a 500 kW gas-turbine alternator and three diesel generators. This new gas-turbine alternator was manufactured by W. H. Allen & Sons, Bedford. *Lincoln* is fitted with controllable pitch propellers, rotating at 200 rpm, which are 12 feet in diameter, manufactured by Stone Marine & Engineering Co Ltd. The full tanks have a compensating system whereby sea water replaces oil fuel as it is consumed.

RECONSTRUCTION. In 1962 the after funnel and lattice mast combination in *Salisbury* was replaced by a single tall funnel with Type 985 aerial on top as a combined mast and stack or "mack". *Chichester* in 1964 was refitted with both fore and main "macks", *Llandaff* completed similarly in 1966, and *Lincoln* in 1968. *Salisbury* also now has two "macks".

RADAR. Search: Type 965 and Type 993. Aircraft Direction: Type 982 and Type 277Q. Fire Control: X Band.

GUIDED MISSILE ARMAMENT. A single 40 mm AA gun, mounted in *Lincoln* as a temporary measure, was replaced by a "Seacat" missile launcher and director. The 40 mm guns in *Salisbury* were replaced by a "Seacat".

NOMENCLATURE. All ships of this class are named after cathedral cities. A fifth ship was to have been named *Exeter*. A sixth ship, to have been named *Coventry*, was originally ordered as *Panther* and was built as *Penelope* ("Leander class"). A seventh ship was to have been named *Gloucester*.

CHICHESTER *1969, Official*

SALISBURY *April 1970, Wright & Logan*

LINCOLN *1970, Official*

LLANDAFF *1971, Official*

FAST ANTI-SUBMARINE FRIGATES (ex-Destroyers)

4 "TYPE 15" 1st RATE
"R" "U" CLASSES
(Fully Converted from Destroyers)

Name	No.	Builders	Laid down	Launched	Completed
GRENVILLE	F 197	Swan, Hunter & Wigham Richardson, Ltd	1 Nov 41	12 Oct 42	27 May 43
RAPID	F 138	Cammell Laird & Co Ltd, Birkenhead	16 June 41	16 July 42	20 Feb 43
ULSTER	F 83	Swan, Hunter & Wigham Richardson, Ltd	12 Nov 41	9 Nov 42	30 June 43
UNDAUNTED	F 53	Cammell Laird & Co Ltd, Birkenhead	8 Sep 42	19 July 43	3 Mar 44

Displacement, tons	2 240 standard; 2 880 full load
Length, feet (metres)	339·5 (103·5) pp; 350·0 (106·7) wl; 362·8 (110·6) oa
Beam, feet (metres)	35·7 (10·9)
Draught, feet (metres)	17·0 (5·2)
Guns, surface	2—4 in (102 mm), 1 twin
Guns, AA	2—40 mm (1 twin)
A/S weapons	"U" class: 2 Limbo 3-barrelled DC mortars (see notes)
Torpedo tubes	Provision for tubes. 8 (4 each side) for homing torpedoes were fitted in Ulster
Boilers	2 Admiralty 3 drum; Pressure 300 psi (21·1 kg/cm²) Superheat 640°F (338°C)
Main engines	Parsons geared turbines; 2 shafts; 40 000 shp
Speed, knots	36·75 designed; 31·25 sea
Radius, miles	1 300 at full power; 2 800 to 3 000 at 20 knots
Oil fuel, tons	570 to 600
Complement	195 (15 officers and 180 men)

RADAR. Search: Type 293 and Type 277 (excluding Grenville)

RAPID   *Official*

"R" CLASS. Of the original flotilla of eight "R" class destroyers, Racehorse was scrapped in 1950 and Raider, Redoubt, and Rotherham (Leader) were transferred to the Indian Navy in 1949 and renamed Rana, Ranjit and Rajput, respectively. Of those converted into frigates Rocket was scrapped in 1967 and Roebuck was expended as a target in 1969. Relentless was on the disposal list in 1970. Rapid is seagoing training ship for marine engineer apprentices at HMS Caledonia, Rosyth. She was converted by Alex Stephen & Sons Ltd, Govan, in 1952-53.

"W" CLASS. Of the original flotilla of eight "W" class destroyers Wessex and Whelp were transferred to the South African Navy in 1950-52 and renamed Jan van Riebeeck and Simon von Stel, respectively, and Kempenfelt and Wager were sold to Yugoslavia in 1957 and renamed Kotor and Pula, respectively. Of those converted into frigates Wrangler was transferred to the South African Navy on 29 Nov 1956 and renamed Vrystaat, and Whirlwind and Wizard were scheduled for disposal in 1966, Wakeful in 1969-70 and relieved by Grenville.

UNDAUNTED   *1969, Official*

"V" CLASS. Of the original flotilla of eight "V" class destroyers, Valentine and Vixen were transferred to the Royal Canadian Navy in 1944 and renamed Algonquin and Sioux, respectively, and the leader Hardy was lost in the Second World War. Of those converted into frigates Vigilant and Virago were sold for scrap in 1965. Venus was scheduled for disposal by scrapping in 1965, Volage was on the disposal list in 1966 (used as Harbour Training Ship, RM) and Verulam in 1971.

"U" CLASS. Converted in 1952-54, Ulster at HM Dockyard, Chatham, Undaunted by J. Samuel White & Co Ltd, Cowes. Ulster has a bowl-shaped sponson at the break and "Leopard" type bridge, Undaunted fitted with helicopter platform aft; she now has deckhouse in place of the twin 4 inch gun. Grenville has no 4 in, one "Limbo", two 40 mm, no helicopter platform; 2 417 tons standard; 13 officers, 190 men. In July 1966 the 20 × 30 ft section from the stern of Urchin was fitted to Ulster, damaged in May, at HM Dockyard, Devonport. Sister ships Ulysses, Undine and Urchin were all listed for disposal by scrapping in 1965 and Urania and Ursa in 1968.

ULSTER   *1969, Wright & Logan*

"T" CLASS. Troubridge was officially approved for disposal in 1970.

"Z" CLASS. Zest was officially approved for disposal in 1969.

GRENVILLE (new column foremast)   *1970, Official*

LOGISTIC LANDING SHIPS

SIR GERAINT

1971, Royal Navy, Official

SIR LANCELOT (ex-LSL 01) Prototype

Displacement, tons	3 370 light; 5 550 load
Measurement, tons	6 390 * gross; 2 180 deadweight
Dimensions, feet	366·3 pp; 412·1 oa × 59·8 × 12·8 mean draught
Main engines	2 Denny/Sulzer 12MD51 diesels; 9 520 bhp
	8 250 bhp at 325 rpm = 17 knots service speed
Oil fuel, tons	811
Aircraft facilities	Wessex forward and aft
Guns	2—40 mm Bofors
Cranes	2 at 20 tons; 2 at 3 tons
Complement	Crew 68 (18 officers 50 ratings) Military passengers 340 (43 officers and warrant officers, 297 sergeants and other ranks)

CONSTRUCTION. Laid down in Mar 1962, launched in June 1963 and completed in Jan 1964 by the Fairfield Shipbuilding and Engineering Co to the order of the Ministry of Transport on behalf of the Ministry of Defence (Army). Transferred to the RFA on 3 Jan 1970.

FUNCTION. Prototype of a class of ship to replace LST (3) for service as a multi-purpose fast troop and roll-on roll-off heavy vehicle carrier.

LOGISTIC. Fitted for bow and stern loading with drive-through facility and deck to deck ramps, the ship is capable of discharging a full load of vehicles on to a beach. Facilities are provided for stowing and operating military pontoon equipment. On-board maintenance of vehicles and equipment and stowage of special military cargo are catered for.

ENGINEERING. Passive tank stabiliser system and bow thrust propulsion unit are fitted. All accommodation is air-conditioned and close circuit television fitted for entertainment and operational use.

AIRCRAFT FACILITIES. *Sir Lancelot* has full capability for operating Wessex helicopters from the after landing platform by day or night. The fore deck is suitable for operating helicopters by day only in favourable weather conditions and sheltered waters.
*Gross tonnage not yet remeasured.

5 PRODUCTION SERIES (LSL 02-06)

Displacement, tons	3 270 light; 5 674 load
Measurement, tons	4 473 gross; 2 404 deadweight
Dimensions, feet	366·3 pp; 412 oa × 59·8 × 13 mean draught
Main engines	2 Mirrlees National Monarch ALSSDM10 diesels; 9 400 bhp
	8 460 bhp at 314 rpm = 17 knots service speed
Oil fuel, tons	816
Aircraft facilities	Wessex forward and aft
Guns	2—40 mm Bofors
Cranes	1 at 20 tons; 2 at 4¼/8½ tons
Complement	Crew 68 (18 officers, 50 ratings) Military passengers 340 (43 officers and warrant officers, 297 sergeants and other ranks)

DESIGN. Similar in size and capacity to class prototype *Sir Lancelot* but layout modified following extensive military probing trials with prototype.

LOGISTIC. Vehicle deck now provides increased vehicle stowage and improved flying facilities forward. Some revision of military accommodation and services carried out.

ENGINEERING. Bridge control of main engines and machinery data-logging equipment fitted.

AIRCRAFT FACILITIES. These five ships have full capability for operating Wessex helicopters from both the after landing platform and the foredeck by day or night. It is estimated that 20 Wessex helicopters can be carried (11 on the Tank Deck and 9 on the Vehicle Deck).

Name	No.	Laid down	Launched	Completed	Transferred to RFA
SIR GALAHAD	ex-LSL 02	Feb 1965	19 Apr 1966	17 Dec 1966	7 Mar 1970
SIR GERAINT	ex-LSL 04	June 1965	26 Jan 1967	12 July 1967	5 Mar 1970

Built by Alexander Stephen & Sons Ltd Linthouse

Name	No.	Laid down	Launched	Completed	Transferred to RFA
SIR BEDIVERE	ex-LSL 03	Oct 1965	20 July 1966	18 May 1967	14 Jan 1970
SIR TRISTRAM	ex-LSL 05	Feb 1966	12 Dec 1966	14 Sep 1967	30 Jan 1970
SIR PERCIVALE	ex-LSL 06	Apr 1966	4 Oct 1967	23 Mar 1968	6 Mar 1970

Built by Hawthorn Leslie (Shipbuilders) Ltd, Hebburn-on-Tyne

SIR TRISTRAM

1970, courtesy DGST

SIR GALAHAD

1970, DGST

SIR BEDIVERE

1970, DGST

HELICOPTER SUPPORT SHIPS

ENGADINE   *1969, Official*

ENGADINE K 08

Displacement, tons	8 000 to 9 000 full load
Measurement, tons	6 384 gross; 2 848 net
Dimensions, feet	424·0 oa × 58·4 × 22·1
Aircraft	4 Wessex and 2 Wasp or 2 Sea King helicopters
Main engines	1 Sulzer two stroke, 5 cyl turbo charged 5RD68 diesel; 5 500 bhp = 16 knots
Complement	RFA: 61 (15 officers, 46 men); RN: 14 (2 officers, 12 ratings) Accommodation for a further RN 113 (29 officers and 84 ratings)

Projected under the 1964-65 Navy Estimates. Built by Henry Robb Ltd, Leith. Ordered on 18 Aug 1964. Laid-down on 9 Aug 1965. Officially named on 15 Sep 1966 (high winds caused postponement of the launching ceremony until 16 Sep). Accepted into service on 15 Dec 1967. Largest ship then built by the company. Intended for the training of helicopter crews in deep water operations against submarines. Fitted with Denny Brown stabilisers to provide greater ship control during helicopter operations, the only RFA vessel so equipped.

The helicopter support ship *Lofoten*, K 07, converted LST(3) 3027, was approved for disposal in 1969.

ENGADINE   *1970, Official*

ENGADINE   *1969, Official*

MINELAYER

ABDIEL

Displacement, tons	1 375 standard; 1 500 full load
Dimensions, feet	244·5 pp; 265 oa × 38·5 × 10
Mines	44 carried
Main engines	2 Paxman Ventura 16 cyl pressure charged diesels; 1 250 rpm; 2 690 bhp = 16 knots
Complement	123 (14 officers, 109 ratings)

Exercise minelayer for the Royal Navy ordered in June 1965 from John I Thornycroft & Co Ltd, Woolston, Southampton. Laid down on 23 May 1966. Launched on 27 Jan 1967. Completed 17 Oct 1967. Main machinery manufactured by Davey Paxman, Colchester. Main gearing supplied by Messrs Wisemans. Her function is to support mine counter-measure forces, maintain these forces when they are operating away from their shore bases, and lay exercise mines. She replaced ageing vessels previously employed on this work. Living accommodation is of a high standard. Cost £1 500 000.

ABDIEL   *1970, courtesy Godfrey H. Walker, Esq*

SONAR TRIALS SHIP (*former "Battle" Class Destroyer*)

Displacement, tons	2 780 standard ; 3 430 full load						
Length, feet (*metres*)	355·0 (*108·2*)pp ; 364·0 (*110·9*) wl ; 379·0 (*115·5*) oa						

Name	No.	Builders	Laid down	Launched	Completed	Converted
MATAPAN	D 43	John Brown, Clydebank	11 Mar 1944	30 Apr 1945	5 Sep 1947	1971-1972

Beam, feet (*metres*)	40·5 (*12·3*)
Draught, feet (*metres*)	18·0 (*5·5*)
Boilers	2 Admiralty 3-drum ; 400 psi (*28·1 kg/cm²*) ; (650°F (*343°C*)
Main engines	Parsons geared turbines ; 50 000 shp ; 2 shafts
Speed, knots	35·75 designed ; 30·5 sea
Radius, miles	1 300 at full power ; 3 000 at 20 knots ; 4 400 at 12 knots
Oil fuel, tons	680
Complement	268 (12 officers, and 256 men)

Before conversion   *Official*

A former "Battle class" destroyer which went into reserve almost immediately after being completed. Being reconstructed at a cost of about £2 500 000. To be attached to the Admiralty Underwater Weapons Establishment at Portland. Above particulars obtained before conversion.

CONVERSION. Taken in hand at HM Dockyard, Portsmouth in Jan 1971 for conversion into a Sonar Trials Ship. The rebuilding involves a new bow, different bridge, remodelled superstructure, extension of the forecastle deck aft all the way to the counter, thus converting her into a flushdecker, erection of deckhouses on the aftercastle, radical structural changes in the keel plating, installation of full air-conditioning, and provision of accommodation for both naval and civil scientific staff. Completion is expected in 2 years.

"MANXMAN" CLASS. The Engineer's Training ship *Manxman* (former Minesweeper Support Ship, ex-Fast Minelayer) was officially listed for disposal in Feb 1971.

Of sister fast minelayers, *Apollo* was scrapped in 1962 and *Ariadne* in 1965 ; and *Abdiel*, *Latona* and *Welshman* were lost during the Second World War.

MATAPAN as originally completed   *Added 1971, Official*

ICE PATROL SHIP

ENDURANCE (ex-*Anita Dan*) A 171

Displacement, tons	*circa* 3 600 (official)
Measurement, tons	2 641 gross
Length, feet (*metres*)	300 (*91·44*) oa ; 305 (*92·96*) including helicopter deck extension
Beam, feet (*metres*)	46 (*14·02*)
Draught, feet (*metres*)	16·5 (*5·03*) ; 18 (*5·5*) max
Aircraft	2 Whirlwind Mk IX helicopters
Guns	2—20 mm
Main engines	B & W 550 VTBF diesels ; 3 220 ihp ; 1 shaft
Speed knots	14·5
Range, miles	12 000 at 14·5 knots
Complement	119 (13 officers, 106 men, including a small Royal Marine detachment) plus 12 spare berths for scientists

ENDURANCE   *1969, Official*

Ten year old ship purchased from J. Lauritzen Lines. Copenhagen (announced on 20 Feb 1967). Strengthened for operation in ice. Converted by Harland & Wolff, Belfast, into an ice patrol ship for southern waters to replace *Protector*, undertaking hydrographic and oceanographic surveys for the Royal Navy, as support ship and guard vessel. New name *Endurance* was announced 27 July, 1967. She was ready for deployment in the Antarctic for the 1968 season by Oct. Refitted May to Oct during the Antarctic winter.

An unusual feature for one of HM ships is her hull painted a vivid red for easy identification in the ice, particularly from the air. Her upperworks and funnel are the traditional white and buff of the naval surveying fleet. Another feature is that the ship can be controlled from the crow's nest so as to give her officers the furthest view of channels through the ice.

"PROTECTOR" CLASS. The ice patrol ship *Protector*, A 146, converted netlayer, was paid off in 1968 after 13 years service in the Antarctic and was officially approved for disposal in 1969. The original sister ship of *Protector*, the netlayer *Guardian*, was disposed of in 1962.

ENDURANCE in pack ice off Grahamland, Antarctic   *1969, Official*

HEAVY REPAIR SHIP (Former *Aircraft Carrier*)

Name	No.	Builders	Laid down	Launched	Completed	Converted
TRIUMPH	A 108 (ex-*R* 16) R & W Hawthorn Leslie, Hebburn		27 Jan 1943	2 Oct 1944	9 Apr 1946	HM Dockyard, Portsmouth 1 Jan 1958 to 7 Jan 1965

Displacement, tons	13 350 standard ; 17 000 full load
Length, feet (*metres*)	630 (*192·0*) pp ; 650 (*198·1*) wl ; 699 (*213·1*) oa
Beam, feet (*metres*)	80 (*24·4*)
Draught, feet (*metres*)	23·5 (*7·2*)
Width, feet (*metres*)	112·5 (*34·3*) overall
Aircraft	3 helicopters in flight deck hangar
Guns AA	4—40 mm
Guns, saluting	3
Boilers	4 Admiralty 3-drum Pressure 400 psi (*28·1 kg/cm²*) Temperature 700°F (*371°C*)
Main engines	Parsons geared turbines 40 000 shp ; 2 shafts
Speed, knots	24·25
Radius, miles	10 000 at 14 knots ; 5 500 at full speed
Oil fuel (tons)	3 000
Complement	500 (27 officers, 473 men) plus 285 (15 officers, 270 men) maintenance staff

TRIUMPH

1969, courtesy Mr. John C. Jeremy

Insulated for tropical service and partially air-conditioned. When she was still an aircraft carrier of the "Colossus" class her accommodation was modified in 1953 to fit her for employment as officer cadets' training ship, but she was converted into a heavy repair ship under the 1956-57 Estimates, and her sponsons removed. Commissioned for service after conversion on 7 Jan 1965. Sailed from Portsmouth on 1 Feb 1965 for the Far East where she is employed as an escort maintenance ship.

CONVERSION. Her reconstruction spanned a period of seven years, but the work actually took less time as her conversion was suspended for about 2·5 years while dockyard commitments of higher priority were met. Although intended for heavy repair the special machinery in the comprehensive workshops for this in the former hangar, 445 feet (*135·6 metres*) long, 52 feet (*15·8 metres*) wide, and 17·5 feet (*5·3 metres*) in depth, is placed in a state of preservation and her main role is escort maintenance, but she has space and facilities to undertake a variety of tasks including the carrying and maintenance of helicopters. She can take four destroyers and frigates alongside, two on each beam. Cost of conversion: £10 200 000, including capital expenditure on the heavy repair plant carried and dockyard and expenses over a protracted period.

CONSTRUCTION. As an aircraft carrier the flight deck, 690 feet (*210·3 metres*) long, 80 feet (*24·4 metres*) wide, and 39 feet (*11·9 metres*) above the water line, was strengthened to take aircraft of over 8 tons in weight. Sponsons could be dismantled to the extent of 3·5 feet on either side if necessary to allow for passage through Panama Canal. Mercantile type hull. Built to Lloyd's specifications up to main deck with the original intention of converting to commercial service after the war. Damage control: No great measure of vertical subdivision on the sandwich system as it was reckoned that it is better for ships to settle evenly in the event of damage and flooding than to foster capsizing.

ENGINEERING. Engines and boilers are arranged *en echelon*, one set of turbines and two boilers being installed side by side in each of the two main propelling machinery spaces, on the unit system, so that the starboard propeller shaft is longer than the port shaft. The maximum designed speed was 25 knots, at 225 rpm. The economical speed is 15 knots at 120 rpm.

APPEARANCE. Distinguished from aircraft carriers by generally lighter appearance, thin funnel, distinctive shape of ship's side forward, absence of sponsons and block deckhouses on the former flight deck.

PHOTOGRAPHS. A starboard quarter view and a dead broadside surface view of *Triumph* appear in the 1965-66 and 1966-67 editions.

CLASS. Of her original sister aircraft carriers, the *Venerable* (renamed *Karel Doorman*) was sold to the Royal Netherlands Navy on 1 Apr 1948 and renamed *Karel Doorman*, and again sold to Argentina on 15 Oct 1968 and renamed *25 de Mayo*; *Colossus* (renamed *Arromanches*) was sold to the French Navy in 1951; and two were completed as maintenance aircraft carriers, *Perseus* (scrapped in 1958) and *Pioneer* (scrapped in 1954). *Vengeance* was lent to the Royal Australian Navy early in 1953, but was returned to the Royal Navy in August 1955, and sold to the Brazilian Navy in 1956 (announced by Admiralty on 14 Dec); she was modernised in 1957-60 and commissioned in 1961 under the name *Minas Gerais*. *Warrior* was sold to the Argentine Navy in July 1958 and commissioned under the name *Independencia* in Jan 1959.

CLASS. Of *Triumph's* sister ships, *Glory* was broken up in 1961, and *Ocean* and *Theseus* in 1962. Of two half-sisters *Pioneer* was scrapped in 1954 and *Perseus* in 1958 (*Unicorn* arrived at Dalmuir to be broken up on 15 June 1959).

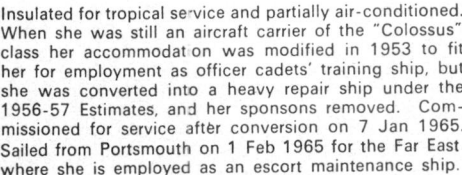

TRIUMPH maintaining four frigates

Official

DESTROYER DEPOT SHIP

1 "TYNE" CLASS

Displacement, tons	11 000 standard; 14 600 full load
Length, feet (metres)	585 (178·3) pp; 613 (186·8) wl; 621 (189·3) oa
Beam, feet (metres)	66 (20·1)
Draught, feet (metres)	20·8 (6·3)
Guns, surface	8—4·5 in (115 mm)
Guns, AA	7—40 mm
Boilers	4 three-drum type
Main engines	Parsons geared turbines 7 500 shp; 2 shafts
Speed, knots	17
Oil fuel (tons)	1 400

Name	No.	Builders	Laid down	Launched	Completed
TYNE	A 194	Scotts' SB & Eng Co Ltd, Greenock	15 July 1938	28 Feb 1940	28 Feb 1941

Complement	520 (normal) as depot ship
	820 as flagship
	Accommodation for 1 000

Built under the 1937 Estimates. Equipment includes two furnaces, each capable of melting 500 lb of metal at any temperature up to 1 500 degrees centigrade; a foundry and machine shops with milling and grinding machines. Refitted from late 1956 to early 1958 with enclosed lower bridge and improved operations room and internal arrangements, etc, seven 40 mm guns replac-

ing former smaller anti-aircraft guns. Was flagship of Home fleet from Autumn 1954 to August 1956, and again from April 1958 to 1960. Also parent ship of the 2nd Submarine Squadron in 1960, and Flagship of the Flag Officer, Flotillas, Home Fleet, until Apr 1961, when she became accommodation ship for Fleet Maintenance Units personnel at Portsmouth, from whence she was towed to Devonport on 18 July 1961 and placed in reserve and used as a living ship. Fleet maintenance S/M Depotship in 1970

TYNE   Added 1968, courtesy Mr. Godfrey H. Walker

SUBMARINE DEPOT SHIPS

Submarine Support Ships
2 "MAIDSTONE" CLASS

Displacement, tons	10 000 standard; 13 000 full load
Length, feet (metres)	497·0 (151·5) pp; 531·0 (161·8) oa
Beam, feet (metres)	73·0 (22·3)
Draught, feet (metres)	21·2 (6·5)
Guns, AA	5—40 mm Bofors (see Gunnery)
Boilers	4 Admiralty 3-drum type
Main engines	Geared turbines (Brown Curtis in Forth: Parsons in Maidstone) 2 shafts; 7 000 shp
Speed, knots	16
Oil fuel, tons	2 300
Complement	695 (45 officers and 650 men) Accommodation for 1 159 (119 officers and 1 040 men) normal; over 1 500 max

Name	No.	Builders	Laid down	Launched	Completed	Reconstructed
FORTH	A 187	John Brown, Clydebank	30 June 1937	11 Aug 1938	14 May 1939	1962-1966
MAIDSTONE	A 185	John Brown, Clydebank	17 Aug 1936	21 Oct 1937	5 May 1938	1958-1962

MAIDSTONE   1969, Official

Equipment includes foundry, coppersmith's, plumbers', carpenters'; heavy and light machine, electrical and torpedo repair shops and plant for charging submarine batteries. Designed for maintaining nine operational submarines, and supplying over 140 torpedoes and a similar number of mines. Repair facilities on board for all material in attached submarines, and extensive diving and salvage equipment. There are steam laundry, hospital, chapel, two canteens, bakery, barber shops, operating theatre and dental surgery. Maidstone was Flagship of the Commander-in-Chief Home Fleet from 16 Aug 1956 until 31 Mar 1958. From 1962 to 1968 she was depot ship for the Third Submarine Squadron but when her function was taken over by the new Clyde Submarine Base, HMS Neptune, at Faslane, she became surplus to naval requirements.

In Oct 1969, Maidstone was restored and recommissioned as an accommodation ship for 2 000 troops and sent to Belfast.

RECONSTRUCTION. Maidstone was extensively reconstructed in HM Dockyard, Portsmouth in 1958-62 as support ship for nuclear powered submarines with a lattice foremast and additional superstructure amidships. The conversion and modernisation included refitting as parent ship for the nuclear-powered submarine Dreadnought. Forth was similarly modernised and converted into a support ship for nuclear powered submarines in HM Dockyard Chatham, in 1962-63.

GUNNERY. As originally designed both ships mounted eight 4·5 inch guns in four twin housings, one forward, one aft, and one sponsoned on each beam between the funnels, but these were removed during their conversion into support ships for nuclear powered submarines. Maidstone formerly also had a light AA gun in the bows and she carried a 4-inch gun on a submarine pattern mounting, for training purposes only, on the starboard side just abaft the midships 4·5 inch turret.

DISPOSAL. The larger and younger submarine support ship Adamant, latterly in reserve at Plymouth, was disposed of in late 1970.

FORTH   1969, Official

MAINTENANCE SHIPS

1 "POINT" CLASS

Displacement, tons	8 580 standard ; 10 200 full load
Length, feet (*metres*)	416·0 (*126·8*)pp ; 441·5 (*134·6*)oa
Beam, feet (*metres*)	57·5 (*17·5*)
Draught, feet (*metres*)	21·0 (*6·4*)
Guns, AA	11—40 mm
Main engines	Triple expansion ; 2 500 ihp ; Pressure 250 psi (*17·6 kg/cm²*) ; Temperature 600°F (*316°C*)

Name	No.	Builders	Laid down	Launched	Completed
HARTLAND POINT	A 262	Burrard Dry Dock N Vancouver	18 July 1944	4 Nov 1944	11 July 1945

Speed, knots	10 approx
Oil fuel, tons	1 000 capacity
Complement	445 (25 officers and 420 men)

Former Landing Ship Maintenance. Extensively refitted externally and internally and modernised as an Escort Maintenance Ship in 1959-60, with lattice foremast, modified bridge, novel short funnel, additional deckhouses, modern cranes, and new armament, messing arrangements and air conditioning. Her task was the maintenance of destroyers and frigates in the Far East at any port required or where the fleet was concentrated. Returned to United Kingdom in May 1965. Sister ship *Dodman Point* was disposed of in 1962.

HARTLAND POINT

1969, Official

BERRY HEAD

1971, Official

3 "HEAD" CLASS

Displacement, tons	9 000 standard ; 11 270 full load
Length, feet (*metres*)	416·0 (*126·8*)pp ; 441·5 (*134·6*)oa
Beam, feet (*metres*)	57·5 (*17·5*)
Draught, feet (*metres*)	22·5 (*6·9*)
Guns, AA	11—40 mm
Boilers	2 Foster Wheeler
Main engines	Triple expansion ; 2 500 ihp
Speed, knots	10 approx
Oil fuel, tons	1 600 capacity
Complement	425

Name	No.	Builders	Laid down	Launched	Completed
BERRY HEAD	A 191	North Vancouver Ship Repairs	15 June 1944	21 Oct 1944	30 May 1945
RAME HEAD	A 134	Burrard DD, N Vancouver	12 July 1944	22 Nov 1944	18 Aug 1945

Escort Maintenance Ships. *Rame Head* was refitted and modernised in 1960-63. *Duncansby Head* on 1 Dec 1962 became "half" of HMS *Cochrane* (Senior Officer Reserve Ships, Rosyth) jointly with *Girdle Ness*. In 1963 *Rame Head* became HQ ship. (Senior Officer Reserve Ships, Portsmouth) but was later accommodation ship in Belfast. *Berry Head* was refitted in 1968-69 to relieve HMS *Triumph* in the Far East, but returned in 1970.

DISPOSALS. *Duncansby Head* was returned to the Canadian Government in 1969 and scrapped.

"MULL" CLASS. *Mull of Galloway* was scrapped in 1965 and *Mull of Kintyre* was for disposal in 1969.

"NESS" CLASS. *Buchan Ness* was scrapped in 1959 and *Girdle Ness* in 1970.

RAME HEAD

Official

SURVEY SHIPS

3 "HECLA" CLASS

Name	No.	Builders	Laid down	Launched	Completed
HECATE	A 137	Yarrow & Co Ltd, Scotstoun	26 Oct 1964	31 Mar 1965	20 Dec 1965
HECLA	A 133	Yarrow & Co and Blythswood	6 May 1964	21 Dec 1964	9 Sep 1965
HYDRA	A 144	Yarrow & Co and Blythswood	14 May 1964	14 July 1965	5 May 1966

Displacement, tons	1 915 light; 2 733 full load
Measurement, tons	2 898 gross
Length, feet (*metres*)	235 (*71·6*) pp; 260·1 (*79·3*) oa
Beam, feet (*metres*)	49·1 (*15·0*)
Draught, feet (*metres*)	15·6 (*4·7*)
Aircraft	1 Wasp helicopter
Main engines	Diesel-electric drive; 1 shaft.
	3 Paxman "Ventura" 12-cyl Vee
	turbocharged diesels; 3,840 bhp.
	1 electric motor; 2 000 shp
Speed, knots	14·35 on trials
Radius, miles	20 000 at 9 knots
Oil fuel, tons	450
Complement	118 (14 officers, 104 ratings)
Accommodation	123 (19 officers, 104 ratings)

New dual purpose deep ocean survey ships for the Royal Navy. The first to be designed with a combined oceanographical and hydrographical role, and the first to be built on commercial lines without a supplementary naval function. Of merchant ship design and similar in many respects to the Royal Research ship *Discovery*, they have range and endurance to fit them for their specialised work. The hull is strengthened for navigation in ice, and a propeller built into a transverse tunnel in the bow for good manoeuvrability. The fore end of the superstructure incorporates a Landrover garage and the after end a helicopter hangar with adjacent flight deck. Equipped with chartroom, drawing office and photographic studio; two laboratories, dry and wet; electrical, engineering and shipwright workshops, and large storerooms. Capable of operating independently of shore support for long periods. High standard of habitability, with library, canteen, laundry, cinema, and hospital. Air conditioned throughout. Ordered from Yarrow & Co Ltd, Scotstoun, in Feb 1964 (Blythswood Shipbuilding Co Ltd, Glasgow, collaborating on two of the three hulls). *Hecla* and *Hecate* were launched from the Blythswood yard.

MODIFIED "BAY" CLASS SURVEY SHIPS. Of the four survey ships of the "Bay" class (modified frigates), *Cook* (ex-*Pegwell Bay*, ex-*Loch Mockrum*) was for disposal in 1965, *Owen* (ex-*Thurso Bay*, ex-*Loch Muick*) in 1966, *Dalrymple* (ex-*Luce Bay*, ex-*Loch Class*) was sold to Portugal in Apr 1966 and renamed *Afonso de Albuquerque*, and *Dampier* (ex-*Herne Bay*, ex-*Loch Eil*) was approved for disposal by scrapping in 1968.

1 ADMIRALTY DESIGN

VIDAL A 200

Displacement, tons	1 940 standard; 2 200 full load
Length, feet (*metres*)	297 (*90·5*) pp; 315·2 (*96·1*) oa
Beam, feet (*metres*)	40 (*12·2*)
Draught, feet (*metres*)	11 (*3·4*) forward; 13·2 (*4·0*) aft
Aircraft	1 helicopter
Main engines	4 ASR-1 diesels (see *Engineering*)
	2 940 shp; 2 shafts
Speed, knots	15·9
Radius, miles	9 500 at 10 knots
Complement	170 (including 17 survey staff)
Accommodation	197 (20 officers, 177 ratings)

Designed by the Royal Navy from the start for hydrographic surveying and chart production. First survey ship to be equipped with a helicopter flight deck and a hangar, designed to enable a helicopter to land on and fly off for air survey photography and transport of personnel to shore observation stations. Air conditioning plant is installed to meet equatorial and polar climatic conditions. The ship carries three survey motor launches equipped with echo sounding apparatus. First British naval vessel to be built equipped from the beginning for cafeteria messing. Cost £1 345 000. Refitted with enclosed bridge in 1961, but the bridge wings were left open. Again refitted in 1962.

CONSTRUCTION. Built by HM Dockyard, Chatham. Laid down on 5 July 1950, launched on 31 July 1951, and completed on 29 Mar 1954.

ELECTRICAL. The latest electronic aids to surveying and navigation are incorporated. Electrical power is provided from 360 kw 220 volt dc diesel generating sets.

HELICOPTER OPERATION. The after end of the forecastle deck extension is a landing apron for the helicopter, housed in the after deck house hangar on the same level.

ENGINEERING. The main propelling machinery was designed in HM Dockyard, Chatham. The four ASR 1 diesels drive two shafts through reverse and reduction gear boxes. Each engine is of the 12 cylinder vee unsupercharged type with a rating of 1 050 hp at 920 rpm.

APPEARANCE. Funnel and fore bridge are pear shaped in plan.

HECLA   1969, Official

HYDRA   1970, Official

HECATE   1971, Official

VIDAL   1969, Official

COASTAL MINESWEEPERS AND MINEHUNTERS

1 NEW CONSTRUCTION GRP TYPE

WILTON

Displacement, tons	450 full load
Dimensions, feet	153 oa × 28·8 × 8·5 (official figures)
Main engines	2 diesels; 2 shafts; 3 000 bhp = 15 knots estimated max
Cost	£1 500 000 to £2 000 000 (official estimate)
Complement	39 (5 officers and 34 ratings)

Contract signed on 11 Feb 1970. Prototype being built of glass reinforced plastic to the existing minehunter design by Vosper Thornycroft at Woolston. Similar to the "Ton" class and fitted with reconditioned machinery and equipment from the scrapped *Derriton*.

BOSSINGTON (Minehunter) WILTON will be similar   *1971, Official*

MAXTON   *1970, Official*

NOMENCLATURE. Named after villages with the suffix "ton". Since 1954 some have been renamed on being allocated to the Royal Naval Reserve, taking the traditional names associated with the divisions (see below). Ships are not permanently attached to one division; on becoming due for refit they revert to their original names and might then be re-allocated to a different division or return to general service. The former Royal Navy and Royal Naval Reserve names are shown in parenthesis above.

APPEARANCE. *Ashton, Chawton, Houghton, Lewiston, Mersey* (ex-*Pollington*), *Nurton, Puncheston, Northumbria* (ex-*Quainton*), *Sheraton, Soberton, Stubbington, Walkerton, Wilkieston, Wiston* and others are fitted with an enclosed or frigate bridge and tripod mast. *Shoulton* covered bridge.

ROLE VARIATIONS. Of this class *Bolton, Soberton, Wasperton* and *Wotton* constituted a division of the Fishery Protection Squadron. *Iveston* was converted to night guard aircraft ship. *Invermoriston* modified for SAR duties, PAS manned, now reserve.

PHOTOGRAPHS. A photograph of *Bildeston* appears in the 1954-55 and 1955-56 editions, of *Highburton* in the 1957-58 edition, of *Wilkieston* in the 1960-61 edition, of *Monkton* in the 1960-61 to 1964-65 editions, of *Wolverton* in the 1961-62 to 1964-65 editions, of *Lewiston* in the 1963-64 to 1966-67 editions, of *Shavington* and *Sheraton* in the 1965-66 to 1967-68 editions, of *Beachampton* and *Laleston* in the 1976-68 and 1968-69 editions, of *Bronington, Iveston* and *Kirkliston* in the 1969-70 and 1970-71 editions.

TRANSFERS. *Dunkerton* and *Hazleton* were transferred to South Africa in 1955 and renamed *Pretoria* and *Kaapstad*, respectively. *Durweston, Overton, Whitton* and *Wennington* to India in 1956, and renamed *Kakinada, Karwar, Connamore* and *Cuddalore*, respectively. *Castleton, Chilton, Dumbleton, Oakington, Packington* and *Stratton* to South Africa in 1958-59 and renamed *Johannesburg, East London, Port Elizabeth, Mosselbaai, Walvisbaai* and *Kimberley*, respectively with *Durban* and *Windhoek*. *Darlaston* was sold to Malaysia in 1960 and renamed *Mahamiru*. *Hexton* in 1963 and renamed *Ledang, Dilston* and *Essington* in 1964 and renamed *Jerai* and *Kinabalu*, respectively, and *Lullington* and *Thankerton* in 1966 and renamed *Tahan* and *Brinchang*, respectively. *Alcaston, Chediston, Jackton, Singleton, Somerleyton* and *Swanston* were transferred to Australia in 1962, and renamed *Snipe, Curlew, Teal, Ibis, Hawk*, and *Gull*, respectively. *Aldington* to Ghana in 1964 and renamed *Ejura, Bevington, Hickleton, Ilmington, Rennington, Santon* and *Tarlton* to Argentina in 1968 and renamed *Tierra del Fuego, Neuquen, Formosa, Chaco, Chubut* and *Rio Negro*, respectively, *Myrmidon* (ex-*Edderton*) to Malaysia in 1968; *Alverton, Blaxton* and *Oulston* to Republic of Ireland in 1971 and renamed *Banba, Fola* and *Grainne*, respectively.

ROYAL NAVAL RESERVE. Eleven units were renamed and attached to Royal Naval Reserve Division Headquarters as follows (Division under *Name*):—

Thames	*Curzon*	*Solent*	*Venturer*	*St. David*	*Mersey*
London	Sussex	Solent	Severn	S. Wales	Mersey
Kilmorey	*Clyde*	*Montrose*	*Killiecrankie*	*Northumbria*	
Ulster	Clyde	Tay	Forth	Tyne	

(Humber Division disbanded in 1958 and HMS *Humber* reverted to original name *Bronington*). The name *Warsash* was superseded by *Solent* in 1969.

49 "TON" CLASS

ASHTON	KELLINGTON	ST. DAVID (ex-*Crichton*,
BEACHAMPTON	KILLIECRANKIE (ex-	ex-*Clyde*, ex-*Crichton*)
BELTON	*Bickington*, ex-*Curzon*,	SHAVINGTON
BILDESTON	(ex-*Bickington*)	SHERATON
BOSSINGTON (ex-	KILMOREY (ex-*Alfriston*,	SHOULTON
Embleton)	ex-*Warsash*, ex-	SOBERTON
BRERETON (ex-*St. David*,	*Alfristcn*)	SOLENT (ex-*Crofton*)
ex-*Brereton*)	KIRKLISTON (ex-	STUBBINGTON
BRINTON	*Kilmorey*, ex-*Kirkliston*)	THAMES (ex-
BRONINGTON (ex-	LALESTON	*Woolaston*)
Humber, ex-*Bronington*)	LEWISTON	UPTON
CHAWTON	MADDISTON	VENTURER
CLYDE (ex-*Repton*,	MAXTON	(ex-*Hodgeston*,
ex-*Ossington*)	MERSEY (ex-*Pollington*)	ex-*Northumbria*,
CURZON (ex-*Fittleton*)	MONKTON (ex-*Kelton*)	ex-*Hodgeston*)
CUXTON	MONTROSE (ex-	WALKERTON
GAVINTON	*Dalswinton*)	WASPERTON
GLASSERTON	NORTHUMBRIA (ex-	WILKIESTON
HIGHBURTON	*Quainton*)	WISTON
HUBBERSTON	NURTON (ex-*Montrose*,	WOLVERTON
IVESTON	ex-*Nurton*)	WOTTON
KEDDLESTON	PUNCHESTON	YARNTON

Displacement, tons	360 standard; 425 full load
Dimensions, feet	140·0 pp; 153·0 oa × 28·8 × 8·2
Guns	1—40 mm AA (removed in some ships); 2—20 mm AA (minehunters 2—40 mm)
Main engines	2 diesels; 2 shafts; 2 500 bhp (JVSS 12 Mirrlees), 3 000 bhp (18A-7A Deltic) = 15 knots (max); see *Engineering*
Oil fuel, tons	45
Radius, miles	2 300 at 13 knots
Complement	27 (36 in minehunters, 5 officers and 31 ratings)

Double mahogany hull and constructed of aluminium alloy and other materials with the lowest possible magnetic attraction to attain the greatest possible safety factor when minesweeping. John I. Thornycroft & Co Ltd, Southampton, were the "parent" firm for the group which built this class of uniform design capable of sweeping both contact and influence type mines and dealing with mines operated magnetically and acoustically. The first, *Coniston*, was completed in Feb 1953. The last, *Lewiston*, in 1960. Vosper stabilisers. *Stubbington* and others have fibre-glass bottom sheathing.

ENGINEERING. High speed diesels, standardised to simplify maintenance. The earlier vessels had Mirrlees diesels, but most of the later units had Napier Deltic light weight diesels. *Highburton*, the first with Deltic diesels was accepted on 21 Apr 1955. Some early ships have undergone conversion from Mirrlees to Deltic diesels. The generators for electrical power are in a separate engine room. Three-bladed propellers, 6 ft diameter, 400 rpm. *Shoulton*, refitted 1965-67 (recommissioned 5 Apr), has pumpjet propulsion.

MINEHUNTING. *Shoulton* was fitted with unique mine-hunting equipment, an all-British sonar development which enables her to locate and classify any mine-like objects on the sea bed with accuracy and range previously impossible. Since then *Bildeston, Bossington, Brereton, Brinton, Bronnington, Gavinton, Hubberston, Iveston, Keddleston, Kellington, Kirkliston, Manton* and *Sheraton* have been refitted as minehunters, with active rudders incorporating electric motors for manoeuvring at slow speed. *Highburton* and *Glasserton* are fitted with Osbourne mine destroyer units.

KEDDELSTON   *1971, Wright & Logan*

DIVING CONVERSION *Laleston* was converted into diving trials ship (recommissioned on 22 Mar 1967).

SURVEY CONVERSIONS. *Edderton* and *Sullington* of this class were converted into coastal survey ships in 1964 and renamed *Myrmidon* and *Mermaid*, respectively. (*Myrmidon* was sold to Malaysia and *Mermaid* approved for disposal in 1968-69).

CLASS. *Calton, Fenton, Floriston* and *Sefton* were officially approved for disposal by scrapping in 1966-67; *Badminton, Caunton* and *Lanton* in 1967-68, *Carhampton, Clarbeston, Derriton, Dufton, Flockton, Kemerton, Kildarton, Maryton, Penston, Picton* and *Roddington* in 1968-69, *Appleton, Boulston, Burnaston, Buttington, Chilcompton, Coniston, Dartington, Fiskerton* and *Letterston* in 1969-70, *Amerton, Houghton* and *Leverton* in 1970-71.

INSHORE MINESWEEPERS

22 "HAM" CLASS

M 2601 M 2701 AND M 2777 SERIES

ARLINGHAM *	TRV (PAS)	EVERINGHAM	PAS	PAGHAM	RNXS
BIRDHAM	RNXS	FLINTHAM *	TRV	PORTISHAM	RNXS
BOTTISHAM	R	FORDHAM	DGV	PUTTENHAM	RNXS
BUCKLESHAM	TRV	FRITHAM	TRV	SHIPHAM	RNXS
CHELSHAM *	R	HAVERSHAM	TRV	THAKEHAM	RNXS
DITTISHAM	TRV	LASHAM	TRV	THATCHAM	DGV
DOWNHAM	TRV	ODIHAM	RNXS	TONGHAM	PAS
				WARMINGHAM	DGV

Displacement, tons	120 standard ; 159 full load
Dimensions, feet	2601 Series : 100 pp ; 106·5 oa × 21·2 × 5·5
	2701 Series : 100 pp ; 107 oa × 21·7 × 5·7
	2777 et seq : 100 pp ; 107·5 oa × 22 × 5·8
Guns	1—40 mm Bofors AA or 1—20 mm Oerlikon AA forward (see Gunnery)
Main engines	2 Paxman diesels ; 1 100 bhp = 14 knots max (9 knots sea speed) see Engineering
Oil fuel (tons)	15
Complement	15 (2 officers, 13 ratings)

Designed to operate in shallow waters, rivers and estuaries. When built they were an entirely new type of vessel embodying novel features resulting from lessons learned during the war and in course of subsequent developments. Named after villages with the suffix "ham". The first inshore minesweeper, Inglesham, was launched by J Samuel White & Co Ltd, Cowes, on 23 Apr 1952. The 2701 series were of wooden construction, whereas the 2601 series were of composite construction. All the M 2701 series had a rubbing strake, unlike the M 2601 and M 2001 series.

*Dittisham and Flintham are in full commission as HM ships and training tenders to H.M.S. Ganges, shore training establishment. Arlingham, formerly PAS is in commission and engaged in TRV duties. Everingham is also TRV.

DGV:—Converted to Degaussing Vessels.
PAS:—Employed in the Port Auxiliary Service.
RNXS:—Adapted for the Royal Naval Auxiliary Service
TRV:—Converted to Torpedo Recovery Vessels.

GUNNERY. Most of the M 2601 series had the 40 mm gun replaced by a 20 mm gun. All the M 2701 series had a 20 mm gun (armament as minesweepers).

ENGINEERING. The main machinery was manufactured by Davey Paxman & Co Ltd. Colchester, or by Ruston & Hornsby Ltd. Lincoln, Foden Ltd, Sanbach, Cheshire, or Ransomes, Sims and Jeffries Ltd, Ipswich, under licence from Davey Paxman. Three-bladed propellers, 600 r.p.m.

NOMENCLATURE. Fordham was originally to have been named Pavenham.

PHOTOGRAPHS
A photograph of Altham appears in the 1957-58 and 1958-59 editions, of Chillingham in the 1958-59 and 1959-60 editions, of Darsham in the 1959-60 edition, of Woldingham in the 1960-61 to 1964-65 editions, and of Polsham in the 1963-64 to 1966-67 editions.

SHIPHAM   1970, courtesy Godfrey H. Walker, Esq.

AUXILIARY SERVICE. Birdham, Odiham, Pagham, Portisham, Puttenham, Shipham, and Thakeham were adapted for the Royal Naval Auxiliary Serivce. Arlingham, Everingham, Tongham and Woldingham were employed in the Port Auxiliary Service. Bucklesham, Dittisham, Downham, Flintham, Fritham, Haversham and Lasham were adapted as Torpedo Recovery vessels.
Fordham, Thatcham and Warmingham were converted into Degaussing Vessels to replace the older degaussing vessels of the converted MMS 1001 type.

R. Chelsham and Bottisham, loaned to the RAF in 1966 for service at Plymouth as Coastal Command range and recovery vessels and numbered HMFA 5000 and HMFA 5001, discarding their former names, were returned to the Royal Navy in 1971, in reserve.

SURVEY CONVERSIONS. Powderham and Yaxham were converted into inshore survey craft in 1964 and renamed Waterwitch and Woodlark, respectively.

DITTISHAM   1971, Official

TRANSFERS
Frettenham, Isham, Kingham, Mersham, Mileham, Petersham, Pineham, Rendlesham, Riplingham, Sparham, Stedham, Sulham, Tibenham, Wexham and Whippingham were transferred to France in 1954-55 ; Hildersham and Littlesham to India in 1955 and renamed Bimlipitan and Bassein, respectively ; Bassingham to East Africa on 25 June 1958, but returned on 9 Oct 1961 ; Bedham to Malaysia in 1958 and renamed Lanka Suka· Cardingham and Etchingham to Hong Kong R.N.V.R. in 1959, but returned on 1 Apr 1966 ; Altham, Asheldham and Brantingham to Malaysia in 1959 and renamed Sri Johar, Sri Perlis and Temasek, respectively, Malham and Ottringham to Ghana at the end of 1959, and renamed Yogoda and Afadzato respectively ; and Harpham and Greetham to Libya in 1963, and renamed Brak and Zuara, respectively, Boreham and Felmersham to Malaysia in 1966 and renamed Jerong and Todak, respectively ; Popham and Wintringham to Australia on 9 June 1966 and renamed Otter and Seal, respectively ; Blunham, Bodenham and Elsenham to South Arabia in 1967 ; Neasham to Australia in 1968.

CLASS. Bisham and Edlingham damaged by fire on 29 Sep 1956 were scrapped in 1959. Bassingham, Brigham (sold in 1964 to Australian Marine Industries Pty Ltd as a Ferry), Chillingham, Cranham (sold in 1967), Halsham (to RAF in 1966 as HMFA 5002), Inglesham, Mickleham, Pulham, (renamed Isis while attached to London RNR), Rampisham (renamed Squirrel while on Fishery Protection), Reedham, Sidlesham, Tresham (handed over to Reardon Smith Nautical College, Cardiff, on 8 Apr 1968 and renamed Margherita II) and Wrentham were on the disposal list in 1964, Cobham Damerham, Darsham, Davenham, Glentham and Hovingham were listed for disposal by scrapping in 1965, Abbotsham, Georgeham, Ledsham, Ludham, Nettleham, Rackham, Sandringham, Saxlingham, Shrivenham and Thornham were officially approved for disposal by scrapping in 1966 (but Sandringham is employed on ferry duties and Thornham is attached to Aberdeen University RN Unit), Ockham and Polsham (sold in 1967 to PLA as Maplin) in 1967 and Woldingham in 1968.

ARLINGHAM   1970, courtesy Michael D. J. Lennon, Esq.

2 "LEY" CLASS. M 2001 SERIES

AVELEY   ISIS (ex-Cradley)

Displacement, tons	123 standard ; 164 full load
Dimensions, feet	100 pp ; 107 oa × 21·8 × 5·5
Guns	1—40 mm AA or 1—20 mm AA forward
Main Engines	2 Paxman diesels ; 700 bhp = 13 knots
Oil fuel (tons)	15
Complement	15 (2 officers, 13 ratings)

The "Ley" class differed from the "Ham" class. They were of composite (non-magnetic metal and wooden) construction, instead of all wooden construction. Their superstructure and other features also differed. They had no winch or sweeping gear, as they were mine hunters, not sweepers. They had smaller engines as less towing power was needed. Aveley is attached to Plymouth. Cradley was allocated to London Division R.N.R. in 1963 and renamed Isis, relieving Pulham (renamed Isis).

CLASS. Broadley, damaged by fire on 29 Sep 1956, was scrapped in 1959, Brenchley and Brinkley were for disposal by scrapping in 1965. Cheiley was on the Sales List in 1965. Squirrel and Watchful (originally named Burley and Broomley, respectively, until allocated to Fishery protection in 1960 and 1958) arrived at Rotterdam to be broken up on 21 Mar 1968. Dingley was sold to Pounds (Portsmouth) in 1968, Brearley for disposal in 1969.

AVELEY   Added 1969, Official

ISIS   1967, Skyfotos

TRIALS SHIP

1 NEW CONSTRUCTION

WHITEHEAD ETV 01

Displacement, tons	3 040 full load (official figures)
Dimensions, feet	291·0 wl; 319·0 oa × 48·0 × 17·0
Main engines	2 Paxman 12 YLCM diesels; 1 shaft; 3 400 bhp = 15·5 knots
Endurance, miles	4 000 nautical at 12 knots
Complement,	10 officers, 32 ratings, 15 trials and scientific staff

Designed to provide mobile preparation, firing and control facilities for weapons and research vehicles. Built by Scotts Shipbuilding Co Ltd, Greenock. Launched on 5 May 1970. Named after Robert Whitehead, the torpedo development pioneer and engineer. Fitted with equipment for tracking weapons and targets and for analysing the results of trials.

CONTROLLED MINELAYERS

3 "MINER" CLASS

Name	Pennant No.	Laid down	Launched	Completed
BRITANNIC (ex-*Miner V*)	Ex-N 15	22 Apr 40	2 Nov 40	26 June 41
MINER III	N 13	18 Jan 39	16 Nov 39	16 Mar 40
STEADY (ex-*Miner VII*)	Ex-N 17	31 Mar 43	29 Jan 44	31 Mar 44

Displacement, tons	300 standard; (355 full load)
Dimensions, feet	110·2 × 26·5 × 8·0
Main engines	Ruston & Hornsby diesels; 2 shafts; 360 bhp = 10 knots

All built by Philip & Son Ltd, Dartmouth, and engined by Ruston & Hornsby Ltd, Lincoln. *Miner V* was converted into a cable lighter and renamed *Britannic* in 1960 with PAS as store carrier. *Miner VII* was adapted as a stabilisation trials ship at portsmouth and renamed *Steady* in 1960 with PAS. *Miner III* was a tender for Clearance Diving Teams attached to HMS *Vernon* shore establishment but was relieved by the coastal minesweeper *Laleston* as diving trials ship in 1967. *Miner IV* and *Mindful* (ex-*Miner VIII*) were sold in 1965, *Minstrel* (ex-*Miner I*) was for disposal in 1965 and *Miner VI* in 1968. *Gossamer* (ex-*Miner II*) was damaged as a target and sunk by Iranian destroyer *Artemiz* off the Dorset coast in 1970. The coastal minelayer *Plover* was scrapped in 1968.

BRITANNIC   *1969, courtesy Dr Giorgio Arra*

MINER III   *1969, courtesy Dr Giorgio Arra*

EMPIRE GULL   *1971, A. & J. Pavia*

SEAWARD DEFENCE BOATS

2 "FORD" CLASS

DROXFORD P 3113 (Clyde RNR)   **DEE** (Ulster RNR)

Displacement, tons	120 standard; 142 full load
Dimensions, feet	110·0 wl; 117·2 oa × 20·0 × 7·0 props
Guns	1—40 mm Bofors AA
A/S weapons	DC rails; large and small DC
Main engines	Davey Paxman diesels. Foden engine on centre shaft. 1 100 bhp = 18 knots max; 15 knots sea
Oil fuel, tons	23
Complement	19

Originally designed to detect, locate and destroy submarines, including midget submarines, in the approaches to defended ports. All built in 1953-57. Had modern electronic equipment, depth charge release gear and flares, and comprehensive electrical installations. *Droxford* was formerly attached to H.M.S. *St. Vincent*, now closed down.

ROYAL NAVAL RESERVE. *Beckford* (renamed *Dee* in 1969) and *Kingsford* were transferred to Mersey and Clyde RNR divisions, respectively, in Dec 1964.

TRANSFERS. *Brayford* was sold to South African Navy in 1954 and *Glassford* in 1955. *Desford* was transferred to Ceylon in 1955. *Elmina* and *Komenda* were built for Ghana in 1962. *Axford, Hinksford* and *Montford* were sold to Nigeria 1 July 1966, *Dubford* and *Gifford* in 1968, and *Bryansford* in 1969.

CLASS. *Camberford, Greatford, Ickford, Marlingford, Mayford, Shalford* and *Tilford* were officially approved for disposal during 1966-67. *Dee* (ex-*Beckford* was sold in 1968 as *Robert Clive*)

DROXFORD   *1967, Wright & Logan*

LANDING SHIPS

2 LST (3) TYPE

STALKER (*LST* (3) 3515)   **EMPIRE GULL** (ex-*Trouncer*, LST (3) 3513)

Displacement, tons	2 140 light; 5 000 full load
Dimensions, feet	330·0 pp; 347·5 oa × 55·2 × 4·7 (forward); 12·0 (max)
Main engines	Triple expansion; 2 shafts; 5 500 ihp = 13 knots max (10 knots cruising)
Boilers	2 Admiralty 3-drum type
Oil fuel, tons	1 400

Stalker, designated submarine support ship in 1958, was at Londonderry until the closure of that base; she is now at Rosyth. *Lofotan*, designated harbour accommodation ship in 1958, was converted into the Royal Navy's first helicopter support ship in 1964 (for disposal in 1969). *Tracker*, designated harbour accommodation ship in 1958, was converted into a net and boom carrier in 1964 and disposed of in 1971.

TRANSFER. Sister ship *Avenger* was transferred to the Indian Navy in 1949 and renamed *Magar*.

NOMENCLATURE. When commercially chartered *Charger* became *Empire Nordic*, *Fighter* became *Empire Grebe*, *Hunter* became *Empire Curlew*, *Trumpeter* became *Empire Fulmar* and *Walcheren* became *Empire Guillimot*, *Attacker* was renamed *Empire Cymric* on commercial charter in 1954.

CLASS. *Smiter* was wrecked off Lagos on 25 Apr 1949. *Searcher* was scrapped in 1949. *Bruiser* was stricken in 1959, *Reggio, Salerno, Suvla* and *Vagso* in 1960, *Puncher* and *Ravager* in 1961, and *Hunter* in 1962. *Chaser*, designated as a submarine support ship in 1958, was listed for disposal in 1962. *Zeebrugge*, employed as a harbour accommodation ship since 1958, was placed on the disposal list in 1963. *Dieppe* designated as a harbour accommodation ship in 1967, was officially approved for disposal by scrapping in 1968, but she was still shown in the spring 1970 Navy list.

STALKER   *1971, Official*

LST(A) TYPE. *Anzio* (ex-LST(A) 3003) was officially approved for disposal by scrapping in 1966 (de-equipped ready for tow in 1967) and *Striker* (ex-LST(A) 3516) in 1967. Both were disposed of in 1971. For disposal of the other ships of this class see 1966-67 edition.

LST(C) TYPE. Of the two LST(C) type tank landing ships, *Narvik* (ex-LST(C) 3044) was officially approved for disposal by scrapping in 1968-69, but is still in service as accommodation ship at Rosyth. and *Messina* (ex-*LST* (C) 3043) was de-equipped in 1967 for tow to shipbreakers.

"BEN" CLASS. Of the two LST(Q) type tank landing ships, *Ben Nevis*, L 3101 (ex-*LST*(Q) 1, ex-*LST* (3) 3012) was scrapped in 1965, and *Ben Lomond*, L 3102 (ex-*LST* (Q) 2, ex-*LST*(3) 3013) in 1960.

LANDING CRAFT

9 LCT (8) TYPE

AACHEN L 4062	**AKYAB** (ex-*Rampart*) L 4037	**AREZZO** L 4128
ABBEVILLE L 4041	**ANDALNES** L 4097	**ARAKAN** L 4164
AGHEILA L 4002	**ANTWERP** L 4074	**AUDEMER** L 4061

Displacement, tons	657 light; 895 to 1 017 loaded
Dimensions, feet	225 pp; 231 2 oa × 39 × 3·2 forward; 5 aft
	Beaching draughts
Main Engines	4 Paxman engines; 1 840 bhp 12·6 knots (9 knots cruising)
Complement	33 to 37

Akyab has lattice mast aft and deckhouse forward. *LCT* (8) 4002 (*Agheila*), 4037 (*Akyab*, ex-*Rampart*), 4041 (*Abbeville*), 4061 (*Audemer*), 4062 (*Aachen*), 4073 (*Ardennes*), 4074 (*Antwerp*), 4085 (*Agedabia*), 4086 (*Arromanches*), which has a large lattice mast forward, 4097 (*Andalnes*), 4182 (*Arezzo*) and 4164 (*Arakan*) were transferred from the Royal Navy to the Army.

PHOTOGRAPHS. A photograph of *Arromanches* appears in the 1960-61 and 1961-62 editions and of *Akyab* in the 1965-66 to 1967-68 editions.

CLASS. *LCT* (8) 4042, 4045, 4050, 4148, 4156 and 4165 were stricken from the list in 1958, and 4025, 4049, 4063 and 4098 in 1960. *LCT* (8) 4063, *Jawada*, on loan to a commercial company, was for disposal at Bahrein. *Redoubt*, L 4001, was sold in 1966 as *Dimitris* 9, and *Sallyport*, L 4064, was sold in 1967 as *Fedra*. *Counterguard*, L 4043 was sold to Malaysia in 1965 and renamed *Sri Langkawi*. *Buttress*, L 4099, was sold to France, in July 1965 and renamed L 9061. *Parapet*, L 4039, was sold to La Société Maseline Ltd (Merchants), Sark, in 1966. *Bastion*, L 4040, was sold to Zambia on 15 Sep 1966. *Citadel*, L 4038, and *Portcullis*, L 4044, which were to have been converted into fleet degaussing vessels, were deleted from the Navy List in 1969. *Agedabia* L 4085 was sold and *Ardennes* L 4073 and *Arromanches* L 4086 were acquired by Singapore in 1970.

ANDALNES   *1969, Skyfotos*

AUDEMER   *1968, Skyfotos*

AGHEILA   *1968, John G. Callis*

L 3507 (see Col 2)   *1969, courtesy Dr Giorgio Arra*

Landing Craft—*continued*

14 LCM (9) TYPE

LCM (9) 700	**LCM (9) 703**	**LCM (9) 706**	**LCM (9) 710**
LCM (9) 701	**LCM (9) 704**	**LCM (9) 707**	**LCM (9) 711**
LCM (9) 702	**LCM (9) 705**	**LCM (9) 708**	**LCM (9) 3507**
		LCM (9) 709	**LCM (9) 3508**

Displacement, tons	75 light; 176 loaded
Dimensions, feet	77 pp; 85 oa × 21·5 × 5·5
Capacity	2 battle tanks or 100 tons of vehicles
Main Engines	2 Paxman 6 cyl. YHXAM diesels; 2 shafts; 624 bhp 10 knots
	Screws enclosed in Kort nozzles to improve manoeuvrability.

LCM (9) 3507 and LCM (9) 3508 were the first operational minor landing craft to be built since the Second World War. Ramped in the traditional manner forward, a completely enclosed radar-fitted wheelhouse is positioned aft. Upon completion they carried out familiarisation trials to perfect the new techniques required in launching and recovering LCMs from the flooded sterns of the parent assault ships. Four of the 700 Series allocated to assault ships.

CONSTRUCTION. The prototype, L 3507, was laid down in Apr. 1962 and accepted on 19 Mar 1963. L 3508 was begun in May 1962 and handed over on 6 June 1963. Both built by Vosper Ltd, Portsmouth. Twelve more of these craft have since been built, 700, 701, 702 and 703 by Brook Marine Ltd, Lowestoft (launched in 1965), 704, 705, 706, 707, 708 and 709 by Richard Dunston Ltd, Thorne (launched in 1965-66), and 710 and 711 by J. Bolson & Sons, Ltd, Poole (launched in Oct 1966).

DESIGN. A new type of Landing Craft Mechanized for operation with the Assault Ships recently built for the Royal Navy. Designed by Vosper Ltd in collaboration with the Royal Navy. The design was evolved as the result of the most exhaustive tank trials ever carried out on a landing craft. Scale models were made and operated by remote control in the Admiralty Experiment Works test tank at Haslar, using simulated wave conditions to prove the design in the roughest possible sea conditions, resulting in a design incorporating new standards of landing craft stability.

ENGINEERING. The Davey Paxman diesels are of the A6YHXAM type, the shafts being geared by a Vee-drive to enable the propulsion machinery to be placed as far aft as possible, an arrangement which provides a clear well deck for tanks and heavy transport carried in the new assault ships.

STEERING. Fitted with Kort rudders, which consist of a swivelling ring surrounding each of the two propellers and which replace conventional rudders. The Kort rudders produce more precise steering and control when going ahead or astern. The ring enclosing each propeller also provides protection when beaching in shallow water during disembarkation or recovery of tanks and heavy transport.

L 702 (F3)   *1967, Wright & Logan*

10 MRC (Ex-LCT)

SIMBANG (MRC 1100)

Maintenance and Repair Craft, former Tank Landing Craft, *Cana*, rated as Naval Servicing Craft (Engineering) was in Singapore reserve, now for disposal. *Medway* (ex-MRC 1110, ex-LCT, see photograph on page 280, 1966-67 edition) a Submarine Support Ship, was base ship Seventh Submarine Division, until relieved by *Forth* in 1966, but she was approved for disposal in 1970. *Simbang*, nominal depot ship, RN Air Station, Singapore. Also *MRC* 1013, 1015, 1023, 1097, 1098, 1119 (for disposal), 1120 and 1413 (ex-LCT (E) 413) used as a power and workshop, Malta, *MRC* 1122 was sold to Ghana in July 1956 and renamed *Asuantsi*. *Cana* (MRC 1109) was removed from the Navy List in 1968.

2 LCM (7) 7,000 SERIES (and NSB)

Displacement, tons	28 light; 63 loaded
Dimensions, feet	60·2 × 16 × 3·7
Main Engines	290 bhp = 9·8 knots

Nos. 7037, 7100. Three are employed as naval servicing boats and store carriers: 7037 (NSB 351), 7100 (NSB 359), 7104 (NSB 358). Some of the LCM (7) type were re-engined with Gray Marine diesels. 7087 and 7104 were removed from the list in 1968 and 7016 in 1969.

29 LCVP 100 SERIES

Displacement, tons	8·5 light; 13·5 full load; LCVP (ex-LCA (2)s 11·5 light, 16 full load
Dimensions, feet	41·5 LCVP (2)s; 43 × 10 × 2·5
Main Engines	130 bhp = 8 knots; LCVP (2)s: 2 Foden diesels, 200 bhp = 10 knots

There are 15 LCVP (1)s Nos 101 to 136 (103 and 118 were deleted from the list in 1969) and 14 LCVP (2)s, Nos 137 to 150. There were also a number of variations and prototypes of about the same length (43 feet).

Raiding Landing Craft, including LCR 5507 and 5508, and Navigational Landing Craft, including LCN 604 (ex-LCR 5505). LCA (1) 1275, 1330, 1481, 1485, 1644, 1678, 1705, 1712, 1733, 1745, 1779 and 1787 were for disposal in 1961, eleven more in 1963, and 1272, 1543, 1639, 1972 and 1891 in 1964, 1485 and 1700 in 1968. LCVP (2)s carried by *Intrepid* and *Fearless* can carry 35 troops or 2 Land Rovers. Crew 4. LCA (2)s were redesignated LCVPs (Landing Craft Vehicle and Personnel) in 1966.

2 LCP (L) 3 500 SERIES

Displacement, tons	6·5 light; 10 loaded
Dimensions, feet	37 × 11 × 3·2
Main Engines	225 bhp = 12 knots

There are two LCP (L) 3s Nos 501 and 503. Aurora gas turbines were installed in LCP (L) 3 No. 502.

LCP (L) No. 556 (6·5 tons light, 10 tons full load, 37 × 11 × 3·2 feet, 225 bhp, speed 12 knots) was officially deleted from the list in 1969.

FAST PATROL BOATS

TENACITY   1971, John G. Collis

1 VOSPER THORNYCROFT MISSILE TYPE

TENACITY

Displacement, tons	165 standard; 220 full load
Length, feet	130·0 wl; 142·0 deck, 144·5 oa
Beam, feet	26·6
Draught, feet	7·8
Missile launchers	4 (2 twin) "Sea Killer" surface-to-surface
Guns	2—35 mm (1 twin)
Main engines	3 Rolls Royce Proteus gas turbines; 3 shafts; 12 750 bhp = 40 knots max
	2 Maybach diesels on wing shafts for cruising = 16 knots
Range, miles	2 500 at 15 knots
Complement	27 (3 officers, 24 ratings)

Built as a private venture by Vosper Thornycroft. Launched on 18 Feb 1969 at Camber Shipyard, Portsmouth. Steel hull and aluminium alloy superstructure. Fully air-conditioned quarters. Taken over by the Royal Navy in mid Mar 1971.

2 "BRAVE" CLASS

BRAVE BORDERER P 1011   **BRAVE SWORDSMAN** P 1012

Displacement, tons	89 standard; 114 full load
Dimensions, feet	90·0 wl; 96·0 hull; 98·8 oa × 25·5 × 7·0 props
Armament	As MGB: 2—40 mm single guns in power operated mountings; 2—21 inch side launched torpedoes
	As MTB: 4—21 inch torpedoes; 1—40 mm gun
Main engines	3 Bristol Siddeley Proteus 1 250 gas turbines; 3 shafts; Fixed pitch propellers; 1 700 rpm; 10 500 shp = 52 knots max (46 knots continuous
Fuel, tons	25 capacity
Complement	20 (3 officers, 17 ratings)

Designed as convertible and interchangeable torpedo boats and gunboats. Built by Vosper Ltd, Portsmouth. The hull is framed in welded aluminium with double skinned planking of mahogany and sheathed with glass fibre below the waterline. An hydraulic operated flap fitted on the transom maintains the running trim. Very beamy in relation to length, the ratio being less than 1 : 4 only. *Brave Borderer* was launched on 7 Jan 1958 and accepted on 26 Jan 1960. Cost: £880 000. *Brave Swordsman* was launched on 22 May 1958 and handed over on 20 July 1960. Cost: £640 000. *Brave Borderer* was decommissioned on 2 Apr 1970 and laid up in reserve at Hythe in the summer and *Brave Swordsman* in the autumn.

BRAVE SWORDSMAN and BRAVE BORDERER   1968. Official

BRAVE SWORDSMAN   1969, Skyfotos

Fast Patrol Boats—continued

SCIMITAR   1971, Official

3 NEW CONSTRUCTION ANTI-FPB TYPE

CUTLAS   **SABRE**   **SCIMITAR**

Displacement, tons	102 full load
Dimensions, feet	90·0 wl; 103·5 oa × 27·7 (over rubbers) × 5·0
Main engines	2 Rolls Royce Proteus gas turbines = 40 knots; 2 shafts (2 Foden diesels for cruising in CODAG arrangement)
Endurance, miles	425 at 35 knots; 1 500 at 11·5 knots
Complement	12 (2 officers, 10 ratings)

Officially designated fast training craft. No armament. Hull of glued laminated wood construction. Design developed from that of "Brave" class fast patrol boats. Launched on 4 Dec 1969 (*Scimitar*), 18 Feb 1970 (*Cutlas*), 21 Apr 1970 (*Sabre*). All built by Vosper Thornycroft Group, Portchester Shipyard.

SABRE   1971, Vosper Thornycroft, Builders

"DARK" CLASS. The construction of the 19th boat, *Dark Horseman* was abandoned *Dark Aggressor*, *Dark Killer*, *Dark Rover* and *Dark Scout* were disposed of *Dark Antagonist*, *Dark Buccaneer*, *Dark Clipper*, *Dark Fighter*, *Dark Highwayman*, in the 1967 Navy List, were scheduled to be scrapped. *Dark Adventurer*, *Dark Hussar* and *Dark Intruder* (photograph in the 1968-69 and 1969-70 editions) in the 1970 Navy List are for sale. In Feb 1968 *Dark Avenger*, *Dark Biter*, *Dark Hunter* and *Dark Invader* were sold to Italy. *Dark Intruder* was in commission in 1966, *Dark Hero* was in commission in 1966 to 1968 and *Dark Gladiator* was in commission in 1967 to 1970 (in the 1st FPB Squadron with *Brave Borderer* and *Brave Swordsman*). Five boats of the "Dark" type were purchased by Burma and two by Finland.

EARIER CLASSES
Of the "Gay" class, *Gay Bruiser*, *Gay Centurion*, *Gay Dragoon* and *Gay Forester* were put on the sales list in 1961, and *Gay Archer*, *Gay Bombardier*, *Gay Bowman*, *Gay Carabineer* and *Gay Cavalier* on the disposal list in 1963. *Gay Charger*, *Gay Charioteer* and *Gay Fencer*, were latterly employed as fast target towing boats, and *Gay Charioteer* was still in the Spring 1970 Navy List. Of the "Bold" class, *Bold Pathfinder* was disposed of in 1962 and *Bold Pioneer* in 1958.

CUTLASS   1971, courtesy Mr. John G. Callis

COASTAL SURVEY SHIPS

FAWN   1969, Wright & Logan

BEAGLE   1969, Official

4 "FAWN" CLASS

BEAGLE A 319   **BULLDOG** A 317   **FAWN** A 325   **FOX** A 320

Displacement, tons	800 approx standard (official figure) ; 1 088 full load
Dimensions, feet	189 oa × 37·5 × 12
Main Engines	4 Lister Blackstone ERS8M, 8 cyl. 4 str. diesels, coupled to 2 shafts, 2 000 bhp = 15 knots max designed, controllable pitch propellers
Range, miles	4 000 at 12 knots cruising
Complement	38 (4 officers, 34 ratings)

A class of coastal survey ships for the charting of shallow waters. Designed for duty overseas, working in pairs. *Fawn* and *Fox* replaced the coastal minesweeper conversions. The names originally allocated were *Albacore, Albatross, Barracouta, Bulldog Fawn* and *Fox*, but these were changed in 1965 to *Beagle, Bulldog, Fawn, Fox, Pelican* and *Porcupine*, and the two latter were cancelled in 1967. The first ship of the class launched was *Bulldog* on 12 July 1967 at Brooke Marine Ltd, Lowestoft, followed by *Beagle* on 7 Sep 1967, *Fox* on 6 Nov 1967 and *Fawn* on 29 Feb 1968. *Bulldog* was commissioned on 21. Mar 1968 and the others by the end of 1968. Built to commercial standards. Lloyd's class 100 A1 and additionally to naval standards where applicable. Fitted with passive tank stabilizer to reduce rolling, most modern echo sounders, precision ranging radar, Decca "Hifix" system, automatic steering. Air conditioned throughout. Carries 28·5 ft survey motor launch in davits. Capable of hydrographic survey anywhere in the world. Designed for maximum habitability.

FOX   1969, Official

BULLDOG   1970, Official

Of the two coastal survey ships of the "Ton" class, modified coastal minesweepers, *Myrmidon* (ex-*Edderton*) was sold to Malaysia in 1968, and *Mermaid* (ex-*Sullington*) was officially approved for disposal by scrapping in 1968-69.

INSHORE SURVEY CRAFT

EGERIA   courtesy Dr. Ian S Pearsall

ENTERPRISE   1970, Official

3 "E CLASS

ECHO A 70   **EGERIA** A 72   **ENTERPRISE** A 71

Displacement, tons	120 standard ; 160 full load
Dimensions, feet	100·0 pp ; 106·8 oa × 22·0 × 6·8 max
Main engines	2 Paxman diesels ; 2 shafts ; controllable pitch propellers ; 700 bhp = 14 knots max ; 12 knots normal
Oil fuel, tons	15 capacity
Endurance, miles	1 600 at 10 knots
Complement	18 (2 officers, 16 ratings) ; accommodation for 22 (4 officers, 18 ratings)

Echo, the first Inshore Survey Craft, was built by J. Samuel White & Co Ltd, Cowes, launched on 1 May 1957, and commissioned on 12 Sep 1958. *Egeria* was built by Wm Weatherhead & Sons Ltd, Cockenzie, and *Enterprise* by M. W. Blackmore & Sons Ltd, Bideford. Of all-wood construction with glued laminated members. *Echo's* main machinery was manufactured by Davey Paxman & Co Ltd, Colchester. No armament, but was fitted with a 40 mm gun for trials and retains her gun seat. In wartime she could be used as an armed inshore minehunter on which her design was based. All built for coastal and harbour hydrographic surveys around the British Isles. Ability to navigate in shoal water, to obtain depths and detect wrecks on the sea bed, and to fix the position with accuracy. Equipped with two echo sounding machines and sonar for wreck location, and survey equipment for triangulation ashore. Modern radar, wire sweep gear, echo sounding launch, and modern chart room.

PHOTOGRAPHS. A photograph of *Echo* without armament appears in the 1968-69 to 1970-71 editions and a photograph as built with gun in the 1960-61 to 1967-68 editions.

WOODLARK   1971, Official

2 "HAM" CLASS

MODIFIED INSHORE MINESWEEPERS

WATERWITCH (ex-*Powderham*) M 304   **WOODLARK** (ex-*Yaxham*) M 2780

Displacement, tons	120 standard ; 160 full load
Dimensions, feet	107·5 oa × 22 × 5·5
Main Engines	Diesels ; 2 shafts ; 1 100 bhp = 14 knots
Endurance, miles	1 500 at 12 knots
Complement	18 (2 officers, 16 ratings)

Former inshore minesweepers of the "Ham" class converted to replace the old survey motor launches *Meda* and *Medusa* for operation in inshore waters at home. *Waterwitch*, ex-*M 2720*, was seconded to Port Auxiliary Service in 1968.

FLEET SUPPLY SHIPS

3 SUPPORT SHIPS (AFS)

LYNESS A 339	**STROMNESS** A 344	**TARBATNESS** A 345

Displacement, tons	circa 16 500 laden (official figure)
Measurements, tons	12 359 gross ; 4 744 net ; 7 782 deadweight
Dimensions, feet	490 pp ; 524 oa × 72 × 25·5
Aircraft	Facilities for helicopters
Main Engines	Wallsend-Sulzer 8-cyl RD.76 diesel ; 11 520 bhp = 17 knots
Complement	184

Ordered on 7 Dec 1964. Designed and built by Swan Hunter & Wigham Richardson Ltd, Wallsend-on-Tyne to meet specific requirements. All fitted with Sulzer type main machinery remotely controlled, and auxiliary machinery manufactured by Wallsend Slipway & Engineering Co Ltd. Lifts and mobile appliances provided for handling stores internally, and a new replenishment at sea system and a helicopter landing platform for transferring loads at sea. A novel feature of the ships is the use of closed circuit television to monitor the movement of stores. All air-conditioned. Lyness was launched on 7 Apr 1966, Stromness on 16 Sep 1966, and Tarbatness on 27 Feb 1967. Lyness was completed on 22 Dec 1966, Stromness on 21 Mar 1967.

LYNESS   1969. Official

TARBATNESS   1969, Official

STROMNESS   1971, Official

1 AIR STORES SUPPORT SHIP

RELIANT (ex-Somersby) A 84

Displacement, tons	4 447 light as built ; 13 737 full load
Measurement, tons	9 290 deadweight (summer), 8 460 gross
Dimensions, feet	440 pp ; 468·8 oa × 61·5 × 26·2
Main Engines	Doxford 6 cyl. diesel ; 8 250 bhp = 18 knots
Complement	110 officers and men

Built by Sir James Laing & Sons Ltd, Sunderland. Launched on 9 Sep 1953. Engined by Hawthorn Leslie. Completed in 1954. Former grain carrier which traded for two years, working between the Gulf of Mexico and the United Kingdom, before purchase from the Ropner Shipping Company. Converted for her now role at North Shields. Sailed from Chatham on 4 Nov 1958 for the Far East as the Royal Navy's first air/victualling stores issuing ship capable of replenishing aircraft carriers at sea. Has an endurance of 50 days steaming at 16 knots, and carries 40 000 different patterns of aircraft spares and general naval stores. Has six holds and the latest automatic tensioning winch for transfer of stores to aircraft carriers in unfavourable weather. Fully air-conditioned for service in the tropics. Her conversion was based on the concept that aircraft carriers should be able to spend more time at sea, independent of shore bases. Originally named Somersby. Renamed Reliant in 1958. As refitted she has a helicopter landing platform built over the poop deckhouse with netting surrounds.

RELIANT   1970, courtesy Godfrey H. Walker Esq.

---

2 REPLENISHMENT SHIPS

REGENT A 486	**RESOURCE** A 480

Displacement, tons	19 000 full load (deep departure)
Measurement, tons	18 029 gross
Dimensions, feet	600·0 pp ; 640·0 oa × 77·2 × 26·1
Aircraft	1 Wessex helicopter
Guns	2—40 mm Bofors (single)
Main engines	AEI steam turbines ; 20 000 shp = 20 knots
Complement	119 R.F.A. service and Merchant Navy officers and ratings ; 52 Navy Dept industrial and non-industrial civil servants ; 11 Royal Navy (1 officer and 10 ratings) for helicopter flying and maintenance

Ordered on 24 Jan 1963. Built by Scott's Shipbuilding & Engineering Co, Greenock, and Harland & Wolff, Belfast. They have lifts for armaments and stores, and helicopter platforms for transferring loads at sea. Designed from the outset as Fleet Replenishment Ships (previous ships had been converted merchant vessels). Air Conditioned. Resource was launched at Greenock on 11 Feb 1966, Regent at Belfast on 9 Mar 1966. Official title is Ammunition, Food, Explosives, Stores Ship (AFES).

RESOURCE   1969, Official

REGENT   1971, Official

2 FLEET REPLENISHMENT SHIPS

RESURGENT (ex-Changchow) A 280	**RETAINER** (ex-Chungking) A 329

Displacement, tons	14 000 (approx) official estimate
Measurement, tons	Resurgent 9 511 gross ; Retainer 9 301 gross
Dimensions, feet	451 pp ; 477·2 oa × 62 × 29 max
Main Engines	Doxford diesel ; 1 shaft ; 6 500 bhp = 15 knots
Oil fuel (tons)	925

Former passenger and cargo motor vessels, both built for the China Navigation Co by Scotts' Shipbuilding and Engineering Co Ltd, Greenock, and completed in 1951 and 1950, respectively. Retainer was formerly a passenger and cargo liner along the China coast. She was purchased in 1952 and converted into a naval storeship during autumn 1954-April 1955 by Palmers Hebburn Co Ltd, where further conversion was carried out Mar-Aug 1957 to extend her facilities as a stores ship, including the fitting out of holds to carry naval stores, the installation of lifts for stores, the provision of extra cargo handling gear and new bridge wings. Resurgent was taken over on completion for employment as a fleet replenishment ship. Official title is Store Support Ships.

RESURGENT   1971, Dr. Giorgio Arra

RETAINER   1970, Official

ARMAMENT SUPPORT SHIPS

2 "FORT" CLASS

FORT ROSALIE A 186   **FORT SANDUSKY** A 316

Displacement, tons	5 250 light; 9 788 normal (13 820 full load)
Measurement, tons	8 570 deadweight; 7 201 to 7 332 gross
Dimensions, feet	416 pp; 424·5 wl; 441·5 oa × 57 × 27
Main Engines	Triple expansion; 2 500 ihp = 11 knots
Boilers	2 Babcock & Wilcox

Both launched in 1944. *Fort Rosalie* and *Fort Sandusky* are Armament Support Ships. Rated as Royal Fleet Auxiliaries. Similar in type to the Maintenance Ships of the "Mull" and "Head" Classes, see earlier page.

PHOTOGRAPHS. A photograph of *Fort Dunvegan* appears in the 1960-61 to 1966-67 editions, of *Fort Duquesne* in the 1957-68 edition, of *Fort Langley* in the 1969-70 edition.

CLASS. *Fort Beauharnois* was scrapped in 1962, *Fort Constantine* was broken up at Hamburg im 1969. *Fort Charlotte* sold in 1968. *Fort Duquesne* was broken up in Holland in 1967. *Fort Dunvegan* in 1969. *Fort Langley* was returned to the Canadian Government, it was officially stated in 1970; she arrived at Bilbao, Spain, to be broken up on 21 July 1970.

FORT SANDUSKY   *1971, Official*

FORT ROSALIE   *1971, Official*

STORE CARRIERS

2 "BACCHUS" CLASS

BACCHUS A 404   **HEBE** A 406

Displacement, tons	2 740 light; 7 958 full load
Measurement, tons	4 823 gross; 2 441 net; 5 218 deadweight
Dimensions, feet	350 pp; 379 oa × 55 × 22 max
Main Engines	Swan Hunter Sulzer diesel; 1 shaft; 5 500 bhp = 15 knots
Oil fuel, tons	720
Complement	57

Built by Henry Robb Ltd, Leith, for the British India Steam Navigation Co. Taken over by the Royal Navy on completion on long term bare boat charter and operated as Royal Fleet Auxiliaries. Rated as dry cargo ships. *Bacchus* was completed in Sep 1962, *Hebe* in May 1962. Crew accommodation and engines aft as in tankers.

BACCHUS   *1970, courtesy Michael D. J. Lennon*

ROYAL YACHT

BRITANNIA A 00

Displacement, tons	3 990 light; 4 961 full load
Measurement, tons	5 769 gross
Dimensions, feet	360·0 pp; 380·0 wl; 412·2 oa × 55·0 × 17·0 max
Main engines	Single reduction geared turbines; 2 shafts; 12 000 shp = 21 knots continuous cruising; 22·75 knots max (trials)
Boilers	2
Radius, miles	2 100 at 20 knots; 2 400 at 18 knots; 3 000 miles at 15 knots
Oil fuel, tons	330 (490 with auxiliary fuel tanks)
Complement	270

Designed as a medium sized naval hospital ship for use by Her Majesty The Queen in peacetime as the Royal Yacht. Built by John Brown & Co Ltd, Clydebank. Ordered in Feb 1952. Laid down on 16 June 1952. Launched on 16 Apr 1953. Completed on 14 Jan 1954. Endurance sufficient to undertake long ocean voyages. Modified cruiser stern, and raked bow. Construction conformed to mercantile practice. The bridge structure and funnel are of aluminium. Fitted with Denny-Brown single fin stabilisers to reduce roll in bad weather from 20 deg to 6 deg. Cost £2 098 000. To pass under the bridges of the St. Lawrence Seaway when she visited Canada, the top 20 feet of her mainmast and the radio aerial on her foremast were hinged in Nov 1958 so that they could be lowered as required.

BRITANNIA   *1969, Wright & Logan*

NUCLEAR DECONTAMINATION VESSEL

MAC 1012

New construciton. Launched at Chatham early in 1971. Length 180 feet, beam 30 feet. To be used in connection with the disposal of radio active waste from the Chatham nuclear powered submarine refitting complex.

TANK CLEANING VESSELS

8 "ISLES" CLASS

2 *Ardrossan Dockyard Co Ltd, Ardrossan*		**1** *A. & J. Inglis Ltd, Glasgow*	
COLL A 333	7 Apr 1942	**SWITHA** A 346	3 Apr 1942
GRAEMSAY A 340	3 Aug 1942	**3** *John Lewis & Sons Ltd, Aberdeen*	
2 *Cook, Welton & Gemmell Ltd, Beverley*		**CALDY** A 332	31 Aug 1943
BERN	2 May 1942	**FOULNESS** A 342	23 May 1943
LUNDY A 366	29 Aug 1942	**SKOMER** A 338	17 June 1943

Displacement, tons	560 standard; 770 full load
Dimensions, feet	150 pp; 164 oa × 27·5 × 14
Main Engines	Triple expansion; 1 shaft; 850 ihp = 12 knots
Boilers	1 cylindrical
Coal, tons	183
Radius, miles	4 200 at 8 knots

Launch dates above. Former minesweeping trawlers converted to tank cleaning vessels. Classed as port auxiliary service craft and have "A" pennant numbers. Sister ship *Bardsey*, also converted, was taken over by Malta Dockyard. For transfers, disposals and other particulars of "Isles" class trawlers see 1961-62 edition.

PHOTOGRAPHS. A large photograph of *Graemsay* appears in the 1959-60 to 1961-62 editions and a port broadside view of *Skomer* in the 1962-63 to 1966-67 editions.

SWITHA   *1967, J. W. Kennedy*

HEBE (see Col. 1)   *1969, Official*

FLEET REPLENISHMENT OILERS

3 "OL" CLASS

OLMEDA (ex-*Oleander*) A 124   **OLNA** A 123
                        OLWEN (ex-*Olynthus*) A 122

Displacement, tons	10 890 light; 33 240 full load
Measurement, tons	22 350 deadweight; 18 600 gross
Dimensions, feet	611·1 pp; 648·0 oa × 84·0 × 34·0
Aircraft	2 Wessex helicopters (can carry 3)
Main engines	Pametrada double reduction geared turbines; 26 500 shp = 19 knots (21·2 on trials)
Boilers	2 Babcock & Wilcox, 750 lbs sq in, 950 deg F
Complement	87 (25 officers and 62 ratings)

Largest and fastest ships when they joined the Royal Fleet Auxiliary Serviec. *Olmeda* was launched on 19 Nov 1964 and completed on 18 Oct 1965 by Swan Hunter, Wallsend, with machinery by Wallsend Slipway & Eng Co Ltd, while *Olna* and *Olwen* were launched on 28 July 1965 and 10 July 1964 and completed on 1 Apr 1966 and 21 June 1965, respectively, by Hawthorn Leslie, Hebburn, engined by Hawthorn Leslie (Engineers) Ltd.
A novel class designed by Hawthorn Leslie and Swan Hunter to meet specified requirements. Designed for support of the Fleet, with handling gear for transferring fuels and stores by jackstay and derricks whilst steaming at speed. A helicopter landing platform and hangar enable ships to collect stores by air. Sophisticated machinery control systems, including bridge control of ahead revolutions. Specially strengthened for operations in ice. Accommodation of a high standard, fully air conditioned. *Olna* has a tranverse bow thrust unit for improved manoeuvrability in confined waters and a new design of replenishment at sea systems. *Olwen*, originally named *Olynthus*, was renamed in Sep 1967 to obviate confusion with the submarine *Olympus* in correspondence and by telephone and *Olmeda*, originally named *Oleander*, was renamed to avoid confusion with the frigate *Leander*.

OLWEN   *1969, Skyfotos*

OLNA   *1969, Official*

OLMEDA   *1971, Official*

2 LATER "TIDE" CLASS

TIDESPRING A 75   **TIDEPOOL** A 76

Displacement, tons	8 531 light; 25 931 full load
Measurement, tons	17 400 deadweight; 14 130 gross
Dimensions, feet	550·0 pp; 583·0 oa × 71·0 × 32·0
Main engines	Double reduction geared turbines; 15 000 shp = 17 knots
Boilers	2 Babcock & Wilcox
Complement	115 (30 officers and 85 ratings)

Built by Hawthorn Leslie, Hebburn with machinery by Hawthorn Leslie (Engineers) Ltd. Highly specialised ships for fuelling (13 000 tons cargo fuel) and storing naval vessels at sea and capable of high performance under rigorous service conditions. Their all-round capability is enhanced by a helicopter platform and hangar. *Tidespring* was laid down on 24 July 1961, launched on 3 May 1962, and accepted on 18 Jan 1963. *Tidepool* was laid down on 4 Dec 1961 and launched on 11 Dec 1962.

TIDEPOOL   *1971, Official*

Fleet Replenishment Oilers—*continued*

TIDESPRING   *1969, Official*

3 "TIDE" CLASS

TIDEFLOW (ex-*Tiderace*) A 97   **TIDESURGE** (ex-*Tiderange*) A 98
                                         TIDEREACH A 96

Displacement, tons	9 040 light; 25 940 full load
Measurement, tons	16 900 deadweight; 13 700 gross
Dimensions, feet	550 pp; 583 oa × 71 × 32 max.
Main Engines	Double reduction geared turbines; 15 000 shp = 17 knots

Tidereach, launched by Swan, Hunter & Wigham Richardson Ltd, Wallsend-on-Tyne, on 2 June 1954, and completed on 30 Aug 1955, was the first of the new Fleet Replenishment Tankers. The main machinery was manufactured by the Wallsend Slipway Co. Designed for the support of the Fleet and replenishment under way at sea. Capacious (15 000 tons of fuel cargo) and fitted with modern handling gear for transferring food, stores, ammunition, oil and jet aircraft fuels by jackstay and derricks. Oil cargo can be discharged at high rate to ships on either beam or astern, while steaming at speed. *Tiderange* (renamed *Tidesurge*) in 1958 was launched at I. L. Thompson & Sons Ltd, Sunderland, on 30 Aug 1954. the main machinery of both being manufactured by North Eastern Marine Engineering Co Ltd, Wallsend. A fourth ship, *Tide Austral*, built for Australia, was renamed *Supply* on 7 Sep 1962.

TIDEREACH refuelling *Hermes*   *1969, Official*

TIDEFLOW   *1969, Wright & Logan*

TIDESURGE   *1970, Official*

Oilers—*continued*
5 "LEAF" GROUP
2 "LONDON" CLASS

BAYLEAF (ex-*London Integrity*) A 79 **BRAMBLELEAF** (ex-*London Loyalty*) A 81

Measurement, tons	17 960 deadweight; 12 123 gross; 7 042 net
Dimensions, feet	526 pp; 556·7 oa × 71·3 × 30
Main Engines	Doxford 6-cyl. diesel; 6 800 bhp — 14·5 knots (*Bayleaf*); 14 knots (*Brambleleaf*)
Oil fuel (tons)	1 470

Both built by Furness S.B. Co Ltd. *Bayleaf* was launched on 28 Oct 1954 and completed in Apr 1955. *Brambleleaf* was completed in Jan 1954. Both from London & Overseas Freighters Ltd, 22 May 1959.

BAYLEAF   *1971, Wright & Logan*

BRAMBLELEAF   *1969, Wright & Logan*

ORANGELEAF (ex-M.V. *Southern Satellite*) A 80

Measurement, tons	17 475 deadweight; 12 481 gross; 6 949 net
Dimensions, feet	525 pp; 556·5 oa × 71·7 × 30·5 mean
Main Engines	Doxford 6-cyl. diesel; 6 800 bhp = 15 knots
Oil fuel (tons)	1 610

Built by Furness Shipbuilding Co Ltd, Haverton Hill on Tees. Launched on 8 Feb 1955. Completed June 1955. From South Georgia Co Ltd, 25 May 1959.

All "Leaf" class tankers have astern fuelling capabilities. *Pearleaf* and *Plumleaf* also have abeam fuelling capabilities.

CLASS. The oiler *Cherryleaf*, A 82 (ex-MV *Laurelwood*) was returned to her original owners (Molasses & General Transport Co Ltd) in 1966 and sold to Greek interests. The oiler *Appleleaf*, A 83 (ex-MV *George Lyras*), the first of the "Leaf" class acquired by the Royal Navy, taken over in 1959, was returned to her original owners in Jan 1970.

ORANGELEAF   *1971, Official*

Oilers—*continued*
"Leaf" Group—*continued*

PEARLEAF A 77

Displacement, tons	24 900 full load
Measurement, tons	18 045 deadweight; 12 139 gross; 7 216 net
Dimensions, feet	535 pp; 568 oa × 71·7 × 30
Main Engines	Rowan Doxford 6-cyl. diesels; 8 800 bhp = 15·8 knots

Built by Scotstoun Yard of Blythswood Shipbuilding Co Ltd, for Jacobs and Partners Ltd, London. Launched on 15 Oct 1959 and completed in Jan 1960. Chartered by the Royal Navy on completion. Can carry three different grades of cargo.

PEARLEAF   *1966, Wright & Logan*

PLUMLEAF A 78

Displacement, tons	24 920 full load
Measurement, tons	18 562 deadweight; 12 692 gross
Dimensions, feet	534 pp; 560 oa × 72 × 30
Main Engines	N.E. Doxford 6-cyl diesels; 9 350 bhp = 15·5 knots

Built by Blyth DD & Eng Co Ltd. Launched 29 Mar 1960. Completed July 1960.

PLUMLEAF   *1969, Wright & Logan*

1 "EDDY" CLASS

EDDYFIRTH A 261

Displacement, tons	1 960 light; 4 160 full load
Measurement, tons	2 300 gross; 2 200 deadweight
Dimensions, feet	270 pp; 286 oa × 44 × 17·2
Main engines	1 set triple expansion; 1 shaft; 1 750 ihp = 12 knots
Boilers	2 oil burning cylindrical

Royal Fleet Auxiliary. Built by Lobnitz & Co Ltd, Renfrew Launched on 10 Sep 1953 and completed on 10 Feb 1954. Constructed on the combined transverse and longitudinal system of framing and classed 100 A1 at Lloyd's for the carriage of petroleum in bulk. Cargo capacity: 1 650 tons oil.

ENGINEERING. The main propelling machinery was built by Lobnitz & Co Ltd, Renfrew and boilers by Caledon Shipbuilding & Engineering Co Ltd, Dundee.

CLASS. *Eddybay*, *Eddybeach*, *Eddycliffe*, *Eddycreek* and *Eddyreef* were disposed of in 1963 and 1964. *Eddyrock* was sold in 1967. *Eddyness* was sold for scrap in 1970.

EDDYFIRTH   *1971, John G. Callis*

For disposal of older naval tankers and other classes of oilers, including the old "Dale" class, see 1966-67 and earlier editions. It was officially stated that the old oil tanker *Bishopdale* of the Early "Dale" class, discarded in 1967, was for disposal by sale in 1969. She was broken up at Bilbao, Spain, in 1970.

Oilers—continued

2 "DALE" CLASS

DEWDALE   *1971, Official*

DERWENTDALE (ex-M.V. *Halcyon Breeze*)

Displacement, fons	88 555 full load
Measurement, tons	28 288 net; 42 343 gross; 72 550 deadweight
Dimensions, feet	761·0 pp; 799·0 oa × 117·8 × 42·3
Main engines	B. & W. 9 cyl diesels; 1 shaft; 20 700 bhp = 15·5 knots
Complement	56

Commercial oil tanker built by Hitachi, Japan. Launched on 8 Jan 1964. Taken over by Great Britain in 1967. Chartered for Royal Fleet Auxiliary Service from the Court Line.

DEWDALE (ex-M.V. *Edenfield*)

Measurement, tons	21 542 net; 35 805 gross; 63 588 deadweight
Dimensions, feet	747·0 pp; 774·5 oa × 107·8 × 41·5
Main engines	B. & W. 9 cyl diesels; 1 shaft; 17 000 bhp = 15 knots
Complement	51

The Ministry of Defence (Royal Navy) chartered three large tankers (announced on 13 July 1967) for service East of Suez, and renamed them, re-introducing traditional "Dale" class names. After limited modifications the ships operated in the Indian Ocean area. But *Ennerdale* sank on 1 June 1970 after striking a submerged hazard in the Indian Ocean. Manned by Royal Fleet Auxiliary personnel and wear the Blue Ensign. Officially rated as Mobile Bulk Tankers.

DERWENTDALE refuelling *Bulwark*   *1969, Official*

DEWDALE   *1969, Wright & Logan*

"SURF" CLASS
It was officially stated in 1970 that the two oilers of the "Surf" class, *Surf Patrol* (ex-*Tatry*) A 357 and *Surf Pioneer* (ex-*Beskidy*) A 365 had been sold.

Oilers—continued

3 "WAVE" CLASS

Name	No.	Builders	Launched
WAVE BARON (ex-*Empire Flodden*)	A 242	Furness SB Co Ltd, Haverton Hill on Tees	19 Feb 1946
WAVE CHIEF (ex-*Empire Edgehill*)	A 265	Harland & Wolff, Ltd Govan, Glasgow	4 Apr 1946
WAVE PRINCE (ex-*Empire Herald*)	A 207	Sir James Laing & Sons Ltd, Sunderland	27 July 1945

Displacement, tons	4 750 light; 8 200 standard; 16 650 full load
Measurement, tons	11 900 deadweight; 8 447 gross
Dimensions, feet	465·3 pp; 492·5 oa × 64·5 × 28·5
Main engines	Double reduction geared turbines; 6 800 shp = 14·5 knots
Boilers	Three-drum type

Classed as Royal Fleet Auxiliaries. Launch dates above. *Wave Baron* and *Wave Chief* are fleet replenishment tankers, *Ware Prince* was a freighter. Turbines of Metrovick type in *Wave Baron*, *Wave Chief*, Parsons in *Wave Prince*. *Wave Baron* and *Wave Prince* were modernised in 1961-62. *Wave Victor* was lent to the Air Ministry as a hulk at Gan Island. *Wave Prince* and *Wave Baron* are in reserve. *Wave Ruler* was reduced to a hulk in Oct 1970.

WAVE BARON   *1969, Official*

WAVE PRINCE   *1969, courtesy Dr. Giorgio Arra*

WAVE CHIEF rigged with replenishment hoses   *Official*

CLASS. *Wave Commander* and *Wave Liberator* were scrapped in 1959. *Wave Conquerer* and *Wave King* were sold in 1960. *Wave Emperor, Wave Governor, Wave Premier* and *Wave Regent* were scrapped in 1960. *Wave Monarch* was sold to foreign interests in 1961. *Wave Protector* was broken up in Italy in 1963. *Wave Knight* was broken up at Antwerp in 1964. *Wave Master* was scrapped in 1964. *Wave Sovereign* was sold in 1967, *Wave Duke* and *Wave Laird* were sold for scrap in 1970.

Oilers—*continued*

3 NEW CONSTRUCTION. "ROVER" CLASS

GREEN ROVER A 269   **GREY ROVER** A 268   **BLUE ROVER** A 270

Displacement, tons	11 522 full load
Measurement, tons	3 185 net; 7 060 deadweight; 7 510 gross
Dimensions, feet	461·0 × 63·0 × 24·0
Main engines	2 Ruston & Hornsby 16 cyl. uni-directional diesels; 1 shaft; controllable pitch propeller; 16 000 bhp = 19 knots
Complement	42 (16 officers and 26 men) of the Royal Fleet Auxiliary

Small fleet tankers designed to replenish HM ships at sea with fuel, fresh water, limited dry cargo and refrigerated stores under all conditions while underway. A helicopter landing platform is provided, served by a stores lift, to enable stores to be transferred at sea by helicopter. Built at Swan Hunter, Hebburn-on-Tyne, *Green Rover* was launched on 19 Dec 1968, *Grey Rover* on 17 Apr 1969, and *Blue Rover* on 11 Nov 1969.

BLUE ROVER   *1971, John G. Callis*

GREY ROVER   *May, 1970, Wright & Logan*

GREEN ROVER   *1970, Official*

1 LATER SMALL "OL" CLASS

ROWANOL (ex-*Cedarol*, ex-*Ebonol*) A 284

Displacement, tons	2 670
Measurement, tons	1 638 deadweight; 1 440 gross
Dimensions, feet	218 pp; 232 oa × 39 × 15·8
Main engines	Triple expansion; 1 140 ihp = 11 knots
Complement	26

Built by Lobnitz & Co Ltd, Renfrew. Launched on 15 May 1946. Officially rated as a port oiler, but in reserve and likely to be disposed of in the near future. Her three sister ships, *Birchol*, *Oakol* and *Teakol* were sold in 1969.

ROWANOL   *courtesy, Dr. Aldo Fraccaroli*

Oilers—*continued*

4 "RANGER" CLASS

BLACK RANGER (22 Aug 40) A 163 **BROWN RANGER** (12 Dec 40) A 169
BLUE RANGER (29 Jan 41) A 157 **GOLD RANGER** (12 Mar 41) A 130

Displacement, tons	6 630 full load
Measurement, tons	3 313 to 3 417 gross. *Gold Ranger*: 3 788 deadweight; others: 3 435 to 3 781 deadweight
Dimensions, feet	*Gold Ranger*: 339·5 pp; 355·2 oa × 47·0 × 20·0 Others 349·5 pp; 365·8 oa × 47·0 × 20·0
Main engines	Burmeister & Wain diesels; 2 750 bhp = 12 knots

Classed as Royal Fleet Auxiliaries. Fleet Attendant Tankers. Built by Harland & Wolff Ltd, Govan, Glasgow, except *Gold Ranger* by Caledon S.B. & Eng Co Ltd, Dundee. Launch dates above. The funnel is on the port side. All fitted with special derrick on the beam to facilitate fuelling at sea. *Gray Ranger* was lost during the Second World War. *Green Ranger* was deleted from the list in 1965. *Blue Ranger* is in reserve and may be disposed of soon.

BLACK RANGER   *1967, courtesy Godfrey H. Walker, Esq.*

GOLD RANGER   *1969, Official*

BROWN RANGER   *1969, courtesy Dr. Giorgio Arra*

BLUE RANGER   *Added 1969, A. & J. Pavia*

6 COASTAL TYPE. "OILPRESS" CLASS

OILBIRD	**OILMAN**	**OILSTONE**
OILFIELD	**OILPRESS**	**OILWELL**

Displacement, tons	280 standard; 530 full load
Dimensions, feet	130·0 wl; 139·5 oa × 30·0 × 8·3
Main engines	1 Lister Blackstone ES6 diesel; 1 shaft; 405 shp at 900 rpm
Complement	11 (4 officers and 7 ratings)

Ordered on 10 May 1967 from Appledore Shipbuilders Ltd. Three are diesel oil carriers and three FFO carriers.

MOORING, SALVAGE AND BOOM VESSELS

4 "WILD DUCK" CLASS

GARGANEY P 194   **GOLDENEYE** P 195   **MANDARIN** P 192   **PINTAIL** P 193

Displacement, tons	950
Measurement, tons	283 deadweight
Dimensions, feet	150 pp; 168·2 excluding horns × 36·5 × 10·8
Main engines	1 Davey Paxman 16 cyl diesel; 1 shaft; controllable pitch propeller; 550 bhp = 10 knots
Complement	24 (6 officers, 6 petty officers, 12 ratings)

Mandarin was the first of a new class of marine service vessels. Launched on 17 Sep 1963 and handed over on 5 Mar 1964. *Pintail* was launched on 3 Dec 1963. Both built by Cammell Laird & Co Ltd, Birkenhead. Designed to be used for mooring, salvage and boom work. Previously these three tasks were separately undertaken by specialist vessels, but the new type is able to give all three services. Capable of laying out and servicing the heaviest moorings used by the Fleet and also maintaining booms for harbour defence. Heavy lifting equipment enables a wide range of salvage operations to be performed, especially in harbour clearance work. The special heavy winches have an ability for tidal lifts over the apron of 200 tons. *Garganey* and *Goldeneye* (port auxiliary service, civilian crew) were built in 1966-67 by Brooke Marine Ltd, Lowestoft.

GOLDENEYE   *1967, Wright & Logan*

MANDARIN   *1969, Official*

GARGANEY   *1969, Official*

LAYBURN   *1967, A. & J. Pavia*

2 "LAY" CLASS

LAYBURN P 191   **LAYMOOR** P 190

Displacement, tons	800 standard; 1 050 full load
Dimensions, feet	160 pp; 192·7 oa × 34·5 × 11·5 feet
Main engines	Triple expansion; 1 shaft; 1 300 ihp = 10 knots
Boilers	2 Foster Wheeler "D" type; 200 psi
Complement	2 officers; 29 to 34 ratings

Both built by Wm. Simons & Co Ltd (Simons-Lobnitz Ltd). The first boom defence vessels designed and built since the Second World War. *Laymoor* was the first and "name" ship of her class. *Layburn*, which cost £565,000 was launched on 14 Apr 1960 and completed on 7 July 1960. *Laymoor* which cost £562,000 was launched on 6 Aug 1959 and accepted on 9 Dec 1959. In addition to minor salvage work and towing net sections, can lay and maintain the latest types of underwater and surface boom defences, first class moorings and navigational buoys. Detailed specifications of the propulsion plant appear in the 1966-67 and earlier editions. Designed for naval or civilian manning. Lifting capacity is greater than that of predecessors, improvement in accommodation enables them to be operated in any climate.

LAYBURN   *1970, Official*

LAYMOOR   *1969, courtesy Dr. Giorgio Arra*

3 "MOOR" CLASS

MOORHEN A 489   **MOORLAND** A 491   **MOORSMAN** P 284

Displacement, tons	*Moorsman:* 1 040 light; 1 510 full load *Moorhen:* 650 standard; 900 full load *Moorland:* 600 standard; 800 full load
Dimensions, feet	*Moorsman:* 196·0 oa × 35·5 × 13·5 *Moorhen:* 149 pp; 159 oa hull × 30 × 12 (196 oa horns) *Moorland:* 135·0 pp; 145·0 oa hull × 30·0 × 12·0
Main engines	*Moorhen, Moorland:* 500 ihp = 9 knots *Moorsman:* 1 000 hp = 10 knots

Built in 1938-46. Displacement and dimensions vary. Employed as Mooring, Salvage and Boom Vessels. Fitted with salvage pumps, air compressors and diving equipment. *Moorsman* is of the larger type built by H.M. Dockyard, Chatham. *Moorland* was built by Goole Shipbuilding & Repair Co Ltd. *Moorhen* and *Moorland* were Port Auxiliary Service craft at Malta and Gibraltar, respectively. *Moorsman*, at Greenock, is also civilian manned. *Moorhen* and *Moorland* were earmarked for disposal in 1970.

CLASS. *Moordale* was sold in 1961. *Moorburn* for disposal in 1962, *Mooress* and *Moorfowl* in 1963. In 1963 *Moorcock* was broken up at Troon, *Moorfield* was sold to Pounds, *Moorfire* was broken up on the Forth, *Moorfly* was sold as *Sophia G*, *Moorgrass* was broken up at Troon, *Moorgrieve* was sold and became *Octopus* in 1965, *Moorhill* was sold as Portuguese mercantile, *Moormyrtle* was broken up at Cork and *Moorside* was broken up on the Forth. *Moorpout* was for disposal in 1968.

MOORHEN   *1967, Wright & Logan*

Mooring, Salvage and Boom Vessels—*continued*

4 "BAR" CLASS

BARBAIN P 201   **BARFOOT** P 202   **BARFOIL** P 294   **BARMOND** P 232

Displacement, tons	750 standard; 1 000 full load
Dimensions, feet	150 pp; 173·8 oa; 182 over horns × 23·2 × 11·5
Main engines	Triple expansion; 850 ihp = 11 knots (Sea speed 9 knots)
Boilers	2 single ended (200 lbs per sq in)
Fuel, tons	214 coal (*Barfoam* and *Barmond* converted to oil in 1966)
Radius, miles	3 000
Complement	32

Launched by Blyth DD & SB Co on 8 Jan 1940, John Lewis & Sons Ltd, Aberdeen on 25 Sep 1942, Philip & Son Ltd, Dartmouth on 18 July 1942, and Wm Simons & Co Ltd, Renfrew on 24 Dec 1942, respectively.
Bow lift of 27 to 70 tons. *Barhill* and *Barndale* were Port Auxiliary Service Craft. *Barfoot* and *Barmond* are also civilian manned.

TRANSFERS. *Barbrake* and *Barcross* were transferred to South Africa, *Barbarian*, *Barbette* (first of this name in the class, launched on 15 Dec 1937) and *Barfair* to Turkey, *Baron* to Ceylon in 1958 (purchased by the Colombo Port Commission).

CLASS. *Barflake* and *Barlight* were lost during the Second World War. *Barbour*, *Bardell* and *Barricade* were discarded. *Barberry*, *Barbrook*, *Barcombe*, *Barford*, *Baritone*, *Barlane*, *Barlow*, *Barmill*, *Barneath* and *Barnwell* were for disposal in 1958, *Barilla* and *Baronia* in 1959, *Bartholm* and *Barstoke* in 1960, *Barbette* (second of this name in the class, accepted into service on 12 July 1943). *Barbridge*, *Barcastle*, *Barcock*, *Barcote*, *Barcroft*, *Bardolf*, *Barlake*, *Barsing*, *Barsound*, *Barthorpe* and *Barrier* in 1962, *Barbourne*, *Barclose*, *Barking*, *Barspear* and *Barwind* in 1963, *Barbastel*, *Barfount*, *Barkis*, *Barleycorn*, *Barmouth*, *Barnaby*, *Barnehurst*, *Barova*, *Barranca* and *Barrhead* in 1964, *Bartisan* in 1966, *Baricarole*, *Barcliffe*, *Barbican*, *Barfoam* and *Barfoss* in 1969, *Barnstone* in 1969, *Barrington* in 1970, *Barbecue*, *Barfield*, *Barglow*, *Barhill*, *Barnard*, *Barndall* and *Barrage* in 1971.

BARFOOT   *Official*

BARRAGE   *1969, courtesy Dr. Giorgio Arra*

SUCCOUR   *1969, John G. Callis*

7 "KIN" CLASS

DISPENSER		**KINGARTH** 22 May 44		**SUCCOUR** 18 Aug 43	
KINBRACE 11 Jan 45		**KINLOSS** 14 Apr 45		**SWIN** 25 Mar 44	
				UPLIFTER 29 Nov 43	

Displacement, tons	950 standard; 1 050 full load
Measurement, tons	775 gross; 262 deadweight
Dimensions, feet	150·0 pp; 179·2 oa × 35·2 × 9·5 mean; 12·0 max
Main engines	*Kinbrace, Kingarth, Kinloss, Uplifter*: 1 British Polar Atlas M44M diesel; 630 bhp = 9 knots; Others: Triple expansion; 1 shaft; 600 ihp = 9 knots
Boilers	1 return tube cylindrical (30 ton) in others
Complement	34

Originally classified as Coastal Salvage Vessels, but re-rated Mooring, Salvage and Boom Vessels in 1971. Launch dates above. Equipped with horns and heavy rollers. Can lift 200 tons dead weight over the bow. *Kinbrace, Kingarth, Kinloss* and *Swin* were built by A. Hall, Aberdeen, *Succour* and *Uplifter* by Smith's Dock Co Ltd. *Uplifter* was the only salvage vessel wearing the White Ensign. She was laid down on 13 Feb 1943, and completed on 6 Apr 1944. (*Kingarth* wore the White Ensign in 1957). *Dispenser* was on charter to Liverpool & Glasgow Salvage Association, but returned in 1971. *Succour* and *Swin* were Royal Fleet Auxiliaries wearing the Blue Ensign. *Kinloss* is in the Port Auxiliary Service as a mooring vessel. *Kinbrace, Kingarth* and *Uplifter* were refitted with diesel engines in 1966-67, and *Kinloss* in 1963-64.
A photograph of *Kingarth* appears in the 1959-60 and earlier editions, of *Swin* in the 1956-57 and earlier editions, and of *Uplifter* in the 1960-61 to 1962-63 editions.

CLASS. *Lifeline* was on the disposal list in 1960. Sister ship *Help* was broken up in Holland in 1968.

KINLOSS   *1966, Wright & Logan*

OCEAN SALVAGE VESSELS

SALVEDA

Displacement, tons	1 250 standard; 1 360 full load
Dimensions, feet	184 pp; 194 oa × 34·5 × 11·2 mean
Main Engines	1 200 hp = 12 knots
Oil fuel, tons	150
Complement	62

Built by Cammell Laird & Co Ltd, Birkenhead, and launched on 9 Feb 1943. Formerly a Royal Fleet Auxiliary ocean salvage vessel on charter to Metal Industries Ltd. In the Spring 1970 Navy List, in reserve.

2 "SALV" CLASS

SALVALOUR   **SEA SALVOR**

Displacement, tons	1 440 standard; 1 700 full load
Measurement, tons	1 122 gross
Dimensions, feet	200·2 pp; 216·0 oa × 37·8 × 13·0 max
Main engines	Triple expansion; 2 shafts; 1 500 ihp = 12 knots
Oil fuel, tons	310
Complement	72

Ocean salvage vessels. Launched in 1942-45. *Salvalour* and *Sea Salvor* were built by Goole Shipbuilding & Repair Co Ltd, and launched on 2 Nov 1944 and 22 Apr 1943, respectively. *Sea Salvor* is a Royal Fleet Auxiliary. *Salvalour* is in reserve.

TRANSFERS. *Salventure* was loaned to the Royal Hellenic Navy and renamed *Sotir*. *King Salvor*, converted to a submarine rescue bell ship in 1953-54 and renamed *Kingfisher*, was sold to Argentina in Dec 1960, sailing to Argentina in Apr 1961 under the new name *Tehuelche* (again renamed *Guardiamarina Zicari* in 1963).

CLASS. *Salvage Duke*, formerly on charter to Turkish Salvage Administration (renamed *Imroz*), was gutted by fire in 1959. *Ocean Salvor* and *Salviola* were disposed of in 1960, and *Prince Salvor* and *Salvigil* were sold in 1968. *Salvestor* and *Salvictor* were sold in July 1970 to Ward (Briton Ferry).

SEA SALVOR   *1970, courtesy Dr. Aldo Fraccaroli*

DIVING TRIALS SHIP
MODIFIED OCEAN SALVAGE VESSEL

RECLAIM (ex-*Salverdant*) A 231

Displacement, tons	1 200 standard; 1 800 full load
Dimensions, feet	200 pp; 217·8 oa × 38 × 15·5
Main engines	Triple expansion; 2 shafts; 1 500 ihp = 12 knots
Oil fuel, tons	310
Radius, miles	3 000
Complement	84

CONSTRUCTION. Built by Wm. Simons & Co Ltd, Renfrew. Engined by Aitchison Blair Ltd. Laid down on 9 Apr 1946. Launched on 12 Mar 1948. Completed in Oct 1948. Her construction was based on the design of a "King Salvor" class naval ocean salvage vessel. She was the first deep diving and submarine rescue vessel built as such for the Royal Navy. She is fitted with sonar, radar, echo-sounding apparatus for detection of sunken wrecks, and equipped for submarine rescue work.
RECLASSIFICATION. Formerly a tender to H.M.S. *Vernon* shore establishment at Portsmouth for deep diving experiments, and subsequently a deep diving vessel in the Portsmouth Squadron. Reclassified as a Mine Countermeasure Support and Diving Trials Ship in 1960, and attached to HMS *Lochinvar*, the minesweeping base at Port Edgar, but her mine countermeasures functions were taken over in 1968 by the minelayer *Abdiel*. Carried out deep diving experiments in the Canary Islands in Jan to Mar 1961.

RECLAIM   1967, Wright & Logan

CABLE SHIPS
2 "BULL" CLASS

BULLFINCH (19 Aug 1940) A 176   **ST. MARGARETS** (13 Oct 1943) A 259

Displacement, tons	1 300 light; 2 500 full load
Measurement, tons	1 524 gross; 1 200 deadweight
Dimensions, feet	228·8 pp; 252 oa × 36·5 × 16·3 mean
Main Engines	Triple expansion; 2 shafts; 1 250 ihp = 12 knots

Royal Fleet Auxiliaries. Both built by Swan, Hunter & Wigham Richardson Ltd. Launch dates above. *Bullfrog* and *Bullhead* of this type were transferred to Cable and Wireless service in 1947. Provision was made for mounting one 4 inch gun and four 20 mm AA guns but no armament is fitted.

BULLFINCH   1970, Official

ST. MARGARETS   1967, A. & J. Pavia

HOVERCRAFT

It was officially announced on 16 June 1967 that:— "A civilian type SRN 6 Hovercraft has been ordered by the Ministry of Defence and will be delivered by the British Hovercraft Corporation within the next few weeks, when the Royal Navy's first operational Hovercraft Unit will be formed. It will be taken in hand for modification for Service use at the Royal Naval Aircraft Yard, Fleetlands, Gosport, including the installation of radar and military communications equipment for its primary role of a fast amphibious communication craft to support Royal Marine units. It will not be armed as its role will not involve belligerent use". Particulars given were:—Length 48 feet, beam 23 feet, Rolls Royce Marine Gnome engines of 900 hp = 50 knots, range 200 miles.
It was stated by the Minister of Technology on 4 Apr 1968 that the Government would order a BH-7 hovercraft as a naval patrol vessel.
It was reported on 15 Feb 1970 that the first "hover warship", costing about £700 000 was to be delivered to the Inter-Service Hovercraft Trials Unit at the Royal Naval Air Station, Lee-on-Solent, in Apr 1970. She could be used as a missile armed fast patrol craft or amphibious assault craft.

EXPERIMENTAL TRIALS VESSELS
1 NEW CONSTRUCTION

CRYSTAL RDV 01

Displacement, tons	3 040 deep (revised official figures)
Dimensions, feet	410·0 wl; 413·5 × 56·0 × 5·5
Complement	60, including scientists

Unpowered floating platform for Sonar Research and Development. Built at H.M. Dockyard, Devonport. Ordered in Dec 1969. Begun in Mar 1970 for completion in Sep 1971. A harbour-based laboratory without propulsion machinery or steering which will provide the Admiralty Underwater Weapons Establishment at Portland with a stable platform on which to carry out acoustic tests and other research projects.

1 LCT TYPE

WHIMBREL (ex-*NSC* (E) 1012)

Displacement, tons	300 (official figure)
Dimensions, feet	190 × 30 × 4·5

Experimental Trials Vessel. Basically of the tank landing craft LCT(3) Type.

WHIMBREL   1968, A. & J. Pavia

1 COASTAL TYPE

ICEWHALE

Displacement, tons	289 standard; 350 full load
Dimensions, feet	120 × 24 × 9
Main Engines	Speed = 9 knots
Complement	12 (Master, Mate and 10 ratings)

Experimental Trials Vessel for the Underwater Weapons Establishment, Portland.

ICEWHALE   1968, John G. Callis

1 TORPEDO TYPE

SAREPTA (ex-*Frieda Peters*)

Displacement, tons	465 standard
Dimensions, feet	150 pp; 157 oa × 27·5 × 12
Tubes	4—21 inch

Ex-German. Launched in 1920. Multi-purpose torpedo experimental, firing, and recovery vessel. Reclassified as RTV in 1966.

SAREPTA   1970, Official

SRN6   1971, Official

STORE CARRIERS

THOMAS GRANT

Displacement, tons	209 light; 461 full load
Measurement, tons	252 deadweight; 218 gross
Dimensions, feet	113·5 × 25·5 × 8·8
Main Engines	2 diesels; Speed = 9 knots

Built as a local store carrier by Charles Hill & Sons Ltd, Bristol. Launched on 11 May 1953 and completed in July 1953. Turned over to the Port Auxiliary Service in 1959 under Dockyard administration at Portsmouth. Converted into a torpedo recovery vessel in 1968.

THOMAS GRANT   *Added 1969, Official*

ROBERT DUNDAS A 204   ROBERT MIDDLETON A 241

Displacement, tons	900 light; 1 900 full load
Measurement, tons	1 000 deadweight; 1 125 gross
Dimensions, feet	210 pp; 222·5 oa × 35 × 13·5 mean
Main Engines	Atlas Polar Diesel; 1 shaft; 960 bhp = 10·5 knots
Oil fuel, tons	60
Complement	17

Coastal store carriers. Both built by Grangemouth Dockyard Co Ltd. Machinery by British Auxiliaries Ltd, Govan. Launched on 28 July and 29 June 1938, respectively. *Robert Middleton* 220 ft oa. Royal Fleet Auxiliaries. A photograph of *Robert Dundas* appears in the 1966-67 to 1968-69 editions.
The degaussing vessels DGV 400, 401 and 403 (ex-MMS 1002, 1003 and 1011, respectively) were deleted from the list in 1969, having been replaced by IMS *Fordham*, *Thatcham* and *Warmingham*. DGV 402 (ex-MMS 1004) was stricken in 1963.

ROBERT MIDDLETON   *1969, courtesy Godfrey H. Walker Esq.*

ARMAMENT CARRIERS

KINTERBURY A 378   THROSK

Displacement, tons	1 490 standard; 1,770 full load
Measurement, tons	600 deadweight
Dimensions, feet	185 pp; 199·8 × 34·3 × 13
Main Engines	Triple expansion; 1 shaft; 900 ihp = 11 knots
Coal, tons	154

Launched on 14 Nov 1942 and in 1943 and completed on 4 Mar 1943 and 22 Dec 1943, respectively. Both built by Philip & Son Ltd. Rated as naval armament carriers. Converted in 1959 with hold stowage and a derrick for handling guided missiles for attending and servicing the guided weapons trials ship *Girdle Ness*. A photograph of *Kinterbury* appears in the 1963-64 to 1966-67 editions.

THROSK   *1968, John G. Callis*

BALLISTA   CATAPULT   MATCHLOCK
BOWSTRING   FLINTLOCK   SPEAR

Of various displacements and particulars. In PAS. *Blowpipe* and *Obus* sold.

Armament Carriers—continued

MAXIM A 377   NORDENFELT A 135

Displacement, tons	604 to 663
Measurement, tons	340 deadweight
Dimensions, feet	131·5 to 144·5 × 25 × 8
Main Engines	Reciprocating; 500 ihp = 9 knots
Complement	13

Built by Lobnitz & Co Ltd, Renfrew. Launched on 6 Aug 1945 and 30 Nov 1945, respectively. *Chattenden* was reduced in 1961 to a dumb derrick lighter. *Snider* was disposed of in 1968. *Enfield* was sold in 1969. *Gatling* was broken up at Cork in 1970.

WATER CARRIERS

4 "WATER" CLASS

WATERFALL Y 17   WATERSIDE Y 20
WATERSHED Y 18   WATERSPOUT Y 19

Measurement, tons	285 gross
Dimensions, feet	123 pp, 131·5 oa × 24·8 × 8
Main engines	Diesels; 1 shaft; 1 100 bhp = 11 knots

Built by Drypool Engineering & Drydock Co, Hull. Launched on 30 Mar 1966, 3 Aug 1966, 20 June 1967 and 29 Dec 1966, respectively.

WATERSHED   *1969, Wright & Logan*

4 "SPA" CLASS

SPALAKE (10 Aug 1946) A 260   SPABROOK (24 Aug 1944) A 224
SPAPOOL (28 Feb 1946) A 222   SPABURN (5 Jan 1946) A 257

Displacement, tons	1 219 full load
Measurement, tons	630 deadweight; 672 to 719 gross
Dimensions, feet	160 pp; 172 oa × 30 × 12
Main Engines	Triple expansion; 675 ihp = 9 knots
Coal, tons	90

Spalake and *Spapool* were built by Charles Hill & Sons Ltd, Bristol and *Spabrook* and *Spaburn* by Philip & Son Ltd, Dartmouth. *Spapool* is with the Port Auxiliary Service. *Spabeck*, high test peroxide carrier for the experimental submarine *Explorer*, was disposed of in May 1966. *Spa* was for disposal in 1970. A photograph of *Spalake* appears in the 1967-68 to 1970-71 editions.

SPAPOOL   *1971, Official*

6 "FRESH" CLASS

FRESHBURN   FRESHMERE   FRESHPOOL
FRESHLAKE   FRESHPOND   FRESHSPRING

Displacement, tons	594
Dimensions, feet	126·2 × 25·5 × 10·8 max
Main Engines	Triple expansion; 450 ihp = 9 knots

Freshspring was converted from coal to oil fuel, in 1961. A photograph of *Freshpond* appears in the 1951-52 to 1953-54 editions and of *Freshlake* in the 1963-64 to 1965-66 editions. *Freshbrook* and *Freshnet* were stricken in 1963, *Freshwater* and *Freshwell* sold in 1968, and *Freshford*, *Freshspray* and *Freshtarn* in 1969. *Freshener* was for disposal in 1971.

FRESHPOOL   *1966, courtesy Dr. Giorgio Arra*

TUGS

3 NEW CONSTRUCTION OCEAN TUGS

ROBUST	ROLLICKER	ROYSTERER

Displacement, tons	1 630 full load
Dimensions, feet	162·0 pp; 178·0 oa × 38·5 × 21·3
Main engines	2 Mirrlees KMR 6 diesels (by Lister Blackstone Mirrlees Marine Ltd); 2 shafts; 4 500 bhp at 525 rpm = 15 knots
Endurance, miles	13 000 nautical at 12 knots
Complement	31 (10 officers and 21 ratings) (and able to carry salvage party of 10 RN officers and ratings)

Roysterer is the biggest and most powerful ocean tug ever built for the Royal Navy. Built by Charles D. Holmes at Beverley Shipyard, Hull. Launched on 20 Apr 1970. Designed principally for salvage and long range towage but can be used for general harbour duties. Sister ocean tugs *Robust* and *Rollicker*, launched on 29 Jan 1971, are being built under the 1969 new construction programme. These vessels are now part of the Royal Maritime Auxiliary Service and no longer Royal Fleet Auxiliary.

TYPHOON A 95

Displacement, tons	800 standard; 1 380 full load
Dimensions, feet	181·0 pp; 200·0 oa × 40·0 × 13·0
Main engines	2 turbocharged vee type 12-cyl diesels; 1 shaft; 2 750 bhp = over 16 knots

Built by Henry Robb & Co Ltd, Leith. Launched on 14 Oct 1958. Completed in 1960. Diesels manufactured by Vickers-Armstrongs Ltd, Barrow-in-Furness. The machinery arrangement of two diesels geared to a single shaft was an innovation for naval ocean tugs. Controllable pitch propeller, 150 rpm. Fitted for fire fighting, salvage and ocean rescue, with a heavy mainmast and derrick attached. Bollard pull 32 tons. Now in the Royal Maritime Auxiliary Service and no longer a Royal Fleet Auxiliary.

TYPHOON   1970, Official

5 "CON" CLASS

ACCORD	ADVICE	CONFIANCE (15 Nov 1955) A 289
	AGILE	CONFIDENT (17 Jan 1956) A 290

Displacement, tons	760 full load
Dimensions, feet	140·0 pp; 154·8 oa × 35·0 × 11·0
Main engines	4 Paxman HAXM diesels; 2 shafts; 1 800 bhp = 13 knots
Complement	29 plus 13 salvage party

Confiance and *Confident* were built by A. & J. Inglis Ltd, Glasgow. Launch dates above. *Confiance* was completed on 27 Mar 1956. Fitted with 2·50 m diam Stone Kamewa controllable pitch propellers. *Accord, Advice* and *Agile*, formerly rated as dockyard tugs, were officially added to the "Confiance" class in 1971 as they are now part of the Royal Maritime Auxiliary Service ocean towing force. See photograph of *Agile* in the 1969-70 and 1970-71 editions.

CONFIANCE   1970, courtesy Godfrey H. Walker Esq

CONFIDENT   1969, courtesy Michael D. J. Lennon Esq.

Of the tugs of the "Envoy" class, *Enticer* was lost on 21 Dec 1946, *Enforcer* and *Enigma* were stricken from the list in 1963, *Envoy* was sold in 1965 as *Matsas*, and *Encore* was sold in 1968 as *Salvaliant*.

Tugs—*continued*

3 "SAMSON" CLASS

SAMSON (14 May 1953) A 390	SEA GIANT (2 June 1954) A 288
	SUPERMAN (23 Nov 1953)

Displacement, tons	1 200 full load
Measurement, tons	850 gross
Dimensions, feet	165 pp; 180 oa × 37 × 14
Main Engines	Triple expansion; 2 shafts; 3 000 ihp = 15 knots

All built and engined by Alexander Hall & Co Ltd, Aberdeen. Launch dates above. A photograph of *Sea Giant* appears in the 1963-64 to 1970-71 editions.

SUPERMAN   Added 1969, Official

SAMSON   1971, Official

3 "NIMBLE" CLASS

CAPABLE (22 Nov 1945) A 508	NIMBLE (4 Dec 1941) A 223
CAREFUL (23 Oct 1945) A 293	

Displacement, tons	890 standard; 1 190 full load
Dimensions, feet	165 pp 175 oa × 35·8 × 13·8
Main Engines	Triple expansion; 2 shafts; 3 500 ihp = 16 knots
Boilers	2 of 3-drum type
Oil fuel, tons	300

Capable was built by Hall Russell, *Careful* by A. Hall & Co, *Nimble* by Flemming & Ferguson. Launch dates above. *Capable* was fitted experimentally with controllable pitch propellers. *Expert* was disposed of in Oct 1968.

NIMBLE   1969, A. & J. Pavia

CAPABLE   1967, Skyfotos

Tugs—*continued*

4 "BUSTLER" CLASS

BUSTLER (4 Dec 1941) A 240   **SAMSONIA** (1 Apr 1942) A 218
CYCLONE (ex-*Growler*, 10 Sep 1942) A 111   **REWARD** 13 Oct 1944) A 264

Displacement, tons	1 118 light; 1 630 full load
Dimensions, feet	190·0 pp; 205·0 oa × 40·2 × 16·8
Main engines	2 Atlas Polar 8-cyl diesels; 1 shaft; 4 000 bhp = 16 knots
Oil fuel, tons	405
Range, miles	17 000
Complement	42

All built by Henry Robb Ltd, Leith. Launch dates above. *Growler*, temporarily renamed *Caroline Moller* while on long term charter, then renamed *Castle Peak*, was returned to RFA service in 1957, then renamed *Welshman* and chartered to the United Towing Co Ltd, and again renamed *Cyclone* on return to Royal Fleet Auxiliary service in 1964. Most of this class, including *Reward*, to United Towing Co Ltd in 1963, and *Turmoil* to Overseas Towage & Salvage Co, were chartered by commercial undertakings. *Bustler* wears the Blue Ensign. Of this class, *Hesperia* was lost during the Second World War, and HMS *Mediator* the last tug to sail under the White Ensign and not the Blue Ensign of the Royal Fleet Auxiliary Service, was paid off in 1964 and sold in 1968 as *Nisos Zakynthos*. *Turmoil* was sold in 1965 as *Nisos Kerkyra*. *Warden* was disposed of in Nov 1969.

CYCLONE   *1969, A. & J. Pavia*

Small fleet servicing and coastal harbour tugs include *Empire Ace* (ex-*Diligent*), *Empire Demon*, *Empire Fred*, *Empire Rosa*, *Frisky* (ex-*Empire Rita*) and *Resolve* (ex-*Empire Zona*), but not all are of the same type.

Tugs in the Port Auxiliary Service include: *Bombshell, Cannon, Chainshot, Diver, Driver, Eminent, Fidget, Foremost, Freedom, Grapeshot, Handmaid, Impetus, Integrity, Prompt, Resolve, Security, Tampeon, Trunnion, Vagrant* and *Weasel*. Also the water tractor *Felicity*, a small Improved "Girl" class small berthing tug for basin work built by Richard Dunstan Ltd, Hull.

BOXER ("Dog" Class)   *1969, Skyfotos*

FORCEFUL   *1969, courtesy, Dr. Giorgio Arra*

Tugs employed on harbour service and in H.M. Dockyards, include the diesel-electric paddle tugs, *Dextrous, Director, Faithful, Favourite, Forceful, Grinder* and *Griper*: twin screw diesel dockyard tug, *Adept*: medium berthing tugs *Airedale, Alsation, Basset, Beagle, Boxer, Cairn, Collie, Corgi, Dalmation, Deerhound, Elkhound, Husky, Labrador, Mastiff, Pointer, Saluki, Setter, Sheepdog, Spaniel, Sealiham*, ("Dog" class); and harbour berthing tugs *Agatha, Agnes, Alice, Audrey, Barbara, Betty, Brenda, Bridget* ("Girl" class); *Celia, Charlotte, Christine, Clare, Daisey, Daphne, Doris, Dorothy, Edith*) Improved "Girl" class).

FLEET TENDERS

6 100 ft "INSECT" CLASS

BEE   **CICALA**   **CRICKET**   **GNAT**   **LADYBIRD**   **SCARAB**

All built by C. D. Holmes Ltd, Beverley, Yorks in 1970-71, first three as stores carriers, two as armament carriers and *Scarab*, due Nov 1971, as mooring vessel.

BEE   *1971, John G. Callis*

35 "ABERDOVEY" CLASS

ABERDOVEY	BIBURY	DATCHET	FINTRY
ABINGER	BLAKENEY	DENMEAD	FOTHERBY
ALNESS	BRODICK	DORNOCH	FROXFIELD
ALNMOUTH	CARTMEL	DUNSTER	FULBECK
APPLEBY	CAWSAND	ELKSTONE	GLENCOVE
ASHCOTT	CLOVELLY	ELSING	GRASMERE
BEAULIEU	CRICCIETH	EPWORTH	LOYAL FACTOR
BEDDGELERT	CRICKLADE	ETTRICK	LOYAL GOVERNOR
BEMBRIDGE	CROMARTY	FELSTED	

Measurmeent, tons	70 gross
Dimensions, feet	75·0 pp; 79·2 oa × 18·0 × 5·5
Main engines	1 Lister Blackstone 4-cyl diesel; 210 bhp = 10·5 knots

Built in 1963-71 by Isaac Pimblott & Sons, Northwich (all six A names, all but two C names, *Glencove* and *Loyal Governor*), J. Lewis, Aberdeen (Cromarty, Dornoch, Fintry, Grasmere), R. Dunston (*Dunster* and three F names), C. D. Holmes (*Cricklade, Denmead, Fulbeck*), *Loyal Factor*, J. Cook, Wivenhoe (all four E names), Vosper Thornycroft (*Datchet*, diving tender). The two "Loyals" are RNXS. J. S. Doig Ltd, Grimsby (all six B names). Built to Lloyd's Register requirements. Designed to carry 25 tons deadweight (or up to 3 000 cu ft) of stores or 200 standing passengers in addition to two 21 inch torpedoes each weighing 1·8 tons. Sixty fleet tenders are being built over ten years to replace the old MFVs. A photograph of *Beaulieu* appears in the 1965-66 to 1967-68 edition, and of *Alness* in the 1968-69 and 1969-70 editions.

APPLEBY   *1971, Wright & Logan*

61 MFV TYPES

MFV 2, 9, 15, 57, 63, 74, 84, 88, 93, 96, 97, 119, 123, 133, 136, 139, 140, 158, 175, 205, 238, 256, 278, 289, 323
     Length: 61·5 feet   25 in port auxiliary service
MFV 642, 658, 686, 687, 715, 737, 740, 742, 767, 773, 775, 815, 816, 867, 911, 944
     Length: 45 feet   16 in port auxiliary service
MFV 1021, 1033, 1037, 1048, 1051, 1057, 1062, 1077, 1079, 1151, 1164, 1190, 1206, 1215, 1219, 1255, 1256, 1257
     Length: 75 feet   18 in port auxiliary service
MV 1527, 1544
     Length: 90 feet   2 in port auxiliary service

MFV 1151, Squirrel and *MVF 1080, Watchful* were used as Fishery Protection Gunboats until replaced. *MFVs* 105, 1021 and 1528 were deleted from the list in 1969, 7, 43, 45, 64, 65, 627, 657, 673 and 1254 in 1970, and 1015 in 1971.

REGARD   *1969, Wright & Logan*

UNITED STATES OF AMERICA

Compiled and Edited by Norman Polmar

ADMINISTRATION

Commander-in Chief:
The President of the United States

Secretary of Defense:
Melvin R. Laird

Secretary of the Navy:
John H. Chafee

Under Secretary of the Navy:
John W. Warner

PRINCIPAL FLAG OFFICERS

Chairman, Joint Chiefs of Staff:
Admiral Thomas H. Moorer, USN

Chief of Naval Operations:
Admiral Elmo R. Zumwalt, Jr, USN

Vice Chief of Naval Operations:
Admiral Ralph W. Cousins, USN

Deputy Chief of Naval Operations (Manpower and Naval Reserve):
Vice Admiral Dick H. Guinn, USN

Deputy Chief of Naval Operations (Submarines):
Vice Admiral Philip A. Beshany, USN

Deputy Chief of Naval Operations (Surface):
Vice-Admiral Benedict J. Semmens, Jnr, USN

Deputy Chief of Naval Operations (Air):
Vice Admiral Maurice F. Weisner, USN

Deputy Chief of Naval Operations (Logistic):
Vice Admiral Ralph L. Shifley, USN

Deputy Chief of Naval Operations (Plans and Policy):
Vice Admiral Francis J. Blovin, USN

*Commander-in-Chief Atlantic and Commander-in-Chief Atlantic Fleet:
Admiral Ephraim P. Holmes, USN

*Commander-in-Chief Pacific:
Admiral John S, McCain, Jr., USN

Commander-in-Chief Pacific Fleet:
Admiral Bernard A. Clarey, USN

Commander First Fleet (Eastern Pacific):
Vice Admiral Raymond E. Peet, USN

Commander Second Fleet (Atlantic):
Vice Admiral Vincent de Poix, USN

Commander Sixth Fleet (Mediterranean):
Vice Admiral Gerald E. Miller, USN

Commander Seventh Fleet (Western Pacific):
Vice Admiral William P. Mack, USN

Commander Military Sealift Command:
Vice Admiral Arthur R. Gralla, USN

Oceanographer of the Navy:
Rear Admiral William W. Behrens, Jnr, USN

MARINE CORPS

Commandant of the Marine Corps:
General Leonard F. Chapman, Jr USMC

Assistant Commandant of the Marine Corps:
General Raymond G. Davis, USMC

Chief of Staff:
Lieutenant General John Chaisson, USMC

MATERIÉL

Chief of Naval Materiél:
Admiral Isaac C. Kidd, Jnr, USN

Commander Naval Air Systems Command:
Rear Admiral Thomas R. McCellan, USN

Commander Naval Electronic Systems Command:
Rear Admiral Joseph E. Rice (ED), USN

Commander Naval Facilities Engineering Command:
Rear Admiral Alexander C. Husband, CEC, USN

Commander Naval Ordnance Systems Command:
Rear Admiral Mark W. Woods, USN

Commander Naval Ship Systems Command:
Rear Admiral Nathan Sonenshein (ED), USN

Commander Naval Supply Systems Command:
Rear Admiral Bernhard H. Bieri, Jr, SC, USN

Diplomatic

US Naval Attaché and Naval Attaché for Air in London:
Rear Admiral Filmore B. Gilkeson

US Naval Attaché and Naval Attaché for Air in Moscow:
Captain Franklin G. Babbitt, USN

US Naval Attaché and Naval Attaché for Air in Paris:
Captain Peter P. Cummins, USN

NOTE: *Unified Command with the Commander-in-Chief directing all US Army, Navy, and Air Force activities in the area. Only naval officers serving as Unified Commanders-in-Chief are listed.

STRENGTH OF THE FLEET

The following table provides a tabulation of the ship strength of the United States Navy and an index to the ship listings within the United States section of this edition. Ship arrangement is based on function and employment; the official arrangement of ship types is contained in the "List of classifications of naval ships and service craft" which appears on a later page in this section. Numbers of ships listed in the table are estimated as of 1 July 1971 based on official and unofficial sources.

Category-Type		Active a	Building b	Reserve
COMMAND AND COMMUNICATION SHIPS				
AGF	Miscellaneous Flagships	1	—	—
CC	National Command Ships	—	—	2
AGMR	Communication Relay Ships	—	—	2
STRATEGIC WARFARE SHIPS				
SSBN	Ballistic Missile Submarines	41	—	—
SUBMARINES				
SSN	Attack Submarines (nuclear)	52	11	1
SSN	Research Submarines (nuclear)	2	—	—
SS'	Attack Submarines (diesel post-war)	12	—	—
SS	Attack Submarines (diesel war-built)	30	—	—
SSG	Guided Missile Submarines (diesel)	—	—	1
LPSS	Transport Submarines	1	—	1
AGSS	Research Submarines	3	—	—
AGSS	Auxiliary Submarines	—	—	5
SST	Training Submarines	3	—	—
AIRCRAFT CARRIERS				
CVAN	Attack Carriers (nuclear)	1	2	—
CVA	Attack Carriers	13	—	1
CVS	Anti-Submarine Carriers	3	—	8
CVT	Training Carriers	1	—	—
SURFACE COMBATANTS				
CG	Missile Cruisers	3	—	—
CGN	Missile Cruisers (nuclear)	1	—	—
CLG	Light Missile Cruisers	4	—	2
DLGN	Missile Frigates (nuclear)	2	2	—
DLG	Missile Frigates	28	—	—
DL	Frigates (all-gun)	—	—	3
DDG	Missile Destroyers	29	—	—
DD	Destroyers (all-gun)	127	9	76
OCEAN ESCORTS				
DEG	Missile Escort Ships	6	—	—
DE-AGDE	Escort Ships (all-gun)	55	21	—
DE-DER	Escort Ships (war-built)	2	—	124
FIRE SUPPORT SHIPS				
BB	Battleships	—	—	4
CA	Heavy Cruisers	1	—	12
LFR	Rocket Ships	—	—	9
AMPHIBIOUS WARFARE SHIPS				
LCC	Amphibious Command Ships	3	—	4
LHA	Amphibious Assault Ships	—	5	—
LPH	Amphibious Assault Ships	7	—	—
LKA	Amphibious Cargo Ships	6	—	13
LPA	Amphibious Transports	3	—	10
LPR	Amphibious Transports (Small)	—	—	11
LPD	Amphibious Transports Dock	15	—	—
LSD	Dock Landing Ships	11	2	11
LST	Tank Landing Ships	27	7	31
LANDING CRAFT				
PATROL SHIPS AND CRAFT				
PG	Patrol Gunboats	17	—	—
PGH	Patrol Gunboats (hydrofoil)	2	—	—
PCH-AGEH	Research Ships (hydrofoil)	2	—	—
PTF	Fast Patrol Craft	18	—	—
RIVERINE WARFARE CRAFT				
SEAL SUPPORT CRAFT				
MINE WARFARE SHIPS				
MCS	Mine Countermeasure Ships	—	—	1
MSO	Ocean Minesweepers	32	—	19
MSC	Coastal Minesweepers	13	—	1
MSF	Fleet Minesweepers (war-built)	—	—	29
MINE WARFARE CRAFT				
UNDERWAY REPLENISHMENT SHIPS		62	6	20
FLEET SUPPORT SHIPS		89	5	63
FLOATING DRY DOCKS				
LOGISTIC SUPPORT SHIPS		96	—	5
EXPERIMENTAL, RESEARCH AND SURVEYING SHIPS		43(c)	3	2
SERVICE CRAFT				
SUBMERSIBLES AND DEEP SUBMERGENCE VEHICLES				

NOTES: (a) Includes ships undergoing overhaul and refuelling in the case of nuclear-powered ships; also includes approximately 30 destroyers, four ocean escorts, and 25 minesweepers assigned to Naval Reserve training. (b) Generally includes only those ships laid down or already being fabricated in the case of DD 963 and LHA 1 classes that are being constructed by modular assembly techniques. (c) Does not include the non-operational carrier Bunker Hill which is a moored test ship.

PERSONNEL

	30 June 1970 (Actual)	30 June 1971 (Estimated)	30 June 1972 (Estimated)
Navy			
Officers	80 536	74 250	73 646
Enlisted men	607 443	554 072	525 659
Naval Academy midshipmen	4 243	4 243	4 243
Marine Corps			
Officers	24 941	21 649	19 863
Enlisted men	234 796	189 899	186 452

MERCANTILE MARINE

Lloyd's Register of Shipping: 2 983 vessels of 18 463 207 tons gross.

SHIP PROGRAMMES

Fiscal Year 1972 New Construction Programme

5 Nuclear-Powered Attack Submarines (SSN 688 class)
1 Nuclear-Powered Guided Missile Frigate (DLGN 38 class)
7 Destroyers (DD 963 class)
1 Replenishment Oiler (AOR 1 class)
2 Submarine Tenders (AS 36 class)
3 Salvage and Rescue Tugs (ATS 1 class)

Fiscal Year 1972 Conversion Programme

2 Guided Missile Frigates (DLG) to improve AAW capability
6 Nuclear-Powered Fleet Ballistic Missile Submarines (SSBN) to Poseidon capability

Fiscal Year 1971 New Construction Programme

1 Nuclear-Powered Guided Missile Frigate (DLGN)
4 Nuclear-Powered Attack Submarines (SSN)
6 Destroyers (DD)
2 Amphibious Assault Ships (LHA)
2 Oceanographic Research Ships (AGOR)

Fiscal Year 1971 Conversion Programme

6 Nuclear Powered Fleet Ballistic Missile Submarines (SSBN) to Poseidon capability
4 Guided Missile Frigates (DLG) to improve AAW capability

The original FY 1971 programme has been modified as reflected above.

Fiscal Year 1970 New Construction Programme

1 Nuclear-Powered Attack Carrier (CVAN)
1 Nuclear-Powered Guided Missile Frigate (DLGN)
3 Destroyers (DD)
3 Nuclear-Powered Attack Submarines (SSN)
2 Amphibious Assault Ships (LHA)

Fiscal Year 1970 Conversion Programme

4 Nuclear-powered Fleet Ballistic Missile Submarines (SSBN) to Poseidon capability
1 Guided Missile Fragate (DLG) to improve AAW capability
5 Ocean Minesweepers (MSO)

The original FY 1970 programme has been modified to reflect the above data.

Fiscal Year 1969 New Construction Programme

5 Destroyers, DX
2 Nuclear-powered Attack Submarines, SSN
1 Amphibious Assault Ship, LHA
4 Fast Deployment Logistic Ships, FDL

Fiscal Year 1969 Conversion Programme

2 Nuclear-Powered Fleet Ballistic Missile Submarines, SSBN, to Poseidon capability
1 Guided Missile Frigate, DLG, to Terrier HT
1 Submarine Tender, AS, to Poseidon support
1 Cargo Ship, T-AK, to Poseidon support
1 Range Instrumentation Ship, T-AGM, to support Poseidon

Of the original FY 1969 programmes, the following ships were either deferred or cancelled; new construction: 5 destroyers (DX), 1 All-Weather Patrol Boat (PB), 1 Destroyer Tender (AD), 1 Submarine Tender (AS), 4 Fast Deployment Logistic Ships (FDL); conversions: 4 Fleet Ballistic Missile Submarines (SSBM) to Poseidon capability, 10 Ocean Minesweepers (MSO).

Fiscal Year 1968 New Construction Programme

2 Nuclear-Powered Attack Submarines, SSN
1 Nuclear-Powered Attack Submarine, SSN, electric drive
1 Nuclear-Powered Guided Missile Frigate, DLGN
2 Ammunition Ships, AE
1 Fast Combat Support Ship, AOE
2 Oceanographic Research Ships, AGOR
1 Submarine Rescue Ship, ASR

Fiscal Year 1968 Conversion Programme

1 Guided Missile Frigate, DLG, to Terrier HT
9 Ocean Minesweepers, MSO
1 Submarine Tender, AS, to Poseidon support
6 Destroyers, DD, improved ASW

Of the original FY 1968 programmes, the following ships were either deferred or cancelled: new construction: 10 Escort Ships (DE), 7 Ocean Minesweepers (MSO), 9 All-Weather Patrol Boats (WPB); conversion: 3 Fleet Ballistic Missile Submarines (SSBN) to Poseidon capability; 1 Destroyer (DD) to improved ASW capability.

SPECIAL NOTES

United States Navy Ships that are in active commission are indicated by an asterisk next to the particular ship's name. It should be noted that this marking for active ships applies ONLY to the United States section of *Jane's Fighting Ships*.

The introductory passages in the United States section of this edition are based primarily on official United States government statements and congressional hearings on the Fiscal Year 1972-1976 Defence Programme and the Fiscal Year 1972 Defence Budget. Any interpretation of these statements and hearings is solely the responsibility of the Compiler and Editor of the United States section, Mr. Norman Polmar.

MAJOR SHIPYARDS

Naval Shipyards

Boston Naval Shipyard, Boston, Massachusetts
Charleston Naval Shipyard, Charleston, South Carolina
Hunters Point Naval Shipyard, San Francisco, California (formerly a division of the San Francisco Bay Naval Shipyard and before that the San Francisco Naval Shipyard)
Long Beach Naval Shipyard, Long Beach, California
Mare Island Naval Shipyard, Vallejo, California (formerly a division of the San Francisco Bay Naval Shipyard)
Norfolk Naval Shipyard, Norfolk, Virginia
Pearl Harbour Shipyard, Pearl Harbour, Hawaii
Philadelphia Naval Shipyard, Philadelphia, Pennsylvania
Portsmouth Naval Shipyard, Portsmouth, New Hampshire (located in Kittery, Maine)
Puget Sound Naval Shipyard, Bremerton, Washington

(Note: Only three of the above shipyards now are engaged in new construction, Mare Island, Philadelphia, and Puget Sound; the others are employed in the overhaul and conversion of warships and auxiliaries).

Commercial Shipyards

Avondale Shipyards, Inc, New Orleans, Louisiana
Bath Iron Works Corp, Bath, Maine
Bethlehem Steel Corp, Sparrows Point, Maryland
General Dynamics Corp, Electric Boat Division, Groton, Connecticut (formerly Electric Boat Company)
General Dynamics Corp, Quincy Shipbuilding Division, Quincy, Massachusetts (formerly Bethlehem Steel Corp Yard)
Ingalls Shipbuilding Corp (Litton Industries), East Bank Yard, Pascagoula, Mississippi
Ingalls Shipbuilding Corp (Litton Industries), West Bank Yard, Pascagoula, Mississippi
Lockheed Shipbuilding & Construction Co, Seattle, Washington
National Steel & Shipbuilding Co, San Diego, California
Newport News Shipbuilding & Dry Dock Co, Newport News, Virginia
Todd Shipyards Corp, San Pedro, California
Todd Shipyards Corp, Seattle, Washington

(Note: All of the above yards are engaged in naval and commercial shipbuilding, overhaul, and modernisation except for the General Dynamics/Electric Boat yard which is engaged only in submarine work).

TREPANG (SSN 674)   *1970, United States Navy*

CLASSIFICATION OF NAVAL SHIPS AND SERVICE CRAFT

The following is the official US Navy list of classifications of naval ships and service craft as promulgated by the Secretary of the Navy.
In actual usage, symbols preceded by the letter "E" indicate the ship or craft is a prototype in an experimental or developmental status; the prefix "T" indicates that the ship is assigned to the Navy's Military Sealift Command and is civilian manned; and the prefix "F" indicates a ship being constructed by the United States for a foreign government.
The following list was promulgated on September 23, 1970.

COMBATANT SHIPS

(1) Warships

Aircraft Carriers:

Attack Aircraft Carrier	CVA
Attack Aircraft Carrier (nuclear propulsion)	CVAN
ASW Aircraft Carrier	CVS

Surface Combatants:

Battleship	BB
Heavy Cruiser	CA
Guided Missile Cruiser	CG
Guided Missile Cruiser (nuclear propulsion)	CGN
Light Cruiser	CL
Guided Missile Light Cruiser	CLG
Destroyer	DD
Guided Missile Destroyer	DDG
Radar Picket Destroyer	DDR
Frigate	DL
Guided Missile Frigate	DLG
Guided Missile Frigate (nuclear propulsion)	DLGN

Ocean Escorts:

Escort Ship	DE
Guided Missile Escort Ship	DEG
Radar Picket Escort Ship	DER

Command Ship	CC

Submarines:

Submarine	SS
Submarine (nuclear propulsion)	SSN
Guided Missile Submarine	SSG
Fleet Ballistic Missile Submarine (nuclear propulsion)	SSBN

Patrol Ships:

Patrol Escort	PCE
Patrol Rescue Escort	PCER
Patrol Gunboat	PG

(2) Amphibious Warfare Ships

Amphibious Command Ship	LCC
Inshore Fire Support Ship	LFR
Amphibious Fire Support Ship	LFS
Amphibious Assault Ship (general purpose)	LHA
Amphibious Cargo Ship	LKA
Amphibious Transport	LPA
Amphibious Transport Dock	LPD
Amphibious Assault Ship	LPH
Amphibious Transport (small)	LPR
Amphibious Transport Submarine	LPSS
Dock Landing Ship	LSD
Tank Landing Ship	LST

(3) Mine Warfare Ships

Mine Countermeasures Ship	MCS
Minesweeper, Coastal (non-magnetic)	MSC
Minesweeper, Fleet (steel hulled)	MSF
Minesweeper, Ocean (non-magnetic)	MSO

COMBATANT CRAFT

(1) Patrol Craft

Patrol Craft (hydrofoil)	PCH
Patrol Gunboat (hydrofoil)	PGH
Fast Patrol Craft	PTF

(2) Landing Craft

Landing Craft, Assault	LCA
Landing Craft, Mechanised	LCM
Landing Craft, Personnel, Large	LCPL
Landing Craft, Personnel, Ramped	LCPR
Landing Craft, Utility	LCU
Landing Craft, Vehicle, Personnel	LCVP
Amphibious Warping Tug	LWT

(3) Mine Countermeasures Craft

Minesweeping Boat	MSB
Minesweeper, Drone	MSD
Minesweeper, Inshore	MSI
Minesweeping Launch	MSL
Minesweeper, River	MSM
Minesweeper, Patrol	MSR
Minesweeper, Special (Device)	MSS

(4) Riverine Warfare Craft

Assault Support Patrol Boat	ASPB
Armoured Troop Carrier	ATC
Command and Control Boat	CCB
Monitor	MON
River Patrol Boat	PBR
Patrol Craft, Inshore	PCF
Quiet Fast Boat	QFB
Riverine Utility Craft	RUC
Strike Assault Boat	STAB

(5) SEAL Support Craft

Landing Craft Swimmer Reconnaissance	LCSR
Light SEAL Support Craft	LSSC
Medium SEAL Support Craft	MSSC
Swimmer Delivery Vehicle	SDV

(6) Mobile Inshore Underseas Warfare (MIUW) Craft

MIUW Attack Craft	MAC

AUXILIARY SHIPS

Destroyer Tender	AD
Degaussing Ship	ADG
Ammunition Ship	AE
Store Ship	AF
Combat Store Ship	AFS
Miscellaneous	AG
Escort Research Ship	AGDE
Hydrofoil Research Ship	AGEH
Environmental Research Ship	AGER
Miscellaneous Command Ship	AGF
Missile Range Instrumentation Ship	AGM
Major Communications Relay Ship	AGMR
Oceanographic Research Ship	AGOR
Patrol Craft Tender	AGP
Radar Picket Ship	AGR
Surveying Ship	AGS
Auxiliary Submarine	AGSS
Technical Research Ship	AGTR
Hospital Ship	AH
Cargo Ship	AK
Cargo Ship Dock	AKD
Light Cargo Ship	AKL
Vehicle Cargo Ship	AKR
Stores Issue Ship	AKS
Cargo Ship and Aircraft Ferry	AKV
Net Laying Ship	ANL
Oiler	AO
Fast Combat Support Ship	AOE
Gasoline Tanker	AOG
Replenishment Oiler	AOR
Transport	AP
Self-propelled Barracks Ship	APB
Repair Ship	AR
Battle Damage Repair Ship	ARB
Cable Repairing Ship	ARC
Internal Combustion Engine Repair Ship	ARG
Landing Craft Repair Ship	ARL
Salvage Ship	ARS
Salvage Lifting Ship	ARSD
Salvage Craft Tender	ARST
Aircraft Repair Ship (Aircraft)	ARVA
Aircraft Repair Ship (Engine)	ARVE
Aircraft Repair Ship (Helicopter)	ARVH
Submarine Tender	AS
Submarine Rescue Ship	ASR
Auxiliary Ocean Tug	ATA
Fleet Ocean Tug	ATF
Salvage Tug	ATS
Auxiliary Training Submarine	ATSS
Seaplane Tender	AV
Guided Missile Ship	AVM
Aviation Supply Ship	AVS
Auxiliary Aircraft Transport	AVT
Distilling Ship	AW
Training Aircraft Carrier	CVT
Fast Deployment Logistic Ship	FDL

SERVICE CRAFT *

Large Auxiliary Floating Dry Dock	AFDB
Small Auxiliary Floating Dry Dock	AFDL
Medium Auxiliary Floating Dry Dock	AFDM
Barracks Craft	APL
Auxiliary Repair Dry Dock	ARD
Medium Auxiliary Repair Dry Dock	ARDM
Deep Submergence Rescue Vehicle	DSRV
Deep Submergence Vehicle	DSV
Unclassified Miscellaneous	IX
Submersible Research Vehicle (nuclear propulsion)	NR
Target and Training Submarine (self-propelled)	SST
Submersible Craft (self-propelled)	X
Miscellaneous Auxiliary (self-propelled)	YAG
Open Lighter	YC
Car Float	YCF
Aircraft Transportation Lighter	YCV
Floating Crane	YD
Diving Tender	YDT
Covered Lighter (self-propelled)	YF
Ferryboat or Launch (self-propelled)	YFB
Yard Floating Dry Dock	YFD
Covered Lighter	YFN
Large Covered Lighter	YFNB
Dry Dock Companion Craft	YFND
Lighter (special purpose)	YFNX
Floating Power Barge	YFP
Refrigerated Covered Lighter (self-propelled)	YFR
Rrfrigerated Covered Lighter	YFRN
Covered Lighter (Range Tender) (self-propelled)	YFRT
Harbour Utility Craft (self-propelled)	YFU
Garbage Lighter (self-propelled)	YG
Garbage Lighter (non-self-propelled)	YGN
Salvage Lift Craft, Heavy	YHLC
Salvage Lift Craft, Light (self-propelled)	YLLC
Dredge (self-propelled)	YM
Salvage Lift Craft, Medium	YMLC
Gate Craft	YNG
Fuel Oil Barge (self-propelled)	YO
Gasoline Barge (self-propelled)	YOG
Gasoline Barge (non-self-propelled)	YOGN
Fuel Oil Barge (non-self-propelled)	YON
Oil Storage Barge	YOS
Patrol Craft (self-propelled)	YP
Floating Pile Driver	YPD
Floating Workshop	YR
Repair and Berthing Barge	YRB
Repair, Berthing and Messing Barge	YRBM
Floating Dry Dock Workshop (Hull)	YRDH
Floating Dry Dock Workshop (Machine)	YRDM
Radiological Repair Barge	YRR
Salvage Craft Tender	YRST
Seaplane Wrecking Derrick (self-propelled)	YSD
Sludge Removal Barge	YSR
Large Harbour Tug (self-propelled)	YTB
Small Harbour Tug (self-propelled)	YTL
Medium Harbour Tug (self-propelled)	YTM
Drone Aircraft Catapult Control Craft	YV
Water Barge (self-propelled)	YW
Water Distilling Barge	
Water Barge (non-self-propelled)	YWN

* Self-propelled barges are indicated.

CLASSIFICATION OF MARITIME COMMISSION SHIP DESIGNS

Ships constructed under the jurisdiction of the US Maritime Commission by private shipyards are assigned Maritime Commission design classifications. These classifications consist of three groups of letters and numbers.

First group letter(s) indicate type of ship and number indicates size class. The letters of Maritime Commission ship classifications now on the US Navy List are:

Cargo	C
Emergency Cargo (Liberty)	EC
Passenger	P
Refrigerator	R
Special Purpose	S
Tanker	T
Victory Cargo	VC

Second group letter(s) indicate type of propulsion and number "2" indicates twin shaft ship and "4" quadruple shaft ship.

Motor (diesel)	M
Motor (diesel) Electric	ME
Steam (reciprocating or turbine)	S
Steam (turbine) Electric	SE

Third group of letters and numbers indicate the design of a particular type of ship, beginning with A1.

NOTE : Drawings are arranged by generic design.

Submarines

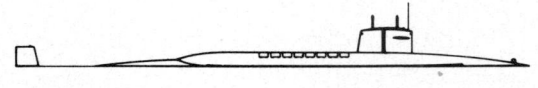

LAFAYETTE (SSBN 616)

GEORGE WASHINGTON (SSBN 598)

STURGEON (SSN 637)

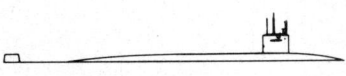

PERMIT (SSN 594)

TULLIBEE (SSN 597)

SCAMP (SSN 588) Skipjack Class

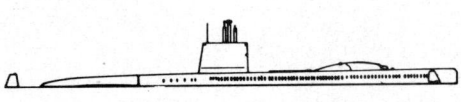

HALIBUT (SSN 587)

TRITON (SSN 586)

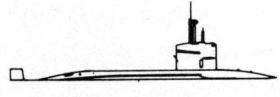

BARBEL (SS 580)

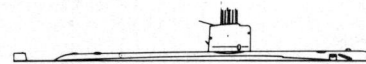

SWORDFISH (SSN 579)

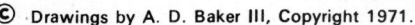

© Drawings by A. D. Baker III, Copyright 1971.

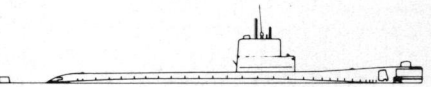

SEAWOLF (SSN 575)

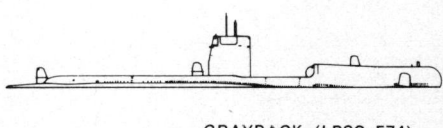

GRAYBACK (LPSS 574)

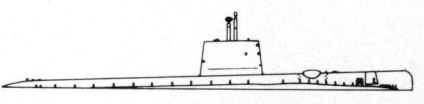

SAILFISH (SS 572)

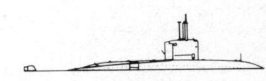

NAUTILUS (SSN 571)

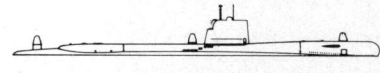

ALBACORE (AGSS 569)

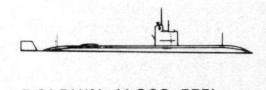

WAHOO (SS 565) Tang Class

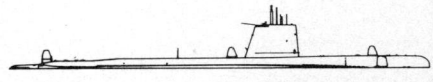

DOLPHIN (AGSS 555)

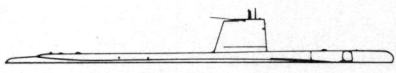

VOLADOR (SS 490) Guppy III Type

THREADFIN (SS 410) GUPPY IIA Type

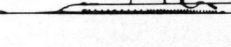

BARRACUDA (SST 3)

MACKEREL (SST 1)

Scale: 1 inch = 150 feet (1 : 1 800)

Aircraft Carriers

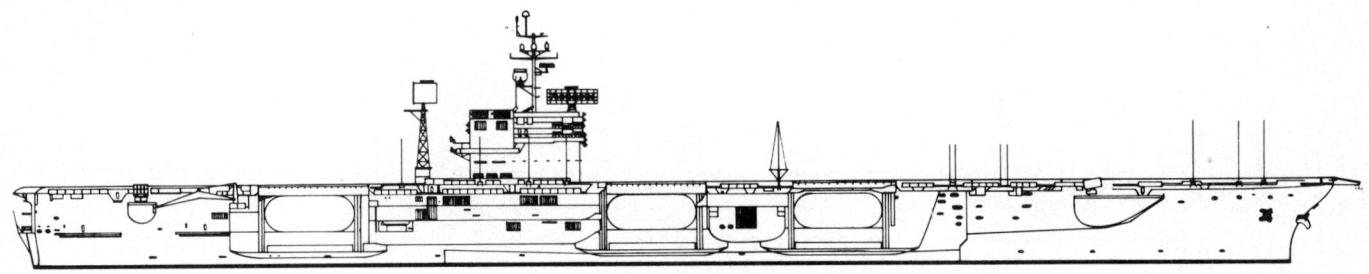

JOHN F. KENNEDY (CVA 67)

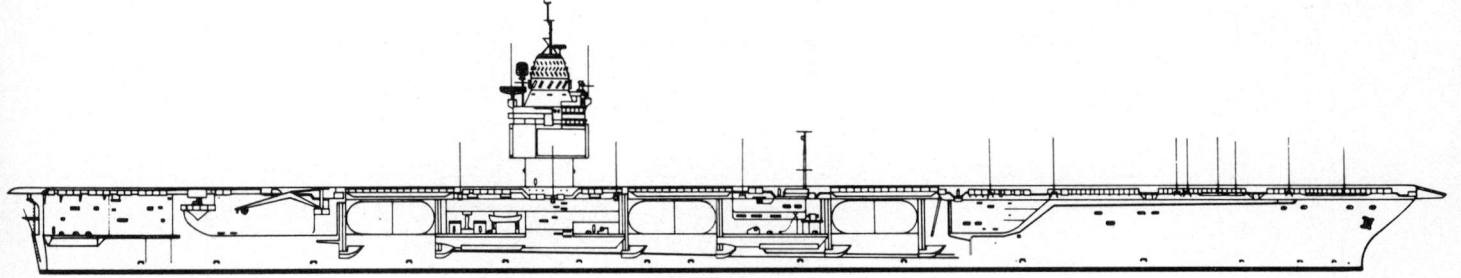

ENTERPRISE (CVAN 65)

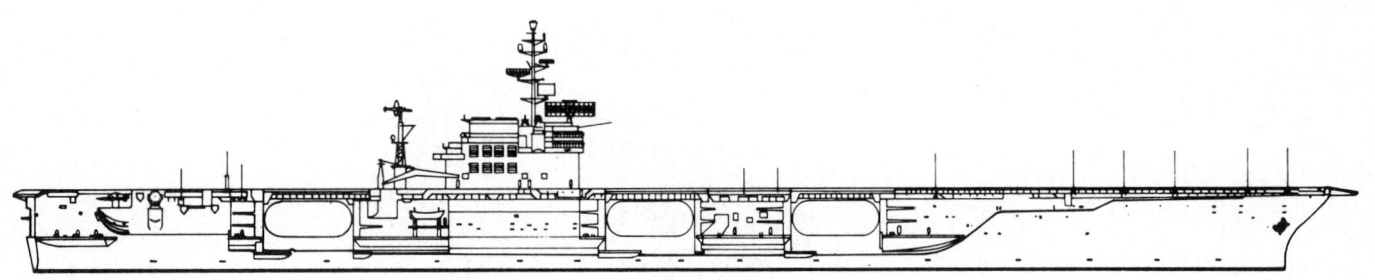

KITTY HAWK (CVA 63)

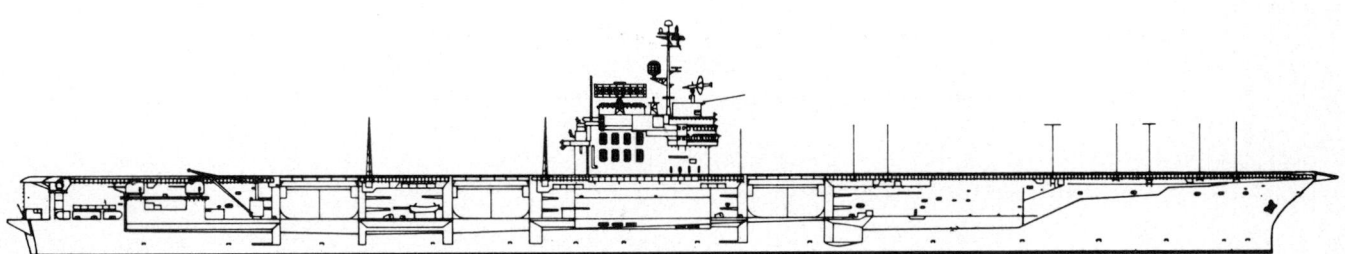

SARATOGA (CVA 60) Forrestal Class

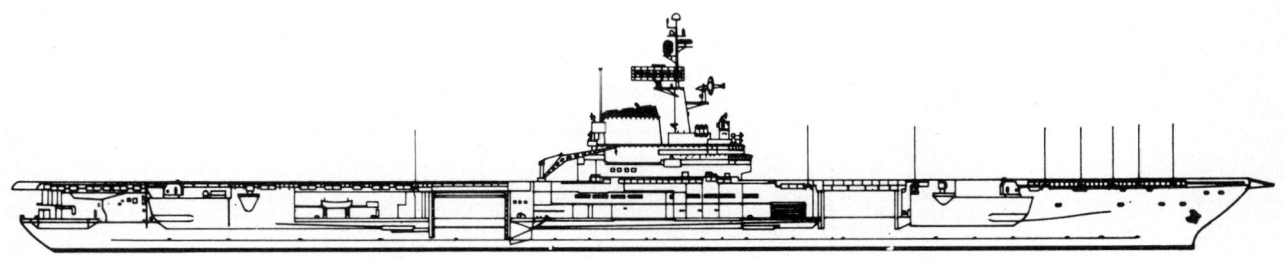

CORAL SEA (CVA 43) Midway Class

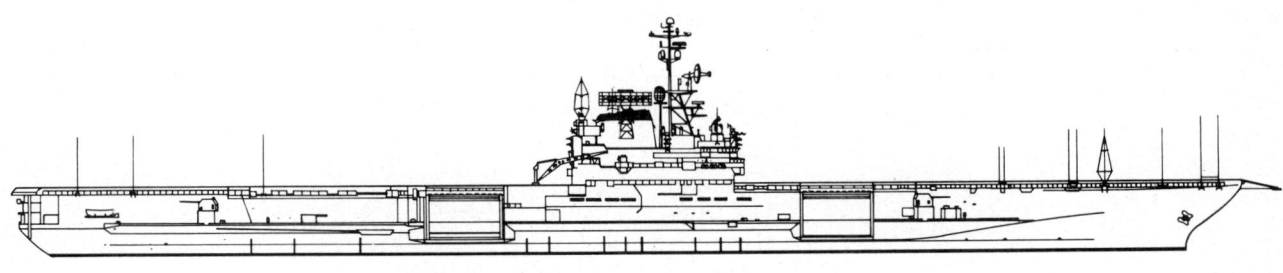

MIDWAY (CVA 41)

Scale: 1 inch = 150 feet (1 : 1 800)

Aircraft Carriers—*continued*

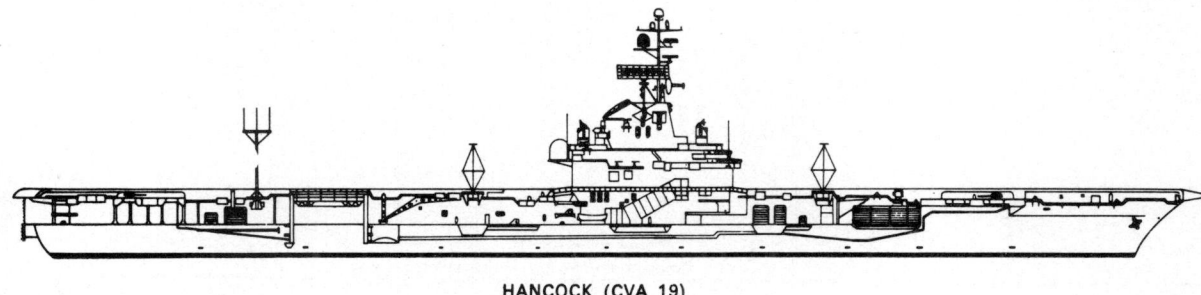

HANCOCK (CVA 19)

Cruisers

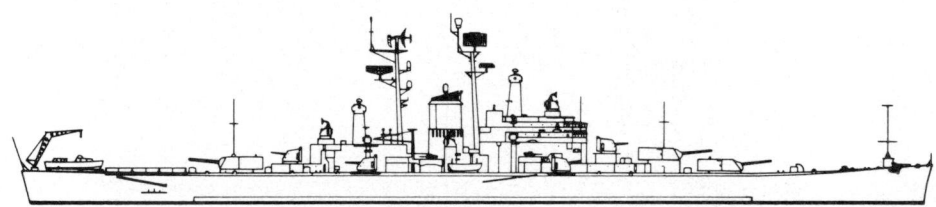

NEWPORT NEWS (CA 148) Des Moines Class

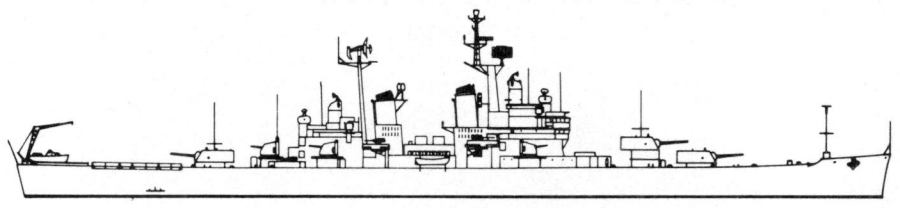

ST. PAUL (CA 73) Baltimore Class

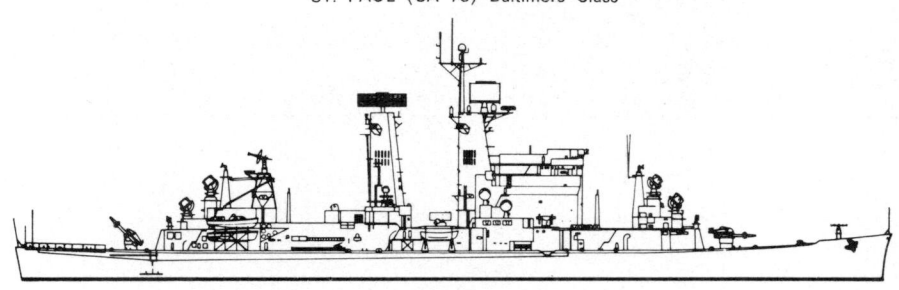

ALBANY (CG 10)

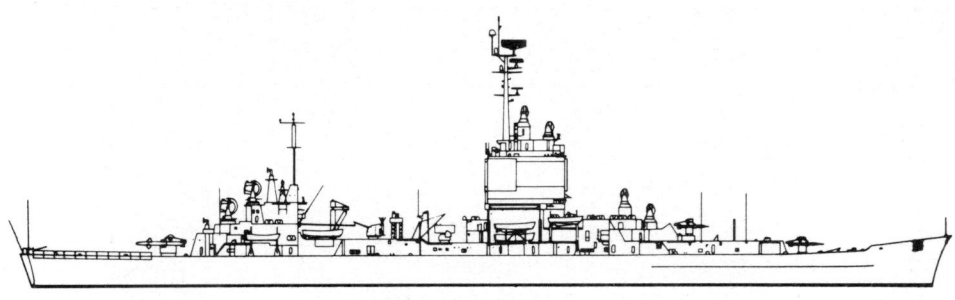

LONG BEACH (CGN 9)

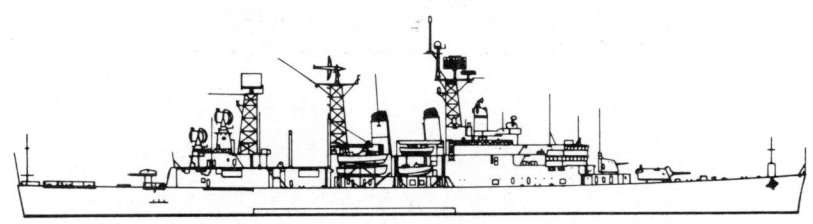

PROVIDENCE (CLG 6) Converted Cleveland Class (Terrier)

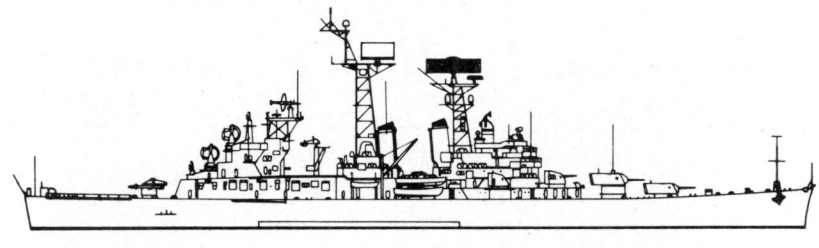

GALVESTON (CLG 3) Converted Cleveland Class (Talos)

Scale: 1 inch = 150 feet (1 : 1 800)

Frigates

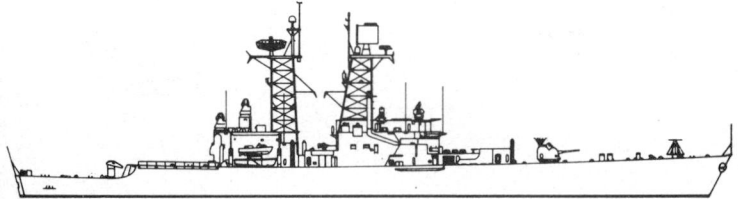

TRUXTUN (DLGN 35)

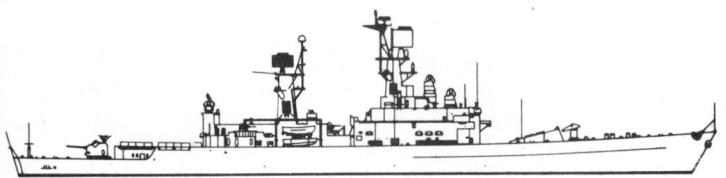

WAINWRIGHT (DLG 28) Belknap Class

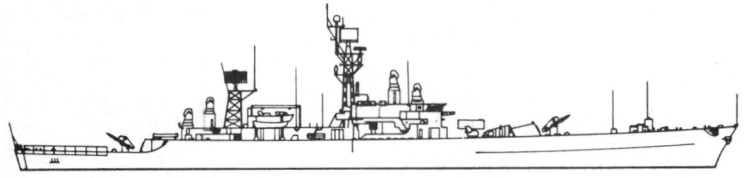

BAINBRIDGE (DLGN 25)

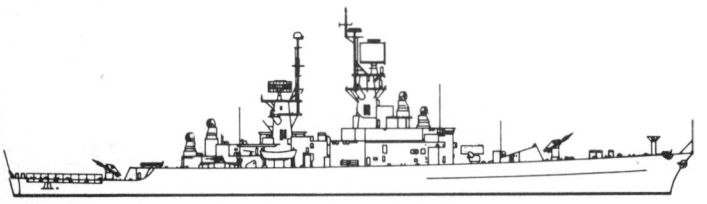

LEAHY (DLG 16)

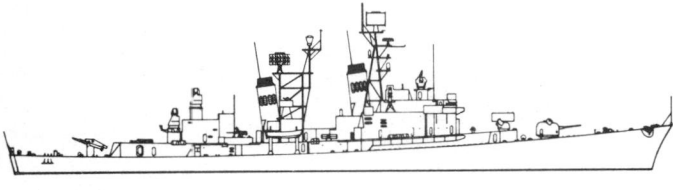

MAHAN (DLG 11) Farragut Class

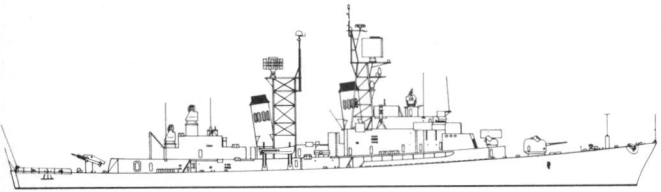

FARRAGUT (DLG 6)

Destroyers

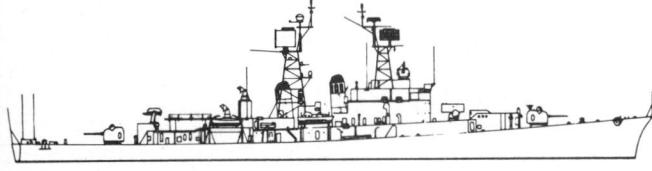

MITSCHER (DDG 35)

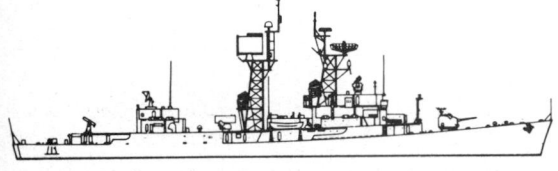

SOMERS (DDG 34) Converted Forrest Sherman Class

Destroyers—*continued*

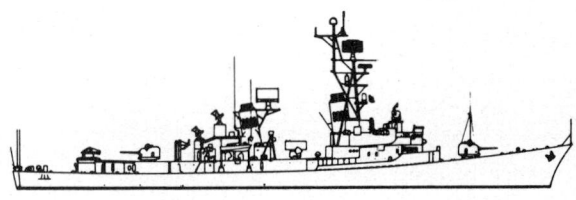

BARNEY (DDG 6) Charles F. Adams Class

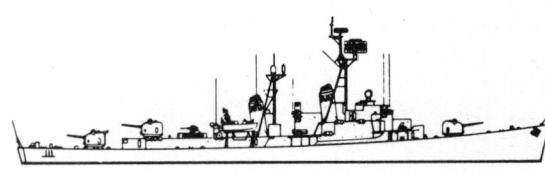

MANLEY (DD 940) Forrest Sherman Class

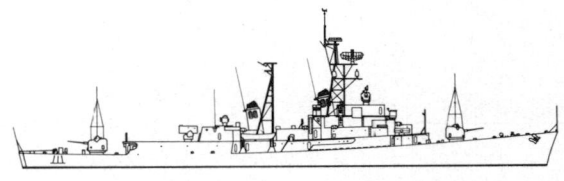

JONAS INGRAM (DD 938) Forrest Sherman Class (ASW)

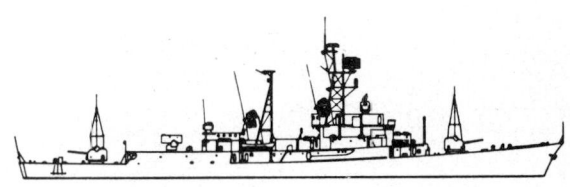

BARRY (DD 933) Forrest Sherman Class (ASW)

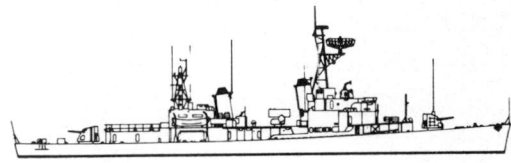

BASILONE (DD 824) Gearing Class FRAM I

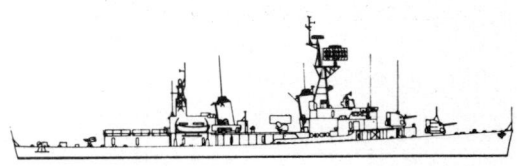

MEREDITH (DD 890) Gearing Class FRAM I

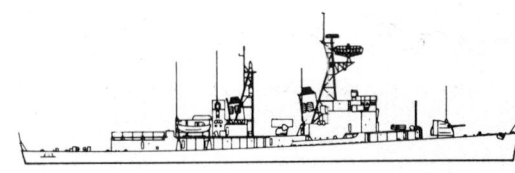

ROBERT A. OWENS (DD 827) Carpenter Type FRAM I

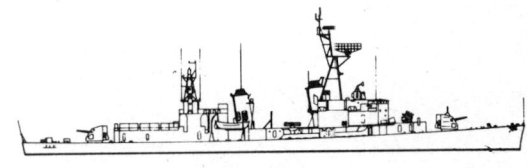

NORRIS (DD 859) Gearing Class ex-Escorts

Scale: 1 inch = 150 feet (1 : 1 800)

Destroyers—*continued*

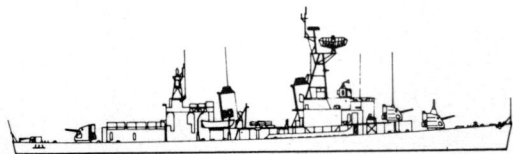

CHEVALIER (DD 805) Gearing Class ex-Radar Pickets

GOODRICH (DD 831) Gearing Class Radar Pickets

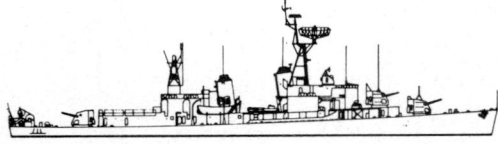

WALLACE L. LIND (DD 703) Allen M. Sumner Class FRAM II

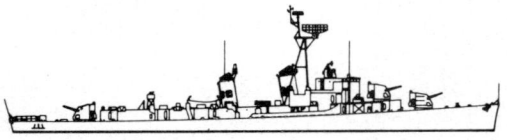

PURDY (DD 734) Allen M. Sumner Class

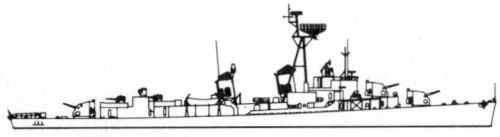

COMPTON (DD 705) Allen M. Sumner Class

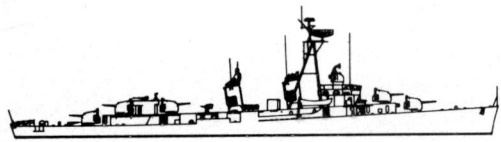

SHIELDS (DD 596) Fletcher Class (5 guns)

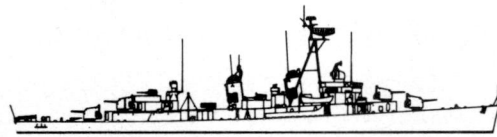

BRAINE (DD 630) Fletcher Class (4 guns)

Escort Ships

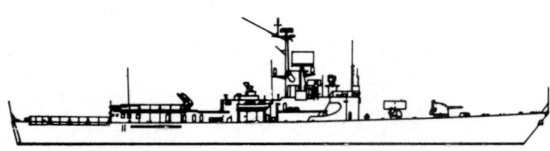

BROOKE (DEG 1)

Escort Ships—*continued*

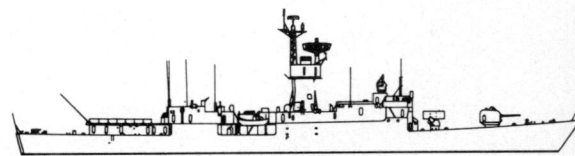

KNOX (DE 1052) Knox Class

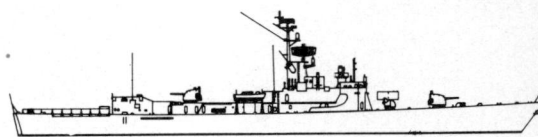

SAMPLE (DE 1048) Garcia Class

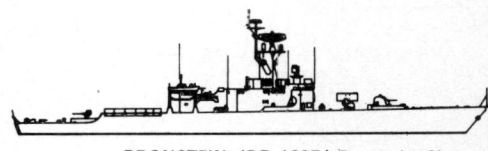

BRONSTEIN (DE 1037) Bronstein Class

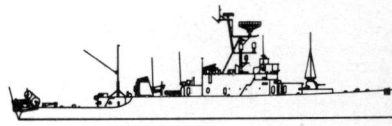

CHARLES D. BERRY (DE 1035) Claude Jones Class

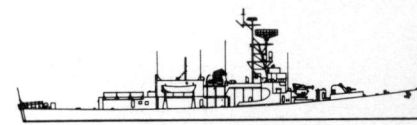

JOSEPH K. TAUSSIG (DE 1030) Courtney Class

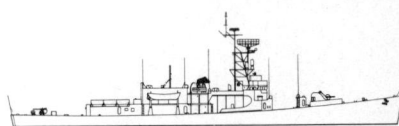

BRIDGET (DE 1024) Courtney Class

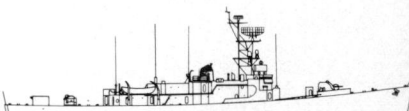

COURTNEY (DE 1021)

CROMWELL (DE 1014) Dealey Class

DEALEY (DE 1006)

CALCATERRA (DER 390) Edsall Class Radar Pickets

Scale: 1 inch = 150 feet (1 : 1 800)

Command Ships

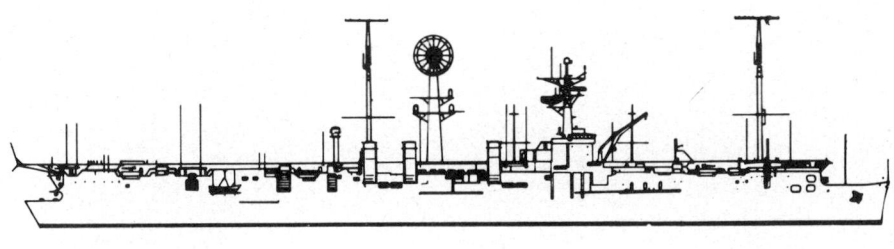

WRIGHT (CC 2)

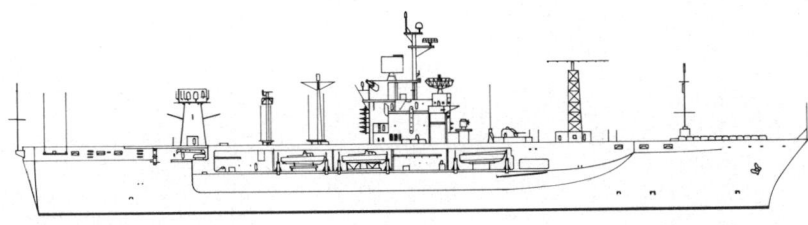

BLUE RIDGE (LCC 19)

Amphibious Warfare Ships

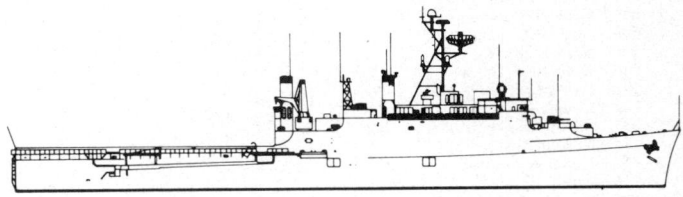

RALEIGH (LPD 1)

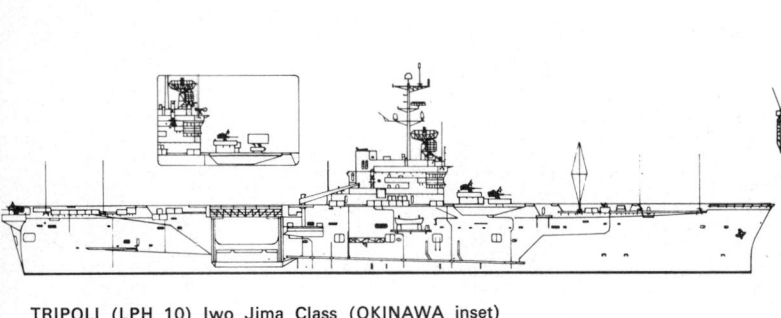

TRIPOLI (LPH 10) Iwo Jima Class (OKINAWA inset)

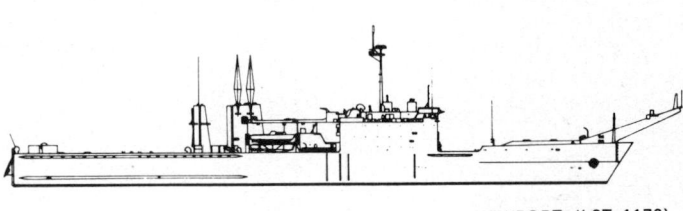

ANCHORAGE (LSD 36)

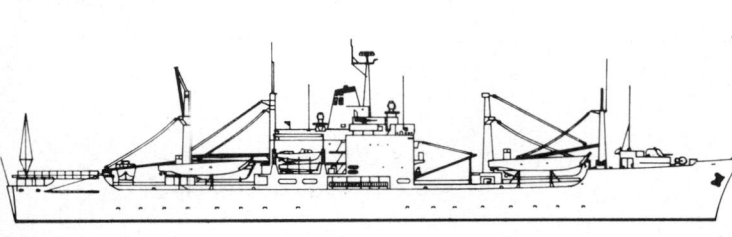

CHARLESTON (LKA 113)

NEWPORT (LST 1179)

Patrol Ships and Craft

ANTELOPE (PG 86) Ashcville Class

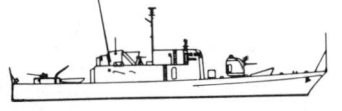

BEACON (PG 99) Asheville Class

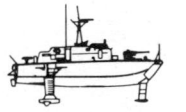

TUCUMCARI (PGH 2)

FLAGSTAFF (PGH 1)

Mine Warfare Ships and Craft

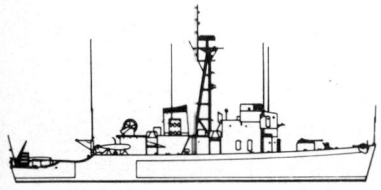

ABILITY (MSO 519) Ability Class

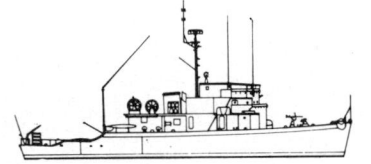

PIVOT (MSO 463) Agile Class

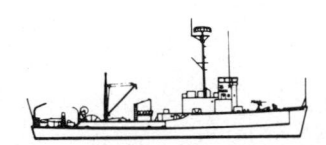

BLUEBIRD (MSC 121) Bluebird Class

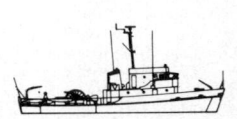

CAPE (MSI 2) Cove Class

Scale: 1 inch = 100 feet
(1 : 1 200)

UNITED STATES SHIP HULL NUMBERS

(Type designations in order of arrangement within this volume; several of the ships listed have been stricken but their hull numbers are retained in this edition for reference and identification).

SSBN—Fleet Ballistic Missile Submarines

"Geo. Washington" Class
598 George Washington
599 Patrick Henry
600 Theodore Roosevelt
601 Robert E. Lee
602 Abraham Lincoln

"Ethan Allen" Class
608 Ethan Allen
609 Sam Houston
610 Thomas A. Edison
611 John Marshall

"Lafayette" Class
616 Lafayette
617 Alexander Hamilton

"Ethan Allen" Class (Cont'd)
618 Thomas Jefferson

"Lafayette "Class (Cont'd)
619 Andrew Jackson
620 John Adams
622 James Monroe
623 Nathan Hale
624 Woodrow Wilson
625 Henry Clay
626 Daniel Webster
627 James Madison
628 Tecumseh
629 Daniel Boone
630 John C. Calhoun
631 Ulysses S. Grant
632 Von Steuben
633 Casimir Pulaski
634 Stonewall Jackson
635 Sam Rayburn
636 Nathanael Greene
640 Benjamin Franklin
641 Simon Bolivar
642 Kamehameha
643 George Bancroft
644 Lewis and Clark
645 James K. Polk
654 George C. Marshall
655 Henry L. Stimson
656 George Washington Carver
657 Francis Scott Key
658 Mariano G. Vallejo
659 Will Rogers

Submarines

**SS SSN—Submarines/
AGSS—Auxiliary Submarines/
LPSS—Transport Submarines/
SSG—Guided Missile Submarines**

"Gato" Class
224 Cod AGSS (T)
240 Angler AGSS (T)
244 Cavalla AGSS (T)
245 Cobia AGSS (T)
246 Croaker (T)
270 Raton AGSS (T)

"Balao" Class
286 Billfish AGSS
287 Bowfin AGSS (T)
287 Ling AGSS (T)
298 Lionfish AGSS (T)
313 Perch LPSS (T)
315 Sealion LPSS
318 Baya AGSS
319 Becuna
322 Blackfin
232 Caiman
324 Blenny AGSS
328 Charr AGSS (T)
331 Bugarass
334 Cabezon AGSS (T)
337 Carbonero SS
338 Carp AGSS (T)
339 Catfish
342 Chopper AGSS (T)
377 Menhaden
382 Picuda
383 Pampanito AGSS (T)
385 Bang AGSS
391 Pomfret
394 Razorback
396 Ronquil
398 Segundo
402 Sea Fox
403 Atule AGSS
406 Sea Poacher AGSS
407 Sea Robin
410 Threadfin
416 Tiru

"Tench" Class
417 Tench AGSS
418 Thornback

419 Tigrone AGSS
420 Tirante
421 Trutta
423 Torsk AGSS (T)
424 Quillback
425 Trumpetfish
426 Tusk
476 Runner AGSS (T)
478 Cutlass
480 Medregal SS
481 Requin AGSS (T)
482 Irex AGSS
483 Sea Leopard
484 Odax
485 Sirago
486 Pomodon
487 Remora
490 Volador
522 Amberjack
523 Grampus
524 Pickerel
525 Grenadier

"Dolphin" Type
555 Dolphin AGSS

"Tang" Class
563 Tang
564 Trigger
565 Wahoo
566 Trout
567 Gudgeon
568 Harder

"Albacore" Type
569 Albacore AGSS

"Nautilus" Type (SSN)
571 Nautilus

"Salmon" Type
572 Sailfish
573 Salmon

"Grayback" Type
574 Grayback LPSS

"Seawolf" Type (SSN)
575 Seawolf

"Darter" Type
576 Darter

"Grayback" Type
577 Growler SSG

"Skate" Class (SSN)
578 Skate
579 Swordfish

"Barbel" Class
580 Barbel
581 Blueback
582 Bonefish

"Skate" Class (SSN)
(Cont'd)
583 Sargo
584 Seadragon

"Skipjack" Class (SSN)
585 Skipjack

"Triton" Type (SSN)
586 Triton

"Halibut" Type (SSN)
587 Halibut

"Skipjack" Class (SSN)
(Cont'd)
588 Scamp
590 Sculpin
951 Shark
592 Snook

"Permit" Class (SSN)
594 Permit
595 Plunger
596 Barb

"Tullibee" Type (SSN)
597 Tullibee

"Permit" Class (SSN)
(Cont'd)
603 Pollack
604 Haddo
605 Jack
606 Tinosa
607 Dace
612 Guardfish
613 Flasher
614 Greenling
615 Gato
621 Haddock

"Sturgeon" Class (SSN)
637 Sturgeon
638 Whale
639 Tautog
646 Grayling
647 Pogy
648 Aspro
649 Sunfish
650 Pargo
651 Queenfish
652 Puffer
653 Ray

660 Sand Lance
661 Lapon
662 Gurnard
663 Hammerhead
664 Sea Devil
665 Guitarro
666 Hawkbill
667 Bergall
668 Spadefish
669 Seahorse
670 Finback
671 Narwhal
672 Pintado
673 Flying Fish
674 Trepang
675 Bluefish
676 Billfish
667 Drum
678 Archerfish
679 Silversides
680 Redfish
681 Batfish
682 Tunny

683 Parche
684 Cavalla

"Quiet" Design
685 Glenard P. Lipscomb

"Sturgeon" Class (SSN)
(Cont'd)
686 L. Mendel Rivers
687 Richard B. Russell

"High Speed" Design
688
689
690
691
692
693
694
695
696
697
698
699

SST—Training Submarines

"Mackerel" Type
1 Mackerel
2 Marlin

"Barracuda" Type
3 Barracuda

CC—Command Ships

1 Northampton
2 Wright

AGF—Miscellaneous Flagship

1 Valcour

AGMR—Major Communication Relay Ships

1 Annapolis
2 Arlington

CVA CVAN—Attack Aircraft Carriers

"Hancock" Class
19 Hancock
31 Bon Homme Richard
34 Oriskany

"Midway Class"
41 Midway
42 Franklin D. Roosevelt
43 Coral Sea

"Forrestal" Class
59 Forrestal
60 Saratoga
61 Ranger
62 Independence

"Kitty Hawk" Class
63 Kitty Hawk
64 Constellation

"Enterprise" Type (CVAN)
65 Enterprise

"Kitty Hawk" Class (Cont'd)
66 America
67 John F. Kennedy

"Nimitz" Class (CVAN)
68 Nimitz
69 Eisenhower

CVS—ASW Aircraft Carriers

"Essex-Hancock" Classes
9 Essex
10 Yorktown
11 Intrepid
12 Hornet
14 Ticonderoga
15 Randolph
18 Wasp
20 Bennington
33 Kearsarge
36 Antietam
38 Shangri-La

CVT—Training Aircraft Carrier

16 Lexington

CG CGN—Guided Missile Cruisers

"Long Beach" Type (CGN)
9 Long Beach

"Albany" Class
10 Albany
11 Chicago
12 Columbus

CLG—Guided Missile Light Cruisers

Converted "Cleveland" Class
3 Galveston
4 Little Rock
5 Oklahoma City
6 Providence
7 Springfield
8 Topeka

DLG DLGN—Guided Missile Frigates

"Coontz" Class
6 Farragut
7 Luce
8 MacDonough
9 Coontz
10 King
11 Mahan
12 Dahlgren
13 William V. Pratt
14 Dewey
15 Preble

"Leahy" Class
16 Leahy
17 Harry E. Yarnell
18 Worden
19 Dale
20 Richmond K. Turner
21 Gridley
22 England
23 Halsey
24 Reeves

"Bainbridge" Type (DLGN)
25 Bainbridge

"Belknap" Class
26 Belknap
27 Josephus Daniels
28 Wainwright
29 Jouett
30 Horne
31 Sterett
32 William H. Standley
33 Fox
34 Biddle

"Truxtun" Type (DLGN)
35 Truxtun

"California" Class (DLGN)
36 California
37 South Carolina
38
39
40

DL—Frigates

"Norfolk" Type
1 Norfolk

"Mitscher" Class
4 Willis A. Lee
5 Wilkinson

DDG—Guided Missile Destroyers

"Chas. F. Adams" Class
2 Charles F. Adams
3 John King
4 Lawrence
5 Claude V. Ricketts (ex-Biddle)
6 Barney
7 Henry B. Wilson
8 Lynde McCormick
9 Towers
10 Sampson
11 Sellers
12 Robinson
13 Hoel

---

14 Buchanan
15 Berkeley
16 Joseph Strauss
17 Conyngham
18 Semmes
19 Tattnall
20 Goldsborough
21 Cochrane
22 Benjamin Stoddert
23 Richard E. Byrd
24 Waddell

Converted "Sherman" Class
31 Decatur
32 John Paul Jones
33 Parsons
34 Somers

Converted "Mitscher" Class
35 Mitscher
36 John S. McCain

DD—Destroyers

"Benson" Class
422 Mayo

"Gleaves" Class
432 Kearny
435 Grayson
437 Woolsey
441 (ex-Wilkes)
443 Swanson

"Fletcher" Class
448 La Vallette

"Gleaves" Class (Cont'd)
455 Hambleton
462 Fitch

"Fletcher" Class (Cont'd)
475 Hudson
478 Stanley
479 Stevens

"Gleaves" Class (Cont'd)
490 Quick

"Benson" Class (Cont'd)
491 Farenholt

"Gleaves" Class (Cont'd)
493 Carmick
494 Doyle
496 McCook
497 Frankford

"Fletcher" Class (Cont'd)
499 Renshaw
501 Schroeder
502 Sigsbee
507 Conway
511 Foote
513 Terry
519 Daly
528 Mullany
530 Trathen
531 Hazelwood
534 McCord
535 Miller
536 Owen
537 Sullivans
538 Stephen Potter
540 Twining
547 Cowell
554 Franks
558 Laws
561 Pritchett
562 Robinson
563 Ross
564 Rowe
566 Stoddard
567 Watts
568 Wren
575 McKee
578 Wickes
585 Haraden
587 Bell
588 Burns
589 Izard
594 Hart
595 Metcalf
596 Shields

"Benson" Class (Cont'd)
598 Bancroft
600 Boyle
601 Champlin
602 Meade
603 Murphy
604 Parker
606 Coghlan
607 Frazier
608 Gansevoort
609 Gillespie
610 Hobby
613 Laub
614 Mackenzie
615 McLanahan
616 Nields
617 Ordronaux

"Gleaves" Class (Cont'd)
618 Davison
619 Edwards

---

621 Jeffers
626 Satterlee
627 Thompson

"Fletcher" Class (Cont'd)
629 Abbott
630 Braine

"Gleaves" Class (Cont'd)
632 Cowie
634 Doran
637 Gerhardi
638 Herndon
641 Tillman

"Fletcher" Class (Cont'd)
643 Sigourney

"Gleaves" Class (Cont'd)
646 Stockton
647 Thorn

Later "Fletcher" Class
649 Albert W. Grant
650 Vaperton
651 Cogswell
652 Ingersoll
653 Knapp
654 Bearss
657 Charles J. Badger
659 Dashiell
660 Bullard
661 Kidd
662 Bennion
665 Bryant
666 Black
667 Chauncey
669 Cotton
671 Gatling
672 Healy
674 Hunt
679 McNair
680 Melvin
682 Porterfield
683 Stockham
684 Wedderburn
685 Picking
687 Uhlmann
688 Remey
690 Norman Scott
691 Mertz

"Allen M. Sumner" Class
692 Allen M. Sumner
693 Moale
694 Ingraham
696 English
697 Charles S. Sperry
698 Ault
699 Waldron
701 John W. Weeks
702 Hank
703 Wallace L. Lind
704 Borie
705 Compton
707 Soley
708 Harlan R. Dickson
709 Hugh Purvis

"Gearing" Class
710 Gearing
711 Eugene A. Greene
713 Kenneth D. Bailey
714 William R. Rush
715 William M. Wood
716 Wiltsie
717 Theo E. Chandler
718 Hammer
719 Epperson

"Allen M. Sumner" Class (Cont'd)
723 Walke
724 Laffey
725 O'Brien
727 De Haven
728 Mansfield
729 Lyman K. Swenson
730 Collett
731 Maddox
732 Hyman
734 Purdy

"Gearing" Class (Cont'd)
742 Frank Knox
743 Southerland

"Allen M. Sumner" Class (Cont'd)
744 Blue
746 Taussig
752 Alfred A. Cunningham
753 John R. Pierce
755 John A. Bole
756 Beatty
757 Putnam
758 Strong
759 Lofberg
760 John W. Thomason
761 Buck
762 Henley

"Gearing" Class (Cont'd)
763 William C. Lawe
764 Lloyd Thomas
765 Keppler

"Allen M. Sumner" Class (Cont'd)
770 Lowry

775 Willard Keith
776 James C. Owens
777 Zellars
778 Massey
779 Douglas H. Fox
780 Stormes
781 Robert K. Huntington

"Gearing" Class (Cont'd)
782 Rowan
783 Gurke
784 McKean
785 Henderson
786 Richard B. Anderson
787 James K. Kyes
788 Hollister
789 Eversole
790 Shelton

Later "Fletcher" Class
(Cont'd)
793 Cassin Young
759 Preston
800 Porter

"Gearing" Class (Cont'd)
805 Chevalier
806 Highbee
807 Benner
808 Dennis J. Buckley
817 Corry
818 New
819 Holder
820 Rich
821 Johnson
822 Robert H. McCard
823 Samuel B. Roberts
824 Basilone

"Carpenter" Type
825 Carpenter

"Gearing "Class (Cont'd)
826 Agerholm

"Carpenter" Type (Cont'd)
827 Robert A. Owens

"Gearing" Class (Cont'd)
829 Myles C. Fox
830 Everett F. Larson
831 Goodrich
832 Hanson
833 Herbert J. Thomas
834 Turner
835 Charles P. Cecil
836 Georges K. Mackenzie
837 Sarsfield
838 Ernest G. Small
839 Power
840 Glennon
841 Noa
842 Fiske
843 Warrington
844 Perry
845 Bausell
846 Ozbourn
847 Robert L. Wilson
849 Richard E. Kraus
850 Joseph P. Kennedy Jr.
851 Rupertus
852 Leonard F. Mason
853 Charles A. Roan
858 Fred T. Berry
859 Norris
860 McCaffery
861 Harwood
862 Vogelgesang
863 Steinaker
864 Harold J. Ellison
865 Charles R. Ware
866 Cone
867 Stribling
868 Brownson
869 Arnold J. Isbell
870 Fechteler
871 Damato
872 Forrest Royal
873 Hawkins
874 Duncan
875 Henry W. Tucker
876 Rogers
877 Perkins
878 Vesole
879 Leary
880 Dyess
881 Bordelon
882 Furse
883 Newman K. Perry
884 Floyd B. Parks
885 John F. Craig
886 Orleck
887 Brinkley Bass
888 Sticknell
889 O'Hare
890 Meredith

"Forrest Sherman" Class
931 Forrest Sherman
933 Barry
937 George F. Davis
938 Jonas Ingram
940 Manley
941 Dupont
942 Bigelow
943 Blandy

944 Mullinnix
945 Hull
946 Edson
948 Morton
950 Richard S. Edwards
951 Turner Joy

"Spruance" Class (tentative)
963 Spruance
964
965
966
967
968
969
970
971

DEG—Guided Missile Escort
Ships

"Brooke" Class
1 Brooke
2 Ramsey
3 Schofield
4 Talbot
5 Richard L. Page
6 Julius A. Furer

AGDE—Escort Research Ship

1 Glover

DE—Escort Ships/DER—Radar
Picket Escort Ships

"Edsall" Class
130 Jacob Jones
131 Hammann
134 Pope
137 Herbert C. Jones
138 Douglas L. Howard
139 Farquhar
140 J.R.Y. Blakeley
141 Hill
145 Huse
146 Inch
147 Blair/DER
149 Chatelain
150 Neunzer
151 Poole
152 Peterson

"Bostwick" Class
162 Levy
163 McConnell
164 Osterhaus
165 Parks
167 Acree
172 Cooner
180 Trumpeter
181 Straub
191 Coffman

"Buckley" Class
202 Eichenberger
217 Coolbaugh
220 Francis M. Robinson

"Rudderow" Class
231 Hodges

"Edsall" Class (Cont'd)
238 Stewart
239 Sturtevant/DER
240 Moore
241 Keith
242 Tomich
244 Otterstetter/DER
245 Sloat
247 Stanton
248 Swasey
249 Marchand
250 Hurst
251 Camp/DER
253 Pettit
254 Ricketts
317 Joyce/DER
318 Kirkpatrick/DER
320 Menges
321 Mosley
323 Pride
342 Falgout/DER
326 Thomas J. Gary/DER
328 Finch/DER
329 Kretchmer/DER
330 O'Reilly
332 Price/DER
333 Strickland/DER
334 Forster/DER
335 Daniel
336 Roy O. Hale/DER
337 Dale W. Peterson

"John C. Butler" Class
340 O'Flaherty
341 Raymond
342 Richard A. Suesens
346 Edwin A. Howard
348 Key
349 Gentry

353 Doyle C. Barnes
354 Kenneth M. Willett
356 Lloyd E. Acree
357 George E. Davis
358 Mack
360 Johnnie Hutchins
262 Rolf
363 Pratt
364 Rombach
367 French
370 John L. Williamson

"Edsall" Class (Cont'd)
382 Ramsden/DER
383 Mills /DER
384 Rhodes/DER
386 Savage/DER
387 Vance/DER
388 Lansing/DER
389 Durant/DER
390 Calcaterra/DER
391 Chambers/DER
392 Merrill
394 Swenning
395 Willis
396 Janssen
398 Cockrill
399 Stockdale
400 Hissem/DER

"John C. Butler" Class
(Contd')
405 Dennis
406 Edmonds
409 La Prade
411 Stafford
414 Le Ray Wilson
415 Lawrence C. Taylor
416 Melvin R. Newman
417 Oliver Mitchell
418 Tabberer
419 Robert F. Keller
420 Leland E. Thomas
421 Chester T. O'Brien
423 Dufilho
438 Corbesier
439 Conklin
441 William Seiverling
443 Kendall C. Campbell
444 Goss
449 Hanna
450 Joseph E. Connolly
508 Gilligan
531 Edward H. Allen
533 Howard F. Clark
534 Silverstein
537 Rizzi
538 Osberg
539 Wagner/DER
540 Vandivier/DER

"Buckley" Class (Cont'd)
577 Alexander J. Luke

"Rudderow" Class (Cont'd)
580 Leslie J. B. Knox
581 McNulty
587 Thomas F. Nickel
589 Tinsman

"Buckley" Class (Cont'd)
639 Gendreau
640 Fieberling
641 William C. Cole
643 Damon M. Cummings
667 Wiseman
681 Gillette
696 Spangler
699 Marsh
701 Osmus
703 Holton
704 Cronin
705 Frybarger

"Rudderow" Class (Cont'd)
707 Jobb

"Bostwick" Class (Cont'd)
742 Hilbert
743 Lamons
744 Kyne
745 Snyder
750 McClelland
765 Earl K. Olsen
767 Oswald

"Buckley" Class (Cont'd)
795 Gunason
796 Major
798 Varian
800 Jack W. Wilke

"Dealey" Class
1006 Dealey
1014 Cromwell
1015 Hammerberg

"Courtney" Class
1021 Courtney
1022 Lester
1023 Evans
1024 Bridget
1025 Bauer
1026 Hopper
1027 John Willis
1028 van Voorhis
1029 Hartley
1030 Joseph K. Taussig

"Claud Jones" Class
1033 Claud Jones
1034 John P. Perry
1035 Charles Berry
1036 McMorris

"Bronstein" Class
1037 Bronstein
1038 McCloy

"Garcia" Class
1040 Garcia
1041 Bradley
1043 Edward McDonnell
1044 Brumby
1045 Davidson
1047 Voge
1048 Sample
1049 Koelsch
1050 Albert David
1051 O'Callahan

"Knox" Class
1052 Knox
1053 Roark
1054 Gray
1055 Hepburn
1056 Connole
1057 Rathburne
1058 Mayerkord
1059 W. S. Sims
1060 Lang
1061 Patterson
1062 Whipple
1063 Reasoner
1064 Lockwood
1065 Stein
1066 Marvin Shields
1067 Francis Hammond
1068 Vreeland
1069
1070 Downes
1071 Badger
1072 Blakely
1073 Conolly
1074 Harold E. Holt
1075 Trippe
1076 Fanning
1077 Ouellet
1078 Joseph Hewes
1079 Bowen
1080 Paul
1081 Aylwin
1082 Elmer Montgomery
1083 Cook
1084 McCandless
1085 Donald B. Beary
1086 Brewton
1087 Kirk
1088 Barbey
1089 Jesse L. Brown
1090
1091
1092
1093
1094
1095
1096
1097

BB—Battleships

"Iowa" Class
61 Iowa
62 New Jersey
63 Missouri
64 Wisconsin

CA—Heavy Cruisers

"Baltimore" Class
68 Baltimore
69 Boston
70 Canberra
71 Quincy
72 Pittsburgh
73 St. Paul
75 Helena

"Oregon City" Class
122 Oregon City
124 Rochester

"Baltimore" Class (Cont'd)
130 Bremerton
131 Fall River
133 Toledo

"Salem" Class
134 Des Moines

"Baltimore" Class (Cont'd)
135 Los Angeles

"Salem" Class (Cont'd)
139 Salem
148 Newport News

LFR—Inshore Fire Support Ships

"Carronade" Type
1 Carronade
LSMR Type
401 Big Black River
405 Broadkill River
409 Clarion River
412 Des Plaines River
512 Lamoille River
513 Laramie River
515 Owyhee River
522 Red River
525 St Francis River
531 Smokey Hill River

Warfare & Amphibious Warfare Ships

LCC—Amphibious Command Ships (ex-AGC)

"Mount McKinley" Class
7 Mount McKinley
11 Eldorado
12 Estes
16 Pocono
17 Taconic

"Blue Ridge" Class
19 Blue Ridge
20 Mount Whitney

LPH—Amphibious Assault Ships

"Iwo Jima" Class
2 Iwo Jima
3 Okinawa
7 Guadalcanal
9 Guam
10 Tripoli
11 New Orleans
12 Inchon

LKA—Amphibious Cargo Ships

"Andromeda" Class
54 Algol
56 Arneb
57 Capricornus
61 Muliphen
88 Uvalde
93 Yancey
94 Winston
97 Merrick

"Rankin" Class
103 Rankin
104 Seminole
105 Skagit
106 Union
107 Vermillion
108 Washburn

"Tulare" Type
112 Tulare

"Charleston" Class
113 Charleston
114 Durham
115 Mobile
116 St. Louis
117 El Paso

LPA—Amphibious Transports

"Bayfield" Class
36 Cambria
38 Chilton
44 Fremont
45 Henrico

"Haskell" Class
194 Sandoval
199 Maggoffin
208 Talladega
213 Mountrail
215 Navarro
220 Okanogan
222 Pickaway
237 Bexar

"Paul Revere" Class
248 Paul Revere
249 Francis Marion

LPR—Amphibious Transports (Small)

55 Laning
86 Hollis
90 Kirwin
100 Ringness
101 Knudson
119 Beverly W. Reid
123 Diachenko
124 Horace A. Bass
127 Begor
132 Balduck
135 Weiss

LPD—Amphibious Transport Docks

"Raleigh" Class
1 Raleigh
2 Vancouver
3 La Salle
"Austin" Class
4 Austin
5 Ogden
6 Duluth
7 Cleveland
8 Dubuque
9 Denver
10 Juneau
11 Coronado

12 Shreveport
13 Nashville
14 Trenton
15 Ponce

LSD—Dock Landing Ships

"Casa Grande" Class
13 Casa Grande
14 Rushmore
15 Shadwell

16 Cabildo
17 Catamount
18 Colonial
19 Comstock
20 Donner
21 Fort Mandan
22 Fort Marion
25 San Marcos
26 Tortuga
27 Whetstone

"Thomaston" Class
28 Thomaston
29 Plymouth Rock
30 Fort Snelling
31 Point Defiance
32 Speigel Grove
33 Alamo
34 Hermitage
35 Monticello

"Anchorage" Class
36 Anchorage
37 Portland
38 Pensacola
39 Mt. Vernon
40 Fort Fisher

LST—Tank Landing Ships
(511-1152 Series)

525 Caroline County
533 Cheboygan County
583 Churchill County
601 Clarke County
722 Dodge County
758 Duval County
762 Floyd County
786 Garrett County
819 Hampshire County
825 Hickman County
826 Holmes County
838 Hunterdon County
839 Iredell County
846 Jennings County
854 Kemper County
901 Litchfield County
902 Luzerne County
980 Meeker County
983 Middlesex County
1032 Monmouth County
1073 Outagamie County
1076 Page County
1077 Park County
1082 Pitkin County
1084 Polk County
1096 St. Clair County
1122 San Jaoquin County
1123 Sedgwick County
1126 Snohomish County
1148 Sumner County
1150 Sutter County

"Talbot County" Type
1153 Talbot County

"Terrebonne Parish" Class
1156 Terrebonne Parish
1157 Terrell County
1158 Tioga County
1159 Tom Green County
1160 Traverse County
1161 Vernon County
1162 Wahkiakum County
1163 Waldo County
1164 Walworth County
1165 Washoe County
1166 Washtenaw County
1167 Westchedter County
1168 Wexford County
1169 Whitfield County
1170 Windham County

"Suffolk County" Class
1171 De Soto County
1173 Suffolk County
1174 Grant County
1175 York County
1176 Graham County
1177 Lorain County
1178 Wood County

"Newport" Class
1179 Newport
1180 Manitowoc
1181 Sumter
1182 Fresno
1183 Peroria
1184 Frederick
1185 Schenectady
1186 Cayuga
1187 Tuscaloosa
1188 Saginaw
1189 San Bernardino
1190 Boulder
1191 Racine
1192 Spartanburg County
1193 Fairfax County
1194 Lamour County
1195 Barbour County
1196 Harlan County
1197 Barnstable County
1198

ADVANCED SHIPBOARD SYSTEMS

ASROC (Anti-Submarine Rocket)
Anti-submarine missile launched from surface ships with homing torpedo or nuclear depth charge as warhead. Launcher is Mk 10 or Mk 26 combination ASROC/surface-to-air missile launcher or Mk 16 eight-cell "pepper box". Installed in US Navy cruisers (CG, CGN), frigates (DLG, DLGN), destroyers (DD, DDG), and escort ships (DE, DEG); Japanese, Italian, West German, and Canadian destroyer-type ships.
Weight of missile approximately 1 000 lbs; length 15 ft; diameter 1 ft; span of fins 2·5 ft; payload: Mk 44 or Mk 46 acoustic-homing torpedo or nuclear depth charge; range one to six miles.
Prime contractor: Honeywell. Designation: RUR-5. Status: Operational.

AEGIS (formerly Advanced Surface Missile System)
Advanced surface-to-air missile system intended for use in US Navy frigates and destroyers to be built during the 1970s and 1980s. To have a capability against high-performance aircraft and air-launched, anti-ship missiles. Launcher is Mk 26 with combined surface-to-air and ASW missile capability. Aegis will have an electronic scanning radar with fixed antennae, and will be capable of controlling friendly aircraft as well as detection. Additional components will include the UYK-7 computer (a component of the Naval Tactical Data System) and "illuminators" for missile guidance.
Prime contractor: RCA. Status: Development (radars only; initially to use Standard missile). Status: Operational.

BPDMS (Basic Point Defence Missile System)
Close-in air defense system employing the Sparrow AIM-7E air-to-air missile (designated Sea Sparrow) and a modified ASROC-type "pepper box" launcher. Mounted in US Navy attack carriers and in the experimental missile ship *Norton Sound* (AVM 1). Reber Sparrow air-to-air missile for basic characteristics.

CAPTOR (Encapsulated Torpedo). Mk 46 torpedo inserted in mine casing. Prime contractor: Honeywell.

Extended-Range ASROC
Programme to extend range of ASROC to maintain surface ASW weapon range on par with Soviet submarine torpedo threat and to provide a weapon compatible with improved sonar range performance.

HARPOON
An air/ship-launched anti-ship missile intended to counter hostile missile-firing ships and small craft; for use in US Navy ships which do not now have a missile capability; quick reaction and conventional warhead. Designation: AGM-84A. Status: Development.

HARPY Advanced shipboard UHF tactical communications system.

Improved SUBROC. (Submarine Rocket). Programme to provide SUBROC with a non-nuclear warhead and capability for use against surface ships. May be part of STAM effort.

JIFDATS (Joint In-Flight Data Transmission System)
Multi-military service system for rapid transmission of reconnaissance data from the collecting aircraft to ship/land-based terminals for immediate use by tactical commanders. To be installed in US Navy attack carriers and possibly certain command ships. Ship-based aircraft include RF-4B Phantom and RA-5C Vigilante; sensors suitable for transmission of data include aerial cameras, infra-red detectors, and side-looking radar. Status: Development with pre-service tests scheduled for late 1970. Prime contractor: Northrop.

LAMPS (Light Airborne Multi-Purpose System)
Ship-launched helicopter intended for anti-submarine and missile-defence missions, with secondary roles of search-and-rescue and utility (e.g., parts and personnel transfer). The helicopter will have an all-up weight of not more than 6 000 lbs to permit operation from escort ships with DASH facilities; to have sensors and weapons in "pods" and modular packages to permit rapid maintenance, re-arming, and changing of mission equipment. For use aboard destroyer-type ships with hangars and certain amphibious warfare ships. Sensors to include dipping sonar, magnetic airborne detection (MAD), and sonobuoys with digital relays to permit control and attack direction by launching ship. Radar will be provided to extend detection range vis-a-vis hostile surface missile ships.
Weapons: 2 Mk 46 ASW torpedoes. Crew: pilot and 2 operators (plus passenger if mission equipment is removed). Endurance: mission goal is 2 hours on station several miles from launching ship.
Status: Approximatey 100 Kaman Seasprite helicopters being modified to SH-2D configuration as interim LAMPS. Initially being deployed on frigates.

NTDS (Naval Tactical Data System)
Combination of digital computers, displays, and transmission links to increase an individual ship commander's capability to assess tactical data and take action by integrating imput from various sensors (e.g., radars) and providing display of tactical situation and the defence or offence options available. Data can be transmitted among NTDS-equipped ships. An automatic mode initiates action to respond to greatest threats in a tactical situation. Also can be linked to Airborne Tactical Data System (ATDS) in E-2 Hawkeye aircraft.
To be fitted to all US Navy attack and ASW carriers, missile-armed cruisers and frigates, new amphibious command ships, and two escort ships (*Voge* and *Koelsch*).
Status: Operational (fitted in 46 ships through Fiscal Year 1971 programme).

PDSMS (Point Defence Surface Missile System). Follow-on to BPDMS with a Target Acquisition System (TAS), powered director, smaller launcher, and control console combined with the Sea Sparrow missile.
Status: Under development; also a NATO co-operative programme (less TAS) with Denmark, Italy, Netherlands and Norway. Intended for ships without larger missile capability.

SAMID (Ship Anti-Missile Integrated Defence)
An immediate effort to provide ships with defence against anti-ship attack missiles (e.g., Styx). SAMID integrates existing shipboard weapons, electronic warfare equipment, and passive and active sensors into a co-ordinated system. Data processing in larger ships will be compatable with NTDS. Effect will be to reduce reaction time from detection of missile to ships' response. (with deceptive electronic warfare and/or weapons). To be installed initially in frigates and aircraft carriers.
Status: Under evaluation.

SECT (Submarine Emergency Communications Transmitter)
Alarm device to warn if a submarine is disabled or sunk. One SECT buoy is to be installed in each US Navy nuclear attack submarine (SSN) and two in each ballistic missile submarine (SSBN), so arranged in the latter submarine that at least one buoy would survive the submarine being hit by a torpedo at any point. The system would release the buoy when (1) the water depth exceeds that of safe submarine operation, (2) subject to an internal pressure that exceeds certain limits, or (3) a "dead-man's switch" is not reset by the crew at two hour intervals. Upon release the buoy would float freely to the surface and transmit pre-set messages on four high frequencies to automatic receivers ashore; it could serve as a homing beacon to locate the *general* area of a submarine in distress.
Status: Advanced development. Prime contractor: Collins Radio.

SHORTSTOP
Advanced shipboard electronic system for anti-ship missile defence. Essentially a follow-on to the SAMID programme, SHORTSTOP is based on an advanced electronic-warfare system with electronically scanned passive receivers, computerised threat recognition, and computer-assisted reactive countermeasure control against anti-ship attack missiles. Officially described as "the most ambitious shipboard electronic warfare project yet undertaken". Initially to be fitted in the frigates. A SHORTSTOP JUNIOR system is being developed for smaller ships.

STAM (Submarine Tactical Missile). Tube-launched anti-ship missile intended for use in mid-1970 design nuclear attack submarine.

SUBROC (Submarine Rocket).
Anti-submarine missile launched from submarines with nuclear warhead. Launched from 21-inch torpedo tube. Carried in US Navy submarines of "Permit" and later classes with amidships torpedo tubes, BQQ-2 sonar, and Mk 113 torpedo fire control systems. The missile is fired from the submerged submarine, rises up through the surface, travels through air toward the hostile submarine, and then re-enters the water to detonate.
Weight of missile approximately 4 000 lbs; length 21 ft; diameter 1·75 ft (maximum); estimated range 25 to 30 miles.
Prime contractor: Goodyear. Designation: UUM-44A. Status: Operational.

VULCAN/PHALANX Rapid-fire, close-in gun system being developed to provide "last-ditch" defense against anti-ship missiles. Probably will be installed initially in frigates. To have "dynamic gun aiming" with fire control radar tracking projectiles and target(s).

TORPEDOES

Designation	Launch Platforms	Weight (pounds)	Length (feet)	Diameter (inches)	Propulsion	Guidance	Notes
Mk 37 Mod 2	Submarines	1 690	13·5	19	Electric	Wire	Anti-Submarine
Mk 37 Nod 3	Submarines	1 400	11·3	19	Electric	Active-passive acoustic homing	Anti-submarine
Mk 44 Mod 1	Surface ships (Mk 32 tubes and ASROC); aircraft	433	8·5	12·75	Electric	Active acoustic homing	Anti-Submarine
Mk 45 Mod 1 & Mod 2 (ASTOR)	Submarines	2 400	19·9	19	Electric	Wire	Anti-submarine; nuclear warhead; 10+ mile range
Mk 46 Mod 0	Surface ships (Mk 32 tubes and ASROC); aircraft	580	8·4	12·75	Solid-propellent	Active-passive acoustic homing	Anti-submarine; successor to Mk 44
Mk 46 Mod 1		512	8·4	12·75	Liquid mono-propellent	Active-passive acoustic homing	Anti-submarine; successor to Mk 44
Mk 48 Mod 0	Submarines	Approx 3 600	19	21	Liquid mono-propellent	Wire/terminal acoustic homing	Anti-submarine; development only; some will convert to Mod 2; 10+ mile range; Westinghouse
Mk 48 Mod 1	Submarines	approx 3 600	19	21	Liquid mono-propellent	Wire/terminal acoustic homing	Anti-submarine and anti-shipping; larger warhead than Mod 0; Clevite
Mk 48 Mod 2	Submarines	approx 3 600	19	21	Liquid mono-propellent	Wire/terminal acoustic homing	Anti-submarine and anti-shipping; production version of Mod 0; Westinghouse

NAVY MISSILES

Name	Prime Contractor	Weight (pounds)	Length (feet)	Diameter (inches)	Range (miles)	Propulsion	Notes
FLEET BALLISTIC MISSILES							
POLARIS A-2 UGM-27B	Lockheed	30 000	31	54	1 725	Solid-propellent	Carried by 5 "Ethan Allen" and 3 "Lafayette" class submarines; to be replaced by A-3 and Poseidon, respectively. 2-stage inertial guidance, nuclear warhead.
POLARIS A-3 UGM-27C	Lockheed	30 000	32	54	2 875	Solid-propellent	Carried by 5 "George Washington" and most "Lafayette" class submarines; to be replaced in latter by Poseidon. 2-stage, inertial guidance, warhead of three re-entry vehicles aimed at same target.
POSEIDON C-3 UGM-73A	Lockheed	65 000	34·2	74	approx 2 900	Solid-propellent	To replace Polaris in 31 "Lafayette" class submarines; increased accuracy and payload over Polaris; range varies with payload. 2-stage, inertial guidance, reportedly carries ten Mk 3 re-entry vehicles that can be *independently* targeted (MIRV)

Name	Prime Contractor	Length (feet)	Propulsion	Speed (Mach)	Range (Miles)	Guidance	Notes
AIR TO AIR							
SPARROW III AIM-7E AIM-7F	Raytheon	12	Solid propellent	3·5+	8+	Semi-active radar homing	Arms carrier fighters providing 360° attack capability; -7E used as Sea Sparrow in Basic Point Defence Missile System (BPDMS) is designated RIM-7H; -7F has solid-state electronics.
SIDEWINDER IC A1M-9D, A1M-9G, A1M-9H, A1M-9L	Philco and Motorola	9·5	Solid propellent	2·5	2	Infra-red homing	Arms carrier fighters; -9H has solid-state electronics; -9C dropped in 1970; -9L in development.
PHOENIX AIM-54A	Hughes	13	Solid propellent			Radar homing	To arm F-14 fighters; used with AWG-9 weapons control system; can attack multiple targets; 2-stage; fitted with electronic countermeasures capability.
AGILE		8	Solid propellent				Close-in "dogfight" missile for F-14 and 1975-era aircraft; 360° attack capability; to replace Sidewinder.
AIR TO SURFACE							
BULLPUP A AGM-12B	Martin and Maxson	11	Storable liquid	1·8	6	Command	250-lb warhead; radio-link command guidance
BULLPUP B AGM-12C	Martin	13·6	Storable liquid		9	Command	1 000-lb warhead
BULLPUP AGM-12E	Martin		Storable liquid			Command	Larger warhead
SHRIKE AGM-45A	Texas Instrument-Sperry	10	Solid propellent		approx 10	Passive-radar homing	Anti-radar missile used on A-4, A-6 and A-7
CONDOR AGM-53A	North American		Solid propellent		approx 40	Television from aircraft; "blind launch"	In "operational development" status; conventional warhead; for use on A-6
WALLEYE AGM-62A	Martin	11·4	Nil (glide bomb)		less than Condor	Television from aircraft; "blind launch"	1 000-lb warhead
STANDARD ARM AGM-78A, AGM-78B AGM-78C	General Dynamics	14	Solid propellant			Radar homing	Homes on enemy radar beams; more sophisticated than SHRIKE for use on A-6
HARPOON AGM-84A							Air and ship-launched anti-ship missile; for use on "non-missile" ships (probably ASROC launchers); characteristics not decided.
SURFACE TO AIR							
TALOS RIM-8G, RIM-8J	Bendix	33	Ramjet with solid propellent booster	2·5+	65+ slant	Beam-riding cruise phase; semi-active homing	Carried by Cruisers; high explosive or nuclear warhead; improved homing capability.
STANDARD (ER) RIM-67A	General Dynamics	27	Solid propellent (Same booster as Terrier)		20+ slant	Semi-active homing	Terrier replacement; compatible with existing launchers; 2 stage (Extended Range); for *Long Beach*, 3 CVA, 30 DLG/DLGN.
STANDARD (MR) RIM-66A	General Dynamics	14	Solid propellent		10+ slant	Semi-active homing	Tartar replacement; compatible with existing launchers; as ER without booster stage; for 3 CG and 35 DDG ships; surface-to-surface variant being developed for use on PG-type ships and launch from modified ASROC "pepper box" on "non-missile" surface combatants (DD-DE).
ADVANCED TERRIER RIM-2F	General Dynamics	26·5	Solid propellent	3·0	20+ slant	Homing all the way	Carried by frigates, carriers, cruisers; replaces earlier Terrier BW and BT series; 2 stages.
IMPROVED TARTAR RIM-24B, RIM-24C	General Dynamics	15	Solid propellent	2·5	approx 12·5 slant	Semi-active homing	Carried by destroyers, escorts, and CG cruisers; replaces RIM-24A model.

NAVAL AVIATION

US Naval Aviation currently is comprised of just over 6 000 operational aircraft: approximately 3 900 fixed-wing aircraft and 550 helicopters flown by Navy personnel, and 1 000 fixed-wing aircraft and 700 helicopters flown by the Marine Corps. These totals do not include aircraft of the Naval and Marine Corps reserve units.

The principal Navy tactical air organizations planned under the 30 June 1972 force levels are:

Eleven Attack Carrier Air Wings (CVW) with 1 300 fighter, attack, reconnaissance, electronic warfare, early warning, and tanker aircraft. (Compositions of air wings and air groups are described in the section on Aircraft Carriers).
Four Anti-Submarine Air Groups (CVSG) with 170 anti-submarine fixed-wing aircraft and helicopters, and early warning aircraft.
Two Readiness Attack Air Wings (RCVW) that operate front-line aircraft for preparing pilots and naval flight officers for assignment to combat squadrons.
Approximately 25 Patrol Squadrons (VP), each with nine P-3 Orion maritime reconnaissance/anti-submarine aircraft.
Two Fleet Air Reconnaissance Squadrons (VQ) that perform specialised reconnaissance with EA-3B and RA-3B Skywarriors, EC-121 and WC-121 Super Constellations, and EP-3 Orions.
One Light Attack Squadron (VAL-4) that operates OV-10A Bronco counter-insurgency aircraft in South Vietnam.
One Light Helicopter Attack Squadron (HAL-3) that operates UH-1 Huey and AH-1 Sea Cobra gunship helicopters in South Vietnam.
One Mine Countermeasures Squadron (HM) that operates RH-53 Sea Stallion minesweeping helicopters.
Seven Helicopter Combat Support Squadrons (HC) that operate SH-3 Sea Kings, SH-2 Sealites UH-2 Sea Sprites, and UH-46 Sea Knights aboard various combatant ships and auxiliaries.
Eight Fleet Composite Squadrons (VC) that operate F-8 and DF-8 Crusaders, DP-2 Neptunes, A-4 Skyhawks, US-2 Trackers, and UH-34 Seahorse helicopters to provide target, electronics calibration, photographic, and other services to ships.
Three Air Test and Evaluation Squadrons (VX) that operate various aircraft in support of Navy experimental and development programmes.
One Oceanographic Development Squadron (VXN-8) that operates NC-121 Super Constellations and an RP-3D Orion on specialised scientific research and electronic missions.
One Antarctic Support Squadron (VXE-6) that operates C-121J Super Constellations, LC-130 Hercules, and LH-34D Seahorse and UH-1D Huey helicopters in support of US scientific efforts in the Antarctic.

One Weather Squadron (VW) flying WP-3A Orions and WC-121 Super Constellations for storm reconnaissance.
Four Fleet Tactical Support Squadrons (VR) that operate C-131 Samaritans, C-130 Hercules, C-118 Liftmasters, CT-39 Sabreliners, C-2 Grayhounds, and C-1 Traders to provide passenger and cargo service for the Fleet.
Two Carrier On-board Delivery Squadrons (VRC) that operate CT-39 Sabreliners, C-2 Grayhounds, and C-1 Traders to provide delivery of passengers and cargo to the Fleet, with the C-2 and C-1 aircraft having a carrier-landing capability.
Two Ferry Squadrons (VRF) that provide ferry services for various naval aircraft.
Twenty Training Squadrons (VT) that operate T-2 Buckeyes, T-34 Mentors, TS-2A Trackers, and TA-4F Skyhawks to provide basic and advanced flight training to Navy, Marine, and Coast Guard pilots.
One Helicopter Training Squadron (HT-8) that operates TH-1 Huey and TH-57 Searanger helicopters for training Navy, Marine, and Coast Guard pilots.

The principal tactical air organizations of the Marine Corp are three Marine Aircraft Wings (MAW) that operate some 1 200 fixed-wing aircraft and helicopters. Each wing has several fighter/attack (F-4 Phantom) and attack (A-6 Intruder and A-4 Skyhawk) squadrons, one refueller/transport squadron (C-130 Hercules), one observation squadron (UH-1 Huey, OV-10A Bronco), heavy helicopter squadrons (CH-53 Sea Stallion), medium helicopter squadrons (CH-46 Sea Knight), and light helicopter squadrons (UH-1 Huey, AH-1 Sea Cobra). One wing normally is assigned in support of each Marine division. A total of 550 carrier-type fighter and attack aircraft are operated by the Marine Corps and periodically these squadrons operate from Navy attack carriers to compensate for reduced Navy aircraft levels and to provide flexibility in planning.

The Marine Corps has begun flying the first of 114 AV-8A Harrier V/STOL attack aircraft that will be acquired. The first 12 aircraft were delivered during 1971 to Marine Attack Squadron (VMA) 513.

The reserve components of Naval Aviation are two Reserve Carrier Air Wings (CVWR) flying F-8 and RF-8 Crusaders, A-4 Skyhawks, and E-1B Tracers; two Reserve Carrier Air Groups(CVSGR) with S-2 Trackers, SH-3 Sea Kings, and E-1B Tracers; 12 Patrol Squadrons (VP) with SP-2H Neptunes and P-3A Orions; three Transport Squadrons (VR) with C-118 Liftmasters; and one Marine Aircraft Wing (MAW-4) with F-8 and RF-8 Crusaders, A-4 Skyhawks, and CH-46 Sea Knight CH-53 Sea Stallion, and UH-1 Huey helicopters. The organization, training, and equipment of the reserve components of Naval Aviation designed to permit rapid activation of the various units and their integration into the operating forces.

SHIP-BASED AIRCRAFT

Name	Manufacturer	Models	Mission (crew)	Engines	Notes
SKYWARRIOR	McDonnell-Douglas	EA-3A, EA-3B KA-3B EKA-3B RA-3B	electronic countermeasures (4-7) tanker TACOS (Tanker Aircraft/Countermeasures Or Strike) Photographic reconnaissance (3-5)	2 Pratt & Whitney J57	Loaded weight approx 82 000 lbs; guns removed; Skywarrior detachments on deployed attack carriers; flown only by Navy; to be replaced by EA-6 and KA-6 variants
SKYHAWK	McDonnell-Douglas	A-4B, A-4C, A-4L TA-4A, TA-4B A-4E, A-4F, A-4J TA-4F A-4M	light attack (1) light attack trainer (2) light attack (1) light attack trainer (2) light attack (1)	1 Wright J65 1 Wright J65 1 Pratt & Whitney J52 1 Pratt & Whitney J52 1 Pratt & Whitney J52	Loaded weight approx 24 500 lbs with 11 000+ lbs bombs, rockets, missiles for A-4F; 2 20 mm cannon (1 gun replaced by ECM gear in Vietnam); A-4C with 2 Sidewinder missiles used as CVS fighter; flown by Navy and Marines; TA-4J carries Shrike, Bullpup, "buddy store" fuel, improved avionics; A-4L carries Walleye and Shrike (A-4C mod); improved A-4M for Marines.
VIGILANTE	North American	RA-5C	reconnaissance (2)	2 General Electric J79	Multi-sensor, all weather reconnaissance; loaded weight approx 61 700 lbs; most remanufactured A-5A, A-5B; RA-5C production reopened 1967-1969; flown by Navy from larger attack carriers
VIGILANTE	North American-Rockwell	RA-5C	reconnaissance (2)	2 General Electric J79	Multi-sensor, all weather reconnaissance; loaded weight approx 61 700 lbs; most remanufactured A-5A, A-5B; RA-5C production reopened 1967-1970; flown by Navy from larger attack carriers
INTRUDER	Grumman	A-6B, A-6E, EA-6A EA-6B KA-6D A-6C	all-weather attack (2) electronic countermeasures (2) electronic surveillance & ECM (4) tankers (2) special TRIM interdiction (2)	2 Pratt & Whitney J52	Loaded weight approx 60 600 lbs with 15 000 lbs bombs, missiles; A-6B carries Standard ARM; flown by Navy and Marines; improved electronics in A-6E. A-6C has special electronics for trail interdiction, some KA-6s converted from A-6As

SHIP-BASED AIRCRAFT—*Continued*

Name	Manufacturer	Models	Mission (crew)	Engines	Notes
CORSAIR II	Ling-Temco-Vought	A-7A, A-7B A-7E	light attack (1) light attack (1)	I Pratt & Whitney TF30 1 Pratt & Whitney TF 41	Loaded weight approx 38 000 lbs with 15 000 lbs bombs, rockets, missiles (including 2 air-to-air) for A-7A; 2 20 mm cannon in A-7A, A-7B, 1 20 mm M61 Gatling gun in A-7E; flown primarily by Navy; Marine procurement deferred
PHANTOM II	McDonnell-Douglas	F-4B, F-4J, F-4G RF-4B, RF-4J	all-weather fighter (2) photographic reconnaissance (2)	2 General Electric J79	Loaded weight approx 54 000 lbs with 13 000+ lbs bombs, rockets, missiles for F-4B; no guns; recon variants flown only by Marines; fighters by Navy and Marines (on larger attack carriers); F-4J has improved avionics, pulse doppler radar (AWG-10); F-4G (few) has special data transmission gear; 6 Sparrows or 4 sparrows and 4 sidewinders
CRUSADER	Ling-Temco-Vought	F-8H, F-8J F-8K, F-8L RF-8A, RF-8G	fighter (1) fighter (1) photographic reconnaissance (1)	1 Pratt & Whitney J57	All except RF-8A remanufactured from earlier models; 4 20 mm cannon in fighters plus four air-to-air missiles and limited bomb/rocket capability (to 4 000 lbs); flown only by Navy from "Essex" class attack carriers; pulse doppler mode APQ-49 radar in F-8J
TOMCAT		AV-8A	V/STOL fighter (1)	1 Rolls-Royce Bristol Pegasus 101	12 aircraft procured for Marines in Fiscal Year 1970; previously tested aboard LPD amphibious ships as XV-6A; no guns; approx 4 500 lbs bombs rockets, missiles with STOL weight of 23 000 lbs; 3 000 lbs external payload as VTOL
HARRIER	Hawker-Siddeley (McDonnell-Douglas)	F-14A F-14B, F-14C	all-weather fighter (2)	2 Pratt & Whitney TF30 2 TF-400 series	Formerly VFX/VFAX designs; replacement for F-111B; F-14A to be operational mid-1973; improved engines in F-14B/C; improved avionics in F-14C; 1 20 mm M61 Gatling gun, 4 sparrow or 6 Phoenix air-to-air missiles plus Sidewinder missiles or bombs; to be flown by Navy and marines; RF-14 planned.
TRACKER	Grumman	S-2E, S-2G	anti-submarine (4)	2 Wright R-1820	Loaded weight approx 29 000 lbs; no guns; variety of bombs, depth charges, torpedoes; flown by Navy from ASW carriers and CVA *Saratoga* in 1971-1972.
—	Lockheed	S-3A	anti-submarine (4)	2 General Electric TF34 turbofan	Former VSX; replacement for S-2 Tracker; improved sensors and data processing equipment
BRONCO	North American-Rockwell	OV-10A	multi-purpose/reconnaissance (2)	2 Airesearch T76	Counter-insurgency aircraft; 9 900 lbs loaded; can carry freight, weapon pods, bombs, 5 troops or 2 litters; has flown from helicopter carriers (LPH); used by Navy and Marines
TRACER	Grumman	E-1B	airborne early warning (4)	2 Wright R-1820	Loaded weight approx 27 000 lbs; no guns; detachments operate from ASW carriers; flown by Navy; saucer-shaped APS-82 radar atop fuselage
HAWKEYE	Grumman	E-2A, E-2B, E-2C	airborne early warning (5)	2 Allison T56	Loaded weight approx 49 000 lb; no guns; detachments operate from attack carriers; flown by Navy, rotating saucer-shaped APS-96 radar atop fuselage; improved avionics in E-2B and planned E-2C
TRADER	Grumman	C-1A	light transport (2+9 passengers)	2 Wright R-1820	Carrier On-board Delivery (COD) transport version of Tracker/Tracer series; flown by Navy
GREYHOUND	Grumman	C-2A	light transport (3+33 passengers)	2 Allison T56	COD transport; wings, engines, subsystems, same as Hawkeye; rear-loading cargo compartment; flown primarily by Navy, few in Marine service

SHIP-BASED AIRCRAFT—*Continued*

Name	Manufacturer	Models	Mission (crew)	Engines	Notes
HUEY (official name IROQUOIS)	Bell	UH-1B, UH-1E UH-1L UH-1N	utility/gunship helicopter (2+7 troops) utility/transport (2+7 troops) utility/transport	1 Lycoming T53 1 Lycoming T53 2 Pratt & Whitney PT6	Loaded weight approx 9 500 lbs; UH-1B/1E have armour; normal armament 2 7·62 mm M60 MG and two pods of 2·75" rockets; flown by Navy and Marines
SEA COBRA	Bell	AH-1J	helicopter gunship (2)	2 Lycoming T53	Loaded weight approx 9 500 lbs; modified Huey design; rapid-fire 20 mm cannon in chin turret; stub wings for additional guns, rockets, missiles; gun improvement planned; flown by Marines and Navy
SEASPRITE	Kaman	UH-2A, UH-2B HH-2C, UH-2C	utility/rescue (2+2 passengers) utility/rescue (2-3+10 passengers)	1 General Electric T58 2 General Electric T58	Loaded weight approx 8 600 lb for UH-2A/B, 10 000 for -2C variants; -2B has auxiliary fuel tanks fitted and some avionics deleted; 12 HH-2C have 7·62 mm MG in chin turret and two waiste MG for Vietnam rescue; flown by Navy
SEALITE	Kaman	SH-2D	anti-submarine	2 General Electric T58	Converted UH-2 type for Light Airborne Multi-Purpose Systems (LAMPS) role; provides ASW capability for destroyer-type ships
SEA KING	Sikorsky	SH-3A, SH-3D HH-3A, HH-3G	anti-submarine helicopter (4) rescue helicopter	2 General Electric T58	Loaded weight approx 18 600 lbs for SH-3D; SH-3A/D have dunking sonar, carry 840 lbs of torpedoes; SH-3A/D assigned to carriers; HH-3A has 7·62 mm MG in turret; HH-3G is non-combat mod; flown by Navy
SEAHORSE	Sikorsky	LH-34D, UH-34E, UH34G	utility helicopter (2-4+ up to 12 troops)	1 Wright R-1820	SH-34 anti-submarine variants discarded by US Navy; LH-34D for Antarctic operations; UH-34D has fired Bullpup missile; no guns, flown by Navy and Marines; few remain
SEA KNIGHT	Boeing Vertol	CH-46A, CH-46D UH-46A, UH-46D CH-46F	cargo/transport helicopter (3+25 troops) utility/replenishment helicopter (3) cargo/transport helicopter (3+33 troops)	2 General Electric T58	Loaded weight approx 21 400 lbs for -46A variants, 23 000 lbs for -46D variants; 4 000 lbs cargo in -46A; CH-46 variants flown by Marines as medium helicopter; UH-46 variants flown by Navy for Vertical Replenishment (VERTREP); no guns; CH-46F has improved navigation gear and avionics
SEA STALLION	Sikorsky	CH-53A CH-53E RH-53	cargo/transport helicopter (3+38 troops) cargo/transport helicopter minesweeping	2 General Electric T64 3 General Electric T64	CH-53A weight approx 37 000 lbs; 8 000 lbs cargo; no guns; flown by Marines as heavy lift helicopter

COMMAND AND COMMUNICATION SHIPS

This category is comprised of command and communication ships operated in support of national and joint US commands. These are different functions than fleet and amphibious command ships that are essentially Navy or Navy-Marine Corp activities.

The only joint command flagship now in commission is the *Valcour* which serves as flagship for the Commander, US Middle East Force who represents US military interests "East of Suez" to the Straits of Malacca where the jurisdiction of the US Commander-in-Chief Pacific begins. The Commander US Middle East Force is generally a Rear Admiral. (In addition to his diminutive flagship—a sister ship to the flagship of the Ethiopian Navy—the

Commander, Middle East Force normally has two destroyers assigned on rotation from the Atlantic Fleet). In reserve are two ships configured to serve as afloat command posts for the President or other national authorities and two communication relay ships. The command ships *Northampton* and *Wright* were designated as National Emergency Command Posts Afloat (NECPA) and operated off the Atlantic coast of the United States, prepared to receive the President or other national authorities in the event a nuclear attack was believed imminent.

The major communication relay ships *Arlington* and *Annapolis* were operated by the Navy to provide mobile

communication facilities for Navy and other service commanders where shore-based communication facilities were inadequate or did not exist. While the command ships *Northampton* and *Wright* are floating command headquarters and their communication facilities are for transmitting and receiving large volumes of voice and teletype communications (as well as electronic data), the communication relay ships *Annapolis* and *Arlington* are equipped to relay large volumes of teletype communications. Further, the two radio relay ships do not have the command centres, theatres, data display facilities, message centres, and staff accommodations that are the keys to the command ships' capabilities.

1 MISCELLANEOUS FLAGSHIP (AGF): CONVERTED SEAPLANE TENDER

Name	No.	Builder	Laid down	Launched	Commissioned
*VALCOUR	AGF 1 (ex-AVP 55)	Lake Washington Shipyard	21 Dec 1942	5 June 1943	5 July 1946

Displacement, tons	1 766 standard; 2 800 full load
Length, feet (*metres*)	300 (*91·4*) wl; 310·8 (*94·7*) oa
Beam, feet (*metres*)	41·1 (*12·5*)
Draft, feet (*metres*)	13 (*4·0*)
Guns	8—40 mm anti-aircraft (1 quad forward, 2 twin amidships)
Main engines	2 diesels (Fairbanks, Morse); 6 080 bhp; 2 shafts
Speed, knots	18
Complement	215

The *Valcour* serves as flagship for the US Commander Middle East Force, operating in the Persian Gulf, Arabian Sea, and Indian Ocean. From 1950 to 1965 the *Valcour* rotated this duty with her sister ships *Duxbury Bay* (AVP 38) and *Greenwich Bay* (AVP 41). All three were fitted with additional communications, radar, and electronic countermeasures (ECM) equipment; painted white, and partially air conditioned. The *Valcour* was reclassified from AVP 55 to AGF 1 of 15 Dec 1965 and is now permanently assigned to the Middle East area.

VALCOUR (AGF 1)

1966, United States Navy

DESIGN. The *Valcour* was one of 35 "Barnegat" class small seaplane tenders built during World War II. Several of these ships survive as Coast Guard cutters and two as Navy auxiliaries, the *Valcour* and the *San Carlos* (ex-AVP 51) in service as an oceanographic research ship (AGOR 1, renamed *Joshiah Willard Gibbs*).

(See Coast Guard section for subsequent disposals and transfers of AVPs listed below as having gone to that service).

DISPOSALS AND TRANSFERS

Barnegat (AVP 10) stricken in 1958; **Biscayne** (AVP 11) converted to amphibious force flagship (AGC 18) in 1944, transferred to Coast Guard in 1946; **Casco** (AVP 12), **Mackinac** (AVP 13), **Humboldt** (AVP 21), **Matagorda** (AVP 22), **Absecon** (AVP 23), **Chincoteague** (AVP 24), **Coos Bay** (AVP 25), **Half Moon**

(AVP 26), **Rockaway** (AVP 29), **Unimak** (AVP 31), **Yakutat** (AVP 32), **Barataria** (AVP 33), **Bering Strait** (AVP 34), **Castle Rock** (AVP 35), and **Cook Inlet** (AVP 36) loaned to Coast Guard in 1948-1949 and subsequently transferred outright; **Mobjack** (AVP 27) and **Oyster Bay** (AVP 28) completed as motor torpedo boat tenders (AGP 7 and AGP 6), the **Mobjack** being transferred to the Coast and Geodetic Survey in 1946 (renamed *Pioneer*; stricken in 1966); **Oyster Bay** to Italy in 1957; **San Pablo** (AVP 30) converted to surveying ship (AGS 30) in 1949; **Corson** (AVP 37) stricken in 1966 (target); **Duxbury Bay** (AVP 38) stricken in 1966; **Gardiners Bay** (AVP 39) to Norway

in 1958; **Floyds Bay** (AVP 40) stricken in 1960; **Greenwich Bay** (AVP 41) stricken in 1966; **Onslow** (AVP 48) stricken in 1960; **Orca** (AVP 49) to Ethiopia in 1961; **Rehoboth** (AVP 50) converted to surveying ship (AGS 50) in 1949.

Shelikof (AVP 52) stricken in 1960; **Suisun** (AVP 53) stricken in 1966 (target); **Timbler** (AVP 54) stricken in 1960; **Wachapreague** (AVP 56) and **Willoughby** (AVP 57) completed as MTB tenders (AGP 8 and AGP 9), both transferred to Coast Guard in 1946; construction of AVP 42-47 and AVP 58-67 was cancelled; planned conversion of AVP 21, 22, and 29 to special-purpose ships (AG 121-123) was cancelled.

NORTHAMPTON (CC 1) See following page

1968, United States Navy

Command and Communication Ships—*Continued*

1 COMMAND SHIP (CC): CONVERTED HEAVY CRUISER

Name **NORTHAMPTON**	No. CC 1 (ex-CLC 1, ex-CA 125)	Builder Bethlehem Steel Co (Quincy)	Laid down 31 Aug 1944	Launched 27 Jan 1951	Commissioned 7 Mar 1953

Displacement, tons	14 700 standard; 17.200 full load
Length, feet (*metres*)	664 (*202·4*) wl; 676 (*206·0*) oa
Beam, feet (*metres*)	71 (*21·6*)
Draft, feet (*metres*)	29 (*8·8*)
Guns	1—5 in (*127 mm*) 54 cal dual-purpose (see *Gunnery* notes)
Helicopters	2 normally carried
Armour	Side 6 in (*152 mm*); Decks 3 in + 2 in (*76 + 51 mm*)
Main engines	4 geared turbines (General Electric); 120 000 shp; 4 shafts
Boilers	4 (Babcock & Wilcox)
Speed, knots	33
Complement	1 191 (68 officers, 1 123 enlisted men)
Flag accommodations	approx 450

The *Northampton* was begun as a heavy cruiser of the "Oregon City" class, numbered CA 125. She was cancelled on 11 Aug 1945 when 56·2 per cent complete. She was re-ordered as a command ship on 1 July 1948 and designated CLC 1 (Task Force Command Ship and later Tactical Command Ship). As CLC 1 she was configured for use primarily by fast carrier force commanders and fitted with an elaborate combat information centre (CIC), electronic equipment, and flag accommodations. She was largely employed as flagship for Commander Second Fleet in the Atlantic prior to her being made available for use by national authorities. Her designation was changed to CC (Command Ship) on 15 April 1961 and she was relieved as Second Fleet flagship on October 1961.

Decommissioned on 8 April 1970 and placed in reserve.

DESIGN. The *Northampton* is one deck higher than other US heavy cruisers to provide additional office and equipment space. Her foremast is the tallest unsupported mast afloat (125 feet). All living and working spaces are air conditioned. Helicopter landing area aft, but no hangar.

ELECTRONICS. Advanced communications, electronic data processing equipment, and data displays are installed; tropospheric scatter and satellite relay communications facilities. As CLC 1 the *Northampton* carried what was believed the largest radar antenna afloat (see 1968-69 and earlier editions); designated SPS-2; removed in 1963.

GUNNERY. As built the *Northampton* mounted 4—5 inch and 8—3 inch weapons. The 5 inch guns were Mk 16 54 calibre weapons capable of firing up to 45 rounds per minute. (Similar weapons are installed in US destroyer-type ships built since World War II). The original 3 inch 50 calibre guns in open twin mounts were replaced by twin 3 inch/70 calibre rapid-fire guns in closed mounts. The latter were removed in 1962 because of high maintenance requirements; removal of the guns and their ammunition hoists, et cetera, provided additional space for berthing, offices, and electronic equipment. When decommissioned she was armed with only one 5 inch gun in the "X" position.

OPERATIONAL. The *Northampton* served as flagship of the US Sixth Fleet in the Mediterranean in 1954-1955, and as flagship of the US Second Fleet in the Western Atlantic from 1955 to 1961.

PHOTOGRAPH. Note final configuration prior to deactivation in the photograph on previous page; superstructure forward of the bridge has been enlarged considerably. Note large radar antenna on forward tower; SPS-37 and SPS-8A search antennae on after tower.

1 COMMAND SHIP (CC) }
1 MAJOR COMMUNICATIONS RELAY SHIP (AGMR) } CONVERTED AIRCRAFT CARRIERS

Name	No.	Builder	Laid down	Launched	CVL Comm	CC-AGMR Comm.
WRIGHT	CC 2 (ex-AVT 7, ex-CVL 49)	New York SB Corp	21 Aug 1944	1 Sep 1945	9 Feb 1947	11 May 1963
ARLINGTON (ex-*Saipan*)	AGMR 2 (ex-CC 3, ex-AVT 6, ex-CVL 48)	New York SB Corp	10 July 1944	8 July 1944	14 July 1945	27 Aug 1966

Displacement, tons	14 500 standard; 19 600 full load
Length, feet (*metres*)	664 (*202·4*) wl; 683·6 (*208·4*) oa
Beam, feet (*metres*)	76·8 (*23·6*)
Draft, feet (*metres*)	28 (*8·5*)
Flight deck width, feet (*metres*)	109 (*33·2*)
Guns	*Wright* 8—40 mm anti-aircraft (twin); *Arlington* 8—3 in (*76 mm*) 50 calibre (twin)
Helicopters	5 or 6 carried by *Wright*
Main engines	4 geared turbines (General Electric); 120 000 shp; 4 shafts
Boilers	4 (Babcock & Wilcox)
Speed, knots	33
Complement	746 plus approx 1 000 on command or communications staff

These ships were built as the light carriers *Saipan* (CVL 48) and *Wright* (CVL 49), respectively. They served as experimental and training carriers for a decade before being mothballed in 1967. Both were reclassified as Auxiliary Aircraft Transports on 15 May 1959, being designated AVT 6 (*Saipan*) and AVT 7 (*Wright*). The *Wright* was converted to a command ship at the Puget Sound Naval Shipyard, 1962-1963; the *Saipan* was to have been similarly converted, but the requirement for an additional ship of this category was cancelled. The *Saipan* subsequently was converted to a major communications relay ship at the Alabama Drydock and Shipbuilding Company in 1953-1965, and renamed *Arlington*. See Conversion and Nomenclature notes. (The survivors of the "Independence" class of light carriers, converted from cruisers during World War II, became Aircraft Transports (AVT); see disposal notes under Aircraft Carriers section).

The *Arlington* was decommissioned on 14 Jan 1970 and placed in reserve; the *Wright* was similarly decommissioned on 22 May 1970 and placed in reserve.

DESIGN. Although both of these ships were laid down with the specific intention of being constructed as aircraft carriers, their hulls and machinery duplicate the design of the "Baltimore" class heavy cruisers. As built they had small island bridge structures and four small funnels aft of the island trunked out at right angles. When aircraft carriers they could operate approximately 50 contemporary aircraft including jets.

CONVERSION. The *Wright* was converted to a command ship under the Fiscal Year 1962 authorisation at a cost of $25 000 000. Like the *Northampton*, she is fitted with elaborate communications, data processing, and display facilities for use by national authorities. The command spaces include presentation theatres similar to those at command posts ashore. The *Wright* has the most powerful transmitting antennae ever installed on a ship. They are mounted on plastic-glass masts to reduce interference with electronic transmissions. The tallest mast is 83 feet high and is designed to withstand 100-mph winds. She was reclassified from AVT 7 to CC 2 on 1 Sep 1962.

The *Saipan* was converted to a major communications relay ship at a cost of $26 886 424. She actually began conversion to a command ship (CC 3) and work was halted in February 1964. Work was resumed for her conversion to a communications ship later that year. She is fitted with elaborate communications relay equipment for the support of major commands afloat or ashore. The *Saipan* was reclassified from AVT 6 to CC 3 on 1 Jan 1964, and to AGMR 2 on 3 Sep 1964; she was renamed *Arlington* in April 1965.

The flat unencumbered deck of an aircraft carrier-type ship facilitates antenna placement for optimum electromagnetic wave propagation. The new "Blue Ridge" class of amphibious command ships has a similar appearance.

WRIGHT (CC 2)

1968, US Navy, PH 1 Arnold A. Clemons

NOMENCLATURE. The Navy's two communications ships are named for the naval radio stations at Arlington, Virginia, and Annapolis, Maryland.

PHOTOGRAPHS. The *Wright* has a large pylon mast supporting a "dish" antenna amidships and two pole antenna masts; *Arlington* has two 3 inch gun mounts at forward and after ends of flight deck. Also, *Arlington* has letters "GMR" preceeding hull number, following identification scheme of deleting initial letter "L" or "A" for US amphibious and auxiliary ships. Note open bow configuration of *Wright* and *Arlington* in comparison with enclosed bow of *Annapolis* (AGMR 1).

Command and Communication Ships—*continued*

1 MAJOR COMMUNICATIONS RELAY SHIP (AGMR): CONVERTED ESCORT CARRIER

Name	No.	Builder	Laid down	Launched	CVE Comm.	AGMR Comm.
ANNAPOLIS	AGMR 1 (ex-AKV 39, ex-CVE 107)	Todd Shipyards (Tacoma)	29 Nov 1943	20 July 1944	5 Feb 1945	7 Mar 1964

Displacement, tons	11 473 standard ; 22 500 full load
Length, feet (*metres*)	525 (*160·0*) wl ; 563 (*171·6*) oa
Beam, feet (*metres*)	75 (*22·9*)
Draft, feet (*metres*)	30·6 (*9·3*)
Flight deck width, feet (*metres*)	106 (*32·5*)
Guns	8—3 in (*76 mm*) 50 calibre anti-aircraft (twin)
Main engines	2 turbines (Allis Chalmers) ; 16 000 shp ; 2 shafts
Boilers	4 (Combustion Engineering)
Speed, knots	18
Complement	710 (44 officers, 666 enlisted men)

The *Annapolis* was built as the escort aircraft carrier *Gilbert Islands* (CVE 107). She was decommissioned on 21 May 1946 and placed in reserve ; again active as a CVE from Sep 1951 to Jan 1955 when she was again decommissioned. While in reserve, on 7 May 1959 she was reclassified as a Cargo Ship and Aircraft Ferry (AKV 39). Converted into a communications ship by the New York Naval Shipyard, 1962-1964.
Decommissioned on 20 Dec 1969 and placed in reserve.

CONVERSION. During conversion the ship was fitted with elaborate communications relay equipment including approximately 30 transmitters providing frequency band coverage from low frequency to ultra-high frequency. The power outputs of the transmitters vary from 10 to 10 000 watts. Numerous radio receivers also were installed as were five large antenna towers. The ship was renamed *Annapolis* and reclassified AGMR 1 on 1 June 1963.
The former escort carrier *Vella Gulf* (AKV 11, ex-CVHE 111, ex-CVE 111) was to have been converted to the AGMR 2 ; her conversion never began because of the availability of the larger carrier *Saipan* for use in this role.

DESIGN. The *Gilbert Islands* was one of 19 "Commencement Bay" class escort carriers built during the latter part of World War II. The surviving ships of this type are classified as cargo ships (AKV) and are listed in the section on Logistic Support Ships.

ANNAPOLIS (AGMR 1)   *1964. United States Navy*

PHOTOGRAPHS. Note enclosed "hurricane bow" installed during conversion to AGMR to improve rough- sea operation. She has a small helicopter landing area on the port side of the former flight deck.

ANNAPOLIS (AGMR 1)   *1966, United States Navy*

ARLINGTON (AGMR 2)—See previous page   *1967, United States Navy*

STRATEGIC WARFARE SHIPS

The US strategic offensive forces now are comprised of 1 054 land-based ICBMs, approximately 450 B-52 and FB 111 bombers, and 41 Polaris-Poseidon submarines carrying 656 missiles. The number of ICBMs will be reduced by 54 and the number of bombers will be reduced by about half during the next few years. However, the number of deliverable warheads will increase as 550 Minutemen III missiles and 496 Poseidon missiles are fitted with Multiple Independently targeted Re-entry Vehicles (MIRV), three per Minuteman and ten per Poseidon. The MIRV concept permits a single missile to deliver small warheads against several separated targets.

With the completion of the Minuteman III and Poseidon programmes in the mid-1970s the United States will have some 8 000 strategic offensive warheads of which 5 120 or approximately two-thirds will be carried by Polaris and Poseidon submarines. (This calculation does not consider the three re-entry vehicles per Polaris A-3 missile in ten remaining Polaris submarines "as separate warheads because they cannot be directed to different targets, but are "shot-gunned" at the same target to increase damage and overcome possible defences).

Although the number of warheads is only one means of tabulating strategic offensive forces, the Polaris-Poseidon submarines also are expected to continue as the least vulnerable strategic system available to the United States. The primary strategic threat to the United States—the capability of the Soviet Union to deliver long-range, nuclear weapons against targets in the United States—continues to be a matter of "grave concern" to US defence officials. The Soviet threat to US nuclear deterrent forces can be divided into three categories: (1) land-based intercontinental ballistic missiles that could destroy most US land-based ICBMs, in a surprise, first-strike attack, (2) submarine-launched ballistic missiles that could destroy most US bomber forces before they could become airborne, and (3) ballistic missile defences that could reduce the effectiveness of surviving ICBMs.

Thus, the US Navy's contribution to strategic offensive forces—fleet ballistic missile submarines (SSBN)—are considered the least vulnerable of the strategic offensive forces. Secretary of Defence Melvin Laird has stated: "According to our best estimates, we believe that our Polaris and Poseidon submarines at sea can be considered virtually invulnerable today. With a highly concentrated effort the Soviet Navy today might be able to localize and destroy at sea one or two Polaris submarines. But the massive and expensive undertaking that would be required to extend such a capability using any current known ASW techniques would take time and would certainly be evident".

ADVANCED SSBN. In anticipation of continued Soviet strategic offensive and defensive buildups, the Navy is proposing development of an advanced submarine missile system known as ULMS (Undersea Long-range Missile System). This system would provide a more survivable offensive capability than either manned bombers or land-based ICBMs within the United States during the period of the next generation of strategic weapons (after 1980). Further, the longer-range missile planned for ULMS would permit the submarines to operate over a much greater ocean area while targeting the Soviet Union, further complicating Soviet attempts to develop an effective anti-SSBN capability.

SURFACE SHIPS. The Navy is proposing the deployment of a Ballistic Missile Ship (BMS) as a means of rapidly increasing US strategic offensive forces should

JAMES MADISON (SSBN 627) awaiting Poseidon missiles   1970, US Navy, PHC B. M. Anderson

such action be required. A force of ballistic missile ships could be constructed in less time than missile submarines could be built and would not interfere with the Poseidon SSBN conversion and SSN construction programmes. Such ships would be less vulnerable to a Soviet pre-emptive attack than strategic offensive forces within the United States. In discussing the survivability of a BMS force, Admiral Thomas H. Moorer, at the time Chief of Naval Operations, stated "In general, the studies have concluded that the force . . . would still retain its effectiveness many hours after an attack began" and "a sufficient number of hours to permit the ship to fire all of its weapons . . . ."

There is a continuing interest in the BMS concept within the Department of Defence, although funding has been minimal. Also considered, but now evoking little interest, is the Sea-based Long-range Missile System (SLMS) that would have a merchant-type ship carrying an advanced-technology missile, providing a more effective system than the proposed BMS concept that would employ the existing Poseidon or Minuteman III missile.

BALLISTIC MISSILE DEFENCE. The final sea-based strategic system now under consideration is a ballistic missile intercept ship. The official position of the Department of Defence is that this concept is being considered only as a "back up" to the fixed Safeguard ABM system now being developed. However, some analyses indicate that a sea-based system could provide

an improved anti-Soviet and Chinese ICBM capability on a more cost-effective basis than could the Safeguard system.

POLARIS. As initially completed, the US Navy's 41-submarine fleet ballistic missile force consisted of five submarines armed with the 1 370-statute-mile Polaris UGM-27A (A-1) missile, 13 submarines with the 1 700-mile Polaris UGM-27B (A-2) missile, and 23 with the 2 875-mile Polaris UGM-27C (A-3) missile. The five "George Washington" class submarines armed with the A-1 missile have been converted to fire the A-3 version as will the five "Ethan Allen" class submarines built with an A-2 capability. The remaining 31 submarines of the "Lafayette" class (with A-2 or A-3 missiles) all are to be rearmed with the improved Poseidon missile.

Of the 41-submarine FBM force, about half is on deterrent patrol at any given time. The remaining operational submarines are alongside tenders undergoing a 28-day replenishment and refit between deterrent patrols or are undergoing overhaul and conversion to the Poseidon capability.

POSEIDON. The first flight test model of the Poseidon UGM-73A (C-3) missile was successfully launched from Cape Kennedy, Florida, on 16 Aug 1968. The first sea firing of the Poseidon occurred on 16 Dec 1969 with a firing from the experimental ship *Observation Island* (AG 154) some seven miles off the coast of Cape Kennedy.

SEA-BASED ANTI-BALLISTIC MISSILE SHIPS: PROPOSED

Displacement, tons	20 000 to 30 000 tons full load
Length, feet	approx 700
Missiles	approx 40 to 60 ABM possibly anti-air and anti-surface weapons
Main engines	Geared turbines; 2 shafts
Nuclear reactors	2 pressurised-water cooled

The US Navy has proposed the sea-based anti-ballistic missile ship as an effective relatively low cost defense against ballistic missiles. The concept provides for tracking/missile-launching ships that could be (1) forward deployed to intercept, enemy ICBMs early in their flight before multiple warheads and penetration aids (decoys and chaff) are fully dispersed, (2) operated in US or allied coastal waters to provide terminal ballistic missile defenses, or (3) sailed with surface naval forces to provide defence against ballistic missiles that could be developed with a terminal manoeuvering capability for use against mobile targets.

The radar to detect an enemy ICBM, the fire control computers, and the ABM missile launchers all would be mounted in a single ship. A small number of ships could provide a low-cost "thin" defence against an "accidental" Soviet or Communist Chinese ICBM launch or the intentional launching of a small number of

missiles. (With existing and predicted technology there appears to be no possibility of providing defence against an all-out Soviet surprise ICBM strike against the United States).

A multi-ship ABM force—the number four has been suggested in the open press—with nuclear-powered escort ships is expected to cost considerably less than the estimated $8 to 40 *billion* Safeguard "thin" ABM defence now proposed for the United States. A sea-based ABM would appear to offer several advantages over a land-based system:

● The problems of detecting and destroying an ICBM during the launch-boost stage are less complicated than seeking to locate and destroy several re-entry packages (warheads and penetration aids).

● The proposed Safeguard ABM is a "sector system" with each of the planned 12 missile sites defending a sector of the United States. Thus, each site must have the capability of intercepting all intercontinental missiles that mainland China is expected to have available in the mid-1970s. However, a single ABM ship could be positioned to intercept virtually all missiles being fired at the United States because of the limited China-to-United

States ICBM trajectory spectrum.

● The ICBM intercept by ship-launched missiles (with nuclear warheads) would take place at sea rather than over populated US and Canadian territory as with Safeguard. Similarly, enemy efforts to destroy the ABM ships would not cause weapons to be aimed at the United States.

● The mobility of a sea-based ABM would enable the defence to be shifted as the threat changed. For example, an ABM system in the United States could not provide for defence against ICBMs aimed at Japan. A sea-based ABM could counter mainland Chinese ICBMs being launched against virtually any target in the Asian littoral.

● Shipboard systems appear to have a longer life than do fixed weapon complexes on land, a result of the long-established technique of adapting a given ship hull to changing missions and equipment.

FISCAL. According to official information, through 1970 only $720 000 had been spent on studies of sea-based ABM systems.

Strategic Warfare Ships—*Continued*

BALLISTIC MISSILE SHIP (BMS): PROPOSED

Displacement, tons	approx 20 000
Length, feet	572 oa
Beam, feet	82
Missiles	Poseidon C-3 or Minuteman III
Main engines	Steam turbine; 1 shaft
Speed, knots	20+ sustained

The ballistic missile ship is proposed as a means of rapidly providing the United States with additional strategic offensive capabilities. The concept of carrying ballistic missiles in surface ships of merchant design was proposed in the mid-1950s for the liquid-fuel Jupiter IRBM and in the early 1960s for the Polaris missile; the latter proposal included multi-national manning of the

ships which would operate under NATO control. Additionally, the installation of ballistic missiles in surface warships has been proposed at various times.

The current Navy ballistic missile ship proposal envisions use of a "Seamaster" (C4-S-86A) merchant ship modified for carrying Poseidon or Minuteman missiles and the related command, control, navigation, and fire control equipment. Such a ship could operate in commercial shipping lanes, increasing the problems of a hostile force in detecting, identifying, and trailing the ships.

MISSILES. The Poseidon C-3 and Minuteman III missiles are being considered for the ballistic missile ship, the latter having a range of approximately 6 000 to 8 000

miles maximum, depending upon payload.

The ship would be fitted with modular missile service-launcher units; presumably a full (16-missile) or half (8-missile) Poseidon SSBN missile system would be installed or a similar number of Minuteman III missiles. The Minuteman III is larger than the Poseidon, being 59·9 feet long, 6 feet in diameter, and weighing 76 000 pounds at launch. (Poseidon data is provided on an earlier page).

FISCAL. According to official information, $332 271 was obligated for ballistic missile ship studies in FY 1970, $414 400 in FY 1971, and $414 000 is requested in FY 1972.

UNDERSEA LONG-RANGE MISSILE SYSTEM (ULMS) SUBMARINE: PROPOSED

Displacement, tons	approx 8 000 surface
Length, feet	approx 450 oa
Main engines	steam turbines, 1 shaft
Reactor	1 pressurised-water cooled
Missiles	20 to 24 long-range, advanced ballistic missiles

The construction of a "dedicated research and development submarine for the ULMS prototype, which could be retained for use in on-going research and development programmes after the ULMS development was complete," has been proposed by the Department of Defense.

The principal characteristics of the proposed ULMS concept are: (1) long-range missile (circa 6 000 miles) to permit targeting the Soviet Union while the submarine cruises in the South Atlantic, South Pacific or Indian Oceans, making effective ASW virtually impossible, (2) extremely quiet submarines, (3) a high at-sea to in-port ratio, (4) high systems reliability, (5) dedicated systems design to provide the most effective submarine, and (6) underwater launch capability. Modular construction techniques would greatly facilitate maintenance, overhaul, and subsequent modernisation.

The above dimensions and particulars are unofficial estimates.

FISCAL. No official cost estimates for the ULMS programme have been published and, indeed, it is unlikely that a realistic estimate could be made at this stage of ULMS development. Unofficial cost estimates are approximately $1 *billion* per submarine, including missiles and ten years of operation; this would mean approximately $25 *billion* for 25 submarines, their missiles, and a decade of operation.

The Fiscal Year 1969 budget provided $5 400 000 for ULMS development, with an additional $10 000 000 in FY 1970, $44 000 000 in FY 1971, and 110 000 000 requested in FY 1972.

31 FLEET BALLISTIC MISSILE SUBMARINES (FBM): "LAFAYETTE" CLASS

Name	No.	Builder	Laid down	Launched	Commissioned
*LAFAYETTE	SSBN 616	General Dynamics (Electric Boat Div)	17 Jan 1961	8 May 1962	23 Apr 1963
*ALEXANDER HAMILTON	SSBN 617	General Dynamics (Electric Boat Div)	26 June 1961	18 Aug 1962	27 June 1963
*ANDREW JACKSON	SSBN 619	Mare Island Naval Shipyard	26 Apr 1961	15 Sep 1962	3 July 1963
*JOHN ADAMS	SSBN 620	Portsmouth Naval Shipyard	19 May 1961	12 Jan 1963	12 May 1964
*JAMES MONROE	SSBN 622	Newport News Shipbuilding & DD Co	31 July 1961	4 Aug 1962	7 Dec 1963
*NATHAN HALE	SSBN 623	General Dynamics (Electric Boat Div)	2 Oct 1961	12 Jan 1963	23 Nov 1963
*WOODROW WILSON	SSBN 624	Mare Island Naval Shipyard	13 Sep 1961	22 Feb 1963	27 Dec 1963
*HENRY CLAY	SSBN 625	Newport News Shipbuilding & DD Co	23 Oct 1961	30 Nov 1962	20 Feb 1964
*DANIEL WEBSTER	SSBN 626	General Dynamics (Electric Boat Div)	28 Dec 1961	27 Apr 1963	9 Apr 1964
*JAMES MADISON	SSBN 627	Newport News Shipbuilding & DD Co	5 Mar 1962	15 Mar 1963	28 July 1964
*TECUMSEH	SSBN 628	General Dynamics (Electric Boat Div)	1 June 1962	22 June 1963	29 May 1964
*DANIEL BOONE	SSBN 629	Mare Island Naval Shipyard	6 Feb 1962	22 June 1963	23 Apr 1964
*JOHN C. CALHOUN	SSBN 630	Newport News Shipbuilding & DD Co	4 June 1962	22 June 1963	15 Sep 1964
*ULYSSES S. GRANT	SSBN 631	General Dynamics (Electric Boat Div)	18 Aug 1962	2 Nov 1963	17 July 1964
*VON STEUBEN	SSBN 632	Newport News Shipbuilding & DD Co	4 Sep 1962	18 Oct 1963	30 Sep 1964
*CASIMIR PULASKI	SSBN 633	General Dynamics (Electric Boat Div)	12 Jan 1963	1 Feb 1964	14 Aug 1964
*STONEWALL JACKSON	SSBN 634	Mare Island Naval Shipyard	4 July 1962	30 Nov 1963	26 Aug 1964
*SAM RAYBURN	SSBN 635	Newport News Shipbuilding & DD Co	3 Dec 1962	20 Dec 1963	2 Dec 1964
*NATHANAEL GREENE	SSBN 636	Portsmouth Naval Shipyard	21 May 1962	12 May 1964	19 Dec 1964
*BENJAMIN FRANKLIN	SSBN 640	General Dynamics (Electric Boat Div)	25 May 1963	5 Dec 1964	22 Oct 1965
*SIMON BOLIVAR	SSBN 641	Newport News Shipbuilding & DD Co	17 Apr 1963	22 Aug 1964	29 Oct 1965
*KAMEHAMEHA	SSBN 642	Mare Island Naval Shipyard	2 May 1963	16 Jan 1965	10 Dec 1965
*GEORGE BANCROFT	SSBN 643	General Dynamics (Electric Boat Div)	24 Aug 1963	20 Mar 1965	22 Jan 1966
*LEWIS AND CLARK	SSBN 644	Newport News Shipbuilding & DD Co	29 July 1963	21 Nov 1964	22 Dec 1965
*JAMES K. POLK	SSBN 645	General Dynamics (Electric Boat Div)	23 Nov 1963	22 May 1965	16 Apr 1966
*GEORGE C. MARSHALL	SSBN 654	Newport News Shipbuilding & DD Co	2 Mar 1964	21 May 1965	29 Apr 1966
*HENRY L. STIMSON	SSBN 655	General Dynamics (Electric Boat Div)	4 Apr 1964	13 Nov 1965	20 Aug 1966
*GEORGE WASHINGTON CARVER	SSBN 656	Newport News Shipbuilding & DD Co	24 Aug 1964	14 Aug 1965	15 June 1956
*FRANCIS SCOTT KEY	SSBN 657	General Dynamics (Electric Boat Div)	5 Dec 1964	23 Apr 1966	3 Dec 1966
*MARIANO G. VALLEJO	SSBN 658	Mare Island Naval Shipyard	7 July 1964	23 Oct 1965	16 Dec 1966
*WILL ROGERS	SSBN 659	General Dynamics (Electric Boat Div)	20 Mar 1965	21 July 1966	1 Apr 1967

Displacement, tons	6 650 light surface; 7 320 standard surface; 8 250 submerged
Length, feet (*metres*)	425 (*129·5*) oa
Beam, feet (*metres*)	33 (*10·1*)
Draft feet (*metres*)	31·5 (*9·6*)
Missiles	16 tubes for Polaris A-2 in SSBN 616, 617, 618 (3 submarines) 16 tubes for Polaris A-3 in others except those submarines converting to Poseidon missiles (see *Missile* notes)
Torpedo tubes	4—21 in (*533 mm*) forward
Main engines	2 geared turbines 15 000 shp; 1 shaft
Nuclear reactor	1 pressurised-water cooled S5W (Westinghouse)
Speed, knots	20 surface; approx 30 submerged
Complement	140 (14 officers, 126 enlisted men)

These Fleet Ballistic Missile (FBM) submarines are the largest undersea craft ever built. Construction plans and design were awarded to the Electric Boat Division of the General Dynamics Corp., Groton, Connecticut, on 24 Mar 1960. The first four SSBNs of this class were authorised in the Fiscal Year 1961 shipbuilding programme with five additional submarines (SSBN 622-626) authorised in a supplemental FY 1961 programme; SSBN 627-636 (ten) in FY 1962, SSBN 640-645 (six) in FY 1963, and SSBN 654-659 (six) in FY 1964. Cost for the earlier ships of this class was approximately $109 500 000 per ship.

CLASSIFICATION. The *Benjamin Franklin* and later submarines officially are considered a separate class; however, differences are minimal (eg, quieter machinery) and all 31 submarines generally are considered as a single class.

JAMES MADISON (SSBN 627)

1970, United States Navy

Strategic Warfare Ships—*Continued*

"LAFAYETTE" CLASS   *continued*

ENGINEERING. The *Benjamin Franklin* and subsequent submarines of this class have been fitted with quieter machinery. All SSBNs have diesel-electric stand-by machinery, snorkels, and "outboard" auxiliary propeller for emergency use.

The nuclear coves inserted in refuelling these submarines during the late 1960s and early 1970s cost approximately $3 500 000 and provide energy for approximately 400 000 miles.

MISSILES. The first eight ships of this class were fitted with the Polaris A-2 missile (1 725 statute mile range) and the 23 later ships with the Polaris A-3 missile (2 880 statute mile range).

The SSBN 620 and SSBN 622-625 (5 ships) were re-armed with the Polaris A-3 missile during overhaul-refuellings from 1968- to 1970. It is planned to subsequently convert these ships to carry the Poseidon missile.

The *James Madison* was the first submarine to undergo conversion to carry the Poseidon missile. She began conversion in February 1969 and was completed in June 1970; ship and missile-firing trials followed, and the submarine began the first deterrent patrol with Poseidon missiles in February 1971. The deployment was delayed briefly because of problems with the submarine's air conditioning equipment and a delay in missile production. Poseidon conversion, overhaul, and reactor refuelling are conducted simultaneously. In addition to changes in missile tubes to accommodate larger Poseidon, the conversion provides replacement of Mk 84 fire control system with Mk 88 system. The Poseidon conversion schedule is given below; should be completed by 1976 or 1977.

LAFAYETTE (SSBN 616)   *General Dynamics, Electric Boat Division*

NAVIGATION. FBM submarines are equipped with an elaborate Ship's Inertial Navigation System (SINS), a system of gyroscopes and accelerometers which relates movement of the ship in all directions, true speed through the water and over the ocean floor, and true north to give a continuous report of the submarine's position. The system includes the capability of both optical and electronic checks. Navigation data produced by SINS can be provided to each missile's guidance package until the instant the missile is fired.

The first 19 submarines have three Mk 2 SINS and the 12 later submarines have two Mk 2 SINS; all have navigational satellite receivers.

NOMENCLATURE. FBM submarines are named for "famous Americans", including South American and Hawaiian leaders as well as Europeans who aided the United States war for independence. The lead ship of the class is named after the French aristocrat who served with George Washington in the American Revolution.

OPERATIONAL. The *Andrew Jackson* launched the first Polaris A-3 missile from a submarine on 26 Oct 1963. The *Daniel Webster* was the first submarine to deploy with the A-3 missile, beginning her first patrol on 28 Sep 1964. The *Daniel Boone* was the first Polaris submarine to deploy to the Pacific, beginning her first patrol with the A-3 missile on 25 Dec 1964.

The **Lewis and Clark** completed 800th deterrent patrol in July 1970.

PERSONNEL. Each FBM submarine is assigned two alternating crews designated "Blue" and "Gold". Each

POSEIDON CONVERSION SCHEDULE

No.	Programme	Conversion Yard	Start	Complete
SSBN 627	FY 1968	General Dynamics (Electric Boat)	3 Feb 1969	28 June 1970
SSBN 628	FY 1970	Newport News SB & DD Co	10 Nov 1969	1 Feb 1971
SSBN 629	FY 1968	Newport News SB & DD Co	12 May 1969	11 Aug 1970
SSBN 630	FY 1969	Mare Island Nav Shipyard	4 Aug 1969	17 Feb 1971
SSBN 631	FY 1970	Puget Sound Nav Shipyard	3 Oct 1969	24 Dec 1970
SSBN 632	FY 1969	Generla Dynamics (Electric Boat)	11 July 1969	19 Nov 1970
SSBN 633	FY 1970	General Dynamics (Electric Boat)	5 Jan 1970	Apr 1971
SSBN 634	FY 1971	General Dynamics (Electric Boat)	15 July 1970	Oct 1971
SSBN 635	FY 1970	Portsmouth Nav Shipyard	19 Jan 1970	June 1971
SSBN 636	FY 1971	Newport News SB & DD Co	22 July 1970	Oct 1971
SSBN 640	FY 1971	General Dynamics (Electric Boat)	Feb 1971	May 1972
SSBN 641	FY 1971	Newport News SB & DD Co	Feb 1971	May 1972
SSBN 642	FY 1971	General Dynamics (Electric Boat)	July 1971	Oct 1972
SSBN 645	FY 1971	Newport News SB & DD Co	July 1971	Oct 1972
SSBN 655	FY 1972	Newport News SB & DD Co	1972	
SSBN 656	FY 1972	General Dynamics (Electric Boat)	1972	
SSBN 658	FY 1972	Newport News SB & DD Co	1972	
SSBN	FY 1972			
SSBN	FY 1972			
SSBN	FY 1972			

crew mans the submarine during a 60-day patrol and partially assists during the intermediate 28-day refit alongside a Polaris tender. The "off-duty" crew is undergoing training or is on leave. All FBM submarines are fully air conditioned and the newer ships have elaborate crew study and recreation facilities.

PHOTOGRAPHS. Fleet ballistic missile submarines converted to Poseidon are virtually indistinguishable from pre-conversion appearance. FBM submarines rarely operate on the surface and photographs are difficult to obtain. Note that the *Mariano G. Vallejo* has her sail number painted out.

MARIANO G VALLEJO (SSBN 658)   *1970, United States Navy, PH3 C. P. Weston*

Strategic Warfare Ships—*Continued*

5 FLEET BALLISTIC MISSILE SUBMARINES (SSBN): "ETHAN ALLEN" CLASS

Name	No.	Builder	Laid down	Launched	Commissioned
*ETHAN ALLEN	SSBN 608	General Dynamics (Electric Boat Div, Groton)	14 Sep 1959	22 Nov 1960	8 Aug 1961
*SAM HOUSTON	SSBN 609	Newport News Shipbuilding & DD Co	28 Dec 1959	2 Feb 1961	6 Mar 1962
*THOMAS A. EDISON	SSBN 610	General Dynamics (Electric Boat Div, Groton)	15 Mar 1960	15 June 1961	10 Mar 1962
*JOHN MARSHALL	SSBN 611	Newport News Shipbuilding & DD Co	4 Apr 1960	15 July 1961	21 May 1962
*THOMAS JEFFERSON	SSBN 618	Newport News Shipbuilding & DD Co	3 Feb 1961	24 Feb 1962	4 Jan 1963

Displacement tons	6 900 standard surface; 7 900 submerged
Length feet (*metres*)	410·5 (*125·1*) oa
Beam, feet (*metres*)	33 (*10·1*)
Draft, feet (*metres*)	30 (*9·4*)
Missiles	16 tubes for Polaris A-2 (see *Missile* notes)
Torpedo tubes	4—21 in (*533 mm*) forward
Main engines	1 geared turbine (General Electric) 15 000 shp, 1 shaft
Nuclear reactor	1 pressurised-water cooled S5W (Westinghouse)
Speed, knots	20 surface; approx 30 submerged
Complement	112 (12 officers, 100 enlisted men)

These submarines were designed specifically for the FBM role and are larger and better arranged than the earlier "George Washington" class submarines. The first four ships of this class were authorised in the Fiscal Year 1959 programme; the *Thomas Jefferson* (which is out of numerical sequence) was in the FY 1961 programme. These submarines and the previous "George Washington" class will not be converted to carry the Poseidon missile because of material limitations and the age they would be after conversion. Also the "George Washington" class submarines are depth limited compared to the later FBM classes which, according to official statements, are based on the "Permit" SSN design.

DESIGN. These submarines and the subsequent "Lafayette" class are deep-diving submarines with a depth capability similar to the "Thresher" class attack submarines; pressure hulls of HY-80 steel.

SAM HOUSTON (SSBN 609)   1967, *United States Navy*

MISSILES. These ships were initially armed with the Polaris A-2 missile (1 725 statute mile range). The *Ethan Allen* launched the first A-2 missile fired from a submarine on 23 Oct 1961. She was the first submarine to deploy with the A-2 missile, beginning her first patrol on 26 June 1962. The *Ethan Allen* fired a Polaris A-2 missile in the Christmas Island Pacific Test Area on 6 May 1962 in what was the first complete US test of a ballistic missile including detonation of the nuclear warhead. All five of these ships will be modified to fire the A-3 missile (2 880 statute mile range).

Fitted with Mk 80 fire control system and compressed air missile ejectors; to have Mk 84 fire control systems and gas-steam missile ejectors with A-3 missile.

NAVIGATION. Fitted with two Mk 2 Ship's Inertial Navigation Systems (SINS) and navigational satellite receiver.

PERSONNEL. Alternating "Blue" and "Gold" crews as in "Lafayette" class submarines.

JOHN MARSHALL (SSBN 611)   1967, *United States Navy*

WOODROW WILSON (SSBN 624)   1969, *United States Navy, PH2 M. B. Sullivan*

Strategic Warfare Ships—*Continued*

5 FLEET BALLISTIC MISSILE SUBMARINES (SSBN): "GEORGE WASHINGTON" CLASS

Name	No.	Builder	Laid down	Launched	Commissioned
*GEORGE WASHINGTON	SSBN 598	General Dynamics (Electric Boat Div, Groton)	1 Nov 1957	9 June 1959	30 Dec 1959
*PATRICK HENRY	SSBN 599	General Dynamics (Electric Boat Div, Groton)	27 May 1958	22 Sep 1959	9 Apr 1960
*THEODORE ROOSEVELT	SSBN 600	Mare Island Naval Shipyard	20 May 1958	3 Oct 1959	13 Feb 1961
*ROBERT E. LEE	SSBN 601	Newport News Shipbuilding & DD Co	25 Aug 1958	18 Dec 1959	16 Sep 1960
*ABRAHAM LINCOLN	SSBN 602	Portsmouth Naval Shipyard	1 Nov 1958	14 May 1960	11 Mar 1961

Displacement, tons	5 900 standard surface; 6 700 submerged
Length, feet (*metres*)	381·7 (*115·8*) oa
Beam, feet (*metres*)	33 (*10·1*)
Draft, feet (*metres*)	29 (*8·8*)
Missiles	16 tubes for Polaris A-3
Torpedo tubes	6—21 in (*533 mm*) forward
Main engines	1 geared turbine (General Electric) 15 000 shp, 1 shaft
Nuclear reactor	1 pressurised-water cooled S5W (Westinghouse)
Speed, knots	20 surface; approx 30 submerged
Complement	112 (12 officers 100 enlisted men)

GEORGE WASHINGTON (SSBN 598)   *United States Navy*

The *George Washington* was the West's first ship to be armed with ballistic missiles. A supplement to the Fiscal Year 1958 new construction programme signed on 11 Feb 1958 provided for the construction of the first three Fleet Ballistic Missile (FBM) submarines. The Navy had already ordered the just-begun attack submarine *Scorpion* (SSN 589) to be completed as a missile submarine on 31 Dec 1957; the hull was redesignated SSBN 598 and completed as the *George Washington*. The *Patrick Henry* similarly was reordered on the last day of 1957, her materials having originally been intended for the not-yet-started SSN 590. These submarines and three sister ships (two authorised in FY 1959) were built to a modified "Skipjack" class design with almost 130 feet being added to the original design to accommodate two rows of eight missile tubes, fire control and navigation equipment, and auxiliary machinery.

MISSILES. These ships were initially armed with the Polaris A-1 missile (1 380 statute mile range). The *George Washington* successfully fired two Polaris A-1 missiles while submerged off Cape Canaveral (Kennedy) on 20 July 1960 in the first underwater launching of a ballistic missile from a US submarine. She departed on her initial patrol on 15 Nov 1960 and remained submerged for 66 days, 10 hours. All five submarines of this class have been refitted to fire the improved Polaris A-3 missile (2 880 statute mile range). Missile refit and first reactor refuelling were accomplished simultaneously during overhaul: *George Washington* from 20 June 1964 to 2 Feb 1966, *Patrick Henry* from 4 Jan 1965 to 21 July 1966, *Theodore Roosevelt* from 28 July 1965 to 14 Jan 1967, *Robert E. Lee* from 23 Feb 1965 to 2 July 1966, and *Abraham Lincoln* from 25 Oct 1965 to 3 June 1967; four at Electric Boat yard in Groton, Connecticut, and *Robert E. Lee* at Mare Island Naval Shipyard. These submarines all have Mk 84 fire control systems and gas-steam missile ejectors (originally fitted with Mk 80 fire control systems and compressed air missile ejectors; changed during A-3 missile refit).

ABRAHAM LINCOLN (SSBN 602)   *United States Navy*

ENGINEERING. The *George Washington* was the first FBM submarine to be overhauled and "refuelled". During her 4½ years of operation on her initial reactor core she carried out 15 submerged missile patrols and steamed more than 100 000 miles.

NAVIGATION. Fitted with three Mk 2 Ship's Inertial Navigation Systems (SINS) and navigational satellite receiver.

PERSONNEL. Alternating "Blue" and "Gold" crews as in "Lafayette" class submarines.

OPERATIONAL. The *Patrick Henry* completed the US Navy's 500th FBM patrol on 13 Feb 1968. It was the *Patrick Henry's* 22nd patrol since her commissioning.

PHOTOGRAPHS. Note that "hump" of hull extension for housing missile tubes is more pronounced in these submarines than later classes. Note the bitts and capstans visible in view of *Abraham Lincoln* while mooring; as in SSNs, most hull projects are removable or retractable to provide a "clean" hull and reduce noise as submarine passes through water.

ROBERT E. LEE (SSBN 601)   *1966, United States Navy*

SUBMARINES

The US Navy's submarine forces consist of two principal categories: fleet ballistic missile submarines (SSBN), listed in the previous section on Strategic Warfare Ships, and attack submarines (SS and SSN).

During 1971 the number of attack submarines in commission was reduced to less than one hundred for the first time in more than a decade. The planned force level provides for 57 nuclear-powered and 36 diesel-electric attack submarines in commission on June 30, 1972 (plus several research submarines and one transport submarine). This represents a 12 per cent reduction in planned attack submarine strength from the 105 units programmed for the past few years. Further, eight of the 57 nuclear submarines no longer are considered first-line submarines, and 24 of the 36 conventional submarines were constructed during World War II.

New attack submarine construction has averaged only 4·4 submarines per year for the past 15 years, too slow a rate to replace older, less-capable diesel and nuclear submarines in countering the increasing Soviet nuclear submarine threat. To further accentuate the situation, during the past few years other US anti-submarine forces have been reduced, specifically the number of ASW aircraft carriers and air groups, the land-based patrol plane squadrons, and the destroyer-type ships. Although there have been significant improvements in quality of equipment in some areas, the current US anti-submarine forces, particularly the attack submarines, should be viewed with caution.

Secretary of Defense Melvin Laird has observed: "Important changes in submarine technology have taken place in both the United States and the Soviet Union in the last ten years, and have compounded the uncertainties inherent in our judgements of our needs for SSNs. However, because of the unique ASW capabilities of submarines and their effectiveness in other missions as well, we believe we should pursue a vigorous SSN construction programme in the near term".

US Navy attack submarines construction is all nuclear and the Fiscal Year 1972 shipbuilding programme provides for five SSN-688 class submarines, the largest number of SSNs in an annual programme since 1967. This rate of five nuclear submarines per year is about the maximum construction rate possible in the United States until at least the mid-1970s because of the Poseidon SSBN conversion programme and the long-lead time for nuclear submarine components. (Current Soviet nuclear submarine construction is officially estimated at 12 to 14 SSN/SSBNs per year on a single-shift basis).

New submarine construction in the United States is comprised of the so-called "high-speed" SSN-688 class and the single "quiet" SSN-685. The lead ship of the SSN-688 class will complete in late 1974, marking the introduction of the first new production submarine propulsion system since the *Skipjack* (SSN 585) went to sea in 1959 with the S5W reactor plant. Hopefully, the SSN-688 class will return the US Navy to the area of high-speed nuclear submarine operations where the Soviet Navy apparently now has the lead.

The SSN 685 represents the US Navy's effort to develop a submarine with a low level of self-generated noise to improve the ability to operate against Soviet undersea craft. This will be a one-of-a-kind submarine with technical and operational benefits accrued from the design being integrated with subsequent SSN and SSBN classes.

ADVANCED SUBMARINES. Beyond the planned SSN 688 class of at least 25 submarines, the Navy is planning a follow-on series of submarines known now as the Mid-1970s design. The development of the SSN 688 and Mid-1970s submarine projects are being directed by a special Project Manager for SSN 688 Class and Later Design Submarines within the Naval Material Command.

ELECTRONICS. Programmes are underway to increase the capabilities of sonars installed in attack submarines. The BQQ-2 sonars of the "Permit"/"Sturgeon"/"Narwhal" classes will receive the BQS-13 DNA search sonar which

BILLFISH (SSN 676)   1971, General Dynamics, Electric Boat Division

provides a digital multi-beam modification with a wide/narrow band processing options, and accelerated active search rate. These submarines also will receive Sub Close Contact Sonar, a mine detection sonar. The BQR-2 passive detecting sonar installed in pre-"Permit" nuclear attack submarines will receive a Digital Multi-Beam Steering (DIMUS) modification to provide a multi-target, automatic track capability and wide/narrow band signal processing option.

MIDGET SUBMARINES. The US Navy's lone "midget" submarine, the USS *X-1*, is listed in the section on Submersibles and Deep Submergence Vehicles.

TRAINING SUBMARINES. Several immobilised submarines are employed for the training of Naval Reserve personnel. Their names and locations are on the last page of the Submarine section. These craft no longer have a seagoing or combat capability.

NOMENCLATURE. Submarines generally have been named for fish and marine life except that fleet ballistic missile submarines have been named for famous Americans. The tradition of naming none-FBM submarines for fish and marine life was broken in 1971 with the naming of the last two "Sturgeon" class submarines for deceased members of the Congress. Previously destroyer-type ships have honoured members of the Congress.

PHOTOGRAPH. The above photograph shows workmen clearing ice from the *Billfish* after her sea trials early in 1971 out of the General Dynamics/Electric Boat yard in Groton, Connecticut. Men on deck and staging alongside sail provide scale. The union jack flying at bow and the national flag at stern indicate the *Billfish* is in commission and is not underway.

12 NUCLEAR-POWERED ATTACK SUBMARINES (SSN): HIGH SPEED DESIGN

No.	Builder	Comm.
SSN 688	Newport News SB & DD Co	1974
SSN 689	Newport News SB & DD Co	
SSN 690	General Dynamics (Electric Boat)	
SSN 691	Newport News SB & DD Co	
SSN 692	General Dynamics (Electric Boat)	
SSN 693	Newport News SB & DD Co	
SSN 694	General Dynamics (Electric Boat)	
SSN 695	Newport News SB & DD Co	
SSN 696	General Dynamics (Electric Boat)	
SSN 697	General Dynamics (Electric Boat)	
SSN 698	General Dynamics (Electric Boat)	
SSN 699	General Dynamics (Electric Boat)	

Displacement, tons	6 900 submerged
Length, feet	360 oa
Beam, feet	33
Draft, feet	32 max
ASW Weapons	SUBROC and Mk 48 ASW torpedoes
Main engines	2 geared turbines; 1 shaft
Nuclear reactor	1 pressurised-water cooled

These are "high-speed" attack submarines intended to counter the new Soviet classes of submarines that went to sea during the late 1960s and early 1970s.

The SSN 688-690 (3 ships) were authorised in the Fiscal Year 1970 new construction programme, SSN 691-694 (4 ships) in FY 1971, and SSN 695-699 (5 ships) in FY 1972. Contracts for the construction of these 12 submarines were awarded on 9 Jan 1971 (prior to authorisation of the FY 1972 programme). See Fiscal notes for cost data.

The Navy has stated that lack of high priority for the SSN-688 programme and the impact of a General Electric Company strike resulted in an "irrecoverable delay" of 11 months for each ship of this class even before construction begins.

Approximately 25 submarines of this design will be constructed under FY 1970-75 programmes before the Navy adopts the so-called Mid-1970s SSN design. Detailed design of the SSN 688 class as well as construction of the lead submarine was contracted to the Newport News Shipbuilding & Dry Dock Company, Newport News, Virginia; the follow-on ships were awarded to Newport News and to the General Dynamics Electric Boat Division yard at Groton, Connecticut.

DESIGN. These submarines will be considerably larger than the previous "Sturgeon" class. All construction features, including sail size, hull shape, propulsion plant design, machinery mounting technique, auxiliary machinery, etc, will be designed to provide the maximum degree of quietness possible. Their sound level will be similar to the "Sturgeon" class when both submarines are travelling at comparable speeds.

ENGINEERING. Unofficial sources indicate that a modified surface ship nuclear reactor plant may be used in this class. The "smallest" surface ship reactor now available for submarine use is the D2G type used in the frigates *Bainbridge* and *Truxtun*; these reactors each produce approximately 30 000 shp.

FISCAL. The FY 1970 shipbuilding programme provided $504 500 000 for the construction of the SSN 688-690 plus $110 000 000 for procurement of long-lead time equipment (primarily reactor components) for five additional submarines. However, the Nixon Administration requested only three SSN-688 class submarines in FY 1971. The Congress subsequently voted four submarines in FY 1971 and appropriated $662 000 000 for their construction plus long-lead time equipment for the FY 1972 programme. The FY 1972 budget request asked $881 000 000 for the SSN 695-699 plus long-lead time equipment for FY 1973.

The total cost of the first 12 submarines of this class is estimated at about $2 *billion* or an average of $166 000 000 per ship.

Submarines—*continued*

1 NUCLEAR POWERED ATTACK SUBMARINE (SSN): QUIET DESIGN

ASW Weapons	SUBROC and ASW torpedoes
Main engines	Turbine-electric drive (General Electric); 1 shaft
Nuclear reactor	1 pressurised-water cooled S5WA (Westinghouse)
Speed, knots	approx 25 submerged

Name	No.	Builder	Laid down	Launch	Commission
GLENARD P. LIPSCOMBE	SSN 685	General Dynamics	June 1971	Sep 1972	early 1974

The Turbine-Electric Drive Submarine (TEDS) is being built to test "a combination of advanced silencing techniques" involving "a new kind of propulsion system, and new and quieter machinery of various kinds", according to the Department of Defense. The noise level produced by an operating submarine is an important factor in its ability to remain undetected by an opponent's passive listening devices and its own ability to detect the opponent. The TEDS project will permit an at-sea evaluation of improvements in ASW effectiveness due to noise reduction. The SSN 685 will be slightly larger than "Sturgeon" class submarines and somewhat slower.

No class of turbine-electric nuclear submarines is planned at this time. Rather, quieting features developed in the SSN 685 which do not detract from speed probably will be incorporated in the SSN 688 design and subsequent SSN classes. (The TEDS design is several years ahead of the SSN 688 design).

Authorised in the Fiscal Year 1968 new construction programme; estimated construction cost will be between $150 000 000 and $200 000 000.

Design of an advanced submarine specifically intended for quiet operation began with Navy studies which commenced in October 1964. Approval to construct the submarine was revoked on at least one occasion by the Department of Defense in an effort to combine several desired characteristics in a single submarine design.

However, high speed and silent operation apparently are not compatible with available technology.

Final Department of Defense approval for construction of the turbine-electric drive submarine was announced on 25 Oct 1968. A contract was awarded to GD/EB for construction of the SSN 685 on 16 Dec 1968.

ENGINEERING. Turbine-electric drive eliminates the noisy reduction gears of standard steam turbine power plants, the major source of noise in a nuclear-powered submarine. The turbine-electric power plant is larger and heavier than comparable steam turbine submarine machinery.

The *Tullibee* (SSN 597) was an earlier effort at noise reduction through a turbine-electric nuclear plant.

1 NUCLEAR POWERED ATTACK SUBMARINE (SSN): "NARWHAL" TYPE

Displacement, tons	4 450 standard; 5 350 submerged
Length, feet (*metres*)	314 (*95·7*) oa
Beam, feet (*metres*)	38 (*11·5*)
Draft, feet (*metres*)	26 (*7·9*)
Torpedo tubes	4—21 in (*533 mm*) amidships
ASW weapons	SUBROC and ASW torpedoes
Main engines	2 steam turbines; approx 17 000 shp; 1 shaft
Nuclear reactor	1 pressurised-water cooled S5G (General Electric)
Speed, knots	approx 20 surface; approx 30 submerged
Complement	107 (12 officers, 95 enlisted men)

Name	No.	Builder	Laid down	Launched	Commissioned
*NARWHAL	SSN 671	General Dynamics (Electric Boat)	17 Jan 1966	9 Sep 1967	14 June 1969

The *Narwhal* is a large attack submarine with an improved propulsion system. She is the largest "straight" nuclear-powered attack submarine yet built by the US Navy (slightly shorter than the pioneers *Nautilus* and *Seawolf*, but wider, deeper, and heavier). Authorised in the Fiscal Year 1964 new construction programme.

DESIGN. The *Narwhal* is similar to the "Sturgeon" class submarines in design.

ELECTRONICS. Fitted with BQQ-2 sonar system. See "Sturgeon" and "Permit" classes for general notes.

ENGINEERING. The *Narwhal* is fitted with the prototype sea-going S5G Natural Circulation Reactor. According to Vice Admiral H. G. Rickover, the Natural Circulation Reactor "offers promise of increased reactor plant reliability, simplicity, and noise reduction due to the elimination of the need for large reactor coolant pumps and associated electrical and control equipment by taking maximum advantage of natural convection to circulate the reactor coolant".

Natural circulation eliminates the requirement for primary coolant pumps, the second noisiest component of a pressurised-water propulsion system after the steam turbines.

The Atomic Energy Commission's Knolls Atomic Power Laboratory was given prime responsibility for development of the power plant. Construction of a land-based prototype plant began in May 1961 at the National Reactor Testing Station in Idaho. The reactor achieved initial criticality on 12 Sep 1965.

NARWHAL (SSN 671)   *1969, General Dynamics, Electric Boat Division*

NARWHAL (SSN 671)   *1969, General Dynamics, Electric Boat Division*

Submarines—*continued*

37 NUCLEAR-POWERED ATTACK SUBMARINES (SSN): "STURGEON" CLASS

Displacement, tons	3 860 standard; 4 630 submerged
Length, feet (*metres*)	292·2 (*89·0*) oa
Beam, feet (*metres*)	31·7 (*9·5*)
Draft, feet (*metres*)	26 (*7·9*)
Torpedo tubes	4—21 in (*533 mm*) amidships
ASW weapons	SUBROC and ASW torpedoes
Main engines	2 steam turbines; approx 15 000 shp; 1 shaft
Nuclear reactor	1 pressurised-water cooled S5W (Westinghouse)
Speed, knots	approx 20 surface; approx 30 submerged
Complement	107 (12 officers, 95 enlisted men)

Name	No.	Builder	Laid down	Launched	Commissioned
*STURGEON	SSN 637	General Dynamics (Electric Boat)	10 Aug 1963	26 Feb 1966	3 Mar 1967
*WHALE	SSN 638	General Dynamics (Quincy)	27 May 1964	14 Oct 1966	12 Oct 1968
*TAUTOG	SSN 639	Ingalls Shipbuilding Corp	27 Jan 1964	15 Apr 1967	17 Aug 1968
*GRAYLING	SSN 646	Portsmouth Naval Shipyard	12 May 1964	22 June 1967	11 Oct 1969
*POGY	SSN 647	Ingalls Shipbuilding Corp	4 May 1964	3 June 1967	Mar 1971
*ASPRO	SSN 648	Ingalls Shipbuilding Corp	23 Nov 1964	29 Nov 1967	20 Feb 1969
*SUNFISH	SSN 649	General Dynamics (Quincy)	15 Jan 1965	14 Oct 1966	15 Mar 1969
*PARGO	SSN 650	General Dynamics (Electric Boat)	3 June 1964	17 Sep 1966	5 Dec 1967
*QUEENFISH	SSN 651	Newport News SB & DD Co	11 May 1965	25 Feb 1966	6 Dec 1966
*PUFFER	SSN 652	Ingalls Shipbuilding Corp	8 Feb 1965	30 Mar 1968	9 Aug 1969
*RAY	SSN 653	Newport News SB & DD Co	1 Apr 1965	21 June 1966	12 Apr 1967
*SAND LANCE	SSN 660	Portsmouth Naval Shipyard	15 Jan 1965	11 Nov 1969	30 Apr 1971
*LAPON	SSN 661	Newport News SB & DD Co	26 July 1965	16 Dec 1966	14 Dec 1967
*GURNARD	SSN 662	San Francisco NSY (Mare Island)	22 Dec 1964	20 May 1967	6 Dec 1968
*HAMMERHEAD	SSN 663	Newport News SB & DD Co	29 Nov 1965	14 Apr 1967	28 June 1968
*SEA DEVIL	SSN 664	Newport News SB & DD Co	12 Apr 1966	5 Oct 1967	30 Jan 1969
GUITARRO	SSN 665	San Francisco NSY (Mare Island)	9 Dec 1965	27 July 1968	early 1972
*HAWKBILL	SSN 666	San Francisco NSY (Mare Island)	12 Sep 1966	12 Apr 1969	4 Feb 1971
*BERGALL	SSN 667	General Dynamics (Electric Boat)	16 Apr 1966	17 Feb 1968	13 June 1969
*SPADEFISH	SSN 668	Newport News SB & DD Co	21 Dec 1966	15 May 1968	31 July 1969
*SEAHORSE	SSN 669	General Dynamics (Electric Boat)	13 Aug 1966	15 June 1968	19 Sep 1969
*FINBACK	SSN 670	Newport News SB & DD Co	26 June 1967	7 Dec 1968	4 Feb 1970
*PINTADO	SSN 672	San Francisco NSY (Mare Island)	27 Oct 1967	16 Aug 1969	29 Apr 1971
*FLYING FISH	SSN 673	General Dynamics (Electric Boat)	30 June 1967	17 May 1969	29 Apr 1970
*TREPANG	SSN 674	General Dynamics (Electric Boat)	28 Oct 1967	27 Sep 1969	14 Aug 1970
*BLUEFISH	SSN 675	General Dynamics (Electric Boat)	13 Mar 1968	10 Jan 1970	8 Jan 1971
*BILLFISH	SSN 676	General Dynamics (Electric Boat)	20 Sep 1968	1 May 1970	5 Mar 1971
*DRUM	SSN 677	San Francisco NSY (Mare Island)	20 Aug 1968	23 May 1970	29 July 1971
ARCHERFISH	SSN 678	General Dynamics (Electric Boat)	19 June 1969	16 Jan 1971	Dec 1971
SILVERSIDES	SSN 679	General Dynamics (Electric Boat)	13 Oct 1969	4 June 1971	mid 1972
REDFISH	SSN 680	Ingalls Shipbuilding (Litton)	4 Aug 1969	Dec 1971	late 1972
BATFISH	SSN 681	General Dynamics (Electric Boat)	9 Feb 1970	Oct 1971	late 1972
TUNNY	SSN 682	Ingalls Shipbuilding (Litton)	22 May 1970	mid 1972	late 1972
PARCHE	SSN 683	Ingalls Shipbuilding (Litton)	10 Dec 1970	late 1972	1973
CAVALLA	SSN 684	General Dynamics (Electric Boat)	4 June 1970	early 1972	1973
L. MENDEL RIVERS	SSN 686	Newport News SB & DD Co	June 1971		1974
RICHARD B. RUSSELL	SSN 687	Newport News SB & DD Co	June 1971		1974

The 37 "Sturgeon" class attack submarines comprise the largest group of nuclear-powered ships built to the same design (followed in the US Navy by the 31 "Lafayette" class missile submarines). These submarines are intended to seek out and destroy enemy submarines. They are similar in design to the previous "Permit" (ex-"Thresher") class but are slightly larger. SSN 637-639 (3 ships) were authorised in the Fiscal Year 1962 new construction programme, SSN 646-653 (8 ships) in FY 1963, SSN 660-664 (5 ships) in FY 1964, SSN 665-670 (6 ships) in FY 1965, SSN 672-677 (6 ships) in FY 1966, SSN 678-682 (5 ships) in FY 1967, SSN 683-684 (2 ships) in FY 1968, and SSN 686 and SSN 687 in FY 1969. The estimated construction cost of the submarines of this class in the FY 1967 and 1968 programmes is $74 500 000 to $84 400 000 per ship. The estimated construction cost of the *Pogy* is $90 200 000 compared to an initial (1961) estimate of $58 000 000.

CONSTRUCTION. The *Pogy* was begun by the New York Shipbuilding Corp (Camden, New Jersey), but was towed to Ingalls Shipbuilding Corp for completion; contract with the New York Shipbuilding Corp was terminated on 5 June 1967; contract for completion awarded to Ingalls Shipbuilding Corp on 7 Dec 1967. The *Guitarro* sank in 35 feet of water on 15 May 1969 while being fitted out at the San Fransisco Bay Naval Shipyard. According to congressional report, the sinking, caused by shipyard workers, was "wholly avoidable". Subsequently raised; damage estimated at $25 000 000 to repair due to interior flooding. Completion delayed more than one year.

DESIGN. These submarines are slightly larger than the previous "Permit" (ex-"Thresher") class and can be identified by their taller sail structure and the lower position of their diving planes on the sail (to improve control at periscope depth). Sail height is 20 feet, 6 inches above deck. These ships incorporate modifications of the submarine safety (SUBSAFE) programme established after the loss of the *Thresher*. These submarines probably are slightly slower than the previous "Permit" and "Skipjack" classes because of their increased size with the same propulsion system as in the earlier classes.

ELECTRONICS. These submarines are fitted with the advanced BQQ-2 sonar system. Principal components of the BQQ-2 include the BQS-6 active sonar, with transducers mounted in a 15-foot diameter sonar sphere, and BQR-7 passive sonar, with hydrophones in a conformal array on sides of forward hull. The active sonar sphere is fitted in the optimum bow position, requiring placement of torpedo tubes amidships. These submarines also have BQS-8 and BQS-13 active/passive sonars; transducers for the former are in small, fin-like domes aft of sail structure. BQS-8 sonar is intended primarily for under-ice-navigation. Sonar suite of *Guitarro* is of an improved design intended for SSN 672 and later submarines of this class. (See *Electronics* notes in the introductory passage to this section).

BPS-14 surface search radar fitted.

These submarines have the Mk 113 torpedo fire control director.

OPERATIONAL. The *Whale, Pargo,* and older nuclear submarine *Sargo* conducted exercises in the Arctic ice pack during March-April 1969. The *Whale* surfaced at the geographic North Pole on April 6, the 60th anniversary of Rear Admiral Robert E. Peary reaching the North Pole. This was believed the first instance of single-screw US nuclear submarines surfacing in the Arctic ice. The *Hammerhead* and the older nuclear submarine *Skate* conducted exercises in the Arctic during November-December 1970, with the *Hammerhead* surfacing at the North Pole on Nov. 20.

PHOTOGRAPHS. The photograph at right shows the *Whale* surfaced at the North Pole on April 6, 1969. Note the position of her diving planes mounted on the sail structure. US nuclear submarines with sail-mounted diving planes can rotate the planes 90 degrees to a vertical position, presenting narrow surfaces facing up when surfacing through ice. The submarine's rudder is at far right. In this photograph the *Whale* has two antenna masts extended.

TREPANG (SSN 674) *1970 United States Navy*

WHALE (SSN 638) At North Pole *1969, US Navy, PHC B. M. Anderson*

Submarines—*continued*

SCULPIN (SSN 590)—"Skipjack" class   *US Navy*

LAPON (SSN 661)—"Sturgeon" class   *US Navy*

FINBACK (SSN 670)   *1969, Newport News SB & DD Co*

BERGALL (SSN 667)   *1969, United States Navy*

Submarines—*continued*
13 NUCLEAR-POWERED ATTACK SUBMARINES (SSN): "PERMIT" CLASS

Displacement, tons	3 750 standard, *Flasher, Greenling,* and *Gato* 3 800 tons; 4 300 submerged except *Jack* 4 500, submerged, *Flasher, Greenling,* and *Gato* 4 600 submerged
Length, feet (*metres*)	278·5 (*84·9*) oa except *Jack* 295·7 (*89·5*), *Flasher, Greenling* and *Gato* 292·2 (*89·1*)
Beam, feet (*metres*)	31·7 (*9·6*)
Draft, feet (*metres*)	25·2 (*7·6*)
Torpedo tubes	4—21 in (*533 mm*) amidships
ASW weapons	SUBROC and ASW torpedoes
Main engines	2 steam turbines, approx 15 000 shp; 1 shaft
Nuclear reactor	1 pressurised-water cooled S5W (Westinghouse)
Speed, knots	approx 20 surface; approx 30 submerged
Complement	107 (12 officers, 95 enlisted men)

Name	No.	Builder	Laid down	Launched	Commissioned
*PERMIT	SSN 594	Mare Island Naval Shipyard	16 July 1959	1 July 1961	29 May 1962
*PLUNGER	SSN 595	Mare Island Naval Shipyard	2 Mar 1960	9 Dec 1961	21 Nov 1962
*BARB	SSN 596	Ingalls Shipbuilding Corp	9 Nov 1959	12 Feb 1962	24 Aug 1963
*POLLACK	SSN 603	New York Shipbuilding Corp	14 Mar 1960	17 Mar 1962	26 May 1964
*HADDO	SSN 604	New York Shipbuilding Cotp	9 Sep 1960	18 Aug 1962	16 Dec 1964
*JACK	SSN 605	Portsmouth Naval Shipyard	16 Sep 1960	24 Apr 1963	31 Mar 1967
*TINOSA	SSN 606	Portsmouth Naval Shipyard	24 Nov 1959	9 Dec 1961	17 Oct 1964
*DACE	SSN 607	Ingalls Shipbuilding Corp	6 June 1960	18 Aug 1962	4 Apr 1964
*GUARDFISH	SSN 612	New York Shipbuilding Corp	28 Feb 1961	15 May 1965	20 Dec 1966
*FLASHER	SSN 613	General Dynamics (Electric Boat)	14 Apr 1961	22 June 1963	22 July 1966
*GREENLING	SSN 614	General Dynamics (Electric Boat)	15 Aug 1961	4 Apr 1964	3 Nov 1967
*GATO	SSN 615	Ingalls Shipbuilding Corp	15 Dec 1961	14 May 1964	25 Jan 1968
*HADDOCK	SSN 621	Ingalls Shipbuilding Corp	24 Apr 1961	21 May 1966	22 Dec 1967

These submarines were the first of a series of advanced attack submarines intended to seek out and destroy enemy submarines. They have a greater depth capability than previous nuclear-powered submarines and are the first to combine the SUBROC anti-submarine missile capability with the advanced BQQ-2 sonar system. The lead ship of the class, the ill-fated *Thresher* (SSN 593), was authorised in the Fiscal Year 1957 new construction programme, the SSN 594-596 (3 ships) in FY 1958, SSN 603-607 (5 ships) in FY 1959, SSN 612-615 (4 ships) in FY 1960, and SSN 621 in FY 1961. Four of these submarines were intended as guided missile submarines (see *Design* notes).

The *Thresher* (SSN 593) was lost off the coast of New England on 10 Apr 1963 while on post-overhaul trials. She went down with 129 men on board (108 crewmen plus four naval officers and 17 civilians on board for trials).

Later submarines of this and subsequent classes were delayed because of safety programme (SUBSAFE) modifications, increased quality control of submarine construction, and specific problems at the New York Shipbuilding Corp and the Portsmouth Naval Shipyard.

CLASS. These submarines are officially listed as belonging to the "Thresher" class in the Naval Vessels Register; generally referred to as the "Permit" class after loss of the *Thresher* in 1963.

CONSTRUCTION. *Greenling* and *Gato* were launched by the Electric Boat Division of the General Dynamics Corp (Groton, Connecticut); towed to Quincy Division (Massachusetts) for lengthening and completion.

DESIGN. The *Plunger, Barb, Pollack,* and *Dace* were ordered as guided missile submarines (SSGN) and were to each carry four Regulus II missiles. They were re-ordered as "Thresher" class attack submarines after the Regulus II programme was cancelled on 18 Dec 1958 (retaining numerical sequence in the submarine series). The *Jack* was built to a modified design to test a different power plant (see *Engineering* notes).

The *Flasher, Gato,* and *Greenling* were modified during construction; fitted with SUBSAFE features, heavier machinery, and larger sail structures.

These submarines have a modified "tear-drop" hull design. Their bows are devoted to sonar and their four torpedo tubes are amidships, angled out, two to port and two to starboard.

The sail structure height of these submarines is 13 feet, 9 inches to 15 feet above the deck, with later submarines of this class having a sail height of 20 feet.

ELECTRONICS. These submarines are fitted with the advanced BQQ-2 sonar system (first installed in the *Tullibee,* SSN 597). Principal components of the BQQ-2 include the BQS-6 active sonar, with transducers mounted in a 15-foot diameter sonar sphere, and BQR-7 passive sonar, with hydrophones in a conformal array along sides of forward hull. The active sonar sphere is fitted in the optimum bow position, requiring placement of torpedo tubes amidships. The advanced BQS-13DNA active/passive sonar will be fitted in these submarines. (See *Electronics* notes in introductory passage to this section). These submarines have the Mk 113 torpedo fire control director.

ENGINEERING. The *Jack* is fitted with two propellers on essentially one shaft (actually a single shaft within a sleeve-like shaft) and a counter-rotating turbine without a reduction gear. Both innovations are designed to reduce operating noises. To accommodate the larger turbine the engine spaces were lengthened ten feet and the shaft structure was lengthened seven feet to mount the two propellers. The propellers are of different size and are smaller than in the other submarines of this class.

Also eliminated in *Jack* was a clutch and secondary-propulsion electric motor.

The *Jack's* propulsion arrangement provides a ten per cent increase in power efficiency, but no increase in speed. All submarines of this and subsequent classes have special machinery mountings to reduce self-generated noise levels.

PLUNGER (SSN 595)   *United States Navy*

HADDOCK (SSN 621)   *1967, United States Navy*

NAVIGATION. These submarines are fitted with the Ship's Inertial Navigation System (SINS).

NOMENCLATURE. Names changed during construction: *Plunger* ex-*Pollack, Barb* ex-*Pollack,* ex-*Plunger; Pollack* ex-*Barb.*

PHOTOGRAPHS. The *Plunger* has her deck equipment "up" as she streams off Hawaii. The sails in these submarines are shorter than in the earlier "Skipjack" class; compare position of sail-mounted diving planes with the later "Sturgeon" class submarines.

Submarines—*continued*

GUARDFISH (SSN 612)

1968, United States Navy

1 NUCLEAR-POWERED ATTACK SUBMARINE (SSN): "TULLIBEE" TYPE

Displacement, tons	2 317 standard ; 2 640 submerged
Length, feet (*metres*)	273 (*83·2*) oa
Beam, feet (*metres*)	23·3 (*7·1*)
Draft, feet (*metres*)	21 (*6·4*)
Torpedo tubes	4—21 in (*533 mm*) amidships
ASW weapons	ASW torpedoes
Main engines	Turbo-electric drive with steam turbine (Westinghouse), 2 500 shp; 1 shaft (Combustion Engineering)
Speed, knots	15 surface ; 20 submerged
Complement	56 (6 officers, 50 enlisted men)

Name	No.	Builder	Laid down	Launched	Commissioned
*TULLIBEE	SSN 597	General Dynamics (Electric Boat)	26 May 1958	27 Apr 1960	9 Nov 1960

The *Tullibee* was designed specifically for anti-submarine operations and was the first US submarine with the optimum bow position devoted entirely to sonar. No additional submarines of this type were constructed because of the success of the larger, more-versatile "Thresher" class. The *Tullibee* was authorised in the Fiscal Year 1958 new construction programme. She is no longer considered a "first line" submarine.

DESIGN. The *Tullibee* has a modified, elongated "tear-drop" hull design. Originally she was planned as a 1 000-ton craft, but reactor requirements and other considerations increased her size during design and construction.

The *Tullibee* has four amidships torpedo tubes angled out from the centreline, two to port and two to starboard. However, she is not fitted to fire the SUBROC anti-submarine missile. She cannot match the "Thresher" and later SSN classes in underwater speed or manoeuvrability.

TULLIBEE (SSN 597)

1960, United States Navy

ELECTRONICS. The *Tullibee* was the first submarine fitted with the advanced BQQ-2 sonar system (see "Permit" class listing for details). The fin-like sonar domes are PUFFs for BQG-4 passive fire control sonar; in the earlier photograph only two PUFF domes are installed (not to be confused with fin-like rudder); later photograph shows three PUFF domes with second dome (aft of sail structure) painted light color.

PUFF is an acronym for Passive Underwater Fire-control Feasibility study.

Fitted with Mk 112 torpedo fire control system.

ENGINEERING. The *Tullibee* has a small nuclear power plant designed and developed by the Combustion Engineering Company. Construction of a land-based prototype plant began at the Atomic Energy Commission's Windsor, Connecticut, test site in June of 1957 and the plant was operated at full power for the first time on 19 Dec 1959.

The *Tullibee* propulsion system features turbo-electric drive rather than conventional steam turbines with reduction gears in an effort to reduce operating noises.

NAVIGATION. The *Tullibee* is fitted with Ships Inertial Navigation System (SINS).

TULLIBEE (SSN 597)

1968, United States Navy

Submarines—*continued*

5 NUCLEAR-POWERED ATTACK SUBMARINES (SSN): "SKIPJACK" CLASS

Name	No.	Builder	Laid down	Launched	Commissioned
*SKIPJACK	SSN 585	General Dynamics (Electric Boat)	29 May 1956	26 May 1958	15 Apr 1959
*SCAMP	SSN 588	Mare Island Naval Shipyard	23 Jan 1959	8 Oct 1960	5 June 1961
*SCULPIN	SSN 590	Ingalls Shipbuilding Corp	3 Feb 1958	31 Mar 1960	1 June 1961
*SHARK	SSN 591	Newport News SB & DD Co	24 Feb 1958	16 Mar 1960	9 Feb 1961
*SNOOK	SSN 592	Ingalls Shipbuilding Corp	7 Apr 1958	31 Oct 1960	24 Oct 1961

Displacement, tons	3 075 standard ; 3 500 submerged
Length, feet (*metres*)	251·7 (*76·7*) oa
Beam, feet (*metres*)	31·5 (*9·6*)
Draft, feet (*metres*)	28 (*8·5*)
Torpedo tubes	6—21 in (*533 mm*) forward
ASW weapons	ASW torpedoes
Main engines	2 steam turbines (Westinghouse in *Skipjack*; General Electric in others); approx 15 000 shp; 1 shaft
Nuclear reactor	1 pressurised-water cooled S5W (Westinghouse)
Speed, knots	20 surface; 30+ submerged
Complement	93 (8 officers, 85 enlisted men)

The "Skipjack" class combines the high-speed endurance of nuclear propulsion with the high-speed "tear-drop" hull design tested in the conventionally powered submarine *Albacore* (AGSS 569). (See *Design* and *Engineering* notes). The *Skipjack* was authorised in the Fiscal Year 1956 new construction programme; the five other submarines of this class were authorised in FY 1957. Although they are now nearing their first decade of service, these submarines are still considered suitable for "first line" service.
Each submarine cost approximately $40 000 000.
The *Scorpion* (SSN 589) of this class was lost some 400 miles southwest of the Azores while en route from the Mediterranean to Norfolk, Virginia, in May 1968. She went down with 99 men on board.

CONSTRUCTION: The *Scorpion's* keel was laid down twice: the original keel laid down on 1 Nov 1957 was renumbered SSBN 598 and became the Polaris submarine *George Washington*; the second SSN 589 keel became the *Scorpion*. The *Scamp's* keel laying was delayed when material for her was diverted to the SSBN 599 (*Patrick Henry*).
This class introduced the Newport News Shipbuilding and Dry Dock Company and the Ingalls Shipbuilding Corporation to nuclear submarine construction. Newport News had not previously built any submarine since before World War I; Ingalls previously had built only one submarine, the *Blueback* (SS 581) launched in 1959.

DESIGN. The *Skipjack* was the first US nuclear submarine built to the "tear-drop" or modified spindle hull design which improves underwater performance. Her length-to-beam ratio is 7·8 : 1 compared to a ratio of 10·7 : 1 for the "Skate" class. (The conventionally powered attack submarine *Barbel* was built to a similar design at the same time as the *Skipjack*). These submarines have a single propeller shaft (vice two in earlier nuclear submarines) and their diving planes are

SNOOK (SSN 592)   *1964, United States Navy*

mounted on sail structures to improve underwater manoeuvrability. No after torpedo tubes are fitted because of their tapering sterns.

ELECTRONICS. Original sonar equipment was modified to provide improved ASW capabilities. (See *Electronic* notes in introductory passage to this section).
These submarines have the Mk 112 torpedo fire control director.

ENDURANCE. The *Scorpion* set an endurance record in 1962 when she maintained a sealed atmosphere for 70 consecutive days.

ENGINEERING. The "Skipjack" class introduced the S5W fast attack submarine-propulsion plant which has been used in all subsequent attack and missile submarines except the *Narwhal*. The plant was developed by the Bettis Atomic Power Laboratory. No land-based prototype was constructed because of the data available from the earlier S3W and S4W nuclear power plants.

PHOTOGRAPHS. Note streamlined shape and lack of projections; all equipment outside of the hull is either recessed or retractable.

SHARK (SSN 591)   *1968, U.S. Navy PHC RM Anderson.*

HALIBUT (SSN 587)   *1968, U.S. Navy PHCM L. P. Bodine*

Submarines—*continued*

1 NUCLEAR-POWERED RESEARCH SUBMARINE (SSN):
FORMER GUiDED MISSILE SUBMARINE

Name	No.	Builder	Laid down	Launched	Commissioned
*HALIBUT	SSN 587 (ex-SSGN 587)	Mare Island Naval Shipyard, Vallejo, Calif	11 Apr 1957	9 Jan 1959	4 Jan 1960

Displacement, tons	3 850 standard ; 5 000 submerged
Length, feet (*metres*)	350 (*106·6*) oa
Beam, feet (*metres*)	29.5 (*8·9*)
Draft, feet (*metres*)	21·5 (*6·5*)
Torpedo tubes	6—21 in (*533 mm*) 4 fwd ; 2 aft
Main engines	2 steam turbines (Westinghouse), approx 6 000 shp ; 2 shafts
Nuclear reactor	1 pressurised-water cooled S3W (Westinghouse)
Speed, knots	15 surface ; 20 submerged
Complement as SSN	97 (9 officers, 88 enlisted men)

The *Halibut* is believed to have been the first submarine designed and constructed specifically to fire guided missiles.

The Soviets began construction of their first built-for-the-purpose ballistic missile submarines ("G" and "H" classes) prior to building dedicated guided missile submarines ("E" and "J" classes).

She was originally intended to have diesel-electric propulsion but on 27 Feb 1956 the Navy announced she would have nuclear propulsion. She was the US Navy's only nuclear-powered *guided* missile submarine (SSGN) to be completed. Authorised in the Fiscal Year 1956 new construction programme and built for an estimated cost of $45 000 000.

The *Halibut* was reclassifed as an attack submarine on 25 July 1965 after the Navy discarded the Regulus submarine-launched missile force. Her missile equipment was removed ; she is no longer considered a "first line" submarine and is employed in experimental work. The submarine's large missile compartment makes her an excellent ship for underwater projects.

The Navy has stated that the *Halibut* and earlier *Seawolf* have been designated as "mother" submarines for the deep submergence research vehicle programme and initially are being modified to accommodate vehicle test simulators. Reportedly the *Halibut* has been fitted with a ducted bow thruster to permit precise control and manoeuvering.

DESIGN. The *Halibut* was built with a large missile hangar faired into her bow. Her hull was intended primarily to provide a stable surface launching platform rather than for speed or manoeuvrability.

MISSILES. The *Halibut* was designed to carry two Regulus II surface-to-surface missiles. The Regulus II was a transonic missile which could carry a nuclear warhead and had a range of 1 000 miles. The Regulus II

was cancelled before becoming operational and the *Halibut* operated from 1960 to 1964 carrying five Regulus I missiles, subsonic cruise missiles which could deliver a nuclear warhead on targets 500 miles from the launching ship or submarine.

As SSGN carried a complement of 11 officers and 108 enlisted men.

During this period the US Navy operated a maximum of five Regulus "guided" (cruise) missile submarines, the *Halibut*, the post-war constructed *Grayback* (SSG 574 now LPSS 574) and *Growler* (SSG 577), and the World War II-built *Tunny* (SSG 282 subsequently LPSS 282) and *Barbero* (SSG 317). The *Grayback* and *Growler* each could carry four Regulus I missiles and the older submarines each carried two missiles.

NAVIGATION. The *Halibut* is fitted with Ship's Inertial Navigation System (SINS).

PHOTOGRAPHS. Note relatively far aft position of sail structure ; modified missile hangar door protruding from forward deck.

HALIBUT (SSN 587)
1968, United States Navy, PHCM L. P. Bodine

TRITON (SSN 586)
1964, United States Navy

Submarines—continued

1 NUCLEAR-POWERED ATTACK SUBMARINE (SSN): FORMER RADAR PICKET SUBMARINE

Name	No.	Builder	Laid down	Launched	Commissioned
TRITON	SSN 586 (ex-SSRN 586)	General Dynamics Corp (Electric Boat), Groton, Conn	29 May 1956	19 Aug 1958	10 Nov 1959

Displacement, tons	5 940 standard; 7 780 submerged
Length, feet (metres)	447·5 (136·3) oa
Beam, feet (metres)	37 (11·3)
Draft, feet (metres)	24 (7·3)
Torpedo tubes	6—21 in (533 mm) 4 forward, 2 aft
Main engines	2 steam turbines (General Electric); approx 34 000 shp; 2 shafts
Nuclear reactors	2 pressurised-water cooled S4G (General Electric)
Speed, knots	27 surface; 20 submerged
Complement as SSRN	172 (16 officers, 156 enlisted men)

The Triton was designed and constructed to serve as a radar picket submarine to operate in conjunction with surface carrier task forces. She is the longest submarine ever constructed and is exceeded in displacement only by the later Polaris missile submarines. Authorised in the Fiscal Year 1956 new construction programme and built for an estimated cost of $109 000 000.

The Triton circumnavigated the globe in 1960, remaining submerged except when her sail structure broke the surface to enable an ill sailor to be taken off near the Falkland Islands. The 41 500-mile cruise took 83 days and was made at an average speed of 18 knots.

The underwater giant was reclassified as an attack submarine (SSN) on 1 Mar 1961 as the Navy dropped the radar picket submarine programme. She is no longer considered a "first line" submarine and was decommissioned on 3 May 1969 to become the first US nuclear submarine to be relegated to the "mothball fleet". There had been proposals to operate the Triton as an underwater national command post afloat, but no funds were provided and there were major operational/technical problems involved in this concept because of the difficulty in communications with a submerged submarine with technology then available.

DESIGN. The Triton was designed to operate as a surface radar picket, submerging when in danger of enemy attack. She was fitted with an elaborate combat information centre and large radar antenna which retracted into the sail structure.

ENGINEERING. The Triton is the only US submarine with two nuclear reactors. The Atomic Energy Commission's Knolls Atomic Power Laboratory was given prime responsibility for development of the power plant. Construction of a land-based prototype plant began in October 1955 at West Milton, New York. The prototype plant's single reactor achieved criticality on 18 Aug 1958. After 2½ years of operation, during which she steamed more than 110 000 miles, the Triton was overhauled and refuelled from July 1962 to March 1964.

PHOTOGRAPH. Note size of sail structure; in this photograph the large sail opening for search radar antenna has been covered. See 1969-1970 and previous editions for earlier photographs.

3 ATTACK SUBMARINES (SS): "BARBEL" CLASS

Displacement, tons	2 145 surface; 2 895 submerged
Length, feet (metres)	219·5 (66·8) oa
Beam, feet (metres)	29 (8·8)
Draft, feet (metres)	28 (8·5)
Torpedo tubes	6—21 in (533 mm) forward
Main engines	3 diesels 4 800 hp (Fairbanks Morse); electric motors (General Electric) 1 shaft
Speed, knots	15 on surface; 25 submerged
Complement	79 (10 officers, 69 men)

Name	No.	Builder	Laid down	Launched	Commissioned
*BARBEL	SS 580	Portsmouth Naval Shipyard	18 May 1956	19 July 1958	17 Jan 1959
*BLUEBACK	SS 581	Ingalls Shipbuilding Corporation	15 Apr 1957	16 May 1959	15 Oct 1959
*BONEFISH	SS 582	New York Shipbuilding Corp	3 June 1957	22 Nov 1958	9 July 1959

These submarines were the last non-nuclear combatant submarines built by the US Navy. All three were authorised in the Fiscal Year 1956 new construction programme.

DESIGN. These submarines have the "tear-drop" or modified spindle hull design which was tested in the experimental submarine Albacore. As built their diving planes were bow-mounted; subsequently relocated to the sail structure.

These submarines introduced a new concept in centralised arrangement of controls in an "attack centre" to increase efficiency; the concept has been adapted for all later US combat submarines.

CONSTRUCTION. The Blueback was the first submarine built by the Ingalls Shipbuilding Corp at Pascagoula, Mississippi, and the Bonefish was the first constructed at the New York Shipbuilding Corp yard in Camden, New Jersey.

BLUEBACK (SS 581)   1967, United States Navy

BONEFISH (SS 582)   1969, United States Navy

Submarines—continued

BARBEL (SS 580)

1962, United States Navy

4 NUCLEAR-POWERED ATTACK SUBMARINES (SSN): "SKATE" CLASS

Displacement, tons	2 570 standard; 2 861 submerged				
Length, feet (metres)	267·7 (81·5) oa				
Beam, feet (metres)	25 (7·6)				
Draft, feet (metres)	21 (6·4)				
Torpedo tubes	6—21 in (533 mm) 4 forward; 2 aft				
ASW weapons	ASW torpedoes				
Main engines	2 steam turbines (Westinghouse) approx 6 600 shp; 2 shafts				
Nuclear reactor	1 pressurised-water cooled S3W (Westinghouse) in Skate and Sargo; 1 pressurised-water cooled S4W (Westinghouse) in Swordfish and Seadragon				
Speed, knots	20 surface; approx 25 submerged				
Complement	95 (8 officers, 78 enlisted men)				

Name	No.	Builder	Laid down	Launched	Commissioned
*SKATE	SSN 578	General Dynamics (Electric Boat)	21 July 1955	16 May 1957	23 Dec 1957
*SWORDFISH	SSN 579	Portsmouth Naval Shipyard	25 Jan 1956	27 Aug 1957	15 Sep 1958
*SARGO	SSN 583	Mare Island Naval Shipyard	21 Feb 1956	10 Oct 1957	1 Oct 1958
*SEADRAGON	SSN 584	Portsmouth Naval Shipyard	20 June 1956	16 Aug 1958	5 Dec 1959

SEADRAGON (SSN 584)

1965, United States Navy

The "Skate" class submarines were the first production model nuclear-powered submarines. They are similar in design to the Nautilus, but smaller. The Skate and Swordfish were authorised in the Fiscal Year 1955 new construction programme, and the Sargo and Seadragon in FY 1956.

The Skate was the first submarine to make a completely submerged transatlantic crossing; in 1958 she established a (then) record of 31 days submerged with a sealed atmosphere; on 11 Aug 1958 she passed under the North Pole during a polar cruise; and on 17 Mar 1959 she became the first submarine to surface at the North Pole. The Sargo undertook a polar cruise during January-February 1960 and surfaced at the North Pole on 9 Feb 1960. The Seadragon transited from the Atlantic to the Pacific via the Northwest Passage (Lancaster Sound, Barrow and McClure Straits) in August 1960. The Skate, operating from New London, Connecticut, and the Seadragon, based at Pearl Harbour, rendezvoused under the North Pole on 2 Aug 1962 and then conducted anti-submarine exercises under the polar ice pack and surfaced together at the North Pole.

The "Skate" also operated in the Arctic Ocean during April-May 1969, conducting exercises under the Arctic ice pack with the later nuclear-powered attack submarines Pargo and Whale.

These submarines are no longer considered "first line" submarines.

DESIGN. The "Skate" design is similar to the Nautilus-Seawolf design with GUPPY hull, bow diving planes, and twin propellers.

ENGINEERING. After the land-based prototype of the Nautilus reactor plant was placed in operation work was begun on a similar but smaller plant suitable for use in smaller submarines. Developed by the Atomic Energy Commission s Bettis Atomic Power Laboratory, the new propulsion system was similar to that of the Nautilus but considerably simplified with improved operation and maintenance. No land-based prototype was constructed because of the similarity to the Nautilus plant. The final propulsion plant developed under this programme had two arrangements, the S3W configuration in the Skate Sargo and Halibut, and the S4W configuration in the Swordfish and Seadragon. Both arrangements have proven satisfactory.

The Skate began her first overhaul and refuelling in January 1961 after steaming 120 862 miles on her initial reactor core during three years of operation. The Swordfish began her first overhaul and refuelling in early 1962 after more than three years of operation in which time she steamed 112 000 miles.

SWORDFISH (SSN 579)

1970, United States Navy, PH1 D. Osborne

Submarines—continued

SKATE (SSN 578)   *United States Navy*

1 GUIDED MISSILE SUBMARINE (SSG): "GROWLER" TYPE

Displacement, tons	2 540 standard; 3 515 submerged	*Name*	*No.*	*Builder*	*Laid down*	*Launched*	*Commissioned*
Length, feet (*metres*)	317·6 (*96·8*) oa	**GROWLER**	SSG 577	Portsmouth Naval Shipyard	15 Feb 1955	5 Apr 1959	30 Apr 1958

Displacement, tons   2 540 standard; 3 515 submerged
Length, feet (*metres*)   317·6 (*96·8*) oa
Beam, feet(*metres*)   27·2 (*8·2*)
Draft, feet (*metres*)   19 (*5·8*)
Torpedo tubes   6—21 inch (*533 mm*) 4 fwd; 2 aft
Main engines   3 diesels (Fairbanks Morse); 4 500 hp/2 electric motors (Elliott); 5 600 shp; 2 shafts
Speed, knots   20 surface; 17 submerged
Complement   84 officers and enlisted men

The *Growler* was authorised in the Fiscal Year 1955 new construction programme; completed as a guided missile submarine to fire the Regulus surface-to-surface cruise missile (see *Halibut*, SSN 587, for *Missile* notes).
When the Regulus submarine missile programme ended in 1964 the *Growler* and her near-sister submarine *Grayback* were withdrawn from service; the *Grayback* subsequently converted to an amphibious transport submarine (LPSS). The *Growler* was scheduled to undergo a similar conversion when the *Grayback* was completed, but the second conversion was deferred late in 1968 because of rising ship conversion costs.
The *Growler* is in reserve as an SSG.

DESIGN. The *Grayback* and *Growler* initially were designed as attack submarines similar to the *Darter*. Upon redesign as missile submarines they were cut in half on the building ways and were lengthened approximately 50 feet, two cylindrical hangars, each 11 feet high and 70 feet long, were superimposed on their bows, a missile launcher was installed between the hangars and sail structure, and elaborate navigation and fire

GRAYBACK (left), GROWLER (right)   *1964, United States Navy*

control systems were fitted, The height of the sail structure on the *Growler* is approximately 30 feet above the deck; the *Grayback's* lower sail structure was increased during LPSS conversion.

1 ATTACK SUBMARINE (SS): "DARTER" TYPE

Displacement, tons	1 720 surface; 2 388 submerged	*Name*	*No.*	*Builder*	*Laid down*	*Launched*	*Commissioned*
Length, feet (*metres*)	268·6 (*81·9*) oa	***DARTER**	SS 576	General Dynamics Corp (Electric Boat)	10 Nov 1954	28 May 1956	20 Oct 1956

Displacement, tons   1 720 surface; 2 388 submerged
Length, feet (*metres*)   268·6 (*81·9*) oa
Beam, feet (*metres*)   27·2 (*8·3*)
Draft, feet (*metres*)   19 (*5·8*)
Torpedo tubes   8—21 in (*533 mm*) 6 fwd; 2 aft
Main engines   3 diesels (Fairbanks Morse); 4 500 shp; 1 electric motor (Elliott); 2 shafts
Speed, knots   17 surface; 25 submerged
Complement   85 (11 officers, 64 men)

Designed for high submerged speed with quiet machinery. Planned sister submarines *Growler* and *Grayback* were completed to missile-launching configuration.

Authorised in Fiscal Year 1954 shipbuilding programme. No additional submarines of this type were built because of shift to high-speed hull design and nuclear propulsion.

DARTER (SS 576)   *United States Navy*

Submarines—*continued*

1 NUCLEAR-POWERED RESEARCH SUBMARINE (SSN): "SEAWOLF" TYPE

Name	No.	Builder	Laid down	Launched	Commissioned
*SEAWOLF	SSN 575	General Dynamics (Electric Boat), Groton, Connecticut	15 Sep 1953	21 July 1955	30 Mar 1957

Displacement, tons	3 720 standard ; 4 280 submerged
Length, feet (*metres*)	337·5 (*102·9*) oa
Beam, feet (*metres*)	27·7 (*8·4*)
Draft, feet (*metres*)	22 (*6·7*)
Torpedo tubes	6—21 in (*533 mm*) forward
Main engines	2 steam turbines (General Electric), approx 15 000 shp ; 2 shafts
Nuclear reactor	1 pressurised-water cooled S2Wa (Westinghouse)
Speed, knots	20 surface ; 20 submerged
Complement	105 (10 officers, 95 enlisted men)

The *Seawolf* was the world's second nuclear-propelled vehicle ; she was constructed almost simultaneous with the *Nautilus* to test a competitive reactor design. Funds for the *Seawolf* were authorised in the Fiscal Year 1952 new construction programme.

The *Seawolf* established a submerged endurance record in 1958 when she remained submerged for 60 consecutive days, travelling a distance of 13 761 miles with a completely sealed atmosphere. She is no longer considered a "first line" submarine and has been engaged primarily in research work since 1969.

ENGINEERING. Initial work in the development of naval nuclear propulsion plants investigated a number of concepts, two of which were of sufficient interest to warrant full development : the pressurised water and liquid metal (sodium). The *Nautilus* was provided a pressurised-water reactor plant and the *Seawolf* was fitted initially with a liquid-metal reactor.

Originally known as the Submarine Intermediate Reactor (SIR), the liquid-metal plant was developed by the Atomic Energy Commission's Knolls Atomic Power Laboratory. A land-based prototype designated SIR Mark I was constructed at the Laboratory's West Milton New York, site. The plant attained initial criticality on 20 Mar 1955 and was operated until dismantled in early 1957.

The SIR Mark II was installed in the *Seawolf*. (The reactor plants were later redesignated SIG and S2G, respectively). The Mark II/S2G in the *Seawolf* achieved initial criticality on 25 June 1956. Steam leaks developed during the dockside testing. The plant was shut down and it was determined· that the leaks were caused by sodium-potassium alloy which had entered the superheater steam piping. After repairs and testing the *Seawolf* began sea trials on 21 Jan 1957. The trials were run at reduced power and after two years of operation the *Seawolf* entered the Electric Boat yard for removal of her sodium-cooled plant and installation of a pressurised-water plant similar to that installed in the *Nautilus* (designated S2Wa). When the original *Seawolf* plant was shut down in December 1958 the submarine had steamed a total of 71 611 miles. She was recommissioned on 30 Sep 1960. The pressurised-water reactor was refuelled for the first between May 1965 and August 1967, having propelled the *Seawolf* for more than 161 000 miles on its initial fuel core.

SEAWOLF (SSN 575)

United States Navy

1 AMPHIBIOUS TRANSPORT SUBMARINE (LPSS): CONVERTED MISSILE SUBMARINE

Name	No.	Builder	Laid down	Launched	Commissioned	LPSS Comm.
*GRAYBACK	LPSS 574 (ex-SSG 574)	Mare Island Naval Shipyard	1 July 1954	2 July 1957	7 Mar 1958	9 May 1969

Displacement, tons	2 670 standard ; 3 650 submerged
Length, feet (*metres*)	334 (*101·8*) oa
Beam, feet (*metres*)	30 (*9·0*)
Draft, feet (*metres*)	19 (*5·8*)
Torpedo tubes	8—21 inch (*533 mm*) 6 fwd ; 2 aft
Main engines	3 diesels (Fairbanks Morse), 4 500 hp/2 electric motors (Elliott) ; 5 600 shp ; 2 shafts
Speed, knots	20 surface ; 17 submerged
Complement	
Troops	67 (7 officers, 60 enlisted men)

The *Grayback* has been fully converted to a transport submarine and is officially classified as an amphibious warfare ship. She was originally intended to be an attack submarine, being authorised in the Fiscal Year 1953 new construction programme, but redesigned in 1956 to provide a Regulus missile launching capability ; completed as SSG 574 in 1958, similar in design to the *Growler* (SSG 577). See *Growler* listing for basic design notes.

CONVERSION. The *Grayback* began conversion to a transport submarine at the San Francisco Bay Naval Shipyard (Mare Island) in November 1967. The conversion was originally estimated at $15 200 000 but was actually about $30 000 000. She was reclassified from SSG to LPSS on 30 Aug 1968 (never officially designated APSS).

During conversion the *Grayback* was fitted to berth and mess 67 troops and carry their equipment including landing craft or swimmer delivery vehicles (SDV). Her torpedo tubes and hence attack capability are retained. As completed (SSG) the *Grayback* had an overall length of 322 ft 4 in ; lengthened 12 ft during LPSS conversion. Conversion was authorised in Fiscal Year 1965 programme completed in June 1969. The conversion was delayed because of higher priorities being allocated to other submarine projects.

ELECTRONICS. Fitted with BQG-4 passive fire control sonar (note three fin-like PUFF sonar domes).

GRAYBACK (LPSS 574)

1969, United States Navy

Submarines—*continued*

2 ATTACK SUBMARINES (SS): CONVERTED RADAR PICKET SUBMARINES

Name	No.	Builder	Laid down	Launched	Commissioned
*SAILFISH	SS 572 (ex-SSR 572)	Portsmouth Naval Shipyard	8 Dec 1953	7 Sep 1955	14 Apr 1956
*SALMON	SS 573 (ex-AGSS 573, ex-SSR 573)	Portsmouth Naval Shipyard	10 Mar 1954	25 Feb 1956	25 Aug 1956

Displacement, tons	2 625 surface; 3 168 submerged
Length, feet (*metres*)	350·4 (*106·8*) oa
Beam, feet (*metres*)	28·4 (*8·8*)
Draft, feet (*metres*)	18 (*5·5*) max
Torpedo tubes	6—21 in (*533 mm*) forward
Main engines	4 diesels (Fairbanks Morse); 9 600 shp/2 electric motors (Elliott); 8 200 shp; 2 shafts
Speed, knots	20·5 on surface; 15 submerged
Complement	95 (12 officers, 83 enlisted men)

Largest non-nuclear submarines built by the US Navy since the *Narwhal* (SS 167) and *Nautilus* (SS 168) completed in 1930. The *Sailfish* and *Salmon* were built as radar picket submarines (SSR) with air-search radar antennas on deck and elaborate air control centres. Both submarines underwent FRAM II modernisation. Authorised in Fiscal Year 1952 programme.

These are believed to be the largest non-nuclear submarines in service.

CLASSIFICATION. Reclassified from radar picket submarines (SSR) to SS on 1 Mar 1961; *Salmon* reclassified AGSS on 29 June 1968 to serve as test and evaluation submarine for Navy's Deep Submergence Rescue Vehicle (DSRV). However, the DSRV programme has been delayed and the *Salmon* reverted to SS designation on 30 June 1969

SAILFISH (SS 572)

1966, United States Navy

As a mother submarine test platform she will evaluate the DSRV's ability to "land on" and "take off" from a moving submarine. (In actual operation the mother submarine would transport the DSRV "piggyback" while travelling submerged to the rescue or work area; see section on Deep Submergence Vehicles). The PUFF sonar domes will be removed from the *Salmon* during the trials; she retains all other combat capabilities (as will DSRV support submarines).

ELECTRONICS. Fitted with BQG-4 passive fire control sonar (note three fin-like PUFF sonar dome

SALMON (SS 573)

United States Navy

GRAYBACK (LPSS 574)

1969, United States Navy

Submarines—*continued*

1 NUCLEAR POWERED ATTACK SUBMARINE (SSN): "NAUTILUS" TYPE

Name	No.	Builder	Laid down	Launched	Commissioned
*NAUTILUS	SSN 571	General Dynamics (Electric Boat) Groton, Connecticut	14 June 1952	21 Jan 1954	30 Sep 1954

Displacement, tons	3 530 standard; 4 040 submerged
Length, feet (*metres*)	323·7 (*98·6*) oa
Beam, feet (*metres*)	27·6 (*8·4*)
Draft, feet (*metres*)	22 (*6·7*)
Torpedo tubes	6—21 in (*533 mm*) forward
ASW weapons	ASW torpedoes
Main engines	2 steam turbines (Westinghouse), approx 15 000 shp; 2 shafts
Nuclear reactor	1 pressurised-water cooled S2W (Westinghouse)
Speed, knots	20 surface; 20+ submerged
Complement	105 (10 officers, 95 enlisted men)

The *Nautilus* was the world's first nuclear-propelled vehicle. She predated the first Soviet nuclear-powered submarine by five years.

The Chief of Naval Operations initially established a requirement for a nuclear-propelled submarine in August 1949 and specified a "ready-for-sea" date of January 1955. The funds for construction of the *Nautilus* were authorised in the Fiscal Year 1952 budget. The *Nautilus* put to sea for the first time on 17 Jan 1955 and signalled the historic message: "Underway on nuclear power".

On her shakedown cruise in May 1955 the *Nautilus* steamed submerged from New London, Connecticut, to San Juan, Puerto Rico, travelling more than 1 300 miles

in 84 hours at an average speed of almost 16 knots; she later steamed submerged from Key West, Florida, to New London, a distance of 1 397 miles, at an average speed of more than 20 knots.

During 1958 the *Nautilus* undertook extensive operations under the Arctic ice pack and in August she made history's first polar transit from the Pacific to the Atlantic, steaming from Pearl Harbour to Portland, England. She passed under the Geographic North Pole on 3 Aug 1958.

The *Nautilus* is no longer considered a "first line" submarine.

DESIGN. The *Nautilus* and *Seawolf* have GUPPY-type hull configurations. The *Seawolf* has a stepped sail and a slight rise at the bow.

ENGINEERING. In January 1948 the Department of Defense requested the Atomic Energy Commission to undertake the design, development, and construction of a nuclear reactor for submarine propulsion. Initial research and conceptual design of the Submarine Thermal Reactor (STR) was undertaken by the Argonne National Laboratory. Subsequently the Atomic Energy Commission's Bettis Atomic Power Laboratory, operated by the Westinghouse Electric Corporation, undertook development of the first nuclear propulsion plant.

Construction of a land-based prototype plant (STR Mark I) began in August 1950 at the reactor test station in Idaho. The STR Mark I was constructed inside a submarine hull, with a surrounding tank of water, to simulate actual submarine operating conditions. Initial criticality was attained on 30 Mar 1953. That June the STR Mark I reached full power and made a simulated 96-hour, full-power crossing of the Atlantic.

A virtually identical STR Mark II reactor plant was installed in the *Nautilus*. (The reactor plants were later redesignated S1W and S2W, respectively). The *Nautilus* Mark II/S2W plant was first operated at power on 20 Dec 1954 and first developed full power on 3 Jan 1955. After more than two years of operation, during which she steamed 62 562 miles, the *Nautilus* began an overhaul which included refuelling in April 1957. She was again refuelled in 1959 after steaming 91 324 miles on her second fuel core, and again in 1964 after steaming approximately 150 000 miles on her third fuel core. (The prototype Mark I/S1W plant was refuelled in 1955, 1958, 1960, and 1967; it remains in operation as an experimental and training facility).

PHOTOGRAPH. Two light areas on deck are emergency, tethered marker buoys (fitted to all US submarines) for localisation of sunken submarine and to winch down McCann submarine rescue chamber.

NAUTILUS (SSN 571)   *United States Navy*

1 RESEARCH SUBMARINE (AGSS): "ALBACORE" TYPE

Displacement, tons	1 500 surface; 1 850 submerged
Length, feet (*metres*)	210·5 (*63·6*) oa
Beam, feet (*metres*)	27·5 (*8·4*)
Draft, feet (*metres*)	18·5 (*5·6*)
Torpedo tubes	None
Main engines	2 diesels, radial pancake type (General Motors) electric motor (Westinghouse) 15 000 shp; 1 shaft
Speed, knots	25 on surface; 33 submerged
Complement	52 (5 officers, 47 men)

Name	No.	Builder	Laid down	Launched	Commissioned
*ALBACORE	AGSS 569	Portsmouth Naval Shipyard	15 Mar 1952	1 Aug 1953	5 Dec 1953

ALBACORE (AGSS 569)   *United States Navy*

High speed experimental submarine. Conventionally powered submarine of radical design with new hull form which makes her faster and more manoeuvrable than any other conventional submarine. Officially described as a hydrodynamic test vehicle. Streamlined, whale-shaped without the naval flat-topped deck. Conning tower resembles a fish's dorsal fin.

EXPERIMENTAL. The *Albacore* has been extensively modified to test advanced submarine design and engineering concepts.

Phase I modifications were made from July 1954 to February 1955 to eliminate the many "bugs" inherent with completely new construction and equipment.

Phase II modifications from Dec 1955 to Mar 1956 during which conventional propeller-rudder-stern diving plane arrangement was modified; the new design provided for the propeller to be installed *aft* of the control surfaces. (At this time a small auxiliary rudder on the sail was removed).

A concave bow sonar dome was fitted for tests in 1960. Phase III modifications from Nov 1960 to Aug 1961 during which an entirely new stern was installed featuring the stern planes in an "X" configuration, a

system of ten hydraulic operated dive brakes around the hull amidships, a dorsal rudder, and a new bow sonar dome. Phase IV modifications from Dec 1962 to Mar 1965 during which a silver-zinc battery was installed and counter-rotating stern propellers rotating around the same axis were fitted.

The *Albacore* conducted trials with towed sonar arrays from May to July 1966.

All modifications were made at the Portsmouth Naval Shipyard.

PHOTOGRAPH. Note stern rudder configuration; rounded hull without superstructure deck common to previous and contemporary submarines. Round electronic "ball" antenna on sail structure. Deck cleats and other equipment are recessed into hull.

Submarines—*continued*

6 ATTACK SUBMARINES (SS): "TANG" CLASS

Displacement, tons	2 100 surface; 2 700 submerged	*Name*	*No.*	*Builder*	*Laid down*	*Launched*	*Commissioned*

Name	No.	Builder	Laid down	Launched	Commissioned
*TANG	SS 563	Portsmouth Naval Shipyard	18 Apr 1949	19 June 1951	25 Oct 1951
*TRIGGER	SS 564	Electric Boat Co, Groton	24 Feb 1949	14 June 1951	31 Mar 1952
*WAHOO	SS 565	Portsmouth Naval Shipyard	24 Oct 1949	16 Oct 1951	30 May 1952
*TROUT	SS 566	Electric Boat Co, Groton	1 Dec 1949	21 Aug 1951	27 June 1952
*GUDGEON	SS 567	Portsmouth Naval Shipyard	20 May 1950	11 June 1952	21 Nov 1952
*HARDER	SS 568	Electric Boat Co, Groton	30 June 1950	3 Dec 1951	19 Aug 1952

Displacement, tons   2 100 surface; 2 700 submerged
Length, feet (*metres*)   287 (*87·4*) oa
Beam, feet (*metres*)   27·3 (*8·3*)
Draft, feet (*metres*)   19 (*6·2*)
Torpedo tubes   8—21 in (*533 mm*) 6 fwd, 2 aft
Main engines   3 diesels (Fairbanks-morse); 4 500 shp/2 electric motors; 5 600 shp
Speed, knots   20 surface; 18 submerged
Complement   83 (8 officers, 75 men)

This design embodied various improvements to provide high submerged speed, based largely on German World War II submarine developments.

These are streamlined deep-diving submarines but have comparatively short hulls. *Trigger* was the first US Navy submarine of the post-war programme to be laid down. *Tang* was the first of the new class to be completed. *Tang* and *Trigger* authorised in Fiscal Year 1947 new construction programme. *Wahoo* and *Trout* in FY 1948, and *Gudgeon* and *Harder* in FY 1949.

The *Gudgeon* was the first United States submarine to circumnavigate the world during Sep 1957-Feb 1958.

ELECTRONICS. BQG-4 "PUFF" sonar domes installed in some of these submarines. See GUPPY III submarine listing for details.

ENGINEERING. *Tang, Trigger, Trout* and *Wahoo* were originally powered by a compact, radial type engine produced after five years of development work, comprising a 16-cylinder 2-cycle plant, mounted vertically with four rows of cylinders radially arranged. These new engines were half the weight and two-thirds the size of the engines previously available for submarines. They proved to be unsatisfactory and were replaced by machinery similar to that in *Gudgeon* and *Harder* which have a Fairbanks-Morse high speed lightweight engine mounted horizontally. The electric motors are Elliott in *Tang* and *Trigger* General Electric in *Wahoo* and *Trout*, Westinghouse in *Gudgeon* and *Harder*.

Snorkel fitted as in all later US nuclear and conventionally propelled submarines.

RECONSTRUCTION. All six submarines of this class were built with an overall length of 269 ft 2 in. The *Tang, Trigger, Trout*, and *Wahoo* had their original diesel engines replaced during the late 1950s. During the process they were cut in half and a 9 ft section inserted amidships. All six submarines were modernised during the 1960s with the installation of improved electronic equipment and other features; additional sections were added to give an overall length of 287 ft.

PHOTOGRAPHS. Note that the *Trigger*, shown at Malta in November 1969, does not have PUFF domes. Her antennas and periscopes are raised.

GUDGEON (SS 567)   *1970, US Navy, PH3 J. B. Land*

WAHOO (SS 565)   *1968, United States Navy, PH1 W. A. Clayton*

TRIGGER (SS 564)   *1969, Anthony & Joseph Pavia*

Submarines—*continued*

1 RESEARCH SUBMARINE (AGSS): "DOLPHIN" TYPE

Displacement, tons	800 standard; 930 full load
Length, feet	152
Beam, feet	19·3
Diameter, feet	18 (maximum)
Torpedo tube	Removed
Main engines	Diesel/electric (2 Detroit 12V71 diesels), 1 500+ hp; 1 shaft
Speed, knots	12+ submerged
Complement	23 (3 officers, 20 enlisted men) plus 4 to 7 scientists

Name	No.	Builder	Laid down	Launched	Commissioned
*DOLPHIN	AGSS 555	Portsmouth Naval Shipyard	9 Nov 1962	8 June 1968	17 Aug 1968

DOLPHIN (AGSS 555)   United States Navy

The *Dolphin* is an auxiliary submarine specifically designed for deep-diving operations. Authorised in Fiscal year 1961 new construction programme, but delayed because of changes in mission and equipment coupled with higher priorities being given to other submarine projects. Operating depth is greater than combatant submarines. Underwater endurance is limited (endurance and habitability were considered of secondary importance in design). On 24 Nov 1968 the *Dolphin* "descended to a depth greater than that recorded by any other operational submarine" according to official statements.

The *Dolphin* is fitted for deep-ocean sonar and oceanographic research. She is highly automated and has three computer-operated systems: a safety system, hovering system, and one that is classified. The digital-computer submarine safety system monitors equipment and provides data on closed-circuit television screens; malfunctions in equipment or trends toward potentially dangerous situations set off an alarm and if they are not corrected within the prescribed time the system, unless overrridden by an operator, automatically brings the submarine to the surface. There are several research stations for scientists in the *Dolphin* and she is fitted to take water samples down to her operating (test) depth.

The single, experimental torpedo tube was removed in 1970. Installation of an externally mounted torpedo tube is planned.

CLASSIFICATION. The *Dolphin*'s number was taken from a block (551-562) authorised but cancelled late in World War II with no construction being assigned. (Submarines built in Norway and Denmark were assigned the hull numbers SS 553 and SS 554, respectively, for financial accounting purposes; hull numbers SS 551 and SS 552 in this series were assigned to the late hunter-killer submarines *Bass*, ex-SSK 2, and *Bonita* ex-SSK 3, respectively).

DESIGN. The *Dolphin* has a constant diameter, cylindrical pressure hull approximately 15 feet in outer diameter, closed at both ends with hemispherical heads. Pressure hull fabricated of HY-80 steel with aluminium and fibre-

glass used in secondary structures to reduce weight, a critical factor in retaining buoyancy at deep depths. No conventional diving planes are mounted; improved rudder design and other features provide manoeuvring control and hovering capability. Access is through a single hatch in the pressure hull (opening into sail structure). Sea-water cooling system replaced by closed-loop system to further reduce hull penetrations; only three "systems" are open to the sea at depth—trim and drain, torpedo tube equalizing, and depth-sensing.

ENGINEERING. Fitted with 330 cell silver zinc battery. Submerged endurance is approximately 24 hours with

an at-sea endurance of 14 days.

STATUS. Completed in early 1969, approximately five years behind official schedule at time of keel laying. The *Dolphin* is in commission and has a commanding officer (correction to previous edition).

PHOTOGRAPHS. Note the *Dolphin*'s rounded, constant-diameter hull configuration in the above photograph; note her small deck area, narrow sail structure, raised periscope. A photograph of the *Dolphin* being launched, showing her stern configuration, appears in the 1970-1971 edition and a photograph of the *Dolphin* design model in the 1969-1970 edition.

DOLPHIN (AGSS 555)   1968, United States Navy

PICKEREL (SS 524)   United States Navy

Submarines—*continued*

9 ATTACK SUBMARINES (SS): GUPPY III TYPE

		Name	No.	Builder	Laid down	Launched	Commissioned
Displacement, tons	1 975 standard ; 2 540 submerged	*CLAMAGORE	SS 343	Electric Boat Co	16 Mar 1944	25 Feb 1945	21 Oct 1944
Length, feet (*metres*)	326·5 (*99·4*) oa	*COBBLER	SS 344	Electric Boat Co	3 Apr 1944	1 Apr 1945	8 Aug 1945
Beam, feet (*metres*)	27 (*8·2*)	*CORPORAL	SS 346	Electric Boat Co	27 Apr 1944	10 June 1945	9 Nov 1945
Draft, feet (*metres*)	17 (*5·2*)	*GREENFISH	SS 351	Electric Boat Co	29 June 1944	21 Dec 1945	7 June 1946
Torpedo tubes	10—21 in (*533 mm*) , 6 fwd, 4 aft	*TIRU	SS 416	Mare Island Navy Yard	17 Apr 1944	16 Sep 1947	1 Sep 1948
Main engines	4 diesels ; 6 400 shp/2 electric	*TRUMPETFISH	SS 425	Cramp Shipbuilding Co	23 Aug 1943	13 May 1945	29 Jan 1946
	motors ; 5 400 shp ; 2 shafts	*REMORA	SS 487	Portsmouth Navy Yard	5 Mar 1945	12 July 1945	3 Jan 1946
Speed, knots	20 surface ; 15 submerged	*VOLADOR	SS 490	Portsmouth Navy Yard	15 June 1945	17 Jan 1946	10 Jan 1948
Complement	approx 86	*PICKEREL	SS 524	Boston Navy Yard	8 Feb 1944	15 Dec 1944	4 Apr 1949

Nine submarines of the "Balao" and "Tench" classes were modernised under the GUPPY III programme in 1960-1962 (see *Design* notes). All previously were GUPPY II submarines. Plans for 15 additional GUPPY III modernisations were dropped in favour of new construction, nuclear-powered submarines.

DESIGN. The Greater Underwater Propulsion Programme (GUPPY) evolved after World War II as a method to improve underwater performance of existing US submarines. The GUPPY concept was based on the German Type XXI submarines which were mass produced in 1944-1945. The Type XXI characteristics included a streamlined hull and superstructure, snorkel, and increased battery power.

The US Navy's GUPPY conversions have similar features, with resulting increases in underwater speed and endurance, plus improved fire control and electronic equipment over their unmodernised sister submarines.

ELECTRONICS. GUPPY submarines are fitted with BQR-2 array sonar. GUPPY III submarines all have BQG-4 sonar (see *Photograph* notes).

ENGINEERING. The GUPPY III submarines have two increased capacity, 126-cell electric batteries as do GUPPY IIA and IA submarines. All GUPPY submarines are fitted with snorkel to permit operation of diesel engines to charge batteries and for propulsion while at Periscope depth. The *Tiru* has only three diesel engines (4 800 shp).

PHOTOGRAPHS. Small, fin-like structures on submarines are antenna domes for BQG-4 fire control sonar (referred to as PUFFS—acronym for Passive Underwater Fire-control Feasibility Study, an anti-submarine targeting system). GUPPY conversions have rounded bows as opposed to "ship bows in streamlined fleet-type submarines."

Note that the *Cobbler's* sail number had been removed when photographed at Malta in Sep 1970. US submarine numbers are often removed when on patrol but returned when in home waters, on training cruises *et cetera* (unlike Soviet submarines which have not had visible pendant numbers on since 1969).

COBBLER (SS 344)   *1970, Anthony & Joseph Pavia*

CLAMAGORE (SS 343)   *1957, United States Navy*

GREENFISH (SS 351)   *1969, United States Navy*

Submarines—*continued*

10 ATTACK SUBMARINES (SS) : GUPPY II TYPE

Displacement, tons	1 870 standard ; 2 420 submerged	
Length, feet (*metres*)	307·5 (*93·6*) oa	
Beam, feet (*metres*)	27·2 (*8·3*)	
Draft, feet (*metres*)	18 (*5·5*)	
Torpedo tubes	10—21 in (*533 mm*) ; 6 fwd, 4 aft	
Main engines	3 diesels ; 4 800 shp/2 electric motors ; 5 400 shp ; 2 shafts	
Speed, knots	18 surface ; 15 submerged	
Complement	Approx 82·	

Name	No.	Builder	Laid down	Launched	Commissioned
*CUBERA	SS 347	Electric Boat Co	11 May 1944	17 June 1945	19 Dec 1945
*DOGFISH	SS 350	Electric Boat Co	22 June 1944	?7 Oct 1945	29 Apr 1946
*TUSK	SS 426	Cramp Shipbuilding Co	23 Aug 1943	8 July 1945	11 Apr 1946
*CUTLASS	SS 478	Portsmouth Navy Yard	22 July 1944	5 Nov 1944	17 Mar 1945
*SEA LEOPARD	SS 483	Portsmouth Navy Yard	7 Nov 1944	2 Mar 1945	11 June 1945
*ODAX	SS 484	Portsmouth Navy Yard	4 Dec 1944	10 Apr 1945	11 July 1945
*SIRAGO	SS 485	Portsmouth' Navy Yard	3 Jan 1945	5 May 1945	13 Aug 1945
*AMBERJACK	SS 522	Boston Navy Yard	8 Feb 1944	15 Dec 1944	4 Mar 1946
*GRAMPUS	SS 523	Boston Navy Yard	8 Feb 1944	15 Dec 1944	26 Oct 1949
*GRENADIER	SS 525	Boston Navy Yard	8 Feb 1944	15 Dec 1944	2 Oct 1951

Fifteen submarines of the "Balao" and "Tench" classes were modernised under the GUPPY II programme in 1948-1950. The *Odax* and *Pomodon* were initially modernised to a GUPPY I configuration; subsequently updated to GUPPY II. The *Cochino* (SS 345) of this type was lost off Norway on a training cruise on 26 Aug 1949 (one civilian on board was lost; no naval personnel aboard *Cochino* were lost but another submarine assisting her had several men washed overboard and lost). General GUPPY notes are found in the GUPPY III listing.

ENGINEERING. GUPPY II submarines have four 126-cell electric batteries. The *Pomodon* has only two 1 600 hp diesels and is fitted with a special 1 500-hp diesel for snorkel operations.

STATUS. All submarines of this type are active.

PHOTOGRAPHS. Note rounded GUPPY type bow in photograph of *Catfish*.

DISPOSALS AND TRANSFERS
Pomodon (SS 486) stricken on 1 Aug 1970, **Diodon** (SS 349) stricken on 15 Jan 1971 and transferred to Argentine ; **Halfbeak** (SS 352), **Catfish** (SS 339) stricken on 1 July 1971 for foreign transfer.

GRENADIER (SS 525)   *United States Navy*

9 ATTACK SUBMARINES (SS) : GUPPY IIA TYPE

Displacement, tons	1 840 standard ; 2 445 submerged	
Length, feet (*metres*)	306· (*93·2*) oa	
Beam, feet (*metres*)	27 (*8·2*)	
Draft, feet (*metres*)	17 (*5·2*)	
Torpedo tubes	10—21 in (*533 mm*) ; 6 fwd ; 4 aft	
Main engines	3 diesels ; 4 800 shp/2 electric motors ; 5 400 shp ; 2 shafts	
Speed, knots	18 surface ; 15 submerged	
Complement	Approx 84	

Name	No.	Builder	Laid down	Launched	Commissioned
*ENTEMEDOR	SS 340	Electric Boat Co	3 Feb 1944	17 Dec 1944	6 Apr 1945
*HARDHEAD	SS 365	Manitowoc Shipbuilding Co	7 July 1943	12 Dec 1943	18 Apr 1944
*JALLAO	SS 368	Manitowoc Shipbuilding Co	29 Sep 1943	12 Mar 1944	8 July 1944
*PICUDA	SS 382	Portsmouth Navy Yard	15 Mar 1943	12 July 1943	16 Oct 1943
*BANG	SS 385	Portsmouth Navy Yard	30 Apr 1943	30 Aug 1943	4 Dec 1943
*THREADFIN	SS 410	Portsmouth Navy Yard	18 Mar 1944	26 June 1944	30 Aug 1944
*TIRANTE	SS 420	Portsmouth Navy Yard	28 Apr 1944	9 Aug 1944	6 Nov 1944
*TRUTTA	SS 421	Portsmouth Navy Yard	22 May 1944	18 Aug 1944	16 Nov 1944
*QUILLBACK	SS 424	Portsmouth Navy Yard	27 June 1944	1 Oct 1944	29 Dec 1944

Sixteen submarines of the "Balao" and "Tench" classes were modernised under the GUPPY IIA programme in 1952-1954. The *Stickleback* (SS 415) of this type was rammed by US escort ship and sunk off Hawaii on 29 May 1958 (no crewmen lost). General GUPPY conversion notes are found in the GUPPY III listing.

STATUS. *Pomfret* not reclassified as AGSS (as stated in previous edition). All submarines of this configuration remain in service.

PHOTOGRAPHS. Note that virtually all GUPPY submarines have had their older "stepped" superstructures replaced by streamlined superstructures constructed of light-weight material. *Threadfin* is one of the few with a "stepped" structure.

DISPOSALS AND TRANSFERS
Razorback (SS 394) transferred to Turkey on 30 Nov 1970, **Sea Fox** (SS 402) transferred to Turkey on 15 Dec 1970 , **Menhaden** (SS 377) and **Ronquil** (SS396) transferred to Spain in July 1971, **Pomfret** (SS 391) and **Thornback** (SS 418) transferred to Turkey on 1 July 1971.

THREADFIN (SS 410)   *1967, United States Navy*

Submarines—*continued*

7 ATTACK AND AUXILIARY SUBMARINES (SS/AGSS): GUPPY IA TYPE

Displacement, tons	1 870 standard; 2 440 submerged				
Length, feet (*metres*)	308 (*93·8*) oa				
Beam, feet (*metres*)	27 (*8·2*)				
Draft, feet (*metres*)	17 (*5·2*)				
Torpedo tubes	10—21 in (*533 mm*) ; 6 fwd, 4 aft				
Main engines	3 diesels ; 4 800 shp/2 electric motors ; 5 400 shp ; 2 shafts				
Speed, knots	18 surface ; 15 submerged				
Complement	approx 84				

Name	No.	Builder	Laid down	Launched	Commissioned
BECUNA	AGSS 319	Electric Boat Co	29 Apr 1943	30 Jan 1944	27 May 1944
*BLACKFIN	SS 322	Electric Boat Co	10 June 1943	12 Mar 1944	4 July 1944
*CAIMAN	SS 323	Electric Boat Co	24 June 1943	30 Mar 1944	17 July 1944
BLENNY	AGSS 324	Electric Boat Co	8 July 1943	9 Apr 1944	27 July 1944
ATULE	AGSS 403	Portsmouth Navy Yard	2 Dec 1943	6 Mar 1944	21 June 1944
SEA POACHER	AGSS 406	Portsmouth Navy Yard	23 Feb 1944	20 May 1944	31 July 1944
TENCH	AGSS 417	Portsmouth Navy Yard	1 Apr 1944	7 July 1944	6 Oct 1944

Ten submarines of the "Balao" and "Tench" classes were modernised under the GUPPY IA programme in 1951. General GUPPY conversion notes are found in the GUPPY III listing.

STATUS. *Becuna, Blenny, Atule, Sea Poacher* and *Tench* were all decommissioned late in 1969 and placed in reserve ; redesignated as AGSS on 1 Oct 1969 while being decommissioned.

Blackfin and *Caiman* to decommission in 1971-1972.

The *Chopper* (AGSS 342) of this type has been decommissioned and serves as an immobilized dockside training submarine for the Naval Reserve.

PHOTOGRAPHS. *Blenny* has later sail structure and three PUFF sonar antennas for BQG-4 sonar.

DISPOSALS
Sea Robin (SS 407) stricken on 1 October 1970.
Chivo (SS 341) stricken on 1 July 1971.

BLENNY (SS 324)

1966, United States Navy

TENCH (AGSS 417)

1968, United States Navy

CAIMAN (SS 323)

1964, United States Navy

HARDHEAD (SS 365)

1970, Anthony & Joseph Pavia

Submarines—*continued*

1 RESEARCH SUBMARINE (AGSS): "TIGRONE" TYPE

Displacement, tons	1 840 standard; 2 400 submerged
Length, feet (*metres*)	312 (*95·1*) oa
Beam, feet (*metres*)	27·2 (*8·3*)
Draft, feet (*metres*)	16·5 (*5·0*)
Torpedo tubes	10—21 in (*533 mm*); 6 fwd, 4 aft
Main engines	4 diesels; 6 400 shp/2 electric motors; 5 400 shp; 2 shafts
Speed, knots	20 surface; 10 submerged
Complement	approx 85

Name	No.	Builder	Laid down	Launched	Commissioned
*TIGRONE	AGSS 419	Portsmouth Navy Yard	8 May 1944	20 July 1944	25 Oct 1944

TIGRONE (AGSS 419)
1968, United States Navy

Originally a "Tench" class submarine refitted as a radar picket submarine in 1947-1948, being provided with elaborate air search radar and air control centre. Reverted to attack submarine status in 1959 with end of submarine radar picket programme. Subsequently fitted with large bow sonar installation and used for research and experimental work.

CLASSIFICATION. *Tigrone* changed from SS to radar picket submarine (SSR) on 31 Mar 1948, reverted to SS designation on 15 Aug 1959; changed to auxiliary submarines (AGSS) on 1 Dec 1963.

ENGINEERING. Fitted with snorkel installation.

PHOTOGRAPH. Note large bow structure housing surface ship sonar installed for research. Two "ball" electronic antennas are fitted atop the sonar structure. Similar antennas are found on the bows of late US nuclear powered submarines and have been seen on a Soviet "W" class submarine.

"TENCH" CLASS

All fleet submarines of the "Tench" class have been stricken except for several immobilised dockside boats for Naval Reserve Training (NRT). Listed separately are "Tench" class submarines converted to the various GUPPY configurations and the research submarine *Tigrone* (AGSS 419).

Twenty-seven "Tench" class submarines were completed as fleet submarines in 1944-1946 and four others were completed to GUPPY configurations in 1949-50. Fourteen other "Tench" class submarines subsequently were converted under the various GUPPY programmes.

A further 101 submarines of this type were cancelled in 1944-1945.

Toro (SS 422) stricken in 1963, **Turbot** (SS 427), **Ulua** (SS 428) not completed, **Unicorn** (SS 429), **Vandace** (SS 430), **Walrus** (SS 431), **Whitefish** (SS 432), **Whiting** (SS 433), **Wolffish** (SS 434) cancelled in 1944, **Corsair** (SS 435) stricken in 1963, **Unicorn** (SS 436), **Walrus** (SS 437) not completed, unnamed SS 438-463 cancelled in 1944, **Chicolar** (SS 464) cancelled in 1944, unnamed SS 465-474 cancelled in 1944, **Argonaut** (SS 475) to Canada 1968, **Runner** (SS/AGSS 476) immobilised NRT, **Conger**

(SS 477) stricken in 1963, **Diablo** (SS 479) to Pakistan 1964, **Medregal** (SS 480) stricken in 1970 (target), **Requin** (SS/SSR/AGSS 481) immobilised NRT, **Irex** (SS/AGSS 482) stricken in 1969, **Sarda** (SS/AGSS 488) stricken in 1964, **Spinax** (SS/SSR/AGSS 489) stricken in 1969, **Pompano** (SS 491), **Grayling** (SS 492), **Needlefish** (SS 493), **Sculpin** (SS 494) cancelled in 1945, unnamed SS 495-515 cancelled in 1944, **Wahoo** (SS 516) cancelled in 1946, unnamed SS 517-521 cancelled in 1944, **Dorado** (SS 526), **Comber** (SS 527), **Sea Panther** (SS 528), **Tiburon** (SS 529) cancelled in 1944, unnamed SS 530-544 cancelled in 1944, unnamed SS 545-550 cancelled in 1945.

1 AMPHIBIOUS TRANSPORT SUBMARINE (LPSS): "SEALION" TYPE

Displacement, tons	2 145 surface; 2 500 submerged
Length, feet (*metres*)	311·5 (*95·0*)
Beam, feet (*metres*)	27 (*8·2*)
Draft, feet (*metres*)	17 (*5·2*)
Torpedo tubes	Removed
Guns	Removed
Main engines	2 diesels (General Motors), 2 305 hp/4 electric motors; 2 shafts
Speed, knots	13 surface; 10 submerged
Complement	74 (6 officers. 68 men)
Troops	160

Name	No.	Builder	Laid down	Launched	Commissioned
SEALION	LPSS 315	Electric Boat Company, Groton	25 Feb 1943	31 Oct 1943	8 Mar 1944

SEALION (LPSS 315)
1967, United States Navy

Originally a "Balao" class submarine converted to underwater transport for carrying Marines, commandos or frogmen in covert operations where surface ships would be too vulnerable. The *Sealion* was to have been replaced by conversion of the *Growler* (SSG 577) to a transport submarine; however, conversion of *Growler* was cancelled because of high cost.
The *Sealion* was decommissioned and placed in reserve late in 1969.

CLASSIFICATION. *Sealion* changed from SS to transport submarine (SSP) in March 1948; changed to auxiliary transport submarine (ASSP) in January 1950; changed to APSS in October 1956; changed again to amphibious transport submarine (LPSS) on 1 Jan 1969.

CONVERSION. The *Sealion* was converted to a transport submarine at the San Francisco Naval Shipyard in 1948. All torpedo tubes and half of her diesel propulsion plant were removed to provide berthing for 160 troops; stowage provided for rubber rafts and other equipment in enlarged superstructure deck aft of conning tower.

ENGINEERING. Fitted with snorkel installation.

GUNNERY. Fitted with two single 40 mm AA guns after conversion to transport submarine; removed during 1960s.

STATUS. In 1960 the *Sealion* was assigned to operational reserve training duties; recommissioned late in 1961 with increase of US conventional warfare capabilities

DISPOSALS
Other US transport-cargo submarines were: **Argonaut** (SM 1/APS 1/SS 166) war loss 1943, **Tunny** (SS/SSG/APSS/LPSS 282) stricken in 1969, **Perch** (SS/SSP/ASSP/APSS/LPSS 313) immobilised NRT, **Barbero** (SS/SSA/ASSA/SSG 317) stricken in 1964.

Submarines—*continued*

"BALAO" CLASS

All fleet submarines of the "Balo" class have been stricken except for several immobilised dockside boats for Naval Reserve Training (NRT). Listed separately are "Balao" class submarines converted to the various GUPPY configurations and the transport submarine *Sealion* (LPSS 315).

One hundred-twenty submarines of this class were completed in 1943-1948. most of which were operational during World War II. Thirty-one submarines were later converted to GUPPY configurations. SS 353-355 were renumbered SS 435-437.

See 1970-1971 and previous editions for dimensions and characteristics.

Balao (SS/AGSS 285) stricken in 1963, **Billfish** (SS/AGSS 286) stricken in 1968, **Bowfin** (SS/AGSS 287) immobilised NRT, **Cabrilla** (SS/AGSS 288) stricken in 1968, **Capelin** (SS 289) war loss 1944, **Cisco** (SS 290) war loss 1944, **Crevalle** (SS/AGSS 291) stricken in 1968, **Devilfish** (SS/AGSS 292) stricken in 1967 (target), **Dragonet** (SS 293) stricken in 1961, **Escolar** (SS 294) war loss 1945, **Hackleback** (SS/AGSS 295) stricken in 1966, **Lancetfish** (SS 296) stricken in 1958 (uncompleted hulk), **Ling** (SS/AGSS 297) immobilised NRT, **Lionfish** (SS/AGSS 298) immobilised NRT, **Manta** (SS/AGSS 299) stricken in 1967 (target), **Moray** (SS/AGSS 300) stricken in 1967, **Roncador** (SS/AGSS 301) immobilised NRT, **Sabalo** (SS 302) stricken in 1971, **Sablefish** (SS/AGSS 303) stricken in 1969, **Seahorse** (SS/AGSS 304) stricken in 1967, **Skate** (SS 305) Bikini target, sunk in 1948; **Tang** (SS 306) war loss 1945, **Tilefish** (SS 307) to Venezuela 1965; **Apogon** (SS 308) Bikini target, sunk 1946; **Aspro** (SS/AGSS 309) stricken in 1962, **Batfish** (SS/AGSS 310) stricken in 1969 (museum), **Archerfish** (SS/AGSS 311) stricken in 1968 (target), **Burrfish** (SS/SSR 312) to Canada 1961, **Perch** (SS/APSS/LPSS 313) immobilised NRT, **Shark** (SS 314) war loss 1945, **Barbel** (SS 316) war loss 1945, **Barbero** (SS/SSG 317) stricken in 1964, **Baya** (SS/AGSS 318) stricken on 14 July 1971.

Bergall (SS 320) to Turkey 1959, **Besugo** (SS/AGSS 321) to Italy 1966, **Blower** (SS 325), **Blueback** (SS 326), **Boarfish** (SS 327) to Turkey 1948, **Charr** (SS/AGSS 328) immobilised NRT, **Chub** (SS 329), **Brill** (SS 330) to Turkey 1948, **Bugara** (SS 331) stricken in 1970, **Bullhead** (SS 332) war loss 1945, **Bumper** (SS 333) to Turkey 1950, **Cabezon** (SS/AGSS 334) stricken in 1970, **Dentuda** (SS/AGSS 335) stricken in 1967, **Capitaine** (SS 336) to Italy in 1966, **Carbonero** (SS 337) stricken in 1970, **Carp** (SS/AGSS 338) immobilised NRT, **Cusk** (SS/SSG/AGSS 348) stricken in 1969, **Dugong** (SS 353), **Eel** (SS 354), **Espada** (SS 355), **Jawfish** (SS 356), **Ono** (SS 357), **Garlopa** (SS 358), **Garruda** (SS 359), **Goldring** (SS 360)

cancelled in 1944, **Golet** (SS 361) war loss 1944, **Guavina** (SS/SSO/AOSS/AGSS 362) stricken in 1967 (target), **Guitarro** (SS 363), **Hammerhead** (SS 364) to Turkey 1954, **Hawkbill** (SS 366), **Icefish** (SS 367) to Netherlands 1953, **Kete** (SS 369) war loss 1945, **Karken** (SS 370) to Spain 1959, **Lagarto** (SS 371) war loss 1945, **Lamprey** (SS 372) to Argentina 1960, **Lizardfish** (SS 373) to Italy 1960, **Loggerhead** (SS/AGSS 374) stricken in 1967, **Macabi** (SS 375) to Argentina 1960, **Mapiro** (SS 376), **Mero** (SS 378) to Turkey 1960, **Needlefish** (SS 379), **Nerka** (SS 380) cancelled in 1944, **Sand Lance** (SS 381) to Brazil 1963, **Pampanito** (SS/AGSS 383) immobilised NRT, **Piranha** (SS/AGSS 344) stricken in 1967, **Pilotfish** (SS 386) Bikini target, stricken in 1947, **Pintado** (SS/AGSS 387),

Pipefish (SS/AGSS 388), **Piranha** (SS/AGSS 389) stricken in 1967, **Plaice** (SS 390) to Brazil 1963, **Sterlet** (SS 392) stricken in 1968 (target), **Queenfish** (SS/AGSS 393) stricken in 1963, **Redfish** (SS/AGSS 395) stricken in 1965 (target), **Scabbardfish** (SS/AGSS A97) to Greece 1965, **Segundo** (SS 398) stricken in 1970 (target), **Sea Cat** (SS/AGSS 399) stricken in 1968, **Sea Devil** (SS/AGSS 400) stricken in 1964, **Sea Dog** (SS/AGSS 401) stricken in 1968, **Spikefish** (SS/AGSS 404) stricken in 1963, **Sea Owl** (SS/AGSS 405) stricken in 1969, **Sennet** (SS 408) stricken in 1968 (target), **Piper** (SS/AGSS 409) stricken in 1970, **Spadefish** (SS/AGSS 411) stricken in 1967, **Trepang** (SS/AGSS 412) stricken in 1967 (target), **Spot** (SS 413) to Chile 1962, **Springer** (SS 414) to Chile 1961.

SEALION (LPSS 315)   *1965, United States Navy*

"GATO" CLASS

Gato (SS 212) and **Greenling** (SS 213) stricken in 1960, **Grouper** (SS/SSK/AGSS 214) stricken in 1968, **Growler** (SS 215) war loss 1944, **Grunion** (SS 216) war loss 1942, **Guardfish** (SS 217) stricken in 1960, **Albacore** (SS 218) war loss 1944, **Amberjack** (SS 219) war loss 1943, **Barb** (SS 220) to Italy 1954, **Blackfish** (SS 221) and **Bluefish** (SS 222) stricken in 1958, **Bonefish** (SS 223) war loss 1945, **Cod** (SS/AGSS 224) immobilised NRT, **Cero** (SS/AGSS 225) stricken in 1957, **Corvina** (SS 226) war loss 1943, **Darter** (SS 227) war loss 1944, **Drum** (SS/AGSS 228) stricken in 1968, **Flying Fish** (SS/AGSS 229) and **Finback** (SS 230) stricken in 1959, **Haddock** (SS 231) stricken in 1960, **Halibut** (SS 232) stricken in 1947, **Herring** (SS 233) war loss 1944, **Kingfish** (SS 234) and **Shad** (SS 235) stricken in 1960, **Silversides** (SS/AGSS 236) stricken in 1969.
Trigger (SS 237) war loss 1945, **Wahoo** (SS 238) war

loss 1943, **Whale** (SS 239) stricken in 1960, **Angler** (SS/SSK/AGSS 240) immobilised NRT, **Bashaw** (SS/SSK/AGSS 241), **Bluegill** (SS/SSK/AGSS 242), **Bream** (SS/SSK/AGSS 243), **Cavalla** (SS/SSR/AGSS 244) stricken in 1969, **Cobia** (SS/AGSS 245) stricken in 1970, **Croaker** (SS/SSK/AGSS 244) immobilised NRT. **Dace** (SS 247) to Italy 1954, **Dorado** (SS 248) war loss 1943, **Flasher** (SS 249) stricken in 1959, **Flier** (SS 250) war loss 1944, **Flounder** (SS 251), **Cabilan** (SS 252), and **Gunnel** (SS 253) stricken in 1959, **Gurnard** (SS 254) stricken in 1960, **Haddo** (SS 255) stricken in 1958, **Hake** (SS 256) stricken in 1968, **Harder** (SS 257) war loss 1944, **Hoe** (SS 258) stricken in 1960, **Jack** (SS 259) and **Lapon** (SS 260) to Greece 1957. **Mingo** (SS 261) to Japan 1955, **Muskallunge** (SS 262) and **Paddle** (SS 263) to Brazil 1957,

Pargo (SS 264) and **Peto** (SS 265) stricken in 1960, **Pogy** (SS 266) stricken in 1958, **Pompon** (SS/SSR 267) and **Puffer** (SS 268) stricken in 1960, **Rasher** (SS/SSR/AGSS 269) immobilised NRT, **Raton** (SS/SSR/AGSS 270) stricken in 1969, **Ray** (SS/SSR 271) stricken in 1960, **Redfin** (SS/SSR/AGSS 272) stricken in 1970, **Rabalo** (SS 273) war loss 1944, **Rock** (SS/SSR/AGSS 274) stricken in 1969.
Runner (SS 275) war loss 1943, **Sawfish** (SS 276) stricken in 1960, **Scamp** (SS 277) and **Scorpion** (SS 278) war loss 1944, **Snook** (SS 279) war loss 1945, **Steelhead** (SS 280) and **Sunfish** (SS 281) stricken in 1969, **Tunny** (SS/SSG/APSS/LPSS 282) stricken in 1969.
Tinosa (SS 283) stricken in 1958, **Tullibee** (SS 284) war loss 1944.

NAVAL RESERVE TRAINING SUBMARINES

The following are immobilised submarines assigned to the training of Naval Reserve personnel at the Naval Districts and home ports indicated. Most of the submarines have had their torpedo tubes welded shut and propellers and/or batteries removed. The designation of Auxiliary Training Submarines (ATSS) was established on 23 Sep 1970, but these submarines had not been redesignated when this edition went to press.

ANGLER	AGSS 240	4th ND	Philadelphia
TORSK	AGSS 423	5th ND	Washington, DC
REQUIN	AGSS 481	6th ND	St Petersburg, Florida
CHOPPER	AGSS 342	8th ND	New Orleans, Louisiana
RUNNER	AGSS 476	9th ND	Chicago, Illinois
PERCH	LPSS 313	11th ND	San Diego, California
CROAKER	AGSS 246	1st ND	Portsmouth, New Hampshire	RONCADOR	AGSS 301	11th ND	San Pedro, California
LIONFISH	AGSS 298	1st ND	Providence, Rhode Island	CHARR	AGSS 328	12th ND	Alameda, California
CARP	AGSS 338	1st ND	Boston, Massachusetts	PAMPANITO	AGSS 383	12th ND	Mare Island, California
LING	AGSS 297	2nd ND	New York	RASHER	AGSS 269	13th ND	Portland, Oregon
COD	AGSS 224	4th ND	Cleveland, Ohio	BOWFIN	AGSS 287	13th ND	Seattle, Washington

Submarines—continued

1 TRAINING SUBMARINE (SST): "BARRACUDA" TYPE

Name	No.	Builder	Laid down	Launched	Commissioned
*BARRACUDA (ex-*K 1*)	SST 3 (ex-SSK 1)	Electric Boat, Groton	1 July 1949	2 Mar 1951	10 Nov 1951

Displacement, tons	756 surface; 1 160 submerged
Length, feet (*metres*)	196 (*59·7*) oa
Beam, feet (*metres*)	24·8 (*7·5*)
Draft, feet (*metres*)	16 (*4·9*)
Torpedo tubes	4—21 inch (*533 mm*), 2 fwd, 2 aft
Main engines	3 diesels (General Motors); 1 050 hp; 2 electric motors (General Motors); 2 shafts
Speed, knots	10 surface; 8 submerged
Complement	50 (5 officers, 45 enlisted men)

Authorised in Fiscal Year 1948 shipbuilding programme. Medium-size, quiet, and highly manoeuverable design intended specifically for anti-submarine operations. Originally had an ungainly bow housing large BQR-4 passive detection sonar; very quiet and small to reduce target image in submarine-versus-submarine encounters. By 1959 this class was considered to be unsuitable in the anti-submarine role, lacking endurance, speed, and range for effective ASW.

Originally three submarines in class; prototypes for mass-production hunter-killer craft to counter large Soviet submarine force (see *Disposals*). Initially given "K" letter names and numbered in separate submarine "hunter-killer" series. "B" names assigned to all three units on 15 Dec 1955.

BARRACUDA (SST 3)   *United States Navy*

DISPOSALS
Bass (ex-*K 2*) SSK 2/SS 551 and **Bonita** (ex-*K 3*) SSK 3/SS 552 were stricken from the Navy List on 1 Apr 1965.

CLASSIFICATION. Designation changed from SSK 1 to SST 3 in 1959 (SSK 2 and SSK 3 were redesignated SS 551 and SS 552, respectively).

2 TRAINING SUBMARINES (SST): "MACKEREL" TYPE

Displacement, tons	303 surface; 347 submerged
Length, feet (*metres*)	131·2 (*40·0*) oa
Beam, feet (*metres*)	13·5 (*4·1*)
Draft, feet (*metres*)	12·2 (*3·7*)
Torpedo tubes	1—21 inch (*533 mm*) forward
Main engines	2 GM diesels; 1 shaft 1 electric motor; 380 hp
Speed, knots	8 surface; 9·5 submerged
Complement	18 (2 officers, 16 enlisted men)

Name	No.	Builder	Laid down	Launched	Commissioned
*MACKEREL (ex-*T 1*)	SST 1	Electric Boat Co. Groton	12 May 1952	14 Oct 1953	20 Nov 1953
*MARLIN (ex-*T 2*)	SST 2	Electric Boat Co. Groton	1 Apr 1952	17 July 1953	9 Oct 1953

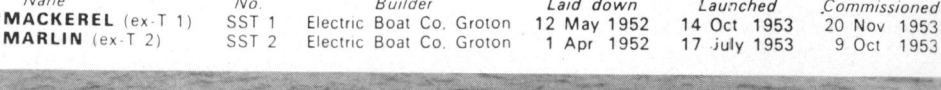

The *Mackerel* and *Marlin* were authorised in the Fiscal Year 1951 and 1952 shipbuilding programmes, respectively. They are the smallest US submarines built since the "C" class of 1909; intended specifically for anti-submarine training. Estimated construction cost was $3 000 000 per submarine.

These submarines and the *Barracuda* primarily operate out of Key West, Florida, as targets for surface and air ASW training exercises.

CLASSIFICATION. The *Mackerel* was ordered as AGSS 570; both submarines were designated SST during construction.

SPECIAL EQUIPMENT. During 1966-1967 the *Mackerel* evaluated equipment for the deep submergence vehicle *NR-1* including keel-mounted wheels for rolling over the ocean floor, thrusters, external television cameras, a manipulator arm, and experimental sonar. The *Mackerel* "bottomed" some 225 times during the nine-month evaluation.
Special equipment was installed at Electric Boat yard in May-June 1966.

NOMENCLATURE. *Mackerel* ex-*T-1* renamed on 15 July 1956 and *Marlin* ex-*T-2* renamed on 15 May 1956.

MACKEREL (SST 1)   *United States Navy*

MACKEREL (SST 1)   *1963, United States Navy*

AIRCRAFT CARRIERS

The US Navy's attack carrier strength is being reduced to its lowest level since 1950, the year that the Korean War began. The planned attack carrier (CVA) force level for 30 June 1972 is 13 ships: nine of post-World War II construction (one nuclear powered), the three "Midway" class ships completed at the end of the war and extensively modernised, and the improved "Essex" class carrier *Oriskany*.

As *Jane's Fighting Ships* went to press the US Navy's attack carrier force consisted of 14 ships, with the war-built *Hancock* in commission in addition to the 13 ships listed above. The *Hancock* was scheduled to be decommissioned late in 1972. However, several plans were being examined for retaining her in commission, including the possibility of having her partially manned with her crew periodically augmented by reserve personnel and sent to sea with a reserve air wing.

There is anticipation in some Navy quarters that an objective evaluation of the role of aircraft carriers in contingency planning for the Jordanian crisis in 1970, coupled with the "low overseas profile" for US military forces under the co-called Nixon Doctrine, will be suitable justification for retaining 14 or 15 attack carriers in service. Hot and cold war crises since 1950—among them the Korean War, Lebanese crisis of 1958, the Berlin crisis of 1961, and the Vietnam War—have kept the number of attack carriers in commission at from 14 to 18 ships. Also, the reduction in the number of anti-submarine carriers (discussed below) that may result in integrated attack-ASW air wings on the attack carriers could make the attack carrier situation even more critical. The Navy would like to retain the *Hancock*, now 27 years old, and the *Oriskany*, now 21 years old, until the mid-1970s when the nuclear-powered attack carriers *Nimitz* and *Dwight D. Eisenhower* join the Fleet. The Navy would then have 11 post-war-built ships (three nuclear powered) plus the three "Midway" class ships that would be completing their third decade of service.

The Navy is seeking a fourth nuclear-powered attack carrier, the CVAN-70 discussed below, to provide 12 post-war carriers in the period 1975-1985 and possibly beyond.

The term "attack carrier" as used above indicates ships capable of operating contemporary high performance fighter, strike, and reconnaissance aircraft. However, because of the reduced number of flight decks now available, the Navy is considering going to a "CV" concept whereby an attack carrier also would regularly embark anti-submarine helicopters and fixed-wing aircraft (at the expense of some fighter and attack aircraft). The attack carrier *Saratoga* began testing this concept in the spring of 1971. Although previously attack carriers have carried anti-submarine helicopters for brief periods since the CVA-CVS classifications were established in 1952, this is the first evaluation of fixed-wing ASW aircraft on CVA deck.

Three anti-submarine carriers (CVS) also are in commission, all of the "Essex/Hancock" class, originally completed in 1943-1945 but extensively modernised. This is the smallest number of anti-submarine carriers in commission since the early 1950s and compares to a maximum strength of nine CVS-type carriers in service during the early 1960s.

Although the Navy maintains a relatively large and modern land-based maritime reconnaissance/ASW air force (20-plus squadrons with P-3 Orion aircraft), the anti-submarine carriers permit ASW operations in areas where land bases are not available, a major consideration today. Of equal importance, the CVS provides for a high concentration of force either for sustained operations or to counter a high-density threat.

Finally, the "Essex/Hancock" class carrier *Lexington* is in service as a training ship (CVT). She officially is classified as an auxiliary ship. On an emergency basis she could embark and operate ASW aircraft; however, her capability of sustained operations would be related to the amount of modification made prior to such employment.

CVAN 70 PROGRAMME. The Navy is seeking construction of a fourth nuclear-powered attack carrier, the CVAN 70. The proposal for this ship dates back to 1967 when then-Secretary of Defence Robert McNamara proposed the construction of three nuclear-powered attack carriers (CVAN 68-70) on the basis of Vietnam War experience and intensive cost-effectiveness studies.

KITTY HAWK (CVA 63) and BEACON (PG 99)

1970, United States Navy

The Fiscal Year 1971 defence budget requested $152 000 000 for long-lead time components for the CVAN-70. Secretary of Defence Melvin Laird told the Congress that "none of these funds will be obligated until the study (of carrier costs and effectiveness) has been completed by the two (Congressional) Armed Services committees and until we have completed our own current review, in the Executive Branch, of future force requirements". The congressional study, held in the spring of 1970, reported 8-to-1 in favour of immediately funding the long-lead time components for the CVAN 70, with the minority voter withholding his decision until the Executive Branch (National Security Council) study was completed.

Despite the Congressional position in favour of the CVAN 70, and full support stated by Secretary of Defence Laird and successive Chairman of the Joint Chiefs of Staff and Chiefs of Naval Operations, the CVAN 70 funds have not been approved, all pending a study by the National Security Council, that appears *not to have been undertaken.*

In presenting the FY 1972 defence budget to the Congress, Secretary Laird stated: "I am convinced that our responsibilities in the Atlantic, the Pacific, the Mediterranean and other ocean areas will require construction of an additional nuclear-powered carrier for the Navy to insure adequate attack carrier capabilities for the 1980s and beyond. The Navy is currently assessing the need for funding to keep the industrial base open with selected long-lead time items in FY 1972. If preservation of the industrial base should be at issue, or if significant savings would be realized, I will seek funds for long-lead time procurement for CVAN 70 in FY 1972 through reprogramming actions or budget amendments . . . This will enable us to keep the option open to authorise the next carrier in FY 1973 or FY 1974".

However, on Apr 27, 1971, Deputy Secretary of Defence David Packard informed the Congress: "I do not propose to make an amendment to the FY 1972 budget or recommend reprogramming of funds for the procurement of long-lead time items for the CVAN 70". He noted: "we

believe we may need one or more additional nuclear carriers. We also recognize the problem of maintaining an industrial base and the cost increases which would result if we defer procurement of long lead time components for the carrier. Nevertheless, we believe that on balance it is desirable at this time to postpone the construction of an additional nuclear carrier."

ATTACK AIR WINGS. Each post-war attack carrier normally operates an air wing of 80 to 90 aircraft comprised of two fighter squadrons with 24 Phantoms, two or three light attack squadrons with 24 or 36 A-7 Corsairs, one attack squadron with 12 A-6 Intruders, and small squadrons or detachments with four RA-5C Vigilantes for reconnaissance, four EA-6A Intruders for electronic warfare, four E-2A Hawkeyes for early warning, and four KA-6 Intruder tankers.

The smaller "Essex/Hancock" class attack carriers that remain in CVA status operate F-8 Crusader fighters, A-7 Corsair and A-4 Skyhawk attack planes, RF-8G Crusader photo-recce planes, EKA-3B Skywarrior tanker/electronic warfare aircraft, and E-1B Tracers in the airborne early warning role.

All attack carriers also have C-1 Trader carrier on-board delivery (COD) cargo aircraft and UH-2 utility helicopters assigned.

ANTI-SUBMARINE AIR GROUPS. Each ASW carrier normally operates an air group comprised of three squadrons with 21 S-2E Trackers, two squadrons with 16 SH-3 Sea King helicopters, and a detachment of four E-1B Tracer early warning aircraft. A fighter detachment of four A-8 Crusaders or four A-4 Skyhawks is embarked for operations in high-threat areas.

COD aircraft and utility helicopters also are embarked.

PHOTOGRAPH. The above photograph shows the attack carrier *Kitty Hawk* refuelling the diminutive patrol gunboat *Beacon*, while the latter ship served as a plane guard escort for the carrier. Since 1970 the US Navy has been evaluating the use of hydrofoil and "Asheville" class gunboats in roles previously carried out by destroyers.

---

2 NUCLEAR-POWERED ATTACK AIRCRAFT CARRIERS (CVAN): "NIMITZ" CLASS

		Name	No.	Builder	Laid down	Launch	Commission
Displacement, tons	95 100 full load	**NIMITZ**	CVAN 68	Newport News	22 June 1968	Apr 1972	Sep 1973
Length, feet (*metres*)	1 040 (*317·0*) wl;	**DWIGHT D. EISENHOWER**	CVAN 69	Newport News	15 Aug 1970	Jan 1974	June 1975
	1 092 (*332·0*) oa						
Beam, feet (*metres*)	134 (*40·8*)						
Draft, feet (*metres*)	37 (*11·3*)						
Flight deck width,							
feet (*metres*)	252 (*76·8*)						
Catapults	4						
Aircraft	approx 90						
Missiles	3 Basic Point Defence Missile System (BPDMS) launchers with Sea Sparrow missiles						
Main engines	Geared steam turbines; 4 shafts; 260 000 shp						
Nuclear reactors	2 pressurised-water cooled						
Speed, knots	30+						

The lead ship for this class and the world's second nuclear-powered aircraft carrier was ordered 9½ years after the first such ship, the USS *Enterprise*. The *Nimitz* was authorised in the Fiscal Year 1967 new construction programme and the *Dwight D. Eisenhower* in the FY 1969 programme. Both ships are being built by the Newport News Shipbuilding & Dry Dock Co, Newport News, Virginia, the only US shipyard now capable of constructing large, nuclear-powered aircraft carriers. Estimated construction costs are $594 000 000 for the *Nimitz* and $616 000 000 for the *Dwight D. Eisenhower* (revised 1971 estimates).

The *Dwight D. Eisenhower* was to have been laid down in April 1970, but was delayed because of difficulties involving contract award. The completion of these two ships is being delayed approximately one year because of delays in the delivery of nuclear plant components. A third ship of this class is planned; see *CVAN 70 Programme* notes above.

ELECTRONICS. These ships will have the Naval Tactical Data System (NTDS) and the following radars: SPS-10 surface search, SPS-43A two-dimensional air search, and SPS-48 three-dimensional air search, and

Aircraft Carriers—Continued

"NIMITZ" CLASS continued

SPN-42, SPN-43, and SPN-44 navigation equipment. These ships will not have sonar as did the last conventionally powered aircraft carriers (the *America* and *John F. Kennedy*).

ENGINEERING. These carriers will each have only two nuclear reactors compared to the eight reactors required for the carrier *Enterprise*. The nuclear cores for the reactors in these ships are expected to provide sufficient energy for the ships to each steam for at least 13 years, an estimated 800 000 to 1 million miles between "refuelling"

FISCAL. It is difficult to trace the funding history of these ships because of continuing reprogramming of funds to meet increasing costs. Total ship costs are given earlier in this listing; ship construction funding for attack carriers since FY 1965 has been: $12 100 000 in 1965, $191 900 000 in 1966, $535 900 000 in 1967, $48 500 000 in 1968, $121 700 000 in 1969, and $377 100 000 in 1970.
No CVAN funding was provided in FY 1971. The FY 1972 budget requests $164 000 000 in additional funding for the CVAN 68 and CVAN 69.

NOMENCLATURE. The *Nimitz* honours Fleet Admiral Chester W. Nimitz who was Commander-in-Chief Pacific

Fleet and Commander-in-Chief Pacific Ocean Areas during World War II, and Chief of Naval Operations from December 1945 to December 1947.

The *Dwight D. Eisenhower* is believed the first major US surface warship to be named for an Army officer; General of the Army Eisenhower commanded Allied forces in Western Europe in 1944-45, subsequently was first Supreme Allied Commander in NATO, and President of the United States from January 1953 to January 1961. The CVAN 69 was named *Eisenhower* on 21 Feb 1970; renamed *Dwight D. Eisenhower* on 25 May 1970, but Secretary of Defence Laird dedicated the ship as the "USS *Eisenhower*" at the keel laying on 15 Aug 1970.

4 ATTACK AIRCRAFT CARRIERS (CVA): "KITTY HAWK" CLASS

Name	No.	Builder	Laid down	Launched	Commissioned
*KITTY HAWK	CVA 63	New York SB Corp, Camden, NJ	27 Dec 1956	21 May 1960	29 Apr 1961
*CONSTELLATION	CVA 64	New York Naval Shipyard	14 Sep 1957	8 Oct 1960	27 Oct 1961
*AMERICA	CVA 66	Newport News SB & DD Co	9 Jan 1961	1 Feb 1964	23 Jan 1965
*JOHN F. KENNEDY	CVA 67	Newport News SB & DD Co	22 Oct 1964	27 May 1967	7 Sep 1968

Displacement, tons	
Kitty Hawk	60 100 standard; 80 800 full load
Constellation	60 100 standard; 80 800 full load
America	60 300 standard; 80 800 full load
John F. Kennedy	61 000 standard; 87 000 full load
Length, feet (*metres*)	990 (*301·8*) wl
Kitty Hawk	1 062·5 (*323·9*) oa
Constellation	1 072·5 (*326·9*) oa
America J.F.K.	1047·5 (*319·3*) oa
Beam, feet (*metres*)	
Kitty Hawk,	
Constellation	129·5 (*38·5*)
America, J.F.K.	130 (*39·6*)
Draft, feet (*metres*)	35·9 (*10·9*)
Flight deck width, feet, (*metres*)	
J.F.K.	252 (*76·9*) maximum
Others	249 (*76·0*) maximum
Catapults	4 steam
Aircraft	80 to 90
Missiles	2 twin Terrier surface-to-air launchers in *Kitty Hawk, Constellation, America; John F. Kennedy* has 3 Basic Point Defence Missile System (BPDMS) launchers with Sea Sparrow missiles
Main engines	4 geared turbines (Westinghouse) 280 000 shp; 4 shafts
Boilers	8—1 200 psi (*83·4 kg/cm²*) (Foster Wheeler)
Speed	35 knots
Complement	2 795 (150 officers, approx 2 645 enlisted men) plus approx 2 150 assigned to attack air wing for a total of 4 950 officers and enlisted men per ship

These ships were built to an improved "Forrestal" design and are easily recognised by their smaller island structure which is set further aft than the superstructure in the four "Forrestal" class ships. Lift arrangement also differs (see design notes). The *Kitty Hawk* was authorised in Fiscal Year 1956 new construction programme, the *Constellation* in FY 1957, the *America* in FY 1961, and the *John F. Kennedy* in FY 1963. Completion of the *Constellation* was delayed because of a fire which ravaged her in the New York Naval Shipyard in December 1960. Construction of the *John F. Kennedy* was delayed because of debate over whether to provide her with conventional or nuclear propulsion.
Estimated construction costs were $217 963 000 for *Kitty Hawk*, $247 620 000 for *Constellation*, and $277 000 000 for *John F. Kennedy*.

CLASSIFICATION. Officially known as the "Kitty Hawk" class; generally referred to as improved "Forrestals". The *John F. Kennedy* is officially a separate one-ship class.

DESIGN. These ships are officially considered to be of a different design than the "Forrestal" class by the Navy's Ship Characteristics Board. The island structure is smaller and set further aft than the superstructure in the newer ships with two deck-edge lifts forward of the superstructure, a third lift aft of the structure, and the port-side left on the after quarter (compared with two lifts aft of the island and the port-side lift at the forward end of the angled deck in the earlier ships). This lift arrangement considerably improves flight deck operations. All four of these ships also have a small radar mast aft of the island structure. The *John F. Kennedy* and *America* have stem anchors because of bow sonar dome.

ELECTRONICS. All four ships of this class have highly sophisticated electronic equipment including the Naval Tactical Data System (NTDS). The *America* and *John F. Kennedy* have bow-mounted SQS-23 sonar, the first US attack carriers with anti-submarine sonar (several ASW carriers have been fitted with sonar during modernisations).

AMERICA (CVA 66)   1970, United States Navy, PH3 L. J. Lafeir

KITTY HAWK (CVA 63)   1968, United States Navy

Aircraft Carriers—*continued*

"KITTY HAWK" CLASS — *continued*

All four ships have SPS-43 search radar antenna on island structure; three ships also have a three-dimensional SPS-52 search radar antenna on island and an SPS-30 search radar antenna on second mast while the *John F. Kennedy* has SPS-48 antenna on second mast; all ships have TACAN navigation pods or "bee-hives".

NOMENCLATURE. US aircraft carriers are generally named after battles and historic ships. However, the *Kitty Hawk* better honours the site where the Wright brothers made their historic flights than the converted aircraft ferry of that name which served in World War II. The *Constellation* remembers a frigate built in 1797 and a later ship still afloat at Baltimore, Maryland, although no longer in Navy commission. The name "America" was previously carried by a 74-gun ship-of-the line launched in 1782 and presented to France, by the racing schooner which gave her name to the America's Cup, and by the German liner *Amerika* which was taken over by the US Navy in World War I, renamed, and used as a troop transport. The *John F. Kennedy* remembers the martyred president who was assassinated in 1963. The destroyer *Joseph P. Kennedy Jr.* (DD 850) honours his older brother who was killed in a bomber explosion over England in World War II.

JOHN F. KENNEDY (CVA 67)   *1969, United States Navy, PH2 R. A. Rima*

AMERICA (CVA 66)   *1970, United States Navy, PH3 L. J. Lafeir*

CONSTELLATION (CVA 64)   *1970, United States Navy*

Aircraft Carriers—*Continued*

AMERICA (CVA 66) and STRONG (DD 758)   *1969, United States Navy, PH3 C. M. Dunn*

AMERICA (CVA 66)   *1970, United States Navy, PH3 L. J. Lafeir*

JOHN F. KENNEDY (CVA 67)   *1968, United States Navy*

Aircraft Carriers—continued

1 NUCLEAR-POWERED ATTACK AIRCRAFT CARRIER (CVAN): "ENTERPRISE" TYPE

Name	No.	Builder	Laid down	Launched	Commissioned
*ENTERPRISE	CVAN 65	Newport News Shipbuilding & Dry Dock Co	4 Feb 1958	24 Sep 1960	25 Nov 1961

Displacement, tons	75 700 standard; 89 600 full load
Length, feet (metres)	1 040 (317·0) wl; 1 123 (341·3) oa
Beam, feet (metres)	133 (40·5)
Draft, feet (metres)	35·8 (10·8)
Flight deck width, feet (metres)	257 (78·3) maximum
Catapults	4 Steam
Aircraft	90+
Missiles	2 Basic Point Defense Missile System (BPDMS) launchers with Sea Sparrow missiles (see Armament notes)
Main engines	4 geared steam turbines (Westinghouse); approx 280 000 shp; 4 shafts
Nuclear reactors	8 pressurised-water cooled A2W (Westinghouse)
Speed, knots	35
Complement	3 100 (162 officers, approx 2 940 enlisted men) plus 2 400 assigned to attack air wing for a total of 5 500

ENTERPRISE (CVAN 65)   1969, United States Navy, JOC R. D. Moeser

The *Enterprise* was the largest warship ever built at the time of her construction and will be rivalled in size only by the nuclear-powered *Nimitz* class ships. The *Enterprise* was authorised in the Fiscal Year 1958 new construction programme. She was launched only 19 months after her keel was laid down. During her first year of operation the *Enterprise* made a six-month deployment to the Mediterranean and took part in the Cuban quarantine of 1962. During that year she recorded more than 12 000 arrested landings a record for non-combat operations. The *Enterprise* was flagship of Task Force One during Operation Sea Orbit when the carrier, the nuclear-powered cruiser *Long Beach* (CGN 9), and the nuclear-powered frigate *Bainbridge* (DLGN 25) circumnavigated the world, in 1964, cruising more than 30 000 miles in 64 days (underway 57 days) without refuelling.

The estimated cost of the *Enterprise* was $393 167 000. The Fiscal Year 1960 budget provided $35 000 000 to prepare plans and place orders for components of a second nuclear-powered carrier, but the money was spent otherwise.

ARMAMENT. The *Enterprise* — "the world's largest warship"—was completed without any armament in an effort to hold down construction costs. Space for Terrier missile system was provided. Short-range Sea Sparrow BPDMS was installed in 1967 because of danger to ship while operating in Gulf of Tonkin. A third Sea Sparrow launcher was installed during the ship's 1970-1971 overhaul.

DESIGN. Built to a modified "Forrestal" Class design. The most distinctive feature is the island structure. Nuclear propulsion eliminated requirement for smoke stack and boiler air intakes, reducing size of superstructure, and reducing vulnerability to battle damage, radioactivity, and biological agents. Rectangular fixed-array radar antennae ("billboards") are mounted on sides of island; electronic countermeasure (ECM) antennae ring cone-shaped upper levels of island structure. Fixed antennae have increased range and performance (see listing for cruiser *Long Beach*). The *Enterprise* has four deck-edge lifts, two forward of island and one aft on starboard side and one aft on port side (as in improved "Kitty Hawk" class).

ELECTRONICS. Fitted with the Naval Tactical Data System (NTDS). In addition to SPS-32 and SPS-33 "billboard" radar antennae, the *Enterprise* has SPS-10 and SPS-12 search radars and various navigation radar antennae atop her island structure; TACAN navigation pod caps mast.

ENTERPRISE (CVAN 65)   1968, United States Navy

ENGINEERING. The *Enterprise* is the world's second nuclear-powered warship (the cruiser *Long Beach* was completed a few months earlier). Design of the first nuclear powered aircraft carrier began in 1950 and work continued until 1953 when the programme was deferred pending further work on the submarine reactor programme. The large ship reactor project was reinstated in 1954 on the basis of technological advancements made in the previous 14 months. The Atomic Energy Commission's Bettis Atomic Power Laboratory was given prime responsibility for developing the nuclear power plant. Construction of a land-based prototype plant (designated A1W) began in April 1956 at the National Reactor Testing Station in Idaho. This plant consisted of two reactors and the associated steam generating equipment to drive one shaft of an aircraft carrier. The first reactor core was installed on 8 Aug 1958 and criticality was achieved on 21 Oct 1958. The second reactor achieved initial criticality on 10 July 1959 and the two-reactor plant was first operated at full power on 15 Sep 1959, demonstrating the feasibility of nuclear propulsion for large ships.

The first of the eight reactors installed in the *Enterprise* achieved initial criticality on 2 Dec 1960, shortly after the carrier was launched. After three years of operation during which she steamed more than 207 000 miles, the *Enterprise* was overhauled and refuelled from November 1964 to July 1965. Her second set of cores provided about 300 000 miles steaming. The eight cores initially installed in the *Enterprise* cost $64 000 000; the second set cost about $20 000 000.

The *Enterprise* underwent an extensive overhaul from October 1969 to January 1971, which included installation of a new set of uranium cores in the ship's eight nuclear reactors. The overhaul and refuelling took place at the Newport News shipyard. Estimated cost of the overhaul was approximately $30 000 000, with $13 000 000 being for non-nuclear repairs and alterations, and $17 000 000 being associated with installation of the new nuclear cores (the latter amount being in addition to the $80 000 000 cost of the eight cores). This third set of cores is expected to fuel the ship for 10 to 13 years, according to Vice Adm H. G. Rickover.

In addition to virtually unlimited high-speed endurance nuclear propulsion for aircraft carriers provides additional space for aviation fuels and ordnance, elimination of stack gases and smoke which have corrosive effects on electronic antennas and aircraft. virtually unlimited electrical power, and the ability to quickly change speed without affecting the number of personnel on watch in the engineering spaces.

There are two reactors for each of the ship's four shafts. The eight reactors feed 32 heat exchangers. The *Enterprise* developed more horsepower during her propulsion trials than any other ship in history (officially "in excess of 200 000 shaft horsepower"; subsequently Navy officials stated that she can generate 280 000 hp).

NOMENCLATURE. Eight US Navy ships have carried the name *Enterprise*. The first was a British supply sloop captured in 1775 and armed for use on Lake Champlain. The seventh *Enterprise* (CV 6) was the most famous US carrier of World War II. She earned 20 battle stars. That "Big E" was sold in 1958 and scrapped.

Aircraft Carriers—*continued*

ENTERPRISE (CVAN 65)   *1969, United States Navy, PH1 W. R. Dappen*

ENTERPRISE (CVAN 65)   *1968, United States Navy*

ENTERPRISE (CVAN 65)   *1968, United States Navy*

Aircraft Carriers—*continued*

4 ATTACK AIRCRAFT CARRIERS (CVA): "FORRESTAL" CLASS

Name	No.	Builder	Laid down	Launched	Commissioned
*FORRESTAL	CVA 59	Newport News SB & DD Co	14 July 1952	11 Dec 1954	1 Oct 1955
*SARATOGA	CVA 60	New York Naval Shipyard	16 Dec 1952	8 Oct 1955	14 Apr 1956
*RANGER	CVA 61	Newport News SB & DD Co	2 Aug 1954	29 Sep 1956	10 Aug 1957
*INDEPENDENCE	CVA 62	New York Naval Shipyard	1 July 1955	6 June 1958	10 Jan 1959

Displacement, tons	
Forrestal	59 650 standard; 78 000 full load
Others	60 000 standard; 78 000 full load
Length, feet (*metres*)	990 (*301·8*) wl
Forrestal, Saratoga	
Ranger	1 039 (*316·7*) oa
Independence	1 046·5 (*319·0*) oa
Beam, feet (*metres*)	129·5 (*38·5*)
Draft, feet (*metres*)	37 (*11·3*)
Flight deck width, feet (*metres*)	
Ranger	260 (*79·2*) maximum
Others	252 (*76·8*) maximum
Catapults	4 steam
Aircraft	80
Guns	4—5 in (*127 mm*) dual-purpose; removed from *Forrestal* (see *Gunnery* notes)
Missiles	1 Basic Point Defence Missile System (BPDMS) launcher with Sea Sparrow missiles in *Forrestal*
Main engines	4 geared turbines (Westinghouse) 4 shafts 260 000 shp in *Forrestal* 280 000 shp in others
Boilers	8 (Babcock & Wilcox) 600 psi (*41·7 kg/cm²*) in *Forrestal* 1 200 psi (*83·4 kg/cm²*) in others
Speed, knots	
Forrestal	33
Others	35
Complement	2 790 (145 officers, approx 2 645 enlisted men) plus approx 2 150 assigned to attack air wing for a total of 4 940+ per ship

SARATOGA (CVA 60)   *1969, United States Navy, PH2 D. S. Sager*

The *Forrestal* was the world's first aircraft carrier designed and built after World War II. The *Forrestal* design drew heavily from the aircraft carrier *United States* (CVA 58) which was cancelled immediately after being laid down in April 1949. The *Forrestal* was authorised in the Fiscal Year 1952 new construction programme; the *Saratoga* followed in the FY 1953 programme, the *Ranger* in FY 1954, and *Independence* in FY 1955.
Estimated construction costs are $189 463 000 for *Forrestal*, $214 387 000 for *Saratoga*, $182 162 000 for *Ranger*, and $222 796 000 for *Independence*.

CLASSIFICATION. The *Forrestal* and *Saratoga* were initially classified as Large Aircraft Carriers CVB 59 and 60, respectively; reclassified as Attack Aircraft Carriers (CVA) in October 1952 to reflect their purpose rather than size. The ill-fated *United States* was a "heavy" carrier (CVA).

DESIGN. The "Forrestal" Class ships were the first aircraft carriers designed and built specifically to operate jet-propelled aircraft. The *Forrestal* was redesigned early in construction to incorporate British-developed angled flight deck and steam catapults. These were the first US aircraft carriers built with an enclosed flight deck to improve seaworthiness. Four large deck-edge lifts are fitted, one forward of island structure to starboard, two aft of island structure to starboard and one at forward edge of angled flight deck to port. Other features include armoured flight deck and advanced underwater protection and internal compartmentation to reduce effects of conventional and nuclear attack. Mast configuration differ; the *Forrestal* originally had two masts, one of which was removed in 1967.

SARATOGA (CVA 60)   *1969, United States Navy, PH2 D. S. Sager*

ELECTRONICS. The primary radar antennae in these ships are SPS-43, SPS-30, and SPS-10 search radars, and SPN-10 navigation radar. Small TACAN navigation pods top the masts of these ships.
Naval Tactical Data System installed in all four ships.

ENGINEERING. The *Saratoga* and later ships have an improved steam plant; increased machinery weight of the improved plant is more than compensated by increased performance and decreased fuel consumption.

GUNNERY. All four ships initially mounted 8—5 inch guns in single mounts, two mounts on each quarter. The forward sponsons carrying the guns interfered with

ship operations in rough weather, tending to slow the ships down. The forward sponsons and guns were subsequently removed (except in *Ranger*), reducing armament to four guns per ship. The guns are 5 inch/54 calibre, rapid-fire, dual-purpose weapons.
The four after 5 inch guns were removed from the *Forrestal* late in 1967 and a single BPDMS launcher for Sea Sparrow missiles was installed forward on the starboard side. Two additional launchers will be installed.

MODERNISATION. During an overhaul in 1963-1964 the width of the *Ranger's* angled flight deck was extended eight feet to accommodate newer aircraft.

NOMENCLATURE. The *Forrestal* honours James V. Forrestal, Secretary of the Navy from 1944 until he was appointed the first US Secretary of Defense in 1947, a post he held until shortly before his death in 1949. The *Saratoga* commemorates the battle at Saratoga, New York, in the American Revolution and five earlier US warships including a carrier of World War II fame (CV 3). The first USS *Ranger* was a sloop built in 1777 and a later ship of that name was the first US built-for-the-purpose carriers (CV 4). The first USS *Independence* was a sloop built in 1775 and a later ship of that name was a light carrier (CVL 22) that saw extensive combat in World War II.

Aircraft Carriers—*continued*

SARATOGA (CVA 60)   *1970, United States Navy, PH1 R. D. Williams*

RANGER (CVA 61)   *1968. United States Navy*

FORRESTAL (CVA 59)   *1970, United States Navy*

INDEPENDENCE (CVA 62)   *1970, United States Navy, PM1 with Bradwell*

Aircraft Carriers—*continued*

3 ATTACK AIRCRAFT CARRIERS (CVA): "MIDWAY" CLASS

Name	No.	Builder	Laid down	Launched	Commissioned
*MIDWAY	CVA 41	Newport News SB & DD Co	27 Oct 1943	20 Mar 1945	10 Sep 1945
*FRANKLIN· D. ROOSEVELT	CVA 42	New York Navy Yard ·	1 Dec 1943	29 Apr 1945	3 Nov 1945
*CORAL SEA	CVA 43	Newport News SB & DD Co	10 July 1944	2 Apr 1946	1 Oct 1947

Displacement, tons
Midway — 51 000 standard
F. D. Roosevelt — 51 000 standard
Coral Sea — 52 500 standard
all approx 64 000 full load

Length, feet (*metres*) 900 (*274·3*) wl; 979 (*298·4*) oa
Beam, feet (*metres*) 121 (*36·9*)
Draft, feet (*metres*) 35·3 (*10·8*)
Flight deck width, feet (*metres*) 238 (*72·5*) maximum
Catapults 2 steam
Aircraft 75
Guns 4—5 in (*127 mm*) dual-purpose in F. D. Roosevelt; three guns in *Midway* and *Coral Sea* (see *Gunnery* notes)
Main engines 4 geared turbines (Westinghouse in *Midway* and *Coral Sea*; General Electric in *F. D. Roosevelt*); 212 000 shp; 4 shafts
Boilers 12—600 psi (*41·7 kg/cm²*) (Babcock & Wilcox)
Speed, knots 33
Complement 2 615 (140 officers, approx 2 475 enlisted men) except *Coral Sea* 2 710 (165 officers, approx 2 545 enlisted men) plus approx 1 800 assigned to attack air wing for a total of 4 400 to 4 500 per ship

MIDWAY (CVA 41) 1970, United States Navy, PH3 A. N. Williams

These carriers were the largest US warships constructed during World War II. Completed too late for service in that conflict, they were the backbone of US naval strength for the first decade of the Cold War. Beginning in 1949 they were modified to store, assemble, and load nuclear weapons, making them the world's first warships with a nuclear strike capability. (P2V-3C Neptunes and AJ-1 Savages were the first delivery aircraft). All three ships operated in the Atlantic and Mediterranean during the Korean War, but subsequently they have operated in the Pacific. The entire class has been in active service (except for overhaul and modernisation) since the ships were completed more than 24 years ago.

CLASSIFICATION. These ships were initially classified as Large Aircraft Carriers CVB 41-43, respectively, reclassified as Attack Aircraft Carriers (CVA) in October 1952.

DESIGN. These ships were built to the same design with a standard displacement of 45 000 tons, full load displacement of 60 100 tons, and an overall length of 968 feet. They have been extensively modified since completion (see notes below). These ships were the first US aircraft carriers with an armoured flight deck and the first US warships with a designed width too large to enable them to pass through the Panama Canal.
The unnamed CVB 44, 56 and 57 of this class were cancelled prior to the start of construction.

ELECTRONICS. Naval Tactical Data System (NTDS) in *Midway* and *Coral Sea*.
The principal radar antennae on these ships are SPS-10, SPS-30, SPS-43, SPN-6, and SPN-10. Note that *Coral Sea* retains large TACAN (Tactical Air Navigation) "bee hive" antenna atop mast compared to smaller antenna domes on *Midway* and *Franklin D. Roosevelt*.

GUNNERY. As built these ships mounted 18—5 inch guns (14 in *Coral Sea*), 84—40 mm guns, and 28—20 mm guns. Armament reduced periodically with 3 inch guns replacing lighter weapons. Minimal 5 inch armament remains. The 5 inch guns are 54 calibre Mk 39, essentially modified 5 inch/38 calibre with a longer barrel for greater range; not to be confused with rapid-fire 5 inch 54s of newer US warships.

MISSILES. During the 1950s these ships were fitted with the Regulus I surface-to-surface missile. Fired by carriers, cruisers, and submarines, the Regulus I had a speed of approx 500 mph, a 500 mile range, and could carry a nuclear warhead.

MODERNISATION. All three "Midway" Class carriers have been extensively modernised. Their most extensive conversion "package" gave them angled flight decks, steam catapults, enclosed "hurricane" bows, new electronics, and new lift arrangement (*Franklin D. Roosevelt* from 1953 to 1956, *Midway* from 1954 to 1957, and *Coral Sea* from 1956 to 1960; all at Puget Sound Naval Shipyard). Lift arrangement was changed in *Franklin D. Roosevelt* and *Midway* to one centreline lift forward, one deck-edge list aft of island on starboard side, and one deck-edge lift at forward end of angled deck on port side. The *Coral Sea* has an improved

CORAL SEA (CVA 43) 1970, United States Navy, PH2 George W. Estaver

Aircraft Carriers—continued

"MIDWAY" CLASS—continued

arrangement with one lift forward and one aft of island on starboard side and third lift outboard on port side aft. The *Midway* began another extensive modernisation at the San Francisco Bay Naval Shipyard in February 1966; she was recommissioned on 31 Jan 1970 and went to sea in March 1970.

Her modernisation included provisions for handling newer aircraft, new catapults, new lifts (arranged as in *Coral Sea*), and new electronics. A similar modernisation planned for the *Franklin D. Roosevelt*, to have begun in Fiscal Year 1970, has been cancelled because the *Midway* modernisation is taking longer and costing more than originally estimated (24 months and $88 000 000 was planned; actual work required approximately 52 months and $202 300 000). The *Franklin D. Roosevelt* completed an austere overhaul in June 1969 which enables her to operate the new A-6 Intruder and A-7 Corsair II attack aircraft; cost of overhaul was $46 000 000.
The *Midway* is now the most capable of the three ships (for example, her lifts can handle aircraft weights to 100 000 pounds compared to 74 000 pounds for the *Coral Sea* and *Franklin D. Roosevelt*).

PHOTOGRAPHS. Note the differing configurations of these three carriers. On the previous page the line cutting the *Midway's* mast is the shadow of the San Francisco Bay "Golden Gate" bridge; the *Midway* retains her lattice tripod mast structure in lieu of the pylon masts of the *Franklin D. Roosevelt* and *Coral Sea*. On the following page the *Coral Sea* is photographed conducting flight operations in the Gulf of Tonkin while under surveillance of the high-speed Soviet intelligence ship *Gidrofon*, a unit of the "Okean" class. The photograph of the *Oriskany* (bottom) also was taken in the Gulf of Tonkin; the camouflaged SH-3 series helicopter on her bow is not part of the ship's attack air wing.

FRANKLIN D ROOSEVELT (CVA 42)   *1969, United States Navy*

MIDWAY (CVA 41), CHEMUNG (AO 30)   *1970, United States Navy, PH3 A. N. Williams*

MIDWAY (CVA 41)   *1970, United States Navy*

Aircraft Carriers—*continued*

CORAL SEA (CVA 43), GIDROFON

1969, United States Navy

FRANKLIN D. ROOSEVELT (CVA 42)

1970, United States Navy

ORISKANY (CVA 34)—See following page

1970, United States Navy, PH3 L. J. Lafeir

Aircraft Carriers—*Continued*

3 ATTACK AIRCRAFT CARRIERS (CVA): "HANCOCK" CLASS

Name	No.	Builder	Laid down		Launched		Commissioned	
*HANCOCK	CVA 19	Bethlehem Steel Co (Quincy)	26 Jan	1943	24 Jan	1944	15 Apr	1944
BON HOMME RICHARD	CVA 31	New York Navy Yard	1 Feb	1943	29 Apr	1944	26 Nov	1944
*ORISKANY	CVA 34	New York Navy Yard	1 May	1944	13 Oct	1945	25 Sep	1950

Displacement, tons	
Oriskany	33 250 standard
Others	32 800 standard
	approx 44 700 full load
Length, feet (*metres*)	820 (*249·9*) wl
Oriskany	890 (*271·3*) oa
Others	894·5 (*272·6*) oa
Beam, feet (*metres*)	
Oriskany	106·5 (*32·5*)
Others	103 (*30·8*)
Draft, feet (*metres*)	31 (*9·4*)
Flight deck width	
feet (*metres*)	
Oriskany	195 (*59·5*) maximum
Others	192 (*58·5*) maximum
Catapults	2 steam
Aircraft	70 to 80
Guns	4—5 in (*127 mm*) 38 cal dual-purpose (single)
Main engines	4 geared turbines (Westinghouse) 150 000 shp; 4 shafts
Boilers	8—600 psi (*41·7 kg/cm²*) (Babcock & Wilcox)
Speed, knots	33
Complement	2 130 (130 officers, approx 2 000 enlisted men) plus approx 1 500 assigned to attack air wing for a total of 3 630 per ship

Twenty-three "Essex" class aircraft carriers were completed between 1943 and 1946, and the modified *Oriskany* was completed in 1950. Fourteen of these ships fought in World War II; many saw combat in the Korean War and Vietnamese War. The above ships remain on the Navy List as attack aircraft carriers embarking fighter and strike aircraft; see subsequent pages for the surviving ships of this type classified as anti-submarine warfare carriers (CVS) and training carriers (CVT).

Because of extensive modernisation since original completion the more-capable "Essex" class ships are considered as the "Hancock" class.

Bon Homme Richard decommissioned on 15 June 1971 and placed in reserve. The *Hancock* was scheduled to be decommissioned late in 1971.

CLASSIFICATION. These ships were initially classified as "aircraft" carriers (CV); reclassified as Attack Aircraft Carriers (CVA) in October 1952. The remaining ships of this type officially are known as the "Hancock" class.

DESIGN. All 24 ships were built to the same basic design with a standard displacement of 27 100 tons, full load displacement of 36 380 tons, and an overall length of 888 or 872 feet. These were the first aircraft carriers built with a deck-edge lift (in addition to two centreline lifts) except for a small outboard platform lift in the carrier *Wasp* (CV 7) launched in 1939.

Two additional ships of this class were cancelled while under construction, the *Reprisal* (CV 35) and *Iwo Jima* (CV 46), and six others were cancelled prior to keel laying, the unnamed CV 50-55.

ELECTRONICS. The *Oriskany* and the frigates *King* (DLG 10) and *Mahan* (DLG 11) conducted the initial sea trials of the Naval Tactical Data System (NTDS) in 1961-1962. NTDS is a highly automated system for collecting, processing, exchanging, and evaluating data on tactical situations. Priorities are assigned to enemy threats and possible courses of action are presented to the commander. The system is intended primarily to deal with the threat of high performance aircraft. The principal radar antennae of these ships include SPS-43, SPS-30, and SPS-10 search radars, and SPN-10 navigation radar. TACAN navigation pods top their masts.

GUNNERY. As built, except for the *Oriskany*, these ships mounted 12—5 inch guns, 68 or 72—40 mm guns, and 52—20 mm guns; the *Oriskany* completed with only 10—5 inch guns and 44—40 mm guns. Armament reduced periodically with 3 inch guns replacing lighter weapons. Minimal 5 inch armament remains on ships in service as carriers (CVA/CVS).

MISSILES. During the 1950s six "Essex" class ships were fitted with the Regulus I surface-to-surface missile (*Randolph*, *Lexington*, *Hancock*, *Bennington*, *Bon Homme Richard*, and *Shangri-La*).

HANCOCK (CVA 19) 1968, United States Navy, PHCM L. P. Bodine

BON HOMME RICHARD (CVA 31) 1969, United States Navy, PH2 L. D. Crouse

MODERNISATION. The completion of the *Oriskany* was delayed after World War II, allowing her to be completed with heavier catapults, improved elevators, reinforced flight deck, increased aviation fuel storage, and other features for operating jets. All of these ships subsequently have been modernised to enable them to operate advanced aircraft including the Mach 1·7 F-8 Crusader fighter and 35-ton KA-3B Skywarrior aerial tanker.

NOMENCLATURE. All 24 "Essex" class carriers are named for early American ships or battles except for *Shangri-La*, which is named for the imaginary locale in James Hilton's novel which President Roosevelt told the press was the base for the Doolittle-Halsey raid against Japan in 1942. Several ships renamed during construction to carry on names of carriers lost in battle. The *Hancock* and *Ticonderoga* exchanged names during construction.

PHOTOGRAPHS. In the **photograph** above forward lift of the *Hancock* is lowered to hangar deck level; the forward lifts of these ships are pointed to accommodate longer aircraft. The carrier *Oriskany* is shown in the Gulf of Tonkin with an E-1B Tracer early warning aircraft being prepared for launch on her starboard catapult forward of the island; the *Bon Homme Richard* is shown entering San Diego after an eight-month deployment in the Western Pacific (a seaward-bound submarine is visible off her port quarter; the *Intrepid* has sub-hunting S-2E Trackers and SH-3 Sea Kings on her flight deck. She also carries E-1B early warning craft and a utility helicopter.

DISPOSALS
Nine "straight-deck" carriers of this class have been stricken: **Franklin** (AVT 8, ex-CVS 13) stricken from the Navy List on 1 Oct 1964; **Bunker Hill** (AVT 8, ex-CVS 17) stricken on 1 Nov 1966, but retained as moored electronic test ship at San Diego, California; **Tarawa** (AVT 12, ex-CVS 40) stricken on 1 June 1967; **Leyte** (AVT 10, ex-CVS 32) stricken on 1 June 1969; **Philippine Sea** (AVT 11, ex-CVS 47), **Lake Champlain** (CVS 39), and **Boxer** (LPH 4, ex-CVS 21) stricken on 1 Dec 1969; **Princeton** (LPH 5, ex-CVS 37) stricken on 30 Jan 1970; **Valley Forge** (LPH 8, ex-CVS 45) stricken on 15 Jan 1970.

Aircraft Carriers—*Continued*

LIGHT AIRCRAFT CARRIERS (CVL)

All light aircraft carriers have been stricken from the Navy List, transferred or reclassified.

Of the nine ships of the "Independence" class converted during construction from light cruisers: **Independence** (CVL 22) used in atomic bomb and radiological experi- ments from July 1946 until sunk on 29 Jan 1951; **Princeton** (CVL 23) sunk in World War II; **Belleau Wood** (CVL 24) to France on 5 Sep 1953 (scrapped); **Cowpens** (AVT 1, ex-CVL 25) stricken on 1 Nov 1959; **Monterey** (AVT 2, ex-CVL 26) stricken on 1 June 1970; **Langley** (CVL 27) to France on 8 Jan 1951 (scrapped); **Cabot** (AVT 3, ex-CVL 28) to Spain on 30 Aug 1967; **Bataan** (AVT 4, ex-CVL 29) stricken on 1 Sep 1959; **San Jacinto** (AVT 5, ex-CVL 30) stricken on 1 June 1970.

The larger, built-for-the-purpose light carriers of the "Saipan" class have been converted to other roles: *Saipan* (AVT 6, ex-CVL 48) converted to major communications relay ship (AGMR 2) and *Wright* (AVT 7, ex-CVL 49) converted to command ship (CC 2).

ORISKANY (CVA 34)　　　　　　　　　　　　　　　*1970, United States Navy*

BON HOMME RICHARD (CVA 31)　　　　　　　　　　*1968, United States Navy*

INTREPID (CVS 11)—See following page　　　　　　　*1969, United States Navy*

Aircraft Carriers—Continued

"ESSEX" CLASS —continued

MODERNISATION. Except for the *Antietam*, all of these ships were extensively modernised while in an attack carrier status. While in a CVS status the *Essex*, *Yorktown*,

Intrepid, *Hornet*, *Randolph*, *Wasp*, *Bennington*, and *Kearsarge* were extensively overhauled under the so-called Fleet Rehabilitation and Modernisation (FRAM II) programme. They received new electronic equipment (CIC), and other features to extend their useful life and (including sonar), remodeled combat information centres

improve their ASW capabilities.

NOMENCLATURE. Ships renamed during construction were *Yorktown*, ex-*Bon Homme Richard*; *Hornet*, ex-*Kearsarge*; *Lexington*, ex-*Cabot*; and *Wasp*, ex-*Oriskany*.

TICONDEROGA (CVS 14)   1970, United States Navy

HORNET (CVS 12)   1968, United States Navy

RANDOLPH (CVS 15)   1968, United States Navy

Aircraft Carriers—Continued

11 ASW SUPPORT AIRCRAFT CARRIERS (CVS)
1 TRAINING AIRCRAFT CARRIER (CVT)

"ESSEX" CLASS

Name	No.	Builder	Laid down	Launched	Commissioned
ESSEX	CVS 9	Newport News SB & DD Co	28 Apr 1941	31 July 1942	31 Dec 1942
YORKTOWN	CVS 10	Newport News SB & DD Co	1 Dec 1941	21 Jan 1943	15 Apr 1943
*INTREPID	CVS 11	Newport News SB & DD Co	1 Dec 1941	26 Apr 1943	16 Aug 1943
HORNET	CVS 12	Newport News SB & DD Co	3 Aug 1942	29 Aug 1943	29 Nov 1943
*TICONDEROGA	CVS 14	Newport News SB & DD Co	1 Feb 1943	7 Feb 1944	10 Sep 1945
RANDOLPH	CVS 15	Newport News SB & DD Co	10 May 1943	28 June 1944	9 Oct 1944
*LEXINGTON	CVT 16 (ex-CVS 16)	Bethlehem Steel Co (Quincy)	15 July 1941	26 Sep 1942	17 Mar 1943
*WASP	CVS 18	Bethlehem Steel Co (Quincy)	18 Mar 1942	17 Aug 1943	24 Nov 1943
BENNINGTON	CVS 20	New York Navy Yard	15 Dec 1942	26 Feb 1944	6 Aug 1944
KEARSARGE	CVS 33	New York Navy Yard	1 Mar 1944	5 May 1945	2 Mar 1946
ANTIETAM	CVS 36	Philadelphia Navy Yard	15 Mar 1943	20 Aug 1944	28 Jan 1945
SHANGRI-LA	CVS 38	Norfolk Navy Yard	15 Jan 1943	24 Feb 1944	15 Sep 1944

Displacement, tons
Intrepid, Shangri-La,
 Ticonderoga   32 800 standard ; 41 726 full load
 Antietam   approx 30 000 standard ;
     approx 38 000 full load·
 Others   approx 33 000 standard ;
     40 600 full load
Length, feet (metres) 820 (*249·9*) wl
 Intrepid, Shangri-La,
 Ticonderoga   894·5 (*272·6*) oa
 Antietam   888 (*270·7*) oa
 Others   890 (*271·3*) oa
Beam, feet (metres)
 Intrepid, Shangri-La,
 Ticonderoga   103 (*31·4*)
 Antietam   93 (*28·4*)
 Others   102 (*31*)
Draft, feet (metres)   31 (*9·4*)
Flight deck width,
 feet (metres)
 Intrepid Lexington,
 Shangri-La,
 Ticonderoga   192 (*58·5*) maximum
 Antietam   154 (*47·0*) maximum
 Others   196 (*59·7*) maximum
Catapults
 Intrepid, Lexington,
 Shangri-La   2 steam
 Others   2 hydraulic
Aircraft   40 to 47 (including 16 to 18
     helicopters)
Guns   4—5 in (*127 mm*) 38 cal dual-
     purpose (single)
Main engines   4 geared turbines (Westinghouse)
     150 000 shp ; 4 shafts
Boilers   8—600 psi (*41·7 kg/cm²*)
     (Babcock & Wilcox)
Speed, knots   33
Complement   1 615 (115 officers, approx 1 500
     enlisted men) plus approx 800
     assigned to ASW air group for a
     total of 2 400 per ship

Five of these ships are in service, four serving with anti-submarine groups and the *Lexington* as a training carrier. Active ships are indicated by asterisk. The *Lexington* relieved the *Antietam* as training carrier in May 1962, the latter subsequently being mothballed. The *Randolph* was decommissioned in Nov 1968 and placed in reserve ; the *Essex* was decommissioned in June 1969 and placed in reserve, the latter ship in active service for 22 years (1943-1947, 1951-1969).
The *Intrepid* operated as a "limited attack carrier" from 1966 to 1969, carrying an air wing of fighter and light attack aircraft ; she reverted to ASW status in August 1969 when she replaced the inactivated *Essex*.
The *Bennington* and *Kearsarge* were decommissioned on 15 Jan 1970, and the *Yorktown* and *Hornet* were decommissioned on 30 June 1970, all placed in reserve. During 1969-1970 the *Shangri-La* operated as a "limited attack carrier" ; she was decommissioned and placed in reserve in 1971.

ANGLED DECK. The *Antietam* was the world's first carrier to have an angled flight deck. The angled deck, a British invention, was provided by adding a small triangular section of flight deck on the port side, rearranging the arresting wires, and repainting the landing lanes. The installation was made at the New York Naval Shipyard, September-December 1952. The scheme greatly increases efficiency and safety of high-speed carrier operations.

(Initial angled deck landing trials were conducted on the British light carrier *Triumph* and then the US large carrier *Midway*, with a simulated angled deck landing lane being painted on their standard flight decks).

CLASSIFICATION. These ships were initially classified as "aircraft carriers" (CV). All were redesignated Attack Aircraft Carriers (CVA) in October 1952 and subsequently became ASW Support Aircraft Carriers (CVS) : *Antietam* in July 1953, *Wasp* on 1 Nov 1955, *Yorktown* on 1 Sep 1957, *Hornet* on 27 June 1958, *Kearsarge* on 1 Oct 1958, *Randolph* on 31 Mar 1959, *Bennington* on 30 June 1959, *Essex* on 8 Mar 1960, *Intrepid* on 31 Mar 1962, *Lexington* on 1 Oct 1962, *Shangri-La* on 30 June 1969, *Ticonderoga* on 21 Oct 1969. Their places in the CVA ranks were

KEARSARGE (CVS 33), ASHTABULA (AO 51), BRONSTEIN (DE 1037)   *1969, US Navy*

INTREPID (CVS 11)   *1969, United States Navy*

taken by new-construction ships. The *Lexington*, a training ship since May 1962, was officially designated as a Training Aircraft Carrier (CVT) on 1 Jan 1969

ELECTRONICS. SQS-23 sonar fitted in eight carriers which have undergone FRAM II work (see *Modernisation*

notes). The primary radar antennas in ships operational during the latter 1960s include SPS-43, SPS-30, and SPS-10 search radars, and SPN-10 navigation radar. The training carrier *Lexington* has SPS-8 height finding radar rather than SPS-30. TACAN navigation pods or "bee hives" top masts of these ships.

Aircraft Carriers—*Continued*

KEARSARGE (CVS 33)   *1968, United States Navy*

LEXINGTON (CVT 16)   *1968, United States Navy*

WASP (CVS 18)   *1968, United States Navy*

SURFACE COMBATANTS

The US Navy has established the category of Surface Combatants to include battleships, cruisers, frigates, and destroyers. The various types of escort ships (DE/DEG/DER) previously addressed within the context of destroyer-type ships now are listed separately in the official category of Ocean Escorts. Also, within *Jane's Fighting Ships* the battleships and non-missile cruisers (CA/CL) are listed as Fire Support Ships because of their limited capabilities for anti-air, anti-submarine, and surface warfare in the context of modern naval operations. The planned Surface Combatant force level provides for approximately 160 cruisers, frigates, and destroyers to be in commission on June 30, 1972: eight missile-armed cruisers (one nuclear powered); 30 missile-armed frigates (two nuclear powered), 29 missile-armed destroyers, 14 all-gun destroyers of post-World War II

construction, and approximately 80 war-built destroyers. In addition, one all-gun heavy cruiser (the *Newport News*) will remain in commission into 1972 and 28 war-built destroyers are employed as operational Naval Reserve training ships.

The above force level represents a reduction of some 80 cruisers, frigates, and destroyers from the US Navy's strength three years ago at the height of the Vietnam War. Still, more than half of the surface combatants remaining in commission are over 25 years of age.

During the 1970s new construction programmes are expected to provide the US Navy with five nuclear-powered, missile-armed frigates (the size of World War II-era cruisers) and 30 essentially all-gun destroyers of

the controversial "Spruance" class. Anticipating the retirement of the seven war-built missile cruisers and 80 war-built destroyers during this period, by the end of the decade the Navy's surface combatant strength will be about 110 ships. Although nine ships will be nuclear powered (giving the Navy two all-nuclear carrier task groups), on balance the oldest of the post-war "Forrest Sherman" class destroyers will be 25 years old.

Thus, it appears that in view of anticipated US commitments about 1980, missions heretofore considered within the purview of destroyers will be given to the less-capable but numerous escort ships and possibly the proposed advanced-design patrol ships. A final factor to be considered in the Surface Combatant equation is the air capable ship, described below.

AIR CAPABLE SEA CONTROL SHIP (DH): NEW DESIGN

The US Navy has begun development of an "air capable ship", tentatively designated DH. Under the express direction of the Chief of Naval Operations, Admiral Elmo Zumwalt, a concept formulation effort is developing general configurations and performance envelopes for a surface warship that will operate aircraft to perform a variety of tactical naval missions.

Admiral Zumwalt announced on May 8, 1971, that the ship officially would be designated as the "sea control ship" in an apparent move to arouse interest and support for the ship.

After the US Navy has undertaken construction of a large number of surface combatants and ocean escorts, the "Spruance" and "Knox" classes, respectively, that are considered inferior in several respects to their foreign contemporaries, the air capable ship concept provides an opportunity for the US Navy and the maritime industry to demonstrate that they still retain the capability to design and produce first-rate fighting ships.

The air capable ship will operate helicopters and vertical/short take-off and landing aircraft, with unofficial sources crediting the ship with six AV-8 Harrier V/STOL aircraft and six SH-3 Sea King helicopters. According to Admiral Zumwalt, the ship will displace approximately 12 000 tons full load and will be "extremely austere . . . with maximum capability in weapons and sensors being

placed in the aircraft (and) minimum in the ship". The ship will not be an "aircraft carrier" because the space and weight requirements for the catapults and arresting gear to operate conventional fixed-wing aircraft would dictate too large a ship. Thus, the air capable ship will be unable to operate the high-performance aircraft found aboard attack and ASW aircraft carriers. This limitation, coupled with the ship's maximum speed of 20+ knots and minimum sensors and armament, would prevent operation in certain high-threat areas without being complemented by more-capable surface combatant ships or land-based or sea-based tactical aircraft.

Primary missions for embarked aircraft would be anti-submarine warfare and limited anti-air warfare. Additional missions being considered for aircraft embarked in the air capable ship include minesweeping, fire support for ground forces, aerial reconnaissance, airborne delivery of small raiding or reconnaissance forces, search and rescue, and underway replenishment.

It is generally thought that the maximum possible flight deck area should be provided to permit the operation of the largest possible number of aircraft and enable short take-off runs (about 300 feet) for heavily loaded VSTOL aircraft. Below the flight deck would be a full-length or partial hangar deck for stowage and maintenance of aircraft. Shop facilities would be provided to increase aircraft availability.

Detailed characteristics of the air capable ship are being determined in a formal concept formulation that was begun in mid-1971. Factors being considered in the concept formulation include the exact ship size, aircraft capacity, propulsion, endurance, speed, armament, and sensors for the ship. The aircraft to be carried will be those expected to be available in the late 1970s.

The final characteristics will determine the eventual classification of the air capable ship: whether a destroyer "type", cruiser, frigate or possibly a new category such as the designation "guided missile helicopter ship" (CHG) that is used by the US Navy and NATO for the Soviet "Moskva" class ships. (The Soviets designate the *Moskva* and *Leningrad* as anti-submarine cruisers).

Assuming full Navy, Department of Defence, White House, and Congressional support for this effort, funds for a prototype air capable ship could be included in the Fiscal Year 1974 new construction programme and the first ship could be completed about 1978. The rate of construction after that would depend upon a number of factors, including the nature of the Soviet and possibly other-nation threats at sea, US Navy missions at the time, the success (or lack thereof) of the "Spruance" class destroyers and Light Airborne Multi-Purpose System (LAMPS).

COLUMBUS (CG 12) 1970, United States Navy, PH3 J. Rose

TRUXTUN (DLGN 35) 1970, United States Navy, PH1 E. L. Goligoski

PHOTOGRAPHS. Above are the US Navy's "last" cruiser and latest frigate. The *Columbus* is one of eight missile-armed cruisers in commission; all except the nuclear-powered *Long Beach* are of World War II construction and were extensively converted to serve as air-defense ships for carrier task groups. Additionally, four of the converted ships were outfitted as flagships for fleet commanders.

The seven older missile cruisers are expected to be stricken during the 1970s, some 30 years after their original completion. Their replacements will be the nuclear-powered, missile-armed "frigates" now under construction and planned. These new warships will be larger than even the *Truxtun*, now the largest "destroyer-type" ship afloat with a displacement of 9 200 tons and and an overall length of 564 feet. She thus exceeds the dimensions of many earlier cruisers, including several

"heavy" cruisers of the 1930s and 1940s built to naval treaty specifications.

Of more significance today, the new US Navy frigates are considerably larger than the Soviet "Kresta" and "Kynda" class cruisers but apparently the US ships have less space and weight allocated to weapons, the *raison d' existence* of fighting ships. However, nuclear propulsion, in part responsible for the size of the US ships, gives them formidable high-speed endurance capabilities.

Surface Combatants—*continued*

3 GUIDED MISSILE CRUISERS (CG): "ALBANY" CLASS

Name	No.	Builder	Laid down	Launched	Commissioned	CG Comm.
* **ALBANY**	CG 10 (ex-CA 123)	Bethlehem Steel Co (Quincy)	6 Mar 1944	30 June 1945	15 June 1946	3 Nov 1962
* **CHICAGO**	CG 11 (ex-CA 136)	Philadelphia Navy Yard	28 July 1943	20 Aug 1944	1 Jan 1945	2 May 1964
* **COLUMBUS**	CG 12 (ex-CA 74)	Bethlehem Steel Co (Quincy)	28 June 1943	30 Nov 1944	8 June 1945	1 Dec 1962

Displacement, tons	13 700 standard; 17 500 full load
Length, feet (*metres*)	664 (*202.4*) wl; 673 (*205.3*) oa
Beam, feet (*metres*)	70 (*21.6*)
Draft, feet (*metres*)	27 (*8.2*)
Missiles	2 twin Talos surface-to-air launchers; 2 twin Tartar surface-to-air launchers
Guns	2—5 in (*127 mm*) 38 calibre dual-purpose (see *Gunnery* notes)
ASW weapons	1 ASROC 8-tube launcher 2 triple torpedo launchers (Mk 32)
Helicopter	utility helicopter carried
Main engines	4 geared turbines (General Electric); 120 000 shp; 4 shafts
Boilers	4 (Babcock & Wilcox) 565 psi
Speed, knots	33
Complement	1 000 (60 officers, approx 940 enlisted men)

These ships were fully converted from heavy cruisers, the *Albany* having been a unit of the "Oregon City" class and the *Chicago* and *Columbus* of the "Baltimore" class. Although the two heavy cruiser classes differ in appearance (see Fire Support Ships), they have the same hull dimensions and machinery. These three missile ships now form a new, homogeneous class.

The cruiser *Fall River* (CA 131) was originally scheduled for missile conversion, but was replaced by the *Columbus*. Proposals to convert two additional heavy cruisers (CA 124 and CA 130) to missile ships (CG 13 and CG 14) were dropped, primarily because of high conversion costs and improved capabilities of newer missile-armed frigates.

CONVERSION. During conversion to missile configuration these ships were stripped down to their main hulls with all cruiser armament and superstructure being removed. New superstructures make extensive use of aluminium to reduce weight and improve stability. Former masts and stacks were replaced by "macks" which support electronic antennas and have machinery exhausts vented from sides near top. These "macks" are covered with plastic material to reduce expansion and contraction with ambient temperature changes which could change alignment of radar and other electronic antennas. Side vents direct machinery exhausts away from electronic gear. The *Albany* was converted at the Boston Naval Shipyard between January 1959 and November 1962; the *Columbus* at Puget Sound Naval Shipyard from June 1959 to March 1963; and *Chicago* at San Francisco Naval Shipyard from July 1959 to September 1964.

ELECTRONICS. These ships are fitted with SQS-23 sonar which is linked to the ASROC fire control system. The Naval Tactical Data System (NTDS) is fitted in the *Albany* and *Chicago*.

The search radar antenna arrangements differ slightly: the *Albany* has SPS-48 three-dimensional and SPS-10 search radar antennas on her forward "mack", an SPS-43 antenna on her second "mack", and an SPS-30 antenna on the after platform (no SPS-30 atop bridge structure); the *Chicago* has SPS-30 antennas forward and aft, SPS-52 and SPS-10 antennas on her forward "mack", and an SPS-43 antenna on her after "mack"; the *Columbus* has SPS-30 antennas forward and aft, an SPS-39 three-dimensional and SPS-10 search radar antenna on her forward "mack", and an SPS-43 antenna on her after "mack".

GUNNERY. No guns were fitted when these ships were converted to missile cruisers. Two single, *open-mount* 5 inch guns were fitted subsequently to provide minimal defence against low-flying, subsonic aircraft or torpedo boat attacks.

Two Mk 56 directors installed for gun control.

MISSILES. One twin Talos launcher is forward and one aft; a twin Tartar launcher is on each side of the main bridge structure. During conversion space was allocated amidships for installation of eight Polaris missile tubes, but the plan to install ballistic missiles in cruisers was cancelled in mid-1959. Reportedly, 92 Talos and 80 Tartar missiles are carried.

MODERNISATION. The *Albany* underwent an extensive anti-air warfare modernisation at the Boston Naval Shipyard; "conversion" began in February 1967 and was completed August 1969. She was formerly recommissioned on 9 Nov 1968. The *Chicago* and *Columbus* will not have AAW modernisations because of plan to discard all conventionally powered cruisers during the 1970s.

The *Albany's* AAW conversion included installation of NTDS, a digital Talos fire-control system which provides faster and more-reliable operation, and improved SPS-48 and SPS-30 air search radars (the *Albany* also has an SPS-43 long-range and SPS-10 short-range search radars, and SPG-51C fire-control radar).

ALBANY (CG 10)   1970, A. & J. Pavia

COLUMBUS (CG 12)   1969, A. & J. Pavia

ALBANY (CG 10)   1970, United States Navy

Surface Combatants—*continued*

LONG BEACH (CGN 9)—See following page

See following page

1968, United States Navy

ALBANY (CG 10)

1969, United States Navy

CHICAGO (CG 11)

1968, United States Navy

Surface Combatants—*continued*

1 NUCLEAR-POWERED GUIDED MISSILE CRUISER (CGN): "LONG BEACH" TYPE

Name	No.	Builder	Laid down	Launched	Commissioned
*LONG BEACH	CGN 9 (ex-CGN 160, CLGN 160)	Bethlehem Steel Co, (Quincy, Massachusetts)	2 Dec 1957	14 July 1959	9 Sep 1961

Displacement, tons	14 200 standard; 17 350 full load
Length, feet (*metres*)	721·2 (*220*) oa
Beam, feet (*metres*)	73·2 (*22·3*)
Draft, feet (*metres*)	29 (*8·8*)
Missiles	1 twin Talos surface-to-air launcher; 2 twin Terrier surface-to-air launchers
Guns	2—5 in (*127 mm*) 38 calibre dual-purpose (see *Gunnery* notes)
ASW weapons	1 ASROC 8-tube launcher 2 triple torpedo launchers (Mk 32)
Helicopter	utility helicopter carried
Main engines	2 geared turbines (General Electric); approx 80 000 shp; 2 shafts
Reactors	2 pressurised-water cooled C1W (Westinghouse)
Speed, knots	approx 35
Complement	1 000 (60 officers, approx 950 enlisted men)

The *Long Beach* was the first ship to be designed and constructed from the keel up as a cruiser for the United States since the end of World War II. She is the world's first nuclear-powered surface warship and the first warship to have a guided missile main battery. She was authorised in the Fiscal Year 1957 new construction programme. Estimated construction cost was $332 850 000. Construction was delayed because of shipyard strike.
No additional new-construction cruisers are planned because of the capabilities of new guided-missile frigates (DLG and DLGN), which are approaching the size of World War II-era light cruisers.

CLASSIFICATION. The *Long Beach* was ordered as a Guided Missile Light Cruiser (CLGN 160) on 15 Oct 1956; reclassified as a Guided Missile Cruiser (CGN 160) early in 1957 and renumbered (CGN 9) on 1 July 1957.

DESIGN. The *Long Beach* was initially planned as a large destroyer or "frigate" of about 7 800 tons (standard displacement) to test the feasibility of a nuclear powered surface warship. Early in 1956 the decision was made to capitalise on the capabilities of nuclear propulsion and her displacement was increased to 11 000 tons and a second Terrier missile launcher was added to the design. A Talos missile launcher was also added to the design which, with other features, increased displacement to 14 000 tons by the time the contract was signed for her construction on 15 October 1956.

ELECTRONICS. The *Long Beach* has fixed-array ("billboard") radar which provides increased range over rotating antennas. Horizontal antennas on bridge superstructure are for SPS-32 bearing and range radar; vertical antennas are for SPS-33 target tracking radar. The SPS-33 uses an "S" band frequency and the SPS-32 is VHF; both frequency scan in elevation. Developed and produced by Hughes Aircraft, they are believed the first operational fixed-array radar systems in the Western world. Also installed in the nuclear-powered aircraft carrier *Enterprise* (CVAN 65).
SPS-12 and SPS-10 search radar antennas are mounted on the forward mast.
The SPS-32/33 "Scanfar" radars and the associated computers were modified in 1970 to improve performance. She is equipped with Naval Tactical Data System (NTDS) and SQS-23 sonar.

ENGINEERING. The reactors are similar to those of the nuclear-powered aircraft carrier *Enterprise* (CVAN 65). The *Long Beach* first got underway on nuclear power on 5 July 1961. After four years of operation and having steamed more than 167 000 miles she underwent her first overhaul and refuelling at the Newport News Shipbuilding and Dry Dock Company from August 1965 to February 1966.

GUNNERY. Completed with an all-missile armament. Two single 5 inch mounts were fitted during 1962-1963 yard period to provide defence against low-flying, subsonic aircraft and torpedo boats.

MISSILES. Initial plans provided for installation of the Regulus II surface-to-surface missile, a transonic missile which carried a nuclear warhead and had a 1 000-mile range. Upon cancellation of the Regulus II programme, provision was made for providing eight Polaris tubes, but they were never installed. Plans to provide Polaris were dropped early in 1961 in an effort to reduce construction costs.
Reportedly, the *Long Beach* carries 40 Talos and 240 Terrier missiles.

OPERATIONAL. Talos missiles fired from the *Long Beach* have downed Communist aircraft in what are believed to have been the first surface-to-air "kills" in combat with ship-launched missiles.

LONG BEACH (CGN 9) *1968, United States Navy*

LONG BEACH (CGN 9) *1963, United States Navy*

While operating in the Tonkin Gulf, the ship's Talos missiles shot down one supersonic MiG fighter on May 23, 1968, and a second MiG in June 1968; both aircraft were over North Vietnam at the time of their destruction. In addition, *Long Beach* radar-aircraft controller personnel are believed to have guided US carrier-based fighters in the destruction of three MiG aircraft during 1968. Official acknowledgement of the *Long Beach* operations was not made until October 1969.

NOMENCLATURE. US cruisers are named for American cities.

Surface Combatants—*continued*

6 GUIDED MISSILE LIGHT CRUISERS (CLG): CONVERTED "CLEVELAND" CLASS

Name	No.	Builder	Laid down	Launched	Commissioned	CLG Comm.
GALVESTON	CLG 3 (ex-CL 93)	Cramp Shipbuilding (Philadelphia)	20 Feb 1944	22 Apr 1945	(see notes)	28 May 1958
*LITTLE ROCK	CLG 4 (ex-CL 92)	Cramp Shipbuilding (Philadelphia)	6 Mar 1943	27 Aug 1944	17 June 1945	3 June 1960
**OKLAHOMA CITY	CLG 5 (ex-CL 91)	Cramp Shipbuilding (Philadelphia)	8 Mar 1942	20 Feb 1944	22 Dec 1944	7 Sep 1960
*PROVIDENCE	CLG 6 (ex-CL 82)	Bethlehem Steel Co (Quincy)	27 July 1943	28 Dec 1944	15 May 1945	17 Sep 1959
*SPRINGFIELD	CLG 7 (ex-CL 66)	Bethlehem Steel Co (Quincy)	13 Feb 1943	9 Mar 1944	9 Sep 1944	2 July 1960
TOPEKA	CLG 8 (ex-CL 67)	Bethlehem Steel Co (Quincy)	21 Apr 1943	19 Apr 1944	23 Dec 1944	26 Mar 1960

Displacement, tons	10 670 standard ; 14 600 full load
Length, feet *(metres)*	600 *(182·9)* wl ; 610 *(185·9)* oa
Beam, feet *(metres)*	66·3 *(20·2)*
Draft, feet *(metres)*	25 *(7·6)*
Missiles CLG 3, 4, 5:	1 twin Talos surface-to-air launcher
CLG 6, 7, 8:	1 twin Terrier surface-to-air launcher
Guns CLG 4-7:	3—6 in *(152 mm)* 47 cal 2—5 in *(127 mm)* 38 cal dual-purpose
CLG 3, 8:	6—6 in *(152 mm)* 47 cal 6—5 in *(127 mm)* 38 cal dual-purpose
Helicopter	utility helicopter carried
Main engines	4 geared turbines (General Electric) ; 100 000 shp ; 4 shafts
Boilers	4 (Babcock & Wilcox)
Speed	31·6 knots
Complement CLG 4-7:	1 680 officers and enlisted men (including fleet staff)
CLG 3,8:	1 200 officers and enlisted men

These ships were converted from light cruisers of the "Cleveland" class (see Fire Support Ships). Although generally similar, the six ships are of four distinct designs: the *Galveston* armed with Talos missiles; the *Little Rock* and *Oklahoma City* armed with Talos and fitted as fleet flagships; the *Providence* and *Springfield* armed with Terrier and fitted as fleet flagships; the *Topeka* armed with Terrier. The flagships normally rotate as flagships of the Sixth Fleet in the Mediterranean and the Seventh Fleet in the Western Pacific.
The *Topeka* was decommissioned on 5 June 1969, the *Galveston* was decommissioned on 25 May 1970; both are in reserve.

The *Little Rock* and *Springfield* are active in the Atlantic-Mediterranean and the *Oklahoma City* and *Providence* in the Pacific.

CLASSIFICATION. The *Galveston* was reclassified CLG 93 on 4 Feb 1956 and CLG 3 on 23 May 1957. All US Navy guided missile cruisers were numbered in a single series, the CAG 1 and CAG 2 having been the *Boston* (now CA 69) and *Canberra* (CA 70) respectively.

CONSTRUCTION. The construction of the *Galveston* was suspended on 24 June 1946 when nearly complete; placed in reserve until 1956 when taken in hand for conversion to a missile ship. She got underway for the first time on 30 June 1958.

CONVERSION. All six of these ships had their two after 6 inch gun turrets replaced by a twin surface-to-air missile launcher, superstructure enlarged to support missile fire control equipment, lattice masts fitted to carry antennas, 5 inch battery reduced (from original 12 guns), and all 40 mm and 20 mm light anti-aircraft guns removed. The four ships fitted as fleet flagships additionally had their No. 2 turret of 6 inch guns removed and their forward superstructure enlarged to provide command and communications spaces for the flag staff.
The *Galveston* began conversion at the Philadelphia Naval Shipyard in August 1956 and was completed in September 1958 ; the *Little Rock* began conversion at the New York Shipbuilding Corp (Camden, New Jersey) in January 1957 and was completed in June 1960 ; the *Oklahoma City* began conversion at the Bethlehem Steel shipyard in San Francisco in May 1957 and was completed in September 1960 ; the *Providence* began conversion at the Boston Naval Shipyard in June 1957 and was completed in September 1959 ; the *Springfield* began conversion at the Bethlehem Steel shipyard in Quincy,

Massachusetts, in August 1957, but was moved to the Boston Naval Shipyard in March 1960 for completion in July 1960 ; and the *Topeka* was converted at the New York Naval Shipyard between August 1957 and March 1960.

ELECTRONICS. The search radar antenna arrangements on these ships differ: the Terrier-armed ships have SPS-43 and SPS-10 antennas on their forward mast, an SPS-30 antenna on the second mast, and an SPS-52 or SPS-39 three-dimensional radar antenna on the third mast; the Talos-armed ships have SPS-43 and SPS-10 antennas on their forward mast, an SPS-52 or SPS-39 three-dimensional antenna on their after mast, and an SPS-30 antenna on the after platform.

The *Little Rock* has had her SPS-39 three-dimensional search radar removed.

These ships have no ASW sonar.

GUNNERY. As converted to missile-gun cruisers these ships each retained one Mk 37 and one Mk 39 gunfire control directors forward; the Mk 39 director has been removed from the *Oklahoma City*.

MISSILES. Reportedly, the three ships armed with Terrier each carry 120 missiles and the three ships armed with Talos each carry 46 missiles.

PHOTOGRAPHS. The four flagships (CLG 4-7) can be identified by their single 6 inch gun turret forward; the ships armed with the Terrier missile have three lattice masts while those with Talos have a short radar-supporting platform in lieu of the third mast.
Note space between second funnel and second lattice mast of *Springfield* compared to *Galveston* and built up structure between the former's funnels.

GALVESTON (CLG 3)   *1966, United States Navy*

SPRINGFIELD (CLG 7)   *1969, United States Navy, PH1 C. F. Witherow*

Surface Combatants—*continued*

2 + 1 NUCLEAR-POWERED GUIDED MISSILE FRIGATES (DLGN): FORMER DXGN

No.	Builder	To Complete
DLGN 38	Newport News SB & DD Co	mid-1975
DLGN 39	Newport News SB & DD Co	1976
DLGN 40	(FY 1972 programme)	1977

Displacement, tons	approx 10 000 full load
Length, feet (*metres*)	585 (*177·3*) oa
Beam, feet (*metres*)	61 (*18·5*)
Draft, feet (*metres*)	29·5 (*9·0*)
Helicopters	2 (see *Helicopter* notes)
Missiles	2 combination twin Tartar-D/ASROC launchers (Mk 26)
ASW weapons	ASROC (*see above*) and torpedo launchers
Guns	2—5 inch (*127 mm*) 54 cal (Light Weight Gun Systems)
Main engines	2 geared turbines; 2 shafts
Reactors	2 pressurised-water cooled D2G (General Electric)
Speed, knots	30
Complement	approx 500 officers and enlisted men

The Navy plans to construct at least eight ships of this class to provide all-nuclear escorts for two nuclear-powered attack carriers. (Additional ships will be requested should the CVAN 70 be approved).
These ships were known as the DXGN during preliminary design. The DLGN 38 was authorised in the Fiscal Year 1970 new construction programme, the DLGN 39 in FY 1971, and the DLGN 40 in FY 1972. The DLGN 41 and DLGN 42 planned for the FY 1973 programme were cancelled on May 6, 1971, because of cost increases.

ANTI-SUBMARINE. The Mk 26 launchers will fire both surface-to-air and the ASROC/Extended-range ASROC missiles; "mixed" magazines are planned for both the forward and aft launcher. Embarked helicopters also will have an anti-submarine capability. A digital ASW fire control system will simplify weapon system interfaces compared to previous ships.

DESIGN. The principal differences between the DLGN 38 class and the "California" class will be the improved anti-air warfare capability, electronic warfare equipment, anti-submarine fire control system, and the combat information centre (CIC) facilities. The deletion of the ASROC "pepper-box" launcher permitted the later ships to be ten feet shorter.

ELECTRONICS. The DLGN 40 and later ships may have the advanced radar systems associated with the Aegis" advanced surface missile system. (The radars for this system now are under development; the development of the associated missile-launching equipment has been deferred and Mk 26 will be retained in the later ships). These ships will have the Naval Tactical Data System (NTDS) with the UYK-7 computer, Mk 116 underwater fire control system, Mk 86 gunfire control system, SQS-26CX sonar, SPS-48 three-dimensional search radar, and SPS-40 search radar.
The "*Aegis*" system in the later ships will have fixed radar antennas that scan electronically rather than

mechanically and "illumination" fire control radars that "bounce" a signal off the target which is detected by the missile for terminal guidance.

FISCAL. The FY 1969 budget provided $52 000 000 for long-lead time components (primarily electronics and propulsion plant) for the DLGN 38 and DLGN 39. The FY 1970 budget provided $196 000 000 to complete the DLGN 38 plus $58 000 000 for long-lead time components for the DLGN 40 and DLGN 41 and $9 900 000 for fire control radars for the DLGN 39 and DLGN 40. The FY 1971 budget rpovided $182 800 000 to complete funding the DLGN 39 plus $28 000 000 for advanced procurement. The FY 1972 budget requested $203 000 000 to fund the DLGN 40 plus $49 000 000 for "programme adjustment" of the entire class.
The estimated cost of the DLGN 38 is $222 000 000 and $213 800 000 for the DLGN 39. with subsequent ships costing an estimated average of $208 000 000 per ship.

GUNNERY. These ships will have the 5 inch Light Weight Gun System (LWGS) of the Mk 45 type also being installed in the "Spruance" class destroyers.

HELICOPTERS. A hangar for helicopters is installed beneath the fantail flight deck with a telescoping hatch cover and an electro-mechanical elevator provided to transport helicopters between the main deck and hangar.

MISSILES. The initial design for this class provided for a single surface-to-air missile launcher; revised in 1969 to provide two Mk 26 launchers that will fire the Standard surface-to-air missiles and ASROC/Extended-range ASROC anti-submarine missiles.

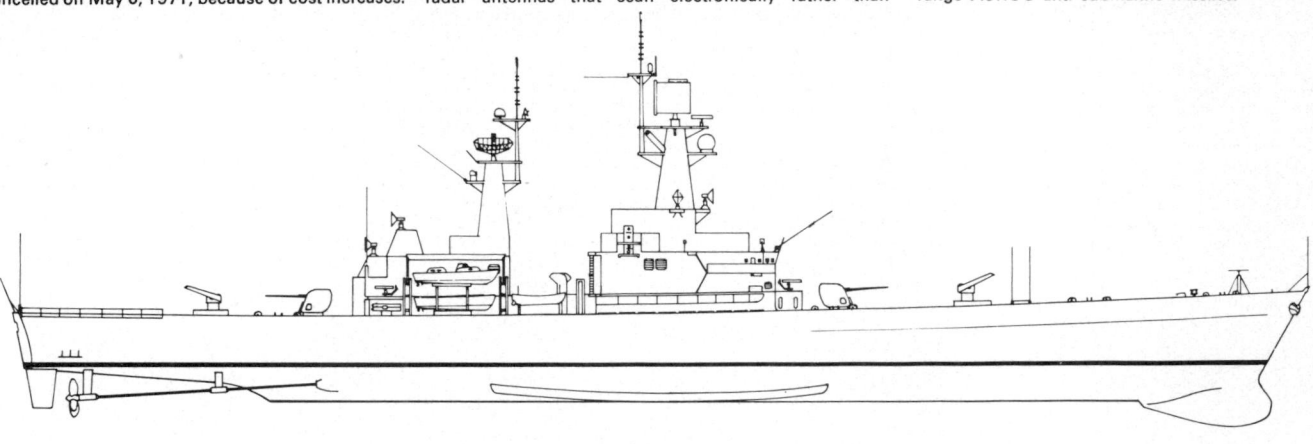

2 NUCLEAR-POWERED GUIDED MISSILE FRIGATES (DLGN): "CALIFORNIA" CLASS

Displacement, tons	10 150 full load
Length, feet (*metres*)	596 (*181·7*) oa
Beam, feet (*metres*)	61 (*18·6*)
Missiles	2 single Tartar-D surface-to-air launchers
Guns	2—5 in (*127 mm*) 54 calibre dual-purpose (single) (Light Weight Gun Systems)
ASW weapons	torpedo launchers 1 ASROC 8-tube launcher
Main engines	2 geared turbines; 2 shafts
Reactors	2 pressurised-water cooled D2G (General Electric)
Speed, knots	30
Complement	approx 550 officers and enlisted men

These are large, multi-purpose warships intended primarily to operate with fast carrier forces. Their high-speed and endurance capabilities also makes them suitable for independent operations.
The *California* was authorised in the Fiscal Year 1967 new construction programme and the *South Carolina* in the FY 1968 programme. The construction of a third ship of this class (DLGN 38) also was authorised in FY 1968, but the rising costs of these ships and development of the DXGN design caused the third ship to be deferred. (See *Fiscal* notes).

Name	No.	Builder	Laid down	Launch	Commission
CALIFORNIA	DLGN 36	Newport News SB & DD Co	24 Jan 1970	July 1971	Dec 1972
SOUTH CAROLINA	DLGN 37	Newport News SB & DD Co	1 Dec 1970	Apr 1972	Aug 1973

The contract for both ships was awarded on 13 June 1968. These two ships together with the three previously built nuclear escort ships (*Long Beach, Bainbridge, Truxtun*) will provide one all-nuclear carrier task group consisting of one attack aircraft carrier and four escorts, with an additional escort undergoing overhaul/refuelling at any given time.

ELECTRONICS. Fitted with bow-mounted SQS-26 sonar and the Naval Tactical Data System (NTDS). These ships will have SPS-48 three-dimensional and SPS-40 Search radars.

ENGINEERING. Estimated nuclear core life for these ships will provide 700 000 miles "range"; estimated cost is $11 500 000 for the two initial nuclear cores.

FISCAL. The DLGN 36 was funded with $20 000 000 for long-lead time components (primarily electronics and propulsion plant) in FY 1966 and $130 500 000 in FY 1967. The DLGN 37 was funded with $20 000 000 for long-lead time components in FY 1967 and $114 800 000 in FY 1968. The estimated cost of these

ships subsequently increased to $200 000 000 for the DLGN 36 and to $180 000 000 for the DLGN 37. (The DLGN 37 was funded only with $20 000 000 for long-lead time components in FY 1968).

MISSILES. Reportedly, these ships will carry some 80 surface-to-air missiles divided equally between a magazine beneath each launcher.

NOMENCLATURE. Destroyer-type ships in the US Navy have traditionally been named for officers and enlisted personnel of the Navy and Marine Corps, Secretaries of the Navy, members of Congress who have influenced naval affairs, and inventors. The frigates generally honour admirals and commodores of the Navy; however, in January 1970 it was announced that henceforth frigates would be named for states of the Union with the first frigate so named honouring California, home state of the incumbent president. The DLGN 37 honours the home state of the late L. Mendel Rivers, chairman of the House of Representatives Committee on Armed Services from 1965 until his death in 1971.

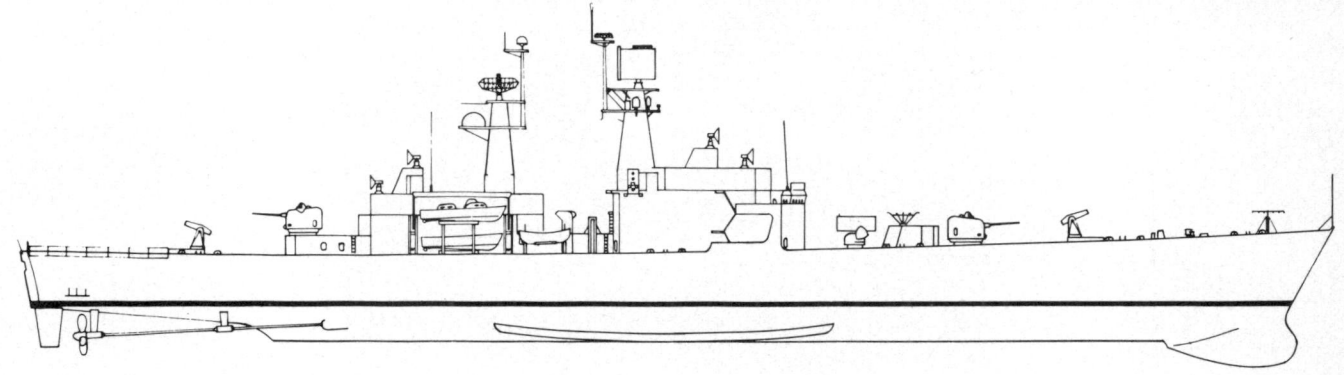

Surface Combatants—*continued*

1 NUCLEAR-POWERED GUIDED MISSILE FRIGATE (DLGN): "TRUXTUN" TYPE

Name	No.	Builder	Laid down	Launched	Commissioned
*TRUXTUN	DLGN 35	New York Shipbuilding Corp (Camden)	17 June 1963	19 Dec 1964	27 May 1967

Displacement, tons	8 200 standard ; 9 200 full load
Length, feet (*metres*)	564 (*171·9*) oa
Beam, feet (*metres*)	58 (*17·7*)
Draft, feet (*metres*)	31 (*9·4*)
Missiles	1 twin Terrier/ASROC launcher (see *Missile* notes)
Guns	1—5 in (*127 mm*) 54 calibre dual-purpose ; 2—3 in (*76 mm*) 50 calibre anti-aircraft (single)
ASW weapons	ASROC (see above) 4 fixed torpedo launches (Mk 32)
Helicopters	Facilities for helicopters
Main engines	2 geared turbines ; 60 000 shp ; 2 shafts
Reactors	2 pressurised-water cooled D2G (General Electric)
Speed, knots	30+
Complement	approx 500 (35 officers, 465 enlisted men)

The *Truxtun* was the US Navy's fourth nuclear-powered surface warship. The Navy had requested seven oil-burning frigates in the Fiscal 1962 shipbuilding prog-ramme ; the Congress authorised seven ships, but stipulated that one must be nuclear powered. Estimated construction cost was $138 667 000.

ANTI-SUBMARINE. Fixed Mk 32 tubes are below 3-inch gun "tubs", built into superstructure. The two Mk 25 torpedo tubes built into her stern are not used.

ELECTRONICS. The *Truxtun* has bow-mounted SQS-26 sonar and the Naval Tactical Data System (NTDS). Fitted with SPS-48 three-dimensional and SPS-10 search radar antennas on forward mast and an SPS-40 search radar antenna and TACAN (Tactical Aircraft Navigation) "pod" on after mast.

ENGINEERING. Power plant is identical to that of the frigate *Bainbridge*.

MISSILES. The twin missile launcher aft can fire both Terrier anti-aircraft missiles and ASROC anti-submarine rockets.

CANCELLATION. A DLGN to be armed with the Typhon missile system was authorised and funded in the FY 1963 programme. When the missile system was cancelled because of high costs the ship also was cancelled. No hull number had been assigned. Announced character-istics included a full load displacement of more than

TRUXTUN (DLGN 35)

1970, United States Navy PH1 E. L. Goligoski

9 000 tons, overall length exceeding 600 feet, one twin launcher for long-range Typhon missiles, two single launchers for short-range Typhon missiles, two 5 inch guns, ASW torpedo launchers, ASROC, and Naval Tactical Data System (NTDS).

NOMENCLATURE. The *Truxtun* is the fifth ship to be named for Commodore Thomas Truxton (sic) who commanded the frigate *Constellation* (38 guns) in her

successful encounter with the French frigate *L'Insurgente* (44) in 1799.

PHOTOGRAPHS. The *Truxtun* can be readily identified by her squared lattice radar masts, empty "B" gun position and lack of funnel. Two chaff rocket (CHAFROC) launchers subsequently have been fitted in the "B" position.

TRUXTUN (DLGN 35)

1970, United States Navy

TRUXTUN (DLGN 35)

1968, United States Navy, J01 James Johnson

Surface Combatants—*continued*

9 GUIDED MISSILE FRIGATES (DLG): "BELKNAP" CLASS

		Name	No.	Builder	Laid down	Launched	Commissioned
Displacement, tons	6 570 standard; 7 930 full load	*BELKNAP	DLG 26	Bath Iron Works Corp	5 Feb 1962	20 July 1963	7 Nov 1964
Length, feet (*metres*)	547 (*166·7*) oa	*JOSEPHUS DANIELS	DLG 27	Bath Iron Works Corp	23 Apr 1962	2 Dec 1963	8 May 1965
Beam, feet (*metres*)	54·8 × (*16·7*)	*WAINWRIGHT	DLG 28	Bath Iron Works Corp	2 July 1962	25 Apr 1964	8 Jan 1966
Draft, feet (*metres*)	28·8 (*8·7*)	*JOUETT	DLG 29	Puget Sound Naval Yard	25 Sep 1962	30 June 1964	3 Dec 1966
Missiles	1 twin Terrier/ASROC launcher	*HORNE	DLG 30	San Francisco Naval Yard	12 Dec 1962	30 Oct 1964	15 Apr 1967
ASW weapons	ASROC (see above)	*STERETT	DLG 31	Puget Sound Naval Yard	25 Sep 1962	30 June 1964	8 Apr 1967
	2 triple torpedo launchers (Mk 32)	*WILLIAM H STANDLEY	DLG 32	Bath Iron Works Corp	29 July 1963	19 Dec 1964	9 July 1966
Guns	1—5 in (*127 mm*) 54 cal dual-purpose; 2—3 in (*76 mm*) 50 cal anti-aircraft (single)	*FOX	DLG 33	Todd Shipyard Corp	15 Jan 1963	21 Nov 1964	8 May 1966
		*BIDDLE	DLG 34	Bath Iron Works Corp	9 Dec 1963	2 July 1965	21 Jan 1967
Helicopters	Facilities for helicopters						
Main engines	2 geared turbines (General Electric in DLG 26-28, 32, 34; De Laval in DLG 29-31, 33); 85 000 shp; 2 shafts						
Boilers	4 (Babcock & Wilcox in DLG 26-28, 32, 34; Combustion Engineering in DLG 29-31, 33)						
Speed, knots	34						
Complement	418 (31 officers, 387 enlisted men) including squadron staff						

These ships are considered excellent anti-submarine and anti-air warfare ships, intended to screen fast carrier task forces. The DLG 26-28 were authorised in the Fiscal Year 1961 new construction programme; the DLG 29-34 in FY 1962 programme.

DESIGN. These ships are distinctive by having their single missile launcher forward and 5 inch gun mount aft. This arrangement allowed missile stowage in the larger bow section and provided space aft of the superstructure for a helicopter hangar and platform. The reverse gun-missile arrangement, preferred by some commanding officers, is found in the *Truxtun*. The "Belknap" class ships have their masts and stacks combined into "mack" structures.

ELECTRONICS. SQS-26 bow-mounted sonar installed. These ships have the Naval Tactical Data System (NTDS). Fitted with SPS-48 three-dimensional and SPS-10 search radar antennas on their forward "mack" and an SPS-37 (first three ships) or SPS-40 search radar antenna on their after "mack".

ENGINEERING. These ships have twin 6-bladed screws and a large single rudder providing an excellent degree of manoeuvrability for ships of their size.

GUNNERY. The 5 inch guns were installed previously on forward sponsons of the "Forrestal" class carriers. They are rapid-fire Mk 42 5 inch guns and the 3 inch guns are Mk 34.

HELICOPTERS. These ships and the nuclear-powered *Truxtun* are the only US frigates now operational that have a full helicopter support capability.

MISSILES. The *Truxtun* and "Belknap" class ships have a twin Terrier/ASROC Mk 10 missile launcher. A "triple-ring" rotating magazine stocks both Terrier anti-aircraft missiles and ASROC anti-submarine rockets, feeding either weapon to the launcher's two firing arms. The rate of fire and reliability of the launcher provide a potent AAW/ASW capability to these ships.

TORPEDOES. As built, these ships each had two 21 inch tubes for anti-submarine torpedoes installed in the structure immediately forward of the 5 inch mount, one tube angled out to port and one to starboard; subsequently removed.

JOSEPHUS DANIELS (DLG 27)   *1970, United States Navy, PH1 Dixon M. Dreher*

JOUETT (DLG 29)   *1969, United States Navy, PHI D. L. Nichols*

STERETT (DLG 31)   *1969, United States Navy*

Surface Combatants—*continued*

1 NUCLEAR-POWERED GUIDED MISSILE FRIGATE (DLGN): "BAINBRIDGE" TYPE

Displacement, tons	7 600 standard ; 8 580 full load	*Name*	*No.*	*Builder*	*Laid down* *Launched*	*Commissioned*
Length, feet (*metres*)	550 (*167·6* wl ; 565 (*172·5*) oa	*BAINBRIDGE	DLGN 25	Bethlehem Steel Co (Quincy)	15 May 1959 15 Apr 1961	6 Oct 1962
Beam, feet (*metres*)	57·9 (*17·6*)					
Draft, feet (*metres*)	29 (*7·9*)					
Missiles	2 twin Terrier surface-to-air launchers					
Guns	4—3 in (*76 mm*) 50 calibre anti-aircraft (twin)					
ASW Weapons	1 ASROC 8-tube launcher 2 triple torpedo launchers Mk 32					
Main engines	2 geared turbines ; approx 60 000 shp ; 2 shafts					
Reactors	2 pressurised-water cooled D2G (General Electric)					
Speed, knots	30+					
Complement	approx 450 (26 officers, approx 425 enlisted men)					

The *Bainbridge* was the US Navy's third nuclear-powered surface warship and the world's first "destroyer type" ship to have nuclear propulsion. She is larger than the light anti-aircraft cruisers the United States built during World War II. Authorised in Fiscal Year 1956 shipbuilding programme.
Estimated construction cost was $163 610 000.

DESIGN. Two heavy lattice radar masts are fitted in place of conventional masts and funnels; can be distinguished easily from the *Truxtun* by twin missile launchers forward and aft whereas later ship has 5 inch gun forward.

BAINBRIDGE (DLGN 25)   *1968, United States Navy*

ELECTRONICS. Fitted with SQS-26 bow-mounted sonar.
The *Bainbridge* has SPS-52 three-dimensional search radar and SPS-10 search radar antennas on her forward mast, and an SPS-37 search radar antenna on her after mast.

ENGINEERING. Development of a nuclear power plant suitable for use in a large "destroyer type" warship began in 1957. The Atomic Energy Commission's Knolls Atomic Power Laboratory undertook development of the destroyer power plant (designated D1G/D2G). Because of the developmental nature of this plant, a land-based prototype was constructed in the 225-foot diameter sphere at West Milton, New York, which previously housed the sodium-cooled propulsion plant developed in conjunction with the submarine *Seawolf* (SSN 575). The D1G plant constructed at West Milton consisted of the reactor and machinery for one of the frigate's two shafts. Initial criticality was achieved on 28 Mar 1962 and the reactor first operated at full power on 9 May 1962.

MISSILES. Reportedly, 80 missiles are carried divided between the forward and after Terrier magazines.

MODERNISATION. The *Bainbridge* is scheduled to undergo an anti-air warfare (AAW) modernisation to improve the capabilities of her electronic and missile system. The Naval Tactical Data System (NTDS) will be installed (not already fitted as stated in previous editions). In addition to the *Bainbridge*, the 19 guided missile frigates of the "Leahy" and "Coontz" classes are being modernised under this programme.

BAINBRIDGE (DLGN 25)   *1968. United States Navy*

GRIDLEY (DLG 21)—see following page   *1970, United States Navy*

Surface Combatants—*continued*

9 GUIDED MISSILE FRIGATES (DLG:) "LEAHY" CLASS

	Name	No.	Builder	Laid down	Launched	Commissioned
Displacement, tons	5 670 standard; 7 800 full load					
*LEAHY		DLG 16	Bath Iron Works Corp	3 Dec 1959	1 July 1961	4 Aug 1962
*HARRY E. YARNELL		DLG 17	Bath Iron Works Corp	31 May 1960	9 Dec 1961	2 Feb 1963
*WORDEN		DLG 18	Bath Iron Works Corp	19 Sep 1960	2 June 1962	3 Aug 1963
*DALE		DLG 19	New York SB Corp	6 Sep 1960	28 July 1962	23 Nov 1963
*RICHMOND K. TURNER		DLG 20	New York SB Corp	9 Jan 1961	6 Apr 1963	13 June 1964
*GRIDLEY		DLG 21	Puget Sound B & D Co	15 July 1960	31 July 1961	25 May 1963
*ENGLAND		DLG 22	Todd Shipyards Corp	4 Oct 1960	6 Mar 1962	7 Dec 1963
*HALSEY		DLG 23	San Francisco Naval Yard	26 Aug 1960	15 Jan 1962	20 July 1963
*REEVES		DLG 24	Puget Sound Naval Yard	1 July 1960	12 May 1962	16 May 1964

Displacement, tons — 5 670 standard; 7 800 full load
Length, feet (*metres*) — 533 (*162·5*) oa
Beam, feet (*metres*) — 54·9 (*16·6*)
Draft, feet (*metres*) — 24·5 (*7·4*)
Missiles — 2 twin Terrier surface-to-air launchers
Guns — 4—3 in (*76 mm*) 50 cal anti-aircraft (twin).
ASW Weapons — 1 ASROC 8-tube launcher; 2 triple torpedo launchers (Mk 32)
Main engines — 2 geared turbines (see *Engineering* notes); 85 000 shp; 2 shafts
Boilers — 4 (Babcock & Wilcox in DLG 16-18; Foster Wheeler in DLG 19-24)
Speed, knots — 34
Complement — 396 (31 officers, 365 enlisted men) including squadron staff

These ships are "double-end" missile frigates, especially designed to screen fast carrier task forces. They are limited in having only 3 inch guns in comparison with 5 inch guns of other DLG classes. The DLG 16-18 authorised in the Fiscal Year 1958 new construction programme; DLG 19-24 in the FY 1959 programme.

DESIGN. These ships are distinctive in having twin missile launchers forward and aft with ASROC "pepper box" launcher between the forward missile launcher and bridge on main deck level. Masts and stacks are combined into "macks".

ELECTRONICS. These ships are being fitted with the Naval Tactical Data System (NTDS) during AAW modernisation. SQS-26 bow mounted sonar installed. These ships have SPS-10 and SPS-48 search radar antennas on forward mast (the latter replacing SPS-39 or SPS-52 in some ships) and an SPS-37 search radar antenna on their after mast.
Halsey, Worden, Richard K. Turner and *Reeves* were completed with only two missile directors; four directors (Mk 76) carried after AAW modernisation.

ENGINEERING. General Electric turbines in DLG 16-18; De Laval turbines in DLG 19-22; and Allis-Chalmers turbines in DLG 23 and DLG 24.

MISSILES. Reportedly, each ship carries 80 missiles divided between the two Terrier magazines.

MODERNISATION. These ships are undergoing an anti-air warfare (AAW) modernisation to improve the effectiveness of their electronic and missile systems. The modernisation includes enlarging superstructure to provide space for electronic equipment, installation of NTDS, the Mk 76 fire control system for Terrier and Standard missiles (including SPG-55B radar and Mk 119 computer), and larger ship's service turbo generators. The *Leahy* was modernised at the Philadelphia Naval Shipyard; others at Bath Iron Works, Bath, Maine; the *Leahy* from Feb 1967 to Aug 1968, *Yarnell* from Feb 1968 to May 1969, *Gridley* from Sep 1968 to Jan 1970, *Reeves* from Apr 1969 to May 1970, *Worden* from Nov 1969 to Jan 1971, *England* from Apr 1970 to June 1971, *Dale* from Nov 1970 to Nov 1971, *Richmond K. Turner* from May 1971 to May 1972, and *Halsey* from Nov 1971 to Nov 1972.
Estimated cost of *Leahy* modernisation was $36 100 000.

NOMENCLATURE. The *England* is the second US warship to honour a sailor killed at Pearl Harbour on 7 Dec 1941; the first *England* (DE 635) sank six Japanese submarines in just 12 days during May of 1944.

GRIDLEY (DLG 21)   *1970, United States Navy*

GRIDLEY (DLG 21)   *1970, United States Navy*

REEVES (DLG 24)   *1970, United States Navy*

Surface Combatants—continued
10 GUIDED MISSILE FRIGATES (DLG): "COONTZ" CLASS

	Displacement, tons	4 700 standard; 5 800 full load
	Length, feet (metres)	512·5 (156·2) oa
	Beam, feet (metres)	52·5 (15·9)
	Draft, feet (metres)	25 (7·6)
	Missiles	1 twin Terrier surface-to-air launcher
	Guns	1—5 in (127 mm) 54 cal dual purpose; 4—3 in (76 mm) 50 cal anti-aircraft (twin) (removed in modernised ships)
	ASW Weapons	1 ASROC 8-tube launcher 2 triple torpedo launchers (Mk 32)
	Main engines	2 geared turbines (see Engineering notes); 85 000 shp; 2 shafts
	Boilers	4 (Foster Wheeler in DLG 6-8; Babcock & Wilcox in DLG 9-15)
	Speed, knots	34
	Complement	370 (22 officers, 348 enlisted men)
	Flag Staff	19 (7 officers, 12 enlisted men)

Name	No.	Builder	Laid down	Launched	Commissioned
*FARRAGUT	DLG 6	Bethlehem Co. Quincy	3 June 1967	18 July 1958	10 Dec 1960
*LUCE	DLG 7	Bethlehem Co. Quincy	1 Oct 1957	11 Dec 1958	20 May 1961
*MACDONOUGH	DLG 8	Bethlehem Co. Quincy	15 Apr 1958	9 July 1959	4 Nov 1961
*COONTZ	DLG 9	Puget Sound Naval Yard	1 Mar 1957	6 Dec 1958	15 July 1960
*KING	DLG 10	Puget Sound Naval Yard	1 Mar 1957	6 Dec 1958	17 Nov 1960
*MAHAN	DLG 11	San Francisco Naval Yard	31 July 1957	7 Oct 1959	25 Aug 1960
*DAHLGREN	DLG 12	Philadelphia Naval Yard	1 Mar 1958	16 Mar 1960	8 Apr 1961
*WILLIAM V. PRATT	DLG 13	Philadelphia Naval Yard	1 Mar 1958	16 Mar 1960	4 Nov 1961
*DEWEY	DLG 14	Bath Iron Works. Maine	10 Aug 1957	30 Nov 1958	7 Dec 1959
*PREBLE	DLG 15	Bath Iron Works. Maine	16 Dec 1957	23 May 1959	9 May 1960

FARRAGUT (DLG 6)　　　　　　1970, United States Navy, PHC F. W. Gotavco

These ships are "single-end" missile frigates intended to screen fast carrier task forces. Their design is based on the "Mitscher" class (DL/DDG). The DLG 6-11 were authorised in the Fiscal Year 1956 shipbuilding programme; the DLG 12-15 in FY 1957 programme. Estimated cost per ship was $51 000 000.

CLASSIFICATION. The Farragut, Luce and MacDonough initially were classified as DL 6-8, respectively; changed to DLG. These ships are known officially as the "Coontz" class; the Coontz was the first to be ordered as a DLG (DLG 9-11 ordered on 18 Nov 1955; DLG 6-8 ordered on 27 Jan 1956).

DESIGN. These ships are the only US guided missile "frigates" with separate masts and funnels. They have aluminium superstructures to reduce weight and improve stability. Early designs for this class had a second 5 inch gun mount in the "B" position; design revised when ASROC "pepper box" launcher was developed.

GUNNERY. These ships have Mk 42 5 inch guns and Mk 33 3 inch guns (latter removed during modernisation).

ELECTRONICS. The King and Mahan along with the aircraft carrier Oriskany (CVA 34) were the first ships fitted with the Naval Tactical Data System (NTDS), conducting operational evaluation of the equipment in 1961-1962.
As completed these ships had an SPS-10 and three-dimensional SPS-39 search radar antennas on their forward mast, and an SPS-37 search radar antenna and TACAN (Tactical Aircraft Navigation) "bee hive" antenna on second mast. Prior to AAW modernisation some ships had the SPS-39 replaced with the SPS-52 radar. During modernisation the SPS-48 three-dimensional search radar is fitted on the forward mast, an improved TACAN "pod" is fitted on the second mast, and NTDS installed.
These ships have SQS-23 sonar.
The Coontz was fitted with the SSM-5 Test Evaluation and Monitoring System (TEAMS) in 1968 for operational evaluation of the electronic check-out system. See Knox (DE 1052) for details.

ENGINEERING. De Laval turbines in DLG 6-8 and DLG 15; Allis-Chalmers turbines in DLG 9-14.

MISSILES. The first five ships of this class were built with Terrier BW-1 beam-riding missile systems; five later ships built with Terrier BT-3 homing missile systems. See Modernisation notes for conversion of earlier ships to improved missile capability. Reportedly, each ship carries 40 missiles.

FARRAGUT (DLG 6)　　　　　　1970, United States Navy, PHCS W. H. Long

PREBLE (DLG 15)　　　　　　　　　　　　1970, United States Navy, Joseph P. Garfinkel

Surface Combatants—*continued*

"COONTZ" CLASS—*continued*

MODERNISATION. These ships all are undergoing anti-air warfare (AAW) modernisations to improve the effectiveness of their electronic and missile systems. All modernised at the Philadelphia Naval Shipyard: *Farragut* from May 1968 to Feb 1970, *Preble* from Jan 1969 to Apr 1970, *Dewey* from Nov 1969 to Mar 1971, *Luce* from Feb 1970 to May 1971, *Coontz* from Feb 1971 to May 1972. Modernisation of others to follow.

The modernisation includes enlarging superstructure to provide space for electronic equipment, installation of NTDS and improved TACAN, converting first five ships to improve guidance capability for Terrier and, Standard missiles (Mk 76 fire control system), provision of larger ships service turbo generators, and removal of twin 3 inch gun mounts.

The *Farragut* also had ASROC reload capability provided and second mast increased in height (see photographs). These modifications are not anticipated for the other ships. Estimated cost of modernisation is $39 000 000 per ship in FY 1970 programme.

NOMENCLATURE. The DLG 7 was to have been named *Dewey*, named *Luce* in 1957.

PHOTOGRAPHS. Note 3 inch gun "tubs" aft of motor launch in photograph of *Dahlgren*.

DAHLGREN (DLG 12)   1969, *United States Navy, PHC B. M. Anderson*

She has improved TACAN "pod" and large SPS-52 three-dimensional search radar installed prior to AAW modernisation. Note ASROC reload structure in front of *Farragut's* bridge.

2 FRIGATES (DL): "MITSCHER" CLASS

Name	No.	Builder	Laid down	Launched	Commissioned
WILLIS A. LEE	DL 4	Bethlehem Steel Co (Quincy)	1 Nov 1949	26 Jan 1952	5 Oct 1954
WILKINSON	DL 5	Bethlehem Steel Co (Quincy)	1 Feb 1950	23 Apr 1952	3 Aug 1954

Displacement, tons	3 675 standard; 4 730 full load
Length, feet (*metres*)	493 (*150·3*) oa
Beam, feet (*metres*)	50 (*15·2*)
Draft, feet (*metres*)	26 (*7·9*)
Guns	2—5 in (*127 mm*) 54 calibre dual-purpose (single)
ASW weapons	2 triple torpedo launchers (Mk 32) 4 torpedo tubes (Mk 23)
Helicopters	Facilities for helicopters
Main engines	2 geared turbines (Westinghouse) 80 000 shp; 2 shafts
Speed, knots	35
Boilers	4—1 200 psi (*84·4 kg/cm²*) (Foster Wheeler)

Four ships of this class of "destroyer leaders" were completed in 1953-54; two ships subsequently were converted to guided missile destroyers: *Mitscher* (DL 2/DDG 35) and *John S. McCain* (DL 3/DDG 36). Both ships were decommissioned on 20 Dec 1969 and placed in reserve. Although fitted with the large SQS-26 sonar, they lacked advanced ASW weapons and fire control equipment to justify their being kept in active service during the Fleet reductions of 1969-1970.

CLASSIFICATION. These ships were originally classified as destroyers (DD 929 and 930 respectively); reclassified as destroyer leaders (DL 4 and 5) on 9 Feb 1951 while under construction; the symbol DL was changed to frigate on 1 Jan 1955.

DESIGN The "Mitscher" class was the first group of destroyer-type ships built by the United States after World War II. The design provided for potent anti-air and anti-submarine capabilities in a ship which could accompany fast carrier task forces. Accommodations and communications equipment provided for a destroyer flotilla or squadron commander.

GUNNERY. As built these ships each had two Mk 42 5 inch/54 calibre guns and four 3 inch/50 calibre guns (plus two 12·75 inch Weapon Able ASW rocket launchers and four fixed 21 inch ASW torpedo tubes). Rapid-fire 3 inch/70 calibre guns were mounted in place of the original 3 inch weapons in 1957-1958. After twin 3 inch mount removed to provide helicopter platform; forward twin 3 inch mount subsequently deleted, leaving only 5 inch armament.

ELECTRONICS. SQS-26 bow-mounted sonar installed, but prototype sonars and not integrated with ASW fire control system.

These ships had SPS-10 and SPS-29 search radar antennas and TACAN on their forward mast and an SPS-8 height-finding radar antenna atop after deckhouse in their final configuration.

WILLIS A. LEE (DL 4)   1967, *United States Navy by PH3 W. F. Bradshaw*

WILKINSON (DL 5)   1968, *United States Navy*

Surface Combatants—*continued*

1 FRIGATE (DL): "NORFOLK" TYPE

Name	No.	Builder	Laid down	Launched	Commissioned
NORFOLK	DL 1 (ex-CLK 1)	New York Shipbuilding Corp	1 Sep 1949	29 Dec 1951	4 Mar 1953

Displacement, tons	5 600 standard ; 7 300 full load
Length, feet (*metres*)	540·2 (*164·6*) oa
Beam, feet (*metres*)	54·2 (*16·5*)
Draft, feet (*metres*)	26 (*7·9*)
Guns	8—3 in (*76 mm*) 70 cal. dual purpose
ASW Weapons	1 ASROC 8-tube launcher
	2 triple torpedo launchers (Mk 32)
Main engines	2 geared turbines (General Electric) ; 80 000 shp ; 2 shafts
Boilers	4—1 200 psi (*84·4 kg/cm²*) (Babcock & Wilcox)
Speed, knots	32
Complement	411 (26 officers, 385 enlisted men)

The Norfolk was one of two cruiser-size anti-submarine ("killer") ships authorised in 1948. Their size was to provide a rough-weather, long-range ASW capability. Construction of the CLK 2 was deferred on 2 Mar 1949 and cancelled on 9 Feb 1951 ; her keel was not laid down. She was to have been named *New Haven*.

The *Norfolk* was decommissioned in 1969 and placed in reserve.

ASW WEAPONS. The *Norfolk* was originally armed with four Weapon Alfa (formerly Weapon Able) rocket launchers. The two launchers aft of the second funnel have been replaced by an ASROC rocket launcher. The *Norfolk* has served as test ship for ASW equipment and was the primary test ship for ASROC. (Original armament included fixed torpedo tubes, but not the two triple torpedo launchers now installed on the main deck alongside the bridge structure).

CLASSIFICATION. The *Norfolk* was reclassified as a Destroyer Leader (DL 1) on 9 Feb 1951 while under construction ; the symbol DL having been changed to Frigate on 1 Jan 1955. While engaged in experimental work she was designated EDL 1.

DESIGN. The *Norfolk* was the first ship fully designed and built by the US Navy after World War II. She has a cruiser hull similar in size to the anti-aircraft cruisers (CLAA) but with a distinctive design including a clipper bow.

ELECTRONICS. An SQS-23 anti-submarine sonar was installed in 1958, the first ship so fitted.

ENGINEERING. The *Norfolk* reached 35 knots on trials ; six-bladed propellers.

GUNNERY. Original gun armament consisted of eight 3 inch/50 calibre guns in twin open mounts and eight 20 mm guns. Faster-firing 3 inch/70s in enclosed mounts were fitted and the lighter weapons were removed. The 3 inch guns are Mk 23 weapons, of a type previously installed in the "Mitscher" class frigates and "Carpenter" class destroyers. They are credited with a rate of fire of 95 rounds per minute.

MISSILES. Conversion to a Terrier DLG configuration was considered, but dropped.

NOMENCLATURE. The *Norfolk* retains her cruiser name ; the only ship in the destroyer "family" named for a city.

PHOTOGRAPHS. Note that the two forward Weapon Alfa ASW rocket launchers previously installed forward of bridge in super-firing position have been removed.

NORFOLK (DL 1)   *1969, United States Navy*

NORFOLK (DL 1)   *1968, United States Navy*

GUIDED MISSILE DESTROYERS (DDG): FORMER DXG TYPE

These ships were a planned variation of the DD 963 class all-gun destroyers but with an improved anti-aircraft capability afforded by a Tartar-D surface-to-air missile system.
Initial Department of Defense planning called for 28 ships of this design. However, construction of these ships was not proposed in the Fiscal Year 1971 shipbuilding programme as previously anticipated. In view of the increasing cost estimates of the non-missile DD 963 class ships *prior* to the start of their construction, and probable new destroyer concepts, this class apparently will not be built. (The missile-armed DDG ships

would, of course have been more expensive than the "straight" DD ships).
The planned DDG/DXG programme provided for a ship similar in many respects to the DD 963 class ships to reduce design and construction costs. The missile-armed design would be similar to the DD type, but somewhat larger. Other differences are noted below.

ELECTRONICS. The Aegis advanced detection and missile guidance radars tentatively were planned for these

ships (formerly designated ASMS for Advanced Surface Missile System). Development of the advanced surface-to-air missile component of Aegis has been deferred.

GUNNERY. These ships were to be armed with one improved 5 inch (*127 mm*) 54 calibre dual-purpose gun (compared to two in the DD 963 class).

MISSILES. These ships were to have a Tartar-D missile system firing the new Standard missile to provided area defence.

Surface Combatants—*continued*

2 GUIDED MISSILE DESTROYERS (DDG): CONVERTED "MITSCHER" CLASS

Name	No.	Builder	Laid down	Launched	DL Comm.	DDG Comm.
*MITSCHER	DDG 35 (ex-DL 2)	Bath Iron Works	3 Oct 1949	26 Jan 1952	15 May 1953	29 June 1968
*JOHN S. McCAIN	DDG 36 (ex-DL 3)	Bath Iron Works	24 Oct 1949	12 July 1952	12 Oct 1953	21 June 1969

Displacement, tons	5 155 full load
Length, feet (*metres*)	493 (*150·3*) oa
Beam, feet (*metres*)	50 (*15·2*)
Draft, feet (*metres*)	26 (*7·9*)
Missiles	1 single Tartar surface-to-air launcher
Guns	2—5 inch (*127 mm*) 54 calibre dual-purpose (single)
ASW weapons	1 ASROC 8-tube launcher 2 triple torpedo launchers (Mk 32)
Main engines	2 geared turbines (General Electric); 80 000 shp; 2 shafts
Speed, knots	35
Boilers	4 — 1 225 psi (*86·1 kg/cm²*) (Combustion Engineering)
Complement	378 (29 officers, 349 enlisted men).

These ships are former "Mitscher" class all-gun frigates which have been converted to a guided missile and improved ASW configuration. They were reclassified as guided missile "destroyers" rather than frigates because of Tartar armament. The *Mitscher* and *John S. McCain* were reclassified as DDG on 15 Mar 1967. See "Mitscher" class for additional notes.

CONVERSION. Both ships were converted to DDG at the Philadelphia Naval Shipyard. The *Mitscher* began conversion in March 1966 and the *John S. McCain* in June 1966. Superstructure was modified with ASROC launcher installed forward of the bridge in "B" position; two heavy lattice masts fitted; triple Mk 32 torpedo launchers retained amidships; and single Tartar Mk 13 launched installed aft (system weighs approximately 135 000 pounds).

ELECTRONICS. SQS-23 sonar installed; SPS-10 and SPS-37 search radar antennae on forward mast and SPS-48 three-dimensional search radar antenna on after mast.

GUNNERY. The original Mk 42 gun mounts have been replaced by modified Mk 42 mounts with local anti-aircraft controls deleted (starboard "bubble" or "frog-eye" on mount removed; port dome is for local anti-surface control).

NOMENCLATURE. Vice Admirals Marc A. Mitscher and John S. McCain commanded the US Navy's fast carrier task forces in the Pacific War during 1943-1945 (Task Forces 38 and 58 of the US Third and Fifth Fleets).

PHOTOGRAPHS. Note rounded bridge facing of *Mitscher*. These ships can be distinguished from the "Forrest Sherman" class DDG conversions at a distance by the larger ships' ASROC launcher in the "B" position and the second 5 inch gun aft. Note old-style TACAN "bee-hive" antenna.

Two photographs of the *Mitscher* appear in the 1970-1971 edition.

JOHN S. McCAIN (DDG 36)　　　　　　*1969, United States Navy*

JOHN S. McCAIN (DDG 36)　　　　　　*1969, United States Navy*

DECATUR (DDG 31). See following page　　　　　　*1968, United States Navy*

Surface Combatants—*continued*

4 GUIDED MISSILE DESTROYERS (DDG): CONVERTED "FORREST SHERMAN" CLASS

Name	No.	Builder	Laid down	Launched	DD Comm.	DDG Comm.
*DECATUR	DDG 31 (ex-DD 936)	Bethlehem Steel Co (Quincy)	13 Sep 1954	15 Dec 1955	7 Dec 1956	29 Apr 1967
*JOHN PAUL JONES	DDG 32 (ex-DD 932)	Bath Iron Works	18 Jan 1954	7 May 1955	5 Apr 1956	23 Sep 1967
*PARSONS	DDG 33 (ex-DD 949)	Ingalls Shipbuilding Corp	17 June 1957	19 Aug 1958	29 Oct 1959	3 Nov 1967
*SOMERS	DDG 34 (ex-DD 947)	Bath Iron Works	4 Mar 1957	30 May 1958	3 Apr 1959	10 Feb 1968

Displacement, tons	4 150 full load
Length, feet (*metres*)	
DDG 31-32	418·4 (*127·5*) oa
DDG 33-34	418 (*127·4*) oa
Beam, feet (*metres*)	
DDG 31-32	45·2 (*13·8*)
DDG 33-34	45 (*13·7*)
Draft, feet (*metres*)	20 (*6·1*)
Missiles	1 single Tartar surface-to-air launcher
Guns	1—5 inch (*127 mm*) 54 calibre dual-purpose
ASW weapons	1 ASROC 8-tube launcher 2 triple torpedo launchers (Mk 32)
Main engines	2 geared turbines (Westinghouse in *John Paul Jones*; General Electric in others); 70 000 shp; 2 shafts
Boilers	4 (Foster Wheeler in *Decatur* and *Parsons*; Babcock & Wilcox in *John Paul Jones* and *Somers*)
Speed	33 knots
Complement	335 (22 officers, 313 enlisted men)

These four ships are former "Forrest Sherman" class destroyers that have been converted to a guided missile and improved ASW configuration. Plans for additional DDG conversions of this class were dropped (the *Turner Joy*, DD 951, was to have been the fifth missile ship of this type). The *Decatur* was reclassified as DDG 31 on 15 Sep 1966; the *John Paul Jones*, *Somers*, and *Parsons* became DDG on 15 Mar 1967. See "Forrest Sherman" class for additional notes.

CONVERSION. The *Decatur* began conversion to a DDG at the Boston Naval Shipyard on 15 June 1965, the *John Paul Jones* at the Philadelphia Naval Shipyard on 2 Dec 1965, the *Parsons* at the Long Beach (California) Naval Shipyard on 30 June 1965, and the *Somers* at the San Francisco Bay Naval Shipyard on 30 Mar 1966. During conversion all existing armament was removed except the forward 5 inch gun; two triple ASW torpedo launchers were installed forward of the bridge; two heavy lattice masts fitted; ASROC launcher mounted aft of second stack; single Tartar Mk 13 launcher installed aft (on 01 level; system weighs approximately 135 000 pounds).
Original DDG conversion plans provided for Drone Anti-Submarine Helicopter (DASH) facilities; however, ASROC was substituted in all four ships as DASH lost favour in the Navy.

ELECTRONICS. SQS-23 sonar installed; SPS-10 and SPS-40 or SPS-37 search radar antenna on forward mast and SPS-48 three-dimensional search radar antenna on after mast.

GUNNERY. The original Mk 42 forward gun mount has been replaced by a modified Mk 42 mount with the local anti-aircraft control deleted (starboard "bubble" or "frog-eye" on mount removed; port dome is for local anti-surface control).

NOMENCLATURE. The *John Paul Jones* honours the Scottish-born father of the American Navy who later served as a rear-admiral in the Russian Navy (1788).

PHOTOGRAPHS. Note SPS-37 radar antenna on *Parsons*; hangar structure aft originally intended for drone helicopters (DASH).

SOMERS (DDG 34)   1969, US Navy, PH2 Stanley C. Wyckoff

PARSONS (DDG 33)   1968, United States Navy

PARSONS (DDG 33)   1970, United States Navy

Surface Combatants—*continued*

23 GUIDED MISSILE DESTROYERS (DDG): "CHARLES F. ADAMS" CLASS

Displacement, tons	3 370 standard; 4 500 full load				
Length, feet (*metres*)	437 (*132·8*) oa				
Beam, feet (*metres*)	47 (*14·3*)				
Draft, feet (*metres*)	20 (*6·1*)				
Missiles DDG 2-14	1 twin Tartar surface-to-air launcher				
DDG 15-24	1 single Tartar surface-to-air launchers				
Guns	2—5 in (*127 mm*) 54 cal dual-purpose				
ASW Weapons	1 ASROC 8-tube launcher				
	2 triple torpedo launchers (Mk 32)				
Main engines	2 geared steam turbines (General Electric in DDG 2, 3, 7, 8, 10-13, 15-22; Westinghouse in DDG 4-6, 9, 14, 23, 24); 70 000 shp; 2 shafts				
Boilers	4 (Babcock & Wilcox in DDG 2, 3, 7, 8, 10-13, 20-22; Foster Wheeler in DDG 4-6, 9, 14; Combustion Engineering in DDG 15-19)				
Speed, knots	35				
Complement	354 (24 officers, 330 enlisted men)				

Name	No.	Builder	Laid down	Launched	Commissioned
*CHARLES F. ADAMS	DDG 2	Bath Iron Wotks	16 June 1958	8 Sep 1959	10 Sep 1960
*JOHN KING	DDG 3	Bath Iron Works	25 Aug 1958	30 Jan 1960	4 Feb 1961
*LAWRENCE	DDG 4	New York Shipbuilding Corp	27 Oct 1958	27 Feb 1960	6 Jan 1962
*CLAUDE V. RICKETTS	DDG 5	New York Shipbuilding Corp	18 May 1959	4 June 1960	6 Jan 1962
*BARNEY	DDG 6	New York Shipbuilding Corp	18 May 1959	10 Dec 1960	11 Aug 1962
*HENRY B. WILSON	DDG 7	Defoe Shipbuilding Co	28 Feb 1958	23 Apr 1959	17 Dec 1960
*LYNDE McCORMICK	DDG 8	Defoe Shipbuilding Co	4 Apr 1958	9 Sep 1960	3 June 1961
*TOWERS	DDG 9	Todd Shipyards Inc, Seattle	1 Apr 1958	23 Apr 1959	6 June 1961
*SAMPSON	DDG 10	Bath Iron Works	2 Mar 1959	9 Sep 1960	24 June 1961
*SELLERS	DDG 11	Bath Iron Works	3 Aug 1959	9 Sep 1960	28 Oct 1961
*ROBISON	DDG 12	Defoe Shipbuilding Co	23 Apr 1959	27 Apr 1960	9 Dec 1961
*HOEL	DDG 13	Defoe Shipbuilding Co	1 June 1960	4 Aug 1960	16 June 1962
*BUCHANAN	DDG 14	Todd Shipyards Inc, Seattle	23 Apr 1959	11 May 1960	7 Feb 1962
*BERKELEY	DDG 15	New York Shipbuilding Corp	1 June 1960	29 July 1961	15 Dec 1962
*JOSEPH STRAUSS	DDG 16	New York Shipbuilding Corp	27 Dec 1960	9 Dec 1961	20 Apr 1963
*CONYNGHAM	DDG 17	New York Shipbuilding Corp	1 May 1961	19 May 1962	13 July 1963
*SEMMES	DDG 18	Avondale Marine Ways Inc	18 Aug 1960	20 May 1961	10 Dec 1962
*TATTNALL	DDG 19	Avondale Marine Ways Inc	14 Nov 1960	26 Aug 1961	13 Apr 1963
*GOLDSBOROUGH	DDG 20	Puget Sound B & DD Co	3 Jan 1961	15 Dec 1961	9 Nov 1963
*COCHRANE	DDG 21	Puget Sound B & DD Co	31 July 1961	18 July 1962	21 Mar 1964
*BENJAMIN STODDERT	DDG 22	Puget Sound B & DD Co	11 June 1962	8 Jan 1963	12 Sep 1964
*RICHARD E. BYRD	DDG 23	Todd Shipyards Inc, Seattle	12 Apr 1961	6 Feb 1962	7 Mar 1964
*WADDELL	DDG 24	Todd Shipyards Inc, Seattle	6 Feb 1962	26 Feb 1963	28 Aug 1964

These destroyers are considered excellent multi-purpose ships. The DDG 2-9 were authorised in the Fiscal Year 1957 new construction programme, DDG 10-14 in FY 1958, DDG 15-19 in FY 1959, DDG 20-22 in FY 1960, DDG 23 and DDG 24 in FY 1961. Three additional ships of this design have been built in US shipyards for Australia (DDG 25-27) and three for West Germany (DDG 28-30).

CLASSIFICATION. The first eight ships were initially assigned hull numbers in the standard DD series (DDG 952-959); renumbered while under construction. The DDG 1 was the *Gyatt* (ex-DD 712), which operated as a missile destroyer from 1956 to 1962.

DESIGN. These ships were built to an improved "Forrest Sherman" class design with aluminium superstructures and a high level of habitability including air conditioning in all living spaces. They do not have the second radar trellis mast nor secondary gun battery of the earlier class. DDG 20-24 have stem anchors because of sonar arrangements.

Several ships have been modified with an extension of the bridge structure on the starboard side on the 02 level, providing additional space for storage (DDG 2, 6, 10, 18, and other ships).

ELECTRONICS. DDG 20-24 have bow-mounted SQS-23 sonar; earlier ships have SQS-23 sonar with hull domes.

DDG 2-14 have SPS-37 and SPS-10 search radar antennae on tripod mast; DDG 15-24 have SPS-40 and SPS-10 antennae. All ships apparently being fitted with SPS-52 three-dimensional search radar antenna on second stack platform; these ships were completed with SPS-39 radar antenna aft.

The *Towers* is the first US Navy ship to be fitted with the Ship Anti-Missile Integrated Defence (SAMID) to counter the Soviet cruise missile threat (Styx, etc); this system integrates existing electronic equipment and weapons to reduce reaction time when under attack. Also fitted with chaff rockets (CHAFFROC).

GUNNERY. These ships have rapid-fire Mk 42 guns. The *Charles F. Adams* has modified mounts with local anti-aircraft controls deleted (starboard "bubble" or "frog-eye" on mounts removed; port dome is for local anti-surface control).

JOHN KING (DDG 3)   *1969, United States Navy*

HENRY B. WILSON (DDG 7)   *1969, United States Navy*

RICHARD E. BYRD (DDG 23)   *1970, Anthony & Joseph Pavia*

Surface Combatants—*continued*

"C. F. ADAMS" CLASS   *continued*

MISSILES. The DDG 2-14 have a twin Mk 11 Tartar missile launcher while the DDG 15-24 have a single Mk 13 Tartar launcher. The Mk 11 launcher installation weighs 165 240 pounds while the Mk 13 weighs only 132 561 pounds. Reportedly, their magazine capacities are 42 and 40 missiles, respectively, and ships equipped with either launcher can load, direct, and fire about six missiles per minute. (The twin Mk 11 launcher is installed in the cruisers CG 10-12; the "Mitscher" and "Forrest Sherman" DDG conversions have a similar Mk 13 launcher which weighs approximately 135 000 pounds).

NOMENCLATURE. The DDG 5 was originally named *Biddle*; renamed *Claude V. Ricketts* on 28 July 1964 to honour the late Vice Chief of Naval Operations who had supported multi-national NATO manning of ballistic missile surface ships. (The name *Biddle* subsequently was assigned to the DLG 34). The DDG 23 honours the famed polar explorer and naval aviator.

PHOTOGRAPHS. In the accompanying illustrations the *John King, Barney, Henry B. Wilson,* and *Robison* have SPS-37 and SPS-52 radar antennae; the *Richard E. Byrd* has SPS-40 and SPS-52 antennae.

ROBISON (DDG 12)   *1968, United States Navy*

RICHARD E. BYRD (DDG 23)   *1970, United States Navy, PH3 W. S. Koenig*

BARNEY (DDG 6)   *1970, United States Navy*

Surface Combatants—*continued*

9 + 7 DESTROYERS (DD) "SPRUANCE" CLASS (FORMERLY DX TYPE)

	Displacement, tons	6 900 full load
	Length, feet (*metres*)	560 (*171·0*)
	Beam, feet (*metres*)	54 (*16·4*)
	Draft, feet (*metres*)	28 (*8·6*)
	Helicopters	Facilities for helicopters
	Missiles	Basic Point Defence Missile System (BPDMS) with Sea Sparrow missiles
	Guns	2—5 inch (*127 mm*) 54 calibre light-weight Mk 45 (single)
	ASW weapons	1 ASROC 8-tube launcher torpedo launchers (Mk 32)
	Main engines	4 gas turbines (General Electric) approx 80 000 shp; 2 shafts
	Speed, knots	30+
	Complement	approx 270

Name	No.	Start Erection	Launch	Commission
SPRUANCE	DD 963	Feb 1973	Jan 1974	late 1974
	DD 964	Aug 1973	mid- 1974	early 1975
	DD 965	Nov 1973	late 1974	mid-1975
DD 966	**DD 968**	**DD 970**		
DD 967	**DD 969**	**DD 971**	**DD 972-978** Proposed FY 1972	

These ships are intended as replacements for the large number of World War II-built destroyers that have undergone extensive modernisation (FRAM) to enable them to serve into the 1970s. According to official statements: "The primary mission of these ships is anti-submarine warfare including operations as an integral part of attack carrier task forces. They also have the capability for shore bombardment and for surface warfare, and will have short range missiles for defense against airborne threats, including enemy missiles. Their effectiveness against submarines is expected to be far greater, particularly at high speeds, than that of current Navy ships due to ship silencing techniques and improved sea-keeping capabilities."
(Also see *Status* notes below).

The Fiscal Year 1969 new construction programme proposed by the Department of Defence requested funding for the first five ships of this class; however, funds were denied by the Congress because of the design status. In the FY 1970 programme the Congress approved funds for five ships, but increasing costs forced the Department of Defence to construct only three ships under the FY 1970 programme (DD 963-965); six ships were authorised in the FY 1971 programme (DD 966-971); and seven ships (DD 972-978) were requested in the FY 1972 programme.
All ships of this class will be built by the Ingalls West shipbuilding facility of Litton Industries at Pascagoula, Mississippi. (See *Construction* notes below).

CONSTRUCTION. The Navy made contract definition awards for the DD 963 class on 3 July 1968 to three shipbuilders: Bath Iron Works Corp, Bath, Maine ($10 500 000); General Dynamics Corp, Quincy, Massachusetts ($9 000 000); and Litton Industries, Pascagoula, Mississippi ($9 000 000) Based on their design and cost proposals, a contract for the development and production of the *entire* DD 963 class was awarded to Litton Industries (Ingalls West Division) on 23 June 1970.

CLASSIFICATION During the early proposal stage these ships were designated as the DX project, the letter "X" signifying that the characteristics were not fully defined.
DD 952-959 initially were assigned to the missile-armed DDG 2-9; DD 960 and DD 961 were assigned to the Japanese *Akizuki* and *Teruzuki*, respectively built with US military aid; DD 962 was assigned to HMS *Charity*, purchased from Great Britain in 1958 and transferred to Pakistan (*Shah Jahan*).

DESIGN. Extensive use of the modular concept is used to facilitate initial construction and bloc modernisation of the ships.
The ships will be highly automated, resulting in about 20 per cent reduction in personnel over a similar ship with conventional systems.

ELECTRONICS. These ships will have SQS-26 sonar and will be the first US warships with a completely digital command and control system. which will reduce complexity and speed up production. (Most existing systems have a mixture of digital and analog components). Advanced electronic countermeasure (ECM) equipment, will be fitted.
To be fitted with SPS-40A and SPS-55 radars, SQS-26CX sonar, and Mk 116 underwater fire control system. The Combat Information Centre (CIC) will provide a centralised location for information and displays for all sensor and weapon systems.
Chaff rocket (CHAFROC) launchers fitted atop bridge, aft of second mast, and at stern.
Provision in stern for eventual installation of SQS-35 variable depth sonar.
Fire control systems for guns are Mk 86.

GUNNERY. These ships may have the 5 inch 54 calibre. light-weight Mk 45 gun. An improved 5 inch/54 calibre Mk 65 gun is being considered for use on later ships in this series.

ENGINEERING. These ships will be the first large US warships to employ gas turbine propulsion. Each ship will have four General Electric LM2500 marine gas turbine engines, a shaft-power version of the TF39 turbofan aircraft engine. Each LM2500 is rated at approximately 20 000 horsepower. The gas turbine was selected because of comparatively low operating costs, smaller space requirements, rapid replacement capability, and cold-start capability (the engines can go from "cold iron" to full power in 12 minutes).
These ships will have controllable-pitch propellers because gas turbine engines cannot use a reversable shaft; to be fitted with advanced self-noise reduction features.
During normal operations these ships will "steam" on two engines, going to three and then four engines for higher speeds.
Endurance is estimated at 6 000 miles at 20 knots.

FISCAL. Under the FY 1969 new construction programme the Congress appropriated $25 000 000 for advanced procurement for the first five ships of this class and completed their funding in FY 1970 with $317 700 000 plus $17 600 000 for advanced procurement for eight ships scheduled for the FY 1971 programme. However. by early 1970 it appeared that these ships would cost "considerably higher than estimated" with anticipated cost of the first five ships increasing from $343 000 000 to $480 000 000; consequently, the Department of Defence decided to construct only three ships with FY 1970 funds ($308 600 000 estimate) and propose the FY 1971 programme of only six ships ($506 800 000 estimate), with $459 500 000 being requested in FY 1971 to complete these six ships. Under this plan $51 700 000 approved by the Congress for the FY 1970 ships and not spent would be used for advanced procurement of FY 1971 and 1972 ships.
The average cost per ship is officially estimated at $85 000 000 but more likely will be in excess of $100 000 000 per ship.

MISSILES. These ships are intended to have the Basic Point Defense Missile System (BPDMS) firing the Sea Sparrow missile from an eight-tube launcher. This will provide a terminal defence capability for the ship against aircraft and some anti-ship missiles; however, BPDMS is not an area or task force defence system.

NOMENCLATURE. The *Spruance* is named for Admiral Raymond A. Spruance, who had tactical command of the US carriers in the Battle of Midway (June 1942)

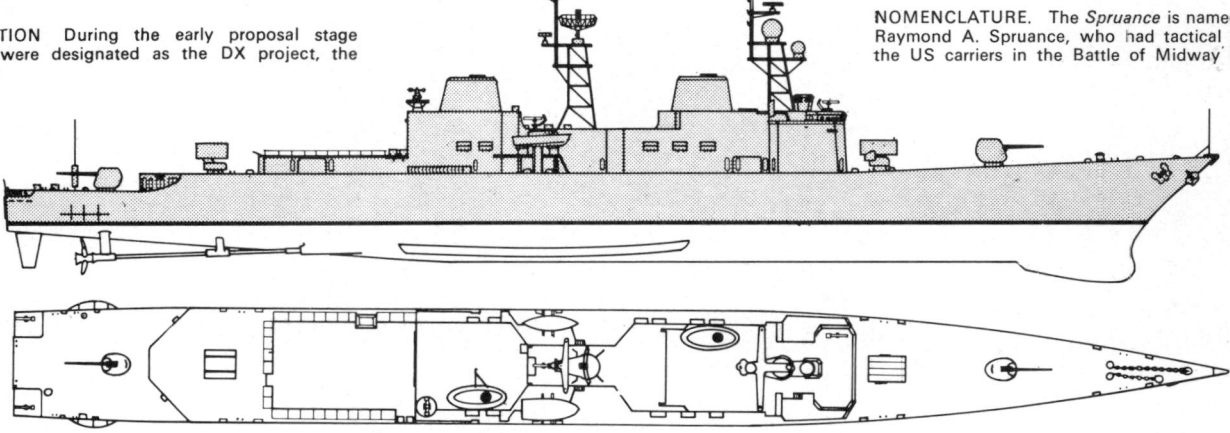

SPRUANCE (DD 963)

Artist's Concept

"SPRUANCE" CLASS — *continued*

and of the US fleet in the Battle of the Marianas (June 1954), two of the major engagements of the Pacific War. He also was considered one of the leading intellectuals of the US Navy.

STATUS. These ships have been criticised by some authorities as being inferior in weapons and general combat capabilities to several foreign contemporaries and earlier ships that are smaller in size, particularly the Soviet "Kresta," "Kynda", and "Kashin" classes. The 1971 prize essayist of the US Naval Institute, Captain Robert H. Smith, US Navy, has described the ships as "even on paper . . . inferior to competitive Soviet ships already alive on the sea".
In view of current US Navy efforts to develop the so-called Air Capable Ship (tentatively designated DH) and plans for new series of ships in the "Patrol" category,

the question has been raised of whether or not the entire "Spruance" class will be constructed in the numbers planned.

PHOTOGRAPH. Artist's concept has been "reversed" with funnels being placed starboard and port going from bow to stern; drawings are based on official design model.

Surface Combatants—*continued*

14 DESTROYERS (DD) "FORREST SHERMAN" CLASS

Name	No	Builder	Laid down	Launched	Commissioned
*FORREST SHERMAN	DD 931	Bath Iron Works	27 Oct 1953	5 Feb 1955	9 Nov 1955
*BARRY	DD 933	Bath Iron Works	15 Mar 1954	1 Oct 1955	31 Aug 1956
*DAVIS	DD 937	Bethlehem Steel Co (Quincy)	1 Feb 1955	28 Mar 1956	28 Feb 1957
*JONAS INGRAM	DD 938	Bethlehem Steel Co (Quincy)	15 June 1955	8 July 1956	19 July 1957
*MANLEY	DD 940	Bath Iron Works	10 Feb 1955	12 Apr 1956	1 Feb 1957
*DU PONT	DD 941	Bath Iron Works	11 May 1955	8 Sep 1956	1 July 1957
*BIGELOW	DD 942	Bath Iron Works	6 July 1955	2 Feb 1957	8 Nov 1957
*BLANDY	DD 943	Bethlehem Steel Co (Quincy)	29 Dec 1955	19 Dec 1956	26 Nov 1957
*MULLINNIX	DD 944	Bethlehem Steel Co (Quincy)	5 Apr 1956	18 Mar 1957	7 Mar 1958
*HULL	DD 945	Bath Iron Works	12 Sep 1956	10 Aug 1957	3 July 1958
*EDSON	DD 946	Bath Iron Works	3 Dec 1956	1 Jan 1958	7 Nov 1958
*MORTON	DD 948	Ingalls Shipbuilding Corp	4 Mar 1957	23 May 1958	26 May 1959
*RICHARD S. EDWARDS	DD 950	Puget Sound Bridge & DD	20 Dec 1956	24 Sep 1957	5 Feb 1959
*TURNER JOY	DD 951	Puget Sound Bridge & DD	30 Sep 1957	5 May 1958	3 Aug 1959

Displacement tons	
DD 931-944	2 780 standard; 3 950 full load
DD 945-951	2 850 standard; 4 050 full load
Length, feet (*metres*)	
DD 931-944	418·4 (*127·5*) oa
except DD 933	425
DD 945-951	418 (*127·4*) oa
Beam, feet (*metres*)	
DD 931-944	45·2 (*13·8*)
DD 945-951	45 (*13·7*)
Draft, feet (*metres*)	20 (*6·1*)
Guns ASW Mod	2—5 in (*127 mm*) 54 calibre dual-purpose
Others	3—5 in (*127 mm*) 54 calibre dual-purpose; 2 or 4—3 in (*76 mm*) 50 calibre anti-aircraft (twin)
ASW weapons	
ASW Mod	1 ASROC 8-tube launcher 2 triple torpedo launchers (Mk 32)
Others	2 hedgehogs; depth charges retained in a few ships 2 triple torpedo launchers (Mk 32)
Main engines	2 geared turbines (Westinghouse in DD 931 and 933; General Electric in others); 70,000 shp; 2 shafts
Boilers	4 (Babcock & Wilcox in DD 931 and 933, 940-942, 945, 946, 950, 951; Foster Wheeler in others)
Speed	33 knots
Complement	292 (17 officers, 275 enlisted men) in unmodified ships; 340 (17 officers, 287 enlisted men) in ASW Mod ships

These ships were the first US destroyers of post-World War II design and construction. Four have been converted to a guided missile configuration and are listed separately. They were authorised in the Fiscal Year 1952-1956 new construction programmes.
(The hull number DD 934 was reserved for the ex-Japanese *Hanazuki*, DD 935 for the ex-German *T-35*, and DD 939 for the ex-German *Z-39*, all 1945 war prizes that were discarded; DD 932, 936, 947, and 949 of the "Forrest Sherman" class were converted to DDG 31-34, respectively).

ARMAMENT. As built all 18 ships of this class had three single 5 inch guns, two twin 3 inch mounts, four fixed 21 inch ASW torpedo tubes (amidships); two ASW hedgehogs (forward of bridge), and depth charge racks.

FORREST SHERMAN (DD 931)   *1969, United States Navy, PH2 G. G. Cottrill*

DESIGN. The entire superstructures of these ships are of aluminium to obtain maximum stability with minimum displacement. All living spaces are air conditioned. The *Decatur* and later ships have higher bows; the *Hull* and later ships have slightly different bow designs. The *Barry* had her sonar dome moved forward in 1959 and a stem anchor fitted.

ELECTRONICS. SQS-23 sonar installed with the *Barry* being the first US warship fitted with bow-mounted sonar. Most of these ships have SPS-37 and SPS-10 search radar antennas on their forward tripod mast, except *Jonas Ingram*, *Mullinnix*, *Dupont* and few others have SPS-40. (Note *Barry* retains older SPS-37).
Several ships fitted with improved electronic warfare equipment (note equipment between *Manley's* funnels). *Barry* has variable depth sonar (VDS) fitted at stern. Structure on fantail of *Jonas Ingram* indicates similar installation planned for her.

GUNNERY. With original armament of one 5 inch mount forward and two 5 inch mounts aft, these were the first US warships with more firepower aft than forward. Note that *Barry* and later ships have their Mk 68 gunfire control director forward and Mk 56 director aft; positions reversed in earlier ships.

MODERNISATION. The 14 non-missile-armed ships of this class all were to have been fitted with "improved ASW systems (to) greatly enhance the effectiveness of these ships against modern high-speed submarines", according to official statements

JONAS INGRAM (DD 938) (ASW Mod.)   *1970, United States Navy*

Six ships (DD 931, 942, 944, 945, 950, and 951) will not undergo modernisation because "the estimated cost of converting these ships has risen substantially since they were originally programmed".

The *Barry* was modernised with FY 1964 funds at the Boston Naval Shipyard in 1967-1968.
Davis and *Dupont* being modernised at Boston Naval Shipyard; *Jonas Ingram*, *Manley* and *Blandy* at Philadelphia Naval Shipyard; *Morton* and *Richard S. Edwards*

at Long Beach (California) Naval Shipyard; all being completed 1970-1972.

NOMENCLATURE. DD 951 was originally named *Joy*; renamed *Turner Joy* on 26 July 1957.

Surface Combatants—continued

BARRY (DD 933) (ASW Modification)

1969, United States Navy, PH1 J. E, Taylor

JONAS INGRAM (DD 938) (ASW Mod.)

1970, United States Navy

MANLEY (DD 940)

1968, United States Navy

TURNER JOY (DD 951)

1970, United States Navy, PH3 Dennis McClosky

Surface Combatants—*continued*

74 DESTROYERS (DD): MODERNISED "GEARING" CLASS (FRAM 1)

Displacement, tons	2 425 standard; 3 480 to 3 520 full load
Length, feet (*metres*)	390·5 (*119·0*) oa
Beam, feet (*metres*)	40·9 (*12·4*)
Draft, feet (*metres*)	19 (*5·8*)
Guns	4—5 in (*127 mm*) 38 calibre dual-purpose (twin)
ASW weapons	1 ASROC 8-tube launcher 2 triple torpedo launchers (Mk 32) facilities for small helicopter
Main engines	2 geared turbines (General Electric or Westinghouse); 60 000 shp 2 shafts
Boilers	4 (Babcock & Wilcox or combination Babcock & Wilcox and Foster-Wheeler)
Speed, knots	34
Complement	274 (14 officers, 260 enlisted men)

Name	No.	Builder	Launched	Commissioned
*GEARING	DD 710	Federal SB & DD Co	18 Feb 1945	3 May 1945
*WILTSIE	DD 716	Federal SB & DD Co	31 Aug 1945	12 Jan 1946
*THEODORE E. CHANDLER	DD 717	Federal SB & DD Co	20 Oct 1945	22 Mar 1946
*HAMNER	DD 718	Federal SB & DD Co	24 Nov 1945	11 July 1946
*WILLIAM C. LAWE	DD 763	Bethlehem (San Francisco)	21 May 1945	18 Dec 1946
*ROWAN	DD 782	Todd Pacific Shipyards	29 Dec 1944	31 Mar 1945
*GURKE	DD 783	Todd Pacific Shipyards	15 Feb 1945	12 May 1945
*HENDERSON	DD 785	Todd Pacific Shipyards	28 May 1945	4 Aug 1945
*RICHARD B. ANDERSON	DD 786	Todd Pacific Shipyards	7 July 1945	26 Oct 1945
*JAMES E. KYES	DD 787	Todd Pacific Shipyards	4 Aug 1945	8 Feb 1946
*HOLLISTER	DD 788	Todd Pacific Shipyards	9 Oct 1945	26 Mar 1946
*EVERSOLE	DD 789	Todd Pacific Shipyards	8 Jan 1946	10 July 1946
*SHELTON	DD 790	Todd Pacific Shipyards	8 Mar 1946	21 June 1946
*JOHNSTON	DD 821	Consolidated Steel Corp	19 Oct 1945	10 Oct 1945
*ROBERT H. McCARD	DD 822	Consolidated Steel Corp	9 Nov 1945	26 Oct 1946
*AGERHOLM	DD 826	Bath Iron Works Corp	30 Mar 1946	20 June 1946
*GEORGE K. MacKENZIE	DD 836	Bath Iron Works Corp	13 May 1945	13 July 1945
*SARSFIELD	DD 837	Bath Iron Works Corp	27 May 1945	31 July 1945
*POWER	DD 839	Bath Iron Works Corp	30 June 1945	13 Sep 1945
*GLENNON	DD 840	Bath Iron Works Corp	14 July 1945	4 Oct 1945
*NOA	DD 841	Bath Iron Works Corp	30 July 1945	2 Nov 1945
*WARRINGTON	DD 843	Bath Iron Works Corp	27 Sep 1945	20 Dec 1945
*PERRY	DD 844	Bath Iron Works Corp	25 Nov 1945	17 Jan 1946
*BAUSELL	DD 845	Bath Iron Works Corp	19 Nov 1945	7 Feb 1947
*OZBOURN	DD 846	Bath Iron Works Corp	22 Dec 1945	5 Mar 1946
*RICHARD E. KRAUS (ex-AG 151)	DD 849	Bath Iron Works Corp	2 Mar 1946	23 May 1946
*JOSEPH P. KENNEDY Jr	DD 850	Bethlehem (Quincy)	26 July 1945	15 Dec 1945
*RUPERTUS	DD 851	Bethlehem (Quincy)	21 Sep 1945	8 Mar 1946
*LEONARD F. MASON	DD 852	Bethlehem (Quincy)	4 Jan 1946	28 June 1946
*CHARLES H. ROAN	DD 853	Bethlehem (Quincy)	15 Mar 1945	12 Sep 1946
*VOGELGESANG	DD 862	Bethlehem (Staten Island)	15 Jan 1945	28 Apr 1945
*HAROLD J. ELLISON	DD 864	Bethlehem (Staten Island)	14 Mar 1945	23 June 1945
*CHARLES R. WARE	DD 865	Bethlehem (Staten Island)	12 Apr 1945	21 July 1945
*CONE	DD 866	Bethlehem (Staten Island)	10 May 1945	18 Aug 1945
*STRIBLING	DD 867	Bethlehem (Staten Island)	8 June 1945	29 Sep 1945
*BROWNSON	DD 868	Bethlehem (Staten Island)	15 Mar 1945	17 Nov 1945
*ARNOLD J. ISBELL	DD 869	Bethlehem (Staten Island)	6 Aug 1945	17 Nov 1945
*FLOYD B. PARKS	DD 884	Consolidated Steel Corp	31 Mar 1945	31 July 1945
*JOHN R. CRAIG	DD 885	Consolidated Steel Corp	14 Apr 1945	20 Aug 1945
*ORLECK	DD 886	Consolidated Steel Corp	12 May 1945	15 Sep 1945
*BRINKLEY BASS	DD 887	Consolidated Steel Corp	26 May 1945	1 Oct 1945
*MEREDITH	DD 890	Consolidated Steel Corp	28 June 1945	31 Dec 1945
(Former Escort Destroyers, ex-DDE)				
*EPPERSON	DD 719	Federal SB & DD Co	22 Dec 1945	19 Mar 1949
*NEW	DD 818	Consolidated Steel Corp	18 Aug 1945	5 Apr 1946
*HOLDER	DD 819	Consolidated Steel Corp	25 Aug 1945	18 May 1946
*RICH	DD 820	Consolidated Steel Corp	5 Oct 1945	4 July 1946
*BASILONE	DD 824	Consolidated Steel Corp	21 Dec 1945	26 July 1949
*ROBERT L. WILSON	DD 847	Bath Iron Works Corp	5 Jan 1946	28 Mar 1946
DAMATO	DD 871	Bethlehem (Staten Island)	21 Nov 1945	27 Apr 1946
(Former Radar Picket Destroyers, ex-DDR)				
'EUGENE A. GREENE	DD 711	Federal SB & DD Co	18 Mar 1945	8 June 1945
*WILLIAM R. RUSH	DD 714	Federal SB & DD Co	8 July 1945	21 Sep 1945
*WILLIAM M. WOOD	DD 715	Federal SB & DD Co	29 July 1945	24 Nov 1945
*SOUTHERLAND	DD 743	Bath Iron Works Corp	5 Oct 1944	22 Dec 1944
*McKEAN	DD 784	Todd Pacific Shipyards	31 Mar 1945	9 June 1945
*HIGBEE	DD 806	Bath Iron Works Corp	12 Nov 1944	27 Jan 1945
*DENNIS J. BUCKLEY	DD 808	Bath Iron Works Corp	20 Dec 1944	2 Mar 1945
*CORRY	DD 817	Consolidated Steel Corp	28 July 1945	26 Feb 1946
*MYLES C. FOX	DD 829	Bath Iron Works Corp	13 Jan 1945	20 Mar 1945
*HANSON	DD 832	Bath Iron Works Corp	11 Mar 1945	11 May 1945
HERBERT J. THOMAS	DD 833	Bath Iron Works Corp	25 Mar 1945	29 May 1945
*CHARLES P. CECIL	DD 835	Bath Iron Works Corp	22 Apr 1945	29 June 1945
*FISKE	DD 842	Bath Iron Works Corp	8 Sep 1945	28 Nov 1945
*STEINAKER	DD 863	Bethlehem (Staten Island)	13 Feb 1945	26 May 1945
*HAWKINS	DD 873	Consolidated Steel Corp	7 Oct 1944	10 Feb 1945
*HENRY W. TUCKER	DD 875	Consolidated Steel Corp	8 Nov 1944	12 Mar 1945
*ROGERS	DD 876	Consolidated Steel Corp	20 Nov 1944	26 Mar 1945
*VESOLE	DD 878	Consolidated Steel Corp	29 Dec 1944	23 Apr 1945
*LEARY	DD 879	Consolidated Steel Corp	20 Jan 1945	7 May 1945
*DYESS	DD 880	Consolidated Steel Corp	26 Jan 1945	21 May 1945
*BORDELON	DD 881	Consolidated Steel Corp	3 Mar 1945	5 June 1945
*FURSE	DD 882	Consolidated Steel Corp	9 Mar 1945	10 July 1945
NEWMAN K. PERRY	DD 883	Consolidated Steel Corp	17 Mar 1945	26 July 1945
*STICKELL	DD 888	Consolidated Steel Corp	16 June 1945	30 Oct 1945
*O'HARE	DD 889	Consolidated Steel Corp	22 June 1945	29 Nov 1945

These ships are enlarged versions of the "Allen M. Sumner" class with an additional 14-foot section amidships for additional fuel tanks. All of the above listed ships have been extensively modernised under the FRAM I programme (see *Modernisation* notes). The *Richard E. Kraus* (ex-AG 151) and *Sarsfield* are used for experimental work (EDD). (The former ship was designated AG 151 from 24 Aug 1949 to 11 Dec 1953). Beginning in 1970 several ships of this class were decommissioned and placed in reserve; the *Arnold J. Isbell* and *Dyess* are operational Naval Reserve training ships.

Eleven "Gearing" class ships were modified in 1949 and 1950 for specialised anti-submarine operations and four others were completed to specialised ASW configurations. Five of these ships which were reclassified as "escort" destroyers (DDE) on 4 March 1950 and subsequently reclassified as "straight" destroyers (DD) on 30 June 1962 are listed here as are the *Basilone* and *Epperson*, changed to DDE on 28 Jan 1948 and again to DD on 1 July 1962. These ships have undergone FRAM I modernisation. The eight other ships of the basic "Gearing" design which were modified or completed to specialised ASW designs are listed separately.

Thirty-six "Gearing" class ships were modified for radar picket operations after World War II. These ships were reclassified DDR between 1949 and 1953. All have been modernised under the FRAM schemes. Twenty-six FRAM I ex-DDRs are listed here; ten FRAM II ex-DDRs are listed separately.
The "Gearing" class initially covered hull numbers DD 710-721, 742, 743, 763-769, 782-791, 805-926. Forty-nine of these ships were cancelled in 1945 (DD 768, 769, 809-816, 854-856, and 891-926); four ships were never completed and were scrapped in the 1950s: *Castle* (DD 720), *Woodrow R. Thompson* (DD 721), *Lansdale* (DD 766), and *Seymour D. Owens* (DD 767).

ARMAMENT-DESIGN. As built these ships had a pole mast and carried an armament of six 5 inch guns (twin mounts), 12 40 mm AA guns (2 quad, 2 twin), 11 20 mm AA guns (single), and 10 21 inch torpedo tubes (quin). After World War II the after bank of tubes was replaced by an additional quad 40 mm mount. All 40 mm and 20 mm guns were replaced subsequently by six 3 inch guns (2 twin, 2 single) and a tripod mast was installed to support heavier radar antennas. The 3 inch guns and remaining torpedo tubes were removed during FRAM conversion.

ELECTRONICS. These ships have SPS-10 and SPS-40 or SPS-37 search radar antennas on their tripod mast; advanced electronic warfare equipment fitted to most ships with an enlarged electronic "stack" atop the helicopter hangar-ASROC magazine structure. Fitted with SQS-23 sonar.

ENGINEERING. Endurance is 5 800 miles at 15 knots.

DENNIS J. BUCKLEY (DD 808)　　　　　　　*1970, United States Navy, PH2 Louis D. Adzima*

Surface Combatants—continued

"GEARING" CLASS FRAM I—*continued*

GUNNERY. The "B" twin 5 inch mount was removed from the experimental destroyer *Sarsfield* in 1959. The other ships lost their "B" or "Y" (after) 5 inch mount during FRAM conversion.

HELICOPTERS. These ships no longer operate drône helicopters, but rely on ASROC and tube-launched torpedoes for anti-submarine weapons.

MODERNISATION. All of these ships have undergone extensive modernisation under the Fleet Rehabilitation and Modernisation (FRAM I) programme. They were stripped of all armament except two 5 inch mounts, new anti-submarine weapons were installed including facilities for operating ASW helicopters, new electronic equipment was installed, machinery was overhauled, living and working spaces were rehabilitiated. For budgeting reasons FRAM I work was officially considered a "conversion". The *Perry* was the first ship to undergo FRAM I conversion, the work being accomplished at the Boston Naval Shipyard from May 1959 to April 1960; her FRAM I cost an estimated $7 700 000.

There are two basic FRAM I configurations: the DD 786, 790, 826, 841, 844, 845, 867, and 890 (eight ships) have twin 5 inch mounts in "A" and "B" positions and Mk 32 torpedo launchers abaft second funnel; others have twin 5 inch mounts in "A" and "Y" positions and Mk 32 launchers on 01 level in "B" position.

The *Herbert J. Thomas* was additionally modified for protection against biological, chemical, and atomic attack; the ship is fully "sealed" with enclosed lookout and control positions, special air conditioning provisions, *et cetera*. (Modified at Mare Island Naval Shipyard from July 1963 to July 1964).

PHOTOGRAPHS. Note the all-gun forward arrangement of the *Noa*; the *Herbert J. Thomas* has a modified bridge structure and enclosed 01 level from forward 5 inch mount to bridge. A starboard-side view of the *Herbert J. Thomas* appears in the 1969-1970 edition.
Note chaff rocket (CHAFROC) launchers between ASROC and second funnel on *Hamner*.

DISPOSALS AND TRANSFERS

Timmerman (DD 828), fitted with experimental lightweight machinery, was reclassified AG 152 on 11 Dec 1953 and stricken on 4 Apr 1958; **Witek** (DD 848), fitted with experimental water-jet propulsion and special sonar, stricken on 17 Sep 1968; **Gyatt** (DD 712, ex-DDG 1), formerly fitted with Terrier missile system as the world's first guided missile destroyer, stricken on 22 Oct 1969; **Fechteler** (DD 870) stricken on 11 Sep 1970; **Samuel B. Roberts** (DD 823) stricken on 2 Nov 1970; **Forrest Royal** (DD 872) to Turkey on 27 Mar 1971.

NOA (DD 841)   1969, United States Navy, by PH2 J. R. Altavena

WILLIAM R. RUSH (DD 714)   1970, United States Navy

HERBERT J. THOMAS (DD 833)   1965, United States Navy

HAMNER (DD 718)   1969, United States Navy

Surface Combatants—*continued*

5 DESTROYERS (DD): "GEARING" CLASS (FRAM II) ex-ESCORTS

	Name	No.	Builder	Launched	Commissioned
*LLOYD THOMAS	DD 764	Bethlehem Steel (San Francisco)	5 Oct 1945	21 Mar 1947
*KEPPLER	DD 765	Bethlehem Steel (San Francisco)	24 June 1945	23 May 1947
NORRIS	DD 859	Bethlehem Steel (San Pedro)	25 Feb 1945	9 June 1945
McCAFFERY	DD 860	Bethlehem Steel (San Pedro)	12 Apr 1945	26 July 1945
*HARWOOD	DD 861	Bethlehem Steel (San Pedro)	24 May 1945	28 Sep 1945

Displacement, tons	2 425 standard; approx 3 500 full load
Length, feet (*metres*)	390·5 (*119·0*) oa
Beam, feet (*metres*)	40·9 (*12·4*)
Draft, feet (*metres*)	19 (*5·8*)
Guns	4—5 inch (*127 mm*) 38 calibre dual-purpose
ASW weapons	1 large, trainable hedgehog (Mk 15) 2 triple torpedo launchers (Mk 32) 2 fixed torpedo tubes (Mk 25) facilities for small helicopter
Main engines	2 geared turbines; 60 000 shp 2 shafts
Boilers	4 (Babcock & Wilcox)
Speed, knots	34
Complement	275 (15 officers, 260 enlisted men)

KEPPLER (DD 765)

1970, United States Navy, PH1 D. M. Dreher

These ships are "Gearing" Class destroyers, some completed with only four 5 inch guns ("A" and "Y" mounts). They were modified for ASW in 1949-1950 with trainable hedgehog installed in "B" position and classification changed to "hunter-killer" destroyers (DDK); changed to "escort" destroyers (DDE) on 4 March 1950. Again classified as "straight" destroyers (DD) on 30 June 1962 with FRAM II modernisation.

Norris and *McCaffery* have been decommissioned and are in reserve. *Harwood* was scheduled for transfer to Turkey in December 1971.

ELECTRONICS. These ships have SPS-12 and SPS-10 search radar antennae on their tripod mast and a small mast atop hangar to support electronic warfare "pods" which differs from other FRAM ships. Fitted with SQS-29 series hull mounted sonar.

ENGINEERING. General Electric turbines in *Lloyd* *Thomas* and *Keppler*; Westinghouse in *Fred T. Berry* and *McCaffery*; Allis-Chalmers in *Norris* and *Harwood*.

DISPOSAL
Fred T. Berry (DD 858) stricken on 15 Sep 1970.

2 DESTROYERS (DD): "CARPENTER" TYPE (FRAM I)

Displacement, tons	2 425 standard; 3 410 full load
Length, feet (*metres*)	390·5 (*119·0*) oa
Beam, feet (*metres*)	40·9 (*12·4*)
Draft, feet (*metres*)	19 (*5·8*)
Guns	2—5 in (*127 mm*) 38 calibre dual-purpose (twin)
ASW weapons	1 ASROC 8-tube launcher 2 triple torpedo launchers (Mk 32) facilities for small helicopter
Main engines	2 geared turbines (Westinghouse in *Carpenter*, General Electric in *Robert A. Owens*); 60 000 shp; 2 shafts
Boilers	4 (Babcock & Wilcox)
Speed, knots	34
Complement	264 (14 officers, 250 enlisted men)

Name	No.	Builder	Launched	Commissioned
*CARPENTER	DD 825	Consolidated Steel Corp	30 Dec 1945	15 Dec 1946
*ROBERT A. OWENS	DD 827	Bath Iron Works Corp	15 July 1946	5 Nov 1949

These ships were laid down as units of the "Gearing" class. Their construction was suspended after World War II until 1947 when they were towed to the Newport News Shipbuilding and Drydock Co for completion as "hunter-killer" destroyers (DDK). As specialised ASW ships they mounted 3 inch (76 mm) guns in place of 5 inch mounts and were armed with improved ahead-firing anti-submarine weapons (hedgehogs and Weapon Able/Alfa); special sonar equipment installed. The DDK and DDE classifications were merged in 1950 with both of these ships being designated DDE on 4 March 1950. Upon being modernised to the FRAM I configuration they were reclassified DD on 30 June 1962.

Drone helicopters are no longer carried.

ELECTRONICS. These ships have SPS-10 and SPS-40 search radar antennae on their forward tripod mast and electronic warfare "pods" on a smaller tripod mast forward of their second funnel.

PHOTOGRAPHS. The *Carpenter* and *Robert A. Owens* are distinguished as the only US destroyers with an ASROC launcher and one twin 5 inch gun mount (forward); note unusual bridge configuration with Mk 56 gunfire control director in lieu of larger Mk 37 found in other FRAM destroyers; Mk 32 tubes on 01 level in "B" position; second tripod mast; and enlarged helicopter hangar-ASROC magazine (enclosing after portion of second funnel). A stern view of the *Robert A. Owens* appears in the 1969-1970 edition.

The *Robert A. Owens* is shown entering Malta; the *Carpenter* is shown alongside the carrier *Hancock* in the Gulf of Tonkin.

ROBERT A. OWENS (DD 827)

1969, A. & J. Pavia

Surface Combatants—continued

4 DESTROYERS (DD): "GEARING" CLASS (FRAM II) ex-RADAR PICKETS

Displacement, tons	2 425 standard; approx 3 500 full load	
Length, feet (metres)	390·5 (119·0) oa	
Beam, feet (metres)	40·9 (12·4)	
Draft, feet (metres)	19 (5·8)	
Guns	6—5 inch (127 mm) 38 calibre dual-purpose	
ASW weapons	2 fixed hedgehogs	
	2 triple torpedo launchers (Mk 32) facilities for small helicopter	
Main engines	2 geared turbines (General Electric except Westinghouse in Perkins); 60 000 shp; 2 shafts	
Boilers	4 (Babcock & Wilcox)	
Speed, knots	34	
Complement	275 (15 officers, 260 enlisted men)	

Name	No.	Builder	Launched	Commissioned
*CHEVALIER	DD 805	Bath Iron Works Corp	29 Oct 1944	9 Jan 1945
*BENNER	DD 807	Bath Iron Works Corp	20 Nov 1944	13 Feb 1945
*EVERETT F. LARSON	DD 830	Bath Iron Works Corp	28 Jan 1945	6 Apr 1945
*PERKINS	DD 877	Consolidated Steel Corp	7 Dec 1944	5 Apr 1945

These ships are "Gearing" class destroyers, modified to serve as radar picket destroyers and reclassified (DDR) on 18 March 1949. Subsequently modernised under the "Gearing" FRAM II programme with special electronics equipment removed; classified as "straight" destroyers (DD) on 30 June 1962. These ships differ from main group of "Gearing" class destroyers by absence of ASROC.

Everett F. Larson is active; Benner, Chevalier and Perkins are operational Naval Reserve training ships.

ELECTRONICS. These ships have SPS-40 and SPS-10 search radar antennæ on their tripod mast. Fitted with SQS-29 series hull mounted sonar.

TORPEDOES. Two single Mk 25 torpedo tubes installed between funnels during FRAM modernisation have been removed from these ships.

PHOTOGRAPHS. Note space between funnels of the "long-hull" Chevalier compared to "short-hull" destroyers of the "Allen M. Sumner" class on subsequent pages. Additional electronic-warfare equipment is fitted on the sides of the after antenna "stack" of the Benner.

BENNER (DD 807)   1969, United States Navy, PH2 S. C. Wyckoff

CHEVALIER (DD 805)   1969, United States Navy, PH2 A. Cuellar

CARPENTER (DD 825)—see previous page   1969, United States Navy

Surface Combatants—*continued*

3 DESTROYERS (DD): "GEARING" CLASS (FRAM II) RADAR PICKETS

Name	No.	Builder	Launched	Commissioned
KENNETH D. BAILEY	DD 713	Federal SB & DD Co	17 June 1945	31 July 1945
GOODRICH	DD 831	Bath Iron Works	25 Feb 1945	24 Apr 1945
DUNCAN	DD 874	Consolidated Steel Corp	27 Oct 1944	25 Feb 1945

Displacement, tons	2 425 standard; approx 3 500 full load
Length, feet (*metres*)	390·5 (*119·0*) oa
Beam, feet (*metres*)	40·9 (*12·4*)
Draft, feet (*metres*)	19 (*5·8*)
Guns	6—5 inch (*127 mm*) 38 calibre dual-purpose
ASW weapons	2 fixed hedgehogs 2 triple torpedo launchers (Mk 32)
Main engines	2 geared turbines (General Electric except Westinghouse in *Frank Knox*); 60 000 shp; 2 shafts
Boilers	4 (Babcock & Wilcox)
Speed, knots	34
Complement	275 (15 officers, 260 enlisted men)

These ships were "Gearing" class destroyers, modified to serve as radar picket destroyers and reclassified (DDR) on 18 March 1949, except *Kenneth D. Bailey* on 9 April 1953. Subsequently modernised under "Gearing" FRAM II programme, but retained special electronic equipment and were not provided with drone helicopter (DASH) facilities; classified as "straight" destroyers (DD) on 1 January 1969.

The three surviving ships of this type were decommissioned in 1969-1971.

ELECTRONICS. These ships have SPS-37 and SPS-10 search radars on forward mast, TACAN (tactical air navigation) "beehive" antenna on short tripod mast forward of second funnel, and SPS-30 search radar atop after deckhouse (except SPS-8 in *Duncan*). During FRAM process these ships were fitted with SQS-29 series hull-mounted sonar; variable depth sonar fitted in all except *Duncan*.

PHOTOGRAPHS. Note smaller, improved TACAN beacon in *Kenneth D. Bailey* compared to earlier "beehive" TACAN antenna in *Goodrich*.

DISPOSALS AND TRANSFERS

Turner (DDR/DD 834) stricken on 26 Sep 1969; **Ernest G. Small** (DDR/DD 838) stricken on 13 Nov 1970 and transferred to Nationalist China in Jan 1971; **Frank Knox** (DDR/DD 742) to Greece on 30 Jan 1971.

GOODRICH (DD 831)   *1965, United States Navy*

KENNETH D. BAILEY (DD 713)   *1968, United States Navy*

ALLEN M. SUMNER (DD 692)—See following page   *1968, United States Navy*

Surface Combatants—*continued*
31 DESTROYERS (DD): MODERNISED "ALLEN M. SUMNER" CLASS (FRAM II)

Displacement, tons	2 200 standard; 3 320 full load			
Length, feet (*metres*)	376·5 (*114·8*) oa			
Beam, feet (*metres*)	40·9 (*12·4*)			
Draft, feet (*metres*)	19 (*5·8*)			
Guns	6—5 in (*127 mm*) 38 calibre dual-purpose			
ASW Weapons	2 triple torpedo launchers (Mk 32) 2 ahead-firing hedgehogs facilities for small helicopter			
Main engines	2 geared turbines; 60 000 shp; 2 shafts			
Boilers	4			
Speed, knots	34			
Complement	274 (14 officers, 260 enlisted men)			

Name	No.	Builder	Launched	Commissioned
*ALLEN M SUMNER	DD 692	Federal SB & DD Co	15 Dec 1943	26 Jan 1944
* MOALE	DD 693	Federal SB & DD Co	16 Jan 1944	26 Feb 1944
* INGRAHAM	DD 694	Federal SB & DD Co	16 Jan 1944	10 Mar 1944
* CHARLES S. SPERRY	DD 697	Federal SB P DD Co	13 Mar 1944	17 May 1944
* AULT	DD 698	Federal SB & DD Co	26 Mar 1944	31 May 1944
* WALDRON	DD 699	Federal SB & DD Co	26 Mar 1944	8 June 1944
* WALLACE L. LIND	DD 703	Federal SB & DD Co	14 June 1944	8 Sep 1944
* BORIE	DD 704	Federal SB & DD Co	4 July 1944	21 Sep 1944
* HUGH PURVIS	DD 709	Federal SB & DD Co	17 Dec 1944	1 Mar 1945
WALKE	DD 723	Bath Iron Works Corp	27 Oct 1943	21 Jan 1944
* LAFFEY	DD 724	Bath Iron Works Corp	21 Nov 1943	8 Feb 1944
* O'BRIEN	DD 725	Bath Iron Works Corp	8 Dec 1943	25 Feb 1944
DE HAVEN	DD 727	Bath Iron Works Corp	9 Jan 1944	31 Mar 1944
MANSFIELD	DD 728	Bath Iron Works Corp	29 Jan 1944	14 Apr 1944
LYMAN K. SWENSON	DD 729	Bath Iron Works Corp	12 Feb 1944	2 May 1944
COLLETT	DD 730	Bath Iron Works Corp	5 Mar 1944	16 May 1944
BLUE	DD 744	Bethlehem (Staten Island)	28 Nov 1943	20 Mar 1944
TAUSSIG	DD 746	Bethlehem (Staten Island)	25 Jan 1944	20 May 1944
ALFRED A. CUNNINGHAM	DD 752	Bethlehem (Staten Island)	3 Aug 1944	23 Nov 1944
JOHN A. BOLE	DD 755	Bethlehem (Staten Island)	1 Nov 1944	3 Mar 1945
* PUTNAM	DD 757	Bethlehem (San Francisco)	26 Mar 1944	12 Oct 1944
* STRONG	DD 758	Bethlehem (San Francisco)	23 Apr 1944	8 Mar 1945
LOFBERG	DD 759	Bethlehem (San Francisco)	12 Aug 1944	26 Apr 1945
JOHN W. THOMASON	DD 760	Bethlehem (San Francisco)	30 Sep 1944	11 Oct 1945
BUCK	DD 761	Bethlehem (San Francisco)	11 Mar 1945	28 June 1946
* LOWRY	DD 770	Bethlehem (San Pedro)	6 Feb 1944	23 July 1944
* JAMES C. OWENS	DD 776	Bethlehem (San Pedro)	1 Oct 1944	17 Feb 1945
* MASSEY	DD 778	Todd Pacific Shipyards	19 Aug 1944	24 Nov 1944
* DOUGLAS H. FOX	DD 779	Todd Pacific Shipyards	30 Sep 1944	26 Dec 1944
STORMES	DD 780	Todd Pacific Shipyards	4 Nov 1944	27 Jan 1945
* ROBERT K. HUNTINGTON	DD 781	Todd Pacific Shipyards	5 Dec 1944	3 Mar 1945

The above 31 ships have been extensively modernised under the FRAM II programme. See the following class listing for basic data.
Frank E. Evans (DD 754) cut in half by Australian carrier *Melbourne* on 2 June 1969; bow section sank with loss of 74 crew. Officially stricken from the Navy List on 1 July 1 969; stern section sunk as target on 10 Oct 1969.
Thirteen of these ships were decommissioned and placed in reserve in 1970-1971. Ten other ships serve as operational Naval Reserve training ships: *Moale, Charles S. Sperry, Ault, Waldron, Borie, Putnam, Lowry, Massey, Douglas H. Fox,* and *Robert K. Huntington.* Only eight ships remain in commission assigned to operating forces.

ELECTRONICS. These ships have SQS-29 series hull-mounted sonar (SQS-29 to -31 designation, depending upon frequency); variable depth sonar in most ships; fitted with SPS-40 or SPS-37 and small SPS-10 search radar antennae on tripod mast.

MODERNISATION. All of these ships have been modernised under the Fleet Rehabilitation and Modernisation (FRAM II) programme. New ASW torpedo launchers were installed as were facilities for operating ASW helicopters and variable depth sonar (VDS). Machinery was overhauled, new electronic equipment was installed, and living and working spaces were rehabilitated.

TORPEDOES. The two single Mk 25 torpedo tubes, installed in these ships during FRAM modernisation have been removed from most units (were between funnels). All have two Mk 32 triple launchers for ASW torpedoes on 01 level between funnels.

TRANSFER
Zellars (DD 777) to Iran on 19 Mar 1971.

PHOTOGRAPHS. The *Lyman K. Swenson* at right has an older SPS-37 search radar on her tripod mast and is one of the few ships of this type without variable depth sonar on her fantail; the *Lofberg* below has SPS-40 radar and VDS at stern; note hedgehog alongside bridge.

LYMAN K. SWENSON (DD 729)

1970, United States Navy, PHC T. J. Taylor

LOFBERG (DD 759)

1970, United States Navy, PH1 Dixon M. Dreher

Surface Combatants—*continued*

10 DESTROYERS (DD): "ALLEN M. SUMNER" CLASS

		Name	No.	Builder	Launched	Commissioned
Displacement, tons	2 200 standard; 3 320 full load	*HANK	DD 702	Federal SB & DD Co	21 May 1944	28 Aug 1944
Length, feet (*metres*)	376·5 (*114·8*) oa	*COMPTON	DD 705	Federal SB & DD Co	17 Sep 1944	4 Nov 1944
Beam, feet (*metres*)	40·9 (*12·4*)	SOLEY	DD 707	Federal SB & DD Co	8 Sep 1944	7 Dec 1944
Draft, feet (*metres*)	19 (*5·8*)	*HARLAN R. DICKSON	DD 708	Federal SB & DD Co	17 Dec 1944	17 Feb 1945
Guns	6—5 inch (*127 mm*) 38 calibre	*MADDOX	DD 731	Bath Iron Works Corp	19 Mar 1944	2 June 1944
	dual-purpose (twin)	*PURDY	DD 734	Bath Iron Works Corp	7 May 1944	18 July 1944
	4—3 inch (*76 mm*) 50 calibre AA	*JOHN R. PIERCE	DD 753	Bethlehem (Staten Island)	1 Sep 1944	30 Dec 1944
	(twin); all removed from *Purdy*	*BEATTY	DD 756	Bethlehem (Staten Island)	30 Nov 1944	31 Mar 1945
	and *Beatty*	*HENLEY	DD 762	Bethlehem (San Francisco)	8 Apr 1945	8 Oct 1946
ASW weapons	2 fixed hedgehogs; depth charges	*WILLARD KEITH	DD 775	Bethlehem (San Pedro)	29 Aug 1944	27 Dec 1944
	2 triple torpedo launchers (Mk 32)					
Main engines	2 geared turbines;					
	60 000 shp; 2 shafts					
Boilers	4					
Speed, knots	34					
Complement	274 (14 officers, 260 enlisted					
	men ((designed wartime 345)					

Fifty-eight destroyers of this class were completed in 1944-1945 with an additional 12 ships completed in 1944 as Light Minelayers (DM). The minelayers are listed in the section on Mine Warfare Ships and 33 destroyers modernised under the FRAM II programme are listed on the previous page.

Nine of these destroyers are operational Naval Reserve training ships; the *Soley* was decommissioned in 1970 and is in reserve.

ARMAMENT-DESIGN. The "Allen M. Sumner" class introduced the 5 inch gun, dual-purpose twin mount on US destroyers.

The 13 US Navy "destroyer leaders" (DD 356-363, 381, 383, 394-396) built during the 1930s had twin 5 inch gun mounts, but they were not capable of sufficient elevation for anti-aircraft fire.

One-hundred six-gun destroyers were planned in the first six-gun destroyer series (DD 692-791); 31 of these were re-ordered as lengthened "Gearing" class. The "later" DD 857 is a short-hull "Sumner".

As built, all ships of this class mounted six 5 inch guns, twelve 40 mm AA guns, several 20 mm guns, and ten 21 inch torpedo tubes.

After the war all ships had the after torpedo bank replaced by a quad 40 mm mount and the 20 mm guns were removed (providing a total of 16 40 mm guns). During the early 1950s most of these ships had the 40 mm guns replaced by two single and two twin 3 inch gun mounts (single mounts on bridge wings and twin mounts aft of second funnel in tandem arrangement) and a tripod radar mast replaced the original pole mast.

During the 1960s most ships of this class were modernised under the FRAM II programme. The non-modernised ships (listed above and in disposals) had their remaining bank of torpedo tubes removed along with the two single 3 inch gun mounts, and two triple Mk 32 launchers for ASW torpedoes were installed.

COMPTON (DD 705)

1969, US Navy, PHC F. W. Gotavco

Most ships now have two 3 inch twin mounts in addition to full main battery of six 5 inch guns.

WAR LOSSES. *Cooper* (DD 695), *Meredith* (DD 726), *Mannert L. Abele* (DD 733), and *Drexler* (DD 741).

DISPOSALS AND TRANSFERS
Hugh W. Hadley (DD 774) stricken 2 Sep 1947 (severely damaged by suicide aircraft in World War II);

Barton (DD 722) stricken on 1 Oct 1968; **Harry E. Hubbard** (DD 748) stricken on 17 Oct 1969; **Hyman** (DD 732) stricken on 14 Nov 1969; **Brush** (DD 745) and **Samuel N. Moore** (DD 747) to Nationalist China on 9 Dec 1969; **Bristol** (DD 857) to Nationalist China on 22 Dec 1969; **Haynsworth** (DD 700) to Nationalist China on 12 May 1970; **English** (DD 696) to Nationalist China on 11 Aug 1970; **Gainard** (DD 706) to Iran on 19 Mar 1971; **John W. Weeks** (DD 701) stricken on 12 Aug 1970.

COMPTON (DD 705)

1969, United States Navy

ZELLARS (DD 777) and QH-50C DASH—See previous page (transferred to Iran)

1969, United States Navy

Surface Combatants—continued

25 DESTROYERS (DD): LATER "FLETCHER" CLASS

Displacement, tons	2 050 standard; 3 500 full load
Length, feet (metres)	376·5 (114·7) oa
Beam, feet (metres)	39·5 (11·9)
Draft, feet (metres)	18 (5·5)
Guns	4 or 5—5 inch (127 mm) 38 calibre dual-purpose
	10—40 mm AA (twin) or 6—3 in (76 mm) AA (twin) see Armament notes)
ASW weapons	depth charges; 2 fixed hedgehogs. 2 triple torpedo launchers (Mk 32) in some ships
Torpedo tubes	5 or 10—21 inch (533 mm) quintuple (removed from some ships)
Main engines	2 geared turbines; 60 000 shp; 2 shafts
Boilers	4
Speed, knots	35
Complement	250 (14 officers, 236 enlisted men) (designed wartime 329)

Name	No.	Builder	Launched	Commissioned
BEARSS (4 guns)	DD 654	Gulf SB Corpn	25 July 1943	12 Apr 1944
BLACK (4)	DD 666	Federal SB & DD Co	28 Mar 1943	21 May 1943
BULLARD	DD 660	Federal SB & DD Co	28 Feb 1943	9 Apr 1943
CAPERTON (4)	DD 650	Bath Iron Works Corpn	24 July 1943	30 July 1943
CASSIN YOUNG	DD 793	Bethlehem Co San Pedro	12 Sep 1943	31 Dec 1943
CHARLES J. BADGER	DD 657	Bethlehem Co Staten Island	3 Apr 1943	23 July 1943
CHAUNCEY	DD 667	Federal SB & DD Co	28 Mar 1943	31 May 1943
COTTEN (4)	DD 669	Federal SB & DD Co	12 June 1943	24 July 1943
DASHIELL (4)	DD 659	Federal SB & DD Co	6 Feb 1943	20 Mar 1943
HEALY (4)	DD 674	Federal SB & DD Co	1 Aug 1943	22 Sep 1943
HUNT (4)	DD 672	Federal SB & DD Co	4 July 1943	3 Sep 1943
JOHN HOOD (4)	DD 655	Gulf SB Corpn	23 Oct 1943	7 June 1944
KIDD	DD 661	Federal SB & DD Co	28 Feb 1943	23 Apr 1944
KNAPP	DD 653	Bath Iron Works Corpn	10 July 1943	16 Sep 1943
McNAIR (4)	DD 679	Federal SB & DD Co	14 Nov 1943	30 Dec 1943
MELVIN	DD 680	Federal SB & DD Co	17 Oct 1943	24 Nov 1943
NORMAN SCOTT	DD 690	Bath Iron Works Corpn	28 Aug 1943	5 Nov 1943
PICKING (4)	DD 685	Bethlehem Co Staten Island	31 May 1943	21 Sep 1943
PORTER	DD 800	Todd Pacific Shipyards	13 Mar 1944	24 June 1944
PORTERFIELD	DD 682	Bethlehem Co San Pedro	13 June 1943	30 Oct 1943
PRESTON (4)	DD 795	Bethlehem Co San Pedro	12 Dec 1943	20 Mar 1944
REMEY	DD 688	Bath Iron Works Corpn	24 July 1943	30 Sep 1943
STOCKHAM	DD 683	Bethlehem Co, San Francisco	25 June 1943	11 Feb 1944
*UHLMANN (4)	DD 687	Bethlehem Co, Staten Island	30 July 1943	22 Nov 1943
WEDDERBURN	DD 684	Bethlehem Co, San Francisco	1 Aug 1943	9 Mar 1944

Fifty-six destroyers of this class were completed in 1943-1944. They are essentially the same as the original "Fletcher" class. All surviving ships of this class are in reserve except the operational Naval Reserve training ship Uhlmann.

ARMAMENT- DESIGN. As built, these ships each mounted five 5 inch guns, ten 40 mm guns, several 20 mm guns, and ten 21 inch torpedo tubes. The twin 40 mm gun mounts were installed just forward of and below the bridge, alongside the second funnel, and atop the after deckhouse.

All secondary guns have been removed from some ships (see photograph of Porterfield).

After World War II a large number of these ships had their pole mast replaced by a tripod mast and five torpedo tubes between funnels were removed. All 20 mm guns also were removed. Twenty ships had their No. 3 ("Q") 5 inch mount removed and the 40 mm guns replaced by six 3 inch guns (twin), the latter installed between funnels and atop after deckhouse. Four-gun destroyers remaining on the Navy List are indicated.

All ships active during the 1960s were fitted with triple Mk 32 launchers for ASW torpedoes.

WAR LOSSES. Callaghan (DD 792), Colhoun (DD 801) and Little (DD 803).

DISPOSALS AND TRANSFERS

Heywood L. Edwards (DD 663) and Richard P. Leary (DD 664) to Japan on 10 Mar 1959; Jarvis (DD 799) to Spain on 3 Nov 1960; McGowan (DD 678) to Spain on 31 Nov 1960; Cushing (DD 797) to Brazil on 20 July 1961; Dortch (DD 670) to Argentina on 1 Aug 1961; Benham (DD 796) to Peru on 8 Oct 1961; Wadleigh (DD 689) and Rooks (DD 804) to Chile on 26 July 1962; Monssen (DD 798) stricken on 1 Feb 1963 (scrapped after running aground while under tow); McDermut (DD 677) stricken on 1 Apr 1965; Gregory (DD 802) stricken on 1 May 1966, but retained as non-seagoing training ship at San Diego (renamed Indoctrinator) until Jan 1971 (sunk as target).

Colahan (DD 658) stricken on 1 Aug 1966 (target); Clarence K. Bronson (DD 668) to Turkey on 14 Jan 1967; Van Valkenburgh (DD 656) to Turkey on 28 Feb 1967; Lewis Hancock (DD 675) to Brazil on 1 Aug 1967; Halsey Powell (DD 686) to South Korea on 27 Apr 1968; Irwin (DD 794) to Brazil on 10 May 1968; Hickox (DD 673) to South Korea on 11 Nov 1968; Bryant (DD 665) stricken on 1 June 1968; Marshall (DD 676) stricken on 12 July 1969; Cogswell (DD 651) to Turkey on 1 Oct 1969; Hopewell (DD 681) stricken on 2 Jan 1970; Mertz (DD 691) stricken on 1 Oct 1970; Albert W. Grant (DD 649) stricken on 14 Apr 1971; Bennion (DD 662) stricken on 15 Apr 1971.

MODERNISED "FLETCHER" CLASS

The 18 standard "Fletcher" class destroyers which were converted to escort destroyers (DDE) in 1949-1951 have been stricken. Their ASW capability was increased; three 5 inch guns and torpedo tubes removed. The Jenkins, Nicholas, and Radford were modernised in 1960 under the FRAM II programme. All 18 ships reclassified DD on 1 July 1962.

Murray (DD 576) stricken on 1 June 1965; Saufley (DD 465) stricken on 1 Sep 1966 (target); Fletcher (DD 445) stricken on 1 Aug 1967; Bache (DD 470) stricken on 1 Mar 1968 (ran aground off Rhodes, Greece, on 6 Feb 1968); Beale (DD 471), Philip (DD 498), Sproston (DD 577) stricken on 1 Oct 1968; Jenkins (DD 447), Cony (DD 508), Eaton (DD 510) stricken on 2 July 1969; Radford (DD 446) and Waller (DD 466) stricken on 15 July 1939; Taylor (DD 468) and Walker (DD 517) to Italy in July of 1969; Conway (DD 507) stricken on 15 Nov 1969; Nicholas (DD 449) and O'Bannon (DD 450) stricken on 30 Jan 1970; Renshaw (DD 499) stricken on 14 Feb 1970.

See 1969-1970 and previous editions for details.

PORTERFIELD (DD 682)　　　　　　　　1965, United States Navy

SHIELDS (DD 596)—See following page　　　　　　　　1966, United States Navy

Surface Combatants—*continued*

35 DESTROYERS (DD): "FLETCHER" CLASS

Displacement, tons	2 100 standard; 3 050 full load		
Length, feet (*metres*)	376·5 (*114·7*) oa		
Beam, feet (*metres*)	39·5 (*11·9*)		
Draft, feet (*metres*)	18 (*5·5*)		
Guns	4 or 5—5 inch (*127 mm*) 38 calibre dual-purpose		
	6—40 mm AA (twin) or 6—3 inch (*76 mm*) AA (twin) (see *Armament* notes)		
ASW weapons	depth charges		
	2 fixed hedgehogs		
	2 triple torpedo launchers (Mk 32) in some ships		
Torpedo tubes	5 or 10—21 inch (*533 mm*) quintuple		
Main engines	2 geared turbines; 60 000 shp; 2 shafts		
Boilers	4		
Speed, knots	35		
Complement	249 (14 officers, 235 enlisted men) (designed wartime 329)		

Name	No.	Builder	Laid down	Launched	Completed
ABBOT (4 guns)	DD 629	Bath Iron Works Corpn	21 Sep 1942	17 Feb 1943	23 Apr 1943
BELL	DD 587	Charleston Navy Yard	24 Feb 1942	24 June 1942	4 Mar 1943
*****BRAINE** (4)	DD 630	Bath Iron Works Corpn	12 Oct 1942	7 Mar 1943	11 May 1943
BURNS	DD 588	Charleston Navy Yard	9 May 1942	8 Aug 1942	3 Apr 1943
*****COWELL** (4)	DD 547	Bethlehem Co. San Pedro	7 Sep 1942	18 Apr 1943	23 Aug 1943
DALEY (4)	DD 519	Bethlehem Co. Staten Island	29 Apr 1942	24 Oct 1942	10 Mar 1943
FOOTE	DD 511	Bath Iron Works Corpn	14 Apr 1942	11 Oct 1942	22 Dec 1942
FRANKS	DD 554	Seattle-Tacoma SB Corpn	8 Mar 1942	7 Dec 1942	30 July 1943
HARADEN	DD 585	Boston Navy Yard	3 June 1942	19 Mar 1943	16 Sep 1943
HART	DD 594	Puget Sound Navy Yard	10 Aug 1943	25 Sep 1944	4 Nov 1944
HAZELWOOD (3)	DD 531	Bethlehem Co. San Francisco	11 Apr 1942	20 Nov 1942	18 June 1943
HUDSON	DD 475	Boston Navy Yard	23 Feb 1942	3 June 1942	13 Apr 1943
LA VALLETTE	DD 448	Federal SB & DD Co	27 Nov 1941	21 June 1942	12 Aug 1942
LAWS	DD 558	Seattle-Tacoma SB Corpn	19 May 1942	22 Apr 1943	18 Nov 1943
MILLER (4)	DD 535	Bethlehem Co. San Francisco	18 Aug 1942	7 Mar 1943	31 Aug 1943
*****MULLANY** (4)	DD 528	Bethlehem Co. San Francisco	15 Jan 1942	12 Oct 1942	23 Apr 1943
McCORD	DD 534	Bethlehem Co. San Francisco	17 Mar 1942	10 Jan 1943	19 Aug 1943
McKEE	DD 575	Consolidated Steel Corpn	2 Mar 1942	2 Aug 1942	31 Mar 1943
OWEN	DD 536	Bethlehem Co. San Francisco	17 Sep 1942	21 Mar 1943	20 Sep 1943
ROBINSON	DD 562	Seattle-Tacoma SB Corpn	12 Aug 1942	28 Aug 1943	31 Jan 1944
ROSS (4)	DD 563	Seattle-Tacoma SB Corpn	7 Sep 1942	10 Sep 1943	21 Feb 1944
ROWE (4)	DD 564	Seattle-Tacoma SB Corpn	7 Dec 1942	30 Sep 1943	13 Mar 1944
SCHROEDER	DD 501	Federal SB & DD Co	25 June 1942	11 Nov 1942	1 Jan 1943
*****SHIELDS**	DD 596	Puget Sound Navy Yard	10 Aug 1943	25 Sep 1944	8 Feb 1945
SIGOURNEY	DD 643	Bath Iron Works Corpn	7 Dec 1942	24 Apr 1943	29 June 1943
SIGSBEE	DD 502	Federal SB & DD Co	22 July 1942	7 Dec 1942	23 Jan 1943
STEPHEN POTTER	DD 538	Bethlehem Co. San Francisco	27 Oct 1942	28 Apr 1943	21 Oct 1943
STODDARD (4)	DD 566	Seattle-Tacoma SB Corpn	10 Mar 1943	19 Nov 1943	15 Apr 1944
TERRY	DD 513	Bath Iron Works Corpn	8 June 1942	22 Nov 1942	26 Jan 1943
THE SULLIVANS	DD 537	Bethlehem Co. San Francisco	10 Oct 1942	4 Apr 1943	30 Sep 1943
TRATHEN (4)	DD 530	Bethlehem Co. San Francisco	17 Mar 1942	22 Oct 1942	28 May 1943
*****TWINING**	DD 540	Bethlehem Co. San Francisco	20 Nov 1942	11 July 1943	1 Dec 1943
WATTS	DD 567	Seattle-Tacoma SB Corpn	26 Mar 1943	31 Dec 1943	29 Apr 1944
WICKES	DD 578	Consolidated Steel Corpn	15 Apr 1942	13 Sep 1942	16 June 1943
WREN	DD 568	Seattle-Tacoma SB Corpn	24 Apr 1943	29 Jan 1944	22 May 1944

One hundred nineteen ships of this class were completed in 1942-45. Eighteen ships subsequently were converted to Escort Destroyers (DDE) and are listed separately. Eleven ships of this class were cancelled: DD 505, 506, 523-525, 542, 543, 548, 549, *Percival* (DD 542), and *Watson* (DD 482). The last two were to have been 2 100-ton destroyers with experimental power plants. (The experimental ships DD 503 and DD 504, of an unspecified type, were cancelled in 1941.)

All surviving ships of this class are in reserve except for the operational Naval Reserve training ships *Braine*, *Cowell*, *Mullany*, *Shields*, and *Twining*

ARMAMENT-DESIGN. These ships marked reversion to flush-deck destroyers by the US Navy after several broken-deck designs built during the 1930s and early 1940s. This design was extremely successful and 56 additional ships of this class were constructed (listed separately).

As built, these ships each mounted five 5 inch guns, six 40 mm AA guns, several 20 mm AA guns, and ten 21 inch torpedo tubes. The twin 40 mm gun mounts were installed on each side of the second funnel and atop the after deckhouse.

After World War II a large number of these ships had their pole mast replaced by a tripod mast and the five torpedo tubes between funnels were removed. All 20 mm guns also removed. Twenty-one ships had their No. 3 ("Q") 5 inch mount removed and the 40 mm guns replaced by six 3 inch guns (twin), the latter installed between Funnels and atop after deckhouse.

Note in photograph of *Shields* that she retained a twin 40 mm gun aft as her only secondary armament in 1966. All ships of this class active during the 1960s were fitted with triple Mk 32 launchers for ASW torpedoes.

HELICOPTERS. The *Hazelwood* was extensively modified to serve as test ship for the Drone Anti-Submarine Helicopter (DASH) programme. Her gun armament was reduced to three 5 inch mounts and a helicopter hangar and platform were fitted amidships (see photograph).

NOMENCLATURE. Three ships were renamed while building: DD 528 ex-*Beatty*, DD 537 ex-*Putnam*, DD 594 ex-*Mansfield*.

WAR LOSSES. *Chevalier* (DD 451), *Strong* (DD 467), *De Haven* (DD 469), *Pringle* (DD 477), *Spence* (DD 512), *Brownson* (DD 518), *Luce* (DD 522), *Abner Read* (DD 526), *Bush* (DD 529), *Hoel* (DD 533) *Johnston* (DD 557), *Longshaw* (DD 559), *Morrison* (DD 560), *William D. Porter* (DD 579), *Halligan* (DD 584), and *Twiggs* (DD 591).

BRAINE (DD 630)   *1970, US Navy, PHC H. W. Browning*

HAZELWOOD (DD 531)   *United States Navy*

DISPOSALS AND TRANSFERS
Capps (DD 550) and **David W. Taylor** (DD 551) to Spain on 15 May 1957; **Anthony** (DD 515) to West Germany on 17 Jan 1958; **Guest** (DD 472) to Brazil on 5 June 1959; **Charette** (DD 581) to Greece on 15 June 1959; **Converse** (DD 509) to Spain on 1 July 1959; **Ringgold** (DD 500) to West Germany on 14 July 1959; **Aulick** (DD 569) to Greece on 21 Aug 1959; **Conner** (DD 582) to Greece on 15 Sep 1959; **Wadsworth** (DD 516) to West Germany on 6 Oct 1959;

Claxton (DD 571) to West Germany on 15 Dec 1959; **Bennett** (DD 473) to Brazil on 15 Dec 1959; **Hall** (DD 583) to Greece on 9 Feb 1960; **Dyson** (DD 572) to West Germany on 17 Feb 1960; **Ausburn** (DD 570) to West Germany on 12 Apr 1960; **Ammen** (DD 527) stricken on 1 Sep 1960 (damaged in collision); **Hale** (DD 642) to Columbia on 23 Jan 1961; **Howorth** (DD 529) stricken on 1 June 1961; **Hailey** (DD 556) to Brazil on 20 July 1961; **Heerman** (DD 532) and **Stembel** (DD 644) to Argentina on 1 Aug 1961; **Isherwood** (DD 520) to Peru on 8 Oct 1961; **Fullam** (DD 474) stricken on 1 June 1962 (target); **Bradford** (DD 545) and **Brown** (DD 546) to Greece on 27 Sep 1962; **Erben** (DD 631) to South Korea on 1 May 1963;

Tingey (DD 593) stricken on 1 Jan 1963 (target); **Smalley** (DD 565) stricken on 1 Apr 1965; **Tingey** (DD 539) stricken on 1 Nov 1965; **Kimberly** (DD 521) to Nationalist China on 1 June 1967; **Halford** (DD 480), **John D. Henley** (DD 553), **Harrison** (DD 573), **John Rodgers** (DD 574), **Young** (DD 580), **Izard** (DD 589), **Paul Hamilton** (DD 590), **Wiley** (DD 597) stricken on 1 May 1968; **Harrison** and **John Rodgers** subsequently transferred to Mexico on 19 Aug 1970; **Yarnall** (DD 541) to Nationalist China on 17 June 1969; **Boyd** (DD 544) to Turkey on 1 Oct 1969; **Pritchett** (DD 561) to Italy on 10 Jan 1970; **Stanley** (DD 478) stricken on 1 Dec 1970; **Metcalf** (DD 595) stricken on 2 Jan 1971; **Stevens** (DD 479) stricken in 1971.

Surface Combatants—*continued*

DESTROYERS (DD): "GLEAVES" CLASS

Displacement, tons	1 700 standard; 2 580 full load
Length, feet (*metres*)	348·2 (*106·1*) oa (see *Design* notes)
Beam, feet (*metres*)	36 (*11·0*)
Draft, feet (*metres*)	18 (*5·5*)
Guns	3 or 4—5 inch (*127 mm*) 38 calibre dual-purpose
	4—40 mm AA (twin) or 12—40 mm AA (two twin, two quad) in rearmed ships
	4 to 7—20 mm AA (single)
ASW weapons	depth charges (removed in former DMS type)
Torpedo tubes	5—21 inch (*533 mm*) quintuple (removed in former DMS type and rearmed DD type)
Main engines	2 geared turbines; 50 000 shp; 2 shafts
Boilers	4 (Babcock & Wilcox)
Speed, knots	37·6
Complement	240 (designed wartime 276 in DD type; 272 in former DMS type)

Name	No.	Commissioned	Name	No.	Commissioned
CARMICK	DD 493	28 Dec 1942	HERNDON	DD 638	20 Dec 1942
DAVISON	DD 618	11 Sep 1942	JEFFERS	DD 621	4 Nov 1942
DORAN	DD 634	4 Aug 1942	KEARNY	DD 432	13 Sep 1940
DOYLE	DD 494	27 Jan 1943	McCOOK	DD 496	15 Mar 1943
EDWARDS	DD 619	18 Sep 1942	QUICK	DD 490	3 July 1942
FITCH	DD 462	3 Feb 1943	STOCKTON	DD 646	11 Jan 1943
FRANKFORD	DD 497	31 Mar 1943	THOMPSON	DD 627	10 July 1943
GHERARDI	DD 637	15 Sep 1942	THORN	DD 647	1 Apr 1943
GRAYSON	DD 435	14 Feb 1941	TILLMAN	DD 641	4 June 1942
HAMBLETON	DD 455	22 Dec 1941	WOOLSEY	DD 437	7 May 1941

Sixty-six destroyers of this class were completed in 1940-1943. Twelve subsequently were converted to High Speed Minesweepers (DMS) in 1944 and another 12 in 1945. This class saw extensive service in World War II with 13 ships being lost to enemy action. The surviving "straight" destroyers (DD) were laid up in reserve in 1946-1948; some of the converted minesweepers remained in service into 1956. The 19 remaining DMS were reclassified DD in 1954-1955.
The *Hobson* (DMS 26, ex-DD 464) was sunk on 26 Apr 1952 in a night collision with the carrier *Wasp* (CVA 18).

All surviving ships of this class are expected to be stricken in 1971-72.

CLASS. These ships often are referred to as the "Gleaves-Livermore" class; officially the "Gleaves" class.

CONVERSION. The 24 ships converted to minesweepers had their aftermost 5 inch gun, all torpedo tubes, and depth charge racks and projectors removed. Minesweep-

ing equipment fitted aft. Of the remaining ships of this class, the following are former minesweepers: *Hambleton* (ex-DMS 20), *Fitch* (ex-DMS 25), *Quick* (ex-DMS 32), *Carmick* (ex-DMS 33), *Doyle* (ex-DMS 34), *McCook* (ex-DMS 36), *Davison* (ex-DMS 37), *Jeffers* (ex-DMS 27), *Thompson* (ex-DMS 38), *Doran* (ex-DMS 41), and *Gherardi* (ex-DMS 30).

DESIGN. This class was built to plans prepared by Gibbs and Cox and differs slightly from the previous "Benson" class. (These ships have rounded funnels). Within this class, the DD 423, 424, 429-444 are 348·3 feet overall and the other ships are 348·2 feet overall.

GUNNERY. The DD 423, 424, 429-444 were armed with five 5 inch guns when completed; subsequently reduced to four guns.

TORPEDOES. The first 18 ships were completed with ten torpedo tubes; subsequently reduced to five.

NOMENCLATURE. The name *Wilkes* was withdrawn from the DD 441 on 16 July 1968 for assignment to the surveying ship AGS 33.

WAR LOSSES. *Gwin* (DD 433), *Meredith* (DD 434), *Monssen* (DD 436), *Ingraham* (DD 444), *Bristol* (DD 453), *Emmons* (DD 457/DMS 22), *Corry* (DD 463), *Aaron Ward* (DD 483), *Duncan* (DD 485), *Glennon* (DD 620), *Maddox* (DD 622), *Beatty* (DD 640), *Turner* (DD 648).

DISPOSALS AND TRANSFERS
Four heavily damaged ships were scrapped after World War II: **Forrest** (DMS 24/DD 461) stricken on 20 Nov 1946, **Harding** (DMS 28/DD 625) on 16 Mar 1947, **Shubrick** (DD 639) on 28 Sep 1947, **Butler** (DMS 29/DD 636) on 10 Jan 1948; **Buchanan** (DD 484) and **McCalla** (DD 488) to Turkey on 28 Apr 1949; **Landsdowne** (DD 484) and **Lardner** (DD 487) to Turkey on 10 June 1949; **Nicholson** (DD 442) to Italy on 15 Jan 1951; **Eberle** (DD 430) and **Ludlow** (DD 438) to Greece on 22 Jan 1951; **Ellyson** (DMS 19/DD 454) and **Macomb** (DMS 23/DD 458) to Japan on 19 Oct 1954; **Rodman** (DMS 21/DD 456) to Nationalist China on 28 July 1955; **Livermore** (DD 429) stricken on 19 July 1956 (target); **Plunkett** (DD 431) to Nationalist China on 16 Feb 1959; **Baldwin** (DD 624) stricken on 1 June 1961 (scrapped after running aground while under tow); **Edison** (DD 439) stricken on 1 Apr 1966; **Knight** (DD 633) stricken on 1 Jan 1967 (target); **Nelson** (DD 623) and **Wells** (DD 628) stricken on 1 Mar 1968;

Niblock (DD 424) stricken on 31 July 1968 (target). **Gleaves** (DD 423) and **Endicott** (DMS 35/DD 495) stricken on 1 Nov 1969 (**Gleaves** retained as memorial); **Earle** (DMS 42/DD 635) stricken on 1 Dec 1969; **Ericsson** (DD 440) stricken on 1 June 1970; **Wilkes** (DD 441) and **Swanson** (DD 443) stricken in 1970. **Cowie** (DMS 39/DD 632) and **Satterlee** (DD 626) Stricken on 1 Dec 1970; **Twining** (DD 540) stricken on 1 July 1971; **Cowell** (DD 547) stricken in Aug 1971; **Mullany** (DD 528) to strike in Oct 1971.

DESTROYERS (DD): "BENSON" CLASS

Displacement, tons	1 620 standard; 2 575 full load
Length, feet (*metres*)	347·7 (*105·9*) oa
Beam, feet (*metres*)	36 (*10·9*)
Draft, feet (*metres*)	18 (*5·5*)
Guns	4—5 inch (*127 mm*) 38 calibre dual-purpose
	4—40 mm AA (twin) or 12—40 mm AA, (two twin, two quad) in some ships as rearmed
	7—20 mm AA (single) reduced in rearmed ships
ASW weapons	depth charges
Torpedo tubes	5 or 10—21 inch (*533 mm*) quintuple, removed from rearmed ships
Main engines	2 geared turbines (Bethlehem); 50 000 shp; 2 shafts
Boilers	4 (Babcock & Wilcox)
Speed, knots	37·6
Complement	230 (designed wartime 276)

Name	No.	Commissioned	Name	No.	Commissioned
BANCROFT	DD 598	30 Apr 1943	LAUB	DD 613	24 Oct 1942
BOYLE	DD 600	15 Aug 1942	McLANAHAN	DD 615	19 Dec 1942
COGHLAN	DD 606	10 July 1942	MACKENZIE	DD 614	21 Nov 1942
FARENHOLT	DD 491	2 Apr 1942	MEADE	DD 602	22 June 1942
FRAZIER	DD 607	30 July 1942	NIELDS	DD 616	15 Jan 1943
GANSEVOORT	DD 608	26 Aug 1942	ORDRONAUX	DD 617	13 Feb 1943
GILLESPIE	DD 609	18 Sep 1942	PARKER	DD 604	31 Aug 1942
HOBBY	DD 610	18 Nov 1942			

Thirty destroyers of this class were completed in 1940-1943. They saw extensive service in World War II, with three ships being sunk by enemy action. The survivors were laid up in reserve in 1946-1948.

All surviving ships of this class are expected to be stricken in 1971-1972.

CLASS. These ships often are referred to as the "Benson-Mayo" class; officially the "Benson" class.

CONVERSION. After World War II two of these ships were to have been converted to Corvettes (DDC) as

prototypes for conversion of this and the "Gleaves-Livermore" classes. Conversion plans provided for removal of two boilers and installation of improved sonar. The ships would be employed as fast convoy escorts. Conversion rescinded.

DESIGN. All of this class were built to Bethlehem-prepared plans and have square funnels.

ENGINEERING. The principal innovation of this class was the alternate grouping of boiler and engine rooms, an arrangement reflected in their separate funnels and greatly increasing their capacity to survive serious damage.

GUNNERY. The first six ships of this class (DD 421, 422, 425-428) initially were armed with five 5 inch guns subsequently reduced to four guns. The five gun ships had an open, forward facing 5 inch mount between the after bank of torpedo tubes and No 4 ("X") gun mount.

TORPEDOES. The first six ships of this class also were completed with ten tubes; later ships built with five

tubes. This class introduced quintuple torpedo tube mounts to United States destroyers.

WAR LOSSES. *Lansdale* (DD 426), *Laffey* (DD 459), *Barton* (DD 599).

PHOTOGRAPHS. These ships have flat-sided stacks while the contemporary *"Gleaves"* class ships have rounded stacks.

DISPOSALS AND TRANSFERS,
Woodworth (DD 460) to Italy on 25 May 1951; **Benson** (DD 421) and **Hilary P. Jones** (DD 427) to Nationalist China on 26 Feb 1954; **Caldwell** (DD 605) stricken on 1 May 1965; **Kendrick** (DD 612) stricken on 1 May 1966 (target); **Madison** (DD 425), **Charles F. Hughes** (DD 428), **Bailey** (DD 492), **Kalk** (DD 611) stricken on 1 June 1968 (**Charles F. Hughes** expended as target); **Murphy** (DD 603) stricken on 1 Nov 1970; **Mayo** (DD 422) stricken on 1 Dec 1970; **Champlin** (DD 601) stricken on 2 Jan 1971.

FRANKFORD (DD 497)

US Navy from James C. Fahey Collection.

OCEAN ESCORTS

Ocean Escorts is the official US Navy classification for escort ships, three variations of which now are on the Navy List: "straight" escort ships (DE), guided missile escort ships (DEG), and radar picket escort ships (DER). The escort research ship *Glover* (AGDE 1) also is included in this section of *Jane's* because of her similarity to other ocean escorts.

From the viewpoint of overall operational capability, these ships fall into three categories:

● The 44 escort ships of the "Brooke", "Knox", "Garcia", "Glover", and "Bronstein" classes that have modern submarine detection equipment (SQS-26 sonar) and medium range anti-submarine weapons (ASROC). These ships may be presumed to have a creditable capability against conventional (diesel-electric) submarines, but their ability to operate against nuclear-powered submarines, especially the later Soviet undersea craft of this type, must be considered extremely marginal. Of particular concern in ASW operations is their maximum speed of about 27 knots and the lack of a helicopter for long-range attack. In both respects these ships are inferior to most foreign contemporaries.

Further, the air/surface combat capability of these ships is limited, consisting of one or two 5 inch 38 calibre guns except for the six "Brooke" class ships armed with the Tartar surface-to-air missiles (with a range of about 15 miles) and two ships armed with only 3 inch guns. Although the Sea Sparrow point-defence missile system is planned for many of these ships, it is many years away from being available. Thus, the six "Brooke" class ships, although limited by a 27-knot speed and lack helicopter, probably are the most capable of the US Navy's escort ships although they are significantly smaller than the later "Knox" class ships.

● The 17 escort ships of the "Claud Jones", "Courtney", and "Dealey" classes are of post-war construction but lack modern submarine detection equipment, ASW weapons, and speed to have an effective capability against nuclear-powered or even modern conventional submarines. However, it is anticipated that several of these ships will be transferred to foreign navies in the near future to replace older, World War II-built escort ships and frigates that no longer are economical to operate.

● The approximately 125 World War II-built escort ships that remain on the Navy List all are in reserve except for two that normally are employed in surveillance of Soviet ships, the *Thomas J. Gary* and *Calcaterra*. These ships have no practical ASW capability against submarines constructed during the past 25 years. However, some were usefully employed in the Vietnamese War as coastal patrol ships, a mission that can be better accomplished by other ships now available to the US Navy.

Twenty-one additional "Knox" class escort ships are under construction or authorised. These will give the US Navy a total of 65 escort ships with SQS-26 sonar and ASROC weapons by 1974, and it is anticipated that no further ships of this category will be built in the foreseeable future.

NOMENCLATURE. Escort ships generally are named for US Navy, Marine Corps, and Coast Guard personnel.

PATTERSON (DE 1061) *1970, United States Navy*

RATHBURNE (DE 1057) *1970, United States Navy*

RATHBURNE (DE 1057) *1970, United States Navy*

Ocean Escorts—*continued*

6 GUIDED MISSILE ESCORT SHIPS (DEG) "BROOKE" CLASS

Displacement, tons	2 640 standard ; 3 425 full load
Length, feet (*metres*)	414·5 (*126·3*) oa
Beam, feet (*metres*)	44·2 (*13·5*)
Draft, feet (*metres*)	24 (*7·3*)
Missiles	1 single Tartar surface-to-air launcher
Guns	1—5 inch (*127 mm*) 38 calibre dual-purpose
ASW weapons	1 ASROC 8-tube launcher 2 triple torpedo launchers (Mk 32) 2 fixed torpedo tubes (stern) (Mk 25) facilities for small helicopter
Main engines	1 geared turbine (Westinghouse) ; 35 000 shp; 1 shaft
Boilers	2—1 200 psi (*83·4 kg/cm²*) (Foster Wheeler)
Speed, knots	27
Complement	241 (16 officers, 225 enlisted men)

Name	No.	Builder	Laid down	Launched	Commissioned
*BROOKE	DEG 1	Lockheed SB & Construction Co	10 Dec 1962	19 July 1963	12 Mar 1966
*RAMSEY	DEG 2	Lockheed SB & Construction Co	4 Feb 1963	15 Oct 1963	3 June 1967
*SCHOFIELD	DEG 3	Lockheed SB & Construction Co	15 Apr 1963	7 Dec 1963	20 Apr 1968
*TALBOT	DEG 4	Bath Iron Works Corp	4 May 1964	6 Jan 1966	22 Apr 1967
*RICHARD L. PAGE	DEG 5	Bath Iron Works Corp	4 Jan 1965	4 Apr 1966	5 Aug 1967
*JULIUS A. FURER	DEG 6	Bath Iron Works Corp	12 July 1965	22 July 1966	11 Nov 1967

These ships are identical to the "Garcia" class escorts except for the Tartar missile system in lieu of a second 5 inch gun mount and different electronic equipment. DEG 1-3 were authorised in the Fiscal Year 1962 new construction programme and the DEG 4-6 in the FY 1963 programme. Plans for ten additional DEGs in FY 1964 and possibly three more DEGs in a later programme were dropped because of the $11 000 000 additional cost of a DEG over DE. See "Garcia" class for additional notes.

CLASSIFICATION. DEG 7-11 are guided missile "frigates" being built in Spain with US assistance.

ELECTRONICS. SQS-26 bow mounted sonar installed. SPS-52 three-dimensional search radar is mounted on the "mack" (combination mast and stack) and SPS-10 search radar is installed on the mast.

BROOKE (DEG 1)   *1969, United States Navy, WO Rodney C. Moen*

HELICOPTERS. These ships were designed to operate Drone Anti-Submarine Helicopters (DASH), but the programme was cut back before helicopters were provided to these ships. Small hangar aft.

MISSILES. These ships have a single Tartar Mk 22 launching system which weighs 92 395 pounds. Reportedly, the system has a rate of fire similar to the larger Mk 11 and Mk 13 systems installed in guided missile destroyers, but the DEG system has a considerably smaller magazine capacity (16 missiles according to unofficial sources).

The DEGs have a single Mk 74-2 missile fire control system whereas the larger DDGs have two such systems, providing a considerably greater anti-air warfare capability.

The DEG 4-6 have automatic ASROC loading system (note angled base of bridge structure aft of ASROC "pepper box" in these ships).

PHOTOGRAPHS. Note stem anchor and second anchor on port side near 5 inch gun, stern tube openings in *Brooke*.

SCHOFIELD (DEG 3)   *1969, US Navy, PH2 J. R. Altavera*

BROOKE (DEG 1)   *United States Navy*

Ocean Escorts—*continued*

46 ESCORT SHIPS (DE): "KNOX" CLASS

Displacement, tons	3 011 standard; 4 100 full load	
Length, feet (*metres*)	438 (*133·5*) oa	
Beam, feet (*metres*)	46·75	
Draft, feet (*metres*)	24 75	
Guns	1—5 inch (*127 mm*) 54 calibre dual-purpose	
ASW weapons	1 ASROC 8-tube launcher 4 fixed torpedo launchers (Mk 32) facilities for small ASW helicopter	
Missiles	space reserved for Basic Point Defence Missile System (BPDMS) (see *Missile* notes)	
Main engines	1 geared turbine (Westinghouse) 35 000 shp; 1 shaft	
Boilers	2—1 200 psi (*83·4 kg/cm²*)	
Speed, knots	27+	
Complement	220 (15 officers, 205 enlisted men)	

Name	No.	Builder	Laid down	Launched	Commission
*KNOX	DE 1052	Todd Shipyards (Seattle)	5 Oct 1965	19 Nov 1966	12 Apr 1969
*ROARK	DE 1053	Todd Shipyards (Seattle)	2 Feb 1966	24 Apr 1967	22 Nov 1969
*GRAY	DE 1054	Todd Shipyards (Seattle)	19 Nov 1966	3 Nov 1967	4 Apr 1970
*HEPBURN	DE 1055	Todd Shipyards (San Pedro)	1 June 1966	25 Mar 1967	3 July 1969
*CONNOLE	DE 1056	Avondale Shipyards	23 Mar 1967	20 July 1968	30 Aug 1969
*RATHBURNE	DE 1057	Lockheed SB & Constn Co	8 Jan 1968	2 May 1969	May 1970
*MEYERKORD	DE 1058	Todd Shipyards (San Pedro)	1 Sep 1966	15 July 1967	28 Nov 1969
*W. S. SIMS	DE 1059	Avondale Shipyards	10 Apr 1967	4 Jan 1969	3 Jan 1970
*LANG	DE 1060	Todd Shipyards (San Pedro)	25 Mar 1967	17 Feb 1968	28 Mar 1970
*PATTERSON	DE 1061	Avondale Shipyards	12 Oct 1967	3 May 1969	14 Mar 1970
*WHIPPLE	DE 1062	Todd Shipyards (Seattle)	24 Apr 1967	12 Apr 1968	22 Aug 1970
*REASONER	DE 1063	Lockheed SB & Constn Co	6 Jan 1969	1 Aug 1970	June 1971
*LOCKWOOD	DE 1064	Todd Shipyards (Seattle)	3 Nov 1967	5 Sep 1964	5 Dec 1970
STEIN	DE 1065	Lockheed SB & Constn Co	1 June 1970	19 Dec 1970	Jan 1972
*MARVIN SHIELDS	DE 1066	Todd Shipyards (Seattle)	12 Apr 1968	23 Oct 1969	Apr 1971
*FRANCIS HAMMOND	DE 1067	Todd Shipyards (San Pedro)	15 July 1967	11 May 1968	25 July 1970
*VREELAND	DE 1068	Avondale Shipyards	20 Mar 1968	14 June 1969	13 June 1970
BAGLEY	DE 1069	Lockheed SB & Constn Co	22 Sep 1970	Apr 1971	May 1972
*DOWNES	DE 1070	Todd Shipyards (Seattle)	5 Sep 1968	13 Dec 1969	Aug 1971
*BADGER	DE 1071	Todd Shipyards (Seattle)	17 Feb 1968	7 Dec 1968	1 Dec 1970
*BLAKELY	DE 1072	Avondale Shipyards	3 June 1968	23 Aug 1969	18 July 1970
*ROBERT E. PERRY	DE 1073	Lockheed SB & Constn Co	20 Dec 1970	June 1971	Sep 1972
*HAROLD E. HOLT	DE 1074	Todd Shipyards (San Pedro)	11 May 1968	3 May 1969	26 Mar 1971
*TRIPPE	DE 1075	Avondale Shipyards	29 July 1968	1 Nov 1969	19 Sep 1970
FANNING	DE 1076	Todd Shipyards (San Pedro)	7 Dec 1968	24 Jan 1970	July 1971
*OUELLET	DE 1077	Avondale Shipyards	15 Jan 1969	17 Jan 1970	12 Dec 1970
*JOSEPH HEWES	DE 1078	Avondale Shipyards	15 May 1969	7 Mar 1970	27 Feb 1971
*BOWEN	DE 1079	Avondale Shipyards	11 July 1969	2 May 1970	May 1971
*PAUL	DE 1080	Avondale Shipyards	12 Sep 1969	20 June 1970	June 1971
AYLWIN	DE 1081	Avondale Shipyards	13 Nov 1969	29 Aug 1970	July 1971
ELMER MONTGOMERY	DE 1082	Avondale Shipyards	23 Jan 1970	21 Nov 1970	Sep 1971
COOK	DE 1083	Avondale Shipyards	20 Mar 1970	23 Jan 1971	Nov 1971
McCANDLESS	DE 1084	Avondale Shipyards	4 June 1970	Mar 1971	Jan 1972
DONALD B. BEARY	DE 1085	Avondale Shipyards	24 July 1970	May 1971	early 1972
BREWTON	DE 1086	Avondale Shipyards	2 Oct 1970	July 1971	mid 1972
KIRK	DE 1087	Avondale Shipyards	4 Dec 1970	Oct 1971	late 1972
BARBEY	DE 1088	Avondale Shipyards	Feb 1971	Dec 1971	late 1972
JESSE L. BROWN	DE 1089	Avondale Shipyards	Apr 1971	1972	1973
	DE 1090	Avondale Shipyards	June 1971	1972	1973
	DE 1091	Avondale Shipyards	Aug 1971	1972	1973
	DE 1092	Avondale Shipyards	Oct 1971	1972	1973
	DE 1093	Avondale Shipyards	Dec 1971	1972	1973
	DE 1904	Avondale Shipyards	Feb 1972	1972	1973
	DE 1095	Avondale Shipyards	Apr 1972	1973	1973
	DE 1096	Avondale Shipyards	June 1972	1973	1974
	DE 1097	Avondale Shipyards	Aug 1972	1973	1974

The 46 "Knox" class escort ships comprise the largest group of destroyer-type warships built to the same design in the West since the end of World War II. These ships are almost identical in design to the previous "Garcia" and "Brooke" classes, but slightly larger. (See those class listings for basic design data). DE 1052-1061 (10 ships) were authorised in the Fiscal Year 1964 new construction programme, DE 1062-1077 (16 ships) in FY 1965, DE 1078-1087 (10 ships) in FY 1966, DE 1088-1097 (10 ships) in FY 1967, and DE 1098-1107 (10 ships) in FY 1968. However, construction of six ships (DE 1102-1107) was deferred in 1968 as US Navy emphasis shifted to the more-versatile and faster DX/DXG ships; three additional ships (DE 1099-1101) were deferred late in 1968 to finance cost overruns of FY 1968 nuclear-powered attack submarines and to comply with a Congressional mandate to reduce expenditures; the last ship of the FY 1968 programme (DE 1098) was deferred early in 1969.

These ships have cost considerably more than originally estimated. The 14 ships built by Todd Shipyards were contracted for $151 000 000 in 1964; as of January 1970 the cost had increased an additional $96 000 000, an average total cost of almost $18 000 000 per ship with several ships not yet built.

CLASS. The DE-1078-1097 officially are considered as the "Joseph Hewes" class for administrative reasons (all ordered under a single contract on 25 Aug 1966). The DEG 7-11 guided missile "frigates" being built in Spain are similar to this design.

CONSTRUCTION. The ships built at Avondale Shipyards in Westwego, Louisiana, are constructed with a mass production technique of fabricating the hulls by using structural carbon steel tees split from wide-flange beams as longitudinal members. The hulls are built keel-up to permit downhand welding with the force of gravity allowing the molten weld to follow the contour of the hull and flow more easily between hull plates. Prefabricated, inverted hull modules first are assembled on a permanent platen, then lifted by hydraulic units and moved laterally into giant turning rings which rotate the hull into an upright position. Avondale, which also builds the "Hamilton" class cutters for the Coast Guard, side launches these ships.

DESIGN. These ships have a very large superstructure and a distinctive, cylindrical "mack" structure combining masts and engine exhaust stacks.

ELECTRONICS. SQS-26CX bow-mounted sonar is installed and there are provisions for SQA-13 variable depth sonar (VDS)

These ships have SPS-40 and SPS-10 search radar antennas on their "mack" structures.

The DE 1078-1097 (20 ships) are being fitted with SSM-5 Test Evaluation and Monitoring System (TEAMS) which continuously checks shipboard radar and sonar systems. If TEAMS detects a malfunction an automatic search will be conducted throughout the subsystems until the fault is found, and the defective component identified for repair or replacement. Up to 5 000 test points in 10 radar and sonar systems can be monitored by TEAMS on a 15-minute cycle with "real time" indication of whether the system is working, not working, or failing but still working. TEAMS can also test itself for malfunction and has a mean time to repair of 10 minutes. The system was evaluated in the frigate *Coontz* (DLG 9).

ENGINEERING. The DE 1101 was to have had gas turbine propulsion plant. According to Secretary of Defense Melvin Laird, the DE 1101, intended as an experimental gas-turbine ship, would not be needed because of the decision to use gas-turbine propulsion in the DD 963-class (DX) destroyers.

The *Peterson* is fitted with Baldwin-Lima-Hamilton controllable-pitch propellers for evaluation for possible use in the "Spruance" class destroyers; her shafts are non-reversible.

HELICOPTERS. These ships were designed to operate drone ASW helicopters. Instead, they now are programmed to receive the Light Airborne Multi-Purpose System (LAMPS) helicopter to become operational in the mid-1970s (two helicopters per ship).

GUNNERY. Gun armament for these ships consists of a single 5 inch/54 calibre Mk 42 mount forward with local anti-surface control (portside "bubble" or "frog-eye") but no local anti-aircraft control capability.

MISSILES. Original planning provided for these ships to have the Sea Mauler, a short-range anti-aircraft missile adapted from a missile being developed by the US Army. However, technical problems forced the Army to abandon the Mauler, terminating the Sea Mauler programme. Weight and space are reserved for eventual installation of a Basic Point Defense Missile System to provide close-in defence against aircraft.

BADGER (DE 1071)

1970, United States Navy

"KNOX" CLASS—*continued*

TORPEDOES. Improved ASROC-torpedo reloading capability as in some ships of previous "Garcia" class (note slanting face of bridge structure immediately behind ASROC "pepper box"). Four Mk 32 torpedo tubes are fixed in the amidships structure, two to a side angled out at 45 degrees. The arrangement provides improved loading capability over exposed triple Mk 32 launchers.

STATUS. These ships are considerably behind schedule, partially because of shipyard labour strikes and delays in Navy acceptance. The Fiscal Year 1964 ships are taking $2\frac{1}{2}$ to 4 years to build; some FY 1965 ships were not to be laid down until 1970, more than four years after the FY 1964 ships.
These ships have been criticised by some authorities as being inferior to their foreign contemporaries. Critics note the delay in providing variable depth sonar and a helicopter capability, the minimal gun armament, and the use of conventional propulsion vice gas turbines or combination diesel-gas turbines.

The 1971 prize essayist of the US Naval Institute, Captain Robert H. Smith, USN, has described this class as "the greatest mistake in ship procurement that the (US) Navy has known".

NOMENCLATURE. The lead ship of this class is named for naval historian Dudley W. Knox (the DD 742 was named for Frank Knox who was secretary of the Navy from 1940 to 1944). The *Harold E. Holt* honours the late Prime Minister of Australia, a firm supporter of U.S. policy in Southeast Asia during the Vietnam War. The *Jesse L. Brown* remembers the first US naval aviator of the Negro race; he was killed in action during the Korean War.

PATTERSON (DE 1061)　　　　　　　1970, United States Navy, PHCS W. H. Long

FRANCIS HAMMOND (DE 1067)　　　　　　　1970, United States Navy

FRANCIS HAMMOND (DE 1067)　　　　　　　1970, United States Navy

Ocean Escorts—continued

10 ESCORT SHIPS (DE): "GARCIA" CLASS

Displacement, tons	2 620 standard ; 3 400 full load				
Length, feet (metres)	414·5 (126·3) oa				
Beam, feet (metres)	44·2 (13·5)				
Draft, feet (metres)	24 (7·3)				
Guns	2—5 in (127 mm) 38 calibre dual-purpose				
ASW weapons	1 ASROC 8-tube launcher 2 triple torpedo launchers (Mk 32) facilities for small helicopter				
Main engines	1 geared turbine (Westinghouse) ; 35 000 shp ; 1 shaft				
Boilers	2—1 200 psi (83·4 kg/cm²) (Foster Wheeler)				
Speed, knots	27				
Complement	247				

Name	No.	Builder	Laid down	Launched	Commissioned
*GARCIA	DE 1040	Bethlehem Steel (San Francisco)	16 Oct 1962	31 Oct 1963	21 Dec 1964
*BRADLEY	DE 1041	Bethlehem Steel (San Francisco)	17 Jan 1963	26 Mar 1964	15 May 1965
*EDWARD McDONNELL	DE 1043	Avondale Shipyards	1 Apr 1963	15 Feb 1964	15 Feb 1965
*BRUMBY	DE 1044	Avondale Shipyards	1 Aug 1963	6 June 1964	5 Aug 1965
*DAVIDSON	DE 1045	Avondale Shipyards	30 Sep 1963	2 Oct 1964	7 Dec 1965
*VOGE	DE 1047	Defoe Shipbuilding Co	21 Nov 1963	4 Feb 1965	25 Nov 1966
*SAMPLE	DE 1048	Lockheed SB & Construction Co	19 July 1963	28 Apr 1964	23 Mar 1968
*KOELSCH	DE 1049	Defoe Shipbuilding Co	19 Feb 1964	8 June 1965	10 June 1967
*ALBERT DAVID	DE 1050	Lockheed SB & Construction Co	29 Apr 1964	19 Dec 1964	19 Oct 1968
*O'CALLAHAN	DE 1051	Defoe Shipbuilding Co	19 Feb 1964	20 Oct 1965	13 July 1968

These ships exceed many of the world's destroyers in size and ASW capability, but are designated escort ships by virtue of their single propeller shaft and limited speed. The DE 1040 and DE 1041 were authorised in the Fiscal Year 1961 new construction programme DE 1043-1045 in FY 1962, and DE 1047-1051 in FY 1963.

All ten ships are active.

CLASSIFICATION. Hull numbers DE 1039, DE 1042, and 1046 were assigned to frigates built overseas for Portugal.

DESIGN. These ships are an enlargement of the previous "Bronstein" design. They have a flush deck, radically raked stem, stem anchor, and mast and stack combined into a "mack" structure. Anchors are mounted at stem and on portside, just forward of 5 inch gun. Fitted with gyrostabilising fins.

ELECTRONICS. SQS-26 bow-mounted sonar installed. SPS-40 and SPS-10 search radar antennas on "mack". The Voge and Koelsch have been fitted with a specialised ASW Naval Tactical Data System (NTDS) ; they conducted operational evaluation of the system with the ASW carrier Wasp.

ENGINEERING. These ships have an advanced "pressure-fired steam generating plant" which generates 70 percent more power than previous steam plants of the same size and weight. Each boiler has an integrated supercharger and associated control system which provides automatic regulation of fuel, air, and water. The boilers can use JP-5 jet fuel or diesel oil which facilitates boiler maintenance and cleaning, and ballasting empty fuel tanks with sea water. Finally, fewer engineering personnel are required to operate the plant.
A small auxiliary boiler is provided to supply steam when in port. Special noise-reduction features are provided.

GUNNERY. Early designs for these ships included a 5 inch/54 calibre gun but existing 5 inch/38 calibre weapons were installed to hold down costs. The older gun is a reliable weapon but has less range and a slower rate of fire than the 5 inch/54 Mk 42 gun.

HELICOPTERS. The Drone Anti-Submarine Helicopter (DASH) programme was cut back before these ships were provided with helicopters. Reportedly, only the Bradley actually operated with DASH.

MISSILES. The Bradley was fitted with a Sea Sparrow Basic Point Defense Missile System (BPDMS) in 1967-1968 ; removed for installation in the carrier Forrestal. The BPDMS "pepperbox" was fitted between funnel and after 5 inch mount. (See photograph).

TORPEDOES. Most of these ships were built with two Mk 25 torpedo tubes built into their ransom for launching wire-guided ASW torpedoes. However, they have been removed from the earlier ships and deleted in the later ships. The Voge and later ships have automatic ASROC reload system (note angled base of bridge structure behind ASROC "pepper box" in these ships) ; earlier ships do not carry reloads.

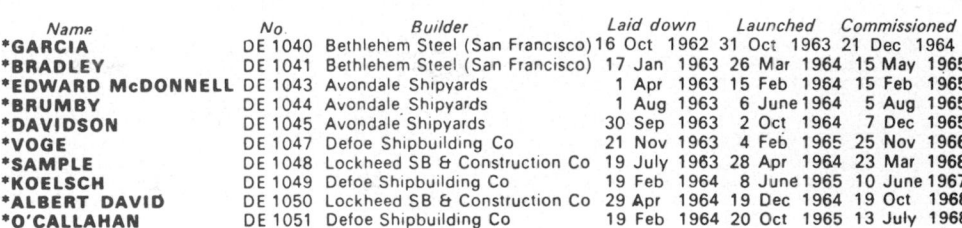

O'CALLAHAN (DE 1051)   1970, United States Navy, PHC T. J. Taylor

EDWARD McDONNELL (DE 1043)   1970, United States Navy, PHC Frederick Gotavco

VOGE (DE 1047)   1967, United States Navy

Ocean Escorts—*continued*

1 ESCORT RESEARCH SHIP (AGDE): "GLOVER" TYPE

Displacement, tons	2 643 standard; 3 426 full load
Length, feet (*metres*)	414·5 (*126·3*) oa
Beam, feet (*metres*)	44·2 (*13·5*)
Draft, feet (*metres*)	14·5 (*4·3*)
Guns	1—5 in (*127 mm*) 38 calibre dual purpose
ASW weapons	1 ASROC 8-tube launcher
	2 triple torpedo launchers (Mk 32)
Main engines	1 geared turbine (Westinghouse); 35 000 shp; 1 shaft
Boilers	2 — 1 200 psi (*83·4 kg/cm²*) (Foster Wheeler)
Speed, knots	27
Complement	225 (14 officers, 211 enlisted men)

Name	No.	Builder	Laid down	Launched	Commissioned
•GLOVER	AGDE 1 (ex-AG 163)	Bath Iron Works	29 July 1963	17 Apr 1965	13 Nov 1965

The *Glover* was built to test an advanced hull design and propulsion system, much the same as the *Albacore*

(AGSS 569) embodied advanced submarine design concepts. However, unlike the *Albacore*, the *Glover* has a full combat capability.

The ship was originally authorised in the Fiscal Year 1960 new construction programme, but was postponed and re-introduced in the FY 1961 programme. Estimated construction cost was $29 330 000.

ACCOMMODATIONS. Provision for approximately 30 civilian scientists and technicians in addition to naval complement.

DESIGN. The *Glover* has a massive bow sonar dome integral with her hull and extending well forward underwater; another "pod" or "nacelle" aft supports counter-rotating propellers mounted on a single shaft. The "pods" at both ends of the ship reduce ship motion at high speeds and move propeller turbulence as far as possible from the bow sonar to increase sonar efficiency. Above the waterline the *Glover* is almost identical to the "Garcia" class escort ships.

ELECTRONICS. The *Glover* has bow-mounted SQS-26 sonar and variable depth sonar (VDS) housed in the bottom of the ship. SPS-40 and SPS-10 search radar antennas on "mack".

PHOTOGRAPH. Stern configuration differs from "Garcia" class escort ships.

GLOVER (AGDE 1)   1968, United States Navy

2 ESCORT SHIPS (DE): "BRONSTEIN" CLASS

Displacement, tons	2 360 standard; 2 650 full load
Length, feet (*metres*)	371·5 (*113·2*) oa
Beam, feet (*metres*)	40·5 (*12·3*)
Draft, feet (*metres*)	23 (*7·0*)
Guns	3—3 in (*76 mm*) 50 calibre (twin forward, single aft)
ASW weapons	1 ASROC 8-tube launcher
	2 triple torpedo launchers (Mk 32)
	facilities for small helicopter
Main engines	1 geared turbine (De Lavel); 20 000 shp; 1 shaft
Boilers	2 (Foster Wheeler)
Speed, knots	26
Complement	220

Name	No.	Builder	Laid down	Launched	Commissioned
*BRONSTEIN	DE 1037	Avondale Shipyards	16 May 1961	31 Mar 1962	15 June 1963
*McCLOY	DE 1038	Avondale Shipyards	15 Sep 1961	9 June 1962	21 Oct 1963

These two ships may be considered the first of the "second generation" of post-World War II escort ships which are comparable in size and ASW capabilities to conventional destroyers. The *Bronstein* and *McCloy* have several features such as hull design, large sonar, and ASW weapons that subsequently were incorporated into the mass-produced "Garcia", "Brooke", and "Knox" classes.

Both ships were built under the Fiscal Year 1960 new construction programme by Avondale Shipyards in Westwego, Louisiana.

DESIGN. These ships have a sharply raked stem, stem anchor, and mast and stacks combined in a "mack" structure. Position of stem anchor and portside anchor (just forward of gun mount) necessitated by large bow sonar dome. Note the deckhouse adjacent to "mack" in photograph of *McCloy*. These ships have a helicopter deck but no hangar.

ELECTRONICS. SQS-26 bow-mounted sonar installed. SPS-40 and SPS-10 search radar antennas mounted on "mack".

GUNNERY. A twin 3 inch closed mount is forward and single 3 inch open mount aft. Later US escort ships all have 5 inch guns.

PHOTOGRAPHS. Note location of helicopter deck forward of after gun mount; later DEs have helicopter deck aft of second gun or missile launcher. Deck breaks aft as in later and larger guided missile frigates (DLG/DLGN). The four "Claud Jones" class DEs have a similar configuration.

McCLOY (DE 1038)   1970, US Navy, PHC Frederick Gotavco

Ocean Escorts—*continued*

4 ESCORT SHIPS (DE): "CLAUD JONES" CLASS

		Name	No.	Builder	Laid down	Launched	Commissioned
Displacement, tons	1 450 standard; 1 750 full load	*CLAUD JONES	DE 1033	Avondale Marine Ways, Inc	1 June 1957	27 May 1958	10 Feb 1959
Length, feet (*metres*)	310 (*95·0*) oa	*JOHN R. PERRY	DE 1034	Avondale Marine Ways, Inc	1 Oct 1957	29 July 1958	5 May 1959
Beam, feet (*metres*)	37 (*11·3*)	*CHARLES BERRY	DE 1035	Avondale Marine Ways, Inc	29 Oct 1958	17 Mar 1959	25 Nov 1959
Draft, feet (*metres*)	18 (*5·5*)	*McMORRIS	DE 1036	Avondale Marine Ways, Inc	5 Nov 1958	26 May 1959	4 Mar 1960
Guns	1 or 2–3 in (*76 mm*) 50 cal see *Armament* notes						
ASW weapons	2 triple torpedo launchers (Mk 32) depth charge rack (removed from *Charles Berry* and *John R. Perry*)						
Main engines	4 diesels (Fairbanks Morse) 9,200 shp; 1 shaft						
Speed, knots	22						
Complement	175 (15 officers, 160 enlisted men)						

These diesel-powered escorts were built in an effort to develop an economical DE suitable for mass production; however, they cannot carry the sonar and weapons necessary to cope with modern submarines. The *Claud Jones* and *John R. Perry* were authorised in the Fiscal Year 1956 shipbuilding programme and the *Charles Berry* and *McMorris* in the FY 1957 programme. The two later ships were ordered originally from the American Shipbuilding Co (Lorain, Ohio) but were completed by Avondale Marine Ways.

ARMAMENT: As built these ships each had two 3 inch guns (single closed mount forward and open mount aft), two ahead-firing hedgehog launchers, two torpedo tubes (Mk 32), and one depth charge rack. The *Charles Berry* and *McMorris* had their hedgehogs removed and were fitted with the Norwegian-developed Terne III ASW missile launcher from 1961 to 1964. Fixed torpedo tubes removed from all ships and triple torpedo launchers installed. After 3 inch gun and depth charge rack removed from *Charles Berry* and *John R. Perry* to compensate for weight of variable depth sonar.

ELECTRONICS. These ships have SPS-12 and SPS-5 search radar antennas. The *Charles Berry* has variable depth sonar (VDS).

DESIGN. These are the only diesel-powered destroyer-type ships built by the US Navy since World War II. They have aluminium superstructure, tripod mast forward and pole mast amidships, and two funnels. Note that *McMorris* has a deckhouse between funnels.

PHOTOGRAPHS. Note unusual twin stack configuration, unique to US ocean escort ships. The *Charles Berry* retains the deckhouse between the forward gun and bridge. All now have built-up section between funnels as in *McMorris*. Note small after mast and the electronic antenna between funnels in *McMorris*.

CHARLES BERRY (DE 1035)   *1964, United States Navy*

McMORRIS   *1969, United States Navy by PH2 B. M. Laurich*

BRONSTEIN (DE 1037)—See previous page   *United States Navy*

Ocean Escorts—continued

13 ESCORT SHIPS (DE): "DEALEY" AND "COURTNEY" CLASSES

Displacement, tons	1 450 standard; 1 914 full load
Length, feet (*metres*)	314·5 (*95·9*) oa
Beam, feet (*metres*)	36·8 (*11·2*)
Draft, feet (*metres*)	13·6 (*4·2*)
Guns	4—3 in (*76 mm*) 50 calibre (twin) in *Dealey, Cromwell* and *Hammerberg*; 2 guns in others; see *Modernisation* notes
ASW weapons	2 triple torpedo launchers (Mk 32) helicopter facilities in DE 1023-1030
Main engines	1 geared turbine (De Laval); 20 000 shp; 1 shaft
Boilers	2 (Foster Wheeler)
Speed, knots	25
Complement	approx 165 (15 officers, 150 enlisted men)

Name	No.	Builder	Laid down	Launched	Commissioned
*DEALEY	DE 1006	Bath Iron Works Corpn	15 Dec 1952	8 Nov 1953	3 June 1954
*CROMWELL	DE 1014	Bath Iron Works Corpn	3 Aug 1953	4 June 1954	24 Nov 1954
*HAMMERBERG	DE 1015	Bath Iron Works Corpn	12 Nov 1953	20 Aug 1954	2 Mat 1955
*COURTNEY	DE 1021	Defoe SB Co, Bay City, Mich	2 Sep 1954	2 Nov 1955	24 Sep 1956
*LESTER	DE 1022	Defoe SB Co, Bay City, Mich	2 Sep 1954	5 Jan 1956	14 June 1957
*EVANS	DE 1023	Puget Sound B & D Co	8 Apr 1955	14 Sep 1955	14 June 1957
*BRIDGET	DE 1024	Puget Sound B & D Co	19 Sep 1955	25 Apr 1956	24 Oct 1957
*BAUER	DE 1025	Bethlehem, San Francisco	1 Dec 1955	4 June 1957	21 Nov 1957
*HOOPER	DE 1026	Bethlehem, San Francisco	4 Jan 1956	1 Aug 1957	18 Mar 1958
*JOHN WILLIS	DE 1027	New York SB Corpn	5 July 1955	4 Feb 1956	21 Feb 1957
*VAN VOORHIS	DE 1028	New York SB Corpn	29 Aug 1955	28 July 1956	22 Apr 1957
*HARTLEY	DE 1029	New York SB Corpn	31 Oct 1955	24 Nov 1956	26 June 1957
*JOSEPH K. TAUSSIG	DE 1030	New York SB Corpn	3 Jan 1956	3 Jan 1957	10 Sep 1957

The *Dealey* was the prototype for the first post-World War II escort ships built by the US Navy. The first three ships are known as the "Dealey" class and the ten others as the "Courtney" class. They were designed for fast convoy escort.

Dealey authorised in the Fiscal Year 1952 shipbuilding programme; DE 1014 and DE 1015 in FY 1953; DE 1021 and DE 1022 in FY 1954; DE 1023-1030 in FY 1955. The *Dealey* cost an estimated $15 000 000.

The *Evans, Bridget, Bauer* and *Hooper* are operational Naval Reserve training ships. The others are in commission (see *Transfer* note below).

ARMAMENT. As built each ship mounted four 3 inch guns (twin closed mount forward, twin open mount aft), one Weapon Able/Alfa rocket launcher, two torpedo tubes (Mk 32), and depth charge racks and projectors. The *Dealey* conducted tests with British "Squid" depth charge launchers (in place of Weapon Alfa). Fixed torpedo tubes have been replaced in all ships by two triple torpedo launchers, depth charge racks removed from most ships. Weapon Alfa rocket launcher (in all except *Dealey*) removed in late 1960s.

CLASSIFICATION. The hull numbers DE 1007-1013 were assigned to *Le Normand* class (Type E-52) frigates built in French shipyards with funds from the US Military Defence Assistance Programme (MDAP); DE 1016-1019 were *Le Corse* class (Type E-50) frigates built in French yards under MDAP; DE 1020 and 1031 were *Centauro* class frigates built in Italian yards under MDAP; DE 1032 was built in an Italian yard for Portugal (*Pero Escobar*). All officially transferred upon completion.

DESIGN. These ships differ radically from the "destroyer escorts" (DE) built by the US Navy during World War II. They have all aluminium superstructures, lattice masts to support extensive electronic antennas, and are single-screw ships. Originally intended for mass production in wartime. Light displacement is 1 280 tons.

ELECTRONICS. These ships have SPS-12 and SPS-10 search radar antennas on their lattice mast.

MODERNISATION. As built these ships were of essentially the same design (with minor variations in weapons, as described under *Armament* notes). Five distinct configurations have now evolved: (1) amidships superstructure built up to provide escort division or squadron flag staff accommodations (Mk 32 tubes atop) 02 deck level), helicopter hangar and flight deck, and after guns removed as *Lester* and *Willis;* (2) same modification but without flag accommodations (Mk 32 tubes atop 01 deck level) as *Bauer;* (3) flag accommodations and helicopter deck but no hangar; (4) flag accommodations without either helicopter hangar or flight deck as *Courtney;* and (5) essentially original configuration as *Dealey.*

Note position of Mk 32 tubes in *Dealey,* between forward 3 inch gun mount and bridge in place of original "Squid" launchers.

Courtney recently has had after 3 inch twin mount removed; special towed sensor equipment fitted on fantail (see 1970-1971 edition for photograph of *Courtney* showing four-gun configuration in 1967).

NOMENCLATURE. *Hooper* ex-*Gatch,* was renamed on 19 July 1956.

TRANSFERS. Reportedly the *John Willis* and *Hartley* of this class were to transfer to New Zealand in 1972.

DEALEY (DE 1006)
1968, United States Navy

CROMWELL (DE 1014)
1970, US Navy, PH3 T. R. Hearsum

JOSEPH K. TAUSSIG (DE 1030)
1970, US Navy, PH3 J. Terry

COURTNEY (DE 1021)

1970, US Navy, PHCS Walter H. Long

LESTER (DE 1022)

1970, US Navy, J. R. Andrews

BAUER (DE 1025)

1969, US Navy, PH1 D. Nichols

JOHN WILLIS (DE 1027)

1970, US Navy, PHC Frederick Gotauco

Ocean Escorts—continued

41 ESCORT SHIPS (DE): "JOHN C. BUTLER" CLASS

Displacement, tons	1 350 standard; 2 100 full load	
Length, feet (metres)	306 (93·3) oa	
Beam, feet (metres)	36·6 (11·3)	
Draft, feet (metres)	11 (3·4)	
Guns	2—5 in (127 mm) 38 cal DP	
	2 to 8—40 mm AA (twin)	
ASW weapons	depth charge rack and throwers	
Main engines	2 geared turbines (General Electric or Westinghouse); 12 000 shp; 2 shafts	
Boilers	2 (Babcock & Wilcox or Combustion Engineering)	
Speed, knots	24	
Complement	190	

Name	No.	Builder	Launched	Commissioned
CHESTER T. O'BRIEN	DE 421	Brown SB Co, Houston	29 Feb 1944	3 July 1944
CORBESIER	DE 438	Federal SB & DD Co, Pt Newark	13 Feb 1944	31 Mar 1944
DENNIS	DE 405	Brown SB Co, Houston	4 Dec 1943	20 Mar 1944
DOYLE C. BARNES	DE 353	Consolidated Steel Corpn, Orange	4 Mar 1944	13 July 1944
DUFILHO	DE 423	Brown SB Co, Houston	9 Mar 1944	21 July 1944
EDMONDS	DE 406	Brown SB Co, Houston	17 Dec 1943	3 Apr 1944
EDWARD H. ALLEN	DE 531	Boston Naval Shipyard	17 Oct 1943	16 Dec 1943
EDWIN A. HOWARD	DE 346	Consolidated Steel Corpn, Orange	25 Jan 1944	25 May 1944
FRENCH	DE 367	Consolidated Steel Corpn, Orange	17 June 1944	9 Oct 1944
GENTRY	DE 349	Consolidated Steel Corpn, Orange	15 Feb 1944	14 June 1944
GEORGE E. DAVIS	DE 357	Consolidated Steel Corpn, Orange	8 Apr 1944	11 Aug 1944
GILLIGAN	DE 508	Federal SB & DD Co, Pt Newark	22 Feb 1944	12 May 1944
GOSS	DE 444	Federal SB & DD Co, Pt Newark	19 Mar 1944	26 Aug 1944
HANNA	DE 449	Federal SB & DD Co, Pt Newark	4 July 1944	27 Jan 1945
HOWARD F. CLARK	DE 533	Boston Naval Shipyard	8 Nov 1943	25 May 1944
JOHN L. WILLIAMSON	DE 370	Consolidated Steel Corpn, Orange	29 Aug 1943	31 Oct 1944
JOHNNIE HUTCHINS	DE 360	Consolidated Steel Corpn, Orange	2 May 1944	28 Aug 1944
KENDALL C. CAMPBELL	DE 443	Federal SB & DD Co, Pt Newark	19 Mar 1944	31 July 1944
KENNETH M. WILLETT	DE 354	Consolidated Steel Corpn, Orange	7 May 1944	19 July 1944
KEY	DE 348	Consolidated Steel Corpn, Orange	12 Feb 1944	5 June 1944
LA PRADE	DE 409	Brown SB Co, Houston	31 Dec 1943	20 Apr 1944
LAWRENCE C. TAYLOR	DE 415	Brown SB Co, Houston	29 Jan 1944	13 May 1944
LE RAY WILSON	DE 414	Brown SB Co, Houston	28 Jan 1944	10 May 1944
LELAND E. THOMAS	DE 420	Brown SB Co, Houston	28 Feb 1944	19 June 1944
LLOYD E. ACREE	DE 356	Consolidated Steel Corpn, Orange	21 Mar 1944	1 Aug 1944
MACK	DE 358	Consolidated Steel Corpn, Orange	11 Apr 1944	16 Aug 1944
MELVIN R. NAWMAN	DE 416	Brown SB Co, Houston	7 Feb 1944	16 May 1944
O'FLAHERTY	DE 340	Consolidated Steel Corpn, Orange	14 Dec 1944	8 Apr 1944
OLIVER MITCHELL	DE 417	Brown SB Co, Houston	8 Feb 1944	14 June 1944
OSBERG	DE 538	Boston Naval Shipyard	7 Dec 1943	17 Dec 1945
PRATT	DE 363	Consolidated Steel Corpn, Orange	1 June 1944	18 Sep 1944
RAYMOND	DE 341	Consolidated Steel Corpn, Orange	8 Jan 1944	15 Apr 1944
RICHARD W. SUESENS	DE 342	Consolidated Steel Corpn, Orange	11 Jan 1944	26 Apr 1944
RIZZI	DE 537	Boston Naval Shipyard	7 Dec 1943	30 June 1944
ROBERT F. KELLER	DE 419	Brown SB Co, Houston	11 Feb 1944	17 June 1944
ROLF	DE 362	Consolidated Steel Corpn, Orange	23 May 1944	7 Sep 1944
ROMBACH	DE 364	Consolidated Steel Corpn, Orange	6 June 1944	20 Sep 1944
SILVERSTEIN	DE 534	Boston Naval Shipyard	8 Nov 1943	14 July 1944
STAFFORD	DE 411	Brown SB Co, Houston	11 Jan 1944	19 Apr 1944
TABBERER	DE 418	Brown SB Co, Houston	18 Feb 1944	23 May 1944
WILLIAM SEIEVERLING	DE 441	Federal SB & DD Co, Pt Newark	7 Mar 1944	1 June 1944

These ships were originally rated as Destroyer Escorts (DE). All surviving ships of this type are in reserve.

ARMAMENT. Designed armament for this class was two 5 inch guns, ten 40 mm guns (one quad, three twin), six 20 mm guns, and one bank of three 21 inch torpedo tubes. (With full armament the designed wartime complement was 15 officers and 207 enlisted men).

CLASS. These ships and those described on the four succeeding pages are the survivors of 561 "destroyer escorts" built in US shipyards during World War II. They were intended to serve primarily as anti-submarine ships in the Atlantic, screening convoys and operating in hunter-killer groups. Ten flying US colours were sunk during the war. Ninety-two were transferred to the Allies during World War II (12 sunk) and 96 were converted to high-speed transports (APD, now LPR, one of which was sunk). The surviving transports are listed with Amphibious Warfare Ships.

Former US war-built destroyer escorts currently serve in the navies of Brazil, Chile, Columbia, Ecuador, France, Greece, Italy, Japan, South Korea, Mexico, Nationalist China, Peru, the Philippines, Thailand, and Uruguay.

The 41 ships of the "John C. Bulter" (WGT) design comprise the largest surviving class of war-built escort ships.

CONVERSIONS. The Wagner (DE 539) and Vandivier (DE 540) of this type were completed as radar picket ships and are listed separately.

DESIGN. This class is officially the WGT design group, the WGT symbol indicating geared turbine drive.

LOSSES. The Eversole (DE 404), Oberrender (DE 344), Samuel B. Roberts (DD 413), and Shelton (DE 407) of this class were lost in World War II.

ROBERT F. KELLER (DE 419)   1962, United States Navy

PHOTOGRAPHS. The Edmonds is shown with a twin 40 mm mount forward of her bridge and a second twin mount at the after end of her deckhouse; there are 20 mm guns alongside her bridge and abaft her funnel with two empty 20 mm gun "tubs" on her fantail. The Robert F. Keller has only a twin 40 mm mount forward of bridge.

DISPOSALS AND TRANSFERS

The incomplete **Oswald A. Powers** (DE 542) and **Sheeham** (DE 541) were scrapped; **Woodson** (DE 359) stricken on 1 July 1965; **Douglas A. Munro** (DE 422) stricken on 1 Dec 1965 and expended as target; **Ulvert M. Moore** stricken on 1 Dec 1965 and expended as target; **Lewis** (DE 535) and **Naifeh** (DE 352) stricken on 1 Jan 1966 and expended as targets; **Heyliger** (DE 510), **Maurice J. Manuel** (DE 351), **Straus** (DE 408) stricken on 1 May 1966, **Cross** (DE 448) and **Hass** (DE 424) stricken on 1 July 1966; **Williams** (DE 372), **Cecil J. Doyle** (DE 368), and **Traw** (DE 350) stricken on 1 July 1967 and expended as targets; **Thaddeus Parker** (DE 369) stricken on 1 Sep 1967 and scrapped; **Jaccard** (DE 355) stricken on 1 Nov 1967 and expended as target; **Abercrombie** (DE 343) stricken on 1 May 1967 (target); **Robert Brazier** (DE 345) and **Jesse Rutherford** (DE 347) stricken on 1 Jan 1968 and expended as targets. **Bivin** (DE 536), **Grady** (DE 445).

EDMONDS (DE 406)   1959, United States Navy

Ocean Escorts—*continued*

"BUTLER" CLASS—*continued*

Jack Miller (DE 410), Presley (DE 371), Richard M. Rowell (DE 403), Richard S. Bull (DE 402), Walter C. Wann (DE 412), stricken on 30 June 1968; Albert T. Harris (DE 447), Alvin C. Cockrell (DE 366), Charles E. Brannon (DE 446), McGinty (DE 365), Walton (DE 361), stricken on 23 Sep 1968. McCoy Reynolds (DE 440) and Formoe (DE 509) transferred to Portugal on 7 Feb 1957; Tweedy (DE 532) stricken on 30 June 1969 (target); John C. Butler (DE 339) stricken on 1 June 1970; Conklin (DE 439), Joseph E. Connolly (DE 450) stricken in 1971 (Connolly target).

HANNA (DE 449)

United States Navy

2 RADAR PICKET ESCORT SHIPS (DER): CONVERTED "JOHN C. BUTLER" CLASS

Displacement, tons	1 745 standard; 2 100 full load	*Name*	*No.*	*Builder*	*Laid down*	*Launched*	*Commissioned*
Length, feet (*metres*)	306 (*93·3*) oa	VANDIVIER	DER 540	Boston Naval Shipyard	8 Nov 1943	27 Dec 1943	1 Dec 1955
Beam, feet (*metres*)	36·6 (*11·2*)	WAGNER	DER 539	Boston Naval Shipyard	8 Nov 1943	27 Dec 1943	31 Dec 1955
Draft, feet (*metres*)	11 (*3·4*)					
Guns	2—5 in (*127 mm*) 38 cal DP					
ASW weapons	1 trainable hedgehog (Mk 15) depth charge rack					
Main engines	2 geared turbines (Westinghouse) 12 000 shp; 2 shafts					
Boilers	2 (Babcock & Wilcox)					
Speed, knots	24					
Complement	187					

These two ships were begun as standard Destroyer Escorts (DE); construction suspended in 1946. Work resumed in 1954 and they were completed as Radar Picket Escort Ships (DER) at the Boston Naval Shipyard. Light displacement 1 260 tons. Both ships are in reserve.

ENGINEERING. These are the US Navy's only steam-driven radar picket escort ships; all others have diesel propulsion.

PHOTOGRAPH. Note tripod masts, TACAN navigation "bee-hive" antenna on after mast and SPS-8 height-finding radar antenna atop after deckhouse.

VANDIVIER (DER 540)

United States Navy

4 ESCORT SHIPS (DE): "RUDDEROW" CLASS

Displacement, tons	1 450 standard; 2 230 full load	*Name*	*No.*	*Builder*	*Launched*	*Commissioned*
Length, feet (*metres*)	306 (*93·3*) oa	HODGES	DE 231	Charleston Navy Yard	9 Dec 1943	27 May 1944
Beam, feet (*metres*)	37 (*11·3*)	LESLIE L. B. KNOX	DE 580	Bethlehem-Hingham	8 Jan 1944	22 Mar 1944
Draft, feet (*metres*)	14 (*4·3*)	THOMAS F. NICKEL	DE 587	Bethlehem-Hingham	22 Jan 1944	9 June 1944
Guns	2—5 in (*127 mm*) 38 cal DP 4 to 8—40 mm AA (two twin, one quad)	TINSMAN	DE 589	Bethlehem-Hingham	29 Jan 1944	26 June 1944
ASW weapons	trainable hedgehog (Mk 15) in some ships depth charge rack					
Main engines	turbo-electric drive (General-Electric geared turbines) 12 000 shp; 2 shafts					
Boilers	2 (Foster Wheeler in DE 580-589; Babcock & Wilcox in DE 224; Combustion Engineering in others)					
Speed, knots	24					
Complement	180					

These ships were originally rated as Destroyer Escorts (DE). Sixty-two ships of this type were built; most converted to High Speed Transports (APD). The *Parle* was the last World War II-built "straight" escort ship remaining in active US service; she was an operational Naval Reserve training ship at Chicago, Illinois, until decommissioned and stricken in 1970 (see 1970-1971 edition for photograph of *Parle* in final configuration).

ARMAMENT. Designed armament for this class was two 5 inch guns, ten 40 mm guns (one quad, three twin), six 20 mm guns, and one bank of three 21 inch torpedo tubes. (With full armament the designed wartime complement was 15 officers and 206 enlisted men).

LESLIE L. B. KNOX (DE 580)

United States Navy

CONVERSIONS. The following ships of this class were converted to high speed transports (see Amphibious Warfare Ships): DE 226-229, 232-237, 590-606, 687-692, and 710-722.

DESIGN. This class is similar to the "Buckley" class of escort ships, the principal difference being the main battery of two 5 inch guns in this class in place of three 3 inch guns in the "Buckley" class ships. The "Rudder-ow" class is officially the TEV design group, the TEV symbol indicating turbine-electric drive with 5 inch guns.

DISPOSALS AND TRANSFERS

Daniel A. Joy (DE 585) stricken on 15 May 1965; George A. Johnson (DE 583) stricken on 1 Nov 1965; Peiffer (DE 588) stricken on 1 Dec 1966 and expended as target in May 1967; Holt (DE 706) transferred to South Korea in 1963; Riley (DE 579), transferred to Nationalist China in 1968; Charles J. Kimmel (DE 584), Eugene E. Elmore (DE 686), Metivier (DE 582), Day (DE 225), stricken on 30 June 1968 (Charles J. Kimmel and Day sunk as targets) De Long (DE 684) stricken on 8 Aug 1969 (target); Jobb (DE 707), Lough (DE 586), Rudderow (DE 224) stricken on 1 Nov 1969, Coates (DE 685) stricken on 30 Jan 1970; Parle (DE 708) stricken on 1 July 1970; McNulty (DE 581) stricken in 1971.

Ocean Escorts—continued

16 ESCORT SHIPS (DE): "BOSTWICK" CLASS

Displacement, tons	1 240 standard; 1 900 full load
Length, feet (metres)	306 (93·3) oa
Beam, feet (metres)	36·6 (11·2)
Draft, feet (metres)	14 (4·3)
Guns	3—3 in (76 mm) 50 cal AA
	2—40 mm AA
ASW Weapons	hedgehogs; depth charges
Main engines	Diesel-electric (4 General Motors diesels); 6 000 shp; 2 shafts
Speed, knots	21
Complement	150

Name	No	Builder	Launched	Commissioned
ACREE	DE 167	Federal SB & DD Co, Pt Newark	9 May 1943	19 July 1943
COFFMAN	DE 191	Federal SB & DD Co, Pt Newark	28 Nov 1943	27 Dec 1943
COONER	DE 172	Federal SB & DD Co, Pt Newark	25 July 1943	21 Aug 1943
EARL K. OLSEN	DE 765	Tampa SB Co	13 Feb 1944	10 Apr 1944
HILBERT	DE 742	Western Pipe & Steel Co	18 July 1943	4 Feb 1944
KYNE	DE 744	Western Pipe & Steel Co	15 Aug 1943	4 Apr 1944
LAMONS	DE 743	Western Pipe & Steel Co	1 Aug 1943	29 Feb 1944
LEVY	DE 162	Federal SB & DD Co, Pt Newark	28 Mar 1943	13 May 1943
McCLELLAND	DE 750	Western Pipe & Steel Co	28 Nov 1944	19 Sep 1944
McDONNELL	DE 163	Federal SB & DD Co, Pt Newark	28 Mar 1943	28 May 1943
OSTERHOUS	DE 164	Federal SB & DD Co, Pt Newark	18 Apr 1943	12 June 1943
OSWALD	DE 767	Tampa SB Co	25 Apr 1944	12 June 1944
PARKS	DE 165	Federal SB & DD Co, Pt Newark	18 Apr 1943	22 June 1944
SNYDER	DE 745	Western Pipe & Steel Co	29 Aug 1943	5 May 1944
STRAUB	DE 181	Federal SB & DD Co, Pt Newark	18 Sep 1943	25 Oct 1943
TRUMPETER	DE 180	Federal SB & DD Co, Pt Newark	18 Sep 1943	25 Oct 1943

These ships were originally rated as Destroyer Escorts (DE). Fifty ships of this type have been transferred to Allied navies (see below). All ships remaining on the US Navy List are in reserve.

ARMAMENT. Designed armament for this class was three 3 inch guns, six 40 mm guns (three twin), several 20 mm guns, and a bank of three 21 inch torpedo tubes. Torpedo tubes removed and light AA guns reduced. (With full armament the designed wartime complement was 15 officers and 201 enlisted men).

DESIGN. This class is officially the DET design group, the DET symbol indicating diesel-electric tandem motor drive.

TRANSFERS. Fourteen ships of this class have been transferred to France, eight to Brazil, six to the Netherlands, four to Nationalist China (Taiwan), four to Greece, three to Italy, three to Peru, two to South Korea, two to Japan and the Philippines and one each to Uruguay and Thailand.

DISPOSALS
Carroll (DE 171) and Micka (DE 176) were stricken in 1965; Neal A. Scott (DE 769) stricken on 1 June 1968; Tills (DE 748), Roberts (DE 749), stricken on 23 Sep 1968 (Tills expended as target).

17 ESCORT SHIPS (DE): "BUCKLEY" CLASS

Displacement, tons	1 400 standard; 2 170 full load
Length, feet (metres)	306 (93·3) oa
Beam, feet (metres)	37 (11·3)
Draft, feet (metres)	14 (4·3)
Guns, varies	3 ships have 2—5 in (127 mm) 38 cal DP; others have 2 or 3—3 in (76 mm) 50 cal AA up to 8—40 mm AA per ship (removed entirely from some ships)
ASW weapons	trainable hedgehog (Mk 15) in ships with 5 inch guns depth charge racks
Main engines	Turbo-electric drive (General Electric turbines); 12 000 shp; 2 shafts
Boilers	2 (Babcock & Wilcox, Combustion Engineering or Foster Wheeler)
Speed, knots	23·5
Complement	180 (185 in ex-DER)

Name	No.	Builder	Launched	Commissioned
COOLBAUGH	217	Philadelphia Navy Yard	29 May 1943	15 Oct 1943
DAMON M. CUMMINGS	643	Bethleham, Warfare	18 Apr 1944	29 June 1944
EICHENBERGER	202	Charleston Navy Yard	22 July 1943	17 Nov 1943
FIEBERLING	640	Bethlehem, San Francisco	2 Mar 1944	11 Apr 1944
FRANCIS M. ROBINSON	220	Philadelphia Navy Yard	29 May 1943	15 Jan 1944
FRYBARGER	705	Defoe Co, Bay City, Mich	25 Jan 1944	18 May 1944
GENDREAU	639	Bethlehem, San Francisco	12 Dec 1943	17 Mar 1944
GILLETTE	681	Bethlehem, Quincy	25 Sep 1943	27 Oct 1943
HOLTON	703	Defoe Co, Bay City, Mich	15 Dec 1943	1 May 1944
JACK W. WILKE	800	Consolidated Steel Corpn, Orange	18 Dec 1943	7 Mar 1944
MAJOR	796	Consolidated Steel Corpn, Orange	23 Oct 1943	12 Feb 1944
MARSH	699	Defoe Co, Bay City, Mich	29 Jan 1943	12 Jan 1944
OSMUS	701	Defoe Co, Bay City, Mich	4 Nov 1943	23 Feb 1944
SPANGLER	696	Defoe Co, Bay City, Mich	15 July 1943	31 Oct 1943
VARIAN	798	Consolidated Steel Corpn, Orange	6 Nov 1943	29 Feb 1944
WILLIAM C. COLE	641	Bethlehem, San Francisco	28 Dec 1943	12 May 1944
WISEMAN	667	Dravo Corpn, Pittsburgh	6 Nov 1943	4 Apr 1944

These ships were originally rated as Destroyer Escorts (DE). Forty-six ships of this type were transferred to the Royal Navy in 1944 under the Lend-Lease where they served as frigates; six of these ships were lost and the remainder were returned to the United States and scrapped.
All surviving ships of this class are in reserve.

ARMAMENT. Designed armament for this class was three 3 inch guns, six 40 mm guns (three twin), several 20 mm guns, and one bank of three 21 inch torpedo tubes. During 1945, 11 ships were fitted with a 5 inch main battery in lieu of 3 inch guns. Torpedo tubes removed and 40 mm and 20 mm weapons reduced (With full armanemt the designed wartime complement was 15 officers and 198 enlisted men). The rearmed ships were DE 217-219, 678-680, 696-698, 700, and 701.

CONVERSIONS. Fifty ships of this type were converted to high speed transports (see Amphibious Warfare ships) The Cronin, Frybarger, and Raby were modified after World War II to direct boat waves during amphibious landings and were designated amphibious control vessels (DEC); all three were mothballed in 1953-1954 and reclassified DE on 27 Dec 1957.
Seven ships of this type were converted to rader picket ships in 1949-1950; they reverted to DE status in Oct 1954 and were mothballed as more efficient radar picket escorts became available. None of those modified to DER configuration remains on the Navy List.

DESIGN. This class is officially the TE design group, the TE symbol indicating turbine-electric drive with 3 inch guns.

ENGINEERING. The Marsh and Wiseman, have been modified to provide electrical power to shore activities and each has two large reels for power cables amidships.

LOSSES. The Fechteler (DE 157) and Underhill (DE 682) of this class were lost during World War II. The Solar (DE 221) was destroyed by internal explosion on 30 Apr 1946.

PHOTOGRAPHS. The Marsh is shown in the power transmission configuration with cable reels aft of funnel depth charge racks on fantail, and a single quad 40 mm mount aft; the Coolbough is typical of 5 inch gun configuration with trainable hedgehog in "B" position, depth charge rack on fantail, and one twin and one quad 40 mm mounts.

MARSH (DE 699) (Power transmission)   United States Navy

COOLBAUGH (DE 217) (5 inch guns)   United States Navy

Ocean Escorts—*continued*

"BUCKLEY" CLASS *continued*

DISPOSALS
Ahrens (DE 575), **Borum** (DE 790), **Durik** (DE 666), **Foreman** (DE 633), **Foss** (DE 59), **Fowler** (DE 222), **Harmon** (DE 678), **Maloy** (DE 791), **Scott** (DE 214), and **Scroggins** (DE 799). stricken in 1965; **Jenks** (DE 665), **Currier** (DE 700) and **Willmarth** (DE 638), stricken in 1966 (**Currier** expended as target); **Earl V. Johnson** (DE 702), **Greenwood** (DE 679), **Lovelace** (DE 198), **Neundorf** (DE 200), stricken in 1967; **Fogg**

(DE/DER 57), **Spangenburg** (DE/DER 223), **William T. Powell** (DE/DER 213), stricken in 1965 (**Lovelace** expended as target); **Buckley** (DE/DER 51), **Raby** (DE 698), **Robert I. Paine** (DE/DER 578), stricken on 1 June 1968; **James E. Craig** (DE 201), **Thomason** (DE 203), **Weeden** (DE 797), **Reuben James** (DE/DER 153), stricken on 30 June 1968; **Manning** (DE 199), stricken on 30 July 1968; **Darby** (DE 218), **Loeser** (DE 680), stricken on 23 Sep 1968; **Whitehurst** (DE

634) stricken on 12 July, 1969; **Vammen** (DE 644) stricken on 12 July 1969; **George** (DE 697), **Otter** (DE 210) stricken on 1 Nov 1969; **Henry R. Kenyon** (DE 683), **Paul G. Baker** (DE 642) stricken on 1 Dec 1969; **J Douglas Blackwood** (DE 219) stricken on 30 Jan 1970; **Alexander J. Luke** (DE/DER 577) stricken on 1 May 1970 (target); **Cronin** (DE 704) stricken on 1 June 1970 (target); **Gunason** (DE 795) stricken in 1971.

23 ESCORT SHIPS (DE): "EDSALL" CLASS

Displacement, tons	1 200 standard; 1 850 full load		
Length, feet (*metres*)	306 (*93·3*) oa		
Beam, feet (*metres*)	36·6 (*11·3*)		
Draft, feet (*metres*)	11 (*3·4*)		
Guns	3—3 in (*76 mm*) 50 cal AA'		
	(2 guns in *Peterson*)		
	up to .8—40 mm AA		
	(removed entirely from some ships)		
ASW weapons	2 hedgehogs; depth charge rack		
	(see *Conversion* notes)		
Main engines	4 diesels (Fairbanks Morse);		
	6 000 shp; 2 shafts		
Speed, knots	21		
Complement	149		

Name	No.	Builders	Launched	Commissioned
CHATELAIN	DE 149	Consolidated Steel Corpn	21 Aug 1943	22 Sep 1943
COCKRILL	DE 398	Brown SB Co. Houston	29 Oct 1943	24 Dec 1943
DOUGLAS L. HOWARD	DE 138	Consolidated Steel Corpn	25 Jan 1943	29 July 1943
FARQUHAR	DE 139	Consolidated Steel Corpn	13 Feb 1943	5 Aug 1943
HAMMANN (ex-*Langley*)	DE 131	Consolidated Steel Corpn	13 Dec 1942	17 May 1943
HERBERT C. JONES	DE 137	Consolidated Steel Corpn	19 Jan 1943	21 July 1943
HILL	DE 141	Consolidated Steel Corpn	28 Feb 1943	16 Aug 1943
HURST	DE 250	Brown SB Co. Houston	14 Apr 1943	30 Aug 1943
HUSE	DE 145	Consolidated Steel Corpn	23 Mar 1943	30 Aug 1943
INCH	DE 146	Consolidated Steel Corpn	4 Apr 1943	8 Sep 1943
JANSSEN	DE 396	Brown SB Co. Houston	10 Oct 1943	18 Dec 1943
KEITH	DE 241	Brown SB Co. Houston	21 Dec 1942	19 July 1943
MOORE	DE 240	Brown SB Co. Houston	21 Dec 1942	1 July 1943
NEUNZER	DE 150	Consolidated Steel Corpn	27 Apr 1943	27 Sep 1943
PETERSON	DE 152	Consolidated Steel Corpn	15 May 1943	29 Sep 1943
PETTIT	DE 253	Brown SB Co. Houston	28 Apr 1943	23 Sep 1943
RICKETTS	DE 254	Brown SB Co. Houston	10 May 1943	5 Oct 1943
STEWART	DE 238	Brown SB Co. Houston	22 Nov 1942	31 May 1943
STOCKDALE	DE 399	Brown SB Co. Houston	30 Oct 1943	31 Dec 1943
SWASEY	DE 248	Brown SB Co. Houston	18 Mar 1943	31 Aug 1943
SWENNING	DE 394	Brown SB Co. Houston	13 Sep 1943	1 Dec 1943
TOMICH	DE 242	Brown SB Co. Houston	28 Dec 1942	27 July 1943
WILLIS	DE 395	Brown SB Co. Houston	14 Sep 1943	10 Dec 1943

These ships were originally rated as Destroyer Escorts Thirty-six ships of this type have been converted to radar picket ships (DER) and are listed separately.
None of these ships are in commission; all in reserve.

ARMAMENT. Designed armament for this class was three 3 inch guns, eight 40 mm guns (one quad, two twin), several 20 mm guns, and a bank of three 21 inch torpedo tubes. Rearmament with two 5 inch guns in place of the 3 inch battery was planned but not carried out. Torpedo tubes removed after World War II and anti-aircraft guns reduced in some ships. (With full armament the designed wartime complement was 15 officers and 201 enlisted men).

CONVERSIONS. The *Peterson* was modified to a special ASW configuration in 1951-1952; two trainable hedge-hogs fitted in the "B" position forward of the bridge, additional sonar installed, and a short second mast fitted; all light AA guns were removed. She was decommissioned in April 1965.

DESIGN. This class is officially the FMR design group, the FMR symbol indicating Fairbanks Morse diesel with reverse gear drive.

PETERSON (DE 152) (see below)   United States Navy

ENGINEERING. The *Mills* (DE 383) was to have been fitted with two British RM 60 gas turbines in place of her diesel engines. The machinery was to reduce plant weight by approximately 15 per cent while providing 67 per cent more power. The conversion was proposed in the Fiscal Year 1955 programme, but the project was abandoned and the *Mills* became a radar picket (DER).

EXPERIMENTAL. The *Brough* (EDE 146), now stricken, and *Huse* (EDE 145) were used for experimental work.

LOSSES. The *Fiske* (DE 143), *Frederick C. Davis* (DE 136), *Holder* (DE 401), and *Leopold* (DE 319) were lost during World War II.

DISPOSALS
Flaherty (DE 135), **Frost** (DE 144), and **Brough** (DE 148) stricken in 1965; **Marten H. Ray** (DE·338) and **Robert E. Peary** (DE 132) stricken in 1966 **Edsall** (DE 129) stricken on 1 June 1968; **Richey** (DE 385) stricken on 30 June 1968 (target); **Howard D. Crow** (DE 252), **Snowden** (DE 246), stricken on 23 Sep 1968; **Stanton** (DE 247) stricken on 1 Dec 1970; **Jacob Jones** (DE 130), **Pope** (DE 134), **J. R. Y. Blakeley** (DE 140), **J. Richard Ward** (DE 243), **Sloat** (DE 245), **Marchland** (DE 249), **Menges** (DE 320), **Mosley** (DE 321), **Pride** (DE 323), **Dale W. Peterson** (DE 337) stricken on 2 Jan 1971; **O'Reilly** (DE 330), **Daniel** (DE 335) stricken on 15 Jan 1971; **Poole** (DE 151), **Merrill** (DE 392) stricken in 1971.

HUSE (DE 145)   Skyphotos

Ocean Escorts—continued

23 RADAR PICKET ESCORT SHIPS (DER): CONVERTED "EDSALL" CLASS

Displacement, tons	1 590 standard; 1 850 full load
Length, feet (metres)	306 (93·3) oa
Beam, feet (metres)	36·6 (11·1)
Draft, feet (metres)	14 (4·3)
Guns	2—3 in (76 mm) 50 cal AA
	2—20 mm AA in Calcaterra and Thomas J. Gary
ASW weapons	2 triple torpedo launchers (Mk 32) in most ships
	1 trainable hedgehog (Mk 15) depth charge rack
	(depth charge rack removed from Calcaterra and Thomas J. Gary); hedgehog removed from Calcaterra).
Main engines	4 diesels (Fairbanks Morse), 6 000 shp; 2 shafts
Speed, knots	21
Complement	169 (19 officers, 150 enlisted men)

Name	No.	Builder	Launched	Commissioned
BLAIR	DER 147	Consolidated Steel Corpn	6 Apr 1943	13 Sep 1943
*CALCATERRA	DER 390	Brown SB Co, Houston	16 Aug 1943	17 Nov 1943
CHAMBERS	DER 391	Brown SB Co, Houston	17 Aug 1943	22 Nov 1943
DURANT	DER 389	Brown SB Co, Houston	3 Aug 1943	16 Nov 1943
FALGOUT	DER 324	Consolidated Steel Corpn	24 July 1943	15 Nov 1943
FINCH	DER 328	Consolidated Steel Corpn	28 Aug 1943	13 Dec 1943
FORSTER	DER 334	Consolidated Steel Corpn	13 Nov 1943	25 Jan 1944
HISSEM	DER 400	Brown SB Co, Houston	26 Dec 1943	13 Jan 1944
JOYCE	DER 317	Consolidated Steel Corpn	26 May 1943	30 Sep 1943
KIRKPATRICK	DER 318	Consolidated Steel Corpn	5 June 1943	23 Oct 1943
KRETCHMER	DER 329	Consolidated Steel Corpn	31 Aug 1943	13 Dec 1943
LANSING	DER 388	Brown SB Co, Houston	3 Aug 1943	10 Nov 1943
MILLS	DER 383	Brown SB Co, Houston	26 May 1943	12 Oct 1943
OTTERSTETTER	DER 244	Brown SB Co, Houston	19 Jan 1943	6 Aug 1943
PRICE	DER 332	Consolidated Steel Corpn	30 Oct 1943	12 Jan 1944
RAMSDEN	DER 382	Brown SB Co, Houston	24 May 1943	19 Oct 1943
RHODES	DER 384	Brown SB Co, Houston	29 June 1943	25 Oct 1943
ROY O. HALE	DER 336	Consolidated Steel Corpn	20 Nov 1943	3 Feb 1944
SAVAGE	DER 386	Brown SB Co, Houston	15 July 1943	29 Oct 1943
STRICKLAND	DER 333	Consolidated Steel Corpn	2 Nov 1943	10 Jan 1944
STURTEVANT	DER 239	Brown SB Co, Houston	3 Dec 1942	16 June 1943
*THOMAS J. GARY	DER 326	Consolidated Steel Corpn	21 Aug 1943	27 Nov 1943
VANCE	DER 387	Brown SB Co, Houston	16 July 1943	1 Nov 1943

Thirty-six ships of this type were converted to radar picket ships between 1951 and 1958; redesignated DER (See Conversion notes). Eleven of these ships were on loan to the US Coast Guard from 1951 to 1954 (they retained Navy names and were designated WDE with hull numbers upped by one hundred to avoid confusion with Coast Guard numbering series): DE 322-325, 328, 331, 334, 382, 387-389 and 391.

Several ships were used in Operation MARKET TIME in the South China Sea and Gulf of Tonkin to halt Communist infiltration of men and arms to South Vietnam; while engaged in MARKET TIME several ·50 calibre machineguns are mounted.

All in reserve except Calcaterra and Thomas J. Gary which are active. Forster is scheduled for transfer to South Vietnam late in 1971.

ARMAMENT. Upon conversion to radar picket ships these ships were fitted with six 20 mm guns; subsequently removed. See "Edsall" class listing for details of original DE configuration.

Forward 3 inch mount is enclosed; after mount open or enclosed, depending upon availability.

CONVERSION. Conversion to radar picket escorts included removal of conventional torpedo tubes and 40 mm guns; installation of mess compartment on main deck and other habitability improvements; fitting of two tripod masts to support radar antennes and TACAN navigation "bee-hive" antenna; installation of SPS-8 height-finding radar antenna atop after deckhouse; combat information centre (CIC) expanded and improved; and aluminium superstructure installed. Note trainable hedgehog fitted in "B" position in place of second 3 inch mount. TACAN and SPS-8 removed from active ships when seaward radar picket barrier was ended in 1965. (See photographs in 1968-1969 and earlier editions for previous configuration).

The DERs in service during the latter 1960s had SPS-28 and SPS-10 or SPS-8 radar antennes on their forward masts; and electronic warfare "pods" on after masts.

ENGINEERING. Maximum operational speed for remaining ships is about 19 knots.

PHOTOGRAPH. Thomas J. Gary shown with large TACAN "bee hive" pod on second mast and SPS-8 radar, both subsequently removed.

CALCATERRA (DER 390)   1970, US Navy, PH2 Thomas W. Woodward

FORSTER (DER 334)   1968. US Navy, PHCM L. P. Bodine

DISPOSALS AND TRANSFERS
Pillsbury (DER 133), Fessenden (DER 142), stricken in 1965 and expended as targets; Sellstrom (DER 255) stricken in 1965; Haverson (DER 316) stricken in 1966 and expended as target; Newell (DER 322), Lowe (DER 325), Brister (DER 327), Koiner (DER 331) stricken on 23 Sep 1968; Haverfield (DER 393) stricken on 2 June 1969, Wilhoite (DER 397) stricken on 2 July 1960 (target); Camp (DER 251) transferred to South Vietnam on 13 Feb 1971 (transfer delayed from July 1970).

RADAR PICKET SHIPS

From 1956 to 1965 the US Navy operated a number of Radar Picket Ships (AGR) converted from Liberty-type merchant hulls to provide radar coverage of the seaward approaches to the United States as part of the continental air defence system. These ships operated in conjunction with the DER-type ships. Sixteen radar picket ships were converted under the Fiscal Year 1955-1959 programmes. Conversion included installation of air and surface search radar, communication equipment, combat information centre (CIC), and suitable berthing and recreation facilities.

The first four ships were initially designated Miscellaneous Auxiliary Craft (YAG); subsequently all were designated Ocean Radar Station Ships (YAGR); and on 28 Sep 1958 they were redesignated Radar Picket Ships (AGR). Names and hull numbers as YAGR/AGR remained the same.

All 16 ships were stricken in 1965 when the seaward extension of the radar barrier was disestablished; they

THOMAS J. GARY (DER 326)   United States Navy

were stripped of electronic equipment and returned to Maritime Administration custody: Guardian (AGR 1, ex-YAG 41), Lookout (AGR 2, ex-YAG 42), Skywatcher (AGR 3, ex-YAG 43), Searcher (AGR 4, ex-YAGR 44), Scanner (AGR 5), Locator (AGR 6), Picket (AGR 7), Interceptor (AGR 8), Investigator (AGR 9), Outpost (AGR 10), Protector (AGR 11), Vigil (AGR 12), Interdictor (YAGR 13), Interpreter (AGR 14), Tracer (ex-Interrupter), AGR 15, Watchman (AGR 16).

FIRE SUPPORT SHIPS

IOWA (BB 61), NEW JERSEY (BB 62), MISSOURI (BB 3), and WISCONSIN (BB 64)   *1954, United States Navy*

The ships listed in this section are those suitable only for gunfire and rocket support of amphibious landings and other coastal operations because of their lack of advanced anti-aircraft, anti-submarine, and command and control capabilities. Under the official (administrative) classification list the battleships and cruisers are rated as Surface Combatants and the rocket ships as Amphibious Warfare Ships.

As of mid-1971 only one fire support ship remained in commission, the heavy cruiser *Newport News*. She was scheduled to be decommissioned and placed in reserve during 1972. In mid-1969, at the height of the Vietnam War, the fire support force was comprised of one battleship, four heavy (8-inch gunned) cruisers, and four rocket ships. With the decommissioning of the *Newport News* the largest gun barrels in the US Fleet will be the three 6 inch guns on each of four cruisers configured as fleet command ships (listed as Surface Combatants). These ships have a limited availability for fire support missions.

There now are no plans to provide the active Fleet with additional ships armed with guns larger than 5 inch calibre and the four surviving 6 inch gunned cruiser-flagships, carrying a total of 12 guns (the armament of one Soviet "Sverdlov" class cruiser), are expected to be decommissioned during the later 1970s.

BATTLESHIPS. The battleship *New Jersey* has been decommissioned after making one deployment to the Western Pacific in the role of fire support ship. She remains on the Navy List in reserve, moored near her sister ship *Missouri* at the Puget Sound Naval Shipyard Bremerton, Washington. The two other battleships of the "Iowa" class, the *Iowa* and *Wisconsin*, remain in reserve at the Philadelphia Naval Shipyard.

There is little likelihood that any of these "super dreadnoughts" will again see active service. There had been several proposals to modify the *New Jersey* to a combination fire support/command/amphibious assault ship, thus justifying her remaining in active service. Her large size, fuel capacity, speed, endurance, and fire power made her an excellent ship for such a role. With the removal of her after 16 inch triple turret and installation of a helicopter flight deck aft, she could easily have carried several hundred Marines and a number of helicopters. With her other attributes, she could have provided a most versatile, one-ship "task force" in remote areas where a US military presence is deemed desirable.

However, such proposals were rejected and the *New Jersey* was decommissioned on 17 Dec 1969. During her third commission, that had begun on 6 Apr 1968, the *New Jersey* made one deployment to the Western Pacific.

CRUISERS. Several all-gun cruisers armed with 8 inch guns remain in reserve in addition to the gun-missile cruisers *Boston* and *Canberra*. These ships are listed here because of their limited capabilities for performing missions other than gunfire support. The *Boston* and *Canberra* have been reclassified as heavy cruisers (CA vice CAG) because of the limited effectiveness of their Terrier BW missiles for task force defence.

The cruisers that remain on the Navy List all are heavy (8 inch gunned) cruisers, and their number is being reduced as periodically one is cut out of a reserve group and towed off to the breakers. The light cruisers (6 inch guns) and anti-aircraft cruisers (5 inch guns) all have been stricken, the last in 1971. The Navy's two large or "battle" cruisers, ships armed with 12 inch guns, were stricken a decade ago.

FIRE SUPPORT SHIPS. Plans developed during the mid-1960s to design and construct a new class of landing force support ships (designated LFS) have been deferred indefinitely. A request for funding of contract definition under the Fiscal Year 1970 budget was denied by the Congress.

The proposed LFS would have combined in one hull an armament of large calibre guns and possibly rocket launchers. The guns were to provide long-range, accurate, and high destructive fire while the rockets would provide saturation fire. The LFS main battery would be three 8 inch Major Calibre Light Weight Guns (MCLWG) that would fire conventional and rocket-assisted projectiles, the latter expected to have a range of more than 50 miles. The ship would have had a relatively large magazine capacity, probably 750 to 800 rounds per 8 inch gun barrel. Secondary gun armament was to be two 5 inch rapid fire guns for close-in support missions and self-defence (possibly supplemented in the latter role by point-defence missiles).

Detailed characteristics of the ship had not been developed; however, Navy officials told *Jane's Fighting Ships* that they expected the ship to displace about 8 000 tons full load, have an overall length of 400 to 500 feet, and be capable of speeds in excess of 20 knots to permit an LFS to accompany post-war amphibious assault ships.

PHOTOGRAPHS. The photograph above is believed the last taken of a formation of battleships, showing the four "Iowa" class super-dreadnoughts underway in the Caribbean. It is expected that these ships will be stricken from the Navy List and scrapped in the near future. Accordingly, the above photograph and the unusual view of the *Wisconsin* in dry dock on the following page are published as a farewell to an era.

NEW JERSEY (BB 62)   *1968, United States Navy, PH3 E. J. Burns*

Fire Support Ships—continued

4 BATTLESHIPS (BB): "IOWA" CLASS

Name	No.	Builder	Laid down	Launched	Commissioned
IOWA	BB 61	New York Navy Yard	27 June 1940	27 Aug 1942	22 Feb 1943
NEW JERSEY	BB 62	Philadelphia Navy Yard	16 Sep 1940	7 Dec 1942	23 May 1943
MISSOURI	BB 63	New York Navy Yard	6 Jan 1941	29 Jan 1944	11 June 1944
WISCONSIN	BB 64	Philadelphia Navy Yard	25 Jan 1941	7 Dec 1943	16 Apr 1944

Displacement, tons	45 000 standard; 59 000 full load
Length, feet (*metres*)	860 (*262·1*) wl; 887·2 (*270·4*) oa except *New Jersey* 887·6 (*270·5*)
Beam, feet (*metres*)	108·2 (*33·0*)
Draft, feet (*metres*)	38 (*11·6*)
Guns	9—16 inch (*406 mm*) 50 cal. 20—5 inch (*127 mm*) 38 cal. dual purpose. several 40 mm guns in all except *New Jersey*
Main engines	4 geared turbines (General Electric in BB 61 and BB 63; Westinghouse in BB 62 and BB 64); 212 000 shp; 4 shafts
Boilers	8 (Babcock & Wilcox)
Speed, knots	33 (all have reached 35 knots in service)
Complement	designed complement varied, averaging 169 officers and 2 689 enlisted men in wartime; *New Jersey* was manned by 70 officers and 1 556 enlisted men (requirements reduced with removal of all light anti-aircraft weapons, floatplanes, and reduced operational requirements) in 1968-1969

These ships were the largest battleships ever built except for the Japanese *Yamato* and *Musashi* (64 170 tons standard, 863 feet overall, 9—18·1 inch guns.) All four "Iowa" class ships were in action in the Pacific during World War II, primarily screening fast carriers and bombarding amphibious invasion objectives. Three were mothballed after the war with the *Missouri* being retained in service as a training ship. All four ships again were in service during the Korean War (1950-1953) as shore-bombardment ships; all mothballed 1954-1958.
The *New Jersey* began reactivation in mid-1967 at a cost of approximately $21 000 000; recommissioned on 6 Apr 1968. The *Iowa* and *Wisconsin* remained in reserve at the Philadelphia Naval Shipyard where the *New Jersey* had been berthed and reactivated; and the mothballed *Missouri* at the Puget Sound Naval Shipyard, Bremerton, Washington.
The *New Jersey* was again decommissioned on 17 Dec 1969 and mothballed at Bremerton with the *Missouri*. Two additional ships of this class were laid down, but never completed: *Illinois* (BB 65), laid down 15 Jan 1945, and *Kentucky* (BB 66), laid down 6 Dec 1944. The *Illinois* was 22 percent complete when cancelled on 11 Aug 1945. The *Kentucky* was 69·2 percent complete when construction was suspended late in the war; floated from its building dock on 20 Jan 1950. Conversion to a missile ship (BBG) was proposed, but no work was undertaken and she was stricken on 9 June 1958 and broken up for scrap.
Approximate construction cost was $114 485 000 for *Missouri*; other ships cost slightly less.

AIRCRAFT. As built, each ship carried three floatplanes for scouting and gunfire spotting and had two quarterdeck catapults. Catapults removed and helicopters carried during the Korean War.

ARMOUR. These battleships are the most heavily armoured US warships ever constructed, being designed to survive ship-to-ship combat with enemy ships armed with 16 inch guns. The main armour belt consists of Class A steel armour 12·1 inches thick tapering vertically to 1·62 inches; a lower armour belt aft of Turret No. 3 to protect propeller shafts is 13·5 inches; turret faces are 17 inches; turret tops are 7·25 inches; turret backs are 12 inches; barbetts have a maximum of 11·6 inches of armour; second deck armour is 6 inches; and the three-level conning tower sides are 17·3 inches with an armoured roof 7·25 inches (the conning tower levels are pilot house, navigation bridge, and flag-signal bridge).

DESIGN. These ships carried heavier armament than previous US battleships and had increased protection and larger engines accounting for additional displacement and increased speed. Design includes clipper bow and long foredeck, with graceful sheer (see photographs).
All fitted as fleet flagships with additional accommodations and bridge level for admiral and staff.

ELECTRONICS. During 1968-1969 the *New Jersey* was fitted with SPS-10 and SPS-12 search radars (not SPS-43 as stated in previous edition).

GUNNERY. The Mk VII 16 inch guns in these ships fire projectiles weighing up to 2 700 pounds (*1 225 kg*) (armour piercing) a maximum distance of 23 miles (*39 km*). As built, these ships had 80—40 mm and 49 to 60 —20 mm anti-aircraft guns (except *Iowa*, only 19 quad 40 mm mounts); all 20 mm guns removed and a reduced number of 40 mm weapons remain on the mothballed ships. During 1968-1969 the *New Jersey* was fitted with two Mk 34 fire control directors in addition to the two Mk 56 and four Mk 37 previously installed. Mk 48 shore bombardment computer installed when reactivated.

NEW JERSEY (BB 62) 1968, United States Navy

WISCONSIN (BB 64) in AFDB 1 at Guam 1952, United States Navy

Fire Support Ships—*continued*

"IOWA" CLASS *continued*

MODERNISATION. The *New Jersey* underwent an "austere" modernisation in 1967-1968, with installation of modern communications equipment, electronic counter-measure (ECM) equipment, a fog foam firelighting system in engine rooms, air conditioning in living spaces, and a new target-designating system. ECM equipment included four Zuni rocket launchers.

OPERATIONAL. The *New Jersey* made one deployment to the Western Pacific during her third (1968-1969) commission.

During the deployment she was on the "gun line" off South Vietnam for a total of 120 days with 47 days being the longest sustained period at sea.

While on the "gun line" the *New Jersey* fired 5 688 rounds of ammunition from her 16 inch main battery guns and a total of 6 200 rounds during the commission, the additional firings being for tests and training. While off Vietnam she also fired some 15 000 rounds from her 5 inch secondary battery guns.

(In comparison, during World War II the *New Jersey* fired 771 main battery rounds and during two deployments in the Korean War and midshipmen training cruises she fired 6 671 main battery rounds).

NOMENCLATURE. US battleships are generally named for states; the exception was the *Kearsarge*, BB 5 launched in 1899 (later *Crane Ship No. 1*, AB 1). Beginning in 1969 the Navy has named frigates for states.

DISPOSALS

Eight World War II-built battleships and large (battle) cruisers have been stricken: **North Carolina** (BB 55), **Washington** (BB 56), **Alaska** (CB 1), and **Guam** (CB 2) on 1 June 1960; **South Dakota** (BB 57), **Indiana** (BB 58), **Massachusetts** (BB 59), and **Alabama** (BB 60) on 1 June 1962. **North Carolina, Massachusetts** and **Alabama** to their states as memorials; others scrapped. Plans to convert the unfinished **Hawaii** (CB 3) to a command ship (CBC 1) were dropped and she was stricken on 9 June 1958.

The five battleships of the "Montana" class authorised on the eve of World War II were never begun and formally were cancelled on 21 July 1943 (60 500 tons standard displacement, 921·25 feet overall, 12—16 inch guns).

NEW JERSEY (BB 62)   *1968, United States Navy*

BOSTON (CA 69) See following page   *1968, United States Navy*

CANBERRA (CA70) See following page   *1968, United States Navy, PH2 R. E. Duggan*

Fire Support Ships—*continued*

2 HEAVY CRUISERS (CA): "BOSTON-CANBERRA" TYPE (ex-CAG)

Name	No.	Builder	Laid down	Launched	Commissioned	CAG Comm.
BOSTON	CA 69 (ex-CAG 1)	Bethlehem Steel Co (Quincy)	30 June 1941	26 Aug 1942	30 June 1943	1 Nov 1955
CANBERRA	CA 70 (ex-CAG 2)	Bethlehem Steel Co (Quincy)	3 Sep 1941	19 Apr 1943	14 Oct 1943	15 June 1956

Displacement, tons	13 300 standard; 17 500 full load
Length, feet (*metres*)	664 (*222·3*) wl; 673·5 (*205·3*) oa
Beam, feet (*metres*)	70·8 (*21·6*)
Draft, feet (*metres*)	26 (*7·9*)
Missiles	2 twin Terrier launchers
Guns	6—8 in (*203 mm*) 55 cal
	10—5 in (*127 mm*) 38 cal dual-purpose
	8—3 in (*76 mm*) 50 cal anti-aircraft
Main engines	4 geared turbines (General Electric), 120 000 shp; 4 shafts
Boilers	4 (Babcock & Wilcox)
Speed, knots	33
Complement	1 273 (73 officers; 1 200 enlisted men)

BOSTON (CA 69) *1968, United States Navy, PH3 D. R. Hyden*

These were the US Navy's first guided missile warships. Originally heavy cruisers (CA) of the "Baltimore" class. Converted 1952-1956 to combination gun-missile configuration and reclassified CAG on 4 Jan 1952. Subsequently reclassified as CA on 1 May 1968, reverting to original hull numbers. They both retained Terrier missile armament but their early BW-1 missile systems were no longer considered suitable for task force defence against high-performance aircraft.

Retention of 8 inch guns forward made these ships valuable in the fire support role during the Vietnamese conflict.

The *Boston* was decommissioned on 5 May 1970 and placed in reserve and the *Canberra* was decommissioned on 16 Feb 1970 and placed in reserve.

CONVERSION. Both ships were converted to a missile configuration at the New York Shipbuilding Corp. Camden, New Jersey. *Boston* conversion ordered on 4 Dec 1951 and *Canberra* on 28 Jan 1952. Conversion included removal of after 8-inch gun turret (143 tons) and after twin 5-inch mount; all 40 mm and 20 mm guns replaced by six 3-inch twin mounts (subsequently reduced to four mounts). Superstructure modified and twin funnels replaced by single large funnel (as in "Oregon City" class cruisers). Forward pole mast replaced by lattice radar mast and radar platform fitted aft of second polemast. Missile system installation includes rotating magazines below decks, loading and check-out equipment, and two large directors aft. Estimated conversion cost was $30 000 000 for the two ships.

ELECTRONICS. The *Boston* has experimental, three-dimensional air search radar on forward mast (topped by

TACAN); a similar antenna was removed from the *Canberra* in mid-1968. Both ships have an SPS-43 search radar antenna atop pole mast and an SPS-30 antenna on platform aft of pole mast.

MISSILES. Reportedly, each ship carries 144 missiles in two rotating magazines. Each launcher can load and fire two missiles every 30 seconds; loading is completely automatic with missiles sliding onto launchers in the vertical position.

NOMENCLATURE. The *Canberra* was originally named *Pittsburgh*; she was renamed while under construction

to honour an Australian cruiser of that name which was sunk with several US Navy Ships in the Battle of Savo Island in August 1942. She is the only US warship named for a foreign capital city.

PHOTOGRAPHS. Twin 3-inch gun mounts abaft missile directors have been removed from both ships. The photographs of the *Boston*, taken in April and September 1968, show her still carrying the "1" of her late CAG 1 designation. The "action" shot shows her firing away from camera at North Vietnamese coastal craft. Note only the *Canberra* has a helicopter "platform" (angled in on starboard side to provide for boat stowage).

3 HEAVY CRUISERS (CA): "SALEM" CLASS

Displacement, tons	17 000 standard; 21 500 full load
Length, feet (*metres*)	700·(*213·4*) wl; 716·5 (*218·4*) oa
Beam, feet (*metres*)	76·3 (*23·3*)
Draft, feet (*metres*)	26 (*7·9*)
Guns	9—8 in (*203 mm*) 55 calibre
	12—5 in (*127 mm*) 38 calibre dual-purpose
	4—3 in (*76 mm*) 50 calibre anti-aircraft in *Newport News*; 20—3 inch guns in others (see *Gunnery* notes)
Main engines	4 geared turbines (General Electric); 120 000 shp; 4 shafts
Boilers	4 (Babcock & Wilcox)
Speed, knots	33
Complement CA 148	approx 1 200

Name	No.	Builder	Laid down	Launched	Commissioned
DES MOINES	CA 134	Bethlehem Steel Co (Quincy)	28 May 1945	27 Sep 1946	17 Nov 1948
SALEM	CA 139	Bethlehem Steel Co (Quincy)	4 June 1945	25 Mar 1947	9 May 1949
✱NEWPORT NEWS	CA 148	Newport News SB & DD Co	1 Oct 1945	6 Mar 1947	29 Jan 1949

NEWPORT NEWS (CA 148) *1967, United States Navy*

These ships were the largest and most powerful 8 inch-gun cruisers ever built. Completed too late for World War II, they were employed primarily as flagships for the Sixth Fleet in the Mediterranean and the Second Fleet in the Atlantic. The *Salem* was decommissioned on 30 Jan 1959 and the *Des Moines* on 14 July 1961. The *Newport News*, normally flagship of the second Fleet, was employed as a fire support ship off Vietnam in 1967-1968; she was scheduled to be decommissioned during 1972.

AIRCRAFT. As completed the *Des Moines* had two stern catapults and carried four floatplanes; catapults removed.

DESIGN. These ships are an improved version of the previous "Oregon City" class. The newer cruisers have automatic main batteries, larger main turrets, taller fire control towers, and larger bridges. The *Des Moines* and *Newport News* are fully air conditioned.

Nine additional ships of this class were cancelled: the *Dallas* (CA 140) and the unnamed CA 141-142, CA 149-153.

ELECTRONICS. The *Newport News* has an SPS-37 search radar antenna and TACAN on her forward mast,

and SPS-8 and SPS-6 antennae on her after mast. (The small antenna on the forward mast is an SPS-10).

Fire Support Ships—*continued*

"SALEM" CLASS *continued*

GUNNERY. These cruisers were the first ships to be armed with fully automatic 8 inch guns firing cased ammunition. The guns can be loaded at any elevation from —5 to +41 degrees; rate of fire is four times faster than earlier 8 inch guns. Mk XVI 8-inch guns in these ships; other heavy cruisers remaining on Navy List have Mk XV guns.

As built these ships mounted 12 5 inch guns, 24 3 inch guns (in twin mounts), and 12 20 mm guns (single mounts). The 20 mm guns were removed almost immediately and the 3 inch battery was reduced gradually as ships were overhauled. (With full armament the designed wartime complement was 1 860).

MODERNISATION. The *Newport News* has been extensively modified to provide improved flagship facilities; note elaborate antennae on masts, forecastle, atop turrets, and on stern crane; superstructure extended outward on both sides between forward 3 inch twin mounts and secondary battery directors; on two 3 inch twin mounts remain (alongside bridge).

PHOTOGRAPHS. Note stern crane of *Newport News* is lowered to provide clear field of fire for after main battery turret. *Des Moines* photograph shows two helicopters and ship's boats on fantail.

NEWPORT NEWS (CA 148)   1967, United States Navy, JO1 W. B. Bass

DES MOINES (CA 134)   *United States Navy*

1 HEAVY CRUISER (CA): "OREGON CITY" CLASS

Displacement, tons	13 700 standard; 17 500 full load
Length, feet (*metres*)	664 (*202·4*) wl; 673·5 (*205·3*) oa
Beam, feet (*metres*)	70·9 (*21·6*)
Draft, feet (*metres*)	26 (*7·9*)
Guns	9—8 in (*203 mm*) 55 calibre; 12—5 in (*127 mm*) 38 calibre dual-purpose; 20—3 in (*127 mm*) 50 calibre AA in *Rochester* (see *Gunnery* notes)
Main engines	4 geared turbines (General Electric); 120 000 shp; 4 shafts
Boilers	4 (Babcock & Wilcox)
Speed, knots	33
Complement	1 700 (designed wartime)

Name	No.	Builder	Laid down	Launched	Commissioned
ROCHESTER	CA 124	Bethlehem Steel Co (Quincy)	29 May 1944	28 Aug 1945	20 Dec 1946

This class is similar in design to the earlier "Baltimore" class but with a single funnel and a more compact superstructure. Three ships of this class were completed the *Albany* (CA 123) was converted to guided missile cruiser (CG 10) in 1958-1962; the *Oregon City* (CA 122) has been stricken; the *Rochester* has been in mothballs since 1961.

AIRCRAFT. As completed the *Rochester* had two stern catapults and carried four floatplanes; catapults removed.

DESIGN. This class is almost identical in design to the "Baltimore" class except for their superstructure.

Seven additional ships of this class were cancelled: the *Northampton* (CA 125), *Cambridge* (CA 126), *Bridgeport* (CA 127), *Kansas* (CA 128), *Tulsa* (CA 129), *Norfolk* (CA 137), and *Scranton* (CA 138); the *Northampton* was later re-ordered as a command ship (CLC 1, now CC 1).

GUNNERY. These ships were designed to mount nine 8 inch guns, 12 5 inch guns, 48 40 mm guns (11 quad and two twin mounts), and 24 20 mm guns. Lighter weapons were replaced by twin 3 inch mounts in *Rochester*.

PHOTOGRAPHS. The *Rochester* is shown shortly after completion (dark "war paint" and catapults on fantail) and in the 1950s.

DISPOSAL
Oregon City (CA 122) stricken on 1 Nov 1970.

ROCHESTER (CA 124)   *United States Navy*

ROCHESTER (CA 124)   *United States Navy*

Fire Support Ships—*continued*

7 HEAVY CRUISERS (CA): "BALTIMORE" CLASS

Displacement, tons	13 600 standard ; 17 200 full load
Length, feet (*metres*)	664 (*204·4*) wl ; 673·5 (*205·3*) oa
Beam, feet (*metres*)	70·9 (*21·6*)
Draft, feet (*metres*)	26 (*7.9*)
Guns	9—8 in (*203* mm) 55 calibre 12—5 in (*127* mm) 38 calibre dual-purpose except 10 guns in *Saint Paul* up to 20—3 in (*76* mm) 50 calibre anti-aircraft (see *Gunnery* notes) except 48—40 mm AA in *Quincy*
Main engines	4 geared turbines (General Electric) ; 120 000 shp ; 4 shafts
Boilers	4 (Babcock & Wilcox)
Speed, knots	33
Complement	1 146 (61 officers, 1,085 enlisted men) in *Saint Paul*; designed wartime complement 1 772 in *Quincy*; 1 969 in later ships

Name	No.	Builder	Laid down	Launched	Commissioned
QUINCY	CA 71	Bethlehem Steel Company, Quincy	9 Oct 1941	23 June 1943	15 Dec 1943
PITTSBURG	CA 72	Bethlehem Steel Company, Quincy	3 Feb 1943	22 Feb 1944	10 Oct 1944
ST. PAUL	CA 73	Bethlehem Steel Company, Quincy	3 Feb 1943	16 Sep 1944	17 Feb 1945
HELENA	CA 75	Bethlehem Steel Company, Quincy	9 Sep 1943	28 Apr 1945	4 Sep 1945
BREMERTON	CA 130	New York Shipbuilding Corporation	1 Feb 1943	2 July 1944	29 Apr 1945
TOLEDO	CA 133	New York Shipbuilding Corporation	13 Sep 1943	6 May 1945	27 Oct 1946
LOS ANGELES	CA 135	Philadelphia Naval Shipyard	28 July 1943	20 Aug 1944	22 July 1945

SAINT PAUL (CA 73)   *1967, United States Navy, PH 1. D. Granthom*

Fourteen ships of this class were completed ; four of the ships have been converted to guided missile cruisers : the *Boston* (CA 69/CAG 1). *Canberra* (CA 70/CAG 2), *Columbus* (CA 74, now CG 12), and *Chicago* (CA 136, now CG 11). The remaining all-gun cruisers were phased out of the active fleet as missile ships became available. The *Qunicy* in 1954, *Pittsburg* in 1955, *Helena* in 1963, *Bremerton* in 1960, *Toledo* in 1960, *Los Angeles* in 1966, and *Saint Paul* in 1971.

AIRCRAFT. As completed these ships had two stern catapults and carried four floatplanes ; catapults removed after World War II.

GUNNERY. These ships were completed with nine 8 inch guns, 12—5 inch inch guns, 48—40 mm guns (12 quad mounts in CA 68-71, 11 quad and two twin mounts in later ships), and 23—20 mm guns. All 20 mm weapons were removed and the 40 mm guns were replaced by 20—3 inch guns (twin mounts) in all above ships but the *Quincy*. The number of 3 inch guns was reduced subsequently in some ships before they were mothballed. (The *Helena* had only 14—3 inch guns when decommissioned ; the *Saint Paul* retained only 12). The *Saint Paul* also lost the twin 5 inch mount forward of her bridge. Prior to being decommissioned the *Saint Paul* used rocket-assisted 8 inch projectiles during shore bombardment firing in the Vietnam conflict ; reportedly, her guns attained a range of 34 miles (approx 60 000 yards), believed to be the longest distance ever fired by a naval gun. It can not be ascertained if this is the maximum range possible with the ship's guns that have been modified to fire the rocket-assisted projectiles that weigh some 113 pounds.

SAINT PAUL (CA 73)   *1967, United States Navy. JO1 B. S. Whitehead*

MODERNISATION. The *Saint Paul*, *Helena*, and *Los Angeles* have been modified to improve their flagship facilities ; advanced electronic equipment fitted and pole foremast replaced by a pylon mast to support additional antennae including "bee-hive" TACAN (Tactical Air Navigation system to guide aircraft). The *Saint Paul's* main radar antennae 'are an SPS-37 forward and an SPS-8 aft ; the *Helena* had a large SPS-43 antenna forward when decommissioned.

NOMENCLATURE. Ships renamed during construction were *Quincy*, ex-*Saint Paul*; *Pittsburg*, ex-*Albany*; *Saint Paul*, ex-*Rochester*; and *Helena*, ex-*Des Moines*.

DISPOSAL
Macon (CA 132) stricken on 1 Nov 1969 ; **Baltimore** (CA 68) and **Fall River** (CA 131) stricken in 1971.

HELENA (CA 75)   *United States Navy*

"WORCESTER" CLASS

The two light cruisers of the "Worcester" class have been stricken, the **Worcester** (CL 144) and **Roanoke** (CL 145), both on 1 Dec 1970. These ships were amongst the largest cruisers ever constructed and were ranked as "light" cruisers only because of their 6 inch main gun battery. Eight additional ships of this class were cancelled : the **Vallejo** (CL 146), **Gary** (CL 147), and the unnamed CL 154-159.
See 1970-1971 and previous editions for details.

Fire Support Ships—*continued*

"CLEVELAND" CLASS

All "Cleveland" class light cruisers have been stricken except for six ships converted to gun-missile cruisers (CLG) and listed in the Fleet Escort Ships section. Of the 36 ships of this class that were completed, 27 were built as light cruisers (including six later converted to CLG) and nine were built as light aircraft carriers (CVL), some of which subsequently were reclassified as aircraft transports (AVT).
See 1970-1971 and previous editions for additional details of this class, including dimensions and characteristics.

Cleveland (CL 55), Columbia (CL 56), Montpelier (CL 57), Denver (CL 58), Santa Fe (CL 60), Birmingham (CL 62), Mobile (CL 63) stricken 1 Mar 1959; CL 59 and CL 61 completed as carriers; Vincennes (CL 64) stricken 1 Apr 1966; Pasadena (CL 65)

stricken 1 Dec 1970; Springfield (CL 66) converted to CLG 7; Topeka (CL 67) converted to CLG 8; CL 76-79 completed as carriers; Biloxi (CL 80) stricken 1 Sep 1961; Houston (CL 81) stricken 1 Mar 1959; Providence (CL 82) converted to CLG 6; Manchester (CL 83) stricken 1 April 1960; CL 84 cancelled 1940; CL 85 completed as carrier; Vicksburg (CL 86) stricken 1 Oct 1962; Duluth (CL 87) stricken 1 Jan 1960; CL 88 cancelled 1940; Miami (CL 89) stricken 1 Sep 1961; Astoria (CL 90) stricken 1 Nov 1969; Oklahoma City (CL 91) converted to CLG 5; Little Rock (CL 92) to CLG 4; Galveston (CL 93) to CLG 3; Youngstown (CL 94) not completed (cancelled 1944); CL 99 and CL 100 completed as carriers; Amsterdam (CL 101) stricken on 2 Jan 1971.
Portsmouth (CL 102) stricken 1 Dec 1970; Wilkes-Barre (CL 103) stricken on 15 Jan 1971.
Atlanta (CL 104) stricken 1 Oct 1962, reinstated 15 May 1964 as IX 304, again stricken 1 Apr 1970 (target); Dayton (CL 105) stricken 1 Sep 1961.

"FARGO" CLASS

The modified "Cleveland" class cruisers Fargo (CL 106) and Huntington (CL 107) stricken 1 Mar 1970 and 1 Sep 1962, respectively. Eleven additional ships of this class were cancelled during construction (CL 108-118); see 1969-1970 and previous editions for details.

ANTI-AIRCRAFT CRUISERS

The World War II-era "anti-aircraft" cruisers all have been stricken or reclassified. "Atlanta" class: San Diego (CLAA 53) and San Juan (CLAA 54) stricken 1 Mar 1959; "Oakland" class: Oakland (CLAA 95), Reno (CLAA 96) stricken 1 Mar 1959; Flint (CLAA 97) stricken 1 Sep 1965; Tucson (CLAA 98) stricken 1 June 1966; "Juneau" class: Juneau (CLAA 119) stricken 1 Nov 1959; Spokane (CLAA 120) reclassified as sonar test ship T-AG 191; Fresno (CLAA 121) stricken 1 Apr 1965.

1 INSHORE FIRE SUPPORT SHIP (LFR):
"CARRONADE" TYPE

Name	No.	Builder	Commissioned
CARRONADE	LFR 1 (ex-IFS 1)	Puget Sound Bridge	25 May 1955

Displacement, tons	1 040 standard; 1 500 full load
Dimensions, feet	245 oa × 38·5 × 10
Guns	1—5 inch 28 cal dual-purpose
	4—40 mm AA (twin) 2—20 mm AA (single)
Rockets	8 rapid-fire launchers for 5 inch rockets
Main engines	2 diesels (Fairbanks-Morse); 3 100 hp; 2 shafts
Speed, knots	15
Complement	139 (9 officers, 130 enlisted men)

The *Carronade* was specifically designed to provide fire support for amphibious landings; she is an improvement over the World War II-era LSMR but lacks big-gun firepower. Built by Puget Sound Bridge & Dredging Co; laid down on 19 Nov 1952; launched on 26 May 1953. Placed in reserve and mothballed from 1960 to 1965 when recommissioned for duty in Vietnam conflict. Subsequently decommissioned and again mothballed on 24 July 1970 (*not* stricken as previously reported by official sources). Designation changed from IFS 1 to LFR 1 on 1 Jan 1969 (both Inshore Fire Support Ship).

ENGINEERING. Fitted with controllable-pitch propellers.

NOMENCLATURE. The *Carronade* is named for the short-range, highly effective weapon developed by the ironworks of the Carron Company, Scotland, and introduced first in the Royal Navy in 1779.

INSHORE FIRE SUPPORT SHIPS —*continued*

These ships were redesigned during construction to provide fire support for amphibious landings. They have pointed bows, bridge structure aft, and 5 inch mount forward of bridge (earlier LSMRs had 5 inch gun aft of bridge). Built by Charleston Navy Yard and Brown Shipbuilding Company, Houston, Texas; originally 48 ships in these series (LSMR 401-412 and LSMR 501-536); all launched 1945; completed 1945-1946. Most mothballed after World War II; LSMR 401, 403, 409, and 412 served in Korean conflict of 1950-1953; the LSMR 512 was active from 1945 to 1955, serving as a training ship during Korean conflict; these ships were named for rivers on 1 Oct 1955.
Original designation of Medium Landing Ship—Rocket (LSMR) changed to inshore Fire Support Ship (LFR) for 11 surviving ships on 1 Jan 1969.
LFR 409, 525, and 536 recommissioned in 1965 for duty off Vietnam; all decommissioned in 1970. With the *Carronade* these ships formed Inshore Fire Support Division 93 for service in the Vietnam conflict.

ROCKETS. The automatic rocket launchers each fire 30 spin-stabilised rockets per minute.

RECLASSIFICATIONS AND DISPOSALS
Full list of stricken ships in 1967-68 edition; one ship remains on Navy List with other designation: Elk River (ex-LSMR 501) as ocean engineering range support ship (IX 501).
Targeteer, YV 3 drone carrier, ex-*Gunnison River* (LSMR 508), was stricken in 1969; Catapult, YV 1, ex-LSM 445, and Launcher, YV 2, ex-LSM 446, were stricken in 1960; Clarion River (LSMR/LFR 409) stricken on 8 May 1970; White River (LSMR/LFR 536) stricken on 22 May 1970; St. Francis River (LSMR/LFR 525) stricken on 17 Apr 1970. AG 335, former LSM 335 operated as supply ship, stricken on 21 Dec 1970 (transferred to Department of Interior).

CARRONADE (LFR 1)   1967, United States Navy

CARRONADE (LFR 1)   1966, United States Navy

8 INSHORE FIRE SUPPORT SHIPS (LFR):
FORMER LSMR

Name	No.	Builder	Commissioned
BIG BLACK RIVER	LFR 401	Charleston Navy Yard	7 Apr 1945
BROADKILL RIVER	LFR 405	Charleston Navy Yard	2 May 1945
DES PLAINES RIVER	LFR 412	Charleston Navy Yard	23 May 1945
LAMOILLE RIVER	LFR 512	Brown Shipbuilding	5 July 1945
LARAMIE RIVER	LFR 513	Brown Shipbuilding	9 July 1945
OWYHEE RIVER	LFR 515	Brown Shipbuilding	16 July 1945
RED RIVER	LFR 522	Brown Shipbuilding	6 Aug 1945
SMOKY HILL RIVER	LFR 531	Brown Shipbuilding	25 Sep 1945

Displacement, tons	994 standard; 1 084 full load
Dimensions, feet	LSMR 401-412 197·2 wl; 203·5 oa × 34·5 × 10
	LSMR 501-536 204·5 wl; 206·2 oa × 34·5 × 10
Guns	1—5 in 38 cal dual-purpose;
	4—40 mm AA (twin)
Rockets	8 twin launchers for 5 in rockets
Main engines	2 diesel (General Motors); 2 800 shp; 2 shafts
Speed, knots	12·6
Complement	137 (7 officers, 130 enlisted men)

ST. FRANCIS RIVER (LFR 525)   1969, U S Navy PH3 W. D. Newton

ST. FRANCIS RIVER (LFR 525)   1967, US Navy, JOC & J. Filtz

AMPHIBIOUS WARFARE SHIPS

The US Navy's amphibious lift capability continues to be reduced although it being extensively modernised. From a peak Vietnam War strength of about 165 ships of this category three years ago, the US Navy will have 75 amphibious ships by 30 June 1972. These ships will be capable of lifting slightly less four brigade/air group assault teams (about 12 rifle battalions plus support, air, and logistic elements for a total of some 20 000 men). The amphibious warfare ships are amongst the most modernised category of the US Navy. By 1975 all (except possbily one command ship) will be of post-World War II construction and about 65 of the 75 ships will be capable of a sustained speed of 20 knots. The "slow" ships in the 1975 force will be mostly 14·5 to 17·5-knot capable LSTs built during the 1950s. There appears to be ample justification for retaining these older ships (and possibly even some of World War II vintage) because the size of the new, 20-knot LSTs will inhibit their use in some areas, especially in a riverine environment such as Vietnam. There are many places that a 522¼-foot ship cannot go that a 328-foot ship can be sent. However, the war-built LSTs are now almost all gone (many to US allies during the past year) and those that remain

are tired after three wars and are not suitable for further service. In some quarters it has been recommended that a successor to the 328-foot, 11·6-knot LST be constructed in small numbers. This proposal does in no way detract from the excellence of design and capability of the 20-knot LSTs of the "Newport" class, that are described in considerable detail in this edition. Despite the development of helicopter assault tactics, large-scale use of helicopters by US forces, and plans for heavy lift helicopters for the Navy and Marine Corps, the LST is still a vital component of amphibious warfare. This was amply demonstrated in Vietnam with some 65 Navy-manned "large slow targets" being employed plus another 40-odd being operated by the Military Sea Transportation Service with civilian crews.

With respect to helicopter assault, most Navy amphibious ships now have a helicopter platform and many also have hangar and maintenance facilities. Assault, gunship, cargo, and medical evacuation ("medevac") helicopters regularly come to roost on their decks. In addition, minesweeping helicopters (RH-53 Sea Stallion) and VSTOL strike aircraft (AV-8A Harrier) will be seen more frequently aboard these ships. The twin-engine, STOL

counter-insurgency OV-10A Bronco did conduct "carrier qualification" landings and takeoffs with one of the late "Essex" class assault ships, but the lack of arresting gear and the take-off run required for these planes make regular LPH/LHA operations unlikely.

During Fiscal Year 1972 one amphibious assault ship (LPH) will be modified to operate a squadron of mine-sweeping helicopters and will be designated as a mine countermeasure helicopter ship (MSH-1). See section on Mine Warfare Ships for additional information.

FIRE SUPPORT SHIPS. The various Surface Combatant Ships (battleships and heavy cruisers) suitable only for gunfire support and the gunfire/rocket support ships officially considered by the Navy as Amphibious Warfare Ships are listed in the immediate previous section of this edition (Fire Support Ships).

TRANSPORT SUBMARINES. The transport submarines of the US Navy are listed in the Submarine section of this edition, in their normal place in the Navy's sequence of hull numbers.

2 AMPHIBIOUS COMMAND SHIPS (LCC): "BLUE RIDGE" CLASS

Displacement, tons	19 290 full load					
Length, feet (metres)	620 (188·5) oa	**Name**	**No.**	**Builder**	**Laid down**	**Launched**	**Commission**

Name	**No.**	**Builder**	**Laid down**	**Launched**	**Commission**
BLUE RIDGE	LCC 19	Philadelphia Naval Shipyard	27 Feb 1967	4 Jan 1969	14 Nov 1970
MOUNT WHITNEY	LCC 20	Newport News SB & DD Co	8 Jan 1969	8 Jan 1970	16 Jan 1971

Displacement, tons	19 290 full load
Length, feet (metres)	620 (188·5) oa
Beam, feet (metres)	82 (25·3)
Main deck width, feet (metres)	108 (33)
Draft, feet (metres)	27 (8·2)
Guns	4—3 in (76 mm) 50 cal AA (twin)
Helicopters	Utility helicopter carried
Main engines	1 turbine (General Electric); 22 000 shp; 1 shaft
Boilers	2 (Foster Wheeler)
Speed, knots	20
Complement	732 (52 officers, 680 enlisted men)
Flag accommodation	688 (217 officers, 471 enlisted men)

These are the first amphibious force flagships of post-World War II design. They can provide integrated command and control facilities for sea, air and land commanders in amphibious operations. The *Blue Ridge* was authorised in the Fiscal Year 1965 new construction programme, the AGC 20 in FY 1966. An AGC 21 was planned for the FY 1970 programme but cancelled late in 1968. It was proposed that the ship combine fleet as well as amphibious force command-control facilities.

CLASSIFICATION. Originally designated Amphibious Force Flagships (AGC); redesignated Amphibious Command Ships (LCC) on 1 Jan 1969.

DESIGN. General hull design and machinery arrangement are similar to the "Iwo Jima" class assault ships.

ELECTRONICS. Fitted with SPS-48 three-dimensional search, SPS-40 and SPS-10 search radar antennas on "island" structure. After "tower" does not have large antenna sphere originally intended for these ships. (See model photo in 1970-1971 edition). Tactical Aircraft

MOUNT WHITNEY (LCC 20)

1971, Newport News Ship Building & Dry Dock Co

Navigation (TACAN) pod tops mast.
Both ships fitted with Naval Tactical Data System (NTDS). Antennas adjacent to helicopter landing area swing out for flight operations.

GUNNERY. At one stage of design two additional twin 3 inch mounts were provided on forecastle; subsequently deleted from final designs. Antennas and their supports severely restricted firing arcs of guns.

BLUE RIDGE (LCC 19)

1970, United States Navy

Amphibious Warfare Ships—*continued*
5 AMPHIBIOUS COMMAND SHIPS (LCC): "MOUNT McKINLEY" CLASS

Displacement, tons	7 510 light; 12 560 full load
Length, feet (*metres*)	435 (*132·2*) wl; 495·3 (*150·5*) oa
Beam, feet (*metres*)	63 (*19·2*)
Draft, feet (*metres*)	28·2 (*8·5*)
Guns	1—5 in (*127 mm*) 38 cal DP
	4—40 mm AA (twin mounts)
Helicopters	Utility helicopter carried
Main engines	1 turbine (General Electric) 6 000 shp; 1 shaft
Boilers	2 (Babcock & Wilcox in AGC 7; Combustion Engineering in others)
Speed, knots	16·4
Complement (ship)	517 (36 officers, 486 enlisted men)

Name	No.	Builder	Launched	Commissioned
MOUNT McKINLEY	LCC 7	North Carolina SB Co	27 Sep 1943	1 May 1944
*ELDORADO	LCC 11	North Carolina SB Co	26 Oct 1943	25 Aug 1944
ESTES	LCC 12	North Carolina SB Co	1 Nov 1943	9 Oct 1944
POCONO	LCC 16	North Carolina SB Co	25 Jan 1945	29 Dec 1945
TACONIC	LCC 17	North Carolina SB Co	10 Feb 1945	17 Jan 1946

Acquired by the Navy in 1943-1944 while under construction to Maritime Commission C2-S-AJ1 design. After 5 inch gun and two twin 40 mm mounts replaced by helicopter platform. The *Pocono* and *Taconic* have a single mast aft in lieu of after king post in earlier ships.

All except *Eldorado* decommissioned 1969-1970 and transferred to Maritime Administration reserve (remain on Navy List).

CLASSIFICATION. Originally referred to as Auxiliary Combined Operations and Communications Headquarters Ships, but designated Amphibious Force Flagships (AGC); five surviving ships redesignated Amphibious Command Ships (LCC) on 1 Jan 1969.

ELECTRONICS. In commission, the *Mount McKinley* *Eldorado*, and *Estes* have an SPS-37 search radar antenna on the forward king post, SPS-30 and SPS-10 antennas on the lattice mast atop the superstructure, and a TACAN "bee-hive" antenna on the after king post; the *Pocono* and *Taconic* have a TACAN antenna on the forward king post, SPS-30 and SPS-10 antennas on the lattice mast atop the superstructure, and an SPS-37 antenna on the after pole mast.

DISPOSALS
Thirteen World War II amphibious force flagships have been stricken from the Navy List: **Appalachian** (AGC 1) on 1 Mar 1959; **Blue Ridge** (AGC 2), **Rocky Mount** (AGC 3) on 1 Jan 1960; **Ancon** (AGC 4) on 25 Feb 1946; **Catoctin** (AGC 5) on 1 Mar 1959; **Mount Olympus** (AGC 8) in 1961; **Wasatch** (AGC 9) on 1 Jan 1960; **Auburn** (AGC 10), **Panamint** (AGC 13) in late 1960; **Teton** (AGC 14), **Adirondack** (AGC 15) in 1961; **Biscayne** (AGC 18, ex-AVP 11) transferred to US Coast Guard on 19 July 1946. The **Duane** (AGC 6) was retained by the Coast Guard. All except the **Ancon**, **Duane**, and **Biscayne** were converted C2 merchant hulls.

MOUNT McKINLEY (LCC 7)　　　　　1969, United States Navy

Several other Coast Guard cutters served as amphibious command ships with WAGC designations (see "Campbell" class).

The yacht **Williamsburg** (ex-*Aras*, ex-PG 56) was designated AGC 369 in 1945, served as presidential yacht until stricken in 1962 (converted to oceanographic research ship, renamed *Anton Bruun*).

POCONO (LCC 16)　　　　　1969, United States Navy

MOUNT WHITNEY (LCC 20)　　　　　1970, Newport News Shipbuilding & Dry Dock Co

Amphibious Warfare Ships—continued

5 AMPHIBIOUS ASSAULT SHIPS (LHA): NEW CONSTRUCTION

No.	Start *	Launch	Commission
LHA 1	10 May 1971	July 1972	mid-1973
LHA 2	Oct 1971	Dec 1972	mid-1973
LHA 3	Mar 1972	Mar 1973	late 1973
LHA 4	Sep 1972	June 1973	late 1973
LHA 5	Jan 1973	Sep 1973	early 1974

Erection of first module

Displacement, tons	39 300 full load
Length, feet	820 oa
Beam, feet	106
Draft, feet	27·5
Guns	3—5 inch (*127 mm*) 54 cal DP (single)
Missiles	2 Basic Point Defence Missile Systems (BPDMS) launchers
Aircraft	Troop helicopters plus possibly AV-8 V/STOL close support aircraft
Main engines	Turbines; 2 shafts
Speed, knots	approx 22 sustained
Troops	1 825 (163 officers, 1 662 enlisted men)

AMPHIBIOUS ASSAULT SHIP   *Artist's concept by G. Meyer*

This is a new class of large amphibious warfare ships combining the characteristics of several previous designs including a full-length flight deck, a landing craft docking well, a large garage for trucks and armoured vehicles, and troop berthing for a reinforced battalion. The LHA 1 was authorised in the Fiscal Year 1969 new construction programme, the LHA 2 and LHA 3 in FY 1970, with two additional ships being authorised in FY 1971. The Navy announced on Jan 20, 1971 that four additional ships of this type previously planned would not be constructed. When the contract was awarded for the LHA programme it included a provision that if the last four ships were not built the government would be charged "cancellation fees" of $109 700 000; this charge—more than half the cost of an LHA—is provided in the FY 1972 budget.

All ships of this class will be constructed by Litton Systems Inc at a new ship production facility known as "Ingalls West". The new yard, located at Pasagoula, Mississippi, was developed specifically for multi-ship construction of the same design.

The cost estimates for these ships were revised in 1969 because of a cost increase and the decision to spread certain non-recurring costs previously charged against the first ship to all nine ships. The LHA 1 estimated cost is now $168 000 000, the LHA 2 and LHA 3 cost estimate is $312 000 000.

CONTRACT. These are the first ships to be procured by the US Navy with the acquisition processes known as Concept Formulation, Contract Definition, and Total Package Procurement. The proposals of Litton Systems

Inc and two other shipbuilding firms were submitted in response to specific performance criteria related to the ships' mission. The firms submitted detailed designs and cost estimates for series production of not less than five ships of this type.

DESIGN. The LHA is intended to combine the features of an amphibious assault ship (LPH), amphibious cargo ship (LKA), and amphibious transport dock (LPD) into a single hull. Beneath the flight deck is a half-length hangar deck, the two being connected by an elevator amidships on the port side and a stern lift; beneath the hangar deck is a docking well capable of accommodating four LCU-1610 type landing craft.

Bow thruster provided for holding position while off-loading landing craft.

ELECTRONICS. Primary radar antennas include the SPS-52 three-dimensional search, and SPS-10 and SPS-40; advanced communications and helicopter navigation equipment provided. Each ship also will have an Integrated Tactical Amphibious Warfare Data System (ITAWDS) to provide computerised support in control of helicopters and aircraft, shipboard weapons and sensors, navigation, landing craft control, and electronic warfare.

Chaff Rocket (CHAFROC) launchers fitted on super-structure.

GUNNERY. These ships will be armed with three 5 inch/54 calibre Mk 45 light-weight, rapid-fire guns.

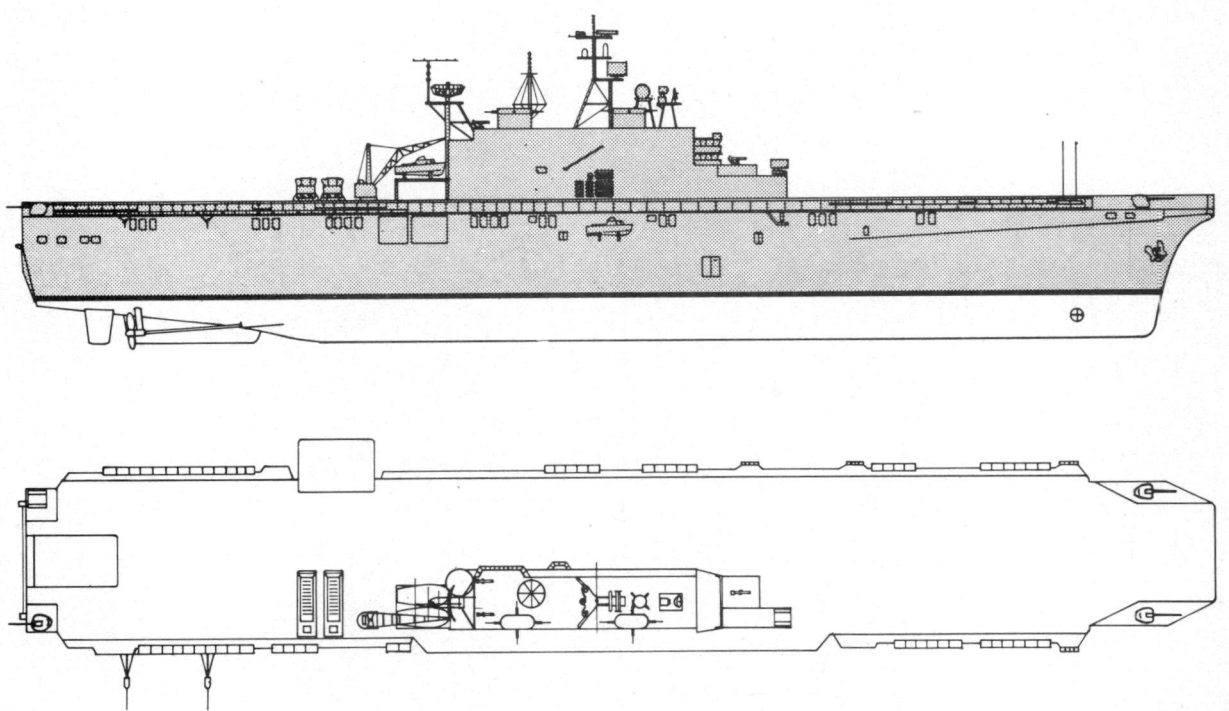

Drawing by A. D. Baker

Amphibious Warfare Ships—*continued*
7 AMPHIBIOUS ASSAULT SHIPS (LPH): "IWO JIMA" CLASS

Displacement, tons	17 000 light; 18 300 full load				
Length, feet (*metres*)	592 (*180·0*) oa				
Beam, feet (*metres*)	84 (*25·6*)				
Draft, feet (*metres*)	26 (*7·9*)				
Flight deck width, feet (*metres*)	105 (*31·9*) maximum				
Helicopters	20-24 medium (CH-46) 4 heavy (CH-53) 4 observation (HU-1)				
Guns	8—3 in (*76 mm*) 50 cal AA (twin) except 6 guns in *Okinawa*				
Missiles	1 Basic Point Defence Missile System (BPDMS) launcher firing Sea Sparrow missiles in *Okinawa*				
Main engines	1 geared turbine, 23 000 shp; 1 shaft				
Boilers	2—655 psi (Combustion Engineering in LPH 2, LPH 3, LPH 7; Babcock & Wilcox in LPH 9)				
Speed, knots	20 (sustained)				
Complement	528 (48 officers, 480 enlisted men)				
Troops	2 090 (190 officers, 1 900 enlisted men)				

Name	No.	Builder	Laid down	Launched	Commissioned
*IWO JIMA	LPH 2	Puget Sound Naval Shipyard	2 Apr 1959	17 Sep 1960	26 Aug 1961
*OKINAWA	LPH 3	Philadelphia Naval Shipyard	1 Apr 1960	19 Aug 1961	14 Apr 1962
*GUADALCANAL	LPH 7	Philadelphia Naval Shipyard	1 Sep 1961	16 Mar 1963	20 July 1963
*GUAM	LPH 9	Philadelphia Naval Shipyard	15 Nov 1962	22 Aug 1964	16 Jan 1965
*TRIPOLI	LPH 10	Ingalls Shipbuilding Corp	15 June 1964	31 July 1965	6 Aug 1966
*NEW ORLEANS	LPH 11	Philadelphia Naval Shipyard	1 Mar 1966	3 Feb 1968	16 Nov 1968
*INCHON	LPH 12	Ingalls Shipbuilding Corp	8 Apr 1968	24 May 1969	20 June 1970

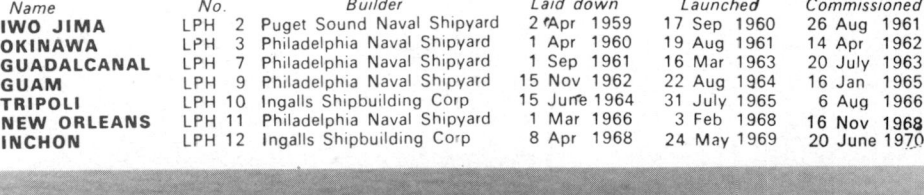

The *Iwo Jima* was the world's first ship designed and constructed specifically to operate helicopters. These ships correspond to Commando Ships in the Royal Navy, except that the US ships do not carry landing craft save for the *Inchon* which has davits aft for two LCVPs. Each LPH can carry a Marine battalion landing team, its guns, vehicles, and equipment, plus a reinforced squadron of transport helicopters and various support personnel. The *Iwo Jima* was authorised in the Fiscal Year 1958 new construction programme, the *Okinawa* in FY 1959, *Guadalcanal* in FY 1960, *Guam* in FY 1962, *Tripoli* in FY 1963, *New Orleans* in FY 1965, and *Inchon* in FY 1966. No additional ships of this type are planned in view of the new LHA capabilities.
Estimated cost of the *Iwo Jima* is $40 000 000.

OKINAWA (LPH 3) 1970, United States Navy, PH3 De Varold Bengston

DESIGN. These ships resemble World War II-era escort carriers in size but have massive bridge structures, hull continued up to flight deck providing enclosed bows, and rounded flight decks. Each ship has two deck-edge lifts, one to port opposite the bridge and one to starboard aft of island. Full hangars are provided; no arresting wires or catapults. Two small elevators carry cargo from holds to flight deck.

GUNNERY. Guns are in four twin mounts, two forward of island structure and two at stern, "notched" into flight deck. The *New Orleans* and *Inchon* have closed gun mounts forward of their islands.

MEDICAL. These ships are fitted with extensive medical facilities including operating room, X-ray room, hospital ward, isolation ward, laboratory, pharmacy, dental operating room, and medical store rooms.

MISSILES. *Okinawa* fitted with BPDMS launcher forward of island structure in early 1970; she was the fifth US ship so armed.

NEW ORLEANS (LPH 11) 1969, United States Navy, PH1 R. Blair

NOMENCLATURE. Amphibious assault ships are named for battles in Marine Corps history. Iwo Jima, Okinawa, Guadalcanal, and Guam were World War II campaigns; the Marines fought Barbary pirates at Tripoli in 1801 and helped stop the British at New Orleans in 1814. There was also a naval battle at New Orleans during the American Civil War. *Inchon* was the near-perfect 1950 amphibious assault in Korea.

DISPOSALS
The **Thetis Bay** (LPH 6, ex-CVHA 1, ex- CVE 90) was stricken in 1966. The **Block Island** (originally CVE 106) was reclassified LPH 1 on 22 Dec 1957 but conversion was cancelled and she reverted to CVE status on 17 Jan 1959; subsequently stricken (as AKV 38) and scrapped.

"ESSEX" CLASS

All three "Essex" class fast carriers employed as amphibious assault ships have been discarded: **Boxer** (LPH 4, ex-CVS 21) stricken on 1 Dec 1969, **Princeton** (LPH 5, ex-CVS 37) stricken on 30 Jan 1970, and **Valley Forge** (LPH 8, ex-CVS 45) stricken on 15 Jan 1970; all are expected to be scrapped.

INCHON (LPH 12) 1970, Ingalls Shipbuilding (Litton Industries)

Amphibious Warfare Ships—continued

GUAM (LPH 9)—See previous page   1970, United States Navy

TRIPOLI (LPH 10)—See previous page   1968, United States Navy

ST. LOUIS (LKA 116)   1969, Newport News SB & DD Co

MOBILE (LKA 115)   1969, Newport News SB & DD Co

ST. LOUIS (LKA 116)   1969, Newport News SB & DD Co

CHARLESTON (LKA 113)   1970, United States Navy

Amphibious Warfare Ships—continued

5 AMPHIBIOUS CARGO SHIPS (LKA): "CHARLESTON" CLASS

Name	No.	Laid down	Launched	Commissioned
*CHARLESTON	LKA 113	5 Dec 1966	2 Dec 1967	14 Dec 1968
*DURHAM	LKA 114	10 July 1967	29 Mar 1968	24 May 1969
*MOBILE	LKA 115	15 Jan 1968	19 Oct 1968	20 Sep 1969
*ST. LOUIS	LKA 116	3 Apr 1968	4 Jan 1969	22 Nov 1969
*EL PASO	LKA 117	22 Oct 1968	17 May 1969	17 Jan 1970

Displacement, tons	20 700 full load
Dimensions, feet	575·5 oa × 82 × 25·5
Main engines	1 steam turbine; 22 000 shp; 1 shaft = 20+ knots
Boilers	2
Guns	8—3 inch (76 mm) 50 cal AA (twin)
Complement	334 (24 officers, 310 enlisted men)
Troops	approx 300

These ships are designed specifically for the attack cargo ship role; they carry 18 landing craft (LCM) and supplies for amphibious operations. Design includes two heavy-lift cranes with a 78·4-ton capacity and helicopter deck aft.
The LKA 113-116 were authorised in the Fiscal Year 1965 shipbuilding programme; LKA 117 in FY 1966 programme.

All built by Newport News Shipbuilding and Dry Dock Co, Virginia. Cost is approximately $21 000 000 per ship.

DESIGN. Note unusual cranes forward and aft; each has a 78·4-ton capacity. Helicopter deck aft.

ENGINEERING. These are the first US Navy ships with a fully automated main propulsion plant; control of plant is from bridge or central machinery space console. This automation enabled a 45-man reduction in complement.

CLASSIFICATION. Originally designated Attack Cargo Ship (AKA). Charleston redesignated Amphibious Cargo Ship (LKA) on 14 Dec 1968; others to LKA on 1 Jan 1969. (Correction from previous edition).

NOMENCLATURE. Amphibious cargo ships are named for counties.

1 AMPHIBIOUS CARGO SHIP (LKA): "TULARE" TYPE

* TULARE (ex- Evergreen Mariner) LKA 112

Displacement, tons	12 000 light; 15 970 full load
Measurement, tons	9 200 gross; 13 400 deadweight
Dimensions, feet	564 oa × 76 ×26
Guns	12—3 inch 50 cal AA (twin)
Main engines	Turbine; 1 shaft; 22 000 shp = 23 knots
Boilers	2
Complement	437 (38 officers, 399 enlisted men)
Troops	approx 135

Built by Bethlehem, San Francisco. Laid down on 16 Feb 1953, launched on 22 Dec 1953; Acquired by Navy during construction. Commissioned on 13 Jan 1956. C4-S-1 B type. Has helicopter landing platform and booms capable of lifting 60-ton landing craft. Carries 9 LCM-6 landing craft. Designation changed from AKA 112 to LKA 112 on 1 Jan 1969.

TULARE (LKA 112)   1969, US Navy, PHCS G. W. Walsh, Jr.

5 AMPHIBIOUS CARGO SHIPS (LKA): "RANKIN" CLASS

Name	No.	Launched	Commissioned
RANKIN	LKA 103	22 Dec 1944	25 Feb 1945
SEMINOLE	LKA 104	28 Dec 1944	8 Mar 1945
UNION	LKA 106	23 Nov 1944	25 Apr 1945
VERMILLION	LKA 107	12 Dec 1944	23 June 1945
WASHBURN	LKA 108	12 Dec 1944	17 May 1945

Displacement, tons	6 456 light; 14 160 full load
Dimensions, feet	459·2 oa × 63 × 26·3
Guns	1—5 inch 38 cal DP (removed from some ships); 8—40 mm AA (twin)
Main engines	Geared turbine (General Electric); 1 shaft; 6 000 shp = 16·5 knots
Boilers	2 (Combustion Engineering)
Complement	247

C2-S-AJ3 type. Ten 20 mm AA guns removed. Designation changed from AKA to LKA on 1 Jan 1969.
All of the above ships are in Navy or Maritime Administration reserve (the latter remain on the Navy List).

DISPOSAL
Skagit LKA 105 stricken on 1 July 1969 (scrap).

VERMILLION (LKA 107)   1970, United States Navy

8 AMPHIBIOUS CARGO SHIPS (LKA): "ANDROMEDA" CLASS

Name	No.	Launched	Commissioned
THUBAN (ex-AK 68)	LKA 19	26 Apr 1943	10 June 1943
ALGOL (ex-James Baines)	LKA 54	17 Feb 1943	21 July 1944
ARNEB (ex-Mischief)	LKA 56	6 July 1943	28 Apr 1944
CAPRICORNUS (ex-Spitfire)	LKA 57	14 Aug 1943	31 May 1944
MULIPHEN	LKA 61	26 Aug 1944	23 Oct 1944
YANCEY	LKA 93	8 July 1944	11 Oct 1944
WINSTON	LKA 94	30 Nov 1944	19 Jan 1945
MERRICK	LKA 97	28 Jan 1945	31 Mar 1945

Displacement, tons	7 430 light; 14 000 full load
Dimensions, feet	435 wl; 495·2 oa × 63 × 24 max
Guns	1—5 inch, 38 cal (removed from some ships); 8—40 mm AA (twin) except Thuban 4—3 inch 50 cal AA in lieu of 40 mm
Main engines	Geared turbines (General Electric); 1 shaft; 6 000 shp = 16·5 knots
Boilers	2 (Foster Wheeler)
Complement	247

C2-S-B1 type. Can carry over 5 200 tons of cargo and 2 200 tons of tanks. Arneb completed refit for Arctic service on 15 Mar 1949. Wyandot. AKA 92, assigned to the Navy's Military Sea Transportation Service and manned by a civilian crew since 1963, was redesignated T-AK 283 on 1 Jan 1969. Designation of other ships remaining on Navy List changed from AKA to LKA on 1 Jan 1969.

All of the above ships are in Navy or Maritime Administration reserve (the latter remain on the Navy List).

TRANSFERS. Whitley AKA 91, was transferred to Italy in 1962, and Achernar AKA 53, to Spain on 2 Feb 1965.

DISPOSALS AND TRANSFERS

Marquette AKA 95 stricken on 9 Jan 1960 (to Maritime Administration reserve), Montagu AKA 99 stricken on 29 Jan 1960 (MarAd), Alshain AKA 55, Andromeda AKA 15, Chara AKA 58, Leo AKA 60, Whitley AKA 91 stricken on 1 July 1960 (all to MarAd; subsequently Whitley to Italy, Chara to AE 30), Diphda AKA 59, Virgo AKA 20, Warrick AKA 89, Whiteside AKA 90 stricken on 1 July 1961 (all to MarAd; subsequently Virgo to AE 31), Archernar AKA 53 stricken on 1 July 1963 (MarAd; subsequently to Spain), Matthews AKA 96, Oglethrope AKA 100 stricken on 1 Nov 1968, Uvalde AKA 99 stricken on 1 Dec 1968.

DISPOSALS OF OTHER CLASSES

"Libra" class (C2-F): Oberon AKA 14 stricken on 1 July 1960, Titania AKA 13 stricken on 1 July 1961, Libra AKA 12 stricken in July 1964 (all to MarAd).
"Bellatrix" class (C2-T): Bellatrix AKA 3 stricken on 1 July 1960 (MarAd; subsequently to Peru); Electra AKA 4 stricken on 1 July 1961 (MarAd).

ALGOL (LKA 54)   1969, US Navy, PH1 R. W. Wilton

MULIPHEN (LKA 61)   1968, United States Navy

Amphibious Warfare Ships—*continued*

MULIPHEN (LKA 61) *1968, United States Navy*

2 AMPHIBIOUS TRANSPORTS (LPA):
"PAUL REVERE" CLASS

Name	No.	Launched	Commissioned
*PAUL REVERE (ex-*Diamond Mariner*)	LPA 248	13 Feb 1954	3 Sep 1958
*FRANCIS MARION (ex-*Prairie Mariner*)			
	LPA 249	11 Apr 1953	6 July 1961

Displacement, tons	10 709 light; 16 838 full load
Dimensions, feet	563·5 oa × 76 × 27
Guns	8—3 inch 50 cal AA (twin)
Main engines	Geared turbine; 1 shaft; 19 250 shp = 22 knots
Boilers	2
Complement	414 (35 officers, 379 enlisted men)

Paul Revere is a C4-S-1 type cargo vessel converted into an Attack Transport by Todd Shipyard Corp, San Pedro, Calif, under the Fiscal Year 1957 Conversion programme. Fitted with helicopter platform. *Francis Marion* was a similar "Mariner" type hull converted into an APA by Bethlehem Steel, Key Highway Yard, Baltimore, Md, under the Fiscal Year 1959 programme. Both ships were built by New York Shipbuilding Corporation, Camden, New Jersey. Designation changed from APA to LPA on 1 Jan 1969.

PAUL REVERE (LPA 248) *1969, US Navy, PHCS G. W. Walsh, Jr.*

FRANCIS MARION (LPA 249) *1969, Anthony and Joseph Pavia*

7 AMPHIBIOUS TRANSPORTS (LPA):
"HASKELL" CLASS

Name	No.	Launched	Commissioned
SANDOVAL	LPA 194	11 Sep 1944	7 Oct 1944
MAGODFFIN	LPA 199	4 Oct 1944	25 Oct 1944
TALLADEGA	LPA 208	17 Aug 1944	31 Oct 1944
NAVARRO	LPA 215	3 Oct 1944	15 Nov 1944
OKANOGAN	LPA 220	22 Oct 1944	3 Dec 1944
PICKAWAY	LPA 222	5 Nov 1944	12 Dec 1944
BEXAR	LPA 237	25 July 1945	9 Oct 1945

Displacement, tons	6 720 light; 10 470 full load
Dimensions, feet	436·5 wl; 455 oa × 62 × 24
Guns	12—40 mm AA (1 quad, 4 twin) forward quad 40 mm mount removed from some ships
Main engines	Geared turbine; 1 shaft; 8 500 shp = 17·7 knots
Boilers	2 (Babcock & Wilcox)
Complement	536
Troops	1 560

VC 2-S-AP 5 "Victory" type, all launched in 1944-45. All have County names. 3 000 tons cargo. Designation of ships remaining on Navy List changed from APA to LPA on 1 Jan 1969.

GUNNERY. The 5-inch gun was removed.

DISPOSALS AND TRANSFERS

Arenac APA 128, **Barnwell** APA 132, **Brookings** APA 140, **Clinton** APA 144, **Crockett** APA 148, **Dane** APA 238, **Edgecombe** APA 164, **Gage** APA 168, **Grimes** APA 172, **Kershaw** APA 176, **Lavaca** APA 180, **Lubbock** APA 197, **McCracken** APA 198, **Menifee** APA 202, **Meriweather** APA 203, **Mifflin** APA 207, **Missoula** APA 211, **Natrona** APA 214, **Neshoba** APA 216, **New Kent** APA 217, **Okaloosa** APA 219, **Oneida** APA 221, **Rawlins** APA 226, **Rockingham** APA 229, **Rutland** APA 192, **San Saba** APA 232, **Sherburne** APA 205, **Sibley** APA 206, **Tazewell** APA 209, all stricken on 1 Oct 1958 and transferred to Maritime Administration; **Shelburne** reacquired by Navy on 22 May 1969 for conversion to Poseidon test instrumentation ship (AGM 22).
Deuel APA 160, **Rockwall** APA 130 stricken in 1959.
Logan APA 196, **Glyn** APA 239, **Sanborn** APA 193, **Sarasota** APA 204 stricken on 1 July 1960.
Bronx APA 236, **Botetourt** APA 136, **Bottineau** APA 235 stricken on 1 July 1961; **Menard** APA 201 stricken on 1 Sep 1961.
Lenawee APA 195, **Renville** APA **Noble** APA 218 transferred to Spain on 1 July 1964. 227 stricken on 30 June 1968; **Rockbridge** APA 228 stricken on 1 Dec 1968. **Montrose** LPA 212 stricken on 2 Nov 1969.

OKANOGAN (LPA 220) *1967, United States Navy*

SANDOVAL (LPA 194) *1969, US Navy, PH3 D. A. Mahalak*

3 AMPHIBIOUS TRANSPORTS (LPA):
"BAYFIELD CLASS"

Name	No.		Launched	Commissioned
*CHILTON (ex-*Sea Needle*)	LPA 38	(ex-AP 83)	24 Dec 1942	7 Dec 1943
FREMONT (ex-*Sea Corsair*)	LPA 44	(ex-AP 89)	31 Mar 1943	23 Nov 1943
HENRICO (ex-*Sea Darter*)	LPA 45	(ex-AP 90)	31 Mar 1943	24 June 1943

Displacement, tons	8 100 light; 15 200 full load
Dimensions, feet	465 wl; 492 oa × 69·5 × 26·5
Guns	1—5 inch (*127 mm*) DP
	8—40 mm AA (twin) in *Chilton* and *Henrico*;
	8—40 mm AA (2 twin and 1 quad) in *Fremont*
Main engines	Geared turbine (General Electric); 1 shaft; 8 500 shp = 18·4 knots
Boilers	2 (Combustion Engineering "D" in *Chilton*; Foster Wheeler "D" in *Fremont* and *Henrico*)
Complement	504 to 581
Troops	1 212 to 1 600
Flag accommodation	151

C3-S-A2 type. *Chilton* built by Western Pipe & Steel Co, San Francisco; *Fremont* and *Henrico* built by Ingalls Shipbuilding Corp, Pascagoula, Mississippi. Designation changed from APA to LPA on 1 Jan 1969.
As built *Chilton* and *Henrico* had two 5 inch guns; *Fremont* carried one.

DISPOSALS

Bayfield APA 33, **Cavalier** APA 37, stricken on 1 Oct 1968 and transferred to Maritime Administration; **Cambria** LPA 36 stricken on 14 Sep 1970.

FREMONT (LPA 44) *1966, United States Navy*

Amphibious Warfare Ships—*continued*

FREMONT (LPA 44)   *1966, United States Navy*

CHILTON (LPA 38)   *1967, United States Navy*

DISPOSALS OF OTHER CLASSES

"Arthur Middleton" class (C3-P): **Arthur Middleton** APA 25, **Samuel Chase** APA 26, stricken in 1958; **George Clymer** APA 27 stricken on 1 Nov 1967.
"President" class (C3-A): **President Jackson** APA 18, **President Adams** APA 19, **President Hayes** APA 20, **Thomas Jefferson** (ex-*President Garfield*) APA 30, stricken in 1958.
"Crescent City" class (C3-Delta): **Crescent City** APA 21 stricken in 1958, **Charles Carroll** APA 28 stricken in 1958, **Calvert** APA 32 stricken on 1 Aug 1966, **Monrovia** APA 31 stricken on 1 Nov 1968 (scrap). **Calvert** retained as a training hulk for cargo handling at Oakland, California.

11 AMPHIBIOUS TRANSPORTS (SMALL) (LPR): CONVERTED DE TYPE

Name	No.		Launched	Commissioned
LANING	LPR 55	ex-DE 159	4 July 1943	1 Aug 1943
HOLLIS	LPR 86	ex-DE 794	11 Sep 1943	24 Jan 1943
KIRWIN	LPR 90	ex-DE 229	16 June 1944	4 Nov 1945
RINGNESS	LPR 100	ex-DE 590	5 Feb 1944	25 Oct 1944
KNUDSON	LPR 101	ex-DE 591	5 Feb 1944	25 Nov 1944
BEVERLY W. REID	LPR 119	ex-DE 722	4 Mar 1944	25 June 1945
DIACHENKO	LPR 123	ex-DE 690	15 Aug 1944	8 Dec 1944
HORACE A. BASS	LPR 124	ex-DE 691	12 Sep 1944	21 Dec 1944
BEGOR	LPR 127	ex-DE 711	25 May 1944	14 Mar 1945
BALDUCK	LPR 132	ex-DE 716	27 Oct 1944	7 May 1945
WEISS	LPR 135	ex-DE 719	17 Feb 1945	7 July 1945

Displacement, tons	1 400 standard; 2 130 full load
Dimensions, feet	300 wl; 306 oa × 37 × 12·6
Guns	1—5 in (*127 mm*) 38 cal DP; 4—40 mm AA (twin) in modernised ships; 8—40 mm AA (twin) in others
ASW weapons	2 triple torpedo launchers (Mk 32) in modernised ships; depth charges in others.
Main engines	Geared turbines (General Electric) with electric drive; 12 000 shp; 2 shafts = 23·6 knots
Boilers	2 ("D" Express)
Complement	204 (designed wartime; 12 or 15 officers, 189 or 192 enlisted men, depending upon DE type)
Troops	162 (12 officers, 150 enlisted men)

These ships are former Destroyer Escorts (DE) converted or completed during World War II to transports for carrying commandoes, reconnaissance troops or frogmen. Fifty-six DEs were completed to this configuration and an additional 38 ships were converted after service as destroyer escorts; nine planned conversions were cancelled (APD 41, 58, 64, 67, 68, 82, 83, 137, 138). Originally designated as High Speed Transports (APD); designation of 13 ships remaining on Navy List as of 1 Jan 1969 changed to Amphibious Transports (Small) (LPR). Converted from TE and TEV type destroyer escorts with troop quarters being provided, single 5 inch gun and six to eight 40 mm guns (twin) replacing previous armament, davits installed amidships for four LCVPs, and 10-ton capacity boom placed aft.
All surviving ships of this type in the US Navy are in reserve, the last to be decommissioned being the *Beverly W. Reid*, *Diechenko*, and *Weiss*, all in 1969.

MODERNISATION. Several of these ships were modernised during the 1960s as part of the FRAM II programme. They have new bridge configurations, additional electronic equipment, tripod mast (in some ships place of forward pole mast), improved habitablity, ASW torpedo launchers, and retain only two 40 mm twin mounts (aft).

WAR LOSS. *Bates* APD 47.

DISPOSALS AND TRANSFERS
Chase APD 54, heavily damaged, stricken in 1946.
Wantuck APD 125, damaged in collision, stricken in 1958.
Cavallaro APD 128 to South Korea in 1959.
Barr APD 39, **Ira Jeffery** APD 44, **Amesbury** APD 46, **Sims** APD 50, **Reeves** APD 52, **Weber** APD 75, **Frament** APD 77, **Tatum** APD 81, **Haines** APD 84, **Runels** APD 85, **Crosley** APD 87, **Cread** APD 88, **Brock** APD 93, **John Q. Roberts** APD

AMPHIBIOUS TRANSPORTS (SMALL) — *continued*
94, **Ray K. Edwards** APD 96, **Upham** APD 99, **William J. Pattison** APD 104, **Myers** APD 105, **Hunter Marshall** APD 112, **Walter S. Gorka** APD 114, **Rogers Blood** APD 115, **Carpellotti** APD 136, **Bray** APD 139 stricken; **Kleinsmith** APD 134 to Taiwan China in 1960.
Bowers APD 40 to Philippines in 1961.
Walter X. Young APD 131 stricken in 1962.
Belet APD 109, **Earheart** APD 113, **Joseph M. Auman** APD 117, **Don O. Woods** APD 118 to Mexico in 1963.
Yokes APD 69, **Bunch** APD 79, **Arthur L. Bristol** APD 97, **Francovich** APD 116, **Gosselin** APD 126 stricken in 1964.
Charles Lawrence APD 37, **Lee Fox** APD 45, **Hopping** APD 51, **Loy** APD 56, **Newman** APD 59, **Earl B. Hall** APD 107, stricken; **Kinzer** APD 91, **Truxtun** APD 98, **Kline** APD 120, **Donald W. Wolf** APD 129 to China; **Tollberg** to Columbia in 1965.
Cofer APD 62, **Lloyd** APD 63, **Scribner** APD 122, **Burdo** APD 133 stricken; **Daniel T. Griffin** APD 38, **Joseph E. Campbell** APD 49, **Odum** APD 71, **Jack C. Robinson** APD 72 to Chile; **Gantner** APD 42, **Bull** APD 78, **Register** APD 92, **Walter B. Cobb** APD 106 (sunk en route while under tow), **Raymon W. Herndon** APD 121 to China; **Harry L. Corl** APD 108, **Julius A. Raven** APD 110 to South Korea in 1966.
Hubbard APD 53, **Liddle** APD 60, **Pavlic** APD 70, **John P. Gray** APD 74, **Walsh** APD 111 stricken; **George W. Ingram** APD 43, **Blessman** APD 48 to Taiwan China; **Kephart** APD 61, **Hayter** APD 80, **William M. Hobby** APD 95 to South Korea; **Enright** APD 66 to Ecuador in 1967.
Burke APD 65, **Bassett** APD 73 to Columbia; **Schmitt** APD 76 to Taiwan China in 1968.
Cook APD/LPR 130 stricken; **Barber** APD 57, **Rendour** APD 102 to Mexico; **Ruchamkin** APD/LPR 89 to Columbia in 1969.

PHOTOGRAPHS. The *Beverly W. Reid* and *Kirwin* have undergone Fleet Rehabilitation and Modernisation (FRAM) process; note enlarged structure between 5 inch gun mount and bridge, modified bridge, additional whip antennas. Both ships retain pole mast (see 1970-1971 edition for photographs of *Ruchamkin* with tripod mast). Neither of these ships has Mk 32 anti-submarine torpedo tubes in these views; normally installed in FRAM transports just forward of boat davits. The *Knudson* retains more broken original configuration with twin 40 mm mount forward of bridge and 20 mm gun "tubs" alongside funnel and aft of boat davits; as completed as transports some ships had a twin 40 mm mount on main deck aft.

BEVERLY W. REID (LPR 119)—Modernised   *1968, United States Navy*

KIRWIN (LPR 90)—Modernised   *1963, United States Navy*

KNUDSON (LPR 101)   *United States Navy*

Amphibious Warfare Ships—continued

12 AMPHIBIOUS TRANSPORT DOCKS (LPD):
"AUSTIN" CLASS

Name	No.	Laid down	Launched	Commissioned
*AUSTIN	LPD 4	4 Feb 1963	27 June 1964	6 Feb 1965
*OGDEN	LPD 5	4 Feb 1963	27 June 1964	19 June 1965
*DULUTH	LPD 6	18 Dec 1963	14 Aug 1965	12 Apr 1966
*CLEVELAND	LPD 7	30 Nov 1964	7 May 1966	21 Apr 1967
*DUBUQUE	LPD 8	25 Jan 1965	6 Aug 1966	1 Sep 1967
*DENVER	LPD 9	7 Feb 1964	23 Jan 1965	26 Oct 1968
*JUNEAU	LPD 10	23 Jan 1965	12 Feb 1966	12 July 1969
*CORONADO	LPD 11	3 May 1965	30 July 1966	23 May 1970
*SHREVEPORT	LPD 12	27 Dec 1965	22 Oct 1966	12 Dec 1970
*NASHVILLE	LPD 13	14 Mar 1966	7 Oct 1967	14 Feb 1970
*TRENTON	LPD 14	8 Aug 1966	3 Aug 1968	6 Mar 1971
*PONCE	LPD 15	31 Oct 1966	20 May 1970	July 1971

Displacement, tons	10 000 light; 16 900 full load
Length, feet (metres)	570 (173·3) oa
Beam, feet (metres)	84 (25·6)
Draft, feet (metres)	23 (7·0)
Guns	8—3 in (76 mm) 50 cal AA (twin)
Helicopters	6 UH-34 or CH-46 (see Helicopter notes)
Main engines	2 steam turbines; 2 shafts; 24 000 shp = 20 knots
Boilers	2
Complement	490 (30 officers, 460 enlisted men)
Troops	930 in LPD 4-6 and LPD 14-16; 840 in LPD 7-13
Flag accommodations	Approx 90 in LPD 7-13

JUNEAU (LPD 10)　　　　　1969, Lockheed SB & Constn Co

These ships are enlarged versions of the previous "Raleigh" class; most notes for the "Raleigh" class apply to these ships. All 12 of these ships are officially considered in a single class; earlier references to separate classes were based on contract awards to builders.

The LPD 4-6 were authorised in the Fiscal Year 1962 new construction programme, LPD 7-10 in FY 1963, LPD 11-13 in FY 1964, LPD 14 and LPD 15 in FY 1965, and LPD 16 in FY 1966. LPD 16 was deferred in favour of LHA programme; formerly cancelled in Feb 1969. No additional ships of this type are planned in view of the LHA capabilities.

LPD 4-6 built by New York Naval Shipyard; LPD 7-8 built by Ingalls Shipbuilding Corp; LPD 9-15 built by Lockheed Shipbuilding & Construction Co, Seattle, Washington. Completion of later ships has been delayed.

DESIGN. These ships are 48 feet longer than the previous "Raleigh" class with the additional space used to carry more cargo, especially vehicles, and more fuel oil. The Cleveland and six later ships differ from the first three and last three in detail (eg, flagship facilities for amphibious squadron commander in LPD 7-13).

AUSTIN (LPD 4)　　　　　1969, United States Navy

HELICOPTERS. These ships do not have integral hangars or aircraft maintenance facilities. The Cleveland and Dubuque were fitted with telescopic helicopter hangars late in 1967; similar hangars later fitted to all other LPDs. The telescopic hangars extend from 25 feet in length to 62 feet.

NOMENCLATURE. Amphibious transport docks are named for United States cities the namesake of which were explorers and developers of America. Some of the names previously were borne by cruisers.

PHOTOGRAPHS. Note only one bridge level in Austin and old style TACAN pod atop mast compared to later ships.

SHREVEPORT (LPD 12)　　　1970, Lockheed SB & Constn Co

NASHVILLE (LPD 13)　　　1969, Lockheed SB & Constn Co

CORONADO (LPD 11)　　　　　　　　　　　　　　　　　　　1970, United States Navy

Amphibious Warfare Ships—*continued*

RALEIGH (LPD 1)

1969, United States Navy, PH3 G. C. Preslar

3 AMPHIBIOUS TRANSPORT DOCKS (LPD):
"RALEIGH" CLASS

Name	No.	Laid down	Launched	Commissioned
✦**RALEIGH**	LPD 1	23 June 1960	17 Mar 1962	8 Sep 1962
✦**VANCOUVER**	LPD 2	19 Nov 1960	15 Sep 1962	11 May 1963
✦**LA SALLE**	LPD 3	2 Apr 1962	3 Aug 1963	22 Feb 1964

Displacement, tons	8 040 light; 13 900 full load
Length, feet (*metres*)	500 (*152·0*) wl 521·8 (*158·4*) oa
Beam, feet (*metres*)	84 (*25·6*)
Draft, feet (*metres*)	21 (*6·4*)
Guns	8—3 in (*76 mm*) 50 cal AA
Helicopters	6 UH-34 or CH-46 (see *Helicopter* notes)
Main engines	2 steam turbines; 24 000 shp; 2 shafts
Boilers	2
Speed, knots	20 sustained; 23 maximum
Complement	490 (30 officers, 460 enlisted men)
Troops	930 except 860 in *La Salle*
Flag accommodations	90 in *La Salle*

LA SALLE (LPD 3)   *1970, Anthony & Joseph Pavia*

5 DOCK LANDING SHIPS (LSD):
"ANCHORAGE" CLASS

Name	No.	Laid down	Launched	Commissioned
✦**ANCHORAGE**	LSD 36	13 Mar 1967	5 May 1968	15 Mar 1969
✦**PORTLAND**	LSD 37	21 Sep 1967	20 Dec 1969	3 Oct 1970
✦**PENCACOLA**	LSD 38	12 Mar 1969	11 July 1970	27 Mar 1971
MOUNT VERNON	LSD 39	29 Jan 1970	17 Apr 1971	Nov 1971
FORT FISHER	LSD 40	15 July 1970	Dec 1971	Mar 1972

Displacement, tons	13 650 full load
Dimensions, feet (*metres*)	555 (*169·0*) oa × 84 (*25·6*)
Guns	8—3 in (*76 mm*) 50 cal AA (twin)
Main engines	2 geared turbines; 2 shafts = 20+ knots
Complement	400
Troops	300+

The amphibious transport dock was developed from the dock landing ship (LSD) concept but provides more versatility. The LPD replaces the Amphibious Transport (LPA) and, in part, the Amphibious Cargo Ship (LKA) and dock landing ship. The LPD can carry a "balanced load" of assault troops and their equipment, has a docking well for landing craft, a helicopter deck, cargo holds and vehicle garages. The *Raleigh* was authorised in the Fiscal Year 1959 new construction programme, the *Vancouver* in FY 1960, and *La Salle* in FY 1961. Built by New York Naval Shipyard. Approximate construction cost was $29 000 000 per ship.

DESIGN. These ships resemble dock landing ships (LSD) but have fully enclosed docking well with the roof forming a permanent helicopter platform. The docking well is 168 feet long and 50 feet wide, less than half the length of wells in newer LSDs: the LPD design provides more space for vehicles, cargo, and troops. Ramps allow vehicles to be driven between helicopter deck, parking area, and docking well; side ports provide roll-on/roll off capability when docks are available. An overhead monorail in the docking well with six cranes facilitates loading landing craft.
The *La Salle* has an additional superstructure level to provide accommodations and facilities for an amphibious squadron commander and his staff. *La Salle* has modified pole mast atop bridge and lighter pole mast amidships; *Raleigh* and *Vancouver* have tripod masts.

HELICOPTERS. These ships are not normally assigned helicopters because they lack integral hangars and maintenance facilities. It is intended that helicopters from a nearby amphibious assault ship (LHA or LPH) would provide helicopters during an amphibious operation. The *La Salle* has successfully operated six SH-3A Sea King helicopters for an extended period. Hangars have been fitted (see "Austin" class notes).

LANDING CRAFT. The docking well in these ships can hold one LCU and three LCM-6s or four LCM-8s or 20 LVTs (amphibious tractors). In addition, two LCM-6s or four LCPLs are carried on the boat deck which are lowered by crane.

PHOTOGRAPHS. Note two bridge levels on *La Salle* indicating she is fitted as an amphibious squadron flagship. Four LCPLs are nested on the *Raleigh* between her superstructure and helicopter deck on the 02 level. LPD flight decks extend to stern counter while LSDs have a significant opening where flight deck ends short of stern.

Improved dock landing ships, slightly larger than previous class; designed to replace earlier LSDs which are unable to meet 20-knot amphibious lift requirement. Similar in appearance to earlier classes but with a tripod mast. Helicopter platform aft with docking well partially open.
LSD 36 was authorised in Fiscal Year 1965 shipbuilding programme; LSD 37-39 in FY 1966 programme; LSD 40 in FY 1967 programme. *Anchorage* built by Ingalls Shipbuilding; LSD 37-40 by General Dynamics (Quincy).
Estimated construction cost is $11 500 000 per ship.

ANCHORAGE (LSD 36)   *1969, Ingalls Shipbuilding*

LA SALLE (LPD 3)   *1970, Anthony & Joseph Pavia*

ANCHORAGE (LSD 36)   *1969, United States Navy*

Amphibious Warfare Ships—continued

8 DOCK LANDING SHIPS (LSD): "THOMASTON" CLASS

Name	No.	Launched	Commissioned
*THOMASTON	LSD 28	9 Feb 1954	17 Sep 1954
*PLYMOUTH ROCK	LSD 29	7 May 1954	24 Jan 1955
*FORT SNELLING	LSD 30	16 July 1954	24 Jan 1955
*POINT DEFIANCE	LSD 31	28 Sep 1954	31 Mar 1955
*SPIEGEL GROVE	LSD 32	10 Nov 1955	8 June 1956
*ALAMO	LSD 33	20 Jan 1956	24 Aug 1956
*HERMITAGE	LSD 34	12 June 1956	17 Dec 1956
*MONTICELLO	LSD 35	10 Aug 1956	29 Mar 1957

Displacement, tons	6 880 light; 11 270 full load; *Alamo, Hermitage, Monticello, Spiegel Grove:* 12 150 full load
Dimensions, feet	510 oa · 84 · 19 max
Guns	12—3 inch 50 cal AA (twin)
Main engines	Steam turbines: 2 shafts; 23 000 shp = 24 knots
Boilers	2
Complement	305
Troops	100

Larger and faster than earlier types. Built by Ingalls Shipbuilding Corp. Fitted with helicopter landing platforms; two 50 ton cranes. 21 LCM (6) or 3 LCU and 6 LCM can be carried.

NOMENCLATURE. Dock landing ships are named for historic sites in the United states except that the *Anchorage, Portland,* and *Pensacola* primarily honour cities.

DONNER (LSD 20)   1968, United States Navy

11 DOCK LANDING SHIPS (LSD): "CASA GRANDE" CLASS

Name	No.	Launched	Commissioned
CASA GRANDE (ex-*Spear*, ex-*Portway*)	LSD 13	11 Apr 1944	5 June 1944
RUSHMORE (ex-*Sword*, ex-*Swashway*)	LSD 14	10 May 1944	3 July 1944
SHADWELL (ex-*Tomahawk*, ex-*Waterway*)	LSD 15	24 May 1944	24 July 1944
CABILDO	LSD 16	28 Dec 1944	15 Mar 1945
CATAMOUNT	LSD 17	27 Jan 1945	9 Apr 1945
COLONIAL	LSD 18	28 Feb 1945	15 May 1945
COMSTOCK	LSD 19	28 Apr 1945	2 July 1945
DONNER	LSD 20	6 Apr 1945	31 July 1945
FORT MARION	LSD 22	22 May 1945	29 Jan 1946
TORTUGA	LSD 26	21 Jan 1945	8 June 1945
WHETSTONE	LSD 27	18 July 1945	12 Feb 1946

Displacement, tons	4 790 standard; 9 375 full load
Dimensions, feet	475·4 oa × 76·2 × 18 max
Guns	8— or 12—40 mm AA (2 quad plus 2 twin in some ships)
Main engines	Geared turbines (Newport News except Westinghouse in *Fort Marion*); 2 shafts; 7 000 shp except 9 000 in *Fort Marion* = 15·4 knots except 15·6 knots in *Fort Marion*
Boilers	2
Complement	265 (15 officers, 250 men)

LSD 13-19 built by Newport News SB & DD Co, Virginia; LSD 20, 21, 26, 27 by Boston Navy Yard; LSD 22 by Gulf SB Corp, Chickasaw, Alabama; LSD 25 by Philadelphia Navy Yard. *Fort Snelling*, LSD 23, and *Point Defiance*, LSD 24, cancelled in 1945; former ship completed for merchant service, reacquired by Navy as cargo ship *Taurus*, T-AK 273, T-AKR 8 (stricken in 1968). LSD 9-12 of this class transferred to Britain in 1943-1944.

Can carry 3 LCUs or 18 LSMs. All ships are fitted with helicopter platforms.

Catamount LSD 17, *Colonial* LSD 18, *Donner* LSD 20, *Fort Mandan* LSD 21, and *Fort Marion* LSD 22, were modernised under the FRAM II programme in 1960-1962. Fitted with helicopter platforms on docking well.

All surviving ships of this class are in Navy or Maritime Administration reserve (the latter ships remain on the Navy List).

ARMAMENT. Arrangement differs; all ships have two quad 40 mm mounts on forward superstructure; some have two twin 40 mm mounts on dock walls aft.

As built, each ship had a single 5 inch DP gun, 12—40 mm AA guns, and several 20 mm AA guns.

TRANSFERS

Fort Mandon LSD 21 to Greece in Jan 1971, **San Marcos** LSD 25 to Spain in July 1971.

DOCK LANDING SHIPS (LSD): "ASHLAND" CLASS

All ships of this class have been stricken: **Ashland** LSD 1 stricken on 25 Nov 1969, **Belle Grove** LSD 2 stricken on 12 Nov 1969, **Carter Hall** LSD 3 stricken on 31 Oct 1969, **Epping Forest** LSD 4 converted to minecraft tender MCS 7 (stricken on 1 Nov 1968), **Gunston Hall** LSD 5 transferred to Argentina on 1 May 1970, **Lindenwald** LSD 6 stricken on 1 Dec 1967, **Oak Hill** LSD 7 stricken on 31 Oct 1969, **White Marsh** LSD 8 transferred to Nationalist China on 17 Nov 1960.

SPIEGEL GROVE (LSD 32)   1968, United States Navy

SPIEGEL GROVE (LSD 32)   1968, United States Navy

SAN MARCOS (LSD 25)—To Spain in 1971

1970, United States Navy

Amphibious Warfare Ships—*continued*

NEWPORT (LST 1179)   *1969, US Navy, Paul Freeland*

20 TANK LANDING SHIPS (LST):
"NEWPORT" CLASS

Name	No.	Laid down	Launched	Commissioned
*NEWPORT	LST 1179	1 Nov 1966	3 Feb 1968	7 June 1969
*MANITOWOC	LST 1180	1 Feb 1967	4 June 1969	24 Jan 1970
*SUMTER	LST 1181	14 Nov 1967	13 Dec 1969	20 June 1970
*FRESNO	LST 1182	16 Dec 1967	28 Sep 1968	22 Nov 1969
*PEORIA	LST 1183	22 Feb 1968	23 Nov 1968	21 Feb 1970
*FREDERICK	LST 1184	13 Apr 1968	8 Mar 1969	11 Apr 1970
*SCHENECTADY	LST 1185	2 Aug 1968	24 May 1969	13 June 1970
*CAYUGA	LST 1186	28 Sep 1968	12 July 1969	8 Aug 1970
*TUSCALOOSA	LST 1187	23 Nov 1968	6 Sep 1969	24 Oct 1970
*SAGINAW	LST 1188	24 May 1969	7 Feb 1970	23 Jan 1971
*SAN BERNARDINO	LST 1189	12 July 1969	28 Mar 1970	27 Mar 1971
*BOULDER	LST 1190	6 Sep 1969	22 May 1970	30 Apr 1971
RACINE	LST 1191	13 Dec 1969	15 Aug 1970	July 1971
SPARTANBURG COUNTY				
	LST 1192	7 Feb 1970	11 Nov 1970	Sep 1971
FAIRFAX COUNTY	LST 1193	28 Mar 1970	19 Dec 1970	Nov 1971
LA MOURE COUNTY				
	LST 1194	22 May 1970	13 Feb 1971	Dec 1971
BARBOUR COUNTY				
	LST 1195	15 Aug 1970	May 1971	Feb 1972
HARLAN COUNTY	LST 1196	7 Nov 1970	July 1971	mid-1972
BARNSTABLE COUNTY				
	LST 1197	19 Dec 1970	Aug 1971	mid-1972
	LST 1198	13 Feb 1971	Oct 1971	late 1972

Displacement, tons	8 342 full load
Dimensions, feet	
(metres)	522·3 (158·7) oa × 69·5 (21·0) × 15 (4·5) (aft)
Guns	4—3 inch (76 mm) 50 cal AA (twin)
Main engines	6 diesels (Alco) ; 2 shafts, 16 000 hp = 20 knots (sustained)
Complement	231 (14 officers, 217 enlisted men).
Troops	430

These ships are of an entirely new design, larger and faster than previous tank landing ships. They will operate with 20-knot LHA LPD LSD amphibious squadrons to transport tanks, other heavy vehicles, engineer equipment, and supplies which cannot be readily landed by helicopters or landing craft. Seven additional ships of this type that were planned for the Fiscal Year 1971 new construction programme have been deferred.

The *Newport* was authorised in the Fiscal Year 1965 new construction programme. LST 1180-1187 (8 ships) in FY 1966, and LST 1188-1198 (11 ships) in FY 1967. LST 1179-1181 built by Philadelphia Naval Shipyard ; LST 1182-1198 built by National Steel & Shipbuilding Co, San Diego, California.

DESIGN. These ships are the first LSTs to depart from the bow-door design developed by the British early in World War II. The hull form required to achieve 20 knots would not permit bow doors, thus these ships unload by a 112-foot ramp over their bow, the ramp is supported by twin derrick arms. A ramp just forward of the super structure connects the lower tank deck with the main deck and a vehicle passage through the superstructure provides access to the parking area amidships. A stern gate to the tank deck permits unloading of amphibious tractors into the water, or unloading of other vehicles into an LCU or onto a pier. Vehicle stowage is rated at 500 tons and 19 000 square feet (5 000 sq ft more than previous LSTs). Full load draft is 15 feet aft and six feet forward.

NOMENCLATURE. LSTs are named for counties and parishes.

PHOTOGRAPHS. Note uneven, staggered funnels, bow opening when ramp is lowered, anchors on starboard side forward and at stern, tunnel opening in super-structure, and helicopter spots marked aft of funnels. Twin 3 inch closed gun mounts are difficult to distinguish in clutter atop superstructure.

NEWPORT (LST 1179)   *1970, US Navy, PH1 Norman P. Plummer*

NEWPORT (LST 1179)   *1969, US Navy, JO1 Craig M. Nuebler*

NEWPORT (LST 1179)   *1969, US Navy, Paul Freeland*

PEORIA (LST 1183)   *1970, United States Navy*

Amphibious Warfare Ships—continued

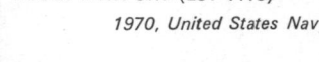

Above: NEWPORT (LST 1179)

1970, United States Navy

Left: FREDERICK (LST 1184)

1970, National Steel & SB Co

7 TANK LANDING SHIPS (LST): "SUFFOLK COUNTY" CLASS

Name	No.	Builder	Launched
*DE SOTO COUNTY	LST 1171	Avondale, New Orleans	28 Feb 1957
*SUFFOLK COUNTY	LST 1173	Boston Navy Yard	5 Sep 1956
*GRANT COUNTY	LST 1174	Avondale, New Orleans	12 Oct 1956
*YORK COUNTY	LST 1175	Newport News SB & DD Co	5 Mar 1957
*GRAHAM COUNTY	LST 1176	Newport News SB & DD Co	19 Sep 1957
*LORAIN COUNTY	LST 1177	American SB Co, Lorrain	22 June 1957
*WOOD COUNTY	LST 1178	American SB Co, Lorrain	14 Dec 1957

Displacement, tons	4 164 light; 8 000 full load
Dimensions, feet	445 oa × 62 · 16·5
Guns	6—3 in, 50 cal (3 twin)
Main engines	Diesels; 2 shafts; controllable pitch propellers; 14 400 bhp (except *Graham County*, 9 600 bhp) = 17·5 knots (except *Graham County*, 14·5 knots); see *Engineering* notes.
Complement	184 (10 officers, 174 men)
Troops	Vary. Approx 575 per ship except *York County* and *Graham County* only 430 troops; see *Design* notes.

Improved LSTs with greater speed and troop capacity than earlier ships of this category; considered the "ultimate" design attainable with traditional LST bow door configuration. Contract for LST 1172 not awarded. *De Soto County* commissioned on 10 June 1958, *Suffolk County* on 15 Aug 1957, *Grant County* on 17 Dec 1957, *York County* on 8 Nov 1957, *Graham County* on 17 Apr 1958, *Lorain County* on 3 Oct 1958, *Wood County* on 5 Aug 1959. *Lorain County* delivered to Todd Shipyards on 11 July 1958 for trials and completion. All of these ships remain in active commission.

DESIGN High degree of habitability with all crew and troop living spaces air conditioned. Can carry 23 medium tanks or vehicles up to 75 tons on 288-foot-long (lower) tank deck. Davits for four LCVP-type landing craft. Liquid cargo capacity of 170 000 gallons (US) diesel or jet fuel plus 7 000 gallons (US) of petrol for embarked vehicles; two ships have reduced troop spaces and carry additional 250 000 gallons (US) of aviation petrol for pumping ashore or to other ships.

ENGINEERING. All except *Graham County* built with six Nordberg diesels. *Graham County* has four Fairbanks Morse diesels, hydraulic couplings and controllable-pitch propellers (9 600 bhp = 14·5 knots). First four ships now have six Fairbanks Morse diesels, electric couplings and reduction gears (14 400 bhp = 17·5 knots). · *Lorain County* and *Wood County* now have six Cooper Bessemer diesels, electric couplings and reduction gears (14 400 bhp = 17·5 knots).

PHOTOGRAPH. The "Suffolk County" class LSTs are identified by their twin fire control towers forward.

YORK COUNTY (LST 1175)   *1969, US Navy, PHC J. R. Weber*

15 TANK LANDING SHIPS (LST): "TERREBONNE PARISH" CLASS

Name	No.	Launched	Commissioned
* TERREBONNE PARISH	LST 1156	9 Aug 1952	21 Nov 1952
· TERRELL COUNTY	LST 1157	6 Dec 1952	19 Mar 1953
TIOGA COUNTY	LST 1158	11 Apr 1953	20 June 1953
* TOM GREEN COUNTY	LST 1159	2 July 1953	12 Sep 1953
TRAVERSE COUNTY	LST 1160	3 Oct 1953	19 Dec 1953
* VERNON COUNTY	LST 1161	25 Nov 1952	18 May 1953
* WAHKIAKUM COUNTY	LST 1162	23 Jan 1953	13 Aug 1953
WALDO COUNTY	LST 1163	17 Mar 1953	17 Sep 1953
WALWORTH COUNTY	LST 1164	18 May 1953	26 Oct 1953
WASHOE COUNTY	LST 1165	14 July 1953	30 Nov 1953
* WASHTENAW COUNTY	LST 1166	22 Nov 1952	29 Oct 1953
* WESTCHESTER COUNTY	LST 1167	18 Apr 1953	10 Mar 1954
WEXFORD COUNTY	LST 1168	28 Nov 1953	15 June 1954
* WHITFIELD COUNTY	LST 1169	22 Aug 1953	14 Sep 1954
* WINDHAM COUNTY	LST 1170	22 May 1954	15 Dec 1954

Displacement, tons	2 590 light; 5 800 full load
Dimensions, feet	384 oa × 55 × 17
Guns	6—3 in, 50 cal (twin)
Main engines	4 GM diesels; 2 shafts; controllable pitch propellers; 6 000 bhp = 15 knots
Complement	116
Troops	395

Design is modification of that of two experimental ships constructed after the Second World War. LST 1156-1160 were built by Bath Iron Works, 1166-1170 by Christy Corporation, and 1161-1165 by Ingalls Shipbuilding Corporation. · Davits amidships for carrying four LCVP-type landing craft.

Several of these ships have been decommissioned since 1969. Seven remained in commission as of July 1971.

TERRELL COUNTY (LST 1157)   *1969, United States Navy*

WAHKIAKUM COUNTY (LST 1162)   *1970, A. & J. Pavia*

Amphibious Warfare Ships—continued

1 TANK LANDING SHIP (LST): "TALBOT COUNTY" TYPE

TALBOT COUNTY LST 1153

Displacement, tons	2 324; 6 000 full load
Dimensions, feet	368 wl; 382 oa × 54 × 17
Guns	2—5 in, 38 cal DP (single); 4—40 mm AA (twin)
Main engines	Geared turbines (Westinghouse); 2 shafts; 6 000 shp = 14 knots
Boilers	2
Complement	190
Troops	197

The *Talbot County* and her sister ship *Tallahatchie County* (LST 1154) were the only steam-driven LSTs built for the US Navy. Built by Boston Navy Yard; *Talbot County* launched on 24 Apr 1947 and commissioned on 3 Sep 1947. Improved arrangements and greater cargo capacity than the war-built LSTs. The *Talbot County* was decommissioned in Apr 1970; in reserve.

CONVERSION. *Tallahatchie County* converted to advance Aviation Base Ship (AVB 2); stricken in 1970.

TALBOT COUNTY (LST 1153)   *A. & J. Pavia*

21 TANK LANDING SHIPS: 511-1152 SERIES

Name	No.	Launched	Commissioned
CAROLINE COUNTY	LST 525	20 Dec 1943	14 Feb 1944
CHEBOYGAN COUNTY	LST 533	1 Dec 1943	27 Jan 1944
CHURCHILL COUNTY	LST 583	5 July 1944	2 Aug 1944
DODGE COUNTY	LST 722	21 Aug 1944	13 Sep 1944
DUVAL COUNTY	LST 758	25 July 1944	19 Aug 1944
FLOYD COUNTY	LST 762	1 Aug 1944	5 Sep 1944
HAMPSHIRE COUNTY	LST 819	21 Oct 1944	14 Nov 1944
HUNTERDON COUNTY	LST 838	8 Nov 1944	4 Dec 1944
KEMPER COUNTY	LST 854	20 Nov 1944	14 Dec 1944
LITCHFIELD COUNTY	LST 901	9 Dec 1944	11 Jan 1945
MEEKER COUNTY	LST 980	27 Jan 1944	26 Feb 1944
MIDDLESEX COUNTY	LST 983	10 Feb 1944	25 Mar 1944
MONMOUTH COUNTY	LST 1032	9 July 1944	1 Aug 1944
PARK COUNTY	LST 1077	18 Apr 1945	8 May 1945
POLK COUNTY	LST 1084	19 Jan 1945	19 Feb 1945
ST. CLAIR COUNTY	LST 1096	10 Jan 1945	2 Feb 1945
SAN JOAQUIN COUNTY	LST 1122	24 Jan 1945	14 Feb 1945
SEDGWICK COUNTY	LST 1123	29 Jan 1945	19 Feb 1945
SUMMIT COUNTY	LST 1146	11 May 1945	30 May 1945
SUMNER COUNTY	LST 1148	23 May 1945	9 June 1945
SUTTER COUNTY	LST 1150	30 May 1945	20 June 1945

Displacement, tons	1 653 standard; 2 366 beaching; 4 080 full load
Dimensions, feet	316 wl; 328 oa × 50 × 14
Guns	8—40 mm AA (2 twin and 2 single) reduced in some ships
Main engines	GM diesels; 2 shafts; 1 700 bhp = 11·6 knots
Complement	119
Troops	147

The US Navy built 1 052 LSTs during World War II in two series: LST 1-150 and LST 511-1152; an even 100 ships were cancelled: LST 85-116, 142-156, 182-196, 232-236, 248-260, 296-300, 431-445. Forty-one were lost during the war. Hundreds of these ships have been transferred to foreign navies or converted to auxiliary configurations.
County or Parish names were assigned to 158 LSTs on the Navy List as of 1 July 1955; 36 Japanese-manned LSTs assigned to the Military Sea Transportation Service (MSTS) at that time were not named.
All of the surviving ships of this series are in reserve except for those operated by the Military Sealift Command (listed separately).

DESIGN. These ships are of the classical LST design developed early in World War II by the British; fitted with bow doors, tunnel-like tank deck with trucks, cargo, or landing craft carried on upper deck; small "island" structure aft with davits for two LCVP-type landing craft. Cargo capacity 2 100 tons. Fitted with tripod masts during postwar period.

RIVERINE SUPPORT. The *Hunterdon County* has been modified to support riverine operations in South Vietnam (as were the now stricken *Jennings County*, *Garret County* and *Harnett County*.)
Changes include installation of 10-ton capacity boom forward of superstructure on starboard side to lift PBR patrol craft, enlargement of cargo hatch to 16 feet by 34 feet to permit lowering of PBRs to tank deck for repairs or transport, strengthening of main deck for operation of UH-1B "Huey" helicopters, and installation of additional communications equipment, helicopter and boat fueling systems, helicopter deck lighting, additional workshops and storerooms, modification of ammunition magazines, and boat booms to permit small craft to moor alongside.
The *Harnett County* and *Garett County* were redesignated as patrol craft tenders (AGP) with some LST hull numbers on 25 Sep 1970 in preparation for transfer to South Vietnam.

MODERNISATION. *Polk County* LST 1084, *Stone County* LST 1141, *Sumner County* LST 1148, were modernised in the 1960 FRAM II programme.

DISPOSALS AND TRANSFERS (Since 1 Jan 1960)
Cape May County LST 521, **Catahouia Parish** LST 528, **Chelan County** LST 542, **Curry County** LST 685, **Douglas County** LST 731, **Juniata County** LST 850, **King County** AG 157, ex-LST 857, **Lake County** LST 880, **Lamoure County** LST 883, **Lee County** LST 888, **Mahoning County** LST 914, **Marinette County** LST 593, **Morgan County** LST 1048, **Ouachita County** LST 1071, **Overton County** LST 1074, **Payette County** LST 1079, **Pima County** LST 1081, **Somervell County** LST 1129, and **Stratford County** LST 1142 stricken in 1960.
Potter County LST 1086, to Greece; **Dukes County** LST 735, to Nationalist China; **Hamilton County** LST 802, to Japan; **Laurence County** LST 887, **Russel County** LST 1090, **Solana County** LST 1128, to Indonesia in 1960.
Jefferson County LST 845, **Steuben County** LST 1138, and **Dunn County** LST 742, stricken in 1961.
Doggett County LST 689, **Hillsdale County** LST 835, **Nansemond County** LST 1064, to Japan; **Greer County** LST 799, **Millard County** LST 987, **Montgomery County** LST 1041, **Rice County** LST 1089, **Saline County** LST 1101, to West Germany; **Sublette County** LST 1144 to Nationalist China; **LST 616, LST 652, LST 657** to Indonesia in 1961.
Calhoun County LST 519, stricken in 1962.
Lincoln County LST 898, to Thailand; **Marricopa County** LST 938, **Marion County** LST 975, to South Vietnam in 1962.
Cayuga County LST 529 to South Vietnam in 1963.
Stark County LST 1134 to Thailand in 1966.
Mahnommen County LST 912 stricken on 31 Jan 1967
Cochino County LST 603 to South Vietnam on 4 Apr 1969; **LST 600** (MSTS) stricken on 1 June 1969; **Caddo Parish** LST 515, **Hickman County** LST 825, **Madera County** LST 905 to Philippines on 26 Nov 1969.
Jerome County LST 848 to South Vietnam on 1 Apr 1970; **Snohomish County** LST 1126 stricken on 1 July 1970; **Clarke County** LST 601, **Iredell County** LST 839 to Indonesia on 15 July 1970; **Luzerne County** LST 902, **Monmouth County** LST 1032 stricken on 12 Aug 1970; **Jennings County** LST 846 stricken on 25 Sep 1970; **Harnett County** LST/AGP 821 to South Vietnam on 12 Oct 1970.
Page County LST 1076 to Greece on 5 Mar 1971; **Holmes County** LST 836 to Singapore in July 1971; **Pitkin County** LST 1082 to Brazil in July 1971; **Outagamie County** LST 1073 to Brazil in 1971; **Garrett County** LST/AGP 786 to South Vietnam on 23 April 1971.

HUNTERDON COUNTY (LST 838)   *United States Navy*

SUMNER COUNTY (LST 1148)   *1968, United States Navy, PH3 R. Ferraro*

1 TANK LANDING SHIP "LST": 1-510 SERIES

BLANCO COUNTY LST 344

Displacement, tons	1 625 light; 2 366 beaching; 4 050 full load
Dimensions, feet	328 oa × 50 × 14·3
Guns	8—40 mm AA (2 twin and 4 single)
Main engines	GM diesels; 2 shafts; 1 700 bhp = 11·6 knots
Complement	119
Troops	147

Built by Norfolk (Virginia) Navy Yard; launched on 15 Oct 1942; commissioned on 29 Nov 1942.

DISPOSALS AND TRANSFERS (since 1 Jan 1960)
Boon County LST 389 and **Bowman County** LST 391 to Greece in 1960; **Alameda County** AVB 1 ex-LST 32 to Italy in 1962; **LST 325** to Greece in 1964; **Bulloch County** LST 509 to South Vietnam on 1 Apr 1970.

BLANCO COUNTY (LST 344)   *courtesy "Our Navy"*

LANDING CRAFT

2 SURFACE EFFECT LANDING CRAFT: AEROJET-GENERAL DESIGN

Weight, tons	162·5 gross
Dimensions, feet	100 oa × 48
Main engines	4 gas turbines (Lycoming), 4 aircraft-type propellers in shrouds mounted atop vehicle for propulsion and steering = approx 50 knots
Complement	6

These are surface effect ships (SES) developed by the Aerojet-General Corp, and being built by the Tacoma Boat Building Co, Tacoma, Washington, under Navy contract. They will be evaluated in competition with the Bell design described below.
Design includes rigid, catamaran side "hulls" with flexible bow and stern seals holding an "air bubble" to reduce surface friction and hence drag; aluminium construction, bow and stern ramps; 75-ton cargo capacity. Company designation is C150-50.

PROJECT. Aerojet-General and Bell Aerosystems were awarded contracts in January 1969 to design competitive assault landing craft employing SES technology. Subsequent awards made to both companies in March 1971 to build and test the craft. Initially a Navy-Maritime Administration project being jointly administered, the Maritime Administration was forced to withdraw its financial support in 1970.
Eventual goal of the Navy's SES programme is to develop large surface effect ships of 4 000 to 5 000 tons and speeds in excess of 80 knots for ocean-going missions. Successful evaluation of these SES landing craft probably will lead to the development of an SES anti-submarine "vehicle" of about 2 000 tons as the next step in this field. (See Patrol Ships and Craft listings).

2 SURFACE EFFECT LANDING CRAFT: BELL DESIGN

Weight, tons	160 gross
Dimensions, feet	87 oa × 47
Main engines	gas turbines = approx 50 knots
Complement	6

These are surface effect ships (SES) developed by Bell Aerospace Division of the Textron Corp, with the hulls being fabricated by the Livingston Shipbuilding Co, Orange, Texas, and fitting out being done at Bell's Michoud facility in New Orleans. The design and project notes given above for the Aerojet-Genreal craft apply to the Bell vehicles. Company designation is SES 100.

Aerojet-General Design, Model

48 UTILITY LANDING CRAFT: LCU 1610 SERIES

LCU 1610	LCU 1619	LCU 1631	LCU 1647	LCU 1657
LCU 1611	LCU 1621	LCU 1632	LCU 1648	LCU 1658
LCU 1612	LCU 1622	LCU 1633	LCU 1649	LCU 1659
LCU 1613	LCU 1623	LCU 1634	LCU 1650	LCU 1660
LCU 1614	LCU 1624	LCU 1637	LCU 1651	LCU 1661
LCU 1615	LCU 1627	LCU 1641	LCU 1652	LCU 1662
LCU 1616	LCU 1628	LCU 1642	LCU 1653	LCU 1663
LCU 1617	LCU 1629	LCU 1644	LCU 1654	LCU 1664
LCU 1618	LCU 1630	LCU 1645	LCU 1655	LCU 1665
		LCU 1646	LCU 1656	LCU 1666

Displacement, tons	200 light; 375 full load
Dimensions, feet	134·9 oa × 29 × 6·1
Guns	2—·50 cal machine guns
Main engines	Diesels; 1 000 bhp; 2 shafts = 11 knots (see Engineering notes)
Complement	12 to 14 (enlisted men)

Improved landing craft, larger than previous series; can carry three M-103 or M-48 tanks (approx 64 tons and 48 tons, respectively).
LCU 1610-1612 built by Christy Corp, Sturgeon Bay, Wisconsin; LCU 1613-1619, 1623, 1624 built by Gunderson Bros Engineering Corp, Portland, Oregon; LCU 1620, 1621, 1625, 1626, 1629, 1630 built by Southern Shipbuilding Corp, Slidell, Louisiana; LCU 1622 built by Weaver Shipyards, Texas; LCU 1627, 1628, 1631-1636 built by General Ship and Engine Works (last six units completed in 1968). LCU 1638-1645 built by Marinette Marine Corp, Marinette, Wisconsin (completed 1969-1970); LCU 1646-1666 built by Defoe Shipbuilding Co, Bay City, Michigan (completed 1970-1971). The one-of-a-kind, aluminium hull, 133·8 ft LCU 1637 built by Pacific Coast Engineering Co, Alameda, California.
LCU 1636, 1638, 1639, 1640 reclassified as YFB 88-91 in October 1969; LCU 1620 and 1625 to YFU 92 and 93, respectively, in April 1971 (see Service Craft section).

ENGINEERING. These landing craft have four 250 bhp diesel engines with Kort-nozzle propellers on twin shafts except for the LCU 1620, 1621, and 1625 which have two 500-bhp diesel engines on vertical shafts fitted with vertical-axis, cycloidal six-bladed propellers. The cycloidal propellers provide thrust in any horizontal direction alleviating the need for rudders. The LCU 1622 was to have been fitted with gas-turbine propulsion machinery, but this project was cancelled.
Endurance is 1 200 miles at eight knots.

TRANSFERS. LCU 1626 was transferred to Burma in 1967.

PHOTOGRAPHS. Note amidships, right-side "island" structure of LCU 1649; LCU 1625 differs with built-up structure aft. All except LCU 1621, 1622, and 1625 have bow and stern ramps.

LCU 1649   1970, Defoe Shipbuilding Co

LCU 1625   United States Navy

LCU 1649   1970, Defoe Shipbuilding Co

29 UTILITY LANDING CRAFT: LCU 1466 SERIES

LCU 1466	LCU 1472	LCU 1485	LCU 1491	LCU 1537
LCU 1467	LCU 1473	LCU 1486	LCU 1492	LCU 1539
LCU 1468	LCU 1477	LCU 1487	LCU 1498	LCU 1547
LCU 1469	LCU 1481	LCU 1488	LCU 1525	LCU 1548
LCU 1470	LCU 1482	LCU 1489	LCU 1535	LCU 1559
	LCU 1484	LCU 1490	LCU 1536	LCU 1609

Displacement, tons	180 light; 360 full load
Dimensions, feet	115 wl; 119 oa × 34 × 6 max
Guns	2—20 mm
Main engines	3 diesels; 3 shafts; 675 bhp = 10 knots
Complement	14

These are enlarged versions of the World War II-built LCTs; constructed during the early 1950s. LCU 1608 and 1609 have modified propulsion systems; LCU 1582 and later craft have Kort nozzle propellers. LCU 1496 reclassified as YFU 70 on 1 Mar 1966; LCU 1471 to YFU 88 in May 1968; LCU 1576, 1582 and 1608 to YFU 89-91, respectively, in June 1970.

CLASSIFICATION. The earlier craft of this series were initially designated as Utility Landing Ships (LSU); redesignated Utility Landing Craft (LCU) on 15 Apr 1952 and classified as service craft.

DISPOSALS AND TRANSFERS

LCU 1478 was transferred to Norway and LCU 1479, 1480, 1501, 1502 were transferred to South Vietnam upon completion; LCU 1504-1593 were built under US Navy contract for US Army; LCU 1594-1607 were built in Japan for the Japanese and Nationalist Chinese navies; LCU 1503 lost accidentally in Aug 1953; LCU 1476, 1483, 1495, 1497, 1499 to Department of the Interior in 1969-1970; LCU 1475 to South Vietnam in 1969; LCU 1493, 1494 to South Vietnam in 1970; LCU 1500 sunk in Vietnam in Mar 1969.

LCU 1468 with mast lowered   1969, US Navy, PH1 A. A. Clemons

Landing Craft—*continued*

LCU 1488   *1965, United States Navy*

23 UTILITY LANDING CRAFT: LCU 501 SERIES

LCU 539	LCU 660	LCU 768	LCU 1045	LCU 1387
LCU 588	LCU 666	LCU 803	LCU 1124	LCU 1430
LCU 599	LCU 667	LCU 871	LCU 1241	LCU 1451
LCU 608	LCU 674	LCU 893	LCU 1348	LCU 1462
LCU 654	LCU 742		LCU 1348	

Displacement, tons	143 to 160 light; 309 to 320 full load
Dimensions, feet	105 wl; 119 oa × 32·7 × 5 max
Guns	2—20 mm
Main engines	Gray Marine diesels; 3 shafts; 675 bhp = 10 knots
Complement	13 (enlisted men)

Formerly LCT(6) 501-1465 series; built in 1943-1944. Can carry four tanks or 200 tons of cargo. LCU 524, 529, 550, 562, 592, 600, 629, 664, 666, 668, 677, 686, 742, 764, 776, 788, 840, 869, 877, 960, 973, 974, 979, 980, 1056, 1082, 1086, 1124, 1136, 1156, 1159, 1162, 1195, 1224, 1236, 1250, 1283, 1286, 1363, 1376, 1378, 1384, 1386, 1398, 1411, and 1430 reclassified as YFU 1 through 46, respectively, on 18 May 1958; LCU 1040 reclassified YFB 82 on 18 May 1958; LCU 1446 reclassified YFU 53 in 1964; LCU 509, 637, 646, 709, 716, 776, 851, 916, 973, 989, 1126, 1165, 1203, 1232, 1385, and 1388 reclassified as YFU 54 through 69, respectively, on 1 Mar 1966; LCU 780 reclassified as YFU 87. YFU 9 reverted to LCU 666 on 1 Jan 1962; LCU 1459 converted to YLLC 4; changes reflect employment as general cargo craft assigned to shore commands (see section on Service Craft).

CLASSIFICATION. Originally rated as Landing Craft, Tank (LCT(6)); redesignated Utility Landing Ships (LSU) in 1949 to reflect varied employment; designation changed to Utility Landing Craft (LCU) on 15 Apr 1952 and classified as service craft.

See 1970-1971 edition for war losses, disposals, and transfers prior to 1965.

MECHANISED LANDING CRAFT: LCM 8 TYPE

Displacement, tons	113 full load (steel) or 105 full load (aluminium)
Dimensions, feet	75·6 or 73·7 oa × 21 × 5·2
Main engines	2 diesels; 2 shafts; 650 bhp = 9 knots
Complement	5 (enlisted men)

Constructed of welded-steel and (later units) aluminium. Can carry one M-48 or M-60 tank (both approx 48 tons) or 60 tons cargo. Also operated in large numbers by the US Army.

LCM-8 carrying M-48 tank   *1970, US Navy, PH1 Robert Woods*

MECHANISED LANDING CRAFT: LCM 6 TYPE

Displacement, tons	55 full load
Dimensions, feet	56·2 oa × 14 × 3·9
Main engines	2 diesels; 2 shafts; 450 bhp = 9 knots

Welded-steel construction. Cargo capacity is 34 tons or 80 troops.

LCM-6 entering LSD 32   *1968, United States Navy*

LANDING CRAFT VEHICLE AND PERSONNEL (LCVP)

Displacement, tons	13·5 full load
Dimensions, feet	35·8 oa × 10·5 × 3·5
Main engines	diesel; 1 shaft; 325 bhp = 9 knots

Constructed of wood or fibreglass-reinforced plastic. Fitted with ·30-calibre machine guns when in combat areas.

LCVP from LST 1157   *1969, United States Navy*

2 WARPING TUGS (LWT); NEW CONSTRUCTION

LWT 1	LWT 2

Displacement, tons	61 (hoisting weight)
Dimensions, feet	85 oa × 22 × 6·75
Main engines	2 diesels (Harbourmaster 6CO-V8-71); 2 steerable shafts; 420 hp = 9 knots
Complement	6 (enlisted men)

These craft are employed in amphibious landings to handle pontoon causeways. The LWT 1 and 2 are prototypes of a new, all-aluminium design completed in 1970. A collapsable A-frame is fitted forward to facilitate handling causeway anchors and ship-to-shore fuel lines. They can be "side loaded" on an LST 1179 class ship or carried in an LPD/LSD type ship.
The propulsion motors are similar to outboard motors, providing both steering and thrust, alleviating the need for rudders.
Built by Campbell Machine, San Diego, California.

LWT 2   *United States Navy*

WARPING TUGS (LWT)

Displacement, tons	approx 120
Dimensions, feet	92·9 oa × 23 × 6·5
Main engines	2 outboard propulsion units = 6·5 knots

These craft are fabricated from pontoon sections and are assembled by the major amphibious commands as required.

LWT 85   *United States Navy*

PATROL SHIPS AND CRAFT

The US Navy has developed an interest in patrol ships and craft for use in direct support of Fleet operations. Heretofore US interests in this area were almost exclusively for inshore warfare. The Chief of Naval Operations, Admiral Elmo R. Zumwalt, has stated: "We have (in November 1970) deployed two patrol gunboats to the Mediterranean to trail Soviet missile ships operating within range of our major combatants. If successful, these will improve our tactical intelligence at less cost than destroyers, releasing the destroyers for other essential duties.

"For the future we are developing plans for a patrol hydrofoil missile boat to carry out the same surveillance mission plus an attack mission. Releasing destroyers for more essential duties, these hydrofoil boats will trail enemy missile ships operating within missile range of our major units and will attack them if they attack our ships.

"The foregoing two initiatives will permit the optimum use of the inadequate number of destroyers we will have in the 1970s in strike carrier task forces and major escort roles."

In addition to the patrol hydrofoil missile boats (PHM) described above, the Navy is seeking to develop a class of relatively small escort ships (PF) and beyond these ships is studying the feasibility of a surface effect ship capable of open-ocean anti-submarine operations. All three of these designs are discussed below.

Some efforts also are being made to improve the combat capabilities of existing US Navy patrol ships and craft. These craft generally are considered inferior in firepower to their foreign contemporaries. Under consideration or development are a series of surface-to-surface missiles and advanced guns. The above photograph shows an "Asheville" class gunboat fitted with a Standard missile modified for use in the surface-to-surface role; several reloads are stowed in the forward portions of the missile tubes. Reportedly, two of these gunboats will be fitted with the Standard missile and may have their forward 3 inch guns replaced by twin 35 mm rapid-fire mounts. The most suitable units for this modification would be the *Antelope* and *Ready* which have the advanced Mk 87 weapons control system.

COASTAL AND RIVERINE CRAFT. Beginning in 1965 the US Navy built up a force of approximately 650 coastal and riverine craft for use in the Vietnam War. These craft were most successful in their efforts to halt Communist infiltration of men and arms into South Vietnam by sea and river, and in support South Vietnamese and US military operations on inland waterways. "Vietnamisation" of the coastal and riverine forces began in June 1968 and by December 1970 some 650 small craft had been transferred to the South Vietnamese forces (including 26 patrol boats from the US Coast Guard).

The US Navy has retained a few riverine craft of various types, primarily for research and use at the Naval Inshore Warfare Training Centre at Mare Island, California. (Several of these craft also have been transferred to the Thai, Philippine, and South Korean navies).

The various riverine mine countermeasure craft are described in the Mine Warfare Craft listing of this edition (M-series classifications).

STANDARD MISSILE-ARMED PATROL GUNBOAT (PGM)   *General Dynamics Corp*

PATROL HYDROFOIL MISSILE BOAT (PHM)

AIR CUSHION VEHICLES. The US Navy conducted two six-month evaluations of three SK-5 type air cushion vehicles in Vietnam. Designated Patrol Air Cushion Vehicle (PACV) in Navy service, the three vehicles encountered varied success. With a general lack of enthusiasm for such craft, especially in view of armed helicopter capabilities, and the reduction of US Navy inshore/riverine forces, the three PACVs have been transferred to the US Coast Guard and are listed in that section of this edition.

MILITARY ASSISTANCE PROGRAMME. The United States has offered four patrol craft designs to foreign navies under the Military Assistance Programme (MAP) in recent years. These craft are the PGM 59 class, a 100-foot, relatively slow but seaworthy craft of about 145 tons; the Sewart 85-foot and 65-foot motor gunboats, armed only with .50 calibre MGs; and the 40-foot Sewart aluminium launch. Bertram 31-foot "Enforcers" with fibreglass hulls have also been provided as local police craft.

PATROL HYDROFOIL MISSILE BOATS (PHM)

Displacement, tons	approx 150 full load
Length, feet	approx 120 oa
Missiles	surface-to-surface
Guns	rapid-fire anti-aircraft
Main engines	Gas turbines; water-jet propulsion = 40+ knots in calm water and 35+ knots in 8 to 13 foot seas

The proposed patrol hydrofoil missile boats (tentatively designated PHM) are intended to serve as high-speed attack and surveillance platforms. This design will be based largely on the US Navy's experience with the hydrofoil gunboat *Tucumcari*. Funding is requested in the Fiscal Year 1972 budget for contractor design and the procurement of long-lead time components. The first PHMs are expected to be funded in the FY 1973 new construction programme and should become operational about 1975. This effort will be undertaken in part in collaboration with NATO allies.

GUNNERY. The PHM will be armed with guns of 3 inch or smaller calibre. Probable candidates include the 35 mm gun developed by Oerlikon-Contraves or an adaption of the 30 mm guns developed by Mauser to be produced in the United States by AMF.

MISSILES. A number of possible ship-to-ship missiles are being considered for the PHM including the Nord MM.38 Exocet, the General Dynamics Standard, and the Contraves Italiana Vulcano/Sea Killer Mk 2.

PHOTOGRAPH. The photograph above (hull number "3") is an artist's concept of one PHM configuration being considered. Note the fully submerged foils and general similarity to the *Tucumcari*. This configuration includes twin 35 mm rapid-fire gun mounts forward and amidships, a five-tube Sea Killer Mk 2 missile launcher aft, and an advanced weapons control system of the M22/Mk 87 type.

ASW SURFACE EFFECT SHIPS

The Navy is studying the feasibility of a relatively large, ocean-going surface effect ship with a primary role of anti-submarine warfare. This ship will be an outgrowth of the experimental surface effect ships now being developed for the Navy by Aerojet-General and Textron's Bell Aerospace Division (see description under Landing Craft section).

It is anticipated that the ASW surface effect ship would have a displacement of approximately 2 000 tons full load and have rigid sidewalls that would "capture" the bubble of air on which the ship rides. Propulsion machinery will be gas turbines to produce speeds in the 60 to 80-knot range.

According to Admiral Zumwalt: "We have placed a very high priority on the surface effect ship on the premise that this offers the potential for destroyer-size ships to conduct anti-submarine warfare on top of the water at speeds two or three times greater than the fastest submarines.

"This will not only complicate the submarine's detection, evasion and weapons solution problems, but will make the surface effect ship much less vulnerable to torpedo attack".

PATROL ESCORT SHIPS (PF)

The largest of the proposed ships in this category will be the patrol escort ship, tentatively designated PF. This ship would be primarily an ocean escort and ASW platform, the latter role indicating the probable use of helicopters. Some anti-air warfare capability would be provided, at least passive (warning and electronic countermeasures) and possibly active (missiles or advanced gun capability). The provision of an anti-ship missile to this ship or embarked helicopters could provide a significant combat capability. It is anticipated that this ship would have a maximum speed in excess of 30 knots to overcome the operational limitations imposed on the "Knox" class escort ships (DE) because of their 27-knot speed. Propulsion for the PF probably will be gas turbines. Sub-classes optimised for anti-air and anti-submarine warfare may be developed. The PF is planned with a maximum full-load displacement of about 3 500 tons. In view of past US Navy efforts in the DE category, there will be a considerable challenge to develop an effective fighting ship within the 3 500-ton constraint.

Ironically, the proposed PF displacement is approximately 400 tons greater than the new Soviet "Krivak" class *guided missile destroyers*; multi-purpose ships with an impressive anti-air, anti-submarine, and possibly anti-ship capabilities.

Funding for design of the PF is requested in the Fiscal Year 1972 budget, with construction of the first units anticipated in the FY 1973 or 1974 shipbuilding programme.

Patrol Ships and Craft—*continued*

17 PATROL GUNBOATS (PG): "ASHEVILLE" CLASS

Name	No.	Builder	Commissioned
* ASHEVILLE	PG 84	Tacoma Boatbuilding	6 Aug 1966
* GALLUP	PG 85	Tacoma Boatbuilding	22 Oct 1966
* ANTELOPE	PG 86	Tacoma Boatbuilding	4 Nov 1967
* READY	PG 87	Tacoma Boatbuilding	6 Jan 1968
* CROCKETT	PG 88	Tacoma Boatbuilding	24 June 1967
* MARATHON	PG 89	Tacoma Boatbuilding	11 May 1968
* CANON	PG 90	Tacoma Boatbuilding	26 July 1968
* TACOMA	PG 92	Tacoma Boatbuilding	14 July 1969
* WELCH	PG 93	Petersen Builders	8 Sep 1969
* CHEHALIS	PG 94	Tacoma Boatbuilding	11 Aug 1969
* DEFIANCE	PG 95	Petersen Builders	24 Sep 1969
* BENICIA	PG 96	Tacoma Boatbuilding	25 Apr 1970
* SURPRISE	PG 97	Petersen Builders	17 Oct 1969
* GRAND RAPIDS	PG 98	Tacoma Boatbuilders	5 Sep 1970
* BEACON	PG 99	Petersen Builders	21 Nov 1969
* DOUGLAS	PG 100	Tacoma Boatbuilders	6 Feb 1971
* GREEN BAY	PG 101	Petersen Builders	5 Dec 1969

Displacement, tons	225 standard; 245 full load
Dimensions, feet	164·5 oa × 23·8 × 9·5
Guns	1—3 in (*76 mm*) 50 cal (forward); 1—40 mm (aft); 4—·50 cal MG (twin)
Main engines	CODAG: 2 diesels (Cummins); 1 450 shp; 2 shafts = 16 knots 1 gas turbine (General Electric); 13 300 shp; 2 shafts = 40+ knots
Complement	24 to 27 (3 officers, 21 to 24 enlisted men)

These are the largest patrol-type craft built by the US Navy since World War II and the first US Navy ships with gas-turbine propulsion plants. They were designed to perform patrol, blockade, surveillance, perimeter defence, and support missions. No anti-submarine capability.

Several of these gunboats were used by the US Navy for coastal patrol operations in the Vietnam War; the *Surprise* and *Defiance* deployed to the Mediterranean in November 1970, the first of the class to operate in the Atlantic and Med areas.

Built by Tacoma Boatbuilding Co of Tacoma, Washington, and Petersen Builders of Sturgeon Bay, Wisconsin. PG 84 and PG 85 authorised in Fiscal Year 1963 new construction programme; PG 86 and PG 87 in FY 1964; PG 88-90 in FY 1965; PG 92-101 in FY 1966. *Ashville* was laid down on 15 Apr 1964 and launched on 1 May 1965; later ships approximately 18 months from keel laying to completion. Estimated cost per ship approximately $5 000 000.

The *Benicia* was virtually destroyed by a shipyard fire in August 1968; material being assembled for the *Grand Rapids* and *Douglas* was extensively damaged. All three ships delayed.

CLASSIFICATION. These ships were originally classified as Motor Gunboats (PGM); reclassified Patrol Gunboats (PG) with same hull numbers on 1 Apr 1967. The term motor gunboats is now applied primarily to craft built for allied navies. PGM 1-32 were submarine chasers modified during World War II. PGM 33-38 were built for the Philippines (delivered in 1955-1956); PGM 39-42 built for Philippines (1960); PGM 43-46, 51, 52 built for Burma (1959-1961); PGM 47-50 built in Denmark ("Daphne" class); PGM 53, 54, 58 built for Ethiopia (1961-1962); PGM 55-57 built for Indonesia (1962); PGM 59-67 built for South Vietnam (1963-1964); PGM 71, 79 built for Thailand (1966); PGM 72-74, 80-83, 91 built for South Vietnam (1966-1967); PGM 75, 76 built for Ecuador (1965); PGM 77 built for Dominican Republic (1965); PGM 78 built for Peru (1966); PGM 102 built for Liberia (1967); PGM 103 built for Iran (1967); PGM 104-106, 108 built for Turkey (1967-1968); PGM 107, 113-117 built for Thailand (1968-1969); PGM 112, 122-124 built for Iran (1969-1971); PGM 109-111 and 118-121 under construction for foreign transfer.

DESIGN. All-aluminium hull and aluminium-fibreglass superstructure. Because of the heat-transmitting qualities of the aluminium hull and the amount of waste heat produced by a gas turbine engine the ships are completely air conditioned.

ENGINEERING. These ships have a Combination Diesel and Gas turbine (CODAG) propulsion system with twin diesel engines for cruising and a gas turbine for high-speed operations. The gas turbine is an LM1500 with the gas generator essentially the same as the J-79-8 aircraft engine (used in the F-4 Phantom and other aircraft). The transfer from diesel to gas turbine propulsion (or vice versa) can be accomplished while underway with no loss of speed. From full stop these ships can attain 40 knots in one minute; manoeuvrability is excellent due in part to controllable-pitch propellers. Speed and propeller pitch is controlled directly from the pilot house console. Either JP-5 or diesel fuel can be used for both the gas turbine and diesels.
Arrangement of gas turbine intake differs on later ships.

GUNNERY. The *Antelope* and *Ready* have the Mk 87 weapons control system for rapid acquisition and tracking of fast-moving targets; the system can also direct and fire appropriate weapons automatically. The Mk 87 can operate in a radar mode or with a stabilised optical sight on the weather decks. No further procurement of this advanced fire control system is planned in the Navy although it is being fitted to a number of foreign warships.
(The Mk 87 is an American-produced copy of the Hollandse Signaalapparaten M22 weapons control system).
Other ships have Mk 63 Mod 29 Gunfire Control System with SPG-50 fire control radar.

NOMENCLATURE. Patrol gunboats are named for small American cities; however, the *Surprise* remembers several earlier US Navy ships.

PHOTOGRAPHS. Note Mk 87 antenna sphere on the *Ready*. The gas turbine air intake is immediately aft of the bridge structure; the adjacent large funnel is the turbine exhaust with a smaller diesel exhaust stack to either side. The *Defiance* is shown in Naples, the *Ready* on the Cua Lon River in South Vietnam.

The *Benicia* is shown as experimentally refitted in 1971 with a surface-to-surface missile. See comments on the weapon modification in the introductory discussion to this section on the previous page.

READY (PG 87)   *1970, United States Navy*

BENICIA (PG 96)   *1971, United States Navy*

DEFIANCE (PG 95)   *1970 US Navy, PH1 Warren Poole*

MARATHON (PG 89)   *1968, United States Navy*

MARATHON (PG 89)   *1968, United States Navy*

Patrol Ships and Craft—*continued*

1 HYDROFOIL GUNBOAT (PGH): "TUCUMCARI" TYPE

*TUCUMCARI PGH 2

Displacement, tons	58
Dimensions, feet	71·8 oa × 19·5 × 4·5 (hull borne) or 13·9 (with foils down)
Guns	1—40 mm; several 20 mm
Main engines	foil borne: 1 gas turbine (Proteus); 3 040 hp; water-jet propulsion = 40+ knots
	hull borne: 1 diesel (General Motors); 150 shp; water-jet propulsion
Complement	13 (1 officer, 12 enlisted men)

The *Tucumcari* is one of two hydrofoil gunboats built by the US Navy as competitive prototypes. Built by Boeing Company in Seattle, Washington, with hull fabricated by Gunderson Brothers of Portland, Oregon. Laid down on 1 Sep 1966, launched on 15 July 1967, placed in service on 7 Mar 1968. Estimated construction cost was $4 000 000. Hydrofoil gunboats are "in service" rather than being in commission. In early 1971 the *Tucumcari* was deployed to the Mediterranean; previously she had operated in Vietnam.

DESIGN. The *Tucumcari* has the canard foil configuration with approximately 30 per cent of the boat's weight supported by the forward foil and 70 per cent by the aft set of foils. The forward foil assembly provides steering by means of rotating the strut about its vertical axis. The foil-borne operation is automatic with a wave-height sensing system to maintain the hull clear of the sea. The foils are fully retractable for hull-borne operations. Aluminium construction.

ENGINEERING. During foil-borne operations the craft's gas turbine drives a water-jet pump instead of a propeller. Water is taken in from the sea through openings in the main pods and carried in ducts within the foil struts to the pump inlet. The water—at the rate of approximately 27 000 gallons (100 tons) per minute—is then pumped out through nozzles under the craft's stern to obtain thrust. The jet pump has a thrust rating comparable to the 18 000-pound thrust of commercial aircraft engines. Hull-borne operation is by means of a diesel-driven water-jet pump.

GUNNERY. Prior to early 1971 deployment to the Mediterranean the *Tucumcari's* 81 mm mortar and two ·50 cal twin MG mounts were replaced by 20 mm cannon.

PHOTOGRAPHS. The *Tucumcari* can be distinguished from the *Flagstaff* by the former's larger deckhouse structure and bow foil strut; the *Flagstaff* has a stern strut and short funnel aft.

TUCUMCARI (PGH 2)   1970, *United States Navy*

1 HYDROFOIL GUNBOAT (PGH): "FLAGSTAFF" TYPE

*FLAGSTAFF PGH 1

Displacement, tons	57
Dimensions, feet	74·4 oa × 21·4 × 4·2 (hull borne) or 12·5 (with foils down)
Guns	1—152 mm guns; 4—·50 cal MG (twin); 1—81 mm mortar
Main engines	foil borne: 1 gas turbine (Rolls-Royce); 3 620 hp; controllable pitch propeller = 40+ knots
	hull borne: 2 diesels (General Motors); 300 hp water-jet propulsion
Complement	13 (1 officer, 12 enlisted men)

The *Flagstaff* is a competitive prototype being evaluated with the *Tucumcari*. Built by Grumman Aircraft Corporation in Stuart, Florida. Laid down on 15 July 1966, launched on 9 Jan 1968, placed in service in July 1968. Estimated construction cost was $3 600 000.

DESIGN. The *Flagstaff* has a conventional foil arrangement with 70 per cent of the craft's weight supported by the forward set of foils and 30 per cent of the weight supported by the stern foil. Steering is accomplished by movement of the stern strut about its vertical axis. Foil-borne operation is automatically controlled by a wave-height sensing system. The foils are fully retractable for hull-borne operations. Aluminium construction.

ENGINEERING. During foil-borne operations the propeller is driven by a geared transmission system contained in the tail strut and in the pod located at the strut-foil connection. During hull-borne operations two diesel engines drive a water-jet propulsion system. Water enters the pump inlets through openings in the hull and the thrust is exerted by water flow though nozzles in the transome. Steering in the hull-borne mode is by deflection vanes in the water stream.

GUNNERY. Rearmed with 152 mm gun in place of single 40 mm gun early in 1971. The 152 mm is a low-velocity weapon mounted on Army's Sheridan armoured reconnaissance vehicle. The cartridge is fully combustible.

TUCUMCARI (PGH 2)   1971, *United States Navy*

FLAGSTAFF (PGH 1)   1971, *United States Navy*

TUCUMCARI (PGH 2)   *Boeing*

FLAGSTAFF (PGH 1)   1968, *United States Navy*

Patrol Ships and Craft—continued

FLAGSTAFF (PGH 1)   *Grumman*

1 HYDROFOIL RESEARCH SHIP (AGEH)

*PLAINVIEW AGEH 1

Displacement, tons	310 full load
Dimensions, feet	212 oa × 40·5 × 10 (foils extended), 26 (withdrawn)
ASW weapons	2 triple torpedo launchers (Mk 32)
Main engines	2 gas turbines (General Electric); 30 000 hp; 2 diesels; 1 200 hp
Complement	20 (6 officers, 14 men)

Aluminium hull experimental hydrofoil. Three retractable foils, 25 ft in height, each weighing 7 tons, fitted port and starboard and on stern, and used in waves up to 15 feet. Initial maximum speed of about 50 knots, with later modifications expected to raise the speed to 80 knots. Fitted with the largest titanium propellers made. The two 15 000 hp gas turbines are General Electric J-79 jet aircraft engines modified for marine use. Power plant and transmission designed to permit future investigation of various types of foils. Built by Lockheed Shipbuilding & Construction Co, Seattle, Washington. Laid down on 8 May 1964, launched on 28 June 1965, and completed in 1968. Delayed because of engineering difficulties. In service vice being in commission.

Two photographs of *Plainview* being fitted out appear in the 1968-1969 edition. The views below show her on builder trials in Puget Sound.

DISPOSAL
The hydrofoil test craft *Denison*, briefly operated by the Navy, has been returned to the Maritime Administration and subsequently sold commercially. Photographs and description appear in the 1970-1971 edition.

PLAINVIEW (AGEH 1)   *1968, Lockheed Shipbuilding*

PLAINVIEW (AGEH 1)   *1968, Lockheed Shipbuilding*

1 EXPERIMENTAL HYDROFOIL (PCH)

*HIGH POINT PCH 1

Displacement, tons	110
Dimensions, feet	115 oa × 31; draught 6 to 17
Guns	2—·50 cal MG (twin). See *Gunnery* notes
A/S weapons	4—21 in torpedo launchers (2 twin); DCT
Main engines	2 Bristol Siddeley Marine Proteus gas turbines; 2 shafts; 6 200 shp = 48 knots max
	Auxiliary diesel propulsion; 600 bhp = 12 knots cruising
Complement	13 (1 officer, 12 enlisted men)

Experimental hydrofoil submarine chaser. Aluminium hull. Four propellers, two pushing, two pulling, fitted on retractable hydrofoils. Forward foil single strut, after foil two struts. Struts extend over 14 ft below hull. With foils retracted draft is about 6 ft. Diesel with retractable propeller. Sonar equipment installed. Provided for under the Fiscal Year 1960 Programme. Cost $3 700 000. Named after High Point, North Carolina.

CONSTRUCTION. Designed by W. C. Nickum & Sons, Seattle, Wn. Built jointly by Boeing Aircraft Corpn, Seattle, Washington, and J. M. Martinac, Tacoma, Washington, at Martinac's Tacoma Yard. Laid down on 27 Feb 1961. Launched on 17 Aug 1962. Completed and placed in service on 3 Sep 1963.

GUNNERY. A single 40 mm gun was mounted forward in 1968; subsequently removed. Machine guns are not normally mounted.

HIGH POINT (PCH 1)   *Boeing*

HIGH POINT (PCH 1)   *Boeing*

4 FAST PATROL BOATS (PTF): PTF 23 TYPE

PTF 23	PTF 24	PTF 25	PTF 26

Dimensions, feet	95 oa
Guns	1—81 mm mortar; 1—·50 cal MG (mounted over mortar); 1—40 mm (aft); 2—20 mm (single)
Main engines	2 diesels; 2 shafts

PTF 23-26 built by Sewart Seacraft Division of Teledyne Inc of Berwick, Louisiana. First unit completed in 1967, others in 1968. Aluminium hulls. Commercial name is "Osprey".
All four units are in service.

PTF 23 TYPE   *United States Navy*

Patrol Ships and Craft—continued

PTF 23 TYPE   *United States Navy*

PTF 13   *1968, United States Navy*

6 FAST PATROL BOATS (PTF): PTF 17 TYPE

PTF 17	PTF 19	PTF 21
PTF 18	PTF 20	PTF 22

Dimensions, feet	80·3 oa × 24·5 × 6·8
Guns (may vary)	1—81 mm mortar; 1—40 mm; 2—20 mm (single); 1·50 cal MG (mounted over mortar)
Main engines	2 diesel (Napier-Deltic); 6 200 hp; 2 shafts

PTF 17-22 built by John Trumpy & Sons, Annapolis, Maryland; lead boat completed in late 1967, others in 1968. Based on "Nasty" design.

All six units are in service (PTF 21 and 22 were given "commissioned" status on 14 May 1969).

8 FAST PATROL BOATS (PTF): "NASTY" TYPE

PTF 3	PTF 6	PTF 10	PTF 12
PTF 5	PTF 7	PTF 11	PTF 13

Displacement, tons	64 light; 69 standard; 76 full load
Dimensions, feet	80·3 oa × 24·5 × 6·8
Guns (may vary)	1—81 mm mortar; 1—40 mm; 2—20 mm (single); 1—50 cal MG (mounted over mortar)
Main engines	2 diesels (Napier-Deltic); 6 200 shp; 2 shafts = 45 knots
Complement	19 (3 officers, 16 enlisted men)

PTF "NASTY" TYPE   *1970, United States Navy*

PTF 3-16 of the "Nasty" type were built by Boatservice Ltd A/S of Mandal, Norway. Same design as the Norwegian Navy's "Tjeld" class torpedo boats. PTF 3 and PTF 4 delivered to USA in December 1962, PTF 5-8 in April 1964, and PTF 9-16 in September 1964. Hulls made of two layers of mahogany which sandwich a layer of fibreglass. British engines. Endurance is 450 miles at 41 knots or 600 miles at 25 knots.

GUNNERY. Guns vary; the PTF 13 has been experimentally fitted with twin Oerlikon rocket launchers (see photograph).

LOSSES. Sunk in Vietnam: PTF 4 on 4 Nov 1965, PTF 8 on 16 June 1966, PTF 9 on 7 Mar 1966, PTF 14 on 22 Apr 1966, PTF 15 on 22 Apr 1966, and PTF 16 on 19 Aug 1966. (Strike dates in 1970-71 edition).

DISPOSALS
PTF 1 (ex-PT 810) and **PTF 2** (ex-PT 811) stricken from the Navy List on 1 Aug 1955 (sunk as targets).

CLASSIFICATION. PT 1-808 were World War II era torpedo boats, many of which went to foreign navies; PT 809-812 were Korean War prototypes (two became PTFs); PT 813-821 were "Flyvefisken" and "Falken" class torpedo boats built in Denmark with US funding.

1 COASTAL INTERCEPTION AND INTERDICTION CRAFT

Displacement, tons	55 to 60
Dimensions, feet	76 oa × 16 × 3
Guns	2—30 mm (twin); 1—106 mm recoilless rifle; 3—·50 cal MG
Main engines	2 gas turbines (TF 35) and 1 diesel (12V71); water jets = 50 knots

The US Navy is planning to construct one Coastal Interception and Interdiction Craft (CIIC) of this type for evaluation and procure an additional number for transfer to South Korea. These craft are intended specifically to intercept infiltration attempts into South Korea by sea. The 30 mm gun is of Hispano Suiza design. The above are preliminary characteristics.

PTF "NASTY" TYPE   *1970, US Navy, Ensign Rodney Moen*

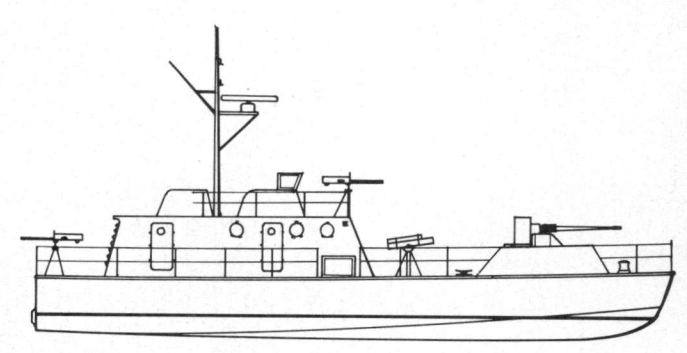

PCF Mark II Type   *1968, United States Navy*

PCF Mark I Type   *1969, United States Navy*

RIVERINE WARFARE CRAFT

13 INSHORE PATROL CRAFT (PCF): "SWIFT" TYPE

3 PCF Mark I series
3 PCF Mark II series
7 PCF Mark III series

Displacement, tons	22·5 full load
Dimensions, feet	50 oa × 13 × 3·5 (Mark III 51 oa × 13½)
Guns	1—81 mm mortar, 3—50 cal MG (twin MG mount atop pilot house and single MG mounted over mortar)
Main engines	2 geared diesels (General Motors); 960 shp; 2 shafts = 28 knots (maximum)
Complement	6 (1 officer, 5 enlisted men)

The "Swift" design is adapted from the all-metal crew boat which is used to support off-shore drilling rigs in the Gulf of Mexico. Approximately 125 built since 1965. Mark II has modified deckhouse; Mark III is slightly larger.
Designation changed from Fast Patrol Craft (PCF) to Inshore Patrol Craft on 14 Aug 1968.

LOSSES. PCF 4, 41, and 97 lost to enemy action off South Vietnam; PCF 77 lost in heavy weather off South Vietnam in November 1966; PCF 14 and 76 lost in heavy weather off South Vietnam in Oct 1967; PCF 19 sunk off South Vietnam on 16 June 1968 in accidental attack by US Air Force aircraft.

TRANSFERS. PCF 33, 34, and 83-86 transferred to the Philippines in 1966. Additional PCFs of this type constructed specifically for transfer to Thailand, the Philippines, and South Korea; not assigned US hull numbers in the PCF series. 104 PCFs formerly manned by US Navy personnel transferred to South Vietnam in 1968-1970.

PCF Mark II Type   1969, United States Navy

64 RIVER PATROL BOATS (PBR): MARK II

34 + 30 PBR Mark II Series

Displacement, tons	8
Dimensions, feet	32 oa × 11 × 2·6
Guns	3—·50 cal MG (twin mount forward; single aft); 1—40 mm grenade launcher; 1—60 mm mortar in some boats
Main engines	2 geared diesels (6V53 Detroit); water jets = 25+ knots
Complement	4 or 5 (enlisted men)

An improved PBR design; fibreglass hull. The first Mark II PBRs arrived in South Vietnam in September 1967. Forward ·50 cal MG mount is lower than in Mk I boats. Approximately 425 built 1967-1970; 30 additional units under construction in 1971. Most transferred to South Vietnam; US Navy retains few for training and development work.

LOSSES. PBR 20 sunk in collision in 1967; PBR 30 stricken in 1967 after being damaged; PBR 55 stricken in 1966 after being damaged; PBR 113 destroyed after being damaged by Viet Cong grenades in 1967; all in South Vietnam area.

PBR Mk II Type   United States Navy

2 ASSAULT SUPPORT PATROL BOATS (ASPB): MARK 2 DESIGNS

Dimensions, feet	50 oa × 20
Guns	1—105 mm howitzer; 2—30 mm; 2—7·62 mm MG; 1—40 mm grenade launcher (see notes)
Main engines	3 gas turbines (United Aircraft of Canada) driving three water jets (Buehler Corp) = approx 40 knots (designed)

The Sikorsky Aircraft Division of United Aircraft Corp, and the Sewart Seacraft Division of Teledyne, Inc, have developed prototype advanced ASPBs for the Navy (designated Mark 2). The Sikorsky craft is described above and shown on trials during March-April 1969 in Long Island Sound. It has a light-weight 105 mm howitzer and two 20 mm cannon mounted in a tank-like turret which has a 360 degree field of fire. The smaller, forward mount is remote controlled and initially contains two 7·62 mm MG and a 40 mm grenade launcher, but Sikorsky has proposed replacing the machine-guns with two 20 mm cannon. Also fitted for minesweeping; note position of radar on tripod mast aft. The Sewart Seacraft ASPB is similar, but initially has an 81 mm mortar in lieu of the 105 mm howitzer. Both craft are heavily armoured with the main turret and engines on shock springs to reduce effects of mine explosions.
No production will be undertaken at this time; reportedly the designed speed has not been achieved.

ASPB MK2   1969, Sikorsky, United Aircraft

ASPB Mk 2   1969, Sikorsky United Aircraft

4 ASSAULT SUPPORT PATROL BOATS (ASPB): PROGRAMME V

Displacement, tons	36·25 full load
Dimensions, feet	50 oa × 15·6 × 3·75
Guns (varies)	1 or 2—20 mm (with 2—·50 cal MG in boats with one 20 mm) 2—·30 cal MG; 2—40 mm high-velocity grenade launchers
Main engines	2 diesels (12V71 Detroit); 2 shafts = 14 knots sustained
Complement	6 (enlisted)

The ASPB was designed specifically for riverine operations and serves as an escort for other Navy river craft, provides mine countermeasures during river operations, and intercepts enemy river traffic. Welded-steel hulls. Armament changed to above configuration in 1968; some boats have twin- ·50 cal MG "turret" forward in place of single 20 mm gun.

Numerous craft of this type transferred to South Vietnamese Navy; four units retained at US Naval Inshore Warfare Training Centre.

Note that open stern well is plated over in the ASPB pictured here (A-131-2); a view of an ASPB with 81 mm mortar/·50 cal MG aft appears in the 1968-1969 edition (programme IV ASPB).

Riverine Warfare Craft—continued

ASSAULT SUPPORT PATROL BOAT (ASPB)   1968, United States Navy

8 ARMOURED TROOP CARRIERS (ATC): PROGRAMME V

Displacement, tons	66 full load
Dimensions, feet	65·5 oa × 17·5 × 3·25
Guns	1 or 2—20 mm; 2—·50 cal MG; 2 to 6—·30 cal MG; 1—40 mm high-velocity grenade launcher; 2—40 mm low-velocity grenade launchers
Main engines	2 diesels (64HN9 Detroit); 2 shafts = 8·5 knots max (6 knots sustained)

These craft were converted from LCM-6 landing craft to transport troops, small vehicles field artillery, and supplies. Heavily armoured. Several have been fitted with light steel helicopter platforms to facilitate evacuation of wounded personnel. Armament changed to the above configuration in 1968.

Numerous craft of this type have been transferred to the South Vietnamese Navy; eight units retained by US Navy at US Naval Inshore Warfare Training Centre.

Note winch on fantail for chain drag equipment used to sweep for command detonated underwater mines.

2 MONITORS (MON): PROGRAMME V

Displacement, tons	80 to 90 full load
Dimensions, feet	60·5 oa × 17·5 × 3·5
Guns	1—105 mm howitzer; 2—20 mm; 3—·30 cal MG; 2—40 mm high-velocity grenade launchers
Main engines	2 diesels; 2 shafts = 8 knots
Complement	11 (enlisted)

These craft provide fire support for riverine operations as well as security for afloat bases. Heavily armoured. Some have two Army M10-8 flame throwers in lieu of one 20 mm gun and howitzer; these craft are dubbed "zippo" monitors. Armament changed to above configuration in 1968. Converted from LCM-6 landing craft. Popularly referred to as the "battleships" of the riverine fleet.

Numerous craft of this type transferred to South Vietnamese Navy; two units retained at US Naval Inshore Warfare Training Centre (one with flame capability and one with howitzer).

ARMOURED TROOP CARRIER (ATC)   1968, United States Navy

MONITOR (MON)   1968, United States Navy

1 COMMAND AND CONTROL BOAT (CCB): PROGRAMME V

Displacement, tons	80 full load
Dimensions, feet	61 oa × 17·5 × 3·4
Guns	3—20 mm; 2—·30 cal MG; 2—40 mm high-velocity grenade launchers
Main engines	2 diesels (64HN9 Detroit); 2 shafts = 8·5 knots max (6 knots sustained)
Complement	11

2 ARMOURED TROOP CARRIERS (ATC): MARK 2

Dimensions, feet	49·75 × 24 × 3·25
Guns	4—·50 cal MG (twim); 2—40 mm grenade launchers
Machinery	2 gas turbines; 1 600 hp; 2 shafts = 15+ knots
Complement	5 (enlisted)
Troops	40

Two craft of this high-speed riverine personnel carrier design were built for evaluation. Built by Sewart Seacraft.

These craft serve as afloat command posts providing command and communications facilities for ground force and boat group commanders. Heavily armoured. Armament changed to above configuration in 1968. Converted from LCM-6 landing craft.

Several units transferred to South Vietnamese Navy; one unit retained at US Naval Inshore Warfare Training Centre.

ARMOURED TROOP CARRIER (ATC/Mk 2)   United States Navy

COMMAND AND CONTROL BOAT (CCB)   1968, United States Navy

Riverine Warfare Craft—continued

RIVERINE UTILITY CRAFT (RUC)

Weight, tons	6·25 full load
Dimensions, feet	20 × 14 × 1·5 (motionless in water)
Guns	1—·30 cal MG; 1—40 mm grenade launcher
Main engines	2 gasoline engines (Chrysler); marsh screw = 10+ knots (ground speed; slower in water)
Complement	2 (enlisted)
Troops	6

The Chrysler Corporation has built ten of these craft for Navy evaluation; propelled by the marsh (Archimedes) screw concept with two propelling cylinders fitted with spiraling vanes installed on the craft's fore-and-aft axis. The vehicles can travel over deep swamps and marshes, rice paddies, as well as water and dry land. It is limited in climbing obstacles. Can carry 6 troops or one ton of cargo.

As of 1971 only six of these craft were in use, two by US Navy and four by US Marine Corps.

COMBAT SALVAGE BOATS (CSB)

The combat salvage boats have been transferred to the South Vietnamese Navy; see 1970-1971 edition for characteristics and photograph.

RIVERINE UTILITY CRAFT (RUC)   *United States Navy*

SEAL SUPPORT CRAFT

The US Navy operates a number of specialised craft in support of its SEAL (Sea-Air-Land) teams and Underwater Demolition Teams (UDT). The SEAL units are counter-insurgency forces organised on 1 Jan 1962 primarily for use in Vietnam; however, SEAL team units also are assigned to the Atlantic Fleet and have given training to naval personnel in several countries other than South Vietnam. The UDT personnel perform reconnaissance of beach areas prior to amphibious assaults and participate in other covert operations.

Four types of SEAL-UDT support craft currently are on the Navy List of classifications: Landing Craft Swimmer Reconnaissance (LCSR), a highly specialised craft intended to pick up swimmers from the water at high speeds; Light SEAL Support Craft (LSSC), a modified 24-foot utility boat; Medium SEAL Support Craft (MSSC), a new design 36-foot craft; and the Swimmer Delivery Vehicles (SDV), essentially two man submersibles intended to carry swimmers from a submarine to their operating area. In addition, several Heavy SEAL Support Craft (HSSC) are in service, these being modified LCM-6 landing craft, heavily armed (including a 106 mm recoilless rifle) and armoured.

In Vietnam SEAL team personnel also employ a variety of riverine warfare craft and helicopters for their activities.

LANDING CRAFT SWIMMER RECONNAISSANCE (LCSR)   *US Navy*

MEDIUM SEAL SUPPORT CRAFT (MSSC)   *US Navy*

LIGHT SEAL SUPPORT CRAFT (LSSC)   *US Navy*

HEAVY SEAL SUPPORT CRAFT (HSSC)   *US Navy*

MINE WARFARE SHIPS

The US Navy has begun a restructuring of its mine warfare forces, essentially shifting away from the techniques and equipment developed on the basis of World War II and Korean War experiences toward the planning of a more realistic capability for future mine countermeasure requirements.

The most obvious manifestation of this shift is the reduction in the number of ocean minesweepers (MSO) in the active fleet from 62 in mid-1970 to about two dozen ships in mid-1971. The other ships have been assigned to Naval Reserve training, transferred abroad or stricken.

Also gone from the active fleet are both of the large mine countermeasure ships (MCS) that had been converted in the mid-1960s.

In a similar move, all of the mothballed World War II-era minelayers have been stricken from the reserve fleet. These ships, the cruiser-design minelayer Terror (MMF 5) and the ten destroyer-minelayers (MMD), also were considered unsuitable for future mine warfare requirements.

Under the Navy's new approach to mine countermeasures the prime minesweeping vehicle will be the RH-53D Sea Stallion helicopter. This is a large, twin-shaft-turbine powered helicopter capable of being refuelled in-flight by tanker aircraft or from surface ships while hovering overhead.

One "Iwo Jima" class amphibious assault ship (LPH) will be refitted to support the RH-53 minesweeping helicopters, with the ship being capable of operating a maximum of about 20 of the helicopters. The assault ship was designed to support helicopters and has adequate accommodations for all flight personnel, and with a sustained speed of 20 knots can keep pace with modern amphibious forces. (In contrast the ocean minesweepers have a maximum speed of about 15 knots and a ten-knot cruising speed, preventing them from transiting to assault areas with amphibious ships).

No additional minesweeping ships are planned at this time. The MSO-523 class, described below, was considered only a marginal improvement at considerable cost compared to the MSO design of Korean War vintage.

Future developments in the field of minesweeprs probably will include surface effect ships (SES) or hydrofoil craft configured for mine countermeasures. These sweeps would have a rapid deployment capability, be highly automated to reduce personnel requirements, and be capable of sweeping or destroying advanced-technology mines.

The US Navy has no surface ships configured for mine-laying and the number of submarines that can plant mines is being reduced as the older, diesel-electric submarines are replaced by nuclear-powered submarines with a more limited selection of tube-launched weapons. (The SSN-688 class will be able to fire only SUBROC and the Mk 48 torpedoes). Navy carrier based attack aircraft and land-based patrol aircraft have a limited aerial minelaying capability; however, the Strategic Air Command operates several hundred B-52 Strato-fortress bombers that are fitted for aerial minelaying.

1 MINE COUNTERMEASURES SHIP (MCS): "CATSKILL" CLASS

Name	No.	Builder	Laid down	Launched	LSV Comm	MCS Comm
OZARK	MCS 2 (ex-LSV 2, ex-CM 7, ex-AP 107)	Willamette Iron & Steel	12 July 1941	15 June 1942	23 Sep 1944	24 June 1966

Displacement, tons	5 875 standard; 9 040 full load
Length, feet (metres)	440 (134·1) wl; 455·5 (138·8) oa
Beam, feet (metres)	60·2 (18·4)
Draft, feet (metres)	20 (6·1)
Guns	2—5 inch (127 mm) 38 cal (single)
Helicopters	2 RH-3A minesweeping helicopters
Main engines	2 geared turbines (General Electric); 11 000 shp; 2 shafts
Boilers	4 (Combustion Engineering "D" type)
Speed, knots	20·3
Complement	586 (47 officers and 539 enlisted men)

OZARK (MCS 2)

1969, United States Navy

The Ozark was one of two ships converted to carry and support minesweeping launches and helicopters. Heretofore this role was performed by modified tank and dock landing ships (see Disposal notes). Sister ship Catskill (MCS 1) has been stricken.

Although extensively converted for the mine warfare role, the Ozark was not considered suitable for advanced mine countermeasures operations (she cannot operate the large RH-53D minesweeping helicopters); decommissioned on 6 Feb 1970 and transferred to Maritime Administration reserve (remains on Navy List).

CLASSIFICATION. Designed as a large minelayer (CM), redesignated as a troop transport (AP), and initially completed as a vehicle landing ship (LSV). Reclassified as a mine warfare command and support ship (MCS) in 1955, changed to mine countermeasures and support ship (MCS) in 1958, to mine countermeasures support ship (MCS) on 25 Aug 1960, and to mine countermeasures ship (MCS) on 14 Aug 1968.

The Ozark was decommissioned and placed in reserve on 29 June 1946; stricken from the Navy List on 1 Sep 1961 but reinstated on 1 Oct 1963 for conversion to MCS configuration.

CONVERSION. Converted to a mine countermeasures ship under the Fiscal Year 1963 shipbuilding and conversion programme at Norfolk Shipbuilding & Dry Dock Corp, Norfolk, Virginia, from Sep 1963 to June 1966. Converted to carry and support 20 minesweeping launches (MSL) and two RH-3A minesweeping helicopters. Maintenance shops, minesweeping equipment stowage, and accommodations for minesweeping crews provided.

DESIGN. As a vehicle landing ship the Ozark was designed to carry amphibious tractors and tanks, unloaded into the water by a stern ramp. Original armament consisted of two 5 inch DP guns and eight 40 mm AA guns.

MINELAYING. The Ozark can be fitted to carry and plant several hundred influence mines. Approximately ten days in a major industrial facility would be required to provide the minelaying capability. (Moored contact mines could not be carried).

DISPOSALS

Five additional ships were built to this basic design: **Saugus** MCS 4 (ex-LSV 4, ex-AN 4) stricken from the Navy List on 1 July 1961; **Monitor** MCS 5 (ex-LSV 5, ex-AN 5) and **Osage** MCS 3 (ex-LSV 3, ex-AN 3) stricken on 1 Sep 1961; **Galilea** (ex-Montauk) AKN 6 (ex-LSV 6, ex-AN 2, ex-AP 161) stricken on 1 Sep 1960; **Catskill** MCS 1 (ex-LSV 1, ex-CM 6, ex-AP 106) stricken on 1 July 1961, reinstated on Navy List on 1 June 1964, and again stricken (after conversion) on 20 Nov 1970.

Epping Forest MCS 7 (ex-LSD 4) stricken on 1 Nov 1968.

Orleans Parish MCS 6 (ex-LST 1069) redesignated as LST on 1 June 1966 (listed with Military Sealift Ships).

FLEET MINELAYER (MMF)

The cruiser-type fleet minelayer **Terror** (MMF 5, ex-MM 5, ex-CM 5) stricken on 1 Nov 1970. (See 1970-1971 and previous editions for characteristics).

FAST MINELAYERS (MMD)

The 12 fast minelayers converted from "Allen M. Sumner" class destroyers have been stricken: **Robert H. Smith** (MMD/DM 23, ex-DD 735) stricken on 26 Feb 1971; **Thomas E. Fraser** (MMD/DM 24, ex-DD 736), **Shannon** (MMD/DM 25, ex-DD 737) stricken on 1 Nov 1970; **Harry F. Bauer** (MMD/DM 26, ex-DD 738 stricken in 1971.

Adams (MMD/DM 27, ex-DD 739), **Tolman** (MMD/DM 28, ex-DD 740) stricken on 1 Dec 1970; **Henry A. Wiley** (MMD/DM 29, ex-DD 749) stricken on 15 Oct 1970; **Shea** (MMD/DM 30, ex-DD 750) stricken in 1971. **J. William Ditter** (DM 31, ex-DD 751), stricken on 11 Oct 1945 (battle damaged); **Lindsey** (MMD/DM 32, ex-DD 771) stricken on 1 Oct 1970; **Gwin** (MMD/DM 33, ex-DD 772) stricken in 1971.

Aaron Ward (DM 34, ex-DD 773) stricken on 11 Oct 1945 (battle damaged).

(See 1970-1971 and previous editions for characteristics).

OZARK (MCS 2)

1966, United States Navy

Mine Warfare Ships—*continued*

2 OCEAN MINESWEEPERS (MSO): "ABILITY" CLASS

Name	No.	Launched	Commissioned
*ALACRITY	MSO 520	8 June 1957	2 Oct 1958
*ASSURANCE	MSO 521	31 Aug 1957	22 Nov 1958

Displacement, tons	810 light; 934 full load
Dimensions, feet	190 × 36 × 14·5
Guns	1—40 mm AA; 2—·50 cal MG
Main engines	2 GM diesels; 2 shafts; controllable pitch propellers; 2 700 bhp = 15 knots
Complement	71 (6 officers, 65 men)

Non-magnetic, wooden hulled vessels built by Peterson Builders Inc, Sturgeon Bay, Wisc. Fitted as mine division commander's flagships. Equipped for all types of mine countermeasures operations. Laid down on 5 Mar 1956, 3 May 1956 and 28 Jan 1957 respectively. Fitted with UQS-1 mine detecting sonar. Endurance is 3 200 miles at 12 knots. Note tripod mast.

Plans to modernise these ships were cancelled (see notes under "Agile" class).

DISPOSAL
Ability MSO 519 stricken on 1 Feb 1971.

ADVANCE (MSO 510)   *1968, United States Navy*

ALACRITY (MSO 520)   *1969, United States Navy*

4 OCEAN MINESWEEPERS (MSO): "ACME" CLASS

Name	No.	Launched	Commissioned
ACME	MSO 508	23 June 1955	27 Sep 1956
*ADROIT	MSO 509	20 Aug 1955	4 Mar 1957
ADVANCE	MSO 510	12 July 1957	16 June 1958
*AFFRAY	MSO 511	18 Dec 1956	8 Dec 1958

Displacement, tons	720 light; 780 full load
Dimensions, feet	173 oa × 35 × 10
Guns	1—40 mm AA; 2—·50 cal MG
Main engines	4 Packard diesels; 2 shafts; 2 800 bhp = 14 knots
Complement	74

This class is different from the "Agile" type but has similar basic particulars. All built by Frank L. Sample, Jnr, Inc, Boothbay Harbour, Maine. Plans to modernise these ships were cancelled (see notes under "Agile" class).
Two ships were decommissioned and placed in reserve late in 1970.

NOMENCLATURE. Ocean minesweepers are named for abstract qualities; coastal minesweepers are named for birds; the older fleet minesweepers carry names of both series ("bird" names were exhausted by World War II mine craft programmes); inshore minesweepers are named for seaboard features.

AFFRAY (MSO 511)   *1969, United States Navy*

45 OCEAN MINESWEEPERS (MSO): "AGILE" CLASS

Name	No.	Launched	Commissioned
AGILE	MSO 421	19 Nov 1955	21 June 1956
AGGRESSIVE	MSO 422	4 Oct 1952	25 Nov 1953
BOLD	MSO 424	14 Mar 1953	25 Sep 1953
BULWARK	MSO 425	14 Mar 1953	12 Nov 1953
*CONSTANT	MSO 427	14 Feb 1952	8 Sep 1954
*DASH	MSO 428	20 Sep 1952	14 Aug 1953
*DETECTOR	MSO 429	5 Dec 1952	26 Jan 1954
*DIRECT	MSO 430	27 May 1953	9 July 1954
*DOMINANT	MSO 431	5 Nov 1953	8 Nov 1954
*ENGAGE	MSO 433	18 June 1953	29 June 1954
EMBATTLE	MSO 434	27 Aug 1953	16 Nov 1954
*ENDURANCE	MSO 435	9 Aug 1952	19 May 1954
*ENERGY	MSO 436	13 Feb 1953	16 July 1954
*ENHANCE	MSO 437	11 Oct 1952	16 Apr 1955
*ESTEEM	MSO 438	20 Dec 1952	10 Sep 1955
*EXCEL	MSO 439	25 Sep 1953	24 Feb 1955
*EXPLOIT	MSO 440	10 Apr 1953	31 Mar 1954
*EXULTANT	MSO 441	6 June 1953	22 June 1954
*FEARLESS	MSO 442	17 July 1953	22 Sep 1954
*FIDELITY	MSO 443	21 Aug 1953	19 Jan 1955
*FIRM	MSO 444	15 Apr 1953	12 Oct 1954
*FORCE	MSO 445	26 June 1953	4 Jan 1955
*FORTIFY	MSO 446	14 Feb 1953	16 July 1954
*ILLUSIVE	MSO 448	12 July 1952	14 Nov 1953
*IMPERVIOUS	MSO 449	29 Aug 1952	15 July 1954
*IMPLICIT	MSO 455	1 Aug 1953	10 Mar 1954
*INFLICT	MSO 456	6 Oct 1953	11 May 1954
*LOYALTY	MSO 457	22 Nov 1953	11 June 1954
LUCID	MSO 458	14 Nov 1953	4 May 1955
NIMBLE	MSO 459	6 Aug 1954	11 May 1955
OBSERVER	MSO 461	19 Oct 1954	31 Aug 1955
PINNACLE	MSO 462	3 Jan 1955	21 Oct 1955
*PLUCK	MSO 464	6 Feb 1954	11 Aug 1954
PRIME	MSO 466	27 May 1954	11 Oct 1954
REAPER	MSO 467	25 June 1954	10 Nov 1954
SKILL	MSO 471	23 Apr 1955	7 Nov 1955
VIGOR	MSO 473	24 June 1953	8 Nov 1954
VITAL	MSO 474	12 Aug 1953	9 June 1955
*CONQUEST	MSO 488	20 May 1954	20 July 1955
*GALLANT	MSO 489	4 June 1954	14 Sep 1955
*LEADER	MSO 490	15 Sep 1954	16 Nov 1955
*PLEDGE	MSO 492	20 July 1955	20 Apr 1956
STURDY	MSO 494	28 Jan 1956	23 Oct 1957
SWERVE	MSO 495	1 Nov 1955	27 July 1957
VENTURE	MSO 496	27 Nov 1956	3 Feb 1958

Displacement, tons	665 light; 750 full load
Dimensions, feet	165 wl; 172 × 36 × 13·6
Guns	1—40 mm AA; 2—·50 cal MG (replaced by 2—20 mm AA in several ships)
Main engines	4 Packard diesels; 2 shafts; controllable pitch propellers; 2 280 bhp = 15·5 knots; *Dash, Detector, Direct* and *Dominant,* have 4 GM diesels; 1 520 bhp (see *Modernisation* notes)
Complement	72 to 76

These ships were built on the basis of mine warfare experience in the Korean War (1950-1953); they have wooden hulls and non-magnetic equipment. *Bold* and *Bulwark* were built by the Norfolk (Virginia) Naval Shipyard; others by private yards. Initially designated as minesweepers (AM); reclassified as ocean minesweepers (MSO) in Feb 1955. Originally fitted with UQS-1 mine detecting sonar.
Beginning in 1970 a number of these ships were decommissioned and placed in reserve or assigned to Naval Reserve training. The ships assigned to the NRT role in 1971-1972 are: *Dash, Detector, Direct, Dominant, Embattle,* and *Reaper.*

ENGINEERING. Diesel engines are fabricated on non-magnetic stainless steel alloy to help reduce possibility of detonating magnetic mines. Endurance is 2 400 miles at ten knots.

MODERNISATION. The 62 ocean minesweepers in commission during the mid-1960s all were to have been modernised; estimated cost and schedule per ship were $5 000 000 and ten months in shipyard. However, some of the early modernisations took as long as 26 months which, coupled with changes in mine countermeasure techniques, led to cancellation of programme after 13 ships were modernised: MSO 433, 437, 438, 441-443, 445, 446, 448, 449, 456, 488, and 490.
The modernisation provided improvements in mine detection, engines, communications, and habitability; four Waukesha Motor Co diesel engines installed (plus two or three

Mine Warfare Ships—*continued*

"AGILE" CLASS *continued*

diesel generators for sweep gear), SQQ-14 sonar with mine classification as well as detection capability provided, twin 20 mm AA mount installed (replacing single 40 mm because of space requirements for sonar hoist mechanism), habitability improved, and advanced communications equipment fitted. Complement in modernised ships is 6 officers and 70 enlisted men.

Some MSOs have received SQQ-14 sonar but not full modernisation (see *Endurance* photo).

TRANSFERS. 36 ships of this type were transferred to NATO navies upon completion; 5 to Belgium: MSO 503, 504, 515, 516, 522; 15 to France: MSO 475-477, 500-502, 505, 512-514, 450-454; 4 to Italy: MSO 506, 507, 517, 518; 6 to the Netherlands: MSO 480-485; 2 to Norway: MSO 498 and 499 (subsequently retransferred to Belgium); 4 ships to Portugal: MSO 478, 479, 486, 487. MSO 451 retransferred to Uruguay in 1970.
Conflict MSO 426, *Dynamic* MSO 432, *Guide* MSO 447, *Pivot* MSO 463 and *Persistant* MSO 491 to Spain in 1971.

DISPOSALS
Prestige MSO 456 stricken on 23 Aug 1958 (grounding); **Stalwart** MSO 493 stricken on 1 Mar 1967 (fire); **Avenge** MSO 423 stricken on 1 Feb 1970 (fire); **Sagacity** MSO 469 stricken on 1 Oct 1970 (grounding); **Notable** MSO 460, **Rival** MSO 468, **Salute** MSO 470, **Valor** MSO 472 stricken on 1 Feb 1971.

ENDURANCE (MSO 435)　　　　　　　　　*United States Navy*

EXPLOIT (MSO 440)　　　　　　　*1969, United States Navy*

ENERGY (MSO 436)　　　　　*1968, United States Navy*

14 COASTAL MINESWEEPERS (MSC): "BLUEBIRD" CLASS

Name	No.	Launched	Commissioned
*BLUEBIRD	MSC 121	11 May 1953	24 July 1953
COMORANT	MSC 122	8 June 1953	14 Aug 1953
*KINGBIRD	MSC 194	21 May 1954	27 Apr 1955
*PARROT	MSC 197	27 Nov 1954	28 June 1955
*PEACOCK	MSC 198	19 June 1954	7 Feb 1955
*PHOEBE	MSC 199	21 Aug 1954	29 Apr 1955
*SHRIKE	MSC 201	21 July 1954	21 Mar 1955
*THRASHER	MSC 203	6 Oct 1954	16 Aug 1955
*THRUSH	MSC 204	5 Jan 1955	8 Nov 1955
*VIREO	MSC 205	30 Apr 1954	7 June 1955
*WARBLER	MSC 206	18 June 1954	16 July 1955
*WHIPPOORWILL	MSC 207	13 Aug 1954	20 Oct 1955
*WIDGEON	MSC 208	15 Oct 1954	28 Nov 1955
*WOODPECKER	MSC 209	7 Jan 1955	3 Feb 1956

Displacement, tons	320 light; 370 full load
Dimensions, feet	138 pp; 144 oa × 28 × 8·2
Guns	2—20 mm AA (twin)
Main engines	2 GM diesels; 2 shafts; 880 bhp = 12 knots (MSC 200-209); Packard engines; 2 shafts; 1 200 bhp = 12·5 knots; (MSC 121, 122, 190-199)
Complement	39

Constructed throughout of wood and other materials with the lowest possible magnetic attraction to attain the greatest possible safety factor when sweeping for magnetic mines. Fitted with UQS-1 sonar. Endurance is 2 500 miles at ten knots.
Only named vessels AMS 121, 122, 190-209 were commissioned into US Navy with MSC 200 and 202 being transferred to Spain in 1959 (replaced by MSC 298 and 290 in US Navy)
An additional 167 coastal minesweepers of this design were built in US private ship-yards for NATO and other allied navies (see *Transfers*).
Of the surviving US ships, all are operational Naval Reserve training ships except *Comorant* which is in reserve.

TRANSFERS. 18 to Italy: AMS 72-76, 79-82, 88-90, 113-137, 280. 18 to Belgium: AMS 63-65, 77, 78, 101, 103, 104, 131, 151-154, 169-171, 259, 260. 8 to Denmark: AMS 127, 128, 129, MSC 221, 256, 257, 263, 264. 30 to France: AMS 66-71, 83-87, 93, 94, 96-99, 113-120, 124-126, 141-142. 14 to Netherlands: AMS 100, 105-112, 148-150, 167, 168. 2 to Norway: AMS 102, 132. 8 to Portugal: AMS 60 (ex-USS *Adjutant*), 61, 62, 91, 92, 145-147. 12 to Spain: AMS 130, 139, 143, 220, 265, 266, MSC 200 (ex-USS *Redwing*), MSC 202 (ex-USS *Spoonbill*), MSC 269, 279, 287, 288. 4 to Japan: AMS 95, 144, 255, 258. 8 to Pakistan: AMS 138, 261, 262, 267, 273, 274, 293, 294. 9 to Turkey: 268, 270, 271, 272, 304, 305, 311, 312, 316. 4 to Iran: MSC 275, 276, 291, 292. 8 to Taiwan, China: AMS 123, 140, MSC 277, 278, 300, 302, 306, 307. 3 to Vietnam: MSC 281, 282, 283. 6 to Korea: MSC 284, 285, 286, 295, 296, 316. 2 to Philippines: MSC 218, 219. 9 to Greece: MSC 298, 299, 308, 309, 310, 314, 317, 318, 319. 4 to Thailand: MSC 297, 301, 303, 313. 6 to Indonesia: *Falcon* MSC 190, *Frigate Bird* MSC 191, *Humming Bird* MAC 192, *Jacana* MSC 193, *Limpkin* MSC 195, *Meadow Lark* MSC 196 (transferred in 1971).

CANCELLATION. AMS 155 to 166 were reserved for German built vessels, but the order and numbers were cancelled.

CLASSIFICATION. All the early vessels formerly known as Auxiliary Motor mine-sweepers (AMS) were reclassified as Coastal Minesweepers, (MSC) in Feb 1955.

DISPOSALS
The **Albatross** (MSC 289) and **Gannet** (MSC 290) of a slightly modified design were stricken on 1 Apr 1970.

PEACOCK (MSC 198)　　　　　　　*United States Navy*

Mine Warfare Ships—continued

BLUEBIRD (MSC 121)   1967, United States Navy

KINGBIRD (MSC 194)   United States Navy

25 FLEET MINESWEEPERS (MSF): "AUK" CLASS

Name	No.	Launched	Commissioned
BROADBILL	MSF 58	21 May 1942	13 Oct 1942
STARLING	MSF 64	11 Apr 1942	21 Dec 1942
HERALD	MSF 101	4 July 1942	23 Mar 1942
PILOT	MSF 104	5 July 1942	3 Feb 1943
PIONEER	MSF 105	26 July 1942	27 Feb 1943
SAGE	MSF 111	21 Nov 1942	23 Aug 1943
SWAY	MSF 120	29 Sep 1942	20 July 1943
SWIFT	MSF 122	5 Dec 1942	29 Dec 1943
SYMBOL	MSF 123	2 July 1942	10 Dec 1942
THREAT	MSF 124	15 Aug 1942	14 Mar 1943
VELOCITY	MSF 128	19 Apr 1942	3 Apr 1943
CHAMPION	MSF 314	12 Dec 1942	8 Sep 1943
CHIEF	MSF 315	5 Jan 1943	9 Oct 1943
COMPETANT	MSF 316	9 Jan 1943	10 Nov 1943
DEFENSE	MSF 317	18 Feb 1943	10 Jan 1944
DEVASTATOR	MSF 318	19 Apr 1943	12 Jan 1944
GLADIATOR	MSF 319	7 May 1943	25 Feb 1944
IMPECCABLE	MSF 320	21 May 1943	24 Apr 1944
SPEAR	MSF 322	25 Feb 1943	31 Dec 1943
ARDENT	MSF 340	22 June 1943	25 May 1944
ROSELLE	MSF 379	29 Aug 1945	6 Feb 1945
SCOTER	MSF 381	26 Sep 1945	17 Mar 1945
SPRIG	MSF 384	15 Sep 1944	4 Apr 1945
TERCEL	MSF 386	16 Dec 1944	21 Aug 1945
WHEATEAR	MSF 390	21 Apr 1945	3 Oct 1945

Displacement, tons	890 standard; 1 250 full load
Dimensions, feet	215 wl; 221·2 oa × 32·2 × 10·8
Guns	1—3 in, 50 cal dp; 2—40 mm AA (single) or 4—40 mm AA (twin) in MSF 314-341 series.
Main engines	Diesel electric; 2 shafts; 3 118-3 532 bhp = 18·1 knots
Complement	9 officers and 96 enlisted men in ships numbered up to MSF 340; 10 officers and 107 enlisted men in later ships.

Steel hulled. This design embraced hull numbers (originally AM) 57-65, 100-131, 100-131, 314-341, and 371-390. All are in the Reserve Fleet. It is anticipated that all of these ships will be stricken from the Navy List in the near future.

RECLASSIFICATION. All the above, formerly known as Ocean Minesweepers (AM) were reclassified as Fleet Minesweepers, (steel-hulled) MSF in Feb 1955. *Prevail* (AM 107), *Pursuit* (AM 108), *Requisite* (AM 109) and *Sheldrake* (AM 62) were reclassified as survey ships (AGS) in 1952 and *Towhee* (MSF 388) in Apr 1964. *Surfbird* (MSF 383) was reclassified as a degaussing vessel (ADG) on 18 May 1957. *Tanager*, MSF 385, was transferred to the Coast Guard on 1 Nov 1963. Designation of *Peregrine*, MSF 373, was changed to AG 176 on 1 Apr 1964.

TRANSFERS. *Strive*, MSF 17, *Sustain* MSF 119, *Seer* MSF 112, and *Triumph* MSF 323, converted and reclassified as coastal minelayers MMC 1, MMC 2, MMC 5, and MMC 3, respectively, transferred to Norway in 1959-60, *Ruddy* MSF 380 and *Shoveler* MSF 382 to Peru in 1960, *Ptarmigan* MSF 376 to Korea on 25 July 1963, *Murrelet* MSF 372 to Philippines in June 1965, *Redstart* MSF 378, *Toucan* MSF 387, to Taiwan China in Dec 1964, and *Waxwing* MSF 389, in Aug 1965, *Chickadee* MSF 59 to Uruguay in Aug 1966, *Dextrous*, MSF 341 and *Speed* MSF 116 to South Korea in 1967, *Vigilance* MSF 324 to Philippines in 1967, *Steady* MSF 118 to Taiwan China in 1968.

"AUK" CLASS continued

DISPOSALS

Auk MSF 57 was stricken from the list of naval vessels on 1 Aug 1959, and **Raven** MSF 55, **Nuthatch** MSF 60, **Heed** MSF 100, **Pheasant** MSF 61, **Motive** MSF 102, **Oracle** MSF 103, **Revenge** MSF 110, **Staff** MSF 114, **Token** MSF 126, **Tumult** MSF 127, **Zeal** MSF 131, **Pigeon** MSF 374, **Pochard** MSF 375 and **Quail** MSF 377 stricken in 1967.

WAXWING (MSF 389) (to Nationalist China)   Ted Stone

4 FLEET MINESWEEPERS (MSF):

"ADMIRABLE" CLASS

Name	No.	Launched	Commissioned
COUNSEL	MSF 165	17 Feb 1943	27 May 1944
CRUISE	MSF 215	21 Mar 1943	21 Sep 1945
SPECTRE	MSF 306	15 Feb 1944	30 Aug 1944
SUPERIOR	MSF 311	11 May 1944	1 Nov 1944

Displacement, tons	650 standard; 945 full load
Dimensions, feet	180 wl; 184·5 oa × 33 × 10
Main engines	2 diesels; 1 701 shp; 2 shafts = 15 knots
Guns	1—3 in 50 cal DP; 4—40 mm AA (twin)
Complement	104

Steel Hulled. Appearance varies according to the builders. Some have a funnel. *Cruise*, completed by Charleston Navy Yard, was armed with only 2—40 mm guns. This design embraced hull numbers (originally AM) 136-165, 214-311, 351-366, and 391-420.
All in the Atlantic Reserve Fleet except *Counsel*, Pacific Reserve Fleet. *Prowess*, MSF 280, employed as a naval reserve training ship and redesignated IX 305 on 18 Feb 1966; transferred to South Vietnam on 4 June 1970.

RECLASSIFICATION. All the above minesweepers, formerly known as Fleet Minesweepers (AM) were reclassified as Fleet Minesweepers MSF in Feb 1955.

TRANSFERS. 34 of this class were transferred to the Soviet Navy in 1943, and 13 to the Chinese Navy. *Gayety*, MSF 329 and *Sentry* MSF 299 were transferred to the Vietnamese Navy in June 1962 and Aug 1962, respectively, and *Serene*. MSF 300 and *Shelter* MSF 301, in Jan 1964, *Crag* MSF 214, *Device* MSF 220, *Diploma* MSF 221, *Dour* MSF 223, *Eager* MSF 224, *Execute* MSF 232, *Facility* MSF 233, *Hilarity* MSF 241, *Instill* MSF 252, *Intrigue* MSF 253, *Invade* MSF 254, *Jubilant* MSF 255, *Knave* MSF 256, *Ransom* MSF 283, *Rebel* MSF 284, *Recruit* MSF 285, *Scout* MAF 296, *Scuffle* MSF 298, *Success* MSF 310 and *Harlequin* MSF 365, to Mexico in Oct 1962. *Report* MSF 289 was transferred to the army in Apr 1963. *Craddock* MSF 356 to Burma on 31 Mar 1967, *Signet* MSF 302 and *Skirmish* MSF 303 to the Dominican Republic in 13 Jan 1965.

LOSSES. *Salute* AM 294, was lost in the Second World War. *Pirate* (AM 275) and *Pledge* (AM 277) of this class struck mines and sank off Wonsan, Korean east coast on 12 Oct 1950.

DISPOSALS

Control MSF 164, was stricken from the Navy List on 13 Mar 1948 and disposed of in 1959, *Clamour* MSF 160, *Climax* MSF 161, *Compel* MSF 162, *Concise* MSF 163, *Incredible* MSF 249, *Mainstay* MSF 261, *Reign* MSF 288, *Dipper* MSF 357, and *Harrier* MSF 366, on 1 Dec 1960. *Change* MSF 159, *Density* MSF 218, *Design* MSF 219, *Garland* MSF 238, *Opponent* MSF 269 and *Scrimmage* MSF 297, at the end of 1960, *Inaugural* MSF 242 in 1961. *Gadwall* MSF 362 on 1 Nov 1966. *Scurry* MSF 304 stricken 1 May 1967. *Hazard* MSF 240 stricken 1 Nov 1967. **Staunch** MSF 307, **Strategy** MSF 308, **Strength** MSF 309, stricken 1 Apr 1967, (subsequently reacquired in late 1968 for use as a salvage hulk in the Potomac River to train divers).
Graylag MSF 364 stricken 1 Oct 1967

DISPOSALS OF OTHER CLASSES

All 29 of the converted minehunters of the underwater locator type (8 former coastal minesweepers of the YMS class and 21 former large infantry landing ships of the LSIL class) were stricken on 1 Nov 1959 or 1 Jan 1960. See names, former numbers, and full particulars on page 433 of the 1959-1960 edition. **Bittern** (MHC 43), a prototype Coastal Mine Hunter built in 1955-1957 has been on loan to commercial operator since July 1966; she remains on Navy List.

All coastal minesweepers of the "Albatross" class have been stricken, the last having been the **Ruff** (MSCO 54, ex-YMS 372), stricken on 14 Nov 1969. These ships are listed in the 1969-1970 and previous editions.

Mine Warfare Craft—*continued*

MSB in South China Sea   MSS 1   1969, United States Navy

1 SPECIAL MINESWEEPER (MSS)

*MSS 1 (ex-*Harry L. Gluckman*)

Displacement, tons	15 000 full load
Dimensions, feet	441·5 oa × 57
Main engines	5 outboard deck mounted diesels = 10 knots
Complement	9 (1 officer, 8 enlisted men)

A "Liberty" ship converted to explode pressure mines. Specially modified to withstand mine explosions and remain afloat and underway. Conversion authorised in Fiscal Year 1966 and work began at American Shipbuilding Co, Lorain, Ohio, in Aug 1966; completed late in May 1969. EC2-S-C1 design.

(Ten "Liberty" ships were partially modified in 1952-1953 to explode pressure mines. Only one ship placed in service, the ex-*John L. Sullivan* as YAG-37. Fitted with four T-34 turbo-prop aircraft engines on deck and stuffed with buoyancy material. She was employed in mine countermeasures experiments until reduced to a floating wreck; scrapped in 1958.)

1 INSHORE MINESWEEPER (MSI): "COVE" CLASS

CAPE MSI 2

Displacement, tons	120 light; 240 full load
Dimensions, feet	105 × 22 × 10
Main engines	2 GM diesels; 1 shaft; 650 bhp = 12 knots
Complement	21 (3 officers, 18 men)
Guns	1—·50 calibre MG

The *Cape* and a sister ship *Cove* (MSI 1) were prototype inshore minesweepers authorised under the Fiscal Year 1956 new construction programme. Both built at Bethlehem Shipyards Co, Bellingham, Washington. *Cape* laid down on 1 May 1957, launched on 5 Apr 1968, and placed in service on 27 Feb 1959. Late in 1969 the *Cape* became an operational Naval Reserve training ship and was taken out of service and placed in reserve in July 1970.

MSI 3-10 were built in the Netherlands for the Dutch Navy under US Military Assistance Programme; MSI 11 and MSI 12 built in Denmark under MAP; MSI 13 and MSI 14 built in United States for Iran; MSI 15-19 built in United States for Turkey.

DISPOSAL

Cove MSI 1 stricken on 31 July 1970 (transferred to Johns Hopkins Applied Physics Laboratory).

CAPE MSI 2   1968, United States Navy

MSB 32   1968, US Navy

Minesweeping Boats—*continued*

MSB in South China Sea   1967, United States Navy

39 MINESWEEPING BOATS (MSB)

MSB 5	MSB 13	MSB 21	MSB 31	MSB 38	MSB 47
MSB 6	MSB 15	MSB 25	MSB 32	MSB 39	MSB 48
MSB 7	MSB 16	MSB 26	MSB 33	MSB 40	MSB 50
MSB 8	MSB 17	MSB 27	MSB 34	MSB 41	MSB 51
MSB 9	MSB 18	MSB 28	MSB 35	MSB 42	MSB 52
MSB 10	MSB 19	MSB 29	MSB 36	MSB 44	MSB 53
MSB 11		MSB 30		MSB 46	

Displacement, tons	30 light; 39 full load except MSB 29, 80 full load
Dimensions, feet	57·2 × 15·5 × 4 except MSB 29, 82 × 19 × 5·5
Guns	several MG (Vietnam configuration)
Main engines	2 geared diesels (Packard); 2 shafts; 600 hp = 12 knots
Complement	6 (enlisted; increased to 7 when deployed)

Wooden-hull minesweepers intended to be carried to theatre of operations by large assault ships; however, they are too large to be easily handled by cranes and assigned to sweeping harbours. From 1966 to Sep 1970 they were used extensively in Vietnam for river operations.

With the post-Vietnam restructuring of the Navy's mine countermeasure forces the MSBs are having their sweep gear removed and are being employed as utility craft. Several are being assigned as operational Naval Reserve training ships, especially in the Great Lakes area.

MSB 1-4 were ex-Army minesweepers built in 1946 (since discarded), MSB 5-54 (less MSB 24) were completed in 1952-1956. MSB 24 was not built. MSB 29 built to enlarged design by John Trumpy & Sons, Annapolis, Maryland in an effort to improve seakeeping ability.

Normally commanded by chief petty officer or petty officer first class.

ENGINEERING. MSB 5 was the first vessel built for the US Navy with gas turbine engines (to provide power for the boat's generators). 48 MSBs fitted with gas turbine generators.

GUNNERY. MSBs serving in South Vietnam were fitted with several machine guns and removable fibreglass armour.

DISPOSALS, LOSSES, AND TRANSFERS

MSB 23 destroyed by fire on 2 Feb 1955 while under construction; rebuilt as an experimental glass-reinforced plastic craft and delivered to the Navy in Aug 1956 for research.

MSB 1 and **MSB 3** stricken in 1958, **MSB 2** to South Korea and **MSB 4** to Taiwan China in Dec 1961, **MSB 12** stricken in 1964, **MSB 54** sunk by mine in Vietnam on 31 Oct 1966, **MSB 14** sunk after collision with merchantman near Saigon on 14 Jan 1967, **MSB 43** sunk after collision with dolphin on 20 Jan 1967, **MSB 45** sunk by mine in Vietnam on 15 Feb 1967, **MSB 49** stricken in Sep 1967 (mine damaged), **MSB 22** stricken in 1968, **MSB 11** and **MSB 37** stricken in 1970.

Mine Warfare Craft—*continued*

MSR controlling MSD in Mekong Delta, South Vietnam

1969, US Navy, PH3 James A. Fallon

MINESWEEPING LAUNCHES (MSL)

Displacement, pounds	23 100 full load
Hoisting weight, pounds	18 500
Dimensions, feet	36 oa × 11·6 × 3·7
Main engines	Gas turbine; 1 shaft; 200 shp=12 knots or geared diesel; 1 shaft; 160 shp = 10 knots
Complement	4 to 6 enlisted men

Versatile minesweeping craft intended to sweep for acoustic, magnetic, and moored mines in inshore waters and in advance of landing craft. They were carried by large amphibious ships to assault areas.

With the post-Vietnam restructuring of the Navy's mine countermeasure forces the MSLs have been stripped of their sweep gear and are being employed as utility launches.

CONSTRUCTION. MSL 1-4 completed in 1946 (wood hull, gas turbine); MSL 5-29 completed in 1948 (wood hull, gas turbine); MSL 30 completed in 1948 (plastic hull, gas turbine); MSL 31-56 completed in 1966 (plastic hull; geared diesel); three wood hull boats converted to geared diesel in 1967.

MSL 11, MSL 17, MSL 14   *1967, United States Navy*

4 PATROL MINESWEEPERS (MSR): MODIFIED ASPB

Dimensions, feet	50 oa × 17
Guns	2—·50 cal MG; 1 or 2—·30 cal MG
Main engines	2 diesels; 2 shafts = 20 knots

Modified ASPB design fitted with bow mine deflector and minesweeping gear to sweep moored and bottom mines in shallow water.

Four of these craft are retained by the US Navy for use at the Naval Inshore Warfare Training Centre.

The photo at the top of the page shows an MSR with four 3·5 inch rocket tubes on either side of the ·50 cal twin "turret".

PATROL MINESWEEPER (MSR)   *1969, United States Navy*

2 RIVER MINESWEEPERS (MSM): PROGRAMME V

Dimensions, feet	56 × 17·5 × 4·5
Guns	2—20 mm; 1—50 cal MG; 2—40 mm grenade launchers
Main engines	2 diesels; 2 shafts = 10 knots (maximum; minesweeping speed is 8 knots)
Complement	4 or 5 (enlisted)

These craft were converted from LCM-6 landing craft for river minesweeping. Heavily armoured. The 20 mm guns are in amidships "turrets", one to port and one to starboard. These craft can sweep moored and bottom mines in shallow water.

Two of these craft are retained by the US Navy.

RIVER MINESWEEPER (MSM)   *1968, United States Navy*

RIVER MINESWEEPER (MSM)   *1968, United States Navy*

4 DRONE MINESWEEPERS (MSD)

Displacement, tons	2·5
Dimensions, feet	23 oa × 8 × 1·5
Main engines	Gasoline engine with outboard drive; 250 hp = 15 to 20 knots in unmanned operation; 30+ knots with operator on board

Small, reinforced plastic minesweeping launch intended for unmanned (drone) operations in river areas; radio controlled; V-8 inboard engine.

Four of these craft remain in US service; others transferred to South Vietnam.

DRONE MINESWEEPER (MSD)   *1969, United States Navy*

UNDERWAY REPLENISHMENT SHIPS

8 AMMUNITION SHIPS (AE): "KILAUEA" CLASS

Name	No.	Laid down	Launched	Commissioned
*KILAUEA	AE 26	10 Mar 1966	9 Aug 1967	10 Aug 1968
*BUTTE	AE 27	21 July 1966	9 Aug 1967	29 Nov 1968
*SANTA BARBARA	AE 28	20 Dec 1966	23 Jan 1968	July 1970
*MOUNT HOOD	AE 29	8 May 1967	17 July 1968	Jan 1971
FLINT	AE 32	4 Aug 1969	9 Nov 1970	late 1971
SHASTA	AE 33	10 Nov 1969	3 Apr 1971	late 1971
MOUNT BAKER	AE 34	13 Apr 1970	Sep 1971	early 1971
KISKA	AE 35	July 1970		early 1972

Displacement, tons	20 500 full load
Dimensions, feet	565 oa × 81 × 25·7
Guns	8—3 in 50 cal AA (twin)
Helicopters	Normally assigned two UH-46 cargo helicopters
Main engines	Geared turbines; 1 shaft = 20+ knots
Boilers	2
Complement	401 (28 officers, 373 enlisted men)

A new class of improved ammunition ships, easily identified by amidships position of superstructure. Fitted with helicopter facilities aft and the Fast Automatic Shuttle Transfer (FAST) system for underway replenishment of missiles to combatant ships. Estimated cost per ship is $32 700 000. AE 26 and 27 authorised in Fiscal Year 1965 shipbuilding programme; AE 28 and 29 in FY 1966, AE 32 and 33 in FY 1967, and AE 34 and 35 in FY 1968. *Kilauea* and *Butte* built by General Dynamics Corp, Quincy Division; *Mount Hood* and *Santa Barbara* by Bethlehem Steel Corp, Sparrows Point, Maryland; AE 32-35 being built by Ingalls Shipbuilding Corp (Litton Systems), Pascagoula.

GUNNERY. 3 inch guns in twin mounts, two closed mounts forward and two open mounts amidships.

NOMENCLATURE. Ammunition ships are named for volcanoes and explosives (eg *Nitro* for nitroglycerine and *Pyro* for pyrotechnic).

KILAUEA (AE 26)   1969, US Navy, J. R. Andrews

5 AMMUNITION SHIPS (AE): "SURIBACHI" CLASS

Name	No.	Laid down	Launched	Commissioned
*SURIBACHI	AE 21	31 Jan 1955	2 Nov 1955	17 Nov 1956
*MAUNA KEA	AE 22	16 May 1955	3 May 1956	30 Mar 1957
*NITRO	AE 23	20 May 1957	25 June 1958	1 May 1959
*PYRO	AE 24	21 Oct 1957	5 Nov 1958	24 July 1959
*HALEAKALA	AE 25	10 Mar 1958	17 Feb 1959	3 Nov 1959

"SURIBACHI" CLASS continued

Displacement, tons	7 470 light; 10 000 standard; 17 500 full load
Measurement, tons	7,500 deadweight
Dimensions, feet	512 oa × 72 × 29
Guns	4—3 in, 50 cal AA (twin)
Main engines	Steam turbines; 1 shaft; 16 000 hp = 21 knots
Boilers	2
Complement	316 (18 officers, 298 men)

CONSTRUCTION. Designed especially to meet the strenuous requirements of rapid replenishment at sea. Built from the hull up as Navy ships. Elevators fitted for internal handling of ammunition and explosives, up-to-date methods of stowage, air conditioning, improved crew quarters. All built by Bethlehem, Sparrows Point, Md Shipyard. Another ship of this class to have been built under the 1959 programme was cancelled. All of these ships are active.

CONVERSION. All five ships of this class have undergone "conversion" to the Fast Automatic Shuttle Transfer (FAST) configuration, the *Haleakala* and *Suribachi* under the Fiscal Year 1963 conversion programme and the three other ships under the FY 1964 programme.
Three holds modified for missile stowage (up to and including Talos), mechanised handling to move missiles from stowage to transfer stations, and FAST to transfer missiles to warships alongside.
Two after 3 inch twin gun, mounts removed and helicopter platform fitted.

HALEAKALA (AE 25).   1968. United States Navy

7 AMMUNITION SHIPS (AE): "WRANGELL" CLASS

Name	No.	Launched	Commissioned
WRANGELL (ex-*Midnight*)	AE 12	14 Apr 1944	28 May 1944
FIREDRAKE (ex-*Winged Racer*)	AE 14	12 May 1944	27 Dec 1944
*VESUVIUS (ex-*Gamecock*)	AE 15	26 May 1944	3 July 1944
*MOUNT KATMAI	AE 16	6 Jan 1945	21 July 1945
*GREAT SITKIN	AE 17	20 Jan 1945	11 Aug 1945
PARICUTIN	AE 18	30 Jan 1945	25 July 1945
*DIAMOND HEAD	AE 19	3 Feb 1945	9 Aug 1945

Displacement, tons	6 350 light; 15 295 full load
Dimensions, feet	435 wl; 459·2 oa × 63 × 28·2
Guns	2 or 4—3 in, 50 cal AA (single)
Main engines	Geared turbines, 6 000 shp; 1 shaft = 16·4 knots
Boilers	2
Complement	267

C2 type. The 5 inch gun and four 40 mm AA guns were removed. *Firedrake, Mount Katmai* and *Paricutin* have helicopter platform installed aft and two after 3 inch guns removed.

All built by North Carolina SB Co. Wilmington, North Carolina. The *Mount Hood* AE 11 of this type was sunk in World War II. Officially considered "Mount Hood" class. Three ships decommissioned and placed in reserve 1970-1971.

BUTTE (AE 27)   1970, United States Navy, PH1 W. M. Welch

Underway Replenishment Ships—*continued*

MOUNT KATMAI (AE 16) *1969, US Navy, PH1 A. Choy*

FIREDRAKE (AE 14) *1967, US Navy*

GREAT SITKIN (AE 17) *1968, US Navy*

1 AMMUNITION SHIP (AE): CONVERTED AKA

Name	No.	Launched	Commissioned
*CHARA	AE 31 (ex-AKA 58)	15 Mar 1944	14 June 1944

Displacement, tons	7 430 light; 14 000 full load
Dimensions, feet	434 wl; 459·2 oa × 63 × 24
Guns	4—3 in 50 cal (single)
Main engines	Geared turbines; 6 000 shp = 15·5 knots
Boilers	2 Foster-Wheeler

Former Attack Cargo Ship. Transferred to Maritime Administration Reserve Fleet in 1961; reacquired by Navy in 1965 and refitted as ammunition ship; recommissioned in 1966. Built by Federal SB & DD Co, Kearney, New Jersey. **Virgo**, AE 30 ex-AKA 20 ex-AK 69, stricken on 18 Feb 1971.

CHARA (AE 31) *1967. United States Navy*

1 AMMUNITION SHIP (AE): "LASSEN" CLASS

Name	No.	Launched	Commissioned
MAUNA LOA	AE 8	14 Apr 1943	27 Oct 1943

Displacement, tons	5 220 light; 14 225 full load
Dimensions, feet	435 wl; 495·2 oa × 63 × 26·5
Guns	2 —3 in. 50 cal AA (single)
Main engines	2 Nordberg diesels; 6 000 bhp = 15·3 knots
Complement	281

Built by the Tampa SB Co. Modified C2 type, converted by Navy. Carries 5 000 tons cargo. *Mauna Loa* transferred to Maritime Administration reserve in 1960; reacquired and returned to the Navy in Sep 1961 and recommissioned on 27 Nov 1961; fitted with helicopter platform aft. Decommissioned and placed in reserve in 1970.

Note helicopter platform in photograph of *Mauna Loa*; shadow from overhang of forward 3 inch gun "tubs".

DISPOSALS
Akutan AE 13 stricken in 1961, **Lassen** AE 3 stricken on 1 July 1961, **Mount Baker** AE 4 stricken on 2 Dec 1969, **Shasta** AE 6 stricken on 1 July 1969, **Rainier** AE 5 stricken on 7 Aug 1970, **Mazama** AE 9 stricken on 1 Sep 1970.
Of the two ammunition ships of the "Sangay" class, **Sangay**, AE 10, was stricken in 1961 and **Formalhaut**, AE 20 ex-AK 22 transferred to Maritime Administration in Sep 1962.

MAUNA LOA (AE 8) *1965. United States Navy*

MAUNA KEA (AE 22) *1968, United States Navy*

Underway Replenishment Ships—continued

5 STORE SHIPS (AF): R2-BV1 TYPE

Name	No.	Launched	Commissioned
ZELIMA (ex-*Golden Rocket*)	AF 49	2 Mar 1945	27 July 1946
***ARCTURUS** (ex-*Golden Eagle*)	AF 52	15 Mar 1942	18 Nov 1961
PICTOR (ex-*Great Republic*)	AF 54	4 June 1942	13 Sep 1950
ALUDRA (ex-*Matchless*)	AF 55	14 Oct 1944	7 July 1952
PROCYON (ex-*Flying Scud*)	AF 61	1 July 1942	24 Nov 1961

Displacement, tons	6 914 light; 15 500 full load
Dimensions, feet	459·2 oa × 63 × 28
Boilers	2
Complement	17 officers, 275 men
Guns	4—40 mm (twin); *Aludra*: 8—3 in 50 cal (twin)
Main engines	Geared turbines; 6 000 shp = 16·4 knots

All built by Moore Dry Dock Co and launched in 1945 and 1946. R2-S-BV1 design reefer type. *Aludra* was acquired for conversion by the Navy. *Pictor* was transferred from Maritime Administration to US Navy. C2-S-B1 type similar to R2-S-BV1 design, except that R2s were built as reefers and C2s as cargo ships. Same type as "Eagle" class. *Procyon* was acquired from the Maritime Administration and commissioned in Nov 1961.

All except *Arcturus* have been decommissioned; in Navy and Maritime Administration reserve fleets with all five ships listed remaining on Navy List.

DISPOSALS
Sirius AF 60 stricken in 1965 (Mar Ad reserve); **Bellatrix** AF 62 stricken on 1 Oct 1968 (scrapped); **Alstede** AF 48 stricken on 31 Oct 1969 (Mar Ad reserve).

PROCYON (AF 61)   *1970, United States Navy*

ALUDRA (AF 55)   *1967, United States Navy*

ARCTURUS (AF 52)   *United States Navy*

2 STORE SHIPS (AF): R3-S-4A TYPE

Name	No.	Launched	Commissioned
***RIGEL**	AF 58	15 Mar 1955	2 Sep 1955
***VEGA**	AF 59	26 Apr 1955	10 Nov 1955

Displacement, tons	7 950 light; 15 540 full load
Measurement, tons	10 850 gross
Dimensions, feet	475 wl; 502 oa × 72 × 29 max
Guns	4—3 in, 50 cal AA (twin)
Main engines	Steam turbine; 1 shaft; 12 500 shp = 18 knots

R3—S—4A TYPE—Continued

Built by Ingalls Shipbuilding Co, Pascagoula. R3-S-4A type. Cost $12 440 000 each. Helicopter platform fitted (two after twin 3 inch mounts removed). 360 000 cu ft of refrigerated space. Both of these ships are active.

RIGEL (AF 58)   *1968, United States Navy*

2 STORE SHIPS (AF): "VICTORY" TYPE

Name	No.	Launched	Commissioned
***DENEBOLA** (ex-*Hibbing Victory*)	AF 56	10 June 1944	20 Jan 1954
***REGULUS** (ex-*Escanaba Victory*)	AF 57	7 June 1944	3 Feb 1954

Displacement, tons	6 700 light; 12 130 full load
Measurement, tons	8 000 deadweight
Dimensions, feet	455·2 × 62 × 28·5
Guns	4—3 in, 50 cal AA, (twin)
Main engines	Westinghouse geared turbines; 1 shaft; 8 500 shp = 17 knots
Boilers	2
Complement	225

Helicopter platforms fitted aft (two 3 inch twin mounts removed). Both of these ships are active.

DENEBOLA (AF 56)   *1964, United States Navy*

1 STORE SHIP (AF): C2-S-E1 TYPE

Name	No.	Launched	Commissioned
HYADES (ex-*Iberville*)	AF 28	12 June 1943	30 Sep 1943

Displacement, tons	6 313 light; 15 300 full load
Dimensions, feet	463·6 oa × 63 × 28
Guns	4—3 in, 50 cal single
Main engines	Geared turbines; 6 000 shp = 15·5 knots
Boilers	2 (Babcock & Wilcox)
Complement	252

Cargo capacity 5 300 tons. The 5 inch gun was removed. The *Hyades* was transferred to the Maritime Administration reserve fleet on 18 Mar 1969 but remains on the Navy List; sister ship *Graffias* AF 29 stricken on 19 Dec 1969 and transferred to Mar Ad reserve.

DISPOSALS OF OTHER CLASSES
Aldebaran, AF 10, transferred to Maritime Administration (decommissioned in June 1968).

HYADES (AF 28)   *Ing Augusti Nani*

Underway Replenishment Ships—continued

CONCORD (AFS 5)   1970, United States Navy

7 COMBAT STORE SHIPS (AFS): "MARS" CLASS

Name	No.	Laid down	Launched	Commissioned
* MARS	AFS 1	5 May 1962	15 June 1963	21 Dec 1963
* SYLVANIA	AFS 2	18 Aug 1962	15 Aug 1963	11 July 1964
* NIAGARA FALLS	AFS 3	22 May 1965	26 Mar 1966	29 Apr 1967
* WHITE PLAINS	AFS 4	2 Oct 1965	23 July 1966	23 Nov 1968
* CONCORD	AFS 5	26 Mar 1966	17 Dec 1966	27 Nov 1968
* SAN DIEGO	AFS 6	11 Mar 1965	13 Apr 1968	24 May 1969
SAN JOSE	AFS 7	8 Mar 1969	13 Dec 1969	23 Oct 1970

Displacement, tons	16 500 full load
Dimensions, feet	581 oa × 79 × 24
Guns	8—3 in, 50 cal AA (twin)
Helicopters	Normally assigned two UH-46 helicopters
Main engines	Steam turbines; 1 shaft; 22 000 shp = 20 knots
Boilers	3 (Babcock & Wilcox) (one spare)
Complement	430 (30 officers, 400 enlisted men)

All built by National Steel & Shipbuilding, San Diego, California. Of a new design with a completely new replenishment at sea system. "M" frames replace conventional king posts and booms, which are equipped with automatic tensioning devices to maintain transfer lines taut between the ship and the warships being replenished despite rolling and yawing. Computers provide up-to-the-minute data on stock status with data displayed by closed-circuit television. Five holds (one refrigerated). Helicopters are carried to provide vertical replenishment (VERTREP) to ships in a task force spread over a wide area.

Automatic propulsion system with full controls on bridge. SPS-40 radar fitted in *Mars* and *Sylvania*, later ships smaller radar; some ships have TACAN (tactical aircraft navigation radar).

Mars authorised in Fiscal Year 1961 shipbuilding programme, *Sylvania* in FY 1962. *Niagara Falls* in FY 1964, *White Plains* and *Concord* in FY 1965, *San Diego* in FY 1966. *San Jose* in FY 1967.

NOMENCLATURE. Combat store ships are named for American cities.

MARS (AFS 1) with UH-46A Sea Knight   1965, United States Navy

1 STORES ISSUE SHIP (AKS): "VICTORY" TYPE

Name	No.	Commissioned
ALTAIR (ex-*Aberdeen Victory*)	AKS 32 (ex-AK 257)	31 Jan 1952

Displacement, tons	4 420 light; 15 580 full load
Dimensions, feet	455·2 oa × 62 × 28·5
Guns	4—40 mm AA (2 twin)
Main engines	Geared turbine; 1 shaft; 8 500 shp = 16·5 knots
Boilers	2
Complement	320 (17 officers, 213 enlisted men)

VC2-S-AP 3 type. Built by Oregon Shipbuilding Corp, Portland, Ore; launched on 30 May 1944; transferred to Navy on 7 July 1951, operating briefly as cargo ship (AK 257) until converted Jan-Dec 1953 to stores issue ship (AKS) at Norfolk Naval Shipyard. Fitted to carry spare parts and dry stores for combatant ships. Fitted with helicopter platform on fantail for "vertical replenishment" (VERTREP) operations. Decommisisoned on 2 May 1969 and placed in reserve.

DISPOSALS
C-2 cargo type: **Castor**, AKS 1, stricken 1 Dec 1968; **Pollux**, AKS 4 ex-AK 54, stricken 1 Jan 1969; **Mercury**, AKS 20 ex-AK 42, stricken 1 Aug 1959.
LST type: **Electron**, AKS 27 ex-AG 146, ex-LST 1070, **Proton**, AKS 28 ex-AG 147, ex-LST 1078, **Colington**, AKS 29 ex-AG 140 ex-LST 1085, **League Island**, AKS 30 ex-AG 149 ex-LST 1097, **Chimon**, AKS 31 ex-AG 150 ex-LST 1102, stricken in 1960.
"Island" class.: **Belle Isle**, AKS 21, **Coaster's Harbor**, AKS 22, **Cuttyhunk Island**, AKS 23, **Avery Island**, AKS 24, **Indian Island**, AKS 25, **Kent Island**, AKS 26, stricken in 1960.

SAN JOSE (AFS 7)   1970, United States Navy

HASSAYAMPA (AO 145)   1968, United States Navy

Underway Replenishment Ships—continued

NAVASOTA (AO 106) (with UH-46A Sea Knight)   1965, United States Navy

PONCHATOULA (AO 148)   1970, US Navy, PH1 E. L. Goligoski

"NEOSHO" CLASS—Continued

AO 143, built by Bethlehem Steel Company, Quincy, Mass. AO 144-148 by New York Shipbuilding Corporation, Camden, New Jersey. Largest Navy oilers built. Carry 180 000 barrels in 24 tanks. The 2—5 inch, 38 cal guns were removed in 1960. A helicopter platform was installed in place of the after 5 inch gun in *Neosho*, *Mississinewa* and *Truckee*. These ships are fitted to carry a service force commander and staff. All of these ships are active.

NOMENCLATURE. Oilers are named after American rivers with Indian names.

5 OILERS (AO): JUMBOISED T3-S2-A3

Name	No.	Launched	Commissioned
* MISPILLION	AO 105	10 Aug 1945	29 Dec 1945
* NAVASOTA	AO 106	30 Aug 1945	27 Feb 1946
* PASSUMPSIC	AO 107	31 Oct 1945	1 Apr 1946
* PAWCATUCK	AO 108	19 Feb 1945	10 May 1946
* WACCAMAW	AO 109	30 Mar 1946	25 June 1946

Displacement, tons	11 000 light; 34 750 full load
Dimensions, feet	646 oa × 75 × 35·5
Guns	4—3 in, 50 cal AA (single)
Main engines	Turbines; 2 shafts; 13 500 shp = 16 knots
Boilers	4
Complement	290 (16 officers, 274 men)

Navasota and *Waccamaw*, jumboised under the 1963 programme, (recommissioned on 28 Dec 1964 and 26 Feb 1965), other three under the 1964 programme. Conversion increased the oil cargo capacity from 100 000 to 150 000 barrels. Helicopter platform fitted forward. All of these ships are active.

6 OILERS (AO): "NEOSHO" CLASS

Name	No.	Launched	Commissioned
* NEOSHO	AO 143	10 Nov 1953	24 Sep 1954
* MISSISSINEWA	AO 144	12 June 1954	18 Jan 1955
* HASSAYAMPA	AO 145	12 Sep 1954	19 Apr 1955
* KAWISHIWI	AO 146	11 Dec 1954	6 July 1955
* TRUCKEE	AO 147	10 Mar 1955	23 Nov 1955
* PONCHATOULA	AO 148	9 July 1955	12 Jan 1956

Displacement, tons	11 600 light; 38 000 to 40 000 full load
Dimensions, feet	640 wl; 655 oa × 86 × 35
Guns	8 or 12—3 in, 50 cal AA (twin)
Main engines	GE Turbines; 2 shafts; 28 000 shp = 20 knots
Complement	300 (fitted to carry squadron staff of 12 officers)

NEOSHO (AO 143)   1966, United States Navy

WACCAMAW (AO 109)   1966, United States Navy

NECHES (AO 47) T2-A TYPE (now stricken)   1970, United States Navy

Underway Replenishment Ships—*continued*

3 OILERS (AO): "JUMBOISED" T3-S2=A1 TYPE

Name	No.	Launched	Commissioned
*ASHTABULA	AO 51	22 May 1943	7 Aug 1943
*CALOOSAHATCHEE	AO 98	2 June 1945	10 Oct 1945
*CANISTEO	AO 99	6 July 1945	3 Dec 1945

Displacement, tons	34 700 full load
Dimensions, feet	644 oa × 75 × 31·5
Guns	4—3 inch 50 cal AA (single)
Main engines	Geared turbines; 2 shafts; 13 500 hp = 18 knots
Boilers	4 (Foster Wheeler)
Complement	300 (13 officers and 287 enlisted men)

Former standard T3-S2-A1 oilers that have been enlarged ("Jumboised") with a new central tank section being added.

ASHTABULA (AO 51) 1970, US Navy, PH1 B. L. Kuykendall

CALOOSAHATCHEE (AO 98) 1970, US Navy, PH3 T. R. Hearsum

3 OILERS (AO): T2-A TYPE

Name	No.	Launched	Commissioned
KENENBEC (ex-Corsicana)	AO 36	19 Apr 1941	4 Feb 1942
TAPPAHANNOCK (ex-Jorkay)	AO 43	18 Apr 1942	22 June 1942
KANKAKEE (ex-Colina)	AO 39	24 Jan 1942	4 May 1942

Displacement, tons	6 013 light; 21 850 full load
Dimensions, feet	502 oa × 68 × 30·8
Guns	2 or 4—3 in. 50 cal AA (single)
Main engines	2 (Babcock & Wilcox)

Cargo capacity 126 000 barrels. The *Tappahannock* is in Navy reserve, *Kankakee* and *Kenenbec* in Mar Ad reserve fleet but remain on Navy List.

15 OILERS (AO): T3-S2=A1 TYPE

Name	No.	Launched	Commissioned
SABINE (ex-Esso Albany)	AO 25	27 Apr 1940	25 Sep 1940
*GUADALUPE (ex-Esso Raleigh)	AO 32	26 Jan 1940	5 June 1941
*CACAPON	AO 52	6 June 1943	21 Sep 1943
*CALIENTE	AO 53	26 Aug 1943	22 Oct 1943
CHIKASKIA	AO 54	2 Oct 1943	10 Nov 1943
*AUCILLA (ex-Escanaba)	AO 56	20 Nov 1943	22 Dec 1943
*MARIAS	AO 57	21 Dec 1943	12 Feb 1944
*MANATEE	AO 58	19 Feb 1944	6 Apr 1944
*NANTAHALA	AO 60	29 Apr 1944	19 June 1944
*SEVERN	AO 61	31 May 1944	19 July 1944
*TALUGA	AO 62	10 July 1944	25 Aug 1944
*CHIPOLA	AO 63	21 Oct 1944	30 Nov 1944
*TOLOVANA	AO 64	6 Jan 1945	24 Feb 1945
*ALLAGASH	AO 97	14 Apr 1945	21 Aug 1945
*CHUKAWAN	AO 100	28 Aug 1945	22 Jan 1946

Displacement, tons	25 525 full load
Dimensions, feet	553 oa × 75 × 31·5
Guns	4—3 inch 50 cal AA (single) in most ships; a few ships retain 5 inch guns of original armament (see notes below)
Main engines	Geared turbines; 2 shafts; 13 500 shp - 18 knots
Boilers	4 (Foster/Wheeler)
Complement	274 (14 officers, 260 enlisted men)

Cargo capacity approximately 142 000 barrels. Original armament varied with one to four 5 inch DP guns, four 3 inch AA guns for ships with fewer 5 inch weapons, and eight 40 mm AA guns.

DISPOSALS

"T3-S2-A1" type: **Salamonie** AO 26 stricken on 2 Sep 1969, **Kaskaskia** AO 27 stricken on 19 Dec 1969, **Platte** AO 24 stricken 25 Sep 1970, **Chemung** AO 30 stricken 18 Sep 1970, **Elokomin** AO 55 stricken Mar 1970.
"T3-S-A1" type: **Enoree** AO 69 and **Niobrara** AO 72 were stricken in Dec 1958.
"T2-A" type: **Merrimack** AO 37 and **Monagahela** AO 42 were stricken in Dec 1958. Distilling ships, ex-oilers, of the "Pasig" class **Abatan** AW 4 (ex-*Mission San Lorenzo* AO 92) and **Pasig** AW 3 (ex-*Mission San Xavier* AO 91) transferred to the Maritime National Defence Reserve Fleet in 1960-61, but **Abatan** was reacquired in Sep 1962 stricken 1 June 1970 but retained as water storage hulk at Guatonamo Bay, Cuba; **Cimarron**, AO 22, stricken on 1 Oct 1968 (scrapped); **Mattaponi** AO 41 stricken 15 Oct 1970, **Neches** AO 47 stricken 1 Oct 1970.

CALIENTE (AO 53) 1970, US Navy, PH2 B. L. Chandler

GUADALUPE (AO 32) 1969, US Navy, PH2 D. W. Dextradeur

CANISTEO (AO 99) 1969, US Navy, PH3 J. C. Cahoon

Underway Replenishment Ships—*continued*

DETROIT (AOE 4)   1970, United States Navy

4 FAST COMBAT SUPPORT SHIPS (AOE):

"SACRAMENTO" CLASS

Name	No.	Laid down	Launched	Commissioned
* SACRAMENTO	AOE 1	30 June 1961	14 Sep 1963	14 Mar 1964
* CAMDEN	AOE 2	17 Feb 1964	29 May 1965	1 Apr 1967
* SEATTLE	AOE 3	1 Oct 1965	2 Mar 1968	5 Apr 1969
* DETROIT	AOE 4	29 Nov 1966	21 June 1969	28 Mar 1970

Displacement, tons	19 200 light; 53 600 full load
Dimensions, feet	793 oa × 107 × 39·3
Guns	8—3 in, 50 cal (twin)
Helicopters	Normally assigned two UH-46 helicopters
Main engines	Geared turbines; 2 shafts; 100 000 shp = 26 knots sustained speed
Boilers	4
Complement	600 (33 officers, 567 men)

DETROIT (AOE 4)   1970, United States Navy

The Fast Combat Support Ships (AOE) are designed to supply task forces. Fitted with "FAST". They combine the functions of ammunition ships, cargo ships and fleet oilers. They carry one fifth more fuel than the latest fleet oilers (black oil, diesel oil and aviation spirit), and one quarter the capacity of the latest ammunition ship, including guided missiles, as well as 250 tons of dry cargo and 250 tons of frozen food. Oil capacity 177 000 barrels. *Detroit*, *Seattle* and *Sacramento* were built by Puget Sound Naval Shipyard, *Camden* was built by New York Shipbuilding Corporation, Camden, New Jersey.
Sacramento authorised in Fiscal Year 1961 shipbuilding programme. *Camden* in FY 1963, *Seattle* in FY 1965, *Detroit* in FY 1966. Construction of AOE 5 in FY 1968 was deferred and then cancelled in November 1969.

ENGINEERING. *Sacramento* and *Camden* have machinery intended for cancelled battleship *Kentucky* (BB 66).

PHOTOGRAPHS. Note large, triple-door helicopter hangars on *Seattle*; fork-lift trucks manoeuver cargo on her helicopter deck. Replenishment equipment is primarily on port side for transfer to carriers; ship's boats are on starboard side of hangar. SPS-40 radar on *Sacramento* and *Camden*; *Detroit* and *Seattle* have smaller SPS-12 antennas; note TACAN pods. Bow and port-side anchors similar to combatant ship arrangement.

NOMENCLATURE. Fast combat support ships are named for American cities.

SEATTLE (AOE 3)   1970, United States Navy

KILAUEA (AE 26) and WICHITA (AOR 1)   1970, General Dynamics Quincy SB Division

Underway Replenishment Ships—continued

8 GASOLINE TANKERS (AOG): "PATAPSCO" CLASS

Name	No.	Launched	Commissioned
PATAPSCO	AOG 1	18 Aug 1942	4 Feb 1943
***ELKHORN**	AOG 7	15 May 1943	12 Feb 1944
GENESEE	AOG 8	23 Sep 1943	27 May 1944
KISHWAUKEE	AOG 9	24 July 1943	27 May 1944
***TOMBIGBEE**	AOG 11	18 Nov 1943	13 July 1944
***CHEWAUCAN**	AOG 50	22 July 1944	19 Feb 1945
***NESPELEN**	AOG 55	10 Apr 1945	
***NOXUBEE**	AOG 56	3 Apr 1945	

Displacement, tons	1 850 light; 4 570 full load
Dimensions, feet	292 wl; 310·8 oa × 48·5 × 15·7 max
Guns	2 or 3 in dp, 50 cal (single)
Main engines	Diesel-electric; 2 shafts; 3 100 bhp = 14 knots
Complement	81 (6 officers, 75 men)

Navy designed small fuel ships originally intended to carry diesel and aviation fuels. All built by Cargill Inc, Savage, Minnesota. Cargo capacity 17 775 barrels. *Kishwaukee Noxubee* and *Patapsco* were reacquired from the Maritime Administration and re commissioned in 1966. Note *Genesee* has only one gun forward; tapering stern and stem anchor. Only five ships remain active.

DISPOSALS
Maquoketa T-AOG 51 was stricken, **Kern** AOG 2, **Wabash** AOG 4, and **Maquoketa** AOG 51 were transferred to Maritime Administration in 1958 and **Susquehanna** AOG 5 in 1959-60. **Ontonagon** AOG 36 was stricken from the Navy List and returned to Maritime Administration on 13 Nov 1957. **Agawam** AOG 6, **Nemasket** AOG 10, and **Rio Grande** AOG 3 were disposed of in 1961. **Chestatee** AOG 49 and **Wacissa** AOG 59 were stricken in 1963 and scrapped. **Mattabesset**, AOG 52, stricken on 1 Oct 1968 and transferred to Maritime Administration.

TRANSFERS. *Natchoug* AOG 54 was transferred to Greece under the MDAP on 1 Aug 1959. *Pinnebcg* AOG 58 is on loan to the US Air Force, *Pecatonica* AOG 57 was transferred to Taiwan China in Apr 1962. *Namakagon* AOG 53 was loaned to New Zealand in 1963.

PATAPSCO (AOG 1)   *1966, United States Navy*

6+1 REPLENISHMENT OILERS (AOR):
"WICHITA" CLASS

Name	No.	Laid down	Launched	Commissioned
***WICHITA**	AOR 1	18 June 1966	16 Mar 1968	7 June 1969
***MILWAUKEE**	AOR 2	29 Nov 1966	17 Jan 1969	1 Nov 1969
***KANSAS CITY**	AOR 3	20 Apr 1968	28 June 1969	6 June 1970
***SAVANNAH**	AOR 4	22 Jan 1969	25 Apr 1970	5 Dec 1970
WABASH	AOR 5	21 Jan 1970	6 Feb 1971	late 1971
KALAMAZOO	AOR 6	28 Oct 1970	May 1970	late 1972

Displacement, tons	38 100 full load
Dimensions, feet	659 oa × 96 × 35
Helicopters	Normally assigned two UH-46 helicopters
Guns	4—3 in, 50 cal, AA (twin)
Main engines	Geared turbines; 2 shafts = 20 knots (18 knots on 2 boilers)
Boilers	3
Complement	345 (20 officers, 325 men)

Fitted with helicopter platform. These ships provide rapid replenishment at sea of petroleum products, ammunition, provisions and fleet freight to task forces. All built by General Dynamics Corporation Quincy. Estimated cost of *Milwaukee* was $27 700 000. Original design provided for eight 3 inch guns.

Wichita and *Milwaukee* authorised in Fiscal Year 1965 new construction programme; *Kansas City* and *Savannah* in FY 1966; *Wabash* and *Kalamazoo* in FY 1967. The Navy plans to attain a force of about 15 ships of this type by 1980 to replace older war-built oilers AOR 7 in FY 1972 shipbuilding programme.

NOMENCLATURE. Replenishment oilers are named after American cities.

DISPOSAL
"Fleet Tanker" **Conecuh** (AOR 110, ex-AO 110, ex-IX 301, former German U-boat tender) stricken 1 June 1960; carried mixed cargoes with fuels; prototype multi-store underway replenishment ship for US Navy.

GENESEE (AOG 8)   *1970, US Navy, PH1 J. D. Osborne*

GENESEE (AOG 8)   *1970, US Navy, PH1 J. D. Osborne*

MILWAUKEE (AOR 2)   *1969, General Dynamics Quincy SB Division*

1970, United States Navy

WICHITA (AOR 1)

FLEET SUPPORT SHIPS

2 DESTROYER TENDERS (AD): "GOMPERS" CLASS

Name	No.	Laid down	Launched	Commissioned
∗ SAMUEL GOMPERS	AD 37	9 July 1964	14 May 1966	1 July 1967
∗ PUGET SOUND	AD 38	15 Feb 1965	16 Sep 1966	27 Apr 1968

Displacement, tons	20 500 to 21 600 full load
Dimensions, feet	643 × 85
Guns	1—5 in, 38 cal DP
Main engines	20 000 hp = over 18 knots
Complement	1 803 (135 officers, 1 668 men)

Samuel Gompers is the first destroyer tender of post-Second World War design. These ships have repair, supply and support facilities for new destroyer types, missile systems, anti-submarine warfare weapons and equipments, advanced communications and electronic systems and nuclear propulsion plants. They are able to furnish in port service to six guided missile destroyers alongside simultaneously. *Samuel Gompers* was authorised under the Fiscal Year 1964 new construction programme; *Puget Sound* in the 1965 programme. Both built by Puget Sound Naval Shipyard. AD 39 in FY 1969 programme was cancelled on 27 Mar 1969 to provide funds for overruns in FY 1969 and FY 1970 programmes (estimated saving was $72 500 000). Additional ships of this type are planned.

NOMENCLATURE. Destroyer tenders generally are named for geographic areas; Samuel Gompers was an American labour leader.

SAMUEL GOMPERS (AD 37)   *1968, United States Navy*

PUGET SOUND (AD 38)   *1968, United States Navy*

PUGET SOUND (AD 38)   *1968, United States Navy*

6 DESTROYER TENDERS (AD): "KLONDIKE" CLASS

Name	No.	Launched	Commissioned
EVERGLADES	AD 24	28 Jan 1945	25 May 1951
FRONTIER	AD 25	25 Mar 1945	2 Mar 1946
∗ SHENANDOAH	AD 26	29 Mar 1945	13 Aug 1945
∗ YELLOWSTONE	AD 27	12 Apr 1945	15 Jan 1946
ISLE ROYALE	AD 29	19 Sep 1945	9 June 1962
∗ BRYCE CANYON	AD 36	7 Mar 1946	15 Sep 1950

Displacement, tons	8 165 standard; 16 635 to 16 900 full load
Dimensions, feet	465 wl; 492 oa × 69·5 × 27·2
Guns	1—5 in, 38 cal DP
Main engines	Geared turbines; 1 shaft; 8 500 shp = 18·4 knots
Boilers	2 (Foster-Wheeler or Babcock & Wilcox)
Complement	778 to 918

These ships are of modified C-3 design completed as destroyer tenders. Officially considered two classes (see below). *Arcadia, Shenandoah, Yellowstone* built by Todd Shipyards, Los Angeles, Calif; *Bryce Canyon* by Charleston Navy Yard; *Everglades, Frontier* by Los Angeles SB & DD Co; and *Isle Royal* by Todd Pacific Shipyards, Seattle, Wash. *Isle Royal* first commissioned on 26 Mar 1946 and placed in reserve before being completely outfitted; recommissioned for service on 9 June 1962 and commenced operations in January 1963.

Originally 14 ships of two similar designs, the "Klondike" class of AD 22-25 and "Shenandoah" class of AD 26-33, 35, and 36. *Great Lakes* (AD 30), *New England* (AD 32), *Canopus* (AD 33, ex-AS 27), *Arrow Head* (AD 35, ex-AV 19) cancelled before completion; *Klondike* (AD 22) reclassified AR 22; *Grand Canyon* (AD 28) reclassified AR 28. Also see *Disposals*.

Frontier decommissioned in 1968 and placed in reserve, *Everglades* and *Isle Royal* in 1970 and placed in reserve.

ARMAMENT. Original armament for "Klondike" class was 1—5 in gun, 4—3 in guns, and 4—40 mm guns; for "Shenandoah" class was 2—5 in guns and 8—40 mm guns.

MODERNISATION. Most of these ships have been modernised under the FRAM II programme to service modernised destroyers fitted with ASROC, improved electronics, helicopters, etc. The tenders' shops were improved and four 3 inch and four 40 mm guns removed.

DISPOSALS
Arcadia AD 23 stricken on 30 June 1969 and transferred to Maritime Administration reserve fleet, **Tidewater** AD 31 transferred to Indonesia in Jan 1971 for use as tender to off-shore oil operations (Navy manned).

SHENANDOAH (AD 26)   *1964, United States Navy*

YELLOWSTONE (AD 27)   *United States Navy*

1 DESTROYER TENDER (AD): "CASCADE" TYPE

Name	No.	Launched	Commissioned
∗CASCADE	AD 16	7 June 1942	12 Mar 1943

Displacement, tons	9 800 standard; 16 600 full load
Dimensions, feet	492 oa × 69·5 × 27·2
Guns	1—5 in; 38 cal DP
Main engines	Turbines; 8 500 shp = 18·4 knots
Boilers	2
Complement	857

Built by Western Pipe & Steel Co, San Francisco, C3-S1-N2 type. Modernised to service FRAM destroyers.
The *Cascade* is in active service.

Fleet Support Ships—*continued*

ISLE ROYAL (AD 29)   *1970, United States Navy*

CASCADE (AD 16)   *1968, United States Navy*

PIEDMONT (AD 17)   *1970, United States Navy*

YOSEMITE (AD 19)   *1968, United States Navy*

5 DESTROYER TENDERS (AD): "DIXIE" CLASS

Name	No.	Launched	Commissioned
* DIXIE	AD 14	27 May 1939	25 Apr 1940
* PRAIRIE	AD 15	9 Dec 1939	5 Aug 1940
* PIEDMONT	AD 17	7 Dec 1942	5 Jan 1944
* SIERRA	AD 18	23 Feb 1943	20 Mar 1944
* YOSEMITE	AD 19	16 May 1943	25 May 1944

Displacement, tons	9 450 standard; 17 176 full load
Dimensions, feet	520 wl; 530·5 oa × 73·3 × 25·5
Guns	1 or 2—5 in, 38 cal DP
Main engines	Geared turbines; 2 shafts; 11 000 shp = 19·6 knots
Boilers	4 (Babcock & Wilcox "A")
Complement	1 076 to 1 698 (total accommodation)

Dixie and *Prairie* built by New York Shipbuilding Corp, Camden, New Jersey; others by Tampa Shipbuilding Co, Florida. All five ships are active. The two after 5 inch guns and the eight 40 mm AA guns were removed.
All five ships are active, amongst the oldest ships remaining in service with the US Navy.

MODERNISATION. All of these ships have been modernised under the FRAM II programme to service destroyers fitted with ASROC, improved electronics, helicopters, etc. Two or three 5 inch guns and eight 40 mm guns removed during modernisation.

DIXIE (AD 14)   *1968, United States Navy*

1 DEGAUSSING SHIP (ADG): Ex-MINESWEEPER

Name	No.	Launched	Commissioned
SURFBIRD	ADG 383 (ex-MSF 383)	31 Aug 1944	25 Nov 1944

Displacement, tons	890 standard; 1 250 full load
Dimensions, feet	215 wl; 221·2 oa × 32·2 × 10·8
Main engines	Diesel electric; 2 shafts; 3 532 bhp = 18 knots
Complement	70

Built by American Shipbuilding Co, Lorain, Ohio. Laid down on 15 Feb 1944. Former Fleet Minesweeper of the steel-hulled type, MSF (ex-AM), reclassified as ADG on 18 May 1957. Decommissioned in 1970 and placed in reserve.

SURFBIRD (ADG 383)   *United States Navy*

3 DEGAUSSING SHIPS (ADG): Ex-PCE

Name	No.	Launched
DEPERM (ex-*PCE* 883)	ADG 10	14 Jan 1944
LODESTONE (ex-*PCE* 876)	ADG 8	30 Sep 1943
MAGNET (ex-*PCE* 879)	ADG 9	1 Sep 1943

Displacement, tons	640 standard; 900 full load
Dimensions, feet	184·5 oa × 33 × 9·5
Main engines	Diesel; 2 shafts; 2 400 bhp = 16 knots

Named on 1 Feb 1955. All out of commission, in reserve. Sister ship *Ampere* ADG 11 (ex-*Drake* AM 359) was stricken from the Navy List on 1 July 1961.

Fleet Support Ships—continued

2 HOSPITAL SHIPS (AH): "HAVEN" TYPE

Name	No.	Launched	Commissioned
REPOSE (ex-*Marine Beaver*)	AH 16	8 Aug 1944	26 May 1945
SANCTUARY (ex-*Marine Owl*)	AH 17	15 Aug 1944	20 June 1945

Displacement, tons	11 141 standard; 15 400 full load
Dimensions, feet	496 wl; 520 oa × 71·5 × 24
Main engines	Geared turbines (General Electric); 1 shaft; 9 000 shp = 18·3
Boilers	2 (Babcock & Wilcox)
Complement	Accommodation for 626 to 698

Built by the Sun SB & DD Co, Chester, Pa. Maritime Commission C 4-S-B2 Type. Beds for approximately 700 patients. Air conditioned throughout. *Consolation* (AH 15) was chartered to a private group, operated by American President Lines, as a floating laboratory and medical school since 1961; she was renamed *Hope* by the People to People Health Foundation Inc. *Benevolence* (AH 13) sank after a collision with a freighter off San Francisco in Aug 1950. *Tranquility* (AH 14) transferred to the Maritime Administration Reserve Fleet in 1961 and *Haven* (AH 12) on 1 Mar 1967. *Repose* was in Sep 1962 transferred to Maritime Administration, but was reacquired and recommissioned on 16 Oct 1965 at San Francisco for naval service with complement of 54 officers, 29 nurses and 543 men and 922 bed capacity. *Sancutary*, was reacquired from Maritime Administration in 1966 and recommissioned on 15 Nov 1966 for naval service. After modernisation by Avondale Shipyard, New Orleans, she has helo platform aft, 760 bed hospital, with 319 staff (24 doctors, 29 nurses, 3 dentists, 263 enlisted hospital corpsmen) and 375 crew (17 officers, 358 men). Both ships were decommissioned in 1971, but the *Repose* remains in service as station hospital in Long Beach, California.

An overhead photograph of the *Repose* appears in the 1970-71 edition.

REPOSE (AH 16)   *1970, US Navy, PH2 Wayne Massie*

1 NET LAYING SHIP (ANL): "COHOES" CLASS

Name	No.	Launched	Commissioned
***COHOES**	ANL 78 (ex-AN 78)	29 Nov 1944	23 Mar 1945

Displacement, tons	650 standard; 855 full load
Dimensions, feet	146 wl; 168·5 oa × 33·8 × 11·7
Guns	3—20 mm AA (single)
Main engines	Busch-Sulzer diesel-electric; 1 shaft; 1 200 shp = 12 knots
Complement	46 (4 officers, 42 enlisted men)

Cohoes built by Commercial Iron Works, Portland, Oregon. Designation changed from Netlayer (AN) to Net Laying Ship (ANL) on 1 Jan 1969. Placed in commission on 23 July 1969. Scheduled to decommission late in 1971.

TRANSFERS. *Tonawanda* AN 89, was transferred to Haiti in 1960. *Marietta* AN 82 to Venezuela in Jan 1961, *Tunxis* AN 90, and *Waxsaw* AN 91 to Venezuela in Jan 1963, *Nahaut* AN 83 to Uruguay in 1968.

DISPOSALS
Manayunk AN 81. **Naubuc** AN 84. **Suncock** AN 80 and **Tunxis** AN 90, were stricken from the Navy List in Sep 1962. **Etlah** AN 79, **Oneota** AN 85, **Passaconaway** AN 86, **Passaic** AN 87, **Shakamaxon** AN 88 and **Yazoo** AN 92, in July 1963. **Suncock** AN 80 was retransferred to the Bureau of Mines in Oct 1964. **Naubuc** AN 78 was reacquired from Maritime Administration in Mar 1967 for conversion to river/harbour as salvage tender; redesignated YRST 4 on 1 Apr 1968 (see section on Service Craft).

NOMENCLATURE. Net laying ships are named for trees.

COHOES (ANL 78)   *1968, United States Navy*

NET LAYING SHIPS (ANL): TREE CLASS

Butternut ANL 9 (ex-AN 9, ex-YN 4) was stricken from the Navy List on 18 July 1969; reinstated on Navy List on 28 Oct 1969 as YAG 60 (see Experimental, Research and Surveying Ships).

7 SELF-PROPELLED BARRACKS SHIPS (APB)

Name	No	Launched
COLLETON	APB 36 (ex-APL 36)	30 July 1945
ECHOLS	APB 36 (ex-APL 37)	30 July 1945
MERCER	APB 39 (ex-APL 39)	17 Nov 1944
NUECES	APB 40 (ex-APL 40)	6 May 1945
DORCHESTER	APB 46 (ex-AKS 17, ex-LST 1112)	12 Apr 1945
KINGMAN	APB 47 (ex-AKS 18, ex-LST 1113)	17 Apr 1945
VANDENBURGH	APB 48 (ex-AKS 19, ex-LST 1114)	20 Apr 1945

Displacement, tons	2 189 light; 4 080 full load
Dimensions, feet	316 wl; 328 oa × 50 × 11
Guns	Vary (see notes)
Main engines	Diesels (General Motors); 2 shafts; 1 600 to 1 800 bhp = 12 knots (*APB* 41-50); 10 knots (*APB* 35-40)
Complement	193 (13 officers, 180 enlisted men)
Troops	1 226 (26 officers, 1 200 enlisted men)

Officially rated as Self-Propelled Barracks Ships (APB). All ex-LST type ships of the same basic characteristics. *Benewah* and *Colleton* recommissioned on 28 Jan 1967 for service in Vietnam; *Mercer* and *Nueces* recommissioned in 1968 for service in Vietnam. All four decommissioned in 1969-71 as US riverine forces in South Vietnam reduced.

Beuewah (APB 35) reclassified as IX 311 on 26 Feb 1971 for use as barracks ship at Subic Bay, Philippines; to be transferred to South Vietnam.

These most-useful ships supported the joint Army-Navy Mobile Riverine Force in the Mekong Delta region of South Vietnam (Navy River Assault Flotilla 1/Task Force 117/River Support Squadron 7). Complement of each ship in this role was 12 officers and 186 enlisted men, and 900 troops and boat crew personnel were carried. These four ships have an armament of two 3 inch guns (single) eight 40 mm guns (two quad mounts), eight ·50 cal MG, and ten ·30 cal MG. They each have troop berthing and messing facilities, evaporators which produce up to 40 000 gallons of fresh water per day, a 16-bed hospital, X-ray room, dental room, bacteriological laboratory, pharmacy, laundry, library, and tailor shop; living and most working spaces are air conditioned. Most ships not activated for Vietnam have eight 40 mm AA guns (quad).

DISPOSALS
Sister ships **Accomac** APB 49, **Cameron** APB 50, **Presque Isle** APB 44, **Wythe** APB 41, **Yavapai** APB 42 and **Yola** APB 43, were stricken from the Navy List in 1959, **Blackford** APB 45 (ex-AKS 16, ex-LST 1111) in 1960, and **Marlboro** APB 38, on 1 Dec 1963.
The barracks ship **Dupage** APB 51 (ex-SS *John R. Weeks*), converted "Liberty" type merchant vessel, was stricken on 1 June 1959.

MERCER (APB 39)   *1968, United States Navy*

BENEWAH (APB 35) (now IX 311)   *1968, US Navy, PH2 Pasco Izzo*

Fleet Support Ships—continued

2 REPAIR SHIPS (AR): Ex-DESTROYER TENDERS

Name	No.	Launched	Commissioned
KLONDIKE	AR 22 (ex-AD 22)	12 Aug 1944	30 July 1945
*GRAND CANYON	AR 28 (ex-AD 28)	27 Apr 1945	5 Apr 1946

Displacement, tons	8 165 standard; 16 635 full load
Dimensions, feet	465 wl; 492 oa × 69·5 × 27·2
Guns	2—3 in, 50 cal AA (single) in *Klondike*
	1—5 in, 38 cal DP in *Grand Canyon*
Main engines	Geared turbines (General Electric in *Klondike*, Westinghouse in *Grand Canyon*); 1 shaft; 8 500 shp = 18·4 knots
Boilers	2 (Babcock & Wilcox in *Klondike*, Foster-Wheeler in *Grand Canyon*)
Complement	826 (48 officers, 778 enlisted men) and 977 (59 officers, 918 enlisted men) designed wartime for *Klondike* and *Grand Canyon*, respectively

These ships are modified C-3 designs completed as destroyer tenders and subsequently reclassified as repair ships, the *Klondike* being redesignated AR 22 on 20 Feb 1960 and the *Grand Canyon* on 10 Mar 1971.
Klondike built by Los Angeles Shipbuilding Corp and *Grand Canyon* by Todd Shipyards, also Los Angeles, Calif. These ships differ in detail, being of slightly different designs; note mast and kingpost arrangements. The *Grand Canyon* has been modernised; note helicopter platform and hangar aft. *Klondike's* designed armament was 1—5 in gun, 4—3 in guns, and 4—40 mm guns; *Grand Canyon's* designed armament was 2—5 in guns and 8—40 mm guns.
Klondike decommissioned on 15 Dec 1970 and placed in service in reserve as station ship at San Diego, Calif; *Grand Canyon* is active.

NOMENCLATURE. Repair ships normally are named for mythological characters.

KLONDIKE (AR 22)　　　　　*1969, US Navy, PH2 S. C. Wyckoff*

GRAND CANYON (AD 28)　　　　*1968, United States Navy*

1 REPAIR SHIP (AR): Ex-DESTROYER TENDER

Name	No.	Launched	Commissioned
MARKAB (ex-*Mormacpenn*)	AR 23 (ex-AD 21, ex-AK 31)	21 Dec 1940	15 June 1941

Displacement, tons	8 560 standard; 14 800 full load
Dimensions, feet	465 wl; 492·5 oa × 69·8 × 24·8
Guns	4—3 in, 50 cal AA
Main engines	Geared turbines (General Electric); 1 shaft; 8 500 shp 18·4 knots
Boilers	2 (Foster-Wheeler)

Built by Ingalls SB Co, Pascagoula, Miss. Former destroyer tender, reclassified as repair ship on 15 Apr 1960 and designation changed from AD to AR. The 5 inch and 4—40 mm guns were removed. The *Markab* was decommissioned on 19 Dec 1969 but remains in service in reserve as station ship at Mare Island, Calif.

MARKAB (AR 23)　　　　　*United States Navy*

1 REPAIR SHIPS (AR): "AMPHION" CLASS

Name	No.	Launched	Commissioned
CADMUS	AR 14	5 Aug 1945	23 Apr 1946

Displacement, tons	7 826 standard; 14 490 full load
Dimensions, feet	456 wl; 492 oa × 70 × 27·5
Guns	Removed
Main engines	Turbines (Westinghouse); 1 shaft; 8 500 shp = 16·5 knots
Boilers	2 (Foster-Wheeler)
Complement	921 (67 officers, 854 enlisted men) designed wartime

Built by Tampa Shipubilding Co. C 3 cargo type. Designed armament was two 5 inch guns and eight 40 mm guns (quad). *Cadmus* decommissioned and placed in reserve in 1971.
The *Amphion* (AR 13) of this class was to be transferred to Iran in 1971.

CADMUS (AR 14)　　　　　*A. & J. Pavia*

AMPHION (AR 13) transferred to Iran　　　*1969, United States Navy*

2 REPAIR SHIPS AR): "DELTA" CLASS

Name	No.	Commissioned
DELTA (ex-*Hawaiian Packer*)	AR 9 (ex-AK 29)	16 June 1941
BRIAREUS (ex-*Hawaiian Planter*)	AR 12	16 Nov 1943

Displacement, tons	8 975 standard; 14 500 full load
Dimensions, feet	465·5 pp; 490·5 oa × 69·5 × 24·3
Guns	4—3 in, 50 cal AA
Main engines	Geared turbines (Newport News); 1 shaft; 8 500 shp = 17 knots
Boilers	2 (Foster-Wheeler) and Babcock & Wilcox, respectively
Complement	688 (29 officers, 559 enlisted men); 903 and 924, respectively, designed wartime

C-3 type built by Newport News SB & DD Co, Newport News, Va. Both launched in 1941 with *Briareus* serving as a merchant ship before being acquired by the Navy. The 5 inch and 4—40 mm guns removed. *Briareus* decommissioned in 1955 and placed in reserve; *Delta* decommissioned in 1970 remains in service in reserve as station ship at Bremerton, Wash.

DELTA (AR 9)　　　　　*1969, US Navy, PH1 Raymond Fitzgerald*

4 REPAIR SHIPS (AR): "VULCAN" CLASS

Name	No.	Launched	Commissioned
*VULCAN	AR 5	14 Dec 1940	16 June 1941
*AJAX	AR 6	22 Aug 1942	30 Oct 1942
*HECTOR	AR 7	11 Nov 1942	7 Feb 1944
*JASON	AR 8	3 Apr 1943	19 June 1944

Displacement, tons	9 140 standard; 16 200 full load
Dimensions, feet	520 wl; 529·3 oa × 73·3 × 23·3
Guns	4—5 in, 38 cal DP
Main engines	Geared turbines; 2 shafts; 11 000 shp = 19·2 knots
Boilers	4 (Babcock & Wilcox 3-drum)
Complement	715 (23 officers, 692 enlisted men); 950 designed wartime

Fleet Support Ships—*continued*

"VULCAN" CLASS—*continued*

Vulcan was built by New York SB Corpn under the 1939 programme and the other three by Los Angeles SB & DD Corpn under the 1940 Programme. All carry a most elaborate equipment of machine tools to undertake repairs of every description. *Jason,* originally designated ARH 1 and rated as heavy hull repair ship, was reclassified AR 8 on 9 Sep 1957. Eight 40 mm AA guns (twin) have been removed. All of these ships are active.

AJAX (AR 6)   1970, US Navy, PH2 Benjamin Startt

AJAX (AR 6)   1970, US Navy, PH2 Benjamin Startt

CABLE SHIPS (ARC); NEW CONSTRUCTION

Navy plans to build two new cable ships during the 1970s to replace two older ships. No details are available.

2 CABLE SHIPS (ARC): "AEOLUS" CLASS

* **AEOLUS** (ex-*Turandot*) ARC 3 (ex-AKA 47)
* **THOR** (ex-*Vanadis*) ARC 4 (ex-AKA 49)

Displacement, tons	7 040 full load
Dimensions, feet	400 wl; 438 oa × 64 × 16
Main engines	Westinghouse turbo-electric; 6 000 shp = 16·9 knots

Aeolus (laid up in the Maritime Administration Reserve Fleet since June 1946) was reacquired by the Navy on 4 Nov 1954. Both converted to Cable Laying or Repair Ships by the Key Highway Plant of Bethlehem Steel, Baltimore, Maryland. *Aeolus* commissioned in May 1955. *Thor,* built by Walsh Kaiser Company, Providence, commissioned on 3 Jan 1956. Unarmed. Helicopter platform aft. Note that the *Aeolus* now has same pole and antenna masts aft as the *Thor.* Both ships are active

THOR (ARC 4)   1964, United States Navy

AEOLUS (AR 3)   1970. US Navy, PH1 E. L. Goligoski

AEOLUS (AR 3)   *United States Navy*

2 CABLE SHIPS (ARC): "NEPTUNE" TYPE

* **NEPTUNE** (ex-*William H. G. Bullard*) ARC 2
* **ALBERT J. MYER** T-ARC 6

Displacement, tons	7 387 full load
Measurement, tons	3 929 gross; 4 860 deadweight
Dimensions, feet	322 wl; 370 oa (T-ARC 6 is 362 oa) × 47 × 18
Main engines	Reciprocating Unaflow engines: 2 shafts; 4 800 hp = 14 knots
Complement	T-ARC 6, 18 officers, 54 enlisted men, 19 scientists

Built by Pusey and Jones Corpn, Wilmington, Del. *Neptune* was launched in 1945 and completed in Feb 1946. Acquired from the Maritime Administration in 1953. Sister ship *Albert J. Myer,* US Army Cable Ship, on loan to the Military Sea Transportation Service, was acquired by the Navy in 1966 and designated T-ARC 6. Both of the S3-S2-BP1 type. Unarmed. Both ships are active. *Albert J. Myer* is used for hydrographic research, operated by Military Sealift Command (ex-MSTS) for the Naval Electronic Systems Command civilian manned.

TRANSFER. *Portunus* ARC 1 (ex-LSM 275) was transferred to Portugal on 1 May 1959.

DISPOSALS

The cable repair ship **Nashawena** YAG 35 (ex-AG 142) was stricken in 1960. The cable repair ship **Yamacraw** ARC 5 (ex-USCG WARC 333, ex-ACM 9, ex-*Trapper*) originally an Army minelayer and subsequently a US Navy auxiliary minelayer, afterwards employed as a US Coast Geard cable layer, then a US Navy cable repair ship until 1959, was stricken on 1 July 1965 and transferred to the Maritime Administration.

NEPTUNE (ARC 2)   *United States Navy*

ALBERT J. MYER (T ARC 6)   US Navy (MSTS)

1 ENGINE REPAIR SHIP (ARG): "LIBERTY" TYPE

Name	No.	Launched	Commissioned
*TUTUILA** (ex-*Arthur P. Gorman*)	ARG 4	12 Sep 1943	8 Apr 1944

Displacement, tons	5 766 standard; 14 350 full load
Dimensions, feet	416 wl; 441·5 oa × 57 × 23
Guns	3—3 in, 50 cal AA
Main engines	Triple expansion (General Machinery Corp); 1 shaft; 2 500 hp = 12·5 knots
Boilers	2 (Babcock & Wilcox)
Complement	434 (19 officers, 415 enlisted men); 528 designed wartime

Liberty ship. "EC 2" type. Built by Bethlehem Steel Co, Fairfield Yard Baltimore, Md. Launched on 12 Sep 1943; commissioned on 8 Apr 1944. Armament reduced with removal of 5 inch gun and four 40 mm guns (twin).
The *Tituila* was scheduled for decommissioning late in 1971.

DISPOSALS

Oglala ARG 1 (ex-CM 4), **Beaver** ARG 19 (ex-AS 5), and **Otus** ARG 20 (ex-A 20) stricken after World War II. **Luzon** ARG 2, **Mindanao** ARG 3 **Oahu** ARG 5, **Cebu** ARG 6, **Culebra Island** ARG 7, **Mavi** ARG 8, **Mona Island** ARG 9, **Palawan** ARG 10, **Samar** ARG 11, **Chourre** ARV 1 (ex-ARG 14), **Webster** ARV 2 (ex-ARG 15), **Kermit Roosevelt** ARG 16, **Hooper Island** ARG 17 all stricken from Navy List between 1959-1963. (ARG 12 and ARG 13 to AG 68 and AG 69 respectively).

Fleet Support Ships—continued

TUTUILA (ARG 4)   *United States Navy*

17 REPAIR SHIPS: CONVERTED LST TYPE

(Battle damage Repair Ships)

ZEUS	ARB 4 (ex-LST 132)	**SARPEDON**	ARB 7 (ex-LST 956)
MIDAS	ARB 5 (ex-LST 524)	**TELAMON**	ARB 8 (ex-LST 957)

(Landing Craft Repair Ships

ACHELOUS	ARL 1 (ex-LST 10)	***SPHINX**	ARL 24 (ex-LST 963)
AMYCUS	ARL 2 (ex-LST 489)	***ASKARI**	ARL 30 (ex-LST 1131)
ATLAS	ARL 7 (ex-LST 231)	**BELLEROPHON**	ARL 31 (ex-LST 1132)
EGERIA	ARL 8 (ex-LST 136)	**INDRA**	ARL 37 (ex-LST 1147)
ENDYMION	ARL 9 (ex-LST 513)	***KRISHNA**	ARL 38 (ex-LST 1149)
***SATYR**	ARL 23 (ex-LST 8521)		

(Aircraft Repair Ships—Aircraft)

FABIUS	ARVA 5 (ex-LST 1093)	**MEGARA**	ARVA 6 (ex-LST 1095)

(Aircraft Repair Ship—Engine)

CHLORIS ARVE 4 (ex-LST 1094)

Displacement, tons	1 625 light; 4 100 full load
Dimenisons, feet	316 wl; 328 oa × 50 × 11
Guns	8—40 mm AA (quad)
Main engines	Diesels "General Motors"; 2 shafts; 1 800 bhp = 11·6 knots
Complement	251 to 286

All launched in 1942-45. Modified from basic LST design with several machine shops, material and ports storage, lifting gear, etc; ARLs cater to small amphibious, riverine, and minesweeping craft.
Indra, Askari Satyr, and *Sphinx* activated for service in Vietnam: all others except *Krishna* are in reserve. *Indra* again decommissioned in 1969. Photographs show *Askari* in Mekong Delta, South Vietnam, servicing small craft of River Flotilla One. Note LST stern anchor, topside clutter of parts and stores, crane for lifting riverine craft, tripod lattice mast, floats and small craft alongside.
ARL 24, 30 and 38 scheduled to decommission in 1971.

DISPOSALS
Demeter ARB 10 (ex-LST 1121), was stricken from the list on 1 Mar 1959, **Adonis** ARL 4, **Daedalus** ARL 35, **Minos** ARL 14, **Pentheus** ARL 20 and **Proserpine** ARL 21, **Crean** ARL 11, **Nenelaus** ARL 13, **Myrmidon** ARL 16, **Numitor** ARL 17, **Stentor** ARL 26 and **Typhon** ARL 28 in 1960, **Amphitrite** ARL 29, **Aristaeus** ARB 1, **Chimaera** ARL 33, **Creon** ARL 10, **Oceanus** ARB 2, **Phaon** ARB 3, and **Poseidon** ARL 12 on 1 July 1961, **Pandemus** ARL 18 stricken on 1 Oct 1968 (target). **Amycus** ARL 2 stricken on 1 June 1970.

ASKARI (ARL 30)   *1967, United States Navy*

ASKARI (ARL 30)   *1967. United States Navy*

13 SALVAGE SHIPS (ARS): "DIVER" CLASS

Name	No.	Launched	Commissioned
*ESCAPE	ARS 6	22 Nov 1942	20 Nov 1943
*GRAPPLE	ARS 7	31 Dec 1942	16 Dec 1943
*PRESERVER	ARS 8	1 Apr 1943	11 Jan 1944
*CURRENT	ARS 22	25 Sep 1943	14 June 1944
*DELIVER	ARS 23	25 Sep 1943	18 July 1944
*GRASP	ARS 24	31 July 1943	22 Aug 1944
*SAFEGUARD	ARS 25	20 Nov 1943	31 Oct 1944
*BOLSTER	ARS 38	23 Dec 1944	1 May 1945
*CONSERVER	ARS 39	27 Jan 1945	9 June 1945
*HOIST	ARS 40	31 Mar 1945	21 July 1945
*OPPORTUNE	ARS 41	31 Mar 1945	5 Oct 1945
*RECLAIMER	ARS 42	25 June 1945	20 Dec 1945
*RECOVERY	ARS 43	4 Aug 1945	15 May 1946

Displacement, tons	1 530 standard; 1 900 full load
Dimensions, feet	207 wl; 213·5 oa × 39 × 43 × 13
Guns	1—40 mm AA (removed from some ships) ; 2—·50 cal MG or 2—20 mm guns fitted in some ships
Main engines	Diesel-electric; 2 shafts; 2 440 shp = 14 knots
Complement	85 (120 designed wartime)

These ships are fitted for salvage and towing; equipped with compressed air diving gear. All built by Basalt Rock Co, Napa Calif. Note position of 40 mm gun forward of funnel and 20 mm guns at bridge level on *Recovery*.
Three additional ships are on loan to private salvage firms, the *Cable* ARS 19, *Curb* ARS 21, and *Gear* ARS 34; they remain on Navy List and support naval requirements as needed. All others are active with Navy crews.

CONVERSIONS. *Chain* ARS 20 and *Snatch* ARS 27 converted to oceanographic research ships, designated AGOR 17 and 18, respectively.

NOMENCLATURE. Salvage ships are named for words relating to salvage activities.

DISPOSALS
Clamp (ex-Atlantic Salvor) ARS 33 stricken in July 1963.

RECOVERY (ARS 43)   *1969, US Navy, PH2 T. W. Woodward*

HOIST (ARS 40)   *United States Navy*

GRAPPLE (ARS 7)   *1970, US Navy, PH3 C. P. Weston*

Fleet Support Ships—continued

2 SALVAGE LIFTING SHIPS (ARSD): CONVERTED LSM

GYPSY ARSD 1 (ex-LSM 549)   **MENDER** ARSD 2 (ex-LSM 550)

Displacement, tons	740 standard; 1 095 full load
Dimensions, feet	224·2 × 34 × 7
Guns	2—20 mm AA
Main engines	Diesel; 2 shafts; 2 800 bhp = 13 knots
Complement	65

Used as diving tenders. Both launched on 7 Dec 1945. In the Pacific Reserve Fleet. Sister ships *Salvager* (ex-LSM 551) ARSD 3 and *Windlass* (ex-LSM 552) ARSD 4 were reclassified as YMLC 3 and YMLC 4, respectively, on 1 Nov 1967. Built by Brown SB Co, Houston, Texas.

2 SALVAGE TENDERS (ARST): CONVERTED LST

LAYSAN ISLAND ARST 1 (ex-LST 1098)   **PALMYRA** ARST 3 (ex-LST 1100)

Displacement, tons	1 653 standard; 4 080 full load
Dimensions, feet	328 × 50 × 11 × 14·3 max
Main engines	Diesel; 2 shafts; 1 800 bhp = 11·6 knots
Complement	289

Former tank landing ships. In reserve. Built by Jeffersonville Bridge & Machinery Co, Jeffersonville, Ind; launched on 27 Jan 1945 and 20 Feb 1945, respectively.

1 HELICOPTER REPAIR SHIP (ARVH): CONVERTED SEAPLANE TENDER

*CORPUS CHRISTI BAY (ex-*Albermarle*) T-ARVH 1 (ex-AV 5)

Displacement, tons	8 671 standard; 13 475 full load
Length, feet (*metres*)	508 (*154·8*) wl; 537 (*163·7*) oa
Beam, feet (*metres*)	69·2 (*21·1*)
Draft, feet (*metres*)	21·3 (*6·5*)
Main engines	Geared turbines (Parsons); 12 000 shp; 2 shafts
Boilers	4 (Babcock & Wilcox)
Speed, knots	19·7
Complement	130 (25 officers, 105 men) plus 310 Army personnel

Built as a large seaplane tender by the New York Shipbuilding Corp, Camden, New Jersey, under the Fiscal Year 1937 shipbuilding Programme; laid down on 12 June 1939, launched on 13 July 1940, commissioned on 20 Dec 1940. She was modernised in 1956-1957 and subsequently converted to a helicopter repair ship in 1964-1965 (see Conversion notes).

DESIGN. As built the *Albermarle* and her sister ship *Curtiss* (AV 4) resembled the "Curituck" class configuration, but with twin funnels. Both of these large seaplane tender designs provided extensive maintenance shops and spare parts, munition, and petrol stowage to support seaplane squadrons; space provided for squadron flight crews and Fleet Air Wing staff; aircraft hangar amidships, open deck aft, and two large aircraft cranes (20-ton capacity in "Curtiss" class; 30-ton capacity in "Curituck" class). As built the *Albermarle* had an armament of 4 5 inch DP guns and 16 40 mm AA guns.

STATUS. The *Corpus Christi Bay* is in service, operated by the Military Sealift Command (formerly MSTS) and manned by a civilian operating crew and army helicopter maintenance battalion.

CONVERSION. The *Albermarle* was converted under the Fiscal Year 1956 programme at the Philadelphia Naval Shipyard to support the P6M Seamaster jet-propelled seaplane. Recommissioned on 21 Oct 1957. Decommissioned in 1960 and placed in the Maritime Administration Reserve Fleet. Stricken from the Navy List in Sep 1962. Reacquired by the Navy in Aug 1964 for conversion to a helicopter repair ship. The *Albermarle* was converted to an aircraft repair ship (helicopter) at the Charleston Naval Shipyard in 1964-1965; fitted with 33 maintenance shops specialising in helicopter repairs, closed-circuit television provided for rapid transmission of drawings and blueprints from central technical library, automatic boiler controls to reduce operating crew, flight control tower (installed on flying bridge), and improved habitability features; amidships hangar structure extended aft and topped with a 50 × 150 ft helicopter platform with four-part steel hatch to permit helicopters to be lowered into hangars; two 20-ton capacity cranes installed aft of second funnel; smaller helicopter deck installed forward. All armament removed. Renamed *Corpus Christi Bay* and designated T-ARVH 1 on 27 Mar 1965. Deployed to South Vietnam to repair Army light fixed-wing aircraft and helicopters.

CORPUS CHRISTI BAY (T-ARVH 1)   *US Navy*

2 + 2 SUBMARINE TENDERS (AS): "L. Y. SPEAR" CLASS

Name	No.	Laid down	Launched	Commissioned
*L. Y. SPEAR	AS 36	5 May 1966	7 Sep 1967	28 Feb 1970
DIXON	AS 37	7 Sep 1967	20 June 1970	Aug 1971
	AS 38	(Fiscal Year 1972 programme)		
	AS 39	(Fiscal Year 1972 programme)		

Displacement, tons	13 000 standard; 22 640 full load
Dimensions, feet	643·6 × 85 × 25
Guns	2—5 in 38 cal DP (single)
Main engines	Steam turbines; 1 shaft; 20 000 shp = 20 knots
Boilers	2
Complement	1 072 (42 officers and 1 030 enlisted men)

Both ships built by General Dynamics Corp, Quincy, Massachusetts. *L. Y. Spear* authorised in Fiscal Year 1965 new construction programme; *Dixon* in FY 1966 programme. AS 38 of FY 1969 programme was cancelled on 27 Mar 1969 to provide funds for overruns in FY 1969 and FY 1970 programmes (estimated saving was $68 600 000).
These ships are especially equipped to support and replenish nuclear-powered attack submarines, providing alongside services to as many as four submarines simultaneously.

NOMENCLATURE. Submarine tenders generally are named after pioneers in submarine development and mythological characters.
Lieutenant G. E. Dixon, an engineer officer, commanded the Confederate submarine *Hunley* when it sank the Union warship *Housatonic* during the American Civil War (1864); Lawrence Y. Spear was a marine engineer who contributed to submarine design in the early 20th century.

L. Y. SPEAR (AS 36)   *1969, General Dynamics (Quincy)*

CORPUS CHRISTI BAY (T-ARVH 1)   *US Navy*

L. Y. SPEAR (AS 36)   *1969, General Dynamics (Quincy)*

Fleet Support Ships—continued

2 SUBMARINE TENDERS (AS):"SIMON LAKE" CLASS

Name	No.	Laid down	Launched	Commissioned
*SIMON LAKE	AS 33	7 Jan 1963	8 Feb 1964	7 Nov 1964
*CANOPUS	AS 34	2 Mar 1964	12 Feb 1965	4 Nov 1965

Displacement, tons	21 450 to 22 250 full load
Dimensions, feet	643·7 × 85 × 30
Guns	4—3 in, 50 cal AA (twin)
Main engines	Steam turbines; 1 shaft; 20 000 hp = 18 knots
Boilers	2 (Combustion Engineering)
Complement	1 075 (55 officers, 1 020 men)

These ships are designed specifically to service Fleet Ballistic Missile Submarines (SSBN), with as many as three submarines alongside being supported simultaneously. The *Simon Lake* was authorised in the Fiscal Year 1963 new construction programme and built by the Puget Sound Naval Shipyard; the *Canopus* was authorised in FY 1964 and built by Ingalls Shipbuilding Corp. AS 35 was authorised in FY 1965 programme, but her construction was deferred. The last ship would have permitted one tender to be assigned to each of five FBM submarine squadrons with a sixth ship available to rotate when another was in overhaul; however, only four SSBN squadrons were established.
Note cranes amidships funnel location (flanked by gun mounts, and helicopter platform).

NOMENCLATURE. Simon Lake was a most-creative submarine designer and builder of the 20th century.

CANOPUS (AS 34) servicing SSBN   1970, US Navy, PH1 Robert Woods

SIMON LAKE (AS 33) servicing SSBN 634   1965, United States Navy

CANOPUS (AS 34)   1965, United States Navy

2 SUBMARINE TENDERS (AS): "HUNLEY" CLASS

Name	No.	Laid down	Launched	Commissioned
*HUNLEY	AS 31	28 Nov 1960	28 Sep 1961	16 June 1962
*HOLLAND	AS 32	5 Mar 1962	19 Jan 1963	7 Sep 1963

Displacement, tons	10 500 standard; 18 300 full load
Dimensions, feet	599 × 83 × 24
Guns	4—3 in, 50 cal, AA (twin)
Main engines	Diesel-electric (10 Fairbanks-Morse diesels); 1 shaft; 15 000 bhp = 19 knots
Complement	1 081 (58 officers, 1 023 men) plus accommodation for 30 officers and 270 men from submarines

"HUNLEY" CLASS   continued

Tenders for serving FBM submarines. *Hunley* was authorised in the Fiscal Year 1960 new construction programme and built by Newport News Shipbuilding & Drydock Co, Newport, Virginia. She provides weapon and nuclear logistic support for ballistic missile submarines. A large hammerhead crane of 32 ton capacity with athwartships bridge travel, the first of its kind aboard a ship, is installed to on and off missiles from submarines. *Holland* was authorised under the 1962 programme and built by Ingalls Shipbuilding Corp for $24 359 800. Equipped with 52 workshops and a helicopter platform. Note amidships funnel position compared to later class of FBM submarine tenders.

NOMENCLATURE. *Holland* is named after John Philip Holland, an Irish emigrant to the United States, and submarine designer and builder. One of his submarines was accepted by the US Navy in 1900 and became Submarine Torpedo Boat No 1, named *Holland*, the first officially accepted US Navy submarine.

OPERATIONAL. US tenders for fleet ballistic missile submarines (Polaris/Poseidon) are based at Holy Loch, Scotland; Rota, Spain; Charleston, South Carolina; and Apra Harbour; Guam. They work with floating dry docks and service craft to replenish and repair SSBN, between 60-day deterrent patrols.

SIMON LAKE (AS 33)   1965 United States Navy

HUNLEY (AS 31)   1967, United States Navy

HUNLEY (AS 31)   United States Navy

Fleet Support Ships—continued

Fulton (AS 11), Skylark (ASR 20), five *SSNs* at New London, Connecticut.

United States Navy

L. Y. Spear (AS 36)

1970, United States Navy

Proteus (AS 19)

1963, United States Navy

Nerevs (AS 17)

United States Navy

Fleet Support Ships—continued

1 SUBMARINE TENDER (AS): "AEGIR" CLASS

Name	No.	Launched	Commissioned
AEGIR	AS 23	15 Sep 1943	8 Sep 1944

Displacement, tons	8 100 standard; 16 100 full load
Dimensions, feet	492 oa × 69·5 × 26·5
Guns	1—5 in, 38 cal; 4—3 in, 50 cal AA
Main engines	Geared turbines (Westinghouse); 1 shaft; 8 500 shp = 14·4 knots
Boilers	2 (Foster-Wheeler "D")
Complement	1 460 (82 officers, 1 378 enlisted men)

Built by Ingalls Shipbuilding Corp. CS-3-A2 type. Original armament also included 4—40 mm guns. Decommissioned in 1946 and placed in reserve.

DISPOSALS

Of three sister ships, **Anthedon**, AS 24 and **Clytle** AS 26 were stricken from the Navy List on 1 Sep 1961, and **Apollo** AS 25, transferred to the Maritime Administration in 1963, was stricken in 1964. **Anthedon** transferred to Turkey on 7 Feb 1969.

1 SUBMARINE TENDER (AS): "EURYALE" CLASS

Name	No.	Launched	Commissioned
EURYALE (ex-Hawaiian Merchant)	AS 22	12 Apr 1941	2 Dec 1943

Displacement, tons	8 282 standard; 15 400 full load
Dimensions, feet	492·5 oa × 69·5 × 25
Guns	1—5 in, 38 cal; 4—3 in, 50 cal AA
Main engines	Geared turbines (De Laval); 1 shaft; 8 500 shp = 16·5 knots
Boilers	2 (Foster-Wheeler "D")
Complement	1 304

Built by Federal SB & DD Co, Kearny, New Jersey. Modified C3 type. Original armament also included 4—40 mm guns. In reserve.

2 SUBMARINE TENDERS (AS): "GRIFFIN" CLASS

Name	No.	Launched	Commissioned
GRIFFIN (ex-Marmacpenn)	AS 13	10 Nov 1939	31 July 1941
PELIAS (ex-Mormacyork)	AS 14	14 Nov 1939	5 Sep 1941

Displacement, tons	8 600 standard; 14 500 full load
Dimensions, feet	492 × 69·5 × 24·2
Guns	4—3 in, 50 cal AA
Main engines	Diesel (Busch-Sulzer); 1 shaft; 8 500 bhp = 16·5 knots
Complement	1 511 and 1 067 respectively

C3 Cargo type. Built by Sun SB & DD Co, Chester, Pennsylvania. Both in the Pacific Reserve Fleet.

FULTON (AS 11) servicing CORPORAL (SS 346) *1965, United States Navy*

BUSHNELL (AS 15) *1967, United States Navy*

7 SUBMARINE TENDERS (AS): "FULTON" CLASS

Name	No.	Launched	Commissioned
*FULTON	AS 11	27 Dec 1940	12 Sep 1941
*SPERRY	AS 12	17 Dec 1941	1 May 1942
BUSHNELL	AS 15	14 Sep 1942	10 Apr 1943
*HOWARD W. GILMORE	AS 16	16 Sep 1943	24 May 1944
*NEREUS (ex-Neptune)	AS 17	12 Feb 1945	27 Oct 1945
*ORION	AS 18	14 Oct 1942	30 Sep 1943
*PROTEUS	AS 19	12 Nov 1942	31 Jan 1944

Displacement, tons	9 734 standard; 18 000 full load *Proteus:* 10 234 standard; 18 500 full load
Dimensions, feet	530·5; *Proteus* 574·5 oa × 73·3 × 25·5
Guns	2—5 in, 38 cal DP (one gun in *Proteus*)
Main engines	Diesel-electric (General Motors); 2 shafts; 11 200 to 11 800 hp = 15·4 knots
Complement	917 (34 officers, 883 enlisted men); except *Proteus* 1 121 (51 officers, 1 070 enlisted men)

Ships vary in detail. *Orion* and *Proteus* built by Moore Dry Dock Co, Oakland, California, others by Mare Island Navy Yard, California. Original armament consisted of 4—5 in guns and 8—40 mm guns. *Bushnell* decommissioned in 1970 remains in service in reserve as station ship at Norfolk, Va.

CONVERSION. *Proteus*, AS 19 was converted at the Charleston Naval Shipyard, under the Fiscal Year 1959 conversion programme, at a cost of $23 000 000 to service nuclear powered Fleet Ballistic Missile Submarine (SSBN) squadron. Conversion was started on 19 Jan 1959 and she was recommissioned on 8 July 1960. She was lengthened by adding a section amidships 44 feet in length, and the bare hull weight of this 6-deck high insertion was approximately 500 tons. Three 5 inch guns were removed and her upper decks extended aft to provide additional workshops.

MODERNISATION. *Bushnell, Fulton, Howard W. Gilmore, Nereus, Orion* and *Sperry* have undergone FRAM II modernisation to service nuclear powered attack submarines. Additional maintenance shops provided to service nuclear plant components and advanced electronic equipment and weapons. After two 5 inch guns and eight 40 mm guns (twin) removed.

NOMENCLATURE. David Bushnell was a submarine inventor whose craft participated in the American Revolution and the Anglo-American War of 1812. Howard W. Gilmore was a submarine commander who lost his life in World War II.

SPERRY (AS 12) *United States Navy*

2 SUBMARINE RESCUE SHIPS (ASR): "PIGEON" CLASS

Name	No.	Builder	Launched	Comm.
PIGEON	ASR 21	Alabama DD & SB Co (Mobile)	13 Aug 1969	mid-1971
ORTOLAN	ASR 22	Alabama DD & SB Co (Mobile)	10 Sep 1969	mid-1971

Displacement, tons	4 200 full load
Dimensions, feet	251 oa × 86 × (see *Design* notes) × 21·25
Guns	2—3 in (76 mm) 50 cal AA; 4—·50 cal MG
Main engines	4 diesels; 6 000 shp; 2 shafts = 15 knots
Complement	115 (6 officers, 109 enlisted men)
Staff accommodation	14 (4 officers, 10 enlisted men)
Submersible operators	24 (4 officers, 20 enlisted men)

These are the world's first ships designed specifically for this role, all other ASR designs being adaptations of tug types. The ASR 21 class ships will serve as (1) surface support ships for the Deep Submergence Rescue Vehicles (DSRV), (2) rescue ships employing the existing McCann rescue chamber, (3) major deep-sea diving support ships, and (4) operational control ships for salvage operations.

The Navy has announced plans to replace the current 10-ship ASR force with new construction ASRs. However, only two ships have been funded with procurement of others deferred. ASR 21 authorised in Fiscal Year 1967 new construction programme; ASR 22 in FY 1968 programme. Estimated cost per ship is approximately $17 000 000.

A shipyard strike delayed completion of the ASR 21 and ASR 22.

DESIGN. These ships will have twin, catamaran hulls, the first ocean-going catamaran ships to be built for the US Navy since Robert Fulton's steam gunboat *Demologus* of 1812. The design will provide a large deck working area, facilities for raising and lowering submersibles and underwater equipment and improved stability when operating equipment at great depths. Each of the twin hulls is 251 feet long and 26 feet wide. The well between the hulls will be 34 feet across, giving the ASR a maximum beam of 86 feet. Fitted with helicopter platform.

ENGINEERING. Space and weight are reserved for future installation of a ducted thruster in each bow to enable the ship to maintain precise position while stopped or at slow speeds. Endurance is 8 500 miles at 13 knots.

ELECTRONICS. Fitted with precision three-dimensional sonar system for tracking submersibles.

Fleet Support Ships—continued

"PIGEON" CLASS—Continued

DIVING. These ships will be fitted with the Mk 2 Deep Diving System to support conventional or saturation divers operating at depths to 850 feet. The system consists of two decompression chambers, two personnel transfer capsules to transport divers between the ship and ocean floor, and the associated controls, winches, cables, gas supplies, et cetera. Submarine rescue ships are the US Navy's primary diving ships and the only ones fitted for helium-oxygen diving.

SALVAGE. During major salvage operations the ASR can serve as a command post for the salvage master. Note two mooring buoys ("spuds") forward of bridge in artist's concept; there are two additional buoys aft. (Precise mooring is required in diving and salvage work, and for operating McCann submarine rescue chamber).

SUBMERSIBLES. Each ASR will be capable of transporting, servicing, lowering, and raising two Deep Submergence Rescue Vehicles (DSRV) (see section on Deep Submergence Vehicles).

NOMENCLATURE. Submarine rescue ships traditionally have carried bird names (the US Navy's first six ASRs were converted "Bird" class minesweepers).

ASR 21 Class   *Official Navy Drawing*

PIGEON (ASR 21)   *1969, Alabama DD & SB Co*

2 SUBMARINE RESCUE SHIPS (ASR)

"PENGUIN" CLASS

Name	No.	Launched
PENGUIN (ex-*Chetco*)	ASR 12 (ex-ATF 99)	20 July 1943
*****SKYLARK** (ex-*Yustaga*)	ASR 20 (ex-ATF 165)	19 Mar 1946

Displacement, tons	1 235 standard; 1 740 full load
Dimensions, feet	195 wl; 205 oa × 38·5 × 15·3
Guns	Removed
Main engines	Diesel-electric (Busch-Sulzer diesels in *Penguin*, General Motors in *Skylark*); 1 shaft; 3 000 bhp = 14 knots
Complement	85 (106 designed wartime)

Former fleet tugs, converted in 1944 and 1947. Built by Charleston SB & DD Co. The *Bluebird* ASR 19 of this type was transferred to Turkey on 15 Aug 1950. These ships are equipped with powerful pumps, heavy air compressors, and submarine rescue chambers. Fitted for helium-oxygen diving. Guns removed; formerly armed with one 3 inch gun. See "Chanticleer" class for additional notes applicable to this class. *Penguin* decommissioned in 1970; *Skylark* was to be decommissioned in 1971
—1972

7 SUBMARINE RESCUE SHIPS (ASR):

"CHANTICLEER" CLASS

	ASR	Launched		ASR	Launched
CHANTICLEER	7	29 May 1942	*****KITTIWAKE**	13	10 July 1945
*****COUCAL**	8	29 May 1942	*****PETREL**	14	26 Sep 1945
*****FLORIKAN**	9	14 June 1942	*****SUNBIRD**	15	3 Apr 1945
			*****TRINGA**	16	25 June 1945

Displacement, tons	1 653 standard; 2 290 full load
Dimensions, feet	240 wl; 251·5 oa × 42 × 14·9
Guns	2—20 mm AA in some ships
Main engines	Diesel-electric (Alco in first 4 ships, GM in others); 1 shaft; 3 000 bhp = 14·9 knots
Complement	85 (102 designed wartime)

Large tug-type ships equipped with powerful pumps, heavy air compressors, and rescue chambers for submarine salvage and rescue operations. ASR 7-10 built by Moore SB & DD Co, Oakland, Calif, and ASR 13-16 by Savannah Machine & Foundry Co, Savannah, Ga. Fitted for helium-oxygen diving equipment (submarine rescue ships are the principal deep-sea diving ships in the Navy and the only ones with a built-in helium capability).
As built each ship was armed with two 3 inch AA guns; removed 1957-1958. Some ships subsequently fitted with two 20 mm AA guns.
One ASR normally is deployed to the Western Pacific and one in the Mediterranean with the others at US submarine bases in the continental United States and Hawaii. The war-built ships were to have been replaced on a one-for-one basis by the ASR-21 class, but latter programme sharply curtailed.
Greenlet ASR 10 of this type transferred to Turkey on 12 June 1970.
Chanticleer decommissioned in 1970.
Florikan has 20 mm gun just forward of funnel on bridge level. port and starboard.
Submarine rescue ships have "fish" symbol on bow next to number.

FLORIKAN (ASR 9)   *1970, US Navy, PH2 Leroy Palmer*

KITTIWAKE (ASR 13)   *1969, United States Navy*

TRINGA (ASR 16)   *1966. United States Navy*

11 AUXILIARY TUGS (ATA): "MARICOPA" CLASS

	ATA	Launched		ATA	Launched
ACCOKEEK	181	27 July 1944	**TATNUCK**	195	14 Dec 1944
SALISH	187	29 Sep 1944	**MAHOPAC**	196	21 Dec 1944
PENOBSCOT	188	12 Oct 1944	**WANDANK**	206	9 Nov 1944
SAMOSET	190	26 Oct 1944	**SAGAMORE**	208	19 Jan 1945
STALLION	193	24 Nov 1944	**CATAWBA**	210	15 Feb 1945
			KEYWADIN	213	9 Apr 1945

Displacement, tons	534 standard; 835 full load
Dimensions, feet	134·5 wl; 143 oa × 33·9 × 13
Guns	1—3 in, 50 cal AA or 4—20 mm AA (twin); all guns removed from some ships
Main engines	2 GM diesel-electric; 1 shaft; 1 500 bhp = 13 knots
Complement	45 (5 officers, 40 men)

Steel-hulled tugs formerly designated as rescue tugs (ATR); renumbered in same series as larger fleet tugs (ATF) when designation changed to ATA in 1944. All above ships built by Livingston SB Corp, Orange, Texas, or Gulfport Boiler & Welding Works, Port Arthur, Texas. During 1948 they were assigned names that had been carried by discarded fleet and yard tugs.
All of the surviving ships were decommissioned in 1970-1971 and placed in reserve. Two ships of this class serve in the Coast Guard.

TRANSFERS. *Bagaduce* ATA 194 and *Wampanoag* ATA 202 to Coast Guard in 1959, *Wateree* ATA 174 to Peru in 1961, *Tankowa* ATA 176 to Nationalist China in 1962, *Sotoyomo* ATA 121 to Mexico in 1963, *Undaunted* ATA 199 to Bureau of Commercial Fisheries, Department of Interior in 1964, *Geronimo* ATA 207 (on loan to Bureau of Commercial Fisheries from 1962 to 1968) to Nationalist China on 8 Feb 1969.
Cahokia ATA 186 loaned to US Air Force on 22 April 1971, *Kalmia* ATA 184 and *Koka* ATA 185 to Columbia in 1971, *Tillamook* ATA 192 to South Korea in 1971, *Umpqua* ATA 209 to Guinea in 1971.

DISPOSALS (since 1 Jan 1965)
Allegheny ATA 179 stricken on 14 Dec 1968, **Sunnadin** ATA 197 stricken on 20 Nov 1969.

ACCOKEEK (ATA 181)   1970, United States Navy

MOSOSPELEA (ATF 158)   1968, United States Navy

CATAWBA (ATA 210)   1970, US Navy, PHCS B. Spang

LUISENO (ATF 156)   1967, United States Navy

1 AUXILIARY TUG (ATA): Ex-US ARMY

ATA 240 (ex-US Army LT 455)

Displacement, tons	534 standard; 835 full load
Dimensions, feet	143 oa × 33·3 × 13·9 max
Main engines	Diesel-electric; 1 500 bhp = 13 knots

The ATA 240 is the last of six Army tugs transferred to the Navy (designated ATA 239-244); see 1970-1971 and earlier editions for disposal of others. All were operated by the Navy's Military Sea Transportation Service (MSTS).

29 FLEET TUGS (ATF): "APACHE" CLASS

	ATF	Launched		ATF	Launched
*APACHE	67	8 May 1942	*MUNSEE	107	21 Jan 1943
*KIOWA	72	5 Nov 1942	*PAKANA	108	3 Mar 1943
*SIOUX	75	27 May 1942	*QUAPAW	110	15 May 1943
*UTE	76	24 June 1942	*TAKELMA	113	18 Sep 1943
*CREE	84	17 Aug 1942	*TAWAKONI	114	28 Oct 1943
*LIPAN	85	17 Sep 1942	*ATAKAPA	149	11 July 1944
*MATACO	86	14 Oct 1942	*LUISENO	156	17 Mar 1945
SENECA	91	2 Feb 1943	*NIPMUC	157	12 Apr 1945
*TAWASA	92	22 Feb 1943	*MOSOSPELEA	158	7 Mar 1945
*ABNAKI	96	22 Apr 1943	*PAIUTE	159	4 June 1945
ARIKARA	98	22 June 1943	*PAPAGO	160	21 June 1945
*CHOWANOC	100	20 Aug 1943	*SALINAN	161	20 July 1945
*COCOPA	101	5 Oct 1943	*SHAKORI	162	9 Aug 1945
*MOCTOBI	105	25 Mar 1944	UTINA	163	31 Aug 1945
*MOLALA	106	23 Dec 1942			

COCOPA (ATF 101)   1970, US Navy, PH2 Donna M. Young

Displacement, tons	1 235 standard; 1 675 full load
Dimensions, feet	195 wl; 205 oa × 38·5 × 15·5 max
Guns	1—3 in, 50 cal AA
Main engines	Diesel-electric drive; 1 shaft; 3 000 bhp = 15 knots
Complement	85 (5 officers, 80 enlisted men)

KIOWA (ATF 72)   1970, United States Navy

Large ocean tugs fitted with powerful pumps and other salvage equipment. ATF 96 and later ships ("Abnaki" class) have smaller funnel. As built these ships mounted 2—40 mm guns in addition to 3 inch gun. All surviving ships built by Charleston SB & DD Co, or United Engineering Co, Alameda, Calif, except Seneca built by Cramp SB Co, Philadelphia, Pa, and Tawasa by Commercial Iron Works, Portland, Oreg. Pakana stricken in 1963 but reinstated on Navy List in 1963.
Two ships of this class serve in the Coast Guard.

CONVERSIONS. Chetco ATF 99, Yurok ATF 164, and Yustaga ATF 165 converted to submarine rescue ships ASR 12, 19, and 20, respectively; Serrano ATF 112 converted to surveying ship AGS 24.

TRANSFERS. Avoyel ATF 150 and Chilula ATF 152 to Coast Guard in 1956, Yuma ATF 94 to Pakistan in 1959, Tekesta ATF 93 to Chile in 1960, Cusabo ATF 155 to Ecuador in 1960, Choctaw ATF 70 to Columbia in 1961, Menominee ATF 73 to Indonesia in 1961, Pinto ATF 90 to Peru in 1961, Arapaho ATF 68 and Cahuilla ATF 152 to Argentina in 1961, Tolowa ATF 116 to Venezuela in 1962, Potawatomii ATF 109 to Chile in 1963, Bannock ATF 81 to Italy in 1954, Chickasaw ATF 83 to Nationalist China in 1966.

DISPOSALS (since 1 Jan 1965)
Hitchiti ATF 103 stricken on 9 Nov 1969.

NOMENCLATURE. US tugs of World War II construction and previous classes were named for Indian tribes and words.

KIOWA (ATF 72)   1970, United States Navy

Fleet Support Ships—*continued*

3 + 3 SALVAGE TUGS (ATS): NEW CONSTRUCTION

Name	No.	Laid down	Launched	Commission
*EDENTON	ATS 1	1 Apr 1967	15 May 1968	23 Jan 1971
BEAUFORT	ATS 2	19 Feb 1968	20 Dec 1968	Oct 1971
BRUNSWICK	ATS 3	5 June 1968	14 Oct 1969	Mar 1972
	ATS 4			
	ATS 5			
	ATS 6			

Displacement, tons	3 125 full load
Dimensions, feet	232·6 × 50 × 14·5
Guns	4—·50 cal MG
Main engines	4 diesels (Paxman); 6 000 shp; 2 shafts = 16 knots
Complement	102 (9 officers and 93 enlisted men)

These tugs are designed specifically for salvage operations and will be capable of (1) ocean towing, (2) supporting diver operations to depths of 850 feet, (3) lifting submerged objects weighing as much as 600 000 pounds from a depth of 120 feet by static tidal lift or 30 000 pounds by dynamic lift, (4) fighting ship fires, and (5) performing general salvage operations.

The ATS 1 was authorised in the Fiscal year 1966 shipbuilding programme; ATS 2 and ATS 3 in the FY 1967 programme. All three ships constructed by Brooke Marine, Lowestoft, England. ATS 4 and ATS 5 planned for FY 1970 programme were deferred to the FY 1972 programme. ATS 1-3 are considerably behind schedule.

A total of 17 ships of this type are planned to replace older ocean-going ATF/ATA/ARS ships.

DIVING. These ships can carry the air-transportable Mk I Deep Diving System to support four divers working in two-man shifts at depths to 850 feet. The system consists of a double-chamber decompression chamber, a personnel transfer capsule to transport divers between the ships and ocean floor, and the associated controls, winches, cables, gas supplies, *et cetera*. The ships' organic diving capability is compressed air.

ENGINEERING. Fitted with controllable-pitch propellers and tunnel bow thruster for precise manoeuvering.

NOMENCLATURE. Salvage tugs are being named for small American cities.

EDENTON (ATS 1) *Artist's concept, photograph by Charles Hodge*

BRUNSWICK (ATS 3) *1969, United States Navy*

EDENTON (ATS 1) *1968, Ford Jenkins*

SEAPLANE TENDERS (AV)

All remaining seaplane tenders on the Navy List were stricken during 1971.

Of the "Currituck" class, the **Pine Island** AV 12 and **Salisbury Sound** AV 13 were stricken on 1 Feb 1971; **Currituck** AV 7 stricken in 1971.

A fourth ship of this class, the **Norton Sound** ex-AV 11, serves as a missile test ship (AVM 1) and is listed with Experimental, Research and Surveying Ships. See 1970-1971 and previous editions for dimensions and characteristics of these ships.

The **Chandeleur** AV 10 of the C3-S1-B1 type was stricken in 1971. See 1970-1971 and previous editions for details.

The **Hamlin** AV 15 and **St. George** AV 16 of the modified C3 type were stricken on 1 July 1963. The latter ship was reacquired from the Maritime Administration reserve fleet and transferred to Italy on 17 May 1969 for use as a transport/command ship.

The *Curtiss* AV 4 was stricken from the Navy List on 1 July 1963. (She had been modified for scientific work in 1951 and subsequently served mainly in support of Atomic Energy Commission experiments until decommissioned in September 1957). Her sister ship *Albemarle* AV 5 has been converted to a helicopter repair ship and renamed *Corpus Christi Bay* (redesignated T-ARVH 1); she is listed with Fleet Support Ships.

ADVANCED AVIATION BASE SHIPS (AVB)

Both advanced aviation base ships, intended to set up advanced bases for land- and sea-based patrol/maritime reconnaissance aircraft, have been stricken from the Navy List.

Tallahatchie County AVB 2 ex-LST 1154 stricken on 15 Jan 1970 (scrapped). See 1969-1970 and previous editions for details. (Her sister ship *Talbot County* LST 1153 remains on the Navy List).

Alameda County AVB 1 ex-LST 32 was transferred to Italy in November 1962 for use as a transport.

SSBN in Richland (AFDM 8) at Guam, Mariana Island

1969, Robert Fudge

FLOATING DRY DOCKS

The US Navy operates a number of floating dry docks to supplement dry dock facilities at major naval activities, to support fleet ballistic missile submarines (SSBN) at advanced bases, and to provide repair capabilities in forward combat areas (such as South Vietnam).

The larger floating dry docks are made sectional to facilitate movement overseas and to render them self docking. The ARD-type docks have the forward end of their docking well closed by a structure resembling the bow of a ship to facilitate towing. Berthing facilities, repair shops, and machinery are housed in sides of larger docks. None is self-propelled.

Twenty-nine floating dry docks are in Navy service (including two partial docks), 15 are out of service in reserve (including two partial docks), 31 are on lease to commercial firms for private use, and 18 are on loan to other US services and foreign navies (including one partial dock). Asterisks indicate docks in active US service.

YFD 69	14 000 tons	Steel (3)	Commercial lease
YFD 70	14 000 tons	Steel (3)	Commercial lease
YFD 71	14 000 tons	Steel (3)	Commercial lease
*YFD 82 (ex-ARD 1)	1 500 tons	Steel	Portsmouth Nav Shipyard
*YFD 83 (ex-AFDL 31)	1 000 tons	Steel	US Coast Guard

LARGE AUXILIARY FLOATING DRY DOCKS

*AFDB 1 (partial)	40 000 tons	Steel (4)	Subic Bay, Philippines
AFDB 1 (partial)	60 000 tons	Steel (6)	Reserve
AFDB 2	90 000 tons	Steel (10)	Reserve
AFDB 3	81 000 tons	Steel (9)	Reserve
AFDB 4	55 000 tons	Steel (7)	Reserve
AFDB 5	55 000 tons	Steel (7)	Reserve
AFDB 6	55 000 tons	Steel (7)	Reserve
AFDB 7 (partial)		Steel (2)	Reserve
*AFDB 7 (partial)	10 000 tons	Steel (1)	US Army
*LOS ALAMOS AFDB 7 (partial)	40 000 tons	Steel (4)	Holy Loch, Scotland

LARGE AUXILIARY FLOATING DRY DOCKS

Name-No.	Capacity	Construction	Notes
*AFDL 1	1 000 tons	Steel	Guantanamo Bay, Cuba
AFDL 2	1 000 tons	Steel	Reserve
*AFDL 6	1 000 tons	Steel	Little Creek, Virginia
AFDL 7	1 900 tons	Steel	Reserve
AFDL 8	1 000 tons	Steel	Commercial lease
AFDL 9	1 000 tons	Steel	Commercial lease
*AFDL 10	1 000 tons	Steel	Subic Bay, Philippines
*AFDL 11	1 000 tons	Steel	Subic Bay, Philippines
AFDL 12	1 000 tons	Steel	Reserve
AFDL 15	1 000 tons	Steel	Commercial lease
AFDL 16	1 000 tons	Steel	Commercial lease
AFDL 19	1 000 tons	Steel	Commercial lease
AFDL 20	1 000 tons	Steel	Loan to Philippines
*AFDL 21	1 000 tons	Steel	Guam, Marianas
*AFDL 22	1 900 tons	Steel	Cameran Bay S. Vietnam
*AFDL 23	1 900 tons	Steel	Danang, S. Vietnam
AFDL 25	1 000 tons	Steel	Reserve
AFDL 26	1 000 tons	Steel	Loan to Paraguay
*AFDL 28	1 000 tons	Steel	Key West, Florida
AFDL 29	1 000 tons	Steel	Commercial lease
AFDL 30	1 000 tons	Steel	Commercial lease
AFDL 33	1 900 tons	Steel	Loan to Peru
AFDL 35	2,800 tons	Concrete	Reserve
AFDL 37	2 800 tons	Concrete	Commercial lease
AFDL 38	2 800 tons	Concrete	Commercial lease
AFDL 39	2 800 tons	Concrete	Loan to Brazil
AFDL 40	2 800 tons	Concrete	Commercial lease
AFDL 41	2 800 tons	Concrete	Commercial lease
*AFDL 42	2 800 tons	Concrete	Long Beach Nav Shipyard
AFDL 43	2 800 tons	Concrete	Commercial lease
AFDL 44	2 800 tons	Concrete	Loan to Philippines
AFDL 45	2 800 tons	Concrete	Commercial lease
AFDL 47	6 500 tons	Steel	Commercial lease
*AFDL 48	4 000 tons	Concrete	Long Beach Nav Shipyard

MEDIUM AUXILIARY FLOATING DRY DOCKS

AFDM 1 (ex-YFD 3)	15 000 tons	Steel (3)	Commercial lease
AFDM 2 (ex-YFD 4)	15 000 tons	Steel (3)	Commercial lease
AFDM 3 (ex-YFD 6)	18 000 tons	Steel (3)	Commercial lease
*AFDM 5 (ex-YFD 21)	18 000 tons	Steel (3)	Subic Bay, Philippines
*AFDM 6 (ex-YFD 62)	18 000 tons	Steel (3)	Subic Bay, Philippines
AFDM 7 (ex-YFD 63)	18 000 tons	Steel (3)	Commercial lease
*RICHLAND AFDM 8 (YFD ex-64)	18 000 tons	Steel (3)	Guam, Marianas
AFDM 9 (ex-YFD 65)	18 000 tons	Steel (3)	Commercial lease
AFDM 10	18 000 tons	Steel (3)	Commercial lease

Figures in parenthesis indicate the number of sections for sectional docks. Each section of the AFDB docks has a lifting capacity of about 10 000 tons. Four sections of the AFDB 7 form the floating dry dock *Los Alamos* at Holy Loch, Scotland, one section is used at Kwajalein atoll by the US Army in support of the Nike-X missile project and two sections are in reserve. (The AFDB sections each are 256 feet long, 80 feet in width, with wing walls 83 feet high; the wing walls, which contain compartments, fold down when the sections are towed.)

The *White Sands* (ARD 20) is employed in support of the deep-diving bathyscaph *Trieste II* (see section on Deep Submergence Vehicles). Early in 1969 the *White Sands*, with *Trieste II* on board, was towed to the Azores to support investigation of the remains of the nuclear-powered submarine *Scorpion.*

All floating dry docks were built during World War II except the YFD 82 (ex-ARD 1) which was built in 1934.

An AFBD was proposed in the Fiscal Year 1970 new construction programme that would be capable of servicing large aircraft carriers (estimated cost $50 000 000); the Congress declined to approve construction of the dock.

AUXILIARY REPAIR DRY DOCKS AND MEDIUM AUXILIARY REPAIR DRY DOCKS

*ARD 5	3 000 tons	Steel	New London, Connecticut
ARD 6	3 000 tons	Steel	Loan to Pakistan
*ARD 7	3 000 tons	Steel	New London, Connecticut
ARD 8	3 000 tons	Steel	Loan to Peru
ARD 9	3 000 tons	Steel	Loan to Nationalist China
*ARD 10	3 000 tons	Steel	Mare Island Nav Shipyard
*ARD 11	3 000 tons	Steel	Key West, Florida
*ARD 12	3 000 tons	Steel	Charleston Nav Shipyard
ARD 13	3 000 tons	Steel	Loan to Venezuela
ARD 14	3 000 tons	Steel	Loan to Brazil
*ARD 15	3 000 tons	Steel	Charleston Nav Shipyard
*ARD 16	3 000 tons	Steel	Davisville, Rhode, Island
ARD 17	3 000 tons	Steel	Loan to Ecuador
ARDM 3 (ex ARD 18)	3 000 tons	Steel	Reserve
*OAK RIDGE ARDM 1 (ex-ARD 19)		Steel	Rota, Spain
*WHITE SANDS ARD 20	3 000 tons	Steel	San Diego, California
WINDSOR ARD 22	3 000 tons	Steel	Loan to Nationalist China.
ARD 23	3 000 tons	Steel	Loan to Argentina
ARD 24	3 000 tons	Steel	Reserve
ARD 25	3 000 tons	Steel	Reserve
*ALAMAGORDO ARDM 2 (ex-ARD 26)		Steel	Charleston South Carolina
ARD 27	3 000 tons	Steel	Reserve
ARD 28	3 000 tons	Steel	Loan to Columbia
*ARCO ARD 29	3 000 tons	Steel	Guam, Marianas
*ARD 30	3 000 tons	Steel	Pear Harbour Nav Shipyard
*ARD 31	3 000 tons	Steel	US Air Force
ARD 32	3 000 tons	Steel	Loan to Chile

YARD FLOATING DRY DOCKS

YFD 7	18 000 tons	Steel (3)	Commercial lease
YFD 8	20 000 tons	Wood	Commercial lease
YFD 9	16 000 tons	Wood	Commercial lease
YFD 15	6 500 tons	Wood	Commercial lease
YFD 23	10 500 tons	Wood	Commercial lease
YFD 54	5 000 tons	Wood	Commercial lease
YFD 55	10 500 tons	Wood	Commercial lease
YFD 68	14 000 tons	Steel (3)	Commercial lease

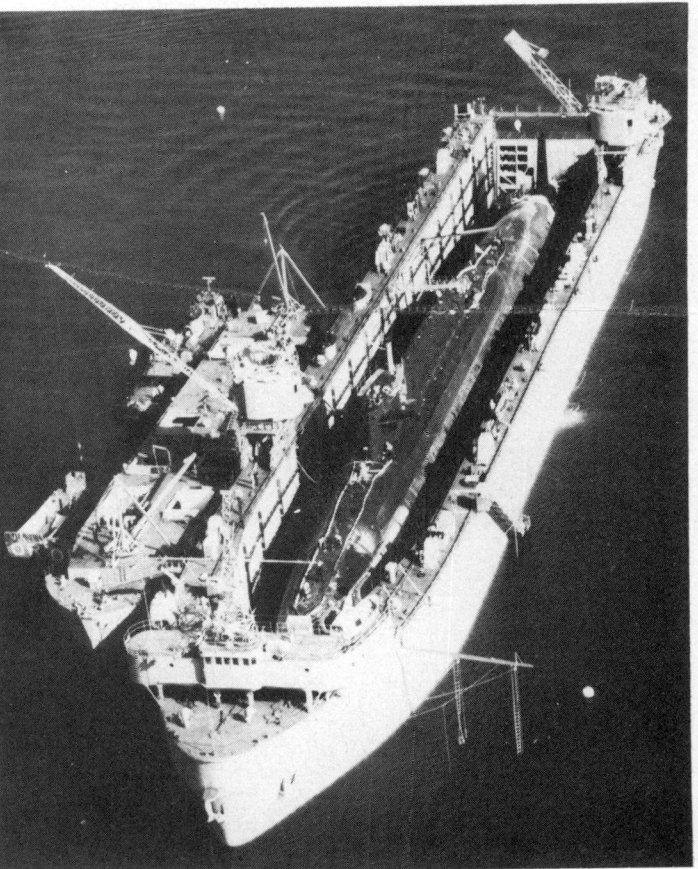

SSBN in OAK RIDGE (ARDM 1)   *1946, United States Navy*

MILITARY SEALIFT SHIPS

Military Sealift Ships provide ocean transportation for all components of the Department of Defense. These ships are operated by the Navy's Military Sealift Command, renamed on 1 Aug 1970 from Military Sea Transportation Service (MSTS).

The cargo ships, tankers, troop transports, landing ships, and aircraft ferries listed below carry military cargo and personnel from port to port except that Military Sealift Command tankers do transfer petroleum to Navy oilers in overseas areas. In addition, the Military Sealift Command directs the chartering of merchantmen owned by shipping lines or private parties to carry government cargo.

The Commander, Deputy Commander, and Area Commanders (Atlantic, Pacific, and Far East) are flag officers

of the Navy on active duty. All ships are civilian manned with most of their crews being Civil Service employees of the Navy. However, the tankers are operated under contract to commercial tanker lines and are manned by merchant seamen and some ships are manned by Japanese and Korean merchant seamen under the command of US personnel (see notes for specific ships). In addition to the ships listed in this section, the Military Sealift Command also operates a number of Special Project ships that support other defence-related activities, mostly research, surveying, and missile-range support ships (see Experimental, Research and Surveying Ships listing). Other Special Project ships are the cable ship *Albert J. Meyer* (T-ARC 6) and helicopter repair ship *Corpus Christi Bay* (T-ARVH 1) listed in the section on

Fleet Support Ships.

A few Navy-manned logistic ships are included in this section although they are not under the control of the Military Sealift Command.

ARMAMENT. No ships of the Military Sealift Command are armed.

CLASSIFICATION. Military Sealift Command ships are assigned standard US Navy hull designations with the added designation prefix "T". Ships in this category are referred to as "USNS" (United States Naval Ship) vice "USS" (United States Ship) which is used for Navy-manned ships.

MULTI-PURPOSE SHIPS

Displacement, tons	28 958 full load
Dimensions, feet	650 oa × 100 × 28
Speed, knots	21·6
Complement	36

The Military Sealift Command proposes to construct ten multi-purpose cargo ships of this design to replace 29 old dry-cargo ships now in service. These ships would cost approximately $25 000 000 each. As proposed, these ships would be built by *private industry* for exclusive military use, being chartered to the Military Sealift Command for ten years with renewal options. With the security of the ten-year charter private financing would be encouraged and the operators would have fully amortised and relatively modern ships after ten years of operation. This already has been done with the roll-on/roll-off ship *Admiral William M. Callaghan*.

These ships are of an advanced design, being fully convertible for carrying break-bulk, roll-on/roll-off or container cargo, or a mix of the three types. Each ship will be capable of carrying a maximum of 1 044 standard freight containers (8 × 8 × 20 ft) or 2 015 000 cubic ft of dry cargo or have 149 000 square ft of deck space available for vehicles. Cargo handling will be facilitated by side and stern ramps and a helicopter deck. One boom with 210-ton capacity, eight with 26-ton capacities, and six with 42-ton capacities.

MULTI-PURPOSE SHIP   *Official artist's Concept*

2 STORE SHIPS (AF): "VICTORY" TYPE

*ASTERION (ex-*Arcadia Victory*) T-AF 63   ***PERSEUS** (ex-*Union Victory*) T-AF 64

Displacement, tons	6 700 light; 12 130 full load
Measurement, tons	8 000 deadweight
Dimensions, feet	455·2 × 62 × 28·5
Main engines	Geared turbines (Westinghouse); 1 shaft; 8 500 shp = 17 knots
Boilers	2
Complement	56 (14 officers, 42 enlisted men)

Victory ships (VC 2-S-AP 3 type). Acquired from the Maritime Administration in 1961, and converted at Portland, Oregon, by Willamette Iron & Steel Co under the 1962 Programme. Of the same type as the Navy-manned replenishment ships *Denebola* and *Regulus*, except they are unarmed and manned by Civilian crews.

ASTERION (T-AF 63)   *United States Navy*

2 STORE SHIPS (AF): "EAGLE" CLASS

BALD EAGLE T-AF 50   **BLUE JACKET** T-AF 51

Displacement, tons	7 430 light; 12 800 full load
Dimensions, feet	459·2 oa × 63 × 24
Main engines	Turbine; 1 shaft; 6 000 shp = 16·4 knots
Boilers	2

Both built by Moore Dry Dock Co. Launched in 1942. C 2-S-B1 type. Sister ship *Golden Eagle* is a Navy-manned replenishment ship (renamed *Arcturus*). These ships were taken out of service in 1970 and placed in the Maritime Administration Reserve Fleet but remain on the Navy List.

BALD EAGLE (T-AF 50)   *United States Navy*

1 STORE SHIP (AF): "ADRIA" CLASS

Name	No.	Launched
*BONDIA	T-AF 42	9 Nov 1944

Displacement, tons	3 139 light; 7 435 full load
Dimensions, feet	320 wl; 338·5 oa × 50 × 21 max
Main engines	Nordberg diesel; 1 700 bhp = 11·5 knots

2 100 tons cargo. R1-M-AV 3 type. Built by Pennsylvania Shipyard, Beaumont, Texas.

DISPOSALS

Adria AF 30, **Arequipa** AF 31, **Corduba** AF 32, **Karin** AF 33, **Kerstin** AF 34, **Latona** AF 35, **Lobia** AF 36, **Malabar** AF 37, **Merapi** AF 38, **Valentine** T-AF 47, **Laurentia** T-AF 44, all transferred to Maritime Administration Reserve Fleet.

BONDIA (T-AF 42)   *Skyfotos*

CARGO SHIP: Ex-LANDING SHIP MEDIUM

The unnamed cargo ship AG 335 (hull number T-AG 335), formerly LSM 335, was stricken on 21 Dec 1970 and transferred to the Department of the Interior. See 1970-1971 and previous editions for description and data on LSM disposals.

Of 558 LSMs constructed during World War II, only 11 remain on the US Navy List: eight inshore fire support ships (LFR), two salvage lifting ships (ARSD), and one test range support ship (IX). Other LSMs now serve the navies of Argentina, Chile, Communist China, Nationalist China, Denmark, Dominican Republic, Ecuador, West Germany, Greece, Japan, South Korea, Peru, Philippines, Spain, Thailand, Venezuela, North Vietnam, South Vietnam.

3 CARGO SHIPS (AG): FORMER DEPOT SHIPS

*PHOENIX (ex-*Arizona*, ex-*Capitol Victory*)	T-AG 172
*PROVO (ex-*Utah* ex-*Drew Victory*)	T-AG 173
*CHEYENNE (ex-*Wyoming*, ex-*Middlesex Victory*)	T-AG 174

Displacement, tons	6 700 light; 2 400 full load
Dimensions, feet	455 × 62
Main engines	Geared turbines; 1 shaft; 6 000 shp = 15·5 knots
Boilers	2

These ships were acquired in 1963 from the Maritime Administration. Initially they were employed as forward depot ships; now used as general cargo ships. Korean manned.

RESCINDED ACQUISITIONS. The twelve "Victory" ships planned as forward depot ships were not acquired from the Maritime Administration Reserve Fleet on 1 Feb 1966 as requested and redesignated T-AG 179 to 190 and given new Navy names (see complete list in the 1966-1967 edition) but were chartered to and operated by commercial shipping companies in Vietnam service under their original "Victory" names.

Military Sealift Ships—continued

PROVO (T-AG 173)   United States Navy

1 CARGO SHIP (AK): Ex-AKA TYPE

*WYANDOT T-AK 283 (ex-T-AKA 92)

Displacement, tons	7 430 light; 14 000 full load
Dimensions, feet	435 wl; 459·2 oa × 63 × 24
Main engines	Geared turbines (General Electric); 1 shaft; 6 000 shp = 16·5 knots
Boilers	2 (Combustion Engineering)

The *Wyandot* is a winterised cargo ship; formerly an Attack Cargo Ship (AKA) of the "Andromeda" class. Built by Moore Dry Dock Co, Oakland, California; launched on 28 June 1944; commissioned on 30 Sep 1944 as AKA 92. Assigned to MSTS and manned by civilian crew since 1963 (T-AKA 92). Designation changed to T-AK 283 on 1 Jan 1969.
Original armament of one 5 inch gun and eight 40 mm guns (twin) removed.

WYANDOT (T-AK 283)   United States Navy

4 FBM CARGO SHIPS (AK): "VICTORY" TYPE

*NORWALK (ex-*Norwalk Victory*)	T-AK 279
*FURMAN (ex-*Furman Victory*)	T-AK 280
*VICTORIA (ex-*Ethiopia Victory*)	T-AK 281
*MARSHFIELD (ex-*Marshfield Victory*)	T-AK 282

Displacement, tons	11 150 full load
Dimensions, feet	455 × 62 × 22
Main engines	Geared turbine; 1 shaft; 8 500 shp = 16·5 knots
Boilers	2
Complement	80 to 90 plus Navy detachment

Fleet ballistic missile resupply cargo ships AK (FBM). VC 2-S-AP 3 type. Designed as a one-stop cargo ship to provide complete resupply of a deployed fleet ballistic missile submarine tender. The logistic support includes "Polaris" missiles, submarine torpedoes; technical spares, packaged petroleum products, bottled gas, black oil and diesel fuel, general cargo, and frozen and dry provisions. No. 3 hold converted to carry 16 Polaris missiles in vertical position, 355 000 gallons of diesel oil and 430 000 gallons of fuel oil carried. *Marshfield* also configured to carry advanced Poseidon FBM.

The *Norwalk* was converted from a standard "Victory" cargo ship by Boland Machine and Mfg Co. and accepted on 30 Dec 1963. Conversion of *Furman* was completed by American Shipbuilding Co in Oct 1964. Conversion of *Victoria* completed by Philadelphia Naval Shipyard in Oct 1965. *Marshfield* converted by Boland Machine and Mfg Co Oct 1968–June 1970. All acquired from the Maritime Administration reserve fleet.

MARSHFIELD (T-AK 282)   1970, United States Navy, Nancy Chutz

1 FBM CARGO SHIP (AK): "VICTORY" TYPE

BETELGEUSE (ex-*Colombia Victory*) AK 260

Displacement, tons	4 420 Navy Light; 15 580 full load (Maritime Commission deadweight 10 850 tons)
Dimensions, feet	455·2 oa × 62 × 28·5
Guns	8—40 mm AA (twin)
Main engines	Geared turbines; 1 shaft; 8 500 shp = 16·5 knots

VC2-S-AP3 type. Reactivated for the Navy in 1951 from the Maritime Administration reserve fleet. Fitted with special equipment to transport material and supplies for fleet ballistic missile submarines (details as in *Norwalk*, above). Decommissioned in 1971 and placed in reserve.

DISPOSALS
Of the "Alcona" class, **Sussex** AK 213, was stricken on 1 Jan 1960, and **Alcona** AK 157, **Beltrami** AK 162, **Faribaulr** AK 179, and **Grainger** AK 184, end 1960. All six vessels of the "Alchiba" class, namely **Alchiba** (ex-*Charles E. Winsor*), **Algorab** (ex-*Elisha Whitney*), **Aquarius** (ex-*John D. Whitney*), **Centaurus** (ex-*Nathanial Brown*), **Cepheus** (ex-*Richard W. Dixie*) and **Serpens** (ex-*William Lester*) AK 261 to 266, respectively, were stricken on 1 Feb 1960.

BETELGEUSE (AK 260)   United States Navy

1 CARGO SHIP (AK): "BLAND" TYPE

*SCHUYLER OTIS BLAND T-AK 277

Displacement, tons	8 918 gross; 10 516 deadweight
Dimensions, feet	478 × 66 × 30
Main engines	Steam turbine; 1 shaft; speed = 18·5 knots
Boilers	2

Acquired from the Maritime Administration by the Military Sea Transportation Service in July 1961. The only ship of the type (C3-S-DX1).

SCHUYLER OTIS BLAND (T-AK 277)   United States Navy

6 CARGO SHIPS (AK): "O'BRIEN" TYPE

*COLONEL WILLIAM J. O'BRIEN (ex-*Maiden's Eye*)	T-AK 246
*SHORT SPLICE	T-AK 249
*PRIVATE FRANK J. PETRARCA (ex-*Long Splice*)	T-AK 250
*FENTRESS (ex-V 206)	T-AK 180
*HERKIMER (ex-V 203)	T-AK 188
*MUSKINGUM (ex-V 208)	T-AK 198

Displacement, tons	2 460 light; 7 450 full load
Dimensions, feet	338·7 × 50 × 21
Main engines	Diesel; 1 shaft; 1 750 bhp = 11·5 knots

C1-M-AV1 Type. *Colonel William J. O'Brien* and *Short Splice* were converted to heavy lift ships with two 80-ton capacity cranes. The *Short Splice* is Korean manned.

DISPOSALS
Hennepin T-AK 187, **Pembina** T-AK 200, **Captain Ario L. Olsen** T-AK 245, **Private John F. Thorson** T-AK 247, **Sergeant George Peterson** T-AK 248 transferred to Maritime Administration.

HERKIMER (T-AK 188)   United States Navy

Military Sea Lift Ships—*continued*

SHORT SPLICE (T-AK 249)   *United States Navy*

1 CARGO SHIP (AK): "ELTANIN" TYPE

*MIRFAK T-AK 271

Displacement, tons	2 036 light; 4 942 full load
Measurement, tons	2 486 gross, 1 300 deadweight
Dimensions, feet	256·8 wl; 262·2 oa × 51·5 × 18·7
Main engines	2 ALCO diesels with Westinghouse electric motors; 2 shafts; 3 200 bhp = 13 knots

Built for MSTS by Avondale Marine Ways, New Orleans, La. Designed for Arctic operation with hull strengthened against ice. C1-M E2-13a type. Launched on 5 Aug 1957. Note icebreaking prow in photo.

CONVERSION. Two other ships of this class converted for oceanographic research: *Eltanin*, reclassified from T-AK 270 to T-AGOR 8 on 15 Nov 1962; *Mizar* T-AK 272 was reclassified T-AGOR 11 on 15 Apr 1964 (see Experimental, Research and Surveying Ships).

MIRFAK (T-AK 271)   *United States Navy*

5 CARGO SHIPS (AK): "VICTORY" TYPE

*GREENVILLE VICTORY	T-AK 237
*LIEUTENANT JAMES E. ROBINSON	
(ex-T-AG 170, ex-T-AK 274, ex-*Czechoslovakia Victory*)	T-AK 274
* PRIVATE JOHN R. TOWLE (ex-*Appleton Victory*)	T-AK 240
*PRIVATE JOSEPH F. MERRELL (ex-*Grange Victory*)	T-AK 275
*SERGEANT JACK J. PENDLETON	T-ÅK 276

Displacement, tons	6 720 light; 12 450 full load
Dimensions, feet	455 oa × 62 × 24
Main engines	Turbine; 1 shaft; 8 500 shp = 16·5 to 17·7 knots
Boilers	2

VC2-S-AP3 type. *Greenville Victory* has been winterised.

RECLASSIFICATION. The former Military Sea Transportation Service Aircraft Cargo and Ferry Ships *Lieut. James E. Robinson*, *Private Joseph F. Merrell* and *Sergeant Jack J. Pendleton*, AKV 3, AKV 4 and AKV 5, respectively, were reclassified as Cargo Ships, AK 274, AK 275 and AK 276 on 7 May 1959. *Kingsport Victory* T-AK 239, was renamed and reclassified *Kingsport* T-AG 164 in 1962 (see Experimental, Research and Surveying Ships).
Lieut. James E. Robinson T-AK 274, was to have been transferred to the Maritime Administration, but was modified for special project work and reclassified as T-AG 170 in 1963, and reverted to the original classification T-AK 274 on 1 July 1964.
Haiti Victory T-AK 238 and *Dalton Victory* T-AK 256 converted to satellite tracking and recovery ships, reclassified and renamed, *Longview* T-AGM 3 and *Sunnyvale* T-AGM 5, respectively.

PVT JOHN R. TOWLE (T-AK 240) in Antarctic   *1961, US Navy*

PVT JOSEPH F. MERRELL (T-AK 275)   *United States Navy*

2 HEAVY LIFT SHIPS (AK): "BROSTROM" TYPE

* PVT. LEONARD C. BROSTROM (ex-*Marine Eagle*)	T-AK 255
* MARINE FIDDLER	T-AK 267

Displacement, tons	13 865 deadweight
Dimensions, feet	520 oa × 71·5 × 33
Main engines	Geared turbine; 1 shaft; 9 000 shp = 15·8 knots
Boilers	2
Complement	57 (14 officers, 43 enlisted men)

These ships have 150-ton-capacity booms, the most powerful lift capacity of any US ships. C4-S-B1 type.

MARINE FIDDLER (T-AK 267)   *United States Navy*

7 CARGO SHIPS (AK): "VICTORY" TYPE

* PRIVATE FRANCIS X. McGRAW (ex-*Wabash Victory*)	T-AK 241
* SERGEANT ANDREW MILLER (ex-*Radcliffe Victory*)	T-AK 242
* SERGEANT ARCHER T. GAMMON (ex-*Yale Victory*)	T-AK 243
* SERGEANT MORRIS E. CRAIN (ex-*Mills Victory*)	T-AK 244
* LT. GEORGE W. G. BOYCE (ex-*Waterville Victory*)	T-AK 251
* LT. ROBERT CRAIG (ex-*Bowling Green Victory*)	T-AK 252
* SERGEANT TRUMAN KIMBRO	T-AK 254

Displacement, tons	6 700 light; 12 400 full load
Dimensions, feet	455 × 62 × 24
Main engines	Geared turbines; 1 shaft; 6 000 shp = 15·5 knots
Boilers	2

T-AK 251, 252, and 254 are VC2-S-AP2, the others VC2-S-AP3 type. (AK-278 authorised in Aug 1962 for the Military Sea Transportation Service, was assigned a new designation and hull number, T-LSV 9, *Sea Lift*; subsequently changed to T-AKR 9).
Pvt. Joe E. Mann T-AK 253, ex-*Owensboro Victory*, was fitted out as a range instrumentation and telemetry ship for the Pacific Missile Range in Oct 1958 and renamed *Richfield* T-AGM 4.
Sagita T-AK 87 (ex-SS *Moses Pike*) and *Vela* T-AK 89 (ex-SS *Charles A. Roulett*) transferred to the Maritime Administration in July 1961 and on 3 Apr 1959 respectively.

DISPOSALS

Sagita T-AK 87; **Vela** T-AK 89 transferred to Maritime Administration.

LT ROBERT CRAIG (T-AK 252)   *United States Navy*

SGT ANDREW MILLER (T-AK 242)   *1963, United States Navy*

Military Sea Lift Ships—continued

SGT MORRIS E CRAIN (T-AK 244)   *United States Navy*

1 DOCK CARGO SHIP (AKD)

* POINT BARROW T-AKD 1

Displacement, tons	5 940 light; 9 415 standard; 14 094 full load
Measurement, tons	12 000 gross; 4 020 deadweight
Dimensions, feet	475 wl; 492 oa × 78 × 22
Main engines	Turbine; 2 shafts; 6 000 shp = 18 knots
Boilers	2
Complement	66
Passengers	42

Built for MSTS by Maryland Shipbuilding & Dry Dock Co. Laid down on 18 Sep 1956, launched on 25 May 1957 and commissioned on 28 Feb 1958. Delivered to MSTS on 29 May 1958. S2-ST-23A type. Originally a Roll-on/Roll-off ship to load vehicles on ramp. Winterised for Arctic service. Ballasting arrangements permit embarking and debarking landing craft as in dock landing ships.

Subsequently refitted with hangar over docking well and employed in transport of large booster rockets to Cape Kennedy space centre. Primarily used to carry the second stage of the Saturn V moon rocket and Lunar Modules.

Placed out of service in reserve on 1 Jan 1971.

POINT BARROW (T-AKD 1)   *1970, United States Navy*

POINT BARROW (T-AKD 1)   *1970, United States Navy*

2 LIGHT CARGO SHIPS (AKL)

Name	No.
*MARK (ex-FS 214, ex-AG 143)	AKL 12
*BRAULE (ex-FS 370)	AKL 28

Displacement, tons	approx 700
Dimensions, feet	176·5 oa × 32·8 × 10
Main engines	1 diesel; 1 000 shp; 1 shaft = 10 knots
Guns	20 mm AA
Complement	varies 21 (designed)

Small cargo ships (freight and supply) acquired from the Army. These ships are Navy manned and are not assigned to the Military Sealift Command.

Both ships scheduled to decommission in 1971 for foreign transfer.

CONVERSIONS. *Banner* (AKL 25), *Pueblo* (AKL 44), and *Palm Beach* (AKL 45) of this type were converted to intelligence ships and reclassified as Environmental Research Ships, AGER 1-3, respectively, on 1 June 1967. *New Bedford* (AKL 17) reclassified as IX 308. They are listed with Experimental, Research, and Surveying Ships.

DISPOSALS AND TRANSFERS
AKL 13, T-AKL 13, 15, 16, 18, 19, 21, 23, 24, 26, 34, 36 stricken in 1959; **AKL 1**, 5, 6, 14, **T-AKL 29** stricken in 1960; **AKL 2**, 9, **T-AKL 20**, 22, 30, 32 stricken in 1961; **T-AKL 43** stricken in 1963; **T-AKL 27** stricken in 1966 and used for salvage training; **T-AKL 35** transferred to Korea in 1956; Korean manned **T-AKL 37-42** formally transferred to Korea in 1960; **AKL 31** stricken in 1907 and transferred to the Department of Interior.
The similar **Redbud** AKL 398 was returned to the Coast Guard in 1970.

MARK (AKL 12)   *1966, United States Navy*

1 VEHICLE CARGO SHIP (AKR): "SEA LIFT" TYPE

*SEA LIFT T-AKR 9 (ex-T-LSV 9)

Displacement, tons	11 130 light; 16 940 standard; 21 700 full load
Measurement, tons	15 750 gross; 12 100 deadweight
Dimensions, feet	540 oa × 83 × 29
Main engines	Geared steam turbines; 2 shafts; 19 400 shp = 20 knots
Boilers	2
Complement	62 plus 12 Passengers

Improved roll-on/roll-off vehicle cargo ship. Maritime Administration C4-ST-67a type. Built by the Puget Sound Bridge & Dry Dock Co, (now Lockheed Shipbuilding and Construction Co), Seattle, Wash, at a cost of $15 895 500. Authorised under the Fiscal Year 1963 programme. Laid down on 19 May 1964 and launched on 18 Apr 1965. Delivered to Navy on 25 Apr 1967 and to MSTS on 19 May 1967. Designed for point-to-point sea transportation of Department of Defense self-propelled, fully loaded, wheeled, tracked and amphibious vehicles and general cargo. Internal ramps, stern ramp and side openings provide for quick loading and unloading. Designation, changed from T-LSV to T-AKR on 1 Jan 1969.

SEA LIFT (T-AKR 9)   *1966, Lockheed Shipbuilding*

1 VEHICLE CARGO SHIP (AKR): "COMET" TYPE

*COMET T-AKR 7 (ex-T-LSV 7, ex-T-AK 269)

Displacement, tons	7 605 light; 18 150 full load
Measurement, tons	12 750 gross; 6 500 deadweight
Dimensions, feet	465 pp; 499 oa × 78 × 28·8
Main engines	Geared turbines (General Electric); 2 shafts; 13 200 shp = 18 knots
Boilers	2 (Babcock & Wilcox)
Complement	73

Roll-on/roll-off vehicle carrier built for MSTS by Sun Shipbuilding & Dry Dock Co. C3-ST-14A type. Laid down on 15 May 1956. Launched on 31 July 1957. Completed on 27 Jan 1958. Has ramp system for loading and discharging. The hull is strengthened against ice. Can accommodate 700 vehicles in two after holds; the forward holds are for general cargo. Equipped with Denny-Brown Stabilisers. Reclassified from T-AK to T-LSV on 1 June 1963, and changed to T-AKR on 1 Jan 1969. LSV 1-6 were World War II-built amphibious ships, subsequently redesignated as mine warfare ships (MCS) or net cargo ship (AKN).

DISPOSALS

Taurus (T-AKR 8, ex-T-LSV 8, ex-AK 273, ex-LSD 23) deactivated in 1968 and subsequently scrapped.

Galilea (AKN 6, ex-LSV 6, ex-AP 161) transferred to Maritime Administration, stricken from the Navy List on 1 Sep 1961.

COMET (T-AKR 7)   *United States Navy*

Military Sealift Ships—continued

4 CARGO AND AIRCRAFT FERRY SHIPS (AKV): "BOGUE" CLASS

Displacement, tons,	9 800 standard ;.15 700 full load
Length, feet (metres)	496 (151·2) oa
Beam, feet (metres)	69·5 (21·2) hull
Draft, feet (metres)	26 (7·9)
Width, feet (metres)	1,12 (34·1) extreme
Flight deck, feet (metres)	450 (137·2)
Aircraft	See General notes
Guns	See Gunnery notes
Boilers	2 (Foster Wheeler)
Main engines	Westinghouse geared turbines; 1 shaft; 8 500 shp
Speed, knots	18
Complement	75

Name	No.	Laid down	Launched	Commissioned
CARD	T—AKV 40 (ex-CVU 11, ex-CVHE 11)	27 Oct 1941	21 Feb 1942	8 Nov 1942
CORE	T—AKV 41 (ex-CVU 13, ex-CVHE 13)	2 Jan 1942	15 May 1942	10 Dec 1942
BRETON	T—AKV 42 (ex-CVU 23, ex-CVHE 23)	25 Feb 1942	27 June 1942	12 Apr 1943
CROATAN	T—AKV 43 (ex-CVU 25, ex-CVHE 25)	15 Apr 1942	3 Aug 1942	28 Apr 1943

All converted from mercantile hulls built by Seattle-Tacoma Shipbuilding Corpn. Vary slightly in appearance. As escort carriers they carried 30 aircraft and had a complement of 800 officers and men. Named after sounds. Equipped with derricks for loading and unloading aircraft at the pierside.

All were active during the 1960s, primarily to support the war in Vietnam, transporting aircraft, vehicles, and other material for all services. Now decommissioned and in Maritime Administration Reserve Fleet but remain on Navy List.

RECLASSIFICATION. Reclassified from Escort Aircraft Carriers (CVE) to Escort Helicopter Aircraft Carriers (CVHE) on 12 June 1955, to CVU on allocation as MSTS aircraft ferries on 1 July 1958 and to AKV on 7 May 1959.

GUNNERY. Unarmed while designated USNS with civil crews. Formerly mounted one or two 5-inch guns, 16—40 mm AA guns, and 20-20 mm AA guns.

DISPOSALS

Sister ships **Altamaha** CVHE 18. **Barnes** CVHE 20 **Bogue** CVHE 9, **Copahee** CVHE 12, and **Nassau** CVHE 16 also half-sister **Prince William** CVHE 31 were stricken from the list in 1 Mar 1959 when **Chenango**, CVHE 28, **Sanntee** CVHE 29, and **Suwannee** CVHE 27 of the "Suwanee" class, were also stricken. The last survivor of the 50 former escort aircraft carriers of the "Anzio" class, **Thetis Bay** LPH6, ex-CVHA 1, ex-CVE 90, was sold for scrap in 1967.

CARD (T-AKV 40)   United States Navy

3 CARGO AND AIRCRAFT FERRY SHIPS (AKV): "COMMENCEMENT BAY" CLASS

Name	No.	Laid down	Launched	Commissioned
KULA GULF (ex-Vermilion Bay)	T-AKV 8 (ex-CVE 108)	16 Dec 1943	15 Aug 1944	12 May 1945
POINT CRUZ (ex-Trocadero Bay)	T-AKV 19 (ex CVE 119)	4 Dec 1944	18 May 1945	16 Oct 1946
RABAUL	AKV 21 (ex-CVHE 121)	29 Jan 1945	14 July 1945	30 Aug 1946

Displacement, tons	11 473 standard; 24 275 full load
Length, feet (metres)	557 (169·8) oa
Beam, feet (metres)	75 (22·9) hull
Draft, feet (metres)	30·7 (9·3)
Width, feet (metres)	105 (32·0) extreme
Aircraft	Originally carried 34
Guns.	1—5 in (127 mm) 38 cal DP; 24—40 mm AA (guns removed in active ships)
Boilers	4
Main engines	Geared turbines 16 000 shp; 2 shafts
Speed knots	18
Complement	Kula Gulf and Point Cruz: 140

All built by Todd Pacific Shipyard, Tacoma. As escort aircraft carriers their complement was 924 officers and men (peace) and over 1 000 (war). Kula Gulf and Point Cruz were reactivated in 1965 for MSTS operation and designated T-AKV, USNS, unarmed with civil service crew; both placed in Maritime Administration reserve fleet in Oct 1969, but remain on Navy List. Rabaul is in naval reserve group.

GUNNERY. Designed armament for these ships was two 5 inch guns and 36 40 mm guns (three quad and 12 twin) plus 20 mm guns.

CONVERSION. Gilbert Islands (AKV 39, CVE 107) was converted into a Major Communications Relay Ship (AGMR 1) in 1963.

RECLASSIFICATION. Seven Escort Aircraft Carriers (CVE) of this class were reclassified as Escort Helicopter Aircraft Carriers (CVHE) on 12 June 1955: Block Island was reclassified as LPH on 22 Dec 1957, but in 1958 her conversion to Helicopter Amphibious Assault Ship was cancelled and she was reclassified as an AKV or 7 May 1959, when all the remaining 18 ships of the class were also reclassified as AKVs, and stricken on 1 July 1959.

CLASS. Sixteen more ships of this class, Bastogne CVE 124, Eniwetok CVE 125, Lingayen CVE 126,

Okinawa CVE 127, and CVE Nos 128 to 139, were cancelled in Aug 1945.

DISPOSALS

Block Island, AKV 38 (ex-LPH 1, CVE 106) was stricken on 1 July 1959, **Mindoro** AKV 20 (ex-CVE 120) on 1 Dec 1959 and **Bairoko**, AKV 15 (ex-CVE 115) **Palau** AKV 22 (ex-CVE 122), **Puget Sound**, AKV 13 (ex-CVE 113) and **Vella Gulf**, AKV 11 (ex-CVE 111) in 1960, **Sicily**, AKV 18 (ex-CVE 118) in 1961 and **Gilbert Islands**, AKV 39 (ex-CVE 107) and **Salerno Bay** AKV 10 (ex-CVE 110) on 1 June 1961. **Vella Gulf** and **Gilbert Islands**, however, were reinstated on the Navy List on 1 Nov 1961. **Siboney** AKV 12 (ex-CVE 112) stricken on 1 June 1970; **Vella Gulf**, **Badoeng Strait** AKV 16 (ex-CVE 116), **Saidor** AKV 17 (ex-CVE 117) stricken on 1 Dec 1970. **Commencement Bay** AKV 37 (ex-CVE 105), **Cape Gloucester** AKV 9 (ex-CVE 109), **Rendora** AKV 14 (ex-CVE 114) stricken on 1 Apr 1971.

POINT CRUZ (T-AKV 19)   United States Navy

Military Sea Lift Ships—continued

SHOSHONE (T-AO 151)   *United States Navy*

1 TANKER (AO): "EXPLORER" TYPE

* AMERICAN EXPLORER T-AO 165

Measurement, tons	16 500 gross; 22 525 deadweight
Dimensions, feet	615 oa × 80 ×44·5
Main engines	Steam turbines; 1 shaft; 22 000 shp = 20 knots

T5-S-RM2a type. Laid down on 9 July 1957; launched on 11 Apr 1958. Built by Ingalls Shipbuilding Corporation, Pascagoula, for the Maritime Administration, but acquired MSTS. Cargo capacity 190 300 barrels.

AMERICAN EXPLORER (T-AO 165)   *United States Navy*

3 TANKERS (AO): "MAUMEE" CLASS

Name	No.	Launched
*MAUMEE	T-AO 149	16 Feb 1956
*SHOSHONE	T-AO 151	17 Jan 1957
*YUKON	T-AO 152	16 Mar 1956

Displacement, tons	25 000 deadweight
Measurement, tons	16 500 gross; 25 000 deadweight
Dimensions, feet	591 wl; 620 oa × 83·5 × 32
Main engines	Turbine; 1 shaft; 20 460 shp = 18 knots
Cargo	203 216 barrels

Yukon, laid down 16 May 1955 by Ingalls, Pascagoula, delivered May 1957. *Maumee* laid down 8 Mar 1955, delivered Dec 1956. *Shoshone* laid down 15 Aug 1955 by Sun Shipbuilding, Chester, delivered Apr 1957. T5-S-12A type. *Potomac* T-AO 150 sank at Morehead, North Carolina, after explosion on 26-27 Sep 1961, but was rebuilt in 1963-1964, renamed SS *Shenandoah* and chartered to MSTS.

Maumee provided with ice-strengthened bow during 1969-1970 modification at Norfolk SB & DD Co; employed in transporting petroleum products to Antarctica in support of US scientific endeavours.

15 TANKERS (AO): "MISSION" CLASS

	T-AO		T-AO
*CACHE (*Stillwater*, 1942)	67	***MISSION SANTA YNEZ**	134
*CHEPACHET (*Eutaw Springs*, 1943)	78	***PECOS** (*Corsicana*, 1942)	65
*COSSATOT (*Fort Necessity*, 1942)	77	***PIONEER VALLEY**	140
*COWANESQUE (*Fort Duquesne*, 1942)	79	***SAUGATUCK** (*Newton*, 1942)	75
*MISSION BUENAVENTURA	111	***SCHUYLKILL** (*Louisburg* 1943)	76
*MILLICOMA (*Conastoga*, 1943)	73	***SHAWNEE TRAIL**	142
MISSION SANTA CRUZ	133	***SUAMICO** (*Harlem Heights*, 1941)	49
		*TALLULAH (*Valley Forge* 1944)	50

Displacement, tons	5 730 light; 22 380 full load
Dimensions, feet	503 wl; 523·5 oa × 68 × 31
Main engines	A 1 type Turbo-electric; 6 000 shp = 15 knots
	A 2 type; 1 000 shp = 16 knots
Boilers	2 Babcock & Wilcox
Cargo	141 158 barrels

T2-SE-A1 and T2-SE-A2 design. These are Navy-owned tankers, operated by commercial shipping firms under contract to the Navy. Several are equipped with an aluminium portable aircraft cargo deck. *Mission Santa Clara* T-AO 132, was loaned to Pakistan in Jan 1963. *Shawnee Trail* T-AO 142 was reacquired from the

Maritime Administration on 20 Jan 1965 to replace *Mission San Antonio* which was stricken. *Mission Capistrano* AO 112, converted into a sound testing experimental ship (T-AG 162), see Experimental, Research and Surveying Ships.

DISPOSALS
Mission San Rafael T-AO 130 stricken on 28 Apr 1970.

SCHUYLKILL (T-AO 76)   *United States Navy*

2 GASOLINE TANKERS (AOG): "ALATNA" CLASS

Name	No.	Launched
*ALATNA	T-AOG 81	6 Sep 1956
*CHATTAHOOCHEE	T-AOG 82	4 Dec 1956

Displacement, tons	5 720
Measurement, tons	3 200 gross; 3 445 deadweight
Dimensions, feet	302 oa × 16 × 19
Main engines	Diesel-electric; 2 shafts; 3 400 hp = 12 knots
Cargo	30 000 barrels

T1-MET-24a type. Built for MSTS by Bethlehem Steel, Staten Island, NY. Laid down on 16 Mar 1956 and 1 May 1956, respectively. Delivered in June and August 1957. Bows strengthened for navigation in ice; equipped with helicopter flight deck.

ALATNA (T-AOG 81)   *United States Navy*

4 GASOLINE TANKERS (AOG): "PECONIC" CLASS

	T-AOG		T-AOG
*NODAWAY (*ex-Belridge*)	78	***PISCATAQUA** (*ex-Cisne*)	80
*PETALUMA (*ex-Raccoon Bend*)	79	***RINCON**	77

Displacement, tons	2 060 light; 6 000 full load
Dimensions, feet	325 oa × 48 × 19 max
Main engines	Diesel; 1 shaft; 1 400 bhp = 10 knots
Complement	33
Cargo	30 000 barrels

T1-M-BT2 design. All built by Todd, Houston. *Nodaway* was reacquired from the Maritime Administration in 1965.

Tonti AOG 76, of this class was transferred to Colombia in 1965.

DISPOSALS
Peconic AOG 68, was transferred to Maritime Administration in 1960.

MISSION SANTA YNEZ (T-AO 134)   *United States Navy*

Military Sea Lift Ships—continued

RINCON (T-AOG 77)   *United States Navy*

3 TRANSPORTS (AP): "BARRETT" CLASS

		Launched	Completed
* **BARRETT** (ex-*President Jackson*)	T-AP 196	27 June 1950	15 Dec 1951
GEIGER (ex-*President Adams*)	T-AP 197	9 Oct 1950	13 Sep 1952
* **UPSHUR** (ex-*President Hayes*)	T-AP 198	19 Jan 1951	20 Dec 1952

Displacement, tons	17 600 standard; 19 600 full load
Measurement, tons	12 660 gross; 10 600 deadweight
Dimensions, feet	533 oa × 73 × 27
Main engines	Geared turbines; 1 shaft; 13 750 shp = 19 to 20 knots (cruising), see *Engineering*
Troops	1 900 (400 officers, 1 500 men)

Maritime Administration type P2-S1-DN1. All three were built by the New York Shipbuilding Corporation, New Jersey. Originally laid down as passenger ships for the American President Lines but taken over by the Navy to be completed as troop transports. Troop carrying capacity of 1 500 plus 396 cabin berths for officers and dependents. Troop lift can be increased by at least 1 000 men if necessary by converting recreation areas into berthing spaces. All spaces are air-conditioned except the engine room and bridge. The *Barrett* and *Upshur* are the only US Navy troop transports in service; the *Geiger* is in Military Sealift Command reserve.

ENGINEERING. On sea trials *Barrett* attained a speed of 21·5 knots at full power.

UPSHUR (T-AP 198)   *Skyfotos*

BARRETT (T-AP 196)   *United States Navy*

TRANSPORTS (AP): P-2 "ADMIRAL" CLASS

General Alexander M. Patch (ex-*Admiral R. E. Coontz*) T-AP 122, **General Simon B. Buckner** (ex-*Admiral E. W. Eberle*) T-AP 123, **General Nelson M. Walker** (ex-*Admiral H. T. Mayo*) T-AP 125, **General Maurice Rose** (ex-*Admiral Hugh Rodman*) T-AP 126, **General William O. Darby** (ex-*Admiral W. S. Sims*) T-AP 127 all stricken in 1969-1970 and transferred to Maritime Administration reserve.
Details and status of other ships of this class given in 1969-1970 and previous editions.

TRANSPORTS (AP): P-2 "GENERAL" CLASS

General John Pope T-AP 110, **General W. H. Gordon** T-AP 117, **General William Weigel** T-AP 119 all stricken in 1969-1970 and transferred to Maritime Administration reserve.
Details and status of other ships of this class given in 1969-1970 and previous editions.

COASTAL TRANSPORTS (APC)

All coastal transports have been stricken from the Navy List, the last being the **Jonah E. Kelley** T-APC 116 stricken on 28 Apr 1970 (earlier transferred to Maritime Administration reserve).
The **Sergeant George D. Keathley** T-APC 117 (ex-*Acorn Knot*, ex-*Alexander R. Niminger, Sr*), and **Sergeant Joseph E. Muller** T-APC 118 (ex-*Check Knot*), were transferred to the Maritime Administration in 1959, but the latter was reacquired in 1962 and reclassified as T-AG 171 in 1963 and the former was reacquired in 1966 and redesignated T-AGS 35 on 1 Dec 1966; see Experimental, Research and Surveying Ships.

FAST DEPLOYMENT LOGISTIC SHIPS (FDL)

The Department of Defense has abandoned plans to construct a class of Fast Deployment Logistic Ships (FDL) that would be pre-loaded with Army combat equipment and supplies and be deployed at overseas locations where the equipment would be "married" to troops flown overseas. The first FDLs originally were requested in the Fiscal Year 1966 shipbuilding programme and each year through the FY 1970 budget request of the Johnson Administration; approval of this programme was continually denied by the Congress and the FDL programme was not included in the FY 1970 budget proposed by the Nixon Administration.
According to the Department of Defense, the most "cost effective" number of FDL ships necessary to meet anticipated requirements in the 1970s would be 30 operating in conjunction with 14 squadrons of C-141 jet cargo aircraft and six squadrons of C-5 jet cargo aircraft. In 1968, because of Congressional opposition to the size of the FDL programme as well as the FDL concept, the Department of Defense requested only a 15-ship programme with the balance of the sealift being obtained through the long-term charter of up to 30 new cargo ships to be privately built according to design criteria specified by the Navy.
These ships were to have been manned by civilian crews with a small Army detachment on board to service vehicles and heavy weapons.
Detailed characteristics and notes, and an artist's concept of the FDL appear in the 1969-1970 edition.

41 TANK LANDING SHIPS (LST)

Name	No.	Name	No.
*LST 47	T-LST 47	*LST 590	T-LST 590
*LST 117	T-LST 117	CLEARWATER COUNTY	T-LST 602
*LST 176	T-LST 176	*LST 607	T-LST 607
*LST 222	T-LST 222	*LST 613	T-LST 613
*LST 230	T-LST 230	*LST 623	T-LST 623
*LST 276	T-LST 276	LST 626	T-LST 626
*LST 277	T-LST 277	*LST 629	T-LST 629
*LST 287	T-LST 287	*LST 630	T-LST 630
*LST 399	T-LST 399	LST 643	T-LST 643
*LST 456	T-LST 456	*LST 649	T-LST 649
*LST 488	T-LST 488	*LST 664	T-LST 664
*LST 491	T-LST 491	*DAVIESS COUNTY	T-LST 692
*LST 530	T-LST 530	*DE KALB COUNTY	T-LST 715
*CHASE COUNTY	T-LST 532	*HARRIS COUNTY	T-LST 822
*LST 546	T-LST 546	*NEW LONDON COUNTY	T-LST 1066
*LST 550	T-LST 550	*NYE COUNTY	T-LST 1067
*LST 566	T-LST 566	*ORLEANS PARISH	
*LST 572	T-LST 572	(ex-MCS 6)	T-LST 1069
*LST 579	T-LST 579	*LST 1072	T-LST 1072
LST 581	T-LST 581	PLUMAS COUNTY	T-LST 1083
LST 587	T-LST 587	*PULASKI COUNTY	T-LST 1088

Displacement, tons	LST 511-1152: 1 653 standard; 4 080 full load
	LST 1-510: 1 625 light; 4 050 full load
Dimensions, feet	328 oa × 50 × 14
Main engines	Diesels (General Motors); 1 700 shp; 2 shafts = 11·6 knots

Former Navy-manned tank landing ships now employed to carry cargo in the Western Pacific. T-LST 287, 532, 590, 626, 643, 664, 692, 822, 1066, 1067, 1069, 1072, and 1088 (13 ships) are manned by South Korean personnel; all others by Japanese personnel. The *Clearwater County* T-LST 602 (ex-US Air Force operated) is in Maritime Administration reserve but remains on the Navy List; others are in Military Sealift Command reserve if not in service. See Amphibious Warfare Ships for detailed data.
Note T-LST 287 has kingposts; T-LST 630 has two sets of boat davits on each side of bridge.

RECLASSIFICATION. The *Orleans Parish* was fitted to support minesweepers and reclassified a Mine Countermeasures Support Ship (MCS 6) on 19 Jan 1959; subsequently reclassified T-LST on 1 June 1966 and assigned to Military Sea Transportation Service.

DISPOSALS
LST 600 stricken on 1 June 1969; **Chesterfield County** LST 551 stricken on 1 June 1970.

LST 287 (T-LST 287)   *United States Navy*

LST 630 (T-LST 630)   *United States Navy*

AIRCRAFT TRANSPORTS (AVT)

All former aircraft carriers redesignated as aircraft transports (AVT) have been stricken from the Navy List. See section on Aircraft Carriers in this edition for details of disposition; see 1970-1971 and previous editions for characteristics.

EXPERIMENTAL, RESEARCH AND SURVEYING SHIPS

EXPERIMENTAL SURFACE EFFECT SHIPS

The large surface effect ships (SES) being built for the Navy by the Aerojet-General Corp, and Textron's Bell Aerospace Division are described in the section on Landing Craft in this edition of *Jane's Fighting Ships*.

1 HYDROGRAPHIC RESEARCH SHIP (AG):
"FLYER" TYPE

*FLYER (ex-SS *American Flyer*, ex-SS *Water Witch*) T-AG 178

Displacement, tons	7 360 light; 11 000 full load
Dimensions, feet	459·2 oa × 63 × 28
Main engines	Turbines; 6 000 shp = 17 knots
Boilers	2
Complement	14 officers, 41 enlisted men

Acquired from Maritime Administration on 9 Feb 1965. C2-S-B1 type. Operated by Military Sealift Command for Naval Electronic Systems Command, civilian manned.

FLYER (T-AG 178)   *US Navy*

1 HYDROGRAPHIC RESEARCH SHIP (AG)
"KINGSPORT" TYPE

*KINGSPORT (ex-*Kingsport Victory*) T-AG 164

Displacement, tons	7 190 light; 10 680 full load
Dimensions, feet	455 oa × 62 × 22
Main engines	Geared turbines; 1 shaft; 8 500 shp = 15·2 knots
Boilers	2
Complement	13 officers, 42 enlisted men, 18 technicians

vC2-S-AP3. Built in 1944 by the California Shipbuilding Corp, Los Angeles. Former cargo ship in the MSTS fleet. Name shortened, ship reclassified, and converted in 1961-1962 by Willamette Iron & Steel Co, Portland, Oregon, into the world's first satellite communications ship, for Project Advent, involving the promotion of a terminal to meet the required military capability for high capacity, world-wide radio communications, using high altitiude hovering satellites, and the installation of ship-to-shore communications, facilities, additional electric power generating equipment, a helicopter landing platform, aerological facilities, and a 30-ft parabolic communication antenna housed in a 53-ft diameter plastic radome abaft the superstructure. Painted white for operations in the tropics. Project Advent Syncom satellite relay operations were completed in 1966, and *Kingsport* was reassigned to hydrographic research. Antenna sphere now removed.
Operated by Military Sealift Command for Naval Electronic Systems Command; civilian manned.
Broadside view appears in 1968-1969 edition; note antenna mast on helicopter platform in photograph; exhaust ducts fitted to funnel.

KINGSPORT (T-AG 164)   *United States Navy (MSTS)*

1 POSEIDON TEST SHIP (AG)

*OBSERVATION ISLAND (ex-*YAG* 57, ex-SS *Empire State Mariner*)   AG 154

Displacement, tons	17 600, full load
Measurement, tons	15 000
Dimensions, feet	529·5 wl; 563 oa × 76·2 × 29
Main engines	Geared turbines (General Electric); 1 shaft; 19 250 shp = 20 knots
Boilers	2
Complement	350

Built by New York Shipbuilding Corp, Camden, New Jersey. Converted by Norfolk Naval Shipyard, Portsmouth, Virginia. Commissioned on 5 Dec 1958. Experimental

OBSERVATION ISLAND *continued*

vessels for firing "Polaris" Fleet Ballistic Missile (FBM); subsequently fitted to fire the improved Poseidon FBM. Navy manned.

MISSILE TESTING. The ship is fitted with complete missile testing, servicing and firing systems. She fired the first ship-launched Polaris missile, at sea on 27 Aug 1959. She was fitted with the second "Polaris" missile launching tube in Sep 1959 at Norfolk Naval Shipyard.
Refitted to fire the improved Poseidon missile in 1969 and launched the first Poseidon test missile fired afloat on 16 Dec 1969.

OBSERVATION ISLAND (AG 154)   *1969, US Navy*

1 EXPERIMENTAL NAVIGATION SHIP (AG)

*COMPASS ISLAND (ex *YAG* 56, ex-SS *Garden Mariner*)   AG 153

Displacement, tons	16 076 full load
Measurement, tons	17 600
Dimensions, feet	529·5 pp; 563 oa × 76·2 × 29
Main engines	Geared turbines (General Electric); 1 shaft; 19 250 shp = 20 knots
Boilers	2

Built by New York Shipbuilding Corp, Camden, New Jersey. Converted by New York Naval Shipyard, Brooklyn, and commissioned on 3 Dec 1956 for the development of the Fleet Ballistic Missile guidance and ship navigation systems. Her mission is to assist in the development and evaluation of a navigation system independent of shore-based aids. (See *Navigation* notes on SINS, Ship Inertial Navigational System, in the 1957-58 to 1963-64 editions). The ship was acquired by the Navy from the Maritime Administration. **Navy manned.**

STABILIZATION. One of the most comfortable riding ships in the Navy. She has the best automatic steering available, and has activated fins for roll stabilization. This system was developed by Sperry Gyroscope Co. When her sister ships roll 15 degrees, *Compass Island*, in the same seaway rolls about 1·5 degrees.

DISPOSALS AND RECLASSIFICATIONS

Acquisition of **AG 155** (C-4 cargo ship) was cancelled; **Hunting** AG 156 (ex-EAG 398, ex-LSM 398) sonar test ship, stricken in 1962; **King County** AG 157 (ex-LST 857) Regulus missile test ship, stricken in 1961; acquisition of research ship **AG 158** was cancelled; **Oxford** AG 159 reclassified AGTR 1; **AG 160** and **AG 161** reclassified AGM 1 and AGM 22, respectively; **Mission Capistrano** AG 162 (ex-AO 112) sound test ship, stricken in 1970; **Glover** AG 163 reclassified AGDE 1.
AG 165-168 reclassified AGTR 2-5, respectively; **Private J. E. Valdez** AG 169 (ex-APC 119) special mission ship, stricken in 1970; **Lieutenant J. E. Robinson** AG 170 (ex-AK 274) reclassified AK-274; **Sergeant Joseph E. Muller** AG 171 (ex-APC) 118 special mission ship, stricken in 1970; **AG 172-174** are in service as cargo ships.
Sergeant Curtis F. Shoup AG 175, survey support ship, stricken in 1970; **Peregine** AG 176 (ex-MSF 373) experimental ship, stricken in 1969; **Shearwater** AG 177 (ex-FS 411) special mission ship, returned to US Army in 1967. **AG 179-190** assigned to 12 "Victory" cargo ship to have been used as floating depot ships; project cancelled; **Spokane** AG 191 (ex-CLAA 120) was to be converted to sonar test ship; project cancelled and probably will be stricken in 1971-1972 (see 1970-1971 edition for details).

ENVIRONMENTAL RESEARCH SHIPS (AGER)

The Navy has stricken the two surviving intelligence collection ships classified as environmental research ships; the **Banner** (AGER 1, ex-AKL 25 ex-FS 345) on 14 Nov 1969, and the **Palm Beach** (AGER 3, ex-AKL 45, ex-FS 217) on 1 Dec 1969. The third ship of this type, the *Pueblo* (AGER 2, ex-AKL 44, ex-FS 344), was boarded and captured by North Korean forces in what were believed international waters off the port of Wonsan in January 1968. Her crew of 80 naval personnel and two civilians were interned for a year (one sailor was killed in the capture). At this writing the ship still was interned by North Korea; her name remains on the US Navy List. These ships are described in the 1969-1970 and previous editions.

1 RANGE INSTRUMENTATION SHIP (AGM):
POSEIDON TEST PROGRAMME

SHERBURNE T-AGM 22 (ex-APA 205)

Dimensions, feet	455 oa × 62 × 24
Main engines	Turbine (Westinghouse); 8 500 hp; 1 shaft = 17·7 knots
Boilers	2 (Combustion Engineering)
Complement	14 officers, 54 enlisted men, 10 technical personnel

Former attack transport converted specifically to serve as a range instrumentation ship in support of the Poseidon Fleet Ballistic Missile (FBM) programme. Built by Permanente Metals Corp, Richmond, California; commissioned on 20 Sep 1944. Stricken from the Navy List on 1 Oct 1958 and transferred to Maritime Administration reserve fleet; reacquired by the Navy on 22 Oct 1969 for AGM conversion.
Recommissioned in Sep 1971 and operated by Military Sealift Command; civilian manned.

Experimental, Research and Surveying Ships—*continued*

2 RANGE INSTRUMENTATION SHIPS (AGM)
T2-SE-A2 TYPE

*VANGUARD (ex-*Mussle Shoals*, ex-*Mission San Fernando*)
T-AGM 19 (ex-T-AO 122)

*REDSTONE (ex-*Johnstown*, ex-*Mission de Pala*) T-AGM 20 (ex-T-AO 114)

Displacement, tons	21 626 full load
Dimensions, feet	595 oa × 75 × 25
Main engines	Turbine-electric; 1 shaft; 10 000 shp = 16 knots
Boilers	2 (Babcock & Wilcox)
Complement	*Vanguard* 19 officers, 71 enlisted men, 108 technical personnel; *Redstone* 20 officers, 71 enlisted men, 120 technical personnel.

Former "Mission" class tankers converted in 1964-1966 to serve as mid-ocean communications and tracking ships in support of the Apollo manned lunar flights. A third ship of this type has been stricken (see *Disposal* notes below).

All built in 1944 by Marinship, Sausalito, California, as tankers. T2-SE-A2 type. Converted to Range Instrumentation Ships (RIS) by General Dynamics, Quincy Division, Massachusetts; each ship was cut in half and a 72-foot mid-section was inserted, increasing length, beam, and displacement; approximately 450 tons of electronic equipment installed for support of lunar flight operations, including communications and tracking systems; balloon hangar and platform fitted aft. Cost of converting the three ships was $90 000 000. Operated by Military Sealift Command for Air Force Eastern Test Range in Atlantic (*Vanguard*) and for NASA Goddard Space Flight Centre (*Redstone*). Civilian crews.

DISPOSAL

Mercury (ex-*Flagstaff, Mission San Juan*) T-AGM 21 (ex-T-AO 126) transferred to Maritime Administration in 1969 (converted to merchant configuration).

VANGUARD (T-AGM 19)   *1966. General Dynamics*

1 RANGE INSTRUMENTATION SHIP (AGM)
C1-M-AV1 TYPE

*SWORD KNOT T-AGM 13

Displacement, tons	8 380 full load
Dimensions, feet	338·8 oa × 50·3 × 12
Main engines	Diesel; 1 shaft = 10 knots
Complement	12 officers, 31 enlisted men, 25 technical personnel

Former merchant ship converted by Air Force to range instrumentation ship. *Sword Knot* built in 1945 by Consolidated Steel Corp, Wilmington, California; C1-M-AV1 type. Assigned to MSTS on 1 July 1964; *Sword Knot* operated by Military Sealift Command for Air Force Space and Missile Test Centre, Vandenberg Air Force Base, California. Civilian manned. She is expected to be stricken in the near future.

The *Coastal Crusader* (T-AGM 16) of this type has been converted to a surveying ship and designated AGS 36. A photograph of the *Coastal Crusader* as a T-AGM appears in the 1969-1970 edition.

DISPOSALS

Four ships of this type have been stricken from the Navy List: **Rose Knot** (T-AGM 14) to Maritime Administration on 26 Mar 1968; **Coastal Sentry** (T-AGM 15), ex-AK 212) stricken on 11 July 1968 (scrapped); **Timber Hitch** (T-AGM 17) to Maritime Administration on 5 Feb 1968; **Sampan Hitch** (T-AGM 18) to Maritime Administration on 24 June 1968 (scrapped).

American Mariner (T-AGM 12), an EC2 "Liberty" ship, was expended as a target in Chesapeake Bay in Oct 1966.

REDSTONE (T-AGM 20)   *1966. General Dynamics*

REDSTONE (T-AGM 20)   *1970, United States Air Force*

SWORD KNOT (T-AGM 13)   *United States Navy*

LONGVIEW (T-AGM 3)   *1970, United States Navy, PH3 J. B. Land*

Experimental, Research, and Surveying Ships—*continued*

2 RANGE INSTRUMENTATION SHIPS (AGM): C4-S-A1 TYPE

*GENERAL H. H. ARNOLD (ex-USNS *General R. E. Collan*) T-AGM 9 (ex-T-AP 139)
*GENERAL HOYT S. VANDENBERG (ex-USNS *General Harry Taylor*) T-AGM 10 (ex-T-AP 145)

Displacement, tons	16 600 full load
Dimensions, feet	552·9 oa × 71·5 × 26·3
Main engines	Geared turbines; 1 shaft; 9 000 shp = 15 knots
Complement	21 officers, 71 enlisted men, 113 technical personnel

Former transports converted in 1962-1963 for monitoring Air Force missile firings and satellite launches.
Both ships built in 1944 by Kaiser Co, Richmond, California, as large troop transports. C4-S-A1 type. Upon conversion to range instrumentation they were placed in service in 1963 as Air Force ships; however, assigned to MSTS for operation on 1 July 1964 (T-AGM 9) and 13 July 1964 (T-AGM 10).
Both ships are operated by Military Sealift Command for Air Force Eastern Test Range in Atlantic. Civilian manned.

GEN. HOYT S. VANDENBERG (T-AGM 10)   *United States Navy*

1 RANGE INSTRUMENTATION SHIP (AGM): AKL TYPE

*RANGE RECOVERER (ex-FS 278) T-AGM 2 (CA-T-AG 161)

Displacement, tons	935 full load
Dimensions, feet	176·5 oa × 32 × 11·5
Main engines	Diesel; 1 shaft = 14 knots
Complement	7 officers, 15 enlisted men, 4 technical personnel

Former Army small cargo ship modified for telemetry of rocket firing from Whallops Station in Chesapeake Bay.
Built in 1944 by Wheeler SB Corp, Whitestone, New York, Assigned to MSTS on 6 Apr 1960; operated by Military Sealift Command for NASA in support of experiments at Whallops Island, Virginia. Civilian manned.

RANGE RECOVERER (T-AGM 2)   *US Navy*

5 RANGE INSTRUMENTATION SHIPS (AGM): "VICTORY" TYPE

*LONGVIEW (ex-*Haiti Victory*)	T-AGM 3 (ex-T-AK 238)
*SUNNYVALE (ex-*Dalton Victory*)	T-AGM 5 (ex-T-AK 256)
*WATERTOWN (ex-SS *Niantic Victory*)	T-AGM 6
*HUNTSVILLE (ex-SS *Knox Victory*)	T-AGM 7
*WHEELING (ex-*Seton Hall Victory*)	T-AGM 8

Displacement, tons	7 190 Navy light; 10 680 full load
Dimensions, feet	T-AGM 6, 7: 455·8 oa × 62 × 28·6;
	T-AGM 3, 5, 8: 455·3 oa × 62·2 × 28 (draft varies)
Main engines	Geared turbines; 1 shaft; 8 500 shp
Speed, knots	T-AGM 6, 7, 16·2; T-AGM 3, 5, 8, 17

All VC2-S-AP3 type; details vary. All extensively modified to serve as Range Instrumentation Ships (RIS) in support of American military and National Aeronautics and Space Administration (NASA) missile and space programmes.
Longview built in 1944 by Permanente Metals Corp, Richmond, California. Assigned to MSTS on 1 Mar 1950 (as T-AK 238); operated in support of Air Force Western Test Range in Pacific; civilian crew of 12 officers, 41 enlisted men, plus 20 technical personnel. Fitted with helicopter hangar and platform aft.
Sunnyvale built in 1944 by California SB Corp, Los Angeles. Assigned to MSTS on 6 Aug 1950 (as T-AK 256); operated in support of Air Force Western Test Range in Pacific; civilian crew of 12 officers, 41 enlisted men, plus 20 technical personnel. Fitted with helicopter hangar and platform aft.

Watertown built in 1944 by Oregon SB Corp, Portland, Oregon. Assigned to MSTS on 11 Aug 1960; operated in support of Air Force Western Test Range in Pacific and NASA; civilian crew of 14 officers, 55 enlisted men, plus 72 technical personnel.
Huntsville built in 1954 by Oregon SB Corp, Portland Oregon. Assigned to MSTS on 1 Mar 1960; operated in support of Air Force Western Test Range in Pacific and NASA; civilian crew of 14 officers, 55 enlisted men, plus 72 technical personnel.
Wheeling built in 1945 by Oregon SB Corp, Portland Oregon. Assigned to MSTS on 28 May 1964; operated in support of Navy Pacific Missile Range; civilian crew of 13 officers, 46 enlisted men, plus 48 technical personnel (accommodation for 64). Fitted with helicopter hangar and platform aft.

ELECTRONICS. The electronic antennae of these ships are regularly changed or modified to support mission requirements.

HELICOPTERS. These ships fitted with helicopter platforms and hangars periodically carry helicopters to assist in recovery packages ejected from orbiting satellites. (These data packages also are "snagged" during re-entry by fixed-wing aircraft fitted with special devices.)

DISPOSALS
Richfield (T-AGM 4, ex-T-AK 253), **Range Tracker** (T-AGM 1, ex-T-AG 160), **Twin Falls** (T-AGM 11) all stricken on 28 Apr 1970.

SUNNYVALLE (T-AGM 5)   *United States Navy*

WATERTOWN (T-AGM 6)   *United States Navy*

HUNTSVILLE (T-AGM 7) 1967, *National Aeronautics and Space Administration*

WHEELING (T-AGM 8)   *United States Navy*

Experimental, Research and Surveying Ships—*continued*

OCEANOGRAPHIC RESEARCH SHIPS (AGOR):
"UTILITY" TYPE

Displacement, tons	950 full load
Dimensions, feet	165 oa × 36 × 10
Main engines	2 diesels; 1 500 bhp; 2 shafts = 11 knots cruising and 13 knots maximum

The Navy plans to construct 12 of these "utility" oceanographic research ships to replace older and obsolescent research ships now operated by civilian research and educational institutions in support of Navy programmes. They will be based on a commercial ship design. The first two units, probably to be designated AGOR 21 and AGOR 22, will be assigned to Texas A & M University and to the University of Hawaii.

CANCELLATION. The planned AGOR 19 and AGOR 20 were cancelled in Feb 1969.

1 OCEANOGRAPHIC RESEARCH SHIP (AGOR):
CATAMARAN TYPE

HAYES T-AGOR 16

Displacement, tons	3 080 full load
Dimensions, feet	246·5 oa × 75 (see *Design* notes) × 18·8
Main engines	Geared diesels; 2 400 shp; 2 shafts = 15 knots
Complement	11 officers, 33 enlisted men, 25 scientists

Authorised in Fiscal Year 1967 new construction programme. The T-AGOR 16 will be the second class of modern US naval ships to have a catamaran hull, the first being the ASR 21 class submarine rescue ships. Under construction at Todd Shipyards, Seattle, Washington; completed in late 1971. Estimated cost is $15 900 000. Laid down 12 Nov 1969; launched 2 July 1970.
The ship will be operated by the Military Sealift Command for the Office of Naval Research under the technical control of the Oceanographer of the Navy; civilian crew.

DESIGN. Catamaran hull design provides large deck working area, centre well for operating equipment at great depths, and removes laboratory areas from main propulsion machinery. Each hull is 246·5 feet long and 24 feet wide (maximum). There are three 36-inch diameter instrument wells in addition to the main centre well.
In Oct 1965 the Chief of Naval Research had proposed that the minelayer *Terror* (MMF 5) be converted to an AGOR to provide a ship of this size; however, the plan was dropped because of excessive conversion costs and a new design was undertaken, resulting in the T-AGOR 16.
The T-AGOR 16 differs in appearance from the ASR 21 class ships by the oceanographic ship having a small deck working space aft of the bridge structure and the absence of stern helicopter platform of the rescue ships.

ENGINEERING. Fitted with controllable pitch propellers. An auxiliary 165-shp diesel is fitted in each hull to provide "creeping" speed of 2 to 4 knots.
Separation of controllable pitch propellers by catamaran hull separation provides high degree of manoeuverability, eliminating the need for bow thrusters.

NOMENCLATURE. Oceanographic research ships and surveying ships generally are named for naval oceanographers, hydrographers, and explorers. (Converted ships generally retain original names).
The AGOR 16 is named for Dr. Harvey C. Hayes of the Naval Research Laboratory, known as the "father of sonar in the US Navy".

PHOTOGRAPHS. Note widely spaced, side-by-side funnels, after mast atop king post-like structure offset to starboard.

HAYES (T-AGOR 16)   *Official Navy drawing*

HAYES (T-AGOR 16)   *1970, Todd Shipyards Corp*

2 OCEANOGRAPHIC RESEARCH SHIPS (AGOR):
"MELVILLE" TYPE

Name	No.	Laid down	Launched	Completed
*MELVILLE	AGOR 14	12 July 1967	10 July 1968	May 1969
*KNORR	AGOR 15	9 Aug 1967	21 Aug 1968	June 1969

Displacement, tons	1 915 standard; 2 080 full load
Dimensions, feet	244·9 × 46·3 × 15
Main engines	Diesel; 2 500 shp; 2 cycloidal propellers = 12 knots
Complement	9 officers, 16 enlisted men, 25 scientists

Oceanographic research ships of an advanced design. AGOR 14 and AGOR 15 authorised in Fiscal Year 1966 new construction programme; AGOR 19 and AGOR 20 of this type in FY 1968 programme, but construction of the latter ships was cancelled. The *Melville* and *Knorr* built by Defoe Shipbuilding Co, Bay City, Michigan. *Melville* operated by Scripps Institution of Oceanography and *Knorr* by Woods Hole Oceanography Institution for the Office of Naval Research; under technical control of the Oceanographer of the Navy.

DESIGN. Fitted with internal wells for lower equipment; underwater lights and observation ports. Facilities for handling small research submersibles. Enlarged and improved version of earlier "Conrad" class.

ENGINEERING. First US Navy ocean-going ships with cycloidal propellers permitting the ships to turn 360 degrees in their own length. One propeller is fitted at each end of the ship, providing movement in any direction and optimum station keeping without use of thrusters. They have experienced engineering difficulties.

KNORR (AGOR 15)   *1965, Defoe Shipbuilding*

8 OCEANOGRAPHIC RESEARCH SHIPS (AGOR)
"CONRAD" TYPE

Name	No.	Laid down	Launched	Delivered
*ROBERT D. CONRAD	AGOR 3	19 Jan 1961	26 May 1962	29 Nov 1962
*JAMES M. GILLISS	T-AGOR 4	31 May 1961	19 May 1962	5 Nov 1962
*SANDS	T-AGOR 6	23 Aug 1962	14 Sep 1963	8 Feb 1965
*LYNCH	T-AGOR 7	7 Sep 1962	17 Mar 1964	22 Oct 1965
*THOMAS G. THOMPSON	AGOR 9	12 Sep 1963	18 July 1964	4 Sep 1965
*THOMAS WASHINGTON	AGOR 10	12 Sep 1963	1 Aug 1964	17 Sep 1965
*DE STEIGUER	T-AGOR 12	12 Nov 1965	21 Mar 1966	28 Feb 1969
*BARTLETT	T-AGOR 13	18 Nov 1965	24 May 1966	15 Apr 1969

Displacement, tons	1 200 standard; 1 380 full load
Dimensions, feet	191·5 wl; 208·9 oa × 37·4 × 15·3
Main engines	Diesel-electric; 1 shaft; 10 000 hp = 13·5
Complement	9 officers, 17 enlisted men, 15 scientists (except *De Steigeur* and *Bartlett*, 8 officers, 18 enlisted men)

This is the first class of ships designed and built by the US Navy for oceanographic research. Fitted with instrumentation and laboratories to measure the earth's gravity and magnetic fields, water temperature, sound transmission in water, and the geological profile of the ocean floor.
Special features include 10 ton capacity boom and winches for handling over-the-side equipment; bow thruster propulsion unit for precise manoeuvrability and station keeping; 620 hp gas turbine (housed in funnel structure) for providing "quiet" power when conducting operations in which use of main engines would generate too high a noise level (gas turbine also can drive the ship at 6·5 knots); endurance of 12 000 miles at 12 knots.
James M. Gilliss operated by the University of Miami (Florida) since 1970 in support of Navy programmes.
Robert D. Conrad built by Gibbs Corp, Jacksonville, Florida. Operated by Lamont Geological Observatory of Columbia University under technical control of the Oceanographer of the Navy.
James H. Gilliss and *Charles H. Davis* built by Christy Corp, Sturgeon Bay, Wisconsin. Operated by Military Sealift Command under technical control of the Oceanographer of the Navy; civilian crew.
Sands and *Lynch* built by Marietta Manufacturing Co, Point Pleasant, West Virginia. Operated by Military Sealift Command under the technical control of the Oceanographer of the Navy. Civilian crew.
Thomas G. Thompson built by Marinette Marine Corp, Marinette, Wisconsin. Operated by University of Washington (state) under technical control of the Oceanographer of the Navy; civilian crew.
Thomas Washington built by Marinette Marine Corp, Marinette, Wisconsin. Operated by Scripps Institution of Oceanography (University of California) under technical control of the Oceanographer on the Navy; civilian crew.
De Steiguer and *Bartlett* built by Northwest Marine Iron Works, Portland, Oregon. Operated by Military Sealift Command under the technical control of the Oceanographer of the Navy; civilian crew.

TRANSFER. *Charles H. Davis* AGOR 5 of this type was transferred to New Zealand on 10 Aug 1970.

PHOTOGRAPHS. Note built-up structure amidships on *De Steigner*; the *Thomas D. Thompson* has side structure built up amidships.

Experimental, Research and Surveying Ships—*continued*

"CONRAD" TYPE—*continued*

THOMAS G. THOMPSON (AGOR 9)   *United States Navy*

DE STEIGUER (T-AGOR 12)   *United States Navy*

SANDS (T-AGOR 6)   *United States Navy*

1 OCEANOGRAPHIC RESEARCH SHIP (AGOR):
Ex-SALVAGE SHIP

Name	No.	Launched	Commissioned
*CHAIN	AGOR 17 (ex-ARS 20)	3 June 1943	31 Mar 1944

Displacement, tons	*Chain:* 2 100 full load
Dimensions, feet	207 wl; 213·5 oa × 39 × 15
Main engines	Diesel electric (4 Cooper Bessemer diesels); approx 3 000 shp; 2 shafts = 14 knots
Complement	*Chain:* 29 + 26 scientists

Converted from a salvage ship for oceanographic research. Built by Basalt Rock Co, Napa, California. Commission date as ARS. Converted to an oceanographic research ship by Savannah Machine & Foundry in 1958. The *Chain* is operated by the Woods Hole Oceanographic Institution for the Office of Naval Research under the technical control of the Oceanographer of the Navy. Civilian crew.

ENGINEERING. Fitted with an auxiliary 250 hp outboard propulsion unit for manoeuvering at low speeds (up to 4·5 knots).

DISPOSAL
Argo AGOR 18 (ex-*Snatch*, ARS 27) was similarly converted; stricken on 1 May 1970. (A photograph of the *Argo* appears in the 1970-1971 and previous editions).

2 OCEANOGRAPHIC RESEARCH SHIPS (AGOR):
Ex-CARGO SHIPS

Name	No.	Launched	Delivered
* ELTANIN	T-AGOR 8 (ex-T-AK 270)	16 Jan 1957	2 Aug 1957
* MIZAR	T-AGOR 11 (ex-T-AK 272)	7 Oct 1957	22 Nov 1957

Displacement, tons	2 036 light; 4 942 full load
Measurement, tons	2 486 gross; 1 300 deadweight
Dimensions, feet	256·8 wl; 262·2 oa × 51·5 × 18·7; (*Mizar* 22·8)
Main engines	Diesel-electric (ALCO diesels, Westinghouse electric motors) 2 shafts; 3 200 bhp = 12 knots
Complement	*Eltanin:* 12 officers, 36 enlisted men, 38 scientists
	Mizar: 11 officers, 30 enlisted men, up to 15 scientists

Built for MSTS by Avondale Marine Ways, New Orleans, La. Designed for Arctic operation with hull strengthened against ice. C1-ME2-13a type. Delivered as T-AK to MSTS (Military Sealift Command).
As research ships the *Eltanin* is operated by Military Sealift Command for National Science Foundations, *Mizar* by Military Sealift Command for Naval Research Laboratory, latter ship under technical control of the Oceanographer of the Navy; civilian crews.

CONVERSION. *Eltanin* was converted in 1961 into a scientific laboratory for Antarctic research programme for the National Science Foundation. Equipped to study meteorology, the upper atmosphere, marine and terrestial biology, physical oceanography, submarine geology, and geomagnetic conditions. Reclassified from T-AK 270 to T-AGOR 8 on 15 Nov 1962.

Mizar converted in 1962 into deep sea research ship. Equipped with centre well for lowering oceanographic equipment including towed sensor platforms, fitted with laboratories and elaborate photographic facilities, hydrophone system and computer for seafloor navigation and tracking towed vehicles. The *Mizar* had key roles in the searches for the nuclear submarines *Thresher* and *Scorpion*, and recovery of the H-bomb lost off Palomares, Spain.

MIZAR (T-AGOR 11)   *United States Navy*

ELTANIN (T-AGOR 8)   *United States Navy*

1 OCEANOGRAPHIC RESEARCH SHIP (AGOR):
Ex-SEAPLANE TENDER

JOSIAH WILLARD GIBBS (ex-*San Carlos*) T-AGOR 1 (ex-AVP 51)

Displacement, tons	1 750 standard; 2 800 full load
Dimensions, feet	300 wl; 310·8 oa × 41·2 × 13·5
Main engines	Diesels (Fairbanks-Morse); 2 shafts; 6 080 shp = 18 knots
Complement	14 officers, 33 enlisted men, 24 scientists

Former seaplane tender converted for oceanographic research. Built by Lake Washington Shipyard, Houghton, Wash. Laid down on 7 Sep 1942, launched on 20 Dec 1942, and commissioned on 21 Mar 1944.
Operated by Military Sealift Command for Naval Research Laboratory under technical control of the Oceanographer of the Navy; civilian manned.

CONVERSION. Converted by Mobile Ship Repair Inc, Mobile, Alabama, in 1958. Fitted with special instrumentation winches, and laboratories for oceanographic research. Auxiliary propeller fitted for precise manoeuvring at speeds to four knots (subsequently removed).

TRANSFER. AGOR 2 was the *H. U. Sverdrup*, built in Norway with US funds.

JOSIAH WILLARD GIBBS (T-AGOR 1)   *United States Navy*

OCEANOGRPAHIC RESEARCH CRAFT:
MISCELLANEOUS TYPES

The Navy also owns a number of smaller oceanographic research craft that are operated by various educational and research institutions in support of Navy programmes; under technical control of the Oceanographer of the Navy; no Navy hull numbers are assigned; all are 100 feet in length or smaller except for the *Lamb*, a converted 136-foot minesweeper (YMS/AMS type) operated by the Lamont Geophysical Laboratory.

HYDROGRAPHIC SURVEYING SHIPS (AGS):
PROJECT HYSURCH

An advanced class of hydrographic surveying ships is planned which will be capable of surveying 1 000 square miles and produce finished charts within a five-day period. Each ship would serve as a "mother" ship for several 20-foot launches to provide capability of mapping 50 square miles of ocean floor in two days. HYSURCH stands for Hydrographic Survey and Mapping System.
Ship construction tentatively is planned for Fiscal Year 1974-1976 new construction programmes.

DISPOSALS

All Navy-manned surveying ships have been stricken:
Pursuit (AGS 17, ex-AM 108) stricken in 1960, **Prevail** (AGS 20, ex-AM 107),
Requisite (AGS 18, ex-AM 109) stricken in 1964, **Towhee** (AGS 28, ex-AM 388)
stricken on 1 May 1969, **San Pablo** (AGS 30, ex-AVP 30) stricken on 1 June 1969,
Tanner (AGSS 15, ex-AKA 34) stricken on 1 Aug 1969, **Maury** (AGS 16, ex-AKA 36)
stricken on 19 Dec 1969, **Serrano** (AGS 24, ex-ATF 112) stricken on 2 Jan 1970,
Rehoboth (AGS 50, ex-AVP 50) stricken on 15 Apr 1970, **Sheldrake** (AGS 19,
ex-AM 62) stricken on 30 June 1968.
The **Littlehales** (AGSC 15, ex-YF 854), the Navy's last coastal surveying ship, was
stricken on 20 Feb 1968 (but not decommissioned until 1 Apr 1968, more than a
month after she was struck).

1 SURVEYING SHIP (AGS): C1-M-AV1 TYPE

COASTAL CRUSADER T-AGS 36 (ex-T-AGM 16)

Dimensions, feet	338·8 loa × 50·3 × 12
Main engines	Diesel 1 shaft 1 750 bhp = 11·5 knots

A former merchant ship converted by the Air Force to a range instrumentation ship
and subsequently converted to a surveying ship in 1969. Built in 1945 by Leatham
D. Smith SB Co, Sturgeon Bay, Wisconsin. C1-M-AV1 type. Taken out of service
and placed in reserve on 1 Dec 1969 as an economy effort.

COASTAL CRUSADER (T-AGS 36 shown as T-AGM 16) *United States Navy*

1 SURVEYING SHIP (AGS): C1-M-AV TYPE

*SERGEANT GEORGE D. KEATHLEY (ex-*Acorn Knot*)
T-AGS 35 (ex-T-APC 117)

Displacement, tons	6 090 full load
Dimensions, feet	338·8 × 50·3 × 17·5
Main engines	Diesel; 1 shaft; 1 750 bhp = 11·5 knots
Complement	11 officers, 32 enlisted men, 15 technical personnel

A former merchant ship assigned to the Army Transportation Services; assigned to
MSTS and renamed in 1950. Refitted to serve as a oceanographic surveying ship in
1966-1967. Built in 1945. C1-M-AV1 type.
Operated by Military Sealift Command for the Oceanographer of the Navy; civilian crew.

ELECTRONICS. During 1969-1970 a high-resolution, electronically stabilised sonar
system was installed for precise navigation on the basis of seafloor terrain features
was installed. Two computers are provided, one for collecting data from various sensors
and the other for processing the data to produce outlines and graphs of seafloor terrain.
Also equipped with satellite-navigation terminal.

2 SURVEYING SHIPS (AGS): "KELLAR" TYPE

Name	No.	Laid down	Launched	Delivered
KELLAR	T-AGS 25	20 Nov 1962	30 July 1964	31 Jan 1969
*S. P. LEE	T-AG192 (ex-T-AGS 31)	27 June1966	19 Oct 1967	13 Dec 1968

Displacement, tons	1 200 standard; 1 400 full load
Dimensions, feet	191·5 wl; 209 oa × 39 × 15
Main engines	Diesel-electric; 1 shaft; 1 200 hp = 15 knots
Complement	9 officers, 19 enlisted men, 13 scientists

This is the first class of ships designed and built for the US Navy for surveying operations.
Same design as the "Conrad" class oceanographic research ships with different instrumentation and equipment. Special features include bow propulsion unit for precise
manoeuvrability and station keeping; endurance of 12 000 miles at 12 knots.
Kellar built by Marietta Manufacturing Co, Point Pleasant, West Virginia, but completed
by Boland Machine-Manufacturing Co, New Orleans (Marietta contract terminated on
14 May 1965; Boland contract awarded 30 July 1966). She was sunk by a hurricane
in Sept 1965, further delaying completion.
S. P. Lee built by Defoe SB Co, Bay City, Michigan. Authorised in Fiscal Year 1962
and 1965 shipbuilding programmes, respectively.
Both ships were built for oceanographic surveying, but the *S. P. Lee* was redesignated
as a research ship (AG 192) on 25 Sep 1970 and assigned to the Naval Undersea
Research & Development Center, San Diego (replacing the PCERs *Marysville* and
Rexburg); note equipment on stern while ship operated in the Mediterranean in 1970-
1971. These ships are operated by the Military Sealift Command (civilian crews);
the *Kellar* is temporarily laid up in Maritime Administration reserve.

S. P. LEE (T-AG 192) *1970, A. & J. Pavia*

KELLAR (T-AGS 25) *1969, Boland Machine Mfg*

2 SURVEYING SHIPS (AGS): "CHAUVENET" TYPE

Name	No.	Laid down	Launched	Delivered
*CHAUVENET	T-AGS 29	24 May 1967	13 May 1968	Oct 1969
*HARKNESS	T-AGS 32	30 June1967	12 June1968	Dec 1969

Displacement, tons	4 200 full load
Dimensions, feet	393·2 oa × 54 × 16
Main engines	Diesel; 1 shaft; 3 600 hp = 15 knots
Complement	13 officers, approx 150 enlisted men and technical personnel, 8 scientists

A new class of large ships designed to undertake extensive military hydrographic and
oceanographic surveys, supporting coastal surveying craft, amphibious survey teams
and helicopters. Fitted with helicopter hangar and platform.
Chauvenet authorised in Fiscal Year 1965 new construction programme; *Harkness*
in FY 1966 programme. Both ships built by Upper Clyde Shipbuilders, Govan Division,
Glasgow, Scotland.
These ships are operated by the Military Sealift Command for the Oceanographer of
the Navy with Navy detachments on board. Civilian crews.

4 SURVEYING SHIPS (AGS): "BENT" CLASS

Name	No.	Laid down	Launched	Delivered
*SILAS BENT	T-AGS 26	2 Mar 1964	16 May 1964	23 July 1965
*KANE	T-AGS 27	19 Dec 1964	20 Nov 1965	19 May 1967
WILKES	T-AGS 33	18 July 1968	31 July 1969	July 1971
WYMAN	T-AGS 34	18 July 1968	30 Oct 1969	Nov 1971

Displacement, tons	1 935 standard; *Silas Bent* and *Kane* 2 558 full load; *Wilkes* 2 540 full load; *Wyman* 2 420 full load
Dimensions, feet	285·3 oa × 48 × 15·1
Main engines	Diesel-electric; 1 shaft; 3 600 hp = 14 knots
Complement	12 or 13 officers, 35 or 36 enlisted men, 30 scientists

Designed specifically for surveying operations. Special features include seafloor
mapping equipment; bow propulsion unit for precise manoeuvrability and station
keeping. All four ships operated by Military Sealift Command for the Oceanographer
of the Navy; civilian crews.
Silas Bent built by American SB Co, Lorain, Ohio; *Kane* built by Christy Corp, Sturgeon
Bay, Wisconsin; *Wilkes* and *Wyman* built by Defoe SB Co, Bay City, Michigan.

SILAS BENT (T-AGS 26) *United States Navy*

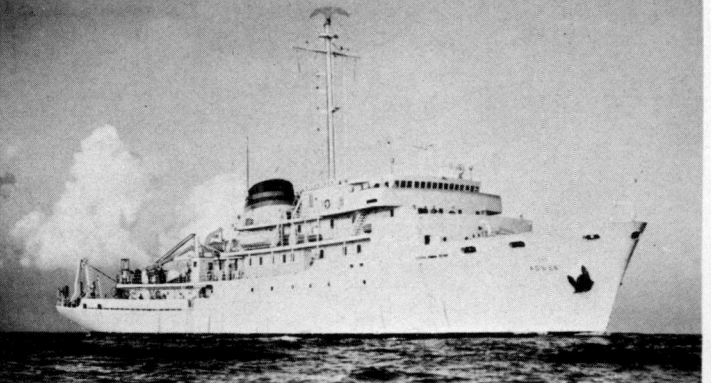

SILAS BENT (T-AGS 26) *United States Navy*

Experimental, Research, and Surveying Ships—*continued*

3 SURVEYING SHIPS (AGS): "VICTORY" TYPE

*BOWDITCH (ex-SS *South Bend Victory*)	T-AGS 21	
*DUTTON (ex-SS *Tuskegee Victory*)	T-AGS 22	
*MICHELSON (ex-SS *Joliet Victory*)	T-AGS 23	

Displacement, tons	4 512 full load
Dimensions, feet	455·2 oa × 62·2 × 25
Main engines	Turbine; 8 500 shp; 1 shaft = 15 knots
Boilers	2
Complement	13 or 14 officers, 47 enlisted men, approx 40 technical personnel

VC2-S-AP3 type built in 1945, *Bowditch* and *Michelson* by Oregon Shipbuilding Co; *Dutton* by South Coast Co, Newport Beach, California. All converted to support the Fleet Ballistic Missile Programme, *Dutton* and *Michelson* at Philadelphia Naval Shipyard 8 Nov 1957 to 16 Nov 1958 and 1 Mar 1958 to 31 Dec 1958, respectively, and *Bowditch* at Charleston Naval Shipyard 10 Oct 1957 to 30 Sep 1958.
Operated by Military Sealift Command for the Oceanographer of the Navy; civilian crews. Designed to chart the ocean floor and to record magnetic fields and gravity to enable vessels to establish locations within a few yards of their actual positions.

MICHELSON (T-AGS 23)   *United States Navy*

TECHNICAL RESEARCH SHIPS (AGTR)

The Navy has stricken the intelligence collection ships that were designated as technical research ships.
The **Oxford** (AGTR 1, ex-AG 159), **Georgetown** (AGTR 2, ex-AG 165), and **Jamestown** (AGTR 3, ex-AG 166) stricken on 19 Dec 1969, **Belmont** (AGTR 4, ex-AG 167) stricken on 16 Jan 1970.
The **Liberty** (AGTR 5, ex-AG 168) was severely damaged by Israeli aircraft and torpedo boat attack in the Eastern Mediterranean on 8 June 1967. She subsequently was decommissioned and placed in reserve until stricken on 1 June 1970. These ships are described in the 1969-1970 edition.

1 TEST RANGE SUPPORT SHIP (IX):

Name	No.	Builder	Commissioned
*ELK RIVER	IX 501 (ex-LSMR 501)	Brown SB Co (Houston, Texas)	27 May 1945

Displacement, tons	1 100 full load
Dimensions, feet	225 oa × 50 × 9·2
Main engines	Diesels; 1 400 shp; 2 shafts = 11 knots
Complement	25
Technical personnel	20

The *Elk River* is a former rocket landing ship specifically converted to support Navy deep submergence activities on the San Clemente Island Range off the coast of Southern California. The ship is capable of supporting the following activities: (1) deep diving for man-in-the-sea programmes (SEALAB), (2) deep diving for salvage programmes, **(3) submersible test and evaluation, (4) underwater equipment testing, and (5) deep mooring operations. Operated by combined Navy-civilian crew.**

CONVERSION. The *Elk River* was withdrawn from the Reserve Fleet and converted to a range support ship in 1967-1968 at Avondale Shipyards Inc. Westwego, Louisiana, and the San Francisco Bay Naval Shipyard.
The basic LSMR hull was lengthened and eight-foot sponsons were added to either side to increase deck working space and stability; superstructure added forward. An open centre well was provided to facilitate lowering and raising equipment; also fitted with 65-ton-capacity gantry crane (on tracks) to handle submersibles and active positioning mooring system to hold ship in precise location without elaborate mooring **and permit shifting within the moor. Five anchors including bow anchor (correction to previous edition).**

DIVING. Fitted with prototype Mk 2 Deep Diving System (see new-construction submarine rescue ships).

ELK RIVER (IX 501)   *1968, United States Navy*

1 INSTRUMENTATION PLATFORM (IX)

*BRIER IX 307 (ex-Coast Guard Cutter)

Displacement, tons	178
Dimensions, feet	100 × 24 × 4½
Machinery	Diesel with electric drive; 2 shafts; 300 bhp = 8·5 knots

Former Coast Guard tender acquired by Navy on 10 Mar 1969 for use as instrument platform for explosive testing.

1 TORPEDO TEST SHIP (IX)

*NEW BEDFORD IX 308 (ex-AKL 17, ex-FS 289)

Displacement, tons	approx 700
Dimensions, feet	176·5 oa × 32·8 × 10
Main engines	Diesel; 1 shaft; 1 000 shp = 10 knots

Small Army cargo ship (freight and supply) acquired by Navy for cargo work and subsequently converted to support torpedo testing. Operated by Naval Torpedo Station, Keyport, Washington.

IX 308 (ex-AKL 17)   *1966, United States Navy*

1 WEAPON TEST SHIP (IX)

*IX 306 (ex-FS 221)

Displacement, tons	906 full load
Dimensions, feet	179 oa × 33 × 10
Main engines	Diesel; 1 shaft = 12 knots

Former Army cargo ship (freight and supply) acquired by the Navy in January 1966 and subsequently converted to a weapon test ship, being placed in service late in 1969. Conducts research for the Naval Underwater Weapons Research and Engineering Station, Newport, Rhode Island; operates in Atlantic Underwater Test and Evaluation Centre (AUTEC) range in Caribbean. Manned by Navy and civilian RCA personnel. Note white hull with blue bow and torpedo tube opening on starboard side just aft of hull number.

IX 306   *1969, United States Navy*

IX 306   *1969, United States Navy*

Experimental, Research and Surveying Ships—*continued*

1 GUNNERY AND GUIDED MISSILE TEST SHIP (AVM): CONVERTED SEAPLANE TENDER

*NORTON SOUND AVM 1 (ex-AV 11)

Displacement, tons	9 106 standard; 15 170 full load
Length, feet (*metres*)	543·25 (*165·2*) oa
Beam, feet (*metres*)	71·6 (*21·5*)
Draft, feet (*metres*)	23·5 (*7·15*)
Guns	1—5 in (*127 mm*) 54 cal experimental (see *Gunnery* notes)
Missiles	1 twin launcher for standard testing 1 Basic Point Defence Missile System (BPDMS) launcher for Sea Sparrow missiles (see *Missile* notes)
Main engines	2 geared turbines (Allis-Chalmers) 12 000 shp; 2 shafts
Boilers	4 (Babcock & Wilcox)
Speed, knots	19·2
Complement	292 (22 officers, 270 enlisted men)

The *Norton Sound* serves as a seagoing weapons laboratory and test centre under the operational control of Commander, Cruiser-Destroyer Force, Pacific Fleet. She was originally a seaplane tender (AV 11) of the "Currituck" class; fitted with helicopter platform forward and missile launching ramp aft during late 1940s and reclassified as Guided Missile Test Ship (AVM 1) on 8 Aug 1951. Subsequently served as test ship for several guided missile systems and, lately, for advanced gun systems. During August and September of 1958 the *Norton Sound* launched missiles which exploded three nuclear weapons at an altitude of about 300 miles to determine effects of nuclear explosions in space on missile defenses (Project ARGUS).

NORTON SOUND (AVM 1)   *1969, United States Navy*

STATUS. Assigned to Operational Development Force as an experimental rocket test ship on 28 Nov 1947 (modified at Philadelphia Naval Shipyard Mar-Sep 1948); currently assigned to Cruiser-Destroyer Force, Pacific Fleet.
From 1963 until 1966 the *Norton Sound* served as test ship for the Typhon advanced fleet air defense system.

CONSTRUCTION. Built by Los Angeles Shipbuilding & Dry Dock Co, San Pedro, Calif. Laid down 7 Sep 1942; launched 28 Nov 1943; commissioned 8 Jan 1945. As built the *Norton Sound* had a 30-ton capacity boom atop her large, amidships aircraft hangar and a second 30-ton boom on her fantail; second boom removed when fitted with missile launching ramp. Original armament consisted of four 5 inch guns, two in single mounts forward and two in single mounts atop hangar, and 20 40 mm AA guns; forward 5 inch guns removed to make space for helicopter platform; all other armament removed prior to modification as Typhon test ship.

GUNNERY. Fitted in 1969 with light-weight 5 inch-54 cal gun and associated Mark 86 Gunfire Control System for operational test and evaluation. The light-weight Mark 45 gun is intended for new-construction ships. It has a rate of fire of 20 rounds per minute, weighs 50 000 pounds, and is operated by a five-man crew none of whom are in the mount. The mount captain initially can fire 20 rounds in the gun's loader drum without the use of ammunition handlers. The gun offers a significant increase in reliability over previous guns of this calibre.

MISSILES. The *Norton Sound* has served as a test platform for several ship-launched rockets and missiles. Currently a twin surface-to-air missile launcher is installed aft for tests of the Standard missile as is a "pepper box" BPDMS launcher for the Sea Sparrow missile.

TYPHON. In 1963-64 the *Norton Sound* was converted to serve as test ship for the Typhon fleet air defense

system. The conversion was undertaken at the Maryland Shipbuilding and Dry Dock Company, Baltimore, Maryland; recommissioned on 20 June 1964. A large, dome-shaped radar installation was erected atop the bridge structure (see photographs in 1968-1969 edition). Typhon system was designed to counter aircraft and guided missile threats of the 1970s. A single, high-powered radar was to automatically and simultaneously search, acquire target, track, and guide ship-launched missiles; system includes high-speed digital computers. However, Typhon was cancelled because of large size, high cost, and relative ineffectiveness. The radar equipment was evaluated in the *Norton Sound*; removed in July of 1966 at Long Beach Naval Shipyard (California).

Complement while Typhon test ship was approx 450 officers and enlisted men.

PHOTOGRAPHS. Note signal yard atop bridge, Standard and Sea Sparrow missile launchers aft. The lightweight 5 inch gun is installed on the forecastle

1 ELECTRONICS TEST SHIP (AVT): Ex-AIRCRAFT CARRIER

BUNKER HILL AVT 9 (ex-CVS 17)

Displacement, tons	27 100 standard
Length, feet (*metres*)	888 (*270·7*) oa
Beam, feet (*metres*)	93 (*28·3*)
Draught, feet (*metres*)	31 (*9·4*)
Width, feet (*metres*)	147·5 (*44·9*) extreme
Complement	1 officer, 25 enlisted men, 36 scientists

The *Bunker Hill* is a former "Essex" class aircraft carrier employed as an electronics test platform for the Naval Electronics Laboratory Centre at San Diego, California. The inactivated ship is moored off the North Island Naval Air Station in San Diego Harbour.

She was completed as a fast carrier in 1943 and saw extensive action in World War II. She was severely damaged by a Japanese suicide plane attack in May 1945 and was not fully rejuvinated. After helping transport allied troops after the war, she was decommissioned on 9 Jan 1947 and placed in the reserve fleet at Bremerton, Washington.
In 1965 the *Bunker Hill* was towed from Bremerton to San Diego and moored off NAS North Island. She was officially stricken from the Navy List on 1 Nov 1966. It is expected that she will be sold for scrap in mid-1972 (unless retained as a memorial).

EXPERIMENTAL. Portions of the *Bunker Hill* have been converted into working areas for scientists and a number of electronic systems have been installed in the ship.

Essentially, she is being used as a test and evaluation platform for the development of integrated electronic systems for naval vessels.
One of the more advanced systems being investigated in the *Bunker Hill* is a computer-controlled message handling and distribution system which receives, transmits, stores, and distributes information.

PHOTOGRAPH. The photograph of the *Bunker Hill* shows her being moved by tugs; a number of antennas subsequently have been installed on her island structure and flight deck. She is moored with non-metallic dacron lines to alleviate the effect of metal anchor chains on the ship's electromagnetic characteristics. As she has been stricken from the Navy List, no flag is flown.

BUNKER HILL (AVT 9) AT NAS NORTH ISLAND   *United States Navy*

DISPOSALS AND RECLASSIFICATIONS

Target ship **Atlanta** IX 304 (ex-CL 104), a converted light cruiser employed in explosive tests, was stricken from the Navy List on 1 Apr 1970 (sunk as target)
Mobile listening barge **MONOB I** IX 309 (ex-YW 87) reclassified as YAG 61 on 1 July 1970 (see Service Craft listing).
Hydrographic research ships **Rexburg** PCER 855 and **Marysville** PCER 857 stricken

on 7 Mar 1970 and 15 July 1970, respectively.
(The research ships *George Eastman* YAG 39 and *Granville S. Hall* YAG 40 are listed with service Craft; the experimental hydrofoil ships *Plainview* AGEH 1 and *High Point* PCH 1 are listed with Patrol Ships and Craft; the research escort ship *Glover* ADGE 1 is listed with Ocean Escorts).

SERVICE CRAFT

Below are listed the self-propelled service craft which support the ships and shore facilities of the US Navy. Listed separately are the target and training submarines (SST), submersible craft (X), and the submersible research vehicle *NR-1*, all designated as Service Craft. Only five service craft are in commission with commanding officers and are entitled to the prefix "USS" before their names: the research ship *George Eastman* (YAG 39), and the floating dry docks *Oak Ridge* (ARDM 1), *Alamagordo* (ARDM 2), *Windsor* (ARD 22), and *Arco* (ARD 29).

The Navy's non-self-propelled floating dry docks are listed separately. In addition to the various service craft listed in *Jane's Fighting Ships*, the US Navy has several hundred non-self-propelled harbour craft, mostly barge-like craft for the transport of material, floating cranes, dredges, power barges, berthing barges, fuel barges, water barges, garbage scows, *et cetera*. The larger non-self-propelled salvage craft are described in the 1970-1971 edition.

1 MOBILE LISTENING BARGE (IX)

MONOB I YAG 61 (ex-IX 309, ex-YW 87)

Displacement, tons	1 390 full load
Dimensions, feet	174 oa × 33

The *Monob I* is a mobile listening barge converted from a water self-propelled barge. Built in 1943 and converted for acoustic research in 1969, being placed in service in May 1969. Conducts research for the Naval Ship Research and Development Centre; based at Port Everglades, Florida.

Designation changed from IX 301 to YAG 61 on 1 July 1970.

MONOB I   *United States Navy*

2 RESEARCH SHIPS (YAG): Ex-MINESWEEPERS

GEORGE EASTMAN YAG 39
GRANVILLE S. HALL (ex-*Iro Nelson Morris*) YAG 40

Displacement, tons	6 000 light, 11 600 full load
Dimensions, feet	422·7 oa × 57 × 34·7 max
Main engines	Steam reciprocating; 1 shaft; 2 500 hp = 11 knots
Accommodation	19 officers, 150 men

Liberty ships of the EC-2-S-C1 type built in 1943-1944, acquired by the Navy in 1952-1953 as Experimental Minefield Sweepers. Several ships of this type have been used as guinea-pig ships in sweeping minefields. Remote engine room controls on bridge. Helicopter platform forward. Replaced in service in 1962. Assigned their former merchant ship names in 1963. Now used as special project and research ships.
The *Granville S. Hall* was taken out of service and placed in reserve in 1971.

DISPOSALS
The experimental minefield sweeper **YAG 37** (ex-*John L. Sullivan*) was scrapped in 1958. **YAG 36** (ex-*Floyd W. Spencer*) and **YAG 38** (ex-*Edward Kavanagh*) were stricken in 1960. The Fleet X-ray examination ship **Whidbey** AG 141, was stricken on 1 May 1959.
The former netlaying ship **Butternut** (ex-ANL 9, ex-AN 9, ex-YN 4) was reinstated on the Navy List as YAG 60 on 28 Oct 1969; after brief service in support of the Pacific Missile Range, she was taken out of service in late 1970 pending disposal.

GRANVILLE S. HALL (YAG 40)   *1966, US Navy*

25 COVERED LIGHTERS (YF)

Lighters used to transport material in harbours; self-propelled; 25 are on the Navy List, six of which are named: **Phoebus** (YF 294), **Lynnhaven** (YF 328), **Suitland** (FY 336), **Little Compton** (YF 864), **Keyport** (YF 885), and **Kodiak** (YF 886).

7 FERRYBOATS (YFB)

Ferryboats used to transport personnel and vehicles in large harbours; self-propelled; one is under construction and seven are on the Navy List, one of which is named; **Aquidneck** (YFB 14). The YFB 88-91 are the former LCU 1636, 1638-1640, all reclassified in October 1969.

YFB 88   *United States Navy*

YFB 87   *1970, US Navy, Kenneth Ollar*

3 REFRIGERATED COVERED LIGHTERS (YFR)

Lighters used to store and transport food and other materials which require refrigeration, three are on the Navy List.

9 COVERED LIGHTERS (RANGE TENDER) (YFRT)

Lighters used for miscellaneous purposes; 9 are on the Navy List. The YFRT 520 is employed in torpedo testing and is fitted with a triple Mk 32 launcher.

YFRT 520   *1969, United States Navy*

10 HARBOUR UTILITY CRAFT (YFU)

YFU 71	YFU 73	YFU 75	YFU 77	YFU 81
YFU 72	YFU 74	YFU 76	YFU 80	YFU 82

Dimensions, feet	125 oa × 36 × 7·5
Main engines	diesels = 8 knots
Guns	2—50 cal MG

Militarised versions of a commercial lighter design. Used for off-loading large ships in harbours and ferrying cargo from one coastal port to another. Built by Pacific Coast Engineering Co, Alameda, California; completed 1967-1968. Can carry more than 300 tons cargo; considerable cruising range. YFU 79 transferred to South Vietnam in Nov 1968; YFU 78 sunk in Vietnam in March 1969; YFU 71-77 and YFU 80-82 loaned to US Army in 1970 for use in South Vietnam.

Service Craft—*continued*

YFU 74   *1969, United States Navy*

36 HARBOUR UTILITY CRAFT (YFU):
FORMER LANDING CRAFT

YFU 4 (ex-LCU 562)	**YFU 53** (ex-LCU 1446)	**YFU 67** (ex-LCU 1232)
YFU 8 (ex-LCU 664)	**YFU 54** (ex-LCU 509)	**YFU 68** (ex-LCU 1385)
YFU 18 (ex-LCU 869)	**YFU 55** (ex-LCU 637)	**YFU 69** (ex-LCU 1388)
YFU 24 (ex-LCU 980)	**YFU 56** (ex-LCU 646)	**YFU 70** (ex-LCU 1496)
YFU 25 (ex-LCU 1056)	**YFU 57** (ex-LCU 709)	**YFU 83** (new; see notes)
YFU 37 (ex-LCU 1283)	**YFU 58** (ex-LCU 716)	**YFU 87** (ex-LCU 780)
YFU 39)ex-LCU 1363)	**YFU 59** (ex-LCU 776)	**YFU 88** (ex-LCU 1471)
YFU 44 (ex-LCU 1398)	**YFU 60** (ex-LCU 851)	**YFU 89** (ex-LCU 1576)
YFU 45 (ex-LCU 1411)	**YFU 61** (ex-LCU 916)	**YFU 90** (ex-LCU 1582)
YFU 47 (ex-LCU 1330)	**YFU 62** (ex-LCU 973)	**YFU 91** (ex-LCU 1608)
YFU 50 (ex-LCU 1486)	**YFU 63** (ex-LCU 989)	**YFU 92** (ex-LCU 1620)
YFU 52 (ex-LCU 743)	**YFU 64** (ex-LCU 1126)	**YFU 93** (ex-LCU 1625)

Former utility landing craft employed primarily as harbour and coastal cargo craft (see section on Landing Craft for basic data). YFU 39 is assigned to Mine Force, Pacific Fleet, and is based at Long Beach, California, to support and sow practice mines for MSBs; YFU 44 is assigned to Naval Undersea Research and Development Centre at Long Beach and is fitted with an open centre well for lowering equipment; YFU 53 also is assigned to the Centre and has an open centre well for handling the CURV tethered torpedo recovery device.

YFU 83 built by Defoe Shipbuilding Co (same design as LCU 1646). YFU 54, 56, 61, 64, 67-70 loaned to US Army in April 1970 for use in South Vietnam.

CLASSIFICATIONS. YFU 1-70 and 84-93 all were former utility landing craft. Several reverted to LCU designations at various times and three were modified for salvage work: YFU 2, 16, and 33 to YLLC 5, 2, and 3, respectively. YFU 87 and 88 so designated in May 1968, YFU 89-91 on 17 June 1970, YFU 92 and 93 on 1 Apr 1971.

DISPOSALS
Recent YFU/LCU disposals include **YFU 12** (ex-LCU 686) stricken in May 1968; **YFU 84-86** formerly on loan to Denmark as LCUs returned and stricken in 1971; **YFU 5, 7, 20,** and **36** stricken in 1970.

YFU 39   *1970, United States Navy*

20 GARBAGE LIGHTERS (YG)

Lighters used to collect garbage and refuse from ships in port, especially those not moored to a pier; popularly known as "honey barges"; self-propelled; 20 are on the Navy List.

1 LIGHT SALVAGE LIFT CRAFT (YLLC):
CONVERTED LANDING CRAFT

YLLC 5 (ex-LCU 529)

Dimensions, feet	139·5 oa × 32·6 × 4·5
Guns	several ·50 cal MG
Main engines	3 diesels; 3 shafts = 6 knots
Complement	15 (enlisted men)

A new design lifting craft, converted from a 119-foot landing craft. She is fitted with a 25-ton capacity shear leg derrick forward, behind which are two 10-ton cargo booms. Beach gear laying is facilitated by the "Eells" anchor "billboards" fitted on each side.

YLLC 5   *United States Navy*

3 LIGHT SALVAGE LIFT CRAFT (YLLC):
FORMER LANDING CRAFT

YLLC 1 (ex-LCU 1388)
YLLC 2 (ex-YFU 16, LCU 788)
YLLC 3 (ex-LCU 1195)

Dimensions, feet	117 oa × 32·6 × 5·6
Guns	several ·50 cal MG
Main engines	3 diesels (Gray Marine); 3 shafts = 6 knots
Complement	16 (1 officer, 15 enlisted men)

Modified landing craft fitted for salvage operations in sheltered waters. These craft are fitted with a 20-ton capacity shear leg derrick forward and can lay beach gear; diver's air compressor, welding equipment, and salvage pumps carried.
The YLLC 4 (ex-LCU 1459) struck a mine and sank in the Ham Luong River, South Vietnam, on 15 Nov 1968 and stricken from the Navy List on 1 Jan 1969.

YLLC 1 type Salvage craft   *United States Navy*

12 GATE CRAFT (YNG)

Specialised craft intended to tend anti-submarine and anti-torpedo nets in harbours; self-propelled; 12 are on the Navy List.

74 FUEL BARGES (YO)

Small liquid fuel carriers intended to fuel ships where no pierside fueling facilities are available; self-propelled; 74 are on the Navy List.

YO 130   *1970, United States Navy*

24 GASOLINE BARGES (YOG)

Similar to the fuel barges (YO), but carry gasoline and aviation fuels; self-propelled; 24 are on the Navy List.

Service Craft—*continued*

27 SEAMANSHIP TRAINING CRAFT (YP)

YP 584	YP 588	YP 654	YP 658	YP 662	YP 666	YP 670
YP 585	YP 589	YP 655	YP659	YP 664	YP 667	YP 671
YP 586	YP 590	YP 656	YP 660	YP 664	YP 668	YP 672
YP 587	YP 591	YP 657	YP 661	YP 665	YP 559	

YP 584 series:

Dimensions, feet	75 oa × 16
Main engines	diesel; 400 hp

YP 654 series:

Displacement, tons	69·5 full load
Dimensions, feet	80·4 oa × 18·75 × 5·3
Main engines	4 diesels (GM); 2 shafts; 660 hp = 13·5 knots

These craft are used for instruction in seamanship and navigation at the Naval Academy, Annapolis, Maryland, and Naval Officer Candidate School, Newport, Rhode Island. Fitted with surface search radar, Fathometer, gyro compass, and UHF and MF radio; the YP 655 additionally fitted for instruction in oceanographic research.

YPs numbered below 645 are older craft of a once-numerous type employed for training and utility work. YP 654-663 built by Stephens Bros, Inc, Stockton, Calif, completed in 1958; YP 664 and 665 built by Elizabeth City Shipbuilders, Inc, Elizabeth City, North Carolina; YP 666 and 667 built by Stephens Bros; YP 668 built by Peterson Boatbuilding Co, Tacoma, Washington, completed in 1968; YP 669-672 built by Peterson completed in 1971-1972.
These craft are of wooden construction with aluminium deck houses.

YP 654 type *United States Navy*

1 SALVAGE CRAFT TENDER (YRST) CONVERTED NET LAYER

NAUBUC YRST 4 (ex-AN 84)
Former "Cohoes" class net layer converted to a self-propelled salvage craft tender for coastal cable laying and salvage support. Launched on 15 Apr 1944 and commissioned on 15 Mar 1945; stricken from the Navy List in Sep 1962, but reacquired in 1967 and converted to YRST. She is the only self-propelled YRST.

NAUBUC (YRST4) *1968, United States Navy*

60 LARGE HARBOUR TUGS (YTB)

EDENSHAW	YTB 752	TONKAWA	YTB 786
MARIN	YTB 753	KITTANNING	YTB 787
PONTIAC	YTB 756	WAPATO	YTB 788
OSHKOSH	YTB 757	TOMAHAWK	YTB 789
PADUCAH	YTB 758	MENOMINEE	YTB 790
BOGALUSA	YTB 759	MARINETTE	YTB 791
NATICK	YTB 760	ANTIGO	YTB 792
OTTUMWA	YTB 761	PIQUA	YTB 793
TUSCUMBIA	YTB 762	MANDAN	YTB 794
MUSKEGON	YTB 763	KETCHIKAN	YTB 795
MISHAWAKA	YTB 764	SACO	YTB 796
OKMULGEE	YTB 765	TAMAQUA	YTB 797
WAPAKINETA	YTB 766	OPELIKA	YTB 789
APALACHICOLA	YTB 767	NATCHITOCHES	YTB 799

ARCATA	YTB 768	EFAULA	YTB 800
CHESANING	YTB 769	PALATKA	YTB 801
DAHLONEGA	YTB 770	CHERAW	YTB 802
KEOKUK	YTB 771	NANTICOKE	YTB 803
NASHUA	YTB 774	AHOSKIE	YTB 804
WAUWATOSA	YTB 775	OCALA	YTB 805
WEEHAWKEN	YTB 776	TUSKEGEE	YTB 806
NOGALES	YTB 777	MASSAPEQUA	YTB 807
APOPKA	YTB 778	WENATCHEE	YTB 808
MANHATTAN	YTB 779	AGAWAN	YTB 809
SAUGUS	YTB 780	ANOKA	YTB 810
NIANTIC	YTB 781	HOUMA	YTB 811
MANISTEE	YTB 782	ACCONAC	YTB 812
REDWING	YTB 783	POUGHKEEPSIE	YTB 813
KALISPELL	YTB 784	WAXAHATCHIE	YTB 814
WINNEMUCCA	YTB 785	NEODESHA	YTB 815

Basic YTB design:

Displacement, tons	350 full load
Dimensions, feet	109 oa × 30 × 13·8
Machinery	2 diesels; 2 shafts; 2 000 hp
Complement	10 to 12 (enlisted)

Large harbour tugs; 60 are in service or under construction. YTB 752 completed in 1959, YTB 753 in 1960, YTB 756-762 in 1961, YTB 763-766 in 1963, YTB 770 and YTB 771 in 1964, YTB 767-769, 776 in 1965, YTB 774, 775, 777-789 in 1966, YTB 790-793 in 1967, YTB 794 and 795 in 1968, YTB 796-803 in 1969, and YTB 804-815 completed in 1970-1971.

TUSKEGEE (YTB 806) *1970, Peterson Builders*

PADUCAH (YTB 758) *United States Navy*

33 WATER BARGES (YW)

Barges modified to carry water to ships in harbour; self-propelled; 33 of these craft are on the Navy List.

145 MEDIUM HARBOUR TUGS (YTM)

All but one of these craft are in service, with one being in reserve; all but five are named; numbered in YTM 128-779 series; several formerly designated YTB or are former US Army tugs.

21 SMALL HARBOUR TUGS (YTL)

Twenty-one of these craft are on the Navy List; unnamed.

MASCOUTAN (YTM 760) *1971, US Navy, PH2 C. Velasquez*

MISCELLANEOUS

1 NAVAL YACHT (AG)

SEQUOIA AG 23

Displacement, tons	110 light
Dimensions, feet	105 × 21 × 5
Main engines	1 diesel; 400 shp

Built in 1925 by J. H. Mathis Co. Assigned to the Secretary of the Navy. The Navy has several small sail training boats at the United States Naval Academy, Annapolis, Maryland. *Highland Light* (IX 48) stricken on 1 Apr 1965 and sold; *Royono* (IX 235) stricken on 1 July 1967 and sold; and *Freedom* (IX 43) stricken in 1968 *Saluda* (IX 87, ex-*Odyssey*) reclassified as YAG 87.

1 SAIL FRIGATE (IX)

CONSTITUTION IX 21 launched 21 Oct 1797

The oldest ship of the US Navy remaining on the Navy List. "In service" status as a relic at Boston. Periodically she is taken out into Boston Harbour and "turned around". Characteristics and photograph appears in the 1970-1971 edition.

SEQUOIA (AG 23)   *United States Navy*

The self-propelled barracks ship **Benewah** (APB 35) was reclassified IX 311 on 1 Apr 1971 pending later transfer to South Vietnam; she is now at Subic Bay, Philippines. The classification **IX 310** has been assigned to a group of barges used at the Naval Underwater Sound Laboratory, Newport, Rhode Island.

SUBMERSIBLES AND DEEP SUBMERGENCE VEHICLES

The US Navy has built only one "midget" submarine, the *X-1*. Although originally intended for evaluation of potential combat roles, the craft has primarily been relegated to scientific research work. The *NR-1* is in many respects a "midget" submarine, but was developed entirely as a test platform for a small nuclear reactor and to perform oceanographic research and work missions.

The US Navy acquired its first deep submergence vehicle with the purchase of the bathyscaph *Trieste* in 1958. The *Trieste* was designed and constructed by Professor Auguste Piccard, the noted Swiss physicist and aeronaut. The US Navy sponsored research dives in the Mediterranean Sea with the *Trieste* in 1957 after which the bathyscaph was purchased outright and brought to the United States.
The *Trieste* reached a record depth of 35 800 feet (*10 910 metres*) in the Challenger Deep off the Marianas on 23 Jan 1960, being piloted by Lieutenant Don Walsh, USN, and Jacques Piccard (son of Auguste). The *Trieste* subsequently was used in the search for wreckage of the nuclear-powered submarine *Thresher* (SSN 593) which was lost in 1963.

Late in 1963 the *Trieste* was rebuilt, the "new" craft being named *Trieste II*. She was employed in 1969 to examine the remains of the nuclear-powered submarine *Scorpion* (SSN 589).

During this period the US Navy sponsored development of the *Alvin*, a deep submergence research vehicle, which served as prototype for the later *Turtle* and *Sea Cliff* submersibles. The *Alvin* subsequently was accidentally lost at sea on 16 Oct 1968, but was salvaged on 30 Aug 1969. She has been rebuilt.

After the loss of the *Thresher* the US Navy initiated an extensive deep submergence programme that includes development of a series of Deep Submergence Rescue Vehicles (DSRV) and Deep Submergence Search Vehicles (DSSV).

Two of the rescue submersibles have been built, but plans for four additional DSRVs and the search vehicles have been dropped.
The deep submergence research craft *Deep View* was designed and built by the Naval Undersea Research and Development Centre, San Diego, California, and appears for the first time in *Jane's Fighting Ships* with this edition.

Finally, in collaboration with the Atomic Energy Commission, the Navy developed the nuclear-powered ocean engineering and research vehicle NR-1.
The Navy has chartered several commercial deep submergence vehicles for research and evaluation, notably the General Dynamics-Electric Boat STAR III, Grumman-Piccard *Benjamin Franklin* (ex-PX-15), Lockheed *Deep Quest;* Perry Cubmarine PC3B, Perry-Link *Deep Diver*, Reynolds *Aluminaut*, and Westinghouse *Deepstar 4000*. (The US Air Force operates the Perry Cubmarine PC3A in support of Pacific missile range activities). The following deep submergence vehicles are Navy-owned craft

1 MIDGET SUBMARINE: "X" TYPE

Displacement, tons	31·5 surface; 36·3 submerged
Dimensions, feet	49·7 oa × 7 × 6·7
Main engines	1 diesel (Hercules); 1 electric motor; 1 shaft
Complement	4

Name	Builder	Laid down	Launched	In Service
X-1	Fairchild Engine & Airplane Corp	8 June 1954	7 Sep 1955	7 Oct 1955

The only "midget" submarine built for the US Navy. Prototype for small submarines intended to penetrate harbours undetected to seek out and destroy enemy shipping with demolition charges. Provisions were made to set and release explosive charges from within the submarine or to lock-out and recover underwater swimmers who would plant or attach the explosives. Designed to be towed to operational area by larger submarine. In service vice being in commission; commanded by an officer-in-charge.

STATUS. Underwent extensive tests and evaluation in 1956-1957. An internal explosion while the *X-1* was at the Portsmouth Naval Shipyard in February 1958 blew off the craft's forward section; remainder of submarine remained intact and was backed away from burning bow section and pier. In reserve from 1958-1960; reactivated in 1960 for experimantel work. Based at Naval Ship Research and Development Centre in Annapolis, Maryland; operates in Chesapeake Bay in support of studies relating to origin and structure of waves, heat balance between water and atmosphere, light penetration of water, underwater visibility, and mixing factors of water. The *X-1* is painted orange for safety considerations because of merchant shipping and pleasure craft in the area.

DESIGN. Modified tear-drop hull design; aircraft type controls; forward diving planes mounted on superstructure forward (just above draft numbers in 1962 photograph).

ENDURANCE. Designed for ten-day missions with crew of four, can carry six men for shorter missions.

ENGINEERING. Originally fitted with diesel/hydrogen-peroxide system which permitted operation of diesel engine while submerged. Small electric "creeping" motor was fitted to diesel for very slow speeds and for battery charging. Hydrogen-peroxide components removed in 1960 and electric motor fitted in 1962 for underwater propulsion ("creeping" motor was retained). Fitted with single five-bladed, five-foot propeller, snorkel installed.

X-1   *1962, United States Navy*

X-1   *United States Navy*

Submersibles and Deep Submergence Vehicles—*continued*

2 DEEP SUBMERGENCE RESCUE VEHICLES

No.	Builder	Launched
DSRV-1	⟨ Lockhead Missiles and Space Co.	24 Jan 1970
DSRV-2	⟩ (Sunnyvale, Caif)	1 May 1971

Weight in air, tons	35
Length, feet	49·2 oa
Diameter, feet	8
Propulsion	Electric motors, propeller mounted in control shroud and four ducted thrusters
Speed, knots	5 (maximum)
Endurance	12 hours at 3 knots
Operating depth, feet	5 000
Complement	3 (pilot, co-pilot, rescue sphere operator) +24 rescuees

DSRV-1 on trailer ("mating skirt" removed)   *1970, United States Navy*

The Deep Submergence Rescue Vehicle is intended to provide a quick-reaction, world-wide, all-weather capability for the rescue of survivors in a disabled submarine. The DSRV will be transportable by road, aircraft (in C-141 and C-5 jet cargo aircraft), surface ship (on ASR 21 class submarine rescue ships), and specially modified submarines (SSN type).

Upon notification that a submarine is disabled on the ocean floor the DSRV and its support equipment (all necessary check-out equipment and spare parts being housed in a mobile van) will be loaded in cargo aircraft and flown to a port near the disabled submarine. The DSRV and van will then be towed to a pier and loaded aboard a "mother" submarine, which had proceeded to the port upon notification that a submarine was disabled.

The mother submarine, with the DSRV attached to her main deck (aft of the sail structure), will then proceed to the disabled submarine and serve as an underwater base for the DSRV which will shuttle back and forth between the disabled submarine and the mother submarine. On each trip the DSRV will carry up to 24 survivors from the disabled submarine. The mother submarine will launch and recover the DSRV while submerged and, if necessary, while under ice. A total of six DSRVs are planned, but only two have been funded and studies now are under way to determine requirements for additional submersibles of this type.

COST. The estimated construction cost for the DSRV-1 is $41 000 000 and for the DSRV-2 $23 000 000. The development, construction, test, and support of both vehicles through Fiscal Year 1975 is now estimated at $220 000 000. This expenditure includes the design and construction of both vehicles, specific research and development associated with the rescue programme, surface support equipment, modifications to "mother" submarines, test and evaluation programmes, procurement of replacement and spare parts, and training of the DSRV operators and support personnel. The DSRV programme has been forced to support research and development into deep-ocean materials equipment, and other technology-related areas not envisioned in earlier programme cost estimates.

DSRV "landing" on mother submarine   *United States Navy*

DESIGN. The DSRV outer hull is constructed of formed fibreglass. Within this outer hull are three interconnected spheres which form the main pressure capsule. Each sphere is 7·5 feet in diameter and is constructed of HY-140 steel. The forward sphere contains the vehicle's control equipment and is manned by the pilot and co-pilot, the centre and after spheres accommodate 24 passengers and a third crewman. Under the DSRVs centre sphere is a hemispherical protrusion or "skirt" which seals over the disabled submarine's hatch. During the mating operation the skirt is pumped dry to enable personnel to transfer between the DSRV and disabled or mother submarine.

ENGINEERING. Propulsion and control of the DSRV are achieved by a stern propeller in a movable control shroud and four ducted thrusters, two forward and two aft. These, plus a mercury trim system, permit the DSRV to manoeuvre and hover with great precision, and to mate with submarines lying at angles up to 45 degrees from the horizontal. An elaborate Integrated Control and Display (ICAD) system employs computers to present sensor data to the pilots and transmit their commands to the vehicle's control and propulsion system.

ELECTRONICS. Elaborate search and navigational sonar, and closed-circuit television (supplemented by optical devices) are installed in the DSRV to determine the exact location of a disabled submarine within a given area and for pinpointing the submarine's escape hatches. Side-looking sonar will be fitted for search missions.

OPERATIONAL. The DSRV-1 and DSRV-2 were to undergo extensive sea trials through 1971, during which time they could be made available for emergency submarine rescue. However, long-range rapid-reaction rescue requires the use of shore facilities support ships, aircraft, and other related equipment that are not yet available.

The first nuclear-powered submarines to be fitted as "mother" submarines to carry and support a DSRV are the *Finback* (SSN 670) and *Hawkbill* (SSN 666).

If a six-vehicle DSRV force is completed two vehicles would be based at each Rescue Unit Home Port (RUHP) in San Diego, California; Charleston, South Carolina; and New London, Connecticut.

The DSRV-1 and DSRV-2 are assigned to Submarine Development Group One at San Diego.

1 NUCLEAR POWERED OCEAN ENGINEERING AND RESEARCH VEHICLE

Name	Launched
NR-1	25 Jan 1969

Displacement, tons	400 submerged
Length, feet	140 oa
Diameter, feet	12 maximum
Machinery	Electric motors, 2 propellers; four ducted thrusters
Reactor	1 pressurised-water cooled
Complement	3 officers, 2 enlisted men, 2 scientists

The NR-1 was built primarily to serve as a test platform for a small nuclear propulsion plant; however, the craft additionally provides an advanced deep submergence ocean engineering and research capability. Vice Admiral H. G. Rickover, USN (Ret), Deputy Commander for Nuclear Propulsion, Naval Ship Systems Command, conceived and initiated the NR-1 in 1964-1965 (the craft was not proposed in a Navy research or shipbuilding budget).

Built by Electric Boat Division of General Dynamics Corp, Groton, Connecticut; laid down on 10 June 1967; launched on 25 Jan 1969; completed late in 1969. Commanded by an officer-in-charge vice commanding officer.

Describing the craft Vice Adm Rickover has stated: "The (NR-1) will be able to perform detailed studies and mapping of the ocean bottom, temperature, currents, and other oceanographic parametres for military, commercial, and scientific use. The development of a nuclear propulsion plant for an oceanographic research vehicle will result in greater independence from surface support ships and essentially unlimited endurance of propulsion and auxiliary power for detailed exploration of the ocean.

"The submarine (NR-1) will have viewing ports for visual observation of its surroundings and the ocean bottom. In addition, a remote grapple will be installed to permit collection of marine samples and other items. With its depth capability, the NR-1 is expected to be capable of exploring areas of the Continental Shelf, an area which appears to contain most accessible wealth in mineral and food resources in the seas. Such exploratory charting may also help the United States in establishing sovereignty over parts of the Continental Shelf".

DESIGN. The NR-1 is fitted with wheels beneath the hull to permit "bottom crawling". This will obviate the necessity of hovering while exploring the ocean floor. Submarine wheels, a concept proposed as early as the first decade of this century by submarine inventor Simon Lake, were tested in the small submarine *Mackerel* (SST 1).

The NR-1 is fitted with external lights, external television cameras, a remote-controlled manipulator, and various recovery devices. No periscope, but fixed television mast. Credited with a 30 day endurance.

Submersibles and Deep Submergence Vehicles—continued

"NR-1" —Continued

ENGINEERING. The NR-1 reactor plant was designed by the Atomic Energy Commission's Knolls Atomic Power Laboratory. She is propelled by two propellers driven by electric motors outside the pressure hull with power provided by a turbine generator within the pressure hull. Four ducted thrusters, two horizontal and two vertical, are provided for precise manouvering.

CONSTRUCTION. Vice Adm Rickover originally planned to construct the NR-1 using "state of the art" equipment, with the cost of such a vehicle estimated to be $30 000 000 in March 1965. During detailed design of the NR-1 the Navy determined that improved equipment had to be developed and a larger hull than originally planned would be required. Consequently, in July 1967 the Navy obtained Congressional approval to proceed with construction of the NR-1 at an estimated cost of $58 000 300. The final estimated ship construction cost at time of launching was $67 500 000 plus $19 900 000 for oceanographic equipment and sensors, and $11 800 000 for research and development (mainly related to the nuclear propulsion plant), for a total estimated cost of $99 200 000.

TURTLE   1968, General Dynamics, Electric Boat

NR-1   1969, General Dynamics Electric Boat

SEA CLIFF   1968, General Dynamics, Electric Boat

NR-1   1969, General Dynamics, Electric Boat

SEA CLIFF stern view   1970, General Dynamics, Electric Boat

2 DEEP SUBMERGENCE RESEARCH VEHICLES: MODIFIED "ALVIN" TYPE

Name	Launched
SEA CLIFF (ex-*Autec I*)	11 Dec 1968
TURTLE (ex-*Autec II*)	11 Dec 1968

Weight in air, tons	21
Length, feet	25 oa
Beam, feet	8
Propulsion	Electric motors, trainable stern propeller; 2 rotating propeller pods
Speed, knots	2·5
Endurance	8 hours at 2 knots
Operating depth, feet	6 500
Complement	2 (pilot, observer)

Both submersibles built by Electric Boat Division of General Dynamics Corp. Groton, Connecticut. Intended for deep submergence research and work tasks. Designated *Autec I* and *Autec II* during construction, but assigned above names in dual launching on 11 Dec 1968. Completed in 1969.

Both vehicles are operated by Submarine Development Group One at San Diego, California.

CONSTRUCTION. Three pressure spheres were fabricated for the *Alvin* submersible programme, one for installation in the *Alvin*, a spare, and one for testing. The second and third spheres subsequently were allocated to these later submersibles.

DESIGN. Twin-arm manipulator fitted to each submersible. Propulsion by stem propeller and two smaller, manoeuvering propeller "pods" on sides of vehicles; no thrusters.

1 DEEP SUBMERGENCE RESEARCH VEHICLE: "ALVIN" TYPE

The research submersible *Alvin* accidentally sank in 5 051 feet of water some 120 miles south of Cape Cod, Massachusetts, on 16 Oct 1968 when a cable broke on her catamaran support ship *Lulu*. Her access hatch was open and the submersible flooded; there were no casualties. She was salvaged on 28 Aug 1969 by the oceanographic research ship *Mizar* (T-AGOR 11) and the commercial submersible *Aluminaut*.

The *Alvin* was operated by the Woods Hole Oceanographic Institution for the Office of Naval Research which designed and funded construction of the *Alvin*. The *Alvin* was built in 1964. See 1968-1969 edition (pp 471-472) for additional details. A photograph of the smashed *Alvin* after salvage appears in the 1970-1971 edition (p 555).

The *Alvin* will be rebuilt and fitted with the world's first submersible titanium pressure hull. Her new operating depth will be 12 000 feet.

1 BATHYSCAPH RESEARCH VEHICLE

Name	No.
TRIESTE II	X-2

Weight in air, tons	84
Displacement, tons	303 submerged
Length, feet	78·6
Beam, feet	15·3
Propulsion	Electric motors, 3 propellers aft, ducted thruster forward
Speed, knots	2
Endurance	10-12 hours at 2 knots
Operating depth, feet	12 000 (see *Design* notes)
Complement	3 (2 operators, 1 observer)

Submersibles and Deep Submergence Vehicles—*continued*

"Trieste II"—*continued*

The *Trieste II* is the extensively rebuilt *Trieste I* which the US Navy purchased in 1958 from Professor Auguste Piccard. Several "modernisations" have resulted in the current vehicle being essentially a "new" craft, the third to be named *Trieste*.

The vehicle is operated by Submarine Development Group One at San Diego, California, and is used primarily as a test bed for underwater equipment and to train deep submergence vehicle operators (hydronauts).

Designated as a "submersible craft" and assigned the designation X-2 on 1 Sep 1969.

DESIGN. The *Trieste II* is essentially a large float with a small pressure sphere attached to the underside. The float, which is filled with aviation petrol, provides buoyancy. Designed operating depth is 20 000 feet but dives have been limited to approximately 12 000 feet. (The record-setting Challenger Deep dive was made with a Krupp sphere which has a virtually unlimited depth capability.)

The bathyscaph was essentially rebuilt for a second time at the Mare Island Naval Shipyard in Sep 1965-Aug 1966 with a modified float, pressure sphere, propulsion system, and mission equipment being fitted. In the broadside view the sphere is now largely hidden by protective supports to keep the sphere clear of the welldeck when the craft rests in a floating dry dock. (Compare with photographs of the earlier *Trieste II* configuration in the 1969-1970 edition).

Fitted with external television cameras and mechanical manipulator; computerised digital navigation system installed.

The photographs below show the *Trieste's* current configuration.

TRIESTE II   *1970, United States Navy*

1 DEEP SUBMERGENCE RESEARCH VEHICLE: "DEEP VIEW" TYPE

Name	Launched
DEEP VIEW	Apr 1971

Weight in air, tons	5·75
Length, feet	16·5
Width, feet	6
Propulsion	4 electric motors (5 hp each), 2 propellers aft, 1 lateral propeller, 1 vertical propeller
Speed, knots	1—2 sustained; 4 maximum
Endurance, hours	4—6
Operating depth, feet	1 500
Complement	2

Designed and built by the Naval Undersea Research and Development Centre, San Diego, California. The *Deep View* is the first submersible that incorporates glass (borosillicate) in the pressure capsule structure with a glass hemisphere capping the forward end of the craft, the remainder of the pressure capsule is fabricated of HY-100 steel. The Glass is 1·125 inches thick.

The power source consists of 20 lead-acid batteries in two pods that can be jettisoned in an emergency to provide the craft with additional buoyancy. Normal and emergency ballast also consists of droppable weights.

The craft is operated by Submarine Development Group One.

TRIESTE II   *1970, United States Navy*

DEEP VIEW   *1971, United States Navy*

DEEP SUBMERGENCE SEARCH VEHICLE (STUDY)

Weight in air, tons	35
Length, feet	50 oa
Diameter, feet	11 (maximum)
Propulsion	Electric motors (powered by fuel cells)
Speed, knots	5 (maximum)
Endurance	30+ hours at 3 knots
Operating depth, feet	20 000
Complement	4 (2 operators, 2 relief operators)

The Deep Submergence Search Vehicle is intended to perform object location and small object recovery missions on the ocean floor to depths of 20 000 feet (an area which encompasses some 80 per cent of the ocean floor). The DSSV will be transportable by aircraft (in C-5 jet cargo aircraft), surface ships, and specially configured support submarines.

Two Search and Recovery Forces have been proposed, each to consist of one DSSV, one set of Unmanned Instrument Platforms (UIP), a specially configured "Mother" submarine, and a surface support ship.

A contract for final design and construction of the DSSV-1 was awarded to the Lockheed Missile and Space Company, Sunnyvale, California.

However, subsequent budget limitations have halted all procurement of DSSV components and, since January 1970, only studies into advanced pressure hull materials, buoyancy materials, and fuel cells are being funded.

ELECTRONICS. To be fitted with side-looking sonar and essentially the same electronics-control "package" as the DSRV rescue submersible.

DESIGN. The external hull of the DSSV will be fabricated of light-weight, corrosion-resistant materials; the internal pressure hull will house two operators, two relief crewmen, control equipment (similar to the ICAD of the DSRV), and the required life-support equipment. A manipulator will be fitted to perform light work, lift objects, and attach surface lift lines.

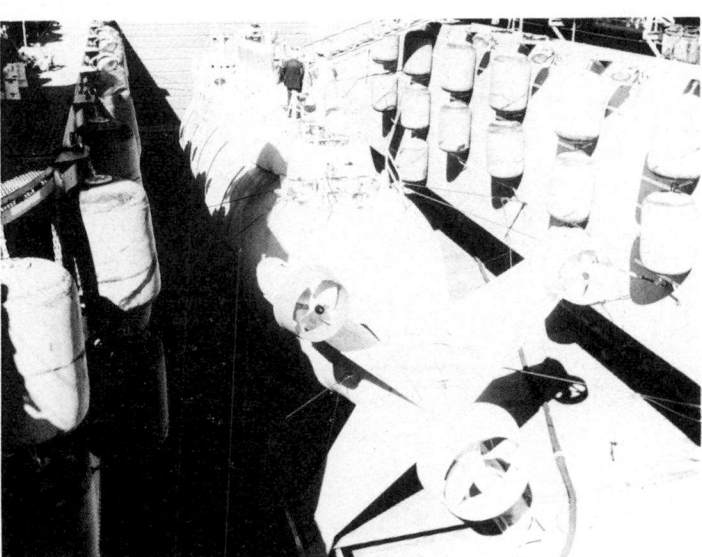

TRIESTE II in dry dock ARD-20   *United States Navy*

UNITED STATES COAST GUARD

Command

Commandant, United States Coast Guard: Admiral Chester R. Bender

Assistant Commandant: Vice Admiral Thomas R. Sargent III

Chief of Staff: **Rear Admiral Ellis L. Perry**

Commander, Eastern Area: Rear Admiral Benjamin F. Engel

Commander, Western Area: Rear Admiral Mark A. Whalen

Establishment

The United States Coast Guard was established by an Act of Congress approved Jan 28, 1915, which consolidated the Revenue Cutter Service (founded in 1790) and the Life Saving Service (founded in 1878). The act of establishment stated the Coast Guard "shall be a military service and branch of the armed forces of the United States at all times. The Coast Guard shall be a service in the Treasury Department except when operating as a service in the Navy".

The Congress further legislated that in time of national emergency or when the President so directs, the Coast Guard operates as a part of the Navy. The Coast Guard did operate as a part of the Navy during the First and Second World Wars.

The Lighthouse Service (founded in 1789) was transferred to the Coast Guard on July 1, 1939.

The Coast Guard was transferred to the newly established Department of Transportation on March 1, 1967.

A Presidential Commission on Marine Science, Engineering, and Resources in 1968 recommended establishment of a National Oceanographic and Atmospheric Agency (NOAA) to consolidate all non-military federal activities in oceanography. The Commission's proposal would transfer the Coast Guard to the proposed NOAA which also would contain the Environmental Science Services Administration (including Coast and Geodetic Survey), the Bureau of Commercial Fisheries, and the National Oceanographic Data Centre. However, NOAA was established within the Department of Commerce and the Coast Guard remained under the Department of Transportation. In January 1971 the President announced another government reorganisation plan that would place components of the Department of Transportation, including the Coast Guard, in a new Department of Economic Development.

Missions

The current missions of the Coast Guard are to (1) enforce or assist in the enforcement of applicable Federal laws upon the high seas and waters subject to the jurisdiction of the United States; (2) administer all Federal laws regarding safety of life and property on the high seas and on waters subject to the jurisdiction of the United States, except those laws specifically entrusted to other Federal agencies; (3) develop, establish, maintain, operate, and conduct aids to maritime navigation, ocean stations, icebreaking activities, oceanographic research, and rescue facilities; and (4) maintain a state of readiness to function as a specialised service in the Navy when so directed by the President.

An analysis of Coast Guard activity prepared for 1970 showed that 65 per cent of the service's funding is related to multi-purpose search, rescue, navigational, port security, and law enforcement activities; 15 per cent to oceanography, meteorology, icebreaking, and other marine sciences; 15 per cent to military activities; and 5 per cent to merchant marine inspection and safety.

The US Navy's five icebreakers (AGB) were transferred to the Coast Guard in 1965-1966 to consolidate this mission under a single service.

Cutters

All Coast Guard vessels are referred to as "cutters". Cutter names are preceded by USCGC. Cutter serial numbers are prefixed with letter designations, the first letter being "W". The first two digits of serial numbers for cutters less than 100 feet in length indicate their approximate length over all. All Coast Guard cutters are active unless otherwise indicated.

Cutter Strength

- 34 High Endurance Cutters
- 16 Medium Endurance Cutters
- 3 Oceanographic Cutters
- 1 Meteorological Cutter
- 80 Patrol Boats
- 3 Hovercraft
- 10 Icebreakers
- 5 Training Ships
- 38 Seagoing Buoy Tenders
- 70 Coastal-River-Inland Tenders
- 1 Supply Ship
- 6 Oceangoing Tugs *
- 29 Harbour Tugs

*Officially classified as Medium Endurance Cutters.

Personnel

1968 Fiscal Year Strength: 36,563 officers and enlisted men
1969 Fiscal Year Strength: 37,565 officers and enlisted men
1970 Fiscal Year Strength: 4,277 officers, 1,250 warrant officers, 32,067 enlisted men (aggregate 37,594) plus 840 cadets at Coast Guard Academy
1971 Fiscal Year Strength: 4 030 officers, 1 179 warrant officers, 32 027 enlisted men (aggregate 37 236) plus 930 cadets at Coast Guard Academy

1972 Fiscal Year Strength: 4 479 officers, 1 338 warrant officers, 32 303 enlisted men (aggregate 38 120) plus 1 047 cadets at Coast Guard Academy

Aviation

The Coast Guard operates a small air arm to support Coast Guard operations. As of June 30, 1971, the Coast Guard operated 64 fixed-wing aircraft and 106 helicopters. Most of the helicopters were HH-52A; HH-3F helicopters are being procured to replace HU-16 Albatross amphibians.

There are nine large and ten small Coast Guard air stations located in the Continental United States; Coast Guard air stations also are located at: Barbers Point, Oahu, Hawaii, Kodiak and Annette, Alaska, Sangley Point, Philippines; San Juan, Puerto Rico, and Naples, Italy.

Vietnam Operations

A number of Coast Guard Cutters were deployed to Southeast Asia to supplement US Navy forces during the Vietnam War. These vessels remained units of the US Coast Guard but were under the operational direction of the Commander US Naval Forces, Vietnam. During 1971 only two large cutters remained in Southeast Asian waters, comprising Coast Guard Squadron Three based at Subic Bay, Philippines. (Two large cutters and 26 small cutters were transferred to the South Vietnamese Navy in 1969-1971).

COAST GUARD CUTTERS

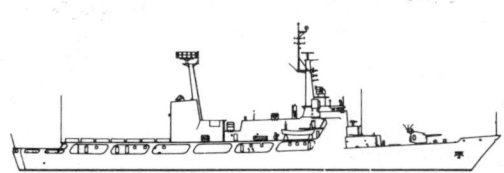

HAMILTON CLASS

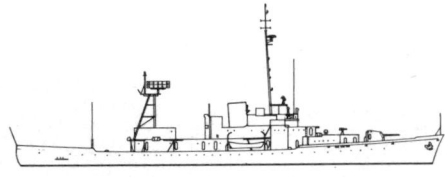

CAMPBELL CLASS

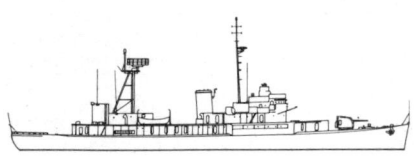

CASCO CLASS

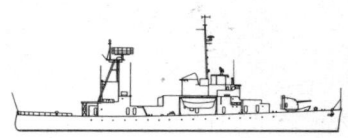

OWASCO CLASS

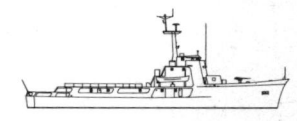

RELIANCE CLASS

USCGC GLACIER

USCGC BURTON ISLAND

© Drawings by A. D. Baker

High Endurance Cutters —continued

12 HIGH ENDURANCE CUTTERS (WHEC): "HAMILTON" (378) CLASS

		Name	No.	Laid down	Launched	Completed
Displacement, tons	2 716 standard; 3 050 full load	HAMILTON	WHEC 715	Jan 1965	18 Dec 1965	20 Feb 1967
Length, feet	350 wl; 378 oa	DALLAS	WHEC 716	7 Feb 1966	1 Oct 1966	1 Oct 1967
Beam, feet	42·8	MELLON	WHEC 717	25 July 1966	11 Feb 1967	22 Dec 1967
Draft, feet	20	CHASE	WHEC 718	15 Oct 1966	20 May 1967	1 Mar 1968
Guns	1—5 inch (127 mm) 38 cal dual-purpose	BOUTWELL	WHEC 719	12 Dec 1966	17 June 1967	14 June 1968
	2—81 mm mortars	SHERMAN	WHEC 720	13 Feb 1967	23 Sep 1967	23 Aug 1968
	4—·50 cal MG	GALLANTIN	WHEC 721	17 Apr 1967	18 Nov 1967	20 Dec 1968
ASW weapons	2 fixed hedgehogs (removed from some ships, see ASW notes)	MORGENTHAU	WHEC 722	17 July 1967	10 Feb 1968	14 Feb 1969
		RUSH	WHEC 723	23 Oct 1967	16 Nov 1968	3 July 1969
Aircraft	1 HH-52 or HH-3 helicopter	MUNRO	WHEC 724	18 Feb 1970	5 Dec 1970	July 1971
Main engines	Combined Diesel and Gas turbine (CODAG): 2 diesels (Fairbanks-Morse) 7 000 hp; 2 gas turbines (Pratt & Whitney), 28 000 hp; aggregate 35 000 hp; 2 shafts.	JARVIS	WHEC 725	9 Sep 1970	Apr 1971	Oct 1971
		MIDGETT	WHEC 726	5 Apr 1971	July 1971	Feb 1972
Speed	29					
Complement	152 (15 officers, 137 enlisted men)					

These are large, attractive, multi-purpose cutters. All built by Avondale Shipyards, Inc, New Orleans, Louisiana.

ASW ARMAMENT. As funding permits, hedgehogs are being removed from earlier ships during overhaul and Mk 309 fire control system for Mk 32 torpedo launchers installed. Hedgehogs deleted in later ships. *Hamilton* dropped hedgehogs and received Mk 309 during 1970 overhaul.

DESIGN. These ships have clipper bows, twin funnels enclosing a helicopter hangar, helicopter platform aft. All are fitted with oceanographic laboratories, elaborate communications equipment, and meteorological data gathering facilities. Superstructure is largely of aluminium construction. Bridge control of maneuvering is by aircraft-type "joy stick" rather than wheel.

ELECTRONICS. Fitted with SQS-36 sonar. Closed-circuit television permits bridge personnel to monitor displays in the Combat Information Centre (CIC).

ENGINEERING. The *Hamiltons* are the largest US 'military' ships with gas turbine propulsion pending completion of the Navy's DD963 class destroyers. The Pratt & Whitney gas turbines are FT-4A, marine variant of the J75 aircraft engine used in the Boeing 707 transport and F-105 fighter-bomber; the Fairbanks Morse diesels are 12 cylinder; variable pitch propellers fitted. Engine and propeller pitch consoles are located in wheelhouse and at bridge wing stations as well as engine room control booth.
A retractable bow propulsion unit is provided for station keeping and precise manoeuvring. (Unit is located directly below hedgehogs, immediately aft of sonar dome). Endurance is 11 500 miles at 20 knots on diesels and 3 000 miles at 25 knots on gas turbines.

NOMENCLATURE. The first nine ships of this class were named for secretaries of the Treasury Department, reflecting the Coast Guard being a part of that department from 1915 to 1967, when it was transferred to the newly formed Department of Transportation. Subsequent ships of this class honour Coast Guard heroes; Signalman First Class Douglas A. Munro was posthumously awarded the Medal of Honour for heroism at Guadalcanal in World War II; Captain David H. Jarvis won a special Congressional Gold Medal of Honour for leading a three-man expedition to save 500 men in Alaska during the winter of 1897-1898; Chief Warrant Officer John A. Midgett won the gold Lifesaving Medal for saving survivors of a torpedoed British tanker in World War I.

Later ships are referred to as "Hero" class.

PHOTOGRAPHS. Coast Guard cutters often are seen in "troubled waters": the *Rush* was photographed in Southeast Asia and the *Sherman* off Cuba. Of three ships on this page only *Sherman* has hedgehogs; others have machineguns in "B" position.

RUSH (WHEC 723)   *1970, United States Navy*

SHERMAN (WHEC 720)   *1970, US Navy, PH3 L. J. Lafeir Jnr.*

MORGENTHAU (WHEC 722)

1969, United States Navy

High Endurance Cutters — *continued*
6 HIGH ENDURANCE CUTTERS (WHEC): "CAMPBELL" (327) CLASS

Name	No.	Laid down	Launched	Completed
BIBB (ex-*George M. Bibb*)	WHEC 31	18 May 1935	14 Jan 1937	19 Mar 1937
CAMPBELL (ex-*George W. Campbell*)	WHEC 32	1 May 1935	3 June 1936	22 Oct 1936
DUANE (ex-*William J. Duane*)	WHEC 33	1 May 1935	3 June 1936	16 Oct 1936
INGHAM (ex-*Samual D. Ingham*)	WHEC 35	1 May 1935	3 June 1936	6 Nov 1936
SPENCER (ex-*John C. Spencer*)	WHEC 36	11 Sep 1935	6 Jan 1936	13 May 1937
TANEY (ex-*Roger B, Taney*)	WHEC 37	1 May 1935	3 June 1936	19 Dec 1936

Displacement, tons	2 216 standard; 2 414 full load
Length, feet	308 wl; 327 oa
Beam, feet	41
Draft, feet	15
Guns	1—5 inch (*127 mm*) 38 cal dual-purpose
	Several ·50 cal MG
ASW weapons	Removed
Main engines	Geared turbines (Westinghouse); 6 200 shp; 2 shafts
Boilers	2 (Babcock & Wilcox)
Speed, knots	19·8
Complement	144 (13 officers, 131 enlisted men)

Rated as 327-foot cutters. All built by Philadelphia Navy Yard except *Bibb*, by Charleston Navy Yard and *Spencer* by New York Navy Yard.

The *Duane* served as an amphibious force flagship during the invasion of Southern France in August 1944 and was designated AGC 6 (Coast Guard manned); the other ships of this class except the lost *Alexander Hamilton* similarly employed but retained Coast Guard number with WAGC prefix (amidships structure built up and one or two additional masts installed); all reverted to gunboat configuration after war (WPG designation).

ASW ARMAMENT. During the 1960s these ships each had an ASW armament of one ahead-firing fixed hedgehog and two Mk 32 triple torpedo launchers; subsequently removed from all ships.

DESIGNATION. These ships were designated as high endurance cutters (WHEC) on 1 May 1966; previously WPG.

GUNNERY. As built these ships had two 5-inch 51 cal guns (single mounts forward) and several smaller guns; rearmed during World War II with an additional single 5 inch 51 cal gun installed aft plus two or three 3 inch 50 cal anti-aircraft guns, and several 20 mm anti-aircraft guns (depth charge racks installed); *Taney* was experimentally armed with four 5 inch 38 cal guns in single mounts. Armament of all ships after World War II reduced to one 5 inch 38 cal gun and two 40 mm guns.

ENGINEERING. Endurance is 8 000 miles at 12·5 knots and 12 300 miles at 11 knots.

NOMENCLATURE. Named for secretaries of the Department of Treasury; names shortened to surnames only in 1942.

LOSS. The *Alexander Hamilton* (WPG 34) was sunk during World War II.

INGHAM (WHEC 35)   *United States Coast Guard*

DUANE (WHEC 33)   *1968, United States Navy*

7 HIGH ENDURANCE CUTTERS (WHEC)
1 METEOROLOGICAL CUTTER (WAGW)
1 OCEANOGRAPHIC CUTTER (WAGO)
"CASCO" (311) CLASS

Name	No.	Builder	Laid down	Launched	Navy Comm.
ABSECON	WHEC 374 (ex-AVP 23)	Lake Washington Shipyard	23 July 1941	8 Mar 1942	28 Jan 1943
CHINCOTEAGUE	WHEC 375 (ex-AVP 24)	Lake Washington Shipyard	23 July 1941	15 Apr 1942	12 Apr 1943
ROCKAWAY	WAGO 377 (ex-WHEC 377, AVP 29)	Associated Shipbuilders	30 June 1941	14 Feb 1942	6 Jan 1943
UNIMAK	WHEC 379 (ex-AVP 31)	Associated Shipbuilders	15 Feb 1942	27 May 1942	31 Dec 1943
BARATARIA	WHEC 381 (ex-AVP 33)	Lake Washington Shipyard	19 Apr 1943	2 Oct 1943	13 Aug 1944
CASTLE ROCK	WHEC 383 (ex-AVP 35)	Lake Washington Shipyard	12 July 1943	11 Mar 1944	8 Oct 1944
COOK INLET	WHEC 384 (ex-AVP 36)	Lake Washington Shipyard	23 Aug 1943	13 May 1944	5 Nov 1944
McCULLOCH (ex-*Wachapreague*)	WHEC 386 (ex-AGP 8, AVP 56)	Lake Washington Shipyard	1 Feb 1943	10 July 1944	17 May 1944
GRESHAM (ex-*Willoughby*)	WAGW 387 (ex-WHEC 387, AGP 9, AVP 57)	Lake Washington Shipyard	15 Mar 1943	21 Aug 1943	18 June 1944

Displacement, tons	1 766 standard; 2 800 full load
Length, feet	300 wl; 310·75 oa
Beam, feet	41
Draft, feet	13·5
Guns	1—5 inch (*127 mm*) 38 cal dual-purpose (removed from *Rockaway*)
ASW weapons	Removed
Main engines	Diesels (Fairbanks Morse), 6 080 bhp; 2 shafts
Speed, knots	18·2
Complement	150 (13 officers, 137 enlisted men)

Rated as 311-foot cutters. These are the survivors of 18 former seaplane tenders transferred from the Navy in 1946-1948 (WAVP/WMEC 370-384 initially on loan and WAVP/WMEC 385-387 permanent transfer). Most of these ships are employed as ocean station ships; fitted for limited oceanographic research except *Rockaway*, modified in 1966 for primary mission of oceanographic research; *Gresham*, modified for ocean station-meteorological work. The *Unimak* is a reserve training ship; the *Barataria* is in reserve.

BARATARIA (WHEC 381)   *1968 US Coastguard, PHC Ralph Sunderlin*

High Endurance Cutters —*continued*

"CASCO" CLASS — *Continued*

ASW ARMAMENT. During the 1960s these ships each had two Mk 32 triple torpedo launchers.

DESIGNATION. These ships were designated WAVP in Coast Guard service until change to high endurance cutters (WHEC) on 1 May 1966.

ENGINEERING. Endurance is 22 000 miles at 11 knots and 8 000 miles at 19 knots.

GUNNERY. As built these ships had one 5 inch gun and eight 40 mm anti-aircraft guns (two twin and one quad), except *Absecon*, *Gresham*, and *McCulloch* had two 5 inch guns (single mounts forward) and fewer 40 mm guns. (ASW weapons installed while in Coast Guard service; hedgehog formerly fitted in "B" position).

DISPOSALS AND TRANSFERS
Coos Bay (WHEC 376, ex-AVP 36) returned to Navy in 1967 and sunk as target; **Dexter** (WHEC 385, ex-AGC 18, ex-AVP 11), **Mackinac** (WHEC 371, ex-AVP 13), and **Matagorda** (WHEC 373, ex-AVP 22) returned to Navy in 1968 and sunk as targets; **Casco** (WHEC 370,

ROCKAWAY (WAGO 377)

1967. United States Coast Guard

ex-AVP 12) returned to Navy in 1969 and sunk as target. **Humboldt** (WHEC 372, ex-AVP 21) and **Half Moon** (WHEC 378, ex-AVP 26) stricken in 1970; **Yakutat** (WHEC 380, ex-AVP 32) and **Bering Strait** (WHEC 382, ex-AVP 34) transferred to South Vietnam on 1 Jan 1971.

12 HIGH ENDURANCE CUTTERS (WHEC): "OWASCO" (255) CLASS

		Name	No.	Laid down	Launched	Completed
Displacement, tons	1 563 standard; 1 913 full load	OWASCO	WHEC 39	17 Nov 1943	18 June 1944	18 May 1945
Length, feet	254 oa	WINNEBAGO	WHEC 40	1 Dec 1943	2 July 1944	21 June 1945
Beam, feet	43	CHAUTAUQUA	WHEC 41	22 Dec 1943	14 May 1944	4 Aug 1945
Draft, feet	17	SEBAGO (ex-*Wachusett*)	WHEC 42	7 Jan 1944	28 May 1944	20 Sep 1945
Guns	1—5 inch (*127 mm*) 38 cal dual-purpose	WACHUSETT (ex-*Huron*)	WHEC 44	3 July 1944	5 Nov 1944	23 Mar 1946
	2—81 mm mortors	ESCANABA (ex-*Otsego*)	WHEC 64	25 Oct 1944	25 Mar 1945	20 Mar 1946
	Several ·50 cal MG	WINONA	WHEC 65	8 Nov 1944	22 Apr 1945	15 Aug 1946
ASW weapons	Removed	KLAMATH	WHEC 66	13 Dec 1944	2 Sep 1945	5 Sep 1946
Main engines	Geared turbines (Westinghouse) with electric drive; 4 000 shp; 1 shaft	MINNETONKA (ex-*Sunapee*)	WHEC 67	26 Dec 1944	21 Nov 1945	20 Sep 1946
		ANDROSCOGGIN	WHEC 68	30 Dec 1944	16 Sep 1945	20 Sep 1946
Boilers	2	MENDOTA	WHEC 69	1 June 1943	29 Feb 1944	2 June 1946
Speed, knots	18·4	PONTCHARTRAIN (ex-*Okeechobee*)	WHEC 70	1 July 1943	29 Apr 1944	28 July 1945
Complement	139 (12 officers, 127 enlisted men)					

Rated as 255-foot cutters. All built by Western Pipe & Steel Company, San Pedro, California, except for the *Mendota* and *Pontchartrain*, built by Coast Guard yard, Curtis Bay, Maryland.

ASW ARMAMENT. During the 1960s these ships each had an ASW armament of one ahead-firing fixed hedgehog and two Mk 32 triple torpedo launchers; subsequently removed from all ships.

DESIGNATION. These ships originally were designated as gunboats (WPG); changed to high endurance cutters (WHEC) on 1 May 1966.

ENGINEERING. Endurance is 12 000 miles at 10 knots.

GUNNERY. As built these ships each mounted four 5-inch guns (twin), four 40-mm anti-aircraft guns (twin), and four 20 mm anti-aircraft guns; subsequently reduced. (Original depth charge racks also removed).

DISPOSAL
Iroquois (WPG 43) was stricken in 1965.

ESCANABA (WHEC 64)

1969. United States Coast Guard

MEDIUM ENDURANCE CUTTERS

16 MEDIUM ENDURANCE CUTTERS (WMEC): "RELIANCE" (210) CLASS

		Name	No.	Launched	Completed
Displacement, tons	950 standard; 1 000 full load except WMEC 615-619 970 fl	RELIANCE	WMEC 515	25 May 1963	20 June 1964
Dimensions, feet	210·5 ca × 34 × 10·5	DILIGENCE	WMEC 616	20 July 1963	26 Aug 1964
Guns	1—3 inch 50 calibre DP;	VIGILANT	WMEC 617	24 Dec 1963	3 Oct 1964
	2—·50 cal MG	ACTIVE	WMEC 618	31 July 1965	17 Sep 1966
Aircraft	1 HH-52 or HH-3 helicopter embarked for missions	CONFIDENCE	WMEC 619	8 May 1965	19 Feb 1966
		RESOLUTE	WMEC 620	30 Apr 1966	8 Dec 1966
Main engines	2 turbo-charged diesels; 2 shafts; 5 000 hp = 18· knots; WMEC 615-619 also have 2 gas turbines (2 000 hp); no speed increase	VALIANT	WMEC 621	14 Jan 1967	28 Oct 1967
		COURAGEOUS	WMEC 622	18 Mar 1967	10 Apr 1968
		STEADFAST	WMEC 623	24 June 1967	25 Sep 1968
		DAUNTLESS	WMEC 624	21 Oct 1967	10 June 1968
Complement	61 (7 officers, 54 enlisted men)	VENTUROUS	WMEC 625	11 Nov 1967	16 Aug 1968
		DEPENDABLE	WMEC 626	16 Mar 1968	22 Nov 1968
		VIGOROUS	WMEC 627	4 May 1969	2 May 1969
		DURABLE	WMEC 628	29 Apr 1967	8 Dec 1967
		DECISIVE	WMEC 629	14 Dec 1967	23 Aug 1968
		ALERT	WMEC 630	19 Oct 1968	4 Aug 1969

Rated as 210-foot cutters. Designed for search and rescue duties. Design features include 360-degree visibility from wheelhouse; helicopter flight deck (no hangar); and engine exhaust vent at stern in place of conventional funnel. Capable of towing ships up to

Medium Endurance Cutters—continued

"RELIANCE" CLASS—continued

10 000 tons. Air conditioned throughout except engine room; high degree of habitability.
WMEC 615-617 built by Todd Shipyards; WMEC 618 built by Christy Corp; WMEC 619, 625, 628, 629 built by Coast Guard Yard, Curtis Bay, Baltimore, Maryland; WMEC 620-624, 626, 627, 630 by American Shipbuilding Co.

AIRCRAFT. The *Alert* was the first US ship fitted with the Canadian-developed "Beartrap" helicopter hauldown system. An HH-52A helicopter conducted trials late in 1969, making 30 successful landings despite winds over 40 mph.
No further procurement of this system has been funded.

DESIGNATION. These ships originally were designated as patrol craft (WPC); changed to WMEC on 1 May 1966.

ENGINEERING. Fitted with controllable-pitch propellers. The first five ships have twin Solar, 2 000 hp gas turbines in addition to the diesels common to all ships of this class.
Diesels are ALCO model 251-B.

Endurance is 6 100 miles at 13 knots for WMEC 615-619 and 6 100 miles at 14 knots for later ships.

DILIGENCE (WMEC 616) landing HH-52A   *1969, US Coast Guard, PH2 J. S. Collins*

"ACTIVE" CLASS

All 33 of the steel patrol cutters of the 125-foot "Active" class have been stricken except the *Cuyahoga*, employed as a training ship and listed on a later page. The "Active" class boats were number WPC/WMEC 125-157; completed in 1926-1927.

TUG TYPE

Six tug-type cutters officially are listed as Medium Endurance Cutters. These ships are listed on a later page under the heading Oceangoing Tugs.

VIGILANT (WMEC 617)   *1969, United States Coast Guard*

PATROL BOATS

26 PATROL BOATS (WPB): 95 ft CLASS

CAPE CARTER	95309	CAPE HORN	95322
CAPE CORAL	95301	CAPE JELLISON	95317
CAPE CORWIN	95326	CAPE KNOX	95312
CAPE CROSS	95321	CAPE MORGAN	95313
CAPE CURRENT	95307	CAPE NEWAGEN	95318
CAPE FAIRWEATHER	95314	CAPE ROMAIN	95319
CAPE FOX	95316	CAPE SHOALWATER	95324
CAPE GEORGE	95306	CAPE SMALL	95300
CAPE GULL	95304	CAPE STARR	95320
CAPE HATTERAS	95305	CAPE STRAIT	95308
CAPE HEDGE	95311	CAPE UPRIGHT	95303
CAPE HENLOPEN	95328	CAPE WASH	95310
CAPE HIGGON	95302	CAPE YORK	95332

CG 95321—95335	CG 95312—95314, 95316—95320	CG 95300—95311
"C" Class (built 1958-59)	"B" Class (built 1955-56)	"A" Class (built 1953)

Displacement, tons	106 (B); 105 (A); 98 (C)
Dimensions, feet	95 oa × 19 × 6
Guns	1—81 mm mortar and 2—·50 cal MG except *Cape Coral*, *Cape Gull*, *Cape Higgon* and *Cape Small* have only machineguns
Main engines	4 diesels; 2 shafts (2 engines in tandem each shaft); 2 200 bhp = 20 knots max
Endurance, miles	1 500 cruising range
Complement	14 (1 officer, 13 enlisted men)

Rated as 95 ft Cutters. Designed and built at Coast Guard Yard, Curtis Bay, Maryland for port security, search and rescue. Steel hulled, twin screws. "C" class boats, for search and rescue, have less electronics.

Diesels are Cummings VT12-600M. Endurance is 2 600 miles for "A" class, 3 000 miles for "B" class, and 2 800 miles for "C" class, all at 9 knots.

TRANSFERS. Nine boats of this type were transferred to the South Korean Navy in 1968: *Cape Falcon* (95330), *Cape Providence* (95335), *Cape Rosier* (95333), *Cape Sable* (95334), *Cape Trinity* (95331), *Cape Darby* (95323), *Cape Florida* (95325), *Cape Kiwanda* (95329), and *Cape Porpoise* (95327).

CAPE CARTER (WPB 95309)   *1968 U.S. Coast Guard*

Patrol Boats—continued

CAPE CROSS (WPB 95321)   1969, US Coast Guard

54 PATROL BOATS (WPB): 82ft CLASS

POINT ARENA	82346	POINT LOBOS	82366
POINT BAKER	82342	POINT LOOKOUT	82341
POINT BARROW	82348	POINT MONROE	82353
POINT BATAN	82340	POINT NOWELL	82363
POINT BENNETT	82351	POINT RICHMOND	82370
POINT BONITA	82347	POINT ROBERTS	82332
POINT BRIDGE	82338	POINT SAL	82352
POINT BROWN	82362	POINT SPENCER	82349
POINT CHARLES	82361	POINT STEELE	82359
POINT CHICO	82339	POINT STUART	82358
POINT COUNTESS	82335	POINT SWIFT	82312
POINT DIVIDE	82337	POINT THATCHER	82314
POINT ESTERO	82344	POINT TURNER	82365
POINT EVANS	82354	POINT VERDE	82311
POINT FRANCIS	82356	POINT WARDE	82368
POINT FRANKLIN	82350	POINT WELLS	82343
POINT GLASS	82336	POINT WHITEHORN	82364
POINT HANNON	82355	POINT WINSLOW	82360
POINT HERRON	82318	POINT BARNES	82371
POINT HEYER	82369	POINT BROWER	82372
POINT HIGHLAND	82333	POINT CAMDEN	82373
POINT HOPE	82302	POINT CARREW	82374
POINT HURON	82357	POINT DORAN	82375
POINT JUDITH	82345	POINT HARRIS	82376
POINT KNOLL	82367	POINT HOBART	82377
POINT LEDGE	82324	POINT JACKSON	82378
		POINT MARTIN	82379

CG 82332—82370
"C" class (built 1962-63
and 1965-67)

CG 82371—82379
"D" Class (built 1969-70)

Displacement, tons	64 standard; 67 full load
Dimensions, feet	78·1 wl; 83 oa × 17·2 × 5·8
Guns	C Class: 1—81 mm mortar and 1—·50 cal MG or 2—·50 cal MG
	D Class: 2—·50 cal MG
Main engines	2 diesels; 2 shafts; 1 600 bhp = 20 knots
Complement	8 (enlisted men)

Rated as 82 ft Cutters. Designed and built at Coast Guard Yard, for law enforcement, search and rescue. Steel hulls, unmanned engine room controlled from the bridge, power steering and air conditioning. "C" class modifications (also 82318) include increase in bhp to 1 600 and speed to 20 knots. In 1965 26 of these craft were deployed with the Navy and transferred to duty in Vietnam (subsequently transferred to South Vietnamese Navy). As a result 17 replacement cutters were added to the construction programme plus nine already planned. Of the latter, *Point Arena, Point Barrow, Point Bonita, Point Franklin, Point Judith* and *Point Spencer* were built under the Fiscal Year 1965 Programme by Martinac SB, Tacoma, Wash, and 82351 to 82370 in the 1966 programme. Nine "D" class cutters built by Coast Guard Yard with first, *Point Barnes,* completed on 19 Dec 1969.

Endurance is 1 500 miles at 9 knots.

NOMENCLATURE. CG 82301-82344 were assigned "Point" names in Jan 1964.

TRANSFERS. All 26 boats of this class that comprised Coast Guard Squadron One in Vietnam have been transferred to the South Vietnamese Navy: *Point League* (82304) *Point Garnet* (82310), *Point Clear* (82315) *Point Gammon* (82328), *Point Comfort,* (82317), *Point Ellis* (82330), *Point Slokum* (82313), *Point Hudson* (82322) transferred in 1969; *Point Arden* (82309), *Point Banks* (82 327), *Point Caution* (82301), *Point Cypress* (82326), *Point Dume* (82325), *Point Glover* (82307), *Point Grace* (82323), *Point Grey* (82324), *Point Jefferson* (82306), *Point Kennedy* (82320), *Point Lomas* (82321), *Point Mast* (82316), *Point Monroe* (82331), *Point Orient* (82319), *Point Partridge* (82305), *Point Welcome* (82329), *Point White* (82308) *Point Young* (82303) in 1970.

PHOTOGRAPH. Photographs of the 82-foot patrol boats in Vietnam area grey paint and special markings appear in 1970-1971 and previous editions.

POINT BONITA (WPB 82347)   1969, United States Coast Guard

AIR CUSHION VEHICLES

3 AIR CUSHION VEHICLES (ACV): SK-5 TYPE

HOVER 01	HOVER 02	HOVER 03

Weight, tons	8·5 normal gross; 10 overload gross
Dimensions, feet	38·8 oa × 23·8 × 16 (height)
Guns	Removed
Main engines	1 gas turbine (General Electric) 1 150 shp; 1 three-bladed, variable-pitch aircraft propeller = 60 knots
Complement	3 + (enlisted men)

These are Americanised versions of the British-developed SR.N5 hovercraft. Built as the SK-5 by Bell Aerosystems of Buffalo, New York, under licence from Saunders-Roe Division of Westland Aircraft Limited. Delivered to US Navy late in 1965 and designated Patrol Air Cushion Vehicles (PACV 1, 2, and 3); transferred to US Coast Guard in Oct 1969 for evaluation in search, rescue, support of navigation aids, and possibly law enforcement missions (see *Operational* notes).

The PACV 1-3 were twice deployed to South Vietnam in 1966-1969. The craft encountered mixed success in their two combat deployments; they were found lacking in coastal operations but were highly successful in the marshy Plain of Reeds during the wet season. After their return to the United States in May 1969 the Navy stated the air cushion vehicles "would not be active in the next calendar year".

In overhaul from July 1970 to October 1970, with operational evaluation commencing in January 1971.

In Coast Guard service the craft are unarmed and can normally carry 15 to 18 passengers in cabin in addition to, minimum three-man crew.

DESIGN. The hard bottom of the ACVs travels on a cushion of air more than four feet thick. Flexible, air-actuated trunks provide obstacle clearance and ditch crossing capability over land and improved riding qualities over water. A large buoyancy chamber subdivided into watertight compartments, provides flotation on water.

ENGINEERING. A General Electric 7LM-100 marine gas turbine engine drives both the lift fan, which forces air downward to create the air cushion beneath the craft, and the aft-mounted propeller which provides propulsion. This is a marine version of the T58-8 aircraft engine.

Unarmed in Coast Guard service.

OPERATIONAL. Two "hovers" are being employed in the San Francisco Bay area in a one-year trials programme; the third vehicle is supporting an Advance Research Projects Agency activity in the Arctic (all Coast Guard manned).

GUNNERY. Armament in Navy service modified to various combinations; official armament during 1968-1969 deployment was 2—·50 calibre MG in a twin mount over the cabin (see photograph), 2—7·62 mm MG (single), and 2 grenade launchers.

HOVER 01   1970, US Coast Guard, PHC Ralph Sunderlin

HOVER 02   1970, United States Coast Guard

ICEBREAKERS

1 ICEBREAKER (WAGB): NEW CONSTRUCTION

Displacement, tons	12 200 full load
Length, feet	385 oa × 78 × 28
Machinery	Diesels supplemented by gas turbines; 3 shafts; 40 000 hp = 17 knots

The Fiscal Year 1971 budget for the Department of Transportation provides $59 000 000 for construction of a new Coast Guard icebreaker, the first ship in a programme to replace the "Wind" class ships. Four new ships are now planned.
The new icebreaker will be the largest Coast Guard-operated ship. The icebreaking capability of this ship with diesel power alone will exceed that of the US icebreaker *Glacier* and approach that of the Soviet *Moskva* and the Canadian *St. Laurent*; with the gas turbines operating, the new US icebreaker's available shaft horsepower will exceed that of any icebreaker afloat including the Soviet nuclear-powered ship *Lenin*.

ENGINEERING. This new WAGB design provides for conventional diesel engines for normal cruising and gas turbines for maximum power situations. The diesel engines will drive generators producing AC power; the main propulsion DC motors will draw power through rectifiers permitting absolute flexibility in the delivery of power from alternate sources. The use of controllable-pitch propellers on three shafts will permit manoeuvering in heavy ice without the risk to propeller blades caused by stopping the shaft while going from ahead to astern.
The Coast Guard had given consideration to the use of nuclear power for an icebreaker, however, at this time the gas turbine-diesel combination can achieve the desirable power requirements without the added cost and operating restrictions of a nuclear powerplant.

COSTS. The cost elements of the new WAGB are identified as $18 780 000 for hull structure, $11 460 000 for propulsion, $11 300 000 for auxiliary systems, $11 405 000 for equipment and furnishings, and $6 055 000 for indirect shipyard costs.

PHOTOGRAPH. Note twin-funnel configuration, change from earlier preliminary design (see photo in 1970-1971 edition).

NEW ICEBREAKER   *1971, United States Coast Guard*

1 ICEBREAKER (WAGB): "GLACIER" TYPE

Name	No.	Launched	Commissioned
GLACIER	WAGB 4 (ex-AGB 4)	27 Aug 1954	27 May 1955

Displacement, tons	8 449 full load
Dimensions, feet	309·6 oa × 74 × 29
Guns	4—·50 cal MG (see *Gunnery* notes)
Aircraft	2 helicopters normally embarked
Main engines	Diesel-electric (10 Fairbanks-Morse diesels and 2 Westinghouse electric motors); 2 shafts; 21 000 hp = 17·6 knots
Complement	231 (15 officers, 216 enlisted men)

The largest icebreaker in US service; designed and built by Ingalls Shipbuilding Corp, Pascagoula, Mississippi laid down on 3 Aug 1953. Transferred from Navy (AGB 4) to Coast Guard on 30 June 1966.

ENGINEERING. When built the *Glacier* had the largest capacity single-armature DC motors ever built and installed in a ship. Endurance is 29 200 miles at 12 knots or 12 000 miles at 17·6 knots.

GUNNERY. As built the *Glacier* was armed with two 5 inch AA guns (twin), six 3 inch AA guns (twin), and four 20 mm AA guns; lighter weapons removed prior to transfer to Coast Guard; 5 inch guns removed in 1969.

GLACIER (WAGB 4)   *1968 U.S Coast guard*

7 ICEBREAKERS (WAGB): "WIND" CLASS

Name	No.	Launched
STATEN ISLAND (ex-*Northwind*)	WAGB 278 (ex-AGB 5)	28 Dec 1942
EASTWIND	WAGB 279	6 Feb 1943
SOUTHWIND	WAGB 280 (ex-AGB 3)	8 Mar 1943
WESTWIND	WAGB 281	31 Mar 1943
NORTHWIND	WAGB 282	25 Feb 1945
BURTON ISLAND	WAGB 283 (ex-ABG 1, ex-AG 88)	30 Apr 1946
EDISTO	WAGB 284 (ex-AGB 2, ex-AG 89)	29 May 1946

Displacement, tons	3 500 standard; 6 515 full load
Dimensions, feet	250 pp; 269 oa × 63·5 × 29
Aircraft	2 helicopters normally embarked
Guns	4—·50 cal MG (see *Gunnery* notes)
Main engines	Diesel-electric (6 diesels); 2 shafts; 10 000 hp = 16 knots
Complement	181 (14 officers, 167 enlisted men)

All seven ships of this class were built by Western Pipe & Steel Co, San Pedro, California. Five ships were delivered to the US Coast Guard during World War II and two to the US Navy in 1946.
Three of the Coast Guard ships were transferred to the Soviet Navy in 1945: *Northwind* (first of name, WAGB 278) renamed *Severni Veter* and returned to US Navy in 1951 and commissioned as *Staten Island* (AGB 5); *Southwind* renamed *Kapitan Belusov* and returned to US Navy in 1950 and commissioned as *Atka* (AGB 3); *Westwind* renamed *Severni Polius* and returned to US Coast Guard in 1951.
The four "Wind" class ships in the US Navy were transferred to the Coast Guard: *Edisto* on 20 Oct 1965, *Staten Island* on 1 Feb 1966, *Atka* on 20 Oct 1966 (renamed *Southwind* in January 1967), and *Burton Island* on 15 Dec 1966.

AIRCRAFT. All of these ships have telescoping hangars to protect helicopters and permit maintenance at night and in inclement weather.

ENGINEERING. These ships were built with a bow propeller shaft in addition to the two stern shafts; bow shaft removed from all units because it would continually break in hard storis ice.
Main engines are Fairbanks Morse 38D81/8.
Endurance is 38 000 miles at 10·5 knots or 16 000 miles at 16 knots.

GUNNERY. As built the five Coast Guard ships each mounted four 5 inch guns (one twin mount forward and one twin mount aft on 01 level) and 12 40 mm anti-aircraft guns (quad); the two Navy Ships were completed with only forward twin 5 inch mount (as built a catapult and cranes were fitted immediately behind the funnel and one floatplane was carried). Armament reduced after war and helicopter platform eventually installed in all ships.
During the 1960s the *Eastwind* carried two 3 inch guns (twin), the *Northwind* two 5 inch guns (twin), and the three other ships each mounted one 5 inch gun; all armament removed in 1969-70.

STATUS. The *Eastwind* is in reserve; all other Coast Guard icebreakers are operational.

BURTON ISLAND (WAGB 283)   *US Coast Guard*

NORTHWIND (WAGB 282)   *1969, US Coast Guard*

Icebreakers—continued

BURTON ISLAND (WAGB 283)   *1971, US Navy, PH2 J. J. Carmerrale*

1 ICEBREAKER (WAGB): "MACKINAW" TYPE

MACKINAW (ex-*Manitowac*) WAGB 83

Displacement, tons	5 252
Dimensions, feet	290 oa × 74 × 19
Aircraft	1 helicopter
Main engines	Diesel; with electric drive; 3 shafts (1 forward, 2 aft); 10 000 bhp = 18·7 knots
Complement	127 (10 officers, 117 enlisted men)

Built by Toledo Shipbuilding Co, Ohio. Laid down on 20 Mar 1943. Launched on 6 Mar 1944. Commissioned on 20 Dec 1944. Completed in Jan 1945. Specially designed and constructed with 1·6 in. plating for service as icebreaker on the Great Lakes. Equipped with two 12-ton cranes. Clear area for helicopter is provided on the quarter deck.

Endurance is 60 000 miles at 9 knots.

MACINAW (WAGB 83)   *1966 U.S. Coast Guard*

1 ICEBREAKER (WAGB): "STORIS" TYPE

STORIS (ex-*Eskimo*) WAGB 38

Displacement, tons	1 715 standard; 1 925 full load
Dimensions, feet	230 oa × 43 × 15
Guns	1—3 in, 50 cal; 2—·50 cal MG
Aircraft	1 helicopter
Main engines	Diesel-electric; 1 shaft; 1 800 bhp = 14 knots
Complement	106 (10 officers, 96 enlisted men)

Built by Toledo Shipbuilding Co, Ohio. Launched in 1942. Ice patrol tender. Helicopter platform aft. Strengthened for ice navigation. Employed on Alaskan service. Search, rescue and law enforcement are primary duties. Makes supply runs to isolated Coast Guard installations within her patrol area. Her designation was changed from WAG to WAGB on 1 May 1966.

Endurance is 22 000 miles at 8 knots or 12 000 miles at 14 knots.

STORIS (WAGB 38)   *1968 US Coast Guard*

TRAINING SHIPS

The Coast Guard operates two training cutters and three reserve training cutters, one of the latter being the *Unimak*, listed earlier with the high endurance cutters. In addition, the reserve training cutter *Lamar* is in Coast Guard reserve pending disposal. The *Eagle*, employed to train cadets at the Coast Guard Academy, is the only sail training ship operated by any US service.

1 TRAINING CUTTER (WTR): Ex-RADIO SHIP

COURIER WTR 410 (ex-WAGR)
(ex-*Coastal Messenger*, ex-USS *Doddridge*, AK 176)

Displacement, tons	5 800 standard; 7 500 full load
Dimensions, feet	338·5 × 50·3 × 18
Armament	None
Main engines	Diesel direct drive (Nordberg 82D diesel); 1 700 bhp = 11 knots
Complement	55 (10 officers, 45 enlisted men)

CI-M-AVI type, launched in 1945. Built as a naval cargo ship but not used by the Navy. Acquired by the US Coast Guard from the US Maritime Commission in 1951, fitted out as an overseas radio relay base, manned by the Coast Guard and operated for the United States Information Agency as a relay station for the "Voice of America" broadcasts from 7 Sep 1952 until 17 May 1964. She was virtually a seagoing radio broadcasting station wirh transmitting equipment the most powerful of its kind ever installed in any vessel. She commissioned on 15 Feb 1952 and began broadcasts on 7 Sep 1952, being stationed at Island of Rhodes, Greece. She returned to the USA in 1964 and was decommissioned on 25 Aug 1964, but was converted and recommissioned on 1 July 1965 and employed as a training "cutter" for the reserve at Yorktown, Va. Her special communication equipment has been removed.

COURIER (WTR 410)   *1968, United States Coast Guard*

1 TRAINING CUTTER (WTR): Ex-PATROL ESCORT

LAMAR WTR 899 (ex-PCE 899)

Displacement, tons	640 standard; 903 full load
Dimensions, feet	180 wl; 184·5 oa × 33 × 9·5
Guns	1—3 inch 50 calibre
ASW weapons	1 hedgehog
Main engines	GM diesels; 2 shafts; 2 000 bhp = 15 knots
Complement	39 plus 57 reserve trainees

Former escort, 180 ft steel type, acquired from the US Navy in 1965, converted for use as Coast Guard Reserve training ship and commissioned in 1965. Built by Willamette Iron & Steel Corp, Portland, Oregon. Laid down 11 Jan 1943. Launched on 11 Aug 1943. Completed (first commission) on 17 Mar 1945.
The *Lamar* now is in reserve pending disposal.

LAMAR (WTR 899)   *1967, United States Coast Guard*

Training Ships—continued

1 TRAINING CUTTER (WTR): Ex-MINESWEEPER

TANAGER WTR 885 (ex-WTR 385, ex-MSF 385)

Displacement, tons	890 standard; 1 077 full load
Dimensions, feet	215 wl; 221 oa × 32·3 × 14
Guns	removed
Main engines	Diesel-electric; 2 shafts; 3 474 bhp = 17·5 knots
Complement	47 (6 officers, 41 men) (plus 80 reserve trainees)

Former fleet minesweeper, large steel-hulled type, acquired from the US Navy in 1964 as a Coast Guard Reserve training ship, at Yorktown, Va. Her minesweeping equipment was removed and a living compartment added. Built by American Ship-building Co, Lorain, Ohio. Laid down on 29 Mar 1944. Launched on 9 Dec 1944 Endurance is 7 200 miles at 9 knots
Armament of single 3 inch gun and ASW hedgehog have been removed.

TANAGER (WTR 885)   1970, United States Coast Guard

1 TRAINING CUTTER (IX): "ACTIVE" CLASS

CUYAHOGA WIX 157 (ex-WMEC 157, ex-WPC 157, ex-WAG 26)

Dimensions, feet	215 oa × 24 × 8
Guns	Removed
Main engines	Diesel; 2 shafts; 800 bhp = 13·2 knots
Complement	11 (1 officer, 10 enlisted men)

Built in 1926 as one of the 33 "Active" class steel patrol boats. The *Cuyahoga* is the only cutter of this type remaining on the Coast Guard list. She is based at Yorktown, Virginia.

CUYAHOGA (WIX 157)   1966, United States Coast Guard

1 TRAINING BARK (IX)

EAGLE (ex-*Horst Wessel*) WIX 327

Displacement, tons	1 634; 1 816 full load
Dimensions, feet	265·8 pp; 295·2 oa × 39·3 × 17
Sail area, sq ft	21 351
Height of masts, feet	150
Speed	As high as 18 knots under full sail alone
Main engines	Auxiliary diesel; 1 shaft; 740 bhp = 10·5 knots
Oil fuel, tons	48
Endurance, miles	3 500 at 10 knots with diesel
Complement	280

Former German training ship for 200 naval cadets. Built by Blohm & Voss, Hamburg. Launched on 13 June 1936. Taken by the United States as part of reparations after the Second World War for employment in US Coast Guard Practice Squadron. Taken over at Bremerhaven in Jan 1946. Arrived at home port, New London, Conn in July 1946. Has made several cruises to European waters to train Coast Guard cadets.

CLASS. Sister ship, *Albert Leo Schlageter*, was also taken by the USA in 1945 but **was** sold to Brazil in 1948 and re-sold to Portugal in 1962.

Training Ships—continued

EAGLE (WIX 327)   *United States Coast Guard*

SEAGOING TENDERS

37 SEAGOING TENDERS (WLB)
1 OCEANOGRAPHIC CUTTER (WAGO) } **"BALSAM" CLASS**

Name	No.	Launched	Name	No.	Launched
BALSAM *	WLB 62	1942	BASSWOOD	WLB 388	1944
CACTUS	WLB 270	1942	BITTERSWEET	W'LB 289	1944
COWSLIP	WLB 277	1942	BLACKHAW*	WLB 390	1944
WOODBINE	WLB 289	1944	BLACKTHORN	WLB 391	1944
GENTIAN	WLB 290	1942	BRAMBLE *	WLB 392	1944
LAUREL	WLB 291	1942	FIREBUSH	WLB 393	1944
CLOVER	WLB 292	1942	HORNBEAM	WLB 394	1944
EVERGREEN	WAGO 295	1943	IRIS	WLB 395	1944
SORREL *	WLB 296	1943	MALLOW	WLB 396	1944
IRONWOOD	WLB 297	1944	MARIPOSA	WLB 397	1944
CITRUS *	WLB 300	1943	SAGEBRUSH	WLB 399	1944
CONIFER	WLB 301	1943	SALVIA	WLB 400	1944
MADRONA	WLB 302	1943	SASSAFRAS	WLB 401	1944
TUPELO	WLB 303	1943	SEDGE *	WLB 402	1944
MESQUITE	WLB 305	1943	SPAR *	WLB 403	1944
BUTTON WOOD	WLB 306	1943	SUNDEW *	WLB 404	1944
PLANTREE	WLB 307	1943	SWEETBRIER	WLB 405	1944
PAPAW	WLB 308	1943	ACACIA	WLB 406	1944
SWEETGUM	WLB 309	1943	WOODRUSH	WLB 407	1944

Displacement, tons	935 standard; 1 025 full load
Dimensions, feet	180 oa × 37 × 13
Guns	1—3 inch 50 calibre in *Citrus, Cowslip, Hornbeam, Sedge,* and *Sorrel* (original armament); replaced by ·50 calibre MG in others; some unarmed
Main engines	Diesel electric ;-1 shaft; 1 000 hp in tenders numbered in WLB 62-303 series except *Ironwood* = 12·8 knots; others 1 200 hp = 13 knots except *Sundew* 1 800 hp = 15 knots
Complement	53 (6 officers, 47 enlisted men)

Seagoing buoy tenders. *Ironwood* built by Coast Guard yard at Curtis Bay, Baltimore, Maryland; others by Marine Iron & Shipbuilding Co, Duluth, Minnesota (20 ships) or Zeneth Dredge Co, Duluth, Minnesota (17 ships).
Eight ships indicated by asterisks are strengthened for icebreaking.
Three ships, *Cowslip, Bittersweet,* and *Hornbeam,* have controllable pitch, bow-thrust propellers to assist in manoeuvering. All WLB have 20-ton capacity boom.
The *Evergreen* has been refitted as an oceanographic cutter (WAGO) and is painted white; the *Cactus* served in a similar role from 1967-1969 (see photograph; a photograph of the *Evergreen* appears in the 1969-1970 edition).

BITTERSWEET (WLB 389) no gun   *US Coast Guard*

Seagoing Tenders —continued

HORNBEAM (WLB 394)   1969, US Coast Guard

CACTUS (as WAGO 270)   1969, US Coast Guard

1 SEAGOING TENDER (WLB): Ex-MINELAYER

MAGNOLIA (ex-*Barricade*) WLB (ex-ACM 3)

Displacement, tons	1 054 standard ; 1 250 full load
Dimensions, feet	188·7 oa × 37 × 12
Main engines	Triple expansion ; 2 shafts ; 1 200 ihp = 11·3 knots
Complement	52 (5 officers 47 enlisted men)

Ex-Army mineplanters, ex-US Navy ACM. Launched in 1942. Redesignated Seagoing Tenders, WLB instead of WAGL on 1 Jan 1965. Fitted with 20-ton capacity boom. Endurance is 4 800 miles at 7 knots.
Heather (WLB 331, ex-ACM 7) stricken in 1967, *qonwuil* (WLB 330, ex-ACM 6), *Ivy* (WLB 329, ex-ACM 5), and *Willow* (WLB 332, ex-ACM 8) stricken in 1969.

HEATHER (WLB 331) (now stricken)   1966, US Coast Guard

COASTAL TENDERS

3 COASTAL TENDERS (WLM): "RED" CLASS

Name	No.	Launched	Name	No.	Launched
RED WOOD	WLM 685	1964	**RED CEDAR**	WLM 688	1970
RED BEECH	WLM 688	1964	**RED OAK**	WLM 689	1971
RED BIRCH	WLM 687	1965			

Displacement, tons	471 standard ; 512 full load
Dimensions, feet	157 oa × 33 × 6
Main engines	2 diesels ; 2 shafts ; 1 800 hp = 12·8 knots
Complement	31 (4 officers, 27 enlisted men)

All built by Coast Guard yard, Curtis Bay, Baltimore, Maryland. *Red Cedar* completed late in 1970 and *Red Oak* late in 1971.

Fitted with controllable-pitch propellers and bow thrusters; steel hulls strengthened for light icebreaking. Steering and engine controls on each bridge wing as well as in pilot house. Living spaces are air conditioned. Endurance is 3 000 miles at 11·6 knots. Fitted with 10-ton capacity boom.

Coastal Tenders—continued

RED BIRCH (WLM 687)   1968, U.S. Coast Guard

3 COASTAL TENDERS (WLM): "HOLLYHOCK" CLASS

FIR WLM 212	**HOLLYHOCK** WLM 220	**WALNUT** WLM 252

Displacement, tons	989
Dimensions, feet	175 × 34 × 12
Main engines	Diesel reduction ; 2 shafts ; 1 350 bhp = 12 knots
Complement	40 (5 officers, 35 enlisted men)

Launched in 1937 (*Hollyhock*) and 1939 (*Fir* and *Walnut*). *Walnut* was re-engined by Willamette Iron & Steel Co, Portland, Oregon, in 1958. Redesignated Coastal Tenders, WLM, instead on Buoy Tenders, WAGL on 1 Jan 1965. Fitted with 20-ton capacity boom.

WALNUT (WLM 252)   1963, United States Coast Guard

1 COASTAL TENDER (WLM): "JUNIPER" TYPE

JUNIPER WLM 224

Displacement, tons	794
Dimensions, feet	177 × 33 × 9·2
Main engines	Diesel, with electric drive ; 2 shafts ; 900 bhp = 10·8 knots
Complement	38 (4 officers, 34 enlisted men)

Launched on 18 May 1940. Redesignated WLM vice WALG on 1 Jan 1965. Fitted with 20-ton capacity boom.

DISPOSALS

Several coastal tenders of various types have been stricken: **Hemlock** (WAGL 217) in 1958, **Violet** (WAGL 250) in 1962, **Arbutus** (WLM 203, ex-WAGL 203) in 1967, **Mistletoe** (WLM 237, ex-WAGL 237) in 1968.

JUNIPER (WLM 224)   United States Coast Guard

1 COASTAL TENDER (WLM): "LILAC" TYPE

LILAC WLM 277

Displacement, tons	770
Dimensions, feet	173 × 34 × 12
Main engines	Reciprocating ; 2 shafts ; 1 000 hp = 11·5 knots
Complement	36 (4 officers, 32 enlisted men)

Launched in 1933. Redesignated WLM vice WAGL on 1 Jan 1956. Scheduled for decommissioning in 1971. Fitted with 20-ton capacity boom.

Coastal Tenders—*continued*

7 COASTAL TENDERS (WLM): "WHITE" CLASS

WHITE BUSH WLM 542	**WHITE PINE** WLM 547
WHITE HEATH WLM 545	**WHITE SAGE** WLM 544
WHITE HOLLY WLM 543	**WHITE SUMAC** WLM 540
WHITE LUPINE WLM 546	

Displacement, tons	435 standard; 600 full load
Dimensions, feet	133 oa × 31 × 9
Main engines	Diesel; 2 shafts; 600 bhp = 9·8 knots
Complement	21 (1 officer, 20 enlisted men)

All launched in 1943. All seven ships are former US Navy YFs, adapted for the Coast Guard. The *White Alder* (WLM 541) was sunk in a collision on 7 Dec 1968. Fitted with 10-ton capacity boom.

DISPOSALS
Of the two "Hawthorne" class coastal tenders. **Hawthorne**. WLM 215 (ex-WAGL 215) was decommissioned on 24 July 1964. and **Oak** WLM 239 (ex-WAGL 239) on 1 Sep 1964. Both were officially deleted from the list in 1965. The larger but older **Cedar** was sold in June 1955.

WHITE HOLLY (WLM 543)   *1968, U.S. Coast Guard*

INLAND TENDERS

TERN WLI 80801

Displacement, tons	168 full load
Dimensions, feet	80 oa × 25 × 5
Main engines	Diesels; 2 shafts; 450 hp = 10 knots
Complement	7 (enlisted men)

The *Tern* is prototype for a new design of inland buoy tenders. A cutaway stern and gantry crane (the first installed in a Coast Guard tender) permit lifting buoys aboard from the stern. The crane moves on rails that extend forward to the deck house. Fitted with 125 hp bow thruster to improve manoeuverability. Air conditioned.
Built by Coast Guard yard at Curtis Bay, Baltimore, Maryland. Launched on 15 June 1968 and placed in service on 7 Feb 1969. She will undergo extensive evaluation to determine if design advantage justifies further craft of this type.

TAMARACK WLI 248

Displacement, tons	400 full load
Dimensions, feet	124 oa × 30 × 8
Main engines	Diesels; 1 shaft; 520 hp = 10 knots

Launched in 1934. Fitted with 10-ton capacity boom. Out of service.

MAPLE WLI 234	**NARCISSUS** WLI 238	**ZINNIA** WLI 255

Displacement, tons	370 full load
Dimensions, feet	122 oa × 28 × 8
Main engines	Diesels; 2 shafts; 980 hp (800 in *Maple*) = 10·3 knots except *Maple* 10 knots
Complement	30 (1 officer, 19 enlisted men)

All launched in 1939. The *Maple* has a 6½-ton capacity boom; others have a 10-ton capacity boom.

COSMOS WLI 293	**BLUEBELL** WLI 313	**PRIMROSE** WLI 316
BARBERRY WLI 294	**SMILAX** WLI 315	**VERBENA** WLI 317
RAMBLER WLI 298		

Displacement, tons	178 full load
Dimensions, feet	100 oa × 24 × 5
Main engines	Diesels; 2 shafts 600; hp = 10·5 knots except *Barberry* 11 knots
Complement	15 (1 officer, 14 enlisted men)

Cosmos launched in 1942, *Barberry* in 1943, *Bluebell* in 1945, others in 1944. The *Barberry* has controllable-pitch propellers. The *Barberry* and *Verbena* are fitted with pile drivers.

AZALEA WLI 641

Displacement, tons	200 full load
Dimensions, feet	100 oa × 24 × 5
Main engines	Diesels; 2 shafts; 440 hp = 9 knots
Complement	14 (1 officer, 13 enlisted men)

Launched in 1958. Fitted with pile driver.

BUCKTHORN WLI 642

Displacement, tons	200 full load
Dimensions, feet	100 oa × 24 × 4
Main engines	Diesels; 2 shafts; 600 hp = 7·3 knots
Complement	14 (1 officer, 13 enlisted men)

Launched in 1963.

Inland Tenders—*continued*

CLEMATIS WLI 74286	**SHADBUSH** WLI 74287

Displacement, tons	93 full load
Dimensions, feet	74 oa × 19 × 4
Main engines	Diesels; 2 shafts; 330 hp = 8 knots
Complement	9 (enlisted men)

Launched in 1944.

BLUEBERRY WLI 65302

Displacement, tons	45 full load
Dimensions, feet	65 oa × 17 × 14
Main engines	Diesels; 2 shafts; 330 hp = 10·5 knots
Complement	5 (enlisted men)

Launched in 1942.

BLACKBERRY WLI 65303	**CHOKEBERRY** WLI 65304	**LOGANBERRY** WLI 65305

Displacement, tons	68 full load
Dimensions, feet	65 oa × 17 × 4
Main engines	Diesels; 1 shaft; 220 hp = 9 knots
Complement	5 (enlisted men)

Launched in 1946.

BAYBERRY WLI 65400	**ELDERBERRY** WLI 65401

Displacement, tons	68 full load
Dimensions, feet	65 oa × 17 × 4
Main engines	Diesels; 2 shafts; 400 hp = 11·3 knots
Complement	5 (enlisted men)

Launched in 1954.

TERN (WLI 80801)   *1969, United States Coast Guard*

BUCKTHORN (WLI 642)   *1966, United States Coast Guard*

BAYBERRY (WLI 65400)   *US Coast Guard*

CONSTRUCTION TENDERS

ANVIL	WLIC 75301	**MALLET** WLIC 75304	**WEDGE**	WLIC 75307
HAMMER	WLIC 75302	**VISE** WLIC 75305	**SPIKE**	WLIC 75308
SLEDGE	WLIC 75303	**CLAMP** WLIC 75306	**HATCHET**	WLIC 75309
			AXE	WLIC 75310

Displacement, tons	145 full load
Dimensions, feet	75 oa (WLIC 75306-75310 are 76 oa) × 22 × 4
Main engines	Diesels; 2 shafts; 600 hp = 10 knots
Complement	9 or 10 (1 officer in *Mallet, Sledge,* and *Vise;* 9 enlisted men in all)

Launched 1962-1965.

Construction Tenders—*continued*

SLEDGE (WLIC 75303) Pushing barge   *US Coast Guard*

RIVER TENDERS

FERN WLR 304   **SUMAC** WLR 311

Displacement, tons	*Sumac* 404, *Fern* 315 full load
Dimensions, feet	115 oa × 30 × 6
Main engines	Diesels; 3 shafts; 960 hp = 10·6 knots
Complement	23 (1 officer, 22 enlisted men)

Built in 1942 and 1943, respectively.

DOGWOOD WLR 259   **FORSYTHIA** WLR 63   **SYCAMORE** WLR 268

Displacement. tons	230 full load, except *Forsythia* 280
Dimensions, feet	114 oa × 26 × 4
Main engines	Diesels; 2 shafts; 2 800 hp = 11 knots
Complement	21 (1 officer, 20 enlisted men)

Dogwood and *Sycamore* built in 1940; *Forsythia* in 1943.

FOXGLOVE WLR 285.

Displacement, tons	350 full load
Dimensions, feet	114 oa × 30 × 6
Main engines	Diesels; 3 shafts; 8 500 hp = 13·5 knots
Complement	21 (1 officer, 20 enlisted men)

Built in 1945.

GOLDENROD WLR 213   **POPLAR** WLR 241

Displacement, tons	235 full load
Dimensions, feet	104 oa × 24 × 4
Main engines	Diesels; 2 shafts; 800 hp = 11·5 knots
Complement	17 (1 officer, 16 enlisted men)

Built in 1938 and 1939, respectively.

LANTANA WLR 80310

Displacement, tons	235 full load
Dimensions, feet	80 oa × 30 × 6
Main engines	Diesels; 3 shafts; 10 000 hp = 10 knots
Complement	20 (1 officer, 19 enlisted men)

Built in 1943.

GASCONADE	WLR 75401	**CHEYENNE**	WLR 75405
MUSKINGUM	WLR 75402	**KICKAPOO**	WLR 75406
WYACONDA	WLR 75403	**KANAWHA**	WLR 75407
CHUPPEWA	WLR 75404		

Displacement, tons	145 full load
Dimensions, feet	75 oa × 22 × 4
Main engines	Diesel; 2 shafts; 600 hp = 10·8 knots
Complement	12 (enlisted men)

Built 1964-1971.

OLEANDER WLR 73264

Displacement, tons	90 full load
Dimensions, feet	73 oa × 18 × 5
Main engines	Diesel; 2 shafts; 300 hp = 12 knots
Complement	10 (enlisted men)

Built in 1940.

OSAGE (WLR 65505)   *US Coast Guard*

River Tenders—*continued*

CUACHITA	WLR 65501	**SCIOTO**	WLR 65504
CIMARRON	WLR 65502	**OSAGE**	WLR 65505
OBION	WLR 65503	**SANGAMON**	WLR 655506

Displacement, tons	139 full load
Dimensions, feet	65·6 oa × 21 × 5
Main engines	Diesel; 2 shafts; 600 hp = 12·5 knots
Complement	10 (enlisted men)

Built in 1960-1962.

SUPPLY SHIPS

1 SUPPLY SHIP (WAK): CI-M-AVI TYPE

KUKUI (ex-USS *Colquitt*, AK 174) WAK 186

Displacement, tons	4 900 light; 5 636 full load
Measurement, tons	5 900 gross
Dimensions, feet	320 wl; 338·5 oa × 50 × 18
Main engines	Nordberg diesel; 1 shaft; 1 750 bhp = 11 knots
Complement	107 (12 officers, 95 enlisted men)

Former naval cargo ship based at Honolulu to perform logistic services for US Coast Guard stations in the Pacific. Built by Froemming Bros, Milwaukee, Wisc Launched in 1944. Maritime Administration type CI-M-AVI.

1 BUOY TENDER : Ex- SUPPLY SHIP

REDBUD WAGL 398 (ex-T-AKL 398)

Displacement, tons	approx 700
Dimensions, feet	108 oa × 37 × 13·7
Main engines	Diesel; 1 shaft; 1 000 hp = 10 knots

Built by Marine Iron & Shipbuilding Co, Duluth, Minnesota. Launched on 11 Sep 1943. Completed as buoy tender (WAGL); transferred to Navy on 20 Feb 1952 for transport and supply work in Greenland area (operated by Military Sea Transportation Service); stricken from Navy List and returned to Coast Guard on 20 Nov 1970. To be employed as buoy tender.

Photograph shows the *Redbud* as T-AKL 398.

TRANSFERS. The cable layer, *Yamacraw* WARC 333, was transferred to the US Navy on a loan basis in 1959, but was stricken from the Navy list on 1 July 1965 and transferred to the Maritime Administration Reserve Fleet; cargo ship *Nettle* WAK 169, ex-FS 396, transferred to Philippines in 1968.

KUKUI (WAK 186)   *1970, US Coast Guard*

REDBUD (WAGL 398)   *United States Navy*

OCEANGOING TUGS

1 MEDIUM ENDURANCE CUTTER (WMEC) } ARS TYPE
1 OCEANOGRAPHIC CUTTER (WAGO)

Name	No.	Launched	Navy Comm.
ACUSHNET (ex-*Shackle*)	WAGO 167 (ex-WAT 167, ARS 9)	1 Apr 1943	5 Feb 1944
YOCONA (ex-*Seize*)	WMEC 168 (ex-WAT 168, ARS 26)	8 Apr 1944	3 Nov 1944

Displacement, tons	1 557 standard; 1 745 full load
Dimensions, feet	213·5 oa × 39 × 15
Main engines	Diesels; 2 shafts; 3 000 hp = 15·5 knots
Complement	*Acushnet* 64 (7 officers, 57 enlisted men)
	Yacona 72 (7 officers, 65 enlisted men)

Large, steel-hulled tugs transferred from the Navy to the Coast Guard after World War II. Both by Basalt Rock Co, Napa, California. *Acushnet* modified for oceanographic research and reclassified WAGO in 1969; *Yocona* reclassified as WMEC in 1969. Armament removed.

Oceangoing Tugs—*continued*

YOCONA (WMEC 168)   1966, US Coast Guard

3 MEDIUM ENDURANCE CUTTERS (WMEC): ATF TYPE

Name	No.	Launched	Navy Comm.
CHILULA	WMEC 153 (ex-WAT 153, ATF 153)	1 Dec 1944	5 Apr 1945
CHEROKEE	WMEC 165 (ex-WAT 165, ATF 66)	10 Nov 1939	26 Apr 1940
TAMOROA (ex-*Zuni*)	WMEC 166 (ex-WAT 166, ATF 95)	13 July 1943	9 Oct 1943

Displacement, tons	1 731 full load
Dimensions, feet	205 oa × 38·5 × 17
Guns	1—3 inch 50 calibre; 2—·50 cal MG
Main engines	Diesel electric (General Motors diesel); 1 shaft; 3 000 hp = 16·2 knots
Complement	72 (7 officers, 65 enlisted men)

Steel-hulled tugs transferred from the Navy to the Coast Guard after World War II; *Chilula* officially on loan since 9 July 1956 until stricken from the Navy List on 1 June 1969. Classification of all three ships changed to WMEC in 1969. *Chilula* built by Charleston Shipbuilding & Dry Dock Co, Charleston, South Carolina; *Cherokee* built by Bethlehem Steel Co, Staten Island, New York; *Tamaroa* built by Commercial Iron Works, Portland, Oregon.
Avoyel (WMEC 150, ex-WAT 150, ex-ATF 150) stricken in 1970.

AVOYEL (WMEC 150)—now stricken   1964, United States Coast Guard

2 MEDIUM ENDURANCE CUTTERS (WMEC): ATA TYPE

Name	No.	Launched	Navy Comm.
MODOC (ex-*Bagaduce*)	WMEC 194 (ex-WATA 194, ATA 194)	4 Dec 1944	14 Feb 1945
COMANCHE (ex-*Wampanoag*)	WMEC 202 (ex-WATA 202, ATA 202)	10 Oct 1944	8 Dec 1944

Displacement, tons	534 standard; 860 full load
Dimensions, feet	143 oa × 33·8 × 14
Armament	2—·50 cal MG
Main engines	Diesel electric (General Motors diesel); 1 shaft; 1 500 hp = 13·5 knots
Complement	47 (5 officers, 42 enlisted men)

Steel-hulled tugs. The *Modoc* was stricken from the Navy List after World War II and transferred to Maritime Administration; transferred to Coast Guard on 15 Apr 1959. *Comanche* transferred on loan from Navy to Coast Guard from 25 Feb 1959 until stricken from Navy List on 1 June 1969. Both ships reclassified as WMEC in 1969.
Modoc built by Levingston Shipbuilding Co, Orange, Texas; *Comanche* built by Gulfport Boiler & Welding Works, Port Arthur, Texas.

MODOC (WMEC 194)   1956, United States Coast Guard

HARBOUR TUGS

MANITOU	WYTM 60	**NAUGATUCK**	WYTM 92
KAW	WYTM 61	**RARITAN**	WYTM 93
APALACHEE	WYTM 71	**CHINOOK**	WYTM 96
YANKTON	WYTM 72	**OJIBWA**	WYTM 97
MOHICAN	WYTM 73	**SNOHOMISH**	WYTM 98
ARUNDEL	WYTM 90	**SAUK**	WYTM 99
MAMONING	WYTM 91		

Displacement, tons	370 full load
Dimensions, feet	110 oa × 27 × 11
Main engines	Diesel-electric; 1 shaft; 1 000 hp = 11·2 knots
Complement	20 (1 officer, 19 enlisted men)

Built in 1943 except WYTM 90-93 built in 1939.

MESSENGER WYTM 85009

Displacement, tons	230 full load
Dimensions, feet	85 oa × 23 × 9
Main engines	Diesel; 1 shaft; 700 hp = 9·5 knots
Complement	10 (enlisted)

Built in 1944.

CAPSTAN	WYTL 65601	**CATENARY**	WYTL 65606	**LINE**	WYTL 65611
CHOCK	WYTL 65602	**BRIDLE**	WYTL 65607	**WIRE**	WYTL 65612
SWIVEL	WYTL 65603	**PENDANT**	WYTL 65608	**BITT**	WYTL 65613
TACKLE	WYTL 65604	**SHACKLE**	WYTL 65609	**BOLLARD**	WYTL 65614
TOWLINE	WYTL 65605	**HAWSER**	WYTL 65610	**CLEAT**	WYTL 65615

Displacement, tons	72 full load
Dimensions, feet	65 oa × 19 × 7
Main engines	Diesel; 1 shaft; 400 hp = 9·8 knots except WYTL 65601-65606 10·5 knots
Complement	10 (enlisted men)

Built from 1961 to 1967.

YANKTON   1969, US Coast Guard

MESSENGER   1969, US Coast Guard

PENDANT   1968, US Coast Guard

NATIONAL OCEAN SURVEY

(National Oceanic and Atmospheric Administration)

Command

Director, National Ocean Survey: Rear Admiral Don A. Jones

Director, Atlantic Marine Center: Rear Admiral Allen L. Powell

Director, Pacific Marine Center: Rear Admiral Norman E. Taylor

Missions

The National Ocean Survey, formerly the Coast and Geodetic Survey, prepares nautical and aeronautical charts; conducts geodetic, oceanographic, and marine surveys; monitors the earth's geophysical fields and seismic activity; predicts tides and currents; and issues tsunami (destructive, long-length ocean wave action) warnings in the Pacific. The National Ocean Survey is a civilian agency that supports national civilian and military survey requirements. During time of war the ships and officers of the National Ocean Survey are subject to military service.

Establishment

The "Survey of the Coast" was established by an act of Congress on Feb 10, 1807. Renamed US Coast Survey in 1834 and again renamed Coast and Geodetic Survey in 1878. The commissioned officer corps was established in 1917. The Coast and Geodetic Survey was made a component of the Environmental Science Services Administration on July 13, 1965, when that agency was established within the Department of

Commerce. The Environmental Science Services Administration subsequently became the National Oceanic and Atmospheric Administration in October 1970 with the Coast and Geodetic Survey being renamed National Ocean Survey and its jurisdiction expanded to include the US Lake Survey, formerly a part of the US Army Corps of Engineers.

President Nixon in January 1971 proposed a far-reaching government agency reorganization that would place the National Oceanic and Atmospheric Administration in a new Department of Natural Resources that would take on certain functions of the Department of Commerce as well as other government departments.

Ships

National Ocean Survey ship designations are: OSS for Ocean Survey Ship, MSS for Medium Survey Ship, CSS for Coastal Survey Ship, and ASV for Auxiliary Survey Vessel. No National Ocean Survey Ships are armed.

Personnel

1971: 241 commissioned officers and approx 2 400 civil service personnel.

Aviation

The National Ocean Survey's Photogrammetry Division operates two aircraft for aerial photographic missions, a twin-engine de Havilland Canada Buffalo and a twin-engine North American Rockwell Aero Commander.

SURVEY SHIPS

1 OCEANOGRAPIC SURVEY SHIP (OSS): "RESEARCHER" TYPE

Name	No.	Launched	Commissioned
RESEARCHER	OSS 03	5 Oct 1968	8 Oct 1970

Displacement, tons	2 875 light
Dimensions, feet	278·25 oa × 51 × 16·25 (*84·7 m × 15·5 m × 4·9 m*)
Main engines	2 geared diesels; 3 200 hp; 2 shafts = 16 knots
Complement	13 officers, 54 enlisted men
Scientists	10 to 13

The *Researcher* was designed specifically for deep ocean research; she is ice strengthened. Estimated cost $10 000 000. Fitted with 20-ton capacity crane, 5-ton capacity crane, four 2½-ton capacity cranes, and an A-frame with 10-ton lift capacity. Built by American Shipbuilding Co, Lorain, Ohio.

DESIGN. Fitted with computerised data acquisition system that automatically samples, processes, and records oceanographic, geophysical, hydrographic, and meteorological data. The 20-ton telescoping crane is designed to handle special sampling equipment and small submersible vehicles as well as small boats. S2-MT-MA74a type.

ENGINEERING. Controllable pitch propellers. A 450-horsepower, 360-degree retractable bow thruster provides sustained low speeds up to seven knots and permits precise positioning. Cruising speed is 14·5 knots with an endurance of 13 000 nautical miles.

2 OCEANOGRAPHIC SURVEY SHIPS (OSS): "OCEANOGRAPHER" CLASS

Name	No.	Launched	Commissioned
OCEANOGRAPHER	OSS 01	18 Apr 1964	13 July 1966
DISCOVERER	OSS 02	29 Oct 1964	29 Apr 1967

Displacement, tons	3 959 light
Dimensions, feet	303·3 oa × 52 × 18·5 (*92·4 m × 15·8 m × 5·6 m*)
Main engines	4 diesels with electric drive; 5 000 hp; 2 shafts = 16+ knots
Complement	13 officers, 80 enlisted men
Scientists	20 to 22

Ice strengthened construction. Fitted with a 5-ton capacity crane and a 3½-ton capacity crane. Built by Aerojet-General Corp, Jacksonville Shipyard, Jacksonville, Florida.

DESIGN. Fitted with computerised data acquisition system. Center well 8 × 6 feet provides sheltered access to sea for SCUBA divers and for lowering research equipment Six ports in submerged bow observation chamber. S2-MET-MA62a type.

ENGINEERING. A 400-horsepower, through-hull bow thruster provides precise manoeuvering. Not equipped for silent operation. Cruising speed is 16 knots with an endurance of 15 200 nautical miles.

RESEARCHER (OSS 03)   *National Ocean Survey*

OCEANOGRAPHER (OSS 01)   *National Ocean Survey*

DISCOVERER (OSS 02)   *National Ocean Survey*

Survey Ships—continued

DISCOVERER (OSS 02)　　　　　　　*National Ocean Survey*

RAINIER (MSS 21)　　　　　　　*National Ocean Survey*

1 HYDROGRAPHIC SURVEY SHIP (OSS):

"SURVEYOR" TYPE

Name	No.	Launched	Commissioned
SURVEYOR	OSS 32	25 Apr 1959	30 Apr 1960

Displacement, tons	3 150 light
Dimensions, feet	292·3 oa × 46 × 18 (88·8 m × 14·0 m × 5·5 m)
Main engines	1 steam turbine (De Laval); 3 520 hp; 1 shaft = 15+ knots
Complement	14 officers, 76 enlisted men
Scientists	8

Specially designed for marine charting and geophysical surveys. Fitted with helicopter platform aft. Ice strengthened. Twin telescoping 2½-ton capacity cargo booms (forward) and 12½-ton capacity crane. Estimated cost $6 000 000. Built by National Steel & SB Co, San Diego, California.

DESIGN. Large bilge keel (18 inches × 70 feet) permits oceanographic observations to be performed up to Sea State 6. S2-S-RM28a type.

ENGINEERING. Retractable outboard motor mounted to stern for precision manoeuvering. Cruising speed is 15 knots with an endurance of 10 500 nautical miles.

FAIRWEATHER (MSS 20)　　　　　　　*National Ocean Survey*

1 HYDROGRAPHIC SURVEY SHIP (OSS 30):

"PATHFINDER" TYPE

Name	No.
PATHFINDER	OSS 30

Displacement, tons	2 000 light
Dimensions, feet	229·3 oa × 39 × 15·5 (66·5 m × 11·9 m × 4·7 m)
Main engines	1 steam turbine; 2 000 ihp; 1 shaft = 14·5 knots
Complement	14 officers, 69 enlisted men
Scientists	4

Specially designed for marine charting. Completed in 1942 and operated for Navy as AGS 1 until 1946 when returned to Coast & Geodetic Survey.

ENGINEERING. Diesel-driven generators provide alternating current. Cruising speed is 12·4 knots with an endurance of 4 250 nautical miles.

SURVEYOR (OSS 32)　　　　　　　*National Ocean Survey*

PATHFINDER (OSS 30)　　　　　　　*National Ocean Survey*

3 HYDROGRAPHIC SURVEY SHIPS (MSS):

"FAIRWEATHER" CLASS

Name	No.	Launched	Commissioned
FAIRWEATHER	MSS 20	15 Mar 1967	2 Oct 1968
RAINIER	MSS 21	15 Mar 1967	2 Oct 1968
MT. MITCHELL	MSS 22	29 Nov 1966	23 Mar 1968

Displacement, tons	1 798 light
Dimensions, feet	231 oa × 42·07 × 13·9 (70·2 m × 12·8 m × 4·2 m)
Main engines	2 diesels; 2 400 hp; 2 shafts = 13+ knots
Complement	12 officers, 62 enlisted men
Scientists	

Ice strengthened. Built by Aerojet-General Corp, Jacksonville Shipyard, Jacksonville, Fla. SI-MT-MA72a type.

ENGINEERING. Fitted with a 200-horsepower, through-bow thruster for precise manoeuvering. Controllable-pitch propellers. Cruising speed is 13 knots with an endurance of 9 000 nautical miles.

2 HYDROGRAPHIC SURVEY SHIPS (CSS):

"McARTHUR" CLASS

Name	No.	Launched	Commissioned
McARTHUR	CSS 30	15 Nov 1965	15 Dec 1966
DAVIDSON	CSS 31	7 May 1966	10 Mar 1967

Displacement, tons	995 light
Dimensions, feet	175 oa × 38 × 11·5 (53·0 m × 11·5 m × 3·5 m)
Main engines	2 diesel; 1 600 hp; 2 shafts = 13·5+ knots
Complement	6 officers, 30 enlisted men
Scientists	

Survey Ships—continued

"McArthur" Class—continued

Designed for nearshore operations. Ice strengthened. Built by Norfolk SB & DD Co, Norfolk, Virginia. SI-MT-MA70a type.

ENGINEERING. Controllable-pitch propellers. Cruising speed is 13·5 knots with an endurance of 4 500 nautical miles.

McARTHUR (CSS 30)   *National Ocean Survey*

2 HYDROGRAPHIC SURVEY SHIPS (CSS): "PIERCE" CLASS

Name	No.	Launched	Commissioned
PIERCE	CSS 28	15 Oct 1962	6 May 1963
WHITING	CSS 29	20 Nov 1962	8 July 1963

Displacement, tons	760 light
Dimensions, feet	164 oa × 33 × 10·1 (*50·0 m × 10·0 m × 3·1 m*)
Main engines	2 diesels; 1 600 hp; 2 shafts = 12·5+knots
Complement	6 officers, 30 enlisted men
Scientists	

Designed for nearshore operations. Ice strengthened. Built by Marietta Manufacturing Co, Point Pleasant, West Virginia. SI-MT-59a type.

ENGINEERING. Controllable-pitch propellers. Cruising speed is 12·5 knots with an endurance of 4 500 nautical miles.

PIERCE (CSS 28)   *National Ocean Survey*

WHITING (CSS 29)   *National Ocean Survey*

WIRE DRAG VESSELS

2 WIRE DRAG VESSELS (ASV); "RUDE" CLASS

Name	No.	Launched	Commissioned
RUDE	ASV 90	17 Aug 1966	29 Mar 1967
HECK	ASV 91	1 Nov 1966	29 Mar 1967

Displacement, tons	214 light
Dimensions, feet	90 oa × 22 × 7 (*27·4 m × 6·7 m × 2·1 m*)
Main engines	2 diesels; 800 hp; 2 shafts = 11·5+ knots
Complement	2 officers, 9 enlisted men

Designed to search out underwater navigational hazards along the coast using wire drags. Built by Jacobson Shipyard Inc, Oyster Bay, New York. SI-MT-MA71a type.

ENGINEERING. Propellers are guarded by shrouds similar to Kort nozzles. Auxiliary propulsion provides 50 horsepower to each propeller for dragging operations. Cruising speed is 11·5 knots with an endurance of 740 nautical miles (provisions carried for eight days.)

RUDE (ASV 90)   *National Ocean Survey*

1 CURRENT SURVEY VESSEL (ASV); "FERREL" TYPE

Name	No.	Launched	Commissioned
FERREL	ASV 92	4 Apr 1968	4 June 1958

Displacement, tons	363 light
Dimensions, feet	133·25 × 32 × 7 (*40·5 m × 9·7 m × 2·1 m*)
Main engines	2 diesels; 820 hp; 2 shafts = 10+ knots
Complement	3 officers, 13 enlisted men

Specially designed to conduct nearshore and estuarine current surveys. Limited surface meteorological observations also are made. Buoy workshop provided in 450-square feet of enclosed deck area with buoy stowage on open after deck. Built by Zeigler Shipyard, Jennings, Louisiana. SI-MT-MA83a type.

ENGINEERING. Fitted with 100-horsepower, electric-driven bow thruster. Cruising speed is 10 knots (provisions for 15 days carried).

FERREL (ASV 92)   *National Ocean Survey*

FERREL (ASV 92)   *National Ocean Survey*

UNION OF SOVIET SOCIALIST REPUBLICS

Administration

Commander-in-Chief of the Navy and First Deputy Minister of Defence:
  Admiral of the Fleet of the Soviet Union
  Sergei Georgiyevich Gorshkov

First Deputy Commander-in-Chief of Navy:
  Admiral of the Fleet Vladimir Afanasevich Kasatonov

Strength of the Fleet

  83 Nuclear Powered Submarines
318 Conventionally Powered Submarines
   2 Cruiser Helicopter Carriers
  26 Cruisers, including missile ships
100 Destroyers, including missile ships
130 Escorts, small frigate type
270 Coastal Escorts, patrol vessels
320 Minesweepers
125 Missile Patrol Boats
325 Torpedo Boats
125 Amphibious Ships
  75 Amphibious Craft excluding LCMs

Support ships, auxiliaries and service craft run into thousands.

Diplomatic Representation

Naval Attaché in London:
  Rear-Admiral Boris D. Yashin

Naval Attaché in Washington:
  Captain Vladimir N. Vashenko

Nomenclature

Helicopter Cruisers after capital cities
Cruisers after statesmen, admirals or heroes
Destroyers after adjectives and ports
Escorts after birds and winds
Minesweepers after weapons and equipment
Survey Ships after astronomical terms and explorers
Depot Ships after naval personalities and rivers
Icebreakers after statesmen and Arctic explorers

The hull or side numerals of warships change periodically, although apparently the pennant numbers of auxiliaries may not change.

State

Most ships are of recent construction. Most modern ships not being refitted are fully manned and operational, but some of the older ships are in reserve. Cruisers, destroyers, submarines and many smaller craft are fitted for minelaying and for launching missiles.

Appearance

Combatant Ships: Painted light grey all over
Auxiliaries: Painted somewhat darker grey
Surveying Ships: Black hulls with red waterlines, yellow funnels with black tops.

Personnel

1971: 500 000 (50 000 officers and cadets, 450 000 ratings)

Mercantile Marine

Lloyd's Register of Shipping:
5 924 vessels of 14 831 775 tons gross

Helicopter Carriers

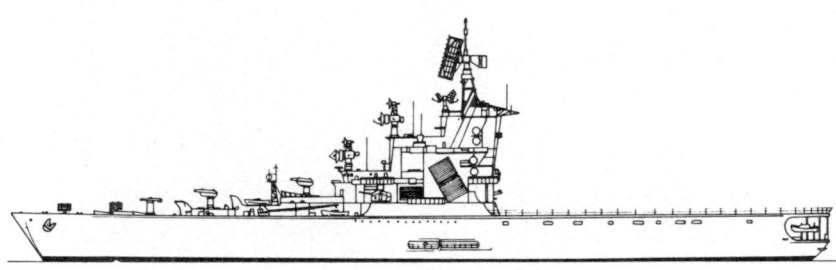

MOSKVA *Class.* Port side   Scale: 150 feet = 1 inch (1 : 1 800)

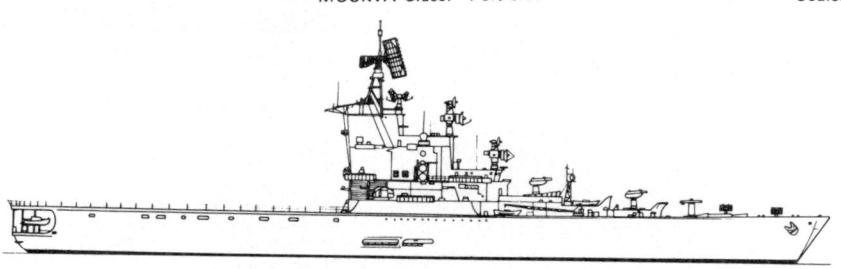

MOSKVA *Class.* Starboard side

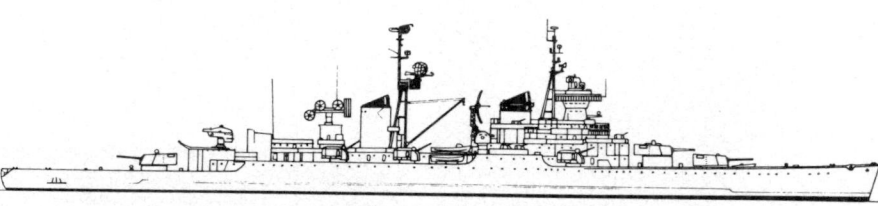

DZERZHINSKI. Twin missile launcher in place of "X" turret   **Cruisers**

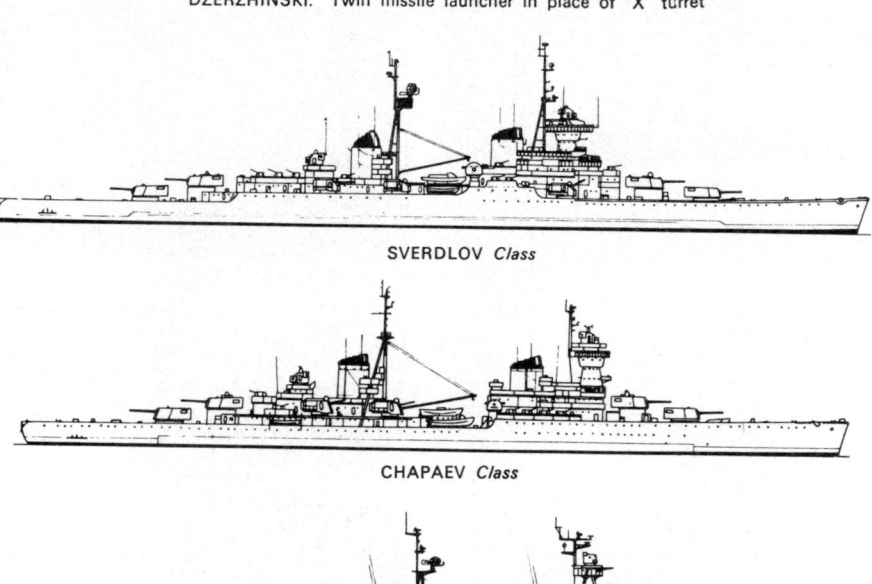

SVERDLOV *Class*

CHAPAEV *Class*

KIROV *Class*

Missile Cruisers, Destroyers

Scale: 150 feet = 1 inch (1 : 1 800)

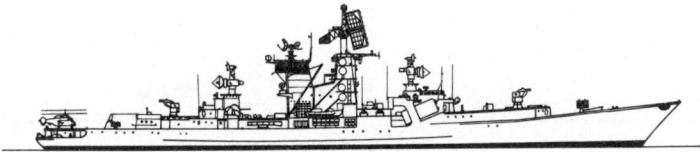

KRESTA II *Class*

KRESTA I *Class*

KOTLIN HELO *Class*

KYNDA *Class*

KOTLIN *Class*

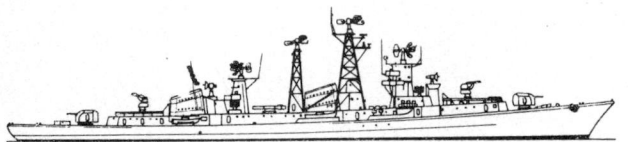

KASHIN *Class*

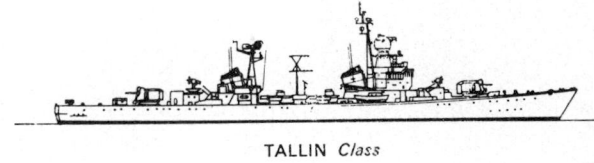

TALLIN *Class*

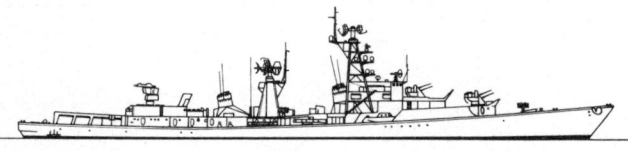

KANIN *Class*

SKORY Modified *Class*

KRUPNY *Class*

SKORY Original *Class*

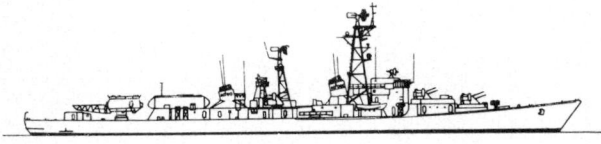

KILDIN *Class*

UGRA *Class*

KOTLIN SAM II *Class*

DON HELO *Class*

KOTLIN SAM I *Class*

DON *Class*

Nuclear, Missile, Submarines

Escorts, Minesweepers

Scale: 150 feet = 1 inch (1 : 1 800)

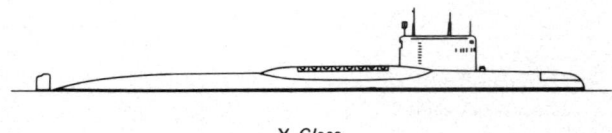

Y *Class*

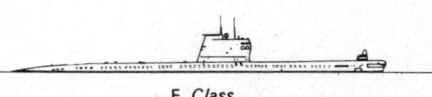

Z V *Class*

C *Class*

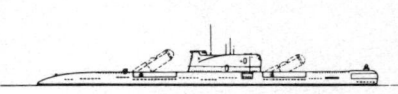

F *Class*

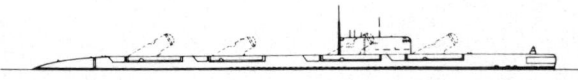

E II *Class*

J *Class*

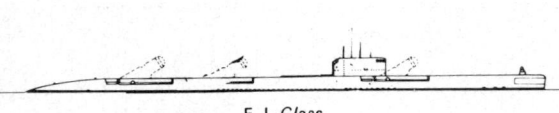

E I *Class*

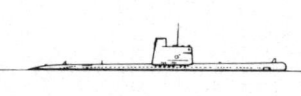

Q *Class*

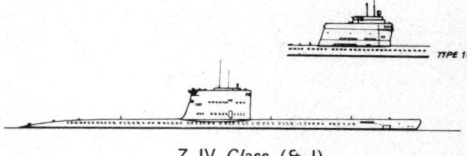

Z IV *Class* (& I)

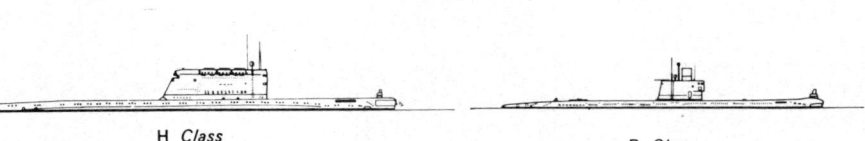

H *Class*

R *Class*

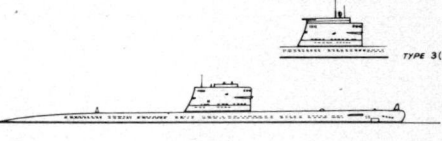

Z II *Class* (& III)

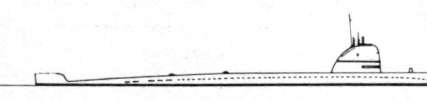

N *Class*

W *Class* Long Bin

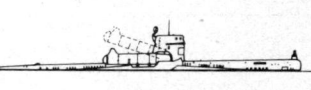

W *Class* Twin Cylinder

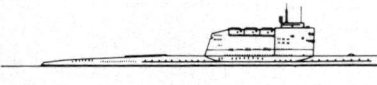

G *Class*

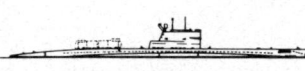

W *Class* One cylinder

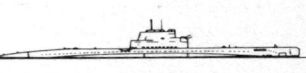

W *Class*

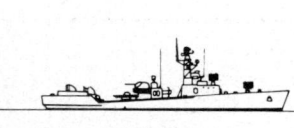

POTI *Class*

PURGA *Class*

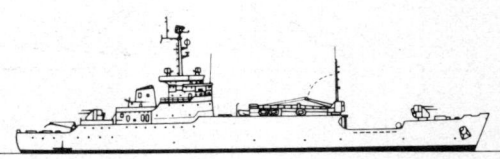

LAMA *Class*

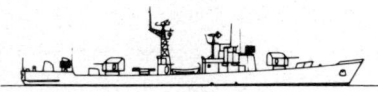

MIRKA *Class*

RIGA *Class*

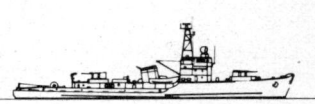

T 58 *Class*

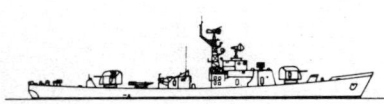

PETYA *Class*

KOLA *Class*

T 43 *Class* (& Radar Picket)

SOVIET NAVAL AVIATION

The Soviet Navy operates some 1 000 fixed-wing aircraft and helicopters in the *Morskaya Aviatsiya*, the world's second largest naval air arm. The primary combat components are (1) medium bombers employed in the anti-shipping and reconnaissance roles, (2) anti-submarine helicopters, and (3) anti-submarine/reconnaissance flying boats. The large number of land-based, turbojet fighter aircraft formerly operated by the Navy were transferred to the air defence organisation of the Soviet Air Force in the 1960's.

The Soviet Navy flies no fixed-wing aircraft from ships, but several destroyers and cruisers, and the cruiser-helicopter ships *Moskva* and *Leningrad* can carry helicopters. The two helicopter ships are the largest built to date by any navy specifically for anti-submarine operations and are the first Soviet warships intended primarily for aviation activities. (A third ship of this type or possibly of an improved design is believed to be under construction according to some reports).

●*Medium bombers.* The Soviet naval air arm has at least 375 medium bombers serving in the anti-shipping and reconnaissance roles. Most of the estimated 300 turbojet Tu-16 Badgers and a smaller number of turbojet Tu-22 Blinders are designed to carry air-to-surface missiles, the "Kipper", "Kitchen" and "Kelt" (A few turboprop Tu-20 Bear bombers remain in Soviet Air Force service as attack bombers carrying the "Kangaroo" air-to-surface missile). Most of the 50 or more Bears remaining in naval service are electronic-laden Tu-20D variant used for long-range maritime reconnaissance.

●*Helicopters.* Over 100 anti-submarine helicopters are believed to be in the naval air arm, mostly Ka-25 Hormones (a twin-turbine craft known as the Harp in the prototype stage) and some of the older Mi-4 Hound helicopters. Anti-submarine helicopters, armed with torpedoes and other weapons, can operate from a number of cruisers and destroyers with a landing area or platform aft. The "Kresta" class cruisers are the first Soviet ships in these categories to have a helicopter hangar; the larger cruiser-helicopter ships *Moskva* and *Leningrad* can each operate some 15 to 20 helicopters, servicing them on a hangar deck below their flight deck, the two decks being connected by two lifts in each ship.

●*Flying Boats.* The Soviet Union is the only nation other than Japan maintaining modern military flying boats, 50 or more Be-6 Madge (piston) and Be-12 Mail (turboprop) aircraft of this type being operational. The latter aircraft, an amphibian often photographed on runways, has an advanced anti-submarine capability evidenced by a radome extending forward, a Magnetic Anomaly Detector (MAD) boom extending aft and a weapons bay in the rear fuselage. The "pure-jet" Be-10 Mallow flying boat, with a minimum military capability, has not been produced in large numbers nor has it entered fleet service.

There also are a few hundred transports, utility, and training fixed-wing aircraft and helicopters under Navy control. A few Il-18 May patrol/anti-submarine aircraft have been sighted, but apparently large numbers of this aircraft are not being procured.

The May is a militarised version of the four-turboprop commercial air freighter (code name Coot) in wide commercial service. The patrol/anti-submarine version has been lengthened and fitted with a MAD boom as well as other electronic equipment and a weapons capability similar to the US Navy's conversion of the Lockheed Electra into the P-3 Orion patrol aircraft.

*Aircraft names are NATO code names; "B" names indicate bombers, "H" names for helicopters, and "M" names for maritime reconnaissance aircraft.

SOVIET NAVAL MISSILES

Category	Designation *	Launch Platform (tubes/launchers)	Range (n. miles)	Length** feet (metres)	Notes
STRATEGIC MISSILES (ballistic missiles)	SS-N-4 SARK	G-I class submarines (3) H-I class submarines (3)	350	35·1 (10·7)	Surface launch; most H-I modified to H-II design
	SS-N-5 SERB	G-II class submarines (3) H-II class submarine (3)	650	35·1 (10·7)	Underwater launch
probably identical {	SS-N-6	"Yankee" class submarines (16)	1 300-1 500	35·1 (10·7)	Underwater launch; two stages
	SS-N-SAWFLY	new submarine class or conversion	1 500	42·7 (13·0)	Underwater launch; two stages
SURFACE-TO-SURFACE MISSILES (cruise missiles)	SS-N-1 SCRUBBER	cruiser *Admiral Nakhimov* (1) (?) "Kilden" class destroyers (1) "Krupny" class destroyers (2)	130	24·9 (7·6)	Subsonic missile; *Admiral Nakhimov* is experimental ship
	SS-N-2 STYX	"Komar" missile boats (2) "Osa" missile boats (4) "Nanuchka" missile corvettes (4-6?)	25	21·3 (6·5)	Transonic missile; sank Israeli destroyer *Elath*; used by Cuba, Algeria, East Germany, Egypt, Indonesia, Syria, Poland, Rumania, Yugoslavia
	SS-N-3 SHADDOCK	"Kynda" class cruisers (8) "Kresta" class cruisers (4) J class submarines (4) E-I class submarines (6) E-II class submarines (8)	450	35·8 (10·9)	Supersonic missile; mid-course guidance required if fired at extreme range; also land launched
	SS-N	C class submarines (8)	26		Possibly underwater launch
SURFACE-TO-AIR MISSILES	SA-N-1 GOA	"Kotlin" class SAM destroyers (1 twin launcher) "Kanin" class destroyers (1 twin) "Kashin" class destroyers (2 twin) "Kynda" class cruisers (1 twin) "Kresta" class cruisers (2 twin)	15	19·3 (5·9)	Also land launched
	SA-N-2 GUIDELINE	cruiser *Dzerzhinski* (1 twin)	25	34·8 (10·6)	Also land launched
	SA-N-3	"Moskva" class cruiser-helicopter carriers (2 twin)			
AIR-TO-SURFACE MISSILES	AS-1 KENNEL	Badger-B bomber	55	26·9 (8·2)	No longer in first-line Soviet squadrons; used by Egypt, Indonesia; subsonic missile
	AS-2 KIPPER	Badger-C bomber	115	32·8 (10·0)	Supersonic missile
	AS-3 KANGAROO	Bear-B bomber	350	48·9 (14·9)	Supersonic missile; used only by Soviet long-range Air Force.
	AS-4 KITCHEN	Blinder-B bomber	400	37·1 (11·3)	Ballistic trajectory; low anti-ship threat
	AS-5 KELT	Badger-B bomber			

*These are NATO designations; "S" names indicate surface-to-surface, "G" names for surface-to-air, and "K" names for air-to-surface.

**Lengths are approximate and include boosters for multi-stage missiles.

NUCLEAR POWERED SUBMARINES

"Y" Class   *1971, S. Breyer*

"E II" Class   *1971*

"C" Class   *1971*

Nuclear Powered Submarines—*continued*

"N" Class (nuclear powered)

1970, MOD, Official

BALLISTIC MISSILE TYPES

18 "Y" CLASS

Displacement, tons	8 000 surface; 9 000 submerged
Length, feet (*metres*)	426·5 (*130·0*)
Beam, feet (*metres*)	34·8 (*10·6*)
Draught, feet (*metres*)	32·8 (*10·0*)
Missile launchers	16 "Sawfly" tubes
Torpedo tubes	8—21 in
Main engines	Nuclear reactors; steam turbines; 24 000 shp
Speed, knots	22

The first units of this class were reported in 1969. The vertical launching tubes are arranged in two rows of eight, and the missiles have a range of 1 500 nautical miles. 15 more submarines are in various stages of construction.

9 "H II" CLASS

Displacement, tons	3 700 surface; 4 100 submerged
Length, feet (*metres*)	344·5 (*105·0*)
Beam, feet (*metres*)	33 (*10·05*)
Draught, feet (*metres*)	25 (*7·6*)
Missile launchers	3 "Sark" or "Serb" tubes
Torpedo tubes	6—21 in (bow); 4—16 in (aft) A/S
Main engines	Nuclear reactors, steam turbines; 22 500 shp
Speed, knots	20
Complement	90

Long range submarines with three vertical ballistic missile tubes in the large "sail", or conning tower. The earlier vessels of the "H 1" class had SS-N-4 missiles with a range of 350 nautical miles, but later units known as the "H II" class have SS-N-5 ballistic missiles with a range of 650 miles.

CRUISE MISSILE TYPES

5 "C" CLASS

Displacement, tons	4 000 surface; 5 000 submerged
Length, feet (*metres*)	385·9 (*117·0*)
Beam, feet (*metres*)	32·8 (*10·0*)
Draught, feet (*metres*)	24·6 (*7·5*)
Missile launchers	8 tubes for new SSM
Torpedo tubes	8—21 in
Main engines	Nuclear reactors; steam turbines; 24 000 shp
Speed, knots	30 approx, submerged
Complement	100

Streamlined submarines designed for high speed. First reported extant in 1969. Developed from the "E" class. Large bulbous bow. Short range missile system of eight topside tubes, four to port and four to starboard.

27 "E II" CLASS

Displacement, tons	5 000 surface; 5 600 submerged
Length, feet (*metres*)	393·7 (*120·0*)
Beam, feet (*metres*)	33 (*10·05*)
Draught, feet (*metres*)	27 (*8·3*)
Missiles, launchers	8 "Shaddock" launching tubes
Torpedo tubes	6—21 in (bow); 4—16 in (aft) A/S
Main engines	Nuclear reactors, steam turbines; 22 500 shp
Speed, knots	20 max; 12 to 14 cruising
Complement	100

Built from 1963-64 onwards. The design of the "E II" sub-group was a development of that of the "E I" sub-group lengthened to accommodate two more missile launchers, arranged four on each side.

4 "E I" CLASS

Displacement, tons	4 600 surface; 5 000 submerged
Length, feet (*metres*)	383·9 (*117·0*)
Beam, feet (*metres*)	33 (*10·05*)
Draught, feet (*metres*)	27 (*8·3*)
Missile launchers	6 "Shaddock" launching tubes
Torpedo tubes	6—21 in (bow); 4—16 in (aft) A/S
Main engines	Nuclear reactors, steam turbines; 22 500 shp
Speed, knots	20 max; 12 cruising
Complement	92 (12 officers, 80 men)

Built from 1961-62 onwards. Long range submarines, with six cruise missiles in launching tubes elevated from the flush deck and arranged two abreast. "E" class submarines in the Pacific were built at Komsomolsk. May be under conversion for the removal of missiles.

"N" Class

1970, MOD, Official

"E II" Class (cruise missiles)

1970

"N" Class

1968, S. Breyer

Nuclear Powered Submarines—*continued*

1971, S. Breyer

"C" Class

"C" Class   *1971*

"N" Class

Nuclear Powered Submarines—*continued*

"N" Class Nuclear Powered Type

USSR

ANTI-SUBMARINE TYPES

7 "V" CLASS

Displacement, tons	3 600 surface; 4 200 submerged
Length, feet (*metres*)	285·4 (*87·0*)
Beam, feet (*metres*)	32·8 (*10·0*)
Draught, feet (*metres*)	26·2 (*8·0*)
Torpedo tubes	8—21 in
Main engines	Nuclear reactors; steam turbines; 24 000 shp
Speed, knots	26 surface; 30 plus submerged

Nuclear powered but otherwise of conventional submarine propensities. First reported in 1969.

13 "N" CLASS

Displacement, tons	3 500 surface; 4 000 submerged
Length, feet (*metres*)	360·9 (*110·0*)
Beam, feet (*metres*)	32·1 (*9·8*)
Draught, feet (*metres*)	24·3 (*7·4*)
Torpedo tubes	6—21 in (bow); 4—16 in (aft) A/S
Main engines	Nuclear reactors, steam turbines; 22 500 shp
Speed, knots	20 surface; 25 submerged
Complement	88

Fleet submarines designed as submarine hunter-killers. The "N" class programme was started in 1958 and completed in 1965 including *Leninsky Komsomol* and *Celjabinsky Komsomol.*

STATE. There are about 400 effective submarines, of which almost half are medium range units and the remainder large oceangoing types.
It is official policy to maintain a four-theatre submarine fleet for operations in the Atlantic, Pacific, Baltic and Black Sea. Some submarines are armed with long range surface missiles with nuclear and hydrogen warheads.

NEW CONSTRUCTION. 28 to 30 submarines are being built in Soviet dockyards. These are of several different types including a nuclear powered class and a missile class.

SONAR AND RADAR. Some submarines have fo'c'sle mounted sonar arrays, others large multi-element sonar arrays in a "forehead" position. Most submarines probably have X band navigation radar with antennae mounted on retractable masts, also passive radar detection equipment.

"N" Class

1970

LENINSKY KOMSOMOL, "N" Class

1967

"Long Bin" (appearance like "N" class at distance, see photo top of previous page)

1970, S. Breyer

MISSILE SUBMARINES

"J" Class   S. Breyer

16 "J" CLASS
CRUISE MISSILE TYPE

Displacement, tons	2 200 surface; 2 500 submerged
Length, feet (metres)	328·0 (100·0)
Beam, feet (metres)	27·2 (8·3)
Draught, feet (metres)	20·0 (6·1)
Missile launchers	4 "Shaddock" tubes; 2 before and 2 abaft the tower
Torpedo tubes	6—21 in (bow); 2 or 4—16 in (aft) for A/S
Main engines	Diesels; 6 000 bhp
	Electric motors; 6 000 hp
Speed, knots	16 surface; 16 submerged.

Medium sized long range submarines with an extended but low sail or conning tower and superstructure fin and high surface freeboard. The prototype was launched in 1962.

22 "G" CLASS
BALLISTIC MISSILE TYPE

Displacement, tons	2 350 surface; 2 800 submerged
Length, feet (metres)	320·0 (97·5)
Beam, feet (metres)	28·2 (8·6)
Draught, feet (metres)	22·0 (6·7)
Missile launchers	3 SS-N-4 (G1); 2 or 3 SS-N-5 (G 2); 3 SS-N-5 (G 3)
Torpedo tubes	10—21 in (bow)
Main engines	3 diesels; 3 shafts; 6 000 hp; Electric motors; 6 000 hp
Speed, knots	17·6 surface; 17 submerged
Radius, miles	22 700 surface cruising
Complement	86 (12 officers, 74 men)

This type has a very large conning tower fitted with three vertically mounted tubes and hatches for launching ballistic missiles. Built at Komsomolsk and Severodvinsk. Building started in 1958 and finished in 1963-65.

"G 1" Class

"G 1" Class Missile Type (side opening hatches open)

"G 1" Class Missile Type

Submarines—*continued*

"Z V" Class

Missile Submarines—*continued*

4 Z "V" CLASS
BALLISTIC MISSILE TYPE

Displacement, tons	2 100 surface; 2 600 submerged
Length, feet (*metres*)	295·3 (*90·0*)
Beam, feet (*metres*)	28·9 (*8·8*)
Draught, feet (*metres*)	19·0 (*5·8*)
Missile launchers	2 tubes for SS-N-4 missiles
Torpedo tubes	10—21 in
Main engines	3 diesels; 3 shafts; 10 000 bhp; 3 electric motors; 3 500 hp
Speed, knots	18 surface; 15 submerged
Complement	85

These were basically of "Z" class design but converted to ballistic missile submarines with larger conning towers and two vertical tubes for missile launching. All boats were converted by 1956-58.

REVERSION. These vessels are possibly being converted back to standard submarines. It is reported that two units have been rebuilt to oceanographic research submarines with the new names *Lyra* and *Vega*.

Z "V" Class

"Z IV" Class

1969, MOD, Official

"Z IV" Class

Submarines—continued

"G" Class   1971

"W" Class Twin Cylinder Type   1971, Col. Borg

"F" Class   1971

Submarines—*continued*

"W" Class "Long Bin" Guided Missile Type

1970, Niels Gartig

"W" CLASS

GUIDED MISSILE GROUP

6 "LONG BIN" TYPE

Displacement, tons	1 300 surface; 1 800 submerged
Length, feet (*metres*)	272·3 (*83·0*)
Beam, feet (*metres*)	24·3 (*7·4*)
Draught, feet (*metres*)	15·7 (*4·8*)
Missile launchers	4 "Shaddock" tubes
Torpedo tubes	4—21 in
Main engines	Diesels; 4 000 bhp;
	Electric motors; 2 500 hp
Speed, knots	17 surface; 15 submerged

Rebuilt in 1959-63. Basically of conventional "W" class submarine design but lengthened by ten metres and converted to carry four missile launchers in an extended but streamlined conning mound housing four inclined tubes.

6 TWIN CYLINDER TYPE

Displacement, tons	1 100 surface; 1 600 submerged
Length, feet (*metres*)	265·7 (*81·0*)
Beam, feet (*metres*)	24·3 (*7·4*)
Draught, feet (*metres*)	15·1 (*4·6*)
Missile launchers	2 cylinders for "Shaddock"
Torpedo tubes	6—21 in (4 bow, 2 aft)
Main engines	Diesels; 4 000 bhp;
	Electric motors; 2 500 hp
Speed, knots	17 surface; 15 submerged

Rebuilt in 1956-60. "W" class converted to "Shaddock" missile carrying submarines with twin cylinders on deck abaft the conning tower.

"W" Class "Long Bin" Type

S. Breyer

"W" Class Twin Cylinder Type

S. Breyer

"W" Class "Long Bin" Type

Submarines—continued

"F" Class   1970

Fleet Submarines

6 "B" CLASS
PATROL TYPE

Displacement, tons	1 000 surface; 1 100 submerged
Length, feet (metres)	239·5 (73·0)
Beam, feet (metres)	21·7 (6·6)
Draught, feet (metres)	14·8 (4·5)
Torpedo tubes	6—21 in
Main engines	Diesel-electric
Speed, knots	16

A new class of submarines of moderate dimensions with conventional propulsion intended for coastal operations. First reported extant in 1969.

45 "F" CLASS
ANTI-SUBMARINE TYPE

Displacement, tons	2 000 surface; 2 300 submerged
Length, feet (metres)	300·2 (91·5)
Beam, feet (metres)	27·2 (8·3)
Draught, feet (metres)	19·0 (5·8)
Torpedo tubes	10—21 in (6 bow, 4 aft)
Main engines	Diesels; 3 shafts; 6 000 bhp; 3 electric motors; 6 000 hp
Speed, knots	20 surface; 15 submerged
Complement	70

Built in 1956 to 1967. Improved version of the "Z" class design. 20 torpedoes carried. Names reported: *Pskovsky Komsomolec, Jaroslavsky Komsomolec, Vladimirsky Komsomolec.*

"F" Class   1968

"F" Class

F" Class

Submarines—*continued*

"R" Class

Fleet Submarines —*continued*

"R" Class   *Skyfotos*

14 "R" CLASS
PATROL TYPE

Displacement, tons	1 100 surface; 1 600 submerged
Length, feet (*metres*)	246·0 (*75·0*)
Beam, feet (*metres*)	24·0 (*7·3*)
Draught, feet (*metres*)	14·5 (*4·4*)
Torpedo tubes	6—21 in bow
Main engines	Diesels: 4 000 bhp
	Electric motors; 4 000 hp
Speed, knots	19 surface; 16 submerged
Complement	65

These are a medium range type of an improved "W" class design with modernised superstructure, conning tower, and sonar installation.   All built in 1958 to 1961.

22 "Q" CLASS
SHORT RANGE TYPE

Displacement, tons	650 surface; 740 submerged
Length, feet (*metres*)	185·0 (*56·4*)
Beam, feet (*metres*)	18·0 (*5·5*)
Draught, feet (*metres*)	13·2 (*4·0*)
Torpedo tubes	4—21 in bow
Main engines	1 diesel; 1 shaft; 3 000 bhp
	3 electric motors; 2 500 hp
Speed, knots	18 surface; 16 submerged
Oil fuel, tons	50
Radius, miles	7 000 cruising range
Complement	40

Short range, single screw coastal submarines.   Built from 1954 to 1960.   Thirteen were constructed in 1955 by Sudomekh Shipyard, Leningrad.

"Q" Class   *1970, B. Borg*

"Q" Class   *S. Breyer*

Submarines—*continued*

"Z" Class

1970. MOD, Official

Fleet Submarines —*continued*
22 "Z" CLASS
OCEANGOING TYPE

Displacement, tons	1 900 surface; 2 200 submerged
Length, feet (*metres*)	259·3 (*90·0*)
Beam, feet (*metres*)	25·9 (*7·9*)
Draught, feet (*metres*)	19·0 (*5·8*)
Torpedo tubes	10—21 in (6 bow, 4 stern); 24 torpedoes carried (or 40 mines)
Main engines	Diesel-electric; 3 shafts 3 diesels; 10 000 bhp 3 electric motors; 3 500 hp
Speed, knots	18 surface; 15 submerged
Radius, miles	20 000 to 26 000
Complement	70

Oceangoing type. Completed from late 1951 to 1957. General appearance is streamlined with a complete row of rapid flooding holes along the casing. This class was stationed in the Baltic and Far East. The first of the class was laid down early in 1951 and most were commissioned during 1954 to 1957. Eighteen were built by Sudomekh Shipyard, Leningrad, in 1952-55 and others at Severodvinsk.

This class was built to the original design in 1950 to 1957, rebuilt to the SSB concept in 1957 to 1958 (Z "V" Class) and converted in 1964-65 with modified tower structure.

A large port quarter oblique aerial view of "Z" Class No. 958 and a port bow surface view appear in the 1960-61 to 1967-68 editions.

"Z" Class

1970, MOD, Official

"Z" V" Class

1970, S. Breyer

Submarines—*continued*

'W" Class   *1970, Niels Gartig*

"W" Class   *1968*

148 "W" CLASS
PATROL TYPE

Displacement, tons	1 030 surface; 1 180 submerged
Length, feet (*metres*)	240·0 (*73·2*)
Beam, feet (*metres*)	22·0 (*6·7*)
Draught, feet (*metres*)	15·0 (*4·6*)
Torpedo tubes	6—21 in (4 bow, 2 stern); 18 torpedoes carried (or 40 mines)
Main engines	Diesel-electric; 2 shafts; Diesels: 4 000 bhp Electric motors: 2 500 hp
Speed, knots	17 surface, 15 submerged
Radius, miles	13 000 to 16 500
Complement	60,

Medium to long range submarines built from 1950 to 1957 in yards throughout the Soviet Union. Stationed in considerable numbers in the Baltic, the North, the Black Sea and the Far East. Equipped with snort. Most are fitted for minelaying.

5 "W" CLASS "CB" TYPE

Displacement, tons	1 100 surface; 1 200 submerged
Length, feet (*metres*)	240·0 (*73·2*)
Beam, feet (*metres*)	22·0 (*6·7*)
Draught, feet (*metres*)	15·0 (*4·6*)
Torpedo tubes	6—21 in (4 bow, 2 stern)
Main engines	Diesels: 4 000 bhp Electric motors: 2 500 hp
Speed, knots	17 surface; 15 submerged

Basically of same design as the "W" class but modified about the superstructure and reported to have been dubbed the "Canvas Bag" type from her conning tower tracking canopy. Converted in 1959 to 1963.

PHOTOGRAPHS. Photographs of No. 12 and No. 25, appear in the 1959-60 to 1966-67 editions.

"W" Class   *1970, Skyfotos*

"W" Class   *1970, MOD, Official*

Submarines—*continued*

"W" Class

Skyfotos

2 MODIFIED "W" CLASS

SEVERYANA	SLAVYANKA
Displacement, tons	1 050 surface; 1 350 submerged
Length, feet (*metres*)	249·3 (*76·0*)
Beam, feet (*metres*)	22·0 (*6·7*)
Draught, feet (*metres*)	15·0 (*4·6*)
Main engines	Diesels: 4 000 bhp
	Electric motors: 2 500 hp
Speed, knots	17 surface; 15 submerged

Converted "W" class submarines specially fitted out for scientific research. *Severyana* is attached to the Soviet Institute for Fisheries and Oceanographic Research. The torpedo compartment was converted into a laboratory. Equipped with observation portholes, top and bottom echo sounders, sonar, long range searchlight, and underwater television camera.

W III CLASS
Submarines of the W III class are no longer in existance in the Soviet Navy.

"W" Class

Skyfotos

"K" CLASS
The few minelaying submarines of the "K" class which survived the Second World War were deleted from the list in 1963-64.

"MV" CLASS
28 boats of the "MV" class, M 205, 206, 209, 211, 212, 214, 215, 216, 219, 234, 235, and 237 to 253, were for disposal in 1962. M 200, 201, 202, 203, 254, 255, 256, 257 and 258 were deleted from the list in 1963, M 204 in 1964, M 259 to M 268 in 1966, and M 269, 270, 271, 272, 273, 274, 275, 276, 277, 278, 279, 280, 281, 282 and 283 in 1966. They are no longer operational A few may be used for static training but these boats are of no further fighting value.

"SHCH" CLASSES
The 19 submarines of the "Shch" IV class were deleted from the list in 1964. The 50 boats of the "Shch" class, including most of the "Sch" I, II and III classes, having become obsolete and worn out, were scrapped in 1960.

"S(C)" CLASS
The 30 old submarines of the "S(C)" class were discarded in 1963.

"W" Class

Skyfotos

"M IV" CLASS
The 18 coastal submarines of the "M IV" class were discarded in 1963.

EX-GERMAN TYPES
The old ex-German submarines N 27 (ex-U 2529), N 28 (ex-U 3035), N 29 (ex-U 3041) and N 30 (ex-U 3515) of the "XXI" types; S 81 (ex-U 1057), S 82 (ex-U 1058), S 83 (ex-U 1064) and S 84 (ex-U 1305) of the VII type and N 31 (ex-U 2353) of the "XXIII" type all taken over by the Soviet Navy as war prizes. were in 1963 reported to have been scrapped.

OTHER CLASSES
For detailed list of disposals of older submarines discarded since the USSR has built so many submarines of her own designs in her own yards, see 1962-63 and earlier editions.

"W" Class

Skyfotos

CRUISER HELICOPTER CARRIERS

2 "MOSKVA" CLASS

LENINGRAD   **MOSKVA**

Displacement, tons	15 000 standard; 18 000 full load
Length, feet (*metres*)	600 wl (*182·9*); 645 oa (*196·6*)
Flight deck, feet (*m*)	295·3 (*90·0*) aft of superstructure
Width, feet (*metres*)	115·0 (*35·0*)
Beam, feet (*metres*)	85·3 (*26·0*)
Draught, feet (*metres*)	24·9 (*7·6*)
Aircraft	20 Ka 25 ASW helicopters; 30 helicopters max capacity
Missile launchers	2 surface-to-air "SA-N-3" systems of twin launchers and 1 twin launcher for either surface or anti-submarine missiles
Guns, dual purpose	4—57 mm (2 twin mountings)
A/S weapons	2—12 tube mortars on forecastle

Torpedo tubes	4 trainable 21 inch (2 twin) anti-submarine
Main engines	Geared turbines; 2 shafts; 100 000 shp
Boilers	4 watertube
Speed, knots	30 max
Complement	800

Both built at Nikolayev. The prototype, *Moskva*, ran her sea trials in July 1967. Would appear to have been designed as a command ship with an air defence and anti-submarine warfare capability. Described as combination helicopter carriers and guided missile cruisers. The foremost dual arm launcher, for either surface or anti-submarine missiles is directed by sonar. The other two dual arm launchers are directed by the surface-to-air radar pedestals on the steps of the bridge superstructure. Both ships are fitted with variable depth sonar aft and prominent radars known as the "Top Sail" (3D) above the crowsnest and "Head Lights" (missile guidance) on the bridge tiers.

ELECTRONICS. Fitted with extensive electronic equipment which includes a large antenna for a 3-D surveillance radar employing electronic scanning mounted amidships on a large tripod. Below, and forward of the tripod, is mounted a V-beam S band 3-D antenna which is probably used for helicopter control and the surface and low angle air surveillance radar. Two missile directors are mounted between the two twin launchers and the upper part of the superstructure. Each director has a pair of cassegrain geometry parabolic antennae for the C band tracking radars. A further pair of X band antennae mounted above the directors are probably for target illumination. The four pods, or radomes, mounted on either side of the funnel probably contain passive electronic detection gear and active jamming equipment.

RADAR. Search/Aircraft Direction: Knightsbridge and Kingsway. Fire Control: Millbank (2). Miscellaneous: Electronic warfare equipment.

MOSKVA   *1969 MOD. RN. Official*

MOSKVA   *1969. S. Breyer*

MOSKVA   *1970, USNFE*

Cruiser Helicopter Carriers—*continued*

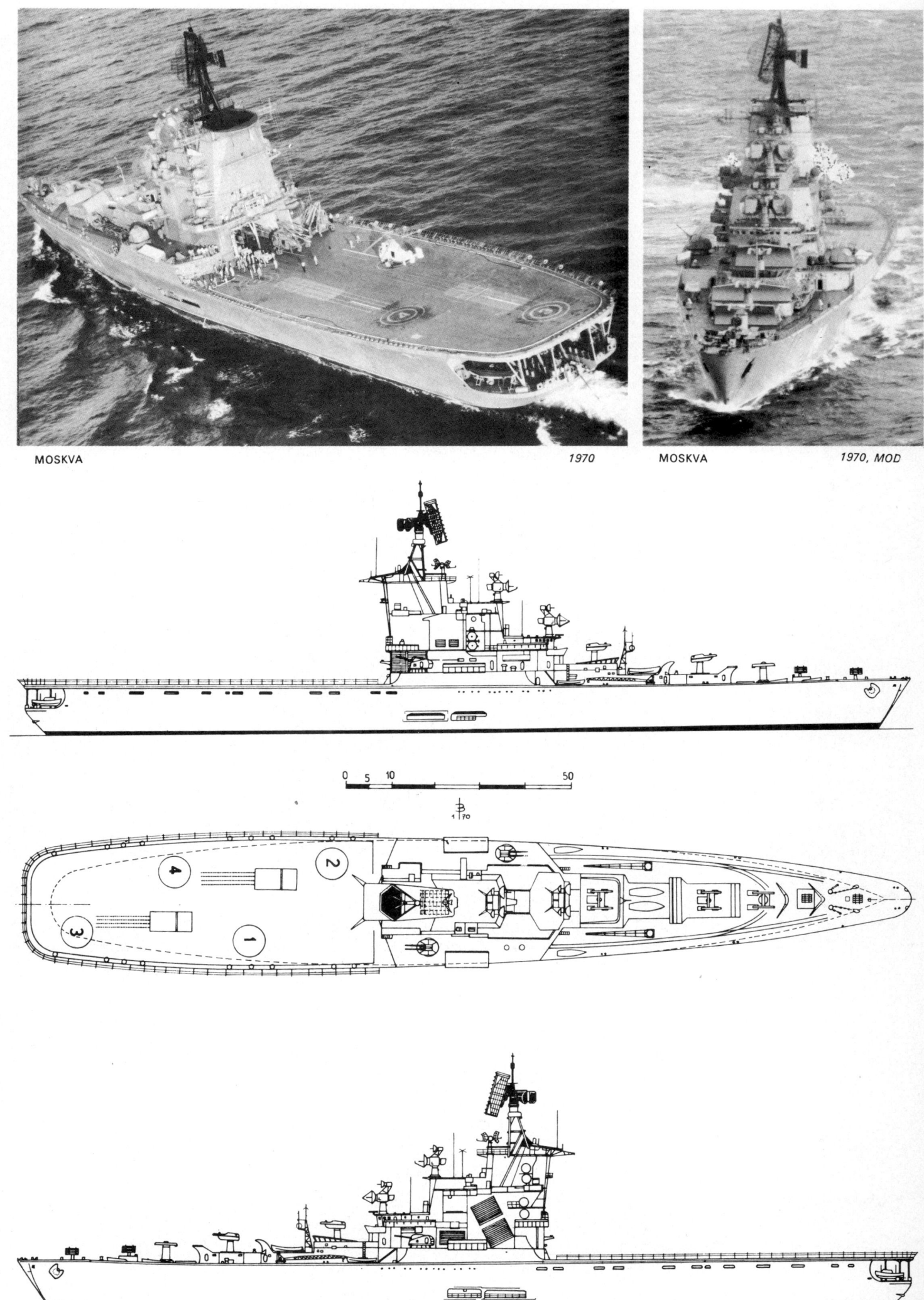

MOSKVA   1970   MOSKVA   1970, MOD

0   5   10   50

Cruiser Helicopter Carriers—*continued*

LENINGRAD   *1970, B. Borg*

LENINGRAD   *1970, MOD. official*

Cruiser Helicopter Carriers—*Continued*

MOSKVA

1969, USN Official

SVERDLOV Class No. 835 (see next page)

1970

CRUISERS

12 "SVERDLOV" CLASS

ADMIRAL LAZAREV	MIKHAIL KUTUSOV
ADMIRAL SENJAVIN	MURMANSK
ADMIRAL USHAKOV	OKTYABRSKAYA
ALEKSANDR NEVSKII	REVOLUTSIYA
ALEKSANDR SUVOROV	SVERDLOV
DMITRI POZHARSKIY	ZHDANOV
DZERZHINSKI	

Displacement, tons	15 450 standard ; 19 200 full load
Length, feet (metres)	656·2 (200·0)pp ; 689·0 (210·0)oa
Beam, feet (metres)	72·2 (22·0)
Draught, feet (metres)	24·5 (7·5) max
Armour	Belts 3·9—4·9 in (100—125 mm) ; fwd and aft 1·6—2 in (40—50 mm) ; turrets 4·9 in (125 mm) ; C.T. 5·9 in (150 mm) ; decks 1—2 in (25—50 mm) and 2—3 in (50—75 mm)
Missile launchers	Twin "Guideline" aft in Dzerzhinski (see Guided Missiles)
Guns, surface	12—6 in (152 mm), 4 triple
Guns, dual purpose	12—3·9 in (100 mm), 6 twin
Guns, AA	22 to 32—37 mm (11 to 16 twin mounts), see Gunnery
Torpedo tubes	10—21 in (533 mm) 2 quintuple (see Torpedoes)
Mines	140 to 250 capacity
Boilers	6 watertube
Main engines	Geared turbines ; 2 shafts ; 130 000 shp
Speed, knots	34
Endurance, miles	8 700 at 18 knots
Oil fuel, tons	3 800
Complement	1 000 average

Of the 24 cruisers of this class originally projected, 20 keels were laid and 17 hulls were launched from 1951 onwards, but only 14 ships were completed by Dec 1960. There were two slightly different types. Sverdlov and sisters had the 37 mm AA guns near the fore-funnel one deck higher than in later cruisers. Most ships were fitted for minelaying. Mine stowage was on the second deck. It was reported that the number of units in this class would be reduced by scrapping.

GUIDED MISSILES. In 1961-62 Dzerzhinski was fitted with a twin long range missile launcher aft in place of No. 3 or "X" turret.

DRAWING. Starboard elevation and plan of Dzerzhinski. Drawn in 1970. Scale: 125 feet = 1 inch (1 : 1 500)

GUNNERY. Dzerzhinski has only nine 6 inch guns in three triple turrets, "X" turret having been replaced by guided missile launcher.

TORPEDOES. Oktyabrskaya Revolutsia and Murmansk no longer have tubes

APPEARANCE. The first ships had their anti-aircraft bridge near the fore-funnel one deck higher than in later ships. Oktyabrskaya Revolutsiya no longer has torpedo tubes. Murmansk has low anti-aircraft bridge near the fore-funnel and no torpedo tubes. Dzerzhinski has a new radar known as "Big Net" on the mainmast.

PHOTOGRAPHS. Photographs of Admiral Ushakov, Aleksandr Suvorov and Sverdlov appear in the 1953-54 to 1957-58 editions, of Oktyabrskaya Revolutsiya (as Molotovsk) in the 1957-58 to 1959-60 editions (also large photograph showing midship details) and in the 1962-63 edition (port bow oblique view), of Sverdlov (counter view showing minelaying stern) in the 1961-62 and 1962-63 editions, of Murmansk (as Zhdanov) in the 1957-58 to 1964-65 editions. of Dzerzhinski in the 1965-66 and 1966-67 editions (port quarter view showing twin guided missile launcher), of Oktyabrskaya Revolutsiya in the 1961-62 to 1966-67 editions.

RADAR. Search: Strand and Minories. Heightfinder: Dzerzhinski only. Fire control: Probably Bankside; but Dzerzhinski is also fitted with Piccadilly.

PROTECTION. Deep and thick side belts of armour from the fore turret to the after turret, tapering to the bow and the stern.

NOMENCLATURE. The ship first named Molotovsk was renamed Oktyabrskaya Revolutsiya in 1957. The ships to have been named Dmitri Donskoi and Kosma Minin apparently never materialised.

TRANSFER. Ordzhonikidze of this class was transferred to the Indonesian Navy in Oct 1962 and renamed Irian.

CLASS. The uncompleted hulls of four "Sverdlov" class cruisers were reported to have been broken up at Leningrad. Several completed ships now surplus to naval requirements are scheduled to be discarded in the near future, and the number of cruisers of this class in commission will gradually be reduced and replaced on active service by the large guided missile armed destroyers or rocket cruisers recently completed. Admiral Nakhimov was deleted from the list in 1969.

MURMANSK (ex-Zhdanov)   Official

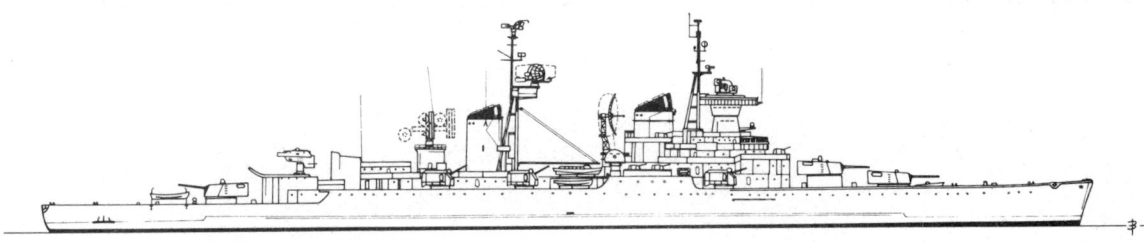

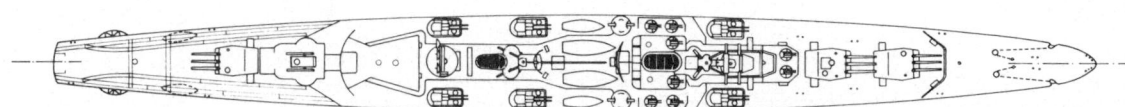

DZERZHINSKI with new radar "Big Net"

Cruisers—*continued*

SVERDLOV Class No. 818 with "Top Trough" radar at masthead

1970, MOD

DRAWING. Starboard elevation and plan of "Sverdlov" class. Drawn in 1970.
Scale: 125 feet = 1 inch (1 : 1 500).

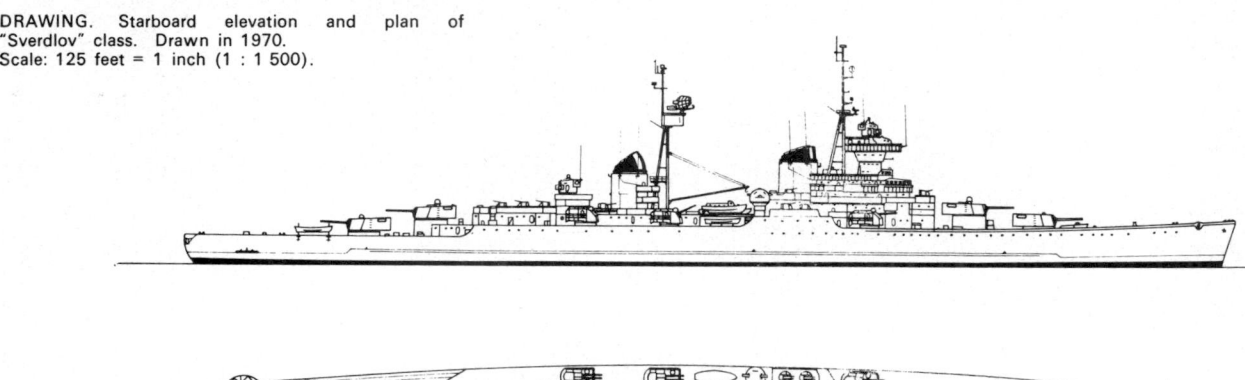

MIKHAIL KUTUZOV with newest radar "Top Trough" at mainmast head

1970

ELECTRONICS. Fitted with a large amount of electronic equipment. A long range L band air surveillance radar antenna is mounted high up on the forward side of the mainmast, and what appears to be an L band height finder antenna aft of the forward funnel in the *Dzerzhinski*. A "cheese" antenna for an S band surface search radar is mounted at the top of the mainmast, and what may be a C band antenna for a low coverage and "Sea skimmer" detection radar at the top of the foremast. Four C band parabolic antennas are mounted on the guided missile director. S and X band navigation radar antennae are mounted before the superstructure. Other electronic detection equipment is fitted and probably active jamming equipment. Earlier ships of the class noticably carry very much less electronic gear than *Dzerzhinski*.

Cruisers—*continued*

SVERDLOV   *1971*

ALEKSANDRA SUVOROV   *1971*

Cruisers—continued

2 "CHAPAEV" CLASS

KOMSOMOLETS (ex-*Chkalov*)   **ZHELEZNYAKOV**

Displacement, tons	11 500 standard; 15 000 full load
Length, feet (*metres*)	659·5 (*201·0*)
Beam, feet (*metres*)	64·7 (*19·7*)
Draught, feet (*metres*)	21 (*6·4*)
Guns, surface	12—6 in (*152 mm*), 4 triple
Guns, dual purpose	8—3·9 in (*100 mm*), 4 twin
Guns, AA	24—37 mm (12 twin)
Mines	100 to 200 capacity
Boilers	6 watertube
Main engines	Geared turbines, with diesels for cruising speeds; 4 shafts; 120 000 shp
Speed, knots	34
Radius, miles	5 400 at 15 knots
Oil fuel, tons	2 500
Complement	834

Laid down in 1939-40. Launched during 1941-47. All work on these ships was stopped during the war, but was resumed in 1946-47. Completed in 1948-50. Catapults were removed from all ships of this type. *Zheleznyakov* serves as a training ship.

GUNNERY. Turret guns are in separate sleeves allowing independent elevation to at least 50 degrees.

APPEARANCE. Heavy director on control tower, pole foremast and tripod mainmast forward of after funnel. Vertical funnels. Higher freeboard and funnels than "Kirov" class. Resemble "Sverdlov" class but forecastle deck breaks abreast forefunnel instead of at quarter deck.

NOMENCLATURE. *Chkalov* was reported to have been renamed *Komsomolets* in 1961.

DRAWING. Starboard elevation and plan. Drawn in 1970. Scale: 125 feet = 1 inch (1 : 1 500).

PHOTOGRAPHS. A port quarter view of *Zheleznyakov* appears in the 1952-53 to 1957-58 editions.

DISPOSALS. *Chapaev*, *Frunse* and *Kuibyshev* of this class were discarded; and the remaining two ships are obsolescent and will probably be laid up in the near future.

RADAR. These ships do not appear to have been fitted with modern electronic equipment. It is reasonable to assume that they have L band long range surveillance radars and X band Gunfire Control tracking radar.

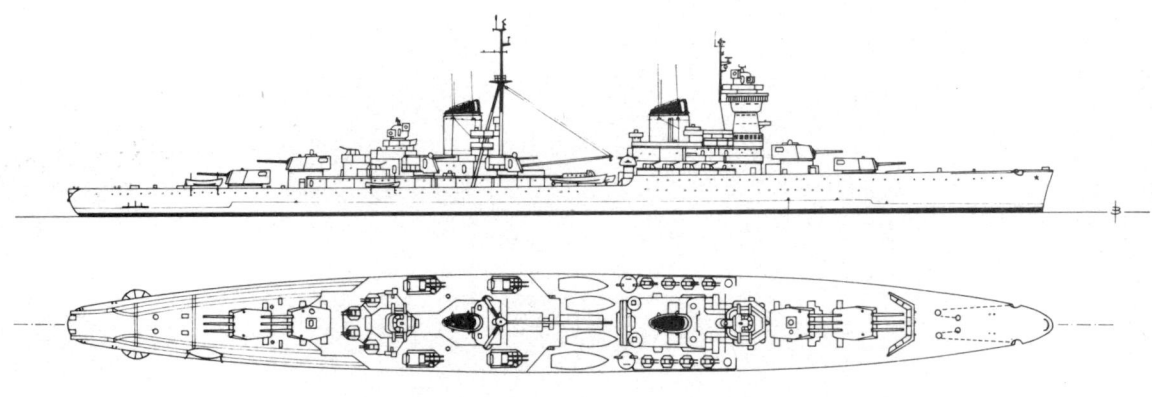

KOMSOMOLETS   *1970, Niels Gartig*

ZHELEZNYAKOV   *Antonov Rogov*

Cruisers—continued

2 "KIROV" CLASS

Displacement, tons	8 500 standard; 11 500 full load
Length, feet (metres)	613·5 (178·0)pp; 626·7 (191·0)oa
Beam, feet (metres)	57·7 (17·6)
Draught, feet (metres)	20·7 (6·3)
Armour	Side 3 in (75 mm); deck 2 in (50 mm); C.T. and gunhouses 3·9 in (100 mm)
Guns, surface	9—7·1 in (180 mm)
Guns, dual purpose	6—3·9 in (100 mm)
Guns, AA	12—37 mm; 6—13 mm
Torpedo tubes	6—21 in (533 mm) removed
Mines	60—90 capacity
Main engines	Geared turbines, with diesels for cruising speeds; 2 shafts; 113 000 shp
Boilers	6 Yarrow
Speed, knots	34
Radius, miles	4 000 at 15 knots
Oil fuel, tons	2 500
Complement	734

Design and technical direction of construction by Ansaldo. Of this class *Ordzhonikidze* under construction at Nikolayev, was wrecked by high explosives before the enemy occupied that port in Aug 1941.

Name	Builders	Laid down	Launched	Completed
KIROV	Putilov DY	1934	1 Dec 1936	26 Sep 1938
SLAVA (ex-*Molotov*)	Marti Yard, Nikolaye	1935	23 Feb 1939	1944

APPEARANCE. *Kirov* has very long forecastle, heavy tripod mast stepped abaft forebridge, light tripod stepped abaft second funnel, very large funnels. *Slava* has high director tower on forebridge, light tripod foremast abaft bridge, heavy tripod mainmast stepped abaft second funnel and generally lighter appearance.

PHOTOGRAPHS. Starboard bow and quarter views of *Kirov*, appear in the 1960-61 to 1962-63 editions, and a port oblique aerial view in the 1959-60 to 1967-68 editions.

GUNNERY. Triple guns are mounted in one sleeve and are incapable of individual elevation. Maximum elevation 40 degrees. For her role as a training ship *Kirov* has 9—7·1 inch, 6—3·9 inch, 8—37 mm and 2 older guns and no torpedo tubes.

DRAWING. Starboard elevation and plan of *Kirov*. Drawn in 1970. Scale: 125 feet = 1 inch (1 : 1 500).

DISPOSALS. *Kaganovich*, *Kalinin*, *Maksim Gorki* and *Voroshilov* of this class are reported to have been scrapped

NOMENCLATURE. *Molotov* was reported to have been renamed *Slava* in 1962.

RADAR. Search: Strand and Minories. Fire Control: Probably Bankside.

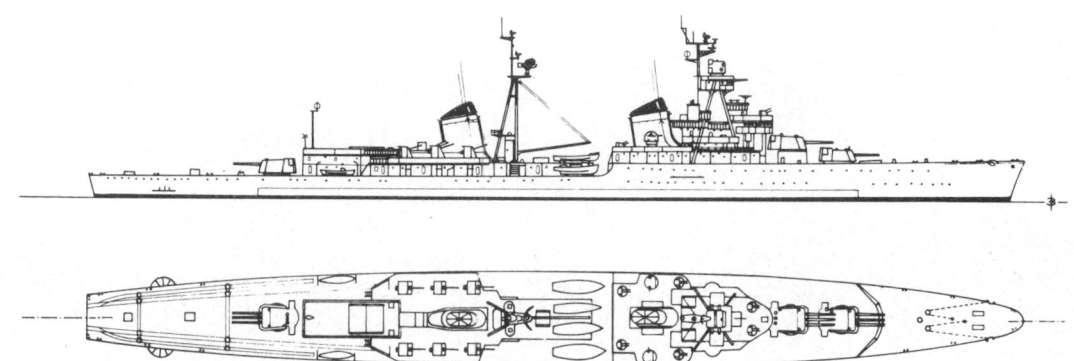

KIROV

1971, MOD, DPR(N), Official

KIROV

1970, Bertil Gard

GUIDED MISSILE CRUISERS

2 "KRESTA II" CLASS

Displacement, tons	6 000 standard; 7 500 full load
Length, feet (metres)	518·4 (158·0)
Beam, feet (metres)	55·8 (17·0)
Draught, feet (metres)	19·7 (6·0)
Aircraft	1 or 2 helicopters
Missile launchers	2 quadruple of a new model for short range surface to surface missiles; 2 twin for SA-N-3 surface-to-air missiles
A/S weapons	2—12 barrelled forward and 2—6 barrelled aft for rocket launchers
Torpedo tubes	10—21 in (two quintuple)
Guns	4—57 mm (2 twin) dual purpose; 8—30 mm (4 twin) anti-aircraft
Main engines	Steam turbines; 2 shafts; 100 000 shp

Boilers	4 watertube
Speed, knots	33
Complement	500

A new class of multi-purpose guided missile armed, anti-submarine and helicopter cruisers. The design was developed from that of the "Kresta" I class, but the layout is more sophisticated and the missile and director and radar complex present a bristling appearance in contrast to the comparatively uncluttered configuration of the "Kresta I" class. Nevertheless there is a distinct family resemblance and the two types might be considered as half-sisters rather than separate classes. The armament scheme is generally similar but with two quadruple short range SSM missiles in place of the "Shaddock" missiles and the rocketry and weaponry has reached a new peak for vessels of the DLG or light cruiser size. Built at Leningrad during 1968 to 1971.

LAUNCHERS. The most interesting and prominent features of the rocketry system are the novel multiple pepper-box trunk launchers tilted from the forecastle deck up to the shelter deck on each beam abreast the forward control position.

FLIGHT. A flight of two helicopters could be operated, although the normal would appear to be one on the apron aft with adjacent low hangar.

ELECTRONICS. The electronic installation appears to have exploited in a smaller compass that fitted in the cruiser helicopter carriers Moskva and Leningrad and is a logical improvement on that in the "Kresta I" class. See previous and following page.

RADAR. The radar installation seems to be a compromise between and combination of that in the "Moskva" class and the "Kresta I" class, with the "Top Sail" 3 D radar of the former and the "Peel Group" fire control radar for surface to air missiles of the latter.

KRESTA II Class No. 585

1971

KRESTA II Class

1971, S. Breyer

KRESTA II Class

1971

Guided Missile Cruisers—*continued*

4 "KRESTA I" CLASS

ADMIRAL DROZD **VLADIVOSTOK**
ADMIRAL ZOZULYA

Displacement, tons	5 140 standard; 6 500 full load
Length, feet (*metres*)	508·5 (*155·0*)
Beam, feet (*metres*)	55·8 (*17·0*)
Draught, feet (*metres*)	18·0 (*5·5*)
Aircraft	Helicopter with hangar aft
Missile launchers	2 twin "Shaddock"; SSM; 2 twin "Goa" SAM
A/S weapons	2—12-barrelled launchers; 2—6-barrelled launchers
Torpedo tubes	10 (two quintuple)
Guns	4—57 mm (2 twin)
Main engines	Steam turbines; 2 shafts; 100 000 shp
Boilers	4 watertube
Speed, knots	34
Complement	400

New construction dual purpose anti-submarine warfare and guided missile armed destroyer leaders or cruisers. The design is a combination of that of the "Kashin" and "Kynda" classes. Provided with a helicopter hangar and flight apron aft. Two ships of the class were reported building at the Zhdanov Shipyard, Leningrad. The prototype ship was laid down in Sep 1964, launched in 1965 and carried out sea trials in the Baltic in Feb 1967. The second ship was launched in 1966, and the others in 1967-68. "Kresta" is the NATO designation for the class.

ELECTRONICS. These vessels illustrate the greatly increased use of electronic equipment in the USSR navy. A long range air surveillance L band radar antenna is mounted above the funnel, whilst a V beam, S band 3-D radar antenna is mounted at the top of the superstructure. This radar is probably used to provide acquisition data for the surface to air missile systems. A pair of what appear to be S band surface surveillance radar antennae are mounted on a sponson forward of the superstructure. These are probably used for surface tactical data acquisition and for surface fire control in a "track-while-scan" mode. The two missile directors each carry C and X band antennas of a type seen in "Precision Approach Radar Systems" where target position is obtained in the horizontal and vertical planes separately, unlike the more orthodox conical scan or monopulse tracking radar systems which employ a circular parabolic antenna. The provision of two separate radar systems, one in C band and one in X band, may indicate that differing types of AA missiles are carried, or that two frequencies are considered necessary for range or ECCM purposes. Four pods, or radomes, are fitted to the sides of the superstructure. These are similar to those fitted in the Moskva class vessels and probably contain passive detection and active jamming equipment. In addition there are what appear to be S band surveillance radar antennae mounted on side sponsons half way up the superstructure.

RADAR. Search, Kingsway and Strand. Fire Control: Cornhill for "Shaddock" system and Piccadilly (2) for "Goa" system.
The all-round radar atop the mast is known as "Head Net-C" and the fire control radar for "SA-N-1" missiles on the forward and after superstructures, see photographs, is known as the "Peel Group".

KRESTA I Class No. 550

1959, MOD RN, Official

KRESTA I Class No. 581

1969, S. Breyer

KRESTA I Class

Guided Missile Cruisers—*continued*

KRESTA I Class No. 542   *1971*

KRESTA I Class No. 563   *1971*

KRESTA I Class No. 550   *1971, MOD, DPR(N), Official*

Guided Missile Cruisers—*continued*

4 "KYNDA" CLASS

ADMIRAL FOKIN   **GROZNY**
ADMIRAL GOLOVKO   **VARYAG**

Displacement, tons	4 800 standard; 6 000 full load
Length, feet (*metres*)	488·8 (*149·0*)
Beam, feet (*metres*)	51·8 (*15·8*)
Draught, feet (*metres*)	17·4 (*5·3*)
Aircraft	Pad for helicopter on stern
Missile launchers	2 "Shaddock" quadruple mounts, 1 fwd, 1 aft for surface-to-surface missiles 1 twin "Goa" mount on forecastle for surface-to-air missiles
A/S weapons	2—12 barrelled rocket launchers on forecastle
Guns, AA	4—3 in (*76 mm*) 2 twin
Torpedo tubes	6—21 in (*533 mm*) 2 triple ASW amidships.
Main engines	2 sets geared turbines; 2 shafts; 100 000 shp
Boilers	4 high pressure
Speed, knots	35
Complement	390

The first DLG or light cruiser (rocket) of this class was laid down in June 1960, launched in Apr 1961 at Zhdanov Shipyard, Leningrad, and completed in June 1962. The second ship was launched in Nov 1961 and fitted out in Aug 1962. The others were completed by 1965. Two enclosed towers, instead of masts, are stepped forward of each raked funnel. Two screws and two rudders.

NOMENCLATURE. Other names reported have not been confirmed.

PHOTOGRAPHS. A starboard broadside aerial view of No. 898 of this class appears in the 1963-64 and 1964-65 editions, and a port broadside surface view of No. 202 in the 1965-66 and 1966-67 editions.

ELECTRONICS. Equipped with a very comprehensive and generous electronics installation. Fitted with duplicated S band combined air and surface search radars, with duplicated antennae at the foremast and mainmast heads. The reason for the duplication may be for redundancy in the event of action damage. The S or C band antennae, mounted in pairs on the sponsons extending forward from the foremast and aft from the mainmast are probably used for surface tracking of targets to be engaged by the "Shaddock" surface-to-surface missiles. The use of four separate antennae for this purpose seems to be because the techniques of Track-while-scan may not be trusted, or yet developed by the Soviet Navy. The "Goa" surface to air missiles, launched from the forward mounting are controlled by the C band radar, whose antennae are mounted on the director above the bridge, whilst the guns are radar controlled from the X band antenna mounted abaft the after funnel.

FLIGHT. There is a helicopter spot landing and take off apron on the stern, but no hangar.

RADAR. Search: Strand (2). Fire Control: Cornhill for "Shaddock" system (2), Piccadilly for "Goa" system and Cheapside for guns.
The fire control radar for "SA-N-1" missiles on the foreward superstructure is known as the "Peel Group"; the fire control radar for the "Shaddock" missiles at each mid-mast is known as the "Scoop Pair"; and the all-round radar atop both masts is known as "Head Net A".

KYNDA Class   *1970*

VARYAG   *1970*

Guided Missile Cruisers—*continued*

KYNDA Class No. 822   1970

KYNDA Class   1968

KYNDA Class No. 299   1967

GUIDED MISSILE ARMED DESTROYERS

15 "KASHIN" CLASS

OBRAZTSOVYI	SLAVNY
OTLITNYI	SOOBRAZITELNYI
OTNASNYI	STEREGUSHCHYI
OTVASHNYI	STOJKYI
PROVEDYONNY	STROGYI
PROVORNYI	

Displacement, tons	4 300 standard; 5 200 full load
Length, feet (metres)	475 (144·8)
Beam, feet (metres)	53 (16·1)
Draught, feet (metres)	19 (5·8)
Missile launchers	4 (2 twin) "Goa" mounted in "B" and "X" positions for surface-to-air missiles
Guns, AA	4—3 in (76 mm), 2 twin, in "A" and "Y" positions
A/S weapons	2—12 barrelled ASW rocket launchers forward; 2—6 barrelled ASW rocket launchers aft
Torpedo tubes	5—21 in (533 mm) quintuple, amidships for ASW torpedoes
Main engines	8 sets gas turbines; each 12 000 hp; 2 shafts; 96 000 shp
Speed, knots	35

A class of guided missile armed destroyers with anti-aircraft and anti-submarine capabilities. Four separate towers carrying radar for missile guidance, anti-aircraft direction, search and gunnery direction.
Built since 1961-62 at the Zhdanov Yard, Leningrad, and the Nosenko Yard, Nikolaev.

These ships have two sets of athwartship twin funnels truncated outwards at an angle off the vertical.

PHOTOGRAPHS. A starboard broadside view of No. 078 appears in the 1964-65 and 1965-66 editions.

RADAR. Search: Either Kingsway and an unidentified L Band radar or two Strand radars. Fire control: Piccadilly (2) for "Goa" system and Cheapside (2) for guns.
There are differing radars atop the mainmast in some ships, see photographs for "Big Net" in No. 545 and "Head Net A" in No. 383.

KASHIN Class — 1970, Hon. Ambrose Greenway

KASHIN Class No. 545 — 1971, MOD, DPR(N), Official

KASHIN Class — 1969, S. Breyer

Guided Missile Armed Destroyers—*continued*

KASHIN Class

1970, Hon. Ambrose Greenway

KASHIN Class

1970, Hon. Ambrose Greenway

KASHIN Class No. 383

1971

Guided Missile Armed Destroyers—*continued*

KANIN SAM Class

S. Breyer

GUIDED MISSILE DESTROYERS
3 "KANIN" CLASS

GREMYASHCHYI

Displacement, tons	3 700 standard; 4 600 full load
Length, feet (*metres*)	456·0 (*139·0*)
Beam, feet (*metres*)	48·9 (*14·9*)
Draught, feet (*metres*)	16·4 (*5·0*)
Aircraft	Provision for helicopter drop
Missile launchers	1 twin "SA-N-1" mounted aft for surface-to-air missiles
A/S weapons	Three 12-barrelled rocket launchers for ASW
Guns	8—57 mm (2 quadruple forward)
Torpedo tubes	10—21 in (*533 mm*) A/S (2 quintuple)
Main engines	2 sets geared steam turbines; 2 shafts; 80 000 shp
Boilers	4 watertube
Oil fuel, tons	900
Speed, knots	43
Complement	350

Converted from 1967-68 onwards at the Zhdanov Shipyard, Leningrad. The first two ships have been in service since 1969. Baltic Fleet. New armament. Longer helicopter flight deck. See photograph above.

DESIGN. Basically of similar design and construction to the "Krupnyi" class guided missile destroyers, see next page, but the plans were modified and the hulls were converted to enable the ships to launch surface-to-air missiles instead of surface to-surface missiles.

NOMENCLATURE. Conveniently identified by the NATO code designation of "Kanin" class, but more specifically known as the converted "Krupnyi" class SAM DLG (ship-to-air guided missile destroyer leaders). Four names reported to be those of the "Krupnyi" class, *Bessposhadnyi*, *Besstrashnyi*, *Gordelivyi* and *Upornyi*, include two ships of the "Kanin" class.

APPEARANCE. As compared with the previous class these ships have enlarged bridge, converted bow (probably a sonar bow) and larger helicopter platforms for landing and take off.

RADAR. Search: Kingsway. Fire Control: Piccadilly for "Goa" fitted ships. Also Barbican and Cheapside for guns.

KYNDA Class

1969, DOD, Official

KRUPNY Class (see revised design of "Kanin" class above)

1970, S. Breyer

Guided Missile Armed Destroyers—*continued*

5 "KRUPNY" CLASS

BOIKI	PLAMYONNY
GNEVNYI	ZORKYI
GORDYI	

Displacement, tons	3 650 standard; 4 650 full load
Length, feet (*metres*)	452·8 (*138·0*)
Beam, feet (*metres*)	47·9 (*14·6*)
Draught, feet (*metres*)	16·5 (*5·0*)
Missile launchers	2 mountings; 1 forward, 1 aft, for "SS-N-1" surface-to-surface missiles
Guns, AA	16—57 mm, 4 quadruple; 2 amidships, 1 forward, 1 aft
Torpedo launchers	6 (2 triple) for A/S torpedoes
Main engines	Geared steam turbines; 2 shafts, 80 000 shp
Boilers	4 high pressure water tube
Speed, knots	34
Complement	360

Flush-decked destroyers designed to carry surface-to-surface guided missiles. Helicopter spot landing apron on the stern. Initial construction started in 1958 at Leningrad. Three ships of this class were converted to carry surface-to-air missiles in 1967-68 and are now known as the "Kanin" class, see previous page.

PHOTOGRAPHS. A port broadside aerial view of No. 526 appears in the 1961-62 to 1963-64 editions, a port broadside surface view of No. 700 in the 1962-63 and 1963-64 editions, a starboard bow surface view of No. 700 in the 1962-63 to 1964-65 editions, and a starboard broadside view in the 1963-64 to 1965-66 editions, and a starboard quarter surface view of No. 703 in the 1962-63 to 1966-67 editions.

RADAR. Search: Either Kingsway or Strand. Fire Control: Cheapside (2).

GNEVNYI with radar "Head Net C" atop foremast   *1969, MOD, RN, Official*

GNEVNYI   *1969, MOD, RN, Official*

KRUPNY Class   *1966, col Borg*

Guided Missile Armed Destroyers—*continued*

KRUPNY Class

KRUPNYI Class

KRUPNY Class

Guided Missile Armed Destroyers—continued

KOTLIN SAM II Class No. 322

1969, MOD, RN, Official

7 "KOTLIN" SAM CLASSES 1 & II

Displacement, tons	2 850 standard ; 3 885 full load
Length, feet (metres)	416·7 (127·0) oa
Beam, feet (metres)	42·3 (12·9)
Draught, feet (metres)	16·1 (4·9) max
Missile launchers	1 twin "Goa" mounted aft for surface-to-air missiles
Guns, dual purpose	2—3·9 in (100 mm), 1 twin
Guns, AA	4—57 mm, 1 quadruple
A/S weapons	6 side thrown DC projectors or 2—12 barrelled ASW rocket launchers
Main engines	Geared turbines; 2 shafts; 72 000 shp
Boilers	4 high pressure
Speed, knots	36
Complement	285

"Kotlin" class destroyers modified with a surface-to-air missile launcher in place of the main twin turret aft and anti-aircraft guns reduced to one quadruple mounting. The first conversion was completed about 1962 and the others during 1966 to 1969.

APPEARANCE. The "Kotlin" SAM II class has a different after funnel and different electronic pedestal to those in the "Kotlin" SAM I class.

RADAR. Search: Strand. Fire Control: Piccadilly for "Goa" system, Cheapside for guns.

KOTLIN SAM I Class No. 165

KOTLIN SAM I Class No. 365

1971, MOD, DPR(N), Official

KOTLIN SAM II Class No. 963 with different radar turret and after funnel

1971, MOD, DPR(N), Official

Guided Missile Armed Destroyers— *continued*

4 "KILDIN" CLASS

BEDOVYY   **NEULOVIMYI**

Displacement, tons	3 000 standard; 4 000 full load
Length, feet (*metres*)	416·7 (*127·0*)
Beam, feet (*metres*)	42·3 (*12·9*)
Draught, feet (*metres*)	16·1 (*4·9*)
Missile launchers	1 for "SS-N-1" missiles
A/S weapons	2—16 barrel rocket launchers on forecastle
Guns, AA	16—57 mm, 4 quadruple

Main engines	Geared turbines; 2 shafts; 72 000 shp
Boilers	4 high pressure
Speed, knots	36 max designed continuous
Complement	350 officers and men

Large destroyers with the "Kotlin" type hull, but redesigned as guided missile armed destroyers with a launcher installed in place of the after gun mountings. Identified by NATO designation as the "Kildin" class.

Bedovyi was rebuilt in 1957-58 in Nakolaev, other three in 1958-59 in Zhdanov Yard, Leningrad. Only *Bedovyi* had 16—45 mm AA (4 quadruple), other three 15—67 mm AA (4 quadruple). *Bedovyi* has a different foremast and funnels from her three sister ships (see photograph).

RADAR. Search: Holborn, Haymarket and Aldgate. Fire Control: Cheapside (2).

BEDOVYI   *1970*

KILDIN Class   *1969, S. Breyer*

KILDIN Class No. 365   *1971*

KILDIN Class   *1964*

DESTROYERS

KOTLIN Class

1970, S. Breyer

20 "KOTLIN" CLASS

BESSLEDNYI	**PLAMENNYI**
BLAGORODNY	**SPRAVETLIVYI**
BLESTYASTCHY	**SVETLIVYIARE**
BURLIVYI	**SVETLYI**
BYVALYI	**VDOKHNOVENNYII**
NAPORISTYI	**VDUMCHIVYI**
NASTROICIVY	**VOZBUSHDONNYI**
	VOZMUSHCHENNY

Displacement, tons	2 850 standard; 3 885 full load
Length, feet (*metres*)	416·7 (*127·0*)
Beam, feet (*metres*)	42·3 (*12·9*)
Draught, feet (*metres*)	16·1 (*4·9*) max
Guns, dual purpose	4—5·1 in (*130 mm*), 2 twin
Guns, AA	16—45 mm (4 quadruple)
A/S weapons	6 side thrown DC projectors or 2—16 barrelled ASW rocket launchers
Torpedo tubes	10—21 in (*533 mm*)
Mines	80 capacity
Main engines	Geared turbines; 2 shafts; 72 000 shp
Boilers	4 high pressure
Speed, knots	36
Complement	285

Improved versions of the "Tallin" design with similar hulls but differing features. These fast anti-aircraft and anti-submarine destroyers, built in 1954-57, were designed for mass production.

MODERNISATION. Several of the "Kotlin" class have been modernised, with extensive modifications in anti-submarine and anti-aircraft armament. Some, including *Svetlyi* were fitted with a helicopter platform abaft the after mounting. Five were fitted with a surface-to-air twin missile launcher aft, installed atop a deckhouse in place of the after guns; with missile radar and tower fitted forward of the after funnel, see previous page.

KOTLIN Class No. 476

1971, R. P. de Kerbrech

KOTLIN Class

Skyfotos

ANTI-SUBMARINE WARFARE. The six depth charge throwers are welded to the deck, three on each beam at the stern, affording only transverse throw. They are apparently charged from deck magazines. The later ships of the class have two 6-barrelled ASW rocket launchers.

RADAR. Search: Haymarket and Minories. Fire Control: Cheapside (2).

PHOTOGRAPHS. Another photograph of a "Kotlin", a port near broadside surface view at sea, appears in the 1957-58 to 1960-61 editions, and starboard broadside view of No. 82 in the 1958-59 to 1964-65 editions.

KOTLIN Class

1966, Skyfotos

KOTLIN Class (helicopter platform aft)

1969, MOD, RN, Official

Destroyers—*continued*

NEUSTRASHIMYI ("Tallin" Class)   *Skyfotos*

1 "TALLIN" CLASS

NEUSTRASHIMYI

Displacement, tons	3 200 standard; 4 300 full load
Length, feet (*metres*)	440·0 (*134·0*) oa
Beam, feet (*metres*)	44·0 (*13·4*)
Draught, feet (*metres*)	16·1 (*4·9*)
Guns, dual purpose	4—5·1 in (*130 mm*) semi-automatic (2 twin)
Guns, AA	16—45 mm (4 quadruple)
A/S weapons	2—16 barrelled ASW rocket launchers and 2 DC rocket launchers
Torpedo tubes	10—21 in (*533 mm*), 2 quintuple
Mines	70 to 90 according to size
Main engines	Geared turbines; 2 shafts; 80 000 shp
Boilers	4 water tube
Speed, knots	38
Radius, miles	2 500 at 18 knots
Oil fuel, tons	850
Complement	340

Built in 1952-54. A multi-purpose anti-aircraft, anti-submarine and minelaying flushdecked prototype destroyer for fleet escort and flotilla leader duties. *Neustrashimyi* means Unfearing.

GUNNERY. The 5·1 inch (*130 mm*) guns in two twin turrets, including firing directors, are fully stabilised. This was the first time such an armament had been contrived in a ship of destroyer size, an experiment in top weight.

CLASS. It is understood that there is only one destroyer of the "Tallin" class, actually the prototype for the "Kotlin" class, see photograph in the 1956-57 to 1960-61 editions with different pennant number 76.

RADAR. Search: Haymarket and Minories. Fire Control: Cheapside (2).

BLESTYASTCHY ("Kotlin" Class)   *1970*

KOTLIN SAM I Class   *1970, MOD, Official*

Destroyers—*continued*

45 "SKORY" CLASS

BESSMENNYI	BEZUKORIZNENNY

Normally in the Black Sea

OTCHAYANNYI	OZHESTOCHENNYI
OTVETSTVENNYI	OZHIVLENNYI

Normally in the Arctic

SERIDTYI	SPOSOBNYI
SERIOZNYI	STATNYI
SMELYI	STEPENNYI
SMOTRYASHCHYI	STOJKYI
SOKRUSHITELNYI	STREMITELNYI
SOLIDNYI	SUROVYI
SOVERSHENNYI	SVOBODNYI

Normally in the Baltic

VDUMCHIVYI	VRAZUMITELNYI

Normally in the Far East

Displacement, tons	2 600 standard; 3 500 full load
Length, feet (*metres*)	393·7 (*120·0*)
Beam, feet (*metres*)	40·0 (*12·2*)
Draught, feet (*metres*)	15·1 (*4·6*)
Guns, surface	4—5·1 in (*130 mm*), 2 twin
Guns, AA	2—3·4 in (*85 mm*), 1 twin;
	8—37 mm (4 twin), formerly
	7—37 mm single see *Modernisation* and *Armament*
A/S weapons	4 DCT
Torpedo tubes	10—21 in (*533 mm*)
Mines	80 capacity
Main engines	Geared turbines; 2 shafts; 70 000 shp
Boilers	4 high pressure
Speed, knots	35
Radius, miles	3 900 at 15 knots
Complement	260

There were to have been 85 destroyers of this class, but construction beyond 75 units was discontinued in favour of later types of destroyers, and the number has been further reduced to 45 by transfers to other countries, translations to other types and disposals.

SVOBODNYI   *1968*

MODERNISATION. Six or so ships of the "Skoryi" class were modified from 1959 onwards under the fleet rehabilitation and modernisation programme, including extensive alterations to anti-aircraft armament, electronic equipment and anti-submarine weapons.

NOMENCLATURE. The names of "Skory" class destroyers are apparently based on their fleet assignment. Those in the Black Sea have names beginning with B, those in the Northern Fleet have names beginning with O, those in the Baltic have names beginning with S and those in the Pacific have names beginning with V.

APPEARANCE. There were three differing types in this class, the anti-aircraft guns varying with twin and single mountings; and two types of foremast, one vertical with all scanners on top and the other with one scanner on top and one on a platform half way.

RADAR. Search: Unidentified S Band and Minories. Fire Control: Obsolescent type.

ARMAMENT. Modernised ships have five 57 mm single, five torpedo tubes and two 16-barrelled ASW rocket launchers.

PHOTOGRAPHS. Photographs of *Stepennyi, Sposobnyi* and *Surovyi* appear in the 1954-55 to 1957-58 editions, a large broadside view of *Smotryahchy* in the 1957-58 to 1959-60 editions, a starboard bow view of *Ozestochennyi* in the 1957-58 to 1962-63 editions, a port broadside view of *Otchaiannyi* in the 1958-59 to 1962-63 editions, a port bow oblique aerial view of *Svabodnyi* (No. 14) and a starboard broadside surface view of *Otretsvennyi* in the 1957-58 to 1966-67 editions.

TRANSFERS. Of this class *Skoryi* and *Smetlivyi* were transferred to the Polish Navy in 1957-58, two to the Egyptian Navy in 1956, four to the Indonesian Navy in 1959, and two (modernised) to Egypt in 1968.

SVOBODNYI   *1967*

OTCHAYANNYI   *Added 1967*

ESCORTS

"Mirka I" Class   1970, Niels Gartig

6 "NANUCHKA" CLASS
MISSILE CORVETTE TYPE

Displacement, tons	800 normal (approx)
Length, feet (metres)	229·7 (70·0) oa
Width, feet (metres)	40·0 (12·2) over missiles
Missile launchers	6 (2 triple) for surface-to-surface missiles (forward)
Guns	2—57 mm AA (1 twin)
A/S weapons	1 or 2 ASW rocket launchers
Main engines	Diesels for 28 to 30 knots sea
Speed, knots	32 max

Enlarged successors of the "Osa" class missile boats. Apparently a development of the "Poti" class submarine chasers but with diesels instead of gas turbines and with SSM launchers as the main armament. Reported to have a very broad beam to length ratio. Built from 1969 onwards.

"Mirka I" Class   1968

21 "MIRKA I" CLASS

Displacement, tons	950 standard; 1 100 full load
Length, feet (metres)	265·7 (81·0) oa
Beam, feet (metres)	29·9 (9·1)
Draught, feet (metres)	9·8 (3·0)
A/S weapons	4—12 barrel rocket launchers (2 forward, 2 aft)
Guns, AA	4—3 in (76 mm) 2 twin
Torpedo tubes	5—16 in anti-submarine (see notes)
Main engines	2 diesels, total 6 000 hp; 2 gas turbines, total 19 000 hp; 2 shafts
Speed, knots	33
Complement	100

Successors and anit-submarine versions of the "Petya" class, of similar design, but with teething problems eradicated. Two built in the Baltic, three others built at Kalingrad in 1964. Two ships fitted with two quintuple 16 inch A/S torpedo tubes instead of rocket launchers aft, the forward rocket launchers being retained, have two 3 inch single guns and two 12-barrelled rocket launchers. Pennant numbers include 891.

"Petya II" Class   1970, MOD, Official

4 "MIRKA II" CLASS

A/S weapons	2—16 barrelled rocket launchers forward
Torpedo tubes	10—16 in anti-submarine (2 quintupled)

Except for the above data these ships have the same general features as their half sisters of the "Mirka I" class.

RADAR. Search: Haymarket. Fire Control: Cheapside

"Petya I" Class   B. Borg

40 "PETYA I" CLASS

Displacement, tons	950 standard; 1 150 full load
Length, feet (metres)	250 (76·2) wl; 265·7 (81·0) oa
Beam, feet (metres)	29·9 (9·1)
Draught, feet (metres)	10·5 (3·2)
A/S weapons	4—16 barrelled rocket launchers, (see notes)
Guns, dual purpose	4—3 in (76 mm), 2 twin
Torpedo tubes	5—16 in (406 mm) see notes
Main engines	2 diesels, total 5 000 hp; 2 gas turbines, total 15 000 hp; 2 shafts
Speed, knots	30
Complement	100

Escort patrol vessels with a low wide funnel. The first ship reported to have been built in 1960-61 by Kaliningrad, Nikolaiev. Construction continued until about 1965. Fitted with two mine rails. Later versions are fitted with two sets of torpedo tubes and two 12-barrelled rocket launchers. "Petya" class pennant numbers include 844, 846, 847, 849.

5 "PETYA II" CLASS

A/S weapons	2—12 barrelled rocket launchers forward
Torpedo tubes	10—16 in anti-submarine (2 quintupled)

Of similar design and general arrangement as the "Petya I" class but with a different scheme of weaponry, see data above. One ship has no 76 mm turret aft but variable depth sonar is mounted instead.

RADAR. Search: Haymarket. Fire Control: Cheapside.

"Petya I" Class   1969, B. Borg

Escorts—*continued*

"Kola" Class

6 "KOLA" CLASS

Displacement, tons	1 500 standard; 1 900 full load
Length, feet (*metres*)	295·3 (*90·0*) pp; 315·0 (*96·0*) oa
Beam, feet (*metres*)	32·8 (*10·0*)
Draught, feet (*metres*)	11·5 (*3·5*)
Guns, dual purpose	4—3·9 (*100 mm*) single
Guns, AA	4—37 mm (2 twin)
A/S weapons	DCT's and racks
Torpedo tubes	3—21 in (*533 mm*)
Main engines	Geared turbines; 2 shafts; 30,000 shp
Boilers	2
Speed, knots	31
Complement	190

Built in 1950-52. In design this class of flushdecked destroyer escort appears to be a combination of the former German "Elbing" type torpedo boat destroyers, with a similar hull form, and of the earlier Soviet "Birds" class frigates. The four 3·9 inch guns were mounted as in the "Gordyi" class destroyers.

"Kola" Class   1969. S. Breyer

48 "RIGA" CLASS

Displacement, tons	1 200 standard; 1 600 full load
Length, feet (*metres*)	278·5 (*84·9*) pp; 285 (*90·0*) oa
Beam, feet (*metres*)	31·5 (*9·6*)
Draught, feet (*metres*)	11 (*3·4*)
Guns, dual purpose	3—3·9 in (*100 mm*) single
Guns, AA	4—37 mm (2 twin)
A/S weapons	2—16 barrelled rocket launchers; 4 DC projectors
Torpedo tubes	3—21 in (*533 mm*)
Main engines	Geared turbines; 2 shafts; 25 000 shp
Boilers	2
Speed, knots	28
Complement	150

Built from 1952-53 onwards. Successors to the "Kola" class escorts, of which they are lighter and less heavily armed but improved versions. Fitted with mine rails. The two 16-barrelled rocket launchers are mounted just before the bridge abreast "B" gun. A photograph of No. 645 appears in the 1956-57 to 1962-63 editions, of No. 168 in the 1962-63 to 1965-66 editions.

RADAR. Search: Haymarket. Fire Control: Obsolescent type.

"BIRDS" CLASSES.
The three of the improved "Birds" class, *Albatros*, *Chaika* (Seagull), and *Krechet* (Buzzard); the seven of the "Birds" class, *Berkut* (Golden Eagle), *Grif* (Griffin), *Kondor*, *Korshun* (Kite), *Orel* (Eagle), *Voron* (Raven) and *Yastreb* (Hawk) were discarded.

ANSALDO TYPE. The two Ansaldo type vessels, *Dzerzhinski* (ex-PS 8) and *Kirov* (ex-PS 26), were deleted from the list on account of age obsolescence or being worn out.

"Riga" Class No. 215   1971

"Riga Class" No. 644   1971, MOD, DPR(N), Official

SUPPORT SHIP

"Ugra" Class No. 922   1970, Niels Gartig

NUCLEAR SUPPORT TYPE
5 "UGRA" CLASS

Displacement, tons	6 750 standard; 9 500 full load
Length, feet (metres)	452·8 (138·0) oa
Beam, feet (metres)	65·0 (19·8)
Draught, feet (metres)	21·3 (6·5)
Aircraft	Provision for helicopter
Guns, dual purpose	8—2·3 in (57 mm), 4 twin mounts, 2 forward, 2 aft
Main engines	Diesels; 2 shafts; 2 × 7 000 bhp
Speed, knots	17

Improved versions of the "Don" class. Built in 1961 to 1968, all in Mikolaev. Support and escort ships of the maintanence and repair, supply and depot type probably for servicing nuclear powered submarines. Built on warship lines. Equipped with workshops and staterooms. Provided with a helicopter platform. Fitted with comprehensive radar. Carries a large derrick to handle torpedoes and warheads. Has mooring points in hull about 100 feet apart, but has side doorways, possibly for coastal craft and submarines.

"Ugra" Class   1964, Skyfotos

RADAR. Search: Haymarket. Fire Control: Cheapside (2).

TRANSFER. The sixth ship, *Amba*, which had four 76 mm guns, was transferred to India.

"Lama" Class

MISSILE SUPPLY TYPE
5 "LAMA" CLASS

Displacement, tons	5 000 standard; 7 000 full load
Length, feet (metres)	370·0 (112·8) oa
Beam, feet (metres)	60·0 (18·3)
Draught, feet (metres)	19·0 (5·8)
Guns, dual purpose	8—57 mm, 2 quadruple, 1 on the forecastle; 1 on the break of the quarter deck
Main engines	Diesels; 2 shafts; 5 000 shp
Speed, knots	15

Support ships of the depot and freighting type. Their features indicate a possible missile supply role. The engines are sited aft to allow for a very large and high hangar or hold amidships for carrying missiles or weapons spares. The main structure is about 12 feet high above the main deck. There are doors at the forward end with rails leading in. This is surmounted by a turntable gantry or travelling cranes for transferring armaments to combatant ships.

PM 131 is a support and repair ship for missile armed surface ships. She can apparently be used for salvage and towing. There are mooring points along the hull for low vessels such as submarines to come alongside. There appears to be a turntable on the deck, which is built up 2 feet above the main deck. The two cranes are in the stowed position and there appear to be pulleyed lifting arrangements, apparently intended to service the well deck and overside. The well deck is about 40 feet

"Lama" Class   1964, Skyfotos

long, enough for a missile to fit horizontally before being lifted vertically for loading in submarines.

RADAR. Search: Haymarket and Minories. Fire Control: Cheapside (2).

Support Ships—*continued*

MAGOMED GADZIEV (guns aft)

1970, Aldo Fraccaroli

VIKTOR KOTELNIKOV (helo deck aft)

1970, Niels Gartig

FAST OCEANGOING SUBMARINE SUPPORT TYPE

6 "DON" CLASS

DMITRI GALKIN   **MIKHAIL TUKALEVSKY**
FEDOR VIDYAEV   **NIKOLAY STOLBOV**
MAGOMED   **VIKTOR KOTELNIKOV**
GADZHIEV

Displacement, tons	6 700 standard; 9 000 full load
Length, feet (*metres*)	449·5 (*137·0*)
Beam, feet (*metres*)	55·1 (*16·8*)
Draught, feet (*metres*)	22·3 (*6·8*)
Aircraft	Provision for helicopter in two ships
Guns, dual purpose	4—3·9 (*100 mm*)
Guns, AA	8—57 mm (4 twin)
Main engines	4 or 6 diesels; 14 000 bhp
Speed, knots	21
Complement	300

Support ships, all named after officers lost in WW II. Built in 1957 to 1962. Originally seven ships were built, all in Nikolaev. One was transferred to Indonesia in 1962. Bow crane with 100 tons capacity. Quarters for about 450 men of submarine crews.

PHOTOGRAPHS. A photograph of *Viktor Kotelnikov*, then bearing No. 701, modified version with helicopter deck aft instead of guns, appears in the 1965-66 to 1967-68 editions.

RADAR. Search: Haymarket and probably Minories. Fire Control: One Barbican and two Cheapside.

MAGOMED GADZHIEV

1968

"Don" Class

1970

OCEANGOING ICEBREAKER TYPE

1 "PURGA" CLASS

Displacement, tons	2 250 standard; 3 000 full load
Length, feet (*metres*)	324·8 (*99·0*)
Beam, feet (*metres*)	44·3 (*13·5*)
Draught, feet (*metres*)	17·1 (*5·2*)
Guns, dual purpose	4—3·9 in (*100 mm*) singles
Mines	50 capacity
Main engines	Diesels
Speed, knots	18
Complement	250

Laid down in 1939 in Leningrad and completed in 1948. Sturdy oceangoing general purpose ship equipped as icebreaker, escort, training ship and tender. Fitted with directors similar to those in the "Riga" class frigates. Modernised in 1958-60.

"Purga" Class

Support Ships—*continued*

2 "ALESHA" CLASS

MMF 075   **MMF 076**

Displacement, tons	3 600 standard; 4 300 full load
Dimensions, feet	337·9 × 47·6 × 15·7
Guns	4—57 mm AA (1 quadruple forward)
Main engines	4 diesels; 2 shafts; 8 000 bhp = 20 knots
Complement	150

Multi-purpose support ship type: minelayer, barrage vessel, rescue ship and tender. MMF 075 has been in service since 1965. Stationed in the Black Sea. Has capacity for 400 mines below decks, with four mine tracks to provide stern launchings for exercises.

"Alesha" Class   *1971*

KUBAN (ex-*Waldemar Kophamel*)

Displacement, tons	4 726 standard; 5 600 full load
Dimensions, feet	446·0 × 52·5 × 14·5
Main engines	4 MAN diesels; 2 shafts; 12 400 bhp = 20 knots

Former German. Launched in 1939. Submarine tender. Salvaged in 1950-51 after being sunk in shallow water by bombing in WW II. Rehabilitated in 1951-1957.

The depot ships ex-*Adolf Luderitz*; *Volga* (ex-*Juan Sebastian de Elcano*) and ex-*Donetz*, ex-*Weichsel*, ex-*Syra*, are reported probably scrapped. The submarine tenders Paysherd (ex-*Otto Wünche*), Terek (ex-*Elbe*), *Irtysh* (ex-*Kronstadt*), and Saratov were in 1971 reported to have been discarded.

COASTAL ESCORTS

"Stenka" Class   *S. Breyer*

30 "STENKA" CLASS

Displacement, tons	170 standard; 210 full load
Dimensions, feet	125·3 × 27·9 × 5·9
Guns	4—30 mm AA (2 twin)
Torpedo tubes	4—16 in (406 mm) anti-submarine
A/S weapons	2 depth charge racks
Main engines	3 diesels; 10 000 bhp = 40 knots
Complement	25

Submarine chasers of a new type. Built from 1967/68 onwards. Five units in service by mid-1969. See photograph above.

"Poti" Class   *1970, S. Breyer*

Coastal Escorts—*continued*

75 "POTI' CLASS

Displacement, tons	550 standard; 650 full load
Dimensions, feet	196·9 × 26·2, × 9·2
Guns	2—57 mm AA (1 twin mounting)
Tubes	4—16 in anti-submarine
A/S weapons	2—12 barrelled rocket launchers
Main engines	2 gas turbines; 2 diesels; 4 shafts; total 20 000 hp = ·28 knots

This class of coastal escort vessels or patrol vessels of the submarine chaser type is reported to have been under series construction since 1961.

"Poti" Class No. 195   *1971*

100 "SOI" CLASS

Displacement, tons	215 light; 250 normal
Dimensions, feet	137·8 × 20·0 × 9·2
Guns	4—25 mm AA (2 twin mountings) see notes
A/S weapons	4 five-barrelled ahead throwing rocket launchers
Main engines	3 diesels; 6 000 bhp = 29 knots
Complement	30

Built since 1957. Steel hulled. Modernised boats of this class have only two 25 mm AA guns but also have four 16 in anti-submarine torpedo tubes.

"SO I" Class No. 58   *1968*

65 "KRONSTADT" CLASS

Displacement, tons	310 standard; 380 full load
Dimensions, feet	167·3 × 19·3 × 9·0
Guns	1—3·9 in; 2—37 mm AA
A/S weapons	Depth charge projectors
Main engines	3 diesels; 3 shafts; 3 300 hp = 24 knots
Complement	65

Built in 1948-56. Flush-decked with large squat funnel, slightly raked, and massive block bridge structure. Now gradually being taken out of service due to age. About 20 boats were rebuilt as communications relay ships of the "Libau" class.

"Kronstadt" Class

"Kronstadt Class No. 512   *1970, courtesy, Godfrey H. Walker Esq.*

FLEET MINESWEEPERS

45 "YURKA" CLASS

Displacement, tons	500 standard; 550 full load
Dimensions, feet	170·6 × 30·2 × 8·9
Guns	4—30 mm AA (2 twin)
Main engines	2 diesels; 4 000 bhp = 18 knots

A class of medium fleet minesweepers with steel hull. Built from 1963 onwards. Reportedly powered with diesels and/or gas turbines.

20 "T 58" CLASS

Displacement, tons	790 standard; 900 full load
Dimensions, feet	220·0 × 29·5 × 7·9
Guns	4—57 mm AA (2 twin)
Main engines	2 diesels; 2 shafts; 5 000 bhp = 18 knots

A class of fleet minesweepers built from 1957 to 1964. Of this class 14 were converted to submarine rescue ships with armament and sweeping gear removed, see later page ("Valdai" class).

T 58 No. 4 with "Muff Cob" fire control radar on the bridge   1968

120 "T 43" CLASS

Displacement, tons	500 standard; 600 full load
Dimensions, feet	191·9 × 28·2 × 6·9
Guns	4—37 mm AA (2 twin)
Main engines	2 diesels; 2 shafts; 2 200 bhp = 17 knots

A handy type of moderately fast madium sized minesweepers built in 1948-57 in shipyards throughout the Soviet Union. Of the original 175 ships ten were transferred to Poland, eight to Albania, six to Egypt, four to Indonesia, three to Bulgaria, and two to Syria. A number of this class were converted into radar pickets (see photograph of No. 55 in the 1965-66 to 1967-68 editions and on a later page) and into rescue ships with no armament.

T 43" Class   1968

T 43" Class   1969, MOD, RN, Official

"T 43" Class   1968

COASTAL MINESWEEPERS

"Vanya" Class   1970, S. Breyer

50 "VANYA" CLASS

Displacement, tons	250 standard; 275 full load
Dimensions, feet	144·4 × 24·0 × 6·9
Guns	2—30 mm AA (1 twin)
Main engines	2 diesels; 2 200 bhp = 18 knots
Complement	30

A coastal class with wooden hulls of a type suitable for series production built from 1961 onwards. Basically similar to NATO type coastal minesweepers.

"Vanya" Class   1968, S. Breyer

35 "SASHA" CLASS

Displacement, tons	245 standard; 280 full load
Dimensions, feet	150·9 × 22·3 × 6·6
Guns	1—57mm dp; 4—25 mm AA (2 twin)
Main engines	2 diesels; 2 200 bhp = 18 knots
Complement	25

Basically similar to NATO coastal minesweepers, but of steel construction. This series did not run into the number at first projected, construction having been discontinued in favour of later types.

"Sasha" Class   1968, S. Breyer

50 "T 301" CLASS

Displacement, tons	150 standard; 180 full load
Dimensions, feet	128·0 × 18·0 × 4·9
Guns	2—37 mm AA; 2 MG
Main engines	2 diesels; 2 shafts; 1 440 bhp = 17 knots

Built from 1946 to 1956. Several were converted to survey craft, and many adapted for other purposes or used for port duty and auxiliary service. Now gradually being withdrawn from service due to age. Twenty reportedly withdrawn in 1971.

"T 301" Class

"TR 40" CLASS

Displacement, tons	50 standard; 70 full load
Dimensions, feet	92·0 × 13·5 × 2·3
Guns	2—25 mm forward; 2 MG (twin) aft
Main engines	Diesels; 600 bhp = 14 knots

"K 8" CLASS

Displacement, tons	40 standard; 60 full load
Dimensions, feet	55·8 × 11·5 × 4·0
Guns	2 MG (1 twin)
Main engines	Diesels; speed 18 knots

Auxiliary motor minesweeping boats of the inshore ("TR 40") and river ("K 8") types.

TORPEDO BOATS

"Shershen" Class   1970, S. Breyer

30 "SHERSHEN" CLASS

Displacement, tons	150 standard; 160 full load
Dimensions, feet	118·1 × 25·3 × 5·0
Guns	4—30 mm AA (2 twin)
Tubes.	4—21 in (single)
A/S weapons	12 DC
Main engines	Diesels; 3 shafts; 1 300 bhp = 41 knots
Complement	16

These large torpedo boats have basically the same hull and layout as the "Osa" class missile boats, but with tubes in the launcher positions. Built from 1962 onwards.

"Shershen" Class   1966, col Breyer

250 "P 6" "P 8" "P 10" CLASSES

Displacement, tons	66 standard; 75 full load
Dimensions, feet	85·3 × 20·0 × 6·0
Guns	4—25 mm AA
Tubes	2—21 in (or mines, or depth charges)
Main engines	Diesels; 4 shafts; 4 800 bhp = 43 knots
Complement	12

The "P 6" class was of a standard medium sized type running into series production. Launched during 1951 to 1960. Known as "MO VI" class in the submarine chaser version (see below). The later versions, known as the "P 8" and "P 10" classes, are powered with gas turbines, and have different bridge and funnel, experimental type. "P 8" boats have hydrofoils.

"P 8" Class en flotille   1969, S. Breyer

25 "PCHELA" CLASS

Displacement, tons	60 standard; 80 full load
Dimensions, feet	88·6 × 18·0 × 0·0
Guns	4 MG (2 twin)
Main engines	Diesels; 6 000 bhp = 50 knots

This class of hydrofoils, probably submarine chasers, are reported to have been built since 1964-65. Also carry depth charges.

20 "P 4" CLASS

Displacement, tons	25 normal max
Dimensions, feet	82·0 × 16·8 × 5·6
Guns	2 MG (1 twin)
Tubes	2—18 in
Main engines	2 Diesels; 2 shafts; 2 200 bhp = 50 knots

Originally a numerically large class of boats with aluminium alloy hulls. Launched in 1951-58. The earlier units are being discarded (30 in 1969-71).

"MO VI" CLASS FAST SUBMARINE CHASERS

Displacement, tons	64 standard; 73 full load
Dimensions, feet	83·7 × 20·0 × 4·0
Guns	4—25 mm AA (2 twin)
A/S weapons	2 depth charge mortars; 2 depth charge racks
Main engines	4 diesels; 4 shafts; 4 800 bhp = 40 knots

Built in 1956 to 1960. Formerly "P-6" class motor torpedo boats.

"P 10" Class   1968, Col Breyer

"P 6" Class   1966, Col Breyer

"P 6" Class   1966, Col Breyer

"Pchela" Class   1970

"Osa" Class (see following page)   1970, S. Breyer

MISSILE BOATS
"OSA" CLASS SERIES

"Osa" I Class   *1969, S. Breyer*

"Osa" II Type (cylindrical missile launchers)   *1969, S. Breyer*

"Osa" I Class   *1969, col Borg*

"Osa" I Class   *1969*

'Osa" I Class   *1969*

"Osa" I Class   *1969*

MISSILE BOATS

"Osa" Class No. 178 — 1970, courtesy Godfrey H. Walker, Esq.

100 "OSA" CLASS

Displacement, tons	165 standard; 200 full load
Dimensions, feet	123·0 × 27·9 × 5·9
Missile launchers	4 in two pairs abreast for "SS-N-2"
Guns	4—30 mm; (2 twin, 1 forward, 1 aft)
Main engines	3 diesels; 13200 bhp = 38 knots

These boats, built since 1959, have a larger hull and four large hood type launchers in two pairs as compared with one pair in the torpedo boat conversions. They have a surface-to-surface missile range of 15 to 18 miles. Later boats have cylindrical missile launchers, probably for new surface-to-surface missiles.

"Osa" Class No. 279 — 1970, S. Breyer

"Osa" Class — 1967, col Breyer

25 "KOMAR" CLASS

Displacement, tons	75 standard; 100 full load
Dimensions, feet	83·7 × 21·0 × 4·9
Missile launchers	2 for "SS-N-2" missiles
Guns	2—25 mm AA (1 twin forward)
Main engines	4 diesels; 4 shafts; 4 800 bhp = 40 knots

A smaller type of boats converted from "P 6" class torpedo boats. Fitted with two surface-to-surface launchers aft in a hooded casing approximately 45 degrees to the deck line with a range of 15 miles. Built since 1960-61.

"Komar" Class — 1968

AMPHIBIOUS SHIPS

8 "ALLIGATOR" TYPE

Displacement, tons	4 100 standard; 5 800 full load
Dimensions, feet	374·0 × 50·9 × 12·1
Guns	2—57 mm AA
Main engines	Diesels; 8 000 bhp = 15 knots

Largest type of Soviet landing ship built in the USSR to date. LST type. First ship built in 1965-66 and commissioned in 1966. These ships have ramps on the bow and stern. Carrying capacity 1 700 tons. "Alligator" is the NATO designation.

"Alligator" type — 1971

50 "POLNOCNY" TYPES

Displacement, tons	780 standard; 1 000 full load
Dimensions, feet	246·0 × 29·5 × 9·8
Armament	2—14 barrelled rocket projectors
Main engines	2 diesels; 5 000 bhp = 18 knots

A type of amphibious vessel basically similar to the US medium landing ship, rocket (LSMR) type. Can carry 8 to 10 tanks. "Polnocny II" type has a modified mast and twin 30 mm AA turret before the bridge. Built in Poland from 1961 onwards.

"Polnochny" Type

"Polnocny II" Type with 2—30 mm AA before bridge and fire control radar on bridge — 1969, S, Breyer

18 "MP" 8 TYPE

Displacement, tons	800 standard; 1 200 full load
Dimensions, feet	239·5 × 34·8 × 15·1
Guns	4—57 mm (2 twin)
Main engines	Diesels; 4 000 bhp = 15 knots

Old type of landing ship with a short and low quarter deck abaft the after castle and a waist between the gun mounting before the bridge and the gun mounting on the high forecastle. Can carry 8 or more tanks. Carrying capacity 400 tons.

"MP 8" Type — 1970, S. Breyer

8 "MP" 6 TYPE

Displacement, tons	1 800 normal; 2 000 full load
Dimensions, feet	246·0 × 37·0 × 14·4
Main engines	Diesels; 2 200 bhp = 12 knots

Two masts, one stepped from the superstructure aft and one in the forecastle. King posts. Mounting in the bandstand on the forecastle has two pairs of barrels in the vertical plane. Can carry 8 to 10 tanks. Several ships serve as transports.

Amphibious Ships—*continued*

25 "MP 4" TYPE

Displacement, tons	800 full load
Dimensions, feet	183·7 × 26·2 × 8·9
Guns	4—25 mm (2 twin)
Main engines	Diesels; 2 shafts; 1 100 bhp = 12 knots

Built in 1956-58. Formerly "Uzka" class. Of the small freighter type in appearance. Two masts, one abaft the bridge and one in the waist. Gun mountings on poop and forecastle. Can carry 6 to 8 tanks. Several ships now serve as transports. Carrying capacity 500 tons.

12 "MP 2" TYPE

Displacement, tons	600 standard; 750 full load
Dimensions, feet	190·3 × 25·0 × 8·2
Guns	6—25 mm (3 twin)
Main engines	Diesels; 1 200 bhp = 16 knots

Basically similar to the British LCT (8) type. Formerly "Adka" class. Gun mountings on after shelter deck abaft funnel and on forecastle. Can carry four tanks. Carrying capacity 200 tons.

AMPHIBIOUS CRAFT

"Vydra" Type   1971

25 "VYDRA" TYPE

Displacement, tons	300 standard; 500 full load
Dimensions, feet	164·0 × 26·2 × 7·2
Main engines	2 diesels; 2 shafts; speed 10 knots

A new class of landing craft of the LCU type. Built from 1967 onwards. No armament.

MP 10/SMB 1 Type   1971

40 "MP 10" "SMB 1" TYPE

Displacement, tons	200 standard; 420 full load
Dimensions, feet	157·5 × 19·7 × 6·5
Main engines	2 diesels; 2 shafts; speed = 11 knots

A type of landing craft basically similar to the British LCT (4) type in silhouette and layout. Can carry 4 tanks. Loading capacity about 150 tons.

"T 4" TYPE

Displacement, tons	80 full load
Dimensions, feet	68·9 × 18·0 × 3·3

Small landing craft of the LCM type with a loading capacity of one tank.

DEPOT SHIPS

6 "ATREK" CLASS

ATREK   AYAT   BAKHMUT   DVINO   MURMATS   OSIPOV

Displacement, tons	3 500 standard; 6 700 full load
Measurement, tons	3 258 gross
Dimensions, feet	336 × 49 × 20
Main engines	Expansion and exhaust turbines; 1 shaft; 2 450 hp = 13 knots
Boilers	2 water tube
Radius, miles	3 500 at 13 knots

Built in 1956-58, and converted to naval use from "Kolomna" class freighters. There are six of these vessels employed as submarine tenders and replenishment ships.

ATREK V(B)-272   1959, Sergei Romanov

Depot Ships—*continued*

"Amur" Class   1971

"AMUR" CLASS

Displacement, tons	6 500 full load
Dimensions, feet	377·3 × 57·4 × 18·0
Main engines	Diesels; 2 shafts

A new class of tenders or depot ships for submarines built since circa 1969.

9 "OSKOL" CLASS

Displacement, tons	2 500 standard; 3 000 full load
Dimensions, feet	282·2 × 37·7 × 14·8
Main engines	2 diesels; 2 shafts; speed = 16 knots

Three series: "Oskol I" class, well-decked hull, no armament; "Oskol II" Class, well-decked hull, armed with 2—57 mm guns (1 twin) and 4—25 mm guns (2 twin); "Oskol III" class, flush-decked hull. Tenders and repair ships. Nine ships built since 1963-64 in Poland.

2 "TOVDA" CLASS

INZA (ex-*Novoshaktinsk*)   **TOVDA**

Displacement, tons	3 000 standard; 4 000 full load
Dimensions, feet	282·1 × 39·4 × 16·0
Guns	6—57 mm AA (3 twin mountings)
Main engines	Triple expansion; 1 300 ihp = 11 knots

Polish built ex-tankers converted in 1958 to 1960. Depot and repair ships. Also known as the "Soldek" class, but the NATO designation is "Tovda" class.

"Tovda" Class   1959

2 "DESNA" CLASS

CHAZHMA   **CHUMIKAN**

Displacement, tons	5 300 light; 14 065 full load
Dimensions, feet	457·7 × 59·0 × 25·9
Aircraft	1 helicopter
Main engines	Triple expansion; 4 000 ihp = 18 knots

Formerly freighters of the "Dzankoy" class (7 265 tons gross). Soviet Missile Range Instrumentation Ships (SMRIS). The "Desna" class have a larger hull than the "Sibir" class and are better equipped. Active since 1963. Large radome on the bridge.

ANGARA (ex-*Hela*)

Displacement, tons	2 115 standard; 2 500 full load
Dimensions, feet	323 × 42·5 × 11
Guns	2—4·1 in; 1—37 mm AA; 2—20 mm AA
Main engines	4 MAN diesels; 2 shafts; 6 300 bhp = 18 knots
Radius, miles	2 000 at 15 knots

Former yacht built by Stülcken, Hamburg. Launched in 1939. In the Black Sea. A photograph of *Angara* appears in the 1947-48 to 1965-66 editions.

KOMMUNA (ex-*Volkhov*)

Displacement, tons	2 400
Main engines	Diesels; 2 shafts; speed = 8 knots

Former submarine salvage vessel. Launched in 1913. Repair ship. Double hull. Refitted at De Schelde Yard, Flushing, Netherlands during May 1950 to July 1951. The repair and depot ship *Elbrus* was in 1971 reported discarded.

KOMMUNA (before last refit)

Depot Ships—*continued*

4 "SIBIR" CLASS

CHUKOTKA	SAKHALIN	SIBIR	SUCHAN

Displacement, tons	4 000 standard; 5 000 full load
Measurement, tons	3 767 gross (*Chukotka* 3 800, *Suchan* 3 710)
Dimensions, feet	475·7 to 493·5 × 56·1 × 20 (ships vary)
Guns	6—45 mm AA; 2 MG
Main engines	Triple expansion; 2 shafts; 3 300 ihp = 15 knots
Radius, miles	3 300 miles at 12 knots

Converted bulk ore carriers employed as Missile Range Ships in the Pacific. *Sakhalin* and *Sibir* have three radomes forward and aft, and carry helicopters. *Suchan* is also equipped with a helicopter flight deck. Launched in 1957-59. Formerly freighters of the Polish "B 31" type. Rebuilt in 1958-59 as missile range ships in Leningrad.

5 "DNEPR" CLASS

PM 17

Displacement, tons	4 500 standard; 5 250 full load
Dimensions, feet	370·7 × 54·1 × 14·4
Main engines	Diesels; 2 000 bhp = 12 knots

Bow lift repair and depot ships for fleet support and maintenance. Built in 1957-66 as repair ships, equipped with workshops and servicing facilities. The last two ships of this class are flushdecked ("Dnepr II" class).

PM 17 ("Dnepr I" Class)   *1965*

RADAR PICKETS

5 "T 43"/AGR CLASS

Displacement, tons	500 standard; 650 full load
Dimensions, feet	192·0 × 28·2 × 6·9
Guns	4—37 mm AA; 2—25 mm AA
Main engines	2 Diesels; 2 shafts; 2 200 bhp = 17 knots
Complement	77

Former fleet minesweepers of the "T 43" class converted into radar pickets with comprehensive electronic equipment. It is reported that there may be six to a dozen vessels of this type. Large "Big Net" radar on after mast.

"T 43" Radar Picket No. 55 ("Big Net" radar on mainmast)   *1970, S. Breyer*

SUBMARINE RESCUE SHIP

14 "T 58" CLASS ("VALDAII" TYPE)

Displacement, tons	725 standard; 850 full load
Dimensions, feet	222·1 × 29·9 ×7·5
Main engines	2 diesels; 2 shafts; 5 000 bhp = 20 knots

Basically of similar design to the "T 58" class larger fleet minesweepers, but the hulls were completed as emergency salvage vessels and submarine rescue ships at Leningrad. Equipped with diving bell, decompresion chamber, lifting gear and emergency medical ward. Known as the "Valdaii type. It has been reported that there may be 12 to 15 of the "T 58" hull type and five or six of the "T 43" hull design.

VALDAII Class   *1970. S. Breyer*

INTELLIGENCE TRAWLERS

ALIDADA	BAROMETR	IZMIRITEL	REDUCTOR
AMPERMETR	DEFLEKTOR	KRENOMETR	PROTRACTOR
AMTR	EKHOLOT	LINZA	VAL
BAKAN	GIDROFON	LOTLIN	VERTIKAL
BAROGRAPH	GIROSKOP	LOTZMAN	VOSTOK
			ZOND

Measurement, tons	684 gross; 226 net; 502 gross; 197 net; 334 gross; 89 net; 293 gross; 88 net; and various other measurements
Dimensions, feet	Length 165 (ships vary)

Most of these trawlers are fitted with electronic interception equipment, with a layout designed for intelligence collection. A considerable number of observation trawlers, equipped with radio aerials and direction-finding apparatus have been sighted by British and NATO warships during international combined sea and air exercises. *Izmiritel* is of "Dnepr" class. *Vostok* was converted for research, see later page.

"LENTRA" CLASS   *1968, Mr Michael D. J. Lennon*

BAKAN   *1970, MOD, Official*

VOSTOK   *1970, courtesy Mr. Michael D. J. Lennon*

GS 239   *1970, Aldo Fraccaroli*

SALVAGE VESSELS

"NEPA" CLASS

Displacement, tons	3 500 light ; 5 000 standard
Dimensions, feet	410·1 × 52·5 × 16·4
Main engines	Diesels ; 2 shafts

New type of submarine rescue and salvage ships similar to the "Prut" class but improved and enlarged and with a special high stern which extends out over the water for rescue manoeuvres. Built since 1969.

"Prut" Class SS 87   1970, S. Breyer

9 "PRUT" CLASS

ALTAI	BRESHTAU	ZHIGULI

Displacement, tons	2 120 standard ; 3 500 full load
Dimensions, feet	296·0 × 36·1 × 13·1
Main engines	Diesels ; 4 200 bhp = 18 knots

Large rescue vessels with raked down flush deck and mainmast derrick. Built since 1960.

"Prut" Class MB 23   1965

"SURA" CLASS

Displacement, tons	3 150 full load
Dimensions, feet	285·4 × 48·6 × 16·4
Main engines	Diesels ; 1 770 bhp = 13·2 knots

Large rescue ships built since 1965 in East Germany.

4 "PAMIR" CLASS

AGATAN	ALDAN	ARBAN	PAMIR

Measurement, tons	1 443 to 2 032 gross
Dimensions, feet	256 oa × 42 × 13·5
Main engines	Two 10 cyl 4 str diesels ; 2 shafts ; 4 200 bhp = 17 knots

Salvage tugs built at AB Gävie, Varv, Sweden, in 1959-60. Equipped with strong derricks, powerful pumps, air compressors, diving gear, fire fighting apparatus and electric generators.

"Pamir" Class   1970, S. Breyer

Salvage Vessels—*continued*

TUG TYPE

	MB 25	MB 26	MB 52
Displacement, tons	835		
Dimensions, feet	134·5 wl ; 143 oa × 34 × 15		
Guns	1—3 in dp ; 2—20 mm AA		
Main engines	2 BM diesels ; 2 electric motors. 2 shafts ; 1 875 bhp = 14 knots		
Oil fuel, tons	187		
Complement	34		

Salvage and rescue tugs. Built by Levingstone Shipbuilding Co., Orange, Texas. Launched in 1944. Former United States ATAs (Ocean Rescue Tugs). In the Baltic.

MB 52   1971, MOD, DPR(N), Official

Fitted with powerful pumps and other apparatus for salvage. Other numbers reported are A 2, 480, 481, 490, 495, 515, 525, 580, 610, 612, 621, and 663. Salvage vessels are designated MSB. The old salvage vessel *Signal*, launched in 1936, was deleted in 1970. Reported to have been worn out and of no further operational value.

TORPEDO RECOVERY/PATROL BOATS

"POLUCHAT I" CLASS

Displacement, tons	100 standard ;
Dimensions, feet	98·4 × 19·0 × 5·9
Guns	2—25 mm (1 twin) or 2 MG (1 twin)

Employed as specialised or dual purpose torpedo recovery vessels and/or patrol boats. Number reported up to 100. They have a stern slipway.

TRANSPORTS

2 "LAKE" CLASS

KAMCHATKA	MONGOL

Former pennant numbers were P-380 and P-242, respectively. The former Japanese cargo ships and military transports, ex-*Hayasaki*, ex-*No. 13*, and ex-*No. 137*, and the former Italian supply ship, ex-*Montecucco*, ex-KT 32, were deleted from the list in 1968, having been discarded on account of age or obsolescence.

6 COASTAL TYPE

SHIM	OLGA	USSURIJ (ex-*Okhotsk*)
OB	SHILKA	VISHERA

Former pennant Nos. were P-247 (*Ob*), P 274 (*Shilka*), P 365 (*Ussurij*), P-379 (*Vishera*), *Olga* and *Ishim* are Coast Guard transports. *Ob* is 1 194 ton diesel electric Antarctic support ship.

RESEARCH TRAWLERS

AYSBERG	ISSLEDOVATEL	OKEANOGRAF	VOSTOK

Measurement, tons	265 gross ; 93 net

All are small converted trawlers for research. *Aysberg* and *Okeanograf* are classed as M-Research. Have visited the United Kingdom. Built in 1956 (*Okeanograf*).

OKEANOGRAF   1970, Michael D. J. Lennon

MISSILE DETECTION SHIPS

KOSMONAUT VLADIMIR KOMAROV   *1970, Michael D. J. Lennon*

2 "KOMAROV" CLASS

KOSMONAUT VLADIMIR KOMAROV   **GENICHVESKI**

Displacement, tons	17 500 full load
Measurement, tons	8 000 approximately
Dimensions, feet	510·8 × 75·5 × 29·5
Main engines	Diesels; 2 shafts; 24 000 bhp = 22 knots

Former freighter of the "Poltava" class, *Kosmonaut Vladimir Komarov* was launched in 1966. Built at the Leningrad Shipyard. Designed for the Soviet Academy of Science as a research vessel to study higher layers of atmosphere in the tropical zone of the western part of the Atlantic Ocean. Prominent features of the ship are the unusual hull sponsons and the radomes, massive plastic spheres enclosing radar arrays. The ship is named in honour of the Soviet astronaut who died when his space craft crashed in 1967. The second ship, *Genichveski*, is reported to have been built in 1967-68.

KOSMONAUT VLADIMIR KOMAROV   *1969, Skyfotos*

KOSMONAUT VLADIMIR KOMAROV   *1969, S. Breyer*

COMMUNICATIONS RELAY SHIPS

20 "LIBAU" CLASS

Displacement, tons	250 standard; 300 full load
Dimensions, feet	170·6 × 22·0 × 5·0
Main engines	Diesels; 2 shafts; 2 200 bhp = 25 knots

Formerly submarine chasers of the "Kronstadt" class rebuilt in 1955-56. Circa 20 units. No armament.

TRAINING SHIPS

ZENIT   *1970, Michael D. J. Lennon*

3 "ZENIT" CLASS

GORIZONT   **HORIZONT**   **ZENIT**

Measurement, tons	4 374 gross; 986 net
Length, feet	344
Beam, feet	47
Main engines	Two 8-cylinder diesels geared to one shaft

Zenit was built in East Germany at Rostock by Schiffswerft Neptune. Mercantile Cadet Training Ship but produces officers for the Navy.

2 "SEDOV" TYPE

KRUZENSTERN   **SEDOV**

Measurement, tons	3 064 gross

Barques. Built in 1921. Employed as sail training ship for midshipmen, cadets and junior seamen. A photograph of *Sedov* appears in the 1968-69 edition.

1 Ex-GERMAN TYPE

TOVARISCH (ex-*Gorch Foch*)

Displacement, tons	1 350
Dimensions, feet	242·8 × 39·3 × 15
Sail area	19 350 sq ft
Guns	2—20 mm AA
Main engines	MAN diesel; 1 shaft; 520 bhp = 8 knots
Oil fuel, tons	25
Radius, miles	3 500 at 8 knots
Complement	260

Barque. Ex-German training ship. Built by Blohm & Voss, Hamburg. Launched in 1933. Of mercantile attachment but produces personnel for the Navy. Sail area: 2 150 sq yds. A photograph of *Tovarisch* appears in the 1968-69 edition.

10 SCHOONER TYPE

ENISEJ   **PRAKTIKA** (ex-*Passat*)   **TOBOL**   **UCHEBA** (ex-*Mousson*)

Displacement, tons	300 approximately (ships vary)

Three masts. In the Baltic. Sailing vessels for training cadets, boys and volunteers. There are about ten three-masted schooners of 300 tons with one square sail on the foremast of the same class as the *Pratika* and *Ucheba*, built in Finland. They are described as very nice little ships.

Some of the above training ships are not strictly rated as naval ships.
The old nominal training ship *Aurora* was deleted in 1963 as although she still exists as a prestige tourist relic (famous to the USSR as the cruiser from which the first round of the October Revolution was fired) she is a museum ship and no longer of military value.

The training ships *Nyeman* (ex-*Isar*, ex-*Puma*) and *Cristoforo Colombo* (ex-Z 18) were in 1971 reported discarded.

SURVEY SHIPS

8 "MOMA" CLASS

ANADIR	**ARKTIKA**	**EKVATOR**	**TAIMYR**
ARKHIPELOG	**ASKOLD**	**PELORUS**	**ZAPOLYARE**

Displacement, tons	1 240 standard; 1 800 full load
Dimensions, feet	219·8 × 32·8 × 13·2
Main engines	Diesels; speed 16 knots

Eight ships reported to have been built since circa 1967-68 (and "Kamenka" class).

"KAMENKA" CLASS

Displacement, tons	1 000 standard
Dimensions, feet	180·5 × 31·2 × 11·5
Main engines	Diesels; speed 16 knots

"SHALANDA" CLASS

Displacement, tons	200 standard
Dimensions, feet	114·8 × 16·4 × 6·6
Main engines	Diesels; speed 12 knots

Shallow draught small surveying craft for coastal operations.

TELNOVSK

Measurement, tons	1 210 gross
Dimensions, feet	229·6 × 32·8 × 13·1
Main engines	Diesels; speed 10 knots

Formerly a coastal freighter, built in Hungary. Refitted and modernised to a new class.

Survey Ships—continued

MICHAIL LOMONOSOV

Displacement, tons	5 960 normal
Measurement, tons	3 897 gross; 1 195 net
Dimensions, feet	336·0 × 47·2 × 14·0
Main engines	Triple expansion; 2 450 ihp = 13 knots

Built by Neptune, Rostock, in 1957 from the hull of a freighter of the "Kolomna" class. Operated not by the Navy but by the Academy of Science. Equipped with 16 laboratories. Carries a helicopter for survey.

MICHAIL LOMONOSOV   1970, Mr. Michael D. J. Lennon

VITYAZ (ex-Mars)

Displacement, tons	5 700 standard
Main engines	Diesels; 3 000 bhp = 14·5 knots
Range, miles	18 400 at 14 knots
Complement	137 officers and men including 73 scientists

Oceanographic research ship. Formerly a German freighter built at Bremen in 1939. Equipped with 13 laboratories. Another non-naval oceanographic research ship, Nereida, was reported to be on operational service in Apr 1965.

NEREIDE

Dimensions, feet	275·6 × 49·2 × 13·1 max

A naval hydrographic and oceanographic surveying vessel designed and built in the USSR.

12 "NIKOLAI" ZUBOV CLASS

A. CHIRIKOV	GAVRIL SARITSHEV	SEJMEN DEZHNEV
A. VILKITSKIJ	KHARITON LAPTEV	T. BELLINSGAUSEN
BORIS DAVIDOV	NIKOLAI ZUBOV	V. GOLOBNIN
F. LITKE	S. CHELYUSKIN	V. OBRUTCHEV

Displacement, tons	2 674 standard; 3 021 full load
Dimensions, feet	295·2 × 42·7 × 15
Main engines	2 diesels; speed = 16·7 knots
Complement	108 to 120, including 70 scientists

"Nikolai Zubov" class, oceanographic research ships were built at Szczecin Shipyard, Poland in 1964. Nikolai Zubov visited London in 1965. Employed on survey in the Atlantic.

NIKOLAI ZUBOV

GAVRIL SARITSHEV   1966, courtesy Mr Michael D. J. Lennon

AISBERG   OKEANOGRAF

Trawlers converted for surveying. Not in the Navy. Visited Glasgow in 1964.

3 "POLYUS" CLASS

BAIKAL	BALKASH	POLYUS

Displacement, tons	6 900 standard
Dimensions, feet	365·8 × 47·2 × 20·7
Main engines	Diesel-electric; 3 400 hp = 14 knots

These ships of the "Polyus" class were built in East Germany in 1961-64.

18 "SAMARA" CLASS

AZIMUT	GORIZONT	RUMB
DEVIATOR	GRADAS	SAMARA
GIDROLOG	HIGROMETR	TROPIK
GIGROMETR	JOUGI	ZENIT
GLOBUS	KOM PAS	VAIGATOR
GOLUVROMETR	PAMYAT MERKURYA	VOSTOK

Displacement, tons	800 standard; 1 000 full load
Measurement, tons	1 276 gross; 1 000 net
Dimensions, feet	180·4 × 32·8 × 11·5
Main engines	Diesels; speed 16 knots

The sister ships of the "Samara" class have been built at Gdansk, Poland, since 1962 for hydrographic surveying and research.

HIGROMETR   1968, Mr Michael D. J. Lennon

ZENIT   1968, Mr Michael D. J. Lennon

KOMPAS   1970, Michael D. J. Lennon

AYTODOR

Displacement, tons	1 200 standard
Measurement, tons	1 217 gross; 448 net

Built in Bulgaria. Naval survey supply ship, formerly a merchant ship.

AYTODOR   1965, Mr Michael D. J. Lennon

3 "MURMAN" CLASS

MURMAN	OKEAN	OKHOTSK

Displacement, tons	1 500 standard; 3 200 full load
Dimensions, feet	265·8 × 42·5 × 18·2
Guns	3—5·1 in; 2—3 in; 2 MG
Main engines	Triple expansion; 2 shafts; 2 400 ihp = 14 knots
Complement	160

Launched in 1937-38. In the Far East. Former minelayers converted into survey ships. Murman was fitted with a helicopter platform in 1962. A photograph of Okhotsk appears in the 1955-56 to 1965-66 edition.

RESEARCH SHIPS

8 "AKADEMIK" CLASS

AKADEMIK KOROLOV (1967)	**DIMITRI MENDELEEV** (1968)
AKADEMIK KURCHATOV (1965)	**PROFESSOR SUBOV** (1967)
AKADEMIK SHIRSHOV (1967)	**PROFESSOR DERYUGIN** (1968)
AKADEMIK VERNADSKY (1967)	**PROFESSOR VIZE** (1967)

Displacement, tons	6 681 full load
Measurement, tons	1 387 net; 1 986 deadweight; 5 460 gross
Dimensions, feet	400·3 to 406·8 × 56·1 × 15·0
Main engines	2 Halberstadt 6-cylinder diesels; 2 shafts; 8 000 bhp = 18 to 20 knots

All built by Mathias Thesen Werft at Wisman, East Germany. Launch dates above.

MORZHOVETS　　　　　　1970, Mr. Michael D. J. Lennon

9 "PASSAT" CLASS

MUSSON	**PASSAT**	**PRILIV**
OCEAN	**PRIBOY**	**VOLNA**

Displacement, tons	2 800 standard
Measurement, tons	962 net; 3 281 gross
Main engines	2 diesels; 2 shafts; speed = 14 knots

Six of the nine research or weather ships built at Szczecin, Poland, since 1968. Aerials differ in certain ships. Formerly freighters of the Polish "B-88" type.

AKADEMIK VERNADSKY　　　　　　1970, Mr. Michael D. L. Jennon

3 "BASLINTCHAK" CLASS

BASLINTCHAK	**DONBASS**	**TAMAN**

Measurement, tons	2 215 net; 6 450 deadweight; 4 896 gross
Dimensions, feet	400·3 × 55·1 × 14·0
Main engines	B & W 9-cylinder diesels; speed 15 knots

Standard timber carriers modified with helicopter flight decks. Built at Leningrad between 1963 and 1966. Entirely manned by naval personnel. Two survey ships, *Baskunchiak* and *Dikson*, sister ships, visited Mombasa in late 1970, navy manned and wearing naval auxiliary ensigns.

PASSAT　　　　　　1970, Mr. Michael D. J. Lennon

2 "LEBEDEV" CLASS

PETR LEBEDEV	**SERGEI VAVILOV**

Measurement, tons	1 180 net; 3 561 gross
Main engines	Diesels

Research vessels with comprehensive equipment and accommodation. Both built in 1954.

BASLINTCHAK　　　　　　1970, Mr. Michael D. J. Lennon

9 "VOSTOK" CLASS

KIRISHI	**SVIRLES**	**VYBORGLES**	**VOSTOK 3**
SUZDAL	**TOSNOLES**	**VOSTOK 2**	**VOSTOK 4**
			VOSTOK 5

As above, but manned by mercantile marine personnel.

PETR LEBEDEV　　　　　　1970, Mr. Michael D. J. Lennon

PROFESSOR DERYUGIN

Measurement, tons	1 166 net; 3 165 gross

Fishery research ship. Built in the USSR in 1968. Sister ship of *Akademik Kurchatov*, see top of column 1.

RISTNA

Measurement, tons	1 819 net; 4 200 deadweight; 3 724 gross
Dimensions, feet	347·8 × 47·9 × 14·0
Main engines	MAN 6-cylinder diesels; speed = 15 knots

Classed as M Research. Converted from a timber carrier. Built in East Germany at Rostok by Schiffswerft Neptun in 1963. Painted white. Fitted with directional aerials on top of bridge wings. Served as Missile Detection Ship.

VOSTOK 3　　　　　　1970, Mr. Michael D. J. Lennon

4 "MORZHOVETS" CLASS

BOROVICHI	**NEVEL**	**KEGOSTROV**	**MORZHOVETS**

As above but completely modified as research vessels with a comprehensive array of tracking, direction finding and directional aerials. Additional laboratories built above the forward holds. Painted white and classed as research vessels. Same measurements as the two classes above, but tonnage increased to 5 277 gross and 967 net.

RISTNA　　　　　　1970, Mr. Michael D. J. Lennon

BOOM DEFENCE VESSELS

18 "NEPTUN" TYPE

Displacement, tons	700 light; 1 230 standard
Dimensions, feet	170·6 × 36·1 × -12·5
Main engines	Oil fuel; speed = 12 knots

Boom defence vessels or netlayers built in 1957-60 by Neptun, Rostock. Has a crane of 75 tons lifting capacity on the bow.

"Neptun" Class No. 13

CABLE SHIPS

5 "JANA" CLASS

DONETS	INGUL	JANA	ZEYA	ZNA

Displacement, tons	6 900
Measurement, tons	3 400 deadweight; 6 000 gross
Dimensions, feet	427·8 × 52·5 × 17
Main engines	5 Wärtsilä Sulzer diesels; 4 950 shp = 14 knots
Complement	118

Ingul and *Jana* were built by Wärtsilä, Helsingforsvarvet, Finland, laid down on 10 Oct 1961 and 4 May 1962 and launched on 14 Apr 1962 and 1 Nov 1962 respectively. *Donets* and *Zna* were built at the Wärtsilä, Abovarvet, Abo. *Donets* was launched on 17 Dec 1968 and completed 3 July 1969. *Zna* was completed in summer 1968. *Zeya* was delivered on 20 Nov 1970.

JANA   1970

PROJECT SHIPS

ZARJA

Measurement, tons	71 net; 333 gross

Auxiliary vessel built in 1952. One of some 50 or so similar schooners built in Finland. Constructed almost entirely of wood. Classed as a research vessel.

NEREY   NOVATOR

Nerey was formerly a small tug. Converted to survey vessel. *Novator* is sister ship.

PETRODVORETSK

Reported to be a former ferry ship converted for special surveying duties.

DISTILLATION SHIPS

"VODA" CLASS

Displacement, tons	2 100 standard
Dimensions, feet	269·0 × 39·4 × 14·1
Main engines	Diesels; speed = 12 knots

Water distillation ships built in 1956 onwards. No armament.

FLEET OILERS

2 "ALTAI" CLASS

ALTAI   **EGORLIK**

Displacement, tons	5 500 standard
Dimensions, feet	344·5 × 49·2 × 19·7
Main engines	Diesels; speed = 14 knots

Built from 1967 onwards. Naval oilers with no armament.

6 "UDA" TYPE

DUNAY	LENA	SHEKSNA	TEREK	SVIR	VISHERA

Displacement, tons	5 500 standard; 7 200 full load
Dimensions, feet	400·3 × 51·8 × 20·3
Main engines	Diesels; 2 shafts; 8 000 bhp = 17 knots

A medium type of Soviet supply ships. Built since 1961. Three ships were transferred to Indonesia in 1963-64.

"Uda" Type   1966, col Breyer

"KONDA" CLASS

KONDA   **ROSHOH**

Displacement, tons	1 178 standard
Dimensions, feet	226·4 × 32·8 × 13·8
Main engines	1 100 bhp = 13 knots

CRYPTON

Measurement, tons	1 769 gross; 559 net

Naval fuel tanker of the "Baskunchak" class. Built in 1965 when she went into Atlantic service.

CRYPTON   1965, Mr Michael D. J. Lennon

"PEVEK" CLASS

OLEKMA   **POLYARNIK**   **ZOLOTOY ROG**

Displacement, tons	4 000 standard
Dimensions, feet	344·5 × 47·9 × 20·0
Main engines	Diesels; 2 900 bhp = 14 knots

A type similar to the United States AOG gasolene carriers. Built in Finland in 1958-64.

20 "KHOBI" CLASS

ALATYR	JAHROVA	LOVAT	SHELON
IRBIT	KRASNOARMEETS	ROSSOSH	SOSVA
	KRASNOFLOTETS	ORSHA	SUJMA

Displacement, tons	800 light; 2 000 approx full load
Main engines	Speed 12 to 14 knots

Of this class numerous units are reported to have been built from 1957 to 1959. Pennant Nos.: P-256 (*Irbir*), P-260 (*Polyarnik*), P-348 (*Rossash*) and P-335 (*Krasnoflotets*). The latter is a Coast Guard tanker. *Alatyr* had pennant number P-393.

"KAZBEK" CLASS

KAZBEK   **VOLKHOV**

Displacement, tons	16 250 full load

Kazbek and *Volkhov* of "Leningrad" class taken over by the Navy as oilers.

ICEBREAKERS

1 PROJECTED. LARGE NUCLEAR POWERED

Main engines   Nuclear reactors; steam turbines; 80 000 hp

According to the Wärtsilä yard the most powerful icebreaker in the world is planned to be built by the Soviet Union.

3 NEW CONSTRUCTION. DIESEL POWERED

Displacement, tons	21 100
Dimensions, feet	445·4 × 85·3 × 36·0
Aircraft	Helicopters
Main engines	9 Wärtsilä-Sulzer 12 cyl 2H 40/48 diesels with Oy Stromberg Ab generators; 3 shafts; 23 000 shp (41 400 bhp main diesel effect = 21 knots max)
Endurance	40 000 miles at 15 knots
Complement	115

The Soviet Union ordered three large and powerful icebreakers on 29 Apr 1970 from Wärtsilä, Helsinki, for delivery in 1974, 1975 and 1976. These will be the largest diesel icebreakers in the world. Seven Wärtsilä 814 TK auxiliary diesels, 8 520 bhp. Propelling and auxiliary machinery controlled electronically.

2 PROJECTED NUCLEAR POWERED

Similar to *Lenin* but 15 000 tons and only two reactors, equal to 30 000 shp.

2 NEW CONSTRUCTION NUCLEAR POWERED

ARKTIKA

Displacement, tons	25 000 standard;
Dimensions, feet	524·9 × 82·0 × 33·5
Aircraft	10 helicopters served by hangar
Main engines	2 nuclear reactors; steam turbines; 30 000 shp = 25 knots

ARKTIKA (Sketch)   1967

1 LARGE NUCLEAR POWERED TYPE

LENIN

Displacement, tons	16 000
Dimensions, feet	440 × 90·5 × 25
Aircraft	2 helicopters
Main engines	3 pressurised water-cooled nuclear reactors. 4 steam turbines; 3 shafts (no shaft in bow); 44 000 shp = 18 knots max
Complement	230

The world's first nuclear powered surface ship to put to sea. Reported to have accommodation for 1 000 personnel.

CONSTRUCTION. Built at the Kirov Elektrosia Works, Leningrad. Launched on 5 Dec 1957. Completed and commissioned on 15 Sep 1959.

ENGINEERING. The nuclear reactors enable her to steam for 18 months without refuelling. Fuel consumption is reported to be only five ounces daily. The turbines were manufactured by the Kirov plant in Leningrad. Three propellers aft, but no forward screw.

OPERATION. With her reinforced prow she is able to force a 100 ft wide ice-free swathe and move continually through solid pack ice 8 feet thick at 3 to 4 knots.

LENIN   *Added 1966*

5 "MOSKVA" CLASS

VLADIVOSTOCK   KIEV   LENINGRAD   MOSKVA   MURMANSK

Displacement, tons	12 840 standard; 15 360 full load
Dimensions, feet	368·8 wl; 400·7 oa × 80·3 × 31 (normal); 34·5 max
Aircraft	2 helicopters
Main engines	8 Suplzer diesel-electric; 3 shafts; 22 000 shp = 18 knots
Oil fuel, tons	3 000
Radius, miles	20 000
Complement	145

DESIGN. Largest diesel-electric icebreakers in the world. Designed to stay at sea for a year without returning to base. The concave embrasure in the ship's stern is a housing for the bow of a following vessel when additional power is required. There is a landing deck for helicopters and hangar space for two machines.

CONSTRUCTION. Built by Wärtsilä-Koncernen A/B Sandvikens Skeppsdocka, Helsinki. *Moskva* was launched on 10 Jan 1959 and completed in June 1960. *Leningrad* was laid down in Jan 1959. Launched on 24 Oct 1959, and completed in 1962. *Kiev* was completed in 1966. *Murmansk* was launched on 14 July 1967, and *Vladivostok* on 28 May 1968.

ENGINEERING. Eight generating units of 3 250 bhp each comprising eight main diesels of the Wärtsilä-Sulzer 9 MH 51 type which together have an output of 26.000 electric hp. Four separate machinery compartments. Two engine rooms, four propulsion units in each. Three propellers aft. No forward propeller. Centre propeller driven by electric motors of 11 000 hp and each of the side propellers by motors of 5 500 hp. Two Wärtsilä-Babcock & Wilcox boilers for heating and donkey work.

OPERATION. *Moskva* has four pumps which can move 480 metric tons of water from one side to the other in two minutes to rock the icebreaker and wrench her free of thick ice.

KIEV   1970, B. Borg

MOSKVA   1960, Wärtsilä-Koncernen A/B Sandvikens Skeppsdocka

KAPITAN MELECHOV (see next page)   1966

Icebreakers—continued

3 "KAPITAN" CLASS

Name	Measurement	Launched	Completed
KAPITAN BELOUSOV	5 360 tons gross	1954	1955
KAPITAN MELECHOV	4 000 tons gross	19 Oct 1956	1957
KAPITAN VORONIN	3 416 tons gross	1955	1956

Displacement, tons	4 375 to 4 415 standard; 5 350 full load
Dimensions, feet	265 wl; 273 oa × 63·7 × 23
Main engines	Diesel-electric; 6 Polar 8 cyl; 10 500 bhp = 14·9 knots
Oil fuel, tons	740
Complement	120

Kapitan Belousov was laid down at the end of 1952 and completed in Sep 1954. All built by Wärtsilä-Koncernen A/B, Sandvikens Skeppsdocka, Helsinki. The ships have four screws, two forward under the forefoot and two aft.

KAPITAN BELOUSOV   *1970, Michael D. J. Lennon*

POLLUKS (ex-*Pollux*)

Displacement, tons	4 500
Dimensions, feet	262·5 × 63 × 23
Main engines	Triple expansion; 6 000 ihp = 13 knots
Boilers	4

Built in the Netherlands by Smit, Rotterdam, in 1943. *Pollux* was German name.

ALIOSHA POPOVICH (ex-German *Eisvogel*)

Displacement, tons	2 090
Dimensions, feet	200 × 49·2 × 21·7
Main engines	2 Triple expansion; 3 200 ihp = 13·5 knots
Boilers	1

Former German icebreaker. Built by Aalborgs. Launched in 1941. In the White Sea.

ILIYA MUROMETS (ex-German *Eisbar*)

Displacement, tons	1 918
Dimensions, feet	180·5 × 49·5 × 21·7
Main engines	Triple expansion; 1 600 ihp = 15 knots
Boilers	1

Former German icebreaker. Built by Eriksberg, Gothenburg. Launched in 1941.

3 "ADMIRAL" CLASS

Name	Builders	Launched	Completed
ADMIRAL LAZAREV (ex-*Yosif Stalin*)	Baltic Works, Leningrad	14 Aug 1937	1939
LAZAR KAGANOVICH	Baltic Works, Leningrad	30 Apr 1937	1938
MIKOYAN (ex-*Otto Schmidt*)	Nikolayev	1938	1939

Displacement, tons	11 000
Measurement, tons	4 866 gross
Dimensions, feet	335·8 pp; 351 oa × 75·5 × 22
Aircraft	1 helicopter
Main engines	Triple expansion with diesel-electric propulsion for cruising; 3 shafts; 10 050 hp = 15·5 knots
Boilers	9
Fuel, tons	4 000 coal; and diesel oil
Complement	142

3 aircraft and 1 catapult were included in the design. All in the White Sea. *Admiral Makarov* (ex-*Vyacheslav Molotov*, was reported in 1967 being scrapped in Spain.

MIKOYAN after refit   *1965, col Breyer*

PERESVET (ex-*Castor*)

Displacement, tons	5 150
Dimensions, feet	295·2 × 69 × 22
Main engines	Triple expansion; 3 shafts; 9 600 ihp = 15 knots
Boilers	4 Wagner

Former German icebreaker. Built by Schichau, Danzig. Launched in 1939. In 1962-63 she was fitted with a helicopter platform. A photograph of *Peresvet* appears in the 1959-60 to 1966-67 editions.

10 "LEDOKOL" CLASS

LEDOKOL 1	LEDOKOL 2	LEDOKOL 6
DOBRINYA NIKITICH (ex-2?)	VASILY POYARKOV (ex-*Ledokol 4*)	
FEDOR LITKE (ex-*Ledokol 10*)	VLADIMIR RUSANOV (ex-*Ledokol 7*)	
IVAN KRUSENSTERN (ex-5?)	YIRI LISYANSKY (ex-*Ledokol 8*)	
	VYOGA (ex-9?)	

Displacement, tons	2 500 standard
Measurement, tons	2 305 gross
Dimensions, feet	223 × 59 × 18
Main engines	3 shafts; speed = 13 knots

All built at Leningrad between 1961 and 1965. Divided between the Baltic, Black Sea and Far East. Name *V. Pronchischev* is also reported.

VLADIMIR RUSANOV   *1970, Mr. Michael D. J. Lennon*

YIRI LISYANSKY   *1968, Mr Michael D. L. Lennon*

FEDOR LITKE   *1970, Mr. Michael D. J. Lennon*

LEDOKOL 7   *Mr. Michael D. J. Lennon*

Icebreakers—*continued*

SIBIRYAKOV (ex-*Jaakarhu*)

Displacement, tons	4 825
Dimensions, feet	246 × 63 × 21
Main engines	Triple expansion; 3 shafts; 9 200 ihp = 15 knots
Boilers	8; oil fuel

Launched by Smit, Rotterdam in 1926. Formerly Finnish. Appropriated by USSR.

SIBIRYAKOV   *1970, Micheal D. J. Lennon*

KRASSIN (ex-*Sviatogor*)

Displacement, tons	9 300
Measurement, tons	4 902 gross
Dimensions, feet	297 wl; 323·2 oa × 71 × 26
Main engines	3 sets triple expansion; 3 shafts; 10 000 ihp = 15 knots
Boilers	10 single-ended
Fuel, tons	3 200 coal
Complement	190

Built by Armstrong and launched in 1917. In the Baltic. Reported to have been converted into a floating museum at Archangel. Photograph in 1951-52 and earlier editions.

VLADIMIR ILYICH (ex-*Lenin*, ex-*Aleksandr Nevskii*)

Displacement, tons	6 260
Measurement, tons	3 828 gross
Dimensions, feet	273 wl; 281 oa × 64 × 19 (mean); 20·5 (max)
Main engines	3 sets triple expansion; 3 shafts; 8 000 ihp = 12 knots
Boilers	8
Fuel, tons	1 200 coal
Complement	122

Launched by Armstrong in 1917. Refitted on the Mersey in 1946-47. In the Baltic.

VLADIMIR ILYICH   *Keith P. Lewis*

MALYGIN (ex-*Voima*)

Displacement, tons	2 070
Dimensions, feet	210·7 × 46·5 × 16·8
Main engines	Triple expansion; 1 shaft; 4 100 ihp = 13·5 knots

Former Finnish icebreaker. Built by Sandvikens and launched in 1917. In the Baltic. Photograph in the 1957-58 and earlier editions.

VOLYNETS (ex-*Suur Toll*, ex-*Vainamoinen*, ex-*Volynets*, ex-*Tsar Mikhail Fyodorovich*)

Displacement, tons	4 000
Dimensions, feet	236·5 × 57 × 18·8
Main engines	3 sets triple expansion; 3 shafts; 5 800 ihp = 13·5 knots
Fuel, tons	800 coal

Former Estonian icebreaker. Launched in 1914. In the Baltic. Photograph in the 1957-58 and earlier editions.

SADKO (ex-*Lintrose*)

Displacement, tons	2 000
Measurement, tons	1 613 gross
Dimensions, feet	255 × 37·5 × 21
Main engines	Triple expansion; 3 500 ihp = 14 knots
Boilers	4

Built by Swan, Hunter and Wigham Richardson, Ltd, Wallsend-on-Tyne. Launched in 1913. Transferred from the Canadian Government in 1915. Sunk during the First World War off the Arctic coast of the USSR where she lay for many years until raised and refitted in the White Sea. Photograph in the 1957-58 and earlier editions.

GEORGII SEDOV (ex-*Beothic*)

Displacement, tons	3 217
Measurement, tons	1 383-1 588 gross
Dimensions, feet	240·5 × 36 × 16·5
Main engines	Triple expansion; 3 000 ihp = 13·5 knots
Fuel, tons	500 coal

Built in 1909 by D. & W. Henderson & Co. Purchased in 1915. In the White Sea. Sister ship *Vladimir Rusanov* (ex-*Bonaventure*) was scrapped.

Most of the above icebreakers are immensely strong in framing and scantlings, with exceptionally thick plating, and decks strengthened for mounting guns in wartime.

Also reported are the icebreaker **PURGA** and the smaller icebreaker **VYUGA**.

Of older icebreakers, *Davidov* (ex-*Krasnyi Oktyabr*, ex-*Nadyazhnyi*) was discarded in 1959 when *Fedor Litke* (ex-*Kanada*, ex-*Earl Grey*) was also scrapped, *Vladimir Rusanov* (ex-*Bonaventure*) was scrapped about 1963, and *Yermak* in 1965. *Sevmorput*, *Stepan Makarov*, *Tamyr*, *Montcalm*, and ex-*Krisjans Valdemaras* were deleted from the list in 1969 as no longer operational or unfit for further service on account of age or obsolescence. *Dobringa Nikitich* was in 1971 reported to have been discarded and her name given to an icebreaker of the "Ledokol" class.

FLEET TUGS

KAPITAN V. FEDETOV

A large and powerful tug which as a naval vessel carried a comprehensive array of radar and radio aerials, but which has since reverted to mercantile use, see photographs in both roles.

KAPITAN V. FEDETOV (mercantile)   *1970, Mr. Michael D. J. Lennon*

There are many other tugs in the Fleet, see under Salvage Vessels on previous page, but numbers of tugs formerly listed have been deleted as they change or are suppressed from time to time according to geographical location or operational requirements.

KAPITAN V. FEDETOV (naval)   *1963*

"Okhtenskiy" Class No. SB 3   *1968*

URUGUAY

Administration	Diplomatic Representation	Mercantile Marine
Inspector General of the Navy: Rear Admiral Pedro Torres Negreira	*Naval Attaché in Washington:* Captain Ademar Torres	1971: Lloyd's Register of Shipping: 41 vessels of 140 657 tons gross

DESTROYER ESCORTS

Name	No.	Builders	Launched	Completed
ARTIGAS (ex-USS *Bronstein* DE 189)	DE 2	Federal SB & DD Co, Pt. Newark	14 Nov 1943	13 Dec 1943
URUGUAY (ex-USS *Baron,* DE 166)	DE 1	Federal SB & DD Co Pt. Newark	9 May 1943	5 July 1943

2 Ex-US DESTROYER ESCORT TYPE (ESCORT SHIPS, DE) "BOSTWICK" CLASS

Displacement, tons	1 240 standard; 1 900 full load
Length, feet (*metres*)	306·0 (*93·3*) oa
Beam, feet (*metres*)	37·0 (*11·3*)
Draught, feet (*metres*)	17·1 (*5·2*)
Guns, dual purpose	3—3 in (*76 mm*) single
Guns, AA	2—40 mm (see *Gunnery* notes)
A/S weapons	Hedgehog; 8 DCT; 1 DCR (see *Torpedo Tubes* notes)
Main engines	Diesel-electric; 2 shafts; 6 000 bhp
Speed, knots	19
Radius, miles	8 300 at 14 knots
Oil fuel, tons	315 (95 per cent)
Complement	160

ARTIGAS   *1971*

Former United States destroyer escorts of the "Bostwick" class, transferred to Uruguay in 1951.

GUNNERY. Formerly also mounted ten 20 mm anti-aircraft guns, but these have been removed.

TORPEDO TUBES. The three 21-inch torpedo tubes in a triple mounting, originally carried, were suppressed.

APPEARANCE. Practically identical, but *Uruguay* can be distinguished by the absence of a mainmast, whereas *Artigas* has a diminutive pole mast aft.

URUGUAY   *1971*

FRIGATE

1 Ex-BRITISH CORVETTE TYPE TRAINING SHIP (*BUQUE ESCUELA*) "CASTLE" CLASS

MONTEVIDEO (ex-HMCS *Arnprior,* ex-HMS *Rising Castle*) PF 1

Displacement, tons	1 010 standard; 1 600 full load
Length, feet (*metres*)	251·8 (*76·7*)
Beam, feet (*metres*)	36·7 (*11·2*)
Draught, feet (*metres*)	17·5 (*5·3*) max
Guns, dual purpose	1—3 in (*76 mm*)
Guns, AA	2—40 mm; 4—20 mm
A/S weapons	Hedgehog; 4 DCT; 1 DCR
Boilers	2 water tube
Main engines	Triple expansion; 190 rpm; 2 750 ihp
Speed, knots	17
Radius, miles	5 400 at 9·5 knots
Oil fuel, tons	480 max
Complement	90

MONTEVIDEO   *1971*

Former successively British and Canadian "Castle" class corvette (frigate). Employed as a training ship.

ESCORT

COMANDANTE PEDRO CAMPBELL, MSF 1 (ex-USS *Chickadee*, MSF 59)

Displacement, tons	890 standard; 1 250 full load
Dimensions, feet	215 wl; 221·2 oa × 32·2 × 10·8
Guns	1—3 in, 50, cal dp; 2—40 mm AA
Main engines	Diesel electric; 2 shafts; 3 118 bhp = 18 knots
Complement	105

Former United States fleet minesweeper of the "Auk" class. Built by Defoe B. & M. Works. Launched on 20 July 1942. Transferred on loan and commissioned at San Diego, Calif on 18 Aug 1966. Employed as PCE, escort patrol vessel, or corvette.

COMANDANTE PEDRO CAMPBELL   *1971*

PATROL VESSELS
1 Ex-US MSO TYPE

MALDONADO (ex-*Bir Hakeim* M 614, ex-USS *AM 451*)

Displacement, tons	700 standard; 795 full load
Dimensions, feet	165·0 wl; 171·0 oa × 35·0 × 10·3
Guns	1—40 mm AA
Main engines	2 GM diesels; 2 shafts; 1 600 bhp = 13·5 knots
Radius, miles	3 000 at 10 knots
Complement	54

Former US ocean minesweeper transferred to France in Feb 1954. Returned to the US Navy and transferred to Uruguay.

MALDONADO, old, being replaced   *Uruguayan Navy, Official*

1 "PAYSANDU" CLASS

SALTO PR 2

Displacement, tons	150 standard; 180 full load
Dimensions, feet	137 × 18 × 10
Guns	1—40 mm AA
Main engines	2 Germania diesels; 1 000 bhp = 17 knots
Oil fuel, tons	18
Radius, miles	4 800 at 10·7 knots
Complement	26

Training ship. Built by Cantieri Navali Riuniti, Ancona, Italy. Launched on 11 Aug 1935. Of two sister ships, *Paysandu* was stricken in 1963 and *Rio Negro* in 1969.

SALTO   *1971*

COASTAL MINESWEEPERS

RIO NEGRO (ex-*Marguerite*, ex-USS *AMS 94*)

Displacement, tons	370 standard; 405 full load
Dimensions, feet	136·2 pp; 141·0 oa × 26·0 × 8·3
Guns	2—20 mm AA
Main engines	2 GM diesels; 2 shafts; 1 200 bhp = 13 knots
Oil fuel, tons	40
Radius, miles	2 500 at 10 knots
Complement	38

Ex-US coastal minesweeper built for France under MDAP. Stricken from the French Navy in 1969 and returned to US ownership. She was transferred to Uruguay at Toulon on 10 Nov 1969.

SURVEY SHIP

CAPITAN MIRANDA CS 10

Displacement, tons	516 standard; 549 full load
Dimensions, feet	148 pp; 179 oa × 26 × 10·5
Main engines	1 MAN diesel; 500 bhp = 11 knots
Oil fuel, tons	37
Complement	52

Built by Sociedad Espanola de Construccion Naval, Matagorda, Cadiz. Launched in 1930. Used as general utility tender.

CAPITAN MIRANDA   *1971*

SALVAGE VESSEL

HURACAN (ex-USS *Nahant*, AN 83)

Displacement, tons	560 standard; 760 full load
Dimensions, feet	146 wl; 163 oa × 30·5 × 11·8
Guns	4—20 mm single
Main engines	Diesel electric; 1 shaft; 1 000 bhp = 11·5 knots
Complement	48

Former US netlayer, purchased in April 1969 for salvage services.

RESCUE LAUNCH

AR1

Displacement, tons	25 standard; 30 full load
Dimensions, feet	63·0 × 15·0 × 3·8
Guns	4 MG
Main engines	2 Hall-Scott Defender; 1 260 bhp = 33·5 knots
Radius, miles	600 at 15 knots
Complement	8

British type rescue launch. Rated as *Lancha de Rescate*. Launched on 4 July 1944. A photograph of AR 1 appears in the 1953-54 to 1957-58 editions.

OILER

PRESIDENTE ORIBE AO 9

Measurement, tons	17 920 gross; 28 267 deadweight
Dimensions, feet	587·2 pp; 620 oa × 84·3 × 33
Main engines	1 Ishikawajima turbine; 12 500 shp = 16·75 knots
Boilers	2 Ishikawajima-Harima Foster Wheeler type
Radius, miles	16 100 at 16 knots
Complement	76

Built by Ishikawajima-Harima Ltd, Japan. Delivered to the Uruguayan Navy on 22 Mar 1962.

PRESIDENTE ORIBE   *1971*

TUG

YTL 589 (ex-US No.)

Transferred from the United States Navy in Sep 1965 under the Military Aid Programme

VENEZUELA

Administration

Commander General of the Navy (Chief of Naval Operations):
  Rear-Admiral Jose Constantino Seijas Villalobas

Chief of Naval Staff:
  Rear-Admiral Alfredo Garcia Landraeta

Strength Of the Fleet

1 Submarine (Diesel Powered)
3 Destroyers
6 Fast Frigates (Light Destroyers)
10 Patrol Vessels (Submarine Chasers)
1 Large Landing Ship
4 Medium Landing Ships
23 Support Ships and Service Craft

Personnel

1971: Total: 7 500 officers and men including 4 000 of the Marine Corps

Diplomatic Representation

Naval Attaché in London:
  Rear-Admiral Pablo Cohen Guerrero

Naval Attaché in Washington:
  Rear-Admiral Luis Ramirez Aranda

Mercantile Marine

Lloyd's Register of Shipping:
96 vessels of 392 576 tons gross

SUBMARINES

1 Ex-US "BALAO" CLASS

CARITE S 11 (ex-USS *Tilefish*, SS 307)

Displacement, tons	1 526 standard; 1 816 surface; 2,425 submerged
Length, feet (*metres*)	312·0 (*91·8*) oa
Beam, feet (*metres*)	27·0 (*8·2*)
Draught, feet (*metres*)	17·0 (*5·2*)
Torpedo tubes	10—21 in (*533 mm*), 6 bow, 4 stern
Main engines	Diesels; 2 shafts; 6 400 bhp; Electric motors, 4 600 hp
Speed, knots	20 on surface; 10 submerged
Radius, miles	12 000 at 10 knots
Oil fuel, tons	300
Complement	80

Former United States submarine of the "Balao" class. Built by Mare Island Navy Shipyard, California. Launched on 25 Oct 1943. Commissioned on 28 Dec 1943. Purchased by Venezuela in 1960 after a four months overhaul in the United States. Transferred from the US Navy at San Francisco on 4 May 1960. Overhauled in San Francisco Navy Yard in 1962.

TRANSFER. The transfer of a second submarine by the USA to Venezuela was approved by the US House Armed Service Committee in Aug 1965 but was rescinded.

PHOTOGRAPHS. A starboard bow view of *Carite* appears in the 1962-63 to 1964-65 editions, and a port quarter aerial view in the 1965-66 to 1968-69 editions.

CARITE   1969, Venezuelan Navy, Official

DESTROYERS

Name	No.	Builders	Laid down	Launched	Completed
ARAGUA	D 31	Vickers Ltd, Barrow	29 June 1953	27 Jan 1955	14 Feb 1956
NUEVA ESPARTA	D 11	Vickers Ltd, Barrow	24 July 1951	19 Nov 1952	8 Dec 1953
ZULIA	D 21	Vickers Ltd, Barrow	24 July 1951	29 June 1953	15 Sep 1954

3 "ARAGUA" CLASS

Displacement, tons	2 600 standard; 3 670 full load
Length, feet (*metres*)	384·0 (*117·0*)wl; 402·0 (*122·5*)oa
Beam, feet (*metres*)	43·0 (*13·1*)
Draught, feet (*metres*)	19·0 (*5·8*)
Missiles	2 quadruple "Seacat" in D 11
Guns, dual purpose	6—4·5 (*114 mm*), 3 twin
Guns, AA	16—40 mm (8 twin)
	4—40 mm (2 twin) in D 11 only
A/S weapons	2 DCT; 2 DC racks ("Squids" in D 11 and D 21)
Torpedo tubes	3—21 in (*533 mm*) triple (none in D 11)
Boilers	2 Yarrow
Main engines	Parsons geared turbines; 2 shafts; 50 000 shp
Speed, knots	34
Radius, miles	5 000 at 10 knots
Complement	256 (20 officers, 236 men)

All built in Great Britain. *Nueva Esparta* and *Zulia* were ordered in 1950. Air conditioned. Two engine rooms and two boiler rooms served by a single uptake. The 4·5 inch guns are fully automatic. *Nueva Esparta* and *Zulia* refitted at Palmers Hebburn Works, Vickers in 1959, and at New York Navy Yard in 1960 to improve anti-submarine and anti-aircraft capabilities. *Aragua* refitted by Palmers Hebburn in 1964-65, *Nueva Esparta* at Cammell Laird in 1968-69 when "Seacat" launchers were fitted and some 40 mm and the torpedo tubes removed.

ARAGUA   1969, Venezuelan Navy, Official

PHOTOGRAPHS. A photograph of *Zulia* appears in the 1966-67 to 1969-70 editions.

RADAR. Search: AWS 2 and (*Nueva Esparta*) SPS 6. Fire Control: X Band.

NUEVA ESPARTA   1970, Venezuelan Navy, Official

FAST FRIGATES

6 "ALMIRANTE CLEMENTE" CLASS
(LIGHT DESTROYER TYPE)

Name	No.	Laid down	Launched	Completed
ALMIRANTE CLEMENTE	D 12	5 May 1954	12 Dec 1954	1956
ALMIRANTE JOSE GARCIA	D 33	12 Dec 1954	12 Oct 1956	1957
ALMIRANTE BRION	D 23	12 Dec 1954	4 Sep 1955	1957
GENERAL JOSÉ DE AUSTRIA	D 32	12 Dec 1954	15 July 1956	1957
GENERAL JOSÉ TRINIDAD MORAN	D 22	5 May 1954	12 Dec 1954	1956
GENERAL JUAN JOSÉ FLORES	D 13	5 May 1954	7 Feb 1955	1956

Displacement, tons	1 300 standard; 1 500 full load
Length, feet (metres)	325·11 (99·1) oa
Beam, feet (metres)	35·5 (10·8)
Draught, feet (metres)	12·2 (3·7)
Guns, dual purpose	4—4 in (102 mm) 2 twin
Guns, AA	4—40 mm; 8—20 mm (modified group 40 mm only)
A/S weapons	2 "Squids", 4 DCT and 2 DC racks in original group; 1 "Hedgehog" 4 DCT and 2 DC racks in modified group
Torpedo tubes	3—21 in (533 mm) triple (original group only)
Boilers	2 Foster Wheeler
Main engines	2 sets geared turbines; 2 shafts; 24 000 shp
Speed, knots	32 max; 28 in service
Radius, miles	3 500 at 15 knots
Oil fuel, tons	350
Complement	162 (12 officers, 150 men)

All built by Ansaldo, Leghorn. The first three were ordered in 1953. Three more were ordered in 1954. Aluminium alloys were widely employed in the building of all superstructure. All six ships are fitted with Denny-Brown fin stabilisers and air conditioned throughout the living and command spaces.

MODERNISATION. *Almirante José Garcia, Almirante Brion* and *General José de Austria* were refitted by Ansaldo, Leghorn, in 1962 to improve their anti-submarine and anti-aircraft capabilities: this group are known as "Modified Almirante Clemente" type. *Almirante Clemente* and *General José Trinidad Moran* were refitted by the Cammell Laird/Plessey group during 1969.

GUNNERY. The 4 inch anti-aircraft guns are fully automatic and radar controlled.

RADAR. Search: MLA 1. Fire Control: X Band.

PHOTOGRAPHS. A photograph of *Almirante Clemente* appears in the 1957-58 edition, of *General Juan José Flores* in the 1957-58 to 1961-62 editions, of *General Jose de Austria* in the 1962-63 to 1964-65 editions, and of *General José Trinidad Moran* in the 1962-63 to 1965-66 editions.

"FLOWER" CLASS. Of the former Canadian "Flower" type frigates, *Carabobo* (ex-*Kamsack*) was lost on passage from Canada, *Libertad* (ex-*Battleford*) ran aground off western Venezuela on 12 Apr 1949 and was discarded, *Independencia* (ex-*Dunvegan*) was stricken from the Navy list in 1953, *Federacion* (ex-*Amherst*) was stricken in 1956 and *Constitucion* (ex-*Algoma*), *Patria* (ex-*Oakville*) and *Victoria* (ex-*Wetaskiwin*) were officially deleted from the Navy List in 1962.

GENERAL JUAN JOSÉ FLORES   1966, Venezuelan Navy, Official

ALMIRANTE JOSE GARCIA (modified group)   1969 Venezuelan Navy Official

PATROL VESSELS

ALBATROS (ex-USS PC 582) P-04	**GAVIOTA** (ex-USS PC 619) P-10
ALCATRAZ (ex-USS PC 565) P-03	**PETREL** (ex-USS PC 1176) P-05
CALAMAR (ex-USS PC 566) P-02	**PULPO** (ex-USS PC 465) P-07
CAMARON (ex-USS PC 483) P-08	**MEJILLON** (ex-USS PC 487) P-01
CARACOL (ex-USS PC 1070) P-06	**TOGOGO** (ex-USS PC 484) P-09

Displacement, tons	280 standard; 430 full load
Dimensions, feet	170·0 wl; 173·7 oa × 23·0 × 10·8
Guns	1—3 in dp; 2—40 mm AA (1 twin); 2—20 mm AA
A/S weapons	Provision for 4 DCT
Main engines	2 Fairbanks-Morse diesels; 2 shafts; 2 800 bhp = 19 knots
Complement	65

Mejillon was refitted and overhauled by Diques y Astilleros Nacionalis, Venezuela, prior to commissioning in the Venezuelan Navy, and from 1962 onwards more ships of this type underwent similar preparation to join the fleet. Altogether twelve of these former United States submarine chasers of the steel-hulled "173-ft" type were purchased from the USA in Oct 1960 for anti-smuggling patrols, namely:—*Cooperstown* PC 484, *Dalhart* PC 619, *Edenton* PC 1077, *Gilmer* PC 565, *Honesdale* PC 566, *Larchmont* PC 487, *Lenoir* PC 582, *Minden* PC 1176, *Paragould* PC 465, *Rolla* PC 483, *Tarrytown* PC 1252 and *Tooell* PC 572, and with these the Navy assumed Coast Guard functions. The latter two ships were not refitted and were discarded.

MEDIUM LANDING SHIPS

4 US LSM TYPE

LOS FRAILES T 15 (ex-USS *LSM* 544)	**LOS ROQUES** T 14 (ex-USS *LSM* 543)
LOS MONJES T 13 (ex-USS *LSM* 548)	**LOS TESTIGOS** T 16 (ex-USS *LSM* 545)

Displacement, tons	743 beaching; 1 095 full load
Dimensions, feet	196·5 wl; 203·5 oa × 34·5 × 8·3
Guns	1—40 mm AA; 4—20 mm AA
Main engines	Direct drive diesels; 2 shafts; 2 800 bhp = 12 knots
Radius	9 000 miles at 11 knots
Complement	59

All built by Brown Shipbuilding Co, Houston, Texas, in 1945. Transferred from the US Navy to the Venezuelan Navy in 1958. The former United States medium landing ships LSM 370, LSM 542, LSM 543, LSM 544, LSM 545 and LSM 548 were sold to Venezuela under MAP in Aug 1958, but only the latter four have been commissioned in the Venezuelan Navy).

PHOTOGRAPHS. A starboard bow oblique surface view of *Los Testigos* appears in the 1963-62 to 1969-70 editions.

CALAMAR   1969, Venezuelan Navy, Official

LOS MONJES   1970, Venezuelan Navy, Official

COAST GUARD VESSELS

8 "RIO" CLASS

RIO APURE	RIO CABRIALES	RIO GUARICO	RIO NEVERI
RIO ARAUCA	RIO CARONI	RIO NEGRO	RIO TUY

Displacement, tons	38
Dimensions, feet	82 × 15 × 4
Main engines	2 Mercedes-Benz MB 820 Bb diesels; 1 400 rpm; 1 350 bhp = 27 knots; 24—25 knots cruising

All built by the Chantiers Navales de l'Estereles, Cannes, during 1954-56.

RIO CABRIALES   1956 Venezuelan Navy, Official

RIO SANTO DOMINGO

Displacement, tons	40
Dimensions, feet	70 × 15 × 6
Main engines	2 GM diesels; 1 250 bhp = 24 knots

RIO TURBIO

Displacement, tons	40
Dimensions, feet	81·3 × 15 × 7·5
Main engines	4 GM diesels; 880 bhp = 20 knots

GOLFO DE CARIACO

Displacement, tons	37
Dimensions, feet	65 × 18 × 9
Main engines	Diesels; speed = 19 knots

TORBES (ex-Felipe Santiago Esteves, LC 12, ex-Brion CS 2) LA 12

Displacement, tons	47
Dimensions, feet	83 × 16 × 4
Guns	1—20 mm; 4 DCT
Main engines	2 petrol engines; 2 shafts; 1 200 bhp = 15 knots
Complement	10

Launched in 1937. Ex-US Coast Guard cutter 56196. Acquired in 1944. Of wooden construction. Brion was renamed Felipe Santiago Esteves in 1957 when LC pennant number was allocated and renamed Torbes No. LA 12, in 1962.

The survey launch Torbes, and the repair launch BT 1 were officially stricken from the list in 1962. Caribe was scrapped in 1956.

Antonio Diaz LC 11 (ex-CS 1, ex-56193), Arismendi LC 14 (ex-CS 4, ex-56194) and Briceno Mendez LC 13 (ex-CS 3, ex-56195) were stricken in 1960.

TRANSPORTS

PUNTA CABANA T 17   **T 19**

Three small troop carriers of about 3 000 tons with a speed of 17 knots for troops.

LAS AVES (ex-Dos de Diciembre) T 12

Displacement, tons	944
Dimensions, feet	234·2 × 33·5 × 10
Guns	4—20 mm (2 twin)
Main engines	2 diesels; 2 shafts; 1 600 bhp = 15 knots
Radius, miles	2 600 at 11 knots

Launched by Chantiers Dubigeon, Nantes-Chantenay, France in Sept. 1954. Light transport for naval personnel. Originally named Dos de Diciembre. Redesignated T 12 in 1958. Renamed Las Aves in 1961.

LAS AVES   Venezuelan Navy, Official

SURVEY SHIPS

3 "PUERTO" CLASS

PUERTO DE NUTRIAS (ex-USS Tunxis, AN 90)		H 02
PUERTO MIRANDA (ex-USS Waxsaw, AN 91)		H 03
PUERTO SANTO (ex-USS Marietta, AN 82)		H 01

Displacement, tons	650 standard; 785 full load
Dimensions, feet	146 wl; 168·5 oa × 33·9 × 10·2 max
Guns	1—20 mm AA
Main engines	Bush-Sulzer diesel-electric; 1 shaft; 1 500 bhp = 12 knots
Complement	46

Former US netlayers of the "Cohoes" class. Puerto Santo was built by Commercial Iron Works, Portland, Oregon. Laid down on 17 Feb 1945, launched on 27 Apr 1945. Loaned from USA in Jan 1961 under MAP and converted into hydrographic survey vessel and buoy tender by US Coast Guard Yard, Curtis Bay, Maryland, in Feb 1962. All ships originally carried one 3-inch 50 cal dp gun. Puerto du Nutrias and Puerto Miranda, built by Zenith Bridge Co, Duluth, Minn, launched in 1944, completed in 1945, were loaned to Venezuela in 1963 under MAP.

PUERTO SANTO   1970, Venezuelan Navy, Official

TRANSPORT LANDING SHIPS

GUAYANA T 18 (ex-USS Quirinus, ARL 39, ex-LST 1151)

Displacement, tons	1 625 light; 3 960 trials; 4 100 full load
Dimensions, feet	316 wl; 328 oa × 50 × 11·2 max
Guns	8—40 mm AA (two quadruple mountings)
Main engines	GM diesels; 2 shafts; 1 800 bhp = 11·6 knots
Complement	81 (11 officers 70 men)

Former US Navy landing craft repair ship. Built by Chicago Bridge and Iron Co, Seneca, Illinois. Laid down on 3 Mar 1945. Loaned to Venezuela in June 1962 and now used as a transport in the Venezuelan Navy, it is officially stated.

GUAYANA   1970, Venezuelan Navy, Official

TUGS

FELIPE LARRAZABAL R 11 (ex-USS Tolowa, ATF 116)

Displacement, tons	1 235 standard; 1 675 full load
Dimensions, feet	195 wl; 205 oa × 38·5 × 15·5 max
Guns	1—3 in; 4—40 mm AA; 2—20 mm AA
Main engines	4 diesels with electric drive; 3 300 bhp = 16·5 knots
Radius	11 500 miles at 12 knots
Complement	85 (4 officers, 81 men)

Former United States fleet ocean tug of the "Apache" class. Built by United Engineering Co, Alameda, California. Laid down on 28 July 1943, launched on 17 May 1944, and completed on 26 Dec 1944. Transferred on loan from the US Navy in Feb 1962. Withdrawn from service in 1971.
The former tug Felipe Larrazabal (ex-USS Discoverer, ex-USCG Auk AM 38) was stricken in 1962 and Esteban Rojas, Dina and Caracas in 1958.

FERNANDO GOMEZ (ex-USS Dadley, YTM 744, ex-Diana, ex-US Army ST 873) R 12

Displacement, tons	161
Dimensions, feet	80 × 19 × 8
Main engines	Clark diesel, 6-cyl, 315 rpm; 380 bhp = 15 knots
Complement	10

A photograph of Fernando Gomez appears in the 1962-63 to 1969-70 editions.

GENERAL JOSE FELIX RIBAS R 13 (ex-USS Oswegatchie, YTM 778, ex-YTB 515)

Large harbour tug. Transferred on 4 June 1965 at San Diego, Calif. There are also medium harbour tugs ex-USS Sassacus (YTM-193) and TYM 385 loaned by USA.

VIETNAM

Administration

Commander-in-Chief and Chief of Naval Operations:
Rear Admiral Tran Van Chon

Diplomatic Representation

Defence Attaché in London:
Colonel Cao Xuan Ve

Naval, Military and Air Attaché in Washington:
Colonel Nguyen Linh Chieu

Strength of the Fleet

 2 Destroyer Escorts (Radar Picket Type)
 2 Frigates (High Endurance Cutters)
 8 Escorts (Including 5 Fleet Minesweepers)
 1 Patrol Vessel (Submarine Chaser Type)
 2 Coastal Minesweepers
20 Coastal Gunboats (Patrol Type)
24 Landing Ships (LST, LSM, LSSL, LSIL)
 4 Oilers
26 Coast Guard Launches
850 Patrol, Coastal and Riverine Craft
161 Auxiliaries

Personnel

1971: 5 000 officers and 34 000 men (official figures)
During 1971 the personnel strength of the South Vietnamese Navy will exceed 50 000, comprising 40,000 Navy and 12 000 Marine Corps. Of the Navy 15 per cent are officers and 35 per cent petty officers. Approximately 16 000 US naval personnel are "in country" assisting the South Vietnamese Navy with planning, maintenance and actual operations.

Mercantile Marine
Lloyd's Register of Shipping:
31 vessels of 27 984 tons gross

---

2 ex-US DER TYPE

CONVERTED "EDSALL" CLASS

TR'AN HUNG DAO (ex-USS *Camp*, DER 251) HQ 1
TR'AN (ex-USS *Forster*, DER 334) HQ

Displacement, tons	1 590 standard; 1 850 full load
Length, feet (*metres*)	306·0 (*93·3*) oa
Beam, feet (*metres*)	36·5 (*11·1*)
Draught, feet (*metres*)	14·1 (*4·3*)
Guns	Two 3-inch (*76 mm*) 50 cal. single
A/S weapons	Trainable "Hedgehogs", DC rack
Main engines	4 FM Diesels, 6 000 bhp; 2 shafts
Speed	20 knots
Oil fuel, tons	300 capacity
Endurance, miles	11 500 at 11 knots
Complement	166 (17 officers, 149 men) Accommodation for 187 officers and men.

Former United States destroyer escorts of the "Edsall" class converted to Radar Picket Escort Ships, DER. Both built by the Consolidated Steel Corporation. *Camp* was launched on 16 Apr 1943 and completed on 16 Sep 1943. *Forster* was launched on 13 Nov 1943 and completed on 25 Jan 1944. Both converted to DER in 1956-57. The three 21-inch torpedo tubes originally carried were removed. *Camp* was transferred from the US Navy to the South Vietnamese Navy in Feb 1971, and *Forster* scheduled to be transferred in July 1971.

TR'AN HUNG DAO *1971, Vietnamese Navy, Official*

FRIGATES (HIGH ENDURANCE CUTTERS)

2 ex-US CG WHEC TYPE

"CASCO" CLASS

TR'AN QUANG KH'AI (ex-US CGC *Bering Strait*, WHEC 382, ex-AVP 34) HQ 2
TR'AN NHAT DUAT (ex-US CGC *Yakutat*, WHE C380, ex-AVP 32) HQ 3

Displacement, tons	1 766 standard; 2 800 full load
Length, feet (*metres*)	311·0 (*94·8*) oa
Beam, feet (*metres*)	41·0 (*12·5*)
Draught, feet (*metres*)	14·1 (*4·3*)
Guns	One 5-inch (*127 mm*) 38 cal, dual purpose. Two 81 mm; six ·50 cal machine guns
Main engines	4 diesels; 6 080 bhp; 2 shafts
Speed, knots	18·2 max
Endurance, miles	22 000 at economical 11 knots; 8 000 at 18 knots
Complement	154 (14 officers, 140 men)

FORSTER *Official*

Former United States Navy seaplane tenders, AVP, of the "Casco" class transferred to the US Coast Guard in 1946-48. *Bering Strait* was built by Lake Washington Shipyard, laid down 7 June 1943, launched on 15 Jan 1944 and completed on 19 July 1944. *Yakutat* was built by Associated Shipbuilders, laid down on 1 Apr 1942, launched on 2 July 1942 and completed on 31 Mar 1944. Both transferred from the US Coast Guard to the South Vietnamese Navy on 1 Jan 1971. In the US Coast Guard they were first known as Patrol Gunboats, WPG, then as Medium Guidance Cutters, WMEC, and finally as High Endurance Cutters, WHEC, but they more nearly approximate to the frigate category in other navies. They are the largest fighting ships ever to be incorporated in the South Vietnamese Navy where they are said to have become South Vietnam's first two "ships of the line". Their five-inch guns are the biggest in the Fleet and will be useful for fire support.

TR'AN QUANG KH'AI *1971, Vietnamese Navy, Official*

ESCORTS

3 Ex-US PCE TYPE

DONG DA II (ex-USS *Crestview*, PCE 895)	HQ 07	18 May 1943
NGOC HOI (ex-USS *Brattleboro*, EPCER 852)	HQ 12	1 Mar 1944
VAN KIEP II (ex-USS *Amherst*, PCER 853)	HQ 14	18 Mar 1944

Displacement, tons	640 standard; 903 full load
Dimensions, feet	180 wl; 184·5 oa × 33 × 9·5
Guns	1—3 in, 50 cal dp; 6—20 mm AA
Main engines	GM diesels; 2 shafts; 2 000 bhp = 15 knots
Complement	7 officers, 83 men

Dong Da II was built by the Willamette Iron and steel Corp, Portland, Oregon. Laid down on 2 Dec 1942 and completed on 30 Oct 1944. Served successively in the US Navy as escort vessel, submarine chaser, weather ship, reserve training ship and anti-submarine warfare evaluation ship. Transferred at Philadelphia Naval base on 29 Nov 1961 and renamed *Dong Da II*. *Ngoc Hoi* was built by Pullman Standard Car Mfg Co, Chicago, laid down on 28 Oct 1943 and completed on 26 May 1944. Formerly on experimental rescue, escort ship in the US Navy, she was transferred on 11 July 1966. Ex-*Amherst* transferred early in 1970 after use as a Reserve training Ship at Detroit, was built by Pulman Standard Car Mfg Co, Chicago, laid down on 16 Nov 1943 and completed on 16 June 1944. Launch dates in table above.

NGOC HOI   *1971, Vietnamese Navy, Official*

5 Ex-US MSF TYPE

CHI LANG II (ex-USS *Gayety*, MSF 239)	HQ 08	19 Mar 1944
KY HOA (ex-USS *Sentry*, MSF 299)	HQ 09	15 Aug 1943
NHUT TAO (ex-USS *Serene*, MSF 300)	HQ 10	31 Oct 1943
CHI LINH (ex-USS *Shelter*, MSF 301)	HQ 11	14 Nov 1943
HA HOI (ex-USS *Prowers*, IX 305, ex-MSF 280)	HQ 13	17 Feb 1944

Displacement, tons	650 standard; 945 full load
Dimensions, feet	180 wl; 184·5 oa × 33 × 9·8
Guns	1—3 in, 50 cal dp; 2—40 mm AA; 8—20 mm AA (4 twin)
A/S weapons	2 DCT
Main engines	Diesels; 2 shafts; 1 710 bhp = 14 knots
Complement	7 officers, 83 men

Built by Winslow Marine Railway and Shipbuilding Co, Winslow, Washington (*Prowess* by Gulf Shipbuilding Corp). Laid down on 14 Nov 1943, 16 May 1943, 8 Aug 1943, 16 Aug 1943 and 15 Sep 1943, and completed on 23 Sep 1944, 30 May 1944, 24 June 1944, 9 July 1944 and 27 Sep 1944, respectively. Launch dates above. *Gayety* was transferred in June 1962 and renamed *Chi Lang II*. *Sentry* was converted into a patrol vessel by the Sun Shipbuilding and Dry Dock Co, Chester, Pennsylvania, the minesweeping gear replaced by increased depth charge storage, and transferred at Philadelphia, Pa in Aug 1962. *Serene* and *Shelter* were transferred on 16 Jan 1964. Employed as escort patrol vessels, not as minesweepers.

KY HOA   *1963, Vietnamese Navy, Official*

PATROL VESSEL

Ex-US PC TYPE

VAN DON (ex-*Anacortes*, PC 1569)	HQ 06	9 Dec 1944

Displacement, tons	280 standard; 380 normal; 450 full load
Dimensions, feet	170 wl; 173·7 oa × 23 × 10·8
Guns	1—3 in dp; 1—40 mm; 4—20 mm AA
A/S weapons	2 DC; 2 RL
Main engines	Diesel; 2 shafts; 2 800 bhp = 19 knots
Complement	6 officers, 45 men

Van Don was built by Letham D. Smit SB Co. Launch date above. Laid down on 26 Sep 1944 and completed on 14 Mar 1945. *Van Don* was transferred ar Seattle, Washington on 23 Nov 1960. *Dong Da* (ex-French *Ardent*, ex-USS PC 1167) was officially stricken from the list in 1961 and *Chi Lang* (ex-French *Mousquet* P 633, ex-USS PC 1144) in 1961, the names allocated to larger vessels, *Tay Ket* HQ 05 (ex-French *Glaive*, ex-USS PC 1146 and *Van Kiep* HQ 02 (ex-French *Intrepide*, ex-USS PC 1130) on 10 July 1965 and July 1965 respectively, and *Tuy Dong* (ex-*Trident*, ex-USS PC 1143) HQ 04, former French *escorteur cotier* transferred in 1956 was officially deleted in 1971.

VAN DON   *1971, Vietnamese Navy, Official*

PATROL GUN BOATS

20 Ex-US PGM TYPE

DINH HAI	HQ 610	**KIM QUI**	HQ 605	**TAT SA**	HQ 615
HOA LU	HQ 608	**MAY RUT**	HQ 606	**THAI BINH**	HQ 612
KEO NGUA	HQ 604	**MINH HOA**	HQ 602	**THI TU**	HQ 613
KIEN VANG	HQ 603	**NAM DU**	HQ 607	**TIEN MOI**	HQ 601
HOANG SA	HQ 616	**PHU DU**	HQ 600	**TO YEN**	HQ 609
PHU QUI	HQ 617	**HON TROC**	HQ 618	**TRUONG SA**	HQ 611
THO CHAU	HQ 619			**SONG TU**	HA 614

Displacement, tons	95 standard; 143 full load
Dimensions, feet	101 wl; 110 oa × 21 × 6
Guns	1—40 mm AA; 2—20 mm AA (1 twin); 2 MG
Main engines	Diesels, 2 shafts; 1 900 bhp = 16 knots

Built in the United States, the first ten, HQ 600-609, five by J. M. Martinac Shipbuilding Corp, Tacoma, Washington (the last of which, PGM 63 was delivered in 1963), and five by Marinette Marine Corp, Wisconsin. The US hull numbers of the above names were PGM 69, 62, 68, 67, 59, 60, 66, 61, 64, 72, 73, 65, 63, 70, respectively.
Thai Binh (ex-PGM 72), *Thi Tu* (ex-PGM 73) and HQ 614 (ex-PGM 74) were transferred on 10 Jan 1966. PGM 74, 80, 81, built in USA for transfer (names reported: *Lam Giang, Le Trong Dam, Nguyen Van Tru*). *Hoang Sa, Phu Qui, Hon Troc* and *Tho Chau* are ex-PGM 82, 83, 91 and 102 taken over on 20 May 1968.

PHU DU   *1963, Vietnamese Navy, Official*

COASTAL MINESWEEPERS

2 Ex-US MSC TYPE

CHU'O'NG-DU'O'NG II (ex-*MSC* 282)	HQ 115
HAM TU II (ex-*MSC* 281)	HQ 114

Displacement, tons	320 standard; 370 full load
Dimensions, feet	138 pp; 144 oa × 28 × 9
Guns	2—20 mm AA
Main engines	2 diesels; 2 shafts; 1 200 bhp = 13 knots
Complement	4 officers, 41 men

United States coastal motor minesweepers of the "Bluebird" class, non-magnetic type, of wooden construction, transferred under the Mutual Defence Assistance Programme in 1959 and 1960. Sister ship *Bach Dang II* (ex-MSC 283) HQ 116 was officially stricken from the list in 1971.

HAM TU II   *1960, Vietnamese Navy, Official*

CHU'O'NG-DU'O'NG II   *1971, Vietnamese Navy, Official*

DISPOSALS

Of the three coastal minesweepers of the ex-US YMS type transferred from the French Navy on 11 Feb 1954, *Ham Tu* HQ 111 (ex-*Aubepine*, ex-*D* 315, ex-YMS 28) was removed from the effective list in 1958. *Bach Bang* HQ 113, (ex-*Belledone*, ex-*D* 318, ex-YMS 78) in 1963, and *Chu'o'ng-Du'o'ng* HQ 112 (ex-*Digitale*, ex-*D* 326, ex-YMS 83) in 1964.

TRAINING SHIP

1 Ex-US FS TYPE

HOA GIANG (ex-*Dinh An*, ex-*Ingenieur en Chef Griod*, ex-*FS* 287, ex-*Governor Wright*) HQ 451

Displacement, tons	950
Dimensions, feet	176 × 32·3 × 10·2
Main engines	2 GM diesels; 1 shaft; 1 000 bhp = 10 knots
Complement	4 officers, 36 men

Former French survey vessel (ex-US Army freighter), sold to Vietnam in Dec 1955. Formerly rated as a light cargo ship (AKL), or supply vessel, but adapted and reclassified as training ship in 1966.

HOA GIANG   *1971, Vietnamese Navy, Official*

LANDING SHIPS

8 Ex-US LST TYPE

CAM RANH (ex-USS *Marion County*, LST 975)	HQ 500
DA NANG (ex-USS *Maricopa County*, LST 938)	HQ 501
THI NAI (ex-USS *Cayugo County*, LST 529)	HQ 502
VUNG TAU (ex-USS *Cochino County*, LST 603)	HQ 503
QUI NHON (ex-USS *Bullock County*, LST 509)	HQ 504
NHA TRANG (ex-USS *Jerome County*, LST 484)	HQ 505
MY THO (ex-USS *Harnett County*, AGP 821, ex-*LST* 821)	HQ 800
CAN THO (ex-USS *Garrett County*, AGP 783, ex-*LST* 783)	HQ 801

Displacement, tons	2 366 beaching; 4 080 full load
Dimensions, feet	316 wl; 328 oa × 50 × 14
Guns	8—40 mm AA
Main engines	GM diesels; 2 shafts; 1 700 bhp = 11 knots
Complement	7 officers, 103 men

Cam Ranh and *Da Nang* were built by Bethlehem Steel Co, Hingham. Laid down on 1 Dec 1944 and 14 July 1944, launched on 6 Jan 1945 and 15 Aug 1944, completed on 3 Feb 1945 and 9 Sep 1944, respectively. Transferred in June 1962. *Thi Nai*, built by Jeffersonville B. & M. Co, Jefferson, laid down on 8 Nov 1943, launched on 17 Jan 1944, completed on 29 Feb 1944, transferred at Guam on 16 Dec 1963. *Vung Tau* transferred on 4 Apr 1969, two further units in 1970. A photograph of *Cam Ranh* appears in the 1963-64 to 1970-71 editions.

MY THO   *1971, Vietnamese Navy, Official*

7 Ex-US LSM TYPE

HAU GIANG (ex-*LSM* 276)	HQ 406
HAN GIANG (ex-*LSM* 9012 ex-US *LSM* 110)	HQ 401
HAT GIANG (ex-*LSM* 9011, ex-US *LSM* 335)	HQ 400
LAM GIANG (ex-*LSM* 226)	HQ 402
HUONG GIANG (ex-USS *Oceanside*, LSM 175)	HQ 404
NINH GIANG (ex-*LSM* 85)	HQ 403
TIEN GIANG (ex-*LSM* 313)	HQ 405

Displacement, tons	743 beaching; 1 095 full load
Dimensions, feet	196·5 wl; 203·5 oa × 34·5 × 8·3
Guns	2—40 mm AA; 4—20 mm AA
Main engines	Diesel; 2 shafts; 2 800 bhp = 12 knots
Complement	5 officers, 70 men

Designed primarily to carry assault troops. First four transferred to French Navy for use in Indo-China, Jan 1954. *LSM 9011, 9012* transferred to Vietnam Navy, Dec 1955. LSM 9014, 9017, 9018, returned to USA in 1955. *Oceanside* LSM 175, transferred at Los Angeles on 1 Aug 1961, LSM 313 in 1962, *Hau Giang* (ex-LSM 276) on 10 June 1965. *Hat Giang* converted into a hospital ship (LSMH) in 1966.

LAM GIANG   *1971, Vietnamese Navy, Official*

4 Ex-US LSSL TYPE

DOAN NGOC TANG (ex-*LSSL* 9)	HQ 228	15 Sep 1965
LUU PHU THO (ex-*LSSL* 101)	HQ 229	2 Oct 1965
NGUYEN DUC BONG (ex-*LSSL* 129)	HQ 231	19 Feb 1966
NGUYEN NGOC LONG (ex-*LSSL* 96)	HQ 230	8 Dec 1965

Displacement, tons	227 standard; 383 full load
Dimensions, feet	158 × 23·7 × 5·7
Guns	1—3 in; 4—40 mm; 4—20 mm; 4 MG
Main engines	Diesel; 2 shafts; 1 600 bhp = 14 knots
Complement	6 officers, 54 men

The dates of transfers of LSSLs from USA are shown above; these were initially transferred to Japan by USA. Renamed after Vietnamese officers who died for their country. *Linh Kiem* (ex-*Arquebuse*, ex-*LSSL* 9092) HQ 226 and *No Than* (ex-*Framee*, ex-*LSSL* 105) HQ 225, both transferred from USA in 1951 for service in Indo-China and retransferred from France to Vietnam in 1955 and 1957, respectively, and *Le Van Binh* (ex-*LSSL* 10) HQ 227, were officially stricken from the list in 1971.

Landing Ships—continued

DOAN NGOC TAMG   1971, Vietnamese Navy Official

5 Ex-US LSIL TYPE

LOI CONG	(ex-*LSIL* 9034, ex-US 699)	HQ 330
LONG DAO	(ex-*LSIL* 9029, ex-US 698)	HQ 327
TAM SET	(ex-*LSIL* 9033, ex-US 871)	HQ 331
THAN TIEN	(ex-*LSIL* 9035, ex-US 702)	HQ 328
THIEN KICH	(ex-*LSIL* 9038, ex-US 872)	HQ 329

Displacement, tons	227 standard; 383 full load
Dimensions, feet	158 × 22·7 × 5·3
Guns,	1—3 in; 1—40 mm; 2—20 mm; 4 MG; and 4 army mortars (2—3·1 in; 2—60 mm)
Main engines	Diesel; 2 shafts; 1 600 bhp = 14·4 knots
Complement	6 officers, 49 men

Former US ships. 9030-9033 were ceded to France at Bremerton; Washington, on 2 Mar 1951, and 9029 and 9034-39 in 1953 and stationed in Indo China. Similar to preceding class. LSIL 9030 (ex-715) was scrapped in 1955. The above vessels were transferred from France to Vietnam in 1956. A photograph of *Thien Kich* appears in the 1962-63 to 1970-71 editions.

LONG DAO   1971, Vietnamese Navy, Officia

UTILITY LANDING CRAFT

13 Ex-US LCU TYPE

HQ 533 (ex-*LCU* 9076) ex-US 1479		HQ 539 (ex-US 1562)
HQ 534 (ex-*LCU* 9089) ex-US 1480		HQ 540 (ex-US 1475)
HQ 535 (ex-*LCU* 9086) ex-US 1221		HQ 541 (ex-US 1477)
HQ 536 (ex-*LCU* 0974) ex-US 1466		HQ 542 (ex-*LCU* 1494)
HQ 537 (ex-*LCU* 9887) ex-US 1501		HQ 543 (ex-*LCU* 1493)
HQ 538 (ex-*LCU*) ex-US 1594		HQ 544 (ex-*LCU* 1485)
		HQ 545 (ex-*LCU* 1484)

Displacement, tons	180 light; 360 full load
Dimensions, feet	115 wl; 119 oa × 34 × 6
Guns	2—20 mm AA
Main engines	3 diesels; 3 shafts; 675 bhp = 10 knots

Built in the USA and transferred under MDAP. Acquired in 1954 from French reparations. All LCT (7) type except HQ 535 (LCT (6) type). The landing ships and landing craft form "naval attack divisions" (*Divisions navale d'assault*) most of which have one LSSL or LSIL as flagships. A photograph of HQ 536 appears in the 1962-63 to 1970-71 editions.

HQ 538   1971, Vietnamese Navy, Official

HQ 536 (ex-*LCU* 9074, ex-US 1466)   **HQ 539** (ex-*LCU*, ex-US 1502)

Displacement, tons	160 light; 320 full load
Dimensions, feet	119 oa × 33 × 5
Guns	2—20 mm AA
Main engines	3 diesels; 3 shafts; 675 bhp = 10 knots

Built under the offshore programme and transferred under the Military Aid Programme.

COAST GUARD LAUNCHES

26 Ex-USCGC "POINT" CLASS

HQ 700 (ex-*Point Garnet* 82310)	**HQ 713** (ex-*Point Kennedy* 82320)
HQ 701 (ex-*Point League* 82304)	**HQ 714** (ex-*Point Young* 82303)
HQ 702 (ex-*Point Clear* 82315)	**HQ 715** (ex-*Point Patrige* 82305)
HQ 703 (ex-*Point Gammon* 32328)	**HQ 716** (ex-*Point Caution* 82301)
HQ 704 (ex-*Point Comfort* 82317)	**HQ 717** (ex-*Point Welcome* 82329)
HQ 705 (ex-*Point Ellis* 82330)	**HQ 718** (ex-*Point Banks* 82327)
HQ 706 (ex-*Point Slocum* 82313)	**HQ 719** (ex-*Point Lomas* 82321)
HQ 707 (ex-*Point Hudson* 82322)	**HQ 720** (ex-*Point Grace* 82323)
HQ 708 (ex-*Point White* 82308)	**HQ 721** (ex-*Point Mast* 82316)
HQ 709 (ex-*Point Dume* 82325)	**HQ 722** (ex-*Point Grey* 82324)
HQ 710 (ex-*Point Arden* 82309)	**HQ 723** (ex-*Point Orient* 82319)
HQ 711 (ex-*Point Glover* 82307)	**HQ 724** (ex-*Point Cypress* 82326)
HQ 712 (ex-*Point Jefferson* 82306)	**HQ 725** (ex-*Point Maromc* 82331)

Displacement, tons	64 standard; 67 full load
Dimensions, feet	83 oa × 17·2 × 5·8
Guns	1—81 mm/50 cal mg and 2—4 ·50 cal mg or 1—20 mm
Main engines	2 diesels; 2 shafts; 1 200 bhp = 16·8 knots
Complement	8 to 10

Transferred from the United States Coast Guard in, five 1969, 11 more in 1970, and ten in 1971.

POINT CLASS   1971, Vietnamese Navy, Official

MINESWEEPING LAUNCHES

10 Ex-US MLMS TYPE

MLMS 150	MLMS 153	MLMS 157	MLMS 159
MLMS 151	MLMS 154	MLMS 158	MLMS 160
MLMS 152	MLMS 155		

Converted 50 foot motor launches acquired from the United States in 1963. 48 others (MSM, MSR, LCMMS, LCPL, skimmer) were used as minesweeping launches. MLMS 156 and MLMS 161 were officially stricken from the list in 1971.

MLMS   1971, Vietnamese Navy, Official

SUPPORT SHIPS

18 AMPHIBIOUS LOGISTIC TYPES

Various landing ships, landing craft and auxiliaries adapted for fleet support.

PCF   1971, Vietnamese Navy, Official

RIVER ASSAULT CRAFT

200 ARMOURED TYPES

A mixed force of various small vessels, see under minor Landing Craft; also River Patrol Boats of the USN PBR Mk 1 and 3, and "Swift" type fast Patrol Craft.

PBR   *1971, Vietnamese Navy, Official*

MINOR LANDING CRAFT

226 ASSAULT TYPES

There were also 14 landing craft (*Commandements*), 69 of the LCM Type, 21 light monitors, 36 LCVP, 42 STCAN, and 27 RPCs. A total of 150 boats of these types were assigned to the River Force in June 1965. These numbers have been much varied by transfers from the USN, as local conditions require.

MONITOR   *1971, Vietnamese Navy, Official*

AUXILIARY GUN BOATS

500 JUNK TYPES

A Coastal Force of motorised junks was organised with United States assistance. This junk fleet was armed with ·50 and ·30 cal machine guns. The junk Force was established on 12 Apr 1960, with 100 junks, 28 groups of junks having been formed by June 1962. Mass production of improved design junks was undertaken to control infiltration of South Vietnam coastal waters by North Vietnamese forces. The latest junks were fitted with armour plate and fibre glass to protect the wooden hull against marine borers, and have diesels equal to speeds up to 15 knots. In June 1969 there were about 500 junks crewed by nearly 4 000 men. The sail junks were disposed of.
The Coastal Force (ex-Junk Force) became part of the Vietnamese Navy, and no longer a para-military organisation in July 1965.

OILERS

4 Ex-US YOG TYPE

HQ 470 (ex-*L'Aulne*, ex-US *YOG* 80)   **HQ 472** (ex-US *YOG* 67)
HQ 471 (ex-*YOG* 33)   **HQ 473** (ex-US *YOG* 71)

Displacement, tons	450 light; 1 253 full load
Capacity, tons	700 deadweight
Dimensions, feet	174·0 × 32·0 × 10·9
Main engines	Diesels; 1 shaft = 10 knots

HQ 470   *1971, Vietnamese Navy, Official*

SUPPLY VESSELS

5 UTILITY TYPE

HA LONG HQ 452	**HQ 454**	**HQ 455**
LONG HAI HQ 453		**HQ 456**

Displacement, tons	90 light; 275 full load
Dimensions, feet	98·0 × 24·0 × 7·8
Guns	3 MG
Main engines	Diesels; 2 shafts; speed = 12 knots
Complement	20 (2 officers, 18 men)

Ha Long and *Long Hai* are supply vessels of the trawler type taken into national service. The others were assigned to Logistic Support Units. Officially rated as Utility Boats.

WATER CARRIER

1 Ex-US YW TYPE

YW 152

Former United States self-propelled water barge transferred under the Military Aid Programme.

TUGS

2 Ex-US YTM TYPE

YTM 193 (ex-USS *Sassacus*)   **YTM 385** (ex-USS *Wannalancet*)

Medium harbour tugs transferred to Vietnam by the USA in Jan 1963. (The large harbour tug USS *Oswegatchie* YTB 515, was transferred to Venezuela and not to Vietnam as originally intended).

12 Ex-US YTL TYPE

HQ 9500	**HQ 9504**	**HQ 9507**	**HQ 9510**
HQ 9501	**HQ 9505**	**HQ 9508**	**HQ 9511**
HQ 9503	**HQ 9506**	**HQ 9509**	**HQ 9512**

Former United States small harbour tugs transferred from the US Navy under the MAP. Nos. 423, 446, 451, 455 and 590 were transferred in Jan 1963, and 587 leased and activated in 1968. 452, 456, 566 and 586 transferred in 1969.

SERVICE CRAFT

2 Ex-YR TYPE

HQ 9601 (ex-US *YR* 24)   **HQ 9610** (ex-US *YRBM* 17)

Displacement, tons	2 271
Dimensions, feet	270·0 × 52·0 × 10·5
Complement	120

There are also 25 LCM (8), 25 LCM 3/6, 20 picket boats, 24 LCPL, 26 Skimmers, 8 MSM, 6 MSR, 6 Coastal Raiders were assigned to Harbour Defence Units.

SKIMMER   *1971, Vietnamese Navy, Official*

VIETNAM (North)

Administration

Commander-in-Chief of the Navy: Rear Admiral Ta Xuan Thu

Strength of the Fleet

3 Patrol Vessels	4 Minesweeping Boats
15 Torpedo Boats	30 Patrol Craft (Launches)
28 Coastal Gunboats	17 Landing Craft
7 Landing Ships	100 Junks and Auxiliaries

Personnel

1971: 3 000 (270 officers and 2 730 men)

Mercantile Marine

Lloyd's Register of Shipping: 5 vessels of 5 002 tons gross

PATROL VESSELS

3 USSR "SOI" TYPE

Displacement, tons	215 light; 250 normal
Dimensions, feet	138 pp; 147 oa × 20 × 10 max
Guns	4—25 mm (2 twin mountings)
A/S weapons	4 ahead throwing rocket launchers; 2 DCT
Main engines	3 diesels; 3 500 bhp = 28 knots
Complement	30

Four submarine chasers of Soviet "SOI" type were originally transferred to North Vietnam, two in 1960-61 and two in 1964-65, but one was sunk by US Navy aircraft on 1 Feb 1966.

TORPEDO BOATS

3 USSR "P 6" TYPE

Displacement, tons	50 standard
Dimensions, feet	82 × 16·8 × 5·5
Guns	4—25 mm AA (2 twin)
Tubes	2—21 in (single)
Mines	4
Main engines	Speed = 40 knots

There are *circa* two to four wooden hulled motor torpedo boats of the "P 6" class built in China and transferred in 1967.

12 USSR "P 4" TYPE

Displacement, tons	50 standard
Dimensions, feet	85·5 × 20 × 6
Guns	4—25 mm AA (2 twin)
Main engines	Diesels; 2 000 bhp = 42 knots

Approximately a dozen aluminium hulled motor torpedo boats were transferred from the Soviet Union in 1961 and 1964. A fast patrol boat, PTF 1, was also reported.

COASTAL GUNBOATS

4 Ex-CHINESE "SHANGHAI" TYPE

Displacement, tons	100 full load
Dimensions, feet	83·5 × 20 × 6
Guns	4—37 mm (2 twin); 2—12·7 mm
A/S weapons	8 depth charges
Main engines	4 diesels; 4 800 bhp = 40 knots
Complement	17

Four motor gunboats were received from the People's Republic of China (Communist) Navy in May 1966.

24 Ex-CHINESE "SWATOW" TYPE

Displacement, tons	67 full load
Dimensions, feet	83·5 × 20 × 6
Guns	2—37 mm; 2—20 mm
A/S weapons	8 depth charges
Main engines	4 diesels; 4 800 bhp = 40 knots
Complement	17

Approximately 30 "Swatow" class motor gunboats built in China were transferred in 1958, and 20 were delivered in 1964 to replace those lost in action. Pennant numbers run in a 600 series.

MINESWEEPING BOATS

4 PATROL TYPE

Four vessels for sweeping, patrol and general purpose duties have been reported delivered in recent years.

PATROL CRAFT

30 MOTOR LAUNCH TYPES

Some thirty motor launches were reported to have been incorporated into the North Vietnam Navy before May, 1966, but not all are still in service.

SERVICE TENDERS

10 GENERAL UTILITY TYPES

Tenders and launches commandeered from private and commercial sources to serve the fleet and naval establishments.

LANDING SHIPS

7 US LSM TYPE

Displacement, tons	743
Guns	2—40 mm AA (1 twin); 4—20 mm AA
Speed	12 knots

One or two of these are reported to be out of operational service.

LANDING CRAFT

5 US LSSL TYPE

Displacement, tons	250
Guns	1—3 in; 4—40 mm AA; 4—20 mm AA
Speed	14 knots

There are also reported to be five of the LCI/LSIL type, one of the LCT(6) type, and six of the LCT (7) type.

AUXILIARY PATROL CRAFT

There are a substantial number of armed junks and similarly adapted craft.

YUGOSLAVIA

Administration

Assistant Secretary of State for National Defence for the Navy:
Vice-Admiral Branko Mamula

Commander-in-Chief of the Fleet:
Vice-Admiral Ivo Purisic

Personnel
1971: 27 000 (2 500 officers and 24 500 men)

Diplomatic Representation

Defence Attaché in London:
Colonel Svetozar Oro

Naval, Military and Air Attaché in Washington:
Colonel Milan Mavric

Naval, Military and Air Attaché in Moscow:
Colonel S. Krivokapic

Strength of the Fleet

5	Submarines	20	Patrol Vessels
2	Destroyers	38	Minesweepers
1	Minelayer	100	Torpedo Boats
10	Missile Boats	26	Support Ships

Mercantile Marine

Lloyd's Register of Shipping:
348 vessels of 1 515 563 tons gross

SUBMARINES (*Podmornice*)

3 "HEROJ" CLASS

HEROJ 821

Displacement, tons	1 068 submerged
Length, feet (*metres*)	210·0 (*6·4*)
Beam, feet (*metres*)	23·6 (*7·2*)
Draught, feet (*metres*)	16·4 (*5·0*)
Torpedo tubes	6—21 in (*533 mm*)
Main engines	Diesels; electric motors; 2 400 hp
Speed, knots	16 on surface; 10 submerged
Complement	55

It is reported that *Heroj* is of a different type from the "Sutjeska" class, and that there are two more submarines of the "Heroj" class in existance.

PENNANT NUMBER. Numbered in an "820" series, see 821 in photograph.

HEROJ *Official*

2 "SUTJESKA" CLASS

NERETVA 812   **SUTJESKA** 811

Displacement, tons	945 submerged
Length, feet (*metres*)	196·8 (*60·0*)
Beam, feet (*metres*)	22·3 (*6·8*)
Draught, feet (*metres*)	16·1 (*4·9*)
Torpedo tubes	6—21 in (*533 mm*)
Main engines	Diesels; electric motors; 1 800 hp
Speed, knots	14 on surface; 9 submerged
Radius, miles	4 800 at 8 knots
Complement	38

Sutjeska was launched on 28 Sep 1958 at Uljanik Shipyard, Pula. The first submarine to be built in a Yugoslav yard. Commissioned on 16 Sep 1960.

PENNANT NUMBERS. Numbered in an "810" series, see 811 and 812 in photographs.

DISPOSALS. The old former Italian submarine *Sava* 802 (ex-*Nautilo*) built during the Second World War, sunk, salvaged and reconstructed, has been scrapped, it was reported in 1971.

NERETVA *1969, Dr Giorgio Arra*

SUTJESKA *1963, Yugoslavian Navy, Official*

DESTROYERS (*Razarac*)

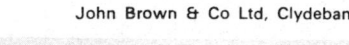

PULA (ex-*Wager*)	R 22	John Brown & Co Ltd, Clydebank	20 Nov 1942	1 Nov 1943	14 Apr 1944

1 Ex-BRITISH "W" CLASS

Displacement, tons	1 730 standard; 2 525 full load
Length, feet (*metres*)	339·5 (*103·5*)pp; 362·8 (*110·9*)oa
Beam, feet (*metres*)	35·7 (*10·9*)
Draught, feet (*metres*)	17·1 (*5·2*)
Guns, surface	4—4·7 (*120 mm*)
Guns, AA	3—40 mm
A/S weapons	4 DCT
Torpedo tubes	8—21 in (*533 mm*) 2 quadruple
Boilers	2 Admiralty 3-drum type
Main engines	Parsons geared turbines; 2 shafts; 40 000 shp
Speed, knots	36·75 designed; 31·25 sea
Radius, miles	2 800 at 20 knots
Oil fuel, tons	580
Complement	186

Former British destroyer of the "W" class. Purchased 1956, with sister ship *Kotor* (ex-*Kempenfelt*), and towed to Yugoslavia in Oct 1956 to be refitted in a northern Yugoslavian shipyard. *Pula* was re-commissioned by the end of 1959.

CLASS. Sister ship of *Wessex*, renamed *Jan van Riebeeck*, and *Whelp*, renamed *Simon van der Stel*, in the South African Navy, and original sister ships of *Wakeful*, *Whirlwind* and *Wizard* in the British Navy, and *Wrangler* in the South African Navy, converted to frigates, see earlier pages.

PULA *Yugoslavian Navy, Official*

APPEARANCE. One director on bridge not so large as in later classes. Tall foremast. Single Bofors mounting high up, abaft funnel, in superfiring position.

DISPOSALS. Sister ship *Kotor* (ex-HMS *Kempenfelt*, ex-*Valentine*), Leader, R 21, has been withdrawn from service, it was officially stated in 1971.

1 "SPLIT" CLASS

SPLIT (ex-*Spalato*, ex-*Split*) R 11

Displacement, tons	2 400 standard ; 3 000 full load
Length, feet (*metres*)	376·3 (*114·7*)pp ; 393·7 (*120·0*)oa
Beam, feet (*metres*)	36·5 (*11·1*)
Draught, feet (*metres*)	12·3 (*3·8*)
Guns, surface	4—5 in (*127 mm*)
Guns, AA	12—40 mm
A/S weapons	2 "Squids", 6 DCT, 2 DC racks
Torpedo tubes	5—21 in (*533 mm*)
Mines	Capacity 40
Boilers	2 watertube type
Main engines	Geared turbines ; 2 shafts ; 50 000 shp
Speed, knots	31·5 max
Oil fuel, tons	590 capacity
Complement	240

Built by Brodogradiliste "3 Maj", Rijeka. The original ship was laid down in July 1939 by Chantieres de Loire, Nantes, in 1939 at Split Shipyard. Launched in 1940. Completed on 4 July 1958. Ready for operational service in 1959. The original design provided for an armament of 5—5·5 inch guns, 10—40 mm AA guns and 6—21·7 inch torpedo tubes (tripled), but the plans were subsequently modified.

Destroyers—*continued*

SPLIT   *Aldo Fraccaroli*

DISPOSALS. The two ships of the light destroyer type (fast frigates), *Biokovo* RE 52 (ex-*Aliseo*) and *Triglav* RE 51 (ex-*Indomito*), former Italian large oceangoing torpedo boats or escort destroyers, have been scrapped, it was officially stated in 1971.

The former Italian large oceangoing torpedo boat or small destroyer *Ucka* (ex-*Balestra*) RE 54, latterly rated as a fast frigate, damaged by bombs on 25 Feb 1945, but completed by Yugoslavia in 1949, was officially removed from the active list in 1968.

The former Italian large oceangoing torpedo boat or small destroyer *Durmitor* (ex-*Ariete*), the only survivor of her class, afterwards reclassified as a fast frigate, was removed from the active list in 1963 and eventually scrapped.

MINELAYER Training Ship (*Skolski Brodovi*)

1 "GALEB" CLASS

GALAB (ex-*Kuchuck*, ex-*Ramb III*) M 11

Displacement, tons	5 182 standard
Measurement, tons	3 667 gross
Length, feet (*metres*)	384·8 (*117·3*)
Beam, feet (*metres*)	51·2 (*15·6*)
Draught, feet (*metres*)	18·4 (*5·6*)
Guns, AA	6—40 mm (mountings)
Main engines	2 diesels ; 2 shafts ; 7 200 bhp
Speed, knots	17

Ex-Italian. Launched in 1938. Refloated and completed in 1952. Now training ship. Also Presidential Yacht. Former armament was four 3·5 inch, four 40 mm and 24—20 mm (six quadruple) guns. The guns were landed.

GALEB   *Yugoslavian Navy, Official*

PATROL VESSELS

2 "MORNAR" CLASS

MORNAR 551   **BORAC** 552

Displacement, tons	330 standard ; 430 full load
Length, feet (*metres*)	170·0 (*51·8*) pp ; 174·8 (*53·3*) oa
Beam, feet (*metres*)	23·0 (*7·0*)
Draught, feet (*metres*)	6·6 (*2·0*)
Guns, dual purpose	2—3 in (single)
Guns, AA	2—40 mm single ; 2—20 mm single
A/S weapons	2 "Hedgehogs" ; 2 DCT ; 2 DC racks
Main engines	4 SEMT-Pielstick diesels ; 2 shafts 3 240 bhp
Speed, knots	20 max ; 16 sustained sea
Radius, miles	3 000 at 12 knots ; 2 000 at 15 knots
Complement	60

Mornar was completed on 10 Sep 1959. Her design is an improved version of that of PBR 581, see next page. *Borac* was launched in 1965. A photograph of *Mornar* appears in the 1968-69 and 1969-70 editions.

BORAC   *Aldo Fraccaroli*

Patrol Vessels —*continued*

1 "FOUGUEUX" TYPE

PBR 581 (ex-P6)

Displacement, tons	325 standard; 400 full load
Dimensions feet	170 pp × 23 × 6·5
Guns	2—40 mm AA; 2—20 mm AA
A/S weapons	1 Hedgehog; 4 DCT; 2 DC racks
Main engines	4 Pielstick SEMT diesels; 3 240 bhp = 18·7 knots
Radius, miles	3 000 at 12 knots; 2 000 at 15 knots
Complement	62

USA offshore procurement. Ordered in France. Built by F. C. Mediterranee (Graville). Launched on 1 June 1954. Transferred to Yugoslavia in 1956.

PBR 581   *Official*

TYPE "134" PATROLNI CAMAC

PC 134

Displacement, tons	85 standard
Dimensions, feet	91·9 × 14·8 × 8·3
Guns	1—20 mm AA; 1—12·7 mm MG
Main engines	2 diesels; 900 bhp = 13 knots sea speed

Patrol boat (Patrolni camac) of new Type 134.

No. 134   *1968, Yugoslavian Navy, Official*

COASTAL MINESWEEPERS

4 "HABRI" CLASS

HRABRI	M 151 (ex-*D 25*)	**SMELI**	M 152 (ex-*D 26*)
SLOBODNI	M 153 (ex-*D 27*)	**SNAZNI**	M 154

Displacement, tons	365 standard; 424 full load
Dimensions, feet	140 pp; 152 oa × 28 × 8·2
Guns	1—40 mm AA; 1—20 mm AA
Main engines	SIGMA free piston generators; 2 shafts. 2 000 bhp = 15 knots
Oil fuel, tons	48
Radius, miles	3 000 at 15 knots
Complement	40

Hrabri, *Slobodni* and *Smeli* were built in France by A. Normand as US "off-shore" orders, launched on 27 Feb 1956, 26 May 1956, 26 June 1956, respectively, and allocated to the Yugoslav Navy at Cherbourg in Sep 1957. *Snazni* was built in Yugoslavia in 1960. A photograph of *Smeli* appears in the 1958-59 to 1965-66 editions.

MINING TENDERS. The three mining tenders of the Yarrow class, M 31 (ex-*Meljine*), M 32, and M 33 (ex-*Mljet*), were officially removed from the list in 1968.

SLOBODNI   *1966, Yugoslavian Navy, Official*

FAST MISSILE BOATS

10 USSR "OSA" TYPE

Displacement, tons	160 standard; 200 full load
Dimensions, feet	131·5 oa × 23 × 6·5
Missile launchers	4 "Styx" in two pairs abreast
Guns	4—25 mm (2 twin, 1 forward, 1 aft)
Main engines	3 diesels; 4 000 bhp = 35 knots

Seven were reported to have been acquired initially and three more were delivered recently.

TORPEDO BOATS (*Torpedni Camci*)

4 NEW CONSTRUCTION SWEDISH "SPICA" TYPE

Displacement, tons	230
Dimensions, feet	141·0 oa × 23·3 × 5·3
Guns	1—57 mm
Torpedo tubes	6—21 in
Main engines	Designed for a speed of 35 knots

Torpedo boats of advanced design based on that of the Swedish "Spica II" class.

10 USSR "SHERSHEN" TYPE

Displacement, tons	150 standard
Dimensions, feet	131·5 oa × 23 × 6·5
Torpedo tubes	4—21 in single
Guns	4—25 mm AA (2 twin)
Main engines	Diesels; 7 500 bhp = 40 knots

90 TYPE "108"

102	115	120	125	157	164	170
103	116	122	126	159	165	174
108	119	124	127	162	167	199
						201

Displacement, tons	55 standard; 60 full load
Dimensions, feet	69 pp; 78 oa × 21·3 × 7·8
Guns	1—40 mm AA; 4—12·7 mm MG
Tubes	2
Main engines	3 Packard motors; 3 shafts; 5 000 bhp = 36 knots
Complement	14

The total number of motor torpedo boats is reported to have reached 100. Under recent programmes if was planned to raise the total to 110. Two of the "108" class were transferred to Ethiopia in 1960 and renamed *Barracuda* P 22 and *Shark* P 21.

TOP 146 as FBP   *1970, Yugoslavian Navy, Official*

MTB 174   *Yugoslavian Navy, Official*

MTB 119   *Yugoslavian Navy, Official*

TRAINING SHIP

JADRAN

Displacement, tons	720
Dimensions, feet	190 × 29·2 × 13·8
Sail area, sq ft	8 600
Main engines	1 Linke-Hofman Diesel; 375 hp = 8 knots

Topsail schooner. Launched in 1932. Accommodation for 150 Cadets. Name means "Adriatic". While in Italian hands she was named *Marco Polo*. A photograph of *Jadran* appears in the 1966-67 to 1969-70 editions.

PATROL BOATS
"KRALJEVICA" CLASS SUBMARINE CHASERS
16 PBR 501-508 and 509-516 TYPES

PBR 509	**PBR 511**	**PBR 513**	**PBR 515**
PBR 510	**PBR 512**	**PBR 514**	**PBR 516**

This second batch of submarine chasers launched in 1957-59 are an improvement on the PBR 501-508 series below, but of similar basic particulars.

PBR 512   *Yugoslavian Navy, Official*

PBR 501	**PBR 503**	**PBR 505**	**PBR 507**
PBR 502	**PBR 504**	**PBR 506**	**PBR 508**

Displacement, tons	190 standard; 245 full load
Dimensions, feet	134·5 × 20·7 × 7
Guns	1—3 in; 1—40 mm AA; 4—20 mm AA
A/S weapons	DC
Main engines	Diesel; 2 shafts; 3 300 bhp = 20 knots
Oil fuel, tons	15
Radius, miles	1 500 at 12 knots
Complement	54

These submarine chasers of the "500" class were launched from 1953 to 1956.

PBR 508   *1969, Dr Giorgio Arra*

SALVAGE VESSEL (*Brod za Spasavanje*)
PS II SPASILAC

Displacement, tons	740
Dimensions, feet	174 × 26·2 × 13
Main engines	Triple expansion; 2 000 hp = 15 knots

Built by Howaldt, Kiel. Launched in 1929. Name means "Salvador". While in Italian hands she was called *Intangible*.

SPASILAC   *1966, Yugoslavian Navy, Official*

YACHT (*Jahta*)
ISTRANKA (ex-*Vilax-Dalmata*)

Displacement, tons	230
Main engines	325 hp = 12 knots

Istranka means Nymph. Named *Fata* whilst in Italian hands during 1941-45.

RIVER PATROL VESSEL
KRAJINA (ex-*Dragor*)

Displacement, tons	250
Dimensions, feet	164 × 26·2 × 3·8
Main engines	480 hp = 10 knots

Launched in 1923. This vessel formerly served as the Royal Yacht on the Danube.

INSHORE MINESWEEPERS (*Minolovci*)
4 NEW CONSTRUCTION

ML 117	**ML 118**	**ML 119**	**ML 121**

Displacement, tons	120 standard; 131 full load
Dimensions, feet	98·4 × 18 × 4·9
Guns	1—40 mm AA; 2—12·7 mm MG
Main engines	2 GM diesels; 1 000 bhp = 12 knots

A new type of small minesweepers built in Yugoslav shipyards.

M 121   *1968, Yugoslavian Navy, Official*

4 US MSI TYPE

M 141	**M 142**	**M 143**	**M 144**

Displacement, tons	123 standard; 164 full load
Dimensions, feet	100 × 21·8 × 5·5
Guns	1—40 mm AA or 1—20 mm AA
Main engines	2 Paxman diesels; 1 100 bhp = 13 knots
Complement	15

Built for transfer to Yugoslavia under the Military Aid Programme. The US Navy hull numbers were MSI 98, 99, 100 and 101.'

M 142   *1968, Yugoslavian Navy, Official*

12 TYPE 101

M 103	**M 106**	**M 111**	**M 113**	**M 115**	**M 120**
M 105	**M 109**	**M 112**	**M 114**	**M 116**	**M 140**

Displacement, tons	90 standard; 95 full load
Dimensions, feet	82 × 19·5 × 6·2
Guns	1—40 mm; 1—20 mm
Main engines	Diesel; 135-175 bhp = 12 knots

Built during 1950-56 in Yugoslav shipyards. Vary in detail. Some used for patrol. M 101, M 102, M 104, M 107, M 108 and M 110 were scrapped in 1966.

M 109   *Yugoslavian Navy, Official*

RIVER MINESWEEPERS
14 RML 300 TYPE

M 301	**M 303**	**M 305**	**M 307**	**M 309**	**M 311**	**M 313**
M 302	**M 304**	**M 306**	**M 308**	**M 310**	**M 312**	**M 314**

Displacement, tons	38
Guns	1—20 mm
Main engines	Speed = 12 knots

All launched in 1951-53. A photograph of M 313 appears in the 1956-57 and 1957-58 editions.

WATER CARRIERS (*Vodonosci*)

PV 6	**PV 11**	**PV 12**

There are 8 water carriers of various types. Also PT 12 and PO 54.

DESPATCH VESSEL

JADRANKA (ex-*Bjeli Orao*)

Displacement, tons	567 standard; 660 full load
Dimensions, feet	213·2 oa × 26·5 × 9·3
Guns	2—40 mm AA; 2 MG
Main engines	2 Sulzer diesels; 1 900 bhp = 18 knots

Built by C. R. dell Adriatico, San Marco, Trieste. Launched on 3 June 1939. Was used as Admiralty yacht and yacht of Marshall Tito. While in Italian hands was named *Alba*, for some days only, then *Zagaria*.

JADRANKA   1970, Yugoslavian Navy, Official

LANDING CRAFT

DTM 233   1970, Yugoslavian Navy, Official

DTM 230   **DTM 233**

Displacement, tons	circa 500
Guns	4—20 mm AA.

Capable of carrying at least two, possibly three of the heaviest tanks. Unlike other tank landing craft in that the lower part of the stern drops to form a ramp down which the tanks go ashore, underneath the prow, which is rigid.

DTM 230   courtesy B. Hinchliffe, Esq

Catamaran Type

Displacement, tons	circa 50

A smaller craft consisting of two pontoons some feet apart, secured to each other by cross-girders on which stand the bridge and cabins, etc. This vessel appears to be capable of carrying one medium tank, to be put ashore by two bridge members which can be seen quite clearly, folded back on the deck.

Catamaran type   courtesy B. Hinchliffe, Esq

DTK 221

Displacement, tons	410
Dimensions, feet	144·3 × 19·7 × 7
Guns	1—20 mm AA; 2—12·7 mm
Main engines	Speed = 10 knots
Complement	15·

A photograph of DTK 221 appears in the 1959-60 to 1969-70 editions.

D 206 (ex-*MZ 713*)   **D 219** (ex-*MZ 717*)

Displacement, tons	225 and 239
Guns	1—20 mm AA; 2 MG AA
Main engines	Speed = 11·knots

Ex-Italian landing craft. Launched in 1942. Capable of carrying three tanks. A photograph of D 219 appears in the 1959-60 to 1965-66 editions.

D 203   **D 204**

Displacement, tons	220
Guns	1—3·4 in (88 mm); 2—20 mm AA
Main engines	Speed = 10 knots

Ex-German landing craft. Two landing craft were launched in 1956.

OILERS

2 "ULJESURA" TYPE

KIT   **ULJESURA**

Displacement, tons	250 standard

1970, Yugoslavian Navy, Official

4 PN 13 TYPE

PN 13 (ex-*Lovcen*)

Displacement, tons	695 standard
Main engines	Speed = 8·5 knots

PN 13 (ex-*Lovcen*) was launched in 1932. For fleet servicing and freighting. PN 17 was transferred to the Sudanese Navy in 1969.

TRANSPORTS

2 PT 71 TYPE

PT 71   **PT 72**

Displacement, tons	310 standard; 428 full load
Dimensions, feet	141·5 × 22·2 × 16
Main engines	300 bhp = 7 knots

The transport *Tum* PT 21 (ex-*Krk*, ex-*Kt. 6*) was removed from the list in 1963.

PT 71   1966, Yugoslavian Navy, Official

TUGS (*Remorkeri*)

PR 52 (ex-*San Remo*)

Displacement, tons	170
Main engines	350 hp = 9 knots

Former Italian tug and multi-purpose vessel. Launched in 1937.

PR 58 (ex-*Molara*)

Displacement, tons	118
Main engines	250 hp = 8 knots

Former Italian tug. Launched in 1937, now used as general transport and towing vessel.

PR 51 (ex-*Porto Cohte*)

Displacement, tons	226

Former Italian tug. Launched in 1936. A photograph appears in the 1951-52 to 1957-58 editions.

PR 55 (ex-*Snazi*)

Displacement, tons	100
Main engines	300 hp = 10 knots

Launched in 1917. Name means "Strong". The Italian name was *Resistance*.

PR 54 (ex-*Ustrajni*)

Displacement, tons	160
Main engines	250 hp = 9 knots

Launched in 1917. Name means "Durable". The Italian name was *Duratero*.

LR II (ex-*Basiluzzo*)

Displacement, tons	108
Main engines	130 hp = 8 knots

Former Italian tug. Launched in 1915. There is also the very old tug PP 1.

ZAMBIA

Mercantile Marine
Lloyd's Register of Shipping: 1 vessel of 5 513 tons gross

The Tank Landing Craft of the LCT(6) type, ex-HMS *Bastion*, L 4040, purchased on 15 Sep, 1966 was sold in Feb 1969 to H. G. Pounds Shipbreakers; and resold for commercial use in the Persian Gulf in Apr 1969.

NAVAL STRENGTHS

ALL THE WORLD'S FIGHTING SHIPS

	Large Aircraft Carriers	Light Aircraft Carriers	Escort Carriers, Helicopter Carriers, Commando Carriers	Command Ships, Communications Ships, Amphibious Force Flag ships	Nuclear Powered Submarines	Conventionally Powered Submarines	Cruisers	Leaders, Large Destroyers, Frigates (DLG)	Destroyers	Destroyer Escorts, Frigates, Escorts (and APD)	Corvettes (including PCE)	Patrol Vessels, Submarine Chasers (PC)	Missile Boats, Torpedo Boats, Fast Gunboats, Fast Patrol Boats	Fleet Minelayers, Fast Minelayers, Mine Support Ships
ARGENTINA		1				2	3		6	3	2	9		1
AUSTRALIA		1	1			4		3	4	7				
BELGIUM														
BRAZIL		1				2	2		11	5	10			
BULGARIA						2				2		8	8	
BURMA										1	2	4	5	
CANADA						4				20		1		
CEYLON										1				
CHILE						2	2		4	4	2	2	4	
CHINA (REP)						35			4	20		24	400	
CHINA (TAIWAN)				2					11	18	4	21		
COLOMBIA									3	4				
CUBA										4	2	18	42	
DENMARK						4				6	4	9	16	4
DOMINICAN R									1	3	5	3		
ECUADOR										4	2			
EGYPT						13			5	4	2	12	65	
FINLAND										3	2	4	16	
FRANCE	2		2		1	20	2	3	17	27		15		
GERMANY (DEM)										2		26	74	
GERMANY (FED)						12			12	21	6		40	2
GREECE						2			9	4	5	5	13	
INDIA		1				4	2		3	22			6	
INDONESIA						12	1		8	12		18	51	
IRAN									1	5	5			
IRAQ												3	12	
ISRAEL						3			2			1	21	
ITALY						10	4	3	4	13	20	1	14	
JAPAN						10			27	13		20	10	
KOREA (N)						2						11	50	
KOREA (S)									3	13	11	6		
MALAYSIA										2			4	
MEXICO									2	10	11	1		
NETHERLANDS						5	2		12	6	6			3
NEW ZEALAND										4				
NORWAY						15				5		2	46	
PAKISTAN						4	1		5	2				
PARAGUAY														
PERU						4	2		4	3	2			
PHILIPPINES										1	7	7		
POLAND						5			3			8	32	
PORTUGAL						4				10	5	14		
ROMANIA												3	13	
SOUTH AFRICA									2	6				
SPAIN			1			5	1		18	4	5	14	3	6
SWEDEN						22			8	6			42	2
THAILAND										5		17		
TURKEY						10			10		18	6	11	1
UNITED KINGDOM	2		3		9	26	3	9	3	65			5	1
URUGUAY										3	2	1		
USA	27		7	12	96	56	23	33	232	198		1	37	1
USSR			2		83	318	26		100	130		270	450	1
VENEZUELA						1			3	6		10		
VIETNAM										4	8	1	22	
YUGOSLAVIA						5			2			3	110	1

Note—Figures include vessels in reserve, but not ships under construction

TABLE SHOWING THE NUMERICAL STRENGTH OF EACH COUNTRY

Ocean Mine-sweepers, Fleet Mine-sweepers	Coastal Mine-sweepers, Mine Hunters	Inshore Mine-sweepers, Minesweeping Boats	Motor Launches, Motor Patrol Craft, River Gun-boats	Landing Ships	Landing Craft	Boom Defence Vessels, Net-layers	Survey Ships	Depot Ships, Repair Ships Maintenance Ships	Transports	Supply Ships	Oilers	Training Ships	Tugs	Miscellaneous	Country
	6		3	5	29		3		4		3	1	13	2	ARGENTINA
	6	3	23				5	1			1		1	6	AUSTRALIA
7	9	12	6					3					6	8	BELGIUM
	2		11				6	1	4	1	2		3	9	BRAZIL
2	4	24			10							1	1	6	BULGARIA
1			34		9				1				4		BURMA
	6					4	6	3		3	2		27	118 *	CANADA
			28										1	1	CEYLON
					5		1	1			2	1	6		CHILE
21	6		22	29	25	6	2	1		8	5		11	375	CHINA (REP)
2	15	2	50	46	29		2	2	6		4		6	13	CHINA (TAIWAN)
			24				2	5			5	1	11	7	COLOMBIA
			27										1	6	CUBA
	8	4	27					2			2			6	DENMARK
2			5	1	2						2		9	5	DOMINICAN R
			8	2			1			1			3	7	ECUADOR
6		2		2	14									5	EGYPT
			14					9					3	11	FINLAND
14	62	15	8	5	18	17	9	9	13	5	8	4	18	47	FRANCE
16	15	18	20		18		2				7	1	10	17	GERMANY (DEM)
	24	51			24		10	8		15	19	2	21	31	GERMANY (FED)
	21			13	8	1	2	2			7		12	9	GREECE
1	4	4	15	5	1		4	2			4		1	5	INDIA
6	14		44	8	10		5	3	2		10	1	5	55	INDONESIA
	4	2	28		2			1			1		1	3	IRAN
			22										1	2	IRAQ
			20		10				1					2	ISRAEL
4	37	20	6	1		2	1	1	5		2	4	26	138	ITALY
	35	6	27	4	48			3			3	2	7	357 *	JAPAN
10		24	26											70	KOREA (N)
	11	1		20			1	1		5	4		2	13	KOREA (S)
	6		24				1							2	MALAYSIA
6			10				1	1			2		5	4	MEXICO
3	36	16	5		12		3	1		2	1	3	8	20	NETHERLANDS
2			12				2			1				2	NEW ZEALAND
	10				2		1	2				1		10	NORWAY
	8		6				1				2		4	3	PAKISTAN
			10										1		PARAGUAY
	2		18	4					3		6		2	3	PERU
	2		28	9				1	1		1		4	20	PHILIPPINES
24		27	38	16			6				7	8	12		POLAND
5	12		47		79		6	1			2	1		5	PORTUGAL
4		30										2		25	ROMANIA
1	10		5			1	1				1	2	2	9	SOUTH AFRICA
13	12		19	3	8	1	4	3			3	1	15	22	SPAIN
	18	17	23		57		7	2		1	1	2		20	SWEDEN
1	4		31	7	9		1	2			6	1	4	3	THAILAND
	13	3	42			6		3			7	1	2	5	TURKEY
	49	24	2	10	24	23	13	5		10	27		91	202	UNITED KINGDOM
	1		1				1				1		1	2	URUGUAY
80	14	1	80	57	100	1	25	54	52	125	72	5	64	940 *	*USA
85	135		120	125	75	18	90	60	25	120	50	20	140	950 †	†USSR
			12	5			3	3					3	3	VENEZUELA
	2	10	896	15	24					5	4	1	14	137	VIETNAM
	4	34	18		8				2		3	1	6	6	YUGOSLAVIA

*Includes Coastguard   † Round figures are estimated

NAVAL AIRCRAFT AND MISSILES

NAVAL AIRCRAFT
SHIPBORNE AIRCRAFT

Br 1050 ALIZE Breguet (France)

Carrier-borne 3-seat anti-submarine aircraft

Max speed at 10 000 ft (*3 050 m*)	254 knots
Patrol speed	210-320 knots
Service ceiling	26 250 ft (*8 000 m*)
Normal range	1 350 n. miles
Normal endurance	5 hr 10 min
Max endurance	7 hr 40 min
Armament	Internal Bay: 3 × 353 lb depth charges or one torpedo Inner wing racks for 2 × 353 lb or 385 lb depth charges Outer wing racks: 6 × 5-in rockets or 2 × AS12 ASM's
Max T-O weight	18 100 lb (*8 200 kg*)
Wing span	51 ft 2 in (*15·60 m*)
Width folded	23 ft 0 in (*7·00 m*)
Length	45 ft 6 in (*13·86 m*)
Height	16 ft 5 in (*5·00 m*)
Power plant	1 × 2 100 eshp Dart R.Da 21 Turboprop

75 were built for the French Navy to equip three squadrons; 12 were supplied to the Indian Navy for service on board "Vikrant".

Alize of the French Navy with underwing rocket rails

BUCCANEER S. Mk 2 Hawker Siddeley (UK)

Carrier-borne 2-seat all-weather strike and reconnaissance aircraft

Max speed at 200 ft	Mach 0·85 approx.
Tactical radius	1 000 n. miles plus
Armament	Internal Bay: Nuclear or conventional weapons (4 × 1 000 lb *453 kg* bombs) or camera pack; four underwing attachments for Bullpup or Martel missiles, 1 000 lb (*453 kg*) bombs (three on each pylon) or rocket packs.
Max weapon load	16 000 lb (*7,257 kg*)
Max T-O weight	62 000 lb (*28 123 kg*)
Wing span	44 ft 0 in (*13·41 m*)
Width folded	19 ft 11 in (*6·07 m*)
Length overall	63 ft 5 in (*19·33 m*)
Length folded	51 ft 10 in (*15·79 m*)
Height overall	16 ft 3 in (*4·95 m*)
Height folded	16 ft 8 in (*5·08 m*)
Power plant	2 × 11 100 lb (*5 035 kg*) st RB.168-1A Spey turbofans

Hawker Siddeley Buccaneer S.Mk.2

Equips four Squadrons of the Fleet Air Arm and is still in production now for the RAF to which the Fleet Air Arm aircraft will eventually go. A land-based version, designated S.50, was built for the South African Air Force to a total of sixteen. An earlier version, the S.1, was powered by 2 × 7 100 lb (*3 220 kg*) BS Gyron Junior turbojets.

A-7 CORSAIR II Ling-Temco-Vought (USA)

Carrier-borne single-seat attack aircraft

Data for A-7E

Max speed at S L	606 knots
Max range (ferry)	2 900 n. miles
Other performance details	Secret
Armament	Fuselage: 1 × 20 mm multi-barrel gun. Six underwing pylons and two fuselage weapon stations. Two outboard pylons on each wing can each accommodate a load of 3 500 lb (*1 587 kg*). Inboard pylon on each wing can carry 2 500 lb (*1,134 kg*). Two fuselage weapons stations, one on each side, can each carry 500 lb (*227 kg*). Weapons include air-to-air and air-to-ground missiles; general-purpose bombs; rockets; gun pods and auxiliary fuel tanks
Max T-O weight	42 000 lb (*19 050 kg*)
Wing span	38 ft 9 in (*11·80 m*)
Width folded	23 ft 9 in (*7·24 m*)
Length	46 ft 1·5 in (*14·06 m*)
Height	16 ft 0 in (*4·88 m*)
Power plant	A-7A 1 × P. & W. TF30-P-6 of 11 350 lb (*5 150 kg*) st A-7B 1 × P. & W. TF30-P-8 of 12 200 lb (*5 534 kg*) A-7D: 1 × Allison TF41-A-1 of 14 250 lb (*6 465 kg*) A-7E: 1 × Allison TF41-A-2 of 15 000 lb (*6 800 kg*)

First A-7E Corsair II delivered to training squadron VA-195 of the US Navy

A-7A entered service with US Navy in November 1967, followed by A-7B. A-7E is a development of the A-7B, initially with TF30-P-8 engine (first 67 aircraft), later with TF-41-A-2. 494 A-7Es ordered.

SHIPBORNE AIRCRAFT

F-8 CRUSADER

Ling-Temco-Vought (USA)

Carrier-borne single-seat fighter

Max speed	F-8A, B, C: 868 knots plus F-8D, E, H, J: Mach 1·7
Combat radius (F-8A)	521·05 n. miles (965 km)
Other performance details	Secret
Armament	Fuselage: 4 × 20 mm Colt cannon and 2 × Sidewinder missiles (4 on F-8C/K, F-8D/H, F-8E/J. Wing Mounts: (2) on F-8E, E(FN), H, J, K and L): 2 × 2 000 lb (907 kg) bombs or Bullpup A or B ASMs or 24 Zuni rockets
Max weight (catapult-launch)	34 000 lb (15 420 kg)
Wing span	35 ft 8 in (10·87 m)
Length	F-8A, B, C, D: 54 ft 3 in (16·54m) F-8E, H, J: 54 ft 6 in (16·61 m)
Width folded	22 ft 6 in (6·86 m)
Height	15 ft 9 in (4·80 m)
Power plant	F-8A, B: 1 × Pratt & Whitney J57-P-4A of 16 200 lb (7 327 kg) st turbojet F-8C: 1 × P. & W. J57-P-16 of 16 900 lb (7 665 kg) st F-8D, E, H, J: 1 × P. & W. J-57-P-20 of 18 000 lb (8 165 kg) st turbojet

RF-8G Crusader, a remanufactured RF-8A

In service with the US Navy since 1957. F-8H, J, K and L are reworked D's, E's, C's and B's respectively. F-8E(FN) is version for French Navy. Reconnaissance versions are RF-8A & RF-8G.

ETENDARD IV-M

Dassault (France)

Carrier-borne single-seat interceptor and fighter bomber

Max speed at 36,000 ft (11 000 m)		Mach 1·02
Max cruising speed at 25,000 ft (7 600 m)		Mach 0·90
Service ceiling	49 200 ft (15 000 m)	
Combat range low level	320 n. miles	
Combat range med. level	870 n. miles	
Armament	Fuselage: 2 × 30 mm Cannon Wing Mounts (4): Up to 3 000 lb (1 060 kg) of rockets, bombs, Sidewinder AAM's or AS.30 ASM's	
Max T-O weight	22 650 lb (10 275 kg)	
Wing span	31 ft 6 in (9·60 m)	
Width folded	25 ft 7 in (7·80 m)	
Length	47 ft 3 in (14·40 m)	
Height	14 ft 1 in (4·30 m)	
Power plant	1 × Atar 8 turbojet of 9 700 lb (4 400 kg) st	

Entered service with French Navy for "Clemenceau" & "Foch" carriers in 1962. 75 aircraft were built. 21 additional aircraft were built as IV-P s dual-role tanker and reconnaissance aircraft with nose and ventral camera positions and flight refuelling equipment.

Etendard IVM of the French Navy

GANNET AEW Mk 3

Westland (UK)

Carrier-borne three-seat early-warning aircraft

Max speed	220 knots approx
Endurance	5-6 hours at 120 knots
Equipment	Early-warning electronic for long-range ship and aircraft detection
Max loaded weight	24 000 lb (10 886 kg)
Wing span	54 ft 6 in (16·61 m)
Width folded	19 ft 11 in (6·07 m)
Length	44 ft 0 in (13·41 m)
Height	16 ft 10 in (5·13 m)
Power plant	1 × Roll-Royce Bristol Double Mamba 102 turboprop of 3 875 ehp

Entered service with the Fleet Air Arm in 1959, equips No. 849 Squadron which provides early-warning flights on each carrier.

Westland Gannet AEW Mk 3 of the Royal Navy's No. 849 Sqdn *Courtesy, Air Portraits*

GANNET AS.4

Five of this variant remain in service with the FAA on COD duties and for training, together with 7 of the T.5 version.

Gannet AS.4 *Courtesy, Peter R. March*

SHIPBORNE AIRCRAFT

C-2A GREYHOUND
Grumman (USA)

Carrier-borne COD (Carrier On-board Delivery) Transport Aircraft

Max speed at 11 000 ft (3 450 m).	306 knots
Cruising speed at 27 300 ft (8 320 m)	258 knots
Range at cruising speed and height	1 432 n. miles
Capacity	39 troops, 20 litters with 4 attendants or 10 000 lb (4 535 kg) of freight
Max T-O weight	54 830 lb (24 870 kg)
Wing span	80 ft 7 in (24·56 m)
Length	56 ft 8 in (17·27 m)
Width folded	29 ft 4 in (8·94 m)
Height	15 ft 11 in (4·85 m)
Power plant	2 × Allison T56-A-8 turboprops of 4 050 ehp

A small number (17) of these COD transports were built, developed from the E-2A Hawkeye, for service aboard US Navy carriers. 8 more were ordered in 1970.

Grumman C-2A Greyhound of US Navy squadron VR-24   *Courtesy, B.M. Service*

E-2A HAWKEYE
Grumman (USA)

Carrier-borne five-seat early-warning aircraft

Max speed at optimum altitude	320 knots plus
Service ceiling	31 700 ft (9 660 m)
Ferry range	1,654 n. miles
Equipment	Early-warning and command electronics including Airborne Tactical Data System (ATDS)
Max T-O weight	49 638 lb (22 515 kg)
Wing span	80 ft 7 in (24·56 m)
Width folded	29 ft 4 in (8·94 m)
Length	56 ft 4 in (17·17 m)
Height	18 ft 4 in (5·59 m)
Power plant	2 × Allison T56-A-8A turboprops of 4 050 ehp

59 produced for service with Squadrons VAW-11 and VAW-12 of the US Navy in 1964. A development, designated the E-2B with more advanced avionics, first flew in February, 1969, and E-2A's are being converted to E-2B standard. The E-2C with new electronics flew for the first time on 20 January 1971.

E-2A Hawkeye of US Navy squadron VAW-11   *Courtesy AiReview (Tokyo)*

A-6A INTRUDER
Grumman (USA)

Carrier-borne two-seat strike and reconnaissance aircraft

Max speed at S L	Mach 0·99
Service ceiling	41 660 ft (12 700 m)
Max range (ferry)	2 800 n. miles
Armament	Weapon mounts (5): Each mount is of 3 600 lb (1 633 kg) capacity to carry bombs, Bullpup missiles and other stores.
Max T-O weight	60 626 lb (27 500 kg)
Wing span	53 ft 0 in (16·15 m)
Width folded	25 ft 2 in (7·67 m)
Length	54 ft 7 in (16·64 m)
Height overall	15 ft 7 in (4·75 m)
Height folded	15 ft 10 in (4·82 m)
Power plant	2 × P & W J52-P-8A turbojets of 9 300 lb (4 218 kg) each

This attack aircraft uses a digital integrated attack navigation system and serves with US Navy and Marine Corps squadrons. It has been developed into the EA-6A electronic countermeasures aircraft and further into the four-seat EA-6B for the same task.

A-6C with TRIM electro-optical equipment under fuselage.

Developments being produced are the A-6B, a special purpose missile carrier, the A-6C with TRIM electro-optical equipment, the KA-6D tanker version and the A-6E with Norden radar.

F-4B PHANTOM II
McDonnell Douglas (USA)

Carrier-borne two-seat all-weather fighter

Max speed	Mach 2·5
Combat ceiling	71 000 ft (21 640 m)
Combat radius	781 n. miles (1 450 km)
Ferry range	1 997 n. miles (3 700 km)
Armament	Fuselage: 4 mountings for Sparrow III and/or Sidewinder AAM's. Wings: 2 mountings for Sparrow III or Sidewinder AAM's Alternatively, 5 mounts for nuclear or conventional bombs and/or missiles up to 16 000 lb (7 250 kg)
Max T-O weight	54 600 lb (24 765 kg)
Wing span	38 ft 5 in (11·70 m)
Width folded	27 ft 6·5 in (8·39 m)
Length	58 ft 3 in (17·76 m)
Height	16 ft 3 in (4·96 m)
Power plant	F-4B, G: 2 × GE J79-GE-2A turbojets of 16 150 lb (7 325 kg) st each, J79-GE-8's for all later models of the F-B F-4J: 2 × GE J79-GE-10 turbojets of 16 500 lb (7 485 kg) st F-4K: 2 × RR Spey RB 168-25R Mk 201 turbofans of 12 500 lb (5 670 kg) st dry

Phantom FG.Mk.1 (F-4K) of Royal Navy taking off from HMS *Ark Royal*   *Courtesy, B. M. Service*

In service with the US Navy and Marines since 1962 in the F-4B form, together with the reconnaissance version, the RF-4B. The F-4G is a development of the F-4B with AN/ASW-21 data link communications equipment; the F-4J is a developed F-4B with more powerful engines, control improvements and advanced electronics; 28 of F-4K version, a developed F-4B, are in service as the Phantom FG Mk 1 with the British Fleet Air Arm.

SHIPBORNE AIRCRAFT

SEA HAWK   Hawker Siddeley (UK)

Carrier-borne single-seat fighter bomber

Max speed at S/L	512 knots
Radius of action	251 n. miles
Armament	Fuselage: 4 × 20 mm cannon
	Wing mounts (4): 2 × 500 lb bombs and/or RP
Max gross weight	16 200 lb (7 355 kg)
Wing span	39 ft 0 in (11·89 m)
Width folded	13 ft 4 in (4·04 m)
Length	39 ft 8 in (12·09 m)
Height overall	8 ft 8 in (2·64 m)
Height folded	16 ft 10 in (5·13 m)
Power plant	1 × RR Nene 103 turbojet of 5 400 lb (2 450 kg) st

The type is operational with the Indian Navy for the carrier "Vikrant".

Sea Hawk Mk. 50 of the Indian Navy with underwing rockets

SEA VIXEN F(AW) Mk 2   Hawker Siddeley (UK)

Carrier-borne two-seat all weather fighter

Max speed at 10 000 ft (3 050 m)	560 knots
Service ceiling	Approx 48 000 ft (14 630 m)
Armament	Fuselage: 2 pods each containing 14 × 2 in rockets
	Wing mounts: (6) Combination of Firestreak, Red Top or Bullpup missiles, bombs, rocket pods or air-to-surface rockets.
Max gross weight	35 000 lb (15 875 kg) approx
Wing span	50 ft 0 in (15·24 m)
Width folded	22 ft 3 in (6·78 m)
Length overall	55 ft 7 in (16·68 m)
Length folded	50 ft 2·5 in (15·30 m)
Height overall	11 ft 0 in (3·35 m)
Height folded	14 ft 11 in (4·55 m)
Power plant	2 × RR Avon Ra.24 Mk 208 turbojets of 11 250 lb (5 100 kg) st

In service with the Fleet Air Arm since 1959, it equips three first-line squadrons.

Sea Vixen F(AW) Mk. 2 of No. 766 Squadron, Royal Navy   *Courtesy, Peter R. March*

SEPECAT JAGUAR M   Breguet/BAC (France/UK)

Single-seat naval tactical aircraft

Max speed at S L	729 knots
Range (ferry, with external fuel)	2 270 n. miles
Armament	2 × 30 mm Aden or DEFA cannon in lower fuselage aft of cockpit. One ventral attachment point on fuselage centre-line and two under each wing. Provision for wingtip attachments for air-to-air missiles. The centre-line and inboard wing points can each carry up to 2 000 lb (900 kg) of weapons, and outboard underwing points up to 1 000 lb (450 kg) each. Typical alternative loads include 2 × Martel AS 37 anti-radar missiles and a drop tank 8 × 1 000 lb (450 kg) bombs; various combinations of bombs, Sidewinder air-to-air missiles, air-to-air of air-to-surface rockets, including the 68 mm SNEB rocket; or a reconnaissance camera pack with two photo-flare pods.
Max T-O weight	29 762 lb (13 500 kg)
Wing span	27 ft 10¼ in (8·49 m)
Length overall	50 ft 11 in (15·52 m)
Height overall	16 ft 0½ in (4·89 m)
Power plant	2 × Rolls-Royce/Turboméca Adour turbofan engines (each 4 620 lb = 2 100 kg st dry) or (6 950 lb = 3 150 kg) with afterburning.

Under development for French Navy. Prototype first flew on 14 November 1969.

Sepecat Jaguar M

SHIPBORNE AIRCRAFT

A-4 SKYHAWK McDonnell Douglas (USA)

Carrier-borne single-seat attack bomber

Max speed at S/L	585 knots (A-4F version)
Max range	1 736 n. miles plus
Armament	Fixed: 2×20 mm cannon in wings. Fuselage and Wing Mounts (5): Up to 10 000 lb (4 535 kg) assorted bombs, rockets, Sidewinder AAM's Bullpup ASM's, Zuni or Mighty Mouse pods, gun pods, torpedoes or ECM equipment
Max T-O weight	24 500 lb (11 113 kg) (A-4F version)
Wing span	27 ft 6 in (8·38 m)
Length	40 ft 3·25 in (12·27 m) (A-4F version)
Height	15 ft 0 in (4·57 m)
Power plant	A-4A: 1 × Wright J-65-W-4 turbojet of 7 700 lb (3 493 kg) st A-4B, C: 1 × Wright J65-W-16A of 7 700 lb (3 493 kg) st A-4E: 1 × P & W J52-P-6A of 8 500 lb (3 855 kg) st A-4F, G: 1 × P & W J52-P-8A of 9 300 lb (4 218 kg) st A-4M, J52-P-408A 11,200 lb (5 080 kg) st

A-4F Skyhawk of Squadron VA-22 of the US Navy

In service with the US Navy since 1956. A-4C and subsequent models have all-weather capability. A-4F inproved controls. A-4G in service with the Rcyal Australian Navy since 1967 (8 aircraft). Delivery of about 50 A-4M's for the US Marine Corps with a more powerful J52-P-408A engine began in Nobember 1970.

A-3B SKYWARRIOR McDonnell Douglas (USA)

Carrier-borne 3-seat attack bomber

Max speed st 10 000 ft (3 050 m)	530 knots
Service ceiling	45 000 ft (13 780 m)
Range, normal	2 520 n. miles
Armament	Fuselage: Weapons bay for bombs, torpedoes, etc. Tail-mounted barbette with 2 × 20 mm cannon (not always fitted)
Gross weight	73 000 lb (33 181 kg)
Wing span	72 ft 6 in (22·07 m)
Length	76 ft 4 in (21·46 m)
Height	22 ft 8 in (6·91 m)
Power plant	A-3B: 2 × P & W J57-P-10 turbojets of 10 500 lb (4 760 kg) st

Entered service with the US Navy in 1957, the A-3B has provision for flight-refuelling. Electronic countermeasures version (24 built) designated EA-3B and thirty RA-3B's entered service with cameras in the weapons bay. Also in service are KA-3 and EKA-3 tankers.

McDonnell/Douglas KA-3B Skywarrior of Squadron VAH-10, US Navy *Courtesy, B. M. Service*

F-14 TOMCAT Grumman (USA)

Carrier-borne two-seat all weather fighter

Max speed	Mach 2 plus
Max T-O weight	(with 4 Sparrow missiles) 53 000 lb (24 040 kg)
Wing span (max)	64 ft 1½ in (19·54 m)
Wing span (min)	33 ft 2½ in (10·12 m)
Length	61 ft 10½ in (18·86 m)
Height	16 ft 0 in (4·88 m)
Armament	1 nose-mounted M-61 six-barrelled cannon, Phoenix, Sidewinder and Sparrow missiles under fuselage and wings
Power plant	F-14A 2 × Pratt & Whitney TF30-P-412turbofans of 23 000 lb (10 432 kg) st F-14B and F-14C, 2 new engines yet to be developed

This aircraft is at present at the advanced development stage as a replacement for the Phantom II in the US Navy. The prototype F-14A first flew on 21 December 1970. Present orders are for 12 development aircraft and 26 production aircraft, with plans for eventual

Mock-up of Grumman F-14A variable-geometry fighter for US Navy

procurement of 463, with first operational squadron in 1973. From the 67th aircraft, designation will be F-14B with P and W F401-P-400 turbofans. New avionics and weapons will be fitted to later F-14C.

E-1B TRACER Grumman (USA)

Carrier-borne four-seat early-warning aircraft

Max speed at S/L	230 knots
Endurance at 10 000 ft (4 545 m) at 156 knots	8 hr
Equipment	A 20 × 30 ft (6·1 × 9·1 m) radar antenna used in conjunction with the APS-82 early-warning system
Gross weight	27 000 lb (12 250 kg)
Wing span	72 ft 7 in (22·04 m)
Length	45 ft 4 in (13·82 m)
Height	16 ft 10 in (5·13 m)
Power plant	2 × Wright R-1820-82 piston engines of 1 525 hp

Developed from the S-2 Tracker. 64 aircraft were built for the US Navy and entered service first in 1960.

E-1B Tracer early-warning aircraft of Squadron VAW-11, US Navy

SHIPBORNE AIRCRAFT

S-2 TRACKER
Grumman (USA)

Max speed at S/L	230 knots (S-2E)
Patrol speed at 1 500 ft (450 m)	130 knots
Service ceiling	21 000 ft (6 400 m)
Ferry range	1 128 n. miles
Max endurance	9 hrs
Armament (S-2D version)	Fuselage bomb bay: 2 × homing torpedoes or 4 × 385 lb (174 kg) depth charges or 1 × Mk 101 depth bomb
	Wing mounts (6): torpedoes or rockets or 250 lb (113 kg) bombs or sonobuoys
Max T-O weight	29 150 lb (13 222 kg)
Wing span	72 ft 7 in (22·13 m)
Width folded	27 ft 4 in (8·33 m)
Length	43 ft 6 in (13·26 m)
Height	16 ft 7 in (5·06 m)
Power plant	2 × Wright R-1820-82WA piston engines of 1 525 hp each

The original variant, the S-2A, entered production in 1954; a total of 755 were built including over 100 supplied to Japan, Italy, Brazil, the Royal Netherlands Navy and other countries. The S-2C (60 built) had enlarged weapons bay. The S-2D (119 built) had increased wing span and improved accommodation. The S-2E is an S-2D with improved ASW equipment, 14 of which were supplied to the Royal Australian Navy. This aircraft was built under licence in Canada with the designations CS2F-1 (S-2A equivalent) and CS2F-2, and CS2F-3 which are developed versions. These are in service with the Royal Canadian Navy and the CS2F-1 with the Royal Netherlands Navy.

Grumman S-2F Tracker—Royal Netherlands Navy

C-1A TRADER

Developed from the S-2 Tracker is the C-1A Trader which is used by the US Navy as a COD transport with accommodation for nine passengers or 3 500 lb (1 590 kg) of freight.

S-3A
Lockheed (USA)

Anti-submarine aircraft

Max speed	430 knots
Ferry range	3 000 n. miles plus
Max T-O weight	41 000 lb (18 597 kg)
Wing span	68 ft 8 in (20·93 m)
Length overall	53 ft 4 in (16·26 m)
Armament	Provision for homing torpedoes, mines, depth charges, rockets, missiles and special weapons in fuselage weapon bay and on underwing pylons
Power plant	2 × General Electric TF34-GE-2 high by-pass ratio turbofan engines of approx 9 000 lb (4 082 kg) st

Lockheed have received contracts from US Navy to build 8 prototypes of a new anti-submarine aircraft under the designation S-3A. The contract also gives the Navy an option to buy 193 production models.

A-5 VIGILANTE
North American Rockwell (USA)

Carrier-borne two-seat tactical reconnaissance aircraft

Max speed at 40 000 ft	Mach 2·1
Service ceiling	64 000 ft (19 500 m)
Normal range	2 000 n. miles
Armament	Wing mountings (4): variety of weapons, including thermo-nuclear bombs
Max T-O weight	approx 80 000 lb (36 285 kg)
Wing span	53 ft 0 in (16·15 m)
Width folded	42 ft 5 in (12·93 m)
Length, overall	75 ft 10 in (23·11 m)
Length folded	68 ft 0 in (20·73 m)
Height	19 ft 5 in (5·92 m)
Power plant	2 × GE J79-GE-10 turbojets of 17 859 lb (8 118 kg) st

In service as the A-5A with the US Navy from 1961. The A-5B was a long-range version with extra fuel in the enlarged fuselage. The RA-5C is a reconnaissance version, carrying cameras and side-looking radar in a ventral fairing. All A's and most B's have been converted to RA-5C standard.

RA-5C Vigilante reconnaissance aircraft of the US Navy

Courtesy, AiReview (Tokyo)

AGUSTA A.106
Agusta (Italy)

Ship-borne single-seat ASW light helicopter

Max speed at S L	96 knots
Max cruising speed	91 knots
Hovering ceiling	8 350 ft (2 545 m)
Normal range	134 n. miles
Endurance	1 hr 40 min
Armament	2 × Mk 44 torpedoes
Max T-O weight	3 086 lb (1 400 kg)
Main rotor diameter	31 ft 2 in (9·50 m)
Length overall	36 ft 0 in (10·97 m)
Power plant	1 × Turbomeca-Agusta TAA-230 of 330 hp

First flown in November 1965. Comprehensive instrumentation and electronic equipment make possible operation of the A 106 in reduced visibility conditions.

Agusta A.106 light anti-submarine helicopter in Italian Navy insignia

HELICOPTERS

AGUSTA-BELL 204B

Agusta (Italy)

Ship-borne ASW helicopter

Max speed at S/L	104 knots
Cruising speed	96 knots
Hovering ceiling (out of ground effect)	4 500 ft (*1 370 m*)
Max range	340 n. miles
Equipment	Dipping Sonar and special electronic equipment for stabilisation etc.
Armament	2 × Mk 44 torpedoes
Max T-O weight	9 500 lb (*4 310 kg*)
Main rotor diameter	48 ft 0 in (*14·63 m*)
Length overall	57 ft 0 in (*17·37 m*)
Power plant	1 × Lycoming T53-11A shaft-turbine engine of 1 100 shp; alternatively 1 × Rolls-Royce Bristol Gnome H.1200 of 1 200 shp or a General Electric T58-GE-3

The Bell UH-1B built under licence in Italy, this aircraft is in service with the armed services of Italy, Spain, Sweden, Holland, Austria, Turkey and Saudi Arabia.

Agusta-Bell 204B — Italian Navy

SE.316 ALOUETTE III

Aérospatiale (France)

Seven-seat general-purpose helicopter

Max speed at S/L	114 knots
Cruising speed at S/L	97 knots
Service ceiling	10 662 ft (*3 250 m*)
Range	290 n. miles
Armament	2 × AS12 missiles or 2 × Mk 44 torpedoes or 1 × torpedo and MAD equipment
Max T-O weight (standard version)	4 850 lb (*2 200 kg*)
Main rotor diameter	36 ft 1¾ in (*11·02 m*)
Length overall	42 ft 1½ in (*12·84 m*)
Length folded	32 ft 10¾ in (*10·03 m*)
Height	9 ft 10 in (*3·0 m*)
Power plant	1 × Turbomeca Artouste IIIB shaft-turbine engine of 870 shp derated to 550 shp

Developed from the standard Alouette III, this version is intended for "plane guard", ASW and attack duties aboard various classes of naval vessels.

Alouette III of the Royal Danish Navy   *Courtesy, Peter R. March*

BELL 47G

Bell (USA)

Two-seat communications light helicopter

Max speed	91 knots
Cruising speed at 5 000 ft (*1 525 m*)	72 knots
Service ceiling	18 400 ft (*5 610 m*)
Hovering ceiling	12 300 ft (*3 758 m*)
Range	217 n. miles
Gross weight	2 950 lb (*1 338 kg*)
Main rotor diameter	37 ft 1·5 in (*11·32 m*)
Length	43 ft 2·5 in (*13·17 m*)
Height	9 ft 3·75 in (*2·83 m*)
Power plant	1 × Lycoming TVO-435-A1A of 260 hp

In use with Chilean, Italian, Mexican, Peruvian and Uruguayan Navies.

Bell 47G

AH-1G HUEYCOBRA

Bell (USA)

Two-seat close-support helicopter

Max speed (in dive)	190 knots
Cruising speed	144 knots
Service ceiling	12 700 ft (*3 870 m*)
Hovering ceiling	9 900 ft (*3 015 m*)
Range	336 n. miles
Armament	XM-28 turret under nose, mounting 2 Miniguns or 2 XM-129 40 mm grenade launchers or 1 Minigun and 1 XM-129
Gross weight	9 500 lb (*4 309 kg*)
Main rotor diameter	44 ft 0 in (*13·41 m*)
Length overall	52 ft 11½ in (*16·14 m*)
Power plant	1 × Lycoming T53-L-13 of 1 100 shp

38 in service with the US Marine Corps. Over 1 000 in service or on order for the US Army. The AH-1J Sea Cobra with Pratt & Whitney T400-CP-400 twin-turbine power plant is in production for the US Marine Corps, with 49 ordered initially.

Bell AH-1J SeaCobra of the US Marine Corps

HELICOPTERS

Ka-15 (code-name "Hen") Kamov (USSR)

Shipborne two-seat general-purpose light helicopter

Max speed	81 knots
Cruising speed	67·5 knots
Service ceiling	9 840 ft (*3 000 m*)
Hovering ceiling	2 230 ft (*680 m*)
Max range	252 n. miles
Max endurance	4 hrs
Gross weight	2 500 lb (*1 136 kg*)
Main rotor diameter	32 ft 8½ in (*9·97 m*)
Length	19 ft 6 in (*6·0 m*)
Power plant	1 × Ivchenko AI-14V radial piston-engine of 255 hp

First flew in 1952.
In service with the Soviet Naval Airfleet

Kamov Ka-15—Soviet Naval Airfleet

Ka-25 (code-name "Hormone") Kamov (USSR)

Shipborne anti-submarine strike helicopter

Max speed	119 knots
Normal cruising speed	104 knots
Service ceiling	11 500 ft (*3 500 m*)
Range with max fuel with reserves	351 n. miles
Equipment	Search radar under nose
T-O weight	16 100 lb (*7 300 kg*)
Main rotor diameter	51 ft 8 in (*15·75 m*)
Power plant	2 × 900 shp Glushenkov shaft-turbine engines

In service with the Soviet Naval Airfleet

Kamov Ka-25 "Hormone" anti-submarine helicopters on the cruiser "Moskva"

S-55 (H-19) Sikorsky (USA)

Carrier-borne and land-based general-purpose helicopter

Max speed at S/L	97 knots
Cruising speed	79 knots
Hovering ceiling	2 300 ft (*700 m*)
Range	313 n. miles
Gross weight	7 900 lb (*3 319.19 kg*)
Main rotor diameter	53 ft 0 in (*16·16 m*)
Length (fuselage)	42 ft 3 in (*12·88 m*)
Height	13 ft 4 in (*4·07 m*)
Power plant	1 × Wright R-1300-3 radial piston-engine of 800 hp

The S.55 is still in service with the US Navy as the UH-19F and the Marine Corps as the CH-19E and with the Japanese navy for training duties.

Sikorsky S-55 in Japanese Maritime Self-Defence Force insignia

HELICOPTERS

S-58 SEABAT
Sikorsky (USA)

Carrier-borne and land-based anti-submarine and general-purpose helicopter

Max speed at S/L	107 knots
Cruising speed	85 knots
Hovering ceiling, out of ground effect	2 400 ft (730 m)
Service ceiling	9 000 ft (2 740 m)
Normal range	226 n. miles
Capacity	16-18 passengers
Max permissible weight	14 000 lb (6 350 kg)
Main rotor diameter	56 ft 0 in (17·07 m)
Length	56 ft 8¼ in (17·27 m)
Height	15 ft 11 in (4·85 m)
Power plant	1 × Wright R-1820-84B/D piston engine of 1 525 hp

In service with the US Navy as the SH-34G and SH-34J Seabat, the LH-34D for cold-weather operation, UH-34G and UH-34J utility aircraft. UH-34D is the US Marines version, also UH-34E amphibious version and VH-34D VIP transport. The S-58 is in service with other navies including the Argentine Navy, Belgian Navy (Sud-built), Indonesian Navy, Royal Netherlands Navy and the French Navy, the latter's aircraft being built in France by Sud-Aviation.

Sikorsky S-58 Royal Netherlands Navy

SH-3 SEA KING
Sikorsky (USA)

Carrier-borne and land-based amphibious all-weather ASW and Transport helicopter

Max speed	144 knots
Cruising speed for max range	118 knots
Hovering ceiling	8 200 ft (2 500 m)
Service ceiling	14 700 ft (4 480 m)
Range with max fuel, 10% reserve	542 n. miles
Equipment	Bendix AQS-13 sonar. Hamilton autostabilisation equipment with sonar coupler. Doppler radar
Armament	Up to 840 lb (381 kg) of weapons including homing torpedoes
Max T-O weight	20 500 lb (9 300 kg)
Main rotor diameter	62 ft 0 in (18·90 m)
Length overall	72 ft 8 in (22·15 m)
Width folded	16 ft 4 in (4·98 m)
Height to top of rotor hub	15 ft 6 in (4·72 m)
Power plant	2 × GE T58-GE-10 shaft turbines of 1 400 shp each.

Two versions built by Sikorsky, the SH-3A, with GE T58-GE-8B engines wihch is also in service with the Japanese MSDF and, under the designation CHSS-2, with the Canadian Armed Forces; and the SH-3D, also in service with the Spanish, Brazilian and Italian Navies and built under licence by Westland Aircraft for the Fleet Air Arm, German and Indian navies, this latter using the RR Bristol Gnome 1400 engine. The Italian Sea Kings are built by Agusta.

Westland Sea King in Royal Navy insignia

SEA KNIGHT
Boeing-Vertol (USA)

Carrier-borne and land-based three-crew transport and utility helicopter

Data for UH-46D

Max speed	144 knots
Cruising speed	140 knots
Hovering ceiling out of ground effect	5 750 ft (1 753 m)
Service ceiling	14 000 ft (4 265 m)
Range at AUW of 23 000 lb (10 433 kg) with 6 750 lb (3 062 kg) payload, 10% fuel reserve	198 n. miles
Capacity	25 troops and troop commander or 15 stretchers plus 2 attendants or up to a 10 000 lb (4 535 kg) load
Max T-O weight	23 000 lb (10 433 kg)
Main rotor diameter	50 ft 0 in (15·24 m)
Length, fuselage	44 ft 10 in (13·66 m)
Height	16 ft 8·5 in (5·09 m)
Power plant	2 × GE T58-GE-10 shaft-turbine engines of 1 400 shp each

In service with the US Marine Corps since 1962 as the CH-46A and US Navy for shore to ship and ship to ship duties as the UH-46A, uprated in 1966 to CH-46D and UH-46D. Three in service with the Royal Swedish Navy as the HKP-4 using Bristol Siddeley Gnome H1200, and six with the Japanese MSDF for mine countermeasures duties.

Boeing-Vertol UH-46D Sea Knight of US Navy Squadron HC-6   *Courtesy, B. M. Service*

HELICOPTERS

SEASPRITE
Kaman (USA)

Ship-borne two-crew all-weather rescue and general-purpose helicopter

Data for UH-2A/B

Max speed at S/L	141 knots
Cruising speed	130 knots
Hovering ceiling	5 100 ft (1 555 m)
Service ceiling	17 400 ft (5 300 m)
Normal range with max fuel	581 n. miles
Capacity	11 passengers or 4 stretcher patients
Max T-O weight	10 000 lb (4 535 kg)
Main rotor diameter	44 ft 0 in (13·41 m)
Length	52 ft 2 in (15·90 m)
Height	13 ft 6.3 in (4·12 m)
Power plant	1 × GE T58-GE-8B shaft turbine engine of 1 250 shp

Entered service with the US Navy in 1962 as the UH-2A, followed by the UH-2B "fair weather" version. A twin-engined version, the UH-2C with two T58 engines, was introduced into service by retrospective modification of UH-2A's and B's. 6 UH-2C's redesignated HH-2C's, were converted into gunships with a chin Minigun, 2 additional machine-guns and additional armour. A total of 67 single-engined models were being converted into HH-2D's, similar to HH-2C but with armament and armour deleted. Ten SH-2D's are interim ship-borne ASW helicopters, with search radar, homing torpedoes and other equipment.

HH-2D Seasprite helicopter of the US Navy

SEA STALLION
Sikorsky (USA)

Carrier-borne and land-based three-crew heavy assault and transport helicopter

Max speed	170 knots
Cruising speed	150 knots
Hovering ceiling out of ground effect	6 500 ft (1 980 m)
Service ceiling	21 000 ft (6 400 m)
Range, with 4 076 lb (1 849 kg) payload 10% reserve at cruising speed and 2 min warming up	223 n. miles
Capacity	38 passengers, 24 stretchers and 4 attendants or 8 000 lb (3 630 kg) of internal or external cargo
Max T-O weight	42 000 lb (19 050 kg)
Main rotor diameter	72 ft 3 in (22·02 m)
Length	88 ft 3 in (26·90 m)
Width, folded	15 ft 6 in (4·72 m)
Height	24 ft 11 in (7·60 m)
Power plant	2 × GE T64-GE-6 shaft turbine engines of 2 850 shp each

Sikorsky CH-53A of the US Marine Corps

Entered service with the US Marine Corps as the CH-53A in 1966, becoming operational in Vietnam in January 1967. The later CH-53D has 3 695 shp T64-GE-412 engines or 3 925 shp T64-GE-413 engines.

SA.321 SUPER FRELON
Aérospatiale (France)

Land-based two-crew heavy assault and anti-submarine helicopter

Max speed at S/L	129 knots
Cruising speed	124 knots
Hovering ceiling out of ground effect	1 814 ft (550 m)
Service ceiling	11 475 ft (3 500 m)
Range at S/L	496 n. miles
Range, ferry with three 146 Imp gallon (666 litre) ferry tanks	730 n. miles
Capacity	30 troops, 15 stretchers and 2 attendants or 9 920 lb (4 500 kg) payload
Max T-O weight	27 557 lb (12 500 kg)
Main rotor diameter	62 ft 0 in (18·90 m)
Length of fuselage, incl tail rotor	65 ft 10¾ in (20·08 m)
Width folded	17 ft 0¾ in (5·20 m)
Height	21 ft 10¼ in (6·66 m)
Power plant	3 × Turbomeca Turmo IIIC6 shaft-turbine engines of 1 550 shp each

Eighteen in service with the French Navy as the SA-321G for ASW duties.

SA-321 Super Frelon—French Navy

HELICOPTERS

UH-1E
Bell (USA)

Land-based single-crew assault support helicopter

Max speed	140 knots
Cruising speed	120 knots
Hovering ceiling out of ground effect	11 800 ft (3 595 m)
Service ceiling	21 000 ft (6 400 m)
Range, max fuel	248 n. miles
Armament	2 × machine guns and 2 × rocket pods, on each side of the cabin
Capacity	8 passengers or 4 000 lb (1 815 kg) of freight
Max T-O weight	9 500 lb (4 309 kg)
Main rotor diameter	44 ft 0 in (13·41 m)
Length	53 ft 0 in (16·15 m)
Height	12 ft 7½ in (3·84 m)
Power plant	1 × Lycoming T53-L-11 shaft-turbine engine of 1 100 shp

Entered service with the US Marine Corps in 1964; the UH-1E is the Marine version of the Iroquois which is in widespread military service. Nine UH-1D's are in service with the Royal Australian Navy. Licence-built by Dornier, 27 UH-1D's will serve with the German Navy. The US Navy is receiving 45 TH-IL trainers and 8 UH-1L.

Bell TH-IL trainer of the US Navy

WASP
Westland (UK)

Shipborne two-crew anti-submarine helicopter

Max speed at S/L	104 knots
Cruising speed	96 knots
Hovering ceiling out of ground effect	8 800 ft (2 682 m)
Range with max fuel and allowances of 5 min for T-O and landing, 15 min cruising with 4 passengers	234 n. miles
Armament	2 × Mk 44 homing torpedoes
Max T-O weight	5 500 lb (2 495 kg)
Main rotor diameter	32 ft 3 in (9·83 m)
Length	40 ft 4 in (12·29 m)
Width folded	8 ft 8 in (2·64 m)
Height, tail rotor turning	11 ft 8 in (3·56 m)
Power plant	1 × RR Bristol Nimbus 503 shaft turbine engine of 710 shp

In service with the Fleet Air Arm since 1963 aboard anti-submarine frigates. Also with the navies of Brazil, New Zealand and South Africa.

Wasp of the Royal Netherlands Navy

WESSEX
Westland (UK)

Ship and carrier-borne two-crew anti-submarine assault and general-purpose helicopter

Max speed at S L	116 knots
Cruising speed	105 knots
Hovering ceiling out of ground effect	HAS.1: 3 600 ft (1 100 m) HU.5: 4 000 ft (1 220 m)
Service ceiling	HAS.1: 14 000 ft (4 300 m)
Range with max fuel 10% reserves	HAS.1: 560 n. miles HU.5: 415 n. miles
Equipment	HAS.1: Doppler radar and dipping sonar HAS.3: as HAS.1 plus new search radar
Armament	HAS.1, 3: 1 or 2 homing torpedoes on fuselage side mounts, alternatively 4 × SS.11 ASM's HU.5: 4 × SS.11 ASM's alternatively various gun/rocket combinations
Capacity	In commando role can carry 16 troops or 8 stretchers or 4 000 lb (1 814 kg) of freight
Max T-O weight	HAS.1: 12 600 lb (5 715 kg) HU.5: 13 500 lb (6 120 kg)
Main rotor diameter	56 ft 0 in (17·07 m)
Length	65 ft 9 in (20·03 m)
Length folded	38 ft 6 in (11·73 m)
Width, folded	13 ft 4 in (4·06 m)
Height	16 ft 2 in (4·93 m)
Power plant	HAS.1: 1 × Napier Gazelle NGa.13 Mk 161 shaft turbine engine of 1 450 shp HAS.3: 1 × Napier Gazelle NGa.22 Mk 165 shaft turbine engine of 1 600 shp HU.5: 2 × RR Bristol Gnome 112/113 shaft turbine engines of 775 shp each

Westland Wessex HU Mk. 5—Royal Navy

Courtesy Peter R. March

In service with the Fleet Air Arm on anti-submarine duties since 1961 (HAS.1) and 1967 (HAS.3), also with Royal Australian Navy as HAS.31, identical to HAS.1 (27 aircraft, since modified to HAS-31B, with new search radar). The HU.5 version is a Marine Commando assault version, in service since 1964 with the Commando carriers.

HELICOPTERS

WHIRLWIND — Westland (UK)

Land-based and Carrier-borne two-crew rescue and general-purpose helicopter

Max speed	92 knots
Cruising speed	90 knots
Hovering ceiling	6 900 ft (2 100 m)
Service ceiling	16 600 ft (5 060 m)
Normal range	260 n. miles
Capacity	Up to 10 troops or 6 stretchers or freight
Armament	4 × SS.11 ASM's
Max T-O weight	8 000 lb (3 630 kg)
Main rotor diameter	53 ft 0 in (16·15 m)
Length fuselage	44 ft 2 in (13·46 m)
Height	13 ft 2·5 in (4·03 m)
Power plant	1 × RR Bristol Siddeley Gnome H.1000 shaft turbine of 1 050 shp

This aircraft is in service with the Fleet Air Arm as the HAR.9 for plane guard and SAR duties and with RAF Strike Command as the HAR.10 for SAR duties. The Brazilian Navy has five.

Westland Whirlwind HAR 10—Brazilian Navy

Drone Helicopter

QH-50 — Gyrodyne (USA)

Max speed	80 knots
Cruising speed	60 knots
Service ceiling	QH-50C: 16 400 ft (5 000 m)
	QH-50D: 16 000 ft (4 875 m)
Hovering ceiling (in ground effect)	QH-50C: 16 900 ft (5 150 m)
	QH-50D: 16 300 ft (4 965 m)
Max range	QH-50C 71 n. miles
	QH-50D 122 n. miles
Armament	2 × Mk 44 torpedoes or 1 Mk 46 torpedo and 1 sonobuoy
Max T-O weight	QH-50C: 2 285 lb (1 036 kg)
	QH-50D: 2 328 lb (1 056 kg)
Rotor diameter	20 ft 0 in (6.10 m)
Power plant	QH-50C: 1 × Boeing T50-BO-8A of 300 shp
	QH-50D: 1 × Boeing T50-BO-12 of 365 shp

The DASH System (Drone Anti-Submarine Helicopter) of which the QH-50 is the mobile weapon-carrying unit is carried aboard many US Navy vessels. The QH-50C went into service in 1962 and the QH-50D in 1965 Take-off and landing are visually controlled by the Deck Control Officer who hands the helicopter over to the control information centre in the ship which flies the drone to the target, actuates the arming and weapon release switches and returns the drone to the ship.

QH-50C drone helicopter, armed with two Mk. 46 torpedoes

LAND-BASED AIRCRAFT

HU-16 ALBATROSS — Grumman (USA)

Land-based five-crew general purpose amphibian

Max speed at S/L	205 knots
Max cruising speed	195 knots
Service ceiling	21 500 ft (6 550 m)
Range	2 475 n. miles
Equipment (ASW version)	MAD gear, nose AS radome, ECM radome in wing
Armament (ASW version)	Torpedoes, depth charges or rockets
Max T-O weight	37 500 lb (12 500 kg)
Wing span	96 ft 8 in (29·42 m)
Length	62 ft 10 in (19·12 m)
Power plant	2 × Wright R-1820-76A radial piston engines of 1 425 hp each

In service with the US Navy as HU-16D and Coast Guard as HU-16E, developed from earlier HU-16C, many of which were converted. Supplied to a number of foreign countries and a special ASW version, produced in 1961, is now operated by the Greek and Spanish Air Forces. CSR-110 is a modified HU-16 with Wright R-1820-82 engines for SAR duties in Canada.

Grumman HU-16A Albatross—No. 333 Sqdn, Royal Norwegian Air Force   *Courtesy, S. P. Peltz*

LAND BASED AIRCRAFT

CP-107 ARGUS
Canadair (Canada)

Fifteen-crew long-range maritime reconnaissance aircraft

Max speed at 20 000 ft (*6 100 m*)	274 knots
Cruising speed	150-175 knots
Service ceiling	20 000 ft (*6 100 m*) plus
Max range	5 124 n. miles at 194 knots
Equipment	Large, nose radome, MAD in tail (for search role)
Armament	15 600 lb of weapons (bombs, torpedoes, missiles) stowed 8 000 lb internally and 3 800 lb under each wing
T-O weight	148 000 lb (*67 130 kg*)
Wing span	142 ft 3·5 in (*43·38 m*)
Length	128 ft 9½ in (*39·25 m*)
Height	36 ft 8·5 in (*11·19 m*)
Power plant	4 × Wright R-3350-EA-1 turbo-compound radial piston engines of 3 700 hp each

In service with four squadrons (Nos. 404, 405, 407, 415 Sqdns) of the Canadian Armed Forces in both Mk 1 and Mk 2 versions which differ in equipment.

Argus Mk. 2 maritime reconnaissance aircraft

Courtesy, B. M. Service

Br.1150 ATLANTIC
Breguet (France)

Twelve-crew long-range maritime reconnaissance aircraft

Max speed at high altitudes	355 knots
Max range	4 850 n. miles
Max endurance at 169 knots (patrol speed)	18 hours
Armament	Fuselage weapons bay: carries standard NATO bombs, 385 lb (*175 kg*) depth charges, homing torpedoes. Wing mounts (4): HVAR rockets, or Martel ASM's
Max T-O weight	95 900 lb (*43 500 kg*)
Wing span	119 ft 1 in (*36·3 m*)
Length	104 ft 2 in (*31·75 m*)
Height	37 ft 2 in (*11·33 m*)
Power plant	2 × RR Tyne R.Ty.20 Mk 21 turboprop engines of 6 105 ehp each

In service since 1966 with French Navy (40 aircraft), German Navy (20 aircraft), Netherlands (9 aircraft), Italian (18 aircraft).

Atlantic in Royal Netherlands Navy insignia

BERIEV M-12 (code-name "Mail")
Beriev (USSR)

Maritime-reconnaissance amphibian

Max speed	329 knots
Max altitude (record attempt)	39 977 ft (*12 185 m*)
Gross weight	65 035 lb (*29 500 kg*)
Armament	Bomb-bay in bottom of hull, aft of step, and pylons for external stores under outer wings.
Equipment	Nose radome and MAD gear in tail
Span	97 ft 6 in (*29·72 m*)
Length	99 ft 0 in (*30·18 m*)
Power plant	2 × Ivchenko AI-20D turboprop engines of 4 000 shp each

In service with the Soviet Naval Airfleet

Beriev M-12 "Mail" of the Soviet Naval Airfleet

Courtesy, Tass

LAND-BASED AIRCRAFT

OV-10A BRONCO
North American (USA)

Two-seat multi-purpose counter-insurgency aircraft

Max speed at S/L without weapons	244 knots
Combat radius, with max weapon load	198 n. miles
Ferry range	1 240 n. miles
Armament	4 × 0·30 in machine-guns in sponsons, which also carry maximum of 2 400 lb (1 088 kg) external ordnance; provision for one Sidewinder AAM under each wing, and for 1 200 lb (544 kg) load under fuselsge
Max weapon load	3 600 lb (1 633 kg)
Max T-O weight	14 466 lb (6 563 kg)
Wing span	40 ft 0 in (12·19 m)
Length	41 ft 7 in (12·67 m)
Height	15 ft 2 in (4·62 m)

OV-10A Bronco light armed reconnaissance aircraft   *Courtesy, S. P. Peltz*

Power plant	2 × Garrett AiResearch T76-G-10/12 turboprops each of 715 shp

96 in service with the US Marine Corps, of which 18 have been loaned to the US Navy for use in Vietnam.

C-121 CONSTELLATION
Lockheed (USA)
Long-range transport and electronic reconnaissance aircraft

Max speed at 20 000 ft (6 000 m)	279 knots
Max range	3 994 n. miles
Capacity	72 troops in transport version 27 crew in electronic recce. version
Gross weight	143 600 lb (65 135 kg)
Wing span	126 ft 2 in (42·03 m)
Height	24 ft 9 in (8·25 m)
Length	116 ft 2 in (38·69 m)
Power plant	4 × Wright R-3350-91 radial piston engines of 3 250 hp each

In service with the US Navy as the C-121J transport, EC-121K/P, EC-121L, EC-121M for early-warning duties with dorsal and ventral radomes, and WC-121N for weather reconnaissance. The earlier version of the Constellation, the L749A, went into SAR service with the French SGAC, and the Indian Air Force is using one squadron of L1049's for maritime reconnaissance.

Lockheed Constellation Maritime reconnaissance aircraft—Indian Air Force   *Courtesy, M. D. West*

AV-8A HARRIER
Hawker Siddeley (UK)

Single-seat V/STOL strike and reconnaissance aircraft

Max speed	over 640 knots
Service ceiling	over 50 000 ft (15 240 m)
Range with one in-flight refuelling	over 3 000 n. miles
Ferry range, unrefuelled	nearly 2 000 n. miles
Armament	Three under-fuselage and four under-wing attachments for up to 8 000 lb (3 628 kg) of bombs, 68 mm SNEB rocket pods, 30 mm gun pods, etc
Max T-O weight	approx 23 000 lb (10 432 kg)
Wing span	25 ft 3 in (7·70 m)
Length	45 ft 6 in (13·87 m)
Height	approx 11 ft 3 in (3·43 m)
Power plant	1 × RR Pegasus 10 (first ten aircraft for USMC) or 1 × Pegasus II of 21 500 lb (9 752 kg) st on later aircraft

Delivery of 30 aircraft for the USMC began in 1971. Another 30 are being requested under the FY 1972 budget. Others serve with the RAF.

Hawker Siddley AV-8A Harrier of the US Marine Corps

C-130 HERCULES
Lockheed (USA)
Medium/long-range transport and reconnaissance aircraft

Max level speed	333 knots
Max cruising speed	320 knots
Service ceiling	21 500 ft (6 550 m)
Range with max load	2 100 n. miles
Capacity	92 troops, 64 paratroops, or 74 stretchers and 2 attendants. Cargo of 26 640 lb (12 080 kg)
Max T-O weight	155 000 lb (70 310 kg)
Wing span	132 ft 7 in (40·41 m)
Length	97 ft 9 in (29·78 m)
Height	38 ft 3 in (11·66 m)
Power plant	4 × Allison T56-A-7A turboprop engines of 4 050 eshp each

This transport is in widespread service with twenty air forces and with the US Navy as C-130E, C-130F and C-130D (for ski operation), the Marine Corps as KC-130F (with flight refuelling equipment) and with the US Coast Guard as HC-130B for SAR duties and EC-130E.

Lockheed HC-130B—US Coast Guard

LAND BASED AIRCRAFT

A32 LANSEN

SAAB (Sweden)

Two-seat all-weather and attack fighter and reconnaissance aircraft

Max speed at S/L	608 knots
Cruising speed at 36 000 ft (*11 000 m*)	470 knots
Service ceiling	52 500 ft (*16 000 m*)
Normal range	750 n. miles
Max range	1 736 n. miles
Armament	Fuselage: 4 × 20 mm cannon Wing mounts (2): 2 × Rb 04 ASM's or 2 200 lb (*997 kg*) of bombs or up to 24 rockets
T-O weight	28 660 lb (*13 000 kg*)
Wing span	42 ft 8 in (*13·00 m*)
Length	48 ft 0¾ in (*14·65 m*)
Height	15 ft 3 in (*4·65 m*)
Power plant	1 × Svenska Flygmotor R.M 5 (RR Avon) turbojet of 9 920 lb st

In service with the Swedish Air Force as the A32A attack fighter, J32B all-weather fighter and S32C photo-reconnaissance aircraft.

Saab A32A Lansen

MB 326GB

Aermacchi (Italy)

Two-seater Trainer-ground attack

Max speed	468 knots
Cruising speed	430 knots
Service ceiling	39 000 ft (*11 900 m*)
Wing span	35 ft 7 in (*10·85 m*)
Length	34 ft 11·25 in (*10·65 m*)
Height	12 ft 2·5 in (*3·72 m*)
Power plant	1 × Rolls Royce Bristol Viper 20 of 3 410 lb (*1 547 kg*) st
Radius of action (fully loaded)	68·2 n. miles
Gross weight	11 500 lb (*5 216 kg*)
Armament	Up to 4 000 lb (*1 814 kg*) of armament can be carried on 6 underwing attachments

Six of this version built as light attack fighters for the Argentine Navy. The Royal Australian Navy is getting 10 MB 326H trainers built in Australia by CAC.

Aermacchi MB 326GB of the Argentine Navy

P-2 NEPTUNE

Lockheed (USA)

Seven-seat long-range maritime-reconnaissance aircraft

Max speed at 10,000 ft (*3 050 m*)	309 knots
Patrol speed at 1,000 ft (*305 m*)	150-180 knots
Service ceiling	22 000 ft (*6 700 m*)
Max range	3 200 n. miles
Armament	Fuselage Weapons Bay: Up to 8 000 lb (*5 000 kg*) of bombs, torpedoes, depth charges. Wing mounts (2): 16 × 0·5 in rockets Optional dorsal turret with 2 × 0·5 guns
Max T-O weight	79 895 lb (*36 497·73 kg*)
Wing span (inc. tiptanks)	103 ft 10 in (*31·65 m*)
Length	91 ft 8 in (*27·94 m*)
Height	29 ft 4 in (*8·94 m*)
Power plant	2 × Wright R-3350-32W radial piston engines of 3 500 hp each Plus 2 × Westinghouse J34 turbojet engines of 3 400 lb st each

This aircraft is in widespread service with the US Navy as the P-2H and with the French Navy, Royal Netherlands

Lockheed Neptune—Royal Australian Air Force

Navy, Royal Australian Air Force and with Argentine. With Brazil and Portugal it serves as the P-2E without the auxiliary turbojets.

A highly-modified version, the Kawasaki P-2J serves with the Japanese MSDF. It is powered by two 2 850 shp IHI/General Electric T64-IHI-10 turboprops plus two 3 085 lb st IHI J3-IHI-7C auxiliary turbojets. It has an extended front fuselage and new sensor systems.

HS.801 NIMROD MR.1

Hawker Siddeley (UK)

Eleven-seat long-range maritime-reconnaissance aircraft

Max cruising speed	over 434 knots
Wing span	114 ft 10 in (*35·00 m*)
Length	126 ft 9 in (*38·063 m*)
Height	29 ft 8·5 in (*9·05 m*)
Power plant	4 × RR RB168 Spey Mk 250 turbofan engines of 11 500 lb st (*5 217 kg*) each
Armament	Forward bay for bombs, mines, depth charges and/or torpedoes 2 wing mounts for Nord AS.12 or Martel ASM Rear weapons bay for active and passive sonobuoys
Equipment	Elliot nav-attack system, Sonar ASV-21 radar, Autolycus Ionisation detector, ECM gear, MAD and searchlight

38 aircraft are in production and in service with RAF Strike Command.

Hawker Siddeley Nimrod MR.Mk.1

Courtesy Air Portraits

LAND BASED AIRCRAFT

N 262   Aérospatiale (France)

Light transport aircraft

Max speed	225 knots
Max and econ cruising speed	220 knots
Service ceiling	26 250 ft (8 000 m)
Range with max payload, FAA reserves	350 n. miles
Capacity	Max seating for 29
Max T-O weight	23 369 lb (10 600 kg)
Wing span	71 ft 10 in (21·90 m)
Length overall	63 ft 3 in (19·28 m)
Height over tail	20 ft 4 in (6·21 m)
Power plant	2 × 1 065 eshp Turboméca Bastan VIC turboprop engines (1 130 ehp Bastan VIIA in Series C and D)

Fifteen of these aircraft are used by the French Navy as aircrew trainers and light transports.

Aérospatiale N 262 transport of the French Navy

P-3 ORION   Lockheed (USA)

Data apply to P-3B

Twelve-seat maritime-reconnaissance aircraft

Max speed at 15 000 ft (4 570 m) at AUW of 105 000 lb (47 625 kg)	413 knots
Patrol speed at 1 500 ft (450 m), same weight as above	200 knots
Max mission radius	2 200 n. miles

Equipment	Sonobuoys, MAD gear, ECM d/f, etc.
Armament	Fuselage weapons bay: accommodates mines, depth bombs, torpedoes. Wing mounts (10): torpedoes, mines or rockets singly or in pods
Max T-O weight	127 200 lb (57 697 kg)
Wing span	99 ft 8 in (30·37 m)
Length	116 ft 10 in (35·61 m)
Height	33 ft 8·5 in (10·29 m)

Power plant	4 × Allison T56-A-14 turboprop engines of 4 910 eshp each (P-3B version)

Produced for US Navy as P-3A (Allison T56-A-10W engines), P-3B and P-3C with A-NEW data processing system. P-3B also serves with Royal Australian Air Force, Royal New Zealand Air Force, and Royal Norwegian Air Force. 3 are being delivered to the Spanish Air Force.

P-3C Orion—US Navy

SHACKLETON MR Mk 3   Hawker Siddeley/Avro (UK)

Ten-seat long range maritime-reconnaissance aircraft

Max cruising speed	220 knots
Service ceiling	19 200 ft (5 850 m)
Range at 150 knots at 1 500 ft (450 m)	3 178 n. miles
Armament	2 × 20 mm cannon in nose (optional) Weapons bay for bombs, mines, depth charge torpedoes, etc Wing mounts (8) for unguided rockets on SAAF aircraft only
Gross weight	100 000 lb (45 360 kg)
Wing span	119 ft 10 in (36·52 m)
Length	92 ft 6 in (28·19 m)
Height	23 ft 4 in (7·11 m)
Power plant	4 × RR Griffon 57A in-line piston engines of 2 455 hp each RAF Phase 3 versions have additionally 2 × RR Bristol Viper 203 turbojet engines of 2 500 lb (1 133 kg) st in outboard nacelles

In service with the South African Air Force in the MR Mk 3 version and the RAF in the MR Mk 3 Phase 3 version and MR Mk 2 which is an earlier tail-wheel version with less tankage.

Hawker Siddeley Shackleton MR Mk 3 Phase 3 of the RAF   *Courtesy, Peter R. March*

LAND BASED AIRCRAFT

SHIN MEIWA PS-1   Shin Meiwa (Japan)
Anti-submarine flying-boat

Max speed at 5 000 ft (1 500 m)	295 knots
Cruising speed at 5 000 ft (1 500 m)	170 knots
Service ceiling	29 500 ft (9 000 m)
Normal range	1 170 n. miles
Gross weight	86 862 lb (39 400 kg)
Wing span	108 ft 8¾ in (33·14 m)
Length	109 ft 11 in (33·5 m)
Height	31 ft 10½ in (9·715 m)
Equipment (Internal)	Dipping Sonar, AQA-3 Jezebel passive acoustic search equipment with 20 sonobuoys, Julie active acoustic echo ranging with 30 charges, four 330 lb (150 kg) anti-submarine bombs and smoke bombs
(External)	Two underwing pods each containing two homing torpedoes and two wingtip launchers for three 5 in (12·7 m) air-to-surface missiles

In production for the JMSDF.

Shin Meiwa Ps-1-JMSDF

TU-16 (code-name "Badger")   Tupolev (USSR)

Long-range medium bomber/reconnaissance aircraft

Max speed at 35 000 ft (10 700 m)	510 knots
Cruising speed	417 knots
Service ceiling	42 650 ft (13 000 m)
Range, max bomb load	2 605 n. miles
Max range at 417 knots with 6 600 lb (3 000 kg) bombs	3 451 n. miles
Armament	Fuselage: 19 800 lb (9 000 kg) bombs carried internally (Badger-A) or "Kipper" stand-off bomb under fuselage (Badger-C). 2 × 23 mm cannon in forward dorsal, ventral and rear turrets and 1 × 23 mm cannon in starboard nose position Wing mounts (2): 2 × "Kennel" or "Kelt" ASMs (Badger-B)
Max T-O weight	150 000 lb (68 000 kg) approx
Wing span	110 ft 0 in (33·5 m)
Length	120 ft 0 in (36·5 m)
Height	35 ft 6 in (10·8 m)
Power plant	2 × Mikulin AM-3M turbojet engines of 20 950 lb (9 500 kg) st each

Tupolev Tu-16 twin-jet bomber of the Indonesian Air Force with underwing "Kennel" missiles

In service with the Soviet Naval Airfleet since 1956 and the Indonesian Air Force since 1961. Badgers D, E and F are electronic reconnaissance versions with under-fuselage blisters or underwing pods.

TU-22 (code-name "Blinder")   Tupolev (USSR)

Medium-range supersonic strike and reconnaissance bomber

Max speed at 40 000 ft (12 200 m)	Mach 1·4
Service ceiling	60 000 ft (18 300 m) plus
Range	1 215 n. miles
Armament	Fuselage: "Kitchen" ASM part-recessed in bomb bay, alternatively internal bomb load
Loaded weight	184 970 lb (83 900 kg)
Wing span	90 ft 10½ in (27·70 m)
Length	132 ft 11½ in (40·53 m)
Power plant	2 × unspecified turbojet engines developing 26 500 lb (12 020 kg) st with reheat

In service with the Soviet Naval Airfleet.

Tupolev Tu-22 "Blinder" of the Soviet Naval Airfleet   *Courtesy, Tass*

TU-95 (code-name "Bear")   Tupolev (USSR)

Long-range strategic bomber/reconnaissance aircraft

Max speed at 41 000 ft (12 500 m)	435 knots
Cruising speed at 32 000 ft (10 000 m)	410 knots
Range with max bomb load	6 773 n. miles
Armament	Fuselage weapons bay: 25 000 lb (11 300 kg) of bombs (Bear-A) Fuselage external mounts: "Kangaroo" ASM, (Bear-B): 2 × 23 mm cannon in dorsal, ventral and tail turrets
Loaded weight	340 000 lb (154 220 kg)
Wing span	163 ft (49·68 m)
Length	150 ft (45·72 m)
Power plant	4 × Kuznetsov NK-12M turboprop engines of 14 795 shp each

In service with the Soviet Naval Airfleet, largely for strategic reconnaissance and ECM roles.

Latest version of Tu-95 (Bear) for ECM roles

LAND BASED AIRCRAFT

VIGGEN SAAB-Scania (Sweden)

Single-seat multi-mission combat aircraft

Max speed at 36 000 ft (10 800 m)	Mach 2 plus
Armament	External mounts 7 (fuselage 3, wings 2): Carries RB04 ASM, RB05A ASM, rockets, bombs, 30 mm gun packs or mines
Max T-O weight	35 275 lb (16 000 kg) approx
Wing span	34 ft 9·2 in (10·60 m)
Length	53 ft 5·8 in (16·30 m)
Height overall	18 ft 4·5 in (5·60 m)
Height, fin folded	13 ft 1·5 in (4·00 m)
Power plant	1 × Svenska Flygmotor (P & W JT-8D-22) RM8 turbojet of 26 450 lb (12 000 kg) st with reheat

This important new aircraft forms the airborne component of System 37 to cover the attack, interceptor and reconnaissance needs of the Swedish Air Force. The seven prototypes are now flying and 175 aircraft are to be delivered between 1971-1974.

A development Viggen with RB05A ASM's

NAVAL MISSILES
SURFACE-TO-SURFACE
Long-range Surface-to-Surface

MSBS Aérospatiale (France)

Submarine-borne intermediate range ballistic missile (IRBM)

Length	34 ft 1½ in (10·40 m)
Body diameter	4 ft 11 in (1·50 m)
Firing weight	39 683 lb (18 000 kg)

This two-stage solid-propellant missile with nuclear warhead was developed in France to equip the "Redoutable" class of nuclear-powered submarines from 1969 onwards, each of 4 submarines carrying 16 missiles becoming operational from 1971. The first stage has 22,050 lb (10 000 kg) of solid propellant in a Norma 904 rocket motor; the second stage is a solid-propellant rocket of 8 820 lb (4 000 kg) weight. The MSBS has inertial guidance.

MSBS missile

POLARIS A2 and A3, UGM-27B and C
Lockheed (USA)
Submarine-borne fleet ballistic missile

Length	A2/3—31 ft (9·45 m)
Body diameter	4 ft 6 in (1·39 m)
Launch weight	30 000 lb (13 600 kg)
Max range	A2—1 500 n. miles
	A3—2 500 n. miles

Both versions are in service as long-range two-stage solid-propellant missiles with nuclear warhead. All 41 US Navy nuclear-powered submarines are operational, each with 16 Polaris missiles, 28 with A3 and 13 with A2 and the A3 serves in 4 Royal Navy submarines. The submarine is positioned by a Ship Inertial Navigation System (SINS), thereafter the missile, after firing relies on its own inertial-guidance system. The first stage ignites as the missile breaks surface, having been ejected by a gas/steam mixture produced by a small solid propellant rocket motor.

POSEIDON C3 ZUGM-73A Lockheed (USA)

Submarine-borne fleet ballistic missile

This is a larger and twice as powerful missile to replace Polaris with twice the payload and longer range. Operational target date is 1971 to equip 31 existing Polaris submarines with Poseidon. First test firing, at Cape Kennedy, was on 16 August 1968 and first vessel to be equipped with Poseidon will be USS "James Madison".

Length	34 ft 0 in (10·36 m)
Body diameter	6 ft 2 in (1·88 m)
Launch weight	65 000 lb (29 500 kg) approx
Range	2 500 n. miles

POSEIDON

SURFACE-TO-SURFACE

SAWFLY (NATO code-name)   (USSR)

Appearing first in 1967 this missile would seem to be a to be a two-stage solid-propellant rocket.

R and D version of a second-generation IRBM with a range of approx 2 000 miles (*3 200 km*). It is thought

Length overall   42 ft 0 in (*12·8 m*) approx
Body diameter   5 ft 9 in (*1·75 m*) approx

Sawfly missile

SERB (NATO code-name)   (USSR)

First seen in 1964, this ballistic missile was said to be capable of underwater launching from submarines.
It appears to be a two-stage solid-propellant rocket.

Serb is thought to be a research and development version of the first-generation Polaris-type weapon carried by Soviet submarines, which have been seen with from two to eight vertical launch tubes for ballistic or cruise missiles. One "G" class ship, with three launch tubes, serves with

the Peoples Republic of China.

Length   33 ft 0 in (*10·0 m*)
Max diameter   5 ft 0 in (*1·5 m*)
Estimated range   330 n. miles

Short-Range Surface-to-Surface

MM-38 EXOCET   Aérospatiale (France)

Surface-to-surface missile

Designed to provide warships with all-weather attack capability against other surface vessels. It can be fitted in all classes of surface warships, including fast patrol boats.
The Exocet missile is in the form of a streamlined body, fitted with cruciform wings and cruciform tail control surfaces indexed in line with the wings. Propulsion is provided by a tandem two-stage solid-propellant motor, and highly destructive warhead. The launch tubes, which are also used as store containers, can be installed in a fixed position or on rotatable mountings.

For operation of the weapon system, the launch ship must be fitted with surveillance and target indicating radar, a vertical reference plane gyro and a log, indicating its speed through the water. Also required is a fire control installation comprising a control panel, fire control computer and junction box.
The missile flight profile consists of a pre-guidance phase during which it travels towards the target, whose range and bearing have been determined by the fire control computer and set up in the missile pre-guidance circuits before launch, and a final guidance phase during which the missile flies directly towards the target under the control of its active homing head. Throughout the flight the missile is maintained at a very low altitude (reported

to be 2 to 3 metres=6·5 to 10 ft) by an FM radio altimeter supplied by TRT. Its range is approximately 20 n. miles (23 miles; *37 km*), cruising at high subsonic speed, and Exocet is intended to operate efficiently in an ECM (electronic countermeasures) environment. The French German, Greek and Royal Malaysian Navies will use Exocet as well as the Royal Navy and Peru.

Length   16 ft 9½ in (*5·12 m*)
Body diameter   1 ft 1½ in (*0·344 m*)
Span of wings   3 ft 3½ in (*1·004 m*)
Span of fins   2 ft 5¾ in (*0·758 m*)
Launch weight   1 587 lb (*719 kg*)
Warhead (over)   220 lb (*100 kg*)
Range   20 n. miles

GABRIEL   Israel Aircraft Industries (Israel)

Operated on the French built "Saar" class gun-boat of the Israeli Navy. It is an automatic homing missile, using sophisticated electronic guidance system and has a high-explosive warhead. Gabriel is subsonic and travels a few metres above S/L to its target.

Length   11 ft 0 in (*3·35 m*)
Max diameter   12·8 in (*0·04 m*)
Launch weight   882 lb (*400 kg*)
Max range   11 n. miles

NETTUNO   ~Contraves/Sistel (Italy)

Short-range surface-to-surface missile,
ship-borne

This missile is installed in a five-round multiple launcher aboard the fast patrol boat "Saetta" of the Italian Navy. Single-stage solid-propellant rocket of 4 410 lb (*2 000 kg*) st thust propels this missile with movable cruciform control surfaces and stabilising tailfins. Guidance is from beam rider/radio command/radar altimeter-systems and the warhead is a high-explosive fragmentation type with proximity Impact fuse.

Length   12 ft 3 in (*3·73 m*)
Body diameter   7·87 in (*0·20 m*)
Wing span   2 ft 9·5 in (*0·85 m*)
Launch weight   370 lb (*168 kg*)
Speed at burn-out   Mach 1·9
Min/max range   1·6/5·4 n. miles (*3/10 km*)

Gabriel missile leaving its launcher

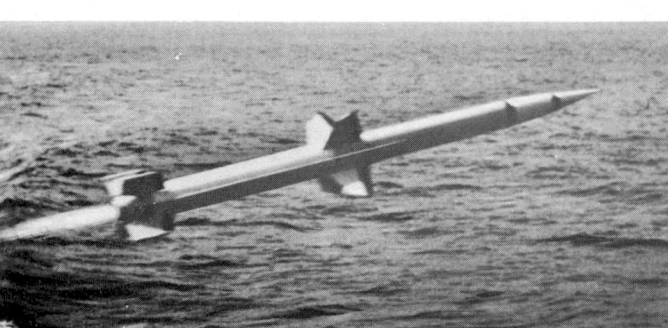

Nettuno

Nettuno multi-round launcher

SURFACE-TO-SURFACE

OTOMAT SA Engines Matra/Oto Melara (France/Italy)

This new weapon is powered by a Turboméca Type 281 turbojet. It is launched with aid of two jettisonable booster rockets and flies to its target at 50 ft above S/L.

It is to be operated by the Italian Navy.

Length	15 ft 9½ in (4·81 m)

Max dia	1 ft 3¾ in (0·40 m)
Launch weight	1 325 lb (601 kg)
Max range	32-54 n. miles

PENGUIN Kongsberg Vaapenfabrikk (Norway)

Penguin uses an inertial guidance system with infra-red terminal homing, and has a 264 lb (119 kg) warhead. 20 "Storm" class gunboats are fitted with 6 launchers aft of decks. It has two-stage solid-propellant propulsion.

Length	10 ft (3·05 m)

Max dia	11 in (0·28 m)
Launch weight	727 lb (329 kg)
Range	10-15 n. miles

RB.08A SAAB (Sweden)

Surface-to-surface cruise missile

This missile is a modification of the French Aérospatiale CT.20 target drone for coastal defence duties. It is ramp-launched by two jettisonable rocket-boosters and thence propelled by a Turboméca Marbore IID turbojet. The warhead is Swedish-designed, and it is both land-based and destroyer-based.

Length	18 ft 9 in (5·71 m)
Body diameter	2 ft 2 in (0·66 m)
Wing span	9 ft 10·5 in (3·01 m)
Span, wings folded	4 ft 5 in (1·35 m)
Launch weight	1 958 lb (900 kg)

Performance details are not publishable, however the following details on the almost identical CT20 are available:—

Speed at 32 800 ft (10 000 m)	512 knots
Mean endurance	60 mins
Practical range	135 n. miles

RB.08A on launching ramp

SAMLET (NATO code-name) (USSR)

This surface-to-surface cruise missile is similar to the "Kennel" air-to-surface missile. It is used by shore units of the Red Banner Northern fleet for coastal defence. Also supplied to Poland and Cuba.

Samlet missile on launch ramp

"SHADDOCK" (NATO code-name) (USSR)

Medium-range surface-to-surface cruise missile

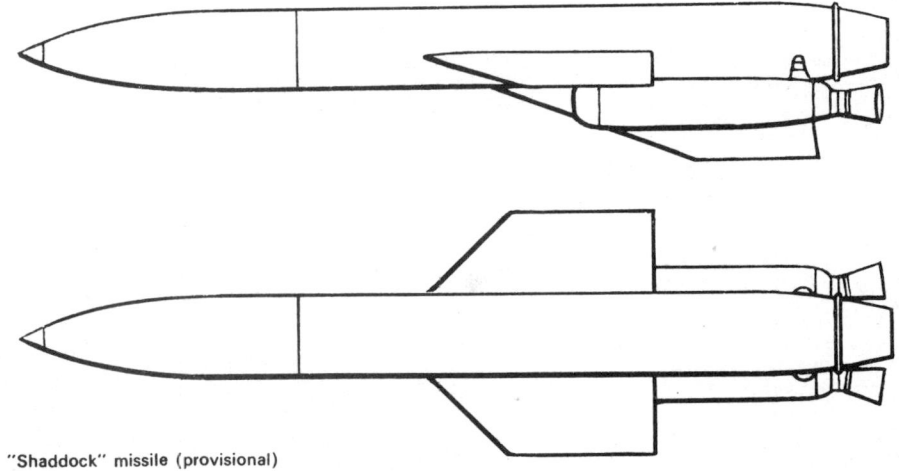

Designed in the same category as "Styx" but at least twice as large, little is known about this missile. It appears to have one main nozzle and two jettisonable booster rockets. The length of the missile is approximately 40 ft (12·2 m) and has a range in the order of 200 n. miles. It cruises at Mach 0·95 or faster, and uses an active radar homing system.

"Shaddock" missile (provisional)

SS-11 (B.1) Aérospatiale (France)

Close-range surface-to-surface wire-guided missile

Developed from the AS-11 (B.1) ASM this missile is in use by French Navy and Army and differs from the AS-11 in launching systems only. It is powered by 2 stage solid propellant rocket with cruciform swept wings on a cylindrical body and can be fitted with a range of war-heads for anti-tank, perforating/exploding or anti-personnel work. The guidance is visual/manual, with a gyrostabilised optical sighting system, through wires from the control. Orders totalled 145 000 by the beginning of 1970, with the production at the rate of 900 per month. France, USA, NATO countries and others use this missile.

Length	3 ft 11 in (1·200 m)
Body diameter	6·4 in (0·16 m)
Wing span	1 ft 7·6 in (0·500 m)
Launch weight	66 lb (30 kg)
Range	9 850 ft (3 000 m)
Cruising speed	313 knots
Endurance	20-21 secs

SURFACE-TO-SURFACE

SS-12M Aérospatiale (France)

Close-range surface-to-surface wire-guided missile

A larger and more powerful derivative of the SS-11, it is used from a twin shipboard launcher and is being developed to use the TCA automatic guidance system of the Harpon anti-tank missile. It is used aboard three Royal Libyan Navy patrol boats. Also used by France and the Royal Netherlands Navy.

Length	6 ft 2 in (*1·875 m*)
Body diameter	7·1 in (*0·18 m*)
Wing span	2 ft 1·5 in (*0·65 m*)
Launch weight	167 lb (*75 kg*)
Range	3·2 n. miles
Endurance	32 secs
Impact speed	182-37 knots

SS-11 and SS-12

STRELA (NATO code-name) (USSR)

Larger and more advanced than "Styx" and is an aeroplane-type cruise missile.
Two launchers, fore and aft, are on 6 of the "Krupny" class and single launchers on 4 of the "Kildin" class of Soviet destroyers.

"STYX" (NATO code-name) (USSR)

Ship-borne surface-to-surface rocket missile

Used for ship-to-ship action this missile has cropped delta wings and a tri-tail with control surfaces. Carried on a twin-rail launcher it is propelled by a solid-propellant rocket with a jettisonable booster. It is carried aboard the "Komar" and "Osa" class fast patrol boats of which more than 150 serve with the Soviet Navy and also serves with many other Navies. Styx missiles from the Egyptian Navy were used to sink the Israeli destroyer "Eilat" on 21st October 1967.

Length	20 ft (*6·10 m*) approx
Wing span	8 ft 10 in (*2·70 m*) approx
Range	13 n. miles plus

TERNE Mk. 8 Kongsberg (Norway)

Short-range ship-borne surface-to-surface missile. Brought to production status by Kongsberg Vaapenfabrikk this anti-submarine missile was originated by the Norwegian Defence Research Establishment for the Royal Norwegian Navy, who now use it operationally. It is a rocket-propelled depth charge with a 110 lb (*50 kg*) warhead, having an ogival nose cone, and cruciform stabilising fins. Propulsion is by two concentric solid-propellant rocket motors and detonation of the warhead by a combined acoustic proximity, impact and time fuse. The system is so installed operationally that a full salvo of six missiles can be fired in 5 seconds.

Length	6 ft 4·75 in (*1·95 m*)
Body diameter	8·0 in (*20·3 cm*)
Launching weight	298 lb (*135·2 kg*)

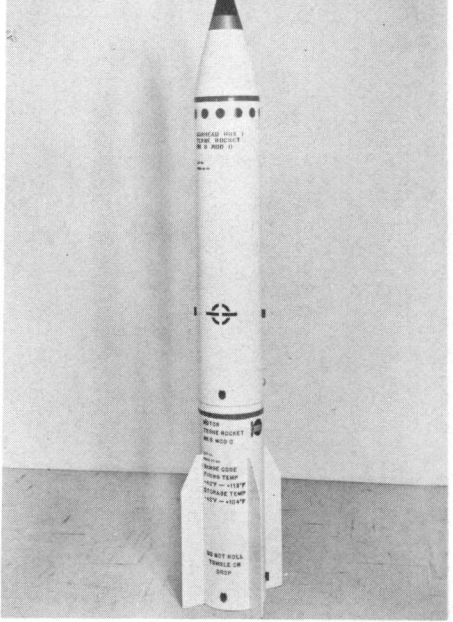

Terne Mk.8 surface-to-surface missile

"Styx" surface-to-surface missile

VULCANO

A two-stage version of Nettuno, to increase operational range. The booster and sustainer are both solid-propellant rocket motors. After burn-out the booster is separated by an aerodynamic drag section.
The missile has the same specification as the Nettuno except for length increased to 14 ft 9 in (*4·50 m*), launching weight to 530 lb (*240 kg*), and max effective range to over 10 n. miles. The first flight trials of Vulcano missiles were carried out in mid 1969.

AIR-TO-SURFACE

AS-11 (B.1) Aérospatiale (France)

Airborne wire-guided missile

This is identical with the SS-11 (B.1) (which see) except that it is air-launched and this increases its range. It is carried by 14 different types of aircraft (fixed and rotary-wing) of 19 nations including all the ASW aircraft of the NATO countries.

AS-12 Aérospatiale (France)

Airborne wire-guided missile

This missile is a companion to the SS-12M (which see) and is already supplementing and replacing the AS-11 (B.1). It is being prepared for automatic guidance with the TCA system for the Harpon missile.

AS-12 missile under wing of Alize of French Navy

AIR-TO-SURFACE

AS-30   Aérospatiale (France)

Tactical air-to-surface missile

This missile has a two-stage solid-propellant rocket power plant and is directed by a pilot-operated radio-command guidance system whereby the pilot steers the missile by means of a small control column in the cockpit. Alternatively this missile can utilise the TCA optical aiming/infra-red automatic guidance system. It is in production for the French Air Force, French Navy, German, Swiss, Israeli and South African air forces and the RAF. It normally carries a 510 lb (230 kg) HE warhead.

Length	12 ft 9·5 in (3·90 m)
Body diameter	1 ft 1·4 in (0·34 m)
Wing span	3 ft 3·5 in (1·00 m)
Launch weight	1 146 lb (520 kg)
Speed at impact	1 475/1 640 ft/sec (450/500 m/sec)
Range	5·9/6·5 n. miles

Aérospatiale AS-30 (inboard) and AS-20 (outboard)

AS-30L   Aérospatiale (France)

Tactical air-to-surface missile

A developed lighter version of the AS-30 for smaller, lighter aircraft. Warhead reduced to 253 lb (115 kg).

Length	11 ft 9·5 in (3·60 m)	Body diameter	1 ft 1·5 in (0·34 m)
		Wing span	2 ft 11·5 in (0·90 m)
		Launch weight	838 lb (380 kg)

BULLPUP AGM-12B   Maxson (USA)

Air-to-surface radio-guided missile

In production and service with the USAF and Navy, the Bullpup has cruciform wings at rear and nose-mounted control planes. Power plant is a Thiokol pre-packaged liquid-propellant motor of 12 000 lb (5 440 kg) st. It is radio-controlled by the pilot in flight with visual flares for guidance. Also with the Royal Navy and with NATO.

Length	10 ft 6 in (3·20 m)
Body diameter	1 ft 0 in (0·30 m)
Wing span	3 ft 1 in (0·94 m)
Launch weight	571 lb (260 kg)
Cruising speed	Mach 1·8
Range	6·07 n. miles

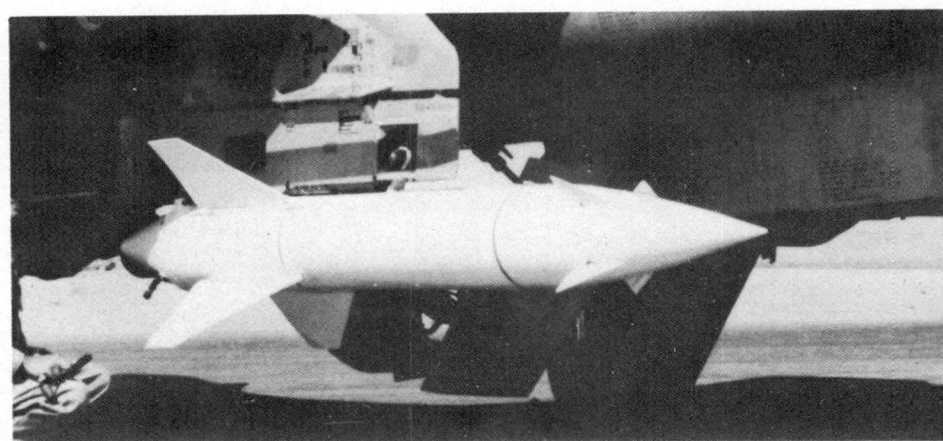

AGM-12B Bullpup air-to-surface missile

BULLPUP AGM-12C   Maxson (USA)

Larger and more powerful version of AGM-12B above

Length	13 ft 7 in (4·14 m)
Body diameter	1 ft 6 in (0·45 m)
Wing span	4 ft 0 in (1·22 m)
Launch weight	1 785 lb (810 kg)
Range	8·7 n. miles

Bullpup B version with larger conventional warhead. The power plant is a Thiokol LR62-2 of 33 000 lb (14 968 kg) st.

AGM-12C Bullpup B missile

CONDOR AGM-53A   North American (USA).

Air-to-surface TV-guided stand-off missile

This missile is under development as a future stand-off weapon for the US Navy for use on the A-6A Intruder and A-7 Corsair II. Its television-guidance system enables its parent aircraft to return to its carrier whilst controlling the missile. It is powered by a Rocketdyne rocket engine and carries a conventional high-explosive warhead. No dimensions or performance details are known other than a reported range of approx 35 n. miles, though one Condor is said to have travelled 50 n. miles after aerial launch.

Condor missile on A-6A aircraft.

AIR-TO-SURFACE

"KELT" (NATO code-name)   (USSR)

Air-to-surface rocket powered missile

Carried by Tu-16 bombers of the Soviet Naval Airfleet

"KENNEL" (NATO code-name)   (USSR)

Air-to-surface turbojet-powered missile

This anti-shipping missile, is operational on the Tu-16 "Badger" aircraft of the Soviet Naval Airfleet and the Indonesian Air Force. It is turbojet-powered and appears to use a radar homing device mounted above its air intake.

Length   28 ft 0 in (*8·5 m*)
Wing span   16 ft 0 in (*4·9 m*)

Two "Kennel" anti-ship missiles loaded beneath the wings of a Tu-16 bomber

"KIPPER" (NATO code-name)   (USSR)

Air-to-surface anti-shipping missile with stand-off capability

"KITCHEN" (NATO code-name)   (USSR)

this is similar to "Kennel" but the ram air intake and radome of the latter missile are replaced by a hemi-spherical nose fairing, probably housing a larger radar. This implies that the "Kelt" is rocket-powered.

Operational with the Tu.16 "Badger" since at least 1961 this missile has a swept-wing aircraft layout with an underslung power plant, presumably a turbojet. Nose radar implies a radar homing device.

Length   31 ft 0 in (*9·5 m*) approx

Little is known about this advanced missile, carried by the Tu-22 "Blinder". It appears to be a stand-off bomb with delta wings and cruciform tail surface and to be about 36 ft (*11 m*) long.

KORMORAN Messerschmitt-Bölkow-Blohm (Germany)

This missile is being developed against a German Navy requirement. Its guidance system has pre-guidance and homing phases, enabling it to approach the target at low altitude. The Kormoran will be carried by F-104G Starfighters of the German Naval Air Arm but can be employed with all aircraft having modern navigation system.

Length overall (approx)   14 ft 5 in (*4·40 m*)
Wing span (approx)   3 ft 3½ in (*1·00 m*)
Launch weight (approx)   1 320 lb (*600 kg*)
Min launch speed   Mach 0·5

Kormoran missile under wing of F-104G Starfighter.

AS-37/AJ.168 MARTEL MATRA/HSD (France/UK)

Air-to-surface television-guided stand-off missile

Developed jointly by Matra and Hawker/Siddeley Dynamics the Martel is in two forms, an anti-radar, all-weather attack missile or a television-guided missile operated by a weapon operator aboard the parent aircraft. The anti-radar version can be launched in a variety of height and mission profiles. Immediately after launch the missile homes automatically on the target radar, the parent aircraft being independent. Its range of tens of miles gives it a stand-off capability. The TV version is guided in the final stages of its run by the weapon operator in the launch aircraft reading from a high brightness monitor in the aircraft displaying the missile's target field.

Martel is to be operational with the British Fleet Air Arm and RAF on Buccaneer and Nimrod aircraft and the French services on Mirage III-E, Jaguar and Atlantic aircraft.

Length   12 ft (*3·6 m*) teleguidance
                      13 ft 1½ in (*4·00 m*) anti-radar
Wing span   3 ft 8 in (*1·09 m*)
Body diameter   1 ft 3 in (*0·39 m*)

Martel development missiles under wing of Buccaneer aircraft

AIR-TO-SURFACE

RB04   Robotavdelningen (Sweden)

All-weather anti-shipping air-to-surface missile

This missile has been operational since early 1959 with the Swedish Air Force but has been under a continuous improvement programme to up-date it to modern needs.

It equips the four attack wings flying A32A Lansens as the RB.04D and will also be used with the Viggen in a later version, the RB.04E. It is powered by a solid-propellant rocket motor giving it a subsonic performance carrying a 660 lb (*300 kg*) warhead.
Details apply to the RB.04C.

Length	14 ft 7¼ in (*4·45 m*)
Body diameter	1 ft 7·75 in (*0·50 m*)
Wing span	6 ft 8 in (*2·04 m*)
Launch weight	1 320 lb (*600 kg*)
Guidance	High-efficiency homing system

RB.04 missile under wing of Viggen aircraft

RB.05A   SAAB (Sweden)

Being developed for the Viggen and Sk.60, this missile is intended for the strike role but can also be used air-to-air. With long-chord cruciform wings and aft-mounted cruciform control surfaces it is powered by a pre-packed liquid propellant rocket motor built by Svenska Flyg-motor. Guidance is by radio command signals from a pilot-operated micro-wave radio link, based on simultaneous observation of both target and missile by the pilot.

Length	11 ft 10 in (*3·61 m*)
Body diameter	1 ft 0 in (*0·30 m*)
Wing span	2 ft 8 in (*0·80 m*)
Launch weight	675 lb (*306 kg*)

RB.05A missiles under the fuselage of a Draken aircraft used for development trials

SHRIKE AGM-45A   NWC (USA)

Air-to-surface anti-radar missile

Built for carrier-based aircraft this anti-radar missile has Texas Instrument's guidance system and has been in service with the US Navy since 1964. Power is provided by a Rocketdyne Mk. 39 Mod 3 solid-propellant motor and it carries a high-explosive warhead.

Length	10 ft 0 in (*3·05 m*)
Body diameter	8 in (*0·204 m*)
Launch weight	390 lb (*177 kg*)
Range	8·7 n. miles approx
Wing span	3 ft 0 in (*0·91 m*)

Shrike anti-radar missile—US Navy

STANDARD ARM   General Dynamics (USA)

Advanced anti-radar missile

This missile is to replace Shrike in the anti-radar role. It will have a better homing head, longer range and more effective protection against ECM. See Standard under Surface-to-Air Missiles.

Length	14 ft 0 in (*4·27 m*)
Launch weight	1 300 lb (*589 kg*)

A Standard ARM fitted to the outboard pylon of a US Navy A-6 aircraft.

AIR-TO-SURFACE

WALLEYE GW Mk 1 Mod-0   Martin (USA)

Television-guided glide-bomb missile

This is an unpowered 1 100 lb (*500 kg*) missile which is released from the parent aircraft and glides to its target with its homing system locked on by television. The guidance system is powered by electrical and hydraulic power from a ram-air turbine and a conventional high-explosive warhead is fitted.

Length	11 ft 3 in (*3·43 m*)
Body diameter	1 ft 3 in (*0·38 m*)
Wing span	3 ft 9 in (*1·14 m*)
Launch weight	1 100 lb (*499 kg*)

Walleye missile—US Navy

SURFACE-TO-AIR

"GOA" (NATO code-name)   (USSR)

Ship-borne anti-aircraft missile

This is a two-stage solid-propellant missile with cruciform wings on both stages and movable control surfaces on the second stage. First seen in 1964. Around 25 Soviet destroyers carry Goa in single or twin launchers.

Length	20 ft 0 in (*6·0 m*)
Body diameter (2nd stage)	1 ft 6 in (*0·45 m*)
Body diameter (1st stage)	2 ft 3 in (*0·7 m*)
Wing span	4 ft 0 in (*1·22 m*)
Range	13 n. miles

MASURCA Mk 2   Marine Francaise (France)

Developed to equip the guided missile frigates "Suffren" and "Duquesne" of the French Navy this missile is a two-stage solid-propellant missile, the first stage being jettisonable. The second stage has controllable tail surfaces in cruciform configuration, in line with the low-aspect ratio wings. A high-explosive warhead with a proximity fuse is fitted. There are two versions of this weapon: Masurca Mk 2 Mod 2 (with a beam riding guidance system) and Masurca Mk 2 Mod 3 (with a self homing guidance system) now superseding Mod 2. In both cases the guidance systems are produced by CFTH/CFS and TRT.

Length	28 ft 2·5 in (*8 600 m*)
Body diameter	1 ft 4 in (*0·405 m*)
Booster fin Span	4 ft 11 in (*1·500 m*)
Launch weight	4 585 lb (*2 079 kg*)
Range	21·7 n. miles plus
Max speed	Mach 2·5

Two Masurca missiles on the launcher of the French Navy's guided missile frigate "Suffren"

The Goa missile which is used as a ship-borne SAM

SURFACE -TO-AIR

SEACAT
Short Bros & Harland (UK)·

Short-range anti-aircraft missile

Seacat is in widespread service and production. It is standard armament aboard Royal Navy ships ranging from "Leander" class frigates to the aircraft carrier "Hermes" and is also ordered for the Royal Australian Navy, Royal New Zealand Navy, Royal Netherlands Navy, Royal Swedisn Navy (with whom it is designated RB 07) Chilean, Brazilian, Federal German, Indian, Argentinian, Libyan, Venezuelan, Iranian and Royal Malaysian navies. It is also under development for use from fast patrol-boats and in a surface-to-surface anti-shipping role. It is propelled by a two-stage solid-propellant IMI rocket and has a high-explosive warhead with contact and proximity fuses. A number of different fire control systems are in use:—Mk 20 Visual (British, Australian and Brazilian navies), Mks 21 and 22 Radar Director (British and New Zealand Navies), M4/3 Radar director (Swedish and Chilean Navies). Normally mounted in a four-round launcher. In 1969 Shorts stated that successful trials had been completed of a system that replaces the optical sighting binocular with a closed-circuit TV system produced by Marconi Co. as the 323 Series.

Further developments now in progress include the use of CCTV for automatic missile tracking operations.

Length	4 ft 10·3 in (1·48 m)
Body diameter	7·5 in (19·05 cm)
Wing span	2 ft 1·6 in (0·64 m)

Seacat being fired from HMAS "Yarra"

SEA DART
Hawker Siddeley (UK)

Medium - range ramjet powered surface - to - air missile

Under development for equipping the Royal Navy's Type 82 and Type 42 destroyers, this missile is a two-stage vehicle with an IMI solid-propellent first stage booster and a second stage comprising the warhead powered by a Rolls-Royce Bristol Odin ramjet. The air duct for this is in the nose with interferometer aerials for the guidance systems around it; it employs semi-active radar homing using the Tracker illuminator radar Type 909. Sea Dart will also arm two type 42 destroyers ordered for the Argentine Navy.

Length	14 ft 3·5 in (4·36 m)
Body diameter	1 ft 4·5 in (0·42 m)
Wing span (max)	3 ft 0 in (0·91 m)
Range	14·8/19·5 n. miles

Hawker Siddeley Sea Dart

SEA INDIGO
Contraves Italiana/Sistel (Italy)

Short-range ship-to-air missile

This is a navalised version of the Indigo. It is intended to utilise an automatic reloading system when installed in ships of more than 500 tons displacement; manual reloading is specified when Sea Indigo is fitted in naval craft of less than 500 tons.

Main features of the missile are similar to those of the Indigo land-based version.

SEASLUG Mk 1/Mk 2
Hawker Siddeley (UK)

Medium-range anti-aircraft missile

The Seaslug, in its Mk 1 and Mk 2 forms, equips the "County" class destroyers of the Royal Navy, initially the Mk 1 with the first four ships although they will be retrospectively fitted with Mk 2 as will be the later ships initially. During test firings a success rate of 90% has been achieved at heights up to 50 000 ft (15 250 m) plus. It has a solid-propellant sustainer rocket which is made by ICI, with four solid-propellant booster rockets around the body. Its guidance system is beamriding in conjunction with Type 901 Radar. The Mk 2 is an improved weapon working on the Type 901M radar, has transistorized electronics, longer range, better low-level capacity and an increase in length of 4 in.

Length (Mk 2)	20 ft (6·10 m)
Body diameter	1 ft 4·1 in (0·41 m)
Wing span	4 ft 8·6 in (1·438 m)
Tail span	5 ft 6·6 in (1·69 m)

Seaslug being launched from HMS "Kent"

SURFACE-TO-AIR

SEA WOLF
BAC (UK)
Short-range anti-aircraft missile

Being developed by BAC and Marconi (for the guidance

SEA SPARROW
Raytheon (USA)
Short-range supersonic anti-aircraft missile

This ship-launched version of the Sparrow AAM is operational with the US Navy. It is a single-stage rocket powered by a Rocketdyne Mk 38 Mod-2 solid-propellant motor and its guidance system is Raytheon-built, a continuous-wave semi-active radar. It has a

and control system) the Sea Wolf, originally designated PX 430, intended as the Royal Navy's Seacat replacement for the 1970's. No further details can be published.

cylindrical body with pivoted cruciform wings and tailfins. Successful test firings have been made from USS "Enterprise". Canada is nearing completion of the development of its close range system with Raytheon Canada Ltd. as prime contractor.

Norway, Denmark, Italy, Netherlands, and the US have joined together in the development of a NATO Sea Sparrow system. Raytheon is the prime contractor.

Contractors in each European country are developing significant portions of the system.

Length	12 ft 0 in (3·66 m)
Body diameter	8 in (0·20 m)
Wing span	3 ft 4 in (1·02 m)
Launch weight	450 lb (200 kg)
Speed	over Mach 3·5
Range	7 n. miles plus

STANDARD RIM-66A/67A|General Dynamics (USA)

Medium-long range supersonic ship-to air-missile

This missile is being developed in two versions, medium-range and extended-range, as a replacement for Tartar and Terrier; 50 destroyers, frigates and escort vessels of the US Navy are scheduled to receive it. Little modification is needed to fit it to the older launchers for the Tartar and Terrier. The MR version is a single-stage integral dual-thrust rocket whilst the ER version has a two-stage motor with jettisonable booster. Both versions have all-electric controls and solid-state electronics and an adaptive autopilot. Standard Missile has a semi-active homing system.

Length	ER: 26 ft (7·92 m) plus
	MR: 14 ft (4·27 m) plus
Launch weight	ER: 3 000 lb (1 360 kg)
	MR: 1 300 lb (590 kg)
Range	ER: 30·4 n. miles plus
	MR: 13 n. miles plus

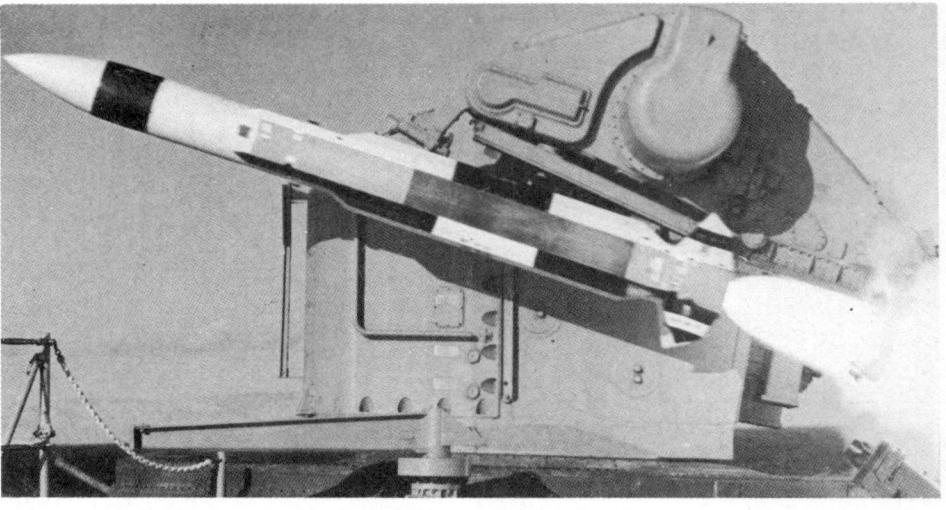

RIM-66A medium-range Standard Missile

TALOS RIM-8G-AAW and RGM-8-H-ARM
Bendix (USA)
Long-range ramjet surface-to-air/surface-to-surface missile

Entered service on USS "Galveston" in 1959 and has since equipped six other cruisers including USS "Long Beach" for which General Electric has developed a special launching and handling system using a computer mechanism by means of which all operations from selecting the particular warhead below decks to the firing of the missile are done automatically. It is a two-stage vehicle with a 40 000 hp Bendix 28 inch (710 mm) ramjet sustainer and an Allegany Ballistics jettisonable solid-propellant booster. It is a beam-riding missile using a semi-active Sperry SPG-49 "lamp" radar and can carry either a nuclear or high-explosive warhead.

It can also be used surface-to-surface. It was reported that the "Long Beach" destroyed two MiG's using Talos over North Vietnam in the summer of 1968, with intercepts in the 61 n. mile range.

Length	38 ft 0 in (11·58 m)
Body diameter	2 ft 4 in (0·71 m)
Wing span	9 ft 6 in (2·90 m)
Launch weight	7 800 lb (3 538 kg)
Speed at burn-out	Mach 2·5
Slant range	60 n. miles plus

Talos

TARTAR RIM-24
General Dynamics (USA)

Supersonic surface-to-air missile

This weapon is in service with the US Navy, the aim being to equip 36 guided missile and several heavy cruisers. In addition it is aboard 4 French "Surcouf" destroyers, two Italian destroyers, three destroyers of the Royal Australian Navy and the Japanese destroyer "Amat-sukaze". It is secondary armament on the larger ships and primary on the smaller ships and has a single-stage solid-propellant Aerojet motor with an initial high-thrust firing followed by a longer low-thrust period maintaining a supersonic speed to the target. It is effective at target heights from 1 000 to 40 000 ft (305 to 12 200 m). It employs a Raytheon guidance system of the homing type.

Length	15 ft 0 in (4·57 m)
Body diameter	13·4 in (0·34 m)
Launch weight	1 200 lb (545 kg) plus
Speed at burn-out	Mach 2·5 plus
Range	10 n. miles plus
Height effectiveness	1 000 to 40 000 ft (305 to 12 200

Tartar on a twin-launcher

SURFACE-TO-AIR

ADVANCED TERRIER RIM-2 General Dynamics (USA)

Shipborne supersonic anti-aircraft missile

Developed from the Terrier the Advanced Terrier is in widespread service. As well as 39 ships of the US Navy, 3 cruisers of the Italian Navy and one of the Dutch Navy are equipped with this missile which is especially effective against low-flying aircraft. Allegany Ballistics supply both the solid-propellant sustainer and booster for this missile and it uses a homing guidance system in conjunction with SPS-48 search radar, the Mk 76 fire control system and the Naval Tactical Data System (NTDS).

Length	27 ft 0 in (*8·23 m*)
Body diameter, missile	1 ft (*0·305 m*)
Body diameter, boosters	1 ft 4 in (*0·406 m*)
Wing span	1 ft 8 in (*0·51 m*)
Launch weight	3 000 lb (*1 360 kg*)
Range	20 n. miles

AIR-TO-AIR

FIRESTREAK   Hawker Siddeley Dynamics (UK)

Interceptor missile

The current standard British air-to-air weapon is used by the RAF on Lightnings and the Fleet Air Arm on Sea Vixens. It has a cylindrical metal body, cruciform wings and tail. It is propelled by a solid-propellant rocket and is homed by an infra-red guidance system and controlled by a proportional navigation system. The 50 lb (*22·7 kg*) warhead can be detonated at a predetermined range.

Length	10 ft 5·5 in (*3·19 m*)
Body diameter	8·75 in (*22·5 cm*)
Wing span	2 ft 5·5 in (*0·75 m*)
Launch weight	300 lb (*136 kg*)
Cruising speed	Mach 2 plus
Range	0·65/4·34 n. miles

A Firestreak AAM being loaded on a Sea Vixen aboard HMS Victorious

MATRA R-530   Matra (France)

Interceptor missile

In quantity production for the French Air Force and Navy, which latter uses it on its F-8E (FN) Crusaders; it is also supplied to Israel and the South African and Royal Australian Air Forces. It has a cylindrical body with cruciform delta wings, two with ailerons and cruciform tail controls and is powered by a two-stage Hotchkiss-Brandt solid-propellant motor of 18 740 lb (*8 500 kg*) static thrust.
It has interchangeable Hotchkiss-Brandt warheads with semi-active radar or infra-red homing, both containing high-explosive warhead of 60 lb (*27 kg*) and fitted with a proximity fuse.

Length	10 ft 9·25 in (*3·28 m*)
Body diameter	10·25 in (*0·26 m*)
Wing span	3 ft 7·25 in (*1·10 m*)
Launch weight	430 lb (*195 kg*)
Max speed	Mach 2·7
Range	9·5 n. miles
Operational heights	0-69 000 ft (*21 000 m*)

R-530 missile with semi-active radar head

AIR-TO-AIR

PHOENIX XAIM-54A   Hughes (USA)
Long-range air-to-air missile

The F-111B aircraft was in mind when the Phoenix was being developed but now it is specified for the Grumman F-14. It has a cylindrical body with long-chord cruciform wings and tail controls. It is powered by a Rocketdyne solid-propellant motor. It is radar-guided (AN/AWG-9) and all-weather operation is envisaged with particular application to long-range targets.

Length	13 ft 0 in (*3·96 m*)
Span	3 ft 0 in (*0·91 m*)
Max dia	1 ft 3 in (*0·38 m*)
Launch weight	838 lb (*380 kg*)
Range	85 n. miles plus

Phoenix missile (extreme right)

RED TOP   Hawker Siddeley Dynamics (UK)

This is in effect a vastly-improved Firestreak with larger wings and control surfaces and a new infra-red guidance unit not limited to pursuit-course attack. Warhead is increased in weight to 68 lb (*31 kg*). The rocket motor is increased in power also. This missile is used by the RAF on Lightnings and the Fleet Air Arm on Sea Vixen FAW.2's.

Length	11 ft 5·7 in (*3·50 m*)
Body diameter	8·75 in (*22·5 cm*)
Wing span	2 ft 11·75 in (*0.91 m*)
Cruising speed	Mach 3
Range	6 n. miles

Red Top missile

SPARROW IIIB AIM-7E   Raytheon (USA)
All-weather interceptor missile

The Sparrow IIIB is in service with F-4B and F-4C aircraft with the US Navy and USAF respectively and will equip the F-4K (Fleet Air Arm) and F-4M (RAF) versions in the UK. It is also carried by the F-104S of the Italian Air Force. Powered by a Rocketdyne Mk 38 Mod-2 solid-propellant motor, it is of standard cylindrical shape with pivoted cruciform wings and tail fins in line with the wings. Homing is by means of a Raytheon continuous-wave semi-active homing system and a 60 lb (*27 kg*) warhead is fitted.

Length	12 ft 0 in (*3·66 m*)
Body diameter	8 in (*0·20 m*)
Wing span	3 ft 4 in (*1·02 m*)
Launch weight	450 lb (*181 kg*)
Speed	Mach 3·5
Range	7 n. miles plus

An advanced version, designated AIM-7F, is being developed.

AIM-7E Sparrow IIIB missiles carried by F-4B of US Navy

AIR-TO-AIR

SIDEWINDER 1A AIM-9B and AIM-9E NWC (USA)

Interceptor missile

Accent in the Sidewinder is on simplicity, with fewer than two dozen moving parts and unsophisticated radio equipment. It is powered by a Naval Propellant Plant solid-propellant rocket and has a 25 lb (11·4 kg) warhead. Control surfaces are at the nose in cruciform configuration, indexed by similar tailfins. It has had limited success in action. As well as being used by the USAF and US Navy it has been exported to Nationalist China, Australia, Japan, Philippines, Spain, Sweden and nine NATO countries and is under licence production in Germany

Length	9 ft 3½ in (2·83 m)
Body diameter	5 in (0·13 m)
Fin span	1 ft 10 in (0·56 m)
Launch weight	159 lb (72 kg)
Speed	Mach 2·5
Range	1·75 n. miles

SIDEWINDER 1C AIM-9C/D   NWC (USA)

Interceptor missile

A developed version of the 1A the 1C is in production for the US Navy and the UK. Power is from the Rocketdyne Mk 36 Mod-5 solid-propellant motor and the aerofoil surfaces have been revised. The AIM-9D version is equipped with infra-red homing guidance (the US Navy and UK version) and the -9C with semi-active radar guidance.

Length	9 ft 6·5 in (2·91 m)
Body diameter	5 in (0·13 m)
Fin span	2 ft 1 in (0·64 m)
Launch weight	185 lb (84 kg)
Range	2 n. miles plus
Speed	Mach 2·5

All figures relate to AIM-9D version.

Sidewinder missile mounted on an A-7A of Sqdn VA-97

ANTI-SUBMARINE SYSTEMS

ASROC RUR-5A   Honeywell (USA)

Surface ship-launched anti-submarine ballistic missile

The complete system comprises a Librascope precision fire control computer fed with data from a Sangamo Electric underwater sonar detector, the Asroc missile and an 8-missile launcher. The missile comprises a ballistic solid-propellant rocket with the weapon (torepdo or depth charge) affixed by a frame. Following a ballistic trajectory after firing, the rocket is jettisoned at a predetermined point and the weapon continues to its target. If a torpedo a parachute opens to lower it into the target area and when submerged behaves as any other homing torpedo. If a depth charge it sinks to a pre-determined depth before detonating.

It is operational aboard cruisers, destroyers and escort vessels of the US Navy and the Japanese destroyer "Amatsukaze".

Length	15 ft 0 in (4·57 m)
Diameter	1 ft 0 in (0·30 m)
Fin Span	2 ft 6 in (0·76 m)
Launch weight	1 000 lb (450 kg)
Range	0·9/5 n. miles

Asroc anti-submarine missile

ANTI-SUBMARINE SYSTEMS

IKARA   Dept of Supply (Australia)

Long-range anti-submarine weapon system

The actual weapon is a dual-thrust, solid-propellant rocket-propelled missile carrying an acoustic homing torpedo launched from a surface ship. Target information from a ship's Variable Depth Sonar or a helicopter's Dunking Sonar feeds into the Action Data Automation system which, with radar/radio tracking and guidance, ensures that the American Type 44 acoustic homing torpedo, separated from the missile and lowered by parachute, enters the sea in the immediate vicinity of the target. The torpedo has an active life of 20 mins for acoustic detection and homing. It is operational on three "Perth" class and six "River" class destroyers of the Royal Australian Navy and will be fitted on "Leander" class ships and the new Type 82 destroyer of the Royal Navy.

Length	11 ft 0 in (*3·35 m*)
Wing span	5 ft 0 in (*1·50 m*)

Ikara missile in launcher on HMAS "Perth"

MALAFON Mk.2   Latecoere (France)

Long-range anti-submarine weapon system

It comprises a cylindrical body containing a 21 inch (*0·533 m*) acoustic homing torpedo and with wings and tail, this weapon is ramp-launched by two solid-propellnt rocket boosters which jettison after 3 sec. The weapon then glides at a height fixed by radio-altimeter. Sonar-detected data is fed into the device so that 875 yards short of its target the torpedo is jettisoned by parachute enters the water and homes on its target. It is in service with the French Navy installed in the anti-submarine vessel "La Galisonniere" and subsequently the frigates "Suffren" and "Duquesne", five T-47 class destroyers and five new corvettes of the "Aconit" class.

Length	19 ft 8 in (*6·00 m*)
Wing span	9 ft 10 in (*3·0 m*)
Launch weight	2 865 lb (*1 300 kg*)
Speed	447·2 knots
Range	1· 0 n. miles

Malafon ASW missile on the French destroyer "Vauquelin"

SUBROC UUM-44A   Goodyear (USA)

Submarine-launched long-range anti-submarine missile

Subroc is part of a complex weapons system including advanced long-range sonar and a specially designed fire control system for use aboard approx 25 US Navy hunter/killer submarines. It is fired conventionally from a submarine's torpedo tube, after which the solid-propellant rocket motor ignites under water at a safe distance from the submarine. Thrust-vectoring controls set the missile on its course, its angle of emergence from the water and control its stability in flight. At a pre-determined range the rocket separates from the depth bomb which continues to its target supersonically, controlled by the inertial guidance system. Upon re-entering the water a shock-mitigating device cushions the impact, the bomb sinks and explodes.

Length	21 ft 0 in (*6·40 m*)
Max diameter	1 ft 9 in (*0·5333 m*)
Launching weight	4 000 lb (*1 815 kg*)
Max range	21·7/26 n. miles

Subroc anti-submarine missile.

ADDENDA

ADDENDA

ARGENTINA

Destroyers

"Hercules" first of two "42" class guided missile destroyers laid down at Vickers, Barrow on 10 June, 1971.

AUSTRALIA

Destroyers

"Daring" class. See silhouette drawings before and after extended refit in 1971-72.

DENMARK

Fast Missile Boats

FPB TYPE

Displacement, tons	circa 240
Guided weapons	To be installed
Guns	1—76 mm Oto Melara or 1—57 mm L 70 Bofors
Torpedo tubes	4—21 in
Main engines	CODAG arrangement of gas turbines plus diesel
Speed, knots	40 max approx

FINLAND

Icebreakers

1 Projected. Wärtsilä Yard planning to build giant icebreaker to be used in the Arctic all the year round. Machinery to cost 36,000,000 Finnish marks. This icebreaker has been offered to the USA for 60,000,000 US dollars, but no negotiations held yet. Possible STAL-LAVAL will deliver the machinery.

Displacement, tons	50 000
Length, metres	195·0 (639·76 feet)
Main engines	140 000 hp

2 NEW CONSTRUCTION

First ordered on 11 Dec 1970. Second ordered 14 Apr 1971 for completion in Jan 1976. Both from Wärtsilä yard.

FRANCE

Guided Missile Frigates

ACONIT. See photograph of ship on builders' trials.

Destroyers

Surcouf forward section sank after collision in Mediterranean on 6 June, 1971.

Minehunters

CIRCE. See photograph of ship on builders' trials.

GREECE

Fast Missile Boats

First units nearing completion. See photograph of **CALYPSO**, launched Apr 1971.

INDIA

Submarines

New class planned to be built at Vishakapatnam dockyard and submarine base. Soviet collaboration may be negotiated to construct the new submarines, the first designed by India to her own requirements. The "pivitol position" of the country in the Indian Ocean is the reason given by the Chief of Naval Staff for India building its own submarines.

IRAN

Frigates

SAAM formally accepted from Vosper Thornycroft on 20 May 1971 (announced).

ITALY

Fast Missile Boats

1 PROJECTED HYDROFOIL MISSILE AND GUN TYPE

Displacement, tons	circa 59
Dimensions, feet	72·0 × 23·0 approx
Missile launchers	2 "Exocet" ship-to-ship
Guns	1 Oto Melara 76 mm automatic anti-aircraft
Main engines	Rolls Royce "Proteus" gas turbine driving waterjet pump; 4 500 bhp; diesel and retractable propeller unit for hullborne propulsion
Speed, knots	50 max, 40 cruising

To be delivered to the Italian Navy in 1973. See photograph of model.

MALAYSIA

Fast Missile Boats

4 NEW CONSTRUCTIONS

Displacement, tons	265 full load
Dimensions, feet	154·2 × 23·0 × 6·3
Missile launchers	2 "Exocet" surface-to-surface
Guns	1—57 mm forward; 1—40 mm aft
Main engines	4 MTU diesels; 12 000 hp = 36·5 knots

All 4 missile gunboats to be built in France, 2 by Constructions Mechaniques de Normandie and 2 by Chantiers Navals Franco-Belges.

CIRCE as completed. French *Navy*   May 1971, courtesy M. Henri Le Masson

CALYPSO as launched. Greek Navy   Apr 1971, courtesy Admiral M. Adam

PROJECTED HYDROFOIL MISSILE BOAT. Italian Navy
1971, courtesy Dr. Giorgio Giorgerini

PROJECTED MINESWEEPER. Swedish Navy
May 1971, courtesy Captain Allan Kull

PROJECTED CORVETTE. Swedish Navy
May 1971, courtesy Captain Allan Kull

NIGERIA
Corvettes

OTOBO. Launched at Vosper Thornycroft Camber Shipyard, Portsmouth on 25 May 1971.

SWEDEN
Cruiser

Discarded cruiser **GÖTA LEJON** may be purchased by the Chilean Navy.

Fast Missile Boats

Under the new naval construction programme starting in 1972 a new series of MTBs will carry guided missiles.

Corvettes

2 PROJECTED

A new type of corvette displacing about 800—1 000 tons is planned to act as flotilla leaders for fast torpedo boats and for escort duties. See adjacent photo-drawing.

Minelayer and Submarine Depot Ship

ÄLVSBORG MO 2. Commissioned on 1 Mar 1971 and taken over by the Swedish Navy on 6 Apr 1971. She will succeed *Patricia* as submarine parent ship and still be able to lay mines. Sister ship MO 3 will succeed *Marieholm* as Command Ship for the Commander-in-Chief of the Active Fleet. A third ship of the Class, MO 3, will replace *Älvsnabben* as minelayer and probably also as training ship. See first photograph of *Älvsborg* as completed and in operational service.

Fast Patrol Boats

24 NEW CONSTRUCTION

Instead of the MGBs projected for a long time there will be two dozen patrol boats. One has been contracted to be built in Norway, and with the same dimensions as the Norwegian gunboats, to be completed at the end of 1972.

Displacement, tons	145
Length, feet	119·75 (*36·5 metres*)
Guns	1—57 mm
Speed, knots	30 plus
Complement	20

Minesweepers

Non-magnetic type projected. See photograph of model.

Icebreakers

Contract for a new icebreaker signed with Wärtsilä, Finland.

UNITED KINGDOM
ADMIRALTY BOARD

Chief of Fleet Support:

Rear-Admiral George Frances Allan Trewby, C.Eng. FIMechE, MIMarE. FRINA will take up his appointment in July, 1971 in the acting rank of Vice-Admiral.

General Officers Royal Marines
Major-General Training Group Royal Marines:

Major-General R. B. L. Oudoun O.B.E. (from 13 Sep 1971).

Guided Missile Destroyers

Second and third ships of "Sheffield" class, "Type 42", ordered from Cammell Laird, Birkenhead on 21 May 1971 (announced). Further ships of the class to be ordered.
At the launch of "Sheffield" on 10 June, 1971 it was officially announced that Vickers are to build a 4th ship of the class.

General Purpose Frigates

"Leander" class. **DIOMEDE** commissioned on 21 May 1971 from new construction.

URUGUAY
Patrol Vessels

MALDONADO (ex-*Bir Hakeim* M 614, ex-USS *AM* 451) Former French ocean minesweeper to join Uruguayan fleet after refit.

U.S.S.R.
Nuclear Powered Ballistic Missile Submarines

Eight or nine reported to have been completed during the past year.

Guided Missile Cruisers

DZERZHINSKI. See adjacent recent photo, Apr 1971.

DARING CLASS. Before and after · *1971, Royal Australian Navy*

ACONIT as completed. French Navy · · · · · · · · · · · · · · · · · · *May 1971, courtesy M. Henri Le Masson*

ÄLVSBORG as completed. Swedish Navy · · · · · · · · · · · · · · · · · *Apr 1971, courtesy Captain Allan Kull*

DZERZHINSKI. Soviet Navy · *Apr 1971, courtesy Admiral M. Adam*

UNITED STATES

Command and Communication Ships

Replacement of *Valcour* (AGF 1) is being considered with the *La Salle* (LPD 3) being favoured for flagship of Commander US Middle East Force when this page closed.

Submarines

SSN 688 named *Los Angeles* introducing "city" names to attack submarines. This is the third name source applied to US attack submarines within a year, indicating the considerable confusion in ship nomenclature in the Navy. The heavy cruiser CA 135 remains on the Navy List (in reserve) as the ex-*Los Angeles*.
Pomfret (SS 391) transferred to Turkey in mid-1971.
Menhaden (SS 377) transferred to Spain in mid-1971.
Icefish (SS 367) on loan to Netherlands Navy stricken from US Navy List on 15 July 1971 for scrapping.
Halfbeak (SS 352) transferred to Brazil in mid-1971.
Diodon (SS 349) stricken on 15 Jan 1971 (scrap): not transferred to Argentina as planned.
Chivo (SS 341) transferred to Argentina in mid-1971.
Tigrone (AGSS 318) is being retained indefinitely in commission (announced May 1971).

Aircraft Carriers

Shangri-La (CVS 38) decommissioned on 20 July 1971 (reserve).

Surface Combatants

Steinaker (DD 863) not assigned to NRT as planned.
James C. Owens (DD 776) assigned to NRT on 1 July 1971.
Wallace L. Lind (DD 703) assigned to NRT on 1 July 1971.
Gherardi (DD 637) stricken on 1 June 1971.
Braine (DD 630) stricken in Aug 1971.
Meade (DD 602) stricken on 1 June 1971.
Boyle (DD 600) stricken on 1 June 1971.
Bancroft (DD 598) stricken on 1 June 1971.
Cowell (DD 547) stricken in Aug 1971.
Frankford (DD 497) stricken on 1 June 1971.
Farenholt (DD 491) stricken on 1 June 1971.
Hambleton (DD 455) stricken on 1 June 1971.
Swanson (DD 443) stricken on 1 Mar 1971.
Wilkes (DD 441) stricken on 1 Mar 1971.
Grayson (DD 435) stricken on 1 June 1971.
Kearny (DD 432) stricken on 1 June 1971.
Jeffers (DD 621) stricken on 1 July 1971.
Edwards (DD 619) stricken on 1 July 1971.
Ordronaux (DD 617) stricken on 1 July 1971.
Gansevoort (DD 608) stricken on 1 July 1971.
Champlin (DD 601) stricken on 1 July 1971.

Ocean Escorts

Bowen (DE 1079) delayed; not commissioned in May 1971 as planned.
Conolly (DE 1073) renamed *Robert E. Peary* on 12 May 1971.

Amphibious Warfare Ships

Rankin (LKA 103) not transferred to Italy as planned.
Arneb (LKA 56) not transferred to Italy as planned.
LST 1198 named *Bristol County*.
Terrebonne Parish (LST 1156), *Vernon County* (LST 1161), and *Washtenaw County* (LST 1166) tentatively scheduled for transfer to Spain in 1972.
Pitkin County (LST 1082) not transferred to Brazil.
Outagamie County (LST 1073) transferred to Brazil in 1971.
Holmes County (LST 836) transferred to Singapore on 1 July 1971.
Garrett County (LST/AGP 786) transferred to South Vietnam on 23 Apr 1971.

Mine Warfare Ships and Craft

King Bird (MSC 194) severely damaged in collision on 12 May 1971; probably will be stricken in near future.
MSC 131 retransferred from Belgium to Turkey.
MSLs 33, 35, 39, and 40 transferred to Greece on 19 May 1971.

Fleet Support Ships

Cohoes (ANL 78) decommissioning scheduled for mid-1972.
Amphion (AR 13) tentatively scheduled for transfer to Iran.
Sphinx (ARL 24), *Askari* (ARL 30), *Krishna* (ARL 38), *Tutuila* (ARG 4) scheduled to be decommissioned late in 1971 (reserve).
Aegir (AS 23) stricken on 1 June 1971.
Chanticleer (ASR 7) decommissioning scheduled for mid-1972.
Seneca (ATF 91), *Utina* (ATF 163) scheduled to decommission late in 1971 (reserve).
Kalmia (ATA 184), *Umpqua* (ATA 209) transferred to Colombia on 1 July 1971.
Cahokia (ATA 186) transferred to US Air Force on 22 Apr 1971.

BENICIA (PG 96) firing Standard missile   *1971, US Navy*

FLAGSTAFF (PGH 1) with 152 mm gun   *1971, US Navy*

EDENTON (ATS 1)   *1971, United States Navy*

Floating Dry Docks

AFDM 7 scheduled to be activated in 1971.

Sealift Ships

Mark (AKL 12), *Braule* (AKL 28) scheduled to decommission late in 1971 (probably for foreign transfer).

Experimental, Research, and Surveying Ships

T-AGM 22 renamed *Range Sentinel*.
Twin Falls (T-AGM 11) in Maritime Administration Reserve to be reacquired and converted into surveying ship AGS 37 commencing in mid-1972.

LATE ADDENDA— SPECIAL SOVIET SUPPLEMENT

No. 500   *May 1971*

NEW CONSTRUCTION

"KRIVAK" CLASS

GENERAL PURPOSE LEADER TYPE

No. 500

Displacement, tons	4 400 standard; 5 600 full load
Length, feet (*metres*)	475·7 (*145·0*)
Beam, feet (*metres*)	52·5 (*16·0*)
Draught, feet (*metres*)	17·4 (*5·3*)
Missile launchers	2 twin (in an angled quadruple bank) of a new model for surface to-surface missile, in "A" position; 2 twin for surface-to-air missiles aft
A/S weapons	2 twelve-barrelled forward for rocket missiles in "B" position
Torpedo tubes	8—21 in (in two quadruple banks) amidships
Guns	4—3 in (*76 mm*) dual purpose automatic (2 twin) in "X" and "Y" positions; 4—30 mm (2 twin) anti-aircraft
Main engines	8 sets of gas turbines; 2 shafts; 112 000 shp
Speed, knots	38 to 40 max

A new class of general purpose fleet escort ship of the super-destroyer of flotilla leader type verging on light cruiser displacement and dimensions. First observed in Western waters in late May 1971.

DESIGN. The hull appears to be a slightly foreshortened modification of that of the "Kynda" class guided missile cruisers combined with the very sharp cutwater of the "Kashin" class guided missile armed destroyers. The bridges and conning positions together form more of a block superstructure than in previous classes. Apparently intended for a general purpose anti-ship, anti-submarine and anti-aircraft role rather than for one specific task, but is reminiscent of the "Kashin" class ships without their aircraft direction propensities. Said to have been designed for both nuclear and conventional warfare.

ENGINEERING. Reported to be powered by gas turbines similar to those fitted in the TU-144 supersonic airliner.

APPEARANCE. The new type presents a more low-lying and less complex appearance than the immediately preceding class of guided missile ships. The mast is lighter and of open lattice construction, instead of being enclosed, and is shorter, this being afforded by the more squat truncated pyramid shaped funnel or gas exhaust casing of considerable area. Much less aggressive looking than the stark and bristling earlier types, with more orthodox and handsome lines.

"Krivak" Class   *May 1971*

GENERAL INDEX

(Named Ships only)

GENERAL INDEX

(Named Ships only)

Abbreviations in ( ) following the name of the ship indicates the country

AbD	Abu Dhabi	Eg	Egypt	Jam	Jamaica	Po	Poland
Al	Albania	ES	El Salvador	J	Japan	Por	Portugal
Alg	Algeria	Et	Ethiopia	Ke	Kenya	R	Romania
A	Argentine	Fin	Finland	Kor	Korea	Sen	Senegal
Aus	Australia	F	France	K.N.	Korea (North)	S.L.	Sierra Leone
Bel	Belgium	G	Gabon	Ku	Kuwait	Sin	Singapore
Br	Brazil	Ger	Germany (Federal Republic)	L	Laos	Som	Somalia
Bru	Brunei	GE	Germany (Democratic Republic)	Leb	Lebanon	S.A.	South Africa
Bul	Bulgaria	Gh	Ghana	Li	Liberia	Sp	Spain
Bur	Burma	Gr	Greece	Lib	Libya	Su	Sudan
Ca	Cambodia	Gu	Guatemala	Ma	Malagasy (Madagascar)	Sw	Sweden
Cam	Cameroon	Gui	Guinea	M	Malaysia	Sy	Syria
Can	Canada	H	Haiti	Mal	Mali	Th	Thailand
Cey	Ceylon	Hon	Honduras	Mau	Mauritania	To	Togo
Chi	Chile	H.K.	Hong Kong	Mex	Mexico	T & T	Trinidad & Tobago
C	China (People's Republic)	Hun	Hungary	Mor	Morocco	Tu	Tunisia
C.T.	China (Taiwan)	Ice	Iceland	N	Netherlands	T	Turkey
Col	Colombia	In	India	N.Z.	New Zealand	U.K.	United Kingdom
Co	Congo	Ind	Indonesia	Nic	Nicaragua	U.S.A.	United States of America
C.R.	Costa Rica	Ir	Iran	Nig	Nigeria	Rus	U.S.S.R.
Cu	Cuba	Ira	Iraq	Nor	Norway	Ur	Uruguay
D	Denmark	Ire	Ireland (Republic of)	Pa	Pakistan	Ven	Venezuela
Dom	Dominican	Is	Israel	Pan	Panama	V	Vietnam
EA	East Africa	I	Italy	Par	Paraguay	V.N.	Vietnam (North)
Ec	Ecuador	I.C.	Ivory Coast	P	Peru	Y	Yugoslavia
				Ph	Philippines	Z	Zanzibar

A. CHIRIKOV—ALMIRANTE

A

	Page
A. Chirikov (Rus)	644
A. Vilkitskij (Rus)	644
A. F. Dufour (Bel)	25
Aachen (U.K.)	370
Aalsmeer (N)	237
Aarøsund (D)	82
Abadia Mendez (Col)	77
Abbeville (U.K.)	370
Abborren (Sw)	301
Abbot (U.S.A.)	477
Abcoude (N)	237
Abdiel (U.K.)	361
Aber-Wrac'H (F)	127
Aberdovey (U.K.)	384
Abete (I)	191
Abhay (In)	163
Abinger (Gr)	384
Abnaki (U.S.A.)	549
Abraham Lincoln (U.S.A.)	410
Absecon (U.S.A.)	576
Abtao (P)	254
Abukuma (J)	212
Acacia (F)	119
Acacia (I)	191
Acacia (U.S.A.)	582
Acadian (Can)	49
Acanthe (F)	119
Acchileus (Gr)	153
Acco (Is)	177
Accokeek (U.S.A.)	548
Acconac (U.S.A.)	569
Accord (U.K.)	383
Acharne (F)	127
Achelous (U.S.A.)	543
Acheron (F)	122
Acheron (Ger)	135
Achilles (U.K.)	350
Achilles (Sw)	309
Achimota (Gh)	146
Achziv (Is)	178
Acme (U.S.A.)	525
Aconit (F)	112, 704
Acre (Br)	32
Acree (U.S.A.)	490
Actif (F)	127
Active (U.K.)	349
Active (U.S.A.)	577
Acushnet (U.S.A.)	584
Acute (Aus)	23
Adamsville (Can)	49

	Page
Adige (I)	196
Adjak (Ind)	166
Adler (GE)	143
Admiral Drozd (Rus)	617
Admiral Fokin (Rus)	619
Admiral Golovko (Rus)	619
Admiral Lazarev (Rus)	611, 648
Admiral Senjavin (Rus)	611
Admiral Ushakov (Rus)	611
Admiral Zozulya (Rus)	617
Adolf Bestelmeyer (Ger)	139
Adroit, L' (F)	120
Adroit (U.S.A.)	525
Adroit (Aus)	23
Advance (Aus)	23
Advance (U.S.A.)	525
Adversus (Can)	49
Advice (U.K.)	383
Aeger (Nor)	246
Aegevs (Gr)	153
Aegir (Ice)	155
Aegir (U.S.A.)	547
Aeneas (U.K.)	340
Aeolus (U.S.A.)	542
Aetos (Gr)	149
Afadzato (Gh)	145
Affray (U.S.A.)	525
Afonso Du Albuquerque (Por)	273
Afroessa (Gr)	151
Agatan (Rus)	642
Agave (I)	191
Agawan (U.S.A.)	569
Agenais, L' (F)	116
Agerholm (U.S.A.)	469
Aggressive (U.S.A.)	525
Agheila (U.K.)	370
Agile, L' (F)	120
Agile (U.K.)	383
Agile (U.S.A.)	525
Aguascalientes (Mex)	228
Aguila (Chi)	60
Aguirre (P)	257
Agusan (Ph)	262
Ahoskie (U.S.A.)	569
Aias (Gr)	153
Aidon (Gr)	150
Aigli (Gr)	150
Aiolos (Gr)	150
Airone (I)	189
Aisberg (Rus)	644
Aitape (Aus)	23
Ajax (U.K.)	350

	Page
Ajax (Sw)	309
Ajax (U.S.A.)	541
Ajay (In)	163
Ajit (In)	163
Ajonc (F)	119
Akaba Ben Naseh (Sy)	310
Akademik Korolov (Rus)	645
Akademik Kurchatov (Rus)	645
Akademik Shirshov (Rus)	645
Akademik Vernadsky (Rus)	645
Akagi (J)	212
Akar (T)	324
Akebono (J)	204
Akhisar (T)	322
Akiyoshi (J)	212
Akizuki (J)	201
Aklan (Ph)	263
Akpinar (T)	324
Akshay (In)	163
Aktion (Gr)	149
Akyab (U.K.)	370
Al Bachir (Mor)	229
Al Harissi (Sy)	310
Al Jala (Tu)	317
Al Mouna (Mor)	229
Al-Mubaraki (Ku)	215
Al Nasser (Eg)	92
Al-Salemi (Ku)	215
Al Thawra (Ira)	174
Al Zafr (Eg)	92
Alabarda (Por)	277
Alacrity (U.S.A.)	525
Alamgir (Pak)	251
Alamo (U.S.A.)	510
Alamogordo (USA)	551
Alano (I)	195
Alanya (T)	320
Alarm (Ira)	174
Alatna (U.S.A.)	557
Alatyr (Rus)	646
Alava (Sp)	292
Albacora (Por)	270
Albacore (U.S.A.)	424
Albany (U.S.A.)	450
Albatros (Ger)	133
Albatros (I)	189
Albatros (Po)	266
Albatros (T)	322
Albatros (Ven)	653
Albay (Ph)	263
Albay Hakki Burak (T)	324
Albert (Ice)	155

	Page
Albert David (U.S.A.)	483
Albert Gast (GE)	142
Albert J. Myer (U.S.A.)	542
Alberto Restrepo (Col)	77
Albin Kobis (GE)	142
Albion (U.K.)	334
Alblas (N)	238
Albufeira (Por)	276
Alcalá Galiano (Sp)	291
Alcatraz (Ven)	653
Alcione (I)	189
Aldan (Rus)	642
Aldebaran (I)	188
Aldebaran (Por)	119
Aldebaran (Por)	276
Aldebaran (Sw)	305
Aleksandr Nevskii (Rus)	611
Aleksandr Suvorov (Rus)	611
Alençon (F)	119
Alert (Ph)	262
Alert (Can)	49, 54
Alert (U.S.A)	577
Alerte, L' (F)	120
Alexander Hamilton (U.S.A.)	407
Alexander Henry (Can)	54
Alexander Mackenzie (Can)	55
Alfange (Por)	277
Alfred A. Cunningham (U.S.A.)	474
Alfredo Cappellini (I)	180
Alfonso Vargas (Col)	77
Algol (F)	119
Algol (Ger)	134
Algol (Por)	276
Algol (U.S.A.)	505
Algonquin (Can)	43
Alholm (D)	83
Alicudi (I)	192
Alidada (Rus)	641
Alidade (F)	122
Aliosha Popovich (Rus)	648
Aliya (Cey)	56
Aljezur (Por) 232	276
Alk (Ger)	133
Alkai (Ind)	169
Allagash (U.S.A.)	535
Allap (Ind)	169
Allen M. Sumner (U.S.A.)	474
Alliance (U.K.)	340
Alloro (I)	191
Almanzora (Sp)	294
Almirante Brion (Col)	75

ALMIRANTE BRION—BARFOOT

CAP GEN PEDRO SANTANA—COSMOS

ENDEAVOUR—GLICINE

LISTERVILLE—MOGANO

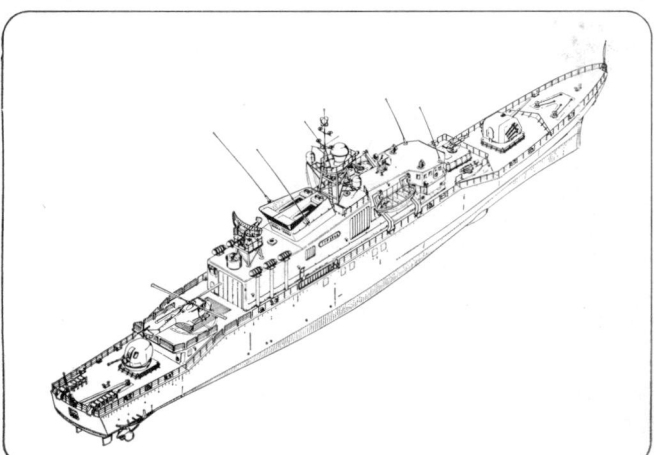

THOMSON-CSF

DIVISION ACTIVITÉS SOUS-MARINES

CENTRE ET DIRECTION : CAGNES-SUR-MER
Chemin du Travail   06 Cagnes-sur-Mer
B.P. 53 - TÉL. 31.35.25
CENTRE DE BREST - CENTRE DE TOULON

- MINE DETECTION SONAR

- NOISE LISTENING AND MEASUREMENT STATION

- **DUMMY** AND **COMBAT MINES**

- **FIXE RANGE MAGNETOMETRIC STATION**

- MAGNETIC DETECTION STATION FOR SUBMARINE

- **IMMUNIZATION SYSTEM**

- **PORTABLE MAGNETOMETER**

- HOMING HEAD AND TORPEDO CIRCUITRY

- LOW FREQUENCY SONAR FOR AVISO

- SUBMARINE PASSIVE SONAR

- SONAR INTERCEPTION UNIT AND UNDERWATER GONIOMETRY

- UNDERWATER TRAJECTOGRAPHY

- SUBMARINE DETECTION EQUIPMENT BY AIRCRAFT

- UNDERWATER TELEPHONY FOR SUBMARINE AND SURFACE SHIP

- OCEANOLOGY EQUIPMENTS

  - SIDE LOOKING SONAR

  - SEDIMENT SOUNDER

  - DYNAMIC POSITIONNING EQUIPMENT

  - MARKING AND LOCATING EQUIPMENT

  - TELEMETRIC EQUIPMENT FOR VESSEL ACCOSTING

- DIVER EQUIPMENTS

  - ACOUSTIC MARKER

  - LOCALISATION RECEIVER

  - PORTABLE SONAR

  - UNDERWATER TRANSCEIVER

ORPHEUS—PORTO EMPEDOCLE

S. RAFAEL—SJÖORMEN

TELUK WORI—VENTURER

Printed in England by
NETHERWOOD DALTON & Co. LTD.
HUDDERSFIELD